THE
1986
JEWISH DIRECTORY
and
ALMANAC

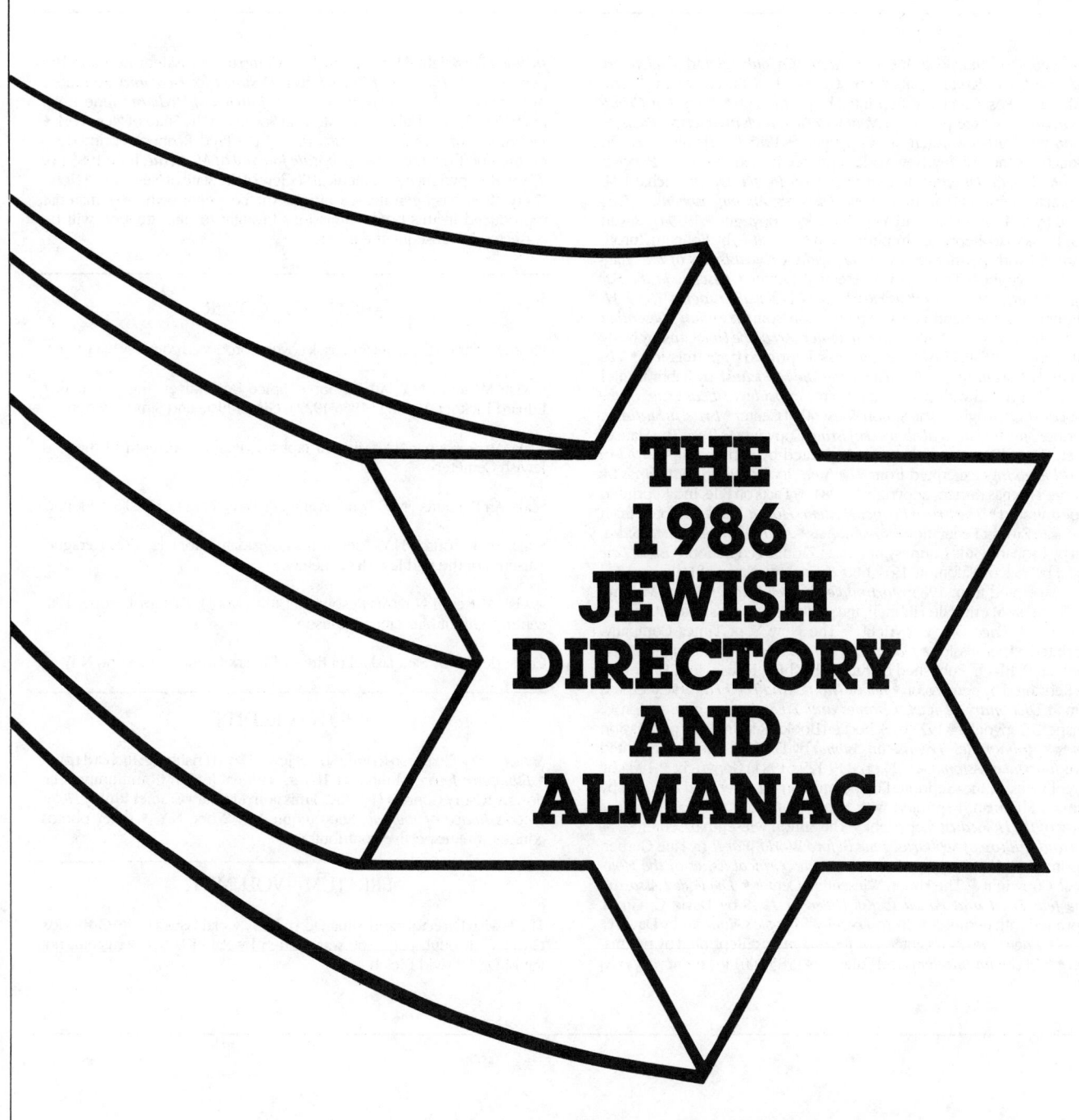

THE 1986 JEWISH DIRECTORY AND ALMANAC

Compiled and Edited by
IVAN L. TILLEM

PACIFIC PRESS
NEW YORK

ACKNOWLEDGMENTS

A Question for Andropov: Where is Raoul Wallenberg? and *Wallenberg and Sweden's Shame (Cont'd.)* by George F. Will, copyright © The Washington Post Company. Reprinted by permission • *Nazi War Criminals In America* excerpted from *Nazi War Criminals in America: Facts... Action* by Charles R. Allen, Jr., Copyright © 1985 Charles R. Allen, Jr. Productions Inc., Albany, New York. Reprinted by permission • *A Perspective on Genetic Diseases Among the Jewish People,* by Dr. Richard M. Goodman. Reprinted from *Genetic Diseases Among Ashkenazi Jews* edited by R.M. Goodman and A.G. Motulsky. Copyright © 1979 by Raven Press Books, Ltd. Reprinted by permission • *Timeline,* by Ephraim Zuroff. Reprinted with permission from *Genocide: Critical Issues of the Holocaust.* Copyright © The Simon Wiesenthal Center • *Rescue via the Far East: The Attempt to Save Polish Rabbis and Yeshivah Students, 1939-41,* by Ephraim Zuroff. Reprinted with permission from the *Simon Wiesenthal Center Annual,* Vol. I. • *Without Surrender: Art of the Holocaust* by Nelly Toll. Copyright © 1978 by Running Press. Reprinted by permission • *The Threefold Covenant: Jewish Belief After the Holocaust,* by Rabbi Daniel Landes. Reprinted with permission from *Genocide: Critical Issues of the Holocaust.* Copyright © The Simon Wiesenthal Center • *Israel in Statistics.* Reprinted from *Statistical Abstract of Israel.* Copyright © 1984. The State of Israel, Central Bureau of Statistics. Reprinted by permission • *Israel in World Rankings* excerpted from *The New Book of World Rankings* by George Thomas Kurian, Copyright © 1984 by Facts on File, Inc. Reprinted by permission • *The Israeli Political System: How It Works,* adapted from American Zionist Federation *Issue Analysis #20: The Israeli Political Situation* by Leonard Fink. Courtesy American Zionist Federation. • *Israel Law Digest* by Yaacov Salomon, Lipschutz & Co., advocates of Haifa and Tel Aviv, excerpted from 1985 *Martindale-Hubbell Law Directory,* Volume VII. Courtesy Martindale-Hubbell, Inc., George E. Krauss, Executive Vice President • *Page One* Copyright © The New York Times Company. Reprinted by permission • *Day by Day in Jewish History.* Copyright © 1983 Abraham P. Bloch. Published by Ktav Publishing House, Inc., Hoboken, N.J. Reprinted by permission • *Jewish Names and Their History* excerpted from *A Dictionary of Jewish Names and Their History* by Benzion C. Kaganoff. Copyright © 1977 by Schocken Books. Reprinted by permission • *Moses Maimonides' Treatise on Asthma* by Dr. Fred Rosner. Reprinted from *Journal of Asthma,* 21(2) pp. 119-129 (1984) Copyright © 1984 by Marcel Dekker, Inc. Reprinted by permission • *Luther and the Jews,* by Franklin Sherman. Reprinted with permission from *Genocide: Critical Issues of the Holocaust.* Copyright © The Simon Wiesenthal Center • *The Life and Culture of Sephardic Jews Before World War II,* by Jane Gerber. Reprinted with permission from *Genocide: Critical Issues of the Holocaust.* Copyright © The Simon Wiesenthal Center • *The Foiled Assassin: One Jew Tried and Failed to Kill Hitler in 1938* by David C. Gross. Reprinted with permission from *The Jewish People's Almanac* by David C. Gross • *Page One* Copyright © *The Jerusalem Post.* Reprinted by permission • *613 Commandments* and Calendars 1985-2001 from *Encyclopedia Judaica* Copyright © Keter Publishing Company, Jerusalem. Reprinted by permission • *The Best of Physicians Is Destined for Gehenna.* Reprinted by permission from the *New York State Journal of Medicine,* June 1983, pp. 970-972, copyright by the Medical Society of the State of New York • *Definition of Death in Jewish Law* by Dr. Fred Rosner, reprinted by permission from the *New York State Journal of Medicine,* June 1983 pp. 973-978, copyright by the Medical Society of the State of New York • Note: Every effort has been made to locate the copyright owners of material reproduced in this book. Omissions brought to our attention will be corrected in subsequent editions.

ABOUT THE COVER

Photographs on the front and back cover reproduced courtesy of (l. to r.):

Jewish Museum N.Y./Art Resource. Spice Box (silver filigree); maker Eduard Lackner, Vienna (1866-1922). Gift of Elsie and Simon Winer.

Scala/Art Resource N.Y. Mizrach tapestry, Prague, Museum of the Old Jewish Cemetery.

Scala/Art Resource, N.Y. Torah Pointer (silver). Prague, Maisl Synagogue.

Scala/Art Resource N.Y. Page from Haggadah (Moravia, 1729) Prague, Museum of the Old Jewish Cemetery.

Jewish Museum N.Y./Art Resource. Tallit (wool), Eastern Europe, 19th century. Gift of Mrs. Linda Brainson.

Cover design by Sara Jaskiel of the Goldmark Group, New York, N.Y.

PHOTO CREDITS

Soviet Jewry: Coalition to Free Soviet Jews; David Frishberg; Richard Lobel • *Ethiopian Jewry:* Abraham J. Bayer, National Jewish Community Relations Advisory Council (NJCRAC) mission; Marriam Cramer Ring • *Hollywood's Image of the Jew:* Phototeque, New York, N.Y. • other photos courtesy the respective contributors.

ERRATUM—VOLUME I

The Jewish Directory and Almanac, p. 359, "Social Issues Unite Orthodox Groups" through page 360 was written by Rabbi Louis Bernstein, not Rabbi Dr. J. David Bleich.

TABLE OF
CONTENTS

TABLE OF CONTENTS

Preface

עשות ספרים הרבה אין קץ (קהלת יב:יב)

Rabbi Israel Salanter, commenting on the words of Ecclesiastes, that "the making of many books is without limit" (Eccl. 12:12), states in a most shrewd observation that not everything a man thinks must he say; and not everything he says must he write; but most importantly, not everything he has written must he publish. The tomes of periodical literature, almanacs, works of reference and handy guides proliferate—apparently without end. While it is true that many in academia must "publish or perish," the fruits of their labor do not always keep pace qualitatively with the initial promise and high expectations that had attended them at their birth. One may therefore ask what can possibly be gained by yet another herculean compilation.

That question was valid one year ago, when The Jewish Directory and Almanac first appeared; it remains valid today, upon the publication of its successor.

The Jewish Directory and Almanac was conceived to fill the need for a concise one-volume compendium of social issues—issues that demand a personal as well as public response from each Jew. No event in Jewish history compares to the Holocaust, yet the end-result of the crisis of two and one-half million Soviet Jews may be similarly fatal, after another generation, denied of its natural culture, passes. Too few of us are sufficiently knowledgeable of the critical issues confronting world Jewry as a civilization—only in 1985 did most American Jews become aware of the plight of their Ethiopian brethren. Tay-Sachs is somewhat known as a Jewish genetic disease—few know that there are actually seven Jewish genetic diseases. We may be aware of the needs of the poor in Israel—too few of us are aware of the needs of the Jewish poor and elderly in our central cities. Forty years after World War II, many Nazi war criminals remain at large—after two more decades pass,

when all of that generation are dead, will we or our children have forgotten their crimes?

Every Jew, regardless of affiliation—or even if totally non-affiliated—must respond to these issues; *no* Jew is immune to their effects. That is only one lesson that we have learned from the Holocaust.

To be a Jew, one must know three things: *How* to be a Jew, *Why* to be a Jew and *What* the essence of a Jew is. How to be a Jew? One must study, understand firsthand and perform the precepts, as outlined by tradition. Why to be a Jew? To improve the world, in a manner to return Man to his primordial, Edenic state.

What, however, is the essence of a Jew? How can one discover his or her Jewish identity?

Ma'ase avot siman l'banim—the deeds of the Patriarchs portend our fate. Why, though, was Abraham chosen to be the first Jew? Was he "chosen" at all, or did *he* do the choosing? And why still do we regard him as the first Jew—why not Adam (for his life is the first in the Torah) or Noah (who was called "righteous," and was the second "father" of humankind) or Moses (who received the entire Torah and spoke to G-d face to face)? What is the singular significance of Abraham?

Abraham lived in a vacuum. G-d's presence, while everywhere, was apparent to no one. Abraham's immediate forebears were idolators. The world of 3700 years ago had forgotten the Creation of two millennia prior. Abraham, totally isolated, discovered the One G-d—without any prompting, prodding, inculcation or outside stimulus—solely through solitary initiative. His "Judaism" was fresh, vibrant; he was the first existentialist. Abraham's second unique testament to his children is *chesed*—lovingkindness. Under the regime where improvident hungry wayfarers were treated as criminals, Abraham, in the heat of the day, while suffering the pain and weakness of *mila* just performed, did not seek the comfort of the shade, but looked for opportunity to invite strangers to the hospitality of the shelter and provision of his tent. The Jewish conception of *Tzedaka*—charity—is not that which makes the giver proud and the recipient humble, nor noblesse oblige, but *responsibility,* to which every necessitous person or cause is given by G-d to claim, to which the poor can stand upright before the rich, and which makes the rich consider themselves merely as administrators of a treasury which belongs to the poor.

Thus, Judaism was founded at the moment of quintessential *chesed.* Abraham was unique for the originality of his mind and the benevolence of his heart. The chapters of Genesis which detail the lives of Abraham, Isaac and Jacob are not mere legends or stories to entertain. From the *avot* we learn the characteristics of a Jew—in order to be "a light unto the nations" in order "to perfect the world."

As Samson Raphael Hirsch wrote in his commentary on Genesis, Jews must form the most definite contrast to the world in general but nevertheless they are always to be found ready for all general humane purposes. Judaism can only be fully appreciated against the backdrop of the world-at-large—Jews can only accomplish their mission in a broader gentile world—an imperfect world. Thus, our responsibility to the issues of intolerance, hunger, totalitarianism, ignorance, in all of their contemporary guises—the Holocaust, antisemitism, sectarianism—must be studied and understood.

I thank Solomon Swimer and his associates, who typeset the text, and I thank The Goldmark Group—Eugene Markowitz and Joseph Goldbrenner—who managed and oversaw the technical aspects of production and design.

Finally, I thank my dear friends Miriam and Joel Lazarus, whose constant encouragement helped enable this project to its fruition.

Ivan L. Tillem
New York, N.Y.
September 1985

For my teacher and dear friend
Rabbi Avrohom Gurewitz

Concerning the Jews

Mark Twain, from Harper's *magazine, September 1898*

Some months ago I published a magazine article descriptive of a remarkable scene in the Imperial Parliament in Vienna. Since then I have received from Jews in America several letters of inquiry. They were difficult letters to answer, for they were not very definite. But at last I received a definite one. It is from a lawyer, and he really asks the questions which the other writers probably believed they were asking. By help of this text I will do the best I can to publicly answer this correspondent, and also the others— at the same time apologizing for having failed to reply privately. The lawyer's letter reads as follows:

> I have read "Stirring Times in Austria." One point in particular is of vital import to not a few thousand people, including myself, being a point about which I have often wanted to address a question to some disinterested person. The show of military force in the Austrian Parliament, which precipitated the riots, was not introduced by any Jew. No Jew was a member of that body. No Jewish question was involved in the *Ausgleich* or in the language proposition. No Jew was insulting anybody. In short, no Jew was doing any mischief toward anybody whatsoever. In fact, the Jews were the only ones of the nineteen different races in Austria which did not have a party—they are absolutely non-participants. Yet in your article you say that in the rioting which followed, all classes of people were unanimous only on one thing—*viz.,* in being against the Jews. Now will you kindly tell me why, in your judgment, the Jews have thus ever been, and are even now, in these days of supposed intelligence, the butt of baseless, vicious animosities? I dare say that for centuries there has been no more quiet, undisturbing, and well-behaving citizens, as a class, than that same Jew. It seems to me that ignorance and fanaticism cannot account for these horrible and unjust persecutions.
>
> Tell me, therefore, from your vantage-point of cold view, what in your mind is the cause. Can American Jews do anything to correct it either in America or abroad? Will it ever come to an end? Will a Jew be permitted to live honestly, decently, and peaceably like the rest of mankind? What has become of the golden rule?

I will begin by saying that if I thought myself prejudiced against the Jew, I should hold it fairest to leave this subject to a person not crippled in that way. But I think I have no such prejudice. A few years ago a Jew observed to me that there was no uncourteous reference to his people in my books, and asked how it happened. It happened because the disposition was lacking. I am quite sure that (bar one) I have no race prejudices, and I think I have no color prejudices nor caste prejudices nor creed prejudices. Indeed, I know it. I can stand any society. All that I care to know is that a man is a human being—that is enough for me; he can't be any worse. I have no special regard for Satan; but I can at least claim that I have no prejudice against him. It may even be that I lean a little his way, on account of his not having a fair show. All religions issue Bibles against him, and say the most injurious things about him, but we never hear *his* side. We have none but the evidence for the prosecution, and yet we have rendered the verdict. To my mind, this is irregular. It is un-English; it is un-American; it is French. Without this precedent Dreyfus could not have been condemned. Of course Satan has some kind of a case, it goes without saying. It may be a poor one, but that is nothing; that can be said about any of us. As soon as I can get at the facts I will undertake his rehabilitation myself, if I can find an unpolitic publisher. It is a thing which we ought to be willing to do for any one who is under a cloud. We may not pay him reverence, for that would be indiscreet, but we can at least respect his talents. A person who has for untold centuries maintained the imposing position of spiritual head of four-fifths of the human race, and political head of the whole of it, must be granted the possession of executive abilities of the loftiest order. In his large presence the other popes and politicians shrink to midges for the microscope. I would like to see him. I would rather see him and shake him by the tail than any other member of the European Concert. In the present paper I shall allow myself to use the word Jew as if it stood for both religion and race. It is handy; and, besides, that is what the term means to the general world.

In the above letter one notes these points:

1. The Jew is a well-behaved citizen.

2. Can ignorance and fanaticism *alone* account for his unjust treatment?

3. Can Jews do anything to improve the situation?

4. The Jews have no party; they are non-participants.

5. Will the persecution ever come to an end?

6. What has become of the golden rule?

Point No. 1.—We must grant proposition No. 1, for several sufficient reasons. The Jew is not a disturber of the peace of any country. Even his enemies will concede that. He is not a loafer, he is not a sot, he is not noisy, he is not a brawler nor a rioter, he is not quarrelsome. In the statistics of crime his presence is conspicuously rare—in all countries. With murder and other crimes of violence he has but little to do: he is a stranger to the hangman. In the police court's daily long roll of "assaults" and "drunk and disorderlies" his name seldom appears. That the Jewish home is a home in the truest sense is a fact which no one will dispute. The family is knitted together by the strongest affections; its members show each other every due respect; and reverence for the elders is an inviolate law of the house. The Jew is not a burden on the charities of the state nor of the city; these could cease from their functions without affecting him. When he is well enough, he works; when he is incapacitated, his own people take care of him. And not in a poor and stingy way, but with a fine and large benevolence. His race is entitled to be called the most benevolent of all the races of men. A Jewish beggar is not impossible, perhaps; such a thing may exist, but there are few men that can say they have seen that spectacle. The Jew has been staged in many uncomplimentary forms, but, so far as I know, no dramatist has done him the injustice to stage him as a beggar. Whenever a Jew has real need to beg, his people save him from the necessity of doing it. The charitable institutions of the Jews are supported by Jewish money, and amply. The Jews make no noise about it; it is done quietly; they do not nag and pester and harass us for contributions; they give us peace, and set us an example— an example which we have not found ourselves able to follow; for by nature we are not free givers, and have to be patiently and persistently hunted down in the interest of the unfortunate.

These facts are all on the credit side of the proposition that the Jew is a good and orderly citizen. Summed up, they certify that he is quiet, peaceable, industrious, unaddicted to high crimes and brutal dispositions; that his family life is commendable; that he is not a burden upon public charities; that he is not a beggar; that in benevolence he is above the reach of competition. These are the very quintessentials of good citizenship. If you can add that he is as honest as the average of his neighbors—But I think that question is affirmatively answered by the fact that he is a successful businessman. The basis of successful business is honesty; a business cannot thrive where the parties to it cannot trust each other. In the matter of numbers the Jew counts for little in the overwhelming population of New York; but that his honesty counts for much is guaranteed by the fact that the immense wholesale business of Broadway, from the Battery to Union Square, is substantially in his hands.

I suppose that the most picturesque example in history of a trader's trust in his fellow-trader was one where it was not Christian trusting Christian, but Christian trusting Jew. That Hessian Duke who used to sell his subjects to George III to fight George Washington with got rich at it; and by and by, when the wars engendered by the French Revolution made his throne too warm for him, he was obliged to fly the country. He was in a hurry, and had to leave his earnings behind—nine million dollars. He had to risk the money with some one without security. He did not select a Christian, but a Jew—a Jew of only modest means, but of high character; a character so high that it left him lonesome—Rothschild of Frankfort. Thirty years later, when Europe had become quiet and safe again, the Duke came back from overseas, and the Jew returned the loan, with interest added.[1]

The Jew has his other side. He has some discreditable ways, though he has not a monopoly of them, because he cannot get entirely rid of vexatious Christian competition. We have seen that he seldom transgresses the law against crimes of violence. Indeed, his dealings with courts are almost restricted to matters connected with commerce. He has a reputation for various small forms of cheating, and for practising oppressive usury, and for burning himself out to get the insurance, and arranging for cunning contracts which leave him an exit but lock the other man in, and for smart evasions which find him safe and comfortable just within the strict letter of the law, when court and jury know very well that he has violated the spirit of it. He is a frequent

and faithful and capable officer in the civil service, but he is charged with an unpatriotic disinclination to stand by the flag as a soldier—like the Christian Quaker.

Now if you offset these discreditable features by the creditable ones summarized in a preceding paragraph beginning with the words, "These facts are all on the credit side," and strike a balance, what must the verdict be? This, I think: that, the merits and demerits being fairly weighed and measured on both sides, the Christian can claim no superiority over the Jew in the matter of good citizenship.

Yet, in all countries, from the dawn of history, the Jew has been persistently and implacably hated, and with frequency persecuted.

Point No. 2.—"Can fanaticism *alone* account for this?" Years ago I used to think that it was responsible for nearly all of it, but latterly I have come to think that this was an error. Indeed, it is now my conviction that it is responsible for hardly any of it. In this connection I call to mind Genesis, chapter xlvii.

We have all thoughtfully—or unthoughtfully—read the pathetic story of the years of plenty and the years of famine in Egypt, and how Joseph, with that opportunity, made a corner in broken hearts, and the crusts of the poor, and human liberty—a corner whereby he took a nation's money all away, to the last penny; took a nation's land away, to the last acre; then took the nation itself, buying it for bread, man by man, woman by woman, child by child, till all were slaves; a corner which took everything, left nothing; a corner so stupendous that, by comparison with it, the most gigantic corners in subsequent history are but baby things, for it dealt in hundreds of millions of bushels, and its profits were reckonable by hundreds of millions of dollars, and it was a disaster so crushing that its effects have not wholly disappeared from Egypt today, more than three thousand years after the event.

Is it presumable that the eye of Egypt was upon Joseph, the foreign Jew, all this time? I think it likely. Was it friendly? We must doubt it. Was Joseph establishing a character for his race which would survive long in Egypt? And in time would his name come to be familiarly used to express that character—like Shylock's? It is hardly to be doubted. Let us remember that this was *centuries before the crucifixion.*

I wish to come down eighteen hundred years later and refer to a remark made by one of the Latin historians. I read it in a translation many years ago, and it comes back to me now with force. It was alluding to a time when people were still living who could have seen the Saviour in the flesh. Christianity was so new that the people of Rome had hardly heard of it, and had but confused notions of what it was. The substance of the remark was this: Some Christians were persecuted in Rome through error, they being *"mistaken for Jews."*

The meaning seems plain. These pagans had nothing against Christians, but they were quite ready to persecute Jews. For some reason or other they hated a Jew before they even knew what a Christian was. May I not assume, then, that the persecution of Jews is a thing which *antedates* Christianity and was not born of Christianity? I think so. What was the origin of the feeling?

When I was a boy, in the back settlements of the Mississippi Valley, where a gracious and beautiful Sunday-school simplicity and unpracticality prevailed, the "Yankee" (citizen of the New England states) was hated with a splendid energy. But religion had nothing to do with it. In a trade, the Yankee was held to be about five times the match of the Westerner. His shrewdness, his insights, his judgment, his knowledge, his enterprise, and his formidable cleverness in applying these forces were frankly confessed, and most competently cursed.

In the cotton states, after the war, the simple and ignorant negroes made the crops for the white planter on shares. The Jew came down in force, set up shop on the plantation, supplied all the negro's wants on credit, and at the end of the season was proprietor of the negro's share of the present crop and of part of his share of the next one. Before long, the whites detested the Jew, and it is doubtful if the negro loved him.

The Jew is being legislated out of Russia. The reason is not concealed. The movement was instituted because the Christian peasant and villager stood no chance against his commercial abilities. He was always ready to lend money on a crop, and sell vodka and other necessaries of life on credit while the crop was growing. When settlement day came he owned the crop; and next year or year after he owned the farm, like Joseph.

In the dull and ignorant England of John's time everybody got into debt to the Jew. He gathered all lucrative enterprises into his hand; he was the king of commerce; he was ready to be helpful in all profitable ways; he even financed crusades for the rescue of the Sepulcher. To wipe out his account with the nation and restore business to its natural and incompetent channels he had to be banished the realm.

For the like reasons Spain had to banish him four hundred years ago, and Austria about a couple of centuries later.

In all the ages Christian Europe has been obliged to curtail his activities. If he entered upon a mechanical trade, the Christian had to retire from it. If he set up as a doctor, he was the best one, and he took the business. If he exploited agriculture, the other farmers had to get at something else. Since there was no way to successfully compete with him in any vocation, the law had to step in and save the Christian from the poorhouse. Trade after trade was taken away from the Jew by statute till practically none was left. He was forbidden to engage in agriculture; he was forbidden to practise law; he was forbidden to practise medicine, except among Jews; he was forbidden the handicrafts. Even the seats of learning and the schools of science had to be closed against this tremendous antagonist. Still, almost bereft of employments, he found ways to make money, even ways to get rich. Also ways to invest his takings well, for usury was not denied him. In the hard conditions suggested, the Jew without brains could not survive, and the Jew with brains had to keep them in good training and well sharpened up, or starve. Ages of restriction to the one tool which the law was not able to take from him—his brain—have made that tool singularly competent; ages of compulsory disuse of his hands have atrophied them, and he never uses them now. This history has a very, very commercial look, a most sordid and practical commercial look, the business aspect of a Chinese cheap-labor cru-

sade. Religious prejudices may account for one part of it, but not for the other nine.

Protestants have persecuted Catholics, but they did not take their livelihoods away from them. The Catholics have persecuted the Protestants with bloody and awful bitterness, but they never closed agriculture and the handicrafts against them. Why was that? That has the candid look of genuine religious persecution, not a trade-union boycott in a religious disguise.

The Jews are harried and obstructed in Austria and Germany, and lately in France; but England and America give them an open field and yet survive. Scotland offers them an unembarrassed field too, but there are not many takers. There are a few Jews in Glasgow, and one in Aberdeen; but that is because they can't earn enough to get away. The Scotch pay themselves that compliment, but it is authentic.

I feel convinced that the Crucifixion has not much to do with the world's attitude toward the Jew; that the reasons for it are older than that event, as suggested by Egypt's experience and by Rome's regret for having persecuted an unknown quantity called a Christian, under the mistaken impression that she was merely persecuting a Jew. *Merely* a Jew—a skinned eel who was used to it, presumably. I am persuaded that in Russia, Austria, and Germany nine-tenths of the hostility to the Jew comes from the average Christian's inability to compete successfully with the average Jew in business—in either straight business or the questionable sort.

In Berlin, a few years ago, I read a speech which frankly urged the expulsion of the Jews from Germany; and the agitator's *reason* was as frank as his proposition. It was this: *that eighty-five per cent.* of the successful lawyers of Berlin were Jews, and that about the same percentage of the great and lucrative businesses of all sorts in Germany were in the hands of the Jewish race! Isn't it an amazing confession? It was but another way of saying that in a population of 48,000,000, of whom only 500,000 were registered as Jews, eighty-five per cent of the brains and honesty of the whole was lodged in the Jews. I must insist upon the honesty—it is an essential of successful business, taken by and large. Of course it does not rule out rascals entirely, even among Christians, but it is a good working rule, nevertheless. The speaker's figures may have been inexact, but *the motive of persecution* stands out as clear as day.

The man claimed that in Berlin the banks, the newspapers, the theaters, the great mercantile, shipping, mining, and manufacturing interests, the big army and city contracts, the tramways, and pretty much all other properties of high value, and *also* the small businesses—were in the hands of the Jews. He said the Jew was pushing the Christian to the wall all along the line; that it was all a Christian could do to scrape together a living; and that the Jew *must* be banished, and soon—there was no other way of saving the Christian. Here in Vienna, last autumn, an agitator said that all these disastrous details were true of Austria-Hungary also; and in fierce language he demanded the expulsion of the Jews. When politicians come out without a blush and read the baby act in this frank way, *unrebuked,* it is a very good indication that they have a market back of them, and know where to fish for votes.

You note the crucial point of the mentioned agitation; the argument is that the Christian cannot *compete* with the

Jew, and that hence his very bread is in peril. To human beings that is a much more hate-inspiring thing than is any detail connected with religion. With most people, of a necessity, bread and meat take first rank, religion second. I am convinced that the persecution of the Jew is not due in any large degree to religious prejudice.

No, the Jew is a money-getter; and in getting his money he is a very serious obstruction to less capable neighbors who are on the same quest. I think that this is the trouble. In estimating worldly values the Jew is not shallow, but deep. With precocious wisdom he found out in the morning of time that some men worship rank, some worship heroes, some worship power, some worship God, and that over these ideals they dispute and cannot unite—but that they all worship money; so he made it the end and aim of his life to get it. He was at it in Egypt thirty-six centuries ago; he was at it in Rome when that Christian got persecuted by mistake for him; he has been at it ever since. The cost to him has been heavy; his success has made the whole human race his enemy—but it has paid, for it has brought him envy, and that is the only thing which men will sell both soul and body to get. He long ago observed that a millionaire commands respect, a two-millionaire homage, a multi-millionaire the deepest deeps of adoration. We all know that feeling; we have seen it express itself. We have noticed that when the average man mentions the name of a multi-millionaire he does it with that mixture in his voice of awe and reverence and lust which burns in a Frenchman's eye when it falls on another man's centime.

Point No. 3.—"The Jews have no party; they are non-participants."

Perhaps you have let the secret out and given yourself away. It seems hardly a credit to the race that it is able to say that; or to you, sir, that you can say it without remorse; more, that you should offer it as a plea against maltreatment, injustice, and oppression. Who gives the Jew the right, who gives any race the right, to sit still, in a free country, and let somebody else look after its safety? The oppressed Jew was entitled to all pity in the former times under brutal autocracies, for he was weak and friendless, and had no way to help his cause. But he has ways now, and he has had them for a century, but I do not see that he has tried to make serious use of them. When the Revolution set him free in France it was an act of grace—the grace of other people; he does not appear in it as a helper. I do not know that he helped when England set him free. Among the Twelve Sane Men of France who have stepped forward with great Zola at their head to fight (and win, I hope and believe[2]) the battle for the most infamously misused Jew of modern times, do you find a great or rich or illustrious few helping? In the United States he was created free in the beginning—he did not need to help, of course. In Austria, and Germany, and France he has a vote, but of what considerable use is it to him? He doesn't seem to know how to apply it to the best effect. With all his splendid capacities and all his fat wealth he is to-day not politically important in any country. In America, as early as 1854, the ignorant Irish hod-carrier, who had a spirit of his own and a way of exposing it to the weather, made it apparent to all that he must be politically reckoned with; yet fifteen years before that we hardly knew what an Irishman looked like.

As an intelligent force, and numerically, he has always been away down, but he has governed the country just the same. It was because he was *organized*. It made his vote valuable—in fact, essential.

You will say the Jew is everywhere numerically feeble. That is nothing to the point—with the Irishman's history for an object-lesson. But I am coming to your numerical feebleness presently. In all parliamentary countries you could no doubt elect Jews to the legislatures—and even *one* member in such a body is sometimes a force which counts. How deeply have you concerned yourselves about this in Austria, France, and Germany? Or even in America for that matter? You remark that the Jews were not to blame for the riots in this Reichsrath here, and you add with satisfaction that there wasn't one in that body. That is not strictly correct; if it were, would it not be in order for you to explain it and apologize for it, not try to make a merit of it? But I think that the Jew was by no means in as large force there as he ought to have been, with his chances. Austria opens the suffrage to him on fairly liberal terms, and it must surely be his own fault that he is so much in the background politically.

As to your numerical weakness. I mentioned some figures awhile ago—500,000—as the Jewish population of Germany. I will add some more—6,000,000 in Russia, 5,000,000 in Austria, 250,000 in the United States. I take them from memory; I read them in the *Encyclopedia Britannica* about ten years ago. Still, I am entirely sure of them. If those statistics are correct, my argument is not as strong as it ought to be as concerns America, but it still has strength. It is plenty strong enough as concerns Austria, for ten years ago 5,000,000 was nine per cent. of the empire's population. The Irish would govern the Kingdom of Heaven if they had a strength there like that.

I have some suspicions; I got them at second hand, but they have remained with me these ten or twelve years. When I read in the *E.B.* that the Jewish population of the United States was 250,000, I wrote the editor, and explained to him that I was personally acquainted with more Jews than that in my country, and that his figures were without doubt a misprint for 25,000,000. I also added that I was personally acquainted with *that* many there; but that was only to raise his confidence in me, for it was not true. His answer miscarried, and I never got it; but I went around talking about the matter, and people told me they had reason to suspect that for business reasons many Jews whose dealings were mainly with the Christians did not report themselves as Jews in the census. It looked plausible; it looks plausible yet. Look at the city of New York; and look at Boston, and Philadelphia, and New Orleans, and Chicago, and Cincinnati, and San Francisco—how your race swarms in those places!—and everywhere else in America, down to the least little village. Read the signs on the marts of commerce and on the shops: Goldstein (gold stone), Edelstein (precious stone), Blumenthal (flower-vale), Rosenthal (rose-vale), Veilchenduft (violet odor), Singvogel (song-bird), Rosenzweig (rose branch), and all the amazing list of beautiful and enviable names which Prussia and Austria glorified you with so long ago. It is another instance of Europe's coarse and cruel persecution of your race; not that it was coarse and cruel to outfit it with pretty and poetical names like those, but that it was coarse and cruel to make it *pay* for them or else take such hideous and often indecent names that to-day their owners never use them; or, if they do, only on official papers. And it was the many, not the few, who got the odious names, they being too poor to bribe the officials to grant them better ones.

Now why was the race renamed? I have been told that in Prussia it was given to using fictitious names, and often changing them, so as to beat the tax-gatherer, escape military service, and so on; and that finally the idea was hit upon of furnishing all the inmates of a house with *one and the same surname,* and then holding the house responsible right along for those inmates, and accountable for any disappearances that might occur; it made the Jews keep track of *each other,* for self-interest's sake, and saved the government the trouble.[3]

If that explanation of how the Jews of Prussia came to be renamed is correct, if it is true that they fictitiously registered themselves to gain certain advantages, it may possibly be true that in America they refrain from registering themselves as Jews to fend off the damaging prejudices of the Christian customer. I have no way of knowing whether this notion is well founded or not. There may be other and better ways of explaining why only that poor little 250,000 of our Jews got into the *Encyclopedia.* I may, of course, be mistaken, but I am strongly of the opinion that we have an immense Jewish population in America.

Point No. 4.—"Can Jews do anything to improve the situation?"

I think so. If I may make a suggestion without seeming to be trying to teach my grandmother how to suck eggs, I will offer it. In our days we have learned the value of combination. We apply it everywhere—in railway systems, in trusts, in trade-unions, in Salvation Armies, in minor politics, in major politics, in European Concerts. Whatever our strength may be, big or little, we *organize* it. We have found out that that is the only way to get the most out of it that is in it. We know the weakness of individual sticks, and the strength of the concentrated fagot. Suppose you try a scheme like this, for instance. In England and America put every Jew on the census-book *as* a Jew (in case you have not been doing that). Get up volunteer regiments composed of Jews solely, and, when the drum beats, fall in and go to the front, so as to remove the reproach that you have few Massenas among you, and that you feed on a country but don't like to fight for it. Next, in politics, organize your strength, band together, and deliver the casting vote where you can, and, where you can't, compel as good terms as possible. You huddle to yourselves already in all countries, but you huddle to no sufficient purpose, politically speaking. You do not seem to be organized, except for your charities. There you are omnipotent; there you compel your due of recognition—you do not have to beg for it. It shows what you can do when you band together for a definite purpose.

And then from America and England you can encourage your race in Austria, France, and Germany, and materially help it. It was a pathetic tale that was told by a poor Jew in Galicia a fortnight ago during the riots, after he had been raided by the Christian peasantry and despoiled of everything he had. He said his vote was of no value to him, and he wished he could be excused from casting it, for indeed casting it was a sure *damage* to him, since no matter which party he voted for, the other party would come straight and take its revenge out of him. Nine per cent. of the population of the empire, these Jews, and apparently they cannot put a plank into any candidate's platform! If you will send our Irish lads over here I think they will organize your race and change the aspect of the Reichsrath.

You seem to think that the Jews take no hand in politics here, that they are "absolutely non-participants." I am assured by men competent to speak that this is a very large error, that the Jews are exceedingly active in politics all over the empire, but that they scatter their work and their votes among the numerous parties, and thus lose the advantages to be had by concentration. I think that in America they scatter too, but you know more about that than I do.

Speaking of concentration, Dr. Herzl has a clear insight into the value of that. Have you heard of his plan? He wishes to gather the Jews of the world together in Palestine, with a government of their own—under the suzerainty of the Sultan, I suppose. At the convention of Berne, last year, there were delegates from everywhere, and the proposal was received with decided favor. I am not the Sultan, and I am not objecting; but if that concentration of the cunningest brains in the world was going to be made in a free country (bar Scotland), I think it would be politic to stop it. It will not be well to let that race find out its strength. If the horses knew theirs, we should not ride any more.

Point No. 5.—"Will the persecution of the Jews ever come to an end?"

On the score of religion, I think it has already come to an end. On the score of race prejudice and trade, I have the idea that it will continue. That is, here and there in spots about the world, where a barbarous ignorance and a sort of mere animal civilization prevail; but I do not think that elsewhere the Jew need now stand in any fear of being robbed and raided. Among the high civilizations he seems to be very comfortably situated indeed, and to have more than his proportionate share of the prosperities going. It has that look in Vienna. I suppose the race prejudice cannot be removed; but he can stand that; it is no particular matter. By his make and ways he is substantially a foreigner wherever he may be, and even the angels dislike a foreigner. I am using this word foreigner in the German sense—*stranger.* Nearly all of us have an antipathy to a stranger, even of our own nationality. We pile gripsacks in a vacant seat to keep him from getting it; and a dog goes further, and does as a savage would—challenges him on the spot. The German dictionary seems to make no distinction between a stranger and a foreigner; in its view a stranger *is* a foreigner—a sound position, I think. You will always be by ways and habits and predilections substantially strangers—foreigners—wherever you are, and that will probably keep the race prejudice against you alive.

But you were the favorites of Heaven originally, and your manifold and unfair prosperities convince me that you have crowded back into that snug place again. Here is an incident that is significant. Last week in Vienna a hail-storm struck the prodigious Central Cemetery and made wasteful destruction there. In the Christian part of it, according to the official figures, 621 window-panes were broken; more than 900 singing-birds were killed; five great trees and many small ones were torn to shreds and the shreds scattered far and wide by the wind; the ornamental plants and other decorations of the graves were ruined, and more than a hundred tomb-lanterns shattered; and it took the cemetery's whole force of 300 laborers more than three days to clear away the storm's wreckage. In the report occurs this remark—and in its italics you can hear it grit its Christian teeth: ". . . lediglich die *israelitische* Abtheilung des Friedhofes vom Hagelwetter *ganzlich verschont* worden war." Not a hailstone hit the Jewish reservation! Such nepotism makes me tired.

Point No. 6.—"What has become of the golden rule?" It exists, it continues to sparkle, and is well taken care of. It is Exhibit A in the Church's assets, and we pull it out every Sunday and give it an airing. But you are not permitted to try to smuggle it into this discussion, where it is irrelevant and would not feel at home. It is strictly religious furniture, like an acolyte, or a contribution-plate, or any of those things. It has never been intruded into business; and Jewish persecution is not a religious passion, it is a business passion.

To conclude.—If the statistics are right, the Jews constitute but *one per cent.* of the human race. It suggests a nebulous dim puff of star dust lost in the blaze of the Milky Way. Properly the Jew ought hardly to be heard of; but he is heard of, has always been heard of. He is as prominent on the planet as any other people, and his commercial importance is extravagantly out of proportion to the smallness of his bulk. His contributions to the world's list of great names in literature, science, art, music, finance, medicine, and abstruse learning are also away out of proportion to the weakness of his numbers. He has made a marvelous fight in this world, in all the ages; and has done it with his hands tied behind him. He could be vain of himself, and be excused for it. The Egyptian, the Babylonian, and the Persian rose, filled the planet with sound and splendor, then faded to dream-stuff and passed away; the Greek and the Roman followed, and made a vast noise, and they are gone; other peoples have sprung up and held their torch high for a time, but it burned out, and they sit in twilight now, or have vanished. The Jew saw them all, beat them all, and is now what he always was, exhibiting no decadence, no infirmities of age, no weakening of his parts, no slowing of his energies, no dulling of his alert and aggressive mind. All things are mortal but the Jew; all other forces pass, but he remains. What is the secret of his immortality?

Postscript—The Jew as Soldier

When I published the above article in *Harper's Monthly*, I was ignorant—like the rest of the Christian world—of the fact that the Jew had a record as a soldier. I have since seen the official statistics, and I find that he furnished soldiers and high officers to the Revolution, the War of 1812, and the Mexican War. In the Civil War he was represented in the armies and navies of both the North and the South by 10 per cent. of his numerical strength—the same percentage that was furnished by the Christian populations of the two sections. This large fact means more than it seems to mean; for it means that the Jew's patriotism was not merely level with the Christian's, but overpassed it. When the Christian volunteer arrived in a camp he got a welcome and applause, but as a rule the Jew got a snub. His company was not desired, and he was made to feel it. That he nevertheless conquered his wounded pride and sacrificed both that and his blood for his flag raises the average and quality of his patriotism above the Christian's. His record for capacity, for fidelity, and for gallant soldiership in the field is as good as any one's. This is true of the Jewish private soldiers and the Jewish generals alike. Major-General O. O. Howard speaks of one of his Jewish staff-officers as being "of the bravest and best"; of another—killed at Chancellorsville—as being "a true friend and a brave officer"; he highly praises two of his Jewish brigadier-generals; finally, he uses these strong words: "Intrinsically there are no more patriotic men to be found in the country than those who claim to be of Hebrew descent, and who served with me in parallel commands or more directly under my instructions."

Fourteen Jewish Confederate and Union families contributed, between them, fifty-one soldiers to the war. Among these, a father and three sons; and another, a father and four sons.

In the above article I was not able to endorse the common reproach that the Jew is willing to feed upon a country but not to fight for it, because I did not know whether it was true or false. I supposed it to be true, but it is not allowable to endorse wandering maxims upon supposition—except when one is trying to make out a case. That slur upon the Jew cannot hold up its head in presence of the figures of the War Department. It has done its work, and done it long and faithfully, and with high approval: it ought to be pensioned off now, and retired from active service.

FOOTNOTES

1. Here is another piece of picturesque history; and it reminds us that shabbiness and dishonesty are not the monopoly of any race or creed, but are merely human:

"Congress passed a bill to pay $379.56 to Moses Pendergrass, of Libertyville, Missouri. The story of the reason of this liberality is pathetically interesting, and shows the sort of pickle that an honest man may get into who undertakes to do an honest job of work for Uncle Sam. In 1886 Moses Pendergrass put in a bid for the contract to carry the mail on the route from Knob Lick to Libertyville and Coffman, thirty miles a day, from July 1, 1887, for one year. He got the postmaster at Knob Lick to write the letter for him, and while Moses intended that his bid should be $400, his scribe carelessly made it $4. Moses got the contract, and did not find out about the mistake until the end of the first quarter, when he got his first pay. When he found at what rate he was working he was sorely cast down, and opened communication with the Post Office Department. The department informed him that he must either carry out his contract or throw it up, and that if he threw it up his bondsmen would have to pay the government $1,459.85 damages. So Moses carried out his contract, walked thirty miles every weekday for a year, and carried the mail, and received for his labor $4—or, to be accurate, $6.84; for, the route being extended after his bid was accepted, the pay was proportionately increased. Now, after ten years, a bill was finally passed to pay to Moses the difference between what he earned in that unlucky year and what he received."

The *Sun,* which tells the above story, says that bills were introduced in three or four Congresses for Moses' relief, and that committees repeatedly investigated his claim.

It took six Congresses, containing in their persons the compressed virtues of 70,000,000 of people, and cautiously and carefully giving expression to those virtues in the fear of God and the next election, eleven years to find out some way to cheat a fellow-Christian out of about $13 on his honestly executed contract, and out of nearly $300 due him on its enlarged terms. And they succeeded. During the same time they paid out $1,000,000,000 in pensions—a third of it unearned and undeserved. This indicates a splendid all-around competency in theft, for it starts with farthings, and works its industries all the way up to ship-loads. It may be possible that the Jews can beat this, but the man that bets on it is taking chances.

2. The article was written in the summer of 1898.—Editor.

3. In Austria the renaming was merely done because the Jews in some newly acquired regions had no surnames, but were mostly named Abraham and Moses, and therefore the tax-gatherer could not tell t'other from which, and was likely to lose his reason over the matter. The renaming was put into the hands of the War Department, and a charming mess the graceless young lieutenants made of it. To them a Jew was of no sort of consequence, and they labeled the race in a way to make the angels weep. As an example take these two! *Abraham Bellyache* and *Schmul Godbedamned.*—Culled from *Namens Studien,* by Karl Emil Franzos.

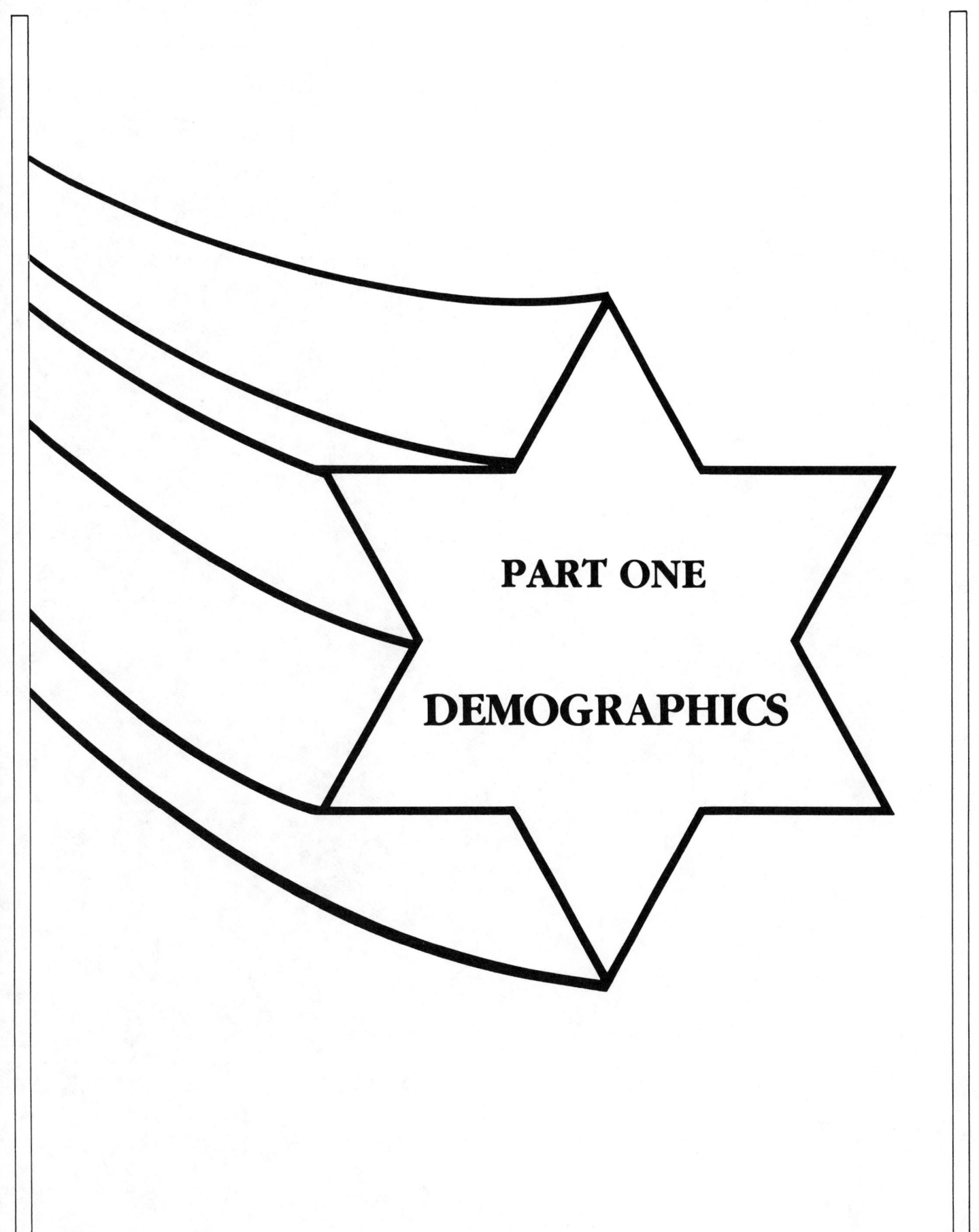

PART ONE

DEMOGRAPHICS

PART ONE

DEMOGRAPHICS

The American Jewish Community in the 21st Century: A Projection

Donald Feldstein, American Jewish Congress

What follows will attempt to describe the likely characteristics of the American Jewish community at the beginning of the 21st century. We will examine what is known and what is predicted about numbers of Jews, age distribution, family, geographic distribution, occupational status, religious and political behaviors and communal organization. Finally, we will explore possible unifying themes which may account for the trends.

I. The Limitations of Forecasting

Since futurism became popular, two dates have served as magnets for predictions about the state of affairs on almost any question—1984 (thanks to George Orwell) and the year 2000. Now 1984 is behind us and the 21st century a scant 14 years away—less than a generation. It should certainly be possible to predict with great confidence, if not certainty, what the American Jewish community will be like in the year 2000. And yet it is realism rather than false modesty which dictates the strongest possible qualification of any predictions about society. The record of futurism is dismal. Writing in the late 1960s about the 70s, only a few years away, Paul Ehrlich wrote in *The Population Bomb*, "In the 70s . . . hundreds of millions of people will starve to death in spite of any crash programs embarked on now." Of course, there were no crash programs and there was no such starvation. Even without any political axe to grind, demographers in the 1930s consistently and dramatically underestimated population growth in the United States; demographers in the 1960s consistently overestimated it.

There are simply so many variables! For instance, one might agree that it is hard to predict American Jewish birth rates for the next fourteen years, but certainly one should be able to estimate the number of Jewish aged in the year 2000; all of them are with us now. And it should be possible except if:

—a hitherto unknown disease takes a great toll among the elderly;

—a new medical breakthrough makes a significant increase in average length of life;

—a wave of immigration from the Soviet Union, Israel or elsewhere swells the adult Jewish population;

—a change in the political or emotional climate results in large-scale *aliyah*, particularly among the elderly, who can live adequately in Israel with Social Security and other dollar pensions.

The likelihood of any of the above four developments occurring may be small. The likelihood that some of the four or another not even considered will occur is greater. Therefore, it is with the greatest trepidation that one should write about the future; it is with sophisticated caution that one should read about it.

Nonetheless, trying to envision conditions in the future is a valuable exercise. It can alert us to trends which, if not acted on, will lead to certain outcomes. Thus it can be a tool for social planning. And since so much of life is a matter of probability, if one can discern *likely* developments, that may be adequate. Often, a variation of five or ten percent from a predicted outcome does not change the functional accuracy of the prediction. And so we will proceed, dealing with general trends, not with many tables or attempts to specify exact numbers or percentages. Where we use them it is because they are the clearest, simplest or most dramatic ways to describe something—not because anyone believes that those numbers are precisely what the outcome will be.

II. Self-Fulfilling and Self-Defeating Prophecies

Much has been written about the self-fulfilling prophecy. An influential investment house predicts that the stock market will rise. This causes people to buy stock, helping to make the market rise. Teachers are told which of their students, based on psychological tests, are likely to succeed, and which to fail. The teachers' attitudes then communicate this expectation, helping it to be fulfilled. Similarly, predictions that a neighborhood will lose its Jewish residents may motivate the residents to leave.

Some of the projections here appear to be pessimistic about the Jewish future. But all are subject to change by strong action. Therefore it is important to bear in mind the "self-defeating prophecy." Jonah predicted the destruction of Nineveh. It was precisely this prediction which caused the citizens to repent and which saved the city. Similarly, predictions that a neighborhood will lose its Jewish residents have also motivated countermeasures which have preserved the neighborhood. Our hope is that the latter attitude will prevail. None of the projections here are so immutable that they cannot be modified by the exertion of will, and their purpose is to help organizations and individuals to move toward the future they desire.

III. American Jewish Trends and American Trends

"Vee ess Kristelt zich, azoy Yidelt zich," goes the old Yiddish expression—"As the Christian world goes, so go the Jews." And this expression appears to describe American Jewry accurately. Many AJ (we will use AJ from here on as an acronym for American Jewish) trends are simply the sectarian reflections of larger American trends. Are we concerned about the declining Jewish birthrate? Well, the AJ birthrate has declined only as the American birthrate has declined. It has traditionally been lower than the American average, and it continues lower, but no more so. Similarly, the rising AJ divorce rate is rising as the American divorce rate rises—approximately no more and no less, and is still lower than the American rate to about the same degree. Even political attitudes follow this pattern. The arguments over whether or not the AJ community has turned to the right or not are generated by the fact that it has turned to the right just as the American community has turned to the right, but it is to the left of the American community to the same degree as Jews have traditionally been; hence the arguments.

These examples should illustrate the difficulty of predicting any AJ trends apart from American trends. The likelihood is that the AJ community will become more like the American community, not less. This suggests that efforts to change AJ behaviors or attitudes to make them more different from overall American behavior and attitude will prove to be very difficult.

Nor can even strict separation protect completely against the American environment. The Orthodox Jewish community twenty years ago prided itself on its immunity from the rising divorce rate. Today, divorce in Orthodox groups may still be lower than elsewhere; but it is a real and growing problem.

It is clear: much of the AJ future will be determined on the American common. How we play our roles on the common will influence the future of American Jewry.

IV. How Many Jews

In 1983, the *American Jewish Year Book* estimated that in 1982 there were approximately 5.7 million Jews in the United States. It is remarkable that most respected demographers using a variety of methods arrive at very similar estimates.

The National Jewish Population Study estimated that there were 5.8 million American Jews in the United States in 1971. If one subtracts non-Jewish members of counted households and adds institutionalized Jews (who were not counted), the 1971 estimate is closer to 5.4 million. But the 5.8 estimate as analyzed was an estimate of an actual number in the range of 5.5 million to 6.0 million. And in 1983, U.O. Schmelz and Sergio Della Pergola estimated that the 1971 figure was 5.6 million and the 1980 figure 5.7 million. (Losses in intermarriage, etc. were more than offset by immigration.) Fred Massarik sees some 1981 erosion from the 1971 figures and estimates that current AJ population is in the range of 5.2 to 5.6 million. And so there seems to be agreement that the current AJ population is 5.5 million give or take five percent.

What about the year 2000? Even when we move to this more speculative question, one is struck more by the agreement than the disagreement among serious demographers. All foresee a long-term and gradual decline in the AJ population. All reject the alarmist notions bruited about in the press, such as only 10,000 American Jews by the Tricentennial Year of 2076, or a 25% decline in the AJ population by the year 2000. There are differences of opinion about the speed and degree of decline. Sidney Goldstein points to the baby boom generation born after World War II. This group is now passing through its child-bearing years and is such a large cohort that even if the fertility *rate* is low, the actual number of births should increase in the '80s. Thus Goldstein sees us entering the 21st century with 5.5 to 5.8 million Jews, much like today. Then he foresees a decline through the first two decades of the 21st century, until we arrive at the Tricentennial, with one to two million fewer American Jews, anywhere from 3.5 to 4.8 millions. Other demographers, considering births, intermarriage, apostasy, immigration and emigration, conclude that American Jews are already losing numbers—from under three percent to over five percent per decade. Thus, if the higher attrition rate is accurate, and the current base is at the low end of estimates, we could enter the 21st century with just over 4.6 million American Jews. If the lower attrition rate is accurate, and the current population is at the higher end of estimates, we could enter the 21st century with 5.5 million American Jews.

We are left then with a most optimistic projection of 5.8 million American Jews in the year 2000, and a most pessimistic (responsible) projection of 4.6 million. Most likely, there will be over 5 million American Jews in the year 2000. But even the most optimistic forecasters see a significant decline from these numbers in the first two decades of the 21st century. Therefore, even if the alarmists are wrong, there does exist a very serious demographic problem for the Jews of the United States. It should also be noted that this decline appears sharper when contrasted with the general American population. In 1937, American Jews were 3.7 percent of the American people. Now they constitute 2.5 percent and by the year 2000, this percentage will be lower.

In the year 2000, it is likely that Israel will contain 4.5 million Jews, assuming no mass immigration, but will continue to have a birthrate higher than that of America's Jews. Thus some time in the first half of the 21st century, the Jewish population of Israel will probably surpass that of the United States, making Israel the numerical as well as the spiritual center of world Jewry.

Do numbers really matter? There are those who argue that undue attention in recent years has been given to the question of Jewish population size. There have been periods in history when there were fewer Jews, and yet the Jewish people have survived. There is little we can do anyway, the argument continues, to offset population size, and therefore, we had best focus on the quality of Jewish life rather than on the number of Jews.

Those who take the other view argue that sheer numbers do matter. While there have been periods with fewer Jews, these have not been in times when the world population was at 4.4 billion. The Jewish people could become so statistically insignificant as to be functionally extinct. In the United States, the argument continues, Jews have managed, in spite of small numbers, to be recognized as one of the three great religious groups, with concomitant benefits. Below a certain critical mass, that may not be possible. It may not be possible to maintain political strength on domestic policy or on behalf of Israel's security. A critical mass is needed for a rich and vibrant cultural and religious life contributing to the Jewish chain. And psychologically the morale and vigor of a group is sapped if it perceives itself as a shrinking or dying community rather than a growing one. Finally, the argument is made that in a free society, losses must inevitably occur through assimilation and intermarriage, inroads which demand countervailing growth policies if the Jews are not to die as a group. Conversionary and pronatal policies, it is argued, can be developed which will make a difference in numbers as well as in quality. Significant population size is a necessary, if insufficient, condition of survival.

V. Age Distribution

The following table, excerpted from the *American Jewish Year Book* 1983, describes the current age distribution of American Jews, how it has changed since 1970, and how it compares with all United States whites:

Jews and Other Population Groups, By Age, 1970 and 1980 (Percent)

Age	1970—U.S. Jews	1970—U.S. Whites	1980—U.S. Jews	1980—U.S. Whites
Total	100.0	100.0	100.0	100.0
0-14	21.2	27.4	16.2	21.7
15-29	23.5	24.2	26.0	26.8
30-44	16.8	17.1	18.2	19.1
45-64	26.5	21.1	24.1	20.6
65+	12.0	10.2	15.5	11.8

The most striking feature of the above table is the increase in the Jewish group 65 and over compared to 1970 and compared to the overall United States white group. There has been a decline in the percentage of Jewish children in the population, but that has been accompanied by a similar decline among all United States whites. The large Jewish pool in the aged category means a higher crude death rate in ensuing years and contributes to the problem of numbers. The over-65 group now also includes a large and significant number of people 75 and over, a more frail group in need of more services. For many people there are now two "generations" or segments of aging—the years 60 to 72, a time of relative health and vigor for most, and 73 plus, a time of failing health and capacity. Thus, people often make retirement plans (to Florida or the Southwest) in terms of their needs at the first stage of aging, and they find the environment particularly ill-suited for the second stage. The 15.5% of the Jewish population which were 65 and over was divided as follows:

—5.7% were ages 65-69
—4.2% were ages 70-74
—5.6% were 75 plus

Females constitute 54% of the 65 plus population. There is also a larger percentage of Jewish females than white females generally in the age range 20-34, the prime child-bearing years. This offers further evidence that even with a low rate of fertility, an increasing absolute number of Jewish babies will be born in the next few years. The number of Jewish schoolchildren is likely to increase into the 1990s and then fall.

Projections of age distribution in the year 2000 vary depending on various estimates for fertility, intermarriage and immigration.

Projections of Jews and All Whites By Age (Percent), 2000

Age	Jews High Proj.	Jews Low Proj.	All Whites High Proj.	All Whites Low Proj.
Total	100.0	100.0	100.0	100.0
0-14	17.0	12.7	25.6	18.5
15-29	18.6	18.9	20.3	19.1
30-44	21.6	22.6	20.8	24.0
45-64	26.4	28.1	21.4	24.8
65+	16.4	17.1	11.8	13.5

One element in the above table which appears most certain is that the percentage of elderly in the Jewish population will continue to rise to the year 2000 and will continue to rise into the 21st century. This is because of the high percentage which in the year 2000 will be between 45 and 64.

VI. Jews on the Move

Immigration in AJ history has been critical to Jewish growth and religious development. The AJ population grew to 5.8 million more as a result of Jewish immigration than of natural increase, and each major move of immigration brought with it new "capital" in Jewish tradition and culture to be invested in the American Jewish amalgam. Hard projections about immigration are impossible to make.

Significant population movements across national borders are usually associated with major convulsions. Who can now predict the future of Soviet Jewish emigration policy, the likelihood or timing of a convulsion in South Africa or Argentina?

Certain realities are clearer:

A. When and if major Jewish populations move transnationally, there will be a strong impetus to encourage settlement in Israel as the first or most desirable choice. The establishment of a Jewish state has created a watershed change in the nature of any future Jewish population movement.

B. In spite of any policies adopted by the organized Jewish community, some Jews will come to the United States and other Western countries rather than to Israel. The larger the emigrating group, and therefore, the less it is restricted to the ideologically committed, the larger the percentage that will come to the West.

C. In spite of popular perceptions and magazine articles, there is apparently nothing like the 300,000 or so Israelis who have been said to have settled in the United States. Recent population studies in New York and Los Angeles and the work of Israeli demographers suggests that the number is probably close to 100,000, only a little more than the number of Soviet Jews who have settled in the United States in the past decade.

D. If new Jewish groups do come to the United States, they will not be bringing large stores of new Jewish capital, learning or religious tradition to enrich the American Jewish community. Rather, it will increasingly become the responsibility of the AJ community to "Judaize" these new immigrants, if they are not to be disproportionately assimilated in America. Work with Russian Jews in the last decade suggests that in communities where a major effort is launched, such a Judaization is possible with a high percentage of immigrants.

E.   Even in the absence of large-scale emigration from any one country, Jews will increasingly be on the move in a world which has shrunk in size and grown in mobility. Some numbers of Jews will continue to move to the United States from all countries of Jewish settlement when they are free to do so—for educational or professional advancement, for economic opportunity, following others in the family, for all the reasons which have created a general brain drain to the United States.

F.   In the absence of near-revolutionary change in economic or social conditions in the United States, there will not be massive United States Jewish *aliyah* to Israel. Intelligent efforts can make for a significant percentage change in the small numbers now making *aliyah*, particularly among the neo-Orthodox. But surveys showing even the strongest pro-Israelism among American Jews do not show any serious readiness to consider *aliyah*.

Internal movement of Jews within the United States—the more significant form of Jewish mobility—will likely continue as such to the year 2000.

American Jews have traditionally been concentrated in the Northeast and in large cities. In 1930, 68% of American Jews were in the Northeast; only 27% of all Americans were in the Northeast. As late as 1970, over 50% of the Jews resided in 12 cities. Of the 3,073 populated counties in the United States, there are 100 or more Jews in only 504 of them.

But change is apparent. In 1982, 54% of American Jews resided in the Northeast, as did 22% of all Americans—the percentage of Jews in the area had dropped by 14 percentage points while the percentage of all Americans had dropped by only five. About 18% of America's Jews and 18% of America's total population are now in the West. The twelve largest cities of Jewish settlement now house under one-third of American Jews. Clearly, America's Jews, still somewhat concentrated, are dispersing, developing a distribution more like that of all America.

Additionally, significant numbers of Jews are moving to small cities. In 1970, 18% of American Jews were in cities of populations under 50,000. In 1980, it was 29%. Much of this shift may simply be from city to suburb. But when the percentage of Jews in towns under 2,500 has gone from one to five percent in ten years, there is obviously something more operating—some dispersion to rural areas, university towns, and elsewhere.

The pattern of mobility of American Jews is much like that of other Americans. Even in 1970, less than one-third were in the city of their birth. While much of this was urban-suburban movement, twenty-five percent were in different states from the ones in which they were born, and only 62% of Jews over the age of 20 were in the same city they were in *four years prior.*

Since mobility is positively associated with higher education, we must assume it will continue for America's Jews. Goldstein argues that mobility must be examined along with fertility and intermarriage among the major factors affecting Jewish demography in the future. Just how to examine it and how to deal with it is less clear.

A.   We must assume on balance that dispersion weakens the Jewish community, providing less Jewish association (which is correlated with intermarriage), and fewer institutional ties. Studies indicate less Jewish affiliation and philanthropy among the mobile in the first years after moving. But in some cases, mobility has led to the reviving of apparently moribund Jewish communities, strengthening institutions and Jewish association. It has provided the necessary critical mass for some communities to go on. Further studies show the Orthodox do not lessen and even increase their Jewish communal involvement inmoving to a new community. For Conservative and Reform Jews, the evidence points the other way. Density within a neighborhood may no longer be a factor in Jewish identity.

B.   Dispersion also threatens to dilute Jewish political power, which is based on concentrating the numbers of a small minority in key states and communities. But it has been argued that, increasingly, Jewish political power is in activity by leaders, contact with and support of legislators, rather than in "delivering votes." Therefore, dispersion could actually increase Jewish power as much as weaken it.

C.   It has been argued that a rich cultural and religious life demands one or more urban centers for the massing of seminaries, libraries, organizations, etc. Happily, the recent New York population study indicates that New York City, although having fewer Jews than it did a generation ago, is holding up as such a center. Fears that the study would show fewer than 3/4 million Jews left in New York City and therefore hurt Jewish influence almost prevented the study from being undertaken. The results show 1.1 million Jews in New York City, a dramatic rise in the Jewish population of Manhattan since 1970, and 1.7 million Jews in the service area of the New York Jewish Federation.

When one adds the metropolitan areas of New Jersey and Rockland Counties, there are about 2 million Jews in the Metropolitan New York area. So at least one vital center remains. While the material has not yet been analyzed, the raw data from the New York study suggests that there are no plans for flight from the city on the part of most of the Jewish residents, and therefore, in the year 2000, New York will still be the center of AJ life, even while individual leaders and organizations will be housed around the country.

In sum, in the year 2000, Jews will continue to be on the move intra- and internationally, will conform more closely to the overall American population distribution, and this will put several items on the American community agenda:

—How to regionalize and nationalize opportunities for Jewish association.

—How to integrate new residents from wherever into local Jewish communities.

—How to nationalize fund raising concerns and efforts. Today, a wealthy Jew in Scarsdale feels responsibility for a poor Jew in Morocco, in Tel Aviv, or in The Bronx (in his own New York area) but he is not likely to feel responsibility for a poor Jew in Albuquerque, New Mexico. Similarly, Jewish federations are increasingly concerned about losing contributors and potential contributors from Jews on the move. This issue is just beginning to be addressed seriously.

—How to maintain the Jewish community's traditional stance of supporting liberal immigration policies as being ultimately in the best Jewish interest.

AJ organizations will need to learn to deal with the permanent and continuing reality of Jews on the move.

VII. Jewish Education

Formal Jewish education has been a major vehicle for the transmission and development of the Jewish heritage. In the United States today, that vehicle is beset by difficulties.

Total U.S.—Jewish School Enrollments, Elementary and Secondary

1946	231,000
1958	554,000
1967	554,000
1971	457,000
1975	391,000
1979	344,000

In part, the rise and fall in enrollment since 1946 reflects the rise and fall in the number of eligible children. But in part it also reflects a smaller percentage of the eligible poor now attending Jewish schools. The Jewish Educational Service of North America estimates that in 1979, 39% of the eligible Jewish children had received or were receiving some form of Jewish education, a much smaller percentage than in the 50s and 60s.

The effectiveness of that education may also be questioned. Of those in Jewish schools in 1979:

—49.2% attended schools with classes once a week;

—24.5% attended schools with classes two or more days per week; and

—26.3% attended day schools.

Since various studies indicate that either a minimum of 1,000 hours or 3,000 hours of Jewish education are needed to have a significant impact on later Jewish identity, fully one-half to three-quarters of those children receiving a Jewish education are not getting an intensive enough education to make a difference in their later lives. When one adds to the above the fact that the AJ education system lacks a cadre of trained teachers, does not by and large pay reasonable salaries and is generally in a constant state of financial crisis, and that relatively few children receive any Jewish education beyond the elementary school level, the message for year 2000 is not hopeful.

However, there are also contervailing trends. That 85 to 90,000 AJ children are enrolled in day schools is a reality few would have predicted in the 1950s. Nor would many have predicted the growth in the number of day schools under Conservative, Reform and communal auspices. This has raised the average number of pupil hours per year from 182 in 1966 to 248 in 1979. There has also been a growth in post-secondary seminaries for advanced Jewish study, particularly among the Orthodox. In the mid-1970s, over 300 American colleges offered courses in Judaism, 40 had Jewish studies majors, and 27 had graduate programs. Jewish federations in the past decade have moved to serious funding of Jewish education under religious auspices and communal sponsorship of Jewish afternoon high schools and even some day schools. The Conference on Alternatives in Jewish Education has grown as a collection of Jewish people interested in new approaches to and lobbying for more aid to Jewish education.

Havurot, camps, and community centers have developed informal and even formal Jewish education even as formal Jewish educational institutions increasingly serve an informal purpose of Jewish association. A small but intense *Baal Tshuvah* or "return" movement has brought several thousand young Jewish men and women into intensive, Jewish study under Orthodox auspices. There is a growing concern for Jewish education as a priority among Jewish communal leaders, for themselves as well as for children. The intensive Jewish identity and educational program of UJA's Young Leadership are a variation on the *Baal Tshuvah* movement; their lives as well as their giving have been influenced.

Therefore, the picture for the year 2000 is particularly cloudy. More than in most areas, it will depend on what is done by the Jewish community between now and then. It appears that there will be more communal involvement and funding in this enterprise which, since the post-World War II period, has been largely synagogue-sponsored. It is one of the ways in which federations will likely begin funding synagogues.

Jewish education may also be a good example of what we will discuss in the summary of bipolarity—the division of the AJ community into two distinct camps. On the one hand, the group receiving no Jewish education seems to be growing and will grow larger into the year 2000, including well over one-half of the Jewish community. On the other hand, the group receiving most intensive Jewish education is also growing rapidly, and could be about 15% of the Jewish community by the year 2000. It is the middle group, somewhat educated and identified, that is shrinking as the extremes grow.

VIII. Income and Occupation

American Jews are among America's wealthiest and most highly-educated subgroups, on the whole. There is no reason to believe that this will change by the year 2000, but within this global continuity, there are important shifts likely. In spite of overall wealth, important pockets of Jewish poverty persist, particularly in the largest cities. About 15% of the Jews in the largest cities are poor, near-poor, or low-income (below 200% of the Federal poverty line).

The aged are the largest segment of Jewish poor. In New York City the Jewish aged poor and near-poor number over 100,000, and suffer the accompanying effects of being subject to high crime, poor medical care, isolation and loneliness. Jews will continue to have a disproportionate number of elderly in their ranks. Jewish communal organizations will continue to focus more attention on serving the elderly, but these services cannot include income maintenance. In the next fifteen years, more and more Jews will enter the ranks of the elderly having been covered by maximum Social Security payments and private pensions. The number of the Jewish aged poor may therefore well decline. However, this will be affected by inflation rates and by the nature of medical insurance. So long as the United States is without universal health insurance or some plan by which middle-class people can contribute partially to continuing medical service, there will be a large number who become poor by using up Medicare benefits and spending down their assets until, pauperized, they are covered by Medicaid.

There is also a class of new Jewish poor, women who are divorced and are trying to raise children in a middle-class environment. House-poor even before separation, these women are driven into poverty by the costs of divorce, separate domiciles, and the accompanying bitterness leading to reluctant alimony and child support. This category of Jewish poor may shrink as more Jewish women are professionally educated and capable of providing support.

A third group of Jewish poor is among Hasidic and other ultra-Orthodox families with many children. Many of these are families still relatively new to the United States—the post World War II immigrants. With each passing generation and its accompanying capacity to function in the United States economy, this group, too, should shrink.

There is also some structural unemployment among Jews disproportionately represented in impacted occupations. Jews are heavily into the human services field, research and development, and academia, all hurt by Reagan administration policies or demographic trends. Thus, Jews as well as others have been touched by the high unemployment rates of recent years. This could change by the year 2000, but there could then be a glut of physicians or lawyers. Some poverty related to gaps between training and needs of the job market is always a possibility.

The changes and cuts in welfare benefits of recent years have hurt poorer Jews. Poor Jews tend to be on the higher end of poverty, and therefore, when eligibility levels for benefits are reduced, the Jewish poor are disproportionately affected in eligibility for low-cost housing, job training, etc.

Finally, every group in the United States produces some case poverty—poverty due to situational tragedy, inability to cope, etc., but this is a very small number.

The Jewish occupational structure is not clear at all. There has certainly been a significant growth in the percentage of Jews in the professions—medical, legal, academic, from a generation ago. In 2000, Jews will still be heavily professionalized, whatever new trends may emerge by then. It is also clear that a new class of Jews is emerging in the corporate executive world in a whole variety of fields, and this group has not yet been adequately reached by Jewish communal organizations. But beyond these understandings, there are questions.

——Are Jews less involved in entrepreneurial work?
——Will occupational change affect Jewish identity and Jewish philanthropy?

Sociologist Steven Cohen, primarily from an analysis of Boston's population studies of 1965 and 1975, sees a significant shift away from self-employment, and a concomitant threat to Jewish philanthropy, since the self-employed are demonstrably the "best givers." Interestingly, Cohen and others find that at least after one generation, these occupational and professional shifts do *not* seem to work against Jewish behaviors or attitudes. The threat that professional subgroup loyalties will replace Jewish subgroup loyalties is always present, but it does not appear to have been fulfilled to date. In fact, certain occupations have become new centers of Jewish association.

As to the occupational shifts and their impact on philanthropy, more study is urgently needed. Most of the data use very broad categories, such as "managerial, sales, clerical, etc.," and do not provide sharp divisions of the Jewish labor force. Does the partner in a law firm describe him/herself as "self-employed" or not? Is the multimillionaire member of an investment firm counted as an "entrepreneur?" What of the physician, the bulk of whose income comes from part ownership of a lab or from real-estate investment? Very carefully structured study is needed.

Even the apparent shift from self-employment may be deceptive. Does a smaller percentage of declared entrepreneurs reflect a closing out of small business—"mom and pop" stores and the like—rather than a shift away from big business? Are the Jewish businessmen whose sons and daughters have become professionals being replaced by what was always a numerically small group of Jewish *big* business people—in high-tech firms such as those in Silicon Valley, in finance, real estate, entertainment and communications? Jews are certainly more likely to be self-employed than are other groups. Is Jewish philanthropy *not* in need of shifting emphasis from major givers? In fact, there may have been an attitudinal shift since the mid-70's, when most of the recent studies were done. Where business was once seen as not of the highest status for Jewish intellectuals, there has, in recent years, been a flocking of some of the best and the brightest of Jewish youth into M.B.A. programs for entrepreneurial as well as corporate purposes.

We do know that in Boston and other places dependence on Jewish philanthropy has been moving toward fewer givers of larger amounts. We do not know if it is necessary to plan for the reverse. The absence of a detailed study of occupation is the major gap that we have noted in our review of the literature on the Jewish population of the United States.

IX. Family and Personal Behavior

In the past decade, the Jewish family has changed much as the American family has changed—in the same directions, in similar proportions, and maintaining similar degrees of difference from the overall American family. To the year 2000 it is likely that AJ family patterns will continue to change as general American family patterns change, perhaps even narrowing the differences between them, as is happening with other subgroups. For instance, among American Catholics, the higher birth rate compared to Protestants has virtually disappeared.

In recent years, American Jews, like other Americans, have been marrying later, divorcing more frequently, and having fewer children. More women are having their first child at age 30 or beyond, and there are about twice as many single person households as there were in 1970.

The question of Jewish fertility is central to Jewish survival, as discussed in the section, "How Many Jews." Family structure, fertility and Jewishness are all intimately connected. Jewish education for children tends to be effective only when there is support for what is being taught. Conversely, the presence of children tends to increase the Jewish behaviors of the family—attending synagogue, holding a seder, etc. And alternative households—single-parent, single non-marital living arrangements, tend to be less Jewish in behavior than the traditional family.

Jews in America have consistently had a fertility rate of about 2/3 that of the rest of America. In fact, even in Europe since the 19th century, at least, Jews have consistently maintained lower fertility rates than their host countries. Given the recent and current American fertility rate, Jews are reproducing below the replacement level. Jews are past ZPG and into the Orwellian "negative population growth," according to most demographers.

While the large number of people in the child-bearing cohort will mask this problem for a decade, it appears to be the single most significant threat to the Jewish future in the long term. A significant turnaround by the year 2000 is probably possible only if there is a significant change in the American attitude to childbearing and family. The large number of late-marrying, professionally-educated, and career-involved Jewish women only underline this reality. While surveys of Jewish women show a continued positive *attitude* toward marriage and children, comparisons of such surveys in the early 1970s with actual behavior show that the former is no longer predictive of the latter.

The Orthodox and ultra-Orthodox communities continue to bear children and to grow. This is hopeful for the maintenance of a core and argues against the most alarmist predictions on Jewish population. We may be approaching a situation like the one in Israel, where 10% of the families bear 40% of the children, but the American Orthodox is not a large enough group to counter the overall direction, and the Orthodox, too, may be influenced by American norms, albeit more slowly, as in the case of divorce. The 8-12 child family becomes rare, and 4-6 children defines the "large" family.

The predicted rate of fertility for Jews in the year 2000 is somewhere between 1.5 and 2.0 (with 2.1 necessary to maintain population at current levels). It may be about 1.7 today.

Abortion, as the almost exclusive method to deal with unwanted pregnancy, is another factor contributing to a lower birthrate. In Israel, where the rate of abortion is about three times that of the United States, it is a major factor. Data is not exact, but if American Jews have an abortion rate not much lower than Americans in general, then about 30,000 Jewish women a year undergo abortion, primarily *not* because of anticipated birth defects. There is no evidence that this pattern is likely to change in the next fourteen years. Jews also use the relatively irrevocable birth control method of sterilization more than do other groups.

Divorce in the Jewish community is rising. "Worst case" projections that by the year 2000, one of every two Jewish marriages will end in divorce, are probably unduly alarmist, based on straight line projections. But divorce interferes with more childbearing and population growth, with Jewish identity and behavior, with economic adequacy, and puts a strain on synagogues and Jewish agencies for services. At the very least, services will need to be refocused to meet the needs of more singles and single parent families. For instance, some synagogues have switched Sunday schools to weekday afternoons, because so many children are away on weekend visitation to a divorced parent. Jewish Agency camps often have over 1/3 of their clientele from single parent families.

But other statistics are slightly more hopeful. Through the 1970s, Jews maintained their traditional ratio of approximately 50% of the divorce rate of American Protestants. If that is maintained, Jews may continue a manageable divorce level to the year 2000—perhaps about 10% and certainly under 20%. And there is evidence that Jews remarry after divorce to a greater degree than others, leading to new quasi-traditional family structures. Social agencies are tooling up for the service needs of such families.

Intermarriage is the traditional enemy in the literature of Jewish survival. It represents the ultimate rejection to traditional Jewish parents, and has been railed against in pulpits more than many other concerns in Jewish life. But it has grown inexorably in the last generation even while its actual effects on the Jewish people are less clear.

Arthur Hertzberg has pointed out that wherever Jews have lived in relative freedom for three generations, the intermarriage rate has been about 33%. This is simply the price, he claims, for living in an open society. The data of the National Jewish Population Study of 1971 created its greatest impact in confirming for the United States the Hertzberg observation. For the college-educated, third generation Jews, AJ intermarriage passed one-third and is likely to have stabilized between 30% and 40%. That rate of intermarriage will be with us into the 21st century. Causes of intermarriage may have changed. Traditionally those with poor relations with their parents were twice as likely to intermarry as those with good relations with their parents. New studies, however, show no connection in the minds of Jewish college students between personal factors, Jewish pride and identity, and willingness to intermarry, if that is the result of open association. Similarly, Jewish men traditionally intermarry at a much greater rate than women, but this, too, may be changing as Jewish women are less protected from and have more access to the full society and its associations. Traditionally, intermarried couples had a 26% lower fertility rate than Jewish couples, but this, too, may be changing. In sum, intermarriage seems to be becoming a viable option for a normative group of Jews in the American value system of individual choice and conscience. Intermarriage has become more a consequence than a cause of assimilation. This is not likely to change by the year 2000.

But the implications for the Jewish community of the continuing high intermarriage rate are less clear. Traditionally, it was assumed that intermarriage was a major component of a demographic disaster facing American Jewry. In recent years, looking at the effects of intermarriage, demographers have been more cautious. Issues of quality aside, there is evidence of little or no quantitative loss to the Jewish people from intermarriage, due to conversion of spouses and Jewish identity of children. But most recently, studies of long-term effects and of children of intermarriages have returned to the older view that intermarriage, at least without conversion, does cut into Jewish population.

The question is easy to understand. If most spouses and children of the intermarriage group join the Jewish group, the losses might be offset by the gains. Since it takes only one rather than two Jews to produce such childen, this could even be a source of numerical expansion. Different studies have provided different figures on conversion and identification rates. It would appear that only a minority of non-Jewish spouses of Jews formally convert. But this percentage is rising, and up to half consider themselves Jewish, formally or informally. As for children, most studies find that a majority are raised as Jews, that those formally inducted into the Jewish religion and those who informally consider themselves Jewish together constitute up to 80% of the children of intermarriage. Therefore, the potential for intermarriage as a source of growth is present. But Dr. Egon Mayer's most recent work on the children of intermarriage indicates critical differences between the children of intermarriage where conversion to Judaism has taken place on the part of the non-Jewish parent, and the children of mixed marriage where no such conversion has occurred. In the former group, over 80% of the children 16 and older identified as Jews; in the latter group, less than 25%. Almost none of the children of non-conversionary marriages married Jews.

Would a conversionary outreach program to mixed marrieds make for Jewish identification on the part of more children, or are the families whose children are likely to identify as Jews the ones already converting? What of the quality of Jewish life among this group of offspring which apparently has only tenuous feelings for Jewish ethnicity and peoplehood rather than for Judaism as a religious belief? Since much of the conversion would likely be non-*halachic,* what kinds of conflicts or legal difficulties in later marriage might this engender within the Jewish group? But one thing is certain: the intermarried, and how to deal or not to deal with them, is one of the major questions now facing American Jews. How it is answered will help shape the nature and size of American Jewry in the year 2000. Today alone there are about 1/2 million children of Jewish intermarriage of various kinds in the United States.

Assimilation and apostasy is another traditional Jewish concern as a source of loss to the Jewish people. Goldstein has pointed out that any attempt to estimate its size on the basis of current data is "guesswork," and no estimate will be attempted here. But we do know something about the nature of contemporary assimilation and the size of some components. In our secular society, there appears to be very little formal conversion of Jews to Christianity as was the case in other times and places. Generalized assimilation is much the larger trend—a Jew is so divorced from Jewish life that his/her children or grandchildren simply do not think of themselves as Jewish in any way, religious or ethnic. Or there is a conscious decision by a Jew to consider him/herself an American, a "human being,"

rather than a Jew. One might have expected more of this phenomenon in the professions with strong and most intensive subgroup professional cultures. But this has not been the case. There is not, apparently, a lower level of Jewish identity in any specific professional group.

While we do not know how many Jews convert out, we have some estimates of those converting in. Probably over 10,000 persons per year go through the conversionary process among the three religious denominations—not a very large group, but not a negligible one, either. Similarly, while Jews are not converting to formal Christian churches in great numbers, there are a number of Jews "converting" to various cults and assorted mystical groups. There has been no definitive study of their numbers, but if, as estimated, over 2 million Americans are in cults, and Jews are involved at their normal percentage of the American population, then over 50,000 American Jews are now in cults. And many believe that Jews are heavily over-represented in the cult culture. It is difficult to translate such numbers into an annual rate, but here, too, we are probably dealing with a phenomenon that is neither overwhelming nor negligible. It is worthy of attention if the mechanization of society continues to produce, to the year 2000, continuing hunger among many for meaningful mystical outlets.

X. Jewish Behaviors and Beliefs

We have previously made reference to bipolarity, the theory that the Jewish community is dividing into two extreme camps, one more assimilated and one more Jewishly identified. Another common belief is that there is less ritual observance and weaker Jewish identity in each succeeding generation on the American scene. There is supportive evidence for these ideas in what has been described here in some areas such as Jewish education. But in the major general area of Jewish identity, even in some specific Jewish behaviors, there is countervailing evidence in recent studies by Steven M. Cohen and one by Neil Sandberg. For the bulk of American Jewry today an evolving form of Jewish identity

—is alive and strong;
—shares a broad middle ground consensus across Jewish denominational lines; and
—does not necessarily continue to decrease, but may even increase by the fourth generation in America.

There does continue to be division in ritual observance between a small but growing Orthodox group and other Jews. And the consensus may be the result of some Jews becoming so bipolarized that they have dropped out of the Jewish community. But none of this detracts from the presence of a strong Jewish consensus on:

—the "theology" of America's civil Judaism;
—the importance of certain rituals and other behaviors, such as philanthropy and visiting Israel;
—a pro-Israelism, formed by a Holocaust consciousness; and
—a continuing political liberalism, at least by the standards of the general American public.

Jonathan Woocher has codified the civil religion of America's Jews as including belief in the following eight basic tenets:

A. The unity and distinctiveness of the Jewish people.

B. The concomitant collective responsibility Jews bear for the security and welfare of other Jews.

C. The Centrality of the State of Israel as a symbol of this unity and responsibility.

D. The enduring value of the Jewish "tradition," however imperfectly defined, and the importance of its perpetuation.

E. The persistence of threats (internal and external) to the survival of the Jewish people and tradition.

F. The importance of *tzedakah*, as charity and social justice.

G. The virtue of participating in the larger society and the compatibility of this with good Judaism.

H. Theological pluralism—the relative unimportance of ritual differences and classic theological concerns; individual conscience as the key to Jewish practice.

The vast majority of American Jews, from the neo-Orthodox to the barely committed, subscribe in large measure to the above eight tenets. It is a package of belief which has evolved over time and is strong. Except for possible changes in pro-Israelism, and liberalism which will be discussed further on, the package appears to be a continuing one, one which is likely to describe civil Judaism in the year 2000.

Rituals and behaviors also exist which are widely observed among Jews. Sociologists have long pointed out how the minor holiday Chanukah has grown in importance as a Jewish companion to Christmas, but other patterns are also strong. More American Jews, probably over 80%, participate in some Passover Seder than even light Chanukah candles (perhaps 70%). Other behaviors common to more than 50% of America's Jews include attending services on Yom Kippur, attending services on Rosh Hashanah, fasting on Yom Kippur, having a *mezuzah* on the door, refraining from bread on Passover, giving to UJA/Federation or other Jewish charities. Half of all American Jews report that all or most of their friends are Jewish. Several of these practices, including Jewish friendships and Yom Kippur observances, show signs of increasing beyond the third generation. Other ritual observance, such as observing *kashruth*, continues to decline. So the case can be made behaviorally as well as attitudinally for a strong and continuing center in the American Jewish population.

Not only does there appear to be a broad consensus in American Judaism, but the components of that consensus are mutually reinforcing. There was a period when many Jewish leaders were believed to be either religiously oriented *or* oriented to secular Jewish organizations. But now Federation leadership is not only synagogue affiliated (as Charles S. Liebman points out for New York), but synagogue affiliation and ritual observance are positively associated with Jewish philanthropic giving. In fact, ritual observance is a better predictor of travel to Israel than age or income! That is, of 1,000 Jews who light candles in their homes every Friday night, and 1,000 who do not, the former are most likely to be contributors to their local Jewish federation and to have visited Israel than the latter.

This pattern of a core of unitary Jewish behaviors and attitudes defining a broad part of the AJ spectrum is likely to be with us in the year 2000.

In the late '50s and early '60s, 80% to 90% of Marshall Sklare's Lakeville Jews belonged to a Jewish organization.

In the 1980s, only 25% of third and fourth-generation Los Angeles Jews belonged to any Jewish organization. Probably just over half of AJ adults, overall, now belong to some Jewish group. In a more "liberated" society, it is not necessary to identify as a Catholic, Protestant or Jew. And along with Jewish education for children, the impetus to be a synagogue member may have declined. Other avenues of affiliation are open to Jews, social or philanthropic. Goldin points out that while Jewish names appear regularly on museum or symphony boards, fewer than 1/2 of American Jewish millionaires contribute to any substantial degree to UJA and their Federation. The membership rolls of the largest Jewish organizations in the United States are not growing, but they are aging. On the other hand, there is some positive correlation between social status and Jewish association, and decline in Jewish association seems to stop after three generations. There are also small but exciting subgroups in AJ life, *havurot* and others, developing affiliation and commitment. The likelihood is that Jewish affiliation with synagogue and communal groups will continue at about current 50% levels to the year 2000, although the forms and motives may change somewhat.

Within the Jewish denominations, national surveys show the following about how Jews identify themselves:

Reform 26%
Conservative 36%
Orthodox 6%
(New York area 13%)
Not affiliated or secular 32%

The last is what is up most sharply from the previous generation, although most of that unaffiliated group is still part of the consensus civil religion. Orthodoxy's percentages in national polls are consistently down from previous generations, despite the apparent growth of orthodoxy. This is not a contradiction. In earlier times, many non-Orthodox-in-practice Jews identified themselves as Orthodox. The synagogues they did or did not attend, the rabbis they would call on only for rites of passage, the Judaism they believed was authentic, was Orthodox. This group is fading. The practicing, committed and religiously-educated Orthodox community is the group that is growing and visible. It is only since World War II that the infrastructure of American orthodoxy began to mature. It should also be noted that identifiable groups like the Orthodox (skullcaps, distinctive dress), Hebrew speaking Israelis and Russian emigres, tend to have their numbers exaggerated because they are so visible.

Bernard Lazerwitz sees a generational progression in how people identify themselves—from Orthodox to Conservative to Reform to unaffiliated, and back largely to Conservative and Reform. How will this pattern develop to the year 2000? The Orthodox will continue to be a small but a larger percentage of the whole as they reproduce and hold onto their own most effectively. As Reform Jewry had adapted to being comfortable with ritual and pro-Israelism, the continued numerical primacy of Conservative Judaism may or may not continue. Some feel that the recent acceptance of equal rights for women in the Conservative movement will give it new strengths; others believe that will simply put the final touch on a left-right Conservative schism. Together, Conservative and Reform Judaism will command the loyalty of more than half of American Jews in the year 2000. A large minority will continue to describe themselves as unaffiliated or secular.

Giving to Jewish causes generally and to UJA/Federations in particular, has become more than a charitable act for American Jews. It has become a form of Jewish identity, a religious or ethnic ritual. There are cities where if one wants to join the Jewish country club, one will not be asked if he is a synagogue member, keeps a kosher home, or even has a Jewish spouse; rather, that person will be required to demonstrate that he contributes to UJA. This has become a badge. Thus, in comparing 1965 and 1975 data, Cohen finds that while affiliation with Jewish organizations has declined, giving to Jewish causes has gone up. About 50% of Jewish households contribute to UJA, more in smaller cities, less in the larger cities. Correlates between synagogue membership and ritual observance demonstrate that over 75% of the more observant contribute to Jewish causes.

There are problems in the form and nature of Jewish philanthropy, which will be discussed further on, and this could cause significant change by the year 2000. But the principle of philanthropic giving as a key element in AJ theology is strong and likely to be present in the year 2000.

Another key element in the Jewish civil religion is pro-Israelism. A remarkable 40% of all AJ adults had visited Israel at least once by 1983 (16% in 1971). One in three report having relatives living in Israel. Surveys consistently show overwhelming consensus (in the 80 and 90% ranges) among American Jews, that Israel is important to them, that if something happened to the state of Israel, this would be one of the great tragedies of their lives, etc. American politicians are very sensitive to the feelings of American Jews toward Israel: their own polling mechanisms confirm the Israel-centeredness of American Jewry. And the outpouring of financial and volunteer support by American Jews when Israel appears to be in crisis is further evidence of its centrality. A number of observers feel that this pro-Israelism is tied closely to a Holocaust consciousness developed in American Jews since the mid-1960s. This consciousness makes for a strenuous defense of Israel as:

—a guarantor against a repetition of Holocausts elsewhere, and

—as a beleaguered state, which must be protected against genocidal forces directed against it.

The active pro-Israelism is legitimized and enhanced by a spirit of pluralism which has developed in American life: the acceptance of the legitimacy of lobbying for group interest.

And yet, it would be a mistake to confuse this pro-Israelism with classical Zionism. Again, by overwhelming majorities, American Jews indicate that they believe their future is in America, that they have a positive and hopeful future in America, and that they do *not* believe that American Jews should seriously consider settling in Israel. In some ways, the pro-Israelism of American Jews is like the feeling among immigrant populations from other countries about the old home.

Other traditional aspects of Jewish belief and behavior in America have been:

—political liberalism; and

—fear of the emergence of more active antisemitism. How pro-Israelism, political liberalism, and fear of anti-

semitism may interact and change between now and the year 2000 is discussed in the next and in the final section. Apart from the impact of possible changes in these areas, there is little reason to question the continuity to the year 2000 of the Jewish beliefs and behaviors described here.

XI. Political Orientation and Behavior

As noted above, Jewish political behavior in America has been marked by:

—political liberalism (at least since the 1930s);

—pro-Israelism (since the establishment of the State of Israel); and

—fear of antisemitism.

In spite of numerous obituary notices, political liberalism is alive and well among America's Jews. This is confirmed by separate work of Cohen, Fisher and Yankelovich & Associates. American Jews continue to describe themselves disproportionately as Democratic, non-Conservative, and as not having voted for Ronald Reagan. They differ significantly from Americans in general in their greater support of spending on social welfare programs and support of liberal attitudes on lifestyle differences. Jews continue to vote for black candidates (Bradley in California, Washington in Chicago and others) disproportionately when compared with other white groups. But there is evidence of a Jewish turn to the political right. Jews are less overwhelmingly democratic and liberal than in the past, but they still stand to the left of where Americans as a whole are now standing, probably with as much difference between them as ever.

There are several theories as to why Jews have been more liberal, and these will not be discussed here. But the evidence is that Jews do *not* vote against their perceived self-interest on the basis of some presumed altruism. On specific issues where apparent self-interest is involved, Jews have parted company from the liberal consensus. Thus, on defense spending (Israel security related?) about the same percentage of Jews as all Americans favor increases. On the death penalty (crime against elderly urban Jews?) Jews are as much in favor as other Americans. And Jews have at least as much fear of affirmative action (quotas which could hurt Jews?) as do Americans in general. So where group interest appears to conflict with liberal positions, Jews will abandon the latter. Liberalism might be the traditional stance because Jews have seen it as in their interest for civil harmony, tolerance, openness, or for other reasons.

While Jews continue to be more liberal than other Americans, this liberalism is not distributed equally among all Jews. There is a particularly interesting distinction. The most ritually observant Jews tend to be significantly more conservative than others. Liberalism grows as ritual observance and identification with the Jewish community lessens. What Cohen calls the "minimalists" are the most liberal Jews, but beyond that, the "secularists" who participate in almost no Jewish behavior are politically conservative. In other words, once Jews fall off the edge of active Jewish identity, they lose whatever distinctive Jewish reasons there may be which make Jews more liberal, and they become like all other Americans. The most observant Jews have little reason to be concerned with integrating into

American society, which appears to be associated with the thrust for liberalism. Liberalism is strongest when there is an active tension between Jewish survivalist and assimilationist tendencies.

For most Jews, the tension between survivalism and assimilation is likely to remain into the 21st century. If that were the only factor, one could predict a liberal Jewish electorate in the year 2000. Much more problematic is how Jews will perceive their group interest in the coming decades, and that is difficult to predict.

Pro-Israelism is generally a consensus feeling among American Jews—a desire to support pro-Israel candidates, concern for Israel's security, etc. But on specifics, there is a real division among American Jews. As Earl Rabb has pointed out, the division is over the same issues on which Israeli Jews are divided. Sixty percent of American Jews would favor some return of territories for real peace. Sixty percent would support criticism by American Jews of specific Israeli policies. For most Jews, it would be a mistake to confuse their specific differences with any diminution of support for Israel.

Thus far, American Jews have been able to avoid confronting possible differences between the United States and Israeli interests. Ninety-three percent of American Jews believe that United States support of Israel is in the United States' interest. Only 29% confess that at times their devotion to the United States and to Israel have come into conflict. But the potential for such conflict is always present, although it has been avoided with great success thus far.

Greater liberalism or income does not produce erosion of support for Israel as some have suspected. But there is erosion in the overwhelming concern for Israel among the younger and better educated Jews. This is a matter of concern when thinking about the year 2000 and the generation removed from the direct memory of the Holocaust and the drama of Israel's birth. Pro-Israelism is now central to AJ civil religion and political behavior. But one can see two differing possible changes by the year 2000:

a. Liberalism could be identified as unfriendly to Israel and become rejected by Jews, although this has not happened to date.

b. Pro-Israelism itself could diminish in the next generation.

Either of these developments would be a major change for American Jewry.

By all reasonable yardsticks, antisemitism, as it has been known in the United States, continues to decline almost inexorably. Surveys show increasing acceptance by Americans of Jews in the workplace and neighborhood, the university, the political arena, and the family. The penetration of Jews in these areas speaks for itself. Jews themselves overwhelmingly see a bright future for themselves in America. And yet 77% of Jews surveyed predict a rise in antisemitism. Commentators seem mostly agreed now that these views are not contradictory. While traditional antisemitism against Jews *qua* Jews has declined and will continue to decline, another kind of antisemitism does threaten to rise. This is based on exploitation by third world ideologues, communists, Arabs and intellectual sympathizers, of the theme of dual loyalty by American Jews. The same surveys which show a decline in antisem-

itic attitudes on the whole by Americans also show some increase in American concern for Jewish power and dual loyalty between the United States and Israel. There is certainly enough residual antisemitism of the older traditional kind for it to be exacerbated and made popular should the new kind of antisemitism succeed. The success or failure of this kind of antisemitism will turn on events between now and the year 2000 difficult to predict, including the American climate for pluralism and the promotion of group interest.

In sum, there are several potential scenarios for Jewish orientation and behavior in the year 2000 which will depend on:

—The American general drift—As in other areas, Jews, although they may differ from the American norm, will drift with the American norm wherever that norm goes, right or left.

—The degree of assimilation—Such an occurrence, in contrast to survivalism in the AJ community, will influence the degree of liberalism and the depth of specific Jewish concern.

—The perceived self-interest of American Jews—The various forms of antisemitism will influence AJ attitudes on a variety of issues.

—Events related to Israel—Liberalism's views on Israel, and the degree to which Israel remains at the center of the AJ civil religion, will influence political behavior.

Jewish ability to influence the political scene in America may be shrinking because of the geographical dispersion mentioned earlier and the shrinking percentage of the American electorate which the Jewish community comprises. Also troubling is some still sketchy evidence that Jews may be becoming like other Americans, ceasing to vote in disproportionate numbers. If this is confirmed as a trend it could be extremely serious and could pose an important agenda item for the AJ community. On the other hand, as has been mentioned earlier, along with the dispersion of the American Jewish community has come broader Jewish influence and political participation; Jewish interest in and penetration of political structures and the acceptance of Jews in the political arena has made it possible for Jewish talent to be exploited and to maximize its influence in the political arena, perhaps as never before. Thus, Jews may continue to have a fair share of influence on the American scene into the 21st century.

XII. Jewish Communal Organization

The Jewish community in the United States has been both envied and ridiculed for its supposed over-organization. Certainly the proverbial visitor from Mars would have a difficult time understanding the alphabet soup of Jewish organizations. Still, most of these perform important functions, and the whole configuration has contributed to the vitality of AJ life. Survey data suggest that the leaders of major organizations are largely in step, ideologically, with the Jewish "masses". The communal structure is as representative and democratic as one is likely to find in a voluntary system.

The level of Jewish charitable giving is most envied. Except for the Mormons, it exceeds by far the average charitable contribution of any other American subgroup or of Americans in general. The UJA/Federation system alone now raises over 3/4 of a billion dollars in annual campaigns, returning to small but steady annual increases after a plateau in the mid- and late 1970s. But to get a fuller picture of Jewish philanthropy, one must add to this the hundreds of millions of dollars contributed each year to one-time capital campaigns, synagogues, Jewish educational institutions, national and local agencies of the Jewish community, scores of Israeli institutions, hospitals, colleges and the like, as well as non-charitable contributions to the American political process based on Jewish interest. All of this happens even while Jews are increasingly overrepresented in the fund raising campaigns of America's universities, museums, health drives, other charitable institutions, and the American political process in general. *Tzedakah* is certainly entrenched as a part of contemporary Judaism, and giving, it has been pointed out, has become more than helping others. It has become a form of Jewish identity, a religious ritual in itself.

And yet there are concerns about the possible erosion of the philanthropic impulse. While Jewish philanthropy depends on a kind of voluntary progressive taxation, that is, it depends most heavily on large gifts, it must also be concerned with the numerical base of its campaign. The growth of direct mail campaigning, and the potential of two-way cable TV contributing indicate that they could become dominant fund raising forms in America, and in New York and other cities the number of contributors shrinks slowly but continually each year. Secondly, in spite of the upward trend of giving, it has not increased in real dollars over the last decade. The competition for Jewish philanthropic dollars has increased as antisemitic exclusion has decreased. Jews are now welcome and command great prestige from participating in the campaigns of universities and the arts. As Milton Goldin points out, there are no Jewish institutional equivalents to the giant gifts in recent years, such as the Annenberg $150 million gift to the Corporation for Public Broadcasting or the Linsky $40 million gift to the Metropolitan Museum of Art. The impulse to *tzedakah* may outlive the automatic translation of this impulse to Jewish causes in general and the UJA/Federation in particular. A post-Holocaust, post-establishment of the state of Israel generation may not contribute automatically to Israel, particularly in a non-crisis atmosphere. As will be suggested further on, how Jewish philanthropies respond to this reality will probably determine the level of Jewish support in the year 2000. Support there will be, and it will be substantial. The direction, growing or shrinking, is an open question.

Despite visionary efforts in the first decade of the 20th century, there is no serious belief that it is possible, even if it were desirable, to organize all of American Jewry under one organizational structure, umbrella, congress or council. At least since World War II, all concepts of the AJ community presumed some degree of pluralism. Within this pluralism, however, questions arise as to who is "more equal."

In the 1950s, there was a great growth of synagogues. Synagogues were the institution *par excellence* of the suburbanizing post-war Jewish community. Herberg, in *Protestant, Catholic, Jew,* saw the need for all Americans to identify under one of these religious umbrellas. Particularly the Conservative movement saw itself, in a variation of Mordecai Kaplan's vision, as a center for an entire gamut of activity of the Jewish community. This notion has changed. In an increasingly secular society, there is less of a demand for individuals to identify with a synagogue; the synagogue never achieved the totality of identification which was sought or imagined possible in the 1950s; an aging society has less demand for synagogue affiliation so long as affiliation came primarily for the Jewish education of children. Synagogues are also beset by financial problems, often with large underutilized plants and no longer ideal locations for a mobile Jewish population. Synagogues are now adjusting rapidly to new realities. They are learning to serve the new alternative family structures which are becoming more common. They are basing affiliation on the associational needs of adults as well as on the Jewish education of the young. Some have experimented successfully with dividing their membership into *havurot,* or small face-to-face associations, providing for a major expressed need for intimacy in the absence of extended family systems. In some way, synagogue affiliation in the year 2000 will be stronger because it will be based more on voluntary choice and identity than on being "the thing to do." But it is not likely that synagogues will be an all-inclusive, dominant or overriding force in the Jewish community in the year 2000.

Another particularly peculiar American institution has been the community center or YMHA. It has succeeded in capturing the loyalty of hundreds of thousands of American Jews with various degrees of intensity. It serves as one of the places within the Jewish community for inter-denominational (Orthodox-Conservative-Reform) Jewish association and interchange, and for some non-religious Jews, may even serve as a primary source of Jewish identity. Increasingly the centers are seen as having Jewish education and the building of Jewish identity as a primary function. However, the centers have never pretended to be nor are they likely to become a primary or dominant force in the organization of American Jewish life.

The early form of Jewish organization in America was the *landsmanschaft* and the "cousin's club." Besides personal services, these groups provided burial, credit unions, and similar social services. The integration and social mobility of American Jews and the coming of social insurance made these groups shrink in size and importance. But giant fraternal or other membership groups replaced them, such as B'nai B'rith and Hadassah. Whether fraternal or Zionist in purpose, large membership groups are aging, if not already shrinking in numbers. It is hard to imagine a scenario for the year 2000 in which they will significantly increase their numbers or influence. Women's organizations or "divisions" or "leagues" of general organizations have largely *not* disappeared in spite of the growing penetration of women into the activities and leadership of previously all male Jewish groups. Women's divisions are often maintained because they still raise significant funds. But with more women in the work force and the continued integration of women in the larger society, the importance of such groups is not likely to grow, and some may disappear altogether by the year 2000.

Major community relations or "defense" agencies continue to play an important role in AJ life. But whatever their origins, they no longer purport to speak for American Jewry. They speak for their constituents, and that is their strength. While Federations and other umbrella organizations deal with consensus, these organizations can be more specific in their ideologies, and show the way toward later consensus and provide outlets for parts of the Jewish community that have a certain orientation. If, as some have argued, there are too many groups in AJ life, certainly it will be impossible for any one of them, even by the year 2000, to deal with all the political and philosophical differences within the AJ consensus.

At least since the mid-1960s it has appeared that if any institution of AJ life were to be dominant, it would be the Federation system. Increasingly it is the collector and disburser of the largest amount of funds. It has attracted the "movers and shakers" of the AJ community. It sees itself as an instrument of the community, but this gives it entry into most of the concerns of the community. Increasingly, it has been turned to by those outside of the Jewish community. Its annual assemblies are the major gathering places of AJ power. At the same time, Federations have never been able, even to the extent that they might want to, to develop discipline within the community, on function or fund raising. Individual fund raising activities proliferate, even as the Federation system flowers. And one or another agency grouping outside of the system could become increasingly important. For instance, the importance and attraction of political work has made AIPAC, in spite of its lack of tax deductibility, a favorite agency for many Jewish philanthropists.

There are two possible scenarios for the year 2000:

A. The Federation system could become more dominant because its power feeds on itself and gives it the potential for continued growth. It has resources which give it the opportunity for new initiatives. There is also an impetus born of financial stringency in the welfare and non-profit fields for greater accountability, avoidance of waste and duplication. And this impetus feeds the Federation system. Finally, so long as there is consensus among American Jews on the major issues, there is great likelihood of leaning on a common institution. All of these factors suggest a stronger federation system in the year 2000.

B. The Jewish community could be torn by specific issues which would strengthen disparate approaches and weaken the Federation—issues such as priorities in funding and developments in Israel. Further, because Federation financial strength has not been growing rapidly enough to keep up with the financial needs of local and national agencies, they may become more independent of the Federation as they become more dependent on their own financial efforts and public funds. Personal needs toward independence and self-determination by lay and professional leaders may also prove very powerful goads to independent community development. There are, after all, no sanctions in voluntary systems, and this is very different from the government within a government which the Jewish communities formed in other times and places.

It is most likely that the scenario which evolves will hinge on whether the large Federation system, sometimes impersonal, can continue to command the personal sense of involvement with a philanthropic product which is smaller and more specific. "Israel" is no longer an automatic stimulus to contributing. Federations will need to create ways (such as they have begun to do with Project Renewal) for contributors to have more access to the governance and therefore the results of philanthropy. If the large system can make this transition, it may continue to grow into the 21st century. Otherwise, the independent and more specialized agencies will probably grow increasingly important.

In any event, Federations will be important into the 21st century, and will evolve in three directions by the year 2000:

A. Federations will continue the trend (which has been evident at least since the mid-60s), toward shifting their resources away from social services to troubled and at-risk populations, and towards community-building activities. The former has increasingly become the public sector's responsibilities, even when money is conduited through private and Jewish agencies. And survivalist concerns mean that a greater percentage of Federation resources will go to Jewish education, culture, informal education, campus services, and other activities designed to maintain the future of the Jewish community. Reagan budget cuts have deflected Federations temporarily to a revived interest in social services, but the long-term trend will continue. Questions of war and peace will determine the proportion of Federation funds going to Israel and spent in the U.S.

B. In some way, shape or form, Federations will evolve, as they have already begun to do, toward synagogues. Circuitous methods may be used. In some cities, Federations now have special funds for particular projects of synagogues. Federations may rent space in synagogue buildings for outstationing various agency services. Certainly Federations will increasingly fund Jewish education, either relieving synagogues of the burden through communal sponsorship, or funding synagogues for that purpose, or a combination of both.

C. There will be increasing development of regional and national systems for the solicitation and rating of potential givers and meeting of domestic needs in a mobile society. The Federations are coming to realize that they cannot afford to operate on a city-by-city basis without articulation among them.

American Jewry will continue to support a variety of organizational forms well into the 21st century.

XIII. General Theories About the Trends

Several theories or themes emerge as the interpretation of all of the above in terms of the future of the AJ community:

A. As America Goes

It is apparent, as was stated earlier, that the future AJ community will be shaped in large measure by the American future. The argument can be made that American trends will not only influence but will determine Jewish trends. For instance, during the post-World War II baby boom, Jewish fertility rates almost caught up, briefly, with the American rate. Jews may be *over*-susceptible to American fashion. Not only in demographics may this be true—fertility, divorce, etc.—but in politics, importance of religion, even attitudes toward Israel. The open questions are the size of a window through which Jews may move despite national trends, and the degree to which the intellectually important AJ community may be able to influence those larger American trends, despite the small size of American Jewry.

B. Limited Options

A variant on the above theme has been sounded by Charles Silberman and others. The case is made for limited ability of American Jews to influence the quantitative trends. Therefore, a counter-emphasis is suggested on improving the quality of Jewish life of those who choose to remain identified. This limits the options and pinpoints the strategies.

C. Bi-Polarity

As has been illustrated earlier, one can interpret much of the data as demonstrating that the AJ community is in the process of separating into two distinct groups. One group, the smaller, will be more Jewishly educated, more identified, more involved in Jewish matters. The other group, the larger, will be largely uneducated Jewishly, less involved, and less identified and dependent upon their stores of Jewish "capital" for their survival as Jews. They will be vulnerable to being lost from the Jewish people, but still Jewish enough to have their attention captured in a crisis, and to be worked on towards winning over their sons and daughters to the other group.

D. Jewish Disaster

There are those who see in the demographic and Jewish education trends an onrushing Jewish disaster. The 21st century will see the elimination of American Judaism as a significant number or force, and the survival of only very few thousands who do not disappear as Jews or make *aliyah* to Israel. We will editorialize at least to the extent of saying that the facts do not appear to support such a scenario.

E. Ebb and Flow

Ebb and flow may be more characteristic of Jewish life than triumphalism or extinction. It is argued that Jews are indeed in the process of shrinking numerically and culturally. But as the group shrinks to a smaller but still sizable core, it is a naturally more committed core which will proceed with the process of growth. Thus, Jewish losses are a kind of natural selection, weeding out and ultimately strengthening the species. This point of view would be more persuasive if Jews were not numerically such a small, endangered species on the planet.

F. Consensus

A different view focuses on the earlier defined American civil Judaism and other areas where a strong majority consensus appears. Without denying the possibility of some numerical shrinkage, this view concentrates on the stronger center which appears capable of evolving for future strength and maintaining an American Jewish community of vigor into the next century.

G. Israel as the Key

It is also possible to review the data and to see all the interplay between AJ and Israeli society as providing the key to the AJ future. Will Jews continue to be liberal? This may depend on whether the liberal establishment becomes identified as the anti-Israel camp. Will antisemitism be a factor in American society? This may depend on political developments in the world regarding Israel as we see the emergence of the new kind of antisemitism. Will AJ philanthropy remain a vital segment of American Jewish communal organizations? This may depend on the relationship and closeness between American Jews and Israel and the continued dependence or independence of Israel on help from outside. Will an American expression of Judaism, culturally and religiously, continue to emerge and be strong? This may depend in part on the dialogue between the AJ community and Israel. American Jews could be separated from a more independent Israel which writes off the Diaspora, a largely Sephardic Israel which does not see itself as connected with American Judaism. American Jews might water down their own vision of Israel's centrality as part of their assimilation. Or these same factors could speed the development of a strong independent culture and religion of American Jewry. At least in some significant ways, the future of the AJ community in the 21st century will be shaped by the future of American Jewish-Israeli relations.

● ● ●

It should be noted that all of the above views are not totally contradictory or mutually exclusive. They are rather questions of emphasis for building strategies. For example, the consensus school may agree that there is some bi-polarity. But this school would suggest that the non-identified part of the bi-polar division is a group that falls off the edge, and the other group is large enough to form a basic consensus. Similarly, almost everyone foresees some numerical shrinkage into the first decades of the 21st century.

On one point, almost all agree. The United States is proving a unique crucible for the confrontation of Jewish identity and modernity. The AJ community has been allowed, and is eager and able, to enter into the American mainstream as has no relatively small Jewish community in a host country before. AJ leaders and organizations have been similarly allowed and eager to maintain Jewish identity as they enter the American mainstream. The ability to do so is the great Jewish adventure of the Diaspora. As Gershon Cohen has written, "The great ages of Jewish creativity have always been the product of the challenge of assimilation and the response of leaders who were to a certain extent assimilated themselves."

Estimated Jewish Population in 172 Cities, Towns, Suburbs and Metropolitan Areas in the United States and Canada

New York, N.Y.	1,734,500	
Los Angeles, Calif.	500,870	
Philadelphia, Pa.	295,000	
Miami, Fla.	253,340	
Chicago, Ill.	248,000	
Boston, Mass.	170,000	
Washington, D.C.	157,335	
Toronto, Ont.	115,000	
Metropolitan New Jersey	111,000	
Baltimore, Md.	92,000	
Montreal, Quebec	90,000	
San Francisco, Calif.	80,000	
Cleveland, Ohio	70,000	
Detroit, Michigan	70,000	
Bergen County, N.J.	69,300	
South Broward, Fla.	60,000	
Orange County, Calif.	60,000	
St. Louis, Mo.	53,500	
Fort Lauderdale, Fla.	50,000	
Pittsburgh, Pa.	45,000	
Palm Beach County, Fla.	45,000	
Boca Raton, Fla.	40,000	
Phoenix, Ariz.	35,000	
Oakland, Calif.	35,000	
San Diego, Calif.	34,000	
Monmouth County, N.J.	33,600	
Atlanta, Ga.	33,500	
North Jersey, N.J.	32,500	
Central New Jersey	32,000	
Denver, Colo.	30,000	
Southern New Jersey	28,000	
Houston, Texas	28,000	
Hartford, Ct.	26,000	
Milwaukee, Wis.	23,900	
Delaware Valley, Pa.	23,000	
Minneapolis, Minn.	22,000	
Rhode Island	22,000	
Cincinnati, Ohio	22,000	
Dallas, Texas	22,000	
New Haven, Ct.	22,000	
Northern Middlesex, N.J.	19,750	
Raritan Valley, N.J.	19,600	
Rochester, N.Y.	19,600	
Seattle, Wash.	19,500	
Kansas City, Mo.	19,000	
North Shore, Mass.	19,000	
Winnipeg, Manitoba	18,500	
Buffalo, N.Y.	18,500	
San Jose, Calif.	18,000	
Bridgeport, Ct.	18,000	
Tucson, Ariz.	18,000	
Las Vegas, Nevada	17,000	
Morris-Sussex Counties, N.J.	16,000	
Orlando, Fla.	15,000	
South County, Fla.	15,000	
Columbus, Ohio	15,000	
Long Beach, Calif.	13,500	
Tidewater, Va.	12,100	
Albany, N.Y.	12,000	
Atlantic County, N.J.	12,000	

Stamford, Ct.	12,000	
New Orleans, La.	12,000	
Springfield, Mass.	11,000	
Tampa, Fla.	10,500	
Indianapolis, Ind.	10,000	
Worcester, Mass.	10,000	
Framingham, Mass.	10,000	
Delaware	9,500	
Ottawa, Ontario	9,500	
Pinellas County, Fla.	9,500	
Englewood, N.J.	9,300	
Louisville, Ky.	9,200	
Memphis, Tenn.	9,000	
Syracuse, N.Y.	9,000	
San Antonio, Texas	9,000	
Portland, Ore.	8,845	
Ocean County, N.J.	8,100	
Richmond, Va.	8,000	
Clifton, Passaic, N.J.	7,700	
St. Paul, Minn.	7,500	
Sarasota, Fla.	7,500	
Sacramento, Calif.	7,000	
Orange County, N.Y.	7,000	
Jacksonville, Fla.	6,800	
Omaha, Neb.	6,500	
Harrisburg, Pa.	6,500	
Toledo, Ohio	6,300	
Akron, Ohio	6,000	
Dayton, Ohio	6,000	
Portland, Me.	5,550	
Schenectady, N.Y.	5,400	
Youngstown, Ohio	5,230	
Nashville, Tenn.	5,080	
Allentown, Pa.	4,980	
Palm Springs, Calif.	4,950	
Albuquerque, N.M.	4,500	
Calgary, Alberta	4,500	
Madison, Wis.	4,500	
Birmingham, Ala.	4,500	
El Paso, Texas	4,500	
Somerset County, N.J.	4,100	
Northwest Indiana	4,000	
Norwalk, Ct.	4,000	
Wilkes-Barre, Pa.	4,000	
Charlotte, N.C.	4,000	
Greenwich, Ct.	4,000	
Hamilton, Ont.	3,750	
Edmonton, Alberta	3,600	
Ft. Worth, Texas	3,600	
Austin, Texas	3,600	
Berkshire County, Mass.	3,500	
Danbury, Ct.	3,500	
Charleston, S.C.	3,500	
Des Moines, Iowa	3,500	
Eastern Connecticut	3,500	
Jersey City, N.J.	3,500	
Scranton, Pa.	3,400	
Broome County, N.Y.	3,000	
Greensboro, N.C.	3,000	
Kingston, N.Y.	3,000	

Manchester, N.H.	3,000	
Tulsa, Okla.	2,900	
Canton, Ohio	2,850	
Waterbury, Ct.	2,800	
Reading, Pa.	2,800	
Cumberland County, N.J.	2,750	
New Bedford, Mass.	2,700	
Savannah, Ga.	2,600	
Newport News, Va.	2,575	
Ft. Myers, Fla.	2,500	
London, Ontario	2,500	
Salt Lake City, Utah	2,500	
Oklahoma City, Okla.	2,400	
Durham-Chapel Hill, N.C.	2,400	
Columbia, S.C.	2,280	
Flint, Mich.	2,200	
Utica, N.Y.	2,100	
Champaign-Urbana, Ill.	2,000	
Lexington, Ky.	2,000	
Chattanooga, Tenn.	2,000	
Fresno, Calif.	2,000	
Daytona Beach, Fla.	2,000	
Windsor, Ontario	2,000	
Peoria, Ill.	1,900	
South Bend, Ind.	1,900	
Lansing, Mich.	1,850	
Quad Cities, Ill.	1,800	
Lancaster, Pa.	1,800	
Montgomery, Ala.	1,800	
Haverhill, Mass.	1,650	
Little Rock, Ark.	1,600	
Augusta, Ga.	1,500	
Grand Rapids, Mich.	1,500	
Knoxville, Tenn.	1,350	
Mobile, Ala.	1,250	
Shreveport, La.	1,200	
Baton Rouge, La.	1,200	
Corpus Christi, Texas	1,200	
Southern Illinois	1,200	
Troy, N.Y.	1,200	
Ft. Wayne, Ind.	1,200	
Evansville, Ind.	1,200	
Steubenville, Ohio	1,200	
Springfield, Ill.	1,100	
Elmira, N.Y.	1,100	
Duluth, Mn.	1,100	
Charleston, W. Va.	1,075	
Roanoke, Va.	1,050	
Lewiston-Auburn, Me.	1,000	
Asheville, N.C.	1,000	
Columbus, Ga.	1,000	
Wichita, Ks.	1,000	

TOTAL UNITED STATES	5,920,890
TOTAL CANADA	305,000

World Jewish Population

1. United States 5,920,890	31. Ethiopia 8,000	61. Singapore 450
2. Israel 3,436,100	32. Denmark 7,500	62. Egypt 400
3. Soviet Union 2,630,000	33. Bulgaria 7,000	63. Japan 400
4. France 650,000	34. Tunisia 7,000	64. Lebanon 400
5. United Kingdom 410,000	35. Greece 6,000	65. Zambia 400
6. Canada 305,000	36. Poland 6,000	66. El Salvador 350
7. Argentina 300,000	37. Yugoslavia 5,500	67. Jamaica 350
8. Brazil 150,000	38. Peru 5,200	68. Albania 300
9. South Africa 118,000	39. New Zealand 5,000	69. Trinidad & Tobago 300
10. Hungary 80,000	40. Syria 4,500	70. Hong Kong 250
11. Iran 70,000	41. Costa Rica 2,500	71. Pakistan 250
12. Australia 67,000	42. Guatemala 2,000	72. Afghanistan 250
13. Uruguay 50,000	43. Panama 2,000	73. Dominican Republic 200
14. Rumania 45,000	44. Zimbabwe 1,960	74. Honduras 200
15. Belgium 41,000	45. Ireland 1,900	75. Nicaragua 200
16. Italy 41,000	46. Cuba 1,500	76. Philippines 200
17. Germany 38,000	47. Paraguay 1,200	77. Zaire 200
18. Mexico 37,500	48. Algeria 1,000	78. Haiti 150
19. Chile 30,000	49. Ecuador 1,000	79. Indonesia 100
20. Netherlands 30,000	50. Finland 1,000	80. Barbados 70
21. Turkey 24,000	51. Luxembourg 1,000	81. Burma 50
22. Morocco 22,000	52. Norway 900	82. Malta 50
23. Switzerland 21,000	53. Bolivia 750	83. China 30
24. Sweden 17,000	54. Curacao 700	84. Cyprus 30
25. Venezuela 15,000	55. Gibraltar 600	85. Libya 20
26. Austria 13,000	56. Portugal 600	Europe 4,102,350
27. Colombia 12,000	57. Surinam 500	Americas 6,839,560
28. Czechoslovakia 12,000	58. Yemen Arab Republic 500	Asia 3,353,810
29. Spain 12,000	59. Iraq 450	Africa 159,340
30. India 8,000	60. Kenya 450	Oceania 72,000

Source: Jewish Information Center, New York, *World Zionist Handbook;* Facts on File.

WORLDWIDE 14,527,150

PART TWO

ANNUAL REVIEW

Highlights of the Year 5745

Jewish Telegraphic Agency

Noah M. Bee,
JTA political cartoonist

THE MIDDLE EAST

September 1984

A flurry of diplomatic activity over south Lebanon suddenly raised hopes that Israel soon may be in a position to pull its forces out. Prime Minister Shimon Peres publicly predicted that the Israel Defense Force will leave Lebanon during the new Hebrew calendar year, 5745.

The new government also seems to have modified the position long held by its predecessor that any pullback of Israeli troops must be accompanied by the simultaneous withdrawal of Syrian forces from Lebanon.

Declaring that the road to peace in the Middle East is "long and hard," President Reagan told the United Nations General Assembly that he is as committed today to his September 1, 1982 peace initiative as he was on the day he issued it.

THE DIGGER AND THE MOURNER

HERE RESTS LEBANON A VICTIM OF TERROR AND DOUBLE-CROSS

DEMOCRACY

"That initiative remains a realistic and workable approach, and I am committed to it as firmly as on the day I announced it," the President declared. He said that the foundation of this plan remains Security Council Resolution 242.

Foreign Minister Abdel Meguid of Egypt told Deputy Prime Minister and Foreign Minister Yitzhak Shamir of Israel that Egypt is interested in improving its relations with Israel. But he made it clear that Israel's continued presence in Lebanon is an obstacle in that direction.

October

A resolution urging the United States to move its Embassy in Israel from Tel Aviv to Jerusalem was approved by voice votes in both the Europe and Middle East and International Operations subcommittees of the House Foreign Affairs Committee.

Opposition to the resolution was expressed only by Reps. George Crockett (D. Mich.), Larry Winn (R. Kan.) and Ed Zschau (R. Calif.). The resolution is a sense of the Senate resolution and does not require the President's signature. President Reagan has opposed moving the Embassy at this time.

The House approved the establishment of a free trade area with Israel by a 416-6 vote. The Senate adopted a similar bill by a 96-0 vote the prior week. Differences between the two bills will be ironed out by a conference committee but the final legislation is expected to be adopted by Congress before it adjourns.

The only concern about the Free Trade Act which was sought by the Reagan Administration, came from some of the areas whose products could be hurt by Israeli competition.

U.S. Trade Representative William Brock has given written assurances that "the import sensitivity of textile apparel, leather goods and footwear, will be taken into account in negotiating with Israel."

Brock, who will be negotiating the FTA with Israel, also said, "the elimination of Israel's export subsidies in these areas will serve as a precondition for U.S. agreement to this free trade zone."

President Reagan, stressing the United States commitment to help in "revitalizing the Israeli economy and putting it on the road to sustained recovery," announced that he and Shimon Peres have agreed to the establishment of a joint economic development group to cooperate toward achieving this goal.

"We have agreed to explore with Israel ways to enhance its growth and development prospects through structural adjustment, increased trade and investment, as well as American aid," Reagan said in a farewell statement in the White House Rose Garden after a two-hour meeting with Peres and Foreign Minister Yitzhak Shamir.

Reagan said that he and Peres have also instructed their negotiators on the Free Trade Area (FTA) between the two countries to reach an agreement within 30 days. The President said this agreement, which he noted was the first FTA between the United States and another country, by expanding Israel's export market will be important in helping Israel on the way to economic recovery and it will also be a boost for the United States. Peres stressed that the new unity government he heads is "determined to tackle our economic difficulties head on." He added that the "support of the President, the United States government and the American people is source of strength and inspiration to all of us."

The Israeli Prime Minister, who met with Reagan previously as the leader of the Israeli opposition, said that his latest meetings in Washington have left him with the belief that "relations between the United States and Israel have reached a new level of harmony and understanding.

The 39th session of the General Assembly overwhelmingly rejected an Iranian proposal to expel Israel from the world body. The vote was 80-41 with 22 abstentions.

This was the third consecutive year that Iran attempted—and failed—to have Israel suspended from the General Assembly by introducing an amendment to reject its credentials. Israel's credentials came up for approval before the 39th session of the General Assembly along with the credentials of 126 other countries.

The Iranian motion was defeated after Denmark introduced a countermotion not to deal with it. The same procedural maneuver was responsible for the defeat of a similar Iranian motion last year. It was undertaken then by Norway. The vote at that time was 79-43 in favor of the Norwegian move with 19 abstentions.

November

A prominent Spanish Socialist politician, Enrique Mujica-Herzog, is preparing himself for the task of becoming his country's first Ambassador to Israel, according to well-informed sources in Madrid. The sources said that Spain is taking seriously warnings by West European nations that failure to establish diplomatic relations with Israel could add to Spain's difficulties in joining the European Economic Community (EEC) at the beginning of 1985.

Israeli and Lebanese military delegations met at the Lebanese border village of Nakura to begin negotiations aimed at the withdrawal of the Israeli Defense Force from south Lebanon.

The talks are held at the headquarters of the United Nations Interim Force in Lebanon (UNIFIL) and are officially under UN auspices. UNIFIL commander, Gen. William Callaghan of Ireland, is attending, but the Israelis and Lebanese disagree sharply on the nature of the UN role.

The Reagan Administration announced that the U.S. and Iraq were resuming diplomatic relations and at the same time stressed that the move will not be harmful to Israel.

"It has no effect on our relations with Israel which continue to be stronger than ever," a senior Administration official said in briefing reporters on the move which took place immediately. The official pointed out that Iraq no longer considers itself a "front line state" in the Arab-Israeli conflict.

December

Israeli officials expressed shock, anger and disappointment over the joint communique issued by Egyptian President Hosni Mubarak and King Hussein of Jordan endorsing the Palestine Liberation Organization as a full partner in negotiations to resolve the Arab-Israeli conflict. There was no official reaction.

The communique, issued simultaneously in Cairo and Amman, followed three days of talks between Mubarak and Hussein in the Egyptian capital, their first summit meeting since Jordan, two months earlier, resumed diplomatic relations with Egypt which it broke in 1979 in protest against the Egyptian-Israeli peace treaty.

Israeli Prime Minister Shimon Peres, returning from Paris, said his three-day visit to France had strengthened Israel's international position as well as Franco-Israeli relations.

Peres said that in his talks with President Francois Mitterand, he raised the issue of Syrian Jewry and there was a possibility that Syria may now allow a limited number of exit visas for Jews. He did not make clear whether he learned this from the French President, who met with President Hafez Assad of Syria in Damascus only a week before Peres arrived in Paris.

Nigeria is prepared to restore diplomatic relations with Israel following Israeli withdrawal "from all occupied Arab territories" and its breaking of links with South Africa, the World Jewish Congress reported.

A United Nations seminar on religious tolerance was used as the platform for an unprecedented attack on Jews and Judaism by the Saudi Arabian delegate who said at one point that Hitler must have had good reasons to want to exterminate the Jews.

The 40-minute diatribe by Dr. Maaruf Al-Mawalibi was allowed to continue uninterrupted. The President of the Seminar, Adam Lopatka of Poland, did not react to it and refused a request by the Israeli delegate, Hebrew University Prof. Eliezer Ravitzki, that the seminar dissociate itself from the attack.

Apart from Israel, only the United States and Costa Rica, among the 26 nations participating, spoke out against the Saudi's remarks. But many of the delegates privately expressed shock after the session.

January 1985

The Israel Defense Force began the first stage of its evacuation of south Lebanon—a pullback from the coastal town of Sidon and its environs to a new line along the Litani River.

A fleet of heavy army trucks arrived in Sidon to begin loading military materiel and equipment, some of which will be offloaded at the Litani line and the rest brought back to Israel. A senior officer said that the equipment move would not affect the operational capabilities of IDF units but the soldiers might experience some discomfort because of the removal of heating appliances and other amenities.

Israeli Defense Minister Yitzhak Rabin indicated that the Reagan Administration has agreed to provide Israel with $1.8 billion in military aid for the 1986 fiscal year, a $400 million increase over this year, but had made no decision on economic aid.

Emerging from a 30-minute meeting with President Reagan at the White House, Rabin would not say directly if the President had approved this figure. But he said while the increase "was not exactly what we wanted," the total

HUSSEIN THE SWINGER

amount will be about $1.8 billion. Israel had asked for $2.1 billion in military aid. The White House confirmed the $1.8 billion sum.

February

The escalation of terrorist activity in the West Bank, including the murder of an Israeli reserve soldier in Ramallah, has sharpened the confrontation between militant Jewish settlers and their Knesset allies and the Labor-Likud unity government.

A no-confidence motion introduced by the ultra-nationalist Tehiya Party, accusing the government of softness and complacency in dealing with terrorists, was easily defeated in the Knesset. But Defense Minister Yitzhak Rabin, speaking for the government, was forced to concede that a serious situation existed in the territory.

On February 16 the Israel Defense Force completed the first stage of its withdrawal from south Lebanon. It is deployed on a line along the Litani River, just north of Tyre and a kilometer or so from the Mediterranean coast, stretching northeast to Jezzine and then turning south toward the southernmost boundary of the Bekaa valley.

The United States and the Soviet Union ended two days of talks on the Middle East in Vienna with no comment from either side.

The talks, which the U.S. repeatedly stressed were an exchange of views and not any form of negotiations, were conducted by delegations headed by Richard Murphy, Assistant Secretary of State for Near Eastern and South Asian Affairs, and Vladimir Polyakov, head of the Soviet Union's Near East Division and the Kremlin's expert on the Mideast. A State Department official, briefing reporters here before the talks began, said that the United States had

HERE HE GOES AGAIN !

ETC

DEFEAT IN LEBANON...

NOWHERE TO GO...

SPLIT WITH SYRIA...

THE BEAR HUG

AMMAN PLO

DAMASCUS PLO

assured Israel and the Arab countries that the U.S. and the Soviet Union were not coming together "to impose a U.S.-Soviet plan on the area." The U.S. remains committed to direct negotiations between Israel and the Arab countries, the official said.

Ambassador Meir Rosenne raised Israel's concerns about the Vienna meeting when he met with Murphy. An Israel Embassy spokesman would not comment on whether Rosenne had felt reassured by Murphy's explanation of the U.S. approach toward the meeting.

This should be viewed in the "context of the management of U.S.-Soviet relations rather than in the context of the Middle East," the State Department official said. He said its purpose is "to help avoid miscalculations and to reduce the potential risk of U.S.-Soviet confrontation.

Prime Minister Peres had a 40-minute meeting with Pope John Paul II at the Vatican. A Vatican spokesman said afterwards that they discussed the Middle East, Jewish-Christian relations and Jerusalem among other topics but the main differences between Israel and the Vatican were not resolved.

Peres told reporters after the meeting that he did not ask the Pontiff for Vatican diplomatic relations with Israel, that he had made it clear that Jerusalem will always be the political capital of Israel with full respect for the religious rights of all faiths and that Israel remains hopeful but cautious with respect to recent Middle East peace moves.

March

Intensive, high level contacts between Israel and Egypt resumed in Jerusalem and Cairo. Prime Minister Shimon Peres and three senior Cabinet ministers met for five hours with an unidentified Egyptian emissary of President Hosni Mubarak. Gen. Avraham Tamir, Director General of the

Prime Minister's Office, was scheduled to leave for Cairo.

In the Egyptian capital, Mubarak received visiting Israeli Energy Minister Moshe Shahal. The latter told Voice of Israel Radio later that the meeting was good and useful but divulged no details.

The Israeli Defense Force adopted an "iron fist" policy in south Lebanon. It is striking back hard and taking pre-emptive and preventive measures against Shiite guerrillas and Palestinian terrorists who have been harassing Israeli forces while they are engaged in their phased withdrawal from Lebanon, and the Israel-backed South Lebanon Army (SLA).

The get-tough tactics were ordered after the IDF sustained serious casualties, including four fatalities among senior and non-commissioned officers, within the first 48 hours of the completion of the first stage of the three-stage withdrawal process on February 16.

The new hard-line policy has yielded results. Defense Minister Yitzhak Rabin told the Knesset Tuesday that no IDF casualties had been reported since it was introduced. He reported further that 15 guerrillas had been killed, 22 wounded and 19 expelled from the areas of south Lebanon still held by the IDF.

Egyptian President Hosni Mubarak concluded three days of talks in Washington, including a White House meeting with President Reagan, apparently unable to gain a commitment from the United States to revive its active involvement in the Middle East peace process.

Mubarak suggested during the course of his meetings and discussions here that the U.S. should seize what he described as a "golden opportunity" presented by the agreement reached last month between Jordan and the Palestine Liberation Organization.

The agreement, concluded in Amman between PLO chief Yasir Arafat and King Hussein on the formation of a joint PLO-Jordanian delegation to negotiate a Middle East settlement, accepts "United Nations Security Council Resolutions" but does not explicitly state Resolutions 242 and 338. The U.S. has refused to recognize the PLO until it accepts those resolutions and specifically recognizes Israel's right to exist. Mubarak has proposed that the U.S. meet with a joint delegation of Jordanian and Palestinian representatives as part of an initial step toward direct negotiations with Israel. But in issuing his appeal, he left himself open to more questions than answers from President Reagan.

The deaths of two CBS television news cameramen in south Lebanon on March 21 brought Israel into sharp conflict with the giant American network.

CBS officials in New York were quick to condemn the Israel Defense Force. They charged on the basis of early eye-witness accounts—later shown to be questionable— that an IDF tank had deliberately fired on the cameramen during a skirmish with Shiite terrorists in Milki village, about 13 kilometers southwest of Tyre. According to the CBS executives, the killing was a manifestation of IDF hostility toward foreign news media.

CBS promptly canceled a series of Passover-Easter week broadcasts which were to have originated in Israel in April. They said this was not to punish Israel but was a gesture of mourning for the slain cameramen, both Lebanese nationals in CBS's employ.

Israeli President Chaim Herzog accused the network of attacking Israel while remaining silent when the same terrorists Israel was fighting killed Americans. He demanded to know why CBS never protested or halted its broadcasts from Lebanon after 250 U.S. marines were killed in a car-bomb attack in west Beirut in 1983 by the same terrorists now harassing the IDF as it is in the process of withdrawing from south Lebanon.

Herzog noted that any journalist who enters a combat zone knows his life is in danger. The two CBS cameramen were killed and a third was wounded by rocket fire from an Israeli tank directed at armed Shiites in the village. Lebanese and foreign media accounts claimed initially that the tank had fired at point-blank range. CBS demanded that Israel establish a commission of inquiry to investigate the incident. This was flatly rejected by Prime Minister Shimon Peres.

April

Hundreds of Arabs detained in the Ansar camp in south Lebanon were released and 1,100 other detainees were transferred to a new camp inside Israel. Most of the 752 persons released are Shiite Moslems who were members of organizations regarded as "hostile" but who had not taken an active part in activities against Israel. The decision to release them is regarded as a goodwill gesture to defuse the explosive situation in the region. The last 752 inmates had hardly left when a fleet of Israel Defense Force bulldozers moved in to level the large tented and hutted area.

The Israel Defense Force withdrew from Nabatiya, a regional military and administrative center in south Lebanon, long a hotbed of Shiite terrorist activities.

Two Israeli soldiers were killed by a teen-age suicide bomber who blew up her car when it drew abreast of their jeep at a road intersection in south Lebanon. Two other soldiers were wounded and a local civilian was killed by the blast.

The suicide bomber was identified as Sana Mohaydaleh, a 16-year-old Shiite from the Zaharani region of south Lebanon. Only recently she appeared on a Beirut television program to declare her desire to become a "martyr" and enter heaven by killing "the highest number possible of our enemies." The Lebanese National Resistance Front claimed responsibility for Mohaydaleh's suicide mission.

Secretary of State George Shultz stressed his commitment to Israel and urged Arab governments to agree to direct negotiations with the Jewish State.

"Those who take risks for peace should know that the United States will help them defend themselves," he told some 1,200 persons attending the opening session of the 26th annual policy conference of the American Israel Public Affairs Committee (AIPAC) at the Hyatt Regency Crystal City Hotel in Arlington, Virginia.

May

Prime Minister Shimon Peres told the Cabinet there was "broad agreement" between Israel and the United States on reviving the Middle East peace process and that Secretary of State George Shultz recognized Israel's position that it is now up to the Arabs to decide on the future of the process.

Shultz and the Israelis are in agreement that the Arabs must put together a joint Jordanian-Palestinian delegation before any new round of negotiations can begin. Peres told

the Cabinet that no list of delegates had been presented to him by Shultz.

The first round of high level talks between Israel and Egypt ended in Cairo with progress reported on some bilateral issues but none in the dispute over Taba, the strip of beach on the Gulf of Aqaba claimed by both Israel and Egypt.

Demands for an official inquiry into the Lebanon war mounted following U.S. Ambassador Samuel Lewis' assertion that Ariel Sharon disclosed plans for the Israel Defense Force to invade Labanon to special U.S. Middle East envoy Philip Habib on December 4, 1981 when Sharon was Defense Minister. The invasion occurred six months later, at the beginning of June 1982.

June

The Reagan Administration's ripple of interest in reviving the Middle East peace process through negotiations involving a joint Jordanian-Palestinian delegation created waves in Israel.

The Administration, in a letter Secretary of State George Shultz sent to Prime Minister Shimon Peres and Deputy Prime Minister and Foreign Minister Yitzhak Shamir, lauded King Hussein of Jordan for his ostensible willingness to negotiate directly with Israel.

Hussein continued to press for U.S. recognition of the Palestine Liberation Organization and its inclusion in the peace process. He also insisted that negotiations between Israel and a joint Jordanian-Palestinian team be held under the auspices of an international conference whose participants would include the five permanent members of the United Nations Security Council.

Prime Minister Shimon Peres outlined in the Knesset a carefully drawn peace plan, proposing a multi-step procedure, and designed to make the United States ease its pressure for Israel to look favorably on Jordanian King Hussein's approach, while warding off Knesset critics.

The plan called for direct talks between Israel and its neighbors, without preconditions but opposing any negotiations with the Palestine Liberation Organization. The first stage would be talks between the United States, Israel, Jordan, Egypt and Palestinian delegates who are not PLO members.

A series of economic liberalization measures in the West Bank will be capped by the establishment of the first Arab bank in the territory, according to the head of the civil administration, Col. Freddie Zachs.

He said the government and the Bank of Israel gave final approval to the project initiated by a prominent Nablus businessman, Zafer Al-Masri. It is aimed at improving the quality of life in the administered territories where the vast majority of the inhabitants are Palestinians. Until now, only Israeli banks were allowed to operate, with the exception of a minor bank, Falastin, in the Gaza Strip.

Zachs said the only remaining obstacle is posed by the Jordanian authorities. The Arab bank will of necessity have strong ties with Jordan because the principal currency used in the West Bank is the Jordanian Dinar. But Amman objects to Israel's insistence that it must operate under the supervision of the Bank of Israel, the country's central bank, which supervises all financial institutions.

The Israel-backed South Lebanon Army (SLA) released 21 Finnish soldiers of the United Nations Interim Force in Lebanon after holding them prisoner for eight days. But UNIFIL sources complained that the SLA continues to harass its troops. The most recent reported incident involved Norwegian UNIFIL soldiers in Ibel Saki village.

Israel released 300 Shiite Moslems from the Atlit detention camp and insisted—as it had repeatedly over the prior two weeks—that there was no linkage to the release of 39 Americans held hostage for 17 days by Shiites in Beirut.

Defense Minister Yitzhak Rabin said the release of the 300 was planned long before Lebanese Shiite extremists hijacked TWA Flight 847 on June 14 and took 39 of its passengers and officers hostage. He said they would have been freed much sooner were it not for the hijacking and an earlier incident in the south Lebanon security zone involving the Israel-backed South Lebanon Army (SLA) and Finnish soldiers of the United Nations Interim Force in Lebanon (UNIFIL).

Israeli officials took two steps clearly aimed at improving relations with the Soviet Union and eastern bloc countries, none of which, with the exception of Rumania, have diplomatic relations with Israel.

Foreign Minister Yitzhak Shamir sent a cable to Eduard Shevardnadze, congratulating him on his appointment as Soviet Foreign Minister. President Chaim Herzog sent a "warm message" to Andrei Gromyko, who has been promoted to be President of the Soviet Union, after setting a record of nearly three decades as Soviet Foreign Minister.

Yediot Achronot reported that contacts between Israeli and East European diplomats have intensified recently, with the latter indicating a possible improvement in Soviet-Israeli relations.

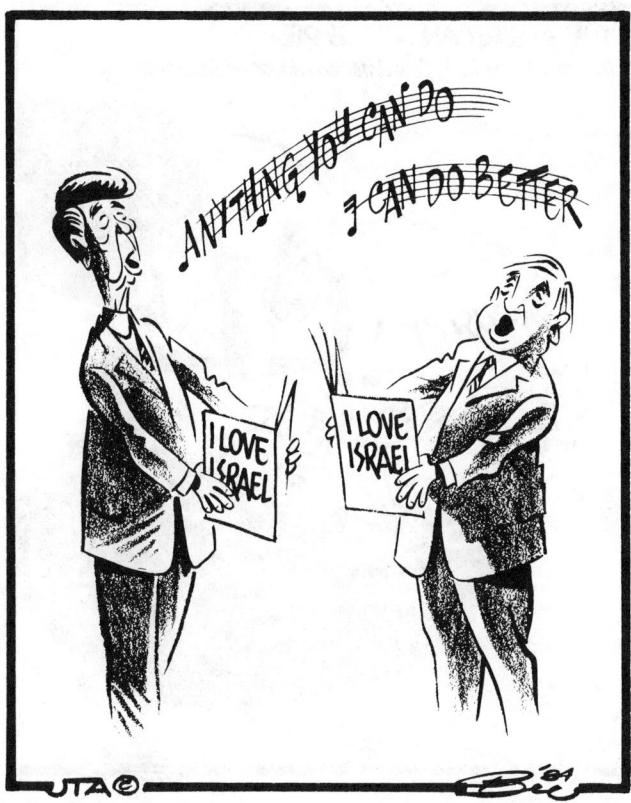

THE AMERICAN SCENE

October 1984

President Reagan brought his re-election campaign to a synagogue in North Woodmere, Long Island, where he donned a *yarmulka* emblazoned with the White House Presidential seal, and unleashed a stinging attack on the Democratic Party for failing to adopt a resolution at its national convention condemning antisemitism.

Noting that the Republican Party at its convention in Dallas last August adopted a resolution as part of its political platform which condemned antisemitism and all other forms of bigotry, Reagan told an enthusiastic audience in Temple Hillel that the Democratic Party "couldn't find the moral courage or leadership to pass a similar resolution." Two weeks after the convention, the Democratic party adopted a resolution condemning antisemitism.

Democratic Vice Presidential candidate Geraldine Ferraro accused President Reagan of a "disgraceful falsehood" when he asserted at a political rally in a North Woodmere, Long Island synagogue that the leadership of the Democratic Party lacked the "moral courage" to denounce antisemitism. "President Reagan's remark is contradicted by the whole history of my party," Rep. Ferraro declared. "It was a Democratic President, Franklin D. Roosevelt, who led this nation in the fight against the Nazis."

November

While President Reagan won a landslide re-election victory, most Jews appear to have voted for his opponent, former Vice President Walter Mondale.

Two major exit polls, conducted by television networks, gave Mondale nearly 70 percent of the Jewish vote. ABC said the Jewish vote was 69 to 31 in favor of Mondale and CBS said its poll showed Jews voted for Mondale by a 67 to 32 majority.

Senators Rudy Boschwitz (R. Minn.) and Carl Levin (D. Mich.), the only two of the eight Jews in the Senate up for election this year, were both re-elected to their second six-year terms. A third Jew running for the Senate, Edythe Harrison, a Democrat, was defeated in Virginia by Sen. John Warner, A Republican.

In the House, Elliott Levitas (D. Ga.), a five-term Congressman, was the only one of 30 Jews seeking re-election to be defeated. The number of Jews in the House stands at 30, with the election of John Miller, a Republican former television commentator in Washington.

This is one less than the number of Jews in the present House because Rep. Richard Ottinger (D. N.Y.) did not seek re-election after 10 years in Congress. Oren Teicher, an aide to Ottinger, was defeated for the seat by Joseph DioGuardi, a Republican.

Israel was not a major issue in the campaign, and the new Congress which takes office in January is expected to be as supportive of the Jewish State as the outgoing one. But several decisions made election day may have some effect.

One of the most important was the defeat of Rep. Clarence Long (D. Md.) after 22 years in the House, by Rep. Helen Bentley. The 76-year-old Long was chairman of the House Appropriations Committee's subcommittee on foreign operations, and had been a leading force in Congress in pushing for aid for Israel.

His replacement as chairman is expected to be Rep. David Obey (D. Wis.), who had been in years past considered lukewarm to Israel, but recently has become "more sensitized," according to sources.

In the Senate, Sen. Charles Percy (R. Ill.) was defeated by Democrat Paul Simon, considered a close friend of Israel during his years in the House. Percy, who had long had the support of Illinois' Jews, lost it this year because of his criticism of Israel and his movement toward the Palestine Liberation Organization, despite his assertion that he supports Israel and his strong leadership in the struggle for Soviet Jewry.

Percy was chairman of the Senate Foreign Relations Committee and his successor may decide how that committee acts toward Israel. With the Republicans maintaining control of the Senate, next in line for the chairmanship is Sen. Jesse Helms (R. N.C.) who, along with Percy, was one of the two Senators targeted by many Jews across the country this year for defeat.

The re-election of Levin, a liberal Democrat, and Boschwitz, a Conservative Republican, means the Jewish contingent in the Senate remains at four Democrats and four Republicans. The other incumbents are: Chic Hecht (R. Nev.); Frank Lautenberg (D. N.J.); Howard Metzenbaum (D. Ohio); Warren Rudman (R. N.H.); Arlen Specter (R. Penn.); and Edward Zorinsky (D. Neb.).

In the House the lineup is now 24 Jewish Democrats and six Republicans. The incumbents re-elected are:

Gary Ackerman (D. N.Y.); Anthony Beilenson (D. Cal.); Howard Berman (D. Cal.); Barbara Boxer (D. Cal.); Sala

Burton (D. Cal.); Ben Erdreich (D. Ala.); Bobbi Fiedler (R. Cal.); Barney Frank (D. Mass.); Martin Frost (D. Tex.); Sam Gejdensen (D. Conn.); Benjamin Gilman (R. N..Y.); Dan Glickman (D. Kan.); Willis Gradison (R. Ohio); Bill Green (R. N.Y.); Ken Kramer (R. Col.); Tom Lantos (D. Cal.); William Lehman (D. Fla.); Sander Levin (D. Mich.); Mel Levine (D. Cal.); James Scheuer (D. N.Y.); Charles Schumer (D. N.Y.); Norman Sisisky (D. Va.); Larry Smith (D. Fla.); Stephen Solarz (D. N.Y.); Henry Waxman (D. Cal.); Theodore Weiss (D. N.Y.); Howard Wolpe (D. Mich.); Ron Wyden (D. Ore.) and Sidney Yates (D. Ill.)

Madeleine Kunin, the Democratic candidate in Vermont, became the state's first woman Governor, defeating State Attorney General John Easton, Jr., a Republican. Kunin had 116,575 or 50.8 percent to Easton's 112,883 or 49.0 percent.

Kunin is from a family of European Jewish emigrants that fled the Nazis in 1940 for the United States. The Swiss-born Kunin became a U.S. citizen in 1947. In 1972, she was elected to the Vermont House of Representatives. She served three terms. She was also Vermont's Lt. Governor for two terms between 1978 and 1982.

Kunin, 51, lost a race for Governor two years ago to Richard Snelling, who is retiring. Significantly, she had in the past weeks gained the endorsement of many of the state's leading newspapers, including the traditionally Republican *Burlington Free Press.* There are about 2,500 Jews in Vermont, out of a state population estimated at 516,000.

Kunin had campaigned against Easton mainly stressing the themes of experience and improving educational opportunities. Easton, 41, stressed the issues of law-and-order throughout the campaign. Kunin becomes only the second woman governor in the U.S. and is only the third Democrat to hold the office in Vermont in 130 years.

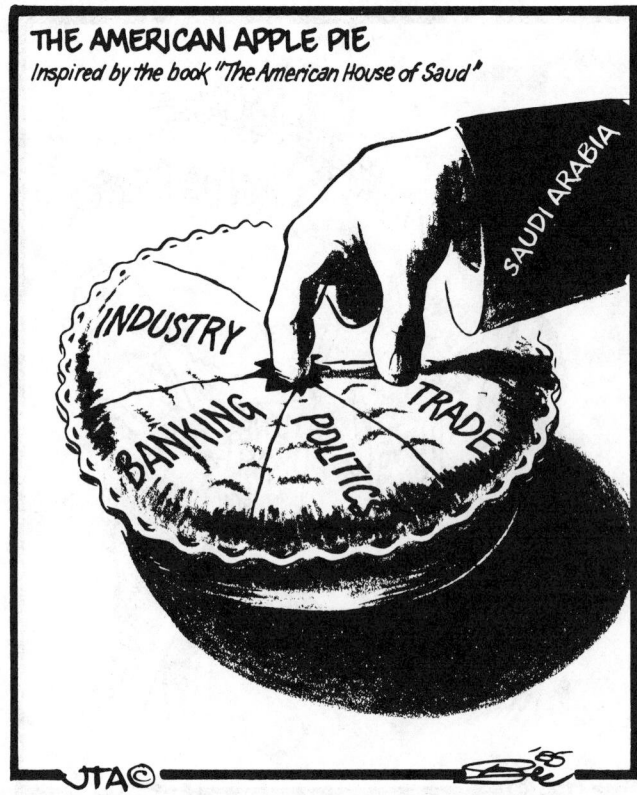

THE AMERICAN APPLE PIE
Inspired by the book "The American House of Saud"

In Missouri, meanwhile, Democratic State Senator Harriet Woods became the state's first woman elected to be Lt. Governor, defeating Republican Mel Hancock.

Woods, who is Jewish, gained national prominence when she staged an unsuccessful bid to oust U.S. Senator John Danforth two years ago.

Also in Missouri, Democrat Lt. Gov. Kenneth Rothman, meanwhile, was defeated by Attorney General John Ashcroft, a Republican, in a fight to succeed retiring Republican Governor Christopher Bond.

The opening plenary of the 53rd General Assembly of the Council of Jewish Federations in Toronto was competely disrupted by 40 protestors demonstrating on behalf of Ethiopian Jewry.

Over the chants of "Let Simcha Speak," a reference to Simcha Jacobovici, producer and director of the award-winning film *Falasha,* Martin Citrin, CJF president, was forced to adjourn the session before it began. Citrin's action came after more than half an hour of uproar that erupted as 2,000 delegates arrived for the plenary that was to have dealt with prospects and challenges of Federation work in the coming period.

Less than four days after its dedication, San Francisco's monument to the Holocaust, one of the few memorials to the Holocaust on public property in the United States, was desecrated.

The target of the vandals was the eleven white plaster bronze figures created by sculptor George Segal, ten of the representations prone and one, a man, staring out of a barbed-wire enclosure. Segal titled the work, "The Holocaust."

The memorial is located in Lincoln Park, overlooking San Francisco Bay. The desecration took place apparently sometime between Saturday night and Sunday morning.

The faces of the ten corpses were found covered with black and yellow spray paint. The memorial was dedicated in a solemn ceremony attended by some 500 survivors and relatives and friends.

Probably the most important result for Israel in the Senate leadership elections was Richard Lugar (R. Ind.) becoming chairman of the Senate Foreign Relations Committee, which became possible after Sen. Jesse Helms (R. N.C.) said he would remain as chairman of the Agriculture Committee.

Helms, during his recent re-election campaign, had promised to remain as chairman of the Agriculture Committee to protect his state's tobacco interests, but there had been strong pressure from the conservative right for him to take the chairmanship of the Foreign Relations Committee upon the vacancy created by the defeat of Sen. Charles Percy (R. Ill.). Helms has consistently opposed all foreign aid, including that to Israel, and has been considered by some to be anti-Israel.

Lugar, who is one of four Senators defeated by Robert Dole for the Majority Leader's position, has been building ties with the Jewish community since coming to the Senate in 1977. He is considered "good" on foreign aid for Israel, but voted for the AWACS sale.

Lugar is expected to go along with most Administration requests. He and the new Senate leadership are expected to look favorably on the expected Administration requests for arms for Jordan and Saudi Arabia.

December

Three American Jewish Congress officials were arrested during an anti-apartheid demonstration at the Embassy of South Africa. Theodore Mann, AJC president, Henry Siegman, executive director, and Theodore Bikel, senior vice president, were handcuffed and taken in a police van to a local police station where they were booked and detained for five hours. They were released on $50 bond each and ordered to appear in court on December 20. The three were charged with trespass.

The leaders of American Reform Judaism have launched a nation-wide appeal to provide emergency shelter and medical care for victims of starvation in Ethiopia.

While no campaign goal had been set, Rabbi Alexander Schindler, president of the Union of American Hebrew Congregations (UAHC), told the UAHC's policy-making Board of Trustees that the UAHC hoped to raise an initial sum of $250,000, which he said was enough to construct and supply a village with 600 tents sheltering 6,000 refugees.

He cited reports that tens of thousands of Ethiopians have uprooted themselves from their homes in search of sustenance, making the need for shelter "almost as desperate as the need for food."

January 1985

A lawsuit filed in Washington seeks to compel the United States government to release four pages of classified Army intelligence documents that may provide key information regarding the reported efforts by Joseph Mengele, the notorious Auschwitz doctor, to gain entry into Canada in 1962.

The suit, filed by Sen. Alfonse D'Amato (R. N.Y.) and Rabbis Marvin Hier and Abraham Cooper, dean and asso-

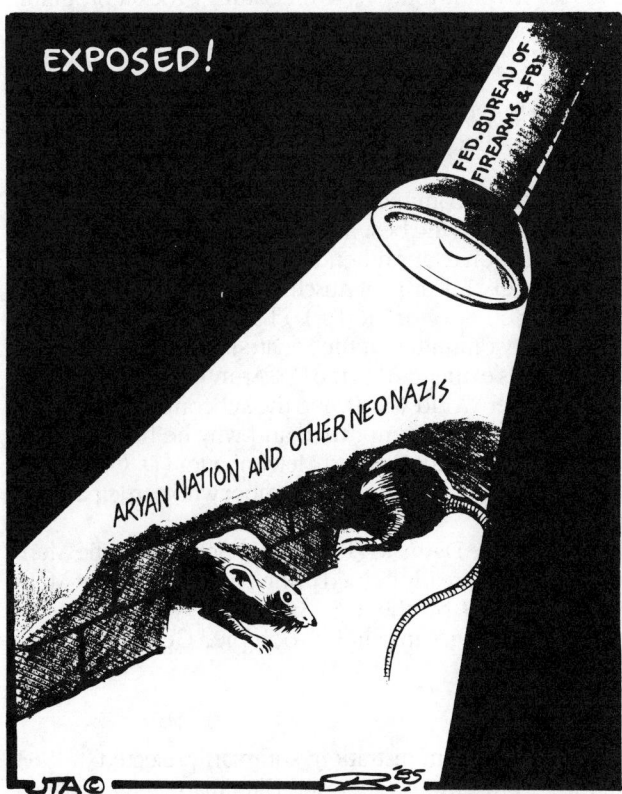

ciate dean, respectively, of the Los Angeles-based Simon Wiesenthal Center, follows the release of documents indicating that, besides attempting to obtain a visa into Canada, Mengele may also have been captured and released in an American occupation zone soon after World War II.

The documents previously released by the government mention that Mengele, considered the most wanted war criminal still at large, may have sought a visa at the Canadian Consulate in Buenos Aires under the alias of "Joseph Menke." There is no knowledge that he ever entered Canada. The documents were obtained under provisions of the Freedom of Information Act.

President Reagan urged the Soviet Union to make known the whereabouts of Raoul Wallenberg, the Swedish diplomat who helped save some 100,000 Jews from the Nazis in Hungary during World War II.

The State Department, which along with the White House released the President's statement, noted that January 17 was the 40th anniversay of Wallenberg's disappearance.

"In the depth of the horror of World War II, Raoul Wallenberg was one shining light of inspiration, upholding the honor of the human race," Reagan said. "The world owes a tremendous and eternal debt of gratitude to this great man. And the Soviet Union owes the world a full and complete accounting of his fate."

February

The National Aeronautics and Space Administration (NASA) has rejected Brooklyn District Attorney Elizabeth Holtzman's call on the Agency and President Reagan to strip Nazi war criminal Arthur Rudolph of NASA's highest award, the Distinguished Service Medal, given to him in 1969 for his contributions to the Saturn V rocket program.

The Justice Department will conduct a full-scale investigation into the whereabouts of Auschwitz death camp doctor Josef Mengele and into reports that he was arrested and then freed in Austria by U.S. occupation forces in 1947, it was announced by Attorney General William French Smith.

A Senate subcommittee was repeatedly told that continuing publicity is the best means of spurring U.S. and international action to apprehend Dr. Josef Mengele, the notorious "angel of death" of Auschwitz.

Sen. Arlen Specter (R. Pa.), chairman of the Juvenile Justice Subcommittee of the Senate Judiciary Committee, said there is evidence that the U.S. Army had Mengele in its custody after World War II, and the subcommittee wanted to know why he was not tried and why he has not been arrested since. Sen. Howard Metzenbaum (D. Ohio) was the only other subcommittee member who participated in the hearing.

Sen. Alfonse D'Amato (R. NY) said publicity of the Mengele case has already helped bring confirmation that Mengele was held by the U.S. Army in 1945 in the Idar-Oberstein prison camp in U.S.-occupied Germany.

April

The Reagan Administration "summarily rejected" a 1983 request from various Baltic and Ukrainian emigre groups

BLACK EYE

TIME

SHARON

JTA©

that the United States impose the administrative equivalent of a "statute of limitations" to prohibit the Justice Department from instituting legal proceedings against alleged war criminals in America, according to the World Jewish Congress.

John Demjanjuk, a retired automobile worker accused of complicity in the murder of hundreds of Jewish inmates while a guard at the Treblinka concentration camp in Poland during the Holocaust, was ordered extradited to Israel to stand trial for war crimes.

The United States Holocaust Memorial Council met in emergency session and expressed its "deep anguish" at President Reagan's planned visit to a German military cemetery during his forthcoming visit to West Germany. But the Council, by unanimous decision, deferred specific action pending a meeting between Council chairman Elie Wiesel and the President.

President Reagan, defending his planned visit to a German military cemetery at Bitburg, said that most of the 2,000 soldiers buried there were 18 year-old boys conscripted into the army and "they were victims just as surely as the victims of the concentration camps."

Elie Wiesel, chairman of the U.S. Holocaust Memorial Council, said that if President Reagan had responded to his plea not to go to a West German military cemetery in May, it would have been seen not as having given in to "pressure" but as a "human response to a human plea."

"I think he would have come out stronger," Wiesel said in an appearance on the ABC-TV "Issues and Answers" program. He added that "At this point, the key is in the hands of Chancellor (Helmut) Kohl." He said Kohl should "release" Reagan from the President's commitment to lay a wreath at the Bitburg military cemetery where some 2,000

German soldiers and 47 members of the Waffen SS are buried.

Reagan did not respond when Wiesel made an emotional plea to the President, at a ceremony at which he received the Congressional Gold Medal, that Reagan not go to the cemetery.

In Philadelphia, The American Gathering of Jewish Holocaust Survivors, for the first time since its inception, forcefully addressed the issue of Nazi war criminals and the role of the American government.

Addressing the issue on three fronts, the Gathering was the site of a Senate Subcommittee hearing where survivors presented eye-witness testimony against Nazi war criminal Josef Mengele and a panel discussion on bringing war criminals to justice, that culminated in a resolution urging Congress to change legal "loopholes" used by war criminals to avoid deportation from the U.S.

A Torah that once belonged to a Jewish community in the Czechoslovak town of Polna, all of whose members were exterminated by the Nazis, is now being used by a five-year-old congregation in Hawaii.

Sen. Daniel Inouye (D. Hawaii) described to the Senate, the event which brought the 200-year-old Torah to Congregation Beth Shalom in Kona, Hawaii. "In 1940, as the country fell under the boots of the Nazis, Polna's Jewish community was deported to the concentration camps never to return," Inouye said.

The Torah and other communal possessions were sent to Prague where they were part of 15,000 Jewish manuscripts, books and other objects with which the Nazis wanted to create "a museum of the extinct race." These items later became part of the Jewish Museum in Prague.

May

Declaring that "the final word has been spoken as far as I am concerned," President Reagan defended his planned visit to the German military cemetery at Bitburg, telling foreign reporters that "I think it is morally right to do what I am doing and I am not going to change my mind about that."

Vice President George Bush, meanwhile, who has refrained from public statements on the Bitburg controversy, told a United States Chamber of Commerce meeting in Washington that "Ronald Reagan has not changed on his abhorrence of the Holocaust—he never will. But the time has come for understanding and support for the President."

Secretary of State George Shultz also defended Reagan's visit to Bitburg. In a satellite news conference from Washington to Bonn, he brushed aside criticism and predicted that the critics "in the end may wind up admiring the person who has stood by his decision." Asked if Reagan would not pay a political price for his decision, Shultz said, "The political price would be heavier if he didn't."

Nevertheless, opposition continued to mount as members of Congress and Jewish organizations scheduled a variety of counter-actions in protest of Reagan's scheduled 15 minute stop at the German military cemetery where at least 47 SS soldiers are buried among the some 2,000 German war dead.

In Washington, the House voted 390-26 for a resolution sponsored by Rep. Dante Fascell (D. Fla.) calling on Reagan to reconsider his itinerary. The Republican-controlled Senate passed a similar resolution by voice vote without opposition. It was sponsored by Sens. Howard Metzenbaum (D. Ohio) and Arlen Specter (R. Pa.). Neither resolution is binding.

The Administration had reportedly asked at least two prominent Jews—Elie Wiesel and Nazi-hunter Simon Wiesenthal—to go along with Reagan when he goes to the military cemetery at Bitburg. Both declined the invitation. Other Holocaust survivors have reportedly been sought to accompany the President. They, too, have reportedly declined.

President Reagan continued to defend his decision to visit the military cemetery at Bitburg while at the same time assuring the victims of the Holocaust, "I promise you, we will never forget."

Reagan and Chancellor Helmut Kohl of West Germany visited the site of the Bergen-Belsen concentration camp, where both leaders spoke, and then flew by helicopter to Bitburg. The two men also made an unscheduled stopover at the grave of Konrad Adenauer, West Germany's first post-war Chancellor who is revered as the architect of its democracy.

Reagan and Kohl spent barely three minutes at the cemetery where the President placed a wreath. He then addressed some 11,000 American servicemen and their families at the U.S. Air Force base nearby.

At Bergen-Belsen, Reagan quoted extensively from the diary of Anne Frank, the publication of which more than a generation ago made the Dutch-born Jewish teenager who perished there one of the most tragic symbols of the Holocaust. The President was clearly seeking to soften the pain and anguish caused Jews and many non-Jews by his decision, at the insistence of Kohl, to pay homage to dead German soldiers, among them the notorious killers of the Waffen SS.

Hundreds of Jewish protesters from the United States, Europe and Israel lined the roads to and from the military cemetery in Bitburg to pour out their anguish and outrage at President Reagan and Chancellor Helmut Kohl for honoring the German soldiers of World War II buried there.

Unlike the scene at Bergen-Belsen earlier in the day where hundreds of other Jewish protestors were removed by police from the concentration camp site hours before Reagan arrived, the authorities at Bitburg were lenient. As a gesture of good-will, in fact, the police laid down their clubs and shields.

A group of Christian leaders urged the United Nations to reconsider "the falsehood promulgated in its 1975 resolution declaring Zionism to be a form of Racism," and called on the Christian community to appreciate the centrality and importance of the State of Israel, as affirmed by the Bible, for the Jewish people.

In a press conference at the Church Center for the United Nations, sponsored by the National Christian Leadership Conference for Israel (NCLCI), a statement, endorsed by Christian leaders from all parts of the U.S., denounced antisemitism and urged Christians to rid themselves of prejudice and hostility "that have been alive among Christians for centuries."

An American Jewish organization has been formed to help suffering non-Jews in Africa, Asia and Central America, it was announced in New York.

Lawrence Phillips, chairman of the new group, the American Jewish World Service, who is also the chairman of the Phillips-Van Heusen Corp., said the service was formed

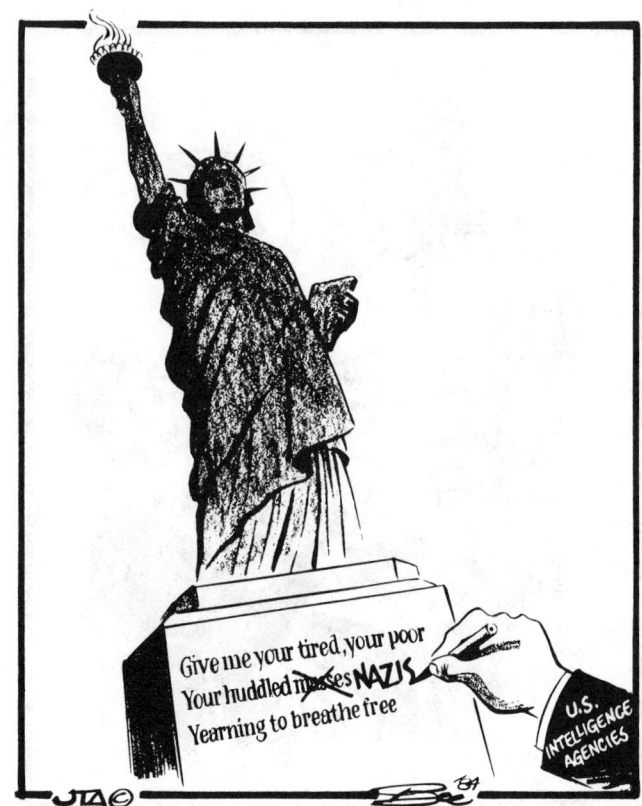

because there was no Jewish organization "dealing exclusively with development projects for non-Jews throughout the world."

The purpose of the organization, he said, and its primary objectives, would be to develop health facilities and peasant agricultural programs. The first project of the organization will be an emergency airlift of a planeload of medical and agricultural supplies to Mozambique, where 100,000 people were reported to have died of famine-related causes last year.

The Rabbinical Assembly, the international organization of Conservative rabbis, has declared 51 members of Israel's Knesset, including Yitzhak Shamir, Ariel Sharon and former Israeli Ambassador to the United States, Moshe Arens, as "not welcome as speakers or honorees in the 850 Conservative synagogues, which they have sought to discredit."

Officials of the Association of Reform Zionists of America said they had adopted, on behalf of the American Reform movement, a resolution disapproving the Conservative rabbinate's declaration that 51 Knesset members are unwelcome as speakers to American Conservative synagogues.

Sen. Jesse Helms (R. N.C.) withdrew his opposition to Senate ratification of an international treaty against genocide, as the Foreign Relations Committee, in a vote of 9-8, approved it for the sixth time in 36 years.

June

The U.S. Supreme Court decision, by a vote of 6-3, striking down an Alabama law authorizing a daily one minute of silence for prayer or meditation to public schools was hailed by four American Jewish organizations.

REFERENCE MATERIAL

THE ABANDONMENT OF THE JEWS DAVID S. WYMAN

The four—American Jewish Committee, American Jewish Congress, the Anti-Defamation League of B'nai B'rith, and B'nai B'rith International—said they view the court's decision as a major victory in the fight against efforts to establish state-sponsored voluntary prayer in public schools.

Dr. Gerson Cohen, chancellor of the Jewish Theological Seminary (JTS) and president of its faculty since 1972, told the JTS board of directors he planned to resign and asked the board to name his successor.

A Jewish ecumenical group has vented serious criticism of a new Vatican document on Catholic-Jewish relations published in Rome which it considers a retrogression from the historic "Nostra Aetate" (Our Times) that emerged from Vatican Council II in 1964 and the December 1, 1974 "Guidelines and Suggestions for the Application of the Declaration Nostra Aetate."

The criticism by the International Jewish Committee on Interreligious Consultations (IJCIC) was more in regret than anger. It referred to a document, "Notes on the Correct Way to Present the Jews and Judaism in Preaching and Catechesis in the Roman Catholic Church." The Notes, three years in preparation, are the work of the Vatican Commission on Religious Relations With the Jews, headed by Johannes Cardinal Willebrands.

They were presented at a Vatican press conference by the Rev. Father Pierre Deuprey and Msgr. Jorge Mejia, vice president and secretary, respectively, of the Commission, and appeared in the Vatican organ, *L'Osservatore Romano*. According to a statement by the IJCIC, the Notes fail to acknowledge the religious significance of the State of Israel to the Jewish people and refer only briefly and superficially to the Holocaust.

The U.S. Supreme Court, by two 5-4 decisions, held as unconstitutional two programs by which, at public expense, remedial educational services have been brought to pupils of all-day religious schools on the premises of the schools.

The majority ruling held in both cases that "even a praiseworthy, secular purpose of providing for the education of school children cannot validate government aid to parochial schools when the aid has the effect of promoting a single religion or religion generally or when the aid unduly entangles the government in matters religious." The general decision was that the programs have the principal effect of advancing religion in violation of the Constitution.

AROUND THE WORLD

September 1984

President Reagan asked seven top Western European leaders to lend their help in efforts to alleviate the plight of Soviet Jews, it was disclosed by Leon Dulzin, chairman of the World Zionist Organization and Jewish Agency Executives.

Dulzin, just returned from a meeting of the presidium of the World Conference on Soviet Jewry in London, also disclosed that future appeals to the Soviet authorities to allow Jews to leave will be based on "repatriation" to Israel rather than family re-unification which has been the rationale until now.

Dulzin said that a senior U.S. diplomat, Max Kampelman, the American Ambassador to the European Security Conference, delivered Reagan's letter to the European statesmen, including Prime Minister Margaret Thatcher of Britain and President Francois Mitterrand of France. Dulzin singled out Thatcher and Mitterrand for warm praise for their actions and intercessions on behalf of Soviet Jews. He said the conditions of Jews in the USSR are "growing worse," and Soviet Jewry's urgent plea to us is: 'Shake the world with your public cry on our behalf.' The London conference, attended by representatives of Jewish communities throughout the free world, expressed grave concern over the deterioration of the situation of Jews in the Soviet Union.

In London, representatives of Jewish communities throughout the free world expressed grave concern about the deteriorating plight of the 2.5 million Jews in the Soviet Union, and appealed to world leaders to intercede on their behalf with the Kremlin.

A lengthy proclamation, issued by the presidium of the World Conference on Soviet Jewry, referred to what it called "a profound crisis" for Jewish life within the Soviet Union.

The statement, issued after three days of discussions by 50 representatives from 20 countries, said that in addition to denying Soviet Jewry's cultural rights and trying to "hermetically seal" it off from the rest of the Jewish world, Moscow was increasingly using antisemitism "as an instrument of domestic and foreign policy.

With fewer than 1,000 Soviet Jewish emigrants expected this year, compared with 50,000 five years ago, the conference expressed concern about the plight of some 300,000 who had unsuccessfully applied to emigrate despite the official claims of the Soviet Union that nearly all the Jews who wished to leave had already done so.

October

Rep. Ted Weiss (D. NY) sharply criticized the State Department for granting a visa to the mayor of an Austrian ski resort community who has been identified as a former sergeant of an SS infantry brigade responsible for the murders of Jews and other civilians in Nazi occupied eastern Europe during World War II.

Franz Hausberger served as an Unterscharfuehrer in the notorious First SS Infantry Brigade which, according to the Anti-Defamation League of B'nai B'rith, was responsible for mopping-up operations behind German lines in the Soviet Union. Later during the war, he was transferred to an administrative post in Amersfoort, a concentration camp in The Netherlands.

The Communist controlled official Polish media is linking West Germany and Israel as "anti-Polish, reactionary allies" in a new propaganda campaign that could trigger a wave of antisemitism in Poland, a country now almost devoid of Jews.

The West German press cited as an example articles in the Polish political journal, *Perspektywy* alleging the existence of a Bonn-Jerusalem "axis" portrayed as "imperialist, revanchist and expansionist." The magazine, which reflects the thinking of Poland's Communist ruling elite, accused West Germany of seeking to change the border of Europe and Israel, of failing to respect the sovereignty and integrity of its neighbors and violating their territory.

West German observers familiar with Poland's problems see the propaganda campaign as an attempt to divert attention from the government's economic and political difficulties. Along with other Eastern bloc countries, Poland is also waging a vigorous propaganda campaign against a possible rapprochement between East and West Germany.

But, according to observers here, the Polish authorities themselves fear the campaign may get out of hand and revive long-standing antisemitic sentiments in the public, with the distinct possibility of violence against the tiny surviving Jewish community.

That possibility was evident recently when soccer fans in Cracow displayed antisemitic banners against a competing team from Lodz, not because the team was Jewish but because a few Jews still live in that city. There have been several unconfirmed reports of violence against Jews in Poland, West German newspapers report.

The International Book Fair in Frankfurt has produced a complaint of discrimination against Israel and charges that the Soviet Union was using the event to disseminate antisemitic propaganda.

The complaint arose from the omission of Israel from a large sign naming the 61 countries which have joint national exhibitions. The name of Israel was added after repeated protests. A spokesman for the Book Fair told the Jewish Telegraphic Agency that the omission was the result of a simple mistake and had no political implications.

M. Biala, of Israel's Ministry of Commerce and Industry, which sponsors the Israeli national exhibition, said he had protested several times to the Book Fair management, but received no explanation.

The Soviet Union was accused of featuring anti-Israel propaganda at its national stand, of a nature that comes close to being antisemitic. The material, printed in German,

includes the latest copy of the Soviet monthly *New Times* which displays a Star of David on its cover against a background of cannons and an American eagle, all under the caption: "Middle East—Pax Americana." It is offered free.

A spokesman for the Soviet stand denied that the material was in any way antisemitic. A Book Fair spokesman said it was long-standing policy to allow exhibitors to select the material to be shown without interference.

The Senate is expected to be bound morally, if not legally, to ratify the United Nations Convention against genocide when the new Congress, the 99th, convenes in January.

Just before adjourning, the Senate accepted, by an 87-2 vote, a resolution expressing the Senate's support for the "principles" of the 35-year-old treaty and asserting that it "declares its intention to act expeditiously" to ratify the Convention next year. Sens. John East (R. NC) and Steven Symms (R. Idaho) voted against the resolution.

The Convention on the Prevention and Punishment of the Crime of Genocide was signed by President Truman on December 11, 1948. Although supported by every President since Truman, except Eisenhower, it has failed ratification in the Senate because of conservative opposition.

New life was given to the treaty this year on September 5 when President Reagan, who had been silent on the issue, announced his support of it on the eve of a speech to B'nai B'rith International.

Sen. Jesse Helms (R. N.C.) and others opposed to ratification want amendments to prevent the treaty from superseding the U.S. Constitution. In the debate, Helms called the treaty just a "noble gesture." But Sen. Christopher Dodd (D. Conn.) noted that symbols are useful in reflecting basic values and stressed that adoption of the Convention would "symbolize a commitment to the significance of human life, to a just world order and to the role of law."

Sen. Rudy Boschwitz (R. Minn.), who led the floor fight for ratification, noted that "most of my family . . . were among the more than six million Jews who perished in the Nazi Holocaust against the Jewish people."

Several of the pro-ratification speakers paid tribute to the late Raphael Lemkin, a Polish-born Jew who emigrated to the U.S. in 1941 and who was an advisor to Supreme Court Justice Robert Jackson when he was a prosecutor at the Nuremburg war crimes trials. Lemkin is credited with introducing the term genocide.

Cesar Milstein, one of the three immunologists who won the 1984 Nobel Prize in Medicine, began his scientific career in Argentina where his father, a Jewish immigrant from the Ukraine, settled in 1897. Among the honors he received prior to the Nobel Prize was the Wolf Prize in Medicine from the Wolf Foundation in Israel, four years earlier.

The other two winners of the $190,000 Nobel Prize were Georges Koehler, 38, of the Basel Institute of Immunology in Switzerland, and Niels Jerne, 72, professor emeritus in the institute. The prize, announced by the Karolinska Institute in Stockholm, will be divided equally between the three recipients.

Milstein was born in Bahia Blanca October 8, 1927. He was educated in the University of Buenos Aires and received his Ph. D. from Cambridge University in 1960. Before settling in England in 1963, he was associated with the National Institute of Microbiology in Buenos Aires from 1961 to 1963.

According to reports in the Argentine press, he left the institute in an act of solidarity with its director who had been dismissed by the government which followed the coup against President Frondizi. The Milstein family was active in Jewish community life and was identified with Jewish causes. Since 1963, Milstein has been associated with Cambridge and now heads its division of protein and nucleic chemistry.

Canada's new Conservative Prime Minister, Brian Mulroney, named Stephen Lewis, a lifelong Socialist active in the Jewish community, to be Canada's next Ambassador to the United Nations. Lewis, 46, is the former leader of the New Democratic Party in Ontario, which his late father also headed. Lewis is also a former chairman of the Histadrut campaign in Ontario and has lectured on the Holocaust.

Secretary of State George Shultz pledged that as the United States attempts to build a "new, more constructive period in Soviet-American relations" following President Reagan's recent meeting with Soviet Foreign Minister Andrei Gromyko, it will continue to stress the plight of Soviet Jews and other human rights issues.

The Executive Council of UNESCO has approved a proposal by the World Jewish Congress that the 850th anniversary of the birth of Maimonides—the great Jewish philosopher and physician—be celebrated during 1985. The resolution, which was unanimously adopted, was submitted by Spain, the native land of Maimonides, and co-sponsored by France, Cuba, Venezuela, Italy, Mexico, and Pakistan.

November

Immigration authorities in Lisbon will have to decide what to do about the notorious cleric, Archbishop Valerian Trifa, who was granted a temporary three-month visa by Portugal, the only country to accept him after he was ordered deported from the United States. Trifa left the U.S. on August 13.

The Portuguese government stated that Trifa's application for a visa had been processed and granted routinely, without knowledge of his controversial background as a leader of the fascist Iron Guard in Rumania who incited a pogrom against the Jewish community in Bucharest in 1941.

His native Rumania refused to accept him, but rumors were rife in Lisbon that Greece may accept him should Portugal decide to oust him next month, and that he may wind up at the celebrated monastery atop Mt. Athos.

Prime Minister Mario Soares of Portugal has declared that if there is proof that Trifa is indeed a Nazi war criminal he will be expelled forthwith. But up to now, no attempt has been made by the government to contact the Justice Department's Office of Special Investigation (OSI) in Washington, D.C. to examine the voluminous evidence that has been compiled with regard to Trifa's wartime activities that had provided for the deportation order.

The successful candidate who emerged from national elections in Uruguay as Vice President of the country, Enrique Tarigo, is a well-known jurist who chairs the Uruguayan Committee for the Right of Soviet Jewry, the World Jewish Congress reported. Tarigo himself is not Jewish.

A communique received from the American Jewish Joint Distribution Committee representative in Ethiopia advised that the overseas relief agency had received permission to operate feeding stations in the Gondar region.

THE OLD MANHOLES OF EUROPE

ANTISEMITISM

JTA

The announcement said the JDC has received donations and pledges exceeding $200,000 from concerned Jews and members of the general public since it "opened its mail box" to contributions on October 23. Half of the sum was committed by the Central British Fund—World Jewish Relief of London.

The Federal Court in Karlsruhe, from which there is no appeal, served notice on lower courts throughout West Germany to end the fairly common practice of suspending prison sentences imposed on neo-Nazis. The court deplored probation for neo-Nazis which can be viewed by the public as unjustified softness toward right-wing extremism.

Paraguay has begun what was described as a thorough nation-wide investigation to locate Josef Mengele, the infamous war criminal and chief doctor at the Auschwitz concentration camp responsible for the murder of tens of thousands of Jews during World War II.

The investigation will be conducted by police authorities in Paraguay under the Ministry of Interior, according to Elizabeth Holtzman, Brooklyn District Attorney, who returned from a three-day visit to Paraguay as a member of a delegation of four persons who travelled there under the sponsorship of the International Network of Children of Jewish Holocaust Survivors.

December

An Alitalia plane left Kennedy International Airport with seven tons of donated new clothing and cloth at an estimated value of $220,000 for distribution in Ethiopia. It was donated to the American Jewish Joint Distribution Committee.

The JDC received permission to operate feeding stations in the Gondar region—one of the areas in Ethiopia hard hit by drought—and is negotiating with the Agency for International Development for the provision of food in coming months. An estimated half a million people face starvation in the Gondar region.

Sixteen North American Jewish leaders who completed a 10-day mission to Ethiopia, under the auspices of the National Jewish Community Relations Advisory Council (NJCRAC), reported that they experienced some of the most significant direct contact with Ethiopian Jewry in many years, including participation in the uniquely Ethiopian-Jewish festival of Seggid, along with 600 Falashas gathered from remote villages in the Gondar province.

The mission members spent almost a full day at the Seggid, a festival combining the joy and religious rites, chanting of prayer and fasting of Yom Kippur and Simchat Torah.

Kiev refusenik Iosif Berenshtein, charged with "resisting arrest," was convicted and sentenced to four years imprisonment on December 10, the National Conference on Soviet Jewry learned. The maximum penalty for the charge is five years. Berenshtein, a 47-year-old engineer, was arrested on November 12 while in nearby Novograd Vilinsky to answer allegations of economic crimes made against his aunt, which have since been dropped.

The French authorities have in custody the alleged leader of a Lebanese terrorist organization who is believed to have masterminded the murder of an Israeli diplomat in Paris more than two years ago.

The suspect, a Lebanese Christian identified as Abdullah Georges Ibrahim, is said to be the head of the Lebanese Armed Revolutionary Fractions which claimed credit for the slaying of the Israeli official, Yaacov Bar Simantov, in the lobby of his Paris apartment building on April 3, 1982.

After a four-hour trial in Moscow, Yuli Edelstein was convicted of allegedly "possessing drugs," and sentenced to three years in a labor camp, the National Conference on Soviet Jewry reported. Only his mother and his wife, Tanya, were permitted inside the courtroom during the trial.

Edelstein, a Hebrew teacher who had long been warned by the KGB to end his teaching activities, was arrested on September 4, after a house search in which Hebrew books and a small container were confiscated. Following the search, Soviet authorities claimed to have found drugs in the container, and claimed that Edelstein was involved with "foreigners who corrupt Jewish youth with medieval and mystical drug rituals."

At least 10 Soviet Jewish families from Moscow, all long-term refuseniks, have received exit visas to Israel, the National Conference on Soviet Jewry reported. The news, which the NCSJ said it sees as a "small but significant reversal in annual emigration trends," marks only the second time in over eight months that Jews from the Soviet capital were granted permission to emigrate. The first visas issued in that city came in November, when 12 Muscovite Jews were permitted to leave.

January 1985

Government and Jewish Agency officials confirmed that large numbers of Ethiopian Jews—probaby the vast majority of that community estimated at about 25,000—are now in Israel.

Save the Falashas!

THE
SAME GARBAGE—
A DIFFERENT
CAN

Der Stürmer
BLAME THE JEWS
1936

PRAVDA ПРАВДА
BLAME THE ZIONISTS
1984

JTA©   '84

While Israel was in an uproar over the importunate "leaks" by its own officials that forced disclosure of the airlift rescue of Ethiopian Jews, sources in Brussels revealed that Trans European Airways (TEA), the Belgian charter company engaged for the task, managed to operate the airlift in absolute secrecy since it began last November.

The pro-Arab weekly *Jeune Afrique* reported that Ethiopian Jews who fled their country to escape famine and persecution suffered a "mini-inquisition" in the nearby countries where they sought asylum—Sudan, Djibouti and North Yemen—because of their religion. The magazine said Ethiopian Christian refugees were subjected to the same treatment.

Israel and Guinea, once the most anti-Israel country in Africa, are moving toward rapprochement and have already exchanged military missions, the Paris-based weekly *Jeune Afrique* reported.

According to the publication, which is considered very reliable, an Israeli military mission visited Conakry, capital of the West African state, earlier this month, and Guinea soldiers have gone to Israel for paratroop and commando training.

The Spanish government and the Spanish Parliament are about to vote a special law recognizing the Jewish community's rights and granting it the same privileges enjoyed by the Catholic church and the various Protestant congregations.

The president of the Spanish Jewish community, Samuel Toledano, announced in Madrid that this special law, which he described as "revolutionary," is slated to be approved "without any difficulties" before the end of the year.

Toledano said the law would take the form of a "Concordat," the special sort of agreement binding the Vatican to various states, and would grant the Jewish community the legal rights enjoyed by the Catholic Church.

The Jewish community would have jurisdiction over matters of personal status concerning its members. Jews, just like Catholics, would be able to undergo only a religious wedding which would automatically be registered with the state registrar's office.

Rabbis would enjoy the same privileges as Catholic priests, would be exempted from military service and would not have to testify in court on any matter related to the ministry. They would also have free access to prisons, hospitals and other state-controlled institutions to which they might be called. Synagogues and religious and cultural Jewish institutions would be tax-exempt and would enjoy other special fiscal privileges.

World Jewish Congress president Edgar Bronfman revealed his plans to go to the Soviet Union towards the end of March for talks with Soviet officials in his dual capacity of business executive and a leader of diaspora Jewry. He is the head of Joseph Seagram and Sons Company.

Bronfman told a news conference at the Hilton Hotel in Vienna, where the WJC Governing Board was winding up its three-day meeting, that the Soviets had extended him an invitation to visit in both capacities and he was practically on his way just before Soviet leader Leonid Brezhnev died.

Austrian-born Nazi war criminal Walter Reder's return to his native country on January 24, following his release from an Italian prison after nearly 40 years' incarceration for mass murder of civilians, threw Austria into political turmoil.

The center of the the storm was Defense Minister Friedhelm Frischenschlager, who personally greeted the 69-year-old former SS Major and shook his hand when he landed at Graz.

This was tantamount to military honors for a convicted killer, an action swiftly repudiated by most of Frischenschlager's fellow ministers in the Socialist-led coalition government of which the Defense Minister's right-leaning Freiheitliche Partei Oesterreichs (FPOE) is a partner.

Adding to the embarrassment of the government of Chancellor Fred Sinowatz was the coincidence of Frischenschlager's reception of Reder with the three-day meeting in Vienna of the Governing Board of the World Jewish Congress, the first gathering of world Jewish leaders in Austria since the end of World War II.

Antisemitic slogans were daubed in the small Jewish cemetery of Antibes in the south of France and on the local synagogue's walls.

The president of the local Jewish community, Leon Allouche, said "local vandals and antisemites probably wanted to celebrate in their own way (Nazi war criminal Walter) Reder's liberation (from Italy) and triumphant return to Austria." Allouche said the incident probably took place after Reder was returned to Austria. He added, "This regularly occurs whenever a Nazi is tried or liberated."

February

The State Department's ninth annual report on human rights throughout the world again praises Israel as an open society with a democratic government, but with human rights problems because of its control of the West Bank and Gaza.

"Each year we note that despite the tremendous security threat against Israel, it maintains a very vigorous democracy," Elliott Abrams, Assistant Secretary of State for Human Rights and Humanitarian Affairs, told a press conference.

Abrams said that the Department's Country Report on Human Rights Practices for 1984 finds that the problems for Israel on the West Bank are the result of its having a military government rule there rather than a democratically elected one. He added that there was an increase in violence in the territories in 1984, but it was occupants against other occupants—apparently a reference to the Jewish and Arab residents—and not the military government against the residents.

The 1,450-page report, covering 164 countries, was submitted to Congress. It is the fifth such report submitted by the Reagan Administration.

In Iran, the report, as it did last year, states that the persecution of Jews that existed in the early days of the Khomeini revolution has abated as it has for Christians and Zoroastrians. "They continue to have problems with the regime over religious practices, and some members of all three groups suffer officially-sanctioned job discrimination," the report added.

Iraq's Jewish community "is believed to have decreased from 150,000 following World War II to about 400," the report notes. "It was severely persecuted in the past, but there is no evidence of recent persecution. In 1983 and in late 1984 Western journalists visited the last known synagogue in Baghdad and confirmed that it is still functioning. Only a handful of people, mostly older men, were seen attending services led by two rabbis."

In Syria, "the 3,000—4,000 Jews are free to practice their religion," according to the report. "The situation of the Jewish community has improved in recent years, despite continuing uncertainty over the community's future, and today it enjoys a relatively good standard of living, access to higher education and entrance into the professions."

However, the report notes that only Syrian Jews are routinely required to post a bond of $250 to $10,000 if they want to travel abroad. "In recent years, Jews have found it somewhat easier to travel overseas, although an official ban on their emigration has continued. The government continues its policy of not issuing passports to all members of a Jewish family at the same time, although there have been some recent exceptions."

The report puts the number of Jews in Morocco at 11,000—14,000, most of them in the major cities. "The Jewish community operates schools and social institutions, as well as 20 major synagogues," the report said. "Publications in Hebrew are permitted," and "the Jewish community has close ties to communities in other nations, including Israel."

In Ethiopia, the report noted the "considerable illegal emigration" by Jews during 1984 since legal emigration is restricted for Jews and other Ethiopians. The report points out that access to the Jewish villages of the Gondar region by foreign Jews and Israelis, which was allowed in 1983, was shut off for most of 1984, although re-opened to some extent in December. "Ethiopian authorities apparently suspected that foreign Jewish and Israeli visitors provided Ethiopian Jews money and encouragement to leave the country," the report said. "They may also hope to prevent the outside world from learning of the frictions that continue to mark government relations with the Ethiopian Jewish community, resulting from government efforts to prevent emigration, lack of Hebrew instruction, and the resistance of Ethiopian Jews to Marxist-Leninist indoctrination.

The report added that while the Ethiopian Jews, because of where they live, are frequently caught in the cross-fire between government troops and insurgents, "stories of 'genocidal' actions by Ethiopian authorities, or highly brutal behavior, appear unfounded."

The human rights report, as in other recent State Department reports, charged that in the Soviet Union, "the Jewish community faced an exceptionally difficult year in 1984 which saw a sharp increase in antisemitic propaganda thinly veiled as anti-Zionism" as well as increased discrimination against Jews. The report speculated that there may be "pressure from some quarters to end Jewish emigration completely."

Abrams said that he did not believe that the urging by Reagan Administration officials at their meetings with Soviet officials for improvement in human rights conditions of Jews and others in the USSR has so far had any effect, but "it is hard to measure," he said.

March

Some 55 tons of food, medication, tents and mobile field kitchens donated by the Magen David Adom (MDA) First

Aid Society, Israel's equivalent of the Red Cross, have arrived in Kenya to aid famine victims in that country.

The relief supplies, shipped from Eilat to the Kenyan port of Mombasa, included 20 tons of flour, 20 tons of sugar, 15 tons of edible oil, five tons of baby food, some half a ton of antibiotics, about 60 family tents and ten mobile field kitchens—all Israeli-made.

Israel is selling "know-how" to the People's Republic of China, employing the promotional services of a local public relations firm and a PR firm in Hong Kong which specializes in translation.

Yonatan Goldberg, head of the Gitam Image Promotion Co., said that Gitam was commissioned to prepare publicity and informational material for the representatives of two Israeli companies who went to China to explain certain processes and to see that they were properly implemented.

Sen. Alan Cranston (D. Calif.) said he believes that all Ethiopian Jews previously stranded in the Sudan when Israel was forced to halt its rescue operation last January are now out of that country following the secret airlift of Ethiopian Jews conducted by the United States.

It has been reported in several leading newspapers that Vice President George Bush successfully laid the groundwork for the airlift when he met with Nimeiry in Khartoum on March 6. The rescue mission is reported to have been conducted by the Central Intelligence Agency, along with the aid of the State Department and the U.S. Air Force.

The new Liberal government taking over in Uruguay on March 1, following elections there three months ago, will include three Jews in prominent posts, the World Jewish Congress reported.

According to the Latin American branch of the WJC, no Jew was elected to national office in the new government, whose main personalities—with President Julio Maria Sanguinetti at the helm—have been for many years proven friends of the Jewish community and of Israel. However, one of the 19 mayors of the country is a Jew. He is Benito Stern in Maldonado, whose jurisdiction includes the famous beach resort of Punta del Este.

In the capital of Montevideo, the mayor chose a Jewish engineer, Luis Lieberman, to head the vitally important department of public works and services. A third Jew, Julio Kneit, was appointed an economic advisor to the new government. Kneit is a former president of the *Kehila*.

The Tunisian League for the Rights of Man elected Serge Edda, a 42-year-old Jewish businessman of Tunis, to its executive committee at the organization's annual general conference, the Tunisian news agency, Tunis Arab Press (TAP) reported.

Edda was confirmed by an overwhelming majority of the 300 delegates who flatly rejected the protest by one of their number that he was "fundamentally opposed to the election of a Jew because all Jews are by definition Zionists."

Ernst Zundel, a resident alien in Canada since 1958, was sentenced to 15 months imprisonment and three years probation by a federal judge for publishing the lie that the Holocaust did not occur.

Zundel, 46, a citizen of West Germany, was convicted under a section of the Canadian criminal code forbidding the dissemination of false information, in his booklet "Did Six Million Really Die?" While the maximum penalty is two

HIS TRIPS AND HIS SKIPS

JERUSALEM

POPE'S TRAVELS

years in prison, any sentence over six months makes him liable to deportation proceedings.

During the three year probation period, Zundel is enjoined from writing, communicating or speaking directly or indirectly on the subject of the Holocaust. The defense is expected to appeal.

A sense of relief swept the 2,000 Jews of the Irish Republic after the government's ban of Pieter Menten, the 85-year-old Dutch millionnaire found guilty of slaughtering Jews in Poland in 1941. Menten owns a large estate near the city of Waterford and was planning to spend the rest of his life there after serving eight years out of a 10-year sentence in a Dutch prison.

But following strenuous protests by the Dublin Jewish representative council, backed by a handful of Jewish members of the Irish Parliament, the Cabinet declared Menten an undesirable alien and prohibited him from entering the Emerald Isle.

The Soviet Union's treatment of Jews was likened to South Africa's apartheid policies by the head of the United States delegation to the United Nations Human Rights Commission, Ambassador Richard Schifter.

Referring to the Commission's earlier discussion of "the phenomenon of discrimination and deprivation of rights on grounds of ancestry practiced in South Africa," the U.S. envoy declared that "similar practices can be identified in the Soviet Union" where "discrimination and persecution is based solely on ancestry and has been on the increase . . . In fact, 1984 has been one of the worst years in recent memory," he said.

Schifter added, "Singled out for such discrimination and persecution are the Soviet Union's Jews and it is because the Soviet media reflects the government's point of view that the increase in antisemitic propaganda is of serious concern. Soviet antisemitism has been offered to the public under the label of anti-Zionism," he charged.

April

Leaders of French political and cultural life and thousands of ordinary Parisians reacted to the latest incident of antisemitic violence in Paris with a mixture of outrage over the act and outpourings of sympathy and solidarity with the Jewish community.

Thousands of demonstrators marched through the center of the city today to protest the bombing of the small Rivoli Beaubourg cinema where the fourth International Jewish Film Festival was taking place.

Three majority candidates in Guatemala's first Presidential election in two decades promised to expand relations with Israel if elected. One of the candidates also called for moving his country's embassy to Jerusalem from Tel Aviv.

Only 97 Jews were permitted to emigrate from the Soviet Union during March, the National Conference on Soviet Jewry reported.

The 850th anniversary of the birth of Maimonides was celebrated in Bucharest. Hundreds gathered for a series of lectures depicting the great Jewish philosopher, doctor, scientist and legislator. The opening lecture was given by Rumanian Chief Rabbi Moses Rosen, who spoke on Maimonides "the legislator." The entire symposium will be repeated, as thousands of would-be listeners did not manage to squeeze into the packed halls.

West German Chancellor Helmut Kohl, speaking at a ceremony in Bergen-Belsen, said that Germans bore "never-ending shame" for the atrocities committed by the Nazis during World War II. Addressing a crowd of some 3,000 people, including Jewish survivors of the camp, Kohl declared: "Reconciliation with the survivors and descendants of victims is only possible if we accept our history as it really was; if we Germans acknowledge our shame."

In his speech, broadcast live on television, Kohl said that Bergen-Belsen "remains a mark of Cain branded in the minds of our nation, just like Auschwitz, Treblinka, Belzec and Sobibor, Chelmno and Majdanek and the many other sites testifying to that mania for destruction."

The Chancellor announced plans to establish an archive for the study of Jewish history in Germany, saying that this was intended to underline the great role played by German Jewish thinkers in past centuries.

Before the ceremonies began, Kohl and President Richard Von Weizaecker both laid wreaths at the memorial to the 100,000 people who died in Bergen-Belsen.

Pope John Paul assailed Nazism as "a mad imperialist ideology" and condemned the atrocities that it bred, including the killings of the Jewish people who were "condemned to extermination."

In an Easter message delivered to more than 200,000 persons gathered in St. Peter's Square, the Pope invoked the 40th anniversary of the conclusion of World War II. He praised the men and women in each country who offered their lives in sacrifice for the right cause, the cause of the dignity of the human person.

"They faced death as defenseless victims, offered in Holocaust, or defending with their arms the free way to

HOME AT LAST!

life," the Pope said. "They fought not to answer violence with violence or hatred with hatred but to affirm a right and a freedom for themselves and others, also for the children of those who were then the oppressors."

"For more than five years," the Pope added, "humanity had lived a horrendous experience. Tens of millions of people massacred, on the battlefronts, cities razed, slaughter in the air and on the sea, populations ruined by hunger and privations."

In addition, he said, "other tens of millions of human beings" were "decimated and destroyed in the concentration camps." The Pope also sent a Passover greeting in Hebrew to the Jewish people.

The Swiss National Bank admitted, in a study written by its former archivist, that it helped finance the Nazi war machine during World War II by accepting more than 1.6 billion Swiss Francs' worth of gold looted by the Nazis from Jews and from the treasuries of occupied countries.

The study, by Robert Vogler, published in the Bank's quarterly bulletin, demonstrated that while the Third Reich had the equivalent of no more than 22 million Swiss Francs' worth of gold when the war started in 1939, it exchanged gold for 1.638 billion Swiss Francs in transactions with Swiss banks between 1939 and 1945.

May

Sudan's new military rulers named a colonel in the now disbanded State Security Department as the man responsible for having permitted the departure by air of thousands of Ethiopian Jews to Israel. The Military Council now ruling Sudan has said it will open an inquiry into "the Falasha affair" and will "severely punish" those responsible for the airlift used by thousands of Jewish refugees.

More Soviet Jews were permitted to emigrate to Israel during April than in any other month since July 1983, with 166 leaving. The total includes more than 100 Jews from Moscow, a city where there has been little emigration movement in recent years.

Black African states that had broken off diplomatic relations with Israel after the Yom Kippur War, largely under Arab pressure, have begun quietly to resume economic and diplomatic ties with the Jewish State, according to the latest issue of *Boycott Report*, an American Jewish Congress publication.

The *Boycott Report*, quoting accounts in the authoritative Paris weekly, *Jeune Afrique*, and in the *Economist* of London, notes that despite the lack of diplomatic relations, Nigeria, Kenya, Ivory Coast, Ghana and Togo all do "lively business" with Israel. About 1,000 Israelis are now working in Nigeria. A Nigerian presidential candidate, Chief Obafemi Awoloho, recently visited Israel.

The Lavi, Israel's second generation all-purpose combat plane, will be seen for the first time outside Israel at the annual Paris Air Show opening at Le Bourget Airport. About a half million visitors are expected.

A synagogue in the heart of Rosario, the second largest city in Argentina, was the target of an arson attempt, the World Jewish Congress reported.

According to the Latin American branch of the WJC, the incident, which was condemned in a published statement by the DAIA, the representative body of Argentine Jewry, has contributed to the climate of concern affecting the Jewish community.

There is a profusion of antisemitic and Nazi material for sale at news kiosks and bookstores, and signs of growing

pro-Arab activity threatening the Argentine-Israeli relationship.

June

The West German government was charged with engaging in what the World Jewish Congress said is a deliberate campaign aimed at restricting entry into the Federal Republic of alleged Nazi war criminals deported from the United States.

The WJC revealed that a letter written in 1984 by the West German Consul General in Washington, Elfriede Kruger, to the Justice Department, confirms West Germany's refusal to accept any deportees that are not of German nationality. The letter is included in court documents filed in connection with the case of accused Nazi war criminal Karl Linnas.

The WJC also charged that German authorities are seeking to force the United States to accept the return of Arthur Rudolph, the former NASA official who surrendered his American citizenship and returned to his native Germany last year after the Justice Department revealed that he had participated in persecuting slave laborers at the Nazi V-2 rocket factory during World War II.

Kharkov Jewish activist Evgeny Aisenberg was convicted of "defaming the Soviet State" and sentenced to two and half years in a labor camp, the Coalition to Free Soviet Jews reported. Aisenberg, 33, had been intensively involved in studying and teaching Hebrew and Jewish culture since 1978, when his pro-emigration activities led him to lose his job as a mechanical engineer. The major evidence used against him was the text of three Purim skits which he participated in last year. Aisenberg will be forced to separate from his wife, Marina, who has breast cancer and requires surgery.

Justice Minister Moshe Nissim announced that Israel will wait on drawing a formal conclusion on the identity of the body exhumed and examined this month in Brazil and believed to be that of Josef Mengele until Israeli experts have examined all the data.

A team of international forensic experts from West Germany, Brazil and the United States indicated that they were convinced that the body exhumed from a grave in a cemetery near Sao Paulo was that of the notorious Nazi death camp doctor, Mengele, known as the "Angel of Death."

Mengele was the target of an international manhunt. He was responsible for the deaths of hundreds of thousands of inmates at the Auschwitz death camp during the Holocaust. He is said to have drowned in a swimming mishap in 1979. His son Rolf Mengele, a West German lawyer, said that the body found in Sao Paulo is that of his father.

A report issued in Sao Paulo by a team of international forensic experts from the United States, Brazil and West Germany concluded that the bones exhumed from the graveyard were those of Mengele. The American delegation issued a separate report concluding that the bones were those of Mengele "within a reasonable scientific certainty."

The U.S. Justice Department said that it supports the conclusions of the international group of experts. "Based on the information available from the forensic examination, these experts have concluded that the body exhumed by Brazilian authorities is in fact Josef Mengele," Attorney General Edwin Meese III said in a statement issued in Washington.

While the only tangible result of the five-day state visit by Israeli President Chaim Herzog to his native land was the decision by the Irish government to abolish the need for visas for Israeli tourists, the Herzog visit was clearly a major success.

A senior Irish government official said it reflected the warmest friendship between Israel and Ireland and "enhanced our mutual friendship and respect."

A federal Canadian commission announced that it has compiled a list of 660 suspected Nazi war criminals who now live in Canada or may have lived here and is weighing evidence against them.

INSIDE ISRAEL

September 1984

The government has imposed harsh new economic measures aimed at absorbing some $900 million from the public sector as a means of curbing inflation.

But the double-barreled approach that went into effect— a one-time property tax and cuts in subsidies for fuel and certain basic commodities that sent prices soaring—has come under fire from some of the country's leading economists.

The cutback on subsidies took effect immediately to avoid hoarding for the High Holidays. The tax, which won final approval by the Cabinet, will apply to private cars, boats, apartments where the owner is not the resident, business premises and securities. Tax collection methods will be tightened and loopholes closed, according to Finance Minister Yitzhak Modai.

But if the government is prepared to tighten the public's belt, it is having difficulty with its own. A major stumbling

THREE FAITHS—ONE FLAG

TIPTOEING THROUGH THE MINEFIELDS

OTHER ENEMIES

LEBANON

ECONOMIC MESS

ARAB TERRORISM

KAHANE SYNDROME

block at the moment is the Education Ministry's budget. Modai and Education Minister Yitzhak Navon agreed to bring their differences before a special ministerial committee headed by Prime Minister Peres, which would have the final say.

The most serious issue is whether or not to continue free high school education. The Education Ministry has proposed raising social insurance payments by 0.2 percent to fund free high school education or, alternatively, impose an overall education tax.

By American and West European standards, Israeli prices are a bargain. A loaf of ordinary bread costs 10 cents. A liter of milk is 30 cents. An egg costs seven cents. A kilo of meat sells from $5.25 and a gallon of premium gasoline is $2.50. But the average Israeli family must now spend $500 a month to cover its basic needs, according to the Central Bureau of Statistics.

October

Former Prime Minister Menachem Begin left Shaare Zedek Hospital after a three-week stay during which he underwent surgery for a prostate condition. He appeared to be in good health, though wan, and in good spirits.

The fact that he spoke to the news media and allowed himself to be photographed immediately raised speculation that Begin will end the self-imposed seclusion that has lasted since his sudden resignation as Prime Minister in September, 1983.

Speaking briefly to reporters before leaving for his home in a Jerusalem suburb, Begin refused to be drawn into comment on current political matters. He said he "wanted to thank" the medical staff and nurses who had "taken such good care of me." He had special praise for Dr. Amitzur Farkas, head of the urology department at Shaare Zedek, who successfully performed surgery on the 71-year-old Begin on September 20.

The former Prime Minister's long-time aide and confidant, Yehiel Kadishai, told the media that Begin may start writing the book he plans, a personal saga of the Holocaust and the birth of Israel tentatively titled *The Generation of Destruction and Redemption.*

Platoons of government price monitors, beefed up by volunteers, closed in on supermarkets and other retail establishments all over Israel to make sure that the six-month price freeze imposed on all consumer goods is being observed.

Early reports from the freeze front said that 40 percent of the businesses in the Tel Aviv area were charging excessive prices. The supervisors found that dozens of small businesses upped their prices to make a quick profit before the freeze can be fully enforced or because the price situation was unclear to them. Excessive prices were found on such basics as cooking oil, margarine, noodles and matches.

The Technion, Israel's institute of technology in Haifa, is the only institute of higher learning in Israel to commence its new school year on time.

All the others, including the Hebrew University in Jerusalem, Tel Aviv University, the Ben Gurion University of the Negev in Beersheba, Bar-Ilan and Weizmann Institute of Science's Feinberg Graduate School, have postponed their openings until November, because of financial difficulties and uncertainty about the extent of government aid they can expect this year.

The Technion said it would open on time because even a delay of a few days in beginning scientific and technical courses might delay a full year's work program.

November

A majority of Israelis expressed shock and revulsion this week over the rocket attack—apparently by Jewish extremists—on an Arab bus enroute to Hebron from Jerusalem. An Arab youth, identified as Ismail El-Mattur, 20, was killed and 10 other passengers, all Palestinians, were wounded.

The assault, by an Israel Defense Force-issue missile, occurred on the Bethlehem Road, near the Jerusalem railway station. A handwritten note, found alongside the abandoned rocket launcher, declared that the attack was in revenge for the murder near Bethlehem a week earlier of an Israeli man and woman, allegedly by a resident of the Daheisha refugee camp.

The Knesset's House Committee and the Ministry of Justice were moving on parallel tracks toward swift action that could deprive Rabbi Meir Kahane, leader of the extremist Kach party, of his Knesset immunity and open the way to prosecute him for racist incitement against Arab citizens of Israel and Arabs on the West Bank and Gaza.

The Justice Ministry is putting final touches to a new law against "racism" which it plans to submit to parliament. The draft bill was reported to have been circulated to other ministries for amendments before a final version is presented to the legislators for enactment.

December

Unemployment in Israel reached a record high of nearly 100,000 jobless, about six percent of the work force. It is the highest rise since the economic slump of the mid-1960's, just before the Six-Day War.

Prime Minister Shimon Peres confirmed that he had received a letter from Secretary of State George Shultz making clear that he would not support Israel's requests for increased U.S. economic aid unless and until the Israeli government produced a comprehensive economic recovery plan.

Peres, addressing Central Bureau of Statistics officials, said it should serve as a warning bell. He said that Shultz complimented the government for doing more to help the economy than its predecessors. But at the same time, the Secretary of State pointed to grave dangers close at hand "unless we act faster and do more," Peres said.

Israel is seeking $4.1 billion in U.S. military and economic aid for the fiscal year 1986, which begins next October 1. This is $1.5 billion more than the $2.6 billion Israel will receive during fiscal 1985, all of it in grants.

The media reports said Shultz's letter advised Peres that his government would have to demonstrate that the increased aid will be put to good use and will not simply fuel inflation. American officials have been demanding a detailed economic plan from Israel to justify its new requests.

Haaretz reported that while Shultz acknowledged to Peres that the unity government has indeed slashed its budget, more remained to be pruned. He urged "structural changes" in the Israeli economy, *Haaretz* said, meaning apparently that the state must stop funding uneconomical businesses and projects.

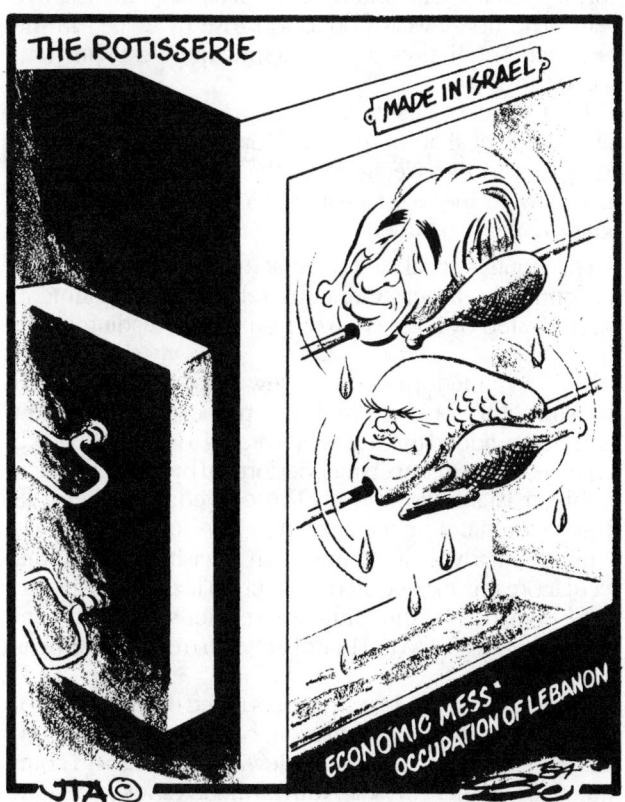

THE ROTISSERIE — MADE IN ISRAEL — ECONOMIC MESS · OCCUPATION OF LEBANON — JTA©

January 1985

The town of Eilat extended a warm, enthusiastic welcome to a group of Ethiopian Jewish immigrants who arrived there to settle.

The newcomers were greeted with smiles, flowers and food when they arrived at the seven-story apartment block that will be their home. They will share the building with government-appointed counselors whose job is to help them adjust and integrate into their new surroundings.

The Army Radio reported that each flat in the Eilat block is equipped with a refrigerator, gas stove and water heater, amenities the immigrants never saw in Ethiopia. Part of the task of the counselors will be to teach them to use these appurtenances of modern living.

But the Ethiopian *olim* are not welcome everywhere in Israel. The town of Yerucham in the Negev has made clear that with the threat of unemployment hanging over its residents, they do not want newcomers competing for jobs with the townspeople.

The report by State Comptroller Yitzhak Tunik on the collapse of publicly-held commercial bank shares in October, 1983, sent shock waves through the economic community and government circles.

Tunik, whose report was over a year in the making, flatly accused the country's major banks of "manipulation" that made the October 6, 1983 crash inevitable, with severe financial losses to investors and the nation as a whole. He held the government's financial institutions responsible for failing to take action to halt "the corrupting phenomenon" which had gone on for more than a decade.

Israel's population stood at 4,235,000 at the end of 1984, according to the Central Bureau of Statistics. Of this total, 3.5 million are Jews. The Jewish population rose by 82,000 during the past year, and by some 500,000 in the last five years. The non-Jewish population rose by 20,000 in the past year. The figures do not include the West Bank and Gaza Strip.

Road accident fatalities in Israel during 1984 were 11 percent fewer than in 1983 and dropped by 32 percent compared to the average over the five preceding years, according to Inspector Eitan Ben-Yehoshua, head of the police traffic department.

The controversial amendment to the Law of Return demanded by Israel's Orthodox religious establishment was defeated by a vote of 62-51 on its first reading in the Knesset.

The Law of Return defines a Jew as a person born of a Jewish mother or converted. The proposed amendment would have added the words "according to halacha" which would invalidate conversions performed by non-Orthodox rabbis in Israel and abroad. The converts and their offspring would not be recognized as Jews in Israel.

Representatives of 21 American Jewish religious and secular organizations called on political leaders in Israel to resist demands by the Orthodox religious establishment for an amendment to the Law of Return to redefine "Who is a Jew."

In addition, the 21 Jewish leaders urged that Israel establish an international commission, composed of representatives of the major branches of Jewish religious and communal life, to meet in Israel with Orthodox spokesmen "in hope of working out an agreement that would prevent the deep divisions in Jewish life we fear if the proposed legislation is passed."

The greatest increase of American tourism to Israel since the establishment of the State in 1948 took place in 1984, it was announced in New York by Moshe Shoshani, Israel's commissioner for tourism for North America. He said that "405,000 Americans visited Israel in 1984, which represents a staggering 15 percent increase over 1983 when 354,000 Americans travelled there." A peak figure of 1.3 million visitors world-wide was also a record achievement.

Orthodox Jews began a boycott of the Bank Leumi, Israel's largest bank, because a luxury hotel under construction by an affiliate of the bank, the Africa-Israel Investment Corp., allegedly is located atop an ancient cemetery near Tiberias where Jewish sages were buried centuries ago.

The bank acknowledged that $10 million had been withdrawn by some 400 Orthodox depositors. Bank officials said this represented a very small portion of its total deposits and turnover.

February

An eight-month economic program to drastically reduce public and private spending, increase government revenues and raise foreign currency reserves, already at a dangerous low, took effect at midnight shortly after it was approved by the Cabinet, meeting in special session.

Immigration from the West fell by about 30% in 1984, but overall immigration to Israel rose by 17% to about 20,000, in 1984 over 1983, according to Absorption Minister Yaacov Tsur. He said that 24% fewer newcomers arrived

GULLIVERS AMONG LILLIPUTS

from North America last year compared with 1983; 33% fewer from South America; and 31% fewer from Western Europe.

Israel's present unemployment rate of 6.3 percent may double by the middle of the year, according to an internal report submitted by the Manpower Planning Authority of the Ministry of Labor and Social Affairs to Minister Moshe Katsav.

The Jerusalem Post suggested that the unemployment figure may then be 170,000 jobless—higher than the 125,000 foreseen in the report if figures of job-seekers compiled by the Central Bureau of Statistics' quarterly labor force survey are taken into consideration.

In addition, another 35,000 youths and demobilized soldiers are expected to join the labor market in 1985, driving the unemployment figure even higher.

March

The cost of living index rose by 13.5 percent during February, the Central Bureau of Statistics announced. The increase was as anticipated, due to price rises at the overlap (known in Hebrew as the seam) between the first and second package deals.

The transfer of the entire Talmud to cassettes has been completed by Rabbi Shabtai Sabbato, 35, of the World Zionist Organization's Beit Midrash Letorah Yeshiva. The achievement was marked this week at a ceremony attended by the two Chief Rabbis, Knesset members, scholars and WZO leaders.

There are 1,000 cassettes containing 1,500 hours of Talmud study. They will enable busy would-be students to imbibe Talmud study while driving or (on Walkman) while engaged in other non-intellectual pursuits.

April

The six million Jews who perished in the Holocaust and those Righteous Gentiles who died while saving Jews will be granted posthumous Israeli citizenship, according to a Knesset declaration. This unprecedented expression is to be officially announced at the 40th anniversary observance of the defeat of Nazi Germany, scheduled for May 5-9 in Jerusalem.

The prices of hundreds of goods and services went up by 10-15 percent as the Treasury introduced a new economic package deal approved by the government, business and the Histadrut.

Israel and the United States signed an agreement—unprecedented in the history of U.S. trade policy—that will remove all trade barriers on goods and services exchanged between the two countries.

In a signing ceremony at the House Ways and Means Committee, Israel's Minister of Commerce and Industry, Ariel Sharon, and special U.S. Trade Representative William Brock, stressed that the agreement would benefit the economies of both the U.S. and Israel and serve as a precedent for future similar agreements with other countries.

A statement read by Brock from President Reagan called the agreement a "milestone in our efforts to liberalize trade."

The U.S.-Israel Trade Area agreement will eliminate tariffs and other trade barriers in phases over a 10-year period.

Leading Knesset members have called for exhaustive parliamentary discussions before Israel decides how to respond to Washington's invitation to participate in "star wars" research. Victor Shemtov (Mapam), acting chairman of the Foreign Affairs and Security Committee, suggested a full debate in that committee. Earlier, Shevach Weiss (Labor) urged discussion in the plenary.

President Reagan had said publicly he would offer the NATO countries, Japan, Australia and Israel a chance to join in the research. The Foreign Ministry said a reply would be sent as soon as possible.

U.S. Secretary of the Navy John Lehman announced in Tel Aviv that Israel will build three diesel-powered submarines for its navy, with financial and technological assistance from the U.S.

More than half the prisoners released—600 Palestinians—were permitted to return to their homes in the West Bank and Gaza Strip. Most security officials agreed they pose a potential menace, if not immediately, then in the long term. But confidence was expressed that the security forces are fully capable of handling any threat that might materialize.

The government won an overwhelming vote of confidence in the Knesset for its controversial prisoner exchange. The Knesset also rejected three opposition motions to establish a commission of inquiry into the Lebanon war.

The question of amnesty for alleged members of a Jewish underground terrorist group now on trial or serving sentences for crimes of violence against Arabs in the West Bank is rapidly building up into an explosive issue in Israel.

The demand for immediate release of the Jewish suspects on trial and those already convicted arose from West Bank settlers in reaction to the controversial and generally unpopular prisoner exchange of May 20. Deputy Prime Minister Yitzhak Shamir, leader of the Likud, went so far as to promise the wives of the defendants that their spouses would be released shortly.

Zaire's President Mobutu Sese Seko ended the official part of his state visit to Israel by signing, with President Chaim Herzog, three cooperation accords—in the areas of aviation, investment, and technical training.

In the 18 years since reunification, Jerusalem has become the largest city in Israel with the largest Jewish population, according to data released by the Central Bureau of Statistics.

At the end of 1984, the population of Jerusalem stood at 445,000, of whom 320,000 are Jewish and about 125,000 non-Jewish. The population of Tel Aviv-Jaffa was 323,000, of which 313,000 are Jews. But Tel Aviv and its commuter suburbs—Petach Tikva, Ramat Gan, Givatayim—constitute the country's largest urban area with a population of 800,000.

The Tel Aviv municipality has declared this year the Rambam Year to mark the 850th birthday of the philosopher Maimonides, known as the Rambam. The city will introduce special lessons in local schools devoted to the personality of the scholar who greatly influenced Jewish thought. His birthday falls on April 5, or Nissan 14 on the Hebrew calendar. About 10,000 people participated in special festivities in Tiberias, near Maimonides' grave.

Israelis celebrated the 37th anniversary of their independence in a less than joyous mood. Festivities were muted. There were far fewer flags on display than in past

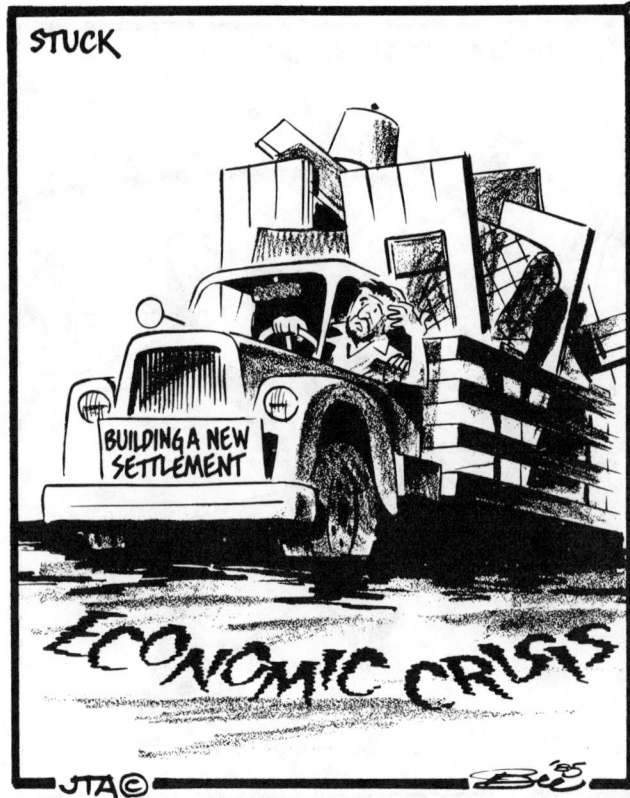

years, less bunting and ribbon-bedecked portraits of national leaders on commercial premises, more modest decorations and fewer colored lights on public buildings, reflecting budget cuts and the high cost of electricity.

For the first time since the anguished days following the Yom Kippur War, the national spirit is low. It was mirrored in President Chaim Herzog's Independence Day address, broadcast on radio and television.

He dwelt on what he saw as the most serious threats to Israeli society: the "grave economic crisis," the "internal problems that give me particular cause for concern"— extremism, fanaticism and racism, which threaten the fabric of Israel's democracy.

Sullen, heavily overcast skies, chill winds and unseasonably low temperatures contributed to the somber mood, though they did not keep tens of thousands of Israelis from the beaches, picnic grounds and camping sites.

May

There can be no reconciliation with history; lessons must be learned from it, President Chaim Herzog declared to representatives from 18 countries who gathered at the Presidential residence to mark the 40th anniversary of the defeat of Nazi Germany.

Prime Minister Shimon Peres, addressing a special session of the Knesset convened for the occasion, said Israel noted with "deep sorrow and pain" the "painful mistake" by the President of the United States who placed a wreath at the war cemetery in Bitburg, West Germany.

Ariel Sharon, the Minister of Commerce and Industry, an outspoken Likud hard-liner, maintained that had Menachem Begin still been Prime Minister instead of Laborite Peres, there would have been "no stuttering reponse" to Reagan's Bitburg visit. Sharon accused the Labor compo-

nent of the national unity government of not knowing how to "stand up to the gentiles."

But Begin, in one of his rare interviews since he retired into semi-seclusion in August 1983, told the Associated Press that Bitburg was one of the saddest days in Jewish history. But he declined to criticize Reagan directly.

The unexpected 19.4 percent hike in the consumer price index in April was conceded by government officials to be a severe setback to economic recovery. But it may have been the shock treatment needed to force the government to take drastic and politically unappetizing measures to correct the nation's severe economic woes.

Officials were predicting that the April price index would not exceed 12 percent. The actual figure, nearly eight percentage points higher, means that inflation is running at an annual rate of 320 percent.

Secretary of State George Shultz solemnly renewed America's pledge to always stand by and support Israel, in a moving speech at the Yad Vashem Holocaust Memorial during ceremonies marking the 40th anniversary of the defeat of Nazi Germany.

A deeply divided Israel was agonizing over the wisdom and dangers of a prisoner exchange carried out in which Israel set free 1,150 Palestinian and other terrorists— among them convicted mass murderers serving life sentences—for the release of three Israeli soldiers held captive for nearly three years by a Damascus-based Palestinian terrorist organization.

June

Israel's three year war in Lebanon ended without official announcements or declarations. According to government statements more than a month earlier, the Israel Defense Force was to be completely out of Lebanese territory by June 6, the third anniversary of its invasion of Lebanon, dubbed at the time "Operation Peace for Galilee."

Israelis generally accept the fact that the war is over. It cost 654 soldiers and other security personnel dead and nearly 6,000 wounded. If it did indeed achieve "peace for Galilee", the settlers in the northern border towns seem hardly less apprehensive over their security now than they were on June 6, 1982 when the IDF plunged into Lebanon.

The last Lebanese soil occupied by the IDF was a security belt several miles deep which roughly parallels the Israel border. The Israel-backed South Lebanon Army (SLA) has been given the task of maintaining security there and preventing the infiltration of Palestinian terrorists or hostile guerillas. A cadre of IDF officers remains to serve as liaison and advisors. The IDF has reserved the right to send fighting units back into Lebanon should a situation develop there threatening Israel's security.

The number of *yordim*—Israelis leaving the country to settle abroad—increased sharply last year with the Bank of Israel reporting that 10,000 left in 1984. The Central Bureau of Statistics, however, put the figure at 17,000. In 1983, only 4,700 Israelis emigrated. Each institution used a different system of calculation for the latest totals.

All of Israel was in mourning for the 18 children and four adults killed when a speeding passenger train slammed into a busload of seventh graders stalled on an unguarded railroad crossing about 12 miles south of Haifa. Seventeen children were injured and hospitalized.

The accident, which transport authorities said was one of the worst in Israel's history, occurred at one of 300 railroad crossings which have no gates or warning lights because they are on little-used secondary roads.

The Mediterranean-Dead Sea canal, a hydro-electric project enthusiastically backed by the former Likud-led government, is dead. The Ministry of Energy and Infrastructure concluded that it was no longer feasible, due in large measure to lack of funds, and ordered a halt to preliminary work which has already cost some $15 million.

The original idea was to use the more than 1,000 foot drop from sea level to the Dead Sea to generate electric power. The canal was supposed to revolutionize Israel's energy systems. On that basis, the Israel Bonds Organization raised substantial funds overseas.

The government adopted a new economic plan, the immediate effects of which will be soaring prices for most consumer goods and reduced compensation for workers. The Knesset, under strict coalition discipline, handed Prime Minister Shimon Peres and Finance Minister Yitzhak Modai a substantial victory when it voted 70-17 to approve the economic package.

Opposition by Histadrut was instantaneous. The powerful trade union federation staged what it called a 24-hour "work stoppage" which halted virtually all business, commercial and productive activity in Israel. Histadrut claimed that 1.5 million people, 90 percent of the country's workforce, were off the job.

The head of Histadrut's trade union department, Haim Haberfeld, and other officials warned that there would be selective strike action by individual unions in the future unless the government is prepared to negotiate elements of the economic program.

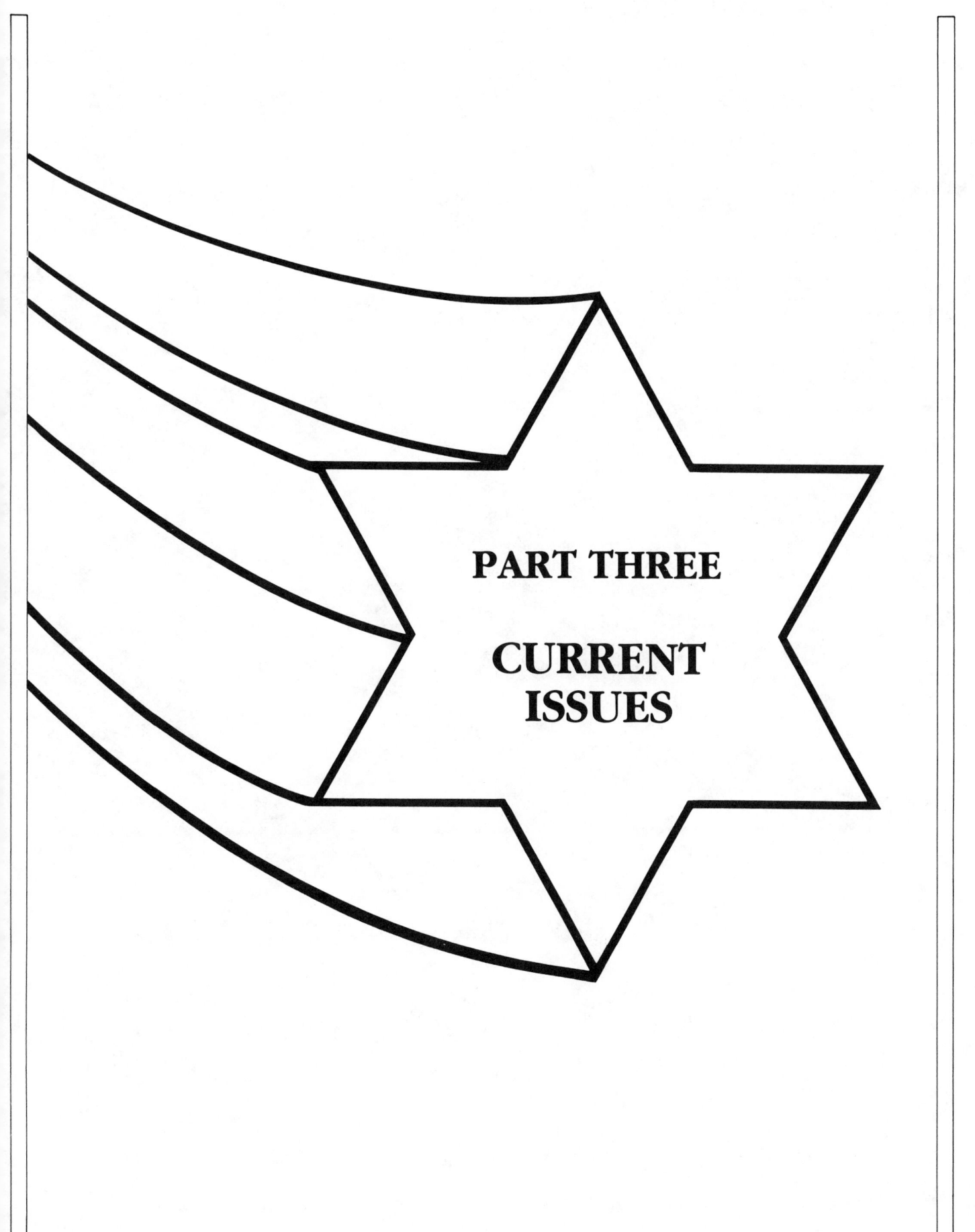

PART THREE

CURRENT ISSUES

The Greatest Jewish Problem

Dennis Prager

It is easier for leaders to tell their people—since it is easier for people to hear—that their problems emanate from outside. But when leaders do this, they are not leading. Indeed they are hurting their group because they are not addressing its greatest problems, which are so often internal.

This applies equally to Jewish life in the free world. While Jews certainly have external enemies who must be fought, the greatest Jewish problem—the rapidly dwindling number of committed or even identifying Jews—is internal. It is not caused by neo-Nazis, Arafat, the Soviets, Jesse Jackson, school prayer, the arms race, or any of the other external problems concentrated upon by Jews and their organizations. The greatest Jewish problem is caused, and can only be solved, by the Jews themselves.

The problem is not survival

Before addressing the problem, its causes and possible solutions, let me put it into perspective. Those of us who hold that the greatest Jewish problem is the disappearing Jew are often criticized as doomsayers. Hasn't every generation of Jews had its predictors of the end of Jewry? Aren't we, as one Jewish philosopher put it, "the ever-dying people?"

In light of this objection, I want to make my position very clear. I do not for one moment fear the end of the Jewish people. So long as there are human beings, I have no doubt that some of them will be Jewish. Should other planets ever be colonized, I am certain that some Jews will be there asking passersby whether they had put on Tefillin that morning.

Nor am I a survivalist. The purpose of Jewish life is not that Jews survive. The purpose of Jewish life is that Jews lead Jewish lives, be "a light unto the nations," and "repair the world under God's rule." Therefore, when I say that the greatest Jewish problem is the diminishing number of Jews, it is not because I am worried about Jewish survival. We will survive.

The problem

I am concerned not that Jews will die out, but that they will become irrelevant. I am concerned that fewer Jews means that Judaism will have less of an impact upon the world. There will always be Jews. The questions are what type of Jews? What quality of Jewish life? What impact will Judaism have on a world increasingly devoid of enduring values? And, of course, how many? As the dean of Jewish historians, Salo Baron, writes in *A Social and Religious History of the Jews*, "Whether the total number of Jews amounts to thousands or to millions makes a calculable difference in their social and hence in their religious life. . . . Quantity here becomes quality. . . ."

Once one understands, to use Herman Wouk's description, that the Jews are an army, one does not ask whether all its soldiers will survive. One asks whether the army is getting stronger or weaker, whether its struggle is nearer to or further from success.

Or, to cite Rabbi Abraham Joshua Heschel's equally accurate description, the modern Jew is "a messenger who forgot his message." Here, too, one does not ask whether the messenger will die—a messenger who forgets his message may very well live, but if he forgot his message, his survival is meaningless. As a messenger he *is* dead.

When Jews understand that they are an army, a messenger, they will recognize that their greatest problem is not Jewish survival but that fewer Jews are fighting, fewer Jews know that they have a message.

The cause

In other words, fewer and fewer Jews know *why* to be Jewish. This is the cause of the greatest Jewish problem. Jews may know how to survive, but they do not know why to survive. This is the overwhelming reason why Jews are assimilating.

This is a relatively new development. In the past, it was often enough to be born a Jew. You knew you were a Jew, that you would marry a Jew, live as a Jew, and die as a Jew. The greatest Jewish problem has often been *how* to survive—in the face of antisemitism, terrible economic conditions, and other problems caused by outside forces. The problem is that Jews continue to act as if this is still their greatest problem. Thus, Jewish life concentrates on *how* to fight antisemites, *how* to rescue persecuted Jews, *how* to feed and clothe the Jewish poor, *how* to gain political support for Israel.

And this emphasis is not only true of secular Jewish life. Religious Jewish life, too, generally ignores the *why* and focuses almost exclusively on the *how*. In my thirteen years of study in three different yeshivas, I learned well *how* to daven, *how* to keep kosher, *how* to study Jewish sources, *how* to keep the Shabbat, and innumerable other *hows* of Judaism. What I rarely learned was *why* I should do any of these things. And despite the fact that the only real answer to why be Jewish is a religious one, in all my years of religious Jewish education, the issue was, for all intents and purposes, ignored.

Jewish life, therefore, has been devoting its energies largely to dealing with the problem of the past, not *the* problem of the present. Without a Jewish *why,* a Jewish *how* strikes most Jews today as irrelevant. As Nietzsche put it, "He who has a why to live can bear with any how." Jews today lack the *why.* Give them that *why,* and they will find the *how* to survive. If Jewish life wants another generation of Jews to fight Israel's enemies or to raise funds for Jewish causes, it had better teach Jews why, in the first place, they ought to lead a Jewish life.

Jews need reasons to be Jewish

In open societies, relatively free of antisemitism, Jews need *reasons* to stay Jewish. Intermarriage provides a perfect example. There have always been two types of arguments against it—positive Jewish ones (why it is so important to perpetuate Judaism), and negative ones (about non-Jews).

In the past, even non-practicing Jews could, if nothing else, often count on the validity of negative arguments: "non-Jews are different," "they don't make good husbands," "they drink too much," "in an argument, they'll revert to antisemitism."

But these arguments no longer hold water. And the differences between irreligious Jews and irreligious non-Jews of the same socioeconomic and educational backgrounds are virtually non-existent. Young Jews therefore now regard those arguments as racist, since they are based on preserving the purity of Jewish ethnicity rather than the purity of Jewish values.

Only if Jewish values are distinctive is there a positive and non-racial reason for Jews not to intermarry or in any other way to maintain a distinct Jewish identity. But Jews have been raised increasingly to believe that Jewish values are not distinctive, that they are essentially identical to liberal, secular humanistic ones. Consequently, many Jews, both in their behavior and their values, have become indistinguishable from the many non-Jews who also have been raised without a distinctive religious value system and who hold the same liberal, secular humanistic values.

None of this should come as a surprise. Haven't a great many Jews been raised to regard most differences among groups—especially in the area of religion—as a reactionary notion to be discarded? Haven't they been taught to be "universalist" by not being "too Jewish?" Haven't they been taught that religion is either irrelevant to ethical values or an actual impediment to them? And once Judaism is no longer a Jew's source of values, does he have a single distinctive Jewish value?

Given such an upbringing, why should an American Jew identify as a Jew, lead a Jewish life, or marry a Jew, or raise Jewish children, or support Israel, or . . .?

The solution

Once the greatest Jewish problem and its cause are recognized, the solution is overwhelmingly clear. Jews must be taught *why* to be Jewish. Jewish life must embark on a campaign to teach this to Jews with the same commitment, resources and sense of life or death as it has in creating and supporting Israel. Even Jews whose dominant Jewish concern is Israel alone should recognize that without such a campaign to fight assimilation, there will be few Jews left in the Diaspora to support Israel.

Why be Jewish? Because the Jewish people has a religious/moral/holy mission to "repair the world under God's rule." Because the Jews are bidden by God to be a "light unto the nations." Because Judaism fills one's life with a holiness, meaning and joy that is not attainable to the uncommitted Jew. And because Judaism has *distinctive* values which if communicated to the world, will reduce human suffering, help to extinguish evil, and prevent holocausts (which are taking place with greater frequency and more apathy—see Afghanistan as an example.)

When Jews understand these reasons, they *will* lead Jewish lives. But they must have the reasons. In an open and free society, Jews need powerful, positive reasons to remain Jewish. They need to know why they should be different when non-Jews are equally well educated and fine, and why Judaism has better moral and personal answers than secular humanism.

And Jews need to learn the answer to a question once posed to me by a holocaust survivor who has completely rejected his Jewish identity, "Why should I bequeath to my child the possibility of another holocaust?"

Jews need *reasons*—intellectual, personal, moral—to be Jewish. Ethnic *feelings* will no longer suffice to keep Jews Jewish.

Ultimate Issues is written and published quarterly by Dennis Prager. Entire contents © Dennis Prager, *Ultimate Issues,* 2265 Westwood Boulevard, Suite 508, Los Angeles, CA 90064. Telephone: 213-204-4290. Subscriptions are $15.00 for one year, $30.00 for two years.

The Global Jewish Community: One Family Indivisible

Norman Lamm

Last year, my wife and I spent Yom Kippur and Sukkot in Jerusalem. I spoke to many people in stations high and low, and returned with one particularly empty, aching feeling: there are many leaders and many competent people, but nobody who is thinking about *all* of us. I found people who were thinking of the Army and people who were thinking of the religious and people who were thinking of the secular, people who were thinking of education and people who were thinking of Likud and people who were thinking of Maarakh. But I found no one whose concern covered all Jews, everywhere.

This is the principal reason I accepted the very kind invitation to speak on the theme of, "Global Jewish Community—One Nation Indivisible." Let us use the shorter and more pregnant term, hallowed by centuries of usage and resonant with both sacred and national sentiment, *Klal Yisrael*—the indivisible global community of the Jewish people.

Before such pious sentiments have a chance to act as sedatives and put you to sleep, dimly expecting the usual sermonic bromides about Jewish unity that are the cliches of our communal discourse, let me assure you that I will not at all dwell upon them. They are true, of course—the Talmud's teaching of *Kol Yisrael arevim zeh ba-zeh,* that all Jews are responsible for each other; that we must learn the lessons of the Holocaust; and that the State of Israel needs us as its only friends. They are true, but I shall not elaborate on them.

Let me ask you to bear in mind that what we take for granted does not necessarily enjoy universal acceptance amongst the Jewish people. We may advocate Jewish unity passionately, but it has not reached the level of a general consensus. Far from it.

A scene just forty-five years ago, aboard a BMT train in Brooklyn: Poland had been invaded by Hitler in September of 1939, five months earlier. A twelve-year-old youngster is shouting above the din and the rattle of the train, appealing for funds for "Vaad Hatzalah" to save Polish Jews. He approaches a middle-aged, obviously Jewish man who snarls at him and says, "I don't care about Polish Jews. I'm a Belgian Jew."

I was that youngster and I shall never forget that rebuff, not because my request for funds had been turned down—I have since grown accustomed to that—but because what I passionately believed in as a self-evident truth was cruelly shattered before my very eyes. The memory of that stupid man's statement will always be an execration that I will never forget. It gave me no joy when three months later Hitler invaded Belgium.

Hence, I have never thought of the concept of *Klal Yisrael* as something that is sufficiently obvious to enjoy the status of a slogan. As an adult I witnessed enough polemics between Israel-oriented and Diaspora-affirming Jews to be confirmed in my belief that Jewish unity still requires a great deal of tender loving care and vigorous affirmation. Such acrimonious debates occasionally are so adversarial and latently hostile that they scare me.

Even this very day the *Klal Yisrael* idea is not universally honored by Jews, in a functional sense, especially by the political and religious extremes; by those who unthinkingly assimilate; and by Israelis who, as part of their anti-Diaspora notions, effectively deny the underlying oneness of the Jewish people. Indeed, an Israeli diplomat told me this week that in Israel the definition of a Zionist Israeli is an Israeli who also identifies with Diaspora Jewry. That implies that all other Israelis bear no such feelings of relationship with the rest of us—surely a cause for worry.

Moreover, even on an open, explicit, and deliberate level, there are those (they used to be called "Canaanites") who deny that Israelis and Jews of other countries constitute one people. A little over a decade ago, I was invited to address an "ideological seminar" of the World Union of Jewish Students some thirty miles north of Helsinki in Finland. An ongoing debate developed between myself and a very debonaire Israeli journalist, publisher of a rather decadent, extremely left-wing newspaper.

Throughout the debate, he kept arguing that, "I am a member of the Hebrew Nation, while you are a member of the American Nation, you are a Belgian national, and you are a French national. I am a Hebrew national—and therefore we are not the same people. We may have some connection in the remote past, like that of the Australians and the British, but we are basically of different nationalities. I am a Hebrew national." I had had just about enough of this particular line and so I said, "I'd like you to know that in the country I come from, 'Hebrew National' is the name of a firm that produces baloney. The only difference is that their baloney is certified as kosher . . ."

Now, if we are to keep away from baloney, especially the non-kosher kind, and if we are to discover a guiding principle for our internal discussion in the studying of priorities and the allocation of resources, we have got to affirm this fundamental philosophic view of *Klal Yisrael.* The commitment to the indivisibility of the global Jewish family must dominate our thinking as and about Jews.

But commitment and affirmation are not enough. What is imperative as well is a clear-headed analysis and sophisticated understanding of the *concept* of Jewish identity.

Permit me to invite you to join me in a brief foray into halakhic discourse, using a Talmudic source as an analogy.

Jewish law places great importance upon the concept of a *neder* or vow. A word once given must be respected. Hence, the Kol Nidre prayer on Yom Kippur eve, which annuls vows, is so very solemn. One who does not keep a *neder* is regarded as utterly beneath contempt. Now there is a kind of vow called *noder hanaah*: a vow not to benefit from someone. I am angry with Mr. X, and I take a vow to have nothing to do with him and to abjure all *hanaah*—pleasure or benefit—from him. The Talmud teaches that if one took a *neder* not to derive any *hanaah* from the people of a particular city, that vow devolves upon all inhabitants who have established residence in that town; and "residence," in turn, is defined as living there for twelve months or more (*Baba Batra* 8a). However, the question arises, what of people who moved into that city and established residence by staying there 12 months *after* I took my vow? Are such new residents included in my previous *neder?* The problem occasioned a controversy between two of the greatest medieval Sephardic scholars. Ran (Rabbenu Nissim), of 14th century Barcelona, maintains that such future residents too are covered by the vow. Ritva (Rabbi Yom Tov B. Abraham), of 14th century Seville, disagrees and avers that the vow covers only past and present inhabitants, not future ones. Here we have a classical *machloket rishonim* (controversy between great medieval Talmudists) that begs for further elucidation and analysis. Such analysis is provided by one of the most brilliant Talmudists of our times, Rabbi Joseph Rosen, known as "The Rogatchover Genius." He suggests (in his *Tzophenat Paaneiach*) that what divides Ran and Ritva is this: a collectivity, such as a city or a town, can be understood in one of two ways. The city can be seen as nothing more than the sum of its parts. All the people who live there—no more, no less—constitute the town. There is no such thing as a "city" other than its population, the collection of inhabitants, the sum of its parts. The other definition of "city" is that a city has a life of its own and is more than the sum of its parts. It is something organic and there is something metaphysical about it—a quality beyond the people who live there. It is an independent entity, one that has a separate, corporate existence of its own. (This is reminiscent of the philosophic dispute of nominalism vs. realism.) Therefore, says the Rogatchover, Ritva holds that the new inhabitants are not included in the vow because he holds the more restricted view of "city" as including only the people who live there and nothing more than the people who live there. Therefore, when the *neder* was made it did not include those who moved into the city afterwards. Ran's opinion that the vow does include future residents results from his larger, more metaphysical or holistic definition of "city" as possessing a separate identity, over and above its residents. Hence, if people later moved into that city and lived there for 12 months, they become part of the "city," and it was this concept of city, not merely the sum total of its then citizens, which is covered by the vow.

This controversy holds true for a city, a town, or a country. But unquestionably, "Israel" as a people is an organic, metaphysical, indivisible entity, and not merely a sociological collectivity that is but the sum of its parts. For analytic reasons, it may be looked upon as a discrete social entity, but essentially it has a life of its own that extends far beyond the sum of the Jews and Jewesses who happen to be alive today.

You have heard it said that Israel and American Jewry are partners. I deny this. Not so! Partnerships are made and partnerships are dissolved, and even when they flourish they exist for specific and limited ends. We Jews the world over are not partners. Whether we like it or not, our destinies are interlinked. As *Klal Yisrael,* the global Jewish community is indeed "one family indivisible." We can argue with each other, and complain about each other—but we are one, and our oneness is not only the oneness that includes every Jew and Jewess alive in the world today all over the globe, but a oneness that comprehends all Jews and Jewesses who ever lived and who ever will live—the dead, the living, the unborn; the whole sweep of Jewish history as well as geography. This is why the Kabbalah teaches that another name for the Shechinah (divine Presence) is *Knesset Yisrael,* a synonym for *Klal Yisrael.* The indivisible unity of God is reflected in the uncompromised oneness of Israel.

So when I wonder, as I said at the outset, "who is thinking about all of us?," our response must be that if indeed no one outstanding figure is obviously doing that, then we must all of us, individually and collectively, do just that. The Mishnah (*Avot*) taught: "In a place where there is no man, you must endeavor to be a man." Where there is *mensch,* each of us must be that *mensch.*

The common denominator of all of us is our commitment to that higher order of Jewish integration—even in today's fragmented world. Knowing that consciously will help us to achieve mutual rapport and to understand intellectually what we already perceive emotionally.

Now, accepting this view of *Klal Yisrael* as our leitmotif does not release us from the obligation to make serious and often painful choices. However, it can and should influence us even on this practical and empirical level. There are three ways in which this interpretation of *Klal Yisrael* can make a difference to us in our own deliberations and in our own work.

The first is *substantive:* Whatever has greater impact on the unity and destiny of our people takes precedence over whatever has lesser consequences for the welfare and integrity of *Klal Yisrael.* I do not mean to imply that we ought to ignore those other causes, all of which are dear to us. After all, a meal consists of appetizer, salads, and desserts as well as entrees. But priority must be assigned by the *Klal Yisrael* test. While I do not want to be guilty of special pleading, it seems to me clear that by this criterion, Jewish education must rise to the very top of the Jewish agenda.

The second way is *psychological.* We are sometimes depressed by the constant bickering, by the clash of interests, biases, and preferences that so often mark our Jewish meetings and deliberations. It can often seem to undo the very basis of our commitment to Jewish world unity. But we should relax. There is nothing wrong with and there is no way to escape the fray and the fracas that frequently accompany the setting of priorities. It is simply a fact of life. That is a major challenge to intelligence and sensitivity in every domain of human life and endeavor. Whether it is a matter of getting married, running a household, shopping, managing a business, going to school, or going to the country, priority decisions must be made. And they must be made every day. Indeed, the basis of American democracy rests upon a principle first formulated by James Madison, father of the American Constitution, in the *Federalist Papers.* Madison believed that the very clash of self-interest groups, passionately advocated, leads to the greatest good for the largest number, and that the very wheeling and dealing necessary to accommodate disparate views eliminated the tyranny of the majority. This indeed is the way America operates to this very day.

Now, while it is true that Madison's ideas work better the larger the polity and the larger the group, and that what is true for government is not necessarily true for a voluntary world-wide community such as the Jewish people, yet enough of it is valid for us not to fear confrontation and to welcome diverse opinions. But, the idea of *Klal Yisrael* establishes these caveats: (a), that all participants acknowledge the primacy of *Klal Yisrael* over its individual parts, and that therefore we reject those views which would undo the unity of *Klal Yisrael;* and (b), that the tone of discourse be civil, respectful, tolerant, sympathetic and, even more, evince concern for the other position, the one we may consider as of only secondary importance.

The third way in which the *Klal Yisrael* concept can influence our practical deliberations is *personal.* Socrates taught that the knowledge of the good will lead people to do good. The Sages of Israel were far too skeptical of philosophical speculation to accept that. They knew that doing good depends more on will and motivation and character than upon one's intellect, and that it is more important to learn *how* to do good than to speculate philosophically on *what* the good really means. Nevertheless, they by no means dismissed knowledge as a critical factor in human moral development, and they taught that "an ignorant man cannot be pious" (*Avot* 2:6). Good intentions alone can lead one to be a "do-gooder," but not to effectuate the good in a consistent manner either in the world around us or internally, in the structure of our personalities.

Hence, our decision-making on the priorities of Jewish life, both philanthropically and in other ways, and our effectiveness in soliciting our fellow Jews, require that we rely upon more than noble intentions and uninformed reason. They require knowledge and constant learning. Kierkegaard once said, "Life must be lived forward, but can be understood only backward." Certainly we have to go forward. We must make decisions for 1986 and 1987 and 1990 and the year 2000. But if they are to be made out of understanding, we must look backward and consult the past—Jewish history, Jewish traditions, Jewish law, the Jewish heritage. And if indeed we act as part of that metaphysical organum called *Klal Yisrael,* then the corpus of knowledge and value system is: the Torah. Whether you choose to feel bound by Torah or not, know it you must if your leadership of the Jewish community is to be *Jewish* leadership and if your choices are to be more than personal or bureaucratic decisions.

Such Jewishly informed leadership cannot be achieved by consulting academicians or by inviting a Torah Sage to lecture or by establishing a panel of scholars as advisors. That is insufficient. In Jewish life, learning is a *mitzvah*

that cannot be relegated or delegated. Expertise can be bought; wisdom must be earned.

The "global Jewish community" did not arise in 1939, with the beginning of the Holocaust, or in 1948 with the creation of the State of Israel. It has a history which is rich in moral, spiritual, emotional, national, and universal dimensions, and even claims that it had at one time a covenant entered into with the Creator of the universe. "One family indivisible" cannot be led if one is ignorant of the family's past and traditions and values. Moreover, if you deny yourself the *mitzvah* of studying, you deny yourself a fabulous source of pleasure, inspiration, challenge, and contentment.

Torah need not be studied in a school. On an adult level learning is best done in small groups—not by yourself, definitely not by yourself, but with one, two, three, or ten other people. Traditional learning was done in a *chavruta*—a small group of co-learners.

I suggest you go back to the sources. Don't just read; study. Keep away from best-sellers and anything that is trendy. And do it regularly.

Enough of our great primary sources are now available in English for you to follow intelligently and creatively. I differ from most of those who preach this doctrine. Leave "conversational Hebrew" for later. We are all busy people, and it may not be worth struggling all these months in an Ulpan in order to order roast chicken from a waiter in Tel Aviv who speaks barely more than a passable—and possibly less than passable—Hebrew . . . study classical Hebrew, the Hebrew of the sources. It may not allow you to read a modern Israeli newspaper with great fluency, but believe me that you will learn more from Rashi than you will from *Haaretz,* and more from Maimonides than from *Maariv.* Most certainly it will be more meaningful than any newspaper in giving you the background of Israel within the context of *Klal Yisrael,* so that your Jewish dimensions will be richer and more authentic and more satisfying.

I am a great believer in "running scared." All the glum and gloomy predictions about Jewish survival that we hear from sociologists and demographers, rabbis, professors, politicians, and economists should really worry us and stimulate us to work harder—but never to fall into despair. A number of years ago a great Jewish historian by the name of Simon Rawidowicz wrote an essay called, "Israel, the Ever Dying People." First he pointed out that throughout Jewish history, from the very beginning, every generation feared it was the last link in the chain of the Jewish people. Our first father, Abraham, complained, "What can you give me, seeing that I am childless?" (Gen. 15:2). He saw himself as both the first and the last Jew! Maimonides (I am, of course, skipping a couple millennia) wrote broodingly to the Jews of Lunel and Marseilles that Torah was all but vanished in Spain, North Africa, Palestine, and Iraq, and that only a couple of southern French Jewish communities were keeping the faith alive. While he was writing this plaintive epistle, his very own works were creating a dynamic body of scholarship that continues to this day, eight and a half centuries later; the great Ashkanazi centers were beginning to form on both sides of the Rhine; and the seeds of Polish and Russian Jewry were being sown. Chapter and verse could be quoted for every generation. We are an "ever-dying people"—and maybe that is why we live so long. It may be a good corrective to our sometimes Pollyannish American faith in the future. But an awareness of the special nature of *Klal Yisrael* will lead us to affirm that while, unfortunately, the parts may sometimes wither and fall off, the whole will always remain. The metaphysically, spiritually unified historical community of *Klal Yisrael* will never cease to exist. So run scared, but deep down remember *ode avinu chai,* as long as there is a God in the world, there will be an Israel in the world. Israel will remain the *am ha-netzach,* the eternal people.

When the great Hasidic Rebbe known as the "Seer of Lublin" died, one of his sons came from some distance to claim his share of the inheritance. All that was left to him was his father's *bekesha,* rabbinic cloak, and his wall clock, one that chimed every hour. On his way home, he stopped at an inn. Unfortunately, it began to rain and because the roads were unpaved, he had to stay there several days longer than he had anticipated. He did not have enough money to pay the innkeeper, and therefore left behind his father's clock in lieu of payment for his lodging.

Many years later, a famous rabbi traveled and stopped by at the same inn and heard the chimes. He saw the clock, and excitedly turned to the innkeeper and asked, "Where did you get that clock?" The innkeeper told him about the Rebbe's son and why he left it there. The Rabbi told the innkeeper that he recognized the clock and told him that it belonged to the "Seer."

How did you recognize it?," asked the innkeeper.

The Rabbi replied, "Every other clock, when it strikes the hour, has its own peculiar and characteristic message. The chime calls out, 'one hour closer to death.' But the clock of the Seer of Lublin has a message different from any other clock in the world. Its chimes sing out, 'one hour closer to redemption.' "

With confidence in the sacred cause of *Klal Yisrael,* and fortified by the high resolve that only such an exalted mission can inspire in us, we shall triumph over all threats and dangers to our communal existence and national life, and bring our people—*all* our people, "one family indivisible"—yet another hour closer to redemption.

5

Soviet Jewry

Shari Rosenfeld,
Coalition to Free Soviet Jews

Today over two-and-a-half million Jews are trapped in a country that's impossible to live in. and impossible to leave.

Since 1979 Jewish emigration from the Soviet Union has plummeted by a shocking 98%. In 1984 only 896 Jews were allowed to leave. This figure represents the first time since the landmark Leningrad Trials of 1970-71 that fewer than 1,000 Jews received permission to leave in a single year. For those Jews who remain behind, life has become more miserable than ever.

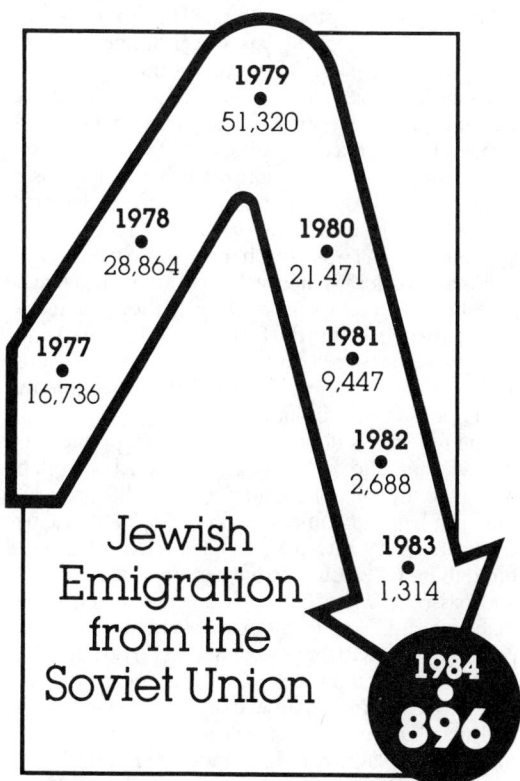

1979 • 51,320
1978 • 28,864
1980 • 21,471
1977 • 16,736
1981 • 9,447
1982 • 2,688
1983 • 1,314
1984 • 896

Jewish Emigration from the Soviet Union

Once a Jew applies to leave the Soviet Union, in order to live freely as a Jew or be reunited with family members in Israel, his or her entire life changes. Would-be emigrants are fired from their jobs, and may then be arrested for not having one. Even if they avoid arrest they become social outcasts, constantly watched and harassed by the KGB. Families who apply for visas together can also expect cruel separations. When The Soviet government does grant a visa, it may be only for a husband but not a wife, or only a mother but not a child.

This living in limbo has lasted years ... for many, the better part of a lifetime.

Of the 20,000 refuseniks who have already been denied permission to emigrate, some have waited for over 15 years. Almost 400,000 have begun the difficult and uncertain emigration process.

Unofficial Hebrew and religious study groups are raided by the KGB. Apartments are stormed and searched. Personal possessions, including books on Jewish history and religion, are confiscated. And almost daily, the official Soviet press attacks Jews as "Zionist traitors."

Jews are arrested and sentenced to prison terms, guilty only of exercising their rights to live as Jews and to live in freedom in the Jewish State.

In recent months, the Soviets have placed enormous pressure on key refusenik leaders and Hebrew teachers. Several important leaders have already been arrested on trumped-up charges as part of this new crackdown, including Aleksandr Kholmiansky and Yuli Edelshtein of Moscow and Yakov Levin of Odessa.

Iosif Begun is now serving 12 years in a Soviet prison and labor camp (to 1995). His crime? Teaching Hebrew. Anatoly Shcharansky, the courageous emigration activist sentenced to 13 years, is still behind bars. His crime? Daring to dream of freedom in Israel. They are just a few of the victims of Soviet "justice."

EMIGRATION: PROCEDURES AND OBSTACLES
Initial steps ...

All applicants for exit visas must submit copies of the following to the local OVIR (visa office):
- *Vyzov*—invitation from relatives in Israel;
- Document of Employment Status—including a character reference;
- Proof of Residency—including validation of housing permit;
- Birth and Marriage Certificates;
- Photographs;
- University Diplomas (where applicable);
- Statement of Intent and Autobiography;
- Parental or Spousal Permissions. If any are deceased, death certificates must be produced;
- Fee. Total emigration cost for a family of four is approximately 4,175 rubles ($5,880), the equivalent of 2 years salary for the average white collar worker. This figure includes payment for baggage, tickets, the visa itself and a special fee for the renunciation of Soviet citizenship.

Obstacles ...

While none of the following rules has been applied universally, all are sufficiently widespread to constitute serious threats to emigration.

- *Denial of visa on the basis of "access to state secrets."* This classification has been applied even to dentists and elevator operators;
- *Minimum five-year waiting period following military service.*
- *Inaccessibility of OVIR officials.* Some offices serving thousands of applicants open for only a few hours a day, two days a week;
- *Vyzovs* mailed from Israel are often confiscated or delayed by Soviet post offices;
- *Three-year employment requirement* following completion of education;
- Restrictions of *vyzovs* (invitations) to "first degree relatives" living in Israel. Because the nuclear families of many applicants reside outside of Israel, often Israeli invitations cannot be produced. Applicants may then be turned down on the basis of "insufficient kinship;"

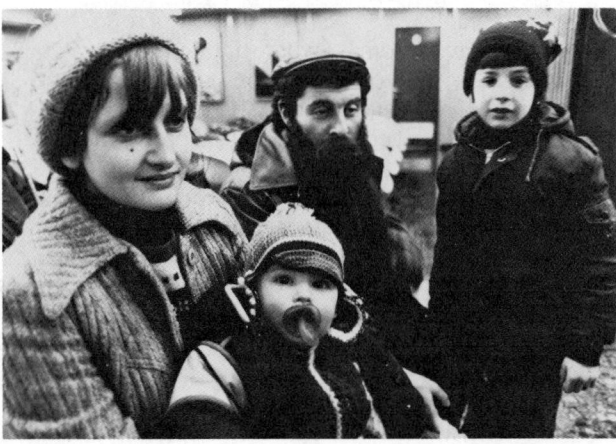

Eugenia Utevskaya with her family, upon their arrival in Israel.

- *Personal and professional risks.* Applicants become vulnerable to job dismissals, school and university expulsion, conscription into the Red Army, withdrawal of residence permit, public denunciation, physical harassment, searches and arrest.

When Permission is Denied . . .

If an application is refused, another cannot be filed for six months. In addition, refuseniks must now submit a completely new set of documents each time they re-apply. In the past, applications could simply be renewed using documents submitted with the first application. In some cases, officials are issuing permanent refusals, closing off every avenue of hope to Soviet Jews.

. . . Try to stop that elderly Jew with the face as white as chalk, fixed eyes and trembling hands, the moment he comes out of the emigration office. Try to speak to that Jewish woman pressing her hand to her heart and looking for a seat, so as not to fall down. They have just received another refusal.

You will hear the Jewish woman speaking:

"It is not life. Life stopped for us. We have lost everything we acquired during fifty years—our money, belongings, job, profession, skill. They call us traitors and double-crossers. We have neither past nor future. We don't plan anything, we don't strive for anything, we don't dream about anything except getting out of here. They keep us under the constant pressure of uncertainty. It is a real torture, indeed. My husband, a well-known electric motor designer works as a night watchman. I work as a postwoman, though I was a teacher. My son, a young engineer, works as a loader. We live with the constant fear that he will be called to military service. Why do they treat us like the fascists treated Jews in the first years of their rule? And what prospects do we have in this country where my husband and I still remember the terror of 1937? Is it true that the world doesn't care about us?"

The refuseniks do not sew yellow six-pointed stars on their clothes. The yellow stars are replaced by work-books, where all the jobs of a man during his life are recorded. This is a basic document in order for a Soviet citizen to obtain a job. "I wanted to get a job in a laundry as a stoker. I fitted there OK. However, after examining my work-book and passport, where my Jewish origin is registered, the manager said. 'You are a doctor of chemistry, an assistant professor, and wish to work as a stoker. You haven't gotten a job for more than two years. That means that you are going to leave for abroad. We do not need such people.' I feel as a refusenik, not only like a leper with a bell, but also like a piano player with his hands severed off."

It is difficult to keep from anger while thinking about the tragedy of the young generation. Young people in their best years are doomed to slowly wasting away—deprived of the right to family life, happiness, joy, and future.

Elderly people are losing hope of returning to professional work as they near the retirement age. Old people are dying, without seeing their relatives abroad, without seeing the deliverance of their relatives here.

Children are being born as refuseniks. Like radiation damage to yet unborn generations, the refusal damages children still in their mother's womb, because they will grow and develop in the atmosphere of fear, alarm and stress, and will live with the consciousness of inferiority.

Listen to our voices. We are the children and grandchildren of those who perished in the tsarist pogroms and the fascist shootings, and who suffocated in the gas chambers. We are the descendants of two victimized generations. We don't want to be the third such generation.

Listen to our voices. It is probable that we will pay for speaking out with our freedom. Forget temporarily all your discussions and unite yourselves for saving living persons.

The American hostages knew that the American people would do anything to rescue them. And the American people greeted them with thousands of yellow ribbons around the trees. Will anybody meet us with blue and white ribbons? Is it true that we are no one's? We address the Jewish people and all people concerned about our plight.

Our ship has been caught by radioactive fall-out from our alarming times. We are Jews. We are deadly sick with "refusal." Save our souls!

—*From "Description of a Disease," an essay written by Yuri Tarnopolsky, a Doctor of Chemistry currently serving a three-year prison sentence for "defaming the Soviet State."*

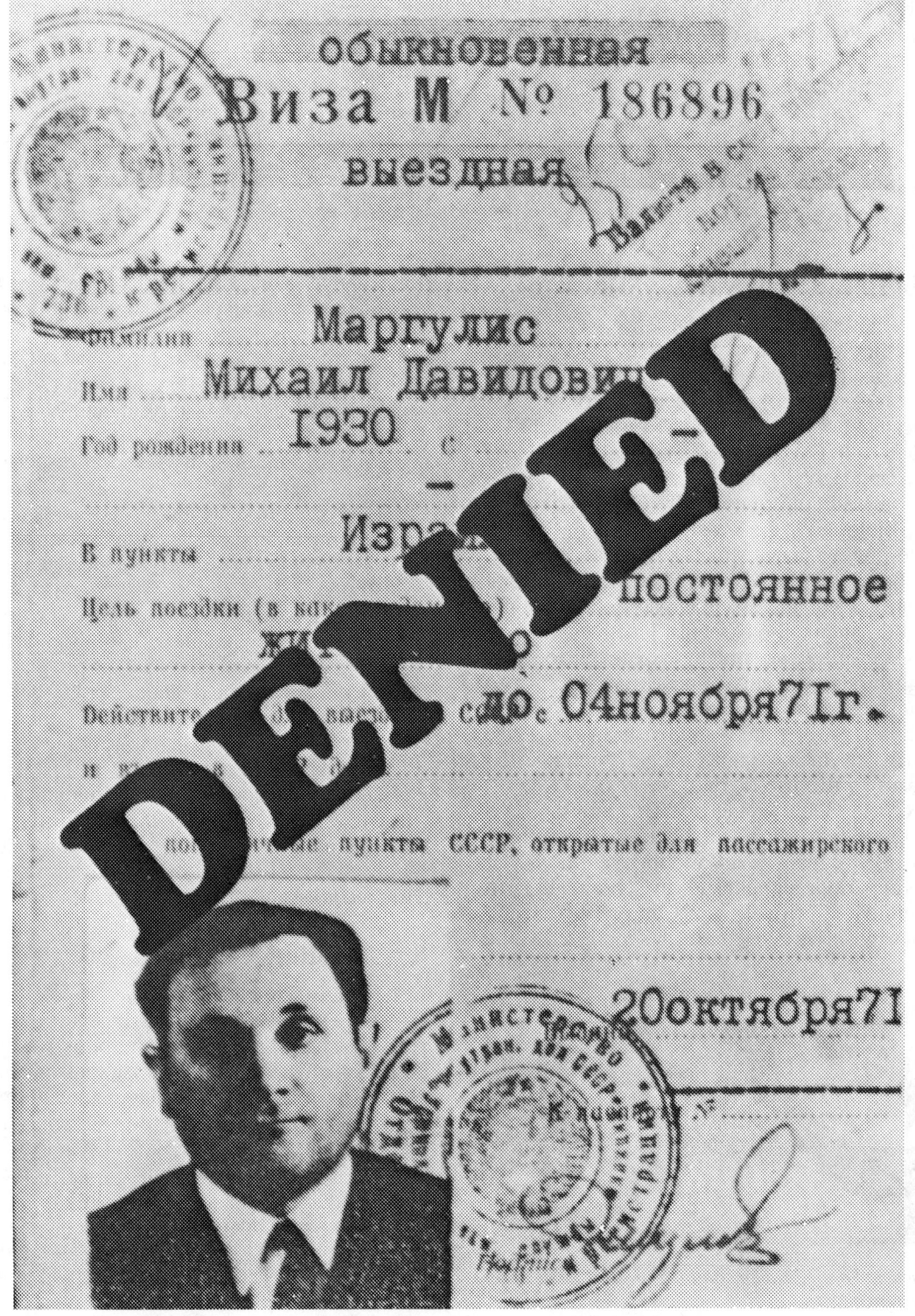

**SOME RELEVANT PROVISIONS IN INTERNATIONAL AGREEMENTS
SIGNED BY THE SOVIETS**

**UNIVERSAL DECLARATION OF
HUMAN RIGHTS:**

Article 13(2)—Everyone has the right to leave any country—including his own—and to return to his country.

**INTERNATIONAL COVENANT ON
CIVIL AND POLITICAL RIGHTS:**

Article 12(2)—Everyone shall be free to leave any country, including his own.

HELSINKI FINAL ACT:
Reunification of families
The participating States will deal in a positive and

humanitarian spirit with the applications of persons who wish to be reunited with members of their family, with special attention being given to requests of an urgent character—such as requests submitted by persons who are ill or old. They will deal with applications in the field as expeditiously as possible. In normal practice they will decide upon these cases within six months of the application. (Six months time frame added in the 1983 Madrid Agreement.) Applications for the purpose of family reunification which are not granted may be renewed at the appropriate level and will be reconsidered at reasonably short intervals by the authorities of the country of residence or destination. . . .

The Right to Cultural Identity: Denied

The Soviet government has been engaged for many years in a methodical effort to sever Soviet Jewry from its cultural heritage, to erase its historical memory and, ultimately, to obliterate its collective identity through a systematic official policy aimed at enforced assimilation.

The attitude of the Soviet authorities toward the study of the Hebrew language among Jews epitomizes their attitude toward Jewish culture generally. Hebrew, the language of the Bible and of the Jewish people in the State of Israel, is the only language which has always been the common property of all Jews everywhere. Knowledge of Hebrew is an integral and essential part not only of the practice of Judaism but also of secular Jewish culture. Yet Hebrew has been rendered virtually inaccessible to Soviet Jews through the vigorous enforcement of an unpublished ban on their study of the language.

Thus, Jews, as a rule, are excluded from those few courses which exist in Soviet universities to train selected Soviet officials in the use of Hebrew. In the USSR, no textbooks of the Hebrew language are published, no teachers of Hebrew are trained, no books in Hebrew have been published for many years, and there are no Soviet newspapers or periodicals published in Hebrew. Efforts to teach Hebrew to Jews privately, unlike the private teaching of other languages, have been ruthlessly suppressed by the

police and teachers of Hebrew have been threatened with punishment on trumped-up charges if they do not cease teaching Hebrew.

Apart from the study of their national languages, Soviet Jewry has not a single school where it can study, in any language at all, its own history, literature, or culture. Such facilities are accorded all other Soviet nationalities, including some that are both more widely dispersed and less numerous than the Jews. No books on Jewish history, literature or culture are published in the USSR in any language, including Russian. Attempts to send books of Jewish content to the USSR by mail lead regularly to their confiscation.

The denial of cultural rights to Soviet Jews by the Soviet government has limited the accessibility that Jewish men, women, and children have to their people and to their culture. But despite the deliberate policy enforced by the Soviets, Jewish culture and education continue to thrive. Hebrew classes are taught in private homes and enormous risks are taken to distribute books and papers on Jewish life. Successful efforts by Jewish cultural leaders bring Soviet Jews together to study, to share frustrations, to celebrate the holidays as a Jewish community. But for every seminar that has been held, there are dozens of others that have been disbanded by the authorities.

Jews of Silence

In 1966, Elie Wiesel wrote *The Jews of Silence,* a moving account of the life of Soviet Jews. Despite the almost twenty years that have passed since the book was written, and despite the many changes that have taken place in Soviet policies towards Soviet Jews, this picture of Simchat Torah, described by Elie Wiesel, depicts a scene similar to one that continues to be seen year after year in Moscow.

Leningrad activist Sarah Fradkin conducts an unofficial Hebrew class for children.

> They came in droves. From near and far, from downtown and the suburbs, from the university and from the factories, from school dormitories and from the Komsomol club. They came in groups; they came alone. But once here, they became a single body, voicing a song of praise to the Jewish people and its will to live.

Two Soviet Jewish refuseniks, temporarily overcoming many obstacles imposed by the Soviet authorities, meet to study the weekly Torah portion.

How many were there? Ten thousand? Twenty thousand? More. About thirty thousand. The crush was worse than it had been inside the synagogue. They filled the whole street, spilled over into courtyards, dancing and singing, dancing and singing. They seemed to hover in mid-air, Chagall-like, floating above the mass of shadows and colors below, above time, climbing a Jacob's ladder that reached to the heavens, if not higher. . . .

The man I was talking to had served as a captain in the Red Army and had been decorated in Berlin. Like his father before him, he was a sworn Communist. But like all the rest, he suffered on account of his Jewishness. Were he Russian he would have long ago been appointed a full professor at the university. He was still holding an instructorship in foreign languages. One day, he said, he decided that as long as they made him feel like a Jew, he might as well act accordingly. It was the only way to beat them at their own game. "Two years ago I came to the synagogue on the night of Simchat Torah. I wanted to see Jews, and I wanted to be with them. I didn't tell my wife, who isn't Jewish, or my sixteen-year-old son. Why should I burden him with problems? There was time enough for that. I came back last year for the second time. The youngsters were singing and dancing, almost like tonight. I found myself suddenly in the middle of a group of youngsters, and my heart stopped. . . . I was standing face-to-face with my son. He said he'd been coming for the past three years, but hadn't dared to tell me."

"Would you like to see him?" he asked me.

"Yes, very much."

"He's here, somewhere," he said, gesturing at the crowd as if to say, "look closely, they are all my sons.". . .

If, on this night of dancing, gladness finally overcame fear, it was because of them. If song triumphed over silence, it was their triumph. And it was through them only that the dream of freedom and community became reality. I am still waiting to see tens of thousands of Jews singing and dancing in Times Square or the Place de l'Etoile as they danced here, in the heart of Moscow, on the night of Simchat Torah. They danced until midnight without rest, to let the city know that they are Jews.

Soviet Antisemitism

During the years of the Cold War between the U.S. and the USSR, the Soviets supported the Arabs and "anti-Zionism" in the press. Jews were attacked in the press as "loathsome and filthy creatures." Israel was described as "hell on Earth" on state radio. Jews were physically beaten in synagogues, their books destroyed, their homes pillaged. Between July 1961 and March 1963, at least 68 Soviet Jews were executed after being convicted of "economic crimes."

Much of this antisemitism, disguised as "anti-Zionism," continues today. In April 1983, in response to the International Conference on Soviet Jewry held in Jerusalem in March, eight Soviet Jews, handpicked by Soviet officials, formed an "Anti-Zionist Committee of the Soviet Public." They have attacked Zionism (and Soviet Jews who have applied to emigrate) as promoting "racial intolerance, armed adventurism, demagoguery, filthy maneuvers and perfidy."

Professor Samuil Zivs, the deputy chairman of the Committee, who is himself Jewish, has claimed that all the Soviet Jews who wanted to leave the USSR have already left. He maintained that Western claims to the contrary represent "juggling of figures by Zionist propaganda." The fact that over 300,000 Soviet Jews have begun the emigration process, and 20,000 of those have been officially refused visas, was dismissed by the Committee as a Zionist fabrication.

U.S. political leaders have expressed alarm over the new developments and the upsurge in anti-Zionist media. State Department officials criticize the Anti-Zionist Committee, condemn the "antisemitic diatribe," and have publicized the fact that Soviet Colonel David Dragunsky, chairman of the Anti-Zionist Committee, is also the head of a Soviet military academy which trains PLO officers. In referring to the current situation in the USSR, one Soviet refusenik said, "It is as bad as 1953."

> "The present generation of Zionists is trying to forget how the Nazi thugs threw Jewish children into the furnaces of the crematoria of the concentration camps or used them as 'material' for experiments of sadist-doctors in S.S. uniforms. However, even then, during the Second World War, business existed when the Zionists collaborated directly with the Hitlerite bosses."
>
> —*Excerpt from "Prompted by an Alien Voice",*
> *published in Moscow, 1982*

Jews in the USSR:
Broken Lives, Unbroken Spirits

Shari Rosenfeld

High contrast, dramatic lighting, revealing portraits: We bring to mind images of Soviet Jews as black and white photographs, stringing together dates and places, painting a picture without a palette.

But Soviet Jews do not live as still life portraits. A refused emigration application, a disrupted Hebrew class, the death of a family member one has not seen for many years, as well as weddings, and holiday celebrations all happen in living color. Tears are wet and laughter is real.

The authorities repeat: "Renounce your desire to emigrate. We will return your job; you will live as you did before." But the refuseniks, those Soviet Jews who have applied to emigrate and have been denied, don't give in, and they don't give up. Stubbornly and repeatedly they bring their application to OVIR, the emigration office. Their reason to emigrate one or three or 15 years ago, their desire to live in Israel, to reunite with their families, is bolstered by a new reason: A person should not live in a country where refusal is possible.

As they wait, new stories unfold, new families are born. And as they wait, their stories continue to be told from afar. Each slice of life presented here depicts not only the story of one individual, though they are true accounts of refuseniks; the stories also document the cycle of Jewish life in the Soviet Union—the waiting, the human grief, the broken families, the unbroken spirits and the small triumphs. As Soviet Jews detail their experiences, they bring their fears to life, they share their troubles, and they

"*Having tread down the resolution of the United Nations demanding a full withdrawal of Israeli forces from captured Arab lands, Tel Aviv extremists continue their aggressive actions against several Arab states." From a Soviet newspaper.*

attempt to communicate, in their own words, a flavor of their lives as Jews in the Soviet Union.

As Jews in the USSR, their life cycles are scarred by scenes of repeated refusal, of inhumane prison conditions, of family separations. Yet they continue to wait, growing up and growing old, dreams surviving the dreamers.

Brit Milah

They were on vacation in Sukhumi, a seaport and health resort in Abkhasia, part of the Soviet Republic of Georgia. In a courtyard sat two old men, who overheard the whispered Hebrew of these two refuseniks. Two more men appeared and invited the vacationers for a *brit milah* (circumcision ceremony) in their home. It was so marvelous and so sudden that they accepted the invitation although these were complete strangers and they were very tired. It was like a dream—to come to a town, find a synagogue and Jews and to see a *brit milah* in a private home. So they went home with them, not too far from the synagogue.

A beautiful house, in a style very different from the Russian, a foreign language, but these were Jews, a Jewish house, where tradition and religion were completely natural. A mezuza on every door, the food strictly kosher. Here they met families where there was no generation gap, where Jews had never stopped living as Jews. And therefore it was completely natural.

Parents & Children:
A New Generation of Refuseniks

Sasha came home from school sullen and withdrawn. Her parents, like all parents, have tried to protect her, but now must listen to reports on how she was ridiculed in front of the whole class as a "traitor" whose parents want to leave the country.

Some young married couples decide to wait before starting a family. It's not fair, they reason, to involve small children in the uncertain and often dangerous life-style of the "refusenik." But after years of waiting and no visa, a new refusenik is born, and a new generation grows up.

"It's hardly the ideal way to plan a family," said Yuli Kosharovsky of Moscow, who has already had two children, "but we've been waiting seven long years and life just has to go on, however hard things are." That was five years ago. Yuli and his family still wait.

Aleksandr and all of his classmates were given a homework assignment to read a new book. When his teacher gave him the book he was to read, the title jumped off the cover and thundered into his head. *The Poison of Zionism.* Feeling that every eye in the room was upon him he pried open the pages. "Zionists are arch imperialists whose sole aim is to undermine and destroy Socialist States," read Aleksandr in the new book which was part of the required reading for school-aged children.

Lionya Barras was only four when his parents received their refusal. For an adult the word refusenik, or "otkaznik" as Soviet Jews call themselves, tells a story. But for a child, the difficulties and problems associated with a denied exit visa are not as apparent.

What does the word "refusenik" mean? wondered Lionya and thousands of other Soviet Jewish children. Leonid, his father, tried his best to explain. But it wasn't easy, particularly as they playfully called the family dog by that name. Slowly and patiently, Leonid groped for words a four-year-old could understand, explaining his dismissal from the newspaper where he had worked as a journalist, recounting his struggle to find another job, describing their isolation from friends and neighbors. For Lionya the solution was simple. "Why don't we change the name of our dog to Visa?"

Yudit Ratner Bialy is proud of her son, and proud of herself for having instilled in him such a strong Jewish identity. "Let me tell you a few things about Misha," she wrote to her mother in Israel. "There are two main things in his life: mathematics and Jewishness. As someone who does everything thoroughly, he approaches these two subjects seriously too. He reads a lot on Jewish literature, studies Hebrew and the Torah.

"On the first day of Chanukah, he gathered his friends (16 of them came), and Misha lit the first candle and everyone said the blessing. He spoke about the history of the festival. Misha is a great patriot of Israel and he, more than all of us, should be living with you; he could contribute a lot to the country."

Living as a Refusenik Unable to Leave . . .

Professors, teachers, engineers, scientists. They become stokers, postmen, baby-sitters, yard keepers—or unemployed. But even unskilled work is difficult to find.

"I consider the time in the state of refusal the most important, the most interesting and the most creative period of my life," wrote Leonid Kelbert, a film director from Leningrad. "Nobody dismissed me, I was even asked to remain at my job. I left it myself because I was not satisfied with the creative level, the conditions of the censorship and with the lack of possibilities to express myself.

"In spite of my higher education I did not know anything about Jewish culture, spiritual heritage, traditions, etc. When I was faced with all this the first time, naturally, I plunged into all of this greedily.

"My first experiments in Jewish Theater were of course *Purimshpiels.* Just during these experiments I sensed the possibilities that were later realized in 'Masada'.

"I built the whole performance around this self-identification: What was the right choice: to die as Jews or to exist as slaves, preserving in this way the people and the possibility for future generations? The impression was so strong that sometimes there were tears in the eyes of the audience.

"After every performance there are some minutes of absolute silence, and only after the actors have changed their costumes and come before the audience, then there is always a lot of generous and sincere applause. And after this there is a discussion. This moment can sometimes be the most exalting one.

"It could be an elderly man standing and telling that there was a time when he was working in the Jewish theater and now he is afraid to give his telephone number because his neighbors are antisemites.

"Or the woman crying, who told us that she survived Babi Yar, and her whole life she tried not to think about it, not to remember, and now she suddenly has understood that it is necessary not to forget and to remind it to others.

"Or a young boy or girl asked to be involved in the theater. Where else could I find such a grateful audience?

"Is there another audience in the world which needs my work so vitally?

"Or some people simply demanded the performances on the *whole* Jewish history—they just demanded and it makes an impression that they *have the right to demand.*"

"The head physician of the so-called 'commission' appeared to be a psychiatrist by the name of Semenova. She was curious—about the reasons for my decision to leave for Israel. After my explanation, she said, 'I don't understand this decision; you should be sent for an examination to the mental hospital' . . . and gave me an appointment."

—A Jew living in Moscow

Tatiana Levinson, whose son lives in Israel, applied for an exit visa in December 1979. "I know that none of the officially recognized obstacles to departure applied to me," she wrote in a letter to a friend. "I never had access to any secrets, I have not been under investigation or on trial, I did not serve in the Soviet army. I am not leaving any persons materially interested in me in the USSR. I intend to go to my only son, the support of my old age."

Then started a series of conversations, letters, visits and telephone calls to "Comrade Burova," who said, "Don't fret, you'll soon leave. Mothers, especially those who are not young and are alone, have preference with us for a positive solution." "Some time later," Tatiana wrote her friend, "I phoned Inspector Kokareva (another official), and she told me that I would receive an answer in a week."

But after still more waiting with no answer, a higher official, Col. Zenchenko, told Tatiana in March 1981, "It is not necessary to cry; submit your application in six months time."

"Two weeks after this conversation," Tatiana continued, "I was summoned to the OVIR authorities. I was told that my case had been examined by higher authorities and it has been decided to confirm the denial, without stating any reasons.

"Months later I was again told that my repeated appeal for permission to be reunited with my family, to see my son, had been denied.

"I have left work, I am afraid to go out on the street—the unknown is the most terrible thing of all. Therefore, I pleaded to be told what are the causes of the inexpediency of the reunification of my family—all in vain. I do not know what there is left for me to do. Everything that I wrote was returned to OVIR, where they arbitrarily decide my fate.

"An OVIR official telephoned me at home and said that she had been instructed to inform me once again that the denial had been confirmed anew. 'For what reason?' I asked. 'For that same one,' was the answer." Tatiana begged to know, "What same reason?" There was none.

... Unable to Live

The right to practice the Jewish religion in the Soviet Union is guaranteed under the Soviet Constitution. This is a fact. It is also a fact that Jewish families who gather to study Hebrew must draw their curtains and disguise their activities to escape the scrutiny and surveillance of the KGB.

Grigory Wasserman was expertly beaten up on his way home from a Hebrew lesson. Although his face, while healing, looked like a multi-colored rainbow, Grigory continued—and still continues—to do what he insists is his constitutional right, to teach Hebrew privately.

"He is an outgoing, friendly man, with a delightful sense of humor," said one of his friends. "He considers himself an expert tea-maker and his tea-time discussions are always a great joy. It is easy to identify his flat. The door still bears the marks of Police boots. And there is a mezuzah on the lintel."

Jewish Holiday Celebrations— Next Year in Jerusalem?

"Why is this night different from all other nights" began five-year-old Moshe Raiz of Vilnius. Fifteen guests at the seder of Carmella and Vladimir, Moshe's parents, joined Moshe in the Passover dialogue. Their baby Saul was still too young to participate.

Passover has a special meaning for refuseniks in the Soviet Union. The story of the wandering, waiting and exodus from Egypt is a parallel of their own waiting, their own formation of a Jewish community in the Soviet Union. The greeting "Next Year in Jerusalem" is a sincere cry repeated throughout the year for which Soviet Jews have risked and sacrificed a great deal.

Mila and Leonid Volvovsky had 17 guests around their seder table in Gorki. For some, it was their first such event. Mila recalled her first seder in 1974 at the home of her Hebrew teacher. "I did not know Hebrew then," she told friends. "Now, of course, the whole ceremony will be conducted in Hebrew."

Averly Kofman, a teacher from Odessa, wrote in a letter, "Our position has not changed yet and exit permits are as far away as ever, but nevertheless we hope for a forthcoming exodus. It may occur only by a miracle, but Jewish history abounds in such miracles. We felt it especially when we celebrated Passover. I am not exaggerating, but just two years ago we did not know that there is such a Jewish festival as Passover and this year we held a real seder, we read the Passover Haggadah, we spoke Hebrew during the whole night; we had nearly all the necessary articles: a special dish, matzah, a goblet for Elijah the Prophet, maror, karpas, a special napkin with the Jewish ornaments. When the seder was over we sang Jewish songs for the rest of the night."

It is repeated: "Soviet Jews dream of freedom." They piece together fragments, things they have seen or heard about, pictures from the postcards sent from Israel, bits of conversation passed on from one to the next." Iosif Radomisilsky, a Leningrad Hebrew teacher who applied to emigrate in 1979, wrote about his dreams of Jerusalem, dreams that have a will stronger than the government trying to destroy them:

"The synagogue itself, the surrounding courtyard and the adjacent street were noisy and overflowing with people. On this day, the day of Simchat Torah, thousands of Jews come to the synagogue from all the corners where Jews reside. Can you picture to yourselves what goes on this day in Jerusalem? No, anyone who has not seen it with his own eyes, can never imagine it. As for me, I have no need to imagine it for I have been there more than once and I have seen with my own eyes the crowded sidewalks, the passersby filling the narrow alleyways. I have seen the Western Wall, the blue sky and the verdant land ... although I have only been there in my dreams. Don't laugh—there are deeds akin to dreams and dreams akin to deeds. Sometimes it is difficult to differentiate between the deed and the dream. Soon, my dream of Jerusalem will become a deed and I will, in reality, come to Jerusalem, to the Western wall and then all of my previous life will become a dream.

"And so, on Simchat Torah in Jerusalem, the skies are blue, the sun shines brightly, while here it is raining and the skies are gray as we stand in the synagogue courtyard. Our synagogue is not in Jerusalem, where I have been only in my dreams, but in Russia, in Leningrad. On this day, the synagogue is a place where Jews can meet their friends, girls and boys. The synagogue is the only place where one can see so many Jews at one and the same time. So we decided to help young Jews become acquainted with a beauty whose first name is 'Culture' and family name 'Hebrew.' We held up a placard above the singing and dancing crowd inviting the Jews to come to us, to our ulpanim to study Hebrew. People stare at the poster, someone approaches and asks about the ulpanim, someone hurriedly jots down the telephone numbers, someone laughs and leaves. But most of them sensed something strange and unusual, were moved by an unknown feeling."

Yizkor: Remembering Those Who Were Unable to Leave

Judith Lerner was buried in a pleasantly shaded Moscow cemetery, her funeral attended by dozens of men and women in a place thousands of miles from where she and her husband sought to be. For 10 years she and Aleksandr, a renowned scientist, waited to emigrate but were refused on the grounds that their departure would be "contrary to the state's interest."

Even after her death, the authorities declined permission for her lifeless body to leave the USSR for burial in Israel.

Instead, Sonia Levin, the Lerners' daughter, who emigrated with her husband and child in 1973, was allowed to return for the funeral in an unprecedented gesture by the Soviet authorities.

After the funeral, Sonia Lerner referred to a conversation she had had with an OVIR official during her return visit to Moscow: "I asked him how soon I would be able to see my father and brother in Israel. I expressed my amazement at the fact that the departure of a single, if very respected, man could harm such a powerful state. He replied that my father's emigration would harm the interests of the Soviet state, and when the interests of the state are at stake, they give them higher priority than the interests of the individual."

Remembering Those Who Continue the Struggle

"All of us Jews are going somewhere. We're either going to the east (Siberia) or to the west (freedom)," refusenik Sofia Kogan said. Until that time, Soviet Jews are acting as regular people would act. Until the time when they can emigrate, they are trying to live their lives as normally as possible. When they succeed, they attempt to accomplish even more. When they fail, they try again.

Marriage Separated by a Common Dream

At 21 years old, Yanna Friedman was a single parent, married to a man who'd never seen his daughter. Months earlier, Yanna, four months pregnant, said goodbye to her husband as he set off for Israel. Mark Abramovich had decided to leave for Israel with the hope that Yanna would be allowed to join him without delay. Yet when Yanna went to apply for an exit visa in April 1980, she was told that Mark was not a member of her family and her papers could not be accepted.

"Because my passport was with the OVIR authorities when I met Yanna, we could not register our marriage in the registrar's office," Mark wrote.

They married in a religious ceremony in the Riga synagogue, but the marriage is not recognized by the Soviet authorities. Three years ago he wrote, "My daughter is now a year old and she is growing up without a father; she has

Refuseniks Chana and Leonid Westfried light homemade Shabbat candles in their Moscow apartment.

never even seen me. My wife is only 22 years old, and she has to live as a 'widow' with her husband being alive, but so far away from her."

Shabbat and Still No Rest

It was Friday evening in the home of Mark Feldman. Fifteen young religious Jews had gathered for Sabbath prayers. A knock on the door and a man appeared who spoke in Hebrew. Before the host could find out what he wanted, the caller gestured and several officials stormed the apartment. The names of those present were listed, and they were informed that such a religious meeting was illegal. Four of them were arrested and held for 15 days for participating in a private prayer service. Shabbat, and there is still no rest.

"The situation one finds himself in here provides one with a wonderful opportunity to become the real master of one's destiny, to feel inner freedom and independence from the chaos outside," Anatoly Shcharansky wrote to his mother in March.

"Shabbat starts soon. I observe it now in the following way: I read parts of Solomon's proverbs and of some other wise books, excerpts from which I had copied when I had, for a short time, the opportunity to read the Bible. Your parcel will, of course, also come in handy at the Shabbat table.

"And where, I wonder, is my wife observing this Shabbat? At Uncle Syoma's? In Los Angeles? Or, perhaps, with our Canadian relatives? If I were with her, there would have been nothing that could induce her to travel. Would it not be nice to lie down somewhere on the beach in Eilat, to go for a swim in the Red Sea! That would be something. And in the meantime—Shabbat Shalom."

Prayers for Freedom

It was the Thursday night before her trial. Maria Slepak, or Masha as she is better known, had just been discharged from the hospital where she was being treated for ulcers and depression. As she herself awaited trial, her husband, Vladimir, awaited the results of his appeal of a five-year sentence of internal exile to Siberia; her son, underground, was avoiding military conscription; another son, living in Israel, was far away from his mother who waits to join him.

Noticing her visitor's *kippah,* she asked, "You are a religious man, tell me what does God want from me? Why is he doing all this to my family?"

She said she did not know how to pray and asked her visitor to guide her. Together they read the Shema, phrase by phrase, two words at a time. And together they recited the 23rd psalm, pausing for a long time after they read, "Yea though I walk through the valley of the shadow of death, I shall know no fear because You are with me."

Prisoners of Conscience
Dream Behind Bars

Isolation in a basement cell. Four stone walls. A cement floor and a plank that serves as a bed. No windows, no electric light, no heat. An air vent in the cell allows a dim light to sneak through during the daytime. Evening, darkness is total. Food is bread and watery soup.

In isolation, a person has to fight for his sanity. Keeping track of the days, sustaining thoughts and memories, seemingly simple tasks, become goals which are difficult to obtain.

"Incidental thoughts pass in a dream, more quickly than they come. If I should wish to recall them, I must discuss them instantly with a neighbor or write them down, otherwise they are forgotten in a matter of seconds," wrote Anatoly Shcharansky in a letter to his wife, Avital. The thoughts escape with no trace, and still Shcharansky holds on.

At age 35, Levi Elbert had already waited seven years to lead his family to Israel. So when he was called up for a second term of military reserve service, he asked that he be given duties which could not later be labeled classified and delay the possibility of his receiving an exit visa for an additional seven or eight years. The authorities refused.

Reject the draft. Go to prison. This is what some military-age refuseniks and others face: the choice of accepting conscription, serving the required two years, and then being automatically categorized as a security risk for an additional five years at least, or they could reject the call up, and go to prison. Like Levi Elbert. Like Aleksandr Panarev. Like Simon Shnirman.

POC Levi Elbert and his wife, Chana.

Lazar Lyubarsky, a former prisoner of conscience who now lives with his wife and two daughters in Tel Aviv, tells the following about Ida Nudel before she was sentenced to four years in exile.

"Ida's apartment consisted of one room and a kitchen. A large bookcase stood in her room, containing, among other things, a thick catalogue with many cards, one for each prisoner. The cards listed all available relevant information about each and every prisoner: date of birth, year of arrest, location, addresses of relatives, education, interests and hobbies.

"A large table which stood in her kitchen was used for preparing material based on the information in the catalogue. Each month she updated the cards with whatever new information she had gathered. She would prepare packages for prisoners a month in advance of dates scheduled for delivery by the authorities, so that when the time for dispatching them arrived, she would be ready. Ida used to send the prisoners letters, pictures and gifts in keeping with each one's interests. Ida would also send all the prisoners and their families greetings, telegrams and souvenirs for their birthdays. She was always up-to-date on everything that concerned the prisoners.

"Included in the information Ida gathered about the prisoners was all the legal material bearing on their respective trials, as well as camp regulations and all that pertained to food allotment, clothing, packages and letters.

"I suddenly realized that Ida's entire life revolved around the prisoners and their problems," said Lyubarsky.

From Russia With Hate: A Bitter Centennial

William Korey, Ph.D.

It was a century ago that international discourse was enriched by the term "pogrom." The word has entered the lexicon of *all* Western languages as defining violence against Jewry, but its roots, linguistically (it comes from the Russian verb "to riot" or "to destroy") and historically, are Russian.

Elizavetgrad, a Ukrainian town of 32,000, was the starting point on April 15, 1881. Prompted by emissaries from the

St. Petersburg aristocracy calling for the "people's wrath" to "be vented on the Jews," the peasants unleashed violence against the Jews in the small city. A wave of killings, rape and pillage spread quickly to hundreds of other towns and then to the large cities of Berdichev and Kiev. By the end of the year it reached Warsaw, an outpost of Tsarism, and moved on to other parts of the Empire.

The record of the 1881-82 pogroms was impressive as an example of frenzied antisemitism. Twenty thousand Jews were made homeless, 100,000 were ruined economically, and Jewish property valued at $80 million was destroyed. A contemporary Russian writer described the trauma as "unending torture." It triggered the mass emigration of Jews to the West even as it spurred the first Zionist movement in Russia—the Biluim and the Hovevei Zion.

The inspiration for this movement came from the distinguished Odessa physician, Leon Pinsker, whose classic work, *Auto-Emancipation,* was published just over a century ago. The pogromist experience prompted him to conclude in his book that "Judeophobia is a psychic disorder" which is "hereditary and, as a disease transmitted for 2,000 years, . . . is incurable." Pinsker was convinced that Jews had no future in Russia.

Like many other oppressors before and after them, the Tsarist authorities blamed the victims for the violence. The Minister of Interior, Count Nikolai P. Ignatyev, in a memorandum to Tsar Alexander III on August 22, 1881, blamed the pogroms upon "the Jews' injurious activities" directed against the peasantry. On May 3, 1882, the Tsarist regime imposed new "temporary rules" forbidding Jews to settle outside towns and hamlets and to carry on any business on Sundays and Christian holidays. Several years later, the rules were augmented with a sharply defined *numerus clausus* for Jews in secondary schools and universities (ten percent within the Pale of Jewish Settlement, five percent outside the Pale and three percent in St. Petersburg and in Moscow).

Hostility toward Jews was not restricted to only the Tsarist aristocracy and the peasantry. The radical populist intellectuals comprising the Narodnaia Volia urged on the pogromists on grounds that the "kikes . . . rob and cheat" the peasant and "drink his blood." To be sure, there was also a small circle of the intelligentsia surrounding the philosopher V. Soloviev and the novelist V. Korolenko that voiced sharp protests against the massacre of Jews. Leo Tolstoy was a supporter of this circle. But these sympathizers were clearly in the minority.

Extraordinary as it may appear, recent major works published in the Soviet Union go as far as to justify the Tsarist pogroms. Vladimir Begun, whose views are highly regarded in certain Kremlin circles, wrote *The Creeping Counterrevolution,* published in 1974 and strongly endorsed in the Soviet media. The book justifies peasant violence against Jews "as the spontaneous reaction of the oppressed strata of the toiling population to their barbarous exploitation by the Jewish bourgeoisie." A dismaying paragraph follows: "We do not grieve today if our fathers, grandfathers and great-grandfathers, in their distress and want, treated their oppressors disrespectfully, regardless of whether they were native or alien by blood."

Even more authoritative is *Zionism As a Form of Racism and Racial Discrimination,* by Lydia A. Modzhorian, a prominent legal scholar active in the Soviet Academy of Sciences. Her 240-page work, which appeared in late 1979, refers to the pogroms of 1881-82 as merely "so-called outbursts of antisemitism." In her view, they were "artificially exaggerated and widely used by Jewish entrepreneurs and rabbis." She acknowledges that there might have been "excesses" against Jews but they were only "a reaction to the exploitation to which the broad masses were subjected in capitalist enterprises."

Modzhorian claims further that the Jewish-dominated press of Tsarist Russia had dubbed the uprisings as "antisemitic pogroms" only when the "bosses were Jews." When the bosses happened to be Christians or Moslems, she writes, the same media used the word "revolt." Clearly, the scholar's bigotry is so intense that it projects onto the late 19th century, in, of all places, Tsarist Russia, recent and current stereotypes about Jewish influence in the media. To speak of a Jewish-dominated press and Jewish "bosses" in Russia at the time is more than a slight exaggeration.

Such attitudes toward the 19th century pogroms, voiced by none other than the currently-favored ideologues, would have caused Lenin himself to tremble. In a classic address, he thundered: "Shame on accursed Tsarism which tortured and persecuted the Jews. Shame on those who foment hatred toward the Jews." He was responsible for the first law in history banning antisemitism and he personally inserted into the statute the phrase that "pogromists and persons inciting to pogroms be outlawed." Nor would he countenance compromise with popular antisemitic views. When Leon Trotsky demurred about taking the position of Commissar of Home Affairs proffered by Lenin, lest it stimulate hostile views toward Jews, Lenin found the argument utterly irrelevant.

"I recommend this—an excellent weapon! It was examined, tried and shot in Auschwitz, in the Warsaw Ghetto. . . ."

But the depth of popular sentiment could not be uprooted that quickly. Perceptions about Jews were integral to Russian society. A Tsarist Commission, comprised of moderates, after five years of lengthy interviews and in-depth study of the Jewish problem, concluded in 1888 that Jews have "a tendency to get control of the economic strength of the population," a tendency to "exclusiveness" (i.e., clannishness), a tendency to "shirk state obligations" and to avoid "physical manual labors." According to the fairly *liberal* commission: "The passion for acquisition and money-grubbing is inherent in the Jew from the day of his birth; it is a characteristic of the Semitic race, manifest from almost the first pages of the Bible."

Such popular views provided the fertile soil for nourishing the notorious Tsarist fabrication, *The Protocols of the Elders of Zion* (first published in 1903 by the reactionary Tsarist publicist, Pavel Krushevan). The impact of the *Protocols* was felt during the Civil War in 1918-20 in the Ukraine, when 30,000 Jews were massacred and 28 percent of Jewish homes destroyed. Later, the *Protocols* would become the basis for Adolf Hitler's Final Solution. Popular antisemitism in Tsarist Russia made possible the extraordinary blood libel trial, the Beilis Case, in Kiev in 1911-12. Clearly, pogromist ideology was a part of the baggage the Russians, and later the Soviets, carried with them into the 20th century.

The vicious stereotyping of Jews persisted even as the Bolshevik leadership of the 1920s tried to eradicate it. The populist Kronstadt uprising against Soviet power in 1921 was based in part upon peasant attitudes toward the "cursed domination" of Jews. In November 1926, the Chairman of the Central Executive Committee of the Soviet regime acknowledged that Soviet white collar workers were "more antisemitic today than . . . under Tsarism." An official "survey of antisemitism among trade union members" conducted in February 1929 in Moscow found that "antisemitic feeling among workers is spreading chiefly in the backward sections of the working class that have close ties with the peasantry. . . ." At the heart of the prejudice, as it had been in the 1880s and afterwards, was "talk of Jewish domination."

The 1950-51 "Harvard Project on the Soviet Social System" was based on interviews with Soviet refugees in the U.S., people who had defected or had been captured during World War II or who had fled during 1946-50. The interviews reflected tremendous hostility toward Jews across the board, though the antisemitism of the Ukrainian refugee population was especially severe. Most of those surveyed agreed that Jews occupied a "privileged and favored position" in Soviet society; that they were "business- and money-minded"; that they were "clannish," "aggressive" and "pushy"; that they don't like to work hard and refuse to serve in the front lines of the armed forces. Despite two to three decades of Bolshevik rule, attitudes of the 1880s had remained unchanged.

Prejudice reached especially intense levels during the "anti-cosmopolitan" campaign of 1949-53, climaxed by the notorious "Doctors' Plot." Ilya Ehrenburg, otherwise an apologist for Stalin's rule, was so shocked by the "ugly survival" of antisemitism that he was convinced "that to cleanse minds of age-old prejudices is going to take a very long time." Had Stalin not died on March 5, 1953, there was certain to be, according to Isaac Deutscher, his distinguished British biographer, "only one sequel: a nation-wide pogrom."

Poet Yevgeny Yevtushenko penetrated to the Russian soul with his "Babi Yar" in 1961. He bemoaned how "the Russian people" were "blemished" by antisemitism and how the Communist song, "The Internationale," can "thunder forth" only when Jew-hatred is "buried for good." When Nikita Krushchev objected to Yevtushenko raising the shameful issue, the poet would not be silenced. The popular hate must be faced, he said, for "we cannot go forward to Communism with such a heavy load as Judeophobia."

"Judeophobia" had already become part of *official* policy by the end of the 1930s, not, as is often assumed, in May 1948 when the State of Israel was 'established. According to Hitler, Stalin told Nazi Foreign Minister Joachim Von Ribbentrop in the fall of 1939 that he would oust Soviet Jews from leading positions the moment he had a sufficient number of qualified non-Jews with whom to replace them. Stalin's promise was more than a mere diplomatic gesture to placate his new racist ally. In 1942, one year after the Nazi invasion of Russia, the Soviet authorities handed down a secret order establishing quotas for Jews in particularly prominent posts.

Igor Gouzenko, a former Soviet diplomatic official in Canada who later defected, related that in 1939 he was told of a "confidential" decree of the Party Central Committee that had been sent to all directors of educational institutions ordering them to establish quotas of admissions for Jews. In the summer of 1945, he said, he was informed by the chief of the secret division of Soviet intelligence that the Central Committee had sent "confidential" instructions to directors of all factories to remove Jews from responsible positions. According to Milovan Djilas, Stalin in 1946 boasted to him that "in our Central Committee there are no Jews!" Stalin's daughter revealed that, after the war, "in the enrollment at the university and in all types of employment, preference was given to Russians. For the Jews, a percentage quota was, in essence, reinstated."

The emergence of anti-Jewish discrimination as state policy in the late '30s and early '40s certainly cannot be considered a function of the foreign policy of the USSR. That policy had swung, pendulum-like, from a pro-West position ("collective security") to a pro-Nazi position (the Nazi-Soviet Non-Aggression Pact) and then back to a pro-West position (the Grand Alliance). On the other hand, official antisemitism (which denied the civil rights of Jews) developed along a single line with little fluctuation. Only in the realm of *collective* ethnic and cultural rights were the Jews accorded equality. The Jewish Anti-Fascist Committee was created in 1942; together with the publication establishment, *Emes,* it was to constitute, until November 1948, the Jewish "address" in the USSR. The Committee was formed in order to win strong Jewish sympathy in the Western world for the Soviet cause.

The government's policy of discrimination against Jews as individuals was largely a function of two internal developments in the Soviet Union at the time: deepening Russian nationalism (bordering on xenophobia) and the formation of a totalitarian structure.

The new Russian nationalism was a dominant characteristic of the struggle against the Old Guard's "internationalism." Suspicion fell equally upon those suspected of harboring sympathies with various non-Russian nationalities of the USSR and those linked, in one way or another, with the West.

Antisemitism came hand in hand with this official Russian chauvinism, as it had during the Tsarist era, at least since the reign of Nicholas I. Certainly it was not accidental that official antisemitism made its first, if then only momentary, appearance at the time, in 1926, when Stalinist forces were attempting to inculcate a national pride in the doctrine of "socialism in one country." Chauvinism catered to and fed upon popular prejudices. The war years were replete with examples of an unleashed bigotry linked to nationalist fervor. Many of the partisan units, for example, were riddled with antisemitism. Krushchev in 1956 acknowledged to a visiting French Socialist delegation that popular prejudice toward Jews did play a role in affecting the state discriminatory policy. In December 1962, he told a Party-organized meeting of artists and intellectuals that if Jews were to occupy top posts, it would tend to create antisemitism.

The other internal development contributing to official antisemitism was the erection of a totalitarian structure aiming to mobilize mass energies for Party-determined purposes. Totalitarianism, of course, could tolerate no genuinely autonomous or corporate social units independent of the central manipulators of power. For territorially-based ethnic groups, dismantling their autonomous communal structures or penetrating into them was a long-term process, difficult to complete. All the more so if the weight of demography, as in the case of the Ukrainians, was added to that of geography. But with the Jewish community, the task was simplified. A dispersed people, the Jews would find that their communal establishment could, simply and literally, be pulverized.

That the Jews were particularly suspect in a totalitarian structure impregnated with a distinct chauvinist character is not surprising, for they indeed *were* a minority with an international tradition and a world-wide religion. Jews everywhere had cultural, emotional and even family ties that transcended national boundaries.

Furthermore, Hannah Arendt has noted that totalitarianism requires an "objective enemy who, like the 'carrier of a disease,' is the 'carrier' of subversive 'tendencies.' " This aspect of totalitarianism had a distinctive impact on the state's relationship to the Jews. The very nature of a system which claims both a monopoly on truth and the control of the "commanding heights" by which the preordained may be reached precludes human error or inadequacy. Only plots and conspiracies by hidden forces could interrupt, hinder or defeat "scientifically" planned programs. Stalin even considered his daughter's marriage to a Jew a "Zionist plot." Other Soviet leaders may not necessarily have perceived the Jew as a "plotter," but, cynically, accepted the functional usefulness of such a perception. Such cynicism enabled the Jew to be cast in the role of scapegoat, to be blamed for failures or difficulties in the regime's internal and foreign policies.

If both chauvinism and totalitarianism lent themselves to the absorption of popular antisemitism at high levels, the background of the Party leadership since the late '30s helps explain the transmission and persistence of folk imagery about the Jew. With the influx of this group, the wide cultural and intellectual horizons which characterized the pre-Purge Party leaders gave way to horizons that were provincial and cramped.

On both national and regional levels, almost half of the top Party executives in the early '60s had peasant fathers. Only six percent had white-collar origins, while a little more than a quarter came from the proletariat. Most likely, many of them learned their negative-Jewish stereotypes in their own homes, their own neighborhoods, their own towns. Moreover, almost 40 percent of Party leaders either had no education beyond secondary school or had attended only a Party school. Of those who completed college, 40 percent studied engineering and 30 percent agronomy—"narrowly specialized and highly applied skills." Training in the broad humanistic disciplines was negligible. About a third of the leaders studied specialized skills in farming, a third in industry, and a third in ideology. Most conjoined their specialized experience with work in the organizational apparatus before reaching their top posts. Clearly, this pattern of training experience did little to broaden their scope.

In the narrow range of outlook, the traditional conception of the Jew, imbibed, as it were, from the environment, emerges as an accepted and acceptable model. That over 90 percent of all top Party posts on the USSR level are held by Russians contributes, indirectly, to the reinforcement of these attitudes. If this figure clearly bares the post-war trend toward Great Russian chauvinism, it just as clearly reflects one of the principal tendencies inherent in such chauvinism—antisemitism.

A (future) Party leader is subjected to totalitarian indoctrination from the day he first embarks upon the course which will enable him to perform the function of a high Party apparatchik, whether in the central secretariat or in the provinces. This creates the classic authoritarian personality—rigid, disciplined, obedient, adoring of the symbol of his own nationality, suspicious of the alien and the outsider. This renders the Jew, especially the "cosmopolitan" and "international Zionist" Jew, the embodiment of all the evil fantasies conspired up to explain the plots and conspiracies which may arise to threaten the socialist "fatherland."

After the Six-Day War and particularly after the Czech reformist "socialism with a human face" movement in 1967-68, official Soviet antisemitism took on an especially virulent form. On one level, it assumed a racist drive in the media—a massive propaganda assault against Jews, launched in August 1967, reacting to the Israeli victory in the Six-Day War. Thinly masked as anti-Zionist, the drive has been directed against Judaism, Jewish tradition and Jewry itself. The Torah and the Talmud have been presented as preaching racism, hatred and violence. A typical comment on the Torah can be found in Vladimir Begun's *Invasion Without Arms,* published in 1977 and republished in 1980. Begun writes: ". . . it proves to be an unsurpassed textbook of blood-thirstiness, hypocrisy, treachery, perfidy and degradation—all the basest human qualities."

This propaganda draws its inspiration from *The Protocols of the Elders of Zion,* which claimed that international Jewry plots world domination through control of the banks and the press and infiltration of the Freemasons. Today in the USSR, Zionism is labeled as a movement seeking "domination over the world" and locked in struggle with the Soviet Union.

The campaign is centrally coordinated and directed. A study of the central and provincial Soviet press revealed that since 1967, the number of articles critical of Zionism has increased sixfold. Zionism has been the main subject of at least half, and as much as two-thirds, of newspaper space on Jewish subjects. The increase in antisemitic books and brochures has been stunning. One study shows that 112 antisemitic books were published in the '60s and '70s, some in editions of 150,000 or 200,000 copies, receiving enthusiastic reviews in the Soviet press.

Especially disturbing is the anti-Zionist campaign in the Soviet military. When a major Soviet military journal, *Sovietskii Voin,* echoed in February 1982, the dark and hoary language of Tsarist antisemitism, it inevitably raised questions about the character of the ideological training in the Soviet armed forces, for every Soviet male over the age of 18, and, beyond that, the perspective of the Kremlin. The periodical described an alleged "Masonic-Zionist strategy" for subverting both Soviet society and the Warsaw Pact structure and for achieving world domination.

The lurid depiction of a vast conspiracy boggles the mind. Free Masonry, "a world-wide semi-public, semi-secret political organization of the bourgeoisie," is described as an instrument for promoting the interests of "international Zionism." Linked to the conspiracy are "activists" in China "who are engaged in the implementation of a secret provocative policy directed against the Soviet Union," NATO espionage in Turkey, political murders in France, terrorist Red Brigades in Italy and the Trilateral Commission headed by "the influential American Mason, D. Rockefeller." The most recent expression of the "Masonic-Zionist strategy," according to the military publication, was the Solidarity movement in Poland. All of its leaders were supposedly "directed by secret instructions and directions" from Masonic Lodges.

More immediately threatening, however, is an anti-Jewish discriminatory pattern in higher education, for it poses a palpable and direct challenge to historic job opportunities and traditional life-styles of Soviet Jews. It is precisely such educational discrimination that has evoked the deepest anxiety in the Soviet Jewish community. Significantly, the USSR has avoided publishing data on university enrollment during the past four years. However, statistics on the city of Moscow, newly published in a Soviet volume, inadvertently throw a glaring light upon this critical aspect of the plight of Soviet Jews. The Moscow data show that in the academic year 1980-81, the number of Jewish students in all Moscow higher education institutions was 9,911, of a total enrollment of 631,888. The percentage was 1.5, an appallingly low amount. Comparison with Moscow data published a decade ago covering the academic year 1970-71 reveals the dramatic decrease in Jewish enrollment. At that time, the number of Jewish students totalled 19,509, in a student body of 617,141. The

percentage of Jews then was 3.16. In the course of a decade, the number of Jews in Moscow higher education plunged by more than 50 percent, both absolutely and relatively.

The current Jewish student percentage is far below the percentage of Jews in the Moscow population. Soviet census data of 1970 shows 251,523 Jews in a total population of 7,061,008—3.56 percent. That the university-age Moscow Jews would be especially attracted to higher institutions is suggested by the 1971 data on Moscow's scientific community (one-quarter of the entire Soviet scientific group). Since roughly 11 percent of the Moscow scientific community is Jewish—an extraordinarily large percentage—the likelihood of their offspring aspiring to higher education is particularly strong.

Certainly the pool of talent available for potential admission to higher education in Moscow would not have been diminished by emigration. The city, until now, has produced a very small percentage of the total emigration group. Careful research indicates that between 1968 and 1980, the total number of Moscow Jews who emigrated was 14,494, only 5.8 percent of the total emigrant population.

According to (unofficial) *samizdat* information, Jews are kept out of the best higher educational institutions in Moscow through the technique of having specially selected examiners give them unusually difficult oral examinations in mathematics and physics. A late 1981 *samizdat* document spells out the impact of discriminatory practices on the graduates of five Moscow high schools specializing in physics and mathematics. Although many Jews from these schools applied, only two were admitted to Moscow State University's Department of Mechanics and Mathematics. In contrast, a large majority of non-Jewish applicants from the high schools were admitted.

The situation in the rest of the USSR, to judge from earlier data, no doubt parallels the Moscow experience. The number of Jewish students enrolled in higher education throughout the USSR plunged downward from 111,900 in 1968-69 to 66,900 in 1976-77 (the last year of published data). The incredible 40 percent decline is certain to have dropped even further since then. (One estimate places it at the 50-55,000 level.) Statistics on the postgraduate level offer a similar pattern. The number of Jewish postgraduate students in 1970 was 4,945; in 1975, it fell to 2,841.

For Soviet Jews, the evidence points to a desperate future. If, until the late '60s, they played a major role in the technological and cultural elite (though not in political, diplomatic or security-related spheres), it was largely a consequence of a fairly open, merit-oriented university admissions policy. That has come to an end. Discrimination is certain to reduce to a minimum the number of Jews permitted to enter the key scientific and higher technical areas. A major and perceptive 5,000-word document prepared by 127 top Jewish refuseniks in February 1981 highlighted the trend: "Access to the highest echelons of power [in science and technology] is practically closed to Jews, a situation reminiscent of the one existing in medieval aristocratic societies."

The profound trauma afflicting Soviet Jews flows from the drastic cutback in emigration—over 95 percent since 1979. Only a trickle is now permitted to leave. With their educational future doomed and antisemitism continuing, it is hardly suprising that the 127 refuseniks warn, "the Jews of the USSR are facing the threat of a national catastrophe."

The 100th anniversary of the pogromist mentality has come and gone, and the situation has reached a desperate turning point. Like Cassandra, Soviet Jews are crying out. Unlike Cassandra's, their cries must be heard.

Soviet Jewish Prisoners of Conscience

Behind the bars of Soviet prisons and isolated in Soviet labor camps sit Jewish political prisoners, detained there solely for their active efforts to obtain a visa to emigrate to Israel.

Officially, they are arrested and tried on charges like "anti-Soviet agitation," "anti-Soviet propaganda," or "defaming the Soviet state." In truth, these Soviet Jewish Prisoners of Conscience (POCs) are guilty only of exercising their rights to live as Jews, to live in freedom. Many of them were leaders or activists in the emigration movement, or served as Hebrew teachers and organizers of Jewish cultural activities.

Soviet Prisons

The inhuman conditions in which a POC serves his sentence inflict not only physical suffering but personal degradation. Once convicted, a POC is either sent to a prison, in which he is confined to a small cell, sent to a labor camp or sentenced to internal exile. In a corrective labor camp, which is surrounded by barbed wire, a prisoner is subjected to the brutal conditions of a small, dank cell, lacking ventilation and insufficiently heated during the cold winter months.

In prison, where regulations are much stricter, a POC is subjected more to punitive measures than to corrective ones. If sentenced to internal exile, the prisoner is confined to another city within the Soviet Union, generally in Siberia, and is allowed neither to return home nor to leave the Soviet Union.

Soviet labor camps are divided into four categories or "regimes." In order of increasing severity they are: standard, reinforced, strict and special. Each regime progressively reduces the spectrum of prisoners' rights. Inmates of prisons are fed differently according to whether they are on ordinary or strict regime. Those on ordinary regime in prisons are on a diet which contains around 2000 calories, the equivalent of one piece of chocolate cheesecake. However, most inmates of prisons spend part of their sentence on strict regime, especially if they are prisoners of conscience who engage in any form of protest against their conditions of confinement. The strict regime diet contains about 1750 calories per day and 49 grams of protein, according to the most detailed available accounts. Furthermore, all prisoners who are put on strict regime serve their first month of this punishment on "reduced rations." This diet reportedly contains around 1300 calories.

All prisoners' mail is censored, and the number of letters which may be sent out is restricted. And, as mail is often the single source of contact with the outside world, these restrictions on mail can sever a prisoner's ties with his/her family. In standard regime labor camps and prisons, POCs are entitled to two letters per month. In strict regime labor

DAILY DIET IN A SOVIET PRISON CAMP

BREAKFAST
14 oz. black bread (full day's ration); 1 cup hot water—no sugar allowed; 1 oz. herring.

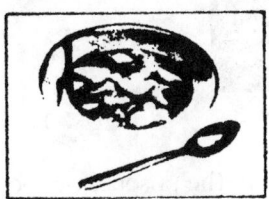

LUNCH
²/₃ cup of soup; boiled cabbage; and ½ medium-sized potato , no fat allowed.

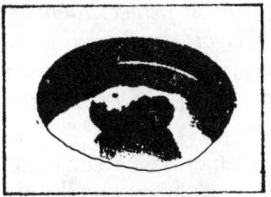

SUPPER
3½ to 5 oz. potato (no fats); or 1 cup raw cabbage and tomato in vinegar.

= 9 Hours at Hard Labor

camps and prisons, one letter per month is allowed. When a prisoner is incarcerated in an internal labor camp punishment cell, he is only allowed one letter every two months; this also applies to prisoners in special regime labor camps and prisons. According to the regulations, there are no restrictions on the number of letters which a prisoner may receive in any of these categories.

However, although a POC's correspondence and visiting rights are supposedly recognized by the authorities, *they are continually violated.* Such was the case with Anatoly Shcharansky in late 1982 and early 1983. The authorities stopped delivering his wife's letters to him, then forbade him to write to her, since she lives in Israel and not in the Soviet Union.

Prison administrators go through the office of the censor in order to restrict prisoners' letters. But with visiting rights, officials can act directly, since permission for a visit depends on the prisoner's "good behavior." If the administration can see to it that he builds up enough infractions to deny him his rights. A common way of provoking a Prisoner of Conscience to commit the necessary offense is to send him to clean up the restricted area by the labor camp's fence, or to repair the fence itself. A POC's ethics forbid him to reinforce or repair the camp fences; the barbed wire is the symbol of their unjust incarceration, so most political

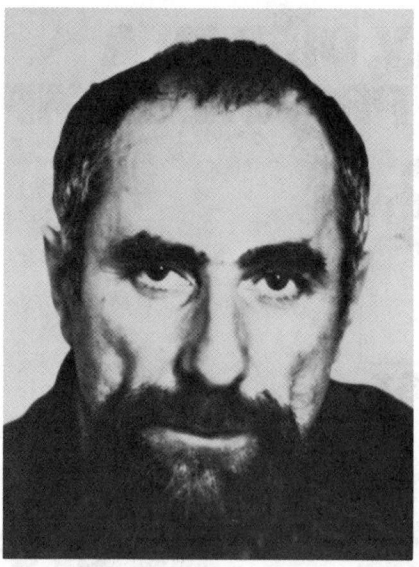

Iosif Begun

Yuli Edelshtein

Aleksandr Kholmiansky

inmates refuse to perform this task. The prisoner can be denied his visits on the basis of this refusal.

Soviet Jewish Prisoners of Conscience are helpless before the prison administrations and the KGB, which directs those administrations' activities. Publicity is the best defense that a POC has. *We must protect them by publicizing the violation of their rights, and urging the Soviet authorities to act in compliance with the Helsinki Accords in granting them the correspondence and visiting rights to which they are entitled.*

> "We are sure that my father's return is the result of his publicity in the West. But it's not freedom. He was released only conditionally. But he says neither prison nor exile and forced labor can change our wish to go to Israel. We will demand it again and again and we hope Jews will help us. . . ."
>
> —*Sasha Lein, daughter of former POC Evgeny Lein*

Following is a list (as of February 1985) of POCs in prisons, labor camps or internal exile in the USSR. Complete biographical information about each POC is available from the Coalition to Free Soviet Jews.

Moshe Abramov. Born in 1955, from Samarkand, Uzbekistan, Abramov taught Hebrew and worked as a shochet (ritual slaughterer) in his home town. He was arrested in late 1983 and charged with "malicious hooliganism." He received a sentence of 3 years imprisonment. Address: Navoi, Uzbek SSR, USSR.

Iosif Begun. Long-time refusenik and Jewish activist Iosif Begun was born in 1932 and lived in Moscow. A mathematician and Hebrew teacher, Begun was arrested for an unprecedented third time in 1982, and charged with "anti-Soviet agitation and propaganda." In the fall of 1983, he was sentenced to 7 years in a labor camp, and 5 years of internal exile. Address: Uchr. VS 389/37, st. Polovinka, Chusovskoi Rayon, Permskaya Oblast 618801, USSR. Wife: Inna Begun, Dmitrievna Raketny Bulvar 11-5-15, Moscow 129243, RSFSR, USSR.

Iosif Berenshtein. Berenshtein, a refusenik from Kiev, was detained during a visit to Novograd Vilinsky in

November 1984. He was charged with "resisting the authorities" and sentenced to 4 years in a labor camp. Address: Entuziastov 35/140, Kiev 252147, UkrSSR, USSR.

Aleksandr Cherniak. Cherniak, a 34-year-old communications engineer from Kiev, was sentenced to four years of imprisonment in April 1984. A refusenik since 1978, he was convicted on trumped-up charges of embezzlement and forgery. Address: Not known. Wife: Polina Cherniak, Vasilkovskaya 4-24, Kiev 40, UkrSSR, USSR.

Yuli Edelshtein. Edelshtein, a 26-year-old Moscow Hebrew teacher, was arrested September 4, 1984 on trumped-up charges of drug possession. Three months later, he was tried and received the maximum sentence of three years. He applied to emigrate to Israel in 1979. Address: Not known. Wife: Tatiana Edelshtein, Yaroslavskoye Shosse 24/1/43, Moscow 129337, RSFSR, USSR.

Yuri Federov. Federov, one of the original non-Jewish defendants in the First Leningrad Trial, was born in 1943 in Moscow. A student at the time of his arrest in 1970, he was charged with "treason," "anti-Soviet agitation and propaganda," "anti-Soviet organization," and "stealing state property." He was tried in 1970 and was sentenced to 15 years (to 6/85). Address: Uchr. VS 389/36, Posiolok Kutchino, Chusovskoy Rayon, Permskaya Oblast, RSFSR, USSR.

Nadezhda Fradkova. Fradkova, an activist from Leningrad, was sentenced to two years for "parasitism" in December 1984. She had been periodically confined to psychiatric hospitals since April 1983. Address: Not known.

Boris Kanevsky. A mathematician by profession, Kanevsky was born in 1945 and lived in Moscow. His arrest in 1982, on the charge of "circulating of fabrications known to be false which defame the Soviet state and social system," resulted in a sentence of 5 years of internal exile (to 6/87). Address: Posiolok Vagai, Tumenskaya Oblast, 626140, RSFSR, USSR. Wife: Elizaveta Kanevsky, 1-YJ Mosfilmovsky 5-14-176, Moscow, RSFSR, USSR.

Aleksandr Kholmiansky. Kholmiansky, 34, a Moscow refusenik and Hebrew teacher, was arrested on July 25, 1984 for a minor infraction of Soviet law. Weeks later, a gun was planted in his home and he was charged with "possession of a weapon." In February 1985 he was sentenced to 18 months in a labor camp for "possession of ammunition."

Feliks Kochubievsky. Kochubievsky, born in 1930, worked as an electrical engineer in Novosibirsk until the time of his arrest in 1982. He was charged with the "circulation of fabrications known to be false which defame the Soviet state and social system." He was sentenced in 1982 to 2½ years in a labor camp (to 3/85). Address: 618 Solikamsk, 2-Permskaya Oblast, P/ya 389/15, Otryad 1, Brigada 13, 618500, RSFSR, USSR. Wife: Valentina Kochubievsky, Vatutina 75-1-45, Novosibirsk 630064, RSFSR, USSR.

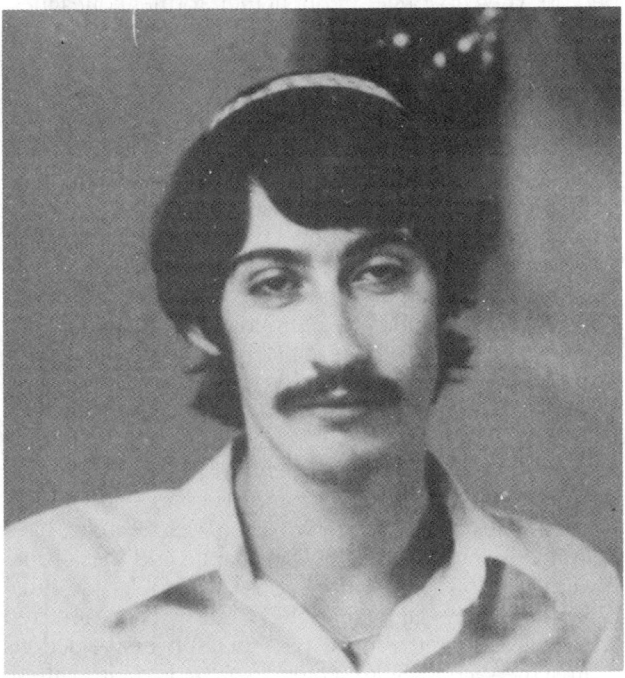

Yakov Levin

Yakov Levin. Levin, a refusenik from Odessa, was arrested on August 10, 1984 just one week before his scheduled marriage to another refusenik, Yehudit Nepomniashchy. He was charged with the "circulation of fabrications known to be false which defame the Soviet state and social system," and received a 3-year sentence in November 1984. Address: Not known. Parents' Address: ul. Zaslavskogo 23/3, Odessa 270020, UkrSSR, USSR.

Yakov Mesh. Mesh, a prominent activist in Odessa and a good friend of Levin, was detained in the fall of 1984 in connection with the investigation of Levin. He may be charged with "refusing to give testimony" and/or "resisting arrest." Mesh was released from confinement, pending his trial, for treatment of severe abdominal and liver injuries sustained during a brutal beating in prison. Address: Ploshchad Martynovskogo 3-4, Apartment 71, Odessa, UkrSSR, USSR.

Mark Nepomniashchy. Nepomniashchy, another Odessa refusenik and the father of Levin's fiancee, Yehudit Nepomniashchy, was arrested around the same time as Mesh and may face the same charge as Levin. His trial is likely to have taken place early in 1985. Address: Pr. Gagarina, 16-4-5, Odessa 39, UkrSSR, USSR.

Mark Ocheretiansky Ocheretiansky, a refusenik from Kiev, first applied to emigrate in 1979. A 44-year-old construction engineer, he was imprisoned in October 1983 for a breach of internal passport regulations. Address: Not known. Wife: Olga Otcheretiansky, ul. Strazhenko 11-49, Kiev 252165, UkrSSR, USSR.

Valery Senderov. Valery Senderov, born in 1944, was arrested with his Jewish colleague Boris Kanevsky in 1982. Senderov worked in Moscow as a mathematician until the time of his arrest. Senderov, who was tried in 1983, received 7 years in a labor camp, and 5 years of internal exile (to 6/94). Address: VS-389/35, Permskaya Oblast, RSFSR, USSR. Wife: Elena Krichagina, Ulansky Per. 14, Apt. 54, Moscow 101000, RSFSR, USSR.

Dan Shapira. Dan Shapira, a Moscow refusenik born in 1962, was arrested in January 1985 and charged with "defaming the Soviet State." His apartment had been searched previously in connection with the investigation of Yuli Edelshtein. During the search, Shapira's mezuzah was ripped from his doorpost, as authorities claimed he was using it to conceal drugs. Also confiscated were his tefillin and all of his books printed in Hebrew, including a Talmud and a Bible. Address: Not known.

Anatoly Shcharansky. Anatoly Shcharansky, a computer technologist from Moscow, was arrested in 1977 and charged with "treason" and "espionage." Shcharansky was tried in 1978 and sentenced to 3 years of imprisonment, and 10 years special regime camp (to 3/90). He was forced to spend considerably more than 3 years in prison, and his health has deteriorated seriously. In December 1984, he was reportedly hospitalized following his transfer from Chistopol Prison to a labor camp in Perm. Address: Not known. Mother: Ida Milgrom, ul. Kooperativnaya 8, Istra, Moskovskaya Oblast, RSFSR, USSR. Wife: Avital Shcharansky, 34 Shderot Herzel, Jerusalem, Israel 96105.

Lev Shefer. An engineer from Sverdlovsk, Shefer applied to emigrate in 1974 and was refused on the basis of "secrecy." He is a Hebrew teacher who has become particularly interested in Judaic history. In September 1981, he was arrested for "anti-Soviet agitation and propaganda" and received a 5-year sentence. Address: Permskaya Oblast, Chusovskoy Rayon, St. Vsesvyatskaya, Posiolok Tsentralny 385/19 (Moscow, Uchr. 5110/1 VS 389/35), RSFSR, USSR.

Simon Shnirman. Shnirman was born in 1957 and worked as a chemical technician in Kerch. He was arrested in 1978 and charged with "draft evasion." He received 3 years in a labor camp as a result of his 1983 trial. Address: Not known. Mother: Faina Shnirman, ul. Kirova 79/31, 334518 Kerch, Krimskaya Oblast, UkrSSR, USSR.

Leonid Borisovich Shrayer. Leonid Shrayer, a refusenik from Moscow, was sentenced on January 3, 1985 to three years for spreading false slanderous fabrications. Address: Not known.

Yuri Tarnopolsky. Tarnopolsky, a chemist from Kharkov, was born in 1936. Charged in 1983 with the "circulation of fabrications known to be false which defame the Soviet state and social system," Tarnopolsky is presently serving 3 years in a labor camp (to 3/86). He too is ailing. Address: 672022 CHITA, P/ya G14/6, 5th Group, RSFSR, USSR. Wife: Olga Tarnopolsky, Per. Krasnoznanemy 2-17, Kharkov 310002, UkrSSR, USSR.

Aleksandr Yakir. Yakir, a 29-year-old engineer and member of a prominent Moscow refusenik family, was arrested in June 1984 and charged with refusing military service. Yakir and his parents have been waiting for permission to emigrate for a decade. Address: Not known. Parents: Evgeny and Rimma Yakir, Profsoyuznaya 96-5-35, Moscow, RSFSR, USSR.

Stanislav Zubko. Stanislav Zubko, from Kiev, was born in 1937. He worked as a chemist until he was arrested in 1981 and charged with the "illegal keeping of arms," and the "illegal possession of drugs." He was tried in 1981 and received a sentence of 4 years in a labor camp (to 5/85). Address: Uchr. MX-224/31, Izyaslav, 281200 Khmelnitskaya Oblast, UkrSSR, USSR.

Zakhar Zunshain. Zunshain, a 33-year-old physicist from Riga, has been a refusenik since 1981. In March 1984, Zunshain, his wife Tatiana, and two friends publicly protested their repeated refusals in front of Moscow's Bolshoi Theatre. Zunshain was subsequently arrested and charged with the "circulation of fabrications known to be false which defame the Soviet state and social system." In June 1984, he was sentenced to three years in prison. Address: IK 272/40, Posiolok 130201, Ekhirit-Bulagatski, 666111 Irkutskaya Oblast, USSR. Wife: Tatiana Zunshain, ul. Lenina 111-22, Riga, Latvian SSR, USSR.

Former Prisoners of Conscience Still Awaiting Exit Visas:

Viktor Brailovsky	Aleksei Murzhenko
Boris Chernobilsky	Mark Nashpitz
Levi Elbert	Ida Nudel
Kim Fridman	Aleksandr Panarev
Grigory Geishis	Aleksandr Paritsky
Semyon Gluzman	Valery Pilnikov
Grigory Goldshtein	Dimitri Shchiglik
Boris Kalendariov	Isaak Shkolnik
Vladimir Kislik	Vladimir Slepak
Evgeny Lein	Moisey Tonkonogy
Osip Lokshin	Vladimir Tsukerman
Aleksandr Magidovich	Aleksandr Vilig

The 'Refuseniks' Need Help

Elie Wiesel

They were the first. The first to reject the reign of terror. The first to defy the Kremlin. The first to claim freely, openly, their right to difference—and to freedom.

I am talking about the Russian Jews. I met them in 1965 during a trip to the Soviet Union. In a work published afterward, I tried to bear witness for them. I described their victories over fear. I told of their Simhat Torah in front of the Choral Synagogue in Moscow: thousands and thousands of young people had gathered to sing and dance and thereby celebrate their devotion to the history of the Jewish people. It was obvious—some 50 years of dictatorship and Communist education had not been able to stifle Jewish memory.

A great number of these young idealists are already in Israel and almost everywhere throughout the free world. But not all. The majority have remained behind. Now they are known as "refuseniks," because they are refused visas. They remain our heroes. How do they manage not to lose hope?

I met with some of them in 1979 during my third visit to their country. We spent a whole night talking about Jewish literature and philosophy. Some had been waiting three years for their visas, others three times that long. From the moment they sent in their request for emigration papers, they lived marginally, in an oppressive atmosphere of unemployment. Still constantly followed, watched, interrogated by the police for trivial matters or for no reason at all, they constitute a separate society within the Russian people. They no longer frequent their former colleagues; they meet among themselves, help each other, let each other know what is happening in the world at large and in the Jewish world in particular. Convinced that eventually they will be able to leave, they live in expectation and spend their time in study. In leaving them, during our last meeting, I asked the usual question: could something be done for them? They answered: send us books.

But their situation is no longer the same. It has considerably worsened. Persecution of all kinds, searches, arrests: the K.G.B. is taking a harder line. All the signs make it impossible to doubt: the intimidation campaign aims chiefly at educators who teach Hebrew, the Bible, Jewish history.

Mark Nepomniashchy, Yaakov Mesh, Yaakov Levin, Polina Green (from Tiraspol), Aharon Munblit (from Kishinev), Mosiey Lieberman (from Bendery), Aleksandr Kholmiansky and Yuli Edelshtein (from Moscow)—and others whose names are not yet known in the West. Searches have been made in the homes of Dan Shapira and Inesa Brokhina in Moscow. The police confiscated books and ritual objects that they claim concealed "drugs." Those arrested are accused, for the most part, of "subversive actions against the state." Severe sentences are to be feared: these victims will be made to serve as examples, as warnings. And these new prisoners will be joining their brave predecessors, Anatoly Shcharansky and Vladimir Slepak, in their prison.

How to explain these measures of the Kremlin? Do they reflect uncertainties at the top? Or, a desire to emphasize its rigidity toward the Western powers? Any hypothesis is likely. On the other hand, what is certain is that the "refuseniks" are entering a dark and threatening time. They are counting on our human solidarity in order to stand fast. If we deny it to them, we are condemning them to solitude and despair. As for ourselves, we shall never be forgiven for any indifference.

"Next Year in Jerusalem"

Anatoly Shcharansky's Words On His Judgment Day

In March and April, during interrogation, the chief investigators warned me that in the position I have taken during investigation, and held to here in court, I would be threatened with execution by firing squad, or at least 15 years. If I would agree to cooperate with the investigation for the purpose of destroying the Jewish emigration movement, they promised me early freedom and a quick reunion with my wife.

Five years ago, I submitted my application for exit to Israel. Now I'm further than ever from my dream. It would seem to be cause for regret. But it is absolutely otherwise. I am happy. I am happy that I lived honestly, in peace with my conscience. I never compromised my soul, even under the threat of death.

I am happy that I helped people. I am proud that I knew and worked with such honest, brave and courageous people as Sakharov, Orlov, Ginzburg, who are carrying on the traditions of the Russian intelligentsia. I am fortunate to have been witness to the process of the liberation of Jews of the USSR.

I hope that the absurd accusation against me and the entire Jewish emigration movement will not hinder the liberation of my people. My near ones and friends know how I wanted to exchange activity in the emigration movement for a life with my wife, Avital, in Israel.

For more then 2,000 years the Jewish people, my people, have been dispersed. But wherever they are, wherever Jews are found, every year they have repeated, "Next year in Jerusalem." Now, when I am further than ever from my people, from Avital, facing many arduous years of imprisonment, I say, turning to my people, my Avital: Next year in Jerusalem.

Now I turn to you, the court, who were required to confirm a pre-determined sentence: To you I have nothing to say.

Anatoly Shcharansky was sentenced to 13 years imprisonment on July 10, 1978. His wife, Avital, lives in Jerusalem. They have not seen each other since they were married on July 4, 1974.

Writing Letters to Soviet Jewish Refusenik Families

Letter-writing provides a lifeline between American Jews who live in freedom and courageous Soviet Jewish activists who must struggle for that opportunity. It establishes a warm, personal relationship between American and Soviet Jewish families.

Letters to Soviet Jews should be warm, personal and sympathetic. They should show concern for the plight of the individual or family to whom you are writing. Keep in mind that your letter should provide encouragement and should stress our solidarity with Soviet Jews.

DO'S

Write about your family, your professions, interests, hobbies and activities. Ask about anniversaries, birthdays, their hobbies, how they spend their vacations, etc.

Send greetings for Jewish holidays. Tell them how you spent a recent Jewish holiday, and describe Jewish experiences. If you've been to Israel, describe your visit.

Send them a picture of your family and ask for one in return.

WRITE REGULARLY, at least once a month, even if you do not receive an answer for several months. KEEP WRITING.

POC Anatoly Shcharansky

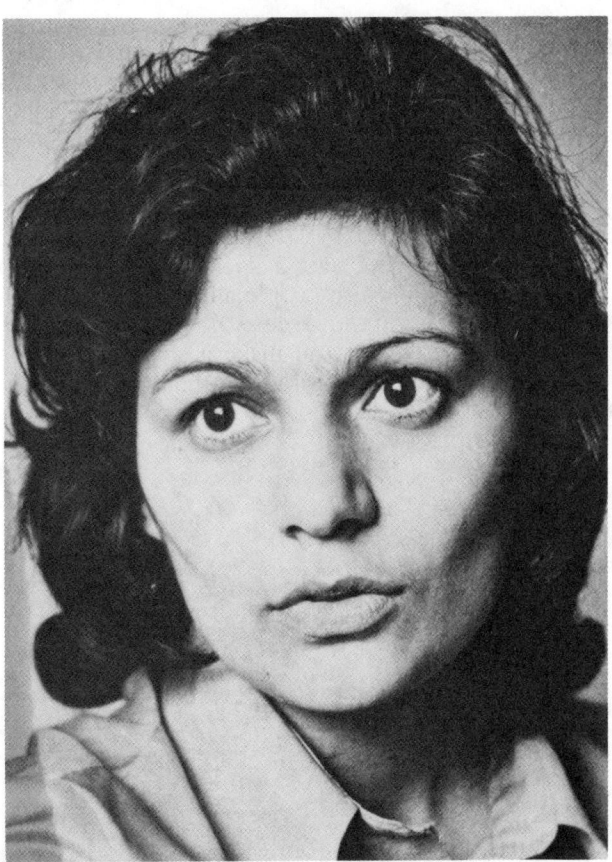

Avital Shcharansky

DON'TS

Do not discuss political topics or name any American organization.

The content of a letter should never be anti-Soviet.

At first, avoid using obvious Jewish symbols—this will increase your chances of a letter being delivered.

You can write to those former Prisoners of Conscience released after completion of their term but not permitted to emigrate:

Vladimir and Maria Slepak

Boris Chernobilsky
Uralskaya 6-3-25
Moscow B-207
RSFSR, USSR

Kim Fridman
Andrievskaya 12-8
Kiev 70
UkrSSR, USSR

Grigory Geishis
Prospekt Stachek 132-2-60
Leningrad 198207
RSFSR, USSR

Grigory Goldshtein
Oktiabraskaya 2nd Mikroraion 2-124
Tbilisi 380080
GruzSSR, USSR

Boris Kalendariov
Ul. Basseinaya 12-81
Leningrad 196070
RSFSR, USSR

Evgeny Lein
Engelsa Prospekt 135-21
Leningrad
RSFSR, USSR

Mark Nashpitz
Ul. Osipenko 17
Strunino, Vladimirskaya Oblast 601601
RSFSR, USSR

Ida Nudel
Yunikh Lenintsev 79/6/28
Moscow
RSFSR, USSR

Dimitri Shchiglik
Ul. Osipenko 17
Strunino, Vladimirskaya Oblast
RSFSR, USSR

Isaak Shkolnik
Ul. Tarnogorodskogo 23-307
Vinnitsa
USSR

Vladimir Slepak
Gordkogo 15-77
Moscow
RSFSR, USSR

Moisey Tonkonogy
Odessa
UkrSSR, USSR

Aleksandr Vilig
Odeskaya Oblast
Aksena Khristeva 52
Bolgrad
MoldSSR, USSR

Soviet Jewry Holiday Calendar

The Jewish Holidays give a special rhythm to the calendar, and unite Jewish people all over the world in shared celebration and with a sense of a common history. During the holidays, we can make a special effort to remember Soviet Jews, to speak out on their behalf, and to send them messages of support.

Rosh Hashanah

The Jewish new year is an occasion which calls for reflection and is a time to renew worthy commitments. On Rosh Hashanah, renew your commitment to help to make freedom for Soviet Jews a reality.

It is customary to eat an apple dipped in honey and say a prayer. This Rosh Hashanah recite a prayer for Soviet Jews at your dinner table.

> May it be your will to
> grant us a good and sweet
> year. May it be your will
> to bless Soviet Jews with
> the sweetness of freedom.

Yom Kippur

Hundreds of synagogues in the USSR have been closed, locking out thousands of Soviet Jews. On the holiest day of the Jewish year, many Soviet Jews have no place to go. To dramatize this, simulate a synagogue lockout at Selichot services. Uniformed guards can block the entrance and the rabbi can deliver his sermon outside the sanctuary.

Sukkot

During Sukkot, invite a Soviet Jewish refusenik or Prisoner of Conscience into your Sukkah and place his or her photograph on a chair to remind your guests of the Soviet Jews who are not able to celebrate the holiday in freedom.

Simchat Torah

On Simchat Torah, we can remember the Soviet Jews who are not here to dance and celebrate with us by incorporating them into our festivities. Dedicate a *hakafah,* a Torah procession, to a refusenik or a Prisoner of Conscience, and choose appropriate readings for the occasion.

Unofficial Simchat Torah celebration.

Chanukah

The holiday of heroes, Chanukah is a time that we remember the Maccabees who fought for the freedom of the Jewish people. In the Soviet Union today, Soviet Jewish heroes are fighting for the freedom to preserve their Jewish heritage by teaching Hebrew and forming Jewish study groups. On each night of Chanukah, you can honor these Soviet Jewish Hebrew teachers who are our modern day heroes by dedicating a candle in their names.

Tu B'Shevat

The 15th of Shevat is the harvest holiday, the Rosh Hashanah of trees. Because the soil is already moistened with the previous winter's rain, it is felt that trees planted on the 15th of Shevat will be firmly rooted and will bear much fruit. On this day, plant a tree in Israel in the name of a Prisoner of Conscience or a refusenik who is not free to settle his or her own roots in the land of Israel.

Fast of Esther

On the 13th of Adar, the fast of Esther is observed in commemoration of the fast undertaken by the Jewish people as they faced destruction by Haman. The purpose of the fast was to affirm that it is not only by physical strength that we prevail, but it is the unity of the Jewish people that overcomes obstacles. On this day, show solidarity with Soviet Jewish refuseniks and Prisoners of Conscience who are persecuted, by fasting in their name.

Purim

On Purim, messages of freedom for the Jewish people were spread throughout the land. This Purim, we Jews who live in freedom should send messages demanding freedom for Soviet Jews to President Mikhail Gorbachev, The Kremlin, Moscow, RSFSR, USSR.

Passover

Because Passover is the holiday on which the Jewish people not only remember their redemption from slavery, but are supposed to re-enact the transition from bondage to freedom on the Seder night, it is appropriate to remember Soviet Jews at the Seder table.

THE MATZAH OF HOPE
מַצָּה זוֹ—עַל שׁוּם הַתִּקְוָה

At an appropriate point during the Seder, the leader takes a matzah and says.

מַצָּה זוֹ, שֶׁאָנוּ מְיַחֲדִים, עַל שׁוּם מָה?

עַל שׁוּם הַתִּקְוָה שֶׁיֵּשׁ לְאַחֵינוּ בְּנֵי יִשְׂרָאֵל, יְהוּדֵי בְּרִית-הַמּוֹעָצוֹת. מַצָּה זוֹ מַעֲלָה עַל לִבֵּנוּ אֶת הַקֶּשֶׁר בֵּינֵינוּ וּלְבֵינָם אֲשֶׁר בַּל יִנָּתֵק לְעוֹלָם.

עַתָּה, בְּחַג הַפֶּסַח שֶׁהוּא זְמַן חֵרוּתֵנוּ, נִזְכֹּר שֶׁיְּהוּדֵי בְּרִית-הַמּוֹעָצוֹת אֵינָם בְּנֵי חוֹרִין.

אֵינָם בְּנֵי חוֹרִין לָצֵאת וְלַעֲלוֹת צִיּוֹנָה. אֵינָם בְּנֵי חוֹרִין לִלְמֹד מָסֹרֶת אֲבוֹתֵינוּ וּלְשׁוֹנָם. אֵינָם בְּנֵי חוֹרִין לְהַכְשִׁיר מוֹרִים וְרַבָּנִים לַדּוֹרוֹת הַבָּאִים.

נִזְכֹּר אֶת אַלְפֵי אֲסִירֵי צִיּוֹן שֶׁבִּקְּשׁוּ חַיִּים יְהוּדִיִּים בְּאַרְצֵנוּ הַקְּדוֹשָׁה וְעַכְשָׁיו נַפְשָׁם יוֹצֵאת בְּבֵית כֶּלֶא הַסּוֹבְיֵטִי. מִלְחַמְתָּם נִמְשֶׁכֶת.

אָנוּ עוֹמְדִים בְּצִדָּם, וְנַעֲמֹד יַחַד אִתָּם עַד שֶׁיִּרְאוּ אֶת הָאוֹר הַגָּדוֹל — אוֹר הַפְּדוּת וְהַגְּאוּלָה.

This matzah, which we set aside as a symbol of hope for the Jews of the Soviet Union, reminds us of the indestructible links that exist between us.

As we observe this festival of freedom, we recall that Soviet Jews are not free to leave without harassment; to learn of their past; to pass on their religious traditions; to learn the language of their fathers; to train teachers and rabbis of future generations.

We remember the scores who sought to live as Jews and struggled to leave for Israel—the land of our fathers—but now languish in Soviet labor camps. Their struggle against their oppressors goes on. They will not be forgotten.

We will stand with them in their struggle until the light of freedom and redemption shines forth.

CHAD GADYA

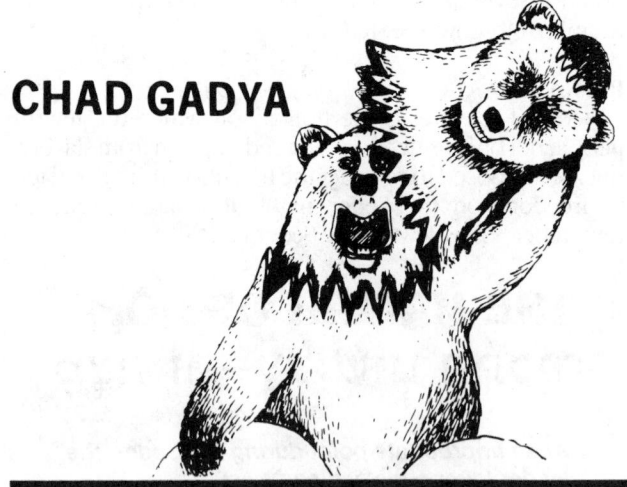

Chad Gadya . . . In the poem "Chad Gadya," the kid is the symbol of the Jew. Each animal represents an oppressor nation in our history: Egypt, Greece, Rome, down the ages through the Crusaders. The Soviet Bear is our present tormentor, creating vicious antisemitic hate campaigns, drastically decreasing the number of Jews allowed to emigrate, repressing Jewish cultural and religious expression, and imprisoning Jews whose only crime is a desire to live full Jewish lives in their homeland Israel.

On Passover, we pray that these policies of the Soviet Bear will meet the same fate as those of the other characters in the poem, that one day soon, Soviet Jews may be able to say "This Year in Jerusalem."

Shavuot

Shavuot, the holiday celebrating the giving of the Torah to the Jewish people, is a time to dedicate a Torah scroll to over two million Soviet Jews who are not free to study the Bible or the Hebrew language in the tradition of their ancestors.

Tisha B'Av

Each year on the ninth day of Av, Jews throughout the world gather to remember the events of long ago; in particular, to remember the destruction of the first and second Temples in Jerusalem. The words which we read on Tisha B'Av also call to mind the potential obliteration of the Soviet Jewish community in our own day. On Tisha B'Av, write to a Soviet refusenik or Prisoner of Conscience and confirm the justness of their cause. Our letters continue to be his/her lifeline.

What You Can Do To Help Soviet Jews

- WRITE to President Reagan right now and demand that he personally intervene to secure the rights denied to Soviet Jews by the Soviet authorities.
- WRITE to Soviet Jews as part of Project Yachad, a letter-writing program which provides a lifeline between refuseniks and American Jews. Biographical information about your refusenik's family and information on how to write to them is available. Refusenik "adoptions" may be made by individuals, families, organizations, camps, schools, or synagogues. Your letters tell refuseniks, and Soviet authorities, that you care.
- CALL the Coalition's 24-hour Actionline (212) 391-0954 for the latest news about Soviet Jewry, appropriate actions you can take regarding new developments, and announcements of upcoming Soviet Jewry events in the New York area.
- ARRANGE for a speaker to talk to your organization, school, or synagogue group about Soviet Jewry. Speakers include teachers, business people, lawyers, scientists and students, many of whom have travelled to the Soviet Union and can recount their firsthand impressions of the struggle for freedom in the USSR.
- BECOME a part of the Bar/Bat Mitzvah Twinning Program, which matches up American Jewish youngsters with their counterparts in the Soviet Union who are unable to mark publicly their entrance into Jewish adulthood.
- MARCH for Soviet Jewry on SOLIDARITY SUNDAY.

A Sample Letter. . .

Mr. Gorbachev:

Thousands of Soviet Jews are waiting to emigrate to Israel, yet you have locked the gates.

Soviet Jews have a right to learn, practice and teach their religion.

We demand that Soviet Jews be allowed to live freely as Jews in the Soviet Union, and that those who wish to emigrate be permitted to do so immediately.

NAME _____

ADDRESS_____

IF YOU DIDN'T MARCH LAST YEAR BECAUSE THINGS WERE GETTING BETTER, MARCH THIS YEAR BEFORE THINGS GET ANY WORSE.

MARCH FOR SOVIET JEWRY

Important Addresses...

President Ronald Reagan
The White House
Washington, D.C. 20500

Mikhail Gorbachev
President
The Kremlin
Moscow
RSFSR, USSR (postage 44¢ per ½ oz.)

Aleksandr M. Rekunkov
Procurator General
Pushkinskaya Street 15-A
Moscow 103009
RSFSR, USSR

Anatoly Dobrynin
Ambassador
Embassy of the USSR
1125 16th Street, N.W.
Washington, D,C. 20036

Ambassador Vernon Jordan
The Representative of the USA
to the United Nations
799 United Nations Plaza
New York, New York 10017

The Hon. (Your Senators)
United States Senate
Washington, D.C. 20510

The Hon. (Your Representative)
House of Representatives
Washington, D.C. 20515

George P. Shultz
Secretary of State
Department of State
2201 C Street, N.W.
Washington, D.C. 20520

Soviet Jewry Timeline: 1967-1984

1967 The Six Day War in the Middle East arouses a new sense of national pride among Soviet Jews; on the last day of the war, the Soviet Union severs diplomatic relations with Israel.

1968 Soviet troops enter Czechoslovakia; the first government-sponsored meeting is held at Babi Yar to condemn Israel; Boris Kochubiyevsky, a young man whose father and grandfather were killed at Babi Yar, protests and is sentenced to three years in prison for "anti-Soviet slander." Kochubiyevsky is the first Soviet Jewish Prisoner of Conscience.

1969 Eighteen Jewish families from the Georgian Republic officially seek to emigrate to Israel.

1970 Thirty-four Soviet Jews are arrested and tried in Leningrad on the charge that they conspired to hijack a plane to Israel. Leningrad Trials spark world-wide activity on behalf of the defendants.

1971 World Jewish Conference held in Brussels, devoted to the problem of Soviet Jewry.
SOVIET JEWISH EMIGRATION: 13,022

1972 A crop failure in the Soviet Union leads to a $750 million grain deal between the USSR and the United States; an education tax is imposed on those Soviet Jews wishing to emigrate; one million Americans petition Richard Nixon to intervene on behalf of

If our voices die so do their hopes.

MARCH FOR SOVIET JEWRY SOLIDARITY SUNDAY

Soviet Jews during his visit to the Soviet Union; the Jackson-Vanik Amendment is passed in Congress, tying "most favored nation" status in trade to Soviet emigration policy; First Annual Solidarity Sunday rally for Soviet Jewry sponsored by the Greater New York Conference on Soviet Jewry.
SOVIET JEWISH EMIGRATION: 31,681

1973 The Soviet Union backs the Arabs in the Yom Kippur War in the Middle East; Jewish emigration grows; in response to world pressure, Soviet authorities suspend collection of the education tax; twelve Jewish activists demonstrating in front of the Ministry of the Interior are arrested.
SOVIET JEWISH EMIGRATION: 34,733

1974 The Soviets begin to clamp down. Emigration drops.
SOVIET JEWISH EMIGRATION: 20,628

1975 Pledging to "respect human rights and fundamental freedoms," thirty-five nations, including the Soviet Union, sign the Helsinki Accords, guaranteeing reunification of families.
SOVIET JEWISH EMIGRATION: 13,221

1976 Brezhnev is reelected; a second World Jewish Conference is held in Brussels.
SOVIET JEWISH EMIGRATION: 14,261

1977 Anatoly Shcharansky, a prominent Jewish activist, is arrested on treason charges, based on allegations that he passed secret documents to Western analysts. He is held in solitary confinement for sixteen months.
SOVIET JEWISH EMIGRATION: 16,736

1978 Shcharansky is sentenced to thirteen years in prison.
SOVIET JEWISH EMIGRATION: 28,864

1979 SOVIET JEWISH EMIGRATION: a record 51,320

1980 Soviet troops invade Afghanistan; a follow-up conference to review the Helsinki Human Rights Accords convenes in Madrid; Viktor Brailovsky is arrested days before the eve of the conference.
SOVIET JEWISH EMIGRATION: 21,471

1981 Emigration continues to decline; number of arrests and visa refusals continues to rise; increase in KGB harassment of Soviet Jewish refuseniks and Prisoners of Conscience, and all those Soviet Jews who apply to emigrate.
SOVIET JEWISH EMIGRATION: 9,477

1982 Shcharansky goes on a hunger strike lasting four months, protesting the isolation from his family; Soviets use the Israel-Lebanon war to fuel their anti-semitic campaign.
SOVIET JEWISH EMIGRATION: 2,688

1983 Third International Conference on Soviet Jewry is held in Jerusalem; in response, Soviet authorities establish an official Anti-Zionist Committee to foster the myth that all Soviet Jews who wanted to leave have already done so; local chapters to spread libel about Soviet Jewish activists are established throughout the country.
SOVIET JEWISH EMIGRATION: 1,314

1984 Thirteen Soviet Jewish activists are arrested and brutalized. These arrests were accompanied by a series of devastating searches and threats. Jews were accused of using drugs in "religious rituals." The state-controlled Soviet media was rife with anti-semitic articles, which culminated in a television program aired in Leningrad which attacked several refuseniks by name and called on Soviet citizens to "beware of the danger posed by Zionism."
SOVIET JEWISH EMIGRATION: 896

If you would like to learn more about how you can help Soviet Jewry, contact one of the following organizations:

Thousands gather on Solidarity Sunday.

Coalition to Free Soviet Jews
8 West 40th Street
New York, New York 10018
(212) 354-1316
Chairman: Herbert Kronish, Esq.
Executive Director: Zeesy Schnur

National Conference on Soviet Jewry
10 East 40th Street
New York, New York 10016
(212) 679-6122
Chairman: Morris Abram, Esq.
Executive Director: Jerry Goodman

Washington Office
2027 Massachusetts Avenue, N.W.
Washington, D.C. 20036
(202) 265-8114

Student Struggle for Soviet Jewry
210 West 91st Street
New York, New York 10024
(212) 799-8900
Chairman: Rabbi Avi Weiss
National Coordinator: Glenn Richter

Union of Councils for Soviet Jews
1411 K Street, N.W.
Washington, D.C. 20005
(202) 393-4117
President: Lynn Singer

Or you can contact the National Jewish Community Relations Advisory Council for information on the Community Relations Council in your area. Their address is 443 Park Avenue South, New York, New York 10016, (212) 684-6950.

This article was prepared by Shari Rosenfeld, Director of Media and Publications for the Coalition to Free Soviet Jews.

All graphic materials appear courtesy of the Coalition to Free Soviet Jews.

This Letter From the Soviet Union Speaks for Itself.
It's a Message We Dare Not Ignore.

We appeal to you in this extremely difficult hour. Many of our friends have been arrested lately and we do not know who the next victim is going to be.

Today we call on you: Do not remain indifferent to our fate! After all, the fate of many of you could have been the same as ours if your grandmothers and grandfathers had not left Russia several decades ago.

Yes, these decades of living in different conditions have left an imprint both on us and on you. And today, we differ from each other, but does this have to divide us? Can several decades cross out the experience of two thousand years and overshadow that which is most important—our common, tragic and glorious past and our historic responsibility for our common future?

Remember! We have a common future!

When you send your children off to a Jewish school, remember that we do not have Jewish schools. When you pick up a Jewish book, remember that we do not have Jewish books. When you lovingly touch a mezuzah, remember that here mezuzot are being torn off during the searches. When you study our beautiful ancient and modern language, remember that here Hebrew teachers are being sent to prison on the basis of trumped-up charges of hooliganism and possession of arms or drugs.

Jewish mothers, remember! Dora Zunshain, the mother of the Prisoner of Conscience Zakhar Zunshain, could not bear the hardship of seeing her son arrested, convicted and sent to prison. She died suddenly after hearing about his suffering and the terrible details of his prison conditions.

Remember! Anatoly Shcharansky, Iosif Begun, Yuli Tarnopolsky and Moshe Abramov might be starting this day in an isolation cell or a punishment ward. Your fate could have been similar to theirs if you were a Soviet Jew wishing to repatriate to Israel.

Remember! A day might come when you sorely miss the hundreds of thousands of us who are doomed to extinction.

Remember! Once, forty years ago, you kept silent. Now, speak out about us and speak out for us. Speak out in spite of the gags they put in our mouths, and shout about the danger we are in. Remember—we are deprived even of this opportunity.

—Signed by 66 Soviet Jews from Moscow, Leningrad, Odessa, Riga and Tbilisi.

6

Ethiopian Jewry

Barry Weise
Abraham J. Bayer
National Jewish Community Relations
Advisory Council (NJCRAC)

After two thousand years, Judaism's sojourn in Ethiopia appears to be ending. Once estimated to number in the hundreds of thousands, the Jewish community of Ethiopia has dwindled to only several thousand souls. Despite heroic efforts to safeguard their religion, poverty, disease, intense missionary activity and war took their toll upon the Jewish community. Today, the remnant community of Jews in Ethiopia finds itself at a crossroads. The Marxist government's policy of forced assimilation threatens the very fabric of Ethiopian Jewish culture. However, with the arrival of thousands of Ethiopian Jews in Israel, despair is giving way to hope. For many, the dream of returning to Zion has been fulfilled. For those yet to come, Jerusalem is now closer than it has been in millennia.

Early History

The early history of the Jews of Ethiopia is shrouded in legend, folklore and speculation. Legendary sources report Ethiopian Jews to be the descendants of the lost tribe of Dan thought to have settled in Ethiopia early in the tenth century B.C.E. Some scholars believe that Ethiopian Jews are descended from indigenous Ethiopians who were converted by Jewish travelers originating from southern Arabia. Although their origin is uncertain, it is known that prior to the fourth century C.E., Judaism was widespread throughout Ethiopia.

The Jewish community fared well in ancient Ethiopia. Jewish life infiltrated Ethiopian society to the extent that traces of Hebraic influences can still be found in modern Ethiopian culture. The ascendancy of Jewish culture ended when the Axum dynasty of Ethiopia was converted to Christianity in the fourth century C.E. Those Jews who remained faithful to Judaism were persecuted and forced to take refuge in the mountainous region of Gondar province.

Within their mountain fortresses, the Jews of Ethiopia established their own independent kingdom. For nearly a thousand years, while most Jewish communities in the world experienced oppression and ghetto life, Ethiopian Jewish culture flourished under the leadership of Jewish kings and queens. The community's political fortunes ebbed and flowed until Ethiopian Christians, motivated by political evangelical ambitions, began a series of wars against them. For three hundred and fifty years, the Jews of Ethiopia fought valiantly to preserve their freedom. Their final defeat in the seventeenth century C.E. resulted in the death, conversion and enslavement of thousands. Those who survived were forced into serfdom upon confiscation of their land. The lot of the Jews of Ethiopia became one of suffering and degradation.

Throughout the medieval period, world Jewry knew little about the black-skinned Jews of Abysinnia. It was not until the eighteenth century C.E. that reports about them began to filter into Europe from African explorers. Stories about a lost tribe of Jews soon inspired Protestant missionary attempts to convert them. Thousands of Jews, struggling with poverty, sickness and hunger, were easy prey.

Rediscovery by World Jewry

Alarmed by the missionaries' work, in 1867 the Alliance Israelite Universelle in Paris sent Orientalist Joseph Halevy to investigate the situation. Ironically, Ethiopia's Black Jews were incredulous that Halevy, a white man, could be Jewish. They had considered themselves the sole-surviving Jews, keeping their religion alive until the advent of the *Moshiach*. Nevertheless, after a thorough investigation, Halevy returned to Europe and announced to the world that the legendary lost tribe of Black Jews had been rediscovered.

Jewish farm woman, village of Attege, Gondar province, Ethiopia.

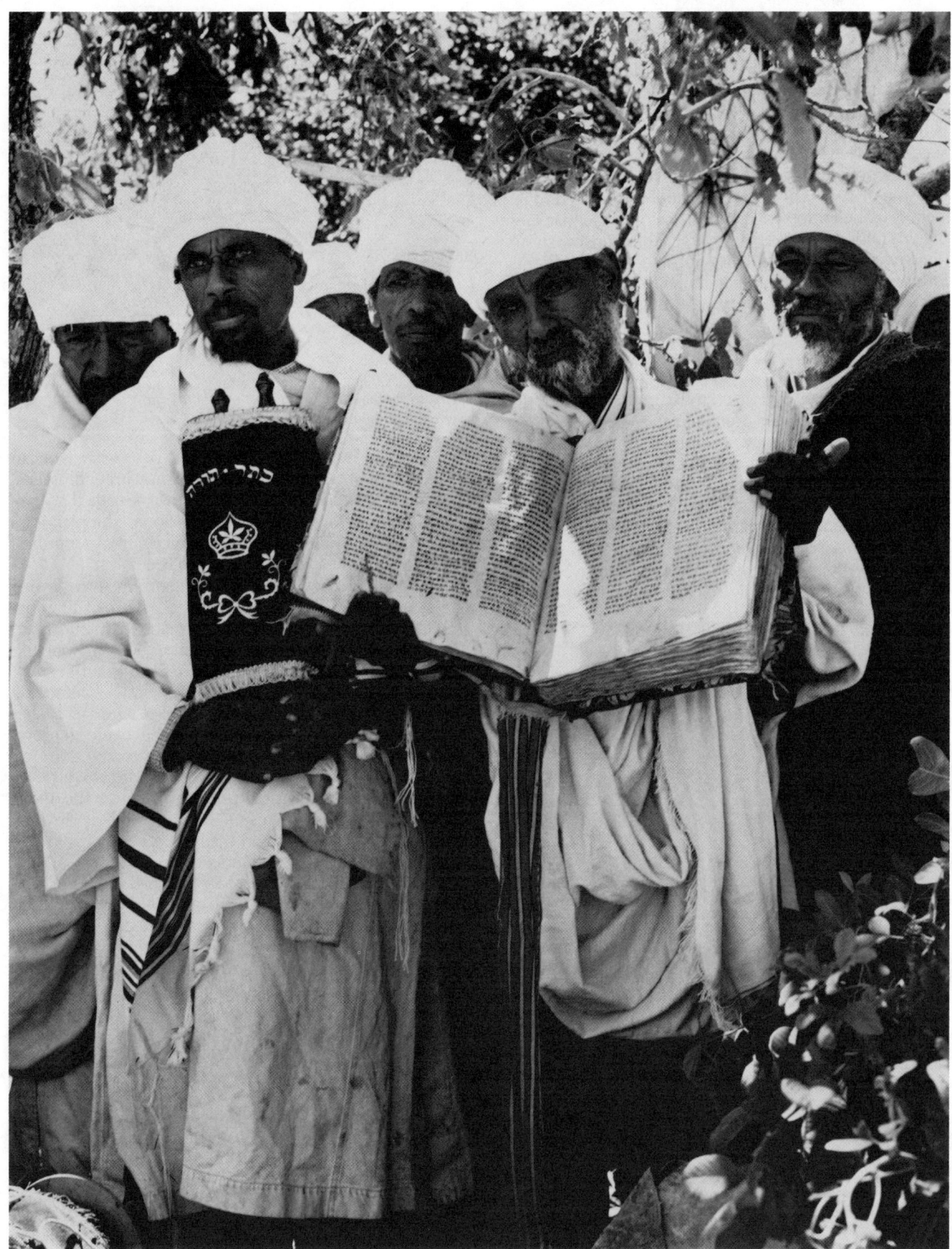

Kesim *(Kohanim), Ethiopian Jewish priests leading the* Sigd *festival, November 22, 1984, Ambover, Ethiopia. Photo Credit: Mariam Cramer Ring, NJCRAC mission.*

In 1904, a student of Halevy's, Professor Jacque Faitlovich, began a lifelong crusade to aid Ethiopian Jewry. He began by preparing future leaders for the community. In the 1920's, he sent several Ethiopian Jews to Europe and Palestine for a secular and Jewish education and opened a boarding school in Addis Ababa. In the 1950's, he persuaded the Jewish Agency for Israel to reopen the Addis Ababa school which had been closed since the Italian invasion of 1936. This time the school was located in the vicinity of the Ethiopian Jewish villages near Gondar. During this period, twenty-seven young Ethiopian Jewish students were sent to Israel. Several returned to Ethiopia, forging a link between Ethiopian Jewry and Israel which would one day lead to the beginning of *aliyah* of Ethiopian Jewry.

The First *Aliyah*

Ethiopian Jewry had longed to return to Jerusalem for centuries. Hundreds had even died en route to Israel in a catastrophic mid-nineteenth century *aliyah* attempt. However, it was not until the students who had studied in Israel returned to their villages that it became known among Ethiopian Jews that it was possible to reach Jerusalem. Until their return, few had imagined that one could ever really reach Jerusalem, and none knew their way there. Those who remained in Israel worked and saved their earnings until they were able to send for their relatives and

Grandmothers, Jewish village of Abba Entonius, Gondar province, Ethiopia.

friends. Those students who returned to the villages began to teach Hebrew and modern Judaism with enthusiasm. Their efforts renewed Ethiopian Jewry's faith that they would one day return to Jerusalem. Soon Ethiopian Jews began to leave their villages for the city, in order to find work and eventually earn a ticket to Israel.

Although by 1960 all but one of the thirty-three Jewish agency schools were closed due to a lack of funding, sufficient impact had already been made for the *aliyah* of Ethiopian Jewry to be set in motion. Throughout the 1960's, Ethiopian Jews began to arrive in Israel in small numbers. As the trickle continued, pressures increased upon the religious authorities in Israel to make a final determination as to whether or not they were full Jews according to *halacha*. Due to Ethiopia's remote location and their consequent isolation, Ethiopian Jewry never received the Talmud, nor did they participate in the development of Rabbinic Judaism. Thus, although in previous years influential rabbis had made declarations affirming that Ethiopian Jews were indeed Jews, doubts still lingered. Finally, in 1973, twenty-five years after the creation of the State of Israel, Chief Sephardic Rabbi Ovadia Yosef declared them to be authentic Jews. The civil authorities followed suit in 1975, when Ethiopian Jews were made eligible to be brought to Israel under the Law of the Return.

Ethiopian Jews, gathered at Ambover, for Sigd *festival.*

Young Ethiopian Jewish children, village of Attege, Gondar province, Ethiopia.

אתה יכול להציל
ילד זה מִמָוֶת!
תרום לקניית מזון ותרופות.
למד״א – סיוע לנפגעי הרעב באתיופיה
חשבון: 184־300 בנק הפועלים סניף 780 ת״א.
✡ מטה המבצע   מגן דוד אדום

Magen David Adom poster in Israel for Ethiopian famine relief.

Revolution in Ethiopia

Although Israel's gates were now open to Ethiopian Jewry, soon political events in Ethiopia took a dramatic turn and closed them shut again. In 1974, Haile Selassie, the emperor of Ethiopia for forty-seven years, was deposed by a military junta. The new regime quickly adopted a Marxist orientation and followed the path of socialist revolution. An all-encompassing land reform was declared which had enormous ramifications for Ethiopian Jewry. Furthermore, under Marxist rule, the limited *aliyah* possibilities under Haile Selassie were now completely lost.

The years following the revolution proved to be terrible ones for Ethiopian Jewry. Although the government's land reforms ended their sharecropper status, Ethiopian Jewry reaped far more suffering than benefits from the new order. From 1977 until 1980, the former landowners raided the Jewish villages, bringing mayhem and destruction. During this period thousands of Ethiopian Jews may have been made homeless and hundreds killed. Like thousands of Christian Ethiopians, Ethiopian Jews began to flee Ethiopia in order to escape the horrors of the revolution. Once across the border, they found themselves in the midst of a foreign climate and culture. Their very survival was threatened by dehydration, malnutrition and endemic diseases.

By 1980, the military regime gained control of most of Gondar province. With the countryside under control, the governor of the province increasingly restricted the freedom of the populace, especially Ethiopian Jews. Viewing Judaism as an archaic religion, and opposing any affiliation with Zionism, measures were instituted to forcibly assimilate Ethiopian Jews. Schools were closed and a Jewish aid program was expelled from the country. The teaching of Hebrew was forbidden. Jews became fearful of attending synagogue or performing other religious activities. Leaders were imprisoned and tortured, along with many caught attempting to flee the country.

Jewish woman artisan, village of Walleka, Gondar province, Ethiopia.

The Role of American Jewry

As Jews living in the free world we are all responsible to do whatever is possible to aid less fortunate Jews in the Soviet Union, Syria, Iran, Ethiopia, or elsewhere. Clearly, different Jewish communities can offer aid in different ways. The Jews of Israel, collectively representing a sovereign state, can accomplish certain goals unattainable by other Jewish communities. The realm of rescue falls under this category. Only a sovereign state has the resources and professionals capable of rescuing the entire community of Ethiopian Jews. However, American Jewry, as a nongovernmental voluntary association, can act in coordination with the State of Israel as a complementary diplomatic force. This role is currently being undertaken through the coordination of the National Jewish Community Relations Advisory Council.

Synagogue entrance, Jewish village of Abba Entonius, Ethiopia (NJCRAC mission visit).

Another critical role American Jewry can fill is the job of traveling to Ethiopia to visit Ethiopian Jews in their villages. There are multiple benefits to such visits. First, they bring encouragement to Ethiopian Jews and let them know that they are not forgotten. Second, they allow us to monitor the situation of Ethiopian Jews vis-a-vis freedom of religion and other basic human rights. Third, they serve notice to the government of Ethiopia that American Jewry is concerned about the Jews of Ethiopia. Finally, they serve to educate the American Jewish community as to the culture, desires and needs of our Jewish brethren in Ethiopia.

The return to Jerusalem is a long and arduous one. Like hundreds of thousands of other Jews before them, each Ethiopian Jew must make the epic decision to leave the country he has called home for centuries. History has left them little choice. However, the road ahead for Ethiopian Jewry will not be chosen by Ethiopian Jews alone. Indeed, the community seems to be caught in a whirlwind of external forces which propel them toward an uncertain future. Although once virtually unknown outside of Ethiopia, today their fate is tied to interests centered in New York, Washington, Jerusalem, Moscow and even Chicago. Finally, one must not limit the analysis to temporal factors. In the following passage, their trust in God is beautifully articulated by one Ethiopian Jew: "Man does not follow the path of his own thoughts. It is the will of God that determines his destiny. The path God chooses for us . . . you can be sure will be the right one."

Young Ethiopian oleh *at Yemin Orde, Youth Aliyah village in Israel.*

Israel's Absorption Program for Ethiopian Jews

After 2,000 years of separation, the long hoped-for aliyah of Ethiopian Jewry has begun. Ethiopian Jews arrive in Israel after a long and dangerous journey, full of hope and potential. Although their difficult trip is behind them, their arrival in Israel signals the beginning of another challenge ahead of them, the challenge of their successful absorption into modern Israeli society.

The realities of the absorption of Ethiopian Jews are vastly different from previous groups. Ethiopian Jews and the government and people of Israel have an enormous task ahead of them. Ethiopian Jews come from one of the poorest countries in the world. They come in need of medical care, clothing and educational training. In order to effectively integrate the large numbers of Ethiopian Jews arriving in Israel, the government is making tremendous investments in their absorption. Examples of the success of the effort are everywhere. In the classrooms, adults are learning to read and write in Hebrew after a lifetime of never holding a pen. On a soccer field or in a swimming pool, children can be seen playing vigorously after arriving in Israel emaciated from malaria or parasites. In bright airy apartments, Ethiopian Jews have space to breathe for the first time in their lives.

In the army, Ethiopian Jews proudly serve their country after years of insecurity and degradation in Ethiopia. And finally, as exemplified by the young Ethiopian Jew who won the National Bible contest in Israel, Ethiopian Jews are able for the first time to freely practice their religion and study Judaism.

Yet, despite all the success stories, some problems still exist in the absorption effort. Israel is beset with severe economic difficulties in addition to its political and military problems. Rampant, triple-digit inflation may limit the resources that the government is able to allocate to the absorption effort. While the Jewish Agency has succeeded in providing such basic services as housing, education, and medical care, Israel's overall need for belt-tightening has kept some enrichment efforts for the community from being implemented. Nevertheless, despite the difficulties the economic situation creates, the degree of success that has been achieved is nothing short of miraculous. On a per capita basis, Israel is exerting more effort and expending more resources for this *aliyah* than for any other previous immigration. Every community in the country has a vital share in the progress through participation in Federation and UJA campaigns.

Beginning Vocational Training

After the first half year is over, most adults begin a vocational course of study. The purpose of the course is to retrain the new immigrants for life in modern Israel. The course is designed to acquaint the Ethiopian immigrants with the basic skills necessary for success in vocational training courses. In addition to arithmetic, intermediate Hebrew and technical terminology, basic work habits and familiarity with machine parts are taught. At the conclusion of the vocational course, the immigrant decides if he will continue on further to a professional training course or if he will go directly to the Israeli work force.

Those who decide to go directly to work are aided in finding jobs by a representative of the Ministry of Labor. The social workers also participate in the job hunt in order to help ensure that jobs with promise are found. In most cases the immigrants are placed in factory jobs that include "hands on" training and possibilities for advancement. Although Ethiopian Jews are in Israel only a short period of time, they have already established a reputation for being dedicated and hard-working employees.

Those who decide to train for a profession continue in courses that last from a few months to a year. All those who are able are encouraged to go on to the professional training. Courses offered enable them to become electricians, automobile body workers, carpenters, garage mechanics, plumbers, seamstresses, beauticians, etc. Lessons in the Hebrew language also continue during the training. At the conclusion of the course, the graduates are given certificates of completion and are aided in job placement.

Out Into the Community

After finishing formal studies at the Ulpan, vocational or professional course, most immigrant families leave the absorption center and move to rent-subsidized apartments. Representatives of the Housing Ministry aid them in their efforts to secure an apartment. The apartments are located in development towns, usually in complexes near other Ethiopian immigrants to promote mutual support systems creating "cluster" formations. In order to avoid the formation of "ghettos," the "clusters" are interspersed within areas where Israelis who come from other parts of the world are living.

In order to ease the transition from life in the absorption center to that of independent living outside of the center, early on in the absorption process the social workers plan projects to promote contact with non-Ethiopian Israelis. The "home hospitality" program with veteran Israeli families is one such project. Ethiopian immigrants are also encouraged to take part in programs offered by local community centers. Finally, day-to-day contact with other Israelis at the store, bank or government ministries increases as the months pass.

Their integration is also helped by government efforts to educate to general Israeli populace about Ethiopian Jews. As Ethiopian Jews are brought to a new town, meetings are held with officials of the various municipal offices to acquaint them with the special needs of Ethiopian immigrants. Also, public meetings are held to educate the general community about the new residents of the town. Lectures are given by the social workers and veteran Israeli Ethiopians about the history and culture of Ethiopian Jews. In many towns the result has been very successful, with public events welcoming the new immigrants and volunteer efforts to aid them in their absorption needs. Finally, special Kabbalat Shabbat and other events are organized by the community so that Ethiopian Jews may join them for the holiday celebration.

Despite all of the challenges, the *aliyah* of Ethiopian Jews maintains an extraordinary potential. Their arrival in Israel is the final step in a 2,000 year journey. They come with the hope and optimism of a community beginning a new life. With their determination, along with the help of the government of Israel and the Jewish people, they will soon be leading productive lives in Israel and be making their special contribution to the Jewish people.

Olim

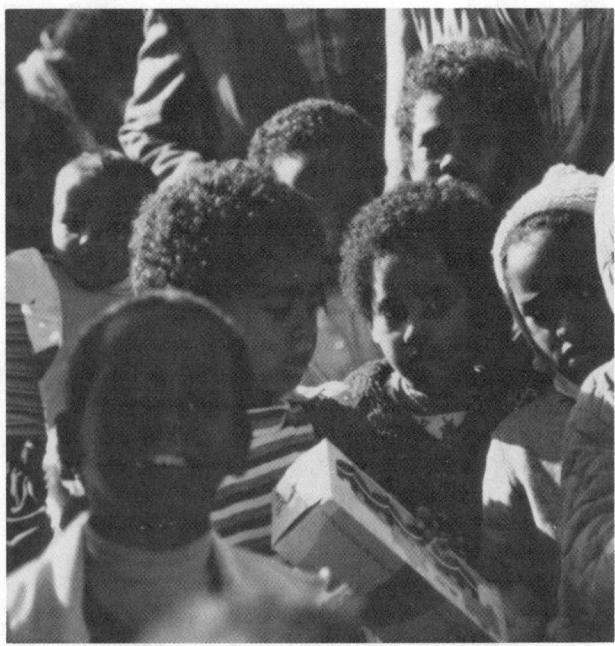

Olim

The Absorption Process

The First Few Weeks

The process of absorption begins shortly after a new immigrant's arrival in Israel. They come exhausted from their long journey and are in need of food, clothes and medical care. Upon arrival, they are interviewed by Jewish Agency workers to determine their family status and medical needs. Some are hospitalized immediately; the rest are taken to absorption centers around the country. The interviews are conducted by teams of social workers and veteran Israeli-Ethiopian *madrichim* (instructors). They organize the immigrants into family units, attempting to place children and elderly immigrants who have been separated from their families with other relatives in Israel.

At the Jewish Agency's absorption centers they are given food and clothes, and are assigned to their new apartments. Paraprofessionals, called *"somchot,"* immediately begin to teach the new immigrants how to properly use gas stoves and electrical appliances. In the following days, medical treatment administered by the Ministry of Health begins. Nearly every immigrant is ill from one tropical ailment or another. Malaria, tuberculosis, pneumonia and intestinal parasites are commonly found. Youngsters and even some adults arrive wearing rags; children under five sometimes come wearing nothing at all.

Somehow, relatives from all over the country learn of the new arrivals and flock to the absorption center. Heart-rending scenes of joy and sorrow occur when relations learn of the fate of their loved ones. During the first few days the new Israelis are left alone to be with their relatives and to adjust to being in Israel.

During the first four to six weeks, the new immigrants learn the basics of dealing with life in a modern society, i.e., how to use money, go shopping, and open a bank account. Medical care continues throughout this period. Informal classes are conducted introducing them to Hebrew, Jewish history and Israeli society.

The Ulpan: Learning To Live in Modern Israel

At the end of the initial acclimatization period, the Ministry of Education begins formal classes in Hebrew, the Ulpan. Except for a limited number of young people who have received upwards to twelve years of education in Ethiopia, most Ethiopian immigrants come with no formal educational background. Most adults are illiterate in their native language, Amharic. Indeed, many times the Ulpan must begin with a lesson on how to hold a pencil.

The Ulpan lasts half a year during which time the new immigrants learn to read, write and speak basic Hebrew. Children learn Hebrew very quickly and as soon as possible they are placed in classes with other Israelis in community schools in order to help preserve the strong religious heritage they bring with them. All immigrant children from Ethiopia attend religious schools. Older children learn in special classes for Ethiopian immigrants. They are extraordinarily motivated to learn and advance themselves. Eventually they are able to "catch up" with their non-Ethiopian Israeli counterparts and enter the religious school system.

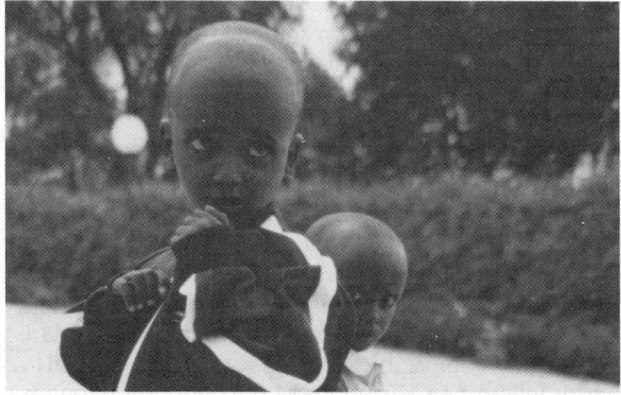

Olim

Unstable conditions in Ethiopia and in the border refugee camps have brought about the arrival in Israel of hundreds of children without their parents. These children are under the care of the Youth Aliyah Department of the Jewish Agency. They live in Youth Aliyah villages designed to deal with the special needs of young immigrants who come to Israel alone.

Bar Mitzvah celebration of new Ethiopian immigrant, Beersheva, Israel, 1984.

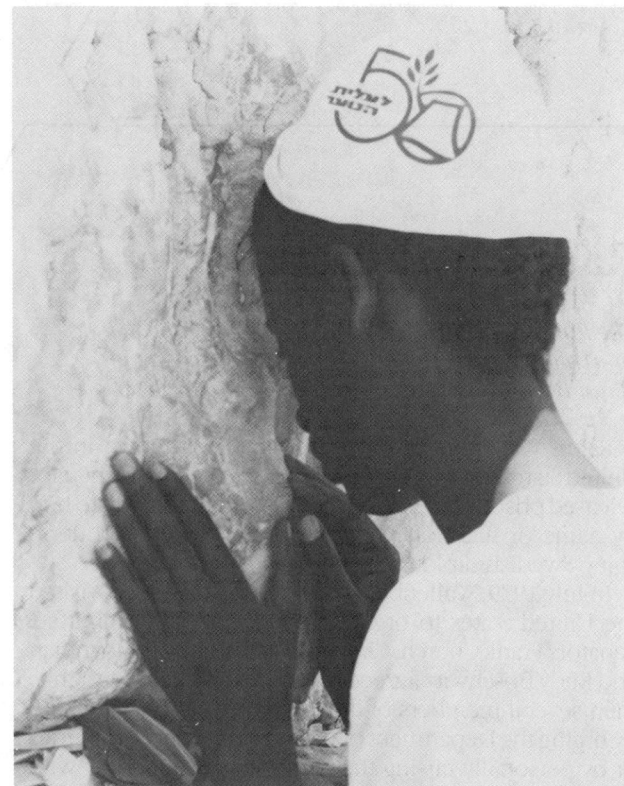

New Ethiopian oleh *at the Western Wall, 1984.*

In addition to training them in Hebrew, the Ulpan provides instruction in government, modern Israeli culture and rituals according to traditional Rabbinic practice. Trips are organized by the director of the absorption center to various parts of Israel. With the assistance of the *somchot* and social workers, the process of learning to deal with the mechanics of life in an industrialized society continues. They learn to cope with the Israeli bureaucracy and to become increasingly independent.

Those young Ethiopian immigrants who have finished several years of elementary and secondary education in Ethiopia are placed in special absorption centers in order to prepare them for post-secondary education. Unlike the majority of Ethiopian immigrants, they are literate and sophisticated. The centers created for them cater to their specialized needs and attempt to bridge the gap between the educational levels of Ethiopian and Israeli schools.

While technical challenges such as learning to operate a gas stove or going shopping are easily met, personal problems relating to the long and hard journey to Israel and the differences in the cultures of Ethiopia and Israel are far more difficult to overcome. The journey to Israel results in frequent disruptions of family units. Children arrive without parents and spouses without mates. Elderly parents often are unable to make the trip and are left behind in Ethiopia. Furthermore, the life style of modern Israel is greatly different from that of traditional Ethiopia. Patriarchical figures of authority are soon displaced by younger, often female, officials of the Jewish Agency or other government offices. The difficulties resulting from these situations can impede successful absorption and thus much attention is given to these problems by the social workers of the Jewish Agency.

7

Raoul Wallenberg

The Raoul Wallenberg Committee of the United States in affiliation with the Anti-Defamation League of B'nai B'rith

Raoul Wallenberg's story was largely unknown in the United States until recent years, when Soviet dissidents and released prisoners reaching the West either referred to him by name or mentioned having seen or heard about an aging Swedish diplomat in prison.

In July 1979, Wallenberg's sister, Nina Lagergren, visited the United States to organize a Wallenberg Committee. Senators Frank Church, Claiborne Pell, Daniel P. Moynihan and Rudy Boschwitz agreed to serve as co-chairmen. Since then several members of the Senate have actively helped by urging the Department of State to make official inquiries or by personally raising the question of Wallenberg with Soviet officials. Under President Carter, the White House also raised the issue with the Soviets. No additional information on Wallenberg has been given by Soviet officials— they have merely repeated the official line that he died in 1947. Nor have they responded to statements by former prisoners that Wallenberg was alive in prison in the seventies.

In the spring of 1980, the American ambassador to Denmark, Warren Manshel, organized a ceremony in Copenhagen at which members of the President's Holocaust Commission honored Raoul Wallenberg.

In November 1980, during the second session of the 96th Congress, Concurrent Resolution Number 434 was passed honoring Wallenberg. This joint resolution called on our delegation to the Madrid Conference on Security and Cooperation in Europe to raise the question of Wallenberg. In Madrid that month Sen. Pell joined members of the U.S. delegation in a press conference with Wallenberg's family, announcing their intent to pursue the question.

On January 15 and 16, 1981, international hearings were held in Stockholm, jointly sponsored by the Wallenberg Committee and the International Sakharov Committee. Members of Wallenberg Committees from several countries reported on their activities and heard the testimony of released Soviet prisoners. Following the hearings, the Swedish minister for foreign affairs received a delegation and accepted a resolution produced by the panel. Minister Olla Ullsten has been very firm on this issue. He delivered a strong human rights speech at the SCE Conference in Madrid in which he referred to Wallenberg, and previously sent an official inquiry to Moscow.

On October 5, 1981 President Reagan signed into law a special bill making Raoul Wallenberg an honorary United States citizen. He is the second such person to be so named, the other one being Sir Winston Churchill.

U.S. Members of UN Human Rights Panel Urge Wallenberg Case Probe
Geneva, Feb. 28, 1982.

GENEVA, Feb. 28 (JTA)—The U.S. delegation to the United Nations Human Rights Commission here has called for an investigation into the case of Swedish diplomat Raoul Wallenberg who saved the lives of some 100,000 Hungarian Jews during World War II and disappeared shortly after Russian forces entered Budapest in 1945.

Michael Novak, head of the U.S. delegation, brought up the Wallenberg case during a debate in the Human Rights Commission on persons who have disappeared under circumstances of a political nature. The U.S., backed by Sweden, proposed that the investigation be conducted by a special five-member UN working group. The head of the Soviet delegation, Valerian Zorin, had no immediate reaction to Novak's proposal.

In 1957, the Soviet government told the Swedish government that Wallenberg died in 1947 in prison, probably of a heart attack. But there have been persistent reports since then that he is alive and has been seen in various Russian prisons or mental institutions. Wallenberg's sister, Mrs. Nina Lagergren, said at a press conference here that the case should be publicized wherever possible but should not become a tool in the Cold War.

In the story of Raoul Wallenberg two issues are tragically linked: the courage of a truly good man and his unjust fate. There are few comparable examples of a man facing evil to save his fellow men. He must not be abandoned as long as there is any question of his survival, however disappointing and frustrating the effort.

The Goals of the Raoul Wallenberg Committee of the United States

There are two goals of the Raoul Wallenberg Committee:
A. To free Raoul Wallenberg and allow him to return to his family in Sweden.
B. To honor Raoul Wallenberg and his accomplishments in the following manner:
   1. To make Raoul Wallenberg's name known throughout the country by serving as a clearinghouse of information and a distributor of a newsletter to everyone interested in the Wallenberg case.
   2. To provide materials for schools, universities, churches, and synagogues to educate future generations about Raoul Wallenberg.
   3. To help coordinate the various activities taking place throughout the United States by assisting individuals and local committees working for Raoul Wallenberg.
   4. To maintain a speakers bureau in order to provide organizations interested in Raoul Wallenberg with lectures.

5. To create a national "Wallenberg Recognition Day."
6. To create national programs that would further the cause of Raoul Wallenberg and attract media attention.

U.S. Committee Services to Local Committees

I— Speakers
II— National newsletter including reports of your local committees
III—Assistance in establishing a local committee
IV— Program plans and publicity
  A. Rallies for Raoul Wallenberg.
  B. Letters to newspapers about his plight.
  C. Resolutions and declarations of Raoul Wallenberg Days by mayors, city councils, governors, state legislators.
  D. School projects, including poster design, focusing on Raoul Wallenberg's heroism.
  E. Naming of public buildings, streets, parks, and playgrounds after Raoul Wallenberg.
  F. Library displays of books about Raoul Wallenberg.
  G. Exhibits about Raoul Wallenberg.

I. EARLY HISTORY

Raoul Gustav Wallenberg was born August 4, 1912. His parents came from two of Sweden's most outstanding families, whose members included diplomats, bankers, and bishops of the Lutheran Church, as well as artists and professors.

Selections from *Righteous Gentile* by John Bierman. Copyright © 1981 by John Bierman. Used by permission of Viking Penguin Inc.

Wallenberg's birth was surrounded by tragedy. His handsome father (after whom he was named), an officer in the Swedish Navy and son of the Swedish ambassador to Japan, died after a brief illness at the age of 23—eight months after his marriage and three months before the birth of his son.

Raoul's mother, Maj Wissing Wallenberg, was only 21 at the time. Three months after Raoul's birth, his grandfather Wissing died suddenly of pneumonia. Many years later, Nina Lagergren, Raoul's half-sister, said, "All of a sudden, in that once-happy house, there were two widows and this baby boy." The two bereaved women focused all their love on the child who, says Nina Lagergren, "gave and received so much love that he grew up to be an unusually generous, loving, and compassionate person."

In 1918 Maj Wallenberg remarried. Her second husband, Frederik von Dardel, was a young civil servant in the health ministry. He later became the administrator of Karolinska, Sweden's largest hospital, world famous for its medical research.

Two more children were born to Maj von Dardel: Guy, a nuclear physicist, and Nina, who serves as an active member of the Swedish Raoul Wallenberg Committee. She is married to Gunnar Lagergren, chancellor to the Royal Court of Sweden and member of the judicial body of the International Court at The Hague.

"We never thought of Raoul as being of a different father," says Nina. "He was completely of us and we of him, and my father adored him as much as the two of us."

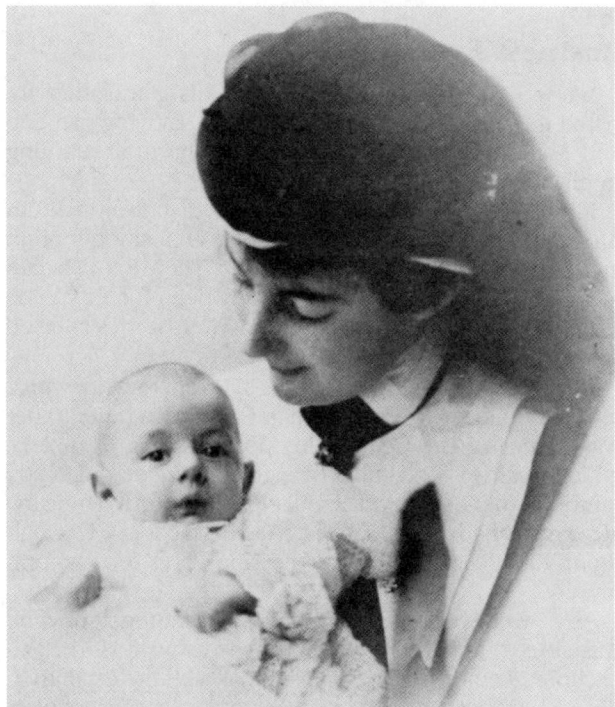

Maj Wallenberg and her infant son.

Raoul, age three, with his grandfather.

Education

Ambassador Gustav Wallenberg, Raoul's grandfather, insisted that Raoul receive an education befitting a member of the Wallenberg family. Accordingly, after high school in Sweden and nine months of compulsory Swedish military service, Raoul was sent to Paris for a year. Then at his own insistence, he attended the University of Michigan in Ann Arbor, where he completed the program at the School of Architecture in three and one half years. He won a medal awarded to only one student out of each class of 1,100. Some years later he entered a national architectural contest in Sweden, where his design placed second—the winner being Sweden's leading architect at the time.

During his summer vacation in 1933, he worked at the Swedish pavilion of the Chicago World's Fair. Another summer found him in Mexico, where he visited Wallenberg relatives. His cousin Birgitta Wallenberg, then eight years old, says of that visit: "Mother adored him; he was her pet. I adored him too. He was wonderful with me, staying with me and trying to teach me chess. He was so unlike most grown-ups; he actually took notice of me, a lonely only child. I remember that his specialty was imitating animal sounds. He was a marvelous mimic and could do twenty-five to thirty different animals. He was good at foreign accents too, and used to keep us all in stitches. It was always fun being with Raoul."

Much later other friends talked of similar memories. Apparently one of Raoul's most successful imitations in the

Raoul Wallenberg, age fourteen.

Portrait. This is the photograph, carried by Swedish newspapers, that first brought Wallenberg to the attention of his countrymen. He was twenty-four and had just won second prize in a national architectural competition.

1930s was of Adolf Hitler. It always brought the house down.

Business Experience

When Raoul returned to Sweden, his grandfather insisted that it was time for him to begin studying banking and commerce. This decision was to have far-reaching implications.

Raoul's first position was with a Swedish firm in South Africa. In 1936 his grandfather arranged a position for him at the Holland Bank in Haifa, Palestine. There Raoul began to meet young Jews who had already been forced to flee from Nazi persecution in Germany. Their stories affected him deeply and left a lasting impression.

In 1939, after several false starts, he went to work with a Jewish refugee from Hungary named Kolman Lauer. Lauer was owner of the Central European Trading Company, which dealt in foodstuffs. In eight months Raoul was a junior partner of the firm. Raoul often traveled to Hungary. His partner had close relatives living in Budapest. Through them, Raoul began to know the Hungarian Jewish community.

As a Swedish Christian from an outstanding family, he was able to travel freely in Germany as well as in Nazi-occupied France. He became familiar with the eccentricities of Nazi bureaucracy and was unusually successful in his required business dealings with Nazi officials.

Michigan. By the time Wallenberg arrived at the University of Michigan he had already seen parts of the globe not normally on any tourist's itinerary.

Wallenberg's vacations while at the University of Michigan were spent seeing America, using his favorite means of transportation: hitchhiking. This photograph was taken on the Golden Gate Bridge.

Home Guard. In 1943, Sweden was an island of neutrality in war-torn Europe. Wallenberg did not take that privileged status for granted, and became an active member of the Swedish Army Reserve.

Events Quicken—The 1940s

Wallenberg was increasingly concerned with the fate of Europe's Jewish communities. Actress Viveca Lindfors, a friend of Raoul's during his bachelor days in Stockholm, recalls an evening when he took her back to his office. There, he began to tell her of the plight of the Jews in Nazi Europe. His stories, told with frightening intensity, sounded impossible to her.

In the United States, at the behest of President Roosevelt, the War Refugee Board was established. Its goal was to save Jews and other Nazi victims. The WRB was well funded. Its top priority, after the partial Nazi Hungarian occupation in June 1944, became the safety of the 750,000 Hungarian Jews.

Soon after, the War Refugee Board came to neutral Sweden, which had an active embassy in Budapest, looking for someone who would agree to go to Hungary. Such a person would work under the auspices of the Swedish government with the protection of a Swedish diplomatic passport, though representing and funded by the War Refugee Board. As a neutral country, Sweden conducted business for many of the warring factions in countries where they no longer had diplomatic representation but often continued to hold property.

The War Refugee Board's representative in Hungary was to be given a large sum of money and would be empowered by the Swedish government to issue passports to as many Jews as possible.

Raoul Wallenberg was chosen to be the War Refugee Board's representative.

The Mission—Budapest

On July 9, 1944, Raoul Wallenberg, age 32, arrived at the Swedish embassy in Budapest. He traveled lightly with a backpack and a small pistol. His primary adversary was SS Lt. Col. Adolf Eichmann. By the time Wallenberg arrived in Hungary, all 437,000 Jews—men, women and children—living outside Budapest had already been deported. The rest of Hungary's Jewish community consisted of the 230,000 Jews living in the capital.

The "Schutzpass"

Wallenberg's first job was redesigning the Swedish protective passport. This new first secretary of the embassy found the document, which was legal and could be issued only by the Swedish legation, physically unimpressive. He knew that the Nazis and their Hungarian counterparts were frequently people of little education, who would be easily impressed by a large, official-looking document. How correct this simple assessment proved to be!

Wallenberg redesigned the "Schutzpass." He used the blue and yellow of the Swedish flag, and emblazoned the document with the symbol of the triple crown of Sweden. This passport saved the lives of tens of thousands of Jews, as well as a great number of anti-Nazi Hungarian partisans.

According to former staff member Agnes Mandl Adachi, Wallenberg printed huge placards and put them up all over

A passport created by Wallenberg.

the city. The billboards, which pictured and proclaimed the validity of the Schutzpass, were designed to make the Nazis familiar with the document and its authority.

In the darkest days of 1944, the Swedish protective passport even provided some humor in the midst of despair. Edith Ernester, who lived through that time, recalls: "It seemed so strange—this country of super-Aryans, the Swedes, taking us under their wings. Often, when an Orthodox Jew went by, in his hat, beard and sidelocks, we'd say, 'Look, there goes another Swede.'"

The Man of Action

A special department was created in the Swedish embassy in Budapest with Wallenberg as its head. It was staffed primarily with Jewish volunteers. Initially, there were 250 workers; later, he had about 400 people working around the clock. Wallenberg seemed to sleep no more than an hour or two a night, and then it was wherever he happened to be working. He was everywhere.

Wallenberg persuaded the Hungarian authorities to free the Jews on his staff from wearing the Yellow Star worn at all times by other Jews. This simple exemption allowed his workers much greater freedom of movement, as well as the protection of anonymity—an essential factor in carrying out many of Wallenberg's missions.

Agnes Adachi recalls the night when she and her co-workers needed to complete about 2,000 Schutzpasses and deliver them before six a.m. when the Nazis would be rounding up several thousand Jewish women. She tells of working by candlelight in a villa on the outskirts of Budapest. Wallenberg came in and very calmly announced that the villa next door was the Gestapo headquarters. He then smilingly assured his staff that they must continue their work and not be alarmed. The Schutzpasses were completed, and each was delivered on foot before six a.m.

According to Mrs. Adachi: "He made a game out of outfoxing the Nazis, but he played it with the utmost seriousness. Most of all, he was like a big brother one looked up to, and he had the most beautiful eyes that I have ever seen. They were so beautiful and they saw everything."

Swedish Protective Housing

Wallenberg's next step was crucial to his ultimate success. In a section of Budapest designated by the Hungarian government as the "International Ghetto," Wallenberg purchased thirty buildings where he flew Swedish flags next to the Jewish Star. These buildings, and others for which he was able to negotiate, were given the full protection of the Swedish government.

In these protected houses Wallenberg set up hospitals, schools, soup kitchens, and a special shelter for 8,000 children whose parents had already been deported or killed.

Generally, the protection of the Swedish flag and the passports held by those living in the houses were protection enough. If his spies told him that a raid was being planned by the Nazis or their Hungarian counterparts, young, blond Jewish men living in the houses would be dressed in Nazi uniforms and put outside to "guard" the houses.

Raoul Wallenberg with his staff: Hugo Wohl, right; Paul Hegedus, left.

Occasionally, however, all efforts failed. On Christmas Day, 1944, a gang of Hungarian Nazis entered a protective Swedish children's shelter; seventy-eight children were machine-gunned and beaten with rifle butts. All died.

Because of Wallenberg's swift action in setting up shelters that offered care and protection, the other neutral legations and the International Red Cross also followed and helped greatly to expand the number of protected houses. After the war it was established that about 50,000 Jews living in the foreign houses of the International Ghetto had survived. Of these, about 25,000 were directly under Wallenberg's protection.

The Nazis and the Arrow-Cross

On October 15, 1944, the legal Hungarian government of Admiral Horthy fell and a pro-Nazi government called the Arrow-Cross was installed. The Germans, who had previously not been so much in evidence, came pouring across the Hungarian border.

The Arrow-Cross gendarmes, an elite, quasi-military corps, were Adolf Eichmann's greatest allies in his march toward the "final solution."

If possible, they were even more sadistic than their German counterparts, and Eichmann used their fervor accordingly.

In late 1944, with the Germans fighting on many fronts, the end of the war and an Allied victory began to seem imminent. This knowledge only seemed to spur Eichmann on to finish his "purification" of Hungary.

In this situation, Jeno Levais recalls, "It was of the utmost importance that the Nazis and the Arrow-Crossmen were not able to ravage unhindered—they were compelled to see that every step they took was being watched and followed by the young Swedish diplomat. From Wallenberg they could keep no secrets. The Arrow-Crossmen could not trick him. They could not operate freely. They were held responsible for the lives of the persecuted and the condemned. Wallenberg's was the 'world's observing eye,' the one who continually called the criminals to account."

The Death Marches

As the Germans found themselves increasingly on the military defensive, they were less able to supply Eichmann with trains and trucks for deporting Jews from Hungary. On November 8, 1944, as the Russian army moved closer to Budapest, Eichmann ordered all Jewish women and children rounded up and marched on foot 125 miles to Hegyeshalom on the Austrian-Hungarian border for deportation to the death camps. The men were brought to a work camp in another location.

It took one week to walk in freezing cold and snow, with no food or heavy clothing. Women in high heels, rounded up in the street, children, and the elderly were forced to keep up with the pace set by the gendarmes. All along the route lay the dead and the dying.

Wallenberg, Per Anger and their driver went along the route of the march by car, giving out food, clothing, fresh water and Swedish protective passports whenever possible. On the first day of the march, they rescued about 100 people with the protective passports. A few others they rescued by sheer bluff.

In the days that followed, Wallenberg made repeated trips along the march route and continued his rescue efforts at the border. He organized Red Cross truck convoys to deliver food and set up checkpoints for those with "Schutzpasses." About 1,500 people were thus rescued from transport to Auschwitz.

At the end of November, Eichmann was ordered back to Berlin by Heinrich Himmler, who was preparing to put out peace feelers to the Allies. The marches were halted and Eichmann was instructed to cease all liquidation efforts.

In December 1944, Wallenberg reported to Stockholm about the death marches. "It was possible to rescue some 2,000 persons from deportation for some reason or another." He added, almost as an afterthought, that the Swedish mission had also secured the return of 15,000 laborers holding Swedish and other protective passes.

A Personal Account

John Bierman, in his book on Wallenberg, *Righteous Gentile,* has included a moving eyewitness account of Wallenberg's work. They are the words of Tommy Lapid, now director-general of the Israeli Broadcasting Authority.

In 1944 Lapid was 13 years old and one of 900 people crowded into a Swedish protected house. His father was dead, and he had been allowed to remain with his mother.

"One morning, a group of Hungarian Fascists came into the house and said that all the able-bodied women must go with them. We knew what this meant.

"My mother kissed me and I cried and she cried. We knew we were parting forever and she left me there, an orphan to all intents and purposes. Then two or three hours later, to my amazement, my mother returned with the other women. It seemed like a mirage, a miracle. My mother was there—she was alive and she was hugging me and kissing me, and she said one word: 'Wallenberg.'

"I knew who she meant because Wallenberg was a legend among the Jews. In the complete and total hell in which we lived, there was a savior-angel somewhere, moving around."

Thwarting a Final Plan

Wallenberg became famous among the Jews of Hungary for his many individual acts of bravery, but it was as a negotiator that he achieved his greatest results. In addition to its International Ghetto, Budapest had a general ghetto, which was guarded and sealed off. The 70,000 Jews kept there as virtual prisoners existed under the most horrible and primitive conditions, unprotected from the violence of the Arrow-Crossmen.

Wallenberg got word in the first days of January 1945 that a final plan, masterminded by Adolf Eichmann before he left Hungary, was soon to be carried out. It was to be

Last-minute rescue. Wallenberg, in a picture taken by his private photographer, is shown here negotiating with the Nazis to win the release of a trainload of Jews bound for the death camps. The X marks Wallenberg.

completed very quickly, before the Russian army could enter Budapest and open the ghetto. The plan called for the total massacre of the ghetto population, by a combined task force of SS men and Arrow-Crossmen led by a priest, Vilmas Lucska. An additional 200 policemen would encircle the ghetto fence, making certain that no Jews escaped.

All the documents for the extermination plan were ready and the German commander in Budapest was prepared to carry out his orders, even as the Russians shelled the city.

Wallenberg had been working behind the scenes for many months with Pal Szalay, a high-ranking Arrow-Crossman who was a senior police official. Szalay was horrified by the atrocities committed by his compatriots, and he quickly became an invaluable ally. In fact, he was the only prominent member of the Arrow-Cross to escape execution after the war by the People's Court; he was set free with no charges. Szalay helped to save many lives in various incidents, but his most important contribution was as Wallenberg's spokesman in negotiations with the German general August Schmidthuber.

Schmidthuber was commander of the SS troops in Budapest, and Eichmann had designated one of his detachments to spearhead the ghetto action. It was far too dangerous for Wallenberg to meet personally with the SS leader; he was already wanted by the Gestapo, and there had been several attempts on his life. Any direct communication with Schmidthuber would mark Wallenberg as a dangerous international witness to the ghetto extermination.

Wallenberg sent Pal Szalay to speak for him with the general. Szalay informed Schmidthuber that, if the planned massacres took place, Wallenberg would see to it that the general was held personally responsible and would be hanged as a war criminal. With the Russian army already approaching the city, the general reconsidered. He issued the order that no ghetto action was to take place. It was Wallenberg's last victory.

A Final Accounting

When the Russian army entered Budapest, they found almost 70,000 Jewish men, women and children alive in the general ghetto. Another twenty-five thousand people were in the protected houses, and an additional twenty-five thousand persons of Jewish origin were found hiding in Christian homes, monasteries, convents, church basements, and other sanctuaries.

In all, one hundred twenty thousand Jews of Budapest survived the "final solution." They were the only substantial Jewish community left in Europe. At least 100,000 of these people owed their lives directly to Raoul Wallenberg.

In Jewish folklore there exists a tale of "36 righteous men." This is the minimum number of anonymous, righteous men who must be living in each generation, as the world exists on their merit. These hidden saints appear in times of great danger to the Jewish community, using their powers to defeat its enemies.

Perhaps such a legendary "Lamed-Vov-Nik"—or "One of the Just"—made his appearance in the person of Raoul Gustav Wallenberg.

The last photograph of Raoul Wallenberg, taken in Budapest on November 26, 1944. Sent by Raoul to his mother.

II. THE ARREST AND DISAPPEARANCE OF RAOUL WALLENBERG

The Russian Explanation

On January 13, 1945 Wallenberg first contacted the Russians, then on the outskirts of Budapest, in an effort to secure food and supplies for the Jews under his protection.

On January 17 Wallenberg and his driver, Vilmos Langfelder, left Budapest for a meeting with the Russian commander, Marshal Malinovsky, in the city of Debrecen, about 120 miles east of Budapest. On the way to the meeting with the Soviet commander he and his driver were taken into "protective custody" by the Soviet NKVD, the secret police later known as the KGB.

The Soviet deputy foreign minister, Vladimir Dekanosov, notified the Swedish ambassador in Moscow that Wallenberg was in Russian hands: "The Russian military authorities have taken measures to protect Raoul Wallenberg and his belongings," said the note.

When he was last seen on January 17 by members of his staff, Wallenberg was already being "protected" by a Russian officer and two soldiers on motorcycles. He was carrying his knapsack, a briefcase containing his own postwar plan, and a large sum of money.

It was the last time anyone ever saw Raoul Wallenberg as a free man.

Imprisonment

In the first week of February 1945, after a trip by train to Moscow, Wallenberg and his driver were placed in separate cells in Lubianka Prison, the principal interrogation center of the Soviet Secret Police.

That month Wallenberg's mother, Maj von Dardel, was informed by the Russian ambassador to Sweden, Alexandra Kollontai, that her son was safe in Russia and would be back soon. The family was asked not to make a major issue of Raoul's absence. His safe return was assured.

On January 21, 1945, Wallenberg was placed in cell 123 of Moscow's Lubianka Prison, where he joined Gustav Richter, a police attache at the German embassy in Rumania until the Russian takeover. Richter testified in Sweden in 1955 that Wallenberg was interrogated only once for about an hour and one half, in the beginning of February 1945. He was accused of spying, perhaps for the United States, since the War Refugee Board was an American-based and funded operation. On March 1, 1945, Gustav Richter was moved and his knowledge of Wallenberg ended.

On March 8, 1945, the Soviet-controlled radio in Hungary falsely reported that Wallenberg had been murdered en route to Debrecen, probably by Hungarian Arrow-Cross or still at-large agents of the Gestapo.

The Swedish Debacle

In April 1945 Averell Harriman, then U.S. ambassador to Moscow, was instructed to contact the Swedish ambassador and offer any assistance necessary to help determine Wallenberg's fate.

Swedish Ambassador Staffan Soderblom declined U.S. help or involvement—potentially a major mistake. A second tactical error was committed during a meeting between Stalin and Soderblom on June 15, 1945. The ambassador told the Soviet chief of state that he personally felt Wallenberg was dead, killed by the Arrow-Cross, but would still appreciate the Soviets' looking into the matter as his government in Stockholm had requested this inquiry. Stalin promised to investigate personally and wrote Wallenberg's name on a pad.

Also, in June 1945, at about the time of the Stalin meeting in Moscow, a Swedish journalist released from Soviet custody told the Foreign Office in Stockholm of a Rumanian and a German who had met Wallenberg in prison. For some mysterious reason, the Foreign Office did not follow up on this report until 1955, when the information was confirmed by the German, Erhard Hiele, on his release.

The Vishinsky Note

On August 18, 1947, the second important Soviet communique about Wallenberg was sent to Sweden. Written by Foreign Minister Andrei Vishinsky in reply to Swedish government inquiries, the message stated that "a search of prisoner-of-war camps and other establishments had turned up no trace of Wallenberg. In short, 'Wallenberg is not in the Soviet Union and is unknown to us.' The note concluded with the 'assumption' that Wallenberg had either been killed in the battle for Budapest or kidnapped and murdered by Nazis or Hungarian Fascists."

For another ten years, the Vishinsky note was the only official Russian word on Wallenberg's fate. When a group of Swedish citizens nominated Wallenberg for the 1948 Nobel Prize for Peace, it elicited the only public statement ever made by the Soviet Union concerning Sweden and the Wallenberg affair: A Soviet journal again accused the Nazis or the Arrow-Cross of murdering Raoul Wallenberg.

The Gromyko Communique

For years thereafter, there was only official Soviet silence. Then as a number of European prisoners were released in 1955, word of Wallenberg's imprisonment began to filter back to Sweden.

On February 2, 1957, a note was delivered to the Swedish government and signed by Deputy Foreign Minister Andrei Gromyko. The note told of a handwritten report by a Col. Smoltsov, head of Lubianka Prison's health service, to Viktor Abakumov, minister of state security. The report was supposedly written on July 17, 1947:

> "I report that the prisoner Walenberg (sic) who is well-known to you, died suddenly in his cell this night, probably as a result of a heart attack. Pursuant to the instructions given by you that I personally have Walenberg under my care, I request approval to make an autopsy with a view to establishing cause of death."

Scrawled across the bottom of the page in the same handwriting was the addendum:

> "I have personally notified the minister and it has been ordered that the body be cremated without autopsy. 17, July. Smoltsov."

Smoltsov and Abakumov were both dead in 1957 when Gromyko delivered the note. It is highly irregular for a Soviet prison doctor to report directly to a minister rather than to the head of the prison. The Russians never produced Col. Smoltsov's note or even a photocopy of it—an important omission, given the Russians' penchant for careful documentation.

Gromyko's communique ended by saying, "The Soviet government presents its sincere regrets for what has occurred and expresses its profound sympathy to the Swedish government as well as to Raoul's relatives."

On February 19, 1957 the Swedish ambassador to Moscow, Rolf Sohlman, delivered a note to Gromyko from the Swedish government, expressing outrage at the facts as reported in the Russian communique. The note continued that the Swedish government felt the investigation was incomplete. It also found it difficult to believe that everything referring to Wallenberg except the Smoltsov note had been completely obliterated. The Swedish government then pressed the Soviets to continue their investigation.

One final comment on the Gromyko letter and its continuing effect on the fate of Raoul Wallenberg is made in an article in the March 1981 issue of McClean's magazine. The author is Yuri Luryi, an expert on Soviet law who now lives and teaches in Canada:

> "The sad thing is that it was Gromyko who signed the letter back in 1957. He was simply a deputy of the foreign minister then, but now he is a member of the Soviet Mount Olympus. He is one of the gods who never makes mistakes. One panelist in Sweden (Wallenberg Hearings, Janu-

ary 1981) said that until Gromyko is out of power, they do not expect any positive change in the Soviet approach to Wallenberg's fate."

III. CONTRADICTORY EVIDENCE

July 17, 1947—Russian date of Raoul Wallenberg's death of a heart attack at age 35.

July 27, 1947—All prisoners who had shared a cell with Wallenberg were questioned by the NKVD, asked with whom they had talked about Wallenberg, and then placed in solitary confinement for a year or more. All were warned never to speak to Wallenberg again.

December 1947—Andrei Skimkevitch, a Soviet prisoner from 1930 to 1957 and stepson of sculptor Jacques Lipchitz, tells of being in a cell with Raoul Wallenberg in December 1947.

April 1945-April 1948—Claudio de Mohr, released Italian diplomat, told of being in a cell next to a Swede named Wallenberg with whom he communicated by tapping code messages on the wall between April 1945 and April 1948.

April 1948—A huge statue honoring Wallenberg was to be dedicated in a major ceremony in Budapest. On the base was a reference to Wallenberg's exploits from July 1944 to January 1945 and a plaque with his profile. There was no ceremony. Russian soldiers removed the statue during the night. Today, it stands in Debrecen in front of a pharmaceutical company, with no reference to Wallenberg on the statue.

August 1948—Corpus II hospital block of Vladimir Prison, a Swiss prisoner named Brugger "talked" by tapping code on his cell wall. "The Swede in the next cell had identified himself as 'Wallenberg, First Secretary Swedish Legation, Budapest, 1945.' " Asked Brugger to contact any Swedish embassy or consulate and report this information if he ever was released.

1951—Abraham Kalinski, former Soviet prisoner, was told of Wallenberg by another prisoner, David Vendrovsky, a Jewish author who had shared a prison cell with Wallenberg. Vendrovsky reported that Wallenberg was both very interesting and exceedingly sympathetic.

February 1952—Swedish communique to Russians demanding an explanation and further information on Wallenberg. This note was based on the evidence provided by Claudio de Mohr.

1953—Abraham Kalinski saw Wallenberg several times exercising in the prison yard with other prisoners.

January 1955—Kalinski reports having seen Wallenberg during a prisoner transfer to Vladimir Prison. They were on the same prison train.

January/February 1955—An Austrian, whose name was not disclosed for fear of Soviet reprisals, tells of having been in a cell with Wallenberg for one night in Corpus II of Vladimir Prison. Wallenberg told him that he had spent years in solitary confinement. He asked the Austrian to contact any Swedish diplomatic mission should he be released and say that they had met: "If you forget my name just say a Swede from Budapest and they'll know who you mean." Prison officials removed the Austrian the next morning and

warned him not to talk to other prisoners about seeing Wallenberg on pain of life imprisonment.

1955—Rigid investigative procedures pertaining to the Wallenberg case were established in Sweden.
1. Hearsay evidence is excluded.
2. Only information from direct contact with Wallenberg or Langfelder is acceptable.
3. Each witness is kept in ignorance as to the testimony of all other witnesses.
4. All statements have to be given under oath and are scrutinized by a veteran criminal investigator.

1956—Kalinski became a cellmate at Vladimir Prison of Simon Gogoberidse, a Georgia Social Democrat who had been kidnapped from Paris by the KGB, where he was a political refugee. Gogoberidse told Kalinski of sharing a cell with Wallenberg. (Wallenberg was always made to share cells with Soviet citizens serving long sentences, never with foreigners. This reduced the risk of evidence about him getting out.)

March 10, 1956—A Swedish note was sent to the Kremlin stating that "complete evidence" existed, and that it was clear Wallenberg had been held as a suspected spy by the USSR. This was accompanied by a statement signed by two Swedish Supreme Court justices saying that "all conditions seemed fulfilled to enable the Russians to trace Wallenberg and send him home."

March 19, 1956—Russian reply to the Swedish inquiry was that a thorough investigation had confirmed that Wallenberg was not, and never had been, in the Soviet Union. The Kremlin added, "that it was impossible to accept the testimony of war criminals whose information was in disagreement with the results of their own thorough investigation."

Easter 1956—Swedish Prime Minister Tage Erlander met with Nikita Khrushchev. In spite of Soviet opposition, he raised the Wallenberg question and handed over copies of the testimony gathered by the Swedish government over the years. He received the stock answer that Wallenberg was not and never had been in the USSR.

April 1956—A German prisoner named Mulle, sent to Vladimir Prison in 1956, shared a cell with Gogoberidse, who told him that Wallenberg had been in solitary for several years as of 1956. He also said that after Prime Minister Erlander's visit to Russia, a prison political officer said, "They'll have to look for a long time to find Wallenberg."

April 1956—Rehemkampf, another German prisoner later released, reports that the same story about Wallenberg was given to him that month by Gogoberidse. This information was given separately from Mulle's report.

April 5, 1956—A Russian communique to the Swedish government stated that the USSR agreed to study the Swedish documentation and added that if Wallenberg was in the USSR, he would "naturally" be allowed to return home.

July 14, 1956—Soviet Ambassador Rodinov informed the Swedish Foreign Office that results could soon be expected.

February 2, 1957—The Andrei Gromyko note arrived reporting Raoul Wallenberg's death on July 17, 1947.

February 19, 1957—Sweden's ambassador to Moscow, Rolf Sohlman, delivered a very strongly worded response to the Soviets, holding them responsible for Wallenberg's fate, urged a continued investigation.

February 1957—Evidence by the unnamed Austrian and his report of having shared a cell with Wallenberg in 1955 was acquired.

March 1959—Abraham Kalinski wrote a postcard, in Yiddish, to his sister in Haifa, Israel. He mentioned a Swede.

August 1959—Kalinski again wrote his sister, this time in Polish, "that the only foreigners now left in the prison, apart from himself, are one Italian and one Swede who saved many Jews in Rumania during the War." (sic)

1959—Swedish/Russian Communiques. The Swedish government, responding to the testimony of the German returnees Mulle and Rehemkampf (April 1956), sent several strongly worded notes to the Russians merely to reiterate the story of Wallenberg's death in 1947. They also accuse elements of trying to poison Swedish-Soviet relations.

1960—Another Swedish communique to the Soviets. Signed by two Supreme Court justices, the message states that evidence clearly points to Wallenberg's survival, at least up to early 1950.

1961—In early 1979 the Soviet dissident Juri Belov passed through Vienna on his way out of Russia. He went with Simon Wiesenthal, the famed Nazi-hunter, to the Swedish embassy. Belov said that Wallenberg had staged a hunger strike in Moscow's Butyrka Prison in 1961. As a result, he was transferred to a psychiatric clinic.

January 27, 1961—Professor Nanna Svartz of Sweden has a routine meeting in Moscow with Professor Aleksandr Miashnikov. Professor Svartz, a physician from Stockholm's Karolinska Hospital, where Wallenberg's stepfather served as administrator, was a close friend of the von Dardel family. Wallenberg's mother, Maj von Dardel, was her patient. Professor Svartz and Professor Miashnikov often discussed medical matters of a highly technical nature together after the conferences. Their language of choice was always German. Dr. Svartz asked on January 27, 1961 to discuss "a matter close to my heart and the hearts of other Swedes." She gave an account of Raoul Wallenberg and asked the Russian doctor if he knew of him and his whereabouts. Dr. Miashnikov replied in a low voice, "that the person inquired about was in a mental hospital." The Russian also told her that he had personally examined Wallenberg. (Revealed by Dr. Svartz in 1980). A Russian colleague was called in for consultation, and it was decided that Dr. Svartz should proceed through diplomatic channels.

January 1961—Professor Svartz returns to Sweden and informs Prime Minister Tage Erlander, an old friend, of her extraordinary conversation.

February 9, 1961—A personal letter from Erlander to Khrushchev is delivered by the Swedish Ambassador.

THE LETTER
"I now wish to inform you that I have been informed by Swedish physician, Professor Nanna Svartz, who visited Moscow at the end of January 1961 ... that Wallenberg was alive at that time and that he was a patient at a mental hospital in Moscow. His health was not good. Dr. Svartz got this information from an internationally known, prominent representative of Soviet medical science."

March 1961—Professor Svartz returned to Moscow. She saw Miashnikov and asked to see Wallenberg in the hospital. He said that this would have to be "decided in higher quarters, unless he is dead." Dr. Svartz then answered that this must have happened quite recently if it had occurred. Professor Svartz sensed that all was not well. Professor Miashnikov, who was so important that he was chairman to Khrushchev's personal physician, said that Professor Svartz should not have told the Swedish government of their conversation. He told Dr. Svartz that he had been summoned before Khrushchev, who had been furious, pounding on his desk and finally ordering him out of his office. He now claimed to know nothing of Wallenberg, and declared that his poor German (which they had used together for years) had caused the misunderstanding.

May 1962—Dr. Svartz again met Professor Miashnikov at a medical congress. When Wallenberg was again mentioned, he said that no further private talks on the subject could be held.

August 17, 1962—Second Erlander letter about Wallenberg to Khrushchev. No reply.

1963—Ex-British spy Greville Wynne told BBC audiences of an incident in Moscow's Lubianka Prison in early 1963. "One day when taken in the tiny cagelike lift to the roof for solitary exercise, Wynne heard another cage coming into the next pen. As the gate opened he heard a voice call out 'Taxi.' Given the filthy condition of the lifts, this piece of defiant humor was greatly appreciated. Five days later when it happened again Wynne called out, 'Are you American?' The voice answered, 'No, I'm Swedish.'" Nothing further could be learned. Guards restrained both prisoners.

1962-1964—Professor Svartz is unable to renew any contact with Professor Miashnikov.

March 1964—Soviet Foreign Minister Andrei Gromyko visits Stockholm. Erlander again presses for an answer and suggests a meeting between Professor Svartz and Miashnikov.

April 29, 1964—Letter from Miashnikov to Dr. Svartz denying any knowledge of Raoul Wallenberg.

May 28, 1964—Professor Svartz writes a letter to Professor Miashnikov reminding him of all their untroubled conversations in the 1950s as well as untroubled discussions after their January 27, 1961 meeting. She also recalls in detail that conversation once again.

July 1965—A meeting was arranged in Moscow between the two doctors. It was held in the presence of Swedish Ambassador Gunnar Jarring and two representatives of the Soviet Foreign Ministry, one of whom acted as interpreter. A three hour discussion conducted in Swedish and Russian (no German) produced no new results. Miashnikov said again that Dr. Svartz must have misunderstood his syntax.

September 16, 1965—A "White Book" was published by the Swedish Foreign Ministry making public the recent interchanges with the Soviet Union, including the Svartz affair. The Swedish public and Swedish press were outraged by the disclosures.

November 1965—Professor Aleksandr Miashnikov died suddenly. He had appeared to be in good health and was in his early sixties.

January 1970—A young Hungarian visiting Stockholm read about Wallenberg for the first time in a Swedish newspaper. He went to Maj von Dardel and told her of a lunch with a woman friend whose father was a senior Hungarian government official. (The Swedes confirmed the existence of both the official and his daughter.) At lunch the father mentioned that a Swedish diplomat named Raoul Wallenberg, who had been active in Budapest during the war, was at the time in a Soviet camp in Siberia.

1974—An unnamed informant said that he had seen Wallenberg in Vadivovo Camp near the Siberian city of Iskutsk from 1966-1967. He was old-looking with thin, white hair and had been very ill. He was called "Roniboni" by the other prisoners.

1978—Conid Lubarsky, a Soviet dissident living in Munich, reported the following information from a reliable source in Moscow: "In 1978, in Blagovischnsk special psychiatric hospital, one old Swede was held. His physical state was very bad. He had been in confinement for a long time, maybe since World War II. His name was unknown to my informants, but they speculated that this man could be Wallenberg."

May 1, 1978—A young Soviet Jewish immigrant to Israel, who wished to remain anonymous because of his family in the USSR, tells of a party at the Moscow home of a senior KGB officer on May Day, 1978: "Much vodka was drunk and the younger men at the party began to speak of dissidents and the rough time they must have in prison. The KGB officer burst out and said, 'Don't you believe it; things aren't so tough nowadays as they used to be. You can live a long time in jail. Why I have a Swede under my charge in Lubianka who's been inside for over 30 years!' " The young Russian heard of Wallenberg in Israel for the first time and then went to the Swedish embassy in Israel where he filed a report.

General Kuprianov 1953-1979

Simon Wiesenthal, at the Wallenberg hearings in Stockholm in January 1981, reported a recent conversation with a Russian he could identify only as "I.L." This I.L. had been a friend of Soviet General G. Kuprianov, a Hero of the Soviet Union who had been jailed during the Stalinist purges of 1948 and remained in prison until 1956 when he was released by Khrushchev.

1953—Kuprianov met Raoul Wallenberg for the first time during a prison transfer.

1955—Met again while being transferred to Vladimir Prison.

1956—Met once more but couldn't speak to one another at the prison dentist's office.

1979—General Kuprianov, now free in Leningrad, learned that Wallenberg had not yet been released. The general was surprised, as he knew that Wallenberg had been sentenced to 25 years in prison in either 1945 or 1956 and should thus have been released no later than 1971.

February 1979—An article about Kuprianov's meeting with Wallenberg appeared in a Russian emigre newspaper in the United States. Kuprianov was interrogated by the KGB and warned to have no further contact with Western journalists.

May 1979—A Swedish newspaper picked up the Kuprianov story about Wallenberg.

May 1979—General Kuprianov is interrogated a second time. The KGB accuses him of collaborating with Western journalists. A KGB colonel demands that Kuprianov help refute these "American-Israeli provocations." Kuprianov refused to deny his statements. The KGB told him that "no doubt he would be ready to give in at the next questioning."

May 1979—Kuprianov said to I.L., "I do not know if I will be able to manage that questioning." The KGB recalled the general a few days after his conversation with I.L.

May 1979—(Five days later)—Mrs. Kuprianov was sent for by the KGB and told that the general had died of a heart attack. While she was at the interrogation center, her apartment was searched, and all the general's papers and documents were removed.

Jan Kaplan— November 1977—August 1979

Jan Kaplan was released from prison in November 1977, after only 18 months of a four-year prison sentence. The former administrator of an operatic studio in Moscow was 66 years old in 1977. He had been jailed for "economic crimes": namely, currency offenses and the illegal purchase of diamonds in preparation for emigration from the Soviet Union.

November 1977—A telephone call from Jan Kaplan in Moscow to his daughter, Anna Kaplan Bilder, a dentist in Jaffa, Israel. When questioned about prison conditions by his daughter, he assured her that conditions were not too difficult. "Why when I was in Butyrka Prison Hospital in 1975, I met a Swede who told me he had been in Soviet prisons for thirty years, and he seemed reasonably healthy to me."

October 1978—Abraham Kalinski, the Polish emigre who had reported seeing Wallenberg from 1955 until 1959, heard about Anna Bilder's conversation with her father via the Russian emigre grapevine. He met her and she gave him a detailed account of the conversation.

December 1978—From the USA, Kalinski telephoned the Kaplan home in Moscow. Kaplan's wife, Eugenia, took the call and said that her husband was not available. She did confirm his report of meeting a Swede in Butyrka Prison in 1975.

December 20, 1978—Abraham Kalinski met with two

Swedish Foreign Office representatives at the Swedish Consulate in New York. Told his own story and then repeated Jan Kaplan's story.

December 1978—The Swedish Foreign Office in Tel Aviv contacted Anna Bilder and invited her in for an interview.

January 1979—Sweden formally re-opened the Wallenberg case, based on this newest evidence.

January 3, 1979—Swedish note to Russians requesting an investigation of new information.

January 24, 1979—Russian reply: "There is not, and cannot be, anything new regarding the fate of Raoul Wallenberg. As already stated on innumerable occasions, he died July 1947, and the assertions that he was in the Soviet Union as late as 1975 are not in accordance with facts."

February 3, 1979—Kaplan home was searched. Jan Kaplan again arrested.

February 1979—Anna Bilder learns that her sick father is again in prison. She receives three anonymous phone calls (two in Russian) warning her not to speak of Wallenberg for her father's sake.

June 14, 1979—Eugenia Kaplan in Moscow writes to her daughter. Anna Bilder receives the letter in July 1979 in Israel. The letter says that Jan Kaplan was again in prison because he had tried to smuggle out a letter to his daughter about Wallenberg. The letter was discovered by the KGB.

May 1979—At Lubianka Prison on a visit to her husband, Eugenia Kaplan was told by the KGB colonel in charge that her husband was accused of anti-Soviet propaganda in Israel. Also said that Jan Kaplan's health and fate depend on Anna Bilder's behavior.

July 23, 1979—Anna Bilder disclosed the contents of her mother's letter to author John Bierman.

July 1979—Mrs. Bilder consulted Abraham Kalinski and together they took the letter to the Swedish embassy in Tel Aviv. It was photocopied and the original went to Sweden by diplomatic pouch. Sweden's Soviet experts after careful study were fully convinced of its authenticity.

August 22, 1979—Swedish Prime Minister Ola Ullsten intervened personally and sent a letter to Soviet Prime Minister Alexei Kosygin. Requested that the Wallenberg case be re-opened and that a Swedish embassy official be allowed to interview Kaplan, if necessary in the presence of Soviet officials.

August 28, 1979—Again Russians stuck by their 1947 story.

August 28, 1979—Prime Minister Ullsten issued a statement calling the Soviet attitude deplorable. He also said that the whole truth of Wallenberg's disappearance was still not at hand and that Sweden would continue its pursuit of the truth.

January 15/16, 1981—Raoul Wallenberg Hearings held in Stockholm, Sweden, under the auspices of the Swedish Wallenberg Committee.

May 1981—Raoul Wallenberg Committee of the United States officially established.

October 5, 1981—President Ronald Reagan signs into law a bill making Raoul Wallenberg an honorary citizen of the United States. This bill was first introduced into Congress by Congressman Tom Lantos (D-Calif),

himself a Hungarian refugee, and a survivor, and in the Senate by Senators Daniel P. Moynihan, Frank Church, Rudy Boschwitz and Claiborne Pell.

November 6, 1981—Ambassador Max M. Kampelman, representing the United States delegation in Madrid, Spain, at a conference reviewing the Helsinki Agreements, spoke of the immediate need to discover the truth concerning Raoul Wallenberg.

February 28, 1982—Ambassador Michael Novak, head of the U.S. delegation to the United Nations Human Rights Commission meeting in Geneva, Switzerland, proposed, with the backing of the Swedish government, a five-member U.N. working group to discover the whereabouts of Raoul Wallenberg. Thus far, the Soviet Union has not responded.

August 3, 1983—A Congressional oversight hearing was called by Representative Gus Yatron, Chairman of the Subcommittee on Human Rights and International Organizations. Rachel Oestreicher Haspel, President of the Raoul Wallenberg Committee of the United States in affiliation with the Anti-Defamation League of B'nai B'rith, requested that the Congress act on the following points:

1. That a question pertaining to Wallenberg be asked of all arriving Soviet immigrants,
2. That Radio Free Europe and the Voice of America be used to help locate Raoul Wallenberg,
3. That all government officials when communicating with the Soviets automatically ask the fate of Raoul Wallenberg,
4. That a United States Postal Stamp be issued to honor the War Refugee Board, bearing Raoul Wallenberg's picture; because he is alive, a memorial stamp would be inappropriate,
5. That the United States Holocaust Memorial Council name a wing in the new Holocaust Memorial Museum in honor of Raoul Wallenberg.

On the State level, the Committee encouraged enactment of the following legislation in all 50 states:

1. To include Raoul Wallenberg's story in school curricula,
2. To designate October 5th a day honoring Raoul Wallenberg.

1983—Efforts on behalf of Raoul Wallenberg continue to be made by Wallenberg Committees and caring individuals throughout the free world. This is an ongoing commitment. Legal actions are being taken on Raoul Wallenberg's behalf. Honors continue to be bestowed on him in countries throughout the world.

He was the *one* shining light in all that darkness. How different our world might have been today had there been a few more heroes like Raoul Wallenberg: a man who acted while the rest of the world watched. The survivors of the Holocaust have a slogan, *"NEVER AGAIN."* Let us take these words and apply them further. NEVER AGAIN will we allow the name RAOUL WALLENBERG or the deeds that his name stands for to be overlooked. NEVER AGAIN will we allow the horrors of the Gulag to totally engulf him. NEVER AGAIN will we remain silent until the true reasons for his imprisonment and his actual whereabouts are made known to his family and to the world.

A Question for Andropov: Where Is Raoul Wallenberg?

George F. Will
The Washington Post, January 6, 1983

The gauze of lies that the Soviet regime wraps around reality has never been thick enough to muffle this question: Where is Raoul Wallenberg?

Now it is asked again, in the wake of the most recent in a long series of tormenting reports. A Russian immigrant in Israel says that when he was hospitalized in 1972 on the way to prison, he met a man who "looked Jewish, so I asked who he was. He answered in accented Russian that he was Swedish and was there because he helped the Jews. He said his name was Raoul Wallenberg." That occurred a quarter of a century after 1947, the year the Kremlin says Wallenberg died.

Last May, when tardily releasing documents about the Wallenberg case, a Swedish official said, "We are working on the supposition that he is still alive." (Sweden's lethargy concerning the case—lethargy born of cowardice—hardly constitutes "working.") If alive, he is 70. It is 38 years since he disappeared from Hungary into the Soviet Union.

On Jan. 17, 1945, he was seized by Soviet forces that were "liberating" Hungary from their former allies, the Nazis. Three weeks later he was in the emblematic institution of the Soviet regime, Moscow's Lubyanka prison.

At 32, representing neutral Sweden, Wallenberg was in Budapest at America's request, working with breathtaking bravery and saving scores of thousands of Jews from Adolf Eichmann's final chapter of the "final solution," the destruction of Hungarian Jews. He bought buildings and draped them with Swedish flags as diplomatically protected territory. He dressed "Aryan-looking" Jewish men in SS uniforms to protect Jewish havens. He distributed fake passports, and used sheer audacity to intimidate Nazi soldiers into opening the doors of cattle cars. Thanks to him, the 120,000 Jews in Budapest were the most substantial Jewish community surviving in Europe when the war ended.

One certainty is that Andrei Gromyko lied in the 1957 memorandum asserting that Wallenberg's "sojourn in the Soviet Union"—Gromyko's words—ended with a heart attack in prison in 1947. This memorandum came after 12 years of Kremlin denials that Wallenberg had ever been in Soviet hands. Gromyko cited the evidence of two Soviet functionaries, both conveniently dead, and said the body had been cremated—a transparent fabrication, given Soviet practices.

There has been a steady trickle of reports about Wallenberg, first from returning German prisoners of war, then from released political prisoners and Jewish emigrants. The reports give dates and places—prisons, cell numbers—that trace a tantalizing trail across the years and through the gulags.

For example, in 1961 a Soviet professor of medicine told a visiting Swedish physician that he had recently examined Wallenberg in a "mental hospital." In 1977 a Muscovite just

released from the gulag called his daughter in Israel and mentioned meeting in a Moscow prison a Swede "who had served 30 years." Two years later the Muscovite was back in prison because, his wife said, he wrote a letter about Wallenberg. Sources in Eastern Europe report that in 1981 Wallenberg was moved to a prison hospital near Leningrad.

Why was he arrested in the first place? The Soviet machinery of brutality operates so automatically it leaves little room for, and certainly does not require, much mind. But Soviet repressors certainly did not want brave witnesses to the breaking of Eastern Europe. Why was he kept? Perhaps, in part, to show contempt for Western disapproval. Why did Soviet troops using horses and ropes drag away the statue erected to him in Budapest in 1948? Because the Kremlin disapproved of what he did.

It is prudent that we insistently ask what happened when Wallenberg ended his dance of death with the Third Reich and fell into the hands of its moral twin. When the Soviet Union gets away with such acts—acts that are as contemptuous as they are contemptible—it gets the idea that it can unleash "yellow rain" and can shoot the Pope with little to fear from the West's fitful disapproval.

Besides, if this case is not America's business, what is? On Oct. 5, 1981, Wallenberg became only the second person (Winston Churchill was the first) to be made an honorary American citizen.

Signing the bill conferring this honor, President Reagan said "we're going to do everything in our power" to locate Wallenberg. But we have not done that. So before Reagan agrees to meet with Yuri Andropov, he should receive an answer, beyond the routine mendacities, to this question: Where is Raoul Wallenberg?

Wallenberg and Sweden's Shame (Cont'd.)

"The Swedish minister said, 'What! Do you believe that Mr. Vyshinsky is lying?' "

George F. Will
The Washington Post, January 16, 1983

Like a northern pike rising at a lure, Sweden's ambassador has risen to defend his country against an accusation in a recent column. I welcome the opportunity to amplify the offending remark.

Writing about Raoul Wallenberg, the savior of thousands of Hungarian Jews, who disappeared into Soviet prisons in 1945, I quoted a Swedish official saying that, "We are working on the supposition that Wallenberg is still alive." I said: "Sweden's lethargy concerning the case—lethargy born of cowardice—hardly constitutes 'working.' "

In a letter to The Washington Post, the ambassador calls this "grossly unfair." He admits Sweden believed initial Soviet lies, but he says Sweden "has pursued this matter with a vigor and perseverance that probably exceeds what any government has done for one of its citizens."

Well.

Sweden's statement about its supposition was made when Sweden released documents pertaining to the case. Rep. Tom Lantos (D-Calif.), who as a boy in Budapest was saved by Wallenberg, wrote to The New York Times (May 26, 1982):

> "It is both ironic and deplorable that Sweden has waited 20 years to release some 42 volumes of reports and eyewitness accounts. . . . Had the information been made public earlier to those in a position to help Raoul Wallenberg, he may have been able to live his life with dignity—with his family—instead of in the infamy of the Soviet gulag. For years, the government of Sweden has engaged in ineffective silent diplomacy. . . . Now they tell those of us who have fought so hard for his release that we can finally see their documents. If . . . the Swedish government is now 'working on the supposition that he is still alive,' then it's about time."

Just after the war, Sweden's foreign minister was urged to press the case and disregard the fact that Soviet Foreign Minister Vyshinsky said that the Soviet Union did not have Wallenberg. The Swedish minister said: "What! Do you believe that Mr. Vyshinsky is lying?" Vyshinsky, the prosecutor in Stalin's show trials, lie? "Absolutely unheard of," said the minister.

The ambassador's claim that Sweden has done more for Wallenberg than any nation has done for a citizen is refuted by many cases, but especially that of Harald Feller, a Swiss diplomat who was in Budapest when Wallenberg was, doing similar rescue work. He, too, wound up in Soviet hands. But he was released in 1946 because his country arrested six Soviet spies and negotiated a swap.

Although Sweden found neutrality profitable between 1939 and 1945, after the war it discovered morality, and ever since has been urging it on others, especially the United States, which frequently falls short of Sweden's exacting standards. Sweden has generally considered swaps beneath its dignity. "Sweden," said a Swedish foreign minister, "does not do such things." By the time (1979) Sweden proposed a swap, the Kremlin reacted with disdain.

Olof Palme, who is again prime minister, and the world's moral tutor (he considers the United States an especially backward student), was prime minister in 1976. When Palme met with Alexei Kosygin, the Wallenberg case was not even on the agenda. Palme's administration dismissed the case in a word: *"utagerad"* (settled).

Even before the invasion of Afghanistan, Wallenberg's supporters urged Sweden to boycott the 1980 Olympics in Moscow. Even after the invasion, Sweden did not boycott.

In October 1981, a Soviet submarine ran aground while violating Swedish territorial waters. Wallenberg supporters urged using the submarine for leverage. When the Soviet Union asked for its boat back, Sweden could have said: Boat? What boat? We know nothing of any boat—just as you know nothing of Wallenberg.

But appearing on ABC's "Nightline" (Oct. 30, 1981), the foreign minister was asked if Sweden "might want to propose a trade." He said that "would certainly not serve any useful purpose." Do Swedes wonder why Soviet submarines show such contempt for Sweden's sovereignty? Cringing neutrality has not noticeably immunized Sweden from the aggressive disdain of Soviet submarines.

In her new biography, "Wallenberg," Kati Marton, a Hungarian-born journalist, concludes that Wallenberg fell victim to "Sweden's near-pathological fear of Russia":

"The scorn with which the Kremlin treated Stockholm's queries about Wallenberg was not altogether unjustified given the Swedes' lack of conviction following his imprisonment. The dim memory of an early 19th-century Russian invasion, Sweden's first and last, is not sufficient explanation for the country's spineless behavior on behalf of its captured diplomat."

Marton also says: "At Wallenberg's expense, Sweden has learned a painful lesson: the price demanded to maintain one's neutrality can sometimes be too high." The lesson certainly has been taught to all of Europe; whether it has been learned is increasingly doubtful.

Monument. A giant St. George slaying the dragon was the monument intended by the people of Budapest to commemorate Wallenberg. The Russians removed it before it was ever unveiled.

For more information, contact:

The Raoul Wallenberg Committee of the United States, in affiliation with the Anti-Defamation League of B'nai B'rith, 823 United Nations Plaza, New York, New York 10017. (212) 490-2525 x331.

8

Nazi War Criminals In America Facts . . . Action

Charles R. Allen, Jr.
COPYRIGHT © 1985 CHARLES R. ALLEN, JR.

Who Are They?

Immediately after World War II, an undetermined number of individuals implicated in Nazi genocides, persecutions and other war crimes made their way to the United States.

Where Did They Come From?

Most of the accused Nazi war criminals and collaborators came from Eastern Europe and the Soviet Union. Many are still wanted there for war crimes and treason. Few are of German origin. Most of the crimes of the Holocaust were committed in Eastern Europe and on the soil of the Soviet Union by Nazi Germany and its collaborators.

How Many War Criminals and Collaborators Are Here?

Estimates vary. The Office of Special Investigations (OSI) of the U.S. Justice Department is charged with investigating and prosecuting alleged Nazi war criminals residing here. Its director has stated that he "works from a file of some 470" cases. The OSI estimates that "somewhat more than a third" of its own official list have died. The author of this article has compiled his own detailed list of 288 individuals against whom substantial war crimes charges have been made. Some 30 percent of the accused on this list are deceased.

Other claims that "more than 3,000 war criminals" have found haven in the U.S. have not been proven. However, it is reasonable to assume that during the nearly four decades since the end of World War II, some 1,000 have come here freely.

As early as 1949, the German-language newspaper *Aufbau* in New York published a listing of 38 individuals that originated with a survivor named Simon Wiesenthal, later the world-famed Nazi hunter.

In 1963, *Nazi War Criminals Among Us* (by Charles R. Allen, Jr.) was the first work to seek out and document charges against sixteen accused Nazi war criminals and collaborators. Evidence obtained by Allen after 1963 suggested that possibly 22 more might have been in the United States at that time. Thus by the mid-1960's, the unofficial estimate was 38. In the late 1960's, the World Jewish Congress had compiled its listing of 59 such individuals, many derived from Allen's published findings.

Thus, from the first reports of 1949 to the carefully checked and computerized listings of the 1980's, the incontestable fact remains: scores, if not hundreds, of Hitlerian genocidists and collaborators made safe passage to the United States. According to an Israeli intelligence report of 1961, the United States was the third largest refuge for Nazi war criminals in the world—after West Germany and Argentina.

Where Do They Live?

No area is "immune" to their presence. Vilis Hazners, an accused Latvian war criminal, lives in an isolated hamlet in upstate New York. Large cities such as New York, Philadelphia, Baltimore, Chicago, Cleveland and Los Angeles have ongoing trials. Valerian Trifa, a denaturalized Romanian Orthodox archbishop, lived in a fortress-like villa in Grass Lake, Michigan. There are proceedings in Florida and Connecticut. Other alleged Nazi war criminals, not yet prosecuted, live throughout the country. Some are at prestigious universities, colleges and corporations.

What Are They Accused Of?

They are accused of various crimes ranging from individual to mass murders, from acts of persecution to high-level responsibility for institutionalizing concentration and death camps; from carrying out experiments on humans to top-level implementation of the Nazi genocide program between 1939 and 1945. Most of those in the United States were low level operators: concentration and death camp guards and guard supervisors, members of execution and punitive squads in collaborator armies, Gestapo agents and informers. Some, however, were complicit at much higher levels: as diplomats, in the secret police, the military, the SS (Schutzstaffel). Many were leaders of the treasonous Fifth Columns of their native lands—the Iron Guard or Green Shirts in Romania, the Arrow/Cross in Hungary, the Iron Wolf in Lithuania, the Thunder-Cross in Latvia, the Black Shirts in Italy, the Ustashi in Yugoslavia, and the like.

Who Made These Charges?

War crimes documentation centers, ministries of justice, concentration camp survivors' and resistance groups from: Poland, Romania, Hungary, Bulgaria, Yugoslavia, Czechoslovakia, the German Democratic Republic and the Soviet Union; Holland, Belgium, France, the Federal Republic of Germany, Denmark, Italy—and Israel.

When Were The Charges First Made?

As early as 1948. In 1951, Yugoslavia formally requested the extradition of one Andrija Artukovic, the Minister of Interior of Nazi-occupied Croatia. He is accused of direct responsibility for the genocide of some 600,000 persons, including 78,000 Jews. The U.S. Justice Department is still seeking his deportation. Substantiated accusations were published by several journalists, including Drew Pearson, Walter Winchell, Milton Friedman of the Jewish Telegraphic Agency (JTA), as well as several U.S. Congressmen in the late 1950's and 1960's. Interest was stirred briefly in the mid-1960's with the publication of *Nazi War Criminals Among Us*. The subject resurfaced in the mid-1970's, and has since become a national issue, as yet unresolved.

Did The United States Government Know?

Yes, from the beginning. Several government agencies—the State Department, the intelligence branches of the Army, Navy and Air Force, as well as the CIA, FBI, Radio Free Europe, Radio Liberty and others—knowingly (and covertly) brought some of them into the country. They were used as "contract agents" and "consultants." From 1948 to the mid-1970's, these government agencies flatly denied their utilization of war criminals.

What Has Congress Done About Them?

In the mid-1970's, Rep. Joshua Eilberg (D-Pa) and Rep. Elizabeth Holtzman (D-NY) of the U.S. House of Representatives Judiciary Committee succeeded in putting the issue on the Congressional agenda. (At about the same time, a former concentration camp guard supervisor, Hermine Braunsteiner Ryan, was extradited to West Germany for trial; Immigration and Naturalization Service (INS) attorney Vincent Schiano and investigator Anthony DeVito left the INS, accusing that agency of years of cover-ups on the Nazi war criminal issue.)

Prodded by the Holtzman-led forces, INS set up a Special Litigation Unit (SLU) in 1977, headed by Martin Mendelsohn. By 1979, there was widespread disaffection with both the INS and its SLU. Rep. Holtzman, by then Chairperson of the Judiciary Subcommittee on Immigration, used her clout to transfer SLU to the Criminal Division of the Justice Department. It became the Office of Special Investigations (OSI).

In January 1977, Congress requested an investigation to determine whether U.S. government agencies had obstructed investigations and prosecutions of alleged Nazi war criminals. On May 15, 1978, the General Accounting Office (GAO), the investigative arm of the U.S. House of Representatives, issued a report. GAO found no evidence of a "widespread conspiracy" within the government to cover up the Nazi war criminal cases, but the FBI and CIA did admit officially for the first time that they had "utilized" Nazi war criminals and collaborators. On July 19-21, 1978, the House Subcommittee on Immigration held hearings on the GAO findings.

On February 6, 1981, Rep. Hamilton Fish (R-NY) and Rep. William Lehman (D-Fla) were joined by over 100 members of the House in signing a letter to President Ronald Reagan, urging the President to give the OSI his full public endorsement. In April 1981, Sen. Christopher Dodd (D-Conn) and eleven other Senators sent a letter to President Reagan, urging him not to cut the OSI's budget for the 1982 fiscal year. The Senators also recommended that Attorney General William French Smith "take a personal interest" in the OSI.

After her November 1980 defeat in a race for the U.S. Senate, Elizabeth Holtzman, as a private citizen, announced formation of "a broadly based Committee of Public Concern." The Holtzman group's purpose is to assure continuance of the OSI, monitor ongoing OSI trials, and "keep the issue before the American people."

Who Is Prosecuting Them?

Beginning in 1973, a series of task forces and prosecution units was set up first in the INS and then in the Criminal Division of the U.S. Justice Department. In 1979 the OSI was launched with a budget (eventually) of $2.3 million. Former Nuremberg prosecutor Walter Rockler was OSI's first director. On April 1, 1980, Deputy Director Allan A. Ryan, Jr. succeeded Rockler. The present staff of 47 includes 18 lawyers, three investigators and six historians. Denaturalization cases are tried in U.S. District courts; deportation hearings are argued before U.S. Immigration and Naturalization administrative courts. A $2.7 million budget was authorized for 1983-84. Neal M. Sher was named OSI director, November 29, 1983.

How Many Cases Are There?

In January 1980, the OSI files contained the names of 413 individuals charged with Nazi pasts. By January 1981, there were 233 "active" cases. By February 1981, the OSI had reviewed for triability and closed a total of 231 cases. Thus 180 cases were being examined in 1981 for triability, according to the OSI. By mid-1981, there were 20 cases in various stages of litigation. Of the 20 cases now pending, six defendants are accused of atrocities in the Ukraine. Six are Latvian, three Lithuanian, two German, and one Estonian. The only two who held positions of any prominence are Archbishop Valerian Trifa, Romanian Iron Guardist, and Andrija Artukovic, Croatian Minister. OSI has filed 37 cases as of January 1, 1984.

How Did They Get Here?

Some Nazi war criminals came here under the Displaced Persons Act of 1948-51, slipping in with legitimate DPs. In some cases, they were secretly requested by various agencies of our government, including the State Department, CIA, FBI, Voice of America, Radio Free Europe and Radio Liberty. They were used for various Cold War activities. Some 1,558 German and Austrian scientists were brought to the U.S. through a Pentagon-State Department-Intelligence operation called Project Paperclip. Most were minimally members of the Nazi party; some were in the SS. Of the OSI's 30 pending cases, seven are implicated in utilization by the U.S. Government. At least 156 alleged Nazi war criminals have been utilized by U.S. intelligence agencies over the past 38 years. Not a single war criminal or collaborator, moreover, was barred at his or her American port-of-entry because of war crimes or collaboration.

When Did They Come Here?

Most arrived in the late 1940's and early 1950's. The earliest arrival of the 30 pending cases is Bronius Kaminskas (May 1947). Artukovic arrived as a "temporary visitor for pleasure" in July 1948; three years later deportation proceedings against him were initiated. The latest entry date listed by the OSI is for Conrad Schellong, in February 1957. Edgars Laipenieks entered the United States for alien residency in 1960, but was in the country as a "tourist" on several occasions as early as 1947.

How Long Will Their Trials Take?

According to former OSI Director Ryan, "If we file an airtight case against a naturalized American citizen tomorrow and there are no judicial delays, it would still take eight years to complete a case." (*JTA Daily News Bulletin,* June 3, 1980.) Deportation proceedings against Artukovic have been outstanding since 1951. After more than 30 years of massive indifference, proven cover-ups and sheer ineptitude, no case is "airtight." Begun on August 15, 1977, the denaturalization case of Feodor Fedorenko was decided in favor of the Government by the U.S. Supreme Court on January 21, 1981. Fedorenko's was the first Nazi war criminal case to be completed at this highest level. Deportation proceedings commenced March 5, 1981.

Who Are They?

(Status of cases as of June 1, 1985. Subject to change. Information based on OSI Digest of Cases in Litigation. Listed alphabetically, last name first.)

Denaturalization Cases

Artishenko, Basil—Accused by OSI of having participated in "execution and persecution of about 100 unarmed gypsies ... women and children" as member of police force in Byelorussia during World War II. OSI complaint filed November 12, 1982. Has since become an OSI witness, thus will not be deported. Artishenko resides East Brunswick, N.J.

Demjanjuk, John—accused of assisting in extermination of thousands of Jews, while uniformed guard with German SS at death camps at Sobibor and Treblinka, Poland. Case completed March 11, 1981; decision pending. Resides Cleveland, Ohio. Ordered denaturalized June 23, 1981.

Dercacz, Mikhail—accused of beatings and executions of unarmed/Jewish civilians in Lvov, Ukraine. Case in discovery phase, with depositions being taken in U.S.S.R. Resides Queens, N.Y. Denaturalized February 2, 1982.

Gudauskas, Vytautus—accused of war crimes in Lithuania. Resides Worcester, Mass.

Hrusitzky, Anatoly—Ukrainian police officer charged on August 9, 1983 by the OSI of having concealed his Nazi past as a collaborator who allegedly participated "in the persecution and murder of unarmed Jewish men, women and children living in and around Cherny, Ostrov" in the Ukraine. OSI has been carrying out audio-visual interviews and depositions of surviving eyewitnesses in the Soviet Ukraine. At pre-trial stage as of December 1, 1983. Defendant resided in Florida; renounced U.S. citizenship; now resides in Venezuela.

Juodis, Jurgis—Charged with "assault, arrest, detention and murder of unarmed Jews and others" in Lithuania and Byelorussia between 1941-1944 as officer in Lithuanian Police Battalion (Schutzmannschaft). OSI complaint filed October 26, 1981. No trial date set as of July 29, 1983. Juodis resides in Florida.

Kairys, Liudas—accused of serving with SS auxiliary guard units in Poland, including Treblinka. Court appointed counsel to represent defendant. On March 13, 1981, OSI responded to defendant's discovery requests, pursuant to a court order. Trial ended July 7, 1982. No decision as of July 29, 1983. Resides Chicago, Ill.

Karklins, Talivaldis—accused of persecution and murder in Madona, Latvia, while member of district police and commandant of Madona concentration camp. Defendant's answer to government's complaint due March 30; defendant requested extension. Resided Los Angeles, California; died 1983.

Katin, Matthew—accused of war crimes in Lithuania. Resides Norwood, Mass.

Kowalchuk, Serge and Mykola—brothers accused of atrocities while members of Nazi-controlled Ukrainian police in Luboml, Poland. Discovery phase to be completed. Reside in Philadelphia, Pa. (Citing death of key witness, OSI moved to dismiss complaint against Mykola Kowalchuk, June 5, 1981. Case against Serge Kowalchuk ongoing). On July 1, 1983, Federal District Court ordered him denaturalized. Appeals court reversed his conviction, 1984. OSI has appealed.

Koziy, Bohdan—accused of murder of unarmed civilians in the Ukraine. Depositions being taken in U.S.S.R. Resides Ft. Lauderdale, Fla. Ordered stripped of citizenship on March 29, 1982. Case on appeal. Oral arguments scheduled for summer 1983.

Kungys, Juozas—Charged with having participated in mass murders of Jews and other peoples in wartime Lithuania as a collaborator "in association with the armed forces of Nazi Germany." OSI complaint filed July 22, 1981. Court ruled for the defendant on September 29, 1983, stating that the government did not sustain burden of proof. U.S. District Judge H. Curtis Meanor accused the OSI of "trying to ram through" the case. Kungys, born in Lithuania on September 21, 1915, lives in a largely Jewish neighborhood in Clifton, N.J. OSI has appealed this ruling. Decision awaited.

Linnas, Karl—accused of supervising and participating in execution of prisoners at concentration camp at Tartu, Estonia. Trial adjourned pending taking of depositions in Estonia, and set for June 1981. Resides Greenlawn, New York.

Osidach, Wolodymir—accused of persecution and murder of Jews in the Ukraine. Citizenship ordered revoked by U.S. District Court on March 17, 1981. If he appeals, deportation proceedings likely to be stayed pending appeal. Resides Philadelphia, Pa. (Osidach died in Philadelphia of natural causes on May 26, 1981. The Court's opinion in Osidach is a key ruling in these kinds of cases.)

Palciauskas, Kazys—(See Predicted Prosecutions—Who Are They?) Federal District Court ordered Palciauskas denaturalized March 23, 1983. Deportation trial ongoing.

Schellong, Conrad—accused of serving as company commander of several SS units in concentration camps and training SS recruits for concentration camp guard duty. OSI filed complaint March 17, 1981. Defendant's answer filed May 14, 1981. September 7, 1982, Federal District Court ordered his denaturalization. Deportation trial ongoing. Resides Chicago, Ill.

Schuk, Mykola—Ukrainian police collaborator accused by OSI of having "beaten and killed unarmed Jews and other civilians" during 1941-1944 period in Nazi-occupied Ukraine. Pre-trial activity began July 25, 1983. Case not assigned as of December 1, 1983. (Schuk is also known as Mykola Zuk or Mike Shuk, and was first written about by the author in 1978 and was also one of those cases developed by Allen during his 1978 testimony before the U.S. Congress.)

Sokolov, Vladimir—Actual name, Vladimir Denisovich Samarin. Denaturalization complaint filed against the former Yale faculty member on January 27, 1982. Pre-trial discovery period ongoing as of December 1, 1983.

Sprogis, Elmars—Latvian Deputy Police Chief during Nazi occupation of that country. Charged on June 23, 1982 by the OSI with having "assisted the Nazis" in carrying out murders and plunder of Jewish property as well as having "killed Soviet POWs (Prisoners of War)." Resident of New York City area. Trial date originally set for October 4, 1983.

Theodorovich, George—OSI charged on August 12, 1983 that defendant as a member of a "Nazi-sponsored Ukrainian police force" in Lvov did murder unarmed Jewish citizens in August of 1942. Deportation trial awaiting verdict.

Trucis, Arnolds—accused of persecuting Jews and others 1941-1943 while member of Latvian Auxiliary Security Police and officer in SS Security Police, and as agent of SS' Sicherheitsdienst (SD, Intelligence). Complaint filed by OSI June 20, 1980. A leader of Daugavas Vanagi (Hawks of the Vanagi), a pro-Nazi Latvian organization in the U.S.A. Defendant died December 6, 1981 before case went to trial. Case formally dismissed December 14, 1981. Resided Philadelphia, Pa.

Virkutis, Antanas—On March 14, 1983, OSI charged that defendant as warden of Lithuanian prison under Nazis carried out "physical torture, abuse, starvation and executions" against civilian prisoners and "Allied POWs from the U.S.S.R." from 1941-1944. Defendant resident of Chicago area. Trial date has yet to be set (December 1, 1983).

Von Bolschwing, Otto Albrecht Alfried—worked as an agent for Eichmann's office in the SS, Subsection IV-B-4 of RSHA (Reichssicherheitshauptamt) the Reich Central Security Office, Jewish Affairs; 1934-1941, agent of the SD (Sicherheitsdienst), SS Security/Espionage. Provided intelligence on Jewish organizations, leaders to prepare for deportations in implementing Final Solution of Europe's Six Million. Born Germany 1909. SS #353603. Entered SS 1932. Entered USA in 1950's, naturalized 1959. Claimed he was double-agent for OSS during SD period and a "contract agent" for the CIA late 1940's-1960's. OSI filed denaturalization complaint May 27, 1981 after more than year's investigation on West Coast and Europe. Von Bolschwing also prefers to be called Baron. Resided Carmichael, Ca., suburb of Sacramento. Died 1982.

Deportation Cases

Artukovic, Andrija—accused of signing decrees authorizing executions and persecutions of thousands of Jews, Serbs, gypsies and others, in his capacity as Minister of Interior, Nazi puppet state of Croatia. Order of deportation outstanding against him since 1952. Board of Immigration Appeals (BIA) to decide whether to reconsider order withholding his deportation because of "physical persecution" in Yugoslavia. On appeal to the Ninth Circuit by defendant, the July 1, 1981 decision by the BIA that the accused mass murderer was amenable to deportation as per its original 1953 findings for deportation was effectively set aside. The Ninth Circuit Court of Appeals ruled on December 1, 1982 that the U.S. Government had to hold an entirely new hearing on the Artukovic matter. On March 21, 1983, that appeals court denied OSI request for a rehearing. This meant that the whole case had to be retried; that the matter reverted back to May 9, 1951. In 1984, Artukovic was ordered extradited to Yugoslavia. Action pending final approval of U.S. Secretary of State. Artukovic continues to reside behind armed walls in Surfside (Seal Beach), California.

Benkauskas, Henrikas—accused of war crimes in Lithuania. Resides Chicago, Ill.

Bernotas, Antanas—On July 8, 1983, the U.S. Justice Department sought this resident alien's deportation, charging that he took part in "the arrest, confinement, forced labor, beating/killing of Jews and suspected anti-Nazi political activists," as a Lithuanian Security Police officer during World War II. No hearing has taken place as of December 1, 1983.

*Demjanjuk, John—(See: Denaturalization Cases.) Appeals court affirmed denaturalization June 8, 1982. Deportation action filed July 2, 1982. Defendant failed to appear for hearing. Tracked down and arrested by OSI on July 14, 1982, Demjanjuk was jailed until August 2, 1982, thus becoming the first charged Nazi war criminal to serve a prison sentence here in the United States in connection with trial involving post-war crimes. Deportation proceedings rescheduled for April 1983. Demjanjuk refused to designate a country to which he could be expelled if found deportable. The OSI thereupon named the U.S.S.R. as the country to which he should be sent. On April 11, 1983, John Demjanjuk's deportation trial began. After months of behind-the-scenes negotiations, Israel formally requested his extradition. On November 18, 1983, Demjanjuk was arrested and then bound over for a hearing on that request scheduled for January 23, 1984. Demjanjuk was set free on his own recognizance, then placed on a $50,000 bond. Demjanjuk thus became the first Nazi war crimes suspect arrested for extradition to Israel. Demjanjuk successfully appealed an order that he be extradited to Israel.

Dercacz, Mikhail—Deportation hearings concluded 1983; died 1983.

Detlavs, Karlis—accused of murder of unarmed civilians, primarily Jews, while serving in Latvian Legion. In February 1980, Immigration judge ruled in favor of defendant. OSI appealed decision to BIA. Appeal argued August 4, 1980. On October 15, 1981, the BIA dismissed OSI's appeal. As of December 1, 1983, the OSI still maintained it was "considering various possible courses of action." Resided Baltimore, Md.; died 1983.

*Fedorenko, Feodor—accused of service as armed guard at Treblinka death camp. Citizenship revoked by U.S. Supreme Court January 21, 1981. OSI commenced proceedings seeking deportation March 5, 1981. On February 23, 1983, U.S. Immigration Court in Hartford, Connecticut ordered Fedorenko deported to the U.S.S.R. The court found specifically that Fedorenko had "assist[ed] in thousands of murders" and had "demonstrat[ed] an immense lack of humanity." The defendant appealed on March 8, 1983. Arguments scheduled on appeal in August 1983. As of December 1, 1983, no decision had been made. Six years have passed since Fedorenko's case began, and he has by no means yet exhausted all avenues of appeal. Resides Miami Beach, Fla.; presently living "somewhere in Connecticut."

Hazners, Vilis—accused of atrocities against Jews of Riga while officer of Latvian "Self-Defense Group" and Schutzmannschaft (Nazi-controlled) police organization. Immigration judge ruled for defendant on February 27, 1980. Oral argument by government on appeal presented September 4, 1980 to BIA. Decision awaited. On July 15, 1981, the BIA dismissed outright OSI's appeal. As of December 1, 1983, the OSI stated it was "considering various courses of action." Resides Dresden, New York.

Kaminskas, Bronius—accused of participating in shooting of some 200 Jews in Lithuania and selection of some 400 Jews for execution. Case adjourned indefinitely because of defendant's poor health. Must submit to periodic mental and physical examinations to determine fitness to stand trial. Resides Hartford, Conn.

Kulle, Reinhold—OSI filed complaint December 3, 1982, charging that as an SS guard leader, he persecuted Jews, Poles, Russians and members of Jehovah's Witnesses at the Gross-Rosen Concentration Camp in Silesia from August 1942 to January 1945. Kulle admitted at a preliminary hearing on January 17, 1983 that he was an SS guard at the camp but denied such "duty" provided grounds for deportation. Trial concluded in November 1983. Ordered deported, 1984. 63-year-old alien Chicago, Ill. resident; a West German citizen.

Laipenieks, Edgars—Latvian police official sentenced to death *in absentia* for war crimes at Central Prison in Riga, where most victims were Latvian Jews. CIA agent since 1950's. OSI filed deportation complaint June 2, 1981. Deportation hearings took place January 26 to February 18, 1982. At sessions, Laipenieks admitted he had "beaten with [my] bare hands" certain prisoners so as to "encourage them" to talk during the Riga Prison period. On June 9, 1982, Immigration Judge John C. Williams in San Diego, California, ruled that Laipenieks, the CIA agent and accused Nazi war criminal, was not deportable. OSI's appeal was, however, upheld by the BIA on September 13, 1983. In the most important decision since the Fedorenko case, the BIA found that Edgars Laipenieks had committed war crimes and carried out persecutions against Communists purely because of their political beliefs. The ruling added another dimension to the findings of the American courts regarding the persecution of peoples because of their race, religion and ethnic origins. A citizen of Chile, Laipenieks requested his return to that country. Deportation order reversed; on OSI appeal. Laipenieks continues to live in San Diego, California.

Lehmann, Alexander—Ukrainian deputy chief of police who is charged with mass murder in OSI complaint of November 23, 1981. Preliminary hearings began December 9, 1981; depositions were taken by way of televised (audio-visual) examinations in summer 1982. Trial was set down for October 24, 1983. Following conviction, deportation order stayed because of ill health. Lehmann is 65 years old and a resident of the Cleveland, Ohio area.

*Linnas, Karl—(See Denaturalization Cases) On July 30, 1981, Federal District Court ordered Linnas stripped of citizenship. The court specifically found that Linnas had personally taken part in "atrocities against men, women and children at the Tartu concentration camp" in Estonia. Linnas lost on appeal on January 25, 1982. Move to deport him was taken by the OSI on the same date. Linnas appealed to the BIA on July 8, 1983. Deportation order upheld; question of return to Estonia for trial holding up expulsion.

Maikovskis, Boleslavs—accused of murders of Jewish and other Latvian citizens and rounding-up of gypsies while police chief in Rezekne, Latvia. Deportation hearings began October 1977. On January 9, 1981, BIA reversed the Immigration judge's decision. BIA ruled that depositions may be taken in Soviet territories, and that their admissibility and evidentiary weight are to be determined by the Immigration judge after they are taken. On January 21, 1981, Immigration judge then ordered that the depositions be taken in Latvia, and they were requested for May 1981. On July 30, 1983, U.S. Immigration Judge Francis J. Lyons ruled defendant was not deportable. The OSI correctly reported that Judge Lyons "found that Maikovskis had indeed participated in mass arrests . . . at Audrini and in the burning of the village. The Court (Lyons) also found that he (Maikovskis) had concealed his (SS-collaborator) police employment in order to procure a U.S. immigration visa." But Judge Lyons ruled Maikovskis' admitted involvement in persecution was not "adequately proved" and his admitted concealment was not "material." The OSI has appealed this case to the BIA. As of June 1985, deportation order on appeal. Resides Mineola, New York.

Palciauskas, Kazys—(See Predicted Prosecutions—Who Are They?) Federal District Court ordered Palciauskas denaturalized March 23, 1983. Deportation trial ongoing.

*Paskevicius, Mecis—accused of murder of Jews and others while admittedly serving in Lithuanian Security Police. By consent judgment, U.S. District Court in Los Angeles on August 23, 1979 revoked citizenship. On December 16, 1980, found mentally incompetent to stand trial. Must submit to periodic mental and physical examinations to monitor fitness to stand trial. Official residence: Los Angeles, Ca. Temporary residence: St. Petersburg, Fla.

Schellong, Conrad—accused of serving as company commander of several SS units in concentration camps and training SS recruits for concentration camp guard duty. OSI filed complaint March 17, 1981. Defendant's answer filed May 14, 1981. September 7, 1982, Federal District Court ordered his denaturalization. Deportation trial ongoing. Resides Chicago, Ill.

Theodorovich, George—OSI charged on August 12, 1983 that defendant as a member of a "Nazi-sponsored Ukrainian police force" in Lvov did murder unarmed Jewish citizens in August of 1942. Deportation trial awaiting verdict.

Cases No Longer Active

Avdzej, John—Charged with war crimes in Byelorussia. Gave up citizenship; today resides in West Germany.

Deutscher, Albert—Ukrainian accused of participating in mass murders as member of a pro-Nazi paramilitary unit there in 1942. OSI filed denaturalization complaint December 17, 1981. On December 18, 1981, Deutscher, a resident of Chicago, was killed by a train. The coroner ruled his death a suicide.

*Fedorenko, Feodor—accused of service as armed guard at Treblinka death camp. Citizenship revoked by U.S. Supreme Court January 21, 1981. OSI commenced proceedings seeking deportation March 5, 1981. On February 23, 1983, U.S. Immigration Court in Hartford, Connecticut ordered Fedorenko deported to the U.S.S.R. The court found specifically that Fedorenko had "assist[ed] in thousands of murders" and had "demonstrat[ed] an immense lack of humanity." Deported to U.S.S.R. in 1984, not to Poland where crimes were committed. Disposition today unknown.

Karklins, Talivaldis (See Denaturalization Cases) Defendant died in a hospital in California on February 9, 1983, one month before his denaturalization trial was slated to start.

Kisielaitis, Juozas—Lithuanian war criminal, deported to Canada 1985, resides in Calgary. Visits U.S. despite ban to entry of any deported war criminal.

Lipschis, Hans J.—Resident alien born on November 7, 1919 in Lithuania. A citizen of West Germany. Admitted ten days before going to scheduled December 23, 1982 trial that he had been an SS-Rottenfuehrer (Corporal) in the SS-Totenkopf Sturmbann (SS-Death's Head Battalion) at the death camp, Auschwitz-Birkenau. Thus he did not contest the order of deportation. He had also been wanted for war crimes by the Allies in 1946. The OSI noted in its July 29, 1983 Summary Report of its ongoing cases that "Lipschis' deportation was carried out on April 14, 1983 when he flew by commercial airliner to West Germany." The OSI did not note that Lipschis successfully avoided the OSI and the FBI and flew off to West Germany, using his own credit card, where he was welcomed by family and friends. The OSI provided the West German prosecutors its evidence on Lipschis. Nothing yet has been done about his possible prosecution in West Germany. After his arrival, Lipschis sent the OSI a bill for his air fare back home. The OSI has vowed not to pay that bill. Lipschis, as the OSI noted, "became the first person deported from the U.S. on Nazi war crimes charges in more than 30 years." Actually, he is the first person to leave for more than 33 years. Technically, he is the first person ever to be deported as the specific object of anti-Nazi war criminals denaturalization/deportation proceedings that began in 1972. In point of fact, he is the first such deported—by his own hand, so to speak—in 38 years since Nazi war criminals and collaborators first reached these shores after World War II.

Osidach, Wolodymir—(See Denaturalization Cases) On May 26, 1981, Osidach died.

Popczuk, Michael—Ukrainian policeman who was charged with persecution of Jews by the OSI in a denaturalization complaint filed on June 28, 1983. On July 6, 1983, Popczuk was found shot to death in his home in Lynn, Massachusetts. His death was ruled a suicide.

Rudolph, Arthur Louis Hugo—Prominent Nazi rocket scientist. Directed use of slave labor; self-admitted participant in crimes against humanity. Chose to leave U.S. in 1984 after years with NASA and major American military contractors. Lives in West Germany; will not face prosecution there.

Soobzokov, Tscherim*,**—In 1979 the OSI filed a complaint seeking his denaturalization for having allegedly concealed his past as a member of proscribed Nazi military units including the Waffen SS during World War II. OSI withdrew action 1980. Utilization by intelligence agencies indicated. Local Democratic Party leader, resident, Paterson, N.J.

*Trifa, Valerian—Iron Guardist accused of persecuting Jews of Romania and inciting January 1941 Bucharest pogrom. Voluntarily consented to denaturalization September 3, 1980, and then filed appeal on consent judgment. Government's motion to dismiss or advance hearing pending before Sixth Circuit Court of Appeals. May 15, 1981, OSI filed for denial of Trifa's appeal. Denial is anticipated, followed by initiation of deportation proceedings on November 3, 1981. On October 7, 1982, Trifa, an Archbishop of the Romanian Orthodox Episcopacy in America, conceded his own deportability in order to avoid a full hearing at which the entire record of his Nazi background would have been revealed. He was promptly ordered deported within a 60-day period (that is, December 7, 1982). His first choice, Switzerland, rejected him. "We do not import war criminals," a Swiss official said. There have been long negotiations with Israel for his extradition to that country. Romania—where Trifa committed his war crimes—has studiously avoided demands for Trifa's return to face justice there. Trifa successfully remained in the United States for more than eight and a half years since the U.S. government moved to expel him. He resided at the Church's luxurious estate, the Vatra, at Grass Lake, Michigan, some 50 miles west of Detroit. More than a dozen Iron Guard veterans of the Holocaust also resided there as "priests." Expelled from U.S. 1983; now in Portugal.

Trucis, Arnolds—(See Denaturalization Cases)—Trucis died on December 6, 1981 at the age of 72 in Philadelphia, Pa. Case formally dismissed on December 14, 1981.

Von Bolschwing, Otto Albrecht Alfried—(See Denaturalization Cases)—He agreed to a consent judgment on December 22, 1981. Case did not go to trial because of von Bolschwing's illness. He died in a Sacramento, California hospital "in early March 1982," according to the OSI. All of the documents concerning his SS and alleged U.S. intelligence involvements have been sealed.

*Case originated as denaturalization action.

Predicted Prosecutions—Who Are They?

In the summer of 1979, Charles R. Allen, Jr. learned the identity of 37 major cases under review by the OSI. In many instances, their common characteristic was indication of formerly hidden U.S. government utilization. When Mr. Allen confronted the OSI with his list (based on his own investigations and analysis), the OSI refused comment.

Arranged alphabetically with brief descriptions, this list follows, containing the charges and allegations against these individuals reflected in the files of the OSI. An asterisk (*) after a name means government utilization is indicated. A double asterisk (**) means the OSI began prosecution *after the fact of Mr. Allen's listing*. (Data from Mr.

Allen's copyrighted article written for the September 1979 *Jewish Veteran*. Jewish War Veterans of the U.S.A. decided editorially not to publish the list in their magazine so as not to preempt the OSI at the start of its work. That list is published here, in abridged, copyrighted form.)

Bryzgys, Vincentas* — Roman Catholic Bishop, accused of collaboration with Nazi occupation and persecution of Jews in Lithuania. Ranking prelate in Chicago, Ill. today.

Caks, Raimunds* — Latvian journalist, Nazi propagandist during Nazi occupation of his homeland. Member of terrorist Perkonkrust. Last known residence Milwaukee, Wisc.

Cenkus, Stasys* — Top Lithuanian Gestapo agent as Chief, Lithuanian State Security Police. Member terrorist Iron Wolf. One of the five top war criminals in U.S. Utilized by at least three U.S. intelligence agencies. Lives Howard Beach, Queens, N.Y. (Grandfather of professional tennis player, Vitas Gerulaitis, who himself has been quoted by the press as using antisemitic slander.)

Dancis, Augustus* — Latvian police collaborator and SD agent charged with murders in Alukene District, Latvia. Last known residence, New York, N.Y.

Ernstons, Janis Arnold* — Former Latvian cleric, Gestapo agent, member terrorist Perkonkrust. Resides San Francisco, Ca.

Futala, Lew* — Ukrainian, member of antisemitic OUN (Organization of Ukrainian Nationalists). Charged with antisemitic acts as Nazi collaborator. Resides Yonkers, N.Y.

Hutyrczyk, Sergis* — Sentenced *in absentia* for crimes as concentration camp guard in Byelorussia, U.S.S.R. Resides New Brunswick, N.J.

Illing, Alexander R.* — Nazi collaborator as Ukrainian police chief. Resides Fresno, Ca.

Kairys, Liudas** — See section on Who Are They?— Denaturalization Cases.

Katkins, Zigurds* — Sentenced to death *in absentia* 1962 for war crimes as Latvian police official and Gestapo agent. Resides Boston, Mass. (since early 1950's).

Klimaitis (Klimavicius), Jonas* — Lithuanian Army officer, member terrorist Iron Wolf, charged with directing murders of 3,800 Lithuanian Jews in Kaunas military forts, July 1941. Gestapo reports list him working with Einsatzgruppen squads, 1941-1942. Has resided in New York, Cleveland, Chicago.

Koreh, Ferenc* — Hungarian lawyer, member of fascist Arrow/Cross Party, wrote antisemitic articles. Found guilty of Nazi collaboration, sentenced in Budapest as a war criminal to one and a half years imprisonment, five years loss of civil rights. Employed by Radio Free Europe. Resides Englewood, N.J.

Mackevicius, Mecislovas* — Lithuanian official of Nazi occupation charged with signing various genocidal decrees. Last known residence, Chicago, Ill.

Macs, Edmund Gustav* — Latvian cleric charged with participation in deportations of Jews. Retired clergyman, resides Tacoma, Wash.

Nesaule, Peter* — Latvian cleric charged with collaboration as Gestapo agent. Employee of Radio Free Europe. Resides San Francisco, Ca.

Palciauskas, Kazys* — Lithuanian official of Nazi occupation. Signed antisemitic decrees, deportation orders. Last known residence, Los Angeles, Ca. (**OSI filed denaturalization complaint mid-June 1981.)

Popov, Ivan* — Ukrainian police officer worked with Einsatzgruppen D, antisemitic murder squads. Poses as "John Nichols" in Miami, Fla. area.

Rabacs, Karlis* — Latvian journalist, Nazi collaborator now editing Latvian language newspaper in New York, N.Y.

Radchenko, Pavel F. — Ukrainian police officer, extreme nationalist, charged with anti-Jewish "actions." Last known residence (1960's) Cleveland, Ohio.

Samarin, Vladimir D.*,** — Russian collaborator as Nazi newspaper editor, Oriel, RSFSR, responsible for antisemitic editorials urging genocide. Faculty member, Yale University, until 1978. Resides New Haven, Conn., lives incognito elsewhere in New England and New York City. (See Who Are They?—Denaturalization Cases)

Sautins, Karlis — Latvian cleric, Gestapo agent, Radio Free Europe employee in 1950's. Last known residence Cleveland, Ohio.

Schatoff, M.B.* — Former Red Army officer, Chief, Personal Security for Gen. Andrei Vlasov (hanged for treason, Moscow, 1946). "Vlasov Army" official wanted for war crimes in U.S.S.R. Member, Columbia University faculty. "Consultant" with CIA and Pentagon. Long-time New York City resident.

Sterns, Alfreds* — Latvian police official, superior of Edgars Laipenieks (see above). Nazi collaborator. Resides New York, N.Y.

Strughold, Hubertus* — World-famous physiologist, retired chief medical scientist, U.S. Air Force. NASA (National Aeronautics and Space Administration) consultant. Charged with complicit knowledge of experiments on human beings at Dachau concentration camp while director of Nazi Luftwaffe (Air Force) Medical Research Center, Berlin. Resides San Antonio, Tex.

Szulc, Johanna* — Guard and guard supervisor at several Nazi concentration camps. Resides New York, N.Y.

Tulis, Peteris — Latvian police official wanted for war crimes in U.S.S.R. Resides Philadelphia, Pa.

Wanko, Annemarie — Austrian physician and Nazi collaborator charged with experiments on camp prisoners. Resides New York, N.Y.

Warvariv, Constantine* — Charged with collaboration as Ukrainian employee of Nazi administration and SS in Rovno. Eyewitness testimonies place him working with SD unit there. Presently official of U.S. State Dept., Washington, D.C.

Woerner, Ottocar Anton — Former Waffen SS officer charged with participation in atrocities on Eastern Front. Last known residence, Lake Grove, N.Y.

Zakevicius, Stasys* — Official of Nazi puppet regime Lithuania. Signed various antisemitic decrees. Resides Los Angeles, Ca.

Zamuels, Voldemars* — Latvian police officer collaborated with Einsatzgruppen A forces in sweeps of Latvia. Resides New York, N.Y.

Zeltins Teodors* — Latvian journalist, Nazi collaborator, founder of "The Antisemitic Institute" during German occupation of his homeland. Last reported (1970's) in Milwaukee, Wisc. and Chicago, Ill. areas.

Action: What Can You Do?

Educate members of your community—Jewish and non-Jewish—about Nazi war criminals in America. The issue should be on the agenda of every concerned organization, including churches and synagogues, civic and veterans groups, Jewish Federations and community relations committees. If you are affiliated with any such organizations, suggest speakers, seminars or audio-visuals about the topic. Urge that the issue be explored in high school and college Holocaust classes. Contact your local media—radio, television and newspapers—to cover this breaking story. (To order copies of this booklet, see Yellow Pages.)

Find out if there are any Nazi war criminals or organizations in your area, and organize appropriately lawful and peaceful action. In addition, search out witnesses to atrocities committed by Nazi war criminals now living here. If a deportation or denaturalization hearing is held in your area, encourage lawful and proper attendance. This serves the two-fold purpose of educating community members and providing moral support for survivor-witnesses. (Witnesses from Israel and elsewhere may also appreciate efforts by your community to welcome them and provide hospitality.) Express your concern to pertinent government officials (listed below).

What Individuals and Organizations Should You Contact?

U.S. Government Officials

- President Ronald Reagan
  The White House
  Washington, D.C. 20500

- Your Congressperson
  House Office Building
  Washington, D.C. 20515

- Your Senators
  Senate Office Building
  Washington, D.C. 20510

- Neal M. Sher, Director
  Office of Special Investigations (OSI)
  U.S. Department of Justice
  P.O. Box 28603
  Washington, D.C. 20005
  (202) 633-2503

- Members of the Judiciary Subcommittee on Immigration, Refugees and International Law, U.S. House of Representatives:
  Rep. Romano Mazzoli, Chairman (D-Ky)
  Rep. Hamilton Fish, Jr. (R-NY)
  Rep. Barney Frank (D-Mass)
  Rep. Sam Hall (D-Tex)
  Rep. Dan Ludgren (R-Ca)
  Rep. Bill McCollum (R-Fla)
  Rep. Patricia Schroeder (D-Col)
  House Office Building
  Washington, D.C. 20515
  Subcommittee telephone: (202) 225-5727

National Organizations

- Office of the National Commander
  AMVETS
  1710 Rhode Island Avenue N.W.
  Washington, D.C. 20036
  (202) 223-9550

- Office of the National Commander
  Jewish War Veterans of the U.S.A.
  1811 R St., N.W.
  Washington, D.C. 20009
  (202) 265-6280

- Mr. Yehuda Hellman, Executive Director
  Conference of Presidents of Major American Jewish Organizations
  515 Park Avenue
  New York, N.Y. 10022
  (212) PL 2-1616

- Mr. Abraham J. Bayer
  National Jewish Community Relations Advisory Council
  443 Park Avenue South
  New York, N.Y. 10016
  (212) 684-6950

- Mr. David Geller
  American Jewish Committee
  165 E. 56 Street
  New York, N.Y. 10022
  (212) PL 1-4000

- Mr. Phil Baum
  American Jewish Congress
  15 E. 84 Street
  New York, N.Y. 10028
  (212) TR 9-4500

- Mr. Abraham Foxman
  Anti-Defamation League of B'nai B'rith
  823 United Nations Plaza
  New York, N.Y. 10017
  (212) 490-2525

- Simon Wiesenthal Holocaust Center
  9760 W. Pico Blvd.
  Los Angeles, Ca. 90035
  (213) 553-9036

- Mr. Albert J. Abrams
  National Association of Jewish Legislators
  45 Thorndale Road
  Slingerlands, N.Y. 12159
  (518) 439-9597

- Mr. John Ranz
  The Generation After
  2747 Throop Avenue
  New York, N.Y. 10469
  (212) 231-5456

- Rabbi Paul B. Silton
  Committee to Bring Nazi War Criminals to Justice
  Temple Israel
  600 New Scotland Avenue
  Albany, New York, 12208
  (518) 438-7858

A Lesson in Duplicity as U.S. Lets Nazi War Criminal Avoid Justice

Charles R. Allen, Jr.

NEW YORK—There can be little gratification here over the expulsion from our shores of the self-certified Nazi war criminal, Archbishop Valerian D. Trifa of Romania.

The 34-year presence here of this inciter of the 1941 Bucharest pogrom has been an insolent mockery of Europe's six million martyred Jews, a travesty of our own laws and presumed commitment to a new post-Holocaust morality.

The curious arrangement which has allowed Trifa, the abettor of genocide, to fly to retirement on the sunny beaches of Portugal grotesquely twists the long-festering issue of Nazi war criminals and collaborators who have found haven in the United States.

Under the legal and moral commitments which we prominently authored in several instances at the height of the Holocaust (the Moscow Declaration of 1943) and after the war (Nuremberg 1946) and in subsequent international compacts, we solemnly covenanted "to pursue them [war criminals/collaborators] to the uttermost ends of the earth and deliver them to their accusers in order that Justice may be done." (Moscow, 1943)

International law developments since then have reinforced this commitment to the point where any legitimately concerned nation may request such criminals to satisfy justice and we are obliged to hand them over.

Trifa committed his crimes—which he in effect admitted when he consented to an order of deportation nearly two years ago—in Romania, not Portugal.

But from the first, Romania had equivocated about him, even though he had been found guilty of war crimes by its own courts.

The U.S. government not once publicly called Romania to account for its evasions in the Trifa matter.

For the past year, discussions have been held with Israel, a logical choice to receive Trifa for trial after Romania's silence. The two nations failed to reach a *modus vivendi.*

For whatever reasons, failure to deport Trifa to stand trial and face justice is in itself morally reprehensible. All parties to this "arrangement" are responsible.

For the past several years, I have warned that the U.S. government might well try to avoid its grave duty to hand over for trial proven Nazi war criminals in our midst.

Stephen S. Trott of the Justice Department announced with satisfaction, "Our mission was to remove Trifa from this country . . . and that has been accomplished."

Our mission, in fact, is to deport them to justice.

The arrangement allowing Trifa to go to Portugal smacks of chicanery, at least. The Justice Department did not publicly and aggressively seek his deportation to be properly tried for war crimes. Indeed, Trifa spent nearly two years shopping around among five countries until he was accepted by Portugal on a 90-day visa.

The State Department knew last December that Portugal gave Trifa a visa. Not a word was uttered to the American people of such knowledge.

The claim by Portugal that it did not know who Trifa was, that his visa application just "floated through routine" procedures, and that the U.S. State Department did not discuss the matter with the nation that originally was the first fascist government in Europe is preposterous.

The meaning of Trifa's escape from justice is undeniably clear for the American people, indeed the world. After nearly 40 years of providing refuge for known Nazi war criminals, after years of using them (including Trifa, who was utilized by the CIA's Radio Free Europe and the FBI), the American government has decided not to ensure final retribution for those found guilty under our own laws of having participated in the Final Solution.

Failure to deport Nazi war criminals to face justice for the crimes they have committed is denial of justice.

This is the meaning of Trifa's escape from justice.

Is this what we are to expect—and accept—with the dozen or so cases of deportation orders that will become final over the ensuing year for the genocidists among us?

Charles R. Allen, Jr.'s latest book, From Hitler to Uncle Sam: How American Intelligence Used Accused Nazi War Criminals, *is scheduled for 1985 release.*

9

The Nature of Holocaust Revisionism

Aaron Breitbart

Despite insightfully accurate descriptions of the Holocaust as history's best documented crime, an insidious effort has been launched to discredit the horrific tragedy as nothing more than a gross exaggeration, if not an outright lie. While the phenomenon commonly known as "Holocaust revisionism" has roots in works dating back to the late 40's, it is only within the last decade that a concerted effort has been made to discredit the victims, liberators, journalists, photographers, jurists, public officials, and historians who bear witness to the Nazi genocide and "Final Solution." Speculating that the general public, especially the post-war generation, will find the crimes of the Third Reich too horrible to be believed, revisionist authors have professed that the crematoria at Auschwitz were used only to bake bread, that Zyklon B gas was dispensed solely to delouse camp inmates, and that the relatively "few" Jews who died were victims of typhus. Indeed, from the revisionist perspective, these deaths should be lain upon the shoulders of the Allies who prevented the S.S. from reaching concentration camps such as Bergen-Belsen with "medical supplies." While not all revisionist claims are quite as bizarre, some impose even greater strains upon the imagination. *The Secret Holocaust,* for instance, published by "Aryan Nations," insists that a 20th century Holocaust did indeed occur and was perpetrated by European Jews against their Gentile neighbors. Interestingly, if not surprisingly, the victims of this massacre are said to number 66 million.

At this point, one must question the motives of the revisionist school. Are these pseudo-historians nothing more than first cousins to the flat earth advocates, whose members seek a harmless means of self expression? Do those who deny the authenticity of Anne Frank's diary realize that two plus two is really four, but cannot make headlines unless they can prove it is five?

To be sure, there are individuals for whom the tragedy of the Holocaust is simply too much to bear. For them, sleep comes much easier by dismissing the ghastly visions of burning flesh as nothing more than a nightmare. The revisionist school, however, includes few if any of those whose denial is therapeutically mandated.

Professor Yehuda Bauer asserts that the goal of Holocaust revisionism is the renewal of Nazi ideology, an ideology that must be cleansed of the stain of the Holocaust before it can hope to gain widespread acceptance; hence the whitewashing of S.S. crimes and the justification of the Hitler state.

An article written by Marvin Perry of New York's Baruch College demonstrates that Holocaust revisionism is a brilliant twist to the age-old Jewish conspiracy theory. In yet another of many attempts to achieve world power, Jews fabricated the Holocaust, hoping to extort millions from guilt-ridden Germans to finance "expansionist" Israel.

In either case, there is little doubt that the underlying core of Holocaust revisionism is the spectre of anti-semitism. In essence, the revisionists are stating that Jews are scheming, pathological liars. By peddling their anti-semitism under the cloak of "research," revisionists hope to portray themselves as academicians rather than neo-Nazi ideologists.

The jewel in the crown of revisionism is the California based Institute for Historical Review. Commonly known as the I.H.R., the Institute, though well-funded, has no official address other than a post office box number. The I.H.R. was the 1978 brainchild of Willis Carto. Carto, a notorious antisemite, also founded the Liberty Lobby, acknowledged by experts as America's best funded hate group. *The Spotlight,* the official publication of the Liberty Lobby, is rife with diatribes against American Jewry and the state of Israel. In addition to the ads it accepts from various hate organizations, *The Spotlight* regularly prints ads for I.H.R. materials and features articles in support of Nazi war criminals living in the United States.

The modus operandi of the Institute for Historical Review includes the publication and distribution of revisionist literature, packaged in a scholarly guise, to individuals and academic institutions who may not be aware of the true nature of the organization. In addition, the I.H.R. sponsors annual conferences which have drawn hundreds of participants. I.H.R. ties to other hate groups are well documented. A recent issue of the Aryan Nations magazine, *Calling Our Nation,* featured an interview with I.H.R. director, Tom Marcellus. It comes as no surprise that virtually every hate organization on either side of the Atlantic has adopted Holocaust revisionism as dogma. Equally obvious is the fact that this pseudo-history is merely the newest symptom of an age old disease.

Who's Who in Revisionists

Butz, Arthur ... Professor of computer science at Northwestern University ... author of *The Hoax of the Twentieth Century,* claiming the fabrication of the Holocaust by Jews seeking to enlist support for Israel by appealing to popular guilt feelings.

Carto, Willis ... founder of the Institute for Historical Review (1978) in Torrance, California. The I.H.R. publishes journals and sponsors conventions designed to whitewash Nazi war crimes by denying the Holocaust. Carto is also the treasurer of the "Liberty Lobby" in Washington, D.C. The "Liberty Lobby" publishes the *Spotlight,* a weekly publication long known for its diatribes against Israel and the American Jewish community.

Degrelle, Leon... author of articles in praise of the S.S., of which he was a member ... currently hiding in Spain to escape a death sentence for war crimes committed in his native Belgium ... contributor to the I.H.R. Journal.

Faurisson, Robert ... holds a Ph.D. from the Sorbonne in Paris ... was dismissed from his position as professor of French at the University of Lyons for revisionist views and convicted by a French court for defaming the victims of the Holocaust ... denies the gassing of Jews at Nazi concentration camps.

Irving, David ... British historian and author of *Hitler's War ...* claims that Hitler had no knowledge of any extermination program ... speaker at I.H.R. conventions.

McCalden, David ... also known as Lewis Brandon, co-founder of the Institute for Historical Review ... sponsor of "Truth Missions," a front for the defamation of Simon Wiesenthal and the propagation of Holocaust revisionism in Manhattan Beach, California.

Smith, Bradley ... publisher of *Prima Facie,* a media oriented monthly geared to the denial of the Holocaust and the libel of Nazi hunters.

Weber, Charles... Professor of German at the University of Tulsa ... author of *The Holocaust: 120 Questions and Answers,* a conglomeration of distortions and half truths trivializing Nazi guilt during World War II. Contributor to the I.H.R. Journal.

Zundel, Ernst ... German-Canadian revisionist and owner of Samizdat Publishing in Toronto ... Distributor of pro-Nazi literature ... convicted on charges for knowingly spreading false information about the Holocaust.

10

Audit of Antisemitic Incidents in America

Anti-Defamation League of B'nai B'rith

The frequency of antisemitic vandalism and of other attacks against Jewish institutions, businesses and homes in the U.S. during 1984 showed a small increase compared to 1983. The number of antisemitic vandalism incidents at Jewish institutions and privately-owned properties reported by Anti-Defamation League offices around the country was 715, an increase of 6.7% compared to the 670 incidents reported during 1983. The 1984 increase interrupted declines of 19.2% in 1983 and 14.9% in 1982. The declines followed two years—1980 and 1981—in each of which vandalism incidents more than doubled: 192% in 1980 and 158% in 1981.

The number of antisemitic vandalisms, including more serious crimes such as bombings, attempted bombings, arsons, attempted arsons and cemetery desecrations, recorded by the ADL Audit in recent years is as follows:

1979—129	1982—829
1980—377	1983—670
1981—974	1984—715

More Serious Incidents

More serious incidents monitored by the ADL as part of the vandalisms in the Annual Audit—bombings, attempted bombings, arsons, attempted arsons and cemetery desecrations—increased during 1984. There were three bombings in 1984 compared to none in 1983; there was one attempted bombing in 1984, the same as in 1983. Arsons rose noticeably; there were nine in 1984 compared to three in 1983, but attempted arsons dropped slightly, to eight in 1984 from 10 in 1983. Cemetery desecrations increased to 11 in 1984 from nine in 1983.

The picture with respect to these more serious violations in recent years is as follows:

	Arsons	Attempted Arsons	Bombings	Attempted Bombings	Cemetery Desecrations	Total
1979	10	0	2	0	0	12
1980	10	2	4	2	5	23
1981	10	6	4	2	15	37
1982	7	7	3	0	15	32
1983	3	10	0	1	9	23
1984	9	8	3	1	11	32

In 1984, as in the past, the overwhelming majority of the incidents reported, based on those cases in which arrests were made, appeared to be the work of teenagers. In only five of the 3,694 vandalisms recorded during the last six years—a fraction over 1%—has there been evidence of organized hate group involvement, the last in 1981.

In a separate category of assaults against Jewish individuals, and threats and harassments in which Jewish individuals or Jewish-owned properties were the victims or targets, the picture in 1984 was also similar to that recorded in 1983: there were 369 such incidents reported in 1984 compared to 350 in 1983, an increase of 5.4%.

Antisemitism in the U.S.

In reading the 1984 ADL Audit of Antisemitic Incidents, it should be borne in mind that while the Audit provides a useful yardstick for measuring an aspect of anti-Jewish hostility in the country, it is not the only such yardstick.

Antisemitism in the United States manifests itself in various ways:

● In national and local political campaigns;

● In the antisemitic rhetoric of various Arab representatives in the halls of the United Nations;

● In the antisemitism promoted around the world by the Soviet Union in the guise of "anti-Zionism";

● In the anti-Israel and anti-Zionist propaganda carried on by pro-Arab and pro-PLO organizations in the U.S. that often tends to mask hostility to Jews;

● In the propaganda activities of organized right-wing anti-Jewish hate groups, such as the KKK, neo-Nazi groups, Willis Carto's Liberty Lobby, and Lyndon LaRouche's operations.

● In the activities of radical leftist organizations such as the Communist Party USA whose propaganda against Israel and Zionism attacks the most basic concerns of the overwhelming majority of Jews in the United States and around the world.

Publicized Incidents

Several incidents in 1984 attracted considerable media attention. In April, a synagogue in Boise, Idaho, was bombed. Damage was estimated at $5,000 to $6,000. Because Idaho rarely has been the scene of antisemitic vandalism or other anti-Jewish violations, the synagogue bombing in Boise was unusual. The militantly antisemitic and violence-prone Aryan Nations organization, which has its headquarters at Hayden Lake, Idaho, disclaimed any connection with the as yet unsolved bombing.

Co-op City, a massive apartment complex in The Bronx, New York, was the scene of antisemitic and racial vandalisms on 17 separate days beginning in April and continuing through November; these remain unsolved. On these days, and at various buildings in the giant complex, antisemitic graffiti, including swastikas and anti-Jewish epithets were smeared on apartment doors; the vandals concentrated mostly on those apartments displaying mezuzahs on their doorposts. Some of the antisemitic—and the racist—graffiti was smeared on hallway walls, elevator walls and stairwells.

In October, a newly-opened synagogue in Manalapan, New Jersey, was vandalized when a bulldozer parked on the grounds was driven into a wall of the building. In addition to the damage caused by the bulldozer, the temple was defaced by antisemitic slogans and epithets. Three teenagers were arrested and charged with the vandalism. A few days later, two teenagers were arrested in connection with an earlier vandalism and attempted arson at another Manalapan synagogue in which a Molotov cocktail was hurled at the house of worship. Two of the teenagers charged in the bulldozing episode were also charged in connection with the earlier arson attempt.

Multiple or Repetitive Incidents

The experience at Co-op City—of multiple and repetitive antisemitic vandalism in apartment houses or in a particular neighborhood—was a pattern reported from some other locations around the country—Philadelphia, Pennsylvania; Salem, Massachusetts; Knoxville, Tennessee; Atlanta, Georgia; Los Angeles and San Francisco, California. No arrests have been reported in connection with any of these episodes.

The 1984 Geographic Breakdown

The 715 incidents of antisemitic vandalism took place in 32 states and the District of Columbia, the same total of states as in 1983. Once again, as in recent years, New York and California were the states reporting the largest number of antisemitic vandalisms—New York with 237 and California with 99. New York increased by 22 incidents compared to 1983 but California decreased by 12. Maryland with 69, an increase of 22 incidents over 1983, moved from fourth place to third. New Jersey, with 56—a decrease of one—dropped from third to fourth place. Florida, with 51 incidents reported—up nine—remained in fifth place.

These five states were followed by Pennsylvania (28, up 9), Massachusetts (20, down 16) and Illinois (19, no change compared to 1983).

The Northeastern region, comprising seven states and the District of Columbia, accounted for roughly 60% of the total number of antisemitic vandalisms reported. In 1983, these states accounted for 58% of the total. The Northeastern states are: Massachusetts (20), Rhode Island (7), Connecticut (5), New York (237), New Jersey (56), Pennsylvania (28), Maryland (69) and the District of Columbia (10).

In nine Southern states, 98 vandalism incidents were reported—13.7% of the 1984 total—compared to 73 such incidents which formed 10.9% of the 1983 total. The nine Southern states are: Florida (51), Georgia (15), Louisiana (9), Virginia (9), Mississippi (5), Texas (5), Arkansas (3), Tennessee (3), and North Carolina (1).

The Midwest—Illinois (19), Minnesota (15), Michigan (7), Ohio (6), Indiana (4), Missouri (2), Iowa (1), Nebraska (1) and Wisconsin (1)—showed a noticeable decline in 1984 compared to 1983. Fifty-six antisemitic vandalisms were reported in these states during 1984 compared to 80 in 1983. The Midwest accounted for 7.8% of the total number of such incidents in 1984 compared to 11.9% in 1983.

The Western region of the country showed practically no change compared to 1983. The seven states of the region—California (99), Arizona (10), Washington (7), Colorado (6), Oregon (2), Idaho (1) and New Mexico (1)—had 126 incidents of antisemitic vandalism which comprised 17.6% of the total. In 1983, there were 127 such incidents reported in these states, which formed 19% of last year's total.

Assaults, Threats and Harassments

Although the total number of assaults against Jewish individuals, and threats and harassments in which Jewish individuals or Jewish-owned properties were the targets remained practically unchanged—369 in 1984 compared to 350 in 1983—there was a near reversal in the "mix" comprising this year's total. The number of incidents in which Jewish institutions were the targets of threats by mail or telephone, or of other anti-Jewish harassment, increased markedly—from 39 in 1983 to 106 in 1984. The number of such incidents in which Jewish individuals were the targets or the victims dropped by 48—from 311 in 1983 to 263 in 1984.

Arrests

During 1984, police and law enforcement authorities arrested 84 persons in connection with 51 of the total number of incidents reported. In 1983, 115 persons were arrested in connection with 55 of the incidents. In 1984, as in previous ADL Audits, the overwhelming majority of those arrested were aged 20 or under; 73 of the 84 persons arrested—87%—were 20 or younger.

ADL Security Handbook

During 1984, the Anti-Defamation League of B'nai B'rith published and distributed across the country a security handbook aimed at preventing—and coping with—destructive violence against persons and property, including such violence motivated by religious or racial prejudice. The document—*Security for Community Institutions*—was prepared in cooperation with the Crime Prevention Section of the New York City Police Department. It was based on ADL's experience in monitoring and countering anti-Jewish vandalism and other crimes aimed at Jews, Jewish institutions, and Jewish-owned property. It reflected the knowledge gained by the League and its 30 regional offices in working closely with law enforcement agencies from coast to coast and in co-sponsoring security conferences and workshops involving police, educators, and community organizations.

The ADL handbook received endorsements from local and Federal law enforcement officials in Boston, Los Angeles, New Jersey and Washington, D.C.

It outlined proper security measures and procedures for community institutions, proper reaction when incidents occur, provided details of security programs carried out by the New York City Police Department's Crime Prevention Section and its Bias Incident Investigating Unit, first of its kind in the nation, a model form for reporting incidents of violence to local police departments, and the text of a model statute developed by ADL as a tool to assist law enforcement agencies to cope with problems such as vandalism against religious and ethnic institutions.

Evaluation and Conclusion

It is disturbing that the declines in antisemitic vandalism recorded in the ADL Audits of 1982 and 1983 have been interrupted by the 6.7% increase recorded in 1984. The latest total of 715 incidents, however, is substantially lower than the peak of 974 recorded in 1981. The 6.7% increase this year is moderate, however, when compared to the skyrocketing increases of 192% and 158% recorded in 1980 and 1981.

That there were 715 incidents of antisemitic violence indicates clearly that counteractive measures and social "preventive medicine" are still very much needed: stricter laws against violence motivated by antisemitic and racial bigotry, stricter law enforcement, greater media attention to the problem of antisemitic violence, more education for understanding and good will in the schools and churches, more community meetings to map counter measures, and more vocal community response to incidents of violence motivated by hate. In short, more hard work, more vigilance, more education and more good will must take place in communities around the country before the nation can be free of the scourge of violence motivated by ignorance and prejudice.

The teenage vandals who appear overwhelmingly to be responsible for much of the anti-Jewish vandalism must be dealt with firmly by American communities, and their offenses punished and repudiated by community and church leaders and by all citizens of good will.

A model can be seen in the response of the community of Manalapan, New Jersey, where the five teenagers were accused in the two assaults against Jewish houses of worship. There, U.S. Senator Frank Lautenberg and Gov. Thomas Kean joined with county and local officials and with local religious and community leaders in expressing outrage; these officials and leaders participated, with 3,000 citizens, in a Solidarity Day that manifested total repudiation of the anti-Jewish violence. The Solidarity Day also expressed the community's commitment to the cause of good will and interreligious understanding. As for the five teenagers arrested in the two synagogue violations, they have been indicted and face trial.

11

Jesse Jackson and the Meaning of Antisemitism

Dennis Prager

Most Americans, Jews included, regard Jesse Jackson's hostility to the Jews as an unfortunate problem—for Jews. This perception is very wrong. Jesse Jackson is a threat to far more than Jews because to the antisemite, the Jews are the embodiment of fundamental moral values of the Western world. It is those values, and ultimately all those who hold those values, that antisemites seek to destroy. The Jews are only their first target.

If this understanding of antisemitism is correct, and if Jesse Jackson is indeed an antisemite, then he is a dangerous man. He is indeed. Jesse Jackson, like other modern day antisemites, is hostile to the Western world and to democracy and sympathetic to tyranny. He is also antagonistic to America, a tragedy for black Americans, and a warning to liberals and Democrats. In view of the Jews' role in the modern world, none of this is surprising.

The Meaning of Antisemitism

Antisemitism is a Jewish problem, but non-Jews make a very self-destructive error when they dismiss it as only the Jews' problem. Treatment of the Jews has served as one of humanity's moral barometers. Watch how nations, individuals, or ideologies react to the Jewish people or the Jewish state, and you have an early and deadly accurate picture of their values and intentions.

The Jews are the world's miner's canary. Miners take canaries down to the mines because canaries are particularly vulnerable to noxious fumes. They die upon exposure to those fumes, well before the miners are aware of them. When the miner sees the canary is dead, he knows there are noxious fumes to be fought.

So it is with the Jews. Moral non-Jews who fail to act against antisemites and anti-Zionists will in due course suffer from them. Jew-haters begin with Jews but never end with Jews. This is why antisemitism and anti-Zionism should be so important to non-Jews. Identifying the Jews' enemies gives civilized societies an unparalleled opportunity to identify the forces that also wish to destroy them. Examples abound.

Hitler and the Nazis. Most dramatic was of course Hitler and the Nazis. During the 1930's, the Western democracies, by dismissing Nazi antisemitism as a Jewish problem, failed to confront Hitler when it might have been possible to stop him. When they finally awoke to the threat that Hitler posed to democracy and Western moral values, it was too late. Fifty-five million lives might have been saved had the democracies understood Jew-hatred.

Idi Amin. When Ugandan dictator Idi Amin became a rabid anti-Zionist, expelled the hundreds of Israelis from Uganda, sent a message to the United Nations Secretary General hailing the Holocaust, and decided to erect a statue to Hitler, nearly everyone either ignored Amin or dismissed his Jew-hatred as the Jews' problem. Soon after, however, he began to decimate Uganda's Christian community and various tribal groups. The man dismissed as merely an anti-Zionist murdered a half million Ugandans before being overthrown.

Mouammar Qaddafi. Libya's Mouammar Qaddafi is one of the world's primary supporters of terrorism against Western democracies and a ruthless tyrant over his own people. He, too, first revealed his hatred of Western democratic and moral values by his hatred of the Jewish state. Arnaud de Borchgrave, former international editor of *Newsweek,* reported that Qaddafi on three separate occasions told him that his greatest aim in life is to develop an atom bomb to drop on Israel.

The United Nations. The clearest indication that the United Nations had betrayed its founding principles to support democracy against tyranny was here, too, revealed by its attitude toward Jews and Israel. The anti-Zionism and antisemitism of the General Assembly, which has devoted more time to delegitimizing Israel than to any other issue, was originally dismissed as the Jews' problem. The moral degradation of UNESCO was also ignored, even when it became so mired in anti-Jewish rhetoric that it declared that Jesus was a Palestinian. Now, however, the United Nations is regarded, as Alexander Solzhenitsyn has pointed out, as a misnomer—it is really the United Governments, most of which enslave their nations.

Islam and the Arabs. The Muslim Arabs' hatred of Israel provides yet another example. Their obsession with destroying Israel tells a great deal about their moral state. Arab regimes that want Israel dead are not otherwise fine, moral, and democracy loving. Not a single Arab Muslim country is a democracy, and most are ruthless dictatorships whose first aim is to destroy the Jewish state. Their war is ultimately against Western values, Christianity, and democracy. That is why Israel's Arab enemies constantly refer to the Jewish state as "an outpost of Western values" in "their" region. That this has not been recognized by Western nations, Christians, and democrats the world over—even after the destruction of a Christian and democratic Lebanon—is only one more example of their unwillingness to understand the meaning of Jew- and Israel-hatred.

The Soviet Union. With regard to the Soviet Union, it is the Jews, more than any other group within the Soviet Union or in the Western world (compare, for example, the recent whitewash of the Soviets by the National Council of Churches) that has consistently reminded the world about Soviet totalitarianism. It makes perfect sense that, after the

United States, Jews are the most frequently attacked group in the Soviet Union.

Jesse Jackson. Jesse Jackson's hostility to the Jews is but the most recent example of anti-Zionism and antisemitism serving to reveal the moral nature of an individual and the threat that he poses to Western democratic values. That Jackson's conflict with the Jews and Israel has been regarded by most people, including many Jews, as primarily a Jewish problem bears witness to the inability, or unwillingness, of good people to learn the single greatest lesson of antisemitism: the Jews are only the first. Like the antisemitic individuals and regimes before him, Jesse Jackson is a threat to far more than the Jews.

Jackson's Antisemitism

Jesse Jackson's hostility to the Jews is long-standing and far deeper than his "Hymies" comment.

As early as 1973, in a speech attacking then-President Nixon, he charged that "Four out of five [of Nixon's advisors, such as Haldeman, Ehrlichman] are German Jews."

When attacked by the press, he said his media critics were "all Jewish."

He has called the relationship between Jews and Democrats "a kind of glorified form of bribery, financial bankrolling and moral bankruptcy."

He has blamed Jewish promoters for boxing matches between a South African white and an American black.

Regarding the Holocaust, he has said that he is "sick and tired of hearing about the Holocaust and having America being put in the position of a guilt trip." And after visiting the Yad Vashem Holocaust Memorial, Jackson said that "Genocide should not be allowed to happen to anyone, not even the Palestinians." When, after hearing such comments, Israeli Prime Minister Menachem Begin refused to meet with him, Jackson termed it "a racist decision based on skin color."

He condemns Zionism as "based on race," and continues to defend his 1980 statement that "Zionism is a kind of poisonous weed that is choking Judaism."

He is one of the only active supporters of the PLO in American public life. "PLO recognition," he said in 1979, "is a human right." He opposed the extradition from the United States of a PLO terrorist who had murdered two Israelis in Tiberias. For good reason Arab PLO supporters carried him on their shoulders and chanted "Jackson! Arafat!"

Finally, he refuses to disassociate himself from Louis Farrakhan, who proudly identifies himself as an antisemite and calls Judaism "a gutter religion."

Despite all this and more, there are those who contend that Rev. Jackson is not an antisemite. They point out that he has Jewish advisors and Jewish friends, and that in his heart does not hate all Jews. Apparently, many people, Jews included, in the aftermath of Nazism and the Holocaust, believe that in order to qualify as an antisemite, one must, as the Nazis did, hate all Jews.

But if antisemitic means having to hate every Jew, then the Nazis were this century's only antisemites. And Stalin, Brezhnev, Arafat, and the sponsors of the U.N.'s Zionism is Racism resolution were not antisemites, since they had or have Jewish friends. That someone does not hate all Jews is

irrelevant to ascertaining whether he is an enemy of the Jewish people. When you say and do what Jesse Jackson has said about and done to the Jewish people, you are an enemy of the Jews, even if in your heart you do not hate every Jew. I do believe that in his heart Jesse Jackson does not hate all Jews. So what?

Louis Farrakhan, on the other hand, does hate the Jews and Judaism, and Jackson's unwillingness to condemn this antisemite and white-hating racist provided yet more evidence of his moral stature. A moral man would disassociate himself from whatever Farrakhan stands for. A man of God would declare Farrakhan a sinner who should repent. He would proclaim his disassociation from Farrakhan as categorically as Ronald Reagan declared his from the Ku Klux Klan. When the Klan endorsed the President, he said he was embarrassed by their support, and that he rejects them and everything they stand for. This is what Jesse Jackson should have said about Farrakhan. But when Jackson is asked about Farrakhan, instead of attacking Farrakhan, he attacks the questioner. He either attacks the press for being under Jewish influence, or he brands the question racist, or protests that Farrakhan is not the issue, or claims that since he, Jackson, is a man of God, he must hold out his hand of reconciliation to everyone.

That Jackson is an enemy of the Jewish people is evident to virtually every Jew. What is not evident to Jews, and needs most forcefully to be articulated, is that Jackson's antisemitism, like that of all other antisemites, tells us far more about the man than just his attitude to Jews.

Jackson Versus Democracy

One consequence of the dismissal of Jackson as the Jews' problem has been the virtual ignoring of his sympathy for anti-democratic regimes. Jesse Jackson likes tyrannies and tyrants (of the Left), and dislikes Western democratic institutions.

When Jesse Jackson travelled around the world to hug Yasser Arafat, nearly everyone, Jew and non-Jew, reacted to the Jewish element, as if hugging the world's leading terrorist is solely a Jewish issue. Those who understand antisemitism, however, suspected that more was involved. Suspicions were confirmed when he later embraced Hafez Assad, just a year after the Syrian tyrant had exterminated 20,000 of his opponents, and when he then embraced Fidel Castro.

Willie Brown, California State Assembly Majority leader, *defending* Mr. Jackson's embrace of Fidel Castro, said that we have to understand that Jesse Jackson has an affinity for Third World people like Castro. While Brown meant it positively, those of us who regard Assad and Castro as unworthy of a decent person's affinity, do not regard Brown's descriptions as complimentary.

After Jackson hugged Yasser Arafat and Assad, William Buckley wrote that we ought to have a rule: If you have to meet with a tyrant who has murdered great numbers of his own people and who governs them ruthlessly, at least do not hug him. Shake his hand, if you must. Why hug him, why give an Arafat a kiss?

The answer is that Jesse Jackson likes such people. Even more than his hugs, his words reveal his admiration for anti-Western tyrants and movements. For example, he praised Arafat as "my friend and the friend of justice and humanity," and the PLO as "a spirit . . . it's bred in children . . . it is a spiritual thing, the PLO." (He is right about its being bred in children. Perhaps Jackson was referring to the graduation exercise for young PLO recruits. To see whether their 15-year-old graduates have mastered the ability not to be squeamish, the boys have to tear apart live chickens or rabbits with their bare hands. That is "the PLO spirit" that is bred in children.)

Mr. Jackson also likes Mr. Assad, who is described by human rights organizations as among the bloodiest dictators in the world. When President Reagan's emissary was to meet with Assad, the emissary publicly explained that in view of the Syrian leader's brutality, it was distasteful to meet him. Jesse Jackson criticized the envoy, saying that unlike Reagan's administration's people, "I feel a kinship" with Assad. Then, on national television, Jackson added that Assad "is really a human at heart."

Those who have lived under tyranny best understand the big lie that underlies Jackson's so-called "moral offensive" in meeting with Third World dictators. Witness the reaction of Andre Vargas Gomez, a former Cuban diplomat and democratic dissident. Despite his joy at being released by Castro to Jesse Jackson after 20 years in a Cuban prison camp, Mr. Vargas Gomez declared that "To go to Cuba to join on 'a moral offensive' with Fidel Castro is a moral offense."

Arafat, Assad, and Castro are not the only dictators and terrorists with whom Mr. Jackson has an affinity. When asked his opinion of the IRA (Irish Republican Army), Jackson replied, "I feel an identity with its mission."

The Khmer Rouge provides yet another example. Though I am a Jew who holds the term Holocaust almost sacred, I am forced to apply that label to what the Khmer Rouge (Communist Cambodians) did to the Cambodian people five years ago. They murdered two million of the six million Cambodians—one out of every three, the same percentage as that of Jews murdered by the Nazis. And what is Jesse Jackson's assessment of the Khmer Rouge? "Unfortunately, sometimes the best of people lose their way."

Given Jackson's values, it was easy to predict his reaction to the Sandinistas. They have all the attributes he most admires—they are Third World, Communist, building a tyranny, and hate America. And indeed Mr. Jackson waxes euphoric over Nicaragua's dictators. "They are," he says, "on the right side of history, and they are leading Nicaragua to democracy."

Perhaps the finest summary of Mr. Jackson's view of tyrants and terrorists, was that of Martin Peretz, editor of *The New Republic:* "Virtually every time Jesse Jackson opens his mouth on foreign affairs, he bolsters the confidence of tyrants and terrorists around the world that they have plenty of friends in America."

Jackson Versus America

If people understood the meaning of Jackson's antisemitism, they would also understand the threat that Jackson poses to America. From his statements and attitudes it is fair to say that he hates this country.

In 1981, when more than twenty black children in Atlanta were murdered, and the black community there was in a state of panic, Jesse Jackson announced that "It is open season on black people. . . . These murders can only be understood in the context of affirmative action and Ronald Reagan's conservative politics." Jesse Jackson publicly blamed white America and the Reagan administration for the murders of black children. This was a libel whose only possible intent was to incite blacks to hate whites. For that charge alone, Jackson should have been drummed out of public life. Yet he has been apparently accountable for nothing he says or does. (A black man was later charged with the murders.)

"America," Jackson told a *Playboy* interviewer, "is not known for her capacity to love and heal but for her capacity to organize and kill."

Jackson's constant references to the Reagan administration as a "repressive regime" are also worth noting. He uses much harsher words for America's democratically elected government than for any Communist or Third World tyranny. "Regime" is also instructive. It is rarely used to describe democracies—which is precisely why he uses the term. In fact, given his sympathy for tyrants, his view of America as "repressive," and his belief that Nicaragua is a democracy, there is every reason to conclude that this man either does not understand democracy or actually opposes it.

A Tragedy for Black Americans

Despite his great popularity among blacks, and the pride he instilled in many of them by being the first black to mount a serious campaign for the presidential nomination of a major party, Jackson is a tragedy for the black people of the United States.

First, he has created or greatly increased black-white tensions. Just as Americans, both black and white, were beginning to believe that healing was taking place after the horror of slavery and the evils of segregation, when Americans were beginning to see one another as Martin Luther King wanted, through colorblind eyes, Jesse Jackson reinjected color into American life.

During the campaign for the Democrats' presidential nomination, almost every time Jackson spoke he increased black-white tensions. Jackson alienates sympathetic whites from both blacks and Democrats. Any major black politician would have received more white votes in the Democratic primaries than Jackson did. Jesse Jackson is part of the reason the Democratic ticket lost 49 states. The "Rainbow Coalition" had no white in it. For blacks to have as their leader a man who is detested by white America may be emotionally cathartic for many black people but it is highly injurious to black progress. Second, Jackson is doing blacks a terrible disservice by leading them to believe that white racism is the root of their problems. We blacks, he is telling them, are hated and even murdered by whites (recall his blaming white America for the murders of the black children in Atlanta). We blacks, he ceaselessly communicates, are *victims. Our problems emanate from white America.* This is unfair to whites, but it is devastating to blacks.

Some blacks, like the Hoover Institute's Tom Sowell, recognize this. They protest that Jackson and white liberals who share Jackson's position are worsening the black plight by telling blacks that they can do little to help themselves; their problems are caused by others—whites, Republicans, Congress—and the solutions will be delivered by others.

I am keenly aware of the pride that Jackson has instilled in innumerable blacks. But beyond that he has helped few blacks but himself. Any minority group can blame its problems on prejudice. But unless that prejudice is truly paralyzing, such notions are a terrible disservice to members of that group.

Thus, while it is bad for whites to be cast as the blacks' villains, most whites go back to a home, a family, and a job. But the poor black who believes a Jesse Jackson and some white liberals, gets it into his mind that he is a victim, helpless until bailed out by others. Jackson is communicating to him that he is not the master of his fate, the white man is. Only the white man and his money can help him. Some black scholars now acknowledge what Senator Daniel Patrick Moynihan long ago noted, that the greatest black problems are no longer white racism and they are rarely solvable by infusions of government funds. Were Jesse Jackson a black leader rather than a black demagogue, he would address those problems which ultimately blacks themselves must solve.

For example, more than half of the blacks born every year in this country are born to unmarried women. Born out of wedlock, the *majority* of black children grow up fatherless. There are more black girls who give birth during high school than black girls who graduate from college. Are these catastrophic problems Ronald Reagan's fault? Are they a result of white racism? If white racism is at fault, the black family should have collapsed during the worst racism—slavery—and during official racial segregation. Yet, as recently as the 1930's, in a much more racist America, the black divorce rate was lower than that of whites.

The fact is that most black problems, such as the crumbling black family, and a violent crime rate four times in excess of the black percentage of the population, are precisely that, black problems. The notion that whites and government must—or even can—solve those problems only serves to prevent blacks from confronting their own problems and to perpetuate black dependence. Had Jesse Jackson confronted the breakdown of values which is at the core of so many black problems, he would have made a seminal contribution to his people and been regarded by most Americans as a leader rather than as a demagogue. With his charisma, he could have led blacks by telling them not what they want to hear, but what they need to hear. Instead, he blames whites, the President, Republicans, and Jews for black problems and focuses on the PLO instead of the disintegrating black family.

Another aspect of the Jackson tragedy for blacks is revealed by an old statement by the black novelist, James Baldwin. "Whenever I go to a white writer's congress," wrote Baldwin, "I have a method for figuring out whether my colleagues are racist. It consists of saying stupid things and supporting absurd theories. If they listen to me respectfully and then burst into applause, there's no doubt about it, a group of racist pigs." Nothing better sums up many Democrats' and liberals' reactions to Rev. Jackson.

Baldwin's statement explains why whites who regard blacks as their equals must feel free to call Jesse Jackson an anti-democratic, anti-American, antisemitic demagogue. When a white who is sympathetic to blacks says that to blacks (not merely to whites when blacks are not around), it is clear that he takes blacks seriously. Jesse Jackson's claims to black leadership through the constant invocation of Martin Luther King, Jr.'s name, as if he is that great man's moral heir, are Orwellian to those who recall King's views on America, Jews, Israel and Communist tyrannies. Contrast the anti-Zionism of Jackson with Martin Luther King's attitude toward Zionism. At Harvard in 1968, when a black radical student said that Zionism is racism, Rev. King angrily told the student that anti-Zionism is merely a codeword for antisemitism and he should never repeat that slander.

In a far tougher time in American history, Martin Luther King knew how to unite black and white and Jew and Christian. In a far better time, Jesse Jackson, claiming King's mantle to black leadership, is working to tear King's painstakingly won unity asunder.

Jackson and the Liberal Democrats

Despite Jackson's antisemitism and anti-Americanism, the Democratic Party's reaction was, in Baldwin's words, to "listen respectfully" because Jackson is black. Democratic leaders felt that if they condemn Jackson's antisemitism, anti-Americanism, or support for terrorists and Third World tyrants, blacks would abandon the Democratic ticket. This was based on one or more of these suppositions:

1. Nearly all black Americans share Jesse Jackson's views.
2. Jesse Jackson is not worth responding to. If we just "listen respectfully" to him irrespective of his values, nearly all blacks will support the Democrats.
3. Nearly all black Americans support Jackson because he is black, not because of his radical views.
4. Many liberal Democrats have little trouble with Jackson's radical views.

If the first is true, Mr. Mondale should have taken issue with Jackson for America's and the Democrats' sake. He should have let black America know that antisemitism, anti-Americanism, and anti-democratic values have no place in his party, and let the electoral chips fall where they may.

If the second is true, the Democrats are precisely the type of racists to which James Baldwin referred. If the third is correct, the Democrats are playing a dangerous game. Big Lies work because they are first perceived as unimportant lies. The fourth *is* true, and worth analyzing.

To most Jews and to all who oppose appeasement of tyrants, Jesse Jackson's trip to Syria and his praise of Assad were reprehensible. But not to many liberal Democrats. Senator Ted Kennedy, for example, perhaps the most popular Democrat and liberal in the country, deeply admired Jesse Jackson's trip to Syria. "This personal initiative by Rev. Jackson," said the Massachusetts senator, "will rank as one of the finest by a private citizen in the history of international relations."

Within the liberal and Democratic establishments, only some Jews took exception to the refusal of liberals to attack Jackson. One of the leading liberals in Jewish life, Rabbi Alexander Schindler, head of the Union of American Hebrew Congregations, and past head of the Conference of Presidents of Major American Jewish Organizations, admitted as much. Even he began to question the moral credibility of his liberal friends. In an essay in the *New York Times*, he asked, "Where are our liberal allies now that we need them; where's the National Council of Churches; where's the National Council of Bishops?"

Rabbi Schindler's question was right but his list was too short. He should have also asked where were all the liberal writers, commentators, politicians? And why did the Democrats reject a platform plank condemning antisemitism and racism? Rabbi Schindler should also have asked an equally revealing question. Where were the conservatives, when the Jews needed them? The answer would have been so embarrassing, however, that the rabbi understandably avoided asking the question. For, by and large, conservatives were writing the truth about Jesse Jackson's antisemitism, anti-Americanism, and hostility to democracy. George Will, William Buckley, William Safire, and *Commentary* Magazine were screaming throughout the campaign that the emperor was naked. Of course there was one liberal exception, Martin Peretz and his magnificent *New Republic*. But Peretz is an anomaly who lives in his own rarefied world, neither liberal nor conservative, just moral.

Let us, then, try to answer Rabbi Schindler's question: Why have liberals and Democrats been so unwilling to confront Rev. Jackson?

One obvious reason is that it is these very same liberal Democrats who have helped bring us to the state where a man with Jesse Jackson's views could run for President of the United States. Too many liberals have made anti-American rhetoric respectable. Liberal Democrats have rendered us accustomed to the morally lopsided view of the world in which the United States, which keeps every democracy on earth alive, is a source of evil, and that Communism is somehow a noble alternative for the Third World. That is why we are not shocked when a man seeking the Democratic presidential nomination visits a Communist state, hails its totalitarian anti-American rulers, and condemns the United States as the major force for evil in Central America.

For Jews there is a critical lesson in this. Jesse Jackson represents the chickens coming home to roost for Jews on the Left. These Jews, who so disproportionately helped to create domestic radicalism and render anti-American radical rhetoric respectable, have created an anti-Jewish Frankenstein. If you constantly attack American foreign policy as immoral, as so many Jews have done from Vietnam to El Salvador, then expect American support for Israel to be attacked as well. Third Worlders like Jesse Jackson are not going to be pro-Sandinista, support anti-Western national liberation movements, and then oppose the PLO. For the Left, for Third World advocates, and for others who condemn American "imperialism," American support of Israel is considered as anti-Third World and reactionary as its policies in Central America.

American Jews should wake up to the reality that American strength and willingness to use that strength are inextricably linked to the survival of Israel and of every other democracy. Too many Jews, in their un-Jewish equation of arms and war with immorality, oppose virtually any strengthening of American defenses, but then demand that America be very strong when it comes to Israel.

Conclusion

Luckily for the Jews, the Democrats did not condemn Jackson once the Jews began attacking him. Just as the Jews were blamed for the downfall of Andrew Young—even though his comments at the United Nations about America having thousands of political prisoners just like the Soviet Union does, and about the saintliness of the Ayatollah Khomeini had already rendered him an embarrassment to the Carter administration—the Jews would have been blamed for the far more serious crime of bringing down a man whom many blacks regard as a virtual messiah.

Jews, however, have suffered enough from denying others' messiahs. With regard to the Reverend Jackson, the Jews for their own sake should now hold their peace. We have said quite enough for those who want to hear to have heard. Now let non-Jews who cherish democracy, wish to improve black-white relations, love America, and want to prevent antisemitism from becoming respectable see to it that Jesse Jackson's absence from the public stage remains permanent.

Jewish problems are humanity's problems, and until non-Jews learn this they will constantly get hurt by the people who hurt us. If I could, as a Jew, make one point to America and the West, it is precisely that. We Jews never asked for this role, but we have it. Unwillingly and unwittingly, it fell upon the Jews of the United States of America, in the year 1984, to be the moral litmus test of a man named Jesse Jackson.

Ultimate Issues is written and published quarterly by Dennis Prager. Entire contents © Dennis Prager, *Ultimate Issues*, 2265 Westwood Boulevard, Suite 508, Los Angeles, CA 90064. Telephone: 213-204-4290. Subscriptions are $15.00 for one year, $30.00 for two years.

Why the Jews?

Dennis Prager
Joseph Telushkin

Why Jew-Hatred Is Unique

Hatred of the Jew has been humanity's greatest hatred. While hatred of other groups has always existed, no hatred has been as universal, as deep, or as permanent as antisemitism.

The Jews have been objects of hatred in pagan, religious, and secular societies. Fascists have accused them of being Communists, and Communists have branded them capitalists. Jews who live in non-Jewish societies have been accused of having dual loyalties, and Jews who live in the Jewish state have been condemned as "racists." Poor Jews are bullied, and rich Jews are resented. Jews have been branded as both rootless cosmopolitans and ethnic chauvinists. Jews who assimilate are often called a fifth column, while those who stay together often spark hatred for remaining different. Literally, hundreds of millions of people have believed that the Jews drink the blood of non-Jews, that they cause plagues and poison wells, that they plan to conquer the world, and that they murdered God Himself.

The *universality* of antisemitism is attested to by innumerable facts, the most dramatic being that Jews have been expelled from nearly every country in which they have resided. Jews were expelled from England in 1290, France in 1306 and 1394, Hungary between 1349 and 1360, Austria in 1421, numerous localities in Germany between the fourteenth and sixteenth centuries, Lithuania in 1445 and 1495, Spain in 1492, Portugal in 1497, and Bohemia and Moravia in 1744-45. Between the fifteenth century and 1772, Jews were not allowed into Russia, and when finally admitted, they were restricted to one area, the Pale of Settlement. Between 1948 and 1967 nearly all the Jews of Aden, Algeria, Egypt, Iraq, Syria, and Yemen, though not officially expelled, fled these countries, fearing for their lives.

The *depth* of antisemitism is evidenced by the frequency with which hostility against Jews has gone far beyond discrimination and erupted into sustained violence. In nearly every country where Jews have lived, they have at some time been subjected to beatings, torture, and murder, solely because they were Jews. In the Russian Empire during the nineteenth and twentieth centuries, mass beatings and murders of Jews were so common that a word, *pogrom,* was coined to describe such incidents. And these pogroms were viewed by their antisemitic perpetrators as being of such significance that they were equated with the saving of Russia.

On a number of occasions even beating and murdering Jewish communities were not deemed sufficient. Anti-semitic passions have run so deep that only the actual annihilation of the Jewish people could solve what came to be called the "Jewish Problem." The basic source of ancient Jewish history, the Bible, depicts two attempts to destroy the Jewish people, the attempt by Pharaoh and the Egyptians (*Exodus* 1:15-22) and that of Haman and the Persians *(Book of Esther).* While it is true that the historicity of these biblical accounts has not been proven or disproven by nonbiblical sources, few would dispute the supposition that in ancient times attempts were made to destroy the Jews. Indeed the first recorded reference to Jews in non-Jewish sources, the Mernephta stele, written by an Egyptian king about 1220 B.C.E., states "Israel is no more." Jewish writings from the earliest times until the present are replete with references to attempts by non-Jews to destroy the Jewish people. *Psalms* 83:5 describes the enemies of the Jews as proponents of genocide: "Come, and let us cut them off from being a nation, that the Name of Israel may no more be remembered." Just how precarious Jews have viewed their survival is reflected in a statement from the ancient and still recited Passover Haggadah: "In every generation they rise against us in order to annihilate us."

On two occasions in the last 350 years annihilation campaigns have been waged against the Jews: the Chmelnitzky massacres in Eastern Europe in 1648-49, and the Nazi destruction of Jews throughout Europe between 1939 and 1945.

For various reasons the Chmelnitzky massacres are today not well known among Jews and virtually unknown among non-Jews; perhaps the Holocaust tends to overshadow all previous Jewish sufferings. Yet without denying the unique aspects of the Nazi Holocaust, we are obliged to cite a number of significant similarities between it and the Chmelnitzky massacres. In both instances all Jews, including infants, were targeted for murder; the general populaces nearly always joined in the attacks; and the torture and degradation of Jews were an integral part of the murderers' procedures. These characteristics are evidenced by the following contemporaneous description of a typical Chmelnitzky massacre:

> Some of them [the Jews] had their skins flayed off them and their flesh was flung to the dogs. The hands and feet of others were cut off and they were flung onto the roadway where carts ran over them and they were trodden underfoot by horse. . . . And many were buried alive. Children were slaughtered in their mothers' bosoms and many children were torn apart like fish. They ripped up the bellies of pregnant women, took out the unborn children, and flung them in their faces. They tore open the bellies of some of them and placed a living cat within the belly and left them alive thus, first cutting off their hands so that they should not be able to take the living cat out of the belly . . . and there was never an unnatural death in the world that they did not inflict upon them.

The *permanence* (as well as depth) of antisemitism is attested to by the obsessive attention given to the "Jewish Problem" by antisemites throughout history. *At one time or another nearly every one of the world's greatest powers that has had a large Jewish population has regarded this group, which never constituted more than a small percentage of the population, as an enemy.* To the Roman Empire in the first century, the Christian world for over fifteen centuries, the Nazi Reich, and to the Arabs, Muslims, and the Soviet Union today, the Jews have been or are regarded as an insufferable threat.

Jews have been perceived as so dangerous that even after their expulsion or destruction hatred and fear of them remain. The depiction of Jews as ritual murderers of young Christian children in Chaucer's "Prioress's Tale" in *The Canterbury Tales* one hundred years after all Jews had been expelled from England, and the characterization of Jews as usurers who wish to collect their interest in flesh in Shakespeare's *The Merchant of Venice* three hundred years after the Jewish expulsion, attest to the durability of antisemitism. A contemporary example is Poland in 1968 when for months the greatest issue on Polish radio, television, and in Polish newspapers was the "Unmasking of Zionists in Poland." Of the 33 million citizens of Poland in 1968, the Jews numbered about 20,000, or less than one-fifteenth of one percent.

How are the universality, depth, and permanence of antisemitism to be explained? Why such hatred and fear of people who never constituted more than a small minority among those who most hated and feared them? Why, nearly always and nearly everywhere, the Jews?

Many answers have been offered by scholars. These include, most commonly, economic factors, the need for scapegoats, ethnic hatred, xenophobia, resentment of Jewish affluence and professional success, and religious bigotry. But ultimately these answers do not explain antisemitism; they only explain what factors have *exacerbated* antisemitism and caused it to erupt in a given circumstance. None accounts for the universality, depth, and persistence of antisemitism. In fact, we have encountered virtually no study of antisemitism that even attempts to offer a universal explanation of Jew-hatred. Nearly every study of antisemitism consists almost solely of historical narrative, claiming implicitly that no universal reason for antisemitism exists.

We reject this approach. To ignore the question of ultimate causation, or to deny that there are ultimate causes for antisemitism, contradicts both common sense and history. Antisemitism has existed too long and in too many disparate cultures to ignore the problem of ultimate cause and/or to claim that new or indigenous factors are responsible every time it erupts. Factors specific to a given society help account for the manner or time in which antisemitism erupts, but they do not explain its genesis—why antisemitism at all? To cite but one example, the depressed economy in Germany in the 1920s and 1930s may help to explain why and when the Nazis came to power, but it does not explain why Nazis hated Jews, let alone why they wanted to murder every Jew in the world. Economic depressions do not account for gas chambers.

The very consistency of the passions Jews have aroused demands a consistent explanation. Ancient Egyptians, Greeks, and Romans, medieval and many modern Christians and Muslims, and Nazis and Communists have perhaps only one thing in common: they have all counted the Jews as their enemy, often their greatest enemy. Why?

This question has been posed only by modern Jews. From the recorded beginnings of Jewish history until the modern age, Jews never asked, "Why the Jews?" They knew exactly why. Throughout their history Jews have regarded Jew-hatred as an inevitable consequence of their Jewishness. Contrary to modern understandings of antisemitism, the age-old Jewish understanding of antisemitism does posit a universal reason for Jew-hatred: Judaism. And the historical record confirms the traditional Jewish view of antisemitism that the Jews were hated because of distinctly Jewish factors. Modern attempts to dejudaize antisemitism, to attribute it to economic, social, and political reasons, and universalize it into merely another instance of bigotry are as opposed to the facts of Jewish history as they are to the historical Jewish understanding of antisemitism.

Antisemites have not opposed Jews because Jews are affluent—poor Jews have always been as hated; or strong—weak Jews have simply invited antisemitic bullies; or because Jews may have unpleasant personalities—kindly Jews have never been spared by antisemites; or because ruling classes focus worker discontent onto Jews—precapitalist and contemporary noncapitalist societies such as those of the Soviet Union and other Communist states have been considerably more antisemitic than capitalist societies. Antisemites have hated Jews because Jews are Jewish. Christian antisemites ceased hating rich Jews when they became Christians. The same has held true for virtually all other antisemites except the Nazis, whom we shall discuss later.

The ultimate cause of antisemitism is that which has made Jews Jewish—Judaism. There are four basic reasons for this and each revolves around the theme of a Jewish *challenge* to the values of non-Jews.

1. For thousands of years Judaism has consisted of three components: God, Torah, and Israel; that is, the Jewish (conception of) God, Jewish law, and Jewish nationhood. Jews' allegiance to any of these components has been a major source of antisemitism because it has rendered the Jew an outsider, and most important, it has been regarded by non-Jews (often correctly) as challenging the validity of the non-Jews' god(s), law(s), and/or national allegiance.

By affirming what they considered to be the one and only God of all mankind, thereby denying legitimacy to everyone else's gods, the Jews entered history—and have often been since—at war with other people's most cherished values. The Jews compounded this hostility by living by their own all-encompassing set of laws in addition to or even instead of the laws of their non-Jewish neighbors. And by continually asserting their own national identity in addition to or instead of the national identity of the non-Jews among whom they lived, Jews have created or intensified antisemitic passions.

2. From its earliest days the *raison d'etre* of Judaism has been to change the world for the better (in the words of an ancient Jewish prayer still recited daily, "to perfect the world under the rule of God"). This attempt to change the world, to challenge the gods, religious or secular, of the societies around them, and to make moral demands upon

others (even when not done expressly in the name of Judaism) has constantly been a source of tension between Jews and non-Jews.

3. As if the above were not enough, Judaism has also held from the earliest time that the Jews were chosen by God to achieve this mission of perfecting the world. This doctrine of the Jews' divine election has been a major cause of antisemitism.

4. As a result of the Jews' commitment to Judaism, they have led higher quality lives than their non-Jewish neighbors in almost every society in which they have lived. This higher quality of life has expressed itself in a variety of ways. To cite but a few examples: Jews have nearly always been better educated; Jewish family life has usually been far more stable; Jews aided one another considerably more than their non-Jewish neighbors aided each other; and Jews have been far less likely to become drunk, beat their wives, abandon their children, and the like. As a result of these factors, the quality of life of the average Jew, no matter how poor, was higher than that of a comparable non-Jew in that society.

This higher quality of life among Jews, which, as we shall show, directly results from Judaism, has challenged non-Jews and provoked profound envy and hostility. In this way, too, Judaism has been the source of antisemitism.

Once we perceive that it is Judaism which is the root cause of antisemitism, otherwise irrational and inexplicable aspects of antisemitism become rationally explicable.

We now understand why so many non-Jews have regarded the mere existence of Jews—no matter how few—as terribly threatening. The mere existence of the Jews, with their different values and allegiances, constituted a threat to the prevailing order.

Since Judaism is the root cause of antisemitism, Jews, *unlike victims of racial or ethnic prejudice,* could in every instance of antisemitism, except Nazism, escape persecution. For thousands of years and until this day, Jews who abandoned their Jewish identity and assumed the majority's religious and national identity were no longer persecuted.*

For these reasons, Jews have always seen antisemitism as the somewhat inevitable and often quite rational, though of course immoral, response to Judaism. Thus, Jews until the modern era, and religious Jews to this day, would describe every Jew murdered by an antisemite not as a victim of ethnic prejudice but as having died *al kiddush hashem,* a martyr to the cause of Judaism, sanctifying the name of God before the world.

Once one understands why Judaism has precipitated antisemitism, the unique universality, depth, and permanence of Jew-hatred also become understandable. It takes infinitely more than economic tensions or racial prejudice to create the animosity—so often to the point of torturing children and murdering whole communities—that Jews have created throughout their long history. Only something representing a threat to the core values, allegiances, and beliefs of others could arouse such universal, deep, and lasting hatred. This Judaism has done.

That Judaism, rather than race or economics, is at the root of antisemitism also helps to explain why totalitarian regimes are inevitably antisemitic. Totalitarian regimes by definition aim to control the totality of their citizens' lives and can therefore tolerate no uncontrolled religious or national expressions, both of which are part of Judaism.

Once the Jewish bases of antisemitism are recognized, the only solutions to the "Jewish Problem," as far as antisemites are concerned, are obvious. The Jews must either convert, be expelled, or be murdered. Indeed, in the 1880s, the Russian czar's procurator of the Holy Synod and architect of Russian government policy at the time, Constantine Pobedonostsev, is said to have offered precisely this advice. One-third of the Jews living in the Russian Empire, he said, should be converted to Christianity, one-third should be expelled from the empire, and one-third should be put to death. In fact, for the last two thousand years, this has repeatedly been the chronological order of antisemitic acts. First, attempts would be made to convert the Jews. When the Jews refused, they were often expelled. And when even expulsion failed to solve the "Jewish Problem," there remained one "Final Solution," which is precisely the name the Nazis gave to their plan to murder all the Jews.

It is also clear that antisemitism is not ethnic or racial prejudice, though it obviously shares certain features with them. Antisemites persecuted Jews for the same reasons Romans persecuted Christians, Nazis tortured members of the Resistance, and Soviets imprison dissidents. In each instance the group is persecuted because its different beliefs represent a threat to the persecuting group. This hatred must be understood as being very different from a prejudice. Blacks in America, for example, have been discriminated against because of the physical fact of their blackness, not because of specific Black ideas or beliefs which they represent. Hatred of Blacks is racial prejudice. Blacks cannot stop being Black. But Soviet dissidents can stop being dissenters, and a Jew has always been able to, and in general still can, stop being a Jew. The single exception to this rule has been Nazi antisemitism. But even this apparent exception confirms the Jewish basis of antisemitism. The Nazis simply maintained that Jews could never really become non-Jews, that no matter how much Jews may consciously attempt to appear and behave like non-Jews, they nevertheless retain the values of Judaism. Nazi anti-Jewish "racism" emanated from a hatred of Judaism and what Jews represent. Nazi racism is *ex post facto;* first came the antisemitism, then came the racist doctrine to explain it.

Antisemitism is, therefore, as Jews have always regarded it: a response to Jews and their way of life. The charges made against Jews, that they poison wells, drink blood, plot to take over the governments of the world, or control world finance, are hallucinatory. But the roots of antisemitism are not. The real reasons antisemites hate Jews and the accusations they make against them are not necessarily the same. This is hardly uncommon. When people harbor hatreds, individually or communally, they rarely articulate rationally the reasons for their hatred.

We should not be so naive as to regard all antisemitic accusations as the reasons for the antisemitism. For example, the modern belief that economic factors cause antisemitism, besides confusing exacerbating factors with causes of antisemitism, grants the accusations of the antisemites far too much credence. It is reminiscent of some historians' preoccupation with determining the historical accuracy of the Christian claim that the Jews killed Jesus, because Christian antisemites called Jews "Christ killers," as if proving one way or another would end Christian antisemitism. The question for those wishing to understand the roots of antisemitism is not whether some Jews helped execute Jesus around the year 30 C.E. or how great a role Jews played in the German economy. The question is why, to begin with, people hate Jews. The answer is Judaism, its distinctiveness and its challenge.

The Meaning of Antisemitism for Non-Jews

Antisemitism is a Jewish problem, but non-Jews make a most self-destructive error when they dismiss it as only the Jews' problem. Treatment of the Jews has served as one of humanity's moral barometers. Watch how a nation, religion, or political movement treats Jews, and you have an early and deadly accurate picture of that group's intentions toward others.

Moral non-Jews who fail to act against antisemites inevitably suffer from them. Nothing about Jew-hatred is clearer than this. Jew-haters begin with Jews but never end with Jews, as antisemitism is ultimately a hatred of higher standards. The antisemites first wish to destroy the perceived embodiment of that higher call to the good, the Jews. But they do not hate the Jews alone. They hate whatever and whoever represents a higher value, a moral challenge. Whoever sees antisemitism as only some aberrational hatred on the part of an otherwise morally acceptable group does not understand antisemitism. So long as there are good people, the Jews will never be the only targets of antisemites.

A particularly clear contemporary example of one such target is the United States. Those who hate the Jewish nation are often the most likely to hate America as well. And almost as consistently as Jew-hatred, America-hatred has become a moral litmus test of nations, regimes, and individuals. America represents freedom, a higher quality of life, and a willingness to fight for its values. These qualities are despised by regimes characterized by tyranny and socioeconomic failure, and by individuals in the West who support such regimes or who wish to denigrate America for reasons akin to those of antisemites in their denigration of Jews. Both supporters and haters of America know that with all its flaws it alone stands between democracy and the ascent of tyranny throughout the world.

Thus, it is small surprise that among tyrannical regimes and their defenders, America and Israel are so often identified as the same enemy. This is not merely a consequence of America's standing alone behind Israel; the United States has aided various Arab countries very generously, and it has on some critical occasions backed Arab regimes (such as Nasser's Egypt in 1956 and Saudi Arabia in 1981) against Israel. This hostility is aroused largely because America and Israel represent democracy, a higher quality of life, and a willingness to confront despotism.

Likewise, within the democratic West itself, so often the individuals who smear America's name attempt to do the same to Israel's. For example, *The Village Voice*'s Alexander Cockburn, a leftist columnist widely known for his scathing attacks on America, has compared Israel in

Lebanon to the Nazis in Poland. There is a desire among opponents of Israel (and America), in the eloquent words of *The New Republic*'s editor Martin Peretz, "to try to establish a parity of immorality" between Israel and its enemies. The reason for this is that the Jewish nation (again, like America) has offered itself, and is perceived, as a moral beacon; hence many individuals wish to portray it as negatively as possible. This explains the unparalleled preoccupation with Israel's (and America's) flaws. And the Jews continue to be aware of their moral challenge: In July 1982, *Newsweek*'s James Pringle asked an Israeli soldier guarding PLO and Syrian prisoners how the latter were treated. "There is no torture," answered the Israeli soldier, "because we are Jews and Jewish people have hearts."

The same mentality which compares a Lyndon Johnson to Nazi war criminals compares a Menachem Begin to Yasser Arafat. Through such exercises of "parity of immorality" America is made to appear morally indistinguishable from the other superpower, the Soviet Union, and Israel is depicted as morally little better than its enemies. To cite one other example, the nationally renowned political cartoonist Conrad depicted these moral equivalences during one week's cartoons in the *Los Angeles Times*. He showed Menachem Begin staring into a mirror which reflected the face of Arafat (July 9, 1982). Later in the week (July 11), the Pulitzer Prize-winning cartoonist drew the Iron Curtain in the form of an American flag. Israel is morally equivalent to the PLO; America is the moral equivalent of the Soviets.

Yet despite all this hatred, America remains the dreamed-for haven of the world's oppressed; and Israel remains an embattled democracy in the midst of authoritarian states, and the birthplace of the kibbutz to which tens of thousands of youth from around the world turn for a living lesson in human equality.**

America today with all its imperfections represents a model of something better, fighting for its ideals and in so doing constituting a moral challenge to others. But the Jews have played this role for millennia. The Jews might be described as humanity's miner's canary. Just as the death of canaries warns miners of noxious fumes, so the death of Jews warns civilized nations of noxious moral fumes. But despite these universal ramifications of Jew-hatred few heed these warnings. Examples abound.

Many in the Western democracies dismissed the Nazis' antisemitism as a bad feature of people who otherwise could be lived with. But had the antisemitism of Hitler and the Nazis been perceived to be the evil it was, had therefore Hitler and the Nazis been perceived to be the evil they were, then good nations would have opposed Hitler earlier and saved not only six million Jews but tens of millions of others.

Before Idi Amin began to butcher hundreds of thousands of Ugandan Christians, he announced his hatred of Israel and his admiration for Hitler's "Final Solution." But only Jews, and America, whose ambassador protested, listened; the rest of the world ignored Amin's antisemitism— that was the Jews' problem. But, as then United States ambassador to the United Nations Daniel Patrick Moynihan pointed out: "It is no accident" that the "racist murderer" Idi Amin called for the extinction of Israel. "For Israel is a democracy and it is simply the fact that despotisms will seek whatever opportunities come to hand to destroy that which threatens them most, which is democracy."

One of the first acts of the Ayatollah Ruhollah Khomeini after assuming power in Iran was the takeover of the Israeli embassy in Tehran. That too was dismissed as the Jews' problem—until the Iranians did the same thing to the American embassy.

The Arab and Muslim hatred of Israel has long been dismissed by many in the West as a Jewish problem which ultimately reveals little about the Arabs or Muslim states. But gradually it has become clear that the hatred of Jewish independence displayed by the Arab Muslim states is not some unrepresentative quirk, but a moral indicator of some precision. As the Christians of Lebanon, who have suffered far worse from Muslim hatred than have the Jews of Israel, have learned, Arab leaders who call for wars to annihilate Zionism are not otherwise tolerant, democracy-loving gentlemen. Indeed, there is often a direct correlation between the ferocity of a Muslim leader's hatred of the Jewish state and his hatred of democracy and other Western values. Iran's Khomeini, Libya's Qaddafi, and Iraq's Hussein are three such examples. Conversely, Arab and other Middle Eastern Muslim societies that are less characterized by despotism and wanton cruelty, such as Tunisia and Turkey, are also characterized by a greater tolerance of the Jews.

The Soviet Union provides another contemporary example of a state whose hostility to Jews is both an indicator of its immoral nature and a warning of the threat it poses to those societies which hold democracy and justice as primary values. Those in the West who regard the Soviet Jewish problem as solely a Jewish problem do a terrible disservice to the other religious groups and nationalities in the Soviet Union whose plights are not as publicized; and they do the West a disservice by preventing it from confronting the evil nature of the Soviet regime.

Jew-hatred and its latest incarnation, Israel-hatred, are the price Jews pay for their role in history. They pay it often unwillingly and they live the role, for the most part, unwittingly. But as the great French Catholic theologian Jacques Maritain noted: "Israel . . . is to be found at the very heart of the world's structure, stimulating it, exasperating it, moving it. Like an alien body, like an activating ferment injected into the mass, it gives the world no peace, it bars slumber, it teaches the world to be discontented and restless as long as the world has not God, it stimulates the movement of history. . . . It is the vocation of Israel which the world hates."

And moral non-Jews who do not heed the universal implications of this hatred are destined to be its victims.

*There is one apparent exception to this rule, the Marranos of Spain. In the fourteenth and fifteenth centuries, Jews who converted to Christianity in Spain were not easily accepted into Christian society. But this was overwhelmingly due to the circumstances of the Jews' conversions. The Christian hierarchy was reluctant to accept these Jewish converts as genuine Christians because it knew that they had converted under threats of expulsion or death, and therefore the sincerity of the Jews' Christianity was questioned. But the Jews who proved by their behavior that they had become religious Christians were accepted. And, in fact, almost all of these tens of thousands of Marranos who remained in Spain did assimilate into Spanish society.

**There is another parallel between Jew-hatred and America-hatred. Both are often perceived as emanating from antagonism to Jews' and Americans' wealth. We have seen how this perception is false regarding Jew-hatred. It is also false as regards America-hatred. Were wealth the major reason for hating a nation, then Switzerland ought to be at least as deeply hated as America, and certainly the Arab oil-exporting nations, whose wealth has increased in direct proportion to a decrease in Third World wealth, should be particularly hated. Yet America, like Israel and the Jews, is hated far more than are these countries. It is what America represents, not merely its wealth, that is loathed.

A Fresh Look at Conversion

Marc D. Angel

Gerut, conversion to Judaism, is one of the most controversial issues confronting us. Judaism has always welcomed sincere converts who wished to become part of the Jewish people and religion and who willingly accepted the responsibility of observing the commandments. However, in our times, many (perhaps most) candidates for conversion are not motivated by an objective love and commitment to Judaism. Rather, they are non-Jews who wish to marry a Jewish partner, or who are already married to a Jew and now wish to convert for the sake of their children. All too often, the candidates for conversion are not seriously interested in accepting the observance of all mitzvot, and may even so indicate. Sometimes it is clear to the rabbis involved that the would-be convert will not in the immediate future be an observant Jew. The question arises: May a Halakhically valid conversion be performed when the motivation is sociological rather than theological, when there is doubt whether the convert will observe the mitzvot?

Rabbinic opinion has varied widely concerning such conversions. Rabbi Abraham Isaac Kook insisted that only converts who will be fully observant of our commandments should be accepted. If we see that a convert does not observe our religious laws and that the conversion was undertaken for ulterior motives, the conversion is not really proper *(ein zo gerut gemurah)*. Moreover, those individuals who accepted such a convert are blameworthy. In one case, Kook ruled that a non-Jewish woman who converted to Judaism for the sake of marriage and clearly had no religious dedication to Judaism remains a non-Jew. The conversion ritual was meaningless. "And happy is the one who stands at the breach to guard the purity of Israel, may a blessing of good come to him."

On the other hand, Benzion Uziel, late Sephardic Chief Rabbi of Israel, argued that not only may we accept such converts, but indeed it is a mitzvah to accept them if we believe this would help create a Jewish home. Even if we know that the convert will not be fully observant, we should perform the conversion in order to prevent intermarriage or loss of children from the Jewish fold.

Between these two positions, there is a wide variety of intermediate opinion, some tending one way, some the other. Since this topic is concerned with the very definition of Jewishness, it has evoked deep emotional reactions. This is not a debate on an abstract point of Jewish law; it touches the source of Jewish existence.

In contemporary Jewish life, the term *giyur kaHalakhah,* conversion according to Jewish law, has become something of a battle cry. From an Orthodox point of view, any conversion which is not done in accordance with traditional Jewish law is an attack on the integrity of the Jewish people. Conversions performed by non-Orthodox rabbis, or even Orthodox rabbis who are not experts in *gerut,* are generally regarded as being invalid. On the other hand, non-Orthodox spokesmen claim that the Orthodox should have no monopoly in determining who is really a Jew, who is an "acceptable" convert. They believe there is more than one way to apply the Halakhah or that traditionally Halakhic guidelines are no longer applicable.

Debates on this topic have frightening implications. On a practical level, many conversions are being performed not in accordance with traditional Halakhah, and these converts marry Jews and have children. Yet in the eyes of Halakhah they are not Jews at all. Thus, we find that a growing number of people who identify as Jews are not Halakhically considered to be Jews. There is great confusion concerning which convert is "really" Jewish and which is not; we are in the process of dividing the Jewish people into two (at least) different peoples, and marriage between members of the two groups might be Halakhically difficult or even impossible. The Jewish people cannot tolerate this situation. On a theoretical level, there are sharp differences of opinion concerning what makes a person Jewish. It is a sad thing when Jews cannot agree even on so fundamental a definition.

What is needed now is a fresh look at the primary sources dealing with conversion. Perhaps if we can understand the sources, we will gain a new perspective on *gerut* and find an answer to the practical and theoretical problems raised above. We must begin at the beginning—with a definition of what makes a person Jewish.

The peoplehood of Israel is inextricably tied to the religion of Israel. Our distinctiveness derives from our Divinely revealed tradition. If it were not for the Torah and its commandments, we would have no raison d'etre, no hope for ultimate messianic redemption. One cannot read the Bible without recognizing the centrality of religion in our life as a people. This article should be read with this observation in mind.

Going back to the Bible, we find no specific mention of a formal procedure for conversion. Various non-Israelites had attached themselves to the people of Israel, e.g., the mixed multitude who joined the Exodus from Egypt. Many laws are stated in the Torah on behalf of the *ger,* the non-Israelite stranger who lived among the Israelites in the land of the Israelites, but the biblical term *ger* does not seem to mean a full-fledged convert in the modern sense. In Kings II 17:32-3 and in Esther 8:17 we find additional references to groups who in some way attached themselves to the people of Israel, but no clear statement describing the conversion procedure.

The classic biblical example of a "righteous convert" is Ruth. She tells her Jewish mother-in-law: "Wherever you go, I shall go; and where you lodge I shall lodge. Your people will be my people and your God will be my God." Ruth has served as a prototype of the ideal convert, one who accepts the Jewish people and religion sincerely and completely. Yet there is no description of Ruth preparing for conversion through study, or telling a Beth Din that she will observe the mitzvot, or immersing in a mikvah. The details of the conversion process are omitted from the text.

Yehezkel Kaufman has described biblical conversion as *giyur ha-artsi-ha-tarbuti,* a non-Israelite's acculturation into the dominant Israelite culture. Non-Israelites living in the Israelite land would naturally become absorbed by the national culture, accepting various social and religious mores in the course of time. Essentially, this was an "ethnic" conversion, in which religion played a part. Kaufman's observation seems fair. Even going back to the case of Ruth, we note that she first identified with the Israelite people and then with the Israelite God.

Who was an Israelite in biblical times? Anyone who was born into an Israelite family, or anyone who attached himself to the people of Israel and became naturalized. The main factor was *Am Yisrael,* the nation or people of Israel. The strictly religious dimension of conversion did not yet exist.

Kaufman asserts that after the Israelites were expelled from their land and lost their national center, a new type of *gerut* came into being—*giyur habrit,* a conversion based exclusively on religion. A non-Jew now had to convert to Judaism, not to the culture and people of Israel. In biblical times, the stranger in the land of Israel gradually adopted Israelite patterns of life; in post-exilic times, the stranger could retain his own language and live in his own land and still convert to Judaism. Religion replaced land and nationality as the definition of an Israelite.

Yet, I believe that if we consider the Talmudic sources dealing with conversion, we shall find that Kaufman errs. The religion of Israel never replaced the people of Israel as the main element of self-definition. Even in Talmudic times, conversion was seen primarily as an act of joining the Jewish people, becoming part of the Jewish national destiny. A procedure was delineated for the conversion process, the religious dimension was stressed, but in the final analysis, peoplehood was more critical than religion alone.

There are two major Talmudic sources on this subject which bear examination.

I. Yebamoth 47a-b:

> Our Rabbis taught: If at the present time a person desires to become a proselyte, he is to be addressed as follows: "Why do you come to become a proselyte? Do you not know that Israel at the present time is persecuted and oppressed, despised, harassed, and overcome by afflictions?" If he replies, "I know and yet am unworthy," he is accepted forthwith, and is given instruction in some of the minor and some of the major commandments. . . . He is also told of the punishment for transgression of the com-

mandments. . . . And as he is informed of the punishment for the transgression of the commandments, so is he informed of the reward granted for their fulfillment. . . . He is not, however, to be persuaded or dissuaded too much. If he accepted, he is circumcised forthwith. . . . As soon as he is healed, arrangements are made for his immediate ablution. . . . When he comes up after his ablution, he is deemed to be an Israelite in all respects.

> In the case of a woman proselyte, women make her sit in the water up to her neck, while two [three] learned men stand outside and give her instruction in some of the minor commandments and some of the major ones.

This passage is noteworthy for several reasons. First, we see that our initial comments to a would-be convert relate to the difficulties of being a member of the Jewish people. We must ascertain that he is willing to share the burdens of our people, to share sincerely in our destiny. Only after we are satisfied on this score do we instruct him "in some of the minor and some of the major commandments." Even when we do give this instruction, it is far from comprehensive, i.e., it does not include all the mitzvot, only some of them.

Moreover, we are not supposed to persuade or dissuade too much, but rather point out the good and the bad aspects and let him judge for himself if conversion is the right choice for him. If he accepts the responsibilities, then he follows the conversion procedure and is accepted as a complete Israelite.

Benzion Uziel, considering this source, concludes that it is apparent that we do not ask the candidate for conversion to fulfill the mitzvot, and it is not even necessary for the Beth Din to know that he will fulfill them. The reason for informing him of some of the commandments is simply to give him a chance to change his mind before it is too late. As long as the candidate is aware in general of what our commandments are, the decision to convert is his.

This source indicates, then, that we are concerned about the convert's becoming a member of our people. One might argue that if a non-Jew agreed to observe all our religious commandments but refused to identify as a member of our people, we would reject his conversion. Accepting Judaism is not identical with becoming Jewish.

We can analyze this point from a different perspective. A person born of a Jewish mother is Halakhically regarded as a Jew. He may be completely unobservant of our commandments, or an atheist, yet Jewish law always regards him as Jewish. If we think of being Jewish solely in terms of adhering to Judaism, this law is absurd; therefore something else is involved, namely, peoplehood. A person born of a Jewish mother is biologically part of our people, regardless of his personal feelings or behavior. By being born Jewish, one is linked to our people by destiny and may never be written off completely. (A parent who disowns a child, or vice versa, does not sever the biological relationship. The relationship is fixed and eternal.) Being Jewish means being part of the Jewish people. Judaism is the religion of our people but it is not the definition of our Jewishness.

II. Yebamoth 24b:

> Mishnah: If a man is suspected of [intercourse] . . . with a heathen who subsequently became a proselyte, he must not marry her. If, however, he did marry her they need not

be separated. Gemara: This implies that she may become a proper proselyte. But against this a contradiction is raised. Both a man who became a proselyte for the sake of a woman and a woman who became a proselyte for the sake of a man . . . are not proper proselytes. These are the words of R. Nehemiah, for R. Nehemiah used to say: Neither lion-proselytes nor dream-proselytes nor the proselytes of Mordecai and Esther are proper proselytes unless they become converted as at the present time. . . . Surely concerning this it was stated that R. Isaac b. Samuel b. Martha said in the name of Rab: the Halakhah is in accordance with the opinion of him who maintained that they are all proper proselytes.

The Talmud is concerned here with people who convert for ulterior motives—marriage, fear, dreams, etc. Rabbi Nehemiah argues that such conversions are not valid. But his opinion is rejected. The conclusion and the accepted law is that such conversions are indeed valid.

What is the basis of this discussion? Rabbi Nehemiah thinks that individuals who do not convert for idealistic, theological, and philosophical reasons are to be rejected. This opinion makes good sense if we view the conversion process as one in which the non-Jew's primary decision is to accept Judaism. If he wants to be Jewish for practical considerations but does not genuinely have a belief in and commitment to Judaism, then the conversion process is a sham, an empty ceremonial.

But Rabbi Nehemiah's opinion is rejected. One who converts even with ulterior motives is a valid convert. The law can be understood only if we assume that conversion means becoming part of the Jewish people, and that if a non-Jew chooses to join our ranks he may do so even if he is not accepting Judaism from theological convictions. A non-Jew who wants to marry someone Jewish and to raise Jewish children has opted to become part of our people, even though the commitment to our religion may be less than perfect.

Another Talmudic passage points in the same direction. Rab and Samuel (Shabbat 68a) speak of a proselyte who became converted among the Gentiles and did not even know fundamental laws of the Sabbath. Rabbi Moshe Feinstein noted that such a convert is valid even if he is still far removed from observing the mitzvot. This proselyte identified with the Jewish people, although his knowledge of Judaism was quite deficient.

In fact, there is no Talmudic legal source that would indicate unequivocally that acceptance of all commandments is a prerequisite for conversion. The central concern of Talmudic as well as biblical times is the proselyte's commitment to the Jewish people.

What does it mean to become part of the Jewish people? How can we measure the commitment of a would-be convert to our people? If a non-Jew donates money to the UJA or in some other way demonstrates a tie to us, is this adequate to make the person Jewish?

Obviously, more than a token or casual commitment to our people is required. To think otherwise is to degrade our people and our history. It is not possible to codify exact guidelines as to what does or does not constitute a genuine commitment to the people of Israel. The final decision in this matter is really left to the rabbis who are involved in each case. Each candidate for conversion has his or her own dynamics, and must be evaluated individually.

Some cases, though, seem clearly to be acceptable. A non-Jewish spouse of a Russian Jew who sacrificed much to migrate to Israel and to join our people is one example. A non-Jewish partner in marriage who wishes to convert in order to raise the children with a Jewish identity is another. Where it can be determined that the non-Jew is sincerely dedicated to sharing our destiny, carrying our burdens, participating in our communal life, there is a good basis for conversion. Certainly, we must make every effort to inform candidates for conversion of the beliefs and principles of Judaism, of our mitzvot and customs. These are basic factors in the life of our people.

In returning to our classic sources in Bible and Talmud, we have arrived at an old but novel understanding of Jewishness. By stressing this view, we can hope to deal more successfully with the contemporary disputes about *gerut*. Certainly, much rabbinic literature has been created since Talmudic times, and the earlier concept of conversion has been blurred in the process. It is all the more important, then, to go back to our primary sources and look at them objectively.

We can defuse the *giyur kaHalakhah* issue. The fact is that the Talmudic Halakhic sources are far more open to receiving proselytes to the Jewish people than some who argue strenuously in the name of Halakhah may want to admit. There is certainly ample support to perform conversions for the sake of marriage if the convert has a genuine commitment to the Jewish people—to identify as a Jew, raise children as Jews, settle in Israel, etc.

Moreover, if the non-Orthodox rabbis who perform conversions would follow the technical procedures of *gerut*, i.e., circumcision and mikvah, while also determining the convert's seriousness in joining our people, there should be a way of considering these conversions as being valid even from an Orthodox viewpoint. If we recognize *gerut* primarily as becoming part of the Jewish people, everyone should be able to admit that Jews of all persuasions belong to *Am Yisrael*. While we may like to see all born Jews fully observant of the mitzvot, and all converts as well, we should understand that one can be Jewish without being fully observant.

It will not be easy for Orthodox and non-Orthodox to come to an agreement on this issue. There is a great deal of pride at stake. But if we do not come to an agreement we will cause the Jewish people to be senselessly divided. This is a prospect which should terrify all of us. It can be avoided. Examining the original sources which define what makes a Jew, we must conclude that Jewishness is more than religion alone. All who sincerely want to join us should be welcome. All who want to divide us will have to answer to God.

14

Combatting Cults and Missionaries

Philip D. Abramowitz

Missionary groups have long sought to convert Jews, using force and bribery to do so. Now, however, they have stepped up their campaign, trying to win the Jews over by the year 2000, when they predict the "Second Coming." They have changed their tactics, substituting charm and friendship for coercion. Groups like "Jews for Jesus" have tried to make Jews believe that Judaism and Christianity can be smoothly combined—provided one simply accepts Jesus as the Messiah. By seeking out Jews on college campuses, in nursing homes, and in Russian neighborhoods, and offering them friendship and assistance, they have won many of them over.

The cults pose an equally dangerous threat. Groups like the Moonies, Hare Krishna and Scientology have courted vulnerable segments of society through deceptions and "mind control" techniques. Jews have seemed especially susceptible to their efforts.

—According to the Federal Bureau of Investigation, there are 8,000,000 Americans in cults, a disproportionate number of them Jews. Estimates of Jewish involvement run as high as 50% for certain groups.

—More than 100 cult and missionary groups have been discovered in the New York area alone. In an effort to step up their campaign in this area, the Jews for Jesus recently purchased a seven-story building in the heart of Manhattan.

—Missionaries have infiltrated hospitals, nursing homes and senior adult residences, sometimes by volunteering to work in these institutions. Thus they are trying to lure not only the young, but also the lonely and vulnerable elderly.

—The leaders of many cults, including the president of the Unification Church (Moonies), are Jews.

—A synagogue was sold to Hare Krishna three years ago, despite desperate pleas not to go through with the sale. Since then, the synagogue has been converted into a world headquarters for this movement. Hare Krishna is not only involved in proselytization, but is reportedly involved in drug peddling and gun-running as well.

—In the summer of 1983, 137 Russian-Jewish youngsters from the Brighton Beach area were found in a Christian camp run by the American Board of Missions to the Jews and the Russo-Slavic Baptist Union. While most were extricated and placed in Jewish camps, nine children were baptized and accepted into the Christian fold.

—Israel is not free from the influence of missionary groups. Missionaries have been found on 37 kibbutzim, and the Scientology Movement, with its bizarre beliefs in mind control from other planets, is reported to control 20% of the educational system in Beersheva. Israelis in the United States have been attracted by this group, which offers them social opportunities they sometimes don't find within the Jewish community. The Mormons have received permission to build an extension of Brigham Young University in Jerusalem and are known to proselytize Jews. Twelve other Christian groups have also petitioned to build large edifices in Jerusalem. This is all being done to prepare for the "Second Coming" of Jesus, which they believe can only be accomplished by the conversion of as many Jews as possible.

—The struggle for the Jewish soul has assumed wide proportions with the holding of large-scale Hebrew-Christian conferences across the country. The Young Messianic Jewish Alliance sponsored a program in Pennsylvania that was attended by 1500 people. United Messianic Jewish Congregations of America held a similar program that lasted four days in St. Louis, Missouri, with over 100 Hebrew-Christian congregations represented.

—The American Board of Missions to the Jews has started a Hebrew-Christian congregation on the University of Pennsylvania campus called "Ohev Melech Yisroel," which sponsors on-campus Sabbath and Holiday services. The Jewish Campus Activities Board in Philadelphia is currently monitoring the situation.

—The Intervarsity Christian Fellowship, which has reached out for many years to both Jewish and non-Jewish college students, has, as of October 1984, begun a ministry that specifically targets Jewish students.

—In an effort to gain credibility, one of the Unification Church front organizations, CAUSA International, has been co-sponsoring conferences with respected organizations. In one New York meeting organized with the Center for International Security, entitled "The Soviet Union and the Middle East," over 300 members of Jewish community organizations participated. The vast majority were unaware they were attending a conference in one of the main Unification Church centers, where the *New York Tribune,* a Unification Church publication, is published. Ads appeared in Jewish publications without mention of the Unification Church tie.

—Among the more alarming recent missionary efforts is a ministry that originates from Oral Roberts University (ORU) in the United States. Headed by Charles Farrah, a professor of theology at ORU, "Project Kibbutz" has been responsible for infiltrating over 30 kibbutzim by sending Christian youth to Israel to work as volunteers. Their motive becomes more apparent when, for example, a Jewish youth stands up during dinner in the dining hall and announces that he/she has accepted Jesus as the Messiah.

—This past summer, Moshe Rosen, head of Jews for Jesus, initiated a strong campaign to convert young Jews at the Western Wall. A popular Jews for Jesus strategy is to take advantage of Jewish youth who are in Israel for a short time, in many cases seeking out their spiritual heritage and thus, emotionally vulnerable. This campaign was thwarted by students from local yeshivot.

Considering the above data, combatting the activities of cults and missionaries should be high on the list of Jewish communal priorities. Unfortunately, this has not been the case.

Many people—and many Jewish organizations—don't react to the problem until they, or their loved ones, are directly and personally affected. There are signs, however, that the rather cavalier attitude of much of the organized Jewish community toward the problem is changing. If that is so, much of the credit can go to the pioneering efforts made by the Jewish Community Relations Council of Greater New York (JCRC) and its Task Force on Missionaries and Cults.

Shortly after the JCRC was formed in 1976, several organizations requested that an investigation be undertaken to ascertain the nature and extent of missionary activity aimed at the Jewish community in the New York metropolitan area. Many individuals, synagogues and organizations reported a more visible public presence of "Hebrew-Christian" groups. The first coordinator of the Task Force, David Mann, spent three months visiting missionary groups and interviewing those who had been or were involved in these activities; meeting with organizations involved in countering missionary work as well as campus, youth and community groups; reviewing all available literature; and finally, preparing a series of recommendations.

Mann found a plethora of missionary organizations, many of them well-financed and professionally staffed in communities throughout the New York area. At that time, he identified more than 40 separate organizations aimed at proselytizing Jews in the Greater New York area. Many of these were part of nationwide movements that have concentrated their activities primarily in New York and California, although they were present in every major Jewish population center. Generally, the primary target population was 15-to 30-year-olds, "loners" with poor family relationships and little Jewish background. But there were groups focusing on every age level, offering everything from meals at nominal cost to "free" nursery schools to attract new members. Mann's findings corroborated the observations of many that the intensity, sophistication and impact of missionary activity had greatly increased. These were no longer street-corner preachers delivering emotional tirades, but part of a well-designed effort that drew support from certain fundamentalist Protestant churches and other sources. This analysis led to the creation of the Task Force on Missionaries, later expanded to include anti-cult activity, under the chairmanship of Dr. Seymour P. Lachman, University Dean for Community Development of the City University of New York and former President of the Board of Education of the City of New York. More than 30 groups and scores of prominent individuals, covering the entire spectrum of Jewish communal life, joined the work of the Task Force, which now represents some 40 constituent member organizations.

Why are these missionary groups and cults proliferating to the extent that they are, and why have they made such deep inroads into the Jewish community?

Several analysts have concluded that the breakdown of the American-Jewish family unit, coupled with the fact that Jewish religious and social institutions are not meeting the intellectual and spiritual needs of young Jews, make the cults a major attraction. Richard Cohen, a leading "Hebrew-Christian" missionary on the West Coast, cited the lack of an adequate Jewish education among assimilated Jews as a factor that enables missionaries to "sell anything" to them. Confusion about their Jewishness, and a need for the attention and spirituality that were missing in their family life, accounts for the vulnerability of many Jews to these groups.

There are also broader social reasons, however, related to general trends in our society such as the yearning for "truth" and meaning and the return to fundamentals. While a significant number of people drawn to cults are those with psychosocial problems, increasingly those attracted are not "on the fringes" but people who could otherwise be described as "normal," but dissatisfied with their lives.

In the case of some of the missionary groups and more often of the cults, followers do not even know the religious sponsorship of the group until after they are lured by clever, deceitful means into a full-time residence in pleasant surroundings away from the city. Others are seeking to fill a void in their lives, and lacking a Jewish education or companionship at a vulnerable time, easily fall prey to superficially warm cult recruiters offering easy answers. While in the cult, they undergo a process of coercive mind control, resulting in complete dependence on the authoritative structure of the group and its totalitarian leader. They are programmed to consider all outsiders, including family members and friends, as evil, satanic and doomed in the coming "Apocalypse." Their families are torn apart by feelings of guilt, shame and helplessness, and they often seek guidance from friends, rabbis and mental health professionals, who, at times, are neither sufficiently familiar with the situation nor equipped to offer proper assistance. Meanwhile, the new cult members, because of a combination of physical and psychological pressures, coupled with their own vulnerability, are unable or afraid to leave.

Several years after the establishment of the Task Force, a Cult Clinic was founded under the Jewish Board of Family and Children's Services (JBFCS) through a grant provided by the Federation of Jewish Philanthropies to counsel distraught families. As an addendum to the Clinic, a 24-hour Hotline was created, coordinated by the JBFCS Cult Clinic. The Hotline meets the growing need for information and professional resources by individuals and families who have suffered distress and disruption caused by missionary and cult activities. Parents, children and families who call the Hotline have immediate access to trained professionals—social workers, psychologists, psychiatrists and rabbis. They are also referred, when necessary, to the special crisis intervention, counseling and rehabilitative services available through JBFCS.

Through the efforts of the Task Force, the government of Israel has been apprised of the growing cult and missionary problem in that country. The Task Force has prepared a report on the activities of these groups in Israel, and has helped set up a parallel Task Force, comprised of various private organizations and government officials, to monitor the problem in the Jewish State.

The Hotline is located at 1651 Third Avenue, New York, N.Y. 10028. Telephone (212) 860-8533 (24-hour number).

15

Why Shouldn't I Intermarry— Doesn't Judaism Believe in Universal Brotherhood?

Dennis Prager
Joseph Telushkin

> Many intermarried parents declare . . . that upon maturity their child will have the right to choose his own identity. This generally means that his identity will be with the majority group. . . . The majority of the children of inter-married Jews, then, will be Gentiles.
> —Marshall Sklare, *America's Jews*

> These people [Jews who assimilate] . . . are lost from Judaism, that is all; lost down a road which has swallowed many more Jews than the Hitler terror ever did. Of course they survive as persons. But from the viewpoint of an army, it makes little difference whether a division is exterminated or disperses into the hills and shucks off its uniforms.
> —Herman Wouk, *This Is My God*

When we write of the centrality of the Jewish role in the world, the Jewish concept of God and man, or the sublime nature of the Shabbat, we appeal to reason. But when we write of our opposition to intermarriage, we must overcome emotions as well as appeal to intellect.

The Issue: Values, Not Ethnicity

Our answer depends entirely on the values you share with us and your prospective mate. Do you care if the Jewish people and its distinctive values survive?

If you do, then sharing common concerns and values, it is relatively easy for us to communicate on the issue of intermarriage. We have only one question: Does the person you are considering marrying also hold these commitments and values? If the answer is yes, marry that person. Judaism welcomes converts.[1]

If your answer is no, however, then logic suggests the exclusion of this non-Jew, just as it would exclude a great many Jews, as a possible mate. In our personal experiences, we (the authors) have been involved in relationships with Jewish women which were eventually ended because to these women Judaism was likely to remain a peripheral concern.

If you are a committed Jew, we do not have to explain why you ought to marry someone who shares this commitment. Unless you subscribe to such romantic notions as "love conquers all" or that you can only love one person, it should be obvious to you that the more values and concerns which you share with your husband or wife, the greater the likelihood of a happy and successful marriage.

But what if you consider Judaism largely irrelevant to your life, or at least not something for which you are prepared to sacrifice a relationship? It is then far more difficult for us to communicate with you concerning intermarriage. Perhaps all we can do is address an appeal to you.

Intermarriage and the Noncommitted Jew

We would begin by asking you not to reject a way of life which you do not know. And please do not fool yourself— you really do not know Judaism. The few hours of bar or bat mitzvah chanting, rote Hebrew, and spitball shooting which you probably experienced each week at Hebrew school simply cannot enable you to know or to judge Judaism. You may be able to judge the Judaism (or lack of it) of your youth, but the Judaism that has survived 3,500 years, the Judaism that bequeathed to the world God and universal morality, the Judaism that survived Pharaoh, Rome, the Crusades, Chmelnitzky (who murdered nearly one-third of the Jewish people in 1648), Hitler and Stalin, and the Judaism that today puts the Jewish people at the vortex of human affairs, is the authentic and powerful Judaism of which, sadly, you know very little.

We therefore appeal to your mind to begin to study authentic Judaism and Jewish history, and we appeal to your heart to begin experiencing Judaism as the beautiful way of life that it is. Once you have studied and developed intellectually and experientially as a Jew, you are, of course, free to reject Judaism. But we think it fair to say that rejection out of ignorance of the most significant moral ideas in history is intellectually unjustifiable; and the rejection of the Jewish people with its embattled 3,500 years of history, and its present battle for survival, is ultimately as self-denying as it is selfish.

In the eyes of the rest of the Jewish community, the intermarrying Jew is abandoning ship while committed Jews are fighting to keep it afloat. In addition to perpetuating the ideal of perfecting the world in a world which increasingly evokes cynicism rather than idealism, committed Jews feel a personal commitment to ensure that the Jewish people survive. Marrying people who share these commitments, creating a Jewish home with them, and raising Jewish children are the core of Jewish survival. In maintaining our ancient struggle on behalf of our ideals and our people, the Jews have answered Hillel's two questions: "If I am not for myself, who will be for me? But if I am only for myself, what am I?" Now you, too, must answer these questions.

The Possibility That You May Change

Consider the following: If you say that being Jewish has no meaning for you, are you certain that this is so? What were your reactions, for example, during the three weeks prior to the Six-Day War when it appeared that Israel might be annihilated? What were your rejections on and after Yom Kippur 1973, when once again the Jewish state was threatened with destruction? How did you feel when Israel freed the Jewish hostages at the Entebbe airport? Did you follow the news on those days with no greater interest or frequency than usual? Do you generally feel as personally uninvolved in Israel's struggles as your non-Jewish friends and co-workers most likely do? How did you react to the television production of *Holocaust?* If indeed your emotional reactions to these events was in no way exceptional, perhaps being Jewish really does mean little or nothing to you.

But, if the Nazi Holocaust, or the possibility of Jews again being slaughtered (in Israel, or elsewhere), or the disappearance of the Jewish people through assimilation affects you emotionally more than it does your non-Jewish friends, chances are that being Jewish means more, perhaps much more, to you than you think. And it is eminently possible that in the near future it will come to mean far more than at present. In fact, should such a change take place, you will be in good company. Many of the foremost Jewish leaders of the last hundred years were people who in their youth were completely disinterested in being Jewish, and who only later in their lives came to realize the centrality of Judaism to themselves and to the world.

Theodor Herzl, the founder of modern Zionism and the man ultimately most responsible for the creation of Israel, was an assimilated Jew until he discovered how profoundly Jewish he was during the Dreyfus case in 1894 when he heard French mobs shouting "Death to the Jews."

When Moses Hess, *the man who converted Friedrich Engels to socialism* and influenced the young Marx, was in his twenties, he considered Judaism irrelevant. Yet within two decades, this father of socialism broke with Marx and Engels over the amoral nature of their ideology, and Moses Hess devoted all his later years to working for Judaism and the Jewish people. His book *Rome and Jerusalem,* written in 1862, begins as follows:

> Here I stand once more, *after twenty years of estrangement,* in the midst of my people; I participate in its holy days of joy and mourning, its memories and hopes, its spiritual struggles in its own house and with the people among which it lives. . . . A thought which I had stifled forever within my heart is again vividly present with me; the thought of my nationality, inseparable from the inheritance of my ancestors, the Holy Land and the eternal city, *the birthplace of the belief in the divine unity of life and in the future brotherhood of all men.* This thought buried alive, had for years throbbed in my sealed heart, demanding outlet. But I lacked the energy necessary for the transition from a path as apparently remote from Judaism as mine was, to that new path which appeared before me in the hazy distance.[2]

Another such Jew was a Russian poet of such extraordinary talent that Maxim Gorki, the father of Soviet literature, predicted that he would become one of the great Russian writers. Yet, with apparent suddenness, Vladimir Jabotinsky decided that it was more important to help fellow Jews establish their own homeland than to devote his life to poetry.

Had you asked any of these men when they were twenty years old if being Jewish was of any significance to them, let alone a reason not to intermarry, they would have probably ridiculed the question. Yet within a few years each of these men discovered that being a Jew was the most important thing in his life.

Since a similar change in your own philosophy of life and identification is a real possibility, consider how you would feel should you discover one day when Israel or Jews elsewhere were in great danger, that while you were deeply troubled, your spouse did not care nearly as much as you, or perhaps not at all. Or consider how you would feel if you wanted to contribute to a Jewish cause and your spouse objected. Or consider how self-conscious you might feel should you decide one day to start reading about Jewish history or Judaism. We are not asking you to imagine the impossible, for we have repeatedly come across sad cases (including marriages between two Jews) wherein one spouse begins to feel much more for Judaism and/or the Jewish people than does the other.

This development can become a major source of tension, for once you have incorporated ideals into your life, they are not easily lost. Unless you are certain that being a Jew is never likely to be a factor of significance in your life, it is advisable that you discuss your present and potential Jewishness with your potential spouse.

You may also wish to take some time out to better know yourself as a Jew or to introduce both you and your potential spouse to Judaism and to Jewish life. Once both of you have studied Judaism and experienced Jewish life, you will be in a far better position to assess how important your Jewishness will likely be to you and to your marriage. You will be able to ascertain which one of three possibilities is likely to materialize: your being Jewish is unlikely to ever be important to either of you; under certain circumstances (such as when you have children, or at Christmas time, or with an eruption of antisemitism in our society) your being Jewish is likely to be important to you and therefore intermarriage is inadvisable; or Judaism has begun to interest your non-Jewish friend, and he or she may want to convert. Whatever your conclusion after studying and experiencing Jewish life, your consideration of the question will greatly reduce the likelihood of your Jewishness becoming a source of marital tension.

Marriage is difficult enough without the added problem of differing values, religions, and roots. Before you intermarry, a dispassionate consideration of this potential source of tension can only help.

The Effect of Intermarriage on Your Children

As a final consideration, we would ask you to recognize the effects which your intermarriage will have on your children. First, and most obvious, you should be aware that your children are not likely to grow up as Jews. This is a fact of contemporary life as reported by the foremost sociologist of American Jewry, Marshall Sklare: "Many intermarried parents declare . . . that upon maturity their child will have the right to choose his own identity. This generally means that his identity will be with the majority group. Only if the child has formed a particularly strong identification with the parent who is Jewish will he be motivated to integrate into the minority community. *The majority of the children of intermarried Jews, then, will be Gentiles. . . .*"

Admittedly, the likelihood of your children not growing up as Jews may not particularly disturb you. But there are two other negative effects of intermarriage upon children which should disturb you irrespective of your present feelings toward Judaism.

No Source From Which to Receive Moral Guidance

Since neither you nor your spouse strongly affirms either of your respective religions and yet neither of you wishes to convert to the other's religion, your children cannot be raised in a religious way of life. In order not to offend either spouse, neither Judaism nor Christianity will be practiced authentically; and it is wrong to assume that some innocuous hybrid of the two religions can be constructed so as to communicate the ethics of both. There are significant differences between Judaism and Christianity, and the attempt to amalgamate the two will not lead to an amalgamated religion, but to no religion at all. In the words of George Santayana, "to attempt to be religious without practicing a specific religion is as possible as attempting to speak without a specific language."

As for ethical instruction without religion, as we have noted on a number of occasions, telling one's children to be ethical does not suffice to render them ethical; an ethical system is needed, it must be based upon religious values, and in any event no comparable secular system of ethical instruction exists.

If not from a religious system in the home, then where else will your children derive ethical values strong enough to withstand a lifetime of challenges? "What contemporary social institution can be counted on to give Western man a strong sense of moral direction? The university? The mass media? The corporation? The country club? The laboratory? The couch? Today only religious faith . . . can provide the basis for a social ethic worthy of the name. . . ."[3]

Existential Loneliness

There is yet another negative effect which intermarriages have on children. You will have effectively cut them off from identification with any community. Instead of affirming for yourself and passing onto your children what so many lost and lonely individuals in modern societies desperately seek, a sense of rootedness and kinship with others, you will have utterly cut yourself and your children off from belonging to anything beyond your immediate family. You are thereby bequeathing to your children the single greatest source of unhappiness in the modern world: alienation.

Consider this empirically based observation of C.G. Jung, one of the most important psychoanalysts of the twentieth century:

> I should like to call attention to the following facts. During the past thirty years people from all civilized countries of the earth have consulted me. I have treated many hundreds of patients, the largest number being Protestants, the smaller number Jews, and [about] five or six believing Catholics. *Among all my patients in the second half of life—that is to say, over thirty-five—there has not been one whose problem in the last resort was not that of finding a religious outlook on life. It is safe to say that every one of*

> *them fell ill because he had lost that which the living religions of every age have given to their followers, and none of them has been really healed who did not regain his religious outlook.*[4]

When we consider the Jewish alternative to this self-imposed alienation, the tragedy of this cutting of Jewish roots is revealed with even greater clarity. Jewish life is communally based (so much so that we possess almost no prayers containing the pronoun *I*) and is structured so as to endow each Jew's life with historical and communal meaning. When the Jewish child is born, it is a major event not only for the immediate family but for the community. When the Jewish boy is circumcised at eight days of age, it is not an antiseptic surgical procedure, but a communal celebration of the entrance of another Jew into the covenant with God. When the Jewish girl reaches her twelfth birthday and the Jewish boy his thirteenth, they do not celebrate it alone or at a party, but with the community as it confirms them as responsible adult members. When two Jews marry, their wedding is sanctified "according to the laws of Moses and Israel," again a community event. Should Israel or Jews elsewhere become targets of hatred and bigotry, Jews will join one another to raise funds, mount political pressure, and do whatever else may be needed to aid fellow Jews—people whom they have never seen, whose country they have never visited, and whose native language they most probably cannot speak. When the committed Jew travels anywhere in the world—from Morocco to Siberia to Alexandria, Louisiana (among the many places where we, the authors, can personally testify to having been beautifully received by fellow Jews)–he or she is not alone but finds brothers and sisters who take him in, feed him, and show him love. Finally, when the Jew dies, the community takes part in this aspect of the life cycle as well. The community ensures a dignified burial, mourns for this Jew, visits and comforts the relatives who are sitting *shiva* (seven days of mourning), and lights annual candles of remembrance for him or her.

The human being is a social animal, and from the beginning of time and in all societies men and women have united to form communities. Whether or not a person finds meaning and happiness in life depends, in part, on having a sense of kinship with others. The community of Israel stands ready to share with all its members its joys and sorrows. They did it for your great-grandmother and great-grandfather in Poland (or Russia, Germany, Syria, etc.) and for your parents in America. They will not do it for your son and daughter, because you have removed them from the Jewish community.

Doesn't Judaism Believe In Universal Brotherhood?

This question is analogous to asking if Einstein believed in relativity. Judaism is the source of the ideal of universal brotherhood. The Jewish Prophets are universally recognized as the earliest and most impassioned advocates of universal peace and brotherhood.

But how are we to achieve universal brotherhood? Is the assimilation of the minority of Jews into majority cultures the answer? Is abandoning Judaism the answer? What sort of universalism is it that demands that small groups give up their identities? That is totalitarianism, not brotherhood. The only way to achieve brotherhood is through all people sharing moral values, while retaining ethnic diversity.

It is precisely due to our commitment to universal brotherhood that we so fervently advocate Judaism, which we believe offers the most viable method for the realization of this ideal. When we ask a Jew to reconsider his or her decision to intermarry, this request has nothing whatsoever to do with negative feelings toward non-Jews, or with automatically positive feelings toward those born as Jews. It is based solely on our commitment to the survival of Jewry and the Jewish way of perfecting the world.

NOTES

1. Judaism so values sincere converts that it believes that the Messiah will be a descendant of a convert, Ruth. But the conversion of which we are speaking must be a sincere commitment to Judaism, not a *pro forma* gesture made to alleviate the bad feelings of anxious in-laws. Conversions that make no demands upon the convert to lead a Jewish life oppose all that Judaism values. Such conversions render Judaism meaningless and render the Jewish people no more than an ethnic society. We enthusiastically welcome converts to Judaism. But a sign-on-the-dotted-line conversion that demands nothing more of the convert is not a conversion to Judaism. It is merely a fraudulent solution to the problem of intermarriage.

2. *Rome and Jerusalem,* M. Waxman, transl. (New York: Bloch Publishing Company, 1918); emphases ours.

3. Unless the home provides a source of firm moral education and guidance, a child will learn his or her values (or nonvalues) from the street and from television. A lack of moral education is common in nonintermarried homes as well. But at least if two Jewish parents realize the error of not rearing their children in a religious-ethical system, the only obstacle they will have to overcome is ignorance of Judaism. In an intermarried home the obstacles are only too obvious.

4. Cited in *Modern Man in Search of a Soul,* C. G. Jung (London: Kegan, Paul, 1933), p. 244; emphasis ours.

16

Review of Church-State Issues in 1985

Marc D. Stern, associate director, legal department
American Jewish Congress

The aggressiveness the Jewish community sometimes displays in asserting its interests, as in the case of the Presidential visit to the military cemetery at Bitburg, is a mark of self-confidence. Paradoxically, it is also a manifestation of insecurity about the Jewish position in the United States. The Jewish community's continued concern about church-state relations—like its reaction to Bitburg—embodies these paradoxical tendencies. The continued importance of the religious liberty issue to American Jews reflects a certainty that speaking out is a wise course, at the same time as it manifests a belief that the liberties Jews enjoy have only a tenuous hold on the American public.

I. Introduction

The last two years have once again seen a heightened level of activity in the church/state area. For the first time since the Kennedy campaign in 1960, religious issues played a major role in a presidential campaign. The news from the Supreme Court has been decidedly mixed as is the news from the Congress. Developments elsewhere, though, are, on the whole, decidedly better.

Public school officials, for example, are decidedly more amenable to complaints about church/state separation than previously. The organized Jewish community has been vigorous in challenging efforts to have government enlist as a pitchman for religion. It has been somewhat less vigorous in protecting the rights of religious observance. And the organized Jewish community has at times seemed more interested in non-establishment as a goal unto itself rather than as a means for protecting religious liberty or the perpetuation of Jewish values.

None of these internal developments is entirely fortuitous. On the contrary, they reflect deeper, more significant, sociological trends. First is an increasing split between the synagogue attending community (Reform, Conservative or Orthodox) on the one hand, and the so-called secular Jewish establishment (Federation, Community Relations Councils, defense agencies and the like) on the other.

These latter agencies most directly speak for the Jewish community in the church/state area. And for this community, it is of particular importance that government not press religious values. This is not to say that Jews who have greater allegiance to the synagogue need not be concerned about separation issues; on the contrary, separation is essential to their well-being, as they too often forget. It is to say that the relative desire to emphasize non-establishment over free exercise is in large part a result of the way communal tasks are assigned.

Second (but related) is the overwhelming fear of the Fundamentalist community, which is seen as the political force behind the efforts to overturn the notion of separation. Those fears are well founded. Prominent spokesmen for the evangelical and fundamentalist communities have frequently called for Christians to reclaim their government or their public schools, or to elect Christian candidates. And many fundamentalist leaders, in their desire to remold America in an older, supposedly more traditional, model, ignore the diversity which makes America what it is and which is a necessary concomitant of freedom in a democratic society.

On the other hand, fundamentalists are not fungible. In some ways they have an admirable record on religious liberties issues. Their institutions adamantly refuse government funds, rather than accept government regulation that comes with it (a position the Jewish community should more seriously consider imitating) and insist on a generous degree of institutional autonomy for their institutions. Moreover, in the last year or two, major spokesmen for this important and growing segment of the American population have begun to somewhat moderate their views, and been more willing to compromise on issues which divide the two communities. The proposed compromises have been inadequate to meet the demands of the Jewish community, but these are trends which the Jewish community would do well to encourage.

II. Legislative Developments

A. Tuition Tax Deductions

There were four major church/state issues debated in the Congress over the last two years. The first of these was a non-development—neither the federal government nor any state enacted a tuition tax deduction for parochial school tuition, despite the Supreme Court's decision in *Mueller v. Allen* (1983) (see Stern, "A Review of Church-State Issues in 1983," in *The Jewish Directory and Almanac* (1984)), upholding the constitutionality of a Minnesota educational expense tax-deduction statute. Such bills were introduced in either Congress and the legislatures of several states. None was enacted; none even reached the floor for a vote. The reasons for this surprising non-development are a combination of budget deficits, concern for the public schools and (the Court's decision notwithstanding) a belief that the states ought not to fund, even indirectly, religious education.

This state of affairs is more than a little surprising. It does point up that a Supreme Court decision that a practice is constitutional is not in itself always enough to persuade legislators that it is good public policy. The failure to enact tuition tax deduction legislation is some indication that the public is still, by and large, in favor of a substantial degree of church/state separation.

B. Constitutional Amendment on School Prayer

In February and March of 1984, the Reagan Administration forced a Senate vote on its proposal for a constitutional amendment to permit voluntary school prayer. Cynics suggested (probably rightly) that the President was seeking to deliver on at least one item on the so-called "social agenda" (abortion, school prayer and tuition tax credits) before the 1984 elections so as to satisfy his evangelical and Catholic supporters.

As originally proposed by the Administration, the amendment would have allowed local school boards to either compose or select prayers for recitation in the local public schools. The former provision met with such overwhelming opposition that it was dropped. The Administration (thankfully) refused all further compromises, including a proposal for a constitutional amendment to permit silent prayer, whose constitutionality was very much at issue at that time. That proposal would have carried the day easily in both houses of Congress.

Still, the Jewish community (which was all but unanimous in its opposition to the President's proposal—the Lubavitch movement and its Rabbi being the only notable exceptions) and numerous allies faced a formidable task. Of the 66 Senators needed to propose a constitutional amendment to the states for ratification, close to 60 were in favor of the proposal at the beginning of the debate. As the extended debate unfolded, however, it became clear that the President's proposal would prove to be unworkable in the public schools, for it was pregnant with opportunities for abuse and religious favoritism. The number of Senators who supported the amendment dropped. It ultimately failed of enactment by a vote of 56-44 (some of the "pro" votes were soft and probably would have gone the other way were the issue close).

The organized Jewish community, working together with a number of Senators, notably Senator Lowell Weicker of Connecticut, played a large role in defeating this ill-considered proposal. It was, however, hard to mobilize Jewish grass roots opposition to the extent that proponents of the amendment were able to generate support for it.

C. Equal Access

"Later troubles," remarks the Talmud, "cause one to forget the earlier ones."

No sooner had the battle over the prayer amendment ended the attention turned to "equal access" proposals. These conditioned federal funding on school policies which allowed student initiated religious clubs to meet on the same basis as other student initiated clubs. These proposals were quite popular in Congress and elsewhere. Because they did not on their face entail government sponsorship of religion, most religious groups which had opposed the prayer amendment supported the equal access proposals. The American Civil Liberties Union was (and remains) ambivalent.

The Jewish community regarded equal access proposals as little more than school prayer in free speech guise, and opposed these proposals vigorously. (The Reverend Jerry Falwell was quoted as suggesting that the prayer amendment was a stalking horse for equal access legislation, which was really what was wanted.) It was joined in these efforts by most educators' groups which feared disruption by extremist groups such as the Nazis. Although the Jewish community was offered substantial opportunities to have the various proposals amended to meet its objections if it would endorse the legislation, it determined, practically unanimously, not to accept these offers and to remain opposed to all forms of equal access legislation.

Notwithstanding the opposition of the Jewish community and education groups (and despite the fact that proponents had to resort to several rarely used parliamentary devices) an equal access law was enacted into law in summer 1984. The statute provides secondary schools with a choice: they may exclude all student initiated clubs which are not curriculum related, or they must permit all such clubs, including religious, political, or ideological ones. Outsiders may not control or regularly attend such clubs. Schools may not sponsor them. Teachers may attend only in a supervisory capacity.

Experience under the law is mixed. Many school districts were slow to decide whether or not to allow student initiated clubs. There have so far (June 1985) been only the most isolated instances of abuses of the law, a not surprising state of affairs given the paucity of experience under it. However, there are indications that church groups are gearing up to use the law as a basis for organizing student religious clubs. If and when that happens, greater controversy can be expected.

As reported in the first edition of the *Jewish Directory and Almanac* (p. 112), the Courts have not been hospitable to claims by religious clubs to equal access. Four Federal Courts of Appeal have held that schools are barred by the Establishment Clause from allowing student initiated religious groups to meet before or after school. (One of those decisions is on appeal to the United States Supreme Court.) It remains to be seen how the Courts will resolve the apparent contradiction between those decisions and the Act. Two cases raising this issue have been brought as of this writing, but the results are, so far, inconclusive.

D. Secular Humanism

During a House-Senate Conference on an omnibus education bill (the most notorious provision of which is the Equal Access Act), Senator Hatch introduced an amendment to a magnet school funding provision prohibiting the expenditure of funds for the teaching of any course of study whose content was "secular humanism." It was left to local school boards to determine what was secular humanism.

Secular Humanism, defined as the rigorous and total exclusion of religion from all human affairs is a religion in the constitutional sense. The public schools may not advocate this viewpoint any more than they may urge more traditional religious views on their students. But the phrase secular humanism is more commonly used by the religious right to denote any course of study which does not advocate religion (particularly Christianity). So defined, secular humanism is a direct attack on the Establishment Clause, which forbids the public schools from advocating religion.

As of June 1, no funds have been distributed under the magnet school program. For this reason—but this reason only—a legal challenge has not yet been brought to the secular humanism provision. No doubt one will be brought as soon as funds are allocated.

This provision cannot be dismissed as a curiosity. It is a significant action in a larger battle for control of the public schools, and, with them, the minds of American youth. The Jewish community cannot and will not remain passive in the face of statutes that create a substantial risk that the public schools will become captive to groups that are intolerant of change and religious and moral differences, and that seek to enlist the public schools as aids in their otherwise unobjectionable efforts to evangelize the community.

III. Litigation

A. Pawtucket Creche Case

The courts have continued to be the focal point of church/state debate. Seven cases were heard by the Supreme Court during its 1984-85 Term, two of which have already been decided. The Court has in addition accepted two additional cases for its 1985-86 Term. Although some of the outstanding cases promise to be important, perhaps none will be as important as the premiere decision of the 1983-84 Term—*Lynch v. Donnelly* (1984), the Pawtucket creche decision.

The City of Pawtucket (Rhode Island) had for forty years at Christmas time erected a creche depicting the birth of Jesus. In recent years, the creche was part of a larger Christmas display, most of which was without particular religious content. In a challenge brought by the American Civil Liberties Union, the lower federal courts ordered the City to stop sponsoring the creche. A closely divided Supreme Court reversed, upholding the right of the municipality to sponsor the creche.

No clear principle emerges from the majority opinion written by Chief Justice Burger. The majority apparently thought that given the ubiquitousness of Christmas, the presence of a municipally sponsored creche added little to the holiday atmosphere and hence did not establish religion. The Court asserted that the Constitution required government to adopt a favorable attitude toward religion. The dissent, written by Justice Brennan, accused the majority opinion of endorsing a rule of law harking back to the day when a Justice of the Supreme Court could write that the United States was a Christian nation.

The Jewish community reacted with shock and anger to a decision which appeared to the Jewish community as indicating that government might give semi-official status to religion. From Agudath Israel to the Zionist Organization of America there was sharp condemnation of the Court. An article attacking the decision, written by one

active member of the Jewish community, was captioned "Strangers In Our Own Land," unwittingly harking back to similar headline over 100 years ago in the Anglo-Jewish press on another church/state issue.

So strong was the reaction to the decision that the overwhelming sentiment within the organized Jewish community was to reject the not unreasonable advice of those who called for the community to seek to have municipalities erect municipal menorahs at Chanukah to counter the impression that, by erecting creches, government was favoring Christianity. Indeed, the Lubavitch organization, which had for years erected menorahs on public land in many cities, was challenged in city after city by spokesmen for the organized Jewish community. Those displays, the argument went, lent credence to the Supreme Court's decision. Whether the Jew-in-the street agreed with the position of the organized community in this regard is a different matter.

B. Scarsdale Creche Case

Lynch v. Donnelly itself held only that a municipality could, if it wanted, erect a creche. It did not mandate that it do so. Much to everyone's surprise, the Jewish community had a fair degree of success in persuading local governments not to sponsor official creches. A more difficult problem arose when private groups sought to erect creches on public land which was made available for the erection of other symbolic displays.

In the period before *Lynch v. Donnelly,* such requests could be combatted by arguing that allowing a religious symbol to stand on public property amounted to government endorsement of that symbol. So long as government endorsement of creches was thought impermissible, this was a persuasive argument. The bottom fell out of the argument with *Lynch.* In the aftermath of that decision, a federal Court of Appeals held that a municipality which allowed non-religious groups (Boy Scouts, community chest, etc.) to erect their symbols on public land denied a religious group freedom of speech when it denied it permission to erect a creche on public land.

The Supreme Court agreed to review this decision, *Bd. of Trustees, Village of Scarsdale v. McCreary* (1985), but, because one of the Justices (Powell) was ill, split four-four. It appears that some of the Justices thought that the appeals court decision did not require the city to permit the erection of the creche (if it barred all free-standing symbols) but only forbade it to rely on the Establishment Clause as a basis for barring the creche.

The decision in *Lynch v. Donnelly* has not resolved all issues about publicly sponsored religious symbols. The lower courts have, despite *Lynch,* barred some displays (creches standing alone, crosses and stars of David) but permitted others (cross on county seal).

C. Other Cases

Among the other cases before the Supreme Court to be decided before the summer are:

• *School District, City of Grand Rapids v. Ball* and *Aguilar v. Felton.* Although they vary slightly in detail, these cases present the question of whether the Establishment Clause prohibits government from providing remedial and supplementary services to parochial schools where the teachers and curriculum are entirely under public control, but the courses take place in the parochial schools.

These are probably the most important Establishment Clause cases of the 1984-85 Supreme Court Term. In deciding these cases, the Court must identify precisely what it is about aid to parochial schools that is constitutionally infirm—is it the bald fact that religious schools are aided in their educational mission, the likelihood that government funds will subsidize religious teaching, or something else?

- *Jensen v. Quaring.* Nebraska, like most other states, requires applicants for drivers' licenses to be photographed. Quaring refused, for religious reasons, to be photographed. The lower federal courts, relying on principles enunciated in earlier decisions of the Supreme Court, held that the state's refusal to issue a driver's license because Quaring would not be photographed interfered with her right to religious liberty, and that interference was not justified by a compelling (that is, overriding) interest of the state.

Nebraska contended that its refusal to issue Quaring a license was justifiable on the grounds that the requirement aided the police to identify motorists, and that to excuse only those who object to photographs on religious grounds would prefer religion over non-religion in violation of the Establishment Clause. (That is not a new claim; the Court has rejected it in the past, although it has never given a satisfactory explanation for that rejection.) The Solicitor General filed an *amicus* (friend-of-the-court) brief in which he urged that, unless Nebraska had a satisfactory alternative which it could apply to all applicants for licenses, and met the objections of persons like Quaring, it was not compelled by the Free Exercise clause to excuse compliance with its law. This test, of course, would, in almost all Free Exercise cases, mean that the government would prevail.

- *Thornton v. Caldor, Inc.* A Connecticut statute requires employers to give employees their Sabbath off. The Connecticut Supreme Court invalidated this statute on the Establishment Clause ground that it conferred a benefit only on some employees, and then only on the basis of religion. If the Supreme Court should uphold the state court decision, all statutes requiring employers to accommodate their employees would be, at a minimum, in constitutional jeopardy. Notwithstanding its position in the Nebraska photo-license case, the Solicitor General, on behalf of the United States, urged a reversal. (June 1985 decision upheld the state court.)

- *Tony and Susan Alamo Foundation v. Secretary of Labor* (decided May 1985). The Court, in a rare unanimous opinion, upheld the constitutionality of applying the federal wage and hour law (Fair Labor Standards Act) to the business operations of the Tony and Susan Alamo Foundation, generally considered a cult group. The decision broke no new ground and was entirely expected.

D. School Prayer

Shortly after the Senate defeated the proposed school prayer amendment, the Supreme Court unanimously, and without oral argument, reaffirmed the ban on school sponsored prayers in *Jaffree v. Wallace* (1984), invalidating an Alabama statute containing a prayer for use in the public schools.

In June, the Supreme Court, by a 6-3 vote, invalidated a review of a different Alabama statute which called on teachers to begin the school day with a moment of silence for "prayer or meditation." The Court observed that the legislative history demonstrated that, in enacting this statute, the legislature intended to encourage students to pray. A majority noted that the Constitution prohibited the state from assuming this role. It also specifically rejected Alabama's argument that the Constitution did not prohibit the state from preferring one faith over another. However, the Court signalled its willingness to uphold statutes which merely set aside a moment of silence to be used as students desired.

Conclusion

It has been a mixed two years on church/state issues. There have been some gains and some more significant losses in the Courts. Public sentiment does not seem to have shifted substantially one way or the other. There remains a broad consensus that government and religion ought to remain separate; there is no consensus on what policies that separation requires.

The Supreme Court appears to be at a crossroads. There is little evidence of a wholesale reevaluation of prior decisions. There is little or no likelihood that the Court will allow government to become a handmaiden of religion. There will remain substantial limits on the forms of aid government can give religious institutions and religion. Nevertheless, the cases coming before the Court now are in many ways closer (and better argued) than ones which came before it earlier. Coupled with an emerging tendency for the Court to defer to the legislative and executive branches in all areas, further defeats at the hands of the Court for the Jewish community must be expected.

Two points bear watching. First, even if the Court is more willing to accept government contact with, and support for, religion, its rationale for doing so will be important. Will it indicate that: 1) Government can support religion so long as it does so fairly (that is, it does not favor one sect or another), and does not coerce participation in religious exercises? 2) Religion may be aided as part of a broader scheme (*e.g.,* tuition tax deduction for public and private school parents, but not for private (parochial) school parents only? 3) Courts should be more deferential to legislative and executive decisions?

The second point follows from the likelihood that the federal courts will be less hospitable to federal constitutional claims. It will be increasingly necessary to vindicate church/state separation in the public arena, or the marketplace of ideas. This will require two things—1) greater attention to the public relations aspects of church/state separation; and 2) a willingness to battle only on important issues, and not on every innocuous technical violation. There are disquieting signs that the Jewish community, for a variety of reasons, will react to a changing jurisprudence by becoming more rigid and doctrinaire, which, while perhaps understandable, would be unfortunate and counter-productive.

17

A Perspective on Genetic Diseases Among the Jewish People

Richard M. Goodman, M.D.

In the early 18th century, physicians in Europe began to write about a number of medical diseases that seemed to occur more frequently in Ashkenazi Jews than in non-Jews. By the early part of the 20th century, numerous reports had accumulated, purporting to show that Jews were indeed more prone to the development of certain diseases, some of which were thought to be of a hereditary nature. However, most of the medical literature during this period concerning diseases in Jews was inundated with biases. Few reports contained controlled studies. Much of the literature was of a testimonial nature. Jewish physicians frequently reported on their Jewish patients. Occasionally, certain studies were designed to convince agencies and governments that Jews were medically and genetically inferior to their host non-Jewish population.

The establishment of the modern State of Israel in 1948 coupled with the rapid growth and interest in medical genetics during the 1950's ushered in a new era in the recognition and understanding of genetic diseases among the Jewish people. The ingathering of Jews from all parts of the world to Israel made that country a natural laboratory for the investigation of hereditary differences among the various Jewish communities. Previously, little had been known about genetic disorders in the non-Ashkenazi communities. As Israeli investigators began to recognize those genetic disorders common to the non-Ashkenazi Jewish communities, their counterparts in the United States and other countries contributed to the understanding of certain hereditary diseases common to Ashkenazi Jewry.

In 1961, an international conference was organized in Jerusalem for the purpose of presenting genetic information on various populations of the world, including newly found observations on the recently settled Jewish communities of Israel. A similar symposium was held in Israel in 1973, in memory of Dr. Chaim Sheba (one of the founders of medical genetics in Israel), which devoted itself to updating information on genetic polymorphisms and diseases in Jews and other ethnic populations of the world. In 1977 the National Foundation for Jewish Genetic Diseases in New York City sponsored the first international symposium devoted solely to the topic of genetic diseases in Ashkenazi Jews.

CLASSIFICATION OF JEWS

For a text dealing with genetic disorders among Jews, the matter of classification of Jews becomes important. According to the *Halacha* (Jewish law), one is a Jew if his or her mother is Jewish, or if an individual converts to Judaism. Despite the controversial aspects of conversion to Judaism, it is apparent that those who do convert probably do not carry mutant genes accounting for the various disorders among Jews.

Religious classification of Jews must be left to rabbinical authorities, but in regard to the nomenclature of Jews, there is need to comment on a few terms that have been used in the past and may also be found today. Some social scientists have spoken of the Jews as a race. In terms of modern anthropology, Jews cannot be so considered because physically they are a heterogeneous group possessing no characteristic racial features. Others have referred to the Jews as a nation—a nation in the tribal sense stemming from biblical times. Such a broad definition is factual in that it points to the early origin of Jews, but it is too nondiscriminating to be used when referring to genetic diseases among Jews. A more acceptable and inclusive term is people. Granted that the Jews are a people composed of various groups, but they are one in that they share a common religion, culture, historic experience, and language, although Hebrew is not spoken by all Jews.

Unfortunately, Jewish historians, linguists, anthropologists, and population geneticists have not pooled their knowledge to produce a unified, acceptable classification of Jews. The main problem in classifying the Jewish communities deals with the many historic events that have molded these groups, and their various migrations with exposure to forces, such as religious conversion, assimilation, and intermarriage. Nevertheless, the amazing fact is the tenacity of the bonds that have kept most of these groups together throughout their difficult periods in history, resulting in the maintenance of distinct ethnic identities. In addition to Judaism serving as a binding force, the various Jewish languages that developed in the Diaspora also aided in uniting the people. Common to all these languages was the use of the Hebrew alphabet. Perhaps the two best known of these Jewish languages are Yiddish (Judeo-German) and Ladino (Judeo-Spanish). Other Jewish languages include Judeo-French, Judeo-Italian, Judeo-Greek, Judeo-Arabic, Judeo-Persian, Judeo-Berber, Tat (Jews of the Caucasus mountains), Gruzinic (Jews of Georgia), and Crimchak (Jews of Crimea). For the linguist, the use of these languages is an ideal means of classifying the Jewish ethnic groups, since the linguistic history of the Jews accurately mirrors their dispersions throughout the world.

Some Jewish historians, on the other hand, prefer to classify Jews according to the political regimen or civilization under which they resided during a given period of time. Thus one can find such broad divisions as Jews under Islamic rule or Jews under Christian rule. Historians also write about Jews under Persian, Greek, Roman, Byzantine, and Ottoman Empires. This method of classification also accurately depicts the time period with its primary influencing factor, be it of a religious or political or a combined nature.

For various reasons, geneticists have not used the method of classifying Jews employed by some historians or linguists but rather have relied on terms such as Ashkenazim, Sephardim, and Oriental, or in some instances speak of the groups by referring to their present or former countries of origin. This is the method of classification that is used in this chapter. However, the terms Sephardim and Oriental are often too broad to reflect the distinct features of a particular subgroup. In such instances, the country or place of origin must also be mentioned. For example, Yemenite and Persian Jews both come under the heading of Oriental Jews, but the genetic traits and diseases of each are so different that it is essential to speak of them in terms of their place of origin. The same situation also exists with Ashkenazi Jewry, although to a lesser extent, so that countries or geographic regions must also be noted. Realizing the inadequacies in classifying Jews, the geneticist frequently must consult the historian and linguist to aid in the interpretation of the data.

DEVELOPMENTAL FEATURES OF THE THREE MAJOR JEWISH COMMUNITIES

Oriental Jewry

The Jewish people are Middle Eastern people. They originated there, and a segment of the population has lived in that part of the world throughout their long history. With the destruction of the first Temple, part of the community moved eastward and became the founders of Babylonian Jewry, which still exists today. The Jews remaining in ancient Israel formed what may be called the Palestinian branch of Oriental Jewry.

Babylonian Jewry has experienced periods of expansion and contraction but has never disappeared. In times of great difficulty, segments of the community left Babylonia (modern Iraq) and established themselves in other parts of Asia—in places known today as Iran, India, Kurdistan, Afghanistan, Bukhara, and regions of the Caucasus mountains. Thus various subgroups developed new cultural ways that came to influence their language and religious customs. Biologic mixing with other populations in turn influenced their physical appearance. Such factors are not unique to Oriental Jewry but can also be noted in Sephardic and Ashkenazi Jewry.

Important developmental features of Oriental Jewry are:
1. Oriental Jewry represents the original "gene pool" of the Jewish people.
2. Their roots were never totally abandoned; although at times small in number, Jews have always remained in the region.
3. The civilization under which Oriental Jewry has lived for the past 1,300 years has been that of Islam.
4. Many subgroups have evolved from Oriental Jewry with distinct environmental and genetic features.
5. The main languages of Oriental Jewry have been Arabic, Persian, and Judeo-Arabic.

Sephardic Jewry

With the rise of the Greco-Roman Empires, Oriental Jewry began to migrate westward. With the advent of Islam and its westward thrust as far as Spain, a segment of Oriental Jewry evolved into what later became known as Sephardic Jewry. Centuries later, following the defeat of the Moslems in the Iberian Peninsula and their return eastward, the Sephardic communities (after their expulsion from Spain) moved mainly toward the eastern basin of the Mediterranean. Prior to the eastward movement of the Sephardic refugees, portions of this population had previously established themselves along the coast of North Africa.

Important developmental features of Sephardic Jewry are:
1. Sephardic Jewry is an outgrowth of Oriental Jewry.
2. The name Sephardi (in Hebrew meaning "Spanish") was acquired after expulsion from Spain.
3. Most Sephardic Jews then came under the rule of Turkish Islam.
4. Many distinct subgroups evolved from Sephardic Jewry with communities along the northern and southern shores of the Mediterranean and also in parts of Western Europe and North and South America.
5. The main language of Sephardic Jewry was Ladino (Judeo-Spanish).

Ashkenazi Jewry

Ashkenazi Jewry also originated from Oriental Jewry, mainly, the Palestinian segment. Although individual Jews made their way into Europe while under Roman rule, most came during the Middle Ages, establishing themselves in France and Germany. Like Sephardim, the Ashkenazim were eventually forced to abandon their roots; they moved into Eastern Europe where they became the largest of the Jewish communities. As they reached a peak in population, persecutions and economic difficulties in early modern times chipped away at their foundations, scattering parts of the community in all directions but mainly westward. This westward migration culminated in the formation of American Jewry. The Holocaust during World War II annihilated more than one-half of the Ashkenazi Jewish population.

Important developmental features of Ashkenazi Jewry are:
1. Ashkenazi Jewry is an outgrowth of Oriental Jewry, mainly its Palestinian segment.
2. The name Ashkenazi was acquired from their early roots in Germany (in Hebrew, Ashkenazi means "German"), and after a period of time they moved into Central and Eastern Europe.
3. The majority of Ashkenazi Jewry grew within the framework of Christian society.
4. Although various regional and ethnic differences can be found, there are no distinct ethnic subgroups, such as those within Oriental and Sephardic Jewry.
5. The main language of Ashkenazi Jewry was Yiddish.

The present-day Jewish population is estimated to be 14,400,000. Table 1 shows the distribution of Jews according to the three major ethnic groups. As noted in that table, 82% of world Jewry is Ashkenazi, while 11 and 7% represent Sephardic and Oriental Jewry, respectively. In Israel, however, only 47% of the Jewish population is Ashkenazi, and 53% is Sephardic and Oriental (30 and 23%, respectively).

Genetic Disorders in the Bible and Talmud

Physicians and medical historians have long been interested in medical diseases mentioned or alluded to in the Bible and Talmud; however, little emphasis has been placed on the possible genetic factors responsible for some of the disorders found in these sources. There are probably two reasons for this relative lack of concern for heredity as a possible cause of these conditions: (a) although there is good evidence to suggest that the ancient Hebrews were aware of the familial nature of certain diseases, they were not knowledgeable about the mechanisms governing inheritance of diseases; and (b) medical scholars in the past who wrote about diseases in the Bible and Talmud likewise did not consider the genetic etiology of diseases. This is understandable when one realizes that genetic thinking as applied to diseases has come to the forefront of medicine only during the past 25 years.

Although a detailed account of genetic disorders in the Bible and Talmud cannot be presented here, it can be stated that none of the hereditary diseases known to be common to Jews today can be traced to these ancient sources. Future scholarly studies, however, may be enlightening.

Table 2 presents a few conditions mentioned or alluded to in the Bible or Talmud whose etiology may be heredi-

tary. A pitfall in dealing with any form of medical material from these sources is that the interpretation or diagnosis may involve an extrapolation beyond acceptable medical boundaries. Thus the term postulated diagnosis (P) has been used in those instances where any doubt prevails.

HEMOPHILIA A

> For it was taught: If she circumcised her first and he died, and she had the second one circumcised and died, she must not circumcise her third child; so stated Rabbi Judah Ha-Nasi. Rabbi Shimon ben Gamliel however said, She may circumcise the third child but must not circumcise the fourth if the third child dies. It once happened with four sisters from Tzippori, where the first had her son circumcised and he died, when the second sister had her son circumcised he died, when the third sister had her son circumcised, he also died and the fourth sister came before Rabbi Shimon ben Gamliel and he told her you must not circumcise your son. (Talmud, Yevamot 64b)

This quotation from the Talmud is the earliest recording of hemophilia A. The fact that the disease presented itself during the ritual of circumcision to a woman with three sons and later to the sons of three sisters strongly supports the genetic features of X-linked recessive hemophilia A.

In their discussion, the two rabbis did not differ about the matter of maternal transmission of the disease but disputed the number of repetitive events necessary to establish a pattern and to remove a subsequent like event from the category of chance. According to the Halachic law of probability *(Hazaka)* when three like happenings (usually of a negative nature) occur to an individual, one is advised to avoid that which would bring about a similar occurrence. In general, three repetitive events are required to establish a pattern; but in matters of life and death, the

TABLE 1.

Estimate of the number* of Jews according to the three major ethnic groups and their world-wide location in 1978

Location	Ashkenazi	Sephardic	Oriental	Total
Asia and Oceania				
Israel	1,400	900	700	3,000
Other	70	50	100	220
Africa				
North	—	40	—	40
South	110	10	—	120
Europe				
U.S.S.R.	2,600	—	80	2,680
Other	1,100	250	20	1,370
America				
North	5,890	210	90	6,190
South	570	180	30	780
Total	11,740 (82%)	1,640 (11%)	1,020 (7%)	14,400 (100%)

* In thousands.

TABLE 2.

A partial list of genetic disorders mentioned or alluded to in the Bible and Talmud

Disorder	Mode of transmission	Source
Alopecia	AD in males	Bible, Kings II, 2:23
Anosmia	V	Talmud, Nezikin, Baba Batra 146a
Astham (P)	M	Bible, Deuteronomy 11:20
Congenital cataract (P)	V	Talmud, Moed, Megillah IV, 6
Cranial malformations	V	Talmud, Kodashim, Bekhorot, 44a
Deaf-mutism	V	Bible, Psalm 38:14
		Talmud (Jerusalem), Moed, Hagigah, 2a
		Talmud, Moed, Hagigah, 3a
Dwarfism	V	Talmud, Kodashim, Bekhorot, 45b
Esophageal fistula and atresia	V	Talmud, Toharot, Nidda 23b
External eye malformations	V	Talmud, Kodashim, Bekhorot, 43b
Facial and body malformations	V	Talmud, Kodashim, Bekhorot 44a
Familial cardiac conduction defect (P)	AD	Talmud, Nashim, Yevamot, 105a
Familial epilepsy	AD and M	Talmud, Nashim, Yevamot, 64b
Gout (P)	M	Bible, Kings I, 15:23
		Bible, Chronicles II, 16:12
Gynecomastia	V	Talmud, Kodashim, Bekhorot 44b
Hemophilia A	XR	Talmud, Nashim, Yevamot 64b
Hermaphroditism	V	Talmud, Zeraim, Bikurin Chapter 4, 5th Mishnah
		Talmud, Nashim, Yevamot 80b
Hirsutism	V	Bible, Genesis 25:25
		Bible, Genesis 27:11
		Bible, Kings II, 1:8
Hypertrophy and atrophy of the upper extremities (P)	V	Talmud, Kodashim, Bekhorot, 3b
Hypothyroidism (P)	V	Talmud, Nashim, Nedarim 66b
Imperforate anus	V	Talmud, Moed, Shabbat, 134a
Left handedness	M	Bible, Judges 3:15
		Bible, Judges 20:15-16
Male genital defects, including cryptorchidism	V	Talmud, Kodashim, Bekhorot VII 5
Night blindness (P)	AD and XR	Talmud, Nashim, Gittin, 69a
Pigmented hairy nevus	AD	Talmud, Nashim, Ketuvot 75a
Red hair	AR?	Bible, Samuel I, 16:12
		Bible, Samuel I, 17:42
Syndactyly and polydactyly	AD and V	Talmud, Kodashim, Bekhorot 44b, 45a
Tall stature and polydactyly	V	Bible, Numbers 13:32-33
		Bible, Deuteronomy 2:10-11
		Bible, Deuteronomy 3:11
		Bible, Samuel II, 21:20-22
Testicular feminization syndrome (P)	XR	Talmud, Nashim, Ketuvot, 10b
Thrombocytopenia purpura (P)	V	Talmud, Moed, Shabbat 134a
Urolithiasis	M	Talmud, Nashim, Gittin 69b

(P), Postulated diagnosis; AD, autosomal dominant; AR, autosomal recessive; M, multifactorial; V, variable; XR, X-linked recessive.

view of Rabbi Judah is upheld that two such events suffice.

Maimonides, the great physician and Talmudist of the 12th century, also discussed hemophilia in his Mishneh Torah. He recognized that a female can transmit the disease to her male offspring even if the latter were conceived from different fathers.

These ancient Jewish writings did not consider the question of circumcision of the child whose maternal uncles died of bleeding after circumcision nor a woman whose brothers also bled to death after this ritual operation. Only the direct maternal transmission of the disease was recognized, whether demonstrated in siblings or in maternal cousins.

Even with modern-day treatment, it is not recommended that a newborn hemophiliac male be circumcised, for his chance of bleeding after the operation is substantially greater than a normal infant. A woman who has a family history of hemophilia cannot have her son circumcised until coagulation studies show her son to be normal. Thus by Jewish law, one must today withhold circumcision and abide by the wisdom enunciated by Maimonides:

> ... One may only circumcise a child that is totally free of disease because danger to life overrides every other consideration.

CLASSIFICATION OF GENETIC DISORDERS AMONG JEWS

The problem of grouping the various genetic disorders thought to be common among Jews is not an easy task. During the past several years, I have recorded over 100 conditions that have at one time or another been considered to be more frequent among the Jewish people. Various methods of classifying these disorders can be employed, including: (a) system involvement, (b) mode of genetic transmission, (c) Jewish communities affected, (d) frequencies, or (e) a mixed system. After considerable thought, a mixed system of classification was decided upon, which consists of the following groups:

1. Genetic diseases in Ashkenazi Jews
2. Genetic diseases in Sephadic and Oriental Jews
3. Rare or isolated genetic syndromes
4. Diseases with complex or unproven inheritance
5. Genetic traits and variants
6. Misconceptions.

Although this system is far from perfect, it is geared to orient physicians to the relative clinical and genetic significance of these disorders.

Table 3 shows the number of genetic disorders appearing in each group and their distribution according to the Ashkenazi and non-Ashkenazi (Sephardic and Oriental) communities. The disproportionate number of non-Ashkenazi Jews with rare or isolated syndromes probably reflects the high rate of consanguineous marriages among these Jewish communities, as compared to the relatively low rate of such marriages in the Ashkenazi community.

The majority of disorders in the group dealing with misconceptions were previously thought to involve Ashkenazi Jews. One reason for this stems from the fact that Ashkenazi Jews resided in a medical environment more advanced than that of non-Ashkenazi Jews during the late 19th and early 20th centuries.

TABLE 3.

Classification and distribution of 120 disorders thought to be common to Jews

Classification	Disorders (N)	Ashkenazi/ Non-Ashkenazi
Genetic diseases in Ashkenazi Jews	11	11/0
Genetic diseases in Sephardic and Oriental Jews	21	0/21
Rare or isolated genetic syndromes	43	4/39
Diseases with complex or unproven inheritance	14	9/5
Genetic traits and variants	13	8/5
Misconceptions	18	16/2
Total	120	48/72

TABLE 4.

Classification of 100 disorders* common to Jews according to system involvement and mode of genetic transmission

System involvement	N	Mode of genetic transmission	N
Metabolic/endocrine	27	Autosomal recessive	58
Central nervous system	12		
Blood	11		
Connective tissue	9		
Musculoskeletal	7	Uncertain	14
Gastrointestinal	7	Autosomal dominant	10
Cardiovascular	6	Multifactorial?	9
Ear	5	X-linked recessive	6
Eye	4	Chromosomal	2
Renal	4	Y-linked	1
Skin	2		
Chromosomal	2		
Neoplastic	2		
Respiratory	2		
Total	100		100

*This excludes the 18 disorders under misconceptions and two categories of disorders listed under the headings of congenital malformations and mental retardation.

Table 4 shows the main areas of system involvement and the various modes of genetic transmission as noted in 100 disorders common to Jews. As one might expect, the inborn errors of metabolism (metabolic and endocrine) form the largest group; concomitantly, autosomal recessive transmission is the most frequent mode of inheritance.

Tables 5 to 7 list some characteristic genetic disorders found among the various Jewish communities. The most outstanding comparative feature is that no one characteristic disease (with the partial exception of familial Mediterranean fever (FMF) in the Sephardic community) can be observed throughout either the Oriental or Sephardic communities. Thus when one speaks of genetic diseases in Oriental or Sephardic Jewry, it is essential to define the community precisely, for each community has its own specific genetic disorders.

TABLE 5.

Some characteristic genetic disorders among Oriental Jewry

Community	Disorder
Kurdistan	*G6PD deficiency*
	Thalassemia (alpha and beta)
India	Ichthyosis vulgaris (autosomal dominant)
	Thalassemia (alpha and beta)
Iran	*Dubin-Johnson syndrome*
	G6PD deficiency
	Pituitary dwarfism, type II
	Pseudocholinesterase deficiency
	Selective hypoaldosteronism
Iraq	Benign familial hematuria
	Bronchial asthma
	Dubin-Johnson syndrome
	FMF
	G6PD deficiency
	Glanzmann thrombasthenia
	Ichthyosis vulgaris (X-linked)
	Meckel syndrome
	Pituitary dwarfism, type II
	Pseudocholinesterase deficiency
Yemen	Celiac disease
	Cystic disease of lung
	Metachromatic leucodystrophy in Habbanites
	PKU
	Thalassemia (alpha)

Italics indicate that the condition is found in more than one Jewish community.

TABLE 6.

Some characteristic genetic disorders among Sephardic Jewry

Community	Disorder
Libya	*FMF*
	Cystinuria
Morocco	Ataxia telangiectasia
	Familial deafness
	FMF
	Glycogen storage disease, type III
Tunisia	*FMF*
	Selective vitamin B12 malabsorption
N. Africa (country not specified)	Celiac disease
	Congenital adrenal hyperplasia
	Cystinosis
	FMF
Turkey and Balkans	*FMF*

Italics indicate that the condition is found in more than one Jewish community.

TABLE 7.

Some characteristic genetic disorders among Ashkenazi Jewry

Mendelian disorders	Disorders of multifactorial or unproven inheritance
Abetalipoproteinemia	Buerger disease
Bloom syndrome	Diabetes mellitus
Familial dysautonomia	Gilles de la Tourette syndrome
Gaucher disease (chronic adult noncerebral form)	Ischemic heart disease
Mucolipidosis type IV	Polycythemia vera
Niemann-Pick disease (infantile type)	Regional enteritis
Primary torsion dystonia	Ulcerative colitis
PTA deficiency (factor XI)	
Spongy degeneration of CNS	
Tay-Sachs disease	

TABLE 8.

Distinguishing features of genetic diseases between Ashkenazi and non-Ashkenazi Jewry

Features	Ashkenazi Jewry	Non-Ashkenazi Jewry (Oriental-Sephardic)
Communities	Genetically less distinct	Genetically very distinct
Diseases	Common to many subgroups comprising the "Jewish genetic diseases"	Not common to all subgroups*
Genetic information on non-Jewish populations (previous residence)	Adequate	Not adequate

*FMF is the exception found in all the Sephardic communities.

TABLE 9.

*Comparative rates of consanguinity for first cousin or closer among some of the Jewish ethnic groups in Israel**

Group	Goldschmidt 1960	Tsafrir 1972
Ashkenazi	1.1	0.8
Non-Ashkenazi		
Iraq	17.5	10.9
Yemen	8.6	4.9
Morocco	7.1	5.9
Syria, Lebanon	4.2	3.1
Egypt	4.2	4.3

*See text for explanation.

Much remains to be learned about the frequency of certain of these disorders among the non-Jewish host populations where Sephardic and Oriental Jewry formerly resided. For example, it is known that phenylketonuria commonly occurs among Yemenite Jews, but adequate data are lacking about this disease in the non-Jewish population of Yemen. In contrast, we know that among most of the 10 genetic disorders found in Ashkenazi Jews, the frequency is much less in the non-Jewish populations of Europe and the Western world. In most instances, more than 50% of all patients with these diseases are Ashkenazi Jews. In disorders such as essential pentosuria, Tay-Sachs disease, and familial dysautonomia, the percentage of Ash-kenazi Jews affected approaches more than 90% of all known cases. Thus it may be concluded that of those disorders definitely of genetic etiology, the most "Jewish" of all the diseases can be found in the Ashkenazi community. Nevertheless, among the non-Ashkenazi Jewish groups, the frequency of conditions such as FMF among Libyan Jews, Dubin-Johnson syndrome among Iranian Jews, and metachromatic leukodystrophy among Habbanite (a region of Yemen) Jews, are among the highest in the world.

Table 8 summarizes the distinguishing features of genetic diseases between Ashkenazi and non-Ashkenazi Jewry.

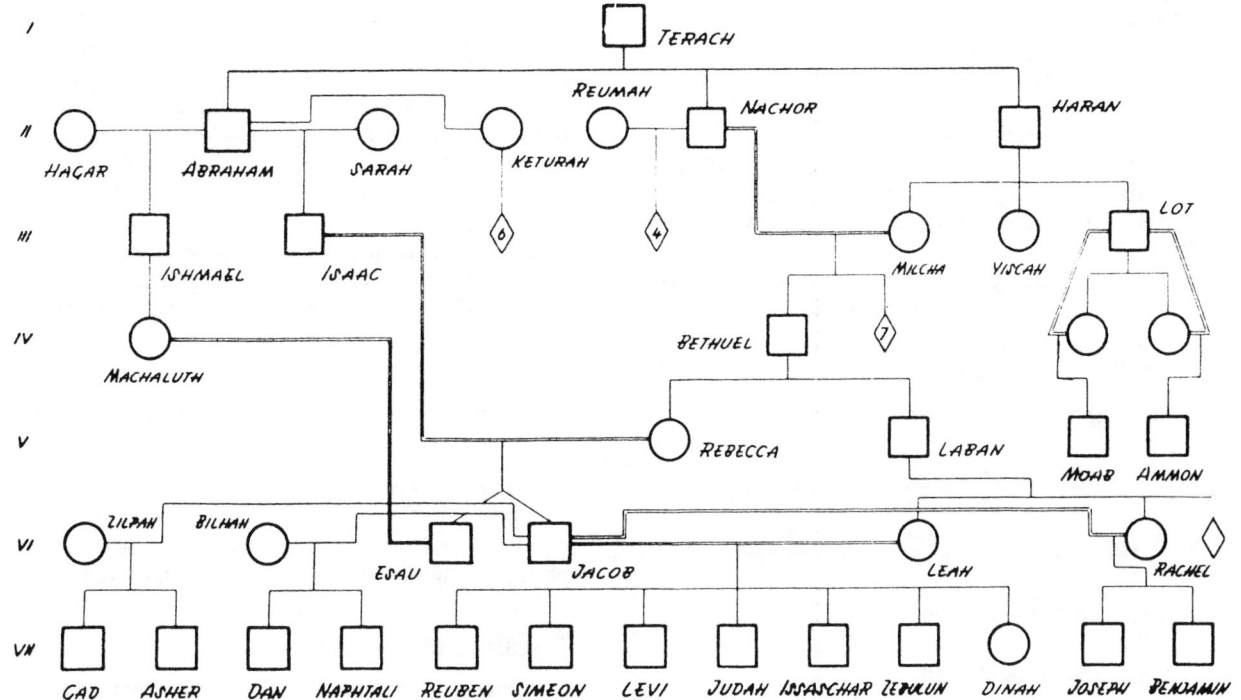

Figure 1. The origin of the Twelve Tribes of Israel beginning with Terach the father of Abraham and proceeding to Jacob with his 12 sons. Note the high degree of consanguinity as indicated by the double lines. Tradition also states that Abraham and Sarah were related.

CAUSATIVE FACTORS

For some time geneticists have been debating those factors responsible for the high frequency of certain genetic diseases among the Jewish people. In view of the historic development of Ashkenazi Jewry, many geneticists tend to favor the mechanism of genetic drift with founder effect as the most likely explanation for the high frequency of Tay-Sachs disease among Ashkenazim. Perhaps such an explanation can also be applied to several other disorders, but it does not answer all questions. Some argue that selective advantage of the heterozygote must be considered when attempting to account for the high gene frequencies of certain disorders common to Jews. It is exceedingly difficult to scientifically prove the existence of selective advantage.

It is not known why three diseases (Tay Sachs, Gaucher, and Niemann-Pick diseases), all sharing a common metabolic pathway, should occur more commonly in the Ashkenazi community. Likewise, our understanding of the high incidence of certain multifactorial diseases among Ashkenazi Jews (e.g., ischemic heart disease, diabetes mellitus, polycythemia vera, regional enteritis, and ulcerative colitis) remains to be clarified.

One causative factor concerns consanguineous matings among Jews. Certainly consanguinity played a crucial role in the early history of the Jewish people, as noted in Fig. 1. The Halacha forbids certain types of consanguineous marriages, but sanctions other forms. The following passages from Jewish sources reflect the thought of scholars on some approved forms of consanguineous marriages within the framework of Jewish Law.

One who married his sister's daughter—him the Bible says: "Then thou will call and God will answer...." (Talmud, order Nashim, tractate Yevamot, 62b).

"It is a mitzvah (a good deed) for a man to marry his sister's daughter or his brother's daughter..." (Shulkan Arukh, Ibn HaEzer, Chapter 2).

In 1960, Goldschmidt et al. studied the marriage patterns in 11,424 Jews from the major Jewish communities residing in Israel. Table 9 shows some of their findings and compares them with a study done by Tsafrir and Halbrecht in Israel published in 1972. Although there is a definite decline in the rate of consanguineous marriages among the Jewish people living in Israel, it is important to stress that the observations of Tsafrir and Halbrecht may not truly reflect the current status, as their sample was quite small and not totally representative of all the communities. However, it may be stated that for the most part, consanguinity does not play a primary role in those genetic disorders characteristically found in the Ashkenazi community, although it does contribute significantly to the occurrence of certain rare genetic syndromes noted among the non-Ashkenazi Jewish groups.

FUTURE TRENDS

There are a number of factors of both a medical and a sociologic nature that will undoubtedly account for a future decrease in the number of Jewish children born with these specific disorders. From a medical standpoint genetic screening programs, prenatal diagnosis, and genetic counseling are all designed to give individuals at risk the opportunity to make decisions that will increase their chances of having healthy offspring. There is every reason to believe that these services will be improved and made available to more people. However, a number of important moral and ethical issues exist. Although advancements in the treatment of genetic diseases are being made, research here is much more complex and probably will not be able to keep pace with the rapid strides being achieved in the area of prevention.

One cannot ignore certain sociologic trends that will also account for a reduction in the number of affected children born. In Israel, for example, two increasing phenomena will tend to lessen the incidence of certain genetic diseases among the Jewish communities. As consanguinity rates continue to decrease (Table 9), fewer children will be born with various rare autosomal recessive syndromes. Second, as rates of marriage between Jews of differing ethnic communities increase (Ashkenazi marrying non-Ashkenazi), there will be a greater dispersal of these mutant genes, with a subsequent reduction in many of these disorders.

In the Diaspora, factors such as increasing rates of assimilation with intermarriage and reduced Jewish family size are destined to lessen the number of affected newborns.

The Seven Most Common Jewish Genetic Diseases

National Foundation for Jewish Genetic Diseases

Familial Dysautonomia

Familial Dysautonomia is the name given to a condition evidenced by abnormal function of the nervous system. Dysautonomia literally means the dysfunction of the autonomic nervous system. The autonomic nervous system controls involuntary functions like temperature and blood pressure regulation. Individuals with dysautonomia cannot regulate these autonomic functions and have certain sensory problems. Children are born with the disease—they do not acquire it later in life.

The most striking manifestations include relative indifference to pain and the inability to cry tears. Severe eye problems are common because of the lack of tearing and the absence of corneal response to foreign objects in the eye. Also, these children have difficulty swallowing properly which can result in poor weight gain as well as repeated pneumonias. Other symptoms include episodic high fever, poor motor coordination, and unstable blood pressure. Many children have stunted height, unclear speech, and scoliosis (curvature of the spine). Forty percent of the children are prone to repeated attacks of vomiting. Intelligence is normal.

Diagnosis is made by using four findings: lack of overflow tears, diminished deep tendon reflexes, smooth surface of the tongue (absence of a flare), and increased responsiveness of the pupil to a drug called methylcholine (miosis with dilute solution).

The disease has so far only occurred in Ashkenazi Jewish families. Sural nerve biopsies have clarified the diagnosis in questionable non-Jewish patients as not being dysautonomia. It is estimated that one out of every 50 Jews in America is a carrier. The risk of recurrence in the family for each offspring to be affected is 1 in 4 (25 percent). The disease afflicts boys and girls in equal numbers.

A better understanding of the disease tends to enable the patient and his family to better cope with the traumatic physiological and psychological difficulties. For further information, you may contact Dr. Felicia Axelrod, Director, Familial Dysautonomia Treatment and Evaluation Center, University Hospital, 530 First Avenue, New York, N.Y. 10016.

The cause of the disease remains a mystery. There is no prenatal diagnosis or carrier identification test.

Torsion Dystonia

The tragedy of Dystonia, a disease affecting movement control, may be best described through the brief case history of a young girl. Early development was quite normal but at age six she complained of difficulty walking. Medical evaluation first revealed no explanation and the problem was mistakenly considered psychological. But the sustained torsion spasms progressed and by ten she could hardly walk. At age eleven, the dystonia was generalized, her limbs were fixed in a twisted posture, and she was confined to a wheel chair. By age twelve, she required help for all her daily living activities; she could not feed or dress herself or get in and out of bed unassisted. However, her voice and her mind remained normal.

In one of its inherited forms, dystonia occurs primarily in Ashkenazi Jews. In this form (transmitted as an autosomal recessive) the disease generally appears between the ages of 4 and 16 years, and has a fairly rapid rate of progression. The sustained spasms may be limited to one limb at first but often spread to other limbs and the trunk. Patients appear to be highly intelligent and mature; in fact, several studies show that affected individuals may have a superior intellect.

In another inherited form (autosomal dominant) the disease strikes families in the population at large; is variable in time of onset; more often affects the trunk or neck first, and has no direct effect on intellect. Dystonia can also be brought about from environmental causes, such as drug reaction, encephalitis or trauma to the head.

The earliest description of autosomal recessive dystonia may have been in 1970 by a psychiatrist-in-training who reported on two brothers and a sister who were hospitalized for "hysterical" torsion spasms. One brother committed suicide in the institution, the sister eventually died of the disease, but the second brother was discharged after several years and later married.

Approximately one out of every 70 Ashkenazi Jews in the United States carries the gene for the recessive form and it occurs in about one of 20,000 Jewish live births. In a geographic breakdown, it was found that 30 percent of the grandparents of Jewish patients had their European origins from the Balkan region, and 20 percent from the Ukraine. The disorder may occur among siblings with no previous family history of the disorder, and is more frequent with intermarriage.

Life expectancy is usually normal. Some medications have been found to be useful in a proportion of patients, particularly children. Cervical cord stimulation is currently being evaluated. Other brain surgery techniques may be useful in some cases.

At present, it is not possible to do genetic screening tests.

Gaucher Disease

Gaucher disease is the most prevalent Jewish genetic disease, afflicting one in every 2,500 Ashkenazi Jews of Eastern and Central European ancestry.

There are three subtypes of Gaucher disease, which are distinguished by their clinical severity and course, and by the presence of neurologic complications. It is specifically Type 1 Gaucher disease that occurs primarily in Ashkenazi Jews, and it is estimated that 1 in every 25 Jewish individuals is a carrier of the recessive Type 1 Gaucher gene.

Type 1 Gaucher disease is characterized by the later age of onset and the absence of any neurological involvement. Type 2 disease has its onset in infancy and is a fatal neurodegenerative disorder, similar to Tay-Sachs disease. This is an extremely rare type and does not occur in any particular ethnic group. Type 3 is a juvenile-onset form which has neurologic involvement. This type is very rare and has been found mainly in Sweden.

Gaucher disease is a biochemical genetic disorder. The basic defect has been shown to be a genetically determined deficiency in the enzyme, acid *beta*-glucosidase. This enzyme normally is involved in the metabolism of a substance called glucosyl ceramide. The inability to break down this substance leads to its progressive accumulation in certain cells and tissues. Measurement of this enzyme permits accurate diagnosis of affected individuals. It is also possible to do prenatal diagnosis early in pregnancy and thus determine the status of the fetus.

In Type 1 Gaucher disease, symptoms may begin in childhood or adolescence and are due to the abnormal accumulation of glucosyl ceramide in Gaucher cells in the bone marrow, spleen and liver. The Gaucher cells in the bone marrow can cause bone and joint pain, fractures, and other orthopedic problems. The presence of Gaucher cells in the spleen and liver causes enlargement of these organs. Blood abnormalities, such as anemia, easy bruising and prolonged bleeding are sometimes seen. Patients with Type 1 Gaucher disease display a wide variety of symptoms. Some may suffer from chronic ill health and debility, while others may experience few, if any, of the disease manifestations.

At present, there is no specific treatment available for Gaucher disease. Recent investigations have been concerned with replacing the deficient enzyme (glucocerebrosidase) in patients with Gaucher disease, with active enzyme obtained from human placental tissue. However, much additional work needs to be done to improve the delivery of the placental enzyme to the cells in which

excessive lipid is stored before the therapeutic effectiveness of this procedure can be evaluated.

Mucolipidosis IV

Mucolipidosis IV is the most recently recognized Jewish genetic disease, having been first described in 1974. To date, about twenty patients, all of Ashkenazi Jewish parents, have been reported. Children with Mucolipidosis IV are normal at birth and develop signs of central nervous system deterioration during the first year of life. Sitting and walking are delayed. The mental deterioration is slowly progressive and usually mild to moderate. Some patients may become more severely retarded in the second or third year of life. The earliest sign is clouding of the corneas. Other eye findings may include esotropia (crossed eyes), and in some patients retinal degeneration develops which may lead to blindness in later years. There is no involvement of the skeleton nor is there urinary excretion of mucopolysaccharides.

The name, Mucolipidosis IV, derives from the presence of diagnostic storage bodies (cytoplasmic inclusions seen under the electron microscope) in certain cells of these patients. The storage bodies are similar to those observed in the *muco*polysaccharide and *lipid* storage diseases; thus, the designation Mucolipidosis. The diagnosis should be considered in mildly to moderately retarded Jewish children who have corneal clouding. The presence of the characteristic storage bodies (observed by electron microscopy) supports the diagnosis.

More recently, a defect in the breakdown of complex fatty substances, called gangliosides, has been described. The enzyme, ganglioside neuraminidase, is presumably defective in these patients. Current research is directed to further characterize the precise nature of this enzyme abnormality and to the development of methods to identify the carriers of the gene which causes Mucolipidosis IV.

The disease is inherited as an autosomal recessive trait. Both parents must be carriers of the disease-causing gene. Although both parents are normal, being carriers, they have a 25 percent risk for an affected child with each pregnancy.

The prenatal diagnosis of this disease has been successfully accomplished by finding the characteristic storage bodies in cultured amniotic cells obtained by amniocentesis early in pregnancy. The prenatal diagnosis is difficult and must be performed in centers with experience in the specialized techniques required for this disease.

At present, no specific therapy is available for this disease. However, optimal supportive care and medical management can significantly improve the quality of life for affected children. Families with affected children should receive genetic counseling and be offered the option of prenatal diagnosis for future pregnancies.

Niemann-Pick Disease

The traditional picture of Niemann-Pick disease is that of a child dying before the age of three, with massive spleen enlargement, striking emaciation and the irreparable disordering of the central nervous system. The age at which the abnormality first appears varies, but most of the children have one or more of the symptoms, such as poor feeding, recurrent vomiting, abdominal protuberance (from the enlarged spleen and liver) and an inability to thrive, before they are six months old. Another typical symptom is a cherry-red spot on the retina of the eye.

The disease, which predominantly affects Ashkenazi Jews, is caused by an abnormal storage of lipids (fatty materials found in tissues of the body and the bloodstream) and cholesterol. The first case was reported in 1914 by the German doctor Albert Niemann, who discovered it in a baby girl born of Polish-Jewish parents. The child died at 18 months, after progressive deterioration.

Three other types of the disease exist besides the classic one. A second group of patients shows the same massive enlargement of the liver and spleen, and the pulmonary changes, but the nervous system is spared. Patients in this group have reached young adulthood, and one young lady has a child of her own who is free of the disease. A third group shows developmental slowdown in late infancy with spleen and liver enlargement, and gradual debilitation leading to death at four to six years of age. The fourth group has been found in individuals of French ancestry whose parents originated from Nova Scotia. In this form the neurological difficulties begin in middle childhood with survival until 12 to 20 years of age.

Family studies strongly support the autosomal recessive nature of the type found in Ashkenazi Jews. It has been estimated that approximately two-thirds of all infants with this form of the disease are of Ashkenazi Jewish descent. The incidence among Ashkenazi Jews is between 1:20,000 and 1:30,000 births per year, or approximately 60 new patients per year, about 25 of whom are born in the United States. The gene frequency of this disorder among Ashkenazi Jews is thought to be greater than 1:100,000 with the frequency for the heterozygote state ranging between 1:100 and 1:140.

Recent strides have been made in controlling this disease. In 1965 researchers identified the specific enzyme absent in those with Niemann-Pick—an enzyme needed to break down fatty materials. From this information, a test was developed for the reliable detection of those afflicted. Similar strides were also made in developing procedures for identifying carriers. In addition, prenatal diagnosis is now possible in the sixteenth week of pregnancy. This is particularly urged when there is a positive family history, or when both parents are shown to be carriers.

Tay-Sachs Disease

Tay-Sachs disease is the most well-known Jewish genetic disease, afflicting about one in every 2,500 Ashkenazi Jewish newborns.

This disease is characterized by the onset of severe mental and developmental retardation during the first 4 to 8 months of life. An early sign of the disease is the cherry-red spot, an unusual abnormality in the retina of the eye observed only by use of an ophthalmoscope. The involvement of the central nervous system progresses rapidly to a state of total debilitation by 2 to 5 years of life. Affected children also develop seizures which are not controllable with anti-epileptic drugs. Death usually occurs by 5 to 8 years of life due to pneumonia or other infections.

Tay-Sachs disease is a biochemical disorder. The basic defect in affected children is the inherited deficiency of the enzyme, hexosaminidase A. This enzyme normally breaks down a naturally occurring substance called G_{M2}—ganglioside. The enzyme deficiency leads to the toxic accumulation of this substance primarily in the cells of the nervous system.

The disease is inherited as an autosomal recessive trait. Each parent of an affected child is a carrier of the disease-causing gene. For such a "carrier couple" there is a 1 in 4 risk of having an affected baby with each pregnancy.

Measurement of the hexosaminidase A activity in plasma, tears or white blood cells can determine if an individual carries the Tay-Sachs gene. The ability to identify carriers by reliable tests has led to large-scale screening programs designed to prospectively identify carriers and particularly couples in which both spouses are carriers of the gene prior to pregnancy. Such programs have become the prototype for disease prevention based on the prospective screening for carriers. To date, Tay-Sachs screening programs have detected over 15,000 carriers, or one in about every 25 Jewish individuals tested. More importantly, over 800 carrier couples at-risk for having a Tay-Sachs child have been identified and counseled as to their 25 percent risk for having an affected child. Since prenatal diagnosis for this disease is possible, these identified at-risk couples have the option to have only normal children.

At present no treatment is available for Tay-Sachs disease. Therefore, emphasis has been placed on public education, carrier screening and prenatal diagnosis for the prevention of this devastating disease.

Chronic G_{M2} Gangliosidosis:

Recently, a new form of *beta*-hexosaminidase A deficiency has been described in adolescents and adults of Ashkenazi Jewish ancestry. This disorder, called chronic (or adult) G_{M2}-gangliosidosis, has been detected in over fifteen individuals from seven unrelated Jewish families residing in both the United States and Israel. Onset of the disease occurs during childhood or adolescence and is characterized by incoordination, tremor and/or slurred speech. Some patients have previously been diagnosed as having Friedreich's ataxia, Kugelberg-Welander disease, or an amyotrophic lateral sclerosis-like disorder. With advancing age, patients develop neurologic symptoms including ataxia, unsteady gait, muscle weakness, and difficulty speaking clearly. In the fourth decade of life, mental and behavioral involvement may become evident.

Chronic G_{M2}-gangliosidosis is inherited as an autosomal recessive trait. Carriers and affected individuals can be diagnosed by the measurement of the enzyme, *beta*-hexosaminidase A. Carriers for this form of *beta*-hexosaminidase A deficiency can be detected in mass-screening programs for Tay-Sachs disease and the prenatal diagnosis is available.

Bloom Syndrome

One hundred and two individuals have been recognized as affected with this syndrome since it was described in 1954 by the New York City dermatologist, David Bloom, a physician long interested in genetics. Bloom syndrome is inherited in autosomal recessive fashion, so that once a couple has had an affected child, thereby proving that they are carriers of the gene, their expectancy for an affected child among their future children is 1 in 4. No test for the carrier state as yet has been developed. The gene is very rare in most populations but is relatively common in Ashkenazi Jews, the carrier rate being greater than 1 in 120.

The affected individual—homozygous for the Bloom syndrome gene—shows the following features: (a) an unusually small size at birth but otherwise a normal degree of maturation; (b) shortness of stature after birth, only rarely reaching 5 feet; (c) redness of the skin of the face, mainly the bridge of the nose and the adjoining upper cheek areas, the lower eyelids, and the lower lip. The skin problem, which is aggravated by sun exposure, varies in severity, being quite disfiguring in some affected persons and mild or even absent in others, but generally improving with age; (d) increased numbers of respiratory tract and ear infections, some of which are life-threatening. Mental ability is usually normal, although mild deficiency has occurred in a few affected persons. Infertility is the rule in men with Bloom syndrome and it appears to be reduced in women. The risk of cancer is considerably greater than normal.

The diagnosis of Bloom syndrome can be confirmed or ruled out by a cytogenetics laboratory, as cultured blood and skin cells show characteristic chromosome "instability," i.e., a tendency to breakage and rearrangement.

No treatment is known for the growth restriction. Affected individuals should be more attentive than usual in surveillance for cancer; i.e., annually to have a complete medical examination and to be particularly attentive of symptoms that could be early evidence of some neoplastic condition.

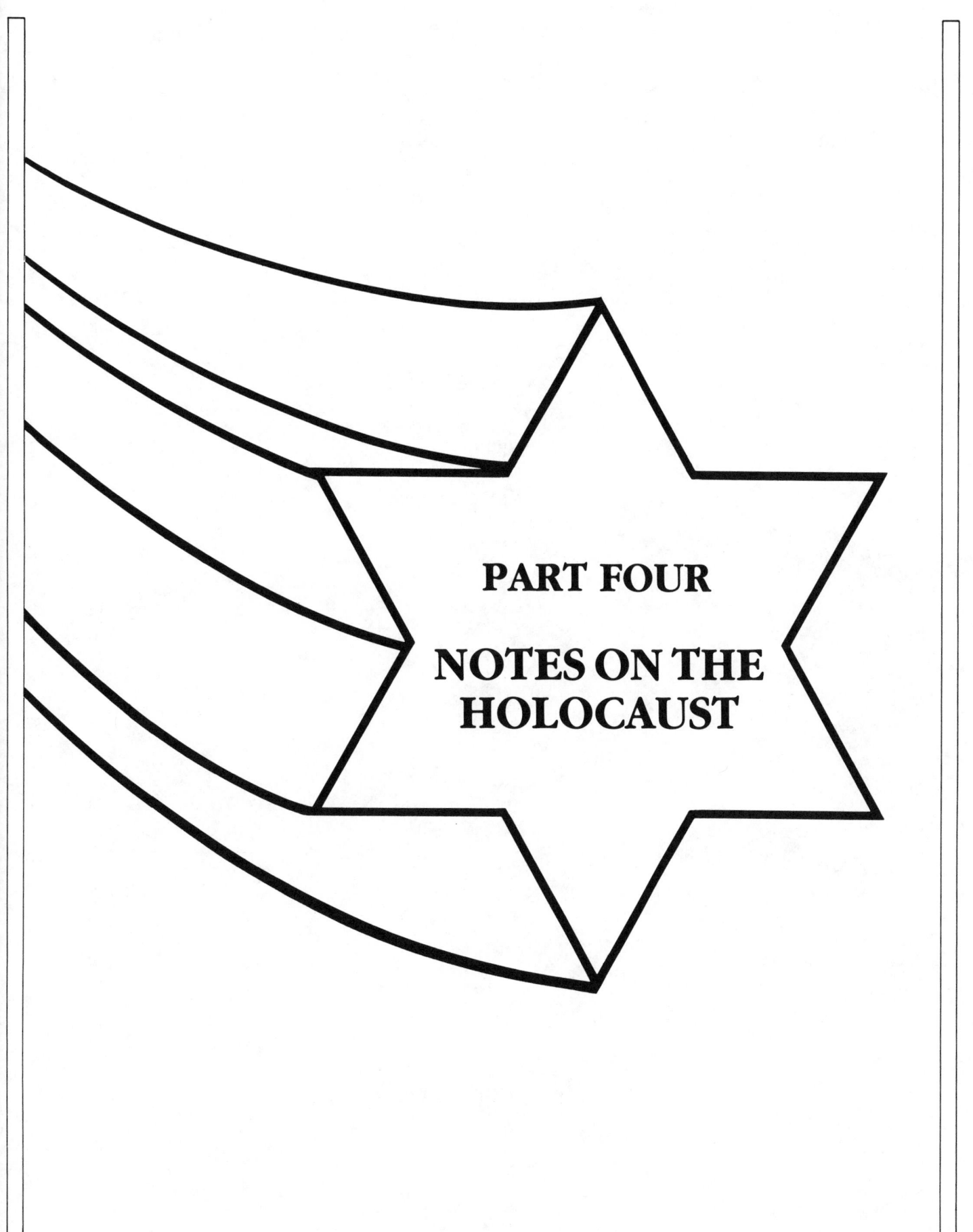

PART FOUR

NOTES ON THE
HOLOCAUST

18

Timeline

Ephraim Zuroff

1933

January 30. Adolf Hitler appointed chancellor of Germany.

February 27. Reichstag fire. Nazis unleash terror to ensure election results.

March 23. First concentration camp—Dachau—established.

March 27. Enabling Act—suspending civil liberties—passed by Nazi-dominated Reichstag.

April 1. Boycott of Jewish shops and businesses. Jewish professionals barred from entering offices.

April 7. First anti-Jewish decree: The Law for the Reestablishment of the Civil Service.

April 21. Ritual slaughter of animals in accordance with Jewish dietary laws prohibited in Germany.

April 26. Gestapo established.

May 10. Public burnings of books by Jews, those of Jewish origin, and opponents of Nazism.

Spring-Summer. Universities and the arts "cleansed" of Jewish influence. Jewish professors expelled, Jewish writers and artists prohibited from practicing their professions.

Spring-Summer. Jewish organizations in America and western Europe protest Nazi persecution of the Jews. A few call for boycott of Nazi Germany.

October 19. Germany leaves the League of Nations.

1934

June 30. "Night of the Long Knives": Nazis purge leadership of Storm Troops (SA) and opponents of Nazism.

August 2. Hitler named president and commander-in-chief of the armed forces following death of von Hindenburg.

1935

March 16. Germany renews conscription, in violation of Versailles treaty.

May 31. Jews barred from serving in German armed forces.

September 15. "Nuremburg Laws": anti-Jewish racial laws enacted. Jews could no longer be German citizens, marry Aryans, fly the German flag, and hire German maids under the age of forty-five.

November 15. Germans define Jew: anyone with three Jewish grandparents; someone with two Jewish grandparents who identifies as a Jew.

1936

February 4. David Frankfurter, young Jewish student, assassinates Wilhelm Gustloff, leader of Nazi party, in Switzerland.

March 3. Jewish doctors barred from practicing medicine in government institutions.

March 7. Germans march into the Rhineland, which had been demilitarized according to treaty.

May 5. Ethiopia occupied by Italy.

June 17. Himmler appointed chief of German police.

July. Germans and Italians join Franco's forces in the Spanish Civil War.

October 25. Hitler and Mussolini form Rome-Berlin Axis.

1937

July 16. Buchenwald concentration camp opens.

1938

March 13. *Anschluss:* annexation of Austria by Germany; all German antisemitic decrees immediately applied in Austria.

April 26. Jews in Reich must register all property with authorities.

August 1. Adolf Eichmann establishes Office of Jewish Emigration to speed up pace of forced emigration.

August 17. Decrees revoke all name changes by Jews and force those Jews who did not have names recognized as Jewish by German authorities to add "Israel" (for males) and "Sarah" (for females) as middle names.

September 29-30. Munich Conference: England and France agree to turn over Sudetenland (part of Czechoslovakia) to Germany.

October 5. Following request by the Swiss authorities, Germans order all Jews' passports marked with large red letter "J" to prevent Jews from smuggling themselves into Switzerland.

October 28. Jews with Polish citizenship living in Germany are expelled to Polish border. Poles refuse to admit them; Germans refuse to allow them back into Germany—17,000 stranded in frontier town of Zbasyn.

November 9-10. *Kristallnacht* (Night of Broken Glass): anti-Jewish pogrom in Germany and Austria. Two hundred synagogues destroyed, 7,500 Jewish shops looted, and 30,000 male Jews sent to concentration camps (Dachau, Buchenwald, Sachsenhausen).

November 12. Decree forcing all Jews to transfer retail businesses to Aryan hands.

November 15. All Jewish pupils expelled from German schools.

1939

January 30. Hitler threatens in Reichstag speech that if war erupts it will mean the *Vernichtung* (extermination) of European Jews.

March 15. Nazis occupy part of Czechoslovakia (Bohemia and Moravia); make Slovakia independent satellite state.

March 22. Germans occupy port of Memel.

August 23. Molotov-Ribbentrop Pact signed: non-aggression pact between Russia and Germany.

September 1. Beginning of World War II: Germany invades Poland.

September 17. Russia invades eastern Poland.

September 21. Heydrich issues directives to establish ghettos in German-occupied Poland.

November 23. Jews in German-occupied Poland forced to wear distinguishing badge.

November 28. First ghetto in Poland established in Piotrkow.

1940

April 9. Germans occupy Denmark and southern Norway.

April 27. Himmler issues directive to establish a concentration camp at Auschwitz.

May 7. Lodz ghetto closed off: approximately 165,000 inhabitants in 1.6 square miles.

May 10. Germany invades Holland, Belgium, and France.

May 20. Concentration camp established at Auschwitz.

June 22. France surrenders to Nazis.

August 8. Battle of Britain begins.

September 27. Rome-Berlin-Tokyo Axis.

November 15. Warsaw ghetto sealed off: approximately 500,000 inhabitants.

November 20-24. Hungary, Rumania, and Slovakia join Rome-Berlin-Tokyo Axis.

1941

January 21-26. Anti-Jewish riots in Rumania by Iron Guard: hundreds of Jews cruelly butchered.

March. Adolf Eichmann appointed head of Gestapo section for Jewish affairs.

April. Germany occupies Greece and Yugoslavia.

June. Vichy government deprives Jews of French North Africa of their rights as citizens.

June 22. Germany invades the Soviet Union.

End of June–December. Nazi *Einsatzgruppen* (special mobile killing units) carry out mass murder of Jews in areas of Soviet Union occupied by German army.

July 31. Heydrich appointed by Goering as responsible for implementation of Final Solution.

September 1. Jews in Third Reich obligated to wear yellow Star of David as distinguishing mark.

September 28-29. Massacre of Jews at Babi Yar—ravine outside Kiev: 34,000 murdered.

October 23. Murder of 19,000 Jews in Odessa.

October. Establishment of Birkenau camp: site of mass extermination of Jews, Gypsies, Poles, Russians, and others.

December 7. Japanese attack on Pearl Harbor.

December 8. Chelmno extermination camp begins operation: 340,000 Jews, 20,000 Poles and Czechs liquidated there by April 1943.

1942

January 20. Wannsee Conference: Heydrich reveals official plan to murder all Jews on European continent.

January. Jewish underground organizations established in Vilna ghetto and Kovno ghetto.

March 1. Extermination by gas begins in Sobibor extermination camp; by October 1943, 250,000 Jews murdered.

March 17. Extermination begins in Belzec extermination camp; by end of 1942, 600,000 Jews murdered.

Late March. Deportations to Auschwitz extermination camp begins.

June 1. Treblinka extermination camp begins operation; by August 1943, 700,000 Jews murdered.

June 30. All Jewish schools in Germany closed.

June. Jewish partisan unit established in forests of Belorussia.

July 28. Jewish fighting organization (ZOB) established in Warsaw ghetto.

Summer. Deportation of Jews to extermination camps from Holland, Poland, France, Belgium, Croatia. Armed resistance by Jews in ghettos of Kletzk, Nieswiez, Mir, Lachwa, Kremenets, and Tuchin.

November. Allied forces land in North Africa.

Winter. Deportation of Jews from Norway, Germany and Greece to extermination camps. Jewish partisan movement organized in forests near Lublin.

1943

January 18-21. Germans attempt to liquidate Jews in Warsaw ghetto; armed resistance by ghetto inhabitants.

February 2. German advance in Russia stopped at Stalingrad.

March. Liquidation of Cracow ghetto.

April 19. Warsaw ghetto revolt begins as Germans attempt to liquidate 70,000 ghetto inhabitants; Jewish underground fights Nazis until early June.

June. Himmler orders the liquidation of all the ghettos in Poland and the Soviet Union.

Summer. Armed resistance by Jews in Czestochowa, Lvov, Bedzin, Bialystok and Tarnow ghettos.

August 2. Armed revolt in Treblinka extermination camp.

Fall. Liquidation of large ghettos: Minsk, Vilna, Riga.

October 14. Armed revolt in Sobibor extermination camp.

1944

March 19. Germany occupies Hungary.

May 15. Nazis begin deporting Hungarian Jews; by June 27, 380,000 sent to Auschwitz.

June 6. Allied invasion of Normandy.

Spring-Summer. Red Army repels Nazi forces.

July 20. Group of German officers attempts to assassinate Hitler.

July 24. Russians liberate Maidanek extermination camp.

Summer. Liquidation of ghettos in Kovno (Kaunas), Shavli (Siauliai) and Lodz; inmates sent to concentration and extermination camps.

October 7. Revolt by inmates at Auschwitz: one crematorium blown up.

October 31. Remnants of Slovakian Jews deported to Auschwitz.

November 8. Beginning of death march of approximately 40,000 Jews from Budapest to Austria.

November. Last Jews deported from Theresienstadt model ghetto to Auschwitz.

1945

January 17. Evacuation of Auschwitz: beginning of death march of camp inmates.

January 25. Beginning of death march of inmates of Stutthof.

April 6-10. Death march of inmates of Buchenwald.

April. Red Army enters Germany from East; Allies enter from West.

April 30. Hitler commits suicide.

May 8. Germany surrenders: end of Third Reich.

19

"Believe the Unbelievable!"

Monty Noam Penkower

One respect in which the blackest of tragedies which we call the Holocaust defies historical analogy is that the victims have been taken to task for their own destruction. The dehumanizing process of any totalitarian regime, Bruno Bettelheim and Hannah Arendt contend, affects persecutors and victims alike. Thus the collaboration of the Jewish councils, a disintegration of personality in the ghettos and concentration camps, and the mindless resignation of a folk that went to its doom "like sheep to the slaughter." Raul Hilberg's pioneering analysis of the Nazi bureaucracy amply refutes Arendt's thesis that Adolf Eichmann and numerous others below him in the Nazi command structure took no initiative in making Europe *Judenfrei.* Yet even his massive volume postulates that the one group marked for complete annihilation during World War II was "caught in the strait jacket" of a four-millennia-old history that "always" reacted to force with "alleviation and compliance," and that the Jews consequently "plunged themselves physically and psychologically into catastrophe." Jewish experience, Edward Alexander has most recently argued, contributed to the fate of the Jews, for it harbors a "deep-seated unwillingness, ultimately, to credit the existence of evil."

Such observations often are factually unreliable, are produced by the dubious gift of hindsight, and suffer from a failure of imagination. Their authors, fortunate not to possess an intimate awareness of what David Rousset termed *l'univers concentraitionnaire,* hazard oversimplified formulations where precise study is especially required. The circumstances that faced each *Judenrat* and community before and after actually comprehending the Nazi design of total murder, as well as the alternatives for rescue then present in and outside Germany's Fortress Europe, are crucial issues that call for examination. These specific questions should also be placed within the context of Jewish traditional values and of the war itself.

Any effort that seeks, while avoiding what Yehuda Bauer properly designates "mystification," to understand how the legions of the swastika attained their ultimate *raison d'etre* must commence with the riddle of human perception, particularly as it operates in time of acute danger. Clinical analysis of behavior in *extremis* indicates that people facing an uncertain threat tend to deny its imminence. Human beings seek to reduce constant tension and actively avoid situations and information that would be likely to increase a feeling of unrelieved stress. The inability to make decisions follows as well, particularly since reaching judgment does not guarantee the reduction of "dissonance." Disbelief and defense mechanisms that dull reaction prevail, especially where cues pointing to calamity are ambiguous and when a disaster-stricken population is uncertain about the means available for escape. And when people are finally devoid of hope, like French Huguenots in the St. Bartholemew's Day Massacre, Turkish prisoners drowned at Napoleon's order, and individuals confronting a hangman's noose or a terrorist's bullet, passivity is also commonplace.

The behavior of non-Jews caught in the Nazi vise illustrates the same pychological responses. Occupied Europe, after all, provided both the administrative apparatus that made possible the invader's continued occupation and the labor force for Third Reich armament factories and large-scale industrial projects. There were no rebellions among the more than seven million foreign workers exploited in Germany itself, where few *Wehrmacht* members of military age could be found. The civilians wiped out in Lidice, Rome's Fosse Ardeatine caves, Oradour-sur-Glane, and Bande did not resist their killers. Uprisings in major cities only began in Polish Warsaw and Paris during the summer of 1944—one year after the Warsaw ghetto revolt. "Poland is not yet lost as long as we live" resounds the first line of the Polish national anthem, yet her Gentile citizens and intelligentsia went without opposition to graves dug by their own hands. Millions of Soviet prisoners of war, notwithstanding much military experience and their slogan "We shall strike the enemy in his own territory," acted in similar fashion whether on the soil of Holy Mother Russia or in Auschwitz. So, too, did the British 2nd Battalion's Norfolk Regiment at Paradis, more than 70 American soldiers near Malmedy, and countless prisoners of war subject to the "Bullet Decree" in Mauthausen.

Viewed in this context, what could have been expected of European Jewry under Hitler's heel?

Irrespective of various uncritical generalizations about their hereditary sensibilities, the march of history from the rise of Adolf Hitler in 1933 until the outbreak of world war six years later fully revealed the Jews as the outcasts of Western civilization. Buffeted by mounting antisemitism wherever they lived, Abraham's seed found possible havens firmly closed. Nations outdid one another at the 1938 Evian conference in professing all good will while refusing entry to a people in its time of greatest need. The serene tenor of life went on for others, outwardly unruffled and complacent, but Jews everywhere could not escape the ominous implications of the Nuremberg laws, *Kristallnacht,* and Hitler's Reichstag declaration in January, 1939, concerning "the destruction of the Jewish race in Europe" in the event of global conflict. On the eve of September 1, 1939, Poland initiated a ruthless program to force out of her borders the largest concentration of Jews on the continent, while His Majesty's Government in England aimed to bar the most obvious available shelter, the Jewish national home in Palestine.

Soon after the huge, finely tuned German war machine lunged eastward, the entire Nazi state apparatus began working with speed and in silence to resolve what it officially designated the "Jewish question." The head of the Security Police, Reinhard Heydrich, issued a "strictly secret" order on September 21 to all *Einsatzgruppen* chiefs that Jews be gathered into the larger cities as "the first prerequisite for the final aim." *Judenraete,* yellow star markings, expulsions from the Reich-Protektorat to the General-government, and ghettoization followed in the search for the so-called "Final Solution." The first mass killings—the last alternative in securing a *Judenrein* Europe, carried out by *SS Einsatzgruppen* immediately after the invasion of the Soviet territories in June 1941— caught the Jews there completely unaware. Limited Jewish groups in Poland, isolated in sealed-off ghettos with no radio or telephone communication to a usually hostile outside world, grasped their true predicament only by the summer of 1942. During the previous year and a half, for example, the Bund had sent "Aryan-looking" Jacob Celemenski from town to town, dispensing funds but also organizing delegations for a scheduled national conference in Warsaw. HeChalutz and other Zionist movements across Europe focused on retraining their youth for a better economic future.

The essential German ministries hitherto uninvolved in the program for total annihilation met covertly on January 20, 1942, in Berlin's Grossen Wannsee suburb to expedite it; not until December 17 did the Allies formally acknowledge the Reich's design. By August 1943, an estimated four million Jews in eastern and western Europe were no more. *Reichsfuhrer* SS Heinrich Himmler felt supremely confident that October in gloating before some district leaders that they were creating "an unwritten and never-to-be written page of glory" in Germany's history. The mass slaughter never stopped. Hungary, which had the last major Jewish community in Europe, lost more than 400,000 from her provinces between May and July 1944. A year later the total number of dead reached six million.

Deception, the most fiendish ingredient in accomplishing the Nazi murder plan, took an especially great toll. Heydrich's concentration order stated that Jews "have most decidedly participated in sniper attacks and plunder action," a pretext that later was amended to include the need to separate the natural disease carriers from clean "Aryans" and to provide the former with a kind of cultural-social autonomy. Before embarking on a full-blown catastrophe, the Nazis introduced the ghetto, yellow star, death from hunger and typhus, and the random bullet as part of a general effort to break the spirit. All these had been encountered by the Jews for generations, however. A Warsaw publication in 1940, for example, could therefore quite reasonably look to past Jewish heroism and suffering for some comfort in the present crisis. Amidst the shock involved in the constant shifting of walled-in boundaries, the brutal caprice of an ever-present armed guard, planted rumors, and abrupt "selections" for "labor" units, the enemy always offered the minutest ray of hope. A plethora of differently stamped exemption cards for work, assurances that only "foreigners" (followed by the sick and old)

would be sent to special "Jewish territories," and improved living conditions after mass deportations all blinded the designated victims. The noble Jewish tradition of collective responsibility was perverted by the German moloch so as to hamper further any thoughts of resistance. Many a *Judenrat* member and young partisan alike struggled, as a result, with the agonizing possibility of heavy reprisals against the community for their actions in a world of permanent terror. "Special treatment," "registration," "transport eastward," "hospital," "resettlement," and hundreds of other phrases also served to conceal the raw reality of diabolic intentions.

The fine art of deceit continued to its fiery completion. "In transit to Bialystok" read the sign over a dummy train station, equipped with a ticket office and a hand-painted lock whose hands pointed to 3:00 for the next departure, as Jews alighted from jammed railroad cars before being driven brutally to Treblinka's gas chambers. A massive Star of David topped a building, called the *"Judenstaat"* by the executioners, which housed ten vaults restricted to one people alone. "Work Makes One Free" *(Arbeit Macht Frei)* greeted all eyes over the main entrance to Auschwitz, where many arrivals printed names and birthdates in bold letters on their suitcases, expecting to get these back. Postcards stamped "Waldsee," each reading, "I am well. I work and am in good health," had to be written on occasion to relatives back home. The strains of fine music, performed by an all-inmate orchestra, accompanied millions on their last walk past a landscaped garden leading to underground chambers. Zyklon-B gas was then delivered to simulated shower rooms in vans with Red Cross markings, and the condemned met their death with cakes of soap in hand.

Under these circumstances, the first Jews who finally realized what ultimately awaited European Jewry as a whole met with a staunch refusal to believe among their own people. Jewish leaders dismissed the first news of Chelmno and other mass slaughter camps from Yehoshua Aronson at the end of 1941 as atrocity propaganda; the head of the Jewish councils in Upper East Silesia (Moses Merin) added that steady jobs in German army workshops alone could save the Jews, while an eminent Orthodox rabbi found traditional consolation in Psalm 23, verse 4: "Yea, though I walk through the valley of the shadow of death, I will fear no evil, for Thou art with me." At about the same time, after receiving testimony from some survivors of the first Ponary massacre, listening to anti-Nazi *Wehrmacht* officer Anton Schmidt, and recalling the grim prophecies of Hitler's *Mein Kampf,* Abba Kovner concluded that the Jews of Europe faced total destruction; on January 1, 1942, he drew up the first call for armed resistance. The United Partisans' Organization (FPO) in Vilna lost its leader, Yitschak Wittenberg, in a confrontation with the ghetto's remaining populace and the *Judenrat* chief six months later; however, a revolt in "the Jerusalem of Lithuania" never took place.

FPO emissaries and a Chelmno survivor reaching the Warsaw ghetto in early 1942 were not believed, while Jewish notables and party chiefs meeting there that April resolved to wait and not let young "provocateurs" bring on harsh German retaliation. Told about Auschwitz-Birkenau in September by a messenger from Sosnowiec, the Vienna

Judenrat responded: *"Unmoglich!"* A realistic appraisal only set in subsequent to the first mass deportations. One year later, after a handful of weapons were obtained against the greatest of odds, militant rebellion remarkably broke out across Poland.

Even then, Jewish communities yet unscathed refused to give credence to reports of complete destruction. The majority in Rumania, Bulgaria, and Denmark discounted reliable information in 1943 that they faced mortal danger. Receiving a letter that same year from Palestinian Jewish representatives in Istanbul about the vast slaughter in Poland, a leader of the Hungarian Zionist movement dismissed the news as mere propaganda, notwithstanding eyewitness accounts from Polish and Slovakian Jewish refugees who had been living in Hungary since 1942. The Budapest *Judenrat,* quickly assured by Eichmann and others they had no need to worry, did not believe an April, 1944, message from Bratislava's Michoel Dov Weissmandel that Europe's last major Jewish center faced deportation. Members of Zionist youth movements, operating from a *Judenrat* office, reached the Hungarian provinces with warnings of imminent disaster—to no avail. Transylvania Jewry, advised by a few of its own leaders to attempt a crossing over the nearby border to Rumania, also refused to assume the worst. Isolated politically and highly vulnerable to native antisemitism, the disoriented Jews of Hungary boarded the cattle cars to Auschwitz denying the certainty of their journey's end.

More decisive than the human response to disaster and German cunning in a hostile environment was European Jewry's natural inability to comprehend the irrationality of the Holocaust. Not that the victims refused to "credit the fact" that they had enemies capable of murder: history had provided them with an overabundance of persecutors. Could most go any further, however, than that heroine of *The Shop on Main Street* who cried out, in a final stab of recognition: "Pogrom!"? The closest parallel would have been the Turkish annihilation of Armenians during World War I, yet not all Armenians were then targeted for death, and, in any case, that act of genocide had receded from the memory of most Europeans by 1939. Moreover, as Emmanuel Ringelblum noted in his Warsaw diary after grasping Hitler's fanatical plan for the Jews, "History *does not* repeat itself. Especially now, now that we stand at the crossroads, witnessing the death pangs of an old world and the birth pangs of a new." Now birth itself constituted the most heinous crime in the Third Reich canon, expiated only by death.

Lacking a complete analogy to draw upon, the Jews could view the enemy's emphasis on survival by work as entirely logical. After all, asked such different *Judenrat* leaders as Adam Czerniakow, Ephraim Barash, Jacob Gens, and Mordecai Chaim Rumkowski, would the Third Reich's military machine sacrifice thousands of valuable laborers, much less divert precious rolling stock for death transports, during the war? Indeed, the labor ghettos enjoyed the longest duration; it is moot whether the halt of the Russian advance during the summer of 1944 prevented the survival of thousands of Jews in Lodz, Kovno, and elsewhere.

Incredulity also stemmed from a deeply rooted belief of many in the culture and conscience of the West. Assimi-lated Jews failed to fathom that the Germany of Kant and Goethe could be capable of humanly unimaginable barbarism. Communist party members were betrayed by the "comrades" with whom they had built up cities like Minsk or by the Soviet partisans in the forests of Byelorussia. Those especially who had taken part in the steady development over the past two centuries toward equality for all, thereby contributing to new Jewish welfare institutions, schools, synagogues, newspapers, movements, and communities across the European landscape, maintained their trust in liberty and humanism. Finally, the Jews clung to the noble but naive faith that if only the Allies knew, the death factories would cease their grisly operation. Alexander Donat spoke for them all, in writing after the war: "We fell victim to our faith in mankind, our belief that humanity had set limits to the degradation and persecution of one's fellow man." The abrupt shattering of this conviction for Czerniakow, the realization that all his liberal and reasonable defenses were illusions and that the Nazis planned to ship every one of "his" charges to Treblinka, led the idealistic head of the Warsaw *Judenrat* to take cyanide rather than sign the second deportation order in July 1942. The transports rolled inexorably ahead.

As for the West, which alone could have checked the tempo of Germany's Final Solution, its political leaders were also slow to grasp the singular nature of the Jewish catastrophe. Reports constantly reached London and Washington of Jewish suffering, but these were scattered and "atrocity" conjured up propaganda stories from earlier wars. Even after realizing that the Third Reich had made starvation a weapon of annihilation, public opinion agreed with Winston Churchill's publicly expressed conviction that "no form of relief can be devised which would not directly or indirectly assist the enemy's war effort." A research paper in January 1942, for Great Britain's Royal Institute for International Affairs surveyed the future possibilities of European Jewish assimilation, "considerable economic stratification," and a "relative decline" in German areas; it offered no word, moreover, regarding the war's possible effects on east European Jewry. Government officials continued their policy of the previous decade to dampen news coverage about Jewry's plight and so avoid the charge of antisemites at home and abroad that the Allies were fighting a "Jewish war." Rumors conveyed through Jewish sources in Switzerland during the summer of 1942 of a Nazi plan to murder all surviving Jews "at one blow" and to use the corpses for soap and fertilizer, recalling British intelligence's admitted fabrication about a German "cadaver conversion plant" during World War I, were thus suspect. Deportation to Poland, both governments taken in by Axis propaganda, meant forced labor at the Nazi war front. This information suited prior expectations, much like American experts erred some months earlier regarding a Japanese attack in the mid-Pacific. Only confirmation from such groups as the Polish government-in-exile and the International Red Cross, as well as mounting publicity from Jewish and other organizations, after more than two million had already perished, led the Allies to declare in December that the perpetrators of this "bestial policy" would not escape retribution.

Still, disbelief continued to the war's end. The chairman of the British Joint Intelligence Committee, upon receiving reports in July 1943, of the use of gas chambers to murder the victims, asserted: "The Poles, and to a far greater extent the Jews, tend to exaggerate German atrocities in order to stoke us up." On July 11, 1944, Jewish Agency spokesman Moshe Shertok felt the need to point out, among other reasons for the bombing of the death installations, that such an act would "go far towards dissipating the incredulity which still persists in Allied quarters with regard to the report of mass extermination perpetrated by the Nazis." Indeed, that very day even the well-informed Churchill expressed his sudden shock at the massacre of Hungarian Jewry, particularly since, as he wrote his foreign secretary, "probably the greatest and most horrible crime ever committed in the whole history of the world" was being carried out "by scientific machinery, by nominally civilized men in the name of a great State and one of the leading races of Europe." The BBC refused to use an eyewitness account by its own correspondent in August 1944, of *liberated* Majdanek, thinking the detailed story "a Russian propaganda stunt." As late as that December the American under secretary of war asked the World Jewish Congress's administrative secretary: "Tell me, do you really believe that those terrible things happened?" "One notable tendency in Jewish reports on this problem," noted an official of the Foreign Office's Refugee Department to his colleagues the following month, "is to exaggerate the numbers of deportations and deaths." It is not surprising that isolated Jewish survivors in Rumania, Belgium, and Greece refused to acknowledge the utter depravity of the Holocaust after their rescue.

Official opinion, even when convinced of the facts, remained skeptical that publicity would have the desired effect. Repeated warnings, various quarters argued, tended to "debase the currency," might result in "increased maltreatment" to the victims, and aid Joseph Goebbels's propaganda that Jews abroad ran the Allied war. But in addition, as the *Reichskommisar* for the *Ostland* had observed to his superior in June 1943, those hearing and reading the facts would not be prepared to give them credence. The Office of War Information did follow a policy of restraint, even attempting to hold up publication in November 1944, of a report on Auschwitz-Birkenau by four Jewish escapees and one Polish officer on the ground that the American public would regard its contents as similar to World War I atrocity tales; as a result, the government's reliability on other information released concerning the war effort would be open to doubt. A Roper poll taken one month later indeed revealed that the great majority of Americans could not believe that millions of Jews had perished in the Nazi onslaught. The British and American people, concluded an official with SHAEF's Plans and War Division in early 1945, were still as a whole not willing to entertain the awful truth. His opposite number in the British Political and Intelligence Division agreed, adding that individuals who would be likely to respond to cruelty to a child or an animal in peacetime "will, after years of being told about brutalities, become anesthetized even to a Lublin." War, after all, entails suffering, while the Holocaust beggared the imagination.

Even those who viewed the annihilation process first-hand found it difficult to internalize it as reality. Three Jews, officially visiting Belzec to examine rumors about the first big "action" from Crakow in March 1942, witnessed that "very hectic work was taking place." Eichmann completely took in an International Red Cross delegation, on an inspection of Theresienstadt in June 1944, with a specially built Potemkin-type village; the report of a second visit several months *after* the liberation of Auschwitz, where most of the camp's Jews had perished, accepted at face value the SS *Obersturmbannfuhrer's* explanation that the Third Reich wished the camp to serve "as a practical experiment, on a small scale, for the future Jewish State to which a certain strip of land should be allotted after the war." Six Jehovah's Witnesses who lived by the side of the gas chambers and crematoria in Birkenau doubted their own eyes; on their return to Holland *during* the war, they, like others before them, were not believed. "How could it be possible for them to burn people, children, and for the world to keep silent?" agonized a young Elie Wiesel after being confronted with Auschwitz. "No, none of this could be true. It was a nightmare. . . ."

This psychological hindrance also affected Palestinian Jewry. As early as October 1939, a meeting in Jerusalem of *chalutz* organizations projected the destruction of Poland's Jews as the first victims of "an awesome holocaust [*shoa ayuma*] which has engulfed the world." Yet a sustained study about the plight of European Jewry, published in Tel Aviv in September 1941, failed to speak of systematic annihilation. One year later, three months after a Bund cable to London gave the first (underestimated) news about the slaughter of 700,000 Jews in Poland, an eminent Polish refugee wrote that "millions" were awaiting salvation. Jewish Agency officials continued to question Geneva reports of mass killings across Europe until survivors from Poland reached the Promised Land in mid-November 1942, just when confirmation came from New York and London. Still, Palestinian emissaries to the Yishuv's rescue committee in Istanbul during the spring and summer of 1943 fully intended to send thousands of letters and parcels to old addresses in Poland. Isaac Gruenbaum, chairman of the rescue committee, asked Istanbul in June 1944, if 150,000 Hungarian Jews had indeed been moved eastward, and if food packages could be dispatched there; after the war he had but one question of Hungarian Zionist Reszo Kastner: why did resistance not take place? The Zionist leadership never wavered to the war's end in publicly supporting the May 1942, Biltmore program (all of Palestine as a Jewish state), although the millions for whom it was intended had obviously perished.

American Jewish organizations were not immune either. Publications hesitated at first to print news of the death centers, and some persisted in writing of continued Jewish life in Poland. The Joint Distribution Committee refused to accept the argument that drastic measures, even if contravening government policy, should be taken. One Agudas Israel executive, opposed to this position, still pleaded for an Allied mercy ship laden with food and drugs to save "millions" in Poland—this on the eve of the Warsaw ghetto uprising. A memorandum to the Bermuda conference on refugees concurrently submitted by the World Jewish Congress, whose centers in New York and abroad also attempted a more radical program of rescue, unconsciously accepted German propaganda in asserting that transports to build fortifications at the Russian front took the heaviest Jewish toll. Most other groups, as epitomized by the umbrella-type American Jewish Conference of August 1943, focused on the postwar relief and reconstruction of European Jewry. As in Palestine, life went on, despair giving way to resignation.

Allied callousness toward the Jewish people reflected a different elementary failure of perception. Having at first misjudged the dimensions of the Holocaust, London and Washington continued to deny Jewry the sense of communal distinction that had accounted for its mysterious survival these past 4,000 years. Heir to the Enlightenment's emphasis on personal freedom and the good inherent in all human beings, the West concluded that according the one people lacking national sovereignty special consideration as an independent entity would mean the vindication of Hitler's philosophy of *das Volk*. Not by accident did Secretary of State Cordell Hull take the occasion of the Balfour Declaration's twenty-fifth anniversary to declare that the postwar world should ensure Jews the full rights of citizens everywhere, a view eagerly applauded by a British government in retreat from its previous pledge of 1917 to establish a Jewish national home in Palestine. Paradoxically, this meant, in point of fact, that the unique fate of Jewry was either concealed under "Poles," "Belgians," etc., or refused sympathy because Jews were classified as "enemy aliens" when found in countries loyal to the Axis. In either instance Hitler—who thought otherwise—secured his primary objective.

Thus it never occurred to the Anglo-American Alliance that European Jewry, like other peoples opposed to the Third Reich, should be assigned any role in the general war strategy. Greeks would obtain relief to avert famine, Poles and Czechs arms for resistance, but not Jews. French youngsters in very impressive numbers could be spirited to safety across the Pyrenees, but not a marked people to Spain and Turkey. Tens of thousands of Yugoslavs and Greeks received a cordial welcome in Middle East refugee camps, yet HMG continued the draconian 1939 White Paper throughout the hostilities for those most needing their national and accessible homeland. Worried lest the Third Reich's leadership "embarrass" the Allies by "flooding" them with unwanted Jews, the two major Western powers sought a joint declaration on Palestine to quash public agitation over that haven in the war years, and mutually consented not to alter their respective limited immigration quotas. (Enemy prisoners fared far better: boats were found to ferry some 430,000 to camps in the United States during the world conflict.) Not a word of the infamous SS death marches appeared in SHAEF directives or in the Western press. The Intergovernmental Committee on Refugees, the British Cabinet Committee on the Reception and Accommodation of Refugees, the Bermuda conference on refugees, and the War Refugee Board all omitted mention in their titles of the one group for which each had been principally created; rarely did Allied statements refer to the persecution of the Jews. For most of World War II, these officially designated nonpersons did not fare better with self-professed guardians of humanitarianism and morality like the International Red Cross and the Vatican, or with the neutral governments. Moscow ignored the entire matter.

Only one Jewish battalion and a tiny parachute unit from the Yishuv saw action, and these grudging concessions from 10 Downing Street and 1600 Pennsylvania Avenue were not granted until toward the end of the war. Nineteen RAF de Havilland Mosquito bombers escorted by Spitfires successfully attacked an Amiens prison in "Operation Jericho" on February 18, 1944, to free nearly 100 members of the French resistance, but the crematoria and the railroad lines leading to them never became prime targets. Reprisals on German cities expressly for atrocities against Jews, the dispatch of funds for underground rescue, and delaying negotiations over the Eichmann "goods for blood" offer were all ruled out by the West. Responses to specific evacuation proposals concerning Jews in Transnistria, France, Rumania, Bulgaria, and Hungary were not commensurate with the urgent need. Szmul Zygielbojm's suicide, meant to move Churchill, Franklin Roosevelt, and the free world to action in mid-1943, went unheeded. FDR fled from 400 Orthodox rabbis who marched on Washington that October; the British prime minister avoided World Zionist Organization president Chaim Weizmann. Instead, to defeat the enemy and have the Jews return to their European "homes" after the war served as the fixed philosophy for the duration. Alas, that policy proved bankrupt for a powerless people.

A few courageous souls attempted to shatter the Allied conspiracy of silence, as well as the prevailing illusion that nothing could be done. Near insuperable difficulties confronted various Jews and Gentiles who responded to the cry of conscience. The Babylonian Talmud prescribes their reward: "Whosoever saves a single Jew, Scripture ascribes it to him as though he had saved an entire world." Yet these individual's valiant race against calculated mass-production death wrested only limited successes. Killers and indifferent bystanders, by depersonalizing the Jews of Europe, marked these innocents for doom. Hitler, Himmler, Eichmann, Antonescu, Horthy, and others of such ilk believed with apocalyptic certainty that a demonic international Jewry controlled Germany's opponents; the West, in whose councils the stateless Jews commanded no political leverage, consigned the Third Reich's primary victim to one category: expendable. Behind the mask called twentieth-century civilization, as a consequence, countless more worlds were destroyed.

Thereafter

Buchenwald, liberated by Combat Team A of the U.S. Army's 6th Armored Division on April 11, 1945, at last allowed mankind to peer into the abyss that had ultimately claimed these six million human beings. Stark horror gripped the parliamentary and congressional missions, soon visiting the camp at the invitation of SHAEF commander Dwight D. Eisenhower, which testified about "the organized crime against civilization and humanity" and "the lowest point of degradation to which humanity has descended." Edward R. Murrow's terse live radio broadcast—"There were two rows of bodies stacked up like cordwood. They were thin and very white"—and a film of bulldozers pushing heaps of dead naked bodies like refuse into a pit shocked people everywhere. The holder of the Keys of St. Peter, who had moved so cautiously to save the Jews, tried to distinguish between a minority of war criminals and a docile, deluded majority of the Germany nation (at least 50 percent Catholic), reported Great Britain's delegate to the Holy See. Eisenhower's son later recalled that it was "impossible actually to believe that what one was seeing was real," just as the distances between galaxies escape full appreciation. Some Polish Jews in Buchenwald even wrote to relatives, long since victims of the Final Solution, asking to look after their affairs and obtain from Gentile neighbors the keys to prewar dwellings.

A barrage of graphic, first-hand accounts from across the blood-soaked soil of Europe could not be denied for long, however. Richard Crossman, then deputy director of SHAEF's Psychological Warfare Division, expressed the sudden transformation of attitudes: "Though we had heard and reported many stories of Nazi massacres of Jews and Slavs, we had never believed in the possibility of 'genocide.' . . . Now we were to realize that our propaganda had fallen far behind the truth." Few had shared Edgar Snow's publicly articulated vision in October, 1944, grasped after his inspecting Majdanek, of the diabolic system which "for the first time made a totalitarian industry out of the reduction of the human being from an upright ambulatory animal to a kilogram of gray ashes." So intense was the trauma that war correspondent Murrow, on reaching Dachau in early May, 1945, began a memorable broadcast with the words, "I pray you will believe me."

The human mind slowly awakened to the reality of the Holocaust after V-E day. The Nuremberg, *Einsatzkommando,* and Eichmann trials, among others, revealed beyond doubt that the Oxford English Dictionary's illustration, printed in the year of Hitler's ascension to power, that "Louis VII once made a holocaust of thirteen hundred persons in a church" would no longer suffice. Man now could not help but "believe the unbelievable!," as the Polish underground frantically cabled London during the summer of 1942. The same liberals who reassuringly thought that Adolf Hitler could be placated in the 1930s now had to grapple with the existence of evil incarnate, as well as their own fundamental inaction at a time when men, women, and children pleaded for the sacred breath of life. This catastrophe is, therefore, far more than the sum of its victims.

A methodical German fervor to destroy not matched by an Allied will to save carried out the inconceivable. In January, 1944, Arthur Koestler warned about the current disbelief in the Nazi *Endloesung:* "A dog run over by a car upsets our emotional balance and digestion; three million Jews killed in Poland cause but a moderate uneasiness. . . . We are unable to embrace the total process with our awareness; we can only focus on little lumps of reality." He should have added that indifference to deeds of barbarism also stemmed from Western civilization's gradual loss of the sense of solidarity. A slow decay of conscience took place in the world before and while the storm clouds of war rolled across Europe. Without that loss of a sense of certain decencies, the Jews, many of whom resisted Nazi attempts at dehumanization and miraculously adhered to their basic values *de profundis,* would not have gone abandoned into the night. Christianity and Western humanism avoided the moral imperative to try to save an innocent people, including 1,500,000 children who perished, and through their silence became accomplice to mass murder. The kingdom of barbed wire and ashes, as a consequence, enjoyed an unbridled reign.

Mankind has forgotten too soon. "Something terrible had fallen like a meteorite into history," as Abba Kovner expressed it years later, when the Holocaust showed the whole world that the blood of a people could be shed with impunity. The seeker after an etiology for modern-day genocides in Tibet, Bangladesh, Biafra, Paraguay, Burundi, parts of southeast Asia, as well as the most recent grave threat to Jewish existence in Israel during October, 1973, should scrutinize Babi Yar, Sobibor, and the diaries of the *Sonderkommando.* The post-Auschwitz recognition of what Emil Fackenheim has denominated "radical evil" must, in turn, be a guide to radical humanist action. Only thus can the victims be snatched from oblivion and complacency give way to personal commitment. Once and for all, the calamitous fallacy that what happens in one part of the globe is not another's affair must be shed, lest one day a brother's keeper be again found wanting in the face of extremity. The madness of an escalating arms race that currently casts a lengthening shadow of omnicide—the transformation of our planet into a universal nuclear crematorium—mandates that active compassion which flows from mutual need replace the crime of indifference.

The cancer of bestiality is the concern of us all, and the infinite preciousness of life requires daily affirmation. *The Plague,* one of the first artistic renditions of the years of France's occupation under the Nazi jackboot, sounded this quintessential lesson of the Holocaust unequivocally in June, 1947. Albert Camus's allegory contains a passage that might well serve as the epitaph for European Jewry's fate during World War II:

> Sometimes at midnight, in the great silence of the sleep-bound town, the doctor turned on his radio before going to bed for the few hours' sleep he allowed himself. And from the ends of the earth, across thousands of miles of land and sea, kindly well-meaning speakers tried to voice their fellow-feeling, and indeed did so, but at the same time proved the utter incapacity of every man truly to share in suffering that he cannot see. "Oran! Oran!" In vain the call rang across oceans, in vain Rieux listened hopefully: always the tide of eloquence began to flow, bringing home still more the unbridgeable gulf that lay between Grand and the speaker. "Oran, we're with you!" they called emotionally. But not, the doctor told himself, to love or to die together—"and that's the only way. They're too remote."

Therein, as well, lies the key to our own *human* survival.

20

Rescue Via The Far East: The Attempt to Save Polish Rabbis and Yeshivah Students, 1939-41

Efraim Zuroff

One of the most interesting, yet least known, of the various rescue projects attempted by Jewish organizations in Allied territory during the Holocaust was the partially successful attempt to rescue several thousand Polish rabbis and yeshivah students. They had escaped to Lithuania shortly after the outbreak of World War II and sought to emigrate from there to the West. This episode deserves careful scrutiny because of the unique circumstances and the relatively large number of people rescued. An analysis of these events helps explain the complex issues of Jewish response and rescue efforts during the Holocaust.

Background

During the interwar period, Poland was the most important center of Jewish learning in the world. After World War I and the establishment of the Polish republic, it became the home of the majority of the world's foremost institutions of higher Talmudic learning *(yeshivot)*, most of which were located in the Kresy region on Poland's eastern border with the Soviet Union.

Most of these *yeshivot* had been established prior to World War I, among them: Mir (founded 1817), Radin (1859), Lomza (1883), and Kamenetz (1897). Others, such as Grodno and Pinsk, were relatively new, established during the interwar period. It should be noted that during World War I, many of these institutions (for example, Mir, Radin, and Nowogrudok) had fled to Russia and returned to Poland after the war. Among the reasons for their return was the establishment of the communist regime, which they knew would not allow them to exist on Soviet soil. Other *yeshivot,* such as Etz Hayim, originally located in Slutzk, preferred when Slutzk became part of the Soviet Union, to move to Poland, where Jewish religious and educational activities were permitted.

The interwar period was a time of unprecedented growth for the Polish *yeshivot,* both in the size of the student body and in the physical expansion of the various institutions.[1] Hundreds of students from all over the world travelled to eastern Poland to engage in intensive Torah study, among them many students from western Europe and the United States.[2] In 1938, over 4,600 young men were enrolled in the *yeshivot* of eastern Poland;[3] this figure indicated the significant increase in the number of students enrolled in these institutions.[4] Moreover, this development occurred despite the rapid deterioration in the political and economic situation of Polish Jewry during this period.

The young men enrolled in the *yeshivot* of eastern poland undoubtedly constituted the elite of those engaged in full-time Torah studies. The Polish *yeshivot,* and the Lithuanian yeshivot (Telshe, Ponevez, and Slobodka), influenced Jewry the world over with their high level of studies and the subsequent work of their graduates. The overwhelming majority of the rabbis and religious leaders active in the orthodox community or in leadership positions in Europe and America were the products of these institutions.[5]

Throughout the interwar period, most of the *yeshivot* in eastern Poland received substantial financial assistance from Jewish communities in Europe and the United States.[6] Funds were transmitted by individuals as well as by the American Jewish Joint Distribution Committee (JDC). To a lesser extent, funds also came from Ezrat Torah, a philanthropic agency established by the Union of Orthodox Rabbis of the United States and Canada (Agudat haRabbanim). The funds sent to these institutions covered a significant part of their budgets.[7] In addition, the various Polish *roshei yeshivot* (deans of the *yeshivot*) frequently travelled abroad to raise funds.[8] In fact, most of the *yeshivot* even opened offices in New York to facilitate their fund-raising activities in the United States.[9]

These activities reinforced the ties between the *yeshivot* and the Jewish communities in western Europe and the United States. As a result, students from abroad went to Poland to study in Mir, Kamenetz, Grodno, Baranowitz, and other *yeshivot,* as well as to Lithuania to study in Telshe and Slobodka.[10]

Another important factor in the relationship between these *yeshivot* and the Jewish communities in the United States was that despite their ostensible orthodoxy, most religious Jews in the United States were far removed from the exacting level of religious observance prescribed by the *yeshivot.* All the leading rabbis and political leaders in the orthodox community in the United States, however, had studied in these *yeshivot* and fully identified with the philosophy espoused by these institutions. The rabbis felt that because of the inroads made by assimilation, it was incumbent upon them to support institutions that were of such vital importance to the growth of what they considered to be the only authentic form of Judaism. The ties between Polish *yeshivot* and Jewish communities in the West were important; they were one reason for rescue efforts during the Holocaust, that saved the lives of hundreds of rabbis and their yeshivah students.[11]

Escape to Vilna, October 1939-June 1940

Seventeen days after the Nazi invasion of Poland, the Soviets also invaded Poland from the east. Within a short time they occupied the eastern half of Poland in accordance with the terms of the Molotov-Ribbentrop agreement (August 1939). The *yeshivot* located in eastern Poland now found themselves under Soviet rule. The rabbis and yeshivah students—many of whom had directly experienced the Soviets' negative attitude to Judaism and Jewish culture—considered the future of their educational institutions to be in jeopardy. Fearing that the Torah centers of eastern Poland would be closed by the Soviet authorities,[12] they began to look for possible escape routes.[13] The news that the Soviets planned to return Vilna (under Polish sovereignty during the interwar period and subsequently in independent and neutral Lithuania) caused many yeshiva students to try to reach Vilna.

The news that Vilna was transferred to Lithuania was announced in early October.[14] Within a week, the first yeshivah students set out for Vilna. Among the first to leave were the students of the Kletzk yeshivah who left on October 14, 1939 (on the Hebrew calendar: Rosh Hodesh Heshvan, the traditional first day of the winter semester following the High Holiday vacation),[15] and the students of the Mir yeshivah, who set out a day later.[16] Each yeshivah made its own decision to flee; there was no coordinated planning among the various institutions. A series of similar decisions made by numerous individuals coincided, and, in most cases, the decision was not made by the *roshei yeshivot* or by the yeshivah's administration on behalf of all the students. Based on the testimonies of those who escaped, almost identical developments took place independently in each yeshivah prior to the decision to flee.[17] The news that Vilna was transferred to Lithuania and that transportation, albeit overcrowded, still existed between eastern Poland and Vilna, galvanized the students into action. In several places, as, for example, at the Mir yeshivah, travel fever was widespread among the students.[18]

It is important to note that students normally did not play a role in determining yeshivah policy. The *rosh yeshivah* decided crucial questions, and his word was binding on both students and faculty. In this particular case, the students generally turned to the *roshei yeshivot* for advice. In most instances, however, the question was rhetorical and was posed only after the decision to go to Vilna had already been made.[19] In effect, the students dragged the rabbis and administrators with them. The latter, due to age, status, and circumstances, were more conservative and less likely to implement rapid or daring moves. It should also be noted that all the *roshei yeshivot,* in contrast to the overwhelming majority of yeshivah students, were married and had children,[20] a factor that contributed to their doubts and hesitations about moving. Moreover, many other people also doubted the wisdom of moving to Vilna; this sentiment was reflected in popular jokes circulating in eastern Poland: for example, "Vilna has indeed been handed over to Kovno (the capital of Lithuania), but Kovno will soon be taken over by Moscow" or "Vilna does not belong to Lithuania, it's just the opposite."[21] Others thought it was a Soviet ploy to discover those opposed to the Communist regime.[22] Despite these doubts, many students regarded the reincorporation of Vilna in Lithuania as a fortuitous opportunity that ought to be exploited quickly before the border was closed. Some considered the matter so pressing that they travelled to Vilna even on the Sabbath.[23]

The decision to flee was made spontaneously; most *yeshivot* did not pursue a policy established by the *roshei yeshivot*. Groups of students began running away; others followed; the *roshei yeshivot,* faculty, administration, and members of their families went in their wake. Apparently, only in the Kamenetz yeshivah were the roles reversed: the students followed their *rosh yeshivah,* Rabbi Boruch Ber Leibowitz.[24]

The Lithuanians entered Vilna on October 28, 1939. During the first half of November, the new border between Lithuania and Soviet-occupied Poland was established, and subsequently civilian travel between the two regions was stopped.[25] At that point, over 1,500 rabbis and yeshivah students had reached Vilna, among them the entire student body and faculty of several yeshivot, including Mir (approximately 300 students), Baranowitz (more than 200), Kletzk (approximately 200), Kamenetz (about 200), and Radin and Grodno (statistics unavailable). Several students of the Volozhin yeshivah also arrived in Vilna simultaneously with students from most major *yeshivot* in eastern Poland. Other arrivals included prominent rabbis,[25] for example, Rabbi Yitzchak Zeev Soloveitchik of Brisk, and also many other communal rabbis from eastern Poland.[26]

The closing of the Lithuanian border in mid-November 1939 made it difficult to reach Vilna. Many who tried were apprehended and arrested by either the Lithuanian or the Soviet border guards. In addition, the winter of 1939-40 was one of the coldest Europe had experienced in the twentieth century. Severe weather conditions impeded travel, a fact reflected in the small number of women and children among the refugees reaching Vilna.[27] Nevertheless, by the end of 1939, approximately 2,100 rabbis and yeshivah students had reached the "Jerusalem of Lithuania,"[28] where they were welcomed by the Jewish community. Their friendly reception undoubtedly encouraged those still in occupied Poland to attempt flight there.[29] Indeed, according to several oral sources, Rabbi Chaim Ozer Grodzinski, the leader of the orthodox community in Vilna and chairman of the local Vaad ha-Yeshivot, sent emissaries to Poland to encourage yeshivah students to flee; there is, however, no documentary evidence to support this.[30]

In January 1940, the Russians tried to seal the border between Lithuania and Soviet-occupied Poland, a factor that resulted in a reduced number of refugees. Many refugees hired professional smugglers and sometimes paid exorbitant fees to cross the border. Despite the numerous obstacles, Jews fled from Poland to Lithuania from late 1939 to June 1940, when Lithuania lost its independence. A total of ca. 14,000 Jewish refugees arrived in Vilna, including many Polish Zionist leaders, e.g., Moshe Kleinbaum (Sneh), Menachem Begin, and Zerach Warhaftig; members of Zionist youth movements;[31] 2,440 yeshivah students;[32] and 171 rabbis.[33] The rabbis included well-known *roshei yeshivot,* for example, Rabbi Aaron Kotler (Etz Hayim of Kletzk), Rabbi Eliezer Yehuda Finkel (Mir), Rabbi Elchanan Wasserman (Ohel Torah of Baranowitz), Rabbi Abraham Yaphin (Beit Yoseph of Bialystok), Rabbi Mendel Zacks (Radin), and Rabbi Shabtai Yogel (Slonim).[34]

Life in Independent Lithuania, October 1939-June 1940

Upon arrival in Vilna, the generally penniless rabbis and yeshivah students turned to Rabbi Chaim Ozer Grodzinski for aid. He wrote and cabled colleagues and former students throughout the world soliciting funds. The refugee scholars were housed temporarily in local synagogues and houses of study where they continued their studies.[35] The United Refugee Committee, consisting of representatives from all refugee groups, was established in Vilna. Headed by Dr. Jacob Robinson, this committee distributed the aid received from the JDC and represented the refugees before Lithuanian authorities. (The Vaad ha-Yeshivot represented the rabbis and yeshivah students on the United Refugee Committee.)[36] The JDC allocated $22 (US) per refugee per month,[37] and Rabbi Grodzinski attempted to obtain additional sums for the rabbis and yeshivah students.

Rabbi Grodzinski's appeal resulted in donations from Jewish communities throughout the world.[38] Clothing was collected in Lithuania and abroad and sent to Vilna for the refugee scholars.[39] Rabbi Grodzinski turned to his former student Rabbi Eliezer Silver of Cincinnati for assistance. Eliezer Silver was a prominent figure in the American orthodox community and a leader of the Agudat ha-Rabbanim, the leading orthodox organization in the United States at that time. Agudat ha-Rabbanim decided at an emergency meeting held in mid-November 1940 to establish an Emergency Committee for war-torn *yeshivot*. The goal of this committee, which eventually became the Vaad ha-Hatzalah (or Vaad Hatzolah, as it was popularly referred to), was to transfer the *yeshivot* from Lithuania to safety abroad; half were to go to Eretz Israel, half to the United States. From its inception, the Vaad had two major tasks: 1) fund raising for assisting students and rabbis in Vilna; and 2) arranging for the emigration of the *yeshivot*.[40]

The financial situation of the refugees was relatively difficult until the committee and various independent individuals raised and sent money to Vilna. Nevertheless, the scholars could continue their studies.[41] Most of the *yeshivot* that had moved to Vilna continued their work. Students from those *yeshivot* that had remained in Poland now attended others.[42] In addition, two *kollels* of refugee Polish rabbis were established in Vilna.[43] Besides financial assistance, Rabbi Grodzinski and the members of the Vaad ha-Yeshivot obtained the necessary permits to allow them to remain in Vilna. Funds were also allocated to help smuggle additional family members from Soviet-occupied Poland into Vilna.[44]

In January 1940, the Lithuanian government decreed that all refugees who had arrived in Vilna after it was annexed by Lithuania had to leave the city. The decree was not directed specifically against Jews but was designed to ensure the demographic and cultural hegemony of the Lithuanians, who had constituted only a relatively small percentage of the city's population during the interwar period.[45] Rabbi Grodzinski and the Vaad ha-Yeshivot actually welcomed this decree.[46] Although relocating the *yeshivot* entailed numerous difficulties (such as their distance

from the center of activity in Vilna), they believed that the atmosphere in rural Lithuania would be more conducive to intensive study and therefore beneficial to the students.[47]

During the winter months, the *yeshivot* began their move to the countryside, and each yeshivah usually moved into a different small village. Thus, for example, the Mir yeshivah moved to Kedainiai; Kamenetz moved to Raseiniai; Baranowitz to Troki; and Beit Yoseph from Bialystok to Birz. In several instances, students from one yeshivah were divided and sent to several different localities. The *yeshivot* forced to relocate their students in different towns were the Radin yeshivah, which moved to Otian and Eisiskiai, and the Etz Hayim yeshivah of Kletzk, which divided its students between Janova, Dushat, and Salok. Many smaller *yeshivot* and some of the independent refugee scholars stayed in Vilna.[48] According to JDC statistics, 1,370 yeshivah students relocated to rural villages, while 607 remained in the city of Vilna; an additional 240 students stayed in the district of Vilna.[49]

Although the *roshei yeshivot* approved the transfer of their institutions to the countryside, they realized that this move was only a temporary expedient. They hoped to relocate to more permanent academies abroad in Eretz Israel and the United States. In fact, several *roshei yeshivot* attempted to obtain visas for either destination immediately upon their arrival in Vilna. For example, as early as mid-November 1939, Rabbi Grodzinski wrote to Rabbi Herzog, the chief rabbi of Palestine, that the Mir and Kamenetz *yeshivot* were ready to go to Palestine.[50] One month later, Rabbi Grodzinski wrote to Rabbi Meir Karelitz in Palestine that Rabbi Aaron Kotler of the Kletzk yeshivah was also interested in immigration to Eretz Israel.[51] During the winter of 1939-40, Rabbi Herzog received many requests for Palestine certificates.[52]

Rabbi Herzog and the Agudat Israel (in Palestine) tried to help rabbis and students stranded in Vilna. Rabbi Herzog proposed a special plan to facilitate the entry of hundreds of rabbis into Palestine. His proposal was rejected by the British, who refused to deviate from their immigration policies under the 1939 White Paper, although Rabbi Herzog had obtained financial guarantees for supporting the prospective immigrants from the American Agudat ha-Rabbanim.

Despite increased support for immigration to Palestine or the United States, many *roshei yeshivot* preferred to stay in Lithuania. They believed, or hoped, that it would be possible to stay where they were for the duration of the war. They hoped that Lithuania would not be overrun by either the Nazis or the Soviets. Rabbi Grodzinski supported this position, although he actively tried to obtain visas to Eretz Israel both for himself and others.[53] It is possible that Rabbi Grodzinski's public stand supporting remaining in Lithuania stemmed from the pragmatic wish to avoid panic and despair among the refugees. He knew that it was virtually impossible to obtain visas for all of the rabbis and students, and thus he publicly opposed efforts for mass emigration. In a letter to Rabbi Silver, Grodzinski stated: "Meanwhile, Torah is lying in the corner."[54] [The reference is to Lithuania.] Apparently, Rabbi Grodzinski believed that the *yeshivot* were temporarily safe, but that this haven could also become a potential trap. Rabbi Joseph Shub, the secretary of the Vaad ha-Yeshivot, also opposed emigration, and the public position of these two leaders moderated communal pressure to leave.[55]

It is likely that several factors affected the yeshiva students: lack of funds to purchase visas and passports, the large amount of time required to deal with bureaucracies, and the absence of simple solutions to the growing threat for those remaining in Lithuania.[56] Throughout the entire period of Lithuanian independence, there were no collective or large-scale attempts by the *yeshivot* to obtain immigration documents. It is noteworthy that the Vaad ha-Hatzalah sent a special emissary to Lithuania to deal with immigration-related issues.[57]

Soviet Invasion of Lithuania and Emigration from the Soviet Union, June 1940-June 1941

The situation changed drastically in June 1940, when the Russians invaded Lithuania; two months later, the independent Baltic republic was formally annexed to the Soviet Union. As a result, many of the *roshei yeshivot* and their students began more urgent attempts to leave Lithuania. Aid from outside organizations for the Torah scholars, the limited number of available Palestine certificates, and the difficulty of obtaining American visas were only a few of the difficulties they faced. There were also many other technical problems: obtaining necessary transit visas, locating adequate means of transportation, and finding safe travel routes from Lithuania to new homes abroad. The technical problems involved in organizing this emigration were magnified when the Russians decreed that all foreign diplomatic offices in Lithuania were to cease operations by September 1, 1940. Another problem was securing Soviet exit permits. The Soviet authorities did not allow free emigration, and the Torah scholars' chances of leaving Russia were not promising. Despite the seemingly hopeless situation, a new and unexpected rescue possibility developed.

In early summer 1940, after the Soviet occupation of Lithuania, Nathan Gutwirth, a Dutch citizen studying at the Telshe yeshivah, sought asylum in one of the overseas Dutch colonies since he could not return to Holland, which had already been conquered by the Nazis in May 1940. Before his departure, Gutwirth approached Jan Zwartendijk, the honorary Dutch consul in Kovno, and they decided that Gutwirth would go to the Caribbean island of Curacao. Since Zwartendijk was only an honorary consul, he could not issue the required visa. Therefore, he turned to L.P. Decker, the Dutch consul in Riga (capital of Latvia). Decker informed Zwartendijk that entry to Curacao was contingent only upon approval of the island's governor and that Gutwirth did not need a visa. Zwartendijk thereupon agreed to give Gutwirth a document confirming that he was allowed to enter Curacao for the regular visa fee of 11 Lithuanian lits (equivalent to $2). At Gutwirth's request, Zwartendijk omitted the qualification stipulating that permission to enter Curacao was contingent upon approval by the island's governor.

Gutwirth showed this visa to Zerach Warhaftig, a prominent religious Zionist in the Polish Mizrachi and one of the leaders of Polish refugees in Lithuania. Warhaftig suggested that Gutwirth ask Zwartendijk if he would be willing to issue such "visas" to non-Dutch individuals. Zwartendijk agreed to help, and Warhaftig informed the Polish refugees of this propitious development. Within a short time, the Dutch consul was deluged with requests for visas to Curacao. The Dutch consulate had, however, received Soviet orders to close, limiting the time when refugees could obtain such visas. Despite the problems, Zwartendijk issued between 1,200 and 1,400 Curacao visas to Jewish refugees, including many to rabbis and yeshivah students.[58]

Once Curacao visas were obtained, the next problem was identifying an exit route. The only route still open to Curacao was via the Far East. Western Europe was already occupied by the Nazis, and thus refugees would have to travel through the Soviet Union and Japan. Several Jewish refugees approached the Japanese consulate in Kovno and applied for transit visas to Curacao. Senpo Sugihara, the local Japanese consul, cabled Tokyo for instructions but did not receive an answer. On August 11, he began issuing Japanese transit visas to all applicants, even to those lacking Curacao visas or other travel documents. Nine days later—on August 20—Sugihara received an emergency cable from the Japanese Foreign Office instructing him immediately to cease issuing transit visas. Sugihara had already planned to close the Japanese consulate at the end of August pursuant to the new Soviet directives, but he continued issuing visas until the end of the month. By August 31, 1940, Sugihara and his two assistants (an ethnic German named Gecke and a student from the Mir yeshivah) distributed visas to almost 3,500 refugees, including many rabbis and yeshivah students.[59]

Once these Japanese transit visas had been obtained, only one obstacle to emigration remained: absence of the Soviet exit permit. This was, however, a formidable obstacle. Several attempts to convince Soviet authorities to allow the refugees to emigrate ensued: Zerach Warhaftig met with the new deputy prime minister of Lithuania, Globetski, and also simultaneously tried to convince the Soviet official in charge of Lithuania affairs, Pozniakov, through the mediation of Pozniakov's Jewish physician, Dr. Elkes. Rabbi Herzog also tried to influence the Russians and corresponded with Ivan Maisky, Soviet ambassador in London; Herzog had met Maisky in February 1940 during his earlier efforts helping Talmud scholars emigrate from Lithuania to Palestine.

Globetski asked Warhaftig to submit a memorandum on the situation of the Polish refugees in Lithuania as well as a list of all potential emigrants from the Soviet Union. Since it was unclear whether those listed would be allowed to leave or would be deported to Siberia, the list was submitted with much trepidation to Soviet authorities. Fortunately, their fears were unfounded, and in August 1940, Globetski and Pozniakov informed them that Soviet exit permits would be given to any Polish refugee possessing a visa. Prospective emigrants were investigated by the secret police and were required to write lengthy essays explaining their desire to leave Russia. Although these bureaucratic procedures were cumbersome and often intimidating, permits were granted enabling departure from the Soviet Union.[60]

The sole remaining problem was raising money for the journey. After granting exit permits, the Soviet authorities decided that travel expenses had to be paid in dollars, although it was illegal to possess foreign currency in the Soviet Union. Under these circumstances, the refugees were once again forced to turn for help to overseas Jewish relief organizations, especially the JDC and the Vaad ha-Hatzalah. These two organizations immediately sent funds to Lithuania to facilitate emigration. Those who obtained the necessary documents and funds set out by train from Kovno to Vladivostok. From there they sailed to the Japanese port of Tsoruga and were afterwards transferred to Kobe, home of Japan's largest Jewish community, which consisted of about fifty families. The refugees were welcomed by representatives from this community and the Committee for Assistance to Refugees (commonly referred to as the Jewcom), which assumed responsibility for the newcomers with the Japanese authorities and also attempted to help the material plight of these refugees.

During the same period, new opportunities also emerged for emigration to Palestine: once the Soviets had agreed to grant exit permits to Polish refugees with visas, those with Palestine certificates were permitted to leave. From August 1940 to April 1941, approximately 1,200 persons went to Palestine via Odessa and Istanbul.[61] This group included several well-known rabbinic personalities, such as Rabbi Eliezer Yehuda Finkel of the Mir yeshivah; Rabbi Shabtai Yogel of Slonim; and Rabbi Eliezer Shach of Kletzk.[62]

The number of certificates allocated to rabbis and yeshivah students was limited; moreover, few Torah scholars had a completely free choice about where to relocate. Although many, perhaps even the majority, of these refugee scholars preferred Eretz Israel over other destinations, few could go there.[63] Despite the efforts of Rabbi Herzog and the Palestinian branch of Agudat Israel, the British refused to increase the allocation of certificates to rabbis. Apart from the previously mentioned *roshei yeshivot* (Rabbis Finkel, Yogel, and Shach), none of the other outstanding Polish *roshei yeshivot* reached Palestine, even though many held valid certificates.[64] Since their students were not granted permits by the British government, their sense of responsibility precluded emigration, unless the entire yeshivah could emigrate together as a unit.[65] It was often already too late to obtain Curacao visas, and the only available option was to route travel via the Far East. Many were thus stuck in Lithuania. Several *roshei yeshivot* succeeded in emigrating to the United States; these held American visas and obviously did not need visas for Curacao or Japan.[66] Their choice was not between Eretz Israel and the Diaspora. In most instances, the pattern of emigration was determined by individual circumstance rather than by ideological considerations.

Parallel to attempts to persuade the Russians to allow Jewish emigration from Lithuania, orthodox organizations lobbied throughout the world to obtain visas for rabbis and students. The most important group was the Vaad ha-Hatzalah, which renewed efforts to bring *yeshivot* to the United States after the Soviet annexation of Lithuania. The Vaad had previously hoped to divide Torah academies equally between Palestine and America, but after their failure to obtain Palestine certificates, they concentrated on the United States. They attempted to influence the State Department, which was the agency responsible for issuing

visas, and they also tried to convince the JDC to assist the transfer of the *yeshivot*.

The Vaad leaders encountered opposition from almost all major American Jewish organizations, to the emigration of approximately 2,500 rabbis, yeshivah students, and family dependents; these American organizations feared that the arrival of such a large group would arouse antisemitism.[67] At a meeting of all major American Jewish organizations on August 15, 1940, in the New York offices of JDC, the leaders of the Vaad ha-Hatzalah presented their plan for the evacuation of the *yeshivot* from Lithuania to the United States. Except for delegates from the orthodox organizations, the others (American Jewish Committee, American Jewish Congress, B'nai B'rith, and HIAS) opposed this proposal for "practical reasons" (in the words of Stephen Wise). The participants decided to establish a committee to study the problem and decide future policies.

This committee recommended that Jewish organizations request only a limited number of visas, and rejected implementation of the Vaad ha-Hatzalah plan.[68] A delegation subsequently sent to Washington met with Assistant Secretary of State Breckenridge Long and submitted lists of individuals for whom visas were requested. In many instances, visas were received.[69] By September 18, 1940, 732 special emergency visas were issued to "leaders of the intellectual thought of the Jewish religion and leading exponents of the Talmudic schools and colleges together with their families," including several *roshei yeshivot*. The Vaad tried to obtain additional visas, but the State Department responded with increasing inflexibility. Long, who had initially approved several emergency visas for rabbis, was no longer willing to help. He advised a delegation of rabbis that those seeking emergency visas should submit applications for regular visas (a process requiring years and with minimal chances of success). Despite State Department intransigence, the Vaad continued its efforts to obtain U.S. visas and to assemble the required financial affidavits for prospective immigrants. These activities became increasingly urgent because of concurrent developments in Soviet Lithuania.

On January 1, 1941, the Soviet authorities in Lithuania announced that by January 25, all refugees in Lithuania had either to accept Soviet citizenship or become stateless.[70] This decree accelerated preparations for departure among many refugee rabbis and students. Very few had already left Lithuania since only a limited number of people had obtained visas for Curacao before the Dutch consulate closed. Although many refugees had obtained Japanese transit visas, these were worthless without visas for a final destination. This problem was solved when the Dutch consul, Decker, prior to his departure from Riga, left instructions that refugees requesting Curacao visas should henceforth submit applications to the Dutch Embassy in Stockholm, which would issue the documents. Consequently, yeshivah students turned for help to Rabbi Schlomo (Wilhelm) Wolbe, a former student of the Mir yeshivah, residing in Stockholm. Rabbi Wolbe contacted A.M. de Jong, the Dutch consul in Stockholm, and submitted applications for refugee rabbis and students. From early January to April 7, 1941, de Jong issued 2,386 Curacao visas; approximately 1,000 of them went to rabbis and students specified by Rabbi Wolbe.[71] With these documents in hand, many of the refugees could obtain Soviet exit permits enabling them to leave for the Far East.

The number of refugees leaving the Soviet Union increased. Funds raised primarily by the JDC and the Vaad ha-Hatzalah covered transportation expenses for those with valid emigration documentation.[72] Approximately 2,200 refugees, including about 650 rabbis, yeshivah students, and their family members left Lithuania for the Far East.[73]

This is perhaps the most appropriate point to deal in a more comprehensive manner with the attitude of the *roshei yeshivot* to emigration attempts via the Far East. As previously mentioned, *roshei yeshivot* sought to transfer their schools abroad immediately after arrival in Vilna. Developments in Lithuania after Soviet annexation reinforced these trends. Almost all of the *roshei yeshivot* opposed efforts to obtain visas for Curacao and Japan, even if they favored emigration in principle. This opposition had two causes: 1) fear of the Soviets, and 2) doubts regarding the feasibility of escape via the Far East. Testimonies by former yeshivah students from Lithuania show that many of the rabbis feared that the emigration scheme was a Soviet ruse, designed to uncover opponents of the Communist regime.[74] Thus, for example, Rabbi Aaron Kotler said that the entire matter was *sakanat nefashot* (a matter of life and death) and reprimanded several of his students who had submitted requests for Soviet exit permits. He claimed that they would be deported to Siberia along with their entire yeshivah.[75] Many rabbis thought it useless to obtain exit documents because of the enormous expense and large amount of time required.[76] A few ridiculed those refugees who obtained such documents and sometimes even tore the documents to pieces, deciding that they were worthless.[77]

It is possible that the desire of the *roshei yeshivot* to arrange collective emigration was an added factor contributing to their skepticism.[78] Each *rosh yeshivah* sought to preserve his own yeshivah and considered its survival as an intact unit his personal responsibility. It is likely that they opposed the Curacao scheme because they considered the possibility of transplanting an entire yeshivah to the Caribbean via Japan highly improbable. Moreover, even if their institutions could reach Curacao safely, that remote island was hardly considered an ideal location. Fear and doubt reinforced each other among the Polish refugees in Lithuania, and this, in turn, prevented more active support of emigration through the Far East and the Caribbean.

We must also remember that after January 1940, most yeshivah students were scattered in rural areas and cut off from Vilna. This diffusion made it difficult to organize any mass emigration. Some of the students acted on their own initiative to arrange for their departure from Lithuania. This was especially true in the Mir yeshivah. Rabbi Eliezer Finkel, the *rosh yeshivah*, began, immediately after his arrival in Vilna, to make arrangements for the transfer of the entire yeshivah to Eretz Israel. Even before the Russians arrived, he adopted tactics unusual in the yeshivah world, in order to arrange for the emigration of his students. For example, he gave yeshivah funds to one student, Eliezer Portnoy, instructing him to go to Kovno to explore emigration possibilities, especially to Palestine. Despite Finkel's pro-emigration stance, he initially opposed the Far East travel

route. His students, however, approved of the idea and enlisted the aid of Zerach Warhaftig in order to convince their *rosh yeshivah* that the idea was feasible. In the end, Rabbi Finkel was convinced and issued instructions to obtain visas for all the students. Although they too feared deportation to Siberia, they nevertheless decided to accept the risk. All of the necessary documents were obtained, and practically all of the students were able to leave the Soviet Union for Japan. Mir was the only yeshivah which left Lithuania almost completely intact.[79]

It is possible that if the *roshei yeshivot* had made a concerted effort to urge their students to obtain visas, the number of those leaving would have been much greater. It should be noted that several *roshei yeshivot* rescued via this route were initially opponents of this plan; these rabbis had left Lithuania with special American emergency visas. By the time they reached Japan, however, it was too late to try to obtain either Japanese or Curacao visas for their students. When it finally became clear that entry into America or Palestine was impossible, it was too late to rectify their earlier indifference to resettlement via Curacao.

Life in Japan, October 1940-Summer 1941

All Jewish refugees arriving in Japan were transferred to Kobe. In most cases, the arriving refugees were practically penniless and in urgent need of financial assistance. The local committee that aided the refugees had limited resources and could not cope with the needs of hundreds of refugees. A more serious problem arose concerning the refugees' presence in Japan. Their entry had been approved on the basis of Curacao visas and the Japanese transit visas issued by Sugihara in Kovno. The latter documents were only valid for two weeks, whereas the former visas were essentially fictitious since the governor of Curacao certainly had no intention of admitting hundreds of Jewish refugees to the island. Most of the refugees were thus stranded illegally in Japan and had no possibility of leaving. The local authorities were aware of their problem, and the refugees feared that the Japanese would deport them to the Soviet Union, stop the entry of additional refugees to Japan, and thereby block any exit channel from the Soviet Union.[80]

Under these circumstances, the leaders of the "Jewcom" turned to Professor Kotsuji, a Bible scholar considered an expert on Jewish affairs and a former employee of the Japanese Foreign Minister Matsuoko. Kotsuji visited his former employer and asked him to permit the refugees to stay in Japan. Matsuoko initially refused to accede to the professor's entreaty but eventually agreed not to take any steps against the refugees as long as the Kobe local police agreed to their presence in the city. Kotsuji also obtained Matsuoko's agreement to allow the entry into Japan of a refugee group that had already been ordered to return to Vladivostok under the new Japanese decrees. After his meeting with Matsuoko, Kotsuji borrowed 300,000 yen (approximately $60,000) from a rich uncle and bribed the Kobe police, who agreed to permit the refugees to remain in the city until they could emigrate, provided they renewed their visas on a weekly basis. The refugees naturally agreed to this arrangement and were thus saved from expulsion to the Soviet Union.[81]

With the temporary solution of their residence problems in Japan, the refugees and Jewish relief organizations increased their efforts to find more secure refuge for those already in Japan as well as for the many stranded rabbis and students in the Soviet Union. The Vaad ha-Hatzalah sent a young American businessman, Frank (Efraim) Newman, as their special emissary to Japan to facilitate the emigration of rabbis and yeshivah students. Newman was friendly with the members of the Zeirei Agudat Israel, an organization closely affiliated with the Vaad ha-Hatzalah, which assisted this rabbinic rescue organization. After approximately four and one half months in Japan, Newman was assisting with the procurement of American visas and in all efforts to extricate additional rabbis and students from Lithuania.[82] During these months, the Vaad ha-Hatzalah raised funds for refugee scholars' transportation expenses from Lithuania to Japan. Between January and April 1941, the Vaad spent more than $80,000; only the JDC spent more.[83] The Vaad ha-Hatzalah specialized in assistance to Torah scholars (with one exception), whereas the JDC helped every Jewish refugee regardless of affiliation or ideology.

In early 1941, the leaders of the refugee community in Japan obtained additional Japanese entry visas by signing an agreement with the Nippon Yushen Kaisha (N.Y.K.) shipping line. This contract allotted a visa for every Jewish refugee purchasing a ticket for one of their ships. N.Y.K. submitted a list of names (provided by refugee leaders in Japan) to the Japanese embassy in Moscow, which then issued the visas. This enabled many refugees, previously unable to obtain Japanese visas from Sugihara during the summer of 1940, to leave the Soviet Union. Technical arrangements with the Japanese stipulated that the Japanese consul in Moscow receive a name list from the shipping company and transmit this list to the Kovno branch of Intourist (the Russian state travel agency), which assumed responsibility for making the necessary travel arrangements to Moscow, where the Japanese visas were finally picked up.[84]

In March 1941, the Japanese government issued orders to suspend the issuance of all entry visas for Jewish refugees and also halted the distribution of transit visas by the Japanese embassy in Moscow.[85] Although this decree did not cause a complete cessation of Jewish immigration to Japan, it did severely hamper efforts to rescue additional Torah scholars. Prior to the issuance of this decree, several hundred rabbis and yeshivah students entered Japan, but an additional 2,000 still remained in Lithuania. Moreover, a group of approximately seventy Jewish refugees (including forty rabbis and students) had reached Vladivostok in the winter of 1940-1941 and were now stranded in the Soviet port city. The Russians threatened to deport them back to Lithuania if they were unable to continue their journey.[86] Frank Newman and Zerach Warhaftig hoped to remove this obstacle by going to Shanghai and obtaining entry permits to this city. They believed that Shanghai permits would: 1) convince the Japanese to cancel the order prohibiting Jewish entry to Japan; 2) open a haven that would enable additional Jews to depart from the Soviet Union; and 3) save those refugees stranded in Vladivostok.[87] Newman and Warhaftig were aided by a local rabbi, Meir Ashkenazi, and succeeded in obtaining several hundred Shanghai permits. These were, however, insuffi-

cient for all the refugee scholars still in Lithuania.[88] The first permits were allocated to the refugees in Vladivostok, and most of them arrived in Shanghai as a group on May 1, 1941. It should be noted that this group included several non-observant Jews as well as rabbis and yeshivah students.[89] It is unclear whether the permits were distributed according to any clear rescue priorities. Despite contrary rumors in Japan, the Soviets acknowledged the validity of Shanghai permits, although it is doubtful that any Jewish refugees left the Soviet Union after May 1941.[90]

Despite decrees prohibiting the entry of Jewish refugees into Japan and the discontinuance of Japanese transit visas by the Japanese Moscow embassy, more than 500 additional Jewish refugees reached Japan by August 1941. During 1940 and 1941, a total of 2,178 Polish Jewish refugees arrived in Japan; this figure included 79 rabbis and 341 yeshivah students as well as their wives and children.[91] Adding to this the number of refugees arriving in Shanghai directly from Vladivostok, it is clear that more than 600 rabbis, yeshivah students, and family dependents reached Shanghai. Many in this group were affiliated with the Mir yeshivah. Some of these refugees reached the United States in 1941, including six famous rabbis: Aaron Kotler (Etz Hayim of Kletzk); Reuven Grazowsky (Kamenetz yeshivah); Mendel Zacks (Radin yeshivah); Abraham Yaphin (Beit Yoseph yeshivah of Bialystok); David Lifschutz (head of the Suwalki rabbinical court); and Moses Schatzkes (head of the Lomza rabbinical court).[92]

Before America's entry into the war, and despite the energetic attempts of the Vaad ha-Hatzalah to secure American visas, very few rabbis and students reached the United States. The Vaad also sought havens in other countries, including Latin American nations. For example, in May 1941, the Vaad sent Dr. Samuel Schmidt to Paraguay, Brazil, and Argentina to obtain entry visas for these countries. Although it was apparently feasible to transfer some refugees to Paraguay, none of the rabbis and yeshivah students went there.[93] The plans for emigration to other South American countries were never realized.[94]

Efforts to have refugee scholars admitted to Canada were somewhat more successful. After extensive lobbying, eighty entry visas for rabbis and yeshivah students were finally obtained.[95] The first group, consisting of twenty-nine refugees, sailed from Shanghai to the United States and arrived in Canada on October 24, 1941. The remaining fifty-one refugees in this group delayed their departure until after the Jewish High Holidays but encountered difficulties in booking a later passage and were forced to remain in Shanghai for the duration of the war.[96]

The Transfer to Shanghai, August-October 1941

The Japanese authorities, never pleased by the arrival of hundreds of Jewish refugees, had attempted to stop their entry. As time passed, the Japanese desire to be rid of the refugees increased. In the summer of 1941, as Japan prepared for war with the United States, they took steps to expel all foreigners, including Jewish refugees. From August to October 1941, the refugees were transferred from Kobe to the International Settlement of Shanghai, where the overwhelming majority remained until the end of World War II.[97] A small group of rabbis and students emigrated to Canada in the fall of 1941 and four others left as part of the Japanese-Allied population exchange in 1942.[98] The remaining 500 refugees remained in Shanghai throughout the war and thus survived.

It is important to summarize those aspects of the rescue of rabbis and yeshivah students in the Far East that are of special significance for our understanding of rescue attempts during the Holocaust. A relatively large number of Torah scholars were ultimately rescued through this route, including a large number of students from the Mir yeshivah. Why were so many rabbis and students saved? Several factors were responsible: 1) the ages of the individuals involved; 2) the unique characteristics of this episode, including outside assistance and group solidarity by rabbis and students in Europe and America; and 3) decisions made by refugee leaders. Each factor will be considered briefly.

Age played an important role in rescue. Most of the individuals saved were relatively young single students between the ages of 16 and 25. Their relative mobility influenced several decisions crucial to survival by emigration. They obviously found it easier to make the initial move to Vilna and subsequently to escape to the Far East, a route that appeared risky and threatening because of its unfamiliarity. Such decisions would have been harder to make when entire families were involved.

A number of unique coincidences and special circumstances were involved in this episode: the temporary return of Vilna to Lithuania, the availability of Curacao and Japanese transit visas, and Soviet willingness to grant exit permits. Torah scholars benefitted from these relatively unusual simultaneous occurrences.

Aid provided by the Vaad ha-Hatzalah and the JDC was crucial to the rescue of scholars. The American Jewish relief organizations maintained the refugees in Lithuania and Japan, and also paid for their transportation from Kovno to Kobe. Moreover, the unceasing efforts of the Vaad to obtain American visas and their continuous pressure to take whatever steps considered necessary for the rescue of rabbis and yeshivah students contributed to their success and resulted in the relatively large percentage of survivors.

Another factor was the solidarity of the entire yeshivah group. This influenced several decisions, as for example the initial decision to move to Vilna in intact schools. Furthermore, they knew that Rabbi Grodzinski would do everything possible to rescue them and this undoubtedly influenced student decisions. It can be assumed also that the rabbis and students knew that they could turn to alumni of these *yeshivot* among orthodox Jews in the United States and Palestine, thereby creating opportunities unavailable to other groups. The group solidarity of the Torah scholars was evident throughout the entire period. After the border between Lithuania and Soviet-occupied Poland was closed, special efforts were made to smuggle Polish rabbis and yeshivah students to Lithuania. Furthermore, the work of the Vaad ha-Hatzalah of the Union of Orthodox Rabbis in the United States, of Rabbi Herzog, Agudat Israel, and other orthodox organizations enhanced the cohesiveness of the *yeshivot*. Their leaders were motivated by a strong sense of personal responsibility to rescue

yeshivot, a feeling stemming from the brotherhood of those who share an ideological commitment to a prescribed way of life. Many advocates of relief and rescue had previously studied in the threatened Polish *yeshivot* and personally knew the *roshei yeshivot* and members of their families.

The final factor that contributed significantly to survival was the role of Jewish leaders in the orthodox world. Given the dominant position of the *roshei yeshivot,* the crucial question is the extent to which their position influenced their students and determined their fate. In most *yeshivot,* the initiative for action came from the students, while the *roshei yeshivot* were initially hesitant and only slowly followed their students' lead. This was true not only for the move to Vilna but applied even more to emigration to the Far East, which many rabbis opposed. We must pose the question whether more yeshivah students would have been saved if the *roshei yeshivot* had not opposed the Curacao scheme. Given their deep-seated fears of the Soviet regime, would the *roshei yeshivot* have been prepared to risk emigration via Japan had they not already held visas to the United States and Palestine, and also had they not hoped that their students could also obtain such visas? The available documentation does not provide unequivocal answers to these questions, but upon careful examination, I believe that we must respond affirmatively.

An analysis of the rescue of Polish rabbis and yeshiva students thus provides us with unique insights into the nature of rescue during the Holocaust. This episode was only one of many initiatives during the period, and a focus on the decision-making problems involved in it helps explain why the number of those rescued was so small. Such analysis contributes crucial elements to our understanding of relief and rescue activities during the Holocaust.

NOTES

Research for this article was made possible by grants from the Memorial Foundation for Jewish Culture, the National Foundation for Jewish Culture, and an award from the Sir Avigdor d'Goldsmid Scholarship Fund.

1. For background on the Polish *yeshivot,* see Shmuel Mirsky, *Mosdot ha-Torah be-Ayropa be-Binyanam u-be-Churbanam* (New York, 1957).

2. In 1937-1938, for example, 100 of the 477 advanced students (age 17-30) at the Mir yeshivah came from outside Poland: 40 from Germany, 28 from the United States, 12 from England, and the rest from Austria, France, Belgium, Sweden, Hungary, Romania, Czechoslovakia, Latvia, and Switzerland. List of the faculty and students sent to the directors of the Central Relief Committee on March 6, 1938, in possession of the author, received from Rabbi Joseph David Epstein, the personal secretary of Rabbi Eliezer Yehuda Finkel, the *rosh yeshivah* of Mir. The author would like to thank Rabbi Epstein for his assistance.

3. Letter of Abraham Horowitz, secretary of the Central Relief Committee to Dr. Cyrus Adler, chairman of the Cultural Committee of the JDC; March 15, 1939; Archives of the JDC, New York [hereafter cited as AJDC].

4. During the 1930s there was a sharp rise in the number of students at several *yeshivot,* especially Kamenetz (From 122 students in 1928-1929 to 326 in 1937-1938); Kletzk (from 149 to 244), Mir (from 350 to 477); Beit Joseph Bialystok (from 210 to 317); and Brisk (from 112 to 207). There was a more moderate

rise in the number of students matriculated at Baranowitz, Grodno, and Slonim. There was no change in the number of students at the other *yeshivot,* with the exception of Ramailes and Kobin, where there was a slight decrease. The statistics for 1928-29 are from *"Yekapa" oyf di Churvos fun Milchomes un Mehumos Pinkas fun Gegent Komitet Yekapa in Vilna, 1919-1930* (Vilna, 1931), 699. The figures for 1937-38 are from the "1938 Digest of Data, Orthodox Higher Educational Institutions Supported by the Joint Distribution Committee through the Central Relief Committee"; Archives of the Central Relief Committee, Yeshiva University, New York.

5. Thus, for example, all the leaders of Agudat ha-Rabbanim studied in either Polish or Lithuanian *yeshivot;* the same applies to leading Ashkenazic rabbis in Eretz Israel. Many of the leaders of orthodox political movements—Mizrachi, Agudat Israel, Hapoel ha-Mizrachi, and Poalei Agudat Israel—also studied in these *yeshivot.*

6. Aaron Sursky, ed., *Achiezer: Kovetz Iggrot shel Rabbi Chaim Ozer Grodzinski ztl* (Bnei Brak, 1970), 134.

7. See the table on aid sent by JDC to Polish *yeshivot* in 1937 in Zosa Szajkowski, "Budgeting American Jewish Overseas Relief, 1919-1939," *American Jewish Historical Quarterly* 59, 1 (Sept. 1969); 111. Figures on the funds sent by Ezrat Torah may be found in *Jubilee Book of Ezras Torah, 1915-1935* (New York, 1936), 26; and Oscar Rand, ed., *Eidut le-Yisrael* (New York, n.d.), 296.

8. Among the *roshei yeshivot* who travelled to the United States to raise funds were Rabbis Eliezer Yehuda Finkel from Mir, Yechiel Michael Gordon from Lomza, Aaron Kotler from Kletzk, Shimon Shkopf from Grodno, Elchanan Wasserman from Baranowitz, and Boruch Ber Leibowitz from Kamenetz.

9. See *Sefer ha-Yovel shel Agudat ha-Rabbanim ha-Orthodoksim de-Arzot ha-Brit ve Kanada* (New York, 1928), 196; Mirsky, 110-116.

10. See above, n. 2.

11. Thus, for example, Rabbi Jacob Levinson, one of the leaders of the Vaad ha-Hatzalah explained the rationale for the special efforts to rescue the *yeshivot:*

> When things were as they should be, the pipe of influence stretched from Europe via the wide sea to us Jews of America, and all the Torah and loyal rabbinate that we acquire in this country comes from there. The *roshei yeshivot,* the great Torah scholars who are spreading the light of their Torah in America . . . are products of the *yeshivot* of Poland and Lithuania. . . . "Hovat ha-Hatzalah." *Ha-Pardes* 14, 11 (Feb. 1941): 11-12.

12. The orthodox journalist Shmuel Rothstein described this feeling: "No one doubted that the Soviet regime would place its heavy hand on the *yeshivot* as it had in Russia. The *roshei yeshivot* and students would be arrested and exiled and what would happen to the Torah?" Shmuel Rothstein, *Achiezer, ha-Gaon Rabbeinu Chaim Ozer Grodzinski mi-Vilna Chayv U-Peulotav* (Tel Aviv, 1960), 51-52. It should also be noted that in the past, religious groups had been involved in many controversies with the socialists regarding the *kehilla,* and, to some extent, this reinforced their apprehensions about the arrival of the Communists.

13. It is interesting to note that after the Soviet occupation, several students of the Kamenetz yeshivah wanted to flee to western Poland, i.e., the German-occupied sector. The Germans had entered Kamenetz at the beginning of the war but subsequently retreated in accordance with the terms of the Molotov-Ribbentrop agreement. During their stay in the city, the Germans had not harmed the yeshivah, and perhaps that explains this strange phenomenon. Yitzhak Edelstein, *Ha-Rav Baruch Ber Leibowitz* (Tel Aviv, 1957), 45.

14. See Elchanan Herzman, *Mofait ha-Dor* (Jerusalem, 1976), which includes a section entitled "The Miracle of the Rescue of the Mir Yeshivah," in which the author recounts his recollections. According to Herzman, the news regarding the return of Vilna to the Lithuanians was received on October 9. This date was confirmed in an interview by the author with Rabbi Yaakov Nayman on June 26, 1977 [hereafter cited as Rabbi Nayman interview]. At that time, Rabbi Nayman was a student at the Baranowitz yeshivah.

15. Hillel Seidman, "Yeshivat Etz Hayim de-Kletzk," in Mirsky, *Mosdot,* 238.

16. Yoseph David Epstein, "Yeshivat Mir," ibid., 117.

17. See the diary of Rabbi Yitzchak Edelstein, "Bi-Yemei Sufa," prepared for publication by Dina Porat, *Galed* 3:329-330 [hereafter cited as Edelstein diary].

18. Interviews by the author with Rabbi Asher Czeczyk (student at the Radin yeshivah), July 5, 1977 [hereafter cited as Rabbi Czeczyk interview]; Rabbi Nayman interview; Rabbi Zelig Epstein (student at the Mir yeshivah), July 7, 1977 [hereafter cited as Rabbi Zelig Epstein interview]; Rabbi Moshe Cohen (student at the Kletzk yeshivah), October 10, 1974 [hereafter cited as Rabbi Cohen interview]; Yad Vashem Archives, 0-31 [hereafter cited as YVA]; and published memoirs such as Herzman, Edelstein diary, and Mirsky.

19. Mirsky, 117; Herzman, 39-40. For information on Kamenetz, see Edelstein diary, 326. See also Rabbi Zelig Epstein, "Yeshivah 'Shaar ha-Torah' be-Grodno," Mirsky, 303; Rabbi Moshe Cohen interview; Rabbi Czeczyk interview; and M. Weisbrod, "Beyn ha-Meitzarim," *Sefer Zikaron le-Kehillat Lomza,* Yom Tov Lewinski, ed. (Tel Aviv, 1952), 83-84.

20. This is evident from lists of Torah scholars whose transportation expenses from Lithuania were paid by the Vaad ha-Hatzalah and from other similar lists submitted for American visas. These lists are located in the archives of the Vaad ha-Hatzalah, Yeshiva University, New York [hereafter cited as AVH], not arranged by file number at the time of access.

21. Edelstein diary, 329.

22. Herzman, 39.

23. Edelstein diary, 330.

24. Ibid., 46.

25. Yitzhak Arad, "Concentration of Refugees in Vilna on the Eve of the Holocaust," *Yad Vashem Studies* 9 (Jerusalem, 1973): 201-206.

26. Letter from Y.D. Zacks, director of the Center and chairman of the Executive Committee of Zeirei Agudat Israel in Lithuania, to Rabbi Moshe Blau, leader of Agudat Israel in Palestine, November 17, 1939; Archives of Agudat Israel in Israel [hereafter AAYEY], file 62; letter of Rabbi Eliyahu Blau, *rosh yeshivah* of Telshe, to Moshe Blau, November 16, 1939, ibid.; Rabbi Nayman interview.

27. Arad, 209; interview with Rabbi Shimon Romm, one of the community rabbis who escaped to Vilna, and formerly a student of the Mir yeshivah, July 27, 1977 [hereafter cited as Rabbi Romm interview].

28. Letter of Rabbi Grodzinski to Dr. Cyrus Adler, December 31, 1939, AJDC.

29. This was true not only for rabbis and yeshivah students, but also for *halutzim* and members of the Zionist youth movements. See Benzion Benshalom, *Be-Salar be-Yom Sufa* (Tel Aviv, 1944), 20-24; Moshe Rothenberg, *Bikurei Aviv* (St. Louis, 1942), 13; Edelstein diary, 335.

30. Rothstein, 53; according to interviews with Rabbi Nayman and Rabbi Zelig Epstein, no emissaries were sent to Poland to encourage the escape of yeshivah students.

31. Arad, 206.

32. Yehuda Bauer, "Rescue Operations through Vilna," *Yad Vashem Studies* 9 (Jerusalem, 1973): 215. This figure constitutes more than half the students studying in the *yeshivot* of eastern Poland, which were under the aegis of the Vaad ha-Yeshivot in Vilna.

33. Bauer, 215. It is possible that the number of Torah scholars

reaching Vilna was actually higher, since a considerable percentage of the community rabbis (in one interview as high as 90 percent) who reached Lithuania returned to Poland following Grodzinski's advice. According to interviews with those in Vilna at that time, Grodzinski's advice was based partly on the belief that rabbis should not leave either their communities or their families. It is believed that Grodzinski thought Lithuania would be occupied by the Soviet Union and thus escaping to Vilna would not solve any problems, since many rabbis would be forced to return to their villages. Another reason was Grodzinski's personal experience during World War I, when he had fled from Vilna and was accused when he returned of having abandoned his community. Rabbi Nayman and Rabbi Zelig Epstein interviews.

34. *Churbn un Rettung: Die Geshichte fun "Vaad Hatzala" in America* (New York, 1957), 156.

35. Ibid., 146.

36. Bauer, 215-217.

37. Edelstein diary, 334.

38. Thus, for example, aid was sent from even relatively small communities in Uruguay. See letter of Rabbi Grodzinski to Rabbi Aaron Milewsky of Montevideo, May 13, 1940; Papers of Rabbi Aaron Milewsky, Jerusalem. The author would like to thank Rabbi Milewsky for his assistance.

39. Rothstein, 56.

40. Eliezer Silver, "Hatzalat Yisrael be-Yameinu," *Churbn un Rettung*, 9-15; "Veida Chatzi-Shanatit Shel Agudat ha-Rabbanim," *Ha-Pardes* 13, 9 (December 1939): 4-9.

41. According to reports from Lithuania, the academic level of the students was outstanding. See letter of Rabbi Block to Rabbi Blau, November 16, 1939; AAYEY, file 62.

42. Rothstein, 54.

43. Rabbi Nayman interview.

44. Rothstein, 54.

45. Arad, 209; Bauer, 216.

46. Letter of Rabbi Grodzinski to Rabbi Herzog, January 26, 1940; Archives of Chief Rabbi Yitzhak Halevy Herzog, Heichal Shlomo, Jerusalem [hereafter cited as AYHH]; file of letters from Rabbi Chaim Ozer Grodzinski.

47. Rothstein, 56; Herzman, 47; Rabbi Nayman interview.

48. JDC report, "Refugees Fed as of June 1, 1940," AJDC, Vaad ha-Hatzalah file.

49. Letter of Rabbi Grodzinski to Rabbi Herzog, November 15, 1939, quoted in Sursky, 225-226.

50. Ibid., 226-227.

51. Numerous requests are located in files 32 (aliyah requests by rabbis, Poland and Lithuania) and 33 (requests for the aliyah of rabbis), AYHH.

52. Jacob Goldman, "Rabbi Herzog's First Rescue Journey, *Niv Ha-Midrashiya* (Winter 1964): 5-7; Dina Porat, "Rikuz ha-Plitim ha-Yehidim be-Vilna bashanim," 1939-1941 (unpublished M.A. thesis; Tel Aviv University), 59-60 [hereafter cited as Porat]; *Churbn un Rettung*, 26-27.

53. In February 1940, Rabbi Herzog went to England to persuade the British to allow the entry of rabbis and yeshivah students who had fled from Poland to Lithuania into Palestine. Herzog met with several prominent personalities, including Halifax, Malcolm Macdonald, and the Archbishop of Canterbury, and requested a special allocation of 1,600 certificates (200 for rabbis and 1,400 for yeshivah students). See letters from Agudat Israel in Palestine to the High Commissioner for Palestine, April 7 and May 7, 1940, about the possibility of enlarging the quotas for rabbis and students; AAYEY, file 106.

See also letters from Rabbi Grodzinski to Rabbi Herzog, April 26 and May 3, 1940; AYHH, file 9 and "Rabbinical Certificates Applications, 1940-1941"; unsigned letter [by Rabbi Moshe Blau] to Jacob Rosenheim, December 17, 1939, AAYEY, file 13; letter from Rabbi Grodzinski to Rabbi Blau, December 15, 1939, AAYEY,

file 44. Also Rothstein, 61-62; and Hillel Seidman, *Ishim she-Hikarti* (Jerusalem, 1970), 257.

54. Letter from Rabbi Grodzinski to Rabbi Silver, February 10, 1940; archives of Rabbi Eliezer Silver. The author would like to thank Rabbi Dr. Aaron Rakeffet (Rothkoff) who made these documents available.

55. Seidman, 257; Rabbi Romm interview.

56. Testimony of Zerach Warhaftig, interview no. 2, November 30, 1965, 2-3; Oral History Division, Institute of Contemporary Jewry, Hebrew University, Jerusalem [hereafter cited as Warhaftig testimony]; Rabbi Romm interview.

57. The emissary, Dr. Samuel Schmidt, was a close friend of Rabbi Silver. Schmidt's reports on his mission were published in *Every Friday*, the Cincinnati Jewish newspaper he edited. He departed on February 8, 1940, and returned to the United States on June 6, 1940. A comprehensive report about this trip appeared in "Vaad ha-Hatzalah," *Ha-Pardes*, 14, 4 (July 1940): 3-4.

58. "Righteous Among the Nations Department," Yad Vashem: file 977 (Zwartendijk); Warhaftig testimony. 7-8.

59. "Righteous Among the Nations Department," Yad Vashem: File 1054 (Sugihara); Mirsky, 122. Moshe Zupnick told the story that the yeshivah student enlisted by Sugihara to help process the applications did not know Japanese, and therefore stamped the visas upside down.

60. Yaakov Edelstein, "Ha-Masa u-Matan ha-Rishon im Shiltonot Brit ha-Rishon im Shiltonot Brit ha-Moetzot al Yitziat Yehudim mi-Russya be-Tekufat ha-Milchama," *Gesher* 1/2, 54-55 (March 1968): 68-72; Warhaftig testimony, 19-23.

61. Bauer, 220.

62. Herzman, 66; "Emergency Committee for war-torn Yeshivot Vaad Hatzala," Budgeting Bulletin for Member Agencies of the Council of Jewish Federations and Welfare Funds, May 1941, AVH [hereafter cited as Federations Report].

63. Letter of Rabbi Grodzinski to Rabbi Herzog, January 26, 1940: AYHH, file "Letters of Chaim Ozer Grodzinski"; Rabbi Hayman interview. Similar information is also found in the numerous requests for certificates submitted to Rabbi Herzog during the war years, and especially in the summer of 1940; AYHH, file 9, "Rabbinical Certificates Applications, 1940-41."

64. See the lists of those granted certificates as rabbis and religious functionaries, AAYEY, file 14; and AYHH, file 9, "Rabbinical Certificates and Applications, 1940-1941."

65. For example, Rabbi Elchonon Wasserman wanted to emigrate to Palestine only if he could bring his students with him. See letter from Rabbi Bloch to Rabbi Moshe Blau, November 16, 1939: AAYEY, file 62.

66. "Vaad ha-Hatzalah," *Ha-Pardes*, 15, 4 (July 1941): 3-4.

67. Bauer, 222.

68. Letter of Moses Leavitt to Samuel Goldsmith, January 27, 1941, AJDC: "Vaad ha-Hatzalah" file.

69. *Churbn un Rettung*, 203, 205.

70. Letter of Breckenridge Long to President Roosevelt, September 18, 1940, *Foreign Relations of the United States* [1940] (Washington, D.C., 1957), 2: 238-240. See also Fred Israel, ed., *The War Diary of Breckenridge Long: Selections from the Years 1939-1944* (Lincoln, Nebraska, 1966), 165.

71. Letter of Moses Leavitt to Samuel Goldsmith, January 27, 1941, AJDC, "Vaad ha-Hatzalah" file; and "Righteous Among the Nations Department," Yad Vashem, file 377 (De Jong); also testimony of Rabbi Schlomo Wolbe, YVA, 0-3/3044, pp. 1-2.

72. During the initial four months of 1941, when the majority of refugees left Soviet Lithuania, the Vaad ha-Hatzalah spent almost $80,000 to cover the transportation expenses of rabbis, students, and family members. During that period, the JDC spent approximately $150,000 for the same purpose. See Federations Report, May 1941, 1-3.

73. Report of the Activity of the Committee for Assistance to Refugees. The Jewish community of Kobe, July 1940-September

1941, 8 [hereafter cited as Jewcom Report]. The author received the report from Rabbi Marvin Tokayer, formerly of Tokyo, and thanks him for his assistance.

74. Rabbi Zelig Epstein interview.

75. Rabbi Moshe Cohen interview.

76. Edelstein diary; Rabbi Romm interview; Epstein as in n. 74.

77. Edelstein diary; Rabbi Nayman interview.

78. For example, Rabbi Finkel initially opposed Curacao visas because he still hoped to organize the emigration of the entire yeshivah to Palestine. Mirsky, 121.

79. Mirsky, 119-124; Herzman, 63-70; Warhaftig testimony, 2-5; Rabbi Zelig Epstein interview; and Rabbi Romm interview.

80. Jewcom Report, 4-22; Porat, 85-88; Warhaftig testimony, interview no. 3, 18.

81. Abraham Kotsuji, *From Tokyo to Jerusalem* (New York, 1964), 162-169.

82. Letter from Frank to author, February 5, 1975; cables from Newman to Vaad ha-Hatzalah headquarters in New York, YIVO Archives, New York, Shanghai file, no. 49.

83. See n. 72.

84. Porat, 90; Warhaftig testimony, interview no. 4, 4-17; Baruch Oren, "Mi-Vilna derech Yapan elha-Olam ha-Chofshi," *Yalkut Moreshet* 11 (November 1969): 44-45.

85. "Japanese transit visas stopped until congestion is eased," *Every Friday* (March 28, 1941), 5.

86. "Report submitted by Rabbi M. Ashkenazi on aid given to European refugees in Shanghai by Vaad Hatzala," February 19, 1948, AVH.

87. Letter from Newman to the author, February 5, 1975; Warhaftig testimony, interview no. 4, 21-24.

88. Approximately 600 permits were received prior to the Nazi invasion of the Soviet Union. See list of Shanghai permit recipients.

89. Letter from Josef Tugendhaft (Rabbi Ashkenazi's assistant) to Newman, May 4, 1941. The author received this letter from Mr. Newman, whom he thanks for his assistance.

90. For an analysis of this problem, see Efraim Zuroff, "The Attempts to obtain Shanghai Permits in 1941: A Case of Rescue Priority during the Holocaust," *Yad Vashem Studies* 13 (Jerusalem, 1979): 322-351.

91. Jewcom Report, 8, 13, 22a.

92. This is evident from documents about the emigration of Torah scholars, such as receipts for ship and train tickets and visa applications, in the AVH collections.

93. "Vaad ha-Hatzalah," *Ha-Pardes* 15, 4 (July 1941): 3-4.

94. Cable of Rabbi Shmulewitz to Rabbi Finkel, July 26, 1941, AYHH, file 8.

95. See Jewcom Report, 22a.

96. Cable from Peters (Federation of Polish Jews in Canada) to Vaad ha-Hatzalah, August 14, 1941, AVH. See letter of Henrietta Buchman (JDC) to David Gross (leader of the Fall River, Massachusetts Jewish community), October 24, 1941, AJDC, Vaad ha-Hatzalah file; "Vaad ha-Hatzala," Budgeting Bulletin No. B-13 of the Council of Jewish Federations and Welfare Funds, February 1943, p. 2, AJDC, Vaad ha-Hatzalah file; Rabbi Zelig Epstein interview.

97. David Kranzler, *Japanese Nazis and Jews: the Jewish Refugee Community of Shanghai, 1938-1945* (New York, 1977), 347; letter of Jewcom to Louis Margolis (JDC emissary to Shanghai), August 12, 1941, AJDC, Shanghai file.

98. Rabbi Romm interview. Romm was among the citizens included in the Allied-Japanese exchange of nationals in 1942. His lengthy journey included stops in Lourence Marques and South Africa before he reached Palestine.

21

Art of the Holocaust

Nelly Toll

Bertolan Gondor. Postcard. 1944.

Drawn in Buchenwald.

A Happy Summer Day. Nelly Toll.

Drawn in Buchenwald.

Drawn in Buchenwald.

Drawn in Buchenwald.

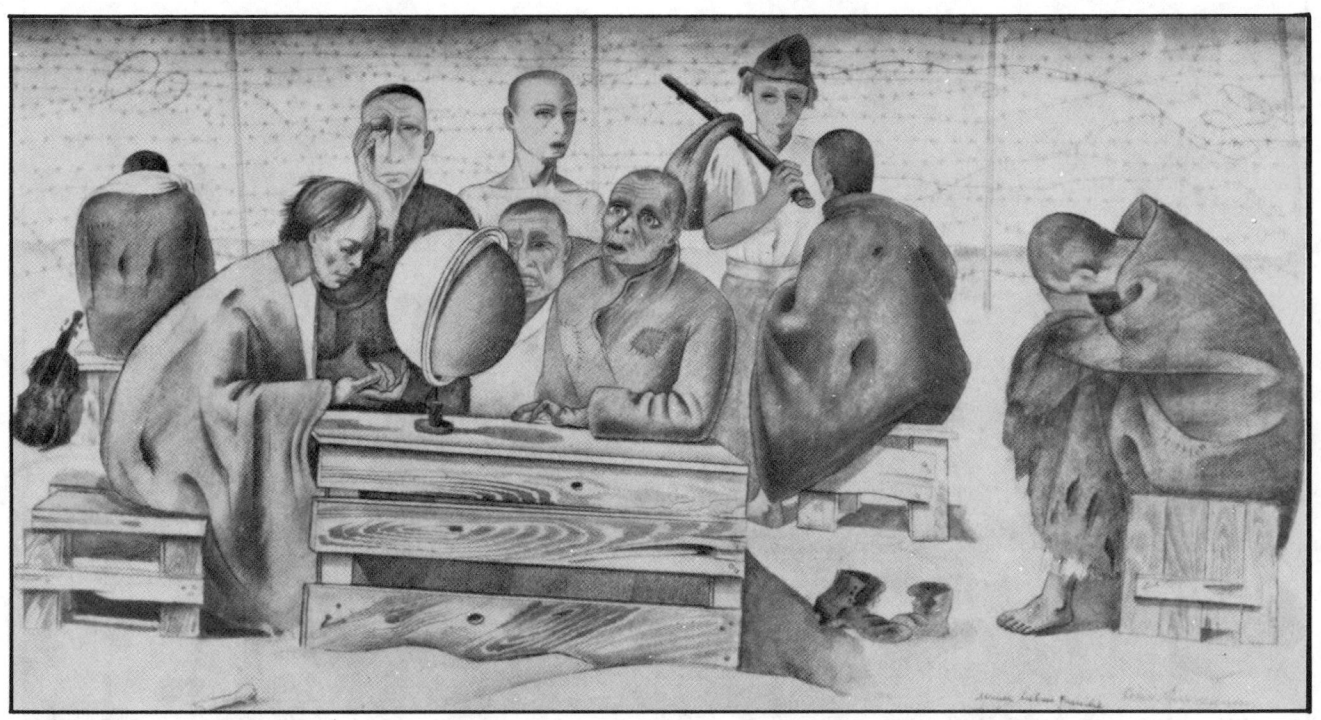

Felix Nussbaum. 1940. Pastel of a scene at Camp Gurs.

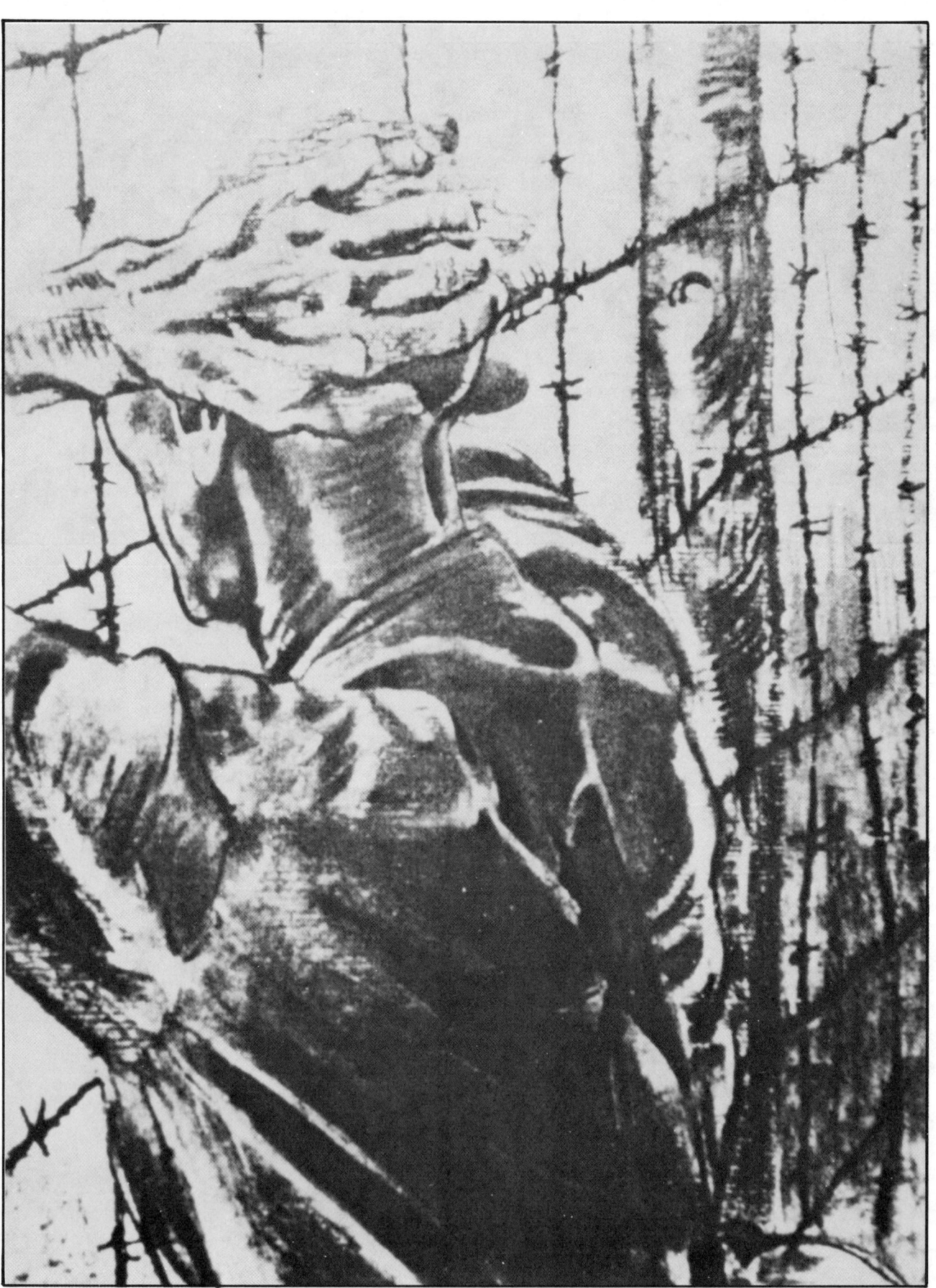

Drawn in Buchenwald.

22

The Threefold Covenant: Jewish Belief After the Holocaust

Daniel Landes

Analysis of Jewish religious self-understanding after the Holocaust must begin with a consideration of Jewish belief before this event. Since the Destruction of the Temple and the subsequent Exile, Jews have existed outside the mainstream of majority history. This position resulted from persecution and the majority's lack of interest in the spiritual life of a formerly great but presently obscure and somewhat mysterious minority. As individuals, Jews continuously contributed to Western civilization, but there was an acquiescense to their communal passivity and invisibility. The lack of prominence had certain advantages: It often kept them out of harm's way; visible, they were endangered. Since they existed outside of power, they did not participate in the violent excesses of the West (even if they were often its victims). Jews did not have to compromise their ideals or distort their faith in the battle for temporal control and earthly wealth.

Even survival, often at crisis, was only seen as a necessary condition for Israel's vocation and not a goal in its own right. Jews considered themselves God's chosen people.[1] This entailed the creation of a society that believed man to be created in the *tzelem elokim* (image of God; "Let us make man in Our image, after Our likeness"—Genesis 1:26). To further this ideal, *halakhah* promoted peace, justice, equity, and congenial relations between men; it also sought to connect man in prayer, ritual, and study with the transcendent. While this was accomplished within the Jewish covenantal community, there was an implicit albeit little proclaimed significance for mankind. *Tzelem elokim,* as man's inheritance and imperative, would at some date be learned from Israel. In exchange for this faithful preservation of *tzelem elokim,* it was the covenantal responsibility of the non-Jew to allow the people of Israel to live. At the same time, it was the pledge of God to preserve Israel for this future destiny.[2]

The Holocaust threatened to sever the bonds tying the Jew with the rest of mankind, his own people, and God. A Jew today knows that in the twentieth century he (or his fellow Jew) stood alone, bereft of support and comfort as a strange "other" in the face of unwarranted, ruthless, and total destruction. This knowledge corrodes trust and fundamental commonality that must serve as the basis of constructive cooperation between Jews and non-Jews in the post-Holocaust world. It is not merely Israel's relationship to mankind that has been imperiled. Ideally and romantically, one expects that shared adversity would lead to complete unity among Jews. Families that suffered major trauma during the war underwent great internal stress with guilt, recrimination, and assignment of blame for the tragedy upon other family members. These intense pressures, which can destroy a family, can also wreak havoc on a people, especially if they expect little or no respite from further trials. Furthermore, the Jew who believes in a God whose providence extends over the world, cannot bear His abandonment of the chosen people during the Holocaust. The covenant that binds Israel to God appears violated by God's refusal to rescue them during their most desperate need.

In fact, many laymen and theologians have concluded that one or more of these bonds were severed. Some gave up hope in Israel and its God and have sought sanctuary in assimilating into other nations. Others committed to Israel felt that salvation was only to be found within, and angrily rejected spirituality as a dead-end leading to irrelevance, quietism, and death. Still others affirmed their bond with God but turned away from the world that rejected them. They are content to await a more propitious moment in history (or messianically, at the end of history). Their radical suspicion of the world extends even to fellow Jews who are active participants in contemporary society.

Jewish belief in the post-Holocaust era is based on an overwhelming choice to maintain these bonds either partly or fully. This resilient faithfulness must be explored. Those who have remained within the Jewish community accept the inescapable condition of their Jewishness, finding succor and support within their own community. The Holocaust is converted from a threat into a prod to Jewish existence. Indeed, in a strange transfiguration it has become a badge of honor: "The people of Israel lives," even if only as a saving remnant. While these feelings have, at times, dissolved into an easy and eventually empty triumphalism, they express the desire not to opt out of Israel and thereby "complete Hitler's work."[3] This essentially negative commitment is transformed when the Jew, explores the significance of his peoplehood. Studying its history, he becomes aware of more than a lachrymose account of suffering and persecution: An epic of many dimensions and a rich heritage is revealed. The Jew thus hopes for a meaningful future, despite the stark and contrary evidence of the Holocaust.

Israel's bond with the rest of mankind similarly has an imposed quality. The Jewish community is inextricably connected economically, politically, and socially with the rest of the world. The nationalistic Jew who wishes the State of Israel to pursue an independent course—for "after the Holocaust, we owe the world nothing"—must acknowledge the web of international relationships and interdependencies that affect, shape, and often govern national policies and decision-making. Even the separatist Jew must react to the values and culture of the "outside world" which inexorably penetrates every household. The only real alternative for the Jew and his community is to participate intelligently within Western society, benefiting from and contributing to its technological and intellectual progress while exerting their own autonomous moral influence. This must be accompanied by a skepticism for the ideological roots of Western civilization, knowing the violent excesses they have either led to or condoned. The Jew recognizes, nonetheless, the greater danger that ensues when he is isolated from the rest of humanity.

Many Jews have also felt desperately compelled to remain faithful to their God. They understand Judaism to enhance life and to affirm its worth. Clinging to Judaism is thus identical with clinging to life. The source of values and meaning within life stems from God. Only He, in His majesty transcendent to the world, is beyond the radical pessimism of the Holocaust and the moral void it has opened. Jews fear that the utter negativity, futility, and deep nihilism that this event represents and induces may engulf all that survives. Their response is to seek meaning grounded in a reality totally distinct from despair. This approach is often interpreted as escapism. Even the most mystical approach to Judaism, however, leads man back to the world, the arena where his Torah is to be fulfilled. In any event, the believer feels compelled to accept God even with the awesome question raised by Auschwitz, rather than reject Him and the basis for value within life.

Jews have felt driven to renew the threefold covenant with mankind, their own community, and God, but this has not resolved the tensions resulting from the Holocaust. The strains are more evident in the affirmation of the covenant "in spite of all that happened" than by its denial. The threefold covenant cannot evade an honest (and not just professed) confrontation with the Final Solution. Refusal, in the long run, is devastating: It denies the Jew's own self-worth, dismissing his significance as a historical being. It is a religious failure, implying that the resources of Judaism are insufficient to meet the harsh challenges of threatening nature. It is dangerous, because it prevents a community from learning the lessons of the past in order to prepare intelligently for future risks. It is morally insensitive, for it closes one's heart to the suffering of the powerless and the innocent. Finally, this leads to the invalid assumption that one can understand the Jew's vocation in post-capitalist civilization without considering its major public event.

The most readily available theory to account for the Holocaust is the traditional teaching of reward and punishment,[4] whose major application until now has been to the Destruction and Exile. In this doctrine, Jews are of central interest to God. He rewards and punishes them according to the morality of their deeds and the purity of their service. The people of Israel's worldly persecutors are unknowing rods of His wrath, but they are not excused for their malicious zeal and ruthless behavior. The doctrine of reward and punishment functions as a theodicy, explaining the existence of evil, shaping events, and clearing God of any fault. The onus is upon Israel, which bears the responsibility for its own actions and thus for its own fate. Despite the harshness of this teaching, there is an implied optimism: Just as a nation can deserve punishment, it can also merit reward. The suffering of the Destruction and Exile was accompanied by prophecy, through which the people of Israel were exhorted to examine their deeds and move to a higher plane in their relationship to others and to God.

The doctrine of reward and punishment applied to the Holocaust results in bizarre and disturbing conclusions. It necessitates the search for a sin that merited the attempted extermination of an entire people. Since a sin of such magnitude is obviously not present, it would have to be manufactured. Speculation in this direction leads to paralleling the antisemitic assumption of the Nazis: The Jews deserve the cruelest of fates. Additionally, the assignment of this responsibility to Israel is inherently a crushing burden, causing inner fragmentation and mutual recrimination.[5] It is not surprising that the most vigorous exponents of this view have distanced themselves from the Jewish community.

This theory also fails as a defense of God, attributing actions to Him which could be ascribed to a monster. It is not adequate to respond that God's punishment of Israel is "beyond our understanding." This ascribed action runs *counter* to our understanding of morality, as formed and shaped by His own Torah. Finally, the application of this doctrine to the Holocaust fails to account for the fact that the Nazis were not unknowing instrumentalities but self-motivated haters whose world program had a unique intentionality directed against the Jews.

No religious doctrine can "explain" why the Holocaust happened. Prior Jewish suffering has been subsumed under the Destruction and Exile. These twin episodes, however, were accompanied by prophecy, which first warned and later determined the reason for punishment. The Holocaust, as a unique occurrence, cannot be understood as a part of these other tragedies. At the same time, no heavenly voice has broken Divine silence to elucidate its meaning. We are left with an historical event which can only be analyzed in those terms. This does not suggest that the Holocaust lacks religious importance. It does mean that a religious understanding of the Holocaust cannot ignore, but must rest on, a profound historical inquiry into the complex and confusing components of the event.

A major element in this approach is the realization that, unlike the Destruction and Exile, the Holocaust was not inevitable. Things could have happened differently if participants and bystanders had made other decisions. The Holocaust as history presumes full human responsibility. It is only within this context that a contemporary meaning of the threefold covenant and Israel's vocation can be found.

An approach to this threefold covenant is suggested by a passage describing the essence of Israel in the writings of Abraham Isaac Kook, the early twentieth-century European talmudist, thinker, and later Chief Rabbi of Israel. Rabbi Kook's works are not readily accessible to many readers. The writing is allusive, evocative, and mystically charged. It posits an underlying unity to reality having been created by One God. His thought, in addition (or, in consequence), conveys an unbounded optimism. Writing before the Holocaust, Rabbi Kook held what in retrospect was a naive confidence in the progress and moral ascent of man.

Rabbi Kook's theory of Israel, nevertheless, presents a vivid depiction of its chosenness in relation to mankind. Further, Kook's mysticism does not obscure but rather heightens Israel as an immanent entity, acting out its destiny within this world. Any definition of chosenness will entail a transcendent purpose, but Rabbi Kook's formulation of this doctrine is accomplished not at the expense of history but rather through it. With this acceptance of history, Kook's theory allows for the Holocaust to be confronted. It does so at the risk of the theory itself being transformed from a spirited optimism to a sober realism redeemed by a radical belief in God and His promise.

> *Knesset Israel* (the people of Israel) is the microcosm of all existence. This refers, in a worldly context, to Israel's material and spiritual dimensions—both its saga and it's faith. Israel's history is the ideal microcosm of universal history. There is no social fluctuation among the peoples of the world that you will not find its prototype in Israel. Its faith is the well-sifted essence as well as the influential source of the good and the ideal of all faiths. In this sense, Israel's faith serves as a resource that reviews belief systems with the goal of elevating their discourse so that all may call in the Name of the Lord; your God, "the Separate One of Israel, shall be called the God of the entire earth."
>
> *Knesset Israel* is the sublime revelation of the spirit, within human existence. One does not doubt that the manifestations of life contained within the brain and the heart are not to be found to a similar degree elsewhere in the body. Identically, one cannot doubt—although a sensitive soul and a thoughtful mind will marvel at—the manifestations of life, wonders, miracles, prophecy, the highest degree of divine inspiration, eternal hope, victory over every obstacle, revealed in an exalted form within Israel. *Knesset Israel* is the revelation of the arm of the Lord within the world, His hand in existence, and His participation within the development of nations. It is intimately connected to all that is exalted, venerable, holy, and lofty within the entire physical and spiritual scope of reality. It is impossible to think otherwise.[6]

Underneath Rabbi Kook's extravagant language is the rejection of any absolute disjunction between Israel and mankind. Israel is not a different form of man; he is man. This is more than a state of being. Israel's vocation and destiny is *to be* human and to share in all that is human, both materially and spiritually. The truth of the Torah is not separate from the truths contained within our systems, nor are the latter considered to be deviant forms of Torah. Rather, it is Israel's task to engage in a critical dialogue with mankind in order to declare monotheism—man's responsibilities to one another and to God. All nations and peoples share in the *tzelem elokim* in that reality is a creation of God, and man the crowning jewel. The meaning of Israel's election is to be the flesh-and-blood bearer of monotheism's message: to cherish the human and the transcendent.

Israel's election does not assure an easy triumph for *tzelem elokim,* despite Rabbi Kook's colorful messianic expectations. The Jewish people were not incidental victims of World War II. The attempt to exterminate them went beyond political expediency and was even counterproductive to the German war effort. Nazi hatred for the people of Israel had a unique intentionality[7] and was the very basis of its ideology and purpose. Standing at the center of mankind, Israel became the target. The Nazi attack upon Israel was thus an attack upon man himself. Nazi hatred of Israel was hatred turned against the image of man. By denying humanity to the Jews, the Nazis denied their own. Ultimately, it was a self-hatred.

From where does this self-hatred derive? Judaism has maintained that violence perpetrated upon man is rebellion against God, in that man is God's image upon earth. The refusal to consider another as in His image is the desire to cast off the yoke of His image that the hater himself bears and the manifold ethical responsibilities that

he is charged with. It is a rejection of meaning and responsibility and a descent into nihilism. A religious understanding of the Final Solution yields this cursed equation: hatred of Israel = hatred of man = self-hatred = hatred of God.

The Holocaust is a paradigmatic event for all mankind. It is a microcosm of ultimate violence and tragedy within the modern nation-states of the West.[8] The Holocaust was not a sacrificial event in which the death of six million Jews expatiates the possibilities of such murder of others. It was, rather, a breakthrough event that threatens its own uniqueness by setting a genocidal pattern for other peoples in other situations. The Holocaust is a dark revelation of man's capacities for participating in (the Nazis and their followers) and acquiescing to (the Allies and others) systematic and total destruction. The Holocaust of that people dedicated to bearing the human and divine image heralds the Nuclear Age, where man's self-destruction is contemplated, planned for, and even played at in wargame scenarios. It announces a technological era in which means of dehumanization and methods of torture are mass produced, increasingly sophisticated, and generally ignored. What befell the Jews now threatens all people.

The Holocaust is revelational *of* man but also *to* man. In that sense, its religious understanding is an historical understanding. Its significance is historical in that it not only provides the background for contemporary society but also points the path where the future may lead. The exploration and teaching of the Holocaust becomes a religious obligation of Israel, who, seeking the continuation of *tzelem elokim,* is the exposed and vulnerable arm of God in history. Man, a morally autonomous and free agent, may reject God and His people.[10] Israel, as the servant of the Lord, has suffered the wrath of those who rebelled against its master. Grievously hurt, Israel has chosen to renew its threefold covenant. For Israel, the Holocaust has imperiled the mission of the chosen people but, paradoxically, has also confirmed it. The renewal of His service takes on a new dimension of desperate urgency in an age when man stands in mutual threat and self-alienation. Israel draws strength from the prophet who charged that he (Israel) "shall not fail nor be crushed until he has rectified the world, for the islands await his teachings" (Isaiah 42:4).

NOTES

1. Judah Halevi, *Kuzari* (standard editions) 3:36.

2. Isaiah 54:10.

3. Emil Fackenheim, *God's Presence in History* (New York: New York University Press, 1969), p. 84.

4. Eliezer Berkovits, *Faith After the Holocaust* (New York: Ktav, 1973), pp. 86-94.

5. Yoel Teitelbaum, *Sefer Vayoel Moshe.* Brooklyn: 5721. p. 5.

6. Abraham Isaac Kook, *Orot* (Jerusalem: Mossad HaRav Kook, 1961), p. 138.

7. Steven T. Katz, "The Unique Intentionality of the Holocaust," *Modern Judaism* (September 1981): 161-183.

8. See "How Unique Is the Holocaust?" by Henry L. Feingold, in *Genocide: Critical Issues of the Holocaust* (Simon Wiesenthal Center, Los Angeles).

9. Irving Greenberg, *Voluntary Covenant* (Monograph) (New York: National Jewish Resource Center, 1982), pp. 21-28.

10. Joseph B. Soloveitchik, *Lessons in Jewish Thought: Adapted from the Lectures of Rabbi Joseph B. Soloveitchik,* ed. Abraham Besdin (Jerusalem: World Zionist Organization, 1979), pp. 31-39; Berkovitz, *Faith,* pp. 94-113.

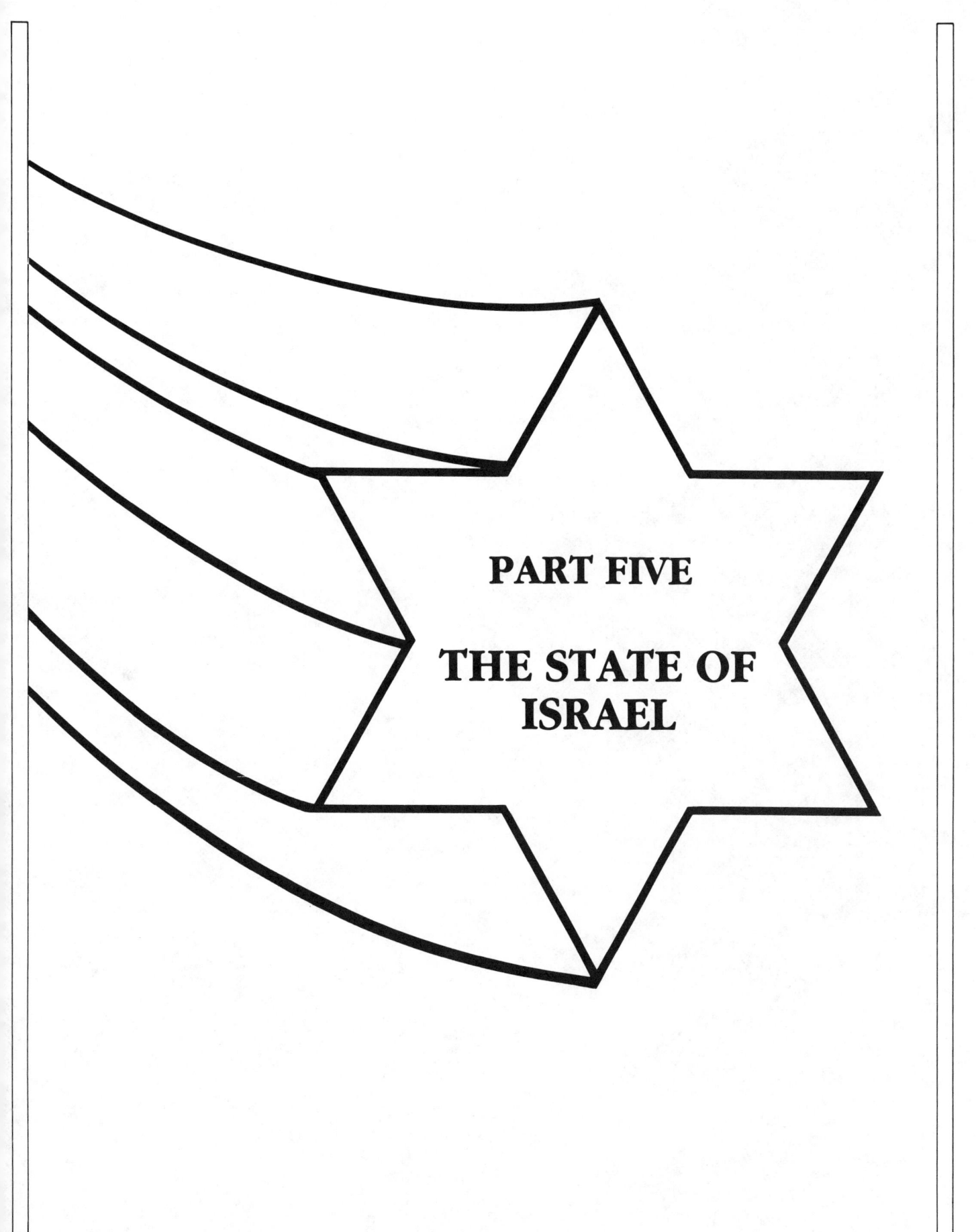

PART FIVE

THE STATE OF
ISRAEL

23

Declaration of Independence of the State of Israel

The Land of Israel was the birthplace of the Jewish people. Here their spiritual, religious and national identity was formed. Here they achieved independence and created a culture of national and universal significance. Here they wrote and gave the Bible to the world.

Exiled from the Land of Israel the Jewish people remained faithful to it in all the countries of their dispersion, never ceasing to pray and hope for their return and the restoration of their national freedom.

Impelled by this historic association, Jews strove throughout the centuries to go back to the land of their fathers and regain their statehood. In recent decades they returned in their masses. They reclaimed the wilderness, revived their language, built cities and villages, and established a vigorous and ever-growing community, with its own economic and cultural life. They sought peace, yet were prepared to defend themselves. They brought the blessings of progress to all inhabitants of the country and looked forward to sovereign independence.

In the year 1897 the First Zionist Congress, inspired by Theodor Herzl's vision of the Jewish State, proclaimed the right of the Jewish people to national revival in their own country.

This right was acknowledged by the Balfour Declaration of November 2, 1917, and reaffirmed by the Mandate of the League of Nations, which gave explicit international recognition to the historic connection of the Jewish people with Palestine and their right to reconstitute their National Home.

The recent holocaust, which engulfed millions of Jews in Europe, proved anew the need to solve the problem of the homelessness and lack of independence of the Jewish people by means of the re-establishment of the Jewish State, which would open the gates to all Jews and endow the Jewish people with equality of status among the family of nations.

The survivors of the disastrous slaughter in Europe, and also Jews from other lands, have not desisted from their efforts to reach Eretz-Yisrael, in face of difficulties, obstacles and perils; and have not ceased to urge their right to a life of dignity, freedom and honest toil in their ancestral land.

In the second World War the Jewish people in Palestine made their full contribution to the struggle of the freedom-loving nations against the Nazi evil. The sacrifices of their soldiers and their war effort gained them the right to rank with the nations which founded the United Nations.

Ben-Gurion proclaims the establishment of the State of Israel, May 14, 1948.

On November 29, 1947, the General Assembly of the United Nations adopted a Resolution requiring the establishment of a Jewish State in Palestine. The General Assembly called upon the inhabitants of the country to take all the necessary steps on their part to put the plan into effect. This recognition by the United Nations of the right of the Jewish people to establish their independent State is unassailable.

It is the natural right of the Jewish people to lead, as do all other nations, an independent existence in its sovereign State.

ACCORDINGLY WE, the members of the National Council representing the Jewish people in Palestine and the World Zionist Movement, are met together in solemn assembly today, the day of termination of the British Mandate for Palestine; and by virtue of the natural and historic right of the Jewish people and of the Resolution of the General Assembly of the United Nations.

WE HEREBY PROCLAIM the establishment of the Jewish State in Palestine, to be called Medinath Yisrael (The State of Israel).

WE HEREBY DECLARE that, as from the termination of

the Mandate at midnight, the 14th-15th May, 1948, and pending the setting up of the duly elected bodies of the State in accordance with a Constitution, to be drawn up by the Constituent Assembly not later than the 1st October, 1948, the National Council shall act as the Provisional State Council, and that the National Administration shall constitute the Provisional Government of the Jewish State, which shall be known as Israel.

THE STATE OF ISRAEL will be open to the immigration of Jews from all countries of their dispersion; will promote the development of the country for the benefit of all its inhabitants; will be based on the principles of liberty, justice and peace as conceived by the Prophets of Israel; will uphold the full social and political equality of all its citizens, without distinction of religion, race, or sex; will guarantee freedom of religion, conscience, education and culture; will safeguard the Holy Places of all religions; and will loyally uphold the principles of the United Nations Charter.

THE STATE OF ISRAEL will be ready to co-operate with the organs and representatives of the United Nations in the implementation of the Resolution of the Assembly of November 29, 1947, and will take steps to bring about the Economic Union over the whole of Palestine.

We appeal to the United Nations to assist the Jewish people in the building of its State and to admit Israel into the family of nations.

In the midst of wanton aggression, we yet call upon the Arab inhabitants of the State of Israel to preserve the ways of peace and play their part in the development of the State, on the basis of full and equal citizenship and due representation in all its bodies and institutions—provisional and permanent.

We extend our hand in peace and neighbourliness to all the neighbouring states and their peoples, and invite them to co-operate with the independent Jewish nation for the common good of all. The State of Israel is prepared to make its contribution to the progress of the Middle East as a whole.

Our call goes out to the Jewish people all over the world to rally to our side in the task of immigration and development, and to stand by us in the great struggle for the fulfillment of the dream of generations for the redemption of Israel.

With trust in the Rock of Israel, we set our hand to this Declaration, at this Session of the Provisional State Council, on the soil of the Homeland, in the city of Tel Aviv, on this Sabbath eve, the fifth of Iyar, 5708, the fourteenth of May, 1948.

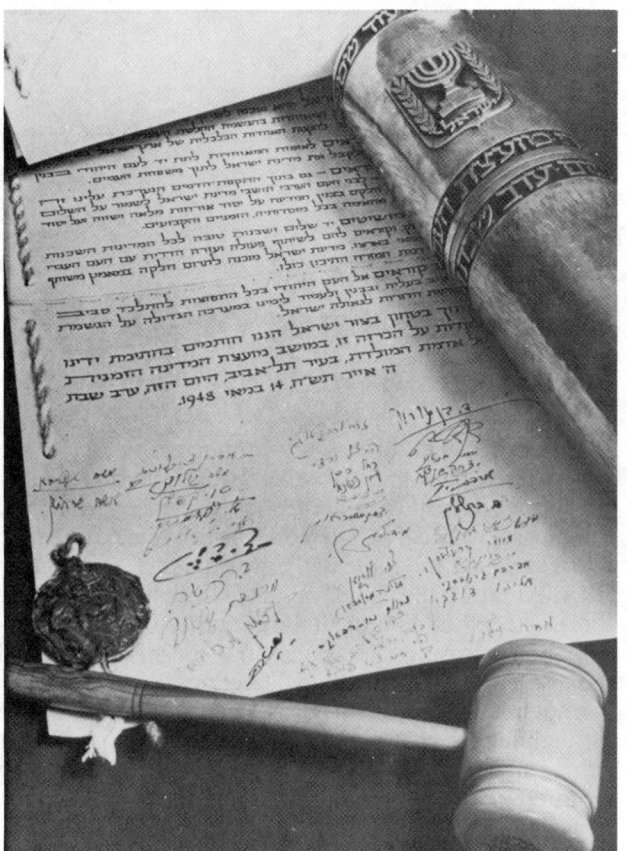

The Scroll of Independence of the State of Israel, signed May 14, 1948.

Israel's Presidents

Chaim Weizmann	(1874-1952)	President 1948-1952
Yitzhak Ben Zvi	(1884-1963)	President 1952-1963
Zalman Shazar	(1889-1974)	President 1963-1973
Ephraim Katzir	(1916-)	President 1973-1978
Yitzhak Navon	(1921-)	President 1978-1983
Chaim Herzog	(1918-)	President 1983-

Israel's Prime Ministers

David Ben-Gurion	(1886-1973)	Prime Minister 1948-1953; 1955-1963
Moshe Sharett	(1884-1965)	Prime Minister 1954-1955
Levi Eshkol	(1895-1969)	Prime Minister 1963-1969
Golda Meir	(1898-1978)	Prime Minister 1969-1974
Yitzhak Rabin	(1922-)	Prime Minister 1974-1977
Menachem Begin	(1913-)	Prime Minister 1977-1983
Yitzhak Shamir	(1915-)	Prime Minister 1983-1984
Shimon Peres	(1923-)	Prime Minister 1984-

Statistical Abstract of Israel

Central Bureau of Statistics, State of Israel

POPULATION — אוכלוסייה

	1983	1980	1970	1960	1950	Unit יחידה
Population—total	4,148.5	3,921.7	3,022.1	2,150.4	1,370.1	10³
Jews	82.9	83.7	85.4	88.9	87.8	%
Non-Jews	17.1	16.3	14.6	11.1	12.2	"
Jews in Israel as % of world Jewry	26.4	25.0	20.0	..	..	%
Jews—total	3,436.1	3,282.7	2,582.0	1,911.2	1,203.0	10³
Israel born	59.1	55.9	45.8	37.6	26.3	%
Born in Asia-Africa	18.2	19.5	26.3	27.6	22.2	"
Born in Europe-America	22.7	24.6	27.9	35.0	51.5	"
Non-Jews—total	712.4	639.0	440.1	239.1	167.1	10³
Moslems	77.0	78.0	74.7	69.6	69.5	%
Christians	13.5	14.1	17.1	20.7	21.5	"
Druze and other	9.5	7.9	8.2	9.7	9.0	"
Population density	[3]187.9	191.8	147.7	106.2	67.7	per km²
Population by district—total	[3,1]100.0	[1]100.0	[1]100.0	100.0	100.0	%
Jerusalem District	11.7	11.4	10.8	8.7	..	"
Northern District	[2]16.2	15.6	15.3	15.7	..	"
Haifa District	14.2	14.4	15.4	17.1	..	"
Central District	20.6	20.1	18.9	17.9	..	"
Tel Aviv District	24.8	25.6	29.4	31.8	..	"
Southern District	11.8	12.1	11.1	7.8	..	"
Population in urban localities—total	[3]3,507.7	3,401.5	2,477.0	1,649.1	..	10³
Jews	86.1	87.2	92.4	96.3	..	%
Non-Jews	13.9	12.8	7.6	3.7	..	"
Jerusalem	428.7	407.1	291.7	164.0	121.0	10³
Jews	71.5	71.8	73.9	98.8	..	%
Non-Jews	28.5	28.2	26.1	1.2	..	"
Tel Aviv conurbation	1,555.4	1,280.4	..	..	..	10³
Thereof: Tel Aviv-Yafo	327.3	334.9	384.0	390.0	335.0	"
Haifa conurbation	387.5	379.1	..	..	..	"
Thereof: Haifa	225.8	230.0	217.1	179.5	140.0	"

1 Including Israeli residents living in Judea and Samaria, Gaza Area and the Golan. 2 Incl. Golan sub-district. 3 Results of the June 1983 census.

POPULATION (cont.) — אוכלוסייה (המשך)

	1983	1980	1970	1960	1950	Unit יחידה
Population in rural localities—total[1]	529.9	520.2	523.5	501.3	..	10³
Jews	62.2	60.5	51.9	64.3	..	%
Non-Jews	37.8	39.5	48.1	35.7	..	"
Thereof: Moshavim and collective moshavim	149.9	151.8	127.8	118.7	71.5	10³
Qibbuzim	115.5	111.2	84.0	78.0	66.7	"
Population by selected age groups						
Jews aged 0–14	30.7	30.4	30.1	35.1	30.0	% of total
65+	9.4	9.7	7.2	5.2	3.7	"
Non-Jews aged 0–14	46.0	47.4	49.7	45.6	..	"
65+	2.9	3.1	3.9	4.5	..	"

VITAL STATISTICS — תנועה טבעית

	1983	1980	1970	1960	1950	Unit יחידה
Jews						
Live births	74,893	71,372	61,209	44,981	36,359	no. מס'
Births per 1,000 population	22.4	22.0	24.2	23.9	33.0	Rate שיעור
Deaths	25,086	23,472	18,425	10,404	7,148	no. מס'
Mortality per 1,000 population	7.4	7.2	7.3	5.5	6.5	Rate שיעור
Infant mortality per 1,000 live births	11.7	12.1	18.9	27.2	46.2	"
Total fertility per woman	2.8	2.7	3.4	3.5	3.9	Average births
Woman born in:						
Israel	2.9	2.8	3.1	2.8	3.9	"
Asia-Africa	3.1	3.0	4.1	5.1	5.7	"
Europe-America	2.8	2.8	2.8	2.4	3.3	"
Life expectation at birth						
Males	[2]72.8	72.5	69.9	70.7	66.3	Years שנים
Females	[2]76.2	76.2	73.3	73.5	69.5	"
Non-Jews						
Live births	23,831	22,949	16,392	11,021	7,072	no. מס'
Births per 1,000 population	34.7	36.5	45.7	50.3	56.0	Rate שיעור
Deaths	2,786	2,806	1,959	1,649	1,552	no. מס'
Mortality per 1,000 population	4.1	4.5	5.5	7.5	..	Rate שיעור
Infant mortality per 1,000 live births	22.0	24.4	37.2	48.0	56.0	"
Total fertility per woman	4.7	5.4	7.7	8.0	..	Average births
Moslem	5.3	6.0	9.0	9.3	..	"
Christian	2.3	2.7	3.6	4.6	..	"
Druze	5.3	6.1	7.5	7.9	..	"

1 Results of the June 1983 census.   2 1982

LIVING COND. (cont.)

	Unit	1983	1980	1970	1960	1950
Daily food consumption per capita[1]						
Calories	Un.	3,069	2,979	2,988	2,772	2,610
Proteins	gr.	97.1	92.2	91.5	85.1	83.9
Fat	gr.	119.6	111.5	104.3	86.7	73.9
Products:						
Wheat and its products		274.2	282.2	285.5	313.7	322.5
Rice		17.3	15.9	18.1	15.6	12.1
Sugar and its products		84.9	82.7	95.9	79.7	47.1
Vegetables		336.4	311.2	331.2	314.0	295.9
Citrus fruit		82.7	95.6	116.2	88.2	134.2
Meat		194.2	170.4	154.3	161.9	51.8
Eggs		59.2	53.7	61.6	50.4	40.0
Milk and dairy products		299.4	272.0	267.7	275.9	264.0

EDUCATION

	Unit	1983	1980	1970	1960	1949
Years of schooling (aged 14+)						
Jews 0 years	%	5.6	6.4	9.3	12.6	6.3
13+ years	"	23.0	20.8	13.0	9.9	..
Non-Jews 0 years	"	16.0	18.9	36.1	49.5	..
13+ years	"	8.2	7.7	2.1	1.5	..
PUPILS — TOTAL	10³	1,305.1	1,203.8	824.5	580.3	140.7
Hebrew education — total	"	1,104.2	1,026.5	713.9	534.0	129.6
Kindergartens	"	254.5	246.6	107.7	75.7	25.4
Primary	"	471.2	436.4	394.4	375.1	91.1
Post-primary — total	"	247.2	216.6	137.3	55.1	10.2
Intermediate	"	87.9	72.8	7.9		
Secondary — total	"	159.3	143.8	129.4	55.1	10.2
General (incl. continuation classes)	"	77.7	68.0	72.2	40.0	8.2
Vocational and agricultural		81.6	75.8	57.2	15.2	2.0
Teacher training colleges		11.5	11.3	5.1	3.1	0.7
Post secondary and other higher institutions		17.1	14.1	6.9	2.7	0.6
Universities — total	"	62.4	57.5	36.2	11.3	1.6
Field of study	%					
— total		100.0	100.0	100.0	100.0	100.0
Humanities	"	30.3	30.1	32.3	44.6	32.5
Social sciences	"	27.4	29.0	25.8		
Law	"	4.0	3.8	5.3	6.6	..
Medicine	"	5.9	5.7	3.9	6.9	3.2
Sciences and mathematics	"	16.6	13.7	14.7	18.4	16.0
Agriculture	"	2.3	2.7	1.5	3.6	4.6
Engineering	"	13.5	15.0	16.5	19.9	43.7
Other institutions	10³	40.3	44.0	26.3	11.0	—

1 Agricultural years.

MIGRATION

	Unit	1983	1980	1970	1960	1950
Immigrants and potential immigrants	no.	16,906	20,428	36,750	24,510	170,215
Residents going abroad	"	771,646	513,459	153,698	63,305	30,018
Residents returning	"	769,015	481,603	146,495	51,256	20,031
Tourists arriving	10³	1,166.8	1,175.8	441.3	117.7	33.1

MANPOWER, EMPLOYMENT AND WAGES

	Unit	1983	1980	1970	1960	1955
Civilian labour force	10³	1,402.6	1,318.1	1,001.4	735.8	631.2
Percent civilian labour force of population aged 14+	%	49.9	49.5	49.3	52.9	53.6
Percent unemployed of civilian labour force		4.5	4.8	3.8	4.6	7.2
Employed persons — total	10³	1,339.4	1,254.5	963.2	701.8	585.7
Agriculture	%	5.5	6.4	8.8	17.3	17.6
Industry	"	22.8	23.7	24.3	23.2	21.5
Electricity and water	"	1.0	1.0	1.2	2.2	2.0
Construction	"	6.5	6.4	8.3	9.3	9.3
Commerce	"	12.8	11.7	13.0	12.3	13.5
Transport	"	6.5	6.9	7.5	6.2	6.6
Finance	"	9.5	8.2	5.2		
Public services	"	29.5	29.6	24.0	22.0	21.2
Private services	"	5.8	6.2	7.7	7.5	8.3
Percent Jews of total employed persons	"	89.3	89.9	90.8	93.1	92.6
Percent employees of total employed persons		78.6	77.5	73.6	67.4	63.2
Percent women of total employed persons		36.9	36.0	29.4	25.6	24.4
Average monthly wage per employee's post	IS ש	37,596	2,810	68	[1]28	..

LIVING CONDITIONS

	Unit	1983	1980	1970	1960	1950
Total annual money income per urban employee's household (beginning of year; at current prices)	IS 10³ ש	513.9	37.6	1.2	[2]0.9	..
Private consumption expenditure per capita (at current prices)	IS ש	223,976	16,277	381	146	27
Thereof:	% of total					
Food, beverages and tobacco		24.9	27.2	29.1	36.4	37.8
Clothing, footwear and personal effects	"	5.2	5.9	8.6	10.2	11.5
Durable goods	"	11.6	9.6	9.6	7.8	7.8
Other products, fuel and light	"	8.3	8.7	7.5	7.5	6.3
Services (incl. housing and non-profit institutions)		50.0	48.6	45.2	38.1	36.6

1 1961　2 1967

ישראל 1980

NATIONAL ECONOMY

	1983	1980	1970	1960	1950	Unit
At 1980 prices						
Gross national product—total	107,733	102,599	62,309	27,140	9,776	IS 10^6
—per capita	26,255	26,459	20,930	12,846	7,742	IS 10^6
Private consumption expenditure—total	80,345	63,117	37,199	17,463	6,820	IS 10^6
—per capita	19,581	16,277	12,509	8,254	5,373	IS 10^6
General government consumption expenditure	35,383	37,098	26,751	6,791	2,980	IS 10^6
Gross domestic capital formation	27,364	24,255	20,874	9,122	5,728	''
At current prices						
Net domestic product—total	100.0	100.0	100.0	100.0	100.0[1]	%
Agriculture, forestry & fishing	5.4	6.4	6.4	11.6	11.4	''
Industry	20.3	20.3	24.0	23.9	21.7	''
Construction, electricity and water	10.6	12.1	12.7	9.4	10.9	''
Commerce, restaurants and hotels	13.0	12.7	11.8	10.6	12.5	''
Transport, storage and communication	7.3	6.8	9.1	8.0	7.4	''
Finance and business services	7.6	8.0	7.0	3.8	2.5	''
Ownership of dwellings	8.9	7.2	6.1	5.9	5.2	''
Public and community services	23.6	23.7	19.1	18.8	18.2	''
Personal and other services	3.3	2.8	3.8	8.0	10.2	''

FOREIGN TRADE

	1983	1980	1970	1960	1950	Unit
Net imports of goods	8,370.0	7,878.3	1,433.5	495.7	300.3	$10^6
Net exports of goods	4,893.8	5,291.9	733.6	211.3	35.1	''
Excess of imports over exports	3,476.2	2,586.4	699.9	284.4	265.5	''
Exports as percent of imports	58.5	67.2	51.2	42.6	11.7	%
Index of import volume	153	167	121	30	..	1972=100
Index of export volume	176	167	76	25	..	''
Agricultural exports	507.5	555.7	129.6	63.1	17.0	$10^6
Industrial exports (excl. diamonds)	3,291.7	3,265.3	393.1	92.6	9.4	''
Diamonds	1,207.7	1,615.1	244.6	60.9	8.8	''
Imports of consumer goods	952.0	544.3	142.6	44.1	76.7	''
production inputs	5,922.0	6,503.7	972.4	353.5	169.1	''
investment goods	1,705.7	969.4	347.0	105.0	56.2	''

[1] 1952

EDUCATION (cont.)

	1983	1980	1970	1960	1949	Unit
Arab education—total	200.9	177.4	110.6	46.3	11.1	10^3
Kindergartens	18.7	17.3	14.2	7.3	1.1	''
Primary	135.3	122.0	85.4	36.9	10.0	''
Post-primary—total	46.4	37.3	10.6	2.0	—	''
Intermediate	18.1	14.8	2.5	—	—	''
Secondary—total	28.3	22.5	8.1	2.0	—	''
General	23.7	19.0	6.2	1.9	—	''
Vocational and agricultural	4.6	3.5	1.9	0.1	—	''
Teacher training colleges	0.4	0.5	0.4	0.1	—	''
Other post-secondary and higher institutions	—	0.1	..	..	—	''
Other institutions	0.1	0.2	..	..	—	''
GRADUATES						
Matriculation	19.1	14.0	11.0	3.6	0.8	10^3
Universities—total	9,891	9,371	5,566	1,237	193	no.
First degree	7,124	6,740	4,064	779	135	''
Second degree	1,943	1,652	807	377	48	''
Third degree	336	378	238	81	10	''
Diploma	488	601	457	..	..	''

HEALTH

	1983	1980	1970	1960	1950	Unit
Beds in hospitals	26.4	26.4	23.7	15.6	8.4	10^3
Beds per 1,000 population	6.4	6.8	7.9	7.3	6.6	Rate
Hospitalization days	8,810	8,926	8,306	5,470	2,271	10^3
Hospitalization days per 1,000 population	2,147	2,301.9	2,878.2	2,583.8	1,792.7	Rate
Live births in hospitals						% of births
Jews	..	100.0	100.0	99.4	94.8	''
Non-Jews	..	98.8	91.2	54.5	..	''

	1983	1980	1970	1960	1955	Unit
Mother and child health centres						
Receptions: Pregnant women	..	74.0	56.7	42.6	16.5	10^3
Infants	..	89.9	72.4	48.7	28.5	''

NATIONAL INSURANCE[1]

	1983	1980	1970	1960	1955	Unit
Insured persons	1,733	1,636	1,060	660	535	10^3
Recipients of benefits and pensions						
Old and survivors	371.1	343.5	176.7	62.2	43.3	''
Maternity grant	102.7	97.3	78.0	49.9	8.7	''
Maternity allowance	42.4	39.8	24.8	13.1	—	''
Children for whom allowances were paid	1,562.7	1,512.9	862.3	83.1	—	''

[1] Budget years.

Upper table

INDUSTRY	Unit	1950	1960	1970	1980	1983
Establishments engaging 100 employees and over	no.	..	198	375	427	446
Industrial production index—total[1]	1978=100.0	..	20	61	102	113
Mining and quarrying		..	30	91	116	115
Food, beverages and tobacco		..	26	58	106	130
Textiles, clothing and leather		..	20	63	99	101
Wood and its products		..	20	77	88	99
Paper and its products, printing and publishing		..	24	66	108	118
Rubber, plastic, chemical and oil products		..	14	56	99	117
Non-metallic mineral products		..	44	82	104	99
Basic metal and metal products		..	25	68	102	111
Machinery, electrical & electronic equipment and vehicles		..	14	50	103	115
Miscellaneous		..	25	62	94	110
ELECTRICITY						
Installed generating capacity	MWT	100	410	1,226	2,737	3,712
Production	10^6 KWH	543	2,205	6,610	12,089	14,047
Consumption						
Household		} 206	} 446	1,448	2,900	3,351
Commerce				782	1,992	2,682
Agricultural		..	196	195	453	558
Industrial		141	669	1,878	3,773	4,079
Water pumping		117	546	1,394	1,678	1,905
WATER[2]						
Household consumption	$m^3 \; 10^6$	..	197	254	367	³385
Industrial		..	54	86	100	³103
Agricultural		..	1,087	1,319	1,212	³1,282
CONSTRUCTION						
Building completed—total	$m^2 \; 10^3$	..	3,485	4,478	5,140	4,970
Building begun—total		..	3,433	5,910	4,930	4,740
Dwellings—building completed		..	31.0	31.4	30.8	30.7
—building begun	no. 10^3	..	26.9	46.7	32.7	26.3
Road construction and widening—completed	km.	..	405.0	348.4	390.8	272.6
—begun		..	501.4	413.2	236.2	227.3
COMMERCE						
Index of sales value in large scale retail trade, at fixed prices	1980=100.0	..	..	56.3	100.0	131.6

1 Excl. diamonds
2 Budget year.
3 1981.

Lower table

BALANCE OF PAYMENTS	Unit	1950	1960	1970	1980	1983
Deficit in goods and services account—total	$10^6	285	346	1,262	3,775	5,039
—excl. direct defence imports		..	298	638	2,120	4,039
Obligations of Israel to abroad		..	946	3,583	22,101	29,313
Israel's foreign assets		..	270	962	10,091	11,573
FINANCE						
Total money supply (end of year)	IS 10^6	..	88	338	7,006	61,335
Thereof: current deposits of the public in banks		..	58	210	4,878	37,432
Exchange rate of the U.S. Dollar	IS	0.04	0.18	0.35	7.55	107.77
PRICES						
Consumer price index	1969=100.0	..	61.7	106.1	3,433.1	40,287.5
Price index of inputs in residential building	1968=100.0	..	..	113.4	3,992.7	47,115.5
Wholesale price index of industrial output (excl. printing and publishing)		..	..	109.3	3,946.9	47,667.8
AGRICULTURE[1]						
Cultivated area	10^3 dunam	2,480	4,075	4,105	4,386	4,370
Thereof: irrigated		375	1,305	1,720	2,003	2,200
Net domestic product (at current prices)	IS 10^6	..	74.8	93.6	4,100.7	⁴4,057.7
Employed persons	10^3	44.1	121.1	89.8	87.7	84.2
Net capital stock (at 1967/68 prices)	IS 10^6	..	139.7	180.6	209.8	204.2
Production:	10^3 tons					
Wheat		27.0	41.3	125.0	253.2	335.0
Sugar beet		—	244.9	237.0	—	—
Vegetables		125.5	296.2	472.3	607.0	778.5
Potatoes		35.3	81.8	137.1	171.7	206.0
Citrus		270.0	609.6	1,261.9	1,542.8	1,530.3
Avocadoes		..	0.2	4.1	32.0	61.6
Poultry meat		7.4	45.7	101.7	200.0	250.3
Beef		1.9	25.1	35.6	40.2	34.3
Cow's milk	1. 10^6 l	92.2	277.3	440.5	670.3	756.2
Eggs	10^6	330.0	1,114.0	1,320.0	1,614.9	1,802.7
Fish	tons 10^3	6.6	13.9	21.8	24.7	21.5
Water consumption[2]	$m^3 \; 10^6$	..	1,087	1,249	1,235	⁴1,282
Tractors	10^3	2.6	7.4	16.3	26.8	27.5

1 Agricultural years.
2 Budget years.
3 At April 1983 prices.
4 1981/82.

ב. אחוז השינוי השנתי הממוצע
B. AVERAGE ANNUAL PERCENTAGE OF CHANGE

Geometric average	1983/1982	1983/1980	1980/1970	1970/1960	1960/1950
Population—total	2.1	1.9	2.6	3.5	4.6
Jews	1.9	1.5	2.4	3.1	4.7
Non-Jews	3.2	3.7	3.8	6.3	3.6
Natural increase rate—total population	1.2	-0.4	-2.6	-1.5	[2]-2.9
Jews	1.4	-0.5	-1.3	-0.8	-3.6
Non-Jews	-3.0	-4.8	-1.5	-0.9	[2]1.4
Infant mortality rates—total population	2.1	-2.0	-4.0	-3.2	[2]-2.9
Jews	-0.1	-1.1	-4.4	-3.6	-5.2
Non-Jews	4.8	-3.4	-4.1	-2.5	[2]-0.2
Immigrants and potential immigrants	23.2	-6.1	-5.7	4.1	-17.6
Tourists	17.0	-0.3	10.3	14.1	13.5
Civilian labour force	2.6	2.1	2.8	3.1	[3]3.1
Employed persons	3.2	2.2	2.7	3.2	[3]3.7
Unemployed	-7.6	-0.2	5.2	1.2	[3]-5.7
Private consumption expenditure per capita—total (at fixed prices)	5.1	6.4	2.6	4.1	4.4
Thereof:					
Food, beverages and tobacco	3.7	4.1	0.9	3.1	4.4
Clothing, footwear and personal effects	-10.8	0.9	2.4	5.3	3.7
Durable goods	13.3	21.0	5.7	9.3	5.8
Other commodities	6.1	5.7	2.1	6.4	6.1
Services	2.1	2.8	3.3	3.4	4.6
Calories per capita per day[1]	1.2	1.0	0.0	0.7	0.6
Protein per capita per day[1]	2.7	1.7	0.1	0.7	0.1
Fat per capita per day[1]	2.2	2.4	0.7	1.9	1.6
Pupils—total	2.9	2.7	4.3	3.3	[4]13.7
Hebrew education	2.5	2.4	3.6	2.6	[4]13.6
Arabic education	3.9	13.2	4.8	9.1	[4]13.9
Students in universities	2.8	2.8	4.7	12.3	[4]19.4

[2] 1960/1951   [3] 1960/1955   [4] 1960/1949

1 Agricultural year.

	1983	1980	1970	1960	1950	Unit יחידה
TOURIST HOTELS						
Hotels	299	302	291	[2]190	..	no.
Rooms	27,183	25,014	15,000	[2]6,501	..	
Person-nights	9.5	9.6	5.1	[2]2.0	..	10⁶
TRANSPORT						
Private cars	572	405	148	24	[3]10	10³
Trucks and other commercial vehicles	111	88	66	22	[3]1.4	"
Buses	7.9	7.1	4.6	2.4	..	"
Bus kilometrage	562	419	372	169	..	km.10⁶
Railways: passengers	2,809	3,300	4,117	4,386	1,557	10³
Railways: tonnage transported	5,822	5,326	3,419	1,949	779	"
Ships of the merchant fleet	94	100	110	50	20	no.
Gross tonnage	1,865	2,463	1,438	288	75	10³ tons
Aircraft landing	9,757	10,933	9,079	2,926	2,272	no.
Air transport: passengers	3,107	2,847	1,051	223	117	10³
freight	125,708	105,802	30,710	$3,516	2,187	tons
Road accidents with casualties	13,785	12,716	13,355	8,356	3,132	no.
Injured	19,867	17,881	19,526	10,542	3,875	"
Thereof: killed	436	434	529	176	228	"
POSTS AND COMMUNICATION[1]						
Mail dispatched and received	..	425	360	165	..	10⁶
Parcels dispatched and received	*2,309	2,029	2,445	1,461	730	10³
Telegrams dispatched and received	920	1,112	$2,208	$1,570	..	"
Telephones	..	1,230	526	123	31	10³
Applications outstanding	257	204	70	20	$13	"
Public telephones	..	7,540	3,740	540	..	no.
BANKS						
Balance sheets of banking institutions (end of year)						
Assets	5,034,970	298,907	1,704	204	..	IS 10⁶
Income	1,631,956	89,304	128	..	..	"
Expenditure	1,635,378	86,091	120	..	..	"
Operational profit	-3,422	3,213	8	..	..	"
INSURANCE COMPANIES						
Premiums received in Israel						
Life insurance	172,595.9	9,591.5	124.3	11.2	1.8	IS 10⁵
General insurance	432,897.1	27,314.4	390.3	57.0	5.4	"
Claims paid in Israel						
Life insurance	51,424.8	3,180.4	40.7	4.0	0.4	"
General insurance	237,813.0	14,395.1	184.9	23.9	2.0	"

1 Budget years.   [2] 1961   [3] 1951

B. AVERAGE ANNUAL PERCENTAGE OF CHANGE (cont.)

Geometric average	1983/1982	1983/1980	1980/1970	1970/1960	1960/1950
Industrial production index—total	3.7	3.5	5.3	11.8	..
Thereof: Food	8.3	7.0	6.2	8.4	..
Textiles, clothing and footwear	-5.7	0.7	4.6	12.7	..
Rubber, plastics, chemicals and oil	11.4	5.7	5.9	14.9	..
Metal and metal products	4.7	2.9	4.1	10.5	..
Machinery, electrical equipment and transport vehicles	3.6	3.7	7.5	13.6	..
Electricity—generation	5.1	5.1	6.2	11.6	15.0
Building completed (area) —total	1.8	-1.1	1.4	2.5	10.2
—dwellings (units)	-8.0	0.0	-0.2	0.9	..
Index of sales in large scale retail trade (at fixed prices)	8.0	9.6	5.9	[1]11.6	..
Tourist hotels—rooms	0.0	2.8	5.2	[2]9.8	..
—person-nights	14.1	-0.2	6.5	[2]11.1	..
Number of computers	..	..	25.1	[3]46.8	..
Motor vehicles	10.3	10.6	7.3	14.3	[4]8.3
Buses—kilometrage	11.9	10.3	1.2	8.2	..
Railways—passengers	-3.5	-5.2	-2.2	-0.6	10.9
Freight loaded at ports	3.8	1.0	6.5	11.0	18.7
Freight unloaded at ports	20.9	17.3	2.5	7.7	3.5
International air passengers	13.1	3.0	10.5	16.8	6.7
Injured in road accidents	7.4	3.6	-0.9	6.4	10.5
Thereof: killed	13.2	0.2	-2.0	11.6	-2.6

[1] 1970/1964   [2] 1970/1961   [3] 1970/1963   [4] 1960/1951

B. AVERAGE ANNUAL PERCENTAGE OF CHANGE (cont.)

Geometric average	1983/1982	1983/1980	1980/1970	1970/1960	1960/1950
Beds in hospitals per 1,000 population	-4.5	-2.0	-1.5	0.8	2.7
Gross national product per capita (at fixed prices)	-0.6	-0.3	2.5	4.9	5.2
General government consumption per capita (at fixed prices)	-6.0	-3.4	0.5	11.1	3.1
Gross capital formation per capita (at fixed prices)	3.9	2.2	-1.3	5.0	-0.5
Deficit in goods and services account in balance of payments	4.4	10.1	11.6	13.4	2.0
Israel's obligations to foreign countries	4.3	9.9	20.0	14.2	[2]12.1
Israel's foreign assets	-8.0	4.5	26.6	33.3	..
Exports of goods	-2.0	-2.6	21.8	13.2	19.7
Imports of goods	5.1	2.0	18.6	11.2	5.1
Excess of imports over exports of goods	17.0	10.4	14.0	9.4	0.7
Exchange rate of the U.S. $	220.3	142.6	36.0	6.9	16.2
Consumer price index	145.6	127.2	41.6	5.6	12.8
Agricultural product [1] (at fixed prices)	6.6	10.5	6.4	6.3	..
Employment in agriculture [1]	2.1	-1.3	-0.2	-2.9	..
Capital stock in agriculture [1] (at fixed prices)	-0.1	-0.9	1.5	2.6	12.2
Production [1] (quantity): Wheat	127.9	9.8	7.3	11.7	4.3
Cotton	20.7	10.6	8.2	13.0	..
Meat	6.2	5.3	5.5	6.5	23.6
Cow's milk	4.1	4.1	4.3	4.4	11.7
Eggs	4.3	3.6	2.0	0.7	12.9
Citrus fruit	17.0	6.3	2.0	7.5	8.5
Other fruit	3.8	14.2	8.4	9.8	17.5

[2] 1955/1960

1 Agricultural year.

25

Israel in World Rankings

		Rank/of Total	First in Rank	Last in Rank
GEOGRAPHY, POPULATION AND VITAL STATISTICS				
Total Land Area	20,720 sq. km./8,000 sq. mi.	135 (188)	Soviet Union	Vatican City
National Coastline	273 km./170 mi.	124 (157)	Canada	Monaco
International Borders	1036 km./643 mi.	102 (138)	China	Gibraltar
Population	4,148,500	97 (187)	China	Vatican City
Est. Population in Year 2000	5,000,000 (Stationary by Year 2060)	96 (125)	China	Trinidad & Tobago
Population Growth Rate	1.9	103 (187)	United Arab Emirates	El Salvador
Birth Rate (per 1,000 inhabitants)	24.7	122 (195)	Rwanda	Norfolk Island
Death Rate (per 1,000 inhabitants)	6.9	152 (192)	Malawi	Christmas Island
Fertility Rate (live births per 1,000 females aged 15-49)	112.7	127 (189)	Mali	Monaco
Population Density	182 per sq. km.	38 (189)	Monaco	Mongolia
Population Density in Agricultural Areas	321 per sq. km. (arable)	53 (163)	Hong Kong	Mongolia
Urbanization	89%	7 (126)	Monaco	Burundi
Annual Urban Population Growth Rate	3.2%	82 (123)	Lesotho	United Kingdom
Marriage Rate (per 1,000 persons)	7.8	39 (134)	Maldives	Guinea-Bissau
Divorce Rate (per 1,000 persons)	1.1	47 (106)	Maldives	Sri Lanka
Divorced Persons as Portion of Population (per 100 married persons)	2.08	79 (117)	Panama	San Marino
Singles (male, aged 45-49)	3.8%	94 (118)	French Guyana	Pitcairn Island
Singles (female, aged 45-49)	2.3%	98 (116)	French Guyana	Pitcairn Island
Male/Female Ratio	50.0	65 (150)	Bahrain	Botswana
Senior Citizens (65+) in Population	8.6%	34 (152)	Sweden	Mali
Widowed Persons of Population (per 100 married)	10.83	68 (121)	Lesotho	Guadeloupe
Average Household Size	3.6 persons	98 (137)	Nigeria	United States
Illegitimate Births as % of Total Births	0.6	100 (102)	Guinea-Bissau	Tunisia
Ethnic Homogeneity	80%	52 (135)	North Korea	Tanzania
Christians (%)	2.2% (85,100)	177 (205)	Vatican	Yemen Arab Republic
Muslims (%)	8.0% (307,400)	63 (77)	Yemen Arab Republic	South Africa
Jews	3,436,100	2 (85)	United States	Libya

		Rank/of Total	First in Rank	Last in Rank

POLITICS AND INTERNATIONAL RELATIONS

		Rank/of Total	First in Rank	Last in Rank
Most Powerful Nations (critical mass + economic capability + military capability) x strategy + will		18	Soviet Union	—
		1/146 of United States	United States	
		4	Soviet Union	
		1	tie w/Taiwan	
Registered Voters, %; Total Number	61.9%; 2,236,000	23 (59)	Finland	South Africa
Age of Nations	36 (1948)	80 (166)	Ethiopia	Vanuatu (3)
Size of Cabinet	19	68 (161)	China (49)	Tuvalu (5)
Civil Disorder Index (incidents since 1948)	313	50 (134)	Vietnam	Gambia (1)
Communist Party Membership (1980)	1,500	68 (94)	China	Saudi Arabia
Deaths from Political Violence (1948-1977)	84	88 (125)	Nigeria	Saudi Arabia (1)
Political Executions (1948-1977)	1	78 (tied with 10 other nations)	China	—
Assassinations (1948-1977)	4	49 (88)	South Vietnam	21 tied with one each

FOREIGN AID

		Rank/of Total	First in Rank	Last in Rank
Per Capita	$216.12	16 (134)	St. Pierre & Miguelon	Venezuela
Total Dollars (1978)	$780,200,000	3 (134)	Egypt	—
Aid from International Organizations (1946-1981)	$305,900,000	70 (141)	India	North Korea
U.S. Economic Aid (1946-1981)	$6,350,000,000	5 (142)	India	Bahamas

MILITARY

		Rank/of Total	First in Rank	Last in Rank
Manpower	400,000	13 (50)	Soviet Union (4,335,000)	—
Men/Women Under Arms (1980)	172,000	33 (132)	China (4,750,000)	Luxembourg (690)
Soldier/Civilian ratio, per 1,000 Inhabitants	44.6	1 (143)	—	Sierra Leone
Defense Expenditures (1980)	$5,540,000,000	10 (134)	United States	Mauritius
Defense Expenditures as % of GNP	29.8%	1 (133)	—	Mauritius
Defense Expenditures, per capita	$1,464	3 (134)	Qatar	Bangladesh
Defense Expenditures, per Soldier	$33,374	23 (132)	Saudi Arabia ($387,909)	Afghanistan ($711)
U.S. Military Aid (1946-1980)	$14,304,200,000	2 (94)	Vietnam	Togo
Civil War & Battle Deaths (1816-1980)	7,570	42	Soviet Union (9.7 million)	—

		Rank/of Total	First in Rank	Last in Rank
ECONOMY				
GNP (1980)	$17,440,000,000	54 (171)	United States	Nive
GNP per capita	$4,500	43	United Arab Emirates	Bhutan ($80)
GNP per capita, growth rate	1.6%	90 (157)	Macao	Angola
Average annual rate of inflation (1970-1980)	39.7%	4 (104)	Chile	Ethiopia
Consumer Price Index (1970 = 100)	15,538 (July 1982)	4 (137)	Argentina	Soviet Union
Public Expenditures, per capita	$3,043.90 (1979)	19 (166)	Qatar	Cuba
Public Expenditures on Social Welfare (% of budget)	19.01% (1980)	27 (97)	Spain	Papua New Guinea
Individual Income Tax as % of total revenue	31.15% (1980)	10 (98)	New Zealand	Nigeria
Corporate Income Tax as % of total revenue	9.54% (1980)	47 (101)	Nigeria	Somalia
FINANCE				
Currency in circulation (per capita)	$100.00	36 (107)	Switzerland	Sri Lanka
Strongest Currency (loss in exchange rate per dollar, 1977-1982)	-3,036.00	136 (137)	Netherlands	Argentina
Gold Holdings	1.147 million fine troy ounces	47 (92)	United States	Upper Volta
External Public Debt (1980)	$12,632,800,000	10 (100)	Brazil	Solomon Islands
External Public Debt as % of GNP (1981)	62.2%	8 (79)	Mauritania	Hong Kong
TRADE				
Balance of Trade (1979)	-$3,302,000,000	109 (125)	Saudi Arabia	United States
Imports per capita (1979)	$1,940.00	23 (125)	Bahamas	Burma
Ratio of Imports to Exports	58.7 (1979)	90 (125)	Brunei	Yemen Arab Republic

Source: *The New Book of World Rankings* by Robert Kurian. © 1984 by Facts on File. Reprinted with permission.

26

The Israeli Political System: How It Works

American Zionist Federation

Israel was founded on May 14, 1948, as an independent and sovereign nation, in accordance with the laws of the United Nations, in the western borders of ancient Palestine. Israel's founding fathers established the country as a democratic republic with a parliamentary system of government. The Knesset is the sovereign legislative body of the republic. The Government (the cabinet) receives its mandate to govern from the Knesset, which has the authority to vote no confidence in the Government at any time. This focuses the Israeli political system on the Knesset and its political parties.

Historically, the predecessors of the Knesset and cabinet in the *yishuv* (pre-state Israel) were the *Asefat ha-Nivharim* (Elected Assembly), *Moetzet Ha'am,* the provisional National Assembly, and the *Vaad Leumi,* the provisional National Council. However, the structure of the Knesset and its predecessors trace their origins to the World Zionist Organization and its legislature, the World Zionist Congress. Inherited from the WZO and casting a major influence on the shape and texture of Israeli political life is the country's electoral system. The electorate votes parties, not individuals, into the Knesset. Legislature seats are apportioned to the parties based on their percentage of the overall popular vote, and then it is up to the President, after consultation, to designate a party leader to form the Government. The Knesset, which has ultimate control over the Government, is actually the apex of a system in which party is supreme.

The Political Parties

The political parties in Israel derive much of their strength from the nation's electoral system. There is no parliamentary districting. The entire country constitutes a single electoral district for the purpose of national Knesset elections. Registered voters, anyone 18 and over regardless of sex, religion or creed, choose their favorite party, from a selection of national party election lists, to represent them in the Knesset chamber.

The parties earn their share of Knesset seats based on the percentage of votes they win in the popular election. Every party capturing at least one percent of the total vote is assured of representation in the Knesset. Also, in local elections, city council candidates are elected proportionally from party lists. Mayors, on the other hand, while they are usually party nominees, are voted in *ad personam.*

Logically, the party has a direct influence over the way its members (MKs) vote in Knesset. Ranking on election lists is controlled by the party—parties may submit up to 120 names on election lists, the first candidates, in order, having the best chance of being seated in Knesset—so that MKs whose records are esteemed by the party, tend to rise upward numerically on the list, better guaranteeing them seating in Knesset. If an MK votes against his party in Knesset, the chance diminishes that the MK's name will be placed in a safe spot (within the number of seats that the party actually expects to capture) in the next general election. If an MK quits his or her party while in Knesset, the MK may retain the Knesset seat, either as a "one-man party" until the next election, or by joining another party in Knesset. When an MK resigns Knesset or dies, the party fills the vacancy with the person whose name next appeared after the cut-off point on the last election list.

Another source of party strength in Israel stems from the early days of the State's development when the huge influx of immigrants depleted the young nation's resources. The parties eagerly came forth to supply many of these needs. They established banks, schools, housing and medical centers. Though the parties no longer run these services today, carry-overs of this phenomenon may be noted in Israel's party-affiliated newspapers, party-aligned settlement-movements, youth and athletic groups, and especially in the Histadrut, the National Labor Union, where parties are elected to union bodies, using the same system of party lists and proportional representation that is used in Knesset elections.

Overall, the system encourages small parties to flourish. The smaller parties' support is often crucial to the larger Knesset party trying to assemble a coalition government. The leaders of the small parties are usually appointed to ministerial positions in the coalition, transforming their political influence into concrete power. The electoral system works to the small parties' advantage by designating the whole country as one electoral district. If small parties had to field candidates district by district their task would be so difficult as to make it impossible for them. Proof of the system's suitability for smaller parties is the fact that 31 parties ran lists for Knesset seats in 1981, 20 of them garnering less than one percent of the national vote.

Israel's polyethnic character provides several sources of political division in the country. Differences between secular and Orthodox Jews cause others. Historically, the most significant ideological debate separating the major parties has been waged over the State's social-economic policies. The Likud Party advocates strong free-market capitalism. The Labor Party and Mapam, the principals of the Labor Alignment, both oppose a State economy left completely to the forces of hierarchy capitalism. However, the Labor Party, when in power, has allowed and even encouraged the development of the private sector. Mapam maintains a strong commitment to developing a cooperative society and economy.

More recently, the question of negotiating the disposition of the territories held by Israel since 1967 (the extent to which territorial compromises should be made in treaties affecting these areas) has arisen as a major source of political dispute in Israel. In 1977, the Likud Party was elected to power advocating the historical right of the Jewish people to these territories of Eretz Israel. The Likud platform maintains that territorial compromise will not necessarily lead to peace. The Labor Alignment, while insisting on defensible borders, deems territorial compromise negotiable. Small parties have sprung up on both sides of the debate.

The Likud Party consists of member parties Herut, the Liberals and Laam. It formed the first non-Labor coalition government following the 1977 elections in which it won a small plurality of the popular vote. The Likud-led coalition then consisted of the National Religious Party, the Orthodox Agudath Israel Party and DASH, the Democratic Movement for Change. Today's Likud coalition includes the religious parties, Tehiya and Tami but not DASH. Herut, the major partner in the Likud Party, is staunchly nationalistic, favors a strong military defense and opposes territorial compromise in Judea-Samaria. The Liberals have steered Likud economic policy toward strong open-market capitalism.

The Labor Alignment (the Maarach) includes the Labor Party, Mapam and the Citizens Rights Party. The Labor Party and Mapam generally share foreign policy views while diverging over social economic policies.

The National Religious Party—Mizrachi and Hapoel Hamizrachi—are committed to a Jewish State based on religious law.

The other Orthodox religious parties, Agudath Israel and Poalei Agudath Israel, refuse to sit as cabinet members in any Government because of their religious interpretations concerning the Jewish State. With the Likud's election to power in 1977, however, the Agudath parties have officially aligned themselves as members of the Likud coalition.

The Knesset is the sovereign parliament of the State of Israel. Upon its formation after the national elections, a Government presents itself before the Knesset with its political platform. When the Government's composition and platform are approved by the Knesset, the Government becomes established through a vote of confidence of the Knesset members and continues in office only as long as it holds the confidence of the Knesset. No-confidence votes are limited, however. Each party is allowed to bring only one no-confidence motion to a vote in a Knesset session. Only the Knesset can vote to dissolve itself or dismiss the Government and set elections. It is the Knesset that has final authority over the Government.

The Knesset consists of a 120-member single chamber elected to a four-year term. However, the Knesset may vote to lengthen or shorten its term by its own special vote. Two sessions of Knesset are held yearly, the first beginning after Succoth (October); the second starting after Israeli Independence Day (April or May). Extraordinary sessions of Knesset can be called at any time at the request of 30 or more Knesset members. Members of Knesset must be 21 years or older. Any Israeli citizen may serve in Knesset, regardless of sex, religion, or political creed. The name and number of seats in the Knesset are derived from the *Knesset ha-Gedolah* of the early Second Temple Period. The permanent Knesset edifice in Jerusalem was opened in 1966.

The first Knesset elections were held on January 25, 1949. Of the total electorate, 505,567 people, 86 percent cast their votes. None of the parties which ran at that time was able to capture a majority of the seats, nor has any party been able to since.

The original coalition, composed of Mapai, Mizrachi, Hapoel Hamizrachi (later, the latter two together, the National Religious Party—NRP) and the progressives (later, Independent Liberals) was to become the backbone of all succeeding Labor coalitions, with variations of additional parties. In 1977, the opposition Likud party captured the popular vote and was able to form its own coalition government, including the NRP.

Although the Knesset was expected to adopt a constitution when it first met on February 14, 1949, the majority of its members felt that it should begin immediately to act as a legislature rather than as a constitutional assembly. On February 16, as its first piece of legislation, the Israeli parliament passed the Transition Act, naming itself the Knesset. Its next action was to vote in a speaker and the President, Chaim Weizmann, who, in turn, charged David Ben-Gurion, leader of Mapai, with the task of forming the first Government, quickly approved by the Knesset.

After several years of debate, the Knesset voted to adopt a constitution gradually by designating certain acts of Knesset as Basic Laws. While the Israeli Supreme Court does not rule on issues of constitutionality, it can rule that Knesset legislation contradicts Basic Law, and it can force the Government to show cause as to why legislation should or should not be enacted.

In the actual legislative process, the Knesset must read a bill three times for it to become law. There is a preliminary reading, followed by a reading in which the bill is debated thoroughly by the full Knesset. After debate, if the bill has enough support, it is sent to be revised or amended in one of the Knesset's standing committees. The committees are composed proportionally according to the parties' percentages in the Knesset chamber. The bill's second reading comes when the committee reports the bill back to the floor of Knesset. Debate then is restricted to committee members only. The third reading is the roll call vote on the bill. Passage comes with a simple majority vote of those present; no quorum is needed. After passage, the bill must have the signatures of the president, prime minister and the cabinet minister responsible for implementing the legislation, before it can become law in the Knesset Book of Statutes, its official entry into Israel's legal codes. No veto powers exist on legislation passed by the Knesset. Only the Knesset itself has the power to rescind, repeal or revise its statutes.

The Speaker of the Knesset often plays a pivotal role in Knesset sessions as the parliamentary chairman who sets the agenda and decides whether or not to entertain urgent Floor motions. The Speaker heads a presidium of party whips through whom he communicates to the parties while Knesset is in session. The Speaker is also proprietor of the Knesset grounds and, as such, can declare individuals persona non grata, preventing them from entering the guarded Knesset gates.

Knesset members have three parliamentary procedures that they can use in the legislative process in addition to the work that they do in committees. They may submit questions in writing to cabinet ministers, make motions to add to the agenda, and they may sponsor private legislation. In practice, all three maneuvers must be cleared with an MK's party beforehand. The number of bills that can be introduced during a legislative session is limited proportionally to the parties, according to their percentage of seats in the Knesset.

While individual Knesset members are not elected by district, giving them no particular constituency to answer to, in practice, the Knesset election lists are composed to elicit votes from as many different areas of the nation as possible and among as many ethnic groups as possible. After election, these groups tend to view these legislators as representing their special interests in Knesset and often turn to them to express their views, or to solicit help on government-related problems.

Herewith is the breakdown of parties in the Knesset, as of the 1984 elections:

BLOC AND PARTY	VOTES	SEATS
Nationalist-Religious		
Likud (Nationalist)	661,302	41
Tehiya (Ultra-Nationalist)	83,037	5
N.R.P. (Religious-Zionist)	73,530	4
Shass (Orthodox-Sephardi)	63,605	4
Agudah (Orthodox-Non-Zionist)	36,079	2
Morasha (Orthodox-Nationalist)	33,287	2
Kach (Kahane-Religious-Ultra-Nationalist)	25,907	1
Labor-Liberal		
Labor Alignment	724,074	44
Shinui (Rubinstein-Liberal)	54,747	3
Ratz (Aloni-Liberal)	49,698	3
Transient		
Yahad (Weizman)	46,302	3
Ometz (Hurwitz)	23,845	1
Tami (AbuHatzera)	31,103	1
Democratic Movement for Change (Yadin)		
Telem (Dayan)		
Predominantly Arab Lists		
Communist	60,815	4
Progressive/Democratic Change (Arab-Nationalist)	38,012	2
Others	58,978	0
TOTAL	2,073,321	120

The Cabinet

The cabinet has day-to-day charge of the State. It conducts foreign and domestic policy through its ministries. Proposed legislation and policy decisions are voted on by the full cabinet and decisions are binding on all its members. The cabinet proposes about 90 percent of the legislation that is passed by Knesset each year. Cabinet ministers are most often the leaders of the parties of the governing coalition, but they may be appointed to sit without portfolios, and they need not be Knesset members.

Generally, cabinet positions are divided among the coalition parties according to their size. First, however, the parties interested in entering into the coalition must come to agreement on the principles that will become the basis for the coalition's formation, functioning and efficacy. For instance, in 1981, coalition parties arrived at specific wording in their platform on the role that Camp David was to play in future foreign policy decisions of the government.

The number of cabinet members varies as Governments change, though one of the electoral reforms proposed in Israel from time to time has been to limit the number of cabinet members to a fixed number. There were 17 cabinet portfolios distributed by the Begin Government at the start of the Tenth Knesset in 1981.

The formation of the coalition Government and the composition of the cabinet are closely related. When the president designates a Knesset member to form a Government, that MK must seek out the support of other parties in order to garner the crucial 61 votes of confidence from the Knesset, whose vote seats the Government. Cabinet positions are used as inducements to have smaller parties join the coalition. If one party were to capture a majority of seats in Knesset in the general election, establishing a coalition government would become, theoretically, unnecessary. Even then, however, the majority party may wish to solicit additional parties to join the Government to strengthen its authority in the Knesset. In fact, every Israeli Government has been comprised by coalition. No party has ever captured a Knesset majority, 61 seats, in the general election.

Within the Knesset, the majority party of the ruling coalition is regarded as the founder and foundation of the Government. Within the Government, the majority party has the authority of being the leadership group with the most cabinet members holding the key ministries.

At the same time, the Government ministers set and execute policy within their respective parties retaining their positions as their parties' senior leaders. This intersection of ministerial functions permits the parties to directly influence the policies of the Government at the pinnacle of the political structure, the prime example of party power in the Israeli political system.

Much cabinet business is discharged through permanent or ad hoc ministerial committees, composed by parties proportionally, according to their strength in the cabinet itself. These committee decisions are final unless challenged by the full cabinet. Ministers, with cabinet approval, may appoint deputy ministers, who must be members of Knesset. They are not cabinet members, but their purview extends from acting as de facto ministers to that of ministerial spokesmen in the Knesset. Most are charged with a particular section of their ministry's work. In addition, cabinet members themselves run an exhausting schedule of working with Knesset committees, attending Knesset sessions and voting as Knesset members (if indeed they are MKs), administering the nation's services and programs and drafting and implementing new laws. In the event of national crisis, the cabinet must steer the State ship.

Ultimately, the cabinet is responsible to the Knesset, which can vote to unseat the cabinet at any time through a simple majority vote of no-confidence. A vote of no-confidence does not cause the dissolution of Knesset, and elections are only held if the Knesset chooses to do so. The cabinet holds no such reciprocal power over the Knesset. Their relationship is based on the concept that it is the Knesset's job to establish an effective Government, to oversee its functioning, and to dissolve it, if and when it has lost the Knesset's confidence to govern the Israeli nation effectively.

The Prime Minister

Legally speaking, the prime minister is first among equals, in the cabinet. Unlike other cabinet members, the prime minister must be a Member of Knesset. The prime minister's vote counts equally as any other member of Knesset. However, there are a number of affairs of state over which the prime minister acts as chief supervisor. The prime minister is in charge of the nation's intelligence services and directs, and often personally conducts, negotiations with foreign countries. The office has final authority on matters of public information concerning the Government.

In the cabinet, the prime minister presides over and determines the agenda. He or she makes cabinet committee appointments too, giving the prime minister enormous influence among the parties in the Government. Since 1981, the prime minister has been given the authority to dismiss any member of the cabinet, though dismissal of a cabinet member outside the prime minister's own party can cause a coalition crisis or even government collapse.

The prime minister acquires his greatest influence over the cabinet by threat of or exercising his resignation. The prime minister's resignation is treated as though the entire cabinet has resigned office. Be this as it may, the prime minister is finally responsible to the Knesset, which can vote at any time to remove the prime minister and the Government by a simple majority vote of its members.

The President

The president is not a member of the Government in Israel and need not be a Knesset member to be elected to serve in the position. While the office is largely ceremonial in character, the president is responsible for signing all laws and treaties and for the appointment of diplomats and judges to the civil judiciary and religious courts, though recommendations for these appointments originate from outside the presidential office. The president accredits his country's diplomatic corps and receives visiting dignitaries from foreign states. The president has the authority to pardon, mitigate or commute sentences.

The president is elected once every five years by a majority vote of Knesset members in secret balloting. The president may not serve more than two terms. In the event of a president's death or absence, the speaker of the Knesset assumes the office until the president's return or until a replacement can be voted in.

A major responsibility of the president is to receive the official resignation of the prime minister, and therefore the Government, either after elections when the Knesset's regular term has expired, or in the case of a Government's loss of confidence voted by the Knesset. In initiating formation of a new Government, the president is required by law to meet with each party in the Knesset to ascertain which Knesset member, based on the recommendations of the party heads, has the greatest chance to form a government. Usually this is the leader of the party with the largest number of Knesset seats. The president then designates that person to the task which must be completed within 21 days, though an additional 21-day extension may be granted by the president.

If a Government cannot be formed, the president has the authority to designate the responsibility to a different Knesset member. In the event that no Government can be formed, only the Knesset has the right to vote to set a new election date. Between elections or Government reformations, the presiding cabinet ministers remain as the interim Government.

Epilogue

A sketch of Israel's political system would be incomplete without mentioning the intensity and diversity that characterize the country's political life. With its numerous parties, its continuously emerging new parties, and these parties' accommodations for special interests, the Israeli political structure is unusually expansive for a nation so small. It is not a surprise that a system so manifold stimulates tremendous debate and dissent from the parliament to the street corner. It is noteworthy, though, that politics in a country composed mainly of immigrants from non-democracies sparks so much public interest and participation. Voter turn-out in national elections regularly exceeds 80 percent of the electorate, one of the highest ratios in the world. Observers would be hard pressed to find another society in which citizens demonstrate a greater awareness and concern about their government's policies, their country's ethnics, their people's historical and future obligations to themselves and the world, in addition to their own routine—and not so routine—problems and dangers that confront them on a daily basis. It is a quilted society of immigrants, from some 75 different countries, in which so many shades of opinion are voiced and make themselves heard that Israelis like to joke that theirs is a land of four million prime ministers.

If the system's efficacy may be gauged, in part, by how often governments change before Knesset terms expire, then the system is becoming more durable as fewer governments are brought down and replaced by Knesset in-between general elections. This would seem to indicate a trend toward political stabilization, as both the public and those in office show increasing stamina to weather storms without precipitating full-scale political crises. Definite proof of the system's resilience was offered after the 1977 election, when Government power was smoothly passed on to the Likud Party from the Labor Party, which had been at the helm of every Israeli Government since the State's beginning in 1948.

The Israeli Political System: How It Works was prepared by Leonard Fink. The American Zionist Federation is headquartered at 515 Park Avenue, New York, New York 10022; (212) 371-7750.

27

Israel Law Digest

Yaacov Salomon, Lipschutz & Co.
Advocates & Notaries, Haifa and Tel Aviv

ABSENTEES:

Apart from Absentees' Property Law, 1950 which deals basically with local problem of care and custody of property belonging to persons who left country at time of 1948 war, there are no specific provisions regarding absentees. Power of attorney may be given for all purposes and, if executed abroad, should be authenticated. See topic Acknowledgments.

Under Protection of Deposited Property Law, 1965 where management or control of property has been committed to another, written notification thereof in form set out in Law, must be given to Administrator General if ten years have elapsed from authorisation or appointment.

ACKNOWLEDGMENTS:

Any deed, power of attorney or other instrument in writing made or executed in any place outside of Israel may be proved in any civil cause or matter in Israel if authenticated (a) before an ambassador, minister, chargé d'affaires or secretary of an embassy or legation, or any consul, vice-consul, pro-consul or consular agent of Israel, and attested by a certificate under the hand of such officer and his official seal, or (b) before a notary public and attested by a certificate under his hand and notarial seal and authenticated by any Israel officer mentioned under (a). (Evidence Ordinance [New Text] §33). See also Affidavits.

ACTIONS:

Civil procedure is governed by Civil Procedure Rules, 1963. In general, courts will only exercise jurisdiction over persons within territorial limits of state and assumption of jurisdiction will depend on validity of service of process. Rules give a list of events in which courts may grant leave to serve outside jurisdiction. Foreign claims are proved in same way as local claims. Foreign law is a question of fact and is proved by evidence of an expert in law in question. See also topics Death; Limitation of Actions; and Practice.

Limitation of.—See Limitation of Actions.

Death.—See topic Death.

ADMINISTRATION:

See Executors and Administrators.

ADOPTION:

Adoption is permitted subject to an order of competent district court. Procedure to be followed is set out in The Children Adoption Law, 1981, and in Civil Procedure Rules. See topic Practice. Interest of child to be adopted is given paramount consideration. Adopted child must be under 18 years of age. Normally adoption of a child will not be allowed if adopting parents live abroad or intend to take child abroad. Secrecy is observed and neither natural parents nor adopting parents know identity of each other unless otherwise ordered by court. Religion of child and adoptive parents must be same (procedure for conversion of child in certain instances set forth in law).

See also topic Descent and Distribution.

ADVERSE POSSESSION:

Land Law 1969 has virtually abolished whole of existing Ottoman legislation and there are now no provisions relating to acquisition of title by adverse possession. See also topic Limitation of Actions.

AFFIDAVITS:

The jurat, which is a memorandum in regard to the place, time and person before whom the affidavit is made, should be without interlineation, alteration, erasure or obliteration, immediately at the foot of the document to be sworn, and towards the side of the paper, and should be signed by the person administering the oath, at the side of the date of the swearing and the place where the document or the instrument is sworn, and should state that the document or the instrument was sworn before the person administering the oath and that warning was given that document was executed under penalty of perjury. See also topic Acknowledgments.

The last paragraph of the affidavit should use words to the following effect: I swear by Almighty God (or I solemnly and sincerely declare and affirm) that this is my name and signature, and that the contents of this, my affidavit (or affirmation of declaration, as the case may be), are true.

In case of a declaration, there should be added the following words: I make this solemn declaration conscientiously believing the same to be true. Declarations may be signed before any advocate authorized to practise in Israel and have same force as an affidavit.

AGENCY: See Principal and Agent.

ALIENS:

Except in regard to elections, aliens are under no disability. Aliens wishing to enter Israel must secure a Traveller's Visa. See topic Constitution and Government, subhead Citizenship.

Corporations Owned or Controlled by Aliens.—Nonresidents may buy and sell Israeli shares provided payments made through authorised dealer, generally bank. Otherwise there are no restrictions on ownership or control of Israeli corporation by alien.

ARBITRATION:

Now governed by Arbitration Law, 1968. All disputes may be submitted to arbitration. No particular form of submission is required, except that submission must be in writing. Award may be enforced by leave of court in same manner as a judgment or order of court to same effect. Award may be set aside if it has been improperly procured, or if arbitrator has misconducted himself or award is bad on face of it. Court will usually stay an action brought in a dispute which it has been agreed should be submitted to arbitration. Where international convention to which Israel is a party, applies to arbitrators, court will stay an action, in accordance with such convention. Schedule is attached to law containing rules relating to procedure of arbitration which will apply unless a contrary intention appears in agreement.

A foreign award is enforceable as a local award and may be relied upon in any legal proceedings. In order that a foreign award may be enforceable in Israel, it must have been (a) made in pursuance of an agreement for arbitration which was valid under the law by which it was governed, (b) made by the tribunal provided for in the agreement or constituted in manner agreed upon by the parties, (c) made in conformity with the law governing arbitration procedure, and (d) has become final in the country in which it was made, and (e) is in respect of a matter which may lawfully be referred to arbitration under the law of Israel, the enforcement thereof not being contrary to the public policy or the law of Israel.

See also topic Executions.

ARCHITECTS:

Under 1958 law all architects must be entered in a register. Qualification: (a) Diploma of Technion, Technical High School; (b) registration abroad entitling to work as architect; (c) actual work for 12 years and examination.

ASSIGNMENTS:

Under Assignment of Obligations Law 1969 right of a creditor, including a conditional or a contingent right, may be assigned without consent of debtor, may be of whole or part of debt and may be conditional or by way of charge. Debtor retains same rights against assignee as he had against assignor and if he pays assignor before receiving notice he is exempt from further payment. Debtor can also assign debt in whole or in part to another with consent of creditor.

ASSOCIATIONS:

The following forms of corporate associations are recognized: (a) partnerships; (b) companies; (c) cooperative societies; (d) societies.

Partnerships.—A partnership is defined in Partnership Ordinance as relation which exists between persons carrying on a business in common with a view to profit. Partnerships are either general or limited.

A partnership formed in Israel may not consist of more than 20 persons. Every partnership formed in Israel must be registered with the Registrar of Partnerships, to whom certain particulars are to be supplied. A small registration fee is payable.

Partners of a general partnership are liable jointly and severally for all debts of the partnership. A limited partnership consists of one or more general partners who are liable for all debts, and one or more limited partners who are not liable for the debts of the firm beyond the amounts contributed by them as capital. A corporation may be a limited partner.

See also topic Business Names.

Companies.—See topic Corporations.

Cooperatives or Cooperative Societies.—A society which has as its object the promotion of thrift, self-help and mutual aid among persons with a common economic need, can be registered as a cooperative society.

No member is entitled to hold more than one-fifth of the capital. Registration fees are nominal.

Non-Profit Associations.—Association having two or more members for non-profit purposes may be registered with Registrar of Non-Profit Associations, provided regulations contain provision for annual meetings, presentation of audited accounts and proper supervision of activities. Registration fee is payable. (Non-Profit Associations Law 1980).

ATTACHMENT:

An application for an attachment may be made in all civil actions whether in contract or in tort. It must be based on a written document or other satisfactory proof as to reasonableness of claim, in which an amount of money is claimed.

An application for attachment may be made prior to or simultaneously with institution of civil proceedings. It can be granted ex parte or in presence of the respondent. It must be supported by an affidavit. A bond or other security is invariably required. Real and personal property may be attached. Property attached may include monies due or property held by third party.

Except in special circumstances such as perishables, property attached cannot be sold before final judgment in action.

Third party claims in opposition to attachment can be heard upon motion in proceedings.

Respondent may obtain release of an attachment against adequate security. See topic Executions.

ATTORNEYS AND COUNSELLORS:

Advocates Ordinance of 1938 which regulated admission of members to Israel Bar was repealed by Chamber of Advocates Law of 1961. Israel Bar has been constituted as a recognised entity by virtue of 1961 Law, and it vested in elected bodies of members of Bar right to admit members to Bar, to regulate discipline and make other appropriate provisions affecting practice of law in Israel.

Only persons who have qualified as lawyers, are residents of Israel, and have reached age of 23 may be admitted to Israel Bar. Persons who qualify as lawyers may be graduates of Law Faculty in Israel or persons who are admitted to a foreign Bar and practiced abroad for not less than two years and/or are graduates of foreign law school. Normal period of apprenticeship prior to admission to local Bar, with reductions for foreign lawyers related to prior experience. There are special provisions for apprenticeship preliminary to admission to local Bar.

A licence to practice as an advocate is renewable annually against the payment of an appropriate fee.

A foreign advocate or attorney may not appear even for the purposes of a particular case, unless he was nominated to defend a foreign citizen accused of a capital punishment crime, and was approved by the Ministry of Justice.

There is a special registration for pleaders before the Rabbinical courts. All advocates may be inscribed on this list upon paying a registration fee.

Under Patents Law, 1967, a patent agent has, with leave of court, right to plead in patent actions, on a nonlegal point.

BANKRUPTCY:

The principal law governing bankruptcy proceedings is Bankruptcy Ordinance (New Version) of 1980, which follows substantially English Bankruptcy Acts of 1914 and 1926.

A debtor is liable to be declared bankrupt and to have his property administered under the Bankruptcy Law upon committing any of the following acts, which are termed Acts of Bankruptcy: (1) If he makes a fraudulent gift or transfer of his property, or any part thereof; (2) if he makes any transfer of his property, or any part thereof, or creates any charge thereon which would be void as a fraudulent preference if he were adjudged bankrupt; (3) if, with intent to defeat or delay his creditors, he departs out of Israel, or being out of Israel remains out of Israel or departs from his dwelling house or absents himself from his usual place of business or abode; (4) if any of his property has been attached and sold in the execution of the decree of any court; (5) if he files in the court a declaration of his inability to pay his debts or petitions to be adjudged bankrupt (debts in such case must exceed IS.1,000 due to at least two creditors); (6) if he gives notice to any of his creditors that he has suspended, or that he is about to suspend payment of his debts; (7) if creditor has obtained final judgment against him for any amount, and execution thereon not having been stayed, has served on him in Israel or by leave of court elsewhere bankruptcy notice requiring him to pay judgment debt, or to secure or compound for it, and he does not within seven days after service of notice (or in case service is effected out of Israel, then within time limited) either comply with requirements of notice or satisfy court that he has counterclaim, set-off or cross demand which equals or exceeds amount of judgment debt, and which he could not set up in action in which judgment was obtained.

The expression "debtor" includes any person of not less than 18 years of age of whatever nationality who at the time when any act of bankruptcy was done or suffered by him: (a) was personally present in Israel; or (b) ordinarily resided or had a place of residence in Israel; or (c) was carrying on business in Israel personally, or by means of an agent or manager; or (d) was a member of a firm or partnership which carried on business in Israel.

A creditor is unable to present a bankruptcy petition against a debtor unless: (a) the debt owing by the debtor to the petitioning creditor, or, if two or more creditors join in the petition, the aggregate amount of debts owing to the several petitioning creditors amounts to IS.1,000, (b) debt is liquidated sum, and (c) act of bankruptcy on which petition is grounded has occurred within three months before presentation of petition. It is also required that debtor be domiciled in Israel, or within a year before date of presentation of petition that debtor (a) has ordinarily resided, or (b) had dwelling house, or (c) place of business, or (d) has carried on business personally or by means of agent or manager, or (e) is or has been member of firm or partnership of persons which has carried on business by means of partner, agent or manager in Israel.

A creditor's petition must be verified by affidavit of the creditor or of some person on his behalf having knowledge of the facts.

At the hearing the court requires proof of the debt of the petitioning creditor, of the service of the petition, and of the act of bankruptcy. A creditor's petition cannot, after presentment, be withdrawn without the leave of the court.

BANKS AND BANKING:

No banking business may be transacted in Israel except by a bank registered under provisions of Companies Ordinance. A foreign company may transact banking business if registered as a foreign company under Ordinance.

Bank may not operate in Israel unless licensed by Governor of Bank of Israel, under Banking Law (Registration) 1981, subject to compliance with Banking Ordinance 1941, as am'd. Purchase and sale of controlling rights in banks require permit of Governor. Banks Law provides for fulfilment of certain conditions preliminary to registration especially in fixing minimum of authorized and paid-up capital of banks operating in Israel. There are also provisions in regard to returns to be furnished. Under Bank of Israel Law 1954, which constituted State of Israel Bank—The Central State Bank—Bank of Israel is given certain powers in regard to control of banking institutions, especially in respect of liquidity, grant of credits, reserves, and rates of interest. 1976 amending law provides for discharge of liabilities, postponement of payments, addition of interest and linkage differences when banking services are disrupted by labour disputes. Banking Law (Service to Customer) 1981 places obligation on banks to give customers proper banking services with penalties for misleading or unfair actions.

BILLS AND NOTES:

Principal statute governing Bills and Notes is Bills of Exchange Ordinance (New Version) 1957 (as amended) which follows substantially English Bills of Exchange Act of 1882.

Inland and Foreign Bills.—An inland bill is one which is, or on its face purports to be (a) both drawn and payable within Israel, or (b) drawn within Israel on some person resident therein. Any other bill is a foreign bill.

Inland bills must be stamped before execution. Foreign bills can be stamped after execution, before presentation for payment. Bill of exchange which has been dishonoured by nonacceptance can now be executed by summary procedure whereby bill of exchange, promissory note or cheque is capable of execution like judgment of court. Amount stated in bill shall be collected in accordance with 1968 Execution Amendment Law with addition of interest so fixed therein, and if no interest is fixed therein, with addition of interest at rate fixed in Adjudication of Interest Law 1961 from date of payment of bill or from date of its presentation for payment. Person wishing to execute bill shall file application to Execution Office supported by affidavit verifying facts stated therein. Debtor may oppose application and Chief Execution Officer shall stay application and refer matter to court. For purposes of hearing in court, opposition shall be regarded as application for leave to defend in summary proceedings under Civil Procedure Regulations 1963. When a bill has been dishonoured by nonacceptance, or by nonpayment, notice of dishonour must be given to the drawer and each indorser, subject to limited exceptions. Notice of dishonour may be given either to the party himself, or to his agent in that behalf. It must be given within a reasonable time, which normally is three days after dishonour of the bill.

The provisions in regard to presentment for acceptance, acceptance, and issue of bills in a set do not apply to promissory notes.

The provisions in regard to presentment for payment apply to promissory notes, only where the promissory note is in the body of it made payable in a particular place, in which case it must be presented for payment at that place, in order to render the maker liable.

Limitation of Actions.—No action on a bill of exchange, cheque or promissory note can be maintained against any party thereto, other than an indorser, after expiration of seven years, or against an indorser after expiration of two years from time when cause of action first accrued to the then holder against such party. Where a bill is payable after sight, presentment for acceptance is necessary in order to fix maturity of instrument. When a bill payable after sight is negotiated, holder must either present it for acceptance, or negotiate it within a reasonable time, provided always that a bill payable after sight must be presented for acceptance within six months of its date, or such shorter period stipulated for either by drawer or by an indorser, or such longer period not exceeding 12 months as may be stipulated by drawer. Failure in regard to presentment discharges drawer and all indorsers prior to holder.

A bill must be presented for payment in accordance with the following rules: (a) where a bill is not payable on demand, presentment must be made on the date it falls due; (b) where a bill is payable on demand, then presentment must be within a reasonable time after its issue, in order to render the drawer liable and within a reasonable time after its endorsement, in order to render the indorser liable. Presentment must be made at a reasonable hour, on a business day, at the proper place, excluding therefore legal holidays. The legal holidays include the State holidays and certain religious days of Jewish, Moslem and Christian communities.

Conflict of Laws.—Where a bill drawn in one country is negotiated, accepted or payable in another the rights, duties and liabilities of the parties are determined as follows: (1) Validity of the bill as regards requisites of form is determined by the law of the place of issue; validity of a supervening contract (e.g., acceptance, endorsement, etc.) is determined by the law of the place where such contract was made. (2) Interpretation of the drawing, endorsement or acceptance is determined by the law where the contract was made, provided that where an inland bill is indorsed in a foreign country the endorsement must, as regards the payer, be interpreted according to the law of Israel.

BROKERS:

There is limited legislation in regard to brokers. Brokers must be licenced by the District Commissioner. Licences are renewable annually. A tariff of brokerage fees for licenced brokers is fixed by law. The usual fees range from 1% to 5%.

BUSINESS NAMES:

Under the Registration of Business Names Ordinance 1935, every individual or firm carrying on business under a business name, namely, a name which does not consist of the true surname of the individual, or of the true names of all partners, must register the name as a business name. Particulars required to be furnished under the Ordinance have to be furnished within 15 days after the person or firm commences business under the business name. A nominal fee is payable.

CHATTEL MORTGAGES:

See topics Mortgages; Pledges.

CHATTELS:

See topic Moveables.

COMMERCIAL REGISTER:

No special registration required but see topics Business Names; Corporations; Licences.

CONSTITUTION AND GOVERNMENT:

A formal Constitution of State of Israel has not yet been promulgated. Present Constitution is based on Declaration of Establishment of State of Israel, dated 14th May, 1948, on Law and Administration Ordinance, 1948, and on Transitional Law of 1949. By a resolution of 13th June, 1950, Knesset resolved to impose upon Constitution, Law and Justice Committee the task of preparing a draft constitution. Constitution would thus be built up chapter by chapter. So far, four such chapters have become law: Basic Law—The Knesset (1958), Basic Laws—Israel Lands (1960), Basic Law—President of the State (1964) and Basic Law—The Government (1968). Further basic Law (1980) substituted reference to principles of Jewish Traditional Law for reference to U.K. common law and equity as prescribed by §46 of Provisional Order in Council 1922 now repealed. (Basic Law—Appointment of Judges [1984]).

The Knesset.—Basic Law—the Knesset, and Knesset Election Law, 1959 combine all previous laws in reference to sovereignty and elections of Knesset, the legislature of Israel. Knesset is elected by all Israeli citizens and residents over age of 18 years. Knesset consists of only one chamber, in which there are 120 members. Term of Knesset is four years. Elections take place on same day all over country and election day is a public holiday. Limits in reference to election propaganda are provided by law, and State officials, army officers, judges, etc., are not allowed to participate in election campaign.

President of Israel is elected by Knesset for a period of five years. 1963 Law forbids holding of office of President for more than two consecutive periods of five years.

Government consists of Prime Minister and Ministers of State. Prime Minister must be a member of Knesset who enjoys confidence of Knesset. A Government which does not enjoy confidence of Knesset must resign. All powers which were formerly vested in British Crown or Mandatory Government, are now vested in Government of Israel, and are exercised through various Ministers of State.

Law and Administration.—Laws which existed on date of establishment of State of Israel on 14th May, 1948, continue to be effective insofar as they are not inconsistent with establishment of State, and insofar as they have not been abrogated or modified by laws passed since establishment of the State of Israel.

Citizenship.—Under Citizenship Law 1952 as am'd 1968, Israel nationality is acquired in one of following ways: (1) Any Jew who has emigrated or emigrates to Israel and expresses his desire to settle there, becomes an Israel citizen automatically unless (a) he ceased to reside in Israel before July 14, 1952 or (b) being a foreign citizen he makes or has made a declaration that he does not desire to be an Israel citizen and in case of an infant, his parents have made such a declaration; (2) former Palestine citizen becomes an Israel citizen if he was resident in Israel on July 14, 1952 and fulfils certain other conditions; (3) any person born in Israel is an Israel citizen if his mother or father is an Israel citizen; (4) stateless person born in Israel after setting up of State may acquire nationality by filing a request to such effect between his 18th and 21st birthdays provided he has resided in Israel five years continuously prior to application; (5) Israel citizenship may also be acquired by naturalization, conditions being (a) residence in Israel at time of and for three out of five years prior to application, (b) intention to reside permanently in Israel, (c) some knowledge of Hebrew language and (d) renunciation of any other citizenship. An infant who is a resident of Israel or one of whose parents is an Israel citizen may apply for grant of citizenship. Israel citizen living abroad may renounce his citizenship. Citizenship acquired by naturalization, may be lost in certain circumstances. Save in case of naturalization, Israel citizenship does not require giving up of any former citizenship. (Book of Laws, No. 95 of 8/4/52).

CONSUMER PROTECTION:

1981 Law forbids dealer in goods or services to mislead consumer by act or failure to act, in writing or verbally in any material matter affecting transaction, inter alia re quality, nature, quantity and type of goods and/or services, measure, weight, form, components, date of delivery of goods or supply of services.

Dealer is likewise forbidden to exploit in any way, reduced circumstances, physical or mental deficiency, ignorance, language, lack of experience or to exercise undue influence to induce transaction on unreasonable or abnormal terms.

Dealer is obliged also to disclose material defects known to him.

Misleading advertisements, or packaging are forbidden.

Detailed Regulations govern credit sales, interest calculation and marking of goods on package.

CONTRACTS:

Israel Law, broadly follows English rules of common law and equity. There are also relics of Turkish laws and there is a growing body of legislation on contracts. Contract requires consensus ad idem which is formed by offer and acceptance. To great extent Israeli legislation has either codified English Common Law or borrowed from models such as American Uniform Commercial Code. One notable departure is absence of any requirement of consideration as basis for contract. (The Gift Law 1968 however retains concept of consideration where gift is defined as ownership of property otherwise than for consideration.) What is paramount under Contracts Law 1973 is intention of parties to enter into agreement.

There are several new laws replacing existing Turkish legislation which lay down general rules in respect of various types of contract. These are Agency Law 1965, Guarantee Law 1967, Pledges Law 1967, Bailees Law 1967 and Sale Law 1968. It is always possible to contract out of these Laws.

New Law.—1973 Law of Contract Act, general part, contains a codification of general part of law of contract, which no longer follows principles of English Law of Contract which have hitherto been accepted by courts. In particular, consideration is no longer required to create enforceable contract. Law came into force on Jan. 1, 1974.

See also topics Consumer Protection; Landlord and Tenant; Mortgages; Moveables; Pledges; Principal and Agent; Restrictive Trade Practices; Sales.

Excuses for Nonperformance.—Contract is void in case of mistake going to root of contract, illegality and impossibility of performance. Impossibility must be literal impossibility. Presence of a material misrepresentation, duress or undue influence may make contract voidable by non-offending party.

Notices Required.—Notice of cancellation of contract for fundamental breach must be given within reasonable time after party becomes aware of breach. If breach is not fundamental, party in breach is given period of grace to make good breach and if necessary notice of breach is given within reasonable time of elapse of such period. Period of grace is not required to be notified in writing. (Law of Contracts [Remedies for Breach of Contract] 1970 §§7-8).

Notice is required for set-off in case of money debts owed by one party to another in same transaction whether liquidated or not, and if not in same transaction, in case of liquidated debts only. (Law of Contracts [General Part] 1973, p. 53).

Purchaser of goods must give immediate notice to vendor after inspection required to be made on delivery if goods are found not to be as ordered, or as soon as defect discovered if concealed, otherwise purchaser has no claim against vendor. (Law of Sale 1968, §14).

Vendor must give notice to purchaser of any third party claim against goods supplied which he knew of or should have known of before delivery. (Law of Sale 1968, §18).

Applicable Law.—English rules of conflict of laws apply and "proper law of the contract" is applicable law: If parties choose a law in contract, this will almost invariably be applicable law. As regards contracts for sale of goods Uniform International Commercial Code applies from Aug. 18, 1972.

Government Contracts.—There are no special forms and Government is generally liable for its contracts and can be sued on them although injunction and specific performance are not available against State.

Remedies for breach of contract have been given statutory force by Contracts (Remedies for Breach of Contract) Law 1970. Subject to provisions of Law, injured party may claim enforcement or rescission of contract and/or damages. Enforcement is similar to equitable remedy of specific performance and is granted except where contract is incapable of performance, where enforcement requires compelling carrying out of personal work, where enforcement requires unreasonable amount of supervision by court or it is inequitable in circumstances of case. Rescission is permissible in case of fundamental breach but where breach is not fundamental, reasonable time must first be given to party in breach to remedy breach. Damages are granted for injury caused by breach and its consequences and which party breaking contract foresaw or should have foreseen as a probable consequence of breach at time contract was made.

Breach of Contract.—Supreme Court has summed up 1970 Law regarding relief on breach of contract (a) that breach of contractual condition, including date of payment, agreed as being "basic" is fundamental breach; (b) on fundamental breach injured party may, and on ordinary breach, he must give an extension which other party may use to fulfil his contractual obligation within reasonable time of grant of extension; (c) right to regard contract as void and must be exercised within reasonable time after lapse of such reasonable period, in case of ordinary breach or immediately in case of fundamental breach; (d) right to regard as void, revives if extension given, even if not obligatory by law, after lapse of reasonable extension period.

Form.—In general, form of contract is immaterial but certain contracts need to be in writing in order to be enforceable, in particular contracts relating to land and to lending of money and partnerships and agreements with building contractors.

Contractors' Agreements.—1974 law regulates work undertaken by a contractor who is not an employee of person ordering work. It regulates liability of contractor to repair defects, contractor's right to refuse delivery until paid according to agreement, and liability to pay contractor.

Warranties.—§11 of Law of Sale 1968 provides that vendor fails to fulfil his obligations under sale agreement if only part of goods or larger or smaller quantity than agreed upon is delivered, if article supplied differs in kind or description from agreement, if article lacks quality or characteristics required for normal or commercial use thereof or for special purpose for which agreement implies it was purchased, or if article is not, by reference to type, description, quality or characteristics, according to sample or specimen submitted by vendor, unless so submitted without any undertaking of conformity to sample. If vendor does not within reasonable time of receiving notice from purchaser, remedy deficiency in fulfilment of his obligations, purchaser may claim specific performance, rescission or deduct from price payable value of deficiency. (§28 of Law of Sale).

CONVEYANCES: See Assignments.

COPYRIGHT:

English Copyright Act of 1911 is incorporated into Israeli Copyright Ordinance.

Nature of Copyright.—Copyright is sole right to produce or reproduce work of literature, music, drama or art or any substantial part thereof in any material form in public. Copyright in lecture exists in delivery. If work is unpublished, it is sole right to publish it wholly or partially and includes sole right to produce, reproduce, perform or publish any translation of work. Copyright exists in conversion of dramatic work into novel or vice versa; and in making of any record, perforated roll, cinematograph film or other contrivance by means of which literary, dramatic or musical work may be mechanically performed or delivered. Publication of any work means issue of copies of work to public. Any unauthorised person who performs above acts infringes copyright. According to 1953 Copyright Amendment Ordinance, copyright in unpublished work exists where author was at time of creation national or resident of Israel.

Infringement.—Copyright in work is infringed when person without copyright owner's consent does anything, sole right to do which, is conferred on owner. Thus copyright is infringed when unauthorised person sells work or lets it for hire or by way of trade exposes or offers it for hire; or where he distributes work either for trade or in manner that prejudices owner of copyright; or when he exhibits work by way of trade in public; or when he imports for hire or sale any work which to his knowledge infringes copyright; or where he for his private profit knowingly permits theatre or other place of entertainment to be used for performance of work without copyright owner's consent.

There are the following exceptions to copyright infringements: (a) Fair dealing with any work for purposes of private study, research, criticism, review or newspaper summary; (b) use by author of work of any mould, cast, sketch, plan, model or study made by him where he is not copyright owner, provided that he does not repeat or imitate main design: (c) making paintings, drawings, engravings or photographs of work of sculpture if permanently situate in public place; (d) publication of non-copyright matter for bona fide use of schools as long as not more than two passages from works by same author are published within five years and source from which passages are taken is acknowledged; (e) publication of report of lecture delivered in public unless printed notice of prohibition of publication is given; (f) reading or recitation in public by one person of any reasonable extract from any published work.

Term of copyright is for life of author and for 50 years from Jan. 1st after his death. Same position obtains in case of any anonymous or pseudonymous work.

Ownership of Copyright.—Author of work is first owner of copyright therein except: (a) In case of engraving or photograph where plate or original was ordered by some other person and was made for valuable consideration in pursuance of that order where person who orders original is first owner; (b) where author was in employ of some other person under contract of service and work was done in course of his employment, employer (in absence of any contrary agreement) is first owner. This provision does not obtain where work is some contribution to newspaper, magazine or periodical where (unless there is contrary agreement) ownership of copyright remains vested in author.

Assignment.—There are no special forms for assignments or licences nor does copyright require registration.

Civil Remedies.—Where there is infringement, owner is entitled to injunction, damages or otherwise as may be conferred by law for infringement of right. Costs are in absolute discretion of court. In action for infringement plaintiff is presumed to be owner unless defendant puts existence of copyright or owner's title in issue. Even if damage resulting from infringement is not proved court may award compensation of not less than IS.250 and not more than IS.15,000 for each infringement.

Copyright Owner's Rights.—All infringing copies and plates used or intended to be used for production of such copies are deemed to be property of copyright owner who may take proceedings for recovery of possession or conversion, except as regards architectural restriction where interdict or injunction cannot be obtained or where demolition cannot be ordered. Infringing structure is not deemed to be property of copyright owner.

Prescription of Action.—According to Prescription Law of 1958 action for copyright infringement expires after seven years from date of infringement.

Protection of Foreign Works.—Where convention relating to copyright protection has been concluded between Israel and another country, or where Israel has acceded to convention, Minister of Justice may direct that works for which protection is required by such convention shall be protected. Israel is signatory of Stockholm B, Brussels and Unesco Conventions. Protection granted by Minister shall not exceed any protection were such work to have been published in Israel. Work published simultaneously in Israel and several other countries shall be considered as having been first published in Israel provided that there is no "colourless" publication.

Privacy.—By an amending Statute of Law of Civil Wrongs, use of name, connotation picture or voice of a person for commercial purposes, constitutes a civil wrong (a tort) rights to relief being given to person affected and after his death to his heirs.

Moral Right.—By 1981 Amendment, author of work has moral right in accordance with Berne Convention to have his work published without distortion, defect or alteration prejudicing its value, or his good name. Infringement of this right is compensated even if financial damage not proved.

CORPORATIONS:

Principal law concerning companies is Companies Ordinance based on English law. Major amendment was made to Companies Ordinance (1929) in Dec. 1980. Table B of Companies Ordinance which granted ancillary powers in addition to aims stated in memorandum has now been abolished. From day on which company has been formed in accordance with date appearing on certificate of association, company assumes all legal rights, duties and acts permitted by law. Any seven or more persons may form public company, and any two or more persons, but not more than 50, private company. Private company is exempt from certain provisions which apply to public company such as annual filing of accounts with Registrar. Both classes of companies must register memorandum and articles of association with Registrar of Companies. Objects of company are set out in memorandum which is company's charter. Any act of company not within objects set out in memorandum is ultra vires. Distinction has been drawn by new 1980 amendment between ultra vires acts and acts in which company directors act outside scope of their authority. Where servant of company acts outside scope of his authority on behalf of company, such acts have no validity vis-a-vis company, unless subsequently authorised by general meeting of company or by decision of board of directors where director has acted outside scope of his authority. According to new 1980 amendment, should company wish to change objects as determined by memorandum of association, such change may now be effected by special resolution and comes into force 21 days after adoption of resolution subject to rights of objection of minority shareholders. Articles set out internal regulations of company. Unless particular set of articles is filed, regulations contained in "Table A" of Companies Ordinance govern internal management of company. Great elasticity is possible in drafting of articles and it is common to include preemption rights and various devices for protecting interests of minority shareholders.

Companies may be: (a) Limited by shares, (b) limited by guarantee, or (c) unlimited. In a company limited by shares, liability of members is limited to amount, if any, unpaid on shares respectively held by them. In a company limited by guarantee, liability of members is limited by memorandum to such amount as members may respectively thereby undertake to contribute to assets of company in event of company being wound up. Company not having any limit on liability of its members is an unlimited company. Company limited by shares is by far most common form of company.

1980 amendment provides for split vote whereby shareholders may vote one way for portion of their shares and other way for rest of their shares at company meetings.

Registration fees are payable in form of registration fees and capital duty. Every company must file annual return with Registrar of Companies containing statutory information in regard to share capital, charges and directors. Public company must also file accounts.

Foreign Company.—1980 amendment defines foreign company as being all companies and associations, except partnerships which have been formed or registered outside Israel. Number of members is now unspecified. Foreign company which establishes place of business in Israel, has to be registered as foreign company. Registration fee is IS.100. Fee is IS.100, if paid by end of Feb., otherwise IS.130 is payable annually with company's annual return.

Application for registration by foreign company has to be made within one month from establishment of place of business and has to be accompanied by following documents: (a) Certified copy of charter, statutes or memorandum and articles of company; (b) list of directors; (c) names and addresses of some one or more persons resident in Israel authorized to accept on behalf of company service of processes and any notices required to be served on company; (d) certified copy of power of attorney enabling some person ordinarily a resident in Israel to act for company in Israel. Fee of IS.100, plus publication fee, or in case of corporation not constituted for purposes of profit fee of IS.50, is payable on registration of foreign company.

New Government Companies Law 1975.—Regulates formation, management and winding-up of companies in which State has more than half voting power or right to appoint more than half directors. Law provides for compensation for minority shareholders in companies which become subject to Law, appointment of directors on behalf of State and of managing directors and appointments to government companies of accountants, legal advisers and internal comptrollers. Resolutions of government companies on certain matters require government ratification. Some of provisions of Law also apply to companies in which State has not more than half voting power or right to appoint not more than half directors.

See also topics Associations; Securities.

COURTS:

The courts of Israel consist of the following: (1) Magistrates' Courts, which deal with civil matters in which the subject matter is of IS.75,000 or less, and recovery of possession and partition of immovable property of any value, and in criminal matters with contraventions and misdemeanours. Claims not exceeding IS.300 where claimant appears in person may be dealt with under simplified procedure. Minister of Justice may, by Order, empower Magistrates' Court to act as Court of Local Matters and deal with defined matters, mainly municipal and local laws and offences. (2) District Courts, which have jurisdiction in all matters save as expressly vested in any other courts, e.g., magistrates' courts. There are five District Courts, one in each of following cities: Jerusalem, Tel-Aviv, Haifa, Beer Sheva and Nazareth. Admiralty jurisdiction formerly vested in Supreme Court, is now vested in district court sitting in Haifa. There is right of appeal to Supreme Court. (3) Supreme Court, which has jurisdiction as High Court of Justice to which application in nature of mandamus, petition of right, habeas corpus and any other petition against Government, or government officer or any other public authority can be made and also as Court of Appeal, i.e., appellate tribunal from decisions of district court. (4) Municipal Courts, which have jurisdiction over any offences against municipal regulations or bylaws and over certain other specified minor offences. (5) Anti-profiteering courts are attached to each magistrates' court and district court. Tribunal is composed of professional judge or magistrate, and two members of public. (6) Rent Tribunals constituted under 1954 Tenant Protection Law, consisting of magistrate and two members of public, assess rent and value of services in relation to tenancies. (7) By Labour Courts Law 1969 court was set up to deal with all matters arising from employer/employee relationships including national insurance claims. Special Juvenile Tribunals were constituted for first time in 1955. Since 1957 Chief Justice may order criminal case to be reheard either by Court of Appeal or by district court if new facts have come to light, another person has been convicted for same offence, or evidence relied on has been declared false or forged. Chief Justice can also decide to rehear any matter decided by Supreme Court if it involves question of importance, difficulty or novelty.

The religious courts of several recognized religious communities have jurisdiction in matters of marriage and divorce of residents. In other matters of personal status these courts have jurisdiction with consent of the parties concerned. The religious courts have no jurisdiction over foreigners except by consent of all parties.

Courts are empowered by Legal Aid to Foreign States Law 1977 to collect testimony, seize documents or articles, conduct searches or carry out other legal proceedings at request of legal authority of foreign country. All such proceedings are to be conducted according to Israel Law. Court is entitled to refuse request for such aid if it is convinced that proceedings are of political character. Law does not apply to extradition proceedings prior to trial or serving of sentence.

See also topic Labour Relations.

CRIMINAL LAW:

Punishments Law 1977 effected comprehensive codification of criminal law and came into force on Apr. 1, 1978. Criminal procedure is codified in Criminal Procedure Law (Consolidated Version) 1982.

Magistrates' Courts can deal with crimes for which penalty is a fine only or imprisonment up to three years. All other offences are within jurisdiction of district courts. In respect of limited offences, private complaint may be filed, otherwise Attorney-General or his representative is in charge of criminal proceedings on behalf of state.

Courts have jurisdiction to release on bail persons charged with any offence except one for which penalty is death or life imprisonment or in respect of certain offences against security of state.

Capital punishment for murder was abolished in 1954, except in respect of a limited number of offences under Nazis and Nazi Collaborators (Punishment) Law, 1950 and it is still in force under Genocide (Prevention and Punishment) Law 1950 and in respect of treason under §96 of Punishments Law.

See also topic Limitation of Actions.

CURRENCY:

Unit of currency is Israel Shekel (IS). New Currency Law of 1980 changes old Israeli Pounds (IL) into Shekels. (Ten IL. have equivalent value of one Shekel.) Since 1955 the Bank of Israel is the central state bank and is the issuing bank of the Government. Dealings in foreign currency are authorized only through approved banks and there are limitations on the export of foreign currency.

Exchange Control is now governed by Currency Control Law 1978 and Currency Control Regulations 1978.

CUSTOMS:

See topic Taxation, subhead Customs Duty.

DEATH:

The Declaration of Death Law implements the United Nations Convention on the subject of declarations of death of persons who disappeared in Europe during the Nazi regime. The same law also provides for declarations of death in a case of persons dying a natural death or through accident and of whom all traces have been lost for more than two years. Application by an interested person, as defined by the Law, is to be made to the competent court, which is the Jerusalem District Court. (Book of Laws, No. 93, of 13.3.53).

A copy of death certificate of a person dying in Israel is obtainable on application to the local authorities of the area in which the death took place.

Actions.—On death of any person any cause of action in respect of a civil wrong subsisting against or vested in him survives against or, as case may be, for benefit of his estate.

Where death is caused by a civil wrong and such person would, had death not ensued, have been entitled at time of his death to recover compensation in respect of bodily injury caused to him by such civil wrong, the husband, wife, parent and child of such deceased person may recover compensation from person responsible for such civil wrong.

These laws, like all other laws, apply equally to foreigners.

See also topic Limitation of Actions.

DEEDS: See topic Real Property.

DEPOSITIONS:

See also Acknowledgments; Affidavits.

For Use Within Israel.—The court or a judge may at any time order that any particular fact or facts be proved by affidavit, or that the affidavit of any witness be read at the hearing, on such conditions as the court or judge thinks reasonable. Where it appears that either party bona fide desires the production of a witness for the court's examination and that such witness can be produced, an order will not be made authorizing evidence of the witness to be given by affidavit.

Affidavits must be in the first person, divided into paragraphs and confined to such facts as the deponent is able of his own knowledge to prove, except on interlocutory applications, in which a statement of the deponent's belief may be admitted provided that the grounds thereof are stated.

Within Israel for Use Elsewhere.—The Foreign Tribunals Evidence Act 1856 (an English Act) has been applied to Palestine and has effect in Israel. Under this Act any court or tribunal of competent jurisdiction in a foreign country before which any civil or commercial matter is pending, may obtain any testimony in Israel in relation to such matter. Application for this purpose may be made to a court or judge in Israel, and such court or judge may order the examination upon oath, upon interrogatory or otherwise, before any person or persons named, of such witness or witnesses as may be required, and the attendance of such witness or witnesses for examination or for the production of any documents may be commanded and other directions given as to time, place or manner of examination.

A certificate under the hand of an ambassador, minister or other diplomatic agent of a foreign state that any matter in relation to which an application is made is a civil or commercial matter pending before a foreign tribunal and that such tribunal is desirous of obtaining the testimony of the witness to whom the application relates, is sufficient evidence of the matter certified.

Further, under the Foreign Tribunals Evidence Rules, where any civil, criminal or commercial matter is pending before a court or tribunal of a foreign country, a district court in Israel is authorized to take the testimony of any person in relation to the matter pending before the foreign court or tribunal. The President of the District Court, if satisfied that the foreign court or tribunal is desirous of obtaining testimony within the jurisdiction, may, on an ex-parte application of any person shown to be duly authorized to make the application and on production of a commission rogatoire or letter of request, make such order as may be necessary to secure the examination of the witness or witnesses. The application should be forwarded to the court through the Israel Minister of Justice.

Under the Extradition Ordinance, depositions or statements on oath taken in a foreign state, and copies of such original depositions or statements and foreign certificates or judicial documents, stating the fact of conviction may, if duly authenticated, be received in evidence in proceedings for extradition.

Outside Israel for Use Within Israel.—On the application of any party to any civil proceedings, the court may make an order for examination upon oath before any person in any place outside jurisdiction of any witness, and court may give directions as to matters connected with examination. Person directed to take any examination may administer oath and report to court on examination, and conduct of any witness.

DESCENT AND DISTRIBUTION:

Comprehensive succession law was enacted in 1965—Inheritance Law of 1965. Former limitations on power of testamentary dispositions in respect of certain classes of immovables were abolished (see topic Wills). Subject to any testamentary dispositions, following are legal heirs entitled to succession: (1) Spouse of deceased; (2) children and their descendants and parents of deceased and their descendants.

Spouse is entitled to home contents including automobile and one-half of rest of estate if there are children of marriage between deceased and spouse, or issue of such children, or surviving parents of deceased if no children of deceased and spouse. Where Financial Relations between Spouses Law results by agreement or by law in surviving spouse being regarded as joint owner with deceased in his lifetime, surviving spouse inherits one-quarter on intestacy. If deceased is survived by children of preceding marriage, spouse takes one-quarter. If parents or brothers or sisters of deceased survive deceased but no children or descendants of children, spouse is entitled to two-thirds of estate. In any other case, surviving spouse is entitled to whole of estate of deceased.

State succeeds in absence of relations.

Adopted child is entitled to same share as natural child. New provisions are embodied in 1965 law entitling needy spouse, needy child or needy surviving parents to maintenance out of estate. Court is entitled to allow widow or widower a one-time grant or periodical maintenance.

Maintenance in respect of children may be granted until they reach age of 18 and in special cases up to 23 years of age, and to parents for life.

Administrator may be appointed by court to administer estate, and court may confirm as administrator an executor appointed by will.

Creditors have to be satisfied first before any distribution is made to heirs.

Spouse, children or parents who lived with deceased in his place of residence are entitled to continue to reside in same premises as lessees of legal heirs for such duration and subject to such terms as may be settled with heirs or as settled by court.

Competent court is entitled to deal with estate of any person who resided in Israel on date of his death or has left property in Israel.

Applicable law is law of residence of deceased on date of his death, except in respect of assets which devolve in accordance with lex situs. Competent court is district court (civil court) where deceased resided at time of his death, or in case of nonresident court having jurisdiction where any assets of deceased are situated in Israel.

Religious courts may exercise jurisdiction when all parties consent to such jurisdiction.

See also topic Marriage.

DESIGNS: See topic Patents.

DIVORCE:

Rabbinical Courts have exclusive jurisdiction in regard to divorce where both parties are Jews, and are either domiciled in Israel or Israeli citizens. Christian recognized Religious Courts have exclusive divorce jurisdiction in regard to Christians who are Israeli citizens. Moslem Religious Courts have exclusive divorce jurisdiction in regard to Moslems who are Israeli citizens or foreigners who, under law of their nationality, are subject in such matters to jurisdiction of Moslem Religious Courts.

Law of Jurisdiction in Dissolution of Marriage in Special Cases, 1969, authorises Chief Justice to direct that an application for divorce (which is not in jurisdiction of any Religious Court) be dealt with either by a Civil Court or a Religious Court. As a result, it is now possible in case of mixed marriages where parties belong to different religious communities, for marriage to be lawfully dissolved. Law also repealed limitation of jurisdiction in divorce cases of foreigners.

Maintenance.—By 1972 Law to ensure payment of maintenance where judgment for maintenance is given in favour of a spouse, a minor child or a parent, resident in Israel, party entitled may apply to be paid by National Insurance Institute, thereby saving himself necessity of execution proceedings. Amount payable is sum adjudged, subject to overriding maximum fixed by regulations. Rights under judgment are subrogated to Institute which may recover from defendant under judgment. Apart from right to maintenance legal separation is not recognized.

Division of Property of Spouses in Divorce.—In absence of agreement each spouse is entitled by 1973 Law of Financial Relations between Spouses to half of total property of both spouses excluding such property as either had before marriage or received as gift or by way of inheritance during marriage or non-assignable rights or property which parties agreed should not be taken into consideration.

EXCHANGE CONTROL:

See Currency; Foreign Trade Regulations; Investment Law.

EXECUTIONS:

Execution Law 1967 provides for various methods of enforcing judgments and for securing defendant's property during course of an action (see topic Attachment). Judgment debtor can be detained or prevented from leaving country if Chief Execution Officer considers he intends to impede execution. There is power to attach movable property but certain items such as foodstuffs for subsistence of debtor and family for 30 days, vital household effects and clothes, religious articles and trade implements are exempt. Attached property may be sold after seven days from date of attachment. Immovable property may also be attached and sold after 30 days. Dwelling house is exempt unless it can be shown that debtor has somewhere else to go. Agricultural land required for subsistence is also exempt. There are also provisions for attachment of property in hands of a third party which includes debts due to judgment debtor. There are certain exemptions, most important being wages up to a certain amount. In certain

limited circumstances a debtor, who has not, after an inquiry into his means, paid the ordered instalments of his debt, can be arrested. Further form of execution commonly used is appointment of a receiver similar in nature to remedy of equitable execution used in Anglo-Saxon systems.

By virtue of a 1968 amendment to Law, bill of exchange may be enforced directly by execution without obtaining judgment.

Execution of Foreign Judgments.—Under Foreign Judgments Enforcement Law 1958, foreign judgment may be enforced in Israel either by action thereon before a district court or by grant of an exequatur issued by a district court. A "judgment" for this purpose means any judgment or order given by a court outside Israel in any civil proceedings, whereby a sum of money is made payable and includes an award in any arbitration, if award is, in pursuance of law enforced in place where it was made. It is enforceable in same manner as a judgment given by a court in that place. Judgment to which an exequatur has been accorded is executory in Israel. There are certain conditions required for enforcement, particularly reciprocity and that judgment was given according to rules of natural justice.

By amendment to above Law in 1977, foreign judgment will be recognized by Israel Court only if following conditions are satisfied: (a) Agreement with country where judgment was given; (b) Israel undertook by such agreement to recognize judgments of same class; (c) such undertaking applies only to judgments enforceable by Israel Law; (d) all conditions of agreement are fulfilled.

By same amendment debts in foreign currency may be paid in that currency or in Israel currency at rate of exchange in force at time of payment.

Special provisions in regard to the enforcement of foreign awards are contained in the (Arbitration) Foreign Awards Ordinance of 1934. The provisions of this ordinance apply only in respect of territories which have made reciprocal provisions. There is as yet no provision for the reciprocal enforcement of awards between Israel and the United States, but it would seem that an award issued and confirmed in the United States may be enforced in Israel under the Enforcement of Foreign Judgment Rules.

EXECUTORS AND ADMINISTRATORS:

See also topic Descent and Distribution.

An administrator may be appointed on the application of any person entitled to an interest of the estate. An administrator is personally liable at the instance of persons beneficially entitled for any wrong committed by him in the course of his administration. An administrator is required to give security, whilst an executor may be exempted from furnishing any security for the due administration of the estate. Executors or administrators are required to file returns in regard to their administration and the discharge is obtained on proper application after the conclusion of the administration or by leave of the court even before the winding up of the estate. The court will, on the application of an administrator, give such direction as may from time to time be required as to the administration of the estate.

The application for probate of a will or for the appointment of an administrator of an estate of a deceased person is made by petition to the court having jurisdiction in the area where the deceased had his last usual residence or place of business; and if the deceased had no place of residence or place of business in Israel, then the petition may be addressed to the court within whose area any part of the estate is to be found.

EXEMPTIONS:

The following are exempt from attachment: (1) a minimum income sufficient to provide the debtor with the necessities of life; (2) things necessary for the support, clothing and lodging of the family of the debtor; (3) machinery and implements used by the debtor in exercising his trade; (4) amount of salary of employees up to IS.357 (after tax) per month; (5) dwelling house of debtor unless reasonable substitute dwelling is available.

FOREIGN EXCHANGE:

See topics Currency; Foreign Trade Regulations; Investment Law.

FOREIGN INVESTMENT:

See topic Investment Law.

FOREIGN TRADE REGULATIONS:

Exchange Control Regulations were imposed during World War II. Although Regulations of 1941 were substantially relaxed, dealings in foreign currency and export of foreign currency are controlled by regulations. Contracts with nonresidents required to be approved by Controller of Foreign Exchange. Tendency in recent years has steadily been a relaxation in control and the streamlining of procedures. Similarly, while for many years all imports were subject to import licences and for protection of local industry, present tendency is towards liberalization of imports including elimination of necessity for import licences on an ever-increasing number of goods and materials. Treaties of friendship and commerce have been concluded with many countries and are renewable annually or at other regular intervals. In Nov. 1977 necessity for import licences was virtually abolished.

Israel has concluded trade and customs agreements with European Economic Community.

See also topics Currency; Investment Law; Taxation.

FRAUDS, STATUTE OF: See topic Contracts.

GARNISHMENT:

See topics Attachment; Executions.

GUARDIAN AND WARD:

Legal Capacity and Guardianship Law of 1962 governs appointment and duties of guardians. Legal acts of persons under 18 and other equally incapacitated persons are subject to ratification by court and where property rights are involved to consent of court. Management of affairs of and care of legally incapacitated persons is entrusted to guardian, subject to general supervision of court. Jurisdiction is vested in District Court but religious courts have jurisdiction if all parties so desire. Law of domicile applies but court has powers over incapacitated person living in Israel or over legal acts performed in Israel relating to property of incapacitated person.

HIRE:

See topic Landlord and Tenant.

HOLIDAYS:

The following are public or legal holidays for the purpose of the Bills of Exchange Ordinance: Independence Day (also day of rest); Jewish holidays (Passover, first and last days, Pentecost, New Year's, two days, Day of Atonement, and First and Eighth day of Feast of Tabernacles); Christian holidays (New Year's Day—according to both Gregorian and Julian calendar, Ascension Day, Christmas Day, and Easter Monday); Moslem holidays (Shaker Bairam, three days, Qurban Bairam, four days, and Maulid al Nabi, one day).

There are also legal rest days. The Jewish rest days are the days mentioned above under "Jewish holidays," as well as Saturdays. These need not be the rest days for non-Jews, as they may rest on their respective holidays and other religious days.

Election day is a public holiday.

HUSBAND AND WIFE:

See topics Divorce; Marriage.

IMMIGRATION:

Substantial rights are granted to new immigrants including income tax concessions, customs and purchase tax exemptions on personal and household effects, investment assistance and housing facilities.

See also topic Constitution and Government, subhead Citizenship.

INFANCY:

Age of majority of both sexes is 18. Parents of a minor (a person under 18) are natural guardians. Natural guardians or any guardians appointed by court may consent to or ratify a contract made by a minor but unless made with such consent or until ratified, contract may be repudiated by minor or by his guardians or by Attorney General. Consent or ratification need not be in writing.

Certain acts of a guardian, such as transfer of real property, charges or mortgages, gifts, donations, guarantees and transactions between a minor and his guardian or his parents, require the approval of court.

An infant is represented in court by his guardian. Court may appoint a guardian ad litem.

Adoption.—See topic Adoption.
See topic Guardian and Ward.

INSURANCE:

The 1981 Insurance Contracts Law has basically legislated much of common law position and now governs law of Commercial (as opposed to State) Insurance in Israel.

Scope.—Law regulates law pertaining to life insurance; personal accident; sickness and disability insurance; regular commercial insurance; and vehicle insurance. (However, 1970 Motor Vehicle Insurance Ordinance is still applicable.) Law does not however apply to Maritime Insurance where 1863 Ottoman Maritime Trade Law still applies (insofar as it has not been repealed). Law does not apply to air insurance, nor does it apply to re-insurance treaties.

1981 Law repeals 1976 Law dealing with rights of third parties but incorporates protection of third parties in case of insolvency of insured. 1981 Law also repeals 1904 Ottoman Insurance Law which dealt with property insurance.

1981 Law provides that should one of parties wish to cancel contract in accordance with said Law or by virtue of conditions of contract, contract is terminated 15 days after notice has been sent to other party.

Claim for insurance payment prescribes three years after occurrence of event insured against.

1981 Law applies concurrently with 1951 Insurance Business (Superintendence) Law. Latter regulates and limits carrying on of insurance business in Israel, deals with grant of licences, lodging of returns by insurance companies and payment of deposits by persons engaging in insurance business in Israel. Maximum deposit in case of Israeli Insurers is IS.280,000 in case of life insurance and IS.210,000 for other types of insurance. Maximum deposit for foreign insurers is IS.450,000. Foreign Insurance Companies licensed before 12/12/79 are liable to maximum deposit of only IS.250,000. Should such company, licensed before 12/12/79, wish to deal in other types of insurance than stipulated

in licence, further deposit of IS.30,000 is due, but total deposit shall not exceed IS.350,000.

See also topics Labour Relations; Consumer Protection.

INTEREST:

Under law of 1957, rate of interest chargeable is restricted. Minister of Finance may by order approved by Finance Committee of Knesset (Israel Legislature) fix maximum rate of interest chargeable in respect of commercial transactions of various categories. There is normally no maximum rate fixed but where repayment is limited to a currency rate of exchange or to an index, maximum permitted rate is 8%. Courts are authorized to reopen usurious transactions and penalties are provided in case of any breach of law.

INVESTMENT LAW:

Law for Encouragement of Capital Investments 1959 as am'd succeeds earlier legislation in regard to encouragement of investments in Israel. Substantial reliefs and exemptions from property tax, local taxes, purchase tax, customs duties, income tax, stamp duties, and inheritance tax are allowed. (See below amended benefits for approvals after July 30, 1978.) Special concessions are allowed to foreign investors whose investments are approved by Investment Centre. These include removal of five year time limit for maximum income tax rate of 25% on dividends from approved investments, exemption from tax on income from investments in foreign currency in securities quoted on Tel Aviv Stock Exchange, provided investor receives no double taxation relief or if Double Taxation Agreement with investor's country allows "tax-sparing."

Law for Encouragement of Capital Investment in Agriculture 1980 provides special tax benefits for approved investment in agriculture.

Foreign currency invested in approved investment and profits earned thereon may be taken out in foreign currency by foreign investor.

Companies owning enterprises approved by Investment Centre are entitled to exemption from income tax and pay profits tax at 28% for five years from first year of chargeable profit (subject to overriding time limit of 12 years from commencement of production). For enterprises approved after Apr. 1, 1980 exemption period is seven years with overriding limit of 14 years. Where approval is granted after 1st Apr. 1971, profits tax is 33%; where approval is granted after Mar. 31, 1976 profits tax is 40%. Enterprises approved after July 30, 1978 pay 30%. Enterprises approved after May 31, 1981 pay 40% reducible to 30% on chargeable income equal to net investment in fixed assets in tax year. Shareholders are exempt from income tax on dividends from profits of approved enterprises on which profits tax has been paid. Dividends out of profits of enterprise approved after Mar. 31, 1976 are chargeable to income tax at 15%. Individuals and Kibbutzim owning approved enterprises pay income tax at 25% if approved before Mar. 31, 1976, 40% if approved between Mar. 31, 1976 and July 30, 1978, and 30% if approved after that date. Approved enterprises with 25% foreign investment being Industrial Companies under Encouragement of Industry (Taxes) 1969 Law are entitled to deduct provision for capital stabilisation, based on dollar exchange rate differences each year. As from tax year 1978, companies where foreign investment exceeds 49% are entitled to alternative capital stabilisation allowances based on adjustment of share capital and profits for exchange rate variation.

Buildings which are assessed approved by Investment Centre completed after 1st Apr., 1968, 70% of area of which is intended for letting and two-thirds of such letting is residential, are granted relief from 80% of property tax, increased depreciation rates and reduced tax rates as for approved enterprises but without time limit.

Industrial enterprises approved between Jan. 1, 1971 and Mar. 31, 1976, and completed by Mar. 31, 1980, or approved between Apr. 1, 1976 and Mar. 31, 1981 and completed by Mar. 31, 1986 are entitled to investment grants from State, amounting to 15% or 30% of amount invested in buildings, machinery and equipment, higher rate being given where enterprise is located in less developed areas of country. Under 1976 amendment, export grants were also paid as percentage of foreign currency earned from exports of approved enterprises up to amount equal to 24% of investment in enterprise. Investments in construction of buildings intended for leasing are also entitled to certain tax exemptions and accelerated depreciation. By Amending Law of July 30, 1978, exemptions from property taxes, local taxes, purchase tax, customs and stamp duties are cancelled in relation to approvals after that date. Export grants are cancelled but investment grants and grants to cover indirect taxes are allowed.

Minister of Finance has power to exempt from income and Companies Tax, international trading concerns, otherwise liable to Israeli taxes only by reason of management and control being situate in Israel.

Investment Encouragement Law (Capital Rich Companies) (1973 Law) provides that any company, capital of which is $100,000,000 of which $20,000,000 was subscribed by signatories to memorandum and purposes of which are to acquire and maintain or enlarge industrial works, finance or agriculture, tourism, transport, land development, building, public services or advance of exports from Israel and recognized by Minister of the Treasury until Dec. 31, 1975, is entitled to extensive benefits. It is free from income tax or capital profits tax within 30 years from first year of income. It will only pay company tax not exceeding 20% and be free from any other tax upon income.

Any person receiving dividends from such a company within 15 years of year when income was obtained will be free from any income tax in addition to income tax paid by company, and any person selling shares out of a series of shares issued by company, will be free from capital profits tax. Shares owned by a nonresident will not be included in his estate for purpose of estate tax. Law contains provisions for cancellation of benefits if capital has not reached $30,000,000 within four years of issue of first series of shares and also if less than 80% of share capital was issued to nonresidents for foreign currency.

JUDGMENTS:

Enforcement of Foreign Judgments.—By a law of 1958, judgments of foreign courts are enforceable if they were given in the foreign country by a court having jurisdiction to act, and are final and not subject to appeal, and their contents are not in contradiction to the laws of Israel or public policy in Israel and they are capable of execution in the country in which they were given. The jurisdiction is based upon mutuality and special rules have been provided. See topic Executions.

LABOUR RELATIONS:

Wages.—1958 Wage Protection Law provides that wages must be paid in cash. Other modes of payment are allowed only under collective agreement; only small portion may be paid in food and lodging. Payment must be directly to labourer. Fixed amount is free from attachments. Time for payment fixed and if delayed, additional sum is payable. This rule was made applicable to compensation for dismissal by 1977 Amendment. Debts due from labourer to employer can be deducted only within limits. 1976 Sickness Pay Law provides for payment of 75% of normal wage in case of sickness for period up to 1 ½ days for each month of service, unless provided otherwise under Collective Agreement.

Employment of Children.—Employment of children and young persons is governed by Law of 1953 Relating to Employment of Youth and Apprenticeship Law of 1953. Employment of persons under age of 14 is forbidden. Minister of Labour has power to prohibit or limit employment of infants in specific occupations or to fix age for employment in certain employments. Minister may also fix work hours and conditions of employment.

The employment of women is also strictly governed by the Employment of Women Ordinance 1945, which restricts the employment and working hours and makes provisions for the protection of women employed in the various undertakings.

Equal opportunity in Employment Law 1981 forbids discrimination in engaging employees on grounds of sex, marital or parental status unless justified by nature of employment or security considerations.

National Insurance Law (Consolidated Version) 1968 as amended contains comprehensive code in regard to payment of old age pensions, payments in respect of compensation to workmen injured by accident, maternity payments, unemployment payments, death benefits and child allowances.

National Insurance Law provides for old age pensions to males of over 65 and females over 60 and for compensation in respect to death or injury during work both to workmen and to independent earners. It also provides certain benefits in respect to childbirth and burial expenses. Law is administered by a National Insurance Board which levies a fixed premium on all residents. The premiums vary according to income and premiums due from employed persons are deducted by employers from their salaries.

Assurance of Income Law, 1980 provides for persons resident in Israel who are unable to work or support themselves sufficiently and who are not eligible for benefits under National Insurance Law. All claims are subject to specific conditions.

National Employment Service.—By the 1959 law, employment agencies have been erected on a national basis and no labourers may be employed except through those agencies, with the exception of certain highly specialized professions or administrative employment. 1976 amending law provides youth occupational guidance and requires notification of dismissals of ten or more employees at one time.

Collective Agreements.—Collective agreements may be entered into between an employer or an organization of employers and between organized labour, regarding conditions and terms of work. Labourers rights under such agreements cannot be waived, and the Minister of Labour may extend its application.

Labour Disputes.—There is no provision in regard to compulsory settlement of disputes between employers and labourers, but the Department of Labour has power to assist the employers and labourers in the settlement of their industrial disputes and it normally intervenes in such disputes with a view of securing an amicable settlement. In case of labour disputes provision is made for settlement by mediation, the mediator possessing far-reaching powers to assemble the parties and ascertain the nature of the dispute. Certain matters are passed to compulsory arbitration, the decision of the arbitrators being binding. There is now a Labour Court which deals with labour disputes.

Under Civil Wrongs Ordinance (New Version) 1963, as amended, master is liable for acts of his servant if he authorized or ratified act or if it was committed by servant in course of his employment.

By Amendments to Law of Settlement of Labour Disputes, following limitations were introduced on right to strike: (a) By §5a of 1969 Amending Law a 15 day notice must be given of any intended strike both to Commissioner of Labour Relations and to employer; (b) by §37 b-d of 1972 Amending Law, special provisions governing public service were introduced. Term "public service" includes labour relations in service of Government, municipalities and local councils, health services, primary and higher education, aviation, oil, water and electricity. In a public service a strike declared without legal notice above-mentioned or whilst a collective agreement is in force is (with few exceptions) an "unprotected strike." Participation by individual labourer in an unprotected strike de-

prives him of protection granted by Collective Agreements Law to effect that a participation in a strike does not constitute a breach of personal agreement of labourer. Person causing labourers to participate in an unprotected strike is liable for procuring a breach of contract. Labour Courts are entitled to issue an injunction prohibiting individual labourers to participate in an unprotected strike. By amending law 1976, Labour Courts are empowered to order proportionate wage reduction in case of unprotected "go-slow" strike in public services. See also topic Banks and Banking.

See also subhead National Insurance Law.

Compensation for Dismissal.—By a 1963 law an employee who has worked continuously for a minimum period of one year with same employer in same job is entitled on dismissal to compensation amounting to a sum equal to one month's pay for each full year of service. No compensation is payable if employee is dismissed for dishonesty. In certain cases, such compensation may be paid even where employee resigns of his own accord, e.g., for health reasons. Female worker who leaves her employment with nine months after birth or adoption of child by her in order to attend to such child is entitled to compensation.

See also topic Wages.

Right of Dismissal.—Supreme Court, as High Court of Justice, set aside a judgment of Labour Court of Appeal ordering an employer to continue employing an employee whom he had dismissed. Rule that court does not order specific performance of a contract of personal employment, is not affected by fact that employment is governed by a collective agreement.

Labour Courts.—By a 1969 Law, special Labour Courts were created and given exclusive jurisdiction in all matters dealing with or arising from labour relations.

There are four District Labour Courts in Jerusalem, Tel-Aviv, Haifa and Beer Sheva, and a State Court in Jerusalem. In every Court there are professional judges and two members of the public, one nominated by employers' association and one by employees' association. In State Court there are three professional judges and two members of public appointed as above. District Courts have exclusive primary jurisdiction in all matters between employers and employees and in collective agreement disputes arising from a special collective agreement (i.e., one dealing with one or a limited number of employers). State Court has primary jurisdiction in disputes arising from general collective agreements (i.e., agreements covering all employers of a certain category) and an appeal jurisdiction from District Court. Both courts have criminal jurisdiction too.

There is no appeal from State Court. It is subject however to a limited "High Court jurisdiction."

Trade Unions.—Supreme Court refused to interfere with decision of Labour Association not to create a trade union consisting of workmen of one branch in certain towns. Labour Association is a voluntary body and, hence, law courts would refrain from interference with a decision, which prima facie constitutes a valid exercise of Association's discretion.

See also topic Wages.

LAND:

Under the "Basic Law—Land of Israel 1960," all the lands which belong to the State Development Authority or J.N.F. are considered as the lands of Israel, the ownership whereof cannot be assigned either by sale or by any other way. Land includes land, houses, buildings and all other appurtenances belonging thereto. Under the Land of Israel Law, 1960, several transactions in reference to these lands are exempted from the prohibition of transfer. These are mainly transactions in the nature of exchange of lands. Special authorities were created in order to manage the lands and to supervise the execution of the provisions of the law.

Land Law is now virtually codified by Land Law 1969. Existing Ottoman legislation has been abolished. Dealings with registered land not valid unless registered, and equitable rights have been abolished. Written document is required for sale or lease of land. Owner of land has right to claim possession against wrongful occupier.

Joint tenancies may only be over an undivided whole. Any joint tenant may require dissolution of joint tenancy which may be carried out by agreement or by order of court. Court may order partition or sale.

Registration.—Land registration now covers most of country except part of Galilee.

Cooperative Houses.—Cooperative Houses Law has been repealed but has been incorporated in Land Law. It facilitates registration of separate dwellings in a jointly-owned house and regulates rights between owners. Urban housing in Israel is largely based on cooperative housing.

Sale of Apartments Law 1973 came into force on 1/10/73 and provides that a sale of an apartment which has been built or is about to be built must be accompanied by a specification in a form prescribed by Minister of Housing. Any deviation from specification or from applicable town planning regulations is regarded as a noncompliance conferring upon purchaser all rights under Sales Law 1968. (See topic Sales.)

Special provisions apply to sale of an apartment in a condominium house or in a property designated to be registered as a condominium house requiring all relevant details as to management of house. Default in attaching specification is punished with a serious money penalty.

See also topic Sales, subhead Sale of Flats.

Securing Purchasers of Apartments.—By 1974-76 Law of Sale (Apartments) (securing investments of apartment purchasers) vendor or lessor by lease for more than 25 years, of an unbuilt apartment, may not receive from purchaser more than 15% of purchase price unless he gave purchaser bank guarantee securing refund of all monies paid, in event of non-delivery of apartment to purchaser as agreed, or has insured himself with an authorised insurance company against such event, with purchaser as beneficiary under policy, or has transferred ownership or long lease of apartment to purchaser or encumbered same in his favour.

Transfers.—Immovable property can only be transferred by execution of a deed which has to be signed either at competent Land Registry in Israel or before any lawyer in Israel who authenticates signatures on deed. Deed is executed before District Land Registrar, when appropriate fees must be paid. Transferee's title is entered on Register in substitution for title of transferor. All transfers of immovable property must now be reported for Betterment Tax purposes.

Recuperation Areas Authority.—By 1973 Statute this authority is set up and authorised to recommend that a certain area having qualities that would attract persons recuperating, be declared a recuperation area, of one of various categories, and any restrictions on undertakings within area. It can also encourage research, advance level of services of existing recuperation areas, encourage housing, supervise and generally regulate exploitation of area. This law contains full supplementary provisions regarding effect of such declaration, and any ensuing rights and liabilities.

Radio and Television Aerial Masts.—Local Authorities (Radio and Television Aerial Masts) Law 1975 empowers local authorities to limit number of radio and television aerial masts on buildings and to require erection of central masts on apartment buildings with compensation for persons aggrieved and financial penalties for infringements.

See topic Taxation. See also topics Adverse Possession; Landlord and Tenant; Limitation of Actions; Mortgages.

LANDLORD AND TENANT:

Land Law 1969 requires written document and registration in Land Registry to effect lease if for more than five years or with option to renew beyond five years. Registration not required for lease of dwellings or business premises unless for period exceeding in all ten years. Subject to agreement lease may be charged with mortgage or easement and tenant may transfer lease or sublet. See also subhead Hire Law 1971, infra.

Duties of landlord to provide services and effect repairs are laid down in Tenants Protection Law 1972. This Law also consolidates previous legislation regarding control of rentals and protection against eviction for tenants of residential and business premises occupying under leases prior to 1958 which have expired or who paid key-money. Protection extends to surviving spouse, children or parents who occupied premises with tenant at least six months prior to decease. Protected tenant continues to hold on terms of expired lease as varied by agreement or by Law.

Rentals of premises within Law may not be increased except within the limits fixed by Regulations issued periodically. In event of dispute between landlord and tenant, local Rent Tribunals have power to fix rental.

Outgoing tenant is entitled to share of key-money to be paid by incoming tenant, amount of which depends on whether his tenancy began before or after 1958, period of occupation and whether he himself paid key-money. Special procedure is provided to settle outgoing tenant's share if disputed.

Law ceases to apply to premises falling vacant and does not apply to buildings completed and let after 1968, nor to buildings of Approved Undertakings (see topic Investment Law).

Principal grounds for eviction of protected tenant are nonpayment of rent, breach of original lease justifying eviction, wilful damage, use of premises for unlawful purpose, molesting neighbours, premises required for own purposes or rebuilding by landlord, public body requiring premises for public purpose. In last two cases alternative accomodation must be provided.

Hire Law 1971.—Law in respect of hire applies to both moveables and immoveables where contrary intention does not appear in agreement. Object hired must comply with specifications in agreement unless lessor knew otherwise at date of agreement or lessee did not notify lessor of unsuitability within reasonable time. Lessor has liability to repair. Where object hired is a chattel, lessor may exchange defective chattel so as to comply with his obligations. Where repair not carried out, lessee may repair and debit lessor with expense or reduce rent in accordance with defect. Where object leased is land and lessee cannot use it for reasons connected with land or access thereto, he is not liable to pay rent. Lessee must give lessor facilities to inspect and repair. Lessor may assign his rights but must notify lessee. Lessee may not assign without lessor's consent, but if lessor unreasonably withholds consent, in case of land lessee may assign without lessor's consent, and in case of any object court may order transaction.

See also topic Sales, subhead Sale of Flats.

LAW REPORTS, CODES, ETC.:

There are official law reports of cases in Supreme Court and in district courts and there are also official reports of cases in rabbinical courts and certain specialised reports such as tax cases.

Certain branches of the law are codified and may be found in books of Mandatory Ordinances and Israeli Statutes. See also topic Statutes.

LEGISLATURE:

See topic Constitution and Government.

LICENCES:

Business Licencing Law of 1968, replacing pre-State legislation empowers Minister of Interior in consultation with Minister of Health to issue Orders requiring certain businesses to obtain licences in order to ensure proper environmental and health conditions, prevention of public nuisances and observation of Town Planning regulations, public safety, prevention of pollution and diseases in livestock. Special provisions are laid down for sale of intoxicating liquors and public entertainments. Comprehensive list of businesses requiring licence has been drawn up in Registration Order of 1973 covering close to 200 kinds of business. Licencing authority is local government or such authority as Minister of Interior may determine. Fine of IS.500 or six months imprisonment is imposed for noncompliance. Companies pay double fine. Court may order temporary or permanent closing of business convicted for noncompliance.

See also topic Foreign Trade Regulations.

LIENS:

There are various forms of liens which basically follow English Law. Maritime liens are provided by Shipping (Vessels) Law 1960.

LIMITATION OF ACTIONS:

Actions must be brought within following periods after respective causes of action, including civil wrongs, accrue: (a) in respect of a debt or chattels, within seven years; (b) in respect of unregistered land, 15 years. There is now no limitation period in respect of registered land. (c) parties may agree in writing to extend the period in case of land, and either to extend it or shorten it in case of movables.

Supreme Court decided in 1955 that suits for specific performance are not barred by any limitation period, but only by laches (delay causing damage).

See topics Bills and Notes; Insurance; also Adverse Possession.

In respect to crimes the following are the periods of prescription: felonies, ten years; misdemeanours, three years; contraventions, one year. Period of prescription runs from date of commission of offence or from date of last step taken in investigation or prosecution of offence in question in respect of felonies or misdemeanours; and in respect of contraventions, from date of commission of offence.

Time limits for bringing of actions under Nazis and Nazi Collaborators (Punishment) Law 1950 and under Genocide (Prevention and Punishment) Law 1950 were abolished in 1966.

Customs prosecutions must be instituted within five years.

Lost Property Law of Return.—By a new law of 1973 which came into force on Aug. 31, 1973, a person finding lost property must either return it to its owner or notify police and may keep property or deliver it to police unless police require such delivery, in which case he must comply with requirement. If owner has not been found within four months, he is presumed to have forfeited ownership, in which case it passes into finder's ownership. If, however, finder did not notify police it becomes State property. Previous owner may, however, within a year redeem lost property on paying its value at time of redemption. Goods liable to destruction or live stock may be sold after notifying police and provisions of Law apply to proceeds.

MAINTENANCE:

See topic Divorce, subhead Maintenance.

MARRIAGE:

Matters of marriage are considered as matters of personal status, which are within exclusive jurisdiction of Rabbinical religious courts in respect of all Jews and religious courts of other denominations in respect of non-foreigners who are members of respective recognized religious communities. In respect of foreigners, who are not Jews, their national law applies, and local courts will recognize as valid any marriage which is valid according to national law.

General consuls, vice-consuls and any other competent consular authority may officiate at marriages where at least one of the parties is of the consul's nationality.

No marriage of a girl under 17 is permitted unless court orders otherwise in special circumstances.

Every marriage must be registered by person performing marriage. Registration is effected by filing a copy of record with District Commissioner of district where marriage is performed. Failure to register involves considerable penalties.

Financial Relations Between Spouses.—1973 Law which came into force on Jan. 1, 1974 provides that spouses may regulate their financial relations by an agreement which requires approval by District Court or by Religious Court having jurisdiction in matters of marriage and divorce of spouses. Failing such an agreement, financial relations and ownership of property of spouses will be regulated as follows: (a) Entry into marriage or its subsistence do not affect spouse's ownership rights and do not confer upon either spouse any right in other spouse's property or any liability for other spouse's debts: (b) upon dissolution of marriage whether by divorce or by death of one spouse, each spouse is entitled to half of total property of both spouses excluding such property as either had before marriage or received as a gift or by way of inheritance during marriage or non-assignable rights or property in respect of which parties agreed that they are not to be taken into consideration. In event of death of a spouse, his heirs succeed to his rights under Law.

Law further contains provisions as to details of assessment of value, of preventing attempts of alienation in order to defeat provisions of law, and confers extensive jurisdiction upon court in application of provisions. Law does not affect such jurisdiction as is conferred upon Religious Courts but these Courts must apply provisions of Law unless both parties agreed to be judged by Religious Law. Law makes necessary amendments in Law of Succession in order to secure spouses rights according to provisions of this Law.

See also Divorce.

MINES:

Mines and minerals are the property of the state and their exploitation is governed by the Mining Ordinance of 1925, as amended. Licences for prospecting or exploring mines or for minerals may be obtained from the competent government department, and concessions are granted by the State. Mining rights or mining leases are obtainable on terms to be agreed with the State.

Oil.—The Oil Law of 1953 provides for prospecting and mining licences and regulations in regard to exploitation of mineral resources in Israel, particularly in respect of prospecting for oil and oil concessions.

National Energy Authority.—Set up by 1977 law to plan, develop and regulate sources and consumption of energy in Israel, taking over Governmental functions under Mining Ordinance and Petroleum Law.

See also topic Taxation.

MONOPOLIES AND RESTRAINT OF TRADE:

See topic Restrictive Trade Practice.

MORTGAGES:

Immovable property may be mortgaged to secure any debt or obligation. Mortgage of immovable property requires registration at District Registry in which land is situate. Mortgage fee of 1% is chargeable. Mortgage on immovable property not registered is not valid. Mortgage on land is realized by order of court or of Execution Office. Any provision denying mortgagor right to repay loan at any time is invalid.

Any mortgage pledge or charge created by company and not registered with Registrar of Companies within 21 days is void against a liquidator or any creditor.

For mortgage of chattels see topic Pledges.

Israel ships may be mortgaged by documents executed: (a) abroad, before an Israel diplomatic or consular delegate and approved by him; (b) in Israel, before Registrar of harbour of registration of ship. Mortgages must be recorded with Registrar of Ships. Mortgage on a ship is foreclosed or executed by order of Admiralty Court.

MOTOR VEHICLES:

Motor vehicles have to be licensed annually. Drivers are also licensed biennially by reference to type of vehicle driven. Age limit is 17½, in respect of all vehicles other than motorcycles. Age limit in respect of motorcycles is 16. All vehicles must carry third party insurance. Transfers of vehicles are effected by Deed of Sale recorded with licensing authority. Identification marks are applied to various types of vehicles, by reference to registry offices. Speed limit is 50 kilometres in built-up areas, 80 kilometres in open country and 100 kilometres (at present restricted to 90 km) on fast motorways. There is detailed road-code and substantial penalties for breaches. Security belt law enacted.

Certain restrictions apply temporarily in regard to the transfer of vehicles as a result of present war conditions. Normally bona fide transactions are approved. Special provisions apply in regard to public vehicles including omnibuses and taxis, and their transfer is substantially restricted.

MOVEABLES:

Moveables Law 1971 grants to owner of moveables same rights against wrongful possession and trespass as Land Law 1969 grants in respect of immoveables. Joint ownership is over undivided whole with right to claim partition. See topic Landlord and Tenant.

NATIONAL SERVICE:

The Security Service Law, 1959, replaces all previous laws in this connection. Under the provisions of the law, every male resident of Israel from the age of 18 to 26 must serve 30 months compulsory service in the Army, and from the age of 27 to 29, 24 months.

Unmarried women from the age of 18 to 26 must serve 24 months. In the Reserves, every man up to the age of 39 years must serve one month per year and from the age of 40 to 49 years, 14 days per year. Unmarried women and married women without children up to the age of 34 years must serve one month per year. All soldiers on the reserve list are paid partly by the Army and partly by their employers.

NOTARIES PUBLIC:

All existing laws and regulations governing Notaries Public have been repealed by a 1976 Notaries Law. Notary must be Israeli citizen, member of Bar, who practises as an advocate in Israel 15 years or, if he is 65 years of age, or is a new immigrant, ten years. New law defines authority of notary, lays down procedure to be followed and code of professional ethics, confers on his confirmations status of lawfully sufficient proof of their contents; and enumerates acts which must be confirmed by him. Notary may be tried in an action before disciplinary courts of Bar, with appeal to Supreme Court. Israel diplomatic and consular representatives overseas are authorised to act as Notaries.

PARTNERSHIPS: See Associations.

PATENTS:

Patent Law was enacted in 1967.

Application.—An inventor or any person deriving title to an invention under him, whether product or process which is new, useful and susceptible of industrial or agricultural application may apply for grant of patent. Patent is granted to person who first validly applied for it in Israel, except that where owner's application for protection has already been filed in one of Convention countries, date of foreign application is deemed to be date of application filed in Israel, if application in Israel has been filed within 12 months after filing of other application.

Patent application is filed at office of Registrar of Patents in Jerusalem, and may be filed through an attorney.

Term of a patent is 20 years from date of application for patent provided that renewal fees are paid on their due dates.

Certain exploitation rights are reserved in favour of persons who prior to application date, have in good faith exploited invention in Israel.

Concept of novelty applied is that of universal novelty.

Opposition and Revocation.—Opposition to grant of a patent may be made within three months from date of publication of application in Reshumot (Government Official Gazette).

Patent may be revoked by Registrar on grounds on which opposition to grant of patent may be made, namely that invention is not patentable or that opponent and not applicant is owner of invention or if there exists another reason for which Registrar is entitled to refuse application in accordance with provisions of Law.

Licences may be granted by patentee. A licence under a patent is not effective in respect of any party other than parties to licence unless licence has been registered.

Certain rights are reserved to State in respect of use of patents which are required for security of State. Appropriate Minister may permit exploitation of patent by Government departments if it is necessary to do so in interest of defence of State or maintenance of essential supply and services. However, when such permission is given, owner of invention is entitled to compensation whether in form of royalties or otherwise, as detailed in Law. If Registrar is satisfied that owners of a patent have a monopoly which is misused he may grant a licence to exploit patent to a person who has applied for and paid prescribed fee, provided application is filed after expiration of three years from date on which patent was granted, or four years from date of filing of patent application, whichever is later.

Compulsory licence may also be ordered if it is necessary to assure public of a reasonable quantity of medical supplies. Detailed provisions are contained in Law in regard to factors to be taken into account in granting a compulsory licence, conditions of licence including payment of royalties.

Patents are assignable. Patentee may also charge patent or income thereof. Assignment and charge have to be registered.

Designs can be registered under Patents and Designs Ordinance of 1925 as am'd in respect of one or more class or classes of goods. A certificate of registration is granted by Registrar. On registration of a design proprietor of design is entitled to copyright in design for five years, and period may be renewed from time to time for five years up to three cycles of five years each.

An amendment to Ordinance brings Israel law in line with Hague International Convention for Protection of Industrial Property to which Israel has now become a signatory. A design may no longer be eliminated from Register because it is in use abroad, and not in Israel. Registration in Israel of a patent or design registered abroad receives preference over an application registered after date of foreign application, if registered in Israel within 12 or six months respectively after registration in any of signatory countries of convention. (Book of Laws, No. 99, of 12.6.52).

PLEDGES:

Law of pledges is contained in a law with effect from Oct. 1, 1967.

Pledge is a charge on chattel as security for debt and creditor may recoup from pledge if debt not discharged. Pledge is created by agreement between debtor and creditor. Pledge serves as security for interest, costs and damages due from debtor. Debtor may repledge chattel to a further creditor, but prior creditor takes precedence; if, however, prior creditor agrees, later creditor may have equal rights (pari passu).

Any profits from pledge are subject to pledge unless agreed otherwise.

In case of nonpayment, execution is obtained by court order, except in case of banks where such order is not required.

On cessation of debt, rights of pledge terminate and debtor may demand return of pledge.

PRACTICE:

Consolidated and revised Rules of Court in civil actions came into effect on Nov. 1, 1963. Actions are commenced by a statement of claim, answered by statement of defense. English procedure is closely followed with rights of request for further particulars, discovery of documents and interrogatories. New rules provide for preliminary settling of issues by court where necessary. Procedure in cases against Government is same as for other cases.

PRESCRIPTION:

See topics Adverse Possession; Limitation of Actions.

PRINCIPAL AND AGENT:

Comprehensive code covering law of principal and agent was recently promulgated as Agency Law of 1965. Law sets out duties and rights of agents. No special formality is required to establish any agency relationship, and agent may be granted unlimited or limited authority. Corporation may be appointed as agent.

Power of attorney authorising person to act as agent in respect of lands or rights in land must be in writing and in certain cases, especially if irrevocable, copy of power of attorney has to be deposited with Betterment Tax Authority and may be subject to payment of Betterment Tax.

Person entrusted with possession of assets or their management, is required, if ten years have passed since grant of authority, to advise Administrator-General of existence of the power or authority. No transaction relating to immovables may be given effect by virtue of power of attorney after expiration of ten years from date of appointment, except with authority of appointor or with leave of court.

Agents for purchase of military equipment of all kinds for Israel Army or Defence Ministry may not receive commission unless permit granted by Defence Minister.

REAL PROPERTY:

See topic Land.

RECEIVERS:

A comprehensive code in regard to liquidators is contained in the Companies Ordinance in respect of winding up of companies. Receivers may be appointed in pending proceedings by way of interlocutory remedy or by judgment. Receivers may also be appointed under a debenture according to its terms. Receivers appointed by a court are officers of the court and must submit certain periodical returns and obtain the discharge from the court. See also topic Executions.

RECORDS:

The only system of formal records is the recording at the District Land Registry of land dispositions, including sales, exchanges, leases exceeding three years and mortgages. There is a limited system of recording of documents before the Public Notary (power of attorney and pledges), and for registration of ships (transfers of ships and mortgages), registration of patents and designs, and registration of trade marks. See also Patents; Shipping; Trade Marks.

REPORTS: See topic Law Reports, Codes, Etc.

RESTRICTIVE TRADE PRACTICE:

Under Restrictive Trade Law, 1959, every "restrictive arrangement" or agreement, i.e., any arrangement or agreement which includes restrictive instructions in reference to price, profits, quality, quantity, marketing, etc., has to be registered with the competent Registrar. Restrictive arrangements which are not so registered and which are not accepted for registration by the Registrar are illegal and considered as an offence for which the offender is liable to receive a penalty. All registered arrangements are open to the public unless otherwise determined by the Registrar. Similar provisions apply in reference to monopolies. By 1963 Law of Standard Contracts, restrictive conditions in standard agreements for supply of goods or services are invalid unless approved by Council set up under Restrictive Trade Practices Law 1959. Restrictive conditions are such as limit normal contractual rights of purchaser as against supplier.

By amending 1973 Law, a monopolist, may not refuse to supply or acquire a commodity or service, in respect of which monopoly exists, except according to accepted trade usage.

SALES:

Sales Law 1968 governs sales of all assets whether movable or immovable but may be contracted out. Usage of parties or of trade may govern sale. Seller is bound to deliver property and transfer ownership therein, delivery being by putting property at disposition of purchaser. If no time is set for delivery there is an implied condition of reasonable time and delivery takes place at place of business of seller. Seller does not fulfil his duty if he does not deliver amount ordered or property of a different nature than that ordered or which does not comply with sample or to accepted usage or which in any other way does not comply with contract. Purchaser may not rely on such unsuitability if he knew of it at time of signing of contract. Purchaser has a duty to inspect property on receipt and must advise vendor immediately of unsuitability. In case of latent defects in goods, purchaser has two years within which to give notice of unsuitability.

Remedies are same as for ordinary breach of contract. In case of unsuitability, purchaser also has right of deduction from price.

International Sale of Goods.—Sale (International Sale of Goods) Law 1971 adopted, for Israel, Uniform Law on International Sale of Goods. Law is now in force.

Purchaser's Bona Fides.—Rule that a bona fide purchaser of movables in ordinary course of vendor's business, acquires clear ownership, is not affected by fact that said movable was pledged and notice was entered in Register of Pledges. Bona fides for purpose of law of sales, is not necessarily excluded by omission to examine Register of Pledges, even if such omission is negligent.

Sale of Flats.—Special 1974 Law regulates mode of securing monies paid by a purchaser of a flat to seller by providing that if purchaser pays more than 15% of price of flat, seller must either give purchaser a bank guarantee securing all sums paid if for any reason transfer cannot take place, or obtain a policy of insurance from an insurance company covering liability to repay in such a case to purchaser sums paid by him or mortgage flat or a proportional part of area on which it is to be built to secure such repayment or enter a note of sale in Land Registry books provided no mortgage is registered, or transfer ownership to purchaser.

Law provides penalties for breach of this provision.

Protection of Consumers Law 1981 provides penalties for exploitation and misleading of customers in sales and services for private purposes. Customers are to be given full and correct information, regarding goods sold and price thereof in credit and instalment sales.

See also topic Contracts.

SEALS:

There is no necessity for seals on private instruments. Corporations are required to have an official seal which is to be fixed on deeds and other documents which by virtue of the statutes of the particular corporation require the corporate seal.

Municipal corporations have a corporate seal. The seal of the State of Israel is affixed to particular instruments of a very special class. The Minister of Justice is in charge of the State Seal.

SECURITIES:

There is a limited supervision by Ministry of Finance on issue of securities in respect of large issues exceeding IS.100,000. License for issue of these securities is required. This limitation was intended as a war measure and is being maintained. In bona fide transactions licence is normally granted. Application is made through Ministry of Justice. These limitations apply to companies only, and do not apply to normal current borrowing without security and similar commercial transactions. Under Mutual Investment Trust Law, 1961, a company, objects of which are to make as trustee mutual investment in securities, must have a paid capital of not less than IS.400,000 and must be connected with another company which will deal with securities.

Securities Law 1968 sets up a Securities Authority to watch over interests of public investing in securities. Offer of securities to public is forbidden except by way of a prospectus permitted by Authority. Law imposes civil liability on directors and experts to purchasers in respect of contents or prospectus. Any person purchasing securities relying on an erroneous statement in prospectus has a right of rescission within a reasonable time. Provisions of law also apply to securities in Israeli companies offered abroad. Authority has power to waive provisions of law in respect of securities of a company registered abroad if satisfied that laws of country of registration adequately safeguard Israeli investors.

By 1981 Amendment "insider trading" by persons holding 10% or more in corporation where shares issued to public or dealt in on Stock Exchange, and by persons holding position in such corporation giving them access to inside information becomes criminal offence punishable by imprisonment or fine; excepted are bona fide transactions, e.g. purchase of qualifying shares, transactions by trustee, liquidator, receiver, transactions by bona fide written contract.

SHIPPING:

A substantial part of the shipping law was embodied in the Shipping (Vessels) Law 1960 dealing primarily with shipping registration and ships' mortgages. Certain parts of the (English) Merchant Shipping Act 1894 have been applied and still apply to Israel.

Ministry of Communications is in charge of maritime matters including the enforcement of the shipping laws. See also topic Mortgages.

Under Ports Authority Law of 1961, Ports Authority was constituted as a separate legal entity and, pursuant to said law, control of ports and their management is vested in Ports Authority.

Shipping (Sailors) Law 1973 regulates conditions necessary to become a sailor both of Israeli and non-Israeli citizens. It provides means of supervision and disciplinary action. Council is appointed to plan, control and supervise examinations. Law defines authority and rights of captain, and regulates his duties both on land and on high seas. It also regulates discipline, and work distribution, salary and other rights of crew and deals with offences.

STATUTES:

Statutes are published regularly in Official Gazette and there are annual volumes. There is an official translation into English of Statutes known as Laws of State of Israel which may be purchased from Government Printer.

TAXATION:

Operation Peace in the Galilee Finance Law 5742–1982.—(a)Levy of 2% is payable on sales of all securities by Israel residents whether same is registered on Tel-Aviv Stock Exchange or on foreign exchange or traded over the counter, and on sales by nonresidents of securities registered on Tel-Aviv Stock Exchange; (b) compulsory loan, repayment of which linked to 80% of increase of cost of living index with linked interest of 1% per annum, or linked to representative rate of exchange between Shekel and U.S. Dollar is deductible from all salaries and income up to defined maximums. Loan is repayable with linkage differentials and interest in four equal annual instalments 1993–1996.

Income Tax.—Income Tax Law was codified in 1961. New Law brings up to date and incorporates in a comprehensive code the provisions of 1947 Ordinance and subsequent amendments.

Income tax is payable on income of any person arising in, derived from or received in Israel from any business, profession or employment as well as from dividends, interest and linkage differences, annuities, rents, premiums, royalties and other profits or gains. Special provisions impose tax on gains from share redemption, bond-washing, waiver of debts, stock options and fringe benefits of employees. Non-capital business expense of obtaining income is deductible, including depreciation at fixed rates on cost of business assets, interest and linkage differences on business loans. Deduction of travel and entertainment expense is restricted.

Capital and revenue expense on approved research projects in industry, agriculture, transport or energy allowed as deduction from tax year 1981. If project not approved, expense allowed in three equal annual instalments from year of outlay.

For tax year 1980, 10% of chargeable income allowed as special inflation deduction. Special inflation deduction extended to tax year 1981 with minimum 10% and maximum 50% of inventories not exceeding 15% of chargeable income. For tax years 1982, 1983, 1984 see Income Tax Law (Taxation in Inflationary Conditions) 5732–1982. Finance Minister has power to extend 1982 Law beyond 1984; otherwise it lapses.

All businesses and professions are required to keep accounts in accordance with rules. Noncompliance involves penalties and loss of tax benefits under law.

Individuals pay tax on chargeable income at progressive rates, i.e.: 25% (earned or rental income), 35%, 45%, 50%, 60%. Amounts charged at each rate are adjusted periodically for index changes. Surtax of 10% is imposed on tax due on income exceeding IS. 3,300,000 for Tax Year 1983 and on this amount adjusted to cost of living index for 1984. Reduced rates may be charged on pay for shift work in industry. Tax credits are allowed for resident taxpayer and wife. Additional credits allowed for new immigrants and for soldiers entering industry or agriculture at end of compulsory military service. Child allowances now given as cash grants by National Insurance. These grants are exempt from tax except where taxpayer entitled to allowances for no more than three children and whose income is liable to tax at 50% rate or more (as from 1/12/83). As to companies and cooperative societies, see below.

Exemptions.—The following persons and institutions are exempt from income tax either totally or partially: municipal and local councils; public institutions for promotion of religion, charity, education and charitable trusts; pension funds; cooperative societies not deriving their income from nonmembers; blind persons in respect of earned income not exceeding IS.70,800; diplomatic representatives and consular officers in regular service of foreign states in respect of salaries and emoluments payable for such services; members of Knesset (Israel Legislature) in respect of salaries and emoluments (there is no similar exemption relating to ministers); war invalids, victims of hostile action or Nazi persecution and dependents of deceased members of fighting services in respect of pensions payable by government; temporary resident in respect of income derived from property abroad, provided he did not reside in Israel for more than six months in year preceding to year of assessment and does not intend to stay permanently in country; linkage differences received by individuals on sale of assets, compensation on expropriation of land, cancellation of sale of assets, claims for damages, private loans to another individual, provided such linkage differences are not liable as trade or professional income; linkage differences on Government loans not held for trading; exchange differences on individual's foreign currency deposits (exemption limited to IS.50,000 if from business); on loan from nonresident, in company if majority of shares in foreign currency held by nonresidents; on foreign currency deposits of payments by nonresidents on account of share purchases; income of nonresident from employment in Israel is exempt if period of stay does not exceed 90 days and amount earned not more than IS.5,000; new residents in respect of income received from abroad for first seven years of residence; nonresidents in respect of interest on foreign currency term deposits; income from agriculture in certain defined development areas. See also topic Investment Law.

Regulations under Oil Law 1953 grant income tax benefits including special treatment for exploration expenses and depletion allowances.

Companies Tax.—Corporate bodies pay Company Tax at rate of 40% of chargeable income and Income Tax at rate of 35% of chargeable income after deducting amount paid by way of Company Tax. Total tax accordingly amounts to 61%. Dividends paid are deducted from income chargeable to income tax (see below as to withholding tax).

Special tax benefits are granted as from 1/4/1968 under Law for Encouragement of Industry (Taxes)-1969 to companies owning industrial undertakings. These benefits comprise deductions for accelerated depreciation, amortisation of patent rights and know-how payments, additional depreciation or revised cost base reflecting change in exchange rates 1967-1975, exchange differences on loan repayments, 10% income tax rate on profits reinvested in development. Reduced income tax rate was withdrawn as from tax year 1975 but renewed at 20% from tax year 1978. Further benefits from tax year 1978 include accelerated depreciation for leased equipment, relief for inflationary increases of inventory values, exemption from capital gains on conversion of private company to public company. Corporate groups may submit consolidated balance sheets for income tax purposes, enabling intercompany set off of losses between industrial members of

group, but only for year of consolidated return. Company amalgamations, where approved by special committee, may be effected with exemption from all taxes on transfers of assets and/or shares arising out of such amalgamation, and with spread allowance of preamalgamation losses against future profits. Supreme Court has confirmed that noncompliance with accounting rules involves loss of benefits under this Law. Company, shareholders of which are all members of one family, i.e. spouse, brothers, sisters, parents, grandparents, grandchildren and their respective spouses, major shareholder may claim treatment as noncorporate taxpayer. For tax year 1980 20% of capital but not exceeding 15% and not less than 10% of chargeable income allowed as special inflation deduction. For tax year 1981 minimum 10% deduction is allowed but ceiling extended to 50% of inventories and for companies within Law for Encouragement of Industry to 75% of capital or 50% of inventories but not exceeding 25% of chargeable income. For tax years 1982, 1983, 1984 see Income Tax Law (Taxation under Inflationary Conditions) 5732–1982.

All arrears of tax are charged with interest and linkage differences which are allowed as deductions from income. Interest and linkage differences are allowed on overpayments but treated as chargeable income.

Income Tax Law (Taxation in Inflationary Conditions) 5732–1982.—This complex law, applicable to tax years 1982, 1983 and 1984, provides mechanism for establishing real values of assets, liabilities and capital of business in determining their taxable income. Encouragement of Industry (Taxes) Law 1969 and Income Tax Ordinance have been amended to conform to this Law.

Main elements of this Law are as follows: In order to compensate for erosion of equity caused by inflation "entitled assessees" are granted deduction from chargeable income up to 50% thereof for tax years 1982, 1983 and 1984. Entitled assessee is body of persons or partnership, keeping proper double entry accounts on which income tax reports are based. Deduction is amount equal to difference adjusted for cost of living index increase during tax year, between "positive components" and "negative components" in entitled assessee's balance sheet. "Positive components" are total of equity if positive and amounts added thereto during year. "Negative components" are equity if negative, "protected assets" and amounts reducing equity during year. Detailed definitions of each of above "components" are provided in Law. "Protected assets" are generally speaking assets which are not considered to decline in value in inflationary conditions or which enjoy special tax benefits or government assistance. Further points to be noted are as follows: Special deduction of 5% for companies and 30% for individuals; index adjustment of depreciation allowances on protected assets; stocks and shares dealt in on Tel-Aviv Stock Exchange or on any other Stock Exchange approved by Minister of Finance, are "unprotected assets" but increase in their market in each tax year is treated as addition to taxable business income. This addition includes sales proceeds during year. Not applicable to shares in companies in which assessee holds 10% voting interest directly or indirectly. Such shares are regarded as "protected assets"; no inflationary amount allowed on sale of unprotected capital assets and capital assets sold in tax year in which acquired; no accelerated depreciation allowed except under Encouragement of Capital Investment Law 1959; special provisions for financial institutions, insurance companies, assessees keeping books on single entry basis or legally unacceptable double entry basis or failing to keep proper books.

Research Investment.—1983 Law grants tax deduction to taxpayers purchasing convertible debentures or shares (participation units) issued by entitled companies with Government approval to finance scientific research on new or improved products for export. Proceeds of issue are held on dollar linked interest bearing deposit by government until required. Research expenditure out of these deposits is not deductible for income-tax but deposits are included in equity for calculation of deduction under Income Tax Law (Taxation in Inflationary Conditions)—(see above). Entitled companies must export goods produced from results of research of prescribed minimum annual value. If license to manufacture outside Israel is granted minimum royalty is payable to Government.

Sanctions are imposed for noncompliance with conditions for benefits.

Dividends.—Income Tax at the rate of 35% is withheld on payment of dividends if company is registered on Tel Aviv Stock Exchange, otherwise 45% unless lower rate fixed by special law, e.g. see topic Investment Law. 25% is withheld from dividends paid to nonresidents.

Capital Profit Tax.—By 1975 new law basis for calculating this tax has been changed. Briefly, purchase price is divided by cost of living index at time of purchase, and multiplied by cost of living index at time of resale. This is called adjusted purchase price. That part of profit on sale, equal to difference between original and adjusted purchase price is called "inflationary excess" and is taxed at 10% of such difference. Balance of profit on sale is taxed at 61% in case of corporations, and at rate of income tax applicable to an individual according to his total income. Where asset sold was acquired by inheritance after 31/3/81, cost of purchase by deceased is taken for calculating profit on sale. Amounts spent on asset sold as taxes, rates, depreciation and repairs are deductible and brought into calculation of adjusted purchase price after index adjustment. Profit on sale of assets purchased before 1948 is taxed at special rate of 12% and rate increases 1% per year for every year after 1948 and up to 1960. Sales of assets purchased after 1960 are taxed at normal rates as above. This is subject to ceiling rate of 50%. New law applies to all transactions completed after July 7, 1975.

Double Taxation.—Agreements are in force with U.K., Sweden, France, Finland, W. Germany, Denmark, Norway, Austria and Singapore, Holland, Italy, Belgium, Canada and South Africa. Mutual exemption has been agreed with many countries with regard to shipping and aviation profits. Unilateral relief may also be granted in certain circumstances.

Estate Tax.—Repealed in relation to estates of persons deceased after 31/3/81. Capital Profit Tax and Betterment Tax Laws adjusted so that profit on sale of asset inherited after 31/3/81 includes increment accrued during lifetime of deceased. See topic Capital Profit Tax.

Property Tax.—As from 1/4/81 Property Tax is charged only on market value of land on Oct. 1, preceding year of assessment.

Purchase tax may be applied by the Minister of Finance to certain commodities. It has been applied to a large range of commodities and the usual rate is 35% of the wholesale price. Purchase tax on certain luxury items increased, as of Aug. 21, 1983.

Imports.—Importers required to deposit 15% of cost of goods imported from abroad, from June 1, 1983.

Betterment Tax.—Imposed on sales of land, house property and rights in land. This tax is calculated on substantially same basis as Capital Profit Tax (see above). As from 10/7/78 sale of private dwellings exempted provided owner has not made exempt sale in previous four years.

Value Added Tax (VAT).—This is an entirely new tax in Israel, and is therefore treated more fully. It is imposed in Israel from July 1, 1976, is in nature of sales tax and is charged on all taxable transactions in Israel and on imports to Israel. Taxable transaction includes sale of asset or supply of services by taxable person in course of his business and also sale of asset used by taxable person in course of his business. Taxable person is person who sells asset or supplies services in course of his business. Isolated transactions of commercial nature and any sale of real estate to taxable person other than financial institution or non-profit organization are also included.

Tax is paid by taxable person as percentage of sale price of asset sold or of service supplied and amount of tax is included in invoice given to customer. Customer in his turn may if he himself is taxable person deduct tax included in invoice and paid by him from amount of any tax which he himself has to pay on sales or services supplied by him. If customer is not taxable person he cannot set off tax which he paid at time of purchase or receipt of services against any other VAT.

Rate of tax in force as from Aug. 1, 1982 is 15%. There are number of transactions exempted from tax such as letting of living accommodation for period not exceeding ten years, letting of any property for key money, transactions of business with annual turnover of less than IS.64,400 and import of goods exempt from customs duty by virtue of international treaties and import of goods for diplomatic staff insofar as exempt from customs.

Certain other transactions are not charged with tax and are described as "zero-rated." These include goods imported by person entitled to purchase them free of Purchase Tax, e.g. an immigrant, hotel accommodation and services including car-hire supplied to foreign tourists, purchase of air and sea tickets, air and sea transport, sale of specified fruit and vegetables. Where taxable person has effected zero-rated transaction as distinct from an exempt transaction, he is entitled to set off any VAT paid by him in connection with any purchases made or services provided by him in connection with such zero-rated transaction.

Financial institutions such as banks and insurance companies are taxed VAT on different basis, namely on percentage of their income chargeable to tax under the Income Tax Ordinance and also on percentage of total salaries and wages as assessed to income tax. Present rate is 12%. Non-profit organizations are also liable to VAT on amount of salaries and wages paid by them unless such amount is less than IS.14,700 annually. Present rate is 5%.

Employer's Tax.—Employer pays 7% on payroll. Exemption granted to industrial undertakings within Encouragement of Industry (Taxes) 1969 Law, farms, companies where 70% of goods sold are exports of Israel industrial or agricultural products, hotels, housing construction. Tax is paid together with income tax deducted from payroll by employer.

Municipal Rates.—Under Municipalities and Local Authorities Ordinances local governments impose tax on buildings and occupied land. Tax is based on area of chargeable assets, location, use and type of building and is payable annually by occupier. Arrears are charged with interest and linkage differences.

Stamp Duty.—A comprehensive system of taxes in the form of a stamp duty is fixed by the Stamp Duty on Documents Law, 1961, which provides for stamps to be affixed on certain classes of documents. Rates of duty are either fixed or ad valorem.

Customs Duty.—Customs are payable in respect of import of commodities subject to substantial list of exempted articles. Duty is either fixed or ad valorem. Many tariffs subject to limitation under General Agreement on Tariffs and Trade with European Economic Community.

Israel has concluded trade and customs agreements with European Economic Community and customs duties are to be progressively reduced on imports from member nations.

TRADEMARKS AND TRADENAMES:

Under Trade Marks Ordinance, trade marks are registered with Registrar of Trade Marks. A trade mark is defined as a mark used upon or in connection with goods for purpose of indicating that they are goods of proprietor of such mark by virtue of manufacture, selection, survey, or dealing with or offering for sale. Trade marks capable of registration must consist of characters, devices or marks or combinations thereof which have a distinctive character. Application for registration is advertised, and opposition may be made within three months of advertisement. Period of duration of trade mark rights is seven years from

date of registration, but this period may be renewed for 14 years from expiration of original registration, or of last renewal.

Under Trade Mark Law of 1965, trade mark may be transferred even if goodwill connected therewith is not transferred. Further, licence to use trade mark may be granted by owner of mark. Such licence is subject to registration with Registrar of Trade Marks. In addition, following Lisbon Treaty of 1958, use of name of place of origin with reference to quality may be protected if product originates from such place and its qualitites are connected therewith.

Under Section 11A of Ordinance, introduced in 1965, Registrar may, subject to certain qualifications, allow registration of a mark registered in its country of origin, notwithstanding that it might not otherwise qualify for registration.

Tradenames.—See topic Business Names.

TREATIES:

Civil Procedure.—Israel is party to Convention on Service Abroad of Judicial and Extrajudicial Documents in Civil or Commercial Matters, and to Convention on Taking of Evidence Abroad in Civil or Commercial Matters. (Regulation for the execution of the Hague Convention [Civil Procedure] 1954).

Israel is party to United Nations Convention on Recognition and Enforcement of Foreign Arbitral Awards.

Extradition Treaties.—Israel has signed following bilateral Extradition Treaties: Belgium (1956), Italy (1956), Luxembourg (1956), Netherlands (1956), France (1958), Switzerland (1958), South Africa (1959), United Kingdom (1960), Austria (1961), U.S.A. (1961), Sweden (1963), Canada (1967), Swaziland (1970).

Double Taxation.—§196 of Income Tax Ordinance empowers Minister of Finance to issue Order giving effect to Treaty made with another State for Relief of Double Taxation, regardless of anything contrary thereto in Ordinance.

Treaties are in force with following countries:

Sweden	—effective 22.12.59 by Order 20.7.61.
Great Britain & N. Ireland	—effective 1.4.61 by Order 25.4.63, revision effective 1.4.68 by Order 18.11.71.
France	—effective 1.4.61 by Order 3.3.66.
Finland	—effective 1.4.65 by Order 12.5.66.
Federal Republic of West Germany	—effective 1.4.61 by Order 19.1.67, revision effective 1.4.70 by Order 26.12.80.
Italy	—effective 1.4.62 by Order 27.6.74.
Denmark	—effective 1.4.65 by Order 20.4.67.
Norway	—effective 1.4.65 by Order 13.6.68.
Austria	—effective 1.4.68 by Order 27.1.72.
Singapore	—effective 1.4.71 by Order 28.5.72.
Holland	—effective 1.4.70 by Order 12.2.75.
Belgium	—effective 1.4.75 by Order 7.7.76.
Canada	—effective 27.7.76 by Order 14.6.77.
South Africa	—effective 27.5.80 by Order 21.5.81.

Customs Duty.—Israel is party to General Agreement on Trade and Tariffs (GATT), and to many Conventions affecting customs duties of which principal ones are Convention concerning creation of International Union for Publication of Customs Tariffs (Brussels) effective 1956, Lisbon Names of Origin Convention effective 1966, Brussels Convention on Nomenclature for Classification of Goods in Customs Tariffs effective 1970, Kyoto Convention for Simplification and Harmonisation of Customs Formalities effective 1977.

Trade Agreements.—Israel signed Agreement with European Economic Community in 1970.

Many bilateral treaties affecting aerial and maritime navigation, commerce, tourism, economic, scientific and cultural cooperation have been signed and are published in Official Treaties Gazette.

TRUSTS:

Nature of trusteeship, duties of trustees, formation of private trusts, charitable trusts and public trusts are defined in Law of Trusteeship 1979.

Trusteeship is defined as relationship to asset requiring trustee to hold such asset or act on behalf of beneficiary or for any other object. Trusteeship may be created by law, by agreement with trustee or by deed of charitable trust, which must be in writing signed in presence of notary or created by will in writing, or bequest under will. If trust is of public nature, registration (with Registrar of Trusts) and publication required. Law also provides for creation of companies for advantage of community requiring licence from Minister of Justice, approval as public institution for tax purposes, declaration by court that its objects are charitable; registration is necessary.

Duties of trustees and supervisory powers of courts are referred to in Law generally, but more detailed regulations are laid down for trusteeship in special cases, e.g. under Law of Inheritance, Law of Guardianship and Legal Capacity.

Trust (Mutual Investment Funds).—Mutual Investment Funds Law of 1961 allows establishment of mutual investment funds. It regulates constitution of the fund and its operations and, subject to compliance with provisions of the law, exempts income of the fund from company tax, and the income tax does not exceed 25%. Income derived from the realisation of securities of an approved mutual fund is free from income tax.

WAREHOUSEMEN:

There are no special provisions in regard to warehousemen, except in respect to licensed warehouses approved by the Director of Customs. There are two classes of licensed warehouses, viz., (a) general warehouses to be used for the warehousing of goods generally, and (b) private warehouses to be used only for the warehousing of goods which are the property of the licensee. Licensed warehouses are only warehouses in which dutiable goods may be warehoused prior to the payment of the duty.

General rules as to bailment are now governed by Bailees Law, 1967.

WATER:

Under the Water Law, 1959 the State acquired ownership of all the water resources in the country. The law entitles all persons to use water only in accordance with the provisions of the law. The objects of the law are to preserve water supplies, to prevent their decrease and pollution and to utilise the water resources for development purposes of the country.

WILLS:

Detailed provisions in regard to capacity to make a will and appropriate form of will are now contained in Inheritance Law 1965.

Will may be in writing or may be made verbally. Holograph will need not be attested. Any other written will must be signed by testator in presence of two witnesses at least. Witnesses must confirm execution of will by testator in their joint presence.

Will may be declared or signed before judge or registrar of civil court or before judge of religious court.

There is no limitation on right of disposition by will. Earlier limitations were abolished.

Capacity to make will is determined by law of place of residence of testator at time will is made, but will is valid in form if made in accordance with Israeli law or in accordance with law of place where it was made or law of residence of deceased when will was made or at time of his death. When testator is not a resident of Israel, will is valid if it is in accordance with form recognised by national law of deceased.

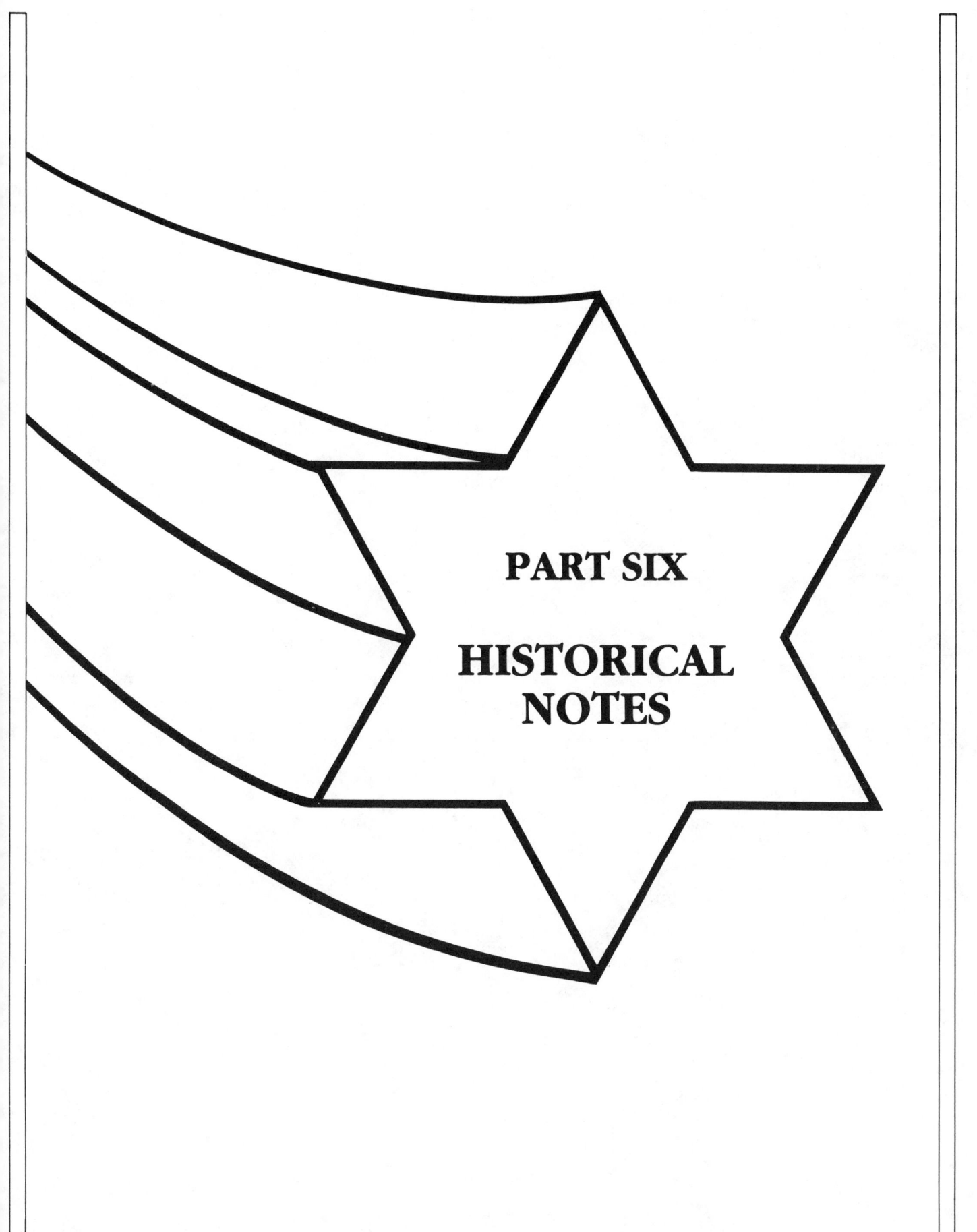

PART SIX

HISTORICAL
NOTES

28

Page One: The State of Israel as Seen in *The New York Times*

"All the News That's Fit to Print"

The New York Times.

LATE CITY EDITION
Cloudy with showers today. Partly cloudy and cooler tomorrow.
Temperature Yesterday—Max., 64; Min., 47
Sunrise today, 5:48 A.M.; Sunset, 7:59 P.M.

Copyright. 1945, by The New York Times Company.

VOL. XCIV..No. 31,881.

Entered as Second-Class Matter,
Postoffice, New York, N. Y.

NEW YORK, TUESDAY, MAY 8, 1945.

THREE CENTS NEW YORK CITY

THE WAR IN EUROPE IS ENDED!
SURRENDER IS UNCONDITIONAL;
V-E WILL BE PROCLAIMED TODAY;
OUR TROOPS ON OKINAWA GAIN

ISLAND-WIDE DRIVE

Marines Reach Village a Mile From Naha and Army Lines Advance

7 MORE SHIPS SUNK

Search Planes Again Hit Japan's Life Line— Kyushu Bombed

By WARREN MOSCOW
By Wireless to The New York Times

GUAM, Tuesday, May 8—In an island-wide American advance on Okinawa yesterday the First Marine Division drove south to the edge of Dakeshi Village, about a mile from Naha, the capital, straightening out the line on our right flank. In the center the Seventy-seventh Army Division used flame-throwing tanks for considerable advances, while the Seventh Army Division moved forward on the left flank.

[Airfields on Kyushu, southern Japan, were bombed Monday and Tuesday by Superfortresses, two of which were lost in heavy air opposition.

[Allied fliers started operating from the Tarakan airfield although fighting continued on that island off Borneo, and in the Philippines American troops made advances on Mindanao and Luzon.]

Japanese Dead at 36,535

As the United States forces on Okinawa resumed their drive, Fleet Admiral Chester W. Nimitz revealed that Japanese killed on the island had mounted to 36,535 on Monday, showing that the Americans were maintaining their rate of 1,000 a day.

The Americans have not yet taken the main Japanese artillery emplacements on Okinawa, which were the principal targets of the fleet off the island. The fleet's guns continued yesterday, along with carrier aircraft, to support the ground movements.

Meanwhile search bombers of Fleet Air Wing 1 continued to give an impressive demonstration of what the "tightening air blockade of Japan will mean. Attacking at mast-head height with bombs and machine guns, these long-range aircraft, based in the Okinawa area, sank four more ships in waters off Korea and damaged five others.

The ships sunk were a large cargo ship, a medium cargo ship, a medium oiler and a large fleet tanker. Two small freighters were

Continued on Page 12, Column 2

Leopold Rescued By 7th Army Troops

By The Associated Press

WITH THE UNITED STATES SEVENTH ARMY, Tuesday, May 8—Leopold III, King of Belgium, and his wife, Princess Rethy, have been liberated by the Seventh Army, it was announced today.

They were found near Strobl, eight miles east of Salzburg. The Americans located two of their whereabouts by civilians.

With the King and his wife were eighteen members of their staff and four children. All were in good health.

Elements of the American 106th Cavalry Group had to overpower German Elite Guards to make the rescue. Seventh Army troops are now closely guarding the royal party.

FOR PROB. NO. 1, PIFC—Courtesy Military

The Pulitzer Awards For 1944 Announced

The Pulitzer Prize awards announced yesterday by the trustees of Columbia University included: For a distinguished novel, to "A Bell for Adano," by John Hersey; for an original American play of the current season, to "Harvey," by Mary Chase.

Among the newspaper awards were those to Hal Boyle, Associated Press war reporter, for distinguished correspondence; to James B. Reston of THE NEW YORK TIMES for his reporting of the Dumbarton Oaks Security Conference; to Joe Rosenthal, Associated Press photographer, for his photograph of marines raising the American flag at Iwo and to The Detroit Free Press for "distinguished and meritorious public service" in its investigation of legislative corruption at Lansing, Mich.

Further details of the awards will be found on Page 16.

MOLOTOFF HAILS BASIC 'UNANIMITY'

He Stresses Five Points in World Charter, but His View on One Is Questioned

By JAMES B. RESTON
Special to The New York Times

SAN FRANCISCO, May 7—The major allies who forced Germany's unconditional surrender have reached "unanimity" on the kind of world security organization which should be created at the United Nations conference to protect their newly won victory, Vyacheslaff M. Molotoff, Russian Foreign Commissar, said today.

While the delegates at the conference celebrated the end of the European war, and three Foreign Ministers, T. V. Soong of China, Paul Henri Spaak of Belgium and Trygve Lie of Norway left the conference to deal with urgent official business elsewhere, Mr. Molotoff told the press that the Soviet Union attached the "greatest importance" to five agreements reached by the heads of the Big Four delegations.

First, he said, these leaders agreed to support the principles of justice, international law, human rights and fundamental freedom for all.

Second, he added, the Big Four agreed not to make provision in the security charter for the revision of treaties.

His statement on this point was ambiguous and led to some speculation as to the unanimity of all four on the question.

Revision Power Called Danger

A reference in the United Nations charter to the necessity of revising treaties, Mr. Molotoff stated, "would play into the hands of enemy countries, which would certainly like to undermine and emasculate these treaties." Furthermore, he declared, to give the new League of Nations authority to consider revision of treaties would be a violation of national sovereign rights, which are guaranteed in the Dumbarton Oaks Charter.

For these reasons, he concluded, "the idea of revising treaties was rejected as untenable."

Third, Mr. Molotoff said, it was agreed among the Big Three that treaties directed against Germany, such as Russia's twenty-year alliances with Britain, France, Czechoslovakia, Yugoslavia and the Warsaw Poles, "should remain in force until such time as the Government concerned felt that the international security organization was really in a position to undertake the accomplishment of the tasks of

Continued on Page 15, Column 2

GERMANY SURRENDERS: NEW YORKERS MASSED UNDER SYMBOL OF LIBERTY

Thousands filling Times Square in spontaneous celebration yesterday

The New York Times

PRAGUE SAYS FOES ACCEPT SURRENDER

Czechoslovak Radio Reports All Fighting in Bohemia Will Be Ended Today

By The Associated Press

LONDON, Tuesday, May 8—The Czechoslovak - controlled Prague radio announced today that the Germans in Prague and throughout Bohemia, a last major holdout pocket of German resistance, had accepted unconditional surrender.

The announcement came as the United States Third Army was reported to have advanced to the outskirts of the Czechoslovak capital, and three Russian armies hammered toward the same goal from the east and north.

"The German military plenipotentiary is negotiating with the Czechoslovak National Council on the modalities of unconditional surrender," said the broadcast, detailing what purported to be the

Continued on Page 11, Column 2

Wild Crowds Greet News In City While Others Pray

By FRANK S. ADAMS

New York City's millions reacted in two sharply contrasting ways yesterday to the news of the unconditional surrender of the German armies. A large and noisy minority greeted it with the turbulent enthusiasm of New Year's Eve and Election Night rolled into one. However, the great bulk of the city's population responded with quiet thanksgiving that the war in Europe was won, tempered by the realization that a grim and bitter struggle still may lie ahead in the Pacific and the fact that the nation is still in mourning for its fallen President and Commander in Chief.

Times Square, the financial section and the garment district were thronged from mid-morning on with wildly jubilant celebrators who tooted horns, staged impromptu parades and filled the canyons between the skyscrapers with fluttering scraps of paper. Elsewhere in the metropolitan area, however, war plants continued to hum, schools and offices and

factories carried on their normal activities, and residential areas were calmly joyful.

One factor that helped to damp-en the celebration was the bewilderment of large segments of the population at the absence of an official proclamation to back up the news contained in flaring headlines and radio bulletins. With ears fresh in everyone's mind, and millions still mindful of the false armistice of 1918, there was widespread skepticism over the authenticity of the news.

By mid-afternoon loudspeakers were blaring into the ears of the exulting thousands in the garment district the news that President Truman's proclamation was being held up by the necessity of coordinating it with the announcements from London and Moscow, and that the formal celebration of the long-awaited V-E Day would be delayed until today.

This sobering note gradually

Continued on Page 7, Column 6

SHAEF BAN ON AP LIFTED IN 6 HOURS

Action Comes After Protests From Newspapers and Public —Writer Still Barred

Suspension of filing facilities of The Associated Press in the European theatre was clamped on by Supreme Headquarters, Allied Expeditionary Forces (SHAEF), yesterday in an unprecedented action and was lifted six hours and twenty minutes later.

The ban was continued, however, on all copy submitted for clearance by Edward Kennedy, chief of the press association's staff on the Western Front, who sent the momentous story announcing Germany's final surrender in a despatch from Reims, France, which was received in New York over the AP wires at 9:35 A. M. (EWT).

It was not until seven hours and fifty-five minutes had elapsed aft-

Continued on Page 4, Column 2

GERMANS CAPITULATE ON ALL FRONTS

American, Russian and French Generals Accept Surrender in Eisenhower Headquarters, a Reims School

REICH CHIEF OF STAFF ASKS FOR MERCY

Doenitz Orders All Military Forces of Germany To Drop Arms—Troops in Norway Give Up —Churchill and Truman on Radio Today

By EDWARD KENNEDY
Associated Press Correspondent

REIMS, France, May 7—Germany surrendered unconditionally to the Western Allies and the Soviet Union at 2:41 A. M. French time today. [This was at 8:41 P. M., Eastern Wartime Sunday.]

The surrender took place at a little red school house that is the headquarters of Gen. Dwight D. Eisenhower.

The surrender, which brought the war in Europe to a formal end after five years, eight months and six days of bloodshed and destruction, was signed for Germany by Col. Gen. Gustav Jodl. General Jodl is the new Chief of Staff of the German Army.

The surrender was signed for the Supreme Allied Command by Lieut. Gen. Walter Bedell Smith, Chief of Staff for General Eisenhower.

It was also signed by Gen. Ivan Susloparoff for the Soviet Union and by Gen. Francois Sevez for France.

[The official Allied announcement will be made at 9 o'clock Tuesday morning when President Truman will broadcast a statement and Prime Minister Churchill will issue a V-E Day proclamation. Gen. Charles de Gaulle also will address the French at the same time.]

General Eisenhower was not present at the signing, but immediately afterward General Jodl and his fellow delegate, Gen. Admiral Hans Georg Friedeburg, were received by the Supreme Commander.

Germans Say They Understand Terms

They were asked sternly if they understood the surrender terms imposed upon Germany and if they would be carried out by Germany.

They answered Yes.

Germany, which began the war with a ruthless attack upon Poland, followed by successive aggressions and brutality in internment camps, surrendered with an appeal to the victors for mercy toward the German people and armed forces.

After having signed the full surrender, General Jodl said he wanted to speak and received leave to do so.

"With this signature," he said in soft-spoken German, "the German people and armed forces are for better or worse delivered into the victors' hands.

"In this war, which has lasted more than five years, both have achieved and suffered more than perhaps any other people in the world."

LONDON, May 7 (AP)—Complete victory in

Continued on Page 3, Columns 2 and 3

Summary of News of the War and German Surrender

TUESDAY, MAY 8, 1945

The war ended in Europe yesterday after five years, eight months and six days of the bloodiest conflict in history. Grand Admiral Karl Doenitz surrendered unconditionally to the Allies in a little red schoolhouse at Reims, France, at 8:41 P. M. Sunday, New York time, Col. Gen. Gustav Jodl signed for the enemy and Lieut. Gen. Walter Bedell Smith, General Eisenhower's Chief of Staff, for the Allies. In the absence of any official announcement there was some confusion as to the compliance with the surrender. Fighting had been going on in Czechoslovakia and nothing had been heard from German pockets along the French coast. [1:7-8.]

President Truman planned a broadcast from the White House at 9 o'clock this morning. Washington, gratified that the war in Europe was over, was confused by lack of confirmation. [2:1.]

Prime Minister Churchill will also broadcast at 9 A. M. from London and Premier Stalin is

expected to make a simultaneous announcement in Moscow. King George will talk over the radio six hours later. [2:3.]

London will celebrate V-E Day today, but, unable to restrain its joy, staged many impromptu celebrations yesterday. [2:7.]

Most New Yorkers took the news calmly and thankfully, sobered by realization that the war in the Pacific was far from over. There were, however, noisy outbursts in such centers as Times Square and Wall Street. Scrap paper showers fluttered from roofs and windows. [1:4-5.]

German Foreign Minister Lutz Schwerin von Krosigk broke the news to his people. The future will be difficult, he warned, and then added: "We must make right the base of our nation. In our nation justice shall be the supreme law" and the guiding principle. We must also recognize law as the basis of all relations between the nations." This sudden, complete reversal of German policy was received with

skepticism by the Allies. [3:1.]

Perhaps one reason for this was the announcement from Moscow that 4,000,000 men, women and children had been done to death by gas, shooting, famine, poisoning and torture in the German extermination camp at Oswiecim, Poland. [12:5.]

The actual situation in Czechoslovakia is obscure. Late last night a Patriot broadcast said the Germans were negotiating with the Czechoslovak National Council details of surrender in Prague. Fighting had continued throughout yesterday and German planes had bombed public buildings and hospitals. [1:3; map F. 11.]

The United States Third Army continued its general advance into Czechoslovakia and the Fifth and Seventh Armies joined again in the Alps. The British Second Army moved to Denmark and Poles entered the shattered part of Wilhelmshaven. [11:1.] Breslau fell to the Red Army after an eighty-four-day siege; 40,000

Germans were captured. [11:5.]

Japan accepted the surrender of her Axis partner with a statement that she never had expected Germany aid and would go on to victory without the Reich. [15:3.]

Infantry and marines on Okinawa scored another general advance after naval bombardment had pulverized German strong-points. Pacific Fleet planes sank or damaged thirteen more ships off Korea and Japan. [1:1; map, P. 12.] B-29's maintained their assault on Kyushu airfields. Two of the big planes were shot down. [1:2-4.]

On Tarakan Allied troops were within a mile and a half of the eastern shore. Americans gained on Mindanao and Luzon in the Philippines. [12:3-4.]

Foreign Commissar Molotoff said in San Francisco that unanimity on amendments to the Dumbarton Oaks proposals was one of the achievements of the conference. He declared that the Big Four consultations had ended. [1:2.]

Continued on Page 3, Columns 2 and 3

"All the News That's Fit to Print"

The New York Times.

LATE CITY EDITION
Partly cloudy and mild today. Occasional showers tomorrow.
Temperatures Yesterday—Max., 64; Min., 41
Sunrise today, 5:56 A. M.; Sunset, 7:51 P. M.
Full U. S. Weather Bureau Report, Page 51

VOL. XCV..No. 32,239. Entered as Second-Class Matter. Postoffice, New York, N. Y. NEW YORK, WEDNESDAY, MAY 1, 1946. THREE CENTS IN NEW YORK CITY

WARSHIP BLOWS UP AT MUNITIONS PIER IN PORT, KILLING 5

0 on Escort Vessel Injured—Blasts Shake New Jersey Towns Near Big Depot

BOMBS ASHORE SET OFF

Sailor Is Only Slightly Hurt as Depth Charge Explodes as He Is Carrying It

By MEYER BERGER
Special to The New York Times.

LEONARDO, N. J., April 30—One officer and four sailors of the destroyer escort Solar's complement of fourteen officers and 136 enlisted men vanished utterly before noon today in an ammunition explosion that tore away one-third of the 306-foot ship's forward structure.

About sixty of the ship's crew were injured, but only thirty-five were hospitalized, and of them only a handful remained tonight for further treatment. The Navy withheld the names of the five missing men and the names of the injured because not all their families had been officially notified.

The explosion happened as the Solar's crew was unloading her ammunition supply in preparation for an overhaul. Normally she carries about fifteen tons of assorted ammunition, including depth bombs and smaller charges, torpedoes and shells for her cannon. Only one-third of this amount was still aboard when the blast occurred.

Tons of Explosives Near By

Near by, when the detonation shook the New Jersey coast in and around the Raritan Bay district, were a number of other vessels preparing to unload ammunition. It was unofficially estimated here that these vessels held, all told, about 25,000 tons of explosives. Tugs dragged these craft out of the danger zone.

Burning fragments from the Solar, hurled at tremendous force against freight cars on the pier, started other explosions. One car in a freight string, filled chiefly with depth charges, blew up and all but vanished in dust and smoke, scattering its parts in all directions. Three strings of cars were hauled shoreward by their locomotive crews, at great risk.

No one seemed certain tonight what had caused the explosion, but what seemed like a possible explanation came from Jack Horne, fireman second class, of Charlotte, N. C. He thought a piece of ammunition carried by Joseph Stuchinski, seaman, of Baltimore, might have done it.

"Ski," the fireman said, "was carrying a 'hedgehog' from the forward magazine. While he was holding it, it just went off. He must have bumped it against something, because those things go off when anything touches them."

Seaman Stuchinski, oddly enough, was not seriously injured. He was deafened, a few minor scratches showed on his chest when he got to the first-aid station and his dungarees were split.

"It went off. The thing just went off," he said.

The "hedgehog" Stuchinski carried was an anti-submarine depth charge. Metal-cased, weighing about sixty pounds, it is generally cylindrical, about thirty inches long and between four and five inches in diameter.

Bow Like Elephant's Trunk

The Solar lay at the northern, or bay end, of the easternmost of the three great piers that jut out from the Navy's Earle Ammunition Depot, when she blew up. She was approximately one and one-half miles from the beach end of the depot. The blast curled her bow in much the same shape as an elephant's back-bent trunk.

The concussion was felt twenty to thirty miles around. The detonation rushed across Raritan Bay to shake homes in Tottenville, Richmond Valley, Pleasant Plains, Princess Bay, Great Kills, Oakwood and New Dorp, all on Staten Island, and shattered panes in some of those communities.

Ground tremors were felt to the west and to the southwest. There were some freakish effects. Residents in Middletown Township, including Rumson, Fair Haven, Red Bank and Little Silver, for example, seemed certain the explosion was local. Several frightened housewives called the police to say, "The boiler just blew up in my cellar."

Dogs raced away from the beach

Continued on Page 2, Column 3

AFTER EXPLOSIONS RIPPED DESTROYER ESCORT

The wrecked U. S. S. Solar at the Navy Ammunition Depot in Earle, N. J., yesterday
The New York Times (U. S. Navy)

BIG FOUR RULE OUT AUSTRIA'S DEMAND FOR SOUTH TYROL

Paris Conference Rejects Any Major Frontier Revision in That Region of Italy

NO PROGRESS ON TRIESTE

Rome and Belgrade Are Asked to Send Delegates—Report of Experts Confusing

By C. L. SULZBERGER
By Cable to The New York Times.

PARIS, April 30—Italy's retention of most of the Province of Bolzano [South Tyrol], which is claimed by Austria, was virtually assured tonight after the Council of Foreign Ministers had agreed that no requests for a major frontier change would be accepted in that area so valuable in hydro-electric power.

At the same time, after examining a verbose and confused report on Trieste and Venezia Giulia, submitted at long last by the special commission sent by the Foreign Ministers' deputies to investigate the Italian-Yugoslav border area, the Ministers agreed to invite the Yugoslav and Italian Governments to send delegates here on Friday to present once again their views on this hotly disputed and vitally important region.

The report showed a complete divergence in opinion between the Soviet investigator and the three other participants on the value of a census taken in 1945 by a Yugoslav, Professor Rodlich. The Soviet member of the commission said the census was fine and the three others said it was just the opposite. Since this census is of vital importance in deciding the ethnic basis for a decision, that leaves everything up in the air.

Suggested by Molotov

The move to widen the scope of the Foreign Ministers' meeting by inviting in the Italians and Yugoslavs was suggested by Vyacheslav M. Molotov. The Soviet Foreign Minister recalled that the Potsdam decisions, the "bible" under which the peace treaties are being drafted, provided that the interested parties should be included when necessary. Thus, the doors have been opened to permit entry of those delegations—Greek, Italian, Yugoslav, Hungarian and Bulgarian—now clamoring for a

Continued on Page 4, Column 2

JOINT PALESTINE BODY BARS A JEWISH STATE, BUT URGES ENTRY OF 100,000 REFUGEES

Arabs 'Outraged' by Report; Jews Are Far From Satisfied

Rival Agencies Reiterate Their Arguments—U. S., British Talks Are Forecast on Easing Burden Too Big for London

By HERBERT L. MATTHEWS
By Wireless to The New York Times.

LONDON, April 30—Now that the report of the Anglo-American Committee of Inquiry on Palestine has been published, one can safely predict tonight that the next step will be for the British to consult the United States Government about it. The British have reached the point at which they consider that Palestine is far too great a burden for them to be forced to handle alone.

No Government spokesman would say anything about the report tonight because the Cabinet and other officials have not had time to study it. One must keep in mind that the members of the committee had a mandate only to make recommendations, which do not in any sense involve Governmental responsibility.

The Arab Office in London has lost no time in issuing a scorching statement condemning the report lock, stock and barrel. The Jewish Agency for Palestine gave the report a mixed reception. It was happy about the proposal to allow 100,000 Jewish refugees to enter Palestine but asserted that without the formation of a Jewish state there could be no solution to the problem of homeless Jews.

On all sides one hears dubious comment about the fact that the committee's report makes no suggestion in terms of any sort of finality nor does it even offer any kind of long-term solution to the Palestinian problem. It is feared that even moderate elements among the Arabs will be more disturbed about that feature of the report than any other.

In their present mood of shocked disgust over the murder of seven British soldiers in Tel Aviv last Thursday the British are inclined to place the most prominence on that part of the report dealing with security and with making it clear that violence and terrorism will be resolutely repressed. The state-

Continued on Page 14, Column 5

TRUMAN FOR ACTION

Inquiry Upholds His Visa Proposal, Urges End of White Paper

WOULD GUARD ARAB RIGHTS

Report for Change in Holy Land Property Curbs—Demands a Firm Stand on Violence

The text of the report of the Anglo-American Committee of Inquiry on Palestine, Pages 15 to 21, inclusive.

FELIX BELAIR JR.
Special to The New York Times.

WASHINGTON, April 30—The Anglo-American Committee of Inquiry on problems of Jews in Europe and Palestine, reporting to the two Governments today on its four-month investigation, urged the admission of 100,000 European Jews into the Holy Land as soon as possible, but flatly rejected the idea of a Jewish state, together with Arab claims for dominance. It asserted Christendom's own interest in the area.

Released simultaneously for publication in Washington and London, the report drew from President Truman an expression of satisfaction that his proposal for the admission of 100,000 Jews into Palestine had been recommended. He added that "the transference of these unfortunate people should now be accomplished with the greatest dispatch."

The President declared it significant that the report aimed at guarantees for Arab civil and religious rights and urged measures to improve Arab cultural, educational and economic position.

Land Changes Asked

"I am also pleased," he said, "that the committee recommends, in effect, the abrogation of the White Paper of 1939."

The report repudiated the 1939 White Paper principles, which made further Jewish immigration dependent on Arab consent and banned Jewish land purchases in a major part of Palestine.

Dependent for its final effect on adoption by both Governments, the report covered a wide range of controversial subjects on which President Truman gave no hint of his attitude except to say that he was taking them under advisement.

However, Mr. Truman seemed to have embraced the major policy statement rejecting "once and for all the exclusive claims of Jews and Arabs to Palestine," which the committee enunciated as follows:

"(I, That Jew shall not dominate Arab and Arab shall not dominate Jew in Palestine. (II) That Palestine shall be neither a Jewish state nor an Arab state. (III) That the form of government ultimately to be established shall, under international guarantees, fully protect and preserve the interests in the Holy Land of Christendom and of the Moslem and Jewish faiths."

Stress on Unique Status

With deliberate emphasis, the Committee of Inquiry declared that "Palestine is a Holy Land, sacred to Christian, to Jew and to Moslem alike; and because it is a holy land, Palestine is not, and can never become, a land which any race or religion can justly claim as its very own."

With equal emphasis, the committee said the same considerations set Palestine apart from other lands, and dedicated it to the precepts and practices of the brotherhood of man rather than to those of narrow nationalism.

The 42,000-word report was signed in Lausanne, Switzerland, by Judge Joseph C. Hutcheson, United States chairman, Sir John E. Singleton, British chairman, Frank Aydelotte, Frank W. Buxton, Bartley C. Crum, James G. McDonald and William Phillips, American members, and W. F. Crick, R. H. S. Crossman, Frederick Leggett, R. E. Manningham-Buller and M. Morrison for Britain.

For the immediate future the

Continued on Page 14, Column 2

BAN BY MUSICIANS BLOW TO TELEVISION

Petrillo Plans to Prolong the Refusal of Union Men to the Industry Indefinitely

By JACK GOULD

The American Federation of Musicians, headed by James C. Petrillo, plans to forbid its members to work in television until some indefinite date in the future when the union can determine the effects of video's advent on present-day radio, it was learned yesterday.

Television broadcasters were agreed that Mr. Petrillo's stand would retard the immediate development of video programs, since it could be a matter of months if not years before anyone could determine to what extent television would supplant or complement sound broadcasting.

Use of "live" musicians was first denied the television industry in February, 1945, by the international executive board of the federation, but yesterday was the first time that Mr. Petrillo explained the action and indicated that the ban would be of prolonged duration.

Musical Films Already Banned

Last week Mr. Petrillo's union and the Hollywood motion picture producers entered into an agreement not to permit films containing music to be used in television, a move leaving the telecasters with only records as a possible source of music. Beginning July 1, under a rule of the Federal Communications Commission, the television stations are scheduled to offer twenty-eight hours of programs a week, but under Mr. Petrillo's edicts they will be forced to rely primarily on talks, sporting events and other non-musical fare.

Coincidentally with stating the union's position on television, Mr. Petrillo also reiterated his stand against permitting standard radio programs containing music to be presented simultaneously on frequency modulation outlets. The union is insisting on double crews of musicians in the event of such duplication.

The re-statement of the union's views on FM were regarded with

Continued on Page 28, Column 2

Stalin Warns of War Plot By 'International Reaction'

By The Associated Press.

LONDON, April 30—Generalissimo Stalin promised tonight that the Soviet Union would be true to a policy of peace and security but charged that what he described as "international reaction" was "hatching plans of a new war." In an order of the day broadcast by the Moscow radio the Russian leader also declared that it was necessary to be constantly vigilant, "to protect as the apple of one's eye the armed forces and defensive power of our country."

TEXT OF STALIN ORDER

His broadcast order, issued in connection with the Soviet Union's May Day celebration, was heard in London by the Soviet monitor, who issued the following text:

Comrades, Red Army and Red Navy men, sergeants and petty officers, comrade officers, generals and admirals, working people of the Soviet Union:

Today, for the first time since the victorious termination of the Great Patriotic War we celebrate May 1—the international holiday of working people—in conditions of peaceful life, won in a hard struggle against the enemies at the cost of heavy sacrifices and privations.

One year ago the Red Army hoisted the banner of victory over Berlin and completed the defeat of fascist Germany. Within four months after the victorious termination of the war against Germany, imperialist Japan downed her arms. The Second World War, prepared by the forces of international reaction and unleashed by the chief fascist states, ended in a full victory of the freedom-loving nations. The smashup and liquidation of the main hotbeds of fascism and world aggression resulted in changes in the political life of the nations of the world, in a wide growth of the democratic movement of the nations.

Taught by the experience of war, the popular masses realized that the destinies of states cannot be entrusted to reactionary leaders, who pursue the narrow caste and selfish anti-popular aims. It is for this reason that nations, which no longer wish to live in the old way, take destinies of their states into their own hands, establish democratic order and actively fight against the forces of reaction, against instigators of a new war. The nations of the

Continued on Page 5, Column 4

INQUIRY FINDS 'PERIL' TO SECRETS OF WAR

Senators Hear Radar Makers on Russian Buying and Urge Law Tightening

By C. P. TRUSSELL
Special to The New York Times.

WASHINGTON, April 30—Need for a tightening of the laws to provide protection for wartime secrets in the electronics and other fields was declared by Senate investigators today to be "very definite." The statement came after a closed-session inquiry into negotiations for sales of radar and similar equipment to Russia.

Members of a special Senate Judiciary subcommittee, conducting the investigation, said that there was no evidence that "classified,"

Continued on Page 3, Column 4

World News Summarized

WEDNESDAY, MAY 1, 1946

Palestine should become neither a Jewish state nor an Arab state, the Anglo-American Committee of Inquiry declared in its report made public simultaneously last night in Washington and London. Admission of 100,000 Jews this year and virtual abrogation of the 1939 British White Paper with its restrictions on land holdings were recommended. Other suggestions included continuation of the present mandate until establishment of a United Nations trusteeship and resolute suppression of violence and terrorism by Jews or Arabs. [1:8.]

Although President Truman expressed pleasure over certain parts of the report, it was felt in Washington that neither the Jews nor Arabs would be satisfied. [13.1.] In fact, Arab leaders threatened to combat any additional Jewish immigration [13:3] and Zionists expressed their opposition. Bartley C. Crum, a member of the committee, predicted that a directive authorizing the entry of 100,000 Jews into Palestine would "issue forthwith." [1:6-7.]

British reaction counted heavily upon American support in whatever was done, but regretted the absence of any long-term solution. [1:6-7.]

Italy will be permitted to retain most of southern Tyrol despite Austrian claims, the Foreign Ministers tentatively agreed at their conference in Paris, but they were as wide apart as ever on what to do about Trieste and the Venezia Giulia area. It was decided to invite Yugoslavia and Italy to present their cases anew. [1:5.]

Britain tried to meet French desires by suggesting internationalization of either the Ruhr or both the Ruhr and the left bank of the Rhine for fifty years. [3:1.] Secretary Byrnes' proposed four-power treaty to keep Germany disarmed was favorably received in the Senate Foreign Affairs Committee. [3:8.]

The United Nations Security Council subcommittee opens its investigation into Franco Spain this afternoon. [1:7.] Europe's ruined industries should be restored before attempts to eradicate world unemployment, the Economic and Employment Commission heard [8:5], while the Transport and Communications Commission debated the relative merits of free enterprise and government control of shipping. [7:1.] The Commission on Human Rights may seek a new international bill of rights and ask authority to supervise its implementation. [8:2.]

Tabriz, capital of Azerbaijan, has been formally evacuated by Russian troops, the Tabriz radio reported. [3:6.] Premier Stalin declared that, while the world must remain vigilant against reaction, it had "no reason to doubt" that Russia would remain steadfast in her devotion to international peace and security. [1:3-4.]

Japan was shocked at the plot to assassinate General MacArthur and the Government offered its apologies. No arrests have been announced. [1:6-7.]

Ammunition being unloaded from the destroyer-escort Solar in Raritan Bay exploded, killing an officer and four sailors. [1:1.]

John L. Lewis served notice that anthracite miners intended to strike on May 31 unless they obtained the same demands that led to the soft-coal strike. Negotiations will start in New York on May 10. No progress was made toward settling the bituminous dispute. [29:1.]

Further restrictions were placed on the use of grain by distillers in order to make more food available for world famine relief. [1:2-3.]

General Motors was authorized by the OPA to raise prices on its cars from $16 to $60 to cover wage increases. [27:6-7.] House members returned to Washington still opposed to extending price control without heavy restrictions. [30:5.]

Truman Said to Plan Start Of Jewish Entry 'Forthwith'

By LAWRENCE RESNER

Bartley C. Crum, one of the six United States members of the Joint Anglo-American Committee of Inquiry on Palestine, predicted here yesterday, on the basis of a discussion he had with President Truman at the White House on Monday, that the directives authorizing the admission of 100,000 European Jews into Palestine would "issue forthwith."

Mr. Crum, a San Francisco lawyer, also expressed the belief that most Jewish groups would endorse the affirmative aspects of the report, although reserving their right to continue a fight for the achievement of their ideological tenets, principally a Jewish state.

An immediate endorsement of the recommendation to obtain the admission of the 100,000 European Jews came from Joseph M. Proskauer, president of the American Jewish Committee, who said the provisions for immediate action were "obviously based on the highest considerations of statesmanship and humanity."

The World Zionist Emergency Council, which speaks for some of the largest and most active Zionist groups in the United States, said a statement outlining its position probably would be issued today, after the report had been studied.

The initial negative response by a Jewish group came from the Political Action Committee for Palestine, whose executive vice chairman, Dr. Baruch Korff, said that despite "the report's few fine points, the commission had proved

Continued on Page 13, Column 4

U. N.'S SPAIN INQUIRY COMMENCES TODAY

5-Man Subcommittee to Meet Here In Secret—No Outside Witnesses at First Session

By W. H. LAWRENCE

The Franco regime in Spain goes on trial today on charges that it is a cause of international friction and a threat to world peace.

Meeting privately at 3 P. M., representatives of Australia, China, France, Poland and Brazil will set in motion the first formal investigation by the United Nations, authorized Monday by a 10-to-0 vote of the Security Council, in which Russia did not participate but refrained from exercising an asserted right to veto the inquiry.

How, where and when the Council subcommittee will function presumably will be decided in the early part of today's meeting, and the members then will turn to analyzing the evidence now before them, listing the specific charges

Continued on Page 7, Column 5

MacArthur Plot Alarms Japanese; They See Possible Repercussions

By The Associated Press.

TOKYO, April 30—News of a frustrated assassination plot against General Douglas MacArthur tonight shocked the Japanese.

Their first reaction was twofold: A feeling that their country had lost face; fears that repercussions might be felt in every household.

The Government officially apologized. Katsuo Okazaki, representing Foreign Minister Shigeru Yoshida, visited General MacArthur's office two hours after Allied Headquarters had announced discovery of the plot. He did not see the general personally, but delivered a verbal message to aides.

Mr. Okazaki expressed "deep regret and concern" and said his Government was "greatly embarrassed." He asked if there was anything his Government could do.

Earlier, Premier Kijuro Shidehara, Mr. Yoshida and Home Minister Chuzo Mitsuchi conferred.

Japanese reporters speculated that they discussed tighter precautions than previously were planned for the May Day demonstrations.

Many Japanese immediately asked, "Will this create more anti-Japanese feeling in America?" They linked this with fear that adverse American reaction might complicate efforts to obtain food and might mean a longer, harsher occupation.

They also expressed regret that the incident might mar the occupation and change the attitude of General MacArthur, whom the Japanese generally respect.

Allied headquarters had previously given some details of the plot. One conspirator was seized and a nation-wide hunt was launched for a die-hard Japanese militarist named as the arch-plotter.

The accused and hunted plot leader was Hideo Tokayama, former member of the dread Kempeitai or "thought police." In the

Continued on Page 12, Column 6

Sharp Restrictions in Distilling Ordered in Food Conservation

By CHARLES E. EGAN
Special to The New York Times.

WASHINGTON, April 30—World famine is more than a short term problem, and plans to meet its reappearance next winter should be drafted immediately, Chester C. Davis, chairman of the President's Special Famine Emergency Committee, asserted today.

Mr. Davis, who conferred with President Truman, later said that emergency measures, taken to insure larger relief shipment of grains and other foods to famine-stricken areas in the next few weeks, could not be considered as final, but were merely "the first sprint" in a continuing race to avert death for millions who otherwise would starve.

Meanwhile, Secretary Anderson issued an order restricting distilleries who operated for five days at full mashing capacity in April to three capacity days in May.

The order still limited the use of grain by the entire distilling industry to [illegible] bushels a month; banned use of wheat in the manufacture of spirits and restricted distillers to the use of corn which is unsuitable for human consumption.

In January, distillers were permitted ten capacity mashing days, but were cut to seven and one-half in February and to five days in March and April.

Brewers, operating on a 30 per cent reduction of grain, were not included in today's order.

"Every report coming before us makes it plain that the present famine is not a short run emergency that ends on July 1," Mr. Davis' statement said, adding:

"The present food shortages have been seriously aggravated by drought in many parts of the world, but even with good weather the wartime destruction of agricultural facilities will be felt for a long time.

"Farm animals and farm machinery have been destroyed. The strength of farm workers has

Continued on Page 28, Column 2

"All the News
That's Fit to Print"

The New York Times.

LATE CITY EDITION
Fair and continued cold today
and tomorrow
Temperature Range Today—Max. 36 : Min. 26
Temperature Yesterday—Max. 45 : Min. 30
U. S. Weather Bureau Report, Page 19, Sect. 1

Section
1

NEWS INDEX, PAGE 78, THIS SECTION

Copyright, 1947, by The New York Times Company.

VOL. XCVII..No. 32,817.   Entered as Second-Class Matter,
Postoffice, New York, N. Y.   NEW YORK, SUNDAY, NOVEMBER 30, 1947.   FIFTEEN CENTS

SCHUMAN BARS DISCUSSION OF FRENCH LABOR OVERTURE; COMMUNIST PAPERS SEIZED

PREMIER ADAMANT

Strikers Must Go Back on Regime's Terms— Labor Curbs Urged

ASSEMBLY SPLIT ON CODE

324 Saboteurs Are Arrested Paris to Expel Aliens Who Help Ruin Economy

By HAROLD CALLENDER
Special to The New York Times

PARIS, Sunday, Nov. 30—Premier Robert Schuman refused early today to meet the leaders of the Confederation of Labor to discuss a strike settlement different from that offered by the French Government.

Meanwhile, the Premier pressed hard for immediate passage by the Assembly of a law to strengthen the Government's hand by enlarging its police force and enabling it to imprison those who would force men to strike or who committed or urged sabotage.

An intense activity continued throughout the night inside and outside the Assembly. It was made clear that the labor leaders who had encouraged the strikes had at last taken the initiative in seeking to end them, and that the Cabinet was divided regarding the policy the Government should adopt.

Early last evening Paris police surrounded the plants of the two Communist newspapers, l'Humanité and Ce Soir, entered the buildings and seized the plates of special editions whose publication had been forbidden. No papers were allowed to leave the premises. Later the police vacated the premises.

The special edition of l'Humanité, in large headlines printed in red ink, proclaimed: "They wish to assassinate the Republic!"

Minister Begins Parley

Shortly after M. Schuman had placed his proposed law before the Assembly early yesterday, Pierre Lebrun, a Communist secretary of the labor confederation, issued a statement urging renewed negotiations and mentioning that the striking workers would have a hard time when the Dec. 1 pay day came on Monday without pay envelopes.

At the same time, Daniel Mayer, Socialist Minister of Labor, who is understood to have opposed the law that M. Schuman sought, opened negotiations with the executive committee of the confederation, which sat most of the night in his office while the Cabinet met in the Palais Bourbon. Through M. Mayer the committee asked to see M. Schuman, but the Premier refused his request and denied that the Government was negotiating with the strike leaders.

A sharp divergence of view de-

Continued on Page 46, Column 2

Major Sports Results

FOOTBALL

With Rip Rowan passing for the first touchdown and dashing ninety-two yards for the second, Army beat Navy yesterday for the fourth straight year. N.Y.U. rallied to beat Fordham. Scores of leading games:

Alabama ...21 Miami, Fla... 6
Army ......21 Navy 0
Florida ....35 Kansas State 7
Fordham ....12 N. Y. U. ...13
Ga. Tech.... 7 Georgia 0
Holy Cross..26 Boston Coll. 6
Maryland ... 0 N. C. State.. 0
Mich. State..58 Hawaii 19
Mississippi ..33 Miss. State. 14
N. Carolina..40 Virginia ...19
Oklahoma ...21 Okla. A.&M. 13
Oregon State..21 Oregon 14
Rice ....34 Baylor 0
S. M. U. ....13 T. C. U. ...13
Tennessee ...12 Vanderbilt.. 7
Texas Tech...14 Hardin-Sim.. 6
West Va.....17 Pittsburgh.. 2

CROSS COUNTRY

Curtis Stone of Philadelphia won the National A.A.U. championship at Van Cortlandt Park, but the New York A. C. took the team title for the third successive time.

HORSE RACING

Inclina outran Gallorette to capture the Bryan and O'Hara Memorial Handicap at Bowie on the last day of the major Eastern season.

(Full details in Section 5.)

U. S. Troops to Stay in Italy Beyond Dec. 3 Sailing Date

Change in Plans Is Linked to Disturbances Led by Communists—Milan Is Calm Following Compromise on Prefect

By ARNALDO CORTESI
Special to The New York Times

ROME, Nov. 29—The United States Army Department today ordered Maj. Gen. Lawrence Jaynes, commanding the Mediterranean Theatre of Operations, and his entire staff to postpone their departure from Italy. This act will remain about 2,500 officers and men who are leading specialists of the United States Army in Italy.

The order is believed to reflect the anxiety with which the Government in Washington views the Communist-fomented disturbances in Italy.

General Jaynes and his officers and men had planned to leave from Leghorn on Dec. 3 aboard the Admiral Sims. Washington ordered a postponement of departure until Dec. 14, the deadline set by the Italian peace treaty. No explanation was given for the change of plans and this strengthened the impression that it was dictated by

outlook.

The officers and men with General Jaynes form the skeleton organization for a large army. They include highly trained specialists, familiar with conditions in Italy. They belong to the Engineer, Signal, Ordnance, Secretariat, Quartermaster, Medical and Military Police Corps and other auxiliary services.

Washington's change of plans came after General Jaynes had said farewell to Pope Pius and President Enrico de Nicola. Ambassador James C. Dunn called on Premier Alcide de Gasperi two days ago, and it is presumed that he informed the Italian Government then of the postponement of the American troops' departure.

Though the American troops should, under present plans, leave

Continued on Page 45, Column 2

No-Parking Area Is Created From City Hall to Canal St.

After a two-hour conference with Mayor O'Dwyer at Police Headquarters, Police Commissioner Arthur W. Wallander announced yesterday two further moves in the department's efforts to ease traffic congestion in the city.

Commissioner Wallander said the section of Manhattan north of City Hall as far as Canal Street and west to but not including West Street to the restricted parking areas already established in a large part of the borough below Fifty-ninth Street.

He also said that a survey was being made throughout the city in an effort to discover additional sites for municipal parking lots like the one established at the old World's Fair parking lot in Flushing, Queens. The lot set up experimentally there "looks promising," he said, reporting that 766 motorists had used it on Friday.

Mayor Explains Needs

The Commissioner announced the moves at a press conference at the end of his talk with the Mayor. Mr. O'Dwyer sat in on the press conference and added some comments of his own after his aide had made the announcement.

About forty traffic policemen will be needed to enforce the parking restrictions in the new area, the Mayor said. Commissioner Wallander has asked for 2,000 additional men for the Police Department to take care of this and other needs, which would add $8,000,000 to the department's budget, he continued.

Continued on Page 13, Column 3

WAR PAY 'RACKET' HUNTED BY TRUMAN

Gen. Vaughan Says President Wants Army, Navy, Air House-Cleaning on Disability Cases

Special to The New York Times

WASHINGTON, Nov. 29—The armed services are preparing to turn over to President Truman at his request the records of 28,000 wartime Army officers who have been retired for disability on tax-free pay normally amounting to three-fourths of their active service remuneration.

This became known as an aftermath of the case against Maj. Gen. Bennett B. Meyers and was confirmed today by Maj. Gen. Harry H. Vaughan, the President's military aide, who said at Philadelphia that Mr. Truman was determined to "wipe out any possible racket" in tax-free disability retirement pay.

The President has already spoken about the matter to James V. Forrestal, Secretary of Defense, and it is expected that a formal directive will be received soon.

Presumably the order will apply also to naval officers retired for disability so that once the President has the records in hand he

Continued on Page 27, Column 1

Congress Action Lags on Aid Bill Despite Warnings Need Is Urgent

By JOHN D. MORRIS
Special to The New York Times

WASHINGTON, Nov. 29—Congress set aside the troublesome problems of European and domestic inflation today and attended the Army-Navy game practically en masse, while pressures for accelerated action on the legislative problems awaited members' return to work Monday.

Despite repeated representations of urgency in both fields, the Congressional machinery faced a slowdown in production of the authorization for winter relief to France, Italy and Austria.

Formulation of anti-inflation legislation still had hardly begun, and completion of the task was far out of sight.

The Senate was prepared to resume consideration Monday of the foreign relief bill, but earlier expectations of passage on that day had been dissipated by failure yesterday to dispose of four amendments proposed by Senator

James P. Kem, Republican, of Missouri.

While some of them are acceptable to the bill's managers, at least one is expected to cause considerable discussion and possible delay of a vote on the bill itself until Tuesday.

This would require detailed, written acknowledgment by every recipient of relief supplies that the goods were gifts of the United States.

Senator Kem successfully proposed action on the amendments yesterday, asserting that it was only Thanksgiving holiday absenteeism that prevented the votes were taken. He thus disrupted leaders' plans for cleaning the slate of all proposed amendments so that the bill itself could be disposed of Monday.

Hope for a final vote Monday

Continued on Page 26, Column 3

VAST GI HOUSING TO RISE NEAR SITE OF WORLD'S FAIR

21 14-Story Apartment Units to Form Nation's Largest Veterans' Cooperative

COST PUT AT $58,000,000

Occupancy on Tenant-Owner Basis—Work Will Start Before End of Year

By LEE E. COOPER

On a fifty-five-acre tract overlooking the site of the World's Fair of 1939, the country's largest veterans' cooperative apartment community soon will begin to take form, it became known last night.

After nearly a year of negotiations, and with the official blessing of the city and of the Veterans Administration, plans for the $58,000,000 project were revealed by Frederick Briggs, chairman of the board of the Communities Redevelopment Corporation, which is sponsoring the enterprise.

The new Queens housing center, which will occupy a large part of the former Arrowbrook Golf Club grounds, will be for occupancy exclusively by veterans of World War II and their families on a tenant-ownership basis.

Plans call for the erection of twenty-one fourteen-story apartment houses of the fireproof type, to accommodate 5,600 families. Each building will have its own garage facilities, to be rented separately, for tenants' automobiles.

Shopping Centers Will Rise

In furtherance of the plan to create a self-contained community, the builders will erect shopping centers at the edges of the property, which is bounded by Main Street, Jewel Avenue and Park Drive East, within the boundaries of Forest Hills. A promenade, with stores beneath it, will be constructed on the hillside overlooking Flushing Meadow Park. The residential buildings will be set amid winding tree-lined walks and landscaped park spaces.

The Board of Estimate gave its unanimous sanction to the over-all plan for the project at a special closed session last Wednesday, after receiving a favorable report on it from Robert Moses, City Construction Coordinator who had been in consultation with the sponsors.

The city's cooperation will be limited to street changes and zoning aids permitting stores and the erection of fourteen-story houses on the site. No municipal financial

Continued on Page 12, Column 3

World News Summarized

SUNDAY, NOVEMBER 30, 1947

The General Assembly of the United Nations yesterday approved the plan for the partition of Palestine by a vote of 33 to 13 with ten abstentions and one absence. After the vote there were repeated statements of bitterness and disillusion from the Arab representatives. One after another they asserted that the Charter had been violated and that their nations would not be bound by the action and would reserve "freedom of action." The Arabs then walked out of the Assembly. [1:8.]

The Arabs subsequently denounced the United Nations "dead," and disavowed any intention of playing a part under the partition plan. They went on to say, however, that this did not mean their retirement from United Nations. Zionist leaders were jubilant over the outcome. [1:6-7.]

Zionists attending the Assembly expressed their joy with tears and excited laughter. Dr. Oswaldo Aranha praised the public for its good behavior. [1:7.]

The Palestine debate concluded the business of the current session of the General Assembly, and Dr. Aranha of Brazil gave his closing address. He declared that this second meeting had made a notable contribution to world peace, and after the delegates had risen to applaud him the meeting adjourned. [1:6.]

In London, Soviet Foreign Minister Molotov demanded the early establishment of a German government to accept the peace treaty. The other Ministers, seeing this as a move to commit them against any possible partition of Germany, opposed him. [1:2-7.] Secretary Marshall and M. Bidault declined to discuss with Bevin Premier Schuman's plan to end the Communist labor agitators in France at next week's meeting of the Foreign Ministers to achieve the economic unification of Germany through the removal of all

sonal barriers in what is expected to be the most important United States pressure at the conference. [50:3.]

In the deputies' meeting the Soviet delegation continued to study the French proposals on Austria and refused to agree on principle at any point. Action was delayed, but it was felt the Russians might accept. [51:1.]

In Paris, Premier Schuman declined to discuss with leaders of the Confederation of Labor any strike settlement on terms other than the Government's. He asked for police powers to suppress Communist agitators and moved against Communist papers. They had charged that a "revolutionary coup" was planned for midnight and that "assassination of the Republic" was the objective. The editions were suppressed. [1:1.]

In Italy, the United States commander and 2,500 American troops were ordered by Washington to postpone departure, presumably because of the troubled situation. The general strike in Milan, however, was ended. [1:2-3.]

The Ronne Expedition in the Antarctic reported the exploration and mapping of a total of about 160,000 square miles of territory in the name of the United States. [56:3.]

A scientific advance that may be important in insect pest control was announced by the United States Army. Ultrasonic waves have been developed that are lethal to mice and small insects. [1:2.]

Defense Secretary Forrestal has been instructed by President Truman to turn over the records of 28,000 wartime Army officers who have been retired for disability on tax-free pay, to determine to wipe out any possible "racket." [1:2.]

ASSEMBLY VOTES PALESTINE PARTITION; MARGIN IS 33 TO 13; ARABS WALK OUT; ARANHA HAILS WORK AS SESSION ENDS

PEACE GAINS NOTED

Brazilian Says Contacts Inspired No Forecast of Imminent War

CITES ROLE OF MINORITY

Lie Regrets That Economic Issues Were Sidetracked —Others Hail Aranha

By MARSHALL E. NEWTON

It is the mission of the United Nations to achieve world peace and the General Assembly made a memorable contribution in that direction, Dr. Oswaldo Aranha of Brazil, president of the Assembly, told the delegates of the fifty-seven member nations yesterday in his speech closing the second regular session in Flushing Meadows.

When he finished his address the delegates rose and applauded Dr. Aranha, whose talents and statesmanlike handling of the difficult task of presiding at the international assembly had been lauded by several preceding speakers.

Dr. Aranha pointed out that the present post-war period had not been marked by the armed conflicts that had followed the Peace of Versailles and he said that we lived today in a different era, in which our minds must turn to the future and not the past.

Calls for Foresight

"But close contact with international political life leads to no forecast of world war in the near future," he said. "The world seeks, however, new forms of political, economic and social integration in which the contact of ideas will not persade the clash of arms. But a reality is rising in sour days, to which we must impart the spirit of the United Nations, the only conception capable of insuring peace, solidarity, dignity and equality of all peoples.

"Our action should not be post factum. Our task is one of foresight and of organized prevention to eliminate the elements and factors capable of disturbing world

Continued on Page 57, Column 2

Molotov Insists on Regime Before Treaty on Germany

By DREW MIDDLETON

LONDON, Nov. 29—Soviet Foreign Minister Molotov urged with new fervor in the Council of Foreign Ministers today the early establishment of a central German government as a precondition of the German peace treaty.

Mr. Molotov's argument was based on the futility of completing a German peace treaty with no German government to sign it or assist in its preparation. But it was obvious that the Soviet delegate was moved by fears that the Western Allies, if this Council meeting failed, would make their own arrangements for a German government and treaty.

With a stridency that disrupted an otherwise decorous meeting, Mr. Molotov declared the Soviet Union would never recognize a peace signed by Western Germany and the Western powers. No government set up in Frankfort on the Main in the United States zone and no "ersatz government for Bizonia" would be a suitable substitute for the Soviet proposal, he asserted.

Secretary of State Marshall and French Foreign Minister Bidault both flatly opposed any tendency to make the establishment of a German government a precondition of signing the German peace treaty.

A compromise proposal presented by British Foreign Secretary Bevin was as abruptly turned down by Mr. Molotov, who said it did not go far enough. Then he proceeded to add a clause that made the British proposal an echo of the Soviet suggestion.

This brisk exchange of German participation in the peace making followed an encouraging agreement by the Big Four on the ad-

Continued on Page 54, Column 3

ZIONIST AUDIENCE JOYFUL AFTER VOTE

Tears, Excited Laughter Mark Tension—Aranha Commends Public's Good Behavior

By WALTER S. SULLIVAN

The attention of the entire Arab and Jewish worlds focused on Flushing Meadow yesterday to hear the verdict of the United Nations General Assembly on the future of Palestine.

The reaction in the packed hall to the decision for partition typified that of listeners far and near. While members of the Arab delegations walked out, Zionists in the audience rejoiced.

It was a rejoicing that started with silence and grew as the meaning neared its end. In the public lobby there were kisses and tears and excited laughter. In the delegates' lounge a rabbi cried, "This is the day the Lord hath made! Let us rejoice in it and be glad!"

The initial silence resulted from a call to order by the Assembly's president, Dr. Oswaldo Aranha. A burst of applause had greeted the affirmative vote of France in favor of partition, and it was that had

Continued on Page 57, Column 2

Arabs See U. N. 'Murdered,' Disavow Any Partition Role

Angry Delegates Stalk From Assembly Hall Before Formal Closing—Silver Voices Gratification, Offers Friendship

By A. M. ROSENTHAL

Bitter Arab delegates walked out of the General Assembly hall at Flushing Meadow last night after the vote for the partition of Palestine and solemnly announced that in their eyes the United Nations had died.

"No, not died," said Faris el-Khouri of Syria, "Murdered."

The representatives of the Arab states swept out of the building without waiting for the formal end of the Assembly and the farewell speeches. But before they announced that their limousines were waiting they expressed their gratitude to the Assembly and especially to the United States and the Soviet Union.

Dr. Silver's statement follows:

"We are deeply gratified with the action of the General Assembly of the United Nations. It marks a turning point in Jewish history. It is an impressive reaffirmation of the just claim of the Jewish people to rebuild its national life in its ancestral home.

"This noble decision to re-establish the Jewish state and restore

Continued on Page 56, Column 2

responsibility would not be theirs but would be on the shoulders of the countries that had pressed for partition.

On the other side of the quarter-century Arab-Zionist dispute there was jubilance and hope for the future. Dr. Abba Hillel Silver, chairman of the American section of the Jewish Agency for Palestine, expressed his gratitude to the Assembly and especially to the United States and the Soviet Union.

There was an open thread of warning running through all the Arab delegates' comments on the Assembly's action. They spoke of bloodshed to come and said the

U. N. REJECTS DELAY

Proposal Driven Through by U. S. and Soviet Will Set Up Two States

COMMISSION IS APPOINTED

Britain Holds Out Hand to It— Arabs Fail in Last-Minute Resort to Federal Plan

By THOMAS J. HAMILTON

The United Nations General Assembly approved today a proposal to partition Palestine into two states, one Arab and the other Jewish, that are to become fully independent by Oct. 1.

The vote was 33 to 13 with ten abstentions and one delegation, the Siamese, absent.

The decision was primarily a result of the fact that the delegations of the United States and the Soviet Union, which were at loggerheads on every other important issue before the Assembly, stood together on partition. Andrei A. Gromyko and Herschel V. Johnson both urged the Assembly yesterday not to agree to further delay but to vote for partition at once.

The Assembly disregarded last-minute Arab efforts to effect a compromise. Although the votes of a dozen or more delegations seesawed to the last, supporters of partition always had more than the required two-thirds majority, or a margin of three.

How Members Voted

The roll-call vote was as follows:

For (33)—Australia, Belgium, Bolivia, Brazil, Canada, Costa Rica, Czechoslovakia, Denmark, Dominican Republic, Ecuador, France, Guatemala, Haiti, Iceland, Liberia, Luxembourg, the Netherlands, New Zealand, Nicaragua, Norway, Panama, Paraguay, Peru, Philippines, Poland, Sweden, the Ukraine, South Africa, Uruguay, the Soviet Union, the United States, Venezuela, White Russia.

Against (13)—Afghanistan, Cuba, Egypt, Greece, India, Iran, Iraq, Lebanon, Pakistan, Saudi Arabia, Syria, Turkey, Yemen.

Abstentions (10) — Argentina, Chile, China, Colombia, El Salvador, Ethiopia, Honduras, Mexico, United Kingdom, Yugoslavia.

Absent (1)—Siam.

All other questions before the Assembly were disposed of a week ago, and it ended its second regular session at 6:57 P. M. after farewell speeches by Dr. Oswaldo Aranha, its President, and Trygve Lie, the Secretary General. The Assembly's third regular session is to open in a European capital on Sept. 21.

The vote on partition was taken at 5:35 P. M. Representatives of Iraq, Saudi Arabia, Syria and Yemen, four of the six Arab member states, announced that they would not be bound by the Assembly's decision and walked determinedly out of the Assembly Hall at Flushing Meadow. The Egyptian and Lebanese delegates were silent but walked out, too.

Britain Seeks Contact

Sir Alexander Cadogan, representative of Britain, which is to terminate the League of Nations mandate over Palestine and withdraw all British troops by Aug. 1, made a brief statement after the vote. He requested the United Nations Palestine Commission to establish contact with the British Government about the date of its arrival in Palestine and the coordination of its plans with the withdrawal of British troops.

The United Nations commission, which will be responsible to the Security Council in the event that the Arab carry out their threats to fight rather than agree to partition, will be composed of representatives of Bolivia, Czechoslovakia, Denmark, Panama and the Philippines.

This state, which is understood to have the backing of the United States Commission, was proposed by Dr. Aranha and approved without opposition by all the Arab delegates but walked out.

The commission, as proposed, has the subcommittee of the

Continued on Page 56, Column 8

Company Asks Rise in Gas Rate From $1.15 to $2 Sliding Scale

The Consolidated Edison Company of New York, Inc., announced yesterday it had applied to the State Public Service Commission for permission to increase the maximum charge for gas from $1.15 to $2 a thousand cubic feet to 12 to 000,000 present customers in immediate schedule of temporary rates, which it estimated would increase its annual revenue approximately $9,520,700 on the basis of estimated gas sales for 1947.

The petition said that neither Consolidated Edison nor any of its predecessor companies had increased its rates since Oct. 1, 1922, and that existing rates were unsufficient of the company's property. It was explained that the company would lose $1,408,500 in 1947 through its gas operations.

According to the company, 87 per cent of the gas it supplies is sold at the maximum rate of $1.15 a thousand cubic feet. The company's service area includes 1,100,000 customers in Manhattan, the Bronx and the first and third wards of Queens—Astoria, Long

Island City, Flushing, College Point, Whitestone, Douglaston, Bayside, Little Neck and Bellerose.

The company proposed an immediate schedule of temporary rates, which it estimated would increase its annual revenue approximately $9,520,700 on the basis of estimated gas sales for 1947.

This increase had been in effect through 1947. In this connection, the company said, it would have provided the company with a net return after taxes of $4,200,000 in connection with its gas operations.

If approved by the Public Service Commission, the new classification would provide a minimum charge of $3 for the first thousand cubic feet or less of gas consumed in any bi-monthly billing period.

For the first 4,000 cubic feet consumed bi-monthly after the initial 1,000-foot block, residential customers would be charged 12 cents a hundred; the next 6,000

Continued on Page 13, Column 1

The New York Times.

"All the News That's Fit to Print"

LATE CITY EDITION
Fair and warmer today and tomorrow.
Temperature Range Today—Max., 65; Min., 48
Temperature Yesterday—Max., 53; Min., 46
Full U. S. Weather Bureau Report, Page 21

Copyright, 1948, by The New York Times Company.

VOL. XCVII..No. 32,984.

Entered as Second-Class Matter,
Postoffice, New York, N. Y.

NEW YORK, SATURDAY, MAY 15, 1948.

Times Square, New York 18, N. Y.
Telephone Lackawanna 4-1000

THREE CENTS NEW YORK CITY

ZIONISTS PROCLAIM NEW STATE OF ISRAEL; TRUMAN RECOGNIZES IT AND HOPES FOR PEACE; TEL AVIV IS BOMBED, EGYPT ORDERS INVASION

NAVY PUSHES PLAN FOR CONSTRUCTION OF MISSILE VESSELS

Sullivan Asks House Committee to Approve Halting Work on Battleship, Destroyer Types

WANTS 65,000-TON CARRIER

Halting 'Submarine Killers' Also Stressed in Plea for Diverting $300,000,000 Fund

By C. P. TRUSSELL
Special to The New York Times.

WASHINGTON, May 14—The Navy asked Congress today for authority to shift sharply its construction of fighting craft from battleship, cruiser and destroyer types to guided missile vessels, a 65,000-ton carrier able to base, for new planes, planes with an operating radius of 1,700 miles, better submarines and floating "enemy submarine killers."

Such new ships, John L. Sullivan, Secretary of the Navy, told the House Armed Services Committee, must have a higher priority—"because of the more immediate need for them in the event of an emergency." The immediate action of the committee appeared to favor prompt action.

For such a shift in construction, Secretary Sullivan brought out, the Navy wanted to halt the building of thirteen naval vessels, including the battleship Kentucky, large cruiser Hawaii, seven destroyers, two destroyer escorts and two submarines. To date this new money was not to be abandoned, Mr. Sullivan emphasized. These craft could be conserved now to the new program, he explained, or be put aside for putting-out later as new weapons are developed.

Aims for $300,000,000 Fund

That the Navy wanted, Secretary Sullivan asserted, was Congressional permission to divert $300,000,000 remaining in the present ship construction account for these purposes:

Starting the 65,000-ton aircraft carrier (the biggest ones now are two of the Midway class, at 45,000 tons), which might cost $124,000,000.

Building, for reproduction later, if the defense program have indicated that Russia has made progress in the submarine field.) A "killer" machine, it is indicated, is developing in line with on the cruiser type of seacraft.

The construction of four submarines of types advanced beyond any now building.

In addition, there was under way a conversion in an unidentified way of a carrier and two submarines.

Secretary Sullivan told the committee that the Kentucky and the Hawaii would not have to stand by the development of new weapons. It is planned, he disclosed, that they be converted into guided missile ships. Apparently to allay the fears in Congress that larger aircraft carriers make easier targets for enemy bombers, Mr. Sullivan drew upon experience in the second World War and the results of atom-bomb tests at Bikini.

Speed Held Bomb Defense

The experiments at Bikini," Mr. Sullivan said, "have proved that a fast-moving fleet is an unsuitable target for an atomic bomb."

He reminded the committee members that even though potential enemy might acquire an atomic bomb, the revised construction program proposed today promised a maximum of safety.

Mr. Sullivan recalled that the carriers in the Pacific, but that we lost three large and four carriers in the Pacific, but that none was sunk by aircraft landed. He indicated that mobility of a fleet, equipped to latest model, would discourage the spending of atomic bombs, even if an enemy had some.

Today, the Senate Republican

Continued on Page 7, Column 4

Heaviest Trading in 8 Years Marks Stock Market Spurt

3,840,000 Shares Change Hands as Wave of Bullish Enthusiasm Increases Securities 1 to 7 Points

The hectic days of the Nineteen Twenties were re-enacted yesterday on the floor of the New York Stock Exchange when the most turbulent session in recent years produced increases of 1 to 7 points in the share list. Accompanied by a burst of bullish enthusiasm not witnessed in almost a decade, the deluge of buying orders so taxed the facilities of the Exchange that the reporting ticker tape lagged behind floor transactions by five minutes.

The cracking of the 1947 high level at the approach of mid-day served as the signal for a buying rush. Public participation suddenly enlarged and buying orders pressed floor traders to the utmost. This condition existed for forty-five minutes in the final hour when 1,350,000 shares were traded.

Accompanied by the broadest market on record with a total of 1,151 issues dealt in, volume on the Stock Exchange spiraled to 3,840,000 shares, the largest since May 21, 1940, in contrast to the Thursday turnover of 2,030,000 shares.

Brokers termed it the "wildest" bull market in twenty years on the premise that at no time in the interval had the industrials and rails advanced with such a unity of force.

While the ground had been well laid for a movement of such scope earlier this week, it was the piercing of the 1947 resistance point that confirmed the presence of a bull market to those who act by the charts, or averages. Early in the day, telegrams were sent by several advisory services to their clients urging the purchase of securities. The response to this advice showed primarily in the late

Continued on Page 23, Column 4

Truman Sees His Election; Calls GOP 'Obstructionist'

By ANTHONY LEVIERO
Special to The New York Times.

WASHINGTON, May 14—President Truman asserted tonight that there would be a Democrat in the White House during the next four years and that he would be the man. He made the statement to a cheering audience of 1,000 young Democrats at their meeting here.

The President's speech was a fighting one in the new Truman manner. He spoke extemporaneously, resorting to whimsy and irony and using forceful gestures of his arms to underscore his points.

Mr. Truman accused the Republican party of stealing Democratic platform planks. "You know," he said, "it has been their habit since 1936 of taking a few planks out of the old Democratic platforms and building a platform and then saying, 'Me, too.'"

[The text of President Truman's speech is on Page 7.]

"What have the Republicans done in the last fifteen and a half years?" Mr. Truman asked, then said:

"They have been obstructionist. They spent most of their time while I was in the Senate—and I was there for ten years—in obstructing progressive legislation that was for the welfare of the common man, and throwing bricks and mud at the greatest President that ever sat in the White House."

Mr. Truman was interrupted by applause at this obvious allusion to President Roosevelt.

"That has been their record," he continued, "and they haven't changed a bit. They were against Social Security. They were against TVA. They were against wages

Continued on Page 7, Column 2

MINNESOTA'S GUARD OUT IN MEAT STRIKE

Governor Acts After 200 Raid Cudahy Newport Plant, Attack 60 Workers and Abduct 25

Special to The New York Times.

ST. PAUL, Minn., May 14—National Guard troops were ordered to South St. Paul and Newport, towns on opposite banks of the Mississippi River near here, by Governor Luther Youngdahl today following violent disorders at strike-bound packing plants in the two areas and the statement of the local sheriffs that their forces could not maintain law and order.

The Governor did not declare martial law but said the troops would take their orders from the civil authorities.

The Governor's action followed a serious outbreak at the Cudahy packing plant in Newport shortly before last midnight in which a group of about 200 men raided the plant with clubs, knives and hammers. In South St. Paul on Thursday strikers forced back pickets who tried to open a way through picket lines at the Swift & Co. plant in

Continued on Page 15, Column 2

Princess Elizabeth, in Paris Talk, Asks Common Effort of 2 Nations

By LANSING WARREN

PARIS, May 14—Speaking in faultless French with just the touch of a British accent to delight French ears, Princess Elizabeth today visited France and Britain to make a common effort to lead Europe to moral and intellectual as well as economic reconstruction.

Her well-worded and discerning speech was cheered, but as her said straight to the hearts of the Parisian throng when, with disarming frankness, she avowed her joy that her first foreign trip since her marriage had brought her here to Paris.

"For a long time," she said, "I have wanted to come to France. More fortunate than I, my husband already knew your admirable capital but he is all the happier to return. This trip is all the more important and agreeable to the warmth of your welcome which has touched us both."

From the time they stepped down from the train at the Gare du Nord early today, Princess Elizabeth and Prince Philip, Duke of Edinburgh, were the center of admiring attention from the throngs that lined the streets and from all the French officials who received them throughout the day.

President Vincent Auriol voiced the general feeling when in a statement issued tonight he said:

"I have been personally struck by her grace, her charm, her modesty and her nobility. I feel sure that the sentiments that she has expressed went straight to the hearts of all the French."

Elizabeth's address, broadcast to the French nation, was delivered from the top of the monumental entry to the Galliera Museum, where she came to open the British Government's exhibition of relics and souvenirs of famous Brit-

Continued on Page 6, Column 5

AIR ATTACK OPENS

Planes Cause Fires at Port—Defense Fliers Go Into Action

BORDER IS BREACHED

Cairo Vanguard Takes Colony—Trans-Jordan Reports a Movement

By The Associated Press.

TEL AVIV, Palestine, Saturday, May 15—Air raiders bombed this all-Jewish city at about dawn today.

First reports said there were "some casualties" near the power and light station.

[Cairo reported that Egyptian armed forces had been ordered to Palestine. Arab armies moved from Trans-Jordan at 12:01 A. M. Saturday to "liberate the Holy Land from Zionism," said a Trans-Jordan communique reported by The United Press from Amman.]

Tel Aviv was under complete blackout all night but no sirens were sounded during the raid. Civil guards were alerted and fifteen to twenty ships in the port area moved out to sea.

The planes swooped over Tel Aviv little more than twelve hours after Jewish leaders proclaimed the existence of a new Hebrew state of Israel.

Some bombs fell in the vicinity of the power station along the Yarkon River near Tel Aviv.

Persons at the scene said there was one hit on or near the power station, causing "some casualties."

TEL AVIV, Saturday, May 15—Some ten bombs were dropped on Tel Aviv by two air craft described as bombers and accompanied by two small fighters. One Jew was killed and three were hospitalized. Jewish Army aircraft took to the skies a few minutes after the enemy planes whizzed over rooftops at an estimated altitude of 300 feet.

Several fires could be seen north

Continued on Page 3, Column 3

U. S. MOVES QUICKLY

President Acknowledges de Facto Authority of Israel Immediately

TRUCE AIM STRESSED

Soviet Gesture to New Nation Anticipated— Others Due to Act

By BERTRAM D. HULEN
Special to The New York Times.

WASHINGTON, May 14—President Truman announced early tonight recognition by the United States of the new Jewish State of Israel. The President acted instantly upon being informed that the new nation had been proclaimed.

"This Government," he announced, "has been informed that a Jewish state has been proclaimed in Palestine and recognition has been requested by the provisional government thereof.

"The United States recognizes the provisional government as the de facto authority of the new State of Israel."

These two paragraphs constituted the text of the President's statement.

Coupled with the announcement was an expression of hope for peace in Palestine. This was made known through a separate White House statement issued by Charles G. Ross, Presidential press secretary.

"The desire of the United States to obtain a truce in Palestine," this said, "will in no way be lessened by the proclamation of a Jewish state.

"We hope that the new Jewish state will join with the Security Council Truce Commission in redoubled efforts to bring an end to the fighting—which has been throughout the United Nations' consideration of Palestine a principal objective of this Government."

[Pending stabilization of the Palestine situation and indications that the State of Israel

Continued on Page 3, Column 2

World News Summarized

SATURDAY, MAY 15, 1948

Several hours after the state of Israel, the first Hebrew nation in 2,000 years, had been proclaimed in a Zionist declaration of independence in Tel Aviv, [1:8.], President Truman announced that the United States recognized the "provisional government" of Israel as the "de facto authority of the new state." A second White House statement expressed the hope that the new regime would cooperate with United Nations efforts to bring about peace in Palestine. [1:5.] The British High Commissioner departed from Palestine and boarded a cruiser at Haifa as Britain's rule over the Holy Land formally ended. [1:7.]

The special session of the United Nations General Assembly ended last night after it had agreed to send a mediator to Palestine to try to arrange a truce. [1:6-7.] The mediation plan for Jerusalem sponsored by the United States was rejected by the Assembly, with the Arab states and the Soviet opposed to the measure. [1:6-7.]

Tel Aviv was bombed at dawn. Egypt ordered her troops to invade Palestine and Trans-Jordan reported her army on the move also. [1:4.] Haganah claimed that its forces captured Acre in the north. [2:8.]

In Moscow the newspaper Pravda, in the first editorial comment on the recent exchange between Washington and Moscow, accused the United States of double-dealing. [4:8.]

Paris crowds gave an enthusiastic welcome to Princess Elizabeth and the Duke of Edinburgh when they arrived for a visit. [1:2-3.]

Congress received a request from the Navy for authority to shift the emphasis in its construction of fighting craft to guided-missile vessels. [1:1.]

President Truman predicted that he would be re-elected next November. [1:2-3.]

Minnesota National Guard troops were rushed to South St. Paul and Newport after 200 persons had raided the Cudahy meat packing plant at Newport, where a strike is in progress, attacking about sixty workers and abducting twenty-five of them. [1:2.]

The New York Stock Exchange enjoyed one of its biggest days in recent years as an avalanche of buying orders sent stocks up from 1 to 7 points. Trading reached a total of 3,840,000 shares, the largest since May 21, 1940. [1:2-3.]

Winston Churchill's War Memoirs

See Page 17 for today's installment, in which Mr. Churchill describes the invasion of Norway and the clash of the British and German fleets.

AT HELM OF THE JEWISH STATE

David Ben-Gurion
Premier

Moshe Shertok
Foreign Minister
The New York Times

U. N. Votes for a Mediator; Special Assembly Is Ended

By THOMAS J. HAMILTON

After hearing both the Soviet Union and the Arab delegates denounce the United States for its sudden recognition of the new Jewish state, the United Nations General Assembly decided last night to send a Mediator to the Holy Land to see what he could to arrange a truce and carry on public services.

The vote was 31 to 7, with sixteen abstentions and four delegates absent, and the General Assembly, which was called into special session at Flushing Meadow on April 16 at the request of the United States, adjourned for good at 8:32 P. M.

The failure of the General Assembly either to repeal the partition resolution of last November or to provide military force to keep the peace means that the fate of Palestine will be decided by the impending war between Jews and Arabs, not by any United Nations action.

The mediation resolution conforms substantially with a United States proposal announced last Wednesday, after it had become obvious that the General Assembly would not accept the original United States plan for a temporary trusteeship.

However, the General Assembly refused to accept a United States plan for a temporary trusteeship over Jerusalem, which was rejected earlier in the evening by a vote of 20 to 15, less than the necessary two-thirds majority.

Two other proposals regarding Jerusalem were rejected, but presumably the provisions of the partition resolution on Jerusalem, which was to have been established as an international enclave under the administration of the Trusteeship Council, still stand.

In addition, the Assembly de-

Continued on Page 4, Column 4

CUNNINGHAM GOES AS MANDATE ENDS

British Commissioner Boards Cruiser Off Haifa—Jews Take Down Union Jack

By The Associated Press.

HAIFA, Palestine, May 15—Britain ended her mandate over the Holy Land last midnight. Lieut. Gen. Sir Alan Cunningham, the last British High Commissioner, sailed from Haifa port, finishing British mandate guidance.

Sir Alan's departure from Palestine's richest port caused little excitement among the Jews, who control most of the city.

The British fired a few rockets and searchlights spotlighted the cruiser as it steamed from the harbor.

Wearing the uniform of a British Army general, Sir Alan walked down a few steps of dock into a launch that took him to the cruiser Euryalus.

Upon getting into the launch, he turned and looked soberly up across the docks. There stood an honor guard of the King's Company of Grenadier Guards and Royal Marine commandos.

The launch pulled away amid the

Continued on Page 2, Column 7

U. N. Bars Jerusalem Trusteeship; Vote Follows Mandate Deadline

By MALLORY BROWNE

The United Nations General Assembly rejected yesterday the United States plan for a temporary trusteeship regime in Jerusalem. Solidly opposed by the Arab States and the Russian bloc, the plan to set up a United Nations Commissioner authorized to protect the Holy City and its holy places failed to obtain the necessary two-thirds majority at the closing session at Flushing Meadow.

The vote, which came just after the bombshell of the United States recognition of the new Jewish State had burst in the Assembly, was 20 in favor, 15 against and 20 abstentions. The balance was turned by the hostility of Britain and most of the Dominions.

The United States fought hard all day, first in the Political and Security Committee of the Assembly, sitting at Lake Success, and then in the evening session of the Assembly, to get the trusteeship plan adopted before the end of the

(mandate at 6:01 P. M. time, New York time.)

An Arab filibuster, aided by the Soviet bloc, defeated this effort. It was well past the zero hour when a roll-call vote showed that the Assembly preferred to leave Harold Evans, newly appointed Jerusalem municipal Commissioner, in sole charge of the Holy City and its treasures.

As one Arab after another filed up to the tribune and took up the maximum five-minute period allowed in repeating the arguments against a trusteeship plan, 6:01 o'clock went by.

At once Awni Khalidy of Iraq, who had led the Arab fight against the trusteeship plan, rushed up to the tribune and exultantly proclaimed that the time had passed; that the mandate was at an end, and that, since, as Francis B. Sayre of the United States had said, the measure must

Continued on Page 2, Column 6

THE JEWS REJOICE

Some Weep as Quest for Statehood Ends —White Paper Dies

HELP OF U. N. ASKED

New Regime Holds Out Hand to Arabs—U. S. Gesture Acclaimed

Text of declaration setting up new Jewish state, Page 2.

By GENE CURRIVAN

TEL AVIV, Palestine, Saturday, May 15—The Jewish state, the world's newest sovereignty, to be known as the State of Israel, came into being in Palestine at midnight upon termination of the British mandate.

Recognition of the state by the United States, which also opposed its establishment at this time, came as a complete surprise to the people, who were tense and ready for the threatened invasion by Arab forces and appealed for help by the United Nations.

In one of the most hopeful periods of their troubled history the Jewish people here gave a sigh of relief and took a new hold on life when they learned that the present national power had accepted them into the international fraternity.

Ceremony Simple and Solemn

The declaration of the new state by David Ben-Gurion, chairman of the National Council and the first Premier of reborn Israel, was delivered during a simple and solemn ceremony at 4 P. M., and new life was instilled into his people, but from without there was the rumbling of guns, a flashback to other declarations of independence that had not been easily achieved.

The first action of the new Government was to revoke the Palestine White Paper of 1939, which restricted Jewish immigration and land purchase.

In the proclamation of the new state the Government appealed to the Jewish people in the building of its state and to admit Israel into the family of nations.

The proclamation added:

"We offer peace and amity to all neighboring states and their peoples, and invite them to cooperate with the independent Jewish nation for the common good of all. The State of Israel is ready to contribute its full share to the peaceful progress and reconstruction of the Middle East."

World Jews Asked to Aid

The statement appealed to Jews throughout the world to assist in the task of immigration and development and in the "struggle for the fulfillment of the dream of generations—the redemption of Israel."

Plans for the ceremony had been laid with great secrecy. None but the hundred or more invited guests and journalists were aware of the meeting until it started, and even then the news leaked out at the only ten minutes before. It was held in the Tel Aviv Museum of Art, a white, modern-design two-story building. Above it flew the blue Star of David, which is the state's flag, and below, on the sidewalk, was a guard of honor of the Haganah, the army of the Jewish Agency for Palestine.

As photographers' bulbs flashed and movie cameras ground out reels of the scene, great crowds gathered and cheered the Ministers and other members of the Government as they entered the building.

The security arrangements were perfect. Sten guns were brandished in every direction and even the hundred selected guests were frisked with thoroughness.

The setting for the reading of the proclamation was a dropped gallery whose hall held paintings by prominent Jewish artists. Many of them depicted the sufferings and joys of the people of the Diaspora, the dispersal of the Jews.

The thirteen Ministers of the

Continued on Page 2, Column 3

"All the News
That's Fit to Print"

The New York Times.

LATE CITY EDITION
Partly cloudy and mild today; fair
tonight and tomorrow.

Temperature Range Today—Max., 65; Min., 47
Temperature Yesterday—Max., 60; Min., 46
Full U. S. Weather Bureau Report, Page 44

Copyright, 1949, by The New York Times Company.

VOL. XCVIII..No. 33,346.   Entered as Second-Class Matter,
Postoffice, New York, N. Y.   NEW YORK, THURSDAY, MAY 12, 1949.   Times Square, New York 18, N. Y.
Telephone Lackawanna 4-1000   THREE CENTS NEW YORK CITY

ISRAEL WINS A SEAT IN U.N. BY 37-12 VOTE

ARABS INDIGNANT

Quit the Assembly Hall After Poll—9 Nations Abstain in Ballot

59TH COUNTRY IN BODY

Israel's Foreign Chief Sharett Pledges Peace Effort—Debate Brings Polish Attack

By THOMAS J. HAMILTON

The General Assembly admitted Israel to membership in the United Nations at 7:28 last night by a vote of 37 to 12, with nine abstentions.

The delegations of the six Arab states—Egypt, Iraq, Lebanon, Saudi Arabia, Syria and Yemen—walked out at the Assembly Hall at Flushing Meadow in protest before the applause over the election of Israel as the fifty-ninth member of the United Nations had died away. They indignantly refused to make any statement to correspondents regarding their intentions, but drove away to New York.

The Arab delegates, who also walked out when the General Assembly adopted the resolution recommending the partition of Palestine on Nov. 29, 1947 gave no hint of their impending action in their speeches in the General Assembly in the afternoon.

Charge Israeli Violation

They protested bitterly, however, that Israel had refused to comply with the provisions of a General Assembly resolution adopted on Dec. 11, 1948, calling for an international regime in Jerusalem and the repatriation of Arab refugees. Also, they challenged the validity of a Security Council recommendation for the admission of Israel, since Britain, a permanent member of the Council, had abstained.

The Charter requires the concurring votes of the Big Five on all except procedural questions, and the Arab delegates insisted that the Assembly should first get a ruling from the International Court of Justice. This procedure was contained in a resolution presented by Iraq yesterday afternoon, but Dr. Evatt ruled it out of order on the ground that the General Assembly could not examine the decision of another United Nations body.

The Yemen delegation returned shortly after 10 o'clock for the night session of the Assembly, and an Egyptian delegate came back into the Assembly later, but the other desks remained vacant.

Immediately after the vote Dr. Evatt summoned to the platform Moshe Sharett, Israeli Foreign Minister, who had arrived by plane from Tel Aviv early yesterday to hear the final speeches.

"We enter this Assembly, which represents the collective statesmanship of the world, in a spirit of humility, anxious for guidance and enlightenment," said Mr. Sharett, who re-stated the Israeli policy of "loyalty to the fundamental principles of the United Nations' Charter and friendship with all peace-loving states, especially with the United States of America and the Union of Soviet Socialist Republics."

New a Working Member

Mr. Sharett took his seat at the desk that had previously been prepared for the Israeli delegation in the back of the Assembly hall, between the Iraqi and Lebanese delegations. United Nations officials said no additional formalities were required, and that Israel would have the right to participate in all further proceedings of the General Assembly on the same basis as the fifty-eight other members.

The vote came too late to permit the Israeli flag to be raised in the area in front of the main delegates' entrance. A flag pole, however, had been prepared in advance, and there will be a ceremony at Lake Success at 10:30 A. M. today.

The General Assembly took up the application at its afternoon session and the debate concluded at 7:30 as a result of the fact that the protests of the Arab delegates,

Continued on Page 18, Column 3

KENNY TO ASK COURT FOR ORDER TO SEIZE JERSEY CITY BOOKS

Mayor-Elect Seeks to Prevent Any Alterations of Records to Shield Old Regime

FULL INQUIRY IS PLANNED

'It's All Right With Me,' Says Hague of Defeat—Fight for State Rule Likely

By LEO EGAN

The political coalition that dethroned Frank Hague as boss of Jersey City has decided to seek a court order barring the outgoing city administration from destroying or altering official records before it leaves office next Tuesday.

John V. Kenny, who headed the coalition and who will become Mayor in the new administration, said a formal application for an order impounding city books and records would be submitted tomorrow to Judge William Brennan in Hudson County Superior Court.

One of the first acts of the new regime, Mr. Kenny added, will be to order a full-scale audit of the records and accounts of the outgoing administration, headed by Mayor Frank Hague Eggers, nephew of the 73-year-old former Mayor, who was one of the last of the old-time bosses in the United States to yield up his political power.

Drive to End State Rule Seen

While the new regime was making its plans for sifting city records for evidence of illegal acts and misuse of public funds on behalf of the Hague machine, Democrats in other parts of New Jersey were contemplating a drive to strip Mr. Hague of his control of the state Democratic party in the state.

Many Democrats fear that unless Mr. Hague's connections with the state organizations are severed the fall elections will result in an overwhelming victory for the Republican State ticket, headed by Gov. Alfred E. Driscoll.

In any reorganization of the Democratic State Committee, Mr. Kenny, who was leader of the Second Ward in Jersey City for many years, is expected to play a leading role. So are former Mayor Meyer C. Ellenstein of Newark, who topped all candidates for City Commissioner there in Tuesday's election, and Mayor George Brunner of Camden.

David Wilentz, who prosecuted Bruno Richard Hauptmann for the Lindbergh kidnapping, and Mayor Michael De Vito of Paterson are also expected to play important parts in any reorganization movement.

In the interview yesterday afternoon in which he told of his plans Mr. Kenny announced also that he would support State Senator Elmer Wene for Governor on the Democratic ticket this fall. Senator Wene won the Democratic nomination with the backing of Mr. Hague in a recent primary.

The interview was ex-sandwiched in between posing for newsreels and making an appearance on a television program. Although he looked tired and his voice was hoarse, Mr. Kenny said he felt "fine."

With respect to his plans on taking over, Mr. Kenny said that

Continued on Page 16, Column 2

WAR PENSION BILL IS SHARPLY LIMITED

House Group Confines Benefit to Unemployable and Reports Measure as Rankin Protests

By JOHN D. MORRIS
Special to The New York Times.

WASHINGTON, May 11—The new veterans pension bill was further watered down in committee today—to such an extent that its author, Representative John E. Rankin, Democrat, of Mississippi, voted, though in vain, against reporting it to the House.

The action was taken by the House Veterans Affairs Committee at a closed meeting that had been scheduled merely to formalize its action yesterday in approving pensions on a more liberal basis.

The committee voted, 14 to 8, to confine the $72-a-month payments to unemployable veterans. By a voice vote, it then cleared the measure formally to the House.

Approval of the limitation was prompted by Veterans Administration estimates, drawn up overnight, that without it the bill would cost $65,000,000,000 to the cost of veterans' benefits over the next fifty years. Yesterday's action had been based on a $12,000,000,000 estimate.

As finally approved, the measure's fifty-year cost was estimated at $8,693,000,000 by Guy H. Birdsall, assistant veterans administrator.

Mr. Rankin was joined by Representative A. Leonard Allen, Democrat, of Louisiana, in voting against reporting the bill. Shortly afterward the Mississippi legislator arose in the House to protest the action of the committee, of which he is chairman.

The employability issue, he asserted, would bar pensions from

Continued on Page 46, Column 4

Johnson Approves Air Force Plan To Distribute Negroes Among Units

Special to The New York Times.

WASHINGTON, May 11—Latest proposals by the Air Force to conform to armed service policy on racial equality were approved today by Louis Johnson, Secretary of Defense.

W. Stuart Symington, Secretary of the Air Force, wrote to Secretary Johnson on April 30 and assured the defense chief that his directive of April 6 asking equality of treatment and opportunity "without regard to race, color, religion, or national origin" would be put into effect.

In his reply to the Army and Navy, Mr. Johnson fixed a deadline of May 25 by which the two services are to provide more details of their plans to conform to the equality policy. The services were instructed to make their replies through Thomas R. Reid, chairman of the National Military Establishment's Personnel Policy Board.

Mr. Johnson made his April 6 directive to the armed service secretaries public on April 30, at which time he stated that he in-

Secretary of the Army at that time, and Dan A. Kimball, Assistant Secretary of the Navy, answering the same April 6 directive, were in effect rejected by Mr. Johnson on the ground that they were too general. The Secretary of Defense asked the two officials to "clarify" the information contained in their responses. Both letters, it was learned, told Mr. Johnson that his policy was already in effect, and did not indicate that additional changes would be made.

One of the principal shows in this direction is an Air Force order disbanding the all-Negro 332nd Fighter Wing at Lockbourne Air Force base at Columbus, Ohio. Its 2,000 officers and men will be distributed throughout the service in non-segregated units, it was stated.

Another assurance given to Mr. Johnson, it was learned, was that "key" positions will be open to Negroes who are individually qualified to hold them.

Letters from Kenneth C. Royall,

BERLIN LAND BLOCKADE IS LIFTED; FIRST TRAIN, AUTOS REACH CITY; ZONE TROOP RETIREMENT STUDIED

U. S. PLAN WEIGHED

Big 3 Would Withdraw to Ports in the North Under Proposal

FRENCH WOULD GO HOME

Presentation of Suggestion Will Depend on Soviet Stand in Paris Talks

By JAMES RESTON
Special to The New York Times.

WASHINGTON, May 11—The United States was reported today to have under consideration a plan under which all occupation troops in Germany would be withdrawn into restricted areas at the North German ports.

Under this plan, which is being discussed with Britain and France, Soviet troops would be situated on the West Bank of the Oder in Stettin, British troops would be restricted to the area of Hamburg, and United States troops would be concentrated in Bremen.

(Stettin was included in the Soviet zone in the Potsdam pact, but under a separate agreement reached Sept. 20, 1947, the Russians turned over control of the former German port to Poland. Bremen is a United States enclave in the British zone.)

These troops, it is understood, would be obliged, under this plan, to use only sea communications, and France, which has a common frontier with Germany, would withdraw her occupation troops into her own territory.

An understanding apparently already has been reached among the Western powers to reject any Soviet proposal at the forthcoming meeting of the Council of Foreign Ministers in Paris for the complete evacuation of all occupation troops from all of Germany.

It is felt here that total withdrawal of these troops would be detrimental to the economic recovery and sense of security of Western Europe.

However, if Soviet Foreign Minister Andrei Y. Vishinsky should demonstrate in Paris that his Government was now prepared to establish a central government in Germany along the lines laid down by the Western powers for the

Continued on Page 3, Column 2

IT'S A REAL HOLIDAY FOR THESE BERLIN YOUNGSTERS

Joyous children hold their lunch boxes over their heads as they get news that there will be no school in celebration of the end of the blockade. The sign reads "blockade free."
Associated Press Radiophoto

ACHESON STILL BARS FRANCO AS FASCIST

Says Spanish Regime Denies Basic Rights in the Pattern of Hitler and Mussolini

Secretary Acheson's remarks on Spanish regime, Page 10.

By BERTRAM D. HULEN
Special to The New York Times.

WASHINGTON, May 11—Secretary of State Dean Acheson declared today that the question of restoring full diplomatic relations with Spain turned primarily upon the attitude of Western European countries that were still opposed to bringing her back into their international family for military and economic cooperation.

This attitude, the Secretary told his weekly news conference, was conditioned by the absence of fundamental freedoms under the Franco regime which, he said, originally and still was patterned on Nazi Germany and Fascist Italy. At one

Continued on Page 10, Column 1

Eisler Reported Stowaway; Seizure in Britain Is Asked

By WILL LISSNER

A man who has identified himself as Gerhart Eisler, native of Germany, is fleeing from the United States aboard the Gdynia-America liner Batory, it became known yesterday. The fugitive—believed to be the former Comintern agent named by the House Un-American Activities Committee as America's No. 1 Communist, jumping $23,500 bail to escape serving a year in jail and other penalties, but his identity has not yet been definitely established.

The Federal Bureau of Investigation and the Immigration and Naturalization Service of the Department of Justice moved yesterday to fix the identity of the fugitive. If the man aboard the Batory is the German-born Communist leader Eisler, he will be placed in custody for eventual return.

The fugitive is bound for Gdynia, but the ship, which sailed last Saturday, will not reach Southampton Saturday. To make sure that Polish Communists aboard the ship do not balk at a return, the State Department, at the request of the Department of Justice, notified Scotland Yard of the incident and asked that top investigators meet the ship on her arrival in the English port. Scotland Yard was asked to hold the suspect.

If Eisler, the convicted Communist agent, has fled the jurisdiction of the Federal District Court, his bail would be forfeited even though the English authorities return him, it was said at the Federal Building.

The forfeiture of the $23,500 bail would be a blow to the Civil Rights Congress and the American Committee for the Protection of the Foreign Born. For a good part of

Continued on Page 4, Column 3

FIRST BERLIN TRAIN FROM WEST SEALED

Officials Lock Doors and Draw Shades to Keep Russians Out and Reporters In

By The United Press.

BERLIN, Thursday, May 12—The first western passenger train since last year arrived in Berlin at 5:11 A. M. today (11:11 P. M. Wednesday, Eastern Daylight Time)—hauled by a Soviet zone locomotive.

A combined British-American train of twelve cars, it carried approximately 140 Western officials, including seventy-three British troops and at least a score of reporters.

Anglo-American officials ordered the doors locked and the shades drawn soon after the train left Helmstedt at 1:23 A. M., the first train to make the West-East run on the Helmstedt-Berlin road since last year.

The train officials said that the "sealing" of the cars was necessary "to keep the Russians out and to keep you newsmen in." The reporters peeked anyway but saw only a moonlit empty landscape during the eventless three hours

Continued on Page 2, Column 2

SIEGE ON 328 DAYS

Leading Car Speeds 102 Miles From the British Zone in 1½ Hours

AIRLIFT PLANES CONTINUE

West Concerned as Russians Turn Back Some Trucks—City's Lights Turned On

By DREW MIDDLETON
Special to The New York Times.

BERLIN, Thursday, May 12—Just as the morning sun rose over the jagged skyline of this broken but defiant city a Soviet zone locomotive chugged wearily into the Charlottenburg Station in the British sector hauling the first train to reach Berlin from the West in 328 days.

Arrival of the train completed the relief of the city from the iron vise of the Soviet blockade.

At some time after midnight (6:01 P. M. Wednesday, Eastern daylight time) two jeeps and a convoy of cars, buses and trucks roared out of the city for the Western zones. An hour and three quarters later the first cars of a flotilla that simultaneously had left Helmstedt, in the British zone at the border of the Soviet zone, swept into Berlin to re-establish the land link with the West broken since the Soviet Military administration established a complete blockade of the city last June.

By morning it was evident that the Russians had observed the letter if not the spirit of the East-West agreement reached in New York. Traffic was flowing freely along the Autobahn.

Although there had been some difficulty over locomotives, the Russians had promised to send sixteen freight trains and one passenger train into Berlin each day. Pending settlement of the dispute the trains will be pulled by Soviet locomotives.

Western Officials Disturbed

To Berliners who awoke in the night to find lights burning in the streets and in their homes and intersector barriers dismantled, the blockade for the moment seemed over. Americans and British in Military Government offices, however, were distinctly disturbed by the turning back at Soviet check-points of trucks bound for the Western zones with Western sector exports.

This refusal to permit trucks to pass stems from a Soviet order of January, 1948. Hence it is not affected by the New York agreement on ending the blockade. But the Western Powers felt that the action indicated that the Russians would not give an inch more than called for by that agreement.

The first railroad train since June of 1948 passed through the checkpoint at Helmstedt, in the British zone at the border of the Soviet zone, at 1:23 A. M., bound for Berlin.

The first car from the West, driven by Walter G. Rundle, United Press manager for Germany, arrived at the American checkpoint outside Berlin at 1:44. Mr. Rundle had driven the distance, which the British declare is 102 miles, in an hour and thirty-seven minutes. He said that the bridge across the Elbe at Magdeburg was in good condition.

Aide's Wife Enters City

The first woman to enter Berlin after lifting of the blockade was Adelaide de Neufville, wife of Lawrence de Neufville, counsel to the civil affairs division of the United States Military Government.

The first two railroad trains to start across the Soviet zone for Berlin since June 17, 1948, left the Russian control point at Marienborn just south of Helmstedt at 1:23 A. M. The first of these was a passenger train. It moved into the moonlit landscape of the Russian zone at 1:55 after an eleven-minute wait at the checkpoint.

Eight minutes later a freight train of forty-two cars carrying thirty tons of coal from the Ruhr for Berlin passed through the checkpoint en route to Berlin, symbolizing the end not only of the Russian block-

Continued on Page 3, Column 5

World News Summarized

THURSDAY, MAY 12, 1949

The 328-day Soviet blockade of Berlin ended on schedule at 12:01 o'clock this morning, Berlin time, and approximately an hour and one-half later the first vehicles from the Western zones entered the city followed by the first train. [1:8; maps P. 2.]

The first Western passenger train to Berlin was sealed; a jeep led the road convoy [1:7.] Russian guards at Berlin ignored automobiles going to Helmstedt; people watched on the Autobahn. [3:1.]

Secretary of State Acheson warned that the end of the blockade did not, in itself, solve the German problem. He said Russia's willingness at the forthcoming Big Four session in Paris to consider proposals that would not erase the progress made in Germany by the Western powers would determine the outcome. He praised the draft constitution for a West German state. [4:2.] The United States was said to be considering a plan for withdrawal of all occupation troops to North German ports, except for French forces, which would return to France. [1:4.]

Guarded optimism was expressed by Moscow's New Times in an editorial on the Big Four meeting. The editorial said the talks could be a "turning point" in East-West relations. [4:6.]

Communists, urging at a Senate hearing in Washington that ratification of the North Atlantic treaty be deferred until after the Paris meeting, likened the pact to "Hitler's Axis." [1:6-7.]

Victorious anti-Hague forces in Jersey City will seek a court order impounding all public records until an audit can be made. [1:3.]

lift the curbs on full diplomatic relations with Spain, Secretary Acheson said, because of the opposition in Western Europe to any change. Explaining this country's position, he denounced the Franco regime as still functioning along Nazi and Fascist lines. [1:5.]

Israel became the fifty-ninth member of the United Nations when the General Assembly voted, 37 to 12, to admit her. The six Arab states left the hall in protest. [1:1.] Foreign Minister Sharett, the first Israeli delegate to the United Nations, pledged his country to work for peace with its Arab neighbors and to remain friendly with both the United States and Russia. [12:3.]

Japan is not what she was ten years ago, Premier Yoshida said in appealing for proper understanding by the world. He asked access to materials and markets to enable Japan to become self-supporting. [19:1.]

Representative Rankin disowned his veterans' pension bill when a "watered-down" version was reported by a House committee. [1:2.]

Labor leaders and President Truman were said to have agreed on pressing passage of the administration's labor bill with some amendments. [24:2.]

A man who has identified himself as Gerhart Eisler, called this country's No. 1 Communist, sailed secretly on a Polish liner now at sea. [1:6-7.]

U.S. Reds Liken Pact to Hitler Axis; Norman Thomas Urges Ratification

By WILLIAM S. WHITE
Special to The New York Times.

WASHINGTON, May 11—The Communist party of the United States, through a statement filed by its general secretary, Eugene Dennis, likened the North Atlantic treaty today to "Hitler's Axis," and demanded that the Senate withhold any action toward ratification until after the Big Four Foreign Ministers' meeting.

However, Norman Thomas, Socialist leader, supported the treaty before the Senate Foreign Relations Committee, but stressed that he did so with much anxiety because of the "dangers" that might lie in it.

He expressed belief that the pact should not be ratified unless the Senate made it "absolutely plain" that Spain would not be included in it, and equally plain that proposed American military aid should not be used against colonial peoples.

Senator Tom Connally, Democrat, of Texas, committee chair-

man, said that Spain's inclusion was "highly improbable" since it could be done only by unanimous consent of the twelve countries that signed the treaty.

Above all, Mr. Thomas recommended that before ratification this country issue "a mighty appeal for an end of the armament race under effective international controls which would make the pact unnecessary."

The Communist party proposal that the pact be held back, first advanced late last week by Henry A. Wallace, was offered also by representatives of the National Council of American-Soviet Friendship and the National Council of the Arts, Sciences and Professions. Witnesses for the three organizations appeared before the committee and further urged Soviet-American race conferences looking toward resolving differences between the two countries.

Their recommendations for de-

Continued on Page 7, Column 3

Index to other news appears on Page 32.

"All the News That's Fit to Print"

The New York Times.

LATE CITY EDITION
Condensation of U. S. Weather Bureau forecast:
Mostly fair today and tomorrow.
Temperature range today: 65—48.
Temperature range yesterday: 62.2—48.1.
Full U. S. Weather Bureau Report, Page 24

VOL. CVI—No. 36,074. Entered as Second-Class Matter, Post Office, New York, N. Y. NEW YORK, TUESDAY, OCTOBER 30, 1956. Times Square, New York 36, N. Y. Telephone LAckawanna 4-1000 FIVE CENTS

ISRAELIS THRUST INTO EGYPT AND NEAR SUEZ; U.S. GOES TO U.N. UNDER ANTI-AGGRESSION PACT

Budapest Rebels Refuse to Yield Until Soviet Troops Leave

EISENHOWER BIDS SOUTH FIGHT BIAS ON A 'LOCAL BASIS'

In Miami He Stresses Roles of States—Hails Byrd in Speech in Virginia

Texts of Eisenhower speeches are on Pages 24 and 25.

By RUSSELL BAKER
Special to The New York Times.

RICHMOND, Va., Oct. 29—President Eisenhower, campaigning in the South today, urged that the problem of achieving racial equality be handled largely "on a local and state basis."

He told a Miami Airport audience he was convinced that progress today in equality of opportunity and equality before the law had "to be achieved finally in the hearts of men rather than in legislative halls."

The President was applauded lightly when he said that "there must be intelligent understanding of the human factors and emotions involved if we are to make steady progress in the matter rather than simply to make political promises never intended to be kept."

In the field of civil rights, he added, he had tried to bring "reason, good sense and good judgment to the performance of clear duty."

Makes 1,800-Mile Trip

Though he delivered three airport speeches in an 1,800-mile aerial campaign in Florida and Virginia, he touched on the civil rights issue only once.

That was in Miami, in the President's first speech today.

In Jacksonville, Fla., and Richmond, Va., where the southern tradition is stronger than in Miami, he did not discuss the racial theme. Nor did he refer directly in any of his speeches to the controversial school integration issue or the Supreme Court decision.

He concentrated instead on three matters: peace, prosperity and attacks on the Democratic ticket.

And at Miami General Eisenhower tried for the first time the handshaking style of campaigning developed to a high art by Senator Estes Kefauver.

Surrounded by several hundred rabid admirers on his way to his plane after speaking, he shook hands by the score with a zest rarely matched by Senator Kefauver and a folksiness as impressive as the Senator's own.

"Hi ya, folks," he said, and

Continued on Page 24, Column 4

Stevenson Says U. S. Gets 'Less Than Truth' on Strife

Charges President Endangered the Nation by 'Good News' From the Mideast—Boston Crowds Hail Candidate

By HARRISON E. SALISBURY
Special to The New York Times.

BOSTON, Oct. 29—Adlai E. Stevenson charged tonight that President Eisenhower had given the nation reassurances about the Middle East that had been "tragically less than the truth."

"The Government has not been

Texts of Stevenson statement and speech, Page 28.

telling us the whole truth," Mr. Stevenson said.

The Presidential nominee addressed an overflow Democratic throng of more than 8,000 in Mechanics Hall in the climax of his drive for Massachusetts' sixteen electoral votes.

Mr. Stevenson's address was televised nationally by the American Broadcasting Company. After the telecast was completed, Mr. Stevenson appended one of his sharpest challenges to President Eisenhower's leadership. The Democrat declared:

"I deeply believe that we cannot afford another four years under a part-time leader of a party which will not plan, which will not create, which will not dare to see the vision of a new America and make that vision come true.

"As a campaigning politician there is none better. It is as a performing politician, as a President who knows how to control his own party, who knows how to grasp the reins of Government that he fails."

Several times Mr. Stevenson's partisan audience booed references to the President. The chorus of boos every time he mentioned Vice President Richard M. Nixon started the moment the crowd sensed that Mr.

Continued on Page 29, Column 3

FIGHTING PERSISTS

Russians Still Pulling Out, With Hungarian Units Taking Over

Text of editorial in Communist newspaper on Page 10.

By ELIE ABEL
Special to The New York Times.

VIENNA, Tuesday, Oct. 30—Soviet troops remained in control of Budapest this morning while the Government of Imre Nagy pleaded with the stubborn revolutionaries to lay down their arms.

But the rebels refused to give up the fight until Mr. Nagy had made good on his promise that the Soviet forces would evacuate the battered city, monitored reports from the Hungarian capital said.

This morning the Budapest radio broadcast the following communiqué:

"While Soviet forces are being withdrawn from Budapest, Hungarian police and armed youth units are maintaining order. Such armed groups as are still resisting will lay down their arms at 9 A. M. [3 A. M. New York time] and will then take part in maintaining order."

[Up to 3 A. M. New York time there had been no further reports on the situation in Hungary.]

Appeal Is Pressed

Earlier this morning the Budapest radio broadcast an appeal by Karoly Janda, Defense Minister, to the rebels to lay down their arms before 9 A. M.

In spite of the gradual Soviet withdrawal, fighting in Budapest flared up again last night. Soviet tank forces engaged in heavy combat in several parts of the city. Latest reports said artillery fire was heard in Budapest all night.

Rebels from eastern Hungary and from the region of Gyor in the west were understood to have joined the insurgents in the capital.

The rebel-held Miskolc radio in northeast Hungary, in a broadcast monitored here, urged anti-Communists in Budapest not to lay down their arms before the last Soviet soldier had left the country.

A general strike called by the rebel leaders appeared to be continuing in many parts of Hungary for the fifth day. Most factory workers, railroad men and miners stayed away from their jobs again this morning despite pressing appeals from Mr. Nagy's Government to resume work.

Nearly complete was an unofficial school strike. Instead of attending classes many teenagers in Budapest did courier work for the rebels and

Continued on Page 10. Column 4

1950 PLEDGE CITED

White House Recalls Promise to Assist Victim of Attack

By DANA ADAMS SCHMIDT
Special to The New York Times.

WASHINGTON, Oct. 29—The United States will take the movement of Israeli forces into Egypt to the United Nations Security Council tomorrow morning.

The planned appeal to the United Nations was announced by the White House tonight after President Eisenhower had held an emergency meeting there with Secretary of State Dulles and six other high officials.

[An emergency meeting of the Security Council was set for 11 A. M. Tuesday.]

The White House statement follows:

"At the meeting, the President recalled that the United States under this and prior Administrations has pledged itself to assist the victim of any aggression in the Middle East. We shall honor our pledge.

"The United States is in consultation with the British and French Governments, parties with us to the tripartite declaration of 1950, and the United States plans as contemplated by that declaration that the situation shall be taken to the United Nations Security Council tomorrow morning.

Special Session in Abeyance

"The question of whether and when the President will call a special session of the Congress will be decided in the light of the unfolding situation."

The statement was read by James C. Hagerty, Presidential press secretary. He said it had the full authority of the President and the other conferees.

Others at the meeting, in addition to Mr. Dulles, were Charles E. Wilson, Secretary of Defense; Admiral Arthur W. Radford, Chairman of the Joint Chiefs of Staff; Sherman Adams, Assistant to the President; Herbert Hoover Jr., Under Secretary of State, Allen W. Dulles, director of the Central Intelligence Agency, and Wilton B. Persons, deputy assistant to the President.

The one-and-a-half-hour meeting at the White House took place immediately after the President's return by air from a campaign trip in Florida and Virginia.

The State Department said Americans "not performing essential services" would be asked to leave the Middle East. Among the first to leave was a group that flew from Israel to Athens.

Earlier, Secretary of State Dulles had initiated the joint steps with Britain and France.

The State Department an-

Continued on Page 3, Column 1

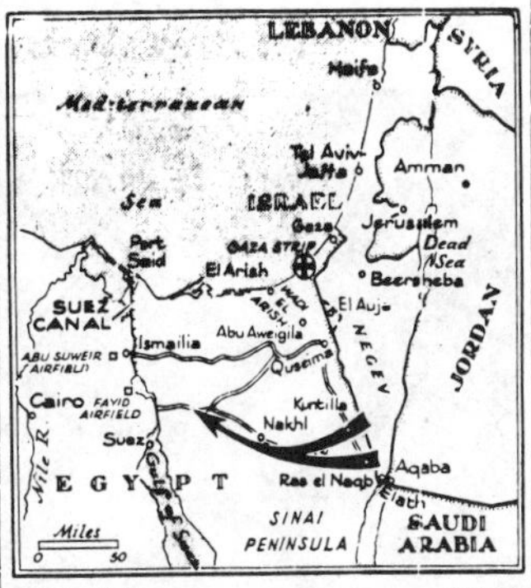

The New York Times Oct. 30, 1956

ISRAELIS OPEN DRIVE: The advance into Egypt was reported made at and below Kuntilla, with a thrust near the Suez Canal. There was a flare-up in Gaza area (cross).

Cairo Says Egyptian Units Have Engaged the Israelis

By The United Press.

CAIRO, Tuesday, Oct. 30—The Egyptian Army said today it had begun "liquidating" an Israeli force that had thrust deep into Egyptian territory toward the Suez Canal. Egyptian army headquarters announced that the Israeli force had suffered "heavy casualties" in the night-long fighting. It gave no precise figures.

"The enemy's plan to penetrate deep inside Egyptian territory failed," the Egyptian communiqué said. "Egyptian armed forces early this morning started liquidating the enemy forces."

[Iraq informed Egypt early Tuesday that Iraqi troops were ready to offer immediate assistance against the Israeli thrust, The Associated Press said. The offer was announced after an urgent morning meeting of Premier Nuri as-Said's Cabinet in Baghdad.]

Leaves Are Canceled

The high command of the Egyptian armed forces recalled all officers and enlisted men on leave to meet the Israeli threat. Orders broadcast by the Cairo radio said all must "report immediately to their units." Reservists were not affected.

The Egyptian communiqué identified the three frontier checkpoints where it said the Israeli raiders had been halted at Kuntilla, Nekhet and El Mimet. All are on the eastern side of the rocky Sinai Peninsula.

[No additional details on the fighting were received up to 5 A. M.]

Suez Canal authorities in Cairo said the situation along the waterway was normal. They said no blackout has been imposed and no emergency alert sounded.

Continued on Page 6, Column 2

FRANCE ACCUSES FIVE OF TREASON

Files Formal Charges Against Algerians Seized in Plane —Sends Aide to Tunisia

By ROBERT C. DOTY
Special to The New York Times.

PARIS, Oct. 29—Five leaders of the Algerian rebellion, seized a week ago, were formally charged today with treason against France. The offense is punishable by death.

The five are Mohammed ben Bella, Mohammed Khider, Mustafa Lachraf, Mohammed Boudiaf and Hossein Ait Ahmed, all members of the Algerian National Liberation Front, which has directed the two-year rebellion against France from headquarters in Cairo.

Their arrest Oct. 22, while aboard a Moroccan plane flying to a conference of North African leaders in Tunis, set off a wave of anti-French protest and violence. Arab anger was based on the theory that the five men were under the protection of Sultan Mohammed V of Morocco, with tacit French consent, at the time of their arrest.

[In the United Nations Security Council, France formally charged Egypt with gun-running for the Algerian rebels.]

As Algerians, the five seized rebel leaders are French citizens, hence subject to a treason

Continued on Page 10, Column 2

DEEP DRIVE MADE

Tel Aviv Declares Aim Is to Smash Egyptian Commando Bases

Text of Israeli statement will be found on Page 4.

By MOSHE BRILLIANT
Special to The New York Times.

TEL AVIV, Israel, Oct. 29—An Israeli military force thrust into the Sinai Peninsula of Egypt today. It was reported to have reached within twenty miles of the Suez Canal.

Army sources said the Israelis were west of the crossroads where the road to Kuntilla branches off from the Suez-Quseima highway.

The Israelis were said to have halted there and to have dug in.

A Foreign Ministry statement said the operation had been started "to eliminate the Egyptian fedayeen [commando squad] bases in the Sinai Peninsula."

Army sources said the Israelis had smashed the Egyptian position at Kuntilla and Ras el Naqb at the southern end of the international border. The forces then advanced more than seventy-five miles.

No fighting was reported on the northern end of the border or in the Gaza Strip, which is heavily populated.

'Too Big for a Reprisal'

Reports from the Sinai area described the fighting as "too big for a reprisal and too small for a war." Details of the fighting were not available tonight, but reliable sources said there had been no aerial bombardment of Egyptian positions.

It was not clear tonight whether the Israelis proposed to push on to the Suez Canal or withdraw to Israeli territory, as they have done after reprisal raids. A high official said: "I do not know. It depends on developments."

Yesterday the Israeli Government attributed its decision to call up reserves to what it said was a renewal of commando activities, to the Egyptian-Jordanian-Syrian military alliance negotiated last Wednesday, to Arab declarations that "their principal concern is a war of destruction against Israel" and to the movement of Iraqi forces to Jordan's border.

According to information here, the Egyptians have a considerable part of their Army in the Sinai Peninsula. Their land forces are reported equipped with the

Continued on Page 5. Column 3

POLAND'S LEADERS BACK HUNGARIANS

Support Demands for Exit of Soviet Troops—Call for End of Strife

By SYDNEY GRUSON
Special to The New York Times.

WARSAW, Oct. 29—The Polish Communist party, differing sharply once again with the Soviet Union, came out formally today in support of Hungarian demands for the withdrawal of Soviet troops from Hungary.

Yesterday the new leadership of the Polish United Workers (Communist) party rejected the Soviet allegation that foreign agents and counter-revolutionaries were responsible for the Hungarian tragedy. Today the Poles stood up again on the side of the Hungarians.

An appeal to those on both sides of the barricades in Hungary to halt fratricidal strife was issued by Wladyslaw Gomulka, the Polish party's First Secretary, and by Premier Jozef Cyrankiewicz.

Emphasizing the growing insistence here for independence in foreign as well as internal affairs, the party statement ignored the Soviet charges of Western interference in Hungary.

For the Poles the statement of solidarity was a means of publicly expressing their apprehension for Hungarian help when Poland was threatened by the Soviet leaders a week ago. Poland escaped Hungary's fate

Continued on Page 22, Column 1

Patrols in Budapest Are Trigger-Happy From Propaganda

By JOHN MacCORMAC
Special to The New York Times.

BUDAPEST, Hungary, Oct. 29—The seventh day of the Hungarian revolution has dawned with Soviet soldiers still patrolling the Budapest streets despite a promise by Hungary's new Government that they would be withdrawn. The Government had qualified its announcement yesterday with the condition "as soon as order has been completely restored."

As far as could be learned, armed resistance in Budapest has ceased, even in the Maria Theresa barracks in Ulloi Ut, which was holding out late yesterday. But that order can ever be completely restored in Budapest as long as the Russians are here seems unlikely because of the fears and propaganda with which the Soviet troops seem to be filled.

At 10 o'clock last night, for instance, a Soviet soldier guarding an area known as Szent Istvan Ut shot and seriously wounded Noel Barber, London Daily Mail correspondent. Mr. Barber had been making a tour of inspection to get the public's reaction to Premier Imre Nagy's announcement that there would be no further firing and that the insurrection had been recognized by his Government at

Continued on Page 15, Column 1

PRESIDENT GIVEN MINNESOTA LEAD

Resurvey Finds Him Moving Ahead in a Close Contest

A Times Team Report

Teams of New York Times reporters have recently surveyed political trends in twenty-seven closely contested states. They are now rechecking the most doubtful states. Following is a resurvey report from Leonard Buder, Donald Janson and W. H. Lawrence.

By DONALD JANSON
Special to The New York Times.

MINNEAPOLIS, Oct. 28—President Eisenhower appears to hold a tenuous lead in the race for Minnesota's eleven electoral votes.

A month ago New York Times reporters found the President and Adlai E. Stevenson running neck and neck in this state. The Eisenhower victory margin of four years ago—155,000 out of 1,379,000 votes cast—had buckled under the impact of defections by farmers who were caught in a cost-price vise.

The farm revolt remains strong today in some areas.

Continued on Page 26, Column 2

Russians Befriend One Hungarian City

By HOMER BIGART
Special to The New York Times.

GYOR, Hungary, Oct. 29—The small Soviet garrison of this industrial city has retired to a near-by wood, giving the townspeople free rein to rally and shout against the Nagy Government and demand democratic national elections.

The Russians here must be credited with sensible behavior. They abandoned their barracks a few days ago under no pressure and took to the wood.

There the Soviet officers are living with their wives and children in tents. They have not shot anyone. The townspeople show their gratitude by taking the Russians eggs and milk.

And although Gyor has

Continued on Page 12, Column 1

Associated Press Radiophoto

AMERICANS LEAVE ISRAEL: Wives and children of State Department personnel boarding Air Force transport plane last night at Lydda Airport near Jerusalem. They were flown to Athens. More dependents are to follow today.

Maria Callas Bows At Opening of 'Met'

By ROSS PARMENTER

Bellini's "Norma" has never been notably popular in this country. But last night, when it opened the Metropolitan Opera's seventy-second season, it established a compound record. Never have so many Americans tried to pay so much money to hear an opera.

The actual sum paid by those who managed to crowd into the opera house was $75,510.50. This exceeded by more than $10,000 the previous box-office record of $65,336, which was set with the opening night "Faust" in 1953. The larger sum, though, was not paid by a larger number of persons. After all, sell-outs have been customary on first nights, and fire regulations re-

Continued on Page 43, Column 4

CITY SCHOOL AIDES SPUR INTEGRATION

District Lines Are Shifted in Some Brooklyn Areas

By BENJAMIN FINE

Without any public announcement, the Board of Education has quietly begun a program to integrate white and Negro pupils in areas where a segregation pattern has existed in the past.

A score of schools in the Bedford-Stuyvesant area of Brooklyn have become interracial since the fall term opened. Children are taken from the all-Negro schools and put into the formerly all-white schools.

At the same time, fairly large groups of children—ranging from fifty to 200—have been taken from a number of all-white schools and placed in the all-Negro schools. In doing this, the board has amended or discarded the old district and school zoning regulations.

This step is part of a "positive program" on integration, Charles H. Silver, Board of Education president, said yesterday. The board has asked its forty assistant superintendents to do everything possible to place Negro and white children in the same schools.

The superintendents are doing

Continued on Page 30, Column 3

"All the News That's Fit to Print"

The New York Times.

LATE CITY EDITION
Condensation of U. S. Weather Bureau forecast: Partly cloudy, little temperature change today and tomorrow.
Temperature range today: 65—51.
Temperature range yesterday: 68.3—53.
Full U.S. Weather Bureau Report, Page 46.

VOL. CVI—No. 36,078. Entered as Second-Class Matter, Post Office, New York, N. Y. NEW YORK, SATURDAY, NOVEMBER 3, 1956. Times Square, New York 36, N. Y. Telephone LAckawanna 4-1000 FIVE CENTS

BRITISH AND FRENCH PUSH TOWARD LANDING; ISRAELIS CAPTURE GAZA AND CONTROL SINAI

Hungary Protests to Soviet Against New Troop Moves; West Urges Action by U.N.; Tension Is Rising in Poland

STEVENSON OFFERS A PROGRAM TO END STRIFE IN MIDEAST

Calls for a Cease-Fire and Israel's Security—Detroit Crowd Boos President

Speech at Detroit and remarks at Cleveland, Page 20.

By HARRISON E. SALISBURY
Special to The New York Times.

DETROIT, Nov. 2—Adlai E. Stevenson offered tonight a program to restore peace in the Middle East, based on the security of Israel and restoration of the Western Alliance.

Mr. Stevenson submitted his program to an enthusiastic overflow audience at the Fox Theatre.

He charged that President Eisenhower did not know what had been happening in the Middle East and that "someone had misled him."

Mr. Stevenson's program called for these steps:

¶A cease-fire in the Middle East.

¶Restoration of the Western grand alliance of the United States, France and Britain.

¶Security for Israel against Arab attack.

¶Establishment of the principle of international concern for the Suez Canal and an end of one-man or one-country control.

¶An all-out attack on resettlement of 900,000 Arab refugees in Middle Eastern lands.

¶A joint program for improvement of economic conditions in the Middle East.

Mr. Stevenson's address was carried on a state TV network. Several thousand persons were unable to gain admission to the theatre.

Earlier today, Mr. Stevenson spoke in Cleveland's Public Square. A huge throng heard him demand United Nations action in behalf of the new Hungarian regime.

Democratic officials put the crowd at 65,000. Newspaper reporters estimated it at closer to 30,000. There was agreement, however, that it was larger than General Eisenhower drew in the same place and time three weeks ago.

Tonight Mr. Stevenson asserted that the first task in the

Continued on Page 20, Column 5

COUNCIL HEARING ON QUINN SLATED

Mayor Backs Tenney Report on Official's Carting Job

By CHARLES G. BENNETT

The City Council will hold hearings soon to consider charges against Councilman Hugh Quinn, Queens Democrat.

In a report to Mayor Wagner on Thursday, Investigation Commissioner Charles H. Tenney found that Mr. Quinn had committed an "apparent" violation of the City Charter and had given grounds for his removal from office.

Yesterday Mayor Wagner said he agreed with the Investigation Commissioner's conclusions.

Council Majority Leader Joseph T. Sharkey, Brooklyn Democrat, said he would call the Councilmen together next week, probably Wednesday, to arrange for hearings in the Quinn case. A question for the Councilmen to determine, Mr. Sharkey said, is whether the hearings will be public or private.

The Council, under the Charter, is the judge of the qualifications of its members. It may expel a member by a two-thirds vote.

Mr. Sharkey said he thought

Continued on Page 42, Column 3

Associated Press Radiophoto

HUNGARIAN PREMIER Imre Nagy, Communist who took office during national anti-Soviet uprising, addressing nation by radio. Date when photograph was taken was not given.

Eisenhower Sees Victory, Leaves Campaign to Nixon

By RUSSELL BAKER
Special to The New York Times.

WASHINGTON, Nov. 2—President Eisenhower now is so confident of re-election Tuesday that he is treating Adlai E. Stevenson's driving campaign finish with a show of indifference. This was emphasized last night in Philadelphia when he indicated that, from his point of view, the campaign was over and that henceforth he would address the nation only in the nonpartisan role of President.

It was pointedly driven home today when the White House noted that Vice President Richard M. Nixon, rather than the President, had been selected to reply tonight to the Democratic nominee's attack on foreign policy.

James C. Hagerty, White House press secretary, said the President's discussion of the Middle Eastern and Central European crises Wednesday had been "nonpolitical." Mr. Stevenson's reply last night, he added, "was strictly political."

Mr. Hagerty's implication was that the President no longer intended to trouble with replies to Mr. Stevenson's "political" charges and that this chore now could be handled adequately by Mr. Nixon.

The President, he added, knew in advance the substance of the Vice President's speech. The White House staff had helped Mr. Nixon get "the facts to refute a lot of misstatements that Mr. Stevenson made last night," Mr. Hagerty said.

The White House also an-

Continued on Page 19, Column 6

PRESIDENT LEADS IN PENNSYLVANIA

Slim Edge Not Widened Yet by Crises Abroad—Clark's Margin for Senate Cut

A Times Team Report

Teams of New York Times reporters have now completed a survey of political trends in twenty-seven closely contested states. They have rechecked eight of those states—the most doubtful ones. Following is a final resurvey report by Leonard Buder, Donald Janson and Wayne Phillips.

By WAYNE PHILLIPS
Special to The New York Times.

PHILADELPHIA, Nov. 2—President Eisenhower is clinging to a lead in this state so insubstantial that it could be washed away by a heavy rain on election day.

Depending upon developments in the Middle East crisis, he may be able to increase that lead in the four days remaining before the election. But at the moment the world crisis has served only to create doubts in the minds of voters on both sides of the fence. Those doubts have not yet crystallized in favor of either candidate.

Two weeks ago a New York Times team found the Pennsylvania Democrats well organized and confident. They were fighting an uphill battle against the appeal of the President's personality, but the odds were on their side in a state that once was a bastion of Republicanism.

They appeared to have won the public—and some Republican newspapers, too—to their Senatorial candidate, Joseph S. Clark Jr. They had created a substantial indecision among the 1952 supporters of President Eisenhower, and had won over enough of them to give some hope of carrying the state for Adlai E. Stevenson.

For Mr. Stevenson this state is the keystone in any arch of triumph he may hope to build. Its thirty-two electoral votes, with various combinations of states, could carry him to a

Continued on Page 18, Column 2

Nixon Hails Break With Allies' Policies

By WILLIAM M. BLAIR
Special to The New York Times.

HERSHEY, Pa., Nov. 2—Vice President Richard M. Nixon hailed tonight this country's break with Anglo-French policies as a "declaration of independence that has had an electrifying effect throughout the world."

Speaking with the full backing of President Eisenhower, he assailed Adlai E. Stevenson for charging that the Administration's foreign policy was a failure and that the President should have averted the Middle East crisis.

He said that the United Nations General Assembly vote gave "the lie to [Mr. Stevenson's] preposterous charge" that the United States stood alone "in an unfriendly world."

The General Assembly early

Continued on Page 19, Column 1

TROOPS REPORTED CROSSING POLAND

Soviet Movement Is Said to Be to East Germany—Panic Buying in Warsaw

By SYDNEY GRUSON
Special to The New York Times.

WARSAW, Nov. 2—Reports reached Warsaw tonight of large-scale Soviet troop movements across Poland from Russia to East Germany. No details were available.

The purpose and the meaning of the troop movements were not disclosed. But even before they had been reported the situation in Poland had reached a point of extreme tension.

All through the day the Polish radio repeated its broadcast of an appeal by the Communist party's new leadership for "calm, discipline and a sense of responsibility" within the nation.

In Warsaw panic buying began. People bought up all the foodstuffs in the stores and then after withdrawing their money from the banks began to buy jewelry and valuables.

Word came from various parts

Continued on Page 14, Column 4

NEW PLEA BY NAGY

Premier Asks That U.N. Defend Neutrality of Hungary

By JOHN MacCORMAC
Special to The New York Times.

BUDAPEST, Hungary, Saturday, Nov. 3—The Hungarian Government made three oral protests yesterday to the Soviet Ambassador in Budapest, complaining that Russian reinforcements were still pouring across the frontier.

[Soviet tanks sealed the main crossings of the Austrian-Hungarian border Friday. This was regarded as a preliminary to dealing sternly with the insurgents.]

Premier Imre Nagy also sent a new appeal to the Secretary General of the United Nations to guarantee Hungary's neutrality and to bring her case before the General Assembly.

Similarly Joseph Cardinal Mindszenty, primate of Hungary, appealed to the West for political support of the revolutionaries and relief for the needy.

Soviet Forces Approaching

Early today, forces at the command of the Revolutionary Council of the Hungarian Army occupied the Foreign Ministry. Other Army units cordoned off the Parliament Building and took up posts on and near all bridges spanning the Danube.

These measures were prompted by information that Soviet forces were approaching the capital.

In his plea to the Secretary General of the United Nations, Premier Nagy said that Hungary's first demand for the withdrawal of Soviet troops had been received favorably by Moscow. In spite of this, he went on, fresh Soviet troops were brought in to Hungary on Tuesday and Wednesday.

The Hungarian Government then denounced the Warsaw Pact, proclaimed Hungary a neutral state and demanded the withdrawal of all Soviet troops. Budapest also proposed the appointment of two joint Hungarian-Soviet committees, one political and one military, to discuss the terms and set the timetable for this withdrawal.

The Premier said that he had protested against any further influx of Soviet soldiers, pointing out to the United Nations that new Soviet units had entered

Continued on Page 15, Column 1

U. S. Protests Refusal by Soviet To Let Americans Quit Hungary

Special to The New York Times.

WASHINGTON, Nov. 2—The United States protested tonight to the Soviet Union against the action of Soviet troops who prevented a convoy of Americans from leaving Hungary.

A report of the incident from the United States Legation in Budapest reached the State Department in early evening. Deputy Under Secretary of State Robert Murphy called in Georgi N. Zaroubin, the Soviet Ambassador, at once.

Mr. Zaroubin told Mr. Murphy he would get in touch with his Government in Moscow about the matter.

A State Department spokesman said Mr. Murphy spoke "energetically" to the Soviet Ambassador against the "interference with American official personnel."

According to the official report, the convoy consisted of dependents—wives and children—of diplomatic personnel at the American Legation. Lincoln White, State Department press officer, said the convoy returned safely to Budapest and would attempt to leave the city again tomorrow.

"We had a report from Budapest that a convoy of our legation dependents was turned back near the Austrian border this afternoon by Soviet tank blocks," said Mr. White. "They returned to Budapest safely."

According to Mr. White, Mr. Murphy told the Soviet envoy he "assumed the incident must be due to an error on the part of the Soviet military commander, although he could not imagine why Soviet forces were in that area."

The Ambassador said he had no information on this, Mr. White told reporters, but added "he would immediately communicate with his Government and that he assumed the matter would be straightened out."

Special to The New York Times.

BUDAPEST, Hungary, Nov. 2—A diplomatic convoy carrying out the wives and children of a United State legation staff in Budapest as well as French, British and American correspondents was turned back from the Austrian border by Soviet troops at 4:30 P. M. today.

"Polemics are useless," a Soviet officer told them. "It is requested that you turn around

Continued on Page 16, Column 3

Israelis Are Mopping Up; Egypt Braces for Landing

12,000 Prisoners Taken

By HOMER BIGART
Special to The New York Times.

TEL AVIV, Israel, Saturday, Nov. 3—Israel's lightning conquest of Egypt's Sinai Peninsula and the Gaza Strip is complete except for minor mopping-up operations. The ancient Philistine capital of Gaza was the last town to fall.

In its drive, Maj. Gen. Moshe Dayan's tough Army had killed, captured or put to flight 30,000 Egyptian troops east of the Suez Canal.

With Israel's southern flank secure after only four days of operations, the Government faced with calm confidence reports that Jordan was being reinforced by Syrian troops and that the Syrian-Jordanian-Egyptian defense pact was about to become operative.

Gaza collapsed after a three-hour fight yesterday morning. A United Nations truce aide,

Continued on Page 3, Column 5

Cairo Defense Held Ready

By The United Press.

CAIRO, Nov. 2—Waves of British and French bombers and fighters blasted Cairo and outlying villages today. An Egyptian communiqué said 100 persons had been killed in one town alone.

Simultaneously, President Gamal Abdel Nasser announced that Egyptian forces in the Sinai desert had "completed their withdrawal safely."

"Now we are waiting for the British and French in the delta," he said. Only "suicide commandos" had been left in Sinai to harass the advancing Israeli forces, he added.

The communiqué asserted that fourteen British and French planes had been shot down in today's raids. An earlier communiqué had claimed three kills in the last twenty-four hours in addition to six reported downed yesterday morning. This would

Continued on Page 3, Column 2

U. N. SPEAKERS ASK HELP FOR HUNGARY

Override Soviet Objections as Security Council Argues International Action

Excerpts from Security Council debate are on Page 16.

By LINDESAY PARROTT
Special to The New York Times.

UNITED NATIONS, N. Y., Nov. 2—The Western powers overrode Soviet objections today and called on the United Nations to take measures against Soviet military action in Hungary.

An emergency meeting of the Security Council heard all nations that spoke, except the Soviet Union, appeal for international action against the reinforcement of Soviet troops in Hungary, where rebel nationalists appear to have taken control. Imre Nagy, Hungarian Premier, asked the United Nations yesterday to guarantee the country's neutralism.

No decision was reached at the two-hour session of the Council tonight. The members will meet again tomorrow afternoon in an attempt to decide on a course of action.

The meeting was sparked by a new message from Mr. Nagy distributed to Council members tonight.

The letter, couched in terms similar to the one Mr. Nagy sent to the United Nations yesterday, charged that "large" Soviet military units had crossed the Hungarian border. Moving toward

Continued on Page 16, Column 5

Eisenhower Offers Relief to Hungary

Special to The New York Times.

WASHINGTON, Nov. 2—President Eisenhower late today offered $20,000,000 worth of food and medical supplies to relieve the suffering in Hungary resulting from the revolt against Soviet domination.

The White House announcement of this offer followed a conference between the President, Secretary of State Dulles, and Under Secretary of State Herbert Hoover Jr.

The aid would consist of $15,000,000 in surplus foodstuffs and $5,000,000 in specially purchased meats, oils, fats, and medical supplies.

The President urged the American people to continue sending their contributions to the American Red Cross, which is pouring relief supplies into

Continued on Page 16, Column 7

PARIS ACTS TO BAR CEASE-FIRE NOW

Fears That Immediate Halt In Military Operations Would Save Nasser

By HAROLD CALLENDER
Special to The New York Times.

PARIS, Nov. 2—The French Government moved fast today to prevent a United Nations cease-fire in the Suez Canal Zone.

It feared a halt in military operation now would save Gamal Abdel Nasser, President of Egypt, whose regime the French and British seek to liquidate. In that case the French would feel deprived of a victory they regard as already within their grasp.

This was the explanation of the hurried trip to London during the day by Christian Pineau, French Foreign Minister, that was given by high political authorities here tonight.

In London, M. Pineau, Prime Minister Eden and Selwyn Lloyd, British Foreign Secretary, were reported to have agreed they would not accept a cease-fire at least until British-French troops had landed. They were expected to land tomorrow.

Action by U. N. Noted

The United Nations General Assembly voted early today for a cease-fire in the Middle East but the question was how it could be carried out.

[Prime Minister Eden rejected a Laborite demand that he order an immediate end to British attacks on Egypt. This was in response to Laborite pressure that he comply with the resolution of the United Nations General Assembly calling for a cease-fire.]

The fear that took posession of French officials was that Prime Minister Eden might agree to a premature cease-fire.

If so, he would do it, according to these officials, because he is harried by the British Labor party to call off the French-British military expedition to Egypt, and because he is pressed by Secretary of State Dulles, who is credited here with desiring a cease-fire before the United States election Tuesday.

It was even suggested that the United States Sixth Fleet, now in the Mediterranean, might be mandated by the General Assembly to occupy the Suez Canal zone, instead of the French-British forces now preparing to occupy it.

This fear arose because Lester B. Pearson, Canadian Secretary of State for External Affairs, proposed yesterday in New York that the General Assembly should authorize the immediate

Continued on Page 6, Column 4

BOMBING PRESSED

Planes Center Attacks on Army After Cairo Loses Airpower

By DREW MIDDLETON
Special to The New York Times.

LONDON, Nov. 2—The neutralization of the Egyptian Air Force, a primary condition to successful landing operations, was claimed tonight by British and French airpower.

More than a hundred Egyptian planes have been destroyed or damaged at airfields by bombers and fighters of Royal Air Force and French Air Force. A high proportion of these were Soviet-built MIG-15 jet fighter planes and Ilyushin-28 twin-jet bombers, R. A. F. sources said.

At the outset of the operations the Egyptian Air Force had ninety MIG's and fifty Ilyushins. Since not all of them were airworthy Wednesday when the attack began, the allies' claim to have neutralized Egypt's airpower appears valid.

Transit Camp Bombed

The British-French air attack is shifting away from air bases onto the Egyptian Army's central forces, now known to be moving slowly northward and northeastward away from the Cairo area.

British air reconnaissance reported the movement of tanks and infantry into the area around Port Said, one of the three sites chosen by the allies for occupation.

One target successfully attacked was a military transit camp, around which tanks and guns were concentrated, about fifteen miles northeast of Cairo in the El Khanka area.

[The British reported that the Egyptians had sunk seven ships in an effort to block the Suez Canal. It was not known in London whether the Egyptian effort had succeeded. No word of an allied landing in Egypt had been received up to 4 A. M., New York time.]

Information that the Syrian Government was placing its armed forces under the commander in chief of the Egyptian forces has not altered British or French planning for forthcoming operations.

As part of the psychological preparation for the allied landing operations the Cairo Radio, the Voice of Arabia, was silenced

Continued on Page 2, Column 3

ARABS SAID TO PUT TROOPS IN JORDAN

Syrian and Iraqi Forces Are Reported on March

By DANA ADAMS SCHMIDT
Special to The New York Times.

WASHINGTON, Nov. 2—Syrian and Iraqi troops are marching into Jordan, according to information telephoned from Cairo, the Egyptian Embassy press counselor announced tonight.

The official, Mohammed Habib, reported also that Lebanese workers had cut one of the pipelines that carry Arabian oil to the Mediterranean.

The report of the troop movements followed announcement by Syria, in a formal note to the State Department, that she had placed her armed forces under Egyptian command. This was done under terms of the Syrian-Egyptian defense pact, the Syrian Chargé d'Affaires, Mamun Jamul, informed the State Department.

"The Syrian armed forces are now taking orders from the Egyptian Commander in Chief, Gen. Abdel Hakim Amer," Mr. Jamul said, continuing, "Syria

Continued on Page 3, Column 3

"All the News That's Fit to Print"

The New York Times.

LATE CITY EDITION
U. S. Weather Bureau Report (Page 54) Forecast:
Mostly sunny, chance of showers.
Clear tonight. Cloudy tomorrow.
Temp. range: 88—68; yesterday: 90—69.

VOL. CXI..No. 38,114.

© 1962 by The New York Times Company.
Times Square, New York 36, N. Y.

NEW YORK, FRIDAY, JUNE 1, 1962.

10 cents beyond 50-mile zone from New York City
except on Long Island. Higher in air delivery cities

FIVE CENTS

SOVIET INCREASES MEAT PRICES 30% TO SPUR FARMING

Butter Is Also Raised 25% in Move to Obtain Funds for Livestock Needs

U.S. ARMS DRIVE BLAMED

Moscow Asserts Threat of Nuclear Attack Prevents Shift of Defense Money

By SEYMOUR TOPPING
Special to The New York Times.

MOSCOW, Friday, June 1—The Soviet Government announced early today increases of 30 per cent in the retail price of meat and 25 per cent in the price of butter.

The announcement called upon the Soviet people to support these "temporary" increases in living costs as a measure directed at stimulating lagging production of agricultural products.

It said that the collective farmers had "not been materially interested in increasing the output of livestock products" because purchase prices had been too low.

A joint statement by the Government and the Central Committee of the Communist party said that the leadership had found it impossible to divert the funds needed for adequate investment in agriculture from defense, heavy industry or housing.

Reference to Kennedy

The Soviet people were told that there was "no other way out," because the Western powers headed by the United States were engaged in an arms race and in "harboring plans for a surprise nuclear rocket attack on the Soviet Union and other Socialist countries."

As alleged proof of the United States' intention, the statement cited the remarks attributed to President Kennedy in a published interview last March that the United States in some circumstances might take the initiative in the use of nuclear weapons.

In recent weeks Soviet leaders and the press here repeatedly have cited President Kennedy's remarks without his qualifying statement that he had no intention of suggesting that the United States might take aggressive action or launch a so-called preventive war.

The President explained that his remarks had been a restate-

Continued on Page 4, Column 4

KOREA SEIZES 41 IN PLOT ON JUNTA

Regime Says They Aimed at Restoring Civilian Rule

By The Associated Press

SEOUL, Korea, Friday, June 1—The South Korean military Government said today it had smashed a plot to overthrow the ruling junta and kill its members. It said forty-one persons were under arrest.

Col. Kim Chong Pil, director of the Central Intelligence Agency, said the organizers of the plot were primarily leaders of the disposed Democratic party of former Premier John M. Chang.

He said the plan of the plotters was for a military coup d'état June 13 with restoration of the civilian Government by Aug. 15.

Colonel Kim disclosed the identity of only fifteen of the forty-one persons he said were under arrest.

If charged and convicted with counter-revolutionary activity, the forty-one could face the death penalty.

The ruling junta took over in a coup last May, ousting Dr. Chang and his party.

On July 3, Gen. Chung Hee Park took control from the officer who had become Premier, Lieut. Gen. Chang Do Young. General Chang was originally sentenced to death for counter-revolutionary activities, but his sentence was commuted to life imprisonment and he was pardoned last month.

The latest arrest list included the former Seoul Mayor, Sang Don Kim, and his wife; Cho Jung Su, Democratic party organization chief, and Kim Dal

Continued on Page 5, Column 5

Eichmann Dies on Gallows For Role in Killing of Jews

Ben-Zvi Rejects Appeal for Mercy by Former Gestapo Officer

By LAWRENCE FELLOWS
Special to The New York Times.

RAMLE, Israel, Friday, June 1—Adolf Eichmann was hanged just before last midnight for the part he played in rounding up millions of Jews and transporting them to their deaths in Nazi camps during World War II.

President Itzhak Ben-Zvi rejected Eichmann's appeal for mercy shortly before the execution.

Eichmann's body was cremated early today, as had been requested in his will. The ashes were scattered in the Mediterranean outside Israeli waters.

Cold and unyielding to the end, Eichmann rejected an appeal by a Protestant minister that he repent. His last words, spoken in German to a small group of witnesses in the execution chamber, were:

"Long live Germany. Long live Argentina. Long live Austria. These are the countries

Associated Press
Adolf Eichmann

So is the fate of all men. I have lived believing in God and I die believing in God.

"After a short while, gentlemen, we shall all meet again.

Continued on Page 2, Column 3

RUSK BRUSHES OFF SOVIET TRADE IDEA

Khrushchev Plan for Parley Called Attempt to Divert West From Its Goals

By MAX FRANKEL
Special to The New York Times.

WASHINGTON, May 31—Secretary of State Dean Rusk brushed aside today Premier Khrushchev's call for a world trade conference, describing it as a "diversion" that betrayed understandable concern about the economic viability of the West.

The Secretary said at a news conference that there was no point in interrupting the "great" movement toward unity in Western Europe merely to talk about larger trade issues that were amply discussed in existing institutions.

The European Economic Community, or Common Market, he said, is flourishing and offers bright prospects not only to its members but also to its trading partners.

He Describes Commitment

Mr. Rusk cited the Common Market in rebutting charges that the Administration pursued a policy of "anything but victory."

He also said, in discussing another phase of Administration policy, that Washington expected a showdown in Laos in a few days.

The United States policy toward the Common Market, foreign aid, and the Western alliance in general, Mr. Rusk said, is evidence of the Administration's commitment "to the notion that the wave of the future lies with freedom."

He challenged Senator Barry Goldwater, Republican of Arizona, who made the "no-win" charge, to offer alternatives other than "unrealistic" notions of hydrogen war or retreat from international commitments.

The Secretary expressed disappointment over the lack of progress in negotiations with the Soviet Union both on disarmament and Berlin.

Continued on Page 4, Column 4

Conciliation Moves Are Made in Algiers As Terrorism Ebbs

By THOMAS F. BRADY
Special to The New York Times.

ALGIERS, May 31—As terrorism here fell well below the daily level of the last two weeks, three steps were taken today in the direction of reconciling the European and Moslem communities of this violent land.

These steps, decidedly preliminary in nature, coincided with reports of contacts between some unidentified Right-Wing European leaders and Abderrahmane Fares, president of the transitional executive that is governing Algeria temporarily under an internal autonomy arrangement until the July 1 referendum on independence.

The steps appeared to be part of a concerted campaign by the Algerian nationalists and the French authorities to check the exodus of Europeans from Algeria.

Europeans at Meeting

In the Moslem section of Belcourt, a working-class district, about 200 Europeans gathered in a tiny movie theatre at 5 P. M. under the "protection of nationalist militants." They asked questions of a spokesman for the Algerian National Liberation Front and adopted a motion of confidence in the future of Algeria.

Three hours later, Roger Roth, a vice president of the transitional executive, spoke on the Algiers television urging his fellow-Europeans to rally round. He accepted on behalf of the peace and self-determination agreements signed at Evian-les-Bains March 18 by the French Government and the Algerian Provisional Government.

He warned that there could be no question of changing or denouncing the Evian agreements, as some Europeans have demanded, but went on to say that the pact was a framework to be filled in and that the Europeans of Algeria could decide, if they would, what the content should be.

Earlier at Rocher-Noir, the fortified administrative capital, Bernard Tricot, the Delegate

Continued on Page 2, Column 2

Kennedy Adopts Buildings Plan To Give Capital a Modern Look

By ADA LOUISE HUXTABLE

President Kennedy directed the Government yesterday to proceed with a large Federal office-building program according to the most advanced principles of modern architectural design, and to make Pennsylvania Avenue a model of the new policy.

These plans are included in a Report to the President on Federal Office Space, approved by the President in Washington and passed on to Government departments for immediate action.

The report prepares the way for a record amount of new Federal building, calls specifically for the improvement of Federal architectural standards and endorses the use of the best modern architecture for all major new construction. Its provisions will have substantial and far-reaching effects on official building in the nation's capital and throughout the country.

The President's directive, however, does not assure smooth sailing for the program. Although his order makes it obligatory for Government departments to follow the new policy in new construction, Congress, which controls appropriations, can still be a stumbling block to its realization. Members of Congress have not been notably hospitable to modern design programs in the past, and have cut back a program of the State Department's Office of Foreign Buildings for contemporary embassies by withholding funds.

Even with these difficulties, however, two parts of the proposal will bring a sweeping new look to Government architec-

Continued on Page 12, Column 2

U.S. AND CITY OPEN 12.6-MILLION WAR ON DELINQUENCY

3-Year Plan Aims to Reform Entire Lower East Side as Example to Nation

By MARJORIE HUNTER
Special to The New York Times.

WASHINGTON, May 31—President Kennedy announced today a $12,600,000 mass social experiment on the Lower East Side of New York. It is part of a program designed to strike eventually at the roots of the national juvenile delinquency problem.

The three-year project, called Mobilization for Youth, will be financed jointly by Federal, city and private funds. It was called "the most advanced program yet devised to combat delinquency on a broad scale."

The announcement was made in the White House garden, just outside the President's office. Attending the ceremony were Attorney General Robert F. Kennedy, chairman of the President's Committee on Juvenile Delinquency; Abraham A. Ribicoff, Secretary of Health, Education and Welfare; Secretary of Labor Arthur Goldberg; Mayor Wagner and members of the New York Congressional delegation.

'Action by All' Urged

The President said juvenile delinquency was a "matter" which requires action by us all in this decade."

Using the Lower East Side area as a giant laboratory, project officials will seek to reform the social patterns of an entire community as a way of guiding youth into conforming with the accepted patterns of American life.

They will cover a broad range of social activities, from organizing the play of 7-year-olds to examining the political structure and community attitudes of adults.

There will be an Urban Youth Service Corps to provide jobs for 16-to-21-year-olds, an Adventure Corps on para-military lines for boys 9 to 16, "cool and jazzy" coffee shops featuring art and folk music, and improved welfare services to "troubled" families.

Special Programs Set

And there will be special school programs for both youths and adults, community development programs, a narcotics demonstration project, and a program to rehabilitate juvenile offenders.

The project is based on a theory, developed by Mobilization for Youth, Inc., of 214 East Second Street, New York City, that there must be a systematic approach to the problems of juvenile delinquency.

The administrative director of the project will be James E. McCarthy, a 45-year-old graduate of the University of Notre Dame who has specialized in youth and social work.

Officials here said that the Federal and state funds for the project would be available July 1 and that the program would

Continued on Page 14, Column 1

Associated Press Wirephoto
ANNOUNCE YOUTH PROGRAM: Attorney General Robert F. Kennedy, left, Mayor Wagner, and President Kennedy discuss Mobilization for Youth project at White House.

REGENTS INCREASE TEACHER TRAINING

5th Year Added to Standard for Elementary Grades— Specialization Stressed

By FRED M. HECHINGER

A substantial tightening of teacher-training standards for New York State's elementary schools was announced by the Board of Regents yesterday.

The new regulations significantly increase the general education required of teachers. They also call for a five-year program of college education for a permanent certificate, compared with the present requirement of a four-year bachelor's degree.

At the same time, colleges and universities were warned that they must improve their teacher-training courses and the quality of their faculties.

The new regulations call for greater breadth of study in the liberal arts and for concentration in at least one selected academic subject. The reform is in line with a nation-wide trend toward greater specialization in elementary schools and toward a declining stress on courses in educational methods apart from practice teaching.

The move, made public by Dr. James E. Allen Jr., State Education Commissioner, follows the raising of academic requirements for high school teachers in September, 1960.

The ruling for elementary school teachers will become effective for those seeking certification after Sept. 1, 1966. However, candidates preparing for elementary-school teaching will still be permitted to begin classroom teaching with a provisional certificate after four

Continued on Page 24, Column 4

Administration Is Hopeful Of Faster Rise in Economy

By JOHN D. MORRIS
Special to The New York Times.

WASHINGTON, May 31—The Administration held out hope today for a faster-than-expected upturn in the national economy in the last three quarters of this year.

Secretary of the Treasury Douglas Dillon and Budget Director David E. Bell cited that possibility as a factor in the Administration's decision to stand by its January forecast of a balanced Federal budget in the fiscal year that starts July 1.

They testified before the House Ways and Means Committee for an Administration bill to fix the national debt limit at $308,000,000,000 for the twelve-month period. The present limit of $300,000,000,000 automatically will drop to $285,000,000,000 July 1 in the absence of Congressional action.

The increase is being sought to cover a budget deficit of $7,000,000,000 in the current fiscal year.

Budget Balance Doubted

Questions by members indicated that the continued forecast of a balanced budget in the coming fiscal year was not wholly convincing to the committee. Words such as "unrealistic" and "highly doubtful" were used by questioners.

Actually, the unofficial position of the Administration is that a balance is now unlikely to be achieved in view of the failure of economic activity to live up to January's expectations in the first three months of the 1962 calendar year. A budget deficit of several billion dollars is now being unofficially predicted.

Secretary Dillon conceded under questioning that the official forecast was now less realistic than it had been in January and would be "much more

Continued on Page 10, Column 1

EMPLOYMENT SETS A RECORD FOR MAY

68,203,000 in Civilian Jobs for Month—Number of Idle Down by 227,000

By JOHN D. POMFRET
Special to The New York Times.

WASHINGTON, May 31—The nation's employment situation improved slightly in May.

The Labor Department announced today that unemployment fell by 227,000 in the month to 3,719,000. Civilian employment, paced by a rise in the number of nonfarm workers to a record level, rose by 1,379,000 to a record of 68,203,000 for May.

The decline in unemployment was about that expected at this time of year. The rise in employment was about 500,000 above the seasonal level.

The effect was to cut the unemployment rate, with seasonal factors eliminated, from 5.5 per cent to 5.4. The rate is the proportion of the labor force that is looking for work and cannot find it.

The last time the rate was as low as 5.4 per cent was in July, 1960. It was 7 per cent last May—its recession high—and has been dropping steadily since.

Secretary of Labor Arthur J. Goldberg, in a statement accompanying the figures, said:

"The fact that employment is at record levels and that unemployment is continuing to go down is encouraging and shows a continued improvement in the economy."

Nonfarm employment rose by 912,000 to 62,775,000 in May. The old record was 62,215,000.

Continued on Page 10, Column 5

STOCKS WIPE OUT MONDAY'S LOSSES IN NEW ADVANCE

Tuesday's Rally Is Extended —Exchange Flooded Again —Volume 10,710,000

INDEX UP 1.59 FOR WEEK

S.E.C. Chief Denies Rigging Inquiry but Says Agency Will Study Fluctuations

By BURTON CRANE

Buy orders surged into the New York Stock Exchange yesterday and erased what remained of the Monday losses.

The gain for the day was about $8,100,000,000, and for the week it was $600,000,000. At the close, aggregate values stood about 6.6 per cent below those of May 18, just before the recent six-day decline began, and 18 per cent below the high point of 1961.

It was not a unanimous advance and many leading issues did not join in it. While American Telephone was rising 4⅜ points, Corning Glass 6 and Sears, Roebuck 3⅞, Eastman Kodak was slipping 4⅝, Beckman Instruments 7⅛, Pittsburgh Plate Glass 5¼ and Polaroid 4¼.

Study in Contrast

But the market's general performance yesterday was in dramatic contrast to that of Monday, when it had its widest one-day loss since "Black Tuesday," Oct. 29, 1929.

The Monday loss, based on the 500-stock index of the Standard & Poor's Corporation, was $20,800,000,000 and volume was the fifth greatest in history at 9,350,000 shares.

On Tuesday, the market rallied sharply to recover $13,500,000,000, or 60 per cent, of Monday's losses. Volume on Tuesday was 14,750,000 shares, second only to the 16,410,930 shares traded on Oct. 29, 1929.

As on Monday and Tuesday, the heavy volume yesterday again swamped the exchange, causing reporting devices to run late. At the close, the ticker was one hour and forty-six minutes late.

News yesterday dealing with economic developments appeared to have mixed implications for the stock market.

On the one hand, Washington reported a slight improvement in the nation's employment picture during May.

And the chairman of the Securities and Exchange Commis-

Continued on Page 33, Column 2

MARYLAND VOTES NEW URBAN SEATS

Adds 19 Delegates Under Order to Reapportion

By The Associated Press

ANNAPOLIS, Md., May 31—The Maryland Legislature gave metropolitan areas nineteen more seats in the House of Delegates tonight in response to a court order requiring reapportionment.

The action was completed only thirty-eight minutes before a constitutional deadline for enactment of the statute. It will replace temporarily a section of the state constitution held invalid by a Federal court.

The Senate accepted the stopgap plan by a vote of 16 to 13, one more than necessary, after it had cleared the House of Delegates, 69 to 51. This was seven more votes than necessary.

A more permanent reapportionment plan, which would take away some of the seats small counties now hold, is to be drafted at the 1963 session of the Legislature and submitted to voters as a constitutional amendment taking effect in 1966.

Legislators were deadlocked on the issue earlier today after Gov. J. Millard Tawes sent a

Continued on Page 12, Column 4

School Contractors To Repay $100,000

By LEONARD BUDER

The Board of Education agreed last night to accept $100,000 in restitution from six plumbing contractors under indictment for allegedly defrauding the school system.

The payment will represent "full and final settlement of all claims by the board for damages or penalties."

Nine officials of the concerns involved were indicted last December by a Queens grand jury on charges of collusive bidding to obtain school contracts. The indictment said that the contractors had defrauded the system of $269,609 on $2,800,000 worth of school work.

The contractors agreed to the school board last night noted that the contractors had "pleaded guilty to misdemeanors with leave to withdraw such pleas and to contest the charges made in event they are unable

Continued on Page 14, Column 4

Associated Press Wirephoto
BEFORE HEARING ON NATIONAL DEBT: Representative Wilbur D. Mills of Arkansas, left, chairman of House Ways and Means Committee, meets with Douglas Dillon, right, Secretary of Treasury, and David E. Bell, Director of the Budget Bureau, prior to committee hearing at which Mr. Dillon and Mr. Bell testified for extension to debt limit.

"All the News That's Fit to Print"

The New York Times

LATE CITY EDITION

Weather: Sunny and warm today; fair tonight and tomorrow. Temp. range: today 83-61; Monday 81-62. Temp.-Hum. Index: 75; Monday 61-72. Full U.S. report on Page 93.

VOL. CXVI..No. 39,945 — NEW YORK, TUESDAY, JUNE 6, 1967 — 10 CENTS

© 1967 The New York Times Company.

ISRAELI AND ARAB FORCES BATTLING; BOTH CLAIM LAND AND AIR VICTORIES; CEASE-FIRE EFFORTS STALLED IN U.N.

4 States Hit by Blackout

JERSEY HURT MOST

13 Million Affected—Power Back Quickly in Philadelphia

By PETER KIHSS

A massive electrical failure along an interconnected system shut off power at mid-morning yesterday for 13 million persons in 15,000 square miles — three-fourths of New Jersey, much of eastern Pennsylvania and eastern Maryland and the northern half of Delaware.

It was more than three hours before power started to come back on in Newark. The restoration of power started in Philadelphia, the nation's fourth largest city, about a half hour after the failure occurred.

Not until 8:15 P.M. did Russell H. Williams, vice president for public relations for the Public Service Electric and Gas Company of New Jersey, report all sections served by his company had regained their electricity.

New York City escaped with only some flickering of lights in Brooklyn and Staten Island and a slight voltage drop when, according to the Consolidated Edison Company, a sensor device at 10:18 A.M. automatically cut off a tie-in to New Jersey across the Arthur Kill.

Source and Cause Sought

Last night, the Federal Power Commission said the precise source and cause—human, mechanical or just too much demand—were still being sought. But Lee C. White, its chairman, said the commission had been worrying for some time about the ability of the Pennsylvania-Jersey-Maryland grid to meet this summer's demand.

The failure — this time fortunately during sunshine, in contrast to the historic Nov. 9, 1965, blackout in New York City and the Northeast—spread with thunderbolt speed from the New Jersey-New York border and Wilkes-Barre, Pa., on the north, to south of Dover, Del., and west to Harrisburg, Pa.

Ingenuity, imagination and a gentle sense of resignation followed in the path of the blackout. Housewives sighed wearily and put away their irons. Subway riders took buses and elevator riders walked.

People sitting in front of radio and television sets listening to the news of the crisis in the Middle East felt new bewilderment as the sets faded out.

One of the last communities to have its power restored, about 7:30 P.M., was Montclair, N. J. During the day stores in the main business area closed—including a barber who finished his last haircut on the sidewalk outside his shop—and residents made thousands of calls to the police asking advice on "everything under the sun,

Continued on Page 42, Column 1

Traffic Is Snarled As Signals Go Out

By PAUL HOFMANN

Motorists blew their horns in self-defense and drove gingerly through intersections where traffic lights were out, 1,500 persons were stranded in the Philadelphia subway and railroad trains in four states rolled to a halt in yesterday's power blackout.

Air traffic over the Northeast generally suffered only little delay and disruption, but Newark Airport was severely crippled for the first hour or so after the power failure started and before emergency equipment could restore partial power.

The Newark control tower was cut off from aircraft on the ground and in the air,

Continued on Page 42, Column 7

U.S. PLANES DOWN 3 MIG'S NEAR HANOI IN RAID ON BRIDGES

Foe Mounts Heavy Defense—Soviet Rejects American Denial of Ship Attack

By United Press International

SAIGON, South Vietnam, June 5—United States planes bombed North Vietnam's war industry today and shot down three MIG interceptors near Hanoi. Military spokesmen said that the North Vietnamese had put up heavy air defenses.

F-105 Thunderchiefs flew into the heart of North Vietnam's industrial triangle and bombed railroad bridges around the Thainguyen manufacturing complex. Other United States planes bombed a manufacturing complex near the Phucyen MIG base, about 20 miles north of Hanoi.

Officials said that all three MIG's had been shot down by Phantoms flying protective cover for the Thunderchiefs. There were no reports of American air losses.

[In Moscow, the Soviet Government rejected a United States denial that American planes had attacked a Soviet merchant ship in a North Vietnamese port Friday. Page 3.]

MIG Total Reaches 77

The enemy losses brought to 77 the total number of MIG's shot down by American aircraft over North Vietnam.

The Soviet press agency, Tass, said that two United States planes were shot down over North Vietnam today, but there was no American confirmation.

Maj. Durward K. Priester, 36 years old, of Hampton, S.C., and Capt. John Pankhurst, 27, of Midland, Mich., both of the Air Force, were credited with one of the MIG's.

Pilots Fly 98 Missions

Special to The New York Times

SAIGON, June 5—Although poor weather covered most of North Vietnam yesterday, pilots flew 98 missions in the Southern Panhandle, the narrow stretch of North Vietnam just north of the border.

Two United States planes were lost: an F-105 Thunder-

Continued on Page 3, Column 5

The New York Times — June 6, 1967

WAR IN MIDEAST: Israelis reported they seized El Arish (1) and Turakumbasis (2). Fighting was heavy in Jerusalem (3) and Gaza Strip (4). Cairo said it repulsed foe at Kuntilla (5) and Khan Yunis (A on inset), but Israel said she took latter and Rafah (B).

Fighting Is Raging In Gaza and Sinai; Action in Air Heavy

Major Mideast Developments

On the Battlefronts

Israel and the Arab nations were locked in full-scale war yesterday along the borders of Israel and in the skies.

Fighting raged from Syria, on the north, to the Sinai Desert, on the south, and on the Jordanian-Israeli border.

Israel claimed major victories in the Sinai Desert and the Gaza Strip, reporting that her troops and tanks had taken El Arish and Khan Yunis, key towns, and asserting that the fall of Gaza city was imminent. In other sectors, the Israelis reported the capture of the Jordanian town of Jenin and said that Syrian land forces had entered the conflict for the first time with an attack on a border village.

Israel also said her pilots had shattered the Egyptian, Syrian and Jordanian Air Forces. Israeli pilots were reported to have destroyed 374 enemy planes, with an additional 34 probably destroyed. Israel put her losses at 19 aircraft.

The United Arab Republic said, however, that Arab land forces had repulsed invading Israeli armor on the Gaza Strip and at two points in the Sinai Peninsula.

In Jerusalem, Jordanian and Israeli troops exchanged machine-gun and mortar fire across no man's land.

In the Capitals

In Tel Aviv, Israeli leaders declared that their goals did not include the conquest of Arab territory.

In Cairo, President Gamal Abdel Nasser said the Arabs sought to "eliminate the shadow of Zionism from Palestine."

In Washington, the Johnson Administration sought to maintain a neutral role in the conflict and, calling on both sides to accept an immediate truce, avoided placing blame.

In Moscow, the Government issued a statement denouncing "Israeli aggression" and demanding withdrawal.

Egypt, Backed by Soviet, Blocks U.N. Call for Truce

By DREW MIDDLETON

Special to The New York Times

UNITED NATIONS, N. Y., June 5—The Security Council recessed tonight after 12 hours of futile effort to frame a resolution calling for a cease-fire and a withdrawal of forces in the Arab-Israeli war.

The refusal of the United Arab Republic to obey any resolution that demanded the withdrawal of its forces beyond the positions they occupied Sunday was the chief reason for the deadlock.

Statements in U.N. debate are printed on Page 17.

The Egyptian intransigence was strengthened, qualified sources said, by the support of the Soviet Union and India. On the other hand, there were indications Nikolai T. Fedorenko of the Soviet Union had asked his Government for further instructions.

"It is quite evident," a Western delegate said, "that the Russians do not like the prospect of another 'eyeball-to-eyeball' confrontation with the United States over what to them is a sideshow."

Denmark's representative on the 15-member Council, Hans Tabor, who is this month's President, announced the recess. He said that the consultations were still going on and would continue tomorrow, and he set 11:30 A.M. as the time for the next meeting.

Mr. Tabor asked members to be available from 10:30 A.M. He had hoped, he said, that when he recessed the first of today's meetings this morning that recess would be shorter than it was.

During the interval between the two brief meetings, the United Arab Republic, backed

Continued on Page 17, Column 3

MOSCOW DEMANDS ISRAEL QUIT EGYPT

Soviet Bids U.N. Condemn 'Aggression' and Repeats Support of Arabs

By PETER GROSE

Special to The New York Times

MOSCOW, Tuesday, June 6—The Soviet Union demanded today that Israel "immediately and unconditionally" halt military operations and pull her troops back from Egyptian territory.

A Government statement condemned "Israeli aggression," asserted the Soviet "right to take all steps that may be necessitated by the situation" and called on states, specifically including the major powers, to work for peace.

The United Nations "must discharge its direct duty: condemn Israeli actions and promptly take steps to restore peace in the Middle East," the statement said.

It expressed the hope that other governments "will do, for their part, everything in their power to extinguish the military conflagration in the Middle East."

This was the first official reaction from the Soviet Govern-

Continued on Page 18, Column 6

U.S. SEEKS TO HOLD A NEUTRAL STANCE

Presses for a Cease-Fire—Many in Congress Oppose a Unilateral Move in Area

By JOHN W. FINNEY

Special to The New York Times

WASHINGTON, June 5—The Administration sought today to maintain a neutral role in the Middle East without formally committing itself to be neutral.

The White House, warning that "tragic consequences" would result if the fighting continued, called on both sides to accept an immediate cease-fire. The dominant Congressional reaction was that the United States should take no unilateral action in the Middle East.

In an attempt to bring about a cease-fire, the Administration deliberately refrained from fixing any blame for the outbreak of fighting.

[In London, the Foreign Secretary said that Britain's policy was "not to take sides." France suspended all deliveries of military equipment to the Middle East. Page 18.]

Confusion Develops in U.S.

The Johnson Administration, in attempting to maintain a position for mediation, became entangled in some confusion over how "neutral" it was.

The State Department spokesman, Robert J. McCloskey, started the confusion by declaring that "our position is neutral in thought, word and deed."

The Administration then spent the rest of the day attempting to tone down the McCloskey declaration by emphasizing that the United States was not neutral in terms of long-standing obligations to support the political independence and territorial integrity of Israel and of the Arab nations.

As it cast around for some way to bring the fighting to an end, the Administration announced that travel by American citizens to Israel and 13 Arab countries was being banned, unless the traveler had the specific permission of the State Department.

As of today, the State Department announced, United

Continued on Page 18, Column 1

Nasser Exhorts Arabs

By ERIC PACE

Special to The New York Times

CAIRO, Tuesday, June 6—The Cairo radio announced last night that the United Arab Republic's forces had invaded Israel after having "wiped out two enemy attacks" in Egyptian territory on the Sinai Peninsula.

The United Arab Republic had declared earlier that its forces had retaliated on land, sea and in the air after Israel carried out surprise ground and air attacks on Egyptian border areas and airbases this morning.

President Gamal Abdel Nasser declared in a statement relayed by the Egyptian Government news service that all Arabs were now fighting to "eliminate the shadow of Zionism from Palestine and to restore its Arabism."

Progress of Fighting Unclear

The over-all progress of the conflict was unclear from the series of military communiqués issued throughout the day by the Cairo radio. But these reported that the United Arab Republic had destroyed 86 Israeli planes by nightfall while they acknowledged only two Egyptian planes lost to the Israelis.

They said that United Arab Republic and Palestinian land forces had repulsed Israeli invaders at Khan Yunis in the Gaza Strip and at Kuntilla and El Aguila on the Sinai Peninsula. Egyptian forces were said

Continued on Page 16, Column 5

Israel Depicts Gains

By JAMES FERON

Special to The New York Times

JERUSALEM (Israel), Tuesday, June 6—The Israeli Air Force indicated early today that it had decimated the Egyptian, Syrian and Jordanian air forces in a sweeping series of air battles and ground attacks.

Israeli pilots reported that they had destroyed 374 enemy planes, and that 34 other aircraft probably had been destroyed.

The Israelis put their losses at 19 planes. Eight pilots were reported killed and 11 were reported missing, including some known to have been captured.

Movement on Sinai

Striking gains were also reported on the Sinai Peninsula where the hostilities began, according to the Israelis, with the shelling of Israeli settlements along the Gaza border at dawn yesterday.

The Israeli Chief of Staff, Maj. Gen. Itzhak Rabin, said in a statement issued at a post-midnight news conference in Tel Aviv that Israeli armor had captured El Arish and was moving rapidly along the El Arish-Abu Aweigila road.

The Gaza town of Rafah was reported captured as well as the junction of Khan Yunis in the disputed Gaza Strip. The fall of Gaza itself was considered imminent.

The Air Force chief, Mordechai Hod, said that most of the damage had been done to the Egyptians, who lost 286 air-

Continued on Page 16, Column 1

HIGH COURT CURBS HOME INSPECTIONS

Backs Right to Deny Entry Not Supported by Warrant —Also Protects Business

By FRED P. GRAHAM

Special to The New York Times

WASHINGTON, June 5 — Property owners may refuse to open their homes or businesses to health, fire and other administrative inspectors unless they have search warrants, the Supreme Court ruled today.

In extending the search warrant requirement beyond law enforcement officials to the routine inspections of administrative authorities, the Court relaxed the traditional standards for the issuance of search warrants.

It ruled that inspectors may obtain warrants to enter premises without having cause to believe that evidence of an ordinance violation would be found inside.

The 6-to-3 opinion by Justice Byron R. White said that such warrants might be obtained for an entire city area simply by showing that a certain period of time had passed since the last inspection, or by showing that the buildings were in a rundown condition.

This provoked a strong dis-

Continued on Page 32, Column 3

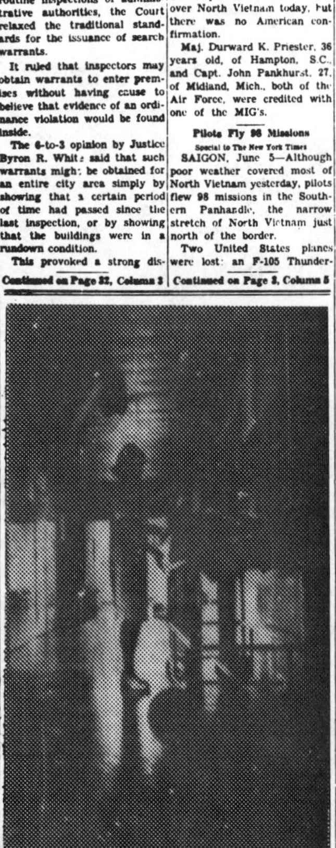

The New York Times

HOSPITAL DIMMED: A nurse comforting a patient in a dark corridor of Jersey City Medical Center yesterday.

U.S. Military Analysts Expect Short War, With Israel Winning

By WILLIAM BEECHER

Special to The New York Times

WASHINGTON, June 5 — A number of American military analysts, while admitting that the situation was still very confused in the Middle East, were of the opinion that the war would probably be short and that Israel would prevail.

Analysts at the Pentagon said that the Egyptian Army was a lot stronger today than in 1956, when Israeli forces swept through the Sinai Peninsula, but that Israel still was believed to have a better-balanced, better-trained, better-led military force.

Several experts, while conceding that predictions are treacherous, said they believed Israel should be able to "punch through" Egyptian forces in one of two directions in Sinai and elsewhere in a week to 10 days.

In 1956, Israel was able to overwhelm opposition in Sinai in 100 hours, but at that time Egypt was fighting on two fronts, with a British-French force pressing in from the north along the Suez Canal.

"Nobody, of course, knows how much better the Egyptian Army has become," said one general, "but we don't think they've had time enough to become a first-class fighting force."

Analysts speculated that Israel might want to fight hold-

Continued on Page 19, Column 1

Speck Is Sentenced To Chair on Sept. 1

By DONALD JANSON

Special to The New York Times

PEORIA, Ill., June 5—Richard F. Speck was sentenced to death in the electric chair today for the murders last summer in Chicago of eight young nurses.

The 25-year-old drifter stood mute and expressionless a foot in front of the bench as Circuit Court Judge Herbert C. Paschen ordered the execution for Sept. 1.

Before sentence was passed, the public defender, Gerald W. Getty, told the judge that the lanky, itinerant seaman had nothing to say in his own behalf.

A jury of seven men and five women found Speck guilty of each of the murders last April

Continued on Page 36, Column 4

Troops and Armor Clash in Jerusalem

By TERENCE SMITH

Special to The New York Times

JERUSALEM (Israel), June 5 — War came to this divided city today at 11:20 A.M., a little more than three hours after the first announcement of the fighting at the Sinai border to the south.

Within minutes of the first shots, Arabs and Israelis were firing at each other with rifles, machine-guns, mortars, tanks and artillery from positions along an eight-mile border through the city.

The fighting continued into the night. In the darkness, the Jordanians threw up a blanket of antiaircraft fire as jets swept overhead.

In early fighting, Jordanian

Continued on Page 16, Column 7

Israeli Planes Raid Airports in Jordan

By DANA ADAMS SCHMIDT

Special to The New York Times

AMMAN, Jordan, June 5—Clouds of black smoke rose over the Amman airport today as four Israeli jet bombers circled and dived, apparently more or less at will. Only light antiaircraft and machine-gun fire appeared to be opposing them as they bombed and strafed aircraft and installations in four attacks.

The Israeli Air Force also was reported to have bombed Jordan's airport in El Mafraq.

Civilians fled the streets as air-raid sirens wailed. Most residents of the leading hotel, the Intercontinental, made for an air-raid shelter in the nightclub. But some watched from

Continued on Page 16, Column 8

NEWS INDEX

	Page		Page
Art	52	Obituaries	44, 47
Books	45	Real Estate	77
Bridge	44	Screen	53-55
Business	63-64, 75-76	Ships and Air	93
Buyers	74	Society	56
Crossword	45	Sports	57-61
Editorials	46	Supreme Court	33, 63
Fashions	51	Theaters	53-55
Financial	65-74	TV and Radio	94-95
Food	51	U. N. Proceedings	17
Man in the News	17	Wash. Proceedings	36
Music	53-55	Weather	93

News Summary and Index, Page 49

A group of Florida executives are in N.Y. today seeking to meet a group of N.Y. VIP's. See adv. pg. 75.—Advt.

"All the News That's Fit to Print"

The New York Times

LATE CITY EDITION

Weather: Fair and warm today and tonight. Partly cloudy tomorrow. Temp. range: today 85-63; Wed. 81-62. Temp.-Hum. Index: mid-70's; Wed. 72. Full report on Page 93.

VOL. CXVI . No. 39,947

NEW YORK, THURSDAY, JUNE 8, 1967

10 CENTS

ISRAELIS ROUT THE ARABS, APPROACH SUEZ, BREAK BLOCKADE, OCCUPY OLD JERUSALEM; AGREE TO U.N. CEASE-FIRE; U.A.R. REJECTS IT

JOHNSON WILL USE CABINET TO COURT STATES' OFFICIALS

Aides Will Seek to Tighten Ties Between Governors and the White House

By WARREN WEAVER Jr.
Special to The New York Times

WASHINGTON, June 7—President Johnson has decided to use the members of his Cabinet as diplomatic agents in his campaign to improve relations between the Administration and state governments.

The President has approved a plan under which each member of the Cabinet would be assigned four or five states as his personal responsibility, with instructions to maintain personal contact between the Governors and the White House.

As part of the same effort, each of the 50 states will be given a "day" in Washington next fall and winter, when a planeload of its key officials will fly here to hold conferences all over the capital, capped by a meeting of the Governors with the President.

Bryant's Work Continued

Both projects reflect Mr. Johnson's continuing determination to build domestic as well as foreign bridges by working to sort out the tangled Federal-state relations that have been increasingly complicated by the administration of the Great Society programs.

Both are attempts to give some permanency to the contacts established during the last four months by Farris Bryant, the President's envoy to the states, on visits to 40 capitals with a squad of Federal experts.

Mr. Bryant, a former Governor of Florida who is now the director of the Office of Emergency Planning, plans to leave his White House post this summer, possibly to return to politics in his home state, and he is eager to help establish more permanent lines of communication before his departure.

As now envisioned, each Cabinet officer would visit all of

Continued on Page 29, Column 2

Rise in Debt Ceiling Rejected in House; Johnson Rebuffed

Special to The New York Times

WASHINGTON, June 7—The House of Representatives dealt the Johnson Administration a sharp setback today by rejecting a bill to increase the ceiling on the national debt $29-billion, to $365-billion.

The vote against passage was 210 to 197, with Republicans voting solidly to kill the bill. Enough Democrats, mostly Southerners, voted with them to turn the tide.

About six Northern Democratic "doves"—opponents of the war in Vietnam—also joined the opposition.

In all, 34 Democrats joined with 176 Republicans to defeat the measure.

Today's action raised the possibility—though a slim one—of financial chaos after June 30. At that time the debt limit reverts to its "permanent" ceiling of $285-billion, though the debt, at $330-billion, is already far above that level. The legal authority of the Treasury to pay its bills would be in doubt.

However, the Ways and

Continued on Page 30, Column 4

U.S. VOWS TO SEEK A DURABLE PEACE

Johnson Recalls Bundy for New Mideast Planning Unit—'Real Chance' Is Seen

By MAX FRANKEL
Special to The New York Times

WASHINGTON, June 7—President Johnson pledged today to do his best to help translate the new Middle Eastern situation into a more lasting settlement between Israel and her Arab neighbors.

Apparently hoping to exploit Israel's lightning military success—which has surprised but not displeased the White House—Mr. Johnson ordered the drafting of special policies for a "new peace" and set up new machinery to deal with the situation.

The President said that the United States, which had worked hard to avoid the war, felt that "there is now a real chance" to turn from "the frustrations of the past to the hopes of a peaceful future."

But Mr. Johnson said the handling of the crisis and the preparations for a lasting settlement would require the most careful consideration in the United States Government. To organize that effort he recalled McGeorge Bundy to temporary duty at the White House as executive secretary to a special subcommittee of the National Security Council.

Mr. Bundy will seek a temporary leave from the presidency of the Ford Foundation, which he assumed last year after serving as special assistant for

Continued on Page 19, Column 1

CONFEREES BLOCK A DRAFT LOTTERY

Compromise Bill Continues Deferment of Students

By United Press International

WASHINGTON, June 7—Senate and House negotiators reached agreement today on a new military draft bill that rules out, for the present, any lottery-like random selection system to determine the order of induction.

The bill was a compromise of differing bills that the Senate and House had passed. It would guarantee the continuance of educational deferments for college undergraduates and students enrolled in apprentice and job training programs.

Senator Richard B. Russell, Democrat of Georgia, who is chairman of the Senate conferees, said the Senate might act on the four-year draft extension bill tomorrow. House action must await approval by the Senate.

Congressional action will clear the way for President Johnson, under current discretionary powers, to reverse the order of induction and take 19-year-olds first from the Selec-

Continued on Page 3, Column 1

Dorothy Parker, 73, Literary Wit, Dies

By ALDEN WHITMAN

Dorothy Parker, the sardonic humorist who purveyed her wit in conversation, short stories, verse and criticism, died of a heart attack yesterday afternoon in her suite at the Volney Hotel, 23 East 74th Street. She was 73 years old and had been in frail health in recent years.

In print and in person, Miss Parker sparkled with a word or a phrase, for she honed her humor to its most economical size. Her rapier wit, much of it spontaneous, gained its early renown from her membership in the Algonquin Round Table, an informal luncheon club at the Algonquin Hotel in the nineteen-twenties, where some of

Continued on Page 38, Column 1

EBAN SEES THANT

Says Acceptance Is Based on Enemy's Reciprocal Action

Excerpts from debate at U.N. are printed on Page 18.

By DREW MIDDLETON
Special to The New York Times

UNITED NATIONS, N. Y., June 7—The Security Council unanimously adopted a Soviet resolution today calling on the combatants in the Middle East to "cease fire and all military activities" at 4 P.M., New York time today.

The Government of Israel shortly thereafter announced that she had accepted the call of the Council for a cease-fire, provided her Arab foes agreed.

In the evening, reports from the Middle East indicated rejection of the call by the United Arab Republic, Syria, Iraq, Saudi Arabia, Algeria and Kuwait. Jordan told Secretary General Thant that she would abide by the cease-fire, except in self-defense.

Says It's in Effect

Abba Eban, the Foreign Minister of Israel, told the Secretary General that a cease-fire was already in effect between Jordan and Israel.

In presenting the resolution, the Soviet delegate, Nikolai T. Fedorenko, made it clear that if Israel failed to heed the Security Council's demands, Moscow would consider severing diplomatic relations. The original Security Council resolution, adopted yesterday, simply called for a cease-fire.

But the reports from the Arab capitals indicate, diplomatic sources here said, that military operations will continue.

According to diplomats, the best hope lies in a draft resolution presented by George Ignatieff, the Canadian delegate. This proposes that the President of the Security Council and the Secretary General take measures to insure compliance with the resolutions.

Today's resolution demanded that the combatants "cease fire and all military activities on 7 June 1967 by 2000 hours Greenwich mean time." The resolution was adopted less than an hour before this time, which is 4 P.M. New York time, 10 P.M. in Jordan and Israel and 11 P.M. in the United Arab Republic and Syria.

The Council adjourned without voting on the Canadian draft largely because Milko Ta-

Continued on Page 18, Column 2

United Press International Radiophoto

OLD JERUSALEM IS NOW IN ISRAELI HANDS: Israeli soldiers in prayer at the Wailing Wall yesterday

Major Mideast Developments

On the Battlefronts

Israel claimed victory in the Sinai Desert after three days of fighting. Sharm el Sheik, guarding the entrance to the Gulf of Aqaba, fell after a paratroop attack, and the Israelis said the blockade of the gulf was broken. Other Israeli units were within 20 miles of the Suez Canal, and one Israeli report placed them in the eastern section of Ismailia, on the canal itself.

In Jerusalem, for the first time in 19 years, Israeli Jews prayed at the Wailing Wall as their troops occupied the Old City. Israeli troops captured Jericho, in Jordan, and sped northward to take Nablus, giving them control of the west bank of the Jordan.

The Egyptian High Command reported that its forces had fallen back from first-line positions in the Sinai Peninsula and were fighting fiercely from unspecified secondary positions. It announced that Egyptian troops had pulled back from Sharm el Sheik to join main defense units.

In the Capitals

In the United Nations, Israel accepted the call for a cease-fire, provided the Arabs complied. Jordan announced that she would accept and ordered her troops to fire only in self-defense. But Baghdad declared that Iraq had refused. There were indications that Syria, Algeria and Kuwait were also opposed.

In Cairo, an Egyptian official said the United Arab Republic would fight on.

In Moscow, the Soviet Union threatened to break diplomatic relations with Israel if she did not observe the cease-fire.

In Paris, the French proposed an international agreement for free passage in the Gulf of Aqaba similar to the one governing the Dardanelles in Turkey.

In Washington, President Johnson promised to seek a settlement that would assure lasting peace in the Mideast.

In London, the British urged the Israelis to halt before they aroused more turmoil in the Arab world and diminished the chances for a settlement.

Israelis Weep and Pray Beside the Wailing Wall

By TERENCE SMITH
Special to The New York Times

JERUSALEM, June 7—Israeli troops wept and prayed today at the foot of the Wailing Wall—the last remnant of Solomon's Second Temple and the object of pilgrimage by Jews through the centuries.

In battle dress and still carrying their weapons, they gathered at the base of the sand-colored wall and sang Hallel, a series of prayers reserved for occasions of great joy.

They were repeating a tradition that goes back 2,000 years but has been denied Israeli Jews since 1948, when the first of three wars with the Arabs ended in this area.

The wall is all that remains of the Second Temple, built in the 10th century before Christ and destroyed by the Romans in A.D. 70.

The Israelis, trembling with emotion, bowed vigorously from the waist as they chanted psalms in a lusty chorus. Most had submachine guns slung over their shoulders and several held bazookas as they prayed.

Among the leaders to pray at the wall was Maj. Gen. Moshe Dayan, the new Defense Minister. He told the troops:

"We have returned to the holiest of our holy places, never to depart from it again."

General Dayan, who was ap-

Continued on Page 17, Column 1

CAIRO ANNOUNCES A SINAI PULLBACK

Blames Foreign Aid to Foe, but Says Troops Fight On in Secondary Positions

By ERIC PACE
Special to The New York Times

CAIRO, June 7—An Egyptian military communiqué reported today that forces of the United Arab Republic had fallen back from some first-line positions on the Sinai Peninsula and were engaged in fierce fighting against Israeli troops from secondary positions.

Another statement of the High Command, broadcast four hours later by the Cairo radio, said Egyptian troops at Sharm el Sheik, guarding the entrance to the Gulf of Aqaba, had joined other Egyptian forces "now concentrated in the Sinai Peninsula."

There was no elaboration, but the communiqué, broadcast about 5:30 P.M., appeared to confirm Israeli reports that the Egyptians had been forced to retreat from Sharm el Sheik.

At night, the High Command reported that Israeli paratroops had dropped over the "second-line Egyptian front" but had been "completely wiped out."

The communiqué also said the Israelis had tried another drop at Sharm el Sheik after the

Continued on Page 17, Column 6

AQABA GULF OPEN

Dayan Asserts Israel Does Not Intend to Capture the Canal

By The Associated Press

TEL AVIV, June 7—Israel proclaimed victory tonight in the Sinai Peninsula campaign against the United Arab Republic. On the eastern front, both the Old City of Jerusalem and Bethlehem were captured from the Jordanians.

"The Egyptians are defeated," said Maj. Gen. Itzhak Rabin, the Israeli Chief of Staff.

"All their efforts are aimed at withdrawing behind the Suez Canal, and we are taking care of that. The whole area is in our hands. The main effort of the Egyptians is to save themselves."

Israel Losses 'Not Great'

Describing the developments through the third day of this third Arab-Israeli war in 19 years, General Rabin made these claims:

¶Sinai, the Egyptian territory between Israel's Negev Desert and the Suez Canal, is taken.

¶Most of the Jordanian territory on the west bank of the Jordan River, including Jericho, is in Israeli hands, and most of Jordan's army has been captured.

¶Relative to what was done, the number of Israelis casualties was "not great."

The Israelis were reported to have swept to the Suez Canal.

[An Israeli delegation source at the United Nations said Israeli troops had seized that part of the canal city of Ismailia that is on the eastern side of the waterway. But this was denied by an army source in Tel Aviv, who said, according to Reuters, that the Israelis had not taken any point along the canal.

[Maj. Gen. Moshe Dayan, the Israeli Defense Minister, declared that there was "no intention" of taking the canal, United Press International reported.]

'Never to Depart'

After the fall of the Old City of Jerusalem, Defense Minister Moshe Dayan said there that the Israelis had reunited their capital and would never "depart from it again."

Israel reported that paratroops aided by naval units had captured Sharm el Sheik, commanding the entrance to the Gulf of Aqaba, and said the blockade that the Egyptians had mounted from that position had been broken.

"The Strait of Tiran is now open," General Rabin said.

Israel's chief of staff said his men had taken on the United Arab Republic, Jordan, Syria and Iraq, knocked out their air forces and overrun their armor and infantry.

"All this the armed forces of Israel did alone," he declared.

The general then turned over the briefing to Brig. Mordechai Hod, commander of the air force, who announced 441 Arab

Continued on Page 16, Column 1

The New York Times — June 8, 1967

CONQUEST IN THE MIDEAST: Israeli troops took Sharm el Sheik (1), drove on to the Suez Canal (2) and seized control of the Old City in Jerusalem (3). Photo was taken in September, 1966, during the flight of Gemini II.

Pentagon Believes Israeli Jets Struck From Sea, Eluded Radar

By WILLIAM BEECHER
Special to The New York Times

WASHINGTON, June 7—At least a part of the Israeli Air Force that caught large numbers of Egyptian aircraft on the ground in the early hours of the war may have slipped through gaps in the United Arab Republic's radar net by flying in over the Mediterranean.

This possibility was raised today by Pentagon analysts. If correct, it would help to explain how Israeli pilots were able to surprise so many Egyptian jets before they could get into the air.

It might also serve to provide part of the explanation behind insistent Arab assertions that carrier-based United States and British jets participated in the raids.

The early blows to Arab, and especially Egyptian, air strength is credited by most military analysts as having been a decisive factor in the Israeli successes on land that followed.

"We know that some of the Israeli planes returned to their bases by way of the sea," one ranking officer said, "and we assume they may have approached from the seaward too."

The officer said it was obvious that Israel had excellent intelligence on weaknesses in the Egyptian radar system and exploited them.

Shortly after the raids, he went on, the Jordanian radio charged that Jordanian radar

Continued on Page 18, Column 8

NEWS INDEX

"All the News That's Fit to Print"

The New York Times

LATE CITY EDITION
Weather: Fair and warm today, tonight and tomorrow. Temp. range: today 85-63; Thurs. 85-64. Temp.-Hum. Index: today 70 to 75; Thurs. 77. Full U.S. report on Page 89.

VOL. CXVI..No. 39,948   © 1967 The New York Times Company.   NEW YORK, FRIDAY, JUNE 9, 1967   10 CENTS

EGYPT AND SYRIA AGREE TO U.N. CEASE-FIRE; ISRAEL REPORTS TROOPS REACH SUEZ CANAL; JOHNSON, KOSYGIN USED HOT LINE IN CRISIS

SENATE APPROVES A TIGHTENED RULE ON REDISTRICTING

33 States Ordered to Bring Population Variant Down to 10% by 1968 Election

By JAMES F. CLARITY
Special to The New York Times

WASHINGTON, June 8—The Senate approved today a bill requiring that by the 1968 election no state have a population variance of more than 10 per cent between its largest and smallest Congressional districts.

The approval, which came in a surprise vote of 57 to 25, was a result of a fight by Senator Edward M. Kennedy, Democrat of Massachusetts, to amend a measure that would have permitted a variance of 35 per cent until the 1972 election.

The Kennedy amendment, which was soundly defeated in committee two weeks ago, is intended, according to the Senator, to make Congressional redistricting conform with the Supreme Court's one-man, one-vote ruling of 1964. The amendment also deleted language giving the states power to determine when the compactness of a district was "practicable."

An Altered Version

The measure, before it was amended today, was an altered version of a bill already passed by the House. The House bill provided for a population variance of 30 per cent, and was amended by the Senate Judiciary Committee to cover four additional states.

The version passed today, which now goes to a Senate-House conference, would apply to 33 states having variances of more than 10 per cent. Nine of these states are under Federal court orders to redistrict. The 17 states not covered by today's Senate action either elect Representatives at large or have variances lower than 10 per cent.

Mr. Kennedy's proposal was approved, first in a crucial 44-to-39 vote as an amendment, then in the final vote on the bill as amended, 57 to 25.

"We knew it would be close.

Continued on Page 26, Column 1

Arms Cost Stress Scored by Rickover

By EVERT CLARK
Special to The New York Times

WASHINGTON, June 8—Vice Adm. Hyman G. Rickover has denounced the cost-effectiveness approach to weapons development as an "ism," a "new religion" and a "fog bomb" that is keeping the nation from gaining technology that would save lives.

In Congressional testimony released today, the head of the nuclear-powered ship program attacked present management techniques in the Pentagon.

By Presidential order, many of these techniques—including the mathematical analysis of cost vs. effectiveness—are now being spread throughout the executive branch of

Continued on Page 2, Column 4

JURY FINDS LAXITY IN BUILDINGS UNIT

Graft, Shirking and Lack of Personnel Training Are Cited—Moerdler Agrees

By JACK ROTH

A New York County grand jury criticized yesterday long-standing conditions in the Buildings Department that it said had resulted in corruption among housing inspectors and landlords.

The jury also said the situation permitted some inspectors and their supervisors to quit work as early as 10:30 A.M. and go to bars and racetracks for the rest of the day.

The jury, in a presentment handed up to Supreme Court Justice Mitchell D. Schweitzer, charged that the department suffered from lack of financial and manpower resources.

It asserted that inspectors were not properly trained for their jobs, that they were unaware of their department's rules and regulations, that there was duplication in inspections, that electronic processing equipment was failing to do its job and that unauthorized persons had access to file rooms and private departmental offices.

The Buildings Commissioner,

Continued on Page 31, Column 1

ALL SINAI IS HELD

U.A.R. Loses 50 Tanks in Actions Termed Fiercest of War

By Reuters

TEL AVIV, Friday, June 9—Israeli troops have reached the bank of the Suez Canal and have taken control of the entire Sinai Peninsula, the Israeli command reported this morning.

The radio broadcast the text of a message from the commander in the southern front, to the Chief of Staff, Gen. Yitzhak Rabin. The message said:

"Happy to inform you that our forces are stationed on the bank of the Suez Canal and the Red Sea. The Sinai Peninsula is in our hands. Greetings to you and to the whole defense forces of Israel."

Battle reports yesterday indicated that the remnants of two Egyptian armored divisions and four infantry divisions were trapped in the western part of that Sinai Desert.

50 Tanks Reported Wrecked

The Israelis' acceptance of the United Nations cease-fire coincided with an announcement by an Israeli spokesman that three battles in the desert yesterday had been "the fiercest in this war."

The Israelis said they had shot down eight Egyptian planes and destroyed at least 50 Egyptian tanks during the fighting.

Other tanks were wrecked and left on the road to Qantara, about 30 miles north of Ismailia, about midway along the 100-mile Suez Canal.

Among the Egyptian planes downed were a Soviet-made Ilyushin bomber and several Soviet-built Sukhoi-7's. Israeli planes also struck Soviet-made missile sites in the Suez Canal zone during daylight raids, the spokesman added.

Despite the continuation of heavy fighting, the Israeli spokesman said that all escape routes for Egyptian armored units had been closed.

He added that Israeli forces had captured oilfields at Ras Sudar, south of the port of Taufiq on the western coast of the Sinai Peninsula. Israeli soldiers said the wells were afire

Continued on Page 17, Column 6

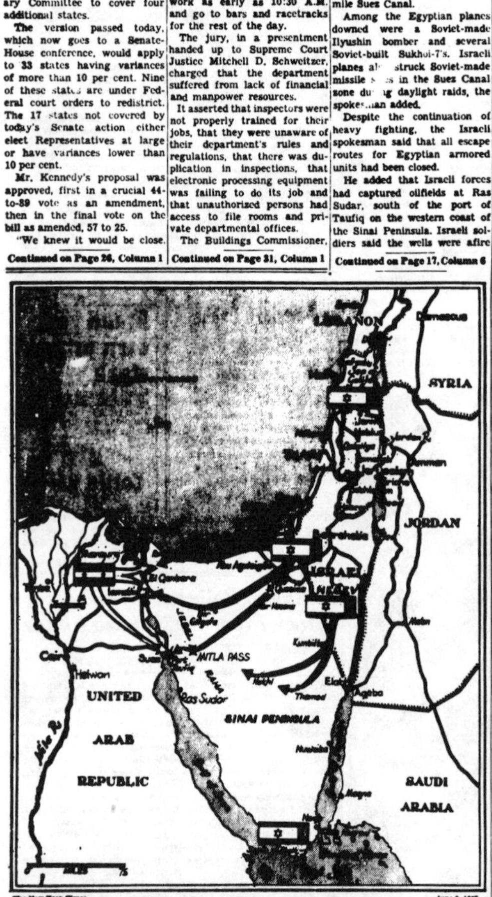

AFTER THE BATTLE: Egyptian prisoners, prone on the sand, their hands behind their heads, are guarded in a compound by Israeli troops at El Arish in the northern Sinai Peninsula. El Arish was taken by Israel Tuesday.
United Press International Cablephoto

EGYPTIANS TOLD OF TRUCE DECISION

Cairo Broadcast Is Terse —Syrians Also Announce Approval of Cease-Fire

By ERIC PACE
Special to The New York Times

CAIRO, Friday, June 9—The Government told the Egyptian people this morning that it had conditionally accepted a cease-fire in the war with Israel.

There was no immediate popular reaction because the Cairo radio waited until early morning before announcing, more than three hours after the fact, that the United Arab Republic had told Secretary General Thant of the United Nations that it would agree to a truce if Israel did so.

[The Damascus radio announced that Syria, too, had accepted the cease-fire, Reuters reported. Page 17.]

Cairo was blacked out as protection against possible Israeli air raids when the news came, but nocturnal strollers reported that policemen were already taking down at least some of the anti-Israeli banners that have festooned the city for the last few weeks.

An early edition of a popular Cairo newspaper, Al Akhbar, put the news on the front page but made no comment. There was also no elaboration from the radio, which broadcast a military communiqué saying that the battle against Israel was continuing at all points along the Egyptian front.

The terse announcement of the cease-fire contrasted with

Continued on Page 17, Column 2

U.S. Planes Batter MIG Base in North

Special to The New York Times

SAIGON, South Vietnam, June 8 — American fighter-bombers knocked out a MIG base near Hanoi yesterday and wrecked a surface-to-air missile storage area 50 miles southwest of the capital, the United States Command reported today.

At the same time, new fighting broke out just south of the demilitarized zone at the border between North Vietnam and South Vietnam, where a battle raged for control of three hills last month.

Navy carrier pilots attacked the Kep Airfield, 37 miles northeast of Hanoi, for the seventh time since April 24. A headquarters spokesman said the airfield was "closed tempo-

Continued on Page 3, Column 6

Major Mideast Developments

In the Capitals

The **United Arab Republic** accepted a United Nations cease-fire. Israel had previously agreed to stop hostilities if her enemies were willing to go along.

In **Damascus**, after a series of militant vows to fight on, the Syrians announced that they would also accept the cease-fire.

President Johnson welcomed the cease-fire agreement and urged prompt action to solve the "many more fundamental" questions in the Middle East.

An **emergency declaration** on oil was being considered by the Johnson Administration after major oil companies reported that a worldwide transportation problem had resulted from the war.

The **hot line** between Washington and Moscow was used this week for the first time during a crisis.

On the Battlefronts

Before the cease-fire went into effect, Israeli planes and torpedo boats mistakenly attacked a United States communications ship about 15 miles off Sinai. The Pentagon reported that 10 Americans had been killed and 100 wounded. Israel sent an apology.

Israel reported that her troops had reached the bank of the Suez Canal and that the entire Sinai Peninsula was under her control. Earlier Israel reported three fierce desert battles in which at least 50 Egyptian tanks had been destroyed.

The **United Arab Republic** announced that its air force had inflicted heavy damage on Israeli armored columns trying to advance westward from El Arish in the Sinai Peninsula.

At the **Strait of Tiran**, a Soviet freighter bound for the Jordanian port of Aqaba was the first ship to pass since Israel declared the waterway open to shipping on Wednesday. Two Israeli ships prepared to follow.

DONATIONS POUR IN FOR ISRAELI FUND

Many Give All They Have— Some Gifts in Millions

By M. S. HANDLER

"You have got it all now," said a brief letter containing a check for $25,000.

The message was from a professor at the Jewish Theological Seminary who said he had gladly stripped himself of his worldly goods and sent the proceeds to the United Jewish Appeal for the Israel Emergency Fund.

The owner of two gas stations arrived at the appeal's offices and turned over the deeds to the stations as his contribution to the multimillion fund drive.

Other Jews walked in the cash-surrender values of their life insurance policies. Still others, possibly moved by the Arab-Israeli war, sold real estate and securities and sent the money to the fund's headquarters, on the Avenue of the Americas at 51st street.

These were some examples of the dramas being played out in the Jewish communities across the United States, U.J.A. officials said yesterday.

The contributions, appeal of-

Continued on Page 11, Column 1

ISRAEL, IN ERROR, ATTACKS U.S. SHIP

10 Navy Men Die, 100 Hurt in Raids North of Sinai

By WILLIAM BEECHER
Special to The New York Times

WASHINGTON, June 8 — An American naval vessel was mistakenly attacked by Israeli planes and torpedo boats today in international waters about 15 miles north of the Sinai Peninsula. Reports tonight listed the toll as 10 dead and 100 wounded. Twenty of the wounded were hurt critically.

The vessel, the Liberty, was on a peaceful, though war-related mission. Pentagon sources said she had been dispatched from Spain to the war zone to provide additional communications to facilitate the evacuation of American citizens from the Middle East and North Africa.

Pentagon officials said it was too early to tell whether indemnification would be asked from Israel for the loss of life and the damage to the Navy ship.

President Johnson, in a letter to the Senate majority leader, Mike Mansfield, noted that the

Continued on Page 19, Column 1

JOHNSON PLEASED BY GAINS ON TRUCE

Looks to a Stable Peace— White House Discloses Use of the Hot Line

Texts of the Mansfield letter and Johnson reply, Page 18.

By MAX FRANKEL
Special to The New York Times

WASHINGTON, June 8—President Johnson welcomed spreading acceptance of a cease-fire agreement in the Middle East today, urged all parties to move promptly toward the "many more fundamental questions" bearing on a stable peace.

While thus pressing for more than merely another frail armistice, the White House also disclosed that its hot-line connection with Moscow had been used for the first time this week in an international crisis.

The United States used the teletype link this morning when it heard of an attack on an American communications ship off the Sinai Peninsula. At the time, the source of the attack was not known.

The Soviet Government, whose warships have been observing the movements of the United States Sixth Fleet in the eastern Mediterranean, was advised that the carrier-based American planes were scrambling into action for the sole purpose of assisting the distressed vessel.

It was later learned that Israeli forces had attacked the American ship in error.

The announcement of quick exchanges to prevent misunder-

Continued on Page 18, Column 1

Russians Continue To Harass 6th Fleet

By NEIL SHEEHAN
Special to The New York Times

ABOARD U. S. S. AMERICA, in the Eastern Mediterranean, June 8—Two Soviet warships, a destroyer and a small, highly maneuverable patrol craft, moved into the formation of this Sixth Fleet carrier task force group this morning and began systematically harassing American ships.

The harassment was undertaken despite a warning in another Soviet destroyer yesterday from Vice Adm. William I. Martin, the Sixth Fleet commander. Admiral Martin warned the Soviet vessel to withdraw from the area of the American formation. He said the Soviet ship, while following the carrier

---

Continued on Page 15, Column 1

A SHIFT BY CAIRO

Thant Notifies Council in Middle of Debate on Resolutions

Excerpts from the U.N. debate are printed on Page 16.

By DREW MIDDLETON

UNITED NATIONS, N. Y., June 8—The United Arab Republic, the leader of the anti-Israel coalition, today accepted the Security Council's demand for a cease-fire in the Middle East provided Israel did the same.

Yesterday, the delegate of Israel said his country accepted the cease-fire provided Israel's foes agreed to it. Reports here yesterday indicated rejection by Cairo.

Syria gave notice tonight that she would also comply, informing the Secretary General after the Security Council recessed.

This afternoon, in his dry, precise voice Secretary General Thant read to the Council a brief letter from Mohamed Awad el-Kony, the Egyptian delegate, disclosing that President Gamal Abdel Nasser's Government had "decided to accept the cease-fire" called for in the two Council resolutions "on the condition that the other party ceases fire."

He Scraps Long Speech

Mr. el-Kony wrote the letter after a long telephone conversation with Cairo shortly before the Council meeting began. After the call, he scrapped a 20-page speech he had prepared and wrote the note to Mr. Thant.

The Israeli Foreign Minister, Abba Eban, hailed the immediate acceptance of a cease-fire as "a notable step" and called on other Arab governments to follow the Egyptian lead.

Cairo's acceptance of the Council resolutions adopted unanimously on Tuesday and Wednesday raised rather than lowered the heat of the debate between the United States and the Soviet Union over the two resolutions each submitted to the Council.

Arthur J. Goldberg, the United States delegate, saying he hoped for a peace "stable and just to all concerned," submitted a draft of a resolution calling for the "withdrawal and disengagement of armed personnel," the renunciation of force, "the maintenance of vital international rights" and the establishment of a durable peace in the area.

The Administration was said

Continued on Page 17, Column 1

SOVIET SHIP SAILS INTO AQABA GULF

Passage Is First Since Israel Lifted Arab Blockade

By Reuters

ELATH, Israel, June 8—A Soviet freighter bound for the Jordanian port of Aqaba passed through the Strait of Tiran today, the first ship to do so since Israel declared the passage an international waterway yesterday.

Two outgoing Israeli freighters were preparing to be the first Israeli ships to pass through the strait since the Egyptians blockaded the Gulf of Aqaba on May 23.

A report from Sharm el Sheik, which dominates the strait, dis-

Continued on Page 17, Column 7

The New York Times   *June 9, 1967*

CRUSHING OFFENSIVES: Israelis thrust westward across northern Sinai (1) to the Suez Canal after sharp fighting at Bir Gifgafa and Mitla Pass, and routed Egyptians at Nakhl and Thamed in drive farther south (2). Soviet ship passed through Strait of Tiran (3), now under Israeli control. Mistaken Israeli attack on U.S. ship in Mediterranean (4) killed 10 men. Israelis held west bank of the River Jordan as far north as Jenin (5).

"All the News That's Fit to Print"

The New York Times

LATE CITY EDITION

Weather: Mostly fair and pleasant today, tonight and tomorrow. Temp. range: today 65-84; Friday 84-67. Temp.-Hum. Index yesterday 75. Full U.S. report on Page 46.

VOL. CXIX..No. 41,104

NEW YORK, SATURDAY, AUGUST 8, 1970

15 CENTS

CEASE-FIRE IN EFFECT ALONG SUEZ; ISRAEL AND EGYPT TO POLICE ZONE; INITIAL TALKS BEGINNING AT U.N.

J m Kean, San Rafael Independent-Journal, via Associated Press

BEFORE JUDGE'S SLAYING: James D. McClaine, convict holding guns against Superior Court Judge Harold J. Haley, his hostage, in San Rafael, Calif. A sawed-off shotgun was fastened to a loop of adhesive tape around the judge's neck. Both men were killed.

NIXON AIDES ISSUE 'INFLATION ALERT' CITING PRICE RISES

But the Economic Advisers Avoid Placing Any Blame on Industry or Labor

By EDWIN L. DALE Jr.

Special to The New York Times

WASHINGTON, Aug. 7—The Nixon Administration's first "inflation alert," issued today, identified several recent price increases, some accompanied by large wage increases, that it said had been important in raising the price level. It pointed no finger of blame, however.

The report attributed the rise in prices this year to a wide variety of causes. Only some of the causes were associated with "concentrated" industries, those dominated by a few large corporations, and with wage increases won by unions.

The basic conclusion of the report was that inflation in the United States always eventually responds to Government policies curbing total spending in the economy. But the longer the duration of the inflation, the slower the response, the report found.

Increases Detailed

Solely because they were important recently, the report discussed in detail price increases for coal and electric power, rubber, cigarettes and trucking.

There was no effort to say whether wage bargains won by unions, or price increases made by the industries involved, were "justified," as was done in the Kennedy and Johnson Administrations.

For 1970 to date, the report mentioned price advances in a variety of sectors of the economy, all different in their causes—steel and construction, medical care and mortgage interest rates, copper and New York City subway fares.

Smaller Union Role

It also pointed out that only 7 per cent of the labor force would have its wages determined by union negotiations this year, although it noted that wage increases in the settlements negotiated so far "have not slowed down."

The most dramatic single price increase identified in the report was that for coal, up 35 per cent in the last year. The cause was a rapid rise in demand, not higher wages, the report found.

So far, electric power rates for consumers have been slow to rise despite the coal price

Continued on Page 10, Column 1

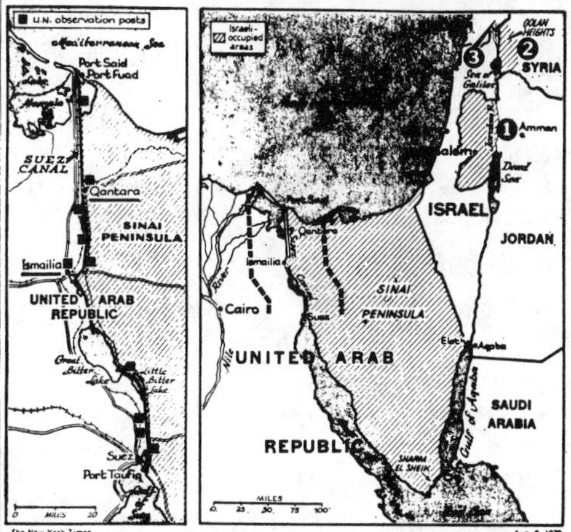

The New York Times

Aug. 8, 1970

MIDEAST TRUCE: U.N. aides are to help police it from posts shown in map at left, with command centers at Ismailia and Qantara. Dotted lines on other map indicate truce zone. U.S. sees truce applying also in area of Jordan (1), Syria (2) and Lebanon (3).

TRUCE OF 90 DAYS

U.S. Acclaims Action —Diplomats Stress Problems Ahead

Texts of related statements will be found on Page 2.

By HEDRICK SMITH

Special to The New York Times

WASHINGTON, Aug. 7—A cease-fire went into effect tonight on the Egyptian-Israeli front along the Suez Canal, and the preliminary phase of a new round of negotiations on peace in the Middle East was under way at the United Nations.

Fighting stopped on this front, where there have been frequent air and ground battles ever since the six-day war of June, 1967, when the Israelis occupied all of the Sinai Peninsula to the eastern shore of the canal. In recent months the fighting has been almost continuous.

Today's cease-fire breakthrough was hailed by President Nixon, Secretary of State William P. Rogers and Secretary General Thant of the United Nations as an important step in the drive for a "just and lasting" peace between the Arabs and Israelis.

Diplomats Are Cautious

At the same time, diplomats cautioned that major differences on the provisions of a peace settlement still divided the Israelis and Arabs, meaning that difficult negotiations lay ahead.

Mr. Rogers, who originally put forward the cease-fire proposal on June 19, was the first to announce that it had been accepted by Israel and the United Arab Republic and would take effect at midnight Israeli time (1 A.M. Saturday in Cairo and 6 P.M. Friday in New York). The 90-day cease-fire is to run until the evening of Nov. 5 in the United States. American officials hope it will lead to a permanent cease-fire.

U.N. Observers to Assist

On the Suez front, Israel and Egypt will police each other's observations of a strict standstill that rules out military build-ups or offensive action within a zone at least 32 miles wide on each side of the canal.

Informed sources said that each side would conduct aerial reconnaissance of the other's positions without actually crossing the canal or flying over the other side's lines. About 100 United Nations observers on the ground will assist in policing the cease-fire.

The depth of the cease-fire zones was described as sufficient to assure Israel that neither Egypt nor the Soviet Union would expand military positions—especially the Soviet SAM-2 and SAM-3 antiaircraft missile sites—into the 32-mile

Continued on Page 2, Column 1

SUBWAY WORKERS QUESTION SAFETY

Supervisors Predict More Serious Mishaps Because of Personnel Shortages

By FRANCIS X. CLINES

The Subway Supervisors Association said yesterday that additional serious accidents were likely on the lines because of a shortage of experienced personnel and an alleged de-emphasis of equipment maintenance by transit officials.

The association's counsel, Moss K. Schenck, said that past warnings to this effect had been ignored by transit officials and that the system, which he described as "basically sound," had deteriorated rapidly in the last two years.

As evidence of this, Mr. Schenck offered copies of Transit Authority data indicating a drop in on-time performance in recent years and listing what he termed a typically poor day of 38 trains abandoned in their runs, 185 others canceled and 953 seriously late of a total of 8,109 scheduled runs.

Personnel Problems

The personnel problems, according to Mr. Schenck, include large-scale retirements of recent years, which transit officials concede have been troublesome, and a consequent lowering, he contends, of employment standards.

The supervisors' group, which says it represents most of the system's 3,000 dispatchers, yardmasters, foremen, stationmasters and other supervisors, echoed recent criticism of subway management that was prompted by a rash of sub-

Continued on Page 34, Column 4

Judge and 3 Slain on Coast As Convicts Hold Up Court

By The Associated Press

SAN RAFAEL, Calif., Aug. 7—An armed man entered a trial court today and touched off a gun battle that took the lives of a judge, the intruder and two convicts he was trying to free.

The intruder and the convicts held the Superior Court at bay for 10 minutes but were shot to death as they fled in a small van carrying the judge and three women jurors as hostages.

Those killed were Judge Harold J. Haley, 65 years old; the convict on trial, James D. McClain, 37; a convict witness, William Arthur Christmas, 27, and the armed intruder, who was tentatively identified as Jonathan P. Jackson, 17.

Others Are Wounded

Deputy District Attorney Gary Thomas was seriously wounded in the back. Also seriously wounded was another convict witness, Ruchell Magee. A juror, Maria Graham, suffered an arm wound and three other persons were less seriously injured.

McClain, who was serving five years to life for burglary in Solano County, was on trial in the stabbing of a San Quentin Prison guard in 1969. McClain and the convict witnesses had been transferred this morning from San Quentin, about five miles away, to the Marin County Hall of Justice.

Lieut. Thomas A. Lightfoot of the Sheriff's office said that, about 11 A.M., a slender man entered the second-floor courtroom where the trial was in progress.

Opening a flight bag containing pistols and road flares taped together to look like dynamite, he tossed a pistol to McClain and covered the crowd with a carbine that he had concealed under his coat.

"This is it," the invader shouted. "Everybody line up."

McClain, with a pistol at the judge's head, forced deputies to remove shackles from himself and Magee, who was on the witness stand. He then sent Magee to the corridor to free Christmas, who was waiting with a guard.

A bailiff slipped out of the courtroom and alerted San Quentin Prison guards and Sheriff's deputies.

McClain got on a telephone, called the Sheriff's office and yelled: "Call off your dog, pigs, or we'll kill everyone in the room."

Judge Haley was put on the telephone briefly and then the four armed men herded the judge, Mr. Thomas and three women jurors to the street by elevator.

McClain had looped adhesive tape around the judge's neck and fastened it to the muzzle of a short, sawed-off shotgun, which one of the fugitives had taken from a deputy in fleeing

Continued on Page 24, Column 3

RATE OF JOBLESS AGAIN RISES TO 5%

Unemployment Among Men in 20-24 Age Group Shows Especially Big Increase

By EILEEN SHANAHAN

Special to The New York Times

WASHINGTON, Aug. 7—The nation's unemployment rate rose in July, again touching the 5 per cent mark, which it had also reached in May.

The Labor Department's monthly report on employment and unemployment, made public today, showed that the rise in unemployment had come about both because there were fewer jobs in most areas of the economy and because there were more job-seekers.

There was a particularly large increase in unemployment among young men in the 20-24 age group. This appeared to indicate, according to department experts, that discharged servicemen were having a hard time finding jobs.

The experts said that while they were not sure how many of the unemployed men in this age group were veterans, the fact that any were reported in the statistics as "re-entering the work force" rather than first-time job-seekers, indicated that many probably were veterans.

The number of men in the 20-24 age group who were looking for work in July and were unable to find it rose to 528,000 from the June level of 515,000. The unemployment rate for this group was up from 7.2 per cent in June to 9.1 per cent in July.

The other category that ex-

Continued on Page 10, Column 7

Mrs. Meir Voices Hope; U.A.R. Notes Assurances

She Looks to Other Fronts

By PETER GROSE

Special to The New York Times

JERUSALEM, Aug. 7—Premier Golda Meir expressed hope tonight that the cease-fire with the United Arab Republic would spread to other fighting fronts and that the truce would have no limit in time.

Her statement came in a message she read on national television in which she informed Israel of the cease-fire agreement.

The Premier's announcement came after a full day of consultations between the two sides—at long distance through United States intermediaries, according to Israeli sources—to work out the terms of the truce and methods of supervision.

None of the arrangements for policing the truce were announced here. Israeli sources indicated their belief, however, that each country's "national means," presumably wide-angle aerial photoreconnaissance without any crossing of the canal line, would be satisfactory assurance against military build-ups. Mrs. Meir read

Continued on Page 2, Column 6

Egypt Emphasizes Security

By RAYMOND H. ANDERSON

Special to The New York Times

CAIRO, Aug. 7—The United Arab Republic agreed today to reinstate the cease-fire along the Suez Canal. It linked the agreement to Israeli acceptance of a timetable for withdrawal from the lands seized in the war of June, 1967.

In a statement, the Foreign Ministry said that Cairo's acceptance of the cease-fire rested on assurances of security for Egypt's Suez Canal front and other Arab fronts.

The reinstatement of the 1967 cease-fire, the Foreign Ministry added, opens the way to a resumption of the mission of Dr. Gunnar V. Jarring, the special United Nations representative for the Middle East, to seek implementation of the Security Council resolution of Nov. 22, 1967.

In the past, President Gamal Abdel Nasser has repeatedly rebuffed appeals by the United States and other Western powers for a return to the 1967 cease-fire agreement, asserting that a cessation of shooting would be a "surrender" to Israeli occupation of the Sinai

Continued on Page 3, Column 1

Jarring Mission Is Reactivated For Middle East Peace Talks

By SAM POPE BREWER

Special to The New York Times

UNITED NATIONS, N. Y., Aug. 7 — Secretary General Thant announced today that the Jarring mission for peace in the Middle East "is now reactivated."

In a report to the Security Council, Mr. Thant said that Dr. Gunnar V. Jarring, his personal representative, was "already intensively at work in this new stage of his peace effort."

Dr. Jarring has been holding consultations with the heads of the three delegations directly concerned—the United Arab Republic, Jordan and Israel—with the United States and Soviet representatives and with high Secretariat officials.

But, as in all of Dr. Jarring's negotiations, almost nothing is known of his actual moves. He is in a 38th-floor office behind all the security the United Nations can muster.

None of his appointments are announced and it is only from other sources that some appointments become known.

Mr. Thant described the renewal of the mission today as "an important step forward in the search for peace in the Middle East," although he forecast a long, hard road ahead.

His report this afternoon added to a spreading feeling here that machinery for making peace might finally be in motion.

Mr. Thant's report included a letter from Dr. Jarring saying the three parties had agreed to name representatives to take part in discussions "at such places and times as I may recommend, taking into account as appropriate each side's preference as to method of procedure and previous experience."

In his earlier negotiations, Dr. Jarring had to travel from capital to capital making suggestions and trying to match positions into something useful.

Mr. Thant said that he and Dr. Jarring believed "there now is a reasonable basis on which to review immediately his contacts with the parties with a view to initiating discussions

Continued on Page 2, Column 1

Burger Finds Courts Imperiled By Breaches of Civility at Trials

By FRED P. GRAHAM

Special to The New York Times

ST. LOUIS, Aug. 7—The Chief Justice of the United States, Warren E. Burger, told the chief justices of the states today that "unseemly, outrageous episodes" in courtrooms and overly long trials were "undermining some of the public confidence in the entire system."

His remarks came during a day in which the issue of the increasing incidence of abrasive tactics by lawyers representing unpopular clients, and the means used by judges to discipline them, dominated several of the sessions at the American Bar Association meeting here.

In extemporaneous remarks to a conference of chief justices, Mr. Burger stressed the theme that he has repeated frequently during his judicial career—the need to maintain courtroom civility, as "the absolutely imperative lubricant for an inherently contentious process."

He advised the chief justices to urge the courts or legislatures in their states to adopt the series of recommendations for administering criminal justice that have been worked out by the A.B.A. during a five-year study that is in its final stages.

Specifically, he said, they should adopt the A.B.A.'s recommendations that attempt to set out the limits to which lawyers can properly go in representing their clients. These rules, including one that forbids opposing counsel to address each other directly dur-

Continued on Page 34, Column 3

Associated Press

PREPARE GAS ROCKETS FOR JOURNEY: Derrick loading concrete-encased rockets of lethal gas in Anniston, Ala. They are to be sunk in the Atlantic. Dispatch, Page 8.

Texas Sued by U.S. On Desegregation

By WILLIAM ROBBINS

Special to The New York Times

WASHINGTON, Aug. 7—The Justice Department filed suits today against the State of Texas and 26 school districts, seeking to compel desegregation for the coming school year in the last large group of holdouts not already under litigation.

The suits, announced tonight by Attorney General John N. Mitchell, named as defendants the Texas Education Agency and the State Commissioner of Education, J. W. Edgar, as well as the 26 districts. They were filed in Federal District Court in Dallas, Houston, Austin and Tyler.

The complaints charged that the school districts had continued to operate dual school systems with both student and

Continued on Page 8, Column 5

Cuba and Chileans Will Exchange TV

Special to The New York Times

MIAMI, Aug. 7 — Cuba and Chile have signed an agreement to exchange television programs. It is believed to be the first of its type between Havana and a Latin-American country since the Organization of American States imposed economic and diplomatic sanctions against the Government of Fidel Castro in 1964

The accord provides for an exchange of news programs between the Cuban Broadcasting Institute and the television channel of the Catholic University of Chile.

An announcement on the Havana radio described Chilean television executives who signed the agreement in Havana as "representatives of Chile." It said that television

Continued on Page 8, Column 4

NEWS INDEX

"All the News That's Fit to Print"

The New York Times

LATE CITY EDITION

Weather: Sunny, cool today; clear, cool tonight. Fair, mild tomorrow. Temp. range: today 60-48; Monday 66-52. Full U.S. report on Page 85.

VOL. CXX . . No. 41,156 — NEW YORK, TUESDAY, SEPTEMBER 29, 1970 — 15 CENTS

NASSER DIES OF HEART ATTACK; BLOW TO PEACE EFFORTS SEEN; NIXON CANCELS FLEET EXERCISE

United Press International

VATICAN CITY: President Nixon with Pope Paul VI during special audience yesterday. Later, he flew by helicopter to U.S.S. Saratoga, with Sixth Fleet in the Mediterranean.

A GESTURE BY U.S.

President Terms Loss Tragic—He Joins Fleet Off Italy

By Reuters

ABOARD U.S.S. SARATOGA, in the Mediterranean, Tuesday, Sept. 29—President Nixon last night ordered cancellation of today's exercises of the United States Sixth Fleet in the Mediterranean because of the death of President Gamal Abdel Nasser of Egypt.

The President, who arrived aboard this aircraft carrier last night, had planned to watch a demonstration of Sixth Fleet firepower, including the launching and recovery of aircraft.

Officials said: "Upon hearing of the death of President Nasser, the President ordered the cancellation of the firepower demonstrations, which were to be held in conjunction with his visit to the Sixth Fleet."

They said that Mr. Nixon's conferences with Sixth Fleet commanders aboard the flagship Springfield would go on as scheduled.

The President flew to this carrier off the coast of Italy by helicopter after a day in which he had conferred in Rome with the President and the Premier of Italy and with Pope Paul VI.

'Tragic Loss'

The President in a statement said that the death of President Nasser was a tragic loss of an outstanding Arab leader.

"I was shocked to hear of the sudden death of President Nasser," Mr. Nixon said. "The world has lost an outstanding leader who tirelessly and devotedly served the causes of his countrymen and the Arab world.

"This tragic loss requires that all nations, and particularly those in the Middle East, renew their efforts to calm passions, reach for mutual understanding and build lasting peace.

"On behalf of the American people I extended deep sympathy to his family and to his people."

Stresses Role of Fleet

Earlier Mr. Nixon had told the men of the Saratoga that never had American military and diplomatic power been used more effectively than in the latest Middle East crisis.

Chatting with sailors who greeted his helicopter on the flight deck, Mr. Nixon spoke of "a hard two or three weeks," which he said had been capped by success. He referred to the Jordanian truce and recovery of the hostages from the hijacked airliners.

"The fact that we were successful is the fact that you were there," he told the sailors. He mentioned their

Continued on Page 19, Column 1

United Press International

President Gamal Abdel Nasser bidding good-by to King Hussein of Jordan after meeting in Cairo yesterday. From ceremony, he returned home where he died of heart attack.

ARAB-WORLD HERO

Vice President Sadat Takes Over as the Interim Leader

Obituary article will be found on Page 16.

By RAYMOND H. ANDERSON
Special to The New York Times

CAIRO, Tuesday, Sept. 29—President Gamal Abdel Nasser, leader of Egypt for 18 years and hero of much of the Arab world, died here yesterday.

The Government radio said the 52-year-old President was the victim of a heart attack.

The death was announced on Cairo's television and radio stations shortly before 11 P.M. by Vice President Anwar Sádat. An hour earlier, regular programs on television and radio were abruptly suspended and replaced with chanting of verses from the Koran. Official mourning was proclaimed for 40 days.

The President suffered the heart attack at 3 P.M. and died three hours later.

No obvious successor to Mr. Nasser was in sight, and no Egyptian seemed in a mood tonight to speculate about the matter.

Funeral Will Be Thursday

Vice President Sadat took over as interim ruler. He reported that emergency meetings had been held by the higher executive committee of the Arab Socialist Union, the political organization created by Mr. Nasser, and the Council of Ministers.

President Nasser's funeral will be held Thursday.

The impact of Mr. Nasser's death will be felt throughout the Arab world. Despite controversies and rivalries during his long years of power, he was the strongest figure of leadership among the Arabs.

Since the battlefield defeat of three Arab armies by Israel in June, 1967, Mr. Nasser was the leader who rallied the Arabs to rebuild their forces for a war of liberation if other means to recover the lands failed.

Favored Political Solution

But he repeatedly emphasized that he favored a political solution of the conflict with Israel if one could be achieved.

Although Mr. Nasser gained a reputation in his early years in power as a fire-breathing radical, in recent years he had become a force for moderation and pragmatism.

Even on the emotional issue of Israel, he was able to swing much of the Arab world behind his acceptance in July of a United States initiative for a cease-fire and he revived efforts for a negotiated settlement. The outlook for pursuing

Continued on Page 17, Column 1

50,000 FLEE BLAZE IN SAN DIEGO AREA

Brush Fire, 30 Miles Long, Is California's Biggest Yet —5 Die in Copter Crash

By United Press International

LOS ANGELES, Sept. 28—The largest brush fire in California history raged today through mountain canyons near the Mexican border, driving thousands of persons from their homes as the flames advanced.

In the San Gabriel Mountains to the north, a helicopter being used by the United States Forest Service to fight another fire crashed late today, killing the five persons aboard.

More than 50,000 persons were evacuated from small communities in San Diego County. The 200-acre fire there erupted in the Cleveland National Forest on Saturday when a falling tree severed a power line. At least 250 structures have been destroyed.

Decreasing winds tonight and a forecast of scattered showers in mountain areas raised hopes that the blaze could be contained tomorrow.

Arson Arrests Made

The enormous blaze, 30 miles from tip to tip, eclipsed in size the Matailaja fire of 1930, which burned 125,000 acres in Kern and Los Angeles Counties.

"We've barely kept up with the situation," said Arlen B. Cartwright of the State Division of Forestry. "The problem seems to come from the fact that fire nuts run around and see flames and smoke and this makes them want to set more fires—which they do."

Arson was suspected in two other major blazes in San Diego County, and five arrests were made in Los Angeles County.

More than 5,000 men worked 36-hour shifts on the fire lines and the neighboring county of San Bernardino was stripped of all but five of its fire engines.

Continued on Page 10, Column 2

Intrepid Wins Series, 4-1, And Keeps America's Cup

By STEVE CADY
Special to The New York Times

NEWPORT, R.I., Sept. 28 — The longest series in 100 years of America's Cup challenges came to a desperately dramatic close today with Intrepid completing a 4-1 conquest of Gretel II.

Once again, the defender of yachting's most famous prize had to fight off almost constant pressure by the chunky Australian challenger.

Until a wind shift put Intrepid in clover starting the final leg of the 24.3-mile race, the action had been about as close as a boat race can produce. The cynics say watching two yachts is like watching grass grow, but the grass was on fire again today, as it was so often during this controversial series.

Stage Set for Upset

When Gretel II closed to within two boat lengths at the fifth mark, the stage was set for another upset of the kind the Australian sloop brought off last Thursday. Then the wind shifted from north to east, Intrepid hit it on the right tack and the suspense evaporated.

With the final windward leg turned into a race, the redesigned 1967 defender opened up and came home safely, 1 minute 44 seconds ahead.

As Intrepid swept majestically across the line about 250 yards ahead of her dangerous rival, the familiar dream of another successful Cup defense began unfolding. Horns, whistles and sirens aboard some 150 spectator boats and Coast Guard patrol vessels cut loose with a noisy salute to the American yacht—the second ever to defend the Cup twice.

A Triumphant Allusion

Bill Ficker, the 42-year-old Californian with the bald head and the bold starting-line maneuvers, shook hands with his young crew. They, in turn, hoisted a "Ficker Is Quicker" flag to the top of Intrepid's mast, a triumphant allusion to the tactical swiftness of their skipper.

In today's race, Ficker and his young stalwarts had to be quicker. Jim Hardy gave Gretel II a slight lead at the start but Ficker took it away early on the opening windward leg. He spent the rest of a cold, overcast afternoon desperately keeping the Aussies from breaking through in the fluky

Continued on Page 53, Column 1

U.S. Officials See Period Of Instability in Mideast

By TERENCE SMITH
Special to The New York Times

WASHINGTON, Sept. 28 — United States officials, startled by the death of Gamal Abdel Nasser, tended to view it today as a blow to peace-making efforts in the Middle East.

A ranking State Department official described the Egyptian President's death as a "critical loss at a decisive moment in history."

The immediate reaction of officials here was that it would bring a period of instability in the Arab world and would therefore reduce the already-thin prospects for negotiating an early resolution of the Arab-Israeli dispute.

[In Moscow, Western diplomats expected the Soviet leaders to assure the United Arab Republic that President Nasser's death would not affect Soviet support for the Arab cause. Page 17.]

An hour before the Cairo radio announcement, a cable from Donald C. Bergus, the senior United States representative in Cairo, reported a rumor that the Egyptian leader was critically ill or perhaps dead. The message was being decoded as the public announcement came.

Six hours earlier Rodger P. Davies, the Acting Assistant Secretary of State for Near Eastern and South Asian Affairs, had told a closed session of the House Foreign Affairs Committee that the Nixon Administration was "leaning toward optimism" about the prospects of getting the United States-sponsored peace initiative in the Middle East back on the track.

The Senate was informed of the news by Senator John C. Stennis, Democrat of Mississippi, who interrupted a debate on election reform. He described Mr. Nasser, the leader in Cairo since 1952, as "superior to most anyone who might have been in power."

"I hope his death does not mean upheaval and turmoil in

Continued on Page 19, Column 1

THE ARAB WORLD IS GRIEF-STRICKEN

Moslems Fire Rifles Into Air as Sign of Mourning —Koran Read on Radio

By JOHN L. HESS
Special to The New York Times

BEIRUT, Lebanon, Sept. 28—The Arab world went into mourning tonight over the loss of its major international figure. Arab distress was heightened by the fear that instability would increase in the area and diminish the already slender prospect of peace.

Television stations went off the air and radio programs were replaced by chants and readings from the Koran. In Beirut, Moslems fired thousands of shots into the air as a sign of emotion for the loss of Gamal Abdel Nasser. Men walked in the streets in impromptu procession declaiming "Allah Akbar!"—"God is great."

Security forces raced to thwart rioting of the kind that followed President Nasser's offer of resignation after the six-day war of June, 1967.

Youths started bonfires of automobile tires and a crowd began collecting outside the United States Embassy.

[A senior Cabinet minister in Israel said that the Israelis now appeared to face an indefinite stalemate on peace negotiations. Page 18.]

Observers here said that President Nasser was the only Arab

Continued on Page 17, Column 7

John Dos Passos Is Dead at 74; Acclaimed for 'U.S.A.' Trilogy

Special to The New York Times

BALTIMORE, Sept. 28—John Dos Passos, the novelist of the post-World War I generation who wrote more than 30 books, including the trilogy "U.S.A.," died today in his apartment.

Mr. Dos Passos, who was 74 years old, had been troubled by a heart ailment in recent years and was released only Saturday from Good Samaritan Hospital. When not away on his extensive travels, he divided his time between his apartment here and a home in Westmoreland, Va.

Mr. Dos Passos is survived by his widow, the former Elizabeth Hamlin Holdridge; their daughter, Lucy, and a stepson, Christopher Holdridge.

A funeral service will be held Thursday at 10 A.M. at the William Cook-Brooks Funeral Home in the nearby town of Towson, Md.

Fame From Early Books

By ALDEN WHITMAN

The life and writings of John Dos Passos were marked by a progression from left to right. "Every day I become more Red," he said in his youth. "My one ambition is to be able to sing 'The International.'" But in middle and old age, he turned against his former ideas, berating liberals, Socialists and Communists with zeal. The one-time writer for The New Masses became a contributor to The National Review; the friend of Ernest Hemingway became that of William F. Buckley Jr.; and the supporter of William Z. Foster turned into the backer of Barry Goldwater.

Gil Friedberg-Pix

John Dos Passos

His novels, too, marched rightward. The trilogy "U.S.A.," completed in 1936 and generally recognized as one of the hinges of modern fiction, was a painstakingly detailed and angry portrait of industrial America between 1898 and 1929. It concluded with the heroine's joining the Communist party in revulsion over what she believed were the injustices of the Sacco-Vanzetti case.

His subsequent trilogy, "District of Columbia," completed in 1949, acerbically chronicled what the author clearly viewed as the failure of the New Deal,

Continued on Page 47, Column 1

Arab Truce Observers Arrive In Generally Peaceful Amman

By ERIC PACE
Special to The New York Times

AMMAN, Jordan, Sept. 28—One hundred foreign Arab officers arrived here today to serve on the peace-keeping observer teams that will be deployed in Amman under the agreement reached yesterday in Cairo to end hostilities between the Jordanian Government and the Palestinian commandos.

The cease-fire instituted last Friday after nine days of civil

Text of Cairo agreement is printed on Page 18.

war seemed generally effective this morning. There were no fires along the capital's skyline, although a few bursts of firing resounded in the center of Amman and on Jebel Luweibda and Jebel Amman, two of the city's seven hills.

Western diplomats also reported that shelling or shooting was continuing in part of the Palestinians' Ashrafiyeh quarter, where many of the airline hostages had been held.

There was no sign that either the army or the commandos had abandoned their positions in Amman, as the Cairo agreement called for. The guerrillas are entrenched in a populous area around the Hussein Mosque at the heart of the city, where gunfire was occasionally heard during the day.

Despite a further provision of the Cairo agreement for a release of detainees, scores were still visible this morning at the army prison camp on the way to the airport. As their women peered in through the barbed-wire fence, they were seated in orderly rows, apparently being indoctrinated by their Jordanian Army captors.

The army appeared yesterday to be trying to finish its clean-up of Ashrafiyeh, once a commando stronghold. Aside from that, no wide-scale military operations were known to be under way. The general calm this morning followed radio broadcasts of the 14-point agreement signed by King Hus-

Continued on Page 18, Column 5

Malpractice Suits Reported Soaring

By LAWRENCE K. ALTMAN

Witnesses at a State Senate public hearing testified here yesterday that a steep rise in medical malpractice suits was forcing physicians to practice "defensive medicine," shirk hazardous modes of treatment that could be of benefit to patients, and pass along the costs of sky-rocketing insurance premiums to patients.

"One physician of every six has been sued for malpractice," State Senator Norman F. Lent told the hearing. And more than 10,000 Americans will initiate medical malpractice suits this year, Senator Lent, who is chairman of the Senate Committee on Health, added.

Because some insurance companies find medical malpractice insurance unprofitable, wit-

Continued on Page 32, Column 1

Anti-Arab Jet Plot Laid to Seized Pair

By MORRIS KAPLAN

An Israeli Army veteran and his wife, accused of trying to board a London-bound plane here with a live hand grenade and four loaded guns hidden in their clothing, were reported yesterday to have planned to hijack an Arab airliner and take it to Israel.

Law-enforcement sources said that the couple reportedly had planned to board a United Arab Airlines plane bound for Cairo at the London airport and divert the flight to Israel "in retaliation" for a recent attempted hijacking of an El Al airliner in London.

The sources said that the veteran, Avraham Hershkovitz, had worked as a "manager" here for the Jewish Defense

Continued on Page 12, Column 3

Fourth Group of Hostages Here After Seeing President in Rome

By ROBERT D. McFADDEN

Thirty-three travel-weary Americans, whose ordinary lives became the focus of international concern during three harrowing weeks while they were hostages in Jordan, arrived at Kennedy International Airport last night and were met by loved ones, friends and a clamoring throng of newsmen.

The passengers—26 men, 6 women and an infant—were brought home safely from an ordeal that began with multiple hijackings Sept. 6. All but two of the 33 were released in Amman over the weekend and were flown home through Nicosia, Cyprus, and Rome.

Their faces were haggard but smiling and their clothes rumpled after a 12-hour flight from Rome, where they met briefly with President Nixon in the morning. They stepped off a chartered flight at the Trans World Airlines terminal shortly after 6 P.M. They were ushered quickly through Customs and led into a private room for a reunion with 175 relatives.

Nearly 1,000 friends greeted them in the corridors and public waiting rooms as they emerged.

Six Americans are still being held of the original group on three hijacked planes. They are someplace in Jordan.

Contrary to the confused reports at three previous returning flights, passengers who were reluctant to talk were not besieged by newsmen thrusting cameras and microphones into

Continued on Page 18, Column 2

NEWS INDEX

	Page		Page
Art	36	Obituaries	46
Books	41	Society	52
Bridge	40	Sports	53-58
Business	61	Theaters	36-39
Crossword	41	Transportation	85
Editorials	42	TV and Radio	86-87
Financial	59-68	U. N. Proceedings	13
Man in the News	52	Washington Record	6
Movies	36-39	Weather	85
Music	36-39	Women's News	50

News Summary and Index, Page 45

"All the News That's Fit to Print"

The New York Times

LATE CITY EDITION

Weather: Sunny and milder today; fair and mild tonight, tomorrow. Temp. range: today 58-77; Tuesday 57-74. Temp.-Hum. Index yesterday 67. Full U.S. report on Page 90.

VOL. CXXI ... No. 41,864 | NEW YORK, WEDNESDAY, SEPTEMBER 6, 1972 | 15 CENTS

© 1972 The New York Times Company

9 ISRAELIS ON OLYMPIC TEAM KILLED WITH 4 ARAB CAPTORS AS POLICE FIGHT BAND THAT DISRUPTED MUNICH GAMES

United Press International

A copter making a test run before picking up Arabs involved in the attack on Israelis. At rear is the Olympic Tower. Sign in German says, "Olympic Village, Gate 6."

MRS. MEIR SPEAKS

A Hushed Parliament Hears Her Assail 'Lunatic Acts'

By TERENCE SMITH

Special to The New York Times

JERUSALEM, Sept. 5—Her voice heavy and trembling with emotion, Premier Golda Meir today denounced "these lunatic acts of terrorism, abduction and blackmail, which tear asunder the web of international life."

Speaking to a hushed and somber parliament before the fate of the Israeli hostages held captive in Munich was known, she said, "It is inconceivable that the Olympic events should continue as long as our citizens are under the threat of being murdered in the Olympic Village."

She called on all the nations participating in the Olympics to do "whatever is necessary" to rescue the nine Israelis taken hostage by Arab guerrillas in an early-morning attack in which two other Israelis were killed.

[Official sources in Jerusalem said early Wednesday that the Cabinet would meet later in the morning and that there would be no statement on the deaths of the hostages until then.]

Cabinet Still Firm

Although she was not explicit, Mrs. Meir left the impression that Israel would continue to refuse the guerrillas' demands for the release of 200 Palestinian commandos held in this country. Cabinet sources said the Government remained committed to its hard-line policy of neither dealing with nor making concessions to the guerrillas.

Most Israelis seemed stunned by the news of the bizarre attack on the Israeli athletes, which was first reported here on a radio broadcast at 9 A.M. (3 A.M. Tuesday, New York time). Although Israeli citizens traveling abroad have been attacked by Palestinian guerrillas before, the Olympics seemed to many an unlikely setting.

"The games were going so well," one Jerusalem news dealer said, "and now this."

In parliament, where the members had gathered in an extraordinary session to confirm the Justice Minister, the attack was the sole topic of conversation.

Cabinet Ministers and members of parliament sat in the building's modern, sun-washed dining room waiting for additional news from Munich. Each hour on the hour, the large room grew silent and the ministers gathered four deep around a radio as the Israeli radio summarized the developments.

The tension was greatest at

Continued on Page 20, Column 2

West German policemen talking with a spokesman, right, for Arabs who invaded Israeli quarters at Olympic Village

Associated Press

A West German Army ambulance passing through the heavily guarded gate at the military airfield in Fürstenfeldbruck, near Munich, after the commandos and the hostages landed in three helicopters.

A 23-HOUR DRAMA

2 Others Are Slain in Their Quarters in Guerrilla Raid

By DAVID BINDER

Special to The New York Times

MUNICH, West Germany, Wednesday, Sept. 6—Eleven members of Israel's Olympic team and four Arab terrorists were killed yesterday in a 23-hour drama that began with an invasion of the Olympic Village by the Arabs. It ended in a shootout at a military airport some 15 miles away as the Arabs were preparing to fly to Cairo with their Israeli hostages.

The first two Israelis were killed early yesterday morning when Arab commandos, armed with automatic rifles, broke into the quarters of the Israeli team and seized nine others as hostages. The hostages were killed in the airport shootout between the Arabs and German policemen and soldiers.

The bloodshed brought the suspension of the Olympic Games and there was doubt if they would be resumed. Willi Daume, president of the West German Organizing Committee, announced early today that he would ask the International Olympic Committee to meet tomorrow to decide whether they should continue.

Policeman Killed

In addition to the slain Israelis and Arabs, a German policeman was killed and a helicopter pilot was critically wounded. Three Arabs were wounded.

There were some reports that two of the hostages said to have been killed might still be alive. "It is a dim hope," said Dr. Bruno Merk, the Interior Minister of Bavaria, "but I am skeptical on this point."

The bloodbath at the airport that ended at 1 A.M. today, came after long hours of negotiaton between German and Arabs at the Israeli quarters in the Olympic Village where the Arabs demanded the release of 200 Arab commandos imprisoned in Israel.

Finally the West German armed forces supplied three helicopters to transport the Arabs and their Israeli hostages to the airport at Fürstenfeldbruck. From there all were to be flown to Cairo.

A Boeing-707 provided by the Lufthansa German Airlines was waiting.

Two of the terrorists, carrying their automatic rifles, walked about 170 yards from the helicopters to the plane. And then they started back to pick up the other Arabs and the hostages.

Positions Cited

As the Arabs were returning, German sharpshooters reportedly opened fire from the darkness beyond the pools of light at the airport. The Arabs returned fire.

The torment of the entire event was heightened by confusion created in the public mind by contradictory reports from German and Olympic officials after the gunfire erupted at the airport.

Dr. Merk, in a press conference at 3 o'clock this morning said:

"In this situation our task and goal to free the hostages was made more difficult by the lack of agreement from Israel to free prisoners or to get guarantees from the Arabs not to take action against the hos-

Continued on Page 18, Column 1

752 Air-Conditioned Cars Ordered for City Subways

By EDWARD RANZAL

Mayor Lindsay announced yesterday that 752 new air-conditioned subway cars had been ordered for $210.5-million. He said the contract was the largest ever signed in the country for the purchase of passenger railroad cars.

The first group of cars, which will be manufactured by the Pullman - Standard Company, are to be delivered by 1973.

The cars will provide a quieter ride than present equipment, according to Dr. William J. Ronan, chairman of the Metropolitan Transportation Authority.

The new equipment, which will be used on the IND and BMT lines, will enable the authority to phase out more than 1,200 pre-World War II cars, which are smaller than the new ones. A study is being made, Dr. Ronan said, to produce an air-conditioned unit that can be used in cars in the smaller tunnels of the IRT system.

20% of Fleet by '75

Each car will cost more than $273,000. The city will provide one-third of the total funds—the money has been provided in the city's 1972-73 capital budget—and the Federal Urban Mass Transportation Administration will supply the rest.

By 1975 more than 20 per cent of the city's fleet of nearly 7,000 subway cars will consist of new air-conditioned cars.

The first order under the contract will be for 454 cars at a cost of $127.4-million. Some of them will be delivered in

Continued on Page 91, Column 2

Berrigan and a Nun Get Prison Terms In Letter Smuggling

By JOHN KIFNER

Special to The New York Times

HARRISBURG, Pa., Sept. 5—The Rev. Philip F. Berrigan—cleared of charges that he led a plot to kidnap President Nixon's adviser on national security affairs, Henry A. Kissinger—was sentenced in Federal District Court here today to four concurrent two-year terms for smuggling letters out of the Lewisburg Penitentiary.

Sister Elizabeth McAlister, also cleared of the plot charges, was sentenced to one year in jail and three years' probation for smuggling letters.

Moments after the sentences were announced, Government attorneys moved to dismiss the first three substantive counts of their indictment, confirming that the Justice Department would not seek a retrial of the controversial "Harrisburg Seven" case.

The Government charged Father Berrigan, Sister Elizabeth, two other Roman Catholic priests, a former priest, a former nun and a Pakistani scholar with conspiracy to kidnap Mr. Kissinger as ransom to force a halt to the bombing in Viet-

Continued on Page 16, Column 1

PARLEY REJECTS HIJACKING TREATY

U.S.-Canadian Project for Penalizing Nations Aiding Air Pirates Rebuffed

By ROBERT LINDSEY

Special to The New York Times

WASHINGTON, Sept. 5—Delegates to a 17-nation conference here rejected today United States-Canadian efforts to negotiate an international anti-hijacking treaty based on a draft proposed by the two nations.

The move for nonacceptance was led by France and Britain and supported by the Soviet Union and Egypt.

Faced with what appeared to be certain defeat of the proposed treaty if it came to a vote, the two North American nations acquiesced in a French proposal to start writing a new treaty from scratch, after debates on what "principles" should be included.

The delegates have eight working days left before the conference is scheduled to end.

Today's rejection was a significant setback for the United

Continued on Page 91, Column 2

IF YOU'RE NOT DRINKING WILLIAM LAWSON'S SCOTCH, DRINK DEWAR'S William Lawson's 86.8 Proof Blended Scotch Whiskies. Imported by Palmer & Lord, Ltd., Syosset, N. Y.—Advt.

Nixon Tightens Security In U.S. Against 'Outlaws'

By TAD SZULC

Special to The New York Times

WASHINGTON, Sept. 5—President Nixon said today that "extra security measures" would be taken in the United States to protect American citizens as well as visiting Israelis from possible attacks by Palestinian guerrillas.

Mr. Nixon, speaking to newsmen in San Francisco, left it unclear, however, whether he meant that this new protection would cover prominent American Jews or only those whom he described as "Americans of Israeli background, American citizens."

Speaking before the gunfight at a military airport in Munich, in which the Israeli hostages were killed, Mr. Nixon discussed the capture of Israeli Olympic team members by Palestinian guerrillas and the slaying of two Israelis. He said:

"Since we are dealing with international outlaws who are unpredictable, we have to take extra security measures to protect those who might be the targets of this kind of activity in the future. That might include Americans of Israeli background, American citizens."

Late tonight, after word was received in Washington of the death of the Israeli hostages and West German policemen, Secretary of State William P. Rogers issued this statement on behalf of the Administration:

"There are no words which can fully express our reaction to today's tragedy at the Olympic Games. I know I speak for all Americans in extending the deepest sympathies of the

Continued on Page 18, Column 4

Reports First Said Israelis Were Safe

Contradictory reports last night about the fate of the Israeli hostages seized by Arab terrorists in the Olympic Village threw the public into confusion all over the world.

Throughout the day, as the tragedy in Munich unfolded, millions of viewers throughout the world watched on live television, which employed circuits that had been intended for the Games. But in the evening, when the events reached their climax, viewers could get no definitive word for hours on how the hostages fared.

At first the West German Government's official spokesman, Conrad Ahlers, announced

Continued on Page 20, Column 1

GAMES SUSPENDED; RITES IN ARENA SET

Halt Is the First Since 1896, When the Classic Resumed —Egypt Team in Forfeit

By NEIL AMDUR

Special to The New York Times

MUNICH, West Germany, Wednesday, Sept. 6 — The Olympic Games were suspended yesterday for the first time since competition in the modern era began in 1896.

Late-afternoon and evening events were called off in the wake of an attack staged by Arab guerrillas before dawn on the Olympic Village in which two Israelis were killed and nine others taken hostage. The hostages were later killed.

After the attack, Mark Spitz, the American swimmer who won seven gold medals at the Munich Olympics and who is Jewish, flew hurriedly to London on his way back to the United States. There were fears before his departure that he too might become a victim. [Page 20.]

The announcement of the suspension, made by the International Olympic Committee, also said that a memorial service would be held for the victims

Continued on Page 18, Column 7

Elizabeth City Hall Under Investigation

By RONALD SULLIVAN

Special to The New York Times

TRENTON, Sept. 5—Law enforcement authorities reported here today that the administration of Mayor Thomas J. Dunn of Elizabeth was the target of a Union County grand jury investigation of alleged municipal corruption.

Mayor Dunn, a Democrat running for a third term, said in an interview that he had "no knowledge of any investigation involving me or my administration." But he said he volunteered last spring to go before a Union County grand jury.

According to official sources, the grand jury is investigating charges of payoffs and kickbacks involving city officials, contracts and businessmen. City license officials have already been subpoenaed, as have a number of city records and contracts.

Karl Asch, the county prosecutor, refused to comment on the nature of the reported investigation. He did say his staff had been instructed to seek indictments before the Nov. 7 elections.

Last week two of Mr. Dunn's three mayoral opponents were indicted in separate matters by a Union County grand jury.

Matthew J. Nilsen, a Republican freeholder in the county, was indicted on charges of atrocious assault in August in a case involving an alleged extortion.

In the other indictment, Michael J. DeMartino, a Democratic City Councilman in Elizabeth, was charged with misconduct in office in a case involving a $3,000 bribe in 1968.

Mayor Dunn recently endorsed President Nixon for reelection. Political observers in Union County noted that the indictments of two of his opponents were sought by a Republican prosecutor, and were seen as aiding the Mayor's re-election chances.

However, Mr. Asch, who has obtained indictments against prominent Union County political figures in recent months, contended today that his anticorruption drive was "absolutely nonpolitical" and that the investigation of the Dunn

Continued on Page 49, Column 6

NEWS INDEX

News Summary and Index, Page 47

"All the News That's Fit to Print"

The New York Times

LATE CITY EDITION
Weather: Partly sunny today; fair tonight. Partly sunny tomorrow. Temp. range: today 53-75; Saturday 53-73. Additional details on Page 91.

SECTION ONE

VOL. CXXIII . . No. 42,260 NEW YORK, SUNDAY, OCTOBER 7, 1973 — 75¢ beyond 50-mile zone from New York City, except Long Island. Higher in air delivery cities. — 50 CENTS

ARABS AND ISRAELIS BATTLE ON TWO FRONTS; EGYPTIANS BRIDGE SUEZ; AIR DUELS INTENSE

Associated Press

REDS, ORIOLES WIN PLAYOFF OPENERS: Johnny Bench after his homer won National League game for Cincinnati from New York, 2-1. Sparky Anderson, manager, is at lower left. Baltimore beat Oakland, 6-0, in the American League. Details in Section 5.

U.S. ASKS A HALT

Pleas by Kissinger to Prevent the Fighting Prove Fruitless

By BERNARD GWERTZMAN
Special to The New York Times

WASHINGTON, Oct. 6—The United States appealed to Israel and Egypt today to halt the fighting.

Secretary of State Kissinger, who was in New York, was caught by surprise when the crisis developed. He made a last-minute effort by telephone with Foreign Minister Abba Eban of Israel and Foreign Minister Mohammed H. el-Zayyat of Egypt to prevent the fighting from breaking out, but it proved fruitless.

Both men had had routine talks with Mr. Kissinger in the last two days without giving any indication that fighting was about to erupt, Administration officials said.

Kissinger Urges 'Restraint'

On instructions from President Nixon, who was in Key Biscayne, Fla., for the weekend, Mr. Kissinger "urged restraint to avoid the undermining and violation of the cease-fire" in effect since August, 1970, "and to avoid any escalation and continuation of the fighting," Robert J. McCloskey, a State Department spokesman, said in New York before Mr. Kissinger returned to Washington this afternoon.

In addition, Mr. Kissinger sent cables to King Faisal of Saudi Arabia and King Hussein of Jordan, both friendly to the United States, expressing the hope that they would "use their good office to urge restraint where they have the influence to do so," Mr. McCloskey said.

Call to Waldheim

Mr. Kissinger telephoned Secretary General Waldheim of the United Nations and Sir Lawrence McIntyre of Australia, this month's President of the Security Council, to discuss possible Council action. He also called the Soviet Ambassador, Anatoly F. Dobrynin, in Washington, Mr. McCloskey said, presumably to urge Soviet restraint as well.

The crisis struck Washington without much warning. American intelligence had routinely reported signs of military build-ups in Egypt and Syria in recent weeks, but the analysts believed these were either

Continued on Page 14, Column 1

United Press International

Army boots slung over his shoulder, an Israeli reservist reports for duty in Tel Aviv

SYRIANS IN CLASH

Fighting Along Canal and Golan Heights Goes On All Night

By ROBERT D. McFADDEN

The heaviest fighting in the Middle East since the 1967 war erupted yesterday on Israel's front lines with Egypt along the Suez Canal and Syria in the Golan heights.

Official announcements by Israel and Egypt agreed that Egyptian forces had crossed the Suez Canal and established footholds in the Israeli-occupied Sinai Peninsula.

A military communiqué issued in Cairo asserted that Egyptian forces had captured most of the eastern bank of the 100-mile canal. An Israeli military communiqué said the Egyptians had attempted to cross the canal at several points by helicopters and small boats and had succeeded in laying down pontoon bridges at two points. Armored forces were pouring across them into Sinai, it said.

Fighting All Night

A communiqué issued early today in Tel Aviv said fighting had raged all night along the canal's eastern bank and along the entire cease-fire line with Syria.

Each side accused the other of having started the fighting. But military observers posted by the United Nations reported crossings by Egyptian forces at five points along the Suez, and said Syrians had attacked in the Golan heights at two points.

Israeli and Syrian artillery dueled in the Golan heights, and on both battlefronts there were air clashes. The Cairo radio said Egyptian forces had shot down 11 Israeli planes and lost 10 of their own in battles over the Sinai and the Gulf of Suez. The Israeli spokesman did not comment on losses but said Israeli planes had shot down 10 Egyptian helicopters carrying troops into the southern Sinai.

Shelling by Syrians

In Damascus, the military command said that Syrian pilots and ground fire had shot down 10 Israeli aircraft in renewed action over the Golan heights this morning.

Syrian artillery was reported by the Israelis to have shelled a number of settlements in the occupied Golan heights and the Hula Valley area.

The Damascus radio said that Syrian forces had reoccupied Mount Hermon in the Golan heights for the first time since 1967, and said Syrian troops were fighting on the ground with Israeli forces along the entire cease-fire line.

An Israeli spokesman said today that Israeli planes had sunk an Egyptian vessel and that the navy had sunk three troop-carrying Egyptian craft during the night.

Gunboats Reported Sunk

As fighting continued into the night, Syrian and Israeli gunboats clashed in the Syrian harbor of Latakia, 110 miles north of Beirut. An Israeli communiqué said that five Soviet-built Syrian vessels were sunk by Israeli sea-to-sea missiles being used for the first time.

In Damascus, however, a military spokesman said that Syrian forces had sunk four Israeli naval vessels and shot down two Israeli helicopters in the sea battle.

No military action involving Jordan or Lebanon was reported, but King Hussein of Jordan placed his armed forces on full alert and conferred by telephone with President Anwar el-Sadat of Egypt and President Hafez al-Assad of Syria. Jordan was a belligerent in the 1967 war won by Israel.

The Government radio stations in Cairo and in Damascus

Continued on Page 2, Column 3

CAB DRIVER SLAIN IN TENSE BOSTON

Found Stabbed to Death in Roxbury Area Following Two Previous Killings

By JOHN KIFNER
Special to The New York Times

BOSTON, Oct. 6—The body of a young white taxi driver who had been stabbed to death was found today in the predominantly black Roxbury neighborhood as this uneasy city tried to come to grips with its racial fears.

The police identified the driver as Kirk Miller, a student at Clarkson College, who was working for the Boston Cab Company. His body was found hidden in some bushes in a vacant lot in Roxbury.

Detectives said that he had multiple stab wounds in his back and head. They said that they "had to assume" that robbery was a possible motive although they could not discount other factors. They said that no money was found on the body.

Mr. Miller was discovered by his sister Sally and a friend, Jeffrey Carter.

Tuesday night, a young white woman was burned to death by six youths in Roxbury, and less than 48 hours later an elderly white man was slain near a housing project. There

Continued on Page 77, Column 3

Tax Agents Compile Data On Net Worth of Agnew

By MARTIN WALDRON
Special to The New York Times

BALTIMORE, Oct. 6—Agents of the Internal Revenue Service are apparently compiling a statement on Vice President Agnew's net worth as part of the continuing investigation into his financial affairs.

Although the purpose of the revenue service's investigation is not known, the service often uses the technique of the net worth audit in an attempt to show that a defendant accused of evading taxes is worth more than the amounts on which he paid taxes.

Earlier this week, the Federal grand jury investigating Mr. Agnew indicted N. Dale Anderson, who succeeded Mr. Agnew as Baltimore County Executive, on income tax charges after revenue agents compiled a net worth statement on Mr. Anderson.

By law, the revenue service is prohibited from commenting on individual income tax reports or on investigations it may have under way.

But in the last few weeks its agents have been collecting data dealing with Mr. Agnew's affairs, even minor transactions, according to sources knowledgeable about the investigations.

On Oct. 3, agents from the Charlotte, N. C., intelligence office of the service subpoenaed records in Asheville, N. C., showing a gift of four yards of homespun cloth worth $16 to Mr. Agnew in 1967 at the time of the Southern Governors Conference, the sources said.

Such gifts are sometimes considered as income for tax purposes.

In making a case charging income tax evasion against an individual, the revenue service sometimes alleges failure to pay tax on specific income items, which it then seeks to prove were received by the individual.

The revenue agents and agents of the Federal Bureau of Investigation are apparently checking every financial transaction that the Vice President

Continued on Page 33, Column 1

U.N. COUNCIL AIDES CONFER ON CRISIS

President of Body Seeks Views on Calling Meeting to Deal With Fighting

By ROBERT ALDEN
Special to The New York Times

UNITED NATIONS, N. Y., Oct. 6—The President of the Security Council, Sir Laurence McIntyre of Australia, opened formal consultations tonight with other members of the Council to seek their views on calling a Council meeting to deal with the fighting in the Middle East.

The Western powers generally favored calling such a meeting, but not prematurely. They said that a premature meeting would result in little more than invective, claim and counterclaim.

Another proposal the Council members were discussing was for the President of the Council to appeal to both sides in the Middle East to halt the fighting. While Western powers generally supported such an appeal, the Chinese and the Russians held back endorsement; the French said they would have to study the idea.

Neither the Israelis nor the Arab states called for an urgent meeting of the Council today, though the Egyptian Foreign Minister, Dr. Mohammed H. el-Zayyat, said he wanted to

Continued on Page 8, Column 1

Israelis and Egyptians Tell Of Beginnings of Conflict

Jerusalem's Report

By TERENCE SMITH
Special to The New York Times

JERUSALEM, Sunday, Oct. 7—Heavy fighting erupted yesterday between Israeli and Arab forces along the Suez Canal and Golan heights cease-fire lines, a military spokesman announced.

The forces were still fighting early this morning in what Defense Minister Moshe Dayan described as "all-out war."

Mrs. Meir's address, Page 5; Dayan excerpts, Page 6.

The fighting began at 2 P.M. yesterday, Israeli time (8 A.M. New York time). Egyptian forces managed to cross the Suez Canal during the afternoon and establish bridgeheads at several points on the Israeli-held eastern bank, but Israeli military spokesmen said last night that Israeli forces had moved into position to block them.

On the occupied Golan heights, a large-scale Syrian force including armor and artil-

Continued on Page 4, Column 1

Cairo Communiques

By HENRY TANNER
Special to The New York Times

CAIRO, Oct. 6 — The Egyptian Government announced today that Israeli ground, sea and air forces attacked Egypt and Syria early this afternoon along the entire length of their front lines with Israel.

In a succession of communiqués read on the Government-controlled Cairo radio, Egypt said that her forces had crossed the Suez Canal in several places and had placed Egyptian flags on the Israeli-held eastern bank.

The radio said that the Egyptians had crossed the canal—the cease-fire line since the 1967 war—after repelling Israeli landing attempts on the Egyptian-held western bank.

The radio interrupted its regular program just after 2 P.M., Cairo time (8 A.M., New York time) saying that the Israeli action had started at 1:30 local time with air attacks on Ain Sukhna, 30 miles south of the town of Suez on the Egyptian shore of the Red Sea, and

Continued on Page 7, Column 1

Queens Sports Center Proposed

QUEENS BLVD.
NORTHERN BLVD.
SKILLMAN AVE.

Race track is flanked by Northern Boulevard at right and Skillman Avenue, left. Hotel rises at center, next to stadium. Queensboro Bridge leads to Manhattan.

By EMANUEL PERLMUTTER

Creation of a $275-million sports complex on air rights over the Sunnyside, Queens, railroad yards of the Penn Central was proposed yesterday by the State Racing and Wagering Board.

The project, which would be competitive with the proposed athletic complex in the New Jersey Meadows, would include two race tracks, an 80,000-seat stadium for football and other entertainments, a 1,000-room resort and convention hotel and parking for 20,000 cars.

No housing or other buildings would have to be demolished for the project since it would be built on a platform over the 300-acre yard site, which is less than a mile east of the Queensboro Bridge at the junction of Queens and Northern Boulevards and just a few minutes from Times Square by subway.

Under the proposal, the project would be financed by a bond issue and proceeds from the sale of Aqueduct Race Track. The air rights would be purchased by the Metropolitan Transportation Authority from the Penn Central and leased to the State Urban Development Corporation, which would build the necessary facilities.

Emil Mosbacher Jr., chairman of the Racing and Wager-

Continued on Page 49, Column 1

Gas Pipeline Contest Develops in Alaska

By GLADWIN HILL
Special to The New York Times

PRUDHOE BAY, Alaska, Sept. 29 — Another Alaskan pipeline dispute is brewing.

While the oil companies with the big petroleum deposits here on the North Slope await a final Congressional go-ahead to build a controversial 789-mile pipeline to Alaska's south coast, a consortium of United States and Canadian concerns is pushing plans to tap the region's rich natural gas reserves via a different but equally controversial 2,000-mile route.

Current exploratory activities of the gas consortium, pointing toward a possible major incursion into the Arctic National

Continued on Page 74, Column 3

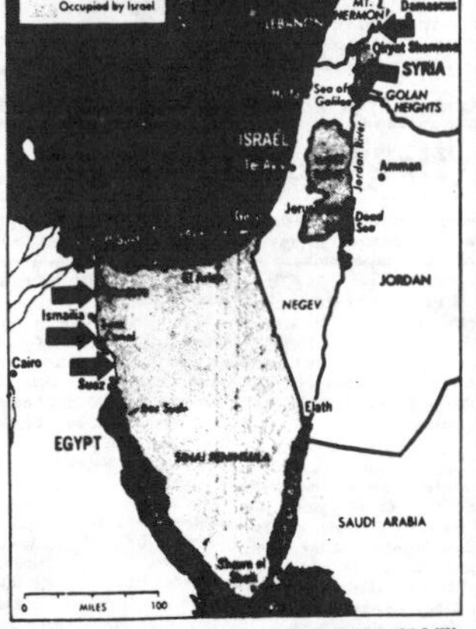
Occupied by Israel
MT. HERMON
Damascus
Qiryat Shemona
SYRIA
Sea of Galilee
GOLAN HEIGHTS
ISRAEL
Jordan River
Amman
Dead Sea
JORDAN
NEGEV
Ismailia
Cairo
Suez
Elath
EGYPT
SAUDI ARABIA
0 MILES 100

The New York Times/Oct. 7, 1973

Heavy arrows (upper right) indicate drive by Syrians and (lower left) crossing of Suez Canal by Egyptians.

Today's Sections

Index to Subjects

"All the News That's Fit to Print"

The New York Times

LATE CITY EDITION

Weather: Chance of rain today; mild tonight. Fair, mild tomorrow. Temp. range: today 53-68; Thursday 51-68. Additional details on Page 86.

VOL. CXXIII . . No. 42,279

© 1973 The New York Times Company

NEW YORK, FRIDAY, OCTOBER 26, 1973

15 CENTS

U.S. FORCES PUT ON WORLDWIDE ALERT LEST SOVIET SEND TROOPS TO MIDEAST; CRISIS EASED AS U.N. SETS UP A PATROL

Associated Press

Mem. ers of a Texas Air National Guard group are briefed at Ellington Air Force Base

ACTION BY COUNCIL

Unit Will Be Made Up of Soldiers From Smaller Nations

By KATHLEEN TELTSCH

Special to The New York Times

UNITED NATIONS, N. Y., Oct. 25—The Security Council voted today to establish a United Nations emergency force to insure a cease-fire in the Middle East, using troops from smaller countries.

The vote was 14 to 0, with China not participating in the adoption of the resolution,

Excerpts from Malik remarks are printed on Page 19.

which asked Secretary General Waldheim to report back within 24 hours on proposals for carrying out the Council's decision.

The vote came in a meeting that was delayed as delegates watched Secretary of State Kissinger's news conference on television amid concern over a possible big-power confrontation in the Middle East.

Threat May Be Averted

The importance of the Security Council's action, as seen by some Western diplomats, was that it could head off the possibility that the Soviet Union might unilaterally send troops to the Middle East.

One Western official said that while the creation of a United Nations peace-keeping force might "be a can of worms," it might also prevent a major-power confrontation.

A quick dispatch of United Nations forces, said a European, "could get all of us off a very painful hook."

Yesterday Egypt had asked that Soviet and American forces be sent to the Middle East to compel Israel to pull back to the positions she occupied Monday when the first cease-fire was ordered. The United States rejected Cairo's appeal that American troops be sent.

Resolution Revised

During the delay this morning, at the insistence of the United States, the eight non-aligned countries sponsoring the resolution agreed to revise it to exclude the five permanent Council members—the Soviet Union, the United States, China, France and Britain—from participation in the emergency force. The original resolution, introduced in a meeting that ended at 12:35 o'clock this morning, did not exclude the major powers.

The willingness of the Soviet

Continued on Page 19, Column 7

Associated Press

President Nixon sees Secretary of State Kissinger off for his Washington news session

KISSINGER SPEAKS

He Cites Ambiguous Signs by Moscow as the Cause

By BERNARD GWERTZMAN

Special to The New York Times

WASHINGTON, Friday, Oct. 26—The United States ordered its military forces on a worldwide "precautionary alert" early yesterday morning, citing concern that the Soviet Union was planning to introduce military forces into the Middle East. But the crisis seemed to abate when the Soviet Union joined later in a United Nations Security Council resolution barring big powers from participating in a Middle East peace-keeping force.

Secretary of State Kissinger said at a news conference in

Transcript of the Kissinger news conference, Page 19.

Washington that the United States was not seeking a confrontation with the Soviet Union.

And a State Department spokesman, noting that Mr. Kissinger had said that such a Security Council vote would ease tensions, termed the United Nations action "a step in the right direction." As of early today the precautionary alert was still in effect.

Other officials said that because of the Council vote some military units might be taken off alert later this morning.

Alert in Soviet Union

The alert was instituted after the Soviet Union gave what Mr. Kissinger called "ambiguous" signs that it might intervene to help out Egyptian forces caught behind Israeli lines and faced with destruction or surrender despite the cease-fire.

Military officials cited an alert of airborne troops within the Soviet Union as one cause of the American alert. [Details on Page 20.]

Intervention by the big powers, Mr. Kissinger warned, could cause major tensions in the world.

The sudden developments unforeseen yesterday when the White House was reporting that the Middle East cease-fire was taking effect, shocked the nation's capital and led President Nixon to postpone his scheduled news conference last evening in which he was expected to defend his actions in the Watergate tapes controversy.

Denial by Kissinger

The crisis, caused by uncertainty in Washington about the ability of the superpowers to avoid a direct confrontation over the Middle East, also produced some speculation that Mr. Nixon might have ordered the alert to distract domestic criticism.

Mr. Kissinger denied such allegations strongly, saying: "It is a symptom of what is happening to our country that it could even be suggested that the United States would alert its forces for domestic reasons."

He added, in his televised news conference, that "the President had no other choice as a responsible national leader" than to follow the advice

Continued on Page 19, Column 1

NEWS INDEX

The Newspaper that likes New York. See the 4 pg. Ad for THE PRESS Inserted in Sunday's Times (Advt.)

FORD BACKS STUDY ON IMPEACHMENT

Says He'll Support Congress if It Insists on Another Watergate Prosecutor

By JAMES M. NAUGHTON

Special to The New York Times

WASHINGTON, Oct. 25—Gerald R. Ford, President Nixon's nominee for Vice President, said today that the House of Representatives should "carry on" with an inquiry into the question of impeaching the President.

Moreover, Mr. Ford said in response to questions that he would support demands for creation of a new Watergate special prosecutor's office if a majority of the Congress insisted on it.

Mr. Ford, who is the minority leader of the House, outlined his views minutes after the House Republican Conference implored three White House officials to persuade Mr. Nixon to name a new special prosecutor and to make public the contents of the secret Watergate tape recordings.

Bryce N. Harlow, a counselor to the President, told newsmen that the Republican requests would be conveyed to Mr. Nixon and that the President would decide "very shortly" whether to name a successor to Archibald Cox, the special prosecutor who was discharged Saturday.

But Democrats in the Senate and the House pressed ahead with plans to enact legislation that would grant Chief Judge John J. Sirica of the United

Continued on Page 24, Column 5

Text of U.N. Resolution

Special to The New York Times

UNITED NATIONS, N.Y., Oct. 2'—Following is the resolution adopted by the Security Council today:

The Security Council,

Recalling its Resolutions 338 (1973) of 22 October, 1973, and 339 (1973) of 23 October, 1973,

Noting with regret the reported repeated violations of the cease-fire in noncompliance with Resolutions 338 (1973) and 339 (1973),

Noting with concern from the Secretary General's report that the United Nations military observers have not yet been enabled to place themselves on both sides of the cease-fire line,

1. Demands that immediate and complete cease-fire be observed and that the parties return to the positions occupied by them at 16:50 hours G.M.T. on 22 October, 1973;

2. Requests the Secretary General, as an immediate step, to increase the number of United Nations military observers on both sides;

3. Decides to set up immediately under its authority a United Nations emergency force to be composed of personnel drawn from states members of the United Nations except permanent members of the Security Council, and requests the Secretary General to report within 24 hours on the steps taken to this effect;

4. Requests the Secretary General to report to the Council on an urgent and continuing basis on the state of implementation of this resolution as well as Resolutions 338 (1973) and 339 (1973);

5. Requests all member states to extend their full co-operation to the United Nations in the implementation of this resolution as well as Resolutions 338 (1973) and 339 (1973).

Smoke Fells 150 on IRT In Crash in South Bronx

By ROBERT D. McFADDEN

More than 150 subway riders suffered smoke inhalation and other minor injuries and hundreds more were trapped in a dark smoky tunnel in the South Bronx for an hour or more last night after an IRT express train struck the rear of another that had been stalled by a fire.

Passengers recounted scenes of confusion, crying, and even instances of hysteria as a northbound train with flames and smoke pouring from a middle car stalled just north of the Longwood Avenue station on the Pelham Bay Park line and was hit by a following train.

The impact of the collision was described by Transit Authority spokesmen as light, but riders on both trains said many had been hurled to the floor. The collision occurred on the express track — the center of three tracks—at the north end of the station, at about 7:20 P.M.

More than a dozen ambulances from hospitals in the Bronx converged on Longwood Avenue and Southern Boulevard in Hunts Point, along with Manhattan and Queens hospital disaster units, a dozen pieces of Fire Department apparatus

Continued on Page 14, Column 3

U.S. Says Mafia Informer Gave Evidence Against Rep. Brasco

By NICHOLAS GAGE

Special to The New York Times

WASHINGTON, Oct. 25—The indictment of Representative Frank J. Brasco on Tuesday came as a result of information given to the Justice Department by John A. Masiello, a Mafia captain who was involved in the case, according to Federal sources.

Masiello is the highest ranking member of the crime syndicate known to have been "turned" — converted into a Government informer or witness.

The sources told The New York Times that Mafia leaders had already learned about Masiello's cooperation with the Government and reportedly had issued a "contract" on his life. He is currently under heavy Government protection in New York.

Representative Brasco was indicted on charges of conspiring to receive $27,500 in illegal payoffs in 1968 for helping Masiello's trucking concern get contracts to haul mail for the Post Office. Masiello was named as co-conspirator with the 41-year-old Democrat and his uncle, Joseph Brasco, but not as a defendant.

Masiello was listed by the Justice Department as a captain

Continued on Page 29, Column 2

WILLCOX & GIBBS has a wholly-owned subsidiary in Tel Aviv (WG-ASE)—Advt.

Beame Recruiting Unit

Controller Abraham D. Beame is so confident of victory in the mayoral election that he is forming a "recruiting" committee to seek out prospective top-level appointees for a Beame administration. Details, Page 31.

EGYPT SAYS ISRAEL CONTINUES FIRING

Sadat's Aide Reports Road From Cairo to Suez City Was Cut During Day

By HENRY TANNER

Special to The New York Times

CAIRO, Oct. 25—Egypt accused Israel today of continuing to violate the cease-fire agreement and said Israeli troops had fired on Egyptian forces wherever they were found.

A foreign-policy adviser to President Anwar el-Sadat said at a news conference that the Israelis cut the vital road from Cairo to the city of Suez at the southern end of the canal during the day.

The adviser, Ashraf Ghorbal, expressed deep bitterness over the shipment of United States matériel to the Israeli forces, "some of it straight to the battlefield." This, he said, enables the Israelis to continue to violate the truce.

Meanwhile, United Nations truce teams took up positions on the Cairo-Suez road 63 miles from Cairo and 12 miles west of Ismailia on the Cairo-Ismailia road. Egyptian officials charged that the Israelis had prevented United Nations observers from taking up a position at the canal site at which Israeli

Continued on Page 21, Column 5

Moscow Exhibits Tension, But No Intent to Intervene

By HEDRICK SMITH

Special to The New York Times

MOSCOW, Oct. 25—The Soviet Union showed new signs of tension with the United States today, but gave no public indication that it was preparing to intervene in the Middle East.

The Soviet leader, Leonid I. Brezhnev, abruptly postponed a scheduled address to 3,000 delegates at the opening session of the World Peace Congress here, in which many had expected him to emphasize the benefits of reconciliation and of Soviet-American cooperation in defusing the Middle East conflict.

He was seen leaving his balcony box for urgent consultations during other speeches and then circulating papers to President Nikolai V. Podgorny. Afterward, Foreign Minister Andrei A. Gromyko left the box.

Moscow signaled acute concern over the fate of Egyptian forces on the east side of the Suez Canal with a string of dispatches by Tass, the official press agency, charging Israel with repeated violations of the Middle East cease-fire and with attempts to capture the city of Suez.

This was in keeping with Soviet efforts to shield Egyptian forces from further defeats along the Suez Canal. The sharpened Soviet line against Washington suggested disillusion with the American moves. It could also have been read as an effort by Moscow to convey

Continued on Page 21, Column 3

Trapped Egyptian Force Held Key Factor in Crisis

By CHARLES MOHR

Special to The New York Times

TEL AVIV, Oct. 25 — The Egyptian III Corps, estimated to number 15,000 to 30,000 men, remained trapped by the Israelis today, unable to acquire fresh supplies of water and food.

It was generally felt here that the plight of the Egyptian force was at the root of the increasingly tense international situation, in which the United States alerted its forces worldwide, citing concern that the Soviet Union was planning to introduce troops into the Middle East.

Israeli spokesmen said that there was no fighting or violation of the cease-fire by either side during the day on either the Egyptian or the Syrian fronts and that the United Nations Truce Supervision Organization's observer teams were moving into position.

Egypt's III Corps is cut off in a narrow pocket on the eastern bank of the Suez Canal south of the Great Bitter Lake and in a small enclave embracing the city of Suez at the southern end of the canal.

If the isolation of the Egyptian force is very much prolonged, the III Corps might be forced to surrender or ask for free passage through Israeli lines.

The surrender during a cease-fire of such a substantial part of the Egyptian armed forces might constitute a stinging political humiliation for the Egyptian Government.

Such a move would reduce Egypt's holdings on the eastern bank of the canal, all of which she had seized soon after the war began on Oct. 6, to a narrow strip running from Qantara to a point opposite

Continued on Page 21, Column 2

United Press International

U.N. observers, in vehicles towing supply trailers, moving to posts in Egypt yesterday

"All the News That's Fit to Print"

The New York Times

LATE CITY EDITION

Weather: Fair today; rain likely tonight. Chance of rain tomorrow. Temp. range: today 61-77; Wed. 62-84. Additional details on Page 82.

VOL. CXXIII ... No. 42,481 · © 1974 The New York Times Company · NEW YORK, THURSDAY, MAY 16, 1974 · 20c beyond 50-mile radius of New York City except Long Island. Higher in air delivery cities. · 15 CENTS

16 YOUNG ISRAELI HOSTAGES DIE AS TROOPS KILL 3 ARAB CAPTORS; KISSINGER TALKS DELAYED A DAY

Young victims being carried from school in Maalot after the clash between Arab guerrillas and Israeli troops — United Press International

TERROR AT SCHOOL

Soldiers Rush Building as Attempt to Trade Prisoners Fails

By TERENCE SMITH
Special to The New York Times

MAALOT, Israel, May 15—A day of terror ended in this northern town this evening with a savage, 10-minute burst of gunfire and grenade explosions that killed three Arab terrorists and 16 of the high-school students they were holding hostage.

Early this morning, terrorists took command of the school, where about 90 students out on an excursion were sleeping. The three Arabs demanded the release of 20 prisoners held by Israel in return for the lives of the students.

An Israeli attempt to meet the demand failed and, as the deadline set by the guerrillas approached, soldiers rushed the school.

On 26th Independence Day

In the fighting that ensued, besides those killed 70 students were wounded, at least nine seriously. In the morning, as the day's terror began, a family of three was cut down by the Arab guerrillas as they entered the town. One soldier was also killed.

It was one of the bloodiest terrorist incidents in Israel's troubled history and it came on the 26th anniversary of the nation's independence.

After the decision to rush the school had been made, soldiers in bullet-proof vests surrounded the three-story building while snipers trained their sights on its shallow horizontal windows.

The firing broke out suddenly, while an officer with an electric megaphone was still pleading with the guerrillas in Arabic to postpone their 6 P.M. deadline.

Two of the three Arabs were hit by the opening burst of fire. One was apparently killed instantly, but the second had the strength to turn his automatic weapon on the students, spraying the second-story classroom indiscriminately.

Sought to Explode School

The third man tossed two grenades out the windows in an attempt to scatter the attacking soldiers. Then, according to one of the officers, the terrorist raced downstairs toward the entrance of the school where explosive charges had been placed. Before he could detonate them, soldiers shot him.

The screams of the terrified teen-agers could be heard a hundred yards away as the shooting erupted. One girl shrieked over and over again, "Up here, he's up here," referring to the wounded terrorist who was still firing.

Even before the shooting

Continued on Page 18, Column 3

A student, wounded in chest and arm, is carried from the Natia Meir school building — Associated Press

SETBACK IS SEEN IN PEACE EFFORTS

Moves for a Compromise on Israeli-Syrian Troops Are Called Impaired

Special to The New York Times

JERUSALEM, May 15—The terrorist attack at Maalot today forced Secretary of State Kissinger to suspend his Middle East peace efforts for one day.

The attack, which occupied the Israeli Cabinet through the day, was denounced by Mr. Kissinger as "this mindless and irrational action." The Secretary made it clear to his aides that he was determined not to let it undermine the progress made so far in this current Middle East negotiating trip.

But the tragic events at Maalot were viewed by both Israeli and American officials as probably having the effect of impairing his efforts to extract any last-minute compromises from either Israel or Syria on disengagement on the Syrian front before his scheduled return to Washington over the weekend.

Mr. Kissinger had been slated to meet with Israeli officials, led by Premier Golda Meir, this morning after an Israeli Cabinet meeting scheduled to discuss Israel's final ideas on disengagement to be conveyed by Mr. Kissinger to Syrian officials.

But this morning, when the dimensions of the terrorist attack became known, Mr. Kissinger put off his plans to leave Israel for Syria, preferring to wait until Mrs. Meir and other Israeli officials could deal with the disengagement problems.

Israeli officials, who spoke from time to time with Mr.

Continued on Page 19, Column 4

Busing of Pupils Upheld In a Senate Vote of 47-46

Ban Urged by Gurney Fails After 6 Hours of Debate—Revision in Aid Formula May Cost Schools Here $23-Million

By RICHARD D. LYONS
Special to The New York Times

WASHINGTON, May 15 — The Senate in effect upheld today the busing of children to end school segregation by a vote of 47 to 46.

The victory for the Senate liberals came only seven weeks after the House of Representatives by a vote of 293 to 117 approved a provision to prohibit Federal courts from ordering long-distance busing of children.

Today's vote followed six hours of often emotional debate. The critical Senate vote tabled an antibusing amendment offered by Senator Edward J. Gurney, Republican of Florida, to the Federal aid to education bill that has been on the Senate floor all week.

The motion to table was made by Senator Jacob K. Javits, Republican of New York.

In a radio address in March, President Nixon supported the antibusing language of the House version of the Gurney amendment, which was introduced in the House by Representative Marvin L. Esch, Republican of Michigan.

After defeating the Gurney amendment, the Senate approved, by a vote of 56 to 36, a more limited provision prohibiting the busing of pupils from one school district into another unless it has been found that discrimination is practiced in both districts or that district lines in both districts were drawn for the purpose of maintaining segregation.

The amendment is aimed at situations such as that in Detroit, where a Federal court has ordered busing between city schools and those in affluent white suburbs. The Detroit case

Continued on Page 9, Column 1

HOUSE UNIT ISSUES 2 NEW SUBPOENAS TO NIXON FOR DATA

Some on the Judiciary Panel Charge Transcripts Omit Significant Material

By JAMES M. NAUGHTON
Special to The New York Times

WASHINGTON, May 15—The House Judiciary Committee issued today two new subpoenas for White House tape recordings and other documents amid charges by some committee members that significant portions of President Nixon's Watergate conversations had been omitted from edited White House transcripts.

In a series of votes on the two subpoenas, the committee

Text of two memorandums on tape subpoenas, Page 26.

demanded this morning that the President turn over to its impeachment inquiry the tape recordings of 11 Watergate-related conversations as well as diaries of Mr. Nixon's White House meetings over more than eight months in 1972 and 1973.

The committee has not received any of this material, either in tape or other documentary form.

Two White House recordings previously obtained by the Judiciary Committee were played for the panel members this afternoon, prompting several Democrats to increase their resolve to obtain tapes, and not transcripts, of the relevant Watergate conversations.

Significance Disputed

Two Democratic members of the panel, Representatives Robert F. Drinan of Massachusetts and Jerome R. Waldie of California, told reporters after hearing the tape of a Sept. 15, 1972, White House conversation that material had been omitted from the White House transcripts not because it was inaudible but, as Mr. Waldie stated it, "because of the content."

Both Democrats declined to specify the nature of the missing material, however, and some Republicans on the committee said that they did not regard the omissions as serious or deliberate.

"The only thing that was deleted was the expletives, nothing of substance," Representative Delbert L. Latta, Republican of Ohio, said after the four-hour closed hearing at which recordings were played for about 40 minutes.

Renewed Effort by Panel

The new subpoenas, which "commanded" Mr. Nixon to supply the recordings and diaries by next Wednesday, were the first step in a renewed and bipartisan effort by the Judiciary Committee to obtain tapes and documents that Mr. Nixon has so far refused to yield.

John M. Doar, the committee's special counsel on impeachment, said that he would meet tomorrow with White House lawyers to get a final answer on whether Mr. Nixon would voluntarily supply recordings of 66 other conversations bearing on pledges of large political contributions to the President's re-election campaign by dairy industry groups and the International Telephone

Continued on Page 26, Column 1

Beame Asks $11.1-Billion For an 'Austerity' Budget

By GLENN FOWLER

Mayor Beame formally presented his first operating budget as the city's chief executive yesterday, labeling it an "austerity" blueprint that calls for spending $11.1-billion to run the municipal government in the fiscal year beginning July 1.

Declaring that he intended to provide "little in the way

Excerpts from Mayor Beame's budget are on Page 34.

of new money for new programs," Mr. Beame detailed in a 67-page message accompanying the basic document his financial acrobatics in overcoming a threatened $1.5-billion gap between income and outgo, enabling him finally to bring the budget into balance, as required by law.

The projected 1974-75 spending level, which is almost 8 per cent higher than the current fiscal year's actual outlay, spreads most of the available money among the areas of concern that have come to absorb much of the municipal treasury: public schools ($2.7-billion), welfare and related programs ($2.6-billion), public safety ($1.3-billion for police and fire) and health services ($1.2-billion).

One unusually large item is $1.5-billion for debt service — money to pay interest and amortization on the city's mounting debt — representing in the new budget a 63 per cent increase over the cost in the current fiscal year.

Mr. Beame placed the blame for the city's fiscal condition on his predecessor, John V. Lindsay, and he had harsh words for the

Continued on Page 34, Column 1

OIL DEPLETION AID FACES HOUSE VOTE

Democrats Mandate Action on Proposal to Repeal 22% Allowance Now

By EILEEN SHANAHAN
Special to The New York Times

WASHINGTON, May 15—Democratic members of the House of Representatives voted overwhelmingly today to force a straight yes-or-no vote in the House on immediate termination of the 22 per cent depletion allowance for the oil industry.

The action by the House Democratic Caucus, though technically only on a procedural matter, brought repeal of the depletion allowance closer than it has ever been in its 50-year history.

The vote in the caucus came about after weeks of intensive strategy planning, lobbying and nose-counting masterminded by three organizations: the American Federation of Labor and Congress of Industrial Organizations, Ralph Nader's tax reform research group and Common Cause, the citizens' lobby.

Rep. Green Is Key

The action of the caucus also brought into prominence a new leader on tax issues among the liberal Democrats in the House, Representative William J. Green of Pennsylvania.

In addition, the vote marked the first time that the new rules of the Democratic Caucus had been used to make sure that the House got to vote on a specific issue. The rules were adopted in February, 1973.

The action was deplored by Frank N. Ikard, president of the American Petroleum Institute. He said that the caucus had displayed a "lynch mob attitude" and predicted that the nation would "suffer a devastating setback in its efforts to attain a reasonable degree of energy self-sufficiency" if the ultimate victory in Congress went to those who, as he put it, "are demanding punitive tax action aimed at petroleum producers."

The caucus voted to permit

Continued on Page 17, Column 1

Police-Killing Mistrial

A mistrial was declared here yesterday in the trial of five reputed members of the Black Liberation Army who were charged with murdering two policemen. Page 45.

CHAPIN SENTENCED TO 10-30 MONTHS

Former Nixon Aide Appeals Prison Term for Lying to Watergate Grand Jury

By ANTHONY RIPLEY
Special to The New York Times

WASHINGTON, May 15 — Dwight L. Chapin, President Nixon's former appointments secretary, was sentenced today to a minimum of 10 months in prison for lying to a Watergate grand jury about political sabotage in the 1972 campaign.

Judge Gerhard A. Gesell imposed two concurrent sentences of 10 to 30 months each, calling it "a punishment sentence for a man who is not likely to repeat and needs no rehabilitation."

When Judge Gesell read the sentence, Mr. Chapin was apparently unmoved as he stood before the bench in United States District Court here. On April 5, he was convicted by a jury on two counts of lying about his dealings with Donald H. Segretti, an old college friend. Mr. Chapin was acquitted on a third count, and a fourth count was dismissed during the trial.

"It appears to the court that your resort to the convenience of swearing falsely when called before a grand jury cannot be condoned," Judge Gesell told the 33-year-old defendant. "I have therefore decided you

Continued on Page 27, Column 4

Threats by Nixon Reported on Tape Heard by Inquiry

By DAVID E. ROSENBAUM
Special to The New York Times

WASHINGTON, May 15—The tape recording of President Nixon's Sept. 15, 1972, conversation with H. R. Haldeman and John W. Dean 3d, which was heard today by members of the House Judiciary Committee, contains at least one long passage that does not appear in the edited White House transcript of that tape, according to a committee source.

In the passage cited by the source, President Nixon threatens to punish The Washington Post and its attorney, Edward Bennett Williams, and notes specifically that The Post owns television stations.

There is the clear implication, according to the source, that the President hoped to take Government action to deprive The Post of its television licenses.

The Post won a Pulitzer Prize last year for its many disclosures about the Watergate case and other scandals in the Nixon Administration.

Reading from a copy of the transcript prepared by the impeachment inquiry staff, the

Continued on Page 28, Column 1

Installation in Lisbon

Gen. António de Spínola took office as President of Portugal and named a left-leaning Government promising democracy at home and in Portuguese Africa. Details on Page 3.

SCHEEL IS ELECTED PRESIDENT IN BONN

Coalition Proves Strength in First-Ballot Victory — Bitterness Dissipates

By CRAIG R. WHITNEY
Special to The New York Times

BONN, May 15 — Walter Scheel was elected to the ceremonial office of the West German presidency today in a demonstration of solidarity between the two governing coalition parties, Mr. Scheel's Free Democrats and the Social Democrats.

The 54-year-old Mr. Scheel, who has been Vice Chancellor and Foreign Minister in the coalition Government since 1969, won a comfortable majority—530 of the 1,036 votes in the presidential electoral college on the first ballot. The fourth President since the formation of the West German Federal Republic in 1949, he is the first to be chosen so easily.

It was clear that despite bickering and fears of a revolt by some Social Democrats because of the resignation of their leader, Willy Brandt, from the chancellorship last week in the wake of a divisive spy scandal, the coalition was holding firmly together. There were only five abstentions and three absences. Mr. Scheel's opponent, Richard von Weizsäcker, received 498 votes, three fewer

Continued on Page 5, Column 5

Haig Said to Testify Simon Warned of Hughes Inquiry

By JOHN M. CREWDSON
Special to The New York Times

WASHINGTON, May 15 — Gen. Alexander M. Haig Jr., reportedly told a closed-door session of the Senate Watergate committee today that he was warned a year ago by William E. Simon, then Deputy Secretary of the Treasury, that a Federal investigation of a $100,000 political contribution from Howard R. Hughes had reached the point where it could eventually prove an embarrassment to President Nixon.

Sources familiar with his testimony said General Haig, the White House chief of staff, had identified Mr. Simon, who was confirmed last week as Secretary of the Treasury, as the individual who told him in the spring of 1973 that an Internal Revenue Service inquiry into the trail of the Hughes money had led to Charles G. Rebozo, Mr. Nixon's close friend.

General Haig's testimony about his knowledge of the Hughes-Rebozo matter was given under oath during an hour-and-a-half session before the Watergate committee members and lawyers, after the President had agreed to waive a claim of executive privilege invoked earlier this month before the committee by the general.

The committee voted unanimously today to ask the full Senate to extend its mandate in the Watergate case through the end of June. Senate Resolution 60, which authorizes the select committee's investiga-

Continued on Page 28, Column 4

Mrs. Meir Pledges Steps To Protect Israeli People

By BERNARD GWERTZMAN
Special to The New York Times

JERUSALEM, May 15—Premier Golda Meir promised a numbed nation tonight that Israel would do everything possible to protect her people against terrorist attacks.

Speaking on television, Mrs. Meir went into detail about

Text of Mrs. Meir's television remarks appears on Page 18.

the "bitter day for all of us" that resulted in the death of three Arab terrorists and 16 teen-aged Israelis in the village of Maalot.

Israel, she said, will "do everything in its power to cut off the hands that want to harm a child, an adult, a settlement, a town or a village."

Mrs. Meir affirmed that Israel had decided during the day to reverse her long-standing policy of not negotiating with terrorists. The Government was prepared to release 23 prisoners in return for the safety of the approximately 90 teen-aged hostages held by three Arab terrorists, the Premier said.

But the deal fell apart, she said, partly out of confusion, when the three terrorists insisted on a code word to begin negotiations. The code word never arrived from abroad for use by the French or Rumanian Ambassadors, who were prepared to begin discussions, she said.

Talking in a firm voice that occasionally faltered, and look-

Continued on Page 18, Column 3

NEWS INDEX

	Page		Page
Art	50	Movies	49-52
Books	39	Music	49-52
Bridge	38	Obituaries	44
Business	59-70	Op-Ed	41
Chess	38	Society	48
Crossword	39	Sports	52-57
Editorials	40	Theaters	49-52
Family/Style	46	Transportation	82
Financial	59-70	TV and Radio	83
Going Out Guide	50	U. N. Proceedings	4
Man in the News	5	Weather	82

News Summary and Index, Page 43

TODAY: SPECIAL ISSUE OF THE MAGAZINE—"AMERICA AT 200"

"All the News That's Fit to Print"

The New York Times

LATE CITY EDITION

Weather: Partly cloudy, mild today and tonight. Fair, mild tomorrow. Temperature range: today 65-80; Saturday 65-86. Details on page 39.

SECTION ONE

VOL. CXXV . No. 43,261 NEW YORK, SUNDAY, JULY 4, 1976

$1.00 beyond 50-mile zone from New York City, except Long Island. Higher in air delivery cities.

75 CENTS

The New York Times/Paul Hosefros

The cruiser Wainwright leads flotilla of ships up the Hudson for Bicentennial celebration. Following the Wainwright are the amphibious command ship Mount Whitney, the Peruvian ship Independencia, the Venezuelan destroyer Zulia, the Spanish missile frigate Asturias and the Dutch destroyer Tromp. Warships were vanguard of review.

HOSTAGES FREED AS ISRAELIS RAID UGANDA AIRPORT

Commandos in 3 Planes Rescue 105—Casualties Unknown

By TERENCE SMITH

Special to The New York Times

JERUSALEM, Sunday, July 4—Israeli airborne commandos staged a daring night-time raid on Entebbe airport in Uganda last night, freeing the 105 mainly Israeli hostages and Air France crew members held by pro-Palestinian hijackers and flying them back to Israel aboard three Israeli planes.

The hostages and their rescuers were due back in Israel this morning after a brief stopover at Kenya's International Airport at Nairobi, where at least two persons were given medical treatment in a field hospital on the runway. No details of the extent of the casualties were available here pending notification of the families.

Only fragmentary reports of the raid were immediately available here. An unspecified number of commandos apparently flew the 2,300 miles from Israel to Entebbe Airport and surprised the hijackers on the ground.

The hijackers were spending the night with their hostages in the old passenger terminal at Entebbe where they have been confined all week. They had commandeered an Air France airliner last Sunday shortly after it had left Athens on its way to Paris.

News agency reports from Entebbe said that a number of large explosions — perhaps bombs — were set off at a distant point on the airport, apparently to divert the ring of Uganda troops that had surrounded the old terminal all week.

The commandos reportedly broke into the old terminal and fought a gun battle with the heavily armed hijackers. Reports from the scene said that the terrorists had been killed in the skirmish, but military sources here declined to confirm or deny this.

The hostages apparently were then rushed to the waiting Israeli planes and flown away before Uganda forces could intervene.

An Israeli radio report said that the raiders were infantrymen and paratroopers dressed in civilian clothes.

Government sources here said that the decision to stage the military operation was approved unanimously by a special Cabinet meeting in Tel Aviv yesterday. The decision was made, the sources said, when it became clear that the hijackers would not relent in their demands and were holding Israel responsible for the

Continued on Page 10, Column 1

LONG TO LET PANEL RESTUDY TAX BILL

Review to Follow Criticism of Many Provisions Put in for Special Interests

By EILEEN SHANAHAN

Special to The New York Times

WASHINGTON, July 3—Senator Russell B. Long, chairman of the Senate Finance Committee, apparently concerned by criticism of the many special-interest provisions contained in the pending tax bill, has decided to take the extraordinary step of giving the committee a chance to reconsider its earlier decisions on the bill.

Senator Long, a Louisiana Democrat, disclosed his plans in an interview just before the Senate recessed for the Fourth of July holiday and the Democratic National Convention, which begins in New York on July 12.

The exact procedures that the committee will use in its reconsideration of the measure have not yet been decided.

For example, it is not yet clear whether the panel will have hearings on the many provisions of the bill that it adopted in May and June without any hearings.

What Mr. Long said was that he was "planning, after the recess, to call the committee together and offer senators an opportunity to express their views

Continued on Page 28, Column 4

Warships of 22 Nations Arrive for Bicentennial

By FRED FERRETTI

An international flotilla of warships sailed under the Verrazano-Narrows Bridge into New York Harbor yesterday, and more than 200 high-masted sailing ships moved into temporary berths at Sandy Hook and Gravesend Bay in preparation for the city's sea and land salute to the Bicentennial celebration today.

At precisely 8 A.M., the cruiser Wainwright, her blue-tipped missiles pointing skyward, moved smartly under the bridge, leading 52 naval ships from 22 countries taking part in the International Naval Review today.

Scores of small pleasure boats scurried about as the warships began moving into New York's lower bay, and the Coast Guard reported that more than 30,000 small boats were in and around the harbor and amid the tall ships off Sandy Hook.

And as the carrier Forrestal, the review ship for today's military sea parade, moved toward its anchorage in the Narrows, the Coast Guard reported "wall-to-wall" pleasure boats around her.

Cannon salutes were exchanged between the Wainwright and Fort Hamilton in Brooklyn, fireboats sprayed arcs of water and helicopters and dirigibles dipped overhead as 17 of the international warships moved into anchorages along the Hudson River from 72d Street to the George Washington Bridge and the 35 other ships sailed into temporary overnight anchor between the Statue of Liberty and Staten Island.

At 1:46 the Forrestal moved into the Narrows.

As the military ships moved into position, the 16 tall ships

Continued on Page 22, Column 1

Oslo Crew Arrives, Bound for Manhood And Tall Adventure

By TONY KORNHEISER

Special to The New York Times

ABOARD THE CHRISTIAN RADICH, July 3—This Norwegian full-rigged ship dropped anchor off Sandy Hook, N.J., at 11:30 A.M. today, ending a six-month, 5,000-mile voyage from Oslo with a crew of boys who have sailed halfway to manhood.

They are 15, 16 and 17 years old—87 cadets in all—and they are full of briny talk and bluster, flushed with adventure and eager to see the America they have heard so much about from a variety of sources.

"The tall lady in the harbor," said 17-year-old Lorentz Kielland. "What is her name? Statue of Liberty? I see her in books ever since I am small guy. I want to see her for real."

Labor and Legends

For Lorentz and his young shipmates, the trans-Atlantic trip from Oslo to Plymouth, England; Tenerife in the Canary Islands; Bermuda; Newport, R.I., and, finally, New York for Operation Sail '76 has been a mixture of routine and the stuff that legends promise.

At sea, life on the Radich is a monotonous cycle of work and sleep—four hours on, four hours off, interrupted only by meals. A regimen to be sure, and planned that way. The cadets sleep in hammocks, in two large areas below decks that give the appearance of bat caves when the hammocks are swung. The bat caves stay quiet because sleep is a necessity and small talk and rock music are luxuries. This is an economy cruise.

"A training ship," said First Mate Fred Hegerstrom, a veter-

Continued on Page 23, Column 6

City Like a Small Town During Holiday Festival

By RICHARD SEVERO

New York was like an old-fashioned small town yesterday, presenting an image of straw hats, little girls in summer prints, unusually orderly boys in proper knee socks and air so clean and fresh you could breathe it without seeing it.

The tall ships of Operation Sail and the gray ships of the International Naval Review glided into a bright harbor where crowds were not overwhelming and where the spirit of the past somehow seemed more real than the present.

The promenade along Battery Park looked more like one of Seurat's impressions of a 19th century Sunday in France than the edge of a great city, teeming with people and the problems of the present, a day away from a gigantic maritime extravaganza.

Indeed, the idyll was challenged only by the fact that somebody forgot to unlock legions of portable toilets in Battery Park with the result that, by midday, a great many tourists and New Yorkers alike had used Beekman Downtown Hospital as a sanitary facility.

"We let them come in but we don't want the word passed around," said Beekman's president, E. Geoffrey High. But Mr. High wasn't complaining. When he got to work yesterday morning, he found that, for the first time in months, the emergency room was empty. "It's absolutely spooky," Mr. High said.

Perhaps it was the salubrious weather or perhaps it was that since everyone had feared huge crowds, the result was a more modest turnout and none of the jostling that can come with a major event in New York.

There were several thousand people at Battery Park, enjoying the passage of the ships in markedly different ways.

For Armando Marrero, a maintenance man at the Columbia Presbyterian Hospital who many years ago was in the merchant marine, it was a chance to watch ships slip by and think about the old days.

"It is so beautiful," he said, "the last time I'll be able to see anything like this."

For Roland Dahlman Jr.,

Continued on Page 22, Column 7

Italy's Major Parties Give Reds Key Legislative Post

By ALVIN SHUSTER

Special to The New York Times

ROME, July 3—The Communist Party won a victory today when the leaders of major parties agreed to give it the job of President, or Speaker, of the Chamber of Deputies.

The decision, which came at a joint meeting of Communist and non-Communist leaders, will give the Communists their most important parliamentary post in the history of the Italian Republic. The Speaker will be elected on Monday when the new Parliament, elected on June 20, assembles.

The Communist leaders had demanded the presidency of either the Chamber or the Senate. They based their demands on their increased parliamentary strength, which rose by 71 seats in both houses in the elections last month.

In the 630-seat Chamber the Communists gained 49 seats. The Christian Democrats, who retained their lead as Italy's largest party, now hold 262 seats to the Communists' 228.

The Communists are also demanding chairmanships of important committees in Parliament. But there was no word today on which they are likely to get.

The Christian Democrats, who have dominated Italian politics for 30 years, will retain the presidency of the 315-member Senate. This is symbolically the more important of the two posts because the Senate president, in effect, is the Vice President of Italy.

In the last Parliament, dis-

Continued on Page 14, Column 4

Pension Law Said to Add Costs for New York City

By FRANCIS X. CLINES

The pension revision law enacted last week in a round of legislative compromise and promises of savings actually will increase New York City's budget expenses and cut into the hopes of attrition in jobs that underlie its austerity plan, the City Actuary cautioned yesterday.

This ironic effect of a bill that the Legislature wrestled with in the name of economy was described by Jonathan Schwartz, the City Actuary, who oversees the city's pension system, as one of a number of negative aspects that make the new law an "absolute monstrosity."

"I kept calling up there to warn them, but no one in Albany seemed interested in hearing from a pension specialist when they were trying to write a pension law," Mr. Schwartz said.

The law produced by the Legislature is a compromise typical of the politically divided body's nature: a three-tiered system that includes some caveats, one of which will have a negative effect on the city budget, at least for the next several years, in Mr. Schwartz's view.

The particular caveat lets city workers enrolled in the old, pre-1973 system transfer to the new 1976 system and thereby extend their mandatory retirement age by five years, from age 65 to 70. Mr. Schwartz figures that about 1,000 city

Continued on Page 32, Column 4

Borg Wins Wimbledon

Bjorn Borg, a 20-year-old Swede, defeated Ilie Nastase of Rumania, 6-4, 6-2, 9-7, yesterday to win the Wimbledon title. Details in Section 5.

Today's Sections

Index to Subjects

U.S. Attorney Calls F.B.I. 'Out of Step'

By SELWYN RAAB

In an unusually sharp attack against the Federal Bureau of Investigation by a high Government law enforcement official, David G. Trager, the United States Attorney for the Eastern District of New York, has described the F.B.I. as "suffering from arteriosclerosis" and of being "out of step" with the major goals of Federal prosecutors.

"Most of the cases they [the F.B.I.] bring to us are insignificant," Mr. Trager said. "They are wasting resources on trivia, and I don't think they have the ability or the people to do the job in the areas we consider priorities — official corruption and white-collar crime."

Mr. Trager, who has been in charge of one of the largest Federal prosecutorial units for more than two years, accused the F.B.I. of refusing to cooperate with his office in several "sensitive areas," such as corruption inquiries. The bureau's investigative methods, he continued in an interview, were "a hangover from the Hoover days," a reference to the late J. Edgar Hoover who was the director of the F.B.I. for 48 years until his death in 1972.

"The whole organization is geared up for gangbuster crime," Mr. Trager said. "It's a hangover from the Hoover days, a mentality of the 1920's and 1930's, and the only things they are capable of investigating are bank robberies, kidnappings and interstate thefts. That may have been important, but they refuse to recognize

Continued on Page 32, Column 1

500,000 View Capital's Bicentennial Parade

By RICHARD HALLORAN

Special to The New York Times

WASHINGTON, July 3—The woman in the yellow jersey may have said it best when she clapped her hands and shouted to her friend marching by: "Everything's O.K.! Lookin' good, lookin' good!"

It was a grand day for the Bicentennial parade in the nation's capital today, and it was a grand parade celebrating the diversity that is America.

It was warm under a hazy sun but not one of Washington's blistering summer days, and 500,000 people, according to the official estimate, turned out to see more than 50 bands, 60 floats and 90 marching units.

President Ford missed the parade because he was playing golf at Burning Tree Country Club in suburban Maryland. But in a series of speeches prepared for the Bicentennial celebrations he paid tribute to the "American adventure" while saying that the blessings of liberty must still be defended. [Page 25.]

In Philadelphia, the influx of visitors to that historic city was much smaller than expected. [Page 26.]

Vice President Rockefeller and Johnny Cash, the singer, led the parade here in separate

Continued on Page 26, Column 4

The New York Times/George Tames

Vice President Rockefeller and his wife, Happy, leading the parade in Washington

"All the News That's Fit to Print"

The New York Times

LATE CITY EDITION

Weather: Cold, snow late today into tonight. Partial clearing tomorrow. Temperature range: today 27-36; yesterday 42-49. Details, page D14.

VOL.CXXVII..No.43,881 | NEW YORK, THURSDAY, MARCH 16, 1978 | 25 cents beyond 50-mile zone from New York City. Higher in air delivery cities. | 20 CENTS

ISRAELIS SEIZE 4-TO 6-MILE 'SECURITY BELT' IN LEBANON AND SAY TROOPS WILL REMAIN; WASHINGTON SEES 'IMPEDIMENTS TO PEACE'

Senate Backers Of Canal Treaty Predict Victory

Say They Have Votes to Win Roll-Call Today

By ADAM CLYMER

Special to The New York Times

WASHINGTON, March 15—Senate supporters of the Panama Canal treaties said today that they had enough votes to win tomorrow's crucial roll-call on the first of the pacts.

On the eve of one of the most important foreign policy votes in many years, Senator Howard H. Baker Jr., Republican of Tennessee, the minority leader, told reporters he now believed that the treaty guaranteeing the neutrality of the canal after American control ends in the year 2000 would be approved. And the effective leader of the treaties' opponents, Senator Paul Laxalt, Republican of Nevada, characterized the situation as "not so good."

Tonight, Vice President Mondale told a Democratic Congressional fund-raising dinner, "Now we have 67 votes for the Panama Canal treaty tomorrow," indicating approval was insured.

Two New Votes in Favor

In a day of intense lobbying, beginning when Mr. Mondale appeared unannounced at the office of Senator Wendell H. Ford, Democrat of Kentucky, at 7:15 A.M., none of the uncommitted senators, including Mr. Ford, announced that they would vote against the treaty.

Two uncommitted senators, Edward W. Brooke, Republican of Massachusetts, and Dennis DeConcini, Democrat of Arkansas, said they would vote for the neutrality treaty. Mr. Brooke, however, said he might vote later against the treaty turning over the canal and the Canal Zone to Panama.

The backing of Mr. Brooke and Mr. DeConcini, plus the expected support of Senator Bob Packwood, Republican of Oregon, gave the treaty supporters 65 votes they could count on. They would not say where they expected to get the two other votes they needed to make up the 67 required for approval.

There were still four uncommitted senators available and at least the chance

Continued on Page A2, Column 1

CAPITAL SYMPATHETIC

U.S. Officials Relieved That Heavy Combat Activity Is Apparently Over

By BERNARD GWERTZMAN

Special to The New York Times

WASHINGTON, March 15—Israel's invasion of southern Lebanon evoked a sympathetic response from the United States today, but Secretary of State Cyrus R. Vance conceded that the Israeli attack and the Palestinian raid that inspired it had raised "impediments to the peace process."

The general mood at the highest levels of the Administration was relief this afternoon that the main fighting seemed at an end.

The evidence that the Israelis were confining their ground operations to a belt up to six miles deep along the border reduced the likelihood that the Syrians would enter the conflict and spread the warfare, one high official said.

Begin Statement Causes Worry

In Beirut, however, Syrian and Lebanese officials appealed for international help in obtaining Israeli withdrawal. [Page A17.] In Cairo, Foreign Minister Mohammed Ibrahim Kamel denounced the Israeli action as "organized genocide" and said that it harmed Egyptian peace efforts. [Page A17.]

American officials said that with Prime Minister Menachem Begin due in Washington next Monday for talks with President Carter on Tuesday and Wednesday, the chances for diplomatic progreess, already dim, were now more remote.

A new problem has now arisen, officials said, over a statement by Mr. Begin today that Israeli forces would remain in the belt of Lebanese territory until an agreement was reached to prevent the Palestinians from returning to the area.

The United States, a strong backer of Lebanon's sovereignty and integrity, wants the Israelis to withdraw as soon as possible and the withdrawal issue undoubtedly will now become a major topic during Mr. Begin's talks with Mr. Carter, officials said.

Late this afternoon, Ambassador Simcha Dinitz of Israel conferred for 90 minutes with Alfred L. Atherton Jr., the Administration's top Middle East negotiator, to discuss the Israeli presence in

Continued on Page A17, Column 1

Associated Press

Israel's Prime Minister, Menachem Begin, left, arriving at the Lebanon border yesterday for a close look at the action. Defense Minister Ezer Weizman is at center, wearing flight jacket and sunglasses.

MAJOR FIGHTING ENDS

Forces Rout the Palestinians in Border Strongholds —Planes Bomb Bases

By WILLIAM E. FARRELL

Special to The New York Times

JERUSALEM, March 15—Israeli forces routed Palestinian guerrillas today from at least seven strongholds in southern Lebanon, and Prime Minister Menachem Begin said the troops would remain until an agreement was reached to insure that the area could never again be used for raids against Israel.

With land, sea and air operations conducted from the Mediterranean to the foothills of Mount Hermon, Israelis occupied what Lieut. Gen. Mordechai Gur, the Chief of Staff, called a "security belt" along the 60 or so miles of its northern border, with a depth of four and a half to six miles. Late tonight, General Gur said the major fighting was over.

[An Israeli military spokesman reported that 11 Israeli soldiers had been killed in the operation and 57 wounded, according to The Associated Press.]

Air Strikes Near Beirut

Mr. Begin's remarks about how long Israelis would remain in Lebanon were echoed by Defense Minister Ezer Weizman, who told reporters:

"We shall continue to clear the area—prevent the area from being attack positions against us as long as we find it necessary."

The ground offensive, the largest that Israel has ever carried out against Palestinians, was accompanied by air strikes against Palestinian enclaves and camps far north of the Israeli border, including at least two in the vicinity of Beirut.

The Israeli Army spokesman announced that Israeli planes had bombed a Palestinian base near Damur, about 20 miles south of Beirut, which he said had been the staging area for the Arab raiders who infiltrated into Israel on Saturday and seized a bus.

Syrians Said to Fire on Planes

The seizure touched off a wild ride on the Haifa-Tel Aviv highway, with shooting and an explosion that led to the death of 34 Israelis and an American and the injury of more than 70 persons.

The army spokesman said that Israeli planes had struck targets at the Mediterranean port of Tyre and at a site near Beirut that the spokesman described as a Palestine Liberation Organization training and supply base "for terrorist naval units and for their equipment."

In the raid at Damur, the spokesman said the Israeli planes had been fired on by a Syrian unit. The Israeli planes did not fire back at the Syrians, he said, and returned safely to base.

The Syrians have a large military

Continued on Page A16, Column 1

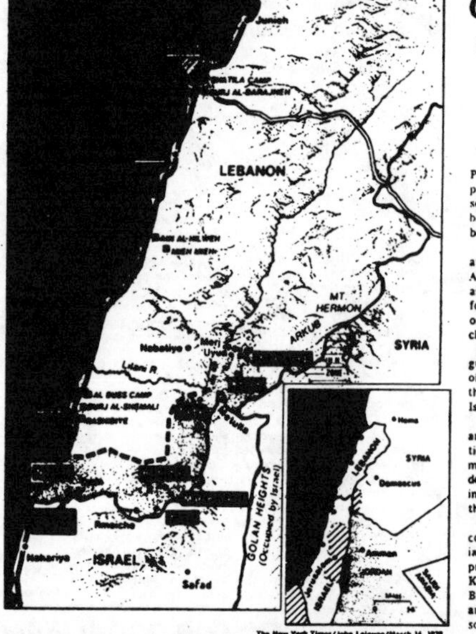

The New York Times/John Lelmone/March 16, 1978

Israelis established "security belt" in southern Lebanon after capturing Palestinian strongholds (marked by panels). Israeli gunboats attacked Tyre, and jets struck there, at Damur and also in Beirut area.

Guerrillas Join Civilian Retreat From Attackers

By MARVINE HOWE

Special to The New York Times

TYRE, Lebanon, March 15 — Many Palestinian and Lebanese families fled in panic today from population centers in southern Lebanon that had been bombarded by Israeli fighter-bombers, gunboats and artillery.

"We're going north, anywhere, to get away from the shelling," said Mohammed Ahmed al-Mohammed, a Lebanese farmer, as he and his family of 12 set out on foot along a road out of Tyre carrying only small bundles of blankets and clothing.

While young Lebanese and Palestinian guerrillas in the towns and villages spoke of their "fierce resistance," it was clear they were retreating in face of the heavy Israeli odds.

"We are not going to let ourselves be annihilated," said a member of the Palestine Liberation Organization's southern military command at Saida. "We cannot destroy the Israeli forces, but we can inflict as many casualties as possible and then make a tactical withdrawal."

The Palestinian military spokesman confirmed reports that the joint Palestinian-Lebanese leftist forces had lost their principal positions in the border area: Khiam, Ibl al-Saqi and Taibe in the east, Bint Jbail and Marun al-Ras in the center and Naqura and Alma al-Chaab in the southwest.

The city of Tyre was a prime target as the main port of entry for arms sup-

Continued on Page A16, Column 4

United Press International

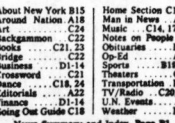

Palestinian refugees fleeing from Damur, Lebanon, following Israeli air strikes yesterday

Soviet Now Termed Cool to Linking Cuban Pullout to Ethiopian Truce

By RICHARD BURT

Special to The New York Times

WASHINGTON, March 15—Contrary to what reporters were told at the State Department last week, the Soviet Union has given little sign that it is prepared to link the end of Somali-Ethiopian fighting with cuts in Cuban forces in Ethiopia, government officials said today.

They said Ambassador Anatoly F. Dobrynin, at a meeting with Secretary of State Cyrus R. Vance on Saturday, declined to commit Moscow on the future of either its own advisers or the Cuban forces in the Horn of Africa.

The previous evening, reporters were told that Moscow said the Cuban forces, estimated at 12,000, would be reduced once Somalia ended its occupation of Ogaden, an ethnic Somali region of Ethiopia. The reporters were also told that the Soviet Union had agreed to have neutral observers monitor a cease-fire. The information was supplied as "deep background," meaning that it could not be attributed.

Pullout Up to Addis Ababa

Today, a high-ranking State Department official said the information had been based on a previous "direct conversation" between Mr. Vance and Mr. Dobrynin. However, at their Saturday meeting, the Soviet envoy said the withdrawal of Cuba's forces from Ethiopia had to be taken up with those two governments, the official said..

The State Department spokesman, Hodding Carter 3d, announced that the Somali pullout, begun last week, was now complete, and he called on Moscow to facilitate the withdrawal of the Cuban troops and of the 1,000 Soviet advisers in Ethiopia.

Privately, State Department and White House officials said the Russians had been unwilling to discuss concrete plans for withdrawing the Cubans or establishing a truce-observation group.

"We have no evidence from Moscow or anywhere else that the Soviets are inclined to be cooperative on the Horn," said one White House official.

Officials expressed doubts over the likelihood of an early reduction in the

Continued on Page A9, Column 1.

6 Guilty in Attack At Washington Sq.

By GREGORY JAYNES

Six of nine young men charged with taking part in a 1976 rampage in Washington Square Park that left one man dead and 13 persons injured were found guilty yesterday—three of manslaughter and three of lesser charges.

The verdict was delivered, after a nine-week trial and six days of deliberation, while a number of the defendants' parents wept in a closed courtroom in State Supreme Court in Manhattan. Parents of the three men found not guilty also cried.

Sentencing was scheduled for April 19 before Justice Robert Haft, in whose court the trial was held. Those convicted of manslaughter could be sentenced to as much as 25 years.

Calling the crime "one of great social severity," Assistant District Attorney John Moscow, the prosecutor, said that "the people will ask for imprisonment for all" those convicted.

During the trial, Mr. Moscow argued that the nine defendants had planned the attack on Washington Square to clear the park of blacks and Hispanic persons.

Of the nine defendants, one, Robert

Continued on Page B17, Column 1

INSIDE

Parking Rules Reinstated

Alternate-side-of-the-street parking regulations are reinstated to let sweepers get at a 62-day accumulation of slushy litter. Page B1.

Miner Council Backs Pact

The bargaining council of the United Mine Workers approved a third tentative contract that now must be voted on by the striking miners. Page D12.

Soviet Bars Rostropovich

The Soviet Union revoked the citizenship of Mstislav Rostropovich, the expatriate cellist, and his wife, Galina Vishnevskaya. Page A10.

CBS Executive Resigns

Robert J. Wussler, former president of the CBS television network and now president of CBS Sports, resigned to form a production company. Page C20.

The New York Times

"All the News That's Fit to Print"

LATE CITY EDITION
Weather: Mostly sunny, cool today; clear, cold tonight. Sunny tomorrow. Temperature range: today 32-48; yesterday 36-49. Details on page C12.

VOL.CXXVIII...No.44,169   Copyright © 1979 The New York Times   NEW YORK, TUESDAY, MARCH 27, 1979   25 cents beyond 50-mile zone from New York City. Higher in air delivery cities.   20 CENTS

EGYPT AND ISRAEL SIGN FORMAL TREATY, ENDING A STATE OF WAR AFTER 30 YEARS; SADAT AND BEGIN PRAISE CARTER'S ROLE

OPEC PARLEY WEIGHS NEW OIL PRICE RISES AND CUTS IN OUTPUT

Saudis Say They Will Try to Resist Big Increases — Carter Puts Off Decisions on Energy

By PAUL LEWIS
Special to The New York Times

GENEVA, March 26 — Pressure for another large increase in world oil prices built up today at the opening of a meeting of oil ministers of the 13 member nations of the Organization of Petroleum Exporting Countries.

The advocates of a sharp new oil price rise, of anywhere from 20 to 35 percent from current levels on April 1, also urged other oil producers to reduce output. The aim would be to keep world markets tight as Iran resumes exports to insure that the new price levels stick.

But Saudi Arabia, the world's largest oil exporter, resisted pressure for price jumps, pointing out that they could do severe damage to the economies of both the developing and the industrialized world. "There is worry particularly about the effects of price changes on developing countries," OPEC's secretary general, René Ortise, said.

Effort to Reduce Increases

Sheik Ahmed Zaki Yamani, Saudi Arabia's oil minister, interviewed after tonight's session, said the ministers faced a "deadlock," with the Saudis feeling that the increases demanded by Iran and Libya were "too steep." Observers here interpreted his stance as an effort to cut probable increases to more moderate levels.

The ministers have not yet voted themselves the power to take any pricing action at the current two-day session but are expected to do so tomorrow. A simple majority vote would grant the meeting such authority.

On the question of possible punitive cutbacks in supplies, reflecting displeasure with some consuming nations' positions on the Palestinian question, Iraqi representatives said such moves were possible, particularly against Egypt. But they carefully noted that no such moves were planned by OPEC, although the "oil weapon" could re-emerge if conditions returned to the situation of 1973.

Carter Decisions Deferred

In Washington, meanwhile, Administration officials said that President Carter's decisions on various energy proposals, expected Thursday, would be deferred, apparently because key White House officials had not been able to devote enough time to the controversial plans. [Page D12.]

When Sheik Yamani entered the OPEC

Continued on Page D12, Column 3

Leaders join hands after signing pact. President Anwar el-Sadat signed first, followed by Prime Minister Menachem Begin. President Carter was witness.
United Press International

Mood of Peace Seems Somber And Uncertain

By BERNARD WEINRAUB
Special to The New York Times

WASHINGTON, March 26 — Shortly after 6 A.M. today, President Anwar el-Sadat arose in the residence of the Egyptian Ambassador and began wandering around the five-bedroom house.

He scanned the morning newspapers, pedaled a stationary exercise bicycle, nibbled a slice of unbuttered toast, sipped a glass of orange juice and, by 7 A.M. turned on the television to watch the morning news.

Less than one mile away, in a guarded ninth-floor suite at the Washington Hilton Hotel, Prime Minister Menachem Begin of Israel peered out the windows at the traffic moving along Connecticut Avenue.

He turned away and, carrying a cup of tea, walked to a writing desk and began working on the emotional speech that he would deliver in mid-afternoon at the White House ceremony ending 30 years of war between Israel and Egypt.

It was the start of a day marked by paradox — a triumphal day of peace that seemed curiously somber, a day of celebration blurred by protests in the heart of Washington, a bright day shadowed by uncertainty.

"There is, you know, a sense of trepi-

Continued on Page A9, Column 1

Treaty Impact Still Unknown

'Hopes and Dreams' but 'No Illusions' for Carter

By HEDRICK SMITH
Special to The New York Times

WASHINGTON, March 26 — The elusive, unprecedented peace treaty that Egypt and Israel signed today has enormous symbolic importance and the potential for fundamentally transforming the map and history of an entire region, but the agreement faces an uncertain future.

News Analysis

Israel has now won what it has sought since 1948 — formal recognition and acceptance from the most powerful Arab state and the ultimate prospect of exchanging ambassadors and entering into a full range of normal relations.

For all the violent denunciations that this historic breakthrough aroused in the Arab world, the best diplomatic estimate here is that the treaty has markedly reduced the risk of a major war in the Middle East for a considerable time by removing Egyptian strength from the active Arab arsenal.

And it has demonstrated American capacity to influence events in the Middle East despite the setbacks Washington has suffered since the overthrow of the

Continued on Page A10, Column 5

CEREMONY IS FESTIVE

Accord on Sinai Oil Opens Way to the First Peace in Mideast Dispute

By BERNARD GWERTZMAN
Special to The New York Times

WASHINGTON, March 26 — After confronting each other for nearly 31 years as hostile neighbors, Egypt and Israel signed a formal treaty at the White House today to establish peace and "normal and friendly relations."

On this chilly early spring day, about 1,500 invited guests and millions more watching television saw President Anwar el-Sadat of Egypt and Prime Minister

Transcripts of statements at signing are on page A11. Texts of treaty and Camp David accords are on pages A12, A13 and A14.

Menachem Begin of Israel put their signatures on the Arabic, Hebrew and English versions of the first peace treaty between Israel and an Arab country.

President Carter, who was credited by both leaders for having made the agreement possible, signed, as a witness, for the United States. In a somber speech he said, "Peace has come."

'The First Step of Peace'

"We have won, at last, the first step of peace — a first step on a long and difficult road," he added.

Later, at a state dinner, Mr. Begin suggested that Mr. Carter be given the Nobel Peace Peace, and Mr. Sadat agreed.

At the signing ceremony, all three leaders offered prayers that the treaty would bring true peace to the Middle East and end the enmity that has erupted into war four times since Israel declared its independence on May 14, 1948.

By coincidence, they all referred to the words of the Prophet Isaiah.

"Let us work together until the day comes when they beat their swords into plowshares and their spears into pruning hooks," Mr. Sadat said in his paraphrase of the biblical text.

'No More War,' Begin Says

Mr. Begin, who gave the longest and most emotional of the addresses, exclaimed: "No more war, no more bloodshed, no more bereavement, peace unto you, shalom, saalam, forever."

"Shalom" and "salaam" are the Hebrew and Arabic words for "peace."

The Israeli leader, noted for oratorical skill, provided a dash of humor when in the course of his speech he seconded Mr. Sadat's remark that Mr. Carter was "the unknown soldier of the peacemaking effort." Mr. Begin said, pausing, "I agree, but as usual with an amendment" — that Mr. Carter was not completely unknown and that his peace effort would "be

Continued on Page A10, Column 1

Judge Bars Hydrogen Bomb Article After Magazine Rejects Mediation

By DOUGLAS E. KNEELAND
Special to The New York Times

MILWAUKEE, March 26 — A Federal District Court judge here, acting only after his suggestion for an attempt at out-of-court settlement was turned down, granted the Government's motion for a preliminary injunction today to keep The Progressive magazine from publishing an article about the hydrogen bomb.

In so doing, Judge Robert W. Warren became the first Federal judge ever to issue an injunction imposing prior restraint on the press in a national security case.

The magazine's attorneys said they would file an appeal shortly with the United States Court of Appeals for the Seventh Circuit in Chicago.

Court's 'Awesome Responsibility'

Before announcing his decision this afternoon, Judge Warren, a former Wisconsin Attorney General, acknowledged that he considered it an "awesome responsibility."

"Stripped to its essence, then," he said, "the question before the court is a basic confrontation between the First Amendment right to freedom of the press and national security."

The judge said "a mistake in ruling against The Progressive will seriously infringe cherished First Amendment rights." However, he added, "a mistake

Continued on Page B12, Column 3

INSIDE

Michigan State Wins
Michigan State became the National Collegiate basketball champion by defeating Indiana State, 75-64, at Salt Lake City. Page C13.

H.R.A. Administrator Quits
Blanche Bernstein, the Human Resources Administrator, resigned rather than accept Mayor Koch's offer to stay in the job without power. Page B1.

Photographs for The New York Times by TERESA ZABALA

Palestinians, Reacting to the Pact, Go on Strike and Denounce Egypt

Special to The New York Times

BEIRUT, Lebanon, March 26 — Vowing revenge, staging strikes and protest marches and calling for punitive measures against Egypt, Palestinians and other Arabs reacted angrily today against the signing of the Egyptian-Israeli peace treaty in Washington.

Yasir Arafat, chairman of the Palestine Liberation Organization, vowed to chase Americans out of the Middle East and to "chop off the hands" of President Carter, President Anwar el-Sadat of Egypt and Prime Minister Menachem Begin of Israel. He spoke to a group of guerrilla recruits at the Sabra Palestinian camp here as effigies of the three signers were burned.

The inhabitants of Lebanon's 15 Palestinian camps protested the signing today by refusing to work, as did many Lebanese Moslems. Similar protests were staged in the occupied West Bank of the Jordan River and the Gaza Strip, and in the Arab Old City of Jerusalem a grenade exploded tonight, wounding five tourists.

Iran Government Condemns Pact

In Teheran, the Iranian Government condemned the treaty, and 30 Arab students took over the Egyptian Embassy there. Protesters also stormed the Egyptian Embassy in Kuwait, where 250,000 Palestinians live, forming the largest foreign community in that small country. In Damascus, Syria, demonstrators occupied the offices of the Egyptian airline, Egyptair.

Meanwhile, foreign and finance ministers of Arab League countries gathered today in Baghdad, Iraq, for a meeting tomorrow on possible economic and political measures against Egypt. The countries had vowed last November to hold such a meeting if the Egyptian-Israeli peace treaty was signed, but Saudi Arabia, Egypt's principal foreign backer, has been trying to exercise a moderating influence.

King Hussein of Jordan flew to Damascus and Baghdad during the day in what was believed to be an effort to coordinate the positions of hard-liners and moderates at tomorrow's Arab meeting.

Gromyko Comments on Treaty

In Damascus, Foreign Minister Andrei A. Gromyko of the Soviet Union ended a three-day visit to Syria today by joining with President Hafez al-Assad in denouncing the peace treaty, saying it appeared bound to increase tension in the Middle East. A joint Soviet-Syrian communiqué said the treaty was aimed at perpetuating the Israeli occupation of Arab lands, the annexation of Arab East

Continued on Page A10, Column 5

"All the News That's Fit to Print"

The New York Times

LATE CITY EDITION

Weather: Cloudy, chance of showers today and tonight. Sunny tomorrow. Temperature range: today 54-66; yesterday 62-67. Details on page 8.

VOL. CXXVIII . . . No. 44,229 | NEW YORK, SATURDAY, MAY 26, 1979 | 20 CENTS

25 cents beyond 50-mile zone from New York City. Higher in air delivery cities.

272 DIE AS JET CRASHES ON TAKEOFF IN CHICAGO AFTER LOSING ENGINE; WORST U.S. AIR DISASTER

Associated Press

Firemen searching through the smoldering wreckage of an American Airlines jet that crashed on takeoff yesterday at Chicago's O'Hare International Airport

NO SURVIVORS FOUND

Los Angeles-Bound DC-10 Narrowly Misses Tract of Mobile Homes

By DOUGLAS E. KNEELAND

Special to The New York Times

CHICAGO, May 25 — An American Airlines jetliner lost an engine and crashed shortly after takeoff from O'Hare International Airport this afternoon, killing all 272 persons aboard. It was the worst disaster in United States aviation history.

Flight 191, a DC-10 bound for Los Angeles at the beginning of the Memorial Day weekend, rose to the northwest from Runway 14 just after 3 P.M., central daylight time. Then, witnesses said, the plane appeared to suffer difficulties with an engine on the left wing, rolled to the left, stalled and plunged into the small abandoned Ravenswood Airport, narrowly missing a mobile home court.

Several witnesses said the engine exploded, and others reported seeing a "huge cylinder" fall from the plane to the runway and burst into flames.

No Survivors Reported

American Airlines officials said there were apparently no survivors of the crash, which scattered debris over an area about 100 by 200 yards. The crash sent up flames and black smoke that could be seen 15 miles away in Chicago's downtown Loop area, and fiery remnants struck some of the mobile homes nearby, severely damaging three of them. Two persons who were apparently working on the ground near the crash site were injured.

The plane narrowly missed a Standard Oil Company gasoline storage facility a block away.

Fire trucks, ambulances and police vehicles from the city and surrounding suburbs rushed to the area and poured water on the flames from the nearly unrecognizable wreckage of the shattered DC-10.

Late this afternoon, ambulances began removing bodies of the victims to a temporary morgue set up in an aircraft hangar. By 11 P.M., 250 bodies had been removed from the wreckage, and Douglas Dreifus, a Federal investigator, said the rest would not be removed before daylight.

Worst Previous U.S. Crash

The worst previous air disaster in the United States occurred last September, when 144 persons died in the collision of a jetliner and a small private plane over San Diego.

William Nickerson, 52 years old, of Elk Grove Village, where the plane crashed, said he saw the DC-10 take off with the left engine smoking. Almost immediately, he said, the engine fell from the plane and the massive jet lost altitude and crashed, sending flames shooting 125 feet into the air.

Danny Niemann, 25, an employee of a

Continued on Page 7, Column 1

ISRAEL LOWERS FLAG, GIVES TOWN IN SINAI BACK TO EGYPTIANS

Inhabitants of El Arish, Conquered in 1967, Cheer, Weep and Jeer at Withdrawal Ceremony

By CHRISTOPHER S. WREN

Special to The New York Times

EL ARISH, Egypt, May 25 — Egyptians cheered, prayed and wept as this town, capital of the Sinai Peninsula, was handed back to Egypt today, after 12 years under Israeli occupation.

The dusty coastal town, separated from the Mediterranean by groves of stately palms amid dunes, became the first still-inhabited Arab town conquered in the 1967 war to be relinquished.

The pullout marked the beginning of Israel's promised withdrawal from Sinai under the peace treaty signed with Egypt March 26 in Washington.

The return of El Arish and a coastal strip westward is the first step of a process that will return to Egypt nearly three-fourths of Sinai within nine months. Israel has agreed to withdraw within three years from the remainder of Sinai, to the border that prevailed before the 1967 war.

Two Sides Meet at Beersheba

As the transfer took place, Egyptian and Israeli negotiators met at Beersheba to begin negotations on a solution to the question of autonomy for Palestinians of the West Bank and Gaza. Secretary of State Cyrus R. Vance, who attended, urged both sides, whose positions were far apart, to show "maximum restraint and farsightedness." [Page 3.]

The turnover ceremony was held in the asphalt parking lot of a former Israeli Army canteen and rest stop a mile and a half east of town. More elaborate festivities are planned tomorrow when President Anwar el-Sadat comes to El Arish.

Egyptians Whistle and Chant

As the blue and white Israeli flag was lowered to bugle accompaniment today, more than a thousand residents watching from across a road began to clap, whistle and chant.

Hundreds of young men ran toward the barbed wire of the compound where the half-hour ceremony was taking place. Armed Israeli troops in combat gear chased them back in jeeps. Four armored half-tracks sent to assist the soldiers sent up plumes of dust.

When the red, white and black Egyptian flag was run up the pole, the nearly hysterical spectators cheered wildly and surged forth again amid cries in Arabic: "God is great!" and "Long live Egypt!"

There was scuffling between some Egyptians and Israeli soldiers, who seemed unprepared for the outburst. Although the scene briefly turned ugly, violence was averted as Egyptian military policemen rushed in to calm the people.

When the Israelis got into their trucks and jeeps and began driving to their new lines a few miles east of town, some

Continued on Page 4, Column 1

FLORIDA EXECUTES KILLER AS PLEA FAILS

Spenkelink, Electrocuted, Is First to Die Since Gilmore in 1977

By WAYNE KING

Special to The New York Times

STARKE, Fla., May 25 — The state of Florida trussed John Arthur Spenkelink immobile in the electric chair this morning, dropped a black leather mask over his face and electrocuted him.

"He simply looked at us and he looked terrified," said Kris Rebillot, a reporter who was one of 32 persons who watched through a window from an adjoining room. "It was just a wide, wide, wide stare."

The execution was carried out a few hours after the last plea in an extended legal battle. It was the first execution in the United States since Gary Mark Gilmore faced a Utah firing squad voluntarily on Jan. 19, 1977, and the first since 1967 in which the condemned person was put to death against his will.

No Final Statement — His Wish

Mr. Spenkelink made no final statement. The prison authorities said that had been his wish.

The prisoner was given three surges of electricity. The first, 2,500 volts, was administered at 10:12 A.M. Mr. Spenkelink jerked in the chair and one hand clenched into a fist.

Then came the second, and the third, by two executioners in black hoods. A doctor stepped forward after the third surge, pulled up the prisoner's T-shirt

Continued on Page 6, Column 2

Flattened Debris and 'Bodies All Over'

By WILLIAM ROBBINS

Special to The New York Times

CHICAGO, May 25 — "The plane just lost power and slowly rolled over on its side," George Owens, a witness to the worst domestic air crash in history, said today shortly after the fiery disaster at O'Hare International Airport here.

Then, he said, he "saw a huge fireball."

Hours after the crash of American Airlines Flight 191, which had just taken off for Los Angeles, smoke was still pouring from the wreckage, which was too hot for removal of many of the bodies of the victims. Red and yellow stakes marked the few charred bodies that firemen could reach. It was nearly 6 P.M. before the first bodies were moved to a nearby hangar.

One of the first physicians to arrive at the scene was Dr. Robert Loguerssio. "There were bodies all over," he said. "There were a lot of corpses on the scene. Obviously there was nothing I could do. Obviously there were no live injuries."

Helplessly, the police and firemen could only mill around the scene, keeping onlookers back and out of possible danger.

Wreckage Carried Off

But immediately after the crash, and before the police could cordon off the site, some small boys arrived and began to carry off bits of wreckage. One was seen walking off with what looked like a fan belt in his hand.

The wreckage of the plane was spread over part of a small abandoned airport, one of the few open areas in the populated region surrounding O'Hare. It ignited three mobile homes situated in a neatly landscaped park at the edge of the field.

A resident of one of the mobile homes, Marie Nikopoulos, had been stretched out on a couch, watching television, when she heard a "big bang."

"It threw me off the couch," she said, "and the force knocked dishes off the shelves and my chandelier fell. I ran and opened the front door and saw part of the plane burning in the street. Thick black smoke filled the neighborhood and turned it pitch black. You couldn't see a foot in front of you."

Residents Ordered Out

Soon officials arrived and ordered the residents out for fear the fires might spread.

One witness, Winnann Johnson, saw what was later determined to have been an engine fall from the wing.

"I saw this silver cylinder thing fall from the plane onto the runway," she said. "It burst into flames and then smothered real quickly."

Larry Roderick saw the flight from about the same vantage point. "The left engine was smoking badly on takeoff," he said. "Then there seemed to be an explosion. There was a burst of flame and the engine fell. The plane appeared to make a steep climb. Then it swung over to the left and plunged to the ground."

President, Angered Over Setbacks, Urges Leadership From Democrats

By TERENCE SMITH

Special to The New York Times

WASHINGTON, May 25 — President Carter, stung by a series of defeats on Capitol Hill, lashed out today at the "demagoguery and political timidity" that he said had made the American people doubt the courage and effectiveness of their political leaders.

Displaying more passion and anger than he normally allows himself on a public forum, the President lectured about 200 members of the Democratic National Committee at their spring meeting here on the need for Congress and the party to confront the difficult choices that face the nation on energy and the economy.

"The American people are looking to us for honest answers and clear leadership," Mr. Carter said. "What they see is a Government which seems incapable of action at all."

In a long answer to a question from the floor, the President also all but declared his candidacy for re-election.

"I haven't made my announcement of

Excerpts from Carter remarks, page 8.

what I'm going to do in 1980," he said, "but I have never backed down from a fight, and I have never been afraid of public opinion polls. And if and when I decide to run, it will be in every precinct in this country, no matter who else ran, and I have no doubt it will be successful."

Mr. Carter also had some thinly veiled criticism for Senator Edward M. Kennedy and the five Democratic Representatives who announced their opposition to the President's re-election earlier this week. "Press conferences will not solve the serious problems we face in energy, in inflation, in maintaining peace in a troubled world," Mr. Carter said.

At a news conference on Monday, Representatives Edward P. Beard of Rhode Island, John Conyers Jr. of Michigan, Richard M. Nolan of Minnesota, Richard L. Ottinger of Westchester and Fortney H. Stark of California announced that they were organizing a campaign to dump Mr. Carter from the Democratic ticket and replace him with Senator Kennedy, who has criticized the President's domestic policies at several meetings with the press in the last fortnight.

Mr. Carter's tone ranged from anger to

Continued on Page 8, Column 5

Gas Lines Touch Off Arguments; Price Hits a Record in Manhattan

By ALAN RICHMAN

Gasoline shortages caused arguments at service stations on Long Island yesterday and forced the posting of police officers to direct a line of waiting motorists in Manhattan. Meanwhile, prices rose to record levels — 56.5 cents a half-gallon at a Getty station in lower Manhattan.

The frantic activity was expected to end soon, because many stations indicated they would run out of gas before Monday night, the end of the Memorial Day weekend.

"My particular situation is that the company is running a day behind in deliveries," said Tim Sullivan, owner of a Sunoco Station at the corner of 220th Street and Horace Harding Boulevard in Bayside, Queens. Mr. Sullivan, who usually sells 1,800 gallons a day, received a 3,000-gallon delivery yesterday morning and sold out by 3:30 yesterday afternoon.

At a Hess station in Manhattan offering regular gasoline for 82.9 cents a gallon, automobiles were lined up from the entrance on 10th Avenue down 44th Street to the corner of 11th Avenue.

Arguments started not only between drivers waiting in line and those pulling in front of the line, but also between drivers waiting in line and those attempting to leave the station. Finally, the Midtown North police precinct dispatched two officers, who spent the rest of the day asking "Leaded or unleaded?" and directing cars to appropriate pumps.

Mostly a Battle of Words

"There's been nothing worse than verbal altercations with some bumping into one another," explained Officer Tony Graffeo, who ordinarily drives a patrol car. "We call that a West Side conversation. Anything short of shooting on the West Side is a friendly discussion."

On Long Island, fist fights started at several stations and Matthew Troy, executive director of the Long Island Gasoline Retailers Association, warned that association members might close for the weekend if drivers did not "behave themselves."

Mr. Troy reported, as of midafternoon yesterday, 50 incidents of verbal abuse by motorists against gas station owners and

Continued on Page 22, Column 5

Associated Press

The Israeli flag being lowered and the Egyptian flag being raised yesterday in the Sinai town of El Arish

INSIDE

Inflation in Double Digits Again

The Consumer Price Index rose 1.1 percent in April, making for an annual rate of 13.9 percent. April prices were up 10.4 percent from 1978. Page 38.

E.P.A. Rules on Coal Burning

The Environmental Protection Agency introduced rules on coal emissions by power plants that will please neither industry nor environmentalists. Page 6.

An Ayatollah Shot in Teheran

An Iranian religious figure believed to be a member of the secret, ruling Revolutionary Council was shot and wounded near his home. Page 2.

Spanish Army Officers Killed

A lieutenant general in the Spanish Army, two colonels and their driver were killed by Basque terrorists who ambushed their car in Madrid. Page 5.

"All the News That's Fit to Print"

The New York Times

LATE CITY EDITION

Weather: Chance of drizzle today and tonight. Partly cloudy tomorrow. Temperature range: today 51-63; yesterday 59-68. Details, page D24.

VOL.CXXXI . . No. 45,094 | NEW YORK, WEDNESDAY, OCTOBER 7, 1981 | 25 CENTS

20 cents beyond 50-mile zone from New York City. Higher in air delivery cities.

SADAT ASSASSINATED AT ARMY PARADE AS MEN AMID RANKS FIRE INTO STANDS; VICE PRESIDENT AFFIRMS 'ALL TREATIES'

Israel Stunned and Anxious; Few Arab Nations Mourning

Worry in Jerusalem

By DAVID K. SHIPLER

Special to The New York Times

JERUSALEM, Oct. 6 — Israel, which had such a high stake in the survival of President Anwar el-Sadat, reacted with stunned anxiety today to news of his assassination in Cairo.

A fear for the peace treaty between Egypt and Israel dominated all emotions. So thoroughly had the Egyptian leader come to personify that peace, and so deeply had Israelis distrusted the motives of other Egyptians, that his death today swept away confidence as swiftly as his historic visit to Jerusalem in 1977 had brought hope.

"The very fact that one bullet can cancel an agreement," said Geula Cohen, who heads the Tehiya Party in Parliament, "is a sign that not only the withdrawal, but all these procedures, must be stopped. There is no doubt that this incident confirms all that we have been saying; there is no stability in this region and one cannot make an agreement which is dependent on a nondemocratic regime and one man."

Question About Treaty

Even in the likelihood that Mr. Sadat's successor will adhere to the treaty's precepts, serious questions are bound to linger for some time, and the Government of Prime Minister Menachem Begin is certain to face rising political difficulties domestically in completing the return of Sinai to Egypt, scheduled for April 1982.

This afternoon, voices on the right were raised in demands that all prepa-

Continued on Page A9, Column 5

Jubilation in Beirut

By JOHN KIFNER

Special to The New York Times

BEIRUT, Lebanon, Oct. 6 — There was no mourning in most of the Arab world today for President Anwar el-Sadat of Egypt, whose separate peace with Israel had led to his isolation.

Public jubilation was reported in Syria, Iraq and Libya, and the streets of mostly Moslem, leftist-dominated West Beirut echoed with gunfire in celebration of the assassination. Most public statements attributed Mr. Sadat's death to discontent with the Egyptian-Israeli peace accord.

However, the Sudan, Egypt's closest friend in the Arab world, condemned the assassination and said it stood with the Egyptian Government against all forms of conspiracy and aggression.

Hope for Arab Unity Expressed

There was little public comment in Saudi Arabia. At the United Nations, Gaafar M. Allagany, the acting head of the Saudi mission, expressed sorrow "that this had to happen at a crucial stage." Noting Saudi opposition to Mr. Sadat's policies, he said, "We hope that our sister country will rejoin the Arab states."

An aide to Yasir Arafat, the leader of the Palestine Liberation Organization, said here on hearing of the shooting of Mr. Sadat, "We shake the hand that fired the bullets."

The aide, Saleh Khalef, better known by the code name Abu Iyad, said that "all attempts at dialogue" with Mr. Sadat had failed and that "it was inevi-

Continued on Page A9, Column 1

Associated Press

As President Sadat watched parade with Vice President Hosni Mubarak, left, and Defense Minister Abu Ghazala . . .

CBS News

. . . uniformed men, apparently part of the assassination team, approached the reviewing stand. Moments later, . . .

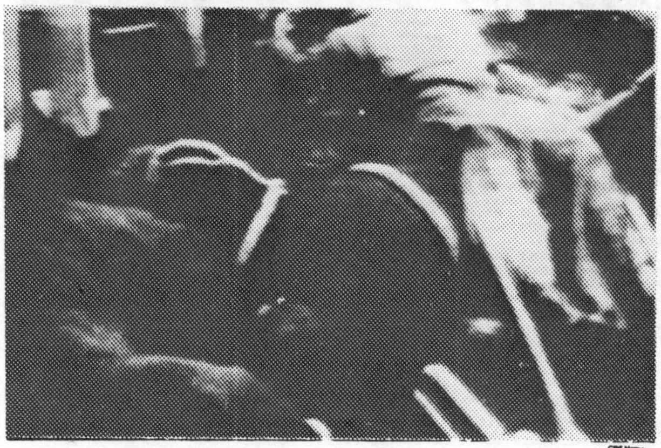

CBS News

. . . after the attack, victims lay sprawled on the floor of the stand.

AT LEAST 8 KILLED

Speaker of Parliament Is Interim President — Election in 60 Days

By WILLIAM E. FARRELL

Special to The New York Times

CAIRO, Oct. 6 — President Anwar el-Sadat of Egypt was shot and killed today by a group of men in military uniforms who hurled hand grenades and fired rifles at him as he watched a military parade commemorating the 1973 war against Israel.

Vice President Hosni Mubarak, in announcing Mr. Sadat's death, said

Mubarak speech excerpted, page A9.

Egypt's treaties and international commitments would be respected. He said the Speaker of Parliament, Sufi Abu Taleb, would serve as interim President pending an election in 60 days.

The assassins' bullets ended the life of a man who earned a reputation for making bold decisions in foreign affairs, a reputation based in large part on his decision in 1977 to journey to the camp of Egypt's foe, Israel, to make peace.

Sadat Forged His Own Regime

Regarded as an interim ruler when he came to power in 1970 on the death of Gamal Abdel Nasser, Mr. Sadat forged his own regime and ran Egypt singlehandedly. He was bent on moving this impoverished country into the late 20th century, a drive that led him to abandon an alliance with the Soviet Union and embrace the West.

That rule ended abruptly and violently today. As jet fighters roared overhead, the killers sprayed the reviewing

Of humble origin, Anwar el-Sadat became a statesman known for daring actions. Obituary, pages A8 and A9.

stand with bullets while thousands of horrified people — officials, diplomats and journalists, including this correspondent — looked on.

Killers' Identity Not Disclosed

Information gathered from a number of sources indicated that eight persons had been killed and 27 wounded in the attack. Later reports, all unconfirmed, put the toll at 11 dead and 38 wounded.

The authorities did not disclose the identity of the assassins. They were being interrogated, and there were no clear indications whether the attack was to have been part of a coup attempt.

[In Washington, American officials said an army major, a lieutenant and four enlisted men had been involved in the attack. The major and two of the soldiers were killed and the others captured, the officials said.]

The assassination followed a recent crackdown by Mr. Sadat against religious extremists and other political op-

Continued on Page A8, Column 1

Egypt After Sadat

Washington's Policies Facing New Problems

By BERNARD GWERTZMAN

Special to The New York Times

WASHINGTON, Oct. 6 — The assassination of President Anwar el-Sadat of Egypt created a new series of problems for future American policy in the Middle East at a time when the Reagan Administration was already worried about the spread of disorder in the region.

Administration officials, concerned about the chaos in Lebanon, the increased subversive activity of Libya and the Soviet inroads in Afghanistan, Southern Yemen and Ethiopia, had viewed Mr. Sadat as a solid, pro-American anchor of stability in the Middle East. With his death, there is now apprehension about the situation in Egypt as well.

At the White House, President Reagan said the United States had lost "a close friend" and "a champion of peace." But the Administration refrained from any public assessment of the possible repercussions of the assassination. [Page A12.]

The mood in Washington was one of shock and sadness at the loss of a leader who had done what would have seemed impossible a decade ago. He replaced the Prime Minister of Israel as the favorite Middle East statesman in Washington.

On virtually every Middle East, African and world issue, the Reagan Administration and Mr. Sadat saw eye to eye. With the expectation that Mr. Sadat would be in control of Egypt's policies

Continued on Page A9, Column 2

Cairo Regime's Plans Now Question Marks

The following article is by William E. Farrell, who has reported on Anwar el-Sadat's diplomacy from Jerusalem as well as Cairo.

Special to The New York Times

News Analysis

CAIRO, Oct. 6 — Anwar el-Sadat's rule in Egypt was that of one man who skillfully engineered, in his 11 years in power, the means of controlling every important facet of Egyptian life.

Although he was dismissed by many as a somewhat feckless interim leader when he became President after the death of Gamal Abdel Nasser, Mr. Sadat gradually showed that he had staying power, political skill and an ability that transformed him into a world statesman when he paid his historic visit to Jerusalem in the search for peace.

Now, with his sudden, violent death, many questions about the future of Egypt and its role in the world are beginning to be raised in this saddened capital and in many other countries.

Over the years, Mr. Sadat controlled his political party, the National Democratic Party; he supervised the Egyptian press, which lauded him; he was commander of the military, a key factor in his rule, and he had a facility for taking the pulse of Egypt's masses — about 43 million people. Some 67 percent of them are illiterate, but he was able to reach them by television and radio. He often did, in long speeches that had a pedagogical tone.

Some Egyptians opposed Mr. Sadat,

Continued on Page A8, Column 5

Other News

'Safety Net' Bill Passes

The House of Representatives approved spending $87.3 billion for social programs, despite President Reagan's threat to veto the bill. Page B10.

Ulster Prison Rule Is Eased

Britain gave inmates in Northern Ireland the right to wear their own clothing but stopped short of meeting the hunger strikers' demands. Page A3.

Runoff Due in Atlanta

Andrew Young, the former diplomat, and a State Representative, Sidney Marcus, won places in a mayoral runoff in Atlanta. Page A20.

Lindbergh Papers Unsealed

Evidence in the kidnapping-murder of the infant son of Charles A. Lindbergh 49 years ago will be opened to review by scholars and others. Page B1.

About New Yrok	B3	Music	C21-22
Around Nation	A20	Notes on People	B8
Books	C25	Obituaries	D23
Bridge	C24	Op-Ed	A27
Business Day	D1-22	Real Estate	D21
Crossword	C25	Shipping	D24
Editorials	A26	Sports	B14-19
Going Out Guide	C30	Theaters	C19-C24
Letters	A26	TV / Radio	C27-28
Living Section	C1-20	Weather	D24
Movies	C25-26	Washington Talk	A24

News Summary and Index, Page B1

Classified Ads	B19-27	Auto Exchange	D24-27

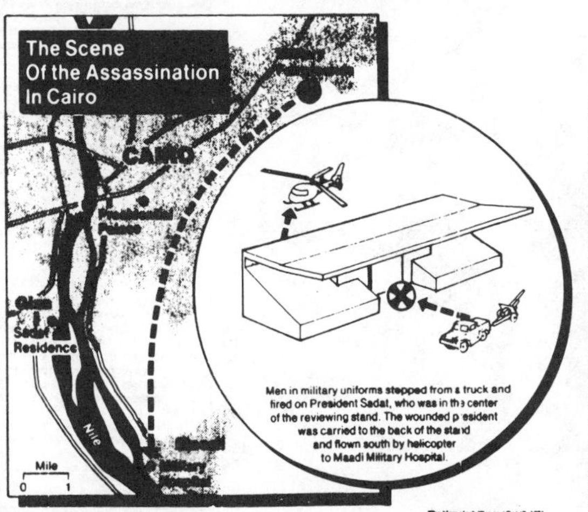
The Scene
Of the Assassination
In Cairo
CAIRO
Sadat Residence
Nile
Mile
0
1
Men in military uniforms stepped from a truck and fired on President Sadat, who was in the center of the reviewing stand. The wounded president was carried to the back of the stand and flown south by helicopter to Maadi Military Hospital.

The New York Times / Oct. 7, 1981

Who Murdered President Sadat?

In the confusion swirling around the assassination of Egypt's President, Anwar el-Sadat, little information was made public in Cairo about the killers. Egyptian authorities were known to have several uniformed men in custody last night, but the Egyptians gave no details about the number or identity of the attackers or the reasons for the attack.

"Islamic fundamentalists" within the Egyptian Army was the characterization offered by Secretary of State Alexander M. Haig Jr. to a group of senators late yesterday afternoon. He also mentioned discontent among some Egyptian officers with the peace treaty that Mr. Sadat signed with Israel.

Reagan Administration officials said their information was that six uniformed men had taken part in the shooting, that three were killed and that the others were captured. They said that at least one was linked to the Takfir Wahigra Society, a radical right-wing Islamic group whose name translates as Repentance and Atonement. Its past actions include the slaying of the Egyptian Minister of Religious Affairs in 1977.

In Beirut, a handful of organizations stepped forward to claim responsibility for the killing, with representatives calling news agencies with their statements. But Reagan Administration officials said they doubted that any of them had been involved in the killing. Details are on page A12.

"All the News That's Fit to Print"

The New York Times

Late Edition
Weather: Rain ending today, mostly cloudy and cool; cloudy and cooler tonight. Partly cloudy and mild tomorrow. Temperatures: today 61-66, tonight 54-56; yesterday 55-60. Details, page B10.

VOL.CXXXI . . No. 45,337

NEW YORK, MONDAY, JUNE 7, 1982 — 30 CENTS

BIG ISRAELI FORCE INVADES SOUTH LEBANON; SHARP FIGHTING WITH GUERRILLAS REPORTED

Limited Summit Agreement Set on Trade and Currency

By RICHARD EDER
Special to The New York Times

VERSAILLES, France, June 6 — The eighth summit conference of the industrialized nations reached limited agreement today on two contentious subjects — East-West trade and the handling of currency fluctuations — and produced something of a breakthrough on North-South relations.

The agreements themselves were the subject of some disagreement: whether they bridged or merely papered over fundamental differences. Prime Minister Margaret Thatcher of Britain described the atmosphere as one of unanimity. Prime Minister Pierre Elliott Trudeau of Canada called it "difficult."

The conference was, in any case, shaded and sometimes interrupted by the fighting in the Falklands and Israel's invasion of Lebanon. Today's final hard bargaining on East-West trade was interrupted by the announcement by President François Mitterrand of France of the Israeli move, and the assembled leaders approved a statement expressing shock.

The accord fell short of American hopes and was seen as having little world impact. News analysis and economic analysis, with text of the communiqué, page D6.

Associated Press
President Reagan at economic meeting yesterday in Versailles.

The Falkland crisis, apart from producing an embarrassing flip-flop over the United States vote in the Security Council, caused Mrs. Thatcher to fly back to London tonight after the state dinner in the Versailles chateau's Hall of Mirrors.

She thus missed the musical masque and ballet and other festivities organized by France to make this the most glittering summit conference, whether or not it will have turned out to be the most productive.

The seven nations — the United States, Japan, Britain, France, West Germany, Italy and Canada — agreed to a compromise on the East-West trade issue. It fell short of American hopes for abolition of government-subsidized financing for such trade. Instead, it calls for "caution" in financial dealings with the Soviet bloc, and it says there is a need for "commercial prudence in limiting export credits."

The Reagan Administration had

Continued on Page D7, Column

United Press International
An armored personnel carrier, part of the Israeli invasion force, breaks through the border with southern Lebanon.

THOUSANDS ATTACK

Some Syrian Units in Area Said to Have Clashed With Raiding Force

By THOMAS L. FRIEDMAN
Special to The New York Times

BEIRUT, Lebanon, Monday, June 7 — The Israeli Army invaded southern Lebanon by land, sea and air Sunday in an attack aimed at destroying the main military bases of the Palestine Liberation Organization.

More than 250 Israeli tanks and armored personnel carriers, as well as thousands of infantrymen, rolled past the observation posts of the United Nations peacekeeping troops in southern Lebanon at 11 A.M. (5 A.M., New York time) and fanned out across the frontier, according to a United Nations spokesman in Beirut.

By late Sunday evening the Israelis had taken several P.L.O. outposts in the craggy hills of southern Lebanon and were engaged in fierce firefights with the Palestinians for control of scores of other strongholds along the 33-mile front, stretching from the port city of Tyre to the foothills of Mount Hermon, the United Nations spokesman said.

Main Targets Besieged

In the first day of the invasion the Israelis besieged all their main targets — Tyre, Beaufort Castle, Nabatiye and Kawkaba — but the Palestinians stood their ground and did not flee north. The number of casualties was not known.

Israel said this morning that Beaufort Castle, a Crusader stronghold overlooking the border that the Palestinians have used as a communications and artillery base, was captured during the night by an Israeli infantry battalion. But the Palestinians denied that the castle had fallen.

It appeared that at least a few elements of Syria's force of about 25,000 men in Lebanon had become involved in confrontations with the Israelis.

The state-run Beirut radio reported Sunday night that Syrian artillery north of Hasbeya was exchanging fire with the Israelis on the eastern route of their advance. This could not be confirmed. In Damascus, a Syrian military spokesman said Israeli forces had come into contact with Syrian troops in three places, but it was not clear whether fighting had occurred. [Page A12.]

The Israel radio broadcast a state-

Continued on Page A12, Column 1

U.N. COUNCIL ASKS ISRAELI PULLBACK

But Delegate, Hinting Refusal, Notes 'Limit of Endurance'

By BERNARD D. NOSSITER
Special to The New York Times

UNITED NATIONS, N.Y., June 6 — The Security Council unanimously demanded tonight that Israel pull its invading forces out of Lebanon. There was, however, no indication that Israel would pay any more attention to this order than to the unanimous Council demand Saturday night for a cease-fire.

Instead, Yehuda Z. Blum, the Israeli delegate, taunted the Council's 15 members for "evincing not the slightest interest" in scores of terrorist acts he attributed to the Palestine Liberation Organization. "How many Israelis have to be killed by terrorists for this Council to be persuaded that the limits of our endurance have been reached?" he asked rhetorically. "Israel cannot expect this body even to deplore P.L.O. barbarism against Israel's civilian population, let alone take any steps with a view towards curbing that barbarism."

Leaders of the major industrial democracies expressed shock at Versailles over Israel's move. Page A14.

Tonight's text, a compromise drafted by Ireland after a day of discussion behind closed doors, directed Israel to withdraw its forces "forthwith and unconditionally." The Soviet Union insisted on that last phrase.

At the demand of the United States, the resolution calls on Israel and the Palestinians to halt all military action "within Lebanon and across the Lebanese-Israeli border." That language was designed to cover P.L.O. shelling into Israel as well as Israeli strikes. The document directs both sides to report

Continued on Page A14, Column 5

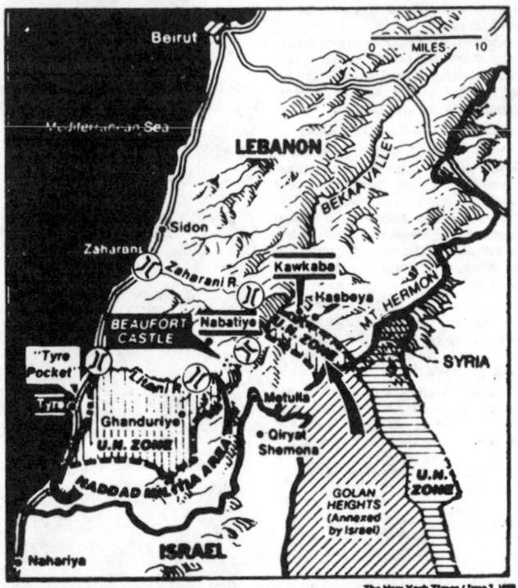

The New York Times / June 7, 1982
Israeli tanks and troops moved into Lebanon in three columns (arrows). The land assaults, together with air and sea attacks, were aimed at the main Palestinian strongholds — Tyre, Beaufort Castle, Nabatiye and Kawkaba. Warships destroyed the Qasmiye Bridge spanning the Litani River north of Tyre, cutting the main Palestinian supply line. Towns shown in northern Israel were among those shelled last week by Palestinian forces.

Britain Confirms the Landing Of 3,000 Soldiers From QE2

By R.W. APPLE Jr.
Special to The New York Times

LONDON, June 6 — British troops besieging the Argentine garrison at Stanley in the Falkland Islands have been reinforced by 3,000 fresh infantrymen from the liner Queen Elizabeth 2, the Defense Ministry announced tonight.

The arrival of the Fifth Infantry Brigade, including a battalion each of Scots and Welsh Guards and Gurkha Rifles, raises British strength on East Falkland Island to about 8,000. About 5,000 paratroops and Royal Marine commandos went ashore last month, and most are drawn up opposite the 7,000 Argentine defenders of Stanley, the Falklands capital.

In Buenos Aires today, Argentina said its planes and artillery had bombarded the British positions surrounding Stanley. Senior military officers said they expected the British to launch a major assault on the Argentine garrison at any moment. [Page A6.]

There were hints in London that the long-awaited assault on Stanley had already begun in a report from Michael Nicholson of Britain's Independent Television News.

"The British push is really on," he said in a broadcast this evening. "There are under way at this moment operations which I can only describe as extraordinarily daring which cannot be revealed until they are completed, but which, almost certainly if they are successful, will surely bring the end of this war that much closer."

Mr. Nicholson reported that the Gurkhas, composed entirely of Nepalese volunteers, were operating on their own, "crisscrossing East Falkland" in a search for Argentine units lurking in the interior, between the British base at San Carlos Bay and their forward headquarters near Mount Kent.

According to unofficial sources, the Fifth Brigade transferred from the Queen Elizabeth to the assault ships In-

Continued on Page A8, Column 3

Why Israelis Invaded Now

Heavy P.L.O. Shelling Said to Tip the Scale

The following dispatch has been subjected to military censorship.

By DAVID K. SHIPLER
Special to The New York Times

JERUSALEM, June 6 — Israel's invasion of Lebanon came today as the culmination of months of military and political calculation in which Prime Minister Menachem Begin repeatedly allowed the troops to be massed and the saber to be rattled, only to pull back at what seemed like the last moment.

News Analysis

Until today the crucial factors favoring a major assault never quite lined up, and the risks seemed greater than the potential benefits.

This time, however, Mr. Begin decided to make the military gamble and to pay the political costs that he and his advisers know exist. The crucial reason was the intensive shelling of northern Israel by forces of the Palestine Liberation Organization, which began Friday afternoon after Israeli air strikes on Palestinian bases near Beirut.

P.L.O. Has Become an Army

The Israeli command described the air raids as retaliation for the shooting Thursday of Israel's Ambassador to Britain, Shlomo Argov, who was critically wounded in London. Five suspects, all traveling on passports from Arab countries, were captured. The P.L.O. denied any responsibility for the attack.

The Palestinian shelling, with artillery and rocket launchers, was the most severe ever directed against Israeli towns and kibbutzim by the P.L.O.,

Continued on Page A13, Column 1

Begin Orders Israelis to Push Palestinians 25 Miles to North

The following dispatch has been subjected to military censorship.

Special to The New York Times

JERUSALEM, Monday, June 7 — Prime Minister Menachem Begin said Sunday that the Israeli Army had been ordered to push the Palestinian forces northward to a distance of 25 miles from the Israeli border, to place their artillery beyond the range of Israeli territory.

Mr. Begin made his statement in a letter to President Reagan, excerpts of which were reported on the Israeli radio. The Cabinet, after an emergency session, issued a statement saying Israel would not attack any Syrian forces in Lebanon or Syria unless the Syrians engaged the Israelis.

The Damascus radio said the Syrian Army was battling the Israelis near Hasbeya, 10 miles north of the border. The Israeli military spokesman said there had been no verification that any such clashes with the Syrians had occurred.

Reagan Urged Restraint

Mr. Begin's letter to President Reagan, disclosing the orders to the army to push the Palestine Liberation Organizaton 25 miles north of the border, came after the President sent a letter to the Israeli leader. That letter, delivered Sunday morning, requested Israeli restraint.

In his reply, as reported by the Israeli radio, Mr. Begin said that "the terrorists aim their weapons only at the civilian population." He went on: "The aim of the enemy is to kill Jews, men, women and children. Is there any people in the world that would accept such a situation?"

The invasion operation, called "Peace for Galilee," would not be aimed at acquiring any Lebanese territory and was not being undertaken against Lebanon, according to Mr. Begin's letter. It was begun after months of sporadic terrorist attacks on Israelis here and abroad, attacks that Israel regarded as violations of the cease-fire that had been negotiated across the Lebanese-Israeli border last July.

As Israeli armored columns swept through the lines of the United Nations peacekeeping forces, a United Nations spokesman in Jerusalem reported, several United Nations units were caught in crossfire. By Sunday evening, one

Continued on Page A12, Column 3

Floods Rampage in Connecticut; 8 Believed Dead

By ROBERT D. McFADDEN

Torrential weekend rains and overflowing rivers swamped wide areas of Connecticut yesterday with the state's worst floods in decades.

The state police said that eight persons were dead or missing in the storm. More than 1,300 others were removed from their homes as floodwaters invaded residential areas, washed out roads and earthen dams and disrupted electric and telephone service and public transportation for tens of thousands of residents.

The floods, accompanied by 5 to 8 inches of pounding rain, struck a wide swath of the state, from Westport and other Fairfield County communities on the west to Waterford and New London on the east. At least 38,000 homes were hit by power blackouts, and 6,000 telephones were knocked out.

Nearly all trains in the state, including those operated by Amtrak between New York and Boston, were halted as Conrail and Amtrak used buses to carry passengers. Commuters and long-distance travelers were expected to face further delays today. Many communities in flooded areas canceled school for today.

The rest of the New York metropolitan area was relatively unscathed. But on eastern Long Island, up to 9.79 inches of rain also triggered heavy weekend flooding. Many traffic accidents were reported, and a stretch of Long Island

Continued on Page B4, Column 1

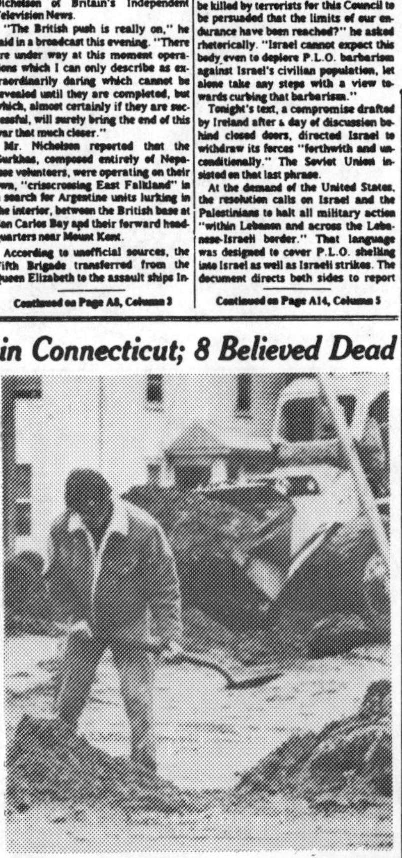

The New York Times / Alan Decker
Matthew Giurintano clearing a storm drain yesterday in Higganum, Conn.

INSIDE

Defeat for Schmidt's Party
The Social Democrats were defeated in state elections in Hamburg in what was considered a direct blow to Chancellor Helmut Schmidt. Page A9.

'Nine,' 'Nickleby' Win Tonys
"Nine," based on "8½," won the Tony award for musicals. The Royal Shakespeare Company's "Nicholas Nickleby" won for plays. Page C11.

Around Nation	A16	Obituaries	D11
Books	C20	Op-Ed	A19
Bridge	C20	Shipping	B9
Business Day	D1-10	Society	B10
Crossword	C20	SportsMonday	C1-10
Dance	C11,C14	Style	B11
Day by Day	B1	Theaters	C11
Editorials	A18	TV / Radio	C19-20
Going Out Guide	C13	U.N. Events	A2
Movies	C11-14	Washington Talk	B6
Music	C12,C14,C20	Weather	B10

News Summary and Index, Page B1

Classified Ads	C14-18	Auto Exchange	C8

"All the News That's Fit to Print"

The New York Times

Late Edition
Weather: Considerable sunshine early today, becoming cloudy by afternoon. Chance of rain tonight and tomorrow. Temperatures: today 77-81, tonight 55-60; yesterday 58-81. Details on page B20.

VOL.CXXXI . . No. 45,340 Copyright © 1982 The New York Times —NEW YORK, THURSDAY, JUNE 10, 1982— 30 CENTS

ISRAEL REPORTS ITS AIR FORCE HAS WRECKED SYRIA'S ANTIAIRCRAFT MISSILES IN LEBANON

U.S. EASES POSITION ON RACIAL BALANCE OF CITY'S TEACHERS

Bell Bars Any Punitive Action Pending Study of Whether New York Follows Law

By JANE PERLEZ
Special to The New York Times

WASHINGTON, June 9 — The Federal Department of Education backed away today from its finding that the New York City Board of Education had failed to comply with an agreement to improve the racial balance of teachers in the city's public schools.

The Secretary of Education, T. H. Bell, promised to review the board's efforts to meet the goals of a 1977 agreement that requires the board to increase the number of minority teachers in predominantly white schools and the number of white teachers in schools attended mostly by minorities.

He also said he would review the legal grounds on which the city contends it complies with the agreement and with the Civil Rights Act of 1964.

Senator Alfonse M. D'Amato, Republican of New York, outlined the department's change of position at a news conference here after a lengthy meeting with Mr. Bell. The Secretary declined to attend the news conference or to comment on the meeting.

Mandatory Transfer Threat

Last week the Department of Education's Office for Civil Rights said that if the Board of Education could not meet the goals of the 1977 agreement by voluntary measures, the mandatory transfer of teachers would be required.

The department also indicated that the city could face the loss of $300 million a year in Federal education funds.

Mr. D'Amato said that the Secretary had indicated today that there would be "no threat of cutoff of funds until this is fully reviewed."

Discussing this threat and also that of mandatory teacher transfers, the Senator said: "This is not what the Reagan Administration is about or what I cam-

Continued on Page B6, Column 1

Reagan Suggests Limit on Troops For 2 Alliances

Expresses Sympathy for Goal of Arms Protests

By HEDRICK SMITH
Special to The New York Times

BONN, June 9 — President Reagan, expressing sympathy with the goal of the European antinuclear movement but differing with its tactics, urged today that East and West agree to a ceiling of 700,000 ground troops for each alliance as "a major step toward a safer Europe."

But with 16 leaders of the Atlantic alliance gathered here tonight, Mr. Reagan also called for the Western allies to strengthen and modernize their conventional forces as the best way of making the possibility of nuclear conflict, or any conflict, "more remote."

The formal proposal on troop ceilings, a modification of an earlier Western position at East-West talks, is to be approved by alliance leaders Thursday. The Reagan Administration considers this session especially significant for projecting alliance solidarity at a time of popular unrest and political division in Europe.

The Warmest Applause

Flying here from London on the fourth and most delicate stop of his European trip, the President drew the warmest applause when he reaffirmed American commitments to Europe's defense and specifically pledged to stand by West Germany.

To the West German Parliament he declared: "We are with you, Germany. You are not alone."

Then, indirectly addressing Moscow, he added, "Our adversaries would be foolishly mistaken should they gamble that Americans would abandon their alliance responsibilities, no matter how severe the test."

But in a carefully modulated speech that balanced firmness with sensitivity for the anxieties of hundreds of thousands of Europeans who have marched in antinuclear demonstrations, Mr. Reagan sought to calm fears that he

Continued on Page A16, Column 3

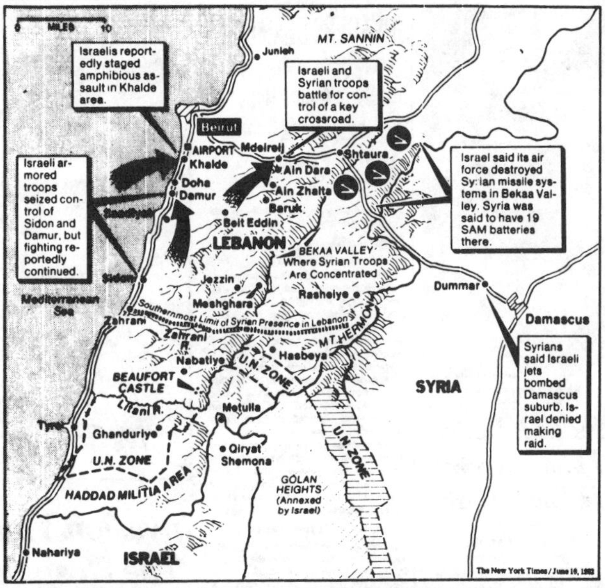

'A TURNING POINT'

22 MIG's Reported Shot Down in the Strikes — Troops Near Beirut

The following dispatch has been subjected to military censorship.

By HENRY KAMM
Special to The New York Times

JERUSALEM, June 9 — Israel said tonight that its air force destroyed the Syrian surface-to-air missile system in the Bekaa Valley of eastern Lebanon "in a concentrated strike" this afternoon. Twenty-two Syrian MIG's were reported shot down in the air battle that accompanied the raid, and seven more were said to have been hit.

Israel said all its planes returned safely. It did not disclose the number of planes involved. [Syria said 90 Israeli planes attacked the SAM batteries. It said 19 Israeli and 16 Syrian planes were shot down.]

An Israeli Army spokesman also said that there was no truth to a report by the official Syrian press agency that Israeli planes had bombed a suburb of Damascus too.

'Brilliant' and 'Complicated'

Defense Minister Ariel Sharon, in a broadcast interview, described the air strikes on the missile batteries as "one of the most brilliant, complicated and intricate operations" ever carried out by Israel.

Mr. Sharon called the raid "a turning point" in the conflict, which began on Sunday with Israeli forces crossing into Lebanon in force.

He said it would enable the Israeli ground forces to mop up quickly the Palestinian guerrillas who he said had sought safety in the valley "under Syrian cover." He said a withdrawal of Syria's ground forces had begun after the raid.

Israelis Seize Palestinian Town

Israeli forces along the Lebanese coast were reported to have seized control of the Palestinian town of Damur, eight miles south of Beirut, and military sources said some Israelis had pushed to a point about half way between Damur and the Lebanese capital.

The principal focus of the Israeli forces, however, appeared to be the Syrian strongholds east and southeast of Beirut.

An official source said tonight that a major "collision" between Israel and Syria was likely if the substantial Syrian ground force in the Bekaa Valley did not withdraw. He added that there was no certainty that such a confrontation would be limited in scope.

Reserves Are Called Up

The official said Israel had begun to bolster its troops in the Golan Heights by a calling up reserve units in preparation for any extended conflict with Syria.

He said Israeli troops were also poised near the Beirut-Damascus highway, the principal supply route for the Syrian troops in Lebanon, but they had so far refrained from moving to cut it. Such restraint may not last, he said, if

Continued on Page A18, Column 5

HAIG SEES A SHIFT IN AIMS OF ISRAEL

Secretary, in Bonn, Suggests Purpose Is to Fight Syrians

By STEVEN R. WEISMAN
Special to The New York Times

BONN, June 9 — Secretary of State Alexander M. Haig Jr., saying that the fighting in Lebanon had grown "somewhat more ominous" in the last 24 hours, suggested today that Israel might be shifting its originally announced objective in Lebanon and was now seeking to take on Syrian forces in combat.

With the Israelis continuing their advance, there were new reports "of the westward movement of Syrian armed forces," Mr. Haig said.

In addition, he reported that in the last 48 hours Syria added to the Soviet-supplied SAM-6 antiaircraft missiles deployed in Lebanon's Bekaa Valley, east of Beirut, by "a rather substantial number."

Israel's Defense Minister, Ariel Sharon, said today that some of the batteries attacked today were moved into Lebanon in the last 24 hours.

Mr. Haig said antiaircraft missiles were being increasingly used against the Israelis.

"If Syrian forces become engaged, then clearly there's a whole new character to the nature of this conflict," Mr. Haig said at a news conference as the leaders of the North Atlantic Treaty Organization opened their conference here.

Mr. Haig noted that Israe' had origi-

Continued on Page A19, Column 1

Syrians Report Major Air Battles; Say They Downed 19 Jets, Lost 16

By HENRY TANNER
Special to The New York Times

DAMASCUS, Syria, June 9 — Israeli and Syrian jets fought two large battles this afternoon over Syrian antiaircraft missile sites in eastern Lebanon, according to communiqués made public here.

A military spokesman reported that 19 Israeli fighter-bombers — F-15's and F-16's — had been shot down. He said the Syrians had lost 16 planes.

A Damascus official said later that the missiles destroyed by the Israeli attacks had "already been replaced."

Late in the evening, a Syrian communiqué said that Israeli planes had bombed a village three miles west of Damascus. Eight civilians were killed and 47 wounded, the communiqué added. Israel denied carrying out such a raid.

A Damascus official reported that Israeli and Syrian ground forces clashed for the third consecutive day as the invaders' tanks tried to push through mountains southeast of Beirut, and up the lower Bekaa Valley toward the important Beirut-Damascus highway.

One Israeli column was said to have been halted, with heavy losses, near Beit Eddein, the principal town in the mountain region, which is known as the Shouf.

Israel's attacks on the missile sites and the push toward the Beirut-Damascus highway were seen here as evidence that Israel's main objective was not, as it had announced, to protect its people from Palestinian rockets. Rather, in the Syrian view, the Israeli aim is to drive Syrian troops from Lebanon and to surround Beirut and destroy the political and military leadership of the Palestine Liberation Organization.

Western diplomats here, who felt until Tuesday that the Israeli invasion had a limited goal, said today that the scope of the invasion clearly was much bigger than they had assumed.

Syria and the Soviet Union signed a 20-year Treaty of Friendship and Cooperation in October 1980. The treaty requires, among other terms, consulta-

Continued on Page A18, Column 1

City Says: No to 'Crisis Relocation'

By LESLIE BENNETTS

The City Council yesterday rejected the Reagan Administration's proposal for the development of a plan to remove New York City residents to "host" areas upstate in the event of a nuclear attack.

In a resolution adopted by a vote of 35 to 5, the Council rejected the Administration's plan to spend $4.2 billion over seven years on what is termed "crisis relocation" planning for urban areas around the United States. The proposal has yet to be approved by Congress.

Despite public antipathy and professional skepticism, the Reagan Administration is pressing its ambitious civil defense program. Page B20.

New York is not the first community to express its disapproval; crisis relocation has been rejected by officials in Marin County, Calif.; Cambridge, Mass.; Boulder, Colo.; Alexandria, Va., and Greensboro, N.C.

The resolution, sponsored by Councilwoman Susan D. Alter, Democrat-Liberal of Brooklyn, condemned the proposal as having "little or no chance of success" and asserted that "the money to develop these plans could be better used to expand health and education services in the inner cities."

Mayor Koch also expressed his opposition to the Reagan plan, saying it would be "impossible to evacuate in any timely, acceptable way."

The resolution was specifically limited to evacuation planning in the event of nuclear attack. However, Federal officials cautioned that those funds would be difficult to extricate from a larger program because as little as 10 percent of the $4.2 billion might be used for nuclear evacuation as opposed to other disaster relief efforts.

"We're not sure whether it could be

Continued on Page B21, Column 1

ISRAELIS IN SIGHT OF CITY OF BEIRUT

Forces Establish a Beachhead Four Miles to the South

By THOMAS L. FRIEDMAN
Special to The New York Times

BEIRUT, Lebanon, June 9 — Israel's ground forces drove to within sight of Beirut today as its fighter-bombers struck heavily at Syrian surface-to-air missile batteries east of here.

An Israeli amphibious force established a bridgehead of five tanks and an undetermined number of infantrymen at Khalde, on the coastal highway four miles south of here near the Beirut International Airport. The bridgehead, which was spotted by reporters, came under machine-gun and mortar fire from Palestinians dug in on the beach and along the highway.

[Israeli planes bombed Beirut's airport Thursday, and fierce battles between Israelis and Palestinians raged along the Lebanese coast south of the capital, according to a Reuters report that quoted the Government radio. The radio said an Israeli attempt to land at the airport had been repulsed.]

Battle for a Key Crossroads

Earlier, Israeli forces pushed into the coastal towns of Sidon and Damur and fighting was said to be continuing. Lebanese Government sources said the Israelis had seized most of Sidon.

Israeli commanders reportedly sent raiding parties north from Damur along the coastal highway as far as Doha, a hillside village three miles south of the Khalde bridgehead.

East of Beirut, Syrian troops using tanks, artillery and truck-mounted Katyusha rocket launchers fought the Israelis for control of a key crossroads on the Beirut-Damascus highway, according to witnesses and the Beirut

Continued on Page A18, Column 3

Refugees in Lebanon Need Food Critically

The following dispatch has been subjected to military censorship.

By DAVID K. SHIPLER
Special to The New York Times

JERUSALEM, June 9 — United Nations observers said today that thousands of Lebanese civilians, uprooted from their homes by the Israeli advance, were in critical need of food and water.

Some supplies have been delivered by the army and the United Nations, but the situation is still serious, the observers said.

Since the Israeli invasion of Lebanon began Sunday, residents of several towns have been warned by Israeli leaflets and announcements over public address systems to gather on the beaches to avoid shelling attacks.

About 41,000 residents of the Tyre area did so, according to a United Nations bulletin, and were left there for two days without food or shelter. But there were apparently few civilian casualties, a United Nations official said; only nine civilians were reported wounded in Tyre.

The United Nations does not have fig-

Continued on Page A20, Column 1

INSIDE

F.B.I. Reports on Donovan

The F.B.I. said a Presidential aide had discouraged it from questioning Raymond J. Donovan about his possible ties to organized crime. Page B8.

British Casualties Reported

Reports from the Falkland Islands said Britain suffered heavy losses when two ships were bombed while landing additional troops. Page A22.

Associated Press

An Israeli soldier directing captured Palestinians yesterday near Tyre in southern Lebanon.

FORMER AFS PARTICIPANTS — Call AFS headquarters, New York 212-661-4550 Ext. 378.—Advt.

The Top-Ranked S.A.T. Review Course in N.Y. can raise your child's scores dramatically. 212-496-8006—ADVT.

MARION GOODMAN IS FIFTY-FIFTY-FIFTY
I could not get the airplane. Love Arnie.—ADVT.

"All the News That's Fit to Print"

The New York Times

Late Edition
Weather: Clearing with northwesterly winds today; clear and cooler tonight. Mostly sunny and warmer tomorrow. Temperatures: today 74-76, tonight 55-60; yesterday 52-54. Details on page D7.

VOL.CXXXI . . . No. 45,344 | NEW YORK, MONDAY, JUNE 14, 1982 | 30 CENTS

NEW BATTLES SHATTER LEBANON CEASE-FIRE; ISRAEL REPORTED TO IMPERIL LAST P.L.O. EXIT

FALKLAND ADVANCE ASSURES VICTORY, BRITAIN DECLARES

Outcome Is Not Now in Doubt, London Says — Argentina Reports a New Assault

By R. W. APPLE Jr.
Special to The New York Times

LONDON, June 13 — Britain's Defense Secretary, John Nott, said tonight that his country's success in ousting Argentine troops from the Falkland Islands had been assured by fighting this weekend.

But he disclosed that the 5,400-ton light cruiser Glamorgan, carrying a crew of 471, had been hit by Argentine gunfire during the assault Friday night on enemy positions west of Stanley, the main Argentine garrison on the islands. Nine British sailors were killed and 17 injured, Mr. Nott added, but the ship remained fit for battle. Buenos Aires had claimed to have sunk a British frigate.

With British troops consolidating their positions, some less than seven miles west of Stanley, in preparation for further offensive operations, there was no news here of further infantry action today. It was not clear when the British would resume their attack, and it appeared possible they were hoping for an Argentine capitulation.

Argentina Reports New Battle

But in Argentina, the military command said that its forces repelled a British assault on Stanley in heavy fighting today and that casualties were high. [Page A8.]

Mr. Nott said: "Our successes on the ground over the weekend mark another significant step to securing the complete and final withdrawal of Argentine forces from the Falkland Islands. There is some way still to go, but the outcome is not in doubt."

He also disclosed for the first time that 50 crew members and soldiers, most of them from the Welsh Guards, had been killed in the Argentine air attacks Tuesday on the landing ships Sir Tristram and Sir Galahad off Bluff Cove and Fitzroy. At least 60 were wounded seriously, he added.

British deaths in the Falkland war have now reached at least 201, not counting those who died in this weekend's fighting. Argentina has lost more than 700 men, according to the most recent tally here.

Mr. Nott acknowledged that the Government had withheld the casualty figures from Tuesday's action in the hope of misleading the Argentines.

"It was important," he said, "that the enemy was not able to assess exactly when, where or in what strength that task force would attack. It is clear that the Argentines greatly overesti-

Continued on Page A8, Column 1

United Press International

King Fahd of Saudi Arabia

Khalid Is Dead; Fahd Succeeds In Saudi Arabia

By STEVEN RATTNER
Special to The New York Times

LONDON, June 13 — King Khalid of Saudi Arabia, ruler of the desert oil nation since 1975, died today of a heart attack in the mountain resort of Taif. The King, 69 years old, was succeeded by Crown Prince Fahd, 59, a half-brother.

Although he had been in ill health for years, the King's death was unexpected. On Saturday the ruler was shown by Saudi television arriving in Taif to spend the summer.

The change in rule came at an awkward time for Saudi Arabia. The country has been a staunch supporter of Iraq, which now appears to be losing its war against Iran. Saudi Arabia has also been active in trying to restore peace in Lebanon, where fighting continues a week after Israel's invasion.

No Immediate Changes Expected

There were differences in personality and outlook between King Khalid and his successor. But the takeover by King Fahd appeared unlikely to have any immediate effect on the country's traditional policies.

It is widely believed that in time, King Fahd, a dynamic man, could move the reclusive nation forcefully into Middle Eastern politics and international affairs.

"We will continue his path, seek to realize his hopes and complete his plan," a sobbing King Fahd said of King Khalid tonight on the Saudi radio. "We seek nothing but the glory of Arabs and Moslems."

Perhaps most immediately, the death of the King appeared likely to bring

Continued on Page A12, Column 4

INVADERS BLAME FOE

No Syria Action Reported in the Daylong Combat With Palestinians

The following dispatch has been subjected to military censorship.

By DAVID K. SHIPLER
Special to The New York Times

JERUSALEM, June 13 — The Israeli military command said today that Israeli artillery and fighter-bombers had attacked Palestinian targets in Lebanon after the Palestinians opened fire on Israeli positions at dawn. The fighting continued all day.

The Israeli truce with Syrian forces, arranged Friday, appeared to be holding, however. No clashes with Syrian forces were reported, and no Syrian planes were reported to have intervened against Israeli aircraft.

The renewed battles with Palestinian forces began just eight hours after Israel declared a cease-fire in the Beirut area. The fighting dashed prospects for a halt to the war that began with an Israeli invasion of Lebanon a week ago.

U.S. Seeks Total Pullout

In Washington, Secretary of State Alexander M. Haig Jr. said the United States would seek the withdrawal of Israeli forces from Lebanon as part of a long-term solution in which Syrian and all other foreign troops would also be pulled out. [Page A14.]

The new fighting appeared to give Israel a chance to continue inflicting damage on the Palestine Liberation Organization's military structure, which has been the principal target of the campaign. Defense Minister Ariel Sharon has said the army will continue clearing Palestinian guerrillas out of areas under Israeli control. The Israeli cease-fire with the Palestinians was intended to apply only to the Beirut area.

During Israeli "mopping up" operations today, fighting was reported in the area of the coastal city of Sidon.

Truce Began Saturday Night

Some Israeli officials had expressed regret that more damage was not done to the P.L.O. in Beirut before the cease-fire, which was firmly requested by the United States, took effect Saturday night.

Despite the devastating assault on P.L.O. forces in the south and the pounding of various P.L.O. headquarters in the Lebanese capital, there had appeared to be enough key Palestinians left in Beirut to retain and possibly rebuild the organization's presence in Lebanon. Military sources said hundreds of Palestinian guerrillas surrendered today after the heavy Israeli attacks.

On the other hand, Israel seems to have little taste for a prolongation of the

Continued on Page A15, Column 1

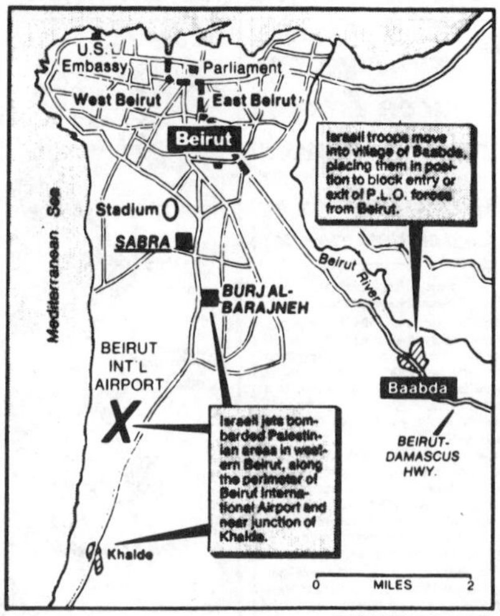

The New York Times / June 14, 1982

Invasion Victims Swamp The Hospitals of Lebanon

By WILLIAM E. FARRELL
Special to The New York Times

BEIRUT, Lebanon, June 13 — The driveway was lined with stretchers. Every so often today ambulances, some of them caked with mud and camouflaged with twigs and greenery, pulled into the driveway, their sirens wailing.

Attendants and medics attached to the American University Hospital here rushed to the vehicles, removing some of the victims of Lebanon's latest bout of carnage, and rushed them to the emergency room.

Other victims straggled in on foot seeking assistance. One elderly woman, tears in her eyes, walked painfully up the driveway today and said to a stranger: "Please, I'm with the diabetes and my home is gone. Where can I get the free help?"

No one knows with any accuracy how many dead and wounded there are in this ravaged and fear-ridden country since the start of the Israeli invasion a week ago.

Regarded as Neutral Territory

The American University Hospital, so far anyway, is regarded as neutral territory and its fatigued and overworked staff have handled hundreds and hundreds of victims of bombings and strafings.

The 10-story building is filled with casualties. Some of them are lying on beds in hallways receiving fluids intravenously.

The hospital is representative of medical facilities all over this battered country where a cease-fire has been declared but the fire has not ceased.

According to the International Commitee of the Red Cross, the medical facilities in southern Lebanon, the scene of fierce exchanges between Israelis and Palestinians, are in a ruinous state. They lack space and medicines, and food hygiene is reportedly deplorable. There is a shortage of water. The wounded are lying in school buildings and hallways.

Because of fierce Israeli shelling around Beirut's International Airport, immobilized since the invasion began, a jumbo jet sitting in Geneva cannot get in to deliver medical supplies.

Private hospitals in Christian East Beirut, which has been untouched during the invasion, have offered aid to overtaxed hospitals in the city's predominantly Moslem western section, the southern outskirts of which have been the target of numerous attacks by Israeli planes and gunboats.

Palestinian Wounded Brought In

Many of West Beirut's hospitals are understaffed because technicians and medical personnel are unable to get to work through the city's dangerous streets.

The Lebanese Red Cross has issued urgent calls for doctors to help in rescue operations and have issued an international call for doctors to help them in the nearly impossible task of providing adequate medical care for the victims.

As armed Palestinian guerrillas carried in their wounded to the Ameri-

Continued on Page A13, Column 1

KEY ROAD AT STAKE

Troops Land Near Home of Lebanese Leader on Beirut's Outskirts

Special to The New York Times

BEIRUT, Lebanon, June 13 — Israeli troops with tanks and armored personnel carriers reportedly moved into a village just five miles southeast of central Beirut tonight. If the troops consolidate their position, it could lead to the virtual encirclement of the capital and the Palestinian guerrilla forces there.

Earlier, a brief cease-fire between Palestinian guerrillas and Israeli forces was shattered in a day of fierce fighting south of the city between Israeli troops and Palestinian guerrillas as well as repeated Israeli air strikes against West Beirut. The cease-fire was worked out Saturday by the Lebanese and United States Governments.

If the Israelis hold their position in the village, Baabda, it would mark a major turning point in their seven-day invasion. It would put Israeli troops astride the strategic Beirut-Damascus highway at the entry of Beirut, choking off the last exit or entry route for the Palestinian guerrilla forces in the capital.

Israeli Ally Controls East Beirut

In effect, the city would be surrounded, for the Palestinians could not be expected to make their way through the area to the north of the highway controlled by Israel's ally, the heavily armed Phalangist Christian militia headed by Bashir Gemayel.

The Israeli troops were reported only a few hundred yards from the palace of Lebanon's President, Elias Sarkis. Mr. Sarkis was in the palace at the time, meeting with 10 of his ministers. The state-run Beirut radio said that the meeting had been called "to consider the formation of a strong government to save the country."

The radio, quoting official Government sources, said the Israeli force had "landed" in the village square. It added that Israeli troops were setting up positions and roadblocks inside Baabda and had commandeered several public buildings, including a police station and a Government hospital.

No Reports on Lebanese Troops

There were no immediate reports of fighting between the Israeli raiding party and Lebanese Army troops, who control Baabda and nearby Yarze, where the Ministry of Defense is situated. Reports near midnight were vague, and there was no indication that the Israelis had tried to enter the presidential palace.

The Phalangist Voice of Lebanon radio reported the Israeli entry into Baabda in the same sketchy manner as the state-run Beirut radio and gave no

Continued on Page A14, Column 4

The New York Times / Fred R. Conrad

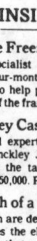

The Calm Restored, Sailors Return to Central Park

Sailboats, with sails and rudders that respond to radio commands, on Conservatory Pond yesterday in a model yacht competition. About 1,000 workers cleared tons of trash from hundreds of thousands of demonstrators who assembled Saturday to protest nuclear arms. Article on the cleanup is on page B1; on the yachts, on page B3.

INSIDE

France Freezes Wages

France's Socialist Government announced a four-month freeze on wages and prices to help prevent a further weakening of the franc. Page A6.

Hinckley Case Is Costly

The medical experts in the trial of John W. Hinckley Jr. have cost his parents and the taxpayers at least $350,000 to $450,000. Page D10.

Aftermath of a Murder Trial

Two children are dead and a 16-year-old boy faces the electric chair in a murder case that continues to cast a shadow over Old Forge, Pa. Page D10.

Power Shifts in Mideast

Israeli Invasion of Lebanon Alters Balance And Jumbles Relations of Friends and Foes

By THOMAS L. FRIEDMAN
Special to The New York Times

News Analysis

BEIRUT, Lebanon, June 13 — The Israeli invasion of Lebanon has recast the balance of power in this corner of the world and created a whole new set of relationships involving Israel, Syria, Lebanon and the Palestine Liberation Organization.

With Israeli forces on the fringes of Beirut and the Israeli Army in control of roughly a fourth of Lebanon's territory, the full political effect of the fighting can now begin to be assessed.

Tensions have already surfaced between the Palestine Liberation Organization and Syria. The Syrians have lost a dominant role in Lebanon. The Soviet Union's clients in the region have been weakened.

Problems for the P.L.O.

Although P.L.O. leaders have apparently not been captured or killed, damage to the organization should not be underestimated.

Southern Lebanon, the P.L.O.'s only independent base of military operations — excluding isolated pockets in Sidon, Tyre and Damur — has been occupied by the Israelis. The P.L.O. has been driven back to West Beirut, well out of striking distance to northern Israel.

This presents the P.L.O. leadership with serious problems. The guerrillas could try to continue operations out of West Beirut, harassing the Israeli occupation forces on the outskirts of the city. But that would expose Beirut's non-Palestinian Moslem and Christian populations to continuous Israeli bombardment.

Moreover, President Elias Sarkis's Government is now eager to get its fragile, but still functioning, army into West Beirut to fill the void left by a nearly total withdrawal of Syrian peacekeeping forces.

Probably the most frequent topic of conversation among the predominantly Moslem inhabitants of West Beirut today was whether the Lebanese Army would finally free the area from the six years of lawlessness presided over by the Syrians and various private militias that operated with Syria's tacit approval.

If and when the Lebanese Army does come in, there will be tremendous pressure on the P.L.O. to maintain an extremely low profile as a military force.

The alternative for the P.L.O. leader, Yasir Arafat, may be to move his military headquarters to Damascus. That appears to be one of Israel's primary objectives in its invasion.

Ever since a war of attrition in 1974 between Israel and Syria in the Golan Heights, the Government of President

Continued on Page A14, Column 1

"All the News That's Fit to Print"

The New York Times

Late Edition

Weather: Sunny today with light southeasterly winds; clear and mild tonight. Cloudy with a chance of rain tomorrow. Temperatures: today 81-83, tonight 63-67; yesterday 54-72. Details, page D24.

VOL.CXXXI. No. 45,345 NEW YORK, TUESDAY, JUNE 15, 1982 — 30 CENTS

BRITAIN ANNOUNCES ARGENTINE SURRENDER TO END THE 10-WEEK WAR IN THE FALKLANDS

Israelis Cut Off West Beirut, Trapping P.L.O. Leaders

ACTION IN LEBANON

Tank Units Push Through the Christian Suburbs Around the Capital

By THOMAS L. FRIEDMAN
Special to The New York Times

BEIRUT, Lebanon, June 14 — Israeli tank columns completely cut off Moslem western Beirut today, trapping the military and political leadership of the Palestine Liberation Organization.

At the same time, other Israeli armored units, greeted by rice and flowers from sympathetic Lebanese Christians, began driving still deeper into Lebanon, apparently in an effort to push Syrian troops northeast of the capital into the Bekaa Valley.

There is a concentration of Syrian troops in the Khalde junction area on the coastal highway south of Beirut near the airport, and fighting was reportedly continuing there today between Israeli forces and Palestinians and Syrians.

The Israeli radio quoted Israel's Chief of Staff, Lieut. Gen. Rafael Eytan, as saying that Israeli troops had trapped guerrilla forces in Beirut and that the troops' mission was to smash the P.L.O.'s political and military nerve center there. [Page A18.]

Lebanese Leader Forms Council

The Israeli siege of guerrilla forces in Beirut came as the Lebanese Government announced the formation of a six-member Council of National Salvation to deal with the political repercussions of the Israeli invasion.

The committee, which was to contain the leading Christian and Moslem militia commanders, was formed by President Elias Sarkis and Prime Minister Shafik al-Wazzan to determine the Government's response to Israeli conditions for withdrawal.

Israel's withdrawal terms were delivered this evening to Mr. Sarkis at the presidential palace in Baabda by the special United States envoy, Philip C. Habib. Mr. Habib arrived by car from Damascus, to which he had flown earlier today from Jerusalem.

Mr. Habib declined to make any statements to the press, but Israel's conditions are reportedly the creation of a demilitarized zone stretching 25 miles north of its border to prevent attacks by Palestinian guerrillas and the withdrawal of the 30,000 Syrian peacekeeping troops from Lebanon.

Leftist Rejects Council

A meeting of the national council to consider the conditions, scheduled for this afternoon, was canceled after one proposed member, Walid Jumblat, leader of the leftist Moslem National Movement, said he would not have anything to do with the group as presently constituted.

Mr. Jumblat, who is under virtual house arrest by Israeli invasion forces occupying his mountain village of Mukhtara south of Beirut, said through a spokesman that the board should be "more comprehensive."

The other proposed council members are Bashir Gemayel, a Chrisian Phalangist militia commander; Nabim Berri, head of Lebanon's Shiite Moslem Party; Nasri Maalouf, another leading Christian political leader; Foreign

Continued on Page A18, Column 1

Associated Press

Israeli soldier atop armored vehicle in position overlooking western Beirut.

In Lebanon, White Flags Fly Amid the Misery and Rubble

By DAVID K. SHIPLER
Special to The New York Times

SIDON, Lebanon, June 14 — Along the battered Lebanese coast, in the wake of the invasion, white flags still fly.

They flutter from the antennas of cars without windows or windshields. They hang from bamboo poles stuck into the shell-pocked roofs and verandas of concrete houses. Even some pedestrians carried torn strips of white cloth to signify their neutrality, their surrender to the storm of war.

The Israeli Army warned residents of Lebanon's picturesque coast to leave their homes before the bombing and shelling began, and many followed the instructions on leaflets dropped from planes.

Battles Silently Traced

But when the fighting was over and they returned home from the beaches and the orange groves and the banana plantations where they had camped for days without food or water, what they saw took the strength out of them.

In Tyre, a stronghold and command center of the Palestine Liberation Organization, not a single building was untouched by the flying shrapnel.

Some high-rise apartments had collapsed like houses of cards, some villas were chewed into piles of dust and rubble.

Many other buildings revealed the course of battle: pits and chips around the doors and windows as Israeli troops fired at guerrillas, then a single gaping hole in a wall where a heavier weapon finished off the resistance.

The Israeli military governor of the town, Maj. Joseph Dana, who in civilian life is a lecturer in Arabic at Haifa University, estimates that 30 percent of all buildings in the town were destroyed.

In Sidon, farther up the coast toward Beirut, the damage was less ex-

Continued on Page A18, Column 4

A MIDEAST WARNING

Soviet Conveys Concern Over Military Activity Near South Border

By JOHN F. BURNS
Special to The New York Times

MOSCOW, June 14 — The Soviet Government warned Israel today not to forget that the Middle East was close to the Soviet Union's southern borders and that developments in that area "cannot help affecting the interests of the U.S.S.R."

The warning was coupled with a demand, apparently directed at the United States, for "urgent effective measures" to halt Israel's "criminal act of genocide" against Palestinians and to bring about a withdrawal of Israeli troops from Lebanon.

Text of Soviet statement, page A20.

The statement, issued through the official press agency Tass, said in part:

"The Soviet Union takes the Arabs' side not in words but in deed and presses to get the aggressor out of Lebanon.

"The present-day Israeli policy makers should not forget that the Middle East is an area lying in close proximity to the southern borders of the Soviet Union and that developments there cannot help affecting the interests of the U.S.S.R. We warn Israel about this."

Implications of Soviet Action

The statement was evidently intended to arouse concern that American inability to arrange an early cease-fire between Israeli forces and Palestinian guerrillas could provoke direct Soviet intervention.

Theoretically, Soviet options would include an emergency airlift of arms to Palestinian guerrillas by way of Syria, which has signed a Treaty of Friendship and Cooperation with Moscow, or a new supply of weapons to the Syrian forces.

As if to underscore the Soviet warning, a Soviet general was reported to have begun talks in the Syrian capital.

Sources in Damascus identified the officer as Col. Gen. Yevgeny S. Yurasov, a first deputy commander of the air defense system. The sending of the general to Syria suggested that the

Continued on Page A20, Column 1

United Press International

Prime Minister Margaret Thatcher after addressing Parliament.

Bus-Only Lanes To Be Increased To Speed Travel

By ARI L. GOLDMAN

Mayor Koch announced yesterday the creation of a system of 10 "red zone" lanes for buses in Manhattan to help relieve traffic congestion, increase bus speeds and reduce what has long been the bane of bus travelers — bus bunching.

Along the pavement at each of the 10 thoroughfares in the program, a bright red eight-inch thermoplastic strip will remind motorists of heavy fines if they park, stand or travel in the bus lane.

"Don't Even Think of Parking Here," a sign along the routes will read. Other signs will warn that fines of at least $100 will be imposed on violators. Only cars preparing to make right turns will be permitted to travel in the lanes, and then only for short distances.

Next Tuesday, the first of the red zone lanes will go into effect, on Third Avenue from 36th to 58th Streets from 7 A.M. to 7 P.M. The others, which will be added over the course of the summer, will be in effect at various times on major thoroughfares in both midtown and lower Manhattan. Fourteen miles of city streets will be affected.

The other streets to get red zone lanes will be: Eighth Avenue from 42d to 57th Streets between 4 P.M. and 7 P.M.; Avenue of the Americas from 40th

Continued on Page B6, Column 1

TRIUMPH BY LONDON

Commander Says Enemy Troops Are Assembled 'for Repatriation'

By R. W. APPLE Jr.
Special to The New York Times

LONDON, Tuesday, June 15 — Argentine forces in the Falkland Islands have surrendered, halting the war in the South Atlantic, Prime Minister Margaret Thatcher's office announced early this morning.

A spokesman quoted Maj. Gen. Jeremy Moore, the commander of British land forces in the archipelago, as saying that enemy troops were being rounded up for eventual repatriation to Argentina. The surrender came at 1 A.M. British time, (8 P.M. Monday New York time), the official announcement said.

There was no confirmation of the surrender from Buenos Aires by early this morning, but the Argentine high command announced Monday afternoon that an unofficial cease-fire had gone into effect on the Falklands. [Page A14.]

'God Save the Queen'

General Moore radioed from his command post on Mount Kent: "Falkland Islands once more under Government desired by their inhabitants. God Save the Queen." It had taken the British three weeks and four days of fighting on the ground to retake the islands following their landings at San Carlos Bay.

The Prime Minister signaled that the end of the conflict, or at least this phase of it, was at hand in a statement to Parliament Monday night in which she said that Argentine forces in Stanley, the last major enemy stronghold in the Falklands, had begun throwing down their arms and hoisting white flags.

As the House of Commons erupted in prolonged cheers, the Prime Minister disclosed that the deputy commander of British land forces, Brig. John Waters, was negotiating surrender terms with the commander of the 6,500 Argentine defenders of the town, Brig. Gen. Mario Menéndez. The surrender terms, she added, would cover both East Falkland, the island on which Stanley is situated, and West Falkland, where two small Argentine forces are based.

Crowds Hail Victory

Within minutes of her statement to the House, crowds gathered outside Mrs. Thatcher's residence at 10 Downing Street, singing "Rule Britannia." When she returned from the House, they cheered her and she said, "What matters is that it was everyone together — we all knew what we had to do and we went out there and did it."

Although it remained possible that fighting would continue on or around

Continued on Page A15, Column 1

United Press International

Yasir Arafat, left, leader of the Palestine Liberation Organization, and an aide yesterday in Beirut.

1,600 Are Arrested In Nuclear Protests At 5 U.N. Missions

By PAUL L. MONTGOMERY

Offering daisies to policemen or chanting prayers for peace, more than 1,600 nonviolent demonstrators for disarmament were arrested in midtown Manhattan yesterday as they tried to block the entrances of the United Nations missions of five countries that have atomic weapons.

In an assembly-line operation that began at 7:30 A.M., the police carried the unresisting demonstrators to rented city buses to be booked for disorderly conduct. Some who had been arrested in the morning were back later in the day, encouraging their friends or sitting down again for another arrest.

The Police Department, which had 3,000 extra officers at the demonstration sites, said the total booked was a record for a civil disobedience campaign in the city. Patrick J. Murphy, the department's chief of operations, said, "almost everybody was very well-behaved — it was a textbook exercise."

The demonstrations, for which the participants were rehearsed and the police were briefed in advance, were a continuation of the protest that brought

Continued on Page A23, Column 1

INSIDE

Sports Pages

The New York Times today introduces Sports Pages, an expanded and redesigned sports section appearing Tuesday through Saturday. It will include added news as well as new columns and features. Today's section begins on page D25.

U.S. Enters Dollar Market

As the dollar reached new highs against the devalued French franc, the Administration intervened in trading to try to restore order. Page D1.

Ruling Due on Copying TV

The Supreme Court agreed to decide whether use of home video recorders to tape television broadcasts violates Federal copyright law. Page D1.

U.S. Challenged in Space

A lack of planning and foreign competition were reported to threaten United States leadership in nonmilitary space technology. Page C1.

17 Fakes at Met Museum

The Metropolitan Museum has discovered that 17 gold vessels it had believed to be ancient Egyptian are modern fakes. Page C9.

U.S. Is Easing '68 Antitrust Guidelines on Mergers

By ROBERT D. HERSHEY Jr.
Special to The New York Times

WASHINGTON, June 14 — The Government, seeking to reduce uncertainty about the types of corporate mergers that it will allow, today published a new set of enforcement guidelines "more lenient" than previous antitrust policy.

Nevertheless, the Justice Department and the Federal Trade Commission, which share antitrust responsibility, said they did not believe that their long-awaited statements would lead to any significant increase in mergers, which have diminished recently.

Attorney General William French Smith described the new guidelines as an "evolutionary change — not a revolutionary change" from actual practices in recent years. William F. Baxter, the Assistant Attorney General in charge of the antitrust division, said that, "in general, the new guidelines would have to be regarded as more lenient." But he added that he did not expect them to encourage more corporate combinations than guidelines that have existed since 1968. Antitrust experts said the new guidelines were more than

Continued on Page D8, Column 4

"All the News That's Fit to Print"

The New York Times

Late Edition
Weather: Overcast and mild today with scattered rainshowers likely through tonight. Cloudy, chance of rain tomorrow. Temperatures: today 73-77, tonight 61-63; yesterday 65-81. Details on page B10.

VOL.CXXXI . No. 45,437 — Copyright © 1982 The New York Times — NEW YORK, WEDNESDAY, SEPTEMBER 15, 1982 — 30 CENTS

GEMAYEL OF LEBANON IS KILLED IN BOMB BLAST AT PARTY OFFICES

Hussein Praises Reagan's Mideast Plan

KING OFFERS HELP

But Jordanian Asserts He Lacks the Authority to Enter Peace Talks

By BERNARD GWERTZMAN
Special to The New York Times

WASHINGTON, Sept. 14 — King Hussein of Jordan, in his first public comment on President Reagan's Middle East peace plan, said in an interview that it was "a very constructive and a very positive move." He added that he would play "a very active part" in trying to bring about a federation between Jordanians and the Palestinians.

But in the interview, aired by the British Broadcasting Corporation on Monday night, the King said he did not have an Arab mandate to join talks with Israel, Egypt and the United States on Palestinian self-rule.

Transcript of interview, page A10.

He said the Arab leaders who met in Fez, Morocco, last week did not alter the 1974 Arab League decision to give the Palestine Liberation Organization, not Jordan, responsibility for negotiations dealing with the Palestinians living in territories occupied by Israel.

'A Very Active Part'

Although the 1974 decision still holds, he said, "I am going to play a very active part in helping, pushing forth every possible attempt for the establishment of a just and durable peace."

King Hussein, in describing his ideas for an eventual settlement of the Palestinian issue, put forth a plan that was very similar to the one proposed by President Reagan in his address on the Middle East on Sept. 1.

In that speech, Mr. Reagan said the United States favored some kind of "association" between Jordan and the Palestinians. He said the United States rejected the idea of Israeli sovereignty over the the West Bank and the Gaza Strip, but would not support an independent Palestinian state in the occupied territories.

Israel captured the West Bank from Jordan and Gaza from Egypt in the 1967 war.

The Fez communiqué repeated the traditional Arab demand for the establishment of an independent Palestinian

Continued on Page A10, Column 1

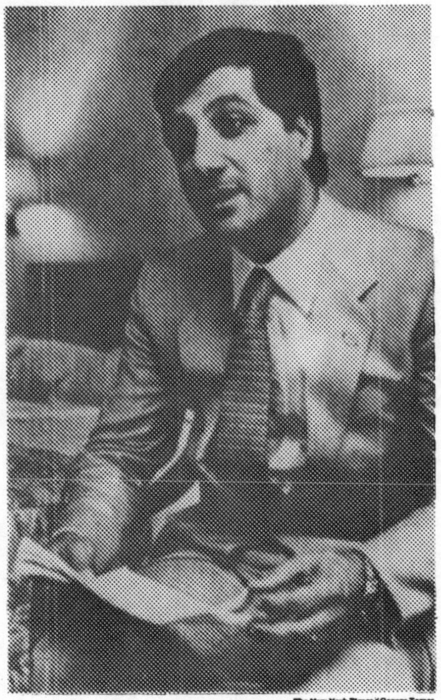

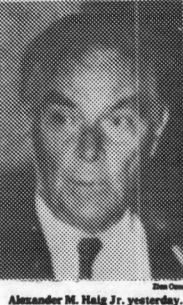

The New York Times/George Tames
Bashir Gemayel during a visit to Washington a year ago.

8 REPORTED SLAIN

President-Elect Was 34 — No Group Reports Making the Attack

By COLIN CAMPBELL
Special to The New York Times

BEIRUT, Lebanon, Wednesday, Sept. 15 — President-elect Bashir Gemayel was killed Tuesday when a bomb shattered the headquarters of his Lebanese Christian Phalangist Party in east Beirut. The Government said he would be buried today.

Mr. Gemayel, 34 years old, who was to have been inaugurated Sept. 23, was said to have died as he was about to address 400 of his followers at a weekly meeting. The state radio said the blast left at least 8 dead, among them other Phalangist leaders, and more than 50 wounded.

Prime Minister Shafik al-Wazzan deplored the killing in a statement, describing it as "a link in a chain of criminal conspiracies against Lebanon at a time when it started to restore its strength."

New Fighting Is Feared

No one took responsibility immediately for the bombing. It raised widespread fears that it would be followed by new fighting between Lebanon's Christian and Moslem militias.

Mr. Gemayel, who had been the commander of the Christian militias, was elected President Aug. 23 at a special session of Parliament that was boycotted by many Moslem legislators. To them, many other Moslems and some Christian groups, he was an enemy and an agent of Israel, whose invading troops made his election possible. [In Israel, there was no immediate official comment on the assassination.]

Until Sept. 23, the current President, Elias Sarkis, will continue as chief of state. Government sources said he could call new elections before then or appoint a presidential council to exercise presidential power until new elections could be called. Since the President in Lebanon is by tradition a Maronite Catholic, the council would also be headed by one.

400 Pounds of Explosives

The sources said another possibility was an extension of the Sarkis term, but this would require a change in the Constitution. The Lebanese President is not allowed under current law to succeed himself.

The blast, involving the detonation of what Phalangist and Government sources estimated to be more than 400 pounds of high explosives, occurred at 4:10 P.M. Tuesday. There was no immediate explanation for how so large an amount of explosive could have been introduced into the building.

For several hours reports circulated that Mr. Gemayel had survived.

There were reports that he had said "God be praised" as he left the scene for treatment of leg bruises at the nearby French-run Hôtel Dieu hospital. Those accounts were broadcast by the Phalangist radio, which quoted wit-

Continued on Page A8, Column 4

Slaying Is Denounced by Reagan; U.S. Fears New Burst of Fighting

Special to The New York Times

WASHINGTON, Sept. 14 — President Reagan said tonight that the "cowardly assassination" of President-elect Bashir Gemayel of Lebanon was a "shock to the American people and to civilized men and women everywhere."

In an unusually sharp statement, Mr. Reagan added, "We condemn the perpetrators of this heinous crime against Lebanon and against their cause of peace in the Middle East."

The White House statement, issued late tonight, expressed deepest sympathy to the Gemayel family, and said, "The tragedy will be all the greater if men in countries friendly to Lebanon permit disorder to continue in this war-torn country."

'U.S. Stands By Lebanon'

Mr. Reagan added that the "U.S. Government stands by Lebanon with its full support in its hour of need."

American officials said earlier that the assassination raised the possibility of new fighting in that country between Mr. Gemayel's Christian Phalangist forces and Moslem leftists.

New internal strife would also raise the possibility that Syrian and Israeli forces, confronting each other in Lebanon, might enter the conflict, destroying hopes for restoring stability.

The Israelis had strongly supported Mr. Gemayel, who was an avowed enemy of Syria. Just today, the Israeli Ambassador, Moshe Arens, called on Secretary of State George P. Shultz to say Israel wanted American assistance in obtaining a peace treaty with Lebanon.

It is the American hope that Elias Sarkis, the Lebanese President, whose term of office officially ends in nine days, will remain in office pending a new consensus choice as President.

The special American Middle East envoy, Morris Draper, arrived in Israel today on his way to Lebanon to help negotiate the withdrawal of Syrian and Israeli forces and the strengthening of the Lebanese Government. His mission is even more precarious now, officials said, given the uncertain future in Lebanon.

There was no fundamental difference between Mr. Sarkis and Mr. Gemayel on the withdrawal of foreign troops from Lebanon, American officials said. They expressed hope that Mr. Sarkis

Continued on Page A9, Column 1

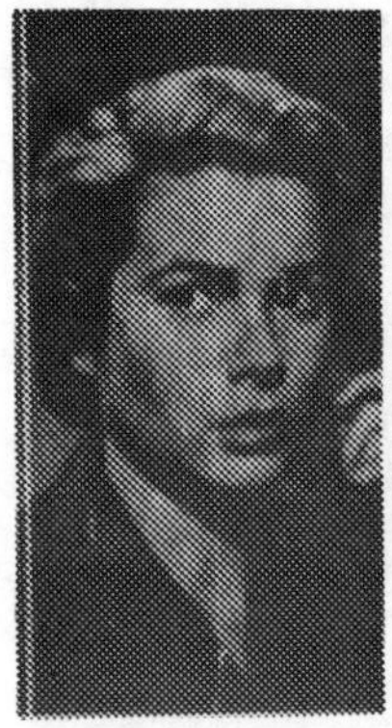

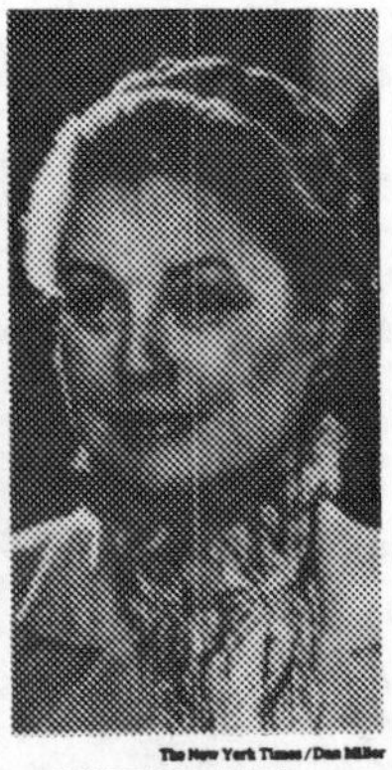

The New York Times / Dan Miller
Grace Kelly, the actress: In "The Country Girl," 1954, for which she won an Oscar. Princess Grace of Monaco: At a tribute in Philadelphia this year.

Princess Grace Is Dead After Riviera Car Crash

By CLYDE HABERMAN

Princess Grace of Monaco, whose stately beauty and reserve gave her enduring Hollywood stardom even long after she ended her film career, died yesterday in Monte Carlo of injuries suffered when her car plunged off a mountain road Monday. She was 52 years old.

The Princess, the former Grace Kelly, died of a cerebral hemorrhage, a palace spokesman said in Monaco.

Princess Grace was driving her British Rover 3500 on a snaking road at Cap-d'Ail in the Côte d'Azur region when she lost control and plunged down a 45-foot embankment. The car burst into flames, and the Princess suffered multiple fractures, including a broken thighbone, collarbone and ribs.

Initial reports gave no sense that her life was in jeopardy. But a Monaco Government announcement yesterday said that her health had "deteriorated during the night."

"At the end of the day all therapeutic possibilities had been exceeded," the announcement said.

With her in the car was Stephanie, 17, her youngest child by Prince Rainier III of Monaco. Stephanie was under observation at a hospital where she had been treated for shock and bruises.

Reagan Praises 'Gentle Lady'

Princess Grace's death brought expressions of grief from former Hollywood colleagues and from residents of her hometown, Philadelphia. President Reagan called her "a compassionate and gentle lady." In Philadelphia, a spokesman for John Cardinal Krol said the Cardinal, who was a close friend, would offer a memorial mass for her at noon Friday.

Alfred Hitchcock, who directed Grace Kelly in three films and was certainly in a position to judge, once said she had "sexual elegance." And it was that very elegance that probably made its most lasting impression on movie audiences of the 1950's.

Whether playing the heiress in "To Catch a Thief" or the Quaker pacifist in "High Noon" or the amusedly detached career girl — a term still in vogue when "Rear Window" was made — Grace Kelly carried herself with straight back and clipped-voice self-assurance. Yet just beneath the frosty exterior lay a sensuality and warmth that cracked the formidable reserve.

It was this delicate balance of contrasts that helped give her legendary status — a remarkable achievement for an actress whose career encompassed only 11 films. She made more of that

Continued on Page C24, Column 1

Primaries Won By Ex-Governor, Two Incumbents

By ADAM CLYMER

A former Massachusetts Governor trying a comeback and two important members of Congress won key tests yesterday as 12 states and the District of Columbia held primary elections.

But another incumbent, Senator Howard W. Cannon of Nevada, was locked in a tight race with Representative James D. Santini as he sought the Democratic nomination for a fifth term.

In Massachusetts, former Gov. Michael S. Dukakis, attacking his successor's administration as corrupt and too supportive of President Reagan, defeated the incumbent, Gov. Edward J. King, for the Democratic nomination for Governor, just as Mr. King did four years ago when Mr. Dukakis was the incumbent. In the heavily Democratic Bay State, Mr. Dukakis will be favored over the Republican nominee in November, John W. Sears, a former Boston City Councilor.

In Vermont, Senator Robert T. Stafford the Republican chairman of the Committee on the Environment and Public Works, defeated two conservative foes trying to end his 11-year Senate career. The two, Stewart M. Ledbetter and John McClaughry, argued that Mr. Stafford had become more interested in Washington than in Vermont.

With 93 percent of the precincts reporting, Mr. Stafford was safely ahead with 23,815 votes, or 46 percent of the

Continued on Page B11, Column 4

I.B.M. Accuses 3 Executives Of Stealing Computer Secrets

By ANDREW POLLACK

The International Business Machines Corporation, following its second undercover investigation in recent months, said yesterday that it had dismissed three of its executives and had sued them on charges of stealing corporate secrets.

The key figure in the month-long I.B.M. investigation, conducted by the company's own security officers, was the president of a small Cleveland computer company who pretended to negotiate a business deal with the I.B.M. executives. While he negotiated, he secretly taped the conversations on recording equipment supplied by I.B.M.

One of the executives had approached the Cleveland company, Tecmar Inc., and had offered to sell designs for products that would enhance I.B.M.'s new and fast-selling personal computer, according to court papers. In some cases, they would compete with still-secret products I.B.M. itself is planning to introduce, the affidavits filed in connection with the lawsuit stated.

The president of the Cleveland company, Martin A. Alpert, reported the approach to I.B.M. and agreed to cooperate when I.B.M. suggested the tape-recording plan.

In one excerpt from the transcript quoted in the court papers, William W. Erdman, an I.B.M. product manager and one of the defendants, said to Mr. Alpert: "I guarantee you that we know more about the way I.B.M.'s going to put it [personal computer products] together than I.B.M. knows, because when the guys that we're talking about leave, a good deal of knowledge leaves with them."

The three men sued in the civil action included two high-level engineers who were heavily involved in the design of I.B.M.'s personal computer and follow-up products. Also sued was Bridge Technology Inc., a White Plains company that I.B.M. asserts was established by the three executives to market their products. The three executives were dismissed by I.B.M. on Monday.

Mr. Erdman, reached yesterday at his home in Stamford, Conn., said he

Continued on Page D7, Column 1

INSIDE

Doctor Shot to Death

A physician was fatally shot as he sat in his car near his Gramercy Park office. The victim, Dr. Philip Wald, 53, was shot once in the head. Page B6.

Tuition Credit Compromise

President Reagan, returning to the theme of social issues, backed legislative compromises aimed to advance a tuition tax credit bill. Page A20.

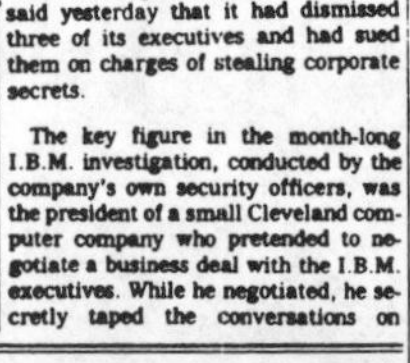

Thomas Victor
JOHN GARDNER IS DEAD: The novelist, killed in a motorcycle accident, was 49. Page D27.

Haig, at U.J.A., Criticizes Reagan's Mideast Plan

By BERNARD D. NOSSITER

Former Secretary of State Alexander M. Haig Jr. attacked President Reagan's Middle East plan yesterday, describing the proposal for a freeze on Israeli settlements in the occupied West Bank as "a very serious mistake."

Mr. Haig also said the Administration's plan for autonomy for the Palestinians in association with Jordan threatened a "gutting session" between Israel and the United States.

"The peace process will only move forward if there is a spirit of cooperation between Israel and the United States," Mr. Haig said. "That has been shaken in recent days."

It was the first time Mr. Haig is known to have criticized the Administration in which he served until June. He spoke without a text to 300 officials of the United Jewish Appeal at the Hilton Hotel in Manhattan.

Mr. Haig made no direct reference to the speech Sept. 1 in which Mr. Reagan announced the Middle East plan, or to his successor, George P. Shultz, who is regarded as the architect of that speech. When Mr. Haig was asked to comment on the Reagan plan, he smiled and said it would be inappropriate to "parse the pros and cons." But he added that his own remarks contained "some pertinent observations."

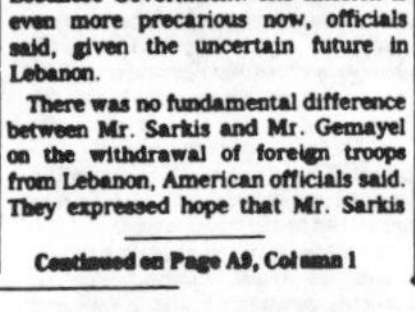

Ziem Ozeri
Alexander M. Haig Jr. yesterday.

The United Jewish Appeal raises funds for needy Jews around the world. It has not taken a formal position on Mr. Reagan's peace plan, but the frequent applause yesterday indicated strong agreement with Mr. Haig's criticism. Mr. Haig, who reportedly received $25,000 for his 45-minute appearance, serves as a consultant for United Technologies, a leading military contractor, and is a senior fellow at the Hudson Institute, a research center.

Mr. Haig received a standing ovation by concluding, "When we are true to Israel, we are true to ourselves."

He had earlier said, "When by our policies we can't deal effectively with our friends in Israel, we are undercutting our effectiveness throughout the Arab world."

Mr. Haig also asserted that "had the credibility" of Israel's invasion of Lebanon "been left undisturbed, the Palestine Liberation Organization would have left weeks earlier, and there would have been less bloodshed."

That was apparently an allusion to

Continued on Page A12, Column 4

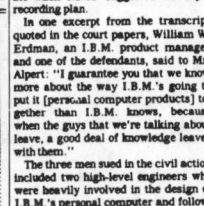

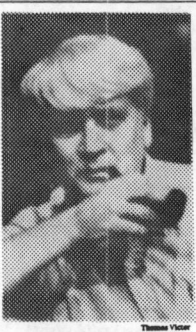

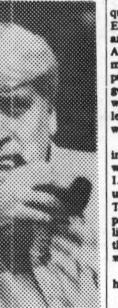

"All the News That's Fit to Print"

The New York Times

Late Edition

Weather: Fair and cold today with gusty winds making it feel much colder; clear tonight. Rain or snow likely tomorrow. Temperatures: today 31-33, tonight 19-23; yesterday 28-35. Details, page D20.

VOL.CXXXII . . . No. 45,584 · NEW YORK, WEDNESDAY, FEBRUARY 9, 1983 · 30 CENTS

ISRAELI INQUIRY GIVES LEADERS 'INDIRECT' BLAME IN MASSACRE; CALLS FOR SHARON'S DEPARTURE

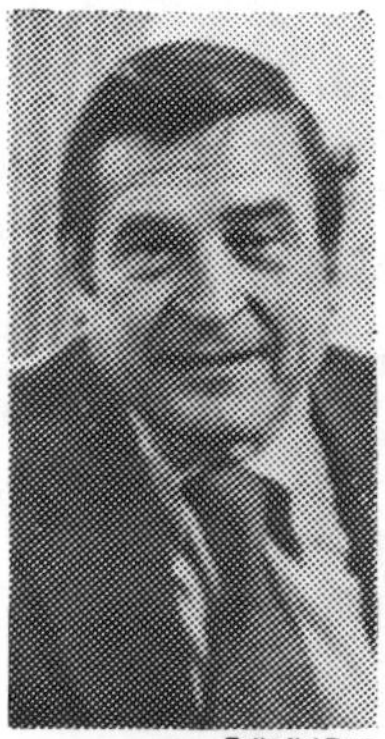

The New York Times

Dan Rostenkowski

Key Democrat Bids Congress Halt Tax Cuts

By EDWARD COWAN

Special to The New York Times

WASHINGTON, Feb. 8 — The chief Democratic tax writer in the House of Representatives, Dan Rostenkowski, proposed today that Congress reduce future budget deficits by the repeal or delay of various tax cuts for business and individuals now scheduled to take effect after 1983.

Mr. Rostenkowski acknowledged, however, that he could not muster a majority on the House floor to repeal the 10 percent cut in individual income taxes scheduled for July 1, 1983, and he indicated that he would not try to do so.

His list of future tax cuts to be forgone included indexing, or the automatic adjustment of tax brackets for wage inflation now scheduled to start in 1985, and reductions in estate, crude oil, tobacco and telephone taxes.

Politically More Attractive

Mr. Rostenkowski, the chairman of the Ways and Means Committee, argued in a speech here to the Securities Industry Association that his "tax freeze" was a politically more attractive way for Democrats and Republicans to raise revenue than President Reagan's proposal for standby tax increases to take effect in 1985.

Because the Chicago Democrat is close to the Speaker of the House, Thomas P. O'Neill Jr., and because he is understood to be willing to negotiate with the Reagan Administration, Mr.

Continued on Page D2, Column 5

U.S. SURVEY CITES RIGHTS VIOLATIONS AROUND THE WORLD

List Ranges From Vietnam to Countries Where Improved Relations Are Sought

By BERNARD WEINRAUB

Special to The New York Times

WASHINGTON, Feb. 8 — The Reagan Administration, seeking what it terms "an active, positive human rights policy," issued an annual human rights report today. The document cited serious human rights violations in nations around the world, including some that are friendly to the United States.

The 1,300-page report to Congress contains long descriptions of human rights violations in the Soviet Union and eastern-bloc nations as well as Middle East and Asian countries with strained ties to the United States. It also lists examples of torture, brutality and violence in South Africa, Pakistan and El Salvador, where the Administration has sought to improve relations.

At a news conference in the State Department, Elliott Abrams, the Assistant Secretary for Human Rights and Humanitarian Affairs, cited improvements and "moves toward democracy" in such countries as Brazil, Uruguay, El Salvador and the Dominican Republic.

Vietnam Termed 'the Worst'

But he said in response to questions that civil liberties seemed to have worsened last year in such countries as Iran, Czechoslovakia, the Soviet Union and Lebanon. And he said the "toughest" section of the document involved Vietnam. "It seemed to me the worst country to live in," Mr. Abrams said.

The annual study draws on reports from United States missions abroad, Congressional studies and human rights groups. It includes a country-by-country examination of political and press rights, freedoms of speech and religion, arbitrary arrest and imprisonment.

In a section on Israel, the report says that although that nation is a parliamentary democracy with full freedom of speech and the press, relations with Arabs in the occupied territories have caused "significant human rights problems." In the West Bank and Gaza, the report said, Israeli forces were observed "roughing up" individuals, freedom of expression was "restricted" and there were cases of Arabs being imprisoned for several months without formal charges or trial.

Although the Reagan Administration

Continued on Page A12, Column 1

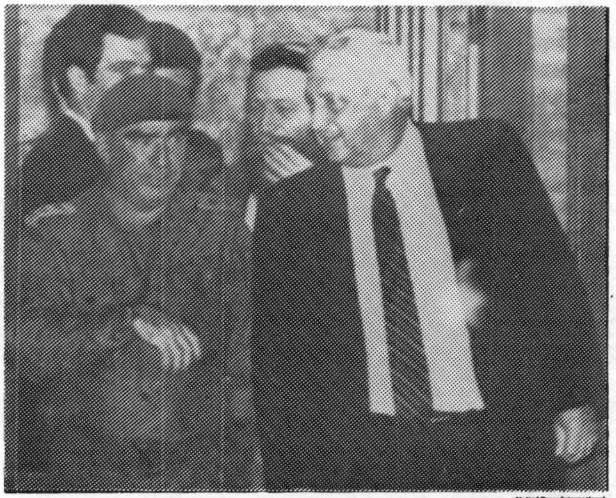

United Press International

Defense Minister Ariel Sharon of Israel, right, and Lieut. Gen. Rafael Eytan, the Army Chief of Staff, leaving a special Cabinet meeting in Jerusalem called to discuss the release of the report on the massacre in Beirut.

REPORT STIRS FUROR

Cabinet Weighs Response — Minister of Defense Refuses to Resign

By DAVID K. SHIPLER

Special to The New York Times

JERUSALEM, Feb. 8 — A special state investigating commission said today that Israel's top civilian and military leaders bore "indirect responsibility" for the massacre of Palestinians by Lebanese Christian Phalangist militia in Beirut last September.

The panel, headed by the Chief Justice of Israel's Supreme Court, recommended the resignation or dismissal of Defense Minister Ariel Sharon.

Key excerpts from the report are printed on pages A18-A20.

Three senior generals were also found to have been seriously at fault. The commission recommended that Brig. Gen. Amos Yaron, division commander in the Beirut district, be relieved of his post as a field commander for at least three years, and that the Director of Military Intelligence, Maj. Gen. Yehoshua Saguy, no longer continue in his post. Its report noted that the Chief of Staff, Lieut. Gen. Rafael Eytan, was retiring in April and that therefore "there is no practical significance to a recommendation with regard to his continuing in office."

Inquiry Took Four Months

The commission's report, issued after a four-month investigation, also criticized Prime Minister Menachem Begin, Foreign Minister Yitzhak Shamir and other officials, and assailed inadequacies in coordination and communication within the Cabinet and the army. These inadequacies, it said, led to faulty reporting and inaction while the Phalangists were in the Sabra and Shatila refugee camps.

The 55,000-word report set off a political furor in Mr. Begin's fractious coalition Government. Key members of the National Religious Party, whose six seats are essential to maintaining the Government's slim majority in Parliament, were reported to have demanded Mr. Sharon's resignation as a condition for remaining in the coalition. Mr. Sharon refused and urged that the army officers named be praised instead of ousted. The Cabinet met in special session to discuss to the report. Most ministers were said to favor following its recommendations, but Mr. Begin was said to oppose dismissal of Mr. Sharon. [Page A21.]

The report and its political consequences could have wide-ranging effects in the Middle East, and on Israel's

Continued on Page A21, Column 1

U.S. Aides Feel if Sharon Leaves, Begin May Show More Flexibility

By LESLIE H. GELB

Special to The New York Times

WASHINGTON, Feb. 8 — Key White House and State Department officials privately expressed the hope today that the findings of the Israeli commission would lead to the departure of Defense Minister Ariel Sharon and new negotiating flexibility on the part of Prime Minister Menachem Begin.

At a meeting in the White House Friday, top Middle East advisers told President Reagan that the commission's report could help break the deadlock over Israeli withdrawal from Lebanon if it placed responsibility principally on Mr. Sharon and only indirectly on Mr. Begin. The general view was that with Mr. Sharon in the Cabinet there was no chance of movement in either the Lebanese or West Bank talks but that, without him, the Begin Government would be somewhat weakened and Mr. Begin might be more amenable to compromise.

Today, neither the White House nor the State Department would publicly comment in detail on the report. Alan Romberg, a State Department spokesman, said, however, "We don't see why the impact of this report, whatever that may be, should affect the Lebanese negotiations or the current Habib mission."

'Issues Are Urgent'

"Our view is clear: The issues being addressed are urgent, and they must be resolved as soon as possible in the interests of Lebanese stability and sovereignty, as well as in the interests of Israeli security," he said.

President Reagan told editorial writers who asked about the report today that "I just don't think we should be commenting or injecting ourselves into that internal problem." He went on to praise Israel as a "strong democracy."

Administration officials were also saying that Secretary of State George P. Shultz was becoming more disposed toward making a trip to the Middle East, perhaps soon. The officials maintained, as President Reagan said Monday, that Israel was primarily responsi-

Continued on Page A21, Column 6

REPORT HIGHLIGHTS PHALANGISTS' ROLE

Inquiry Says Israeli 'Ordered' Christians Into the Camps

By THOMAS L. FRIEDMAN

Special to The New York Times

JERUSALEM, Feb. 8 — The report of the Israeli commission of inquiry into the killings in the Palestinian camps in Beirut contains new details of the events of September and of the workings of the Christian Phalangists who carried out the operation.

For the first time, the Israeli commission officially confirmed the name of the Phalangist officer in charge of the operation in the Sabra and Shatila camps — Elie Hobeika, the head of intelligence. The report also disclosed that the Israeli Chief of Staff, Lieut. Gen. Rafael Eytan, made a personal appeal to Phalangist commanders after the massacre to admit their guilt and try to explain their behavior publicly, but they did not do so.

According to the report, when the Israeli Army entered West Beirut on Wednesday, Sept. 15, after the assassination of President-elect Bashir Gemayel — the former commander of the Phalangist militia — General Eytan went to the Phalangist military headquarters. There, it said, he "ordered the Phalangist commanders to effect a general mobilization of all their

Continued on Page A22, Column 4

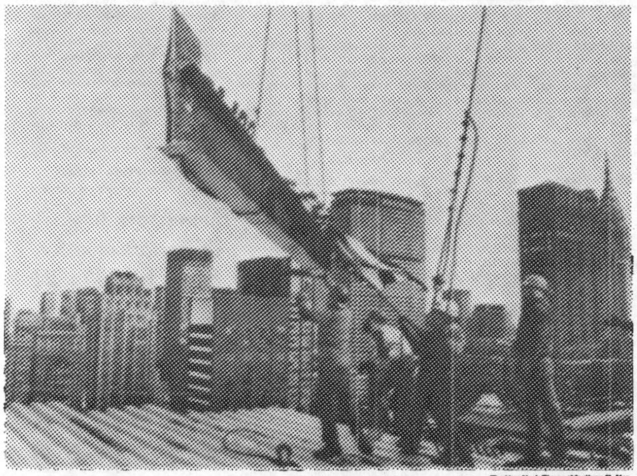

The New York Times/Marilynn K. Yee

FIFTH AVENUE BUILDING TOPPED OUT: Workers placing a flag-draped girder on the addition to the Republic National Bank building. A Fifth Avenue Association official called it "the first real, meaningful construction" on the avenue below 42d Street since the Empire State Building. New York Day by Day, page B3.

Sentry Inquiry Leads to $1 Million

By SELWYN RAAB

A green plastic garbage bag stuffed with about $1 million has been found in the home of relatives of one of the suspects in the theft of $11 million from a Bronx armored-car company, the Federal Bureau of Investigation said yesterday.

F.B.I. agents came across the money after interviews Monday with Mr. and Mrs. Thomas Skiadas, the father- and mother-in-law of Demetrious Papadakos, who was arrested Saturday in Miami, law-enforcement officials said.

According to the officials, Mr. and Mrs. Skiadas said they had no idea how the bag and its 60 pounds of money in denominations of $100 and smaller had got into a closet at their home in Westport, Conn.

A spokesman for the F.B.I., Joseph Valiquette, said investigators were trying to determine whether the money was some of that stolen from the Sentry Armored Car Courier Company in December. If the money is part of the loot, it would be the first recovered from the crime.

The F.B.I. has said that the 35-year-old Mr. Papadakos, who lived in Norwalk, Conn., until two months ago, was probably the "main motivator" in the Sentry theft. Three other men were also arrested last week in the case.

As part of background checks of all the suspects, F.B.I. agents interviewed Mr. and Mrs. Skiadas in their home at 6 Fermily Lane.

A law-enforcement official said that after the interviews, the couple let the agents "look around" their home, and the bag with the money was found.

After the discovery, the F.B.I. got a search warrant from a Federal judge in Bridgeport to allow them to seize the money.

There have been no charges against

Continued on Page B7, Column 1

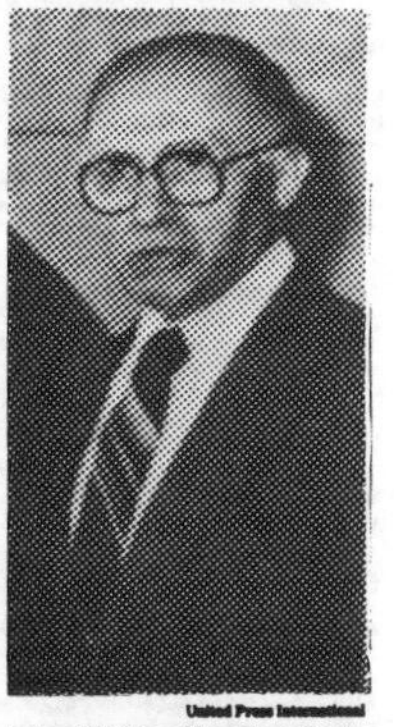

United Press International

Prime Minister Menachem Begin of Israel, whom report criticized.

E.P.A. Counsel Accused of Impeding Inquiry

By DAVID BURNHAM

Special to The New York Times

WASHINGTON, Feb. 8 — The general counsel to the Environmental Protection Agency was accused by a House subcommittee chairman today of violating the law by seeking to impede a Congressional investigation.

The allegation by Representative John D. Dingell, Democrat of Michigan, arose one day after President Reagan dismissed Rita M. Lavelle, a top official of the agency, and after the House of Representatives held Anne M. Gorsuch, the agency's administrator, in contempt of Congress for failure to turn over information.

In a letter to Mrs. Gorsuch, he said that his committee was being hampered in efforts to question agency employees to investigate strong evidence that waste site cleanup funds had been "manipulated for political purposes."

Representative Dingell is chairman of the Oversight and Investigations Subcommittee of the House Energy and Commerce Committee. He charges that the environmental agency's general counsel, Robert M. Perry, sought to block the subcommittee's inquiry into how the agency handled the case of the Stringfellow Acid Pits in California. That case had been supervised by Miss Lavelle, who was dismissed Monday by Mr. Reagan as assistant administrator in charge of the toxic waste cleanup program.

The Stringfellow Acid Pits site is a large toxic waste dump near Los Angeles; negotiations are under way over what steps should be taken to clean it up and who should pay for the cleanup.

A spokesman for the agency said Mrs. Gorsuch had received Mr. Dingell's letter but would have no comment

Continued on Page B13, Column 4

INSIDE

New Holocaust Report

A Jewish organization's report concludes American Jews were slow to react to the dangers Nazi Germany posed to European Jews. Page B11.

Agee Out at Bendix

William M. Agee resigned as president of the Allied Corporation and chairman of Bendix, which was acquired by Allied last year. Page D1.

"All the News That's Fit to Print"

The New York Times

Late Edition

Weather: Partly sunny and cool today, northwesterly winds; partly cloudy tonight. Partly sunny, milder tomorrow. Temperatures: today 45-50, tonight 43-47; yesterday 38-48. Details on page 25.

VOL.CXXXIII . . . No. 45,853

NEW YORK, SATURDAY, NOVEMBER 5, 1983

60 cents beyond 75 miles from New York City, except on Long Island

30 CENTS

AT LEAST 39 DIE AS TRUCK BOMB RIPS ISRAELI POST IN LEBANON; JETS STRIKE PALESTINIAN SITES

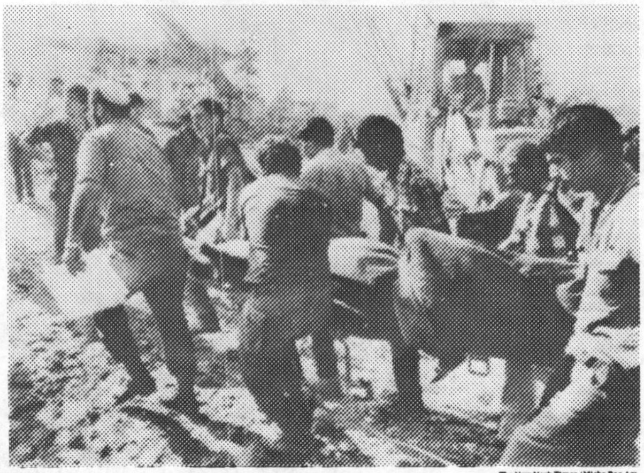

The New York Times / Micha Bar-Am

An Israeli Army rabbi, left, helping to carry the body of an Israeli soldier from site of bombing in Tyre, Lebanon.

ARABS AMONG DEAD

Sentries Shot the Driver but Were Not Able to Divert the Vehicle

By TERENCE SMITH

Special to The New York Times

TYRE, Lebanon, Nov. 4 — A truck loaded with explosives crashed through the entrance to an Israeli headquarters compound here today and detonated near the main building, killing at least 39 people and wounding 32.

A few hours later, Israeli jets struck at Palestinian targets along the Beirut-Damascus Highway, knocking out a command post and a number of tanks and artillery pieces. Some reports said they also attacked Syrian positions. As many as 60 people were reported killed. [Page 8.]

In Tyre, Defense Minister Moshe Arens visited the site of the explosion and told reporters Israel would continue to "hit back" at the terrorists.

The Beirut radio reported that responsibility for the incident had been claimed by the so-called Moslem Jihad, or Moslem Holy War, one of the two groups that claimed responsibility for the Oct. 23 truck bombings in Beirut of the American Marine headquarters and a French barracks.

Sentries Opened Fire

An Israeli Army spokesman said two sentries opened fire at the green Chevrolet truck as it crashed through the main gate of the headquarters compound. The Israelis estimated that the truck was carrying 800 to 1,000 pounds of explosives.

The sentries said they believed that they had hit the driver, but the truck careered on toward the main building. One of the guards was quoted as saying the truck swerved easily around three concrete blocks set as obstacles in the driveway.

Despite the shots fired by the sentries, the truck rolled into the center of the compound to the spot where it exploded, just a few yards from the main building. Officials said it was not clear exactly what set off the explosion.

Building Collapsed

The shockwave caused the building to collapse and blew down the tents of a 35-man medical team bivouaced nearby, according to Lieut. Col. Yona Gazit, a spokesman for the Israeli Army's Northern Command. He said the blast dug a crater 15 yards deep.

The Israeli Army said at least 29 of those killed today were Israeli soldiers or security personnel. Also reported killed were 10 Arabs who were being held in detention cells in the building for interrogation as suspected Palestinian guerrillas.

As the rescue operations got under

Continued on Page 8, Column 5

'We'll Hit Back,' Israel's Defense Minister Vows

By DAVID K. SHIPLER

Special to The New York Times

JERUSALEM, Nov. 4 — Israel reacted to the bombing of its headquarters in Tyre, Lebanon, today with a series of military steps and statements designed to regain a posture of determination and resolve.

Defense Minister Moshe Arens indicated that retaliation might be taken beyond the two air strikes conducted against Palestinian factions near the Beirut-Damascus highway.

"We'll hit back against those who commit these criminal acts," he said on the army radio. "We, of course, will investigate what happened, how it happened, what must be done in order to assure that this won't happen in the future." He ordered the appointment of a commission of investigation.

Stiffer Measures Promised

The Chief of Staff, Lieut. Gen. Moshe Levy, promised stiffer measures against the local population in southern Lebanon.

"We shall have to think about additional arrangements that will surely make life in general in that region more difficult — not only for the security forces — in order that even more extreme actions can be prevented," he said.

Officials said the bridges across the Awali River, Israel's northern defense line in Lebanon, were closed to vehicles after the bombing.

In fashioning its reaction, officials here indicated that the Government was anxious to destroy illusions as well as military targets.

In recent weeks officials in Jerusalem have expressed worry that Syria and Palestinian factions in Lebanon have been seeing an irresolute Israel, weakened by domestic political objections to the involvement in Lebanon

Continued on Page 7, Column 5

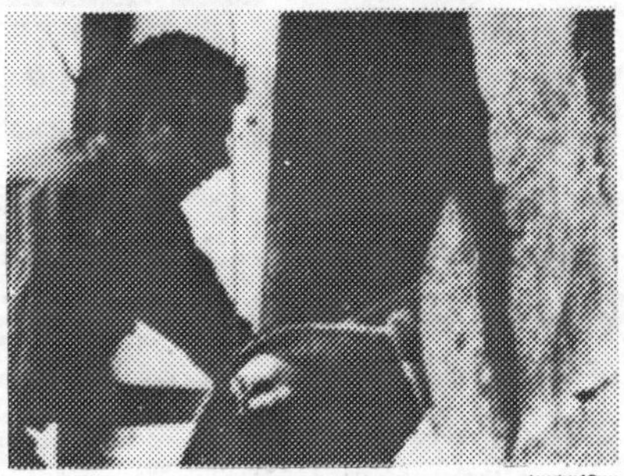

Associated Press

An Israeli soldier covering the body of a comrade in demolished building.

U.S. and Israeli Interests

By BERNARD GWERTZMAN

Special to The New York Times

News Analysis

WASHINGTON, Nov. 4 — The suicide attacks on American, French and Israeli forces over the last 12 days have quickened Washington's determination to alter its policy in Lebanon by forging a closer strategic bond with the Israelis, American officials said today.

They said they hoped to create such a bond now to take advantage of what they regard as a growing convergence of American interests with Israel's.

By coincidence, Under Secretary of State Lawrence S. Eagleburger was in Israel winding up a mission aimed at reducing the misunderstandings and distrust of the last two years when the terrorist explosion occurred at an Israeli compound in Tyre. A goal of his trip was to persuade the new Prime Minister, Yitzhak Shamir, to make an early trip to Washington for discussions on how the two countries can collaborate in these tense times in Lebanon and the Middle East.

A Major Shift for U.S.

This represents a major shift in American thinking about Lebanon, a shift caused both by the diplomatic stalemate over the country's future and a major buildup of Syrian forces. Ever since Israel pulled its troops back from the Shuf Mountains against the advice of the American and Lebanese Governments in early September, the Administration has feared that the Syrians may be under the impression that they can force Israel and the United States out of Lebanon without making any concessions themselves.

In the American view, this could make it impossible to reach a diplomatic solution for the withdrawal of all foreign forces from Lebanon, and increase the risk of another Middle East war by miscalculation, a conflict that could also involve the United States and the Soviet Union.

When the American Marines and the other Western members of the multinational force were sent to the Beirut area in September 1982, after the massacres at the Palestinian camps of Sabra and Shatila, the goal was to bring about a speedy withdrawal of Israeli forces from Lebanon.

The Americans held Israel morally responsible for allowing the Christian Phalangist militiamen into the camps, and Washington wanted to distance it-

Continued on Page 8, Column 1

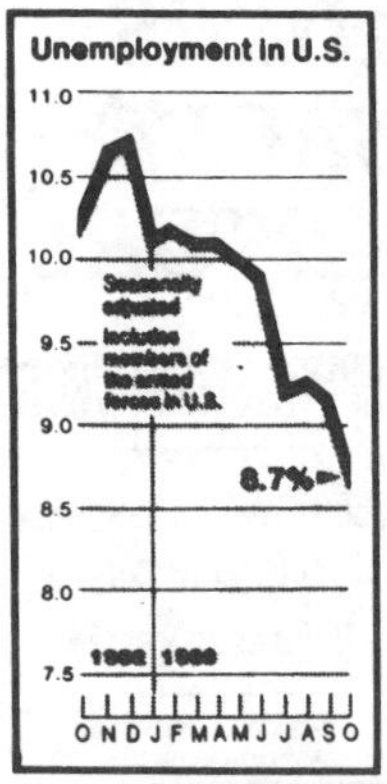
Unemployment in U.S.
11.0
10.5
10.0
9.5
9.0
8.5
8.0
7.5
Seasonally adjusted Includes members of the armed forces in U.S.
8.7%
1982
1983
O N D J F M A M J J A S O

The New York Times / Nov. 5, 1983

Unemployment Drops to 8.7%; Payroll Jobs Up

By SETH S. KING

Special to The New York Times

WASHINGTON, Nov. 4 — The national unemployment rate fell four-tenths of a percentage point in October, to 8.7 percent of the labor force from 9.1 in September, the Labor Department reported today.

The Bureau of Labor Statistics said there was an increase of 320,000 payroll jobs, many of them in durable goods manufacturing and construction, two sectors hit hardest by the recession. The Government said one reason for the rise might be that employers hired more workers instead of extending work hours.

Big Decrease for Jersey

The jobless rate for civilians alone, not counting members of the armed forces in the United States, also declined, falling to 8.8 percent from the 9.3 percent recorded in September.

In New Jersey, the October unemployment rate dropped to 6.8 percent from 8.2 in September. New York City's unemployment rate dropped to 9.2 percent from 10.1 percent. The state rate declined to 8 percent from 8.6. [Page 16.]

The Bureau of Labor Statistics said 101,928,000 civilians were employed last month, down from 101,945,000 in

Continued on Page 16, Column 1

U.S. MAKES PUBLIC ARMS PACTS IT SAYS GRENADIANS MADE

Asserts Soviet, North Korea and Cuba Were to Deliver $37 Million in Weapons

By PHILIP TAUBMAN

Special to The New York Times

WASHINGTON, Nov. 4 — The Reagan Administration made public today copies of what it said were five secret military cooperation agreements concluded by the former Government of Grenada with Cuba, the Soviet Union and North Korea.

Administration officials said the documents called for the delivery of $37 million in military equipment to Grenada and the permanent basing of 27 Cuban military advisers there.

Administration officials said the documents, which were found by American forces that invaded the island last week, supported President Reagan's assertion that Cuba and the Soviet Union were turning Grenada into a military bastion.

49 Russians Leave Grenada

Early today the 126 occupants of the Soviet Embassy in Grenada, including 49 Soviet citizens, 53 Cubans and 15 North Koreans, were flown off the island and taken to Mérida, Mexico. [Page 4.]

The five treaties made public by the State Department this evening show that the Soviet Union planned to ship $25 million in military equipment to Grenada, that North Korea had agreed to provide $12 million worth of supplies and that Cuba expected to send advisers to help Grenada train and expand its armed forces.

Arms to be provided by the Soviet Union, according to the agreements, included 4,000 submachine guns, 2,500 rifles, 7,000 mines, 15,000 grenades and 60 armored-personnel carriers.

'Free Offer of Assistance'

A three-page document, dated April 14, 1983, is designated an agreement regarding "the free offer of military assistance to the People's Revolutionary Government of Grenada by the Government of the Democratic People's Republic of Korea," or North Korea. The name Maurice Bishop appears in handwriting in the signature block, alongside a signature that appears to be in Korean characters.

This agreement, which contains little detail, appears to provide for the sup-

Continued on Page 4, Column 6

U.S. Presses Salvador to Act On Men Tied to Death Squads

By LYDIA CHAVEZ

Special to The New York Times

SAN SALVADOR, Nov. 4 — The United States Embassy here is pressing the Government to take action against a number of army and security officers who are said to be "highly suspected" of involvement in assassination squads, according to high-ranking embassy officials.

The officers said to be involved include the head of security for the Constituent Assembly, two provincial commanders and the directors of intelligence for two of the country's security forces.

Héctor Antonio Regalado, the head of security for the Constituent Assembly, is said to be the "head of the thing," according to well-placed officials here.

Many Thousands Killed

Mr. Regalado is known as a close friend of Roberto d'Aubuisson, the president of the Assembly, and was hired by Mr. d'Aubuisson to direct security for the Assembly.

The death squads, which are believed to be in the pay of right-wing elements, have been blamed for many thousands of civilian deaths in El Salvador over the last four years.

Embassy officials say the death squads are believed to be responsible for the kidnapping of Amilcar Martínez, the third-highest-ranking member of the Foreign Ministry. The officials say the squads are also believed to have assassinated 10 Salvadoran labor union members and to have threatened the two highest-ranking officials in the Roman Catholic Church here, Archbishop Arturo Rivera y Damas and Msgr. Gregorio Rosa-Chávez.

Diplomats here say they believe that unless the Government takes action against these suspects it will be increasingly difficult for the United States Congress to approve further aid to El Salvador.

Some embassy officials said they had expected some of the suspects to be relieved of their duties at the beginning of this month. But the high command issued general orders concerning per-

Continued on Page 10, Column 5

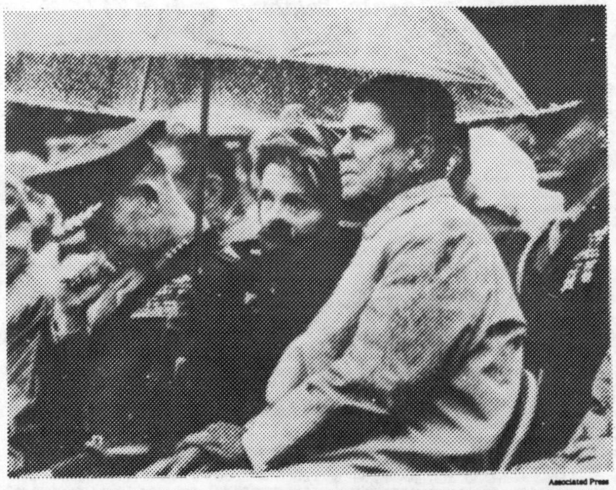

Associated Press

MARINES REMEMBERED: President Reagan and his wife, Nancy, at memorial service at Camp Lejeune, N.C., to honor marines killed in Beirut and Grenada. Gen. Paul X. Kelley, Marine commandant, is at left. Page 7.

INSIDE

Medicare Overhaul Urged

A Federal advisory panel says that to avert Medicare bankruptcy, the eligibility age should go up to 67 and premiums should be raised. Page 12.

Soviet Sub Still on Surface

Officials said the submarine off South Carolina may have been forced up by a collision with a sonar device towed by a U.S. destroyer. Page 10.

Burma Says Agents Of North Korea Set Blast That Killed 21

By The Associated Press

RANGOON, Burma, Nov. 4 — The Burmese Government said today that it had "firmly established" that North Korean agents planted the bomb that killed 17 high-ranking officials of the South Korean Government here last month.

The state radio said that as a result Burma had cut diplomatic relations with North Korea and ordered North Korean Embassy personnel to leave within 48 hours. The two countries had previously had warm relations.

The broadcast said evidence examined by Burmese investigators "firmly established" that the explosion Oct. 9 during a state visit by President Chun Doo Hwan of South Korea was "the work of saboteurs sent by the Democratic People's Republic of Korea."

Four of President Chun's Cabinet members and 13 other presidential aides were killed, along with four Burmese reporters. Forty-six other people were injured.

The radio said the investigators had reached their conclusions from confessions by two men captured by the Burmese police shortly after the bomb attack. The broadcast said the evidence also included equipment seized from the two men and from an associate who

Continued on Page 10, Column 3

"All the News That's Fit to Print"

The New York Times

Late Edition

Weather: Light rain or rain and snow today; snow likely tonight. Partly cloudy, with flurries likely tomorrow. Temperatures: today 37-42, tonight 20-23; yesterday 26-40. Details on page B9.

VOL.CXXXIV . . . No. 46,282 NEW YORK, MONDAY, JANUARY 7, 1985 — 60 cents beyond 75 miles from New York City, except on Long Island — 30 CENTS

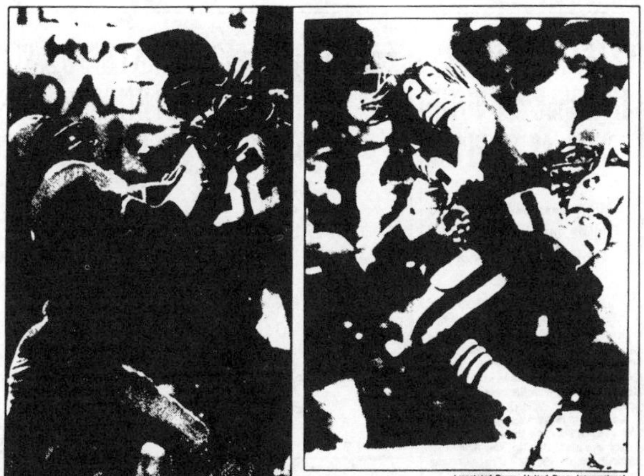

Associated Press; United Press International

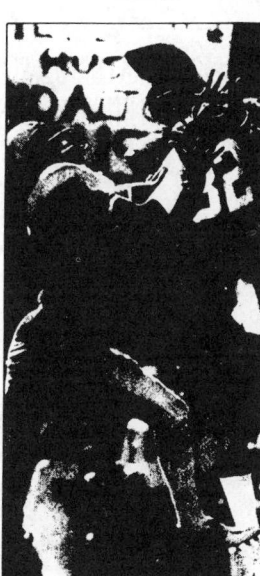

Dolphins and 49ers Win

In American Conference championship, Dolphin's William Judson, left, intercepted pass intended for Steelers' John Stallworth in first quarter. Miami won, 45-28. In National Conference game, 49ers' Wendell Tyler, with Bears' Al Harris in tow, crossed goal line for touchdown in team's 23-0 victory. The Dolphins and the 49ers will meet in Super Bowl XIX in Palo Alto, Calif., on Jan. 20. SportsMonday, page C1.

ISRAEL-RUN AIRLIFT OF ETHIOPIA'S JEWS FROM SUDAN HALTS

Spokesman Says Relief Group Hopes the End of Flights Will Be Just Temporary

By THOMAS L. FRIEDMAN

Special to The New York Times

ASHKELON, Israel, Jan. 6 — The covert airlift of Ethiopian Jews to Israel has been halted because of the publicity given to the operation, a spokesman for the Jewish Agency, a semiofficial Government body, announced today.

"The flights have stopped," said Zvi Eyal, the spokesman for the Jewish Agency, the Israeli-Jewish relief organization that has been coordinating the rescue. "The last planeload arrived Saturday night. We hope this will only be temporary. We are now looking for other airlines."

On Saturday the Belgian charter carrier Trans European Airways — which had reportedly been paid to ferry some 7,000 Ethiopian Jews to Brussels by way of the Sudan since late November — announced it was ending its part in the secret airlift.

Public Disavowals

The announcement of the halt was apparently due to publication of — and fears of repercussions from — the fact that many of the flights of Ethiopian Jews to Israel reportedly began in the Sudan, an Arab country that has no diplomatic relations with Israel. Ethiopia and the Sudan have publicly disavowed the operation. There was no independent confirmation that the airlift had been halted.

News of the airlift was reported in December in two Jewish publications in New York and Washington. Later, on Dec. 11, The New York Times published an account of the increased airlift and then other news organizations around the world published their own reports. The Israeli Government officially acknowledged the airlift for the first time last Thursday.

Thousands Still Stranded

Meanwhile, Libya announced today that it would call for an emergency Arab League meeting to discuss the Israeli airlift of Ethiopian Jews, the official Libyan press agency reported.

The reported abrupt end to the rescue effort has left 6,000 to 8,000 Ethiopian Jews still inside drought-ridden Ethiopia and at least 4,000 Ethiopian Jews stranded in refugee camps outside Ethiopia, according to Mr. Eyal.

As for the 12,000 Ethiopian Jews already in to Israel, many of them re-

Continued on Page A6, Column 1

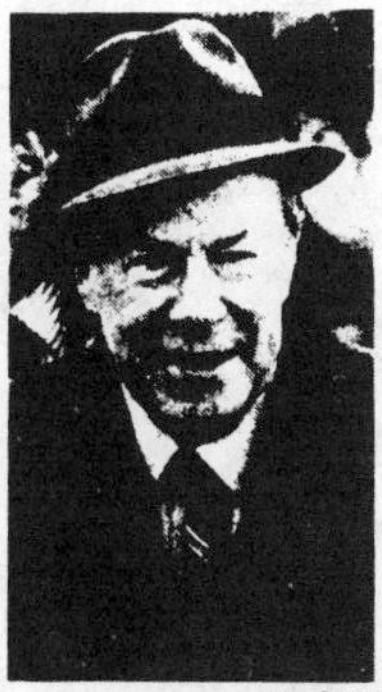

Reuters

Secretary of State George P. Shultz arriving yesterday in Geneva.

Geneva Meeting Is an Encounter On Three Fronts

By LESLIE H. GELB

Special to The New York Times

GENEVA, Jan. 6 — The superpower meeting here on arms control is taking shape in three arenas: a public propaganda battle as a backdrop to businesslike private exchanges, intertwined with throngs of journalists ready to record and judge success and failure.

In the arena of public diplomacy, Moscow is trying to fan concerns about a new arms race in space, and Washington is trying to play down the issue and expectations about the results of the meeting generally.

Polite and Ritualized

In the arena of private diplomacy, the talks that begin Monday between Secretary of State George P. Shultz and Foreign Minister Andrei A. Gromyko are expected by both sides to be polite, ritualized and largely predetermined by deliberations in Washington and Moscow. Mr. Shultz is said to hope that Mr. Gromyko will invite him to visit Moscow in a few months.

The third arena emerges from the interplay between the diplomats and the journalists from around the world who are gathered here. From grimaces, nods and cryptic remarks by diplomats, the journalists pass on what they think is happening behind the closed doors. Sometimes an American official or Soviet reporter is assigned the task of disclosing a particular piece of information.

The Administration began the latest

Continued on Page A8, Column 4

SHULTZ PROMISES A 'REASONABLE' U.S. AT ARMS MEETINGS

HE MEETS GROMYKO TODAY

Secretary Is Said to Be Given New Flexibility in Talks on Antisatellite Weapons

By BERNARD GWERTZMAN

Special to The New York Times

GENEVA, Jan. 6 — Secretary of State George P. Shultz said today that he was carrying "some very interesting and reasonable positions" to present to Foreign Minister Andrei A. Gromyko when Soviet-United States arms control talks resume here on Monday.

He did not specify, in a news conference aboard his plane on his way here, what those "positions" were. But some American officials said Mr. Shultz was given additional flexibility by President Reagan two days ago in discussing possible restraints on development of an antisatellite weapons system, something that Moscow seeks to halt.

'We Have No Illusions'

In his arrival statement this morning, Mr. Shultz said he had been sent here on "a mission for peace," but he was deliberately cautious about predicting the outcome of the first important Soviet-American arms control exchange in 13 months.

"We have no illusions that progress will be easy to achieve," he said.

Mr. Gromyko, who like Mr. Shultz was wearing a fedora and a heavy overcoat against the unusually bitter Geneva weather, arrived eight hours after Mr. Shultz.

He was restrained in his remarks, which he made in English. He repeated the Soviet Union's desire for progress in the meetings and affirmed the Soviet goal, stated again on Saturday by Konstantin U. Chernenko, the Soviet leader, to have the two days of talks here Monday and Tuesday result in an agreement to orient future negotiations toward preventing "an arms race in outer space" as well as achieving "radical reduction" of nuclear arms.

Soviet Focus on Space Arms

The purpose of these talks, which have drawn hundreds of journalists to Geneva from all over the world, is to agree on a format for future negotiations covering both nuclear arsenals and space weapons. But there has already emerged what appears to be a significant difference over how to deal with the American plan for long-range research on defensive space weapons.

Mr. Shultz is working under instructions from President Reagan not to agree to negotiations that might inhibit such research, while Mr. Chernenko and Mr. Gromyko seem to be giving priority to having future negotiations focus on "the nonmilitarization" of space, as Mr. Chernenko put it on Saturday, which would mean a ban on development programs.

Washington made clear last week that it sees such weapons, known by critics as "Star Wars," as a way of enhancing stability, while Moscow re-

Continued on Page A8, Column 5

Zaccaro Indictment Is to Be Announced Today, Lawyers Say

By RALPH BLUMENTHAL

The Manhattan District Attorney is to announce the indictment of John A. Zaccaro today on several misdemeanor counts involving a failed real estate deal in Queens, lawyers close to the case said yesterday.

Elkan Abramowitz, a lawyer for one of three other men reported to have been indicted along with Mr. Zaccaro, said he had been notified to surrender his client, Harold Farrell, today at the office of District Attorney Robert M. Morgenthau for booking and arraignment. At that time, he said, Mr. Farrell and the three others are to be informed of the charges.

Considering Guilty Plea

A lawyer for Mr. Zaccaro, John B. Koegel, said in an interview Saturday that Mr. Zaccaro was considering pleading guilty to one of the charges in return for the dropping of the others. Mr. Koegel declined to say which charge Mr. Zaccaro might plead guilty to, and Mr. Zaccaro would not discuss the matter.

Mr. Koegel did not repond yesterday to numerous messages left at his Manhattan apartment and law office. But other lawyers familiar with the discussions said such a plea was likely today.

Jerome Blitzer, counsel to the credit union of the Port Authority of New

Continued on Page B2, Column 5

Water That Enriched Valley Becomes a Peril in California

By ROBERT LINDSEY

Special to The New York Times

FRESNO, Calif., Jan. 2 — Farmers in the Central Valley of California are facing a cruel irony: the irrigation water that transformed a desert into the nation's most bountiful agricultural area is now threatening to make much of it worthless again.

"There's already some areas of the valley where you can't grow anything," said John Pucheu, who farms 2,300 acres near the hamlet of Tranquillity, 30 miles west of here.

The reason: irrigation water has picked up salt and other chemicals from the soil, and there is no natural outlet from the valley for the tainted water. A hard layer of clay concentrates the polluted water near the surface, making the soil infertile.

'We're Facing Disaster'

"If we don't solve the problem, we're facing disaster," said Mr. Pucheu, a third generation farmer in this valley. "The way it's going, it could affect half a million acres."

The Federal Bureau of Reclamation, which built the system of canals and dams that helped turn the valley into a productive farming region, acknowledges that unless the problem is solved, vast sections of the west side of the valley now farmed by more than 12,000 growers will have to be taken out of production within a few years.

Man's efforts to drain the brackish water from the valley have been snagged in politics. One plan was put into effect, with the result that some of the poisons are now being dumped into a wildlife refuge, where they are blamed for causing thousands of birds to be born with twisted wings, misshapen hearts, warped spines and other defects.

The only other option that seems feasible in the near term, building a pipeline to the Pacific Ocean, is opposed by coastal communities.

Solution May Take 20 Years

The Bureau of Reclamation says that it is looking for ways to drain the valley but that finding a solution could take as long as 20 years and cost as much as $5 billion.

Although there has been no indication that toxins in the irrigation water pose a hazard to humans, some environmentalists have warned that, in

Continued on Page A12, Column 1

Philadelphia Is 'on the Move,' Mayor Says of His First Year

By WILLIAM ROBBINS

Special to The New York Times

PHILADELPHIA, Jan. 6 — W. Wilson Goode likes to describe Philadelphia as "a city on the move," an expression that many people here would also apply to the outgoing, perpetually busy man who has now served a year as Mayor.

For both Mayor Goode and the city he leads, it was a year of highly visible successes and few setbacks, a year in which so many people found his enthusiasm for his job infectious and in which comment from the press here was so favorable that one critic complains he is being "deified."

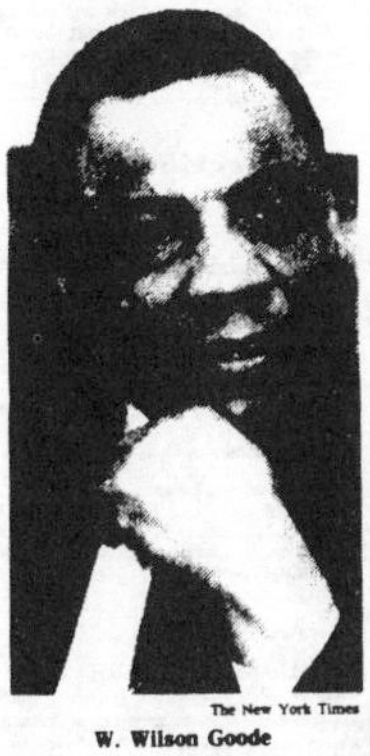

The New York Times

W. Wilson Goode

Such criticism as the Mayor has encountered has been muted, generally involving suggestions that his assertions were overstated and he had been too quick to compromise.

Sometimes the drama of setbacks has worked in his favor. A sequence of events last month could hardly have been improved if he had written a script himself. On a single day, Dec. 15, he emerged successful in a struggle to resolve a transit crisis and in a fight to prevent the Eagles football team from moving to the Sun Belt.

Symbolic Incidents

"There were some crises that permitted me to demonstrate leadership," he acknowledged in an interview.

There was much that was symbolic of Philadelphia and its Mayor in those incidents and in his responses.

One of the year's most highly publicized events was the opening of the Center City commuter tunnel in mid-November after decades of argument over the concept and expenditures of more than $330 million.

Amid the euphoria, few people paid attention to critics who pointed out that the new tunnel connected two rundown and long-neglected commuter-rail systems. The cost of the neglect became evident a week later after an old rail

Continued on Page A15, Column 1

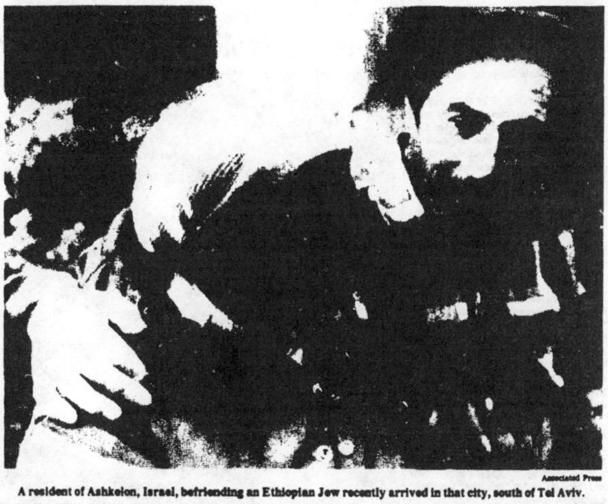

Associated Press

A resident of Ashkelon, Israel, befriending an Ethiopian Jew recently arrived in that city, south of Tel Aviv.

Head of Corruption Inquiry Is Slain in El Salvador

By JAMES LeMOYNE

Special to The New York Times

SAN SALVADOR, Jan. 6 — The head of a Government commission investigating official corruption was shot to death early today, and President José Napoleón Duarte said followers of a far-right party were responsible.

Two men were killed, including one of the reported assailants, and another man was seriously wounded in what was described as a fierce shootout and car chase after the slaying.

The slain Government investigator, Pedro René Yanes, was the head of the Presidential Commission on Ethics, established last year by Mr. Duarte to look into official corruption under previous governments that were controlled by conservative parties. Government officials said Mr. Yanes had found many cases of wrongdoing.

"The cause is obviously of a political character," Mr. Duarte said this evening after attending a wake for Mr. Yanes. "This was a very important person charged with investigations of corruption in all of the country."

Although several Government officials are reported to have received death threats, Mr. Yanes is the first member of Mr. Duarte's Government to be slain. Government ministers have feared such attacks amid growing tension between the Christian Democratic Party, led by Mr. Duarte, and its conservative opponents as the Government pursues peace talks with leftist rebels and prepares for legislative elections in March.

Mr. Yanes was reportedly shot by two assailants. President Duarte did not name them, but one was tentatively identified by Government officials as Reinaldo Osorto, the mayoral candidate for the far-right National Republican Alliance in the rural town of Concepción de Oriente, where the shooting occurred.

The National Republican Alliance is

Continued on Page A5, Column 1

15 Years of Talks

Charts and tables summarize the negotiations between the United States and the Soviet Union. Page A9.

INSIDE

Vietnam Resistance in U.S.

Groups opposed to Communist rule in Vietnam are gaining followers among refugees in the United States, but their strength is uncertain. Page A11.

Cuomo at Midterm

The Governor has made his mark on New York State, and on the nation, as much for what he has said as for what he has done. News Analysis, page B1.

Purchasers Cite Slowdown

New industrial orders fell last month, according to purchasing managers, who paint a bleaker economic picture than other recent reports. Page D1.

2 SPECIAL SECTIONS TODAY: MEN'S FASHIONS AND HIGH-TECHNOLOGY CAREERS

"All the News That's Fit to Print"

The New York Times

Late Edition

Weather: Light rain likely today; chance of light snow tonight. Partly sunny, windy and chilly tomorrow. Temperatures: today 40-42, tonight 30-32; yesterday 35-49. Details on page 37.

VOL. CXXXIV . . . No. 46,358 Copyright © 1985 The New York Times NEW YORK, SUNDAY, MARCH 24, 1985 $1.60 beyond 75 miles from New York City, except on Long Island. $1.25

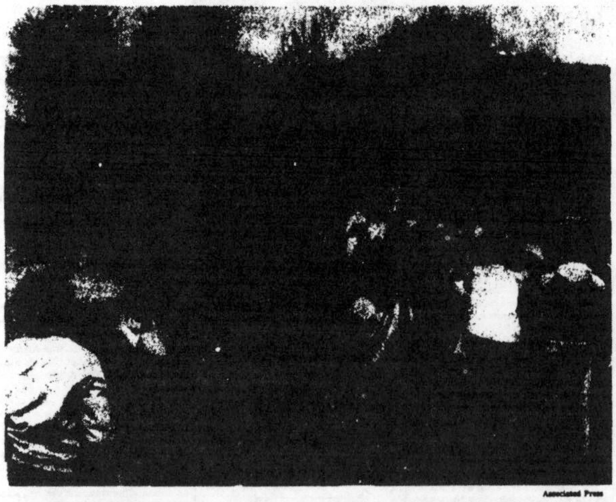

Associated Press

Customers standing in line yesterday outside Molitor Loan and Building Company branch in suburban Cincinnati.

INSURANCE URGED FOR NURSING CARE

Study Says Plan Can Cut Cost of Medicaid and Medicare

By ROBERT PEAR

Special to The New York Times

WASHINGTON, March 23 — Reagan Administration officials say they plan to encourage the development of private insurance for nursing home care for the elderly to help save money for Medicaid and Medicare.

The Department of Health and Human Services commissioned a study of the subject, which concluded that there was a large potential market for such insurance.

The study also said the use of private insurance could produce substantial savings for the Government.

"Long-term care insurance could have a significant impact on Medicaid expenditures" by substituting private for public financing, it said, adding, "Significant savings would occur even if only 20 percent of the elderly purchase the insurance."

The study did not give exact figures for possible savings but said Medicaid costs for a group of elderly people ranging from 67 to 69 years old could be reduced by more than 20 percent over a 35-year period.

A separate report, by the department's National Center for Health Services Research, concluded that there was "a clear need" for private insurance to protect against the costs of nursing home care.

Medicaid, the medical assistance

Continued on Page 25, Column 1

46 Thrift Units Reopen in Ohio; Level of Activity Is Called Normal

By GARY KLOTT

Special to The New York Times

CINCINNATI, March 23 — Forty-six more savings and loan institutions reopened in Ohio today to a steady stream of customers who had access to their accounts for the first time since Gov. Richard F. Celeste ordered 71 state-chartered, privately insured thrift units closed March 15.

State officials said a survey of thrift units open today found brisk but not unusually heavy business. They said more money was withdrawn than deposited but the level of withdrawals was not a cause for concern.

"It was excellent — beyond belief," said Robert B. McAllister, Ohio's superintendent of savings and loans. He said there were "heavy runs" on only two of the thrift institutions, which he did not name. He said, however, that these runs did not approach the magnitude of those last week when mounting concerns over insurance covering deposits at the thrift units led to a run on deposits at several of the institutions.

Only four institutions had to borrow funds today from the Federal Reserve Bank in Cleveland to meet withdrawals.

100 Customers in Line

There were reports of lines at some institutions. The longest was reported at the Molitor Loan and Building Company branch in suburban Cincinnati, where the police watched as the doors opened at 10 A.M. to about 100 customers.

There was a line of 35 to 40 depositors, some of them chanting, "We want our money," outside the Charter Oak Savings Association branch, also in suburban Cincinnati. Both institutions experienced a run on deposits before the Governor ordered the 71 thrift units closed.

At the Charter Oak Savings Association in Columbus today, two private security guards allowed 10 customers at a time into the lobby to make withdrawals limited to $750 or less, to cash checks or to make deposits. About an hour after opening about 15 people were waiting in line outside.

"This is my only bank and I've got some bills to pay," said Jim Knoblauch, a 38-year-old toolmaker who was waiting on line to replenish his checking account.

T. B. Neighbors, 29, said she planned to withdraw some of her savings from a Columbus Charter Oak branch and "put it elsewhere, so I don't have all my eggs in one basket."

Normally Closed Saturday

In downtown Cincinnati, one small thrift institution had no customers in the lobby at midday despite a large sign in the window saying, "We're Open." At another a few blocks away, only one customer was making a transaction. At the Molitor branch near the

Continued on Page 31, Column 1

REAGAN'S MARGIN IN HOUSE MX VOTE SEEN AS SLIPPING

2 Camps Say Odds Still Favor Missile, but Backers Now Fear Chance of Defeat

By STEVEN V. ROBERTS

Special to The New York Times

WASHINGTON, March 23 — As the House prepares to vote Tuesday on President Reagan's request for 21 new MX missiles, both sides say the Administration's once-comfortable margin is slipping.

Opponents of the huge intercontinental weapon concede that the odds still favor approval, but for the first time supporters of the MX are worrying openly that it could be defeated.

Representative Les Aspin of Wisconsin, a leading Democratic proponent of the missile, assessed the fight as "very, very close."

Speaker Sees Gains

In an interview reported by The Associated Press today, House Speaker Thomas P. O'Neill Jr. said opponents of the MX had gained ground in recent days with "ones who were wavering."

"It's an uphill battle, but it's close," Mr. O'Neill said.

Another senior Democrat who backs the missile said: "There are some very ominous signs that give me concern. I think it's going to lose." He said those signs included growing opposition to the cost of the weapon at a time of budget austerity; the united efforts of the House Democratic leadership to defeat the weapon, and a backlash among some Democrats against Republican campaign tactics.

Only a Few Undecided

Opponents of the missile say they can count on a minimum of 190 Democrats and 19 Republicans, or 209 votes. Mr. O'Neill told the A.P. that a recent count by the House leadership found 198 Democratic votes solidly against the missile. Since the House has two vacancies, 217 represents a majority if all members vote.

Only 15 to 20 members still profess genuine indecision, and they have been subject to ferocious lobbying by both sides.

"This is the most intense struggle for votes I've ever seen," said David Cohen, former president of the public affairs lobby Common Cause, who is a strategist for the MX opponents. "It's one on one, member to member."

As part of that struggle, the Administration Friday night summoned home Max M. Kampelman, the chief negotia-

Continued on Page 18, Column 1

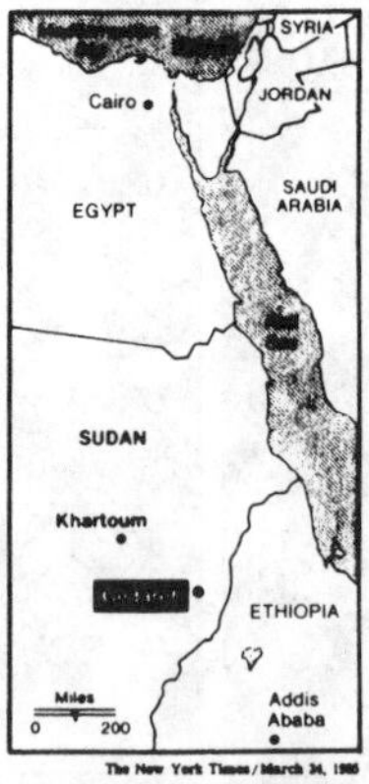

The New York Times/March 24, 1985

U.S. planes picked up Ethiopian Jews near Gedaref, the Sudan.

7 Die as Unrest Flares Up Anew In South Africa

By ALAN COWELL

Special to The New York Times

JOHANNESBURG, March 23 — The police reported today that black activists had killed five fellow blacks they suspected of being Government stooges and that two other blacks were shot and killed by a black policeman.

Five of the slayings were apparently in revenge for the police killing of 19 blacks Thursday in Langa township near the southern automotive center of Uitenhage. Many blacks in South Africa feel that blacks who work with the white authorities share responsibility for the authorities' actions.

Thus, in the vengeful mood that followed the shootings Thursday, such figures would be seen as candidates for retribution. In the violence today, the homes of black policemen were set on fire.

Three of those killed today were said by the police to be friends or relatives of the township's last remaining community councilor.

In townships near Uitenhage, the focus of recent unrest that has raised the number of deaths in the last year to almost 250 across the nation, thousands of blacks massed in the streets. Witnesses said that policemen ringed the tense areas in armored vehicles and that air force helicopters were flying

Continued on Page 17, Column 1

SUDAN LETS U.S. FLY 800 ETHIOPIA JEWS TO ISRAELI REFUGE

SECRET 3-DAY OPERATION

Evacuation of Last Refugees Was Arranged by Bush in Meeting With Nimeiry

By BERNARD GWERTZMAN

Special to The New York Times

WASHINGTON, March 23 — The United States, in a secret operation, today completed the evacuation of virtually all the Ethiopian Jews who were left in the Sudan after an Israeli-sponsored airlift was halted, Administration officials said.

The operation was directed by the Central Intelligence Agency, and involved the State Department and the Air Force, the sources said. In a three-day period, 800 people were flown by C-130 Hercules transports to Israel, the officials said.

Because of the sensitivity of the issue, the United States Government would not officially comment. Israel has also refused to discuss the matter and has imposed censorship on news dispatches related to it, saying that the lives of people involved were at risk.

Reporter in the Sudan

According to United Press International, President Reagan was asked about the matter today as he and his wife, Nancy, were greeting children involved in the Special Olympics for the disabled. Mrs. Reagan looked at him and whispered, "I don't know." He then told reporters, "No comment."

Information was gained from several officials aware of the airlift who spoke on condition that there would be no attribution to them or their agency.

The operation was first disclosed by The Los Angeles Times, whose reporter was in the Sudan. As a result of that account, people who might not otherwise have spoken were willing to provide additional information.

They said the plan had been worked out when Vice President Bush met with President Gaafar al-Nimeiry of the Sudan this month. Mr. Nimeiry agreed, as long as the Jews were not evacuated by Israeli planes.

Nimeiry Coming to the U.S.

The Sudan, which has dire economic problems, has already received nearly 400,000 refugees from the famine in Ethiopia, including 8,000 Jews.

Mr. Nimeiry has relied on American military and economic aid, even though much of the aid has been held up until the Sudan carries out needed economic changes.

It was announced today that he is scheduled to come to the United States and will see President Reagan at the White House on April 1.

"It was obviously convenient for Nimeiry to win some points on the Falashas," an official said. Ethiopian Jews are sometimes called Falashas, an Amharic word for "stranger" that they find derogatory.

State Department officials said they did not believe that Mr. Nimeiry's visit was conditional on his cooperation in the airlift. They said he had been scheduled to visit earlier this month, but the date was postponed because of

Continued on Page 15, Column 1

Court Weighs Suit by Parents In Birth of an Unsought Child

By DAVID MARGOLICK

For most parents, there are few events more joyous than the arrival of a healthy, normal baby. But for Brian and Susanne O'Toole of Queens, things were not so simple.

Five years ago Mr. and Mrs. O'Toole decided that for their financial and physical health, three children were enough.

Mr. O'Toole, who was 25 years old at the time, brought home barely $200 a week as a subway car cleaner for the Metropolitan Transportation Authority. His family was already jammed into a one-bedroom apartment. And Mrs. O'Toole, who was about to undergo her third Caesarian section, had been told that any more such deliveries could endanger her life.

So, in January 1980, after the birth of her third child, she was sterilized. She said the doctors at Jamaica Hospital who performed the operation, known as a tubal ligation, had assured her that she would never become pregnant again.

Child-Raising Costs Sought

But about one year later, Mrs. O'Toole became pregnant. KellyAnne Marie O'Toole was born in November 1981, two months after her parents had filed a malpractice claim against the doctors who performed the surgery and against the hospital where it was done. What distinguishes the O'Toole case from other "wrongful pregnancy" cases is the damages they seek: the costs of raising KellyAnne until she reaches adulthood.

KellyAnne and the lawsuit that revolves around her have grown together. She is now 3 years old, a pretty strawberry blonde with bright blue eyes. And the case of O'Toole v. Greenberg et al. is before the state's highest court, which has been asked, in effect,

Continued on Page 30, Column 1

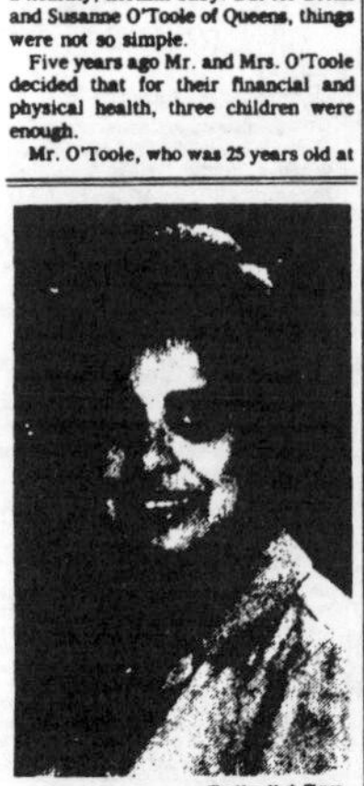

The New York Times

PATRICIA R. HARRIS DIES: Former Secretary of H.E.W. and H.U.D. in the Carter Administration died in Washington. Page 36.

Koreans Hold Chinese Boat on Which 6 Died

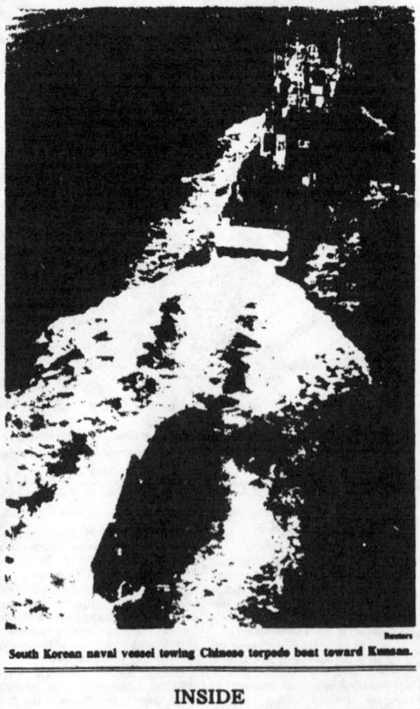

Reuters

South Korean naval vessel towing Chinese torpedo boat toward Kunsan.

By CLYDE HABERMAN

Special to The New York Times

TOKYO, March 23 — South Korea continued tonight to hold a Chinese torpedo boat that drifted into its waters with six dead crew members, killed in what some reports described as a mutiny after some crewmen tried to defect.

The South Korean Government made no direct response to a Chinese request for the return of the naval vessel and its crew "as soon as possible."

[China and South Korea were reportedly holding talks on the return of the boat and crew through officials they maintain in Hong Kong.]

2 Reportedly in Hospital

Two crew members, reportedly shot but not critically wounded, were in a hospital in the South Korean port of Kunsan, on the Yellow Sea. A total of 10 or 11 other crewmen were also believed to have been taken to Kunsan, but their whereabouts could not be determined. Their boat was apparently offshore.

It was not clear whether any of the sailors sought political asylum in South Korea or preferred to be sent home.

South Korean officials seemed to deal cautiously with the episode, which threatened to undercut recent attempts by the two countries to pursue friendly contacts even though they have no diplomatic relations.

'A Simple Scuffle'

A statement issued tonight in Seoul by the Minister of Culture and Information, Lee Won Hong, did not mention a mutiny or any deaths.

"It was determined, based on facts so far obtained, that casualties aboard the Chinese torpedo boat were due to a simple scuffle among the crewmen and that no political reason was involved," Mr. Lee said.

Officials interviewed by telephone from Seoul declined to give details. But several foreign diplomats in South Korea described the incident as a mutiny that seemed to have begun on

Continued on Page 14, Column 1

INSIDE

Accord in Pan Am Strike

Pan American World Airways has reached a tentative settlement with striking ground workers after a 24-day walkout. Page 23.

Zoot Sims Dies

The saxophonist, the exemplar of "swing" as he played in the bands of Benny Goodman, Woody Herman and Stan Kenton, died at 59. Page 36.

Today's Sections

Index to Subjects

"All the News That's Fit to Print"

The New York Times

Late Edition
Weather: Mostly sunny and warm today; cloudy, chance of showers tonight. Partly cloudy and mild tomorrow. Temperatures: today 80-85, tonight 50-55; yesterday 45-67. Details on page C4.

VOL.CXXXIV . . . No. 46,384 | NEW YORK, FRIDAY, APRIL 19, 1985 | 30 CENTS

50 cents beyond 75 miles from New York City except on Long Island.

ECONOMIC GROWTH FELL TO 1.3% RATE IN FIRST '85 PERIOD

LEVEL BELOW FORECASTS

Import Rebound and Drop in Exports Cited — Interest Rates and Dollar Slide

By ROBERT D. HERSHEY Jr.
Special to The New York Times

WASHINGTON, April 18 — The economy slowed sharply to a weak 1.3 percent annual growth rate in the first three months of the year, the Commerce Department reported today.

That was the smallest growth since the recovery began in late 1982 and was far below the 4.3 percent rate of the final 1984 quarter.

According to most economists, the report dashed hopes that the United States could achieve the Reagan Administration's 3.9 percent growth target for 1985. One of the implications is an adverse effect on the Federal budget deficit because lower economic activity, among other things, implies lower incomes, profits and Treasury revenues.

Frantic Currency Trading

Today's report spurred a sharp fall in interest rates. It also led to frantic trading in the currency markets as the dollar suffered one of its sharpest plunges in the 12-year history of floating exchange rates. [Pages D1 and D16.]

Although some analysts shaved their estimates recently for the first-quarter gross national product, the nation's total output of goods and services, the 1.3 percent growth rate fell well below expectations. The department's "flash" estimate last month was that growth would run at a 2.1 percent rate for the quarter.

The main reason for the first-quarter slowdown was the drag from the international sector. Imports, which tumbled in the preceding quarter, rebounded, while exports fell.

"I see this as part of the longer-range trend that began in the summer of 1984 when the strength of the dollar really began to bite into economic activity,"

Continued on Page D4, Column 1

New York City And Key Union Agree on a Pact

Contract Would Cover 115,000 for 3 Years

By JOSH BARBANEL

Mayor Koch and the leader of the city's largest municipal union announced a tentative agreement yesterday on a three-year contract covering 115,000 city employees.

The agreement, with District Council 37 of the American Federation of State, County and Municipal Employees, was reached in a hastily convened four-hour bargaining session that caught other labor leaders by surprise after nearly a year of sporadic negotiations. The last contract expired June 30.

Under the tentative pact, most workers would receive 5 percent wage increases in each of the first two years of the contract and 6 percent in the third year. The average salary for members of the union is $16,000, union officials said.

Reductions in Vacations

The union also gained the right to a 12th paid holiday in honor of the birthday of the Rev. Dr. Martin Luther King Jr. and other benefit increases.

The union agreed to sharp reductions in the vacations for new employees for the first four years on the job, beginning with a cut from four weeks to two weeks in the first year.

Mr. Koch and the head of the union, Victor L. Gotbaum, announced the tentative agreement in separate news conferences. Mr. Gotbaum said that this reflected the bitterness of the often-stalled negotiations, especially Mr. Koch's refusal to grant a paid holiday last January for Dr. King's birthday.

Voting Next Thursday

"I didn't want to smile down his teeth," Mr. Gotbaum said. "I didn't feel like saying to the Mayor, 'Now everything is ginger peachy.'"

Mr. Koch declined to comment on Mr. Gotbaum's remarks, except to say, "You know when you know a real victor — when they're gracious."

The accord was unanimously approved by the union's board, and it is to be put to a vote by union delegates next

Continued on Page D19, Column 2

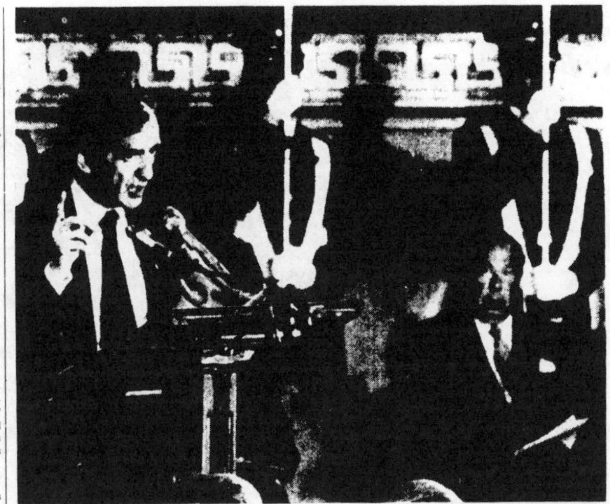

The New York Times/Paul Hosefros

Elie Wiesel speaking yesterday during a memorial service in the Rotunda of the Capitol marking the anniversary of the liberation of the Nazi concentration camps. Seated at right is Secretary of State George P. Shultz.

Reagan Likens Nazi War Dead To Concentration Camp Victims

By GERALD M. BOYD
Special to The New York Times

WASHINGTON, April 18 — President Reagan, standing by his decision to lay a wreath at a German military cemetery next month, said today that most of the soldiers buried there were as much victims of the Nazis as the inmates of the concentration camps.

The President's remarks immediately stirred a new burst of criticism from American Jewish groups and others, who reiterated demands that he cancel the cemetery visit.

"I think that there is nothing wrong with visiting that cemetery where those young men are victims of Nazism also, even though they were fighting in the German uniform, drafted into service to carry out the hateful wishes of the Nazis," Mr. Reagan said. "They were victims, just as surely as the victims in the concentration camps."

His remarks, made in response to a question at a White House session with regional editors and broadcasters, were his most detailed explanation yet of the decision to visit the cemetery at Bitburg, near the Luxembourg border. The cemetery has the graves of nearly 2,000 German soldiers, including 47 members of the SS, the Nazi elite guard.

As the new protests erupted, several resolutions were introduced in the House of Representatives urging Mr. Reagan not to go to the cemetery. On Wednesday, 53 senators urged him in a letter to omit the Bitburg ceremony.

Protests over preparations for President Reagan's five-day trip to West Germany next month began when he said at a news conference on March 21 that he would not visit a Nazi concentration camp site. The criticism mounted when it was announced last week that the itinerary included a stop at the Bitburg cemetery.

The protests from Jewish organizations and veterans' groups prompted Mr. Reagan to agree to add a Nazi camp site to his itinerary after all.

The camp is expected to be chosen after the President confers Friday with Michael K. Deaver, his deputy chief of staff, who has been in West Germany inspecting possible sites. Bergen-Belsen appears to be favored, according to reports from Bonn.

Today Mr. Reagan appeared to be prepared for a question on his visit to West Germany and sought to explain his decision to lay a wreath in Bitburg.

He said it would be "very hurtful" to

Continued on Page A13, Column 1

Transcript of remarks, page A13.

REAGAN'S REMARKS STIR NEW DEBATE

President's Visit to Germany Is Assailed at Ceremony

By FRANCIS X. CLINES
Special to The New York Times

WASHINGTON, April 18 — Elie Wiesel, chairman of the United States Holocaust Memorial Council, pleaded today with Secretary of State George P. Shultz to dissuade President Reagan from inflicting "pain and shame" on Americans by visiting a cemetery where Nazi war dead are buried.

"Mr. Secretary, please be our emissary," Mr. Wiesel said, turning to Mr. Shultz at a mournful Capitol ceremony honoring the American liberation of the German death camps of World War II. "Tell those who need to know that our pain is genuine, our outrage deep and our perplexity infinite."

Mr. Wiesel spoke before learning of remarks today in which the President contended that both the Jews slain in the Holocaust, and some of the soldiers, many of them draftees, who are buried in the German cemetery that he intends to visit, were victims of Nazism.

This evening, about 25 of the 55 Presidential appointees to the Holocaust Memorial Council voted unanimously to send a telegram to Mr. Reagan saying,

Continued on Page A10, Column 1

REAGAN REPORTED TO POSTPONE MOVE ON REBEL ARMS AID

MOVE TO 'NONLETHAL' HELP

But Attempt to Send Weapons to Nicaraguan Guerrillas Would Be Renewed

By STEVEN V. ROBERTS
Special to The New York Times

WASHINGTON, April 18 — Faced with almost certain defeat in Congress, President Reagan has agreed for now to accept a compromise proposal to postpone military aid to the rebels fighting the Nicaraguan Government, a White House official said tonight.

The official said the President would accept an arrangement under which any American aid to the rebels between now and Oct.1 could be used only for "nonlethal" purposes. That would include trucks and uniforms, the official said, but not guns and ammunition.

Republicans and Democrats in both houses were still working on various compromises tonight and many of the details remained uncertain. But the Democrats favor legislation that would provide only nonmilitary aid, such as food and clothing, and would be more restrictive than the compromise backed by the White House.

Byrd Proposes Talks

This evening, Senator Robert C. Byrd of West Virginia, the Democratic leader, met Democratic lawmakers and then telephoned President Reagan with an offer to discuss possible compromises. The President replied that such a meeting would be a "good idea," according to a spokesman for Mr. Byrd.

All parties to the negotiations, however, seem to have accepted the principle that no military aid will be provided for the rest of the fiscal year, which ends Sept. 30.

Asked if military aid to the Nicaraguan rebels was now dead for this fiscal year, Representative Trent Lott of Mississippi, the Republican whip, said, "I think so."

Senator James A. McClure, an Idaho Republican handling the issue in the Senate, said, "It's pretty clear that military aid is dead for an extended period of time."

Renewed Fight Is Seen

But the Republicans indicated that the Administration would renew its fight for military aid to the rebels when Congress allocates foreign assistance for the next fiscal year. "This is not the last vote on this issue," Mr. Lott said.

Last year, the Administration requested $14 million in military funds for the rebels, to be funneled through the Central Intelligence Agency. The lawmakers allocated the money but said it could not be released until the

Continued on Page A8, Column 1

Turner Makes Offer for CBS; Wall St. Skeptical on Success

By SALLY BEDELL SMITH

Ted Turner, the Atlanta broadcasting entrepreneur, yesterday made his expected offer to buy CBS Inc. But the view on Wall Street was that he stood only a slim chance of succeeding.

Richard MacDonald, an analyst for the First Boston Corporation, an investment house, called the proposal "a brilliant idea, a fabulous blueprint for someone who wants to take over CBS." But he added, "It will never happen."

CBS, the dominant television network in ratings and also a power in radio, magazines and records, is certain to fight for its independence. Yesterday, though, it declined to comment until it could study the proposal, which it characterized as "complex."

In his offer, Mr. Turner, acting without financial partners, offered to buy 67 percent of the broadcasting giant, but he would pay no cash. Instead, he would give CBS stockholders a package of stock in his much smaller company, Turner Broadcasting System Inc., as well as bonds and other notes paying high interest. Later he would offer to buy the rest of CBS on the same terms.

Mr. Turner estimated the value of his offer at $175 a share, although analysts said it was more realistically worth from $150 to $160 a share. At a value of $150 a share, a 67 percent holding would cost Mr. Turner about $3 billion.

The price of CBS stock gyrated yesterday, as it has in the weeks since Mr. Turner's interest became known. It ended the day at $106.25, down $3.50.

Most Wall Street analysts expressed doubts about Mr. Turner's offer. But

Continued on Page D9, Column 5

New York Developer Seeks to Evict 1,200 Under Rent Controls

By MICHAEL deCOURCY HINDS

A New York developer who recently purchased a block of 26 walk-up buildings on the Upper East Side has announced plans to evict more than 1,200 tenants so he can demolish the buildings and replace them with four high-rise towers.

The announcement has intensified what is likely to be a long and bitter battle between those who live in the six-story, beige-brick buildings, where the rents are regulated, and the developer, Peter Kalikow, who wants to put 1,676 luxury rental apartments in their place.

Regulatory officials say that if Mr. Kalikow is successful, it would be one of the largest dislocations of tenants ever in New York State.

A Sharp Contrast

The walk-ups, for which Mr. Kalikow paid $43 million, are in the heart of one of the most desirable and expensive areas of the city, on a block bounded by 78th and 79th Streets and York Avenue and Franklin D. Roosevelt Drive. Some apartments in the neighborhood carry million-dollar price tags, in sharp contrast to the $300 average monthly rent in the 85-year-old tenements.

Until now, the rent-regulated status of these and similar projects has shielded them from the intense development pressures in Manhattan. As the owner of the property, Mr. Kalikow can

Continued on Page B2, Column 1

U.S. Program in Honduras Helps Families of Nicaraguan Guerrillas

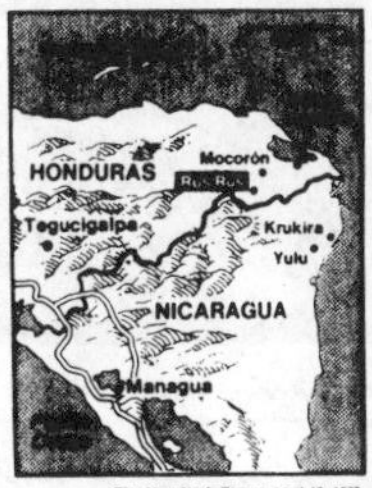

The New York Times/April 19, 1985

The main Nicaraguan Indian guerrilla base is near Rus Rus.

By JAMES LeMOYNE
Special to The New York Times

RUS RUS, Honduras — The United States Government has begun to provide $7.5 million in medical and other nonmilitary aid to an area near a main camp in Honduras for guerrillas fighting the Nicaraguan Government.

A private American relief agency, Friends of America, is working in the same zone, near the Nicaraguan border, supported by conservative United States legislators and private church groups.

Officials in charge of the relief programs strongly denied in interviews that their intention was to assist guerrillas fighting the Sandinista Government, and a reporter found no evidence that either program has directly helped armed rebel fighters. But the projects appear to offer an example of how humanitarian assistance can indirectly support guerrilla fighters.

Over 20,000 Miskito Indian refugees have crossed into the border region in northeastern Honduras over the last three years, fleeing repression in Nicaragua. Indian rebels, drawn from the refugees, have waged a determined guerrilla war against Sandinista troops from bases like the one at Rus Rus, tucked safely inside Honduras.

The chief manner in which the American aid programs appear to assist the rebels is by helping to attract Indian refugees to the border and by providing food and medical care to the families of Indian fighters.

Miskito guerrilla leaders have sought for three years to persuade refugees to move to the border in order to provide food, shelter and new recruits

Continued on Page A8, Column 1

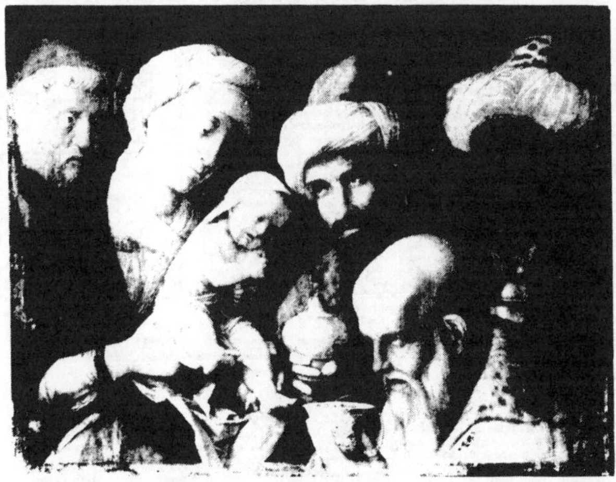

A
B
C
D
E
F

Renaissance Masterpiece Fetches a Record Price for a Painting

Andrea Mantegna's "Adoration of the Magi," which was purchased yesterday by the J. Paul Getty Museum for $10.4 million at a Christie's auction in London. The museum must still get an export license for the work. Page C14.

INSIDE

Conviction in Taiwan

A military court in Taiwan convicted the former head of military intelligence of plotting the murder of a Chinese-American writer. Page A3.

'Tilted Arc' Opposed

A Federal panel urged removal of the controversial Richard Serra sculpture in Foley Square, but a final decision is still to come. Page C4.

U.S. Criticizes Willowbrook

The Government, citing violations of health rules, plans to deny nearly $22 million to the Staten Island center once called Willowbrook. Page B1.

U.S. Relaxes G.E. Ban

Much of General Electric's eligibility to bid for contracts from the Government is being restored by the Air Force. Page D1.

"All the News That's Fit to Print"

The New York Times

Late Edition

Weather: Partly sunny and mild today, light, northerly winds; partly cloudy tonight. Partly sunny and mild tomorrow. Temperatures: today 68-72, tonight 50-55; yesterday 65-88. Details on page 42.

VOL.CXXXIV . . . No. 46,385 Copyright © 1985 The New York Times NEW YORK, SATURDAY, APRIL 20, 1985 — 50 cents beyond 75 miles from New York City, except on Long Island — 30 CENTS

Wiesel Confronts Reagan on Trip; President to Visit Bergen-Belsen

Survivor of Holocaust Urges Him Not to Stop at German Cemetery

By BERNARD WEINRAUB

Special to The New York Times

WASHINGTON, April 19 — President Reagan listened intently today as Elie Wiesel, chairman of the United States Holocaust Memorial Council, implored him to cancel a visit to a German cemetery where Nazi war dead are buried.

"That place, Mr. President, is not your place," Mr. Wiesel told Mr. Reagan at White House ceremonies honoring the 56-year-old writer. "Your place is with the victims of the SS."

White House Announcement

The moment, in the silence of the packed Roosevelt Room, came on a day when the White House announced that Mr. Reagan would visit the Bergen-Belsen concentration camp site.

Elie Wiesel's day in Washington began at 4 A.M. It would end many hours later with Mr. Wiesel saying, "I am still hopeful." Page 4.

His visit to the camp, where Anne Frank died, will be made on the same day that he attends ceremonies at the Bitburg military cemetery, which includes the graves of 47 SS soldiers, members of the Nazi elite guard.

Despite Mr. Wiesel's plea, the White House said Mr. Reagan would not change his plans to lay a wreath at Bitburg, accompanied by Chancellor Helmut Kohl, who requested the visit.

Reagan Is 'Obviously Moved'

But the White House spokesman, Larry Speakes, said that "the President was obviously moved" by Mr. Wiesel's speech.

Drama surrounded Mr. Wiesel's appearance at the White House, where he received the Congressional Gold Medal of Achievement, the highest honor that the Government gives to civilians.

Even when he entered the Roosevelt Room after a 26-minute meeting with Mr. Reagan, it was unclear what he would say and how Mr. Reagan would react. Mr. Wiesel told friends that although he worked on his speech through the night, he remained uncertain this morning if he would actually give it or boycott the ceremonies.

Tension was heightened further when Mr. Wiesel told friends that Marshall J. Breger, a White House liaison officer for Jewish affairs, had sought to limit his speech to three minutes and to

Continued on Page 4, Column 4

Kohl Praises Plan to Honor War Dead — Calls Decision 'Final'

By JAMES M. MARKHAM

Special to The New York Times

BONN, April 19 — Chancellor Helmut Kohl said today that he was gratified President Reagan had reaffirmed his intention to visit a German military cemetery next month, saying it showed he was "a friend of the Germans."

Mr. Kohl told a West German television interviewer that he and Mr. Reagan had discussed the President's revised plan to visit both the Bitburg cemetery and the site of the Bergen-Belsen concentration camp and that Mr. Reagan's decision on his German itinerary was "final." The Bergen-Belsen visit was announced today by the White House.

The Chancellor added that Germans "ought to be very reserved" in regard to the American debate over Mr. Reagan's plan to visit the cemetery, which has sparked strong criticism from American veterans' organizations as well as Jewish groups in West Germany and the United States.

'Hard Decision' for Reagan

"I know that this was a hard decision for the President," the West German leader said, adding that he understood the reaction of American Jews and victims of what he called "the Nazi barbarity."

Chancellor Kohl, describing an "extensive" telephone talk he had today with Mr. Reagan, said: "It was really a conversation among friends. And I am gratified that the American President, 40 years after the war, is ready to make this gesture of reconciliation."

Mr. Kohl, who was interviewed in a Bonn television studio, looked subdued as he spoke. The controversy over the Reagan visit has deeply embarrassed his Government.

Cites 'Collective Shame'

The Chancellor said that he was opposed to the conception of "collective guilt" for the crimes of the Nazis but that he embraced the notion of "collective shame." He said he hoped the visit to the Bitburg cemetery would become "a symbol of peace."

Widespread protests began after the White House announced April 11 that Mr. Reagan would lay a wreath at the cemetery, but would hold to his decision, announced the month before, not to visit the site of a concentration camp. Criticism mounted further when Mr. Reagan, at a state dinner Wednes-

Continued on Page 5, Column 1

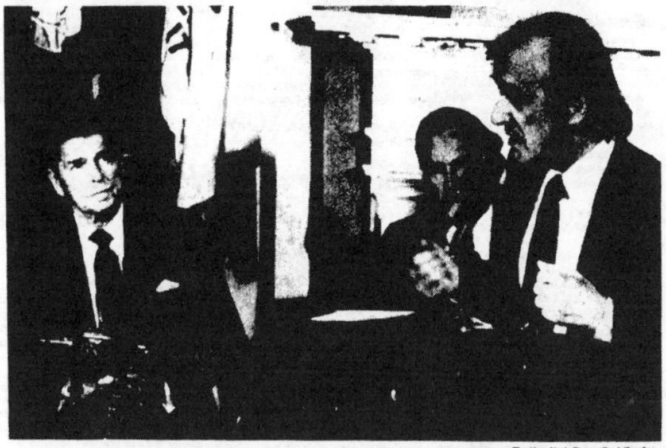

The New York Times/Paul Hosefros

President Reagan and Vice President Bush listening to Elie Wiesel during ceremony at the White House.

East Harlem 'Renovators' Build Trap for Grafters

By SELWYN RAAB

In the summer of 1983, a new construction company called Concor Associates began renovating dilapidated tenements in East Harlem.

Yesterday, the full name and real purpose of the company were disclosed. Concor stands for Construction Corruption, and the company was established by the State Commission of Investigation to uncover racketeering and payoffs in the city's construction industry.

In addition to finding graft among union officials and city inspectors, the commission said, it stumbled onto a major organized-crime gambling ring that rented a room in an apartment building Concor was renovating and used it as a headquarters to redistribute bets from bookmakers in five states.

The commission has turned over evidence of extortion by union officials and city inspectors to the United States Attorney's office in Manhattan for possible prosecution. Although authorized to look into corruption and irregularities affecting state or local governments, the commission has no prosecutorial power.

According to Thomas J. Staffa, the commission's chief counsel, the union leaders demanded bribes for allowing nonunion workers to be employed, and inspectors wanted payments for certifying that city building and electrical codes were met.

"Corruption seems to be the normal way of life in the construction industry," Mr. Staffa said. "Our major purpose was to get information about the extent of it. As a sidelight, we stumbled onto a huge gambling operation."

The inquiry, Mr. Staffa said, showed how profitable the construction business could be. After legitimate expenses for renovating three apartment buildings, the fake company earned $150,000, he said. Mr. Staffa said the profits would be turned over to the Federal Government.

"We made money even though we had no experience," Mr. Staffa said. "We learned on the job."

Concor Associates, Mr. Staffa said, was an outgrowth of a broader investigation of the construction industry that began in 1982. Because contractors are reluctant to disclose extortion for fear of reprisal, Mr. Staffa said, the commission decided to try to get "first hand" information about corrupt practices by establishing a dummy corporation.

Three commission investigators were assigned to run Concor as a general contracting concern that renovated apartment buildings. The company obtained three contracts from the Federal Department of Housing and Urban Development and began work in the summer of 1983, Mr. Staffa said.

Officials at the Federal agency, Mr. Staffa said, were aware of the under-

Continued on Page 27, Column 4

What's Sunday without The New York Times? Unthinkable! Delivery is now available in many parts of the U.S. Just call toll-free: 1-800-631-2500 — ADVT.

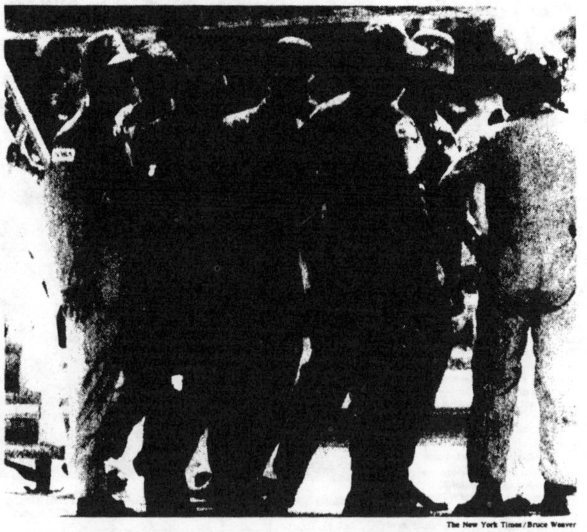

The New York Times/Bruce Weaver

Standing under Discovery after landing were, from left, Senator Jake Garn; George Abby, director of flight operations; Capt. Donald E. Williams of the Navy, Dr. Jeffrey A. Hoffman, Col. Karol J. Bobko of the Air Force, mission commander, and S. David Griggs. Man with sunglasses at rear was not identified.

SEVEN ASTRONAUTS MAKE SAFE LANDING IN SPITE OF MISHAPS

LOCKED BRAKES BLOW TIRE

Damage on Final Day Includes Loose Heat-Shield Tile and a Hole at Tip of Wing

By JOHN NOBLE WILFORD

Special to The New York Times

CAPE CANAVERAL, Fla., April 19 — The space shuttle Discovery landed safely today, despite a tire blowout and a gaping hole at the end of one wing, ending a seven-day mission remarkable for the unexpected things that kept happening at every turn.

Like the flight itself, the landing did not go exactly as planned. It was delayed an extra orbit because of rain clouds. When the 100-ton spaceship finally touched down here, at 8:55 A.M., the brakes on one landing gear locked, shredding two tires and causing a blowout. Two other tires were badly worn.

Technicians who examined the Discovery found a hole the size of a dinner plate at the tip of the left wing where the elevon, a maneuvering and control flap, hinges to the wing. A heat-shielding tile had come loose, and the fiery temperatures of re-entry melted some of the exposed aluminum and other components of the elevon.

First Serious Damage

Although a few of the tiles have been nicked, loosened or lost on each mission, this was the first time a tile malfunction has led to possibly serious structural damage to a shuttle. And, although the shuttles have experienced numerous problems with brakes and landing gear, this was the first failure of the brakes.

At a news conference this afternoon, Robert Sieck, the launching director at the Kennedy Space Center, called the damage major and said a thorough investigation would be necessary before proceeding with future missions.

Mr. Sieck said the problems would be reviewed Tuesday to see if they warranted delaying the next mission, the flight of a sister ship, the Challenger, carrying a large laboratory for scientific experiments. The Challenger is on the launching pad and scheduled for liftoff April 29.

No Setbacks Are Seen

Jesse W. Moore, head of the shuttle program for the National Aeronautics and Space Administration, said that "as of now," he did not foresee any setbacks to future missions.

The Discovery is to make its next flight June 12, and Mr. Sieck said, "The only threat at this time could be the damage to the elevon."

Officials and engineers said the causes of the damage had not been determined. They said the Discovery's crew of seven was never in any danger. In fact, the crew was reported to be unaware of the problems until the right outboard tire blew a few feet before the shuttle came to a stop on the concrete runway.

If the elevon had been left inoperable, it would still have been possible for the shuttle to land, but it would have been more difficult to control the craft

Continued on Page [illegible], Column 1

Officials Drafting a Plan to Merge New York City and Transit Police

By SAM ROBERTS

City and transit officials say they are negotiating the details of merging the transit police force into the New York City Police Department.

A report ordered earlier this year by Mayor Koch recommends that the transit police, a separate force for half a century, be absorbed at first as a bureau within the City Police Department.

A combined force would be more efficient in fighting crime, proponents of the proposal say.

Several city officials are optimistic that an agreement will be reached, perhaps in a matter of weeks, if transit officials are assured that their concerns will be addressed.

The report, delivered to the Mayor two months ago but not yet released publicly, says a merger can be accomplished administratively by the city and the board of the Metropolitan Transportation Authority.

Some officials have said, however, that a merger would require approval of the State Legislature, where the police unions, which have opposed consolidation, wield considerable influence.

"The city clearly has been disposed toward merger or consolidation for a long time," Robert R. Kiley, the M.T.A. chairman, said yesterday. "I'm convinced that the process we're going through is a useful one. I remain to be convinced merger is the way to go."

Housing Police Left Out

According to officials familiar with the mayoral report, a merger of the city and housing police has not been recommended at this time because it may require Congressional approval and could jeopardize a Federal subsidy for the housing police.

The report indicates that although there would be additional costs associated with the merger — combining the separate communications systems, for one — the merger would lead to more police efficiency and a coordinated response to crime.

Under the existing agreement between the Transit Authority and the city police, the transit police chief, James B. Meehan, reports to Police Commissioner Benjamin Ward on operational matters. But Mr. Meehan reports to David L. Gunn, the Transit Authority president, on policy matters.

Officials from the Mayor's office and the City Police Department have been seeking to assuage the concerns of

Continued on Page 28, Column 1

JAPANESE TO EASE TECHNOLOGY CURBS

Pact, Strongly Sought by U.S., to Increase Some Imports

By SUSAN CHIRA

Special to The New York Times

TOKYO, April 19 — Japan has agreed to simplify some of its telecommunications regulations, making them comparable to those in the United States, a team of American trade negotiators said today.

The agreement appears to fulfill Prime Minister Yasuhiro Nakasone's recent commitment that Japan would change regulations that American companies regarded as barriers to trade. The Japanese Government praised the agreement, which was reached well before a June deadline.

The five-day talks were held amid mounting trade frictions between the two nations, political pressures that the negotiators said had helped to speed their progress.

One Part of Market

They emphasized that the agreement covered only part of Japan's $4.5 billion telecommunications market and that they could not say that Japan's telecommunications markets were as open as those in the United States. The new rules, they said, may allow certain products to enter Japan, but other barriers such as distribution systems may continue to hinder sales.

The changes apply to equipment such as modems that link computers or telecommunications networks, one of

Continued on Page 35, Column 5

Fire Altering the Evolution of Darwin's [illegible]es

By MALCOLM W. BROWNE

Special to The New York Times

PUERTO AYORA, Galápagos Islands — A fire that has been charring Isabela Island for the last month has made life precarious for nesting birds, giant tortoises and other forms of wildlife unique to the Galápagos Islands. But for some of the human residents of this Ecuadorean archipelago, the blaze has created a modest boom.

Firefighting experts, pilots, scientists, journalists, volunteers, yachtsmen and tourists have been flocking to the Pacific islands, some to help put out the fire, some to observe the proceedings, others merely to savor the excitement. But whatever their reasons for coming, they have been spending money, and the results are visible in this dusty little fishing village.

Big Fire on Isabela Island

Sooner or later, nearly everyone who visits the Galápagos Islands ends up here, at least for a few days. Puerto Ayora on Santa Cruz Island is not the archipelago's capital town — Baquerizo Moreno on San Cristóbal Island has that distinction — nor does it command a view of the big fire on Isabela, which lies 60 miles to the west. But Puerto Ayora is where one finds soft beds, cold beer and good talk, not to mention tame tortoises, Darwin's finches and iguanas.

This archipelago, of course, has long been known as a unique natural laboratory of evolution. Thrust up from the Pacific floor by volcanic action three million to four million years ago, the Galápagos were at first lifeless islands of hardened lava. Over time, however, birds and pollen from the South American mainland were occasionally blown in by freak storms, and land animals arrived on seaweed rafts carried by ocean currents.

Cut off from the outside world by 600 miles of ocean, creatures here followed independent paths of evolutionary development — paths that caught Darwin's attention when he visited the islands in 1835. What he saw led to his theory of evolution.

But the attraction of fascinating wildlife has not flooded the islands with tourist money.

The two main hotels, the Galápagos

Continued on Page 5, Column 1

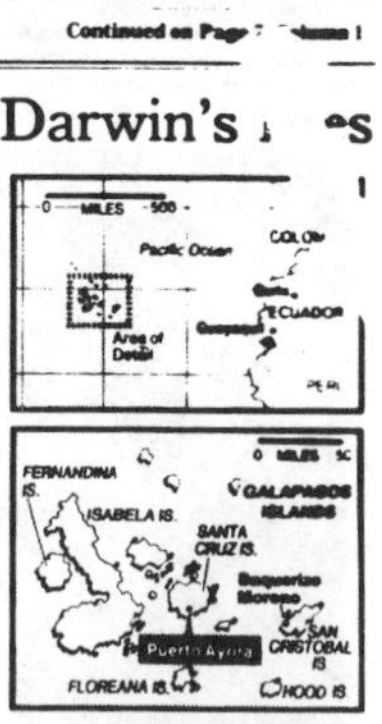

The New York Times April 20, 1985

Soft beds, cold beer and good talk are to be found in Puerto Ayora.

INSIDE

U.S. Halts Use of Hormone

The Federal Government halted the distribution of a hormone used to treat severe growth deficiencies as a precaution after three deaths. Page 7.

58 Seized in Drug Dragnet

American and Bahamian officials arrested 58 people in a major drug-trafficking sweep in the Bahamas and along the Florida coast. Page 6.

About New York	27	Movies	12
Around Nation	6	Music	9,12
Books	13	News Quiz	13
Bridge	13	Obituaries	28
Business Day	30-42	Op-Ed	23
Crossword	8	Relig. Services	29
Dance	12	Sports Pages	43-46
Day by Day	26	Style	48
Editorials	22	TV / Radio	46-47
Going Out Guide	13	Washington Talk	8
Letters	22	Weather	42

News Summary and Index, Page 25

Classified Ads	*13-21*	*Auto Exchange*	*45*

HAPPY BIRTHDAY GEORGE TO A WONDERFUL Guy on his 55th! Love George — ADVT

A B C D E F

"All the News That's Fit to Print"

The New York Times

Late Edition

Weather: Mostly sunny and warm today; southeasterly winds; partly cloudy tonight. Sunny and warm tomorrow. Temperatures: today 80-82, tonight 53-57; yesterday 52-83. Details on page C7.

VOL.CXXXIV . . . No. 46,387 NEW YORK, MONDAY, APRIL 22, 1985 50 cents beyond 75 miles from New York City, except on Long Island. 30 CENTS

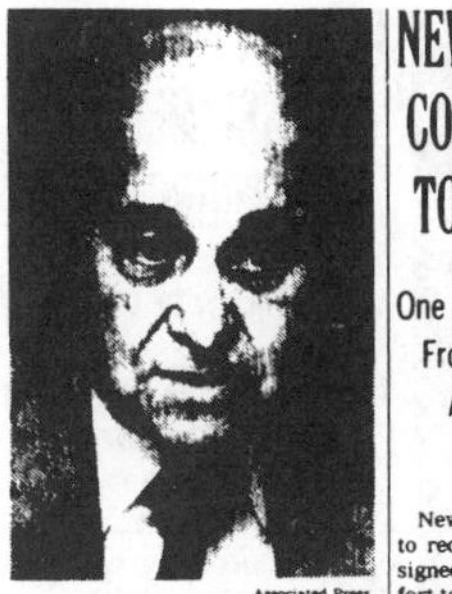

Associated Press

Tancredo Neves

Brazil's Leader Dies at Age 75; Never Sworn In

By MARLISE SIMONS

Special to The New York Times

RIO DE JANEIRO, April 21 — The Brazilian President-elect, Tancredo Neves, died tonight from complications following intestinal surgery that had prevented him from taking office as the country's first civilian ruler in 21 years. He was 75 years old.

The Vice President, José Sarney, who was sworn in as acting President in place of Mr. Neves on March 15, automatically became President tonight, although many politicians believe that new elections may be held within two years.

In an address to the nation tonight, Mr. Sarney said he would carry out the program of Mr. Neves. "The promised changes will take place," he said. "We will carry out a government of harmony, change, work, morality and austerity, and we will be implacable against corruption."

To Lie in State in Capital

Mr. Neves's death, at 10:23 P.M., ended a five-week-long vigil during which Brazil was both paralyzed and traumatized by his deteriorating health.

Mr. Neves's body will be flown Monday from São Paulo, where he has been treated over the last three weeks, to Brasília, the capital, where he will lie in state in the Presidential Palace. He is expected to be buried Wednesday in his home town of São Joao del Rei in the state of Minas Gerais. The Government has declared eight days' official mourning.

Although Mr. Neves had been a prominent political figure in Brazil for much of the last half-century and was

Continued on Page B12, Column 1

NEW YORK TO SHIFT COURT PROCEDURES TO SPEED DECISIONS

One Judge Would Hear a Case From Start to End — More Accountability Is Seen

By SAM ROBERTS

New York State court officials intend to reorganize the way judges are assigned criminal and civil cases in an effort to speed dispositions, better measure judicial productivity and hold lawyers and prosecutors more accountable.

Cases now are often disposed of piecemeal. They bounce to different sets of courtrooms, which are designated to handle particular legal procedures such as motions or trials — each presided over by different judges.

To relieve caseloads elsewhere and to spread work and experience, the judges assigned to those courtrooms, or "parts," are rotated, too.

Switch Planned This Year

Under the new approach cases would generally be handled by one judge from start to finish within each level of the court system.

Court officials say they expect to begin phasing in the system selectively before the end of the year, perhaps as soon as this fall.

Sol Wachtler, the state's new Chief Judge, is as adamant in supporting the concept as his predecessor, Lawrence H. Cooke, was in opposing it. Mr. Wachtler says the objective of the old system, known as master calendaring, was to reduce backlogs but had not worked.

Speech Scheduled Today

"This is not a question of whether or not, but how," said Judge Wachtler, who was sworn in last January. He plans to outline the approach, known as the individual calendar system, in his State of the Judiciary Message to the Legislature today. [Page B1.]

Court officials say they must remain flexible in putting the change into effect, and it is uncertain how many aspects of the present system may be retained.

All state courts could ultimately be affected by the shift, including State Supreme Court, county courts upstate, the Criminal Courts in New York City and the civil courts. At present, many of the state courts outside New York City already operate on an individual calendar basis.

The shift would have its biggest impact on New York City. The present system was imposed gradually through the state and has been in place in New

Continued on Page B4, Column 1

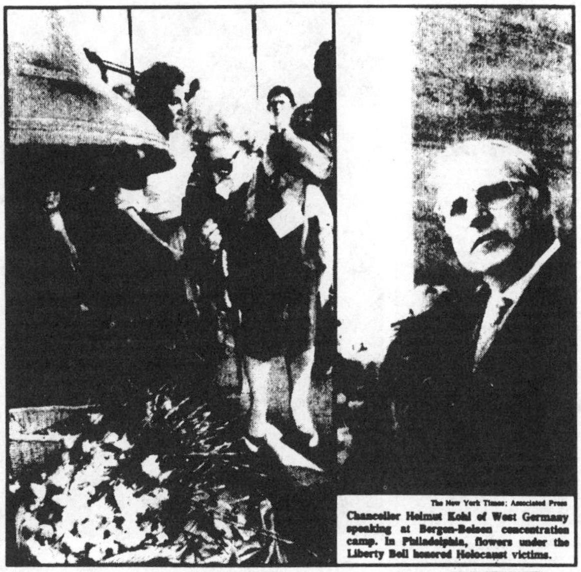

The New York Times; Associated Press

Chancellor Helmut Kohl of West Germany speaking at Bergen-Belsen concentration camp. In Philadelphia, flowers under the Liberty Bell honored Holocaust victims.

Reagan Cemetery Visit Criticized At Holocaust Survivors Ceremony

By WILLIAM K. STEVENS

Special to The New York Times

PHILADELPHIA, April 21 — Survivors of the Holocaust cheered loudly and lustily today as one of their most prominent children called for an intensified campaign to persuade President Reagan to cancel a visit to a German cemetery containing the graves of Waffen SS troopers.

"The time for soft-spoken words and appeals is over," said Menachem Z. Rosensaft of New York, a son of concentration-camp victims who is chairman of the International Network of Children of Jewish Holocaust Survivors. "For the sake of history, we must prevent him from going to Bitburg." He argued that the visit next month would be exploited by "revisionist historians, neo-Nazis and their sympathizers."

If Mr. Reagan visits the military cemetery at Bitburg, West Germany, he went on, "we must see to it that survivors, children of survivors and American war veterans will be waiting for him at the gates of that cemetery."

He said that his plea, contained in one of the strongest statements of protest yet made against the proposed visit, was designed to ignite renewed efforts to force Mr. Reagan to cancel the Bitburg visit or substitute another cemetery. There was no immediate indication as to what response it would draw from other Jewish leaders.

But one of them, Benjamin Meed, the president of the American Gathering and Federation of Jewish Holocaust Survivors, the group of survivors now gathered here, told the crowd after Mr. Rosensaft had spoken, "I can feel the heat, your heartbeat, and the emotions, and the message is coming through."

Ceremony at Independence Hall

The speech took place in the shadow of Independence Hall, where, in a moving ceremony minutes before, thousands of Holocaust survivors had laid white carnations beneath the Liberty Bell in a symbolic linking of American freedom and their own liberation from Nazi captivity and torture 40 years ago.

The ceremony opened what is called the Inaugural Ceremony of the American Gathering of Jewish Holocaust Survivors. The group plans to establish a permanent mechanism to perpetuate the memory of the Holocaust. The assembly first met four years ago in Jerusalem, and again two years ago in Washington. Mr. Rosensaft was invited to take part in today's ceremonies.

Commemorative activities continued tonight with a program of poems and other writings read by entertainment figures, and a documentary film, "The Final Solution." At intermission, Elie Wiesel, the author and historian

Continued on Page A8, Column 1

KOHL SAYS SHAME OF NAZIS PERSISTS

At Belsen Rites, He Accepts Responsibility for Crimes

By JAMES M. MARKHAM

Special to The New York Times

BELSEN, West Germany, April 21 — Chancellor Helmut Kohl, at a ceremony marking the 40th anniversary of the liberation of the Bergen-Belsen concentration camp, said today that he accepted Germany's "historical responsibility for the crimes of the Nazi tyranny."

Standing beside a looming stone obelisk on the site of the Nazi camp where more than 50,000 people died, the Chancellor declared: "This responsibility is reflected not least in never-ending shame. We shall not let anything to do with this be falsified or made light of."

Camp Was Burned Down in '45

The Chancellor gave his speech — one of the most forthright and unflinching a West German leader has made about the Hitler era — surrounded by senior political figures, ambassadors, local people and survivors of the camp. The survivors had made emotionally painful pilgrimages here from Israel, the United States and other countries.

After its capture by British troops on April 15, 1945, the Bergen-Belsen camp, built on the north German flatlands, was burned because a typhus epidemic among its 58,000 surviving prisoners made it a health hazard. Some 14,000 emaciated survivors died after the liberation.

The memorial to the camp is a vast open park punctuated with raised

Continued on Page A8, Column 1

SHULTZ SAYS ARABS HURT PALESTINIANS BY BLOCKING TALKS

ADDRESSES ISRAEL LOBBY

He Calls on Mideast Leaders to Support Jordan's Move for Direct Negotiations

By BERNARD GWERTZMAN

Special to The New York Times

WASHINGTON, April 21 — Secretary of State George P. Shultz declared today that Arab leaders were prolonging the suffering of Palestinians by not supporting direct negotiations between Israel and Jordan.

"How ironic and tragic it is," he said, "that those who claim to act on behalf of the Palestinians have continued to block negotiations — the only course that can achieve a just settlement for the Palestinians."

With Richard W. Murphy Jr., the Assistant Secretary of State for Near Eastern and South Asian Affairs, arriving in Syria today as part of his two-week trip Middle East trip, Mr. Shultz said recent statements by King Hussein of Jordan and President Hosni Mubarak of Egypt had been encouraging.

Praise Mixed With Annoyance

"Today, for the first time in years," he said, "there are signs of a new realism and a new commitment on the part of key regional actors."

But his remarks seemed to reflect the Administration's annoyance with the failure of most Arab leaders to encourage King Hussein to negotiate with Israel. Syria is leading an effort to try to block King Hussein's participation.

King Hussein has said he was willing, through a joint Jordanian-Palestinian delegation, to seek a negotiated accord with Israel on the West Bank, if he is given the support of key Arab leaders. But only Mr. Mubarak has publicly endorsed the Hussein moves.

No Alternative to Talks

"Now is the time for the Arabs to let King Hussein come forward," Mr. Shultz said. "There is no alternative to direct negotiation; the longer the truth is evaded, the longer the Palestinian people are the victims."

The Israelis have said they would not negotiate with a joint delegation that included prominent Palestine Liberation Organization members. Mr. Murphy has been urging the Arabs to produce a list of Palestinians who would be acceptable to Israel.

So far he has not been given such a list, State Department officials said,

Continued on Page A9, Column 1

Israel Says It Sank A 'Terrorist Vessel'; 20 Presumed Dead

Special to The New York Times

TEL AVIV, Monday, April 22 — An Israeli gunboat sank an Arab "terrorist vessel" with 28 people aboard in an exchange of fire off the Israeli coast Saturday night, a military spokesman announced early today.

Eight Arabs were captured, one body was recovered and 19 people were missing and presumed drowned, according to a communiqué.

In another development, Defense Minister Yitzhak Rabin announced that the Israeli Cabinet decided Sunday to complete the withdrawal of troops from Lebanon by early June but to retain temporarily a military presence for the defense of the border region.

The report on the sinking of the boat said the guerrillas were to have landed in the Tel Aviv area to stage attacks during the Israeli Independence Day celebrations starting Wednesday night.

A deep-water patrol boat detected the guerrillas' vessel and ordered it to halt and identify itself, the communiqué said.

When it refused to do so, the Israelis fired warning shots, it added. The guerrillas then fired on the Israeli vessel with small arms and rocket-propelled grenades as they tried to escape, the communiqué said. The Israelis then sank the boat.

"Initial interrogation of the terrorists established that the vessel was

Continued on Page A10, Column 1

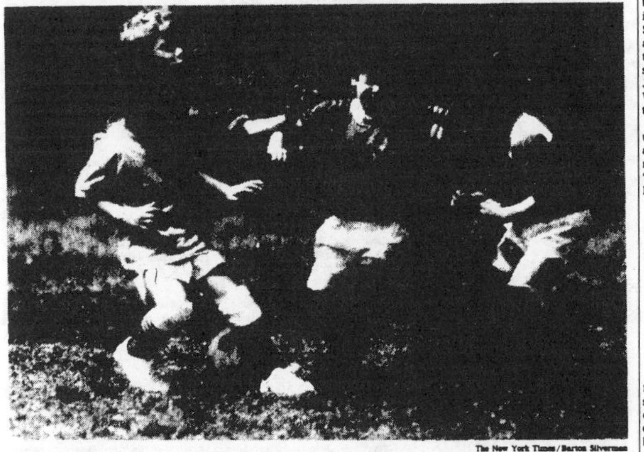

The New York Times/Barton Silverman

TENSE COMPETITION FOR 4-YEAR OLDS: The Warriors, in light jerseys, battled the Explorers under sunny skies as the teams met in Dix Hills, L.I., in a game sponsored by the Huntington Boys Club. The youngsters played to a sort of tie; no score was kept. Today should also be sunny, with a high in the low 80's.

Farmers Shaken as Credit Cooperatives Fail

By WILLIAM ROBBINS

Special to The New York Times

O'NEILL, Neb., April 18 — Richard Flannery is surrounded by farmers who are losing money and losing their land. But until last November, by watching his expenses and debts closely, he survived the mayhem of a distressed agricultural economy with relatively few scars.

But then, on Nov. 9, trouble from an unforeseen source came for Mr. Flannery and about 500 of his neighbors here in the Sand Hills region of north-central Nebraska. Together they lost nearly $6 million in the collapse of what they once regarded as rock-solid credit institutions.

The institutions were the Production Credit Associations here in O'Neill and about 100 miles west at Valentine, Neb. They are two of 370 such associations around the country, local affiliates of a national network of credit cooperatives and institutions known as the Federal Farm Credit System.

The associations have consistently provided about 20 percent of all short-term financing for farmers. Last year they lost money for the first time since the Depression, according to Ronald H. Erickson, the Farm Credit Administration's associate director of Congressional and public affairs.

Over the last two years, with more than 8 percent of their loans becoming delinquent at one point, they lost about $800 million on bad loans, nearly as much as they had in their previous 50 years of existence.

For the half-century from 1933 to 1983, Mr. Erickson could cite only one failure of an association. Since Sept. 1, 1983, 11 have collapsed, including those at O'Neill and Valentine, and 39 others with financial problems have been merged into stronger associations.

Federal Land Banks, another major part of the Federal Farm Credit Sys-

Continued on Page B7, Column 1

A
B
C
D
E
F

Issue of Missing in Vietnam Has Not Faded After Decade

By ANDREW H. MALCOLM

Special to The New York Times

LINTHICUM, Md. — Donald Shay's father is retired now. Donald's little sister has two young children of her own. His fiancée finally married someone else. And Donald's mother doesn't bake his favorite apple pie much anymore; the good smell brings back too many bad memories.

Mr. Shay doesn't know any of this. And he may never know. In fact, his family may never know where he is, or where he was when he died, if he died. For Mr. Shay is one of 2,477 Americans still missing in action from the Vietnam War.

Ten years after the fall of Saigon and 15 years after that smiling, 24-year-old lacrosse player flew off a radar screen into his family's memory somewhere over Indochina, no one knows for sure what happened to any of the missing Americans.

But in one of the more mysterious legacies of that painful era in American history, these men who went off to war as individuals have now become, as a group, much more than simply a sad statistic. They are the subject of movies, books and songs, the object of angry demonstrations, earnest petitions and solemn vigils, the focus of intense Presidential interest, microscopic analysis and secret satellite photography and the heart of some delicate diplomatic exchanges trying to bridge broad cultural chasms.

The alleged remains of some missing men, reduced to bones and fragments after years in the jungle, have even become the currency of a ghoulish, clandestine commerce that preys on the hopes and fears of families and refugees.

"Somehow," said one United States Government official, "the mystery of their disappearance and their deaths

Continued on Page B8, Column 1

INSIDE

Changes in Publishing

The hard-cover book is losing its commanding position in the publishing world to the paperback, which is reshaping the industry. Page C13.

Rudi Gernreich Dies

Rudi Gernreich, the country's leading avant-garde fashion designer in the 1950's and 60's, died in Los Angeles. He was 62 years old. Page B12.

"All the News That's Fit to Print"

The New York Times

Late Edition

Weather: Mixed sun and clouds today, increasing humidity; chance of showers tonight. Fair and breezy tomorrow. Temperatures: today 70-79, tonight 43-47; yesterday 57-77. Details, page C16.

VOL.CXXXIV . . . No. 46,401 Copyright © 1985 The New York Times NEW YORK, MONDAY, MAY 6, 1985 — 60 cents beyond 75 miles from New York City, except on Long Island. 30 CENTS

ASTRONAUTS STOW GEAR AS THEY HEAD FOR COAST LANDING

MISSION TERMED SUCCESS

Weight of Spacelab in Cargo Bay Is a Factor in Shifting Touchdown to Mojave

By RICHARD D. LYONS

Special to The New York Times

EDWARDS AIR FORCE BASE, Calif., May 5 — The seven astronauts aboard the space shuttle Challenger ended experiments today and stowed equipment in preparation for their scheduled landing here Monday at the end of what has been hailed as a highly successful seven-day mission.

The Challenger is due to swoop in from the South Pacific, rake Los Angeles with a sonic boom from 90,000 feet and alight on the dry lake bed of the Mojave Desert here shortly after 9 A.M. (noon, Eastern daylight time).

The landing was originally scheduled to take place at Cape Canaveral, Fla., but the hard landing of the Discovery spacecraft there last month, which damaged that shuttle's brakes, blew one of its four main tires and seriously frayed the other three, led officials of the National Aeronautics and Space Administration to switch sites as a precaution.

Reason for Switching Sites

With the Spacelab scientific laboratory nestled in its cargo bay, the Challenger is 12 tons heavier than the Discovery, and the almost endless dry lake beds here provide more flexibility in case of trouble.

NASA officials have attributed problems of the last landing, at least in part, to the fact that Discovery had to make a landing bucking a stiff crosswind, which put added strain on its braking system.

The crosswind blew the Discovery 50 feet off course in the landing, which forced Col. Karol Bobko of the Air Force, the commander of that mission, to stand on the brakes much harder than had been planned.

Loss of Information

Because of the switch from Florida to California, scientists will lose some valuable information that they had hoped to obtain from the 24 white rats that are riding aboard Challenger.

The rats were to have been unloaded,

Continued on Page B11, Column 4

Demonstration For Soviet Jews Jams Fifth Ave.

Bitburg Visit Denounced as 'Denial of the Past'

By WILLIAM R. GREER

Tens of thousands of people marched down Fifth Avenue and gathered near the United Nations yesterday in a demonstration of support for Soviet Jewry that participants said was colored by anguish over President Reagan's visit to a military cemetery in Bitburg, West Germany.

"Why not admit it, today we are wounded," said Elie Wiesel, addressing the rally in Dag Hammarskjold Plaza at 47th Street and First Avenue. Mr. Wiesel is chairman of the United States Holocaust Memorial Council.

Placards and Chants

"Is there a connection between Bitburg and this rally?" he asked. "Yes, there is. What was attempted at Bitburg — a denial of the past, a disregard of Jewish agony — the same but on a larger scale has been attempted in Russia."

The organizers of the demonstration, the 14th annual Solidarity Sunday for Soviet Jewry, said it was the largest held so far in New York to protest the Soviet Union's treatment of Jews. The police estimated that 240,000 people either marched, lined the route down Fifth Avenue from 70th to 47th Street or gathered at the plaza.

Archbishop John J. O'Connor and many elected officials, including Mayor Koch, Governor Cuomo and United States Senators Alfonse M. D'Amato and Daniel Patrick Moynihan, spoke at the rally as demonstrators waved placards bearing the photographs of Soviet Jews, often behind bars, and chanted "Let my people go."

Archbishop Addresses Rally

Herbert Kornish, the chairman of the Coalition to Free Soviet Jews, which sponsored the demonstration, said that harassment of Soviet Jews had grown since 1979, when 51,320 Jews were allowed to emigrate, and that last year only 896 were allowed to emigrate.

The Archbishop, who has been designated a cardinal by Pope John Paul II, greeted the marchers as they passed St. Patrick's Cathedral and later addressed the rally.

"To all who may know or who came to learn of my presence among you," he said, "I say to destroy Jews anywhere is to destroy Christians everywhere. Let those who would write your

Continued on Page A10, Column 1

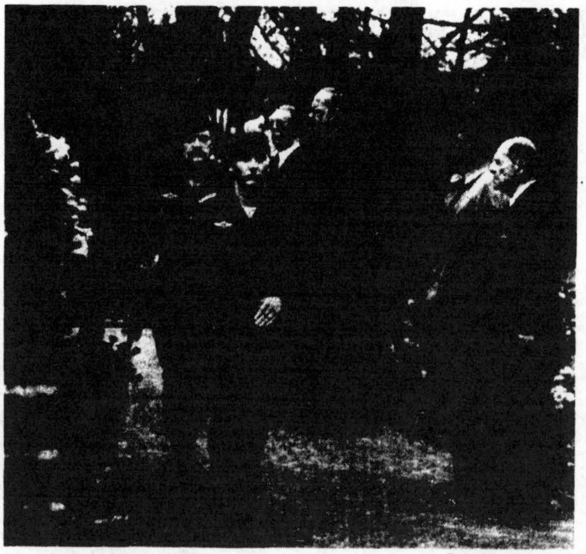

The New York Times/Paul Hosefros

President Reagan and Chancellor Helmut Kohl at ceremony at Bitburg cemetery. Accompanying them are two former Generals, Matthew B. Ridgway, right, and Johannes Steinhoff.

REAGAN JOINS KOHL IN BRIEF MEMORIAL AT BITBURG GRAVES

VISIT STIRS WIDE PROTESTS

President Voices Regret Over Continuing Controversy — Goes to Bergen-Belsen

By BERNARD WEINRAUB

Special to The New York Times

BITBURG, West Germany, May 5 — President Reagan presided over a wreath-laying today at the base of a brick cemetery tower looming over the graves of nearly 2,000 German soldiers, including 49 SS troops.

Alluding to the controversy aroused by his visit to the cemetery, Mr. Reagan voiced regret in remarks at an American air base afterward that "old wounds have been reopened."

Texts of speeches, pages A8 and A10.

Accompanied by Chancellor Helmut Kohl, Mr. Reagan walked slowly through the narrow, hilltop cemetery, ablaze with tulips and marigolds. Mr. Reagan did not glance at the graves during his eight-minute visit. Mr. Kohl brushed tears from his eyes. Neither made a speech at the cemetery.

Hours earlier, Mr. Reagan stood before an obelisk at the site of the Bergen-Belsen concentration camp, where 50,000 victims of the Nazis are buried in mass graves under mounds of heather.

"Here they lie," Mr. Reagan said in a trembling voice. "Never to hope. Never to pray. Never to love. Never to heal. Never to laugh. Never to cry."

Merging Past and Present

Mr. Reagan's visit to Bergen-Belsen, in addition to the Kolmeshöhe Cemetery at Bitburg, was designed to merge past and present — to pay homage to the millions of victims of Nazi Germany and to honor West Germany's emergence as a powerful democracy and ally of the United States.

"We who were enemies are now friends," Mr. Reagan told about 5,000 American military personnel, their families and local German residents at the Bitburg Air Base, less than one mile from the military cemetery.

"We who were bitter adversaries are now the strongest of allies," Mr. Reagan said. "In the place of fear we have sown trust, and out of the ruins of war has blossomed an enduring peace."

Jewish demonstrators from the United States, France, Britain, West Germany, Belgium, the Netherlands, Israel and other countries protested the President's visit to Bergen-Belsen as well as the stop at Bitburg. They were joined by groups of veterans and politicians, many of them weeping.

Rabbis Refuse to Attend

Although Roman Catholic and Protestant clergymen took part in the ceremonies at the Bergen-Belsen site, German rabbis refused to attend because of the Bitburg visit.

The Israeli Ambassador to West Germany, Yitzhak Ben-Ari, came to the Bergen-Belsen ceremony — despite anguish, he said, about Mr. Reagan's visit to Bitburg. "I believe the new Germany can be trusted," he said.

White House aides have acknowledged that the Bitburg visit is probably the biggest fiasco of Mr. Reagan's Presidency. The visit, which was made at the insistence of Mr. Kohl, was overwhelmingly opposed by both houses of Congress, Jewish organizations, veterans' groups and others.

Up to the last moment, White House

Continued on Page A9, Column 1

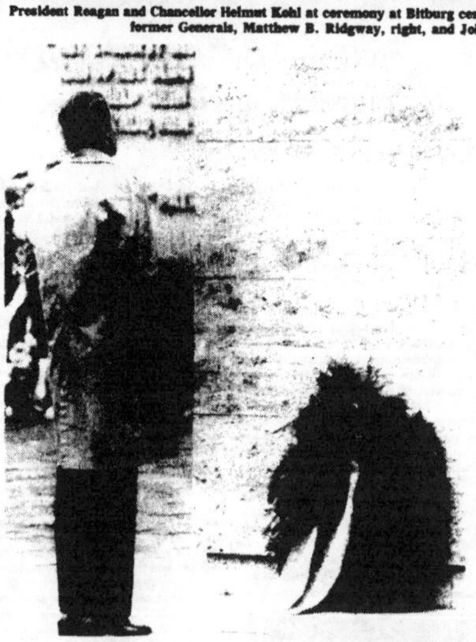

Associated Press

Mr. Reagan pays tribute to victims of Bergen-Belsen concentration camp.

For Bitburg, Day of Anger Ends Quietly

By JAMES M. MARKHAM

Special to The New York Times

BITBURG, West Germany, May 5 — It was the scene that many had feared. At the main crossroads of this small town, policemen with plastic antiriot shields confronted an advancing crowd of Jews, many of them wearing the badge that accompanied their parents and grandparents to their deaths: a six-pointed yellow star bearing the word Jude.

The Jews came from 21 countries, but many were from France, Belgium and the Netherlands. One big blue banner hoisted in their midst read in French, "Neither hate nor forgetfulness."

Another hand-painted banner, in English, said: "Don't honor SS murderers. My brother's blood cries out to me from the ground."

'They Haven't Learned'

When the protesters reached the police line they halted, some of them only inches from the policemen. Among them was Irene Quetting, 67 years old, from Traben-Trarbach, West Germany, who said she was half-Jewish.

"If you want to know my impression about the Germans," she said, nodding toward Mötscherstrasse, where Chancellor Helmut Kohl and President Reagan would shortly pass, "they haven't learned from history."

She said she was not speaking of the policemen in green uniforms who were holding back the protesters. "No," she said, "I am talking about my generation and Kohl's, who should have learned but didn't."

The policemen were correct and polite, and clearly uncomfortable. "Personally," said a dark-haired policeman, holding his white helmet to his

Continued on Page A8, Column 5

Atlanta's Years of Progress Temper New Racial Disputes

By WILLIAM E. SCHMIDT

Special to The New York Times

ATLANTA, May 5 — In the 1950's and 60's, when the civil rights movement was challenging the old order across the South, a group of white civic leaders in Atlanta began preaching a gospel of accommodation rather than confrontation.

They took to describing Atlanta as "the city too busy to hate," and with the help of local blacks like the Rev.

Race Relations: The Changing South

Last of six articles that have appeared since March 1.

Martin Luther King Sr., they set out to dismantle the legal barriers of segregation in hotels, lunch counters, jobs, schools and government, with little of the disruption and none of the violence that occurred elsewhere in the region.

"When they were putting dogs on people and beating them up in Birmingham," said Mayor Andrew Young, who plans to seek a second term this fall, "blacks and whites in Atlanta sat down together and worked out their differences around a table."

That spirit of cooperation may have had less to with racial enlightenment that it did with an abiding pragmatism among civic leaders here who argued that racial strife was bad for business. Still, over the last two decades, this cooperation has worked some powerful truths in Atlanta.

This city of 427,000 people, which is two-thirds black, has emerged not only as the booming financial capital of the Southeast, but as a national beacon of black political and economic opportunity.

However, Atlanta is not colorblind: race continues to be a constant and frequently divisive factor in the conduct of business, government and day-to-day social intercourse. And, as in the rest of the nation, there is a large economic gap between blacks and whites.

"Over the last 20 years, we have ac-

Continued on Page B8, Column 1

Rising Brutality Complaints Raise Questions About New York Police

The following article is based on reporting by Jane Perlez and Selwyn Raab and was written by Mr. Raab.

For decades, the tough methods used against criminals by a Prohibition-era detective, Johnny Broderick, were widely sanctioned in New York City's police force. Roaming the streets of Manhattan, Detective Broderick clubbed suspected gangsters and hoodlums with a lead pipe wrapped in a newspaper.

Police officials in the late 1960's tried to end that type of brutality. In response to public complaints about pervasive police misconduct, training programs were established that emphasized sensitivity and civil rights in dealing with suspects and the public in general.

But a recent string of incidents, including purported assaults with an electric stun gun, has raised questions about overall police behavior and the effectiveness of Police Department programs to prevent misconduct. Last year, 6,698 complaints were filed against city police officers for purported mistreatment and excessive force — about 600 more than in 1983.

Sociologists and police experts say policy and personnel shifts in the city's 26,000-member Police Department may have contributed to the increase in brutality allegations.

More Inexperienced Officers

Among the chief contributing factors cited by the experts are these:

¶An influx of inexperienced officers who have been assigned mainly to high-crime precincts, where conditions can be most stressful. About half of the force — 13,000 men and women — have less than five years' experience. Last year, 58 percent of the complaints filed with the Civilian Complaint Review Board were against officers on the force for three years or less.

¶A lack of adequate programs to raise morale and provide career incentives for older officers who, according to some sociologists, may become abusive after years of job frustration.

¶A failure to give periodic psychological tests to all officers and supervisors. Although precise figures are not available, sociologists say police officers generally have higher rates of suicide, alcoholism and divorce than peo-

Continued on Page B5, Column 1

Salvador Defense Lawyer Charges Cover-Up in Slaying of U.S. Nuns

By LARRY ROHTER

A lawyer who defended a Salvadoran national guardsman convicted of murdering four American churchwomen said yesterday that he had been forced to take part in a "conspiracy" aimed at preventing higher-ranking military officers from being implicated in the case.

The lawyer, Salvador Antonio Ibarra, said that another defense lawyer had pressed him not to contradict a statement that "the possibility of a cover-up had been thoroughly investigated" and rejected. Mr. Ibarra said that declaration was "an outright lie" and added that he was specifically warned not to pursue the case on his own.

After it became clear he would not cooperate fully in the plan, Mr. Ibarra said in an interview, he was abducted by Salvadoran security forces, held prisoner at National Guard headquarters and tortured. The objective, he said, was to get him off the case, either by killing him or forcing him to flee the country.

Mr. Ibarra's remarks involved one of the most controversial aspects of the murder of the three American nuns and a lay worker, who were shot by Salvadoran security forces after being stopped at a roadblock near San Salvador International Airport in December 1980.

Human rights groups and some United States diplomats have long argued that the guardsmen were not acting on their own, but carrying out orders issued by their superiors. They have also charged that the Salvadoran Government sought to hide the involvement of those high-ranking officials.

A spokesman for the United States Embassy in El Salvador, when asked yesterday about Mr. Ibarra's remarks, declined to comment on their substance, saying he did not know specifics of the statements. Speaking of the court case, the spokesman, Donald Hamilton, said, "We believe the judicial verdict was a fair and accurate one."

Maj. Salazar Brenes, a personal ad-

Continued on Page A6, Column 4

Nonpayers Hurt Long-Distance Companies

By ERIC N. BERG

Americans are paying their long-distance telephone bills later and later. And — in what communications industry experts are calling one of the seamier effects of the extraordinary competition that has broken out in long distance — many people are not paying their bills at all.

The runup in delinquent and totally uncollectible bills has already translated into higher telephone rates for consumers, according to many industry experts.

"It's adding $1 a month to phone bills in California," reports Harry Strahl, an engineer who has studied the problem for the California Public Utility Commission.

The problem in New York is difficult to gauge, because data are not readily available. Last summer, however, the New York State Public Service Commission permitted the New York Telephone Company to disconnect the telephone service of those customers who do not pay their American Telephone and Telegraph Company long-distance bills. That is cutting down on bad debt to A.T.&T., but it has been no help to the dozens of A.T.&T. rivals doing business in the state.

A.T.&T. has a similar edge in most other states, where local Bell companies handle its billing. But A.T.&T. plans to do its own bookkeeping in the future. The effect of that change, industry experts say, is that A.T.&T. will

Continued on Page D4, Column 3

INSIDE

Labor Plan Explained

The steel industry's national approach to labor bargaining eroded because of concessions at the local level, industry leaders say. Page B11.

Sikh Leadership Is Split

Prime Minister Rajiv Gandhi's attempt to soothe relations with India's Sikhs has stalled because of factionalism among the Sikhs. Page A3.

A B C D E F

What's Sunday without The New York Times? Unthinkable! Delivery is now available in many parts of the U.S. Just call toll-free: 1-800-631-2500 — ADVT

FOR THOSE FAVORING CREMATION WOODLAWN CEMETERY OFFERS A FREE PAMPHLET GIVING COMPLETE INFORMATION CALL 212-920-0600 - ADVT

HAPPY BIRTHDAY HOWIE. I LOVE YOU, DORIS — ADVT

"All the News That's Fit to Print"

The New York Times

Late Edition

Weather: Partly sunny today, southerly winds; chance of showers tonight. Chance of a shower tomorrow morning. Temperatures: today 80-85, tonight 67-69; yesterday 59-79. Details on page 45.

VOL.CXXXIV . . . . No. 46,448 · NEW YORK, SATURDAY, JUNE 22, 1985 · 80 cents beyond 75 miles from New York City, except on Long Island. · 30 CENTS

Copyright © 1985 The New York Times

SCIENTISTS DECIDE BRAZIL SKELETON IS JOSEF MENGELE'S

INQUIRY RULES OUT A HOAX

Experts From U.S. and 2 Other Countries Say They Have 'Absolutely No Doubt'

By RALPH BLUMENTHAL

Special to The New York Times

SAO PAULO, Brazil, June 21 — American, Brazilian and West German scientists announced jointly today that a skeleton recently exhumed from a graveyard near here was unquestionably that of Dr. Josef Mengele.

A separate report by American experts concluded that the bones were those of the long-sought Nazi death-

Text of Americans' report, page 8.

camp doctor "within a reasonable scientific certainty."

Under questioning, the Americans said they had "absolutely no doubt" of their findings and ruled out any possibility of a hoax.

In Washington, Attorney General Edwin Meese 3d said the Justice Department accepted the group's conclusion, while in Los Angeles, officials of the Simon Wiesenthal Center for Holocaust Studies said they were "99 percent" satisfied that the skeleton was Dr. Menegle's. [Page 8.]

There was no immediate response from the Israeli authorities, who had said last month that they would await the forensic experts' reports before drawing a conclusion on whether or not the remains were those of Dr. Mengele.

"I came here not knowing whether it was or wasn't Josef Mengele," said Dr. John J. Fitzpatrick, acting chairman of the radiology department at Cook County Hospital in Chicago and a forensic radiologist selected as an independent expert by the Wiesenthal Center. "I go home fully convinced that it was Mengele."

Brazilians Also Emphatic

Brazilian Government authorities were equally emphatic. "It is our scientific opinion that this exhumed skeleton belongs to Josef Mengele," said Romeu Tuma, the federal police chief of São Paulo, who has headed the investigation since a burst of evidence from West Germany led here three weeks ago.

Today's announcements, accompanied by considerable scientific data, appeared to mark a formal end to the 40-year mystery of the whereabouts of Dr. Mengele, whose grisly medical experiments and selections for the gas chambers at the Auschwitz death camp made him perhaps the most hunted man in history.

As unlikely as many skeptics believed the story to be when it first be-

Continued on Page 8, Column 1

Vendors of Food Face New Limit On Street Sales

Crowding in 3 Boroughs Cited in Council Vote

By ROBERT D. McFADDEN

The New York City Council voted yesterday to widen restrictions on food peddlers in the congested streets of midtown Manhattan and to extend similar limits to crowded sections of lower Manhattan, Brooklyn and Queens.

Mayor Koch said he would sign the measure, which is aimed at reducing the crush of pushcarts selling hot dogs, ice cream, knishes, pretzels and other foods during daylight hours on some of the world's busiest sidewalks and street corners.

Merchants, theater organizations and other business interests had backed the bill, contending that congestion was becoming overwhelming in some areas. Representatives of thousands of street vendors had opposed the bill, saying it would hurt peddlers and their customers. Vendors who violate the regulations face having their merchandise confiscated by the police.

'We Can't Make a Living'

"Many of the city's vending operations will go out of business, because we can't make a living if we're allowed to work only outside the prime midtown and downtown areas," said Chris Ferencsik, president of the Big Apple Food Vendors Association.

Mr. Ferencsik, in an interview, estimated that 25 percent of the city's 3,000 licensed pushcart food vendors would be forced out of business by the new law. Ripple effects, he said, would hurt the manufacturers and processors of foods sold on the carts.

Acting without debate in an unusual Friday meeting, the City Council — which usually meets on Tuesdays or Thursdays — approved the bill by a vote of 31 to 0, with 2 abstentions. Several other minor actions were taken by the council during the afternoon session.

No Vendors at Session

Vendors groups, which have staged protests and filed lawsuits against the restrictions, were caught by surprise. They had no representatives at City Hall when the vote took place, and spokesmen later said they had not expected action before next Tuesday.

"It was very strange that they acted in such a hurry," said Mr. Ferencsik. "We were under the impression the vote was going to be next week."

A spokesman for the Council said there had been no intent to pass the bill without fair notice. The Council met yesterday because action was needed

Continued on Page 33, Column 2

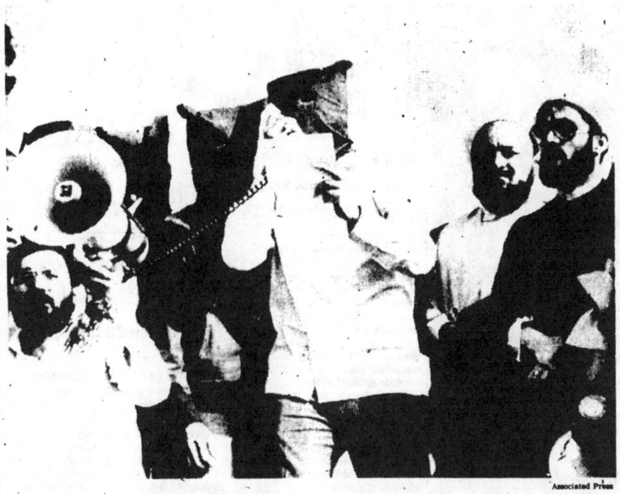

Associated Press

At Beirut International Airport, a masked hijacker addressed about a thousand Shiite Moslems who approached the T.W.A. airliner to express their support yesterday during a demonstration. The hijackers and Shiite clergymen denounced the United States and insisted that Israel free the Lebanese prisoners it holds.

SHULTZ AND PERES AGREE TO OPPOSE SHIITES' DEMANDS

SEEK TO EASE TENSIONS

In First High-Level Contact of Crisis, Israel Assures U.S. of Complete Support

By BERNARD GWERTZMAN

Special to The New York Times

WASHINGTON, June 21 — As the Beirut hostage crisis entered its eighth day, Prime Minister Shimon Peres of Israel and Secretary of State George P. Shultz agreed on the importance of not yielding to the demands of the hijackers holding 40 Americans hostage in Beirut, the State Department said.

Their conversation, by telephone, was said to be the first high-level Israeli-American contact since the Athens-to-Rome T.W.A. Flight 847 was hijacked by Lebanese Shiite gunmen last Friday, with 153 passengers and crew aboard. It appeared to be part of an effort to reduce the strain in relations that has developed since the hijacking.

Reagan Sees Limit to Restraint

With no visible progress in achieving the release of the hostages, Administration officials were cautioning that the crisis could continue indefinitely if Nabih Berri, the Amal Shiite leader, who has become the central intermediary, refuses to free the Americans unconditionally.

In Dallas, President Reagan said the United States would continue to show restraint in the aftermath of recent terrorist acts, but warned that "no one" should doubt America's resolve to counter such attacks. [Page 4.]

The Administration has been seeking support from many foreign governments, particularly those with possible influence on Mr. Berri. A major effort has been concentrated on persuading President Hafez al-Assad of Syria, who is currently in the Soviet Union, to support the unconditional release of the Americans.

'Support and Admiration'

State Department officials said that on Thursday, Richard R. Burt, Assistant Secretary of State for European and Canadian Affairs, met with Oleg M. Sokolov, the No. 2 diplomat at the Soviet Embassy, to discuss possible use of Soviet influence in freeing the hostages. Soviet commentaries since the hijacking have focused on the American military movements in the region, suggesting that Washington was trying to use the crisis to intimidate Arab nations.

Mr. Shultz has said publicly and told foreign governments privately that if the Americans are freed, the Israelis would return to Lebanon the 766 detainees whose release has been the princi-

Continued on Page 4, Column 4

8 Days of Mideast Terror: The Journey of Flight 847

This is the story of the hijacking of Trans World Airlines Flight 847 up to this point, as told by those who have been freed so far. Those who spoke withheld some details, and some said they were doing so because Federal authorities had warned them that the remaining hostages could be jeopardized by their remarks.

By JOSEPH BERGER

As Trans World Airlines Flight 847 waited to take off from Athens International Airport on the hot, windless morning of Friday, June 14, few passengers gave any thought to a minor commotion that had taken place at the terminal just before boarding.

A young, slender, Arabic-speaking man named Ali Atwa had gotten into an argument with T.W.A. ticket agents because they refused to let him board. The jet, they told him, was already full with 145 passengers.

Rudely Aggressive Behavior

One of those passengers, Dr. Benjamin Harris, a 62-year-old professor of education at the University of Texas, may have missed the commotion because his attention was caught by two sharply dressed men who stuck out from the mélange of tourists, military personnel, students and religious pilgrims boarding the plane.

"They were too well-dressed," he said remembering their tan Palm Beach suits, silk shirts and Italian shoes. He had also been struck by their rudely aggressive behavior. After arriving at the last minute and buying tickets at the transfer gate, they twice pushed past him, once on the line to clear security, and once at Gate 8 while waiting for buses to the jet.

As it turned out, that minor commotion and the aggressive behavior of those well-dressed men were the only signals that Flight 847 might be a troubled one. But troubled it would be. For, once the Boeing 727 had lifted off, it was taken on a flight of terror, a drama that continues nine days later. A band of Shiite Moslems commandeered the plane, forcing it to zigzag across the Mediterranean between Beirut and Algiers on a tortuous odyssey of 8,300 miles.

The passengers were compelled at gunpoint to spend up to seven hours with their arms raised and their heads

Continued on Page 7, Column 1

1,000 SHIITES RALLY AT BEIRUT AIRPORT

Supporters of the Hijackers Chant 'Death to America'

By IHSAN A. HIJAZI

Special to The New York Times

BEIRUT, Lebanon, June 21 — Hundreds of Moslem demonstrators chanting "Death to America' and "Death to Reagan" held a mass rally at the international airport here today, where they cheered the hijackers of the T.W.A. airliner.

The march was organized by the pro-Iranian Shiite group called the Party of God, whose members were believed to have commandeered the Boeing 727 last Friday.

In some ways, it was a scene reminiscent of the Iranian hostage crisis that ended in 1981. Many of the demonstrators carried huge posters of Iran's fundamentalist Shiite leader, Ayatollah Ruhollah Khomeini.

Meanwhile, the Lebanese police said they could not confirm a report by the Christian radio, the Voice of Lebanon, that the T.W.A. passengers with Jewish-sounding surnames had been transferred by the hijackers to the Shiite city of Baalbek, 50 miles east of here. The radio said those hostages, believed to number 7 to 9, were being held by the Party of God.

Eastern Lebanon, which is predomi-

Continued on Page 4, Column 1

N.C.A.A. APPROVES STIFFER PENALTIES

Collegiate Body Seeks to End 'Integrity Crisis' in Sports

By GORDON S. WHITE JR.

Special to The New York Times

NEW ORLEANS, June 21 — The National Collegiate Athletic Association today overwhelmingly approved the strongest sanctions it has ever enacted against colleges and coaches who violate rules governing recruiting, amateurism, academic standards and ethics.

The sanctions, approved by N.C.A.A. member institutions at a special convention here, will take effect Sept. 1.

Excerpts from speech, page 49.

They include suspension for an athletic team for as long as two seasons if it is found guilty of major infractions twice in a five-year period.

Facing what some convention delegates have described as an "integrity crisis" in collegiate athletic programs, the representatives also agreed to suspend or dismiss any coach involved in major violations and to suspend the college's right to recruit athletes in the sport. A repeat offender would also be prohibited from awarding new athletic scholarships in the sport for two years.

The special meeting — only the fifth the N.C.A.A. has held since its founding in 1906 — was called by the association's 44-member Presidents' Commission, which was concerned about a

Continued on Page 49, Column 1

IN THE LONG RUN, YOU'RE THE WINNER, when you advertise in The New York Times City Marathon® Official Spectator's Guide, an all advertising supplement to The New York Times, Sunday, October 20. Please call Margaret Porter at (212) 556-7201.—ADVT.

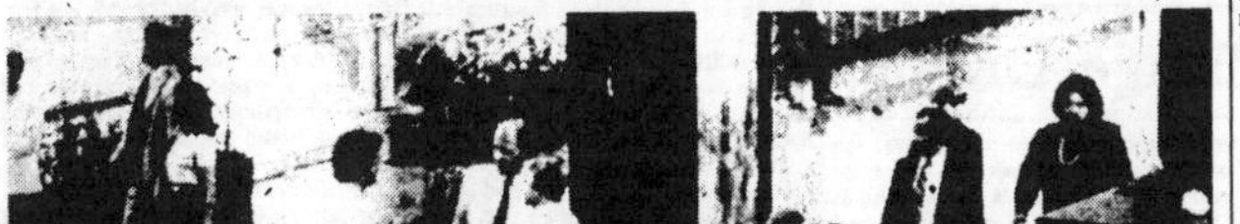

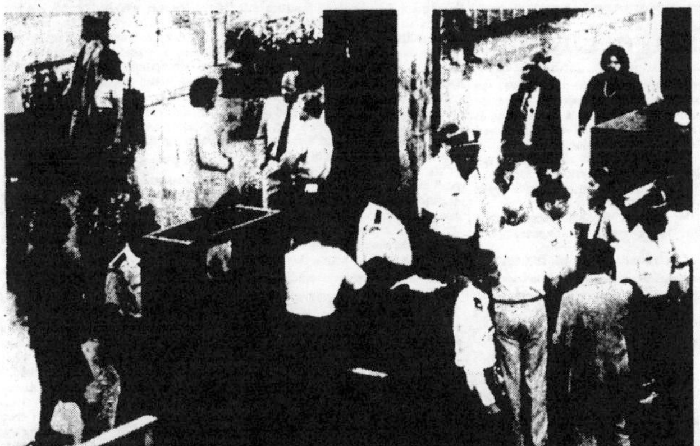

The New York Times/Marilynn K. Yee

Guards standing at security gate in the lobby of the State Department building yesterday after shooting.

Man Kills Mother and Himself at State Dept.

By NEIL A. LEWIS

Special to The New York Times

WASHINGTON, June 21 — A young man shot and killed his mother and himself today on the seventh floor of the State Department, about 100 feet from the office of Secretary of State George P. Shultz, officials reported.

The District of Columbia police said the man, 20-year-old Edward Steven Doster, killed his mother, Carole Doster, 44, just after noon. The two lived at different addresses in Alexandria, Va. Mrs. Doster was a secretary in the office of Edward J. Derwinski, a former Republican Congressman from Illinois who is the State Department counselor.

A senior State Department official said Mr. Doster had a history of mental illness.

Mr. Shultz was in his office at the time of the shooting, speaking by telephone with Prime Minister Shimon Peres of Israel about the 40 Americans being held hostage in Lebanon by Shiite Moslems, an official said. Mr. Derwinski was traveling in Japan.

"At no time was there a threat to the Secretary of State or other senior officials," the department spokesman, Bernard Kalb, told reporters. "This was not a terrorist incident."

Nonetheless, the shooting raised questions about security at the State Department, and a senior official said procedures were being quickly reviewed. Some changes, including searches at department entrances of such hand-carried items as purses and attaché cases, were instituted within hours of the shooting.

According to a well-placed State Department official, Mr. Doster brought an unassembled rifle into the building and put it together in a men's bathroom. The official, who asked not to be identified, said Mr. Doster was able to enter the building using a card that identified him as a family member of a State Department employee.

According to one source, a witness saw Mr. Doster assembling the gun in

Continued on Page 32, Column 2

The Quandary for Israel

Second Thoughts on Its Own Prisoner Swap Seen as Causing Strains Over U.S. Hostages

By THOMAS L. FRIEDMAN

Special to The New York Times

News Analysis

JERUSALEM, June 21 — Israel finds itself in a quandary over how to respond in the Beirut hostage crisis, and Israeli experts on terrorism say they believe it is an indirect result of the Government's decision last month to trade 1,150 prisoners, most of them Palestinians, for 3 Israeli prisoners of war.

The experts say that by giving in to the demands of a Palestinian guerrilla leader, Ahmed Jabril, last month — a move widely viewed here as a blunder — Israel helped to create the atmosphere in which the Beirut hijacking took place.

Now, the experts argue, Israel is trying to compensate for this by refusing to concede to the hijackers' demands for the release of 766 detainees unless the United States formally appeals to the Israeli Government to, in effect, "cave in" to the demands.

Friction Between Allies

This has created a great deal of strain between Jerusalem and Washingtion, and officials here acknowledge that coordination between the two Governments has been inconsistent.

The result, said Zeev Schiff, the military editor of the daily newspaper Haaretz, is that the hijackers have already won a major victory: Israel and America, instead of fighting the hijackers jointly, are at odds with each other.

The connection between the Beirut hijacking and the Israeli-Palestinian prisoner swap last month is multifold, the experts say.

To begin with, said Ariel Merari, Israel's leading civilian expert on terrorism, there is the price the hijackers have demanded. This is not the first time Shiites have hijacked an airplane, he noted, but it is the first time they have made such enormous demands on Israel. The hijackers requested not

Continued on Page 5, Column 1

FOR HOME OR OFFICE DELIVERY of The Times in New York, Boston, Hartford, Washington and Philadelphia, call 1-800-631-2800.—ADVT

INSIDE

Test Laser Hits Shuttle

A laser beam from Hawaii hit the shuttle Discovery in what the Pentagon called a "successful test" for the proposed antimissile shield. Page 11.

Rhode Island Reprimand

Rhode Island's Chief Justice was told by an ethics panel to step down for four months because of friendships with reputed criminals. Page 10.

Officers Reported Cleared

An admiral and a captain, relieved of command because of a purchasing scandal, were later reported cleared of blame by an inquiry. Page 32.

"All the News That's Fit to Print"

The New York Times

Late Edition

Weather: Mostly cloudy today, chance of showers; cloudy, chance of showers tonight. Chance of showers tomorrow. Temperatures: today 73-77, tonight 63-67; yesterday 61-78. Details, page B2.

VOL.CXXXIV.. No. 46,458   Copyright © 1985 The New York Times   NEW YORK, TUESDAY, JULY 2, 1985   30 cents beyond 75 miles from New York City, except on Long Island.   30 CENTS

HIGH COURT BARS PUBLIC TEACHERS IN CHURCH SCHOOLS

REMEDIAL CLASS AT ISSUE

Strict Separation of Religion and State Affirmed, 5 to 4, in New York City Case

By LINDA GREENHOUSE
Special to The New York Times

WASHINGTON, July 1 — The Supreme Court ruled today that public school systems may not send teachers into parochial school classrooms to provide remedial or enrichment instruction.

Such programs, the Court said, forge a "symbolic union of government and religion," that is forbidden by the Constitution.

In two cases, decided by 5-to-4 votes on most questions, the Court struck down two programs of public aid to parochial schools.

New York Program Invalidated

One was a program administered by New York City with Federal funds earmarked for "educationally deprived" children from poor neighborhoods. The

Excerpts from opinions, page A14.

other was a state-subsidized program of remedial and enrichment classes for parochial school children in Grand Rapids, Mich.

Similar remedial programs are run by hundreds of school districts across the country, especially in urban areas. Educators said that parochial school students might have to be bused to public schools for after-hours help or the remedial services might have to be delegated to contractors, in order to comply with the Supreme Court ruling as well as with their legal responsibility to provide the services to students in both public and parochial schools. [Page A14.]

Defeat for Administration

New York City's program is the largest in the country under a $3.2 billion Federal program of remedial instruction for impoverished children, which is known as Title I of the Elementary and Secondary Education Act. The New York program serves 300,000 students, about 25,000 of them in parochial schools.

The opinions, both written by Associate Justice William J. Brennan Jr., marked the third recent Supreme Court defeat for the Reagan Administration's views on the relationship between religion and government.

In its term scheduled to end Tuesday, the

Continued on Page A14, Column 3

Supreme Court Historical Society
Justice William J. Brennan Jr. wrote decisions in school cases.

New York City Weighs Tapping Hudson Water

By ALEXANDER REID

Rain was plentiful in the New York City area last month. But watershed areas upstate that supply most of the city's water were abnormally dry, and the prospect for even stricter water-conservation measures has increased, officials said yesterday.

The normal level for the city's reservoirs for this time of year is 96 percent of capacity, but with the current level at 87.6 percent, environmental officials are taking steps to pump water from the Hudson River and are considering tougher restrictions on water use in homes and businesses.

In northern New Jersey, where water rationing has been imposed on 93 communities, the situation has improved. More than 11 inches of rain have fallen since April in the watershed serving that area, pushing reservoir levels close to 80 percent. [Page B2.]

Worst Since 1960's

A spokesman for New York City's Environmental Protection Department, William Andrews, said: "We haven't been this far into a drought since the 1960's. Since then, we really never had to devise measures for something this severe."

Within the next several days, he said, the City Environmental Protection Commissioner, Joseph T. McGough Jr., and Mayor Koch will discuss what measures are to be taken to handle the drought. Among the measures likely to be considered are more severe cutbacks in water use for businesses and

Continued on Page B2, Column 5

AUSTERITY IMPOSED ON ISRAEL IN PLAN TO CURB INFLATION

Labor Federation Reacts With Call for a General Strike — Shekel Devalued 18.8%

Special to The New York Times

JERUSALEM, July 1 — After a 20-hour Cabinet meeting, the Israeli Government declared an economic emergency today and imposed sweeping austerity measures intended to break the country's 200 percent inflation.

The Histadrut, Israel's labor union members, immediately responded by calling a nationwide general strike for Tuesday. It said the Government "has gone too far."

With 90 percent of the labor force in the Histadrut, the entire country, including harbors and airports, is expected to be shut down by the strike. Services will operate on an emergency Sabbath schedule.

Plan's Principal Elements

The key elements of the 200-point economic reform package are an immediate 18.8 percent devaluation of the shekel, making it 1,500 to the dollar; price increases in Government-subsidized products such as gasoline, which now sell for $3.44 a gallon; the dismissal of 9,000 Government employees within 30 days; a Government spending cut of $750 million, and a Government-ordered three-month wage freeze and price freeze for most goods.

Israel's economic deterioration has its roots in a decade-long combination of mismanagement by several administrations and heavy spending on the Lebanon war and the West Bank settlements and other factors.

But this is the first time an Israeli Government has used its powers of emergency decree — which do not require parliamentary approval — to take such comprehensive economic measures.

Failure of Previous Efforts

What prompted the Government to do so were mounting indications that voluntary wage-price arrangements the national unity Cabinet had worked out with the nation's manufacturers and the Histadrut in the past year had not stemmed the economic deterioration or dampened inflation.

After having slowed for a few months, inflation was projected to hit a monthly record of 30 percent for June.

Meanwhile, foreign currency reserves fell to less than $2 billion in June, well below the $3 billion regarded as a safe minimum.

Having struggled with the economy for nine months and having unsuccess-

Continued on Page D6, Column 1

ISRAELIS SET TO RELEASE 300; U.S. OPENS DIPLOMATIC DRIVE TO 'ISOLATE' BEIRUT AIRPORT

NONMILITARY MOVES

Washington, Responding to Hijacking, Will Bar Lebanese Carriers

By BERNARD GWERTZMAN
Special to The New York Times

WASHINGTON, July 1 — The United States announced today that in response to the hijacking of a Trans World Airlines plane last month by Lebanese Shiite extremists, it was beginning a diplomatic campaign "to isolate" Beirut International Airport.

There was no sign that immediate military action would be taken. Reagan Administration officials said they were holding in reserve several military options in response to the hijacking, but that diplomacy would be pursued first.

Meeting at White House

After a meeting at the White House of President Reagan and members of the National Security Council, a senior State Department official said Mr. Reagan had decided, as a first step, to end air service to the United States by Lebanon's two air carriers, Middle East Airlines and Trans-Mediterranean Airways, a cargo carrier.

Secretary of State George P. Shultz said tonight that "the purpose is to place off limits internationally that airport until the people of Beirut place terrorists off limits."

In an interview on the Public Broadcasting Service program "The MacNeil-Lehrer Newshour," Mr. Shultz

Continued on Page A6, Column 1

Agence France-Presse
Blake Synnestvedt after being reunited with wife, Jane. Dr. Arthur W. Toga, below left, was greeted by brother, Jim.
The New York Times/Fred R. Conrad

Ex-Captives Say Gunmen Planned To Kill Military Men One by One

By JOHN TAGLIABUE
Special to The New York Times

WIESBADEN, West Germany, July 1 — The hijackers of the Trans World Airlines jet separated the American servicemen from the other passengers and intended to kill them one by one, some of the former hostages said here today.

They said the decision to kill the Navy diver Robert Dean Stethem was part of an effort to force the Shiite Amal militia to cooperate in the hijacking. Mr. Stethem was beaten, then shot to death by the gunmen in the early hours of the hijacking.

The former hostages said that Mr. Stethem and the others had been brought to the first-class section of the aircraft to be killed, and that the diver was apparently chosen at random.

"We weren't told the specific reason," said Dr. Arthur W. Toga, a 33-year-old researcher in the neurology department of the Washington University School of Medicine in St. Louis. "But he was the sacrificial lamb. They weren't getting the action they needed

at the airport. It seemed to me that man was picked almost at random."

Mr. Toga and others said the hijackers decided that they needed the help of the Amal militia to assure that the hijacking would not be halted.

In interviews broadcast last week on American television during their captivity, the men who had been taken hostage declined to criticize the conditions of their imprisonment. Women who had been held and were later released were also reticent, apparently fearing that they would jeopardize the safety of those remaining.

But today, freed from confinement, they laid bare details of physical and psychiatric abuse.

'They Were Going to Kill Them'

"I think they had all the military guys lined up," said Blake Synnestvedt, a former hostage from Bryn Athyn, Pa. "They had them in first class. They were going to kill them off one by one."

Mr. Synnestvedt said the killing was intended to "accelerate the process" of negotiation between the hijackers and the more moderate Amal.

"They were panicked," he said of the hijackers. "They were running up and down the aisles screaming. They were panicked, and so we were panicked."

Robert Gordon Brown, a sales executive from Stow, Mass., agreed. "Hesbollah wanted to pull it off, but they could not handle it," he said, using the Arabic name for the extremist Shiite Party of God. "So they drew in the Amal by the threats."

Most of the hostages said they did not see the killing, which occurred in the cockpit, but learned of it later. The

Continued on Page A7, Column 1

ACTION BY CABINET

Freeing of Rest May Be Delayed to Emphasize No Deal Was Made

By THOMAS L. FRIEDMAN

JERUSALEM, July 1 — The Israeli Cabinet decided today to release 300 of its 735 mainly Shiite Moslem detainees over the next two days, officials here said.

Freedom for the detainees, whom Israel has been holding without charges for as long as 20 months, was the principal demand of the Lebanese Shiites who hijacked a Trans World Airlines jet June 14 and held a group of Americans hostage. The Americans were freed Sunday.

There were indications that Israel would probably extend the release of the other detainees over a longer period of days, if not longer, to drive home the point that it was not responding to the hijackers' demands.

Key Cabinet Ministers Meet

The Israeli radio said key Cabinet ministers met this afternoon and decided to free the 300 detainees "in accordance with Government policy that was set out before the June 14 T.W.A. hijacking crisis."

Cabinet sources said the closed-door vote by the inner Cabinet was unanimous. The inner Cabinet is made up of five Labor Party ministers led by Prime Minister Shimon Peres and five Likud-bloc ministers led by Foreign Minister Yitzhak Shamir.

After the 300 are turned over to representatives of the International Committee of the Red Cross in southern Lebanon in the next two days, "the Cabinet will consider the release of the other detainees given the security situation in south Lebanon," the Israeli radio reported.

No Timetable From U.S. Reported

Senior officials said it clear that Israel was not involved in any deal for the release of the 39 American hostages, and that at no time did the United States either ask Israel to free the 735 prisoners in return for the hostages or suggest a timetable under which the release of the detainees should take place.

A senior official said the Americans had only sought confirmation from Israel that it would go ahead with its plans to release the 735 men on its own schedule once the hostages were free.

Israel has already prepared a list of the 300 detainees to be released, officials here said. They are the same men who were scheduled to be freed three

Continued on Page A6, Column 3

U.S. REMAINS WARY DESPITE SYRIAN AID

Help on the Hostages Doesn't Allay Concern Over Policy

By JUDITH MILLER

American officials say that the role of Syria's President, Hafez al-Assad, in resolving the Beirut hostage crisis has improved his image in Washington for the moment and led to hopes that better relations between the two Governments might be possible.

But it has failed to allay concern within the Reagan Administration and among moderate Arab governments about Syria's foreign policy, its support for terrorism and its close ties to the Soviet Union, according to Arab officials in the Middle East and Administration officials in Washington.

A senior State Department official said yesterday that the Administration was "highly appreciative" of Syria's help in securing the release of the 30 Americans held by Lebanese Shiites.

In a subsequent State Department briefing, however, Bernard Kalb, the department spokesman, said that despite Syria's assistance, the Administration still listed Syria as a supporter of terrorism.

Citing what he called "reliable reports," Mr. Kalb said Syria had aided "a number of terrorist organizations" by permitting them to maintain headquarters or training camps in Syria or

Continued on Page A8, Column 1

New York's Rescue: The Offstage Dramas

By MARTIN GOTTLIEB

If there was one 24-hour period during New York City's long fiscal crisis when it seemed as if bankruptcy might finally be at hand, it began on the evening of Oct. 16, 1975.

The drama was played out in evening clothes, because Gov. Hugh L. Carey, Mayor Abraham D. Beame and others were called into it from the annual Alfred E. Smith political dinner at the Waldorf-Astoria Hotel.

Before it was over, the city had gone so far as to get an order from Justice Irving Saypol in State Supreme Court — an order that was never executed — allowing it to default temporarily on payment of notes that were coming due.

Deadline Approached

But as with so much else during the long crisis, the reality was different

Back From the Brink
The Enduring Legacy
of New York's Fiscal Crisis
Second of five articles

from the public's perception, because of a quiet conversation, unreported and away from center stage.

The problem of the moment was this: By 3 P.M. on Oct. 17, the city had to come up with $440 million, to pay off bondholders and a state loan and to cover a payroll. But Albert Shanker, the president of the United Federation

of Teachers, was balking at investing $150 million in teacher retirement funds in Municipal Assistance Corporation bonds, something that government officials were counting on as a key part of their money-raising efforts.

State officials alerted the White House to the prospect of a bankruptcy, and millions of New Yorkers went to sleep with the prospect of the largest governmental default in American history dangling before them.

But unknown to state officials or

other negotiators, not too late into the evening Mr. Beame put in a telephone call to an old friend. It was to John J. DeLury, the head of the Uniformed Sanitationmen's Association.

"John, I need this one," the Mayor said, in the recollection of Sidney J. Frigand, who was the Mayor's press secretary.

Mr. Beame recalled recently that Mr. DeLury swore him to secrecy but

Continued on Page B4, Column 1

Touch-Up Work Up on the George Washington Bridge

The New York Times/Ruby Washington

Robert Lachman painting New York tower of George Washington Bridge yesterday; in the distance across the Hudson River is Fort Lee, N.J. The touch-up, part of regular maintenance by the Port Authority of New York and New Jersey, is expected to continue until October, the 54th birthday of the 3,500-foot-long bridge.

INSIDE

Blasts in Madrid and Rome
A woman was killed and 20 people were wounded in attacks at airline offices in Madrid, and 12 were hurt in a Rome airport blast. Page A3.

Shake-Up in the Kremlin
Andrei A. Gromyko becomes Soviet President and Grigory V. Romanov, once a potential top leader, is out of the Politburo. Page A10.

Happy Fifth of July
Many offices will close Friday to create a four-day Fourth of July weekend. One economist called it "a ghost day." Page D20.

Time Capsule of the First 2½ Millennia

Day One	Light and Darkness
Day Two	The Firmament
Day Three	Division of Earth and Seas; grasses and trees
Day Four	The Two Great Lights
Day Five	Living Creatures
Day Six	Man
Day Seven	The Sabbath

	Adam; lives 930 years
130	Seth; lives 912 years
235	Enosh; lives 905 years
325	Kenan; lives 910 years
395	Mehalalel; lives 895 years
460	Jared; lives 962 years
622	Enosh; lives 365 years
687	Methuselah; lives 969 years
874	Lamech; lives 777 years
1056	Noah; lives 950 years
1558	Shem; lives 600 years
1656	The Flood
1658	Arpachshad; lives 438 years
1693	Shelah; lives 433 years
1723	Ever; lives 464 years
1757	Peleg; lives 239 years
1787	Reu; lives 239 years
1819	Serug; lives 230 years
1849	Nahor; lives 148 years
1878	Terah; lives 205 years
1948	Abram (Abraham) born
1958	Sarai (Sarah) born
1996	Tower of Babel
2006	Death of Noah, aged 950
2018	The Covenant with Abram; birth of Judaism
2034	Ishmael born
2047	Circumcision of Abraham and Ishmael Destruction of Sodom and Gomorrah; Lot's wife
2048	Isaac born

2085		Binding of Isaac Rebekah born Death of Sarah, aged 127
2108		Esau and Jacob born
2123		Death of Abraham, aged 175
2158		Death of Shem, aged 600
2171		Isaac blesses Jacob instead of Esau
2193-		
2206		Birth of Twelve Tribes Sons of Leah: Reuben (firstborn), Simeon (2), Levi (3), Judah (4), Issachar (9), Zebulun (10) Sons of Bilhah: Dan (5), Naftali (6) Sons of Zilpah: Gad (7), Asher (8) Sons of Rachel: Joseph (11—father of Ephraim and Manasseh), Benjamin (12)
2216		Joseph sold
2228		Death of Isaac, aged 180
2229		Joseph becomes prime minister of Egypt
2238		House of Israel, numbering 70 souls, enters Egypt, due to famine in Canaan
2255		Death of Jacob, aged 147
2309		Death of Joseph, aged 110 End of Book of Genesis
2368	7 Adar	Birth of Moses
2448	15 Nisan	Exodus from Egypt
	21 Nisan	Splitting and crossing of Sea of Reeds
	16 Iyar	Provision of Manna
	6 Sivan	Torah given
	7 Sivan	Moses ascends Mt. Sinai
	17 Tammuz	Golden Calf; First Tablets destroyed
2449	10 Tishrei	First Yom Kippur; Second Tablets
	11 Tishrei	Construction of Tabernacle
	25 Kislev	Tabernacle completed
	1 Iyar	Census begins
	20 Iyar	Designation of tribal banners
	29 Sivan	Spies sent to scout Land of Israel
	9 Av	Spies return
2487	10 Nisan	Death of Miriam
	1 Av	Death of Aaron
2488	1 Shevat	Book of Deuteronomy
	7 Adar	Death of Moses; conclusion of the Torah
	10 Nisan	Crossing of the Jordan

Day By Day In Jewish History

Abraham P. Bloch

Tishri 1

First day of Rosh Ha-Shanah (Lev. 23:24).

Creation of Adam and Eve (*Sanhedrin* 38b).

Adam and Eve were expelled from the Garden of Eden (ibid.).

Birth of Cain (ibid.) and Abel (*Bereshit Rabbah* 22).

Noah dispatched the dove and removed the cover of the ark (Gen. 8:5, 8:13, Rashi).

Falasha holiday named "The Commemoration of Abraham" or "The Festival of the Light Has Appeared" (Leslau, *Falasha Anthology*). Falasha interpretation of the Bible is in substantial agreement with the views of other nonrabbinic sects, such as the Samaritans, Sadducees, and Karaites. They did not accept the traditional view of Rosh Ha-Shanah as the New Year and the Day of Judgment. Since it is the only holiday in the Bible described as a "memorial" day (Lev. 23:24), the Falashas apparently linked this "memorial" with an ancient tradition, preserved in the Talmud, that Abraham was born and died in the month of Tishri (*Rosh Ha-Shanah* 10b). Their alternate name for this holiday, "The Festival of the Light Has Appeared," reflects a legendary account of the light which filled the cave when Abraham was born (*Sotah* 12a). According to the Falasha epic *Teezaza Sanbat*, Abraham was born on Tishri 8.

Sarah, Rachel, and Hannah prayed for offspring. According to the Talmud, their prayers were granted on Rosh Ha-Shanah (*Yevamot* 61b). The Midrash says that the prayers of Rebecca and Leah were also granted on this day (*Tanhuma, Vayera*). The biblical accounts of Sarah's and Hannah's conceptions are read in the synagogue on the first day of Rosh Ha-Shanah.

Joseph was released from prison (*Rosh Ha-Shanah* 10b).

Pharaoh freed the Jews from slavery (ibid. 11a).

Ezra read the Torah to the assembled Jews at the water-gate in Jerusalem, 444 B.C.E. (Neh. 8:2).

Yahrzeit of Rabbi Amnon, author of the liturgical poem *U-Netanneh Tokef* (*Zikhron Yemot Olam*).

Tishri 2

Second day of Rosh Ha-Shanah. The story of the *Akedah*, the 'binding' of Isaac (Gen. 22), is the subject of the Torah portion on the second day of Rosh Ha-Shanah. The association is derived from the rabbinic interpretation of the shofar as a symbolic reminder of the ram which was substituted for Isaac (*Rosh Ha-Shanah* 16a). The *Zohar* explains the association by the coincidence of this holiday with Isaac's birthday. This contradicts a Talmudic source which alleges that he was born on Nisan 15 (*Rosh Ha-Shanah* 10b; *Tanhuma, Vayera*).

On Tishri 2 "God blessed the seventh day and sanctified it because on it he had rested from all his work . . ." (Gen. 2:3; *Sanhedrin* 38b).

Tishri 3

Gedaliah b. Ahikam, governor of Judea after the destruction of the First Temple, was assassinated on Tishri 3 (2 Kings 25:25). A fast day was decreed to commemorate his murder and the dispersal of the remnants of Judea's population (Zech. 7:5; *Megillat Taanit* chap. 7; *Rosh Ha-Shanah* 18b). The Karaites observe the Fast of Gedaliah on Tishri 24. The Bene Israel of India call the fast of Tishri 3 "Navuyacha Roja," New Year's Fast. See Neh. 9:1.

Tishri 4

Bene Israel of India celebrate a holiday called "Kiricha San" (Pudding Festival).

Tishri 5

Birthday of Jacob's son Naphtali (*Yalkut Shimoni*).

Tishri 6

The Jewish community of Berlin, Germany, was organized on September 10, 1671.

Tishri 7

Birthday of Dinah, twin of Zebulun (*Book of Jubilees*).

Tishri 8

Birthday of Abraham in the Falasha tradition (Leslau, *Falasha Anthology; Teezaza Sanbat*). The Falasha tradition is in accord with the view of Rabbi Eliezer in the Talmud that the birth and death of Abraham occurred in the month of Tishri (*Rosh Ha-Shanah* 10b). This comes close to some rabbinic sources which place Abraham's birthday on Tishri 10.

Tishri 9

Traditional birthday of Rabbi Judah ha-Nasi, editor of the Mishnah, ca. 135 C.E. (*Seder ha-Dorot*). *Seder ha-Dorot* adopts a literal interpretation of the Talmudic statement: "When Rabbi Akiva died, Rabbi Judah ha-Nasi was born" (*Kiddushin* 72b). However, it was most likely a figurative expression of a belief in the uninterrupted continuity of Jewish scholarship.

Tishri 10

Yom Kippur. There is a rabbinic tradition which links the date of Moses' descent from Mt. Sinai, carrying the second Tablets of the Law, with the date of Yom Kippur (*Seder Olam Rabbah* 6; Tishri 10:8). The new tablets were a token of God's forgiveness in answer to Moses' plea after the golden calf incident: "And pardon our iniquity and our sin" (Exod. 34:9). This date was therefore set aside as a day of forgiveness for all time. The Book of Jubilees alleges that on Tishri 10 Jacob mourned and wept upon receiving a false report of Joseph's death. That date was for that reason designated a day of fasting and weeping. Bene Israel of India call Yom Kippur "Darfalnicha San," the Festival of the Closing of the Doors. No one leaves his home on this day. This custom may be related to the injunction to the Jews in Egypt to stay indoors when the angel of death appears (Exod. 12:22). On Yom Kippur, too, life and death are decreed.

Birthday of Abraham and Ishmael (Gen. 17:26, Rashi).

Abraham was circumcised and admitted into the covenant *(Pirkei de-Rabbi Eliezer* 29). There are two dates mentioned for the day of Abraham's circumcision, Nisan 13 *(Bereshit Rabbah* 50) and Tishri 10. According to Rashi, Abraham was circumcised on his birthday (Gen. 17:26). It would therefore follow that Abraham was born either on Tishri 10 or Nisan 13. See Nahmanides on Exod. 17:27; *Daat Zekenim miBaalei Tosafot,* Gen. 17:26.

Abraham placed Isaac on the altar on Mt. Moriah *(Pirkei de-Rabbi Eliezer; Akedat Yitzhak, Asarah Maamarot* 3).

Jacob's sons reported Joseph's death to their father (Book of Jubilees). After the restoration of the tablets, Moses ordered an obligatory contribution of half a shekel per person for the construction of the sanctuary. A midrash *(Tanhuma, Ki Tissa* 10) views this tax as an atonement for the golden calf, for which many Jews had contributed half a shekel each, and for the sale of Joseph, for whom the brothers had each received a coin.

Moses brought down from Mt. Sinai the second Tablets of the Law (Exod. 34:29-30, Rashi). He recited part of the Torah to the Jewish people *(Seder Olam Zuta).*

Egyptian and Syrian forces opened the Yom Kippur War on October 6, 1973, with invasions of Sinai and the Golan Heights.

Tishri 11

Bene Israel of India celebrate Shila San, post-holiday. Gifts are sent to the poor and friends exchange visits.

Tishri 12

Angels informed Abraham that Sarah would bear a son.

Tishri 13

Destruction of Sodom and Gomorrah. Abraham was circumcised on Tishri 10 and visited by the angels on Tishri 12 *(Bava Metzia* 86b). Sodom was destroyed one day later, Tishri 13. According to a second rabbinic tradition, Abraham was circumcised on Nisan 13. It would therefore follow that Sodom was destroyed on Nisan 16.

Operation Magic Carpet, which transferred the entire Jewish community of Yemen to Israel, was completed on September 24, 1950. Yemenite Jews, given to mysticism and Kabbalah, were emotionally receptive to messianic movements to speed the return to Zion. They eagerly grasped at the reports of the pseudo-messiah Shabbetai Zevi and hastened to make preparations for mass emigration to Palestine. The Yemenite government suppressed the movement with harsh severity. It was not until 1882 that the first group of Yemenite Jews secretly left for Palestine. The process was completed 68 years later, in 1950.

Tishri 14

The dedication ceremony of Solomon's Temple was completed (2 Chron. 7:9).

Tishri 15

First day of Sukkot (Lev. 23:34).

Tishri 16

Simhat Beit ha-Shoevah, the ritual of the libation of the altar, was performed on the second day of Sukkot, according to the statement of Rabbi Judah b. Bathyra in the Talmud *(Ta'anit* 3a). According to the prevailing Talmudic view, the ritual of libation began on the first day of Sukkot and was performed on each successive day of the festival *(Sukkah* 42b).

Tishri 17

David Ben-Gurion, founding father and first prime minister of Israel, was born on October 16, 1886.

Tishri 18

Death of Jacob (Lowenstein, *Dor Dor ve-Dorshav).*

Tishri 19

The first organizational meeting of the Order of B'nai B'rith was held at Sinsheimer's Cafe, 60 Essex Street, New York City, on October 13, 1843.

Tishri 20

The crossing of Israeli forces to the western side of the Suez Canal on October 16, 1973, marked a turning point in the Yom Kippur War.

Tishri 21

Hoshana Rabbah.

Tishri 22

Shemini Atzeret (combined with Simhat Torah in Israel).

Tishri 23

Simhat Torah (outside Israel).

Tishri 24

Ezra and Nehemiah convened the Jewish community in Jerusalem to purge its heathen elements and to renew the ancient covenant, 444 B.C.E. (Neh. 9:1).

Tishri 25

Rabbi Moses Sofer, leading Talmudist and founder of the yeshivah of Pressburg (Bratislava), author of *Hatam Sofer,* died on October 3, 1839.

Tishri 26

Simon Bar Giora inflicted heavy losses upon the Roman forces at Bet Horon, 66 C.E.

Tishri 27

Fighting was resumed in the Yom Kippur War on October 23, 1973. Egypt, Syria, and Israel announced their acceptance of a second cease-fire passed by the U.N. Security Council. Fighting continued until October 26. The estimated losses up to February 12, 1974 were: Israel—2,522 killed, 1,578 wounded, 107 planes, 840 tanks, 1 ship; Egypt—7,500 casualties, 242 planes, 895 tanks, 20 ships; Syria—7,300 casualties, 179 planes, 880 tanks, 9 ships. In the War of Independence (1948-49) 6,200 Israelis died, among them 1,700 civilians. The total wounded was put at 12,500. In the 1956 Suez campaign, 190 were killed. In the war of 1967, the death toll was 806, including 26 civilians; 3,006 were wounded, including 195 civilians.

Tishri 28

Rabban Gamaliel VI, last patriarch (*nasi*) of Palestine, was removed from office by a joint decree of Emperors Honorius and Theodosius II on October 17, 415. With the removal of Rabban Gamaliel VI, the last vestiges of Jewish autonomy in Palestine disappeared. The publication of the British White Paper, 1,515 years later, sought to accomplish the same ends.

Tishri 29

Traditional *yahrzeit* of Simeon the Just, high priest and member of the *Knesset ha-Gedolah* (*Yoma* 39b).

Tishri 30

A Roman legion under the command of Cestius entered the suburbs of Jerusalem, forcing the Jewish defenders to retreat behind the walls of the inner town, 66 C.E. The foundation stone of the Knesset in Jerusalem was laid on the anniversary of this attack, which eventually led to the loss of Jewish independence.

Heshvan 1

The opening of the sowing season in Palestine (Rabbi Simeon, *Bava Mezia* 106b).

The seventh and last of the Christian Crusades was brought to an end by a treaty concluded by King Louis IX of France and the Berbers of North Africa on October 18, 1270.

Heshvan 2

Purim Mo'ed Katan was annually celebrated by the Jews of Shiraz, Persia, in commemoration of their escape from forced conversion upon the sudden death of the apostate Jew, Abu Al Hasan, on Heshvan 2.

Heshvan 3

King Cyrus of Persia formally occupied the city of Babylon in 539 B.C.E. The Babylonian empire, which had crushed Judea in 586 B.C.E. came to an end 47 years later.

Heshvan 4

Maimonides reached Jerusalem on October 12, 1165, six months after his arrival in Palestine. In commemoration of this event, he set aside Heshvan 4 as a private holiday for himself and his family.

Heshvan 5

The British government of Palestine announced, on October 17, 1920, that Hebrew would become one of the official languages in the courts of the land.

Heshvan 6

Rabbi Joseph Leib Bloch, dean of the Yeshivah of Telz, died on November 9, 1929. The Yeshivah of Telz was one of the outstanding Talmudical academies of Eastern Europe. Its official existence came to an end in 1940, when the Russians closed it. Some of its leaders, who happened to be on a tour of the United States at that time, were fortunately able to found a new Telz Yeshivah in Cleveland, Ohio, and thus assure the perpetuation of the Telz academic program. Rabbi Joseph Leib Bloch, dean of the yeshivah, died on Heshvan 6. Rabbi Hayyim Rabinowitz, a successor, died on Heshvan 8. Rabbi Simon Shkop, a former dean of the school, died on Heshvan 9. The American Telz Yeshivah was founded on Heshvan 7.

Heshvan 7

On November 3, 1878, the first settlers arrived at the site of Petah Tikvah to prepare the ground for a new colony.

Heshvan 8

Jewish insurgents returned to Jerusalem from their victorious pursuit of the defeated Roman forces under Cestius, 66 C.E. (Josephus, *Jewish Wars*, 2, 19).

The House of Bishops of the Protestant Episcopal Church issued a proclamation in St. Louis, Mo., on October 14, 1964, clearing Jews of the charge of deicide.

Heshvan 9

King Casimir III of Poland, on October 9, 1334, renewed Jewish privileges granted by his predecessors. Unlike the Jews of Western Europe, who were decimated by the Crusaders and Black Death rioters, the Jews of Poland and Lithuania enjoyed comparative peace and freedom until the 16th century. Casimir III granted important privileges to the Jews of his realm.

Heshvan 10

Asser Levy was granted a butcher's license on October 15, 1660. The supply of kosher meat in New Amsterdam was thus assured.

Heshvan 11

Yahrzeit of Rachel. Rachel is the only biblical woman whose *yahrzeit* is commemorated by posterity.

Heshvan 12

A requirement of corroboration of Jewish witnesses in all blood-ritual accusations was published in a papal decree on October 8, 1272.

Heshvan 13

The Nazi governor of Poland prohibited Jewish ritual slaughtering of animals, on October 26, 1939. Agitation against ritual slaughtering of animals, allegedly on humane grounds, received its most ardent support from antisemitic circles. The hypocrisy of the anti-*kashrut* campaign was brazenly demonstrated by the Nazi governor of Poland, who prohibited kosher slaughtering even as he proceeded to exterminate millions of Jews, calling to mind the bitterly sarcastic outcry of the prophet Hosea: "They that sacrifice men kiss the calves" (13:3).

Heshvan 14

The British government gave its final approval to the Balfour Declaration on October 30, 1917. The Balfour Declaration, according to some historians, derived from several factors. 1. The top-secret Sykes-Picot agreement, negotiated by Britain with France and Russia, provided for the partition of the Ottoman Empire. As soon as the agreement was signed, however, Britain sought to invalidate its terms by keeping the French out of the Middle East, particularly out of Palestine. The British felt that their espousal of Zionism would lead to a demand by world Jewry that Britain alone should protect Jewish interests in Palestine. This would provide the pretext for a repudiation of the secret agreement with France. Exclusive British sovereignty over Palestine would assure the security of the Suez Canal. 2. There was hope in some British circles that the Balfour Declaration would draw the Russian Jewish intellectuals away from the leftist parties and win their support for Russia's continued participation in the war on the side of the allies. 3. The segment of the British people which drew its inspiration from the Bible saw in the restoration of a Jewish state in Palestine the fulfillment of biblical prophecy. To them, the geographical demarcation, "From Dan to Beersheba," was still a relevant phrase. The Balfour Declaration, dated November 2, was released on November 9. By that time the British Foreign Office had lost interest in the document. The British Army had entered Gaza and the Bolshevik Revolution had broken out in Russia. It had been justly concluded that if the declaration had not been approved by October 30, it never would have been approved at a later date.

Heshvan 15

A huge Nazi pogrom, which later became known as *Kristallnacht* (the Night of the Broken Glass), took place throughout Germany and Austria on the night of November 9-10, 1938. Officially sparked by the murder by a Jew of a German embassy official in Paris, *Kristallnacht* was thinly disguised as a "spontaneous" act of retaliation by the "Aryan" population. Hundreds of Jewish businesses and homes, as well as nearly three hundred synagogues, were destroyed. Among the ruins was the famous Rashi Chapel of Worms. The Rashi chair was hidden in 1938 in the museum of Worms and thus escaped destruction.

Heshvan 16
General Ulysses S. Grant, on November 9, 1862, issued the first in a series of orders barring Jews from entering the military department under his command.

An order to suspend extermination and dismantle the crematoria was sent to Auschwitz from Berlin on November 2, 1944.

Heshvan 17
Beginning of the biblical flood (Gen. 7:11; Rabbi Eliezer, *Rosh Ha-Shanah* 111b). According to Rabbi Joshua, the flood began on Iyar 17 (ibid.)

Heshvan 18
Hovevei Zion, the pioneer Russian Zionist movement, was founded on November 6, 1884, at the first international Zionist convention, in Kattowitz (Katowice), Poland. Hovevei Zion was the first to link the nationalist movement with the term Zion. Ninety-one years after the adoption of "Zion" as the emblem of Jewish nationalism, the U.N. condemned Zionism by equating it with racism.

Heshvan 19
The first B'nai B'rith lodge was organized on November 12, 1843 in New York.

Heshvan 20
In 407 B.C.E., Jedoniah, head of an ancient Jewish colony in Egypt, petitioned the Persian governor of Judea for permission to rebuild the destroyed Jewish temple at the fortress of Yeb (Kobler, *Letters of Jews Through the Ages,* Vol. I, p. 23).

Heshvan 21
Chaim Weizmann, the father of the State of Israel and its first president, died on November 9, 1952.

Heshvan 22
The British captured Gaza, Palestine, from the Turkish army on November 7, 1917.

Heshvan 23
The stones of the altar, which had been defiled by the Greeks, were removed from the Temple (ca. 164 B.C.E.). The anniversary of this day was designated a holiday (*Megillat Ta'anit* 8).

Heshvan 24
Israeli forces crossed into Egyptian territory in the Sinai Peninsula on October 29, 1956, and occupied El-Kuntilla.

Heshvan 25
King John Hyrcanus reduced Samaria, the capital of the Samaritans, in the year 109 B.C.E. The anniversary of this victory was designated a holiday. The Samaritans, an ancient sect which has survived to the present day, had posed a serious threat to the political and religious integrity of the Jewish community in the land of Israel for several centuries. The Hasmonean conquest of Samaria put an end to this internal threat.

Heshvan 26
The first antisemitic attack over a radio network in the U.S. was broadcast by Father Coughlin on November 20, 1938.

Heshvan 27
Noah left the ark a little over a year after the beginning of the flood (Gen. 8:14). The Talmud and Midrash occasionally refer to the 12 months' duration of the flood (*Edduyot* 2:10; *Bereshit Rabbah* 28:9), which appears to be in conflict with the biblical account of the flood ending on the eleventh day after the first anniversary of its inception (Gen. 7:11, 8:14). However, the 11 additional days following the lunar year make up a complete solar year, or 12 solar months. It is likely that the rabbis were referring to 12 solar months inasmuch as the Bible links the solar seasons to the flood.

Heshvan 28
Jews' College, a seminary in London, England, for the training of rabbis and Hebrew teachers, was founded by Rabbi Nathan Adler on November 9, 1855.

Heshvan 29
Jews were permitted to continue to reside in Alexandria by the treaty of November 8, 641, which sealed the Arab conquest of Egypt. Jews settled in Alexandria at the time of its founding in 332 B.C.E.

Heshvan 30
American forces marched into New York on November 25, 1783. The Jewish residents, who had fled the city in 1776 because of their revolutionary sympathies, were able to return soon after the retreat of the British.

Kislev 1
The beginning of winter in Israel (Rabbi Judah, *Bava Metzia* 106b).

Kislev 2
Kislev 2 was proclaimed a day of fast and prayer in ancient Palestine if no rain had fallen by that date.

Kislev 3
Purim of Amtchislav (Mstislavl, Belorussian S.S.R.) was annually observed by that community in commemoration of a happy event on November 13, 1844.

Kislev 4
A delegation of Babylonian Jews arrived in Jerusalem in 518 B.C.E., to inquire from the prophet Zechariah whether the fast of Av should be discontinued (Zech. 7:1). It took five years to construct the Second Temple, from 520 to 516 B.C.E. The Babylonian delegation arrived in 518 B.C.E., two years after the construction had begun. Their inquiry mentioned only the fast of Av, which was the principal postexilic fast day. The discontinuation of this fast would, ipso facto, have led to the elimination of the other three fast days.

A private Purim was observed by the Jewish community of Tiberias to commemorate the lifting of a siege by Suleiman Pasha of Damascus, on December 1, 1742 (Ya'ari, *Zikhronot Eretz Yisrael,* vol. 1, p. 96).

The first Reform Prayer House of Berlin was closed by Emperor Frederick William III of Prussia, on December 6, 1815, on the ground that it was detrimental to the established rights of the Jewish "Church."

Kislev 5

Fast day of the Jewish community of Posen, Poland, in commemoration of assaults on their quarters by antisemitic gangs on November 10, 1687. The Jewish quarters were successfully defended by the Jews, and the attackers were repulsed (Berenfeld, *Sefer Ha-Dema'ot,* vol. 3). The fast day of Posen commemorates one of the earliest successful self-defense actions engaged in by a medieval Jewish community. Jews fought heroically to repel Chmielnicki's murderous hordes in the 17th century, but they rarely succeeded in saving their lives. Only in the few exceptional instances when the Polish nobility supported the Jews were they able to escape destruction. In the Posen mob violence of 1687, the Jews fought a battle which lasted for three days and they emerged triumphant.

Kislev 6

The U.N. Assembly, on November 10, 1975, adopted a resolution defining Zionism as "a form of racism and racial discrimination."

Kislev 7

King Jehoiakim burned the scroll which had been dictated by Jeremiah to Baruch b. Neriah in 603 B.C.E. (Jer. 36:23). This date was proclaimed a fast-day (*Megillat Ta'anit,* concluding chap.).

Death of King Herod the Great, 4 B.C.E. The anniversary of this date was proclaimed a holiday (*Megillat Ta'anit* 9). According to Josephus, Herod the Great died in the month of Adar. Some historians amended the text of *Megillat Ta'anit* by substituting the name of King Alexander Jannaeus the Hasmonean, who died in the year 76 B.C.E. Professor Zeitlin suggests that the ancient holiday of Kislev 7 commemorated the victory of the Jews over the Roman general Cestius on November 25, 65.

An armistice, marking the end of World War I, was proclaimed on November 11, 1918. World War I broke out on Tishah be-Av. It came to an end on Kislev 7, an ancient Jewish holiday.

Kislev 8

The U.N. General Assembly passed a resolution, on November 22, 1974, approving the right of the Palestinians to a sovereign state, at the expense of Israel.

Kislev 9

Jews of Paris and the entire royal domain of France were expelled by Charles VI for the last time on November 3, 1394. This expulsion brought to an end the medieval Franco-Jewish community, although the Jews of Lyons continued undisturbed for another 25 years. The last remnants of French Jewry, the Jews of Provence, were expelled in 1493. It is curious that almost exactly a century elapsed between each of the major expulsions of the large West European Jewish communities: English Jewry was expelled in 1290, French Jewry in 1394, and Spanish Jewry in 1492.

The American Jewish Joint Distribution Committee for the relief of Jewish war sufferers was established on November 27, 1914. The Joint was organized on the eve of Sabbath Va-Yezei. It is in the portion of the Bible read that week that the classical expression of Jewish voluntary charity was first enunciated: "And of all that thou shalt give me, I will surely give the tenth unto thee" (Gen. 28:22).

Kislev 10

President Anwar el Sadat of Egypt addressed the Knesset in Jerusalem on November 20, 1977.

Kislev 11

The charter of Yeshiva College was amended by the New York State Board of Regents on November 16, 1945, making it the first American university under Jewish auspices. Christian universities were closed to Jewish students throughout the Middle Ages. There were very few exceptions to this rule. The most famous schools were in countries from which Jews had been expelled so that Jewish students had no access to them. Furthermore, universities were primarily ecclesiastical schools, closely linked to the Church, and as a result, Jewish students were inevitably excluded, even in countries where Jews enjoyed the right of residence. The University of Padua, Italy, was a notable exception. From the middle of the 16th century it attracted Jewish students from all over Europe. The University of Leyden, Holland, adopted a similar liberal policy in the 17th century. The earliest known effort to establish a university under Jewish auspices was made in Sicily. King John granted authorization, on January 17, 1466, to open such a school but the project never materialized. Rabbi Abraham Provencal attempted to found a Jewish university in Italy in the 16th century, but he too failed. The first Jewish university was established in Jerusalem. It opened on April 1, 1925. Yeshiva University was the first Jewish university in America, established in the tradition of the American pluralistic cultural pattern.

Kislev 12

Solomon Schechter, discoverer of the Cairo Genizah and founder of the United Synagogue of America, died on November 19, 1915.

Kislev 13

Ravina, co-editor of the Babylonian Talmud, died in 499. His death marked the end of the Talmudic period (*Iggeret Rav Sherira Gaon*).

Kislev 14

The first plane in Operation Magic Carpet, the transportation of Yemenite Jews to Israel, left Aden on December 16, 1948.

Kislev 15

An altar dedicated to Zeus Olympius was set up by Athenaeus, the Syrian in charge of public worship, in the Temple of Jerusalem, 167 B.C.E.

Kislev 16

Hermann Ahlwardt, apostle of modern German antisemitism, was elected to the Reichstag on December 5, 1892. Nazi antisemitism was an offshoot of 19th-century modern German racism, of which Ahlwardt was a leading figure. His election to the Reichstag marked the beginning of political antisemitism through its involvement in national politics. With singular foresight he linked the success of German antisemitism with American sympathy and support. In furtherance of this objective, he undertook, in 1896, a personal lecture tour through the United States in order to spread his gospel of hate. The tour ended in complete failure and brought about his decline.

Kislev 17

The U.N. voted in favor of the partition of Palestine on November 29, 1947.

The Arab terrorist campaign opened in Palestine on November 30, 1947.

Kislev 18

The directory council on the district of Strasbourg, Alsace-Lorraine, decreed, on November 22, 1793, the prohibition of the rite of circumcision and the wearing of beards. It also ordered the burning of all books written in Hebrew. This prohibition is illustrative of the frenzy of the extremists of the French Revolution in their anti-religious campaign. Not since the days of the Roman Emperor Hadrian and the persecutions of Yezdegerd II in the year 456 during the neo-Persian period, were Jews subjected to such legislation. The Nazis banned circumcision in most of the ghettos and concentration camps.

The first kibbutz, Deganyah Alef, was founded in Palestine on December 1, 1909. The colony played an important part in the War of Independence. Left defenseless in the face of advancing Syrian forces, since the only trained Israeli forces were withdrawn to aid in the defense of Jerusalem, the Deganyah defenders repulsed the attempt of the enemy to continue its westward advance. The U.N. resolution to internationalize Jerusalem was passed on the anniversary of the founding of Deganyah, but was never implemented.

Kislev 19

Rabbi Shneur Zalman, author of the *Tanya*, the philosophy of Habad Hasidism, and the founder of the Lubavitch hasidic movement, was released from the St. Petersburg jail on November 27, 1798.

Kislev 20

Rabbi Manasseh ben Israel, the famous rabbi of Amsterdam who was responsible for the resettlement of Jews in England, died on November 26, 1657. Manasseh ben Israel believed that the restoration of Israel hinged upon the prior total dispersion of Jews throughout the world. This belief motivated his successful efforts to gain the readmission of Jews into England. His eagerness to discover Jews in every part of the world led to his willing acceptance of the theory that the Indians of North America were the descendants of the lost ten tribes.

Kislev 21

Mt. Gerizim Day, an ancient festival, marked the Jewish victory over the Samaritans in the year 331 B.C.E. (*Megillat Ta'anit* 9).

Kislev 22

Charles IV issued Letters of Protection to the Jews of Strasbourg, Alsace, on November 25, 1357. The Letters of Protection proved worthless two years later. An enraged mob, stirred by rumors of well-poisoning, burned 1,000 Jews and forced the remainder into baptism.

Kislev 23

Anti-Jewish riots broke out in the protectorate of Aden on December 6, 1947; 75 Jews lost their lives.

Kislev 24

The foundation of the Second Temple was completed in 520 B.C.E. (Hag. 2:18). The eve of Chanukah marks three important anniversaries: (1) the completion of the foundation of the Second Temple; (2) the prophecy of Haggai predicting the restoration of Israel; (3) the liberation of Jerusalem by the British.

Kislev 25

First day of Chanukah.
Cain killed Abel (*Bereshit Rabbah* 22).
The construction of the Tabernacle was completed by Moses (*Numbers Rabbah* 13). Two important Second Temple anniversaries coincide with two anniversaries of the Tabernacle: the dedication of the Second Temple was on

Adar 23 (1 Esdras 7), which is also the anniversary of the dedication of the Tabernacle, and the Hasmonean reconsecration of the Temple took place on the traditional anniversary of the completion of the construction of the Tabernacle. 1 and 2 Maccabees as well as Josephus stress the significance of the coincidence between the dates of the profanation of the altar and its rededication by the Maccabees. There seems to be a subtle implication that the Maccabees chose Kislev 25 for its historical significance.

The first pagan sacrifice was offered on the altar of Zeus Olympius in the Temple in Jerusalem, 168 B.C.E.

Judah Maccabee cleansed the Temple and offered the daily sacrifice on the new altar, 165 B.C.E.

Kislev 26

The First Crusade was proclaimed by the Council of Clermont on November 26, 1095.

Kislev 27

The biblical flood rains stopped (Gen. 8:3; Rashi, according to Rabbi Eleazar).

Kislev 28

Rabbi Abraham Dov of Avritz, author of *Bat Ayin,* comments on the Pentateuch, died on December 23, 1840. Rabbi Abraham Dov was rabbi of the Ashkenazic community of Safed. He was captured by the Druze and held for ransom. When the money was not forthcoming, they placed a sword at his throat and threatened to use it if there was no immediate payment. The rabbi, calm and courageous, asked to make a last request. His captors were so impressed when, instead of pleading for his life, the rabbi asked for water to wash his hands so he could recite his final prayers, that they thereupon released him from captivity.

Kislev 29

King Manuel I, on December 5, 1496, ordered the expulsion of all Jews from Portugal.

Kislev 30

A congress of Hungarian Jews which convened on December 14, 1868, resulted in the splitting of the Jewish community into three religious factions. The congress, dominated by sympathizers of Reform, organized a liberal community, known as the Israelite Chancery. The Orthodox followed in 1871 with the establishment of the Orthodox Israelite Chancery. In 1929, those communities which had remained independent of either national group formed their own national organization.

Tevet 1

Esther was presented to King Ahasuerus (Esther 2:16). The marriage of Esther to Ahasuerus is a unique event in Jewish history, reflecting social and political conditions completely devoid of racial and religious discrimination. Even after Esther's disclosure of her origin, her position and influence at the court were in no way prejudiced or undermined. The intermarriage of Esther was viewed by traditionalists as an exceptional event, divinely ordained to effectuate the salvation of Israel. It is ironical to note that Tevet 1, the anniversary of Esther's presentation to the king, is also the anniversary of Ezra's convocation, summoned to undo the threat to Judaism posed by the widespread intermarriages in his period.

Ezra opened a convocation on the problem of intermarriage, 456 B.C.E. (Ezra 10:16).

Tevet 2

The first written proposal to introduce Reform Judaism in America was published in a memorial signed by 47 members of

Congregation Beth Elohim of Charleston, S.C., on December 23, 1824. The Reform movement gained momentum in the wake of the growing political and economic emancipation of Jews in Europe and America. Unlike the ancient dissident sects of Israel, which introduced new dogmas and, at times, a strict fundamentalism, modern Reform sought merely the liberalization of Orthodox traditions. It reflected, to a large extent, a universal trend emanating from the Renaissance which aimed at the lessening of religious discipline and practices. Reform Judaism early evolved into a social rather than a theological creed, providing a modus vivendi for the non-observant Jew in the midst of a non-Jewish society.

Tevet 3

The first printed edition of the Siddur of Rabbi David b. Joseph Abudarham was published in Lisbon on November 25, 1489. The popularity of Abudarham's work is attested to by the nine editions which were published in the four centuries following its initial publication. Much of the information included in the Siddur was culled from rare ancient manuscripts which are no longer in existence.

Tevet 4

The Cairo Peace Conference, with the participation of Egypt, Israel, the U.S. and the U.N., opened on December 14, 1977.

Tevet 5

Empress Catherine of Russia issued a ukase, on December 31, 1791, restricting the right of Jewish residence in Russia, the beginning of the notorious Pale of Settlement.

Tevet 6

A special Jewish badge was introduced for the first time in the Middle Ages, by a decree of Pope Innocent III on November 30, 1216. The badge was not a Christian innovation. It was used by the Sassanid rulers of Persia in the 3rd century in their persecution of Christians. Caliph Haroun al-Rashid, in 807, ordered that Jews wear a yellow badge, Christians a blue badge, and Magians a black badge. The badge introduced by Pope Innocent III was enforced in most Catholic countries for five centuries. It had disappeared by the end of the 18th century, but was reintroduced by the Nazis in 1939.

Tevet 7

The Prussian government, on December 9, 1823, decreed that "the divine service of the Jews must be conducted in accordance with the traditional ritual and without the slightest innovation in language, ceremonies, prayers and songs." The decree was aimed at the fledgling Reform movement in Germany, which had provoked the fierce opposition of Orthodoxy. Its purpose was twofold, support of traditionalism in all segments of society, and maintenance of law and order. The intervention of the authorities came at the behest of traditionalist Jewish leaders who failed to perceive the inherent danger of government aid in the suppression of dissident religious views. Unfortunately, historical precedence has established the lesson that intervention by the authorities in internal Jewish affairs is eventually detrimental to the Jewish community.

Tevet 8

Ancient fast day, commemorating the completion of the Greek translation of the Pentateuch, known as the Septuagint *(Megillat Ta'anit)*. The translation of the Bible into Greek was considered a tragic event by the early rabbis. Although its purpose was to meet the needs of Greek-speaking Jews in Alexandria, Syria, Mesopotamia and Asia Minor, it was extensively used by early Christian missionaries. Widespread Jewish proselytizing in the declining period of paganism was not hampered by the lack of a translation of the Bible. Judaism attracted the intellectual elite. Christianity went after the masses, to whom the language barrier would have been insurmountable. The rabbis deplored the need for the Septuagint both as a symptom of the growing Jewish ignorance of the Hebrew text and as a bridge to the outside world which was destined to drain some of the Jewish vitality and strength. The Talmud attributed the publication of the Septuagint to the initiative of King Ptolemy *(Ta'anit* 9a).

Tevet 9

Death of Ezra *(Selihot of Asarah be-Tevet, Ezkerah Mazok)*. Ezra holds a very prominent place in Jewish history generally, and in the development of rabbinic Judaism, in particular. Tradition ascribes to him many innovations which have become part of the Jewish religious way of life. He was crowned with the title of "Restorer of the Torah," and is regarded as the founder of the Great Assembly, a body in which was vested supreme religious authority to interpret the law. He adopted the square Hebrew script which is still in use today. He instituted the scriptural readings at services on Monday and Thursday mornings and Saturday afternoons. Above all, he is said to have established the synagogue in its all-important central position in Jewish life.

Tevet 10

Fast of Asarah be-Tevet. The fast of Asara be-Tevet is one of four commemorative fast days mentioned by the prophet Zechariah (8:19): Tevet 10 (siege of Jerusalem); Tammuz 9 (breach of the city walls); Av 9 (destruction of the Temple); Fast of Gedaliah (assassination of the Jewish governor). These fast days were discontinued after the return from Babylonia and the rebuilding of the Second Temple (Zech. 8:19; *Rosh Ha-Shanah* 18b). Upon the destruction of the Second Temple, the four fast days were reinstated. The fast of the 10th of Tevet and the fast of Gedaliah were reintroduced to commemorate the tragic events before and after the first destruction. Tammuz 9 was replaced by Tammuz 17 to commemorate the breaching of the walls of Jerusalem by the Romans *(Ta'anit* 28b). Av 9 was retained as a commemorative day for the destruction of both Temples.

Death of the prophet Malachi, the last of the prophets of Israel.

Memorial Day for the 6 million Jews killed by the Nazis (by proclamation of the Chief Rabbinate of Israel).

Tevet 11

Purim of Lepanto was annually celebrated on Tevet 11 by the Jews of Lepanto (Naupaktos), Greece, to commemorate a miraculous escape from destruction.

Tevet 12

Mordecai and Esther, residents of Medzibezh, saved the Jewish inhabitants from Chmielnicki's army on December 27, 1648. The day was designated "Mordecai Purim."

Tevet 13

The first Jewish censor was appointed by the Russian government on January 1, 1798, to censor all Hebrew books printed in Russia or imported from other countries.

Tevet 14

Window Purim, a private festival of the Sephardic community of Hebron, was observed annually on Tevet 14 in commemoration of the community's delivery from a crushing tax.

Tevet 15

The first printed edition of *Sefer Mitzvot Gadol*, a popular work by Rabbi Moses b. Jacob of Coucy, was published in Soncino, Italy, on December 9, 1488.

Tevet 16

The ship *The 29th of November*, carrying illegal Jewish immigrants to Palestine, was driven off the coast by the British on December 29, 1947.

Tevet 17

Rabbi Abraham b. Moses, author of *Zera Avraham*, commentary on the midrash, and a *maggid* (itinerant preacher), died on December 21, 1725. The 18th century brought two innovations to the Jewish scene—Hasidism and "Maggidism." The widespread ignorance of rural Jews scattered through the Ukraine and other countries led to lax religious observance. Hasidism stepped into the breach, with a strong appeal to the emotions and enthusiasm of the common people. Like Hasidism, the appeal of the *maggid* was also directed to the general masses who were outside of the small circle of scholars and students. The immediate impact of the *maggidim* was strong, but their influence was not enduring. Tevet 17 is the anniversary of two *maggidim*: Abraham b. Mose, the son of a famous preacher and author, whose homiletical work won great popularity, and the Dubno Maggid, Rabbi Jacob Kranz.

Congregation Shearith Israel of New York purchased, on December 17, 1728, a lot on Mill Street, lower Manhattan, for the purpose of erecting the first synagogue structure in New York. Shearith Israel, organized in 1656, is the oldest congregation in North America. Its first synagogue was dedicated on April 8, 1730. The six oldest congregations in the United States are: (1) Shearith Israel, New York City; (2) Yeshuat Israel, Newport, R.I., organized in 1677; dedicated its synagogue in 1763; (3) Mikveh Israel, Savannah, Ga., organized in 1733; built its first synagogue in 1820; (4) Mikveh Israel, Philadelphia, Pa., organized in 1745; built its first synagogue in 1782; (5) Beth Elohim, Charleston, S.C., organized in 1749; built its first synagogue in 1794; (6) Beth Shalom, Richmond, Va., organized in 1789.

Tevet 18

Pope Martin V issued a bull, on December 23, 1420, banning the conversion of Jewish children under 12 without the consent of their parents.

Tevet 19

Emile Zola published his famous open letter entitled "J'Accuse" on January 13, 1898, forcing a revision of the Dreyfus trial.

Tevet 20

Rabbi Moses b. Maimon (Rambam; also known as Maimonides), outstanding Talmudist, codifier, and philosopher, died on December 13, 1204.

The first printed edition of the tractate *Berakhot*, of the Babylonian Talmud, was published in Soncino, Italy, on December 19, 1483. This historic edition included the commentary of Maimonides on the Mishnah. A precedent was thus set for most of the later publications of the Talmud. The tractate was published on Maimonides' 279th *yahrzeit*.

Tevet 21

Jews of Galicia, Austria, were ordered to adopt fixed and hereditary family names by January 1, 1788. The Austrian decree ordering Jews to adopt family names was motivated by the policy of Emperor Joseph II, which aimed at the Westernization of Austrian Jewry. The state officials, however, used this decree to force degrading animal names upon the poor, who could not afford to pay the extortionist prices for desirable names.

Tevet 22

Moses b. Hanokh Altschul, the *shammash* of the Meisel synagogue in Prague, designated Tevet 22 Curtain Purim, in commemoration of the escape of Joseph Thein from the gallows in the year 1622.

Tevet 23

A fire broke out on January 14, 1711, in the house of Rabbi Naphtali Katz of Frankfort on the Main. The resulting conflagration practically destroyed the entire Jewish ghetto.

Tevet 24

Mt. Sinai Hospital of New York, the first hospital in America under Jewish auspices, was founded on January 16, 1852.

Tevet 25

The first critical edition of *Hovot ha-Levavot*, the classical work on Jewish ethics by Rabbi Bahya b. Joseph ibn Paquda, was published in Mantua, Italy, on January 4, 1559.

Tevet 26

Maryland's "Jew Bill," which went into effect on January 5, 1826, qualified Jews for public office if they subscribed to a belief in rewards and punishments in the hereafter. It was not until 50 years after the establishment of the United States that Maryland permitted its Jewish citizens to hold public office. Ever since the founding of the colony as an asylum for Catholics in 1634, the denial of the validity of Christianity had been a crime punishable by death. Theoretically, every Jew residing in Maryland was liable to legal execution for professing Judaism. The practice of Judaism was legalized in Maryland in 1776, but many civic restrictions had remained in force.

Tevet 27

Rabbi Samson Raphael Hirsch, theologian and philosopher, dynamic leader of German Orthodox Jewry, died on December 31, 1888. Rabbi Hirsch was one of the chief architects of modern Orthodoxy in Germany. In a country where State and Church were not separated and the Jewish communal representatives controlled the religious life of every Jew, he found it necessary to fight for "separatist Orthodoxy" so that the Orthodox element could survive in the midst of a rapidly assimilating Jewry. The following anecdote is a fitting epitaph to his life. It was his custom to receive three months' salary in advance. When he made out his will he inserted a clause requiring his family to make restitution to the community of part of his salary in the event of his death within the three-month period. His family was spared the effort. He died precisely on the last day of the three-month period.

Tevet 28

Rabbi Simon b. Shetah reorganized the Sanhedrin by eliminating its Saducean members. The anniversary of this Pharisaic victory was observed as a holiday (Skolion, *Megillat Ta'anit*, ch. 10).

Tevet 29
End of winter (Rabbi Judah, *Bava Metzia* 106b).

Shevat 1
Moses began to review the Torah; the instructions continued until the day of his death, 36 days later (Deut. 1:3).
God commanded Moses to observe the Promised Land from the top of a mountain; he was also instructed to prepare Joshua for the leadership of Israel (Deut. 3:27-28; *Midrash Petirat Moshe Rabbenu*).

Shevat 2
The Nazi Gestapo leader, Reinhard Heydrich, on January 20, 1942, met with top representatives of the German police, the SS, and the Nazi Party in the Wannsee section of Berlin to discuss implementation of the "final solution of the Jewish question." Hitler was appointed chancellor of Germany on Shevat 3, 1933. On Shevat 10, 1939, he announced in his annual speech that Jews would be exterminated in the event of war. On Shevat 2, 1942, Heydrich outlined the implementation of the final liquidation of the Jewish people. He was appointed head of the Jewish Emigration Office on Shevat 4, 1939.

Shevat 3
Mordecai M. Noah, American Jewish diplomat, petitioned the legislature of the state of New York, on January 19, 1820, for the sale of Grand Island in the Niagara River for the purpose of founding a settlement there for Jewish immigrants from Europe.

Shevat 4
Yeshivat Kol Ya'akov, a seminary for religious functionaries to provide religious leadership for Russian Jewry, was established in Moscow on January 6, 1957. Yeshivat Kol Ya'akov, which was founded in Moscow with the approval of the Soviet authorities, was a token seminary designed to counter charges of Soviet antisemitism and suppression of religion. It is of interest to note that the opening of the Moscow yeshivah came close to the 65th anniversary of the dissolution by the Russian government of the Yeshivah of Volozhin, the oldest and most famous of all the yeshivot of Russian Jewry.

Shevat 5
Bilu, early Russian Zionist organization, was founded in Kharkov, Russia, on January 25, 1882. Several important Palestinian anniversaries fall on the fifth day of Hebrew months. On the positive side of the calendar: Elul 5, 1809—the disciples of the Gaon of Vilna arrived in Safed; Shevat 5, 1882—Bilu was founded, marking the beginning of Zionism; Heshvan 5, 1920—Hebrew became one of the official languages of Palestine; Iyar 5, 1948—the State of Israel proclaimed its independence; Kislev 5, 1948—the Road of Valor, which defeated the Arab siege of Jerusalem, was officially opened; Av 5, 1970—a cease-fire went into effect on the Egyptian, Jordanian, and Lebanese fronts. On the negative side: Tevet 5, 586 B.C.E.—the news of the destruction of Jerusalem by the Babylonians reached the Jews of the diaspora; Sivan 5, 68—the Roman general Vespasian left Caesaria to begin his assault on Jerusalem; Tammuz 5, 70—the innermost wall around Jerusalem was captured by the Romans; Nisan 5, 1917—the Jews of Tel Aviv and Jaffa were expelled from Palestine; Adar 5, 1957—Israeli forces completed their withdrawal from the Gaza Strip.

Shevat 6
Jews of Majorca were guaranteed protection in an edict issued by the governor on January 21, 1393. The edict was issued in order to reassure the Jewish populace after the horrible massacres of August 24, 1391. The Majorca edict, like most medieval protective decrees, was soon forgotten. Ferdinand of Aragon renewed the persecution by a decree issued on March 20, 1413. The Jewish community was destroyed in 1435.

Shevat 7
A decree requiring compulsory attendance of the Jews of Sicily at conversionist services was repealed on January 1, 1430.

Shevat 8
The first invocation by a rabbi at the opening of a session of the U.S. Congress was delivered by Rabbi Morris J. Raphall on February 1, 1860.

Shevat 9
Jews of Toulouse, France, who had buried a convert to Christianity who returned to Judaism in the Jewish cemetery, were tried by the Inquisition on January 4, 1278. Rabbi Isaac Males was condemned to the stake. Medieval Christian authorities meted out capital punishment not only to Christians who had converted to Judaism but also to the Jews who had offered them aid and refuge after their conversion. Rabbi Isaac Males was martyred for permitting the burial of a convert's body in a Jewish cemetery. The severity of the punishment demonstrated the need of a deterrent against those who might feel drawn to Judaism. Among the famous Roman pagans who were attracted to the Jewish faith were Sabina Poppaea, the wife of the Emperor Nero; the Consul Flavius Clemens, nephew of Emperor Vespasian; and his wife, Domitilla Flavia. King Yusuf Dhu Nuwas, the ruler of Yemen, embraced Judaism in the year 515. The royal court of the Khazars was converted to Judaism in the 8th century.

Shevat 10
Hitler announced, in his annual speech on January 30, 1939, his intention to exterminate the Jewish race in the event of a war in Europe.

Shevat 11
Hebrew books and manuscripts which had been confiscated by Church authorities in Rome were burned on January 14, 1601.

Shevat 12
Jews of the ghetto of Warsaw put up their first resistance to the Nazis' final liquidation efforts on January 18, 1943. The early attack in the Warsaw ghetto by a few Jews who were in a column of deportees was merely a prelude to the full-scale uprising which broke out two months later.
The Russian army liberated 2,819 survivors of the Auschwitz camps on January 26, 1945.

Shevat 13
The French National Assembly, on January 28, 1790, granted full equality and citizenship to the Portuguese and Avignonese Jews. France became the first European country to pass such liberal legislation. France pioneered in many phases of Jewish legislation and public relations. It was the first European country to grant full citizenship to Jews. Napoleon was the first modern statesman to promise the restoration of Palestine to Jews. France was also the first European country to grant financial support to the religious institutions of the Jewish community.

Shevat 14
The National Federation of Temple Sisterhoods was organized on January 22, 1913. American women have played a much

greater role in the policy making and fund-raising activities of American congregations than their sisters in the Old World. The social and economic emancipation of the American woman offered a greater opportunity for participation in synagogue and church affairs. The tendency of many American men to leave all religious and educational problems to their wives left a vacuum which women were quick to fill. The National Federation of Temple Sisterhoods, representing the Reform wing, was organized on January 22, 1913. The Women's League of the United Synagogue of America, representing the Conservative wing, was organized on January 21, 1918.

Shevat 15

Hamishah-Asar bi-Shevat (Tu bi-Shevat), the New Year of the Trees (*Rosh Ha-Shanah* 2a).

Shevat 16

Markus Edinger, first Jew of Mayence to serve as a juror, died on February 9, 1879.

Shevat 17

Purim of Saragossa was celebrated by the Jews of that city in commemoration of their escape from destruction on February 4, 1428. Purim of Saragossa was one of many special Purim-type festivals which were instituted in the course of time by individuals or communities in commemoration of happy events. The biblical Purim set the pattern for the manner of celebrating the special holidays. Some communities decreed only the holding of a feast on the anniversary of the event. Others (including Saragossa) prescribed the reading of a scroll in the synagogue and the recitation of psalms as an added feature of the celebration. Most communities also called for the distribution of gifts to the needy and the exchange of presents. There were also a few communities which ordained a fast on the day preceding the festival.

Shevat 18

Chaim Weizmann was elected the first president of Israel on February 17, 1949. The official title conferred on Dr. Chaim Weizmann upon his election to the presidency of Israel was "Nasi." The first Jew in post-biblical history to be honored with the title "Nasi" was Hillel (*Pesahim* 66a). The title was borne by the heads of the Patriarchate, most of them direct lineal descendants of Hillel, until the year 425, when Emperor Theodosius II abolished the office.

Shevat 19

Jews of Basle, Switzerland, were burned alive on January 9, 1349, in a wooden house, erected for that purpose on an island in the Rhine. Basle, Switzerland, was a hotbed of antisemitism in medieval times. In modern history it became the host city of the 1st Zionist Congress, and subsequently extended similar hospitality to many other congresses. The Zionist program formulated at Basle provided a blueprint for the State of Israel. Six hundred years after the horrible massacre of the Jews of Basle, the new State of Israel elected its first president.

Shevat 20

The first printed edition of *Zeror ha-Mor,* popular commentary on the Pentateuch by Rabbi Abraham Sebag, was published in Venice on February 5, 1523. Rabbi Abraham Sebag sought refuge in Portugal upon his expulsion from Spain in 1492. Instead of refuge, he met with persecution. His two sons were forcibly baptized and taken away from him. His only remaining treasure, the manuscripts of his exegetical work on the Bible, had to be buried for fear of confiscation and destruction. Among these papers was the manuscript of *Zeror ha-Mor.* He never saw the manuscripts again. When Rabbi Sebag finally reached Africa, after his release from a Portuguese prison, he assumed the laborious task of rewriting some of his works. It was the second manuscript of *Zeror ha-Mor* which was published in Venice in 1523. Its appearance symbolized Jewish perseverance and determination to rise from the ruins.

Shevat 21

Oliver Cromwell granted the right of residence in England to Luis Carvajal on February 4, 1657. This day became known in Anglo-Jewish history as Resettlement Day. The tolerant attitude of the English government toward its Jewish residents was a major factor in the early history of the Jewish settlers in the British colonies in America and other parts of the empire. Cromwell's grant of the right of residence to Carvajal in 1657 was considered by historians to be the earliest official British act of tolerance in favor of the Jews. However, the eminent historian Dr. Cecil Roth made the momentous discovery that the British Council of State, on June 25, 1656, had already granted Rabbi Manasseh ben Israel's petition for the right to practice Judaism in England.

Shevat 22

A decree by Caius Caligula, providing for the placing of pagan images in the Temple, was voided upon his death by assassination on January 24, 41. The anniversary was observed as a holiday (*Megillat Ta'anit* 11).

Shevat 23

The Israelites assembled to wage war on the tribe of Benjamin (Judg. 20:1; *Megillat Ta'anit,* concluding chap.). The ancient battle of the Hebrew tribes was practically reenacted by modern French Jewry. In their desperate efforts to coax equality out of the reluctant French National Assembly, the Jews of Spanish and Portuguese descent, concentrated in Bordeaux, put forth the claim that they were the only pure-blooded descendants of the tribe of Judah, while the Alsatian Jews, like all German Jews, were descended from the ten lost tribes. The National Assembly happily accepted this legend, and on January 28, 1790, granted equality to the Sephardi Jews only. The Alsatian Jews, however, continued to clamor for their rights. Their efforts were rewarded a year later when the assembly extended equality to them on January 28, 1791.

Shevat 24

The prophet Zechariah, in 519 B.C.E., predicted the restoration of Zion and encouraged the resumption of the construction of the Temple building (Zech. 1:7). Exactly 2,415 years after the prophecy of Zechariah, Theodor Herzl's *Der Judenstaat* appeared, predicting the third restoration of Zion.

Shevat 25

Louis Bonaparte, on February 23, 1808, freed the Jews of Emden, Germany, of all restrictions, and granted them the privileges enjoyed by French Jews.

Shevat 26

Russia broke diplomatic relations with Israel on February 11, 1953.

Shevat 27

The Jewish community of New Amsterdam was granted a site for burial purposes by an order dated February 22, 1656.

Shevat 28

King Antiochus V lifted the siege of Jerusalem, 163 B.C.E. The anniversary was observed as a holiday (Zeitlin, *Megillat Ta'anit*).

Shevat 29

Henrietta Szold, founder of Hadassah and Youth Aliyah, died on February 12, 1945.

Shevat 30

A humiliating medieval practice, to which the Jews of Rome had been annually subjected, came to an end on February 14, 1667, when they ran the foot-races at the Roman carnival for the last time. The Monday on which the Roman carnivals usually opened was known to the Jews of Rome as the Black Monday. Beginning with the 14th century, Jews were compelled to contribute heavily to the expense of the carnival. In the 15th century, a note of indignity was added by the authorities. Jewish runners were forced to open the foot-races. Eight scantily clad Jews had to run the entire course of 400 yards amid shouts and blows. The exertion not infrequently proved fatal to Jewish runners. Following the initial race, the rabbis and leading Jews had to walk the length of the course on foot to submit to the insults and derision of the howling mob.

Adar 1

The Common Council of New York City passed an ordinance, on February 1, 1813, restricting the right to sell kosher meat to butchers licensed by Congregation Shearith Israel. The colonial Jewish community depended upon gentile butchers to supply it with kosher meats. The discovery of fraud led to a Jewish request for the legislation passed by the Common Council. The ordinance was repealed one week after its adoption due to a split which had developed among the members of Shearith Israel.

Adar 2

The Knesset passed a bill, on March 10, 1970 (Adar II), defining a Jew as one born to a Jewish mother or a convert to the Jewish faith. The legal definition of a Jew adopted by the Knesset is in accord with halakhic interpretation. It rejects the secular contention that the Jewish religion and nationality are divisible. By implication of this definition, conversion to another faith results in the loss of Jewish nationality.

Adar 3

The building of the second Temple of Jerusalem was completed in 515 B.C.E. (Ezra 6:15).

Adar 4

Vespasian occupied the city of Gadara, 68 C.E.

Adar 5

Sara Coppio Sullam, Jewish poetess, died on February 14, 1641. (Kobler, *A Treasury of Jewish Letters,* p. 436). Sara Coppio Sullam was not the first Jewish woman to write Italian poetry. Deborah Ascarelli, a Roman Jewish woman, had her work of Italian verse published in Venice as early as 1602. Her book consisted mainly of translations into Italian of ancient Hebrew liturgical poems for use in the synagogue. Rachel Akerman of Vienna, Austria (1522-44), was the first Jewish woman to write poetry in the German language.

Adar 6

Moses completed his review of the Torah, which began 36 days earlier on Shevat 1 (*Seder Olam* 8). The anniversary of the completion of Moses' instruction of the Torah appropriately coincides with the anniversary of the first printing of a comprehensive edition of the Pentateuch in 1482. Rashi's commentary on the Pentateuch was the first dated printed Hebrew work. The book reflected the indispensability of Rashi to the Bible student. It was unsatisfactory, however, because the publishers failed to include the text of the Pentateuch in the same work. This glaring fault was corrected by the Bologna edition, which became the standard form for most subsequent Pentateuchal editions everywhere, for centuries to come. It fully met the traditional requirements, relating to the reading of the weekly portion of the Torah. By the use of this book, one was able to read, understand, and chant the scriptural text as well as read the Targum which was ritually required.

Adar 7

Birth of Moses (*Sotah* 12b). The birthday and *yahrzeit* of Moses were fixed by the Talmud and universally accepted by tradition. *Midrash Ge'ulat Esther* offers a dissenting opinion: Moses was born in the month of Nisan and died on Adar 1.

Death of Moses (*Kiddushin* 38a).

The fall of manna came to an end (ibid.).

Adar 8

Yeshiva Etz Chaim, the first elementary yeshivah with a secular department in the U.S., was established on March 15, 1886 (Adar II). Yeshiva Etz Chaim was merged in 1915 with Yeshivat Rabbi Isaac Elchanan to form the principal Orthodox rabbinic school in the U.S.

Adar 9

Adar 9, traditionally accepted date of the first controversy between the schools of Shammai and Hillel, was observed as a fast-day in ancient times.

Adar 10

Jews of the Austrian Empire were granted equal civil and political rights on March 4, 1849. The joyous anniversary of Adar 10 was subsequently overshadowed by the grim anniversary of Hitler's march into Austria on Adar 9, 1938.

Adar 11

Pope Eugenius IV issued a bull on February 20, 1434, prohibiting anti-Jewish sermons.

Adar 12

Dedication of the Temple built by King Herod the great at Jerusalem, 19 B.C.E. (*Zikhron Yemot Olam*).

Adar 13

Fast of Esther.

The ten sons of Haman were hanged (Esther 9:7).

Adar 14

Purim (Esther 9:21).

Adar 15

Shushan Purim (Esther 9:21).

Adar 16

King Agrippa I began the construction of a gate for the wall of Jerusalem, 42 C.E. The day was designated a holiday (Zeitlin, *Megillat Ta'anit*).

Adar 17

The arrival of Josephus in the year 66 to assume command of the Jewish insurgent forces in the Galilee saved the local Jewish population from assault by the gentiles. The day was designated a holiday (Zeitlin, *Megillat Ta'anit*). The official outbreak of the rebellion against Rome took place, according to some historians, on Iyar 17 of the same year.

Adar 18

David Emmanuel, the first Jewish governor in the United States, was sworn in as governor of Georgia on March 3, 1801.

Adar 19

The restriction of the sale of Arab land to Jews in Palestine, published in the MacDonald White Paper, went into effect on February 28, 1940. The Balfour Declaration, which held out the promise of the establishment of a Jewish homeland in Palestine, was practically voided by the MacDonald White Paper. The capture of En-Gedi, which terminated the War of Liberation of Israel on the anniversary of the Mac-Donald Paper, brought final fulfillment to the Balfour Declaration.

The capture of En-Gedi by Israel, on March 20, 1949, brought to a conclusion the military engagements of the War of Independence.

Adar 20

The first Maccabiad was held at Tel Aviv on February 27, 1932.

Adar 21

Purim of Narbonne was celebrated by the Jewish community of Narbonne to commemorate its escape from a rampaging mob on March 1, 1236. Purim of Narbonne is the oldest private Purim on record.

Adar 22

The Purim Association of the City of New York was organized on March 24, 1862 (Adar II), for the purpose of arranging annual Purim balls.

Adar 23

The Second Temple was dedicated in 516 B.C.E. (1 Esdras, 7).

Adar 24

An attack on Petah Tikvah on March 1, 1886, was the first organized Arab assault on a Palestinian Jewish settlement (*Zikhronot Eretz Yisrael,* vol. 1, p. 317).

Adar 25

A petition initiated by Rev. William E. Blackstone was sent, on March 5, 1891, to President Harrison, requesting the aid of the U.S. government in the reestablishment of Palestine as a sovereign Jewish state (AJHSP, no. 36, p. 42). The petition was signed, among others, by Cyrus H. McCormick, J. Pierpont Morgan, William McKinley, John D. Rockefeller, Russell Sage, and Cardinal Gibbons. It was a spontaneous expression of American sympathy for Zionism, totally independent of Jewish Zionist activities. The petition was motivated by biblical influences and by intense indignation aroused by Russian pogroms.

Adar 26

The Jewish community of Newport, R.I., on February 28, 1677, purchased a plot of land for a burial ground. Whenever Jews settled in a new land, the patterns of communal life soon began to emerge. The essential requirements of a new Jewish community were a synagogue, a school, and a cemetery. Thus, the first Jewish settlers of New Amsterdam bought a cemetery in 1656, two years after their arrival. The earliest record of a synagogue in New Amsterdam dates from about 1666. The Jewish community of Newport was

established in 1658. Its first cemetery was acquired in 1677. The land for the Touro Synagogue was purchased in 1759, a full century after the establishment of the community.

Adar 27

King Zedekiah, the last king of Judea, died in captivity in Babylonia, 561 B.C.E.

Adar 28

Purim of Cairo was observed annually on Adar 28 in commemoration of an escape from massacre on March 4, 1524.

Adar 29

Napoleon captured the city of Jaffa, Palestine, on March 6, 1799.

Adar 30

The headquarters of the Jewish Agency at Jerusalem was bombed on March 11, 1948, resulting in the death of many Jews. The Hebrew poet Leib Yaffe was among the victims.

Nisan 1

The erection of the Tabernacle was completed (Exod. 40:17; *Numbers Rabbah* 13). The construction work of the Tabernacle was completed, according to rabbinic tradition, on Kislev 25 (*Numbers Rabbah* 13).

Moses completed the consecration rites of Aaron and his sons (Lev. 9:1, Rashi). Aaron performed the first sacrificial rites on Nisan 1.

Death of Nadab and Abihu, sons of Aaron (*Megillat Ta'anit* 1). According to *Midrash Petirat Aharon,* the deaths of Nadab and Abihu took place on Nisan 2.

The plot of Bigthan and Teresh to assassinate King Ahasuerus was discovered by Mordecai (Apocrypha; Book of Esther).

Nisan 2

Moses performed the first *parah adumah* (red heifer) rite (*Gittin* 60b, Rashi).

Nisan 3

A decree expelling Jews from Spain and Sicily was published on March 31, 1492.

Nisan 4

The first Young Men's Hebrew Association was organized in New York on March 22, 1874.

Nisan 5

Joshua sent scouts to survey Jericho and the surrounding territory (Josh. 2:1, Rashi).

Menachem Begin visited Cairo, Egypt, on April 2, 1979. It was the first visit of an Israeli prime minister to Egypt.

Nisan 6

The Arab Yarmuk Army, under the command of Fawzi al-Kaukji, was defeated in the battle of Mishmar ha-Emek on April 15, 1948. The battle of Mishmar ha-Emek was the first major military engagement between Arab and Jewish forces prior to the establishment of Israel.

Nisan 7

Jews of York, England, committed mass suicide on March 16, 1190, rejecting an invitation to submit to baptism.

Nisan 8

The Zion Mule Corps, consisting of Jewish volunteers from Palestine, was formed on March 23, 1915. The Zion Mule Corps was the first Palestinian Jewish military unit attached to a reular army in the Christian era. It was the forerunner of the Jewish Legion, which was formed in 1918 and committed to combat at Es-Salt, Transjordan.

Nisan 9

Anti-Jewish riots broke out in Seville, Spain, on March 15, 1391. The anti-Jewish riots which broke out in Seville on Ash Wednesday of 1391 initiated a wave of violence which spread rapidly over the Iberian Peninsula and claimed 50,000 victims before the year was up. A substantial number of Jews escaped with their lives only at the cost of converting. This marked the emergence of Marranos, said to number 200,000, in the kingdoms of Aragon and Castile. They were to provide countless martyrs in the Old and New Worlds for centuries to come.

Nisan 10

Death of Miriam (*Seder Olam* 10). According to *Midrash Petirat Aharon,* Miriam died and the well dried up on Nisan 1.

The Jews, under the leadership of Joshua, crossed the Jordan and erected 12 monuments at Gilgal (Josh. 4:20). According to Rabbi Simon (*Sotah* 36a), the following events took place on that day: the Jews lined up on Mt. Ebal and Mt. Gerizim; the pertinent Torah portion relating to the blessings and curses was recited; Joshua erected an altar on Mt. Ebal and brought offerings; the entire Torah, with multilingual translations, was inscribed on it (Josh, 8:30-34); and Joshua composed the second paragraph of the after-meal grace (Berakhot 48b).

Nisan 11

The generation of Jews born in the desert submitted to the rite of circumcision upon entering Palestine (Josh. 5:3; *Seder Olam* 11).

Nisan 12

The Russian revolutionary government, on April 4, 1917, granted equality to all Russian Jews for the first time in Russian history. In the first decade of the 20th century Russia had, under its effective control and domination, about 50 percent of the total world Jewish population. The grant of equality by the Russian revolutionary government affected, therefore, a major part of world Jewry. By the end of the second decade, Russia had under its jurisdiction only about 18 percent of the total Jewish population.

Nisan 13

Haman published a decree calling for the extermination of all the Jews of the Persian Empire (Esther 3:12). Esther ordered a three-day fast for all the Jews of Shushan (ibid. 4:16).

The German Workers' Party, on April 1, 1920, was renamed the National Socialist German Workers' Party; this marked the emergence of the Nazi Party. The Nazi Party emerged on the anniversary of the day that Haman published his decree of extermination of the Jews.

Nisan 14

Rabbi Moses b. Maimon (Rambam; also known as Maimonides), codifier and philosopher, was born on March 30, 1135.

Nisan 15

God made a covenant with Abraham (Gen. 15:18, *Seder Olam* 5).
Birth of Isaac (*Rosh Ha-Shanah* 10b).
Moses saw the burning bush (Exod. 3:2, Bahya, *Bo*).
The Egyptian first-born were slain (Exod. 12:29).
First day of Passover. The beginning of the Exodus (Exod. 12:37).
Queen Esther appeared before King Ahasuerus to plead for the Jews (Esther 5:1; *Seder Olam* 29).
The defenders of Masada committed suicide, 73 C.E. The last resistance to the Roman conquest of Palestine came to an end (Josephus, *Wars* 7:9).

Nisan 16

Haman was hanged (Esther 7:10; *Seder Olam* 29). Mordecai was appointed chief minister by King Ahasuerus to replace Haman (Esther 8:2).

Nisan 17

Mother Maria of Paris, a Russian nun who had saved many French Jews by providing them with hiding places, was killed by the Nazis in the Ravensbrueck camp on March 31, 1945. (Friedman, *Their Brothers' Keepers.*)

Nisan 18

Pharaoh was informed that the Hebrew slaves had escaped (Exod. 14:5, Rashi). When Moses was sent to liberate the Jews from Egyptian slavery, he set out to attain three objectives: emancipation, religious education, and national independence (Exod. 6:7-8). The first objective was achieved with the exodus from Egypt. The next goal was reached at Mt. Sinai. The final aim was accomplished upon the military conquest of Palestine.

Nisan 19

Pharaoh set out in pursuit of the Jews (Exod. 14:5, Rashi). Adolf Hitler made his first appearance on the anniversary of the day on which the first antisemite in Jewish history set out in pursuit of the Jewish people.

Adolf Hitler was born in Braunau-am-Inn, Austria, on April 20, 1889.

Nisan 20

Pharaoh and his pursuing army caught up with the Jews encamped at Pi-hahiroth by the sea (Exod. 14:5; Rashi).

Nisan 21

Jews crossed the Red Sea. (Exod. 14:22; *Sotah* 12b).

Nisan 22

The Kishinev pogrom broke out on April 19, 1903. The massacres led to world-wide protests. The Kishinev pogrom sparked widespread efforts to organize Jewish self-defense. Ha-Shomer, an early Palestinian Jewish self-defense organization, was founded on Nisan 21, 1909.

Nisan 23

Haganah captured the strategic village of Katamon, southwest of Jerusalem, on May 2, 1948.

Nisan 24

The Jews paused at Marah after their crossing of the Red Sea (Exod. 15:23). It was at Marah that the Jews paused on their first Sabbath in the desert (*Shabbat* 87b).

Nisan 25

The first Jewish American national organization of women, the United Order of True Sisters, was organized on April 21, 1846.

Nisan 26

Israeli postal service was esablished on May 5, 1948.

Nisan 27

Nisan 27 was designated Holocaust Day, in commemoration of the martyred six million Jews and the fighters of the ghettos, by a resolution of the Knesset on April 12, 1951.

Nisan 28

The Society for the Education of Poor Children and Relief of Indigent of the Jewish Persuasion in the City of New York was incorporated on April 11, 1831.

Nisan 29

U.S. forces liberated the Buchenwald concentration camp with its 20,000 inmates on April 12, 1945.

On April 10, 1975, the government of Israel recognized Falashas as Jews under the law.

Nisan 30

The first yeshivah in America was established on March 15, 1886.

Iyar 1

An Israelite gathered wood on the Sabbath (*Yalkut,* Num. 15:32). This act marked the first public violation of the Sabbath (Ibid.). There are two traditional dates for the first Sabbath, Nisan 24 and Iyar 15. Rabbi Simon's opinion that the wood-gatherer violated the Sabbath on Iyar 22 (*Yalkut,* Num. 15:32), is in accord with the second tradition. The author of the hymn of Dayenu (Passover Haggadah), who lists the manna ahead of the Sabbath, also follows the second tradition.

Moses was ordered, in the second year of the exodus, to take a census of the Jewish people (Num. 1:1).

Iyar 2

German forces marched into Holland on May 10, 1940. The diary of Anne Frank, the young Dutch Jewish girl, attracted universal attention to the suffering of Jews in Nazi-occupied territories. Anne Frank died in the Belsen concentration camp. The British army liberated the Belsen camp and its 40,000 inmates on April 15, 1945, the fifth anniversary of the Nazi invasion of Holland.

Iyar 3

A Spanish royal proclamation, issued on April 30, 1492, warned Jews that their departure must begin on May 1 and be completed by the end of July.

Iyar 4

Rabbi Meir b. Baruch's (Maharam of Rothenburg) body was released by the authorities for Jewish burial on April 19, 1306, 13 years after his death in prison. Rabbi Meir of Rothenburg was buried in the old Jewish cemetery of Worms. The tombstone, which marks his grave and the adjoining grave of Alexander Susskind, miraculously escaped the Nazi ravaging of the cemetery.

Iyar 5

Israel was proclaimed an independent state on May 14, 1948.

The first legislative act of the provisional government of the State of Israel, passed on May 14, 1948, provided for the repeal of the British White Paper of 1939, which had restricted Jewish immigration and the acquisition of land in Palestine. The Haftarah on the Sabbath following the promulgation of the law of unrestricted Jewish immigration into Israel was the ninth chapter of Amos. It reads: "And I will return the captivity of my people Israel. And they shall build the waste cities and inhabit them . . . and they shall no more be plucked up out of their land which I have given them, saith the Lord thy God."

The U.S. granted Israel de facto recognition on May 14, 1948.

Iyar 6

Anti-Jewish riots broke out in Kiev, Russia, on May 5, 1881. The Russian pogroms of 1881 led to the spread of Zionist ideas in Eastern Europe and the formation, in 1882, of Hovevei Zion, the first organized modern Zionist movement in the world. The subsequent publication, in 1896, on the anniversary of the Kiev pogrom, of an English edition of Herzl's *Der Judenstaat,* helped spread Zionism among the English-speaking, emancipated Jews.

An English edition of Herzl's *The Jewish State* was published for the first time on April 19, 1896.

The British mandate over Palestine went into effect on April 24, 1920. This date became known as San Remo Day. The coincidence of the dates of the publication of the English edition of Herzl's *The Jewish State* and the beginning of the British mandate over Palestine, charged with the establishment of a Jewish home in Palestine, is noteworthy.

The British mandate over Palestine came to an end on May 15, 1948. The British mandate over Palestine went into effect on Iyar 6, 1920, and it came to an end exactly 28 years later on Iyar 6, 1948.

The armies of Egypt, Jordan, Syria, Iraq, and Lebanon invaded Israel on May 15, 1948.

Iyar 7

Chaim Weizmann was elected first president of the State of Israel on May 16, 1948.

Iyar 8

Venice became the first city in the world where the term *ghetto* was associated with the Jewish quarter, when the Jews were compelled, on April 10, 1516, to move into a restricted area (Roth, *Personalities and Events in Jewish History,* p. 232). The area was formerly the site of a foundry which manufactured weapons for the government of Venice. The Italian term for "new foundry" is *geto nuovo.* The first official document which uses the word *ghetto* to describe an area restricted to the residence of Jews exclusively was a papal edict dated February 27, 1562. (Teaff, *Getto-Ghetto; American Sephardi,* vol. 6, nos. 1-2).

Iyar 9

A three-month period of grace, given by the Portuguese to the Jews of Brazil to leave the country, terminated on April 26, 1654. Those who remained after this deadline were surrendered to the Inquisition.

Iyar 10

Theodor Herzl, the founder of modern Zionism, was born on May 2, 1860.

Iyar 11

The Israeli air force went into action for the first time in Israel's War of Independence on May 20, 1948.

The Syrian army, which had advanced to Deganyah, was halted and repulsed on May 20, 1948. The defeat of the Syrians at Deganyah was Israel's first significant victory in the War of Independence. It came on the anniversary of the end of the Warsaw ghetto uprising.

Iyar 12

Israel was admitted as the 59th member nation of the U.N. on May 11, 1949.

Iyar 13

By a decree issued on May 10, 1427, all Jews were ordered expelled from Berne, Switzerland. Expulsions of Jewish communities continued unabated throughout the 15th century. The following is a partial list of expulsions in the 15th century: Treves, 1419; duchy of Austria, 1421; Cologne, 1424; Zurich, 1436; archbishopric of Hildesheim, 1457; Schaffhausen, 1472; Mayence, 1473; Warsaw, 1483; Geneva, 1490; Thurgau, 1491; Spain, Sicily, Sardinia, and Lithuania, 1492; Mecklenburg and Arles, 1493; Portugal, 1497; Nuremberg, 1499; Provence, 1500.

Iyar 14

Thousands of books written by Jewish and liberal non-Jewish authors were publicly burned by the Nazis on May 10, 1933.

Berlin was declared "Judenrein" on May 19, 1943. Berlin was declared free of Jews on the tenth anniversary of the day when Berlin was declared free of the influence of Jewish authors.

Iyar 15

The supply of matzah, taken along by the Jews upon their exodus from Egypt, was exhausted (Yonatan b. Uziel, Exod. 16:2).

Iyar 16

The U.S. 7th Army liberated the Dachau concentration camp on April 29, 1945.

Iyar 17

Beginning of the biblical flood (Gen. 7:11; Rabbi Joshua, *Sanhedrin* 108b).

Iyar 18

Lag ba-Omer.

Iyar 19

By a government decree issued on May 28, 1948, Haganah was converted into the regular Israeli army.

Iyar 20

A community of Jewish slaves, captured over a period of two centuries and held for ransom by the Knights of St. John on the island of Malta, was officially dissolved on May 15, 1800 (Roth, *Personalities and Events in Jewish History*).

Iyar 21

The Jewish agricultural settlement, Alliance, was founded in New Jersey on May 10, 1882.

Iyar 22

The first Sabbath, the observance of which was made obligatory for all Jews, was dated Iyar 22 in the first year of the Exodus. It was violated by some Jews who had gone to collect manna (Exod.16:27; *Seder Olam* 5).

Iyar 23

The Arab states and Israel agreed to a cease-fire on June 1, 1948. By the time of the first truce, Israel had already scored substantial victories over the Syrian and Egyptian armies, though greatly outnumbered by the enemy. The biblical portion of that week includes the following verses: "And I will bring peace in the land . . . and you shall chase your enemies . . . and five of you shall chase a hundred . . ." (Lev. 26:6-8).

Iyar 24

An Israeli attack on Egyptian positions at Ashdod, on June 2, 1948, marked the turning point in the war between Israel and Egypt. The battle forced Egypt to change its military strategy. It gave up its plans to attack Tel Aviv and made the isolation of the Negev from the rest of Israel its prime objective.

Iyar 25

Alliance Israelite Universelle of Paris was organized on May 17, 1860, for the purpose of defending Jewish civil rights throughout the world.

Iyar 26

War broke out between Israel and the Arab nations on June 5, 1967. The important Egyptian base at El-Arish, in the Sinai Peninsula, was captured by the Israeli army on the same day.

Iyar 27

Demetrius I, in the year 143 B.C.E., relinquished to the Jews of Palestine the crown money which he had annually levied. This marked his recognition of the independence of Judea under Simon the Hasmonean (Zeitlin, *Megillat Ta'anit*).

Iyar 28

The White Paper, which reversed the policy of the Balfour Declaration, was published on May 17, 1939.

Israel captured the Old City of Jerusalem on June 7, 1967, uniting the city for the first time since the establishment of the state. It also captured, on the same day, Jericho, Bethlehem, and Sharm-el-Sheikh, and lifted the blockade of the Gulf of Aqaba. The entire Jordanian bulge on the western bank of the Jordan came under Israeli control.

Iyar 29

Death of the Prophet Samuel (*Megillat Ta'anit,* concluding chap.).

Sivan 1

The flood waters began to recede (Gen. 8:3, Rashi).

Sivan 2

Moses ascended Mt. Sinai (Exod. 19:3, Rashi).

Sivan 3

The aliyah of Iraqi Jews began on May 19, 1950. The first deportation of Jews to Babylonia took place in 597 B.C.E. The bulk of Palestinian Jewry followed them to Babylonia 11 years later, in 586 B.C.E. The first return of some Babylonian Jews to Palestine took place in 539 B.C.E. The majority, however, remained in Babylonia, where they were destined eventually to make a major contribution to Judaism through the creation of the Babylonian Talmud and the Geonic responsa. It was not until 1951, 2,548 years after the arrival of the first Jewish deportees in Babylonia, that this ancient Jewish community began its own liquidation through an aliyah to Israel.

Sivan 4

Moses wrote the first part of the Torah, from Genesis to the revelation on Mt. Sinai, in the first year of the Exodus (Exod. 24:4, Rashi).

Bogdan Chmielnicki's anti-Polish warfare, which resulted in the massacre of more than 300,000 Jews, broke out on May 25, 1648. (Hanover, *Yeven Mezulah* 4).

Representative Louis T. McFadden of Pennsylvania delivered a Nazi-type attack on Jews as a race on May 29, 1933. It was the first antisemitic speech made in Congress. McFadden published his speeches in the *Congressional Record* and then used his congressional frank to disseminate thousands of reprints through antisemitic organizations. The exposure of McFadden's fraudulent past led to his defeat by the electorate and to an end of his public antisemitic career.

Sivan 5

Israel bombed and destroyed the Iraqi nuclear reactor in Baghdad on June 7, 1981.

Sivan 6

First day of Shavuot.

Moses was placed by his mother in a basket and was left floating on the river *(Sotah* 12b). This entry follows the view of Rabbi Aha bar Hanina. According to Rabbi Hanina bar Papa, the infant Moses was placed on the river on Nisan 21 *(Sotah* 12b).

The Ten Commandments were proclaimed on Mt. Sinai *(Shabbat* 86b).

Sivan 7

Moses ascended Mt. Sinai to receive the first Tablets of the Law (Exod. 32:1, Rashi).

Death of King David (Jer. Talmud, *Hagigah* 2:3).

Sivan 8

The extermination camp of Auschwitz was opened on June 14, 1940. In the course of the existence of the notorious camp at Auschwitz, two and a half million people were exterminated there and another half-million died of disease and starvation.

Sivan 9

The ancient Jewish community of Khonia, Crete, dating from Roman times, came to an end on May 31, 1944, when the ship *Danai,* into which all the Jews had been herded, was towed out of the port of Iraklion 12 miles to sea and sunk.

Sivan 10

Reuben Siegel laid the cornerstone of the first house in Tel Aviv, Palestine, on May 30, 1909.

Sivan 11

A resolution introduced in the U.S. House of Representatives on June 2, 1879, requested the president to have all international treaties which impair the rights of American citizens because of religion amended to secure equal rights *(AJHSP,* no. 41, p. 168). This resolution marked the first action taken by Congress affecting Russo-American relations. It was prompted by Russian discriminatory policies against American Jews.

Sivan 12

The Festival of the First Fruits (Shavuot) is observed by Falashas on Sivan 12 (Leslau, *Falasha Anthology).* The Falashas observe Shavuot on Sivan 12 because it is the fiftieth day after the conclusion of Passover. Thus they agree with the rabbinic interpretation of the term *Sabbath,* mentioned in the biblical injunction to count 50 days (Lev. 23:15), as a reference to the festival of Passover rather than the day of the Sabbath. However, according to the Falasha tradition, the counting is to begin on the conclusion of the festival of Passover and not at the end of the first day of the festival.

Sivan 13

The central system of the underground water supply was dedicated in the northern Negev in Israel on June 17, 1951.

Sivan 14

The Allies marched into Rome on June 5, 1944. Jews emerged from their hiding places, and the gate of the great synagogue was opened.

Sivan 15

Israeli forces crossed into Lebanon on June 6, 1982, to destroy P.L.O. military bases.

Sivan 16

God appeared to Jacob at Beersheba and said: "Fear not to go down to Egypt, for I will make thee there a great nation" (Book of Jubilees; Gen. 46:3).

Sivan 17

Noah's ark came to rest on Mt. Ararat (Gen. 8:4, Rashi).

Sivan 18

The Union of Orthodox Jewish Congregations of America was organized on June 8, 1898.

Sivan 19

The first Jewish hospital in America, Jews' Hospital of New York, admitted its first patient on June 5, 1855. The Jewish community of Berlin maintained a small hospital in the 16th century. The Jewish community of Rome had its own hospital in the 17th century. The first Jewish hospital in England was opened in 1743. The first French Jewish hospital was opened in 1836. Russian Jewry maintained 112 hospitals prior to World War I. Some East European countries restricted the right of Jews to build hospitals and also restricted the number of Jewish patients admitted into public hospitals. When a Bucharest Jew died in 1896 because he was denied admission to the city hospital, the Jewish community petitioned the government for permission to build its own hospital. The petition was denied.

Sivan 20

34 Jewish men and 17 Jewish women were burned at the stake in Blois, France, on May 26, 1171, in the first ritual-murder charge on the European continent.

The fast of Sivan 20 was decreed by Rabbenu Tam in memory of the martyrs of Blois who were burned on charges of ritual murder. The fast of Sivan 20 was originally ordained by Rabbenu Tam in the 12th century to commemorate the first blood-ritual charges in France and the subsequent burning of the innocent Jewish victims in Blois. The fast was observed in France, in the German province of the Rhine, and most likely also in England. The same day was also declared a fast-day in Poland in the year 1650 to commemorate the Chmielnicki pogroms. Sivan 20 was designated a memorial day because it was the anniversary of the massacre of the Jews of Niemirow, early in the uprising. The fact that this day had already been observed as a fast-day in the 12th century, and that special prayers had already been composed for the occasion, was an important factor in the selection of this date.

Sivan 21

Sultan Mohammed II, the conqueror of Constantinople, granted equal rights to Jews and other non-Muslim subjects of the Ottoman Empire on May 29, 1453. The liberal policy of the Turkish government toward its Jewish population was announced upon the capture of Constantinople on Sivan 21, 1453. This policy providentially provided one of the principal havens of refuge for the mass immigrants who were to pour into Muslim countries 40 years later, after the expulsion from Spain in 1492.

Sivan 22

The directors of the West India Co. instructed Governor Peter Stuyvesant, on June 14, 1656, to suggest to the Jews of New Amsterdam that they restrict their residence to a self-imposed ghetto where they might exercise their religion in the privacy of their homes; to permit Jews to trade along the South River (Delaware River); and to grant them the right to own real estate in New Amsterdam *(AJHSP,* no. 10, p.48). A petition by the Jews of New Amsterdam for permission to build a synagogue was denied by the local authorities on Adar 16, 1656. History made amends for this mistake. The United Synagogue of America was founded on Adar 16, 1913. The early Jewish community of New Amsterdam never succeeded in obtaining a permit to build a synagogue during the 10 years of its existence under Dutch rule. On September 7, 1664, New Amsterdam became New York. We do not know when the first public synagogue was dedicated. There is positive proof, however, of the existence of a synagogue in 1697.

Sivan 23
Mordecai issued a royal decree calling upon Jews to defend themselves against attack (Esther 8:11). This is the oldest record of an organized Jewish self-defense in the diaspora.

Sivan 24
The Jewish Publication Society of America was organized on June 3, 1888.

Sivan 25
Geviha ben Pesisa, Jewish delegate, emerged victorious from his debate with the Samaritans in the presence of Alexander the Great· (*Megillat Ta'anit* 3).

Sivan 26
The German army was defeated at El-Alamein, North Africa, on June 11, 1942, ending the threat to Palestine. The defeat of General Erwin Rommel at El-Alamein brought to an end the worst crisis facing the Jewish community of Palestine in World War II. The turning point came one day short of the first anniversary of the Nazi attack on Russia, which led to the destruction of a great part of Russian Jewry.

Sivan 27
Germany invaded Lithuania and Latvia in its opening attack on Russia on June 22, 1941.
Sivan 27 has been designated a Memorial Day by the survivors of Lithuanian Jewry.

Sivan 28
Yeshivat Hakhmei Lublin, an academy for the training of rabbis and teachers, was opened by its founder, Rabbi Meir Shapira, on June 24, 1930.

Sivan 29
The first public warning of rising antisemitism in the U.S. was given by Henry Ward Beecher in a sermon entitled "Jew and Gentile," delivered on June 24, 1873.

Sivan 30
In a letter to Louis Marshall, dated June 30, 1927, Henry Ford retracted and apologized for the publication of the spurious *Protocols of the Elders of Zion* in the *Dearborn Independent.*

Tammuz 1
Jacob and his family arrived in Goshen, Egypt (Book of Jubilees). Tammuz 1, according to the Book of Jubilees, is the anniversary of the establishment of the first Jewish voluntary diaspora. A moshav established on this day in modern Palestine, in the year 1940, was appropriately given the name of She'ar Yashuv ("the remnant will return").

Tammuz 2
Palestine was rocked by an earthquake on July 2, 1927.

Tammuz 3
Lydda Airfield was captured by the Israeli army on July 10, 1948.

Tammuz 4
Jerusalem was bombed from the air for the first time in its history on July 11, 1948.

Tammuz 5
A bloody pogrom at Kielce, Poland, the first post-Nazi massacre of Polish Jews, broke out on July 4, 1946.

Tammuz 6
Israeli commandos, in a daring and spectacular raid on July 4, 1976, rescued about 100 Jewish passengers held hostage at Uganda's airport of Entebbe.

Tammuz 7
Israel bombed Cairo on July 14, 1948.

Tammuz 8
Queen-Mother Maria Christina of Spain abolished the Spanish Inquisition on July 15, 1834. The last auto-da-fe was held on April 1, 1826, in Valencia, Spain.

Tammuz 9
King Nebuchadnezzar's army breached the walls of Jerusalem and entered the city 586 B.C.E. (Jer. 39:2). According to the Babylonian Talmud (*Rosh Ha-Shanah* 18b), Tammuz 9 was one of the four commemorative fast-days established by the Babylonian Jewish community.
Pompey captured Jerusalem in the year 63 B.C.E. and killed 12,000 Jews (Zeitlin, *Megillat Ta'anit,* p. 27). This was the first military confrontation between Rome and Judea.

Tammuz 10
A conference of Reform rabbis, which opened at Frankfort on the Main, Germany, on July 15, 1845, adopted a resolution to eliminate from the prayerbook all "prayers for the restoration of a Jewish State." The classic anti-Zionism of the early Reform movement preceded the birth of Zionism. The naive faith in the liberal orientation and progress of modern society was to be shattered within the century by their host-country.

Tammuz 11
Colonel Alfred Dreyfus, victim of French antisemitism and militarism, died on July 12, 1935.

Tammuz 12
Pope Boniface VIII issued a bull on June 13, 1299, which allowed Jews denounced to the Inquisition the right to have the names of their accusers revealed to them. By the terms of an order issued by the Inquisition on November 18, 1297, accused Jews were not entitled to demand a confrontation with their accusers. The denial of the right of confrontation was also one of the worst features of European totalitarianism and of McCarthyism in modern America. Extremism, religious or political, produces the same evils. It is ironical that the Roman Emperor Trajan, one of the most tyrannical persecutors of early Christianity, specifically rejected anonymous charges as inconsistent with equity and fair play. He directed all magistrates to allow every person accused of practicing Christianity the right to face his accuser (Gibbon, *Decline and Fall of the Roman Empire,* chap. 16).

Tammuz 13
The Anglo-Jewish Association was founded in England on July 2, 1871. The Association was patterned after the Alliance

Israelite Universelle, founded by French Jewry 11 years earlier. Both Jewish communities had been emancipated and enjoyed full civil rights. Having won equality for themselves, they set out to extend protection to Jewish communities in other lands still subjected to discrimination and oppression.

Tammuz 14

Francis Salvador, a plantation-owner of South Carolina, the first Jew to lose his life in the American Revolution, was killed on July 1, 1776.

Tammuz 15

Hur, the son of Miriam, was killed when he attempted to dissuade the Israelites from demanding a golden calf (*Shemot Rabbah* 48). Tradition assigns to Hur the distinction of being the first Jewish martyr to die in defense of his faith.

Tammuz 16

Aaron made a golden calf (*Seder Olam* 6).

Tammuz 17

Fast of Tammuz 17.

Moses broke the Tablets of the Law (Exod. 32:19; *Ta'anit* 28b).

The *korban tamid* was discontinued in the second Temple on August 8 (approximation), 70 C.E. (*Ta'anit* 28b; Josephus, *Jewish War* 6:2).

The American colonies declared their independence on July 4, 1776. The American Declaration of Independence, with its momentous potential for the future of Jewry, marks a ray of light against the tragic background of Tammuz 17. Similarly, Columbus' journey into history (Av 10) brightened the darkness of Tisha be-Av.

Tammuz 18

Moses destroyed the golden calf (Exod. 32:20; *Seder Olam* 6; Rashi, *Ta'anit* 30b).

Tammuz 19

Moses ascended Mt. Sinai for the second time. He remained there for 40 days, pleading for the Jews who were guilty of the sin of the golden calf (Rashi, Exod. 33:11).

Tammuz 20

A Fair Sabbath Law, covering the entire state of New York, was signed into law on July 20, 1965.

Tammuz 21

The remains of 25 members of the Zealot community of Masada, who died by suicide in the year 73, were interred with full honors at the foot of the rock-fortress on July 7, 1969.

Tammuz 22

The poet Henry Wadsworth Longfellow visited the Jewish cemetery in Newport, R.I., on July 9, 1852. Shortly thereafter, he wrote the poem, "The Jewish Cemetery at Newport."

Tammuz 23

Crusaders captured Jerusalem on July 15, 1099.

Tammuz 24

Crusaders herded the Jews of Jerusalem into a synagogue on July 16, 1099, and set it aflame. All the Jews perished in the fire. Jerusalem remained under the control of the Crusaders for 88 years. Jews were barred from the city throughout that period.

Tammuz 25

Napoleon, on July 20, 1808, issued a decree requiring all Jews of the French Empire to adopt family names. The first country to introduce compulsory adoption of family names for its Jewish population was Austria. It was enacted as part of the sweeping reforms of Emperor Joseph II in 1785. The French-created Kingdom of Westphalia followed with a similar decree in 1808. Napoleon extended the decree, in the same year, to all of France. Poland made family names compulsory in 1821, and Russia, in 1844.

Tammuz 26

Israeli airmen over the Suez front shot down four Migs flown by Russian pilots on July 30, 1970. The brief engagement marked the first encounter between Israeli and Russian military forces.

Tammuz 27

Pope Innocent III promulgated, on July 15, 1205, a Church doctrine which held Jews doomed to perpetual servitude and subjugation due to the crucifixion of Christ. The first official effort to remove this classic charge of deicide was made in a document presented to the Vatican II ecumenical council on November 8, 1963.

Tammuz 28

Jewish settlers, bringing with them a Torah and other religious articles, arrived from London on July 11, 1733, on the second ship to reach Savannah, Ga. The availability of religious articles made it possible for the new arrivals to organize Congregation Mikveh Israel within a month after their arrival. The congregation dissolved in 1740. Services were resumed in 1750 and continued sporadically until they were reorganized on a more permanent basis in 1774. Jewish life was once again disrupted with the occupation of Savannah by the British in 1778. Congregation Mikveh Israel was reestablished on July 7, 1787.

Tammuz 29

Rabbi Shlomo Yitzhaki (Rashi), celebrated Talmudic commentator and Bible exegete, died on July 13, 1105. Rashi was one of the outstanding intellectual giants produced by medieval Jewry. As the commentator of the Talmud par excellence, he has no peer in the long post-Talmudic history. His comments illumine the most complex and obscure passages of the Talmud with logic and incisive analysis. The popularity of his work may be gauged from the fact that the first dated printed Hebrew book was his commentary on the Pentateuch.

Av 1

Peaks of high mountains emerged above the receding flood waters (Gen. 8:5, Rashi).

Av 2

Pope Gregory X, on July 7, 1274, confirmed a bull of 1272, banning blood-ritual charges. Papal bulls banning ritual accusations were obviously ineffective. The bull of Pope Gregory X, issued on Av 2, 1274, was preceded by a similar bull by Pope Innocent IV issued on Av 1, 1247. About three centuries later, Pope Paul III issued a bull on May 12, 1540, banning blood accusations. That bull, too, failed to halt the flood of ritual libels in Christendom.

Av 3

The first shipload of Russian Jewish immigrants, opening the mass immigration of Russian Jews following the pogroms of 1881, arrived in New York on July 29, 1881.

Av 4
The first envoy of Soviet Russia arrived in Israel on August 9, 1948.

Av 5
Pope Clement VI issued a bull on July 5, 1345, forbidding forcible baptism of Jews. The Roman Curia ruled, on October 22, 1597, that a Jewish child baptized without the permission of his parents, as required by canonical law, must be brought up as a Catholic. This ruling required the removal of the child from its parents. Pope Benedict XIV confirmed this decision 250 years later in a bull issued on February 28, 1747.

Av 6
A bill for the emancipation of the Jews of England passed its third reading in the House of Commons on July 22, 1833. The bill was rejected by the House of Lords and not approved until July 31, 1845.

Av 7
King Nebuchadnezzar occupied Solomon's Temple, 586 B.C.E.
Hermann Goering ordered Reinhard Heydrich on July 31, 1941, to "take all preparatory measures . . . required for the final solution of the Jewish question in the European territories under German influence." This order launched the official and systematic Nazi policy of mass extermination of Jews.

Av 8
Civil war broke out in Jerusalem in the year 66 between the activists and peace party. The activists were in control of the Temple Court and the Lower City at the time of the outbreak of the civil war. The struggle continued for nine days and ended in the defeat of the forces of King Agrippa.

Av 9
Fast of Tishah be-Av (Zech. 8:19).
The 12 scouts dispatched by Moses to survey Palestine returned with an unfavorable report *(Ta'anit* 29a).
The exodus generation was condemned to die in the desert (Deut. 1:35; *Ta'anit* 26b). More than 15,000 died annually on Av 9 (Jer. Talmud, *Ta'anit* 3:7).
Nebuchadnezzar set fire to the Temple, 586 B.C.E.
The Romans destroyed the Second Temple on August 29, 70 C.E.
Betar, the last independent outpost under Bar Kokhba, fell to the Romans on August 5, 135 *(Ta'anit* 26b).
King Edward I of England ordered the expulsion of all Jews on July 18, 1290.
The period of expulsion of the Jews from Spain commenced on August 2, 1492.
World War I broke out on August 1, 1914.

Av 10
The First Temple was destroyed by a fire which had started on the preceding evening, 586 B.C.E. (*Ta'anit* 29a).
The Second Temple was set aflame on August 30 (approximation), 70 C.E. (Josephus, *Jewish War* 6:4).
Columbus set sail for the new world on August 3, 1492. The coincidence of the departure of the Jews from Spain and the sailing of Columbus for the new world was noted by the explorer himself in his diary. There was another coincidence linking the two events. The decree expelling the Jews from Spain was publicly announced on April 30, 1492. On the same day Columbus was given the royal commission to equip a fleet for the voyage.

Av 11
The Common Council of New York City suppressed the butcher license of Nicholas Smart, a non-Jew, on August 15, 1796,

for affixing Jewish seals to nonkosher meats. This action marked the earliest intervention of the law in protection of kashrut *(AJHSP,* no. 25, p. 32). New York was the first state to prohibit the sale of nonkosher meat which was represented as kosher. The statute became law in 1915 and was upheld by the U.S. Supreme Court in 1924.

Av 12
The famous disputation between Nahmanides and the apostate Pablo Christiani opened on July 20, 1263.

Av 13
Sir Moses Montefiore, outstanding philanthropist and Jewish leader, died on July 25, 1885.

Av 14
Arabs wrested control of most of Palestine from the Byzantine Emperor Heraclius, in the decisive battle of the Yarmuk on July 23, 636. The three major religions successively lost their supremacy in the Holy Land in the month of Av. Judaism suffered its setback on Av 9, 70; Christianty, on Av 14, 636, and Islam, on Av 26, 1920. Judaism was dominant for about 13 centuries, Islam about 11 centuries, and Christianity about four and one-half centuries.

Av 15
The last of the exodus generation, which was barred from entering Palestine, died in the desert *(Bava Batra* 121a).
Intertribal marriage was permitted to post-exodus generations *(Ta'anit* 30b).
Permission was given to the young men of the tribe of Benjamin to marry young women of other tribes, and thus the tribe of Benjamin was saved from extinction (Judg. 21:21; *Bava Batra* 121a).
An ancient folk-festival was celebrated on Av 15 by the youth of Palestine, featuring annual dances for young men to choose prospective brides *(Bava Batra* 121a).

Av 16
The Jewish Theological Seminary of Breslau, Germany (now Wroclaw, Poland), was opened on August 10, 1854.

Av 17
The extended Fast of Av, observed by the Falashas commencing with Av 1, is terminated on Av 17 (Leslau, *Falasha Anthology).*

Av 18
Gerhart Riegner, representative of the World Jewish Congress in Switzerland, was informed by a German industrialist, on August 1, 1942, that Hitler had ordered the extermination of all European Jews. It was the first reliable report of the impending mass murder of Jews to reach Western Europe. Riegner sent two reports through diplomatic channels to Rabbi Stephen Wise in New York and Mr. Sidney Silverman in Liverpool on August 8, 1942. The State Department suppressed the report until August 28, when the British draft had reached Rabbi Wise. (Morse, *While Six Million Died,* chap. 11).

Av 19
Bar-Ilan University, the first secular institution of higher learning under religious auspices in Israel, was founded on August 7, 1955.

Av 20
Titus ordered the raising of banks in preparation for the attack on Mt. Zion, on August 9 (approximation), 70 C.E. (Josephus, *Jewish War,* 6:8).

Av 21

24 of the foremost Yiddish writers of Russia, including David Bergelson, Itzik Fefer, and Perez Markish, were executed by the Soviet government on August 12, 1952. These executions marked the liquidation of Yiddish culture in Russia.

Av 22

A violent earthquake rocked Palestine on July 23, 501. The city of Acre was totally destroyed.

Av 23

A pogrom broke out in Zhitomir, Russia, on August 24, 1905.

Av 24

The Jewish agricultural colony of Woodbine, N.J., was established on August 28, 1891. The establishment of a Jewish agricultural colony at Woodbine, N.J., was one of several attempts of the Baron de Hirsch Fund to found Jewish agricultural settlements in North and South America. The failure of most of these projects confirmed the pessimistic view of early Zionists regarding the practicability of Jewish farming in areas divested of historical and religious sentiments linking the Jew to the soil.

Av 25

Many Jews of Copenhagen lost their lives in the British bombardment of the city on August 29, 1807. The anniversary of this date was set aside as a memorial day.

Av 26

A group of 70 people, led by the disciples of the Gaon of Vilna, arrived in Palestine on August 8, 1809.

Av 27

S.A. Bierfield was lynched by the Klan in Franklin, Tenn., on August 15, 1868, in the first such incident involving a Jew.

Av 28

Moses came down following his second ascent to the top of Mt. Sinai *(Bava Batra* 121a, Rashbam).

Av 29

Moses hued out of stone the second Tablets in preparation for his third ascent to Mt. Sinai on the following morning (Exod. 34:4).

Av 30

Moses ascended Mt. Sinai to receive the second Tablets of the Law (Exod. 33:11, Rashi).

Elul 1

Elul 1 marked the beginning of the fiscal year for the purpose of determining tithes of cattle *(Rosh Ha-Shanah* 2a).

Elul 2

Pope Julius III ordered the confiscation and burning of the Palestinian and Babylonian Talmuds on August 12, 1553. The banning of the Talmud was officially justified by the claim that it contained anti-Christian statements. The real reason, however, was the belief that the destruction of Talmudic Judaism would hasten the conversion of Jews to Christianity.

Elul 3

The first news of Nazi mass extermination reached the outside world on August 16, 1942, when a group of Polish women who had been exchanged for German war prisoners arrived in Palestine.

Elul 4

A decree issued on September 5, 1750, provided for the annual search of every Jewish home in Paderborn, Prussia, for stolen or "doubtful" goods.

Elul 5

Mussolini canceled the civil rights of Italian Jews and ordered the expulsion of all foreign-born Jews on September 1, 1938.

Elul 6

Italian planes bombed Tel Aviv on September 9, 1940, and killed 117 people. Italy adopted Nazi anti-Jewish laws on Elul 5, 1938. Its planes bombed Tel Aviv, a nonmilitary target, on Elul 6, 1940.

Elul 7

King Agrippa I dedicated the new gate of the Jerusalem wall, 42 C.E. *(Megillat Ta'anit* 6). The anniversary of this date was observed in ancient times as a holiday.

Elul 8

The walls of the upper city of Jerusalem were battered down by the Romans and all resistance came to an end on September 27 (approximation), 70 C.E. The leaders of the resistance, Simon and John of Giscala (Gush Halav) were captured (Josephus, *Jewish War* 6:9).

Emperor Alexander III appointed a commission on September 2, 1881, to study the "injurious influences of Jews upon the Russian native population."

Elul 9

Rabbi Moses b. Nahman (Nahmanides) arrived in Jerusalem on September 1, 1267, and soon thereafter reestablished a Jewish community (Kohler, *A Treasury of Jewish Letters,* 225). After the defeat of Bar Kokhba in the year 135, the Romans razed Jerusalem and built a smaller city on its site which they named Aelia Capitolina. Jews were barred from residing in this city. A Jewish community was reestablished in 637 and continued to exist until Jerusalem fell to the Crusaders in 1099. A new community was established again in 1187, but it was forced to dissolve in 1260 when the Tartars overran the city. Nahmanides renewed the community seven years later. It enjoyed an uninterrupted existence until 1948 and was reestablished in 1967, 700 years after the arrival of Nahmanides.

Elul 10

Noah opened the window of the ark and sent out the raven (Rashi, Gen. 8:5).

Elul 11

Operation Magic Carpet, which transported 45,000 Yemenite Jews to Israel, was officially concluded on August 24, 1950.

Elul 12

One of the earliest recorded Church censorships of Hebrew writings was ordered by King James I of Aragon on August 19, 1263. Russia was the last feudal government to introduce censorship of Hebrew books. It was decreed on October 17, 1796. The ban on Hebrew and Yiddish periodicals was lifted by the revolutionary government of Russia on July 21, 1918.

Elul 13

Governor Dongan was petitioned by the Jews of New York on September 12, 1695, for liberty to exercise their religion in public. The Charter of Liberties granted by James I of England on October 30, 1683, limited the free exercise of religion to Christians only. Accordingly, Governor Dongan declined the Jewish petition.

Elul 14

The Knesset passed Israel's draft law on September 8, 1949, making it obligatory for every Jewish youth in Israel to serve a term in the military forces. Israel's draft law, passed on Elul 14, 1949, was the first such law since the loss of Jewish independence. Jews were ineligible for military service in the medieval period. With the coming of emancipation, they were gradually incorporated in all national armies. The most shocking draft law affecting Jews was enacted by the Russian government on Elul 15, 1827. Under the provisions of that law, Jewish minors were drafted into battalions of cantonists. They were educated until the age of 18 and thereafter had to serve in the army for 25 years. It is estimated that 100,000 Jewish boys became cantonists and that at least half of them were baptized.

Elul 15

The study of Hebrew as a modern language was introduced for the first time into the public schools of New York on September 8, 1930. Hebrew was taught at Harvard College almost from the very inception of the school in 1636.

Elul 16

The forged *Protocols of the Elders of Zion* were serially published for the first time in the Russian paper *Znamia,* beginning with the issue of August 26, 1903. The spurious *Protocols of the Elders of Zion* were exploited by antisemites throughout the world in their dissemination of anti-Jewish slanders. Articles based on the *Protocols* were serialized in Henry Ford's *Dearborn Independent,* beginning with May 22, 1920. Thirty years after the original publication of the work at Kishinev, Congressman Louis T. McFadden spread the charges contained in the *Protocols* in the *Congressional Record.*

Elul 17

World War II broke out on September 1, 1939.

Elul 18

Falashas designated Elul 18 "The Festival of the Eighteenth" to commemorate the death of the patriarchs Abraham, Isaac, and Jacob (Leslau, *Falasha Anthology*).

Elul 19

Anti-Jewish riots broke out in Stockholm, Sweden, on September 3, 1852.

Elul 20

Charles VI issued a decree on September 17, 1394, ordering the expulsion of Jews from France.

Elul 21

Many Jews of London, England, lost their lives in anti-Jewish riots which broke out during the coronation of King Richard I on September 3, 1189.

Elul 22

General Tadeusz Kosciuszko appointed Berek Joselewicz commander of the Jewish regiment fighting with the Polish revolutionary army on September 17, 1794. It was the first Jewish fighting force in modern times.

Elul 23

Rabbi Jacob Frankel, head of Philadelphia's Congregation Rodeph Shalom, was appointed a military hospital chaplain on September 18, 1862. He was the first American rabbi in the U.S. Chaplaincy (Korn, *American Jewry and the Civil War,* 77).

Elul 24

Rabbi Israel Meir Kagen, author of *Chofetz Chaim,* founder of the Yeshivah of Radin, Talmudist and moralist, died on September 15, 1933. Rabbi Israel Meir Kagen, known the world over as the Chofetz Chaim, was the most revered person of his generation. His emphasis on ethics and moralism and his exemplary life made him a legendary figure in his lifetime. Even the Communist officials of Russia treated him with great deference and respect.

Elul 25

The beginning of the Creation *(Seder ha-Dorot).*

Elul 26

The Congress for the Safeguarding of Non-Jewish Interests, which opened at Dresden, Germany, on September 10, 1882, was the first international conference assembled to promote antisemitism. The conference was attended by close to 300 delegates. They represented antisemitic parties in Germany, Austria, Moravia, Hungary, and Russia.

Elul 27

The General Assembly of New York passed a resolution on September 23, 1737, that "persons of the Jewish religion be not admitted to vote for representatives in this colony."

Elul 28

The first synagogue in South Africa, Tikvat Israel, was dedicated in Cape Town on September 15, 1849.

Elul 29

Remnants of the Jewish community of Plungyan (Plunge), Soviet Lithuania, consisting of 18 families, were pogromized, on September 14, 1948, by a mob inflamed by rumors of a ritual murder.

31

Jewish Names and Their History

Benzion C. Kaganoff

Note: *Kinnui* is a noun that first appears in the Talmud. It means "surname," "by-name," or "substitute name." It derives from the Biblical verb meaning "to give an epithet." In the Middle Ages, Jews made a distinction between a Hebrew or sacred first name *(shem hakodesh)* and a secular name that related to it in some way. The secular name is called the *kinnui*.

ABA An Aramaic personal name from the Talmudic period. Some families adopted this name as an acronym for *Avo Begevurot Adonai* (Psalm 71:16), "may I come into thy strength, Lord" ("strength" is symbolically associated with the age of eighty).

ABEL Sometimes a diminutive of Abba, but most often a diminutive of Abraham (Avraham). Avraham becomes Avril, Avil, Abil, Abel. Sometimes this last form appears as Apel or Appel, since the letters "b" and "p" are interchangeable.

ABZUG This word means "copy-sheet," "proof-sheet," and is taken from the printing trade.

ADLER There were actually two houses in Frankfurt with the sign of the eagle *(Adler)*, No. 27, the black eagle, and No. 86, the golden eagle.

ALBUM Latin for "white," a translation of Weiss.

AMSTER From the word meaning "hamster." A name given to a diligent, industrious individual.

ANTMAN "Handy-man," one who works with his hands.

ARFA The Polish word for a tool used to separate the chaff from the grain. Name assumed by a grain merchant.

ASTRUC In Provencal it means "born under a lucky star," and is the equivalent for the Hebrew names Mazal Tov or Gad. A similar Latin name Asterius appears on Jewish catacombs in Rome. Astruc first appears as a personal name in southern France in the eleventh century and eventually became a family name.

AUSTERN When a man whose name or whose father's name was Pesah (Passover) appeared before the Austrian officials, they often insisted that he select a German name. He solved the problem by taking the name Austern which is a garbled version of the German *Ostern*, which means Easter. Even today a number of Jews refer to Passover as the Jewish Easter.

AVRECH, AVERIK, AFRICK The word *avrekh* appears as a tribute to Joseph (Genesis 41:43). A rabbinic interpretation reads the word as an acronym for *av behokhmah* rakh *beshanim*, "old in wisdom and tender in years." Perhaps this name was assumed by a person called Joseph in reference to his Biblical namesake.

BARON A form of *bar Aron* ("son of Aaron"), telescoped into one word; it indicates priestly descent.

BAUM Although the word is "tree" in German, the name has nothing to do with a tree. It is a shortened form for *Schlagbaum*, the tollgate on a highway or road.

BERNSTEIN *Bernstein* is German for "amber." Some Bernsteins may have derived their name from their dealings in amber. However, almost all the Bernsteins are descendants of a person called Berko or Berish, a diminutive for Ber, the *kinnui* for Issachar.

BESSER From Besserer, the title of a German officer of the court who levied fines. As a Jewish name, it indicates either the tax collector of the Jewish community or a rabbinic judge.

BETTSACK A garbled version of Pesah. Or the acronym for *ben tehorim zera kedoshim*, "a son of pure lineage, a descendant of martyrs." Or it may be phonetically associated with Bettsack, the German for mattress and indicate a dealer in, or maker of, mattresses.

BICKEL Either from *Bickel*, the German for pick-axe, and denoting someone who used this tool in his work, or an acronym for *bene yisrael kedoshim leadonai*, "the children of Israel are holy unto God."

BLASER Sounding the ram's horn is an important ritual in the synagogue, and the one who performs this ritual is called the *shofer-blozer*, in Yiddish, or just *blozer* or *blaser*. It is retained in the name Blaser or Blazer.

BLEIER One who smelts lead.

BORER Although the name sounds like the German *Bohrer*, "drill," "bore," it has nothing to do with any occupation using that tool. It is, rather, a title of honor to distinguished individuals in the community who served as the electors and participated in the selection of the head of the community. Borer in Hebrew means "one who chooses."

BORODATY "Bearded," in Russian. It was conferred by officials upon Jews. Since all eastern European Jews wore beards, the name was rather widespread.

BRANDEIS From the town of Brandeis, in Bohemia, where Jews from Germany first settled in 1440. The name appears in the form of Brandes and Brandys, Brandiss, and among Russian Jews it is spelled Barondes.

BRANDLER The production of alcohol was a government monopoly, and the privilege to engage in this trade was leased to individuals who enjoyed a certain status in the community. Brandler is the name for such a distiller.

BRONFMAN *Bronfn* is the Yiddish for the German *Branntwein*, "spirits," "whiskey." The name was originally Bronfen-man, the man who made or sold whiskey.

CALISCH (KALISCH) From Kalisz, a town in Poland, or from *kalich*, the Yiddish for "lime." A dealer in lime.

DAVIS Davis is an English name which means "son of David." Some Jews in English-speaking countries assumed this patronymic form.

ECKSTEIN Eckstein means "a cornerstone" and is a reference to Psalm 118:22; "The stone that the builders rejected has become a cornerstone." This has been traditionally viewed as a reference to the tragic fate of Israel and expressed the hope that in the future its fortune would rise.

EHMANN "Husband," in German. In many communities no marriage licenses were granted until military service was completed. As a result, many Jews were married by the rabbi only, and their marriages were never officially registered. This name was selected by one who could officially be registered as a "husband," and indicated that all the military requirements were met.

FLEISCHER It is the German word for "butcher" or "meat dealer." The trade of butcher was very important in the Middle Ages. First of all, it was the source of supply of kosher meat, which was the only kind available to Jews, for religious reasons. Secondly, the butchers in the ghettos of medieval Europe were often an unofficial Jewish army and self-defense group, since they were the only ones familiar with the handling of knives and axes.

GASTER The late Dr. Moses Gaster was of the opinion that his family name was a garbled version of De Castro, a widespread Sephardic name that is found in many countries of Europe, North, Central, and South America. This name is quite common among Christians of Spain and South America and is probably derived from a number of localities called Castro. The Jewish name is derived from the town of Castro near Cordova, Spain.

GEDULD In present-day German, *Geduld* means "patience." However, an older German vernacular meaning is "peace." When Warsaw was occupied by the Prussians from 1794-1806 and imposed German-sounding names on the Polish Jews, the Prussian authorities used *Geduld* in the sense of "peace," and the name is the Prussian translation of Solomon, which in other areas was often translated into Friedman or Fried.

GINSBURG From Gunzburg, a town in Bavaria. The name was first assumed by Jews exiled from Bavaria in the sixteenth century. In 1804 many Russian Jews who had to assume family names selected the name Gunzburg in various forms, even though they were not related to the original family. The name had become popular in Russia because of the family of St. Petersburg bankers, philanthropists, and spokesmen for the Jewish community. There are records of some of the original bearers going to court to prohibit strangers from assuming the name. They did not succeed, however, and as a result, thousands of families assumed the name Ginsburg. Some Jews selected the name Gunzburg as a garbled version of Koenigsberg, formerly capital of East Prussia.

GOLDBERG Goldberg is one of the most widespread Jewish family names. There is actually a place called Goldburgh in Silesia, where the first Goldberg lived more than six hundred years ago, and this is the source of the name. When the Jews were expelled from Silesia in the fourteenth century, a number of them took Goldberg as their family name. This, however, does not explain why there are more than 60,000 Goldbergs in the United States alone; they certainly are not all descended from those few families. Actually, the name was adopted by many others who had no relationship to the original Silesian Jews. Many Jews honored a matriarch by the name of Golda by assuming the family name Goldberg.

GROBTUCH The kind of clothes worn by an individual often determined the name given him by the authorities. Grobtuch indicates that the person named was wearing a coarse material, just as Feintuch describes the fine material of his garment.

HEIFETZ Heifetz is a family name derived from Hefetz which means "desire," "delight." It was formerly a popular first name among eastern Jews. Another form of the name is Keyfetz.

KAFKA Kafka or Kavka is Czech for "crow" and may indicate a person who lived in or near a house with the sign of this bird. In Polish, Kawka is a dealer in coffee. Some have derived Kafka as a nickname from Yaakov (Jacob). Yaakov becomes Koppel, which becomes Kopke, and this in turn is transformed to Kapke and Kafka.

KATZ Katz has nothing to do with cats but is an acronym for *kohen tzedek,* "priest of righteousness." It is based on Psalm 132:9 which says "Your priests will be clothed in righteousness." Kohen Tzedek appears as the name of the Gaon of Pumbedita in the tenth century. As a family name, it first appears in the seventeenth century.

KAVINOKY This name is based on a Talmudic expression *kav venaki,* which means "only a *kab* (a small quantity) but *naki* ('pure')." This name was given as tribute to a person small in size but with many qualities of character.

KEMMELMAN A seller of combs and other notions. *Kemml* is "comb" in Yiddish.

KIMMELMAN A seller of caraway and other spices; a retail grocer or food merchant. *Kimmel* is "caraway." Spices provide a number of family names to indicate one involved in merchandising them: Gewirtz, Gewirtzman *(gewirtz* is Yiddish for "spice"), Fenichel (from *Fenchel,* "fennel," in German), Muskat (the leaf of nutmeg), Zimring, Zimmet, Zinneman ("cinnamon"), Pepper and Feffer, Nelken ("cloves").

KIRSTEIN, KIRSTEN As a Gentile name, it is derived from an ancestor whose name was Christian. As a Jewish name it is a veiled form for the name Gershon or Gershom. The disguise of the name was further developed in the form Kirsche, and a variety of combinations were created: Kirchstein, Kirchen, Kirschheim, Kirschdorf, Kirschenberg, Kirschenzweig, Kirschenblatt, and Kirschenbaum.

KRATCHMER Kratchmer is the Yiddish for the operator of a *kretchme* ("country inn"). Inns were practically a Jewish monopoly in Poland. The name sometimes appears as Kretchmer or Krachman.

KRAUS Kraus in German means "curly." Kraus, Krauss, and Krause describe a curly-headed person. So do the family names Kraushaar ("curly hair") and Krauskopf ("curly head").

KRUPNICK A manufacturer of groats, popularly known among Jews as *kasha.*

LEHMAN/LEHMANN Lehman is a technical term from the Middle Ages and means a vassal of a feudal lord. As a Jewish family name it is derived from the profession of banking or money lending. In German *leihen* means "to lend," and *Leihhaus* is a pawnshop and *Leihman* was the pawnbroker. This became Lehman(n). The name may also be a disguised name for a Levite. Lehman was understood as Levi-man.

LIEBERMAN This name is a curious development from Eliezer. Eliezer became Eliezerman, which was abbreviated to Lieserman. Lieserman ultimately became Lieberman.

LIPMAN Lipman is a *kinnui* of Eliezer. Eliezer was often associated with the German name Gottlieb. Gottlieb was shortened to Lieb, which was in turn lengthened to Liebman or Lipman. Lipman appears as Lipa or Lapman. Variations of this name are Lipkin and Litman. Lipis or Lipes is another patronymic form.

LURIA One tradition traces the name from Luria, a town in the province of Treviso, Italy. Due to religious persecution, the Jews of Luria left Italy for Germany and thence to Poland, Lithuania, and Russia. Another tradition traces the name to Loria, a town near Bassano, Italy. The name first appears in Alsace in the fifteenth century. Luria appears in the forms Lurje and Lurie.

LUZZATTO The name of a distinguished Italian family. It goes back to the sixteenth century when the first members of the family came to Italy from the German province of Lausitz, which was called Lusatia and became in Italian Luzzatto. Some members of the family called themselves Luzzatti.

MANISCHEWITZ Manisch is either a short form of Menahem or of Menashe, and Manischewitz means "son of Manisch."

MANKUTA From the Polish *mankut,* "left-handed."

MAPU The family name of Abraham Mapu, who first introduced the novel into Hebrew literature. He fashioned the name out of his own first name, the names of his grandfathers, and the town the family came from. The name is an acronym of *M*oshe, *A*braham, *P*inhas, and the town *V*asiloshok.

MARAM Maram, or Marum, was originally the *kinnui* of Meir and was an acronym for *M*orenu *H*a*rav M*eir, in honor of Rabbi Meir of Rothenburg, the greatest Jewish scholar in Germany in the thirteenth century. Members of families who traced their descent from him and many of his disciples named their sons in his honor. This name has continued for more than seven centuries, first as a personal name and later, when family names were adopted, as a family name. Beginning in South and West Germany, the name was carried among families into Bohemia and Moravia and followed the movement of German Jews into other places.

MARKS Marcus is an ancient Roman name and means "belonging to the god Mars." It has continued as a name to this day as Marcus, as Mark in English, and as Marco in Italian and Spanish. Jews with a Hebrew name of Moshe or Mordecai often selected Marcus or Mark as the non-Hebrew name. This became the family name Marks or Marx.

MEHLMAN A flour merchant.

MESSINGER *Messing* is German for "brass." A dealer or worker in brass.

MISHKIN Mishke is an affectionate form for Miriam. Mishkin means descended from Miriam.

MONTAGU Montagu is the family name of Shakespeare's Romeo and in French it means "peaked mountain." There is in England a famous Jewish family by the name of Montagu. Moses Samuel was given the name Montagu as his non-Hebrew first name and became Montagu Samuel. He later reversed his names to become Samuel Montagu, and this has remained the family name for the past one hundred fifty years.

MONTALBAN A city in Aragon with a Jewish community going back to the fourteenth century. There is also a city by that name in Castille.

NASATIR Many Jews kept their business books in the Hebrew language. One page was designated *natati* (*nasati,* in Ashkenazic pronunciation), "I gave," and another page was marked *kibalti,* "I received." From *natati* we get a name for a money lender or banker. We also get a family name Kibaltic.

NASHELKA Nashelka is a Russian word meaning "stretcher," but the name is actually an acronym for *ni*srefu *a*l *k*iddush *h*ashem, "burned in martyrdom." This name was selected by a family in Russia to commemorate the martyrs in a pogrom.

NERENBERG Among Austrian and Galician Jews, Nerenberg was a kind of merchandise which included all kinds of notions—toys, buttons, needles, etc. A seller of such items assumed this name.

OSTROW There are hundreds of villages and towns in Russia and Poland named Ostrow, from which the family names Ostrow and Ostrower are derived.

PACIFICO It means "peaceful" and is a translation of Shlomo (Solomon) or Shalom among Sephardic Jews.

PASTERNACK This is the word for parsnip in Russian and the name was assumed by a dealer in vegetables or by one who served food.

PERGAMENT In German *Pergament* is "parchment" and preserves the original Latin word which referred to Pergamon, an ancient city in Asia Minor, where this item originated. The name was assumed by a scribe.

PINSK, PINSKER, PINSKY Pinsk is a city in the area of Minsk. The Jewish community goes back as early as 1506. Originally it was part of Lithuania, later becoming part of Poland, and later still becoming part of Russia.

PLOTKIN *Plotka* is Russian for a kind of whitefish. Plotke, Plotka, and Plotkin signify a dealer in fish.

PORATH In Genesis 49:22, Joseph is given the descriptive title Porath and thus a Joseph took this as a family name.

PORTNOY "Tailor," in Russian. Other translations are the Polish and Ukranian Kravitz, the German Schneider, the Yiddish Sherman, and the Hebrew Chait, Hait, Hayt.

RASKIN Raske is a nickname for Rachel, and Raskin means "a descendant of Rachel."

ROTHMAN It would be a name given to a redhead. Or it may be an extended form of Roth.

SACHS Sachs, Zaks, and Saks are family names that perpetuate the memory of martyrs. The acronym is *z*era k*odesh* sh*emo* ("his name descends from martyrs"). A number of families trace their descent from Speyer in western Germany, which suffered much during the Crusades. Others trace the family name to martyrs in Stendal, in Prussia, where Jews were martyred in the early sixteenth century. Still others selected the name in honor of some martyr in the past without specifying the city. But these names could also mean "one coming from Saxony," and one such name appears as early as the fourteenth century. The variation would depend on the Hebrew spelling.

SAHL For *Z*alman *Ha*levi or S*a*nder *Ha*levi.

SALANT Salant, Salanter, Salander, Sollender indicates one from Salanty, near Kovno, Lithuania.

SARFATTI Sarfatti, or Zarfatti, was the name of an Italian Jewish family originating in France. Tzarfat, an ancient community mentioned in the Bible, became the Hebrew word for France during the Middle Ages.

SCHEIER Scheier, Schayer, and Schauer are variations of Schorr, a symbolic reference to the name Joseph (Deuteronomy 33:17 compares Joseph to an ox—*shor*, in Hebrew).

SCHICK Schick, Shick, or Shik is either the acronym Sh*em* Y*israel* K*odesh*, "the name of Israel is holy," or it may be a name assumed by descendants of the famous sixteenth-century Italian rabbi, S*h*muel *Y*ehudah *K*atzenellenbogen.

SCHRAM Schram, or Schramm, means "slight facial scar" and was probably the reason that this name was given to the bearer.

SCHUPACK Schupack means "pickerel" in Russian and signifies a dealer in fish. Another form of the name is Schupakevitch. In Polish there is a word *Szupak*, which means "sandpaper" and would indicate cabinet worker.

SCHWEID From the Polish *Szwed*, "Swede." This would indicate a person who came to Poland from areas in Germany occupied by the Swedes in the seventeenth century.

SHAPIRO The city of Speyer in Rhenish Bavaria, Germany, has given us many name forms. The Jews first settled there at the end of the eleventh century and were compelled to leave in the middle of the fourteenth century. Large numbers of these Jews settled in Poland, Bohemia, Hungary, and Russia, and their name variants are: Shapiro, Spira, Spire, Spier, Spiro, Spero, Chapiro, Sprai, Szpir, Saphir, and Spear.

SHERMAN A dealer in woolen cloth. Since the cloth had to be cut with shears *(Scher* or *Sher)*, this is how the name developed.

SHTULL *Shtul* is Yiddish for "steel" and symbolizes the inner strength and faith of the Jew.

SIEGEL Siegel is the German for "seal." An engraver of seals would be called Siegel or Siegler. Jews were very prominent in the occupation of seal engraving in the eighteenth century. Other variations are Ziegler, Ziegelman, Ziegel, Siegelman. This name should not be confused with Segal which is an acronym for a Levite, although Segal and Siegel are often pronounced alike in English.

SIROTA Sirota in Slavic means "orphan," and may describe one who actually was an orphan or one who looked sad and depressed.

SOROKA Soroka means "magpie" in Russian and was applied by the naming commission to a talkative person.

SUKENIK Sukenik is the Russian for "a dealer in cloth."

TALESNICK Talesnick, Talisnick, or Talisman refers to one who sells or makes prayer shawls.

TALMACH Tolmach is the Russian adaptation of the German *Dolmetsch,* "interpreter." One form of the name is Talmach, which is often anglicized to Talmadge.

TANZER This is the German-Yiddish for "dancer." Some individuals achieved the distinction of being very adept at dancing, especially at community weddings.

TELLER Teller is the dish which identified the barber-surgeon in eastern Europe (like the striped pole in front of the present-day barber shop). This name was taken by a barber-surgeon.

TENDLER Tendler, or Tandler, denotes a dealer in second-hand furniture or clothes. It is a name especially found among Austrian and Galician Jews.

del VECCHIO The oldest Italian Jewish families traced their descent from a number of families who had been brought to Rome by Titus after the destruction of Jerusalem and who remained there. These families are, in Italian, Rossi ("reds"), Adolescenti ("youths"), Pomis ("apples"), and Anav ("humble," in Hebrew). (The Anav families took on Italian versions of their names, Pietosi and Piatelli.) Another old family was named Bethel in Hebrew, which was translated to the Italian Casadio ("house of God") and Degli Mansi ("of the house") and De Synagoga (*bet hakneset*, in Hebrew). However, there was one family that traced its descent to Jews who were in Rome *before* Titus, and these called themselves del Vecchio, which means "old-timers" in distinction from the newcomers.

VIGODA Vigoda or Wygoda means "inn" or "tavern," in Polish. There were hundreds of such places all over Poland and Jews were almost always in charge of them. Other names derived from this occupation are Wigodar, Wigodney.

WACHTEL Wachtel means "quail" in German and may refer to one who lived near a place with a sign of the quail. However, it may be a name that was selected by a Jew who recalled God's mercy and providence in providing quail to the Israelites in their march through the wilderness.

WINKLER The owner of a shop located at a corner (*Winkel*, in German) was called Winkler.

WOLFISH Wolfish or Walfisch, which means "whale," is the *kinnui* for Ephraim, whose descendants were to multiply like fish.

YARMAK An acronym for y*ehe* r*aavo* m*in* k*odomoh*, "may it be Thy will." This was selected as a prayer by the person assuming the new name.

ZELEZNIKOV "Dealer in iron," in Polish.

ZUNDER The German for "tinder." Before the invention of matches, tinder was used for kindling fire. A seller of tinder.

32

Moses Maimonides' *Treatise on Asthma*

Fred Rosner

Moses, son of Maimon (Rambam in Hebrew, Abu Imran Musa Ibn Maimun in Arabic, and Maimonides in Greek), was born in Cordova, Spain on March 30, 1135, corresponding to Passover eve of the Hebrew year 4895 (Figure 1). Maimonides' mother died in childbirth and consequently his father Dayan (judge) Maimon, raised him. Persecution by the Almochades, a fanatical group from North Africa, forced the Maimon family to flee Cordova in 1148. The family wandered through southern Spain and northern Africa for the next ten years and finally settled in Fez, Morocco in 1158.

Little is known of Maimonides' early life and medical education. There are no sources indicating that Maimonides had any formal medical education. In his *Medical Aphorisms,* he mentions "the elders before whom I have read"; this is the only allusion to some semiprivate study of medicine.

Maimonides must have been an avid reader, since his medical writings show a profound knowledge of Greek and Moslem medical works. Hippocrates, Galen, and Aristotle were his Greek medical inspirations and Rhazes of Persia, Al Farabi, and Avenzoar are Spanish-Arabic physicians frequently quoted by Maimonides.

The Maimon family left Morocco in 1165, and traveled to Palestine, landing in Acco, and from there to Egypt, where they settled in Fostat (old Cairo). Maimonides turned to medicine as a livelihood only after the death of his father in 1166 and the death of his brother in a shipwreck shortly thereafter. Maimonides was left with his brother's wife and children to support, and, after a year's illness following his father's death, entered into the practice of medicine. In 1174, at age 39, he was appointed Court Physician to Visier Alfadhal, Regent of Egypt during the absence of the Sultan, Saladin the Great, who was fighting the Crusaders in Palestine. It was at this time that Richard the Lion-Hearted, fighting in the Crusades, is reported to have invited Maimonides to become his personal physician, an offer which Maimonides declined. His reputation as a physician grew in Egypt and neighboring countries, and his fame as theologian and philosopher became worldwide.

In 1193, Saladin died, and his eldest son, Al Afdal Nur ad Din Ali, a playboy, succeeded him. As a result, Maimonides' medical duties became even heavier, as described in the famous letter he wrote to his friend, disciple, and translator, French Rabbi Samuel Ibn Tibbon, in the year 1199:

Generally accepted likeness of Moses Maimonides.

. . . I live in Fostat and the Sultan resides in Cairo; these two places are two Sabbath limits [marked off areas around a town within which it is permitted to move on the Sabbath; approximately one and one half miles] distant from each other. My duties to the Sultan are very heavy. I am obliged to visit him every day, early in the morning, and when he or any of his children or concubines are indisposed, I cannot leave Cairo but must stay during most of the day in the palace. It also frequently happens that one or two of the officers fall sick and I must attend to their healing. Hence, as a rule, every day, early in the morning I go to Cairo and, even if nothing unusual happens there, I do not return to Fostat until the afternoon. Then I am famished, but I find the antechambers filled with people, both Jews and Gentiles, nobles and common people, judges and policemen, friends and enemies—a mixed multitude who await the time of my return.

I dismount from my animal, wash my hands, go forth to my patients, and entreat them to bear with me while I partake of some light refreshment, the only meal I eat in twenty-four hours. Then I go to attend to my patients and write prescriptions and directions for their ailments. Patients go in and out until nightfall, and sometimes, even as the Torah is my faith, until two hours and more into the night. I converse with them and prescribe for them even while lying down from sheer fatigue. When night falls, I am so exhausted that I can hardly speak.

Maimonides was also the spiritual leader of the Jewish community of Egypt. At age 33, in the year 1168, shortly after settling in Fostat (old Cairo), he completed his first major work, *Commentary on the Mishnah*. In 1178, ten years later, his magnum opus, *Mishneh Torah* or *Code of Maimonides*, was finished. This monumental work is a 14-book compilation of all Biblical and Tamudic law and remains a classic to this day. In 1190, Maimonides' great philosophical masterpiece, the *Guide for the Perplexed*, was completed.

Maimonides died on December 13, 1204 (Teveth 20, 4965 in the Hebrew calendar) and was buried in Tiberias. Legend relates that Maimonides' body was placed upon a donkey and the animal set loose. The donkey wandered and wandered and finally stopped in Tiberias. That is the site where Maimonides was buried.

Moses Maimonides' *Treatise on Asthma*, as all his medical works, was originally written in Arabic, with the title *Makalah Pi Alrabo*. An original Arabic version with Arabic lettering is manuscript No. 601⁹ in the Madrid library (formerly Escorial No. 888). Additional Arabic manuscripts but in Hebrew letters are manuscript No. 1211 of the National Library in Paris, and Bodleian (Neubauer) manuscript No. 1202 in Oxford. The Parisian catalog only lists this work with the notation "a few pages are not in proper order," but in reality the Parisian manuscript No. 1211 also contains three other Maimonidean medical treatises: *Treatise on Poisons, Treatise on the Regimen of Health,* and *Medical Responses.*

Maimonides' *Treatise on Asthma* was twice translated into Hebrew and once into Latin. However, not all extant manuscripts in the various libraries throughout the world have been adequately studied.

The first Hebrew translation, in 1320, apparently prepared from the Latin version, is that of Samuel Benveniste, a Spanish physician from Saragossa. He was physician in the house of Don Manuel, brother of King Don Fredo the fourth of Aragonia. Benveniste's translation is extant in the following manuscripts: Parma-Rossi No. 1208, Bologna No. 20⁵, Paris No. 1173, Paris No. 1175, Paris No. 1176, Vienna No. 151 (folio 163, Gold folio 86). There are differences among these manuscripts. In only one of the six manuscripts is the name of the translator (Benveniste) mentioned, in Chapter 12. The Vienna manuscript is briefer than the others and the Paris manuscripts are incomplete. The Bologna manuscript has the additional title *Sefer Hamisadim* (literally, book of nourishments), probably because the unknown patient for whom the book was written asked for and was given nutritional advice in regard to which foods he should select and which he should avoid and which regimen he should follow to be cured of his asthma. Steinschneider points out that *Treatise on Asthma* contains parallel phrases and verbatim wording of various sections of Maimonides' *Regimen of Health.*

Gravesite of Moses Maimonides in Tiberias, Israel.

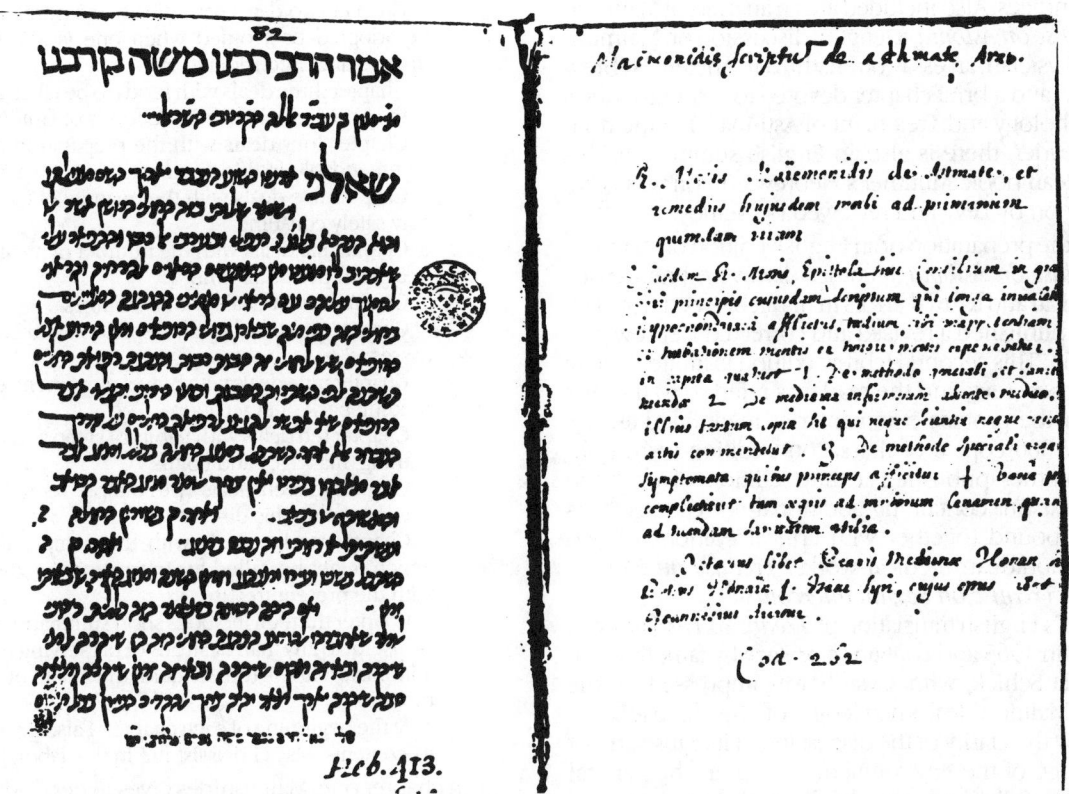

First folio page of Maimonides' Treatise on Asthma *from Hebrew Manuscript No. 1173 in the National Library, Paris, France.*

Steinschneider also points out that a fragment of Benveniste's translation was extant in the private library of Joshua H. Schorr.

The second Hebrew translation of Maimonides' *Treatise on Asthma* is that of Joshua Shatibi from Xativa, about the end of the fourteenth century. He translated directly from the original Arabic into Hebrew. Shatibi was called "the scholar in every field of knowledge, especially medicine." A copyist's note in Munich manuscript No. 280 states that Shatibi translated this treatise for an unknown Jewish apostate of high standing in the court of King Juan the first of Castille who reigned from 1379 to 1390. The translator did not translate the title nor much of the Arabic text except for the names of therapies. Only two manuscripts of Shatibi's Hebrew version of Maimonides' *Treatise on Asthma* are extant today: Munich manuscript No. 280, folio 35 (copy also in Munich manuscript No. 43 from the middle of the sixteenth century) and Steinschneider manuscript No. 30, folios 66 to 92b. The latter is now in the national library in Berlin as manuscript No. 232, and also contains several other Maimonidean medical treatises, including *Commentary on the Aphorisms of Hippocrates, Regimen of Health, Treatise on Sexual Intercourse, Treatise on Hemorrhoids, Medical Responsa,* and *Medical Aphorisms of Moses.*

Maimonides' *Treatise on Asthma* was translated into Latin by Armengaud de Blaise, a French scholar, in May 1302. The Latin version exists in Cambridge (Smith Catalog, p. 92) as manuscript St. Peter, Cambridge 209[8] under the title *Tractatus Contra Passionem Asthmatis* or *De Regimine Egrorum et Sanorum et Specialiter de Asinate* (should be *asthmate*). An additional Latin manuscript is described by Friedenwald, who states that this work is "not found elsewhere in Latin translation . . . This anonymous translation differs from that of Armengaud and is otherwise unknown." It would thus appear that this manuscript, which is now part of the Friedenwald collection of the Hebrew University in Jerusalem, differs from the Cambridge Latin manuscript described above.

Muntner writes that Dr. L. Bertolot in the Vatican discovered a fifteenth century Latin manuscript containing translation of six of Maimonides' medical writings, including his *Treatise on Asthma*. The others are his *Regimen of Health, Medical Responsa, Poisons and Their Antidotes, Treatise on Hemorrhoids,* and *Treatise on Sexual Intercourse.* This Latin manuscript is probably identical to the Friedenwald manuscript, which also contains the other five Maimonidean medical works in the same sequence. Both the Vatican and Friedenwald manuscripts begin and end with identical phrases: *Inquit Moyses filius Maymonis filii Abdelle cordubensis yspanus—Narravit nobis dominus rex . . . Finis. Explicit Tractatus Alrabo idest asmatis.*

Maimonides' *Treatise on Asthma* remained dormant for several hundred years until the early part of the twentieth century when Dr. Herman Kroner, rabbi in a small town in Germany, began editing this work and translating it into German. Unfortunately, he died in 1930 before the task was completed. Ten years later, Suessman Muntner published the first critical Hebrew edition of the *Treatise on Asthma,* based mainly on the Paris Hebrew manuscript No. 1173, which represents Benveniste's Hebrew translation. Muntner's edition is complete with introduction, bibliography, remarks, commentary and Hebrew, Arabic, Greek, and Latin indices. Also included are an analysis of Maimonides' *Treatise on Asthma,* a lengthy discussion on Maimonides the physician, an essay on "Asthma in Ancient Hebrew Literature," and a brief chapter devoted to "Modern Views on the Pathology and Treatment of Asthma." For the non-Hebrew reader, there is also an English summary of this Maimonidean book. Muntner's Hebrew edition was commented upon by Levy and reviewed by Nemoy.

During the preparation of an English edition of Maimonides' *Treatise on Asthma,* Muntner discovered numerous typographical and textual errors in his Hebrew edition. He, therefore, published a revised and corrected Hebrew edition in 1963. This second Hebrew edition is limited solely to the Hebrew text, and the reader is referred to the first edition for the profuse commentaries mentioned above. Since only 300 copies of the second edition were published, Muntner published a third edition of only the Hebrew text but containing additional corrections. This edition is bound together with critical editions of two other Maimonidean medical works. *Treatise on Hemorrhoids* and *Treatise on Sexual Intercourse.*

Muntner's English translation of *Treatise on Asthma* was published in 1963 and contains a preface by famed pediatrician Bela Schick, who says: "I was impressed by the depth of Maimonides' knowledge of the disease (i.e., asthma), by the clarity of the discussion of its cause and of the influence of the environment, as well as the general health of the individual upon the disease." In an introduction to the English version, noted allergist M. Murray Peshkin points out that "in spite of spectacular modern advances made in the theoretical and practical aspects of the allergies, the studies of the asthmatic state, written in the 12th century by Maimonides, still merit our attention."

Shortly after the appearance of the English edition of Maimonides' *Treatise on Asthma,* Muntner, in collaboration with Isidore Simon, founder and editor of the Parisian-based *Revue D'Histoire de la Medicine Hebraique,* published a French version, but without notes, commentary or index.

From the time of the Greeks to the era of Maimonides to the present time, the *name* asthma has changed its significance several times. The *disease* itself has changed even more, as physicians looked for different sets of symptoms that changed with their theoretical concepts for causality. It is, therefore, possible that Maimonides' *Treatise on Asthma* may not refer to what is today known as asthma. All one can say is that asthma was a difficulty of breathing or a pain in the chest.

In the introduction of this book, Maimonides praises his benefactor for having asked him to write the book. Maimonides points out that asthma should be treated according to the various causes that bring it about. He further states that one can only manage the disease properly if one has thorough knowledge of the patient's constitution and his individual organs, the age and habits of the patient, the season and the climate. Maimonides asserts that in this book he intends to include general principles which might be useful to all people to preserve their health and to prevent disease. He then lists the 13 chapters and their headings:

> Chapter one advises on the best course of personal conduct in general.

> Chapter two deals with dietary measures which should be adopted or avoided when one is afflicted with the disease under consideration.

> Chapter three deals with foods to be taken or eschewed, with special emphasis on the foods of familiar origin.

> Chapter four deals with the preparation of the dishes commendable in this disease.

> Chapter five deals with the quantity of food the patient may safely consume.

> Chapter six deals with the number of meals to be taken in a given period of time.

> Chapter seven deals with beverages.

> Chapter eight deals with respiration and emotional processes.

> Chapter nine deals with bowel movement, eventuality of holding back of evacuation.

> Chapter ten deals with habits of sleep and waking up, of bathing, massages and coitus.

> Chapter eleven deals with simple remedies and their use in treating this disease.

> Chapter twelve deals with the composition of drugs which might be called for in treating this disease in line with the present treatise.

> Chapter thirteen includes short summaries which might be useful to any man desirous of preserving his health and administering to the sick, in the form of concise admonitions.

> At the beginning of each chapter, I also give a preview of its contents. May G-d assist me in this labor.

In chapter one, Maimonides gives general advice regarding illnesses which are characterized by acute attacks such as arthritis, migraine, asthma, kidney stones and the like. He cites Galen who recommends dietary means to treat and even to prevent these maladies. Maimonides states that hygienic principles can be grouped into seven categories of which the first six are obligatory and the seventh is commendable: clean air, correct eating and drinking, regulation of one's emotions, exercise and rest, sleep and wakefulness, excretion or retention of wastes, and bathing and massaging. To these he adds the regulation of coitus as an important factor in a general health regimen. These are discussed in detail in the subsequent chapters.

Chapter two deals with nutritional and dietary measures to be adhered to or avoided by the patient suffering from asthma. Maimonides recommends that food be consumed in moderate amounts and should be easily digestible. He states that a fattening diet is objectionable and may endanger life, especially in an asthmatic patient. Gas-generating foods and scalding-hot foods should also be avoided.

In chapter three, Maimonides lists a variety of poorly digestible foods such as grossly sifted wheat flour, flour pudding, macaroni, and spaghetti, especially when these are fried, in oil or treated with cane sugar or dipped in honey and fried since all flour dishes which fatten the body are detrimental because they generate thick juices which block the body vessels and passageways. Rather, flour should be finely ground and unadulterated. One should avoid gas-producing foods such as black beans, peas, rice, lentils, nuts, onion, and garlic. Maimonides also describes the virtues and detriments of a variety of other foods such as different types of meat and fowl, cheese, eggs, fish, vegetables and fruits. Chicken soup is recommended for patients suffering from asthma, as is fresh-water fish. Also efficacious for asthmatics are fennel, parsley, mint, penny-royal, origanum, watercress, and radish, whereas lettuce, pumpkin, cauliflower, and turnip are harmful. Figs, quinces, and raisins in moderate amounts are beneficial, whereas watermelon, peaches, apricots, cucumbers and fresh dates should be avoided.

Chapter four presents numerous recipes for the preparation of dishes helpful to the asthmatic patient. One example is a soup made from rue, beet, and chicken, cooked with or without beans.

Chapter five deals with the quantity of food one should consume. This quantity varies from person to person and from season to season. A person should cease eating before experiencing a sense of repletion or fullness. Overeating is one of the prime causes of many diseases and maladies such as heartburn, diarrhea, and fainting. One should also not consume a large variety of foods during a single meal. Not only are the quality and quantity of food consumed important but also the sequence of its consumption. Galen is cited as recommending that light dishes be consumed before heavy ones. Other authors are of the opposite view. Maimonides suggests that a single uniform dish, not too light or heavy, is preferred. He then points out the virtues of moderate exercise prior to eating and advises against such exercise immediately following a meal. He, therefore, calls sexual intercourse, bloodletting, or the taking of a hot bath immediately after eating as an offense against one's health because they involve strenuous physical and emotional exercise. Finally, Maimonides enumerates a variety of ailments which occur in people who insufficiently or inadequately digest their food: heartburn, loose stools, impotence, insomnia, lethargy, depression, urinary retention, fever, or inflammation of the kidneys, spleen, liver, or joints.

Chapter six deals with the timing and number of meals one should eat. Maimonides suggests that healthy people should eat a single meal daily and that the elderly and debilitated and those convalescing from illness should consume small quantities at frequent intervals. One should only eat when the stomach is empty. The time to eat again is when the food has left the stomach, when there is no aftertaste from eructation and when one feels real appetite and salivates in the mouth—even then one should wait another half hour. Maimonides then recounts his personal eating habits. He used to eat only once in 24 hours, except on the Sabbath. In the winter he drank a little wine, depending on the degree of cold, before going to bed. For Moslems, to whom wine is prohibited, Maimonides suggests a fine honey drink.

Chapter seven deals with beverages. Excessive imbibition of wine is said to be injurious in that it makes the drinker feel heavy, affects his brain and hearing, gives rise to severe diseases and aggravates others such as asthma. However, a small quantity of wine during or after meals is useful in the diet of the healthy and an excellent cure for many disorders in that it aids digestion, increases natural body warmth, and removes superfluities in the form of sweat and urine. Maimonides again offers a substitute for wine for Moslems to whom wine is forbidden: honeyed drink (i.e., mead) seasoned with spices. He also lists spices which stimulate urination: lentils, borax, mint, anise, ginger, mastic, muscat nuts, and nard. Recommendations

regarding the drinking of water include the following: it should be sweet, clear, and pure, boiled a little, and drunk from a clean vessel after it cools down. The best time to drink water is about two hours after eating.

Chapter eight is concerned with rules of conduct regarding fresh air and psychic or emotional moods. Not only should air be fresh and clean but its temperature is important. On hot days, the air should be conditioned by spraying and sprinkling the floor with aromatic water, by flowers, heat-abating leaves, and draft. Conversely, on cold, rainy days, the air should be fumigated with perfumes which warm the body. Maimonides asserts that if a person is emotionally upset or mentally agitated, his physical well-being suffers and eventually he becomes physically ill. This statement is perhaps an early description of psychosomatic medicine indicating that a deranged psyche can profoundly affect the somatic or physical well-being of an individual. Conversely, continues Maimonides, gaiety and joy gladden the heart, and stimulate the blood and mental activity. Excessive indulgence in the pursuit of pleasure, however, is injurious to one's health. The avoidance of illness induced by such excesses is by conducting oneself according to ethical and moral principles.

In chapter nine, Maimonides discusses constipation, urinary retention, and other forms of retention of body superfluities. A variety of oral cathartic preparations and antidiarrheal concoctions are described. One should try to regulate one's bowels by maintaining a regular and normal diet. Very potent cathartics should be avoided. Numerous types of enemas to cleanse the bowels are cited and various emetics to cleanse the stomach are listed. The conditions under which all these remedies are to be used are clearly enunciated. For example, vomiting is best effected when the patient is in a raised position, so that nothing remains in the stomach. Maimonides then describes a series of experiments that he conducted on himself to regulate his bowels. Finally, he posits that urine stimulation, bloodletting, and purgation do not preserve health and should not be done on healthy people but should be reserved for cases of illness.

Chapter ten deals with the effects of sleeping, waking, bathing, massage, and coitus on asthma. Sleeping immediately after meals is said to be harmful, as is washing with cold water. Sleeping after bathing is efficacious. The bath water should be warm and contain some salt. Massaging the body upon awakening in the morning and before going to bed at night is highly recommended. Several types of massaging are described as are certain forms of exercise for the young and the elderly. The final portion of this chapter is devoted to a discussion of coitus, an excess of which is injurious even to healthy people. A man who indulges excessively in coitus suffers from memory lapses and decline in mental capacity, faulty digestion, and defective vision. Coitus should be avoided soon after a bath, soon after physical exercise or bloodletting, at daybreak, when a person is hungry or fully satiated, or seriously ill.

In chapter eleven, Maimonides discusses simple medicinal therapy for asthma. He advises one to use an experienced and expert physician who develops a rational treatment plan and implements it. He counsels against the use of "empiricists who do not think scientifically" but who succeed or fail purely by chance in treating patients.

רבינו משה בן מיימון

ספר הקצרת

או «ספר המסעדים»

مقالة في الربو

(מקאלה פי אלרבו)

בתרגומו העברי של הרופא

ר' שמואל בנבנשתי

איש סרגוססה

עס״י כ״י פריס מ' 1173

י״ל בפעם הראשונה בצרוף מבוא וביאורים

מ א ת

זיסמן מונטנר

הוצאת ראובן מס ירושלים ת״ש

Figure 4. Title page from the 1940 Hebrew edition by Suessman Muntner of Maimonides' *Treatise on Asthma.*

Title page from the 1940 Hebrew edition by Suessman Munter of Maimonides' Treatise on Asthma.

He cites the following parable: a patient who puts his life in the hands of an experienced physician who is lacking in scientific training is like a mariner who places his trust in good luck, relying on the sea winds which sometimes blow in the direction desired by the mariner but which sometimes spell his doom. Maimonides is obviously cautioning against consultation with and treatment by medical quacks. In support of his position, he cites Galen and Hippocrates who assert that medicines should be compounded scientifically and logically, according to the individual qualities of the patient. Specifically for asthma, Maimonides recommends enemas "to drain the thick juices," and aromatic herbs "to fortify the brain and dry out any humidity herein." These should be employed once or twice a year. During an acute attack, chicken soup is advised if the patient is afebrile, and sweetened barley porridge if the patient has fever. Should these be insufficient to allay the attack, an enema should be used. For the most severe cases, an emetic may be necessary. The patient should sleep as little as possible and in a sitting position. Excessive bathing and strenuous physical exercise should be avoided, but light exercise may be beneficial.

Chapter twelve describes compound remedies for asthma in ascending order of potency. The mildest remedy is made from liquiritia, althaea, fleabane, and fennel boiled and strained into freshly made rosewater syrup. Maimonides endorses a remedy of Rhazes to clear the lungs of moisture, ease respiration, and eliminate the cough: soak wheat bran overnight in hot water, filter, and add sugar and almond oil; place on the fire until it resembles a julep and drink when lukewarm. A mild remedy of Galen for asthma consists of equal parts of seeded raisins and fenugreek cooked in clear water, sifted, strained and left standing for a prolonged period. More potent remedies of Galen are also described.

Maimonides cautions against the use of opiates except for severe cases of asthma. He details at some length the case of one of his patients who suffered from asthma, a young, thin unmarried woman with a moderately warm constitution, for whom he prepared a remedy containing numerous ingredients. His purpose was "to cleanse her lungs, fortify her brain and stop her catarrh." He states that no mention of this remedy is found in any of the medical texts written by ancient or modern physicians but that he had great success therewith. Maimonides again asserts that chicken soup assists in the expectoration and expulsion of pulmonary phlegm. He points out that Ibn Zohr preferred powders to oily pastes for "fortifying the brain" in asthmatic patients. Various formulas for ointments, fumigations, enemas, and purgatives are then described and their varying degrees of potency are cited. Most of these formulae were taught to Maimonides by "Western (i.e., Moroccan) Masters" and only a few are recorded in medical books. He concludes this chapter by stating that he only listed those remedies for asthma whose ingredients are easily available and whose preparation is simple.

The last and most important chapter of Maimonides' *Treatise on Asthma* is concerned with concise admonitions and aphorisms which he considered "useful to any man desirous of preserving his health (i.e., the patient) and administering to the sick (i.e., the physician)." The chapter begins as follows: "the first thing to consider . . . is the provision of fresh air, clean water and a healthy diet." Fresh air is then described in some detail:

> . . . city air is stagnant, turbid and thick, the natural result of its big buildings, narrow streets, the refuse of its inhabitants . . . one should at least choose for a residence a wide-open site . . . living quarters are best located on an upper floor . . . and ample sunshine . . . toilets should be located as far as possible from living areas. The air should be kept dry at all times by sweet scents, fumigation and drying agents. The concern for clean air is the foremost rule in preserving the health of one's body and soul . . .

These air pollution control measures advocated by Maimonides nearly 800 years ago seem appropriate indeed to the twentieth century reader of this essay.

Healing of illness is said to be dependent not only upon the therapeutic measures prescribed by the physician but also the nature and constitution of the patient. In mild cases of illness, the physician should not interfere but allow nature to heal. If the physician errs and prescribes a therapy which is contrary to the course of nature, he may impede the cure or even aggravate the illness. Even if the physician prescribes correctly and even if the patient follows the prescription precisely, it is possible that cure will not be effected because nature may not cooperate. The same may happen to the farmer, he does everything that is expected of him yet the seed brings forth no fruit if nature does not cooperate. Maimonides then quotes the famous aphorism of Rhazes who said:

> When the disease is stronger than the natural resistance of the patient, medicine is of no use. When the patient's resistance is stronger than the disease, the physician is of no use. When the disease and the patient's resistance are equally balanced, the physician is needed to help tilt the balance in the patient's favor.

This rule of *primum non nocere* was already enunciated centuries earlier by Hippocrates who said that the physician should help the patient and not harm him. If one cannot help him, at least do not harm him. Maimonides then criticizes "famous physicians who commit grave errors on patients who later succumb..." Maimonides says he often observed a physician prescribe the use of a strong purgative for a patient who did not even need a mild one. Some physicians commit gross blunders, according to Maimonides, yet the patient survives; others commit seemingly small errors and the patient dies. Anyone with common sense should keep this in mind. The genuine physician is always beset with doubts whereas the charlatan thinks that everything is clear.

Maimonides cites Rhazes' aphorism which considers medicine to be an art, and Galen's assertion that "the medical art seems easy and simple to men of limited vision but how profound and far-reaching was this art in the eyes of a man like Hippocrates." Maimonides makes reference to his *Commentary on the Aphorisms of Hippocrates.* He also quotes Aristotle who said that most people die of the remedies given them, a clear reference to iatrogenic disease. This observation, however, should not lead one to abandon appropriate remedies. Medicine is a science essential to man at all times and in all places, not only for the ill but also for the healthy. However, one should seek out and consult with expert physicians who have complete mastery of theoretical and practical knowledge. An unlearned physician should be avoided; if an expert physician is not available one should rely only on nature, confirming Hippocrates' assertion that "nature cures disease ... she takes no orders from man ..." Where a diagnosis is in doubt, it is best to rely on nature to cure the illness.

The humble Maimonides then addresses himself to the Sultan for whom he wrote his *Treatise on Asthma* saying:

> Do not assume that I am the right person in whose hands you might place your body and soul for treatment. Heaven be my witness that I myself know well that I am one of those who are not perfect in this art [of medicine] and who shrink from it because it is enormously difficult to attain its vastness ...

The chapter continues with the observation that therapeutic measures developed by practical experience are more frequently employed than those arrived at by theoretical reasoning. Maimonides again warns against the use of "experienced" quacks. The genuine physician has at his disposal not only his own experience but that of all physicians over many generations up to the time of Galen and Hippocrates as recorded in medical books. Another cardinal rule is that the physician should not treat the disease but the patient who is suffering from it.

The case of a young Moroccan patient who was wrongly treated and whose care was then taken over by one of Maimonides' teachers is cited in detail. Other cases of erroneous treatment with fatal outcome are also mentioned. Another case described in detail is the illness of the Sultan Amrael Muselmin in Marakesh, Morocco, treated by four of the greatest professors of medicine: Abu Ali Ibn Zohr, Serapion, Abu Alchassan Ibn Kamniel of Saragossa, and Abu Ayub Ibn Elmualim of Seville. The strong young Sultan recovered from his illness but later died, probably of an incorrect dosage of medicine. Maimonides investigated the circumstances surrounding the Sultan's death and comments thereon at some length. Maimonides expresses admiration for the fundamental rules of medical practice in Egypt and enumerates several reasons for his admiration. Finally, he lists the circumstances where such multiphysician consultation should be avoided.

Chapter thirteen and the entire treatise end with the following prayer:

> May G-d the Gracious and Truthful guide us on the right path to our salvation in eternity. Praise be to G-d forever and ever.

Maimonides' logical and systematic approach to the prevention, diagnosis, and treatment of illness, is typical of all his medical and other writings. One should note his allusions to psychosomatic medicine and his discussion of iatrogenic medicine and his discussion of iatrogenic disease, seemingly modern concepts. His teachings that a bad physician is worse than none, that one should treat patients and not diseases, and that *primum non nocere,* among others, should be taken to heart by all students of medicine and medical practitioners of the present era. It is hoped that this essay describing Maimonides' *Treatise on Asthma* will stimulate the reader to read this important Maimonidean medical work as well as his other nine medical books, nearly all of which are now available in English.

33

Luther and the Jews

Franklin Sherman

Title page from Martin Luther's 1543 tract, On the Jews and Their Lies.

Martin Luther did not really know what he was starting when he nailed his "Ninety-Five Theses" to the church door in Wittenberg that late October day in the year 1517. The effects of his action spread beyond his wildest imagining, and later ages would mark that event as the beginning of the Protestant Reformation.

Similarly, Luther could not know, as he published his writings on the Jews, that some four centuries later his words would be cited in support of the antisemitic measures of a violent neopaganism that had seized the heart of Europe. Yet, so sharp were his words, and so pervasive his influence, that he cannot be absolved of all responsibility for what happened, despite the vast historical gap between his time and ours.

It is ironic that Luther, in his later life, should have become known as a foe of the Jews (his major treatise on the subject was published in 1543, just three years before his death), for in his early years it was just the opposite. Jewish leaders hailed the work of Luther and the Reformation as the dawn of a new day, in which they might experience a greater freedom and justice than they had known in medieval Christendom. They noted the new interest in the study of Scripture in the original languages, and the establishment of professorships of Hebrew in the Protestant universities.

The young Luther, for his part, fully reciprocated this new sense of cordiality. This may be seen most clearly in his treatise of 1523, significantly entitled, "That Jesus Christ Was Born a Jew," in which Luther stressed the Jewish origins of Christianity and, especially, the Jewishness of Jesus. An appreciation of this indebtedness, he indicated, would induce an attitude of affection and respect towards contemporary Jews. "We are aliens and in-laws," he reminded his fellow Gentiles; "they are blood relatives, cousins, and brothers of our Lord."

A closer examination of the text of the treatise, however, reveals the deep ambiguity of Luther's attitude towards the Jews, even in this earlier period. On the one hand, he was sharply critical of traditional prejudices, and proposed, in effect, that Christendom make a fresh start, adopting policies based on an affirmation and appreciation, not a denigration and rejection, of the Jews and their faith. On the other hand, it is plain that his eventual hope was for their conversion. Note how these two motifs intertwine as Luther wrote, in his usual colorful style:

> Our fools, the popes, bishops, sophists, and monks ... have hitherto so treated the Jews that anyone who wished to be a good Christian would almost have had to become a Jew. If I had been a Jew and had seen such dolts and blockheads govern and teach the Christian faith, I would sooner have become a hog than a Christian.... I hope that if one deals in a kindly way with the Jews and instructs them carefully from Holy Scripture, many of them will become genuine Christians.... They will only be frightened further away from it if their Judaism is so utterly rejected that nothing is allowed to remain, and they are treated only with arrogance and scorn.

The same duality of motive—genuine human concern and the hope for conversion—is evident in Luther's concluding recommendations in the 1523 treatise.

> Therefore, I would request and advise that one deal gently with them and instruct them from Scripture; then some of them may come along. Instead of this, we are trying only to drive them by force.... So long as we thus treat them like dogs, how can we expect to work any good among them? Again, when we forbid them to labor and do business and have any human fellowship with us, thereby forcing them into usury, how is that supposed to do them any good? If

we really want to help them, we must be guided in our dealings with them not by papal law but by the law of Christian love ... If some of them should prove stiff-necked, what of it? After all, we ourselves are not all good Christians, either.

Compared to the foregoing, Luther's treatise, written twenty years later, exhibited a very different attitude, from its title, "On the Jews and Their Lies." Here, we find Luther treating the Jews with the "arrogance and scorn" that he had earlier condemned. Rather than "dealing gently" with them, he advocated exceedingly harsh measures. As to the Jews' economic role, he overlooked the fact that the restrictions which a Christian society had played on them may have forced them into usury; he now blamed solely their avarice and cunning. In short, his image of the Jews and his recommendations became almost entirely negative.

How is this transformation to be explained? A variety of theories have been propounded to account for it. Reference has been made to Luther's declining health in his later years; to his frustration over the obstacles being met by the Reformation and the splintering of the movement; to his fear of what he considered "Judaizing" tendencies within the Church itself. The most important factor, however, was clearly the disappointment of the hopes expressed in Luther's earlier treatise, that is, *the Jews' failure to convert.*

Thus, the Jews fell afoul of Luther's wrath for the same reason they had remained a "problem" ever since the emergence of Christianity—their steadfast maintenance of the integrity of their faith. Originally, of course, it had been the Christians who were the minority, a small sect that had burst forth from the womb of Judaism. But as the Christian mission advanced, transcending the ethnic base of Judaism and appealing to all peoples, the proportions were reversed, until in time Christianity was acknowledged as a separate religion in its own right, and eventually as the official religion of the Roman Empire. Now Christianity had at its disposal not only the sword of the spirit but also the sword—in the literal sense—of the secular power as well. This would remain true throughout the Middle Ages and down to the rise of modern democratic pluralism (far after Luther's time).

Within this framework, all the "dynamics of prejudice" were free to operate. Thus, the rivalry between Jews and Christians during this period can be viewed in several dimensions: (1) sociologically, it represented a classic case of in-group/out-group tension, one group in the possession of privilege and power and the other struggling to gain a share of it; (2) psychologically, it showed all the signs of scapegoating—the projection onto a hapless individual or group of the blame for untoward events for which there is no ready explanation, or for which others wish to escape responsibility. This was greatly intensified by the dark undercurrent of superstition in the late Middle Ages, which could attribute all sorts of demonic powers and practices to the Jews; (3) economically, there was the resentment of the Jewish role as moneylenders, and of the wealth that some Jews were able to achieve; (4) ideologically, the Jews suffered from being the one most glaring exception to an otherwise universally accepted set of sym-bols that served to give cohesion to the whole social order—in this situation, "heresy" was considered very close to "treason"; and finally, (5) religiously, the two faiths may be viewed as locked in a sibling rivalry, each claiming to be the true heir of the prophets and patriarchs of ancient Israel. To the Jews, the Christians were a people who, although sprung from Jewish loins, had forsaken the law of Moses, the Torah, for the sake of a messianic faith that lacked confirmation in reality (did the world look redeemed?). To the Christians, the Jews were those who, out of willful blindness, rejected and crucified the true Messiah.

Luther's treatise reflected all these factors. The greater part of it was taken up with the interpretation of numerous passages from the Hebrew Bible (the Old Testament) that Luther claimed must be interpreted as prophecies of Christ, but which the Jews interpreted in a different sense (hence their "lies," in Luther's view). here, Luther was continuing a debate that had gone on for centuries between Jewish and Christian scholars; but he lent it the special harshness of his own rhetoric. Elements of superstition and half-truths about Jewish practices and alleged anti-Christian rituals were passed in review with mounting ire on Luther's part, until finally he issued his infamous list of proposals—that their synagogues and houses be destroyed, their prayer books seized, and their rabbis forbidden to teach, etc. Although many of these proposals parallel, in a chilling manner, the antisemitic measures later undertaken by the Nazis (not to speak of the many intervening persecutions and pogroms), it should be made clear that Luther did not envision anything like genocide. Luther advised pastors to admonish their parishioners to be wary of the Jews, but he added, "They should not curse them or harm their persons." His ultimate penalty was to expel them from the country.

Luther's treatise of 1543 has caused embarrassment and dismay from the first day of its publication; it is known, for example, that his closest colleague, Phillip Melanchthon, was unhappy with its severity. Fortunately, his proposals met with very little response among the authorities. In two nearby provinces, the right of safe conduct of Jews was withdrawn, and in another, Jews were prohibited from moneylending and were required to listen to Christian sermons. In no cases were his harsher suggestions followed. As to the treatise itself, it did not sell widely, in contrast to the more benign treatise of 1523. For the most part, it has remained buried in obscurity, although selected quotations from it—the worst parts, of course—have been circulated by antisemitic movements.

There is no way to undo what has been done or to unsay what has been said, but some comfort can be taken in the fact that this aspect of Luther's thought has been so vigorously repudiated by contemporary Christians, including official Lutheran church bodies. We live in a day of ever-deepening dialogue and the growth of mutual respect between Jews and Christians. Yet, we are living also just one generation after the Holocaust. Facing the stark facts of Jewish-Christian conflict in the past, such as in Luther's time, can serve to remind us of the need for eternal vigilance against the forces of racial and religious hatred.

34

The Golem

Howard Spielman
Arnold Fine

Many stories have been written about the Golem. According to legend, the Golem would roam the streets of Prague at night, keeping a watchful eye over Jews who were in danger of attack by antisemites.

What follows is the legend of the creation of the Golem by Rabbi Loew, the Maharal of Prague.

WHEN THE STEAM CLEARED - THEY SAW THAT HAIR HAD GROWN ON ITS HEAD.

IT HAS ALSO GROWN *NAILS* ON ITS HANDS AND TOES!

NEXT THE MAHARAL HIMSELF BEGAN TO CIRCLE AROUND THE GOLEM SEVEN TIMES.

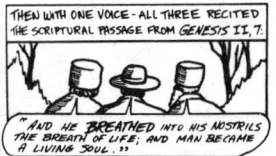

THEN WITH ONE VOICE - ALL THREE RECITED THE SCRIPTURAL PASSAGE FROM *GENESIS II, 7:*

"AND HE *BREATHED* INTO HIS NOSTRILS THE BREATH OF LIFE; AND MAN BECAME A LIVING SOUL."

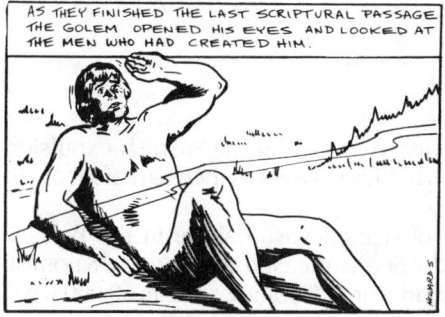

AS THEY FINISHED THE LAST SCRIPTURAL PASSAGE THE GOLEM OPENED HIS EYES AND LOOKED AT THE MEN WHO HAD CREATED HIM.

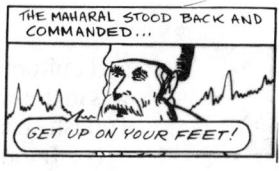

THE MAHARAL STOOD BACK AND COMMANDED...

GET UP ON YOUR FEET!

SLOWLY THE GOLEM BEGAN TO RISE.

IMMEDIATELY, THE GOLEM OPENED HIS EYES...

AND LOOKED AT THE THREE MEN WONDERINGLY.

HE STOOD BEFORE THE THREE MEN, SILENTLY WAITING FOR THE MAHARAL'S NEXT ORDER.

REB ISAAC AND REB JACOB LOOKED AT THE GOLEM IN COMPLETE AWE.

THE MAHARAL BROKE THEIR TRANCE-LIKE STATE BY SHOUTING...

DRESS HIM! IT WILL BE LIGHT SOON!!!

REB ISAAC AND REB JACOB QUICKLY DRESSED THE GOLEM IN THE CLOTHES THEY HAD BROUGHT WITH THEM, CLOTHES THAT WERE FITTING FOR A SHAMMES.

FOLLOW US!

THE GOLEM SEEMED TO UNDERSTAND AND QUICKLY OBEYED THE MAHARAL'S EVERY ORDER.

MOST WONDERFUL TO RELATE - WHEN THEY HAD LEFT THE CITY TWO HOURS BEFORE THEY WERE ONLY THREE, NOW THERE WERE *FOUR* RETURNING.

ON THE WAY HOME THE MAHARAL SPOKE TO THE GOLEM.

WE HAVE CREATED YOU FOR A *PURPOSE!*

YOU ARE TO *PROTECT* DEFENSELESS JEWS AGAINST THEIR ENEMIES.

YOUR NAME IS *JOSEPH* AND YOU WILL SERVE ME AS SHAMMES IN THE HOUSE OF JUDGEMENT.

YOU MUST *OBEY* ME NO MATTER WHAT I TELL YOU TO DO...

...EVEN SHOULD I ASK YOU TO JUMP INTO *FIRE* AND *WATER!*

THE FOUR MEN CONTINUED THEIR WALK HOME, BUT NOW THE MAHARAL WALKED A LITTLE FASTER BECAUSE HE WANTED TO CATCH UP TO REB ISAAC AND REB JACOB AND SPEAK WITH THEM.

THE GOLEM HAD UNDERSTOOD EVERY WORD THE MAHARAL HAD SPOKEN TO HIM.

HE ALSO HAS A *REMARKABLE SENSE OF HEARING* AND CAN DETECT SOUNDS FROM A VERY GREAT DISTANCE.

THE GOLEM *CANNOT SPEAK,* FOR THE POWER OF SPEECH IS G-D'S ALONE TO GIVE.

ALSO, I HAVE *NAMED* HIM *JOSEPH* BECAUSE I HAVE IMPLANTED IN HIM THE *SPIRIT* OF JOSEPH SHIDA...

HE WHO WAS *HALF-MAN* AND *HALF-DEMON,* AND WHO HAD *SAVED* THE SAGES OF THE TALMUD FROM MANY TRIALS AND DANGERS!

THE FOUR FIGURES REACHED THE OUTSKIRTS OF THE CITY JUST AS THE FIRST MORNING LIGHT BROKE.

35

The Life and Culture of Sephardic Jews Before World War II

Jane Gerber

One of the main components of the Jewish people is the Sephardim, Jews who trace their origin to medieval Spain. Living under Christian and Muslim overlords for over 1,000 years in Spain, the Jews of the Iberian Peninsula developed a unique culture, both secular and religious, and an articulated sense of a proud and brilliant history. Sephardic Jews in Spain, despite their many centuries of persecution, experienced periods of economic efflorescence and social integration, feeling quite at home in their Jewish culture as well as in the broader culture of the wider non-Jewish society. Open to philosophical concepts, receptive to Arab scientific and geographic discoveries, and enamored of the Hebrew language and its abilities to express lofty as well as mundane notions, Sephardic Jews developed an outlook and civilization unique in the annals of the Jewish people. This civilization was violently uprooted with the pogroms of 1391, the expulsion from Spain in 1492, and the expulsion from Portugal in 1497. Thousands of Spanish Jews sought refuge wherever possible, while smaller numbers chose to remain in Spain as clandestine Jews until escape was more propitious. But the doors of Europe were almost entirely shut to practicing Jews. Thus, the Jewish community of Spain was forced to flee to distant lands, bringing with them their cultural baggage and fierce nativist loyalties of a dispossessed people.

Sephardic Jews were warmly welcomed in the Ottoman Turkish Empire. Indeed, the Ottoman sultan is reported to have been incredulous that the king of Spain had ousted such a talented population element. From the 1490s, and in increasing numbers throughout the first quarter of the sixteenth century, boatload after boatload of Sephardic Jews arrived in the Ottoman Empire: Sephardim came to Rhodes after it was conquered by the Turks in 1523; the first documents attesting to a Jewish presence in Sarajevo date from 1565 and relate to Sephardic Jews; Sephardim quickly overwhelmed and dominated the old Ashkenazic and Romaniot (Greek-speaking) Jews of Bulgaria, so that the separate Jewish communities joined into a single Sephardic enclave in the sixteenth century. With the conquest of Belgrade by the Turks in 1521, older Jewish settlements in the city were revivified by Sephardic refugees. By far, the greatest concentration of Sephardic Jewish life and culture in Europe soon after the Spanish expulsion was in the city of Salonica in Greece (then part of Ottoman Turkish suzerainty).

For hundreds of years, Jewish culture in the Balkans emanated from the Sephardic cultural center of Salonica. On the eve of World War II, Salonica, with its 60,000 Jews, its printing presses and newspapers, its schools and scholars, its craftsmen and merchants, was the greatest Sephardic Jewish center in Europe. This premier place of Salonica had been established in the early sixteenth century, as waves of refugees settled there and dynasties of great rabbinic scholars and personalities issued legal decrees from its academies. While to the outside world these refugees were simply "Sephardim," internally they were divided by geographic origin, their synagogues bearing the names of Saragossa, Barcelona, Gerona, Gerush Portugal, Castille, Aragon, and a score of other Iberian place names. Each of the separate congregations boasted its own nexus of self-help institutions, such as alms chests, burial societies, sick care, and chests for orphans and widows. In addition, each congregation took pride in its academy of learning. Sixteenth-century Salonica was a center of learning of the Talmud that attracted students from abroad, its luminaries including such Jewish personalities as Solomon Alkabez and Samuel da Medina. It was also famed as a center of Jewish mysticism and provided instruction to Jews in medicine, natural sciences, liturgical poetry, and song. Although the city was weakened by successive plagues and conflagrations in the seventeenth century, its Jewish population still comprised half the population of the town throughout this period.

Salonican Jews were severely traumatized by the false messianic movement of Shabbetai Zevi in the seventeenth century, particularly as the impostor had preached in the city and had a strong personal following there. After Zevi's conversion to Islam and subsequent death, 300 Jewish families in the city converted to Islam, severely weakening the unity of Salonican Jews. In general, the Jewish communities of the Ottoman Empire began to decline as the empire grew more anarchic.

The spread of European influence and consular protection of Jews in the Balkans ushered in a new era for Sephardic Jews. The nineteenth century witnessed many signs of Westernization among the Jews, the introduction of secular subjects in the newly founded schools of the French *Alliance Israelite Universelle,* and a quickening of Jewish political life, as Zionism captured the imagination of Sephardic Jews in Greece, Bulgaria, and Yugoslavia. So vital was the Jewish community to the economy of the city of Salonica that the whole town and its port were closed on the Sabbath at the beginning of the twentieth century. (It is interesting to note that fishermen, sailors, and stevedores of Salonica played a conspicuous role in the development of maritime life in Haifa and Tel Aviv in the 1920s and 1930s, encouraged to emigrate by Palestinian leaders Yitzhak Ben Zvi and Abba Khoushi.)

Sephardic Jews had not labored under the same restrictive economic system as their Ashkenazic coreligionists. While they distinguished themselves in commerce, utilizing their widely dispersed family connections to their commercial advantage, the Sephardim were an economically variegated community in Europe, equally distributed among rich and poor, modest blacksmiths and bankers or textile magnates. They were not housed in ghettos, but rather shared in the modernization and incipient industrialization of their states.

The cultural and communal life of Sephardic Jews, up until the eve of the Nazi onslaught, was richly textured and colorful. Despite differences among them, the Sephardim of the Balkan nations shared an underlying cultural unity. A lively Ladino and Hebrew press could be found in Sephardic lands, frequently tracing its origins back to the great Sephardic printing houses of Lisbon via Italy. Romances or ballads conveying vibrant, lyrical, and frequently courtly and sensual Iberian traditions could be heard at family and communal gatherings in Rhodes or Greece, Sarajevo or Sofia. Music and poetry were staples of community life.

Religious institutions and edifices were sources of pride in the Jewish communities. New and majestic synagogues dotted the communities, such as the great Sephardic synagogue built in Sarajevo in the late 1920s, and benevolent societies flourished. Zionist politics added lively debates to community discussions. The Sephardim of Sarajevo could even boast of a Jewish Workers' Union and a Jewish choir *(Lyra Sociedad de Cantar de los Judios-Espanoles).* The great cemetery of Salonica's half-million graves was a living archeological treasurehouse of Jewish history in the area. This cemetery was desecrated and destroyed by the Nazis in the general pillaging of all the Jewish historical and cultural treasures of the city.

How does the historian measure the cultural and human loss when a community is wiped out? How does one comprehend the measure of destruction of communities that date their beginnings back to approximately 140 B.C.E., as was the case in Salonica? In the mosaic of Jewish communities, the dazzling jewels of the Sephardic Jews added a special luster to the whole. All that remains today are the oral traditions and ballads laboriously collected by anthropologists and folklorists among emigres in Israel, Paris, and New York as literary testimony of the fidelity of Sephardic Jews to their Jewish and Spanish heritages.

The Foiled Assassin: One Jew Tried and Failed to Kill Hitler in 1938

David C. Gross

The story of this one Jew's unsuccessful effort to change the course of history came to light in a brief eulogy delivered at his gravesite on a kibbutz *in Israel.*

By 1938 the threat of Nazism had become widespread. Germany was rearming. The Sudetenland had been seized from Czechoslovakia. Barbaric anti-Jewish legislation had been promulgated in Germany, threatening the very existence of that country's 600,000 Jews, as well as the Jewish community of Austria that had been "annexed" by Germany.

Like Jews elsewhere, the Jews in British-mandated Palestine were deeply worried about their coreligionists. They urged those who would listen to leave Europe and join them, and of course the Youth Aliyah movement did succeed in bringing out of Germany many thousands of youngsters. But beyond that, it was a situation of waiting and watching—and hoping.

There was one Palestinian Jew, a member of the Haganah, a member of a *kibbutz,* who took a much more serious view of things. He thought Hitler was only at the beginning of his career of murder and destruction. He believed that if the Nazi tyrant could be eliminated, many Jews would be spared suffering, and humanity's prospects would be enhanced.

At a meeting of his Haganah group, he proposed that a squad of volunteers be sent to Germany for the sole purpose of assassinating the Nazi chief. His proposal was discussed, evaluated, and rejected. Haganah said it would be an impossible task, no matter how desirable it was. The meeting went on to the next topic on the agenda.

But this particular Haganah member was not satisfied. The threat that he saw in the growing Hitler movement would not let him rest. He brooded about it for days and weeks, and then one day, he made up his mind to act. He was a taciturn man, but he held strong convictions.

He bade his family goodbye and said he was being sent on a mission abroad, without specifying any details. He packed a few clothes and secreted two guns and ammunition in his bags. In 1938 there was no direct flight from Palestine to central Europe, so the way he traveled was by train, crossing many borders, with only one goal in mind. He first crossed the border into Lebanon and then Syria,

and then the train headed west—to Turkey. The trip continued across the Bosporus, into Greece, across the Balkans, and eventually to Austria, to the country's capital, Vienna. He found a room in a modest hotel and began his period of waiting—a matter of ten days.

A parade led by Hitler was scheduled to be held in the main street of the Austrian capital, and the Haganah man's plan was very simple: to get a front-line position among the crowds sure to come out to hail their great "liberator" and to pump Hitler full of bullets. He knew he would be arrested, tried, and probably executed. He also knew he might even be shot to death on the spot by enraged Nazi followers—but he was also convinced that the deed was worth his life. He was convinced there was an impending catastrophe for mankind in general, and for the Jews in particular.

He had seen newsreels of Hitler standing up in his open car, waving at the crowds as he passed through various cities. He was a Haganah marksman, familiar with arms, and felt he could carry off his mission.

The fateful day arrived. As planned, he was among the first to arrive and found a front-line position. He was careful to stand on the side of the street where the sun would not impede his view. He felt the two pistols in his belt and knew they were ready, for he had checked them thoroughly the night before.

At last the parade began. First came the swastika-emblazoned motorcyclists. They were followed by several bands, with Nazi flags flying in the wind. The crowds all around him cheered and applauded. He remained watchful, calm, and waited. At last, there was a tremendous uproar—the Austrian Hitler-lovers were cheering; the car carrying the Fuhrer was driving slowly down the avenue.

The Haganah man followed the people's gaze—and his hands froze on the guns stuck in his belt. He felt cold sweat break out all over him, for he saw that the car with Hitler was not the usual open vehicle but a bulletproof, closed car, through which a figure of Hitler could barely be discerned. All his plans, all his hopes, all his waiting—it was all in vain.

Filled with a sense of dismay, he left the crowd and went back to his room, packed, and retraced his steps to Palestine. Only a few close friends and his wife had known of his mission. He returned to his *kibbutz,* deeply grieved in spirit, totally convinced that his unsuccessful mission was an omen of a terrible Holocaust that lay in store.

From then until his death at an advanced age, he nurtured a feeling of profound anguish. He never said those two words, but they were inscribed on his face for the rest of his life: "If only . . ."

Simon Wiesenthal: The Man, The Mission, His Message

Abraham Cooper

"I am not a speaker on Days of Remembrance, because for me, every day is a Day of Remembrance . . ."

I believe in G-d and in the world to come. When each of us comes before the six million, he will be asked what we did with our lives. One will say he became a watchmaker and another will say that he became a tailor . . . but I will be able to say, 'I did not forget you.'

Some of you may have read about Simon Wiesenthal in the newspapers, seen him on television, or even heard him lecture. Still others may only have heard about the famed "Nazi hunter."

Simon Wiesenthal's personal story closely parallels the tragedy and rebirth of the Jewish people in many ways. At the end of World War II, millions of the victors and the vanquished tried to piece together their dislocated personal, communal, and national lives. For the remnant of European Jews, this was especially difficult. Two out of every three Jews on the continent had been murdered in the Final Solution, and a once-vibrant European Jewish life and culture had been effectively wiped out.

A large number of the survivors left Europe, looking to start anew in Israel, the Americas, and Australia. One of those who chose to remain was Simon Wiesenthal. Living in Vienna, he could most effectively hunt the murderers and obtain the documents necessary to prosecute them.

The Man

Simon Wiesenthal was born in Lvov, Galicia (today the Soviet Union) in 1908 and was educated as an architectural engineer at the University of Prague. A politically involved student, he recalls that in the 1920s the response of his circle of friends to Adolf Hitler was to tell jokes: "No one was prepared to take Hitler seriously—then."

At the onset of World War II, the world changed rapidly and prospects for the Wiesenthal family deteriorated, as they did for all European Jews. Simon's stepfather was arrested by the Soviet secret police and eventually died in prison; his stepbrother was shot; he barely managed to save his mother, wife, and himself from deportation to Siberia. When the Germans invaded Russia in 1941, he was interned in a concentration camp near Lvov. Both Simon and his wife were then assigned to a forced labor camp. In Europe, the Final Solution had begun. It exacted a heavy toll on the Wiesenthal family—eighty-nine members perished without a trace. Simon Wiesenthal arranged for the Polish underground to spirit his wife, Celia, out of the camp in the fall of 1942. For two years, the blond woman passed as an Aryan in Warsaw.

The Escape

Wiesenthal escaped in October 1943, but was recaptured in June 1944. He was then sent to a camp where he certainly would have been murdered, had it not been for the German retreat from the eastern front. The SS guards, fearing that they would be transferred to the front if they had no prisoners to guard, kept a handful alive. Out of an original population of 149,000, only thirty-four remained. Wiesenthal was one of them.

Very few survived the long winter march west that ended for Wiesenthal at the Mauthausen concentration camp in upper Austria. It was there, on May 5, 1945, that an American armored unit liberated him.

The Mission

"First you will go to a sanitorium, then you will go home, and then you can build houses again." Such was the friendly advice of a United States Army captain to Mr. Wiesenthal just weeks after liberation. Not knowing that his wife was alive, Wiesenthal cried for the first time in years. There was no one from the prewar period "with whom or for whom I could live. . . . People like me don't

Simon Wiesenthal (center) is pictured in 1923 with a group of boy scouts of which he was the leader in Buchach, Poland. Only one of these boys survived the Holocaust.

need houses. We lost more than houses. We lost more than families—we lost belief in humanity, in friendship, in justice, and without these, I couldn't begin anew."

It was then that he decided to devote "a few years" to bringing the murderers to justice. "When justice would be served—then I can go back to building houses again," Wiesenthal explained. Within weeks, working for the War Crimes Section of the United States Army, along with the OSS (Office of Strategic Services) and OIC (Counter-Intelligence Corps), Wiesenthal captured the first of over 1,100 Nazi murderers.

The "few years" have evolved into half a lifetime. It has been a long and lonely journey. Many eyewitnesses never survived; tons of incriminating evidence were destroyed by the Nazis before the Allied victory; criminals often escaped prosecution after the war through Nazi underground groups such as Odessa, Six, Star, and Spider to safe havens in the Americas and elsewhere. The most frustrating fact was that, for the crucial years following the Nurenberg trials, most countries, including the United States, not only did not actively bring these people to trial, but, under the pressure of the cold war, opened their doors to thousands of these newfound "anti-Communists."

By 1954, Wiesenthal's volunteers and co-workers at his Jewish Historical Documentation Center in Linz, Austria, drifted away, and he closed his office there. Although Wiesenthal sent most of his files to Israel, he kept the dossier on Adolf Eichmann. Wiesenthal never relaxed his efforts and, with information provided by him and others, Israeli agents captured Eichmann in Argentina (May 1960) and brought him to Israel for a trial that received international attention and coverage. Eichmann was found guilty of mass murder and crimes against humanity, and was executed in May 1962.

Encouraged by this startling success, Wiesenthal re-opened the Jewish Documentation Center in Vienna, Austria, yards away from the former Gestapo headquarters. Wiesenthal now works in a country which was home to countless, unrepentant "ex"-Nazis and within a postwar society which, unlike West Germany, has never systematically tried its compatriots for crimes related to the Holocaust.

The Message

People have often asked, "What motivates Wiesenthal? Why does he persist in hunting Nazis so many years after the Holocaust? What purpose can it serve?"

Simon Wiesenthal and his wife Cyla in 1936.

Self-Portrait by Simon Wiesenthal while incarcerated in the Mauthausen concentration camp, March 1945.

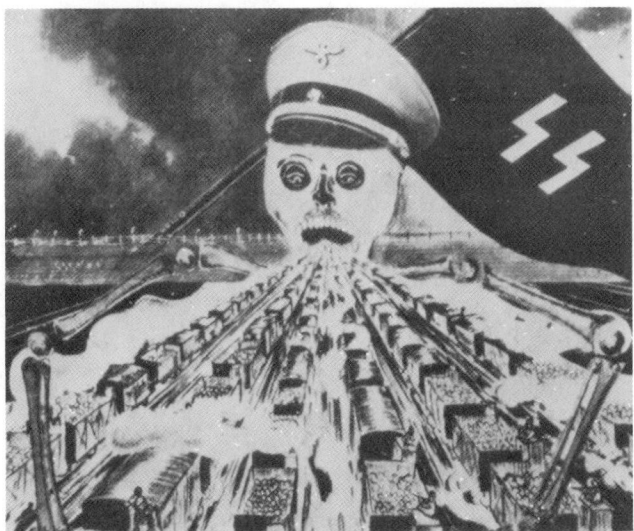

Simon Wiesenthal passed some of the time he spent in concentration camps sketching and drawing. Pictured above is one of his renderings.

"I am neither a Jewish James Bond nor a crazy Don Quixote," Wiesenthal declares. Revenge is not the aim. Wiesenthal has always opposed vigilante justice. What measure of revenge can match the crimes of a Dr. Josef Mengele, the infamous "Angel of Death" responsible for the death of 200,000 children at Auschwitz? Wiesenthal states that "It is impossible to punish these crimes. No, we need Mengele today as much as a witness as we do to try him for his unspeakable crimes. While arranging someone's death on a street in South America may be simple, it would serve no useful purpose. What we need are sentenced criminals, not martyred Nazis."

I Am My Brother's Keeper

Another way to explain Wiesenthal's motivation is by recounting the following story:

He had just delivered his third lecture in as many days. This last appearance in a moderate-sized Midwestern city drew an audience larger than the total local Jewish population. Counting the initial flight from Vienna, Wiesenthal had flown over 20,000 miles in a week. Although forty years his junior and having only to join him from Los Angeles for this tour, I was exhausted. Yet, as we sat in another airport lounge, Wiesenthal clearly relished the challenge of another appearance 800 miles away that night. My face must have betrayed my thoughts, because it was then that he told me the story of the siddur (prayer book).

"Six months after the war, I was approached by an American Polish-born rabbi serving as a chaplain in the United States Army. He had heard a rumor that somewhere deep in the forests of Bavaria, there existed a medieval castle which housed Jewish holy objects, memorabilia, prayer books, and Torah scrolls.

"It was rumored that the Nazis had planned to create museums for the 'Thousand Year Reich,' which would teach future generations about an extinct group known as Jews. The army had finally allowed them to travel there and they asked me to go along as translator. Eight hours later, after driving through the snow, we reached this castle. As

the door swung open, we knew instantly that the rumor was true. Thousands of volumes, candelabra, and other holy objects were stacked to the ceilings throughout the vast rooms. For some time, we said nothing, standing in awe of the only surviving remnants of entire communities. Finally, it was decided that we would each review a section of the castle.

"But as I ascended the staircase to check out the second floor, I heard a crashing sound. I rushed downstairs to find that the rabbi had collapsed with a small siddur in his hand. When I revived him, he could not speak—he only pointed to the Yiddish inscription in the book. It read in part: 'Whoever finds this siddur, please give it to my brother. The murderers are among us. They are in the next house. I do not know how much longer I will remain alive. Please, do not forget us—and do not forget our murderers.'"

Wiesenthal turned to me and added, "It was signed by the chaplain's sister.

"Some years later the chaplain passed away and his family sent me that precious book. It is the only prayer book in my home—I keep it on my night table next to my bed. ..."

**Excerpted from *GENOCIDE: Critical Issues of the Holocaust*, pages 384-387.

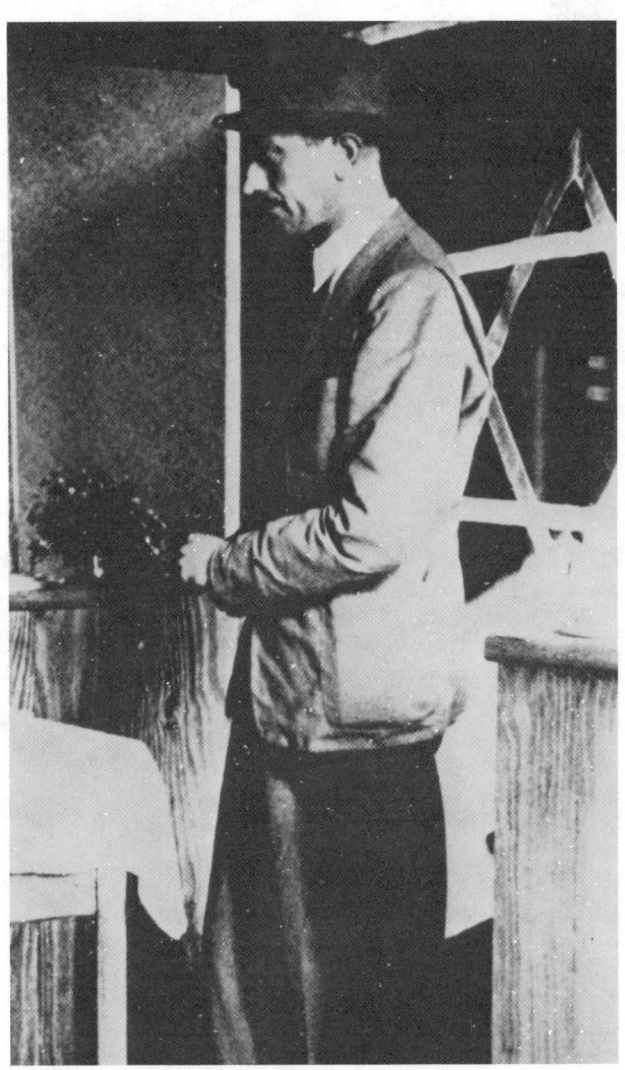

Simon Wiesenthal in the first displaced persons' synagogue in 1946.

The final scene of the film, GENOCIDE, shows Simon Wiesenthal in Israel (where his only daughter and grand-children live) at the Western Wall, the holiest of Jewish shrines, placing between the cracks of the Wall his prayer: "I am my brother's keeper." This is an apt summary of Wiesenthal's calling and his hope for young people every-where not to allow the repetition of the tragedies of past generations. Ultimately, it is they who stand to gain the most from his incredible odyssey.

Books by Simon Wiesenthal

Max and Helen, New York: William Morrow, 1982
The Sunflower, New York: Schocken Books, 1976
Sails of Hope, New York: Macmillan Publishing Co., 1973
The Murderers Among Us: The Wiesenthal Memoirs, Edited by Joseph
     Wechsbergj, New York: McGraw Hill, 1967

Honors

The list of honors received by Simon Wiesenthal:

Diploma of Honor of the Internationale of the Resistance
Dutch Medal for Freedom
Medal for Freedom of Luxemburg
Needle of Honor of the Austrian Resistance Movement
Diploma of Honor of the League of the United Nations
Dr., honoris causa, Hebrew Union College, New York, 1974
Dr., honoris causa, Hebrew Theological College, Skokie, Illinois
     (Chicago), 1976
On April 24, 1977, the foundation was laid for the Simon Wiesenthal
     Center for Holocaust Studies at Yeshiva University of Los
     Angeles, California
Annual Award of Merit for 1977 of the Decalogue Society of Lawyers,
     Chicago, Illinois, 1978
Diploma of Honor of the City of Los Angeles
Diploma of Honor of the State of California
Diploma of Honor of the Organization of the Jewish War Veterans of
     the USA
Honorary Member of the French "Institut de Recherches de
     Psychotherapie"

Simon Wiesenthal is pictured speaking at a memorial meeting before the coffin containing the ashes of Austrian Jews was taken to Israel.

Simon Wiesenthal and his daughter, Pauline, at Mauthausen in 1961.

Jean-Moulin-Medaille, Medal of the French Resistance
Kaj-Munk-Medal (Denmark)
Honorary Member of the Dutch Resistance
Honorary Member of the Danish Association of Freedom Fighters
Decoration of Honor for the meritorious Action of liberating Austria
Commander of Oranje-Nassau, given by Queen Juliana of the
     Netherlands, 1978
Commendatore de la Republica Italiana, given by the Italian President,
     Mr. Pertini, 1979
Honorary Citizen of Dallas, Texas, May 1979
Henrietta Szold Award, August 21, 1979
Honorary Citizen of Louisville, November 1979
Justice Louis D. Brandeis Award, November 11, 1980
Gold Medal of the American Congress, presented by President Carter in
     the White House, August 1980
Jerusalem Medal, 1980 presented by the town council of Jerusalem
Medal of Honor of the Yad Vashem Foundation (Jerusalem)
Proclamation of the City of New York, March 31, 1981, Day of
     Solidarity with Mr. Wiesenthal
Dr., honoris causa, Washington University, St. Louis, 1981
Commandeur de ordre pour le merite, Luxemburg, 1981
David Award, Prize of the Diaspora Jewry for outstanding
     achievements, 1981
Dr., honoris causa, of Criminal Justice, Colby College, Waterville, 1981
Dr., honoris causa, of Criminal Justice, John Jay College, New York,
     1982
Member of the International Council of Yad Vashem, Jerusalem
Grand Cross of Merit, Federal Republic of Germany, 1985

Jewish Nobel Prize Winners

Peace
1911 Tobias Michael Carel Asser (Holland)
1911 Alfred H. Fried (Austria)
1968 Rene Cassin (France)
1973 Henry Kissinger (U.S.A.)
1978 Menachem Begin (Israel)

Physics
1907 Albert A. Michelson (U.S.A.)
1908 Gabriel Lippmann (France)
1921 Albert Einstein (Germany)
1922 Niels Bohr (Denmark)
1925 Gustav Hertz (Germany)
1925 James Franck (Germany)
1938 Enrico Fermi (U.S.A.)
1943 Otto Stern (U.S.A.)
1944 Isidor I. Rabi (U.S.A.)
1952 Felix Bloch (U.S.A.)
1954 Max Born (U.K.-Germany)
1958 Igor Y. Tamm (U.S.S.R.)
1959 Emilio Segre (Italy)
1960 Donald Glaser (U.S.A.)
1961 Robert Hofstadter (U.S.A.)
1962 Lev Davidovich Landau (U.S.S.R.)
1965 Richard Phillips Feynman (U.S.A.)
1965 Julian Seymour Schwinger (U.S.A.)
1967 Hans Albrecht Bethe (U.S.A.)
1969 Murray Gell-Mann (U.S.A.)
1971 Dennis Gabor (U.K.)
1971 Gerhard Herzberg (Canada)
1973 Brian D. Josephson (U.K.)
1975 Benjamin R. Mottelson (Denmark)
1975 Aage Bohr (Denmark)
1976 Burton Richter (U.S.A.)
1978 Pyotr Kapitsa (U.S.S.R.)
1978 Arno Penzias (U.S.A.)
1979 Sheldon Glashow (U.S.A.)
1979 Steven Weinberg (U.S.A.)

Literature
1910 Paul J.L. Heyse (Germany)
1927 Henri Bergson (France)
1958 Boris Pasternak (U.S.S.R.)
1966 Shmuel Yosef Agnon (Israel)
1966 Nelly Sachs (Sweden)
1976 Saul Bellow (U.S.A.)
1978 Isaac Bashevis Singer (U.S.A.)
1981 Elias Canetti (Bulgaria)

Economics
1970 Paul A. Samuelson (U.S.A.)
1971 Simon Kuznets (U.S.A.)
1972 Kenneth J. Arrow (U.S.A.)
1975 Leonid Vitalyevich Kantorovich (U.S.S.R.)
1976 Milton Friedman (U.S.A.)
1978 Herbert A. Simon (U.S.A.)
1980 Lawrence Klein (U.S.A.)

Chemistry
1905 Adolph von Baeyer (Germany)
1906 Henri Moissan (France)
1910 Otto Wallach (Germany)
1915 Richard Willstatter (Germany)
1918 Fritz Haber (Germany)
1943 George de Hevesy (Hungary/Denmark)
1961 Melvin Calvin (U.S.A.)
1962 Max Perutz (U.K.)
1971 Gerhard Herzberg (Canada)
1972 William H. Stein (U.S.A.)
1979 Herbert C. Brown (U.S.A.)
1980 Paul Berg (U.S.A.)
1980 Walter Gilbert (U.S.A.)
1981 Roald Hoffman (U.S.A.)
1982 Aaron Klug (South Africa)

Medicine and Physiology
1908 Paul Ehrlich (Germany)
1908 Elie Metchnikoff (Russia)
1914 Robert Barany (Austria)
1923 Otto Meyerhoff (Germany)
1930 Karl Landsteiner (Austria/U.S.A.)
1931 Otto Warburg (Germany)
1936 Otto Loewi (Austria/U.S.A.)
1944 Joseph Erlanger (U.S.A.)
1944 Herbert Gasser (U.S.A.)
1945 Sir Ernst Boris Chain (U.K.)
1946 Herman Joseph Muller (U.S.A.)
1950 Tadeus Reichstein (Switzerland)
1952 Selman Waksman (U.S.A.)
1953 Sir Hans Krebs (U.K.)
1953 Fritz Albert Lipmann (U.S.A.)
1958 Joshua Lederberg (U.S.A.)
1959 Arthur Kornberg (U.S.A.)
1964 Konrad Bloch (U.S.A.)
1965 Francois Jacob (France)
1965 Andre Lwoff (France)
1967 George Wald (U.S.A.)
1968 Marshall Nirenberg (U.S.A.)
1969 Salvador Luria (U.S.A.)
1970 Julius Axelrod (U.S.A.)
1970 Sir Bernard Katz (U.K.)
1972 Gerald Edelman (U.S.A.)
1975 David Baltimore (U.S.A.)
1975 Howard Temin (U.S.A.)
1976 Baruch Blumberg (U.S.A.)
1977 Rosalyn Yalow (U.S.A.)
1978 Daniel Nathans (U.S.A.)
1980 Baruj Benacerraf (U.S.A.)
1984 Cesar Milstein (U.K.)

Judaica in U.S. Postage Stamps

Murray Frost

Jerome Kern (1885-1945) wrote the music for *Showboat,* which included "Ol' Man River" among its hits. He also won Academy Awards for "The Way You Look Tonight" and "The Last Time I Saw Paris." This stamp was the first 22¢ stamp issued in 1985.

George Gershwin (1898-1937) served as the rehearsal pianist for Jerome Kern early in his career. He went on to compose such hits as "Sewanee" and "I Got Rhythm" for such shows as *Funny Face* and *Girl Crazy.* His greatest works included *Porgy and Bess, Rhapsody in Blue,* and *An American in Paris.* The stamp was issued in 1973.

Adolph S. Ochs (1858-1935) took over the ailing *New York Times* in 1896 and built it into the nation's leading newspaper. The stamp was issued in 1976.

Rabbi Alexander Goode (1911-1943) was one of the Four Chaplains on the S.S. Dorchester who gave up their life jackets to others on board the torpedoed troopship. The stamp was issued in 1948.

Samuel Gompers (1850-1924) was the founder of the American Federation of Labor. Gompers, born in London, came to the United States as a youth and worked as a cigarmaker. The stamp was issued in 1950.

Albert Einstein (1879-1955) was born in Germany and fled to the United States in 1933. He was the winner of the 1921 Nobel Prize in Physics. His formula, $E=mc^2$, contributed to the nuclear age. Stamps depicting him were issued by the United States in 1966 and 1979. Thirty-two other nations have honored Einstein on stamps.

Haym Salomon (1740-1785) was considered the "financier of the American Revolution." His contribution was recognized with a stamp issued in 1975 as part of a set honoring "Contributors to the Cause." The glu-side of the stamp includes a description of his contribution.

David B. Steinman (1886-1960) was born in New York and went on to design many bridges around the world. One of his greatest achievements was the Mackinac Bridge connecting the upper and lower peninsulas of Michigan. A stamp picturing that bridge was issued in 1958.

Leon S. Moisieff (1872-1943) came to the United States from Riga. He became a bridge designer and his works included the George Washington Bridge connecting New Jersey and New York City. It is pictured on a 1952 stamp.

The New York Coliseum was the site of the 1956 International Stamp Exhibition. To commemorate that event, the United States issued a postage stamp. The design used was the building itself which was the creation of Leon and Lionel Levy, two unrelated architects.

The 1977 stamp to commemorate the 50th anniversary of the first talking movie has several Judaica connections. That movie, *The Jazz Singer,* was produced by the Warner brothers and starred Al Jolson. The story focused on a cantor's son who goes into show business.

Part of the poem by Emma Lazarus (1849-1887) at the base of the Statue of Liberty was quoted on a stamp issued by the United States in 1978.

In 1944 the United States commemorated the 100th anniversary of the first telegraph message. The words, "What hath God wrought . . ." are from Numbers 23:23.

In 1969 the United States commemorated the Apollo 8 mission which orbited men around the moon. In addition to the photo of the Earth and the surface of the moon are the opening words of Genesis: "In the beginning, God . . ."

In 1976 a definitive stamp depicting the Liberty Bell quoted the words on the bell which are from Leviticus 25:10, "Proclaim liberty throughout the land." Another Judaica connection for the Liberty Bell is that it was brought to America aboard a ship owned by a Jew.

The Newport Rhode Island synagogue was pictured on a stamp issued in 1982. The synagogue is known as the Touro Synagogue, named after its benefactor Abraham Touro. Although the quote on the stamp is from President George Washington's address to the congregation, the phrase had been used in the congregation's greetings to the President by Moses Seixas.

40

The First Stowaway

Arthur Schreiber

Editor's Note: What follows is the story of a young Jewish boy, the first stowaway in the history of aviation.

In those days, aircraft capable of spanning the Atlantic nonstop were extremely rare. Cruising speeds averaged 120 M.P.H. and weight factors were crucial, particularly in the tail-end of any aircraft.

On the afternoon of June 12, 1929 in the company of three friends, I went to Old Orchard Beach from my home in Portland, Maine, to look at two airplanes that were to attempt flights across the Atlantic Ocean the next day. One, the "Green Flash," was piloted by Americans Capt. Yancey and Roger Williams, and was destined for Rome. The second was flying to Paris, and had a crew of three, consisting of Armand Lotti, co-navigator and financier of the flight; Jean Assolant, chief pilot, and Rene Lefevre, co-pilot and navigator.

While looking over the two ships, my friends and I exchanged opinions, indulged in some dares and challenges out of which grew my idea to fly in one of them.

I worked with crews of mechanics and technicians through the night trying to make myself useful carrying cans of fuel, oil and water and performing odd chores in an attempt to ingratiate myself in the hope that the fliers might take me with them. In my complete ignorance of aviation, I thought that an airplane, like an auto, could take as many as could get aboard.

The next morning, June 13, at about 7:00 A.M., the crews of both planes arrived, together with reporters, camera men and hundreds of observers. I asked the two Americans to take me with them, but they pointed out that theirs was a two-place, open-cockpit plane. That finished my hopes for that flight.

Next, I asked Armand Lotti of the French plane, called the "Yellow Bird," and his negative reply to my request to accompany them left me chagrined and somewhat lessened in enthusiasm.

At about nine o'clock a call was made for volunteers to push the two planes about a mile up the beach preparatory to the take-off. I found myself on the side of the "Yellow Bird" holding the door handle for leverage. An order was given to push and as I applied my weight to the door, it swung open. This was my invitation. In full view of hundreds of people I scampered into the plane and looked for some place to secrete myself.

The Yellow Bird.

Pre-flight inspection. Note the primitive landing gear.

The Yellow Bird was a Bernard-designed high-winged monoplane powered by a 500 H.P. water-cooled Hispano-Souza engine. It had a stand-up cabin eight or ten feet long and about seven feet wide. I went to the rear of the cabin where it tapered to about three feet in diameter and where a double hinged door led to the tail. I settled my 120 pounds in a contorted position so that I would not interfere with the cables that ran through that sector.

I was aware of the ship's motion while it was being pushed; and the next sensation I perceived was the tremendous vibration when the engine was started. I remained crouched in the tail until I became so uncomfortable that I had to come out from my hiding place.

At this point I decided that I had achieved my desire to be in an airplane and feel the thrilling sensation of power delivered by the engine. I was satisfied that I could have also flown, but because of the discomfort, I decided just to get out of the plane and call it an adventure. My excitement caused me to lose all sense of time.

As I went through the swinging door into the cabin, I saw Armand Lotti seated at a little table with a map on it. He was in the front of the cabin and his back was to me. The door to the plane was on the left which made it ideal for me to

get out without disturbing Mr. Lotti. No one would be the wiser and I would have a great story to relate to my friends.

Then, the first shock. I stealthily reached for the door handle when I saw through the window that we were airborne and the shore was about five miles away.

Now I had no choice—I had to reveal my presence aboard—and I was frightened. For the first time during the venture I had misgivings about my actions. Mr. Lotti had refused when I asked him to take me along. Now how would he and the crew react? I was still oblivious to the hazards my weight caused to the plane's balance and fuel consumption.

I turned to the right and tapped Mr. Lotti on his shoulder. He turned his head and looked at me incredulously in open-mouthed amazement. He shook his head and spoke to me, words I could not hear. He then wrote a note asking me to explain myself. I answered by note, reminding him that I did ask him to take me along. He then placed me in the center of the cabin and motioned me to stand there while he went forward through a catwalk between fuel tanks to Jean Assolant and Rene Lefevre. I saw Mr. Lotti point to me and then, alternately, Lefevre and Assolant looked back to inspect me. At this point I would have evaporated if I could. The three exchanged communications after which Mr. Lotti wrote me that they had decided to make me a member of the crew. He then brought out a bottle of cognac and poured four drinks into thermos bottle caps and offered a toast, thus initiating me as a member of the crew. Their decision, I now realize, was in effect their concession to me of my chance to live or die with them. And for that I will never stop being grateful.

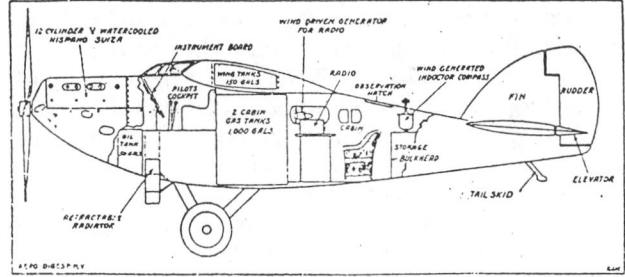

Cross-section of the Yellow Bird.

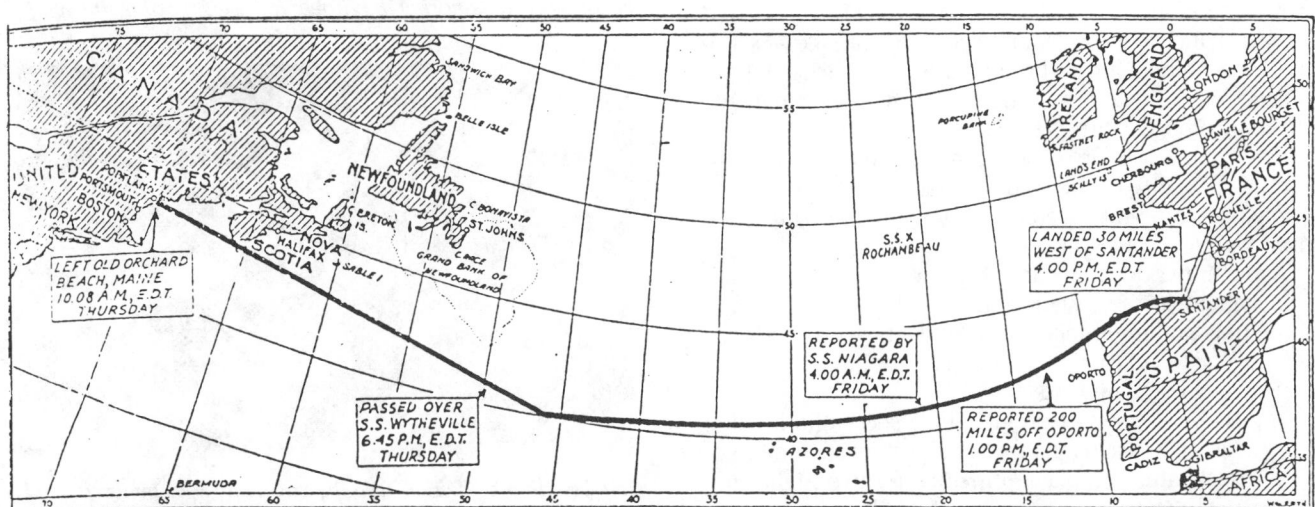

Map showing the course taken by the Yellow Bird *in flying from Old Orchard, Maine, to Santander, Spain.*

The Yellow Bird.

flew to a military base at Cazieux and from there, to LeBourget.

When my idea to fly first took form a few days before, I went home and donned a discarded outfit that my elder brother had used when experimental parachute jumping with the U.S. Air Corps. I was influenced by the motion pictures of that era when fliers all wore butterfly trousers, leather boots or puttees, jackets, helmets and goggles. I was so attired when we arrived in Paris and, ironically, the three fliers all wore business suits.

I was also invited to many receptions and was treated very kindly by the French people and the press. I was Mr. Lotti's guest at the Hotel Lotti for four days. I then returned to the U.S. by boat arriving in New York on June 26, 1929, after the thirteen most glorious days of my life.

That I am able to recount that great adventure is testimony to the graciousness and thoughtfulness of those three gallant pioneers of the sky, Assolant, Lefevre and Lotti.

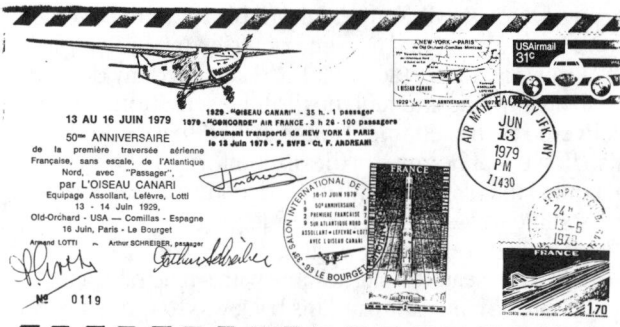

First-day cover honoring the fiftieth anniversary of the flight of the Yellow Bird.

I was assigned some duties including reeling out an antenna and setting a wind-driven generator for power when the radio was put to use and returning them to their stationary positions after use. I was briefed by Mr. Lotti and my first solo performance resulted in the loss of a panel which had to be removed from the side of the cabin to permit the generator's blade to catch the wind. The resultant cold air that came in from the opening was another handicap that I imposed on the brave gentlemen.

We experienced both fair and bad weather, and when the plane quivered and lurched and because of tense excitement, I was more than a little frightened. I remember seeing two ships and the Azores, and after passing the islands a violent electrical storm was encountered. At one point the plane fell so fast and far that Mr. Lotti and I clasped hands in expectation of crashing into the sea. The two fliers at the controls brought the plane back to a level position and Mr. Lotti told me that we were less than 100 meters from the water. He also informed me that, many hours back, our course had been changed from Paris to Portugal because of the storms. And, he added, the three compasses on board were in disagreement and calculations were complicated.

After thirty-odd hours and the storms behind us, land was sighted in the distant horizon—thanks to God and three outstanding French fliers! Mr. Lotti again produced the cognac to celebrate. Our hearts were lighter with the prospect of reaching land.

Shortly before sunset on June 14, a successful landing was made on a beach near the small fishing settlement of Comillas, Spain. The plane remained for two nights and one day at the beach where it was refueled for the next leg, to Mimizan, France. At Mimizan we re-fueled again and

The three Frenchmen allowed the stowaway to be honored at all the celebrations. In his leather jacket, Arthur Schreiber looked more like an aviator than they did.

THE PALESTINE POST

INCORPORATING The Palestine Bulletin

Telephone Numbers 733 & 734

IX. No. 2343. JERUSALEM, TUESDAY, JANUARY 31, 1933 (Sh'vat 4, 5693 — Shawwal 4, 1351.) Price: 10 Mils.

ERR HITLER NEW GERMAN CHANCELLOR

K OF PARLIAMENTARY ORITY CAUSES APPOINTMENT OF NAZI CHIEF

he New Cabinet Confirmed

rlin, Monday.— Following a rence of President von Hinburg, Dr. Alfred Hugenberg, f Hitler, and Fritz von PaHitler was appointed Chanr of Germany, von Papen deng that the formation of a rnment on the basis of a parntary majority was impos-

is expected in political circles Hitler will be given the auty to dissolve the Reichstag set new elections. The new net is composed of Herr Frick, ster of Interior, von Neurath, ster of Foreign Affairs, Seldte sident of the Stahlhelm,) Mir of Labour, and Dr. Hugen, Minister of Economics and culture.

l ministerial appointments been confirmed. Von Papen been appointed Reichscomioner of Prussia, and Count erin von Krosigk, Minister of nce.

Reuter/P.T.A.

mer German Colonies in Africa

r Lindequist on the Way to Capetown

ndon, Sunday. — Herr von equist declares that there is olitical significance to be atd to his African visit. terviewed by Reuter aboard Watussi he said that he was g to see old friends in old s. "I do not even know", he d, "how long I shall be there. ay be two months but the is a private affair."

tterdam, Saturday.— Herr quist, the former German rnor of South West Africa, is the leader of a movement ermany for the return of the er German Colonies in Africa. passenger aboard the Watussi Capetown.

proposes to visit South West a and Tanganyika. He reely declined to interview Reucorrespondent, who was not allowed on board the Wa
Reuter/P.T.A.

T TURKISH EXPOSITION

Turkish Ministry of Economy Finance is occupied now with reparation and construction of

De Lodier Heads French Cabinet

LEFT WING RADICAL ACCEPTS PREMIERSHIP

Paris, Monday. — Despite the first report stating that he had reserved his reply, which is the usual procedure in such circumstances, M. de Lodier, left wing Radical, who was Minister of War in the Boncour cabinet, has definitely accepted the French premiership.

M. de Lodier, in a statement to the press, declared that he was quite aware of the difficulties of the moment, but believed that their solution was only a question of determination and energy.

Reuter/P.T.A.

Lancashire Cotton

MANCHESTER GUARDIAN ON EXPLOITATION

London, Sunday. — Commenting on the Manchester Chamber of Commerce report, the Manchester Guardian says that the Chamber will only have itself to blame if its word are used to foment Nationalist feeling and to prove that Lancashire is ready for selfish interests to go to the lengths of wrecking the Government's schemes for Indian self-government.

The words of the Chamber's report may be taken to imply that Lancashire is not content with the method of friendly negotiation begun at Ottawa, which bore fruit in preference for Lancashire, but insists that her right to exploit the Indian market is superior to the rights of the Indian Legislature.

Why do not the directors of the Chamber, asks the journal, admit and make the best of the fact that the day has gone when Westminster can dictate what India buys.

Reuter/P.T.A.

PACIFIST ACQUITTED BY FRENCH COURT

Paris, Saturday. — The French Military Court has acquitted the radical pacifist, M. Gilbeaux, of the charges of having spread anti-French propaganda in other countries, and of having inflicted ill-treatment on French subjects when they were in Russia. M. Gilbeaux, who is an ex-officer, a veteran of the French delegation sent to Russia during the war, has since become a bolshevist. In 1919 he was condemned to death for desertion. Since then, he has lived in exile. He had only recently returned to France, to ask a rehearing of his trial. B.P.O.

AUSTRALIAN TENNIS CHAMPIONSHIP

Melbourne, Sunday. — Australian Tennis Championships, Semi-finals— Gledhill beat McGrath 6/4, 6/1 6/1. Crawford and Moon beat Allison and Van Ryn 10/8, 6/3, 6/4. Vines and Gledhill beat Cummings and Hassett 6/2, 6/3, 7/5. Reuter/P.T.A.

INTERNATIONAL SOCCER

THE COMING WASHINGTON MEETING

STATEMENT BY MR. ROOSEVELT AND BRITISH AMBASSADOR

Preliminary Understanding

New York, Monday.— Mr. Franklin D. Roosevelt and Sir Roald Lindsay, British Ambassador in Washington, after a conference, issued a joint statement to the effect that they had conversed satisfactorily concerning tentative arrangements for the meeting with British and other representatives in Washington, which they hoped to begin early in March.

Newspapers are of the opinion that Mr. Roosevelt wants to reach a preliminary debt understanding with Britain on the same pattern as the Hoover-MacDonald naval parity agreement.

Reuter/P.T.A.

RAISING WHOLESALE COMMODITY PRICES

U. S. A. and Britain Cooperating

London, Monday (B.O.W.P.)— Sir Robert Horne, a former Chancellor of the Exchequer, in a broadcast speech to the United States last night, said that the British Government had declared its intention to employ all legitimate measures to raise wholesale commodity prices. For, as he could judge, the policy of United States has been directed to the same object. The joint declaration by America and Great Britain that such was their object and that the monetary policy would be designed to that end would of itself start and stimulate the movement in the desired direction.

FOG FOLLOWS FROST IN ENGLAND

Royalty Enjoy Skating

London, Monday (B.O.W.P.)— There was a general thaw throughout Great Britain yesterday, although in some parts it was still possible to skate, and today the frost was succeeded by fog locally.

The Prince of Wales and the Duke of York enjoyed about an hour of skating on Virginia water, Windsor Great Park, on Saturday. They moved freely with hundreds of skaters on the ice which was in an excellent condition. The Prince again watched skating on lake yesterday but did not participate.

ABYSSINIAN EMPEROR AT ADEN

Aden, Saturday. — A great welcome was accorded to Haile Salassie, Emperor of Abyssinia, on his arrival here on board the British sloop Penzance on a brief private visit.

The Emperor, who will visit

Removal of Irish Partition Urged

DE VALERA DISCUSSES ANGLO-IRISH PEACE

Mr. De Valera, interviewed by Reuter, said that the removal of the partition of Ireland was a necessary preliminary to the establishment of true and lasting peace between Ireland and Great Britain. Nevertheless, there would have to be a different temper before proposals were made to the six Northern counties.
Reuter/P.T.A.

Settling the Oil Dispute

UNDERSTANDING REACHED

Geneva, Monday.— It is reported that M. Benes has reached a basis of understanding with both parties in the Anglo-Persian dispute. It is understood that an agreement has been submitted to the two governments, and if they confirm it, the Council of the League will merely have to give its benediction to the arrangement. Reuter/P.T.A.

LADY BAILEY MISSING

London, Monday (B.O.W.P.)— No news has been received of Lady Bailey since early on Saturday. She left San Xavied on the South Coast of Spain, bound for Paris.

GALSWORTHY NOT BETTER

London, Monday (B.O.W.P.)— Mr. John Galsworthy, the famous novelist, who from some weeks has been seriously ill, was reported to be not quite so well this morning following a restless night.

Centenary Of Gordon's Birth

SERVICE IN ST. PAUL'S

London, Saturday. — The base of the statue of General Gordon in Trafalgar Square was decked with flowers to-day on the occasion of the centenary of Gordon's birth.

A special memorial service was held in St. Paul's Cathedral, the congregation including the Duke and Duchess of York, officers and men of the Royal Engineers, Chelsea Pensioners, and several officers and men who served in the relief expedition to Khartoum in 1884-1885. Reuter/P.T.A.

GENERAL WHO FOUGHT WITH BIBLE AND SWORD

Men who took part in the relief expedition to Khartoum in 1885, when British troops fought their way into the town only to find that General Gordon had been killed by the Mahdi after a siege of 317 days, took part in the celebrations of the centenary of Gordon's birth.

They were among the members of the Old Comrades' Association of the Royal Engineers, the corps in which Gordon served for 30

PROGRESS OF HAIFA LAST YEAR

CITY'S PROSPERITY UNAFFECTED BY HARD TIMES

Chamber of Commerce Report

Haifa, Monday.— The world crisis which reached its peak in 1931, although it showed signs of mitigation in 1932, is still sowing its seed of economic evil, Mr. Nathanson, Chairman of the Jewish Chamber of Commerce of Haifa, declared in opening the annual meeting at the Anglo-Palestine Bank last night. His report contained a review of economic conditions in the world in general and in Palestine in particular. The export trade of most countries is still on the downgrade, said Mr. Nathanson, budgets of various governments still show huge deficits, and the world-wide problem of unemployment remains as yet unsolved. Instability of currency, insecurity of stocks and bonds, inability to pay debts, whether national or international, all these circumstances characterise the condition of the world at large today.

In Palestine, however, the reverse is true. Foreign trade is on the increase, the government treasury shows a large surplus, and unemployment is at a minimum, despite the constant growth of the population caused by the large influx of immigrants during the past year. Foreign capital has also been streaming into the country, a sign of confidence in the economic future of Palestine.

(Continued on page 5.)

centenary celebration and in the evening General Sir Bindon Blood, senior colonel commandant of the R.E.'s, broadcast an appreciation of Gordon, whom he knew in the sixties.

Few events created such a sensation in the England of the last century as the death of Gordon. Gordon, the soldier who fought "with a sword in one hand and a Bible in the other" had won a great hold on the affections of the public and the progress of the expedition for his relief had been followed with the deepest interest

"Chinese" Gordon was one of the most romantic figures in the annals of British military history. He served against the Chinese in the war of 1860-2 and was subsequently made a commander of their forces and a first class mandarin.

Disgusted, however, by their breach of faith in executing captured rebel leaders, he refused the gifts and honours offered him by the Emperor of China.

His great work was the abolition of the slave trade in the Suda

THE PALESTINE POST

INCORPORATING The Palestine Bulletin

l. IX. No. 2379.   JERUSALEM, WEDNESDAY, MARCH 15, 1933.   (Adar 17, 5693 — Zu (a) 1 Qadeh 18, 1351.)   Price: 10 M

TELEPHONE
Your News
To Us
CALL 733

3.44 Dollars – £

BUSINESS AS USUAL IN 12 CITIES

LONDON MARKET REOPENS

TREASURY SELLING SHORT TERM ISSUES

Washington, Monday.— President Roosevelt has explained that the Federal Reserve member banks will be licensed to open to-day, the Clearing House member banks to-morrow and the banks of the smaller communities on Wednesday.

A progressive plan has been adopted to afford time for the necessary shipments of new currency.

The twelve cities that have been permitted to resume banking operations on Monday are Boston, New York, Philadelphia, Cleveland, Richmond, Atlanta, Chicago St. Louis, Kansas City, Minneapolis, Dallas, and San Francisco.

In the meantime Mr. Woodin has announced that the Treasury would sell short term issues (totalling 800 million dollars) of Treasury certificates on March 15, to meet the maturing indebtedness on certificates totalling 695 million dollars and raise about 59 million dollars to meet public debt payments. The issues will bear four and four a half per cent interest respectively.   Reuter/P.T.A.

London, Monday (B. O. W. P.)— On the London Exchange, dealings were restored in dollars this afternoon, and the New York cable rate was quoted at 3.44 which compares favourably with the rate of 3.44 3/4 at the close of Friday, March 3, the last occasion on which dealings took place. Business began at the same time in other centres, at an hour corresponding with the opening of the 52 United States banks authorised to begin business today.

The London Stock Markets generally closed on the dull side. Internationals were weaker, and Kaffir shares improved. War Loan 3 1/2 per cent closed at 99.

19 YEAR OLD AIRMAN FOUND

160 MILES FROM CAPETOWN

London, Monday (B. O. W. P.) - Victor Smith, the 19 year old South African airman, has been found in the Vanrhynsdorp district only 160 miles from Capetown. He left Walvis Bay, 800 miles from Capetown, yesterday evening with a fair chance of lowering Amy Johnson's record of 4 days and 7 hours for the England-Cape flight. He encountered fog, however, and ran short of petrol, being forced to land in the dark. When he failed to arrive in Capetown, several planes set out to search for him.

Rates of Exchange

As will be seen from the quotations below, the dollar was given on Monday for the first time since March 3, on exchange notices. The British Official Wireless Press quoted 3.39 per pound sterling; another message says the New York cable rate was quoted at 3.44, comparing favourably with the rate of 3.44 3/4 which was the quotation at the close of Friday, March 3, the last day on which dealings took place.

The Anglo-Palestine Bank quoted the New York rate as fluctuating between 3.40 and 3.44.

	B. O. W. P.	A. P. B.
Paris	86 7/8	87 1/4
New York	3.39	3.40 - 3.44
Zurich	—	17.75
Trieste	—	.67 1/8
Brussels	24.45	24.50
Prague	—	115
Berlin	—	14.4
Montreal	4.15 1/2	—
Geneva	17.65 1/2	—

A Reuter cable from Berlin states that Reichsbank shares have dropped on rumours that the German Government intends to strengthen the state control of and even to nationalise the bank.

Doctor Luther's early resignation is expected in financial circles.

California Shocks Now Number 35

PNEUMONIA AMONG REFUGEES

New York, Monday.— Three shocks in California early yesterday morning brought the total number of shocks to thirty-five.

Twenty-nine cities in South California are reported to have been seriously damaged to the extent of between thirty and fifty milion dollars. The inhabitants of the affected area spent a second sleepless night in the chilly open air huddled around camp fires. Many of them are developing pneumonia.   Reuter/P.T.A.

NEW AMERICAN AMBASSADORS

Mr. Jesse Straus To France

London, Monday (B. O. W. P.)— The retiring United States Ambassador in London, Mr. Andrew Mellon, sails for home in the s.s. Leviathan on Friday.

President Roosevelt today sent to the Senate the nominations of Mr. Bingham as Ambassador to London, Mr. Jesse Strauss as Ambassador to France and Mr. Josephus Daniels as Ambassador to Mexico.

The Oil Pipe Line

WORK ON PALESTINE SECTION

Work on the Palestine section of the Iraq Petroleum Company pipe line from Iraq will commence in May, it is understood.

The continuation of the line from Trans-Jordan will cross a good part of the Plain of Jezreel on its way to Haifa.

ANOTHER PIPE LINE

Baghdad, Saturday.—It is learned from reliable sources that the British Oil Development Company intends to lay a new pipe-line in its zone of concession west of the river Tigris, ending in Lattakiah, in Syria, on the Mediterranean.   B.P.O.

NEW GOVERNMENT APPOINTMENTS

It is officially notified for general information that the following appointments to the Public Service of Palestine have been made by the Secretary of State:—

Mr. F. J. Salmon, Director of Land Registration and Survey, Cyprus, to be Director of Surveys.

Mr. T. Dawe, O. B. E., Director of Agriculture, Cyprus, to be Director of Agriculture and Forests.

Mr. C. E. de B. Biden, Deputy Auditor, Gold Coast, to be Auditor.

The official announcement of these appointments was foreshadowed in the Palestine Post on March 12.

LAND TAX LAW IN TRANS-JORDAN

Amman, Monday. — A land tax law, repealing the old Turkish law and consolidating the tithe, the road, and the house and land taxes, has been passed by the Legislative Council, approved by the Emir, and will be promulgated on April 1.

The new law is said to be an improvement over the old and will make for a more just incidence of taxation.

The present session of the Legislative Council has been prolonged until March 30.

Constable Convicted on Assault Charge

Police Constable Lodge, convicted yesterday on the charge of assaulting Abraham Betromovitch, a taxi driver, on the night of February 13, was sentenced by Mr. P. E. F. Cressall, in the Chief Magistrates' Court to pay a fine of L. P. 5 or serve a month's imprisonment.

Mr. Cressall, in delivering judgment, said that "The complainant's story and that of his witnesses must be believed. . . . The accused could not be said to have acted reasonably in the circumstances."

Further details of the case will be found on Page 4, in the Law Courts section.

ARAB CONGRESS POSTPONED

The Falastin reports that the Arab Congress scheduled to be held in Baghdad will be postponed until the fall, because of lack of

JEWS FLEE NAZIS' REIGN OF TERROR

LONDON HEARS OF APPALLING PERSECUTIONS AND ANTI-JEWISH MEASURE

MAX REINHARDT FORCED TO FLEE

Berlin, Tuesday.— London newspapers describing the appalling anti-Semitic Nazi reign of terror, declare that the bodies of Jews are daily recovered from the Spree, the Berlin canal.

Nazis in Koeln have ordered the immediate suspension of Jewish slaughter houses, confiscating all ritual appurtenances and driving Jewish butchers from the market.

Jacob Leshchinsky, who was arrested on Saturday, was released today and ordered to leave the country by Thursday.

Political police raided the Jewish Telegraphic Agency office here, finding nothing of an incriminating nature in an hour and a half search. Normal work has been resumed by the news agency.

Max Reinhardt, the famous theatrical producer, it is reported, has fled to Vienna.   P.T.A.

Appeal to Polish Government

Warsaw, Tuesday.— 2,000 Polish Jews living in Saxony have requested the Polish Government to grant them passports, to enable them to leave Germany.

More than a hundred Leipzig Jews have already crossed the German border to enter Poland. So far, more than five hundred Polish Jewish families have re-entered their native country.

Republican Flag Definitely Discarded

Berlin, Monday.— The Republican black, red and gold flag has been discarded. The old Imperial black, white and red has been restored as national colours by a Presidential decree. This was announced by Herr Hitler by broadcast. The Swastika flag shares full equality with the Imperial flag and will be flown simultaneously on public buildings.

Herr Hitler described the flag order as "symbolic of the marriage of tradition and the young national revolution." He was commanded all public buildings in Germany to fly both flags for three days.

The Imperial Prussian flags were flying in Berlin on Sunday as a sign of mourning for Germany's war dead, memorial services for whom were held throughout Germany. President Hindenburg in the uniform of a Field-Marshal with Herr Hitler, and other Ministers took the salute of the Reichswehr, Steel Helmets and Nazi Storm Troops after the memorial service in the Opera House of Berlin.

Nazi Chancellor Against Terrorism

Herr Hitler again has sternly from terrorism. He says that Nazi victory is so overwhelming that they "cannot stoop to petty revenge." It was their to restore a feeling of absolute curity in the interests of the ple, and especially for busin "Only when our enemies com acts of violence will you be missioned to smash resist ruthlessly."

And "Unknowns" Shoot Solicitor

Herr Kiels Spiegel, a well known solicitor, who acted for the man Socialist party in coun political lawsuits was shot at his home at 2 a.m., on Sun by what the police describe "unknown" assailants.   Reuter/P

French Alarmed by Nazi Inva Of Demilitarised Zone

London, Monday.— The N penetration into the demilitar zone, which alarmed France, been extended by the occupa of Speyer and Cologne where troops have taken possession the Rathaus. The chief bu master, Herr Adenaurer, has suspended by the Nazi Herr R   Reuter/P

35 EXECUTIONS IN MOSCOW

SHOT FOR ALLEGED WRECKAGE

Moscow, Monday.— Thirty persons described as "descend ants of the bourgeois and l owner classes" have been shot, cording to an announcement m by the O. G. P. U. They w sentenced on charges of coun revolutionary activity and wr age in connection with So farms in the Ukraine, North casus and White Russia.

Twenty-two others were s enced to ten years' imprisonm and eighteen to eight years pectively.   Reuter/P.T.

JAPAN TO ANNEX MANDA ISLANDS

Tokyo, Monday.— Following decision of the Cabinet to w draw from the League of Nati it was also decided to annex Caroline Islands, which are u Japanese mandate.

This decision has been submi to the Emperor for approval.   B.P.O

CRICKET

M. C. C. v. South Australia

Adelaide, Monday.— Lunch sco M. C. C. second innings 96 fo Tea Score: M. C. C. 208 for wickets.

Close of play:
M. C. C. 371/8. Leyland 152

THE PALESTINE POST

Vol. IX. No. 2565. JERUSALEM, SUNDAY, OCTOBER 29, 1933. (Hshvan 9, 5694 — Ragha'b 11, 1352.) Price: 10 Mils.

ROYAL PLOT IN AUSTRIA

SENSATIONAL DISCOVERY IN RAID ON PRINCES' CASTLE

Vienna, Saturday.— A sensational discovery, which is alleged to connect German princes with the last attempt on the life of Herr Dolfuss, the Chancellor, was made this afternoon in a raid on the castle of Princes Rainer and Ernst of Sachsen-Coburg-Gotha, at Redning, Styria, and the residence of Dr. Guenther, the stepfather of Herr Dollfuss. The assailant is stated to be Rudolf Dertil.

A letter has been found from Rudolf Dertil's brother Kurt begging for financial support, the purport of which is not yet clear.

Kurt Dertil has been arrested. The distant relatives of Hitler's are among others arrested on the charge of alleged connivance.

Reuter/PTA.

FRENCH CABINET FORMED

Paris, Friday.— The Cabinet has been composed as follows:—

Premier and Minister of Marine, M. Sarraut.

Foreign Affairs, M. Paul Boncour.

Interior, M. Chautemps.

War, M. Daladier.

Finance, M. Bonnet.

Budget, M. Abel Gardey.

Agriculture, M. Queuille.

Commerce, M. Laurent-Eynac.

Public Works, M. Paganon.

Labour, M. Frot.

Education, M. de Monzie.

Colonies, M. Pietri.

Air, M. Pierre Cot.

Justice, M. Dalamier.

Merchant Marine, M. Jacques Stern.

Health, M. Lisbonne.

The Cabinet is mainly Radical with slight extensions to either side.

Reuter.

KING'S CHRISTMAS BROADCAST

London, Saturday.— His Majesty the King will broadcast a Christmas message again this year.

Reuter P.T.A.

PALESTINE POST EXTRA

ORTHODOX JEWS' PROTEST

A delegation of Orthodox Jews who posted themselves at the door of the pressroom in the Hassolel Building last Friday afternoon and protested against work being done on the eve, contributed to the difficulties of the Palestine Post in issuing the Government bulletin relating the situation in Jaffa. They were dispersed by police whom it was necessary to summon to allow the bulletin to be printed.

The cries of the protestors which were uncontrolled as they asked the publishers should have "Have pity on Jerusalem," attracted crowds of passers by to the scene. The necessity for issuing the bulletin was explained to the delegation who would not desist from the demonstration.

The Bulletin, it is believed, had a quieting effect on the population of this city which had received no other reliable news.

We appreciate the comments received, of which the following is one.

Jerusalem, Oct. 27, 1933.

Dear Editor,

Congratulations and appreciation for your prompt issue of the Extra on Friday and thereby relieving an anxious population...

NAZIS CHARGE BRITISH JOURNALIST

"DAILY EXPRESS" CORRESPONDENT TO BE TRIED FOR TREASON

London, Friday. (BOWP.) — The British Consul-General in Munich, Mr. Gainer, who since Tuesday has been denied access to Mr. Noel Panter, the Munich Correspondent of the "Daily Telegraph," was to-day permitted to visit him at Munich Police Headquarters where he has been held under "protective custody."

Panter is to be charged at Leipzig under Article 92 of the penal code with high treason and espionage the penalty for which is death or penal servitude for life. It is assumed that Panter's arrest is in connection with his descriptive report reproduced in last Monday's "Daily Telegraph" of the parade of storm troops which Chancellor Hitler addressed at Kelheim on Sunday. The German journalist Herr Ackermann has been arrested on a similar charge.

Article 92 of the criminal code provides for punishment by penal servitude for not less than two years of

(Continued on page 4, col. 1.)

ALARM AT LORD RATENDONE'S HOME

London, Friday. The police are investigating a mysterious occurrence at the house in Victoria Square of Viscount Ratendone, the Viceroy's heir, who it is understood will be leaving for India on Monday.

Lord Ratendone's neighbour, Miss Dorota Flattau, the novelist, was giving a party. She went to her study, heard a noise outside the window, and on investigating saw a man, whom she describes as an "Indian" crouching on a flat roof outside Lord Ratendone's bathroom with an eighteen inch curved knife in his hand. She challenged him and he threatened her, whereupon she threw a flower-pot at him and called the police.

A thorough search was made and the knife was found; also some lead piping which the intruder threw at Miss Flattau. Lord Ratendone was not at home at the time.

The police state that "there is no question of any attempt on Lord Ratendone."

After exhaustive inquiries the police no longer entertain the theory of an Indian or coloured man being concerned in the alarm raised at Victoria Square.

ARAB DEMONSTRATIONS CAUSE MANY FATALITIES

Violence And Bloodshed In Jaffa, Haifa, Nablus

DEATH TOLL MAY MOUNT TO FIFTEEN

For about a fortnight the seed of sedition was recklessly sown by the Arab leadership in this country and on Friday the crop of violence and bloodshed was reaped in Jaffa.

Friday's official death toll for Jaffa is one policeman and ten rioters. The number of seriously injured is two policemen and twenty rioters.

These figures are not claimed to be complete, and if to Friday's fatalities and grave injuries in Jaffa are added the gravely and dangerously wounded in Haifa and Nablus, in the former both Friday and yesterday, in the latter on Friday only, the number of killed may well mount to fifteen, with the fate of the injured still in the lap of the gods.

Of the police, at least one other was known to have succumbed in Jaffa on Friday, and the Haifa communique tells of a constable dangerously stabbed yesterday.

A fully authenticated account of what happened in Jaffa may not be had for some time. The police authorities have been far too preoccupied with the situation to take time to prepare a comprehensive report. But what happened in Jaffa had its repercussion elsewhere and, fortified by exaggerations of fatalities which are serious enough without them, the mobs in other places created situations which only the prompt action of the police prevented from becoming as critical as was that at Jaffa.

There have been attacks on police stations at Nablus and Haifa, and attacks on the railway station and trains at Haifa. The attacks have been repulsed not without loss of life and limb, and no serious trouble is reported from other centres.

In Jaffa it was the expected that happened. The officies' statement which "The Palestine Post" late on Friday afternoon printed in an extra edition, and which appears in this issue, gives the report which we are able to supplement from eye-witnesses' accounts.

A crowd began collecting in and near the Great Mosque in the neighbourhood of the Government Offices at an early hour. By eleven o'clock the mob numbered several thousand. Foot and mounted police were on duty in considerable numbers, with the military in reserve. Access to Government Offices was blocked by barbed wire. The arrival from Jerusalem of a number of women to join in the demonstration caused a disorderly demonstration among the crowd. Police were sent to disperse it, and one constable (No. 870), either was dragged from his horse, or the animal tripped and the rider was thrown. The constable was set upon by the crowd and severely beaten. At this point the first baton charge was made.

At mid-day, it is understood, Mr. Pollock, the Assistant District Commissioner, accompanied by the District Officer, Azmi Eff. Nashashibi, called at the meeting place of the Arab Executive Committee and delivered what was meant to be a final warning, that if the crowd did not disperse quietly, force would be used to disperse them. A large number of the members of the Committee were in conference, but the warning evidently fell on deaf ears, as did the High Commissioner's reminder last Wednesday of "their responsibility as leaders if they did not take all possible measures to stop action which might lead to conflict with the police."

It is believed that following Mr. Pollock's warning, counsel among the Committee became divided.

Whereas the Jaffa people were inclined to do what they could to call off, or at least limit, the demonstration, the Jerusalem agitators insisted on the original plan being carried out.

At 12.30 the crowd poured out of the Mosque, Arab Executive members, the committee of the youth associations and the boatmen, some carrying their oars, in the lead. The crowd formed into what was intended to be two processions — one by way of Salahi Road and Suq el Der to King George's Boulevard, the other through Manshieh. The crowds were ordered to disperse. The mob replied by hurling stones and by

(Continued on page 5.)

OFFICIAL STATEMENTS

The first official statement was issued on Friday evening just before sundown as follows:

The Arab Executive Committee announced their intention of holding on Friday, October 27, a political demonstration in Jaffa, similar to that which was disallowed in Jerusalem on October 13. The High Commissioner received the President and members of the Arab Executive on October 25 and informed them that no political procession or demonstration would be allowed in Jaffa; but that members of the Executive would be permitted to proceed to the District Offices and there hand a written protest or manifesto to the District Commissioner for transmission to His Excellency.

In spite, however, of the High Commissioner's prohibition a procession was formed today at 12.30 p.m. in the neighbourhood of the Government Offices, Jaffa, which moved towards King George Avenue. The procession was ordered to disperse but disobeyed the injunction and assaulted the Police. The Police were compelled to make baton charges, to disperse the mob, who, however, reformed and again attacked the Police. Shots were fired from the street at the Police, who were compelled in self-protection, to fire a few rounds under control. By 2 p.m. the rioters had been dispersed by the Police and quiet restored in Jaffa.

All reports show that the Police throughout acted with the greatest control and forebearance.

The Military were not called upon to intervene, as the Police had the situation in hand.

One member of the Police and 3 rioters were killed, and 7 other rioters were reported to be killed.

Two of the Police suffered serious injuries.

The estimated number of rioters seriously wounded is 20. The injured are receiving medical attention.

A large number of arrests have been made.

Complete quiet prevailed throughout Palestine, with the exception of Jaffa.

We understand that curfew has been declared in the Jaffa-Tel Aviv district from 6 p.m. to 5 a.m.

The second communique was issued at noon yesterday as follows:

At about 6 p.m. Friday night a riotous crowd gathered at Nablus

(Continued on page 4, col. 4.)

FEATURED IN LONDON NEWS

London, Saturday.— The reports of unrest in Palestine were most prominently featured in the morning and afternoon issues of the entire London Press, without comment.

POLISH PRESIDENT AND PALESTINE

Warsaw, Saturday.— President Moscicki received Deputy Gruenbaum today and discussed with him the Palestine question, prior to his departure for Palestine as member of the Jewish Agency...

NO ADVANCE OR NO RETREAT IN NAZI TREATMENT OF JEWS

Berlin, Saturday.— Herr Goebbels, addressing a meeting at Dresden last night...

Dissolution of Parliament
PAGE THREE

THE PALESTINE POST
JERUSALEM
MONDAY, OCTOBER 28, 1935
VOL. XI. No. 2870
PRICE TEN MILS.

Nazis Apply Nuremberg Laws Against the Jews in Germany

Wave of Protest Spreads

"NON-ARYANS" LOSE MUNICIPAL RIGHTS

(From Palestine Telegraphic Agency)

BERLIN, October 25. — Jews in Germany may no longer participate actively or passively in municipal elections, although they must continue to pay municipal taxes, it was announced today. The decision was taken by the authorities on the basis of the Nuremberg laws.

The announcement explained that since the Jews are no longer citizens of the Reich, they are automatically deprived of their municipal citizenships rights.

JEWISH BLOOD PERMISSIBLE

BERLIN. — An Aryan need fear no risk of "racial defilement" if he accepts a transfusion of blood from a Jew.

Professor Loeffler, of the Radical Political Department of the Nazi Party, declares there is no foundation for the belief that such a transfusion would affect the Aryan's "purity of race."

He remarks that persons guilty of spreading such an idea as that Jewish blood is not permissible for transfusions may cause damage to the health of the people since it might result in unnecessary restrictions at a moment when quick action was essential.

"Jews Will Never Forget Nuremberg"

(From Palestine Telegraphic Agency)

LONDON, Sunday. — "Whatever else the Jews may forget, they'll never forget the 'Ghetto' laws of Nuremberg and their authors," Mr. Leonard G. Montefiore, president of the Anglo-Jewish Association, said last night in an address at a meeting here of the Jewish Board of Guardians.

The speaker defended Italy against the charge that anti-Semitism flourishes in that country. He asserted that the movement is non-existent there.

LOCAL PROTEST AGAINST "GHETTO" LAWS

A conference of Jewish youth in Palestine to protest against enactment of the Nuremberg laws and against the persecution of the Jews in Germany will be called, according to a decision taken at a meeting of representatives of all sections of the Jewish youth at the Jerusalem club-house of the Hebrew Students' federation on Wednesday night.

The representative of the German boycott committee proposed that besides the protest conference the Palestinian youth should work towards strengthening the boycott without going into the question of the "transfer."

His motion was carried with only two negative votes, one from the representatives of the Y.W.H.A. and the other from Betar. The Betar representatives left the meet-

18,000 PERSONS ATTEND HYDE PARK DEMONSTRATION

(From Palestine Telegraphic Agency)

LONDON, Sunday.— A huge anti-Nazi demonstration was held here today in Hyde Park. It is estimated that about 18,000 persons attended.

The crowd adopted a resolution condemning the persecutions of the Jews in Germany and Reichsfuehrer Adolf Hitler, and in addition a resolution supporting the boycott of products imported from Germany.

GERMANY VOICES NEED FOR COLONIAL EMPIRE

(From a Special Correspondent)

BERLIN, October 26. — The efforts of the Third Reich to regain Germany's former colonies were again brought to the fore today at the opening of the colonial exhibition at Hanover.

Hitler's slogan "We Need Colonies Like Any Other Country" was the motif of the exhibition and was hung in large letters on all the walls. Dr. Gessner, the President of the Chamber of Commerce, opened the exhibition and stated that Germany suffers from over-population and needs colonies which would supply her with raw materials.

FORMER GERMAN COLONIES UNDER BRITISH AEGIS

(From Our Own Correspondent)

LONDON, October 22. — Correspondence which took place between Lord Apsley, M.P., and the Secretary of State for the Colonies, will be read with interest in Palestine. On October 5 Lord Apsley wrote to Mr. Malcolm MacDonald as follows:

"I notice the enclosed News Agency message in the paper with regard to Germany's Former Colonies.

"You will see that General Ritter von Epp, the speaker at Dusseldorf, seemed to anticipate that the colonial issue would be re-opened either by Great Britain or Germany. May I ask whether there is any likelihood of this, or whether the British Government still maintain the attitude that there is no possibility of the retrocession of German Colonies which are held by Great Britain?"

Surrender Not Contemplated

The Secretary of State replied as follows this week:

"Thank you for sending me the press cutting on the question of the desire of Germany to reopen the Colonial question.

"It has been repeatedly stated in Parliament that His Majesty's Government have never contemplated the surrender of the mandates for the former German colonies which are now under British administration; and as recently as the 9th April the then Prime Minister said, in a reply to a question in the House of Commons, that he had no reason to suppose that the German Government is under any misappre-

SYRIAN ANXIETY OVER INTERNATIONAL SITUATION

(From Our Own Correspondent)

DAMASCUS, Oct. 26.— The panic that arose out of the unstable international political situation has subsided and the price of foodstuffs has returned to normal.

LONDON OPINION DISCOUNTS ARAB ALLEGATIONS

Arms Believed to be Destined for Ethiopia

Following the seizure in Palestine of a consignment of arms concealed in a ship carrying cement, the leaders of the Arab Party in Palestine are accusing the Jews in Palestine of secretly arming against the Arabs, the Morning Post's Diplomatic Correspondent wrote on Oct. 23.

In London this allegation is not taken seriously, the Correspondent added. There is no evidence that the arms in question were intended for use in Palestine and it is thought quite possible that their eventual destination was Abyssinia.

The British authorities are making a thorough investigation into the matter and the High Commissioner has given the Arab leaders complete assurances as to the impossibility of any such plot as they allege materialising.

Anniversary of Bible Translation

The 1500th anniversary of the translation of the Bible into Armenian was celebrated this weekend in Jerusalem.

The three day festival took place at the Armenian Patriarchate of St. James and culminated with a celebration in the hall of the Theological Seminary at which were present His Beatitude the Armenian Patriarch, the Bishops and vartabeds of the community; the Vicar of the Armenian Catholic Patriarch; Archdeacon Stewart, representing the Anglican Bishop; Mr. Shiraganian, representing the British and Foreign Bible Society; and notables of the Armenian lay community.

In his concluding address, the Patriarch reviewed the celebrations which had taken place throughout the world in the Jubilee year, particularly mentioning his gratification with the celebration in London arranged at the request of His Grace the Archbishop of Canterbury and addressed by Bishop Graham Browne of Jerusalem. His Beatitude also commented on the fine unanimity with which Armenian Catholics and Protestant Armenians united to honour the translation made so many centuries ago.

The programme of the Jerusalem festival included addresses by Mr. Shahan Berberian and the Rev. Diran vartabed Uersoyian on the translation of the Bible; a pageant

Fascist Anniversary to be Marked by Huge Offensive

Ethiopian Commanders Warned

NEWS SUPPLY CUT OFF FROM GORAHAI

13TH ANNIVERSARY OF MARCH ON ROME

About fifty Fascists in uniform from Jerusalem, Jaffa and Tel Aviv attended a meeting yesterday morning at the Fascist club in Jerusalem commemorating the thirteenth anniversary of the Fascist era and the march on Rome.

The Italian Consul-General was the first speaker. He was followed by the Secretary of the Fascist club in Jerusalem who delivered a long speech on the Italo-Ethiopian conflict.

(Leader on Page Four.)

CO-ORDINATION PLAN FOR BRITISH MINERS

LONDON, October 25. — As a result of the Government's intervention with the owners, Captain Crookshank, the Secretary of Mines, announced last night to the Executive Committee of the Mine Workers' Federation that he expects to receive next Thursday a definite undertaking that selling organisations will be established in all coalfields with central coordination before next July.

Capt. Crookshank asked the Executive to consider this undertaking very carefully as signifying a substantial and permanent contribution to the structure of the industry as well as to the well-being of work-people in the industry.

Selling organisations, he said, were something practical and held out prospect of benefits to the mine workers more tangible than the arbitration tribunal, which by itself, would bring them nothing of value.

The Executive privately considered Capt. Crookshank's statement and at midnight issued a reply stating that they regretted the attitude of the Government in declining the miners' offer to submit their claims to an arbitration court and adding that they will therefore proceed with the ballot on the question of a strike as originally suggested.

A further meeting of the Executive was held this morning to consider what other steps should be taken before putting the ballot into operation.

The Miners' Grievances

Following a meeting of the Miners' Federation Executive this morning it was announced that the strike ballot will be taken on November 11, 12 and 13, that is, just before the General Election.

The Executive statement says that they regret no attempt has been made to meet the miners' demands for an increase in wages. They welcome the suggestion for a selling organisation but feel that this alone offers no solution to the problem as it will only succeed in increasing the production costs and thus prevent the owners from making advances in wages. In conclu-

(Reuter/P.T.A.)

ADDIS ABABA, Sunday. — [To] mark the thirteenth anniversa[ry of] the Fascist march on Rome, [which] occurs tomorrow, the Italians [are] preparing a great offensive [on] the Aksum-Adowa-Adigrat lin[e].

The news of tomorrow's adv[ance] was communicated by the E[mpe]ror to Ras Seyoum, command[er of] the troops in the Tigre secti[on].

Orders have also been issue[d to] the Ethiopian commanders on [all] fronts warning of a general It[alian] offensive which may be laun[ched] tomorrow.

From Harar comes a mes[sage] that it is believed that the Ita[lians] have attacked Gorahai, the [...] centre of the Ogaden district, [which] is in line of the approach [of the] Italian troops in the Webbe [Shi]beli offensive. It is also tho[ught] that the wireless station in [the] town has been bombed and dest[roy]ed.

Authorities in Addis Ababa [are] considerably perturbed over the [ab]sence of news from Gorahai. [The] station usually wirelesses twic[e a] day and for the past twenty-[four] hours there has been no messa[ge].

A RECONNAISSANCE FLI[GHT]

Major Barnes, Reuter, repre[sen]tative at Asmara, who accompa[nied] an Italian squadron led person[ally] by Count Ciano, describes a [...] mile flight over the Northern [...] with Signor Mussolini's "deat[h or] glory boys." The 'planes dived within a few hundred feet of Ethiopian machine-gun det[ach]ments, opening fire on the sol[diers] manning the guns. The Ethiop[ians] returned fire but the Italian 'pl[anes] were not damaged.

A reconnaissance failed to di[sco]ver the whereabouts of Ras [Sey]oum's forces and no large nuc[leus] of the Ethiopian force was obs[erv]ed anywhere.

Rains Handicap Offensive

The Italian offensive which [was] reported to have started on [the] Webbe Shibeli river, came to [an] early standstill last Thursday ow[ing] to the sodden character of [the] country, after the recent he[avy] rainfall, but is expected to oper[ate] again with the general offen[sive].

(Continued on Page Eight)

Last Minute New[s]

The British Government has anno[unc]ed that the sanctions prohibiting l[oans] and credits to Italy will be enfo[rced] from Tuesday, October 29. The ex[port] of arms and certain raw materials [will] be prohibited from the same day.

The French Government will not [en]force sanctions before the meeting [of] the Sanctions Committee in Geneva [on] October 31. French newspapers bel[ieve] that the early enforcement of sanct[ions] by Great Britain will have a discou[rag]ing effect on the peace efforts which [are] at present being undertaken by M. La[val].

The U. S. State Department has [re]plied to the invitation of the League [to] join the States applying sanct[ions] against Italy. The U.S. Government, [it is st]ated, has already applied an arms [...]

THE PALESTINE POST

JERUSALEM
THURSDAY, NOVEMBER 26, 1936

VOL. XII No. 3202
PRICE: TEN MILS

Dr. Weizmann's Statement
LEADER, PAGE FOUR

Russia to Elect Her First Democratic Parliament

New Constitution Adopted

13,721 Amendments to Original Draft

(Reuter)

MOSCOW, Wednesday. — The adoption today by the All-Union Congress of Soviets of the new Constitution of Russia is the prelude to the election of the first democratic Parliament since the Bolshevik Revolution.

At an extraordinary session held at the Kremlin the Congress signed its own death-warrant by

BULLETIN

The death sentence of Herr Stickling and of two Russians, MM. Leonenko and Kovalenko, have been commuted to that of ten year's imprisonment each. In the case of the six other Russians accused of "criminal wrecking and diversionist activities of counter - revolutionary groups" the death sentences will be carried out.

abdicating power to a Parliament of two Chambers.

As a result of the discussions of the past few months, attended by 25,000,000 people, the Central Executive Committee made 13,721 amendments to the original draft, affecting every chapter and article.

The grant of full civil rights to all Soviet citizens under this new Constitution was made on June 12 last when the Presidium of the C.E.C. approved of the text now adopted.

The Supreme Legislature was designed to consist of two Chambers — the Soviet of United Republics and the Soviet of Nationalities. The former was to have one representative for every 300,000 population, and the latter 10 representatives from every Federal Republic, five from each Autonomous Republic, and two from each Autonomous Province.

The Legislature was to be elected for four years, and elections, by secret ballot.

Three Germans Arrested

A Berlin message from Moscow says that three more Germans have been arrested by the Soviet authorities.

They are Herr Friedrich Boesherz, Herr Reinhold Schindler, an engineer, and Herr Herman Stammer.

The German Embassy is trying to obtain further information in regard to these arrests which took place on Saturday.

When the German-Japanese agreement to coordinate action against the activities of the Communist International was read to assembled diplomats in Berlin today, it was noteworthy that the Soviet Ambassador was absent.

The absence of an invitation had aroused the belief that the announcement would be much more grave than it actually turned out to be.

A categorical denial is given in British quarters (says BOWP) to a

Reich - Japanese Military Alliance

ANNOUNCED IN BERLIN

(Reuter)

LONDON, Wednesday. — British circles suspect that the agreement between Japan and Germany, which has been announced in Berlin, goes farther than the published terms.

It may indeed resemble an iceberg — reaching further below the surface than above. Well-informed quarters, however, have no news confirming reports that the two countries have agreed to a defensive military alliance. Such a step, if true, would naturally weaken the position of Great Britain in the Far East.

There is readiness to credit reports of a barter agreement under which German arms would be exchanged for Japanese raw materials.

Taking the published terms alone, it is felt that the agreement does not alter the situation, and it is regarded as an announcement, made for political reasons, of an old-standing affinity between the contracting parties.

Nevertheless, the agreement is not liked by Great Britain insofar as it represents a further accretion to the system of a bloc representing opposing ideologies, and any such alignment runs counter to British policy, as has been frequently made clear by Mr. Eden and Mr. Baldwin.

A message from Rome states that the Italian Government is not affected by the German-Japanese agreement and that no accord exists between Rome and Tokyo although there is an identity of views.

The Acting-Secretary of State in the United States, Mr. Walton Moore, stated yesterday that the United States is only academically interested in the German-Japanese pact.

Spain Rejects Plan For a Neutral Zone

TO BOMB FASCISTS

According to a Lisbon message, the Spanish Government has refused to cooperate in the establishment of a neutral zone in Madrid.

The Government radio station reports that Senor Del Vayo, the Foreign Minister, declared that the suggestion of the International Red Cross to this effect would mean that the Government agreed to the bombardment of the remaining districts of the capital in

DR. WEIZMANN'S ADDRESS

The Jewish problem was a two-fold problem: it was one that could be expressed in the word "homelessness" and also one of considerable world importance.

There are about 6,000,000 Jews in Central, Eastern, and South-Eastern Europe condemned to be penned up in places where they are not wanted.

Here is a people which is a minority everywhere, a majority nowhere.

Uganda was refused as a Jewish home because "it was never Palestine, it would never be Palestine."

The Jews have conferred, indirectly, considerable benefits on the Arab population.

"A Certificate for Palestine Is a Certificate for Freedom"

PRESS COMMUNIQUE NO. 13.

Wednesday, November 25.

The Royal Commission sat in public session from 10.30 a.m. to 1 p.m. and heard the evidence of Dr. Chaim Weizmann.

Dr. Weizmann stated that he is the President of the Jewish Agency for Palestine and the President of the Zionist Organization. The Zionist Organization is the Agency referred to in paragraph 4 of the Mandate. Later, in 1929, the Jewish Agency was formed. The Council of the Jewish Agency consists of 50 Zionists and 50 of others who are not Zionists but are interested in the upbuilding of Palestine. The Zionist members are elected by the Zionist Congress and the non-Zionist members are appointed by their respective groups in various countries. The Council of the Jewish Agency has an Administrative Committee, composed also of 50 Zionists and 50 non-Zionists and the Administrative Committee has an Executive Committee in Palestine composed of similar proportions which conducts the current business.

In outlining the background of the Zionist movement Dr. Weizmann stated that the Jewish problem was two-fold. The first one is the homelessness of the Jewish people. Although it may be said that there are individual Jews with homes and many comfortable homes in countries in Western Europe, East of the Rhine, in Poland, Germany, Austria, Rumania, Lithuania and Latvia, there are about 6,000,000 Jews who are condemned to be penned up in places where they cannot live and where they are not wanted.

The Jews and Palestine

The other problem is one of world importance namely, the presence of 6,000,000 people who don't know what will happen tomorrow. The young man in a depressed area in England feels that there is the State which is interested in his welfare and that there is some outlook but the Jew

Dr. WEIZMANN SPEAKS For the JEWISH PEOPLE

TESTIFIES BEFORE THE ROYAL COMMISSION

"Gov't Should Introduce Dynamic Development"

(From a Staff Correspondent)

. A vivid and profoundly moving account of the world Jewish tragedy of "homelessness" and the moral background and spiritual forces of the Zionist Movement was given to the Royal Commission yesterday morning by Dr. Chaim Weizmann, President of the Jewish Agency and World Zionist Organization.

From 10.30 until after 1 o'clock, Lord Peel and his colleagues listened to Dr. Weizmann's introduction of the Jewish case, which will be later amplified by statistical data and other material submitted by the Jewish experts.

Dr. Weizmann was accompanied by Mr. Moshe Shertok, head of the Political Department of the Jewish Agency Executive, and Mr. Leonard Stein, the Agency's honorary adviser. Visitors included Mr. David Ben Gurion, Dr. Vera Weizmann, Mr. Isaac Ben-Zvi, Mr. Nevill Barbour, Mr. N. Kirschner (of South Africa), and Dr. B. Joseph, Mr. D. G. Harris and Mr. L. Andrews, on liasion duty with the Royal Commission, also attended.

Composition of Jewish Agency

At the request of Lord Peel, the witness described the composition and functions of the Jewish Agency, its constituent bodies, and the method of their election.

Dr. Weizmann then proceeded to give what he called "a bird's-eye view" of the Jewish position and of Zionism. It was a problem, he said, which could best be expressed in the word "homelessness." Individual Jews and individual groups of Jews might have a home and be comfortably placed, but drawing the geographical line across Europe, in the eastern section one found the Jewish populations in a political and economic state which was "something neither life nor death."

No Emigration

The means of migration westwards, mostly to America, had been closed. Only recently Colonel Josef Beck, Polish Foreign Minister, had said in Geneva that there were a million Jews too many (out of 3,000,000) in Poland. Where could they go? Was there a place in the world which could rapidly absorb a million people? The witness narrated some of the causes which were ousting Jews from economic life in Poland,— principally the migration of poor Polish peasants into the towns.

A similar position existed in other "Succession States," territories formerly part of the old Russian Empire, as well as in Central and Eastern Europe.

"It is no exaggeration on my part to say," declared the Zionist leader, "that there are about 6,000,000 Jews in this part of the

In dealing with the past history of the Jews, Dr. Weizmann pointed out that there was not one period where the Jews did not try to come back to Palestine and there have always been movements of Jews into Palestine whenever the opportunity arose. The connection of Great Britain with the return of the Jews to Palestine extends over a period of 300 years and the Balfour declaration is but the final link in the chain.

The Balfour declaration was not lightly made, its form and words were the subject of serious discussion by the British Cabinet, even at a time of stress, and suggestion that it was a mere war-time expediency which might thereafter be whittled down, was unfounded. The Balfour declaration was hailed by Jewry throughout the world as the Magna Carta of the Jewish people and meant, to quote the word of Lord Cecil, "The Jews are restored to Judaea." When he ((Dr. Weizmann) was asked at the Peace Conference "What do you mean by a Jewish National Home?" he replied impromptu "To build up something in Palestine which will be as Jewish as England is English."

Referring to the conditions under which their work was begun, Doctor Weizmann stated that seldom in the history of colonization has work of the kind been carried out by private organization. He spoke from per-

(Continued on Page 8, Col. 2)

After Midnight

Dr. Chaim Weizmann will continue his evidence this morning before the Royal Commission in camera.

Six shots were fired near Napoleon Hill, Ramat Gan, last night. Police are investigating.

The French Government is making an appropriation of 10,500,000,000 francs on armaments in 1937. This is

SUBSCRIPTIONS: Local: LP.1.250 a year; LP.1.350 a half year:— Foreign: £3.- a year. The rate for display advertisements is 150 mils per column inch. Other rates supplied on request. The right is reserved to make changes in wording or to decline or discontinue any advertisement or to postpone insertions when space is not available.

THE PALESTINE POST

JERUSALEM Hasselel Road P. O. Box 81, Telephone 4233

Tel Aviv - Jaffa: 65 Allenby Road, P. O. Box 1125, 'Phone 4251-4252.

Haifa: Khayat Square, opposite the Post Office entrance, P.O.B. 66, 'Phone 1290.

SUNDAY NOVEMBER 13 1938 JERUSALEM VOL. XIV. No. 3798 PRICE 10 MILS.

NEW NAZI SAVAGERY SPELLS DOOM OF JEWISH LIFE IN GERMANY

MILITARY AND POLICE ACTION IN SEARCHES

TWELVE KNOWN ARAB CASUALTIES IN 3 DAYS

Military and police operations throughout the country during the past three days included searches in eight different localities.

One member of his Majesty's Forces was killed and three were injured in various localities.

Three Jews have been wounded, and 12 Arabs known to have been killed or wounded including a small girl, as a result of terrorism and military action since Thursday.

PLANE FORCED DOWN

When an R.A.F. machine cooperating with the military in an engagement at Beit Furik village east of Nablus, made a forced landing the pilot, Sergeant Pilot Tebbs, was seriously hurt, while Corporal George Wickens, of the Green Howards, was slightly injured in the same engagement in which heavy casualties were inflicted on the band.

Many arrests were made as a result of these searches, and over a thousand rounds of ammunition seized together with several rifles, bombs and detonators, some documents and a camera.

Shots were fired yesterday afternoon at troops who were on duty at a Traffic Control Post in the Bab Zeitun Quarter of Gaza. One British soldier was killed and another severely wounded. A 24-hour curfew was imposed as from 3 p.m.

EXPLOSION KILLS FIVE

An explosion which occurred on Thursday night in the house of Khalil el Awoor in Al Majdal, north of Gaza, completely wrecked the building, killing the owner and four other persons.

Yesterday afternoon a party of British police in a tender were fired on near Jenin police station. They returned the fire and killed an Arab who was subsequently found to be in possession of a rifle and more than 250 rounds of ammunition.

CUSTOMS GUARD SHOT DEAD

Yesterday afternoon a customs guard named Abdul Hafiz of Kalkania was shot dead by unknown assailants while walking in the Nazareth Road, Haifa.

An Arab of Kabatiya village, Samaria, Nasser el Kassem was shot

(Continued on Page 2)

AFTER MIDNIGHT

A decree was issued in Paris last night providing for the revaluation of the gold stock in the Bank of France at the rate of 170 francs to the £. Gold is now valued about 110 francs to the £. Another decree provides that agricultural production be nationalised by agreements to be reached between the parties concerned.

"We shall solve the political Catholic problem with the same consequences as the Jewish Question," declared Gauleiter Jury, the Regional Leader of Lower Austria, in addressing a Nazi meeting yesterday in Gaenserndorf.

"A BLACK DAY FOR GERMANY"—TIMES

BRITISH PRESS CONDEMN NAZI OUTRAGES

LONDON, Saturday (R. and Palcor).— The entire British press devotes space today to the riots and pillaging of Jewish houses and businesses in Germany. Comment takes the form of unprecedentedly strong condemnation, even in journals 'friendly' to Germany.

"The Times" heads its editorial with the words "A Black Day for Germany" and states that no amount of foreign propaganda could have done Germany so much harm as the events which have taken place. Similar views are expressed by other leading morning papers.

CRUELTY AND DESTRUCTION

The Archbishop of Canterbury in a letter to "The Times," expresses the feeling of indignation with which he claims Christians in Britain have "read of the deeds of cruelty and destruction which were perpetrated last Thursday in Germany and Austria."

Adding that whatever provocation may have been given by the deplorable act of a single irresponsible Jewish youth, reprisals on such a scale, so fierce, cruel and vindictive, could not possibly have been justified.

Dr. Lang calls for the remembrance in prayers offered in Churches tomorrow of those who have suffered in this fresh onset of persecution.

Sir Archibald Sinclair, leader of the Liberal Party, in a speech last night said that the treatment of the German Jews was Germany's business only so long as she did not expel them after having robbed them.

Sir Archibald said that the refugee problem must be tackled in a general spirit, and that in the light of recent events British obligations towards the Jewish National Home must be interpreted in a generous spirit.

NAZI ARMS FOR ARABS

He said that the Arabs who were incited by German and Italian propaganda, and aided by German arms, should not be allowed to frighten the British Government from fulfilling its pledges towards the Jewish National Home. He insisted that there was room in Palestine for the Jews, and that the Arab complaints were unreasonable since Jewish immigration had helped development, and the Jews must find a home.

The Foreign Under-Secretary, Mr. R. A. Butler, yesterday received a deputation consisting of Mr. Neville Laski, Chairman of the Board of Jewish Deputies, and Mr. C. G. Montefiore, President of the Anglo-Jewish Association, together with Mr. L. H. Glueckstein, M.P.

PILLAGED OF 84 MILLION POUNDS TO "PAY" FOR MURDER OF GERMAN OFFICIAL

BERLIN, Saturday (R).—Jews in Germany have been ordered to pay one milliard marks (over 80 million pounds sterling) as compensation for the murder of Herr von Rath, the secretary of the German Embassy in Paris.

The indemnity will be levied in the form of a special tax on all Jewish property. Since this property is officially valued at about 10 milliard marks, the tax will be at a rate of ten per cent.

MINISTERS' CONFERENCE

The decision was taken at a conference presided over by Field-Marshal Goering, attended by Dr. Frick, Reich Minister of the Interior, Dr. Goebbels, Minister of Propaganda, Dr. Guertner, Minister of Justice, and Count von Krosigk, the Minister of Finance.

Furthermore, all the damage "caused through the indignation of the people over the agitation by international Jews, on November 8, 9, and 10" must be made good by Jewish occupiers or Jewish businessmen, while sums derived from insurance companies will be confiscated for the benefit of the Reich.

The official communique which announces these decisions also contains the announcement that "further drastic measures for driving the Jews out of Germany's economic life and the elimination of provocative conditions will shortly be taken, in the form of laws and decrees." It is stated that "a number of the most drastic measures will be taken," the first of which have already been announced.

ELIMINATION PROCESS

From January 1, 1939, Jews will not be allowed to engage in

retail trade,
export businesses,
commercial offices or
independent handicraft businesses, and
will not be permitted to occupy managerial posts.

The decree forbidding Jews to own weapons is implemented by new measures announced today.

Further, a decree was issued by Dr. Goebbels, forbidding Jews to visit theatres, concerts, cinemas, music halls, dance entertainments, museums and exhibitions of any kind.

It was stated by Dr. Goebbels that there was no reason why Jews should visit such entertainments or exhibitions since they had their own cultural organizations. The activities of the latter have however been brought to a complete standstill, as all Jewish theatre, concert and cinema performances have been prohibited.

Jewish schools and newspapers have been closed down.

Ruin

EFFECT OF NEW DECREE

(By Our Commercial Correspondent)

The decree ordering Jews in Germany to pay a milliard Reichsmarks and the decision to levy this amount in the form of a ten per cent capital tax clearly reveals the intention to destroy whatever economic assets are left to the Jews.

The execution of this decree means irreparable ruin for every Jewish business in Germany and this apart from the order forbidding Jews to engage any longer in retail trade, since it is normally impossible for owners of businesses to raise ten per cent of their capital in cash.

Landlords, shopkeepers and security holders will thus be compelled to sell their property or shares, provided they can find buyers. To sell buildings has become extremely difficult. The market value is not taken into account, and the price is fixed by an "arbitrator," usually appointed by the Nazis.

In the case of securities the market has contracted to such an extent owing to forced investments in Government securities that small sales inevitably lead to heavy drops in prices. What will happen when large blocks of securities are suddenly offered for sale can readily be imagined.

Altogether the decrees amount to nothing less than the complete spoliation of what property still remains in Jewish hands.

PARIS, Saturday (R). — The funeral service for Herr von Rath took place here today at the Lutheran Church in the German Colony.

The French Foreign Minister, M. Bonnet, was present, and the Government, the President, and the President of the Chamber, were represented.

JEWS HIDING IN BERLIN WOODS

REPORTS OF TORTURE AND MURDER

LONDON, Saturday (R). — Mass arrests of Jews are still the order of the day in Berlin and other German towns. It is estimated that several thousand Jews were arrested in Berlin, while thousands, according to a report received here, are hiding in the woods round Berlin.

In Frankfort-on-Main all Jewish men between the ages of 18 and 60 were arrested and herded into concentration camps, where, like all other Jewish internees, they will have to pay for their own board and lodging, as well as for that of those Jews among them who are without funds.

Further to the demonstrations which took place on Tuesday, Wednesday and Thursday, it is now learned according to reports received here, that the worst disorders occurred in small towns where the entire population took part in smashing and looting Jewish shops. Warnings were published in the local newspapers that anybody who failed to take part would be regarded as an enemy of the regime.

QUESTION IN HOUSE

Notice was given today by Mr. Attlee, Leader of the Opposition, of a question regarding the events in Germany. This fact has caused reports in the German press that Parliament is to debate the riots.

German newspapers react to this report with an outburst of abuse, several stating that if Parliament is to debate the position of the Jews in Germany, the Reichstag will be called to debate British policy in Palestine.

TORTURED TO DEATH

A leading personality who witnessed some of the scenes in Berlin and arrived here yesterday (reports Palcor), stated that no Jewish business was left intact and many Jewish houses were damaged and looted. Scores of Jews, according to him, were not only beaten but literally tortured to death.

Officially it is stated in Berlin that a Polish Jew was killed in Munich, where 1,400 Jews are now stated to have been arrested, over half of whom were brought to Dachau concentration camp.

The announcement that one Jew was killed was made in Munich today by the Gauleiter, Herr Wagner, at a mass meeting. This accident occurred, he said, "because he could not keep his mouth shut."

Herr Wagner also expressed satisfaction that the last synagogue in Munich had now finally been got rid of. "I hope foreigners of all kinds in Munich will now keep out of our affairs," said Herr Wagner.

ATTACK ON CATHOLICS

In another part of his speech he attacked the Roman Catholic Church which he accused of giving shelter to the Jews. Following his speech a mob went to the palace of Cardinal Faulhaber, known as an opponent of the regime, and smashed a number of windows.

Only brief and casual reports of the disturbances were published in the German press. The Berlin streets were cleaned overnight, and apart from paneless windows and closed shops there was nothing yesterday to remind passers-by of the demonstrations. The damage in Berlin alone is estimated at tens of millions of marks.

The Zionist Organization's Offices in Berlin were destroyed by a mob and leading Zionists were arrested.

ONE HUNDRED JEWS FLEE PERSECUTION

LONDON, Saturday. — One hundred Jews, men, women and children, from Germany and Austria sailed from Liverpool last night in the Canadian Pacific liner, Duchess of Bedford, for Montreal on their way to Australia and New Zealand.

All the men are skilled workers and all have received permits to enter the Dominions. Some had sufficient means to pay their fares. Others have been assisted by Jewish Aid Societies.

Some of the women had to leave their husbands in Germany, because they had not enough money for both fares.

RECOGNISES ITALY'S CONQUEST

CAIRO, Saturday (R). — Egypt has decided to recognise the Italian conquest of Abyssinia. An announcement to this effect was made here today.

GEN. INUENU NEW TURKISH PRESIDENT

REGARDED AS ATATURK'S LOGICAL SUCCESSOR

ISTANBUL, Saturday (R).— General Ismet Inuenu, former Prime Minister and close collaborator of Kemal Ataturk, was unanimously elected President of the Republic by the National Assembly in Ankara today.

Following the election, a reshuffle of the Cabinet was announced.

Dr. Rushdi Aras, the Foreign Minister is replaced by the former Minister of Justice, Shukru Aracaghu, while the Minister of the Interior, M. Shukru Kaya is replaced by the former Minister of Health, Refik Saydan.

Dr. Aras has held the post of Foreign Minister continuously since 1925, and was a well-known figure at Geneva where he represented Turkey since she became a member of the League in 1932.

The new President of Turkey was born in 1882 and served a distinguished career in the Army, before joining the Nationalist movement led by Kemal in 1919 and taking over command of the army that defeated the Greeks.

He represented Turkey at the Lausanne Conference in 1923 where she was finally recognised by the former Allied Powers.

In 1925 Inuenu became Prime Minister, a post he occupied for 12 years. He was then known as Ismet Pasha.

His resignation last year was reported to have been due to differences of opinion with the President on Turkey's foreign policy, but his unanimous election is proof that he continues to be regarded as the logical successor to Kemal Ataturk.

In connection with the death of Kemal Ataturk, the Turkish Consulate in Jerusalem on Friday received visits from members of the Consular Corps, including the Consuls of Iran, Iraq and Yugoslavia.

Mr. L. Kohn and Mr. E. Epstein called on behalf of the Jewish Agency and Mr. E. Elmaleh on behalf of the General Council of Palestine Jews.

The latter has also telegraphed to the new President of the Turkish Republic expressing the sorrow of Palestine Jewry on the news of the death of Kemal Ataturk.

The Chief Rabbinate of Palestine has sent the following message signed by Chief Rabbi Herzog and Rabbi Meir to the Prime Minister of Turkey:

"Palestine Jewry's profoundest sympathy and condolence with Turkish nation in serious loss sustained through untimely death of great leader and regenerator of Turkey, Gazi Kemal Ataturk."

INSURGENTS RAID BARCELONA

BARCELONA, Saturday (R). — Barcelona was raided today by Insurgent planes which dropped a number of bombs in the centre of the town. The number of casualties is stated to have been very small.

Fighting on land is progressing

"WE OPEN OUR SESSION TO THE LIGHT OF SYNAGOGUE FIRES"

WEIZMAN OVERCOME WITH EMOTION AT GENERAL ZIONIST MEETING IN LONDON

LONDON, Saturday (Palcor). Meeting under the shadow of the tragic events in Germany, the session of the Zionist General Council opened here at 11 o'clock yesterday morning in the presence of 73 delegates from all parts of the world, including the United States and Palestine.

The Council observed the two minutes' silence customary on Armistice Day, prior to Mr. Ussishkin opening the meeting with a tribute to the victims of the Palestine disturbances, to Dr. F. Rottenstreich and to Mr. L. Motzkin, on the occasion of the fifth anniversary of his death.

Recalling the desecration of the Wailing Wall, Mr. Ussishkin went on to describe the happenings in Europe during the last few days and closed with an appeal for unity.

"Reality overcomes all internal differences," he said, "let us unite for the sole salvation of the Jewish people which is 'Palestine."

U. S. JEWS THANKED

Mr. Ussishkin paid a special tribute to the Jews of America for their recent great efforts which would not be forgotten in Zionist history. Act-

In a hushed silence, Dr. Weizman began his opening address with a reference to the losses recently suffered by the Jews in Palestine, among whom he named with particular sorrow the son of his colleague, Dr. Mossinsohn.

"NO PEACE" — WEIZMAN

Proceeding, Dr. Weizman said that while millions of people of all nations celebrated the Armistice today, there was no peace for the Jews. "We open this session in the light of synagogue bonfires now burning throughout Germany and to the groans of the murdered and cries of thousands of Jews in the concentration camps," he said.

Dr. Weizman was overcome by emotion and a few moments passed before he was able to continue. They had been trying, he said, during the last few days, to influence persons whom them believed to be powerful, but their efforts had been in vain.

They had obtained sympathy but they were unable to do anything. The forces of shameless cruelty could not be checked.

Zionists were not accustomed, however, to weep and wail, he said. The world in which they had been brought up when justice prevailed was breaking up, but there were

Dr. Weizman then referred to the Palestine situation and said that the partition scheme had been dropped, though they had not been responsible either for its presentation or for its withdrawal. The establishment of a Jewish State would have been impossible now, even if the report of the Partition Commission had been favourable, because the enemies of the Jewish people and of justice were too strong at the moment.

CYNICAL DOCUMENT

He had rarely seen a more cynical document than the Woodhead report, and he was unable to understand the mentality of its members with the exception of one who seemed to possess human feelings. The Report aimed at breaking up what the Jews had already acquired with superhuman effort.

The so-called Jewish State was apparently to be charged with the financial upkeep of the Arabs and British States which were admittedly unable to maintain themselves. Altogether the Report was a sign of the times and significant of the way in which small nations were being treated, of which Czechoslovakia was an example.

The Report, however, was now

nified and courageous stand of the Jewish community in Palestine, which, he stated would remain as glorious as the struggle of the Maccabeans, second only to the united efforts of the Jews all over the world, especially in the United States, where Jews had manifested an unexampled unity and reacted to the danger in a manner which was a consolation — if consolation was possible in these days.

MANDATE IN FORCE

Dr. Weizman stressed the fact that the Balfour Declaration and the Mandate were still in force, but they were entering a period of difficulties in continuing and maintaining their work. The central theme of the immediate struggle was the question of immigration, which continued although in a thin stream.

They had received an invitation to negotiate with the Arabs, which they did not wish to refuse, but negotiations were possible only on the basis of the Balfour Declaration and the Mandate.

Concluding, Dr. Weizman said that although the project of a Jewish State had been temporarily dropped, he was convinced that it would come up again in due course. In the meantime Jewry must unite in strengthening the Jewish position in Palestine and its only instrument, the Zionist Organization.

THE FOUR POWER FUNK

AN ARMISTICE DAY INTERVIEW WITH

G. B. SHAW

TOMORROW

IN

SUBSCRIPTION: Local: LP.2.250 a year; LP.1.250 a half year:— Foreign, £3.- a year. The rate for display advertisements is 150 mils per column inch. Other rates supplied on request. The right is reserved to make changes in wording or to decline or discontinue any advertisement or to postpone insertions when space is not available.

THE
PALESTINE POST

JERUSALEM
Hassolel Road
P. O. Box 81,
Telephone 4233

Tel Aviv - Jaffa:
55 Allenby Road,
P. O. Box 1125
'Phone 4251-4262.

Haifa: Khayat Square, opposite the Post Office entrance, P.O.B. 66.
'Phone 1296.

THURSDAY MAY 18 1939 JERUSALEM VOL. XV. No. 3955. PRICE 10 MILS

NEW POLICY WINDS UP MANDATE AND JEWISH NATIONAL HOME

BRITAIN'S BLOW WILL NOT SUBDUE JEWS

Statement of the Jewish Agency for Palestine

A Statement was issued by the Jewish Agency in Jerusalem last night, in reply to the White Paper, as follows:

The new policy for Palestine laid down by the Mandatory in the White Paper issued on May 17th denies to the Jewish people the right to reconstitute its National Home in its ancestral land. It hands over the government of the country to the present Arab majority and places the Jewish community of Palestine at the mercy of that majority. It decrees the stoppage of immigration as soon as the Jewish inhabitants of the country have become one-third of the total population. It sets up a territorial ghetto for Jews in their own homeland.

The Jewish people regard this breach of faith as a surrender to Arab terrorism, a delivery of England's friends into the hands of its enemies. It widens the gulf between Jews and Arabs and destroys any prospect of peace in the country.

The Jewish people will not acquiesce in such a policy. The new regime envisaged in the White Paper will be a regime of mere coercion devoid of all moral basis and contrary to international law. Such a regime can only be established and maintained by force.

The Royal Commission, invoked by the White Paper, indicated the dangers inherent in such a regime. "Convinced as they (the Jews) are" they wrote "that an Arab Government would mean the frustration of all efforts and ideals, that it would convert the National Home into one more cramped and dangerous ghetto, it seems only too probable that they

(Continued on Page 2)

POLICY IMPOSED UPON JEWS

ZIONIST LEADERS EXPLAIN ATTITUDE

LONDON, Wednesday (Reuter and Palcor). — Professor Brodetsky and Mr. M. Shertok addressed a press conference at the Savoy Hotel here this afternoon in connection with the Government's Statement of Policy. Professor Brodetsky dwelt on the breach of the Government's international obligations and emphasised the fact that the new Policy had not been negotiated with the Jews but imposed on them.

Mr. Shertok, in giving an analysis of the situation, stressed the fact that the White Paper gave expression to a policy of crystallising the National Home instead of developing it in accordance with the obligation under the Balfour Declaration; it restricted immigration, proscribed settlement on the land, subordinated the Jews to Arab domination and completely disregarded the Jewish Agency which possessed an official status under the Mandate.

He announced Jewish resistance which would not be malicious and not unfriendly to Britain but to the Government's Policy.

REUTER COMMENT

The main purpose of the Government's declaration of Palestine policy is to remove uncertainty as to the intentions and objectives of the Government, as uncertainty is felt to be one of the major causes of the trouble in Palestine, Reuters lobby correspondent understands.

The fact that the policy is definite is expected to produce criticisms from both sides. These will be faced, however, in the belief that the proposals represent a just solution which pays regard to the obligations to the Arabs and Jews alike. The Government specifies as an alternative to extreme Jewish and Arab claims an independent state in which Jews and Arabs will share in the authority of Government in a manner serving the interests of both sides.

No arbitrary decision is taken on the form of the new State which can be federal or unitary. It will be shaped in consultation with the League of Nations. The White Paper contains a reference to protecting the interests of foreign countries, which is understood to refer especially to American missions. Under the arrangements for the admission of 25,000 refugees it is expected that 10,000 children will be involved.

The whole scheme is subject to ap-

"DAY OF VISITATION"

WHITE PAPER CASTS DARK SHADOW; P.B.S. STAFF TO RAMALLAH IN ARMOURED CAR

At 8 o'clock last night, at the moment when the Arabic broadcast of the summary of the White Paper was to begin, the transmission was interrupted, and the broadcast was not resumed for an hour and a half. Rumours of a last-moment postponement immediately began to circulate, although many people had heard the summary broadcast from Daventry.

The interruption was apparently caused by sabotage to the land line between Jerusalem and Ramallah, where an announcement was immediately made in the three languages that the programme would be given later. It was resumed at 9.25, the P.B.S. Staff, headed by the Programme Director, travelling to Ramallah in armoured cars for the purpose.

"BLACK PAPER"

The White Paper, which the Jewish population, at any rate, on the basis of the numerous forecasts, have dubbed the "Black Paper," cast its shadow over the country yesterday.

The Vaad Leumi (National Council of Palestine Jews) in a statement entitled "Day of Visitation" yesterday said:

"Confronted by the declaration of the British Government announcing its new policy for Palestine and which decrees that the Jewish settlement must never exceed a third of the population, thus degrading the Jewish National Home to a Jewish ghetto in an Arab Palestine State," the Yishuv in its hundreds of thousands declares its opposition to the "policy of betrayal" and to the Government based upon such a policy.

"This is not a day for mourning or lamentations," (the statement proceeds) "but a day of enumeration and consolidation of the Yishuv's forces, a day on which will be demonstrated the determination and the readiness of the people to resist this brutal attack."

"On this day we shall, to a man, enter upon this great political struggle for the fate of our people and homeland — a struggle not for one day, and not of words, but a struggle which may call for heavy sacrifices from us."

The name chosen for the day is from Isaiah 10: 3:

"And what will ye do in the day of visitation, and in the desolation which shall come from far? to whom will ye flee for help?

DAY OF PROTEST

The Vaad Leumi also proclaimed a complete stoppage of work, including transport and schools, but excepting Government services, water and power supply, health services and the Haifa Port.

It was made generally known, by posters on hoardings and through the newspapers, that today would be a day of protest against the new Policy, the protest to take the form

(Continued on Page 2)

LAND RESTRICTIONS OPERATIVE TODAY

No Immigration After Five Years Without Arab Consent

ARABS EXPECTED TO SAY "NO"

FIRST SIGNS OF REJECTING PALESTINE WHITE PAPER

BAGHDAD, Wednesday (R). — It is understood that the Iraqi and Saudi-Arabian Governments have informed the British Government that they consider the British proposals regarding future policy in Palestine as a refusal of the demands of the Arab States.

Writing on Friday last the diplomatic correspondent of "The Times," London, foreshadowed the rejection of the White Paper by the Arab States. Commenting on the wish of the Mufti of Jerusalem, who has been staying with a large suite at Zok, Lebanon, to settle in Baghdad, the correspondent said that important personages in Iraq favoured the visit.

CLAIMING THE KUDOS

The article proceeded that the competition displayed among some of the Arab Governments to take the credit of having extricated the Mufti and his party from their increasing difficulties has been keen, as several incidents during the recent conferences on Palestine indicated.

There are imaginative politicians in Iraq who would like to see an Arab State of Palestine linked in some way to Iraq, in spite of the geographical and political difficulties of such a union.

The Mufti, too, is probably tired of the close surveillance which the French and Lebanese authorities have maintained over his movements for several months, the more so as this has probably become closer since two of his near kinsmen left for Berlin.

(Reuter's Summary)

The establishment of an independent Palestine State within ten years and the limitation of Jewish immigration to 75,000 over five years with its cessation thereafter, is envisaged in the far-reaching declaration of the Government's intentions contained in the White Paper issued last night.

The new State will be in treaty relations with the United Kingdom, providing satisfactorily for the commercial and strategic requirements of both countries. Consultation with the League would be necessary with

FULL TEXT OF WHITE PAPER ON PAGE 3

a view to the termination of the Mandate. The independent State would be one in which Arabs and Jews will share in the Government (in proportion to their respective population), in such a way as to ensure that the essential interests of both communities are satisfied.

TRANSITION PERIOD

The establishment of an independent State would be preceded by a transitional period throughout which His Majesty's Government would maintain responsibility. During the transitional period, the people of Palestine would be given an increasing part in the Government and the process carried on whether or not Arabs and Jews avail themselves of the opportunity.

As soon as peace was sufficiently restored, steps would be taken to give Palestinians an increasing part in the Government with the object of placing Palestinians in charge of all the departments of the Government, with the assistance of British advisers and subject to the control of the High Commissioner. The Palestinian heads of Departments would sit on the Executive Council which advises the High Commissioner, and Arab and Jewish representatives would be invited to serve in proportion to their respective populations.

TOWARDS INDEPENDENCE

Five years from the restoration of peace an appropriate body representing Palestine and His Majesty's Government would be established to review the working of constitutional arangements during the transition period and to make recommendations regarding the constitution of an independent Palestine.

His Majesty's Government would do everything to create conditions enabling the independent State to come into being in ten years, but if the circumstances required a postponement, they would consult with Palestinians and the League of Nations as well as the neighbouring Arab States, before deciding on a postponement.

MAXIMUM OF 75,000

During the next five years, Jewish immigration would be at a rate to bring the Jewish population to approximately one third of the whole. This would allow as from April of this year of some 75,000 immigrants in the next five years. For each of the next five years a quota of 10,000 would be allowed, and as a contribution towards the Jewish refugee problem an additional 25,000 would be allowed, making an aggregate of 75,000. After five years no further Jewish immigration, would be permitted without the permission of the Arabs.

The High Commissioner is given powers to regulate transfers of land.

NOVEMBER, 1917

Foreign Office,
November 2nd, 1917.

Dear Lord Rothschild,

I have much pleasure in conveying to you, on behalf of His Majesty's Government, the following declaration of sympathy with Jewish Zionist aspirations which has been submitted to, and approved by, the Cabinet.

"His Majesty's Government view with favour the establishment in Palestine of a national home for the Jewish people, and will use their best endeavours to facilitate the achievement of this object, it being clearly understood that nothing shall be done which may prejudice the civil and religious rights of existing non-Jewish communities in Palestine, or the rights and political status enjoyed by Jews in any other country."

I should be grateful if you would bring this declaration to the knowledge of the Zionist Federation.

Yours sincerely,
(Sgd.) *ARTHUR JAMES BALFOUR.*

MAY, 1939

. . . . His Majesty's Government do not read either the Statement of Policy of 1922 or the letter of 1931 as implying that the Mandate requires them, for all time and in all circumstances, to facilitate the immigration of Jews into Palestine subject only to consideration of the country's economic absorptive capacity. Nor do they find anything in the Mandate or in subsequent Statements of Policy to support the view that the establishment of a Jewish National Home in Palestine cannot be effected unless immigration is allowed to continue indefinitely . . .

The alternatives before His Majesty's Government are either (i) to seek to expand the Jewish National Home indefinitely by immigration, against the strongly expressed will of the Arab people of the country; or (ii) to permit further expansion of the Jewish National Home by immigration only if the Arabs are prepared to acquiesce in it . . .

Therefore His Majesty's Government, after earnest consideration, and taking into account the extent to which the growth of the Jewish National Home has been facilitated over the last twenty years, have decided that the time has come to adopt in principle the second of the alternatives referred to above.

T.A. CROWD RAIDS DISTRICT OFFICES

CURFEW DECLARED

TEL AVIV, Wednesday.—Twenty-five persons were injured, four of them seriously, when police dispersed a crowd of 5,000 which stormed the District Offices, at the bottom of Allenby Road, here tonight and set fire to the building. Following the attack, curfew was imposed in Tel Aviv until further notice.

Crowds carrying flags and banners began to collect towards 8 o'clock and converged on the square in front of the Great Synagogue in Allenby Road. There speakers addressed the crowd which had swollen to several thousands, mostly youths. "Hatikvah" was sung and all those present raised their right arm and repeated the words: "If I forget thee, oh Jerusalem, may my right hand forget her cunning."

Shouts of "Down with Weizman" and "Up, Jobotinsky" were raised amongst the crowd.

The demonstration then proceeded to the District Offices, and forced the doors, wrecking the furniture and setting fire to the records, while others hoisted the blue-and-white flag on the roof of the building. Heavy pieces of furniture were hurled into the street and set on fire by the crowd. Considerable damage was also done to the Land Registry and Migration Department Offices.

British police soon appeared on the scene and dispersed the crowd, after firing a volley of shots into the air.

BOMBS AND FIRE AT IMMIGRATION OFFICES

A series of loud explosions shortly before 11.30 last night gave the first indication of an attack upon the building of the Government Department of Migration in Queen Melisande Road, Jerusalem. The whole building could be seen lit up by several flashes before fire broke out over the whole of the upper storey.

Police were on the spot immediately, and the alarm siren was sounded continuously for a few minutes. Two bound and unconscious Jewish ghaffirs were found near the gate to the side entrance of the building and taken to the Hadassah Hospital.

After recovering consciousness, shortly after being brought in, one man said that he and his companion had been on duty inside the main entrance, when a rap was heard on the door, and a voice said in English "C.I.D. Inspection. Open the door."

This was a nightly routine, and he went forward to unbar the door. As it opened the ghaffirs distinguished four figures with masked faces, but were then struck over the head and bound, and must have been bundled out of the building by their captors.

Both ghaffirs went to make their

that the fire in other parts of the building was caused by similar bombs, and a passer-by stated that he had seen the whole of the building light up briefly after each explosion.

The fire brigade arrived shortly after the alarm had been given and succeeded in putting out the flames, though not before the major part of the building had been gutted.

AFTER MIDNIGHT

The Tel Aviv Municipality issued a manifesto at one o'clock this morning, deeply deploring the demonstration in the town as a breach of discipline. Pointing out that the Municipality had assumed responsibility for the maintenance of order, it appealed to all inhabitants to demonstrate their strength through unity and discipline.

The Mayor, Mr. Rokach, was slightly bruised in the leg by a stone thrown at him as he alighted from his car outside the District Offices to persuade the demonstrators to disperse. He did not require medical attention.

Arab circles in London express grave disappointment in the transitional period, expressing the opinion that the utmost limit should have been three

INDEFINITE EXILE FOR HAJ AMIN

LONDON, Wednesday (R). — The Mufti of Jerusalem, Haj Amin al Husseini, is to be excluded indefinitely from Palestine.

This statement was made by Mr. Malcolm MacDonald in the House of Commons this afternoon in answer to a questioner who asked if it was the Government's intention to allow the Mufti to return to Palestine.

Replying in the negative, the Colonial Secretary said that His Majesty's Government, in deciding to exclude him from Palestine indefinitely, could not lose sight of the fact

SUBSCRIPTION: Local: LP.3.350 a year; LP.1.350 a half year.— Foreign, 85/- a year. The rate for display advertisements is 150 mils per column inch. Other rates supplied on request. The right is reserved to make changes in wording or to decline or discontinue any advertisement or to postpone insertions when space is not available.

THE PALESTINE POST

JERUSALEM Hassolel Road P. O. Box 81. Telephone 4233
Tel Aviv - Jaffa: 65, Allenby Road, P. O. Box 1125. 'Phone 4251-4252.
Haifa Khayat Square, opposite the Post Office entrance, P.O.B. 66. 'Phone 1594-1595

MONDAY SEPTEMBER 4 1939 — JERUSALEM — VOL. XV. No. 4047. PRICE 10 MILS

ANGLO-FRENCH WAR ON HITLER

NAZIS BLAME BRITISH "INTERVENTION"

Wanted 'Reasonable Solution'

BERLIN, Sunday. — The outbreak of war with Great Britain was announced to the German people here today in the form of a broadcast quoting a memorandum which had been handed earlier by the German Government to Sir Nevile Henderson, the British Ambassador.

The statement declares that the German Government and the German people refuse to accept or fulfil any ultimative demands from the British Government and will meet force with force.

It is claimed that a virtual state of war has existed on the eastern frontier of Germany for many months and but for the intervention of Britain a reasonable settlement of the Polish-German dispute would have been found. The memorandum declares,

DEFENCE IN THE WEST

"Germany neither had the intention not has she put forward a demand to annex Poland. The Reich has only demanded the revision of those articles in the treaty of Versailles which farseeing statesmen of all nations regarded at the time it was drafted as intolerable. The memorandum severely attacks Britain's "blank cheque" to Poland and accuses her of being chiefly responsible by this action for Polish terrorism. It is then alleged that Britain rebuffed Signor Mussolini's proposal "which could still have saved the peace of Europe, though the German Government declared itself willing to accept it."

Germany was also unwilling to tolerate further ill-treatment from Poland.

The memorandum continues, adding that therefore the Government refuses all efforts to force Germany by means of ultimatums to recall her troops.

"We shall therefore answer any British aggression with like arms and in a like way."

Herr Hitler in a proclamation to the western army calls on them to protect the frontiers of the Reich "unshakeable as a wall of steel or iron" against every attack. If they did their duty, battle in the east would reach a successful conclusion in a few months. The proclamation concluded "I am going with confidence in you to the army in the east."

A protest against allegations in some foreign newspapers that the German forces had already started using poison gas and incendiary bombs was today issued by the German News Agency, which described the report as the "first "atrocity" story in the military sphere.

"Voelkischer Beobachter" stated today that the restrictions on listening to foreign broadcasts were necessary "in order to ensure a German victory in the war of nerves."

BREMEN SEIZED

French wireless stations last night announced that a British warship had seized the German luxury liner, Bremen, on her way back from New York without passengers and was escorting her to an unnamed British port.

THE KING'S MESSAGE TO THE EMPIRE

His Majesty the King broadcast a message to the people of the British Empire at 5 o'clock G.M.T. yesterday afternoon (7 o'clock Palestine time). The message was relayed by the P.B.S. from Jerusalem.

His Majesty said:

"In this grave hour, perhaps the most fateful in our history, I send to every household of my people, both at home and overseas, this message, speaking with the same depth of feeling to each one of you as if I were able to speak to you myself.

"For the second time in the lives of most of us, we are at war. Over and over again we have tried to find a peaceful way out of the differences between ourselves and those who are now our enemies, but it has been in vain.

"We have been forced into a conflict, for we are called with our allies to meet the challenge which, if it were to prevail, would be fatal to any civilized order in the world.

"It is the principle which permits a state in selfish pursuit of power to disregard treaties and solemn pledges, which sanctions the use of force or the threat of force against the sovereignty and independence of other States.

"Such a principle, stripped of all disguise, is merely the primitive doctrine that might is right.

"If this principle were established throughout the world, the freedom of our own country and of the whole British Commonwealth of Nations would be in danger.

"But far more than this, the peoples of the world will be kept in the bondage of fear and all hope of a settled peace and of the security of justice and liberty among nations would be ended. This is the ultimate issue which confronts us.

"For the sake of all that we ourselves hold dear and of the world order and of peace, it is unthinkable that we should refuse to meet the challenge.

"It is for this high purpose that I now call my people at home and my people across the seas who will make our cause their own. I ask them to stand firm and calm, and unite in this time of trial. The task will be hard. There may be dark days ahead. War can no longer be confined to the battlefield. But we can only do the right as we see the right and reverently commit our cause to God.

"If one and all will keep reverently faithful to it, ready for whatever service or sacrifice, then with God's help we shall prevail. One and all we are resolutely faithful to the cause, ready for whatever sacrifice may be demanded. May He bless and keep us all."

WAR CABINET AFTER TWENTY-ONE YEARS

Churchill and Eden Included

LONDON, Sunday (R). —Britain's new War Cabinet was formed today with the inclusion of Mr. Winston Churchill as First Lord of the Admiralty and Mr. Anthony Eden as Dominions Secretary with special access to the Inner Cabinet. The latter is now composed of the following:

Mr. Neville Chamberlain — Prime Minister;
Sir John Simon — Chancellor of the Exchequer;
Lord Halifax — Foreign Secretary;
Lord Chatfield — Minister for the Coordination of Defence;
Mr. Winston Churchill — First Lord of the Admiralty;
Mr. Hore Belisha —Secretary for War;
Sir Kingsley Wood — Secretary for Air;
Sir Samuel Hoare — Lord Privy Seal;
Lord Hankey — Minister without Portfolio.

Sir John Anderson becomes Home Secretary in place of Sir Samuel Hoare and also remains Minister for Civilian Defence. Sir Thomas Inskip becomes Lord Chancellor and Lord Stanhope is moved from the Admiralty to the Lord Presidency. Lord Hankey, the former Sir Maurice Hankey, was Secretary to the Cabinet in the World War.

CONSCRIPTION

In the House of Commons last night, Mr. Ernest Brown, Minister of Labour, moved the second reading of the National Service Armed Forces Bill providing for the enlistment of men between 18 and 41. Mr. Arthur Greenwood supported the second reading of the Bill, which was carried by 340 votes to 7.

The Minister of Pensions introduced the Personal Injuries Emergency Provisions Bill, which is to make loss or damage due to war including accidental injuries sustained while on duty a State liability. Payments are to be immediate to tide the victims over the first emergency, and serious injury or disablement may receive pensions on service lines.

The British Cabinet, which met on Saturday afternoon, was summoned for the second time on Sunday night and sat for 45 minutes.

BRITAIN UNITED AGAINST NAZI TYRANNY

FRENCH ULTIMATUM EXPIRED AT FIVE O'CLOCK YESTERDAY AFTERNOON

LONDON, Sunday (R). — The Commons and Lords were both informed at noon today by the Prime Minister and the Foreign Secretary, respectively, that Great Britain was at war with Germany.

Mr. Chamberlain arrived at Westminster shortly before midday, having 45 minutes earlier broadcast his message (given in an adjoining column) to the United Kingdom, the British Empire and the world.

ALL-DAY CONSULTATIONS

The Premier's statement was as follows:

"When I spoke to the House last night, I could not but be aware that in some parts of the House there were doubts or bewilderment as to whether there would be hesitation or vacillation on the part of His Majesty's Government. But in the circumstances I make no reproach. If I had been in the same position as members on the other benches, and not in possession of all the information, I might have felt the same.

"We were in consultation all day yesterday with the French Government and we felt that the intensified action which the Germans were taking against Poland allowed of no delay in making our own position clear. Accordingly we decided to send our Ambassador in Berlin instructions which he was to hand at 9 o'clock this morning to the German Foreign Minister."

Mr. Chamberlain then read the terms of the instructions sent to Sir Nevile Henderson, which had been issued earlier in the morning as a communique from No. 10 Downing Street as follows:

11 O'CLOCK THE ZERO HOUR

'On September 1, His Majesty's Ambassador in Berlin was instructed to inform the German Government that unless they were prepared to give His Majesty's Government in the United Kingdom satisfactory assurance that the German Government had suspended all aggressive action against Poland and were prepared promptly to withdraw their forces from Polish territory, His Majesty's Government in the United Kingdom would without hesitation fulfil their obligations to Poland.

'At 9 o'clock this morning, His Majesty's Ambassador informed the German Government that unless not later than 11 o'clock B.S.T. today, September 3, satisfactory assurances to the above effect would

(Continued on Page 2)

German Air Onslaught on Poland

LONDON, Sunday (R). It was announced by the Polish Embassy tonight that the German Government had proposed to Poland that aerial bombardments should be limited to military objectives, but although the Polish Government accepted, German airplanes had bombed 24 towns of Poland.

The Polish Embassy in London claims that the Polish forces are holding their positions, the most serious threat being in the concentration of the main mass of the German Air Force against Poland.

Not only were military objectives being bombed, but it was certain that towns and villages were being indiscriminately and continuously raided although they were of no military importance.

A Warsaw message states that 26 people were killed when 15 bombs were dropped on the town of Lublin 250 miles south-east of Warsaw.

The German radio today claimed that the town of Czenstochowa 130 miles south-west of Warsaw and a famous place of pilgrimage for the Poles had been captured by the German forces.

Last night the Polish Government reported Czenstochowa to be in flames as a result of having been bombed several times by German aircraft on Friday and Saturday.

GERMAN REPORTS

The German Army High Commands in a communique claims that a whole

confined to military objectives.

The communique declares that after units of the German armoured cars reached the Vistula at noon, German forces effectively attacked points for the passage of the river, and asserts that one bridge and another under construction were destroyed by numerous bombs.

An important railway station was also bombed. It adds that while military objectives were being attacked and destroyed, there was resistance by Polish anti-aircraft and pursuit planes.

The new Russian Ambassador to Berlin arrived last night in company of a Russian general and members of his staff.

SUCCESS CLAIMED

Another wireless communication in Germany claims that German troops in the Corridor sector have reached the Vistula and Polish army contingents in the northern part of the Corridor have been cut off and are being mopped up.

The German army is also stated to have reached the Vistula from east Prussia though for several miles the river forms a frontier on this side.

It is believed in London that these claims of successes are probably exaggerated.

HIGH COMMISSIONER'S BROADCAST TODAY

His Excellency the High Commissioner will broadcast to Palestine at 9 p.m. today.

Translations of the address into Arabic and Hebrew will follow immediately.

PALESTINE JEWRY'S STAND

STATEMENT BY JEWISH AGENCY AND VAAD LEUMI

Palestine Jewry's loyalty to Britain and readiness to take its share in the defence of Palestine and support of the British forces was proclaimed yesterday in a statement issued by the Jewish Agency Executive and a joint decision taken by the Jewish Agency and the General Council of Palestine Jews.

The Executive of the Jewish Agency issued the following statement last night:—

His Majesty's Government has today declared war against the Germany of Hitler.

At this fateful moment, the Jewish community has a threefold concern: the protection of the Jewish homeland, the welfare of the Jewish people, the victory of the British Empire.

The White Paper of May, 1939, was a grave blow to us. As heretofore we shall defend to the utmost of our ability the right of the Jewish people in its National Home. Our opposition to the White Paper was, however, never directed against Great Britain or the British Empire.

The war which has now been forced upon Great Britain by Nazi Germany is our war, and all the assistance that we shall be able and permitted to give to the British Army and to the British People we shall render wholeheartedly.

We do not know what will be in store for our country in this war. Our first duty is to ensure the survival and the welfare of the Jewish community, to strengthen it materially and morally, and to prepare it for the great and difficult [illegible] have devoted our forces to constructive effort. If need be, we shall now show our strength in war also.

Let us close our ranks, let us unite in a spirit of responsibility and mutual help, discipline and national devotion, and let us be prepared.

EMERGENCY MEASURES

A joint meeting of the Executives of the Jewish Agency and of the General Council of Palestine Jews, (Vaad Leumi) was held yesterday at the Offices of the Jewish Agency.

The meeting dealt with the emergency created by the declaration of war. Among other matters, it was decided to carry out a registration of volunteers, (men and women) for national service during the period of the emergency. Volunteers will be registered:

(a) to serve the needs of the Jewish Community as regards security, economic life and other public requirements.

(b) to be at the disposal of the British military authorities in Palestine for such services as they may require.

All men and women between the ages of 18 and 50, who register for such voluntary service, will be required to furnish full details of their technical qualifications and special experience, and to indicate the tasks in which they are prepared to serve the Jewish Community or the British Army in Palestine.

Details of the registration will shortly be announced.

It was further resolved to set up, under the auspices of the Jewish Agency, an Economic Council composed of prominent members of the Jewish Community whose function will be to deal with the requirements of the Jewish economy in Palestine, in the fields of agriculture, industry, labour, supplies, credit, transport, import, export, etc.

Tokyo Staying Out

U.S. EXPECTED TO INVOKE NEUTRALITY ACT

SHANGHAI. —It is reliably learned here that the Japanese Government will give assurances to Great Britain of Japanese neutrality.

WASHINGTON, Sunday (R). —A White House proclamation says that legislation has been drawn up to invoke the Neutrality Act which bans shipment of munitions to belligerents.

President Roosevelt will broadcast tonight at 2.00 a.m. G.M.T. and his speech will afterwards be broadcast in six different languages.

A wonderful impression of calmness and sincerity has been created here by Mr. Chamberlain's speech and the instructions broadcast by the B.B.C., declared a responsible U.S. official today. He added that once again the American people would contrast the voice of Britain with that of Germany "and from such a comparison our people can only draw one conclusion, and the people of Britain know what that conclusion is."

BRUSSELS. — It is officially announced that Belgium has sent a declaration of neutrality to all the countries concerned.

AFTER MIDNIGHT

Australia and New Zealand last night followed the lead of the Mother-country by declaring war on Germany.

Zero hour in France passed quietly without any outward manifestation that France was at war. The weekly rest day has been abolished and a seven-day week has been established in all concerns working for National defence.

"France and Britain are with us," were the cries of thousands of demonstrators outside the British and French Embassies in Warsaw yesterday.

The Admiralty announces that Rear-Admiral the Duke of Kent has taken up a war appointment.

Residents of the United Kingdom

THE PALESTINE POST

FRIDAY
DECEMBER 12, 1941

VOL. XVII. No. 4742
PRICE 10 MILS

AMERICA AT WAR WITH GERMANY

AXIS FOLLOWS TOKYO -- CONGRESS' UNANIMOUS REPLY

President Roosevelt at 3.05 p.m. Eastern Time yesterday (11.05 in Palestine) signed America's Declaration of War Against Germany and at 3.06 Against Italy. Both resolutions were voted unanimously by Congress, following Hitler's and Mussolini's declarations of war against the U.S.

"ITALIANS' DECISION"

GENEVA, Thursday.— Speaking from the balcony of the Palazzo Venezia in Rome today to a mass meeting assembled in the square below, Mussolini announced Italy's "decision" to follow Germany and Japan in declaring war on the United States.

Neither the Axis Powers nor Japan had desired this latest extension of the war, said the Duce, adding that "only one man wanted it and has been working for it with diabolical tenacity for two years — the American despot, Franklin Delano Roosevelt."

Italy, he continued, was making a solemn decision today in the face of great and memorable events which would change the history of mankind. She was ranging herself by the side of Germany and Japan in a tripartite alliance of 250 million people "united in their determination to bring the Anglo-Saxon tyranny to an end."

Russia Not Mentioned

"Italy is proud to fight shoulder to shoulder with Japan." Mussolini concluded. "Italians — you are on your feet again. You are worthy of this great hour. We shall win!"

No mention is made in the tripartite military alliance announced by both Mussolini and Hitler of the war against Russia. The document contains three clauses as follows:

Article one. Italy, Germany and Japan will wage the common war which was imposed on them by the United States and Great Britain by all the means at their disposal until the conclusion of hostilities.

Article two: Japan, Germany and Italy undertake to conclude neither an armistice nor any peace whatever with the United States or Great Britain without a full reciprocal agreement.

Article three: "Japan, Germany and Italy will continue even after the victorious conclusion of the war to collaborate very closely in the sense of the Tripartite Pact which they concluded in September, 1940, with the object of accomplishing an equitable order.

PREMIER REVIEWS POSITION ON FOUR FRONTS

HOW THE ALLIES STAND

LONDON, Thursday (R). — Following are the main points made by Mr. Churchill in the House of Commons this afternoon on the position of Britain, the United States and her Allies:

Libya The Libyan offensive did not take the expected course, but General Auchinleck set out to destroy the entire armed forces of the Germans and Italians. Now it seems very probable that he will do so. From the viewpoint of drawing weight from the vast Russian front, the continuance of the fighting in its severity is not to be regarded as evil.

"The first phase is over. The enemy has been swept out of the positions which barred our western advance. Tobruk is definitely disengaged. Substantial British reinforcements and fresh troops are close at hand."

Atlantic November fully maintained the great recovery of the previous four months, as regards shipping losses in the Atlantic.

Russia Paying tribute to Russia's "glorious steadfastness," Mr. Churchill said, "German losses have been immense. The Russians have now regained definite superiority in the air over large parts of the front.

"Although our position has changed in important ways, not all favourable, we must faithfully and punctually fulfill the very serious undertakings that we have made to Russia."

Far East "The Japanese onslaught has brought upon the United States and Britain very serious injuries to our naval power. I cannot remember a naval blow so heavy as the sinking of the Prince of Wales and Repulse. The naval power of Britain and the United States is still largely superior to the combined forces of the three Axis Powers.

"For the next few months at any rate, we must expect that the volume of American supplies reaching Britain and the degree of help given by the United States Navy will be reduced."

Marked Improvement in Atlantic Battle; Russian Air Superiority Over Nazis; Libya Drew Weight from Eastern Front, Auchinleck's Great Battle; Reduced Help from America, Serious Blows in The Pacific but Naval Superiority Maintained

LONDON, Thursday (R). — Mr. Churchill, making his review of the war situation in the House of Commons today, said that the military spokesman in Cairo had been pretty well justified in what he said having regard to how things seemed to stand when he said it. If anybody based his hopes on what he said, that man would find today that he had not been misled. The Prime Minister went on:

"The Libyan offensive did not take the course that General Auchinleck and others expected, though it will reach the end at which they aimed. Still when all is said and done, on November 18 General Auchinleck set out to destroy the entire armed forces of the Germans and Italians in Cyrenaica and now on December 11 it seems very probable that he will do so.

"The Commanders beforehand had an idea that the whole German armoured forces would be encountered by our armoured forces in mass at the outset. However, the sudden surprise and the success of our advance prevented any such main trial of strength.

"Almost at the first bound, we reached right up to Sidi Razegh, dividing the enemy armoured forces and throwing them into confusion. In consequence, a very large number of fierce detached actions took place over an immense space of desert country, and the battle, though equally intense, became both dispersed and protracted.

"For us the foundation of everything was supply and mechanized transport, and this was provided on what has until now been considered a fantastic scale. Also we had to rely on our superiority in armour and in the air.

Generals and Men

"Most of, well, everything depended for us upon the absolutely unrelenting spirit of the offensive, not only in the generals, but in the troops and every man. That has been forthcoming and is still forthcoming. All troops have fought all the time in every circumstance of fatigue and hardship with one sincere and insatiable desire to engage the enemy and destroy him if possible.

"But behind all this has been the persisting will-power of the Commander-in-Chief, General Auchinleck. Without that will-power, we might easily have subsided to the defensive and lost the precious initiative to which here in this Libyan theatre we have for the first time felt ourselves strong enough to make claim.

"On November 24, General Auchinleck proceeded to Battle Headquarters and on the 26th he decided to relieve General Cunningham and appoint Major-General Ritchie, a comparatively junior officer, to command the Eighth Army in his stead.

"General Cunningham rendered a brilliant service in Abyssinia and was also responsible for the planning and organization of the present offensive in Libya, which began with a surprise and success, and which has now definitely turned the corner. He has since been reported by the medical authorities to be suffering from serious overstrain and has been granted sick-leave. Since November 26, therefore, the Eighth Army has been commanded with vigour and skill by General Ritchie.

General Auchinleck — "a military figure of the first order."

Although the battle is not yet finished, I have no hesitation in saying that for good or ill it is General Auchinleck's battle. I believe we have found in him, as we have also found in General Wavell, a military figure of the first order.

"British armoured corps, the New Zealand Division, the South African Division, and the Indian Division, the British 17th Division and the rest of Tobruk garrison, including the Poles, all played an equally valiant and active part.

"At the beginning of the offensive, I told the House that we should for the first time be fighting the Germans on equal terms in modern weapons. This was quite true.

"Naturally there have been some unpleasant surprises and some awkward things have happened. Those who fight the Germans fight a stubborn and resourceful foe — a foe in every way worthy of the doom prepared for him.

Tanks Four-Pounders

"Some of the German tanks carried as we know, a six-pounder gun, which, though it fires much fewer shots, is sometimes more effective than the gun with which our tanks are mainly armed," continued Mr. Churchill.

"Our losses in tanks were a great deal heavier than we expected and it may be that at the outset, before it was disorganized, the enemy's recovery process for damaged vehicles worked better than ours. I am not so sure of it, but it may be so. We had good superiority in the numbers of armoured vehicles. We gradually obtained mastery as far as the first phase of the battle is concerned.

Our air force was undoubtedly superior throughout in number and quality, and although the Germans have drawn in a most extravagant manner upon reinforcements from many quarters, including the Russian front, that superiority has been more than maintained.

"The greatest satisfaction is expressed by the troops and by the military authorities about the way in which they have been helped and protected by the action of the R.A.F. None of the complaints of the previous enterprises have reached us here upon that score.

"It may be that this wearing down battle will be found in the end to have inflicted deeper injury upon the enemy than if it had all been settled by manoeuvre and in a few days. In no other way in this Libyan attack could a second front have been brought into action under conditions more costly to the enemy and more favourable to ourselves. Remember that about half, and sometimes more, of everything, men, munitions and fuel, which the enemy sends to Africa is sunk before it gets there by our submarines, cruisers, destroyers and our Air Force acting from Libya and Malta.

From the viewpoint of drawing weight from the vast Russian front, the continuance of fighting in its severity is not to be regarded as an evil.

"The first stage of the battle is now over. The enemy has been driven out of the positons which barred our Western advance. Everything has been swept away except certain pockets at Bardia and Halfaya which are hopelessly cut off.

"It may definitely be said that Tobruk has been disengaged. The enemy is still strong but severely mauled and largely stripped of his armour and is retreating to a defensive line west of Tobruk fortress. The clearance of the approaches to Tobruk by the establishment of our air power this far forward to the west in the new air fields, enables the great supply depots of Tobruk which have been carefully built up, to furnish support for the second phase of our offensive with great economy on our lines of communication.

"Substantial reinforcements and fresh troops are available close at hand. It may be that the second phase will gather more easily the fruits of the first than has been our experience in the fighting that has taken place so far.

All the dangers of the Army of the Nile not being able to celebrate Christmas and the New Year in Cairo have been decisively removed.

Mr. Churchill went on to say that the Atlantic Battle in November and the first ten days of December had fully maintained the great recovery of the previous four months.

Turning to Russia, the Prime Minister said that Hitler was not only brought to a standstill everywhere but his losses had been immense -- and this was only the beginning of the winter. The Russians had now regained definite superiority in the air over large parts of the front.

The launching of the Nazi campaign on Russia was one of the outstanding blunders of history. "Nevertheless, we must remember the great munition capacities which have been lost to Russia by the German invasion and our pledges to the Russians for heavy monthly quotas of tanks, aeroplanes and vital raw materials."

(Continued on Page 3)

TIRADE ON ROOSEVELT

By a Staff Correspondent

Hitler's speech to the Reichstag yesterday, delaying for some minutes the announcement of his and Mussolini's declaration of war on the United States, was another exercise in the art of trying to picture himself as an ardent lover of peace whom the wickedness of the Democracies had forced to fight for "a new world order."

Starting out with a survey of the feats accomplished by the Axis armed forces, among which he was careful to include the Italians and the small vassal states which have sent contingents to the Russian front, he gave a detailed time-table of the course of the war since the collapse of France and some highly fanciful accounts of the fighting in Russia.

The most remarkable point of his speech was the fact that the lion's share of praise went not to the much-advertised Panzer divisions which, oddly enough, were not even mentioned, but to the infantry. While carefully avoiding any mention of the recent reverses suffered in Russia, he also announced that the peculiarities of the Russian climate made it necessary for military operations to come to a standstill during the winter.

"Self-Defence"

This uninspiring opening was followed by what must have been an intolerably boring part for even his most devoted listeners, namely a lengthy account of the negotiations on the Polish question which took place immediately prior to the outbreak of the war. Hitler did not spare his audience the reading of a long and complicated document designed to show that in attacking Poland, Germany acted only in self-defence and after having made the most generous offers for a peaceful arrangement between the two countries.

But while acting in self-defence, Germany at the same time fought not only for her own interests but for those of Europe as a historical and cultural entity. To prove this point, Hitler ventured into the intricacies of ancient, medieval and modern history, claiming that what he called his "European Crusade" was in line with, and of a similar importance as the fight of the Greeks against the Persians, and of Rome against Carthage

Here he took occasion to announce that Europe cannot be limited by political or geographical frontiers in the East. It was incorrect to say that it ended at the Ural Mountains; the Europe of the future would be as large as the "European Spirit" can make it

Roosevelt the Arch Scoundrel

At this point, Hitler finally came round to the villain of the piece. In the beginning there was some doubt whom he meant, but soon it became clear that Mr. Churchill had now been relegated to second place, while President Roosevelt has advanced to the role of arch-scoundrel.

It was at that point that Hitler, who had spoken up to then with an emotional and oratorical restraint unusual with him, reverted to the pristine purity of his Beer Cellar style. President Roosevelt was deliberately taking the U.S.A. into war to save himself and his "Jewish advisers" from the political and economical bankruptcy of their regime.

In referring to the President and incidentally to Mrs. Roosevelt as well, Hitler became his old ego again. He sentimentalized about the difference between himself and the President whom he pictured as, of all things, the representative of the American plutocracy.

By a long chain of unlawful and dishonourable acts, he declared, President Roosevelt had step by step brought the United States into a ostate of quasi-belligerency, until his shooting order to the U.S. Navy had brought things to a climax. From his interference and his overbearing meddling into affairs which were none of his concern, all the authoritarian countries had had to suffer likewise, though straining their patience and love of peace to the utmost.

It was therefore with deep satisfaction that he and the German people had received the news that Japan had decided to defend herself against the attempts of the United States to cripple her existence and to deny what Japan regarded as her right to live. Even were he not compelled to do so by existing treaties, he would not hesitate to range Germany at the side of those who had called President Roosevelt's bluff, thus making the struggle for the "New Order" truly world-wide. Hitler declared that he was burdened with his task by the will of God by whom he was inspired to fulfil it.

Jap Battleship, Cruiser And Destroyer Sunk

NEW YORK, Thursday (R). The Navy Department has confirmed the sinking of the Japanese battleship, Haruna.

The U.S. Navy also sank one Japanese cruiser and one destroyer in defending Wake Island. Four separate attacks on Wake Island have been repulsed during the past 48 hours.

Three hits were scored on the 29,000 ton Japanese battleship Haruna which was set on fire north-east of Northern Luzon. The warship was burning fiercely as the planes left the scene.

The attack occurred ten miles north-east of Northern Luzon.

The Haruna has a displacement of 29,300 tons and a complement of 980. She was launched in 1933 and belongs to the Kongo class of four ships.

Her armament includes eight 14-inch guns, 16 six-inch guns and 8 5-inch anti-aircraft guns. The warship was refitted between 1926 and 1930. Three planes were added to her equipment.

Making the official announcement at a press conference, Mr. Stimson, the Army Secretary, said that determined resistance by American Forces confined the Japanese landings on Luzon to the vicinity of Aparri at the extreme northern tip of the island. (A Manila report, however, states that parachutists have landed near Iligan, in Eastern Luzon).

Mr. Stimson said that there were continued attacks by Japanese aircraft in the vicinity of Manila yesterday. Losses in planes during the attack on Hawaii, on Sunday, although heavy, are already being replaced. "They can be made good and are being made good."

Mr. Stimson said that a flight of four-engined bombers arrived in Hawaii during the Japanese attack. The first was shot down but the crews of the remainder, with a few seconds warning, landed safely in various air fields, only two suffering damage.

Regarding the attack on Hawaii, Mr. Stimson said that the War Department itself had not yet a complete report, but this was no time for recrimination or accusations of blame. "It seems to me that anything like that is the sign of an immature Government and people.... The present time is one for action and preparation."

Luzon Landing

Mr. Stimson added that the Army was engaged in strengthening its defences everywhere — "In Hawaii and everywhere else."

It was reported from Manila earlier that the Japanese troops which landed early on Wednesday on Luzon Island were immediately engaged by American and Phillipine troops.

A large fire was seen emanating from Nicholls airfield. Moderate anti-aircraft fire was put up, and one plane was seen to be brought down with smoke issuing from its tail.

After the first two attacks, nine more bombers, flying at a high altitude, bombed Cavite and merchantmen anchored in the harbour. The final assault was made eight minutes later by eight more bombers. More than 100 bombs were dropped at Manila and Arza. Citizens watched the raiders without any signs of panic.

It is also announced that a Filipino division has repulsed an attack by Japanese troops 100 miles from Manila. The attack, which was not heavy, was made in the neighbourhood of Lingayen, on the West coast of Luzon. Apart from this fighting, the situation is completely in hand.

ENEMY WITHDRAWING WESTWARD, BUT STILL UNBROKEN

By B. Z. GASTER,
Our Cairo Correspondent

CAIRO, Thursday Evening.— The enemy is still moving west and northwest in Libya, but shows no sign of breaking.

The movement is still orderly, and controlled, though the main concentration forces are spreading out; smaller columns thus avoid affording too marked a target for bombing attacks.

One of these tank columns attempting to halt a southwest flanking movement being carried out by a mixed force of Sikhs, Punjabis and the Royal Sussex Regiment was engaged by a group of our armoured forces which came up in time to drive them off.

Further south other pockets of enemy infantry and armoured cars are being mopped up.

The Germans have been sending a certain amount of air reinforcements to Libya and air attacks against Tobruk, despite a raging duststorm, are somewhat stronger, though largely ineffective. Reports *that these reinforcements are being sent from the Russian front are unconfirmed, though the news that any of our moves in this part of the world would help relieve the pressure of the Soviet front by forcing them to send machines elsewhere would naturally be welcome.*

Earlier Dispatch—Page Three

M.E. Communiques

G.H.Q., CAIRO — Thursday

Throughout the day our mobile forces continued successfully to attack the enemy, whose general trend of movement was northwest and west from El Adem. A number of engagements took place, but owing to the wide area covered and difficulties of communications detailed reports have not been received.

Enemy troops and transport sheltering behind defences immediately west of El Adem were attacked by British armoured units, while further to the west British and South African mobile columns pressed the enemy back all day in a north-westerly direction. Small pockets of enemy infantry and armoured cars left in the area north of Bir Hakeim are being dealt with.

In the late afternoon our armoured forces attacked and drove off a number of German tanks which were endeavouring to interfere with operations being carried out west of El Adem by Sikhs, Punjabis and the Royal Sussex Regiment. Some miles southwest of Acroma, British armoured units shelled a concentration of enemy motor transport, burning some and damaging others.

At Tobruk, Polish units maintaining pressure on the enemy, captured two posts on the Western Defences. Enemy air action against Tobruk yesterday was on a somewhat increased scale, but ineffective.

Further east, South African troops continued to clear up the area north of Trigh Capuzzo, where a few enemy stragglers are being captured. New Zealanders are also engaged in mopping-up operations in the area immediately east of Tobruk.

In addition to the 27 abandoned German tanks found between Bardia and Tobruk the day before yesterday, a further ten German tanks have been discovered.

In the frontier area our artillery is persistently harassing enemy detachments isolated in various defended localities.

Supporting our ground forces, our air forces carried out continual sweeps over the whole area of operations. Enemy concentrations and motor transport were attacked and near Acroma a particularly large number was damaged and set on fire. Ground troops shot down one German ME 110.

R.A.F. MIDDLE EAST—Thursday

Bomber aircraft of the Royal Air Force raided objectives at **Tripoli** and the landing grounds at **Derna** and **Gazala** during Tuesday night.

At **Tripoli**, considerable damage was caused to military buildings and many explosions occurred. A number of fires which broke out developed into a blaze which was seen many miles from the target.

Our aircraft also machine-gunned motor transport vehicles and bombed storage buildings. **At Derna and Gazala** the results of the raids could not be observed owing to unfavourable conditions of visibility.

During yesterday, bad weather seriously hampered operations but in the course of fighter patrols a number of enemy aircraft was damaged.

From these and other operations three of our aircraft are missing, but two pilots are safe.

AFTER MIDNIGHT

Edinburgh will replace both the Prince of Wales and Repulse. The Admiralty previously agreed to allocate the battleship Howe, sister ship of the Prince of Wales, to Edinburgh which has now expressed the intention of replacing the Repulse also. The money invested during Edinburgh's Warships Week last night reached £12,500,000. The original aim was £10,000,000.

BLACKOUT:	Sunset in
Jerusalem, 5.36	Sunrise, 7.30

JAP TRANSPORT SUNK

ATTEMPTED LANDING

U.S. War Communiques—Thursday

Out of six Japanese transports escorted by a large naval force which attempted a landing between Vigan and San Fernando (Philippines), three received direct hits, one capsizing and sinking. It is presumed that other attempts were made at various points.

On Wednesday morning all communications with Aparri, Vigan and Toguegarao were interrupted. The news of the fighting caused great excitement in Manila, but there was no panic, business in the city continuing normally, though some people fled to the hills.

Military and naval installations on Luzon Island have been subjected to intermittent Japanese air attacks throughout the day with particularly heavy attacks on the naval base at Cavite.

Initial Japanese attacks against the West coast of Luzon, north of San Fernando, were repulsed with apparent heavy enemy losses, but the Japanese effected landings along the northern coast of the island. The Japanese attacks are of considerable strength and are supported by heavy naval forces.

No action is reported in the Hawaiian Islands since the initial attack on December 7.

BLAMEY BACK IN M.E.

General Sir Thomas A. Blamey, Deputy Commander-in-Chief, Middle East Forces, arrived back in Beirut on Wednesday.

Gen Blamey in Australia. — Picture — Page 2.

AUSTRALIA'S FIRST WAR COMMUNIQUE

The first war communique ever issued in Australia comes from the R.A.A.F. It states:

There is nothing of major importance to report. Seaward reconnaissances have been carried out by the R.A.A.F. since the Pacific hostilities broke out. One of our aircraft has failed to return.

THAILAND SIGNS

LONDON, Thursday (R). — The conclusion of an alliance between Japan and Thailand was announced today in a Tokyo statement which said:

"It is reported that an agreement of views concerning the conclusion of an offensive and defensive alliance between Japan and Thailand was reached between the Japanese Ambassador at Bangkok, Teiji Tsubokami and the Thai Prime Minister, Luang Pibul Songgram."

2,330 SAVED FROM BATTLESHIPS

ADMIRAL PHILLIPS MISSING

LONDON, Thursday (R). — The Admiralty announces that approximately 130 officers and 2,200 ratings have been saved from the Prince of Wales and Repulse.

It is also announced that Admiral Sir Tom Phillips is reported missing, from H.M.S. Prince of Wales.

The survivors have arrived at Singapore.

At least seven aircraft were destroyed during the attack.

It is now learned that the Prince of Wales and the Repulse were sunk by bomber attacks and three waves of torpedo planes.

The total complement of both ships was approximately 2925 officers and ratings.

WAR FLASHES

President Roosevelt's message to Congress yesterday asking for a Declaration of War against Germany and Italy said in part: "The forces endeavouring to enslave the entire world are now moving toward this hemisphere. . . A rapid and united effort by all the peoples of the world who are determined to remain free will ensure world victory for the forces of justice and righteousness over the forces of savagery and barbarism."

According to Manila newspapers, 30 were killed and 300 wounded in Wednesday afternoon's raids.

The U.S. Senate's declaration of war against Germany was 90 votes to nil, and the House of Representatives 393 to nil. The Senate also passed a Bill enabling American expeditionary forces to be sent to any part of the world. The vote was 86 to nil.

Japanese troops are reported to have landed at the airport six miles from Llagan in Isabela Province 80 miles south of Aparri. The Filipino Constabulary are organising to repel them.

THE PALESTINE POST

LATE Edition

WEDNESDAY NOVEMBER 25, 1942

VOL. XVII. No. 5035
PRICE 12 MILS

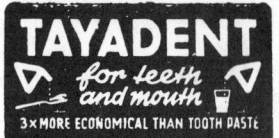
ALLIES ADVANCE ON TUNIS, BIZERTA

HOPE OF 'GERMAN DUNKIRK'

ALLIED HEADQUARTERS, NORTH AFRICA, Tuesday — Fighting spread over the greater area of Tunisia today in the form of local engagements.

An American-French force drove back the German advance screen south-west of Tunis, while the British battered a similar screen along the coast.

Tonight's U.S. communiqué reads:

Local engagements were reported by forward troops of the Allied Force. French patrol activity continued in the southern sector.

In the northern sector the Allied patrols gained some ground against an enemy mechanised column and captured prisoners. Our fighter planes shot down four enemy aircraft and attacked an enemy troop train near Gabes.

Southern bases carried out night raids on Bizerta and Tunis. None of our aircraft is missing from these operations.

Allied columns advancing along the valley of the Nedjerda River have encountered and overcome the resistance of a German light armoured column, while small German detachments are reported to be infiltrating between Kairouan and Gafsa.

The persistence and tenacity of these German landings in the Gabes and Sfax regions would seem to indicate that Rommel is determined to establish land communication between Tripoli and Tunis. It is also believed that many German planes coming from Rommel's camp.

Speaking at a press conference here today, General Clark after asserting that the Allied position was better than expected with the prospect of North Africa becoming a "German Dunkirk" also revealed that the Allies intend to make Oran a gigantic supply base as it is comparatively out of range of German planes.

Referring to the present operations, he said: "Now we are greedy and we want Tunisia without a fight. But we must realise that we can't have it that way."

He added that while the situation was favourable it was, as yet, "a sure thing" because the Germans had been able to reinforce their positions.

DAKAR TO BE USED AS ALLIED BASE

MADRID, Tuesday (UP). It is reported that Darlan's first order to the Governor of West Africa, M. Boisson, was to forbid any ship to leave Dakar harbour. The warships there include the battleship Richelieu, a cruiser, and 21 submarines.

Darlan is also dispatching a special staff mission to Dakar to establish cooperation and to grant facilities to the British and Americans.

A dispatch which took 11 days in transmission, sheds some light on the situation in West Africa before Boisson joined up with Darlan.

Donald Coe. UP. correspondent at an Allied base in West Africa, cabling on November 13, said that four young French aviators arrived at the base on that day in a battered American-built plane after incapacitating other planes on an airfield near Dakar and dismantling the aerodrome's radio-station.

They said that for many weeks they had planned to escape from Vichy rule when the American occupation of North Africa gave them a chance, and requested permission to join the United States Air Force.

The flyers asked that their comrades at Dakar be informed of the warm reception they had received, and expressed the hope that many would join the Americans.

MR. EDEN DENIES DIFFERENCES WITH PREMIER

LONDON, Tuesday (R). — Mr. Eden, who was loudly cheered on entering the House of Commons this afternoon for the first time as Leader of the House, dealt with the allegation that the script of a proposed broadcast by General de Gaulle was suppressed by Mr Churchill after Mr Eden himself had approved it.

Mr Eden promised a full reply at the earliest moment to the allegation, adding that there was no difference whatever between Mr. Churchill and himself.

The British Government is not aware that the former French ministers M Pierre Flandin and M Pierre Pucheux both formerly connected with Vichy, have arrived in North Africa and the Leader of the House of Lords. Lord Cranborne, answering questions today in the House of Lords.

He added. "They have certainly received no assistance or encouragement to proceed there from any British authority."

THOSE IN COMMAND

CAIRO, Tuesday (R) — The names of the Eighth Army Corps Commanders were disclosed in Cairo today They are: Lieutenant-General H Lumsden, commanding the 10th Corps. Lieutenant-General Sir O.W.H. Leese commanding the 30th Corps and Lieutenant-General B.G Horrocks, commanding the 13th Corps.

U-BOAT TORPEDOED BY BRITISH PLANE

ORAN, Tuesday. — An Allied anti-submarine patrol operating some miles off Oran by depth charges forced a U-boat to the surface, after which a British plane blew it up with a torpedo. Two members of the crew were rescued.

The Seafire, a slight modification of the Spitfire used for aircraft carriers, has been playing an important part in protecting Allied troopships.

(United Press and Reuters)

FIGHTING WEST OF EL AGHEILA

CAIRO, Tuesday (R). — The Allied forces have entered Jedabya and occupied Jalo oasis, on the road to Agheila while the Axis forces have continued to withdraw.

Fighting is now going on 30 miles west of El Agheila, according to one report.

Today's joint Middle East war communiqué reads:

LAND: Our forces entered JEDBAYA early yesterday and are maintaining contact with the enemy who are continuing their withdrawal towards EL AGHEILA.

The enemy has evacuated JALO Oasis which has been occupied by our troops.

AIR: Air activity over Cyrenaica yesterday was on a small scale. On the night of November 17-18 our torpedo aircraft successfully attacked an enemy merchant vessel south-east of Sardinia. The ship received a direct hit amidships and was subsequently sunk.

BIZERTA was bombed on the same night and dispersed aircraft at PALERMO, Sicily. Yesterday at least three large enemy aircraft were shot down by our fighters off the east coast of TUNISIA, and no damage was attached with our forces.

From the above operations, two of our aircraft did not return.

The Bizerta Raid

Royal Air Force medium bombers operating from Malta in the raid on Bizerta harbour, reported in today's communiqué, defied German anti-aircraft fire and swooped down to release their bombs. A number of fires were lit; burning on the docks and a particularly heavy bomb was seen to burst near a dockside goods station.

Other aircraft, while attacked the aerodrome at Palermo in Sicily shot up several planes dispersed on the ground. Hundreds of wrecked aircraft in Libya have shown the effectiveness of such tactics.

Flying operations were still bad in the Tunisia battle area yesterday and reduced air activity to a minimum.

KNOX HOPEFUL OF SOLOMONS ISSUE

U.S. FORCES KEEP SHARP LOOKOUT

WASHINGTON, Tuesday (UP).—Colonel Frank Knox, the Secretary for the Navy, told the press here today that it was unlikely that the Japanese would now be able to get reinforcements ashore at Guadalcanal due to the United States forces maintaining a day and night watch.

The enemy might be able, he said to get in small reinforcements and aircraft at night, but while this was possible, it was improbable.

The Secretary said that the Solomons situation appeared to be progressing satisfactorily along the lines which he had outlined at his last press conference when he said that the operations were progressing satisfactorily with the United States forces holding a firm grip on Guadalcanal.

The U.S. forces were widening their area of control to about seven to nine miles west of Henderson Field, although they actually controlled only three per cent of the total area of the island.

The western front line lay along 20 miles from Cape Esperance, on the south-western tip of the island, where the Japanese had earlier landed their largest concentrations.

Asked whether he believed that the Japanese forces could be wiped out, he replied: "That is our objective."

ALLIES STORM NEW GUINEA KEYPOINTS

By CURTIS HINDSON
Reuters Special Correspondent at General MacArthur's Headquarters.

Australian forces have entered Gona in strength following the first penetration by their patrols on Sunday afternoon.

There is still some resistance, according to General MacArthur's spokesman, though it should be only a matter of time before the village is completely in Allied hands. The Australians now were merely cleaning up stragglers.

On the right flank a U.S. column, after capturing a landing strip at Buna, pressed on to Cape Endaidere. This position was taken against strong opposition, the Japanese having well-prepared machine-gun positions and snipers hidden in the trees.

Fighting is now narrowed down to focal points at Buna village and Buna mission, which are being stormed jointly by the Australian and United States forces. The enemy's resistance here is officially stated to be heavy. Some Japanese attempting to escape down the Kumusa river on rafts have been wiped out.

Marauders and Havocs have again bombed and machine-gunned Japanese positions, especially those at Sananda Point.

Japanese on Timor

It is now revealed that the Japanese have occupied the villages of Beco and Raimean on the south coast of Timor. This is the first mention of Japanese forces on the south coast of the island A spokesman disclosed that the Japanese came over from the centre of the island a few days ago. Beco on the south-west coast—and Raimean—one mile south-west of Beco—were both bombed and strafed by Hudsons and Beaufighters.

The Allied H.Q. communiqué this morning says:

BUNA-GONA: On the left, our troops entered Gona, advancing on Sananda; on the night of November 22, Cape Endaidere was captured. Heavy resistance around Buna itself continues. Our air forces are supporting the attack.

VITIAZ STRAITS: An Allied reconnaissance unit shot down a Zero Japanese aircraft which attempted interception. TIMOR: Allied medium bombers raided the enemy-occupied Beco and Raimean. (Vitiaz Straits are between New Guinea and New Britain).

SOVIET ARMY SCORES SMASHING VICTORY

It was officially announced in Moscow last night that the Russians have captured three enemy divisions, which had been previously surrounded, together with three Generals and their staffs. Sweeping away all German resistance, Russian troops north-west of Stalingrad have continued their successful advance. In a north-westerly direction the Russians advanced 10 kilometres. South of Stalingrad they advanced between 15 and 20 kilometres.

Russian forces yesterday took 12,000 prisoners, bringing the total to 36,000. Fifteen thousand Germans were killed in the latest fighting. The Germans in their retreat are abandoning large quantities of supplies including ammunition, fuel and food dumps.

GERMANS FACE DISASTER

By Reuters Special Correspondent
STOCKHOLM, Tuesday — If the Germans cannot check the Russian advance north and south of Stalingrad some 400,000 Axis troops who for the past three months have been held while at the doors of the Volga fortress will be trapped and annihilated, it is believed here.

Some observers think that the Germans are no longer in a position to do real damage, others that they may launch counter-attacks in order to halt the progress of the Russian armies.

If the Russians continue their advance or even if they only succeed in maintaining their positions acquired in the past four days, it is felt that the Germans will not be able to establish a winter line either on the Don or the Chir.

In the Russian advance yesterday, one success overshadowed all others—the capture of Cherymchevskaya on the Chir river. Describing the plight of the Rumanian fighting in this sector the Germans say they fought until the last man and the last hand grenade.

The Last Outlet

The gap between Kalach and Abganerovo is probably the only outlet through which the Germans in the Don-Volga corridor can escape. The Russians are now in an excellent position to close the German "sack" before Stalingrad. But the cleaning up of this "sack" may take some time, because the Germans will probably put up a desperate defensive fight.

In the five-day Soviet offensive the Germans have lost 27,000 dead. The Germans are not yet to hand, the authorities made it clear that in many places the German defeat has been a total rout.

The German Command has been caught out more effectively than last year at Rostov. Hitler evidently prevented it from cutting its losses and withdrawing from Stalingrad in time. Now it appears definitely too late and the Germans stand under the threat of their greatest military defeat of the war.

A German communiqué says that Soviet troops have broken through the defensive front south-west of Stalingrad and in the great Don bend. In the Caucasian area unfavourable weather conditions prevented large scale fighting.

Counter-measures are now in progress. In the last two days several hundred enemy tanks have been destroyed, states the communiqué, adding that in Stalingrad itself there was only local fighting.

300,000 NAZIS TRAPPED AT STALINGRAD

By HAROLD KING, Reuters Special Correspondent

The armies of Generals Romanenko and Batov are smashing their way from north and south to close the iron ring which the victorious Soviet forces are throwing round the Germans at Stalingrad.

The movement has been beautifully timed and excellently carried out, and the double Soviet attack appears completely to have overwhelmed the enemy and disorganised him.

Three armies are now swiftly and inexorably closing round German forces rallied at some 300,000 men. Cut off from their far-away bases the Germans in the 40-mile strip of steppe between the Don and Volga at Stalingrad now appear to be hopelessly trapped.

The original blows struck at the vital eastern and southern railroad supply lines for the Germans attacking the Volga city have been reinforced threefold and the heroic garrison inside Stalingrad, after three months of grim defensive battles, has joined in the offensive in the last 24 hours. General Rodimtsev's troops are slowly advancing westward from the northern factory belt as well as from the southern suburbs of the city.

Advance Continues

Meanwhile the main offensive is going according to plan and the tempo of the advance is not slackening. The troops of Major-General Chistiakov are chasing the Germans at top speed inside the Don elbow, after the big battles. The Germans are being rolled back in the direction of the southern arm of the Don.

At the southern end the Soviet advance has broken the Red Army 60 miles back along the Caucasian railway which only a few days ago was still practically entirely in German hands.

The big lines of the operational strategy of the Red Army are unfolding themselves as the rapid advance across the Don steppes continues. It is significant that the latest report is that the Germans are retreating, indeed fleeing precipitately southward from Chernyshevskaya. On Monday night, one army already stood no further than 40 miles from Kotelnikovo and during the night of Monday/Tuesday, this army made a further successful advance.

DECISIVE BATTLE RAGING

By HENRY SHAPIRO
U.P. Correspondent in Moscow

Great possibilities are foreseen for the decisive battle now raging in the Stalingrad region as the battered German forces, fearing entrapment in the Red Army's iron ring, are trying to rally for a counter-attack.

The Soviet offensive meanwhile is gaining momentum. One army moving southward has reached the village of Pogodinsky, well inside the Don River bend, in a drive to achieve a junction with the Russian forces hammering the enemy to the west, while a third army advancing from the southern sector has cut the railroad to Rostov.

While the Russians have crushed many German divisions, others are still concentrated in the Stalingrad area, occupying fortified villages and whose strong points show their determination with a increasingly difficult. General Timoshenko's offensive whose momentum, but General von Bock's attempts to launch a counter-offensive have thus far failed with the virtual loss of two divisions.

The situation has apparently become a race between Bock's effort to make a counter-attack and the Soviet ability to reinforce the two principal advance columns in order to prevent a German break-out.

Artillery and Infantry

Aviation played a minor role in the last day's fighting on account of dense screening fog which, however, furnished excellent cover for artillery and advancing infantry.

Front-line dispatches indicate that the Russian offensive began with diversionary attacks, whereby the enemy was deceived, causing him to throw his forces against unimportant sectors. The Russians then struck powerfully in two principal directions.

Soviet forces massed southward of Stalingrad, on the east bank of the Volga, only a few days ago hurriedly crossed the river in pontoons thrown across the freezing water and struck early in the morning following an intensive 21 hours artillery bombardment. The infantry cleared the minefields for the passage of tanks which crushed one line after another. Mobile heavy and medium-sized artillery played an important part in widening the breach.

After a full day of these operations, Soviet cavalry fanned out cut the railroads to Tikhoretsk, smashed numerous German groups, and advanced 14 miles. From then on there was no stopping them.

Freezing Prisoners Surrender

In the steppes south of Stalingrad there are now clusters of with overturned and bogged out enemy machines and thousands of green-uniformed bodies. Endless columns of frost-bitten prisoners conveyed by Russian cavalrymen attest to the east, while the victors are picking up propaganda leaflets such as "Hitler has never been beaten: the German Army remains invincible."

The entire steppe is now frozen and covered with snow. Large German and Rumanian units poorly clad and wrapped in blankets, are roaming the icy steppes, frequently surrendering without a fight.

MUSSOLINI SEEKS A WAY OUT

GERMAN GENERALS CONFLICT AMONG

LONDON, Tuesday (ANA) Reliable information reaching London suggests that Mussolini is trying to set up a National Defence Cabinet, now that he doubts his ability to maintain the unity of Italy and the prolongation of resistance at a time where the Allied threat to Italy is growing.

The Fascist leader Viduzoni, the former Liberal Minister Orlando, and Catholic leaders have been contacted for this purpose, it is stated.

Mussolini is also reported to have established contact with the leaders of the former trade union movement, as well as with some leaders of the Banned Socialist Party, but the latter as any rate have declined to cooperate.

In the meantime, increased German pressure is being brought to bear on Italy. Mass arrests are taking place throughout the country.

Hitler and Rommel

While trouble is thus brewing in Italy, there are indications that a serious conflict exists among Germany's military leaders.

For reasons of personal prestige, in an attempt to maintain the myth with which Rommel's alleged military genius had been surrounded Hitler has ordered the organisation of a propaganda campaign intended to explain away the defeat inflicted on the Afrika Korps.

Official German propaganda continues to strike the familiar note that Rommel is invincible, and that the British have been surprised by his western retreat the pursuit of which has been beyond their power.

The motive underlying this campaign is understood to be Hitler's desire to maintain the leadership of the Army, as Rommel is the only general field in high esteem by Hitler and he is represented to the public as an outstanding strategist.

REINFORCEMENTS RUSHED TO ITALY

By DANA SCHMIDT
U.P. Staff Correspondent in Ankara

Reports from the Balkans quoted in military quarters here show that all the indications of hurried German troop and air movements after the Allied landings in North Africa and the British break-through in Libya took down to the fact that reinforcements have been almost exclusively directed towards Italy.

These indications contain only one specific report involving German divisions which moved through the Balkans from Russia to Africa. These reached Greece too late for their transport to Cyrenaica and have been shipped on to Italy.

A considerable though unestimated number of planes was withdrawn from Russia and flown across the Balkans to Italy and Sicily.

Reliable sources understand that the full tide of this German troop movement from the Balkans to Italy and Sicily were greatly hindered by Chetnik raids.

As no per cent increase in the price of civilian rail transport was announced in Sofia this week-end and similar increases are scheduled for Hungary and Croatia from January.

U.S. Troops Push On

WASHINGTON Tuesday (R). It is officially announced that the American westward advance on Guadalcanal continues.

Today's communiqué says:

During the night of November 22, United States aircraft attacked enemy positions on Guadalcanal island. During November 22, United States units advanced westward of the Matanikau River.

General Sigurah has taken over the command of all Greek forces in the Middle East after a spectacular escape from Greece.

Lieutenant-General Sir Hubert Huddleston, the Governor-General of the Sudan, and Lady Huddleston have arrived in Cairo by air from Khartoum.

Mass-Butchery of Poland's Jews

LONDON, Tuesday (R). — The most ruthless methods are being used in Poland to give effect to the order made by Himmler that the whole Jewish population must be exterminated by the end of this year, says a report reaching the Polish Government in London.

Special battalions commanded by SS men seize the victims, including old people and cripples, who are taken to cemeteries and shot there.

The remainder are loaded in goods trucks at the rate of 150 to a truck covered with a thick layer of lime or chlorine sprinkled with water and the doors of the trucks are sealed. Wherever the trains pull up half the people arrive dead.

Those surviving are sent to special camps Once there, the so-called "settlers" are massacred Only the young and relatively strong are left alive for they provide valuable slave labour for the German. By the end of September a quarter of a million Jews had been "eliminated."

Norwegian Clergy Condemn Pogroms

STOCKHOLM, Tuesday (R). — Norwegian churchmen have sent to Quisling a solemn protest against the persecution of Norwegian Jews, says the Swedish-Norwegian Press Bureau.

The protest is signed by the Provisional Church Council of all affiliated Church organisations and the Theological Faculty of Oslo University It states:

"These measures have provoked unheard-of horror throughout the country. We do not intend to start any political action or to defend Jews who have committed crimes, but if they are guilty, they must be tried according to Norwegian law."

Norwegian Government circles in London (quoted by Palcor) report that 2,300 Norwegian aged 15 and over have been interned by the Nazi authorities and are to be sent to forced labour gangs partly in the far north and partly in Poland.

All Jewish property in Norway has been confiscated.

ARRESTS IN TANGIER

LONDON, Tuesday (Palcor). Many arrests among the Jewish community in Tangier, now part of Spanish Morocco, after the Allied landings in North Africa are reported in a message which has just arrived here.

The arrested persons were sent to concentration camps on the ground that the movement was discovered among the Jews of Spanish Morocco to cross the border clandestinely and join the Allies in occupied territory.

TEL AVIV MEETING

TEL AVIV, Tuesday. — Local journalists met here today to express their indignation and horror at the unspeakable atrocities inflicted on European Jews by the Nazis.

In the presence of leaders of Polish Jewry, the pressmen heard authenticated reports of the mass butchery of hundreds of thousands of men, women and children under the German yoke and of the veritable hell under which others live.

Even the findings of an Italian Red Cross Commission, it was stated protested against the inferno trained of Jews in Warsaw.

FEEDING THE LIBERATED AREAS

WASHINGTON, Tuesday (R) President Roosevelt gave a clear intimation today that he will explain this programme for the rehabilitation of liberated countries in a radio speech shortly.

He defended his policy of feeding liberated areas and said that the policy would continue. He added that it would prove sound both from the standpoint of the American pocketbook and from that of defence.

Author of Political Thriller Arrested

NEW YORK, Tuesday (UP) — Upon the order of the Attorney General, Julius Herman Krebs, who under the name of Jan Valtin wrote the best-seller "Out of the Night" describing Gestapo methods has been arrested for the duration of the war, after the termination of which he is scheduled to be deported.

The order was issued following the publication of findings by the Immigration Board to the effect that Krebs' life had been so marked by violence and treachery that it would be difficult, if not unwarranted to conclude that his present reliability and good character had been established.

According to a Chicago message, the father of one of the recently convicted German saboteurs Hans Haupt, a certain Walter Frehling, and one Otto Wergin, have all been sentenced to death for treason and have been convicted of aiding Herbert Haupt in landing from a U-boat.

His mother, Mrs Wergin, and Mrs Frehling were sentenced to 25 years' imprisonment.

It will be recalled that Haupt was recently executed at Washington together with five saboteurs. The Chicago sentence pronounced on six naturalised German-born accused has now climaxed the greatest treason trial in U.S. history.

GOVERNMENT TO BUY CITRUS

At least 25,000 tons of citrus will be purchased at a price for good quality fruit of LP.3.500 per ton on the tree by the Food Controller this season. The object of this step is to absorb any surplus citrus by stimulating consumption, it is officially announced.

In view of the altered citrus marketing circumstances according to a communiqué just issued the Government has decided with the approval of the Secretary of State to abandon the Disposal Permit this was inaugurated at a time when supply was far in excess of demand and when aimed at reducing the price level of that portion of the crop which could be marketed.

Normal Trading Resumed Four days' grace are given from today to enable those who have bought fruit on which the fee has been paid to dispose of their stocks. After November 29 the normal channels of trade will operate unrestricted so far as internal civilian requirements are concerned. The Citrus Marketing Board will afford any necessary and practicable assistance in this and other directions.

Intermediate charges will be subject to strict regulations to ensure a maximum benefit. It is hoped that the fullest and most beneficial use of the fruit will be made and that the relief obtainable by the destruction of any portion of the crop will no longer arise.

The Food Controller will publish shortly details of the methods of purchase and distribution.

The first consignment of Palestinian citrus, consisting of about 1,000 cases, was dispatched by Arab citrus-growers this week in accordance with the agreement with the military authorities.

CHEERFUL WELCOME HOME FOR SMUTS

PRETORIA, Tuesday (R) — Field Marshal Smuts returned home today from his visit to London. In an interview with Reuter on his arrival he said:

I am very glad to be back and pleased to see everybody looking so cheerful. I am very satisfied and pleased with my visit overseas and my visit to troops in North Africa.

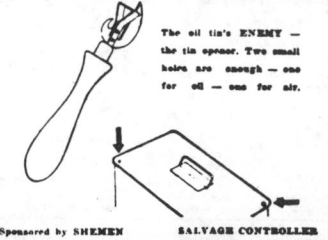

LATE Edition

THE PALESTINE POST

TUESDAY MARCH 30 1943

Vol. XVIII No. 5142 PRICE MILS

ROMMEL IN FULL RETREAT

BRITISH BREAK AND OUTFLANK MARETH LINE

ALLIED HEADQUARTERS IN N. AFRICA, Monday (R). — With the Mareth Line broken and the Afrika Korps in full retreat to the north to avoid encirclement, British, American and French troops are attacking in all sectors on a 300-mile front.

Rommel is falling back to the Gabes area, under tremendous ground and air pressure and with the loss of much equipment and thousands of prisoners. Mareth, Matmata and Toujane are in British hands. At El Hamma, on his flank, first-class German troops were defeated and yielded control of the town to the Eighth Army, while the Gabes area has been heavily bombarded by Allied naval forces.

French and American troops are converging on Kairouan and the American column which took Fondouk continues to advance towards the coast. In the north the First Army continues its offensive in the Djebel Abiod region.

Thaw Holds Up Major Fighting At Smolensk

Russians Reach Main Defences

MOSCOW, Monday. — The Russians have now reached the main defence line of the Smolensk fortifications system and scouts are already probing into the enemy positions.

Reports related steady progress by both Soviet forces in the two-pronged Smolensk drive — one thrusting from Byeli and the other south-westward along the Moscow-Smolensk railway. But the spring thaw and the generally deteriorating climatic conditions are likely to become the predominant factor in the central front operations for several more weeks.

It is admitted that it is now problematical whether the Red Army will undertake an assault on the main enemy line before the weather improves. New gains have been made by the Soviet forces striking for Smolensk but because of thaw fighting has been reduced to local operations.

In a frontal advance towards the great German base, the Russians during the night occupied an inhabited locality in hand-to-hand fighting. Using hand grenades and bayonets, they killed over 100 Germans. Three places south of Byeli were occupied by Soviet troops engaged in a thrust from the north-east, and Guardsmen defeated a German counter-attack in this sector, killing 150 Germans.

In the Middle Donetz area, the Russians flattened out a wedge driven into their lines at one point. By encircling movements on flanks, the Germans were surrounded and over 200 wiped out. Elsewhere another German attempt to cross a river was repulsed.

(UP and Reuter)

Nazis Raze Country in Retreat

MOSCOW Monday (UP) — The Metropolitan Nicolai of Kiev, one of the most prominent leaders of the Russian Orthodox Church, who has just returned from an extensive tour of the reoccupied area in the Smolensk district, states that the retreating Germans have carried out a devastating "scorched earth" policy.

The Germans, he said, systematically massacred thousands of civilians, burned down hundreds of towns and villages, and destroyed churches, schools, and other public buildings.

A vast area had been turned into a wilderness and many historic towns and villages levelled to the ground.

Puppets to Pay

LONDON, Monday (R). — A Czechoslovak officer broadcasting from London last night said that the puppet Government of Slovakia, as well as the German Army would be held responsible for the decimation of the Slovak Regiment which recently mutinied on the Russian front.

Reports reaching Czechoslovak circles in London state that the regiment decided to go over to the Russians when the Slovak division to which it belonged was ordered to retreat in the Tuapse sector. The Germans were warned of the plan and every tenth man of the regiment was shot.

Underground Army Ready

A leading article in "The Times" today says:

"The underground struggle in Europe is taking on a fiercer note. Premature risings can only serve German ends but once the moment has been chosen and the call given there is no doubt that the assault on the enemy from the front will be powerfully assisted from within Hitler's so-called European fortress.

"All over Europe a great army is preparing to take the field when the hour strikes for a decisive blow."

LEASE-LEND SHIPMENTS IN FEBRUARY

WASHINGTON, Monday (R). The Lend-Lease Administrator, Mr. Stettinius reports that almost all Lease-Lend food shipped to America's allies during January and February went to Russia and Britain in about equal proportions.

Shipments over this period, he said, showed an increase in 11 items and a decrease in 9, as compared with last year.

QUARTER CENTURY OF AIR ARM

Air Minister Pays Tribute to RAF

LATEST RAID ON BERLIN 'A SHATTERING ASSAULT'

LONDON, Monday. — The Secretary for Air, Sir Archibald Sinclair, in a broadcast tribute to the R.A.F. last night on its silver jubilee — the service will be 25 years old on Thursday — described Saturday night's R.A.F. raid on Berlin as "a shattering assault."

"British and Dominion airmen, with their superb British aircraft and equipment, have established their ascendancy over the airmen of the Axis," said the Air Minister "The present role of the R.A.F. is destructive. It may yet win fame and laurels in constructive work for the service of mankind."

Sir Archibald traced the growth of the RAF from the Royal Naval Air Service and Fleet Air Arm, and paid a tribute to Lord Trenchard, "whose genius, foresight, leadership, and driving force fused the naval and military elements of air power into one mighty service" and to "three other great men of action"—Lloyd George, Field Marshal Smuts, and the Prime Minister, Mr. Churchill, for the part they played in the formation of the service 25 years ago.

Panic in Berlin

The Berlin press now admits that panic and inefficiency was responsible for much of the damage caused during the last R.A.F. raid on Berlin.

Newspapers are admonishing the citizens of Berlin for their behaviour, openly stating that if the people had kept their heads and gone about their fire-fighting duties in a proper manner there would have been much less damage and loss of life.

Following this raid the municipal authorities in Berlin were forced to grant a special allocation of clothing coupons to the thousands of homeless Berliners.

So great was the damage that professional workers were mobilized to clear the blocked roads and repair damaged buildings.

Nuremberg Hard Hit

More facts have now come to light showing how extensively Nuremberg's factories were damaged during the big R.A.F. raid on the night of March 8.

Fire appears to have been the chief cause of the devastation. One area with timber and goods covering 16 acres and another of 30 acres were set ablaze. At the Siemen's plant, two-thirds of the main workshops covering five acres have been destroyed.

The Air Ministry announced tonight that when the Brown House the headquarters of the Nazi Party was hit in the raid on Munich on March 9 the top floor was burned out

On this floor was Hitler's office A bust of Mussolini used to stand in the wall facing the door and a head of Napoleon used to be on a small bookcase behind the Fuehrer's chair.

(Reuter and ANA)

Eden-Hull Talks Concluded

WASHINGTON, Monday (UP) — Mr. Anthony Eden is concluding his conferences here, the atmosphere indicating that great progress has been made towards Anglo-American understanding on the issues of war and peace.

The Foreign Secretary will be Mr. Hull's guest of honour at a banquet tonight. He is scheduled to arrive at Ottawa tomorrow.

A War Department statement says: "Meetings have been arranged by the Joint Chiefs of Staff to acquaint the Commanders in the Pacific with the policies and plans decided upon at the recent Casablanca conference which concerned future action in which their theatres will be involved.

"At the same time, the Chiefs of Staff will be able to obtain first-hand knowledge of the developments in the Pacific to learn the views of the commanders in the field."

Half Million Jews Killed in Warsaw

BALTIMORE, Monday. — According to Rabbi Maurice Perlzweig, President of the British Section of the World Jewish Congress, all of Warsaw's half a million Jews have been killed by the Germans.

Addressing a mass meeting here yesterday, he declared that the destruction of the entire Jewish population of Warsaw and millions of other Jews by the Nazis had been substantiated by both the British Foreign Office and the U S State Department This was the last phase of Hitler's drive to exterminate European Jewry.

Minority Rights

The U.S. Government and the United Nations generally were urged to clarify the position regarding the restoration of rights of Jewish minorities in European countries by Dr. Israel Goldstein, speaking at a dinner given in his honour in New York today, at which Dr. Weizman spoke.

Senator Barkley backed Dr Weizman's demand for a national home in Palestine, while Governor Dewey sent a message hailing Palestine's contribution to the war effort.

(Reuter and PAT)

ONLY 20 MILES TO GABES

8th Army Hurdles Another Obstacle

By ALAN HUMPHREYS
Reuters Special Correspondent

For the third time since the Eighth Army started from El Alamein, General Montgomery has overcome a very difficult prepared defence line by an outflanking movement. He used these tactics at El Agheila, at Wadi Zeumzem before Tripoli, and now at Mareth.

Battering its way forward against very fierce opposition in the El Hamma sector, the British column was so threatening to the rear of the Axis forces in the Mareth position that they were compelled to withdraw in the direction of Gabes.

This is not a rout. The Axis Command is making a withdrawal which, though forced, is nevertheless in some order, and the Eighth Army is still having to fight its way forward. At El Hamma, the British are opposed by first class German troops. Pockets of resistance which have been left behind by the retreating enemy make the rearguard fighting very tough.

It is generally believed that Rommel will retreat to a line north of Sousse since his position in the plains bounded by the Shott Djerid, Kairouan, Sousse and Gabes is undefendable.

On the northern front, the First Army's attack in the hilly sector after going like clockwork in its initial stages up to last night, was temporarily slowed down by the weather, rain and hail storms being experienced. On the flank the British troops are being heavily engaged

On the southern front, fighting went on in the El Guettar valley, where Axis resistance appears to be stiffening. The Americans made some headway in the hills on either side of the valley but Axis strong points are making progress difficult.

Brisbane Cheers The Ninth

BRISBANE, Monday (R).— Elements of the A.I.F. Ninth Division recently home from two years' campaign in the Middle East paraded through the main streets of Brisbane today.

Thousands lined the route, cheering and waving flags and breaking the police cordons to scatter confetti over column after column of bronzed troops.

Sir Leslie Wilson, Governor of Queensland, took the salute from the steps of Brisbane's beflagged Town Hall.

Twenty-three Service personnel, including three members of the R.A.A.F., were killed when an R.A.A.F. transport plane crashed in the darkness near Brisbane early on Saturday.

The victims included 17 R.A.A.F. men one Australian Army officer, and two United States Army officers. There were no survivors.

Squadron Leader Keith Truscott is reported missing believed killed He crashed off the Australian coast today during a practice flight.

NEW ZEALAND DEFENCE MINISTER HERE

New Zealand's Minister of Defence, the Hon. Frederick Jones, arrived in Jerusalem yesterday at the conclusion of his tour of the Middle East.

Mr. Jones, who brought greetings and messages to troops from the Government and people of New Zealand, previously visited Egypt, Syria and the Lebanon

W.A.A.F. Recruiting in M.E. Soon

CAIRO, Monday (R). — It is learned that young British women living in Middle East countries, including Egypt and Palestine, may shortly be recruited for service in the Women's Auxiliary Air Force.

AMERICANS DRIVE ON TO COAST

By VIRGIL PINKLEY U.P. Correspondent at Allied H.Q. North Africa

The pressure of the Allied flanking movement behind the Mareth Line has forced Rommel to abandon his positions and the Eighth Army, smashing through the fortifications, has rolled on to capture Matmata, only 22 miles from the big Axis base of Gabes.

All along the battle-front, even in the far north where the British First Army had been biding its time, the Allies are on the march. The American forces continue to advance to the east from El Guettar, and altogether there are six columns pressing the Afrika Korps relentlessly towards the sea.

General Montgomery inflicted a heavy defeat on Rommel in his battering-ram attack on the Southern Tunisian defence system when the enemy was forced to give up the entire Mareth Line and retire towards Gabes. The combination of a frontal attack against the main Mareth Line, a heavy drive against El Hamma, and pressure on the El Guettar, Maknassy and Fondouk areas, forced Rommel to pull out of Mareth and start for Gabes, which is now really a bottleneck, with the Eighth Army driving from the south and other forces at the edge of El Hamma, only 16 miles away.

Combined Blitz

The pressure of combined land and air attack and the gains at El Hamma have caused Rommel to leave a considerable quantity of undamaged guns, tanks and motor transport behind. The air forces and artillery pounded the region so hard that the enemy — mostly crack German troops of the Afrika Korps — were forced to flee before they could destroy their equipment.

The Americans continue to hold the initiative in the El Guettar, Maknassy and Fondouk sectors. Much of this terrain of rocky hills and semi-desert is covered in some places with scrub. The pressure from these American field areas played a great part in the Eighth Army advances against El Hamma and the forcing of the Mareth Line.

Allied air power, built up painstakingly in the past three months, is making itself felt throughout the front as the Axis forces are harassed and threatened on all sides. This power is being applied methodically in accordance with the over all master plan worked out carefully by General Eisenhower and General Alexander with their affiliated land, air and sea commanders.

The air forces teamed with the ground forces to keep pressure on Rommel from every direction — land and air. It was a magnificent powerhouse attack. The retreating Axis forces were blasted, bombed and hammered by the air forces which, in addition to strafing and bomb-plastering the ground troops, continued their attacks against landing grounds, harbours, docks, railways, highways and Axis bases in Sicily, Sardinia, and Italy.

The New Line

In the far north, British and French troops pushed deeper into Axis territory as they advanced some miles north and north-east of Djebel Abiod. Allied forces recaptured important parts of the Tamera-Sedjanene roads. North Moroccan "Goums" commanded by French officers fought exceedingly well in this action.

The Allies today hold a huge, inverted horse-shoe position starting at the sea end of the Mareth Line, swinging round south-west, and then north-east to El Hamma. Inside this horse-shoe are Rommel's forces. Still further north, the Americans hold a large arc, swinging through points east of El Guettar, Sened and Maknassy, and a similar arc in Central Tunisia, west of the "holy city" of Kairouan, running roughly through Fondouk, Pichon and Ousseltia.

The Americans are less then 40 miles at their forward positions east of Maknassy to Mahares on the coast. From Fondouk to Kairouan is 20 miles while from Pichon to Kairouan is 25 miles. Kairouan and Sousse are 32 miles airline and about 41 miles by road.

Nazis Plough Up Gabes Field

By BERTHA GASTER
Our Cairo Correspondent

The threat to Rommel's rear represented by the advance of two Allied columns from Fondouk and El Hamma respectively, is strikingly confirmed by the report that the west and main landing grounds at Gabes have been ploughed up by the Germans.

Whether that indicates preparations for an early withdrawal or only that the landing grounds are now useless under the day and night hammering of Allied planes is not clear. What is clear is that they have no further hope of using them again.

While news of the Mareth battle front has flared up dramatically into the headlines the air offensive over the Gabes area continues in spite of bad weather and swirling dust-storms

The battle is now over, with Rommel retreating through the Gabes gap, while the British force on his flank which took El Hamma is harassing his columns. The Mareth victory was won largely by this outflanking movement in which the air force played a large part.

(UP).

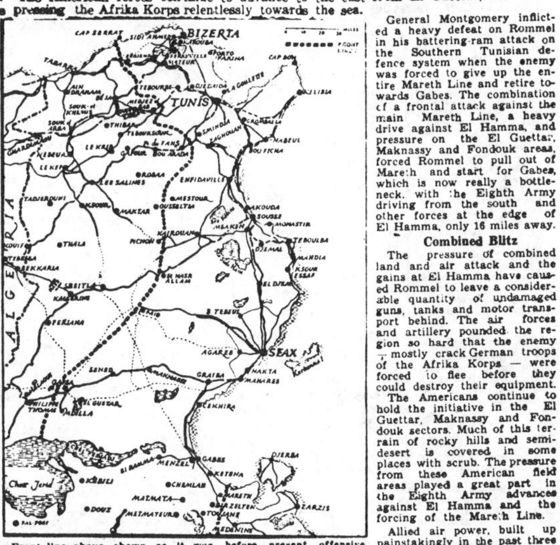

Front line above shown as it was before present offensive.

LUFTWAFFE ABSENT FROM DJEBEL BATTLE

By PHIL AULT
U.P. Correspondent with the U.S. Forces beyond El Guettar (Delayed)

The American troops, opening the big push to the sea, struck the German mountain line at three places on Sunday in an attempt to break through the last hill barriers before the Tunisian coastal plain.

The biggest attack was a strong thrust through the hills along both sides of the Gabes road, nine miles south-east of El Guettar. At the southern end of the sector, American troops developed a threat to Kairouan in a second attack.

The third action involved an artillery duel for the high ground east of Maknassy where the troops crept forward over the naked hills up the ravines under mortar and shell fire south-east of El Guettar and slowly gained ground against stubborn German resistance which lasted all day. The Germans who were favoured by rugged terrain obviously intend to resist to the utmost.

From a captured Italian observation post on top of a wind-blown dusty ridge I watched the Americans edge forward under a German barrage from guns concealed on the north side of the Gabes road. The attack began at dawn. Some troops advanced along the northern slope of Djebel Berda towards the low hills overlooking the road where the supply road south to Kevili crosses the salt lake and joins the Gabes road. Others infiltrated over the high ground skirting the bases of the mountains forming the northern edge of the valley.

Djebel Mcheltat Fight

The key point in this sector — a German stronghold — is the Djebel Mcheltat a bald, 1,500-foot hill forming a horse-shoe with its points eastward. The rock is deeply cut by ravines At dusk the Americans had captured the northern half of the horse-shoe and the Germans were stubbornly holding the southern end. The troops then swung south to aid those trying a frontal assault.

The German air force was entirely absent from the battle, while American planes were handicapped by a mist covering the ground for much of the day. In my observation post, lying on an Italian overcoat left by a former occupant when he fled hurriedly several days ago, I could look forward across the semi-arid valley to the southern shoulder of Mcheltat. To the right rose the Djebel, barren-topped The American vehicles crept forward along the foot of the mountains, raising clouds of dust and dodging into a gully as German artillery laid salvoes along their path

During a one-minute period in mid-morning, a concentrated American barrage laid on Mcheltat 1,000-lbs. of explosives dropped on the heights but the Germans clung to the position.

The Germans, on higher ground than the Americans, had the advantage of superior observation posts and gun positions enabling them to lay direct fire on jeeps and trucks scouting across the valley. Captain Percy L. Smith, assistant regimental surgeon, told of driving in a jeep around a bend into an exposed position, immediately after which a shell burst 40 yards away. He hopped from the jeep and took cover, several other bursts following quickly.

Capt Smith said: "Our boys taking cover behind the rocks in small natural caves and gulleys were trying to work forward against the German shell-fire but it was tough going. A number of them were injured and lay in the valley but the shell-fire was so intense that stretcher-bearers were unable to reach them. They had to lie there until dark."

Axis Runs Tunisian Gauntlet

By FERGUS J. FERGUSON,
Reuters Military Correspondent

LONDON, Monday. — It was the threat to the Gabes bottleneck from the British outflanking column at El Hamma that forced Rommel's hand. The German Commander must now draw out as fast as he can if he does not wish to be cornered.

He is believed to have with him the remains of two German armoured divisions and some motorized troops of the 90th Light Division who have had abundant experience in making a quick get-away.

At all costs he has to try to hold his flank between El Hamma and Gabes while the withdraws to the north, but this is going to be a costly experience involving the sacrifice of much material and many prisoners. If he does get through the bottleneck, he has a long and narrow coastal road to traverse before he joins forces with von Arnim in the north.

Here too his flank is threatened at four points, where the roads lead through the coastal range to the coastal plain. The Americans are at Maknassy, at Faid Pass, and now at Fondouk, south-west of Kairouan so that Rommel will find himself beset by the Allies practically along the whole 150 miles to Sousse where he may hope to link up with von Arnim.

It is of course possible that General Alexander may also have some surprise up his sleeve that will make Rommel's route more onerous than his retreat from El Alamein to Tripoli.

Premier of Bengal Dismissed

CALCUTTA, Monday.— Mr. Fazlul Huq, formerly General Secretary of the Indian National Congress, has resigned as Prime Minister of Bengal.

In a statement, Mr. Fazlul Huq said that various proposals were put forward during talks with the Governor last night, some of which he could not accept consistently with self-respect, whereupon the Governor suggested that he should resign.

The growing strength of the Moslem League has just been shown in Bengal, where in six elections for Moslem seats in the Legislative Council five were won by the League.

The Ministry, which is based on a coalition of non-League Moslems and Hindus survived a motion of censure last week in the Assembly by 30 votes in a House of 202.

The motion accused the Ministry of weakening the administration by not accepting responsibility for the actions of its officials It was supported by the Moslem League, which is in opposition and by the European group, which is independent but generally supports the Ministry

(Reuter and ANA)

Curtin Foresees Long War

SYDNEY, Monday (UP). The Prime Minister, Mr. Curtin, in a speech here today, warned that the war would probably last three more years.

He pointed out that "Japan, tireless, formidable and unrelenting, knows that if she cannot win this time, it will be impossible for her to win in centuries."

The Premier also stressed Australia's vital military importance for the Allies.

War Flashes

A police inspector and another policeman were among ten Belgian hostages shot by the Germans for the killing of several members of the German Army Transport Corps, an SS man, and a Rexist (Belgian Fascist).

Several German E-boats were sunk in a clash in the Channel yesterday in which light British naval forces suffered no losses.

Ventura bombers with fighter escort yesterday attacked shipping at Rotterdam. Industrial objectives in Holland and railway yards at Abbeville, without loss.

AIR BLITZ PAVED THE WAY

Gen. Montgomery Thanks R.A.F.

ALLIED H.Q., NORTH AFRICA, Monday (R). — General Montgomery has signalled the following message of thanks to Air Vice Marshal Broadhurst, Air Officer Commanding the Western Desert Allied Air Force:

I would like to convey to you my great appreciation of the support to the land battle that has been given by the air forces under your command yesterday and, in fact, every day since the battle began. Such intimate support has never to my knowledge been achieved before and it has been an inspiration to the troops. The results have been first-class.

I sincerely trust that you have not suffered many losses. Please convey to all concerned the grateful thanks of myself and the whole Army for the truly magnificent effort.

The air action which General Montgomery singled out was 2½ hours' intense attack on Axis positions at El Hamma on Friday afternoon. Three big attacks by light bombers and seven strafing and bombing attacks by large formations of fighter-bombers and fighters were made in that time — an average of one every quarter of an hour.

Before the 2½ hours were ended, the Axis forces were in retreat and the British troops had broken through the German positions. The last few attacks were switched on to the road north of El Hamma, which was jammed with retreating enemy transport.

Heaviest Combined Attack

This was the heaviest and most concentrated air attack which the Air Force had ever delivered in combination with Army operations. It was more devastating than anything which had been achieved during the Battle of Egypt at El Alamein. A conservative estimate is that 80 to 100 vehicles were destroyed and another 200 damaged.

Damage to Axis shipping and vital supply lines in rear areas inflicted last week by Flying Fortress, Marauder and Mitchell aircraft was the heaviest of any week in the campaign. Nine ships were sunk in convoys or harbours and 60 others badly damaged.

These losses were inflicted despite the bad weather. A total of 16,496 bombs were dropped on Axis targets during the week.

Today's Communique also pays a special tribute to the Air Force, It says:

Eighth Army Front: The attack which was launched on the afternoon of March [illegible] on the enemy's strong positions south of El Hamma has forced the enemy to withdraw from the Mareth area. This attack, with powerful and very effective support from our Air Forces, caused the enemy heavy losses in tanks, guns, motor transports and men. Many Germans were taken prisoner.

Fierce fighting continued in this area during March 27 with our troops making good progress. The whole of the strongly organized defences of the Mareth positions are now in our hands and our troops on March 28 occupied Mareth, Toujane and Matmata. Prisoners taken by the Eighth Army since March 20 now total over 6,000.

East of El Guettar, our troops made progress yesterday in difficult country. In the Maknassy and Fondouk areas, our patrols were very active. In the north in the Djebel Abiod, successful advances were made and a considerable number of prisoners were taken.

In spite of bad weather over the Tunisian front, fighters and fighter-bombers of the Western Desert Air Force maintained their attacks on enemy transport in the Gabes area. In the course of these operations, four enemy aircraft were destroyed. Fighters carried out sweeps in the central sector and made attacks on enemy positions and vehicles. From all these operations, two of our aircraft are missing.

RUMOURED RECALL OF SPANISH SHIPS

WASHINGTON, Monday (UP). — State Department and Spanish Embassy officials have both disclaimed any knowledge of unconfirmed radio reports that all Spanish vessels at sea have been called home.

THE PALESTINE POST

LATE Edition

JERUSALEM SUNDAY, JULY 9, 1944.

PRICE : 15 MILS — VOL. XIX. Number 5533

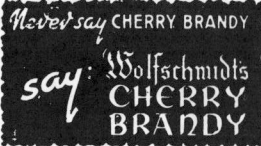
ADVANCE ON REICH ON 3 FRONTS

By JOHN KIMCHE, Reuters Military Correspondent

LONDON, Saturday. — Three Allied Armies are today 300 miles from the frontier of Greater Germany.

General Montgomery in Normandy, is 300 miles from the Rhine at Cologne, General Zhukov, before Lwow, is 300 miles from Silesia. General Alexander, outside Leghorn, is the same distance from Villach and Innsbruck.

General Bagramyan's advance on East Prussia is a case by itself. The German High Command now faces its greatest threat. Its overriding need is to stop the leak in the front in the East.

The Germans have lost 20 divisions in a fortnight. Troops must be sent to stiffen the Russian front. Kesselring's armies in Italy are the obvious hope. Given time for reorganization Kesselring should be able to produce 20 to 22 divisions. Italy is a secondary theatre of the war. Therefore troops must somehow be spared from the Italian front.

From the Italian frontier come reports which tend to confirm this suspicion. Widespread German preparations for the total evacuation of Northern Italy are said to be under way, the bulk of the Luftwaffe has been withdrawn.

General Alexander's order to the Partisans on Monday was couched in a language of importance and urgency. If Alexander and the Partisans succeed, they will disorganise German communications so as to make a big transfer of troops almost impossible and certainly too late to have much effect on the present crisis.

Alternatively, the Germans may pull out of Italy using the present stubborn defence of the Gothic Line screen. This would provide General Alexander with a first-rate opportunity as his armies are no further from the borders of Austria than either Marshal Zhukov or General Montgomery is from the Reich frontier.

RUSSIANS FIGHT IN VILNA STREETS

BARANOVICZE JUNCTION LIBERATED

MOSCOW, Saturday Midnight (R). — The capture of Baranowicze, the important junction of the Minsk-Warsaw railway, a break-through into the city of Vilna, where street-fighting is taking place, and the loss to the Germans of 43,000 killed and prisoners in the past four days, including three German generals who surrendered, are announced here tonight.

After reporting the capture of Baranowicze, tonight's Soviet Communique states:

"Our troops developing their offensive, fought their way forward late more than 300 inhabited localities including 11 railway stations. Thus our troops cut the railway line from Vilna to Dvinsk.

"Our troops have broken into the town of Vilna and engaged the enemy in street fighting. North of Baranowicze our troops continuing their offensive, captured Lyachka, and Gorodische, district centres of the Baranowicze region, and fought their way late more than 100 other inhabited localities. East of Minsk our troops continued the mopping-up of the encircled enemy group."

According to preliminary reports, the enemy lost in this area between July 4 and 7 54 tanks, 210 guns of various calibres, 915 machine-guns, and 1,674 lorries. The enemy left more than 25,000 dead on the battlefield ; 15,105 German officers and men were taken prisoner.

During the same period, our troops captured the following booty: 54 tanks, 172 guns of various calibre, 54 mortars, 599 machine-guns, 1,652 lorries, 60 tractors and trailers, 838 carts with war material and 1,567 horses.

In the 7 following German airfields, surrendered: the Commander of the 41st German Tank Corps, Lieutenant-General Hoffmeister; the Commander of the 60th German Motorised Division Major-General Steinhuber; the Commander of the 221st German Infantry Regiment Major-General Hiel.

The fighting for the extermination of isolated and dispersed German troops continues.

The communique then repeats the Order of the Day and adds that the Russians occupied a number of places east of Pinsk.

The fall of Baranowicze paves the way for a Soviet drive west to Bialystok and southward toward the approaches to Warsaw.

General Zakharovsky's tanks and storm troops have moved on Vilna along a 60-mile front while heavily-armoured spearheads thrust ahead to threaten the German lines of withdrawal from the north-east and south-east. The Russians are rolling on at an average speed of at least ten miles a day.

It is the same above Polotsk on the Dvinsk front, where the Germans are counter-attacking fiercely. Every wood is thick with mines and the undergrowth is festooned with barbed wire. North-west of Minsk the Russians have their spearhead within 35 miles of the key junction of Lida.

Due west of Minsk the front in 50 miles away. Most of the German front has crumbled and the Germans will be fortunate to extricate the remnants of their garrison, as strong groups of Cossacks are thrusting round the town to cut their escape routes.

Bitter fighting continues in the two sectors east of Minsk where Red Army men's fury is rising at the reports now confirmed that encircled units were told by the German Command to go forward with one arm raised in surrender and the other grasping a weapon to open fire on the Russians.

In a fortnight of uninterrupted fighting in which it has moved 150 miles the Red Army has taken nearly 100,000 prisoners and left over 180,000 German dead in marshlands.

A less conservative estimate of not less than 250,000 makes the German total well over half a million German casualties.

The Finnish Front

In the north, the recent progress of the Red Army in advancing west of Petrozavodsk places them within striking distance of the important communications centres of Suojarvi and Sortavala. The capture of these two towns would greatly simplify the movement of supplies and reinforcements for developing the offensive into Finland proper.

RUSSIA SEEN AS MAIN FRONT

LONDON, Saturday (BOP). — The latest dispatches from the Eastern front give the impression of an overwhelming advance, in spite of German efforts to slow the Russian drive and to save their retreating supply columns by throwing-in fresh troops, (writes "The Times").

The chief spokesman in Berlin are now declaring that the Eastern front, for the time being, is front number one. They frankly state that the defence system in White Russia has broken down with far greater speed than the Nazi Command had expected, but that countermeasures have already been taken and that developments in the next few days are likely to be as dramatic as in the preceding fortnight. What these will be is left obscure.

One Berlin report dwells on the nearness of East Prussia to the present front, pointing out that General Bagramyan has little more distance to cover to Koenigsberg than the distance already covered since the advance started east of Vilna a fortnight ago. This is true, but it indicates the direction in which the German mind is now working.

All Arms Cooperate

A feature of the whole Russian offensive so far has been the masterly coordination of all arms. Thus Stormoviks are giving such close support to the infantry that Red Army men are following up within 500 to 1,000 yards of ground-strafing formations, and Soviet artillery is always at hand to prepare the ground for a special breakthrough.

The speed of the advance has made it necessary (says "The Times") that progress of the German people and its way of life, root and branch. There is no possibility (for us to renew this conflict say in 10, 20, or 50 years if we should prove incapable of resisting the onslaught in this decisive time.

"The major untapped reserve in the unbombed areas of Germany must be now mobilised and each German must now take as a measure of his own way of life the much reduced standard of living which prevails in the districts threatened by the air war."

The Prime Minister, when asked in the House of Commons on Thursday if the Government would inform the German people that if the Nazi government was displaced by a democratic regime in which the Allies would have faith they would be opened toward a settlement on the basis of the Atlantic Charter, replied:

"So far as His Majesty's Government is concerned it is repeatedly made it clear in public statements that we shall fight until Germany is forced to capitulate, until Nazism is extirpated and it is for the German people to draw a logical conclusion."

German Civilians Flee from Lithuania

LONDON, Saturday (R). — German officials and settlers and their families are fleeing panic-stricken from Vilna area where Soviet troops are breaking through in their new offensive, it is stated by the Polish Telegraphic Agency today. Vilna railway station is packed with refugees and their belongings, and special evacuation trains are being run.

The agency adds that the speed of the Soviet offensive has taken the Germans by surprise. Roads are full of cars and horse-drawn vehicles laden with possessions of German stock, wayward. The Germans are looking everywhere, carrying furniture from factories, offices and private houses as well as household goods and clothing.

Chaos on the roads is increased by the activities of Polish underground army units carrying out sabotage on railway lines and roads, causing even more anxiety among the terrified German residents.

Florence Held by Italian Partisans

The administration of Florence has been taken over by Italian patriots since Germans and Italian Fascists evacuated the city, according to reports from the Italian frontier published in Berne newspapers.

Allied troops have captured Rosignano, Catellina, and Colledivalle, three outposts of the German defence line below Volterra, in bitter hand-to-hand fighting with high casualties on both sides. Volterra is now under assault.

Eighth Army forces still maintain pressure on Arezzo and have made small gains of about six miles, repulsing three counter-attacks.

In the Tiber valley, the village of Carpini, six miles northeast of Umbertide, was captured by Indians who also took Monte Cuzzo and forced the Germans out of Montone also. Polish forces are four miles north-west of Osimo, within 5½ miles of Ancona.

Today's communique states:

ARMY: After overcoming protracted enemy resistance, American troops of the Fifth Army have occupied Rosignano and Castellina and have now progressed just south of Pegli. General Troops of the Eighth Army have repulsed a number of counter-attacks in the vicinity of Arezzo and have made further limited gains. In the upper Tiber Valley, Indian troops of the Eighth Army, advancing beyond Umbertide, are now in the outskirts of Montone. In the Adriatic sector in advance has been made northwest from Osimo against the enemy who is stubbornly defending the port of Ancona.

AIR: Strong forces of light aircraft bombers yesterday again attacked three systematic rail plants in German Silesia, and Blechhammer and another at Odertal, as well as aerodromes and railyards at Zagreb in Yugoslavia. Medium bombers struck at rail bridges and fuel supplies in Northern Italy. Fighter bombers were active against communications and gun positions in or near the battle area.

Rocket firing fighters attacked railways and rolling stock in Salonica (Greece) area. In the day's operations 61 enemy aircraft were destroyed. Twenty-four of our heavy bombers and three other aircraft are missing. In night operations on July 6/7, five enemy aircraft were destroyed and 13 of ours are missing. The MAAF flew approximately 2,300 sorties.

(UP and Reuters)

Attack in South Reported

LONDON, Saturday. — The launching of a new Red Army offensive on a wide front at the approaches to the Carpathians in Rumania and east of Lwow was reported tonight by the German News Agency correspondent, Colonel Ernst von Hammer. The correspondent stated:

"At least five Soviet rifle divisions and a tank corps are being hurled against the German positions in a bid to breach their lines and shatter the southern wing of the German Eastern Front."

"German Nation In Danger"

LONDON, Saturday (R). — Speaking in a "town in Eastern Germany" today the Propaganda Minister Goebbels, said: "The German nation is in danger."

"Germany's enemies," Goebbels said, intend to "eradicate"

400,000 Hungarian Jews Sent to Death Camps

LONDON, Saturday (R). — The Polish Government has received from its delegate in Poland details of the fate of more than 400,000 Hungarian Jews who were sent to Poland, mainly to the concentration camp in Oswiecim.

On May 15 the Germans sent from Hungary 62 railway carriages loaded with Jewish children aged between 2 and 4 years. Every day since, for a considerable period, six railway transports with Jewish adults passed through the stations of Plazsa and Krakow. They were sent to Oswiecim where most of them have been put to death in gas chambers. Before deportation they were told that they would be exchanged in Poland for prisoners of war.

The news has been confirmed in despatches received by the Polish Council for the Rescue of Jews in Poland and a Jewish member of the Polish National Council. The German entered in Oswiecim, in 1942, gas chambers with installations enabling them to kill 6,000 and even more of their victims daily. Later two more death camps were erected. In these three camps the bulk of the over 2,000,000 Polish Jews, who have died since, 1939, were murdered.

Surete Transfer In Lebanon

BEIRUT, Saturday. — Transfer of the Sureté from the French to the Lebanese and Syrian authorities was the subject of a protocol signed yesterday at Sofar by representatives of the three parties.

The Acting Delegate-General M. Yves Chataigneau, and the French delegate to the Syrian Government represented the French authorities; the Syrian Premier, Saadallah Bey Al-Jabiry, and the Foreign Minister, Jamil Bey Mardam, represented the Syrians; while their Lebanese "Opposite Numbers," Riadh Bey as-Solh and Saleem Bey Takla, signed for the Lebanese Republic.

Northern Italy Boils Over

CHIASSO, Saturday (R). — Partisans in Tuscany have begun a general attack on German lines of communication. It is announced by their High Command. At Leghorn, street fighting is taking place and all Fascist chiefs have left the town.

The strikes at Turin have spread to a new centre in Piedmont and Lombardy. Patriots have taken over the administration of Florence since the Germans and Fascists evacuated the city, according to frontier reports.

NEW YUGOSLAV CABINET

By ALFRED GRANT, Reuters Balkan Correspondent

LONDON, Saturday. — A Yugoslav Cabinet of six members under the premiership of Doctor Ivan Subasic was formed last night, I understand. Two of Marshal Tito's associates are joining the Cabinet. They are now on their way from liberated Yugoslav territory.

The two are Stein Vukosavlye, professor of Belgrade University and member of the executive committee of the Independent Democratic Party, well-known as an expert on agricultural questions, and Drago Marusic, a Slovene politician and examiner and Governor of Slovenia.

Vukosavljevich will hold the important Ministry of Supply as well as the former Ministry of Agriculture, Forests and Minerals in the new Cabinet, while Marusic will be Minister of Justice and Communications.

Doctor Subasic, in addition to being the Premiership, will hold the portfolios of Foreign Affairs and War. The deputy Premier Sava Kosanovic becomes Minister of the Interior, Social Welfare, Health and Public Works. He is at present in the United States.

The Slovene University professor and member of the Slovene Catholic Party, Izidor Cankar, becomes Minister of Education. He was Yugoslav Minister to Canada, but resigned office in protest against the policy of the Purich Government. Doctor Juraj Sutej, a leading member of the Croatian Peasant party, becomes Minister of Finance. Altogether the Cabinet consists of two Serbs, two Croats, and two Slovenes. A declaration of policy by M. Subasic is expected today.

GERMANS SHOOT BRITISH PRISONERS

By MARSHALL YARROW, Reuters Special Correspondent with British Forces in Normandy. — (Delayed).

Authenticated statements by French civilians show that small groups of captured British soldiers have been shot by Germans as reprisals for the alleged shooting of German prisoners by British.

Such incidents have been definitely reported from Audrieu and Bronay where bodies discovered by civilians leave no doubt of the soldiers' fate. The numbers killed are not great.

Paris and Berlin Raided

By IAN MUNRO, Reuters Special Correspondent

S.H.A.E.F., Saturday. — A few hours after a smashing attack on German positions outside Caen last night in which 450 Lancasters and Halifaxes dropped 2,300 tons of bombs, Bomber Command heavies went out again to plaster railway yards at Vaires on the eastern outskirts of Paris.

Conditions were good and soon the whole area was seething with explosions which later lay hidden by a huge pall of smoke thousands of feet high. The Germans sent up many night fighters in an unsuccessful attempt to beat off the bombers.

At the same time as the attack on Vaires was on squadrons of Mosquitoes, carrying 4,000-lbs bombs were over Berlin. The bombers had come and gone before the defences had had a chance to ward off the attack.

VIENNA BOMBED

ROME, Saturday (UP). — Over 500 heavy bombers attacked oil plants and airfields in the Vienna area today.

Japan Raided By Super-Bombers

WASHINGTON, Saturday. — No planes were lost when the Japanese naval base at Sasebo was attacked by Super-Fortresses last night.

Bombs were also dropped on industrial objectives at Yawata, which was the target of Super-Fortresses on June 16. Both cities are on the island of Kyushu, part of the Japanese mainland.

The mission was flown from Chinese bases on the seventh anniversary of China's declaration of war against Japan.

The Domei News Agency states that Nagasaki, as well as Sasebo and Yawara, were attacked. It added that three American planes were shot down by air defence units. The Agency reports that the raiders dropped incendiary bombs, but claimed they "practically no damage was done."

First Raid on Yawata — Pg. 4

Jap Losses on Saipan

WASHINGTON, Saturday (R). — The Americans who landed on Saipan Island have buried 8,914 Japanese dead since the campaign began, the Commander-in-Chief of the Pacific, Admiral Nimitz, reported last night.

American forces are now within two miles of the northeast tip of the island.

BID TO CLEAR ROAD TO PARIS

WHY RUNDSTEDT STEPPED DOWN

By ROBERT LLOYD, Special to The Palestine Post

LONDON, Saturday. — Von Rundstedt had to abandon his command because he considered that Germany has lost the war and said so. This, and not quarrels about the conduct of the campaign in France, was the issue, in the view of experts who follow German affairs closely.

Their opinion is based on these facts and considerations:

(1) According to reliable Allied intelligence reports, a highly-placed German General told officers of one coastal defence regiment on an inspection visit shortly after D-Day: "Unless we can expel the Allies from France within one month, Germany has lost the war." Rundstedt's fall was announced precisely one month after D-Day.

(2) The public announcement that the C.-in-C. had been deposed in the middle of Germany's most critical battle must have been a terrific shock to the German Army and people, and particularly to the officers' corps. Even Hitler would do his utmost to avoid it if at all possible.

For the past two months the Nazi leaders have, indeed, been most careful to spare the susceptibilities of the military. Even now Rundstedt has not been replaced by his old rival Rommel, who would be the obvious candidate for a strategy of intuition, but by a man of the same tradition as Rundstedt who has a reputation for successful defensive fighting.

(3) Rundstedt is the most far-sighted of the German Generals. He was the man who asked for a transfer to the West in the spring of 1942 because he did not believe in the second Russian offensive and was convinced that timely preparation against invasion was of decisive importance. After one month of fighting he is quite capable of judging coolly that German plans have miscarried and that the armies cannot be expected to hold once the Russians enter Reich territory from the East.

Some Germans Leave Paris

LONDON, Saturday (R). The Germans are evacuating their civil services from Paris to France, according to French sources. The evacuation began a few days ago. So far it includes the archives of the Gestapo, of the Todt organisation and of the Economic Control.

Storms Almost Caused Disaster

By RONALD CLARK, U.P. Correspondent with the Allied Forces

A high naval authority revealed yesterday that unbelievably bad weather nearly terminated Allied invasion plans in catastrophe two weeks after D-Day.

In the first comprehensive description of the mid-June gale that swept the beach-head positions for four days this spokesman said that there had been some losses in small craft. A large number of river barges and motor craft were sent to the beaches for unloading tanks and a few of these were "lost." Repair of essential craft damaged in this storm is now going on apace.

The four-day gale came at the high tide period and consequently carried some craft so high on the beaches that refloating was a major problem.

The speaker indicated that the weather was still more of a problem to the Allies than other enemy operations. German E-boats caused some trouble but Allied activities gradually reduced the threat. The capture of Cherbourg was of material assistance in this respect.

S.S. Divisions Identified

By JAMES McGLINCY and SAMUEL HALES, U.P. Correspondents

NORMANDY, Saturday. — British forces advanced yesterday within half a mile of Caen from the north after the forces had dropped 2,000 bombs on the German front and some 2,000 tons on the five-mile rear lines.

The ease with which the ribsey area was taken was one of the biggest surprises in the day's British advance, which was preceded by as big operation. It was gathered greater Caen, straightening out the lightening the ring of defences around it to the desert areas.

By mid-afternoon one hour had moved his way into the huge of Galmanche and, fanning outward fighting around Epron, Lebun and light bombers delivered low-level attacks with good results on troop concentrations, batteries, and strong points just ahead of our troops near Caen, and on communication targets as far south as Nantes.

Others reported into a two-way bridge over the Elle at Nojent le Rotrou spanning the Loire just an hour. One modern missing. Escorting fighters destroyed three enemy aircraft. Heavy day bombers with strong escort of fighters searched out openings in the clouds and bombed targets of opportunity east of the bombers.

Early on Friday morning a force of enemy E-boats and R-boats with two M-Class minesweepers and one other identified vessel was intercepted in an attempt to enter the eastern anchorage and was brought into action. One German vessel was seen to blow up. One E-boat and one R-boat was sunk and another set on fire.

Advance in Carentan Sector

S.H.A.E.F., Saturday (R) Tonight's communique No. 66 says:

Steady gains have been made on all the active portions of the front. Our patrols are now in the town of La Haye du Puits and we command all the high ground in this area. The bridgehead over the Vire river has been extended beyond Saint Jean de Daye, and between that village and Carentan Allied troops have advanced to the Vire of Taute canal. Much of Caen, in heavy fighting the enemy has been driven from the villages of Saint Contest, Epron and Morenville.

Our progress everywhere owns much to the Allied air forces which operated in strength. Medium and light bombers delivered low-level attacks with good results.

American forces from occupied south to the next village Grouby while patrols again entered La Haye du Puit. Americans completed their isolation of the west side of La Montostere within through the east side, west of Carentan, slow progress were achieved again stout resistance.

The American front in near early static, with striking distance all along this line.

The Germans are throwing in reserves "Das Reich" S.S. Division has now been identified at several spots against the Americans. A total of three S.S. divisions have fighting from Russia are now in Normandy.

BRITISH DRIVING ON CAEN

By VIRGIL PINKLEY, U.P. Correspondent

S.H.A.E.F., Saturday. — The British Second Army launched an all-out offensive at dawn today on the defences of Caen in an all-out offensive evidently designed to clear the road to Paris. They are reported to be battling deep into the enemy lines against stout resistance.

General Montgomery has unleashed his offensive against the strongest-held sector on the Normandy front, defended by nearly seven crack enemy Panzer divisions. He is crashing through where attempting a full offensive effort unless he has a better-than-even chance of succeed, and he has had weeks to build up his forces.

It is understood that the Germans are moving big guns and armour south of Caen. Reports show heavy movements of German vehicles along the Caen roads which they are attempting a full-scale withdrawal. The British and Canadians have now cut 12 out of 14 roads leading into and out of Caen.

The attack began early today after bombing by hundreds of planes last night. Early morning artillery began to pound the German defences in and the German barbed minefields, strong-points, other defence positions barrage surpassed the heaviest on this front against assault on the beaches on D-Day.

The size of the operation can be gauged from yesterday's German estimate that 400,000 men and 60,000 tanks are engaged in a bitter battle frontal area of 12 miles.

High Commissioner Says Goodbye at School Prize-Day

Distributing the prizes and certificates at the Bishop Gobat School in Jerusalem on Friday, H.E. the High Commissioner announced that he was leaving Palestine in a month's time.

After prayers in Arabic led by Archdeacon A.C. McInnes, the principal the Rev. R. Iliff, reviewed the year's scholastic achievements. There were 10 nationalities and 12 religious denominations among the pupils, he said, and the school was contributing towards international understanding. Music had been introduced as a voluntary subject, there had been many academic distinctions, and the school had excelled in sports as well.

The Anglican Bishop in Jerusalem, stated that almost all Arabic Anglican clergy in this country were graduates of the Bishop Gobat School. Mr. Nikola Saba, District Officer at Ramle and an Old Boy, addressed the students, in Arabic and Wadi Rumman made the valedictory address.

Big Air Battle Over Central Reich

LONDON, Saturday (R) — Yesterday's air fighting over Central Germany cost the Luftwaffe 114 planes—75 shot down by fighters and 39 by bombers. Allied losses were 38 bombers and six fighters.

It was the greatest kill since D-Day, and over 1,000 bombers took part. One American fighter pilot shot down six single-handed.

It is stated at SHAEF today that the Luftwaffe have been losing 250 planes weekly since D-Day, but the Allies have been losing [illegible]

Siege of Moscow

M. Palecius, the President of the Lithuanian Supreme Soviet, states in the Moscow "Izvestia" that the Lithuanian countryside is in a state of turmoil and attacks by partisan detachments and acts of sabotage are increasing against Assassinations of German soldiers are increasing in Kaunas. Twenty bodies of soldiers were found in March alone.

In the past two months Lithuanian patriots have killed several dozen German officials. Following large-scale disturbances the Germans arrested 5,000 people in Vilna.

AFTER MIDNIGHT

The Russians have again heavily bombed Brest Litovsk. Dozens of fires were started.

Classifieds
Everyone's Column
Effective and Economical

LATE Edition
THE PALESTINE POST
JERUSALEM
Wednesday, May 2 1945
PRICE: 15 MILS
VOL. XX. No. 5781

The suit with the beautiful fit— as cut by ROSENBLUM ladies' & gents' garments 44 HERZL ST. HAIFA

HITLER'S DEATH ANNOUNCED

DOENITZ SUCCEEDS FUEHRER: SAYS GERMANS WILL FIGHT ON

LONDON, Tuesday (R.) — Hitler died this afternoon, and the former C.-in-C. of the German Navy, Admiral Doenitz, is his successor, the German radio announced tonight. Doenitz, speaking over the radio later, said: "The Fuehrer has fallen at his command post. My first task is to save the German people from destruction by Bolshevism. If only for this task the struggle will continue."

The announcement which preceded the proclamation by Doenitz said: "It is reported from the Fuehrer's headquarters that our Fuehrer, Adolf Hitler, has fallen this afternoon at his command post in the Reich Chancellery fighting to the last breath against Bolshevism and for Germany. On April 30 the Fuehrer appointed Grand Admiral Doenitz as his successor. Our new Fuehrer will speak to the German people." Then followed a talk by Doenitz.

Column One
By
David Courtney

SAN Francisco is full of problems and vexations already and there is a feeling among the small countries that they are in danger of being rushed. It looks as if the Big Three had left too many preliminaries undone before they set out for California. It is also felt that security decisions cannot be taken on the basis of a Europe much of which, at the moment, is little more than a charred jig-saw puzzle. It would probably be as well if the delegates went home to deal with unconditional surrender on their own ground and came back again when things have sorted themselves out a bit. The brief sojourn in San Francisco will have done them no harm; it has at least raised the kind of preliminary problem, like Poland and Argentina, which the Great Powers ought to be able to solve among themselves. A series of disputes which create "bloks" (with ideological foundation) around the major contestants, as in the case of Argentina, will do post-war security no good. The idea of San Francisco was more valuable than the fact. For the fact, more and better preparation is essential.

WHATEVER may be happening in Denmark, there is still a lot of fighting inside Germany. With the red flag of the Soviets hoisted above the Reichstag, Berlin can be regarded as captured. The "death battalions of wild-eyed women" resisting fanatically at the order of Goebbels are hardly likely to delay the end. It would be interesting to know what Russia proposes to her hand. Having settled the do when Berlin is definitely in political affairs of Vienna to her own satisfaction, will she be as hasty in Berlin? Military occupation will be more severe in Germany proper than in Austria. Germany, let us hope, for a long time to come will not be given the opportunity to answer back.

With the Fifth Army at the Southern approaches to the Brenner and the Seventh coming down on Innsbruck at the northern end, Vietinghof cannot hope to get more than a handful of his men through the Alps. The speed and completeness of the Italian move are prime factors in Himmler's despairing conclusion that the game is up; and we should never forget it. Meanwhile the Eighth is on its way to Trieste, where Yugoslav troops are now battling for control of the port. The Romans are choosing this moment to shout slogans reminiscent of d'Annusio. The Yugoslavs, in possession, don't need to shout slogans Anyway, the grim fact remains, for all the horrid details of Mussolini's end, that Italy is an ex-enemy State; and the Yugoslavs have a big score up against her.

ONE of today's most striking news items is that the heavy bomber offensive in Europe has come to an end. The targets have been overrun. R.A.F. Bomber Command finished off its long and obdurate campaign last week with a load of 12,000-pound bombs on Berchtesgaden. That was the end of four years' terrific effort to break, by strategic air operations, the power of the enemy to wage war. The success of the campaign has been obvious in the rapid diminution of the Wehrmacht's resources, until today it has neither oil nor adequate arms; and in the slowing down of communications to a point where the High Command could no longer maintain cohesion or prevent those disastrous encirclements in the East and in the West, which robbed it of whole armies at a time.

THE end of the heavy bomber offensive in Europe is no pleasant omen for the Japanese. The Fourteenth Army in Burma, and the American Fleet in the Pacific, can do with the long-range heavy bombers from European airfields. The miraculous advance of the Fourteenth from the Indian frontier to within a few miles of Rangoon naturally has not had the bomber support given to our armies in the West: and when such support comes it is hard to see how the Japanese can avoid a disintegration very like that of the German armies. It is the effect on Japan proper, however, that should provide the drama. The Americans in the Pacific have seen to it that airfields within range are availabe. The transfer of the U.S. and British fleets from the West to the East will help to spell for Japan a doom as great as that of her European partner's. Will Japan, for all her spirit of hara-kiri, submit to the obvious doom or to the equally obvious warning?

Jerusalem, May 8, 1945

HELPING HOLLAND

LONDON, Tuesday (UP).— About 400 Eighth Air Force Fortresses today dropped food supplies to the Dutch in the vicinity of The Hague and Rotterdam.

NO OFFER FROM HIMMLER

STOCKHOLM, Tuesday (R) — During his latest visit to Copenhagen, from which he returned today, Count Bernadotte met not Himmler, but Werner Best, the German Minister to Denmark. He was not given any surrender terms.

Count Bernadotte told a press conference today: "I have not seen Himmler during my last visit to Germany and Denmark, and I have not forwarded any message from Himmler or any other authoritative German to the Allies."

The Swedish radio, shortly after denying reports of the German evacuation of Denmark, reported in a broadcast in Danish the "partial withdrawal" of German troops from the towns of Zealand — the island between the mainland and Sweden on which Copenhagen stands, while Free Danish underground sources at Malmoe report that the Germans have begun to move out of Copenhagen today with the apparent intention of abandoning Denmark.

Last night it was expected that the withdrawal from the towns — which would also include the capital — would be continued during the night.

So far it is only the military who are withdrawing from the towns. German police are still functioning. A Danish spokesman in a broadcast from Sweden said: "German forces are still remaining ready for action in Denmark. Avoid provocation and quietly await immediate developments."

Nazi Day of Atonement

LONDON, Tuesday (R). — Lord Vansittart, who advocates a "hard peace" for Germany, wants January 30, the anniversary of Hitler's accession to power, to be observed in Germany as a day of national repentence or atonement.

He made this proposal today in the Lords debate on German atrocity-guilt in which Lord Denham urged that the whole German race must be made to feel remorse for their responsibility for Nazi crimes.

Resistance Broken Everywhere

LONDON, Tuesday.— With the Soviet flag flying from the Reichstag building in Berlin, and Marshal Stalin declaring in his May Day Order to the fighters and workers of Russia, "The collapse of Hitlerite Germany is a matter of the very near future," a Hamburg radio speaker announced today:

The war will probably last only a few more hours.

The latest cables show that there is still stubborn resistance in fragments of the Reich particularly at the northern edge around the ports. But in the south, Munich has been captured undefended and American troops could find nobody in authority.

From the main Elbe bridgehead, British Second Army patrols have thrust out 10 miles and the bridgehead area is seven miles wide and six miles deep. The new bridgehead achieved yesterday 10 miles west of Lauenburg by the U.S. Airborne Division is now two miles wide by two deep. Field Marshal Montgomery's armies are moving in for the kill and the big ports of Hamburg, Bremerhaven, Wilhelmshaven and Emden are entering their last days of life.

Red Army troops are sweeping across the northern plain and have taken important towns west of Stettin, including Neustrelitz in the lake country, and Geifswald, a Baltic port. Marshal Rokossovsky is now 50 miles from Rostock.

In Czechoslovakia, Russian forces took the arms centre of Moravska Ostrava, a key point in the German defence system.

In the south, United States tanks are attacking along a 20-miles' stretch of the Austrian border between the Danube and the Swiss frontier. The American Seventh Army is reported 18 miles north of Innsbruck.

French and Third Army troops and armour have clambered into the northern fringes of the redoubt without meeting the hysterical opposition which would be expected if the Bavarian Alps were planned to be the scene of a "do or die" last stand. Difficult country, road blocks and demolitions are proving more of an obstacle than the Germans, leading to the belief that the plan to establish a Bavarian fortress has been nipped in the bud by the swift and daring Allied sweep.

LEAVING THE NORTH

LONDON, Tuesday (R). — The "Evening News" understands that the Count Bernadotte's negotiations referred to the question of withdrawal from Denmark and the surrender of 300,000 German fighting men in Norway and that the Swedish Government, in agreement with the Allies, is ready to send Swedish armed forces to supervise the German capitulation.

Certain German forces in Norway are understood already to have approached the Norwegian Government in London through a Swedish intermediary regarding their capitulation.

German Naval Last-Ditchers

By PAUL SCOTT RANKINE
Reuters Correspondent

WITH THE CANADIANS, Tuesday. — The German Navy has refused to take any part in Himmler's peace negotiations, according to unconfirmed rumours filtering from Western Holland and N.W. Germany.

The centres of Germany's naval establishments, such as the E-boat bases at Ijmuiden in Holland and the submarine bases like Wilhelmshaven, do not want to yield. German naval officers who want to fight to the end claim they have enough supplies to carry on for another two months from Denmark and Norway if necessary.

2,500,000 LIBERATED

S.H.A.E.F. Tuesday (R). — More than 2,500,000 refugees, displaced persons and liberated prisoners of war have been recovered since the Allied entry into Germany.

The Russians constitute 40% of its total, the French 25%, the Poles 15%, the Belgians 4 per cent, the Dutch 4%, the Italians 8%. The rest are largely, Czechs and Yugoslavs.

It is estimated that between three and six million displaced persons remain in German hands.

NIGHT LIKE DAY IN BURNING BERLIN

ROCKETS AND FLAMES LIGHT UP DESTRUCTION

By DUNCAN HOOPER,
Reuters Special Correspondent

MOSCOW, Tuesday. — Katushas, rockets and flames from fires blazing in the city make the nights like day in Berlin. With the main sections of Berlin in the hands of the Red Army, the struggle through the streets of the Capital has become a mopping up battle with every hour speeding the complete annihilation of the remnants of the German garrison.

The roar of battle is still resounding through the central streets of the city, as the Red Army storms them. The German defence is disorganized and broken and its fire everywhere is being smothered by the overwhelming concentrations of Soviet artillery and small arms.

German transport planes are attempting to break through to the central area of Berlin to parachute supplies to the defending forces, but few have succeeded.

The Germans are still fighting on like automatons. White flags, and then red flags are going up over the city each time Russian troops approach buildings. The final stage of this greatest of all street battles is marked by such destruction as few cities have endured since the days of Pompeii. It is becoming simpler to pick out the relatively undamaged buildings rather than those which are wrecked.

So far the Red Army does not appear to have reached the German Headquarters, but its location is believed to be known, and every effort will be made to secure any German war leaders remaining in the capital when the last shots are fired.

The Berlin battle has developed into a gigantic mopping-up operation. The defenders are disorganized and broken, although some Germans still fight on fanatically. Volkssturm units are laying down their arms in increasing numbers and sometimes lining whole streets with white surrender flags. Some S.S. battalions, however, have made suicide pacts to go down with the buildings they are defending.

1918—1945

END OF A MYTH

By a Staff Correspondent

Hitler's death marks the end of an epoch and, for all Doenitz' ranting about a last-ditch fight, the end of German resistance. It does not matter that the "Fuehrer" in all probability did not die a soldier's death in Berlin but a gangster's death in some Gestapo cellar. Even if it should turn out that he was not despatched by Himmler's gangsters but spirited away, it would not matter. For the Germans, and the world, he is dead. And that means that his followers have been released from their obligation to fight on. Himmler and Doenitz — the German Badoglio — can now capitulate if they choose.

Hitler had to die when the Third Reich died. If he refused to die he had to be killed. For Hitler had declared that he would never surrender, and surrender has become inevitable. Therefore Hitler died or was despatched, and Doenitz, Admiral of the Fleet and a "respectable" German nationalist, steps forward to declare that he is only fighting against "Bolshevism," while Himmler remains silent and probably organizes his underground. That is the political meaning of the announcement that Hitler is dead.

But Hitler's death is more than the formal dissolution of the alliance between the German Army, which fought this war, and the Nazi Party, which prepared it and is already preparing the next one. It is the final apotheosis of the Hitler myth. The pervert from the slums of Vienna who covered Germany with filth before drenching Europe in blood is destined by the Nazi propagandists to become their biggest asset after his death. His "heroic" death in Berlin is his last and biggest lie, uttered from the grave. It is also his most dangerous lie.

Full Circle

At the very end, Hitler returns to his beginnings. He began as a slum boy in Vienna who hated his socialist fellow-workers. He started his political career in Vienna as a spy set to ferret out ex-soldiers holding radical views. He rose by exploiting the reaction against the Republic and the Peace. He came to power by claiming to deliver Germany from a "Communist danger" which never existed until he created the myth that every anti-Nazi must be a Communist. He won power for Germany by proclaiming himself the bulwark against Bolshevism. He reached the high point of his career when, with all Europe at his feet and the reactionaries hailing him as their saviour, he attacked Russia. Now that the Red Army has hoisted the Red Flag over the flaming ruins of Berlin, he repeats from the grave that his mission consists in defending Germany against the "Red Peril." Having with his own hands torn down every bulwark against the flood, he proclaims himself, or is proclaimed by his lieutenants, the dyke-builder of Europe.

The arch-nihilist who planned to erect a slave state on the ruins of Europe's civilization is dead. His dictatorship has lasted 12 years. For six year he prepared war, then for six years he waged it until every corner of Europe had been turned into a slaughter-house. In the final phase he brought the war to Germany where it had started and thus fulfilled his destiny and that of the deluded nation which followed him into the abyss.

RED PERIL STILL THE KEYNOTE

LONDON, Tuesday (R). — "The Fuehrer has appointed me as his successor," said Doenitz, in his broadcast tonight. "Fully conscious of the responsibility I take over the leadership of the German people at this fateful hour. It is my first task to save the German people from destruction by the Bolshevists and it is only to achieve this that the fight continues.

"As long as the British and Americans hamper us on reaching this end we shall fight and defend ourselves against them as well. Britain and America do not fight for the interests of their own people but for the spreading of Bolshevism.

"I shall do my utmost to make life bearable for our brave men, women and children. To achieve all this I need your help. Trust me. Keep order and discipline in towns and the countryside. Everybody must do his duty. Only then we shall be able to alleviate the sufferings which the future will bring to each of us and avoid collapse."

Twilight

The announcement of Hitler's death was preceded by the playing of solemn Wagnerian music including the "Twilight of the Gods." Then came "Achtung: in a few minutes you will hear a serious and important message to the German people. We are now going to play the slow movement of Bruckner's seventh symphony." Finally came the report of Hitler's death. All this time the Southern German radio network went on broadcasting light music.

Where is Goering?

In the event of his death Hitler, on the historic date of September 1, 1939, before leaving Berlin for an "undisclosed destination"—the Polish front—appointed Goering as his successor. If Goering was not available, Hess was to have succeeded Admiral Doenitz is the man who launched the U-boat warfare against the Allied Atlantic lifeline.

The last German reference to Hitler was in today's German communique which said: "In the heart of Berlin the gallant garrison gathered round the Fuehrer and herded together in a very narrow space is defending itself heroically."

Count Bernadotte today said in Stockholm he was sure Hitler was in Berlin, but whether he was dead or alive he did not know. Himmler is said to have told him that Hitler was dying of cerebral haemorrhage, while Dittmar told his captors on Wednesday that Hitler refused to leave Berlin and would die there.

Duce Buried in 'Potter's Field'

By JAMES ROPER,
U.P. Correspondent

MILAN, Tuesday. — Benito Mussolini, Clara Petacci and Achille Starace were secretly buried in unmarked graves in the "Potter's Field" in Milan's Maggiore cemetery at 8.30 yesterday evening.

The only witnesses were 12 members of the cemetery staff, and the exact locations are being kept secret in order to prevent the mob from exhuming the remains. Officials also filled several empty graves to thwart possible attempts of this kind.

It is now known that the partisans placed Mussolini and his mistress in the bedroom of a peasant's house, where they stayed 14 hours, after which they were taken out and stood against a wall. When the executioner announced the death sentence, Clara Petacci threw her arms around Mussolini. They were separated and then killed by several shots. Mussolini slumped when shot through the chest, and the executioner gave him the coup de grace by shots through the head. His brain has taken from the body for study by psychiatrists and criminologists.

111,000 LIBERATED

MUNICH, Tuesday. — Seven high-ranking Russian officers were freed when Third Army tanks burst into the great "United Nations" prison camp at Moosburg on the banks of the Isar river north of Munich and freed 111,000 war prisoners.

PALESTINE POLICY ATTACKED

WASHINGTON, Tuesday—England had forfeited the trust placed in her by the League of Nations in administering the Palestine Mandate, and Palestine should be placed under international trusteeship, wrote Representative Emanuel Celler (Democrat, New York) to the American delegation at the San Francisco Conference.

Mr. Celler stated that England was no longer entitled to be the sole administrator of Palestine, adding:

An international trusteeship instead of a sole trusteeship of Mandates has awakened widespread interest. Such an international trusteeship of Mandated territories applies most significantly to Palestine.

Another strong attack on British policy in Palestine was launched at yesterday's mass Zionist demonstration by Senator Robert F. Wagner at the Lewisohn Stadium in New York (as reported briefly).

"The power which is preventing the development of a Jewish Commonwealth in Palestine is the British power," he said. "Britain's policies in Palestine are the tragic survival of the disease of appeasement."

Urging that the nations of the world should "put their hand to the neglected task of constituting a Jewish Commonwealth in Palestine," Senator Wagner added:

"I say to our British friends and allies, — You have not fulfilled your obligations to Palestine. The American people believe that it is high time that you redeem your pledge."

Concluding, he said: "While the primary responsibility for the development of Palestine is British, I have never forgotten that America has a responsibility as well to make known its position on the Palestine question."

Wise-Silver Reunion

An outstanding feature at the demonstration was the tremendous reception given to Rabbi Abba Hillel Silver when he was introduced by Dr. Stephen Wise. The great gathering rose spontaneously and sang "Hatikvah." It is thought that this appearance marked Rabbi Silver's return to the American Zionist Emergency Committee.

(R., UP & JWN)

TRUSTEESHIP TALKS BEGIN

SAN FRANCISCO, Tuesday. — The Big Five have begun their long-awaited consultations on the problem of international trusteeships.

The first meeting was held last night, and another is scheduled for tomorrow night. The discussions are on the "technical level" but delegates from each nation have been invited. Commander Harold Stassen heads the U.S. delegation on discussions of the question.

The U.S. group last night presented the American plan for trusteeships to Russia, Britain, France and China. It is understood that the plan is designed to provide for control of territory captured from the Japanese in the Pacific.

None of the other Powers has so for presented any trusteeship plan to take care of territory taken from the enemy or territory placed under the League of Nations after the last. They expect, however, to have a lot to say about the U.S. plan at the next meeting.

ARABS SEEK PLACES ON REGIONAL COUNCIL

By FAY BICK,
Palcor Correspondent

SAN FRANCISCO, Tuesday. — Arab delegations at the United Nations Conference here are seeking places not only on the International Trusteeships Commission, but also on the Regional Council likely to be set up in Mandated areas.

The object of the Regional Council is to provide an instrument for consultation among Powers with interests in a given area, and with the Mandatory Power entrusted with the actual administration of that area.

MOLOTOV WILL GO HOME

CONFERENCE TO CARRY ON

By PAUL SCOTT RANKINE,
Reuters Correspondent

SAN FRANCISCO, Tuesday — The Soviet Foreign Commissar, M. Molotov, informed Mr. Stettinius, Mr. Eden and Mr. Soong at a meeting late last night that he would like to return to Moscow at the end of this week or the beginning of next week in view of the war situation, I am authoritatively informed today.

It is understood that the Soviet delegation will continue to use its full rights and privileges as a sponsoring nation and will act on direct instructions from Moscow after M. Molotov's departure. M. Molotov stated that he would stay until the main problems of the conference had been settled but he hoped they would be settled by the beginning of next week.

Mr. Eden is understood to be planning to stay here for the three or four weeks which he originally fixed for his visit, unless some totally unlooked-for situation arises, while Mr. Stettinius is expected to stay for the duration of the conference.

Informed quarters express themselves satisfied with the progress made today and the Big Four are reported to be in an optimistic mood regarding the speed with which matters are proceeding.

Argentina Invited

In a scene of extraordinary emotion. the United Nations today accepted Argentina as a member of the World Security Conference.

It was an open defeat for the Soviet Foreign Commissar, M. Molotov, and in the final vote, which was an exciting climax to a debate of intense fervour, only three delegates voted with Russia— Czechoslovakia, Greece and Yugoslavia. Immediately after the vote had been taken, M. Molotov left the theatre where the conference is taking place.

Answering a request from the president of the session — the British Foreign Secretary, Mr. Eden—whether there were "any observations" on the Steering Committee's proposal that the Argentine be immediately admitted to the conference, M. Molotov, speaking through an interpreter, declared that Argentina's admission to the conference should be postponed for a few days.

Poland's Right

M. Molotov added that several Latin-American countries thought the situation in Argentina had changed for the better but "I think our delegation should be given time to be shown that the situation has changed. I think that will take some time."

Referring to Poland's right to be present at the conference, M. Molotov affirmed that it was well known that Poland had been one of the most active participants on the side of the Allies. He recalled that the Poles made immense sacrifices and added:

"We must not forget that, and if we invite Argentina, which helped the enemy throughout, and do not invite the Polish Provisional Government, we will prejudice the prestige of this conference."

Giving a possible hint that a Polish solution might be produced if the Argentine matter were delayed, the Soviet Foreign Commissar said:

"We should at any rate provide a seat for Poland at this conference no later than we do with regard to Argentina.

"It might perhaps be said that Argentina committed certain sins and they may be forgotten. May be that is true but I wonder why we should forget the sins committed by Argentina and, on the other hand, forget the services rendered by Poland to the common cause."

He noted that India and the Philippines were participating in the conference, although not fully independent, and that Russia had not objected, adding:

"Up to now all invitations for this conference were accepted unanimously by the four sponsor governments. This we consider a very good rule and should not like to depart from it."

Support for Argentina was also given by the leader of the Peruvian delegation, Manuel Gallagher, and Carlos Alberto Liaras, chief of the Colombian delegation. M. Henri Spaak, the Belgian Foreign Minister, spoke in favour of M. Molotov's protest.

War Flashes

The Rome radio has broadcast a proclamation by Marshal Graziani, now in Allied hands, calling to the trapped Ligurian Army of three German and three Fascist-Italian divisions to lay down their arms.

General Patton's tanks have pushed 25 miles south today to reach the river Inn on the Austrian-German frontier near Braunau, Hitler's birthplace.

HORTHY IN "PROTECTIVE CUSTODY"

S.H.A.E.F., Tuesday (R). — The former Regent of Hungary, Admiral Nicholas Horthy, and his family have been taken into protective custody by troops of the U.S. Seventh Army, it was announced today.

They were found in a castle at Weilheim, in Bavaria.

NAZIS FLED FROM MUNICH

The American Seventh Army completed the occupation of Munich last night against surprisingly light resistance.

Munich was so relieved that the war was over for it that people greeted the Seventh Army with cheers. The Nazi leaders had long since fled, and only a few small fry remained in the Party buildings around the famous Beer Cellar where Hitler and his henchmen plotted the "putsch" which brought them control of Germany.

A WIDE SELECTION OF LADIES DRESSES

THE PALESTINE POST

JERUSALEM, SUNDAY, DEC. 16, 1945

PRICE: 15 MILS — VOL. XX, No. 5973

Never say CHERRY BRANDY — say Wolfschmidts CHERRY BRANDY

Column One
By David Courtney

WASHINGTON and Mr. Byrnes are apparently insuring against failure at Moscow. Their utterances are intended to give the impression that discussions will be informal and decisions merely provisional. They say in effect that if nothing decisive comes of Moscow no one should be surprised. Nobody will be. At the same time, despatches from London make it clear that Mr. Bevin expects something to happen, and has a pretty full dossier to draw out when he sits in front of M. Molotov. He intends to raise the central problem of Germany and, it is believed, to insist upon reaching a workable basis for the final disposal of Italian colonies and other debatable territories formerly under Italian rule. One report says that Mr. Bevin is in obstinate mood, and ready himself to lay all sorts of surprising cards on the table, is determined to force M. Molotov to display his. A Reuter message from Moscow provides further evidence to discount the American suggestion that the meeting is only to exchange views, not to unify them. It says that fixing a settlement of the Persian problem is definitely on the agenda, and that the Russians will call for a realignment of policies in the Far East.

WHAT Moscow anticipates is indicated to a certain degree by her official and semiofficial press and radio. Since the announcement of the conference of the three Foreign Secretaries, press and radio campaign have been opened affecting Persia, the Far East, Turkey, Spain, Poland and South-East Europe. The line on Persia has become much clearer. In simple terms it is this: Russia has as much right to keep her troops there as Britain to keep hers in Egypt, Palestine or Iraq, not to mention Indonesia; and since the withdrawal of all troops from Persia means virtually the political status quo, with Britain exercising supreme diplomatic influence at Teheran, the British demand that all foreign troops should clear out of the country is suspect anyway. The argument, of course, is weak; but only to those who know the facts — and even then its weakness is probably legal rather than moral. On Persia, Russia has at any rate the advantage of going to the Conference with, as it were, Azerbaijan in her pocket. There, the second town of Persia, has fallen to the Democrats and practically the whole rich province is now independent of the capital.

WHAT Russia seems to be seeking all over the world is not a balance of power on the basis of old-fashioned political and strategic values, but an equilibrium of forces designed to create stability. She regards world stability as her main defence, and probably is less avid of imperial power than anxious to diminish the imperial power of her major competitors. It is probable that she has no desire to occupy Persia; but would rather do that than submit to a frontier State under what she conceives to be the subjection of Britain. Some circles trace Russia's policy in China to the same nervous motive — to reduce Anglo-Saxon hegemony rather than impose Soviet hegemony. If these are the facts, and there is a lot to be said for them, it looks as if there is a clear basis for international unity and collaboration; and if they are put that way to Mr. Bevin, instead of in the petulant imputation of British troop movements appearing in Friday's "Pravda", there is some reason to hope that Britain will react. It has been said in this column before, and I repeat it now, that Britain, for all her impoverishment and financial vassalage to the United States, is still the key to world unity. She has greater flexibility than the other great powers, and her present Government has a foot in both camps. If Mr. Bevin uses the opportunity, he can raise this country's prestige and advance world progress and security. There is still a chance that he may.

WHAT, meanwhile, are we to say of the happenings in Indonesia? Not Mr. Bevin or Mr. Attlee or any other member of the Labour Government will find that easy to explain away. "Pravda" may exaggerate concerning the purpose behind the presence of British troops in Indonesia, Saigon, Egypt, Palestine and elsewhere; but nothing that can be said in malice is as bad in its effect on public opinion as such factual reports as have been published the last day or two on the burning and bombing of villages in Indo-China and Java. These punitive raids cannot fail to shock progressive opinion everywhere, and to cast suspicion upon British foreign policy wherever it is applied. To be sure, far worse has been done, and is being done, by other powers; but that is not the point: the point is that far better is expected of Britain and is needed if she is to retain her voice as a moral factor in world affairs.

Jerusalem, December 16.

U.N.O. JOB FOR MRS. ROOSEVELT

WASHINGTON, Saturday (UP) — Mrs. Eleanor Roosevelt is being considered by President Truman for a post with the United Nations Organization.

NAZIS ADMIT MURDERING 6 MILLION JEWS IN EUROPE
NOT ENOUGH TO SATISFY HIMMLER

By ERIC BOURNE, Reuters Special Correspondent

NUREMBERG, Saturday. — The Germans killed 6,000,000 Jews in the East, according to an S.S. Sturmbann-fuehrer (Major), Dr. Wilhelm Hoettl, whose affidavit was offered as evidence before the War Crimes Tribunal yesterday.

Hoettl's affidavit said that in August last year, he talked in Budapest with S.S. Obersturmbann-fuehrer (Lt.-Col.) Adolf Eichmann (Hebrew - speaking Nazi German born in Sarona near Tel Aviv), who "certainly had the best record of Jews who had been murdered."

Eichmann told Hoettl that he reported to Himmler that approximately 4,000,000 Jews had been killed in various extermination camps, while an additional 2,000,000 met their deaths in other ways, the majority being shot by the Security police.

Himmler was not satisfied with this report, since in his opinion the number of Jews who had been killed must have been more than 6,000,000. "I have reasons to believe, however, that Eichmann's information was correct," Hoettl added.

Major Walsh, U.S.A. Deputy prosecutor, cited evidence that 1,765,000 Jews were exterminated at the Auschwitz and Birkenau death-camps, between April, 1942, and April, 1944.

According to a document from the U.S. President's War Refugee Board files, the Jews murdered were of the following nationalities:

900,000 Poles; 100,000 Dutch; 45,000 Greeks; 150,000 French; 50,000 Belgians; 60,000 Germans; 50,000 Yugoslavs, Italians and Norwegians; 30,000 Lithuanians; 30,000 Bohemians, Moravians and Austrians; 30,000 Slovaks; and 300,000 of various nationalities taken from scattered camps in Poland.

Starving of Millions

Major Walsh introduced a new series of German documents and directives clearly showing the calculated plan to starve millions of Jews to death by shutting them off from all sources of supply and certain areas, and forbidding them to participate in agriculture where they might get food.

So widespread did the executions of the Jews become that the S.S. police at Berlin wrote to Rosenberg complaining that some 5,000 Jews killed by the police and S.S. might have been used for forced labour.

The document added that it should be possible "to avoid atrocities and bury those who have been liquidated. To lock men, women and children into barns and set fire to the structures, does not appear to be a suitable method of combating these bands, even if it is desired to exterminate the population. This method is unworthy of the German cause and hurts our reputation."

S.S. Death Vans

S.S. death vans were mentioned by Major Walsh in his evidence when he produced a report on their operations at Kiev, written by S.S. officials on May 16, 1942. Another report from Riga complained that the existing three death vans were incapable of handling the Jews being brought in for execution, and requested another five vans to cope with the numbers.

Major Walsh then gave details of the German extermination camp for Jews at Treblinka, in Poland. This was part of the indictment of Hans Frank by the Polish Government for

---

establishing in March, 1945, an extermination camp at Treblinka intended for mass killings of Jews by suffocating them in steam-filled chambers.

The Polish charge added: "It may be assumed that several hundreds of thousands of Jews have been exterminated at Treblinka. Exposed to the most cruel sufferings of body and soul, their death in the steam chambers must have come almost as a welcome relief.

"Their only crime consisted in fact of belonging to a race condemned by Hitler to death."

Major Walsh read an extract from a British War Office report stating that, during an interrogation, a French student deposed: "During July 1944 at the Auschwitz concentration camp, Hungarian Jews were being liquidated at the rate of 12,000 daily, and the crematoria could not deal with such numbers. Many bodies were thrown in large pits and covered with quick-lime."

"Germanizing Europe"

When Major Walsh closed the case on the murder of six million Jews, another U.S. assistant prosecutor, Mr. Sam Harris, took up the evidence on the spoliation and "Germanization" of the occupied countries.

The first document underlined the German intention to make the conquered Poles slaves of Germany and to rob the country of all its industrial assets.

Frank in a report explained how he intended to govern Poland under Hitler's directive which provided that Poland could only be administered by utilizing the country through the means of ruthless exploitation of all supplies of raw materials, machines and factory installations; making available all labour for work in Germany; and reducing Polish

---

economy to the bare minimum for existence.

It also provided for the closing of all educational institutions lest they breed a new race of intellectuals, and for reducing Poland to "the status of a German colony, with the Poles becoming the slaves of the Great German world empire."

Poland as Test Ground

Poland was used as a testing ground, said Mr. Harris. Secret documents, introduced in Court, showed that the Nazis had plans for wholesale migrations and re-shuffling of European populations to provide a solid German race for the Reich. The Czech problem was to be solved by absorbing half of the population into Germany and stripping the other half of power and shipping it off.

This last order agreed it would take years to "Germanize" Czechoslovakia, but "all elements which resist the plan-ned 'Germanization' are to be handled roughly and should be eliminated."

At the conclusion of yesterday's hearing, Mr. Justice Jackson, the U.S. prosecutor, announced that he proposed to seek a declaratory judgment by the Tribunal that the six Nazi organizations named in the indictment — the Reich Cabinet, the Leadership Corps of the Nazi Party, the S.S., including the Sicherheitsdienst (S.D.), the Gestapo, the S.A., and the General Staff and High Command of the German armed forces — be named in the indictment as criminal organizations.

Such findings, he pointed out, might constitute the basis for proceedings against individuals in other Courts.

The United States was anxious to present as much as possible of the evidence against these organizations before the Christmas recess, he said, in order that the defence might have an opportunity for examining it.

Court Shown Grim Exhibits of Terror

By GEORGE LICHTHEIM, Palestine Post Correspondent

NUREMBERG, Dec. 13 (delayed) — Lampshades made of the human skin of victims slain for this purpose by concentration camp guards, and shrunken human skulls used as mascots by Nazis in the same camp, figured among the exhibits when the prosecution this afternoon concluded its case against Nazi terrorism. A sharp change was then opened when the Nazi extermination of the Jewish people was detailed by Major Walsh, the American Military prosecutor, with the aid of captured evidence, including photographs of the Ghetto liquidation taken by an S.S. member.

Going back to the original Nazi programme and outlining the gradual intensification of the campaign against the Jews, the Prosecutor gradually prepared the Court for the climax of the extermination campaign in the actual liquidation of the Polish ghettoes.

Campaign of Horror

Showing the gradual development of the anti-Jewish campaign, beginning with Streicher's ritual murder ravings 20 years ago, and ending with a diary entry of Governor Frank of Poland on August 24, 1942, "that we sentenced 1,200,000 Jews to die of hunger should be noted only marginal-ly," the prosecutor built up a case notably against Frick, who signed most of the early anti-Jewish decrees; Goering, who organized the 1938 confiscations; Streicher and Rosenberg, who supplied the ideological basis; and Frank, who directed the massacres in Poland.

Despite the somewhat sketchy and superficial presentation of the evidence, which mostly ignored the historical background of the campaign, leaving the sources of this outburst unexplained, the prosecutor succeeded in impressing upon the Court the full horror of the final extermination drive, which served the double purpose of ridding the Reich of superfluous consumers, and serving the Nazi political purpose as well as the insatiable bloodlust of Himmler's S.S.

The full S.S. report on the liquidation of the Warsaw ghetto was also issued, giving a detailed day-by-day account of the extermination, resulting in the killing of many tens of thousands of Jewish civilians, mostly unarmed.

A marked feature of the report, which was prefaced by the words, "For the Fuehrer and their Country: The following fell in the battle for the destruction of the Jews and bandits in the former ghetto of Warsaw" followed by fifteen names and then the words "They gave their utmost, their lives. We shall never forget them" is the apparent conviction of the S.S. murderers that their "operation" with tanks, flame-throwers, and grenades against helpless humanity was a serious and dangerous military action.

Though many of the Jews were armed with primitive weapons smuggled in by Poles and others, the great majority were simply slaughtered, and evidenced by the comparison of losses on both sides.

The accused lost lots of their buoyancy during the recital but showed no sign of shame.

TRUMAN URGES TRUCE IN CHINA

WASHINGTON, Saturday (R) — President Truman today called for an immediate end to hostilities in China between the National Government and the Communist forces, and the summoning of a national conference of representatives of all major political elements of the Chinese nation to seek an early solution to the present internal strife.

The President issued a comprehensive statement of United-States policy towards China within two hours of the departure of General George C. Marshall, new American diplomatic envoy to Chungking. President Truman reiterated that America would continue to recognize Generalissimo Chiang Kai Shek's Government

---

U.N.O. CHOOSES U.S. FOR HEADQUARTERS

LONDON, Saturday (R.). — The United Nations executive committee's recommendations that U.N.O. headquarters should be in the United States was today endorsed by the Preparatory Commission with the recommendation that the headquarters be somewhere in the vicinity of New York.

The vote was later made unanimous on a motion by the Canadian delegate seconded by Mr. Philip Noel-Baker, for the United Kingdom, who had led the case for Europe.

Voting was by roll-call after a motion to vote by secret ballot had been defeated.

The Commission's decision for the United States was reached after prolonged and, in some cases, bitter debates.

BRITISH DOCKERS ACCEPT TERMS

LONDON, Saturday (Reuter). British dockers have accepted proposed terms of settlement of their wage dispute made under the Government Investigation committee's report, and authorized union representatives to enter into an agreement with the employers.

Dockers' delegates from all over Britain, at a conference in London yesterday, accepted the basis of a 19/- minimum daily wage to date back to November 26, new piece rates, and a medical scheme.

The question of a 48-hour week was left in abeyance because it is being dealt with by the trade unions on a national basis.

BRITISH ADVANCE IN BATAVIA

By NOEL BUCKLEY, Reuters Correspondent

BATAVIA, Saturday. — British forces have taken over the Batavian railways and telephone exchange at Buitenzorg, about 40 miles from Batavia along the Bandoeng road. The Indonesian "Resident" had fled the town after declaring himself unable to maintain order.

On the whole, the present Indonesian administration is doing its utmost to end the disturbances, especially in West Java. The Indonesian Peace Preservation Corps at Bandoeng, a hill station and internee centre in Western Java, are cooperating in full military action against extremists.

Leading members of the Indonesian "Republican" Government will shortly undertake a tour of Central and Eastern Java to induce the local leaders, who wield real power, to accept its discipline.

In Eastern Java, British troops continue to fan out south and west of the Naval base of Sourabaya, and are now clearing towns about 15 miles from the port against the hostilities by Japanese guards, have taken over by air, on his way to confer with his home Government. He was expected to return in about three weeks to resume his talks with Indonesian leaders.

A British paratroop battalion which won fame at Arnhem and two companies of Gurkhas have arrived in Batavia. Allied military police arrested the editor of the popular Indonesian newspaper "Merdeka" and his wife, a graduate of Columbia University. The editor was later released but his wife was detained.

At Singapore, Mr. Moberly Dening, British Foreign Office adviser, stated that it was necessary that Siam "should make restitution for the damage done to British interests and in particular to the international character of territories bordering on Siam, for the welfare of which Britain is responsible. Siam must realize that treaties are not to be lightly broken." Mr. Dening has resumed negotiations at Singapore to end the hostilities.

Batavia today for The Hague

POLICE SWOOP IN LONDON

Palestine Post Cable

LONDON, Saturday. — The results of last night's police round-up was announced as follows by Scotland Yard tonight:

Total number of persons stopped — 15,161;
Deserters handed over to military escort — 32;
Arrests for alleged house-breaking — 2;
Arrests for alleged larceny — 4;
Arrests for alleged unlawful possession — 9.

In addition to these arrests, one person was detained on a charge of being found on enclosed premises, two others were R.A.F. personnel said to be wearing false decorations, and another was an escaped Italian prisoner of war. (Earlier Story, Page 3.)

ELEVEN BELSEN BANDITS HANGED

HAMBURG, Saturday (Reuter). — All eleven men and women of the Belsen concentration camp staff sentenced to death were hanged on Thursday, it was announced yesterday.

The executions took place in the presence of the prison governor and one British doctor. Only one scaffold was used and the executions were carried out in accordance with British practice. Witnesses from the Court at Lueneburg were present to identify the condemned persons.

German Catholic and Protestant prison chaplains were in attendance. All eleven went quietly to their death and there were no scenes outside the prison.

Chief of those executed were Josef Kramer, commandant; Irma Grese, 21 years old S.S. woman; Elisabeth Volkenrath, an S.S. guard at the camp; Fritz Klein, the camp doctor who made gas-chamber selections; and Juana Bormann, stated at the trial to have turned a dog loose on prisoners.

Five days before the executions General Field-Marshal Montgomery refused an appeal for mercy. Sentences of death were passed on November 16.

TALKS BEGIN IN MOSCOW
INTEREST CENTRES ON PERSIA

MOSCOW, Saturday. — Both Mr. Ernest Bevin, British Foreign Minister, and Mr. James Byrnes, U.S. Secretary of State, have arrived in Moscow after delay and some anxiety due to bad flying weather, and have already been received by the Foreign Commissar, M. Molotov.

Though official statements have specified only atomic energy as one of the subjects to be discussed, it is definite that Persia will be on the agenda, Sir Reader Bullard, the British Ambassador to Iran, and Mr. J. D. Jernegan, U.S. Embassy Representative, having left Teheran for Moscow by Soviet plane.

Another major question up for discussion appears to be Allied relations in the Far East centring round control of Japan.

The talks were "an exploratory exchange of views" and need not necessarily lead to the announcement of any major decisions, Mr. Byrnes told the press.

Meanwhile, at least as far as Persia is concerned, facts are being created which might in themselves become decisions. The latest news from Teheran is that insurgent forces have captured Tabriz, the chief town of Azerbaijan, and Ardabil, the Caspian port 30 miles from the Soviet frontier. All Persian battalions were stopped by the Red Army from moving into the "trouble province" and have returned to the capital on orders from their headquarters.

Azerbaijan Lost

"Azerbaijan seems definitely lost to Persia," said Nurteza Qualkhan Bayatt, Governor of the province, who arrived in Teheran from Tabriz on Friday and who stated that he had been advised to leave by Jafar Pishevari, president of the newly formed provincial government and leader of the Democratic Party. It appears, states one commentator, that the insurgents hope to confront the Government with a fait accompli before the Moscow Conference can make any decision.

In Teheran itself, although everything looks calm, measures have been taken to prevent disturbances, it being rumoured that several illegal groups are in existence. In spite of this, M. Hakimi, the Iranian Prime Minister, is reported to be optimistic and great hopes are placed on his coming visit to Moscow accompanied by his Foreign Minister. Whether the visit will coincide with or impinge on the talks of the three Allied Foreign Ministers remains for the latter to decide.

The actual military operations in Azerbaijan are expected to develop in intensity in the Spring.

Persian Government circles point out that the province's present rulers are neither Democrats nor Central Government, but Russian occupation authorities. Since these are pledged to evacuate Iran by March 2 at the latest the situation is likely to develop to a grim climax.

If the Foreign Ministers in Moscow agreed that the foreign forces leave Iran appreciably in advance of that date, it is claimed that the Iran Government would be capable of restoring order, even if it involved a certain amount of fighting there.

The next week or two would show to what lengths Russia is prepared to go. It is believed in Teheran that that has already been indicated by the Soviet reply of November 24 to the Iran Government's Note, when it was stated in effect that should the Iran Government despatch troops to Azerbaijan and precipitate bloodshed, it would be necessary to send additional Red Army forces from Russia to restore order.

A strong case to be consulted and represented at talks at which decisions affecting Persia are taken, was advanced by the Iranian Government two days ago. The State Department disclosed in Washington the American view that Persia should be able to use her own forces wherever and in whatever manner necessary to preserve its authority and security, but reiterating that British troops could not be withdrawn without similar action on the part of Russia.

U.S. Interest

The United States would press for evacuation of the Iranian question within an international frame rather than by agreement between two countries, well-informed circles in Washington state.

The Iranian crisis is part of the general situation in the Middle East, and its solution will influence public opinion in that part of the world as to the real intentions of the Big Powers in the international questions of the future. It is the United States' wish, according to these circles, that the Moscow discussion of the Iran problem should be only preliminary, and that the final solution should be left to the Security Council of the U.N.O. Although the United States did not sign the agreement fixing the date of the Anglo-Russian evacuation, American Government support is behind the closest interest in the Persian question and also in Russian aims in the Near and Middle East.

(Reuter, U.P. and AFP)

American Securities Suffer Setback

(Reuters Economic Service)

NEW YORK, Saturday. — Wall Street this week suffered its biggest setback since mid-July. Undoubtedly, the market was discouraged by the lack of a conciliatory attitude among either labour or management. The fact that the setback was led by steels and motors was indicative of the market's temper, and the factors affecting these groups spread their depressing influence to other shares.

If the slump was technical, as some assert, the market should partly regain its equilibrium, but if it represents a growing fear about the national labour and price riddle, reaction may extend.

PATTON IMPROVING

FRANKFURT, Saturday (R). — Today's bulletin on the state of health of General George Patton, Commander of the U.S. 45th Army in Germany, who was injured in a car accident last Sunday, said that his general condition was excellent.

"There has been a slight but significant improvement in his condition during the past 24 hours," the bulletin added. The General continues alert and cheerful.

RUSSIANS CLAIM RIGHTS IN PERSIA

LONDON, Saturday (R). — The presence of British troops in Palestine, Egypt, the East Indies, and several European countries was challenged today by a "Pravda" commentator, David Zaslavski, according to the Moscow radio.

M. Zaslavski stated that the U.S.S.R. had the right to station its troops in Persia under its treaty with that country, continuing:

"Just as simple is the answer concerning Soviet troops in other countries. This can arouse no doubt or perplexity.

"It may seem that the question concerning the presence of British troops in Persia, in accordance with the 1942 agreement, is relatively simple. Are there not in Persia British troops who were stationed there before the 1942 agreement?

"If so, when did they appear? For what purpose? Where are they stationed? What is their number? What are the duties? Do the conditions of the 1942 agreement extend to them also? We do not hear the answers to these questions.

"Other Countries

"The Egyptian press almost daily raises the same question: When will Great Britain at last withdraw her troops from Egypt? Truly, ancient Oedipus encountered less difficulty in extracting a reply from the Egyptian State than the contemporary Egypt has in receiving an answer from the British State," the writer added.

Truman Sees U.S. Inquiry Members

WASHINGTON, Saturday (PTA). — The six American members of the Committee of Inquiry are being received by President Truman today, the White House press secretary announced.

They are impressed with the importance of taking up their work with all possible despatch (he said) and therefore wished to talk over the whole matter with the President.

LONDON, Saturday (Reuter). — The constitution of the Joint Anglo-American Committee of Inquiry on Palestine into the Palestinian problem was the subject of an exchange of Notes between the British Ambassador, Lord Halifax, and the Secretary of State, Mr. James F. Byrnes. The text was published here yesterday.

Mr. Byrnes wrote to Lord Halifax on December 10:

"I have the honour to inform Your Excellency with reference to our conversations on the subject that the Government of the United States agrees to constitute, in cooperation with the Government of the United Kingdom, a joint Anglo-American Committee of Inquiry with the following composition:

"The Committee should be composed of six nationals of the United States appointed by the Government of the United States, and six nationals of the United Kingdom appointed by the Government of the United Kingdom, and shall operate

expedition in dealing with the subjects committed to it for investigation and shall request that they may be furnished with the reports within 120 days of the inception of the inquiry.

"Committee's Procedure

"The procedure of the Committee shall be determined by the Committee itself and it will be open to it, if it thinks fit, to deal simultaneously through the medium of sub-committees with any of the subjects entrusted to its consideration.

"Such Government might be responsible for compensating its own members of the Committee and such expenses as are not susceptible of being jointly shared by the two Governments, all other expenses of the Committee shall be borne jointly by both Governments in equal proportions."

Lord Halifax wrote to Mr. Byrnes on December 10:

"I have the honour, in reply to Your Excellency's note of December 10 about the terms of reference of the Joint Anglo-American Committee of Inquiry to report on the position of Jews in certain countries of Europe and in Palestine."

(American sources, Page 8)

LORD CHORLEY

Lord Chorley, who took part in the debate on Palestine in the House of Lords last Monday, is

THINK! LOOK FORWARD!

INDUSTRY IS MAKING POST-WAR PLANS. WHAT ARE YOU DOING ABOUT YOUR FUTURE?

If your job is a temporary one and if you want to consolidate it, earn a bigger pay, and build a career with a future, you must read "Commercial Opportunities" which shows how you can qualify for a permanent and highly paid post in peace-time.

This valuable guide to success outlines courses for recognized University and Professional Diplomas in all branches of Commerce such as B. Com., and A.C.C.A. etc., and also Matriculation.

OUR GUARANTEE IS: NO PASS, NO FEE.

Whatever your age or position, you can use your spare time to ensure your future career. A copy of this valuable handbook will be sent FREE on application to:

THE PALESTINE POST

LATE Edition

JERUSALEM
TUESDAY, JULY 23, 1946

PRICE 15 MILS
VOL. XXI. No. 6135

Column One
By David Courtney

THE dust of irresponsible bombs raises a curtain through which the events of the larger world are seen dimly. The bloody foreground to yesterday's events is foreground only to those near at hand; and the perspective on the other side of the curtain will be less distorted than on this side. The world today comprehends violence as violence only: it has suffered too much of it to be deceived by the extenuations of its fraudulent politics. The outrage committed yesterday in Jerusalem has neither sense nor apology. It was unqualified evil and will be judged as such by honest men in every part of the world. At this moment, it is nothing less than a challenge to the Jewish cause itself, a challenge that must be taken up in the interest of the cause.

IT is permissible to argue that the events of yesterday are of a piece with the chaos of a world groping frantically for values. If other world events of the last twenty-four hours have been less spectacular, their implications have been in many cases hardly less terrifying. It is a tale of violence from Trieste to Manchuria and of unwisdom from Berlin to Athens. No one event excuses the other and all of them are symptoms of a Peace which is less than an uncontrollable projection of the war. It is obvious that Hitler has had greater success in his long-term plans than in his short-term ambitions. That fact needs to be borne in mind. The tendency to consider the German war as over and the penalty largely paid grows alarmingly.

THE latest evidence of this is the Anglo-American plan to flout the Soviet and, bowing to the pressure of Big Business in Britain and the United States, to re-establish a vast German economic system on lines which can lead to nothing else but the renewed domination of industrial Germany. General McNarney talks plain American. If the Russians won't collaborate in a scheme of economic unity for the whole of Germany and largely for the benefit of German heavy industry, their acquiescence will not be sought for a scheme of partial union. One gets the impression from General McNarney's statements of a too-eager readiness to profit by the apparent intransigence of the Soviet.

THE Anglo-American case has persuasive merits. Administration of the two western zones is a heavy financial liability on the British American taxpayer, and may well remain so until a scheme of German inter-zonal and international trading is adopted and applied. In practice this can only mean vast German sovereignty based on the revived heavy industries of the Ruhr and therefore fundamentally opposed to the terms of the Potsdam agreement. It is not sufficient to argue that the Soviet itself has failed to honour the Potsdam agreement. It has not been honoured by any one of the occupying Powers. The Russians have claimed that Britain and America's interpretation of its spirit, and that even with the American twenty-five year plan added to it, the ultimate result would be the restoration of a Germany little different from the one that has gone to war twice in the last twenty-two years.

AT successive conferences of the Big Three during and immediately after the war, it was laid down as a unified principle that the victorious Allies would accept the responsibility for the demilitarisation of Germany in every sense including the economic; and for the rehabilitation of the country in a fashion that would make it a welcome and peaceful member of the community of nations. It was, and is, a tremendous job: it may be a forlorn job. But the war has been over barely a year and it is too soon to grow tired or even parsimonious in the task which, if unfulfilled, would make a mockery of Allied victory. It is natural that the British, and especially the Americans should want to get quit of such a responsibility at a time when their own internal problems are almost unbearable; but Germany in defeat is still the major problem of international security. That problem will only be exacerbated if General McNarney and those who advise from Wall Street and the City of London get their way.

Jerusalem, July 23.

41 DEAD, 53 INJURED, 52 MISSING, IN TERRORIST ATTACK ON SECRETARIAT
NOON-HOUR OUTRAGE BY GANG; BOMBS IN MILK CANS; SIR JOHN SHAW AND SOME SENIOR OFFICERS SAFE

At least 41 men and women were killed, 53 were injured, and another 52 were still reported missing at midnight, as a result of a terrorist attack shortly after noon yesterday which destroyed a large section of the offices of the Secretariat of the Palestine Government housed in the south-west corner of the King David Hotel.

It was officially announced last night that the following officers in the Secretariat at the time of the morning's outrage were known to be safe.

Sir John Shaw, Mr. Gibson, Mr. J. Gutch, Ruhi Bey Abdul Hadi, Mr. J. Cornes, Mr. A.M. Dryburgh, Mr. J. Smith, Mr. M. Browne, Mr. Bradley, Mr. Ford, Mr. N.W. McClellan, Mrs. Small, Miss M. King, Mrs. Cassell, Miss R. Walsh, Mr. Antippa, Mr. Forrest, Mr. Bayliss, Mr. R. Newton.

The dead whose bodies have so far been recovered and identified include :

Mr. Z. Shimshi; Mr. Yanowsky; Mr. E. Sperling; Mr. Mughannam; Mr. I. Farraj; Mr. Y. Mormilstein; Mr. L.J. Barder; Mr. Jamil Barder; Mr. A.M. Suleiman; Mr. E. Krantz; Mr. M. Atizeh; Mr. D.M.A.S. Khatib; Mr. Eissa Isis; Mr. G. Paragenian; Mr. T. Mansour; Mr. M.A. Khadir; Mr. S. Yitshaiah; Mr. Bada Abdul Farrah Abu Lahab; Mr. Mohammed H. Salah; Mr. R.S. Tamimi; Mr. F. Stein; Mr. S. Kharoufi; Miss R. Salman.

The Civil Service Second Division Association has called for the observance of a 15-minute silence by all officers at noon today in sign of mourning.

Arrangements have been made to answer inquiries concerning those missing as a result of the explosions at the King David building. Inquiries may be made by telephone to Number 4437 Extension 5.

Troops and civilian workers were digging in the debris under the glare of searchlights in the early, post-midnight hours of this morning. An R.A.F. bulldozer was brought up early in the evening to remove wreckage, as several people were believed to be still alive beneath the debris.

Curfew was imposed from 12.45 on the whole municipal area of Jerusalem but was later in the afternoon restricted to the central area of the city in which most Jewish residential quarters are situated. The curfew lasted until 5 o'clock this morning, when it was lifted completely. Patrol wireless cars and armoured cars assisted in the hunt for suspect cars. Within a few minutes of the explosions, as the sirens went, the police had telephoned all Government buildings and ordered the complete evacuation of staffs until searches for further bombs could be carried out.

THREE EXPLOSIONS

There was first an explosion about 12 o'clock, some 50 yards from the southern end of the hotel building. Almost simultaneously another detonation took place in the lane along the northern end of the hotel, leading to the French Consulate General. Shop-fronts and windows were blown in.

At the same time, a truck drove into the sunken driveway which leads from the northern lane to the service entrance to the basement and kitchens. A number of men — put variously at four or five to seven or eight — alighted and several began unloading milk-cans and buckets. Others went inside and held up the kitchen staff — cooks, waiters, mechanics and dishwashers.

The men deposited the milk-cans and buckets, now known to have been full of explosives, in the hallway outside the Regence cafe at the southern end of the long corridor and then escaped, leaving the hotel staff to scramble to safety as best they could.

According to one report, an anonymous woman caller telephoned to the switchboard operator at the King David and told him that the building must be evacuated as there would be an explosion "in a few minutes." About 12.35, The Palestine Post was told, also by a woman, in English, that the Government offices were about to be blown up, and that the people there had been warned to evacuate the building.

A mysterious woman caller telephoned the French Consulate General and said, "In a few minutes there will be an explosion in your neighbourhood. We suggest that you open all your windows." This was done and no one was hurt there.

The third explosion came at 12.37 with a heavy shattering roar. An eye-witness at a window in the P.I.O. offices high up in the David Building, across the field, stated that after the explosion, the walls of the south-west corner seemed to bulge, there was a thick and heavy cloud of brown-grey smoke, and then the masonry swayed and collapsed. The screaming of men and women trapped by the debris rose above the din of crumbling stone, iron girders and woodwork.

GAPING HOLE

The dense column of acrid smoke spiralled several hundred feet into the air, completely hiding the southern wing of the hotel. When the billowing smoke started to drift off into the sunny, cloudless sky, there was a huge, gaping chasm where the six-storey corner had been. Wounded troops and civilians, their clothes spattered with blood, their faces covered with white dust and streaked with blood, staggered out of the wreckage dazed by shock.

Inside the hotel, all electric clocks had stopped at 12.37. The entire southern wall at the end of the corridor was blown out and the wall behind the bar was demolished. The bar itself was a shambles of broken bottles, windows and furniture.

The lobby was caked with dust and a good deal of sand blown up through the loosened marble floor, which was covered with glass splinters. A whole row of tiles from the entrance hall to the south wing was raised a few inches. Broken woodwork was scattered about and pell-mell in the lobby.

LEAKING PIPES

Down the stairs, in the basement, water pipes were twisted and leaking, the whole looking like the interior of a torpedoed ship.

The annexe building in the southern grounds, where the War Supply Board offices were housed, had its roof knocked in by falling stones. A large iron safe was hurled by the blast into Julian's Way, killing a passer-by.

Within a few minutes after the first explosion, police radio cars, armoured cars, and jeep-borne infantry converged on the spot. The anti-terrorist sirens had sounded and traffic halted, at first somewhat uncertainly. A few minutes later, as C.I.D. experts and Army sappers were examining the wreckage of shop-windows and fronts, the All Clear sirens went and traffic was resumed. The police and infantry withdrew some distance, but then came the third and heaviest into play. Police later found it contained a Sten-gun.

A sentry who saw a man throw the first bomb fired at him and the man, throwing explosion and the sirens went away a sub-machine gun, limp-

Senior and Junior Civil Servants

Senior and Junior Civil Servants — British, Jewish, and Arab — are among the dead. Of those identified, the names of 23 Palestinians were released for publication, but the identity of five British officials and seven Army and Police personnel will not be disclosed until tonight, after their next-of-kin have been notified.

ATTACKERS OUTLAWED BY JEWISH HEADS

The following joint statement was issued last night by the Jewish Agency and Vaad Leumi.

The Executive of the Jewish Agency and the Executive of the Vaad Leumi express their horror at the dastardly crime perpetrated by the gang of desperadoes who today attacked the Government offices in Jerusalem, and shed the innocent blood of Government officers and other citizens, British, Jewish and Arab.

They express their deepest sympathy to the relatives of those who have been murdered and to those who have been injured.

The Yishuv in Palestine is called upon to rise up against these abominable outrages.

Statements by Tel Aviv Municipality and Histadrut Page 3

Official Army H.Q. Account

In a statement issued from H.Q. Palestine late last night, it was stated that at 12.10 on Monday a civilian truck drove up to the basement of the King David Hotel and a number of Jews dressed as Arabs got out and held up the civilian doorkeeper at the service entrance.

This party of Jews then entered the hotel and held up the kitchen staff before unloading several milk-churns through the service door into the hotel.

They pushed these milk-churns along towards the far end of the building, past the Signal exchange, and deposited them by the Regence restaurant, directly below the Secretariat. A Royal Signals officer working in the exchange, hearing a good deal of noise, came out to investigate and was confronted by a man dressed as an Arab, pointing a revolver at him.

Before the officer had time to make a sound, the man covered with a layer of dust. One member of the kitchen staff told The Palestine Post that he was held up by two men dressed as Arabs who entered the basement door, and told him in Arabic to keep still and not move.

Sir John Shaw permitted press photographers to take pictures at all angles, and it is understood that a special plane was flown to Cairo for pictures to be radio-wirelessed to England. One high military officer on the scene was heard to say, "This is mass murder."

The Jerusalem Fire Brigade and Army Fire Service engines were on the scene to cope with possible outbreaks of fire.

Thirty-one bodies were brought to the Government Hospital at 7 o'clock yesterday evening, but only 21 could be identified. According to the P.B.S. at 9.30, five Britons and 28 Palestinians had lost their lives. The radio also stated that 15 Britons and 27 Palestinians were injured, and that a number of persons were not yet accounted for.

The following persons were admitted to hospital:

Government Hospital:
Mr. A. Southworth, Crown Counsel; Emile Marroum; Fazid Abu Ghosh; Assa Aref Musha'sha; P/C Mahmud Abdul Sabe; Gablan Mifekl; Youssef Mustafa Jeddah; Jabra Bader Abdul Lati Maghrabi; Musaa Hussein Ali Nouri; Mohammed Abdul Haj; and an unidentified person.

French Hospital:
George Bushad; Yacub Abdul Muneim; Bibhi Hassan Hamude; Mohammad Fatteah Rabbah; Awad Sayed Mantoul; Hassan Abdul Rahman; and Herman Freidman.

General Military Hospital:
Miss Leeba Walsh; Miss Julia Jessel; Miss Victoria Rafaeian; Miss Marie Green-berg; Miss Rose-Anne Trindel; Miss Jean Khoury; Miss Adi Bitar; Miss Jean Cattough; man named Artih; and Mr. Richard Mower.

More than 50 persons were given first aid treatment at Government Hospital, the French Hospital, and the Hadassah clinic and were sent home.

'Monty' Summoned to Cabinet on Palestine

LONDON, Monday. — Field Marshal Montgomery, Chief of the British General Staff, was summoned to Downing Street today when the British Cabinet met to consider the critical Palestine situation.

While it is doubtful whether the Cabinet had yet received detailed of the blasting of the Palestine Administration's Headquarters in Jerusalem, Mr. Attlee is believed to have given an account of recent developments in Palestine.

Informed quarters now confirm that there will be both an official statement and a White Paper on Palestine before Parliament rises, probably in the first week of August.

The Government has still to fix a date for the statement, which will be of an interim character so far as general policy is concerned, but will cover the "public order" side of the present situation about which most of the facts are now known.

It is understood that documents found in the Jewish Agency offices in Jerusalem will be published in a White paper next week.

LP.100,000 Damage

The King David Hotel was built in 1929 and opened in 1931. It cost a quarter of a million pounds at that time, but the value is now of course considerably more.

The section of the building destroyed yesterday is valued at LP.100,000.

Rental paid by Government to the hotel management is LP.1,000 monthly.

Mr. Benjamin Chaikin, F.R.I.B.A., who designed the building, was brought yesterday to examine the damage after the explosion.

Guests were allowed to return last night to sleep there.

Federalness Lesser Evil

There are signs that the Joint Palestine Report's vision of a unitarian Palestinian state is proving impossible of fulfilment, says the "Daily Telegraph", referring to the suggestion of a federal Palestine with Jewish, Arab and "mixed" cantons.

The paper says, "as far as to object to a federal or any solution unwelcome to either the Arab leaders or the more extreme Zionists among the Jews. No ingenuity could devise a scheme to satisfy either. Therefore, the first duty of the Mandatory Power must be to restore order as has been done; and the second, to apply some scheme morally and materially defensible. If there is only a choice of evils, we must choose the lesser."

A federal system for Palestine, dividing the country into Arab and Jewish states, is also forecast as the solution towards which the British and United States experts have been moving during their meetings in London, by the London Correspondent of the "Yorkshire Post".

EYE-WITNESS STORIES

The Officer Administering the Government, Sir J.V.W. Shaw, was sitting in his office at the south-eastern corner of the hotel when the explosion occurred. Immediately afterwards, he was seen rushing from one room to another in the hotel and later carrying a ladder to take part in the rescue work. The O.A.G. was joined by the Inspector-General of Police, Colonel W. N. Gray. The G.O.C. Lt.-General E.H. Barker, and members of the Staff were also soon on the scene.

Sir John had been trapped in his room but was rescued after the door was broken open. His office was not damaged as it was in the opposite wing, but the desk and floor were covered with falling plaster.

The Superintendent of Police, Jerusalem District, Mr. K.P. Hadingham, was investigating the cause of the first two apparently diversionary, explosions when the third occurred. He was badly injured about the hands and later returned to the scene bandaged. He also received a cut under the right eye. Mr. Dan Ben-Dor, R.E. garrison engineer, who was driving by at the time of the explosion, escaped with minor cuts, while his Great Dane, which was sitting at his side, was so badly hurt by fragments that it had to be destroyed. The motor of his car was smashed.

Two correspondents who were standing in the main lounge of the hotel had a narrow escape. Mr. T.S. Steele, "Daily Telegraph," and Mr. Stanley Bishop, "Daily Herald," threw themselves to the ground, and were unhurt. Mr. R. Catling, Deputy Superintendent at the C.I.D., who had arrived to investigate was with them but was also unhurt.

Mr. Richard Mowrer, "New York Post" correspondent, was walking across the street in front of the hotel when he was hit and suffered a broken leg.

One man who emerged from the Secretariat with only slight cuts was praying aloud and weeping. "My sister is under there. Lord, send her out alive." he repeated. He, his father and his sister were all employed in the Secretariat. His father was alive. He was still repeating his prayer half an hour later.

Mr. Robert Newton, of the political section of the Secretariat, said: "The whole side of my room fell away to the ground six storeys below and I was left suspended above the wreckage." He made his escape and helped to take charge of the rescue work.

As the "Daily Telegraph" correspondent was standing with Sir John Shaw, the figure of a civilian covered in dirt and with torn clothes emerged from the wreckage, walked up to the O.A.G., and said, "I have got the cyphers and locked the safe, sir."

Responsible Jewish sources put the blame for the attack on the Irgun Zevai Leumi or Stern Gang (according to a news agency report from Jerusalem). The Haganah was absolved of blame by both the Jews and the British, the message added.

The police reported they had arrested two men on suspicion a short distance from the hotel but would give no further details.

One Jewish source quoted by a news agency stated the attack was "an attempt to hamper Dr. Weizmann in his present talks with the British Government."

Attlee Statement Expected Today

LONDON, Monday. — The Prime Minister said in the House of Commons tonight that he can make a statement on the blowing up by Jewish terrorists of the British Army Headquarters at the King David Hotel in Jerusalem.

Mr. Attlee will, almost certainly, make a statement on the situation, though this may be fairly short pending the completion of the inquiries and the receipt in London of an official report on what has occurred.

There will be no demand for a debate at once, as it is already known that the Government meant propose to have a full debate on Palestine next week.

Mr. Hall, in a written reply today, refused Mr. Crossman's demand for a statement on the release of the Jewish leaders detained without charge, either entirely or pending their committal for trial.

(Reuter & PTA)

SUBMARINES OFF HAIFA

HAIFA, Monday. — The Cruiser HMS Liverpool, which has been in Haifa since Thursday, left today for Tel Aviv and Jaffa. Two submarines, the HMS Templar and HMS Totem off Port, and are here for a few days for exercises.

THE PALESTINE POST

LATE Edition

JERUSALEM
WEDNESDAY, July 31, 1946

PRICE: 15 MILS
VOL. XXI. No. 6165

PALESTINE'S BIGGEST CITY BESIEGED
TEL AVIV'S 200,000 BEING CHECKED BY TWO DIVISIONS

THE TWO COMMUNIQUES

No. 76, July 30.

The following communication was received from H.E. the High Commissioner (Gen.-Sir Alan Cunningham) this morning:

I wish to make it clear that the military operations now proceeding in the Tel Aviv area have as their objective the search for and detention of terrorists and are a direct result of the vile and horrible crime committed on Monday, July 22, 1946, through which over one hundred innocent civilians lost their lives, including women and boys, of British, Arab and Jewish birth.

There is clear evidence of the existence of terrorists in Tel Aviv and that some if not all of those who took part in the Jerusalem crime come from that town.

In making this announcement I do not depart one iota from my statement of June 22.

It has been and is my earnest wish that if as a result of violence directed against the Government, military action is forced on us, it should have as its objective the force responsible for that violence, and that military operations and restrictions should interfere as little as possible with the normal life of the country.

The remedy, therefore, is plain to see. Should violence be eschewed, normal occupations will take no harm, and the endeavour of all for the betterment of the future of Palestine can continue in peace. However, I would remind all the peoples of Palestine of the great and urgent activity now proceeding to find an early solution of the Palestine problem.

Discussions are to be held with both Arabs and Jews. Violence can only make the task more difficult and lengthy, if not impossible.

Palestine Post Staff

TEL AVIV, Tuesday. — Nearly 20,000 British troops and Palestine Police were engaged here today in the most intensive and most complete search operation ever undertaken in Palestine or perhaps in any other part of the world, with the object of finding members of terrorist gangs.

Some 25,000 persons were estimated to have been interrogated by evening, of whom 133 men and 10 girls were sent to Rafa and Latrun camps for further investigations. The G.O.C. Sir Evelyn Barker, and the Inspector General of Police, Colonel W. N. Gray, inspected the operations.

The search was so thoroughly planned that every adult in Tel Aviv will be questioned, every building searched, and even patients in hospitals examined during the four or five days it will last. X-ray photographs will be taken of patients in plaster casts to determine if their injuries are genuine.

Completely cut off from the rest of Palestine by land and sea, the city was placed under an absolute curfew from 5 o'clock in the morning.

Residents were warned that anyone breaking the curfew was liable to be shot on sight.

The troops and police appeared to know for whom they were looking. They had been furnished with a long alphabetical list of suspected members of the Irgun Zevai Leumi and the Stern Gang, and with photographs of some of the leading members of the two groups.

NO RESISTANCE

As far as could be observed in Tel Aviv yesterday by visiting press correspondents, there was no resistance to the search, not even passive. Men and women submitted quietly, and seemingly without showing resentment.

Before dawn, troops of the Sixth Airborne Division placed a cordon around the entire city. All traffic was prevented from entering or leaving. Traffic jams piled up at the cross-roads outside. When the foreign press correspondents arrived on a conducted tour from Jerusalem they found Tel Aviv to be a dead city, at first glance appearing to be entirely deserted except for the red-bereted troops and an occasional scavenging dog. Correspondents of the local press were prevented from joining the tour, though they were given special permit authorizing them to move freely in the town.

Every shop and office, including newspaper offices, was closed and not a single civilian could be seen on the streets under a lender escort of soldiers or in barbed-wire pens.

Within the city, a series of inner cordons were established. At 4.55 the search began, house by house, shop by shop, building by building and block by block. When the foreign press correspondents arrived on a conducted tour from Jerusalem they found Tel Aviv to be a dead city, at first glance appearing to be entirely deserted except for the red-bereted troops and an occasional scavenging dog. Correspondents of the local press were prevented from joining the tour, though they were given special permit authorizing them to move freely in the town.

British Police with a Jewish policeman attached as interpreter. Screening teams were set up at tables on the shady sides of streets or in shops. Each person was required to produce an identity card. Those who had no papers or whose papers or replies seemed suspicious were detained for further questioning by more expert interrogators at Brigade H.Q.

List of Suspects

Of 16 men detained at one Brigade command post all were young, some of them youths in their teens. Two girls, in bright summer print frocks, age say chiffon handkerchiefs over their heads, were held in a covered driveway with a wrought-iron gate. Both hid their faces when press photographers approached.

(Continued on Page 2 Col. 2)

Habimah Theatre Is Brigade H.Q.

TEL AVIV, Tuesday. — A Brigade Headquarters was established in the Habimah Theatre, which was surrounded by barbed wire. Police and army interrogators sat at a table in the entrance to question suspects brought for a second screening. Back stage, maps were laid out on tables erected from the theatre's props for "Hamlet".

In this instance a shameful and barbarous crime has been committed. It must be evident to every right-minded man that mere protests are not sufficient to remove stains of this kind. No movement of terrorist character would have a chance of survival against the wishes of the people from whom it springs. Preventive measures have been set in motion. It lies with the Yishuv to decide whether they will help or hinder the design of rooting out a canker which, if it remains, can only recoil on the heads of the Yishuv under whatever conditions the future may hold for them.

No. 77 July 30, 9.30 p.m.

Following the outrage at the Secretariat on July 23, the most extensive operations yet carried out against Jewish terrorists commenced at dawn today when some twenty thousand British troops of the 6th Airborne Division and the 1st British Infantry Division, working in conjunction with the Palestine Police, established close inner and outer cordons around Tel Aviv, isolating the town from the remainder of Palestine. Within the cordons a thorough search is being conducted.

The operations are under the command of Major-General A.J.H. Cassels, C.B. D.S.O. G.O.C. 6th Airborne Division. A complete curfew has been imposed and all telephone communication in and out of the town has been suspended. All traffic in and out of the town has been suspended. Seaborne traffic has also been stopped.

Searches proceeded throughout the day according to plan. Large numbers of Jews were screened and of these 133 males and 10 females have so far been held for further questioning. Apart from minor cases of stone throwing by Jews no incidents occurred. There were no casualties. The operations were attended by a large party of foreign correspondents.

Troops Patrols

Patrols of troops moved down one street of Tel Aviv after another, entering every door. Every abladbodied man between 15 and 50 years and every woman between 15 and 30 years, with the exception of pregnant women or mothers with small children, were ordered out of their homes to the nearest "screening" point.

Although intolerance reared its ugly head at times on all sides during the day and tempers frequently frayed, there was evident also genuine co-operation by both searched and searchers.

In Balsamh Road, however, our correspondent saw soldiers armed with heavy clubs, forcing detainees to double and prodding stragglers. The detainees appeared nervous and one man who dropped his hat did not stop to pick it up.

For every "Get back inside there!" harshly yelled by police or Tommies to curious spectators standing on the balconies over the quiet streets, however, there was always a harmonious counter, such as a young cherry-bereted paratrooper offering a "screened" girl a half hearted "Shalom" for her homeward way.

Searchers Civil

The searchers were civil on the whole, and an attempt was made to keep husbands, wives and children together.

Small groups shepherded the streets made a queer collection — orthodox Jews in long coats and round hats, men in shorts and shirts, women in house-dresses — and one lady in a dressing gown carrying a parasol.

Except for those detained for further interrogation, the screening took only a few minutes, sometimes a minute only. Each company of troops had its own "screening" team of

"I'm Sorry"

As a result of the search, a great many people in Tel Aviv would be put "to serious inconvenience within the next few days," he said, adding: "I that I can only say I'm sorry,

---

Dangerous Corner

REPRISALS Rd.

FEDERATION: TRUMAN'S TALK

WASHINGTON, Tuesday (R) — President Truman today examined the full report and recommendations of the London Anglo-American conference for 40 minutes with a party of New York Congressmen, headed by Mr. Emanuel Celler, Democratic representative from Brooklyn, and with members of his special Cabinet committee on Palestine.

While press reports published here today said that Mr. Byrnes in his conference with Mr. Attlee in Paris over the week-end had already approved the plan and had agreed to recommend it to Mr. Truman, Mr. Celler left the White House condemning the scheme as "outrageous."

"The report is dead before it is published, because it has already been rejected in advance by both Arabs and Jews," he said, today.

Referring to the proposed provision of a loan to the Arab world, Mr. Celler said: "This is outrageous when the Arabs did not lend a penny or a donkey to the war effort. Why should we reward them with 300,000,000 dollars? The American people will not stand for it."

He was confident that Congress would not approve such a proposal.

(More on Page 3 Col. 1)
Debate Prospects — Page 4.

"PRELIMINARY STEP" — CASSELS

The search operations begun in Tel Aviv yesterday were "a preliminary step" towards wiping out the terrorist gangs, declared tall, youthful-looking Major-General A. J. H. Cassels, Area Commander and commander of the Sixth Airborne Division, to foreign press correspondents at "Lydda" Police Headquarters in Jaffa yesterday morning.

Major-General Cassels acknowledged that the search would involve serious inconvenience to large numbers of people. Nineteen units of battalion strength, totalling 14,000 to 15,000 men, and some 600 British police were participating in the search. They would enter "every house, every shed, and every place where a man might be."

The commander explained that arrangements were being made to bring food into the city, that persons ill in bed were not being moved, and that a central post of ambulances had been formed to assist the sick during the searches.

Jewish policemen were engaged in finding people needed to maintain essential services and teams of sappers were sent to the Power Houses and water-supply to keep the services running.

Hospitals were being searched but they would thereafter be given special facilities to continue their work. He added that plaster casts on hospital patients would be X-rayed to determine whether they covered genuine injuries. Even hospital nurses were being interrogated.

"Rough Idea"

Giving foreign correspondents a "rough idea" of what's behind the house-to-house search," General Cassels said: Last Monday week there was a very serious, murderous outrage against the community as a whole.

It has been determined that by hook or by crook we must try and find, and detain, these terrorist gangs.

As a preliminary step, I was given orders to institute a speedy and detailed search of Tel Aviv, the idea being to go through every building in the city with the help of experts in the police force, in the hope of capturing some of these terrorists.

It is not a task that anyone wants to do, but I hope you'll all agree that it's a task which has to be done.

but I feel that any steps that can be taken to deal with these terrorists and to stop the outrages which have been going on are well worth while."

The object was, he summed up, to check up on everybody in Tel Aviv with the hope of removing as many members of the Irgun Zevai and the Stern Gang as we can." Major-General Cassels indicated that the operations were not directed against the "Haganah".

Asked whether British soldiers had been given any special orders concerning their behaviour to the public during the operation, he replied, "Five thousand times."

PEACE CONFERENCE OPENS WITH
EVATT-MOLOTOV CLASH ON RULES

By FRASER WIGHTON, Reuter's Special Correspondent

PARIS, Tuesday. — The conference of the 21 nations opened its second day with a clash at the first meeting this morning of the Procedure Committee.

Dr. Herbert Evatt of Australia proposed M. Paul Henri Spaak (Belgium) as chairman of the committee, but was promptly opposed by the Soviet Foreign Minister, M. Molotov, who declared that in his view the leader of the Yugoslav delegation, M. Edvard Kardelj, was better qualified for the office.

OPPOSING VIEWS

A warm discussion is believed to have followed reflecting the opposing views of the followers of Dr. Evatt and those of the Soviet Union on the Big Powers' right in drawing up the peace treaties. Greece, Holland and Britain, supported the nomination of M. Spaak, and the Ukraine and Poland supported M. Kardelj.

"ONE OPERATION"

The Chinese delegate, M. Wang Shih Chih advanced that the President and Vice-President be elected in one operation — the one with the majority vote being the President and the other the Vice-President.

A vote on this proposal resulted in its rejection and subsequently a ballot was taken resulting in the election of M. Spaak, who took the chair and proposed that M. Kardelj be elected Vice-President. This proposal was passed unanimously.

DISCUSSION

Discussion over the election of office holders occupied the major portion of the proceedings and apparently the question of a two-thirds majority — proposed by the "Big Four" — as the basis of voting on all matters has not yet been broached.

SOVIET CONFERENCE PLAN FOILED

PARIS, Tuesday (Reuter). — The Soviet delegation attempted to arrange a conference of the heads of all the delegations half an hour before the procedure committee met this morning, presumably to discuss in advance the procedural questions raised by Dr. Evatt at yesterday's opening session, but their plan had to be abandoned because not all heads of delegations were available at such short notice.

This morning's committee meeting carried with it the first real challenge facing the conference. The issue is whether the smaller powers, championed by Dr. Evatt, will agree to the draft rules of procedure drawn up by the "Big Four".

"Very Seriously"

Dr. Evatt made it clear at yesterday's session that the Australian delegation at least is prepared to take very seriously the duties and rights of these Allied powers so far as excluded from the active share in the peace-making. The discussion of the rules of procedure will provide the first opportunity for the lesser powers to challenge the joint decisions of the "Big Four".

The basic question is whether the "Big Four" will feel bound to preserve a united front in defence of the draft rules of procedure, including that which proposed voting by a two-thirds majority on all questions of substance.

Britain's position is of particular interest. On the one hand, being a member of the "Big Four", she is to that extent committed to support the "Big Four" proposals.

On the other hand, she is under heavy pressure from the majority of the smaller members of the British Commonwealth who follow the lead of Dr. Evatt, in seeking to secure a simple majority as the basis of the conference voting procedure.

Draft Treaties, Page 3 Col. 1

First Session
NO MORE U.S. ISOLATION

PARIS, Tuesday (Reuter). — Speaking at the first plenary session of the Conference of Paris tonight, the United States Secretary of State, Mr. James F. Byrnes, declared that after World War No. 1, the differences between the Allies all led to weaken and destroy their will to co-operate in the maintenance of peace.

"The United States unwisely decided to return to a policy of isolation rather than co-operate and improve the peace, which fell short of its expectations," he said.

"Other Governments also shifted into a policy of isolation, or appeasement. That must not happen again. However difficult may be the path of international co-operation, the United States is determined not to return to the policy of isolation. We must try to understand one another, even when we cannot agree with one another."

Mr. Attlee was greeted with ringing applause as he mounted the rostrum.

He said: "As States, Germany and Japan can hardly be said to count at present, but let us never forget that they are still there and that their capacity for making trouble if there is any disunion in the Allied ranks, is still very real.

"The spirit of militant totalitarian nationalism that animated Hitler, Mussolini and the Japanese war lords, has not yet been altogether killed.

Proposals

In speaking of the proposals which were before the Conference, Mr. Attlee said: "We should not be devoting ourselves to examining historical claims or supposed interests of particular states. We should keep before our minds the simple objective of removing from the brooding fear of another war (cheers and loud applause)."

K.D. DEATH TOLL NOW 85

With the recovery of the body of Mr. F.W.G. Blenkinsop on Monday the King David bomb toll stood at

85 DEAD
19 MISSING

Mr. Blenkinsop was the last of the British victims to be found.

The search of the wreckage

TRANSFERS TO SECRETARIAT

Five officers in other branches of the Public Service have been transferred to posts in the Secretariat to take the places of men killed in the King David Hotel explosion on July 22.

In addition, Mr. D.H. Mackay has been appointed to act as Postmaster General during Sir John Shaw's absence. Mr. R. Scott, C.M.G., will act as Chief Secretary and Mr. J. Gutch as Financial Secretary, with Mr. R. Newton as Under Secretary.

Mr. C.M. Pirie Gordon, formerly of the Haifa District Administration who has been Assistant British Resident in Trans-Jordan since January,

will be continued until the bodies of all victims of last Monday's outrage have been recovered, it is officially stated.

The demolition yesterday was carried out in order to remove part of the building which was endangering the work of excavation, and the search was resumed as quickly as possible.

becomes an Assistant Secretary. Transfers from the District Administration include Mr. A.G. Dalgleish, Deputy District Commissioner in Galilee, to act as Principal Assistant Secretary and Mr. J.V. Prendergast, Gaza Administrative Officer, as Assistant Secretary.

Two transfers have been made from other departments, Mr. D.R. Lockhart, Assistant Controller of Heavy Industries, and Mr. H. Beides, Assistant Intelligence and Research Officer. Department of Labour, becoming acting Administrative Assistants. Mr. M. Bachrach, of the Secretariat staff, whose sister was killed in the explosion, has received a similar acting appointment.

T.A. Mayor Sees General

The Mayor of Tel Aviv, Mr. Israel Rokach, was summoned at midday yesterday to Major-General Cassels' headquarters at Jaffa, where the Military Commander explained to him the reason for the current searches in Tel Aviv and asked him to urge the inhabitants to co-operate with the authorities in the arrest of the terrorists.

Mr. Rokach strongly objected to the allegation that the terrorist attack on the King David Hotel had been committed by residents of Tel Aviv. He asked to be allowed, to convene a meeting of the Municipal Council and also to ensure the city's food supply during the curfew period.

The commander agreed to allow a meeting of the Municipal Council at 11 o'clock this morning, and told Mr. Rokach that arrangements had been made for the delivery of bread and milk to residents, on the order of the military, as from today.

LATE Edition

THE PALESTINE POST

JERUSALEM
TUESDAY, AUGUST 13, 1946

PRICE: 15 MILS
VOL. XXI. NO. 6275

REFUGEES NOT TO BE LANDED IN PALESTINE

LONDON ORDERS ILLEGAL IMMIGRANTS TO BE SENT TO "CYPRUS OR ELSEWHERE" PENDING DECISION ON THEIR FUTURE

LONDON, Tuesday Morning (Reuter). — The British Government have given instructions to the Palestine authorities that reception into Palestine of illegal immigrants must cease, an official Government statement declares. Immigrants arriving illegally will be conveyed to Cyprus or elsewhere and housed in camps there until a decision can be taken as to their future.

Column One

By David Courtney

THAT swift-flowing channel of contention, the Dardanelles, is about to overflow its banks: nothing else was to be expected. The Foreign Office has confirmed the announcement from Ankara that Russia has made a formal demand for the revision of the Montreux Treaty; and without or within any existing international machinery, a conference will be called soon: the chant of Macbeth's witches will be heard over still another cauldron. The Dardanelles in its immediate implications, link with the Danube; but like the Persia problem, which will probably stay quiescent for a week or two, its future status is a matter of very real interest to Palestine: the two problems together are gradually shifting the powder barrel of international politics from the Balkans to the Middle East. Behind them rival interests are assembling with modern manuals of strategy in their pockets and conflicting ideologies with which to bribe their way among the people.

■

THE validity of the Montreux Treaty lies in the assumption that the Straits are a dividing line, not a bridge, between Russia and the West. By reducing Russia's belligerent rights in the Straits to an equality with those of Britain and France and their lesser Allies, it ignored the special position of Russia as a State dependent on the Dardanelles for outlet and missed the natural, inevitable and legitimate tendency of the industrializing Soviet to extend its interests to the Eastern Mediterranean. The treaty revision which the Russians are demanding is likely to amount to a virtual scrapping of the original terms; and a new treaty will be proposed under which the Soviet would be given privileges on a par with those which Britain is relinquishing in Egypt and taking up in Trans-Jordan.

■

DOUBTLESS, the Sovereignty of Turkey is threatened: that is the line Ankara will take; and it is probable that Britain and the United States will toe it also, with a great show of moral indignation. It is as good, or as bad, an argument as the line of security along which the Russians will marshal their forces. But however much they keep their tongues in their cheeks, in their minds will be the problem of strategy in relation to possible Danube, Middle East and Mediterranean developments. The current that races turbulently down the Straits divides at Cyprus to sweep on the one side to the Persian Gulf and on the other to Trieste; in short, the Mediterranean and its pendant problems are gradually, portentously taking their old shape. The legacy of Czarist and Tory Imperialism is too much for its Socialist inheritors; and neither Britain nor Russia has the courage to experiment in its own faith. There is one sensible answer to the problems of these great waterways: it is the same answer for the Straits as for the Suez Canal, for the Danube as for the Rhine — their full and positive internationalization. But if the old order is to remain, Russia has as much right to favoured treatment in the Dardanelles as America to favoured treatment through the Panama Canal; and on much the same principles as those which animate the Monroe Doctrine.

■

THE Dardanelles, with their direct and immediate bearing on the Danube and their indirect but unmistakeable bearing on the Middle East as a whole; the oil and Southward highways of Persia: these are part of the terrifying concatenation of portents through which the delegates to the Paris Conference have to pick their way, as through barbed wire, to the problems set them. Whether the addition of Albania, Cuba, Egypt and Mexico to their counsels will help or hinder there is no knowing; but it is clear that Russia has had to pay a trifle heavily for its championship of Albania. Dr. Evatt, bent on his role as the White Knight of small nations, keeps his vizor closed so tightly that he fails to see that at a certain stage of their smallness, the small states are little more than food for the bellies of the Big Powers. Neither Albania, Cuba, Egypt nor Mexico are in Paris as independent units; and half the voices raised at the Luxembourg Palace are no better confusing echoes. They play their part in Big Power politics as diligently as their masters; and if Dr. Evatt feels he has a crusade to lead, let it be rather for the weeding out of the Conference than for its cluttering up.

Jerusalem, August 13.

Mr. Acheson's Recommendations

U.S. COMPROMISE PLAN

The American compromise plan for Palestine, said to have been prepared under the supervision of Mr. Dean Acheson, is reported to provide for a Jewish zone of 4,900 sq. kilometres, instead of 2,900 sq. kms., as in the British plan. Another source speaks of an increase in the area of only 30 percent over the British proposal.

Larger local autonomy is also proposed, with the powers of the British High Commissioner limited, the immigration quota to be fixed by the Jews themselves, and the United States to help finance the execution of the entire plan — for both the Arab and Jewish provinces — for a period still to be decided on.

According to the New York correspondent of the London "Evening News," the experts are urging the quickest acceptance by President Truman of these suggestions, in order to avoid the grave consequences which might result from the measures taken by the British Government against illegal immigration.

"Yedioth Ahronot" reports from "a source close to the White House" that America will demand the addition of the Negev to the Jewish zone and make it a prior condition of American participation that 100,000 Jews be allowed to immigrate immediately.

From the same quarter it is said that America would agree to federalization only as a step towards definite partition of Palestine into independent Jewish and Arab States within two or three years, with bases for Britain by treaty on the lines of the Anglo-Iraqi Treaty.

The British Ambassador, Lord Inverchapel, is reported to be leaving shortly for London with details of this American scheme.

On the other hand, UP reports from London that British circles are sceptical about President Truman approving the Federal Plan.

In Baghdad, Jamil Bey el Madfai, President of the Iraqi Senate, described the partition plan as an act against the Arab world and a help to the Zionists in the use of Palestine for spreading their influence in the Arab world. "I believe Arabs will definitely refuse to attend the London conference, he added, especially after the British declaration approving the partition proposals."

In a note handed by the British Minister in Damascus to the Syrian Foreign Minister yesterday it is stated that the partitioning of Palestine would not form the basis for discussion at the London conference, and the Arab Governments would be able to make any suggestions for the solution of the Palestine problem (says AFP).

The American Labour Committee for Palestine, which has the support of both the A.F.L. and the C.I.O., has sent a telegram to the British Labour Party protesting against the present Palestine policy of the Labour Government: "So long as it continues with its present policy it cannot count on the support of the American Labour movement".

(R., PTA., Palcor, AFP., UP.)

Haifa Bulletin

HAIFA, Tuesday (3 a.m.). — The two small vessels, Yagour and Szold, are still anchored outside the breakwater, and two cruisers, the Ajax and the Mauritius (the latter had arrived today from Malta) have left the harbour and are anchored near them.

The "deportation ships" are still at their moorings and are brightly illuminated.

Some shops were opened on Hadar Hacarmel after the curfew announcement, and people are queueing up to buy food.

Pauley Scheme

2ND EXODUS

By GEORGE LICHTHEIM
Palestine Post Correspondent

LONDON, Monday. — A minor sensation was caused today by Washington cables concerning a report to President Truman by Mr. E.D. Pauley, U.S. Reparations Commissioner.

Mr. Pauley apparently suggested that pending an over-all solution of the refugee problem, in which America must play a part, the European Jews now trekking west might well organize their own exodus to Italy in "caravans," carrying their own medical supplies, etc. Mr. Pauley, reportedly, feels there is no reason why Germany should not contribute reparations to the Jews in the form of building materials useable in Palestine and elsewhere for the rapid construction of houses.

Generally, the Pauley Report suggests that half a million or a million Jews might well be settled during the coming year in the United States and other overseas countries, including Palestine. There has been no comment here so far. The mere fact that someone is capable of approaching the problem in other than nagging and pettifogging terms seems to have struck Whitehall and Printing House Square alike.

An interesting contrast to Pauley was provided by Miss Maude Royden in a letter prominently displayed by "The Times" on Saturday, wherein, after declaring that all countries must share the burden, she adds that there is no reason why, for example, "Jewish Communists" who are now shooting British soldiers in Palestine might not be sent to Siberia, while others could find homes in East Africa and other tropics.

The prominence lent by "The Times" to these aberrations bears out the impression created by earlier excursions into a political no-man's land. Concerning the major issue, earlier predictions that President Truman is likely to sponsor a modified Federation scheme are now supported by the latest despatches from Washington and unofficial information.

Agency Marking Time

It is understood that the Agency Conference in Paris is awaiting publication of the American views this week before considering the possibility of attending a round-table, but little doubt is felt that President Truman will accept the scheme in principle, but with substantial modifications, stressing the urgency of immediate entry of the immigrants and also for a larger area of the Jewish province and greater Jewish control of immigration.

Observers believe that the scheme with these modifications is acceptable as a basis for discussion as far as the Agency is concerned, while the British reaction is doubtful. The failure of the original attempt to rush Washington into an acceptance of the original scheme is still rankling in Whitehall, where a fortnight ago Jews were already regarded as a negligible factor.

The new development may necessitate greater activity on the part of the Arab League moderates to curb the extremists' wild talk of dragging Russia into the controversy.

Rundstedt in Box

By WILLIAM HAMSHER,
Reuters Special Correspondent

NUREMBERG, Monday (R) — Field Marshal von Rundstedt, Hitler's commander-in-chief on the Western Front during the Ardennes counter offensive of Christmas, 1944, told the tribunal today that he was opposed to this attack because "all the conditions for success were lacking despite the stroke of genius behind the idea."

Von Rundstedt explained his own idea was to attack the American troops east of Aachen from several sides. This idea was turned down in favour of the Ardennes offensive which had to start with inadequate forces.

"In my opinion the war could not be won after Stalingrad. It was lost, I consider, after the Allies had established a strong bridgehead on French soil."

Rundstedt said that he and Field-Marshal Rommel wanted to bring the front back to Germany, but Hitler would not listen. Declaring that he had never entertained the idea of overthrowing Hitler by violence, Rundstedt said that such an attempt would not have been successful. If he had brought it about with the aid of the Allies, it would have been exactly the same, and he would have been considered for all time a traitor to the Fatherland.

GOVERNMENT STATEMENT

Continuance of illegal immigrant traffic at the present time, the statement says, "is likely to have an adverse effect on the hope of a general settlement in Palestine. In announcing this decision, the British Government wish to make it clear that while they cannot tolerate this attempt by a minority of Zionist extremists to exploit the sufferings of the unfortunate people in order to create a situation prejudicial to a just settlement, they are deeply sensible of the sufferings undergone by the Jewish community and are anxious to bring them to an end as soon as possible."

The statement adds that recent developments had revealed illegal immigrant traffic as a "widely ramified and highly organized movement supported by very large financial contributions from Zionist sources, which has been built up and put into operation by unscrupulous persons in an attempt to force the hand of the British Government and anticipate their decision on future policy in Palestine.

UNDERGROUND RAILWAY

"The organizers maintain a closely knit network of agents in countries of Eastern and Southern Europe by whom considerable numbers of Displaced Jews are moved from points of departure as far distant as Poland down to the Mediterranean seaboard. Thence, herded into overcrowded and unseaworthy ships with insufficient food and in conditions of utmost privation and squalor, they are brought across the Mediterranean, inspired by the conviction carefully instilled into them that this is their only road to safety.

"In all this process, the laws and regulations of the countries concerned are ignored; identity and ration cards, travel documents etc. are forged on a large scale; food, clothing, medical supplies and transport provided by UNRRA and other agencies for the relief of suffering in Europe, are diverted to the maintenance of what is openly described as 'the underground railway to Palestine'."

The other points made were: Illegal immigration "threatens both civil war and a breakdown of the Government in Palestine."

From Eastern Europe

The British Government was concerned at the reports of prosecution and pogroms against the Jews in Eastern and South-Eastern Europe, and hoped that the countries concerned would "bring this shame to a sharp and decisive end."

The statement also expressed concern that a large proportion of these immigrants came from Eastern Europe and not from Displaced Persons centres in Germany, Austria and Italy, which it was hoped to empty.

Illegals

The statement added: apart from its illegality, immigration and traffic to Palestine is a source of grave danger to law and order in Palestine. The reception and guarding of large numbers of illegal immigrants places a severe strain on the administration.

Their arrival has greatly increased the tension between the Arab and Jewish communities in Palestine. And since there is evidence that the terrorist element among the Jews has been reinforced from the ranks of illegal immigrants, their promiscuous introduction clearly cannot be tolerated any longer. As the mandatory power for Palestine, H.M. Government have responsibilities towards the population of that country.

It is obviously not in the interests of Palestine generally that such illegal activities should be allowed to continue.

The recent increase in illegal immigration, which sets aside considerations of priority and equity, the statement continues, is also operating with great unfairness towards those Jews who would otherwise have been able to enter Palestine legally under the quota. All potential legal immigration has been pushed aside by this illegal traffic.

The statement recalls that the British Government has accepted as basis for negotiation the plan drawn up by the British and American experts in London, which is designed to "provide for increased immigration into Palestine under conditions which would not disturb the peace and economy of the country."

Giving the background of their decision about illegal immigration into Palestine, the British Government in their statement say:

Not a country in the world has been a better or more consistent friend of the Jewish people than Britain. Wherever Jews were persecuted, the voice of Britain was lifted in protest, and wherever possible action was taken to mitigate their lot.

The statement says that under the British Mandate, nearly 500,000 Jews settled legally in Palestine. In December 1945, the quota of 75,000 Jewish immigrants permitted to enter Palestine under the provisions of the White Paper, was exhausted. Nevertheless, pending final decision on the future policy for Palestine, the British Government authorized the continuance of Jewish immigration at the rate of 1,500 monthly.

Yet there has been an increasing flow of illegal immigration and their numbers have to be set off against the monthly quota. Those already held in camps in Palestine or on ships in Haifa Harbour are more than sufficient to absorb the whole quota for many months ahead. Moved by sympathy for the suffering of the Jewish people in Europe, the British Government have hitherto allowed illegal immigrants to land, in spite of the great embarrassment caused to the Palestine authorities.

"The patience, forbearance and humanity thus shown by the British Government has, however, been interpreted by those responsible for the traffic as a sign of weakness and as an encouragement to redouble their efforts to increase the flow of illegal immigrants still further.

Harmonizing Claims

"A point has now been reached when it is clear that the present illegal traffic is not, as has been maintained, a movement arising spontaneously among European Jews who see in Palestine their only hope for the future. Nor are those who encourage and direct it inspired solely by the sympathy which is so widely felt for their suffering."

Concluding the statement says: "It is clear that a permanent solution of this complicated question can only be brought about if Jews and Arabs are prepared to enter upon discussions in a realistic and constructive spirit in order to evolve a practical scheme for harmonizing the claims of these two historic peoples."

STOP PRESS

CURFEW IN HAIFA

The High Commissioner announced at 2.30 this morning that those illegal immigrants who arrived at Haifa before August 11 will be sent to Athlit and not to Cyprus.

(This means that passengers in the Hagana and Hahayal Haivri, who are still on board ship in Haifa Harbour, will be landed, but those who arrived yesterday in the Yagour and Henrietta Szold will be deported.)

Curfew has been imposed on the entire Haifa Municipal Area as from one o'clock this morning until further notice. The announcement was made by loud-speaker cars touring the town shortly after one.

"Optimism" In London

From . ur Political Correspondent

News from Jewish Agency quarters in London yesterday had a quality of astringent "optimism" as regards the future. In part, this was based on more hopeful news, from the Jewish point of view, brought from Washington by Dr. Nahum Goldman, the member of the Executive who had flown over to confer with President Truman's Cabinet Committee.

As reported in another column, the more hopeful outlook is based on not much more than somewhat better proposals, or rather counter-proposals, from the White House.

But a matter causing grave concern in London is the continued detention of the Jewish Agency members in Latrun. The absence from the present important consultations of Mr. Shertok and Dr. Joseph, who have been responsible for the Agency's political work for several years, is acutely felt. To this lack must be added the complication that the Agency is precluded from entering into any official consultations with the Government so long as the Jewish leaders are incarcerated.

This complication, to which Dr. Weizmann, while still in Palestine, referred as a "vicious circle," not only hampers or prevents consultations with the Colonial Office concerning the proposed Round-Table, but is also in the way of urgent, if less important, day-to-day questions that have to be negotiated with the authorities, whether in London or Jerusalem.

Other Nations to State Their Views

PARIS DELEGATES ACTUALLY AGREE

PARIS, Monday (UP). — The Peace Conference today unanimously agreed to invite Albania, Mexico, Cuba and Egypt to "state their views" here at the plenary sessions and the Commissions on the Italian peace treaty.

The vote came after more than two hours' wrangling over procedure and how to vote on various amendments.

Britain tried to amend the resolution to include Austria among the invited states but it withdrew the proposal and no one moved to include Iran on the list. Both Austria and Iran had made a belated request to be admitted.

Persia's Application

Iran's application was received by the Conference Secretariat late on Saturday night and was made public this morning just before the plenary session opened.

The conference session ended a two days' debate on methods of permitting nations outside the 21 to express their views. The action almost certainly opens the flood-gates to other requests, probably from most of those nations which declared war on the Axis.

General Agreement

Originally Yugoslavia had asked that Albania should be admitted with full voting privileges. This request was withdrawn early in the Conference and there was general agreement that additional states should be invited to state their views on the Italian treaty.

The Conference proceeded by acclamation to elect M. Fouques du Parc of France as permanent Secretary-General.

Vyshinsky vs. Australia

PARIS, Monday (Reuter).— When Australia was proposed as a member of the Conference secretariat, M. Vyshinsky (U.S.S.R.) objected, declaring:

"Australia has shown herself a rather temperamental member of our meeting and has taken part with great energy in our debates. It would perhaps be better to have at the secretariat, for which other qualities are required, a representative of a calmer nation and therfore I propose Ethiopia."

The Ethiopian delegation indicated that it did not wish to stand. Norway, proposed by Byelo-Russia, also declined and ultimately the British proposal that Australia, Brazil, China and Yugoslavia be represented on the secretariat in addition to the "Big Four" was accepted without a vote.

Diplomatic Moves against Refugees

GREEK PORTS TO BE BLOCKED

Palestine Post Staff

Greece has been added to the list of countries requested by Britain to assist in controlling illegal Jewish immigration to Palestine, a Foreign Office spokesman announced yesterday.

No reply has yet been received by Britain from the Soviet Union. The majority of the countries approached are said to have promised to do all in their power to help.

Last week the Mexican and Panama embassies in London were requested to make a careful check on the issue of visas to Jewish refugees in Europe.

In view of more reassuring reports reaching leading Jewish circles at present in Paris regarding American measures connected with the entry of Jewish refugees into the American zone of Germany, the proposed visit of Dr. Stephen Wise to Frankfort has been postponed.

It is understood that the Salsburg-Munich route used by refugees entering the American zone of Germany from the American zone of Austria is now open again. The frontier between Czechoslovakia and the American zone remains, however, temporarily closed. The Czech authorities appear to want guarantees that the number of Jewish refugees allowed to enter the American zone will not be deducted by the Americans from the number of Sudeten Germans which the Czechs are permitted to send across the border.

The Americans, on the other hand, apparently considered that the arrival of Jewish refugees from across the Czech border complicated their task of screening of the Sudeten Germans before the latter are allowed to proceed further inland. In these circumstances, the only route open to refugees from Czechoslovakia to Vienna — from where they are sent to the American zone of Austria — is across the Russian zone of Austria. On several occasions recently, the Russians have interfered with refugees crossing their zone, but it is not certain whether this is a settled policy.

Approach to America

As part of her diplomatic campaign, Britain has made representations to the U.S.A. about the publication of Zionist appeals for money to transport Jewish refugees which have been appearing in American papers. While the network which has been passing Jews illegally into Palestine has grown up inside Europe, writes Reuters Diplomatic Correspondent, there is reason to believe that most of the funds which have financed the movement have come from Zionist organizations in the U.S.A. who have been conducting their appeals quite openly in columns of American newspapers. It is believed that the U.S. authorities have agreed to look into the matter.

A categorical denial of reports that refugees reaching Palestine were terrorists was made by a Jewish Agency spokesman yesterday at a press conference in Jerusalem with foreign newspaper correspondents.

"On the contrary, they are people who oppose terrorism in any form," the spokesman said. He added that there were 3,700 people on board the refugee ships at Haifa, and not 8,000 as was stated by the B.B.C. Over half of the refugees at Haifa were children.

When asked how many more refugees were known to be at sea, the spokesman replied that it was believed there were another 1,300 on their way to Palestine.

The Public Information Officer, Mr. R. Stubbs, told journalists at his weekly Press Conference in Tel Aviv yesterday that the Palestine Government still had no confirmation of reports that camps were being prepared in Famagusta, Cyprus, for Jewish immigrants. He also stated that he had no information about the floating cages in the Haifa Port.

3rd Ship Sighted

1,298 ARRIVE

HAIFA, Monday. — "Yagur" and the "Henrietta Szold," two sailing vessels carrying illegal immigrants arrived in Haifa Port this morning. The two ships, have a total of 1,298 men, women and children on board.

A third vessel, believed to be carrying 1,300 refugees, is also reported to be approaching Haifa.

First to be escorted into port was the "Yagur," which anchored outside the main breakwater among the warships there at about 7.30 this morning.

Though for the first time Jewish Agency officials were not allowed to board the ship, some facts were ascertained by an official who spoke to the passengers from the police launch which took police officers alongside.

Aboard the ship are 758 immigrants consisting of 350 women, 10 old people and about 400 younger people, some of whom are members of the Youth Aliyah.

Among the women 50 are expectant mothers, 13 of them being in the last month of pregnancy.

The ship is reported to have been at sea for 20 days. The crew of about 10, including several Turks and one Lebanese, have been arrested.

The Henrietta Szold, a smaller sailing ship with an auxiliary motor, was sighted about two hours later. She has 540 passengers on board, including some 150 women and 250 young people, 30 infants and 15 old men and women. Fifteen of the women are expectant mothers. The trip from the port of embarkation is said to have taken 15 days.

Preparations which are believed to presage the deportation of the refugees are meanwhile progressing in Haifa Port. The cargo jetty has been cleared of all civilians and placed under army guard.

Two Liberty ships, the Empire Rival and the Empire Weywood, are moored to the jetty and barbed wire cages have been constructed on the decks and around the hatches.

The ships have also been fitted with searchlights which are used to illuminate the port at night. Work on the landing barges which, as reported yesterday, have been converted into floating cages, has now been completed, and the craft are at the western end of the Harbour where they have been camouflaged. It is assumed that the expected transfer will take place within the next [illegible] hours.

One of the new arrivals, 25-year-old woman from Greece named Naomi Furt, was rushed today at noon by a Red Shield Society Ambulance to the Maladah Maternity Hospital on Mt. Carmel, suffering from childbirth complications.

USSR ASKS BRITAIN FOR STRAITS TALKS

By Reuter's Diplomatic Correspondent

LONDON, Monday. — The Soviet Government has informed Britain that it wishes the Montreux Straits Convention of 1936 to be revised, a Foreign Office spokesman stated in London this morning.

This announcement follows the unconfirmed reports from Ankara during the week-end that the Turkish Government had been informed that the Soviet Union intended to secure the revision of the terms.

The Montreux Convention, which since 1936 has governed navigation conditions in the Dardanelles, is valid for a period of 20 years from November 9, 1936, the date on which it came into force through the ratification by all the signatories, except Japan.

THE PALESTINE POST
LATE Edition

JERUSALEM TUESDAY, DEC. 10, 1946

PRICE: 15 MILS
VOL. XXI. No. 6374

PERSIAN DISPUTE COMES TO HEAD
FIGHTING BREAKS OUT IN KURDISTAN HILLS

TEHERAN, Monday. — Tanks, artillery and trench-mortars have been used in a battle between Persian Government troops and Azerbaijan forces, Radio Teheran stated tonight.

The battle took place in the mountainous district of Qardasht in Kurdistan, which the Central Government troops occupied after it had changed hands twice.

"Our casualties were one killed and 17 wounded," the Azerbaijan radio station said. "According to villagers, the Government troops lost 30 men, who were killed in the first offensive. Two peasants were seriously injured in the aerial bombardment of a village near the town of Miyanduab.

"During the battle villages and industrial enterprises were continuously bombed by Government planes," Radio Tabriz added.

Radio Tabriz also stated that Persian Government planes are "mercilessly bombing Kurd villages," adding that many peasants' houses had been destroyed, but that the casualties were not yet known.

Planes of the Central Government have again flown over Tabriz and dropped leaflets signed by M. Ghavam Sultaneh which said: "If Azerbaijan really belongs to Iran then the soldiers of the Central Government have the right of free movement in their own homes."

The Iranian Government is following "a dangerous path suggested to it from the outside" in sending troops to Azerbaijan, writes "Pravda" today. The troops are not being sent. "Pravda" asserts, "for the purpose of securing order but with the intent to liquidate the national democratic freedom of Azerbaijan, to disband the Democratic Party there and to reverse the election of its representatives to the Central Parliament."

The new development, "Pravda" says, is welcomed not only by Iranian reactionaries but also by certain foreign circles. As an instance for this "Pravda" quotes a public statement by the American Ambassador in Iran in which he said that here is "nothing unusual in sending troops for the maintenance of order during elections." The Azerbaijan government had invited the Central Government to send observers and journalists to the elections but "the Iranian Government did not accept this sensible suggestion," "Pravda" concludes.

(U.P. and Reuter)

T.J. STUDENTS AGAINST MONARCHY

BEIRUT, Monday (A.F.P.) — Trans-Jordan students from the universities of Beirut and Damascus at a meeting held here today passed a resolution affirming their determination to work for the replacement of King Abdullah by a republic.

750 DEPORTEES LEAVE CYPRUS

Palestine Post Correspondent

KYRENIA, Monday. — Seven hundred and fifty immigrants of the January quota, three capital cases from the December quota, and three people with individual entry permits embarked on the Olenen Vigour at 6 o'clock this evening and sailed for Palestine.

Another 750 deportees were transferred to winter quarters at Xylotymbou today, and the remainder of the first batch of 2,000 are expected to be transferred tomorrow.

REST of the NEWS

CHRISTMAS MAIL will be flown by R.A.F. Transport Command to the tune of fifty tons per week to ensure that troops everywhere are receiving it on time.

THE U.S. CRUISER FARGO, the aircraft carrier Randolph, the destroyer Perry and a landing craft have left Piraeus harbour after a three-days' visit to Greece.

PASTEUR. — The fiftieth anniversary of the death of Louis Pasteur, the founder of modern bacteriology, is celebrated by French scientists this week.

Owing to the slight indisposition of David Courtney "Column One" will not appear for the next two or three days.

TREATY TALKS CRISIS

By JON KIMCHE
Palestine Post Cable

LONDON, Monday. — Hopes of an early conclusion of the Anglo-Egyptian treaty were dashed today when a Foreign Office spokesman read a dramatic communique to a crowded press conference, thus virtually ruling out the possibility of any revision of the treaty unless either the British or Egyptians drastically change their present standpoints.

"The Governor of the Sudan, Sir Hubert Huddleston," said the spokesman, "was compelled to make his statement—assuring the Sudanese that nothing in the proposed new Egyptian treaty could prejudice their right to achieve independence nor bind a people in search of liberty—owing to partial disclosures in Egypt of the Sidky-Bevin talks.

Continued silence by the British Government, in view of one-sided interpretations, might have led to bloodshed or even worse in the Sudan. In these circumstances neither H.M. Government nor the Sudanese Government can be blamed for clearing up the situation.

"It should be noted that all the British Government want to do is to establish a situation under which, when the time is ripe, the Sudan can choose to become an independent state. Clearly, this is only one of several choices open to the Sudan.

"They can seek union with Egypt if they wish. It would be manifestly impossible for the British Government in its treaty discussions with Egypt to deny the rights of a free people to the Sudan."

This statement is considered in diplomatic circles as writing "finis" to the treaty discussions. It is considered unlikely here that any Egyptian Government can renew the talks in the present atmosphere.

Boycott of Conference

There has been some discussion here with the embassies of other Arab States but there is no definite indication of what attitude they will take in view of the Arab League's commitment to support Egypt.

One form of Arab reaction considered possible is an Arab boycott of the Palestine Conference next month. The other most likely is reference to UNO Parliamentary circles, particularly in the Labour Party, were surprised by the firmness of the British statement, but not altogether displeased by it.

Statement on Sudan

The statement by Sir Hubert Huddleston to which the Egyptian Government has taken exception read as follows:

"Whatever the results of the Anglo-Egyptian negotiations, Mr. Attlee has authorized me in writing to give the Sudanese assurances that the British Government is determined that nothing shall be permitted to deflect the Sudanese Government from preparing the Sudanese for self-government.

"The Sudanese protocol provides that the Sudanese when ripe for self-government shall be free to choose the future status of the Sudan. H.M. Government considers that, in the words used by the Egyptian Premier to the British Foreign Secretary, nothing in the proposed treaty can prejudice the right of the Sudanese to achieve independence."

Police Stand By

Troops and police stood by in Cairo today. The city was calm but some anxiety was felt lest the resignation of Sidky Pasha should lead to disorders.

Political talk centred round the question whether Sidky Pasha's resignation in effect meant a breakdown in the Anglo-Egyptian negotiations for the revision of the treaty. Circles in close touch with Sidky suggest that he interpreted the statement by the Governor General of the Sudan as tantamount to the breaking off of the negotiations by Britain.

Nokrashy Forms Government

CAIRO, Monday. — Nokrashy Pasha, the leader of the Saadist Party, tonight formed a coalition Cabinet of Saadists and Liberals. The Wafd are excluded.

The Cabinet was approved by King Farouk.

When he was asked whether any change would take place in the Egyptian Government's attitude towards the Anglo-Egyptian Treaty Draft, Nokrashy replied: "This question will be studied by the new Cabinet."

Lebanese Cabinet Goes

BEIRUT, Monday (Reuter). — Saadi el Mulla, Premier of the Lebanon, today confirmed that his Cabinet would resign tomorrow (as already reported on Sunday).

According to parliamentary circles the resignation is due to the severe criticism of the Government's economic policy and to the intention of some deputies to press for a vote of non-confidence.

WEIZMANN OPENS FIRST POST-WAR ZIONIST CONGRESS
NATIONAL HOME MUST BECOME JEWISH STATE

WHITE PAPER DIRECTLY RESPONSIBLE FOR PALESTINE TROUBLES

BASLE, Monday. — Dr. Chaim Weizmann, President of the World Zionist Organisation and the Jewish Agency for Palestine, opening the 22nd Zionist Congress this afternoon, declared that if Britain could not return to the original spirit of the Mandate she should, before retiring, vest the Jewish National Home with the full authority and status of a Jewish State. He rejected the Morrison federal plan "without hesitation or reserve, in principle and in detail", since it entirely excluded 85 percent of Palestine from the scope of Jewish colonization without even assuring complete freedom in the remaining 15 percent. The Jewish community, he said, will never surrender its national attributes and tradition in order to merge them into the attributes and traditions of another people. He held the White Paper of 1939 largely responsible for the present desperate situation of the Jewish people and directly responsible for the present troubles in Palestine. "Few documents in history have worse consequences for which to answer".

The Zionist President began his address, which lasted an hour, at this turning point in Jewish history, in a quiet voice that carried to the ends of the great Exhibition hall, the Mustermesse, in which were seated close on 400 delegates, representing the Jewries of 61 countries of the world, and over 2,000 visitors. The hundreds who could not find place in the main hall overflowed into one adjoining, to which the speech was relayed by radio.

Seated on the platform behind the President were the leaders of the Zionist Organization and representatives of the Swiss Federal Government, the Cantonal authorities and Basle Municipality. In a special gallery were the diplomatic representatives of 23 countries. Special interest was aroused by the presence of the Soviet, United States, and Vatican representatives, but regrets at his inability to attend had been received from the British Minister through the Vice-Consul in Basle. A party of refugees from camps in Germany arrived at the last moment.

Dominating the assembly was a huge portrait, flanked by the Jewish blue-white colours, of Theodor Herzl, founder of the Zionist Movement, who had opened the first Congress in the same city in 1897; while significant of the changes wrought on the Jewish people by the intervening fifty years were the massed delegations from Palestine and the United States contrasting with the handful from the once great communities of Eastern Europe.

Dr. Weizmann recalled that the condition stipulated for the National Home by Arab leaders such as King Feisal and British advisers such as Colonel Lawrence, was that the Arabs outside Palestine should be enabled to achieve independence. The Arabs now possess seven independent sovereignties and a generous measure of international representation.

How can it be moderate for them to claim seven States and extreme for us to claim one? By what tortuous logic can our morsel be stolen and added to their feast?

Other nations are liberated and can rebuild their ruins, but the survivors of our holocaust languish without liberty and hope, and when, in desperate bid for these, they strike out towards their homeland, they are barred from its shores and herded behind barbed wire, once again on foreign soil, Dr. Weizmann said.

Turning to Britain, he said that the bond of friendship between the Jewish people and Britain had been all but destroyed, but not by the Jews, and it could not be healed by the Jews themselves but the strain could be eased by the Government's undertaking to carry out the provisions of the Mandate in its spirit and letter.

STERN WARNING AGAINST TERRORISM

The Zionist President uttered a stern warning against the effects of terrorism. Terrorist acts, he said, are morally abhorrent and also barren of all advantage. Against suicidal 'heroics' he urged the courage of endurance and the heroism of superhuman restraint.

Finally, after a tribute to the American nation and to President Truman for his unfailing understanding of the Jewish problem, Dr. Weizmann said:

"Believing as we do that our claim to establish a Jewish State is justified by the Mandate and by the relative positions of the Arab world and ourselves, we cannot contemplate a solution falling short of that claim. The Jews must be vested with the privileges and responsibilities of direct government. Once secure in possession of full national status, we shall strive to enter into a free and harmonious relationship with the other States in the Middle East.

Dr. Weizmann was followed by Mr. David Remez, Chairman of the Vaad Leumi, who said the Jews wanted peace and not conditions of war in Palestine. They wanted an alliance with the Arabs. He invited the next Congress to meet in Palestine.

(Full text of Dr. Weizmann's address begins on Page Two)

U.S. Army Was Ready for D.P.'s

LONDON, Monday (Palcor). — "In May and June of this year, the U.S. Army was prepared, under President Truman's direction, to move the D.P.s from Europe's pestholes to Palestine within 30 days," stated Mr. Bartley Crum, speaking to 2,000 Jews and non-Jews at the Portland (Oregon) Municipal Auditorium.

"Mr. John Dugdale, Financial Secretary of the British Admiralty, recently expressed on the Ohel Shem hall hatred for the Jews.

"Mr. John Dugdale, Financial Secretary of the British Admiralty, recently expressed the concern about those Jews who were brave enough to try to reach Palestine by underground route, and were risking their lives in unseaworthy hulks which were likely to founder in the winter gales.

"Since I am somewhat familiar with the situation, Mr. Dugdale's words fail to move me, and I think that if Mr. Dugdale will consult British intelligence, he will find that the determination of those stateless and oppressed people is unshakeable and that, if necessary, they will go to Palestine on rafts.

"I respectfully suggest to Mr. Dugdale that American ships, perfectly seaworthy and still available in sufficient numbers, transport these people in safety and comfort to Palestine."

General Zionists Debate Partition

BASLE, Monday. — The most important of the pre-Congress party debates, that of the Confederation of General Zionists, developed on Sunday into sharp differences of opinion regarding participation in the London Conference and future Zionist policy.

Rabbi Abba Hillel Silver (as reported in The Palestine Post yesterday) and Mr. M. Sneh attacked the trend of the Jewish Agency Executive's recent talks with the British Government, while Dr. Nahum Goldmann and Professor S. Brodetsky advocated participation.

Recalling that in 1939 he had opposed Partition, Professor Brodetsky said that now he saw no solution except in a Jewish State wherein Jews would be masters of their destiny.

Dr. Goldmann said that Jews could not force the British to allow such mass immigration as was needed. Even the friends of Zionism in the Government were not prepared to agree to 100,000 immigrants except as part of a final solution. There were three alternatives: Britain might give up the Mandate and undertake a trusteeship instead, which would perpetuate the present situation; or there would be a joint trusteeship, making the Jews a pawn in the game between the Great Powers; or the Jews could bring forward their plan for a viable state. The last was "a tragic compromise", but it would be a historic decision which would bring rejoicing to Jewish people, Dr. Goldmann concluded.

Mr. Sneh opposed participation in the London Conference on such terms. Why, he asked, should Jews serve as ornaments at a British conference which only sought an anti-Zionist decision?

Changes of Front

Possibility of a change of front in the present attitude of the Zionist Organization of America who have hitherto opposed partition is indicated in a decision of the Organization to agree to Jewish participation in negotiations at the London Conference "with the purpose of discussing the creation of a Jewish State." The significance of this decision is that it does not insist on the inclusion of all Jewish people in such a State. Mr. Daniel Frisch, one of the principal members until now against the Jewish Agency's present leadership, said that he accepted Dr. Weizmann's thesis of a "viable State capable of absorbing the remnants of European Jewry in ten years."

(PTA, Palcor, U.P., Reuter)

TERRORIST TRUCE REPORTED

It was reported from Tel Aviv yesterday that both the Irgun Zvai Leumi and the Stern Group would cease all terrorist activities until after the close of the sessions of the Zionist Congress.

CONGRESS OPENING CELEBRATED

TEL AVIV, Monday. — To mark the opening of the Zionist Congress at Basle, over 1,000 people attended a ceremony in the Ohel Shem hall here tonight, arranged by the Jewish National Fund, the Palestine Foundation Fund and the Municipality. Speakers were the Mayor, Mr. I. Rokach; Dr. A. Shalit, who was Dr. Herzl's secretary; Dr. A. Goldstein; and Dr. A. Geiher. A programme of Zionist songs was given by the choirs of the Histadruth and the Teachers' Seminary.

AFTER MIDNIGHT

MR. LA GUARDIA will announce his resignation as Director-General of UNRRA today, when the council of the organization holds its sixth annual meeting in Washington.

15,000 CHINESE Communist troops have crossed the frozen river Sungari in what a Nanking message describes as the beginning of the Communist winter offensive.

BRITISH WANT ARMS CENSUS AUDIT

FLUSHING MEADOW, N.Y., Monday (Reuter). — In a five-hour night session the Uno General Assembly last night held a debate on the census of troops, during which Sir Hartley Shawcross (Britain) urged that information furnished should be verified by an "auditing committee" and M. Molotov asked that the question of troops at home should be kept separate from that of troops abroad. A census of troops at home without a tally of armaments, he said, would give an incomplete picture.

When Britain submits her return on troops, Sir Hartley promised, there would be a surprise at the smallness of the forces she maintains. "But," he added, "we should like our figures certified, so that nobody will be able to challenge them."

"If we are not prepared to agree to the simple processes of verification now, in regard to this comparatively unimportant matter, what confidence would the time come when we shall be ready to put into operation a far more rigid and far more elaborate system of control for the prohibition of atomic warfare?", Sir Hartley asked.

'Test of Sincerity'

"This is perhaps a test of our sincerity in the matter," he said. "A perfectly simple system of international audit could be set up quickly by the Military Staffs Committee. "Who ever heard of the requirement that accounts should be submitted and compared with other accounts without a provision that they should also be audited?" The job of the auditing committee would be to put figures which meant different things in different countries on a comparable basis, which could represent them in the proper perspective.

M. Molotov, who started speaking after midnight, said:

"We put forward the suggestion that all member States should report to the United Nations on their armed forces stationed outside their country. According to our proposal, all States would have to report on the forces which they still have on territories of other Uno members. The presence of foreign troops on other nations' territory can be used by a State to exert pressure on the internal affairs of another and in influencing relations between the occupied State and its neighbours. It is obvious that such a situation cannot be permitted to last."

M. Molotov repeated the Soviet argument that the question of troops at home should not be mixed up with the census of troops in foreign territories. Home troops, he said, should be dealt with separately when the United Nations took up the whole wider issue of disarmament.

M. Molotov pointed out that the request for a census of home troops did not include the census of armaments, and therefore it would give an incomplete picture.

Yesterday at U.N.

The South African demand that the dispute between India and the Union should be referred to the International Court of Justice was defeated in the General Assembly. First the Assembly decided by 31 votes to 24 that the South African amendment should require a two thirds majority. After that the amendment was defeated by 31 votes to 11 with two abstentions.

The American proposal on Franco Spain was amended by the political sub-committee to include the demand for the breaking off of diplomatic relations with Franco. The American version of the resolution had called on Franco to surrender her power to a provisional government but had refrained from demanding the rupture of diplomatic relations. Sunday night's amendment, submitted jointly by Mexico, Venezuela, Guatemala, Panama, and Chile demands the break-off as well. It was carried by 11 votes to 6 with one abstention.

Overriding Russian objections the Political and Security Committee yesterday decided to call upon the Security Council to curb the use of the veto.

1000-MILE MISSION OF MERCY
R.A.F. FLIES TO AID OF STRANDED REFUGEES

Palestine Post Reporter

Despite bad flying weather, six tons of food, medical supplies and clothing for the ship-wrecked immigrants on the Dodecanese island of Syrina, 500 miles from Haifa, were dropped at dawn yesterday by a flight of three four-engined Halifax transports of No. 113 Royal Air Force Airborne Support Squadron.

'READY AND GENEROUS ASSISTANCE'

Describing the relief measures that had been taken and were being planned, a Jewish Agency spokesman in Jerusalem yesterday said: "We should like to put on record the ready and generous assistance which we have received from the Palestine Government Secretariat, the security authorities, the R.A.F., the people who deal with passports, and others.

"We have been helped very considerably and with great readiness by everybody concerned. We should like that to be made known."

A British member has reported late last night to have reached the island, where she stood by waiting for the arrival of H.M.S. Chevron which left Haifa last night.

The Chevron, which was accompanied by a minesweeper, is expected to arrive at 3 o'clock this morning with doctors, nurses, medical supplies and food on board.

A medical mission consisting of three doctors and two nurses is to leave Palestine by air for Rhodes this morning, and will sail for Syrina to attend the refugees, some of whom are likely to have been injured during the shipwreck.

The planes took off from Aqir airport at 4 a.m. and returned at 11.40 after the 1000-mile journey. A fourth Halifax left just after noon with a further two tons of supplies.

Working all night, the R.A.F. ground crews prepared the machines for their special mission and the handling and packing of the stores was carried out by men of the 6th Airborne Division. Two paratroopers flew in each plane to carry out the actual dropping of the supplies, which included a six volt wireless battery in case the stranded refugees have a radio transmitter.

The story of the trip was told by F/Lt. Alan Ross, of Wembley, Middlesex, who was in command of the flight, a few minutes after he had touched down.

"It was pitch-black when we took off from Aqir," the Flight Lieutenant said, "and, though weather conditions were very bad — the worst I've ever known — we sighted the island just after first light."

The airmen saw no trace either on the shores of the island or at sea of the vessel that had foundered. They noticed a few white stone houses and barns in which they thought some of the refugees might have found shelter.

Tree-less and barren, Syrina's 650 ft. hills are split by a valley which the R.A.F. observers could see the immigrants — 400 or 500 was the estimate — sheltering.

With only 200 or 300 yards in which to drop their supplies, the aircraft had to make several runs over the wadi and the job took just under an hour. They came down as low as 50 feet over the hill-tops to do it.

Smoke-Fires Lit

"As soon as the people in the wadi saw us," the R.A.F. officers continued, "they spread out, lit bonfires, waved and signalled to us. The smoke from the fires gave us our course and as we went to drop the supplies. We landed everything that (Continued on Page 8 Col. 1)

FRANCO STAGES PROTEST

MADRID, Monday (UP). — General Franco today addressed a crowd of 100,000 people on the occasion of the "Day of National Protest" against what is called the "interference of Uno in Spain's internal affairs." The movers of the motion to break off diplomatic relations with Spain were called by General Franco "enemies of our crusade."

He was speaking from the balcony of the Oriente Palace and said that Spain would not tolerate any foreign interference in her internal affairs. Spain had the right to benefit from her internal victory, he said.

Many thousands had marched in procession for two miles along Madrid's avenues until they reached the plaza before the Oriente Palace. At the climax of the rally, Franco appeared on the balcony and received a long ovation. He spoke for only five minutes.

'Forced Demonstration'

Many workers were given half-tickets and ordered to retrieve the other half at certain assembly centres of the procession so as to assure their attendance. Unidentified persons phoned the United Press offices at Madrid and shouted: "Tell the world that this is a forced demonstration."

Despite today's demonstration reliable diplomatic observers believe that General Franco may accept mediation in the Latin American Republics in his differences with the United Nations. The Spanish Foreign Office is reported to be in favour of the Colombian resolution submitted at the Uno which recommends that the Latin American nations should offer their good offices towards the solution of the Spanish question by the Spaniards themselves. Although the resolution was rejected in the Political and Security Sub-Committees on Sunday, Colombia is planning to submit it again to the full committee.

M.R.P. WIN POLL

PARIS, Monday (R). — The Popular Republicans (M.R.P.) beat the Communists by exactly 1500 votes to the first place in the Council of the Republic — the new French Upper House — in the elections held yesterday.

The elections were for the first 214 out of 315 members to be chosen for the Council. The struggle between the M.R.P. and the Communists has there by been taken a step further, the M.R.P. emerging as the strongest party though by the scant margin — in the Upper House, while the Communists are the strongest in the Chamber.

Results published this morning (including North African seats) were as follows:

Popular Republican 61 seats
Communists 61 seats
Socialists 50 seats
Radicals 25 seats
Independent Republicans 10 seats
Liberty Party (Right-wing) 8 seats
Other Metropolitan Parties 2 seats
Algerian Manifesto List 2 seats
Franco Muselman 2 seats

Nearly 85,000 electors were chosen in the primary elections a fortnight ago. They gave 27,250 votes to the Communists.

The remaining 101 members are to be elected by electoral colleges. The National Assembly will elect 62 of them; another 37 will be chosen by overseas assemblies, some of which have not yet been constituted, while eight will be designated by means yet to be determined to represent Frenchmen living in Tunis.

750 DEPORTEES LEAVE CYPRUS

(continued in left column)

INDIAN CONSTITUENT ASSEMBLY MEETS

NEW DELHI, Monday (R). — The Indian Constituent Assembly met here this morning in the brilliantly lit domed circular library hall of the Central Legislature under the chairmanship of the 75 years old Dr. Sinha.

The 74 Moslem League members did not attend the League's decision to boycott the Assembly. The 205 members present made a colourful gathering dressed in the many different garbs of Indian provinces.

In his inaugural address Dr. Sinha strongly recommended the United States Constitution to the Assembly for careful study.

He held it up to the members as an ideal constitution, one "built for immortality, and whose strength which will outlast and overcome all destructive tendencies."

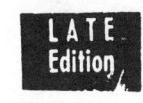

THE PALESTINE POST

LATE Edition

JERUSALEM
MONDAY, MARCH 3 1947

PRICE 15 MILS
VOL. XX
No. 6345

TEL AVIV OUTLAWED
MARTIAL LAW OVER HALF YISHUV

PARALYSIS TILL TERROR IS ENDED; PART OF JEWISH J'LEM BESIEGED

Palestine Post Staff

Tel Aviv, Ramat Gan, Bnei Brak and Petah Tikva, with about a quarter of a million inhabitants, together with a small area of northeast Jerusalem have been completely isolated and outlawed since dawn yesterday, when 10,000 troops of the First Infantry Division and the Ninth Infantry Brigade launched "Operation Hippo".

The curfew imposed on Tel Aviv at midnight on Saturday is to be lifted at 5 o'clock this morning, the Area Commander, Brigadier J.W.R. Moore, announced last night.

The nature and background of Operation Hippo was described at his Divisional Headquarters in Tel Litwinsky to a party of local and foreign correspondents by Major-General R. N. Gale, in command of the operation. "For some time past the authorities had been preparing to take vigorous steps to put down illegal activities against the State," the General declared.

"Certain preliminary steps, such as cantonment and evacuation of British subjects, have already taken place, but the problem which faces us now is to know what to do in the event of sabotage and murder, and, obviously, our purpose is to get hold of the perpetrators with as little inconvenience as possible to the public. Yet, unfortunately, indirectly, the community must suffer. This is regretted as much by us as by them," he said.

The isolated area has been completely cut off from the rest of the world. Communications have ceased. The railway system, with the exception of certain food and through trains, has been dislocated, and road transport has been stopped. Posts, telegraphs and telephones have ceased functioning, and the distribution of food will be made through the Food Control authorities, with military transport at their disposal. Tel Aviv Port has ceased functioning, and six freighters waiting to be unloaded must go elsewhere.

A number of destroyers have been patrolling off the shore today.

A special system of Military Courts will be set up to deal with all offenders. This, however, was not Martial Law, the General emphasized, and the military were only assisting the police in this operation, which was primarily directed towards the search for individuals.

Essential Services

All facilities would be given to essential services as well as to the press whose duty it was "to make it clear that this operation was not a punitive measure, but a drastic step against illegal organisations which must be paralyzed."

General Gale told the hushed press conference that measures will continue until the terrorists have been put to earth, even if this takes weeks. This most drastic action ever taken in Palestine was the Government's answer to Saturday's terrorist attacks on the military and the police.

All evidence we have as to who carries out these attacks tends to show that they come from the area we have isolated. In order to eradicate them, we shall try to prevent as far as is humanly possible any movement in or out of the area. The objective of this plan is to search for and arrest the law-breakers within it, however long that may take.

"The operation's objective is not punitive," the General emphasized. "There is absolutely no quarrel with the community as a whole. In fact, what I know of the community, which is quite a lot, makes me think they would be as glad to get rid of the bad souls."

The General made it clear that he was not going to have any wholesale searches, such as the four-day house-to-house search last July which angered the population and achieved next to nothing. The police have their suspicions, and I have told them to go after the men they want. They cannot get out of the area except by sea, and the Navy is looking after that. This means a terrific paralysis, I know, but it cannot be helped. This thing has got beyond the control of the police, and we have got to help them.

When asked what would happen if the terrorists lay low during the operation, and what would happen in fact if the plan failed, the General said:

Frankly, I don't know. We can only hope that in the unwer, and it will work, but how soon is impenetrable. It may take a week or a month, I just don't know.

Traffic between Jaffa and Haifa yesterday was diverted through Beit Dujan, and roads leading into the Controlled Area were blocked by tanks and barbed-wire barriers. Wire entanglements were stretched across fields and troops posted every two hundred metres around the perimeter.

A number of Hebrew newspapers, normally printed in Tel Aviv, have transferred their offices to Haifa and will publish one-sheet editions.

RED HIPPO

Special orange - coloured identification cards, labelled "Hippo" and stamped across the back, with the picture of a hippopotamus in red, have been issued to 16 residents of the Controlled Area in Jerusalem.

The cards which permit entry and departure from the zone, must be held overhead in clear view of the patrols. They have been issued to mukhtars of the Quarter, Government officials, and two doctors.

Deserted City

Palestine Post Reporter

A deathly stillness reigned in the streets of Tel Aviv yesterday. Patrols closely checked military vehicles circulating in the city but both police and troops were out by the khamsin, sought shade whenever possible. Even roving cars also seemed to sense the new order and hardly ventured on the streets.

In some parts of town, as patrolling was relaxed towards evening, people began to move cautiously about.

Of the city's 6,000 telephones, only two lines were operating—one to the Public Information Office and the other to the Mayor's residence. Neither nurses nor doctors were allowed on the streets. Sanitary and other services were suspended.

Very few screenings or searches were carried out and, with the announcement that the curfew would be lifted at 5 o'clock this morning, it seemed unlikely that intensive searches would take place.

Instead of the usual 30 buses on the Tel Aviv-Petah Tikva route, 25 will be allowed to operate daily between 6 and 8 o'clock in the morning, and from 4 to 8 in the evening. No other buses will leave Tel Aviv.

By 11 o'clock no order had been received instructing factories and other industrial undertakings to close, and employees still walk to work this morning. Schools will function as fully as possible.

VAAD LEUMI STOPPAGE CALLED OFF

The self-imposed curfew which the Jewish communities of Haifa and Jerusalem had planned for last night was cancelled, and cafes and restaurants were open.

Communists Accuse Chiang Kai Shek

NANKING, Sunday (Reuter). — In a telegram to Generalissimo Chiang Kai Shek from General Chou En-Lai, the Communist leader, the Generalissimo is accused of "bolting the door to any negotiations," and is charged with determination to wage civil war to the end.

This follows the order that Communist representatives leave Nationalist territory, signed, according to General Chou En-Lai, by Marshal Chiang Kai Shek himself.

The first group of Communist liaison officials left Nanking for Yenan in an American plane today. About 180 men, women and children are to be evacuated by March 7.

CHILD KILLED

A four-year-old girl, Ketti Shalom, was fatally injured when she was shot in the head as she appeared on the balcony of her parents' house in the Stauri Building in the Mea Shearim Quarter of the Controlled Area) at 3 o'clock yesterday afternoon.

The child died almost immediately after admission to hospital.

Her older sister, Mrs. B. Mazon (22), was shot in the leg, but was not permitted to go to the Red Shield Society clinic for treatment.

It was stated later that a court of inquiry is to be held to investigate the circumstances in which the girl was killed. The P.I.O. said that the shot was fired at the girl's father when he tried to leave the house. The bullet "penetrated the balcony wounding Mrs. Mazon in the leg, and the child was hit by the ricochet."

Another official statement, issued at 6 o'clock, said that warning shots were fired during the day in the Mea Shearim Quarter under Statutory Martial Law, and that no casualties occurred.

Tel Aviv Mayor Urges Courage

Nothing will be allowed to stop the building of Palestine out of Tel Aviv, declared the Mayor of the city, Mr. I. Rokach, in a statement last night.

Referring to the restriction on movement and the withdrawal of Government services, the Mayor warned that "other severe blows may follow," and were likely to weaken the economic position of the Yishuv, on which further development depended.

Mr. Rokach said that the Municipal Council was about to take steps, in conjunction with the economic and public institutions, to prevent or at least reduce the suffering of the population.

Calling on the citizens to refrain from panic action likely to weaken Jewish powers to overcome the present difficulties, the Mayor declared that the private individual must "from now on at the disposal of the public — and the public will look after the individual."

25,000 ISOLATED IN JERUSALEM QUARTERS

Palestine Post Staff

Statutory Martial Law was brought into force in the north-eastern quarters of Jerusalem at 8 o'clock yesterday — Mea Shearim, Bokharian Houses, Sanhedria, Beth Israel, Beth Israel Hahadasha, Geulah and Kerem Avraham.

The announcement that the measure had been applied to the large areas which includes, Tel Aviv, Bnei Brak, Ramat Gan and Petah Tikva was made five hours later, at 1.15 p.m.

The official figure of the number of people affected by Operation Hippo is 238,210: 180,000 in Tel Aviv; 17,260 in Petah Tikva; 10,380 in Ramat Gan; 5,760 in Bnei Brak, and 25,000 in Jerusalem.

The New Order was enacted in a supplement to the "Palestine Gazette" yesterday and announced in two official communiques.

The curfew imposed on other Jewish quarters of Jerusalem at 7 o'clock on Saturday night was lifted at 1 o'clock yesterday afternoon, 18 hours later, but in the Martial Law area remains in force until 10 o'clock tomorrow morning, when it will be lifted for only three hours.

Statutory Martial Law differs from full martial law in that it prescribes the powers and regulations by which a Military Commander can govern certain areas. These powers are

Continued On Page 5, Col. 1.

20 KILLED ON SATURDAY

Palestine Post Staff

Terrorist activities throughout Palestine on Saturday took toll of 20 lives — two British officers, eight British other ranks, a British police clerk and nine civilians. Twenty-five other people were wounded - seven British officers, 12 British other ranks, two British policemen and six civilians.

In addition to the series of outrages reported yesterday, two British soldiers were killed when the scout car in which they were patrolling was blown up north of Petah Tikva on Saturday night. One soldier on road patrol nearby was killed and another wounded.

Two soldiers were wounded, one seriously and the other slightly, yesterday afternoon when the truck in which they were travelling struck a mine on the Tel Aviv-Haifa highway two kilometres south of the Hadera junction.

A third member of the party of four Military Police lance-corporals, whose jeep was blown upon on Mountain Road in the Tel Aviv area on Saturday, died on Saturday, the fourth N.C.O. is not out of danger and has been transferred to the Military Hospital at Sarafand.

The funeral of Mr. George Beynon, a police clerical officer, who was killed in the Goldsmith Club outrage, took place at the Zion cemetery in Jerusalem yesterday afternoon. The three British Army victims of the same outrage will be buried at the Military Cemetery in Ramle this morning.

The identities of the seven NAAFI employees killed in the Club have been established. They are:

Germano Mazzoti, the manager;
Emil Gandour, assistant manager;
Olga Petrowycznski, receptionist;
Hassan Yussef el Bakhri;
Elias Yussef Korra;
Hanna Elias Hasboun;
Mussa Mohammed Abu Diab.

The two NAAFI employees injured are - Stadios Andronini and Rushdi Murrad Masud.

Export-Import Bank Stops Credits
WILL CONTINUE TO FINANCE TRADE

WASHINGTON, Sunday (Reuter). — The Export-Import Bank has informed the U.S. Congress that it "had decided to bring to an end its programme of emergency reconstruction credits, and this decision would apply especially to countries which have access to facilities of the International Bank."

America's Terms For Greek Aid

LONDON, Sunday (Reuter). — Receipt of an aide-memoire from the U.S. outlining the terms on which it would be prepared to provide economic assistance for the Greek Government, was confirmed by a Foreign Office spokesman tonight.

The communication is now being considered. It is reliably understood to have urged that British troops should continue to stay in Greece, if economic assistance is to be supplied from Washington.

Germans Escape To S. America

LONDON, Sunday (Reuter). — The International Committee for the Study of European Questions, in a fresh report issued today on underground Nazi plots, says many Germans are still escaping to South America through Sweden and Italy some having changed their passports, identity and names as many as three times.

The report has been sent to the Prime Ministers and Foreign Secretaries of Britain, France, Belgium, Denmark, Norway, the U.S. and Russia. "In spite of recent denials," it says, "a great part of the economic potential hidden abroad by the Axis powers has neither been handed over to former Allied countries nor liquidated. The Argentine Government, after having supported Axis policy during the war, definitely refuses to hand over their assets to former Allied nations."

Anglo-French Alliance
BRITAIN'S SECOND STEP

PARIS, Sunday (Reuter). — Mr. Bevin and M. Bidault, the British and French Foreign Ministers, are both expected to make speeches when they sign the Anglo-French Treaty of Alliance at Dunkirk on Tuesday.

The pact will be signed at the Sub-Prefecture at 1500 hrs G.M.T. and three hours later the text will be published.

The "Observer" says in a leading article today the alliance with France was the "second big step to improve things Britain has taken since the end of the war" — the first having been her agreement with the U.S. to unite their two zones in Germany. A diplomatic correspondent of the "Sunday Times" makes the suggestion that the formula used in the Treaty may serve as a model for a revised Treaty of Alliance with Russia which Mr. Bevin is expected to sign in Moscow.

France Welcomes Pact

An enthusiastic welcome to the Treaty was also given in editorials of the French press, which were broadcast to the nation today as the Paris newspaper workers' strike is still going on.

United Nations Army Under Discussion

LAKE SUCCESS, Sunday (AFP). — The Committee appointed to study the deployment of the armed forces to be controlled by the United Nations has completed its work, and is now examining the organization of these armed forces.

Speaking at a reception given by the League for Industrial Democracy in New York yesterday, Mr. Trygve Lie said that the United Nations would have succeeded in its aims if belief in the possibility of another war were banished for ever from the minds of men.

The German and Japanese peace treaties should be signed as soon as possible, he said, to avoid antagonisms between the big and small nations.

Mr. Lie said that workers of the world should know that the United Nations was their one organization, and have confidence in it. Their fate was linked to that of the U.N.

BIG 4 MAY DISCUSS DARDANELLES

ANKARA, Sunday (Reuter). — Turkey's dispute with Russia over the control of the Dardanelles will "most probably" be discussed at the Big Four meeting in Moscow, Turkish political quarters stated today.

Eight days before the opening of the conference, the Embassies of the participating powers had not been informed today where the meeting was to take place.

"RESULT of LACK of COOPERATION"

OFFICIAL COMMUNIQUE
No. 110, March 2, 7.45 a.m.

Following on extensive outrages on March 1, 1947, the High Commissioner has made regulations under the Palestine (Defence) Order in Council, 1937, which provide for the imposition of statutory martial law in areas specified by the High Commissioner. These Regulations are considered by the High Commissioner to be expedient for the maintenance of public order and their effect, in areas to which they are applied, is to provide for the withdrawal from the population of such areas of the normal facilities of civil government. Government offices and courts will be closed; banks may be closed by order of the military commander; telephone and postal services may be suspended. The movement of persons and vehicles may be prohibited. Exclusive jurisdiction in respect of criminal offences committed in areas specified by the High Commissioner is vested in military courts.

These regulations have been applied with effect from 8 a.m. on March 1, 1947 to the following areas of Jerusalem: —

From a point in Mea Shearim Street at the northeast corner of the Syrian Orphanage property, in a northerly direction along the eastern boundary of the Syrian Orphanage property to a point adjacent to Survey cairn No. 798.2; thence in a northeasterly direction following the middle of the road to a point on the Nebi Samwil road approximately 100 metres north west of Survey cairn No. 766.5; thence in a southeasterly direction in a straight line to the culvert on the Nablus road in the Sheikh Jarrah quarter; thence in a southerly direction along the middle of Saint George's Road to its junction with Mea Shearim Street; thence along Mea Shearim Street to the point at the southeast corner of the Syrian Orphanage property.

OFFICIAL COMMUNIQUE
No. 111, March 1, 1.15 p.m.

A month ago the Government invited the Jewish Agency and Vaad Leumi to call upon the Yishuv to cooperate in bringing to justice members of the terrorist groups. These institutions refused their cooperation. Renewed warnings were therefore given of the serious consequences which any further outbreaks of terrorism would entail. The newest measures now necessary are the result of the lack of cooperation against bloodshed and terrorism

which these institutions have themselves condemned.

Since the invitation to cooperate was issued, 48 outrages have occurred in which 20 people have lost their lives and 31 people have been wounded, including 18 killed and 25 injured in yesterday's incidents. Included in these casualties are 15 civilians.

There is distinct evidence to link the attacks carried out on March 1 with the Tel Aviv area, from which it is well known that operations by the dissident groups are conducted. In the attacks in Jerusalem and Haifa were stolen yesterday in Tel Aviv.

The regulations providing for the imposition of Statutory Martial Law are therefore being applied with effect from 1.15 p.m. today, March 2, to an area including Tel Aviv, Ramat Gan, Bnei Brak and Petah Tikva.

"Fight Against Terror Will Be Intensified"
OUTRAGES A "NUMBING SHOCK"

Expressing the Yishuv's "numbing shock" at the latest outrages, a statement issued by the Jewish Agency and the Vaad Leumi last night declared the determination of the Yishuv to intensify its fight to stamp out terror.

Both bodies point out that they have made consistent efforts to combat terrorism; but the failure of the Government to ease the immigration restrictions had not helped to relieve the tension in the country. The statement read as follows:

The Jewish Agency and the Vaad Leumi are filled with horror at the outrages which have been perpetrated in Palestine during the past 24 hours. These murderous and senseless crimes have come as a numbing shock to the entire Yishuv and its leaders. For some considerable time past the disciplined elements in the Yishuv, hampered though they have been by lack of adequate powers, have been making efforts to combat the terrorist groups and to undermine their organisation. These efforts are continuing and will be intensified, for the Yishuv is determined that the shedding of innocent blood shall play no part in its national struggle.

The Executive of the Jewish Agency and the Executive of the Vaad Leumi deplore the loss of life caused by these latest crimes. These sections of Palestine Jewry which are new under martial law remain an integral part of the Yishuv, which declares its complete solidarity with them both in the common fight against terrorist outrages and in the toll which they have been called upon to endure as scapegoats for an evil that is not their making.

It was stated in its official statement that not linked the "government measures now necessary" with the Jewish National Institutions' "lack of cooperation."

They would point out, for their part, that the Jewish Agency has, as stated above, made consistent efforts to combat terrorism. It regrets however that in the course of lengthy negotiations it had failed to secure from the Government any measure of help in solving the burning question of illegal immigration, a matter which, apart from its intrinsic urgency, would no doubt also have relieved the existing tension. The Government has steadily refused concessions of any kind, and no amount of pleading has made any account of the hard facts of the situation have so far availed to move the Government one inch. The Government is now retaliating against the Yishuv as a whole for the crimes of a few desperate gunmen, and is seeking by the imposition of martial law, which is unlikely to deter the terrorism, to punish an entire community.

The Jewish Agency and the Vaad Leumi wish to stress once again that the disciplined forces of the Yishuv will intensify their action against terrorism so as to bring to an end all manner of bloodshed in this country. They call upon the Yishuv in this hour of crisis to rally round the National Institutions which are now under martial law and to maintain an integral part of the Yishuv in their midst in order to overcome the present difficulties, the Mayor declared that the private individual must "from now on at the disposal of the public — and the public will look after the individual."

Germans Escape / Invitation

ATLANTA, (Georgia), Sunday (Reuter). — A proposal that England, Scotland, Ireland and Wales should be admitted as member states of the U.S.A. was made by Senator Richard Russel, (Georgia Democrat) in an interview with Ralph McGill, the editor of the "Atlanta Constitution," a Democratic morning paper.

The newspaper quoted the Senator as saying that his proposal was based on the threatened break-up of the British Empire and its probable inability to carry out world commitments. He proposed that the commonwealths within the Empire should consider some form of association with the U.S. if Britain acted to become part of the U.S.

Senator Russel added that the King and Queen would be able to retire on their incomes "and the King could, if he wished, remain in politics and run for the Senate as could Mr. Churchill.

MR. BEN-GURION IN HOSPITAL

Mr. David Ben-Gurion, Chairman of the Jewish Agency Executive who arrived in Palestine on Thursday, was admitted to the Surgical Section of the Hadassah Hospital in Jerusalem yesterday morning. He was brought from the Kallia Hotel in an ambulance to be treated for a leg ailment.

Dr. Milevitsky said that his condition is not serious, and that within a week or 10 days of treatment and rest are necessary, it is unlikely that an operation will be needed.

LATE Edition

THE PALESTINE POST

JERUSALEM
Wednesday, July 30, 1947

PRICE 20 MILS
VOL. XXII. No. 6471

Column One

By

David Courtney

MR. Attlee will have to stand up to some sharp heckling when he faces the Parliamentary Labour Party today. Morrison will be there to help and can be relied upon to crack his whip. Between them, the Prime Minister and the Leader of the House will make it clear that the country's crisis is the Party's crisis and that the ranks had better stay solidly in formation unless willing to risk defeat in the Commons and a sharp reaction against the Government outside. Driven by the fear of bankruptcy and of failure in Germany and the rest of Europe, the lukewarm support of the Liberals for the Government's planned economy schemes is turning to hostility; and the big Middle Class vote, which gave Labour the extra seats that made the difference between a bare, perhaps unworkable majority and a majority with hardly any risk of defeat as long as the Party voted together, is getting ready to turn back to its old, safe loyalties. Whether this will frighten the conscientious Socialists of both front bench and back into acceptance of a compromise policy of go-slow in the home-schemes of nationalisation remains to be seen. Those who refuse to accept it may also refuse to admit the need of subservience to the American demand that Britain should quit its plans for nationalization in the Ruhr and should share control of its zone with the United States.

■

SHORTLY after the elections in the summer of 1945, Mr. Attlee, as much frightened by some of the elements which made up his own majority as by the problems ahead of him, decided upon a policy of gradualness. "We need at least one full term of office to work ourselves in," he is reported to have said. "He is a modest man," Mr. Churchill has said of the Prime Minister; "with a good deal to be modest about." His modesty and his policy of Socialist gradualness would have served well enough in fair weather. In the foul tempests to which Britain has been subjected, in common with the rest of the old world, they have not been enough. Some of his Cabinet colleagues and an increasing number of his supporters on the back benches have become critical. If in the present crisis, gradualness is to become still more gradual and modesty to develop into appeasement to the Tory Opposition as well as subjection to the Marshall planners, ructions will start in the Labour Party. It looks as if Mr. Attlee must decide today between more Socialism and less; and whatever the decision, it cannot fail to bring about big Ministerial changes.

■

JON Kimche says that Aneurin Bevan, Minister for Health and Housing, has his resignation in his pocket. Kimche should know. He is editor of the political weekly, "Tribune," which is largely owned by Bevan and has consistently warned the Government against giving in to the steel interests on the question of the nationalisation of the industry they control, and against selling the Ruhr trade unionists down the river at the behest of Americans. Bevan's prestige is high. He has done more than he might have done in this field; and in the field of Public Health has carried out some of the most important reforms in the social legislation of the present Government. He is politically more consistent then a Crossman, has more skill and experience than Michael Foot, and none of the pseudo-Communist taint attributed to that conscientious and courageous politician, Zilliacus.

■

FOREIGN policy, apart from the future of the Ruhr and the necessity to apply such policy at crippling cost in men and money, may not be a major subject today. Critics will keep most of their fire for the debate. But if a process of self-accounting has set in among the members of the Labour Party, it is difficult to see how Mr. Bevin can escape the consequences. His long record of failure has brought him the sympathy of an easy-going people ready to forgive much for the sake of at least one vivid personality among a drab collection of apparent dullards. But no people will go on being made a fool of for very long; and it begins to look as if Mr. Bevin is by way of doing just that.

Jerusalem, July 30.

"NONE BUT DEAD MEN WILL BE LANDED HERE", SAY EXILES

REFUGEES REFUSE TO LEAVE THE SHIPS

PORT DE BOUC, Tuesday.— Saying that they wanted to go to Palestine, the 4,500 Jewish immigrants of the "Exodus 1947," who arrived here today in three British transports, refused to land and, thanking the French for their hospitality, declared, "None but dead men will be landed here." A French official said that his Government would not force the Jews to disembark.

The three British vessels anchored half a mile apart, about a mile off this tiny harbour. The French health officer who went aboard the first transport, quickly ran up a flag signalling that no signs of an epidemic had been found.

The French had intended to register the refugees at the rate of one shipload a day. They prepared invitations to land in French, Hebrew, and Yiddish, and promised each refugee that he would be fed, given medical attention and moved swiftly to camps or hospitals. Trucks, field kitchens and ambulances gathered at the docks before dawn to attend to the refugees' needs.

The harbour area was cordoned off to prevent incidents, but hundreds of Frenchmen crowded into this little holiday village. The first of the refugee freighters arrived just before 8 o'clock. French authorities did not permit either newsmen or representatives of Jewish aid associations to board the ships.

FLOATING CAGES

The ships were described as "floating cages" by eye-witnesses who approached them in small craft. The cargo holds had been converted into dormitories and the decks surrounded by 12-feet high barbed wire.

M. Rene Colaveri, the Secretary-General of the local prefecture, went out to meet the ships, and on his return spoke to the French Premier, M. Paul Ramadier, in Paris by phone. He is understood to have delivered a message from the emigrants that they were unwilling to land.

According to a PTA message, a British Colonel on the Runnymede Park told the head of the French delegation to "return tomorrow morning when more than a thousand refugees would be willing to get off."

The ships had been cruising the French waters, just out of sight of land for three days, awaiting instructions.

As soon as the first of the three ships entered the roads a special police boat left the harbour with a boarding party of French officials and Mr. S. E. Kay, the British Consul-General in Marseilles, who is representing the British Government. In the wake of the police boat was another small craft carrying French medical officers.

M. Colaveri declared that the launch conveying representatives of the Foreign Affairs, Interior and Public Health Ministries, M. Gouineau of the "Entr'aide Francaise," M. Blumer, special Government Delegate, Admiral Decoux and the adviser to the British Embassy in Paris, first proceeded to the "Runnymede Park" and then to the "Ocean Vigour," anchored a few hundred metres farther.

"We were greeted on board by a British Officer, and by Col. Gregson, to whom we expressed our desire to speak to the immigrants. They were assembled behind grilles on the forecastle. They apparently did not understand what it was all about, as they all went to starboard and port, where we followed them in the company of British officers. In the holds, where it was terribly hot, I read to the few hundred men and women the French Government's declaration offering them hospitality in the following words:

The French Government informs the immigrants on board the Exodus 1947 that, with their consent, they will be given asylum on the national soil, where they will enjoy all the liberties which France traditionally endows upon all citizens who fought for the freedoms of the human being. Immediately after landing ashore, they will be provided with food and immediate material needs.

One of the immigrants, on

(Continued on Page 2)

"We Would Rather Starve than Land"

By BOYD FRANCE, Reuters Special Correspondent

PORT DE BOUC, Tuesday. — The Jewish refugees aboard the British ship Ocean Vigour who arrived here today told me that they refused to land.

When I pulled alongside the ship and asked the immigrants, through a Hebrew interpreter, whether they would land, there was a deathly silence. Then as one man, they chorused, "No."

"We would rather starve to death than land anywhere except in Palestine," they shouted.

Although my boat was unable to approach the other two immigrant ships lying ouside the port, I was told that the immigrants there, too, were refusing to disembark.

Only one immigrant had landed by this afternoon a woman suffering from tuberculosis, whose condition made it necessary to send her to Marseilles Hospital.

The control of ships' movements in and out of the port was strict. Privately owned vessels were told that they would not be allowed to set out to sea. My boat ran the police blockade, but as we tried to approach the 'Runnymede Park,' lying one kilometre off the entrance of the port with refugees on board, we were overtaken by the police boat and threatened with a fine of 15,000 francs and a term of imprisonment if we persisted in our attempt.

Instead, we proceeded to follow the Ocean Vigour, which had weighed anchor and was making for the open sea. About 15 miles offshore we overtook her and drew alongside.

We asked them four times "Are you going to get off?"

Suddenly the crowd burst into a loud cry of "Nein, nein," and began to sing "Hatikvah."

At strategic points along the railing of the ship's deck British Paratroopers with red berets stood in silent guard over their unwilling passengers.

About 32 kms. offshore we could distinguish the outlines of the four British warships which had escorted the immigrants back to France. With them was the third immigrant ship, Empire Rival.

FRANCE DENIES DEAL TO LIMIT MIGRATION

Palestine Post Reporter

The Jewish Agency was officially informed by the French Government yesterday that no agreement had been made by France with Britain to limit Jewish immigration to Palestine. The full text of the message, which was given to correspondents at a press conference in Jerusalem yesterday morning, is as follows:

"According to a growing number of rumours coming from the foreign press it would appear that the taking to France of the refugees on board the "Exodus 1947" by the British authorities has been done in agreement with the French Government. Foreign correspondents also maintain that France and Great Britain have concluded a secret agreement limiting Jewish immigration into Palestine. In reply to these rumours, the French Ministry of Foreign Affairs stresses that, following upon repeated British notes, the Government of the Republic has simply issued the following order to the relevant authorities:

(1) To verify the authenticity of visas for any destination.

(2) To assure the application of the conventions concerning the safeguarding of human lives at sea.

"These orders are obviously applicable without distinction of race or religion to any emigrants leaving French territory.

"An exchange of letters between France and Great Britain is the *only document* in which the two Governments have treated the question of Jewish refugees. There is no foundation to the statement by some news agencies concerning an agreement for the limitation of Jewish immigration into Palestine, in connection with decisions taken solely by the British authorities.

"I would like to add that the French Government is about to apply to the refugees on board the "Exodus 1947" the liberal attitude which has already been publicly announced."

PLEAS FOR 2 SERGEANTS

A strongly-worded warning against possible reprisals against the two kidnapped sergeants was issued by the Executive of the Vaad Leumi at its meeting in Jerusalem yesterday morning.

Appeals for the release of two British Army Sergeants were voiced yesterday by the Chief Rabbis, Dr. I. H. Herzog and Rabbi B. Z. Uziel, the Vaad Leumi Executive and the Hebrew press, while an appeal from Sgt. Paice's father was transmitted to the Jewish Agency for publication by the Zionist Federation in London.

The Vaad Leumi's statement ran as follows:

The Yishuv, which has been hurt and shocked by the Government's lack of response to all the appeals for clemency and by the execution of the three young men sentenced to death for the attack on Acre Prison, will regard any act of reprisal taken against the two innocent Britons as a bloodthirsty deed contrary to all human standards and as an unforgivable sin against the Yishuv and the Jewish people.

Mr. Paice's appeal was transmitted at 2.45 by telephone from the Chief Secretary's Office to the Jewish Agency:

Most immediate. Following from Zionist Federation of Great Britain for the Jewish Agency Jerusalem: Just received telephone call from Mr. Paice, father of one of the two British sergeants held as hostages by the Irgun, who asks us if humanly possible to transmit message to Palestine in attempt to save life of son stressing that neither he, nor son ever anti-Zionists and completely innocent participants in tragic political situation. Have explained to him how strongly you and we disapprove action Irgun and deplore present terrible situation. Premised transmit this message urgently for publication Palestine in last minute attempt influence Irgun to exercise compassion.

The Chief Rabbis expressed deep grief that the appeals of the Yishuv and its leaders for the commutation of the death sentences of the three Jewish youths had not been heeded. These men had not been convicted of murder, they stressed, and that the sentences were carried out at a time when the Jewish and Palestine problems were being judged by the United Nations.

At the same time, Their Eminences appealed, in the name of all that was sacred and dear to Israel, to those in whose hands lay the fate of the two kidnapped Britons to suppress any urge for revenge and to strengthen in their hearts the feeling of common humanity.

They called on them to release the two men immediately and to sanctify their religion, people and land.

In a leading article, "Davar" wrote that if there was still a vestige of common sense and national responsibility in the minds of those who directed the acts of the dissidents, they must now release the two men.

Not to Blame

"Haaretz" also appealed to "the comrades of the executed men."

"They have done all they could to save their comrades' lives; they even trespassed the limit; and failed. They know as well as we do that the two British boys who have fallen into their hands by chance are not to blame for this morning's tragedy. They too are but victims of the hidden hand that has engineered all this"

BRITAIN ASKED WHAT WAS GAINED

LONDON, Tuesday. — The whole press has given prominence to the arrival at Port de Bouc of the deportation convoy and also to this morning's executions in Palestine and the Irgun Zvai Leumi's threats of reprisals.

There might be ugly scenes around Marseilles, apart from a new wave of terrorism in Palestine, said the "News Chronicle." It condemned Zionists in France, whose "unscrupulous temper is clear from their clamour to board the British transports to inspect living conditions," while "the people who raise this cry are those who condemned 4,000 of their co-religionists to the squalor of the President Warfield (the Exodus 1947)."

"In such an atmosphere," the "Chronicle" continued, violence may be avoided by a miracle, but bitterness and recrimination will be planted in many hearts and minds. We have fanned the flames in Palestine. We have thrust friendly France into a situation which at the very least must be most embarrassing to her."

The "Chronicle" then asked: "What have we gained by this sudden decision about one shipload of Jews among the many? What did we think we were going to gain? It is high time somebody told us."

The "Daily Mail" featured an

brought to Palestine. Explaining the tragic position of the Jewish DP's, he said that they were escaping from Gehenna, not, as described, being placed on the road to Gehenna.

The Paris correspondent of the B.B.C. criticized the decision of the British authorities not to allow press representatives at the disembarkation.

800 DISEMBARK IN CYPRUS

By SHAHE GUEBENLIAN

NICOSIA, Tuesday. — The Empires Shelter and Comfort arrived here this morning with 387 men, 228 women and 187 children from the two ships "Return to Zion" and the "Fourteen."

They were taken to Caraolos Camp by road. About 400 of the party are Arabic-speaking Jews from North Africa.

There is still no news of the fate of the remainder of the July quota of repatriates, some of whom had already embarked for the return journey on July 23, but were removed from the ship again.

The "Empire Comfort" returned to Haifa late last night and took on board 223 refugees from the "Fourteen"—165 men,

Prison Raiders Hanged at Acre

Palestine Post Bureau

HAIFA, Tuesday. — "Do not grieve too much, what we have done we did out of conviction." This last message from the three men executed this morning to their families was given to Chief Rabbi Nissim Ohana, who was brought to Acre by the police last night at the request of the condemned men.

The parents and brother of Nakar, the mother, father and sister of Habib, and Weiss' sister were not permitted to see the men before they died, but, having been brought to Haifa in the middle of the night, were kept at C.I.D. Headquarters until morning, when they were escorted to Safad for the funeral.

Rabbi Ohana, who did not know that the hanging were imminent, was awakened after midnight by a Police Inspector accompanied by constables, who told him why he was needed.

When he arrived at Acre, the three men were awakened. He was brought first to the cell of Nakar, who was alone, and heard his confession through the heavy grilled door, with a prison inspector and two Arab policemen standing by. He gave Nakar a skull-cap for the prayer. He was then taken to Habib and Weiss who were together in one cell, and again carried out the last rites with the men on the other side of bars.

All three men were composed and steadfast, the Rabbi told *The Palestine Post,* and their main concern was for their families.

The prison authorities asked Rabbi Ohana to wait and witness the execution, but he chose to return to Haifa where he saw the Police Inspector before going home.

A police sergeant came to the house where Edith Weiss lives in the Neve Shaanan Quarter here shortly before 11 o'clock, where they found that she had gone to friends in Ramat Gan. She last saw her brother on Saturday.

There was a guard of about 200 soldiers and police outside the Police H.Q. at Mt. Cana'an. The taxis bringing the relatives were thoroughly searched from top to bottom after the people alighted.

The bodies were accompanied to Safad by a convoy of about 10 armoured cars, but

BURIALS AGAIN AT SAFAD

Palestine Post Reporter

SAFAD, Tuesday. — For the second time this year Safad was designated as the burial place for Jews executed at Acre, and at four o'clock this morning, Rabbi M. Podhorzer, Chairman of the Jewish Community Council, was officially informed that the bodies of the three condemned men would be brought here.

The four men executed in April, Dov Gruner, Rosenbaum, Kashani and Alkoshi, had also been sent here for burial.

The families of the three men executed today — Nakar's parents and brother, Habib's parents, brother and sister-in-law, and Weiss' sister, his only surviving relative, arrived at seven o'clock this morning and were taken to police headquarters on Mount Canaan, where the bodies were brought from Acre at 8.15, each in a separate police tender. The Haifa Burial Society came at the same time.

Small bundles consisting of the men's clothing and articles found on them at the time of their capture were handed over to the relatives.

The funeral set out at 10 o'clock from Mt. Canaan to the cemetery, headed by the police tenders bearing the three bodies. The streets of the Jewish quarter through which it passed were shuttered and lined with silent men and women, while hundreds waited at the cemetery. The Prayer for the Dead for Nakar and Habib was spoken by their fathers, while for Weiss the prayer was recited by Mr. Podhorzer.

The families left the town at one o'clock to return home.

Rabbi A.L. Zilberman and Rabbi Podhorzer made brief addresses.

Only Jewish constables and

Searches for N.C.O. Hostages

Palestine Post Staff

Eighteen days after the kidnapping of Sergeants Paice and Martin, no trace has yet been found of them, although searches were carried out with renewed vigour in various parts of Palestine yesterday. The Nordiah Quarter in Tel Aviv was cordoned off and searched in the afternoon, but nothing was found. In the morning, Kfar Avihayil, near Nathanya, was also searched.

Civilian patrols were also formed all over the Nathanya area last night to conduct renewed searches for the two missing men.

Throughout the day rumours that the two men had been found were current all over the country, but none of them was substantiated.

British Policemen and Military Police guarded Zion Square in Jerusalem all day, taking up positions early in the morning and leaving them only after the curfew came into force.

In Tel Aviv, people continued to buy food against possible curfews, and there were long queues at ice factories and bakeries.

Cinema and theatre performances were stopped and cafes and restaurants closed.

In Nathanya, a memorial service was held in the afternoon for the three men executed in the morning.

"UNNECESSARY DANGER"

LONDON, Tuesday (PTA). — "The House of Commons watches with anxiety and sympathy the position of our men in Palestine, and with horror the danger to which they are unnecessarily exposed," declared the Rt. Hon. Oliver Stanley, during a brief reference to Palestine in a debate on the Colonies today.

Cabinet to Review Military Needs

EARLY SHOWDOWN IN CRISIS EXPECTED

By JON KIMCHE, Special to The Palestine Post.

LONDON, Tuesday.— Field-Marshal Montgomery's sudden recall from his Pacific tour is said to be due to the Cabinet's request to the War Office for an immediate reassessment of British military requirements in the Middle East and Germany, with a view to drastically cutting them down.

The crisis atmosphere lessened somewhat today with an inspired editorial in the "Daily Herald" entitled "Crisis" which acknowledged the seriousness of the situation, but stated categorically that there will not be a coalition.

Meanwhile, Mr. Attlee has had discussions with leading Ministers and received a long letter signed by Messrs. Crossman and Ben Levy, making serious categorical demands. In Downing Street it is stated that there is no Cabinet crisis as such, but it is known that on a number of specific issues serious differences have arisen among the Ministers.

The campaign in the Conservative press and also among some Trade Union M.P.'s for "Bevin for Prime Minister" is discounted in Government circles, where it is suggested that whatever changes Mr. Attlee may make, it is out of the question that he will give up the Premiership.

City Reacts

The crisis is also reflected in a general unsettling of the stock exchange and the marking down of all types of shares, but there is nothing that can be called panic-selling. The Government still has the financial situation firmly in hand, although there is now also a propaganda campaign in certain Opposition circles for the devaluation of the sterling.

In view of the accumulation of these factors, an early showdown between the Government and the Opposition is expected, and tomorrow's meeting may take the form of an appeal by Mr. Attlee to the Party, to unite to face this Opposition drive against the Labour Government. Critics are, however, at present not in the mood to accept this, unless it is combined with undertakings by the Government to take firm measures on outstanding domestic and foreign policy issues.

New York Stocks Break

NEW YORK, Tuesday (UP). — Stocks broke sharply on a heavy volume of late afternoon trading.

Shortly after 2 p.m. the tape was two minutes behind, with prices down one to four points. Wheat broke as much as 5-5/8 cents a bushel. Cotton lost $4.50 a bale.

INDONESIANS BOMB 2 DUTCH-HELD TOWNS

BATAVIA, Tuesday. — The Indonesian "Air Force", in its first combat operation, bombed two Dutch-held towns in Java today, one of them Samarang on the North Coast, and the other Salatiga, in the eastern sector of the island. This was announced by Jogjakarta radio, which stated that the raiding aircraft had evaded two Dutch fighter planes and returned to their base undamaged. Pamphlets as well as bombs were dropped on Semarang, it is stated.

An Indonesian communique said that Republican ground troops had shot down two Dutch fighter planes near Mantoep, in Eastern Java, and that the area north of Mantoep was now in control of Indonesian troops.

According to today's Dutch communique, two oil wells in the Socony Vacuum fields at Pendopo, 100 miles south-east of Palembang in Sumatra, have been set on fire.

An Indonesian radio report, picked up in Sumatra, states that two days ago, a Dutch submarine had shelled the Japanese coast in the Sunda Strait (between Java and Sumatra) and had fired on the town or Labuan.

The radio also said that an Indonesian mercy plane, flying medical aid to the beleaguered Republican capital of Jogjakarta had been shot down by two Dutch Mustangs tonight as it was landing on an airport just outside the city. All seven occupants, including two British pilots and a woman, are reported to have been injured.

UP. & Reuter)

Russia Accepts Invitation

By SYLVAIN MANGEOT, Reuters Diplomatic Correspondent

LONDON, Tuesday. — The Soviet Government has accepted Britain's invitation to a conference of the Foreign Ministers Deputies, to meet in London at the beginning of October, it was officially stated by a Foreign Office spokesman today. The invitation was sent simultaneously three weeks ago to Washington, Paris and Moscow.

The Russian reply is the first official answer, though the French Government has given its approval in principle to the Deputies' meeting in London, without the mention of a fixed date. No American reply has yet been made.

NO UNSCOP COMMENT ON TRIPLE HANGING

GENEVA, Tuesday (UP). — Members of the U.N. Special Committee on Palestine refrained from official comment on the execution of the three Irgun members at Acre this morning. Individual delegates said that the matter was an internal Palestine issue.

The Yugoslav member said, however, that he personally regretted the executions, especially since the three condemned men had not killed anybody while attempting to aid the escape of prisoners from the Acre fortress.

After Midnight

A Dutch spokesman said yesterday his Government saw no reason to oppose the request to bring the Indonesian conflict before the U.N.

M. Gromyko, in the Security Council, yesterday vetoed the entire U.S. proposal to keep the Border Investigating Commission in the Balkans.

Reversing its declaration of independence made over six weeks ago, Travancore, has decided to join the Dominion of India.

Pandit Nehru, will be the Indian Union's first Prime Minister, Mahatma Gandhi told a prayer meeting last night.

THE PALESTINE POST

JERUSALEM
SUNDAY, NOV. 30, 1947

PRICE: 20 MILS
VOL. XXII. No. 6571

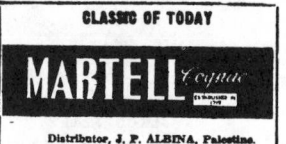

PARTITION APPROVED BY MORE THAN 2/3; 33 TO 13

FLUSHING MEADOW, Saturday (U.P.) — When the plan for the Partition of Palestine and the setting up of Jewish and Arab States appeared certain of enough votes to pass the General Assembly today, the Arab States in a last-ditch effort to prevent this, proposed the establishment of a federated state based on the canton system in which the Jews and Arabs would be separated as far as possible.

The Arab motion, which was attacked as a move to sabotage the U.N. Partition plan, was opposed by the rapporteur of the Ad Hoc Committee, Mr. Thors, and by the delegate of the United States, Mr. H. Johnson, who asked the Chairman, Dr. Aranha, to call for a vote on the Ad Hoc Committee's recommendation for Partition. Mr. Aranha ruled that the delegates would have to vote on the partition plan after hearing last minute appeals by Iran and Syria. Mr. Johnson, said:"There is nothing conciliatory in this," and he was supported by the Soviet Delegate. The vote was taken; 33 said Yes, 13 No and 10 abstained; One was absent.

24-Hour Delay Follows Colombian Resolution

FLUSHING MEADOW Saturday. — The Colombian delegate, Senor Alfonso Lopez, opened yesterday afternoon's session of the U.N. Assembly with a surprise manoeuvre, suggesting that the U.N. defer its vote and make a last-minute attempt at guiding the Arabs and Jews to a settlement.

"With so many abstentions and negative votes registered in the Ad Hoc Committee," he said, "Partition will remain a minority plan, even if it got the required two-thirds majority in the Assembly." It was irrelevant at the last minute to try and influence another few delegates to endorse the proposal — that would not give it world backing. One should not ignore the fact that the Moslem delegations opposed it en bloc, and it was significant in the Ad Hoc Committee China and France had not seen eye to eye with the U.S. and U.S.S.R. His new plan would leave the question of Palestine in the consideration stage until well into Spring next year.

His proposal was to give the Ad Hoc Committee the character of an interim subsidiary organ of the General Assembly, to carry on the study of the Palestine question with a view to finding a satisfactory solution. This Committee should be authorised

to take necessary steps to bring about agreement between the Arabs and Jews as to the future Government of that country;

to request, if it deems necessary, the advisory opinion of the International Court of Justice;

to formulate complete recommendations as to the manner in which the U.N. may give effect to its unanimous recommendations and to report on its work not later than February 29, 1948.

He proposed that member states shall advise not later than April 15, 1948, whether they wish to consider the matter at a special Assembly session.

"We have limited but ample time, as the Mandatory will not complete the evacuation until August next year." Thus, if the Palestine Committee was allowed to continue its work and report before the end of February, that would give ample time to convene — if necessary — a special session in Spring.

When the Colombian delegate left the rostrum, the President of the Assembly, Dr. Aranha, announced that the proposal would be put to the vote later in the session.

M. Alexandre Parodi, of France, then sprang the second surprise in proposing a 24-hour adjournment in the hope of some last-minute conciliatory move. He based his proposal on the statements of Sir Mohammed Zafrullah Khan (Pakistan) and Dr. Fahdil Jamali (Iraq) who earlier in the debate had suggested that the door to conciliation was still open.

"This overture comes quite late in the game, and it might be asked whether it is not merely an attempt to delay the moment of decision," he said later. However, he considered the question too grave and complicated to allow any chance to be left aside, "even a faint one," of making a peaceful settlement based on agreement.

M. Parodi opened his short statement with explaining the present position was — either Partition or nothing, and that he did not like being pushed to this extremity.

After the Ethiopian delegate declared he would abstain, the Chairman declared the debate closed and put the French proposal to the vote. The Assembly decided by 25 votes to 15 votes to adjourn for 24 hours, after M. Oscar Lange of Poland had made a short but ardent plea against the deferment, and so did the Colombian delegate — for different reasons.

(Reuter, UP, Palcor)

ARABS PROPOSE ALTERNATIVE

FLUSHING MEADOW, Saturday. — The tenseness of the last few hours at the U.N. Assembly when it was believed that voting on the Palestine question would finally be taken was evidenced tonight by the packed public galleries, with crowds larger than ever in the chequered history of the United Nations.

For the first time in the history of the United Nations, uniformed police appeared at all strategic points of the public and press galleries.

M. Chamoun's soft spoken approach reportedly did not have the support of Jamal Eff. Husseini, who as spokesman for the Arabs of Palestine, recently threatened to hurl the entire Arab world of 70 million persons against any Jewish State created in the Middle East. The Arabs had held off until the last possible moment and until passage of partition seemed assured.

Mr. Johnson said: "I submit that the conditions outlined by the delegate of France have not been fulfilled. The purpose of the adjournment was to permit conciliation. No conciliation plan is before the Assembly now. The Lebanon "has no more to do with conciliation than Austria or China. There is no mention of conciliation between the Jewish Agency and the Arab Higher Committee."

The Iran delegate suggested that the question should be referred back to the Ad Hoc Committee for further study during a "number of weeks." The Chairman ruled the proposal to be put in writing and called on Faris Bey el-Khoury, Syria, who appealed to the delegates to look for a solution other than Partition, which he said was impossible of implementation.

The Syrian delegate read a letter from Dr. Evatt to Prince Feisal of Saudi Arabia dated November 1, inviting him to confer with Mr. George Marshall on conciliation efforts. The Saudi reply accepted the suggestion but, Faris Bey maintained, nothing was done, the Ad Hoc Committee concentrating on partition. He therefore appealed for further time for conciliation efforts, in order to avert violenve and bloodshed.

The Chairman announced he could not put the Iranian motion — which he considered a new one — until the Partition proposal was voted and decided. "Now we proceed to vote" said Dr. Aranha, at 12.20 a.m. (Palestine time) when M. Chamoun for the Lebanon was given the floor on "a point of order."

Dr. Aranha ruled that the Lebanese proposal was out of order. Voting began at 12.27 a.m. Palestine time and was concluded by 12.30 a.m.

Mr. Gromyko was the last speaker pending the written translation of the Iranian adjournment motion. He said nothing was changed in the 24 hours during which the Assembly stood adjourned: it was a question that had remained unsettled for 25 years. The Lebanese proposals did not change the position "one iota," although it was the same proposal as the UNSCOP alternative which the Arabs, for reasons of their own, had not even wished to discuss. The U.N. had taken the question on itself and must settle it; the Assembly must proceed to a vote without delay. The Soviet delegation would support Partition in the Assembly as it had done in the Ad Hoc Committee.

The Chairman then read the Iranian motion asking for adjournment until January 15, 1948.

ARAB STATES PREPARE TO FIGHT ABDULLAH

By JON KIMCHE, Special to The Palestine Post

LONDON, Saturday.—Representatives of the Arab States here express serious disquiet following reports that King Abdullah's Arab Legion will occupy the Arab State sector of Palestine when the British withdraw. One British source normally very close to these representatives has stated, however, that what will happen, according to his information, is rather different.

The Arab Legion, together with a token force from Iraq will occupy, he said, the central sector of the Palestine Arab State. Syria and the Lebanon will occupy the coastal stretch of the Arab State north of Acre, and Egypt, with a token Saudi Arabian force, will occupy parts of the Negev and the desert frontier area.

What will happen after such a "partition of partitioned Palestine," he added, is anybody's guess, but one thing is certain: that the Arab States will not accept Trans-Jordan taking over by itself, and that Trans-Jordan will oppose Syrian and Lebanese inroads.

British Personnel

This has raised again more acutely the question of the position of British officers and personnel seconded for service in Trans-Jordan. The position is that the status of these military and civilian officials is still not decided. When the British Administration leaves Palestine, a new agreement with Trans-Jordan is to be negotiated on lines similar to that negotiated with India, which would allow for continued service by British officials in Trans-Jordan. Special consideration, however, is to be given to the position of Glubb Pasha.

The Colonial Office is at present engaged in straightening out this situation, but a Foreign Office source today stated categorically that the British Government would not allow a situation to arise where a high British officer would be responsible for leading a foreign army against either the prospective Jewish State or against other Arab States or against a U.N. force. This has been interpreted as foreshadowing the probable early withdrawal of Glubb Pasha and other high-ranking officers in executive positions in the Trans-Jordan army. The possibility, however, that they may remain in Trans-Jordan's service in a purely advisory capacity is now under consideration.

PAKISTAN, IRAQ TALK OF RECONCILIATION

FLUSHING MEADOW, Saturday. — The first speaker in yesterday's debate was the delegate of Pakistan, Sir Mohammed Zafrullah Khan, who recalled the "mortal struggle" in which the Allies had been drawn not long ago, when the Arabs were called upon to redress the balance in the Middle East, and they threw in their lot with the Allies.

What legal right had the world to cut up Palestine, he asked, warning the nations of the West that tomorrow they might need friends and allies in the Middle East. "I appeal to you," he said, "not to wrong your friends."

From North Africa to Central Asia, Sir Mohammed said, there were doubts and distrust of the motives and statements of the Western Powers. "You take the gravest risks of impairing any chance of real cooperation between East and West by thus forcibly driving what amounts to a western wedge into the heart of the Middle East."

UNSCOP had recommended that all UN members take refugees and D.P.'s to alleviate their lot. What had the General Assembly done in that respect? Sub-Committee Two had put forward the same recommendation; it had asked that D.P.'s and refugees "shall be distributed among member states according to their capacity to receive them." The U.S., which was "so humanitarian" had made no effort to take refugees but recommended that they go to Palestine. That was the contribution to the solution of the problem by that "august power."

The proposed Jewish and Arab States would each consist of three parts. Was that justice? And Jerusalem would remain forever under international jurisdiction. The Holy City would never belong to the Arabs, she would always be different. "What authority, legal authority, have you to do this," he asked. The whole scheme lacked legal and constitutional authority, Sir Mohammad asserted, imploring delegates not to accept it. "Will you take the responsibility?"

Economic Board

The Joint Economic Board was as illegal as the U.N. administration of Jerusalem. Sir Mohammad then went into detail as concerns boundaries, minorities etc. to claim that injustice was being done to the Arabs, and he drew particular attention to the Negev where far more Arabs were now living, but which was to be given to the Jews.

He also invited the attention of delegates to "that eminent, highly respected Jew," Dr. Magnes, who had always stood for political unity. It was a fallacy, he said, to think that once economic unity was established, political unity would follow. But the Arabs of Palestine and the Arab States would not cooperate.

Mr. Johnson of the U.S., he said, had expressed the hope that, given the support of the surrounding Arab States and the people of Palestine, the experiment might work. "But the Arabs of Palestine have declared that they are not going to cooperate—and remember," he warned, "this is not an experiment; it is proposed as a permanent solution."

"The United Nations was in honour bound to seek to unite and bring together, rather than divide," he concluded. Let it make a last attempt at bringing together. "Let us decide here today to promote and foster peace, prosperity and welfare for all, Jew, Arab and Gentile alike, which shall redound to our glory forever."

In a brief statement, the Chinese delegate informed the Assembly that as per instructions received from Nanking, China would not support Partition, but abstain from voting. His country maintained that any solution of the problem must be based on the consent of the peoples immediately concerned.

China's Abstention

China had right from the beginning of the Ad Hoc Committee's work sought to bring about cooperation between the Jews and the Arabs in search of a settlement. Unfortunately, the two plans submitted by the Sub Committees represented a set of diametrically opposed views that could not be reconciled. It had then been hoped that the plan of Sub-Committee One could be modified in such a way as to be "if not satisfactory to both, at least less objectionable to either." That, too, had not been achieved.

Dr. G. Granados, of Guatemala recalled that the Arab Higher Executive would not even listen to UNSCOP's chairman, Judge Sandstrom, and had intimated that they did not seem to be in favour of conciliation. "UNSCOP went out to call at the doors of the Arabs and were received in villages, where it did not notice the hostility accorded to them by Arab leaders."

He gave instances of the Arab boycott against the Jews, to prove that conciliation was not possible, not because the Jews did not want it, but because of the Arabs' animosity.

The unitary system proposed by the Arab Higher Executive and supported by the other Arab States would mean immediate persecution and enslavement for the Jews. A Jewish State had to be established; the world owed that to the Jews. There was no alternative, he concluded.

Mr. Ernest Dihigo announced that Cuba would oppose Partition "despite the pressure brought to bear upon us." Cuba had shown sympathy to the Jews and appreciated their qualities. "We have allowed into our own territory thousands of Jews, and they live amongst us free and without discrimination of any kind. We cannot, however, vote here according ordinate position" who had previously been the rightful owners of the country. Cuba urged that the Assembly should wait a few months, rather than hurry a bad solution.

Dr. Fahdil Jamali, the Iraqi delegate, spoke for over an hour alleging that "great pressure" was being brought to bear on the anti-Partitionists and that power politics were "playing havoc" with the independence of UN members.

Laughter broke out, and Dr. Aranha pounded his gavel on the table, when Dr. Jamali asserted that 150,000 Jews in Iraq shared "equal rights with the Arabs," and again when he asserted that some power was using "infiltration methods as the Nazis did in the past"; and that immigrants from Black Sea ports were "subversive discordant elements."

He warned that any injustice imposed on Palestine "will have serious effects on the harmony between the Jews and non-Jews of Iraq." Palestine was a Holy Land, and Partition would only dissect its holiness. Why did the Jews not fight for the retention of Jerusalem in their State, he asked. Jerusalem was said to be their Holy City, and if the Jews "acquiesce in having Jerusalem separated from the Jewish State, then why don't they want to establish their Jewish State in another part of the world, such as the U.S., Australia or Birobidjan?"

Three times during his speech, Dr. Jamali referred to great power pressure trying to make the Partition plan work. Asserting that no serious attempt had been made at conciliation, Dr. Jamali referred to Article 14 of the Charter which recommended peaceful adjustment. "No member here present can claim that an effort at peaceful settlement has been made," he declared.

Where, he asked, would the armed force to implement Partition come from. The States who would be asked to send troops to Palestine would be considered enemies of the Arab world. Thus, the plan would achieve nothing but breed prejudice and hatred.

Was it not better to let both parties sort out their disputes by themselves? That could not produce more chaos, not only in Palestine, but all around it. However, Dr. Jamali asserted,

MASS ESCAPE TUNNEL FOUND IN LATRUN

A tell-tale crack in the floor of a hut led to the uncovering on Friday morning of a mass-escape plan from the Latrun Detention Camp.

Inspecting the camp shortly before noon, a Senior Police Officer noticed a crack in the flooring of one room. Probing, he found an escape chamber linked to a shaft, about 100 metres long, leading to the perimeter fence. Inside were an electric drill, electric lighting and air ventilation.

The Officer raised the alarm, and some of the detainees stoned the Police, slightly injuring a British Sergeant and Constable.

Meanwhile, four detainees were released from Latrun on Friday after their parents had posted LP.500 bonds for each of them. They are to remain under police supervision.

Three are from Haifa and one from Jerusalem.

Lebanese Mission Arrives in Baghdad

BAGHDAD, Saturday. — The Lebanese President, Sheikh Bishara Khouri, arrived here this morning accompanied by his Premier, Riad Bey es Solh, the Defence Minister, Emir Majid Arslan and a number of other Deputies.

The party was met at the airport by the Regent of Iraq, Emir Abdul Illah, the Premier, Saleh Jabr, and other Senators

Paris Police Get Reinforcements
FRANCE CONSIDERS ANTI-STRIKE BILL

PARIS, Saturday (Reuter). — Paris police were reinforced and on the alert for trouble tonight as news was received of four big Communist meetings to be held in the capital while the Assembly debated the Government's new severe anti-strike bill.

This followed police confiscation of special editions of the Communist newspapers "Humanite" and "Ce Soir." The latter described the bill as "a reactionary coup d'etat" and announced in bold headlines "the republic is in danger."

"Humanite" said: "The 'American party' is about to tear up the Constitution. A coup d'etat is to be carried out tonight at midnight. Workers, Democrats, Patriots—you have the power to prevent this crime."

In the Assembly, Premier Schuman, introducing the Bill to restrain strikers, declared that responsibility for it lay with the Communists. They in turn claimed that it was "worse than anything Napoleon thought of."

With about two million workers idle, crippling industries and public services, Mr. Schuman asked for an immediate passage of the Bill which provides for the call up of 80,000 more reservists to service in the Mobile Republican Guard, and prison terms and fines of up to 500,000 francs for people found guilty of obstructing workers.

Official sources said that the Bill, if passed today, would become effective at 2300 hours GMT tomorrow, November 30, and remain in force until 2300 hours, GMT., May 31, 1948.

The door for renewed negotiations between the Government and the General Confederation of Labour was left open by M. Pierre Lebrun, the Secretary General of the C.G.T., who indicated that there might be negotiations between the Government and the Confederation before the Assembly began debating the anti-strike Bill. Many informed observers believed that the Government might accept the overture.

CAIRO PAPER COMES OUT FOR PARTITION

CAIRO, Saturday.—While Azzam Pasha, Secretary-General of the Arab League, repeated his threat of the use of force against Partition if it is decided on by the United Nations, the influential daily "Al Mokattam" came out today with an editorial supporting Partition.

This is the first time that any important Arab voice in the Middle East has pronounced publicly for Partition, and Arab circles in Cairo are reported to be amazed at the article.

The paper wrote: "We stand for Partition because we believe that it is the best final solution for the problem of Palestine. If rejection of Partition would solve the problem we would have welcomed it, but in fact it will lead to further complications and will give the Zionists another space of time to complete their plans of defence and attack."

Failure of the U.N. to come to a decision now would, "Al Mokattam" considers, lead to a delay of one more year, which would not benefit the Arabs but would benefit the Jews, especially after the British evacuation, when, the paper thinks, the U.N. would be unable to keep order in the country.

Azzam Pasha, who returned to Cairo from Saudi-Arabia, told pressmen that a decision in favour of Partition would lead to war in the Middle East.

Activity has been evident at Arab League headquarters here in connection with the forthcoming meeting of the League's Council. Sheikh Sami El Khoury, the Lebanese Minister, consulted his Government by telephone on Thursday. Dr. Fawzi Bey El Mulky, the Trans-Jordan Minister, had a long conference at the League's offices. It is reported that Faris Eff. El Khoury, the Syrian delegate at Lake Success, and Camille Eff. Chamoun, the Lebanese representative, have been called to the Arab League Council's meeting.

In Damascus, a communique from the Ministry of the Interior reminds the press that no news concerning troop movements may be published.

(ANA, Reuter, AFP)

("Al Mokattam" is owned and published by Dr. Nimr, father of Lady Smart, whose husband was for many years Oriental Secretary at the British Embassy in Cairo, and of Mrs. Kate Antonius of Jerusalem).

British Lobbying

FLUSHING MEADOW, Saturday (UP). — Feverish last-minute lobbying is going on in the Assembly hall and the corridors.

Although Britain has officially professed a position of neutrality, a tall blond Britain busily mingled with the Latin American delegation urging them to refrain from supporting Partition.

The Briton was the British Legation's liaison officer for the Latin American nations.

CAIRO STUDENTS STONE POLICE

CAIRO, Saturday (AP). — Students shouting against capitalism, the Egyptian Prime Minister, Nokrashi Pasha, and the "Truman-Attlee Axis" engaged in a stone throwing bout with the police today at Fouad University which opened this morning after being closed during the cholera epidemic.

The police tried to limit the students admitted to the small number who have paid University fees and had identity cards, but the remainder forced the police cordon at one of the University's iron doors.

Inside they roamed the halls shouting "Capitalism evacuate... education for all... long live Russia our ally . . . mobs are the leaders of the people . . . no education by dollars . . . down with the Truman-Attlee Axis... Nokrashi, enemy of the people . . . where is evacuation?"

A force of about 500 police, armed with rifles and clubs, was attacked by stone-throwing students and some policemen threw the stones back despite contrary orders from their officers. The exchange lasted for 15 minutes until a police officer raised a white handkerchief and a truce was arranged.

1,420 VISALESS IMMIGRANTS COME BACK TO PALESTINE

Palestine Post Bureau

HAIFA, Saturday. — Their number carefully checked, 1,420 mothers, fathers and infants had boarded the Ocean Vigour in Cyprus on a special transfer to Palestine, but 1,421 left Haifa Harbour yesterday.

One of them was born in the Port itself, in the Quarantine Section of the Health Department.

His mother, Mrs. Simha Nahmani, was rushed over in a lighter while the ship was still standing in the roadstead, and later she was taken to Moladah Hospital.

The morning was high, and hot as midsummer, by the time the Ocean Vigour (on its first trip here since Hamburg) was moored, its caged human cargo singing and cheering. There was a large party on the jetty to meet the young parents and their babies, who had been sent out of their turn through the generosity of other refugees. Ambulances of the Red Shield Society waited alongside the ship as an oblong wooden "bucket" was slowly lowered by a boom, with a cargo of three — a mother, her three-day-old baby and a soldier who held the stretcher steady. To avoid the jarring trip down the long, steep gangplank, eight such loads of women and their babies born this week were swung off in a smooth transfer. Four were taken to the Ezra Hospital here and four to Moladah. Six infants were sent to the Hadassah Hospital in Tel Aviv.

Tubs from Tins

Then the refugees marched down the gangplank, fathers holding tightly to well-padded tubs made from petrol tins in which babies bobbed up and down. Mothers, many with childish faces themselves, followed. Soldiers carried the bigger children. One man, balancing a tub with a baby on his head, oriental-fashion, brought watchers hearts to their mouths, but he seemed to know what he was about. Some of the women were met by their husbands, who, for reasons of health, had not been deported to Cyprus.

An old woman waited for hours on the jetty. She wore a heavy black dress, a black woollen coat and a long black lace shawl. She told how seven sons and daughters had been killed in Poland, by bayonets, bullets, gas-chamber. An eighth son, Mordechai Sorin, had fled. She had come to Palestine only a few weeks ago "on a proper ship, like a princess," because she had been told her son was here. And now he was coming ed her came down the gangplank, and then he held her hard in his arms, and kissed her mouth to stifle her wailing, and everyone turned away. Her daughter-in-law and granddaughter were among those sent to hospital.

Cheering Rhythm

The cheerful rhythm of refugees filing down the gangplank was resumed, and the fleet of 33 Egged buses filled with quietly contented people and squalling babies. At 2.30 the first bus reached Raanana, where the Jewish Agency transit camp had been prepared for their arrival. Thirty six nurses and assistants, graduates of the WIZO Mothercraft School and the institutions of the Working Mother's Organization, will take care of the babies, and 40 women from Raanana and nearby kibbutzim have been enrolled. Dr. J. Roth, pediatrician of the Hadassah Hospital in Jerusalem will spend the first 10 days there, and medical service will be provided by the Jewish Agency.

The Government has waived immigration certificates for the 467 babies under two who came yesterday, but deducted them for the 912 parents and 41 older children.

The Jewish Distribution Committee, which had been responsible for the Cyprus Children's Camp, will continue to take care of the more than 150 babies who remained there and the newborns who are coming at the rate of two and three a day.

The immigrants were accompanied from Cyprus by Dr. W. Falk and five Palestinian nurses. On the quay they were met by Mrs. Goldie Myerson, Mr. Eliahu Dobkin, Dr. Grushka, and Mr. P. Litvak of the J.D.C.

(Raanana — Page 3)

TWO DEAD IN PLANE CRASH

Palestine Post Reporter

NATHANYA, Saturday.— Two men were killed when a private Czech-made "Bi-Bi" single-engined bi-plane, belonging to Mr. Z. Levinson, co-owner of the "Michael" silversmith[illegible], crashed near Beit [illegible] smallholders settlement shortly after noon today. The victims were Mr. Levinson, who piloted the aircraft, and his friend, Mr. Ernst Mendelson, a BOAC engineer who took the flight while off duty.

The plane took off from Lydda Airport before noon and turned towards Beit Itshak, 25 kilometres away. Mendelson had informed his brother, Walter, a settler there, that he would be flying over.

The plane cruised over the houses, and settlers came out of their homes waving. While the plane was in a steep bank, and flying low, its engine stopped suddenly.

The machine was then seen to rise to about 50 metres, and then crashed to the earth between the village well and central stores. Both men were thrown out of the plane, Mr. Mendelson being killed instantly. Mr. Levinson died shortly afterwards.

"Hunch" Disregarded

Mr. Levinson, who was a R.A.F. engineer during the war, purchased the plane some years ago and used it at least twice weekly. It was tested twice before it took off this morning. A pilot friend P. Constable Gruenberg, of Tel Aviv Div. H.Q., who flew along on the test flight, insisted that he had a "hunch" and begged Levinson not to fly. The two friends discussed the matter heatedly, and finally Levinson pushed Gruenberg aside and switched on the engine. Thirty minutes later, Gruenberg, who was waiting at the airport for the plane to return, was informed that it had crashed.

Levinson leaves a wife and three children.

KAPLAN LEAVES FOR U.S.

Dr. Moshe Sneh, of the Jewish Agency Executive, returned by Air France to Palestine from Paris on Friday morning.

Mr. Eliezer Kaplan, the Agency Treasurer, left by air for America, where he is to take part in the United Jewish Appeal conference.

After Midnight

THE PALESTINE POST

SPECIAL EDITION

JERUSALEM
Monday, Feb. 2, 1948
PRICE: 20 MILS
VOL. XXIII No. 6627

Printed for the Jerusalem Press Ltd. at Hamadpis Liphshitz Press Jerusalem

COLUMN ONE

By

David Courtney

THE truth is louder than TNT and burns brighter than the flames of arson. It will win in the end. Last night's bomb smashed machinery, burned precious records, made people homeless, injured some; but the target was plain truth. It is surprising what some men will do to destroy truth. The tyrant, the Fascist, the fool and the ignorant victims of any one or all of these have tried to suppress the truth since history began; and tried vainly. They are still at their monstrous folly.

WHAT was done last night is an incident among many in the brutal history of this land. It was nothing new to see flames and hear the groans of hurt men. It was nothing new to see little children and old women and stumbling men silhouetted against fire as they hurried silently away from their homes. That is the modern history of Palestine. It is the recent history of the Mandate. It will be said in London that it is the consequence of the judgment of the earth's United Nations. To say just that accusingly, is to be in part responsible for the evil that is done.

THE bomb in Hassolel Street for a moment closed the mouths of the messengers of the world; and shut off, as a telephone is shut off, the news from a score of capitals. It did but throw into still sharper relief, and sound with still farther-reaching voice, the truth of this land and the sureness of its triumph. And that truth will be told. The men who did last night's deed probably overlooked that. There is nothing they can do about it now or at any time. It has escaped them. It makes their triumph short-lived and hollow.

Jerusalem, February 2.

COMMISSION'S FIRST REPORT

Palestine Post Correspondent

LAKE SUCCESS, Sunday. — Tomorrow will be a crucial day for the Yishuv — as the Five-Nation Palestine Commission hands its first report to the Security Council.

If the Commissioners are determined to see the Assembly's resolution implemented, the report will contain a strong indictment of Britain, who has in all her actions obstructed the Commission's work rather than helped.

The five Commissioners will hold a press conference at 3 o'clock in the afternoon (10 p.m. Palestine time)).

At the same time, the sixth session of the U.N. Social and Economic Council opens tomorrow, and Dr. Charles Malik of the Lebanon is certain to be elected Chairman. The only opposition will come from countries of the Slav Bloc and some Latin American Republics who want to see a delegate of their blocs elected.

Dr. Malik has long been held in great esteem by U.N. members, because of his intellectual abilities and wide experience. As chairman of the Social and Economic Council he will be responsible for the establishment of economic unity in partitioned Palestine.

Dr. Malik's appointment as such would not be of vital importance to the Jews, but the fact that his candidacy is being supported by the U.S., may be another pointer of America's intention to follow a bi-partisan policy which would in the end bring about some sort of Morrison-Grady plan.

The Jerusalem Working Committee has been busy completing its report which is due to be submitted to the Trusteeship Council on February 11. Here the Jerusalem delegates, Dr. Eliash and Mr. Auster have done a great deal of constructive work and sheer logic has succeeded to some extent in face of the considerable lack of enthusiasm of the delegates which has been evident there.

PALESTINE POST PRESS AND OFFICES DESTROYED

Bomb and Fire Gut Three Buildings

EXPLOSION ROCKS JERUSALEM

The Palestine Post and two adjacent buildings at the top of Hassolel Street were wrecked by an explosion and a fire that followed last night. A five-ton army-type lorry drove up the narrow street shortly after 10.45 and parked outside the press room. An explosion a few minutes later rocked a large part of the city and smashed windows and doors within a radius of almost a mile.

As *The Palestine Post* goes to press this morning, prepared in borrowed office space, its editorial offices and the Jerusalem Press are smoking ruins.

About 20 persons were hurt by the blast and flying glass, nine of them seriously. It is not yet known whether the United Press wireless operator who is usually in the building at that time reached safety or not.

The pressmen seriously hurt are: Zalman Levin, Shimshon Lifshitz, Aharon Tanachi, Yitzhak Tawil and Nathan Rabinovitz.

Others wounded are: Benjamin Meyuhas, Victoria Meyuhas, Judith Ash, Zipora Shimoni, Banin Tamanni, Weinberg (watchman), Harry Mardler, Zina Mardler, Jaacov Shtrevneh, and Ruth Shtrevneh.

The blast came with a dull red flash that reached the level of the upper stories of the two buildings, sending glass spinning across the rooms, shaking workers and tenants, cutting them about the face and toppling furniture. On some floors the lights went out adding to the confusion.

Workers and tenants hurried out of the buildings. The slightly wounded and uninjured helped the seriously hurt to the Hadassah Clearing Clinic a few metres up the road, edging past a blazing ambulance. In the Jerusalem Press, on the ground floor of the building, the blast sent pieces of lead flying through the air.

The last injured man to be brought out of the press, when it was thick with smoke and dust and stiflingly hot, was rescued by Mr. John Donovan, the Jerusalem correspondent of the N.B.C., who was on his way to *The Palestine Post* when the explosion occurred. Another foreign correspondent who helped in the rescue work was Mr. Fitzhugh Turner of the "New York Herald-Tribune," who climbed the stairs into the burning building in search of victims, together with three British constables and had to jump from an upper story when he was cut off from the stair

(*Continued on page 2*)

Nehru Weeps For Gandhi

NEW DELHI, Sunday (AP). — Pandit Nehru wept tonight when he placed a floral tribute beside Gandhi's ashes.

Part of Gandhi's ashes will be cast into the sacred Jumma River at Delhi near where he was cremated, but some of the bones will be carried later to other sacred rivers and cast there to symbolize the universal love between him and the people.

Crowds gathered today near Birla House. Some knelt down to touch the ground with their heads as an indication of grief and as a symbolic act signifying their desire to transfer to themselves what they consider to be Ghandi's saintliness.

MAHASABHA ACCUSED

Police refused to discuss anything which might have been told them by Narayan Vinayak Godse, who is held as Gandhi's assassin. They identified him as active in the Hindu Mahasabha leadership and as a vigorous critic of Gandhi.

Delhi newspapers carried stories today asserting that they had learned that Godse had made statements implicating several persons in several parts of India as members of a conspiracy to kill Gandhi. His statement was said to have uncovered the existence of a gang operating in Delhi, Bombay, East Punjab and West Bengal. The newspaper alleged that this group was responsible for placing the bomb which exploded near Gandhi not many days before the assassination.

The paper also linked this group with the man found with a hand grenade in his pocket who was arrested at a meeting addressed in Amritsar recently by Nehru. Both men are still held incommunicado.

Bombay Police Fire at Rioters

BOMBAY, Sunday (Reuter). — Police opened fire early today to disperse angry crowds which persisted in attacking the residences of Hindu Mahasabha leaders and supporters in northern Bombay. A tense situation was reported to have developed and police reinforcements, supported by military, were sent to the areas.

Gandhi's accused assassin, Naturam Vinyak Godse, once belonged to the Mahasabha. Rioting, looting and burning of Mahasabha members' homes and business premises ocurred in Bombay, Poona and Kolhapup, after Ghandi's cremation yesterday.

In north Bombay, several casualties were reported and police opened fire several times.

At Poona today, an angry crowd attempted to set fire to the house of a leader of a militant Hindu organization soon after the curfew in the city was lifted. Troops and police intervened.

USTACHIS JOIN ARABS

By SAM SOUKI, U.P. Correspondent

BEIRUT, Sunday. — Twenty-five Yugoslav Moslems, said to have been members of Pavlevitch's Ustachis who during the war fought alongside the Nazis against the Allies, have arrived in Beirut and have gone on to Syria for training as volunteers to fight against the Jews of Palestine.

One of them, however, has been arrested, as it was alleged that he was a "Jewish spy."

Altogether there are now 40 Yugoslav Moslems in camps in Southern Syria. The Syrian authorities are determined to keep them there, despite

280 Deported To Cyprus

HAIFA, Sunday. — On the day on which Britain was to have opened a free port to Jewish immigration, as recommended by the United Nations General Assembly, the Royal Navy today intercepted a small schooner with 280 men, women and children on board. The Navy was more vigilant in maintaining its blockade than the Army in guarding the land frontiers across which a steady stream of armed Arabs has been coming for the past month.

The ship, called the "35 Heroes of Kfar Etzion," was boarded without incident early this morning. It was brought into Haifa shortly after noon.

Transhipment to the Empire Rival was a sea-borne operation. The refugees were taken from the schooner aboard the cruiser, Phoebe, alongside which they were moored, and after passing through fumigation tents, were taken across to the Empire Rival which sailed for Cyprus in the afternoon.

CABLES IN BRIEF

STUDENTS from the Farouk I University in Alexandria yesterday staged anti-Government demonstrations and stoned the police who fired at them.

A TURKISH motor-boat was attacked and boarded by an armed motor-boat of unknown nationality off Samos island yesterday. Turkish coastguards opened fire and the ship escaped out to sea.

THE FRANCO-SPANISH frontier will probably be reopened in the next fortnight. The desirability of a change in Spanish-French relations is understood to have been agreed upon in semi-official talks in Madrid.

ITALY and the U.S. will today sign a trade and financial agreement which will re-open economic cooperation between the two States after a lapse of ten years.

SOVIET revenue exceeded expenditure in 1947 by 24,000 million roubles, said the Soviet Finance Minister in a budget speech to the Supreme Soviet yesterday.

THREE THOUSAND Singapore workers struck yesterday as a protest against the new federation of Malaya.

Syrian Currency Breaks from Franc

DAMASCUS, Sunday (AP). — The Syrian currency was separated definitely from the French franc as from this morning, and it is now intended to create a purely national currency backed by a healthy export-import policy.

Rumours that this separation was sought in order to attach Syria to the sterling area were authoritatively denied. The Syrian pound, it was stated, will conserve its equivalent with the sterling rate.

In Beirut, the Lebanese Premier issued a communique last night regarding a financial agreement now being negotiated with France. It stated that France had not fulfilled her obligations and that the Lebanon was determined to recover the debt due to her.

Cominform Meets In Secret

BELGRADE, Sunday (AP). — The Cominform held its first meeting in Yugoslavia in the middle of January, according to a communique published in the sixth issue of the Cominform Bulletin, which appeared on the streets of Belgrade today.

The meeting was held in the closest secrecy, and it is believed that the formation of a permanent editorial board was the major issue under discussion.

GREAT BRITAIN "RESPONSIBLE FOR BLOODSHED"

LONDON, Sunday (Reuter). — The Zionist Federation Conference here today passed a resolution deploring the "present attitude of the British Government to the implementation of the United Nations Palestine decision."

"By impeding the defence of the Yishuv (the Jews of Palestine), allowing Arab preparations for warfare, refusing to permit a gradual transference of power and failing to cooperate

NEW YORK SHORTAGE OF OIL CRITICAL

NEW YORK, Sunday. — Offices in New York had to close down on Friday, when Mayor O'Dwyer banned the supply of fuel oil to all but private homes and certain priority industries.

This is a hard blow to business, coming as it does in one of the coldest winters in U.S. history.

The reason for the shortage is said to be the expansion of home building, but even during the war, when half of America's oil supplies were reserved for the forces, no such breakdown ever occurred.

Observers think that one of the causes may be the Administration's

If you can't come to town,
please telephone 4607
Lighting, Heating, Cooking, Refrigeration
CARL MARX
3 PRINCESS MARY AVE., JERUSALEM

THE PALESTINE POST
JERUSALEM
SUNDAY, MAY 16, 1948
PRICE: 25 MILS
VOL. XXIII. No. 6714

THE PALESTINE POST
THE SUBSCRIPTION DEPARTMENT
has returned to The Palestine Post offices, Hassolel Street, Jerusalem, Tel. 4233.

STATE OF ISRAEL IS BORN

The first independent Jewish State in 19 centuries s born in Tel Aviv as the British Mandate over Palestine ne to an end at midnight on Friday, and it was immedely subjected to the test of fire. As "Medinat Yisrael" ate of Israel) was proclaimed, the battle for Jerusalem ged, with most of the city falling to the Jews. At the same time, President Truman announced that the United States would accord recognition to the new State. A few hours later, Palestine was invaded by Moslem armies from the south, east and north, and Tel Aviv was raided from the air. On Friday the United Nations Special Assembly adjourned after adopting a resolution to appoint a mediator but without taking any action on the Partition Resolution of November 29.

Yesterday the battle for the Jerusalem-Tel Aviv road was still under way, and two Arab villages were taken. In the north, Acre town was captured, and the Jewish Army consolidated its positions in Western Galilee.

Most Crowded Hours in Palestine's History

Between Thursday night and this morning Palestine through what by all standards must be among the crowded hours in its history.

For the Jewish population there was the anguish over fate of the few hundred Haganah men and women in Kfar Etzion bloc of settlements near Hebron. Their ender to a fully equipped superior foreign force des-ely in need of a victory was a foregone conclusion. t could not be known, with no communications since eday morning, was whether and to what extent the Cross and the Truce Consuls would secure civilised itions for prisoners and wounded, and proper respect he dead. Doubts on some of these anxious questions now been resolved.

Friday afternoon, from Tel came the expected an-ement of the Jewish State, s official naming at birth, nat Yisrael"—State of Is-ith the swearing in of the ouncil of Government. The nation of the State was at midnight, coinciding with ing from Haifa of Britain's igh Commissioner. Within ur, President Truman and in Washington that the ment of the United States cided to give *de facto* re-on to the Jewish State, with such recognition implied. ssembly of the United Na-neeting since the middle of for "further study" of the e problem was thus left, means or another, to ratify vo-States decision of No-last year, or dissolve with concrete to its credit. The ly adjourned with the re-to appoint a mediator the Jews and Arabs, to te with the Security Coun-ruce Commission in Jeru-

an Recognition Awaited

a and her allies had given ssurance of their intention gnize the Jewish State, else did or did not. As t of Washington's action Eastern Bloc's stand, ountries are expected to ex-eir recognition to the new-state.

did the Arab Bloc remain rue to their promises, or the members of the Arab completed their plans for cale invasion of Palestine has been described as a "crusade" against the el Aviv was bombed twice y by Egyptian war planes. f the enemy planes was own by a Jewish fighter and the pilot taken prison-ving that this move against lian population was not a , and that the Jewish pre-s include anti-aircraft de-

lack-out has been ordered whole of Jewish Palestine viv itself having blacked Friday.

he same time, the air was with reports of two Egypt lumns on the move from th towards Gaza and Beer and of intensified shell-m across the northern border of Jewish settlements in North-Eastern Galilee.

The Security Council met yesterday in a special session to consider action on the invasion of Palestine by member states of the U.N.

In the afternoon, Jerusalem was subjected to shelling from the northwest.

Haganah forces throughout the country continued mopping up, and Jewish sources claimed most of Western Galilee safe against attack. Naharayim, near Jisr el Majamie, inside Trans-Jordan, where the Jordan River works of the Palestine Electric Corporation are, is claimed by the Arab Legion. The battle for the Tel Aviv-Jerusalem Road at Bab el Wad is still on, Haganah taking two villages — Abu Shusha and Kubab — between Ramleh and Latrun.

Converging on Old City

In Jerusalem the "cease fire" observed on both sides for six days was broken on Friday, although the more strategic buildings in Princess Mary Avenue, the Russian Compound, and Jaffa Road passed to the Jews without a shot being fired, as did the David Building commanding the road to the German Colony and Railway Station. By yesterday evening, Jewish forces were approaching some of the gates of the Old City. The Police Training School on Mt. Scopus and Sheikh Jarrah are in Jewish hands.

On Friday morning, the Truce Commission met at the French Consulate and invited Jewish and Arab representatives to confer with them. Jewish Agency delegates agreed that the "cease fire" be extended in Jerusalem for eight days. Arab representatives could not attend, they said, because of the firing in Julian's Way, and a two-hour respite was arranged from 5 to 7 in the evening. Whether they agreed or not, became academic as by that time the battle for Jerusalem had been renewed.

To Jerusalem's tension was added the aggravation of electric power failing in most parts of the city, as nearly all of the Electric Corporation's lines had been shot down. This meant, on top of the other heardships to a fuel-less city, no broadcast news yesterday, when there were no newspapers. For more than a week the city was also without piped water.

RE CAPTURED

, the sea-coast town s the bay from Haifa, was red by Jewish forces yes-y, the Haganah Radio re-d. The surrender of the and subsequently two vil-to the north, came after ong Jewish attack. es dumps containing enor-quantities of military ment were captured. B.B.C. stated yesterday almost all of Western Ga was in Jewish hands, but Naharayim, on the Jor-had been occupied by the n.

Double Summer Time in Jerusalem

At midnight tonight all clocks in Jewish Jerusalem will be advanced two hours.

The Emergency Committee has instituted double summer time in order to save fuel. The measure does not apply to the rest of the country.

The Jerusalem Electric Corporation will cut off current to the Jewish Quarters from 1 to 9 p.m. as from today.

JEWS TAKE OVER SECURITY ZONES

The Battle for Jerusalem, which began when the British forces withdrew on Friday morning, continued all day Friday and yesterday. The crackle of small-arms fire and explosions of mortar shells were still being heard in the early hours of this morning as the battle entered its third day.

Repeated efforts on Friday evening and again on Saturday by the U.N. Truce Commission to bring about a "cease fire" were brought to nought when the Arab representatives failed to agree within the specified time limit.

On Friday morning, Jewish forces entered the Russian Compound and Zone C to re-occupy the buildings requisitioned from Jews last year. This operation was almost bloodless, but beyond the western edge of Zone C, Arabs engaged the Jews in Jaffa Road. The Arabs were forced back and the Barclays Bank area was taken.

In other parts of the city fighting flared up. Jews overran one after another the areas evacuated by the British. By last night, the quarters and strongpoints held by Haganah included the German Colony and part of the Baka'a Quarter in Zone A, all of Zone B except for the Red Cross area, Sheikh Jarrah (where the Jewish flag was flown from the Mufti's House), the Mea Shearim Police Station and Allenby Barracks on the Bethlehem Road. The I.Z.L. were in occupation of the Scopus Police Billet.

Yesterday afternoon eight cannon shelled Jewish Jerusalem from the Arab village of Nebi Samwil, more than 100 shells falling in the north-western quarters. Several persons were injured.

Jewish casualties in the two days of fighting were eight killed and a number of wounded. Arab casualties are not known.

EMERGENCY

A state of emergency in the Jerusalem area was declared to exist by the Haganah Area Commander as from yesterday in what is the first Order of the Day to be issued in almost 2,000 years by a Jewish Military Commander of the city.

The Order said:

With the declaration of the establishment of Medinat Israel (the State of Israel) and the setting up of its Provisional Council of Government, the Jews of Palestine have entered upon the decisive phase of the war.

In order to obviate any disturbance during the difficult time that confronts us, I hereby declare a state of emergency to exist in the Jerusalem District as from 00.01 hours on Saturday, May 15, and I hereby give the following instructions:

1. Every inhabitant must place himself at the disposal of the authorized security forces of Medinat Israel and obey their orders.
2. All property required for the needs of the Military Command may be expropriated by the security forces acting through officers carrying proper documents. Compensation for such expropriated property will be paid according to evaluation by the Jerusalem Committee and at such time as the latter shall decide.
3. The areas evacuated by the forces of the Mandatory Government and now held by the security forces are hereby declared to be Military Occupation Areas under the authority of Military Governors.
4. No person may enter any such area without permission of the Military Governor.
5. Any person found looting or committing any criminal act will be brought before a Military Court and punished with all the rigour of the law.

The Palestine Post

Despite the power failure in Jerusalem, the Electric Corporation succeeded in providing these offices with power about 10.15 last night. There was another failure about 11.15 but again the Corporation was able to restore the current.

Before the linotype machines could begin to work, however, it was 1 a.m., and in order to be able to appear this morning, The Palestine Post is published, for the third time in as many weeks, in two pages.

Egyptian Air Force Spitfires Bomb Tel Aviv; One Shot Down

Kol Israel, the Tel Aviv broadcasting station, reported at 2 o'clock yesterday afternoon that Tel Aviv had been bombed three times in the previous evening and morning, and that one plane had been shot down and its Egyptian pilot taken prisoner.

In the first raid, four planes attacked from a height of 300 feet. Two dropped bombs, while the others strafed the city. Little damage was caused. In the second attack two hours later, the airport to the north of the city was bombed, and an Air France plane parked there was damaged. The third raid was launched shortly before midday, but the planes were driven off without causing any damage.

Two settlements in the Negev had also been attacked from the air, the radio reported.

A country-wide blackout was ordered by Air Raid Precaution Headquarters in Tel Aviv.

Mr. David Ben Gurion, the Prime Minister, broadcast from Tel Aviv to the people of America yesterday morning. As he spoke, Egyptian planes were bombing the city.

In the north, the settlements of Ein Gev and Shaar Hagolan and Dan had been shelled, but no further details were available.

Kalandia airfield was taken by the Jewish army on Friday morning, shortly after the High Commissioner had left there by plane for Haifa. The field was evacuated, together with the neighbouring settlement of Ataroth, on Friday night. The settlement itself was burnt by Arabs yesterday.

2 Columns Cross Southern Border

By WALTER COLLINS
U.P. Correspondent

CAIRO, Saturday. — A communique issued today by the Egyptian Ministry of National Defence reported that two columns of Egyptian troops, including infantry and artillery, had struck across the Palestine border, preceded by aircraft.

One column was reported to have crossed the frontier 30 miles inland and to have attacked the "Jewish village of Auja on the road to Beersheba, wiping it out because its inhabitants had refused to surrender." (Auja is a police post near the frontier, about 25 miles from the nearest Jewish settlement). The column then entrenched itself on heights east of Gaza.

Meanwhile, according to this Cairo report, another column crossed the border at midnight, travelling north along the coast road towards Gaza.

Egyptian sources later reported that their forces had reached the Negev settlements of Nirim and Kfar Darom, but could give no further details.

In Cairo, at midnight, 2,000 Egyptian Police, commanded by 370 Officers, started a round-up of suspected Zionist sympathizers and arrested 600 persons within six hours.

According to Haganah sources, Jewish soldiers beat off an Egyptian "amphibious operation," an attempt to land troops near Ashdod, 20 miles north of Gaza. The ship which attempted to make the landing was forced to turn back, these sources said.

Arab Legion Cross Border

It was reported in Jerusalem last night that troops of the Arab Legion had crossed the border into Palestine in two places, over Allenby Bridge and near the Palestine Electric power station at Naharaim.

According to Reuters, the long convoy of the first route of lorry-borne troops, artillery and armoured cars, was headed by King Abdullah, who fired a symbolic pistol shot towards Palestine and wished his troops success in their campaign.

In Cairo, a group of journalists have asked the Egyptian Premier, Nokrashi Pasha, for an interview to discuss the proposed blackout of news, the Cairo Radio has reported.

A Good Thing

CAIRO, Saturday (UP). — The Egyptian Premier, Nokrashi Pasha, told the press that advance units of the Egyptian army had entered Gaza 12 hours after crossing the frontier.

"This is a very good thing," he added.

Etzion Settlers Taken P.O.W.

Fighting in the Kfar Etzion bloc continued throughout Friday, after Kfar Etzion itself had surrendered to the Arabs on the previous day. The wounded from the settlement were evacuated to Massuot Itzhak.

The fighting was broken off on Friday on the intervention of a Red Cross representative, accompanied by a Jewish Medical Officer, who went out to the settlements and supervised the transfer of the Jews from Revadim and Ein Zurim, the wounded and women being taken to Bethlehem, and the other settlers to prison.

The settlers from Massuot Itzhak, including the wounded from the first day's fighting at Kfar Etzion, were removed yesterday.

The terms of surrender agreed on by the Jews and Arabs were:

All able-bodied soldiers to be taken as prisoners of war, and kept in special camps, to be supervised by the International Red Cross.

Women, non-combatants and wounded to be brought to Jerusalem by the Red Cross.

War Office Says Legion Had Left

LAKE SUCCESS, Saturday. — Sir Alexander Cadogan, Britain's delegate to the UN, read in the Security Council a telegram from the War Office today, stating that *all units of the Arab Legion had left Palestine for Trans-Jordan prior to the end of the Mandate.*

EGYPTIAN INVASION BEFORE U.N. SECURITY COUNCIL

LAKE SUCCESS, Saturday. — Israel today appealed to an emergency meeting of the Security Council to order a halt to Arab invasions into Palestine and, if necessary, to impose economic and military sanctions.

Dr. Mordechai Eliash, representing the day-old Jewish State, appealed to the Council to act fast against the invading Arab States, because "every hour counts." He stated that King Abdullah of Trans-Jordan, through the instrument of the Arab Legion, was clearly committing an act of aggression.

At the beginning of the session, Dr. Issa Nakhleh, of the Arab Higher Committee, declared that Egyptian forces had been invited by the A.H.C. to assist in the establishment of law and order. He asked: "What right has the Jewish Agency, which represents world Jewry, to complain against this action before the Security Council?"

Mahmoud Bey Fawzi, of Egypt, declared in explanation of a cable which he had earlier read to the Council that Egyptian troops had entered Palestine by invitation and with the unequivocal consent of the Palestine people. Egyptian forces were not going to Palestine to conquer anybody, but just to restore peace.

The invasion was "not directed against the Palestine

(Continued on Page 2, Col. 7)

GROMYKO TO BE REPLACED

LAKE SUCCESS, Saturday. (UP). — M. Andrei Gromyko, the Soviet Deputy Foreign Minister and his country's representative at the U.N., will soon be replaced — probably permanently.

The 38-year-old Soviet diplomat will be replaced by M. Jacob A. Malik, Deputy Foreign Minister and a major figure in the conduct of Russian Foreign policy in the Far East. M. Malik, is already en route here by plane from Berlin.

U.S. RECOGNIZES JEWISH STATE

WASHINGTON, Saturday. —Ten minutes after the termination of the British Mandate on Friday, the White House released a formal statement by President Truman that the U.S. Government intended to recognize the Provisional Jewish Government as the *de facto* authority representing the Jewish State.

The U.S. is also considering lifting the arms embargo but it is not known whether to Palestine only or the entire Middle East, and the establishment of diplomatic relations with the Jewish Provisional Government.

The White House press secretary, Mr. Charles Ross, told correspondents today that reaction so far to the recognition had been overwhelmingly favourable. He said this step had been discussed with Mr. Marshall and Mr. Lovett before action was taken, and it had their complete support.

Mr. Ross said that the President had decided several days ago to grant American recognition to the new Jewish State, but due to protocol regulations he could not announce his policy until a formal letter arrived. "We were able to move very quickly when the messenger brought the letter," he said, "because the President had already determined the course of action to be taken."

Provisional Government

A few minutes before five (midnight Palestine time), Mr. Eliyahu Epstein, of the Jewish Agency's Washington Office, handed a letter to the White House, requesting the U.S. to recognize the new Jewish State. "With the full knowledge of the deep bond of sympathy which existed and has been strengthened over the past 30 years between the U.S. Government and the Jewish people of Palestine," the letter said, "I have been authorized by the Provisional Government of the new State to tender this message and express the hope that your Government will recognize and welcome Israel into the community of nations."

In Frankfurt, General Lucius D. Clay, the U.S. Military Commander of Germany, said today that Jews in Germany and Austria would be assisted to leave for the State of Israel as soon as official word of America's recognition was to hand.

Proclamation by Head Of Government

The creation of "Medinat Yisrael", the State of Israel, was proclaimed at midnight on Friday by Mr. David Ben Gurion, until then Chairman of the Jewish Agency Executive and now head of the State's Provisional Council of Government.

David Ben Gurion, Prime Minister

The first act of the Council of Government, as announced by its head, was to abolish all legislation of the 1939 White Paper of the late Mandatory Power, particularly the Ordinances and Orders relating to immigration and land transfer.

In the declaration of independence, Mr. Ben Gurion called on the Arabs of Palestine to restore peace, assuring them full civic rights and full representation in all governmental organs of the State.

Mr. Ben Gurion prefaced the declaration with a review of the historic connection of the Jewish people with the Land of Israel and of their efforts to return, which never ceased throughout the generations of their dispersal, until the Nazi holocaust proved anew the urgency of the need for a Jewish State.

The Balfour Declaration of 1917, confirmed by the League of Nations, had given explicit international recognition to the right of the Jewish people to reconstitute its National Home in Palestine, he said.

"On November 29, 1947," continued the declaration, "the United Nations decided on the establishment of a Jewish State and an Arab State in Palestine and called upon the inhabitants of the country to take all steps necessary for the establishment of the two States.

Historic Rights

"This decision cannot now be changed. Accordingly, we, the members of the Provisio-

(Continued on Page 2, Col. 6)

Special Assembly Adjourns

FLUSHING MEADOWS, Saturday. — The Special U.N. Assembly, called four weeks ago to discuss the U.S. proposal for a temporary Trusteeship for Palestine, adjourned yesterday until its next regular meeting in September without taking any decision to alter the resolution of November 29, which called for the setting up of two states in Palestine. The Assembly adopted only one motion — to appoint a special mediator to go to Palestine and cooperate with Truce Commission.

President Truman's announcement that the U.S. was proposing to recognize the new Jewish State reached newsmen during the session before the American delegation itself knew about it.

All the afternoon, the Assembly had been tied up in knots. After much filibustering it rejected the Franco-U.S. proposal for a special administration for Jerusalem. As the debate dragged on, correspondents sat with stopwatches to see whether a decision would be taken before the six o'clock deadline (N.Y. Summer Time) when the Mandate terminated. As zero hour was reached without a vote, they rushed to the booths, and about ten minutes later, the tickers in the local news agency offices flashed President Truman's recognition.

Gromyko and Jessup

The Assembly floor was half deserted and the American delegation had not been officially informed. The first to mention the Jewish State from the restrum was M. Gromyko, who said he saw no need for further action on the American mediator proposal, since the Jewish State had been recognized as a reality by the U.S. He asked what was being proposed for the Arab area of Palestine which was still without a government.

Shortly afterwards, Mr. Philip Jessup, the anti-Partition fighter, mounted the rostrum and officially announced U.S. recognition of the Jewish State, insisting, however, that the passage of the American mediator proposal was more necessary now than ever.

The Assembly passed it.

Between the flash from the White House and the final vote there was an eerie atmosphere in Flushing Meadows. The lights of the television cameras played on the rostrum, lighting up one Arab speaker after another who mounted the steps and expressed in a low voice frustration and anger.

To the last minute, officials of the State Department had been lobbying right on the floor against the Jewish State, even while the President's statement was already on the wires.

The Assembly did not adopt any resolution at all which altered the U.N. decision of November 29, 1947.

2 Villages Taken In Road Battle

In the battle for the Tel Aviv-Jerusalem road, the Haganah on Friday night took Kubeib and Abu Shusha villages between Latrun and Ramle. In engagements elsewhere along the route positions near Latrun and Bab el Wad changed hands.

Jewish casualties in this area in the last two days are about 40 killed. The Iraqis suffered greater losses, but their exact number is unknown.

It was reported that Iraqi troops had entered the Trappist Monastery at Latrun, and had set up strongpoints on the grounds and the building itself.

Sir Alan Sails From Palestine

The High Commissioner's departure from Palestine on Friday went according to plan — he appeared on the steps of Government House at 8 o'clock in the morning, wearing a full General's uniform. There he reviewed a guard of honour, consisting of 50 men of the Highland Light Infantry, the last British troops to leave Jerusalem.

Sir Alan Cunningham then drove to Kalandia airfield and boarded a plane for Haifa. Spitfires and Lancasters covered his short car journey.

The last British civil servants left Jerusalem together with Sir Alan: including Sir William Fitz-Gerald, the Chief Justice, and Sir Henry Gurney, the Chief Secretary.

Sir Alan's plane was piloted to Haifa by the Air Officer Commanding in Palestine, Air Com-

If you can't come to town, please telephone 4607
Lighting, Heating, Cooking, Refrigeration
CARL MARX
3 PRINCESS MARY AVE., JERUSALEM

THE PALESTINE POST

FIVE A.M.

JERUSALEM
SUNDAY, MAY 30, 1948

PRICE: 25 MILS
VOL. XXIII. No. 6724

THE PALESTINE POST
SUBSCRIPTION RATES
Monthly ... ... L.P. 0.675
Three Months ... ... L.P. 2.000
Six Months ... ... L.P. 3.900
One Year ... ... L.P. 7.800

Column One
By David Courtney

THE blandness of Sir Alexander Cadogan lies thinly upon the surface of his embarrassment. He is a man with a code, born of a family with a code; and the code must conflict painfully with Sir Alexander's loyalty to a master who distorts, falsifies and deceives; and whose performance of his Ministry is a corruption not merely of the Parliamentary traditions, but also of the public life of England. The plan put up to the Security Council by Sir Alexander Cadogan was a transparent move to neutralize that body and at the same time to provide a foxhole for Bevin to hide in. The Chinese delegate, with the leisurely whimsy of his race, gave the plan his blessing; but the British Cabinet, even with the full strength of the Kuomintang behind it, once more has failed to get itself taken at its word: the word of England, which this Government has made a lie. And time is getting short, for the British Government. There sits Mr. Bevin in his Whitehall chambers. He strains his ears for sound of the messenger with news of the victory of his Allies; and fills in the anxious time doodling time-savers for U.N., to which Sir Alexander Cadogan, drawing comfort from the tireless encouragement of the Chinese delegate, gives the accent if not the substance of his training as a Christian Gentleman. But time, quite definitely, is getting short. Mr. Bevin's messenger seems much delayed. The planned victory, on which the Government depends to save its thick skin, seems a very uncertain prospect. Even Cadogan's blandness is no longer an effective covering to the sham piety of London. The world sees through it.

*

THE other day Mr. Bevin recalled Britain's strategic interests in the Middle East. We are getting our soldiers out, he said, but that doesn't mean that we have not a deep commitment in the Middle East. He has lost Palestine and lost the whole Middle East. By the manner of his losing Palestine, he has lost Britain's influence in every part of Arabia and the Eastern Mediterranean; for it is no use being wicked and stubborn if you are unsuccessful; and no use offering treaties to countries you have led into disaster. Mr. Bevin has persuaded himself that his policy is a flail to beat the Jews with. It has proved itself to be a lie to fool the Arabs with; for the British Government, and the British Government alone, is responsible for the extravagant adventure into which the States of the Arab League have plunged. How will Mr. Bevin get them out of their fix? It is his own fix as well as their fix. It is the British people's fix as well as the Arabs'. Mr. Bevin had better resign. He cannot go on boasting of his failures: even "The Times" begins to count the cost and resent the tedium of this puffed-up and perfidious ignoramus.

*

AGAINST the background of London's cheap manoeuvring and U.N.'s whistling of every tune it can think of, to keep up its spirits, the battle scorches the earth of the Holy Land and welds the future with blood and fire. The word is not with London or with Lake Success but with the man gasping under the hot sun and the woman waiting at dawn. The chatter of London and Lake Success is like pebbles thrown against the Homeric shield raised by young men in the name of a people's freedom. Whatever, from now on, politics may do or say, the problem of Palestine has become, grimly, Palestine's problem and the solution lies here, in the hands and hearts of the people. Bevin has forfeited his country's right to any part in the counsels of this land; and what part has U.N. deserved? Or the Archbishop of Canterbury, or His Holiness the Pope: or any of these magnificent gentlemen who speak holiness and condone desecration; and would preserve a stone but stand aside indifferently at the slaying of souls? No matter. The proud men and nations have been stripped to their nakedness: one knows them; and that, for the future should be half the battle. They go about naked and men, increasingly, will turn from them in disgust. This, then, is a cleansing war. Its implications may be greater than any of the great wars of the past: and

OLD CITY DEFENDERS YIELD AFTER EPIC RESISTANCE

Exhausted after two weeks of incessant lane-to-lane and house-to-house fighting, and overcome by fresh Arab troops who greatly outnumbered them, the Jewish garrison in the Old City of Jerusalem accepted the Arab Legion's surrender terms on Friday afternoon, while 290 able-bodied men from 15 to 50 were taken prisoner, and 1,200 women, children and aged were passed to the Jewish lines outside the walls with the cooperation of the U.N. representative and the Red Cross. Among the prisoners were 54 slightly wounded, including four nurses.

GARRISON'S LAST DITCH STAND

By AP & Reuter Correspondent in the Old City

The surrender of the Jews in the Old City, after 14 days of house-to-house fighting, was offered before noon on Friday when two men of the religious community came out with a white flag, and asked for terms. The terms were accepted in the afternoon.

The evacuation went on through the night. The Jews appeared to be reassured when the Legion threw a strong protective cordon round them, brought in the Red Cross, and provided food, water, and attention for the sick, wounded and aged.

A convoy of 14 buses from the Jordan Valley reached the Old City at dawn yesterday to take prisoners to a prisoners' camp in Trans-Jordan for screening. During the night, 294 men of military age had been held temporarily in the Jaffa Gate (Kishleh) Police Station. In the Armenian School, 150 wounded were sorted out, the seriously wounded to be delivered to the Jewish lines, the others to be kept as prisoners of war.

Weapons Seized

The Legion Headquarters reported the seizure of about 400 assorted Jewish weapons. The Commander claimed that the Jews mined the last buildings they held on surrendering, and when the mines exploded they caused big fires.

Long queues of civilians — women, children, and the aged —passed through Zion Gate, held by the Legion, crossed the shell-scarred garden of the Church of Dormition, and entered the Haganah lines. It required more than six hours for the 1,200 people to leave the walls of the Old City and return to Jewish care, carrying bundles of their few wordly goods.

Many sad-eyed Jewish grandfathers, women and children who were sealed up, living on meagre rations for weeks, carried small bags holding personal belongings. But other personal things, like children's toys, clothes, shoes, photographs, combs and books, were left behind.

A Legion soldier was wounded at 8.30 p.m. at Zion Gate, when sniping suddenly broke out there. Dr. Pablo Azcarate, representing the Secretary General of the United Nations in Palestine, was at the side of the Legion's Old City Commander when word came of the soldier casualty.

"It is only provocation. Please keep pushing the civilians right along," Dr. Azcarate pleaded, and the Arab Officer complied.

"Sticking to the Rules"

Armed women were among the Jews captured, the Legion Commander said, but had been allowed to go. Mr. A. M. Weingarten, Mukhtar of the Jewish Community, was also among those released. The Legion Commander said: "These people were told we would massacre them. I am letting such men as Weingarten go because we want the Jews as a whole to know that the Arab Legion is sticking to the rules and abiding by international conventions." (Later, reports stated that Weingarten had been taken prisoner.)

"It was quite a job protecting 2,000 Jews from the 40—50,000 Arabs, but the Legion saw to it that not a single Jew was harmed on the way out," he said.

(For more than an hour, Reuter's Correspondent, Doon Campbell, tramped over the stumps of walls that were once homes, and piles of rubble that were once a synagogue. It must have been like life in Belsen in this crowded, fly-ridden and shell-ripped quarter towards the end. The scene was like Stalingrad or Berlin. Roofless walls leaned crazily. Alleys were wrist-high with debris.

A Swiss official of the International Red Cross who remain-

At 11 a.m. on Friday, Rabbis Reuven Hazan, 70 and Israel Mintzberg, 83, walked from one of the Jewish positions toward the Arab lines. They carried a white flag made out of a bit of once-festive table cloth tacked to a stick. Although he was shot at and wounded by a sniper, Rabbi Hazan called out in Arabic, "Good morning. We have come to talk to you, and we want to see your commander."

They were led into the Armenian Convent of St. James, the Arab H.Q., where they were given cigarettes and tea. The Commander appeared, followed by about 80 Britons, many of them tattooed, and wearing only khaki shorts.

The Arabs asked for the Haganah chief and Mr. A. M. Weingarten, Chairman of the Jewish Community of the Old City. Rabbi Hazan replied that he and his colleague had come to negotiate, but were not authorized to conclude terms.

Rabbi as Hostage

Holding Rabbi Mintzberg as hostage, the Arabs sent Rabbi Hazan back to the Jewish lines to return with a Haganah representative. When the Haganah man appeared, the Arab demands were presented. All able-bodied men from 15 to 50, including the slightly wounded, were to collect at the Armenian School, with their arms, as prisoners of war. Non-combatants were to be evacuated out of the Old City, and the Legion was to accept responsibility for protecting the Jews from Arab mobs.

Informed by the Jewish Agency of the negotiations, the Red Cross delegation in Jerusalem, which was meeting with the World President, Mr. Paul Ruegger, at the time, sent three men into the Old City, including, at the Agency's request, Dr. K.S. Krikorian of the Red Crescent Society

The Legion's terms were accepted, and through intervention of the Red Cross "cease fire" was agreed upon to evacuate the non-combatants.

The evacuation of civilians through Zion Gate began on Friday evening, and lasted until 2 o'clock on Saturday morning. At the same time, the prisoners of war, among whom were 39 men carrying arms, were taken to the Armenian School. Fifty-one of the captives were wounded, and three physicians and four nurses volunteered to accompany the prisoners.

Another "cease fire" was arranged for 5.30 p.m yesterday, and Red Cross ambulances and

(Continued on Page 3, Col. 8)

HELD OUT UNTIL AMMO RAN OUT

By DANIEL DE LUCE, AP Correspondent

INSIDE THE OLD CITY, Saturday. — In a shadowy prison near Jaffa Gate an Arab Policeman chatted pleasantly with a Haganah Commander early this morning — blood enemies, but observing the ancient formalities after the surrender.

A few feet away Eric J. Apter, a Jewish agricultural expert before he became a Haganah Liaison Officer, leaned wearily against the steel bars and tried to reconstruct the history of the battle which had made him a captive.

"Our fighting men were too few—our arms were too few—finally our position was hopeless and our casualties very heavy," said Mayer, the Haganah Commander." "We kept hoping for a new linkup with our people outside Zion Gate." We had this link on the evening of May 17, and brought in new fighters and ammunition. But when the Legion came into the Old City on May 18, the link-up was broken and never restored. We surrendered yesterday because we were at the end of our resources. We were finished.

Short of Drugs

"Our greatest shortage was weapons and ammunition. We had three physicians from the Hadassah Hospital and rather large stocks of medical supplies, although we ran short of some drugs towards the end.

"Our biggest burden was civilians, 1,500 of them. They kept below ground most of the time so that their casualties were low, but they were a heavy weight on us."

Wounded American

Mayer said the Jewish garrison had learned to spot all types of shells which the Legion hurled into the siege zone. He said demolitions were most feared, "because you never knew when your house would tumble down around you."

He said that one American Jew, who had served in the U.S. Navy and had a family in San Francisco, had been wounded in the fighting and was in the hospital when surrender came.

ISRAEL CHARGES VANDALISM

TEL AVIV, Saturday (Reuter). — Israel today accused the Arabs of deliberately destroying the Hurva Synagogue in Jerusalem's Old City, where the Jews made their last stand before surrender.

They said it was the first time a Holy Place had been destroyed deliberately, and not hit by accident during fighting.

LEBANESE UNITS ROUTED BY JEWS

ROSH PINAH, Saturday — In a combined operation last night, Israel's Army — artillery, armour and infantry — captured the Lebanese border villages of Malkieh and Kadesh after a fierce engagement with units of the Lebanese Army there. Three enemy armoured cars and a number of supply vehicles were destroyed.

Jewish forces pursued the Lebanese soldiers fleeing from these two key points on the road to northern Galilee, penetrated about three kilometres inside the Lebanon. Thirty of the Lebanese were killed and large quantities of arms and ammunition were captured. One Jew was killed and 13 were wounded.

The Haganah reported that the whole of the Western Galilee was safe from invasion following this operation.

The Lebanese villages of Eitarou, Ein Abel and Aalma were bombed by the Air Force. Jewish infantry later cleared the area of Eitarou, and other units silenced enemy resistance in two Police Posts on the Syrian frontier. Both stations — near Lehavoth Hazaahan and Amir — put up stiff resistance. A quantity of arms and ammunition was captured, and the buildings were blown up.

Jewish forces raided enemy concentrations in the Banias area, over the Syrian border, and villages in the area were evacuated.

A bridge near the Arab village of Zara'in, in the Valley of Jezreel, was captured on Thursday night. The enemy had fortified the village as a strongpoint on the northern edge of the Jenin-Tulkarm-Nablus triangle, and the Jewish forces met stiff opposition. Israel's soldiers broke through the fortifications and remained in possession despite counter-attacks by guns and armoured vehicles.

Arabs Try To Fan Out From Old City

Arab forces tried to break into Jewish Jerusalem in two sectors on Friday night, under cover of a barrage, but both attempts were fought off.

The Arabs struck out simultaneously from Sheikh Jarrah toward the northern quarters, and from the Damascus Gate toward the New Gate, but withdrew when they met heavy fire.

Meanwhile, the shelling of Jerusalem continued on Friday and yesterday.

Local and foreign correspondents were yesterday shown Jewish hospitals which had received direct hits during the past week. Most severely hit was the Hadassah Clinic. Other hospitals badly damaged were Bikur Holim and the Hadassah at the English Mission

Marshall's Wishes To State Of Israel

In a telegram to Mr. Moshe Shertok on Friday, Mr. George Marshall expressed the hope that the new Jewish State would prosper in the years of peace.

Mr Marshall formally acknowledged the appointment of Mr Eliahu Epstein as Israel's representative in Washington

TRIANGLE BOMBED

The Jewish Air Force made daylight air raids yesterday on the three apexes of the "dangerous Triangle" —Nablus, Jenin and Tulkarm.

Direct hits on troop concentrations were observed in the first two towns, the Haganah reported. In Tulkarm, a fuel dump in the Arab Legion camp went up in flames.

Earlier, Kfar Yona and Ein Vered settlements west of Tulkarm had been attacked by artillery and infantry, but both attacks were repulsed. An attack on Friday on the settlement of Kfar Yaavetz was also beaten off.

At one point in the fighting, Bnei Geulim settlement in this area was overrun by Arabs, but was re-taken by the Haganah.

A U.P. despatch from Amman, quoting 'frontline advices,' said that Iraqi troops had occupied Kfar Yona, marking "the first Iraqi push towards Nathanya in an effort to puncture the Jewish coastal strip between Tel Aviv and Haifa."

Jewish aircraft yesterday and on Friday night bombed Arab Legion artillery positions in the Jerusalem area and transport north of the city. Troop concentrations at Ramallah were also raided, and fires were started there.

In the south, Jewish aircraft bombed an Egyptian ammunition train coming from Egypt.

All Israelean planes returned safely.

A twin-engined Anton Iraqi bomber was brought down over the Jordan Valley on Friday

Bombs dropped by the enemy in the Dan sector failed to explode.

Ramat Naphtali was bombed on Friday. Our planes raided Kuneitra, El Hama and Lubia, scoring a number of direct hits.

There was a fighter-bomber attack on Tel Aviv on Friday.

IRAQIS CONQUER ARAB TOWNS

KYRENIA, CYPRUS, Saturday (Reuter). — Iraqi forces today claimed they had advanced to within 15 miles of Tel Aviv, reports said here,

The Iraqi troops, advancing from the northeast, occupied Nablus, Tulkarm and "Kalkilya," the reports said.

Syrian and Iraqi troops raided Degania, the large Jewish settlement to the south the Sea of Galilee, and dropped leaflets on Tiberias.

In the fighting on the Tel Aviv-Jerusalem road, Jewish troops had encircled a large force of Arabs south of Latrun.

SECURITY COUNCIL ADOPT[S] BRITISH FOUR-WEEK TRUC[E]

Cadogan Proposed World-Wide Arms Embargo

By RICHARD WITKIN, UP Correspondent

LAKE SUCCESS, Saturday. — At Thursday night's session of the Security Council, Britain suggested a world-wide embargo on arms shipments to the Middle East and asked the U.N. Security Council to appeal once again for a truce in Palestine.

Britain offered to cut off the flow of British armaments to Iraq, Trans-Jordan and Egypt, if the U.N. laid down an effective and universal ban on arms to both Jews and Arabs. Sir Alexander Cadogan, the British delegate, formally proposed a four-weeks' cessation of hostilities in Palestine, during which time both Jews and Arabs should stop importing arms and men of military age into Palestine.

During the "cease-fire" period, Britain suggested, the U.N. mediator, Count Bernadotte, should try to work out a settlement between the Arabs and Jews. If this new appeal were to fail Britain would be willing to go along with the American and Russian view that the Palestine war should be declared a "breach of the peace" under the punitive sections of the U.N. Charter. This theoretically would open the way to the use of economic blockades or military sanctions force against the Arabs or Jews, in case either or both failed to comply with the "cease fire" order—a tougher measure than a mere "appeal."

Britain's delegate said his country would review subsidy payments to the Trans-Jordan Government "in the light of decisions by the U.N." and would immediately withdraw 21 of the 37 British officers at present helping to direct the operations of the Arab Legion. Sir Alexander said that Britain had no power to withdraw the other 16 officers, including Brigadier Glubb Pasha, since they were employed by King Abdullah as private individuals.

He heatedly denied statements that Britain had the power to halt the Legion's operations if it wanted to. Saying that Russia and the Jewish Agency had particularly charged "that the foreign policy of King Abdullah ... is controlled by my Government," Cadogan declared "I entirely repudiate this misconception. Trans-Jordan is a Sovereign State."

Britain Accuses Jews

He bitterly attacked the Jews at several points in his speech and charged that the Stern Group was responsible for the breakdown of the "cease-fire" agreement in force for a short time last month in Jerusalem. He also accused the Jews for responsibility for the failure of the Red Cross attempt to arrange a truce with King Abdullah for the evacuation of doctors and patients from the Hadassah Hospital.

A Jewish spokesman, rejecting the new British proposal, said that "the British Government's aim is to tie Israel's hand behind its back so that the Arabs can be free to strike Israel down."

He said that Sir Alexander Cadogan "apologetically repeated Arab excuses for not observing the "cease fire, and associated his Government with them. The alliance between the British Government and the Arab aggressors, now complete both in the political and military spheres, can be no better expressed than in the suggestion for a world-wide arms embargo. This is not a neutral proposal ... it is an attempt to perpetuate the advantage which the Arab States gained through stock-piling British arms for months and years, while denying the State of Israel, claim any access to the means of defence."

The Jewish spokesman said the British proposal was a "maneouvre to create the best conditions for the Arabs to pursue their aggression successfully for the next four weeks and at the same time to twist the U.N. Charter so that the punitive section of the Charter becomes a weapon against the State of Israel, instead of an instrument for its defence."

225 BRITONS IN LEGION—EBAN

LAKE SUCCESS, Saturday (UP) — The number of British officers and technicians serving with the Arab Legion was 225, and not, as stated by Mr. Bevin recently 37, said Mr. Aubrey Eban, Israel's representative at Lake Success, today. He was referring to Sir Alexander Cadogan's announcement yesterday that 21 British officers serving with Abdullah's Army had been recalled

That announcement was an empty gesture, Mr. Eban said, which "should not lead the public into believing the U.K. is effectively withdrawing support from Abdullah's drive to rule and ruin Jerusalem."

Without those British officers and technicians, he declared, the Legion could not effectively maintain and operate its destructive equipment. "Top British officers remain in command," he added.

STOP PRESS —5 A.M.

The Security Council called on the Jews and Arabs to send their acceptance of the cease-fire by 2200 GMT on Tuesday and stating that the Council would take direct action under Chapter 7 of the Charter against whichever party rejected it. The Soviet and the Ukrainian delegates consistently abstained on all the parts of the British resolution. The Council adjourned until Wednesday.

SOVIET MOTI[ON] FOR SANCTIO[NS] DEFEATED

LAKE SUCCESS, Satu[rday]. — The British propos[al for] a 4-week cease-fire in [Pal]estine was adopted by [the] Security Council by [...] votes, with three abst[entions] tonight (3.15 a.m. Su[nday] Palestine Time).

The Council adopted by [...] votes, with four abstentio[ns a] French amendment to the [Brit]ish text calling on all gov[ern]ments and authorities [con]cerned to undertake that [they] will not introduce fighting [per]sonnel into Palestine, E[gypt], Iraq, the Lebanon, Syria, T[rans-]Jordan, Saudi Arabia and Yemen during the Cease F[ire] and calling on all gov[ernments] and authorities, "if men of [mi]litary age are introduced [into] the countries or territories [un]der their control during [the] cease fire not to mobilis[e or] submit them to military tr[ain]ing during that period."

By nine votes with two [ab]stentions the Council adop[ted] an American amendment [to] the British text calling on [all] governments and author[ities] concerned "to refrain from [im]porting or exporting war [ma]terial into or to Pales[tine], Egypt, Iraq, the Lebanon, Sy[ria], Trans-Jordan, Saudi A[rabia] and the Yemen during [the] cease-fire." The Council ad[opt]ed unanimously a clause [...] "all governments and a[utori]ties to take every possible [pre]caution for the protection [of] thes Holy Places and the [city] of Jerusalem, including a[ccess] to all shrines and sanctua[ries] for those who have an [esta]lished right to visit and w[or]ship at them."

Earlier, the Soviet [...] calling for an [...] cease-fire within 36 hours [...] the imposition of Sanctions [un]der Article 7 of the Charter [...] only five votes [...] failed to pass.

The continuing aggression [of] the Arabs and their failure [to] obey the Council's [...] cease fire orders constitut[e a] direct threat to internatio[nal] peace, the Soviet resolu[tion] said.

France put forward a [pro]posal for a cease fire for J[eru]salem only.

Both Senator Austin and [the] Colombian delegate [...] recalled that on five diffe[rent] occasions had the Cou[ncil] already tried to negotiate [a] truce and failed. Stern[er] measures were now imperat[ive,] they said.

"Scandalous Mockery"

Today, the American deleg[ate] vigorously attacked the Bri[tish] attitude in the Security Cou[ncil] and denounced Britain's [...] in Palestine. Mr. Aubrey E[ban,] the representative of Isr[ael,] called Britain's attitude to U.N. a scandalous mocke[ry] aimed against the very existe[nce] of the Jewish State and UN's Partition decision, [by] giving weapons to the Arab[s to] destroy Israel.

There was a heated excha[nge] between M Gromyko and [Sir] Alexander at this morni[ng's] session. The Soviet deleg[ate] made a bitter attack on [Bri]tain's Middle East pol[icy,] charging that her latest p[ro]posal —if adopted — would only complicate the situat[ion] in Palestine, but intensify [the] struggle and intensify the blo[od]shed."

Moreover, the proposal we[re to] be illegal, as "the Secu[rity] Council had no power to ad[opt] any decision except one wh[ich] would implement the decis[ion] of the General Assembly."

Sir Alexander Cadogan [dis]missed the Soviet charge t[hat] Britain was pursuing a po[licy] of "hypocrisy and cynicism" [as] a "vulgar, base and gene[ral] vilification." He counter-cha[rg]ed that the Soviet demand [for] an unconditional "cease f[ire"] would only worsen the sit[ua]tion.

This afternoon, Fares [el] Khoury defended the "legal[ity"] of the Arab invasion of [Pal]estine, claiming that the A[rab] armies had been "invited" [by] the Palestine Arabs to hel[p.] The U.S. and Russia [had] power to suppress whate[ver] they wanted to suppress, [he] charged, adding: "They [sup]pressed Germany." Howe[ver,] force could not solve the p[rob]lem, el Khoury said. "W[hen] you base peace on justice, [you] may get it," he added.

Criticizing the British res[olu]tion, Mr. Eban declared: [...] other State in the world w[ould] allow its immigration to be [in]terfered with." And he [...]

SMUTS DEFEATED; MALAN HEADS GOVERNMENT

LONDON, Saturday. — Following his victory at the polls, Dr. D.F. Malan, leader of the South African Nationalist Party, has been invited by the Governor-General, Mr. Van Zeel, to form a new Government.

Field Marshall Jan C. Smuts, who tendered his resignation as soon as the results were announced, will remain in office until the new Government is formed.

General Smuts' United Party was defeated by a narrow majority of five seats, although it polled more individual votes in the country as a whole than its opponents. The arrangement of the constituencies, however, is such that the United Party gained 65 seats and the Nationalist Party 70. Supporting General Smuts are also three Labour members and six Coloured Africans, while supporting Dr. Malan are nine members of the Afrikaner Party so that the grouping in the House of Assembly is 79 to 74.

The defeat of General Smuts came as a surprise after the first polls, which had convinced observers that he would have a large majority. The rural counts later changed the picture.

The principal issue of the elections was the colour question. It is now feared that Dr. Malan will introduce a strict colour bar and that he might even force the coloured people of the cities back into their re- had the support of 110 members against the Opposition's 43.

AP quotes political observers in Johannesburg as saying that another general election in South Africa is inevitable in the next few months.

They pointed out that the nationalist Afrikaner coalition majority of only five seats in Parliament will become increasingly embarrassing for the Government.

Field Marshal Smuts is not likely to avail himself of offers by elected members of Parliament to stand down in his favour, said newspaper reports today. More than a score of successful United Party candidates offered their seats to their defeated leader.

The "Rand Daily Mail" states that it is doubtful whether Marshal Smuts will go to Capetown at all during the next parliamentary session, and Mr. J.H. Hofmeyr, the former Deputy Prime Minister, is expected to be the new leader of the Opposition.

Speculation about the legislative programme of the victorious and traditionally anti-British Nationalists in the new Parliament was marked by returning confidence today.

lish factories in South Africa should not do so.

Dr. Malan's accession to power in South Africa will save 218 Germans from deportation from the Union to Germany.

The Government of Field Marshal Smuts appointed a commission to examine the cases of 5,000 Germans, mainly resident in South Africa, who had been interned during the war and recommended 218 for deportation. The deportations were confirmed on the day that Dr. Malan came into power.

In Parliament, as leader of the opposition, Dr. Malan had pleaded vigorously against the proposed deportations. Now he can simply wash out the whole thing.

WORLD BANK LOAN

WASHINGTON, Saturday (PTA).— The Security Council requested the arms embargo several months ago, and the U.S. could not modify the ban until the Council lifted the embargo, President Truman told a press conference yesterday.

Mr. Truman said that Israel had not formally requested a loan, and if made, such a request would have to be dealt with like any other loan application, through the World Import and Export Bank.

The President shrugged his shoulders when a reporter pointed out that the Bank's

THE PALESTINE POST

JERUSALEM
Thursday, Feb. 17, 1949

PRICE: 25 MILS
VOL. XXV. No. 6940

LEBANESE TALKS BEFORE T.-J.

Our Diplomatic Correspondent, Copyright, The Palestine Post

KIRYA, Wednesday. — It is thought probable that the Lebanon may precede Trans-Jordan as the next Arab state to negotiate an armistice agreement with Israel. The questions of armistice are understood to have been considered at length between Israel and Lebanese representatives some weeks ago, and to present relatively few difficulties.

On the other hand, protracted and delicate discussions are anticipated with Trans-Jordan, especially as agreement between this Arab state and Israel, covering military terms affecting a long area, including Jerusalem, is regarded as of the utmost importance from the national angle. It is expected in some quarters that these will be raised at a later at to Ministerial level.

Same Level

The earlier phases of talks with Trans-Jordan, may begin toward the end of next week, Israel will ably be represented at a similar to that of the delegation now at Rhodes. Walter Eytan, head of present Israel delegation, but it is thought, take as his services are needed at the Foreign Ministry, of which he is Director-General. Among military leaders expected to Rhodes for the talks on Trans-Jordan is Lt.-Col. Commander of the Jerusalem Area.

satisfaction is felt at fortunate turn of events Israel-Egyptian talks at the Rhodes. The concluding phase of negotiations will almost surely take another week perhaps longer. While the outstanding problem, covers the military future, Auja, has been settled and has to be ironed out before agreement, which is now in draft form, will have been drawn up and made ready for important questions are said.

whether the armistice agreement is to be temporary or of permanent nature, further, if at all, it can be brought up as of political consequence;

further, is to be the extent of the subject to the same agreement as for the post of itself;

much of the area on both sides of the Gaza-Rafa strip would be subject to the demilitarisation terms; and extent of that demilitarisation.

It is thought that it may at least a full week before these details are satisfactorily worked out.

Egyptians Battles In Burma

RANGOON, Wednesday (AP). Fierce battle was fought on the outskirts of Karen, Irrawaddy, north of on, in which strongly changed hands several as Government forces to penetrate the hard of the Karen defences.

ernment troops were in session of a monastery is a strategic point, the Karens were preparing yet another counter-offensive, official sources said afternoon. Karens have slashed a series of road behind the monastery.

town of Bassein, 70 west of Rangoon, is infested with Communist insurgents, who are harassed by Government troops, according to a Government communique released tonight. Karens are reported to regrouping east and west Bassein. Fifty Karens were killed during the fighting, miles north of Ran, the communique said.

CLAY AGAINST ANTI-SEMITISM

FRANKFURT, Wednesday A). — General Lucius D. Clay, U.S. Military Commander here, addressing a conference today, vigorously denounced members of the U.S. Military Government who show anti-Semitic inclinations.

persons in the army found guilty of anti-Semitic statements they would

LONDON, Wednesday (PTA) afternoon following the receipt

RED CROSS CHIEF COMES TO ISRAEL

Dr. Paul Ruegger, President of the International Red Cross, who arrived in Israel on Tuesday, visited Jerusalem yesterday and was the guest of the Foreign Minister, Mr. M. Shertok, at lunch.

Other guests were the Middle East directors of the Red Cross; Dr. Avraham Katznelson, Director of the Government Health Department; Mr. Berl Locker, chairman of the Jewish Agency Executive; Mr. Juda Gaulan, of the Foreign Ministry; and Dr. Steinberg and Dr. Hochman, Israel Army Liaison Officers with the Red Cross.

Dr. Ruegger had earlier erroneously been reported missing in a flight from Beirut to Amman.

Dr. Ruegger later went to the Old City and met Lt.-Col. Abdullah el-Tel.

SEARCH FOR U.N. PLANE

HAIFA, Wednesday. — U.N. and Israel Air Force planes continued to search today for the missing U.N. Consul plane. (One plane, and not two, as reported earlier, is missing).

The craft left Beirut for Amman on Monday, piloted by a Briton, Mr. Whitehead; its radio operator was Mr. Borden.

Several Israel planes carried on the search this morning over Israel territory and two U.N. Dakotas scoured the snow-covered mountains to the north.

U.N. Headquarters here did not make any statement to the press.

Commission Revises Schedule of M.E. Tour; Now in Saudi Arabia

The Conciliation Commission's schedule has been revised, and it will complete its tour of the Middle East on February 26, when it will return to Jerusalem, it was announced by the Commission's Press Officer, Mr. Hamilton Fischer, at a press conference in Jerusalem yesterday. The Commission has as yet no detailed plan for its future programme.

The Commission visited Jedda yesterday, and will go to Riadh today to continue official talks with Saudi Arabian representatives. Mr. Fischer was unable to say whether members of the Commission had been received by King Ibn Saud. From Riadh the Commission will fly to Baghdad for conversations with the Iraqi Government, and on February 20 it will begin official talks with the Trans-Jordan Government at Amman. The Commissioners will fly to Damascus on February 21, and then to Beirut.

They will visit Tel Aviv on February 24 for official talks with the Israel Government, returning to Jerusalem two days after.

Asked whether the Commission had had talks with the Egyptian Government or the

WEIZMANN FIRST PRESIDENT OF ISRAEL

Jerusalem Will Come Into Its Own

After a dramatic debate, the Knesset decided last night to hold a special session in Tel Aviv after the new Government was formed to discuss the possibility of transferring the seat of the Knesset and the Government to Jerusalem.

During the debate on the "small constitution," Mr. Menahem Begin proposed a clause naming "Jerusalem, the capital, as the seat of the Knesset and of the Government." When this motion had been brought before the ad hoc Legislative Committee, the majority decided that the question was not one to be resolved in the "small constitution."

When he addressed the plenary session in the evening, Mr. Begin referred to his late mentor, Ze'ev Jabotinsky, and recalled that his proposal for a Jewish State formula at the 17th Zionist Congress had been turned down by the majority; the State was nevertheless forged. So, too, if the majority voted against Mr. Begin's current proposal, history would show that in any case Jerusalem would come into its own.

Jerusalem's Place

Mr. Shertok replied that those who had voted against Jabotinsky's motion at the 17th Zionist Congress had in the final analysis established the Jewish State. Thus, those who voted against Mr. Begin's proposal, would in the end ensure that Jerusalem received its due place in the State of Israel. This was not a matter to be decided in interim legislation, the Foreign Minister declared.

Nevertheless, a considerable part of the House appeared reluctant to vote against Mr. Begin's motion. There was something of a commotion and a number of Members pleaded for the floor, despite the fact that a general debate on a question that had been through a sub-committee was against procedure.

Compromise Proposed

Rabbi Avraham Zvebner (Mizrahi), white-bearded and dignified in his knee-length black cloak, proposed a compromise formula. He said he could not vote against the Herut proposal but suggested instead a resolution calling on the Government to do everything possible to establish Jerusalem as the seat of the Knesset and the Government.

Mr. Eliahu Eliachar (Sephardim) criticized Mr. Begin for having caused the stir in the House.

Finally, Mr. Pinkas, one of the shrewdest parliamentarians in the defunct State Council, showed the chairman a way out of the impasse. He suggested that the issue be reverted to the ad hoc Committee on the ground that Rabbi Zvebner, a Member, had been unable to participate in the discussion on that point.

Mr. Pinkas's suggestion was received with laughter, but the chairman, Mr. Sprinzak, gracefully picked it up. He put it to a vote and the Knesset passed it unanimously, with the Herut faction and Mr. Friedman-Yellin (Fighters) abstaining.

KNESSET ADOPTS "SMALL CONSTITUTION"

Before choosing the new President, the Knesset, at a five-hour session adopted a "Small Constitution," which also defined the powers and duties. With the approval of the Knesset or the ministers concerned, he will sign treaties, make diplomatic appointments, receive foreign diplomats and confirm foreign diplomatic representations. He will also have the power of amnesty. Every presidential act, however, will require the counter-signature of the Prime Minister.

The President's duties will not necessarily be limited to these. This was made clear during the debate by Mr. Israel Idelson (Mapam), chairman of the ad hoc parliamentary Legislative Committee. He said that these powers were defined in the "small constitution" because they concerned urgent matters. But when the State Constitution is adopted, it may give the President broader powers.

Mr. Idelson made this statement when he replied to Mr. Menahem Begin (Herut) who had proposed that the State President should be empowered to veto and return bills to the Knesset if he did not wish to sign them. Only after they passed the Knesset a second time, would they become law against the President's wishes, according to Mr. Begin's proposals.

The Knesset defeated, the Herut motion (60-13) and upheld the view expressed by Mr. Idelson that the people's chosen representatives should

exclusively enjoy powers of legislation.

Mr. Begin also sought to amend the text of the Presidential oath, in which the President is to pledge allegiance to "the State of Israel and its laws." Mr. Begin proposed the substitution of "people" for "State" and objected to the pledge of allegiance to the State laws, on the grounds that some emergency laws had been carried over from the British Administration.

Mr. Idelson opposed these amendments on the grounds that not all the people of Israel were Jews and not all the Jews were in Israel. He further said that the pledge

to uphold the laws referred to the laws which the Knesset would enact. In the vote on these points, Herut obtained some support from Orthodox members, but their motions were defeated (78-18).

A motion by a Progressive Member, Mr. Izhar Harari, designed to give the President the sole power of signing bills was defeated by an overwhelming majority. Hence, bills will require the signatures of the Prime Minister as well as the ministers charged with their execution.

The President will receive the resignation of the Provisional Government and will ask them to remain in office until a new Government is formed. He will then ask Mr. David Ben Gurion to form a new Government.

Mapam sought to introduce a clause which would give the man charged to form a government only seven days in which to bring his recommendations to the Knesset for a vote of confidence. If he were then unable to do so, the President should charge someone else, according to the proposal. Mapam was backed by Herut and the Communists, but the motion was defeated (52-31).

There was a close vote on the question of whether persons who were not members of the Knesset could be included

in the Cabinet. The Provisional Government had recommended that others be eligible, but the ad hoc Legislative Committee confined its recommendation only to Knesset members. Mr. Shertok defended the Government view which prevailed (49-39). Another Herut motion for a Cabinet of eight was decisively defeated.

Second Thoughts

At the second reading of the draft "small constitution," the Knesset passed a motion giving the name of "Megilot Hamedina" (State Scrolls) to Official Gazettes. It was passed unanimously.

A few hours later, however, Mr. David Pinkas (Mizrahi) reconsidered and objected to the name. "Megilot" was the Hebrew name for five Books of the Bible, and Mr. Pinkas thought it was improper to use the same nomenclature for a publication which would report such mundane things as bankruptcies.

He received unexpected support from the Mapai benches when Dr. Yosef Lamm proposed that this question was not so urgent that it had to be included in the interim legislation. Other Assemblymen offered alternative names, and it was decided to postpone the decision for a week.

(Constitution Text — Page 3)

Silver and Neumann Resign from Agency

By JESSE ZEL LURIE, Copyright, The Palestine Post

NEW YORK, Wednesday. — Dr. Abba H. Silver, Chairman of the American Section of the Jewish Agency, and Dr. Emanuel Neumann, President of the Zionist Organization of America, resigned from the Agency Executive today but their resignations have not yet been accepted.

Dr. Silver cancelled a trip to see Mr. Henry Morgenthau, former Chairman of the United Jewish Appeal, when Mr. Morgenthau wired that he could not change his minimum demand to be given full control of the U.J.A. campaign if he resumed the Chairmanship.

The Agency proceeded to vote on returning to office Mr. Morgenthau and Mr. Henry Montor, former Executive Director of the campaign, and the vote is still going on. All absent members are being polled by cable.

Only the Z.O.A. representatives opposed acceptance of Mr. Morgenthau's terms, while

the Mizrahi members of the Agency abstained from voting. The votes of members absent from the sessions are expected to increase the majority for Mr. Morgenthau, and unless Dr. Silver and Dr. Neumann withdraw their resignations, they will be announced after the final vote is published.

Dr. Silver and Dr. Neumann intimated that they will appeal to the Zionist General Council. A statement which they issued declared that they "cannot accept the responsibility for the consequences if the U.J.A. campaign is headed by a divisive personality such as Mr. Montor, who has created ill-will in the Jewish communities and whose appointment to high office is sure to jeopardize the success of the campaign."

Dr. Silver returned to Cleveland today. Meanwhile the Agency resumed its sessions in camera. An official spokesman indicated that there is a feeling of optimism regarding the eventual solution of the new crisis.

THREE MORE RECOGNITIONS

Three states announced their recognition of Israel yesterday — Argentina, Peru and Sweden. The Argentine and Peruvian recognitions were de jure.

The Argentine recognition was announced by the Argentine Government in Buenos Aires. In Lima, members of the Jewish mission called on the President and thanked him for his government's recognition.

The Swedish recognition, which was de facto, was communicated to the Foreign Minister, Mr. Shertok, by the Swedish Consul-General in Jerusalem, Mr. WidarBagge.

U.S. Minister to Leave Hungary

BUDAPEST, Wednesday (AP). — The U.S. Minister to Hungary, Mr. Selden Chapin is considered "persona non-grata" by the Hungarian Government, and will leave Budapest tomorrow morning, a spokesman for the U.S. Legation revealed today.

Mr. Chapin's plans were not disclosed, but it is believed that he will stay in Paris for a time. The spokesman said that "activities aimed at destructing the instigating certain elements of the

2 MORE HANGED IN IRAQ

BAGHDAD, Wednesday (Reuter). — Two more men, Zakki Mohammed Basim and Yaluda Ibrahim Sedik, under sentence of death for security offences, were hanged yesterday.

Two others, Yusif Salman Yusif and Hussain Mohammed al Shabiby, were executed on Monday on the same charges — "activities aimed at destructing the State's foundations and in

Wins over Klausner on first Ballot-83:15

DR. CHAIM WEIZMANN WAS ELECTED ISRAEL'S FIRST PRESIDENT AT 1.15 THIS MORNING ON THE FIRST BALLOT IN THE KNESSET (the new official name for the Constituent Assembly). HE OBTAINED 83 VOTES AGAINST 15 FOR PROFESSOR YOSEF KLAUSNER, WHOSE CANDIDACY WAS SPONSORED BY HERUT AND SUPPORTED BY MR. FRIEDMAN-YELLIN.

The result was announced by the Knesset Speaker, Mr. Yosef Sprinzak, who rapped three times with his gavel and announced "Chaim Ben Ozer Weizmann has been elected first President of the State of Israel."

The meeting then rose and sang the national anthem, and the Knesset adjourned until today, when Dr. Weizmann will be ceremoniously inaugurated.

Fifteen envelopes were empty to represent opposition to both candidates. One vote was not valid, and six Assembly members were absent.

The midnight session lasted an hour and 20 minutes, and was packed with drama and studded with heated outbursts. There had been intense lobbying after the adjournment of the evening session at 9 o'clock to ensure that Dr. Weizmann would get the required 61 votes on the first ballot. The meeting has been called for 10.15 but no agreement had been reached, and it was postponed for an hour. However, there was a further delay until five minutes before midnight, when the chairman of the Steering Committee, Mr. Zalman Rubashov, announced that there were two candidates: Professor Chaim Weizmann and Professor Yosef Klausner.

Party leaders then made brief statements explaining how they would vote, although the actual balloting was secret. Mr. Eliezer Pra'i (Mapam) read a declaration that his party would vote for Dr. Weizmann out of recognition of his stature in the Zionist Movement, especially his support for pioneering. It also wanted to show its determined opposition to the candidate of the Herut Party. At the same time, it declared that it did not agree with Dr. Weizmann's policy.

Uproar in House

When the Herut spokesman, Mr. Arieh Ben Eliezer, concluded his declaration nominating Professor Klausner with the words "We won't argue with collaborators," there was an uproar. Mapam members rose in their seats calling "Shame" at the Herut group seated on benches directly behind them, and the Herut members shouted back for several minutes until the Chairman succeeded in restoring order.

There followed declarations by Mr. Meir Wilner (Communists) and Mr. Nathan Friedman-Yellin, both of whom expressed opposition to Dr. Weizmann. The Communist also opposed Professor Klausner, and indicated that his party would abstain.

Ballot by Roll Call

The roll call of 120 names took a quarter of an hour, each Member casting his vote into the ballot-box as his name was called. There were absentees, including the Prime Minister who was confined to bed with a chill, the Finance Minister, Mr. Eliezer Kaplan, who is in Washington, and Mrs. Goldie Myerson, Envoy to Moscow. It took 15 minutes to count the votes, and the results were then announced.

A few minutes later, the Presidential Private Secretary, Mr. Yigal Kimche, was on the phone to Rehovot informing Dr. Weizmann of his election. Dr. Weizmann will come to Jerusalem today for his inauguration.

810,000 Refugees From Palestine

LONDON, Wednesday (AP). — The Minister of State, Mr. Hector McNeil, said today that there were about 810,000 Arab refugees from the Palestine fighting.

In a written reply in the House of Commons to Brigadier R. Rayner (Cons.), Mr. McNeil said that there were 210,000 in the Gaza area, 320,000 in Palestine and 280,000 in neighbouring Arab states.

Mr. McNeil said that the U.N. Relief groups were aiding about 600,000.

Egypt Must Refer Text to Cairo

RHODES, Wednesday (Reuter). — Although Israel-Egyptian agreement on an armistice is expected to be reached next week, a slight delay in the signing is expected, as the Egyptians have to send the completed text to Cairo for approval. This should, however, not take more than 24 hours, and the Egyptian delegation is reported to have told Dr. Ralph Bunche that it was a "formality."

Both delegations were today putting the finishing touches to that part of the agreement affecting Auja, and are next due to consider the question of Beersheba, where Israel forces are expected to remain. An Egyptian demand for a civil administration in Bir Asluj is reported to have been dropped, after the Israel delegation had convinced the Egyptians that the place was little more than a few huts, needing no "administration."

No Britons

While no details are known about the composition of the Trans-Jordan delegation which is expected here next week, Israel circles have pointed out that they would refuse to meet it if it included any British officers such as Glubb Pasha or Brigadier Norman Lash.

A source close to the Israel delegation said here today that an armistice with the Lebanon was "very close," the main point of dispute between the two countries — the return of nine Israel-held Lebanese villages — having been settled by Israel's agreement to hand them back. An agreement between the two sides had been "virtually drafted," it was said.

(Reuter.)

THE JERUSALEM POST

THURSDAY, July 6, 1950

PRICE: 28 PRUTA
VOL. XXVI. No. 7299

Column One
By
David Courtney

IN Japan, events are moving according to plan. Korea has made no difference. A week ago, on the day President Truman announced the sending of U.S. warships and air units to South Korea, all members of the Tokyo Cabinet, except the Prime Minister, resigned. Mr. Yoshida, the Prime Minister, is an amiable man; and wanted about him amiable men, who could be persuaded to accept without too much fuss a separate peace treaty with America and the other Western powers, which would leave the strategic control of the Japanese islands to the United States. General MacArthur and his friends at Washington have long insisted upon this. The Chiefs of Staff Mission recommended it. They said that Russia's possession of the atom bomb made the Okinawa advance bases indefensible, and left America with no alternative to bases in Japan.

■

PUBLIC opinion in Japan dislikes the idea. A large part of the Japanese Parliament opposes it. But Mr. Yoshida's recent victory in the elections has given him strong backing in both houses for a decision to accept the American terms. He still needs to have a few of the other main right-wing party, the People's Democratic Party, in his Cabinet, and to that end he has been talking matters over during the past week with Mr. Ashida, leader of the Democrats and a former Prime Minister. Three Cabinet posts are available for Mr. Ashida's group. The rest of the Cabinet posts have been filled. Nearly all of the Ministers are new men. General MacArthur is said to be satisfied.

■

UNTIL now, the U.S. State Department strongly opposed the military insistence upon retaining, permanently, bases in Japan. The Korea incident has made the political chiefs at Washington catch up with the military chiefs and Mr. Yoshida has been told to prepare his Houses of Parliament to take the consequences. Matters will not, of course, go as simply as that.

■

THE Japanese Press is saying that the Americans will have to double their forces in the area if they want to beat the North Koreans. Most of the newspapers are urging General MacArthur to double and even treble his forces at once; for they fear that if South Korea falls, it will be next to impossible for the Japanese to get a peace treaty of any kind, separate or collective. What worries the Japanese people is the fear that an extension of the Korean war might, because of American bases on the Emperor's territory, either force Japan into a state of belligerency or make her the object of attack as a result of armed intervention by interested Powers. It is not a nice prospect for the Japanese, who have among them the monuments of Hiroshima and Nagasaki.

■

THERE is a good deal of anti-American feeling in Japan just now. Visitors to that country have come back to tell that General MacArthur, who very rarely sees any Japanese and, until Korea, hardly ever moved outside Tokyo, has no real conception of the extent of the people's resentment. Misconceptions are, of course, the rule in Asia. It is unlikely that armed intervention on behalf of the crumbling South Koreans will do much to remove the misconceptions; or that it will make the Japanese more docile. Mr. Yoshida is, of course, a useful ally, and his new Cabinet should make him still more useful. It is a pity we have to make do with the Yoshidas and the Chiang Kai Sheks and the Bao Dais, when what we really need is the friendship of the Asian peoples.

Tel Aviv, July 6.

Law of Return Passed by House

By MOSHE BRILLIANT

The Law of the Return which records the right of every Jew to migrate to Israel was yesterday written into the State Legislation. The Knesset passed it unanimously and some members rose to their feet spontaneously in acclamation.

Charter of Entry

The Law of the Return states:

1. Every Jew has the right to immigrate to the country.

2 (a) Immigration shall be on the basis of immigrant visas.

(b). Immigrant visas shall be issued to any Jew expressing a desire to settle in Israel, except if the Minister of Immigration is satisfied that the applicant

(1) acts against the Jewish nation; or

(2) may threaten the public health or state security.

3. A Jew who comes to Israel and after his arrival expresses a desire to settle there, may, while in Israel, obtain an immigrant certificate.

(b) The exceptions listed in Article 2(b) shall apply also with respect to the issue of an immigrant certificate, but a person shall not be regarded as a threat to public health as a result of an illness which he contracts after his arrival in Israel.

4. Every Jew who migrated to the country before this law goes into effect, and every Jew who was born in the country either before or after the law is effective enjoys the same status as any person who migrated on the basis of this law.

5. The Minister of Immigration is delegated to enforce this law and he may enact regulations in connection with its implementation and for the issue of immigrant visas and immigrant certificates.

There was a feeling in the House that the passage of the law marked a milestone in Jewish history, and the atmosphere was heightened by the fact that yesterday was the anniversary of Herzl's death.

The passage of the law on Herzl Day was made possible by special dispensation from the Knesset at the opening of yesterday's session. The bill had been introduced to the Knesset by the Prime Minister on Monday and the general debate had not yet been completed. But the House yesterday unanimously agreed to the unusual procedure of considering the first reading closed and going ahead with the final reading.

The Law of the Return is linked with the proposed Nationality Act, which is before the House. The Nationality Bill naturally does not discriminate between Jewish and other citizens, pledging equal rights to all regardless of race, creed or colour. The bill passed yesterday deals with the inherent rights of the Jewish people in Israel.

The "Challenge"

Mr. Ben Gurion, who on Monday described it as a "charter" to the Jews of the world, came out yesterday with a second interpretation. Saying he could not find an adequate Hebrew term to express what he wanted to say, he resorted to English, calling it a "challenge" to the Jews of the world for whom the way to Israel was no longer barred.

The Mapam, Herut and Communist opposition factions expressed support for the principle but appeared to feel that the law was not sufficiently water-tight and might be abused by the Government. Dr. Yohanan Bader (Herut) and Mr. Israel Bar Yehuda (Mapam) proposed amendments providing that no Jew may be deported from the country, and making the clause affirming every Jew's right to migrate irrevocable.

Mr. Ben Gurion fought both proposals. He said the question of deportation had no place in the Law of Return. It should be dealt with by special legislation and whatever decision was reached would apply equally to all citizens. Mr. Bar Yehuda accepted this argument but Dr. Bader insisted on a vote. His amendment was defeated.

With respect to the motion that the article should be irrevocable, Mr. Ben Gurion said that a future Knesset could amend that clause as well as any other. Only if the House should grant the Supreme Court power to declare Knesset legislation unconstitutional, could the immutability of any legislation be assured. But, he added, the House had rejected this principle in the recent voting on the Constitution issue.

Force vs. Force

Mr Ben Gurion then said it was inconceivable that any future elected government should wish to reverse this decision. The danger, he said, was that an anti-Zionist minority might seize power by force. This, he said, could not be obviated with words. Other means would be necessary.

(Continued on Page 3, Col. 5)

France Gives $15m. Credit, to Double It

TEL AVIV, Wednesday. — France has extended $15m. credits to Israel and discussions are proceeding for credits of an additional $15m., according to M. M. B. Eliacheff, Commercial Counsellor to the French Legation here. Payments will be made in dollars. Discussions are also proceeding for a commercial agreement between the two countries which may be concluded soon.

France has agreed that part of the payments would be in the form of the transfer of capital of future immigrants to Israel and in payments from Jewish funds collected in France. The $15m. credits were given from January to June 1950 by private banks for a five-year period, and have been guaranteed by the French Government to the extent of 80 to 90 per cent under the French credit insurance scheme to foster exports. Israel will receive equipment for industry and agriculture, rails and sleepers for the Hadera-Tel Aviv line, construction iron, cement, woollen yarns and chemicals. The other $15m. credits are for the purchase of foodstuffs.

When the commercial agreement is signed, many very solid French enterprises will be willing to invest money here on a purely commercial basis, M. Eliacheff said. The amount of Jewish capital in France which would be invested in Israel is variously estimated and no predictions can be made as to the probable extent of such investments, he said.

M. Eliacheff was commercial counsellor to the French mission here shortly after the establishement of the State. He later returned to France, and is now back here for a period of one year.

After Midnight

The Foreign Relations Committee of the Syrian Constituent Assembly has recommended that Syria should remain neutral in the Korean conflict, parliamentary circles in Damascus reported last night.

TURKISH TRADE PACT SIGNED

TEL AVIV, Wednesday. — A trade and payments agreement, in the nature of an open exchange agreement, was signed between Israel and Turkey in Ankara yesterday.

Credits to the value of IL.300,000 will be opened by both countries for the exchange of goods. No details of what particular goods will be exchanged have yet been announced, but it is understood that Israel is to purchase from Turkey cattle, fodder and foodstuffs against manufactured articles, including pharmaceutical products, medical supplies, ice boxes and — when the motor truck assembly plant is in operation — also trucks and truck parts.

M. P.R. Zorlu, Economic Assistant to the Turkish Minister for Foreign Affairs, signed the agreement on behalf of his Government and Mr. Eliahu Sasson, Israel's Minister to Turkey, signed on Israel's behalf.

Sweden Says Bernadotte Issue Closed

STOCKHOLM, Wednesday, — (Reuter). — Sweden's early de jure recognition of Israel is expected shortly following a note from Foreign Minister Gesten Unden to the Israel Government, saying that the two countries' exchange of views on the murder of Count Bernadotte "is now considered closed."

Sweden's note said:

"The Swedish Government notes with satisfaction that the Government of Israel admits without circumlocution and expresses its regrets at the shortcomings of the original Israel police inquiry in the case which have been pointed out by the Swedish authorities.

"The Swedish Government notes further that the Government of Israel accepts full responsibility for what has occurred in this respect. The Swedish Government finds further evidence for this in the fact that the Government of Israel has paid to the U.N. the sum claimed as reparations for the monetary damage borne by the U.N. in connection with the murder of Count Bernadotte."

"The Swedish Government wishes to stress that it attaches special importance to the declarations that the inquiry of the Israel army is still in progress and in particular that the Government of Israel does not regard the case as closed.

"The Swedish Government wishes to express its expectation that, since conditions in Israel have now been stabilised, continued investigations will one day throw full light on the whole case. In accepting the expressions of regret and the apology which Dr. Eytan conveyed on behalf of his Government, the Swedish Government considers the exchange of views terminated."

Cabinet on Korea

The Foreign Minister, Mr. Moshe Sharett, reviewed the development of the struggle in Korea and its repercussions on the world at a Cabinet meeting in Jerusalem yesterday.

A Ministerial Committee was appointed to clarify some of the problems connected with travel abroad.

Questions concerning the jurisdiction of local authorities, wages of policemen and grading of police employees, the allocation of additional areas for the University buildings and Hadassah Hospital; and financial problems of immigration absorption were also discussed.

The Cabinet decided to appoint additional judges to the Aniti-Profiteering Courts.

French Socialists Talk with Other Parties on Gov't

PARIS, Wednesday (Reuter). Secretary-General Guy Mollet, of the Socialist Party, today accepted President Vincent Auriol's invitation to "undertake a mission of information" with a view to forming a new French Government.

The President took this step in the course of his efforts to find a government to take the place of the still-born Cabinet of Radical-Socialist Henry Queuille, out-voted last night at its first appearance before the Assembly.

Political observers here said M. Mollet had no chance of being accepted by the Assembly as Prime Minister, but that the President had made the first offer to the Socialist leader because it was the Socialists who provoked the fall of the Government last night.

Programme Sought

M. Mollet made it clear that he had accepted the mission with a view to reaching agreement between the so-called "governmental parties" on a possible programme and not with a view to himself becoming Premier-designate.

Observers interpreted this as meaning that the Socialists might be prepared to enter the next Government if they could agree with th Popular Republicans and Radicals on an acceptable wages policy.

Sterling Area Dollar Surplus at $180m.

LONDON, Wednesday (Reuter). — Sir Stafford Cripps, Chancellor of the Exchequer, announced in Parliament today that the sterling area's gold and dollar surplus amounted to $180m. in the second quarter of 1950.

This compared with a surplus of $40m. in the first quarter of the year.

It compared also with a deficit of $31m. in the fourth quarter of 1949 and a deficit of $632m. in the second quarter of 1949.

Sir Stafford gave these reasons for the improvement in the country's economic affairs: Britain and the other Commonwealth countries, together with other states like Burma, Iraq and Iceland which make up the sterling area, have stuck by the programme of restrained dollar spending which they agreed to do last year. The U.S. Economic Recovery Programme helped to make up the major part of the rise.

President Given Warm Send-Off On Leaving for Switzerland

HAIFA, Wednesday. —Haifa gave President and Mrs. Weizmann an official yet affectionate send-off in the Port this afternoon when they arrived from Rehovot to board the s.s. Kedmah for Genoa en route to Switzerland where they will remain for two months. The visit has been arranged for reasons of the President's health.

The Port, festooned with the flags of all nations and the emblem and the blue-white colours of the State, teemed with uniforms of civil, military, naval, port and customs police. A guard of honour supplied by the Navy and Haifa police was stationed outside the passenger quai and the band of the Volunteer Fire Brigade played martial music as the guests arrived and the guards presented arms.

At 4.15 sharp, the Presidential car drove up, and as the President, Mrs. Weizmann and the Military Adjutant, Sgan-Aloof M. Arnon, stepped out they were greeted by the Hatikva. The guard of honour presented arms and a swarm of cameramen rushed about snapping the President from all possible angles.

Personal Flag

Visibly tired and in need of rest, the President shook hands with Mr. David Remez, Minister of Communications, and Mr. Y. Sprinzak, Speaker of the Knesset. In a brief ceremony Mr. Remez, in his capacity as Chairman of the Committee of State Symbols, presented Dr. Weizmann with his personal flag, dark blue with the State emblem embroidered on it, which will fly from the mast of the s.s. Kedmah during the trip.

Mr. Remez then unveiled the Presidential standard. He wished the President and Mrs. Weizmann farewell and a

Amidst the thunder of 21-gun salvos, the President slowly walked up the gangplank to the ship assisted by the Adjutant. During this trip, the President and Mrs. Weizmann will occupy the Captain's quarters and the upper deck of the vessel.

21-Gun Salute

As the ship moved away from the quayside, the President waved to the crowds below which applauded and fighter planes roared low above the Port escorting the Kedmah out to Haifa Bay. There the ship was met by a flotilla of Israel warships which will accompany it.

Among those who went aboard to bid the President and Mrs. Weizmann farewell were Mr. Y. Sprinzak, who will now be Acting President; Mr. Remez; Sgan-Aloof N. Argov, representing the Prime Minister; Mr. Z. Sharef, Secretary to the Government; Mr. Berl Locker, Chairman of the Jewish Agency Executive; Mr. James G. McDonald, U.S. Ambassador and doyen of the Diplomatic Corps; and Mrs. McDonald; the Chief Rabbis, Dr. I. H. Herzog and B. Z. Uziel; Rav-Aloof Ya'akov Dori, of the Scientific Research Council; Mr. Gershon Agron, Director of the Information Services; Mr. S. Eisenberg, Secretary of the Jewish Agency; Dr. M. Simon, Chief of Protocol; the Inspector-General of Police, Mr. Y. Sachar; the Mayor of Haifa, Mr. S. Levy; Mr. George Weidenfeld, Political Secretary to the President; Mr. M. Weisgal, Executive Chairman of the Weizmann Institute, and Mrs. Weisgal; Dr. B. M. Bloch, a director of the Institute; the District Representative, Mr. Y. Bergman; the Chief Rabbis of Haifa, B. Marcus and Y. Ohana; District Superintendent of Police; Mrs. Flora Solomon, of London; and members of the President's family as well as senior military officers and consular officials.

The entire crew of the s.s. Kedmah went on strike today when they learned that representatives of the port workers had not been invited to the farewell ceremony. After the Army promised to investigate the circumstances which had led to the omission, the crew agreed to return to work.

After the s.s. Kedmah steamed out of the harbour, her place was taken by the s.s. Nazar, a Turkish luxury ship carrying 221 passen-

U.S., S. Korean Troops Retrea[t] In Face of Northern Offensive

U.S. Arms for Europe Diverted to Korea

WASHINGTON, Wednesday— (Reuter). Mr. Roger Tubby, a State Department spokesman, said today that some arms and military supplies destined for the defence of Western Europe may be diverted, as a temporary measure, for the use of American forces fighting in Korea.

He said any materials diverted to Korea would be replaced later so that the American arms programme for Western Europe would not suffer.

He categorically denied a press report here that a secret decision had been made to divert many millions of dollars worth of American weapons from Europe to the Philippines, Indo-China, Siam, Burma and Indonesia.

"No decision on any level has been made about this," Mr. Tubby said.

India Mediation Plea Wasn't Official

LONDON, Wednesday (Reuter). — A British Foreign Office spokesman told a press conference today that "no official approach" had been received from India proposing mediation over Korea.

15 U.N. Members Don't Back Korean Stand

LAKE SUCCESS, Wednesday, (Reuter). —Communist and Arab countries are predominant among the 15 U.N. members who have either opposed or so far withheld support from the U.N. Security Council resolution on Korea.

Until today 43 member nations have extended support.

Among Arab countries Egypt has abstained and the Yemen merely acknowledged receipt of the resolution.

Iraq, Lebanon, Saudi Arabia, Syria, Afghanistan, Burma Byelo-Russia, Liberia and the Ukraine have not yet replied.

U.S., SYRIA CONFER

DAMASCUS, Wednesday (Reuter). — U.S. Minister to Syria James Keely yesterday interrupted a Syrian Cabinet meeting for 45-minutes to confer with the Premier, Nasem el Kudsi. It was understood they discussed Syria's attitude to the Korean war, which is still undecided.

LEAGUE ON KOREA

The Near East Aram Broadcasting Station reported yesterday that Secretary-General Azzam Pasha of the Arab League was contacting member nations on the advisability of holding a meeting to work out a joint policy on the U.N. stand on Korea.

American Unit Cut off By Enem[y] Tanks South of Suwon

TOKYO, Wednesday. — General Douglas MacArthur headquarters announced officially that North Korea[n] forces today drove back American and South Korea[n] forces to higher ground north of Osan, 11 miles south[east] of Suwon, and appeared ready for a further advance.

The American communiq[ue] said: "North Korean forc[es] launched a frontal attack on the Suwon line as other el[e]ments continued an envelop[ing] attack on the Yonog[...] Inchon-Suwon triangle. Nor[th] Korean forces drove the d[e]fenders on to high ground [...] Osan.

"They continue to pre[ss] South Korean forces from th[e] north while at the same tim[e] extending columns around th[e] east flank of the defendin[g] forces with the apparent ob[jective] of cutting off the avenue of retreat.

"Reported movements [of] troops and material acro[ss] the Han River from Seoul in[to] recently captured areas [in]dicates preparation for fu[r]ther Northern action. Nor[th] Korean columns are report[ed] headed from Yoju to Inch[on] 23 miles east of Suwon. Nor[th] Korean troops in Wonju a[re] reported advancing towa[rd] Chungju. Their light t[...] have been active on the [...] coast near the 38th parall[el]. Other light reinforcements a[re] reported in the vicinity [of] Samchok.

"Air strikes against Nor[th] Korean targets inflicted hea[vy] damage at Haeju, Pyongyan[g] and Chinampo. The U.S. air [...] continued to move suppli[es,] munitions and personnel [by] air and sea from Japan [to] Korea. Air Force bomber[s] flew 16 sorties against rail road tracks northwest of O[...]nan with reported good re[sults]. Fighter units flew [...] sorties with trucks, buses, [lo]comotives and a railro[ad] trestle as objectives. One [...] car train was set on fire, o[ne] locomotive damaged, railro[ad] tracks and a bridge we[re] rocketed and strafed.

"The Navy continued [to] patrol the east and we[st] coasts."

Reach Americans

North Korean tanks and in[fantry], defying artillery a[nd] the blazing guns of Americ[an] and Australian fighter plane[s] thrust within small arm[s] range of forward America[n] troops, which may herald th[e] first major battle.

Cutting off an America[n] infantry unit in a sweepi[ng] outflanking movement fro[m] Suwon, three of four Norther[n] divisions were feeling the[ir] way towards the main bod[y] of American troops straddli[ng] their path ahead.

In teeming rain, the fron[t] line American units called [up] reinforcements of men a[nd] anti-tank weapons to stiffe[n] the front for the inevitab[le] clash — hourly awaited.

No news came of the fa[te] of the American outpost by[-]bassed by Communist tan[ks] which rumbled on down th[e] main highway from Suwo[n] after their fist taste of Ame[r]ican artillery fire.

Stepping up the air atta[ck] on the North Korean comm[u]nication links, fighter plan[es] of British and American [air]craft carriers completed [a] two-day hammering of bri[d]ges, trains aid airfield inst[al]lations with no losses and [no] casualties.

They shot down two North[ern] fighters and strafed eig[ht] others on the ground.

But muddy, wet weath[er] with low clouds, alternati[ng] with brighter flying cond[i]tions, threatened to peg ba[ck] the airmen, now near [...] chalking up their 1,000[th] sortie of the war.

With the Northerners push[]ing on in the centre of t[he] front, South Koreans fallin[g] back from evacuated Suw[on] were regrouping round t[he] American advanced positio[ns].

(Reuter, AP, U[P])

Commons Backs Korea Policy

LONDON, Wednesday (Reuter). —Mr. Winston Churchill today called for new talks with the Russians to seek a settlement before they possess the "devastating power" of atomic weapons.

"It is my belief that the American superiority in atomic warfare is, for the time being, an effective deterrent against a general Communist onslaught" he told the House of Commons, debating tho Korea war.

The House approved the Government's action in giving aid to South Korea without a vote.

The Conservative opposition leader joined Prime Minister Clement Attlee in declaring that British and American action in Korea gave the best chance of maintaining world peace.

Mr. Attlee said that the world was "indebted to the United States Government" for its prompt action in defending South Korea against "naked aggression."

Defending Britain's swift support for the U.S., he said delay might have allowed the aggressor to "get away with it" and to confront the United Nations with a *fait accompli*.

"The broad principle is that all states may be endangered if the aggressor is allowed to get away with the fruits of aggression in any part of the world," he said.

"To my mind, the danger of war would be increased were action not taken in this case. I have no doubt that this matter has got to be carried through and settled to show that aggression does not pay."

Mr. Stephen Davies, Labour, said the Government had talked about unprovoked aggression by the North Koreans. "That is an abuse of the English language. Were it not for the unprovoked aggression of the United States, this conflict would have been finished in a week."

Iraqis to Oil Talks

BAGHDAD, Wednesday. — (Reuter). Three Iraqi delegates left today by air for London for negotiations with British oil companies holding concessions in Iraq.

The delegation consists of ex-Premier Nuri Pasha Said, Dr. Ohia Jafar, Economics Minister, and Dr. Nadim el Pachachi, Director General of Oil Affairs.

Sicily's Bandit King Killed in Action

CASTELVETRANO, Sicily (Wednesday). — Salvatore Giuliano, notorious Sicilian bandit "king" reputed to have killed 105 policemen, died in a hail of police bullets here at dawn today.

After a fierce gun battle on the outskirts of this little village in south-west Sicily, the 27-year-old bandit leader was shot from the back as he crouched behind a barricade of felled treetrunks piled up in a farmhouse doorway.

Giuliano, wearing a diamond ring, khaki battledress, and a pair of brand new sandals, was ambushed at the farmhouse which he and a few faithful henchmen were attempting to hold after slipping through a police cordon surrounding their headquarters further north. Giuliano was apparently the only bandit casualty.

Gambled Career

After the fight, Colonel Luca, veteran Italian soldier, took off his steel helmet and murmured: "It was a good fight."

For Colonel Luca it was the end of a fight which he had gambled his career on. Virtually unknown, he was picked out last year by Interior Minister Mario Scelba to lead the special anti-bandit force set up to eliminate Guiliano.

Friends warned him that the job was "political suicide." They said Guiliano had influential friends, particularly secret society. They said also that if Giuliano's bullets did not kill him, he would "fall with political stabs in the back."

Colonel Luca ignored them, and pledged his career on killing Guiliano. And for the past months he had been patiently hacking away at the supports of Guiliano's "kingdom," pursuing and capturing his followers until today's final victory.

Only eight hours after his death, Giuliano was buried in a rough, pine wood coffin in the local cemetery. There were no mourners.

His 52-year-old mother was not given a last chance to see her son.

JUDEA INSURANCE COMPANY LTD.
THE FIRST ISRAEL INSURANCE COMPANY

THE JERUSALEM POST

The Daily News — All Israel Views

POST

THURSDAY, SEPTEMBER 11, 1952

PRICE: 70 PRUTA
VOL. XXVIII, No. 7360

Marginal Column
By A. V. SHERMAN

ASSAM'S resignation is a measure not only of Egypt's crisis but also of the Arab League's. His resignation was not unforeseen. During the past few years he has been engaged in a series of conflicts, partly political, partly personal, with many delegations, governments, and personalities; only recently the representatives of Libya, his second homeland, declared him persona non grata. Even had the internal Egyptian scene not changed as abruptly as it has done, it is doubtful whether a reform movement inside the League which has met so many defeats under Assam's leadership, would not have pushed him out sooner or later.

BECAUSE Assam was a prominent and representative figure, almost an institution in the Arab world, his rise and fall in themselves epitomize its recent unhappy history. He was born in 1891 in Egypt still nominally part of the Ottoman Empire. A brilliant but emotionally unstable youth, he went to England to study medicine, but found the discipline of continued study irksome, and soon was caught up in the Arab nationalist movement which was gaining strength at that time among the young intellectuals. Even at that time the basis of the movement was largely negative; the young men felt that they and their people were undervalued, and that independence was the thing. But they lacked a general philosophy and orientation to guide them amid the rapid world changes which were soon to come about. For most Syrians and others under Turkish rule the Turk was the main enemy, the blight which held back their countries from progress. For Assam, however, the Europeans were the enemy, and Turkey was to spearhead the East's revival. While other Arab nationalists aided the Entente against the Turks, Assam joined the Turkish Armies in Libya, showing himself a talented chief but poor collaborator.

AFTER the 1936 Anglo-Egyptian Treaty he served as Minister to several Middle Eastern countries, later joining the Cabinet as Minister for Social Welfare. He was one of the generation which took up high posts in the administration, as a reward for years of successful opposition. But they had become far too set in their habits and could only oppose, cherish old enmities and make new ones. His policy with regard to Palestine "illustrated the duality of his c a ract r. His claim that the Jews were his "cousins" and that he desired peace and co-operation with them were no less sincere than his fire-eating oratory, when he threatened that Arab power would push the Jews into the sea. Even his fellow-orators complained that he was carried away by his own oratory.

THE Palestine defeat was only one of the causes which led to the League's splintering and his own growing unpopularity. Indulging in his old feud against the Senussi, Assam used his position and power to try to gain for himself the post of "Viceroy of Tripolitania," thereby setting up a barrier between Egypt and Libya, which has remained outside the League. In 1949 the feud between him and Iraq grew nearly strong enough to make his position untenable, and only Egyptian intervention saved him. After 1951, when the Wafd brought the Anglo-Egyptian crisis to a head, Assam's efforts to embroil the whole Arab League in Egypt's troubles led to further League crises, with Iraq, Syria, Lebanon and Jordan objecting on one score or another and Assam becoming ever fiercer and more irreconcilable in his imprecations against imperialism and Zionism. His removal opens the way for a changed attitude on the part of the Arab League. If it survives. There is no reason why the League under sober guidance could not become an instrument of Arab co-operation and political stability in the Middle East. The surest course about only if Assam's mistakes are not repeated. Peace with Israel is only one of the steps the League needs to take now that Assam — who, like one of his collaborators, staked his reputation on Palestine — has

Assam Quits; New Secretary Sought

CAIRO, Wednesday (Reuter) — Leading candidates for the vacant post of Secretary-General of the Arab League are former Egyptian Foreign Ministers Mohammed Salah e-Din and Abdul Khalek Hassuna, it was reported here.

Egypt Plans New Approach to U.K.

CAIRO, Wednesday (Reuter). — Egypt is planning a new approach to solve the Anglo-Egyptian question, an Egyptian Foreign Office spokesman said last night.

He said that although no immediate action was contemplated, because the Egyptian Government is busy implementing social, political and economic reforms at home, "we shall turn to foreign affairs in the not too distant future."

The spokesman made this comment after British Ambassador Sir Ralph Stevenson paid a courtesy call on the new Sovereign Minister, Ahmed Farag Tayeh.

The Wafd's executive today announced the formation of a three-man committee to draw up the rules for the Party's reorganization in accordance with the new law governing political parties.

Searches Continue

Special Army and police squads, continuing the search for "hostile elements" in Egypt, have raided scores of houses in Cairo and Alexandria in the past 48 hours, it was disclosed today.

They seized masses of documents which are now being studied. One of the main objectives raided was the premises of the Royal Automobile Club in the two cities. The homes of many prominent personalities under the old régime, many of them under arrest since last Saturday, were also searched.

The Government today ordered three clubs where ex-King Farouk and his associates used to meet to close down immediately. They are the Royal Automobile, the Mohammed Aly and the Nile Boat clubs.

General Naguib last night announced the appointment of Brigadier Mohammed Ibrahim, Director of Military Training, as Deputy Commander in Chief of the Army.

Brigadier Ibrahim will carry out the day to day military routine of the commander in chief which General Naguib, as Premier, no longer looks after himself.

Mexico Proposes Korea Compromise

MEXICO CITY, Wednesday. — President Aleman, of Mexico, has formulated a compromise proposal on Korea which was officially submitted yesterday to the U.N. The proposal is designed to break the bottleneck preventing an armistice in Korea, and provides a compromise on the question of prisoners of war. Its main points are as follows:

1) Prisoners detained by either side, and who have expressed the wish to return to their country of origin, will be exchanged.
2) Other prisoners will be given the right to work and will be received by U.N. member countries which agree to receive them.
3) After restoration of a normal service in Korea, the governments of the countries of origin of these prisoners will extend the necessary facilities necessary for their immediate return to their country; those Governments will agree to repatriate prisoners, who wish to return to their country of origin under the restoration of normal conditions in Korea. In this latter event, U.N. will provide the necessary assistance.

Mr. Trygve Lie, U.N. Secretary-General, said at his press conference at the U.N. today that he supported the Mexican plan.

Manoeuvres End in South
By Sraya Shapiro
POST Military Correspondent

TEL AVIV, Wednesday. — The southern war games ended at 4.15 p.m. today. They formed the fifth and last link in the summer manoeuvres this year, which included three Army war games and large-scale Navy and Air Force manoeuvres. In autumn, a test of the preparedness of area defences will be held, while on the higher Army level there will be an internal trial of combined staff operations without the participation of soldiers.

These will virtually end a three-year plan. During this year to test the preparedness of the Israel Defence Forces; their composition, training and warfare principles, the Chief of the General Staff, Rav Aluf Yigael Yadin, told military correspondents today. To learn the lessons of the manoeuvres and translate them into proper instructions in the Army Train-

Nobody was more conscious of the defects revealed than Headquarters, Rav Aluf Yadin said. There was a marked improvement over last year's performance.

Parachutists' Ability

The Air Force and the Navy, in particular, deserved praise for their technical ability and the fighting spirit of the crews whose job was almost as perilous in peacetime as it is in war. The parachute unit was able to stand comparison with any group abroad, according to expert testimony.

Unreserved praise from the Chief of Staff also went to the Reservists. They proved to be as tough and dependable as regular soldiers. The same compliment went to the owners of the civilian vehicles which had been drafted for the war games.

The Deputy Chief of Staff, Aluf Mordechai Makleff, could be considered the head of the "aggressive progress" in the Army plan, a seven months obscure observer.

In the last day of the southern war games the newly introduced airborne troops took part, as did a large number of aircraft. Its main task was to destroy "enemy" positions in face of harassing fire from enemy guns. The manoeuvre ended with a large number of

SHARETT, ADENAUER SIGN PACT IN MUTE, SECRET 13-MINUTE CEREMONY

'Blow to Nazism, Triumph for Israel'

WASHINGTON, Wednesday (Reuter). — Official and diplomatic quarters here regard the West German-Israel agreement as a personal triumph for Chancellor Adenauer.

These sources point out that a decisive part in the negotiations was played by Dr. Adenauer, who had the support of democratic and liberal groups in Germany, but was strongly opposed by neo-Nazi elements.

One source stated that the signing of the agreement "is also a triumph for the forces genuinely anxious to promote the cause of Democracy in Germany."

Historic Achievement

The agreement is also regarded in diplomatic quarters here as an historic achievement for the new State of Israel in that it has been able to emphasise the changed status of Jews and defend their rights in Europe.

It is further pointed out here that recompense for confiscated Jewish property is to be paid by a foreign state for the first time since ancient days.

Acheson Hopes For Quick Ratification

WASHINGTON, Wednesday (AP). — Secretary of State Dean Acheson said today that West Germany's agreement with Israel to compensate its Jewish victims of Nazi persecution is proof that the "vast majority of the German people intend to make redress for the sufferings of the Jews under the Nazis."

Mr. Acheson said that the U.S. hoped the agreement signed in Luxembourg today will be ratified without delay. He told a news conference that the U.S. is pleased the negotiations ended successfully.

German Envoy in U.S. 'Deeply Satisfied'

WASHINGTON, Wednesday (AP). — West German Chargé d'Affaires Heinz Krekeler today issued a statement expressing his "deep satisfaction at the successful outcome of the Hague negotiations."

"I am very well aware of the load that human suffering has no relation to material claims and their restitution," the statement said, "but material means are often a way to express an attitude of mind and spirit, and this is certainly what is happening here."

Referring to the attitude of Hitler and his associates against the Jewish people, Krekeler said, "We consent that the crimes committed by those who wronged this people were so great that they may never happen again. It is with profound respect for the victims of terror and persecution that we present this pledge to the people of the world."

Preamble to Agreement

WHEREAS unspeakable criminal acts were perpetrated against the Jewish people during the National Socialist régime of terror

AND WHEREAS by a declaration in the Bundestag on September 27, 1951, the Government of the Federal Republic of Germany made known their determination, within the limits of their capacity, to make good the material damage caused by these acts

AND WHEREAS the State of Israel has assumed the heavy burden of resettling so great a number of uprooted and destitute Jewish refugees from Germany and from territories formerly under German rule and has on this basis advanced a claim against the Federal Republic of Germany for global recompense for the cost of the integration of these refugees

NOW THEREFORE the State of Israel and the Federal Republic of Germany have agreed:

(The preamble is followed by the 17 articles of the agreement which are summarised on Page 4 and which will be published textually tomorrow.)

First Goods to Arrive In 1953, Oil in Few Weeks

TEL AVIV, Wednesday. — The first German goods under the reparations agreement will probably arrive in Israel at the beginning of next year, shortly after formal ratification of the agreement, but oil purchased with German Sterling balances will probably come within the next few weeks.

At a press conference here tonight, Dr. Jacob Robinson, Legal Adviser to the Israel delegation to the U.N. and Legal Adviser to the Reparations Delegation, said that the Government's formal ratification would follow a day or so after ratification by the German parliament, probably about the end of November. The instruments of ratification will then be exchanged by the representatives of the two Governments before the Secretary-General of the U.N. in New York. An unofficial Israel delegation will probably start administrative work in Germany preparing for the establishment of the official Israel mission even before the formal ratification.

Agency and Malben

Part of the 450m. marks to be paid to Israel for the benefit of the Conference on Jewish Material Claims Against Germany will be spent by the Jewish organizations, principally the Jewish Agency and the American Joint Jewish Committee, in Israel for the absorption and rehabilitation of Jewish refugees.

Two-thirds of the entire sum of 3,450m. marks will be used directly by Israel, while 18.5 per cent will be used by the Jewish Agency and the Joint, through Malben, in Israel. The balance of about 15 per cent will be used abroad by the 20 Jewish organizations for the relief of former victims of the Nazis.

Germany still being under the control of the Occupying Powers, the agreement, as all contracts entered into by Germany, must be sent to the three High Commissioners. If no objections are raised by them within 21 days, the agreement is regarded as having the consent of the Occupying Powers.

In an exchange of letters between the two delegations, and incorporated in the agreement as an annex to the agreement, arrangements are made for reparations goods to be shipped to Israel in Israel vessels, in which case shipping charges are to be paid by Israel, or by ships of a third party, which payment to be made in German marks out of the sum set aside for services. In no case will goods be brought to Israel in German vessels.

Eban and Blaustein Sign Contract
By Jesse Zel Lurie
POST Correspondent

NEW YORK, Wednesday (Reuter). — The reparations agreement signed with West Germany is "a moral victory, a victory of conscience over the dictates of brute force," Israel Ambassador Abba Eban said this morning. He was speaking at a contract with the Jewish Conference on Material Claims against Germany providing for Israel's payment to the Jewish organizations of their share of the reparations.

"The Germans, who wanted to wipe the Jews off the face of the earth, are now signing a contract of compensation with a sovereign Jewish State," Mr. Eban said.

Mr. Jacob Blaustein, President of the American Jewish Committee, stated that it was the Conference's intention to use the share of the reparations for relief of victims outside Israel, but it did not exclude spending some of the funds in Israel.

Much of the Conference's funds, he said, will probably be given to the Joint Distribution Committee.

(Continued on Page 2, Col. 6)

Payments to Gird State and Lead To Economic Freedom — Lavon

The reparations agreement — a great moral and political victory — will strengthen the country and help make us economically independent, Mr. Pinhas Lavon, Minister without Portfolio, told the nation last night over Kol Yisrael.

No amount of reparations could wipe out the wrong done to the Jewish people, he emphasised, and noted that reparations would increase the State's future safety by placing it on a firmer economic basis. "Weakness arouses the lust of tyrants and extortioners," he said.

Mr. Lavon noted the benefits the nation could draw from $715m. — to be paid directly and the $110m. given to world Jewry — by comparison with the $800m. the nation has received from all sources — in the past four years — in reparations, private and national loans, grants, private investments, property of new immigrants, and non-payment imports. With the latter we, he said, we fought and were victorious in the War of Liberation; we re-equipped our Defence Forces; we brought 650,000 Jews of different countries and assured accommodation to hundreds of thousands; we established many hundreds of agricultural settlements and equipped older

ties in various parts of the country; we laid pipelines and built irrigation works on hundreds of thousands of dunams; and we enlarged Haifa harbour and built Kishon port.

The Minister emphasised that the goods to be received from West Germany would further the process of development. They would permit us to exploit the Negev mines, broaden agriculture, develop transportation, shipping and fishing, increase electrical output, develop basic industries, and build homes for ma'barot residents.

Mr. Lavon reminded the nation that "the people who wanted to exterminate us is forced to bear some of the burden involved in creating a new Jewish centre of strength and a place of rebirth."

It was not by chance that some Germans, those openly and those secretly anti-Semitic, tried to block the agreement. It was not by chance that the Arab countries tried many times to prevent the signing. Both knew that this agreement would strengthen the State of Israel and the feeling of security of world Jewry.

This is the first time in the history of mankind that an unwritten law was broken — the law that only force can assure just claims. The agreement establishes a new principle, in international relations, he said.

3,450m. Marks in Reparations

LUXEMBOURG, Wednesday. — At a secret, silent ceremony that lasted 13 minutes, Israel and Germany signed an agreement here today under which the Bonn Government agrees to pay 3,450m. marks as reparations for material damage suffered by the Jews at the hands of the Nazis.

Contacts First Made 18 Months Ago
POST Political Correspondent

TEL AVIV, Wednesday. — The signing of the German reparations agreement by the Israel Foreign Minister and the head of the West German Federal Government is in accordance with the wish of the Israel Government to underline the historic importance of the agreement, regarded as unique in that it represents restitution by a plunderer for past actions.

The agreement follows 16 months of contacts and negotiations. It was completed seven years after the end of the war. Without the establishment of the State of Israel, it is pointed out in Mapai circles, such agreement would have been impossible.

Ratification by the West German Parliament is expected by the end of this year. As far as Israel, this agreement requires the ratification of the Cabinet alone, but it is understood that when Foreign Minister Sharett reported to the Knesset Foreign Affairs Committee on the agreement he stated that the Cabinet would present a full report to the Knesset after the summer recess and might then initiate a debate on the subject. West German law, on the other hand, lays down that such agreements must be ratified by the Parliament.

First contact on a reparations agreement was made in March, 1951, when the Israel Government appealed to the three occupying powers. The initial reply was positive, and on September 27, 1951, the German Chancellor, Dr. Konrad Adenauer, stated in the German Bundestag that the West German Government was prepared to enter into negotiations with Israel regarding reparation for the wrong done to world Jewry under the Nazi régime. In December, 1951, Dr. Adenauer sent a private letter to Dr. Nahum Goldmann, stating that he was prepared to accept the Israel demands as a basis for negotiations. Formal talks began between delegates of the West German Government and the Israel Government on March 20, 1952, and were temporarily suspended on April 7. They were resumed on June 24, and a draft agreement was completed last week.

The first stage — the negotiations

Tension at Signing
By Nora Beloff
Special to The POST

LUXEMBOURG, Wednesday (OFNS). — An atmosphere of tension created by threats of Jewish extremists and the need for security measures enveloped the ceremony of signature of the Israel-German reparations agreement here today. Nevertheless, when the silent ceremony was ended and the text signed, Mr. Sharett accepted Chancellor Adenauer's invitation to a private talk, which could no longer have been just a matter of terms of payments since these had been settled, but must have covered a wider political field.

The contents of the agreement were in no way surprising. The six months of negotiations which started in The Hague and ended in Luxembourg were in part technical through in economics, many of whom are university professors whose job was to set Israel's claims against Germany's capacity for payment and to formulate an acceptable compromise.

The background of the talks which brought Jews and Germans together was memories of the kind of evil which cannot be paid for in cash: the evil of gas chambers and the mass slaughter of millions of men, women and children, the murder of whole communities in the death camps and concentration camps.

There were still antagonist Nazis loose in the country denouncing the talks, but the German delegation was able to announce that they had received "encouragingly few" letters of protest against the talks begun.

AFTER MIDNIGHT

Freezing of C-o-L Considered
Jerusalem POST Reporter

Commodity prices and the cost-of-living index featured in a series of conferences in Jerusalem yesterday.

Mapai, Government and Histadrut leaders met for several hours in the morning at the Ministry of Finance. It was reported that the C-o-L allowance was thoroughly aired, with Cabinet members generally favouring a halt in further increases, and Histadrut representatives reluctant to agree to such a policy.

Among those who participated in the conference were Minister of Finance Levy Eshkol, Minister of Commerce and Industry Dov Joseph, Minister of Agriculture Perets Naphtali, Minister Without Portfolio Pinhas Lavon; Mr. A. Becker and Mr. Z. Onn, of the Histadrut, and Mr. H. Dan, of Solel Boneh.

No Shoe Tender

At still another meeting, shoe manufacturers accepted a Commerce Ministry proposal for the production of 40,000 pairs of shoes at last April's prices, thus guaranteeing no immediate increase. Ministry spokesman declared that the tender system had been rejected in this instance because of a "shortage of materials," although it was reported that the tenders had begun to be cancelled. Another Ministry source stated that although a tender for the production would have dropped the price, it was feared that several manufacturers would have been forced to close down for lack of materials.

Dr. Joseph also conferred with Mr. A. Shenkar, President of the Manufacturers' Association, on the "problems of industry." Among the questions discussed were the difficulty of business to pay wages and the continuing raw material shortage.

SOCIALISTS SAY ALL GERMANS CONCERNED

BONN, Wednesday (Reuter). — The press service of the Social Democrats (opposition) today declared that the West German-Israel reparations agreement should be ratified by the West German Parliament as soon as possible.

Material and moral reparation to the Jews concerned all Germans. The German people would only then be reconciled with its neighbours when it had brought proof of its good will in making good the crimes of the Third Reich, the statement said.

But there remained the task of fighting and killing all movements which were liking for the dictatorship, including Nazi excesses, made them unsuitable for service to humanity and the German people. This was an obligation which could not be laid down in treaties but must

THE JERUSALEM POST

SUNDAY
NOVEMBER 4, 1956

PRICE: 120 PRUTA
VOL. XXXII, No. 8646

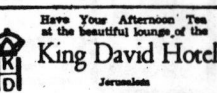

Nagy Forms New All-Party Gov't

BUDAPEST, Saturday. — Premier Imre Nagy formed a new Government today and opened negotiations with Russia on withdrawing the Red Army from Hungary. The new Government is said to contain all major Hungarian parties and is "truly representative."

These parties include the Conservative Smallholders Party, the Social Democrats, the Liberal Peasants Party and the Communists, who this week changed their name to the Socialist Workers Party.

With the formation of the new Cabinet, it was announced that negotiations had been opened with a Soviet military mission on the withdrawal of the Red Army. The Soviet delegates consists of three Russian generals and four colonels.

There were no reports of fighting today although news of Soviet troop movements was widespread.

In New York, the U.N. Security Council met today, over the objections of Russia, to discuss the situation in strife-torn Hungary.

The U.S. delegate, Mr. John Cabot Lodge, said, "We must give honest consideration to what the U.N. can do that will help the brave Hungarian people in their struggle for freedom."

Dr. Carlos Blanco, of Cuba, said he could not believe that any member would resist the demands of the Hungarian people for self-determination. He recalled that the Soviet delegate yesterday spoke eloquently during the Middle East debate of the right of all people to choose their own governments and against armed intervention by foreign powers.

Dr. Blanco appealed a resolution to appeal immediately to Moscow to withdraw Soviet troops from Hungarian territory; to reiterate the right of the Hungarian people to determine by free elections the type of government they wanted; and to establish a Commission of the Council to supervise and see that these measures were carried out.

US Tempts Hungary With $20 m. Aid

WASHINGTON, Saturday (Reuter). — The U.S. yesterday offered an initial allocation of $20m.-worth of food and medical supplies to Hungary.

The White House Press Secretary, Mr. James Hagerty, said the offer would be transmitted immediately to the Hungarian Government. President Eisenhower took the final decision to make this offer at a meeting yesterday afternoon.

The U.S. protested to Russia that demands of American legation officials being evacuated from Budapest were turned back at the Austrian-Hungarian border after Russian military road blocks yesterday.

Russian troops armed with tommyguns turned back four American mothers and 10 children for the second straight day today when the dependents of Legation personnel in Budapest tried to reach homes in Austria.

A State Department spokesman said that the Deputy Under - Secretary of State, Mr. Robert Murphy, summoned the Soviet Ambassador, Mr. Georgi Zarubin, and "protested energetically against the interference with American official personnel.

DULLES TAKEN TO HOSPITAL

WASHINGTON, Saturday (Reuter). — Mr. John Foster Dulles, Secretary of State, entered the Walter Reed Army Hospital early today and doctors reported that he might be suffering from appendicitis.

The State Department said 68-year-old Mr. Dulles is "resting comfortably," and was carrying on some of his work by telephone from his hospital bed. The Under-Secretary of State, Mr. Herbert Hoover, Jr., was in charge at the State Department as Acting Secretary.

A later announcement said that Mr. Dulles would have an immediate operation for acute appendicitis.

Dulles Would Like Bonn To Halt Reparations

WASHINGTON, Saturday (INA). — The State Department has notified West Germany that the U.S. Government would take a sympathetic view if Germany was to withhold reparations shipments to Israel. This was made known here yesterday by State Department sources.

Such a move would be seen by the State Department as clearly in spirit with the U.N. General Assembly resolution adopted on Thursday night and would be consistent with the efforts of the international community to restrain Israel.

It was made known that earlier this week the matter had been discussed in a meeting between the German Ambassador, Mr. Heinz Krekeler, and Mr. Robert Murphy, Deputy Under Secretary of State.

Eden Promises Israel Withdrawal

LONDON, Saturday (Reuter). Prime Minister Sir Anthony Eden in a nation-wide broadcast tonight said, "Once British and French forces have occupied the key points on the Canal, the Government will ensure that the Israel forces withdraw from Egyptian territory.

"I have no doubt that this is their intention, but they will not do so unless we are there to keep the peace, to give the necessary guarantee and prevent a repetition of these events."

CABINET MEETS

The Cabinet met yesterday to discuss the U.N. General Assembly resolution and the security situation.

Fedayeen Make Last Attacks

REHOVOT, Saturday. — The remnants of the fedayeen gangs fleeing from Gaza committed acts of sabotage on Friday and tonight, in the Rehovot area.

A woman member of Kibbutz Givat Brenner was knifed three times early tonight by an assailant who jumped out of a wood near the kibbutz school. He tried to drag her away and when she flashed her torch he stabbed her. She is being treated for her injuries at the hospital.

The railway line from Tel Aviv to Beersheba was blown up near Kfar Yavneh on Friday evening, but workers soon came to repair it. Telephone lines were also cut in the vicinity. Police and defence forces have gone to comb the whole area for fedayeen.

The Army spokesman announced that on Friday night a number of shots were fired on a bus on the Wadi Ara road. A Border Police car which rushed to the place hit a mine. There were no casualties.

On Thursday night a considerable number of fedayeen bands were active in the Negev, the spokesman said. A number of vehicles were attacked, and waterlines were blown up.

Uri Osen, aged 25, a member of Kibbutz Eres died today from wounds sustained when his car hit a mine laid by fedayeen on Thursday last. He leaves a pregnant wife.

Osen is the third victim of this attack. The other two, Simha Korichman and Shlomo Glickstein, were killed instantly.

Battle for Gaza — Edgar Hirshbein, photographer of The Jerusalem Post, went into action with his camera along with Israel troops on Friday morning in their attack on Gaza. Top photo shows Israelis advancing on strongpoint at Al Mashahira, north of Gaza. Smoke rises from exploding Israel mortars. After the action was over, Hirshbein took picture (below) of Egyptians captured at the outpost. (See other photos on Page 3.) The Post photographer was forced to take cover behind a tank when cross-fire was opened up on Army jeep in which he was riding.

Eden: We'll Stop If U.N. Force Enters

LONDON, Saturday (Reuter). — Sir Anthony Eden told an extraordinary session of the House of Commons today that Britain has informed the United Nations she will willingly stop military action in Egypt if the U.N. will put in a force to keep peace between Egypt and Israel. A condition was that both Israel and Egypt would agree to accept forthwith limited detachments of Anglo-French troops to be stationed between the combatants.

The Prime Minister said he had been in consultation with the governments of Australia and New Zealand. "I have good reason to believe that these governments will welcome my statement" he said. The substance of the statement had also been communicated to Canada, the United States, and the United Nations Secretary-General.

Sir Anthony began by saying that this sitting of the Commons had been arranged so that he could make a statement on the reply British proposed to send to the resolution of the U.N. Assembly.

The House will first recall the statement which I made in the course of my speech on November 1, when I said that the first and urgent task is to separate the combatants and to stabilise the position. That is our purpose. If the U.N. were then willing to take over the official task of maintaining peace in the area nobody would have been better pleased than I.

"Since that statement was made I have had consultations in London with the French Foreign Minister. As a result the British and French Governments are sending the following reply to the resolution of the U.N. General Assembly:

(An Israel Embassy spokesman in Paris reported the Army had got within 15 kilometres of the Suez Canal at one point.

(He also said Israel had taken about 15,000 Egyptian prisoners in the Sinai Peninsula and captured about 100 tanks, 500 guns of various calibres and considerable stocks of munitions and petrol. Final figures had not yet been established.)

France Elated by Israel Victory

By MAURICE CARR, Jerusalem Post Correspondent

PARIS, Saturday. — Franco-British determination to bring their military move into the Suez Canal to a successful and speedy conclusion remains "absolute," it was authoritatively learned here. Nothing happening at the diplomatic sphere can change that determination, it was said.

A team of technicians and appropriate equipment is already being assembled for the clearance of the blocked Canal with a minimum of delay as soon as the occupation of the Canal Zone is completed. It is intended that the French and British forces will serve as the spearhead and nucleus of future U.N. police, paving the way for international control of the Canal and an Israel-Arab peace settlement.

Expressing "very great satisfaction" with the brilliantly successful Israel operations, the same sources pointed out that the apparent slowness of the Franco-British campaign is due to the fact that for reasons of international propriety it was impossible to embark troops, let alone order troopships to sail, before the expiration of the ultimatum.

The Egyptian Air Force is described as "virtually dead." Its installations are destroyed, all rendering Egyptian night flights impossible, and by day the Egyptians are capable at most of individual sorties, but not of coherent actions. The first phase of the Franco-British campaign is regarded as successfully terminated.

France and Britain said today they will halt their military operations against Egypt only when Israel and Egypt accept intervention of United Nations police force until peace is achieved and a "satisfactory arrangement" for the Suez Canal arrived at.

The Quai d'Orsay officially refuses to take a tragic view of the American attitude, underlining the more positive aspects of Eisenhower's television address, notably his allusion to friendship for Britain and France and recognition of Israel's action under serious provocation.

The French press, however, is exceedingly critical of the U.S. attitude. Thus, Roger Massip, diplomatic editor of the Conservative "Figaro," writes: "Mr. Dulles has deliberately permitted aggravation of the menace which has pressed on Israel since the accession of the military dictatorship in Cairo."

SINAI BATTLE WON

TEL AVIV, Saturday. — The Sinai Campaign is virtually over. Israel troops are within sight of the Suez Canal. In the South, the capture of the village, Tor, on the Gulf of Suez, 250 kilometres south of the Canal on the western banks of the peninsula, was announced this morning.

The two islands which block the Tiran straits are included in the term "the whole of the peninsula" used by the army spokesman tonight, although their occupation was not yet officially announced today.

Two Tiran Islands Next to Fall

TEL AVIV, Saturday. — The Government and Army spokesman said this evening that the whole of the Sinai Peninsula is "or shortly will be" occupied by the Israel Army. This included the two Tiran islands blocking the entrance to the Gulf of Akaba, the spokesman said.

Israel troops, moving along three fairly parallel roads across the Peninsula, have halted some 15 kilometres from the Suez Canal, the spokesman added. "I am sure reconnaissance patrols have come up to the Canal itself," he said.

There was no Egyptian air activity today. Asked if the Government intended to deny the troops one kilometre nearer the Canal than the 16 kilometres mentioned in the Anglo-French ultimatum, the spokesman said he did not know.

The number of Israel casualties in the campaign may be announced in a day or two. The only indication of the number of enemy prisoners was that they were "thousands." Comparatively few officers were among them, and it appears from what Egyptian soldiers said that the bulk of the officers fled as quickly as they could, leaving their troops behind.

Arabic "Mein Kampf"

About 100 tanks and self-propelled guns have been taken as booty. They were mostly T-34's, with a number of Shermans among them. The self-propelled guns were mostly SU 100's (Russian-made). The number of vehicles of various makes runs into hundreds. Very large dumps of ammunition were discovered near the frontier.

Among the standard equipment of the Egyptian officers captured there was a two volume paper-back edition in Arabic of Hitler's "Mein Kampf."

500 Cairo Jews Said Arrested

More than 500 Jews have been rounded up by the Egyptian authorities in Cairo and its suburbs and sent to concentration camps, Beirut Radio reported on Friday. The Jews were said to be "well-known for their Zionist sympathies."

The same source declared that 450 British technicians who remained in Egypt to tend the Suez Canal Zone military bases after the British evacuation, were also arrested and sent to detention camps. More than 100 British firms and some 30 French businesses registered in Egypt have been confiscated and their assets placed under the control of the Egyptian Government, the Radio reported.

Nutting Quits As Minister of State

LONDON, Saturday (Reuter). — Mr. Anthony Nutting, Minister of State at the Foreign Office, has resigned because he disagrees with the policy of the Conservative Government.

Two days ago Mr. Nutting denied reports that he was going to resign. Nutting, 36, became Minister of State two years ago — then the youngest-ever man to hold the post of second in command at the Foreign Office.

In that capacity he negotiated the 1954 agreement with Egypt on the British evacuation of the Suez Canal Zone base. He was Foreign Under-Secretary from the age of 31.

Landing in Canal Expected

LONDON, Saturday (Reuter). — British and French amphibious landings at each end of the Suez Canal were expected this weekend after Britain and France jointly reaffirmed their determination to go ahead with their "police action" in Egypt.

A junior Minister in the Government declared in a public speech at Wolverhampton last night that within a few hours British and French troops would be occupying territory in the Suez Canal area. But spokesmen for the Prime Minister and the Ministry of Defence both declined to comment on the speech by Mr. Enoch Powell, Parliamentary Secretary to the Ministry of Housing.

Mr. Anthony Head, the Minister of Defence, told the House of Commons today that no landing had taken place so far by the Anglo-French forces.

He said reports indicated that Egyptian forces were withdrawing in some disorder to Kantara and Suez. There were also indications that some had reached the Canal area. He added that the Egyptians had sunk four block ships so far in the Port Said approach to the Suez Canal.

Mr. Head reported that "Egyptian armoured units are moving from the Delta to the Canal area."

He reported that the plan to neutralise the Egyptian Air Force had been largely accomplished by means of bombing attacks on airfields by Valiant and Canberra jet bombers followed by low-level ground attacks.

The plan was devised to achieve maximum destruction of Egyptian aircraft with the minimum loss of Egyptian life. "A very high degree of accuracy was achieved."

He said that after this phase, attacks were being switched to other purely military targets, particularly armour and successful attacks had been made in the past 24 hours. Many hundreds of sorties were flown. He added that repeated warnings had been given to the Egyptian civil population to keep away from purely military installations and airfields.

Allied Air Forces suffered their first casualty in the Mid-East conflict today when a Royal Air Force "Venom" failed to return from dawn strikes against Egyptian military objectives.

Allied Headquarters in Nicosia said a heavy attack by R.A.F. Valiant and Canberra bombers from Cyprus and Malta pin-pointed Luxor Airfield on the Nile about 400 miles south of Cairo. An indefinite night curfew has been imposed on all Cyprus main towns as from tonight following a fresh outbreak of bomb incidents on the island.

On Friday British Canberra bombers attacked Cairo Radio's transmitters.

A French Defence Ministry spokesman said on Friday that 100 Egyptian planes were believed destroyed or badly damaged.

A British Ministry of Defence communique said on Friday night that French naval aircraft attacked and set on fire an Egyptian "Skoryi" class off Alexandria on Thursday morning. The "Skoryi" class destroyers are of 3,000 tons.

Nasser Says Army Has Left Sinai

CAIRO, Saturday (UP) — Abdul Nasser announced today that Egyptian forces had completed the withdrawal from the Sinai Peninsula, leaving only suicide commandos behind.

Meanwhile, in London, British Defence Minister, Mr. Anthony Head, said that latest reports "indicated that Egyptian forces were withdrawing in some disorder in Kantara and Suez, and that some have reached the Canal."

Iraq Orders Army Into Jordan

The Iraqi Government yesterday ordered its troops to enter Jordan immediately to reinforce the Arab Legion against a possible Israel attack.

The order followed an urgent request from King Hussein of Jordan, it was reliably learned in Baghdad. The troops would come under the orders of the Jordan Commander-in-Chief, who would dispose of them according to his requirements.

According to Reuter correspondent Ronald Batchelor, who left Jordan for Syria with a U.N. convoy on Friday, Syrian tanks were moving over the border in a steady stream.

Meanwhile, the Syrian Embassy in Washington informed the U.S. Government on Friday that Syria had "decided to implement immediately the joint Egyptian-Syrian defence pact."

The note said that the Syrian forces are now under the command of the Egyptian Chief-of-Staff, General Abdul Hakim Amer, and all her resources are from this moment devoted to the common cause," it concluded.

In Damascus, Acting Prime Minister Khalil Kallas announced yesterday that Syria has broken off consular relations with Britain and France.

The Soviet President, Marshal Klementi Voroshilov, told President Kuwatly of Syria yesterday in Moscow that Russia is "ready to supply the necessary assistance to help Syria surmount the vestiges of colonialism and reinforce its independence."

Speaking at a reception the Syrian President, whose cut short his visit to the Russian capital, Marshal Voroshilov said that "aggression against Egypt by one of the founders of the Baghdad Pact proves once again that the alliance is an aggressive bloc."

The Old City daily "Falastin" reported on Friday that the Arab Legion had taken over Mafrak Airport near the Iraqi border. Earlier, the paper had reported that the R.A.F. had evacuated Amman Military Airport.
— (Reuter, UP.)

I.P.C. Stops Pumping Oil Through Syria

BAGHDAD, Saturday (Reuter). — The Iraq Petroleum Company today suspended the pumping of crude oil through Syria, a company spokesman announced here. He said this was due to a breakdown in the company's transport between Iraq and Syria. It was through a wise under present circumstances to stop pumping from Iraq to Mediterranean ports through Syrian territory.

At an Egyptian spokesman said tonight he had received unconfirmed reports that three of the Company's pumping stations in Syria had been blown up.

Holland to 'Protect' Israel P.o.W.'s

THE HAGUE, Saturday (UP) — The Netherlands will act as "protecting nation" for Israel prisoners - of - war in Egypt, it was officially announced here this afternoon.

Published daily except on Saturday by The Post Ltd. Founded in 1932 by GERSHON AGRON. ...ed at the G.P.O. Copyright of ...ntal reserved; reproduction ...ted only by arrangement. ...itor: TED R. LURIE
...Offices: 9 Rehov Havatzelet, ..., P.O.Box 81, Tel. 4233. ... 52 Rehov Nahlat Binyamin, ... 1125, Tel. 64251/2. ...4 Rehov Herzl, Tel. 4304/5. ...Subscription: IL. 28. ...Copy: 17 Agorot.

...SDAY, MAY 24, 1960 ...5720. ... 28 Iyar ... 1379 ...L. XXXVI, No. 9720

THE JERUSALEM POST

...OLF EICHMANN, ...hose detention in an ... prison the Prime ...er announced to an amazed ...FINAL ...TION Knesset yesterday, is the most sought-after survi... the leaders of the ...murder machine. His guilt remains to be ..., but for over a de... his name has been a ...rd, the symbol that ... for war crimes. The ...s attributed to him innumerable. There ... doubt in the minds ... historians of that ...ous period that he ... the Gestapo office ...rge of carrying out ...nal solution," a mo... paraphrase for the ...d physical destruc... the Jews of Europe. ... mind today shrinks ... recalling these hor... The sudden confron... with one of the men ...deeply involved with ...drives us back to the ...s. Belsen. The ... between hydrogen ...e gas or motor ex...fumes. The selection, ... and sex, of victims ...special action," or ... All children unde... ... men over 50. The ...sal" of typhoid pa... These were the kind ...oblems with which ...ann, according to the ... had to deal.

...ite the ghastly me... it evokes, the ar... Eichmann also gives ...s for the profound... ...sfaction. The desire ...troy the Jews could ...even in the diseased ...of a Hitler, only be... they were a scatter...ion. Hitler could de... ...hem of their elemen... right to live and ..., to work, to mar... ...ir children, even to ... decency. Even in so ... the other European ... were prepared to ...ny action to save the ...before the outbreak ... war, they could not ... do so because Ger... ... treatment of the ... was part of its "in... policy." The deaths ... six million victims ... an important part ...paring the world for ...alization of the need ... independent Jewish ...s the only means of ...ng the Jews to es... their equality of ... as Jews. The State ... and it has proved ...ess to defend those ...wish to become part

... a punishment ...ely fitting to the ... that it is here, in ... that Eichmann ... stand trial for his ...r the murder of ... by their hundreds ...housands. He will be ... with the greatest ...liousness, but also ...he full rigour of the ...Ten years ago a law ...haped to fit precise... ...h a case, and make ...sible to try a Nazi ...criminal if the occa...rose. When the death ...y was abolished for ...categories of capital ...es, it was retained ...his one, inhuman, ... At the time, Eich... ...s name was frequent... the lips of the legis...

...remains to be said ...he finding of Eich... ... and his successful ...ging to trial here ...e Security Services ...achievement of that ...ned determination, ...ity and courage in ...nall measure. For ...a decade, Eichmann ...een sought all over ...orld, and he was on ... wanted list of ... Germany ever since ...d of the war. With... ...e State, a Jew ... have been found to ...nate him. Now, be... ..., an act of justice ...dress the insult to ...ation, if never the

Gromyko Asks U.N. To Condemn Spying

UNITED NATIONS. — The Soviet Union yesterday asked the Security Council to condemn the American U-2 flights over its air space as aggression and to state that "such actions create a threat to universal peace."

In addition, a resolution tabled in the Council by the Soviet Foreign Minister, Mr. Andrei Gromyko, would have the 11-member body request the U.S. Government to "take steps forthwith to put an end to such actions and to prevent their recurrence."

In his reply, U.S. Ambassador Henry Cabot Lodge, offered to negotiate an "open skies" treaty with Russia and other countries to "obviate forever such measures of self-protection" as the admitted U-2 spy flights.

Mr. Lodge said: "The U.S. has not committed any aggressive act against the Soviet Union or any other country, neither through its air force nor any other agency of the U.S. Government."

Mr. Gromyko charged the U.S. with "unprecedented cynicism" in claiming that the "aggressive spy flights" over Russia were both justified and endorsed by President Eisenhower.

Spying for Years

He declared that the U.S., "without batting an eyelash," had admitted that espionage was an integral part of its foreign policy and that President Eisenhower's administration had been pursuing it for years.

The Foreign Minister warned, "The entire might of the Soviet Union will be used, if required, in defence of its borders and the sovereign rights of the State." It cannot be doubted that the Soviet Union "has the facilities to defend its borders," he told the Council meeting which began its debate on Russia's demand to condemn the admitted U-2 flights.

He accused the Eisenhower administration of carrying on a "pirate-like" policy.

Mr. Gromyko said the Soviet Government had made careful plans for the Paris Summit meeting and approached the talks with a feeling of great responsibility. But the flight of the U-2 spy plane on May 1 clearly showed that the U.S. wanted to torpedo the conference before it began.

The Soviet Prime Minister, Mr. Khrushchev, had "done everything to provide the U.S. President with an opportunity to find a way out of the deadlock," and to make the holding of the conference possible, he said.

Opening the session, the President of the Council, Sir Claude Corea, of Ceylon, urged an early resumption of great-power negotiations "in a renewed spirit of good will."

After Mr. Lodge's reply, the Council adjourned its debate until this evening.

(Reuter, UPI)

Ike to Broadcast On Summit Tomorrow

WASHINGTON (Reuter). — President Eisenhower will make a 30-minute coast-to-coast radio-television address tomorrow night on the abortive Summit talks, the White House announced yesterday.

Mr. James Hagerty, the White House Press Secretary, said: "He will make a report to the American people on the events at Paris and the future aims and goals of the U.S., and indeed, of its allies in the free world."

Gaitskell Defends Stand on A-Bomb

GREAT YARMOUTH (Reuter). — Mr. Hugh Gaitskell, leader of the British Labour Party, said here yesterday the urgent necessity for Britain was to remain in Nato and for nuclear weapons to be available as long as Russia has them.

But he told the annual conference of the General and Municipal Workers' Union that he wanted to see a greater reliance on conventional and a smaller reliance on nuclear weapons in Europe.

"I want to be sure that nuclear weapons are effectively subject to control by the governments concerned and not just left in the hands of the generals," he added.

Mr. Gaitskell continued: "We believe that if Western Europe does not stand together and stand with America, we should each one of us be hopelessly weak in the face of any possible Soviet threat."

He did not think much of the point of view which said: "We will have nothing to do at all with nuclear weapons" and "Yank go home, but please protect us if there is any trouble."

Referring to the Labour Party split over defence matters, Mr. Gaitskell said the Party must decide clearly questions of principle.

Demonstrators Clash With Tokyo Police

TOKYO. — Police on Monday clashed with over 1,000 students who tried to break into the Diet (Parliament) grounds in a demonstration against the U.S.-Japanese security treaty.

Eighty-two policemen and more than 50 students were injured.

The leader of the students — most of whom were members of the fanatic and violent *Zengakuren* Student Federation — vowed that the students would burn down the official residence of Premier Kishi and the Foreign Ministry building "when the time is ripe."

NEHRU TO BURIAL FOR 2-DAY STAY

Premier Nehru of India will arrive in the Lebanese capital from Istanbul today for a two-day visit, according to Beirut Radio last night.

AFTER MIDNIGHT

Moscow Radio in an Arabic broadcast last night detailed two routes by which it alleged American planes were carrying out spy flights over the Middle East. "The first runs from Adana along the Turco-Syrian border to Mardin, in Turkey, and thence over Iraq to Dharan, Saudi Arabia. The other route runs southwards from Adana over Syria, Lebanon, Israel and el Arish and thence to Port Sudan and Dharan."

MOROCCAN KING BECOMES PREMIER

RABAT, (Reuter). — King Mohammed V of Morocco announced last night that he himself would take over government of the country.

In a radio message to the Moroccan people, the king said. "It is difficult to form a government. We will take the government in hand and preside over it."

He announced that Crown Prince Moulay Hassan would be his deputy Premier.

New Tremors Shake Chile

SANTIAGO (Reuter). — Another strong earthquake rocked Southern Chile yesterday after a weekend of terror, adding new casualties to a reported toll of 400 dead and over 500 injured.

New fires were started in the partially-destroyed city of Castro on Chiloe Island, and fire fighters lacking water had to use dynamite to control them.

Ancud, in the north of the island, where 100 persons were believed swept away in Sunday's tidal wave, suffered anew. So did Puetro Montt, 500 km. south of devastated Concepcion. About 60 persons are reported missing and at least 100 severely injured there.

Massive aid by ship and plane is being rushed to the thousands left homeless by the weekend quakes, fires and tidal waves.

The army provided tents for the panic-stricken population of Concepcion, a town of 180,000 persons 440 km. south of here, who fled to the woods and fields when the second quake struck the already battered city on Sunday night.

Many trying to escape were trapped in their crumbling homes. Bridges, roads, railway and telephone lines were cut, and the desolated city was cut off from the world. Many smaller communities were devastated in an area of 70,000 square miles between Santiago and Chiloe Island.

A six-foot tidal wave, thought to have been triggered off by the Chilean earthquakes, struck the tropical paradise of Hawaii early yesterday, bringing death to the palm-ringed islands.

The main brunt of the rushing waters was borne by Hilo, largest city on the island, where at least four persons were known to have lost their lives.

There were also tidal waves in San Francisco Bay, but no damage was caused.

Four Murdered in Congo Elections

LEOPOLDVILLE, Belgian Congo (Reuter). — Four African voters were hacked to death at Kamina, near Jadotville, during the first major round of the Belgian Congo's general election on Monday.

Fourteen other voters were injured during a clash between tribesmen belonging to rival political parties. The authorities immediately clamped a military occupation regime over the area. Minor incidents were also reported in Elisabethville, Jadotville and Leopoldville, the capital.

Results in these three cities — described as "test areas" by election organizers — will be known today.

Eichmann Found by Security Services; To be Tried Here for Crimes Against Jews

Adolf Eichmann, one of the most notorious Nazi war criminals, who has been in hiding for 15 years, was found recently by the Israel Security Services and is now under arrest in Israel, where he will shortly be put on trial. This dramatic announcement was made by the Prime Minister in the Knesset yesterday afternoon. It caused unprecedented excitement in the Chamber and shortly thereafter in the streets outside.

Official Government sources have so far declined to release any details on the circumstances that led to Eichmann's apprehension. However, at a press conference one hour after Mr. Ben-Gurion's statement, the Minister of Justice, Mr. Pinhas Rosen, repeated his reply to a parliamentary question several months ago, which quoted a British denial of reports that the notorious Nazi criminal was hiding in Kuwait. The only other reports on Eichmann's whereabouts during recent years spoke of his hiding in a Latin American country.

Mr. Rosen said that no request had been made for Eichmann to be extradited to this country.

Mr. Ben-Gurion's announcement read as follows:

"I have to inform the Knesset that a short time ago one of the greatest of the Nazi war criminals, Adolf Eichmann, who was responsible, together with the Nazi leaders, for what they called "the final solution of the Jewish question," that is, the extermination of six million of the Jews of Europe, was found by the Israel Security Services.

"Adolf Eichmann is already under arrest in Israel, and will shortly be placed on trial in Israel under the terms of the Law for the Punishment of Nazis and Nazi Collaborators, 5710-1950."

The news of Eichmann's arrest spread quickly to Jerusalem's adjacent business centre and at 4.30, only half-an-hour after Mr. Ben-Gurion's announcement, both evening papers came out in Tel Aviv with special editions which were in demand faster than newsboys could sell them.

With the five o'clock news over Kol Yisrael, the entire nation could listen to the Prime Minister's statement and the story of Eichmann's capture had become the talk of the country.

At 3.30 p.m., half-an-hour prior to yesterday's Knesset session, the Cabinet convened in special session so that the Prime Minister could inform all his colleagues of the news.

Speculation Rife

Speculation on the content of Mr. Ben-Gurion's statement began when the Prime Minister entered the Knesset building accompanied by the Inspector-General of Police and the Chief of the Security Services.

It is now learned that as far back as January 27, Mr. Yitshak Navon, the Prime Minister's Political Secretary, had written to Mr. Perets Bernstein, M.K., General Zionist, asking him to withdraw a parliamentary question to the Prime Minister concerning the Eichmann affair. The letter stated that certain steps were being undertaken which would assist in Eichmann's extradition and that the Prime Minister considered that a public reply in the Knesset would harm these efforts. The letter also said that the Chief of the Security Services, would be prepared to give Mr. Bernstein certain details on the matter in person.

At a press conference in the Knesset building, given by the Minister of Justice and the Inspector General of Police, Mr. Rosen stressed that everything would be done to hasten Eichmann's trial. He presumed that he would be charged with crimes against the Jewish people, under the Law of Punishment of Nazis and their Collaborators, for which the penalty is death.

Mr. Rosen said that West Germany was the only other country to have issued a warrant of arrest against Eichmann. Asked whether another country could ask for Eichmann's extradition, Mr. Rosen said that he would first have to serve the sentence pronounced against him here before an extradition request could be considered.

Eichmann is entitled to, and will receive, full legal defence, even if he should request legal counsel from abroad, Mr. Rosen said. Up to now he has not been fully interrogated and the charge sheet against him would soon be prepared, Mr. Rosen added.

Other States Not Told

No other government has been officially informed of Eichmann's arrest, Mr. Rosen said, and Mr. Ben-Gurion's statement in the Knesset should be considered as an official announcement to all interested governments.

Mr. Nahmias stated that Eichmann was "absolutely fit" and that special security precautions are being taken for his custody. The press would not be allowed to meet him for the time being, Mr. Nahmias stated.

Mr. Rosen declined to say how long the place of Eichmann's arrest would be kept secret, saying only that he was from now on in the hands of the police.

The 14-day remand order would be renewed whenever necessary, Mr. Rosen said.

Leading members of all Knesset factions were unanimous in terming the arrest a "tremendous operation." Dr. Y. Bader (Herut) said that the security services deserve high praise, and Mr. M. Ya'ari (Mapam) said that the arrest proved the organization was outstanding.

Mr. Y. Bar-Yehuda (Ahdut Ha'avoda) said that he had been deeply moved when he heard the news of the arrest and added his praise to that expressed by other M.K.'s.

(Portrait of a Killer—Page 4)

ADOLF EICHMANN, YOU ARE CHARGED...

Jerusalem Post Reporter

TEL AVIV. — Clean-shaven, well groomed, and looking younger than his 54 years, S.S. Colonel Adolf Eichmann appeared before Chief Magistrate Yedidya Halevy in Jaffa at 11 o'clock yesterday morning, to hear the charges against him.

"Adolf Eichmann, you are charged with causing the death of millions of Jews in Germany and the occupied countries in the years 1933 to 1945. Are you he, Adolf Eichmann?" he was asked.

This was translated to the accused by Rav-Pakad Shmuel Roth, head of the C.I.D. at police headquarters. Rav-Pakad Roth told *The Jerusalem Post* that Eichmann was composed, but turned pale as he heard the charge.

He replied distinctly:

"Ich bin Adolf Eichmann."

He had nothing more to say at present, other than that he would ask to be defended. Eichmann speaks no language but German, Rav-Pakad Roth said.

Chief Magistrate Halevy remanded the accused for 14 days. The proceedings, at which the Inspector-General of Police, Mr. Yosef Nahmias, was present, lasted 20 minutes.

Eichmann had been brought to Jaffa in handcuffs. These were removed as he appeared before the Magistrate. He stood to rigid attention, and was escorted by armed police guards.

Penalty is Death

Paragraph 1 of the Nazis and Nazi Collaborators (Punishment) Law 1950 stipulates that: persons, who during the period of the Nazi regime committed crimes against the Jewish people and humanity in general or during the Second World War committed war crimes, will be liable to the death penalty.

A crime against the Jewish people is defined as the commission of any of the following with the intent of destroying the Jewish people in whole or in part:

- killing Jews;
- causing serious bodily or mental harm to Jews;
- placing Jews in living conditions calculated to bring about their physical destruction;
- imposing measures intended to prevent births among Jews;
- forcibly transferring Jewish children to another national or religious group;
- destroying or desecrating Jewish religious or cultural assets or values;
- inciting to hatred against Jews.

The above crimes were excluded from the provisions of the later law abolishing the death penalty in Israel.

Eichmann in the uniform of an S.S. Colonel

Chief Rabbi Asks Stern Justice

Chief Rabbi Nissim, in a statement last night, described Eichmann as a criminal "whose like had not been known in all Israel's history of persecutors and enemies...

"Hundreds of thousands of the children of Israel who were bereaved and tortured by this oppressor look to the courts to judge him with all the severity of the law."

'Most Wanted' In Germany

FRANKFURT, (AP). — Adolf Eichmann is the Nazi wartime criminal most wanted in Germany. He once headed a Nazi office named after him. It was charged with the systematic extermination of Jews.

An arrest warrant for the German-born former Lt. Colonel of the S.S., for murder had been circulated through the country for years. German prosecution officials dealing with wartime crimes asked Israel officials last year to check reports that Eichmann was in the Middle East, possibly in Israel.

El Al Plane Delayed Three Hours in Brazil

LYDDA AIRPORT. — The El Al plane that took the Israel delegation to the Argentine independence celebrations, returned early on Sunday morning from Buenos Aires.

En route to Argentina, crew members related, the plane made a brief stop at Recifa airport in Brazil. The aircraft was held up three hours by the airport manager there who, for reasons that are unclear, tried to prevent the plane from taking off.

After the seriousness of his action was pointed out, in view of international aviation regulations, the manager allowed the plane to proceed on its way. (Itim)

Meir Stands by Statement On Dag's Suez Assurance

Jerusalem Post Knesset Reporter

Foreign Minister Golda Meir yesterday stood by her statement of last December 22, when she told the Knesset of Mr. Hammarskjold's advice to Israel regarding the shipment of cargoes through the Suez Canal.

She was reviewing the activities of the Foreign Ministry, in the context of the debate on the State Budget for 1960/61.

Mrs. Meir quoted from Mr. Hammarskjold's press conference of May 5, in which he said:

"The fact is that there has never been any agreement (with Nasser on the shipment of Israel cargoes). And that is well known to all parties... No understanding preceded the despatch of the Astypalea."

The Foreign Minister noted that she had been asked time and again concerning the apparent contradiction between this and her statement, which she quoted as follows:

"Following on these efforts with the Egyptian authorities, the U.N. Secretary-General told us that he had reason to believe that, if Israel would agree to send her export cargoes through the Canal in the ownership of the purchaser (that is, f.o.b.), and to import goods intended to pass through the Canal towards her own ports under the ownership of the seller (that is, c.i.f.), the U.A.R. authorities would not obstruct the passage of ships carrying these cargoes."

"That is how I then summed up what was said to us by Mr. Hammarskjold, and I have nothing to add or detract," Mrs. Meir declared yesterday.

Relations with U.S.S.R.

Referring to our relations with the Soviet Union, Mrs. Meir said that, despite all our efforts, the U.S.S.R. has not permitted relations of substance with us. In this it has displayed a marked attitude of discrimination in contrast with its declared policy of willingness to maintain commercial and cultural relations with all countries.

Mrs. Meir noted that our attempt to have talks with the heads of the Soviet Government were unsuccessful. The reason given by the Soviet Government when it refused to agree to a meeting between Mr. Ben-Gurion and Mr. Khrushchev was statements allegedly made in Israel which were not conducive to peace.

With regard to the last sentence of the U.S.S.R. reply, which states that "the U.S.S.R. wishes good relations with all countries of the Middle East, if mutual aspiration and mutual interest of that kind exist," the Foreign Min-

(Continued on Page 2, Col. 3)

POST Published in Jerusalem, Israel, daily except on Saturday by The Palestine Post Ltd. Founded in 1932 by Gershon AGRON. Registered at the G.P.O. Copyright of all material reserved; reproduction permitted only by arrangement.
Editor: TED R. LURIE
Editorial and Business Office: 9 Rehov Havatselet, Jerusalem, Israel P.O.B. 81, Tel. 24233, 24321.
Tel Aviv: 52 Rehov Nahlat Binyamin, P.O.Box 1125, Tel. 30141.
Haifa: 34 Rehov Herzl, Hadar Hacarmel, P.O.Box 4810, Tel. 64584.
VOL. XXXVI, No. 11356
PRICE : 28 AGORA

THE JERUSALEM POST

WEDNESDAY, MAY 19, 1965 • 17 Iyar, 5725 • 18 Muharam, 1385

TO hang a man in a public square and leave his body suspended for half a day with the charge pinned on his chest is a demonstration, not an execution. To order a man to be executed after passing a special "law" that he shall not be permitted legal aid for his defence, and to keep him incommunicado after declaring that he has confessed, is simple vengeance, and not a trial. The way the Syrians dealt with Eli Cohen was barbarous even by Syrian standards of justice, and these are not high.

ELI COHEN

Public executions are not the exception there, and arbitrary arrest and the killing of political opponents are common enough. But there was a significant difference here, in the fact that Eli Cohen was not a Syrian. In many parts of the world — even Israel in wartime — a citizen who commits treason against his own country is sentenced to death. A man from another country is not executed on a political charge, however grave. If he is declared to have been working for a foreign power he is in some sense a soldier, and not a criminal. He may be imprisoned for long periods, but not infrequently he is in time exchanged for some other person arrested under similar circumstances.

Not long ago, the U.S. and the Soviet Union exchanged two of their most conspicuous spies — Abel and U2 pilot Powers. Every conceivable effort was made by Israel to have this view presented to Syria by intermediaries of high standing, and all the Syrians held in Israel were offered in exchange for Eli Cohen's life. Unhappily the Syrians have too little regard for their own citizens' lives to be inclined to accept such an offer, and the relatives of these men were unable to make their voices heard.

Despite the tragic ending to this episode, the people of Israel will remain warmly grateful to the many distinguished and authoritative persons and organizations who attempted to use their good offices to cause the Syrians to reprieve their prisoner. It is clear that these interceders felt strongly that this act of pseudo-legal barbarism was totally inacceptable. They also understood that while the hanging might be due to feuds among different sections of the Ba'th party in Syria, its result would be to increase immeasurably the bitterness already felt in this country against the Syrians for their long series of acts of cruelty against individual Israelis. The torture of the border crossers and other minor offenders whom they returned last year as broken men is one item on this list. Another is the long and harsh detention of the Israeli members of the boating party captured on the shores of Lake Tiberias. In the long run, between nations, such inhumanity counts as heavily as political intransigence, for it has no national purpose to explain it.

It is small comfort to accept that Cohen had built up something akin to a public position for himself. Obviously he had become an embarrassment within the Syrian ruling clique, where one group was only too anxious to expose mistakes made by their rivals. Thus while one side made sure that all proper defence would be denied lest Cohen reveal the Ba'th party's weakness, the other side made sure that he should not be allowed to be exchanged or spirited away without anything discreditable to his associates being uncovered.

In the eyes of the world, Eli Cohen remains a man of rare courage, and no part of the Ba'th has emerged with any credit at all.

U.S. air attacks on N. Vietnam resumed

WASHINGTON. — The U.S. resumed its air attacks on North Vietnam yesterday after a five-day lull.

Authoritative sources in Washington said that during the lull the Johnson Administration made a peace move to Hanoi through a third party. There was speculation that the third party was either Canada or India.

Meanwhile the North Vietnamese authorities yesterday rejected the reported U.S. attempt to start peace negotiations, according to Radio Hanoi.

U.S. air attacks on targets within South Vietnam continued unabated yesterday, with 150 missions flown.

About 2,000 South Vietnamese troops yesterday launched a massive assault on a key Vietcong supply base at Ba Long, 20 miles south of the North Vietnam frontier. *(Reuter, UPI)*

UN peace man in Dominica

SANTO DOMINGO (Reuter). — Rival Dominican factions continued block - by - block fighting yesterday in the northwest sector of Santo Domingo as the line of battle moved close to U.S. troop positions.

The fighting, in the fourth week of the civil war, continued as the special U.N. representative, Dr. Jose Antonio Mayorre, arrived to negotiate in an attempt to end the conflict.

At least one U.S. military officer was seen by reporters with the "reconstruction" forces of Brigadier-General Antonio Imbert Barreras.

U.S. military spokesmen declined to comment. *(Inter-American Press, Page 2)*

Jordan rejects Eshkol offer

Jordan rejected yesterday the offer made by Israeli Premier Levi Eshkol on Monday to negotiate a peace settlement with the Arabs.

A Government spokesman said in Amman that Jordan rejected the proposals "because our firm policy rejects the Zionist presence itself in Palestine."

In Cairo, Mr. Eshkol's offer was front-paged by all Arabic newspapers, but there was no editorial comment or official reaction.

"Al Ahram" published the story under the headline, "Israel's official reply to Bourguiba's proposals," and "Al Gomhouriya" declared: "Eshkol offers peace terms to Bourguiba."

The Tunisian news agency, Tunis Afrique Presse, said that Israel's offer was "far from accepting the proposals of President Bourguiba."

The difference

President Bourguiba considered that the application of the U.N. resolutions should be a starting-point in "defreezing Arab-Israel relations," while Mr. Eshkol spoke "only of minor readjustments of the frontiers," reports Reuter.

A spokesman of the "Palestine Liberation Movement" said in Cairo that "the Palestine people have always rejected negotiations with the Zionist gang," the movement's radio, Saut Falastin, reported last night.

'Peace plan' aired as Eban meets Soviet envoy

The Deputy Prime Minister, Mr. Abba Eban, yesterday discussed Israel's peace plan outlined in the Knesset Monday by Prime Minister Eshkol, with the Soviet Ambassador, Mr. Dmitri Chuvakhin.

The meeting was requested by Mr. Chuvakhin.

General international problems were discussed and Mr. Eban took the opportunity to explain in greater detail the proposals for peace and cooperation in the Middle East made in the Knesset by Mr. Eshkol, a spokesman said.

QUEEN GETS BIG WELCOME IN BONN

BONN (Reuter). — Thousands of West Germans yesterday gave Queen Elizabeth of Britain an enthusiastic welcome on the first day of a state visit aimed at ending the bitterness of two world wars.

Crowds ten and 12 deep greeted the British monarch in this small capital city when she drove to call on President Luebke. They pitched flowers at her car, spilled into the roadway and delayed the royal procession of automobiles and outriders by about seven minutes.

(Radiophoto — Page 2)

Bonn envoy quits Syria

DAMASCUS (Reuter). — The West German Ambassador to Syria, Dr. Hans Mangold, left Damascus for Bonn yesterday.

Syria formally announced the severance of diplomatic relations with West Germany last Thursday after Bonn had agreed to establish diplomatic relations with Israel. France has since then been looking after West Germany's interests in Syria.

The West German Ambassador to Jordan will leave Amman tomorrow.

It was stated that officials in charge of consular, commercial and cultural affairs would remain in Amman to carry on their work.

The French Embassy in Amman has been looking after West German interests in Jordan since the diplomatic break.

The last minutes of Eli Cohen, 40, shown during three moments of his hanging in public in Damascus yesterday. (AP radiophoto)

Chief Chaplain joins family in mourning

The Chaplain of the Army, Aluf Shlomo Goren, accompanied the family of Eli Cohen yesterday evening in the ritual of tearing their clothes in mourning and reciting the *kaddish*.

Rabbi Goren was the first to enter on Tuesday the modest little flat in Bat Yam in which the Cohen family lives. During the course of the day, ever since the announcement of the execution came over the radio in the morning, neighbours and friends who had congregated outside were kept away by security officers.

After the visit of Aluf Goren, the doors were opened to all who wished to express their condolences to the mother, the widow, the five brothers and two sisters.

According to "Itim," Cohen's two daughters, Sofia, 4, and Irit, 2, had joined the family around the television set to follow the daily course of their father's trial.

Damascus spurned countless appeals for fair trial

POST Diplomatic Reporter

Heads of state, the Vatican, world statesmen, and countless other people appealed to the Syrian authorities during the last few months to spare the life of Eli Cohen and to give him a fair trial. Throughout the trial the French lawyers engaged by Eli Cohen's wife, Nadia, were even refused permission to attend the hearing as observers.

To save Cohen's life, Israel offered, through intermediaries, to repatriate several Syrians in custody here, even if Cohen were to be imprisoned in Syria. For months Israel diplomatic missions abroad did their utmost to arouse public opinion.

News withheld

The news of the case was withheld in Israel because of a fear of prejudicing the efforts to save Cohen.

In January, when Cohen's arrest was announced, Syria passed a special decree which deprived Cohen of the elementary rights of counsel and appeal. The trial dragged on with continuous delays.

The Syrian insistence on taking Cohen's life, despite enlightened world opinion, is attributed partly to a desire to counter charges of "weakness" from the Nasserist press in Lebanon and particularly because of factional rivalries in the Syrian ruling junta.

The fight for Cohen's life was waged on a number of fronts. On the legal side, his wife obtained the services of two noted French lawyers, M. Jaques Mercier and Paul Arrighi, who appealed to Syrian President Hafez, the Supreme Court, and the Syrian Ambassador in Paris. Mercier even went to Damascus twice, once before the verdict and sentence — 10 days ago — and again after the sentence, on Sunday.

Promised interview

On Sunday, the Syrian military authorities promised him that he or his colleague would be received by Hafez before the sentence was approved by the Supreme Revolutionary Council. Returning to Paris the next day, Monday, Mercier told Mrs. Cohen's representatives that Hafez might receive him. At midnight the lawyer learnt from press reports that the sentence had been ratified, and shortly afterwards Cohen was executed.

The French lawyers were

(Continued on Page 6, Col. 2)

Hafez offers Yemen military aid

DAMASCUS. — Lieutenant-General Amin Hafez, chairman of the Presidency Council, has announced that Syria is ready to offer "material and moral aid and support to the Yemeni revolution" in the political, military, economic, and social spheres.

General Hafez sent a cable to this effect to the Yemeni Prime Minister in reply to an appeal to the Arab heads of state for help to restore stability in Yemen.

Meanwhile the former Foreign Minister of the Yemen Republic, Abdul Qawae Hameen, said in Al Hauta, in the South Arabian Federation yesterday, that Yemen's Prime Minister, Ahmed Mohammed Noman had used "heavy weapons to destroy our homes, our town."

He told Reuter: "The Noman Government first attempted our arrest and assassination. When it failed, it sent a military force to overcome opposition elements."

The former Foreign Minister arrived in Al Hauta, about 20 miles north of Aden, on Monday.

Mameem said Prime Minister Noman wanted to establish a "one-man tribal system of rule, as in the past, whereas we opposition want a national, democratic, progressive system of government." *(Reuter, UPI)*

Syria claims Israel opens fire on border

DAMASCUS (Reuter). — Syrian and Israeli troops exchanged sporadic fire for more than two hours across the armistice line yesterday, a Syrian military spokesman said last night.

The spokesman accused Israeli forces of starting the firing and said the Syrians returned the fire.

There were no casualties among the Syrians and Syria had filed a complaint with the U.N.

Syria hangs Eli Cohe[n] in public square, as sp[...]

Sense of shock and outrage in Jerusalem

The Foreign Ministry in Jerusalem yesterday expressed "shock and outrage at the fact that an Israeli citizen has been executed in Syria after a travesty of a trial, without any opportunity for legal defence, in defiance of the most elementary precepts of justice and in spite of the appeals by scores of personalities and organizations in enlightened countries asking the Syrian authorities to abide by the customary rules of justice and clemency."

The Ministry's statement added:

"Without entering into the details of the vague and unsubstantiated indictment, it is a fact that in no enlightened country is a foreign citizen executed in peace time on charges of espionage."

Eulogy in Knesset

POST Knesset Reporter

The first speaker in yesterday's foreign policy debate in the Knesset, Mr. Israel Galili of Ahdut Ha'avoda, prefaced his remarks by eulogizing Eli Cohen.

"Israel and the Jewish people will long remember this loyal son who sacrificed his life for the sake of the State of Israel, its existence and its independence," he said.

He described Syria's hanging of Eli Cohen as despicable barbarity, and said it was carried out after the accused had been denied legal counsel, and after all the appeals of leading world figures that his life be spared had been ignored.

ISRAELI DENIED DEFENC[E]

DAMASCUS (Reuter). — Eli Cohen, convicted of [...]ing an Israeli spy ring in Syria, was executed by p[...] hanging before dawn yesterday.

He was the first Israeli citizen to be executed in Syria.

The execution was attended by Lt.-Col. Salah al-Dilli, head of the special military court which sentenced Cohen to death on May 8, members of the court, newsmen and Rabbi Nissim Andbu, religious head of the Jewish community in Syria.

Earlier Cohen was driven in a heavily guarded military car from the Mazza prison down to police headquarters in the very heart of the city. The nearby Marja Square (Martyrs Square) looked like a battlefield with red-capped military police and troops throwing two parallel cordons around the gallows erected in the square garden.

In reply to questions by Col. Dilli, Cohen said, "I am sorry for what I have done and I confirm all my previous confessions." Questioned in the presence of Rabbi Andbu, Cohen said he had left no savings or debts.

Letter to wife

In a letter which he wrote in Arabic and French, Cohen asked his wife, Nadia, to remarry and not to leave their children fatherless. He appealed to her to look after the children, educate them and keep in constant touch with members of his family.

After writing the letter he repeated a prayer which the Rabbi read, and then walked for a distance of 30 metres to the gallows accompanied by Dilli and members of the special military court.

The executioner held Cohen's arm and helped him onto the platform of the gallows and fastened the rope around his neck. He died after 90 seconds.

The body, to which was attached the verdict of the court, remained hanging in public for six hours, and was later driven off in a small truck.

Its final disposition was not known.

Soldiers kept crowds from approaching too near.

The verdict said that Eliahu Ben Saul Cohen was sentenced to death in [the] name of the Arab peop[le of] Syria after being f[ound] guilty of entering a mil[itary] place in disguise and o[b]taining classified inform[ation] and passing it to an ene[my].

Cohen, who was 40, wa[s ar]rested early this year. [The] trial began in February [and] lasted 40 days.

He came to Syria by [way] of Beirut in 1962, car[rying] the passport of a Leba[nese] emigrant in Argentina [and] assuming the name of K[...] Amin Thabet.

PRAISED BY FRIEN[DS]

Eli Cohen's friends ye[ster]day highly praised his [per]sonality.

"Intelligent and quick[...] always kept his own co[unsel] and was not talkative[," a] childhood friend recalled.

Cohen, born in Alexa[ndria,] Egypt in 1924, attended [the] elementary school of the [Cai]ro Jewish community, t[rans]ferred later to the Alexa[ndria] Lycee and completed his [edu]cation at the Farouk Un[iver]sity in Cairo (engineerin[g).]

He joined the Zionist [move]ment in 1941 and was a [mem]ber of Hehalutz Hatzair [from] 1941 to 1946. He subsequ[ently] undertook various securit[y as]signments for Israel, eve[n be]fore the establishment o[f the] State.

After reaching Israel h[e was] immediately given specia[l as]signments which, accordi[ng to] his superiors, were all [suc]cessfully carried out, [with] brilliance and persisten[ce.]

"Eli Cohen knew wha[t he] wanted and reached [his] goals," *The Jerusalem [Post]* was told in Tel Aviv yeste[rday.] "He was always ready to [take] on new assignments — k[now]ing that most of these put [him] in great personal danger[.]

"I see no reason wh[y he] should refuse. I am afte[r all] no better than anyone e[lse,"] Cohen was accustomed to [say.]

A relative of Cohen, [now] serving in the Defence [For]ces, told Itim yesterday [that] the victim had been [ar]rested by the Egyptian [au]thorities in 1954 in connec[tion]

(Continued on Page 6, Col. [...])

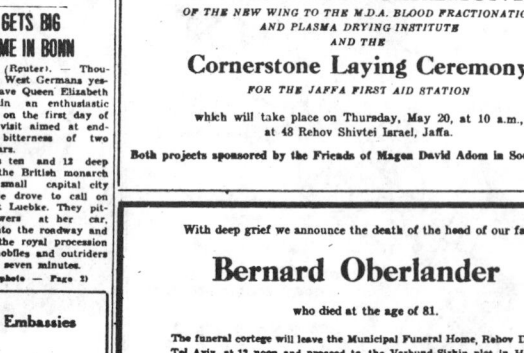

IR FORCE WINS SUPREMACY AS ARMY DRIVES
GYPTIANS BACK INTO SINAI AND GAZA

THE JERUSALEM POST

Published in Jerusalem, Israel, daily except on Saturday by The Palestine Post Ltd. Founded in 1932 by Gershon AGRON. Registered at the G.P.O. Copyright of all material reserved; reproduction permitted only by arrangement. Editors TED R. LURIE

TUESDAY, JUNE 6, 1967 • EYAR 27, 5727 • SAFAR 28, 1387 • VOL. XXXVII, No. 11973*

PRICE: 35 AGORA

BULLETIN:

The army spokesman announced that 374 enemy planes were destroyed yesterday. Nineteen Israeli planes were lost.

Jordan shells Jerusalem; 10 dead, houses damaged

ESHKOL: ARAB AIR FORCES DEFEATED

Jerusalem Post Reporter

Prime Minister Eshkol told the Knesset yesterday that the Egyptian Air Force was "heavily defeated." During the day the Syrian and Jordanian Air Forces also started to attack, and they also suffered heavy blows from our Air Force.

"Since morning our forces were compelled to beat back the enemy in order to rout the forces of the aggressor's Egyptian dictator. The battle is still in full swing. Our army has not disappointed expectations — it is standing the test."

We had declared, Mr. Eshkol went on, that we would not attack unless others attack us. Nevertheless, the Syrians and the Jordanians opened fire on Israel territory and sent aircraft over our towns and villages. The Egyptian Army Commander issued an Order of the Day which was broadcast over Cairo Radio on June 1, stating that the Egyptian forces are launching an historic and holy war to retrieve the Arabs' "stolen" territory.

Nasser's troops were concentrated near Sinai in a bid to cut off the Southern Negev. When the Egyptian war machine started moving, we took action to protect our territory. The forces facing the Arab armies are Israeli in their entirety — and there are no others.

Mr. Eshkol's statement, to have been made at 7 p.m., was postponed while he conducted a short meeting of the Ministerial Security Committee. The Knesset was crowded with Members and foreign and local pressmen. Shortly after 8 o'clock, a bomb fell right by the building, shattering windows in the canteen. All present were shepherded into the shelter, where eminent personalities such as Mr. Kadish Luz, Mr. Ben-Gurion and Mrs. Golda Meir sat with senior officials, clerks, cleaning workers and a British TV technician clutching his tapes — all in high spirits and good humour.

As the Knesset session was announced, people streamed out of the shelter and neighbouring corridors, to find Mr. Eshkol, trapped by a British television interviewer, on his way to the Assembly hall. He readily answered questions in English, such as: "Have you any territorial claims to make against the Arabs?" Answer: "None. All we want is security within our own frontiers."

He then announced the expansion of the Cabinet to include three new Ministers. Two of them came up to take oath of office — Mr. Menahem Begin, who put on a skull cap, and Mr. Yosef Saphir, both of Gahal. Mr. Moshe Dayan, of Rafi, co-opted as Minister of Defence, had come at the scheduled time of 7 p.m., but was compelled to leave before the delayed induction ceremony, to resume his duties.

MESSAGE FROM TEDDY KOLLEK, MAYOR OF JERUSALEM

Citizens of Jerusalem!

You, the inhabitants of our Holy City, were called upon to suffer the vicious onslaught of the enemy, while our determined airmen and soldiers were battling with him in the air and in the South. Your homes also became a battlefield.

In the course of the day I travelled throughout Jerusalem. I saw how its citizens, rich and poor, veteran and new immigrant alike, children and adults, stood steadfast. Nobody flinched; nobody failed. You remained cool, calm and confident, while the enemy launched his assault upon you.

You have proved worthy inhabitants of the city of David. You have proved worthy of the words of the Psalmist: If I forget thee, O Jerusalem, may my right hand forget its cunning. You will be remembered for your stand in the hour of danger.

Citizens have paid the price with their lives; many have been wounded. We mourn our dead and will care for their families. We will tend our wounded.

The enemy inflicted much damage on houses and property. But we will repair the damage, and we will rebuild the City so that it will be more beautiful and more treasured than ever.

I pay special tribute to the police, Haga, the volunteers, and all those who contributed to the defence of the city.

Eban: took arms in self-defence

TEL AVIV. — Foreign Minister Abba Eban said yesterday that the events of the day culminated in the pattern of aggression which had forced Israel to defend her territory and her integrity. "Never in history has there been a more righteous use of armed force," Mr. Eban told the press at Beit Sokolow.

Enumerating the main stages in the provocative actions against Israel, Mr. Eban pointed out the hundreds of tanks sent to the southern frontier of Israel; the large tank force opposite Eilat in a plan to sunder the Southern Negev from the rest of the country; the blockade of the Straits of Tiran; the threat of strangling encirclement, which resulted in the pact with Jordan; the placing of Iraqi troops in Jordan; the order of the day of the Egyptian Commander, General Mourtagi, calling on his troops in Sinai to wage a holy war against Israel. The acts of sabotage and terrorism from Syria and Sinai and, finally, yesterday morning, the movement of Egyptian regular troops against Israel, and the bombardment of the villages of Ramat Hakovesh and Nahal Oz, were also part of the pattern of aggression.

At noon, the Jordanians initiated an attack. Mr. Eban maintained that he was discussing...

Gov't House taken

Israeli forces occupied Government House (the headquarters of the U.N. Truce Supervision Organization) in Jerusalem yesterday afternoon — 11 minutes after the compound had been occupied by Jordanians.

The Jordanian authorities had earlier demanded from Gen. Odd Bull that he leave the Headquarters. It is understood Gen. Bull refused and cabled U.N. Secretary-General U Thant, who in turn appealed to King Hussein to refrain from attacking the Headquarters. But the Jordanians occupied the Headquarters.

Around 4 p.m. Israeli forces got word to the U.N. personnel that they intended to recapture the compound. In eleven minutes the fight was over. The U.N. personnel was safely ushered away, and in a long convoy were later seen leaving Jerusalem.

The U.N. personnel in residence were removed to safety and installed in the Eden and President Hotels last night. Some of them wanted to be allowed to cross into Jordan but their request was refused.

The U.N.T.S.O. Chief of Staff, Gen. Odd Bull, asked to have the building restored to U.N. control; but this was refused on the grounds that the U.N. was unable to hold it.

The Jordanians kept the Norwegian General and his staff virtual prisoners for almost three hours.

The building evidently was hit, heavily damaged, and showed signs of interior fires. The courtyard was strewn with the wreckage of U.N. and Jordanian vehicles.

The Israel Defence Forces yesterday morning repelled an attempted Egyptian air and tank attack and smashed into Sinai as the Israel Air Force appeared to have won total supremacy.

Before nightfall an Israeli task force had captured the key town of Khan Younis, thereby cutting off the Egyptian forces in the Gaza Strip.

(The British Broadcasting Corporation last night reported that Israel armour has sliced through the Gaza Strip to the Mediterranean and that Arab forces in the area "are no longer a fighting factor.")

At the same time, Jordanian positions yesterday morning began firing and shelling in Jerusalem and on Mt. Scopus — a battle which continued intermittently throughout the day. Effective Israel counter-action silenced most of the Jordanian positions by the end of the day. Ten civilians were killed and about a hundred wounded.

Three Syrian airplanes also went into action briefly yesterday morning, in the Megiddo area. Two were shot down.

Deganta was shelled by both Syrian and Jordanian flat trajectory fire. The bombing in the north was mostly between Haifa and Acre, in the Bayside area. One of the targets apparently was the refinery, but was no damage caused.

Further to the south, places shelled or bombed were Megiddo, Nahsury, Ramat Hakovesh, Eyal, Kfar Syrkin, and the area around Kfar Saba and Kfar Yavetz.

Artillery shells began falling in the Tel Aviv area in the evening hours, one shell falling apparently near Kfar Masaryk. Other targets were Tel Baruch and the Lydda region. It seems all these were shelled from the Kalkilya region.

Ruling the skies

By ZE'EV SCHUL, Jerusalem Post Military Reporter

TEL AVIV. — The Israel Air Force appears to have achieved almost complete supremacy in its counter-strikes against the Egyptian, Jordanian and Syrian air forces during the daylight hours. If this is confirmed, the Defence Forces will have solved one of its main, and most urgent, problems. The Egyptian supply lines will be at the mercy of Israel's Air Force and the Egyptians will have increasing difficulties in maintaining their already scanty water and food supplies.

The Egyptians were the first to be dealt with. According to Baghdad Radio at 8.50 a.m., the Israel Air Force swung out against bases in the Canal and Cairo areas. Syrians made a number of forays against Eilabun (Central Galilee), Megiddo, and Haifa Bay. Two out of three Mig-17s were shot down over Megiddo. Later another Syrian plane crashed over Tuwafik, near Kibbutz Ein Gev, east of Lake Kinneret.

Not a single bomb fell on Tel Aviv or its vicinity throughout the day. The Jordanians massed across the 15 kms. to Netanya to bomb the southern outskirts of this seaside resort.

As far as the tactical situation of the advancing Armoured Corps and infantry units is concerned, the situation still appears rather vague, beyond the basic fact that the Defence Forces turned the Egyptian head-on assault. Egyptian reports say that the Israel forces were in action in the Kuntilla and other regions some 20-30 kms. inside Sinai.

By the early evening hours, it seemed that the Gaza Strip had been cut off at Khan Yunis.

As far as the Jordanian and Syrian frontiers are concerned, the Jordanians have put on a token show in Jerusalem, but shown no inclination for a massive entanglement with the Israel Defence Forces.

The Syrians, who started it all, have shown the least desire to fight Israel. Apart from sorties by their Air Force there has been no report of serious Syrian artillery engagements so far, and other Syrian units have stuck to their trenches — as of the early morning hours of yesterday. It is difficult to believe that the Syrians will remain passive, but there is every reason to believe that they will be more swiftly dealt with, and put on the defensive within hours if they venture into an open engagement.

peace through war

EL. has sought peace, and war has been forced upon her for the time. The events of yesterday un in no doubt that those who wise to live in peace are indeed wise to vs for war.

We have full information yet from three fronts on which the battle aped. Counter-attacks took the Israeli forces deep into Egyptian territory wreaked utter havoc with the tian air force and their airfields; battle around Jerusalem devel- Israel forces also struck into Jordan to eliminate the positions from which attack had come, and those from parts of the centre of the country were attached. The Jordanian forces under Egyptian command and their's plan provided for the placing of Egyptian forces in Jordan within four days, thus surrounding us and making effective defence infinitely more difficult and perilous — if not impossible.

yesterday's battles Egypt's leadership were clearly discernible. It was who sent orders to Jordan and Syria to begin attacking on the morning the Egyptian forces were hardened. If the Jordanian forces did not go forward quite as hard as they might have done, being inferior in numbers to Nasser's, if small in numbers comparison, this may be because the Jordanian commander sent there did not have too much prestige for Hussein's which might help to keep him on throne. If they occupied the U.N. quarters in the old Government near Ramat Rachel in Jerusalem, they may have been as a result of Nasser's urgent appeal that they occupy small corner of Arab territory in the make of Arab prestige. It is curious to note that the army of that Jordan who 'that of so..., although it was their persistent mando attacks which led to the...

1.30 a.m.

The Israel Defence Forces have occupied El Arish after taking Rafah and Sheikh Zuweid. Other towns taken were Khan Yunis, Der el-Balagh. At midnight we were engaged in a battle on the outskirts of Gaza.

In the central sector of the southern front, Anja el-Khafir was captured, and fighting was going on around the Um-Kalof positions. Kuntilla also was captured. Israel has taken a large number of prisoners as well as guns and tanks. The enemy suffered heavy casualties. Israel casualties are comparatively light.

On the Jordanian front, where shelling and bombing continued during the entire day, Israel forces counter-attacked, and Sur Baher, south of Jerusalem was captured. Also taken were Kadar and Sheikh Aziz near Kibbutz Ma'ale Hamisha. A number of villages elsewhere, particularly in the north, were captured. Israel forces are also sealing off Jenin.

"Our air force dealt a decisive blow to the enemy in an achievement without parallel," Rav Aluf Rabin announced in a broadcast at 1 a.m. this morning.

"Egypt has lost 300 planes, of which almost 200 were destroyed on the ground and 30 were downed in aerial combat. The Syrians lost 50 planes, Jordan 27 and Iraq nine. There were also 24 probables.

Eight Israel pilots were killed, and eleven have been listed as missing."

U.N. move for cease-fire

UNITED NATIONS. — Brazil's chief U.N. delegate, Dr. Jose Sette Camara, sought support yesterday, in backstage consultations with other Security Council members, for an immediate call for a cease-fire in the Middle East. Informed sources said that the proposed Brazilian initiative countered a bid by India to have the Council call for the return of both sides to the positions they held before fighting began.

The Argentine was also reported to be backing the Brazilian move.

The council, which met in the afternoon, was still in recess as this report was written, having heard brief opening statements at its opening session. Private talks were going on behind the scenes and in the Council chamber itself, which remained packed despite the official recess.

When the Council first assembled, at 1 p.m. Israel time, U Thant reported that Jordanian troops had captured Government House, the Jerusalem headquarters of the U.N. Truce Supervision Organization, and Israel forces had killed three Indian members of the deactivated U.N. Emergency Force at Rafah in the Gaza Strip area. India immediately asked condemnation of Israel for the air attack in which three of its nationals died.

Council President Hans Tabor, of Denmark, with support from the U.S. and Canada, wanted a resolution simply ordering an immediate cease-fire on all sides. Indian Ambassador Gopalaswami Parthasarathi wanted the measure to condemn Israel.

Soviet Ambassador Nikolai Fedorenko, with considerable support, wanted the cease-fire resolution to include an order to all forces to withdraw at once to positions they held on Sunday.

Mr. Tabor read to the Council the communications he had received from Israel, at 10.10 Israel time, and from Egypt, 30 minutes later.

Israel Ambassador Gideon Rafael told the 15-nation Council, "it is evident that in the early hours of this morning, Egyptian armoured columns moved in an offensive thrust against our border and at the same time Egyptian planes took off from airfields in Sinai and struck out against Israel." He said Egyptian artillery shelled four Israel villages as the fighting began. Egyptian Ambassador Mohammed Awad...

U.S. 'neutral' in conflict

Jerusalem Post — Near East Report 1.

WASHINGTON. — President Johnson yesterday condemned the war engulfing the Middle East as "needless and destructive" and gave first priority to trying to end it through the U.N. Security Council. For the time being it appeared that the U.S. would not intervene directly to try to halt the fighting.

Mr. Johnson conferred with Secretary of State Dean Rusk and Secretary of Defence Robert McNamara. There was an unconfirmed report that he spoke to British Prime Minister Harold Wilson in London. Mr. Rusk and Mr. McNamara briefed Congressional leaders on the flare-up in a secret session.

Meanwhile, the U.S. yesterday officially declared itself neutral. "Our position is neutral in thought, word and deed," said State Department Spokesman Robert J. McCloskey. He said all military and civilian aid to countries in the immediate area or involved in the conflict "are urgently under review."

At 10.30 a.m., the Ambassadors of Iraq, Lebanon, Saudi Arabia, Egypt, Yemen, Tunisia, Libya, Algeria, Morocco and Sudan met Under-Secretary of State Eugene Rostow in a group. Earlier, Israel Charge d'Affaires Ephraim Evron met Mr. Rostow for 30 minutes. The French and the British Ambassadors also met Mr. Rostow.

In London, British Foreign Secretary George Brown summoned the U.S., Soviet

(Continued on Page 8, Col. 2)

Sabotage units

The Army spokesman said late last night that a small unit of saboteurs penetrated from the Gaza Strip near Nir Am junction, opened fire on a private car, and then opened fire on an ambulance. At 11.15 an electric pylon near Beisan was sabotaged, and fire opened on an ambulance going from Bet Aza to Yad Mordechai.

At 11.15 p.m. Jordanian artillery opened fire on Sde Eliyahu in the Beisan Valley.

Reports say airports of 3 Arab Capitals strafed

CAIRO. — An Egyptian Foreign Ministry statement said Israel planes attacked Egyptian airfields in the Cairo area and Suez Canal zone. Heavy gun and anti-aircraft fire could be heard on the desert outskirts of the city.

The wail of air raid sirens brought traffic in Cairo, a city of four million, to a halt shortly after 9 a.m. Army military trucks and cars, including taxis commandeered by officers, raced through the streets. Thousands of people braved the alert to throng the streets listening to first communiques over transistor radios. They wildly cheered and danced in the streets at the first announcement claiming 23 Israel planes had been destroyed. Later, Cairo Radio interspersed martial music with slogans, including a call: "All Arabs — we have a rendezvous in Tel Aviv."

There were three other air raid alerts in Cairo during the day. Cairo Radio alleged triumphantly that at least 23 Israeli planes had been brought down in an air raid on the El Arish airport.

But then, Cairo Radio went on to urge all citizens to observe restraint, remain quiet, and ignore rumours.

The Cairo authorities imposed censorship on all news out of Egypt.

The "joint Arab command" in Amman announced that Jordanian, Iraqi and Syrian air forces were conducting joint air operations against targets inside "Occupied Palestine." A Syrian military communique said "the Syrian Air Force is bombarding enemy airports and strategic targets. The...

FRENCH SAID HALTING AID TO ISRAEL

PARIS (UPI). — France has suspended the delivery of all war materials to Israel and to all Arab countries involved in the Middle East conflict, informed sources said last night.

The sources said the decision was made following a meeting between Premier Georges Pompidou and Gen. Michel de Brébisson, Secretary-General of the National Defence Office which is in charge of sales and supplies of French war material to foreign countries.

SCOPUS ROAD OPENED, OLD CITY ENCIRCLED

THE JERUSALEM POST

Published in Jerusalem, Israel, daily except on Saturday by The Palestine Post Ltd. Founded in 1932 by Gershon AGRON.
Registered at the G.P.O. Copyright of all material reserved; reproduction permitted only by arrangement. Editor: TED R. LURIE.

Jerusalem: 9 Rehov Havatzelet, P.O.B. 81, Telephone 24255, 24521
Tel Aviv: 55 Rehov Rehov Magen-ha, P.O.Box 1125, Tel. 65925
Haifa: 16 Rehov Herzl, Hadar Hacarmel, P.O.Box 4333, Telephone 66386

PRICE: 35 AGORA

WEDNESDAY, JUNE 7, 1967 • IYAR 28, 5727 • SAFAR 29, 1387 • VOL. XXXVII, No. 11979*

OTHER WAR NEWS, pages 2, 3, 4

200 EGYPTIAN TANKS SMASHED; GAZA FALLS

Only 36 hours after the start of fighting, Israel forces were deep in Sinai, had captured Gaza, made sweeping gains on the Jordan front, and had encircled the Old City of Jerusalem.

The Israel forces in Sinai destroyed 200 Egyptian tanks on Monday and yesterday, the Defence Establishment's spokesman told foreign correspondents last night. One hundred and fifty Egyptian tanks were destroyed yesterday and 50 the day before. The spokesman said that there were tank battles in Sinai yesterday as well as some air engagements. In general, the Egyptian forces were on the retreat.

Spearheads of Israel Armoured Corps units were last night reported to be well beyond El Arish, and engaged in large-scale tank battles along the Sinai coastal plain, with the Egyptians retreating westwards.

Israel Air Force units shot down eight Egyptian planes yesterday. The first six were brought down during the morning.

They were all of the Sokhoi-7 type, the most modern planes in use by the Egyptians. The other two were Mig-21s. A TU-16 of the Iraqi Air Force was shot down over Megiddo, after attempting a bombing run on Netanya. The plane was brought down by anti-aircraft fire.

The mechanized units appeared to have advanced more rapidly than those during the Sinai Campaign. An Army spokesman said here yesterday. The Gaza Strip has been completely occupied; a sizeable part of the north-central section of Sinai was in Israel hands, and Israeli armour was engaging what seemed to be the last major Egyptian armoured unit still intact, southwards in the Kuntilla area.

KALKILYA, JENIN TAKEN

In Jordan, Israel units captured Kalkilya, Latrun and Jenin and reached the vicinity of the Samaria mountains in addition to its successes in Jerusalem. Jordanian units appeared to be retreating eastwards.

Reports of street fighting in the Old City were denied by the Army spokesman yesterday. However, with the conquest of Sheikh Jarah and the so-called French Hill, Israel has been able to relieve the defenders of Mt. Scopus, who had been besieged since the fighting started.

Some localities, like Abu Agheila, were yesterday captured by the Israel Defence Forces for the third time. Veteran commanders are also familiar with a good many of the others, notably Latrun and Jenin.

Yesterday's most significant development, however, was not any specific conquest but the noticeable westward movements of Egyptian units now abandoning the Kuntilla-Abu Agheila axis, the Egyptian "Maginot line" which had been reinforced by a crack armoured division. Observers here yesterday afternoon saw in the new Egyptian troop movements the first signs of a crack up and possible general retreat by the Egyptians to new positions further to the south.

LATRUN'S IMPORTANCE

Most important of yesterday's gains were the capture of Latrun and the artillery positions surrounding it, and seizure of Abu Agheila, the "impregnable" Egyptian position in Sinai. From Latrun the Jordanians had lobbed shells into Lydda. Artillery positions at Kalkiliya also fired some shells into central and northern Tel Aviv (suburbs).

In the Jerusalem area, Israeli troops last night outflanked the Jordanian held part of the city, taking Nebi Samuel in the North, with the fall of Ramallah considered to be only a matter of hours.

With the fall of the Old City, Ramallah and Latrun this entire-front could be rolled back, possibly splitting the western half of Jordan by separating the Hebron and Nablus districts.

SYRIAN GUNS SILENCED

The Syrians' massive artillery bombardments of settlements along the entire length of the Upper Jordan Valley was countered by Air Force strafings and return to Israel continues to be on the defensive in Upper Galilee, with the Syrians once again gaining time, thanks primarily to the relative military insignificance.

The conflict with Jordan is primarily aimed against Jordanian artillery positions which continue to shell Jerusalem as well as settlements along the entire length the central frontier — from Latrun northwards.

Armoured units succeeded in cutting the Gaza Strip during the first few hours of hostilities, sweeping across the 14 kilometres separating Israel from the Mediterranean at this point. This was followed by the piecemeal whittling down of resistance, culminating with the surrender of Gaza at noon yesterday. Small pockets of resistance are expected to be mopped up within the next 24 hours.

Following the surrender of El Arish and Abu Agheila, the Egyptians are now withdrawing their remaining troops stationed in the Kuntilla area and are heading west. Much will now depend on the speed of Israeli pursuit — whether this will give the Egyptians enough time to reform.

EGYPTIAN COMMANDOS

The introduction of Egyptian commandos in the Jordanian army has unfortunately compelled Israel to take stronger measures than were initially anticipated. Prisoners taken at Latrun yesterday include a number of Egyptian commandos officers and men. The highest ranking officer was a major who said that two commando battalions arrived in Jordan on June 3, immediately after the signing of the Egyptian-Jordanian military agreement. Their mission, they said, had been the sabotage of airfields in Israel.

(Amman Radio broadcast the Jordan Army's communiqué No. 36, which admitted heavy fighting is proceeding in the area of Kalkilya, Bethlehem and Hebron. The communiqué said Israeli bombers raided Jordanian air installations, troop concentrations and reinforcement convoys, and alleged that napalm bombs and rockets were used.)

Observers here said yesterday that fighting was entering a concluding phase on the Jordan front, and perhaps also the Sinai.

JERUSALEM

THE battle for Jerusalem has been won. Its brave, heroic, and weary citizens are unlikely to have to spend a third night in their hot and cramped shelters. The death toll in the fighting has not been low among civilians, though many of these deaths and injuries could have been avoided with more care.

It was a brief taste of the drawn-out trial of 1948, when the city remained on starvation rations and almost without water for many weeks. But there is a difference. In 1948 there was a deep fear that Jewish Jerusalem might fall — as the Jewish Quarter of the Old City had fallen after long and heroic resistance, when its ammunition gave out. There was no such fear this time and the aimless shelling was doubly resented as mere obedience to Nasser's order for a diversionary move that would cause Israel forces to be withdrawn from the Sinai front for the protection of their Capital.

But the current battles have a bitter logic, bitter for Nasser's strategy of domination of all Arab countries, and doubly bitter for his unwilling supporters, who have been dragged into a battle that is not of their own choosing. There were no indications during the past few years that Jordan's King Hussein had any intention of attacking Israel in force, or of making any move in Jerusalem. Presumably he knew himself that the result was likely to be disastrous for him, and likely to cost him his position in Jerusalem, if not his crown or his life.

Israel has had an account of its own with Jordan ever since 1948 for its failure to observe the Armistice Agreements. First of all, the free access to the Western Wall in the Old City, which was part of the Agreement, has never been implemented, and scarcely even debated. Access to the old Hadassah Hospital and Hebrew University buildings on Mount Scopus has not been free, but limited to fortnightly convoys for supplies and the exchange of the police guard in the buildings, and in times of tension the passage of the convoy has often been delayed or stopped. On Monday morning, when the battle in the South had begun, but the shooting in Jerusalem not yet started, security authorities were wondering whether this meant that the convoy, due today, would be held up, and whether perhaps the Jordanians would try out a lesser Titan blockade themselves and create new difficulties in contact with the Mount Scopus area.

The massed attack launched by Jordan upon Israel Jerusalem was unexpected, but its result could have been foreseen, despite the comparative strength of the Arab Legion forces, who are a very different body of men to Nasser's troops. There was no way of protecting Jerusalem against Jordanian shelling except by capturing the outlying positions from which this fire was directed, and some of them are deep in Jordanian territory. The Old City itself is a very much more delicate issue, for although some of the fire came from positions right inside the City, Israel was not prepared to shell this close-packed warren of old buildings containing some of the most treasured religious monuments of the three faiths, and so was severely hampered in dealing with the attack coming from this area. In a hard and costly fight, the City has been surrounded, and it is not expected to resist very long in this condition. The Jews of Israel will once more practise the ancient custom of visiting the Western Wall of the ancient Temple for prayer and remembrance.

Israel cannot permit itself to be locked out of the Old City again or to rely on the uncertain services of the U.N. for its right of access. The division of the city has been a painful and expensive anomaly for 20 years. Now it looks as though some entirely new solution to this problem will have to be found.

NEW YORK STOCK EXCHANGE

Closing Tuesday, June 6, 1967

Dow Jones Industrial Average 902.71 +14.94
Volume of shares traded 9,750,000

Admiral	22⅛	Int'T&T	81⅞
Alcoa	87⅜	Jlt'cn	37¾
Am T&T	56⅛	McTson	43½
Anacon	93⅝	MinnMM	83⅝
BethStl	34	Monsan	48⅝
Boeing	97	OlinMath	57⅜
Burrough	127⅛	PacGelec	76¾
Chrysler	40⅝	P&R	64⅝
Comsat	82⅜	Polaroid	215
CrownCork	51⅜	RCA	51⅜
DowCh	78⅛	PennToh	57⅜
duPont	156⅞	Sperry	35⅞
ElKodak	135	SperRd	31⅞
FairCam	94¼	StONJ	61⅜
FordMot	50⅛	TransW	69⅝
Gen Elec	85¼	U.SStel	43⅜
GenMot	80	Westghl	57¼
Homestke	49	Woolwrth	23
IntBusM	477¼	Xerox	282⅛
IntPap	29⅜	ZenithRad	58¼

Supplied by Albert Kaplan, Israel Rep.

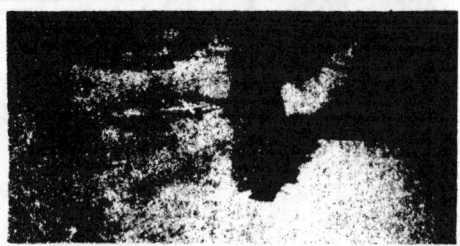

Soviet-built Egyptian TU-16 bomber belches black smoke after Israel Air Force set it afire at an air base in Sinai.

Six Arab countries sever ties with U.S.; Egypt closes Canal

Egypt, Syria and Algeria last night broke off diplomatic relations with the U.S., and Arab oil-producing states cut off supplies to both the U.S. and Britain after Arab charges that the two nations provided air cover to Israel during Monday's hostilities. They were followed by Yemen, Sudan and Iraq. Both the U.S. and Britain vigorously and angrily denied the charges. Syria, Yemen, Sudan and Iraq also severed relations with Britain. Egypt and Algeria had done so earlier.

In addition, Egypt announced yesterday that it has decided to halt navigation in the Suez Canal so that the waterway will not be a target for Israeli air attack. Cairo Radio linked this decision with the allegations.

In Cairo, Alexandria, Damascus and Baghdad there were prolonged demonstrations in front of U.S. missions. Baghdad demonstrators set fire to the U.S. Information Service Library and the British Council. Mobs sacked and burned the U.S. Consulate in Alexandria. Another mob tried to force its way into the British Consulate. Demonstrators shouted "Down with Johnson, down with Wilson," outside the U.S. Embassy in Cairo.

In Beirut, Lebanese security forces dispersed a crowd of demonstrators outside the U.S. Embassy. Reports abroad that the U.S. Embassy was burned were denied as "not true."

In Amman, troops squashed anti-American and anti-British demonstrations. The troops headed off demonstrators marching on the embassies of the two countries.

In another development, British Prime Minister Harold Wilson announced the suspension of all British arms shipment to the Middle East for 24 hours pending reassessment of the situation. Mr. Wilson, addressing the Commons, urged the Arabs not to disrupt commercial arrangements on the basis of false statements.

The nations imposing a ban on oil shipments to the U.S. and Britain were Kuwait and Algeria. Iraq ordered a halt yesterday in the pumping of oil to British and U.S. customers. Iraq's pipelines cross Syria en route to the Mediterranean.

The U.S. State Department confirmed that Egypt had broken diplomatic relations and said it intended to make this action reciprocal. The new U.S. Ambassador to Cairo, Mr. Richard Nolte, who was originally due to submit his credentials to President Nasser on Monday. (Reuter, UPI, AP)

U.S. and Soviets seek accord in U.N. Council

UNITED NATIONS (Reuter). — The U.S. and Soviet delegates discussed the Middle East crisis for almost an hour yesterday while the start of a scheduled meeting of the Security Council was delayed at least until midnight last time. Mr. Arthur Goldberg, the American representative, and his Soviet opposite number, Dr. Nikolai Fedorenko, met in the office of the Council President, Mr. Hans Tabor.

It was understood that they were trying to reconcile their differences on how the Council should go about calling for a ceasefire. Informed sources said Mr. Tabor was trying to obtain the agreement of the two super powers to a draft resolution which would enable the Security Council during the night to call for an immediate ceasefire.

Russia obstructed this bid all day Monday by insisting on adding other clauses to the simple appeal favoured by the U.S. and Britain. In particular the Russians want the Council to call for the withdrawal of Arab and Israel troops to the positions they occupied before fighting began on Monday. The Western powers objected to this because, they said it would freeze the status quo, particularly Egypt's blockade of the Tiran Straits.

The Soviet Ambassador in London, Mr. Mikhail Smirnovsky, had a 10-minute meeting with Prime Minister Harold Wilson yesterday. No details were immediately available about the call, made at the envoy's own request shortly after Britain had denied Arab charges that British planes were involved in Arab-Israel fighting. Mr. Wilson has been in continuous contact with world leaders, including Soviet Prime Minister Alexei Kosygin, over the past few days as part of Britain's drive to get Russia to work with the Western Big Three to end the fighting.

Eshkol appeals to Kosygin

Mr. Eshkol has appealed to the Soviet Prime Minister a second time to show understanding for Israel's necessity to repel Nasser's "wicked aggression" and foil his declared and planned intention to destroy this country. In a letter to Mr. Kosygin, dated June 5, he also appealed to the Soviet Union to join an effort to pacify the Middle East. (Text of letter on page 2)

The Kremlin in a statement early yesterday, quoted by Reuter, demanded that Israel stop its "aggression" against Arab countries and withdraw its troops to behind the lines held before fighting broke out.

Prime Minister Kosygin yesterday told talks in Moscow with the Egyptian Ambassador, Mr. Mohammed Ghaleb. An official announcement by Tass said they had "a friendly conversation in which questions of mutual interest were discussed."

Tass breaks out with Israel version

MOSCOW (UPI). — Soviet news media reported for the first time last night that Israeli troops might be winning battles in the Middle East war. Tass broke into its usual strung of Arab communiqués to report Israeli claims of victories in Sinai and Jerusalem. The agency quoted a radio report by Israeli generals in Israeli advances in northern Sinai, its capture of these towns "on the road to the Suez Canal," its taking of Jenin, Gaza and the...

Syrian attacks repulsed

By DAVID SLAV
Jerusalem Post Reporter

TIBERIAS. — Syrian infantry and an armoured column tried to penetrate the Sh'ar Yashuv and Tel Dan areas yesterday, but were beaten back by Israel armour and the Air Force. During the 90-minute battle the Syrians shelled Dan, Daphne, Sh'ar Yashuv, Ma'ayan Baruch, Lehavot Habashan, Gadot and Yesud Hama'alah. They used long-range artillery against Rosh Pina and the frontier station at the Bnot Ya'acov Bridge. Shrapnel fell in Moshav Eliphelet.

In Rosh Pina, one resident was slightly wounded and 15 buildings hit. One house went up in flames, set alight by a brush fire. Telephone lines were cut. At Dan a resident was slightly wounded. In the southern sector, the Syrians attacked Ein Gev and Tel Katzir with artillery fire. One person at Ein Gev was killed and several wounded. The concert hall and other buildings were damaged. At Tel Katzir one building was hit.

SYRIANS BOMBED

Israel Air Force planes strafed and bombed the Syrian fortified emplacements on the slopes, silenced the guns and damaged most of them. At the same time, Israel artillery hit them from below. Tel Aznaiat and Tel Hamra, said "acquaintances" of the settlers, were wrecked. All day and night, fire and smoke were seen rising from the Syrian positions. No Syrian planes were seen above the area all day.

At 2 p.m. the whole front was quiet. In all the settlements near the border, including Tiberias, people spent hours in shelters. They emerged in the afternoon to enjoy the cool air.

Syrian plane crashes on petrol station, kills nine

AFULA. — Nine were killed and a number were wounded when a Syrian Dushin bomber was shot down by an Israeli fighter at 5.35 yesterday morning before it could drop any bombs.

The bomber was flying very low in a southerly direction over the rooftops of the buildings at Rehov Habaim and the Government housing quarter. Hit by the Israel plane, the bomber fell in flames near a petrol station on the outskirts of the town and exploded together with its load of bombs. Nine Israelis were killed instantly. The pilot and the co-pilot were also killed.

B.B.C. SEES JORDAN ARMY COLLAPSING

The British Broadcasting Corporation (B.B.C.) last night quoted "reliable sources" in Amman as saying that the Jordanian armed forces were "on the point of collapse." In a report by its diplomatic correspondent, the broadcast said Jordanian ground forces were "pinned down in isolated points" along the area bordering Israel. With "its air cover destroyed in the first hours of the attack, Jordan's forces must either stand their ground and be destroyed or pull out in a full-scale retreat across the river Jordan," the report said.

Mt. Scopus relieved

By CHARLES WEISS, Jerusalem Post Reporter

After bitter fighting that lasted throughout Monday night and well into yesterday, all Jordanian Jerusalem outside the Old City Wall — including the "French Hill" adjacent to Mt. Scopus, Sheikh Jarrah and the road to Mt. Scopus — were in Israeli hands. The garrison on Scopus was relieved after a 24-hour siege

In addition, the villages of Beit Iksa, Nebi Samuel and Shu'afat and the radar station above Ma'aleh Hahamisha to the north were captured. But snipers were still being mopped up in the Old City until last night.

As the troops being relieved drove out of Mandelbaum Gate into the Mea Shearim neighbourhood yesterday morning, they were greeted by large crowds of excited residents from the neighbourhood, clapping and cheering them on. The men were dog-tired; they just smiled.

Among the vehicles were a number bearing Jordanian licence numbers.

Mayor Teddy Kollek, in the company of the O.C. Central Command, made a quick tour of Jordanian Jerusalem outside the walls yesterday afternoon.

One soldier said to Mr. Kollek: "We've made your city bigger." His reply: "A bigger headache, you mean." The Commander of the Southern District Police, Mr. Shani Rosolio, showed up at 3 p.m. to ask about getting his border control police station at Mandelbaum Gate back. They told him he could have it at 14.00 hours today. Aside from the danger of sniper fire (still very real — a soldier was fatally wounded several minutes after Mayor Kollek reached the crossing point on his way out), there is the danger of looting, which must be prevented.

A party of three experts visited the Palestine Museum (known as the "Rockefeller") outside the Herod's Gate Quarter. They were the Government Director of Antiquities and Museums, Dr. A. Biran; the Director of the Hebrew University Archeology Institute, Prof. Nahman Avigad; and the Secretary of the Israel Exploration Society, Mr. Yosef Aviram.

Walking a hundred metres past the control point on the Jordanian side of Mandelbaum Gate, we came across the body of a Jordanian soldier killed in the break...

(Continued on Page 2, Col. 6)

I would like to thank all of those who have expressed their good wishes on my appointment as Minister of Defence.

I would ask my friends to forgive me for not being able to reply to each one personally in view of the needs of the hour.

To all of Israel and to the Israel Defence Forces I extend my wishes for victory in our struggle.

**GENERAL MOSHE DAYAN,
Minister of Defence**

Egyptian-Syrian attacks held

Tanks battle as Syrians penetrate Golan line, Egyptians cross Canal, Israel planes maintain air supremacy

Syrian shells explode in a kibbutz in northern Galilee. (AP photo)

THE JERUSALEM POST

SECOND EDITION

Price: 65 Ag.

SUNDAY, OCTOBER 7, 1973 • TISHRE 11, 5734 • RAMADHAN 11, 1393 • VOL. XLIII, No. 13911*

By HIRSH GOODMAN, Jerusalem Post Military Correspondent

Israel forces yesterday contained invading Egyptian and Syrian units which crossed into Sinai and the Golan Heights under heavy artillery and air cover. The attack began shortly before 2 o'clock.

Two positions, one on the northern tip of the Canal and the other on Mount Hermon, which were taken by Arab forces in the late afternoon, were recaptured yesterday evening. No casualty figures were available last night, but Syrian and Egyptian losses were reported to be "heavy."

Israel will be fighting an estimated 350,000 troops on both fronts—250,000 of them along the Egyptian front alone. According to Defence Minister Moshe Dayan, the Egyptians have 2,000 tanks, 1,500 artillery pieces and 700 planes readied for the battle, while the Syrians have mobilised 800 tanks and 800 long-range and medium-range guns along the front.

Only limited Egyptian and Syrian forces managed to cross over the cease-fire lines as Israel maintained supremacy in the skies. The Egyptians crossed the Suez Canal at several points, attacking sparsely defended Israeli forward positions, while the Syrians brought troops by helicopter to positions on the Hermon and along the Golan Heights. The attacks were coordinated with massive artillery bombardments aimed at Israeli forces.

Throughout last night, Egyptian forces were attempting to build bridgeheads across the Canal, in an attempt to bolster commando and infantry units, which had taken positions on the Israeli side during the afternoon.

According to the army spokesman, an attempt by the Egyptians to transport troops by helicopter into Abu Rodeis in southern Sinai at 6 p.m. was fought off when Israeli Air Force planes destroyed eight (unconfirmed reports claim 10) of the helicopters in flight. Each helicopter carries an average of 30 men and their equipment.

Air raid sirens sounded off three times in Tel Aviv. According to Defence Minister Dayan, the sirens were in response to enemy planes flying in the direction of the city from the sea. Mr. Dayan said in reply to a question that the planes were equipped with missiles, but he would not elaborate.

Throughout the afternoon there was heavy aerial fighting both in the north and in Sinai. No losses for either Israeli or Arab planes were given. Mr. Dayan said last night there were no Israeli air raids on enemy positions beyond the battle front.

Up to last night Jordanian forces had remained out of the war, and in the administered territories, Mr. Dayan reported, life was normal. Mr. Dayan strongly advised the Jordanians not to enter the battle.

Israeli towns and settlements suffered in no significant way according to Mr. Dayan, who reported that there had been one fatality in the northern town of Kiryat Shmona.

No Israeli settlements had been evacuated, apart from the civilian oil town of Abu Rodeis in southern Sinai, where families were flown north yesterday morning before actual hostilities commenced.

There was no gauging last night how long the war was likely to last, or what it's scope would be. Israel is thought to have lost a certain advantage, observers point out, by not staging a pre-emptive attack. Defence Minister Dayan would not commit himself to a time limit last night, but stated the war would take neither months nor weeks.

The Syrians' air attack was directed in part against the Golan's Druse — several men and women were killed by strafing and 15 were injured, in the villages of Majdal Shams, Bukata and Mas'ade. The residents told an Israel Radio reporter the planes swooped on them while they were in the fields, strafing them mercilessly, then went on to spray fire at their homes.

Decision against pre-emptive attack

Jerusalem Post Reporter

The joint Egyptian-Syrian attack began just before 2 p.m. yesterday, timed deliberately for Yom Kippur. Israel learned earlier that the attack would take place. The Cabinet was called into extraordinary session, and Prime Minister Golda Meir informed U.S. Ambassador Kenneth Keating that the assault was imminent.

The Cabinet decided not to preempt the planned Arab assault, authoritative sources said. The decision was taken for political not military reasons to make it clear who was responsible for starting the war. The Israeli decision was taken deliberately, despite the military disadvantage involved, out of confidence that the situation of Israel's borders provided the additional security needed to make up for leaving the initiative to the enemy.

The attack was planned by Cairo and Damascus for some time, and was designed as a "maximum effort." The Egyptian aim, it is believed, is to regain parts of Sinai, especially the Mitla area, Sharm e-Sheikh and Abu Rodeis, while the Syrians apparently set their war aim as to retake all of the Golan Heights.

The Egyptians have amassed a huge tank force, said to number two thousand vehicles and have all of their airplanes estimated at about 500 in the air. Their aim yesterday was to establish beachheads west of Suez before nightfall and bolster them under cover of darkness.

Israel sources believe the Egyptians may also be seeking to attack Israel cities from the air.

The troop concentrations along the Syrian and Egyptian fronts were noted last week. However, it was first believed that the Arab forces were arrayed in a defensive alignment.

This changed into an offensive pattern at the end of the week. Even before that, however, Russian civilians in both Syria and Egypt began to be evacuated, indicating that an attack was in the wind.

5 Syrian ships sunk

Jerusalem Post Military Correspondent

Four Syrian missile boats and one torpedo boat were sunk in a naval battle between Israel and Syrian vessels near the Syrian port of Latakia yesterday evening. The Israeli naval unit suffered no losses.

The Syrian vessels, of the Soviet-built Comar and Osea classes, were sunk with Israel-made Gabriel sea surface-to-surface missiles used in combat for the first time.

U.S. seeks cease-fire

NEW YORK. — Secretary of State Henry Kissinger, on instructions from President Nixon, yesterday sought an immediate cease-fire in the Middle East, the State Department spokesman said in New York.

The spokesman, Mr. Robert McCloskey, said that U.S. attempts to prevent the outbreak of war had failed, but Dr. Kissinger was under orders from the President to "make every effort to see that it is brought to a stop."

Kissinger flew back to Washington from New York — where he had been attending the U.N. session — after a series of urgent telephone consultations with the President.

Dr. Kissinger was to meet with a special task force set up within the State Department as soon as fighting broke out, McCloskey told newsmen.

One White House official said the President was "very, very concerned," and was giving direct guidance to Kissinger in their frequent telephone conversations.

At the direction of the President, he said, Kissinger immediately got in touch with the Foreign Ministers of Israel, Egypt and Syria and Soviet Ambassador Anatoly Dobrynin. The President ordered Kissinger to make a major diplomatic effort to prevent the fighting from spreading and to restore the cease-fire.

In each appeal, Dr. Kissinger had urged restraint and efforts to avoid escalation or continuation of the fighting.

McCloskey said although Kissinger spoke to U.N. Secretary-General Kurt Waldheim and the Security Council President, Sir Laurence McIntyre of Australia, there were no plans at the moment to call an emergency meeting. The U.S. would not oppose such a move.

McCloskey said that Kissinger

(Continued on page 2, col. 3)

Victory in few days: Dayan

Jerusalem Post Reporter

Defence Minister Moshe Dayan predicted last night that Israel would smite the Egyptians and Syrians "hip and thigh," but said it might take a few days.

In a television and radio address to the nation, Mr. Dayan said the Egyptians had inflicted some casualties on Israel forces on the eastern bank of the Canal, and had managed to capture a number of Israel strongholds, but the overall situation was somewhat better than had been expected under the circumstances.

In the Golan Heights the Syrians got a few of their tanks across the cease-fire lines, and broke through in several places, but scored no meaningful successes, and the situation there was fairly satisfactory.

The Defence Minister argued that the initial Arab advantage could only have been forestalled if Israel had resorted either to a huge per-

(Continued page 2, col. 1)

Arabs claim success

By ANAN SAFADI
Jerusalem Post Arab Affairs Reporter

The Egyptians last night said they had poured reinforcements into the eastern bank of the Suez Canal, and claimed they had captured most of the Israeli-held side of the waterway.

The dispatch of reinforcements was announced shortly after an army spokesman in Cairo said the Egyptian forces had "succeeded in storming the Suez Canal all along the confrontation line and capturing most of the eastern bank of the waterway." The spokesman said the Egyptian flag had been hoisted over several positions captured during the afternoon.

Similar claims of success were made last night by the Syrians, who said they had "liberated" several positions across the cease-fire line on the Golan Heights. The Syrians said they succeeded in repelling an Israeli attack and moving into the offensive. They said fighting was being waged on the Israeli side of the cease-fire line late last night. The Syrians claimed to have "liberated" several positions, including one on Mount Hermon, and said three Israeli planes were shot down.

There were no reports of fighting at sea, although the Egyptians said late last night that their navy had gone into action. "Our naval forces also protected the flank of our forces on the Mediterranean coast, hitting important enemy targets on the northern shore of the Sinai Peninsula and scoring direct hits."

Both Egypt and Syria earlier warned all ships to stay out of their territorial waters. The two countries also closed off their air space.

As darkness fell, Cairo Radio repeated civil defence measures, including a complete blackout. A state of emergency has been declared throughout Syria.

Jordan's King Hussein ordered the commanders of his armed forces to keep in close touch with Egypt and Syria. He placed his forces under a state of alert.

There were no indications at this stage of Jordanian or Lebanese involvement, but Palestinian terrorist spokesmen claimed their own forces were "intercepting the enemy" along Lebanon's southeast border, which neighbours Syria's cease-fire line with Israel.

The war was first reported by Cairo, whose state-run radio interrupted its regular programme at 2.10 p.m., claiming an Israeli air and naval force had attacked two Egyptian positions on the western coast of the Suez Canal 40 minutes earlier. The two positions were named as Sokhneh and Za'afarana.

In a later broadcast, the Syrians announced their positions had been attacked at 2 p.m. Subsequent communiques reported the development of fierce clashes on land and in the air. Egypt said it had lost one plane and later amended the figure to ten, while claiming to have downed eleven Israel fighters.

Amid the broadcast of martial music, Cairo radio reported President Sadat has moved to military headquarters to personally supervise operations.

Syrian President Hafez Assad too was reported to have taken over the army headquarters. In a nationwide broadcast Assad accused Israel of launching a "blitzkreig" against Egypt and his country.

"We do not want to kill anyone, but we are repulsing those who want to kill us. We are fighting the battle of honour and dignity," Assad added.

Arab radio reported the progress of fighting with evident jubilation. Nevertheless, Cairo Radio later in the evening demonstrated caution, confining its reports to official statements. Cairo broadcast several code "appeals," the first of which urged "all our friends in beloved Sinai" to report to Cairo. "We are awaiting your news. God be with you and victory to all." Ten other messages

STRONGER ARAB FORCES THAN '67

Russians flee scapegoat role

By ZEEV SCHUL
Jerusalem Post Reporter

TEL AVIV. — The total deployment of the Syrian and Egyptian armies — including mobilisation of all of their reserve units — into the so-called front line offensive jumping-off platform was accomplished gradually during the past few weeks.

The total strength of the two armies by noon yesterday was believed to exceed the combined might of the Arab armies during the Six Day War by some 30 per cent. There was a similar increase in the number of guns, tanks and aircraft available to the two Arab countries.

The strongest indication of all that more than a mere jockeying for tactical positions was involved came when the Russian advisers started a wholesale exodus from both Syria and Egypt.

Russian civilian and military personnel, believed to number several thousand in Syria and a few hundred in Egypt, were evacuated with their families in an intensive airlift begun just over 40 hours ago and was expected to be completed by yesterday evening.

The reasons for the Russian departure are believed to have been their reluctance to become involved in another Arab fiasco, or even to be blamed for it by a vengeance-bent Arab population as the only available scapegoats. Then there was also the omnipresent threat of Israel Air Force counter bombings.

Finally a continued Soviet presence might also compel the Russians to intervene in the fighting at a certain stage in order to rescue their citizens.

Both the Syrian and Egyptian deployments were carried out during the past few weeks in accordance with Russian tactics, involving a multi-purpose deployment with medium-range tanks and artillery being brought forward.

When the total strength of the Syrian and Egyptian armies was poised and ready to strike, Israel Army H.Q. yesterday morning sent out its first mobilization orders. The Egyptians are understood to have advanced bridging equipment to the frontline and their attempt to cross the Canal took nobody by surprise here.

There was no plausible explanation for the timing of yesterday's two-pronged Arab strike. Commentators here pointed out that the Egyptian-Syrian attack could not be traced to any particular political pressure (internal or foreign) in either country. They apparently chose the Day of Atonement because they hoped to be able to achieve some measure of surprise on this most sacred day in the Jewish calendar.

The Observers pointed out the parallel of the period preceding the Six Day War, when at first nobody took the Egyptian war threats seriously — coming as they did when

(Continued on page 2, col. 3)

Meir: Israel first asked friendly quarters to act

Jerusalem Post Reporter

Prime Minister Golda Meir went on radio and television within a little more than four hours of the start of the Arab offensive, to voice full confidence in Israel's victory over the Egyptian and Syrian aggressors.

(The broadcast of Mrs. Meir's address — and of Mr. Dayan's, later in the evening — was, technically, in violation of the Broadcasting Authority's earlier decision to bar radio and television appearances by political leaders until after the Knesset elections. The technical rule was waived, however, in view of the unusual situation.)

Following is the text of Mrs. Meir's address:

Shortly before 2 p.m. today, the armies of Egypt and Syria started an offensive against Israel. They launched a series of air, armoured and artillery atacks in Sinai and on the Golan Heights. The IDF has entered the fight, and is beating back the offensive. The enemy has suffered grave losses.

The rulers of Egypt and Syria have long planned this violation of the cease-fire. Contemptibly, the aggressors are now spreading the lie that it was Israel which opened fire. But the responsibility for the renewal of the fighting and for the bloodshed lies with them alone.

Our enemies had hoped to catch the citizens of Israel by surprise on Yom Kippur, when so many of our people are fasting and praying in the synagogues. Our attackers thought that on Yom Kippur we would not be prepared to hit back at them. We were not caught by surprise.

For several days now, our intelligence services had been apprised that the armies of Egypt and Syria were lining up for a joint offensive. IDF patrols discovered that large armed forces were massing in offensive deployment in the vicinity of the Suez Canal and on the Golan Heights. The findings of the patrols checked with the reports already received. Our forces were duly ar-

MEIR SPEAKING ON TV LAST NIGHT

be victorious. We are also convinced, however, that this renewal of Egyptian-Syrian aggression is an act of madness. It was our desire to prevent this outbreak. We appealed to a number of influential political quarters to intercede so as to frustrate the criminal initiative of the rulers of Egypt and Syria. While there was still time, we brought to the attention of friendly political quarters the information in our possession with regard to the plans for the launching of the offensive. We called upon them to act for the prevention of the war. For all that, the offensive has been launched.

As I said, the IDF is all set to repel the enemy's attack. Early this morning, a partial call-up of reserves was approved and begun.

Having regard to the gravity of the news, I was obliged to convene a meeting of the Cabinet on Yom Kippur. The offensive started

Blackout in force

Civil defence measures were ordered into effect yesterday evening. Residents were told to:

- Observe a total blackout;
- Fill all available containers with water;
- Remove all flammable materials from homes and shelters;
- Tape windows;
- Prepare first-aid kits and fire-fighting equipment for immediate use;
- Store mirrors and non-essential glass items;
- Avoid using cars and phones unless necessary;
- Be familiar with air-raid sirens: a rising and falling tone orders residents to go to the shelters and remain there until the all-clear, a steady, continuous blast lasting at least one minute.

For several hours after the sirens began sounding yesterday, phone service was disrupted, due to an overloading of the lines as relatives and friends called each other to exchange information.

Schools will be closed today and will remain closed until further notice, the Education Ministry announced at 11 o'clock last night, following a decision by the Government. The decision applies to all educational institutions, from kindergarten and elementary schools to high schools, with the exception of boarding schools, where studies will continue.

Parents are asked to keep their children off the streets and to tell them to listen to instructions by *Haga* men. Principals are to go to their schools and act in accordance with standing instructions.

Arabs fail to convene special Assembly session

UNITED NATIONS. — The Arab states yesterday unsuccessfully sought to convene a special weekend session of the General Assembly on the Middle East fighting but apparently avoided a Security Council meeting because of fear of another U.S. veto.

U.N. men confirm crossing of lines

UNITED NATIONS. — U.N. military observers on the spot confirmed that Egyptian troops had crossed the Suez Canal at five points yesterday and that Syrian forces crossed the Golan Heights cease-fire line at two places, a U.N. spokesman said.

The observers said they had not seen any attempt by Israeli forces to cross the cease-fire lines during Friday night, as alleged by the Arabs.

He said that none of the parties had laid any complaint of a violation of the cease-fire before the U.N. truce supervision organization, which controls observers' operations

DAYAN: FINISH SYRIA SOON

Defence Minister Moshe Dayan last night predicted that the Syrian front would be "finished for all practical purposes" last night or during the night.

Mr. Dayan told a Shidurei Yisrael reporter: "I think the Syrians are practically broken. You can see their forces on this front withdrawing or running away. Those which remain have no military value on this front.

"We have to teach the Syrians a lesson — that the road fom Damascus to Eretz Yisrael, also leads from Eretz Yisrael to Damascus. Our forces are now moving on the road from Kuneitra to Damascus."

Israel drives 10 kms. towards Damascus

800 tanks destroyed, taken; Israeli planes blast targets

Battery of Isra[illegible]22mm. guns in action during the Golan Heights offensive.

THE JERUSALEM POST

SECOND EDITION

Price: IL1.50

FRIDAY, OCTOBER 12, 1973 • TISHRE 16, 5734 • RAMADHAN 16, 1393 • VOL. XLIII, No. 13915*

By RONNIE HOPE and ZE'EV SCHUL, Post Military Correspondents

TEL AVIV. — Israel armoured spearheads and infantry yesterday pierced through the Syrian defences beyond the Golan and by the evening had penetrated 10 kilometres inside enemy territory, advancing northeast along the Kuneitra-Damascus axis, the army spokesman announced here last night.

The two forces locked yesterday morning, following a 24-hour lull, in what was probably the largest single tank battle in this arena until now. The principal engagement, involving hundreds of tanks, focused on the northern sector of the front, around the Kuneitra-Damascus highway — where the Syrians lost 800 tanks destroyed or captured intact.

While capturing Damascus is one of the options open to the I.D.F., it is by no means certain that it will be taken up. Conquering the city and holding it would tie up large forces required elsewhere. It would also involve Israel in complex political problems.

Military circles said last night that Israel was close to reaching the turning point in the battle against Syria, in which Israel's aim is to break Syria's ability and will to fight. The importance of crushing Syrian resistance lies not only in that this will make it possible to put more pressure on Egypt, but also to deter Iraq and Jordan from active involvement in the war.

The air force, in addition to supporting the advance, devoted some efforts to bombing eight Syrian airfields, including Damascus International, which is now used only for military purposes. There was little interference. Altogether 11 enemy planes were shot down yesterday on both the Syrian and Egyptian fronts. The airfields bombed received "very basic and intensive treatment," a military source said. The aim was to prevent what is left of Syria's air force from interfering in the ground war.

The Israeli thrust was concentrated in the northern sector between Kuneitra and Mt. Hermon on a number of axes. Last night infantry units were clearing enemy pockets of resistance left behind by the rapidly advancing armour.

The break-through came after very heavy fighting. The Syrians had fallen back into their highly fortified line which they had build and held since the 1967 war. The ground offensive was preceded by heavy artillery and aerial softening up.

Well informed sources confirmed that the Rusians are flying arms into Syria, but said that this is of no great significance. The raids on airfields could disrupt this flow of supplies, it was pointed out.

Throughout the day, Syrian soldiers left behind by their retreating forces on the Israel side of the cease-fire line continued to surrender to IDF units. Roaming among the more than 800 destroyed and abandoned tanks left behind by the Syrian army, the Syrian infantry and tank men held out until noon Wednesday, in the hope that their units would be able to mount a counter-attack and reclaim some of the Heights they captured earlier in the week.

The Israeli spearheads, enjoying massive air support, were reported earlier in the day to be advancing on a wide front along the entire length of the Golan Heights.

Yesterday's counter-offensive was preceded by an intensive artillery barrage to soften the Syrian defences, during which Israeli gunners reportedly established new "records" in the swift pacing of their rounds. In addition to the artillery, the advancing columns also had a covering "airumbrella."

The continued pursuit of the Syrians across their home frontier arises from more than purely military considerations. The Chief of Staff's pledge on Sunday to pursue the Syrians whenever and wherever they could be found is now a reality. Politically, Israel will not be cowed into blind respect for the armistice lines.

Latest estimates of the Syrian line count a possible 2,000 tanks — five times the number they had in the Six Day War. Subtracting the estimated 800 tanks the Syrians lost this week, there is still a substantial number to account for. It may be assumed that a certain percentage consists of vintage armour and units that cannot be moved from where they are now stationed for internal-political reasons.

A Syrian T-62 tank captured intact in the Golan Heights, was shown yesterday to foreign correspondents in an Armoured Corps base. It is the first time that this tank, the most modern in the Soviet arsenal, has ever been seen outside the Soviet bloc and the Arab countries.

It is essentially similar to the T-54 and T-55 but carries a 115mm. instead of 105mm. gun and weighs 36.5 tons.

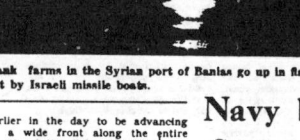

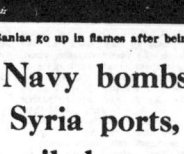

Tank farms in the Syrian port of Banias go up in flames after being hit by Israeli missile boats.

Attrition war in Sinai

Jerusalem Post Military Reporters

TEL AVIV. — Israeli forces continued their "war of attrition" against the massive Egyptian deployment along the Suez Canal during the past two days, keeping up a constant artillery bombardment, air force harassment and sniping at the enemy concentrations.

Informed sources said the steady pressure on the Egyptian concentrations at their Canal bridgeheads was beginning to show results. The Egyptians yesterday made no attempts to bring more reinforcements across the Canal, although some supplies may have been ferried across.

While the two main armies facing each other along the Canal front remained largely static, several minor engagements ended with Israeli victories on Tuesday and Wednesday.

Israeli commandos crossed the Canal and raided Egyptian supply lines and ordnance dumps on Wednesday night. The raid, in the southern sector, caused severe disruptions and heavy damage, informed sources said.

In another action, IDF forces on Wednesday broke through to an Israeli fortified position in the northern Canal sector on the Mediterranean coast. The men holding the position for five days had fought off Egyptian tank attacks under heavy artillery bombardment.

The relieving force pushed back an entrenched Egyptian force, armed with anti-tank missiles, which had blocked its advance.

The Egyptians left behind several of their dead on the battlefield. A later Egyptian attempt to capture the Israeli position was beaten off.

On Tuesday, an Egyptian drive towards Ras Sudar, south of the Canal, was blocked by Israeli infantry and armour. Then the Air Force was called in and the Egyptian force was wiped out. An Egyptian aircraft bombed Abu Rodeis, further south along the east coast of the Gulf of Suez on Tuesday night. There were some casualties and damage to buildings, but the oil installations were not hit.

Inside the Egyptian bridgeheads, the Egyptian units were reportedly still digging in, lining their approaches with anti-tank gun and missile emplacements.

Military correspondent Eli Landau, reporting from the southern sector on Wednesday, said the Egyptians were using infantry units armed with anti-tank missiles in their attempts to repel the Israeli armoured columns. He said the Egyptians were storming the tank formations in waves and were being literally mowed down. Their corpses were strewn over areas facing the Israeli lines for many kilometres.

U.S. resupply to Israel reported as Soviets send arms to Arabs

By News Agencies

WASHINGTON. — The U.S. appears to be laying the groundwork for a major resupply effort for Israel, But knowledgeable officials stress that no decision has been made. They say the U.S. is concentrating on a diplomatic drive to find a consensus with the Soviet Union and other powers for at least a cease-fire to end the fighting, and more preferably for a framework for a lasting negotiated settlement.

"We're in close and continuing contact with the Government of Israel," said Robert J. McCloskey, the State Department spokesman. At the same time, he said that a massive airlift of Soviet supplies to Egypt and Syria, reportedly under way, "would tend to put a new face on the situation" both for Israeli forces in the field and for the U.S.

But a highly placed Pentagon source said, "They've got scores of aircraft en route. It's not their normal shuttle to Cairo."

Witnesses reported, meanwhile, that a Boeing 707 transport plane bearing Israeli markings was loaded with Sparrow and Sidewinder air-to-air missiles at the Oceana Naval Air Station near Norfolk, Virginia. Officials described this as a resupply effort. Other observers said Israel undoubtedly already has asked Washington to speed up delivery of F-4 Phantom jets and other weapons promised in contracts for shipment this year and next.

McCloskey also pointed to a statement made on Monday by Secretary of State Henry Kissinger, that, "detente cannot survive irresponsibility in any area, including the Middle East." McCloskey said that "still stands."

A source at the Oceana Air Station told the Norfolk, Virginia, newspaper "Ledger-Star," another Boeing 707 with Israeli markings was loaded with arms last Saturday, the first day of the war.

The Pentagon's official spokesman declined to discuss anything to do with the resupply of Israel. But other officials said a moderate level of resupplies was continuing to flow.

The White House yesterday refused to respond to questions about whether the U.S. was resupplying Israel with arms. Presidential spokesman Gerald Warren also skirted a question on whether President Nixon had been in contact again with Soviet leader Leonid Brezhnev, saying instead that Dr. Kissinger "continues to be in direct contact" with major powers as well as the warring parties.

In Ramstein, West Germany, U.S. Air Force spokesmen yesterday, under orders to maintain silence, declined to comment on the report the Air Force was readying 48 F-4 Phantom jets in Germany to resupply the Israel Air Force. The spokesmen also declined to say whether

(Continued on Page 3, Col. 2)

Zayyat says 500 killed in Delta raids

UNITED NATIONS (Reuter). — Egyptian Foreign Minister Mohammed Hassan el-Zayyat told the General Assembly that he had word from Cairo yesterday that 500 people had been "murdered" in Israeli raids on the Nile Delta and the capital's suburbs. He spoke in the 135-nation body on the final day of its general policy debate.

"We still stand respectfully and bound by the charter, by U.N. resolutions and by its findings," he said. "We refuse, however, to be dictated to. We refuse, however, to be subjugated by long occupation and we simply refuse to stay occupied.

"We struggle, not because we guarantee success, but because we have no other option. It is our national duty. It is the only diktat we are obeying and are going to obey."

The Security Council, originally scheduled to meet on the war at 9.30 p.m. Israel time, postponed its session until 12.45 a.m. today. It was also supposed to hear a statement by Zayyat.

Earlier, Secretary-General Kurt Waldheim said in a written statement to the Council that the conflicting governments in the Middle East should "consider alternative courses before it is too late, so that fighting and bloodshed may cease."

Breaking the silence he had preserved since the war erupted last Saturday, he also urged the deadlocked Council members to make another effort to overcome "the obstacles to effective and peaceful action."

Lebanon: We downed an Israeli Phantom

Navy bombs Syria ports, oil depots

Jerusalem Post Military Correspondent

TEL AVIV. — The Israel Navy bombed the Syrian coast on Wednesday night, setting fire to fuel installations and tank farms at Latakia, Banias and Tartus.

The Navy also suceeeded in sinking two more Soviet-built missile boats. All told, five Syrian-Soviet missile boats have been sunk in the war.

A military correspondent on one of the Israeli vessels described "the rather uncanny feeling" he had in seeing the Syrian missiles repeatedly zeroing in on the Israeli task force. In most cases the Israeli Gabriel missiles hit the Syrian ships first, sending the manually-controlled Styx missiles careening off course. Other Styx missiles were brought down by anti-aircraft fire.

Reuter reported from Banias that Syria has issued no casualty figures, but townspeople said the Israeli bombardment caused deaths and injuries. All along the coast, the normally bustling little towns and villages were sombre. Most of the shops were shuttered and blue black-out paint was splashed on windows and car lamps.

Syrian refinery destroyed

By MALEK AL-HUSSEINI

HOMS. — Israeli aircraft destroyed a major power station and put a still-blazing oil refinery out of action for years to come during raids on this central Syrian town, officials said here yesterday.

I saw great pillars of black smoke and flames rising from the wrecked oil refinery more than 24 hours after the last Israeli bombing attack on Wednesday.

Experts said 80 per cent of the £20m. refinery was destroyed and it would not he in operation again for several years. Annual production at the refinery was estimated at one million tons.

The power station produced a fifth of Syria's electricity supplies. The director of the plant said at least 30 of his 450 workers were killed and about 100 injured.

Rescuers were unable to approach the inferno of flames and explosions that the oil refinery had become.

(Reuter)

AFTER MIDNIGHT

CAIRO (UPI). — U.S. Phantoms from an aircraft carrier in the Mediterranean have joined in Israeli raids on Egyptian positions, the Middle East News Agency said yesterday, quoting "Arab diplomatic sources."

The claim of direct U.S. involvement in the Arab-Israeli fighting was reminiscent of similar claims made by the late President Abdul Nasser during the Six Day War.

Agnew resigns as Vice-President

WASHINGTON. — Spiro T. Agnew resigned abruptly as U.S. Vice-President on Wednesday "in the best interest of the nation," and pleaded no contest to a charge of

as December, 1972, when he was Vice-President. He was the second Vice-President in U.S. history to resign.

Attorney-General Elliot Richard-

Agnew appeared yesterday morning at his office in the Executive Office Building adjacent to the White House to close out his affairs.

The White House said Nixon,

Israel task force crosses Canal

Knesset members stand in mourning for the fallen at the start of yesterday's special session. (Weiss)

THE JERUSALEM POST

SECOND EDITION

Price: 65 Ag.

EDNESDAY, OCTOBER 17, 1973 • TISHRE 21, 5734 • RAMADHAN 21, 1393 • VOL. XLIII, No. 13919*

SYRIA LOSES 105 TANKS, 10 PLANES

POST Military Correspondents

TEL AVIV. — Israeli forces on the Syrian front yesterday morning destroyed 105 tanks and downed 10 aircraft as they repulsed three counter-attacks by enemy armour and commandos.

The enemy attacking forces included a number of Iraqi tanks, the remnants of the Iraqi division which was virtually wiped out on Monday.

The enemy left behind 40 knocked out tanks on the battlefield near Beit Jann, at the northern corner of the Israel-held bulge in Syrian territory, and some 65 tanks in the central sector of the enclave, near Tel Shams.

The Syrians also attacked Israeli forces from the air, and 10 enemy planes were shot down, mostly by small arms fire from the Israeli ground units.

The Israeli Air Force provided close support for the ground forces and also bombed military and strategic targets deep inside Syria, including two bridges near Tartous, missile bases, and radar installations.

Israeli forces in Syria are now concentrating on consolidating their positions in the area they now hold, an area which has a topographic advantage, making it relatively easy to defend.

The airlift of Soviet arms and ammunition into Syria continues.

'Jordan in action on Syrian front'

AMMAN (Reuter). — Jordanian troops, sent to the Syrian front on Saturday, went into action there for the first time yesterday, the official Jordanian Radio said.

The reports said that the Jordanians repulsed Israeli forces at several places.

Anti-aircraft missile batteries destroyed

By ZE'EV SCHUL and RONNIE HOPE, Post Military Correspondents

TEL AVIV. — An Israeli task force crossed the Suez Canal in the central sector early yesterday to attack the Egyptians to the rear of their positions on the west bank of the Canal.

Its targets included surface-to-air missile sites, and artillery batteries.

Anti-aircraft missile batteries were reported to have been destroyed.

No details of the strength and further aims of the raiding force were available.

Ground operations in Sinai were limited yesterday to local artillery and tank duels.

The Air Force continued to give close support to the ground units. The Egyptians lost 12 planes in dogfights. With the Syrian loss of 10 yesterday, the total of enemy aircraft downed so far is 222.

Enemy interference with Air Force sorties is largely restricted to the missile systems. The Air Force is in turn concentrating on disrupting Egyptian and Syrian supply lines, the destruction of missile batteries and maintaining close ground support for the front line units.

Naval activity was limited to attempts by Egyptian missile boats to bombard Sharm e-Sheikh with a number of missile salvoes on Monday night. All missed their targets.

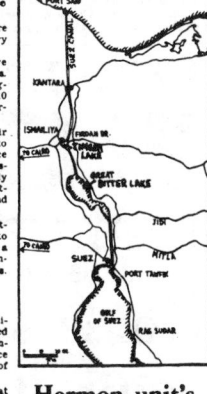

Cairo confirms

CAIRO (UPI). — The Egyptian military command yesterday confirmed Prime Minister Golda Meir's announcement that an Israeli force raided Egyptian positions west of the Suez Canal.

In a special communique issued at 9.50 p.m., it described this as "a desperate raid," which it said took place at 2.30 p.m.

It said Egyptian artillery destroyed three out of seven Israeli tanks which made a "desperate bid to raid some positions on the West Bank" of the Suez Canal.

Hermon unit's fate unknown

KIRYAT SHMONA. — Following the official announcement of the fall of an IDF outpost on Mount Hermon in the first day of the war, the fate of the defenders is still unknown.

The men are still listed as missing because the Syrian authorities refuse to give details on the prisoners of war they have taken.

An Itim reporter who spoke with area Druse yesterday heard from them that three Syrian helicopters appeared there on Yom Kippur and circled above the outpost. After a while, one of the helicopters went up in flames.

It has also been learned that a Syrian helicopter pilot who fell into Zahal's hands told interrogators that a commando force had been flown in to take the outpost. He said the Israeli soldiers in the outpost fortified themselves as best they could.

But, the Itim reporter adds, there are doubts about the veracity of this account, and meanwhile the fate of the outpost's defenders remains unknown. (Itim)

No U.S. troops but 'firm support' of Israel's arms needs

WASHINGTON. — The U.S. does not intend to send American military forces into the Middle East but will firmly support Israel's weapons needs, U.S. officials said yesterday. The statement followed a reported comment by Secretary of State Henry Kissinger at a White House dinner that if the Soviets introduced troops, the U.S. would follow suit.

Similarly, Melvin Laird, Domestic Adviser to President Nixon, was reported to have told a group of newsmen at a breakfast that the situation is becoming one of confrontation with the USSR.

U.S. Air Force C5A Galaxies, the world's largest military transports, landed one after the other at an Israeli air base yesterday, carrying U.S. military supplies.

The Lockheed C5A Galaxy, according to "Jane's World's Aircraft," is 75.5 m. long and 19.85 m. high, with an 11-ton payload. A typical load includes two M60 tanks or 16 three-quarter ton trucks or one M60 tank and two Bell Iroquois helicopters, five M113 personnel carriers, one M59 two-and-one-half ton trucks and 4 M151 quarter-ton truck.

At mid-afternoon, U.S. Ambassador Kenneth Keating drove onto the airfield.

"I'm just out here to take a look around," he told a reporter.

Washington officials yesterday said about 30 U.S. Air Force flights resupplied Israel with about 500 tons of war material during the first two days of the U.S. arms airlift.

They said the shipments amounted to about 3,000 tons of the supplies the U.S.S.R. has flown to Egypt and Syria in the last six days.

The officials, who asked not to be identified, said the U.S. tonnages did not include aircraft the U.S. also is sending to Israel.

The U.S. resupply effort was launched on Sunday, the officials said, to keep the U.S.S.R. from upsetting the power balance in the Middle East.

In Norfolk, Virginia, the Israeli cargo ship Aben Dat prepared to sail yesterday to the Middle East with a load of U.S. bombs, jet fighters, and perhaps tanks, rushed aboard on Monday at the naval base here.

Witnesses reported seeing four holds of the ship packed with 250 and 500 pound bombs and three U.S. A4 Skyhawk jet fighters lashed to the ship's deck. All markings on the planes were obliterated.

Other sources said U.S. Air Force C5 and C141 jet transports are flying tanks and ammunition to Tel Aviv. In addition, they said F4 Phantom fighter bombers, withdrawn from U.S. units, also are being sold to Israel and delivered here.

U.S. air chief: 'We won't match Soviet airlift'

WASHINGTON (UPI). — U.S. Air Force Chief of Staff George S. Brown told a news conference the U.S. did not plan to match the Soviet airlift "ton for ton."

He estimated Israel was losing one plane for every two Arab fighters.

"The point is, Israel will run out of airplanes before the Arabs will," Brown said.

He said the U.S.S.R. has deployed its strongest-ever force in the Mediterranean — 60 combat ships.

Nixon meets four Arab foreign ministers today

WASHINGTON. — President Nixon will meet four Arab Foreign Ministers today to discuss the Middle East war, the White House announced yesterday.

Presidential spokesman Gerald Warren said the ministers — Abdelaziz Bouteflika of Algeria, Sheikh Sabah al-Ahmad al-Jaber al-Sabah of Kuwait, Ahmed Benhima of Morocco and Omar Sakkaf of Saudi Arabia — had requested the meeting.

Mr. Warren said that Dr. Kissinger, who discussed the Middle East crisis at an hour-long conference with President Nixon yesterday, would attend the meeting with the four Foreign Ministers.

Diplomatic sources said the Arab ministers intended to express their concern over the U.S. decision to send arms to Israel.

The announcement came amid reports that the envoys were carrying a message from King Feisal of Saudi Arabia, who has been under intense pressure from other Arab leaders to deny oil to the U.S.

It is understood that Nixon and Feisal have exchanged messages since the outbreak of the war.

(Reuter, AP)

Belgian solidarity

BRUSSELS (INA). — A Belgian "Committee of solidarity with Israel" has been set up here under the presidency of former premier Gaston Eyskens. Several former ministers are among the many political figures who have joined the group.

AFTER MIDNIGHT

One person was slightly hurt and two houses and six cars were damaged as Katyusha rockets fired from Lebanese territory hit Kiryat Shmona at 11 o'clock last night. The occupants of the houses were in their shelters and none of them was hurt.

THE JERUSALEM POST will not appear tomorrow Simhat Tora. The next issue, on Friday, will contain a 16-page magazine including Lea Ben Dor's analysis — Why We Didn't Know, Philip Gillon on Tending the Wounded, Helga Dudman on the Home Front, Abraham Rabinovich Following the Golan war trail, Hadassah Bat Haim's Thoughts in the Queue, reviews of books about the Dreyfus Case, Ellis Island, and others, art and theatre notes and broadcasting reviews.

'All the aid needed to repel our attackers'

MEIR THANKS THE U.S.

By ASHER WALLFISH
Jerusalem Post Knesset Reporter

Premier Golda Meir said yesterday that in the name of the Israeli nation she wished to thank the President and the people of the United States for acting in the American tradition of helping a State which was struggling to withstand aggression.

In a 60-minute statement on the conduct of the war delivered at a special session convened during the recess — Premier Meir said she was convinced that the U.S. would do all that was necessary to deter dangerous trends in the policies and the actions of the Soviet Union and give Israel all the aid required to defend its existence and repel its attackers.

The U.S. was continuing to reply to Israel's requests for weapons and equipment in the quantities, categories and tempo dictated by the situation, she said. (Excerpts from Mrs. Meir's speech on page 2.)

She made these points:

• Israel does not want anybody else to fight in its place.

• The British and French arms embargo constitute cynical and immoral bias by enlightened states or selfish ends.

• She assumed that Soviet advisers and experts are arriving in Syria and Egypt with the airlift of weapons.

• Discussion of a cease-fire is pointless as the Arabs have made no proposals. They will be ready for a cease-fire only after they have been hit harder, it seems, and then they will have many fiends to propose a truce.

• Any truce must include a full prisoner-of-war exchange.

• Israel's well-wishers must be made to realise that the Arab aim is to destroy the State of Israel. Israeli Arabs have offered aid for the war effort in many ways — which augurs well for the future.

• Israel does not want to fight the Kingdom of Jordan.

Knesset Speaker Yisrael Yeshayahu opened the session, in the presence of President Ephraim Katzir, with a minute's silence for the nation's fallen, and expressed profound condolences to the next-of-kin and hopes for the speedy recovery of the wounded.

When the packed Chamber was seated once more, the Speaker appealed once more, the Speaker appealed this with that the prisoners-of-war return home soon.

Opposite the Speaker's dais, prominent in the Diplomats' Gallery, were the ambassadors of Britain, Finland, Denmark, Norway and Sweden.

Premier Meir spoke at first in a low and sombre tone and with firmness and confidence throughout.

Defence Minister Moshe Dayan was conspicuous by his absence — down in Sinai. Three or four M.K.s came in army uniform. From outside the Knesset building was blacked out.

Before the session ended Speaker Yeshayahu announced that the Knesset would convene again next week, in special session, for legislation to deal with the postponement of the elections (which were due to be held on October 30).

Gahal leader Menahem Begin, who opened the three-hour debate on the Prime Minister's statement, matched a bitter attack on Britain and France with warm praise for the U.S. and touched briefly on some of the lessons to be learned from the present war.

Gahal was firmly resolved to keep its questions about the events leading up to the war till after victory — "and there are questions," Mr. Begin said. All the Opposition, as well as the Alignment's two Coalition allies — the National Religious Party and the Independent Liberals — said that queries were inevitable but that now was not the time.

Mr. Begin said that Britain's violation of formal contracts in its refusal to send vital equipment to Israel threw a strange light on British Prime Minister Edward Heath's statement after his visit to Israel three years ago, that "now he understood Israel's security needs better." The Jewish People had paid with six million lives because Britain disavowed the Balfour Declaration, and now the latter was denying vital equipment to a country facing an aggression supported by the Communist Empire.

Turning to France, Mr. Begin said that while it was sending weapons to Israel's enemies till the present day, it was denying this fact in a way that heaped obloquy upon itself.

Both Britain and France, he said, were trading their own destinies for immediate advantage and for a barrel of oil, for they were facilitating the Soviet Union's aims of breaking through the Suez Canal to link up its Mediterranean and Indian Ocean fleets, to dominate Aden and Somalia and to spread over the Persian Gulf.

The U.S., on the other hand, merited all possible gratitude for standing behind Israel.

Mr. Haim Zadok (Labour Alignment) said the Soviet Union had not committed such a massive act of deception since the Cuba missile affair in 1962. Today, when detente prevailed — and not the cold war of those days — the deception was all the graver.

Mr. Zadok said the solid support which Israel was receiving from the U.S. stemmed not only from friendship between the two peoples, but also from the profound awareness

(Continued on page 2, col. 2)

Sadat: Cease-fire after Israel withdraws

Jerusalem Post Arab Affairs Reporter

Egyptian President Anwar Sadat yesterday said he would accept a cease-fire and subsequent peace only after Israel withdrew from all territories it captured in the 1967 war. Otherwise, Sadat said, he would go on fighting. Warning Israel against bombarding deep inside Egypt, he announced that Egyptian long-range ground-to-ground missiles were "ready to strike the very depths of Israel at any moment."

Sadat identified the ground-to-ground missile as the Zafer, the smallest of three Egyptian-made rockets which is said to have a range of 500 kilometres and be capable of carrying a 500-kilogram warhead. (Full story on page 2.)

"Our Egyptian Arab missiles are of the Zafer type, which can cross Sinai, are now on their pads ready to be launched by a single order into the farthest depths of Israel," Sadat said. He warned Israel to remember what I have cautioned against in the past: an eye for an eye, a tooth for a tooth and a depth for a depth."

Sadat said that Egypt could have used these missiles "the very first minute" of the war, but "we are not advocates of extermination as the Israelis claim."

The Egyptian President said he began the war "for the sake of peace that is based on justice." He said Egypt had two aims: Israel's withdrawal from the occupied territories and the restoration of the Palestinian people's "legitimate rights."

Sadat said that once these two ends are guaranteed he would agree to a cease-fire and subsequent peace talks at "an international conference" where he would try to persuade other Arab leaders and Palestinian representatives to join him.

He made his "peace proposals" in the form of "an open letter" to U.S. President Richard Nixon. The letter contained five points expressing Egypt's position, the last of which stated Cairo's preparedness to reopen the Suez Canal. Sadat said he has already ordered the chairman of the Canal authority to make initial preparations in this direction.

Sadat offered nothing to indicate a change in his basic demands. What was new was that he appeared to feel that this time he was speaking from a position of strength.

The Egyptian President spoke at an extraordinary session of the National Assembly (parliament). His ceremonial address was broadcast over all Egyptian radio networks. Wearing a field marshal's uniform as supreme commander of the Egyptian armed forces, Sadat was received with wild applause. So was his

(Continued on page 2, col. 1)

ISRAEL OBSERVERS:

Sadat's aim: dismemberment of Israel

Jerusalem Post Diplomatic Correspondent

President Sadat's speech of yesterday was seen in Jerusalem as clearly revealing his ultimate aim: the dismemberment of the Jewish State. He spoke of two stages in Egyptian policy. First, to force a cease-fire with Israel undertaking to withdraw to the pre-'67 lines; and then to summon an international peace conference to discuss "restoring" the rights of the Palestinians" — which is a euphemism for taking apart the State of Israel.

If the peace conference failed to materialize, observers in Jerusalem pointed out, Egypt could then launch an attack similar to the Yom Kippur attack — but this time from the pre-'67 lines — with imaginable results.

A top Israeli diplomat currently in New York referred to the Sadat speech as "the speech of a man who wants neither ceasefire nor peace."

Strengthening this assessment was the tone of the Egyptian leader's address. He simply did not re...

Kissinger, Tho win Nobel Prize for arranging Vietnam cease-fire

OSLO (UPI). — Henry Kissinger and North Vietnamese chief negotiator Le Duc Tho yesterday won the 1973 Nobel Peace Prize, the Norwegian Nobel Committee announced.

Kissinger, the new U.S. Secretary of State, and Le Duc Tho negotiated the Vietnam cease-fire during a series of secret meetings in Paris which stretched over several years. The agreement was finally signed in January of this year.

The decision came as a complete surprise here, since the two men had never been mentioned as possible candidates.

The committee said, "For more than three years they have used all their strength and good will to achieve a negotiated solution, a peaceful solution of the Vietnam war.

"Thereby, they have performed a feat which is in the best accordance with Alfred Nobel's thoughts, that conflicts should be solved through negotiations and not through war."

The Vietnam war was described as "the most gruesome and long conflict the world has experienced after the Second World War. It was a gruesome war that not only forced upon the Vietnam civilian population enormous sufferings but that also poisoned the atmosphere in and between other countries in the whole world.

"It is our hope that all parties in this conflict will feel the moral responsibility that the treaty on a...

Le Duc Tho and Henry Kissinger after their final talks in Paris in January. (AP)

accused each other of continuing me in public life has moved me

---

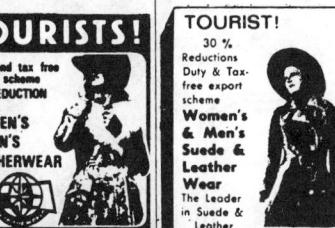

View from the room in the Kiryat Shmona building in which the three Arab terrorists were blown up yesterday. In background is school. On left, is the hill from which the murderers came. (AP)

Eighteen murdered in Kiryat Shmona terror

Three Arabs butcher women and children, then die in blast

By HIRSH GOODMAN, Jerusalem Post Military Correspondent

Eighteen persons — mainly women and children — were massacred by terrorists in the northern Galilee town of Kiryat Shmona by three terrorists who crossed the border into Israel from Lebanon on Wednesday night. The three men infiltrated at a point between Metula and Misgav Am, and it is believed that they reached the outskirts of Kiryat Shmona under cover of darkness, waiting until the morning before "attacking" an apartment block on the perimeter of the town with the objective of killing any man, woman or child whom they found there. The three died in an explosion as troops stormed the building.

Ahmed Jibril's Popular Front for the Liberation of Palestine: General command claimed credit for the attack yesterday in an announcement from Damascus. Israeli army trackers on a routine patrol along the northern frontier noticed the infiltrators' tracks at 6.40 yesterday morning. It was quickly established that the three-man terrorist group had followed a rocky ridge running from the border near the vicinity of Misgav Am to a school on the outskirts of the town. According to the Acting Chief of Staff, Aluf Yitzhak Hofi, the army immediately notified regional defence authorities — including the Kiryat Shmona police — that terrorists had crossed the border, and that regional forces should be placed on maximum alert. The army also dispatched two limited units to the town to help the 20-man police force try and track down the terrorists.

Shortly before 8 a.m. the first evidence was uncovered that the terrorists had entered the town. A two-man police patrol was fired on from the entrance to a block of apartments about 200 metres from the school which, as far as can be ascertained, the terrorists never entered. The encounter with the police seems to have sparked off a massacre the proportions of which only became apparent later in the morning.

As soon as they left their night hiding places early in the morning, the terrorists entered two ground level flats and cold-bloodedly murdered five persons there. They then ran to the next building where they systematically entered each flat, killing almost every living soul in the four-storey building before coming to an empty apartment on the fourth floor. From there they began sniping at passers-by in the street below. By the time they had reached the apartment at approximately 8 a.m. the terrorists had killed 16 persons — including eight children, and wounded more than a dozen others. Two Israeli soldiers were killed later in the morning while trying to flush the terrorists out of the flat.

According to Aluf Hofi, Israel had no prior intelligence that the terrorists were planning any specific acts against Israeli population centres "or anything of that sort." He further told military correspondents that no unusual terrorist activity had been noticed on the Lebanese side of the border over the past few weeks.

The Acting Chief of Staff said that it was very difficult to prevent terrorist infiltration into Israel from Lebanon in that particular area because of the harsh topographical conditions and rocky terrain. He added that the short distance from the border to towns and villages in the area made track-

(Continued on page 2, Col. 1)

Names of the victims

Shimon Biton, 30, his son Avi, five, and his two-and-a-half-year-old daughter; Ya'acov and Miriam Gueta, both 30; Esther Cohen, 40, her son David, 17, and her daughter Shula, 14; Fannie Shitrit, 30, and her children Yocheved, 11, Aharon, 8, and Motti, four; Hansa Stern, 47, and her daughter Rachel, eight; Shaul Ben-Eliahu, 30; Esther Wozana, 60; Acting Officer Mordechai Grady, 20, of Ramat Hasharon; Rav-Turai Suahil Abdak, 20 of Tarshiha.

Another 16 wounded were brought to Government Hospital in Safad, including one who was seriously wounded, Kamal Haboushi, 21, a Druse soldier from Julis.

Four had medium injuries. Mrs. Shoshana Biton, 27, fell off the balcony when she was shot at close range as she tried to get her three children out of their fourth floor flat. The others are Na'if Ma'arouf, 27, a Druse border policeman from Hurfeish; David Cohen, 29, a soldier, and Yosef Ben-Dror, 29, a border policeman, from Haifa.

Of the slightly injured, Albert Mishali, 19, a border policeman from Kiryat Tivon, was discharged. Those kept for treatment are Rani Moses, a five-year-boy from Tirat Carmel who was visiting relatives; Yoel Noel, 19, and Binyamin Sulimani, 22, both border policemen from Kiryat Shmona; Shlomo Rouif, 24, deputy commander of the Kiryat Shmona police; Eliyahu Ayesh, 43, of Kiryat Shmona; Yitzhak Hanukah, 27, of Kiryat Shmona; Hajaj Sinai, 41, of Kiryat Shmona; David Aboutbul, 24, a Kiryat Shmona soldier; Michael Meirowitz, 25, of Kiryat Bialik and David Zaguri, 26, of Kiryat Shmona.

THE JERUSALEM POST

40 PAGES including 28-Page MAGAZINE

OCTOBER ELECTION SEEN Page 2

Price: IL1.75

FRIDAY, APRIL 12, 1974 • NISAN 20, 5734 • RABI AWWAL 21, 1394 • VOL. XLIV, No. 14069*

'THERE IS MINISTERIAL RESPONSIBILITY'

Golda says she had to quit after public ire

Jerusalem Post Staff

Prime Minister Golda Meir briskly followed up her resignation announcement to the Knesset yesterday by noting that Israel has a fully functioning government pending formation of a new one and that the Cabinet would continue in its efforts to achieve peace.

On the internal political front, she noted that the Cabinet was dealing with the question of individual Ministerial responsibility in the wake of the interim Agranat report. She said that in resigning she could not ignore the public ferment.

As to the Agranat report, Mrs. Meir said that in her view there was no doubt that a Minister was responsible for the activities of his Ministry. "This principle is part of our constitutional concept of the reciprocal relations between the executive and the legislature. The matter is thus on the agenda of the Cabinet."

The Cabinet, she said, had also determined procedures for considering and acting upon the recommendations of the Agranat Committee in connection with arriving at a clear definition of authority in defence matters, setting up a Cabinet security committee, ensuring secrecy of Cabinet security discussions and ensuring effective operation of the intelligence community.

Mrs. Meir, wearing a blue suit and looking fit and well, read out her statement in a composed voice. The chamber was packed and in the VIP section sat the families of many Members, including the Prime Minister's son.

The six-hour debate that followed her statement was milder than had originally been expected when the special session was called during the Passover recess — at the request of both the Government and Likud — in connection with the Agranat report.

Explaining her resignation, Mrs. Meir said the public ferment could not be ignored: after much thought she had come to the conclusion that the public and its representatives should be given another chance to choose a new government.

But she added that the present Cabinet was vested with full authority until a new Government was chosen either by this Knesset or the next. "Our envoys abroad have been authorized to explain this. She added: "The Government will continue in political efforts to bring about peace between Israel and the Arabs."

(Statement text — page 12; Debate — page 2)

Yesterday morning, Mrs. Meir informed the Cabinet officially of her decision to resign. At noon she called on President Katzir to hand in her formal letter of resignation which said:

"In accordance with the provisions of section 23 of the Basic Law: The Government, and having informed the Cabinet of my intention, I herewith tender my resignation from the post of Prime Minister."

Mrs. Meir handed her resignation to the President exactly one month after she had presented to him her new Government on March 10. The forming of the short-lived Government was preceded by protracted coalition negotiations with the National Religious Party, which got bogged down several times over the question of "Who is a Jew."

The difficulties in the coalition talks were compounded by an earlier decision of Rafi leaders Moshe Dayan and Shimon Peres not to join the new Cabinet, in the wake of which Mrs. Meir had decided to return her mandate to the President, relenting afterwards to party pressure.

Following his half-hour-long talk with Mrs. Meir, the President made a public statement, formally announcing the Prime Minister's resig-

(Continued on page 2, Col. 1)

U.S. blasts massacre

WASHINGTON. — The State Department yesterday condemned the "brutal and senseless slaughter" in Kiryat Shmona, "particularly the murder of women and children, as we deplore all terrorist activity."

Spokesman George Vest added that "in this instance it is particularly regrettable" because the murders came "when the process of peace is already in motion. This attack underlines even more the urgent need for U.S. Secretary of State Henry Kissinger's continued efforts to bring peace to this region."

Vest said it is too early to say that the raid plus the political disruptions in Israel will delay Kissinger's planned trip to the Middle East later this month.

However, he said, "the events in the area are not slowing down his sense of urgency or efforts" to arrange a military disengagement between the Syrians and Israelis.

In that connection, Vest said a time has not yet been fixed for a meeting between Kissinger and the Syrian delegation to discuss disengagement.

(AP, JTA)

Two hurt in North

Two Israeli soldiers were wounded by Syrian artillery fire yesterday.

The Syrians opened fire — for the 31st consecutive day — at 9 a.m. on Israeli positions in the southern sector of the bulge and on positions west of the pre-October cease-fire line. Positions in the area were shelled intermittently throughout the day, and by 8 last night, after several shells had fallen on the Israeli Hermon, quiet returned to the area.

Photo distributed by the PFLP: General Command in Beirut yesterday showing the three terrorists who attacked Kiryat Shmona. Left to right, Monir Moghrabi, Ahmed e-Sheikh Mahmoud and Yassin Mousa el-Mouzani. (AP radiophoto)

MEIR PUTS BLAME ON LEBANON

By MALKA RABINOWITZ
Jerusalem Post Reporter

Prime Minister Golda Meir said yesterday Israel placed responsibility for yesterday's slaughter in Kiryat Shmona on the Lebanese Government and on inhabitants of that country who aided the terrorists.

Addressing a packed Knesset chamber after presiding over an extraordinary session of the Cabinet, Mrs. Meir said it was the nation's duty to defend and help the residents of that northern border town.

The 18 dead, she said, included eight children, five women, two soldiers and three male civilians.

It was not a movement of liberation that had perpetrated the attack but a movement of murder for the sake of murder. "This nation has suffered much through the generations," said Mrs. Meir. "And we are in an independent Jewish state capable of defending itself and its citizens."

A circular left behind by the terrorists in Kiryat Shmona was signed by the "Popular Front: General Command" and declared that the armed struggle would continue until Israel was destroyed and replaced by a "democratic Palestinian state of Jews and Arabs." To the surprise of the House, Mrs. Meir read out in full the text of the fairly lengthy terrorist outpouring, explaining — after Geula Cohen (Likud) called out, "Why are you reading that out?" — that it was to demonstrate the true nature of the terrorist movement.

The session opened with the House rising in tribute to the victims of the attack in Kiryat Shmona after Speaker Yisrael Yeshayahu condemned the "animal cruelty" of the murderers.

Mrs. Meir extended the condolences of the Government and the Knesset to the bereaved families.

Earlier, Foreign Minister Abba Eban issued the following statement:

"The full scope of the atrocity committed by Arab terrorists against men, women and children at Kiryat Shmona is still not fully clear, but it is already plain that an immense brutality has been perpetrated in violation of every law of civilization and humanity. Every civilized man and woman in the world must be asking to what lengths this peril will go.

"The lesson must be: implacable resistance to the terrorists and an end to the deplorable indulgence with which these organizations have been surrounded in many places."

EXTREME JIBRIL GROUP CULPRIT

By ANAN SAFADI
Jerusalem Post Arab Affairs Reporter

Responsibility for the Kiryat Shmona terrorist operation was claimed yesterday by Ahmed Jibril's Popular Front for the Liberation of Palestine-General Command which is a splinter group of George Habash's PFLP.

As three terrorists took over the building in Kiryat Shmona, the PFLP-General Command issued statements in Damascus and Beirut claiming that the operation was carried out by one of its "suicide squads." It said that the three men were holding hostages and that they were demanding the release of 100 terrorist prisoners within six hours, with 2 p.m. as the deadline.

The PFLP-General Command gave the following identifications and details on the three sabotuers:

Monir Moghrabi, 20, code-named Abu Khaled, a Palestinian born in Damascus. He joined the front shortly after graduating from a Syrian secondary school in 1971; Ahmed e-Sheikh Mahmoud, 20, code-named Abu Shaker, a Syrian who joined the front in 1972; Yassin Mousa el-Mouzani, 27, code-named Abu-Hadi, an Iraqi construction worker who served in the Iraqi army before joining the front in 1972.

The movement emphasized that they wanted Japanese terrorist Kozo Okamoto released among the 100 terrorists. Okamoto is serving a life sentence for his role in the May 1972 Lod airport massacre. The PFLP-General Command further demanded the release of all female terrorist prisoners.

The statement issued by it showed that the three saboteurs were instructed to take over a nearby school building which, however, was closed for the Pessah holiday.

But as the terrorist operation came to an end, it issued a communiquqe saying that its three men had set off explosive belts killing them with their hostages. The movement blamed the Israel authorities for "failing to heed warnings" against assaulting the building.

The PFLP-General Command claimed that the three belonged to a unit operating "inside the occupied territory." It denied that they had set out from Lebanon.

The terrorist attack came a few days after Fatah chief Yasser Arafat claimed to have instructed all terrorist members grouped in the Palestine Liberation Organization to avoid launching operations from Lebanese territory to prevent retaliation by Israel against Lebanon.

The Kiryat Shmona attack was viewed as part of operations planned by a number of terrorist groups

(Continued on Page 3, Col. 3)

AFTER MIDNIGHT

A car with Gaza licence plates blew up in Rishon Lezion at 11.30 last night. Two Arabs inside were seriously injured and were taken to Assaf Harofe Hospital. Police are investigating.

Likud leader Menahem Begin last night said his party has asked for a special Knesset session next week to debate the security arrangements in Kiryat Shmona.

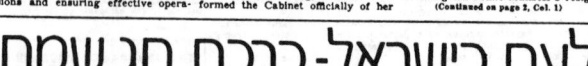

THE JERUSALEM POST

LATE EDITION 2.30 A.M.

IL7.00 (inc. Vat)

TUESDAY, MARCH 27, 1979 • ADAR 28, 5739 • RABI THANI 27, 1399 • VOL. XLIX, No. 14581

Israel and Egypt sign peace treaty declaring end to 30-year state of war

Prime Minister Begin and Egyptian President Sadat put their signatures to the Israel-Egyptian peace treaty in Washington yesterday. (UPI telephoto)

A triple clasp for peace unites an elated President Jimmy Carter, Prime Minister Menahem Begin and President Anwar Sadat following the signing of yesterday's treaty. (UPI telephoto)

Begin, Sadat and Carter pledge shalom, salaam at White House ceremony

By ARI RATH, WOLF BLITZER, DAVID LANDAU and MALKA RABINOWITZ

WASHINGTON. — President Anwar Sadat and Prime Minister Menahem Begin yesterday signed the Israeli-Egyptian peace treaty at a formal White House ceremony on the North Lawn. President Jimmy Carter, whose mediating was instrumental in achieving the agreement, signed as a witness.

It was Israel's first-ever peace treaty with a neighbouring Arab state.

The signing represented the dramatic culmination of 16 months of arduous negotiations beginning with Sadat's visit to Jerusalem in November 1977. All three men, during their remarks delivered at the simple but moving one-hour ceremony, stressed the significance of the occasion, but they also acknowledged the pitfalls on the road ahead.

"Today we celebrate a victory," president Carter declared, "not of a bloody military campaign, but of an inspiring peace campaign."

Only the night before, Carter had predicted that the signing of the treaty would eventually represent the most important achievement of his term in office.

Prime Minister Begin said it was the third "greatest day in my life," explaining that the establishment of the State of Israel on May 14, 1948, and the unification of Jerusalem during the 1967 Six Day War were the first and second greatest days of his life.

Sadat omitted at the last minute a powerful call for Palestinian rights from the text of his address at the White House ceremony. His speech as delivered made no specific reference to the Palestinians, although the prepared text distributed to newsmen earlier had contained a strong appeal to President Carter and the U.S. to support the Palestinians' aspirations for "self-determination and statehood" and to ensure the full implementation of the autonomy plan.

Two hours later the president's spokesman, Saad Zaghloul Nassar, said Sadat's omission had been inadvertent. He said two pages of the speech had been stuck together and the president had turned them both at once.

But some observers wondered whether Sadat's omission of the passage had nevertheless been a deliberate reaction to a noisy demonstration by Palestinian students and supporters, whose chorused slogans could be clearly heard during the ceremony. The demonstrators were kept by police about 300 metres away from the White House grounds.

While Sadat made no reference to Begin, but dwelt on President Carter's role in "performing the miracle," the Israeli leader paid generous tribute to Sadat as a man of "great civil courage" and referred to him as "our friend."

But Sadat did have praise for "the hundreds of thousands of Israelis who remained unwavering in their commitment to peace" — a clear reference to the "Peace Now" movement which, Sadat believes, had a major impact on Israeli policymaking.

President Carter's remarks were carefully uncontroversial. But he underscored "the obstacles that lie ahead" and added: "We must rededicate ourselves to the goal of a broader peace with justice for all who have lived in a state of conflict in the Middle East."

Carter called on other Arab states to join the peace process. "I am convinced," he said, "that other Arab people need and want peace; but some of their leaders are not yet willing to honour these needs and desires."

The omitted passage from Sadat's address asserted that "no one is more entitled to your support and backing than the Palestinian people. A grave injustice was inflicted upon them in the past. They need a reassurance that they will be able to take the first step on the road to self-determination and statehood. A dialogue between the U.S. and the representatives of the Palestinian people will be a very helpful development... We must be certain that the provisions of the Camp David framework... are carried out. There must be a genuine transfer of authority to the Palestinians in their land. Without that the problem will remain unsolved."

But Sadat did remind President Carter of his pledge that "the U.S. is committed without reservation to seeing the peace process through, until all parties to the Arab-Israeli conflict are at peace."

Begin's speech was in many ways the most moving — certainly the most personalized — of the three. He recalled his parents who had perished in the Holocaust, and his voice almost cracked as he declaimed in sonorous tones the words (in Hebrew) of Psalm 126.

Begin spoke of the peace treaty as "the cornerstone of cooperation and friendship" between Israel and Egypt. He, alone among the three leaders, did not dwell on the challenges and difficulties that still lie ahead, nor refer to their common pledge to reach a comprehensive settlement that would embrace Israel's other fronts.

There was, however, one common reference in all three addresses: Isaiah's immortal swords-into-ploughshares prophesy.

Begin raised the only laugh during the hour-long ceremony when he said he agreed with Sadat's praise of Carter as the "unknown soldier" — "but, as usual, with an amendment." Carter's efforts for the peace would be "remembered and recorded for generations to come," he said.

When the prime minister spoke of the day Israel took the Old City as the "second greatest day" of his life, there was applause only from a group of American Jewish leaders sitting together to the left of the signing dais. Most of the audience reacted in stolid silence. They seemed to feel that in making this remark Begin was uttering a pledge, on this most solemn occasion, that Jerusalem would remain reunited under Israel's rule at any cost.

The ceremony started exactly on schedule. Between 1,200 and 1,500 people gathered on the front lawn of the White House and heard the three leaders — "the president of the United States of America, the president of the Arab Republic of Egypt, and the prime minister of Israel" — introduced. There was steady applause as the three men walked together, Carter in the middle, to the heavy table and sat down behind three microphones. All three were smiling.

As a U.S. military band began to play the Egyptian national anthem, the three men, and later the rest of the assembled guests, stood at attention. Carter placed his hand across his heart. Afterwards the Israeli and U.S. anthems were played. Begin was seen singing along in Hebrew and later Carter in English. Sadat's lips did not move during the Egyptian anthem.

It was probably the last major occasion for the Egyptian anthem, since a new one has been commissioned by Sadat and is expected to be released shortly.

The U.S., Israeli and Egyptian flags flapped in the steady breese behind the three men under partly sunny skies. It was chilly outside with temperatures hovering in the mid-50s (about 13 centigrade).

Throughout the ceremony the constant chanting of protestors, who had assembled across Pennsylvania Avenue, could be heard. They had interspersed themselves among the

(Continued on page 2, col. 5)

BEGIN, SADAT, CARTER SPEECHES ON BACK PAGE

Begin: Open border with Egypt in two months

Jerusalem Post Staff

Free border crossings between Israel and Egypt will start two months after the peace treaty is ratified and El-Arish is handed over to Egypt, Prime Minister Menahem Begin said yesterday. He was briefing the Israeli press in Washington four hours after signing the peace treaty.

Begin said it could take up to three weeks for the Egyptian Peoples Assembly (parliament) to ratify the treaty because of precedural complications. Israel, Begin said, could ratify the treaty within a day.

Begin said that in the last two days of talks wiith President Jimmy Carter and administration officials the U.S. had given Israel a firm commitment that it "won't tolerate violations of the treaty...It is clear that the reference was not to Israel but to other bodies."

Begin said the U.S. commitments included a promise to ensure arms supplies to Israel in the event of war, an assurance that the U.S. would "step up its presence, in the area" and take action to lift naval blockades, and that the U.S. would block attempts to subvert the treaty in the UN Security Council.

Negotiations with Egypt over the form of the autonomy to be granted to the West Bank and Gaza Strip will start within seven to eight weeks, Begin said. The talks will start after instruments of ratification are exchanged and after Israel's ministerial "committee of 11" prepares detailed proposals for autonomy as Israel envisages it.

Negotiations over West Bank and Gaza Strip autonomy will take place in El-Arish, Begin said.

Begin confirmed that he will fly to Cairo next Mondat for what he said would probably be a one-day visit. He said he had raised the proposal to Sadat in his meeting with him yesterday and Sadat had said "for sure" to his idea.

Begin referred to a "gesture" by Israel following the signing, but said he preferred not to make this public now. It would not harm Israel's security one iota, he added.

Agreement was also reached on the supply of oil from wells off the Sinai shore which Israel is due to evacuate. Israel will withdraw from the Alma field seven months after the treaty ratified, and will immediately start to buy oil from the wells. Before Begin and Sadat's meeting the Egyptians had insisted on a seven-month gap between the evacuation of the field and the first shipments of Sinai oil to Israel, Begin said.

On the 15-year U.S. guarantee on oil supplies, he said "We are grateful, but would not want to activate it, in view of the U.S. own energy crisis. He would not like to hear it said in the U.S. one day that Americans freeze because we gave oil to Israelis — or to Jews."

He disclosed that British Premier James Callaghan told him at their recent meeting that Britain would take Israel into account with regard to North Sea oil next year.

Begin also declared he was against calling early general elections. It would not be right to exploit the peace move, he said, and anyway he

(Continued on page 2, col. 4)

Peres invited to Cairo

WASHINGTON (Itim). — Labour Party leader Shimon Peres has been invited by President Anwar Sadat to visit Egypt. The invitation was tendered yesterday when the two met for an informal chat at the Egyptian Embassy here, before the peace signing ceremony.

Israel to move Gaza army headquarters out of town

By ASHER WALLFISH
Jerusalem Post Reporter

Israel has agreed to move the Gaza headquarters of the military government out of the town and into a relatively uninhabited part of the Gaza Strip, at Egypt's request.

Prime Minister Menahem Begin told Acting Prime Minister Zevulun Hammer of this and other gestures requested by Egypt through the medium of the U.S. — some of which were accepted in full or in part. Others were rejected.

After Israel received the original Egyptian request to shift the military government from Gaza over to Beersheba, Israel said "no." The compromise was to keep the headquarters inside the strip, but not in the town, whereupon Egypt sought a fixed date from Israel when the transfer would be carried out. Begin told Hammer that he had not agreed to set a date at this point since it was hard to estimate how long the construction would take. So the Israeli agreement had been given in principle.

Israel rejected an Egyptian request that the IDF stay away from urban areas entirely, but agreed that the presence of soldiers in town would be kept to the minimum level for ensuring law and order.

Israel had rejected an Egyptian request for absolute freedom of political expression, Begin told Hammer, but agreed to allow moderate local expression of a nature not calculated to cause incitement.

Begin said Israel had turned down

(Continued on page 2, col. 6)

Crowds brave bad weather to mark peace

Jerusalem Post Staff

Israelis turned out in the thousands last night to participate in public peace celebrations which were held in most major cities. By far the biggest crowd — between 80,000 and 100,000 — gathered in Tel Aviv's Kikar Malchei Yisrael. Rather smaller crowds, estimated at about 2,000 people, attended ceremonies at the Western Wall in Jerusalem and in Haifa.

The Jerusalemites braved biting winds and unseasonably cold weather to participate in the celebrations. Children and adults joined in spontaneous dances, all for the benefit of the TV cameras that were covering the event for viewers throughout the world. About 100 high school pupils bearing flaming torches were interspersed among the crowd.

A discordant note was struck by some 200 anti-peace demonstrators, mostly Gush Emunim members and students at Jerusalem yeshivas, who held a pray-in at the wall. They said they were demonstrating not only against the signing of the treaty, but also against the "desecration of this holy place by holding a ceremony here."

Yehudi Menuhin topped the list of musicians who entertained the crowd in the plaza. The chief army chaplain, Aluf Gad Navon, recited a

(Continued on page 2, col. 3)

Warmly dressed crowd at Western Wall plaza listens to violinist Yehudi Menuhin serenade the Israel-Egypt peace treaty being signed in Washington. (Rahamim Israeli)

Nine hurt in Old City grenade attack

By DAVID RICHARDSON
Jerusalem Post Reporter

The restrained tone of yesterday's general strike in East Jerusalem was shattered when a grenade exploded in the centre of the Old City a few minutes before the peace treaty signing ceremony last night. Seven tourists and two Arabs were slightly injured.

Security forces already on high alert sealed off the area within minutes and arrested a number of people. This was the only serious incident reported yesterday.

Shortly before nine o'clock the grenade was hurled at a small Old City restaurant and hotel known as "Halil Rahman."

The wounded, among them tourists from the U.S. and Europe, were first taken to the Hospice Hospital in the Old City but were later moved to Shaare Zedek and Hadassah Hospitals.

Rebel tanks surround Amin in Entebbe

NAIROBI. — President Idi Amin was reported yesterday to be threatened by tanks or to have already fled from his residence near Entebbe airport in the face of advancing forces seeking to overthrow him.

A presidential aide, speaking by telephone from the Ugandan capital of Kampala, quoted the president as saying this morning that he could see 12 tanks from his house.

Ugandan exile sources said the tanks were Ugandan and were commanded by Minister of State for Defence Brig. Emilton Mondo, who had staged a coup against Field Marshal Amin.

But other exile sources said the president had fled Entebbe for the northwestern town of Arua which had been prepared for a final stand against the approaching Tanzanian and rebel Ugandan forces.

Travellers from Uganda said Entebbe was under shellfire from Tanzanian guns at the hill town of Mpigi.

The high ground at Mpigi, from which Tanzanian artillery can reach both the capital and the airport, was said to be the deepest advance of the Tanzanians in the five-month war. Fighting began in October when Ugandan soldiers occupied a large area of northwestern Tanzania and Amin claimed it for Uganda.

Other exiles said Amin offered his own resignation twice during the weekend to military advisers in his defence council, and it was rejected both times.

Despite the reports, Entebbe residents said there were no tanks and no fighting. They said the road from Entebbe to Kampala was open.

Exile leaders, meanwhile, wound up a meeting in Moshi, in northern Tanzania, and announced agreement on the structure of a provisional government after the possible defeat of Amin.

About 120 exiles travelled from the

(Continued on page 4, col. 7)

Anti-peace camp meets in Baghdad

Jerusalem Post Staff and Agencies

Arab opponents of the Israel-Egyptian peace treaty began gathering in Baghdad yesterday to take action against the government of Egyptian President Anwar Sadat.

Iraq, hosting today's anti-peace pact conference, called on Arab governments to take "concrete measures against Sadat on political, economic, informational and mass mobilization levels."

The conference of Arab League foreign and economic ministers took on expanded significance with the arrival in the Iraqi capital last night of Jordan's King Hussein, who is believed to be pushing for an alignment with Syria and Iraq. Hussein flew into Baghdad from Damascus after day-long consultations with Syrian leaders who had just wound up three days of talks with Soviet

only heighten tension in the Middle East. The seven-page statement was released by the official Tass news agency. Soviet Foreign Minister Andrei Gromyko returned from Syria yesterday.

"The main attention at the talks was devoted to the dangerous developments in the Middle East in connection with the conclusion of a separate treaty between Israel and Egypt with the active participation of the United States," the communique said. "The sides have resolutely condemned the treaty as one directed against the interests of the Arabs, including the Egyptian people."

Much of the credibility of the anti-Egyptian camp depends, however, on Saudi Arabia, whose position was swinging between maintaining economic ties with Egypt and joining other Arabs in imposing comprehen-

believed "Saudi Arabia will fulfil joint Arab resolutions."

Iraq's official newspaper "A-Thawra" yesterday warned that "those who continue supplying financial aid to Egypt are themselves traitors."

The government-inspired Saudi newspapers yesterday came out with surprisingly outspoken attacks on the peace treaty signed in Washington. "A-Riyadh" daily said that yesterday was a "black day for the White House."

The signing of the treaty was yesterday greeted by protest action including demonstrations and assaults on Egyptian embassies in a number of countries.

Yasser Arafat, whose Palestine Liberation Organization sponsored demonstrations and strikes in western Beirut, vowed to chop off the

THE JERUSALEM POST

Wednesday, October 7, 1981   VOL. LI, No. 15347   IS6.50

Sadat salutes his troops yesterday only minutes before falling victim to an assassins' shots. (UPI telephoto)

Sadat assassinated

Mubarak pledges continuity on peace

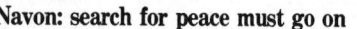

Begin: Won't halt our drive for peace

By DAVID LANDAU
Post Diplomatic Correspondent

Israel will continue with its part of the peace process undeterred by the death of President Sadat, a source close to Premier Begin asserted last night.

The source said this resolve was the intended significance of the premier's statement, issued yesterday evening that "We hope that the peace process, despite the cruel act of its enemies, will continue — as we know President Sadat would wish with all his heart."

The premier's statement came at the end of a message of mourning and condolence that Begin read out in a hushed voice after the news of Sadat's death became official.

"I have lost today not only a partner in peace but also a friend," Begin lamented, saying that during their many meetings a real "personal friendship" had evolved between them.

The source close to Begin said there was no significance in the fact that the premier had couched his reference to the future of the peace process in terms of "hope" rather than making an outright pledge on Israel's part that the process will go forward.

Such a pledge was indeed made later in the evening by President Yitzhak Navon in a television tribute to Sadat (see story below). "We must continue the peace process and do everything possible to ensure its successful conclusion," Navon declared.

The source close to Begin said that while the president's words had not been specifically cleared with the premier, they reflected Begin's thinking precisely. The two men spoke by telephone immediately after Sadat's death was officially announced in Cairo, the source added.

The cabinet is to meet in special session this morning, and is expected to issue a fuller statement of Israel's reaction to Sadat's death.

Whatever the wording of cautious

(Continued on Page 2, Col. 2)

Navon: search for peace must go on

President Yitzhak Navon said last night that the factors that brought Anwar Sadat and the Egyptian leadership to strive for peace have not vanished with his death, and that Israel "must continue the peace process, doing whatever has to be done to bring it to a positive conclusion."

Speaking on Israel Television, Navon said that "we did not make peace with one man — however great — but with the Egyptian people, which on various occasions has expressed its support for peace."

The president said that it was difficult for him to speak of Sadat in the past tense, because ever since

Sadat's historic visit to Jerusalem he has become "part of our lives." In their personal meetings, Navon added, they formed a warm, close relationship.

When he visited Egypt a year ago, Navon said, he met with the top leadership, including Vice-President Hosni Mubarak, and found that they fully supported Sadat's peace policy.

Egypt has lost a great leader who dedicated his life to his people's welfare, Navon said. On behalf of himself and his family, Navon sent his condolences to Jehan Sadat and her family, and expressed their deep shock at Sadat's tragic death. (Itim)

Attackers shoot Sadat and aides at army parade

CAIRO. — The attack on President Anwar Sadat and his aides took place at about 12:40 p.m. yesterday when soldiers participating in a parade threw two hand-grenades and sprayed machinegun fire at the reviewing stand.

The Egyptian leader was hit in the chest and shoulder. He was rushed by helicopter from Nasr City, an eastern Cairo suburb, where the parade was being staged, to the Ma'adi armed forces hospital, south of Cairo, where he underwent emergency surgery.

The president later died of his wounds, officials and hospital sources said. He was 63. He is to be buried on Saturday.

The sources said the president died between 2:15 and 2:30 p.m. Defence Minister Abdel Halil Abu Ghazalla also was hit, but Vice-President Hosni Mubarak, who was on the other side of Sadat in the reviewing stand, was unharmed, reports said.

The raiders were said to have killed nine persons besides Sadat, and 22 others were reported wounded.

Fawzi Abdel-Hafez, Sadat's personal secretary, was killed, an Egyptian official said. A number of foreign diplomats, who were in the reviewing stands with Sadat, also were reported hit.

An Israeli security man on the reviewing stand was wounded slightly, according to a high-ranking Israeli official accompanying Foreign Minister Yitzhak Shamir in New York. It was not made clear whether the security man was guarding the Israeli ambassador, who was not wounded.

A well-placed State Department source said late last night the U.S. had firm evidence that at least one

of the assassins had been captured and had been identified as having ties with a Moslem fundamentalist group (related story below).

Reports said a group of men began firing at Sadat from a truck towing artillery as it passed the grandstand.

Two of the men jumped off the back of a truck and charged the reviewing stand.

"No one was sure it was real for a few seconds, then all hell broke loose," one witness said.

A brief but fierce gunbattle erupted between the blue-bereted soldiers and the guards around Sadat, and bullets sprayed into the grandstand behind the president.

Several people were seriously wounded, among them Belgian Ambassador Claude Ruelle and Australian Embassy First Secretary John Woods, as the crowd dived for cover among tumbling chairs, eyewitnesses said. Two Korean diplomats were reported wounded, as was Irish Defence Minister James Tully. Three U.S. military officers were also said to be injured, but an official report on exactly who was injured in the attack was not available as of late last night.

Spectators continued to flee in panic as the young soldiers in olive drab fatigues fired their weapons from the shoulder at the low platform. Many people lay bleeding on the stand. It was unclear if the assailants were caught.

Ambulances and security vehicles rushed to the stand and carried away the wounded, who included military men and Moslem and Christian leaders.

The soldiers charged at the same instant that six low-flying jetfighters

(Continued on Back Page)

Egyptian exile group claims it was behind the killing

BEIRUT (AP). — An exiled Egyptian opposition group claimed responsibility here yesterday for the assassination of Egyptian President Anwar Sadat.

An anonymous telephone caller identifying himself as the spokesman for the "Rejection Front for the Liberation of Arab Egypt" told the leftist Beirut newspaper Al-Liwa its secret "free officers" branch within the Egyptian armed forces staged the attack on Sadat.

The caller described the group as the military arm of a group formed by former Egyptian Army chief of staff Saad Eddin Shazli, known as the Egyptian "National Front." The

mar Gaddafi, Sadat's most implacable Arab foe, has branch offices in Syria, Lebanon and Algeria.

PLO sources said their latest information was that Shazli, who is in Algiers, capital of Algeria, although Libya's state-run Tripoli Radio said he would shortly make a statement on Sadat's assassination through the Libyan station.

The Libyan News agency JANA claimed yesterday that the assassination was part of an attempted military coup that was still underway. It said the rebels had killed many pro-Sadat officers.

The alleged coup attempt was apparently being led by a group called "the free officers," JANA said.

U.S. lauds Egyptian renewed peace pledge

By WOLF BLITZER
Jerusalem Post Correspondent and agencies

WASHINGTON. — The U.S. yesterday welcomed what a White House spokesman said was Egypt's readiness to continue the Camp David peace process following President Anwar Sadat's assassination.

White House spokesman David Gergen told reporters: "We are pleased that the Egyptian government is pursuing its constitutional processes with regard to succession and are pleased by the continuity of Egyptian policy including the continued dedication of that nation to the Camp David accords."

Gergen, asked to explain how he could so confidently say that Egypt would continue Sadat's peace policies, replied that Secretary of State Alexander Haig had personally instructed him to issue the statement, based on the latest information reaching Washington from Cairo.

President Ronald Reagan, standing on the steps of the White House after assembling his senior national security advisers for urgent meetings, said the assassination of President Anwar Sadat was "an act of infamy, cowardly infamy, that

fills us with horror. America has lost a close friend. The world has lost a great statesman. Mankind has lost a champion of peace. In a world filled with hatred, he was a man of hope. He helped improve a world tormented by malice and pettiness. He was a humanitarian unafraid to make peace."

Spokesman Gergen, asked about the impact of Sadat's death on the administration's proposed Saudi AWACS sale, said the president remained convinced of its crucial importance. "The president views this tragedy as in no way lessening the urgency of the sale," he said. "Indeed, he views it more urgently." Reagan remains "dedicated to support the sale," he added. (See related story, page 4)

Several U.S. officials and former presidents Jimmy Carter and Gerald Ford warned of the consequences Sadat's death could have on America, the Middle East and the world.

Carter, who negotiated the peace accord with Sadat, said he thought Sadat had been "crucial to stability in the Middle East."

Former secretary of state Henry Kissinger said if there was an "indispensable man" in the Middle

(Continued on Page 2, Col. 6)

Arab capitals celebrate

Post Mideast Affairs Reporter and agencies

There was jubilation in several Arab capitals yesterday following the news of President Anwar Sadat's assassination, with Syrians dancing in the streets of Damascus, militiamen in Beirut firing joyful salvos into the air and crowds of people laughing and singing in the streets of Tripoli.

Only in the Sudan and Oman, the

audience rose to its feet, while the speaker described the eventful day out ... the great Egyptian ... with us the arrogant ... liberation ...

The ... JANA ...
Reuters ...
upon an ...
surrendered ...

The agency denounced ...

Hosni Mubarak

Mubarak a 'puzzle' in Egypt

Post Mideast Affairs Editor

The assassination of President Anwar Sadat yesterday has brought his deputy, Hosni Mubarak, to the forefront of the Egyptian leadership — at least temporarily.

Like his predecessor who took over following a stormy power struggle on the death of Gamal Abdul-Nasser in 1970, Mubarak is bound to face challenges for the presidency. These will either come from within the ruling hierarchy or army officers who see themselves as senior to the 53-year-old taciturn Soviet-trained airman.

Mubarak has been something of a puzzle, even to knowledgeable Egyptians who differ over what an Egyptian administration controlled by Mubarak would be like. A majority, however, was virtually unanimous in the assessment that Mubarak would certainly bring

(Continued on page 3)

Vice-President now in control of Egypt

By DAVID BERNSTEIN
Post Mideast Affairs Reporter and Agencies

Anwar Sadat's heir-apparent, Vice-President Hosni Mubarak, vowed last night that Egypt would remain committed to the dead president's goal of a comprehensive peace in the Middle East and would continue to honour "all international charters, treaties and commitments which Egypt has concluded."

Mubarak, who assumed effective control of the country soon after Sadat was gunned down while reviewing a military parade yesterday held to mark the anniversary of the 1973 Yom Kippur War, announced that, in accordance with the Egyptian constitution, Parliamentary Speaker Sufi Abu Taleb would be acting president for a maximum of two months, during which a new president must be elected.

Abu Taleb's first move as acting president was to declare a nationwide state of emergency, to remain in force for one year.

He also confirmed Mubarak in his post as vice-president and authorized him to act as commander-in-chief of the armed forces.

As such, Mubarak will continue to wield effective power until he is confirmed as president in a national referendum within two months.

Mubarak was being groomed by Sadat to be his successor, and few doubt that he will be the next president. The political bureau of the ruling National Democratic Party met late yesterday and decided unanimously to nominate him for the presidency, a nomination certain to be approved by a sweeping majority in the NDP-dominated parliament. The nationwide referendum will be

held shortly afterwards to confirm his election.

In his address to the Egyptian people last night, Mubarak left no doubt in the mind of his listeners that although Sadat had departed, his regime remained intact and his policies would continue to be pursued.

"In the name of the great departed and the name of the people, its constitutional institutions and its armed forces," Mubarak said, "I declare that we will honour all international charters, treaties and commitments which Egypt has concluded.

"Our hands will not cease to push the wheel of peace in pursuance of the mission of the departed leader," he continued. "We will remember with pride when our banners are hoisted over the whole of Sinai (next April) and when a comprehensive peace is realized throughout the region."

He told a stunned nation that Sadat had been assassinated "by criminal and treacherous hands," noting that "God had willed that the leader should be martyred on the day that is his own symbol and among his soldiers and heroes."

It remained unknown as night who exactly was behind the assassination. The "Free Officers of the Opposition Front for the Liberation of Egypt," headed by exiled former chief of staff Sa'ad Eddin Shazli, who led the Egyptian forces in the

(Continued on Page 4)

Obituary — page 4
Related reports and pictures — pages 2 and 10

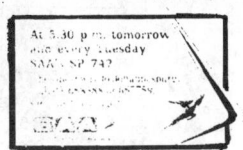
Israeli forces advance 'on schedule' in massive thrust into South Lebanon

Israel yesterday sent armoured columns and infantry deep into Southern Lebanon, in a massive thrust aimed at pushing PLO terrorist gunners back from the northern border. At midnight last night, UN spokesmen said that Israeli units had advanced to six kms. north of the Litani River, and had encountered stiff resistance on the coast near Tyre, and in the Arkoub region on the slopes of Mt. Hermon.

Reports from Israeli sources were still sketchy, but the Israel Defence Forces spokesman confirmed that two aircraft — an attack helicopter and a Skyhawk fighter-bomber — had been shot down over Lebanon.

Damascus said it had ordered its forces to "confront" the Israeli troops, and there were reports of "contact" at three points.

Begin to Reagan:
40km. push to end threat to Galilee

By BENNY MORRIS
Post Diplomatic Reporter

Prime Minister Menachem Begin yesterday informed U.S. President Ronald Reagan that the Israeli forces invading Lebanon will push back the PLO units "forty kilometres to the north."

"The army has been instructed to push back the terrorists to a distance of forty kilometres to the north so that all our civilians in the region of Galilee will be set free of the permanent threat to their lives," Begin wrote Reagan.

Observers noted that the terminology used by Begin is vague, probably deliberately so. The prime minister did not state from where the 40 kilometres begin — from the Israel-Lebanese border, from the Christian enclave-UNIFIL border, or from the UNIFIL-PLO- "state border."

Western sources in Israel last night said that during his recent visit to the U.S., Defence Minister Ariel Sharon said that Israel envisages a 72-hour campaign against the PLO in Lebanon, after which a reinforced UNIFIL, with an expanded zone, would keep the peace and secure Israel's northern border from long-range attack.

Meanwhile, in the major diplomatic initiative so far to halt the fighting, the U.S. is sending special Middle East envoy Philip Habib to Jerusalem in an effort to restore the cease-fire he helped negotiate in July, 1981 between Israel and the PLO. Habib is due to meet Begin and Foreign Minister Yitzhak Shamir this morning.

Habib yesterday met with and received instructions from U.S. Secretary of State Alexander Haig and President Reagan in Versailles, where the American leaders were attending the 7-nation summit of leaders of the major industrial Western states.

In his response yesterday to Reagan's messages of June 4, which urged "restraint" upon Israel, and of June 6, sent before the start of the ground invasion, Begin said that Reagan's "words of sympathy, friendship and understanding touched me deeply."

Begin went on to tell the American President that he had been in constant contact with the surgeon who operated on the wounded Israeli ambassador to Britain, Shlomo Argov, and gave Reagan a possible prognosis.

"I feel it is my duty...to convey to you the real situation," he went on. "For the last seventy-two hours, twenty-three Israeli settlements" in

(Continued on back page)

Heavy fighting reported

Post Mideast Affairs Reporter and agencies

UN reports from Lebanon last night suggested that Israeli forces were running into stiff PLO resistance, mainly in the major PLO stronghold of Tyre but also near Nabatiyeh in the central sector of the battle-front.

UNIFIL spokesman Timur Goksel said in Naqoura last night that tank-led Israeli infantry had to by-pass Tyre, one of their main objectives, and press on for easier targets in the surrounding villages.

Earlier reports had spoken of heavy fighting along all three axes of Israel's advance into Lebanon.

For the first time since the latest round of hostilities began on Friday, there were indications last night that Syria had become involved in the fighting, with Damascus Radio confirming earlier reports that its forces had made contact with Israeli troops in the eastern sector.

Lebanon's state radio later said Syrian positions were pounding the advancing Israeli forces in the central sector of the invasion front with long-range heavy artillery.

implying infantry or tank combat was involved.

A UN spokesman in Beirut, Samir Sanbar, yesterday provided what appears to th be the most detailed account of the Israeli offensive which followed more than 48-hours of intensive air and artillery bombardment of PLO positions in Beirut and some 15 other centres in South Lebanon.

Sanbar reported that at 11 a.m. yesterday, Israel launched a three-pronged offensive — up the Mediterranean coast, through the central sector, and from the south-east — apparently aiming for the major PLO strongholds of Tyre and Nabatiyeh.

UNIFIL spokesman Timur Goksel said in Naqoura last night that, by nightfall, it was estimated that three Israeli armoured brigades and one mechanized infantry brigade were in action. The PLO put the number of invading troops at 20,000.

Sanbar said an Israeli column of 100 tanks and 100 armoured personnel carriers had reached al-Bass on the coastal road opposite Tyre. He reported heavy clashes there between the PLO, aided by their leftist Lebanese allies, and the Israeli forces.

To reach Tyre, one of the main PLO bases in the region, the Israeli forces had to drive through a four-kilometre strip controlled by Dutch troops of the UN Interim Force in

(Continued on Page 2, Col. 2)

Syria orders army to 'confront' Israel

BEIRUT (AP). — Syria said last night it had ordered its army in Lebanon "to confront the Israeli forces," and claimed that "direct contact" had been made in three separate sectors of the central and eastern fronts.

A communique issued by Sana, the official Syrian news agency, did not say that there had been major fighting between elements of the 30,000-man Syrian force in Lebanon and the Israel force, estimated at 20,000 men, which moved across the border yesterday morning. But it did report contact at the Jarmak mountain range, in the central sector, and at Burghos and the Hasbaya intersection in the eastern Arkoub region, on the foothills of Mt. Hermon.

Industrial powers urge cease-fire

VERSAILLES (Reuter). — Leaders of the seven major Western industrial powers yesterday reached broad agreement on monetary stability and credits to the eastern bloc.

As the Versailles summit — held in the shadow of crises in the Middle East and the Falklands — drew to a close, heads of state and government worked on the wording of their economic communique and issued a strong statement on the new outbreak of violence in Lebanon.

They called on both Israel and the Palestinians to "cease immediately and simultaneously all military activities."

Special U.S. Middle East envoy Philip Habib flew to Versailles to confer with President Ronald Reagan on the crisis and was expected to fly to Israel after the meeting.

The monetary accord, as European leaders have urged, is likely to commit the industrial countries to intervene, if necessary, on the exchange markets to counteract disorderly conditions.

But summit sources said the

(Continued on Page 4)

Israel loses plane, 'copter

By HIRSH GOODMAN
Post Military Correspondent

ON THE NORTHERN BORDER. — The Israeli advance into Lebanon was last night reported to be on schedule. But few details were available from Israeli sources.

The Israel Defence Forces spokesman declined to divulge casualty figures for the attack. He would confirm that Israel has lost one Skyhawk fighter and an attack helicopter, and that two helicopter pilots were missing, with the fighter pilot thought to be a captive of the PLO.

According to foreign sources, at 11 a.m. yesterday, Israeli forces entered Lebanon on three main axes.

The declared goal of the operation is to push back terrorist artillery and rockets from Israel's frontier. The government and the army made it clear that it is not the IDF's intention to engage the Syrians in any form of battle, and this message was also passed on to the Syrians by diplomatic means.

Judging from reports reaching Israel from the battlefield, it was clear last night that there are three major prongs in the Israeli attack. Mixed ... ... infantry forces were reported to be moving along the coastal highway and said to have reached the Tyre area, where fierce fighting was raging. A second force of ... armour had entered via the central ... and says last night said to have taken the town of Nabatiyeh.

A third force was moving in the Arkoub (mountain) area in the eastern sector.

It was last night there was no official Israeli confirmation of these reports, the government's policy is to refrain from any specific information being given out until the operation is completed.

There was also no official announcement on Israeli casualties in addition to the lost pilots.

Yesterday's attack was a combined land, air and sea operation, with Israel's armoured thrust passing through territory being held by the Dutch, Norwegian and French UNIFIL detachments. In contradiction of UNIFIL spokesmen's reports, IDF officers deny that there were any exchanges of fire with UNIFIL during the day.

Army sources said that the air force flew many dozens of sorties against terrorist and all air strikes were directed against terrorist sources of fire. They noted that the terrorists used hundreds of Strela missiles against the attacking aircraft.

Undoubtedly, the most complicated part of yesterday's mission was ... along the prongs from ... source ... and ... and Sidon and Tyre. This coastal city has a population of about 17,000, and ... sources said last night

(Continued on back page)

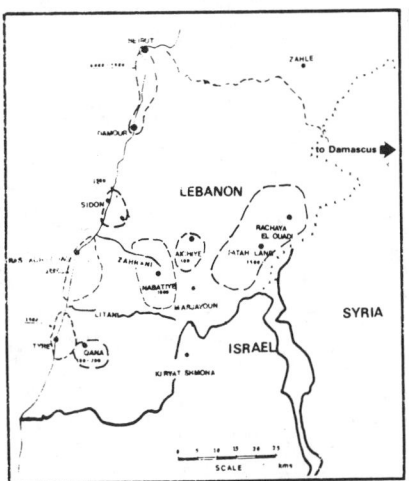

PLO concentrations in South Lebanon. The Zahrani River, south of Sidon, is approximately 40 kilometres north of the Israel-Lebanon border in Western Galilee. In his letter to U.S. President Reagan, Premier Begin writes that the army was instructed to push back the terrorists 40 kms.

'Peace for Galilee' move decided Saturday night

Jerusalem Post Reporter

The cabinet decided at a 3½-hour session on Saturday night to move into southern Lebanon. But it announced the decision at 4 p.m. yesterday, five hours after Israeli forces had launched a major multipronged push across the border.

The announcement by cabinet secretary Dan Meridor said that "Operation Peace for Galilee" had been launched "to place all the civilian population of the Galilee

beyond the range of terrorist fire from Lebanon." It said that Israel will not attack the Syrian army "unless it attacks our forces" and that Israel continues to aspire to the signing of a peace treaty with independent Lebanon."

A last minute attempt by Ambassador Samuel Lewis at 6 a.m. to forestall any Israeli action against the terrorists failed.

The government met tonight in

(Continued on Page 7)

Peres, Rabin support government's action

Jerusalem Post Reporter

Labour Party leaders who yesterday were called to a meeting with Prime Minister Menachem Begin after operations in Lebanon had begun, later expressed support for measures taken by the government

to defend the northern settlements from bombardment.

Labour Party chairman Shimon Peres and MK Yitzhak Rabin were among those at the meeting. Rabin later declared: "Now is the time for unity." (See fuller report, p. 3)

3 Arabs charged with shooting in court today

Jerusalem Post Correspondent

LONDON. — Three Arabs charged with the attempted murder of Israel Ambassador to Britain Shlomo Argov will appear in court here today, police said.

They are Ghassan Hasan Ahmed Said, 22, a Jordanian student, Marwan al-Banna, 21, also of Jordan, and Nowaf Nagib Miflih Rosan, 36, an Iraqi businessman. Said was also charged with the at-

tempted murder of a policeman, co/in Simpson.

A Syrian was arrested in connection with the shooting on Friday but has since been released. An Iranian was still being held, but police said he was not likely to be charged.

Queen Elizabeth has sent a personal letter of sympathy to Hava Argov, the wife of the Israeli Ambassador, a Buckingham Palace spokesman told JTA last night.

(Argov's condition — page)

Facing the enemy in southern Lebanon

By JOSHUA BRILLIANT
Jerusalem Post Reporter

TEL AVIV. — Implementation of the cabinet decision to "place all the civilian population beyond the range of terrorist fire from Lebanon" will require the clearing of a strip nearly 30 kilometres deep along Israel's northern border. The 130-millimetre cannon, longest-range weapons in the hands of terrorist forces in southern Lebanon,

have a maximum range of 28 kms.

This will bring the Israel Defence Forces very close to a Syrian brigade at Meshki northeast of Metulla, and stretch a line at some points crossing the Zaharani River, east to somewhere between the Lebanese coastal cities of Tyre and Sidon.

Terrorist forces in southern Lebanon number 6,000 armed men, about half of the PLO's total

strength in Lebanon. According to military sources, the terrorist concentrations include a string of heavily fortified positions, each housing a platoon-strength force.

It is believed that some areas are heavily mined, some with unmarked minefields, and that there are many booby-traps in the area as well.

Only a few of the terrorist positions are in villages, according to

(Continued on Page 7)

Israeli troops move across the border into Lebanon yesterday.   (IPPA)

THE JERUSALEM POST

Wednesday, August 31, 1983 | Vol. LI, No. 15411 | IS35

Prime Minister Menachem Begin speaks yesterday to coalition leaders who tried to convince him to change his mind about resigning. (GPO)

Begin resignation final; Shamir leads Herut succession hopefuls

Begin agrees to postponement to permit Likud coalition to pre-empt Labour try at government. • Herut ministers back Shamir, press for rapid decision • Levy isolated in ministers' forum, demands decision by Herut central committee • Possibles: Aridor or Levy — Foreign Minister; Moda'i — Finance; Arens to continue at Defence

By ASHER WALLFISH

The succession struggle within the Herut Party was on with a vengeance last night in the wake of Prime Minister Menachem Begin's announcement to his colleagues that his decision to resign was irrevocable.

Two and perhaps three Herut ministers emerged as likely candidates, and unless they can compromise on a shareout of the political spoils, the party seems headed for an upheaval which could threaten the coalition.

Begin acceded to his colleagues' plea to hold off his resignation letter to President Chaim Herzog for a few days, to enable his colleagues to approach Herzog with an agreed candidate to form a new coalition. Begin said he would probably tell his colleagues today how much time they had at their disposal.

Foreign Minister Yitzhak Shamir, deputy Prime Minister and Housing Minister David Levy — and possibly Minister without Portfolio Ariel Sharon — appeared to be in the running last night.

When the eight Herut ministers met yesterday afternoon and again in the evening to decide on the next step, Shamir emerged as the man with the most support. However, Levy insisted that he had as much right as anyone to run for the top job. He urged that the decision on a candidate not be taken by the eight Herut ministers, but be left to an open and democratic contest in the Herut Party central committee.

Between the afternoon and evening meetings of the eight ministers, when Sharon went to Shamir's bureau in the Foreign Ministry and conferred with him for an hour, speculation had it that Sharon was offering to support Shamir's candidacy against Levy provided Shamir paid him off. Sharon is reportedly seeking the post of chairman of the Ministerial Settlement Committee, a job held by the late deputy premier and agriculture minister Simha Ehrlich. Deputy Agriculture Minister Pessah Grupper has insisted on inheriting the chairmanship when he becomes minister.

At last night's meeting, Levy got no support from his colleagues for his proposal to leave the choice of candidate to the central committee. He dismissed his colleagues' apprehension that a contest would not be dignified and would create a vacuum in time as well as in leadership, which could be exploited by the Alignment to snatch power from Herut.

Shamir spoke little at the meeting. But he stressed that the candidate must be the man with most prospects of support in the coalition as a whole, and not only the man with backing inside Herut.

Sharon did not play a big role in the discussion. He said Herut had to remain in a position in which it could achieve its national goals and decide its candidate in that light. He said nothing to hint that he would stand against Levy if Levy ran in an open contest.

The ministers took no vote last night but decided to meet with their Liberal party and La'am faction colleagues this morning, to see which candidate and which procedure for naming the candidate they preferred.

The seven men who oppose Levy intend to use the Liberals' and La'am preference for Shamir as a weapon, either to deter Levy from going to the central committee, or to influence members of the central committee against Levy, should there be a contest.

By and large, the Liberals don't like Levy's social and economic policies. La'am finds him too dovish. So Levy's opponents in Herut are sure their partners will plump for Shamir.

The eight Herut ministers decided to meet again tonight and ... on the procedure for selecting the candidate: either by unanimous recommendation from themselves to the central committee or in open contest.

As of last night, Levy was adamant about an open contest.

Levy's supporters in the central committee were reported to be organizing for a contest, on the grounds that even if Levy lost, he

(Continued on Page 2, Col. 2)

Tough coalition talks look likely for Likud

By JOSHUA BRILLIANT
Jerusalem Post Reporter

TEL AVIV. — After the Likud chooses its candidate to succeed Menachem Begin as prime minister, it will probably face some tough negotiations with prospective coalition partners.

By last night, the Likud was still the faction with which the National Religious Party, Agudat Yisrael and Tami preferred to form a government, but none of these parties ruled out going with the Labour-Mapam Alignment.

Problems are expected over the question of division of portfolios and the policies the new government should implement.

Leaders of the potential coalition parties agreed it was the Likud's prerogative to nominate the prime minister. But that acquiescence did not extend to the division of portfolios — even those which would go to the Likud.

Some criticism was raised following reports that Yitzhak Moda'i was being spoken of as finance minister and Yoram Aridor as foreign minister. "The man is famous for his communicative qualities," one source said sarcastically about Aridor.

"Our deal was with Begin. If somebody replaces him and they want to change portfolios, there are partners who must express their views, he added.

In a similar vein, Education Minister Zevulun Hammer said yesterday the division of portfiolios must be discussed with his National Religious Party, although it was not demanding any more portfolios. "We haven't grown in size in the past month to be able to ask for more. I think we'll want to continue in the same roles," he said.

Problems are also expected over the joint platform. Tami leader MK Aharon Abuhatzeira said his party will demand changes in the cabinet's recent economic decisions. He recalled Tami was on the verge of quitting the present coalition because it believed the economic burden was not divided justly between the affluent and other sectors.

MK Menahem Porush of Agudat Yisrael said his party will demand that the candidate for the premiership sign an undertaking to implement all the commitments to the Aguda in the last coalition agreement.

Senior sources in Agudat Yisrael explained they wanted binding assurances because they did not expect Begin's successor to have as positive an attitude towards religious affairs as Begin had. "The Likud without Begin will be like the Alignment," one Aguda source said.

In an interview on Israel Television, Aguda MK Avraham Shapira said "Whatever happens, this will be a second government. If they really want to continue with the coalition, we must first know who will form it. We should know if we're taking the same path, with the same coalition agreement. A serious person does not sign any blank (papers)."

MK Abba Eban (Labour) smiled as he watched the live broadcast. It seemed as though Labour may have a chance of winning the ultra-Orthodox party's support for an alternative government.

But leaders of the small coalition parties said last night they believed talk of a coalition with Labour was "not realistic" and "not pr... ."

Abuhatzeira said he believed it was not realistic because he did not see where the Alignment would get the minimum 61 votes. Tami, he explained, would not join a coalition with the Rakah Communist list.

Meanwhile, The Council of Jewish Settlements in the territories yesterday decided to oppose the return of former defence minister Ezer Weizman to the cabinet.

Four French soldiers killed

Fighting intensifies in Beirut

BEIRUT. — The Lebanese Army mounted a navy-supported counter-attack against Shi'ite and Druse militiamen in mostly Moslem West Beirut yesterday, as U.S. Marines battled with rebel irregulars around the city's international airport.

Three French soldiers in the multinational peace keeping force in Lebanon and a para-military policeman at the French Embassy were killed in Beirut yesterday, the French Defence Ministry in Paris confirmed last night.

A ministry spokesman said two soldiers and the policeman were killed at the French embassy in a shelling attack that also injured several other people. Earlier yesterday, another French soldier was killed and two others injured at the Galerie Semaan crossing point between East and West Beirut.

There have now been 12 deaths among French soldiers since France sent 2,000 troops into Beirut last September.

State and privately owned radios said hundreds of troops landed by helicopters and boats at the Cadmos Hotel beach, just 400 metres from U.S. Marines protecting the six-storey building that now houses most U.S. Embassy personnel.

News agencies gave conflicting reports of the fighting. Reuter quoted U.S. marines at the scene as saying that American Embassy buildings on the Beirut seafront came under sustained attack by rocket-propelled grenades and

(Continued on Page 2, Col. 5)

Shouf postponement vexes IDF officers

By HIRSH GOODMAN
Post Defence Correspondent

ALEY. — The news that the redeployment of the Israel Defence Forces to the Awali line had been post... again yesterday, could not have been received by Israeli forces stationed in Lebanon.

Yesterday was the third postponement in recent days. For weeks now, forces on the front line have been living under harsh field conditions, waiting for the move. When the order finally comes, the move will be completed within a matter of hours — if there are no hitches.

The chances of a smooth redeployment are remote. Apart from the logistical problems involved in moving the army down the narrow and pothol'd axis leading down from the Shouf, the probability that the IDF may have to withdraw under fire is considered high.

The renewed fighting in Beirut, coupled with the sporadic shelling and exchanges between Druse and Phalangists in the Shouf, have brought tension in this area to a breaking point. Aley, and the roads leading to it, are deserted, sandbags covering shuttered windows.

The Christian quarter of the town has been boarded up; only very few of the Christian residents have dared to remain in this predominently Druse town strategically located on the Beirut-Damascus Highway

Despite constant contacts with the Druse, including a meeting yesterday morning, Israeli officers in the Shouf have been unable to obtain any sort of guarantee that the Druse will hold their fire once the IDF starts pulling back. The Druse are determined to physically resist any attempt by the Lebanese army to deploy here, unless an ironclad political agreement has been

(Continued on Page 2, Col. 7)

Begin agrees to a further delay in Shouf pullback

Post Diplomatic Staff

Prime Minister Menachem Begin yesterday acceded to U.S. President Ronald Reagan's request that Israel once again delay its planned withdrawal from the Shouf Mountains of central Lebanon.

Begin met with U.S. special Middle East envoy Robert McFarlane just before telling the heads of the government coalition that he was firm in his resolve to resign. He agreed during the meeting to a limited postponement of the pullback.

Well-informed sources in Jerusalem said that Begin had agreed to a postponement of "a few more days," and that this postponement was the final one.

McFarlane returned to Beirut yesterday to renew his efforts to obtain an agreement between the rival Druse, Moslem and Christian factions before the partial Israeli pullback to the new Awali River line.

McFarlane handed Begin a personal message from Reagan asking for the postponement. The Americans, according to reliable sources, are convinced that the chances for achieving a Druse-Christian agreement in the Shouf have increased.

Such an agreement is vital, McFarlane reportedly told Begin, Foreign Minister Yitzhak Shamir and Defence Minister Moshe Arens at the meeting in Jerusalem. An Israeli pullback prior to the achievement of an agreement may well put paid to any chance of reaching such an agreement, he added.

The Americans, focusing their efforts on achieving agreement between the warring Lebanese factions, fear that the Israeli pullback from the Shouf will be followed by full-scale factional fighting and, possibly, a bloodbath, endangering the existence of President Amin Jemayel's government.

Arens has repeatedly said in the past that the achievement of an agreement between the warring Lebanese factions is not a precondition for the Israeli withdrawal.

Israeli officials have reportedly said that the IDF pullback from the Shouf will be completed by September 7, the eve of Rosh Hashana.

Opposition plays it cool

Alignment-led coalition is possible, Peres declares

Jerusalem Post Staff

TEL AVIV. — Labour Party chairman Shimon Peres believes it is possible to establish an Alignment-led government. In an interview on the Mabat television programme last night, Peres said that the Alignment, with its 50 members, is the Knesset's largest and most stable bloc and it is prepared to create as wide a coalition as possible to cope with the country's problems.

Asked about the basis of this conviction, Peres said: "The basis is need and possibility.

"I think that more and more Knesset factions are becoming convinced that this must be done quickly on as wide a foundation as possible, and there is no wide foundation without the Alignment."

The Likud government has collapsed and its successor must step into office as quickly as possible, Peres said. "I have confidence in the sense of responsibility of other Knesset members," he said.

Asked how he justifie[d] his conviction that the Alignment can create a coalition when leaders of the National Religious Party, Tami and Agudat Yisrael have rejected the prospect, Peres answered: "Yesterday was yesterday, when a somewhat pathetic attempt was made to influence Begin. A different situation exists today and it will be different tomorrow. All parties must respond to the problems of today and tomorrow, and not to those of yesterday."

To a question whether the Alignment was maintaining formal contacts with party leaders, Peres said that informal talks were taking place and that they would continue.

Labour leaders would like to form a government — even if it is short-lived — until early Knesset elections are held. One party source explained that this would deny the Likud the ability to repeat election "stunts" such as it had pulled before the last elections when the price of colour TV sets was reduced and the Iraqi atomic reactor was bombed

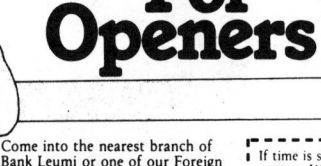

Kohl visit off until situation becomes clear

Jerusalem Post Diplomatic Staff

West German Chancellor Helmut Kohl will put off his visit to Israel until the political constellation in this country becomes more stable, political sources said last night in Jerusalem. Kohl was supposed to arrive today.

Informed sources in Bonn said yesterday it was unlikely that Kohl would be able to travel to Israel before 1984, Associated Press reported.

Kohl's visit taking place at a time of great political uncertainty in Israel.

Yesterday's statement by the prime minister's media adviser Uri Porat that Israel and the Federal Republic of Germany had mutually agreed to postpone the visit signalled a sharp change of direction. Until noon, everything was still uncertain. Preparations for the visit have been going forward in Bonn and Jerusalem for some time

leaders had not yet ended, reporters waiting outside the Prime Minister's Office where the meeting took place, concluded that the Bonn report meant that Begin had decided not to step back from his decision.

The decision to postpone the Kohl visit was taken during a number of telephone conversations between Foreign Minister Yitzhak Shamir and West German Foreign

THE JERUSALEM POST
INTERNATIONAL EDITION
The perfect gift for your friends and relations overseas

THE JERUSALEM POST

Vol. LIII, No. 15803 Sunday, January 6, 1985 • Tevet 13, 5745 • Rabia Tani 13, 1405 IS280

Drive Carefully
better to *be* late
than *the* late

Defence Minister Yitzhak Rabin visits Israeli soldiers in Lebanon last week.

Airline stops Ethiopian rescue

Both the Israel and Sudanese governments yesterday denied reports of collusion between them in the rescue of Ethiopian Jews and their aliya. The Ethiopian government "accused" the Sudan – a member of the Arab League – of cooperating with Israel in arranging the illegal exit of Ethiopian nationals. In response, Khartoum accused the communist Ethiopian regime of "trading Jews for arms."

The Belgian charter airline which has been ferrying the Ethiopian Jews to Israel for the last few weeks announced that its part in the airlift was now over. A planeload arrived yesterday.

Unidentified U.S. officials accused the Israel authorities of endangering the rescue operation by the "premature" lifting of censorship of the issue, while the Jewish Agency chairman said he hoped the worldwide publicity would, on the contrary, ensure the continuity of the scheme.

A local "affair" is brewing over the "Jewishness" of the latest olim, with suspicion in some rabbinic quarters that their ancestry might have included marriages that are forbidden by halacha with consequent risk of *mamzerut* among them.

And meanwhile, a son was born on Friday to a very new Ethiopian olah in a Jerusalem hospital. He was reported healthy despite weighing only 1.8 kilograms.

U.S. officials angered by lifting of censorship

By WOLF BLITZER
Jerusalem Post Correspondent

WASHINGTON. – Senior White House and State Department officials, as well as American Jewish leaders, claim to have been shocked and deeply irritated by Israel's decision on Thursday to lift military censorship on the sensitive operation.

The American officials said this had been done without coordination with Washington, despite extensive U.S. diplomatic financial and other involvement in planning the operation in recent months.

There was widespread confusion over Israel's reasoning.

Some U.S. officials and Jewish leaders were even raising the possibility that Israel may have deliberately hoped to curtail the rescue operation at this point because of the mounting social and financial problems in absorbing the Ethiopians.

This charge was strongly rejected by Israeli officials who insisted that the government had permitted the publication only of the absorption of the Jews – and not details of the airlift.

It was only last Wednesday that visiting Absorption Minister Ya'acov Tsur appealed to U.S. officials, Congressional leaders and staffers, journalists, and American Jewish leaders for strict silence on Operation Moses, the name for the airlift.

"I can tell you that there is significant irritation in Washington," a U.S. official said yesterday. "We stuck our necks out on this operation and suddenly Israel changes the rules without consulting us. The whole thing now looks as if it has been torpedoed. We don't know

(Continued on Page 2, Col. 3)

Belgian charter firm: 'Publicity stopped us'

Jerusalem Post Staff
and agencies

Another planeload of Ethiopian immigrants arrived in Israel yesterday, immigration officials said – even as the Belgian charter airline that ran the massive airlift of the immigrants announced that the operation had ended.

"The operation has ended as far as we are concerned," a spokesman for Trans European Airways (TEA) said in Brussels.

The company had expected to continue flying refugees for another two weeks, as thousands more Ethiopian Jews were said to be waiting for flights to Israel, BBC reported yesterday.

Asked by the BBC why the airlift had ended, a TEA spokesman said the widespread publicity about the previously secret operation had made it impossible to continue.

The spokesman said he had seen a blue and white Boeing arrive in Brussels yesterday morning. No one got in or out, and after four hours the plane took off for Israel, BBC reported.

The spokesman said yesterday's flight was the last. Brussels airport confirmed that no more TEA flights were scheduled on that route, BBC reported.

The Jerusalem Post has learned that the charter airline does a large business flying Moslem pilgrims to Mecca.

A Brussels airport official said the Italian airline Alitalia was involved in a similar operation via Rome.

In Israel, the cabinet secretary said that in the wave of publicity here and abroad on the immigration of Ethiopians, "many details were re-

(Continued on Page 2, Col. 4)

Assad 'assumes leadership' of 'Palestinian struggle'

DAMASCUS (AP). – President Hafez Assad said yesterday that he no longer believed the PLO led by Yasser Arafat was representative of the Palestinian people, thus in effect withdrawing Syria's recognition of the PLO as it now exists.

Assad made the comment as he opened a long-awaited meeting of Syria's ruling Ba'ath Party, criticizing both PLO chairman Arafat and Jordan's King Hussein for cooperating with Egypt, though he mentioned neither directly by name.

The Syrian president, who opposed Arafat's convening of the Palestinian parliament-in-exile last month in Jordan, accused the PLO chairman and Hussein of "conducting the biggest conspiracy" against the Palestinian people.

He said Syria will lead "the Palestinian struggle henceforth."

"We were the ones to make the PLO the sole representative at the Rabat 1974 summit while he (Hussein) was in the other camp," Assad said. "We will refuse to believe that those people are the representatives of the Palestinian people and that they reflect the aspiration of this people."

The reference was to an Arab summit in Morocco which recognized the PLO as the sole legitimate representative of the Palestinian people. This came after Hussein's army had driven PLO terrorists out of Jordan in 1970.

Assad's speech was filled with references to those who "want to meet with the Egypt of Camp David," referring to Arafat and Hussein, who have both moved recently toward the government of Egyptian President Hosni Mubarak.

Assad pledged Syrian support for Beirut against the Israeli occupation of South Lebanon.

He said: "We support the Lebanese resistance (against Israel) with all our strength and work with our Lebanese brothers for improving security conditions in Lebanon, because security creates a better climate for the Lebanese resistance.

"Israel knows that, and this is why it is doing its best not to let security be maintained in any Lebanese area."

Halachic tangle faces Ethiopian immigrants

By HAIM SHAPIRO

In their confrontation with halachic Judaism, the Ethiopian Jews may well find themselves being lifted out of the frying pan of a conversion ceremony, only to fall into the fire of being considered possible *mam[illegible]rim*.

This was revealed on Friday by Dr. Michael Corinaldi, chairman of the International Committee for Ethiopian Jews and an attorney specializing in the halachic problems of esoteric groups of Jews.

Regarding the conversion ceremonies, Corinaldi told *The Jerusalem Post* that despite a recent ruling of the chief rabbinate, restricting this ceremony to ritual immersion and eliminating the need to draw a drop of blood in a symbolic circumcision, the Ethiopians are still adamantly opposed to undergoing the ceremony – and, in fact, all such conversion ceremonies have been stopped.

"They see themselves as 'complete Jews and won't tolerate any procedure that questions this," he said. He added that as a result of an appeal by his group to the High Court of Justice, the Interior Ministry is now registering the Ethiopian Jews as Jews and not as converts to Judaism.

But the Ethiopian Jews also face another and possibly more explosive halachic problem – although their marriages are considered perfectly in order by the rabbis, some rabbinical authorities view their divorces as invalid.

This could place the entire community under the stigma of being possible *mamzerim*, children of a married woman and a man other than her husband, who are only allowed to marry other *mamzerim*.

Ironically, the symbolic conversion ceremony, to which the Ethiopians object so strenuously, could erase any question of this stigma, Corinaldi noted. Thus, if they were not complete Jews before their arrival in Israel, any irregularity in their marriage ritual would be irrelevant.

Corinaldi stressed that rabbinical views on the subject are still mixed and it is not clear which view will become dominant. As eminent an authority as former Sephardi chief rabbi Ovadia Yosef ruled that there is no suspicion of *mamzerut* among the Ethiopians.

Corinaldi roundly censured the recent publication of the facts of the Ethiopian Jewish airlift. He said his group is planning to call for a commission of inquiry into what he described as only the latest in a 30-year series of obstacles to their being

(Continued on Back Page)

Mubarak and Hussein meet on Palestinians

CAIRO (Reuter). – Egypt's President Hosni Mubarak said he discussed the Palestinian problem and his forthcoming visit to the U.S. during a meeting with Jordan's King Hussein yesterday.

The two leaders had three hours of talks during Mubarak's four-hour stay at Akaba, on his second visit to Jordan in less than three months.

Mubarak said on his return to Cairo: "We discussed the Palestinian issue... There must be movement on the Palestinian issue or else it will die."

Prime Minister Kamal Hassan Ali said yesterday he hoped Mubarak's visit to Washington in March would give impetus to a Middle East peace settlement.

The Mubarak-Hussein talks followed by two days a session Hussein held with PLO Chairman Yasser Arafat, with whom the monarch hopes to forge a common Middle East policy.

Hussein had met three times with Arafat during the past week and also made a brief trip to Saudi Arabia, where he talked with King Fahd.

Hussein has been calling for a UN-sponsored peace conference on the Middle East, and has Egypt's support in this.

Only 896 Jews left Soviet Union in 1984

NEW YORK (Reuter). Jewish emigration from the Soviet Union last year dropped to its lowest level since 1970, American Jewish groups have reported.

In a joint statement issued Thursday, the National Conference on Soviet Jewry and the Greater New York Conference on Soviet Jewry said only 896 Jews had left in 1984.

The figures suggested that Moscow had "effectively closed the gates" on Jewish emigration.

The statement said over 260,000 Jews had left the Soviet Union since 1970 when Moscow began allowing large-scale emigration.

There were 20,000 "refuseniks," Soviet Jews who have been refused exit permits, it added.

Dulzin hopes publicity will help rescue

By JERRY LEWIS
Jerusalem Post Correspondent

LONDON. – Yehuda Dominitz, the Jewish Agency official at the centre of the Ethiopian Jews news leak who was suspended from his post last week, has been reinstated.

Arye Dulzin, chairman of the Jewish Agency, told *The Jerusalem Post* that Dominitz's suspension was "a little holiday which I will call a punishment." He was asked to return by Dulzin after the matter had been discussed with Immigration Department head Haim Aharon, Dominitz's boss.

Asked whether the leak had harmed the chances for rescuing the remaining Ethiopian Jews, Dulzin said: "We are just keeping our fingers crossed and hope that the saving action will not be interrupted." He thought the press coverage might even protect the rescue mission by arousing public opinion in the Western world.

Dulzin said that a major part of the operation had been completed.

First Sabra born to airlifted Ethiopian

An Ethiopian baby was born on Friday in Jerusalem to a woman who arrived in Israel only five days before. The boy only weighed 1,800 grams, but is reported in good condition at Bikur Holim hospital.

The mother has already gone through 10 pregnancies, three of which were aborted. Two of the seven babies she bore died within one day of birth. (Itim)

Informal package deal talks expected to start today

By ROY ISACOWITZ
Jerusalem Post Reporter

TEL AVIV. – Government, Histadrut and manufacturers' representatives are expected to begin their informal contacts today, with the aim of reaching a package deal extension agreement by the middle of the month, Histadrut sources said last night.

The contacts will be held in small subcommittees of the trilateral Economic Council, which met last Thursday. The subcommittees will attempt to reach agreement on a wide range of issues, such as subsidies, taxes and unemployment. The agreements will then be brought to the council for approval.

According to the sources, representatives of the three sides over the weekend prepared its position for the negotiations.

Thursday's meeting was restricted to opening statements from the three sides and did not include negotiations, the sources said.

However, the government and the manufacturers reportedly accepted in principle a proposal by Histadrut Secretary General Yisrael Kessar that the current package deal remain in force until a follow-up deal is signed. A decision on the proposal will be made if the present agreement expires with no successor in sight.

Syrian soldier infiltrates, killed by IDF

By MENAHEM HOROWITZ

KIRYAT SHMONA. – A Syrian soldier who crossed the border on the Golan Heights early yesterday morning was killed later in an exchange of fire with Israeli troops.

IDF units in the area went on alert after finding the man's tracks near the border fence. Border settlements were warned, with residents told to stay indoors and lock their homes. Soldiers guarded the settlements.

Around 2 p.m., the man shot at an IDF vehicle and was killed by the soldiers' return fire.

He was described as about 20, dark and short. He was wearing sneakers and carrying a Syrian Army card complete with personal army number. A grenade, discovered in his possession and thought to be booby-trapped, was safely dismantled. Kalashnikov rifles, two grenades, eight magazines and medicines were found in his possession.

Military sources said they regarded the incident as exceptional and not reflecting any change in Syrian policy. They believe the man may have been mentally unbalanced.

Haifa top league at half-way stage

Post Sports Staff

The National soccer League reached the half-way stage yesterday with the champions Maccabi Haifa climbing back to the top of the table in impressive fashion.

While Betar Jerusalem managed only a 1-1 draw against Hapoel Beersheba, Haifa scored a convincing 3-0 away win in Kfar Sava. That lifts them a single point ahead of Betar in their dramatic two-way battle for honours, a repeat of last season's yo-yo act.

The innovation of staging several top fixtures on Friday afternoon rather than, as traditionally, on Saturdays has met with mixed reactions. There were larger crowds than usual at the three grounds where games were played on Friday but some aficionados have complained that spreading the weekend fixture list over two days dilutes the excitement of all matches being contested at the same time.

Match report – Sports page 7.

Soviets apologize about missile

MOSCOW (AP). – The Soviet Union yesterday published an apology to Finland and Norway, admitting that a target missile fired during [illegible] the Soviets had apologized for the incident after saying that a target drone fired from Soviet vessels might have strayed into their airspace and went into the territory of Finland," Tass said.

"The target drone did not have on board any explosive matter or toxic materials.

The Israel Experience

All First International Bank personal current account holders (not just those on salaries) can now overdraw up to IS 50,000 at the prime interest rate (currently 10,3% per month.)
Have you started banking at First International Bank?
Details in All Branches

Kesher Barel & Assoc.

"IN TOPSY-TURVY TIMES, THINK ALONG NEW LINES"
"THAT'S VERY TRUE. I BANK FIRST INTERNATIONAL TOO"

THE JERUSALEM
POST
Vol. LIII, No. 15903 Monday, May 6, 1985 • Iyar 15, 5745 • Shaban 15, 1405 IS430

Reports from Madrid:

Spain has agreed to diplomatic ties

By MICHAEL EILAN
Jerusalem Post Reporter

Spanish Prime Minister Felipe Gonzalez has agreed to establish diplomatic relations with Israel, according to reports reaching the Foreign Ministry last night.

According to these reports, Gonzalez made his statement to American reporters here to cover Reagan's visit to Spain beginning today (story page 4). There was no other confirmation of the statement.

There has been consistent pressure on Spain to establish diplomatic relations with Israel ever since Spain started serious negotiations over its accession to the European Community.

David Kimche, director-general of the Foreign Ministry, visited Spain on April 21 for talks on diplomatic relations. Spain recognizes Israel but has no diplomatic links with it, and had previously indicated that it would establish such ties only when it formally joins the EC in January 1986.

Inner cabinet approves Cairo visit of 3 officials

By MICHAEL EILAN
Jerusalem Post Reporter

The inner cabinet yesterday approved a visit of three senior officials to Cairo. But it appears that considerable negotiation is necessary both inside Israel and with the Egyptians before a summit meeting can take place.

Prime Minister Peres and Vice Premier and Foreign Minister Shamir had agreed on the proposals brought before the inner cabinet before the meeting, according to senior officials. But apparently the agreed positions are not such as can lead to a quick resolution of the issues of Israeli interest – such as the return of the Egyptian ambassador to Tel Aviv – or those of Egyptian interest, mainly Taba.

Israel Radio yesterday quoted Egyptian sources as saying that no summit could take place before July.

Avraham Tamir, the director-general of the Prime Minister's Office, and David Kimche, the director-general of the Foreign Ministry, presented a position paper to the inner cabinet. The two are to go to Egypt with Aluf Menahem Einan, head of the Israel Defence Forces Planning Division. But this position paper was worked out in previous negotiations between their seniors, mainly Peres and Shamir.

According to senior government sources, the delegation's brief is to open a broad dialogue on all the issues under dispute between the two countries. Unlike previous descriptions of this mission, planned ever since Minister without Portfolio Ezer Weizman returned from Cairo on April 18, the delegation is now not charged with preparing a summit meeting between Peres and Egyptian President Hosni Mubarak.

There have been several proposals on the most contentious part of the delegation's brief, which is the Egyptian demand to hand the Taba issue over to arbitration. Government officials were understandably reluctant to reveal what the delegation's fallback positions were before the actual negotiations start, but it appears that they fall short of what the Egyptians have consistently demanded. Possibly because of the prior coordination between Peres and Shamir, the three-hour debate in the 10-man inner cabinet was not held on strictly partisan lines.

At the same time the Egyptians, in briefings to their local press, have said that they believe a summit meeting cannot take place before July. Earlier Israeli assessments had said

(Continued on Page 2, Col. 4)

Beirut battles rage on

BEIRUT (AP). – Christian and Moslem militias fought tank, mortar and rocket-propelled-grenade battles along Beirut's dividing Green Line yesterday, lobbing rounds into residential districts in the worst shelling since the fighting began eight days ago.

Police said six people were killed and 30 wounded in the fighting overnight and during the day.

A French Defence Ministry statement issued in Paris said an *aide de camp* of French Defence Minister Charles Hernu suffered slight wounds at the Residence Des Pins on the Green Line when the compound was hit by a "few shells" overnight.

The new casualties raised the overall toll to 29 dead and 183 wounded since last Sunday.

Moves were made to reconvene the nine-man coalition Lebanese cabinet which last week split over sectarian differences as president Amin Jemayel sought ways to end the bloodshed in the capital.

But with the year-old government paralyzed, there was no immediate sign of a halt in the fighting.

President and Mrs. Reagan and Chancellor Helmut Kohl and his wife walk past honour guard of U.S. and West German soldiers as they enter the Bitburg cemetery yesterday. (Reuter telephoto)

Back-to-work orders sought at hospitals

By D'VORA BEN SHAUL
Jerusalem Post Reporter

Jerusalem Labour Court Judge Nehemiah Guttman last night was still deliberating the Health Ministry's request to issue back-to-work orders to the administrative, nursing and housekeeping staff of the government's 37 hospitals.

The government workers who started yesterday to implement sanctions that placed the government hospitals on weekend schedules and closed the emergency rooms of all facilities will, if the order is given, return to work this morning.

Emergency patients were received in most government hospitals yesterday by a reinforced staff of doctors only. Last night pressure was described as heavy on Kupat Holim Clalit and private hospitals, since the government emergency facilities were closed during the night.

Earlier yesterday Professor Dan Michaeli, director-general of the Health Ministry, tried to alleviate the situation by asking hotel work-

(Continued on Page 2, Col. 4)

High-school teachers to dismiss pupils at 11 today

By LEA LEVAVI
Jerusalem Post Reporter

TEL AVIV. – Teachers belonging to the Secondary School Teachers Association intend to dismiss their pupils at 11 am. today to protest against cuts in teaching hours, threatened dismissal of teachers and pressure on the Association to postpone for a year increases scheduled for September.

Today's sanctions are to affect some junior high classes and most high schools.

The Secondary School Teachers Association also stopped all preparations for *bagrut* (matriculation) exams as of yesterday.

A scheduled meeting between Education Minister Yitzhak Navon and Histadrut Teachers Union Secretary-General Yitzhak Wellber was not held yesterday because Wellber was ill. But the union leadership met last night and instructed principals and inspectors among its members not to cooperate with the ministry in planning the coming school year when such plans involve dismissing teachers.

The leaders also warned the ministry that they would take every action up to and including a general strike to protect their members' jobs. But the union said last night that it would not take any strike action this week.

In a meeting between Navon and Secondary School Teachers Association chairman Shoshana Bayer yesterday, she also promised that her union's partial strike would not be stepped up this week.

Tears, anger as Reagan visits Belsen and Bitburg

BITBURG (Reuter). – Emotional protests accompanied U.S. President Ronald Reagan yesterday when he visited the site of Bergen-Belsen concentration camp and laid a wreath at a German war cemetery containing the graves of 49 SS soldiers.

Young European Jews, U.S. war veterans and politicians, many of them weeping, gathered in this small town to express outrage at the visit.

"We want reconciliation but not with the SS," Moshe Ronen, president of the North American Jewish Students Network, said.

His group unfurled a blue-and-white banner by the roadside as Reagan sped past towards the Bitburg cemetery. It read "no rehabilitation of the SS. They are murderers, not victims."

About 300 young Jews from France, the Benelux countries, West Germany, Britain and the U.S. demonstrated peacefully in the town centre. They jeered and shouted, "Reagan out," as the president's cavalcade went past.

"We want to show the world how horrified Jews are that Reagan should be equating those who perpetrated the Holocaust with those who were its victims," said Mike Isaacs, head of the British Union of Jewish Students.

Nearer the cemetery, about 20 members of the New Jersey Senate and State Assembly linked arms and sobbed as Reagan passed.

"I happen to be Jewish. I happen to be a veteran, but I'm here as an American to protest," said New Jersey State Senator Matthew Feldman. "Reagan is trying to rewrite the history of World War II."

But there was a warm welcome for Reagan from the 12,000 people of Bitburg who live with 11,000 U.S. airmen and their families in this town in the Eifel Hills.

"Thanks for liberty," said a placard carried by West German Herbert Dzur. "I'm [illegible] President Reagan [illegible] against fascism or any other kind of dictatorship," he said.

About 20 minutes before Reagan passed through the centre of Bit-

(Continued on Page 2, Col. 5)

At death camp: 'Never again'

Reagan admits Bitburg visit opens wounds

BITBURG (Reuter). – U.S. President Reagan stood in silence at a memorial to German war dead yesterday and later acknowledged his decision to visit Bitburg cemetery, containing the remains of 49 SS men, had reopened old wounds.

Reagan, with West German Chancellor Helmut Kohl at his side, remained at attention for two minutes before a plain stone tower in the tiny graveyard as a lone trumpeter sounded a melancholy salute to the fallen.

Before flying to Bitburg, a grim-faced Reagan had stood before the bleak mass graves of the former Bergen-Belsen concentration camp and pledged that "the hell of the Holocaust would never again "yawn forth its awful contents."

But in both places, Jewish protesters chanted slogans against Reagan and charged that his visit to the Bitburg graveyard amounted to a rehabilitation of Nazism.

Speaking at a U.S. airbase in Bitburg after his seven-minute stay in the cemetery, he said it had marked a reconciliation between Germans and Americans.

"On this fortieth anniversary of World War II we mark the day when the hate, the evil and the obscenities ended and we commemorate the rekindling of the democratic spirit in Germany," he told American and German servicemen.

But he added: "This visit has stirred many emotions in the American and German people...some old wounds have been reopened and this I regret very much because this should be a time of healing."

To the survivors of the Holocaust, he said: "Many of you are worried that reconciliation means forgetting. I promise you we will never forget."

Reagan called the crimes of the SS "among the most heinous in history," but he said others buried at Bitburg were simply soldiers in the German Army.

Nazism had turned all human values upside down, he declared. "Nevertheless we can mourn the German war dead today as human beings crushed by a vicious ideology."

Earlier, under solemn grey skies at Bergen-Belsen, Reagan spoke of his "painful walk into the past" and said the horror of the Holocaust was "for ever burned" upon his memory.

"Rising above all this cruelty, out of this tragic and nightmarish time, beyond the anguish, the pain, and the suffering and for all time we can and must pledge – never again," he said.

Kohl struggled to fight back tears as he thanked Reagan at the Bitburg base for going ahead with the cemetery visit.

"I thank you Mr. President from the whole German people and I thank you as a friend that you made this step together with me," he said.

Earlier, at Belsen the president and Mrs. Reagan prayed at the former concentration camp Bergen-Belson, where scores of thousands, mostly Jews died. Nancy Reagan appeared to be holding back tears as the couple walked along the mass grave sites to a stark monument where Reagan made his comments.

The president spoke from a small lectern at the base of the camp monument after he had joined Kohl and 400 invited guests in prayer. They included Israel's Ambassador to West Germany Yitzhak Ben-Ari.

Roman Catholic, Protestant and Jewish clergymen were originally due to take part, but only two Christian priests were present after Jewish leaders announced on Saturday they were boycotting the ceremony in protest.

In his speech, Reagan said: "Here lie people, Jews, whose death was inflicted for no reason other than their very existence. Above all, we are struck by the horror of it all, the monstrous, incomprehensible horror."

Shi'ites join effort to defend South Lebanese security strip

By JOSHUA BRILLIANT
Post Defence Reporter

TEL AVIV. – Local militias have been organized in nearly 80 per cent of the Shi'ite villages in the security belt in South Lebanon, political and defence sources have reported.

The sources also said that hundreds of Shi'ites have volunteered for the South Lebanon Army (SLA) and that the defence establishment is confident it will overcome the problems that have hampered the recruitment of Druse for the force.

However, SLA commander General Antoine Lahad could become a problem because he appears to come to regard himself as a protector of the Christian community, when Israel is seeking to abandon its policy of favouring the Christians, military sources said.

Village militias have been established in more than 40 of the 50-odd Shi'ite villages in the strip just north of the Israeli border. Once a village agrees to the establishment of a militia, there is no problem finding recruits, the defence sources said.

The readiness of Shi'ites to volunteer for the militias and the SLA was attributed by the sources to their conclusions that Israel will strike back rigorously if subjected to more attacks.

The examples of Nabatiya and al-Khiyam, whose residents fled because of attacks before the Israeli invasion of 1982, must still be vivid in their minds, the sources said. There were only 4,000 people in Nabatiya when the IDF entered it then, compared with 60,000 now. Al-Khiyam was deserted until the Shi'ite residents were permitted back. It had been sacked by the late South Lebanese militia under the late Major Sa'ad Haddad, who "knew" Israel wanted a *cordon sanitaire* in that area, then called Fatahland, the sources said.

(Continued on Page 2, Col. 7)

Moshe Mandelbaum at yesterday's hearing of the Bejski commission. (Dan Landau)

At Bank Shares Inquiry

Mandelbaum tells of 'master-plan'

By PINHAS LANDAU
Post Finance Reporter

Bank of Israel Governor Dr. Moshe Mandelbaum yesterday revealed how the "master-plan" to change the face of the Israeli economy was formulated in the summer of 1983. This scheme, better known as the dollarization plan of former finance minister Yoram Aridor, was eventually leaked in October 1983, a few days after the bank shares' regulation system collapsed, and brought Aridor's resignation the same day.

Nevertheless, as Mandelbaum made clear in his testimony yesterday to the Bejski Commission, he pinned his hopes of economic recovery on this programme and worked on it through the summer of 1983. It was, he maintained, in the background of all the discussions that took place in those months, as the bank share crisis steadily worsened.

But Justice Moshe Bejski and his fellow-members were unmoved by the story of the master-plan, and forced Mandelbaum back to the reality of those days. Bejski repeatedly asked the governor the same question, in different formulations: "What practical steps did you take to deal with the 'gathering storm'?"

Mandelbaum was the first witness to explain the formulation of the "master-plan," although it may be expected that Aridor and his director-general, Professor Ezra Sadan, will refer to it in their evidence. It was thus the first public recounting of some aspects of the now-infamous dollarization plan that has continued to cause controversy in academic and government circles since its premature publication on October 13, 1983.

"After the crisis in the stock market in January 1983," Mandelbaum told the commission, we analysed the situation that had been created. At that time the "5-5" plan was the centre of economic policy (the Aridor-Plessner policy that envisaged holding the rates of both inflation and devaluation to 5 per cent monthly, introduced in September 1982, P.L.). There was a need to change the whole basis of economic policy. The report of the International Monetary Fund experts who visited them painted a very gloomy

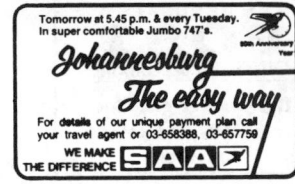

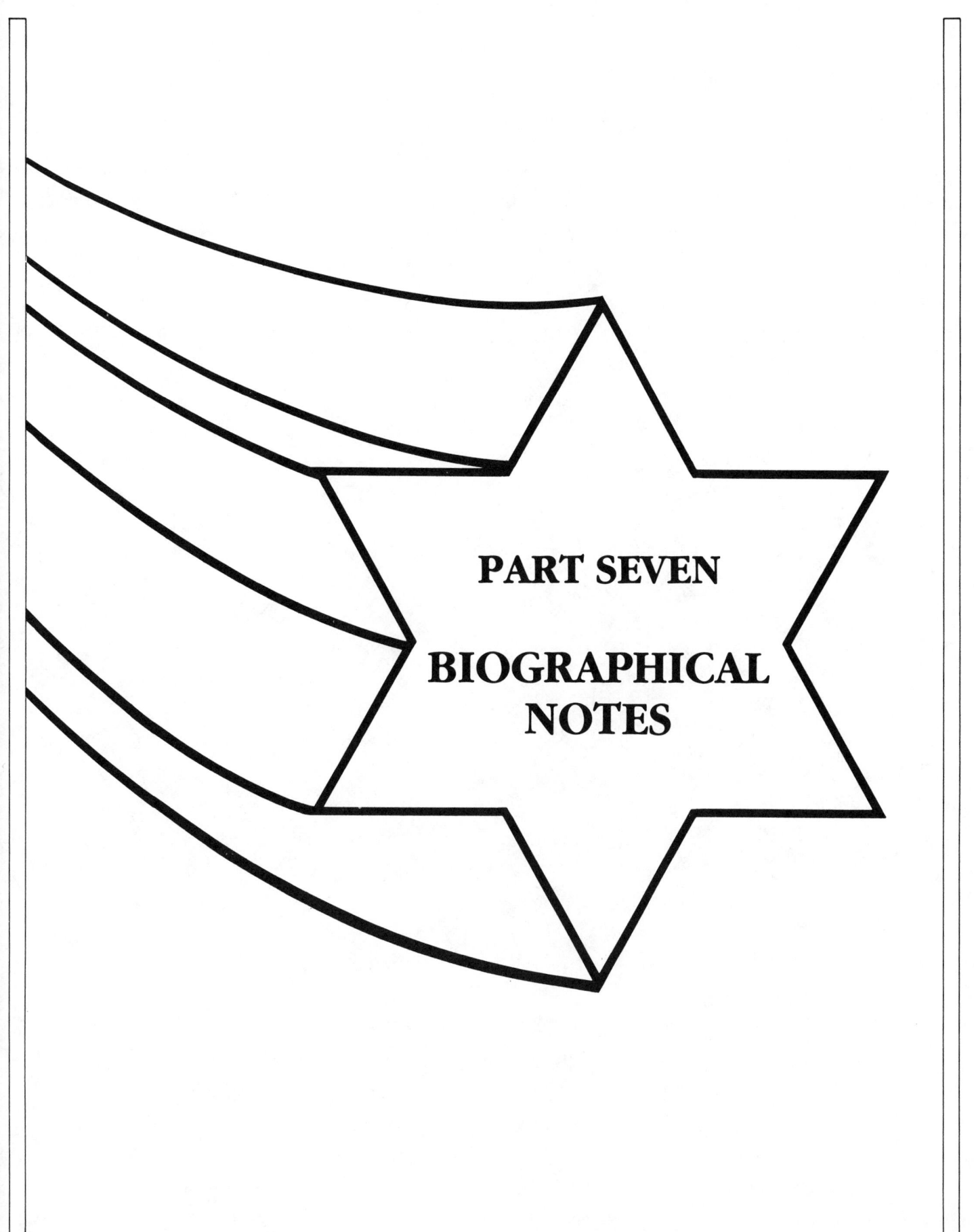

PART SEVEN

BIOGRAPHICAL
NOTES

Current Biography

Academics; Historians; Scholars; Educators

Alter, Robert B.; b. 1935; professor of Hebrew and comparative literature at Berkeley; critic of Judaica and modern Jewish fiction

Baron, Salo W.; b. 1895; professor of Jewish studies at Columbia; prolific scholar of Jewish social history

Boorstin, Daniel J.; b. 1914; historian; educator; author; Librarian of Congress, 1975-present; recipient of 1974 Pulitzer Prize for History

Botstein, Leon; b. 1946; Zurich-born educator, historian, musician; former president of Franconia (New Hampshire) College; president of Bard College, New York

Chomsky, Noam; b. 1928; linguist; political writer; revisionist historian; early opponent of Vietnam War; professor of linguistics at MIT

Elazar, Daniel J.; b. 1934; political scientist; professor at Bar-Ilan University and Temple University; author of *Community and Polity: The Organizational Dynamics of American Jewry*

Chyet, Stanley Franklin; b. 1931; historian; Reform rabbi; editor; professor of American Jewish history at HUC-LA.

Cohen, Arthur A.; b. 1928; novelist; publisher; scholar of fiction, nonfiction, theological, philosophical and spiritual issues.

Cohen, Gerson David; b. 1924; historian; Conservative rabbi; chancellor of the Jewish Theological Seminary of America since 1972

Cohen, Naomi W. (Naomi Weiner); b. 1927; specialist of 20th century American and American Jewish history; professor at Hunter College; author of *Not Free to Desist*

Cremin, Lawrence; b. 1925; educator; historian; president of Teachers College, Columbia University since 1974; winner of 1981 Pulitzer Prize for History

Dawidowicz, Lucy (Lucy Schildkret); b. 1915; historian; author; professor at Yeshiva University; major scholar of the Holocaust era

Edel, Leon (Joseph Leon Edel); b. 1907; biographer of Henry James, James Joyce, Henry David Thoreau and Willa Cather; winner of 1963 Pulitzer Prize for biography

Ehrlich, Paul R.; b. 1932; geologist; biologist; evolutionist; leader in the international crusade for population control; professor of biology at Stanford U.; author of *The Population Bomb* (1968)

Falk, Richard Anderson; b. 1930; professor of international law at Princeton University; questioned legality of U.S. role in Vietnam; spokesman for international human rights

Feingold, Henry L.; b. 1931; German-born historian; authored *Politics of Rescue: The Roosevelt Administration and the Holocaust 1938-1945,* which questioned official efforts to save European Jewry; editor of *American Jewish History* (American Jewish Historical Society)

Finkelstein, Louis; b. 1895; rabbi; former chancellor of Jewish Theological Seminary of America; authored *The Jews: Their History, Culture and Religion*

Friedberg, Maurice; b. 1929; Polish-born professor of Russian literature and Slavic languages at University of Illinois (Urbana-Champaign); expert on role of Jews in Russian literature

Gay, Peter; b. 1923; Berlin-born professor of history at Yale University; expert on the Enlightenment and on pre-war German cultural life

Gershman, Carl; b. 1943; author; lecturer; counselor to the United States representative to the United Nations since 1981

Glatzer, Nahum N.; b. 1903; Austrian-born historian; professor of Judaic studies and religion at Boston University (previously at Brandeis)

Goldman, Eric; b. 1915; historian; professor at Princeton University; former special consultant to President Lyndon Johnson; scholar of 20th century American liberalism and reform

Gordon, Cyrus H.; b. 1908; historian; Semitic scholar and archaeologist; authored *Before Columbus: Links Between the Old World and Ancient America*

Gutman, Herbert; b. 1928; historian; professor at the Graduate School of the City University of New York; specialist in social history and Afro-American history

Halpern, Ben; b. 1912; scholar; activist; Zionist thinker; professor of Near Eastern and Judaic Studies at Brandeis University

Handlin, Oscar; b. 1915; historian; scholar of the emotional and social impact of immigration, especially of Jews in America; professor at Harvard; winner of 1952 Pulitzer Prize for History

Jakobson, Roman; b. 1896; Moscow-born linguist; taught in Czechoslovakia in the 1930's, Scandinavia and Colombia in the 1940's, Harvard from 1949 until retirement; studied culture and language of Jewish communities in Slavic countries.

Katsh, Abraham I.; b. 1908; educator, scholar; pioneered the teaching of Hebrew in American colleges; former president of Dropsie University

Kohl, Herbert; b. 1937; educational reformer; author of *36 Children;* advocate of the "open classroom"

Kozol, Jonathan; b. 1936; educational writer and critic, especially of inner-city school practices

Lachman, Seymour P.; b. 1933; educator; former president of the New York City Board of Education; leading advocate for Soviet Jewry

Lamm, Norman; b. 1927; rabbi; philosopher; prolific writer; president of Yeshiva University; founder of *Tradition* quarterly

Luttwak, Edward; b. 1942; Rumanian-born military scholar and writer; associate of Georgetown University's Center for Strategic and International Studies; wrote *A Dictionary of Modern War, The Israeli Army* (with Dan Horowitz), *Coup d'Etat: A Practical Handbook;* frequent contributor to Commentary

Marcus, Jacob Rader; b. 1896; historian; rabbi; founder and director of the American Jewish Archives in Cincinnati; professor at Hebrew Union College; former president of the Central Conference of American Rabbis

Marcus, Steven; b. 1928; scholar of 19th century English literature; professor at Columbia University

Miller, Israel; b. 1919; rabbi; vice-president of Yeshiva University; former chairman of the Conference of Presidents of Major American Jewish Organizations

Nagel, Ernest; b. 1901; Hungarian-born scholar of philosophy; professor at Columbia University since 1931; known for his application of systematization to knowledge

Neusner, Jacob; b. 1932; scholar of ancient Jewish history; professor at Brown University; prolific author, particularly of Mishnaic law; outspoken advocate of *aliyah*

Nozick, Robert; b. 1938; philosopher; professor at Harvard University; authored *Anarchy, State and Utopia,* in which he argues for limitation of governmental functions and authority

Patai, Raphael; b. 1910; Budapest-born anthropologist; authored *The Jewish Mind;* in *The Myth of the Jewish Race,* he argued that Jews are not a single race, but take on characteristics of their host peoples

Rackman, Emanuel; b. 1910; rabbi; attorney; president of Bar-Ilan University since 1977; former professor of political philosophy and jurisprudence at Yeshiva University

Rivkin, Ellis; b. 1918; historian; scholar of Pharisaic Judaism; professor at Hebrew Union College

Rubenstein, Richard L; b. 1924; theologian; rabbi; leading thinker and writer on the Holocaust; leading designer of Holocaust curricula; professor at Florida State University

Sachar, Abram; b. 1899; historian; first president of Brandeis University; leading architect of the growth of the Hillel Foundation; author of *A History of the Jews* and *The Course of Our Times*

Sarna, Nahum; b. 1923; London-born scholar of Biblical history; professor at Brandeis University; authored *Understanding Genesis;* leading translator of the simplified JPS version of *The Writings*

Schapiro, Meyer; b. 1904; Lithuanian-born art historian; professor emeritus at Columbia University; author of *Romanesque Art; Modern Art*

Schappes, Morris Urman; b. 1907; Ukrainian-born historian and editor; professor of American Jewish history at Queens College; author of *A Documentary History of Jews in the U.S.A.: 1654-1875;* editor of *Jewish Currents*

Schiff, Alvin; b. 1926; educator; executive vice-president of the Board of Jewish Education of Greater New York; author of *The Jewish Day School in America;* editor of quarterly *Jewish Education*

Schrag, Peter; b. 1931; writer; education system critic; author of *Decline of the WASP*

Silverman, Ira; b. 1945; president of the Rabbinical Reconstructionist College

Sovern, Michael I.; b. 1931; president of Columbia University; former professor and dean of the Columbia University School of Law; specialist in civil rights and labor law

Tuchman, Barbara; b. 1912; historian; journalist; won Pulitzer Prizes for *The Guns of August* and *Stilwell and the American Experience in China, 1911-1945*

Urofsky, Melvin; b. 1939; historian; professor at Virginia Commonwealth University; authored *American Zionism from Herzl to the Holocaust; A Voice that Spoke for Justice: The Life and Times of Stephen S. Wise*

Weiss-Rosmarin, Trude; b. 1908; Frankfurt-born scholar; writer; Hebraist; founder and editor of *The Jewish Spectator;* leading Jewish feminist

Zinn, Howard; b. 1922; historian; professor at Boston University; stresses experiences of neglected groups—women, blacks, manual laborers; author of *A People's History of the United States*

Art; Architecture

Amen, Irving; b. 1918; woodcut artist

Baskin, Leonard; b. 1922; anti-abstractionist; sculptor and graphic artist

Glaser, Milton; b. 1929; graphic designer; illustrator

Goodman, Percival; b. 1904; architect; major designer of synagogues and Jewish community centers

Gross, Chaim; b. 1904; sculptor and graphic artist, especially of Judaic and Hasidic themes

Levine, David; b. 1926; caricaturist; painter

Nevelson, Louise (Louise Berliawsky); b. 1899; Kiev-born abstract sculptor; has used her art to make significant political statements

Segal, George; b. 1924; sculptor of neo-realist school

Sendak, Maurice; b. 1928; illustrator; set designer

Steinberg, Saul; b. 1914; Rumanian-born artist, who created *The New Yorker* view of New York and beyond

Commerce and Industry

Annenberg, Walter; b. 1908; communications; Triangle Publications; former ambassador to Great Britain; philanthropist

Bernstein, Robert; b. 1923; publisher; president of Random House; leading human rights activist

Bronfman, Edgar; b. 1929; Montreal-born industrialist; president of Distillers Corporation; president of World Jewish Congress; naturalized American; philanthropist

Davis, Marvin; b. 1925; industrialist; America's most successful independent oil wildcatter; co-owner of 20th Century Fox; philanthropist

Fisher, Max M.; b. 1908; industrialist; former board chairman of United Brands and Aurora Gasoline; the leading Jewish Republican during the Nixon and Ford Administrations; philanthropist; former chairman of the Jewish Agency, and of the Council of Jewish Federations

Goldenson, Leonard; b. 1905; chairman and chief executive officer of ABC

Hammer, Armand; b. 1898; industrialist; art collector; president of Occidental Petroleum; pioneer (since 1921) in Soviet trade

Hess, Leon; b. 1914; industrialist; chairman of Amerada Hess Corporation; principal owner and chairman of the New York Jets football team

Krim, Arthur B.; b. 1910; former president of United Artists, former chairman of Transam Corporation; attorney (Phillips, Nizer, Benjamin, Krim and Ballon); active in Democratic party fund-raising and policy-making

Lefrak, Samuel J.; b. 1918; realtor; developer of middle-class communities in New York; philanthropist

Marcus, Stanley; b. 1905; chairman emeritus of Neiman-Marcus Company

Paley, William; b. 1901; founder and former chairman of CBS, Inc.; trustee of the Federation of Jewish Philanthropies

Pritzker, Jay; b. 1922; industrialist; attorney; leading figure in Chicago-based Pritzker family, owners of Hyatt International Corp.; chairman of the family corporation, the Marmon Group

Sarnoff, Robert W.; b. 1918; chairman of RCA; helped develop use of color broadcasting

Shapiro, Irving S.; b. 1916; attorney; former chairman of E. I. du Pont de Nemours & Company; head of the Business Roundtable

Stern, Leonard; b. 1940; industrialist; head of Hartz Mountain Industries

Straus, Roger; b. 1917; publisher; founder and president of Farrar, Straus and Giroux, Inc.

Sulzberger, Arthur Ochs; b. 1926; publisher of *The New York Times*

Tisch, Laurence A.; b. 1923; financier; chairman of the Loew's Corporation; past president of the United Jewish Appeal of New York

Werblin, David "Sonny"; b. 1910; entertainment and sports entrepreneur; former owner of the New York Jets; developer of the Meadowlands Sports Complex

Winter, Elmer Louis; b. 1912; attorney; co-founder of Manpower, Inc.; former president of the American Jewish Committee

Communal Affairs

Bayer, Abraham J.; b. 1932; community relations and international affairs activist; director, international commission of NJCRAC; former coordinator of American Jewish Conference on Soviet Jewry

Berger, Graenum; b. 1908; communal executive and planner; defender of Ethiopian Jewry; founding president of AAEJ

Berman, Julius; b. 1936; attorney; former president of the Union of Orthodox Jewish Congregations of America; chairman of the Conference of Presidents of Major American Jewish Organizations, 1982-84

Bialkin, Kenneth; b. 1929; attorney; national chairman of the Anti-Defamation League of B'nai B'rith; chairman of the Conference of Presidents of Major American Jewish Organizations, 1984-

Bookbinder, Hyman; b. 1916; Washington director of American Jewish Committee; longtime associate of Hubert H. Humphrey; former official of HUD

Commoner, Barry; b. 1917; biologist; ecologist; educator; 1980 Presidential candidate on Citizens Party ticket

Decter, Midge; b. 1927; writer; editor; leader of neo-conservative movement; a founder of the Committee for the Free World

Evans, Eli N.; b. 1936; president of the Charles H. Revson Foundation; attorney; student of the Jewish experience in the South

Friedan, Betty; b. 1921; feminist leader; authored *The Feminine Mystique* (1963), which helped create the women's movement; former president, National Organization for Women

Glasser, Ira; b. 1937; executive director of ACLU since 1978

Gold, Bertram H.; b. 1916; Canadian-born former executive vice-president of the American Jewish Committee; reversed AJC's policy of non-Zionism and assimilationism

Goodman, Naomi (Naomi Ascher); b. 1920; leading pacifist and feminist historian; president since 1972 of the Jewish Peace Fellowship

Haddad, Heskel; b. 1928; Baghdad-born physician; Sephardic leader; clinical professor of ophthalmology at New York Medical College; founder (1968) and president of the American Committee for the Rescue and Resettlement of Iraqi Jews; president since 1978 of the World Organization of Jews from Arab Countries

Hier, Marvin; b. 1939; rabbi; founder and dean of Yeshiva University of Los Angeles; founder and dean of the Simon Wiesenthal Center; leading spokesman for Holocaust and genocide-related issues

Hoenlein, Malcolm; b. 1944; executive director, Jewish Community Relations Council of New York, was founding executive director of the Greater New York Conference on Soviet Jewry; served as Middle East Specialist at the Foreign Policy Research Institute; special advisor, United States Holocaust Memorial Council

Jacobson, Charlotte; b. 1914; Zionist leader; president of the Jewish National Fund; former president of the World Zionist Organization; former president of Hadassah; critic of those (especially HIAS) who aid Soviet Jewish emigres who refuse to move to Israel

Kahane, Meir; b. 1932; rabbi; founder and leader of the militant Jewish Defense League; holds degrees in law and international relations from New York University; critic of the Jewish establishment; founder of Israeli Kach party in 1976; member of Knesset

Klutznick, Philip M.; b. 1907; businessman; former secretary of commerce under Jimmy Carter; former president of the World Jewish Congress

Korey, William; b. 1922; scholar; director of policy research for the B'nai B'rith International Council; leading expert on Soviet Jewry and related human rights issues; prolific journalist; authored *The Soviet Cage: Anti-Semitism in Russia*

Levine, Irving M.; b. 1929; communal executive; founder of the Institute of Pluralism and Group Identity of the American Jewish Committee; urban affairs specialist

Levine, Naomi (Naomi Bronheim); b. 1923; attorney; former executive director of the American Jewish Congress; currently vice-president for external affairs at New York University

Lowell, Stanley H. (Stanley H. Lowenbraun); b. 1919; attorney; a founder of the New York City Commission on Human Rights; former chairman of the National Conference on Soviet Jewry

Neier, Aryeh; b. 1937; Berlin-born civil libertarian; former executive director of the NYCLU and ACLU; defended right of American Nazi Party to march in Skokie, Illinois in 1978; later wrote *Defending My Enemy* regarding that experience

Novick, Ivan J.; b. 1927; former president of the Zionist Organization of America; leading advocate of defense buildup by the United States

Perlmutter, Nathan; b. 1923; national director of the Anti-Defamation League of B'nai B'rith; has guided ADL back into advocacy of Jewish concerns; has made extensive efforts to improve Catholic-Jewish relations

Pollack, Allen; b. 1938; leading Labor Zionist; former professor of Russian history at Yeshiva University; former president of the Labor Zionist Alliance; helped create American Professors for Peace in the Middle East

Regenstein, Lewis; b. 1943; conservationist; heads the Fund for Animals; lobbied for the Marine Mammal Act and the Endangered Species Act; helped save the bowhead whale from extinction

Rudin, A. James; b. 1934; rabbi; national director for interreligious affairs at the American Jewish Committee; expert on effect of cults on Jewish youth

Schindler, Alexander M.; b. 1925; rabbi; president of the Union of American Hebrew Congregations; former chairman of the Conference of Presidents of Major American Jewish Organizations

Sherer, Morris; b. 1921; rabbi; president of Agudath Israel of America; first Jewish leader to support federal aid to parochial schools

Squadron, Howard; b. 1926; attorney; former president of the American Jewish Congress; former chairman of the Conference of Presidents of Major American Jewish Organizations

Taub, Henry; b. 1927; co-founder of Automatic Data Processing; former president of the American Jewish Joint Distribution Committee

Vorspan, Albert; b. 1924; writer; vice-president of the Union of American Hebrew Congregations

Wishner, Maynard I.; b. 1923; attorney; former president of the American Jewish Committee

Economics

Arrow, Kenneth J.; b. 1921; economist; professor at Stanford University; equilibrium and welfare theorist; winner of 1972 Nobel Prize

Bergson, Abram; b. 1914; economist; professor at Columbia and Harvard; expert on the Soviet economy

Burns, Arthur (Arthur Frank Burnseig); b. 1904; Austrian-born chairman of the Federal Reserve Board, 1970-78; his policies later became famous as "Reaganomics"

Cherne, Leo M.; b. 1912; management specialist; attorney; sculptor

Drucker, Peter; b. 1909; Vienna-born management consultant; former professor of political science and philosophy

Friedman, Milton; b. 1912; economist; proponent of free enterprise; opponent of state intervention in business and trade; winner of Nobel Prize, 1976

Ginzberg, Eli; b. 1911; economist; professor of economics at Columbia; manpower advisor to seven U.S. presidents

Goldman, Marshall; b. 1930; economist; professor at Wellesley College; expert in Russian studies as well as the economics of pollution

Greenspan, Alan; b. 1926; economist; confidant of Presidents Nixon, Ford and Reagan; supporter of fiscal restraint and a balanced budget; chairman of the Council of Economic Advisors, 1974-77

Heilbroner, Robert; b. 1919; economist; best-selling author of economics texts; professor of economics at the New School for Social Research in New York

Klein, Lawrence R.; b. 1920; economist; developer of econometrics; 1980 Nobel Prize winner

Kuznets, Simon S.; b. 1901; Russian-born economist; theorist of the gross national product; professor emeritus at Harvard University; 1971 Nobel Prize winner

Lekachman, Robert; b. 1920; economist; professor at Lehman College and at the Graduate Center of the City University of New York; prolific writer, especially regarding the social aspects of economics

Samuelson, Paul; b. 1915; economist; leading Keynesian theorist; consultant to the Rand Corporation and the Eisenhower, Kennedy and Johnson Administrations; professor at MIT; author of the all-time best-selling economics textbook; winner of 1970 Nobel Prize

Silk, Leonard; b. 1918; economics editor for *The New York Times;* author of *The American Establishment*

Stein, Herbert; b. 1916; economist; leading policy maker in the Nixon Administration as chairman of the Council of Economic Advisers; professor at the University of Virginia

Weidenbaum, Murray; b. 1927; economist; chief economic advisor to President Reagan; professor at Washington University in St. Louis; specialist on government regulation

Williams, Harold; b. 1928; managerial specialist; former head of the Securities and Exchange Commission; former dean of the Graduate School of Business and Management at UCLA; former attorney and executive with Hunt-Wesson Inc. and Norton Simon Inc.; president of the J. Paul Getty Museum

Journalism and Media

Abel, Elie; b. 1920; professor of journalism at Stanford University; former dean, Columbia School of Journalism; former NBC correspondent

Agronsky, Martin; b. 1915; PBS commentator

Alexander, Shana (Shana Ager); b. 1925; formerly commentator for *60 Minutes, Newsweek*

Bernstein, Carl; b. 1944; ABC news commentator; formerly reporter for the *Washington Post;* broke Watergate story; winner 1973 Pulitzer Prize

Block, Herbert L. (Herblock); b. 1909; editorial cartoonist for the *Washington Post;* three-time Pulitzer Prize winner

Broder, David; b. 1929; columnist for the *Washington Post;* winner of 1973 Pulitzer Prize

Buchwald, Art; b. 1925; nationally syndicated social and political satirist; winner of 1982 Pulitzer Prize

Cosell, Howard (William Howard Cohen); b. 1920; ABC radio and television sportscaster

Cowan, Paul; b. 1940; journalist and author; former staff writer for the *Village Voice;* authored *An Orphan in History;* active in Havurah movement in New York

Drew, Elizabeth; b. 1935; writer and television commentator; analyst of the human element within the national political scene

Epstein, Jason; b. 1928; editor and publisher; co-founder of *The New York Review of Books;* vice-president of Random House; supporter of individual rights in America and abroad

Feiffer, Jules; b. 1929; political cartoonist; playwright; *Village Voice* regular; authored *Little Murders* and *Carnal Knowledge*

Fein, Leonard; b. 1934; writer; political activist; editor and founder of *Moment;* critic of Menachem Begin's government; Reform theorist and planner

Frankel, Max; b. 1930; German-born *New York Times* editorial page editor; promoted 1971 publication of the Pentagon Papers

Friendly, Fred (Frederick Wachenheim); b. 1915; former executive producer of CBS, president of CBS News; professor of journalism at Columbia University; proponent of honesty and ethics in broadcast journalism

Gelb, Arthur; b. 1924; deputy managing editor of *The New York Times*

Goodman, Ellen (Ellen Holtz); b. 1941; syndicated (over 700 newspapers) columnist (*At Large*); 1980 Pulitzer Prize winner

Goodman, Walter; b. 1927; former *New York Times* editor; directed humanities programming for public television (WNET in New York City); authored *The Committee,* a study of HUAC

Grunwald, Henry Anatole; b. 1922; Vienna-born editor-in-chief of Time Inc.

Halberstam, David; b. 1934; journalist; author; former *New York Times* reporter; authored *The Best and the Brightest* and *The Powers That Be;* 1964 Pulitzer Prize winner

Hechinger, Fred Michael; b. 1920; president of The New York Times Company Foundation; former education editor of *The New York Times*

Hentoff, Nat; b. 1925; journalist; commentator; jazz expert; *Village Voice* columnist since 1957, especially focusing on civil liberties issues

Hersh, Seymour; b. 1937; Pulitzer Prize-winning journalist who broke the My Lai massacre story; also noted for reportage regarding Henry Kissinger, secret B-52 bombings in Cambodia and domestic spying operations of the C.I.A.

Himmelfarb, Milton; b. 1918; researcher; director of information for the American Jewish Committee; editor of the American Jewish Yearbook; advocate of traditional Jewish values, conservatism, preservation of Jewish population

Isaac, Rael Jean (Isaacs); b. 1933; journalist and writer; leading factor in disintegration of Breira movement; fierce defender of conservative Israeli policies

Kael, Pauline; b. 1919; film critic for *The New Yorker* magazine

Kalb, Bernard; b. 1922; news correspondent; author; State Department correspondent for NBC; co-author of *Kissinger* with brother Marvin; since 1984, Assistant Secretary of State for Public Affairs

Kalb, Marvin; b. 1930; television journalist; chief diplomatic correspondent for NBC News; author; leading chronicler of events in Eastern Europe; leading reporter of events of Iranian revolution

Kauffman, Stanley Jules; b. 1916; theater and film critic

Kraft, Joseph; b. 1924; widely syndicated columnist; writer for the *Washington Post;* specialist on foreign affairs and on the executive branch of American government

Lerner, Max; b. 1902; Minsk-born journalist; long-time *New York Post* columnist

Lewis, Anthony; b. 1927; editorial columnist for *The New York Times;* winner of 1955 Pulitzer Prize for articles on a McCarthy era victim; severe critic of Menachem Begin's government

Lewis, Flora; b. 1920; journalist; editorial columnist for *The New York Times*

Lukas, J. Anthony; b. 1933; journalist; won 1968 Pulitzer Prize for coverage of the trials of the Chicago Seven; former *New York Times* reporter; professor of journalism at the Kennedy School of Government at Harvard

Mankiewicz, Frank; b. 1924; journalist; attorney; president of National Public Radio; former press secretary to Robert F. Kennedy; leading critic of television programming

Mitgang, Herbert; b. 1920; journalist; cultural correspondent for *The New York Times;* biographer of Abraham Lincoln; playwright (*Mr. Lincoln,* 1980)

Navasky, Victor; b. 1932; journalist; editor of *The Nation;* leading liberal and advocate of freedom of expression in America; author of *Naming Names,* a study of the 1947 HUAC investigation

Newfield, Jack; b. 1939; investigative reporter for the *Village Voice,* with focus on New York City corruption

Newman, Edwin; b. 1919; television commentator for NBC; author of two books on language art, *Strictly Speaking* and *A Civil Tongue*

Peretz, Martin; b. 1939; editor and publisher of *The New Republic,* lecturer in political science at Harvard University; active spokesman for liberal causes and Israel

Podhoretz, Norman; b. 1930; editor of *Commentary* since 1960; leading neo-conservative voice; authored *The Present Danger, Why We Were In Vietnam*

Pogrebin, Letty Cottin; b. 1939; founding editor of *Ms.* magazine; *Ladies Home Journal* columnist

Polner, Murray; b. 1928; journalist; editor of *Present Tense;* prolific writer; author of *Branch Rickey: A Biography, Rabbi: The American Experience,* editor of *American Jewish Biographies*

Porter, Sylvia (Sylvia Feldman); b. 1913; syndicated financial columnist

Raskin, A. H. (Abraham Henry Raskin); b. 1911; long-time labor correspondent and editor for *The New York Times*

Rosenthal, A. M. (Abraham Michael Rosenthal); b. 1922; executive editor of *The New York Times;* responsible for publication of the Pentagon Papers; winner of Pulitzer Prize in 1960

Safire, William; b. 1929; columnist; formerly speechwriter for President Nixon and Vice-President Agnew; leading conservative voice at *The New York Times;* humorous analyst of spoken English; won Pulitzer Prize in 1978 for his probe into the financial affairs of Bert Lance

Schanberg, Sydney; b. 1934; journalist; winner of 1976 Pulitzer Prize for his reportage of Cambodian atrocities for *The New York Times;* currently op-ed page columnist for the *The New York Times*

Schoenbrun, David; b. 1915; television correspondent

Schorr, Daniel; b. 1916; journalist; known for Watergate and CIA investigation coverage in the 1970's

Shapiro, Harvey; b. 1924; poet; editor of *The New York Times Book Review*

Shawn, William (William Chon); b. 1907; editor-in-chief of *The New Yorker*

Silvers, Robert B.; b. 1929; editor and founder of *The New York Review of Books*

Stone, I. F. (Isidor Feinstein); b. 1907; prototypical investigative journalist; publisher of *I. F. Stone's Weekly,* which attacked Defense Department corruption and waste

Syrkin, Marie; b. 1899; Swiss-born journalist and writer; leading Labor Zionist; former editor of the *Jewish Frontier;* former professor of humanities at Brandeis University

Szulc, Tad; b. 1926; Warsaw-born journalist; specialist in Latin American affairs and known for coverage of Czechoslovakia in 1968; former foreign affairs reporter for *The New York Times*

Wallace, Mike (Myron Leon Wallace); b. 1918; television journalist; host of *60 Minutes;* formerly narrator of *Biography*

Walters, Barbara; b. 1931; television journalist

Wattenberg, Ben; b. 1933; editor; author; former aide to Lyndon Johnson; former Democratic party official

Weber, Simon; b. 1911; Polish-born editor-in-chief of the *Jewish Daily Forward*

White, Theodore H.; b. 1915; journalist; author of *The Making of the President 1960* and its sequels of 1964, 1968 and 1972, and other political histories; winner of 1962 Pulitzer Prize

Labor

Chaikin, Sol "Chick"; b. 1918; attorney; president of ILGWU; member of Trilateral Commission and the Council on Foreign Relations

Finley, Murray Howard; b. 1922; attorney; president of the Amalgamated Clothing and Textile Workers Union of America; leading labor organizer in the Sunbelt

Gotbaum, Victor; b. 1921; leader of New York City's District Council 37, the largest union of public employees; liberal, reformer; powerful influence in municipal government

Kheel, Theodore; b. 1914; mediator; attorney; helped settle New York newspaper strike (1962-63), transit strike (1966), sanitation strike (1968), etc.

Miller, Marvin; b. 1917; executive director of the Major League Baseball Players Association; spearheaded the 1972 and 1981 baseball players strikes

Shanker, Albert; b. 1928; president of the American Federation of Teachers; AFL-CIO vice president; leader of the 1968 teachers strike against the Ocean Hill-Brownsville Governing Board in Brooklyn

Tyler, Gus (Gus Tilve); b. 1911; ILGWU official; writer on labor history

Law

Abram, Morris B.; b. 1918; attorney; former American Jewish Committee president; chairman, National Conference on Soviet Jewry

Amsterdam, Anthony G.; b. 1935; professor (N.Y.U.) of constitutional law

Bazelon, David; b. 1909; judge, U.S. Court of Appeals, District of Columbia Circuit; pioneer of insanity defense (*Durham Rule*)

Dershowitz, Alan M.; b. 1938; attorney; civil libertarian; Harvard Law School professor; author

Dorsen, Norman; b. 1930; attorney; civil libertarian; author; past general counsel, chairperson of the ACLU

Freedman, Monroe H.; b. 1928; attorney; former dean, Hofstra University School of Law; former director of the United States Holocaust Memorial Council

Garment, Leonard; b. 1924; attorney; special counsel to President Nixon, 1969-1974; prepared defense of Watergate

Ginsburg, Ruth Bader; b. 1933; judge, U.S. Court of Appeals, District of Columbia Circuit; professor at Columbia University Law School; specialist in constitutional law, civil procedure, sex discrimination

Goldberg, Arthur J.; b. 1908; attorney; former Secretary of Labor, Supreme Court Justice, U.S. representative to the United Nations

Hauser, Rita E. (Abrams); b. 1934; international lawyer; former U.S. representative to the United Nations

Kampelman, Max; b. 1920; attorney; chairman of the U.S. delegation to the Conference on Security and Cooperation in Europe (Madrid 1980, 1982); former protege of Hubert Humphrey; leading advocate for Soviet Jewry; chief U.S. negotiator, arms control talks, Geneva, 1985

Kaufman, Irving; b. 1910; judge, U.S. Court of Appeals, Second Circuit; chiefly known for presiding over the controversial 1951 Rosenberg spy case

Kunstler, William; b. 1919; attorney; defender of civil liberties and civil rights cases; defender of the Chicago Seven, Rev. Philip Berrigan, the Black Panthers, etc.

Levi, Edward H.; b. 1911; scholar; U.S. attorney general, 1975-77 under Gerald Ford; president of the University of Chicago 1968-75; integrated social sciences into curriculum while dean at University of Chicago Law School

Lewin, Nathan; b. 1936; Washington, D.C.-based constitutional lawyer, particularly regarding rights of Orthodox Jews

Nizer, Louis; b. 1902; London-born attorney; leading trial counsel; general counsel for the Motion Picture Association of America; author of *My Life in Court, What To Do With Germany* (1944) and *The Implosion Conspiracy*, in which he argued the guilt of Ethel and Julius Rosenberg

Pfeffer, Leo; b. 1910; Hungarian-born attorney; leading supporter of the separation of church and state; authored *Church, State and Freedom*; professor of constitutional law at Long Island University

Pilpel, Harriet (Harriet Fleishl); b. 1911; attorney; civil libertarian; general counsel for Planned Parenthood and the ACLU; successfully litigated *New York Times v. Sullivan,* in which the scope of protection for the press against libel suits was significantly enlarged

Rapps, Dennis; b. 1942; attorney; executive director, National Jewish Commission on Law and Public Affairs (COLPA); leading advocate for the protection of civil rights for practicing Jews

Rauh, Joseph L., Jr.; b. 1911; attorney; helped move Democratic party into field of civil rights in 1948; defended many 1950's loyalty and HUAC-related cases; early opponent of U.S. policy regarding Vietnam; defended University of California in Bakke case (1978)

Rifkind, Simon H.; b. 1901; Russian-born attorney and former federal judge; leading civil libertarian and devotee to Jewish causes

Shestak, Jerome; b. 1925; attorney; helped found Legal Services Corporation; founder of the Lawyers Committee for International Human Rights

Literature

Bellow, Saul (Solomon Bellows); b. 1915; novelist; Nobel laureate, 1976; *Mr. Sammler's Planet, Humboldt's Gift, To Jerusalem and Back* and others

Caras, Roger; b. 1928; naturalist; author of books on wildlife, conservation and humane treatment of animals

Charyn, Jerome; b. 1937; novelist; educator

Colwin, Laurie; b. 1944; short story writer and novelist

Doctorow, E.L. (Edgar Lawrence Doctorow); b. 1931; novelist; editor; *The Book of Daniel, Ragtime,* etc.

Elkin, Stanley; b. 1930; novelist and short-story writer, particularly of Jewish-American black humor

Fast, Howard; b. 1914; widely-translated writer, formerly blacklisted following non-compliance with HUAC; authored *Spartacus, The Jews, The Immigrants* and several novels of the American Revolutionary period

Frank, Gerold; b. 1907; biographer of Dr. Martin Luther King, Jr., Sheila Graham, Lillian Roth, etc.; authored *The Deed* (1963), which examined Jewish terrorist groups in Palestine

Ginsberg, Allen; b. 1926; poet; 1960's activist; best known for *Howl* and *Kaddish*

Gold, Herbert; b. 1924; novelist; essayist; visiting professor at various universities; themes include racial discrimination, violence, alienation

Gottlieb, Robert; b. 1931; publisher; editor; president of Alfred A. Knopf, Inc.; responsible for developing works of Joseph Heller, John Updike, Chaim Potok and others

Green, Gerald; b. 1922; writer; novelist; author of *The Last Angry Man* and the screenplay of *Holocaust.*

Greenberg, Joanne; b. 1932; novelist; author of *I Never Promised You a Rose Garden, A Season of Delight*

Harris, Mark (Mark Finkelstein); b. 1922; prolific author; *Bang The Drum Slowly, The Goy,* as well as theater, television and films

Heller, Joseph; b. 1923; novelist; *Catch-22, Something Happened, Good As Gold, God Knows*

Hellman, Lillian; b. 1907; playwright; author of *The Children's Hour, The Little Foxes, Toys in the Attic;* outspoken anti-Fascist, opponent of HUAC

Howe, Irving; b. 1920; editor; critic; author of *World of Our Fathers, How We Lived, We Lived There Too,* and editor (with Yiddish poet Eliezer Greenberg) of a series of translated Yiddish works; professor of English at the Graduate Center of the City University of New York

Jong, Erica (Erica Mann); b. 1942; novelist; poet; author of *Fear of Flying, How to Save Your Own Life*

Kahn, Roger; b. 1927; sportswriter; author of *The Boys of Summer*

Kaplan, Justin; b. 1925; biographer; won 1966 Pulitzer Prize for *Mr. Clemens and Mark Twain*

Kazin, Alfred; b. 1915; literary critic; literary historian; professor of English at Hunter College and the Graduate Center of the City University of New York; authored *New York Jew* and other memoirs

Koch, Kenneth; b. 1925; poet; playwright; professor of English at Columbia; has taught poetry to nursing home residents as well as to children

Kosinski, Jerzy Nikodem; b. 1933; Polish-born author of *The Painted Bird, Being There* and other novels; has taught English at Princeton and Yale

Kotlowitz, Robert; b. 1924; author of *Somewhere Else* and *The Boardwalk;* programming executive in public television

Kumin, Maxine (Maxine Winokur); b. 1925; Pulitzer Prize-winning poet and writer

Kunitz, Stanley; b. 1905; Pulitzer Prize-winning poet; professor of English at numerous universities

Lash, Joseph P.; b. 1909; biographer of Helen Keller, Eleanor Roosevelt and Dag Hammarskjold; former editorial page writer for *The New York Post;* Pulitzer Prize winner

Levin, Ira; b. 1929; author of *Rosemary's Baby, The Boys from Brazil;* playwright, *No Time for Sergeants, Critics Choice, Deathtrap*

Levine, Philip; b. 1928; poet; professor at California State University (Fresno)

Lurie, Alison; b. 1926; novelist; authored *The War Between the Tates; The Language of Clothes,* and others; professor of English at Cornell University

Mailer, Norman; b. 1923; novelist; essayist; helped found the *Village Voice;* writings include *The Naked and the Dead, Barbary Shore, Miami and the Siege of Chicago; The Executioner's Song;* a leader of the anti-Vietnam War movement; winner of 1969 Pulitzer Prize

Malamud, Bernard; b. 1914; novelist; writings include *The Assistant, The Magic Barrel, The Fixer* (Pulitzer Prize); teaches at Bennington College part-time; advocate of literary freedom in the Soviet Union and South Africa

Mamet, David; b. 1947; playwright; created *American Buffalo* and *The Water Engine*

Michaels, Leonard; b. 1933; novelist; authored *The Men's Club;* professor of English at Berkeley

Miller, Arthur; b. 1915; playwright; won Pulitzer Prize for *Death of a Salesman,* 1949; also *The Crucible, A View From the Bridge, After the Fall, Playing for Time*

Nemerov, Howard; b. 1920; Pulitzer Prize-winning poet (*Collected Poems,* 1977); professor of English at Washington University

Nissenson, Hugh; b. 1933; author of short stories and a novel, *My Own Ground,* on the Jewish condition

Olsen, Tillie (Tillie Lerner); b. 1913; authored *Tell Me a Riddle;* focuses on problems of working people and on women trying to cope with their pre-determined roles

Ozick, Cynthia; b. 1928; novelist; authored *The Pagan Rabbi, The Cannibal Galaxy*

Paley, Grace; b. 1922; author of short stories; peace activist

Potok, Chaim; b. 1929; novelist of Hasidic life; authored *The Chosen, The Promise, My Name Is Asher Lev, Wandering—Chaim Potok's History of the Jews;* special projects editor for the Jewish Publication Society

Rosenthal, M.L. (Macha Louis Rosenthal); b. 1917; poet; critic; professor of English at New York University

Rosten, Leo; b. 1908; Polish-born author of *The Education of H*Y*M*A*N K*A*P*L*A*N, The Joys of Yiddish, Captain Newman, M.D.*

Roth, Philip; b. 1933; novelist; author of *Goodbye, Columbus, Portnoy's Complaint, Our Gang, Zuckerman Unbound, Zuckerman Bound* and others

Schulberg, Budd; b. 1914; screenwriter; novelist; author of *What Makes Sammy Run?, On the Waterfront, The Harder They Fall*

Shaw, Irwin; b. 1913; novelist; playwright; author of *The Young Lions, Rich Man, Poor Man, Beggarman, Thief* and others

Singer, Isaac Bashevis; b. 1904; Polish-born writer; author of *In My Father's House, Crown of Feathers, Gimpel the Fool* and others; winner of 1978 Nobel Prize for Literature

Sontag, Susan; b. 1933; writer; critic; essayist; author of *Against Interpretation;* early opponent of the Vietnam War

Stone, Irving (Irving Tennenbaum); b. 1903; biographical novelist; author of *Lust for Life, The Agony and the Ecstasy, The Origin* and others

Uris, Leon; b. 1924; novelist; author of *Exodus, Battle Cry, Mila 18, QB VII* and others

Wiesel, Elie; b. 1928; Transylvanian-born writer and philosopher of the Holocaust as well as Hasidic and Kabbalistic themes; titles include *Night, Dawn,* and most recently *The Fifth Son;* chairman of the United States Holocaust Memorial Council

Wouk, Herman; b. 1915; writer; won Pulitzer Prize in 1952 for *The Caine Mutiny;* also—the *Winds of War, War and Remembrance, This Is My God* and in 1985, *Inside, Outside*

Performing Arts

Allen, Woody (Allen Konigsberg); b. 1935; actor; director; writer

Alpert, Herb; b. 1935; composer

Arkin, Alan; b. 1934; actor; director; writer

Asner, Ed; b. 1929; actor

Bacall, Lauren (Betty Joan Perske); b. 1924; actress

Bacharach, Burt; b. 1929; composer; pianist

Bakshi, Ralph; b. 1938; Palestinian-born film animator; director

Berle, Milton (Milton Berlinger); b. 1908; comedian; actor

Bernstein, Leonard; b. 1918; conductor; composer; pianist

Bikel, Theodore; b. 1924; Vienna-born actor; folk singer

Borge, Victor (Borge Rosenbaum); b. 1909; Danish-born entertainer

Brooks, Mel (Melvyn Kaminsky); b. 1926; comedian; actor; film director

Burns, George (Nathan Birnbaum); b. 1896; comedian; actor

Caan, James; b. 1940; actor

Cahn, Sammy; b. 1913; lyricist

Clayburgh, Jill; b. 1944; actress

Cohen, Alexander; b. 1920; theatrical producer

Comden, Betty; b. 1919; actress; songwriter

Copland, Aaron; b. 1900; composer; conductor; critic; performer

Cosell, Howard (William Howard Cohen); b. 1920; sportscaster

Diamond, Neil; b. 1941; singer; songwriter

Douglas, Kirk (Issur Danielovitch); b. 1918; actor; producer

Dreyfuss, Richard; b. 1947; actor

Feld, Eliot; b. 1942; dancer; choreographer (ballet)

Friedkin, William; b. 1939; film director

Garfunkel, Art; b. 1941; singer; actor

Goodman, Benny; b. 1909; clarinetist; band leader

Gould, Elliot; b. 1938; actor

Green, Adolph; b. 1915; lyricist

Greene, Lorne; b. 1915; actor

Grey, Joel; b. 1932; actor; singer; dancer

Hamlisch, Marvin; b. 1944; composer

Heifetz, Jascha; b. 1901; Vilna-born violinist

Hodes, Art; b. 1904; Russian-born blues pianist

Hoffman, Dustin; b. 1937; actor

Horowitz, Vladimir; b. 1904; pianist

Kaye, Danny (Daniel David Kominski); b. 1913; entertainer

Kidd, Michael (Michael Greenwald); b. 1917; choreographer

King, Alan (Irwin Alan Kniberg); b. 1927; comedian

King, Carole (Carole Klein); b. 1941; singer; songwriter

Kramer, Stanley; b. 1913; film producer

Kubrick, Stanley; b. 1928; film director

Lear, Norman; b. 1922; producer; writer; director

Leinsdorf, Erich; b. 1912; conductor

Lerner, Alan Jay; b. 1918; lyricist

Levine, James; b. 1943; conductor

Lewis, Jerry (Joseph Levich); b. 1926; comedian; actor; director

Manilow, Barry; b. 1946; singer; composer

Mann, Herbie (Herbert Solomon); b. 1930; jazz flutist

Matthau, Walter; b. 1920; actor

May, Elaine (Elaine Berlin); b. 1932; actress; playwright; director

Mazursky, Paul (Irwin Mazursky); b. 1930; director; screenwriter

Menuhin, Yehudi; b. 1916; violinist

Merrick, David (David Margulies); b. 1912; theatrical producer

Merrill, Robert (Moishe Miller); b. 1919; opera singer

Milstein, Nathan; b. 1904; Odessa-born violinist

Nichols, Mike (Michael Igor Peshkowsky); b. 1931; Berlin-born director and producer

Papp, Joseph (Joseph Papirofsky); b. 1921; theatrical producer and director

Penn, Arthur; b. 1922; director

Perahia, Murray; b. 1947; pianist; conductor

Perlman, Itzhak; b. 1945; violinist

Peters, Roberta (Roberta Peterman); b. 1930; opera singer

Picon, Molly; b. 1898; actress

Polonsky, Abraham; b. 1910; film director; screenwriter

Prince, Harold; b. 1928; producer; director

Randall, Tony (Leonard Rosenberg); b. 1920; actor

Raskin, Judith; b. 1928; opera singer

Reiner, Carl; b. 1922; actor; writer; producer; director

Ritt, Martin; b. 1920; film director; producer

Robbins, Jerome (Jerome Rabinowitz); b. 1918; choreographer

Sahl, Mort; b. 1927; satirist

Schneider, Alexander; b. 1908; Vilna-born violinist; conductor

Segal, George; b. 1934; actor

Sills, Beverly (Belle Silverman); b. 1929; opera singer; opera company director

Silver, Joan Micklin; b. 1935; director; producer

Simon, Paul; b. 1941; songwriter; singer

Sondheim, Stephen; b. 1930; composer

Spielberg, Steven; b. 1947; film director; producer

Stern, Isaac; b. 1920; Russian-born violinist

Streisand, Barbra; b. 1942; singer; actress

Susskind, David; b. 1920; producer

Tureck, Rosalyn; b. 1914; pianist; symphony director

Wallach, Eli; b. 1915; actor

Wilder, Gene (Jerome Silberman); b. 1935; actor; director; producer; scriptwriter

Winkler, Henry; b. 1945; actor

Winters, Shelly (Shirley Schrift); b. 1923; actress

Wolper, David; b. 1928; film producer

Zukerman, Eugenia; b. 1944; flutist

Zukerman, Pinchas; b. 1948; Tel-Aviv born violinist

Photography

Avedon, Richard; b. 1923; preeminent fashion photographer

Capa, Cornell (Cornell Friedmann); b. 1918; photojournalist; creator of "Concerned Photography"

Newman, Arnold; b. 1918; official photographer to several U.S. presidents; specialist of environmental portraiture

Penn, Irving; b. 1917; leading portraitist

Vishniac, Roman; b. 1897; Russian-born photographer; photomicrographer; scientist; author of *A Vanished World,* 180 photographs of pre-war Polish Jewry

Politics and Government

Abrams, Elliot; b. 1948; attorney; head of State Department's Latin American bureau; formerly Assistant Secretary of State for Human Rights and Humanitarian Affairs

Abzug, Bella (Bella Savitzky); b. 1920; attorney; Congresswoman from New York, 1970-76

Boschwitz, Rudy; b. 1930; Berlin-born businessman (retail lumber); Republican U.S. Senator from Minnesota, 1978-present

Eizenstat, Stuart E.; b. 1943; attorney; presidential adviser for domestic affairs during the Carter Administration

Feinstein, Dianne; b. 1933; mayor of San Francisco, 1978-present

Garth, David (David Goldberg); b. 1930; media consultant for politicians; foreign clients include Menachem Begin

Harris, Louis; b. 1921; pollster

Hecht, Chic; b. 1928; Republican U.S. Senator from Nevada, 1983-present

Hoffman, Abbie (Abbott); b. 1936; political activist; writer; 1960's civil rights and anti-war movement figure; founder of the Youth International Party, the Yippies

Holtzman, Elizabeth; b. 1941; attorney; former U.S. Congresswoman from Brooklyn; currently Kings County District Attorney (Brooklyn)

Javits, Jacob; b. 1904; attorney; politician; leading liberal Republican in U.S. Senate (1956-1980); activist in civil rights and social issues; staunch defender of Israel

Kissinger, Henry (Heinz Alfred Kissinger); b. 1923; Bavarian-born former U.S. Secretary of State; 1973 Nobel Prize winner (with North Vietnamese negotiator Le Duc Tho); currently heads U.S. Commission on Central America

Koch, Edward I.; b. 1924; attorney; mayor of New York City, 1978-present; former congressman

Lautenberg, Frank; b. 1924; businessman, Democratic U.S. Senator from New Jersey, 1982-present; founder and former chairman of Automatic Data Processing; former chairman of the United Jewish Appeal

Levin, Carl; b. 1934; attorney; Democratic U.S. Senator from Michigan, 1978-present; leading human rights activist

Linowitz, Sol M.; b. 1913; attorney; roving ambassador; former chairman of Xerox Corporation; former U.S. representative to the Organization of American States; President Carter's representative on Middle East negotiations, 1979-1981; leading communal leader

Metzenbaum, Howard; b. 1917; businessman; attorney; Democratic U.S. Senator from Ohio, 1976-present

Minow, Newton; b. 1926; attorney; former chairman of the Federal Communications Commission; media critic

Myerson, Bess; b. 1924; consumer consultant; political aspirant; television personality; former New York City Commissioner of Consumer Affairs

Ottinger, Richard; b. 1929; attorney; Congressman from New York, 1965-1971, 1975-1984; leading advocate of liberal and Jewish causes

Ravitch, Richard; b. 1933; businessman; attorney; former chairman of the Metropolitan Transportation Authority (MTA) of New York

Ribicoff, Abraham A.; b. 1910; attorney; former congressman, governor and senator from Connecticut; former Secretary of HEW; leading liberal; staunch defender of Israel

Rickover, Hyman; b. 1900; admiral, U.S. Navy; controversial "father" of the nuclear Navy; supervised development of the first nuclear submarine

Rohatyn, Felix; b. 1928; Vienna-born financial consultant; corporate merger specialist; as chairman of the Municipal Assistance Corporation (MAC), helped avert New York City's bankruptcy during the mid-1970's fiscal crisis

Rostow, Eugene; b. 1913; legal scholar; former undersecretary of state for political affairs under President Johnson; former director of the Arms Control and Disarmament Agency under President Reagan; former dean of Yale Law School; leading supporter of Israel's West Bank policy

Rostow, Walt Whitman; b. 1916; economist; historian; special assistant for national security affairs under President Johnson; considered the most significant influence on Vietnam policy, 1961-1969

Rudman, Warren; b. 1930; attorney; Republican U.S. Senator from New Hampshire, 1980-present; former New Hampshire attorney general

Solarz, Stephen; b. 1940; Congressman from New York, 1975-present; Israel's most outspoken supporter in Congress

Sonnenfeldt, Helmut; b. 1926; Berlin-born senior aide to Henry Kissinger; chief planner of the detente policy toward the Soviet Union in the Nixon Administration

Specter, Arlen; b. 1930; attorney; Republican U.S. Senator from Pennsylvania, 1981-present; assistant counsel to Warren Commission, 1964

Strauss, Robert S.; b. 1918; attorney; former chairman of the Democratic National Committee; former U.S. ambassador to the Egyptian-Israeli talks on Palestinian autonomy; recipient of the Medal of Freedom

Yarmolinsky, Adam; b. 1922; attorney; leading figure in the formation of domestic policy in the Kennedy and Johnson Administrations;

professor at University of Massachusetts; author of *The Military Establishment: Its Impact on American Society*

Zorinsky, Edward; b. 1928; businessman; Democratic U.S. Senator from Nebraska, 1976-present

Rabbinate

Agus, Jacob Bernard; b. 1911; Conservative; scholar in the philosophy of Jewish history; Baltimore

Angel, Marc; b. 1945; Orthodox; leader of Sephardic Jewish community; New York

Axelrad, Albert S.; b. 1938; Reform; Hillel, civil-rights leader; Boston

Beerman, Leonard I.; b. 1921; Reform; civil rights and anti-nuclear activist; Los Angeles

Berkowitz, William; b. 1924; Conservative; pioneer in adult Jewish education, prayer-service innovation; New York

Bleich, J. David; b. 1936; Orthodox; theorist on bioethics issues; professor at Yeshiva University; New York

Borowitz, Eugene B.; b. 1924; Reform; theologian; editor of *Sh'ma;* New York (HUC-JIR)

Brickner, Balfour; b. 1926; Reform; social activist; New York

Carlebach, Shlomo; b. 1926; Orthodox (Hasidic); "singing Rabbi"; New York

Cohen, Gerson David; b. 1924; Conservative; fifth chancellor of Jewish Theological Seminary of America, 1972-85; professor of history; New York

Eisenstein, Ira; b. 1906; Reconstructionist; past president of the Reconstructionist Rabbinical College in Philadelphia

Feinstein, Moshe; b. 1895; Orthodox; leading world authority on halacha; dean of Mesivta Tifereth Jerusalem in New York; serves on presidium of the Union of Orthodox Rabbis and the Mo'ezet Gedolei ha-Torah of Agudath Israel; New York

Finkelstein, Louis; b. 1895; Conservative; former professor, president and chancellor of the Jewish Theological Seminary of America; pioneer in interreligious dialogue

Freifeld, Shlomo; b. 1926; Orthodox; dean of Shor Yoshuv Institute in Far Rockaway, New York; leader in "kirov rechokim" movement

Gordis, Robert; b. 1908; Conservative; professor of biblical studies at Jewish Theological Seminary; founder and editor of *Judaism* magazine

Gottlieb, Lynn; b. 1949; Conservative (privately ordained) minister in sign language to deaf congregations; leader in efforts for ordination of women; New York

Gottschalk, Alfred; b. 1930; Reform; president of Hebrew Union College—Jewish Institute of Religion; ordained first woman rabbi; member of the United States Holocaust Memorial Council; Cincinnati

Greenberg, Irving; b. 1933; Orthodox; director of the National Jewish Resource Center; a founder of Yavneh; a founder of the Center for Russian Jewry; president of the United States Holocaust Memorial Council; leading proponent of interdenominational dialogue; New York

Hertzberg, Arthur; b. 1921; Conservative; former president of the World Jewish Congress, former president of the American Jewish Congress; professor of history at Columbia University since 1961; leading Zionist spokesman

Horowitz, Levi Isaac; b. 1921; Orthodox; the *Bostoner Rebbe;* head of the New England Hassidic Center; developed significant outreach program to assimilated Jews; Boston

Jung, Leo; b. 1892; Orthodox; long-time rabbi of the Jewish Center in Manhattan's Upper West Side; professor emeritus at Yeshiva University; prolific writer, was only American contributor to Soncino translation of the Talmud; wrote on ethics, against intermarriage; New York

Kamenecki, Yaakov; b. 1891; Orthodox; dean of Mesivta Torah Vodaath; formerly rabbi of Zitavian in Kovno province; serves on presidium of the Union of Orthodox Rabbis and the Mo'ezet Gedolei ha-Torah of Agudath Israel; Monsey, New York

Kelman, Wolfe; b. 1923; Conservative; executive vice-president of the Rabbinical Assembly; formerly director of the United Synagogue of America; New York

Klaperman, Gilbert; b. 1921; Orthodox; vice-president of the Rabbinical Council of America; spiritual leader of Cong. Beth Sholom, Lawrence, New York

Priesand, Sally; b. 1946; Reform; first woman to be ordained by Hebrew Union College (1972); first woman to head a congregation (Congregation Beth El, Elizabeth, New Jersey, 1979)

Riskin, Shlomo; b. 1940; Orthodox; founded Lincoln Square Synagogue; leader in return to active participation in Jewish life by thousands of Jews; founder of two Hebrew high schools and New York's most extensive adult education courses; New York and Israel

Ruderman, Jacob I.; b. 1901; Orthodox; dean and founder of Baltimore's Ner Israel Rabbinical College

Schachter, Zalman; b. 1924; Polish-born mystic; a founder of the Havurah movement; professor of religion at Temple University; founder of B'nai Or; Philadelphia

Schindler, Alexander M.; b. 1925; Reform; president of the Union of American Hebrew Congregations; former chairman of the Conference of Presidents of Major American Jewish Organizations; New York

Schneerson, Menahem Mendel; b. 1902; Orthodox; seventh *Lubavitcher Rebbe;* New York

Schulweis, Harold; b. 1925; Conservative; leader of Havurah movement; Encino, California

Serotta, Gerold; b. 1946; Reform; president of the New Jewish Agenda; former leader of Breira and Dorot; New York

Sherer, Morris; b. 1921; Orthodox; president of Agudath Israel of America; leading promoter of safeguards to Jewish religious life; New York

Siegel, Seymour; b. 1927; Conservative; professor of ethics and theology at the Jewish Theological Seminary; chairman of the Committee on Jewish Law of the Rabbinical Assembly; favors opening of rabbinate to women; New York

Soloveitchik, Joseph Dov; b. 1903; Orthodox; *rosh yeshiva* of Rabbi Isaac Elchanan Theological Seminary of Yeshiva University; leading Jewish philosopher and thinker; New York

Tanenbaum, Marc; b. 1925; Conservative; director of international affairs of the American Jewish Committee; leading advocate of Christian-Jewish dialogue; co-founder of the National Conference on Race and Religion; New York

Wurzburger, Walter S.; b. 1920; Orthodox; theologian; president of the Synagogue Council of America; former president of the Rabbinical Council of America; professor at Yeshiva University; editor of *Tradition;* New York

Science; Medicine

Asimov, Isaac; b. 1920; chemist; popular science fiction writer

Benacerraf, Baruj; b. 1920; physician; Harvard professor; Nobel laureate, 1980, in physiology for research in immunology

Berg, Paul; b. 1926; chemist; Stanford professor; 1980 Nobel laureate

Blumberg, Baruch; b. 1925; physician, anthropologist; U. of Pennsylvania professor; 1976 Nobel laureate in physiology

Cohen, Bernard L.; b. 1924; physicist; U. of Pittsburgh professor; leading force in the development of safe nuclear energy

Djerassi, Isaac; b. 1925; Bulgarian-born physician, cancer researcher, especially of leukemia

Feld, Bernard T.; b. 1919; physicist; leading spokesman for nuclear arms control, pacifism and civilian control of atomic energy

Gell-Man, Murray; b. 1929; theoretical physicist; professor at California Institute of Technology; leader in classification of subatomic particles

Hiatt, Howard H.; b. 1925; physician; dean of the Harvard School of Public Health; proponent of nuclear freeze and disarmament

Hoffman, Jeffrey A.; b. 1945; astronaut; astrophysicist; member of crew of space shuttle Discovery, April 1985

Hofstadter, Robert; b. 1915; physicist; professor at Stanford, won 1961 Nobel Prize for designing a device that enabled physicists to measure the size and shape of protons and neutrons

Kline, Nathan S.; b. 1916; psychiatrist; introduced use of modern tranquilizers in the early 1950's; was the first to test anti-depressant drugs on mental patients

Lederberg, Joshua; b. 1925; geneticist; demonstrated sexual reproduction in microorganisms; president of Rockefeller University; co-recipient of 1958 Nobel Prize in physiology

Rabi, Isidor; b. 1898; physicist; winner of 1944 Nobel Prize; was active in development of the atomic bomb, and later was active in seeking its peaceful uses

Rosner, Fred; b. 1935; physician; leading scholar and lecturer on Jewish medical ethics and Jewish medical history; professor of medicine, State University of New York at Stony Brook

Sabin, Albert B.; b. 1905; physician; developer of oral vaccine against polio; developed lesser-known vaccine against dengue fever in the Pacific during World War II; former professor of research pediatrics at University of Cincinnati

Salk, Jonas; b. 1914; physician; developed first effective polio vaccine in 1954; founded the Salk Institute of Biological Studies in La Jolla, California, where he currently is researching a cure for multiple sclerosis

Teller, Edward; b. 1908; Budapest-born nuclear physicist; "father" of the hydrogen bomb; helped create Manhattan Project; senior research fellow at Stanford University

Wald, George; b. 1906; biologist; humanist; professor at Harvard University; recipient of 1967 Nobel Prize in physiology; leading opponent of the Vietnam War and nuclear weaponry

Weisskopf, Victor; b. 1908; Vienna-born physicist; leading opponent of nuclear arms proliferation; formerly professor at MIT

Wiesner, Jerome; b. 1915; electrical engineer; early developer of radar; former president of MIT; adviser to Presidents Kennedy and Johnson; early proponent of nuclear disarmament

Yalow, Rosalyn S.; b. 1921; medical physicist; pioneer in radioimmunoassay; second woman to win a Nobel Prize, in Medicine in 1977

Sociology; Public Policy; Psychology; Political Science; Public Affairs

Aronowitz, Stanley; b. 1933; activist; labor organizer; leader of anti-war movement in the 1960's

Barnet, Richard J.; b. 1929; political analyst; critic of American foreign policy

Bell, Daniel (Daniel Bolotsky); b. 1919; professor at Columbia and Harvard; leading social critic

Bettelheim, Bruno; b. 1903; child psychologist; scrutinizer of social behavior under stress; professor of education at University of Chicago

Chesler, Phyllis; b. 1940; psychologist; author; feminist theorist

Epstein, Edward Jay; b. 1935; political scientist and critic of the Warren Commission and network media

Erikson, Erik H.; b. 1902; German-born pyschoanalyst; pioneer in child development; biographer of Luther and Gandhi (Pulitzer Prize winner); coined phrase "identity crisis"

Gaylin, Willard; b. 1925; psychoanalyst; clinical professor of psychiatry at Columbia; expert in bioethics

Glazer, Nathan; b. 1923; sociologist; professor at Harvard; authored *The Lonely Crowd*, co-authored *Beyond the Melting Pot;* leading student of ethnicity in America

Goodwin, Richard N.; b. 1931; author; attorney; speechwriter for JFK, confidant of LBJ, for whom he helped create "The Great Society"

Harris, Louis; b. 1921; pollster

Hess, Stephen; b. 1933; political scientist; prolific political writer; former White House staff member under Eisenhower and Nixon; senior fellow at the Brookings Institution

Hoffman, Stanley; b. 1928; Vienna-born political scientist; chairman of the Western European studies department at Harvard

Horowitz, Irving Louis; b. 1929; sociologist; professor at Rutgers University; prolific writer, especially in areas of Latin American development, militarism and upheaval and Jewish-Israeli relations

Hurewitz, Jacob C.; b. 1914; political scientist; Middle East specialist; professor at Columbia University

Janowitz, Morris; b. 1919; sociologist; professor at University of Chicago; analyst of effect of technology on society

Karpatkin, Rhoda; b. 1930; attorney and civil rights advocate; executive director of the Consumers Union of the United States

Kristol, Irving; b. 1920; writer; prolific journalist; leading neo-conservative; professor at New York University; highly influential advocate of capitalist theory

Lifton, Robert Jay; b. 1926; psychiatrist; psychohistorian; his *Death in Life, Survivors of Hiroshima* studied the impact of war and barbarism on survivors

Lipset, Seymour; b. 1922; sociologist; political scientist; professor of political science at Stanford University; national president of American Professors for Peace in the Middle East

Mayer, Egon; b. 1944; Swiss-born sociologist; student of Jewish family life in America, particularly education and intermarriage; associate professor at Brooklyn College; author of *From Suburb to Shtetl* and numerous monographs

Mayer, Martin; b. 1928; writer; critic of the American school system and the American economy

Melman, Seymour; b. 1917; industrial engineer; peace activist; co-chairman of SANE: A Citizen's Organization for a Sane World; professor at Columbia University

Pipes, Richard; b. 1923; Polish-born Russian expert; serves on National Security Council; professor of history at Harvard; influenced mid-1970's reevaluation of the Soviet Union as a far greater threat than previously believed

Raskin, Marcus; b. 1934; political scientist; co-founder of the Institute for Policy Studies; early critic of U.S. policy in Vietnam

Riesman, David; b. 1909; sociologist; attorney; authored *The Lonely Crowd* (1950); professor of social sciences at Harvard University

Rothenberg, David; b. 1933; prison reformer; founder and executive director of the Fortune Society in New York; teacher of criminology and of prisoners themselves, as well

Shulman, Marshall D.; b. 1916; Sovietologist; special advisor to Secretary of State Cyrus Vance in the Carter Administration; leading supporter of SALT II; director of the Russian Institute at Columbia University

Silberman, Charles Eliot; b. 1925; social analyst; lecturer; journalist; author of *Crisis in the Classroom: The Remaking of American Education* and *The Open Classroom Reader*

Sklare, Marshall; b. 1921; sociologist; professor at Brandeis University; commentator on the condition of American Jewry; author of *Not Quite at Home: How an American Jewish Community Lives with Itself and its Neighbors* and others

Steel, Ronald; b. 1931; author; political and foreign policy analyst; author of *Walter Lippman and the American Century*

Szasz, Thomas; b. 1920; Budapest-born psychiatrist; writer; defender of the civil rights of the mentally ill; professor of psychiatry at Upstate Medical Center in Syracuse

Toffler, Alvin; b. 1928; writer; futurist; author of *Future Shock, The Third Wave*

Walzer, Michael; b. 1935; social scientist; professor at the Institute for Advanced Study in Princeton; author of *Just and Unjust Wars*

Waskow, Arthur; b. 1933; writer; theologian; organizer of Trees for Vietnam, the Farbrangen Community; author of *Godwrestling*

Wildavsky, Aaron; b. 1930; political scientist; head of the Survey Research Center at Berkeley; scholar on the power of the American presidency and of public policy

Yankelovich, Daniel; b. 1924; pollster; sociologist; research professor of psychology; co-founder of the Public Agenda Foundation

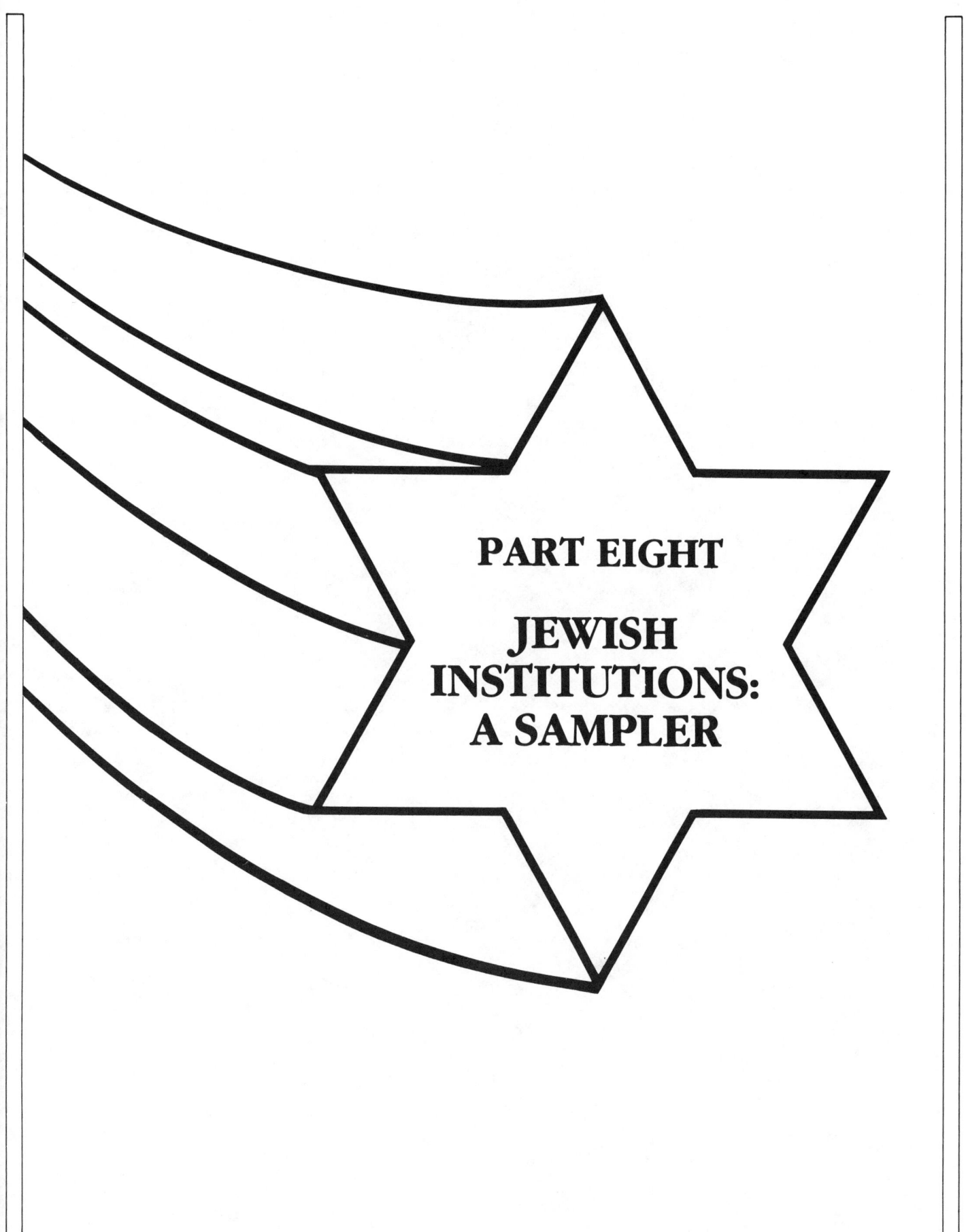

PART EIGHT

JEWISH INSTITUTIONS: A SAMPLER

Jewish Organizations at a Glance

	RECONSTRUCTIONIST	REFORM	CONSERVATIVE	"Modern Orthodox"	ORTHODOX "Strictly Orthodox"	"Hasidic"
CONGREGATIONAL ORGANIZATIONS	—Federation of Reconstructionist Congregations —Jewish Reconstructionist Foundation	—Union of American Hebrew Congregations	Synagogue Council of America (umbrella) —United Synagogue of America —Union for Traditional Conservative Judaism	—Union of Orthodox Jewish Congregations of America —National Council of Young Israel (not a member of Synagogue Council)	—Agudath Israel of America	—Hasidic groups: —Ger —Lubavitch —Munkatch —Satmar —Bostoner —Stolin —Sigeter —Bobov —Skulener —Skverer —Viznitz —Pupa —Belz
RABBINIC ARM		—Central Conference of American Rabbis	—Rabbinical Assembly	—Rabbinical Council of America —Council of Young Israel Rabbis	—Agudath Harabbonim —Igud Harabbonim	—Hisachdus Horabbonim
RABBINICAL SEMINARIES	—Reconstructionist Rabbinical College—Wyncote, Pa.	—Hebrew Union College— Cincinnati New York Los Angeles Jerusalem	—Jewish Theological Seminary— New York —University of Judaism— Los Angeles	—Yeshiva University (RIETS)— New York —Hebrew Theological College— Skokie, Ill.	—Beth Medrash Govoha— Lakewood, N.J. —Mesivta Rabbi Chaim Berlin— Brooklyn, N.Y. —Ner Israel—Baltimore, MD. —Torah Vodaath—Brooklyn, N.Y. —Mirrer Yeshiva—Brooklyn, N.Y. —Telshe—Wickliffe, Ohio —Mesivta Tifereth Jerusalem— New York, N.Y. —Chofetz Chaim—Forest Hills, N.Y. —Yeshivas Brisk—Skokie, Ill.	—Lubavitch—Brooklyn, N.Y. —Satmar—Brooklyn, N.Y.
PUBLICATIONS	—Reconstructionist	—Reform Judaism —CCAR Journal	—United Synagogue Review —Conservative Judaism	—Tradition —Young Israel Viewpoint	—Jewish Observer —Jewish Press—Brooklyn, N.Y. —Algemeine Journal	
YOUTH ORGANIZATIONS		—National Federation of Temple Youth	—United Synagogue Youth	—National Conference of Synagogue Youth —Bnai Akiva	—Pirchei Agudath Israel —Bnos Agudath Israel	—Pirchai Chabad —Bnos Chabad
CANTORIAL ORGANIZATIONS		—American Conference of Cantors	—Cantors Assembly	—Cantorial Council of America		
COMMUNITY RELATIONS, SOCIAL, POLITICAL AND LEGAL ORGANIZATIONS			National Jewish Community Relations Advisory Council (umbrella) Conference of Presidents of Major American Jewish Organizations (umbrella) —American Jewish Congress —American Jewish Committee —B'nai B'rith —Anti-Defamation League of B'nai B'rith —Jewish Labor Committee —Jewish War Veterans of the U.S.A. —National Council of Jewish Women —Women's American ORT —Hadassah		—National Jewish Commission on Law and Public Affairs (COLPA) —Commission on Legislation and Civic Action of Agudath Israel —Association of Orthodox Jewish Scientists	
ZIONIST ORGANIZATIONS		—ARZA—Association of Reform Zionists of America	American Zionist Federation (umbrella) —Mercaz —Bnai Zion —Pioneer Women —Labor Zionist Alliance	—Mizrachi —Hapoel Hamizrachi —AMIT Women —Emunah Women —Religious Zionists of America		

The Role of Israel Bonds in Israel's Economic Development

Since its founding in 1951, the Israel Bond Organization has been an important source of development capital for Israel, providing more than $7 billion to help build every aspect of the nation's economy.

Bond proceeds were used to help construct Israel's National Water Carrier; to build oil pipelines; to construct highways and harbors. Israel Bonds helped finance extension of rail and communications systems, the construction of new power plants, the building of new towns and the development of new sources of energy.

Among the many projects which Bonds have helped complete in recent years was Maor David, the giant coal-burning electric power plant at Hadera. Ground for the 1,400 megawatt facility had been broken at an Israel Bond Prime Minister's Conference in 1977.

By operating on coal, the Hadera plant saves Israel a great deal of money that would otherwise be spent on costly imported oil.

Israel Bond proceeds are currently helping to construct another new power station—this time the huge $700 million "Darom" facility near Ashkelon.

Since every dollar of Israel Bond money is channeled through the Development Budget of Israel's Finance Ministry and since the Finance Ministry is the source of research and development monies for Israel's high-technology industries, the Bond Organization can be credited with providing start-up funds for many of the products of these promising industries of the future.

Because Israel is relatively poor in natural resources, it made a decision to capitalize on its greatest resource—brainpower. As a result, Israel's high technology-based exports increased from $40 million in 1973 to $1.7 billion in 1984—or 40% of the nation's total exports.

More and more of Israel's exports are the result of local research and development, thanks in part to R & D funds provided through Bonds. This relates not only to com-

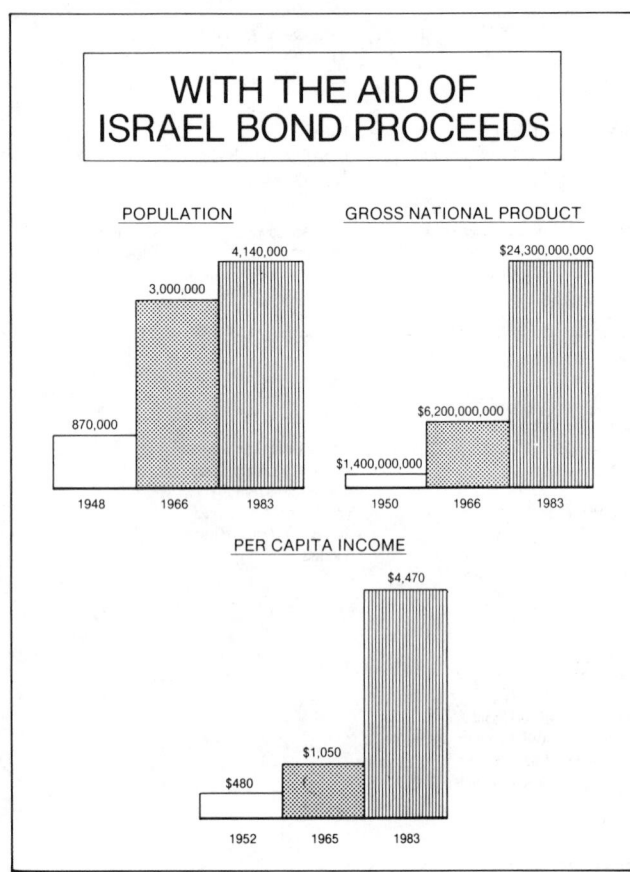

WITH THE AID OF ISRAEL BOND PROCEEDS

POPULATION
870,000 — 1948
3,000,000 — 1966
4,140,000 — 1983

GROSS NATIONAL PRODUCT
$1,400,000,000 — 1950
$6,200,000,000 — 1966
$24,300,000,000 — 1983

PER CAPITA INCOME
$480 — 1952
$1,050 — 1965
$4,470 — 1983

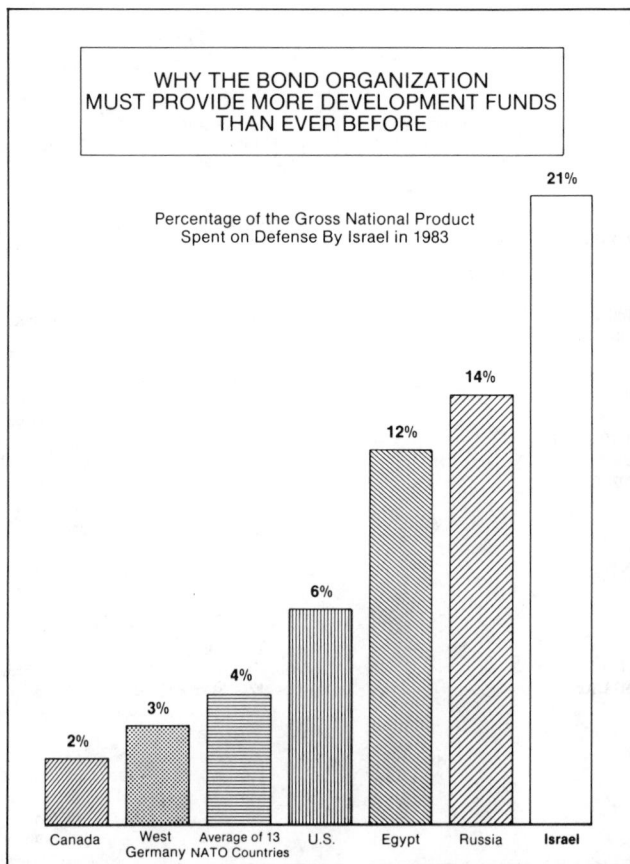

WHY THE BOND ORGANIZATION MUST PROVIDE MORE DEVELOPMENT FUNDS THAN EVER BEFORE

Percentage of the Gross National Product Spent on Defense By Israel in 1983

Canada — 2%
West Germany — 3%
Average of 13 NATO Countries — 4%
U.S. — 6%
Egypt — 12%
Russia — 14%
Israel — 21%

WITH THE AID OF ISRAEL BOND PROCEEDS

ISRAEL HIGH TECHNOLOGY EXPORTS

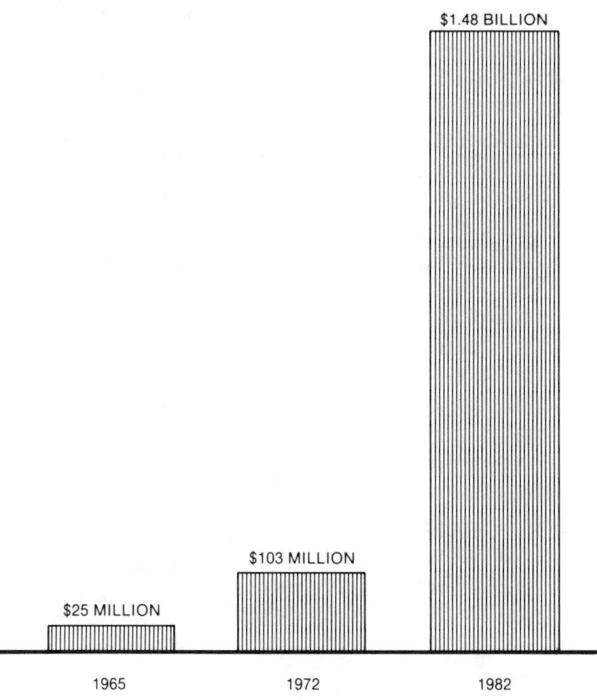

puter-based industries but to out-of-season farm produce grown for the European market and other high-quality products in textiles, diamonds and the metal industry.

The Israel Bond campaign has been a highly productive partnership between the people of Israel and world Jewry. It has also gained new friends for Israel in the non-Jewish community who support Israel through the Bond program.

Of the more than $7 billion in Israel Bonds and other financial instruments sold since the inception of the Bond efforts, some 80 percent were sold in the United States.

Since 1951, each Israel Bond which has matured has been redeemed fully and on time, and all interest payments have been made promptly.

In addition to more than a million individual purchasers, thousands of banks, pension funds, trade unions, insurance companies and other fiscal and communal institutions have bought Israel Bonds.

The Bond Organization offers a variety of financial instruments. These include Seventh Development Issue Current Income Bonds which pay 4% interest. The minimum purchase is $500.

The newest instrument in the Bond Organization's portfolio of Israeli securities is the Individual Variable Rate Instrument (IVRI), which was issued in response to requests from friends of Israel who wanted a larger-denomination Bond with a higher yield which can be held in a personal portfolio.

WITH THE AID OF ISRAEL BOND PROCEEDS

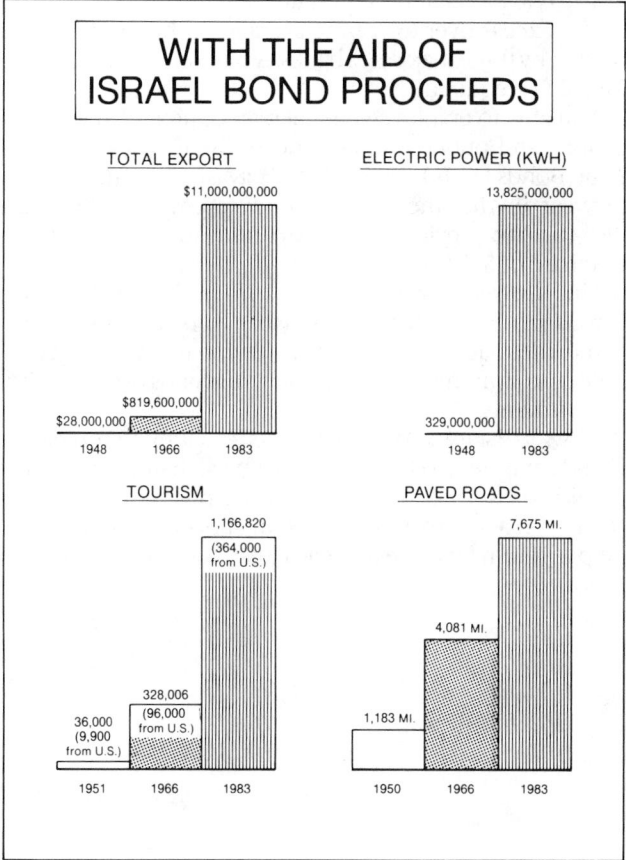

WHY THE BOND ORGANIZATION MUST PROVIDE MORE DEVELOPMENT FUNDS THAN EVER BEFORE

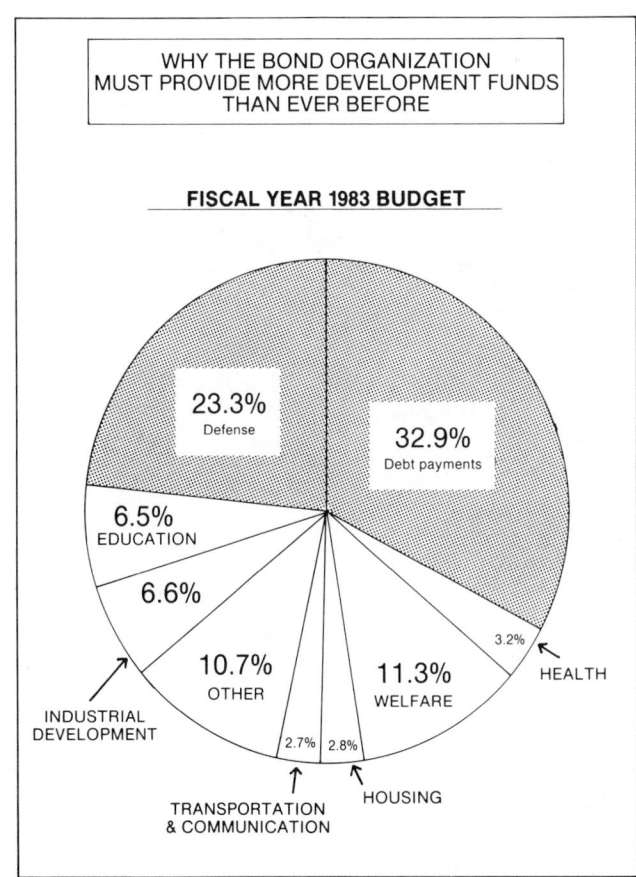

The IVRI pays a minimum annual interest of 6% plus 50% of the excess over 6% of the average of the prime rates quoted by three major U.S. banks. A minimum purchase of $10,000 is required.

Available to employee benefit plans, union plans, foundations and public endowment funds are Variable Rate Issue Bonds (VRIs). These Bonds pay a minimum of 7½% per year plus half the excess of the average prime rate over 7½% on the previous October 1 and April 1. An initial purchase of $25,000 is required.

Fifth Development Investment Issue Current Income Bonds pay 5.5%. They are available to banks, insurance companies, labor unions, employee benefit funds, credit unions, community funds, and building funds of charitable organizations.

Now, as Israel is overcoming its economic problems, friends of Israel can help develop high tech industries and provide jobs for Israelis through the purchase of Israel Bonds. This in turn will improve the nation's exports and help to return Israel on the road to economic progress and peace.

WITH THE AID OF ISRAEL BOND PROCEEDS

ISRAEL EXPORTS (In millions of dollars)	1970	1982
GOODS TO THE USA	149.1	1,119.2
METAL PRODUCTS	28.2	514.6
HIGH TECHNOLOGY	103.	1.48 Billion
TRANSPORT EQUIPMENT	9.1	439.9
ELECTRICAL AND ELECTRONIC EQUIPMENT	12.8	465.7
PETROLEUM AND CHEMICAL PRODUCTS	52.9	580.1

45

A Concise English-Yiddish-Hebrew Dictionary

Jonathan Geffner

Transliteration Key

a = a in *arm*.
o = o in *come*, or o in *phone*.
e = e in *end*.
i = i in *it*.
ee = ee in *week*.
ey = a in *ate*.
ay = i in *fine*.
u = oo in *good* or oo in *food*.
ch = ch in *chip*.
kh = ch in *Bach*.
zh = s in *measure*.

English	Yiddish	Yiddish (transliteration)	Hebrew	Hebrew (transliteration)
abandon	אָפּלאָזן	óplozn	נטש	natásh
able	פֿעיִק	féik	מסוגל	mesugál
abolish	אָפּשאַפֿן	ópshafn	ביטל	beetél
about	וועגן, אַן ערך	vegn, an érekh	על, בערך	al, be-érekh
above	איבער	íber	מעל	me-ál
abroad	אין אויסלאַנד	in óysland	חוץ לארץ	khuts la-árets
absent	פֿעלנדיק, ניטאָ	félndik, nitó	חסר	khasér
absorb	אײַנזאַפֿן	áynzapm	ספג	safág
accept	אָננעמען	ónnemen	קיבל	keebél
accident	(דער) צופֿאַל, (דאָס) אומגליק	(der) tsúfal, (dos) úmglik	תאונה	te-uná
accompany	באַגלייטן	bagléytn	ליווה	leevá
accomplish	דערגרייכן	dergréykhn	ביצע	beetséya
accomplishment	(דער) דערגרייך	(der) dergréykh	השלמה	hashlamá
account	(דער) חשבון	(der) khézhbm	חשבון	khezhbón
accuse	באַשולדיקן	bashúldikn	האשים	he-esheém
across	אויף יענער זײַט, אַריבער	(prep) oyf yéner zayt, (adv) aríber	מעבר	me-éver
act	שפּילן אַ ראָלע	shpiln a róle	שׂיחק במחזה	seekhék bemakhazé
actor	(דער) אַקטיאָר	(der) aktyór	שחקן	sakhkán
actually	בעצם	be-étsem	בעצם	be-étsem
add	צוגעבן	tsúgebm	הוסיף	hoseéf
address	(דער) אַדרעס	(der) adrés	כתובת	ketóvet
admire	האַלטן פֿון	haltn fun	העריץ	he-ereéts
adult (n.)	(דער) דערוואַקסענער	(der) derváksener	מבוגר	mevugár
advertisement	(דער) אַנאָנס	(der) anóns	מודעה	moda-á
advice	(די) עצה	(dee) éytse	עצה	eytsá

English	Yiddish	Yiddish (transliteration)	Hebrew	Hebrew (transliteration)
affair (matter)	דער ענין	(der) ínyen	ענין	inyán
afford	פֿאַרגינען זיך	fargínen zikh	היה יכול	hayá yakhól
afraid	דערשראָקן	dershrókn	מפחד	mefakhéd
after	נאָך	nokh	אחרי	akharéy
afternoon	(דער) נאָכמיטאָג	(der) nókhmitog	אחר־הצהריים	akhár-hatso-haráyim
again	נאָך אַ מאָל	nokh a mol	עוד פעם	ód pá-am
against	קעגן	kegn	נגד	néged
age	(דער) עלטער	(der) élter	גיל	geel
aggressive	אַגרעסיוו	agreseév	תוקפני	tokfaneé
agree	מסכים זײַן	máskim zayn	היסכים	heeskéem
agriculture	(די) אַגריקולטור	(dee) agrikultúr	חקלאות	khaklaút
aim (n.)	(דער) ציל	(der) tseel	מטרה	matará
aim (v.)	צילן	tseeln	כיוון	keevén
air	די לופֿט	(dee) luft	אוויר	aveér
air-conditioner	(דער) לופֿטקילער	(der) lúftkeeler	מיזוג־אוויר	meezúg-avír
airplane	(דער) אַוויאָן	(der) avyón	אווירון	avirón
airport	(דער) אַעראָפּאָרט	(der) aeropórt	נמל תעופה	nemál teufá
alive	לעבעדיק	lébedik	חי	khay
all	אַלע, אַלץ	ále, alts	כל	kol
allow	דערלויבן	derlóybm	הירשה	heershá
almond	(דער) מאַנדל	(der) mandl	שקד	shakéd
almost	כּמעט	kimát	כמעט	keemát
alone	אַליין	aleyn	לבד	levád
although	כאָטש	khoch	אף־על־פי	af-al-peé
always	תמיד	tómed	תמיד	tameéd
ambassador	דער אַמבאַסאַדאָר	(der) ambasádor	שגריר	shagrír
amount	(דער) סכום, (די) סומע	(der) skhum, (dee) súme	סכום	skhum
amusement	(די) פֿאַרווײַלונג	(dee) farváylung	שעשוע	shaashúa
ancestors	אבות	óves	אבות	avót
and	און	un	ו	ve
angel	(דער) מלאך	(der) málekh	מלאך	malákh
angle	(דער) ווינקל	(der) vinkl	זווית	zaveét
angry	בייז, אין כּעס	beyz, in káas	כועס	koés
anguish	(די) פּיַן	(dee) payn	ייסורים	yeesureém
animal	(די) חיה	(dee) kháye	חיה	khayá
ankle	(דאָס) קנעכל	(dos) knekhl	קרסול	karsól
annoy	דערקוטשען	derkúchen	היטריד	heetreéd
another	אַן אַנדער, נאָך אַ	an ánder, nokh a	אחר	akhér
answer (v.)	ענטפֿערן	entfern	ענה	aná
answer (n.)	(דער) ענטפֿער	(der) éntfer	תשובה	teshuvá
ant	(די) מוראַשקע	(dee) muráshke	נמלה	nemalá
anti-Semitic	אַנטיסעמיטיש	antisemítish	אנטישמי	antishémee
anxious	אומרויק	úmruik	מודאג	mudág
anybody	יעדער איינער	yéder éyner	כל אחד	kol ekhád
apartment	(די) דירה	(dee) deére	דירה	deerá
apathetic	אַפּאַטעטיש	apatétish	אדיש	adeésh
appetite	(דער) אַפּעטיט	(der) apeteét	תיאבון	te-avón
apple	(דער) עפּל	(der) epl	תפוח	tapúakh
apple sauce	(דער) עפּל־צימעס	(der) épl-tsímes	רסק־תפוחים	rések-tapukheém
appointment	די באַשטימונג	(dee) bashtímung	מינוי	meenú-ee
appreciate	אָפּשאַצן	ópshatsn	העריך	he-ereékh
approve	באַשטעטיקן	bashtétikn	היסכים ל	heeskéem l'
approximately	אַן ערך	an érekh	בערך	be-érekh
apricot	(דער) אַפּריקאָס	(der) aprikós	משמש	meésh mesh
Arab	(דער) אַראַבער	(der) Aráber	ערבי	araveé

English	Yiddish	Yiddish (transliteration)	Hebrew	Hebrew (transliteration)
architect	(דער) אַרכיטעקט	(der) arkhitékt	אדריכל	adrikhál
area	(דער) שטח	(der) shétekh	שטח	shétakh
arm (n.)	(דער) אָרעם	(der) órem	זרוע	zeróa
army	(די) אַרמיי	(dee) arméy	צבא	tsavá
arrange	אַראַנזשירן	aranzhírn	סידר	seedér
arrive	אָנקומען	ónkumen	הגיע	heegeé-a
arrow	(די) פּײַל	(dee) fayl	חץ	khets
art	(די) קונסט	(dee) kunst	אומנות	omanút
article	(דער) אַרטיקל	(der) arteékl	מאמר	maamár
artificial	קינסטלעך, געקינצלט	kínstlekh, gekíntslt	מלאכותי	melakhuteé
artist	(דער) קינסטלער	(der) kínstler	אומן	omán
ask	פֿרעגן	fregn	שאל	sha-ál
asparagus	(די) ספּאַרזשע	(dee) spárzhe	אספרג	aspárg
athlete	(דער) אַטלעט	(der) atlét	אתלט	atlét
atrocious	גרוייליק	gróylik	ניתעב	neetáv
attach	צוטשעפּען	tsúchepen	חיבר	kheebér
attack (v.)	באַפֿאַלן	bafáln	התקיף	heetkeéf
attic	(דער) בוידעם	(der) bóydem	עלייה	aliyá
attorney	(דער) אַדוואָקאַט	(der) advokát	עורך־דין	orékh-deén
aunt	(די) מומע	(dee) múme	דודה	dóda
author	(דער) מחבר	(der) mekháber	מחבר	mekhabér
authority	(דער) אויטאָריטעט, (דער) בעל־דעה	(der) oytoritét, (der) baal-déya	סמכות	samkhút
automatic	אויטאָמאַטיש	oytomátish	אוטומטי	otomátee
automobile	(דער) אויטאָ	(der) óyto	מכונית	mekhoneét
autumn	(דער) האַרבסט	(der) harbst	סתיו	stav
available	פֿאַראַן	farán	ניתן להשיג	neetán lehaseég
avoid	אויסמײַדן	óysmaydn	נימנע	neemná
awake	וואַך	vakh	ער	er
away	אַוועק	avék	הלאה	hála
awful	שרעקלעך	shréklekh	נורא	norá
awkward	אומגעלומפּערט	úmgelumpert	מגושם	megushám
baby	(דאָס) עופֿעלע	(dos) éyfele	תינוק	teenók
back	(דער) רוקן	(der) rukn	גב	gav
backward	הינטערשטעליק, אויף צוריק	híntershtelik, oyf tsurík	מפגר, לאחור	mefagér, le-akhór
bad	שלעכט	shlekht	רע	ra
bag	(דער) זאַק	(der) zak	שק, תיק	sak, teek
bake	באַקן	bakn	אפה	afá
baker	(דער) בעקער	(der) béker	אופה	ofé
bakery	(די) בעקעריי	(dee) bekeráy	מאפייה	maafeeá
balance (n.)	(די) גלײַכוואָג	(dee) gláykhvog	איזון	eezún
balcony	(דער) באַלקאָן	(der) balkón	מרפסת	mirpéset
bald	ליסע, פּליכעוואַטע	líse, plikheváte	קרח	keréakh
ball	(דער) באַל, (די) פֿילקע	(der) bal, (dee) pílke	כדור	kadúr
banana	(דער) באַנאַן	(der) banán	בננה	banána
bandage	(דער) באַנדאַזש	(der) bandázh	תחבושת	takhbóshet
bank	די/דער באַנק	(dee, der) bank	בנק	bank
barefoot	באַרוועס	bórves	יחף	yakhéf
bargain (n.)	(די) מציאה	(dee) metseé-e	מציאה	metseé-á
barley	גערשטן	(pl) gershtn	שעורה	seorá
barn	(דער) שײַער	(der) sháyer	אסם, רפת	asám, réfet
barrel	(די) פֿאַס	(dee) fas	חבית	khaveét
bashful	שעמעוודיק	shémevdik	ביישן	bayshán
basket	(דער) קוישׁ	(der) koysh	סל	sal
basketball	(דער) קוישבאָל	(der) kóyshbol	כדור־סל	kadúr-sál

English	Yiddish	Yiddish (transliteration)	Hebrew	Hebrew (transliteration)
bath	(די) וואַנע	(dee) váne	אמבט	ambát
bathrobe	(דער) באָדכאַלאַט	(der) bódkhalat	מעיל רחצה	me-eél rakhtsá
bathroom	(דער) וואַשצימער	(der) váshtsimer	חדר־אמבט	khadár-ambát
bathtub	(די) וואַנע	(dee) váne	אמבטיה	ambátya
battery	(די) באַטעריע	(dee) batérye	סוללה	solelá
be	זיַן	zayn	היה	hayá
beach	(די) פּלאַזשע	(dee) plázhe	חוף	khof
beans	(די) בעבלעך (די) פּאַסאָליעס	(dee) béblekh, (dee) fasólyes	שעועית	she-ueét
bear	(דער) בער	(der) ber	דוב	dov
beard	די באָרד	(dee) bord	זקן	zakán
beautiful	שייַן	sheyn	יפה	(m) yafé, (f) yafá
because	ווייַל	vayl	כי	kee
become	ווערן	vern	היה ל	hayá l'
bed	(די) בעט	(dee) bet	מיטה	meetá
bedbug	די וואַנץ	(dee) vants	פשפש	peeshpésh
bedroom	(דער) שלאָפֿצימער	(der) shlóftsimer	חדר־שינה	khadár-sheyná
bee	(די) בין	(dee) bin	דבורה	devorá
beef	(דאָס) רינדפֿלייש	(dos) rindfleysh	בשר בקר	basár bakár
beer	(דאָס) ביר	(dos) beer	בירה	bíra
beet	(דער) בוריק	(der) búrik	סלק	sélek
before	פֿאַר	far	לפני ש	leefnéy sh'
beg	בעטן	betn	התחנן	heetkhanén
beggar	(דער) שנאָרער	(der) shnórer	פושט יד	poshét yad
begin	אָנהייבן	ónheybm	התחיל	heetkheél
beginning	(דער) אָנהייב	(der) ónheyb	התחלה	hatkhalá
behavior	(דער) אויפֿפֿיר	(der) úffir	התנהגות	heetnahagút
behind (prep.)	הינטער	hinter	מאחורי	me-akhoréy
belch (v.)	גרעפּצן	greptsn	גיהק	geehék
belief	(דאָס) גלויבן	(dos) gloybm	אמונה	emuná
bell	(דער) גלאָק	(der) glok	פעמון	paamón
belly	(דער) בויך	(der) boykh	בטן	béten
below (prep.)	אונטער	únter	למטה מן	lemáta meen
below (adv.)	אונטן	untn	למטה	lemáta
belt	(דער) פּאַס, (דער) גאַרטל	(der) pas, (der) gartl	חגורה	khagorá
bench	(די) באַנק	(dee) bank	ספסל	safsál
benefit (n.)	(דער) נוצן	(der) nutsn	תועלת	toélet
bet (v.)	וועטן זיך	vetn zikh	התערב	heetarév
betray	מסרן, בוגד זיַן	másern, bóyged zayn	בגד	bagád
between	צווישן	tsvishn	בין	beyn
Bible	(דער) תּנך	(der) tanákh	תנך	tanákh
bicycle	(דער) ביציקל	(der) bítsikl	אופניים	ofanáyim
bill (of fare)	שטר	shtar	שטר	shtar
bird	(דער) פֿויגל, (דאָס) פֿייגעלע	(der) foygl, (dos) féygele (dim)	ציפור	tseepór
birth	(די) געבורט	(dee) gebúrt	לידה	leydá
birthday	(דער) געבורטסטאָג	(der) gebúrtstog	יום־הולדת	yom-hulédet
bite (v.)	בייַסן	baysn	נשך	nashákh
bite (n.)	(דער) ביס	(der) bis	נשיכה	neshikhá
bitter	ביטער	bíter	מר	mar
black	שוואַרץ	shvarts	שחור	shakhór
blackboard	(דער) טאָוול	(der) tovl	לוח	lúakh
bladder	(דער) פּענכער	(der) pénkher	שלפוחית	shalpukheét
blame (v.)	אַרויפֿוואַרפֿן די שולד אויף	aroýfvarfn dee shuld oyf	האשים	he-eshém
blame (n.)	(די) שולד	(dee) shuld	אשמה	ashmá
blanket	(די) קאָלדרע	(dee) kóldre	שמיכה	smeekhá
bleach (v.)	אויסבלייכן	oýsbleykhn	הלבין	heelbeén

English	Yiddish	Yiddish (transliteration)	Hebrew	Hebrew (transliteration)
bleach (n.)	(דאָס) בלייכעכץ	(dos) bléykhekhts	חומר מלבין	khómer malbeén
bless	בענטשן	benchn	בירך	beyrékh
blind	בלינד	blind	עיוור	eevér
blood	(דאָס) בלוט	(dos) blut	דם	dam
bloom	בליִען	bleé-en	פרח	parákh
blouse	(די) בלוזקע	(dee) blúzke	חולצה, חליקה	khultsá, khaliká
blow	בלאָזן	blozn	נשב	nasháv
blow (nose)	שנײַצן די נאָז	shnaytsn dee noz	גרף את האף	garáf et ha-áf
blue	בלוי	bloy	כחול	kakhól
blueberry	(די) שוואַרצע יאַגדע	(dee) shvártse yágde	אוכמנית	ukhmaneét
boat	(דאָס) שיפֿל	(dos) shifl	סירה, ספינה	sirá, sfeená
body	(דער) גוף, (דער) קערפער	(der) guf, (der) kérper	גוף	guf
boil	קאָכן, זידן	kokhn, zidn	הרתיח	heerteéakh
boiler	(דאָס) קעסל	(dos) kesl	דוד הרתחה	dud hartakhá
bomb	(די) באָמבע	(dee) bómbe	פצצה	petsatsá
bone	(דער) ביין	(der) beyn	עצם	étsem
book	(דאָס) בוך	(dos) bukh	ספר	séfer
border	(דער) גרענעץ, (דער) ברעג	(der) grénets, (der) breg	גבול	gevúl
boring	נודנע	núdne	נימאס	neemás
bother (n.)	(די) דאגה	(dee) dáyge	טרחה	tirkhá
bother (v.)	טשעפּען	chépen	היטריד	heetreéd
bottle	(די) פֿלאַש	(dee) flash	בקבוק	bakbúk
bottom (n.)	(דער) דנאָ	(der) dno	תחתית	takhteét
bow (n.)	(דער) בויגן	(der) boygn	קשת	késhet
bow (v.)	פֿאַרנייגן זיך	farnéygn zikh	ניכנע	neekhná
bowl	(די) שיסל	(dee) shisl	קערה	ke-ará
box	(די) פּושקע	(dee) púshke	ארגז	argáz
boy	(דאָס/דער) ייִנגל	(der, dos) yingl	ילד	yéled
bracelet	(דער) בראַסלעט	(der) braslét	צמיד	tsemeéd
brain	(דער) מוח	(der) móyekh	מוח	móakh
brake	(דער) טאָרמאַז	(der) tormáz	בלם	bélem
brass (n.)	(דאָס) מעש	(dos) mesh	פליז	pleez
bread	(דאָס) ברויט	(dos) broyt	לחם	lékhem
break (n.)	(די) הפֿסקה	(dee) hafsóke	הפסקה	hafsaká
break (v.)	צעברעכן	tsebrékhn	שבר	shavár
breakfast	(דאָס) איבערבײַסן, (דער) פֿרישטיק	(dos) íberbaysn, (der) frishtik	ארוחת־בוקר	arukhát-bóker
breast	(די) ברוסט	(dee) brust	חזה	khazé
breath	(דער) אָטעם	(der) ótem	נשימה	nesheemá
breathe	אָטעמען	ótemen	נשם	nashám
brick	(דער) ציגל	(der) tsigl	לבנה	levená
bride	(די) כּלה	(dee) kále	כלה	kalá
bridegroom	(דער) חתן	(der) khosn	חתן	khatán
bridge	(די) בריק	(dee) brik	גשר	gésher
bring	ברענגען	brengen	הביא	heveé
broken	צעבראָכן	tsebrókhn	שבור	shavúr
brooch	(די) בראָש	(dee) brosh	סיכת תכשיט	seekát takhsheét
broom	(דער) בעזעם	(der) bezem	מטאטא	mataté
brother	(דער) ברודער	(der) bruder	אח	akh
brotherhood	(די) ברידערשאַפֿט	(dee) breédershaft	אחוה	akhavá
brother-in-law	(דער) שוואָגער	(der) shvóger	גיס	gees
brown	ברוין	broyn	חום	khum
brush (n.)	(דער) פענזל, (די) באַרשט	(der) penzl, (dee) barsht	מכחול, מברשת	meekhekhol, meevréshet
brush (v.)	בערשטן, פּוצן, פֿאַרטשעפּען זיך	bershtn, putsn, farchépen zikh	בירש, צחצח, נגע קלות	berésh, tsikhtsekh, nagá kalót
bucket	(דער) עמער	(der) émer	דלי	dlee
budget	(דער) בודזשעט	(der) bujét	תקציב	taktseév

English	Yiddish	Yiddish (transliteration)	Hebrew	Hebrew (transliteration)
buffoon	(דער) לץ	(der) lets	לץ	lets
building	(דער) בנין	(der) bínyen	בנין	beenyán
bullet	(די) קויל	(dee) koyl	כדור, קליע	kadúr, kalee-á
bum	(דער) שלעפּער	(der) shléper	שתיין	shatyán
bundle	(דאָס) בינטל	(dos) bintl	חבילה	khaveelá
burn (v.)	ברענען	brenen	בער	ba-ár
bury	באַגראָבן	bagróbm	קבר	kavár
business	(דאָס) געשעפֿט, (דער) עסק	(dos) geshéft, (der) eýsek	עסק	ések
butcher	(דער) קצבֿ	(der) kátsev	קצב	katsáv
butcher shop	(די) יאַטקע	(dee) yátke	אטליז	eetleéz
butter	(די) פּוטער	(dee) púter	חמאה	khemá
butterfly	(דאָס) פֿלאַטערל	(dos) fláterl	פרפר	parpár
button	(דאָס) קנעפּל	(dos) knepl	כפתור	kaftór
buy	קויפֿן	koyfn	קנה	kaná
by	פֿון, לעבן	fun, lebm	מאת, על-יד	me-ét, al-yád
cabala	(די) קבלה	(dee) kabóle	קבלה	kabalá
cabbage	(דאָס) קרויט	(dos) kroyt	כרוב	krub
cabin	(די) כאַטע, (דאָס) ביידל	(dee) kháte, (dos) baydl	ביתן	beetán
café	(דער) קאַפֿע	(der) kafé	בית-קפה	beyt-kafé
cage	(די) שטייג	(dee) shtayg	כלוב	kluv
cake	(דער) קוכן	(der) kukhn	עוגה	ugá
calendar	(דער) לוח	(der) lúekh	לוח	lúakh
calf	(דאָס) קאַלב	(dos) kalb	עגל	égel
call	רופֿן	rufn	קרא	kará
camel	(דער) קעמל	(der) keml	גמל	gamál
camera	(דער) אַפּאַראַט	(der) aparát	מצלמה	matslemá
camp	(דער) לאַגער	(der) láger	מחנה	makhané
can	(דאָס) בלעכל	(dos) blekhl	שימורים	sheemureém
canal	(דער) קאַנאַל	(der) kanál	תעלה	te-alá
candle	(דאָס) ליכט	(dos) likht	נר	ner
candy	(דאָס) צוקערל	(dos) tsúkerl	סוכרייה	sukáriya
cane	(דער) שטעקן	(der) shtekn	מקל הליכה	makél halikhá
cannon	(דער) האַרמאַט	(der) harmát	תותח	totákh
canopy (wedding)	(די) חופה	(dee) khúpe	חופה	khupá
capital	(די) הויפּטשטאָט	(dee) hoýptshtot	עיר בירה	eer birá
capture	פֿאַרכאַפּן	farkhápm	שבה	shavá
card	(דאָס) קאַרטל	(dos) kartl	כרטיס	karteés
care (v.)	אויפּפּאַסן, אָרן	óyfpasn, arn	טיפל	teepél
careful	פֿאָרזיכטיק	fórzikhtik	זהיר	zahír
cargo	(דער) פֿראַכט	(der) frakht	מטען	meetán
carpenter	(דער) סטאָליער	(der) stólyer	נגר	nagár
carpet	(דער) טעפּעך	(der) tépekh	שטיח	shateéakh
carrot	(די) מער	(dee) mer	גזר	gézer
carry	טראָגן	trogn	נשא	nasá
cash	(דאָס) מזומן	(dos) mezúmen	מזומנים	mezumaneém
castle	(דער) שלאָס	(der) shlos	מבצר	meevtsár
cat	(די) קאַץ	(dee) kats	חתול	khatúl
catch	כאַפּן	khapm	תפס	tafás
cattle	בהמות	behéymes	בקר	bakár
cauliflower	(דאָס) בלומענקרויט	(dos) blúmenkroyt	כרובית	kŕuveét
caution	(די) אָפּגעהיטקייט	(dee) opgehítkeyt	זהירות	zehirút
cave	(די) הייל	(dee) heyl	מערה	meará
celebrate	פֿראַווען	práven	חגג	khagág
celebration	(די) שׂימחה	(dee) símkhe	שימחה	seemkhá

English	Yiddish	Yiddish (transliteration)	Hebrew	Hebrew (transliteration)
cellar	(דער) קעלער	(der) kéler	מרתף	martéf
cemetary	(דער) בית־עולם	(der) besóylem	בית־עלמין	beyt-almeén
century	(דער) יאָרהונדער	(der) yorhúndert	מאה	meá
certainly	אודאי	aváde	בודאי	bevadáy
chain	(די) קייט	(dee) keyt	שרשרת	sharshéret
chair	(די) שטול	(dee) shtul	כיסא	keesé
chairman	(דער) פֿאָרזיצער	(der) fórzitser	יושב־ראש	yoshév-rosh
chalk	(די) קרייַד	(dee) krayd	גיר	geer
chance	(די) געלעגנהייט	(dee) gelégnhayt	אפשרות	efsharút
change (v.)	ענדערן	éndern	שינה	sheená
chaos	(דער) כאַאָס	(der) kháos	תוהו ובוהו	tóhu vavóhu
charity	(די) צדקה	(dee) tsedóke	צדקה	tsedaká
charm	(דער) חן	(der) kheyn	חן	kheyn
charming	חנעוודיק	khéynevdik	נחמד	nekhmád
chat	שמועסן	shmúesn	שׂוחח	sokhéakh
cheap	ביליק	bílik	זול	zol
check (n.)	(דער) חשבון	(der) khezhbm	חשבון	khezhbón
cheek	(די) באַק	(dee) bak	לחי	lékhee
cheese	(דער) קעז	(der) kez	גבינה	gveená
chemistry	(די) כעמיע	(dee) khémye	כימיה	keémya
cherry	(די) קאַרש	(dee) karsh	דובדבן	duvdeván
chess	(דער) שאָך	(der) shokh	שח	shakh
chest	(די) ברוסט	(dee) brust	חזה	khazé
chew	קייַען	káyen	לעס	laás
chicken	(די) הון	(dee) hun	תרנגלת	tarngólet
child	(דאָס) קינד	(dos) kind	ילד	yéled
chimney	(דער) קוימען	(der) kóymen	ארובה	arubá
chin	(די) גאָמבע	(dee) gómbe	סנטר	santér
chocolate	(דער) שאָקאָלאַד	(der) shokolád	שוקולד	shokolád
Christian (n.)	(דער) קריסט	(der) krist	נוצרי	notsreé
Christmas	(דער) ניטל	(der) nitl	חג המולד הנוצרי	khag hamolád hanotsreé
church	(די) קירך	(dee) kirkh	כנסייה	knesiá
cigarette	(דער) פּאַפּיראָס	(der) papirós	סיגרייה	sigáriya
circle	(דער) קרייַז	(der) krayz	עיגול	eegúl
circumciser	(דער) מוהל	(der) móyel	מוהל	móhel
circumcision (ceremony)	(דער) ברית	(der) bris	ברית	breét
citizen	(דער) בירגער	(der) bírger	אזרח	ezrákh
class	(דער) קלאַס	(der) klas	כיתה	keetá
clay	(די) ליים	(dee) leym	חומר	khómer
clean	רייַן	reyn	נקי	nakeé
clear	קלאָר	klor	ברור	barúr
clever	קלוג	klug	פיקח	peekéyakh
climb	קלעטערן	klétern	טיפס	teepés
clock	(דער) זייגער	(der) zéyger	שעון	shaón
close (adj.)	נאָענט	nóent	קרוב	karóv
close (v.)	פֿאַרמאַכן	farmákhn	סגר	sagár
clothing	(די) קליידער	(dee) kléyder	בגדים	begadeém
cloud	(די) כמאַרע	(dee) khmáre	ענן	anán
coach (n.)	(דער) אייַנלערנער	(der) áynlerner	מאמן	meamén
coal	קוילן	koyln	פחם	pekhám
coat	(דער) מאַנטל	(der) mantl	מעיל	me-eél
cockroach	(דער) טאַראַקאַן	(der) taraкán	תיקן	teekán
coffee	(די) קאַווע	(dee) káve	קפה	kafé
cold (adj.)	קאַלט	kalt	קר	kar
cold (n.)	(די) פֿאַרקילונג	(dee) farkeélung	הצטננות	heetstanenút

English	Yiddish	Yiddish (transliteration)	Hebrew	Hebrew (transliteration)
collapse	אײַנברעכן זיך	áynbrekhn zikh	התמוטט	heetmotét
collar	(דער) קאָלנער	(der) kólner	צווארון	tsavarón
collect	קלײַבן	klaybm	אסף	asáf
color	(דער) קאָליר	(der) koleér	צבע	tséva
comb	(דאָס) קעמל	(dos) keml	מסרק	masrék
come	קומען	kúmen	בא	ba
comedian	(דער) קאָמיקער	(der) kómiker	קומיקן	komeekán
comedy	(די) קאָמעדיע	(dee) komédye	קומדיה	komédya
comfort	(די) באַקוועמלעכקייט	(dee) bakvémlekhkayt	נוחיות	nokheeút
comfortable	באַקוועם	bakvém	נוח	nóakh
commission	(די) קאָמיסיע	(dee) komísye	ועדה	vaadá
common	געוויינטלעך	gevéyntlekh	רגיל	rageél
common sense	(דער) שכל	(der) seykhl	שכל	sékhel
community	(דער) ציבור	(der) tsíber	קהילה	keheelá
compare	פֿאַרגלײַכן	fargláykhn	הישווה	heeshvá
comparison	(דער) פֿאַרגלײַך	(der) fargláykh	השוואה	hashvaá
competition	(די) קאָנקורענץ	(dee) konkurénts	תחרות	takharút
complain	קלאָגן זיך	klogn zikh	התאונן	heetonén
complaint	(די) טענה	(dee) táyne	תלונה	tluná
complicated	קאָמפּליצירט	komplitsírt	מסובך	mesubákh
compliment (n.)	קאָמפּלימענט	(der) komplimént	מחמאה	makhmaá
composer	קאָמפּאָזיטאָר	(der) kompozitor	מלחין	malkheén
computer	(דער) רעכענער	(der) rékhener	מחשב	mekhashév
conceited	גדלותדיק	gádlesdik	גאוותן	gaavtán
concentrate	קאָנצענטרירן	kontsentrírn	התרכז	heetrakéz
concept (n.)	(דער) באַגריף	(der) bagríf	מושג	muság
concert	(דער) קאָנצערט	(der) kontsért	קונצרט	kontsért
condition	(דער) תנאי	(der) tnay	תנאי	tnay
confused	צעמישט	tsemísht	מבולבל	mevulbál
congratulations	(דער) מזל־טוב	mázltov	מזל־טוב	mazál-tóv
connection	(די) פֿאַרבינדונג	(dee) farbíndung	קשר	késher
console (v.)	טרייסטן	treystn	ניחם	neekhém
continuation	(דער) המשך	(der) hémshekh	המשך	hémshekh
continue	ממשיך זײַן	mámshekh zayn	המשיך	heemsheékh
contribution	(דער) צושטײַער	(der) tsushtayer	תרומה	trumá
control (v.)	קאָנטראָלירן	kontrolírn	שלט	shalát
conversation	(דער) שמועס	(der) shmúes	שיחה	seekhá
convert (n.) (to Christianity)	(דער) משומד	(der) meshúmed	משומד	meshumád
convert (n.) (to Judaism)	(דער) גר	(der) ger	גר	ger
cook (n.)	(דער) קוכער	(der) kúkher	טבח	tabákh
cook (v.)	קאָכן	kokhn	בישל	beeshél
cookie	(דאָס) קיכל	(dos) kikhl	עוגית	ugeét
copper	(דאָס) קופער	(dos) kúper	נחושת	nekhóshet
copy (n.)	(די) קאָפּיע	(dee) kópye	העתק	heték
corkscrew	(דער) פּראָפּן־ציִער	(der) própn-tsee-er	מחלץ	makhaléts
corn	(די) קוקורוזע	(dee) kukerúze	תירס	teéras
correct (adj.)	ריכטיק	rikhtik	נכון	nakhón
correct (v.)	פֿאַרריכטן	farríkhtn	תיקן	teekén
cost (n.)	(דער) פּרײַז	(der) prayz	מחיר	mekhír
cotton	(דער) באַוול	(der) bavl	כותנה	kutná
couch	(די) קאַנאַפּע	(dee) kanápe	ספה	sapá
cough (v.)	הוסטן	hustn	השתעל	heeshtaél
count	ציילן	tseyln	ספר	safár
country	(די) מדינה	(dee) medeéne	מדינה	medeená
couple	(די) פּאָר	(dee) por	זוג	zug

English	Yiddish	Yiddish (transliteration)	Hebrew	Hebrew (transliteration)
courage	(דער) קוראַזש	(der) kurázh	גבורה	gevurá
cousin	(דער) קוזין	(der) kuzeén	בן־דוד	ben-dód
cover (n.)	(דער) צודעק	(der) tsúdek	מיכסה	meekhsé
cover (v.)	דעקן	dekn	כיסה	keesá
cow	(די) קו	(dee) ku	פרה	pará
coward	(דער) פּחדן	(der) pakhdn	פחדן	pakhdán
cozy	היימיש	héymish	נוח	nóakh
crack (n.)	(דער) שפּאַלט	(der) shpalt	סדק	sédek
cracker	(דאָס) פּלעצל	(dos) pletsl	פכסם	pakhsám
cranberry	(די) זשורעכלינע	(dee) zhurekhleéne	אוכמנית	ukhmaneét
crawl	קריכן	krikhn	זחל	zakhál
crazy	משוגע	meshúge	משוגע	meshugá
cream	(דער) קרעם	(der) krem	שמנת	shaménet
create	שאַפֿן	shafn	יצר	yatsár
crib	(די) וויג	(dee) vig	עריסה	areesá
crime	(דער) פֿאַרברעך	(der) farbrékh	פשע	pésha
cripple	(דער) קאַליקע	(der) kálike	נכה	nakhé
crooked	קרום	krum	עקום	akóm
cross (n.)	(דער) צלם	(der) tséylem	צלב	tseláv
crowd	(די) מאַסע	(dee) máse	המון	hamón
crude	פּראָסט	prost	גס	gas
cruel	אכזריותדיק	akhzóryesdik	אכזרי	akhzareé
cry	ווײנען	véynen	בכה	bakhá
cucumber	(די) אוגערקע	(dee) úgerke	מלפפון	melafefón
culture	(די) קולטור	(dee) kultúr	תרבות	tarbút
cunning	כיטרע	khítre	ערום	arúm
cup	(דאָס) טעפּעלע	(dos) tépele	ספל	séfel
curse (n.)	קללה	klóle	קללה	klalá
curtain	(דער) פֿירהאַנג	(der) fírhang	וילון	veelón
custom	(דער) מינהג	(der) mínheg	מינהג	meenhág
cut	שנײַדן	shnaydn	חתך	khatákh
cute	חנעוודיק	khéynevdik	מלא־חן	malé-khéyn
dairy (adj.)	מילכיק	mílkhik	חלבי	khalaveé
dam (n.)	(די) דאַמבע	(dee) dámbe	סכר	sékher
damage	(דער) שאָדן	(der) shodn	נזק	nézek
damp	פֿײַכט	faykht	לח	lakh
dance (n.)	(דער) טאַנץ	(der) tants	ריקוד	rikúd
danger	(די) סכנה	(dee) sakóne	סכנה	sakaná
dark	פֿינצטער	fíntster	חשוך	khashúkh
date (fruit)	(דער) טייטל	(der) teytl	תמר	tamár
date (time)	(די) דאַטע	(dee) dáte	תאריך	taareékh
daughter	(די) טאָכטער	(dee) tókhter	בת	bat
daughter-in-law	(די) שנור	(dee) shnur	אשת הבן	éshet-habén
dawn	(דער) קאיאָר	(der) kayór	שחר	shakhár
day	(דער) טאָג	(der) tog	יום	yom
deaf	טויב	toyb	חירש	kheyrésh
dear	טײַער	táyer	יקר	yakár
death	(דער) טויט	(der) toyt	מוות	mávet
debt	(דער) חובֿ	(der) khoyv	חוב	khov
deceive	אָפּנאַרן	ópnarn	רימה	reemá
decide	באַשליסן	bashlísn	החליט	hekheleét
decorate	דעקאָרירן	dekorírn	קישט	keeshét
decoration	(די) דעקאָראַציע	(dee) dekorátsye	קישוט	keeshút
dedicate	אָפּגעבן	ópgebm	הקדיש	heekdeésh

English	Yiddish	Yiddish (transliteration)	Hebrew	Hebrew (transliteration)
deep	טיף	teef	עמוק	amók
deer	(דער) הירש	(der) hirsh	צבי	tsveé
defective	דעפֿעקטיוו	defekteév	פגום	pagúm
defend	באַשיצן	bashítsn	הגן	hegén
definite	באַשטימט	bashtímt	מסוים	mesuyám
definition	(די) דעפֿיניציע	(dee) definítsye	הגדרה	hagdará
deformity	(דער) מום	(der) mum	עיוות צורה	eevút tsurá
degree	(דער) גראַד	(der) grad	דרגה	dargá
delicious	באַטעמט	batámt	ערב ביותר	arév beyotér
delightful	מחיהדיק	mekháyedik	מהנה	mehané
deliver	אָפּגעבן	ópgebm	מסר	masár
demand (n.)	(די) פֿאָדערונג	(dee) főderung	תביעה	teveeá
dentist	(דער) דענטיסט	(der) denteést	רופא שיניים	rofé shináyim
deny	לייקענען	léykenen	הכחיש	heekhekheésh
depart	אַוועקגײן	avékgeyn	עזב	azáv
department	(די) אָפּטײלונג	(dee) ópteylung	מחלקה	makhalaká
depend	פֿאַרלאָזן זיך	farlózn zikh	סמך	samákh
depressed	פֿאַרקלעמט	farklémt	מדוכא	meduké
derma	(די) קישקע	(dee) kíshke	מעיים	meaeém
descendants	קינדסקינדער	kindskínder	צאצאים	tse-e-tsaeém
desert	(די) מידבר	(dee) mídber	מידבר	meedbár
design (n.)	צייכענונג	tséykhenung	תרשים	tarsheém
despair	(דער) ייאש	(der) yíesh	ייאוש	yeúsh
desperate	פֿאַרצווייפֿלט	fartsvéyflt	נואש	noásh
dessert	(דער) דעסערט	(der) desért	פרפרת	parpéret
destiny	(דער) גורל	(der) goyrl	גורל	gorál
destroy	צעשטערן	tseshtérn	הרס	harás
develop	אַנטוויקלען	antvíklen	פיתח	peetéakh
devil	(דער) טײַוול	(der) tayvl	שד	shed
diarrhea	(דער) שילשול	(der) sheelshl	שילשול	sheélshul
diary	(דאָס) טאָגבוך	(dos) tógbukh	יומן	yomán
diaspora	(דאָס) גלות	(dos) góles	גלות	galút
dibbuk	(דער) דיבוק	(der) díbek	דיבוק	deebúk
dictionary	(דאָס) ווערטער בוך	(dos) vérterbukh	מילון	milón
die	שטאַרבן	shtarbm	מת	met
different	אַנדערש	ándersh	שונה	shoné
dig	גראָבן	grobm	חפר	khafár
digest	פֿאַרדײַען	fardáyen	עיכל	eekél
dining room	(דער) עסצימער	(der) éstsimer	חדר־אוכל	khadár-ókhel
dinner	(דאָס) אָנבײַסן	(dos) ónbaysn	ארוחה עיקרית	arukhá eekareét
direction	(די) ריכטונג	(dee) ríkhtung	כיוון	keevún
dirty	שמוציק	shmútsik	מלוכלך	melukhlákh
disappear	נעלם ווערן	nelm vern	נעלם	ne-elám
disappointed	אַנטוישט	antóysht	מאוכזב	meukhzáv
disaster	(דאָס) אומגליק	(dos) úmglik	אסון	asón
discount	(די) הנחה	(dee) hanókhe	הנחה	hanakhá
disease	(די) קראַנקייט	(dee) kránkayt	מחלה	makhalá
disgrace	(דער) בזיון	(der) bizóyen	קלון	kalón
disgusting	חלשותדיק	khalóshesdik	מגעיל	mageél
dish	(די) שיסל	(dee) shisl	קערית	kaareét
distance	(דער) מהלך	mehálekh	מרחק	merkhák
distinct	בולט	bóylet	מובהק	muvhák
distribute	פֿאַרשפּרייטן	farshpréytn	הפיץ	heféets
divide	צעטיילן	tsetéyln	חילק	kheelék
divorce (n.)	(דער) גט	(der) get	גט	get

English	Yiddish	Yiddish (transliteration)	Hebrew	Hebrew (transliteration)
dizzy	שווינדלדיק	shvíndldik	סחרחר	skharkhár
do	טאָן	ton	עשׂה	asá
doctor	(דער) דאָקטער	(der) dókter	רופֿא	rofé
document	(דער) דאָקומענט	(der) dokumént	מסמך	meesmákh
dog	(דער) הונט	(der) hunt	כלב	kélev
doll	(די) ליאַלקע	(dee) lyalke	בובה	búba
donkey	(דער) אייזל	(der) eyzl	חמור	khamór
door	(די) טיר	(dee) tir	דלת	délet
dot	(דאָס) פּינטל	(dos) pintl	נקודה	nekudá
doubt	(דער) ספֿק	(der) sófek	ספק	safék
dough	(דאָס) טייג	(dos) teyg	בצק	batsék
down	אַראָפּ	aróp	למטה	lemáta
drag	שלעפּן	shlepm	סחב	sakháv
draw (v.)	צייכענען	tséykhenen	שירטט	sirtét
draw (n.)	(דער) רעמי	(der) remeé	תיקו	téyku
dream	(דער) חלום	(der) khólem	חלום	khalóm
dress	(דאָס) קלייד	(dos) kleyd	שׂימלה	seemlá
drive	טרײַבן	traybm	נהג	nahág
driver	(דער) טרײַבער	(der) tráyber	נהג	nehág
drop (v.)	אַפּפֿאַלן	ópfaln	הפיל לארץ	heepeél laáretz
drop (n.)	(דער) טראָפֿן	(der) tropm	טיפה	teepá
drown	דערטרינקען	dertrínken	הטביע	heetbéea
drug	(דער) נאַרקאָטיק	(der) narkótik	סם	sam
drum	(די) פּויק	(dee) poyk	תּוף	tof
drunk	שיכּור	shíker	שיכּור	sheekór
dry	טרוקן	trukn	יבש	yavésh
duck	(די) קאַטשקע	(dee) káchke	ברווז	barváz
dumplings	קניידלעך	knéydlekh	כופתות	kuftót
during	בעת	beys	במשך	beméshekh
dusk	(דער) פֿאַרנאַכט	(der) farnákht	בין-השמשות	beyn-hashemashót
dust	(דער) שטויב	(der) shtoyb	אבק	avák
duty	(דער) חובֿ	(der) khoyv	חובה	khová
dwarf	(דער) קאַרליק	(der) kárlik	גמד	gamád
eager	האָבן חשק	hobm khéyshek	להוט	lahút
eagle	(דער) אָדלער	(der) ódler	נשר	nésher
ear	(דער) אויער	(der) óyer	אוזן	ózen
early	פֿרייִק	freé-ik	מוקדם	mukdám
earring	(דאָס) אוירינגל	(dos) óyringl	נזם אוזן	nézem ózen
earth	(די) ערד	(dee) erd	אדמה	adamá
east	מיזרח	mízrekh	מיזרח	meezrákh
eat	עסן	esn	אכל	akhál
echo	(דער) אָפּקלאַנג	(der) ópklang	הד	hed
economy	(די) עקאָנאָמיע	(dee) ekonómye	חסכנות	khaskhanút
ecstasy	(דאָס) התלהבֿות	(dos) hisláyves	התלהבות	heetlahavút
editor	(דער) רעדאַקטאָר	(der) redáktor	עורך	orékh
education	(די) דערציִונג	(dee) dertseéung	חינוך	kheenúkh
eel	(דער) ווענגער	(der) vénger	צלופה	tselofá
effect	(די) פּעולה	(dee) peúle	פעולה	peulá
efficient	בריהש	béryesh	יעיל	yaeél
effort	(די) מי	(dee) mee	מאמץ	maamáts
egg	(דאָס) איי	(dos) ey	ביצה	beytsá
eggplant	(דער) פּאַטלעזשאַן	(der) patlezhán	חציל	khatseél
elbow	(דער) עלנבויגן	(der) elnboygn	מרפק	marpék
election	וואָלן	valn	בחירות	pkheerót

English	Yiddish	Yiddish (transliteration)	Hebrew	Hebrew (transliteration)
electricity	(די) עלעקטריע	(dee) eléktrye	חשמל	khashmál
elephant	(דער) העלפֿאַנד	(der) helfánd	פיל	peel
elevator	(דער) ליפֿט	(der) lift	מעלית	maaleét
embarrass	פֿאַרשעמען	farshémen	הביך	heveékh
emergency	(דער) גוואַלד	(der) gvald	חרום	kheyrúm
empty	ליידיק	léydik	ריק	reyk
end	(דער) סוף	(der) sof	סוף	sof
enemy	(דער) שׂונא	(der) sóyne	אויב	óyev
energy	(די) ענערגיע	(dee) enérgye	מרץ	mérets
engineer	(דער) אינזשעניר	(der) inzhenír	מהנדס	mehandés
English	ענגליש	énglish	אנגלית	angleét
enjoy	הנאה האָבן	hanóe hobm	נהנה	nehená
enlightenment	(די) השׂכּלה	(dee) haskóle	השׂכלה	haskalá
enough	גענוג	genúg	מספיק	maspeék
entrance	(דער) אַרײַנגאַנג	(der) aráyngang	כניסה	keneesá
envelope	(דער) קאָנווערט	(der) konvért	מעטפה	maatafá
era	(די) תּקופֿה	(dee) tkúfe	תקופה	tkufá
escape	ניצול ווערן	nitsl vern	ברח	barákh
especially	דער עיקר	der eéker	במיוחד	bimeyukhád
eulogy	(דער) הספּד	(der) hésped	הספד	hésped
evening	(דער) אָוונט	(der) ovnt	ערב	érev
event	(דאָס) געשעעניש	(dos) geshé-enish	מאורע	meorá
Evil Eye	(דער) עין־הרע	eyn-óre	עין־הרע	eyn-hará
exactly	פּונקט	punkt	בדיוק	bideeúk
exaggeration	(די) גוזמא	(dee) gúzme	גוזמא	guzmá
examine	באַקוקן	bakúkn	בדק	badák
example	(דער) משל	(der) moshl	דוגמא	dugmá
excellent	אויסגעצייכנט	oysgetséykhnt	מצוין	metsuyán
exception	(דער) אויסנעם	(der) óysnem	יוצא מן הכלל	yoŧse min haklál
exchange	אויסבײַטן	óysbaytn	החליף	hekheleéf
exciting	שפּאַנענדיק	shpánendik	מרגש	meragésh
excommunication	(דער) חרם	(der) khéyrem	חרם	khéyrem
excuse (n.)	(דער) תּירוץ	(der) térets	תירוץ	teyrúts
exit	(דער) אַרויסגאַנג	(der) oróysgang	יציאה	yetseeá
exodus	(די) יציאה	(dee) yetseé-e	יציאה	yetseeá
expense	(די) הוצאה	(dee) hetsóa	הוצאה	hotsa-á
expensive	טײַער	táyer	יקר	yakár
expert	(דער) מבֿין	(der) meyvn	מומחה	mumkhé
expire	אויסגיין	óysgeyn	פקע	paká
explain	דערקלערן	derklérn	הסביר	heezbeér
export (v.)	אַרויספֿירן	aróysfirn	ייצא	yeetsé
exposition	(די) אויסשטעלונג	(dee) óysshtelung	תצוגה	tetsugá
express (v.)	אויסדריקן	óysdrikn	הביע	heebeéa
extreme	עקסטרעם	ekstrém	קיצוני	keetsoneé
eye	(דאָס) אויג	(dos) oyg	עין	áyin
eyeglasses	ברילן	briln	מישקפיים	meeshkafáyim
face	(דאָס) פּנים	(dos) pónim	פנים	paneém
fact	(דער) פֿאַקט	(der) fakt	עובדה	uvdá
factory	(די) פֿאַבריק	(dee) fabrík	בית־חרושת	beyt-kharóshet
fail	דורכפֿאַלן	dúrkhfaln	נכשל	neekhshál
faint	חלשן	kháleshn	התעלף	heetaléf
fairy tale	(די) באָבע־מעשׂה	(dee) bóbe-máyse	מעשייה	maaseá
faith	(דער) בטחון	(der) bitókhn	אמונה	emuná
family	(די) משפּחה	(dee) mishpókhe	משפחה	meeshpakhá

English	Yiddish	Yiddish (transliteration)	Hebrew	Hebrew (transliteration)
famous	באַרימט	barímt	מפורסם	mefursám
fancy	געצאַצקעט	getsátsket	קישוטי	keeshuteé
far	ווײַט	vayt	רחוק	rakhók
farm	(די) פֿערמע	(dee) férme	משק	méshek
fast (adj.)	גיך	geekh	מהר	mahér
fast (n.)	(דער) תּענית	(der) tónes	צום	tsom
fat	פֿעט	fet	שמן	shamén
father	(דער) טאַטע	(der) táte	אב	av
favor	(די) טובֿה	(dee) tóyve	טובה	tová
fear	(די) מורא	(dee) móyre	פחד	pákhad
feast	(די) סעודה	(dee) súde	סעודה	seudá
feather	(די) פֿעדער	(dee) féder	נוצה	notsá
feel	פֿילן	feeln	הרגיש	hirgéesh
feeling	(דאָס) געפֿיל	(dos) geféel	הרגשה	hargashá
fence	(דער) פּלויט	(der) ployt	גדר	gadér
ferry	(דער) פּראָם	(der) prom	מעבורת	mabóret
few	ווייניק	véynik	אחדים	akhadeém
fig	(די) פֿײַג	(dee) fayg	תאנה	te-ená
fight (n.)	(דער) קאַמף	(der) kamf	נלחם ב	neelkhám b'
find	געפֿינען	gefínen	מצא	matsá
finger	(דער) פֿינגער	(der) fínger	אצבע	étsba
fingernail	(דער) נאָגל	(der) nogl	ציפורן	tseepóren
finish	ענדיקן	éndikn	גמר	gamár
fire	(דער) פֿײַער	(der) fáyer	אש	esh
first	ערשט	ersht	ראשון	reeshón
fish	(דער) פֿיש	(der) fish	דג	dag
fist	(די) פֿויסט	(dee) foyst	אגרוף	egróf
flat	פֿלאַך	flakh	שטוח	shatúakh
flatter	חנפֿענען	khánfenen	החניף	hekheneéf
flavor	(דער) אַראָמאַט	(der) aromát	טעם	táam
flea	(דער) פֿלוי	(der) floy	פרעוש	parósh
flee	אַנטלויפֿן	antlóyfn	ברח	barákh
flirt	קאָקעטירן	koketírn	חיזר	kheezér
flood	(די) פֿאַרפֿלייצונג	(dee) farfléytsung	מבול	mabúl
floor	(דער) דיל	(der) dil	רצפה	reetspá
flour	(די) מעל	(dee) mel	קמח	kémakh
flower	(די) בלום	(dee) blum	פרח	pérakh
flute	(די) פֿלייט	(dee) fleyt	חליל	khaleél
fly (n.)	(די) פֿליג	(dee) flig	זבוב	zevúv
fly (v.)	פֿליִען	fleé-en	עף, טס	af, tas
fog	(דער) נעפּל	(der) nepl	ערפל	arafél
follow	נאָכגיין	nókhgeyn	עקב	akáv
food	(דאָס) עסן	(dos) esn	אוכל	ókhel
fool	(דער) נאַר	(der) nar	טיפש	teepésh
foot	(דער) פֿוס	(der) fus	רגל	régel
football	(דער) פֿוטבאָל	(der) fútbol	כדורגל	káduregel
for	פֿאַר	far	בשביל	beeshveél
forbidden	פֿאַרבאָטן	farbótn	אסור	asúr
foreign	פֿרעמד	fremd	זר	zar
forget	פֿאַרגעסן	fargésn	שכח	shakhákh
fork	(דער) גאָפּל	(der) gopl	מזלג	mazlég
fox	(דער) פֿוקס	(der) fuks	שועל	shuál
fragile	ברעכעוודיק	brékhevdik	שביר	shavír
free	פֿרײַ	fray	חופשי	khofsheé
freedom	(די) פֿרײַהייט	(dee) fráyhayt	חרות	kherút

English	Yiddish	Yiddish (transliteration)	Hebrew	Hebrew (transliteration)
freeze	אײנפֿרירן	áynfrirn	קפא	kafá
fresh	פֿריש	frish	טרי	tareé
friend	(דער) פֿרײַנד	(der) fraynt	חבר	khavér
frog	(די)זשאַבע	(dee) zhábe	צפרדע	tsefardéya
from	פֿון	fun	מן	min
front	(דער) פֿאָרנט	(der) fornt	חזית	khazeét
frozen	פֿאַרפֿרוירן	farfróyrn	מוקפא	mukpá
fruit	(די) פֿרוכט	(dee) frukht	פרי	pree
frustrated	פֿרוסטרירט	frustrírt	מתוסכל	metuskál
fry	פּרעגלען	préglen	טיגן	teegén
fun	(די) הנאה	(dee) hanóe	הנאה	hanaá
funeral	(די) לוויה	(dee) leváye	לוויה	levayá
funny	קאָמיש	kómish	מצחיק	matskheék
fur	(דער) פֿוטער	(der) fúter	פרווה	parvá
futile	אומזיסט	umzíst	עקר	akár
future	(די) צוקונפֿט	(dee) tsúkunft	עתיד	ateéd
gain	געווינען	gevínen	הרוויח	hirveéakh
gallows	(די) תליה	(dee) tleé-e	תליה	tleeá
galoshes	(די) קאַלאָשן	(dee) kalóshn	ערדלים	ardaleém
gamble	אײַנשטעלן	áynshteln	הימר	heemér
game	(די) שפּיל	(dee) shpeel	משחק	meeskhák
gang	(די) חבֿרה	(dee) khévre	חברה	khévre
gang (rag-tag)	(די) כאַליאַסטרע	(dee) khalyástre	כנופיה	knufiyá
garden	(דער) גאָרטן	(der) gortn	גן	gan
garlic	(דער) קנאָבל	(der) knobl	שום	shum
gasoline	(דער) בענזין	(der) benzeén	דלק	délek
gasp	סאַפּען	sápen	התאמץ לנשום	heetaméts leenshóm
gate	(דער) טויער	(der) tóyer	שער	sháar
gather	קלײַבן	klaybm	אסף	asáf
gauge (n.)	(די) מאָס	(dee) mos	מד	mad
general (adj.)	אַלגעמײן	álgemeyn	כללי	klaleé
generous	ברייטהאַרציק	bréythartsik	נדיב	nadeév
genius	(דער) גאָן	(der) góen	גאון	gaón
gentile	(דער) גוי	(der) goy	גוי	goy
gentle	צאַרט	tsart	אציל	atseél
gesundheit!	צו געזונט!	tsu gezúnt!	לבריאות	labreeút
ghetto	(די) געטאָ	(dee) géto	גטו	géto
ghost	(דער) שד	(der) shed	שד	shed
gift	(די) מתּנה	(dee) matóne	מתנה	mataná
girl	(דאָס) מיידל	(dos) meydl	ילדה	yaldá
give	געבן	gebm	נתן	natán
glad	צופֿרידן	tsufrídn	שמח	saméakh
glass (n.)	(דאָס) גלאָז	(dos) gloz	כוס	kos
glory	(די) גדולה	(dee) gdúle	גדולה	gedulá
glove	(די) הענטשקע	(dee) hénchke	כפפה	kefafá
glue	(דער) קליי	(der) kley	דבק	dévek
glutton	(דער) פֿרעסער	(der) fréser	זוללן	zolelán
go	גיין	geyn	הלך	halákh
goal	(דער) ציל	(der) tseel	מטרה	matará
goat	(די) ציג	(dee) tsig	עז	ez
God	גאָט	got	אלקים	elokeém
godfather	(דער) קוואַטער	(der) kváter	סנדק	sandák
gold	גאָלד	gold	זהב	zaháv
good	גוט	gut	טוב	tov

English	Yiddish	Yiddish (transliteration)	Hebrew	Hebrew (transliteration)
goodbye	זײַ געזונט	zay gezúnt	להתראות	leheetraót
goose	(די) גאַנדז	(dee) gandz	אווז	aváz
gossip	(דאָס) רכילות	(dos) rekhíles	רכילות	rekheelút
government	(די) רעגירונג	(dee) regírung	ממשלה	memshalá
grab	כאַפּן	khapm	תפס	tafás
graceful	גראַציעז	gratsyéz	חינני	kheenaneé
gradually	ביסלעכווײַז	bíslekhvayz	בהדרגה	behadragá
graduate	גראַדוירן	graduírn	סיים	see-ém
grammar	(די) גראַמאַטיק	(dee) gramátik	דיקדוק	deekdúk
granddaughter	(דאָס) אייניקל	(dos) éynikl	נכדה	nekhdá
grandson	(דאָס) אייניקל	(dos) éynikl	נכד	nékhed
grape	(די) ווײַנטרויב	(dee) váyntroyb	ענב	enáv
grapefruit	(דער) גרייפּפֿרוקט	(der) gréypfrukht	אשכולית	eshkoleét
grass	(דאָס) גראָז	(dos) groz	עשב	ésev
grave (n.)	(דער) קבֿר	(der) kéyver	קבר	kéver
gravy	(די) יויך	(dee) yoykh	רוטב	rótev
gray	גרוי	groy	אפור	afór
green	גרין	green	ירוק	yarók
greet	באַגריסן	bagreésn	בירך	berékh
groan	קרעכצן	krekhtsn	נאנח	ne-enákh
ground	(די) ערד	(dee) erd	אדמה	adamá
grow	וואַקסן	vaksn	גדל	gadál
guard (n.)	(דער) שומר	(der) shóymer	שומר	shomér
guess (v.)	טרעפֿן	trefn	ניחש	neekhésh
guide	(דער) מדריך	(der) mádrikh	מדריך	madreékh
guilty	שולדיק	shúldik	אשם	ashém
gun	(דער) פּיסטויל	(der) pistóil	אקדח	ekdákh
Gypsy	(דער) ציגײַנער	tsigáyner	צועני	tsoaneé
habit	(די) געוווינהייט	(dee) gevóynhayt	הרגל	hergél
haggard	אויסגעדאַרט	óysgedart	כחוש	kakhúsh
haggle	דינגען זיך	díngen zikh	התמקח	heetmakéakh
hail (n.)	(דער) האָגל	(der) hogl	ברד	barád
hair	(די) האָר	(dee) hor	שערות	saarót
hair-splitting (n.)	(דער) פֿילפּול	(der) pilpl	פילפול	peelpúl
half	האַלב	halb	חצי	khétsee
hamantash	(דער) המן־טאַש	(der) hómen-tash	אזן־המן	ózen-hamán
hammer	(דער) האַמער	(der) hámer	פטיש	pateésh
hand	(די) האַנט	(dee) hant	יד	yad
handkerchief	(דאָס) נאָזטיכל	(dos) nóztikhl	ממחטה	mimkhatá
hang	הענגען	héngen	תלה	talá
harbor	(דער) האַוון	(der) havn	נמל	namál
hard (not soft)	האַרט	hart	קשה	kashé
hard (difficult)	שווער	shver	קשה	kashé
harm (v.)	פֿאַרשאַטן	farshátn	הזיק	heezeék
harvest	(דער) שניט	(der) shnit	קציר	katseér
Hasid	(דער) חסיד	(der) khósed	חסיד	khaseéd
hat	(דער) הוט	(der) hut	כובע	kóva
hate (v.)	פֿײַנט האָבן	faynt hobm	שנא	sané
hate (n.)	(די) שינאה	(dee) seéne	שינאה	seená
have	האָבן	hobm	היה ל	hayá l'
hazy	פֿאַרנעפלט	farnéplt	אביך	aveékh
he	ער	er	הוא	hu
head	(דער) קאָפּ	(der) kop	ראש	rosh
headache	(דער) קאָפּווייטיק	(der) kópveytik	כאב־ראש	ke-év-rósh

English	Yiddish	Yiddish (transliteration)	Hebrew	Hebrew (transliteration)
health	(דאָס) געזונט	(dos) gezúnt	בריאות	breeút
healthy	געזונט	gezúnt	בריא	bareé
hear	הערן	hern	שמע	shamá
heart	(דאָס) האַרץ	(dos) harts	לב	lev
heartache	(דער) האַרצווייטיק	(der) hártsveytik	כאב לב	ke-év lév
heat (n.)	(די) היץ	(dee) hits	חום	khom
heaven	(דער) הימל	(der) himl	שמים	shamáyim
heavy	שווער	shver	כבד	kavéd
heel	(די) פּיאַטע	(dee) pyáte	עקב	akév
height	(די) הייך	(dee) heykh	גובה	góva
heir	(דער) יורש	(der) yóyresh	יורש	yorésh
hell	גיהנום	gehénem	גיהינום	geyhinóm
hello	שלום־עליכם	shólem-aléykhem	שלום	shalóm
help (v.)	העלפֿן	helfn	עזר	azár
here	דאָ	do	כאן	kan
heretic	(דער) אפּיקורס	(der) opikóyres	אפּיקורס	apikóres
herring	(דער) הערינג	(der) héring	מליח	maleéakh
hesitate	קווענקלען זיך	kvénklen zikh	היסס	heesés
hide	באַהאַלטן	baháltn	החביא	hekhbeé
high	הויך	hoykh	גבוה	gavóha
highway	(דער) שאָסיי	(der) shoséy	כביש ראשי	kveesh rosheé
hill	(דאָס) בערגל	(dos) bergl	גבעה	geevá
hint (n.)	(דער) רמז	(der) rémez	רמז	rémez
history	(די) געשיכטע	(dee) geshíkhte	היסטוריה	heestóriya
hit (v.)	שלאָגן	shlogn	הכה	heeká
hobby	(דער) צײַטפֿאַרברענג	(der) tsáytfarbreng	תחביב	takhbeév
hodgepodge	(דער) מיש־מאַש	(der) mísh-mash	בילבולת	beelbólet
hole	(די) לאָך	(dee) lokh	חור	khor
holiday	(דער) יום־טובֿ	(der) yóntef	חג	khag
holocaust	(דער) חורבן	(der) khurbm	שואה	shoá
holy	הייליק	héylik	קדוש	kadósh
home	(די) היים	(dee) heym	בית	báyit
homemaker	(די) בעל־הביתטע	(dee) balebóste	עקרת־בית	akéret-báyit
honest	ערלעך	érlekh	ישר	yashár
honey	(דער) האָניק	(der) hónik	דבש	devásh
honor	(דער) כּבֿוד	(der) kóved	כבוד	kavód
hope (v.)	האָפֿן	hofn	קיווה	keevá
hope (n.)	(די) האָפֿענונג	(dee) hófenung	תקווה	teekvá
hopeless	פֿאַרפֿאַלן	farfáln	חסר תקווה	khasár teekvá
horse	(דאָס) פֿערד	(dos) ferd	סוס	sus
horseradish	(דער) כריין	(der) khreyn	חזרת	khazéret
hospital	(דער) שפּיטאָל	(der) shpitól	בית־חולים	beyt-kholeém
hotel	(דער) האָטעל	(der) hotél	מלון	malón
hour	(די) שעה	(dee) sho	שעה	shaá
house	(דאָס) הויז	(dos) hoyz	בית	báyit
how	ווי	vee	איך	eykh
however	אָבער	óber	בכל אופן	bekhól ófen
hug (v.)	אַרומנעמען	arúmnémen	חיבק	kheebék
huge	ריזיק	rízik	ענקי	anakeé
hum	ברומען	brúmen	זמזם	zeemzém
humane	מענטשלעך	ménchlekh	אנושי	enosheé
humble	הכנעהדיק	hakhnóedik	עניו	anáv
humid	פֿײַכט	faykht	לח	lakh
humiliation	(די) בושה	(dee) búshe	בושה	bushá
humor	(דער) הומאָר	(der) humór	הומור	humór

English	Yiddish	Yiddish (transliteration)	Hebrew	Hebrew (transliteration)
hungry	הונגעריק	húngerik	רעב	raév
hunt (v.)	יאָגן זיך נאָך	yogn zikh nokh	צד	tsad
hunt (n.)	(דאָס) געיעג	(dos) geyég	ציד	tsayd
hurry (v.)	אײַלן	ayln	מיהר	meehér
hurt	וויי טאָן	vey ton	פגע	pagá
husband	(דער) מאַן	(der) man	בעל	báal
hypocrite	(דער) צבֿוּעק	(der) tsvuák	צבוע	tsavúa
ice	(דאָס) אײַז	(dos) ayz	קרח	kérakh
ice cream	(דער) אײַז קרעם	(der) áyz krem	גלידה	gleéda
idea	(דער) אײַנפֿאַל	(der) áynfal	רעיון	rayón
identity	(די) אידענטיטעט	(dee) identitét	זהות	zehút
if	אויב	oyb	אם	eem
ignoramus	(דער) עם־האָרץ	(der) am-órets	עם־הארץ	am-haárets
ignore	איגנאָרירן	ignorírn	התעלם מן	heetalém meen
ill	קראַנק	krank	חולה	khole
illegal	אומלעגאַל	úmlegal	לא חוקי	lo khukeé
illness	(די) קרענק	(dee) krenk	מחלה	makhalá
illusion	(די) אילוזיע	(dee) ilúzye	אשליה	ashlayá
imagination	(דער) כּוח־הדמיון	(der) kóyekh-hadímyen	כּוח־הדמיון	kóakh-hadimyón
imitate	נאָכמאַכן	nókhmakhn	חיקה	kheeká
immigrant	(דער) אימיגראַנט	(der) imigránt	מהגר	mehagér
import (v.)	אַרײַנפֿירן	aráynfirn	ייבא	yibé
important	וויכטיק	víkhtik	חשוב	khashúv
impossible	אוממיגלעך	ummíglekh	אי־אפשר	ee-efshár
impression	(דער) רושם	(der) róyshem	רושם	róshem
improve	פֿאַרבעסערן	farbésern	שיפר	sheepér
in	אַרײַן	aráyn	ב	be'
income	(די) הכנסה	(dee) hakhnóse	הכנסה	hakhnasá
increase	פֿאַרגרעסערן	fargrésern	הגדיל	heegdeél
indeed	טאַקע	táke	באמת	be-emét
independent	אומאָפֿהענגיק	úmophengik	עצמאי	atsmaeé
indulge	פֿאַרגינען	fargínen	התמכר	heetmakér
industry	(די) אינדוסטריע	(dee) indústrye	תעשייה	taaseeá
infection	(די) אָנשטעקונג	(dee) ónshtekung	אילוח	eelúakh
inflation	(די) אינפֿלאַציע	(dee) inflátsye	אינפלציה	inflátsya
influence (n.)	(די) השפעה	(dee) hashpóe	השפעה	hashpaá
information	(די) אינפֿאָרמאַציע	(dee) informátsye	מידע	meydá
inherit	ירשענען	yárshenen	ירש	yarásh
injury	(דער) שאָדן	(der) shodn	פצע	pétsa
ink	(די) טינט	(dee) tint	דיו	dyo
innocent	אומשולדיק	úmshuldik	חף מפשע	khaf meepésha
Inquisition	(די) אינקוויזיציע	(dee) inkvizítsye	חקירה	khakirá
insect	(דער) אינסעקט	(der) insékt	חרק	kharák
inside	אינעווייניק	inevéynik	בפנים	beefneém
insight	(דער) אײַנבליק	(der) áynblik	תובנה	tovaná
inspire	באַגײַסטערן	bagáystern	השרה	heeshrá
instrument	(דער) אינסטרומענט	(der) instrumént	כלי	klee
insult (v.)	באַליידיקן	baléydikn	העליב	he-eleév
insult (n.)	(די) באַליידיקונג	(dee) baléydikung	עלבון	elbón
insurance	(די) פֿאַרזיכערונג	(dee) farzíkherung	ביטוח	beetúakh
intelligent	אינטעליגענט	inteligént	אינטליגנטי	inteligéntee
intentionally	בכיוון	bekívn	בכוונה	bekhavaná
interesting	אינטערעסאַנט	interesánt	מעניין	meanyén
intermission	(די) הפֿסקה	(dee) hafsóke	הפסקה	hafsaká

English	Yiddish	Yiddish (transliteration)	Hebrew	Hebrew (transliteration)
international	אינטערנאַציאָנאַל	internatsyonál	בין-לאומי	beyn-leumeé
interpret	פֿאַרטײַטשן	fartáychn	פירש	perésh
introduce	פֿאָרשטעלן	fórshteln	הציג	heetseég
invasion	(די) אינוואַזיע	(dee) invázye	פלישה	pleeshá
invention	(דאָס) אויסגעפֿינס	(dos) óysgefins	המצאה	hamtsaá
investigate	פֿאָרשן	forshn	חקר	khakár
invite	פֿאַרבעטן	farbétn	הזמין	heezmeén
iron (n.)	(דאָס) אײַזן	(dos) ayzn	ברזל	barzél
iron (v.)	פרעסן	présn	גיהץ	geehéts
irritate	רײַצן	reytsn	הרגיז	hirgeéz
island	(דער) אינדזל	(der) indzl	אי	ee
Israel	ישראל	yisróel	ישראל	yisraél
it	עס	es	זה	ze
itch	לאָפּטשען	lópchen	חש גירוי	khash geyrúee
jacket	(די) יאַק	(dee) yak	מיקטורן	meektóren
jack-of-all-trades	(דער) כּל-בוניק	(der) kol-bóynik	מומחה לכּול	mumkhé lakól
jam	(דאָס) אײַנגעמאַכטס	(dos) áyngemakhts	ריבה	reebá
jar	(דער) סלוי	(der) sloy	צנצנת	tseentsénet
jealous	אייפֿערזיכטיק	éyferzikhtik	קנאי	kanaeé
jester	(דער) מאַרשעליק	(der) márshelik	ליצן	leytsán
Jew	(דער) ייִד	(der) Yid	יהודי	Yehudeé
jewel	(דער) אייידלשטיין	(der) éydlshtyn	אבן טובה	éven tová
Jewish	ייִדיש	Yídish	יהודי	yehudeé
job	(די) שטעלע	(dee) shtéle	מישרה	meesrá
join	פֿאַרבינדן (זיך מיט)	farbíndn (zikh mit)	הצטרף	heetstaréf
joke	(דער) וויץ	(der) vits	בדיחה	bedeekhá
journalist	(דער) זשורנאַליסט	(der) zhurnaleést	עיתונai	eetonaeé
journey	(די) נסיעה	(dee) neseé-e	נסיעה	neseeá
judge	(דער) ריכטער	(der) ríkhter	שופט	shofét
juice	(דער) זאַפֿט	(der) zaft	מיץ	meets
jump	שפרינגען	sphríngen	קפץ	kafáts
justice	(דער) יושר	(der) yóysher	צדק	tsédek
keep	האַלטן	haltn	החזיק	hekhezeék
key	(דער) שליסל	(der) shlisl	מפתח	maftéakh
kick	בריקען	bríken	בעט	baát
kidney	(די) ניר	(dee) nir	כליה	keelyá
kill	הרגענען	hárgenen	הרג	harág
kind	ליב	leeb	טוב-לב	tóv-lév
king	(דער) קיניג	(der) kínig	מלך	mélekh
kiss (n.)	(דער) קוש	(der) kush	נשיקה	nesheeká
kitchen	(די) קיך	(dee) kikh	מטבח	meetbákh
kite	(די) פֿלישלאַנג	(dee) fleéshlang	בז	baz
knee	(דער) קני	(der) knee	ברך	bérekh
knife	(דער) מעסער	(der) méser	סכין	sakéen
knock	קלאַפּן	klápm	דפק	dafák
know (facts)	וויסן	visn	ידע	yadá
know (persons)	קענען	kénen	היכר	heekár
knuckle	(דאָס) קנעקל	(dos) knekhl	פרק אצבע	pérek étsba
kosher	כּשר	kósher	כשר	kashér
ladder	(דער) לייטער	(der) léyter	סולם	sulám
lake	(די) אָזערע	(dee) ózere	אגם	agám
lamb	(דאָס) לעמל	(dos) leml	טלה	talé

English	Yiddish	Yiddish (transliteration)	Hebrew	Hebrew (transliteration)
lamp	(דער) לאָמפּ	(der) lomp	מנורה	menorá
land	(דאָס) לאַנד	(dos) land	אדמה	adamá
language	(די) שפּראַך	(dee) shprakh	שפה	safá
large	גרויס	groys	גדול	gadól
last (adj.)	לעצט	letst	אחרון	akharón
last (v.)	געדויערן	gedóyern	נמשך	neemshákh
late	שפּעט	shpet	מאוחר	meukhár
laugh (v.)	לאַכן	lakhn	צחק	tsakhák
laundry	(דאָס) וועש	(dos) vesh	כביסה	keveesá
law	(דאָס) געזעץ	(dos) gezéts	חוק	khók
lawyer	(דער) אַדוואָקאַט	(der) advokát	עורך־דין	orékh-deén
lazy	פֿויל	foyl	עצל	atsél
lead (adj.)	(דאָס) בלײַ	(dos) blay	עופרת	oféret
lead (v.)	פֿירן	firn	הוביל	hoveél
leaf	(דער) בלאַט	(der) blat	עלה	alé
leak (v.)	רינען	rínen	דלף	daláf
learn	לערנען	lérnen	למד	lamád
leather	(די) לעדער	(dee) léder	עור	or
leave	פֿאַרלאָזן	farlózn	עזב	azáv
lecture	(די) לעקציע	(dee) léktsye	הרצאה	hartsaá
left	לינק	link	שמאל	smol
leg	(דער) פֿוס	(der) fus	רגל	régel
legal	לעגאַל	legál	חוקי	khukeé
legend	(די) לעגענדע	(dee) legénde	אגדה	agadá
lemon	(די) לימינע	(dee) límine	לימון	leemón
lend	אויסלײַען	óyslayen	השאיל	heesheél
less	ווייניקער	véyniker	פחות	pakhót
lesson	(די) לעקציע	(dee) léktsye	שיעור	sheeúr
letter	(דער) בריוו	(der) briv	מכתב	meekhtáv
library	(די) ביבליאָטעק	(dee) bíbleeoték	ספריה	seefreeá
lie (v.)	ליגן	lign	שיקר	sheekér
lie (n.)	(דער) ליגן	(der) lign	שקר	shéker
life	(דאָס) לעבן	(dos) lebm	חיים	khayeém
lift	הייבן	heybm	הרים	hereém
light (adj.)	ליכטיק	líkhtik	בהיר	baheér
light (weight)	לײַכט	laykht	קל	kal
lightning	(דער) בליץ	(der) blits	ברק	barák
limit	(דער) גרענעץ	(der) grénets	גבול	gvul
line	(די) ליניע	(dee) línye	שורה	shurá
linen	(די) לײַוונט	(dee) layvnt	לבנים	levaneém
lion	(דער) לייב	(der) leyb	אריה	aryé
lip	(די) ליפּ	(dee) lip	שפה	safá
liquid (adj.)	פֿליסיק	fleésik	נוזל	nozél
liquor	(דער) בראָנפֿן	(der) bronfn	משקה מזווקק	mashké mezukák
list	(די) רשימה	(dee) reshéeme	רשימה	resheemá
literature	(די) ליטעראַטור	(dee) literatúr	ספרות	seefrút
little	קליין	kleyn	קטן	katán
live	לעבן	lebm	חיה	khayá
liver	(די) לעבער	(dee) léber	כבד	kavéd
living room	(דער) וווינצימער	(der) vóyntsimer	טרקלין	trakleén
lizard	(די) יאַשטשערקע	(dee) yáshcherke	לטאה	letaá
lock (v.)	פֿאַרשליסן	farshleésn	נעל	naál
lock (n.)	(דער) שלאָס	(der) shlos	מנעול	manúl
long	לאַנג	lang	ארוך	arókh
look	קוקן	kukn	הסתכל	heestakél

English	Yiddish	Yiddish (transliteration)	Hebrew	Hebrew (transliteration)
loose	לויז	loyz	רפה	rafé
lose (v.)	פֿאַרלירן	farlírn	איבד	eebéd
lost	פֿאַרלוירן	farlóyrn	אבד	avúd
lost (completely)	פֿאַרבלאָנדזשעט	farblónjet	אבד לגמרי	avúd legámrey
loud	הויך	hoykh	בקול רם	bekól rám
love (n.)	(די) ליבע	(dee) leébe	אהבה	ahavá
low	נידעריק	neéderik	נמוך	namókh
luck	(דער) מזל	(der) mázel	מזל	mazál
luggage	(דער) באַגאַזש	(der) bagázh	מזוודות	meezvadót
lung	(די) לונג	(dee) lung	ריאה	reá
luxury	(דער) לוקסוס	(der) lúksus	מותרות	motarót
machine	(די) מאַשין	(dee) masheén	מכונה	mekhoná
magazine	(דער) זשורנאַל	(der) zhurnál	ירחון	yarkhón
magic	(דער) כישוף	(der) kíshef	קסם	késem
magician	(דער) כישוף־מאַכער	(der) kíshef-mákher	מכשף	mekhashéf
maid	(די) דינסט	(dee) dinst	משרתת	mesharétet
mail	(די) פּאָסט	(dee) post	דואר	dóar
main	הויפּט	hoypt	עיקרי	eekareé
majority	(דאָס) רובֿ	(dos) royv	רוב	rov
make	מאַכן	makhn	עשׂה	asá
man	(דער) מאַן	(der) man	איש	eesh
manager	(דער) פֿאַרוואַלטער	(der) farválter	מנהל	menahél
map	(די) מאַפּע	(dee) mápe	מפה	mapá
mark (n.)	(דער) צייכן	(der) tseykhn	סימן	seemán
market	(דער) מאַרק	(der) mark	שוק	shuk
marry	חתונה האָבן	khásene hobm	נשׂא אישה	nasá eeshá
martyr	(דער) מאַרטירער	(der) martírer	מקודש שם	mekudásh shem
mask	(די) מאַסקע	(dee) máske	מסכה	masekhá
match	(דאָס) שוועבעלע	(dos) shvébele	גפרור	gafrúr
match (people)	(דער) שידוך	shídekh	שידוך	sheedúkh
matchmaker	(דער) שדכן	(der) shatkhn	שדכן	shadkhán
material	(דער) מאַטעריאַל	(der) materiál	חומר	khómer
mattress	(דער) מאַטראַץ	(der) matráts	מזרן	meezrán
mature	דערוואַקסן	derváksn	מבוגר	mevugár
maybe	אפֿשר	éfsher	אולי	uláy
meal	(דער) מאָלצייט	(der) móltsayt	ארוחה	arukhá
mean (v.)	מיינען	meynen	התכוון	heetkavén
mean (adj.)	בייז	beyz	שפל	shafál
meaning	(דער) באַטייט	(der) batáyt	מובן	muván
measure (v.)	מעסטן	mestn	מדד	madád
meat	(דאָס) פֿלייש	(dos) fleysh	בשׂר	basár
medal	(דער) מעדאַל	(der) medál	מדליון	medalyón
medicine	(די) מעדיצין	(dee) meditsín	רפואה	refuá
meet	טרעפֿן	trefn	פגש	pagásh
meeting	(די) זיצונג	(dee) zítsung	פגישה	pegeeshá
melon	(די) דיניע	(dee) dínye	מלון	melón
melt	שמעלצן	shmeltsn	נמס	namás
member	(דער) מיטגליד	(der) mítgleed	חבר	khavér
memorial	(דער) אָנדענק	(der) óndenk	אזכרה	azkará
memory	(דער) זכּרון	(der) zikórn	זכרון	zeekarón
merchandise	(די) סחורה	(dee) skhóyre	סחורה	skhorá
merchant	(דער) סוחר	(der) sóykher	סוחר	sokhér
merry	לעבעדיק	lébedik	עליז	aleéz
mess	(דער) באַלאַגאַן	(der) balagán	בלגן	balagán

English	Yiddish	Yiddish (transliteration)	Hebrew	Hebrew (transliteration)
message	(דער) אָנזאָג	(der) ónzog	הודעה	hodaá
metal	(דער) מעטאַל	(der) metál	מתכת	matékhet
middle	אין מיטן	in mitn	אמצע	émtsa
milk	(די) מילך	(dee) milkh	חלב	khaláv
mind (n.)	(דער) מוח	(der) móyekh	מוח	móakh
mine	מײַנער	máyner	שלי	sheleé
minute	(די) מינוט	(dee) minút	דקה	daká
miracle	(דער) נס	(der) nes	נס	nes
mirror	(דער) שפיגל	(der) shpeegl	מראה	mará
mischievous person	מזיק	mázek	תככן	takhekhán
miser	(דער) קמצן	(der) kamtsn	קמצן	kamtsán
miss (long for)	בענקען נאָך	bénken nokh	התגגע	heetgaagéya
mistake	(דער) טעות	(der) tóes	טעות	taút
mix	מישן	mishn	עירבב	eerbév
modest	באַשיידן	bashéydn	צנוע	tsanúa
moment	(די) רגע	(dee) rége	רגע	réga
money	(דאָס) געלט	(dos) gelt	כסף	késef
monkey	(די) מאַלפּע	(dee) málpe	קוף	kof
monster	(דאָס) פֿאַרזעעניש	(dos) farzé-enish	מפלצת	meeflétset
month	(דער) חודש	(der) khóydesh	חודש	khódesh
mood	(דאָס) געמיט	(dos) gemít	מצב־רוח	matsáv-rúakh
moon	(די) לבֿנה	(dee) levóne	ירח	yaréakh
more	מער	mer	עוד, יותר	od, yotér
morning	(דער) פֿרימאָרגן	(der) frimórgn	בוקר	bóker
mosquito	(דער) קאָמאַר	(der) komár	יתוש	yatúsh
most	מערסטע	mérste	ביותר	beyotér
mother	(די) מאַמע	(dee) máme	אמא	eéma
mountain	(דער) באַרג	(der) barg	הר	har
mouse	(די) מויז	(dee) moyz	עכבר	akhbár
mouth	(דאָס) מויל	(dos) moil	פה	pe
mouthwash	(דאָס) שוװענקעכץ	(dos) shvénkekhts תמיסה לשטיפת פה		temeesá leeshteefát pe
move	באַוועגן	bavégn	הניע	heneéa
move (household)	איבערציִען זיך	ibertsíen zikh	עבר דירה	avár dirá
movie	(דער) פֿילם	(der) film	סרט	séret
movie theatre	(דער) קינאָ	(der) kinó	קולנוע	kolnóa
much	אַ סך	a sakh	הרבה	harbé
mud	(די) בלאָטע	(dee) blóte	בוץ	bots
muscle	(דער) מוסקל	(der) muskl	שריר	shreer
mushroom	(דאָס) שוועמל	(dos) shveml	פיטרייה	peetreeá
music	(די) מוזיק	(dee) muzeék	מוסיקה	múseeka
musician	(דער) מוזיקער	(der) múziker	מוסיקאי	museekáy
musician (Jewish music)	(דער) כלי־זמר	(der) klézmer	כלי־זמר	klézmer
mustard	(דער) זענעפֿט	(der) zéneft	חרדל	khardál
mute	שטום	shtum	אילם	eelém
my	מײַן	mayn	שלי	sheleé
mystery	(די) מיסטעריע	(dee) mistérye	תעלומה	taalumá
nail (hardware)	(דער) טשוואָק	(der) chvok	מסמר	masmér
naked	נאַקעט	náket	ערום	aróm
name	(דער) נאָמען	(der) nómen	שם	shem
napkin	(די) סערוועטקע	(dee) servétke	מפית	mapeét
narrow	שמאָל	shmol	צר	tsar
nasty	פּאַסקודנע	paskúdne	מטונף	metunáf
nature	(די) נאַטור	(dee) natúr	טבע	téva
navel	(דער) פּופיק	(der) pupik	טבור	tabúr

English	Yiddish	Yiddish (transliteration)	Hebrew	Hebrew (transliteration)
near	נאָענט	nóent	קרוב	karóv
necessarily	דווקא	dáfke	דווקא	dávka
necessary	נייטיק	néytik	דרוש	darúsh
neck	(דער) קאַרק	(der) kark	צוואר	tsavár
necklace	(די) האַלדז־באַנד	(dee) haldz-band	ענק	anák
need (v.)	דאַרפֿן	darfn	הצטרך	heetstarékh
needle	(די) נאָדל	(dee) nodl	מחט	makhát
neglect	פֿאַרלאָזן	farlózn	הזניח	heezneéakh
neighbor	(דער) שכן	(der) shókhen	שכן	shakhén
neighborhood	(דער) געגנט	(der) gegnt	שכונה	shkhuná
nervous	נערוועז	nervéz	עצבני	atsbanée
neutral	נייטראַל	neytrál	ניטרלי	neytrálee
never	קיין מאָל ניט	keyn mol nit	לעולם לא	leolám lo
new	נײַ	nay	חדש	khadásh
newspaper	(די) צײַטונג	(dee) tsáytung	עיתון	eetón
next	נאָענסט	nóenst	הבא	habá
night	(די) נאַכט	(dee) nakht	לילה	láyla
nightmare	(דער) קאָשמאַר	(der) koshmár	סיוט	seeút
no	ניין	neyn	לא	lo
noise	(דער) רעש	(der) rash	רעש	ráash
nonsense	(די) נאַרישקייט	nárishkayt	שטויות	shtuyót
noodle	(דער) לאָקש	(der) loksh	איטרייה	eetreeá
noon	מיטאָגצײַט	mítogtsayt	צהריים	tsoharáyim
north	צפֿון	tsófn	צפון	tsafón
nose	(די) נאָז	(dee) noz	אף	af
notebook	(די) העפֿט	(dee) heft	מחברת	makhbéret
nothing	גאָרניט	górnit	כלום	klum
now	איצט	itst	עכשיו	akhsháv
nuisance	(דאָס) אָנשיקעניש	(dos) ónshikenish	מטרד	meetrád
number (counting)	(דער) נומער	(der) númer	מספר	meespár
number (quantity)	(די) צאָל	(dee) tsol	מספר	meespár
nurse	(די) קראַנקן־שוועסטער	(dee) kránkn-shvéster	אחות	akhót
nut	(דער) נוס	(der) nus	אגוז	egóz
oak	(דער) דעמב	(der) demb	אלון	alón
oar	(דער) רודער	(der) rúder	משוט	mashót
oath	(די) שבֿועה	(dee) shvúe	שבועה	shvuá
oatmeal	(דער) האָבערגריץ	(der) hóbergrits	קמח שבולת־שועל	kémakh sheebólet-shuál
obey	פֿאָלגן	folgn	ציית	tsee-ét
obnoxious	דערווידערדיק	dervéederdik	נתעב	neetáv
obscene	ניבול־פּהיק	níbl-péik	מגונה	meguné
obsession	(דאָס) באַנעמעניש	(dos) banémenish	שגעון	sheegaón
obstacle	(די) מניעה	(dee) meneé-e	מכשול	meekhshól
obtain	קריגן	krign	השיג	heeseég
occupation	(דער) פֿאַך	(der) fakh	משלח יד	meeshlákh yád
occupy	פֿאַרנעמען	farnémen	תפס	tafás
of	פֿון	fun	של, מ	shel, me
off	אָפּ, אַראָפּ	op, aróp	רחוק, מעל	rakhók, meál
offend	באַליידיקן	baléydikn	פגע ב	pagá b'
offer (v.)	אָנבאָטן	ónbotn	הציע	heetseéa
office	(דאָס) ביוראָ	(dos) byuró	משרד	meesrád
official (adj.)	אָפֿיציעל	ofitsyél	רשמי	reeshmeé
often	אָפֿט	oft	לעתים קרובות	le-eeteém krovót
oil	(דער) אייל	(der) eyl	שמן	shémen
old	אַלט	alt	ישן	yashán

English	Yiddish	Yiddish (transliteration)	Hebrew	Hebrew (transliteration)
olive	(די) מאַסלינע	(dee) masleéne	זית	záyit
on (prep.)	אויף	oyf	על	al
onion	(די) ציבעלע	(dee) tsíbele	בצל	batsál
only (adj.)	איינציק	eýntsik	יחידי	yekheedeé
only (adv.)	נאָר	nor	רק	rak
open	אָפֿן	ofn	פתוח	patúakh
opinion	(די) מיינונג	(dee) méynung	דעה	deyá
opportunity	(די) געלעגנהייט	(dee) gelégnhayt	הזדמנות	heezdamnút
opposite	פֿאַרקערט	farkért	מול, הפך	mul, héfekh
oppress	באַדריקן	badríkn	דיכא	deeké
option	(די) ברירה	(dee) bréyre	ברירה	breyrá
or	אָדער	óder	או	o
orange (n.)	(דער) מאַראַנץ	(der) maránts	תפוז	tapúz
orange (color)	אָראַנזש	oránzh	תפוז	tapúz
orchestra	(דער) אָרקעסטער	(der) orkéster	תזמורת	teezmóret
order (arrangement)	(די) אָרדענונג	(dee) órdenung	סדר	séder
order (command)	(דער) באַפֿעל	(der) bafél	פקודה	pekudá
order (to be delivered)	באַשטעלן	bashtéln	הזמין	heezmeén
ordinary	געוויינטלעך	gevéyntlekh	רגיל	rageél
organization	(די) אָרגאַניזאַציע	(dee) organizátsye	ארגון	eergún
orphan	(דער) יתום	(der) yósem	יתום	yatóm
other	אַנדער	ánder	אחר	akhér
our	אונדזער	úndzer	שלנו	shelánu
out	אַרויס	aróys	החוצה	hakhútsa
outside	אין דרויסן	in droysn	בחוץ	bakhúts
oven	(דער) אויוון	(der) oyvn	תנור	tanúr
over	איבער	íber	מעל ל	meál l'
owe	זײַן שולדיק	zayn shúldik	חב	khav
owl	(די) סאָווע	(dee) sóve	ינשוף	yanshúf
ox	(דער) אָקס	(der) oks	שור	shor
package	(דאָס) פּעקל	(dos) pekl	חבילה	khaveelá
page	(די) זײַט	(dee) zayt	דף	daf
pail	(דער) עמער	(der) émer	דלי	dlee
pain	(דער) ווייטיק	(der) véytik	כאב	ke-év
painter	(דער) מאָלער	(der) móler	צייר	tsayár
painting	(דאָס) מאָלערײַ	(dos) moleráy	ציור	tseeúr
pair	(די) פּאָר	(dee) por	זוג	zug
palace	(דער) פּאַלאַץ	(der) paláts	ארמון	armón
pan	(די) פֿאַן	(dee) fan	מחבת	makhvát
pancake	(די) לאַטקע	(dee) látke	לחם־דפוסים	lékhem-defuseém
panic	(די) בהלה	(dee) behóle	בהלה	behalá
pants	הויזן	hoyzn	מכנסיים	meekhnasáyim
paper	(דאָס) פּאַפּיר	(dos) papír	ניר	neyár
parcel	(דאָס) פּעקל	(dos) pekl	חבילה	khaveelá
parents	עלטערן	éltern	הורים	horeém
park (v.)	פֿאַרקירן	parkírn	חנה	khaná
parsley	(די) פּעטרישקע	(dee) pétrishke	כרפס־נהרות	karpas-neharót
part	(דער) טייל	(der) teyl	חלק	khélek
participate	אָנטייל נעמען	ónteyl némen	השתתף	heeshtatéf
particularly	(דער) עיקר	(der) eéker	במיוחד	bemeyukhád
partition	(די) מחיצה	(dee) mekhítse	מחיצה	mekheetsá
partner	(דער) שותף	(der) shútef	שותף	shutáf
party	(די) וועטשערינקע	(dee) vechereénke	מסיבה	meseebá
pass	דערלאַנגען	derlángen	עבר	avár

English	**Yiddish**	**Yiddish (transliteration)**	**Hebrew**	**Hebrew (transliteration)**
pass (exam)	אויסהאַלטן	óyshaltn	עמד	amád
passionate	ליַידנשאַפֿטלעך	laydnsháftlekh	רגשני	ragshaneé
Passover	פּסח	péysakh	פסח	pésakh
past	(די) פֿאַרגאַנגענהייט	(dee) fargángenhayt	עבר	avár
path	(דער) שטעג	(der) shteg	שביל	shveel
patience	(די) געדולד	(dee) gedúld	סבלנות	savlanút
pawnshop	(דער) לאָמבאַרד	(der) lómbard	בית־עבוט	beyt-avót
pay (v.)	צאָלן	tsoln	שילם	sheelém
peace	(דער) שלום	(der) shólem	שלום	shalóm
peach	(די) פֿערשקע	(dee) férshke	אפרסק	afarsék
peacock	(די) פּאַווע	(dee) páve	טווס	tavás
peak	(דער) שפּיץ	(der) shpits	שיא	see
pear	(די) באַר	(dee) bar	אגס	agás
peas	אַרבעס	árbes	אפונות	afunót
peasant	(דער) פּויער	(der) póyer	איכר	eekár
peculiar	מאָדנע	módne	מוזר	muzár
peel (n.)	(די) שאָלעכץ	(dee) shólekhts	קליפה	kleepá
pen	(די) פֿעדער	(dee) féder	עט	et
pencil	(דער) בלַייער	(der) bláyer	עפרון	eeparón
people (ethnic)	(דאָס) פֿאָלק	(dos) folk	עם	am
people	מענטשן	menchn	אנשים	anasheém
pepper	(דער) פֿעפֿער	(der) féfer	פילפל	peelpél
performance	(די) פֿאָרשטעלונג	(dee) fórshtelung	הצגה	hatsagá
perhaps	אפֿשר	éfsher	אולי	uláy
permitted	דערלויבט	derlóypt	מותר	mutár
perplexed	געפּלעפֿט	gepléft	מבולבל	mevulbál
persecution	(די) רדיפֿה	(dee) redeéfe	רדיפה	redeefá
person	(די) פּערזאָן	(dee) perzón	איש	eesh
personal	פּערזאָנלעך	perzénlekh	אישי	eesheé
personality	(די) פּערזאָנעלעכקייט	(dee) perzénlekhkayt	אישיות	eesheeút
perspire	שוויצן	shvitsn	הזיע	heezeéa
persuade	איַינרעדן	áynredn	שכנע	sheekhnéa
pharmacist	(דער) אַפּטייקער	(der) aptéyker	רוקח	rokéakh
phonograph	(דער) פֿאָנאָגראַף	(der) fonográf	מקול	makól
photograph	(די) פֿאָטאָגראַפֿיע	(dee) fotográfye	תצלום	tatslúm
piano	(די) פּיאַנע	(dee) pyáne	פסנתר	psantér
picture	(דאָס) בילד	(dos) bild	תמונה	temuná
piece	(דאָס) שטיק	(dos) shtik	חתיכה	khateekhá
pig	(דער) חזיר	(der) kházer	חזיר	khazír
pigeon	(די) טויב	(dee) toyb	יונה	yoná
pillow	(דער) קישן	(der) kishn	כר	kar
pin	(די) שפּילקע	(dee) shpéelke	סיכה	seeká
pine tree	(די) סאָסנע	(dee) sósne	אורן	óren
pink	ראָז	roz	ורוד	varód
pipe (tobacco)	(די) פּיפּקע	(dee) pipke	מיקטרת	meektéret
pipe	(די) רער	(dee) rer	צינור	tseeńor
pity	(דאָס) רחמנות	(dos) rakhmónes	רחמנות	rakhmanút
place	(דער) אָרט	(der) ort	מקום	makóm
plan (n.)	(דער) פּלאַן	(der) plan	תוחנית	tokhneét
plant (n.)	(דאָס) געוויקס	(dos) gevíks	צמח	tsémakh
plate	(דער) טעלער	(der) téler	צלחת	tsalákhat
play (v.)	שפּילן	shpeeln	שׂיחק	seekhék
playing cards	קאָרטן	kortn	קלפים	klaféem
please	זיַיט אַזוי גוט	zayt azóy gut	בבקשה	bevakashá
pleasure	(דאָס) פֿאַרגעניגן	(dos fargenígn	הנאה	hanaá

English	Yiddish	Yiddish (transliteration)	Hebrew	Hebrew (transliteration)
plow	(דער) אָקער	(der) áker	מחרשה	makhreshá
plum	(די) פלוים	(dee) floym	שזיף	shazeéf
pocket	(די) קעשענע	(dee) késhene	כיס	kees
point (n.)	(דאָס) פינטל	(dos) pintl	נקודה	nekudá
poison	(דער) סם	(der) sam	רעל	ráal
polite	העפֿלעך	héflekh	מנומס	menumás
pond	(דער) סטאַוו	(der) stav	בריכה	breykhá
pool	(דער) באַסיין	(der) baséyn	בריכה	breykhá
poor	אָרעם	órem	עני	aneé
poorhouse	(דאָס) הקדש	(dos) hégdesh	הקדש	hekdésh
population	(די) באַפֿעלקערונג	(dee) bafélkerung	אכלוסיה	ukhlóseea
positive	פּאָזיטיוו	poz“teév	חיובי	kheeuveé
possible	מעגלעך	méglekh	אפשרי	efshareé
postcard	(דאָס) פּאָסטקאַרטל	(dos) póstkartl	גלויה	geluyá
postpone	אָפּלייגן	ópleygn	דחה	dakhá
pot	(דער) טאָפּ	(der) top	סיר	sir
potato	(דער) קאַרטאָפֿל	(der) kartófl	תפוח־אדמה	tapúakh-adamá
pour	גיסן	geesn	שפך	shafákh
powder	(דער) פּראָשיק	(der) próshik	אבקה	avká
power	(דער) כוח	(der) kóyekh	כוח	kóakh
pray	מתפלל זײַן, דאַוונען (Jewish)	mispalel zayn, davnen (Jewish)	התפלל	heetpalél
precise	גענוי	genóy	מדויק	meduyák
pregnant	טראָגעדיק	trógedik	הרה	hará
prepare	גרייטן	greytn	הכין	hekheén
pressure	(דער) דריק	(der) drik	לחץ	lákhats
pretend	מאַכן אַן אָנשטעל	makhn an ónshtel	העמיד פנים	he-emeéd paneém
prevent	פֿאַרהיטן	farhítn	מנע	maná
price	(דער) פּרײַז	(der) prayz	מחיר	mekhír
pride	(דער) שטאָלץ	(der) shtolts	גאווה	gaavá
print (v.)	דרוקן	drukn	הדפיס	heedpeés
prison	(די) תפיסה	(dee) tféese	בית־סוהר	beyt-sóhar
private	פּריוואַט	preevát	פרטי	prateé
privilege	(די) זכיה	(dee) skheé-e	זכות	skhut
prize	(דער) פּריז	(der) preez	פרס	pras
probably	מסתמא	mistóme	יתכן	yeetakhén
profession	(דער) פֿאַך	(der) fakh	מיקצוע	meektsóa
profit	(דער) רווח	(der) révekh	רווח	révakh
program	(די) פּראָגראַם	(dee) prográm	תוכנית	tokhneét
project	(דער) פּראָיעקט	(der) proyékt	תוכנית	tokhneét
promise	צוזאָגן	tsúzogn	הבטיח	heevteéakh
proof	(דער) דערווײַז	(der) derváyz	הוכחה	hokhekhá
propaganda	(די) פּראָפּאַגאַנדע	(dee) propagánde	תעמולה	taamulá
proper	געהעריק	gehérik	מתאים	mateém
property	(דער) פֿאַרמאָג	(der) farmóg	רכוש	rekhúsh
prophet	(דער) נבֿיא	(der) nóvee	נביא	naveé
propose	פֿאָרלייגן	fórleygn	הציע	heetseéa
protect	שיצן	shitsn	הגן	hegén
proud	שטאָלץ	shtolts	גאה	ge-é
publish	אַרויסגעבן	aróysgebm	הוציא לאור	hotseé laór
punishment	(די) שטראָף	(dee) shtrof	עונש	ónesh
purse	(דאָס) בײַטל	(dos) baytl	ארנק	arnak
push (v.)	שטופּן	shtupm	דחף	dakháf
pushcart	(דאָס) שטופֿוועגל	(dos) shtúpvegl	עגלת־יד	eglát-yád
put	שטעלן, לייגן	shteln, leygn	שם, נתן	sam, natán
puzzle	(דאָס) רעטעניש	(dos) rétenish	חידה	kheedá

English	Yiddish	Yiddish (transliteration)	Hebrew	Hebrew (transliteration)
quality	(די) קוואליטעט	(dee) kvalitét	איכות	eykhút
quantity	(די) קוואנטיטעט	(dee) kvantitét	כמות	kamút
quarter	(דאָס) פערטל	(dos) fertl	רבע	réva
queen	(די) מלכה	(dee) málke	מלכה	malká
question	(די) פֿראַגע	(dee) frage	שאלה	she-elá
quick	גיך	geekh	מהר	mahér
quiet	שטיל	shtil	שקט	shakét
quiver	צאַפּלען	tsáplen	רטט	ratát
quote	ציטירן	tsitírn	ציטט	tseetét
rabbi	(דער) רבֿ, רבי	(der) rov, rébe (Hasidic)	רב	rav
rabbit	(דער) קראָליק	(der) królik	שפן	shafán
race	(די) ראַסע	(dee) ráse	גזע	géza
race (contest)	(דאָס) געיעג	(dos) geyég	מירוץ	meyróts
radio	(דער) ראַדיאָ	(der) rádio	רדיו	rádio
radish	(דער) רעטעך	(der) rétekh	צנון	tsenón
rag	(די) שמאַטע	(dee) shmáte	סמרטוט	smartút
rain	(דער) רעגן	(der) regn	גשם	géshem
rainbow	(דער) רעגן־בויגן	(der) regn-boygn	קשת	késhet
raincoat	(דער) רעגן־מאַנטל	(der) regn-mantl	מעיל-גשם	me-eél-géshem
raise (v.)	אויפֿהייבן	óyfheybm	הרים	hereém
raisin	(די) ראָזשינקע	(dee) rózhinke	צימוק	tseemúk
rake	(די) גראַבליע	(dee) gráblye	מגרפה	magrefá
rare	זעלטן	zeltn	נדיר	nadír
rascal	(דער) יונגאַטש	(der) yungách	נוכל	nokhél
raspberry	(די) מאַלענע	(dee) málene	פטל	pétel
rat	(דער) ראַץ	(der) rats	חולדה	khuldá
raw	רוי	roy	גולמי	golmeé
razor	(דער) גאָלמעסער	(der) gólmeser	תער	táar
reach	דערגרייכן	dergréykhn	הגיע	heegéea
read	לייענען	léyenen	קרא	kará
ready	גרייט	greyt	מוכן	mukhán
really	טאַקע	táke	באמת	be-emét
reason	(די) סיבה	(dee) síbe	סיבה	seebá
rebellion	(דער) אויפֿשטאַנד	(der) oýfshtand	מרד	méred
receipt	(די) קבלה	(dee) kabóle	קבלה	kabalá
receive	קריגן	krign	קיבל	keebél
recently	אנומלט	anúmlt	לאחרונה	laakharoná
recognize	דערקענען	derkénen	הכיר	heekeér
recommend	רעקאָמענדירן	rekomendírn	המליץ	heemleéts
record (n.)	(דער) דיסק	(der) disk	תקליט	takleét
red	רויט	royt	אדום	adóm
reduce	אַראָפּלאָזן	aróplozn	הקטין	heekteén
reflect	אָפּשפּיגלען	ópshpiglen	החזיר	hekhezír
refrigerator	(דער) פֿרידזשידער	(der) frijidér	מקרר	mekarér
refugee	(דער) פּליט	(der) pólet	פליט	paleét
regime	(די) ממשלה	(dee) memshóle	משטר	meeshtár
register	רעגיסטרירן	registrírn	רשם	rashám
regret (v.)	חרטה האָבן	kharóte hobm	הצטער	heetstaér
rehearsal	(די) רעפּעטיציע	(dee) repetítsye	חזרה	khazará
relatives	קרובֿים	króyvim	קרובים	kroveém
relax	רוען זיך	rúen zikh	הרפה	hirpá
relevant	שייך	sháyekh	שייך	shayákh
religion	(די) רעליגיע	(dee) relígye	דת	dat
remain	בלײַבן	blaybm	נשאר	neeshár

English	Yiddish	Yiddish (transliteration)	Hebrew	Hebrew (transliteration)
remember	געדענקען	gedénken	זכר	zakhár
remind	דערמאָנען	dermónen	הזכיר	heezkír
remove	צונעמען	tsúnemen	סילק	seelék
rent	דירה־געלט	díre-gelt	דמי שכירות	deméy sekirút
repair	פֿאַרריכטן	farríkhtn	שיפץ	sheepéts
repeat	איבערחזרן	iberkházern	חזר על	khazár al
report	(דער) באַריכט	(der) baríkht	דוח	dúakh
reputation	(דער) שם	(der) shem	שם	shem
request	(די) בקשה	(dee) bakóshe	בקשה	bakashá
rescue	ראַטעווען	ráteven	הציל	heetseél
resign	רעזיגנירן	rezignírn	התפטר	heetpatér
responsibility	(דאָס) אַחריות	(dos) akhráyes	אחריות	akhrayút
rest (v.)	רוען	rúen	נח	nakh
restaurant	(דער) רעסטאָראַן	(der) restorán	מסעדה	meesadá
result	(דער) רעזולטאַט	(der) rezultát	תוצאה	totsaá
revenge	(די) נקמה	(dee) nekóme	נקמה	nekamá
revenue	(די) הכנסה	(dee) hakhnóse	הכנסה	hakhnasá
review (n.)	(דער) איבערקוק	(der) íberkuk	סקירה	skirá
revive	אויפֿלעבן	óyflebm	החיה	hekheyá
revolution	(די) רעוואָלוציע	(dee) revolútsye	מהפכה	mahapekhá
rice	(דער) רײַז	(der) rayz	אורז	órez
rich	רײַך	raykh	עשיר	asheér
ridicule	חוזק מאַכן פֿון	khóyzek makhn fun	לעג	laág
ridiculous	לעכערלעך	lékherlekh	מגוחך	megukhákh
rifle	(די) ביקס	(dee) biks	רובה	rové
right	רעכט	rekht	ימין	yameén
ring (n.)	(דאָס) פֿינגערל	(dos) fíngerl	טבעת	tabáat
riot	(די) מהומה	(dee) mehúme	פרעות	praót
ripe	צײַטיק	tsáytik	בשל	bashél
risk	(די) ריזיקע	(dee) rízike	סיכון	seekún
river	(דער) טײַך	(der) taykh	נהר	náhar
road	(דער) וועג	(der) veg	דרך	dérekh
roast	בראָטן	brotn	צלה	tsalá
robber	(דער) גזלן	(der) gázlen	שודד	shodéd
rock (n.)	(דער) פֿעלדז	(der) feldz	סלע	séla
roll (n.)	(די) בולקע	(dee) búlke	לחמניה	lakhmaneeá
roof	(דער) דאַך	(der) dakh	גג	gag
room	(דער) צימער	(der) tsímer	חדר	khéder
root	(דער) וואָרצל	(der) vortsl	שורש	shóresh
rope	(דער) שטריק	(der) shtrik	חבל	khével
rose	(די) רויז	(dee) royz	ורד	véred
rotten	פֿאַרפֿוילט	farfóylt	רקוב	rakúv
round	קײַלעכיק	káylekhik	עגול	agól
row	(די) ריי, (די) שורה	(dee) rey, (dee) shúre	שורה	shurá
rub	רײַבן	raybm	שפשף	sheefshéf
rubber	(די) גומע	(dee) gúme	גומי	gúmee
rug	(דער) טעפעך	(der) tépekh	שטיח	shateéakh
rumor	(די) שמועה	(dee) shmúe	שמועה	shmuá
run	לויפֿן	loyfn	רץ	rats
rush	אײַלן	ayln	חפז	khafáz
rust	(דער) זשאַווער	(der) zháver	חלודה	khaludá
ruthless	אַכזריותדיק	akhźoryesdik	אכזרי	akhzareé
rye	קאָרן	korn	שיפון	shifón
Sabbath	(דער) שבת	(der) shábes	שבת	shabát

English	Yiddish	Yiddish (transliteration)	Hebrew	Hebrew (transliteration)
sacrifice	מקריב זיַין	mákrev zayn	הקריב	heekreév
sad	טרויעריק	tróyerik	עצוב	atsúv
saddle	(דער) זאָטל	(der) zotl	אוכּף	ukáf
safe	זיכער	zíkher	בטוח	batúakh
safety	(די) זיכערקייט	(dee) zíkherkayt	ביטחון	beetakhón
sage	(דער) חכם	(der) khókhem	חכם	khakhám
sailor	(דער) מאַטראָס	(der) matrós	מלח	malákh
saint	(דער) צדיק	(der) t̂sadik	צדיק	tsadeék
salary	שכירות	skhíres	משׂכּורת	maskóret
salesman	(דער) פֿאַרקויפֿער	(der) farkóyfer	זבן	zabán
salt	(די) זאַלץ	(dee) zalts	מלח	mélakh
salvation	(די) גאולה	(dee) geúle	גאולה	geulá
same	זעלביק	zélbik	אותו	otó
sample	(דער) מוסטער	(der) múster	דוגמא	dugmá
sand	(דאָס) זאַמד	(dos) zamd	חול	khol
satisfaction	(די) צופֿרידנקייט, (דאָס) נחת	(dee) tsufrídnkayt, nákhes	סיפוק, נחת	seepúk, nakhát
satisfy	באַפֿרידיקן	bafreédikn	סיפק	seepék
saucer	(דאָס) טעצל	(dos) tetsl	תחתית	takhteét
save (rescue)	ראַטעווען	ráteven	הציל	heetseél
save (money)	שפּאָרן	shporn	חסך	khasákh
saw	(די) זעג	(dee) zeg	מסור	masór
scale	(די) וואָגשאָל	(dee) vógshol	משקל	meeshkál
scapegoat	(דאָס) כּפרה־הינדל	(dos) kapóre-hindl	שׂעיר־לעזאזל	saeér-leazazél
scare	דערשרעקן	dershrékn	הפחיד	heefkheéd
scarf	(די) שאַל	(dee) shal	סודר	sudár
scene	(די) סצענע	(dee) stséne	סצנה	stséna
schedule	(דער) צײַטפּלאַן	(der) tsáytplan	מערכת	maarékhet
scholar	(דער) געלערנטער	(der) gelérnter	למדן	lamdán
science	(די) וויסנשאַפֿט	(dee) vísnshaft	מדע	madá
scientist	(דער) וויסנשאַפֿטלער	(der) vísnshaftler	מדען	madán
scissors	(דאָס) שערל	(dos) sherl	מספריים	meesparáyim
scrambled eggs	(די) פּרעזשעניצע	(dee) prézhenitse	ביצה טרופה	beytsá trufá
scratch	קראַצן	kratsn	גרד	garád
scream	קוויטשען	kvíchen	צווח	tsavákh
screw	(דער) שרויף	(der) shroyf	בורג	bóreg
sea	(דער) ים	(der) yam	ים	yam
search	זוכן	zukhn	חיפש	kheepés
secret	(דער) סוד	(der) sod	סוד	sod
secretary	(דער) סעקרעטאָר, (די) סעקרעטאָרשע	(der) sekretár, (dee) sekretárshe	מזכיר, מזכירה	mazkír, mazkirá
section	(דער) חלק	(der) khéylek	חלק	khélek
seduce	פֿאַרפֿירן	farfírn	פיתה	peetá
see	זען	zen	ראה	raá
seed	(דער) זוימען	(der) zóymen	זרע	zéra
seem	דאַכטן זיך	dakhtn zikh	נדמה	needmé
sell	פֿאַרקויפֿן	farkóyfn	מכר	makhár
send	שיקן	shikn	שלח	shalákh
sense (physical)	(דער) חוש	(der) khush	חוש	khush
sense (judgement)	(דער) שכל	(der) seykhl	שׂכל	sékhel
sensitive	סענסיטיוו	sensiteév	רגיש	rageésh
sentence	(דער) זאַץ	(der) zats	משפט	meeshpát
separate (adj.)	באַזונדער	bazúnder	נפרד	neefrád
serious	ערנצט	erntst	רציני	retseeneé
serve	דינען	deénen	שירת	sheyrét
several	עטלעכע	étlekhe	כמה	káma
sew	נייען	néyen	תפר	tafár

English	Yiddish	Yiddish (transliteration)	Hebrew	Hebrew (transliteration)
sex	(דער) מין	(der) meen	מין	meen
sexton	(דער) שמש	(der) shámes	שמש	shamásh
shabby	אָפּגעטראָגן	ópgetrogn	מרופט	merupát
shadow	(דער) שאָטן	(der) shotn	צל	tsel
shake	שאָקלען	shóklen	נענע	neená
shame	(די) בושה	(dee) búshe	בושה	bushá
share	טיילן זיך	teyln zikh	התחלק	heetkhalék
sharp	שאַרף	sharf	חד	khad
shave	גאָלן זיך	goln zikh	התגלח	heetgaléakh
she	זי	zee	היא	hee
sheep	(די) שאָף	(dee) shof	צאן	tson
shelf	(די) פּאָליצע	(dee) pólitse	מדף	madáf
shephard	(דער) פּאַסטעך	(der) pástekh	רועה	roé
ship	(די) שיף	(dee) shif	אונייה	oneeá
shirt	(דאָס) העמד	(dos) hemd	חולצה	khultsá
shiver	ציטערן	tsítern	רעד	raád
shock	(דער) שאָק	(der) shok	הלם	hélem
shoe	(דער) שוך	(der) shukh	נעל	náal
shoot	שיסן	sheesn	ירה ב	yará b'
shop (v.)	אײַנקויפֿן	áynkoyfn	ערך קניות	arákh kneeót
short	קורץ	kurts	קצר	katsár
shoulder	(די) פּלייצע	(dee) pléytse	כתף	katéf
shout	שרײַען	shráyen	צעק	tsaák
shovel	(די) לאָפּעטע	(dee) lópete	יעה	yaé
show (v.)	ווײַזן	vayzn	הראה	herá
show (n.)	(די) פֿאָרשטעלונג	(dee) fŏrshtelung	הצגה	hatsagá
shy	שעמעוודיק	shémevdik	ביישן	bayshán
sick	קראַנק	krank	חולה	kholé
side	(די) זײַט	(dee) zayt	צד	tsad
sigh	זיפֿצן	ziftsn	נאנח	ne-enákh
sign	(דער) סימן	(der) símen	סימן	seemán
signature	(די) חתימה	(dee) khseéme	חתימה	khateemá
silent	שטיל	shtil	שותק	shoték
silk	(די) זײַד	(dee) zayd	משי	méshee
silly	נאַריש	nárish	טיפשי	teepsheé
silver	(דאָס) זילבער	(dos) zílber	כסף	késef
similar	ענלעך	énlekh	דומה	domé
simple	פּשוט	póshet	פשוט	pashút
sin	(די) עבירה	(dee) avéyre	עבירה	aveyrá
since	זינט	zint	מאז	meáz
sing	זינגען	zíngen	שר	shar
sink (n.)	(דער) אָפּגאָס	(der) ópgos	בור שופכים	bor shofkheém
sister	(די) שוועסטער	(dee) shvéster	אחות	akhót
sit	זיצן	zitsn	ישב	yasháv
size	(די) גרייס	(dee) greys	גודל	gódel
ski	נאַרטלען זיך	nártlen zikh	החליק במיגלשיים	hekhleék bemeeglasháyim
skin	(די) הויט	(dee) hoyt	עור	or
skinny	דאַר	dar	כחוש	kakhúsh
sky	(דער) הימל	(der) himl	שמיים	shamáyim
slap	פּאַטשן	páchn	סטר	satár
slave	(דער) שקלאַף	(der) shklaf	עבד	éved
sled	(דער) שליטן	(der) shlitn	מיזחלת	meezkhélet
sleep	שלאָפֿן	shlofn	ישן	yashán
slowly	פּאַמעלעך	pamélekh	לאט	leát
sly	כיטרע	khítre	ערמומי	armumeé

English	Yiddish	Yiddish (transliteration)	Hebrew	Hebrew (transliteration)
small	קליין	kleyn	קטן	katán
smell (n.)	(דער) ריח	(der) réyekh	ריח	réyakh
smell (v.)	שמעקן	shmekn	הריח	hereéakh
smoke (n.)	(דער) רויך	(der) roykh	עשן	ashán
smoke (v.)	רייכערן	réykhern	עישן	eeshén
smooth	גלאט	glat	חלק	khalák
snack	(דער) נאש	(der) nash	ארוחה קלה	arukhá kalá
snake	(די) שלאַנג	(dee) shlang	נחש	nakhásh
sneeze	ניסן	neesn	התעטש	heetatésh
snore	כראָפען	khrópen	נחר	nakhár
snow	(דער) שניי	(der) shney	שלג	shéleg
so	אזוי	azoy	כל-כך	kol-kákh
soap	(די) זייף	(dee) zeyf	סבון	sabón
society	(די) געזעלשאַפֿט	(dee) gezélshaft	חברה	khevrá
sock	(דער) זאָק	(der) zok	גרב	gérev
soft	ווייך	veykh	רך	rakh
soldier	(דער) סאָלדאַט	(der) soldát	חיל	kayál
solid	סאָליד	soleéd	מוצק	mutsák
solution	(די) סגולה	(dee) sgúle	פתרון	peetarón
something	עפעס	epes	משהו	má-shehu
sometimes	א מאָל	a mol	לפעמים	leefameém
son	(דער) זון	(der) zun	בן	ben
song	(דאָס) ליד	(dos) leed	שיר	shír
soon	באַלד	bald	בקרוב	bekaróv
sorrow	(דער) טרויער	(der) tróyer	צער	tsáar
sorry	באַנג טאָן אויף	bang ton oyf	הצטער	heetstaér
soul	(די) נשמה	(dee) neshóme	נשמה	neshamá
sound	(דער) קלאַנג	(der) klang	צליל	tseleél
soup	(די) זופ	(dee) zup	מרק	marák
sour	זויער	zóyer	חמוץ	khamúts
south	דרום	dórem	דרום	daróm
space	(דאָס) אָרט	(dos) ort	מקום	makóm
speak	רעדן	redn	דיבר	deebér
special	ספּעציעל	spetsyél	מיוחד	meyukhád
speech	(די) רעדע	(dee) réde	הרצאה	hartsaá
spell	אויסלייגן	óysleygn	אית	eeyét
spend	פֿאַרברענגען	farbréngen	בילה	beelá
spice	בשמים	psómim	תבלין	tavleén
spit	שפּייַען	shpáyen	ירק	yarák
spite	אויף צו להכעיס	oyf tselókhes	מרי	mree
spoon	(דער) לעפֿל	(der) lefl	כף	kaf
spot	(דער) פֿלעק	(der) flek	כתם	kétem
spring	(דער) פֿרילינג	(der) fríling	אביב	aveév
spy	(דער) שפּיאָן	(der) shpeeón	מרגל	meragél
square	קוואַדראַט	kvadrát	רבוע	ravúa
squeak	(דער) סקריפ	(der) skrip	ציוץ	tseeúts
squeeze	קוועטשן	kvechn	סחט	sakhát
squirt	שפּריצן	shpritsn	התיז	heeteéz
stairs	טרעפּלעך	tréplekh	מדרגות	madregót
stammer	שטאַמלען	shtámlen	גמגם	geemgém
stamp (mail)	(די) מאַרקע	(dee) márke	בול	bul
stand	שטיין	shteyn	עמד	amád
star	(דער) שטערן	(der) shtern	כוכב	kokháv
start	אָנהייבן	ónheybm	התחיל	heetkheél
state	(דער) שטאַט, (די) מדינה	(der) shtat, (dee) medeéne	מדינה	medeená

English	Yiddish	Yiddish (transliteration)	Hebrew	Hebrew (transliteration)
station	(די) סטאַנציע	(dee) stántsye	תחנה	takhaná
steal	גנבֿענען	gánvenen	גנב	ganáv
steel	(דאָס) שטאָל	(dos) shtol	פלדה	pladá
steps	טרעפלעך	tréplekh	מדרגות	madregót
stick	(דער) שטעקן	(der) shtekn	מקל	makél
stiff	שטײַף	shtayf	קשיח	kasheéakh
sting	שטעכן	shtekhn	עקץ	akáts
stingy	קאַרג	karg	קמצן	kamtsán
stink	שטינקען	shtínken	הסריח	heesreéakh
stomach	(דער) מאָגן	(der) mogn	קיבה	keyvá
stone	(דער) שטײן	(der) shteyn	אבן	éven
stop (n.)	(דער) אָפּשטעל	(der) ópshtel	עצירה	atsirá
stop!	הער אויף	her oýf	תפסיק	tafseék
store	(די) קראָם	(dee) krom	חנות	khanút
storm	(דער) שטורעם	(der) shtúrem	סערע	seará
stove	(די) הרובע	(dee) hrúbe	כירה	kirá
straight	גלײַך	glaykh	ישר	yashár
straw	(די) שטרוי	(dee) shtroy	קש	kash
strawberry	(די) טרוסקאַפקע	(dee) trúskafke	תות־שדה	tut-sadé
street	(די) גאַס	(dee) gas	רחוב	rekhóv
stretch	אויסציִען	óystsee-en	מתח	matákh
string	(דאָס) שטריקל	(dos) shtrikl	חוט	khut
strong	שטאַרק	shtark	חזק	khazák
stubborn	פֿאַרעקשנט	farákshnt	עקשני	akshaneé
student	(דער) סטודענט	(der) studént	סטודנט	studént
study	שטודירן	shtudírn	למד	lamád
suburbs	(די) פֿאָרשטעט	(dee) fŏrshtet	פרברים	parbareém
success	(די) הצלחה	(dee) hatslókhe	הצלחה	hatslakhá
suddenly	פלוצלינג	plútsling	פתאום	peetóm
suffer	לײַדן	laydn	סבל	savál
sugar	(דער) צוקער	(der) tsúker	סוכר	sukár
suggestion	(דער) פֿאָרלייג	(der) fŏrleyg	הצעה	hatsaá
summer	(דער) זומער	(der) zúmer	קיץ	káyits
sun	(די) זון	(dee) zun	שמש	shémesh
supper	(די) וועטשערע	(dee) véchere	ארוחת־ערב	arukhát-érev
support	שטיצן	shtitsn	תמך	tamákh
sure	זיכער	zíkher	בטוח	batúakh
surprise	(דער) חידוש	(der) khídesh	הפתעה	haftaá
surround	אַרומרינגלען	arúmringlen	הקיף	heekeéf
suspect (v.)	חושד זײַן	khóyshed zayn	חשד	khashád
sympathy	(דאָס) מיטגעפֿיל	(dos) mítgefeel	אהדה	ahadá
sweet	זיס	zees	מתוק	matók
swim	שווימען	shvímen	שחה	sakhá
synagogue	(די) שול	(dee) shul	בית־כנסת	beyt-knéset
table	(דער) טיש	(der) tish	שולחן	shulkhán
tail	(דער) ווײדל	(der) veydl	זנב	zanáv
tailor	(דער) שנײַדער	(der) shnáyder	חיט	khayát
take	נעמען	némen	לקח	lakákh
talent	(דער) טאַלאַנט	(der) talánt	כשרון	keesharón
talk	רעדן	redn	דיבר	deebér
tall	הויך	hoykh	גבוה	gavóha
target	(דער) ציל	(der) tseel	מטרה	matará
taste (n.)	(דער) טעם	(der) tam	טעם	táam
taste (v.)	פֿאַרזוכן	farzúkhn	טעם	taám

English	Yiddish	Yiddish (transliteration)	Hebrew	Hebrew (transliteration)
tasty	געשמאַק	geshmák	טעים	taeém
tax	(דער) שטײַער	(der) shtáyer	מס	mas
tea	(די) טיי	(dee) tey	טה	tey
teabag	(דאָס) סענצערל	(dos) séntserl	שקית־טה	sakeét-tey
teach	לערנען	lérnen	לימד	leeméd
teacher	(דער) לערער	(der) lérer	מורה	moré
teapot	(דער) טשײַניק	(der) cháynik	קומקום	kúmkum
tear (v.)	רײַסן	raysn	קרע	kará
tear (n.)	(די) טרער	(dee) trer	דימעה	deemá
tedious	נודנע	núdne	משעמם	meshaamém
television	(די) טעלעוויזיע	(dee) televízye	טלוויזיה	televízya
tell	דערצײַלן	dertséyln	סיפר	seepér
tendency	(די) טענדענץ	(dee) tendénts	נטיה	neteeá
tense	געשפּאַנט	geshpánt	מתוח	matúakh
tent	(דאָס) געצעלט	(dos) getsélt	אוהל	óhel
terrible	שרעקלעך	shréklekh	איום	ayóm
thank you	אַ דאַנק	a dánk	תודה	todá
the	דער, די, דאָס	der, dee, dos	ה	ha
theatre	(דער) טעאַטער	(der) teáter	תיאטרון	teatrón
then	דעמאָלט	démolt	אז	az
there	דאָרט	dort	שם	sham
therefore	דערפֿאַר	derfár	לכן	lakhén
they	זיי	zey	הם	hem
thick	גראָב	grob	עבה	avé
thief	(דער) גנבֿ	(der) gánef	גנב	ganáv
thigh	(די) פּאָלקע	(dee) pólke	ירך	yarékh
thin	דין	deen	רזה	razé
thing	(די) זאַך	(dee) zakh	דבר	davár
think	טראַכטן	trakhtn	חשב	khasháv
thirsty	דאָרשטיק	dórshtik	צמא	tsamé
thread	(דער) פֿאָדעם	(der) fódem	חוט	khut
threaten	סטראַשען	stráshen	איים על	eeyém al
throat	(דער) האַלדז	(der) haldz	גרון	garón
through	דורך	durkh	דרך	dérekh
throw	וואַרפֿן	varfn	זרק	zarák
thumb	(דער) גראָבער פֿינגער	(der) gróber fínger	בוהן	bóhen
thunder	(דער) דונער	(der) dúner	רעם	ráam
ticket	(דער) בילעט	(der) bilét	כרטיס	karteés
tie (v.)	בינדן	bindn	קשר	kashár
tie (n.)	(דער) שניפּס	(der) shnips	עניבה	aneevá
tiger	(דער) טיגער	(der) tíger	נמר	namér
tight	ענג	eng	צר	tsar
time	(די) צײַט	(dee) tsayt	זמן	zman
tin	בלעך	blekh	פח	pakh
tiny	קלײנטשיק	kleýnchik	קטנטן	ktántan
tire (n.)	(דער) רייף	(der) reyf	צמיג	tsameég
tired	מיד	meed	עיף	ayéf
to	צו	tsu	ל	le'
toast	(דער) טאָסט	(der) tost	פת קלויה	pat kluyá
tobacco	(דער) טאַביק	(der) tábik	טבק	tabák
today	הײַנט	haynt	היום	hayóm
toe	(דער) פֿינגער פֿון פֿוס	(der) fínger fun fas	אצבע של רגל	étsba shel régel
together	צוזאַמען	tsuzámen	יחד	yákhad
tomato	(דער) פּאָמידאָר	(der) pomidór	עגבניה	agvaneeyá
tomb	(דער) קבֿר	(der) kéyver	קבר	kéver

English	Yiddish	Yiddish (transliteration)	Hebrew	Hebrew (transliteration)
tomorrow	מאָרגן	morgn	מחר	makhár
tongue	(די) צונג	(dee) tsung	לשון	lashón
tooth	(דער) צאָן	(der) tson	שן	shen
toothbrush	(דאָס) ציינבערשטל	(dos) tséynbershtl	מיברשת שיניים	meevréshet sheenáyim
top	(דער) שפיץ	(der) shpits	פסגה	peezgá
torture	פּייניקן	páynikn	עינה	eená
touch	אָנרירן	ónrirn	נגע	nagá
towel	(דער) האַנטעך	(der) hántekh	מגבת	magévet
town	(דאָס) שטעטל	(dos) shtetl	עיר	eer
toy	(די) צאַצקע	(dee) tsátske	צעצוע	tsaatsuá
trade (v.)	בייטן זיך	baytn zikh	החליף	hekhleéf
tradition	(די) טראַדיציע	(dee) tradítsye	מסורה	masorá
tragedy	(די) טראַגעדיע	(dee) tragédye	אסון	asón
train	(די) באַן	(dee) ban	רכבת	rakévet
translate	איבערזעצן	íberzetsn	תירגם	tirgém
transparent	דורכזעיק	dúrkhzeik	שקוף	shakúf
trap	(די) פּאַסטקע	(dee) pástke	מלכודת	malkódet
travel	פאָרן	forn	נסע	nasá
tray	(די) טאַץ	(dee) tats	מגש	magásh
treasure	(דער) אוצר	(der) óytser	אוצר	otsár
tree	(דער) בוים	(der) boym	עץ	ets
trial	(דער) משפט	(der) míshpet	משפט	meeshpát
trick	(די) קונץ	(dee) kunts	תחבולה	takhbulá
trip	(די) נסיעה	(dee) neseé-e	נסיעה	neseeá
trouble	(די) צרה	(dee) tsóre	צרה	tsará
trousers	הויזן	hoyzn	מיכנסיים	meekhnasáyim
trust	געטרויען	getróyen	האמין ב	he-emeén be'
truth	(דער) אמת	(der) émes	אמת	emét
try	פרווון	pruvn	ניסה	neesá
tumult	(די) מהומה	(dee) mehúme	מהומה	mehumá
turkey	(דער) אינדיק	(der) índik	תרנגול הודו	tarngól hódu
turn	דרייען, קערעווען	dréyen, kéreven	פנה	paná
twin	(דער) צווילינג	(der) tsvíling	תאום	teóm
type (v.)	טיפירן	tipírn	תקתק	teekték
type (n.)	(דער) טיפ	(der) teep	טיפוס	teepús
typewriter	(די) שרייבמאַשין	(dee) shráybmasheen	מכונת-כתיבה	mekhonát-keteevá
ugly	מיאוס	meé-es	מכוער	mekhoár
umbrella	(דער) שירעם	(der) shírem	מטרייה	meetreeá
uncanny	טשודנע	chúdne	מוזר	muzár
uncle	(דער) פֿעטער	(der) féter	דוד	dod
under	אונטער	unter	תחת	tákhat
understand	פֿאַרשטיין	farshtéyn	הבין	heveén
unemployed	אַרבעטלאָז	árbetloz	מובטל	muvtál
unfortunate	אומגליקלעך	úmgliklekh	אומלל	umlál
unique	איינציק	éyntsik	יחיד-במינו	yakheéd bemeenó
unite	פֿאַראייניקן	faréynikn	איחד	eekhéd
unlucky person	שלימזל	shlimázl	איש רע-מזל	eesh ra-mazál
until	ביז	biz	עד	ad
up	אַרויף	aróyf	מעלה	mála
upset	צערודערט	tserúdert	נרגז	nirgáz
upstairs	אויבן	oybm	למעלה	lemála
urgent	אייליק	áylik	דחוף	dakhúf
use (v.)	נוצן	nutsn	השתמש ב	heeshtamésh b'
useful	נוציק	nútsik	שימושי	sheemusheé

English	Yiddish	Yiddish (transliteration)	Hebrew	Hebrew (transliteration)
useless	אַרויסגעוואָרפֿן	aróysgevorfn	חסר תועלת	khasár toélet
usual	געוויינטלעך	gevéyntlekh	רגיל	rageél
utensil	(דער) מכשיר	(der) mákhsher	מכשיר	makhshír
vacation	(די) וואַקאַציע	(dee) vakátsye	חופש	khófesh
vague	אומקלאָר	umklór	מעורפל	meurpál
value (n.)	(די) ווערט	(dee) vert	ערך	érekh
vanish	נעלם ווערן	nelm vern	נעלם	nelám
various	פֿאַרשיידן	farshéydn	שונים	shoneém
vegetables	גרינסן	greensn	ירקות	yerakót
velvet	(דער) סאַמעט	(der) samét	קטיפה	keteefá
verify	קאָנטראָלירן	kontrolírn	אימת	eemét
very	זייער	zéyer	מאד	meód
vicious	רציחהדיק	retseékhedik	מושחת	moshkhát
victim	(דער) קרבן	(der) korbm	קרבן	korbán
victory	(דער) נצחון	nitsókhn	נצחון	neetsakhón
village	(דאָס) דאָרף	(dos) dorf	כפר	kefár
villian	(דער) רשע	(der) róshe	רשע	rashá
vinegar	(דער) עסיק	(der) ésik	חומץ	khómets
violent	רציחהדיק	retsíkhedik	אלים	aleém
violin	(דער) פֿידל	(der) fidl	כינור	keenór
violinist	(דער) פֿידלער	(der) fídler	כנר	kanár
virtue	(די) מעלה	(dee) máyle	מידה טובה	meedá tová
visit	באַזוכן	bazúkhn	ביקר	beekér
voice	(דאָס) קול	(dos) kol	קול	kol
vomit	ברעכן	brekhn	הקיא	hekeé
vote	אָפּשטימען	ópshtimen	הצביע	heetsbeéa
vulgar	פּראָסט	prost	גס	gas
waist	(די) טאַליע	(dee) tálye	לסוטה	lesutá
wait	וואַרטן	vartn	חיכה	kheeká
waiter	(דער) סאַרווער	(der) sárver	מלצר	meltsár
waitress	(די) סאַרווערין	(dee) sárverin	מלצרית	meltsareét
walk	שפּאַצירן	shpatsírn	הלך	halákh
wall	(די) וואַנט	(dee) vant	קיר	kir
wallet	(דאָס) בײַטל	(dos) baytl	ארנק	arnák
wander	וואַנדערן	vándern	שט	shat
wanderer	(דער) נע־וונדניק	(der) navenádnik	נודד	nodéd
want	וועלן	veln	רצה	ratsá
war	(די) מלחמה	(dee) milkhóme	מלחמה	meelkhamá
warm	וואַרעם	várem	חמים	khameém
warn	וואָרענען	vórenen	הזהיר	heezhir
wash	וואַשן	vashn	רחץ	rakháts
waste (v.)	פּטרן	pátern	בזבז	beezbéz
watch (v.)	באַטראַכטן	batrákhtn	צפה	tsafá
water	(דאָס) וואַסער	(dos) váser	מיים	máyim
wave	(די) כוואַליע	(dee) khválye	גל	gal
way	(דער) וועג	(der) veg	דרך	dérekh
wax	(דער) וואַקס	(der) vaks	שעווה	shaavá
we	מיר	mir	אנחנו	anákhnu
weak	שוואַך	shvakh	חלש	khalásh
wealthy	רײַך	raykh	עשיר	ashír
weapon	(דער) וואָפֿן	(der) vofn	כלי־נשק	klee-néshek
wear (v.)	טראָגן	trogn	לבש	lavásh
weather	(דער) וועטער	(der) véter	מזג אוויר	mézeg avír

English	Yiddish	Yiddish (transliteration)	Hebrew	Hebrew (transliteration)
wedding	(די) חתונה	(dee) khásene	חתונה	khatuná
weight	(די) וואָג	(dee) vog	מישקל	meeshkál
weird	משונהדיק	meshúnedik	מוזר	muzár
welcome	באַגריסן	bagreésn	קידם בברכה	keedém beevrakhá
well (n.)	(דער) ברונעם	(der) brúnem	באר	be-ér
west	מערב	máyrev	מערב	maaráv
wet	נאַס	nas	רטוב	ratóv
what	וואָס	vos	מה	ma
wheat	(דער) וווייץ	(der) veyts	חיטה	kheetá
wheel	(די) ראָד	(dee) rod	גלגל	galgál
when	ווען	ven	מתי	matáy
where	ווו	vu	איפה	éyfo
which	וואָסער	vóser	איזה	éyze
while (conj.)	בעת	beys	בעוד	beód
whine	פּישטשען	píshchen	ייבב	yeebév
whisper	שעפּטשען	shépchen	לחש	lakhásh
whistle	פֿײַפֿן	fayfn	שרק	sharák
white	ווײַס	vays	לבן	laván
who	ווער	ver	מי	mee
why	פֿאַר וואָס	far vós	למה	láma
wide	ברייט	breyt	רחב	rakháv
widow	(די) אַלמנה	(dee) almóne	אלמנה	almaná
widower	(דער) אַלמן	(der) álmen	אלמן	almán
wife	(די) פֿרוי	(dee) froy	אישה	eeshá
wild	ווילד	vild	פראי	peereé
win	געווינען	gevínen	ניצח	neetséakh
wind	(דער) ווינט	(der) vint	רוח	rúakh
window	(דער) פֿענצטער	(der) féntster	חלון	khalón
wink	ווינקען	véenken	קרץ בעינו	karáts be-eynó
winter	(דער) ווינטער	(der) vínter	חורף	khóref
wipe	ווישן	vishn	מחה	makhá
wire	(דער) דראָט	(der) drot	תיל	tayl
wise	קלוג	klug	חכם	khakhám
wish	וווּנטש	vunch	רצון	ratsón
wit	חכמה	khókhme	בינה	beená
witch	(די) מכשפֿה	(dee) makhshéyfe	מכשפה	mekhashefá
with	מיט	mit	עם	eem
without	אָן	on	בלי	blee
witness	(דער) עדות	(der) éydes	עד	ed
wolf	(דער) וואָלף	(der) volf	זאב	ze-év
woman	(די) פֿרוי	(dee) froy	אישה	eeshá
wonderful	וווּנדערלעך	vúnderlekh	נפלא	neeflá
wood	(דאָס) האָלץ	(dos) holts	עץ	ets
wool	(די) וואָל	(dee) vol	צמר	tsémer
word	(דאָס) וואָרט	(dos) vort	מילה	meelá
work (n.)	(די) אַרבעט	(dee) árbet	עבודה	avodá
work (v.)	אַרבעטן	árbetn	עבד	avád
worry (v.)	זאָרגן זיך	zorgn zikh	דאג	daág
worse	ערגער	érger	יותר רע	yotér ra
worth	(די) ווערט	(dee) vert	ערך	érekh
worthwhile	כּדאי	kedáy	כדאי	kedáy
wound	(די) וווּנד	(dee) vund	פצע	pétsa
wrap	ווייקלען	víklen	עטף	atáf
wrinkle	(דער) קנייטש	(der) kneych	קמט	kémet
wrist	געלענק	gelénk	פרק כף היד	pérek kaf hayád

English	Yiddish	Yiddish (transliteration)	Hebrew	Hebrew (transliteration)
write	שרײַבן	shráybm	כתב	katáv
wrong	פֿאַלש	falsh	לא נכון	lo nakhón
yard	(דער) הויף	(der) hoyf	חצר	khatsér
yawn	געענעצן	génetsn	פיהק	peehék
year	(דאָס) יאָר	(dos) yor	שנה	shaná
yearn	בענקען	bénken	התגעגע	heetgaagéa
yell	שרײַען	shráyen	צרח	tsarákh
yellow	געל	gel	צהוב	tsahóv
yes	יאָ	yo	כן	ken
yeshiva	(די) ישיבה	(dee) yesheéve	ישיבה	yesheevá
yesterday	נעכטן	nekhtn	אתמול	etmól
Yiddish	ייִדיש	yídish	ייִדיש	yéedish
you (sing.)	דו	du	אתה	atá
you (pl.)	איר	eer	אתם	atém
young	יונג	yung	צעיר	tsaeér
zeal	(דער) ברען	(der) bren	קנאות	kanaút
zero	נול	nul	אפס	éfes
Zionism	(דער) ציוניזם	(der) tsee-enízm	ציונות	tseeonút
Zionist	(דער) ציוניסט	(der) tsee-eníst	ציוני	tseeonée
numbers	נומערן	númern	מספרים	meespareém
one	איין	eyn	אחת	akhát
two	צוויי	tsvey	שתים	shtáyim
three	דרײַ	dray	שלש	shalósh
four	פֿיר	fir	ארבע	árba
five	פֿינף	finf	חמש	khamésh
six	זעקס	zeks	שש	shesh
seven	זיבן	zibm	שבע	shéva
eight	אַכט	akht	שמונה	shmóne
nine	נײַן	nayn	תשע	tésha
ten	צען	tsen	עשׂר	éser
eleven	עלף	elf	אחד־עשׂרה	akhát-esre
twelve	צוועלף	tsvelf	שתים־עשׂרה	shtéym-esre
thirteen	דרײַצן	draytsn	שלש־עשׂרה	shlósh-esre
fourteen	פֿערצן	fertsn	ארבע עשׂרה	arbá-esre
fifteen	פֿופֿצן	fuftsn	חמש־עשׂרה	khamésh-esre
sixteen	זעכצן	zekhtsn	שש־עשׂרה	shésh-esre
seventeen	זיבעצן	zibetsn	שבע־עשׂרה	shvá-esre
eighteen	אַכצן	akhtsn	שמונה־עשׂרה	shmoné-esre
nineteen	נײַנצן	nayntsn	תשע־עשׂרה	teshá-esre
twenty	צוואַנציק	tsvantsik	עשׂרים	esreém
thirty	דרײַסיק	draysik	שלושים	shlosheém
forty	פֿערציק	fértsik	ארבעים	arbaeém
fifty	פֿופֿציק	fúftsik	חמשים	khameesheém
sixty	זעכציק	zékhtsik	ששים	sheesheém
seventy	זיבעציק	zíbetsik	שבעים	sheeveém
eighty	אַכציק	ákhtsik	שמונים	shmoneém
ninety	נײַנציק	náyntsik	תשעים	teesheém
hundred	הונדערט	húndert	מאה	méa
thousand	טויזנט	toyznt	אלף	élef
million	מיליאָן	milyón	מליון	milyón

English	Yiddish	Yiddish (transliteration)	Hebrew	Hebrew (transliteration)
week	(די) וואָך	(dee) vokh	שבוע	shavúa
Sunday	זונטיק	zúntik	יום ראשון	yom reeshón
Monday	מאָנטיק	móntik	יום שני	yom sheneé
Tuesday	דינסטיק	deénstik	יום שלישי	yom shleesheé
Wednesday	מיטוואָך	mítvokh	יום רביעי	yom revee-eé
Thursday	דאָנערשטיק	dónershtik	יום חמישי	yom khameesheé
Friday	פֿרײַטיק	fráytik	יום שישי	yom sheesheé
Saturday	שבת	shábes	שבת	shabát
months	חדשים	khadóshim	חדשים	khadasheém
January	יאַנואַר	yánuar	ינואר	yánuar
February	פֿעברואַר	fébruar	פברואר	fébruar
March	מאַרץ	marts	מרץ	merts
April	אַפּריל	apríl	אפריל	apríl
May	מײַ	may	מאי	may
June	יוני	yúnee	יוני	yúnee
July	יולי	yúlee	יולי	yúlee
August	אויגוסט	oygúst	אוגוסט	ogúst
September	סעפּטעמבער	septémber	ספטמבר	septémber
October	אָקטאָבער	október	אוקטובר	október
November	נאָוועמבער	novémber	נובמבר	novémber
December	דעצעמבער	detsémber	דצמבר	detsémber
seasons	סעזאָנען	sezónen	עונות	onót
spring	(דער) פֿרילינג	(der) fríling	אביב	aveév
summer	(דער) זומער	(der) zúmer	קיץ	káyits
fall	(דער) האַרבסט	(der) harbst	סתיו	stav
winter	(דער) ווינטער	(der) vínter	חורף	khóref

Colleges and Universities Under Jewish Auspices

Brandeis University

Founded in 1948, Brandeis University is recognized as one of the finest private liberal arts universities in the United States. It received accreditation within five years, the shortest possible time, and was awarded recognition by Phi Beta Kappa in 1961, only 13 years after its founding—the youngest institution so honored in over 100 years. It is the only Jewish-sponsored, nonsectarian institution of higher learning in America and was named for United States Supreme Court Justice Louis Dembitz Brandeis (1856-1941).

Of the approximately 2,000 accredited colleges and universities in the nation, Brandeis is one of only 100 recognized as research universities. As such, Brandeis combines the breadth and range of academic programs usually found at much larger universities with the intimate educational atmosphere of an undergraduate college.

The four schools—Science, Social Science, Humanities, and Creative Arts—offer about 900 semester courses during the academic year, 32 fields of concentration, and several specialized programs. In addition, undergraduates are able to participate in research normally restricted to graduate programs. Undergraduates number about 2,850 men and women from nearly every state in the union and over 40 foreign countries.

The Graduate School of Arts and Sciences

The Graduate School of Arts and Sciences offers courses of study leading to the master's and doctoral degrees. Graduate areas include anthropology, biochemistry, biology and photobiology, biophysics, chemistry, classical and oriental studies, comparative history, Jewish communal service, English and American literature, history of American civilization, literary studies, physics, politics, psychology and cognitive science, sociology, and theater arts.

Rosenstiel Basic Medical Sciences Research Center

The center is one of the nation's leading centers for research programs in the basic medical sciences embracing work in biochemistry, biology, chemistry, microbiology, physics, biophysics and immunology.

The Florence Heller Graduate School for Advanced Studies in Social Welfare

The Heller Graduate School, founded in 1959, is Brandeis' internationally known professional school. It offers a master's degree in Management of Human Services and a doctoral program in Social Policy Analysis. The faculty, which represents a broad spectrum of the social sciences and related professions, conducts a multidisciplinary policy-oriented research program on a wide range of health and welfare issues. Six research centers anchor a variety of projects that involve collaborative activity between faculty members and advanced students. They are: the Center for Health Policy Analysis and Research, which conducts studies in long-term care, health care quality and effectiveness, and regulation and reimbursement; the Levinson Policy Institute, which focuses on the long-term care needs of the elderly and disabled individuals and their families; the Center for Human Resources, which consolidates the research and training activities in the area of employment training and income maintenance and develops training programs for employee benefit managers; the Policy Center on Aging, which focuses on major federal and state policies that affect the aged; the National Institute for Sentencing Alternatives, which concentrates on developing new programs for criminal offenders and evaluating the effectiveness of existing programs; and the new Center for the Study of Social Problems in the Middle East, which focuses on the many interrelated social problems of countries in that region, including Israel and Egypt. The Heller School also supports major research projects in alcoholism, mental retardation, mental health, children's issues, and a new venture which analyzes the factors influencing social change.

THE BRANDEIS LIBRARIES

With the opening in 1983 of the new Leonard L. Farber Library as part of an $8.5 million library building and expansion program, Brandeis today has four libraries with a combined collection of about 1,000,000 books, 600,000 microtexts, 150,000 documents, 3,400 periodicals and 55 newspapers.

The Farber Library is the centerpiece of the main library complex which includes the Jacob and Bertha Goldfarb Library and the Rapaporte Treasure Hall, all joined together by a common entrance. The fourth library—Gerstenzang Science Library—is located in the science complex and contains materials supporting the natural sciences.

The Judaica Department's reading room houses one of the country's most important collections of reference materials and basic texts in major areas of Judaic studies, the ancient Near East, and the modern Middle East. Access to the collection is open to undergraduate and graduate students.

ACADEMIC SCHOOLS AND INSTITUTES

*Crown School of Graduate Studies in
American Civilization*

*Danielson School of Philosophy, Ethics,
and Religious Thought*

Fierman School of Chemistry

Fisher School of Physics

Kutz School of Biology

Lown School of Near Eastern and Judaic Studies

The school encompasses an intensive teaching and research program in all the main areas of Judaic studies, the ancient Near East and the modern Middle East. In addition, the Lown School has programs which prepare students for Jewish communal service and programs of research in areas of direct concern to the American Jewish community.

The Department of Near Eastern and Judaic Studies is the primary teaching and research unit in the Lown School. In this department the university has assembled an unusual array of distinguished scholars who offer an extremely broad curriculum. A second unit in the Lown School is the Benjamin S. Hornstein Program in Jewish Communal Service which provides graduate education for students interested in professional careers in Jewish communal service and Jewish education. The school also includes the Center for Modern Jewish Studies which is devoted to the study of contemporary American Jewish life. The center currently engages in research and teaching in three major areas: Jewish population studies, Jewish identity, and the Jewish family.

Benjamin Michtom School in Computer Science

Swig School of Political Science

The Tauber Institute

The Tauber Institute is an independent, multidisciplinary research institute that seeks to set into the context of modern history the causes, nature and consequences of the crisis of European society in the second quarter of the twentieth century with a particular focus on the origins of the European Jewish catastrophe. The institute undertakes research into broad aspects of modern European intellectual, diplomatic, social, and political history. Among the areas of study with which it is concerned are: nationalism and racialism in modern Europe, European Jewish history since the Enlightenment, refugee problems, and the roots and development of Nazism, fascism, and antisemitism. The institute is engaged in both research and teaching. Its government includes a distinguished Board of Overseers. Distinguished scholars are invited to visit the institute. It also awards fellowships for advanced doctoral study and for postdoctoral research. Lectures, symposia and conferences are arranged under the auspices of the institute which initiates and sponsors major research projects.

Joseph and Esther Foster Visiting Professorships

Established in 1974, the Foster fund underwrites visiting professorships for distinguished Israeli scholars in many different academic fields. Its objective is to promote scientific and intellectual exchanges between Brandeis and Israel.

Fannie Hurst Visiting Professorships

*Shirley and Maurice Saltzman
Artists-in-Residence*

Jacob Ziskind Professorships

Dropsie College, Philadelphia

Dropsie College was founded in Philadelphia in 1907 as a graduate institution for Near Eastern and Judaic learning.

The founder was Moses Aaron Dropsie, an eminent citizen and lawyer of Philadelphia who died in 1905. During his lifetime he had been deeply interested in Hebrew lore and Semitic studies. In his will, dated September 17, 1895, he directed "that there be established and maintained . . . a college for the promotion of, and instruction in, the Hebrew and cognate languages and their respective literatures." He also directed "that in the admission of students there shall be no discrimination on account of creed, color or sex." A charter was granted to the College on June 6, 1907, under the name of The Dropsie College for Hebrew and Cognate Learning.

The College is the only independent graduate institution in America, nonsectarian and nontheological, completely dedicated to Hebrew, biblical, Judaic, and ancient and contemporary Near Eastern studies.

From its founding, Dropsie occupied a site in North Philadelphia. On January 1, 1984, the College moved to its new quarters on the Main Line. Its relocation to a suburban setting within the vicinity of several academic institutions such as Bryn Mawr College, Haverford College, Swarthmore College, and St. Joseph's University, places Dropsie in an environment particularly conducive to promoting scholarship.

A reciprocal agreement on student exchange at the graduate level between Temple University and Dropsie

Moses Aaron Dropsie (1821-1905), the founder of Dropsie College.

A Biblical fragment with Masorah from the Cairo Genizah now housed at Dropsie.

College permits full-time graduate students enrolled at either institution to take courses at the other without additional fees and without requesting formal transfer of credits. Dropsie students may also attend undergraduate courses in the Classics department at Temple University, as well as in the French, German, and Hebrew departments. An informal and close agreement has always been in existence between Dropsie and the University of Pennsylvania's departments of Religious Studies and Oriental Studies.

The Tomshinsky Library contains more than 150,000 volumes of books and periodicals and is particularly rich in publications on biblical and rabbinical learning, the Semitic languages, Jewish history, Assyriology and Egyptology. Special collections have been developed in the fields of Palestine and the modern Middle East.

The library includes 600 fragments from the Cairo Genizah, in Hebrew and Arabic; 275 Oriental manuscripts in Arabic, Ethiopic, Hebrew, Samaritan, Coptic, Persian, Sanskrit and Turkish; some fragments of Coptic papyri; 32 incunabula; 290 sixteenth-century books, and other rarities. In the Abraham I. Katsh Center for Manuscript Research there are microfilm collections of rare Hebraica manuscripts and documents from the USSR, Poland, and Hungary. Also available for research are microfilms of the Vatican Hebrew collection.

The archives of the library are strong in American-Jewish history. Included are the papers of Isaac Leeser, Sabato Morais, Mayer Sulzberger, Cyrus Adler, and Abraham Neuman. Recently, the library acquired the papers of B.Z. Goldberg dealing with the American Jewish labor movement.

Dropsie College continues to publish the *Jewish Quarterly Review,* which had been founded in England in 1888 as the sole English-language scholarly journal devoted to the study of Judaism. In 1910 publication was assumed by the College. The *Jewish Quarterly Review* has been a leading force in the field, shaping and reflecting the nature of scholarly inquiry. *JQR* provides a medium for the publication of ancient and medieval texts, serves as a forum of interpretation and investigation, and critically reviews recent publications. The Editorial Board consists of Dropsie's faculty.

Dropsie College conceived the project of publishing a new edition of these writings with translations and commentaries under the title *Jewish Apocryphal Literature.* The work has been undertaken by faculty members of the College in collaboration with other recognized authorities, and consists of a series of volumes, each containing the text and translation of a single apocryphal or pseudepigraphic writing, together with introduction, commentary, and textual *apparatus criticus.* In the translations, special emphasis has been placed upon the recovery of the original sense through critical reconstruction of the underlying Hebrew or Aramaic, while in the commentaries the subject matter has been elucidated with special reference to Jewish sources.

Dropsie College believes this project will contribute materially towards a better understanding and evaluation of the Apocrypha and Pseudepigrapha and of their importance for the interpretation of both the Jewish and Christian religions.

Thus far, the following volumes have appeared:
- *The First Book of Maccabees.* Translation by Sidney Tedesche, Introduction and commentary by Solomon Zeitlin (1950)
- *The Second Book of Maccabees.* Translation by Sidney Tedesche, Introduction and commentary by Solomon Zeitlin (1954)
- *The Third and Fourth Books of Maccabees.* Translated and edited with Introduction and commentary by Moses Hadas (1954)
- *The Book of Wisdom.* Translated with Introduction and commentary by Joseph Reider (1957)
- *The Book of Tobit.* Translated and edited with Introduction and commentary by Frank Zimmerman (1958)
- *The Book of Judith.* Translation, commentary and critical notes by Morton S. Enslin; General Introduction and appendices by Solomon Zeitlin (1972)

Dropsie College offers programs of study leading to the graduate degrees of Master of Arts and Doctor of Philosophy. Departments include Ancient Near Eastern Studies, including Ugaritic, Syriac, Akkadian, Eblite, Sumerian and Egyptian; Biblical Studies; Hellenistic Studies; Rabbinic Studies; Arabic and Islamic Studies; Medieval Jewish Studies; Hebrew Language and Literature; Modern Jewish History and Middle Eastern Studies; and Religious Thought.

Alumni of Dropsie College include Bernard Revel, first president of Yeshiva College, Solomon Zeitlin, Solomon Grayzel, Robert Gordis and Nahum Sarna.

Gratz College, Philadelphia

Gratz College in Philadelphia is the oldest general non-denominationally affiliated College of Jewish Studies in the Western Hemisphere. It owes its existence to the benevolence of Hyman Gratz, who by a Deed of Trust executed in 1856, shortly before his death, conveyed his estate to his trustees to pay the income to designated beneficiaries during their lives, and upon termination of these trusts, to transfer the entire fund to the Kahal Kadosh Mikveh Israel of Philadelphia "in trust for the establishment and support of a college for the education of Jews residing in the city and county of Philadelphia." When the

Gratz College building, Philadelphia.

fund came into the possession of the Congregation as Trustee in 1893, it was decided, in view of the needs of the community, to establish the College as an institution for preparing teachers for Jewish religious schools.

Hyman Gratz was a distinguished member of the historic family whose name he bore. He occupied an important place in the Jewish community of Philadelphia and was prominent in the civic and financial affairs of that city. He was, for many years, a member of the Adjunta of Mikveh Israel Congregation, as well as its treasurer.

The Board of Trustees of the College was constituted in 1895 in accordance with the provisions of the Deed of Trust. In the latter part of that year the first course of lectures under the auspices of the Board of Trustees was delivered by Dr. Solomon Schechter, then of Cambridge University, England. Other scholars of distinction—Dr. Aaron Friedenwald, Dr. Marcus Jastrow, Dr. Kaufmann Kohler, and Sabato Morais—lectured under the same auspices during the following year. The College formally opened for regular instruction in November 1897, and during the greater portion of the time until 1909 held its sessions in the assembly rooms of the Mikveh Israel Synagogue on 7th Street above Arch. In September 1909, the College moved to its own building on York Street, east of Broad, immediately adjacent to the new synagogue of Mikveh Israel Congregation.

In 1909, a School of Observation and Practice was established under the supervision of the College, and it held its sessions in the College building. It subsequently came to be known as "The Gratz College School of Observation and Practice at Mikveh Israel."

Moses A. Dropsie, Esq., founder of Dropsie College, was the first President of the Board of Trustees of Gratz College, continuing in office until his death in July 1905.

Gratz College offers a broad range of bachelor's, master's, certificate, teacher training, and continuing education programs in Judaic, Hebraic, and Middle East Hebrew Literature and B.A. degrees in Jewish studies plus joint B.A. degree programs with Temple University and Beaver College; Hebrew and Jewish Teacher's diplomas; Certificates in Judaica Librarianship, Sephardic Studies, and Jewish Chaplaincy; and Master of Hebrew Literature and M.A.'s in Jewish Music, Jewish Education, and Jewish Studies. The College runs courses in Jewish studies for Jewish Communal Workers and a joint Gratz-Federation Young Leadership Institute in Jewish Studies. Summer Pre- and Regular Sessions are offered.

The Samuel Netzky Adult Institute for Jewish Studies, the continuing education arm of the College, conducts Hebrew Ulpan classes, adult education courses in Jewish studies and in-service courses for teachers of Jewish studies in fifteen locations throughout the city, its suburbs and in Wilmington, Delaware.

The College Preparatory Division includes Gratz College High School, a five-year, comprehensive supplementary high school program, as well as its Isaac Mayer Wise Department, a two-year, post-confirmation track for graduates of Reform religious schools.

The College's Division of Community Services is the central agency for Jewish education in Philadelphia and is affiliated with the Jewish Education Service of North America. The Division provides a variety of consultative services and resources to Jewish schools, organizations, communal agencies, and individuals. One of its major goals is to enhance the quality of Jewish education through setting standards, certifying teachers and principals, and providing individual and group consultation to teachers and administrators.

The College's vast educational resources include the main library, the renowned Schreiber Jewish Music Library, the Chomsky Educational Resource Center, the Audio-Visual/Film Library, the Holocaust Oral History Archives, and the Educational Games Center, exceeding in total over 100,000 volumes.

The 1984-85 school year marked a record enrollment at Gratz College with over 1,400 full and part-time students in all of its divisions, an increase of 23% from 1983-84. This growth trend is expected to continue as the College prepares to move to its new location, a thirty acre, wooded site in Melrose Park, an upper middle class Philadelphia suburb. This will be the College's first "green, suburban" campus in its ninety year history and will offer the most updated and modern facilities, including a planned new multi-million dollar library/resource center.

Hebrew Theological College/ Jewish University of America— Skokie, Illinois

In 1919, a group of rabbis met to evaluate the priorities of Jewish education in Chicago. The Bet Midrash L'Rabonim was founded at this meeting with a total of ten students. Rabbi Ephraim Epstein, one of the original founders, served as the first president. On October 15, 1921, the name of the school was officially changed to the Hebrew Theological College/Bet HaMidrash LeTorah, and was chartered by the State of Illinois.

The school was established on the West Side of Chicago in 1922, and a new building was erected to accommodate the growing student body. At this time, the Teachers Institute for Women was established, where young women could study Torah and earn a teaching certificate.

From 1922 to 1946, the Hebrew Theological College was led by Rabbi Saul Silber. One of Rabbi Silber's major goals was the training of Orthodox rabbis in the spirit of modern

Hebrew Theological College, Skokie, Illinois.

American culture, to meet the needs of the American Jewish community. A baccalaureate degree was required of all students in addition to ordination.

The Graduate School was opened in 1950 to enable ordained rabbis to pursue advanced theological studies leading to higher degrees in Hebrew Literature, Religious Education and Pastoral Counseling. The continuing growth of the Yeshiva and the population shift made it necessary to relocate. In 1958, a new building was completed in suburban Skokie, and operations in the new location began at once.

The School of Liberal Arts and Sciences was established in 1959, and in that year, in accordance with the expanding program of the Yeshiva, the additional name, Jewish University of America, was adopted.

In February 1961, Yeshiva High School was opened as a preparatory school on the Skokie campus.

The Hebrew Theological College consists of five major divisions:

1. Rabbinic Division
2. The Max Bressler School of Advanced Hebrew Studies
3. School of Liberal Arts and Sciences
4. The Anne M. Blitstein Teachers Institute for Women
5. The Graduate School of Advanced Hebrew Studies

Hebrew Union College— Jewish Institute of Religion

Hebrew Union College was founded in 1875 in Cincinnati, the first institution of Jewish higher learning in America. Its founder was Rabbi Isaac Mayer Wise, the architect of American Reform Judaism, who had established the Union of American Hebrew Congregations two years earlier for the primary purpose of supporting a seminary to train rabbis for the Reform Movement.

In 1922, Rabbi Stephen S. Wise established the Jewish Institute of Religion in New York. The similar orientation of the two schools led to their merger in 1950.

A third center was opened in Los Angeles in 1954 to serve the growing Jewish community on the West Coast. A fourth branch was established in Jerusalem, Israel, in 1963.

Beginning in 1880, this former Cincinnati mansion served as the home of Hebrew Union College for 30 years.

Isaac Mayer Wise, founder of Hebrew Union College.

From modest beginnings, Hebrew Union College-Jewish Institute of Religion has developed into an institution providing a wide variety of academic programs. In addition to its Rabbinic School, the College includes a School of Graduate Studies, a School of Biblical Archaeology and Schools of Education, Jewish Communal Service and Sacred Music.

The Klau Library in Cincinnati is one of the most extensive Jewish libraries in the world. It contains approximately 330,000 volumes, among them 150 incunabula, and over 2,000 manuscript codices and many thousands of pages of archival documents. Special collections include Jewish Americana, music, an outstanding Spinoza collection, and extensive microforms. It also houses the American Jewish Periodical Center, which preserves American Jewish periodicals and newspapers on microfilm. More than 700 titles, representing over 10,000,000 pages, are available in the Center.

The American Jewish Archives is a major center of study and research in the field of American Jewish history. The Archives systematically collect and catalogue material, both published and manuscript, reflecting the life and history of American Jewry. The archives now have approximately 8,000,000 pages of documents. Two million of these are from the archives of the World Jewish Congress. This collection makes the Archives a central research institution on the Holocaust in the United States.

The Hebrew Union College Skirball Museum in Los Angeles is one of the foremost Jewish museums in the world. Its approximately 14,000 objects, comprising artifacts of biblical archaeology, Jewish ceremonial art and fine arts, reflect 4,000 years of Jewish history, culture and art.

The Rabbinic School operates in Cincinnati, New York, Los Angeles and Jerusalem. It offers a five-year program leading to the Master of Arts degree and ordination. The Year-in-Israel Program, mandatory for all entering rabbinic students, is offered at the Jerusalem School. The Cincinnati and New York Schools offer the subsequent four years of the program leading to ordination. The Los Angeles School offers the second and third years of the rabbinic program, after which students transfer either to Cincinnati or New York for the fourth and fifth years.

The Graduate Programs offer doctoral and master's degrees. The doctoral programs lead through advanced and specialized studies to advanced scholarship in Judaic and cognate subjects. The College confers the Doctor of Philosophy degree in Cincinnati at the School of Graduate Studies; the Doctor of Philosophy degree in Jewish Education in Los Angeles at the Rhea Hirsch School of Education; and the Doctor of Hebrew Letters in Cincinnati, New York and Los Angeles.

The School of Sacred Music in New York, which trains cantors and synagogue music directors, awards the degree of Master of Sacred Music.

The Program in Sacred Music in Los Angeles offers special courses for synagogue professionals, organists and choir directors.

The Rhea Hirsch School of Education in Los Angeles offers a program leading to the Doctor of Philosophy degree in Jewish Education and a Master of Arts degree in Jewish Education. Undergraduate programs leading to the Bachelor of Science in Hebrew Education and the Bachelor of Science in Jewish Education are available on a limited basis.

The School of Education in New York offers a program leading to the degree of Master of Arts with specialization in religious education. Adult courses on a graduate level are offered leading to the Judaic Studies Certificate. The School of Education also sponsors and supervises an extensive outreach program offering accredited courses at host congregations throughout the greater New York area.

The Jerome H. Louchheim School of Judaic Studies in Los Angeles offers a program which leads to the Bachelor of Arts in Judaic Studies. Under a cooperative arrangement with USC, its students may pursue a course of study in the Louchheim School leading to the Bachelor of Arts with specialization in Judaic Studies.

The School of Jewish Communal Service in Los Angeles offers graduate programs for those preparing for or already engaged in Jewish communal work. The School awards a Graduate Certificate and the Master of Arts in Jewish Communal Service. Under a cooperative program with the University of Southern California School of Social Work, the George Warren Brown School of Social Work, Washington University, St. Louis, and the University of Pittsburgh, students may earn both the Master of Social Work and Master of Arts in Jewish Communal Service degrees. Under a cooperative program with the Leonard Davis School of

Many HUC alumni served as chaplains during World War II. They entered the concentration camps alongside American combat troops, and remained in Europe after the war to work with the displaced Jewish refugees and organize hospitals, clinics, farms, schools, synagogues and newspapers. Rabbi Alexander D. Goode, '37, was one of the memorable heros of World War II. On February 3, 1943, the S.S. Dorchester, a United States Army troop ship, was struck by enemy torpedos in the mid-Atlantic. As the ship began to sink and the men were ordered over the side, the four chaplains on board gave up their life preservers to soldiers struggling in the water, and standing hand in hand, went down with the ship. The four chaplains were a Catholic priest, Methodist and Baptist ministers, and Rabbi Goode.

Gerontology of the University of Southern California, students may earn both the Master of Science in Gerontology and the Master of Arts in Jewish Communal Service. In addition, there is a program leading to the degree of Master of Public Administration.

The School of Jewish Studies in Jerusalem serves rabbinic and other students of the American campuses of the College and is the center for the National Federation of Temple Youth undergraduate programs. A program leading to rabbinic ordination, designed for Israeli graduate students, offers preparation for the rabbinate in the Israel Movement for Progressive Judaism.

The Nelson Glueck School of Biblical Archaeology, at the Jerusalem School, is an American center for postgraduate study in the fields of Bible, archaeology and the history of ancient Israel. The School conducts archaeological excavations of historic sites in Israel.

The Hebrew Union College Annual, established in 1924, is a scholarly journal in the fields of Hebraica and Judaica. *Studies in Bibliography and Booklore* is published in Cincinnati by the Library of the College. *American Jewish Archives,* published by the American Jewish Archives, is a journal devoted to the preservation and study of American Jewish historical records. Dr. Jacob Rader Marcus is the editor.

Jewish Theological Seminary

In 1886, The Jewish Theological Seminary of America was founded for "the preservation in America of the knowledge and practice of historical Judaism." In 1902, its original charter was revised to include "the perpetuation of the tenets of the Jewish religion, the cultivation of Hebrew literature, the pursuit of biblical scholarship, the establishment of a library and the education and training of Jewish rabbis and teachers."

Today the Seminary is comprised of five schools at its New York campus, a sixth in Israel, and the University of Judaism as its Los Angeles affiliate. Its student-body exceeds 900 and it has a faculty of some 150 scholars.

The new Ivan F. and Seema Boesky Family Library, at the Seminary's 3080 Broadway campus, is a state-of-the-art complex containing the largest collection of Judaica in the western hemisphere. Housed in the library are over 250,000 books, 10,000 manuscripts and the latest periodicals in the Jewish field. The world-famous Rare Book Room holds, among other treasures, a signature of Maimonides and one of the largest collections of fragments from the Cairo Genizah. The library is open to the public.

A summer school program is offered by the Seminary including a variety of courses in both Hebrew and English. Courses include elementary, intermediate and advanced Hebrew language instruction (4 hours of Hebrew instruction, 4 days a week), "The History of New York City Jewry," introductory Talmud, Midrash and philosophy. The Melton Research Center also conducts sessions to help educators hone their teaching skills.

Seminary College of Jewish Studies, founded 1909, offers a complete college program in Judaica leading to the B.A. degree; conducts joint programs with Columbia University and Barnard College allowing students to receive two B.A. degrees after four years.

Main entrance, Jewish Theological Seminary.

Cantors Institute and Seminary College of Jewish Music, founded 1952, trains cantors, music teachers and choral directors for congregations. Offers programs leading to degrees of B.S.M., M.S.M., and D.S.M., and diploma of Hazzan.

Rabbinical School. A program of graduate studies leading to a degree in Masters of Arts in rabbinics and ordination. Study focuses on advanced reading in Talmud, Bible, Jewish history, philosophy and Hebrew literature. Women were admitted to the program in 1984, and the first conservative woman rabbi was ordained in May 1985.

Graduate School: Institute for Advanced Study in the Humanities, founded 1968. A graduate program leading to the M.A. degree in all aspects of Jewish studies and the Ph.D. in Bible, Jewish education, history, literature, philosophy or rabbinics; offers a dual degree in social work.

American Student Center in Jerusalem, founded 1962. The center offers programs for rabbinical students, classes in Judaica for qualified Israelis and Americans, and Midreshet Yerushalayim, an intensive program of Jewish studies for undergraduates.

SEMINARY AFFILIATE INSTITUTES

University of Judaism (1947) 15600 Mulholland Drive, Los Angeles, Calif. 90024 (213) 476-9777. West Coast school of Jewish Theological Seminary. Serves as center of undergraduate and graduate study of Judaica; offers pre-professional and professional programs in Jewish education and allied fields, including a pre-rabbinic program and joint program for students to receive a B.A. from UCLA and B.H.L. from University of Judaism after four years; offers a broad range of adult education and Jewish activities.

Institute for Religious and Social Studies (N.Y.C. 1938; Chicago 1944; Boston 1945). Serves as a scholarly and scientific fellowship of clergymen and other religious teachers who desire authoritative information regarding some of the basic issues now confronting spiritually minded individuals.

Elton Research Center, founded 1960, devises new curricula and materials for Jewish education; offers intensive program for training curriculum writers; recruits, trains and retains educators through seminars and in-service programs; maintains consultant and supervisory relationship with a number of pilot schools.

Schocken Institute for Jewish Research, founded 1961, 6 Balfour Street, Jerusalem, Israel, incorporates Schocken library and its related research institutes in medieval Hebrew poetry and Jewish mysticism.

Department of Radio and Television, founded 1944, produces radio and TV programs expressing the Jewish tradition in its broadest sense, with emphasis on the universal human situation. "Eternal Light" (a weekly radio program) seven "Eternal Light" TV programs produced in cooperation with NBC, and 12 "Directions" telecasts with ABC are broadcast on network television. Scripts and related program material are distributed to the public.

Prozdor, founded 1951, is an advanced Hebrew high school program offered throughout the New York Metropolitan area. Classes meet twice a week concentrating on classical Jewish studies.

The Bernstein Center and The Brand Institute, founded 1964, is a pastoral psychiatry program introducing rabbinical students to the dynamics of mental health and basic concepts of psychiatry and psychoanalysis. Internships are available at selected social and mental health agencies.

The Ramah Camps, founded 1947, provide an eight-week summer camp program, including instruction in Jewish classical texts, Hebrew language and contemporary Jewish problems. A full range of craft, athletic and art activities are offered. Programs are instructed by Seminary students. Applicants are required to have some previous Hebrew education.

The Reconstructionist Rabbinical College

The Reconstructionist Rabbinical College was established by Charter in 1968 "to train and ordain Rabbis for service in every aspect of the Jewish community and at the same time to equip them with the necessary academic training which would qualify them to teach Jewish studies at a college or university; to provide facilities, administration and faculty to implement the training and ordination of Rabbis as aforesaid; to confer the title of Rabbi; and to confer the Doctor of Hebrew Letters Degree and such other degrees as may be approved in accordance with such curricula as shall be established by the governing board and faculty of the corporation and as approved by the proper authorities of the Commonwealth of Pennsylvania from time to time."

The curriculum at the Reconstructionist Rabbinical College is based on the conception of Judaism as "an evolving religious civilization." The students concentrate each year upon a specific period: the first year, Biblical Civilization; the second, Rabbinic Civilization; the third, Medieval Civilization; the fourth year, Modern; and the fifth, Contemporary Civilization.

RRC combines a university program of graduate studies with rabbinic studies. Students are required to enroll in the Graduate Department of Religion at Temple University, or its equivalent in the University of Pennsylvania.

The Reconstructionist Rabbinical College is committed to facilitating the needs of the Jewish deaf community in life cycle and ritual matters and, accordingly, has developed a two-year para-professional training program. Ap-

Home of the Reconstructionist Rabbinical College.

Rabbi Mordecai M. Kaplan affixes the mezuzah at the dedication of the Reconstructionist Rabbinical College, October 1968.

plicants for this program must be qualified interpreters and must be able to reverse interpret as well.

Since its inception the College has accepted men and women.

The College maintains an active library including over 25,000 volumes with extensive collections in Biblical Studies, Jewish History and Judaism. In addition, over 150 general and scholarly periodicals are available. The library is named in honor of the founder of Reconstructionism, Rabbi Mordecai M. Kaplan. His personal library and papers are housed in the Molly and Julius Fligelmen Center for the Kaplan Archives at the College and are being organized through the generosity of a Friend of the College. Other special collections include the library of Rabbi Ira Eisenstein, President Emeritus of the Reconstructionist Rabbinical College, and the Hendler Bible Collection of illustrated Bibles dating from 1653 to 1918.

The College maintains an academic press and publishes materials which range from the popular to the technical. The RRCP has published *Shiv'im: Essays and Studies in Honor of Ira Eisenstein; A Catalog of the Correspondence in the Mordecai M. Kaplan Archives; Teaching Medical Ethics to Theological School Students, A Syllabus and Study Guide;* and the ongoing series, *Jewish Civilization: Essays and Studies.*

Spertus College of Judaica, Chicago

Established in 1925 as the College of Jewish Studies, the College provided high school graduates with a basic knowledge of Judaic studies. Since 1964, the College has become a liberal arts institution offering undergraduate and graduate degree programs in Jewish and Hebrew studies. In 1970 the College was renamed in recognition of the generosity of the Spertus family of Chicago.

Since the early seventies, Spertus College of Judaica has provided several colleges and universities in the Chicago area with major programs in Jewish studies. The college is the largest, non-theological, secular institution of higher Jewish learning in the Midwest.

The Asher Library is one of the largest circulating libraries of Judaica in the Midwest. Its resources include exten-

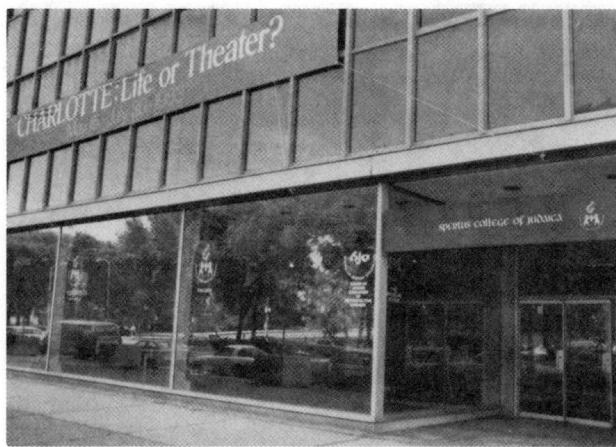

Spertus College of Judaica, Chicago.

sive collections in Judaica and Hebraica; a distinguished rare book collection; the Badona Spertus Library of Art in Judaica; and the Chicago Jewish Archives, which hold the archives of the Jewish Federation of Metropolitan Chicago. Current library holdings exceed 75,000 volumes.

Maurice Spertus Museum of Judaica

The Maurice Spertus Museum of Judaica is the Midwest's most comprehensive Jewish Museum. Established in 1967, the Museum serves as an educational adjunct of the College; as a research resource for students, faculty, and other scholars in the field of Jewish studies; and as a cultural center for the Jewish and non-Jewish communities.

The original collection presented to the College by Mr. Maurice Spertus has been substantially augmented by numerous other gifts. Currently, the Museum houses several thousand works of art, including ceremonial objects, ethnographic materials, paintings, sculpture, graphics, textiles, coins, and medals tracing the history of Judaism from ancient to modern times. The collection also contains special materials on the Holocaust, some of which are displayed in the Zell Holocaust Memorial exhibit. In addition, the Museum serves as a center for the display of special exhibitions organized by the Museum and in cooperation with other museums and cultural centers.

Cooperative University Programs

Since the late 1960s, Spertus College has entered into cooperative agreements with several Chicago colleges and universities. The purpose of these agreements is twofold: (1) To provide Spertus students with the opportunity to complete B.A. requirements in general studies (Spertus offers the major in Judaica exclusively); (2) To provide general university students the opportunity to major, minor, or take elective Humanities courses in Jewish Studies. This unique "consortium" arrangement has been highly successful over the years, both for the opportunities for learning it has offered and for the division of academic resources it has engendered.

Currently the College maintains full major programs at two Chicago universities, the University of Illinois at Chicago and Northeastern Illinois University. Students at these universities may take Jewish Studies as part of their B.A. programs; and Spertus students may register at these universities for the general-studies half of their B.A. programs.

Spertus College currently also has cooperative programs with Roosevelt University, De Paul University, Mundelein College, and the Chicago Cluster of Theological Schools. Spertus also staffs the Hebrew language program at Northern Illinois University at DeKalb. Consortium students may take Spertus courses in Judaica at the several university locations where they are offered and earn credit at their home institutions.

A similar type of academic cooperation is maintained at the level of graduate studies. Spertus College and the Loyola University School of Social Work offer a joint program leading to the M.A. in Jewish Communal Service and to the M.S.W. degree. The College of Education at the University of Illinois at Chicago provides access to graduate courses to complement the M.A. in Jewish Education program at Spertus. For the M.A. in Jewish Studies, required cognate (non-Judaic) courses are taken at area graduate schools in the individual student's area of concentration.

About half of the Spertus student community consists of undergraduates taking Judaic courses at the cooperating academic institutions. A good number of the students coming to Spertus are over thirty and working. Five percent are from abroad, mainly from Israel; five percent are senior citizens. The result is that classes have an interesting blend of student populations.

The Bachelor of Judaic Studies program is offered mainly to individuals who already possess a bachelor's degree in a field other than Jewish Studies. The candidates for the Bachelor of Judaic Studies for the most part are returning students who have an academic interest in Judaica to the extent of wishing to complete a degree program.

GRADUATE PROGRAMS

The Marvin and Joan Holland Program in Jewish Education

The overall objective of the Holland Program is to train individuals in the competencies necessary to work in and administer Jewish schools of all types.

M.A. In Jewish Communal Service

The graduate course of study in Jewish Communal Service is a professional degree program designed to train individuals as administrators and managers in Jewish social service agencies.

M.A. In Jewish Communal Service/ Master of Social Work: Dual Degree Program

The School of Social Work of Loyola University of Chicago and Spertus College have developed a parallel degree program for persons who intend to do direct practice in Jewish communal agencies. The parallel degree program, through an integrated, individualized course of study, makes it possible for a student to work concurrently toward the M.S.W. degree at Loyola and the M.A.J.C.S. degree at Spertus. Participation in the dual program allows students to earn both degrees in a shorter period than if each degree were to be pursued separately.

M.A. In Jewish Studies

Spertus College offers a master's program in the Jewish Humanities leading to the M.A. in Jewish Studies. Students may select major and minor areas of concentration from the following: Bible, Hebrew Literature, Jewish History, Jewish Thought, and Rabbinic Literature.

M.S. In Human Services Administration

Responding to the personnel needs of the helping professions, Spertus College has developed a one-year evening master's program in the field of Human Services Administration. The program is offered to individuals already working in the field who are seeking positions on a managerial level. Applicants may also include individuals who wish to explore careers in Human Services Administration. The basic goal of the program is to provide the requisite skills for administrative and managerial positions in hospitals, social service agencies and other institutions involved in the helping professions.

The Joseph M. Levine Program of Extension Studies

In response to the educational needs of the wider Chicago community, Spertus College offers an Extension Studies program in suburban areas of Chicago. These courses are designed mainly for adults who wish to develop an awareness and appreciation of Jewish culture, thought, and history.

Touro College

Touro College was chartered in 1970 and admitted its first class of 35 students in 1971. Founded by the sociologist and educator, Dr. Bernard Lander, who serves as the college's president, Touro's stated mission since its inception has been to emphasize the relevance of the Jewish heritage to modern society.

The college drew its name from Judah and Isaac Touro, leaders of colonial America. The Touro family provided substantial endowments to universities, hospitals and pioneering settlements in Israel. It was at the Touro Synagogue in Newport, Rhode Island that George Washington in 1790 enunciated his famous commitment to religious freedom in the United States.

The College serves a wide range of Jewish needs. Touro has specialized programs for Hasidic and yeshivah students, and it has a variety of programs for students with no background in Jewish studies at all. Touro's goal of enriching Jewish life in the United States and Israel is coupled with the desire to serve the broader citizenry as well. To paraphrase Hillel's teaching, "If we were not concerned with the enrichment and preservation of our own heritage, who will be? If we are concerned only with our own needs, what are we?" This philosophy of service gave rise to the establishment of a variety of schools not oriented specifically to the Jewish community. These include the School of Health Sciences, whose first program was established in 1972; the School of General Studies, organized in 1974; and the School of Law, located in Huntington, Long Island, established in 1979.

The Herzliah-Jewish Teachers Seminary merged with Touro College in 1979. Out of this merger the Graduate School of Jewish Studies was founded to further scholarship and teaching at an advanced level. In 1982 Yeshivah Ohr HaChayim was founded. This affiliate of Touro, located in Queens, provides students with the opportunity

Midtown campus, Touro College.

to study full-time in yeshiva during the day, while enrolling in college courses in the evening. The Touro-Technion medical education program admitted its first class in 1983. This program for pre-med graduates from colleges and universities around the country includes 1½ years of study at Touro's Center for Biomedical Education, located at Touro's Long Island campus, and 2½ years of study at the Technion in Haifa, one of the world's leading technological universities. Following an additional year of advanced clinical rotations, students receive the M.D. degree.

In 1985, total enrollment at Touro reached 3,500, with students from close to 30 states, Canada, Israel and a number of other foreign countries. In fourteen years, the college's enrollment has increased a hundredfold.

College of Liberal Arts and Sciences

The College of Liberal Arts and Sciences, based in midtown Manhattan, offers majors and pre-professional options in twenty-five fields. Its 600 students in the coordinate Men's and Women's divisions receive a highly personalized education in which the average class size is ten to fifteen. The setting is informal and friendly and relationships between faculty and students are cordial and close-knit. All students must enroll in a minimum of six hours per week of Judaic study courses. Many students take advantage of the Intensive Talmud track, in which students enroll in a daily Talmud study curriculum lasting the entire morning. A second and distinctive curricular requirement in the College of Liberal Arts and Sciences is the Humanities Core Curriculum, a 24 credit sequence in the history and literature of Western civilization from antiquity to the modern period. This sequence provides a strong liberal arts foundation for all Touro graduates, whether their major is accounting, chemistry or history.

Jewish Studies at Touro College

Jewish Studies at Touro is offered on the undergraduate and graduate levels, as well as through the Israel program, the Law School, and the Jewish People's University of the Air.

At the undergraduate level, classes are offered for beginners as well as for students with an advanced Jewish education.

Each semester, the college offers more than sixty courses in the field of Judaic Studies in such areas as Bible, Jewish Law, Jewish History, Jewish Heritage and Talmud. Hebrew language and literature courses are also given. Bible courses stress textual analysis and commentaries. Jewish law courses are based on particular topics (Kashrut, Sabbath and Festivals, Medical Ethics, The Family). Most Talmud classes involve detailed study of a particular tractate with classical commentaries and codes.

Qualified undergraduates may be admitted to a limited number of courses in the Touro Graduate School of Jewish Studies for undergraduate credit. Students also have the option, with departmental approval, of pursuing a Jewish Studies program at another school of Jewish higher education such as a *yeshiva gedolah* or a seminary.

Men students may elect to enroll in Touro's intensive Talmud Program. Those who participate in this program register for two Talmud courses every semester. In addition to attending two classes Monday through Thursday, students also spend time learning in pairs in the Touro study hall.

In addition, a Touro-affiliated full-time yeshiva in Queens enables students to spend a full day immersed in Jewish Studies. Students enrolled at the Yeshiva may take general college courses in the evening and can prepare themselves for careers in accounting, law, management and computer science. Students who live in Brooklyn may attend local yeshivot or seminaries during the day and enroll in a specially designed Touro College evening program, located in Flatbush.

In keeping with Touro College's commitment to higher Jewish studies, the College has established the Year Abroad/Israel Option to enable students to spend one year of intensive study at selected seminaries and yeshivot in Israel towards their baccalaureate degree. Students may earn up to a maximum of 36 college credits for a full year of studies, or up to a maximum of 18 credits per semester.

The Graduate School of Jewish Studies offers a M.A. degree to highly qualified students. The program specializes in the history of the post-Talmudic period; electives are also offered in Jewish philosophy, Hebrew and Yiddish literature, Jewish education and Jewish communal service.

The Jewish Law Institute of the School of Law, the first of its kind in the United States, offers a variety of courses in Jewish Law at the Law School, and serves as a center for research and scholarship in the field.

The Jewish People's University of the Air (JPUA), an educational outreach program of Touro College and its Herzliah-Jewish Teachers Seminary Division, offers recorded courses in Jewish studies for radio broadcast and on cassettes. JPUA courses are broadcast by independent radio stations and via National Public Radio satellite to over 300 affiliates across the country. JPUA courses on cassettes are being used by more than 50 colleges and universities as well as the U.S. Armed Services and numerous organizations and institutions in their adult-study programs. The blind and handicapped are also served by this project.

JPUA lecturers are outstanding authorities in their particular fields and have been selected from the faculties of Touro College and other institutions of higher learning. JPUA offerings include courses in Jewish history and literature, the entire Jewish cultural heritage, and trends and problems of contemporary Jewish life in this country, in Israel and throughout the world. JPUA presently maintains a curriculum of 20 courses, and new courses are developed at the rate of about four per year.

University of Judaism, Los Angeles

The University of Judaism, affiliated with the Jewish Theological Seminary of America, was founded in Los Angeles in 1947 as a teachers college and a school for adults who wished to continue their Jewish education.

Now nearing the beginning of its fifth decade, the UJ has evolved into a leading center of Jewish education on the West Coast. On its magnificent Familian Campus in the Santa Monica Mountains, there now exist four degree-granting schools, a broad range of adult education courses, and a series of outreach programs that involve Jewish communities from Calgary to El Paso.

Lee College, established in 1982, is a small, challenging, innovative liberal arts college, which combines opportunities for the integration of the study of Jewish and Western civilizations with professional career preparation in a variety of fields. The UJ's Graduate Management Program offers a unique MBA (Master of Business Administration) degree, focusing on the administrative leadership needs of Jewish community institutions and not-for-profit organizations.

University of Judaism, Los Angeles.

The nationally recognized M.A. degree-granting program in Education has a comprehensive curriculum in education and Judaica to prepare Jewish education professionals for teaching, administration, research, and curriculum design. In addition, the UJ offers both undergraduate and graduate programs in Judaic studies.

The UJ is housed in the modern Fingerhut Academic Building and the Ziegler Administration Building. The new residence halls and apartments complex, including the Rochlin Student Residence Hall, Taper Hall, and the Lee College Residence Hall, was completed in Spring 1985, anabling students from Jewish communities world-wide to come to Los Angeles to study and live in a Jewish ambience.

Among the elements which contribute to the academic excellence of the UJ are the Ostrow Library, which houses more than 160,000 volumes, as well as a documentation center, containing in its topically arranged files more than 600,000 clippings, brochures, and other sources of information covering all aspects of contemporary Jewish life throughout the world; and the Clejan Educational Resources Center, with its state-of-the-art audiovisual and computer equipment. Additionally, the UJ sponsors the Center for the Arts, featuring the 500-seat Gindi Auditorium; two summer institutes for college students and educators; and joint programs with UCLA and other leading centers of higher education. The UJ's Zimmer Conference Center in Ojai, California, is the site of Camp Ramah during the summer, and hosts a variety of seminars, weekends, colloquia, and other activities throughout the rest of the year.

The UJ also offers a number of programs designed to meet the changing social and cultural needs of the Jewish community: the Department of Continuing Education, an extensive adult education program; *Elderhostel,* week-long, in-residence educational programs for adults aged 60 and up; the Wagner Memorial Program for Jewish Family Living; Making Marriage Work; and "Commitment," a weekly public affairs television program.

The University of Judaism publishes *Direction,* a bi-monthly newspaper.

Yeshiva University

Marking its 100th anniversary in 1986, Yeshiva University has an enrollment of 7,000 (41% women) from all parts of North America as well as Latin America, Europe, the Middle East, and Africa, with a full-time faculty of 1,300. The University has awarded 25,000 degrees and diplomas, and maintains four major centers in Manhattan and the Bronx, with affiliated units in Los Angeles and Jerusalem. With a current operating budget of $175,000,000, Yeshiva University maintains graduate and undergraduate academic programs as well as service projects benefitting the city, the Jewish community, and the nation in such areas as medical care, Jewish education, the aged, mental health, and youth services.

Yeshiva University began in 1886 as Yeshiva Eitz Chaim, an elementary day school offering Jewish and general studies, on New York's Lower East Side. Ten years later, the Rabbi Isaac Elchanan Theological Seminary was founded there, and in 1915 the two schools merged under the name of the latter—eliminating the elementary school program

Rabbi Isaac Elchanan Spektor (1817-96), noted Rabbi of Kovno, Lithuania, one of the outstanding rabbinic scholars of the 19th century, for whom RIETS was named.

and concentrating on high school and more advanced levels. Liberal arts studies were initiated in 1928, and university status was achieved in 1945.

Dr. Norman Lamm was elected as the institution's third president—the first American born—in August 1976. He succeeded Dr. Samuel Belkin, who served from 1943 to 1976. Dr. Bernard Revel was the first president, 1915 to 1940.

Yeshiva University comprises 15 schools, divisions, and affiliates. There are 5 undergraduate schools—4 for men, 1 for women; 7 graduate and professional schools, and 3 affiliates, with a total enrollment of 7,000 men and women and full-time faculties numbering 1,300. The four major teaching centers in New York are valued at $126,000,000, at cost. Three of these, the Main, Midtown, and Bronx Centers, have dormitory and dining facilities.

Yeshiva College, (founded 1928) (Main Center, 500 West 185th Street, N.Y. 10033) provides liberal arts and sciences curriculums for men; pre-professional programs are offered; students may pursue interdepartmental majors, honors work, independent study, and joint bachelor's-master's programs; grants Bachelor of Arts and Bachelor of Science degrees.

Isaac Breuer College of Hebraic Studies (1917) offers programs of Hebraic studies for men who wish to train for educational leadership, self-improvement, and effective participation in communal life; awards Hebrew Teacher's Diploma and Associate in Arts, Bachelor of Arts, and Bachelor of Science degrees.

James Striar School of General Jewish Studies (1956)—offers a special program of Jewish studies for men with limited Hebraic background; courses are provided at several levels; students may apply credits toward their bachelor's degrees; grants Associate in Arts degree.

Yeshiva Program/Mazer School of Talmudic Studies (1970)—offers a four-year course of study for men with an advanced background in Jewish studies, emphasizing intensive analysis of Talmudic texts and commentaries in the original Hebrew and Aramaic; students may apply credits toward their bachelor's degrees.

Stern College for Women (1954)—(Midtown Center, 245 Lexington Avenue, N.Y. 10016) provides liberal arts and sciences curriculums including courses in Judaic studies; pre-professional programs are offered; students may pursue interdepartmental majors, honors work, independent study, and joint bachelor's-master's programs; awards Bachelor of Arts and Bachelor of Science degrees; students may also receive Associate in Arts degree and Hebrew Teacher's Diploma.

Stern College offers a Shaped Major, through which a student may design a major specifically to meet her needs and interests. The school's intensified Jewish studies program is designed to equip students with broader knowledge and a stronger grasp of basic Jewish texts. The program's core segment includes required periods of study of Tanakh and Halakhah for all students; additional courses are geared to a range of language skills; an elective segment enables students to broaden their studies in areas of particular interest. The Stern College Shanah program of intensive Jewish studies is available to women from other colleges and college graduates, with any level of prior Jewish education.

> *Teachers Institute for Women* (1952)—amalgamated with Stern College; trains professional personnel for positions of leadership in education and community agency work; awards Hebrew Teacher's Diploma and Bachelor of Science in Education degree.

GRADUATE AND PROFESSIONAL SCHOOLS

Bernard Revel Graduate School (1937)—(Main Center) offers graduate work in Judaic studies and Semitic languages, literatures, and cultures; confers Master of Science, Master of Arts, and Doctor of Philosophy degrees.

David J. Azrieli Graduate Institute of Jewish Education (1945)—(Midtown Center) offers Master of Science programs in Jewish elementary education and Jewish secondary education, and Specialist's Certificate and Doctor of Education programs in the administration and supervision of Jewish education. Block Education Program under a grant from the L.A. Pincus Fund for the Diaspora, Jewish Agency, trains Jewish education administrators for service throughout the United States; grants Doctor of Education degree.

Albert Einstein College of Medicine (1955)—(Bronx Center, Eastchester Road and Morris Park Avenue, Bronx, N.Y. 10461) prepares physicians through programs leading to Doctor of Medicine degree stressing interdisciplinary collaboration and interaction; conducts research in every major medical specialty and area of biomedical research, with a level of achievement that has brought Einstein more federal funding for research and training than all but a few other academic medical centers; provides patient care through clinical affiliations encompassing a network of decentralized, community-based facilities including such major resources as the Bronx Municipal Hospital Center,

Studies at Yeshiva Eitz Chaim, the forerunner of Yeshiva University, circa 1900.

comprising two units, Abraham Jacobi Hospital and Nathan B. Van Etten Hospital; Montefiore Hospital and Medical Center, which also administers the Hospital of Albert Einstein College of Medicine; Bronx-Lebanon Hospital Center, Bronx Psychiatric Center, Bronx Children's Psychiatric Center, and Bronx Developmental Services.

Student exchange programs are offered with four institutions in Israel—School of Medicine, Ben-Gurion University of the Negev; Hadassah Medical School, Hebrew University; Shaare Zedek Medical Center; and Shalom Hartman Institute—one in West Germany, Medizinische Hochschule Hanover; and one in the People's Republic of China, Beijing Medical College. The Shaare Zedek-Einstein agreement also calls for faculty participation as well as joint symposia and publications.

Sue Golding Graduate Division of Medical Sciences (1957)—(Bronx Center) offers advanced study in the biological sciences, including biochemistry, genetics, and pathology; awards Doctor of Philosophy degree; six-year medical Scientist Training Program prepares students for a research or teaching career, and offers combined Doctor of Medicine degree from Einstein—Doctor of Philosophy degree from Sue Golding.

Wurzweiler School of Social Work (1957)—(Main Center) offers graduate programs in social group work, social casework, and community social work; grants Master of Social Work and Doctor of Social Welfare degrees; the two-year, full-time Concurrent Program combines classroom study and supervised field instruction; the Extended Program permits a period of up to five years to complete requirements for some Master's degree candidates.

Yeshiva University Gerontological Institute (1976)—offers an interdisciplinary program for professionals holding master's degrees in such fields as social work, psychology, counseling, or nursing, or holding ordination; fosters and coordinates University-wide research, study, and activities related to the process and problems of aging; grants Post-Master's Certificate in Gerontology.

Ferkauf Graduate School of Psychology (1957)—(Bronx Center, 1165 Morris Park Avenue, Bronx N.Y. 10461) offers Master of Arts program in general psychology; Doctor of Psychology programs in clinical and school psychology; and Doctor of Philosophy programs in clinical, developmental-experimental, school, social, health, and bilingual educational-developmental psychology.

Benjamin N. Cardozo School of Law (1976)—(Brookdale Center, 55 Fifth Avenue, N.Y. 10003) offers innovative programs in trial advocacy, critical writing and thinking, and judicial internships, providing both a practical and theoretical legal education for students preparing for a career in law and other areas where a legal education has relevance; grants Doctor of Law (J.D.) degree.

AFFILIATES

Rabbi Isaac Elchanan Theological Seminary (1896)—(2540 Amsterdam Avenue, N.Y. 10033) the Western Hemisphere's largest center for higher learning in the Orthodox tradition of Judaism; program of intensive Torah study in the classic spirit of Judaism leads to *Semikhah* (ordination) and trains rabbis to minister to the multi-faceted spiritual needs of Jewish communities in the United States and other countries; prepares leaders for a broad range of communal services and provides scholars and researchers with a rich grounding in original sources to carry on the noble tradition of Torah scholarship; a major service center for synagogues and Jewish schools, social agencies, and community groups through a network of auxiliary programs and special projects; a center for *Torah Lishmah*—study for its own sake.

Rabbi Joseph B. Soloveitchik Center of Rabbinic Studies offers the core academic program of RIETS—the *Semikhah* program consisting of three years of intensive study of Talmud and Codes; Supplemental Rabbinics prepares students for the practical problems faced in the rabbinate; second- and third-year students select tracks of study for the pulpit rabbinate, education, chaplaincy, and other communal positions—serving an apprenticeship in one of those tracks through the *Shimush* program; students are required to attend a concurrent graduate program relating to their chosen track, or pursue either Kollel studies or a specialized program in Jewish thought.

Caroline and Joseph S. Gruss Institute in Jerusalem (Rehov Havaad Haleumi, Givat Mordechai, Jerusalem, Israel 93721), a center in Israel for advanced Talmudic studies, offers programs for pre-*Semikhah, Semikhah,* and post-*Semikhah* students.

Maybaum Sephardic Fellowship Program trains rabbis for service in Sephardic communities here and abroad; they pursue courses in Sephardic Halakhah, Spanish or Arabic, and other pertinent areas.

Philip and Sarah Belz School of Jewish Music provides professional training of cantors and other music personnel for the Jewish community, and awards Associate Cantor's Certificate and Cantorial Diploma.

RIETS programs for the community are:

Max Stern Division of Communal Services serves Jewish communities in the United States and Canada, as well as Israel, South and Central America, Australia, and South Africa, with special attention to outreach to the young, service to the elderly, and other educational, communal, religious, and social programs.

Camp Morasha, a children's summer camp at Lake Como, Pa., is sponsored by the Metropolitan New York Commission on Torah Education and the Rabbinic Alumni of RIETS.

Yeshiva University High Schools—(The Marsha Stern Talmudical Academy—Yeshiva University High School for Boys [1916], 2540 Amsterdam Avenue, N.Y. 10033; Tonya Soloveitchik Yeshiva University High School for Girls [1959], Olga Gruss Lewin Educational Center, 425 Fifth Avenue [at 38th Street], N.Y. 10016) offer a four-year college preparatory curriculum, with a complete Jewish studies program, leading to an academic High School Diploma with New York State Regents endorsement; graduates of High School for Girls receive a Hebrew Certificate as well.

P'TACH Program enables boys and girls with learning disabilities to receive the full benefit of a regular Jewish all-day high school education. The program, offered in cooperation with P'TACH (Parents for Torah for All Children), integrates these students into the YU High Schools' regular classes and activities through various resource-center services.

Yeshiva University of Los Angeles (1977)—(9760 West Pico Boulevard, Los Angeles, Calif. 90035) with Menachem Begin School of Jewish Studies, Yeshiva Program, Beit Midrash Program, Kollel; students pursue Bachelor of Arts degree at a college of their choice.

Simon Wiesenthal Center for Holocaust Studies at YULA offers programs of lectures, discussions, and films, bringing to students and communities the history and lessons of the Holocaust; a major resource, it includes a reference library, documentation and exhibit area, lecture hall, and multimedia facility.

YULA High School, with boys' and girls' divisions, serves the needs of the Los Angeles community.

LIBRARIES

The University's libraries house some 850,000 volumes, periodicals, and other materials in all branches of the arts and sciences and Judaica, and have interlibrary exchanges and loans. The University's libraries have been named a Government Selective Depository Library by the U.S. Government Printing Office.

The Mendel Gottesman Library at the Main Center is a six-story, block-long central library. Components include the Pollack Undergraduate Library, Mendel Gottesman Library of Hebraica-Judaica, Landowne-Bloom Library, Science Library, Archives, and Rare Book and Manuscript Room. The Hedi Steinberg Library at the Midtown Center strengthens undergraduate academic programs there. The collection pertaining to the David J. Azrieli Graduate Institute of Jewish Education is also housed at the Midtown Center. Libraries that serve other special needs are the Lillian and Rebecca Chutick Law Library of Benjamin N. Cardozo School of Law and the D. Samuel Gottesman Library of the Albert Einstein College of Medicine.

Yeshiva University Museum (endowed by Erica and Ludwig Jesselson), located in the Mendel Gottesman Library, is of tri-level design, offering a permanent display of 10 scale-model "Synagogues Through the Centuries"—spanning the 3rd to 19th centuries—created especially for the Museum; reproduction of frescoes from the Dura-Europos Synagogue (ancient Assyrian city dating back to the third century); ceremonial objects and rare books; wall-size cybernetic map, the only one of its kind, tracing Jewish migration from Abraham to the 20th century; audiovisual presentations and film theater; and Torah Scroll of the Baal Shem Tov, founder of Hassidism—one of two known to exist.

The *Huppah*

Lillian Burg

Huppah—the canopy under which the most sacred and joyous of Jewish sacraments takes place. It is symbolic of the couple's first home.

There are no halakhic rules or specifications for a *huppah*. *Huppah* was merely a curtain placed upon poles, and the bride and groom were led thereunder, where the consecration and benedictions of betrothal and marriage are expressed.

In Talmudic times and considerably earlier, a marriage was in two parts. The first was *kiddushin* or *erusin* (betrothal). The second part of the ceremony took place at a later date and was called *nissu'in* (marriage proper). It was also called *Huppah* after either the bridegroom's house to which the bride was led, or the *canopy* symbolic of that house under which the ceremony took place. Post-Talmudic times found the two parts of the marriage ceremony joined into one, performed at one time.

In ancient times, the *huppah* was the tent or room of the groom, into which, at the end of the betrothal period, the bride was brought, in festive procession, for the marital union. Therefore, the term *"huppah"* originally referred to the bridal chamber and sometimes to the wedding itself.

It became customary to make the canopy under open skies as a blessing, for it is written: "Thus shall thy children be, like the stars of the heaven."

There are as many varied customs of *huppah* as there are variations of Jews. In Talmudic times, the father of the bridegroom erected the *huppah*. In Bethar (near Jerusalem), the poles of the *huppah* were made from the cedar and pine trees which had been planted specifically for this purpose at the birth of male and female children, respectively. The canopy itself was of precious scarlet and gold fabric.

In the early Middle Ages, however, no *huppah* was used at all. In France, the groom covered the bride's head with his *tallit* as a symbol of sheltering her. In the late Middle Ages, the *huppah* consisted of a cloth spread on four posts and was placed inside the synagogue. Later on, it was moved to the courtyard.

In modern Israel, for weddings of soldiers on active duty, the *huppah* often consists of a *tallit*, supported by four rifles held by friends of the bride and groom.

Truly symbolic of their first home, this huppah *was designed and constructed by bride and groom Myra J. Burg and Ronald A. Milberger (both architects) for their wedding on April 21, 1985 in Los Angeles, California. They intend to loan this magnificent, easily assembled structure to other Jewish couples.*

Jewish Humor is No Laughing Matter

Sy Kleinman

From time immemorial, humor has defied definition. Jewish humor has defied definition even longer. Some analysts say we Jews laugh in order that we not cry while others cry because they don't know how Jews can laugh with pride at prejudice and in the teeth of persecution and pain. Jews know why. But they can't explain it either. It is my belief that humor is a key to Jewish survival and that we laugh to prove our survival to those who would have preferred otherwise. But, even more significantly, we also laugh, in fear and trembling, at the threatening tragedy, to show our persecutors that we are fully confident that, in the end, we will have a longer and more enjoyable last laugh when our adversary cannot hear our joy and exultation because he did not survive.

Conclusion? As victims, we laugh at today's adversity knowing that, as survivors, we will again laugh in retrospect, in nostalgia, relief and in gratitude to God. Non-survivors do not laugh. Spend an hour in any cemetery and you'll agree. Only survivors laugh.

In sum, Jewish laughter, like business, operates primarily on credit. We laugh today, secure in our belief that today's sadness will be tomorrow's humor. And, if not tomorrow, then eventually for sure. If we wept with each adversity, our persecutors would be convinced they won. By laughing, we confuse them and destroy their premise. Little do they know we may be laughing with *yastchikas* ("butterflies in the stomach"). Tears may be prologue to laughter in the very same sense that joyous laughter will evoke tears as epilogue.

Our Torah contains many references to laughter and its wisdom has indeed survived. Abraham laughed ironically when he was informed, by angelic messenger, that, at age 100, he would be catering a *pidyon-haben*. When Sarah, then 90, got the news, she laughed hysterically in embarrassment. "What will the neighbors say? Can I shop in the A & P with such a belly yet?" And then, of course, *Yitzchok* emerged "conceived in laughter." And many references to humor follow in Biblical parable, pun and purpose until *Koheleth* reminds us that there is a time to weep and a time to laugh.

Conclusion? Our holiest Book recognizes the reality and necessity of laughter to endure the slings and arrows of outrageous fortune as God's chosen tribe and man's chosen target. No other compendium of ethical life can claim the same. Search as you will, you'll never find an "Anthology of Assyrian Wit", a "Synopsis of Sumerian Satire", a "Bibliography of Babylonian Banter" or even a

pamphlet of "Philistine Fun and Frolic." Even if such publications once existed, they obviously had no staying power.

We can more readily illuminate Jewish humor by illustrating what it is and isn't than by defining it. A "for instance" is always more instructive than an elaborate explanation. Analysis will not reveal the magic formula of its conception but does yield some useful labels. Jewish humor is unique unto itself because, unlike all other forms, it is *always* clean (i.e., not dirty), cerebral (i.e., not stupid), calm (i.e., not violent, impatient or intolerant) *and* clever (i.e., not illogical per se but sometimes logically faulty or faultlessly illogical). As a performer, I sense the *chochma* (wise word), or *shtick* (ploy) that reminds and uplifts a Jewish audience, knowledgeable of tradition or not, by the reminder that our heritage is proud and noble. Whether I address an audience of Orthodox, Conservative or Reform leaning, I know for certain they have one thing in common. None of them know all of the words to the Hatikvah. And, getting serious, I hit them where it hurts when I point out that the most binding force in Judaism, from generation to generation is, *matzoh.* And there we have another lever unique to Yiddish humor—The *shtoch!* No story can qualify as Jewish humor (despite the characters or dialect) if it doesn't make some comment, either in palatable criticism of a failing, in deserved derogation of a pomposity or in excessive praise of a virtue.

Our humor seeks truth by stripping away all veneer of pretension and pomposity so that the realities of the

emperor's nakedness can be revealed. Without that comment, which I call the deft *shtoch,* or thrust, the story makes no contribution to *Yiddishkeit* and may, because of its use of Jewish characters or dialect, be an anti-Yiddish story. Too many performers fail to see this line of demarcation and leave a non-Jewish audience more convinced of their inbred prejudice than disabused. Yiddish humor must, like all things, teach, however subliminally, and we learn most palatably through wisdom within laughter.

Two students engage in debate over the "greatness" of their respective rabbis. "Mine," says one, "is such a great rabbi, he can give a sermon for an hour, on *any* topic." His challenger counters with: "My rabbi is even greater. My rabbi gives a sermon for an hour, no topic!" *(Shtoch!)*

A cantor pompously advises his congregants that his voice was insured by Lloyds of Warsaw for one million dollars. When the tumultuous applause simmers down, a voice from the rear asks: "So, what, *Chazan,* did you do with the money?" *(Shtoch!)*

Jewish humor is rarely based on a contrived premise because contrivances are not reality. Talking animals are rarely featured unless some cerebral comment is made. For example, a cat and her kittens are confronted by an angry bulldog. The kittens run in fright to the mother cat who, protecting her brood, *barks* angrily at the dog. The dog, hearing a cat bark, turns and runs. The cat then addresses her kittens: "Now, children, you see the value of a second language?" *(Shtoch!)* A generic nostalgic story reminds each member of the audience of a personal experience and evokes laughter merely because it stirs a memory of an event that might not have seemed humorous then. Who has not had a mother who tells her son to go to the grocer and buy "for five cents cockroach powder." She then adds the following injunction: "But don't tell him why we need it."

A good Jewish humorist is more than a story teller because he will palatably weave into the story a social comment. "Today, children don't go to synagogue unless you give them a new fringe benefit—a Tallis by Adidas." *(Shtoch!)* Consider the difference between yesterday and today implicit in the following comment: "Would you believe that my kids don't even know the taste of kosher soap? With me it was a 'forshpeis'." Or the obvious criticism implicit in the following: "Here's a new way to raise money. A group of Cadillac dealers got together and raffled off a synagogue."

All ethnic humor strikes out against hypocrisy, prejudice and social vices. Humor, properly structured, is a most

effective form of criticism. Our long exposure to and experience in this area has given us an expertise in such structure. Not self-demeaning stories, as some commentators suggest, but stories with substantive *shtoch.* Some trendy, non-Jewish 'humor' will feature a fall guy—a common victim. Currently, the trend is anti-Polish, and all Poles are depicted as non-intellectual or stupid. For example: A patient, desirous of a brain transplant is offered a choice—the brain of an astrophysicist who had been a Nobel Laureate or the brain of an unidentified Polish peasant. The first brain has a price tag of $750 and the second will cost $2500. The puzzled patient asks why the difference, and the doctor explains: "The Polish brain was never used." Or, did you hear about the "Polish certified public accountant who absconded with his firm's accounts payable?" Stories of that genre are readily adaptable next year to another hapless target. As humor, they really make no comment. They are demeaning to an entire people and, as such, have no redeeming social value.

In a certain sense, the Polish story of today may trace its origin to the Jewish Polish story of yesterday, but those originals had another purpose. I refer, of course, to the legendary fables dealing with the fools of Chelm. All the residents of that mystical Polish *shtetl* were foolish because, as legend has it, God ran out of brains before He ran out of bodies and, therefore, decided to put all the brainless bodies in Chelm where they could live in peace and harmony. If He had distributed brainless bodies elsewhere, proportionate to the bodies with brains, the latter would take advantage of them. Although the residents of Chelm were presumptively brainless, they were lovingly dubbed "the wise men of Chelm" because their brainless logic had an illogic of its own. The story is told of the Chelmers who ran to their Rabbi (by hypothesis, the most foolish in all Chelm) to tell him of an amazing incident. "Rabbi, a piece bread already smeared with butter fell from the table and landed buttered side up. We all know that when buttered bread falls from a table, it always lands buttered side down. So this is either a sign from God or a defiance of the laws of gravity. Which is it, our beloved

By permission of the artist.

Rabbi, and please explain." The Rabbi of Chelm, on the horns of a dilemma, knows there is only one out. With deep profundity, he explains: "It's neither a sign from God nor a defiance of the laws of gravity. The reason this bread fell buttered side up is because it was buttered on the wrong side." A passerby saw four Chelmers trying to hold a pole erect while a fifth Chelmer clambered up to measure it. Halfway up the pole, it toppled. The visitor suggested they lay the pole on the ground and then measure it. To which the climbing Chelmer said: "We want the height— not the width."

Note the difference between the pure Polish story and the Chelm fables. The latter do not demean the entire group because the story has made a redeeming and elevating comment.

I am often asked if Israeli humor is Yiddish. The answer is "No." The laughter of Israel is, like the people of Israel, self-serving, arrogant and as bitterly sweet as the sabra fruit they eat. Jewish virtues are not necessarily featured; political implications are. Thus, in response to a poster announcing a monetary reward for the capture of PLO terrorists, two Israelis go out in pursuit. Asleep in the desert, one awakes at dawn's early light and sees they are surrounded by 5,000 PLO terrorists. Excitedly, he rouses his sleeping friend and says: "Avram, get up, *we're rich!*" (*Shtoch!*)

Or, consider the story of Prime Minister Thatcher who invited the Israeli delegation to her home but was deeply concerned about the non-controversial topics she should raise during the course of the dinner. She was advised by the British Cabinet to limit small-talk to history so as to avoid any conflict. Casually, at one point during the meal, she posed the following question: "I wonder what the course of history would have been if, instead of President Kennedy, Chairman Brezhnev had been assassinated in office." There was a hush and a somewhat embarrassed silence, following which one of the Israeli delegates said: "I don't think Mr. Onassis would have married Mrs. Brezhnev." (*Shtoch!*)

We can highlight the difference between the Polish story and Israeli humor with a similar parable. The story is told of a Polish soldier who, in the course of cleaning an old bottle, freed a genie and was granted three wishes. The first wish was for a bottle of Polish vodka that "never emptied." The genie waved his right hand and, lo, there was a bottle of Polish vodka on the table. The excited soldier uncorked

the bottle, poured out its contents and then watched as the bottle refilled itself. He did this again, with the same result. The genie then said: "You have two more wishes," and the Polish soldier replied: "I want two more bottles, *just like that one.*" (*Shtoch!*)

In Israeli context, the logic changes. The Israeli's first wish is expressed as follows: "I would like Red China to invade Israel and then withdraw." For the second wish, he replies again: "I would like Red China to invade Israel and then withdraw." And when the third wish was exactly the same, the genie disgustedly said: "You're just like the Polish soldier I met the other day. He had everything he wanted with the first wish and then wasted two perfectly good wishes. Why did you waste the second and third wishes?" The Israeli replied: "I didn't waste those wishes. Can you imagine how Syria and Jordan will look after Red China marches back and forth six times?" (*Shtoch!*)

An Israeli complained when the State of Israel began in 1948, that Ben Gurion was an ineffective leader. Here he was on a line-up for food. Line-ups were everywhere. For theatre, transportation, school, funerals, etc., etc. Building up a complaint against Ben Gurion, he turned to the chap behind him and said: "Hold my place on the line. I'm going to kill Ben Gurion." When he returned an hour later, he was asked: "Nu, did you kill him?" His reply: "Impossible. There was such a line-up." (*Shtoch!*)

A Texan, impressed with Israel, expresses a desire to go into business there, "franchisin' kibbutzes. But," he said, "how can I be certain of endin' up with a small fortune?" The Israeli reply: "Bring with you a big one." (*Shtoch!*)

Performers are often cautioned against using material that features dialect. The sensitivities that give rise to such

cautions are often suspect. Is it necessary to use a Yiddish dialect to tell a Jewish story? It's not even necessary to use fish to make *gefilte* fish. If the cook uses tofu as a synthetic substitute, the resulting *"gefilte* fish" will taste like a *"gefilte* tofu," or, to make the dish more binding—*"glatt traif."* The better answer, if the use of dialect is the sole reason for laughter, that story is then an anti-whatever dialect is used.

Sometimes dialect is absolutely necessary to make the comment. Perhaps the best illustration is the following story: "Vot a vunderful country is America. I came here a immigrant boy. Not a penny in the pockets. Today, I am a pottner in McCarthy and Schmulowitz. Nu, vare except in America could you have it a firm McCarthy and Schmulo-witz and on the best from terms? Never a harsh void between us and I got for you another surprise: "I'm McCarthy."

That story, without the use of dialect, would fall flat because it makes no comment. It's like the complaint of a businessman who, after trying a dictating machine on approval, said: "Get that rotten machine out of here. It's defective. It talks with an accent." Or, my grandfather's remark: "What a strange country is America. Would you believe it, before I came here, I didn't talk with an accent?"

As a performer, the best examples of Jewish humor are those stories which, like Gaul, are tripartite in nature. Each of its three segments makes a separate comment. It demonstrates Talmudic training by emphasizing alternatives— "on the one hand, this; on the other hand, that, and, on still another hand, something else." On analysis, these stories are based on climax, superclimax and the topper, establishing that each section, which may be laughter-provoking in itself, could still be improved. For example, a proposal is made to authorize the purchase of an expensive crystal

Drawing by George Price. © 1938 The New Yorker Magazine, Inc.

chandelier for the synagogue. The membership is unanimous in its approval, except for one dissident who states three objections:

> "First, I am the recording secretary of this meeting and I have to make the minutes. I can't spell the words 'crystal chandelier.'
>
> Second, if we got a crystal chandelier for the synagogue, there's probably no one here who knows how to play it.
>
> Third, what we really need here is *more light.*"

Jewish humor is uniquely non-violent. Even Jewish curses are often less violent than they were intended to be because they are extended to such a point that all malediction is extracted and the convoluted logic of the final statement converts the threat to something else. To illustrate the point: "You should get so poor, you shouldn't have a piece bread in the house to eat. You should have to come to me, I should give it to you and I shouldn't have it to give it to you."

The same sort of illogical logic is featured in comments like: "If medical science made so much progress in the past 25 years, so how come I felt better 25 years ago?" Or, "When you lose your memory, forget it."

"In the olden days, so money talked. Now, it goes without saying."

"Alright, you forget it, and I'll forget it. But I'll remember it and don't you ever forget it."

"The next time I take *your* kids anyplace, I'm gonna leave them home."

"Listen carefully. I can only tell you this once because I swore to the one who told me that I wouldn't repeat it."

"How can I tell you more? I already told you more than I know."

More than any other ethnic humor, Yiddish stories are often defensively cerebral. Thus, for example, when President Nixon, the greatest President ever to resign that high office, met Golda Meir, he sought to ingratiate himself by noting that Israel and the United States had the only two Jewish Secretaries of State—Abba Eban and Henry Kissinger, respectively. Golda Meir said: "That's true. But mine speaks better English." *(Shtoch!)*

A dyed-in-the-wool WASP arrogantly told a Jewish audience that his great, great, great-grandfather fought with

Drawing by S. Gross. © 1978 National Lampoon, Inc.

© 1980 by The New Yorker Magazine, Inc

George Washington, his great, great-grandfather fought with Ulysses S. Grant, his great-grandfather fought with Theodore Roosevelt, his grandfather fought with General Pershing, his father fought with Dwight Eisenhower, and he fought with Douglas MacArthur. To all of which, a member of the audience replied: "Your family doesn't get along with anybody?" *(Shtoch!)*

That response reflects a quick witted cerebral reaction designed to strip away the WASPish claim of "superiority." When my own father was told by a Catholic that Jews are not really devout, pointing out that we pray *after* we eat, whereas Catholics pray *before* each and every meal, my father replied: "Well, your people have to. You're eating *traif!*" *(Shtoch!)*

Humor is basically a search for truth, and often, by *reductio ad absurdum,* reveals falsity. It might be said that Jews think fast because they can't run fast. Thus, we resort to humor to establish parity and avoid violence.

Some analysts claim that Jewish humor is self-demeaning and designed to prove to the adversary that he need not make jokes about us because we are already doing so. Although Freud subscribed to that view, it is far from elevating. True Jewish humor does not demean the Jew. In some cases, the point of the story is only understandable by other Jews and may, indeed, be a secret method of inner communication. There was, for example, a special lexicon of quasi-German Jewish words in the concentration camps which meant one thing to a Jew and another thing, quite harmless in nature, to Nazi personnel.

Jewish humor, true to Talmudic training, is gentle and logical. It stresses virtue, not vice, and is used lovingly to make a comment. It rarely depends on vulgarity or sex, although it sometimes seems to come dangerously close. A *yeshivah bucher* who returns from a European vacation is greeted by friends who are surprised to see him dressed in drag. When they asked him: "What's with the dress, Bernie?", he replied, now more effeminately than ever: "From now on, my name is Bernice. When I was in Sweden, I took advantage of the operation and now, I'm a woman." His friends refused to accept that statement. "Come on, Bernie,

you left a man, how could you now be a woman?" His reply was insistent. "The name is Bernice. From now on, I sit upstairs. I'm a regular woman." But, they all said, "How could you be a regular woman? You were once a regular man. Isn't that mixed up? Don't you ever get a masculine feeling?" To which Bernice, nee Bernie, replied: "Well, you're all my best friends. So I'll tell you in confidence. Yes. Once in a while, I do get up in the morning with a tremendous urge to *laig tefilin!*"

Or take the current story of an Israeli who seeks female companionship in New York. He is recommended to a house of ill repute, but, with its Mayflower madame, of *high* ill repute. He asks the madame if he can talk privately with the girls and she introduces him to one of the girls to whom he whispered something. The latter turned on him with fast rejection: "Get lost, buddy, that's not my thing." After another introduction, the young lady smacked the Israeli and said: "Not me, buster. I don't do that." When he asked for another prospect, the madame, now beside herself with curiosity, said: "No, sir. Not until you tell me what you're asking my girls to do." The Israeli's bland reply was "I'm only asking them if they'll accept Israeli currency."

No human condition is exempt from exposure to laughter. Even tragedy can be its target. Indeed, the line of demarcation between tragedy and comedy is rarely pikestaff clear, and even when we weep, we are comforted by the promise that we will ultimately laugh when we recall what once caused our tears. And so, we find reason to laugh, even at death, because laughter, not tears, is the only hope of survival after death.

A dying husband begs his wife to remarry as quickly as possible after his demise. She asks why and he explains: "Because I want someone to be sorry I died."

Or consider the bittersweetness of the Messiah discussions: "When Messiah comes, the world we know ends. Everyone who ever died is redeemed and we all go to Israel—El Al." "That's wonderful for El Al. But what happens to Israel? 'Everyone who ever lived.' That's billions of people. Israel today can't support three million people. With billions, it'll be worse than India. It'll fall into the Mediterranean." "Stop worrying. The good Lord in His Infinite wisdom delivered us from Pharaoh. He saved us from Haman. So, He'll surely protect us against the Messiah."

"LOOK! JOE COLLEGE!"

"Dad," said a devoted son to his dying parent, "Which cemetery would you like? Your old shul has a plot for you in a cemetery we couldn't even find. Mama's cemetery is over 30 miles away, and we have a family plot in our synagogue cemetery which is very convenient for the family. Which would you like?" The old man thought and then said: "Tell you what, my son, surprise me."

The *shtoch* in Yiddish humor is multi-purposed. It may be the devastating destroyer of pretense, the palatable offense or calculated defense to insult or criticism, the moral admonition or the instructive teaching tool so basic to Judaic tradition. A mother gets a long-awaited phone call with the preface: "Ma, I was gonna call you last week." Her inevitable reply: "And who didn't let you?" admonishes both the son and his wife without the direct charge of neglect. A mother greets her son, on furlough from Talmudic studies. He is dressed in black *kaftan* and *strammel*, beard and curled sidelocks. "Look," she proudly says, "Joe College." A criticism of both worlds in one. "Rabbi," asks the class, "why is the sea so salty?" With every desire to teach, the Rabbi says: "I think it's because so many herring live in it.'

If the story has no purpose, no thrust, no *shtoch,* then it may just be a funny story, devoid of Yiddish content, even though its characters have Jewish names and Yiddish dialect is dominant. In fact, it has been my experience that a story parading as such, on the strength of characters and dialect alone, without a comment, is too often an anti-Semitic story pretending to be otherwise.

Dissent in humor is not as punishable as outright criticism. Thus, the Russian Jew explains. "Americanskis make beeg fuss over freedom of speech. We got it freedom of speech in Soviet Union. We got, da, freedom of speech. But we don't got freedom *after* speech." Or the announcement that Pravda is having *beeg* contest for best political picture. First prize: "Twenty years in Gulag." In an interview, the Soviet Commissar estimated there were 2,000,000 Jews in the Soviet Union. If they were all allowed to leave, how many Jews would leave? "Oh," said the Commissar, "about 4 to 5 million."

The *shtoch* can be as direct as a right jab, as powerful as an uppercut or as devastating as a knockout, and no Yiddish story ever leaves home without it. It can also be as indirect as a Roumanian excuse, as subtle as a French sauce or as deft as an Italian stiletto. The "modern" beggar who is told to come back tomorrow and replies by saying he doesn't give credit is like the beggar of old who told the banker Rothschild, "If I had your money, Mr. Rothschild, I'd be richer yet than you are because I won't give up schnurring." Moral lessons are updated by the flexible *shtoch.* In the older generation, divorce was a *shanda* (a shame) because we believed in the sanctity of a mistake. Currently, a husband seeking a divorce may refuse to pay alimony but offers to give his ex-wife a "nice letter of recommendation." The wife may demand that her husband leave her "exactly as he found her." When told that the law cannot order such unusual relief, she counters with the statement that the law can. "He found me a widow, let him leave me a widow." Indeed, the *shtoch* readily adjusts to changing morality. Thus, we have the story of the mother who is congratulated on her daughter's marriage to a dentist. "Oh, no," the proud mother replies. "Not a dentist, a doctor. A dentist was my daughter's second husband." When her friend inquires about the first, she is told that her daughter's first mate was a C.P.A. Her friend then enviously says: "First a C.P.A., then a dentist, now a doctor? Such *nachas* from one *shtickel kind!*" The moral lesson is still the same.

Whatever the subject matter of the jest, a true Yiddish story involves some aspect of Judaism, its traditions or an alleged virtue or foible in the genetic chain linking generation to generation. The anti-Semitic import of an alleged Jewish story leads non-Jews to laugh *at* faith. Jews, on the other hand, sense that no story qualifies as Yiddish humor unless it generates laughter *with* faith. I once did a performance, prior to introducing a black sports hero as guest of honor. Halfway through, someone at the dais reminded me that I had ended a story with a Yiddish witticism and that our guest of honor needed a translation. However, he was laughing just as heartily at the Yiddish punchline as the audience. I asked whether he understood Yiddish, and he said: "No, but I have a lot of confidence in you people."

In summary, the quest to discover why we laugh is as futile as the alchemist's search for a magic formula for gold. Whatever the chemistry, we laugh for a variety of reasons, none of which is clear. If we dissect a songbird to find out why it sings, it will sing no more and we will learn nothing thereby except how to stop its beautiful melodies for all time. So, let it sing on and enjoy it while it lasts. Life without the enjoyment and relief of laughter would be meaningless, and surely life must have meaning. It would be laughable to think otherwise. Jews without laughter would be Jews without tradition, without hope and without faith in survival.

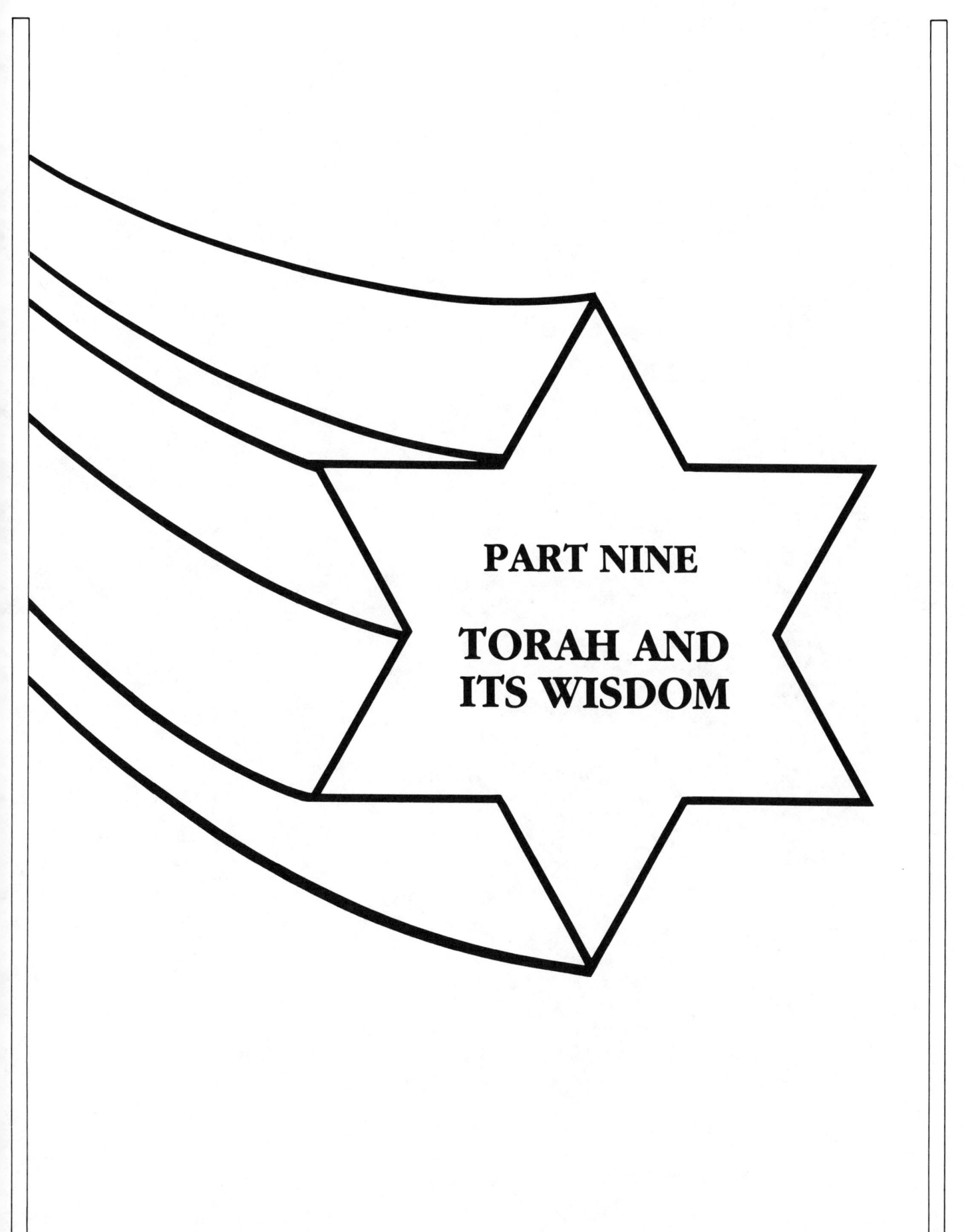

PART NINE

TORAH AND
ITS WISDOM

The Bible *(Tanakh)*

The Law *(Torah)*—Pentateuch

	Chapters	Verses	Letters
Genesis	50	1534	78,064
Exodus	40	1209	63,529
Leviticus	27	859	44,790
Numbers	36	1288	63,530
Deuteronomy	34	955	54,892
	187	5845	304,805

The Prophets *(Nevi'im)*
Former Prophets
Joshua	24
Judges	21
I Samuel	31
II Samuel	24
I Kings	22
II Kings	25

Latter Prophets
Isaiah	66
Jeremiah	52
Ezekiel	48
The Twelve Prophets	
Hosea	14
Joel	4
Amos	9
Obadiah	1
Jonah	4
Micah	7
Nahum	3
Habakkuk	3
Zephaniah	3
Haggai	2
Zechariah	14
Malachi	3

The Writings *(Ketuvim)*—Hagiographa
Psalms	150
Proverbs	31
Job	42
Five Scrolls *(Megillot)*	
Song of Songs	8
Ruth	4
Lamentations	5
Ecclesiastes	12
Esther	10
Daniel	12
Ezra	10
Nehemiah	13
I Chronicles	29
II Chronicles	36

The 613 Commandments

Mandatory Commandments.

God.

The Jew is required to [1]believe that God exists and to [2]acknowledge His unity; to [3]love, [4]fear, and [5]serve Him. He is also commanded to [6]cleave to Him (by associating with and imitating the wise) and to [7]swear only by His name. One must [8]imitate God and [9]sanctify His name.

1. Ex. 20:2		2. Deut. 6:4
3. Deut. 6:5		5. Ex. 23:25;
4. Deut. 6:13		Deut. 11:13
6. Deut. 10:20		(Deut. 6:13 and
7. Deut. 10:20		also 13:5)
9. Lev. 22:32		8. Deut. 28:9

Torah.

The Jew must [10]recite the *Shema* each morning and evening and [11]study the *Torah and teach it to others. He should bind *tefillin* on his [12]head and [13]his arm. He should make [14]*zizit* for his garments and [15]fix a *mezuzah* on the door. The people are to be [16]assembled every seventh year to hear the Torah read and [17]the king must write a special copy of the Torah for himself. [18]Every Jew should have a Torah scroll. One should [19]praise God after eating.

10. Deut. 6:7		
11. Deut. 6:7		
12. Deut. 6:8		14. Num. 15:38
13. Deut. 6:8		15. Deut. 6:9
16. Deut. 31:12		
17. Deut. 17:18		
18. Deut. 31:19		19. Deut. 8:10

Temple, and the Priests.

The Jews should [20]build a *Temple and [21]respect it. It must be [22]guarded at all times and the [23]*Levites should perform their special duties in it. Before entering the Temple or participating in its service the priests [24]must wash their hands and feet; they must also [25]light the candelabrum daily. The priests are required to [26]bless Israel and to [27]set the shewbread and frankincense before the Ark. Twice daily they must [28]burn the incense on the golden altar. Fire shall be kept burning on the altar [29]continually and the ashes should be [30]removed daily. Ritually unclean persons must be [31]kept out of the Temple. Israel [32]should honor its priests, who must be [33]dressed in special priestly raiment. The priests should [34]carry the Ark on their shoulders, and the holy anointing oil [35]must be prepared according to its special formula. The priestly families should officiate in [36]rotation. In honor of certain dead close relatives the priests should [37]make themselves ritually unclean. The high priest may marry [38]only a virgin.

20. Ex. 25:8		21. Lev. 19:30
22. Num. 18:4		23. Num. 18:23
24. Ex. 30:19		
25. Ex. 27:21		
26. Num. 6:23		27. Ex. 25:30
		28. Ex. 30:7
		29. Lev. 6:6
30. Lev. 6:3		
31. Num. 5:2		32. Lev. 21:8
33. Ex. 28:2		
34. Num. 7:9		
35. Ex. 30:31		
		36. Deut. 18:6–8
		37. Lev. 21:2–3
		38. Lev. 21:13

Sacrifices.

The [39]*tamid* sacrifice must be offered twice daily and the [40]high priest must also offer a meal-offering twice daily. An additional sacrifice *(musaf)* should be offered [41]every Sabbath, [42]on the first of every month, and [43]on each of the seven days of *Passover. On the second day of Passover [44]a meal offering of the first barley must also be brought. On *Shavuot a [45]*musaf* must be offered and [46]two loaves of bread as a wave offering. The additional sacrifice must also be made on [47]*Rosh Ha-Shanah and [48]on the Day of *Atonement when the [49]*Avodah must also be performed. On every day of the festival of [50]*Sukkot a *musaf* must be brought as well as on the [51]eighth day thereof.

Every male Jew should make [52]pilgrimage to the Temple three times a year and [53]appear there during the three pilgrim Festivals. One should [54]rejoice on the Festivals.

On the 14th of Nisan one should [55]slaughter the paschal lamb and [56]eat of its roasted flesh on the night of the 15th. Those who were ritually impure in Nisan should slaughter the paschal lamb on [57]the 14th of Iyyar and eat it with [58]*mazzah* and bitter herbs.

Trumpets should be [59]sounded when the festive sacrifices are brought and also in times of tribulation.

Cattle to be sacrificed must be [60]at least eight days old and [61]with-

39. Num. 28:3		40. Lev. 6:13
		41. Num. 28:9
43. Lev. 23:36		42. Num. 28:11
44. Lev. 23:10		
46. Lev. 23:17		45. Num. 28:26–27
47. Num. 29:1–2		48. Num. 29:7–8
49. Lev. 16		
50. Num. 29:13		
51. Num. 29:36		
53. Ex. 34:23;		52. Ex. 23:14
Deut. 16:16		
54. Deut. 16:14		55. Ex. 12:6
56. Ex. 12:8		
57. Num. 9:11		
		58. Num. 9:11;
59. Num. 10:10;		Ex. 12:8
Num. 10:9		
60. Lev. 22:27		61. Lev. 22:21

out blemish. All offerings must be [62]salted. It is a *mitzvah* to perform the ritual of [63]the burnt offering, [64]the sin offering, [65]the guilt offering, [66]the peace offering and [67]the meal offering.

Should the *Sanhedrin err in a decision its members [68]must bring a sin offering which offering must also be brought [69]by a person who has unwittingly transgressed a *karet* prohibition (i.e., one which, if done deliberately, would incur *karet*). When in doubt as to whether one has transgressed such a prohibition a [70]"suspensive" guilt offering must be brought.

For [71]stealing or swearing falsely and for other sins of a like nature, a guilt offering must be brought. In special circumstances the sin offering [72]can be according to one's means.

One must [73]confess one's sins before God and repent for them.

A [74]man or [75]a woman who has a seminal issue must bring a sacrifice; a woman must also bring a sacrifice [76]after childbirth. A leper must [77]bring a sacrifice after he has been cleansed.

One must [78]tithe one's cattle. The [79]*first born of clean (i.e., permitted) cattle are holy and must be sacrificed. The firstborn of man must be [80]redeemed. The firstling of the ass must be [81]redeemed; if not [82]its neck has to be broken.

Animals set aside as offerings [83]must be brought to Jerusalem without delay and [84]may be sacrificed only in the Temple. Offerings from outside the land of Israel [85]may also be brought to the Temple.

Sanctified animals [86]which have become blemished must be redeemed. A beast exchanged for an offering [87]is also holy.

The priests should eat [88]the remainder of the meal offering and [89]the flesh of sin and guilt offerings; but consecrated flesh which has become [90]ritually unclean or [91]which was not eaten within its appointed time must be burned.

Vows.

A *Nazirite must [92]let his hair grow during the period of his separation. When that period is over he must [93]shave his head and bring his sacrifice.

A man must [94]honor his vows and his oaths which a judge can [95]annul only in accordance with the law.

Ritual Purity.

Anyone who touches [96]a carcass or [97]one of the eight species of reptiles becomes ritually unclean; food becomes unclean by [98]coming into contact with a ritually unclean object. Menstruous women [99]and those [100]lying-in after childbirth are ritually impure. A [101]leper, [102]a leprous garment, and [103]a leprous house are all ritually unclean. A man having [104]a running issue is unclean, as is [105]semen. A woman suffering from [106]running issue is also impure. A [107]human corpse is ritually unclean. The purification water *(mei niddah)* purifies [108]the unclean, but it makes the clean ritually impure. It is a *mitzvah* to become ritually clean [109]by ritual immersion. To become cleansed of leprosy one [110]must follow the specified procedure and also [111]shave off all of one's hair. Until cleansed the leper [112]must be bareheaded with clothing in disarray so as to be easily distinguishable.

The ashes of [113]the *red heifer are to be used in the process of ritual purification.

Donations to the Temple.

If a person [114]undertakes to give his own value to the Temple he must do so. Should a man declare [115]an unclean beast, [116]a house, or [117]a field as a donation to the Temple, he must give their value in money as fixed by the priest. If one unwittingly derives

---

63. Lev. 1:2
66. Lev. 3:1
67. Lev. 2:1; 6:7
71. Lev. 5:15, 21–25; 19:20–21
72. Lev. 5:1–11
73. Num. 5:6–7
74. Lev. 15:13–15
75. Lev. 15:28–29
77. Lev. 14:10
78. Lev. 27:32
80. Ex. 22:28; Num. 18:15
82. Ex. 13:13
84. Deut. 12:14
85. Deut. 12:26
86. Deut. 12:15
88. Lev. 6:9
89. Ex. 29:33
90. Lev. 7:19
92. Num. 6:5
94. Deut. 23:24
95. Num. 30:3
96. Lev. 11:8, and 24
98. Lev. 11:34
99. Lev. 15:19
101. Lev. 13:3
102. Lev. 13:51
105. Lev. 15:16
107. Num. 19:14
108. Num. 19:13, 21
111. Lev. 14:9
112. Lev. 13:45
113. Num. 19:2–9
114. Lev. 27:2–8
117. Lev. 27:16, 22–23

62. Lev. 2:13
64. Lev. 6:18
65. Lev. 7:1
68. Lev. 4:13
69. Lev. 4:27
70. Lev. 5:17–18
76. Lev. 12:6
79. Ex. 13:2
81. Ex. 34:20
83. Deut. 12:5–5
87. Lev. 27:33
91. Lev. 7:17
93. Num. 6:18
97. Lev. 11:29–31
100. Lev. 12:2
103. Lev. 14:44
104. Lev. 15:2
106. Lev. 15:19
109. Lev. 15:16
110. Lev. 14:2
115. Lev. 27:11–12
116. Lev. 27:14

442

119. Lev. 19:24
120. Lev. 19:9
121. Lev. 19:9
123. Lev. 19:10

125. Ex. 23:19
126. Deut. 18:4

128. Deut. 14:22
129. Num. 18:26

131. Deut. 26:13

133. Num. 15:20

136. Lev. 25:10

138. Lev. 25:24
139. Lev. 25:29–30

140. Lev. 25:8
141. Deut. 15:3

144. Deut. 18:4

147. Lev. 17:13
148. Deut. 22:7
150. Deut. 14:11
151. Lev. 11:21
152. Lev. 11:9

154. Ex. 23:12

159. Ex. 12:16
160. Ex. 12:16
161. Lev. 23:35
163. Lev. 23:24
165. Lev. 16:29, 31

169. Lev. 23:40

benefit from Temple property [118]full restitution plus a fifth must be made.

The fruit of [119]the fourth year's growth of trees is holy and may be eaten only in Jerusalem. When you reap your fields you must leave [120]the corners, [121]the gleanings, [122]the forgotten sheaves, [123]the misformed bunches of grapes and [124]the gleanings of the grapes for the poor.

The first fruits must be [125]separated and brought to the Temple and you must also [126]separate the great heave offering (terumah) and give it to the priests. You must give [127]one tithe of your produce to the Levites and separate [128]a second tithe which is to be eaten only in Jerusalem. The Levites [129]must give a tenth of their tithe to the priests.

In the third and sixth years of the seven year cycle you should [130]separate a tithe for the poor instead of the second tithe. A declaration [131]must be recited when separating the various tithes and [132]when bringing the first fruits to the Temple.

The first portion of the [133]dough must be given to the priest.

The Sabbatical Year.

In the seventh year (shemittah) everything that grows is [134]ownerless and available to all; the fields [135]must lie fallow and you may not till the ground. You must [136]sanctify the Jubilee year (50th) and on the Day of Atonement in that year [137]you must sound the shofar and set all Hebrew slaves free. In the Jubilee year all land is to be [138]returned to its ancestral owners and, generally, in a walled city [139]the seller has the right to buy back a house within a year of the sale.

Starting from entry into the land of Israel, the years of the Jubilee must be [140]counted and announced yearly and septennially.

In the seventh year [141]all debts are annulled but [142]one may exact a debt owed by a foreigner.

Concerning Animals for Consumption.

When you slaughter an animal you must [143]give the priest his share as you must also give him [144]the first of the fleece. When a man makes a herem (a special vow) you must [145]distinguish between that which belongs to the Temple (i.e., when God's name was mentioned in the vow) and between that which goes to the priests. To be fit for consumption, beast and fowl must be [146]slaughtered according to the law and if they are not of a domesticated species [147]their blood must be covered with earth after slaughter.

Set the parent bird [148]free when taking the nest. Examine [149]beast, [150]fowl, [151]locusts and [152]fish to determine whether they are permitted for consumption.

The *Sanhedrin should [153]sanctify the first day of every month and reckon the years and the seasons.

Festivals.

You must [154]rest on the Sabbath day and [155]declare it holy at its onset and termination. On the 14th of Nisan [156]remove all leaven from your ownership and on the night of the 15th [157]relate the story of the exodus from Egypt; on that night [158]you must also eat mazzah. On the [159]first and [160]seventh days of Passover you must rest. Starting from the day of the first sheaf (16th of Nisan) you shall [161]count 49 days. You must rest on [162]*Shavuot, and on [163]*Rosh Ha-Shanah; on the Day of *Atonement you must [164]fast and [165]rest. You must also rest on [166]the first and [167]the eighth day of *Sukkot during which festival you shall [168]dwell in booths and [169]take the *four species. On *Rosh Ha-Shanah [170]you are to hear the sound of the *shofar.

118. Lev. 5:16

122. Deut. 24:19
124. Lev. 19:10

127. Lev. 27:30;
Num. 18:24

130. Deut. 14:28

132. Deut. 26:5

134. Ex. 23:11
135. Ex. 34:21

137. Lev. 25:9

142. Deut. 15:3

143. Deut. 18:3

145. Lev. 27:21, 28

146. Deut. 12:21

149. Lev. 11:2

153. Ex. 12:2;
Deut. 16:1

155. Ex. 20:8
156. Ex. 12:15
157. Ex. 13:8
158. Ex. 12:18

162. Lev. 23
164. Lev. 16:29
166. Lev. 23:35
167. Lev. 23:36
168. Lev. 23:42
170. Num. 29:1

171. Ex. 30:12–13	
172. Deut. 18:15	
174. Deut. 17:11	173. Deut. 17:15
	175. Ex. 23:2
	176. Deut. 16:18
	177. Lev. 19:15
178. Lev. 5:1	
179. Deut. 13:15	
180. Deut. 19:19	
181. Deut. 21:4	
	182. Deut. 19:3
	183. Num. 35:2
184. Deut. 22:8	

Community.

Every male should [171]give half a shekel to the Temple annually. You must [172]obey a prophet and [173]appoint a king. You must also [174]obey the Sanhedrin; in the case of division, [175]yield to the majority. Judges and officials shall be [176]appointed in every town and they shall judge the people [177]impartially.

Whoever is aware of evidence [178]must come to court to testify. Witnesses shall be [179]examined thoroughly and, if found to be false, [180]shall have done to them what they intended to do to the accused.

When a person is found murdered and the murderer is unknown the ritual of [181]decapitating the heifer must be performed.

Six cities of refuge should be [182]established. The Levites, who have no ancestral share in the land, shall [183]be given cities to live in.

You must [184]build a fence around your roof and remove potential hazards from your home.

187. Deut. 20:17	185. Deut. 12:2; 7:5
188. Deut. 25:19	186. Deut. 13:17
	189. Deut. 25:17

Idolatry.

Idolatry and its appurtenances [185]must be destroyed, and a city which has become perverted must be [186]treated according to the law. You are commanded to [187]destroy the seven Canaanite nations, and [188]to blot out the memory of *Amalek, and [189]to remember what they did to Israel.

190. Deut. 20:11–12	191. Deut. 20:2
	192. Deut. 23:14–15
	193. Deut. 23:14

War.

The regulations for wars other than those commanded in the Torah [190]are to be observed and a priest should be [191]appointed for special duties in times of war. The military camp must be [192]kept in a sanitary condition. To this end, every soldier must be [193]equipped with the necessary implements.

194. Lev. 5:23	195. Deut. 15:8; Lev. 25:35–36
197. Ex. 22:24	196. Deut. 15:14
198. Deut. 23:21	199. Deut. 24:13; Ex. 22:25
	200. Deut. 24:15
	201. Deut. 23:25–26
204. Deut. 22:1; Ex. 23:4	202. Ex. 23:5
205. Lev. 19:17	203. Deut. 22:4
207. Deut. 10:19	206. Lev. 19:18
208. Lev. 19:36	

Social.

Stolen property must be [194]restored to its owner. Give [195]charity to the poor. When a Hebrew slave goes free the owner must [196]give him gifts. Lend to [197]the poor without interest; to the foreigner you may [198]lend at interest. Restore [199]a pledge to its owner if he needs it. Pay the worker his wages [200]on time; [201]permit him to eat of the produce with which he is working. You must [202]help unload an animal when necessary, and also [203]help load man or beast. Lost property [204]must be restored to its owner. You are required [205]to reprove the sinner but you must [206]love your fellow as yourself. You are commanded [207]to love the proselyte. Your weights and measures [208]must be accurate.

	210. Ex. 20:12
209. Lev. 19:32	211. Lev. 19:3
212. Gen. 1:28	213. Deut. 24:1
	214. Deut. 24:5
215. Gen. 17:10; Lev. 12:3	
216. Deut. 25:5	217. Deut. 25:9
	218. Deut. 22:29
219. Deut. 22:18–19	
220. Ex. 22:15–23	
221. Deut. 21:11	
222. Deut. 24:1	
	223. Num. 5:15–27

Family.

Respect the [209]wise; [210]honor and [211]fear your parents.

You should [212]perpetuate the human race by marrying [213]according to the law. A bridegroom is to [214]rejoice with his bride for one year. Male children must [215]be circumcised. Should a man die childless his brother must either [216]marry his widow or [217]release her (ḥaliẓah). He who violates a virgin must [218]marry her and may never divorce her. If a man unjustly accuses his wife of premarital promiscuity [219]he shall be flogged, and may never divorce her. The seducer [220]must be punished according to the law. The female captive must be [221]treated in accordance with her special regulations. Divorce can be executed [222]only by means of a written document. A woman suspected of adultery [223]has to submit to the required test.

Judicial.

When required by the law [224]you must administer the punishment of flogging and you must [225]exile the unwitting homicide. Capital punishment shall be by [226]the sword, [227]strangulation, [228]fire, or [229]stoning, as specified. In some cases the body of the executed [230]shall be hanged, but it [231]must be brought to burial the same day.

Slaves.

Hebrew slaves [232]must be treated according to the special laws for them. The master should [233]marry his Hebrew maidservant or [234]redeem her. The alien slave [235]must be treated according to the regulations applying to him.

Torts.

The applicable law must be administered in the case of injury caused by [236]a person, [237]an animal or [238]a pit. Thieves [239]must be punished. You must render judgment in cases of [240]trespass by cattle, [241]arson, [242]embezzlement by an unpaid guardian and in claims against [243]a paid guardian, a hirer, or [244]a borrower. Judgment must also be rendered in disputes arising out of [245]sales, [248]inheritance and [246]other matters generally. You are required to [247]rescue the persecuted even if it means killing his oppressor.

Prohibitions.

Idolatry and Related Practices.

It is [1]forbidden to believe in the existence of any but the One God. You may not make images [2]for yourself or [3]for others to worship or for [4]any other purpose.

You must not worship anything but God either in [5]the manner prescribed for His worship or [6]in its own manner of worship.

Do not [7]sacrifice children to *Molech.

You may not [8]practice necromancy or [9]resort to "familiar spirits" neither should you take idolatry or its mythology [10]seriously.

It is forbidden to construct a [11]pillar or [12]dais even for the worship of God or to [13]plant trees in the Temple.

You may not [14]swear by idols or instigate an idolator to do so, nor may you encourage or persuade any [15]non-Jew or [16]Jew to worship idols.

You must not [17]listen to or love anyone who disseminates idolatry nor [18]should you withhold yourself from hating him. Do not [19]pity such a person. If somebody tries to convert you to idolatry [20]do not defend him or [21]conceal the fact.

It is forbidden to [22]derive any benefit from the ornaments of idols. You may not [23]rebuild that which has been destroyed as a punishment for idolatry nor may you [24]have any benefit from its wealth. Do not [25]use anything connected with idols or idolatry.

It is forbidden [26]to prophecy in the name of idols or prophecy [27]falsely in the name of God. Do not [28]listen to the one who prophesies for idols and do not [29]fear the false prophet or hinder his execution.

You must not [30]imitate the ways of idolators or practice their customs; [31]divination, [32]soothsaying, [33]enchanting, [34]sorcery, [35]charming, [36]consulting ghosts or [37]familiar spirits and [38]necromancy are forbidden. Women must not [39]wear male clothing nor men [40]that of women. Do not [41]tattoo yourself in the manner of the idolators.

You may not wear [42]garments made of both wool and linen nor may you shave (with a razor) the sides of [43]your head or [44]your beard. Do not [45]lacerate yourself over your dead.

225. Num. 35:25
226. Ex. 21:20
229. Deut. 22:24
230. Deut. 21:22

224. Deut. 25:2
227. Ex. 21:16
228. Lev. 20:14
231. Deut. 21:23

232. Ex. 21:2
234. Ex. 21:8

233. Ex. 21:8
235. Lev. 25:46

236. Ex. 21:18
237. Ex. 21:28
241. Ex. 22:5
242. Ex. 22:6–8
243. Ex. 22:9–12
246. Ex. 22:8
247. Deut. 25:12
248. Num. 27:8

238. Ex. 21:33–34
239. Ex. 21:37–22:3
240. Ex. 22:4
244. Ex. 22:13
245. Lev. 25:14

1. Ex. 20:3
4. Ex. 20:20

2. Ex. 20:4
3. Lev. 19:4

5. Ex. 20:5
6. Ex. 20:5

7. Lev. 18:21
8. Lev. 19:31

9. Lev. 19:31
10. Lev. 19:4

11. Deut. 16:22
13. Deut. 16:21
14. Ex. 23:13

12. Lev. 20:1

15. Ex. 23:13
16. Deut. 13:12

17. Deut. 13:9
18. Deut. 13:9

19. Deut. 13:9
20. Deut. 13:9

21. Deut. 13:9
22. Deut. 7:25
23. Deut. 13:17

24. Deut. 13:18

25. Deut. 7:26
26. Deut. 18:20
27. Deut. 18:20

28. Deut. 13:3, 4
    Deut. 13:4
29. Deut. 18:22
32. Deut. 18:10

30. Lev. 20:23
31. Lev. 19:26;
    Deut. 18:10
35. Deut. 18:10–11
36. Deut. 18:10–11
40. Deut. 22:5

33. Deut. 18:10–11;
    Deut. 10–26
34. Deut. 18:10–11
37. Deut. 18:10–11
38. Deut. 18:10–11
39. Deut. 22:5
41. Lev. 19:28

42. Deut. 22:11
45. Deut. 16:1;
    Deut. 14:1;
    also Lev. 19:28

43. Lev. 19:27
44. Lev. 19:27

Prohibitions Resulting from Historical Events.

It is forbidden to return to Egypt to [46]dwell there permanently or to [47]indulge in impure thoughts or sights. You may not [48]make a pact with the seven Canaanite nations or [49]save the life of any member of them. Do not [50]show mercy to idolators, [51]permit them to dwell in the land of Israel or [52]intermarry with them. A Jewess may not [53]marry an Ammonite or Moabite even if he converts to Judaism but should not refuse (for reasons of genealogy alone) [54]a descendant of *Esau or [55]an Egyptian who are proselytes. It is prohibited to [56]make peace with the Ammonite or Moabite nations.

The [57]destruction of fruit trees even in times of war is forbidden as is wanton waste at any time. Do not [58]fear the enemy and do not [59]forget the evil done by *Amalek.

Blasphemy.

You must not [60]blaspheme the Holy Name, [61]break an oath made by It, [62]take It in vain or [63]profane It. Do not [64]try the Lord God. You may not [65]erase God's name from the holy texts or destroy institutions devoted to His worship. Do not [66]allow the body of of one hanged to remain so overnight.

Temple.

Be not [67]lax in guarding the Temple. The high priest must not enter the Temple [68]indiscriminately; a priest with a physical blemish may not [69]enter there at all or [70]serve in the sanctuary and even if the blemish is of a temporary nature he may not [71]participate in the service there until it has passed.

The Levites and the priests must not [72]interchange in their functions. Intoxicated persons may not [73]enter the sanctuary or teach the Law. It is forbidden for [74]non-priests, [75]unclean priests or [76]priests who have performed the necessary ablution but are still within the time limit of their uncleanness to serve in the Temple. No unclean person may enter [77]the Temple or [78]the Temple Mount. The altar must not be made of [79]hewn stones nor may the ascent to it be by [80]steps. The fire on it may not be [81]extinguished nor may any other but the specified incense be [82]burned on the golden altar. You may not [83]manufacture oil with the same ingredients and in the same proportions as the annointing oil which itself [84]may not be misused. Neither may you [85]compound incense with the same ingredients and in the same proportions as that burnt on the altar. You must not [86]remove the staves from the Ark, [87]remove the breastplate from the *ephod or [88]make any incision in the upper garment of the high priest.

Sacrifices.

It is forbidden to [89]offer sacrifices or [90]slaughter consecrated animals outside the Temple. You may not [91]sanctify, [92]slaughter, [93]sprinkle the blood of or [94]burn the inner parts of a blemished animal even if the blemish is [95]of a temporary nature and even if it is [96]offered by Gentiles. It is forbidden to [97]inflict a blemish on an animal consecrated for sacrifice.

Leaven or honey may not [98]be offered on the altar, neither may [99]anything unsalted. An animal received as the hire of a harlot or as the price of a dog [100]may not be offered. Do not [101]kill an animal and its young on the same day. It is forbidden to use [102]olive oil or [103]frankincense in the sin offering or [104], [105], in the jealousy offering (*sotah). You may not [106]substitute sacrifices even [107]from one category to the other. You may not [108]redeem the *firstborn of permitted animals.

Source references (left column):

47. Num. 15:39
50. Deut. 7:2
53. Deut. 23:4
54. Deut. 23:8
55. Deut. 23:8
56. Deut. 23:7
57. Deut. 20:19
59. Deut. 25:19
60. Lev. 24:16; rather Ex. 22:27
62. Ex. 20:7
65. Deut. 12:4
67. Num. 18:5
71. Lev. 21:18
73. Lev. 10:9–11
74. Num. 18:4
75. Lev. 22:2
77. Num. 5:3
80. Ex. 20:26
83. Ex. 30:32
86. Ex. 25:15
89. Deut. 12:13
90. Lev. 17:3–4
94. Lev. 22:22
95. Deut. 17:1
99. Lev. 2:13
100. Deut. 23:19
101. Lev. 22:28
104. Num. 5:15
105. Num. 5:15
106. Lev. 27:10

Source references (right column):

46. Deut. 17:16
48. Ex. 23:32; Deut. 7:2
49. Deut. 20:16
51. Ex. 23:33
52. Deut. 7:3
58. Deut. 7:21
61. Lev. 19:12
63. Lev. 22:32
64. Deut. 6:16
66. Deut. 21:23
68. Lev. 16:2
69. Lev. 21:23
70. Lev. 21:17
72. Num. 18:3
76. Lev. 21:6
78. Deut. 23:11
79. Ex. 20:25
81. Lev. 6:6
82. Ex. 30:9
84. Ex. 30:32
85. Ex. 30:37
87. Ex. 28:28
88. Ex. 28:32
91. Lev. 22:20
92. Lev. 22:22
93. Lev. 22:24
96. Lev. 22:25
97. Lev. 22:21
98. Lev. 2:11
102. Lev. 5:11
103. Lev. 5:11
107. Lev. 27:26
108. Num. 18:17

It is forbidden to [109]sell the tithe of the herd or [110]sell or [111]redeem a field consecrated by the *herem* vow.

When you slaughter a bird for a sin offering you may not [112]split its head.

It is forbidden to [113]work with or [114]to shear a consecrated animal. You must not slaughter the paschal lamb [115]while there is still leaven about; nor may you leave overnight [116]those parts that are to be offered up or [117]to be eaten.

You may not leave any part of the festive offering [118]until the third day or any part of [119]the second paschal lamb or [120]the thanksgiving offering until the morning.

It is forbidden to break a bone of [121]the first or [122]the second paschal lamb or [123]to carry their flesh out of the house where it is being eaten. You must not [124]allow the remains of the meal offering to become leaven. It is also forbidden to eat the paschal lamb [125]raw or sodden or to allow [126]an alien resident, [127]an uncircumcised person or an [128]apostate to eat of it.

A ritually unclean person [129]must not eat of holy things nor may [130]holy things which have become unclean be eaten. Sacrificial meat [131]which is left after the time-limit or [132]which was slaughtered with wrong intentions must not be eaten. The heave offering must not be eaten by [133]a non-priest, [134]a priest's sojourner or hired worker, [135]an uncircumcised person, or [136]an unclean priest. The daughter of a priest who is married to a non-priest may not [137]eat of holy things.

The meal offering of the priest [138]must not be eaten, neither may [139]the flesh of the sin offerings sacrificed within the sanctuary or [140]consecrated animals which have become blemished.

You may not eat the second tithe of [141]corn, [142]wine, or [143]oil or [144]unblemished firstlings outside Jerusalem. The priests may not eat the [145]sin-offerings or the trespass-offerings outside the Temple courts or [146]the flesh of the burnt-offering at all. The lighter sacrifices [147]may not be eaten before the blood has been sprinkled. A non-priest may not [148]eat of the holiest sacrifices and a priest [149]may not eat the first-fruits outside the Temple courts.

One may not eat [150]the second tithe while in a state of impurity or [151]in mourning; its redemption money [152]may not be used for anything other than food and drink.

You must not [153]eat untithed produce or [154]change the order of separating the various tithes.

Do not [155]delay payment of offerings—either freewill or obligatory—and do not [156]come to the Temple on the pilgrim festivals without an offering.

Do not [157]break your word.

Priests.

A priest may not marry [158]a harlot, [159]a woman who has been profaned from the priesthood, or [160]a divorcee; the high priest must not [161]marry a widow or [162]take one as a concubine. Priests may not enter the sanctuary with [163]overgrown hair of the head or [164]with torn clothing; they must not [165]leave the courtyard during the Temple service. An ordinary priest may not render himself [166]ritually impure except for those relatives specified, and the high priest should not become impure [167]for anybody in [168]any way.

The tribe of Levi shall have no part in [169]the division of the land of Israel or [170]in the spoils of war.

It is forbidden [171]to make oneself bald as a sign of mourning for one's dead.

#	Reference	#	Reference
109.	Lev. 27:33	110.	Lev. 27:28
		111.	Lev. 27:28
		112.	Lev. 5:8
113.	Deut. 15:19	114.	Deut. 15:19
		115.	Ex. 34:25
117.	Ex. 12:10	116.	Ex. 23:10
119.	Num. 9:13	118.	Deut. 16:4
		120.	Lev. 22:30
123.	Ex. 12:46	121.	Ex. 12:46
124.	Lev. 6:10	122.	Num. 9:12
125.	Ex. 12:9	126.	Ex. 12:45
		127.	Ex. 12:48
		128.	Ex. 12:43
130.	Lev. 7:19	129.	Lev. 12:4
131.	Lev. 19:6–8	132.	Lev. 7:18
133.	Lev. 22:10	134.	Lev. 22:10
135.	Lev. 22:10	136.	Lev. 22:4
137.	Lev. 22:12		
139.	Lev. 6:23	138.	Lev. 6:16
140.	Deut. 14:3		
144.	Deut. 12:17	141.	Deut. 12:17
145.	Deut. 12:17	142.	Deut. 12:17
146.	Deut. 12:17	143.	Deut. 12:17
147.	Deut. 12:17		
149.	Ex. 29:33	148.	Deut. 12:17
150.	Deut. 26:14		
151.	Deut. 26:14	152.	Deut. 26:14
153.	Lev. 22:15	154.	Ex. 22:28
155.	Deut. 23:22		
156.	Ex. 23:15		
157.	Num. 30:3		
158.	Lev. 21:7	159.	Lev. 21:7
		160.	Lev. 21:7
161.	Lev. 21:14		
162.	Lev. 21:15	163.	Lev. 10:6
164.	Lev. 10:6	165.	Lev. 10:7
166.	Lev. 21:1		
		167.	Lev. 21:11
		168.	Lev. 21:11
170.	Deut. 18:1	169.	Deut. 18:1
171.	Deut. 14:1		

Dietary Laws.

A Jew may not eat [172]unclean cattle, [173]unclean fish, [174]unclean fowl, [175]creeping things that fly, [176]creatures that creep on the ground, [177]reptiles, [178]worms found in fruit or produce or [179]any detestable creature.

An animal that has died naturally [180]is forbidden for consumption as is [181]a torn or mauled animal. One must not eat [182]any limb taken from a living animal. Also prohibited is [183]the sinew of the thigh (gid ha-nasheh) as is [184]blood and [185]certain types of fat (helev). It is forbidden [186]to cook meat together with milk or [187]eat of such a mixture. It is also forbidden to eat [188]of an ox condemned to stoning (even should it have been properly slaughtered).

One may not eat [189]bread made of new corn or the new corn itself, either [190]roasted or [191]green, before the *omer offering has been brought on the 16th of Nisan. You may not eat [192]*orlah or [193]the growth of mixed planting in the vineyard (see: *Mixed Species). Any use of [194]wine libations to idols is prohibited, as is [195]gluttony and drunkenness. One may not eat anything on [196]the *Day of Atonement. During *Passover it is forbidden to eat [197]leaven (*hamez) or [198]anything containing an admixture of such. This is also forbidden [199]after the middle of the 14th of Nisan (the day before Passover). During Passover no leaven may be [200]seen or [201]found in your possession.

Nazirites.

A *Nazirite may not drink [202]wine or any beverage made from grapes; he may not eat [203]fresh grapes, [204]dried grapes, [205]grape seeds or [206]grape peel. He may not render himself [207]ritually impure for his dead nor may he [208]enter a tent in which there is a corpse. He must not [209]shave his hair.

Agriculture.

It is forbidden [210]to reap the whole of a field without leaving the corners for the poor; it is also forbidden to [211]gather up the ears of corn that fall during reaping or to harvest [212]the misformed clusters of grapes, or [213]the grapes that fall or to [214]return to take a forgotten sheaf.

You must not [215]sow different species of seed together or [216]corn in a vineyard; it is also forbidden to [217]crossbreed different species of animals or [218]work with two different species yoked together.

You must not [219]muzzle an animal working in a field to prevent it from eating.

It is forbidden to [220]till the earth, [221]to prune trees, [222]to reap (in the usual manner) produce or [223]fruit which has grown without cultivation in the seventh year (*shemittah). One may also not [224]till the earth or prune trees in the *Jubilee year, when it is also forbidden to harvest (in the usual manner) [225]produce or [226]fruit that has grown without cultivation.

One may not [227]sell one's landed inheritance in the land of Israel permanently or [228]change the lands of the Levites or [229]leave the Levites without support.

Loans, Business and the Treatment of Slaves.

It is forbidden to [230]demand repayment of a loan after the seventh year; you may not, however, [231]refuse to lend to the poor because that year is approaching. Do not [232]deny charity to the poor or [233]send a Hebrew slave away empty-handed when he finishes his period of service. Do not [234]dun your debtor when you know that he cannot pay. It is forbidden to [235]lend to or [236]borrow from another Jew at interest or [237]participate in an agreement involving interest either as a guarantor, witness, or writer of the contract. Do not [238]delay payment of wages.

You may not [239]take a pledge from a debtor by violence, [240]keep a poor man's pledge when he needs it, [241]take any pledge from a widow or [242]from any debtor if he earns his living with it.

Kidnaping [243]a Jew is forbidden.

Do not [244]steal or [245]rob by violence. Do not [246]remove a land-marker or [247]defraud.

It is forbidden [248]to deny receipt of a loan or a deposit or [249]to swear falsely regarding another man's property.

You must not [250]deceive anybody in business. You may not [251]mislead a man even verbally. It is forbidden to harm the stranger among you [252]verbally or [253]do him injury in trade.

You may not [254]return or [255]otherwise take advantage of, a slave who has fled to the land of Israel from his master, even if his master is a Jew.

Do not [256]afflict the widow or the orphan. You may not [257]misuse or [258]sell a Hebrew slave; do not [259]treat him cruelly or [260]allow a heathen to mistreat him. You must not [261]sell your Hebrew maidservant or, if you marry her, [262]withhold food, clothing, and conjugal rights from her. You must not [263]sell a female captive or [264]treat her as a slave.

Do not [265]covet another man's possesions even if you are willing to pay for them. Even [266]the desire alone is forbidden.

A worker must not [267]cut down standing corn during his work or [268]take more fruit than he can eat.

One must not [269]turn away from a lost article which is to be returned to its owner nor may you [270]refuse to help a man or an animal which is collapsing under its burden.

It is forbidden to [271]defraud with weights and measures or even [272]to possess inaccurate weights.

Justice.

A judge must not [273]perpetrate injustice, [274]accept bribes or be [275]partial or [276]afraid. He may [277]not favor the poor or [278]discriminate against the wicked; he should not [279]pity the condemned or [280]pervert the judgment of strangers or orphans.

It is forbidden to [281]hear one litigant without the other being present. A capital case cannot be decided by [282]a majority of one.

A judge should not [283]accept a colleague's opinion unless he is convinced of its correctness; it is forbidden to [284]appoint as a judge someone who is ignorant of the law.

Do not [285]give false testimony or accept [286]testimony from a wicked person or from [287]relatives of a person involved in the case. It is forbidden to pronounce judgment [288]on the basis of the testimony of one witness.

Do not [289]murder.

You must not convict on [290]circumstantial evidence alone.

A witness [291]must not sit as a judge in capital cases.

You must not [292]execute anybody without due proper trial and conviction.

Do not [293]pity or spare the pursuer.

Punishment is not to be inflicted for [294]an act committed under duress.

Do not accept ransom [295]for a murderer or [296]a manslayer.

Do not [297]hesitate to save another person from danger and do not [298]leave a stumbling block in the way or [299]mislead another person by giving wrong advice.

238.	Lev. 19:13
239.	Deut. 24:10
242.	Deut. 24:6
243.	Ex. 20:13
244.	Lev. 19:11
245.	Lev. 19:13
247.	Lev. 19:13
248.	Lev. 19:11
250.	Lev. 25:14
252.	Ex. 22:20
253.	Ex. 22:20
254.	Deut. 23:16
255.	Deut. 23:17
256.	Ex. 22:21
258.	Lev. 25:42
264.	Deut. 21:14
265.	Ex. 20:17
266.	Deut. 5:18
267.	Deut. 23:26
268.	Deut. 23:25
269.	Deut. 22:3
270.	Ex. 23:5
271.	Lev. 19:35
272.	Deut. 25:13
273.	Lev. 19:15
275.	Lev. 19:15
276.	Deut. 1:17
280.	Deut. 24:17
281.	Ex. 23:1
283.	Ex. 23:2
285.	Ex. 20:16
287.	Deut. 24:16
289.	Ex. 20:13
290.	Ex. 23:7
291.	Num. 35:30
292.	Num. 35:12
293.	Deut. 25:12
295.	Num. 35:31
297.	Lev. 19:16
298.	Deut. 22:8

237.	Ex. 22:24
240.	Deut. 24:12
241.	Deut. 24:17
246.	Deut. 19:14
249.	Lev. 19:11
251.	Lev. 25:17
257.	Lev. 25:39
259.	Lev. 25:43
260.	Lev. 25:53
261.	Ex. 21:8
262.	Ex. 21:10
263.	Deut. 21:14
274.	Ex. 23:8
277.	Lev. 19:15, rather Ex. 23:3
278.	Ex. 23:6
279.	Deut. 19:13
282.	Ex. 23:2
284.	Deut. 1:17
286.	Ex. 23:1
288.	Deut. 19:15
294.	Deut. 22:26
296.	Num. 35:32
299.	Lev. 19:14

300. Deut. 25:2-3	It is forbidden [300]to administer more than the assigned number of lashes to the guilty.

301. Lev. 19:16 — Do not [301]tell tales or [302]bear hatred in your heart. It is forbidden to [303]shame a Jew, [304]to bear a grudge or [305]to take revenge.

302. Lev. 19:17
305. Lev. 19:18

303. Lev. 19:17
304. Lev. 19:18 — Do not [306]take the dam when you take the young birds.

306. Deut. 22:6 — It is forbidden to [307]shave a leprous scall or [308]remove other signs of that affliction. It is forbidden [309]to cultivate a valley in which a slain body was found and in which subsequently the ritual of breaking the heifer's neck (*eglah arufah) was performed.

307. Lev. 13:33

308. Deut. 24:8
309. Deut. 21:4

310. Ex. 22:17 — Do not [310]suffer a witch to live.

311. Deut. 24:5 — Do not [311]force a bridegroom to perform military service during the first year of his marriage. It is forbidden to [312]rebel against the transmitters of the tradition or to [313]add or [314]detract from the precepts of the law.

312. Deut. 17:11
313. Deut. 13:1
314. Deut. 13:1

315. Ex. 22:27 — Do not curse [315]a judge, [316]a ruler or [317]any Jew.

316. Ex. 22:27
317. Lev. 19:14

318. Ex. 21:17 — Do not [318]curse or [319]strike a parent.

319. Ex. 21:15

320. Ex. 20:10
321. Ex. 16:29 — It is forbidden to [320]work on the Sabbath or [321]walk further than the permitted limits (*eruv). You may not [322]inflict punishment on the Sabbath.

322. Ex. 35:3

It is forbidden to work on [323]the first or [324]the seventh day of *Passover, on [325]*Shavuot, on [326]*Rosh Ha-Shanah, on the [327]first and [328]eighth (*Shemini Azeret) days of *Sukkot and [329]on the Day of *Atonement.

325. Lev. 23:21
327. Lev. 23:35
328. Lev. 23:36

323. Ex. 12:16
324. Ex. 12:16
326. Lev. 23:25
329. Lev. 23:28

Incest and Other Forbidden Relationships.

330. Lev. 18:7
331. Lev. 18:8
332. Lev. 18:9
335. Lev. 18:10
338. Lev. 18:17
339. Lev. 18:17
340. Lev. 18:12
341. Lev. 18:13
343. Lev. 18:15

It is forbidden to enter into an incestuous relationship with one's [330]mother, [331]step-mother, [332]sister, [333]half-sister, [334]son's daughter, [335]daughter's daughter, [336]daughter, [337]any woman and her daughter, [338]any woman and her son's daughter, [339]any woman and her daughter's daughter, [340]father's sister, [341]mother's sister, [342]paternal uncle's wife, [343]daughter-in-law, [344]brother's wife and [345]wife's sister.

333. Lev. 18:11
334. Lev. 18:10
336. Lev. 18:10
337. Lev. 18:17
342. Lev. 18:14
344. Lev. 18:16
345. Lev. 18:18

It is also forbidden to [346]have sexual relations with a menstruous woman (see *Niddah).

346. Lev. 18:19

347. Lev. 18:20 — Do not [347]commit adultery.

348. Lev. 18:23 — It is forbidden for [348]a man or [349]a woman to have sexual intercourse with an animal.

349. Lev. 18:23

350. Lev. 18:22
352. Lev. 18:14 — Homosexuality [350]is forbidden, particularly with [351]one's father or [352]uncle.

351. Lev. 18:7

It is forbidden to have [353]intimate physical contact (even without actual intercourse) with any of the women with whom intercourse is forbidden.

353. Lev. 18:6

A *mamzer may not [354]marry a Jewess.

354. Deut. 23:3

355. Deut. 23:18 — Harlotry [355]is forbidden.

356. Deut. 24:4 — A divorcee may not be [356]remarried to her first husband if, in the meanwhile, she had married another.

A childless widow may not [357]marry anybody other than her late husband's brother (See *Levirate Marriage).

357. Deut. 25:5

358. Deut. 22:29
359. Deut. 22:19 — A man may not [358]divorce a wife whom he married after having raped her or [359]after having slandered her.

An eunuch may not [360]marry a Jewess.

360. Deut. 23:2

361. Lev. 22:24 — Castration [361]is forbidden.

The Monarchy.

362. Deut. 17:15 — You may not [362]elect as king anybody who is not of the seed of Israel.

The king must not accumulate an excessive number of [363]horses, [364]wives, or [365]wealth.

363. Deut. 17:16

364. Deut. 17:17
365. Deut. 17:17

The Talmud

Orders and tractates of the Mishnah and Talmud

	Mishnah No. of Chapters	Babylonian Talmud * No. of Folios	Folios Munich Ed.	Jerusalem Talmud No. of Folios	Subject Matter
Order Zera'im					
Berakhot	9	64	19	14	Benedictions and daily prayers
Pe'ah	8	—	3	7	Gleanings (Lev. 19:9-10)
Demai	7	—	3	6	Doubtfully tithed produce
Kilayim	9	—	4	7	Diverse kinds (Lev. 19:19; Deut. 22:9-11)
Shevi'it	10	—	4	7	The Sabbatical Year (Ex. 23:10-11)
Terumot	11	—	4	9	Heave offering (Lev. 22:10-14) assigned to the Kohanim
Ma'aserot	5	—	2	5	Tithes (Num. 18:21)
Ma'aser Sheni	5	—	3	5	Second tithe (Deut. 14:22 ff.) of the first, second, fourth and sixth years
Hallah	4	—	2	4	Dough offering (Num. 15:17-21) given to the Kohanim
Orlah	3	—	2	4	The fruit of young trees (Lev. 19:23-25)
Bikkurim	3	—	3	3	First fruits (Lev. 26:1-11)
Order Mo'ed					
Shabbat	24	157	28	18	The Sabbath
Eruvin	10	105	17	9	The fusion of Sabbath limits
Pesahim	10	121	18	11	Passover
Shekalim	8	—	6	7	The Shekel dues (Ex. 30:11-16)
Yoma	8	88	16	8	The Day of Atonement
Sukkah	5	56	9	5	The Feast of Tabernacles
Betzah	5	40	11	5	Festival laws
Rosh Ha-Shanah	4	35	7	4	The four new years, particularly Rosh Ha-Shanah
Ta'anit	4	31	8	7	Fast days
Megillah	4	32	9	7	Purim
Mo'ed Katan	3	29	7	4	The intermediate days of festivals
Hagigah	3	27	6	5	The Festival offering (Deut. 16:16-7)
Order Nashim					
Yevamot	16	122	24	16	Levirate marriage (Deut. 25:5-10) and halitzah
Ketubbot	13	112	20	12	Marriage contracts
Nedarim	11	91	10	7	Vows (Num. 30)
Nazir	9	66	8	8	The Nazirite (Num. 6)
Sotah	9	49	11	9	The suspected adulteress (Num. 5:11 ff.)
Gittin	9	90	16	7	Divorce
Kiddushin	4	82	14	9	Marriage; legal acquisition of bondsmen, chattel and real estate.
Order Nezikin					
Bava Kamma	10	119	22	7	Torts: cases of compensation for theft, robbery or violence
Bava Metzia	10	119	20	6	Civil law: found property; bailments; hiring; leasing; joint ownership
Bava Batra	10	176	21	6	Property law, including rights & restrictions
Sanhedrin	11	113	24	14	Judges: courts; arbitration; procedure; capital cases; dogma
Makkot	3	24	5	3	Flagellation (Deut. 25:2): treatment of perjurers; cities of refuge
Shevu'ot	8	49	9	7	Oaths
Eduyyot	8	—	4	—	Traditional testimonies
Avodah Zarah	5	76	13	7	Idolatry
Avot	5	—	2	—	Ethical maxims and aphorisms
Horayot	3	14	4	4	Erroneous ruling of the court (Lev. 4:22 ff.)

	Mishnah	Babylonian Talmud *		Jerusalem Talmud	
	No. of Chapters	No. of Folios	Folios Munich Ed.	No. of Folios	Subject Matter

Order Kodashim

Zevahim	14	120	21	—	Animal offerings and their procedure; conditions of acceptability
Menahot	13	110	21	—	Meal and drink offerings
Hullin	12	142	25	—	Slaughtering of animals & birds
Bekhorot	9	61	13	—	Firstlings (Deut. 15:19 ff) and tithing (Lev. 27:32-33)
Arakhin	9	34	9	—	Vows of valuation (Lev. 27:1-8)
Temurah	7	39	8	—	The substituted offering (Lev. 27:10)
Keritot	6	28	9	—	Excisions (Lev. 18:29)
Me'ilah	6	22	4	—	Sacrileges (Lev. 5:15-16)
Tamid	7	9	4	—	The daily sacrifice (Num. 28:3-4) and Temple service
Middot	5	—	3	—	Dimensions of the Temple
Kinnim	3	—	2	—	The Bird offering (Lev. 5:7 ff.)

Order Tohorot

Kelim	30	—	11	—	Uncleanness of vessels (Lev. 11:33-35)
Oholot (Ahilot)	18	—	7	—	Uncleanness through presence under same roof (Num 19:14-15)
Nega'im	14	—	7	—	Leprosy (Lev. 13, 14) and purification
Parah	12	—	5	—	The Red Heifer (Num. 19)
Tohorot	10	—	5	—	Contact with sources and grades of impurity
Mikva'ot	10	—	5	—	Ritual immersion
Niddah	10	73	14	4	The menstruant (Lev. 15:19-31)
Makhshirin	6	—	3	—	Liquid that predisposes food to become ritually unclean (Lev. 11:37-38)
Zavim	5	—	2	—	Fluxes (Lev. 15)
Tevul Yom	4	—	2	—	Ritual uncleanness between immersion and sunset (Lev. 22:6-7)
Yadayim	4	—	3	—	The ritual uncleanness of the hands
Uktzin	3	—	2	—	"Stalks" parts of plants susceptible to uncleanness

*The number given is the last page number. The pagination, however, always begins with page 2; one page should therefore be deducted.

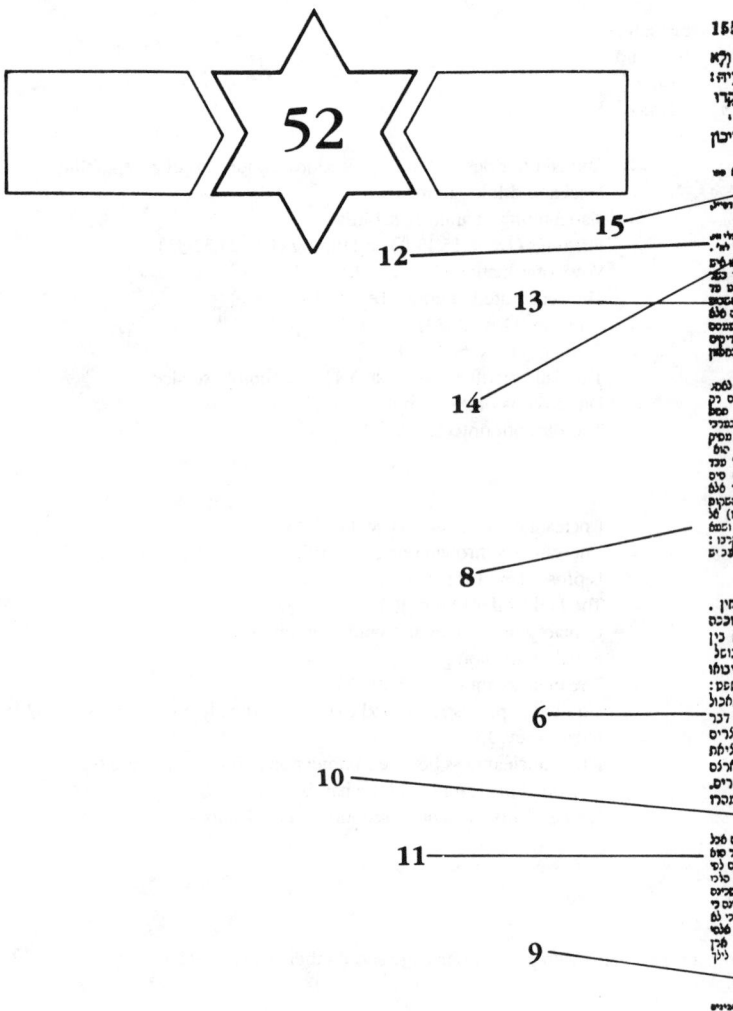

A Guide to Torah Texts

Shlomo Berger

CHUMASH

1. Original text of the Torah, or Chumash. (Chumash: A word that refers to the number five, there being Five Books of Moses.)

2. Onkelos—An Aramaic translation of the Torah made by the proselyte Onkelos at about the end of the first century C.E. In ancient life it was read along with the Torah so that everyone was able to understand what was being read. Occasionally, the text is rendered in a Midrashic way.

3. Toldot Aharon—An invaluable work of reference which locates the folio page in the Talmud so that the reader can find the discussion of the matter in rabbinic literature. The author is Rabbi Aharon M'Pisaro, an Italian Jewish scholar of the early 17th century.

4. Rashi—An acronym for Rabbi Shlomo Ben Yitzchak (Yarchi), who lived in Provence, France, 1040-1105. The importance of this commentary, first among

equals, cannot be overstated. It approaches the text, by turns, and only where the need arises, in a homelitic, literal, and pietistic way. The style is terse. Many works have already been compiled as supercommentaries on Rashi. (see #5)

5. Sifethey Chakhamim—A brilliant work on Rashi's commentary, dialectical in nature, the essence of which, was to find out what question Rashi was asking or answering, The author, Rabbi Shabathai (Meshorer) Bass (1641-1718), was a cantor in Prague.

6. Ibn Ezra— *Rabbi Avraham ben Meir.*
The Ibn Ezra was a famous poet, grammarian, and biblical exegete. Born in Toledo, Spain in 1089, he usually seeks to establish the plain, literal meaning through an examination of the etymological roots of the word or phrase in question. He died in 1164 having established his work as a mainstay of textual scholarship.

7. Ramban—An acronym for Rabbi Moses Ben Nachman (Nachmanides). Born in Spain in 1194. Ramban was truly a master of exegesis and one of the greatest Torah scholars of his or any age. This commentary on the Torah is considered a masterpiece at many levels. Taking issue with Rashi and the Ibn Ezra on many occa-

אונקלוס · · · · · · · · · · · · · · שמות יב בא · · · · · · · · **154**

[Hebrew Torah text — Shemot 12 (Bo), with Onkelos, Rashi, Sifsei Chachamim, Ibn Ezra, and Ramban commentaries arranged in the traditional Mikraot Gedolot layout]

אונקלוס

רש"י

שפתי חכמים

אבן עזרא

רמב"ן

— 1
— 2
— 3
— 4
— 5
— 7
— 6

---

sions he discusses literary as well as Midrashic interpretations while often adding a mystical dimension as well. His talent at etymology, grammar and his vast erudition make this work one of the primary resources on Chumash study. Ramban died in Acco in 1270.

8. **Daat Z'Kenim**—This is a Midrashic approach to the text which is believed to have been compiled by the tosafists, yeshiva academicians of the 12th & 13th centuries. Some of these great names were descendants of Rashi.

9. **Sforno**—*Rabbi Ovadia Ben Yaakov.* This commentary was named for the city of the author, Sforno, Italy. Rabbi Ovadia flourished in the 15th to 16th centuries and had one of the greatest libraries of his time. While the Sforno can be said to be chiefly concerned with the plain meaning, he can be quite philosophical at times.

10. **Ohr HaChaim (Ha-Kadosh)**—This commentary written by Rabbi Chaim Ben Moshe (Ibn Attar) who lived from 1696 to 1743. Born in Sale, Morocco Ibn Attar earned the title of Hakadosh (the Holy one) because of his piety and saintly character. His work is much savored by the chassidic community. He favors answering simple questions with in-depth analysis

which bring to the fore fundamentals of Jewish thought.

11. **K'li Yakar**—*Rabbi Shlomo Efraim of Luntschitz,* Poland, 1550-1619. This work is prized for its almost aesthetic beauty as well as its wonderful elucidation of difficult concepts by way of profound symbol juxtaposition. The author was a student of the great Maharal of Prague and was widely known in Poland.

12. **Rashbam**—An acronym for Rabbi Shmuel Ben Meir, c. 1080-1174. This work is almost solely concerned with the plain meaning of the text. The author was a grandson of Rashi and elder brother of Rabbi Yaakov Tam, the great Tosafist.

13. **Baal Ha-Turim**—written by Rabbi Yaakov Ben Asher 1268-1340. This is a group of associations, numerical values, symbols and word plays on the text. Very popular and extremely thought-provoking.

14. **Targum Yonatan**—This is an Aramaic translation of the form which some have attributed to Yonatan Ben Uzziel c. 50 C.E. Others have stated that it is of unknown origin.

15. **Targum Yerushalmi**—Aramaic translation of the Torah.

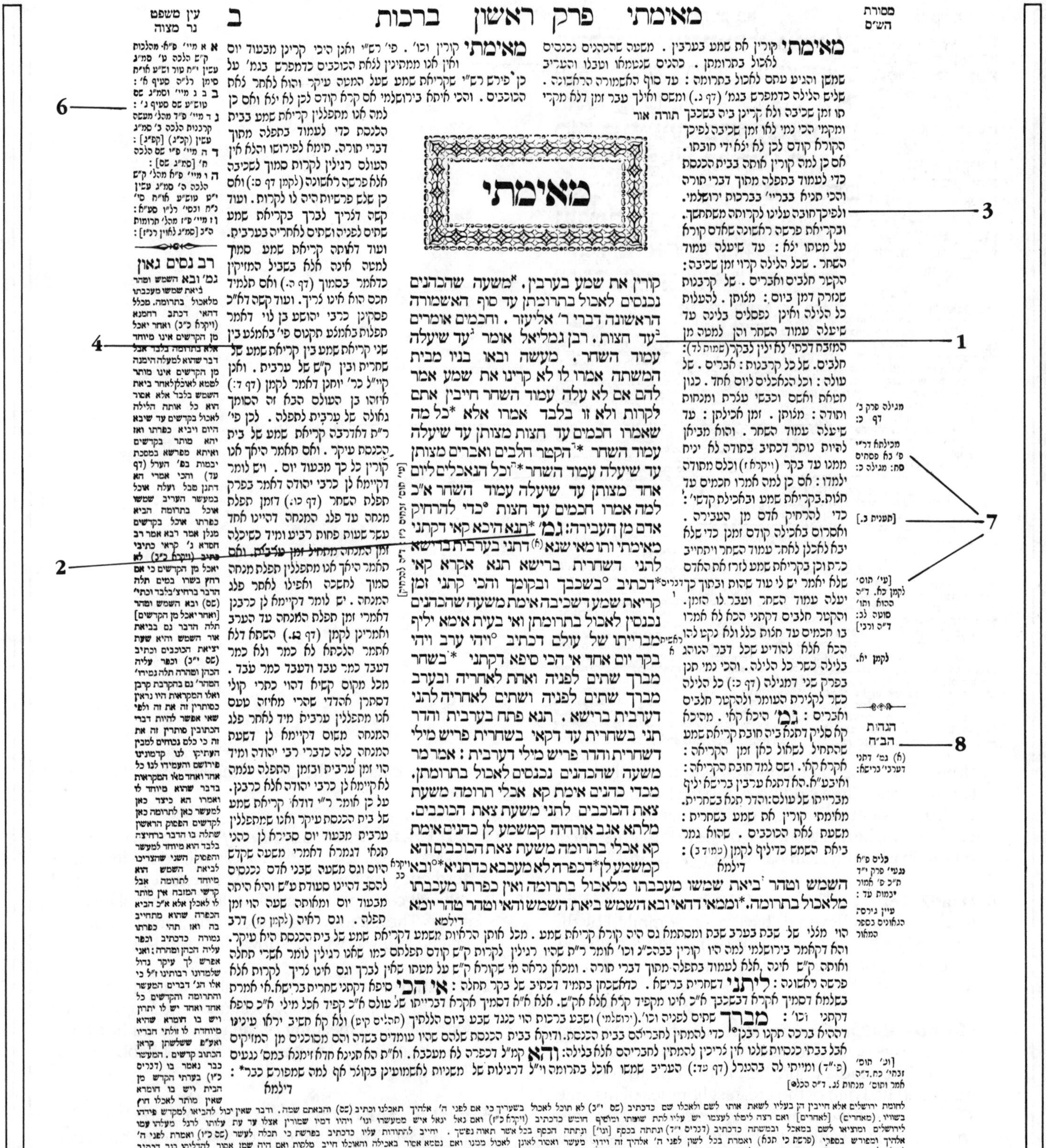

מאימתי פרק ראשון ברכות ב

עין משפט נר מצוה

מסורת הש"ס

מאימתי

מאימתי קורין את שמע בערבין. משעה שהכהנים נכנסים לאכול בתרומתן עד סוף האשמורה הראשונה דברי ר' אליעזר. וחכמים אומרים עד חצות. רבן גמליאל אומר עד שיעלה עמוד השחר. מעשה ובאו בניו מבית המשתה אמרו לו לא קרינו את שמע אמר להם אם לא עלה עמוד השחר חייבין אתם לקרות ולא זו בלבד אמרו אלא כל מה שאמרו חכמים עד חצות מצותן עד שיעלה עמוד השחר הקטר חלבים ואברים מצותן עד שיעלה עמוד השחר וכל הנאכלים ליום אחד מצותן עד שיעלה עמוד השחר א"כ למה אמרו חכמים עד חצות כדי להרחיק אדם מן העבירה: גמ' תנא היכא קאי דקתני מאימתי ותו מאי שנא (א) דתני בערבית ברישא לתני דשחרית ברישא תנא אקרא קאי דכתיב בשכבך ובקומך והכי קתני זמן קריאת שמע דשכיבה אימת משעה שהכהנים נכנסין לאכול בתרומתן ואי בעית אימא יליף מברייתו של עולם דכתיב ויהי ערב ויהי בקר יום אחד אי הכי סיפא דקתני בשחר מברך שתים לפניה ואחת לאחריה ובערב מברך שתים לפניה ושתים לאחריה לתני דערבית ברישא. תנא פתח בערבית והדר תני בשחרית עד דקאי בשחרית פריש מילי דשחרית והדר פריש מילי דערבית: אמר מר משעה שהכהנים נכנסים לאכול בתרומתן. מכדי כהנים אימת קא אכלי תרומה משעת צאת הכוכבים לתני משעת צאת הכוכבים. מלתא אגב אורחיה קמשמע לן כהנים אימת קא אכלי בתרומה משעת צאת הכוכבים והא קמשמע לן דכפרה לא מעכבא כדתניא ובא השמש וטהר ביאת שמשו מעכבתו מלאכול בתרומה ואין כפרתו מעכבתו מלאכול בתרומה. וממאי דהאי ובא השמש ביאת השמש והאי וטהר טהר יומא דילמא

רב נסים גאון

הגהות הב"ח

גליון הש"ס

TALMUD

1. **Mishna**—The mishna was the first great codification of the Oral Law, which was compiled by Rabbi Yehudah HaNasi around the year 200 C.E. Every area of Jewish law is treated although in a very concise manner. Legal arguments are recorded but rarely are the implications of these arguments made clear. The authorities quoted are called Tannaim (lit. 'Teachers who repeat')—memory up until that time being the only device for learning and transmitting the oral law.

2. **Talmud**—(Gemara): (lit. 'The study or the teaching'). The Babylonian Talmud was arranged and completed around 500-550 C.E. The authorities quoted are, of course, the earlier Tannaim as well as the Amoraim (lit. 'The speakers' or 'interpreters') of Babylonia. The Talmud is a record of thousands of discussions, debates and directives regarding Jewish law, philosophy and ethics.

3. **Rashi**—an acronym for Rabbi Shlomo Ben Yitzchak (Yarchi), who lived in Provence, France, 1040—1105 Rashi's explanation of the Aramatic text is indispensible. He enters into many discussions with his contemporaries on the interpretation of questions, answers, suppositions and conclusions. One simply cannot imagine the study of Talmud without his aid.

4. **Tosafot**—This collection of erudite dialectics by the great yeshiva academicians of France (and Germany) spans the entire range of the Talmudic corpus. If a contradiction appears in the Talmud and especially in Rashi's interpretation of the Talmud, the Tosafists will put on a display of intellectual fireworks. Chief among them was Rabbi Yaakov Tam, Rashi's grandson.

5. **Gilyon HaShas**—*Rabbi Akiva Eger*
Born in Eisenstadt, Hungary 1761. These are seminal notes and novellae on the Talmud by the father-in-law of the Chasam Sofer. His genius and piety were legendary and his works are required reading (study) at every level of higher learning. He died in Pozen, Poland in 1838.

6. **Ein Mishpat, Ner Mitzvah**—*Rabbi Yehoshua Boaz*, 16th century.
Wrote these footnotes to the entire Talmud. They indicate the legal texts where the law can be found. This is a massive undertaking which uses the Mishna Torah of Maimonides, The Sefer Mitzvot Gadol, the Tur Shulchan Aruch and the Shulchan Aruch of Rabbi Yosef Karo.

7. **Mesoret HaShas**—cross-reference work in the Talmud itself which helps locate where else the issue is discussed.

8. **Hagahot HaBach**—Textual inaccuracies and emendations of Rabbi Yoel B. Shmuel Sirkes 1570-1640. The word 'Bach' is an acronym for Bayit Chadash, the other famous work of this author. His son-in-law was the Taz. (See Shulchan Aruch).

א   עיקר תוי"ט   ברכות פרק א   ר"ע מברטנורה

מָאֵימָתַי קוֹרִין. משעה שהכהנים נכנסים לאכול בתרומתן. כהנים שנטמאו וטבלו אין יכולים לאכול בתרומה עד שיעריב שמשן, דהיינו צאת הכוכבים. והא דלא תני משמע לאה כוכבים, מלתא אגב אורחיה קא משמע לן שאם נטמאו הכהנים בטומאה שסופה טהרה תלויה בקרבן,גבן זב ומצורע,אין הכפרה מעכבתן מלאכול בתרומה,דכתיב (ויקרא' כב) — **1**
ובא השמש וטהר ואחר יאכל מן הקדשים, ביאת שמשו מעכבתו מלאכול בתרומה, ואין כפרתו מעכבתו מלאכול בתרומה: **עד סוף האשמורה הראשונה**.שליש הראשון של לילה, שהלילה נחלק לשלש משמרות(ד'). ומשם ואילך לא מקרי זמן קריאת שמע דשכיבה,ולא קרינא ביה בשכבך,ומקמי צאת הכוכבים נמי יממא הוא ולאו זמן שכיבה. והמקדימים וקולוס קש על צרבית מבעוד יום, סומכים אהא דר' יהודה דאמר לקמן בפרק תפלת השחר תפלת המנחה עד פלג המנחה שהוא שעה ורביע קודם הלילה, וקיימא לן דעבד כרבי

מֵאֵימָתַי קוֹרִין (א) אֶת שְׁמַע בְּעַרְבִית, מִשָּׁעָה שֶׁהַכֹּהֲנִים נִכְנָסִים לֶאֱכֹל בִּתְרוּמָתָן (ב), עַד סוֹף הָאַשְׁמוּרָה הָרִאשׁוֹנָה, דִּבְרֵי רַבִּי אֱלִיעֶזֶר. וַחֲכָמִים אוֹמְרִים, עַד חֲצוֹת. רַבָּן גַּמְלִיאֵל אוֹמֵר, עַד שֶׁיַּעֲלֶה עַמּוּד הַשָּׁחַר (ג). מַעֲשֶׂה שֶׁבָּאוּ בָנָיו מִבֵּית הַמִּשְׁתֶּה, אָמְרוּ לוֹ, לֹא קָרִינוּ אֶת שְׁמַע. אָמַר לָהֶם, אִם לֹא עָלָה עַמּוּד הַשָּׁחַר, חַיָּבִין אַתֶּם לִקְרוֹת. וְלֹא זוֹ בִלְבַד, אֶלָּא כָּל מַה שֶּׁאָמְרוּ חֲכָמִים עַד חֲצוֹת, מִצְוָתָן עַד שֶׁיַּעֲלֶה עַמּוּד הַשָּׁחַר. הֶקְטֵר חֲלָבִים וְאֵבָרִים, מִצְוָתָן עַד שֶׁיַּעֲלֶה עַמּוּד הַשָּׁחַר. וְכָל הַנֶּאֱכָלִין לְיוֹם אֶחָד, מִצְוָתָן עַד שֶׁיַּעֲלֶה עַמּוּד הַשָּׁחַר. אִם כֵּן, לָמָּה אָמְרוּ חֲכָמִים עַד חֲצוֹת, כְּדֵי לְהַרְחִיק אֶת הָאָדָם מִן הָעֲבֵרָה: ב מֵאֵימָתַי קוֹרִין אֶת שְׁמַע בְּשַׁחֲרִית, מִשֶּׁיַּכִּיר בֵּין

* ס"א [אמרו].

(א) **מאימתי כו'.** תנא אקרא קאי דכתיב (דברים ו) בשכבך ובקומך, משם למד שחובה על אדם לקרות שמע בערב ובבקר. ואל עכשיו מאימתי זמן, ומדכתיב בשכבך ברישא,הקדים של ערבית. גמ' ו: (נ) דהקרא ואחר יאכל מן הקדשים מוקמינן לה בתרומה כדאיתא דף ע"ב. והכי משמע קרא, עד שיעריב שמש כרקיע מן האחוך, והיינו כשיאלח הכוכבים. הכי: (נ)בחצומן.כלומר שמוקנת לפמרים וכלום חקר כי אם לאכול תורים: (ד) משמוסה, עבודה של מלאכים וביר שלא כה נחלק לשלש חלקים, כאלאבים לכם אחה וכו'. רש"י: (ה) עמוד השחר. יש רגילין לפותחו כוכב השחר,וקן כתב כרד"ק במזמור אילת השחר, שום מפרשים אילת שם לכוכב השחר. ועי"ש: (ו) כלומר. בפירוש בשכבן,כוומר קביעא לכו, דסילילו של כללו, ולא בכריחו, והא וכקאמרי כו',שהם שמו קיות, ונכא שלינו עלי. ואפילו קבילניו אין הלכה כב"ב. ולא כהנא הלכה כב"ב אלא עיקר דין חובה. תוריס: (ז) ואפי"ג דמפמרה דקרא בכל עולה כתיב, ולא דוקא בעולה תמיד,ובד"ח ס"ד דמתמים מוכח דכל אמורי קדשים דיק דכל הלילה, אלא נקפי מלחא פסיקא. תוי"ס: (ח) שם רגילות המשניות למתנה בקולל מס שכתוב בסירוס

ר"נ

יהודה עבד, ומיד כשתכלה זמן כשמנה מחמיל זמן קש של ערבית: **עד שיעלה עמוד השחר.** דכל הלילה מקרי זמן שכיבה.והלכה כרבן גמליאל,שבס חכמים מודים לו,ולא אמרו עד חצות אלא כדי להרחיק את האדם מן העבירה, ומרא לכחמלה משניע עונת קש של ערבית דמחמיין **2** דהיינו מלאת הכוכבים, מקור לקפוד ,וכל שכן ליום עד שיקבא קש ויתפלל: **מעשה שבאו בניו מבית המשתה.** בני רבן גמליאל שמעינהו לרבנן דאמרי עד מלת,והכי קאמרי ליה,הא דפליגי רבנן עלך, דוקא קאמרי עד מלת וחו לא, ומיד ורבים הלכה עד כרבנן,או דלמא רבנן כותך קבירא להו, והאי דקאמרי עד מלת, כדי להרחיק את האדם מן העבירה. ואמר להו, רבנן כוחי קבירא להו(א), והאי דקאמרי עד מלת, כדי להרחיק את האדם מן העבירה, וחייבים אחם לקרות: ולא זו בלבד. כולה מלתא דרבן גמליאל היא דאמר לבניו: **הקטר חלבים. ואברים.** של קרבנות. של תמיד של בין הערבים שמרק דמו ביום, מלוה להעלות הנתחים כל הלילה, דכתיב (ויקרא ו) היא העולה על מוקדה על המזבח כל הלילה עד הבוקר (ז): **וכל הנאכלין ליום אחד.** כגון חודה ומנחא ואשם וכיולא בהם, שכם נאכלים ליום ולילה, אין אכילתן עד שיעלה עמוד השחר. והוא מביא לידי נותר: **אם כן למה אמרו חכמים עד חצות.** בקש ובאכילת קדשים: מלבים ואברים לא אמרו בו מכמים עד מלת כלל, ולא נקט ליה בכאללה אלא להודיע שכל דבר שמלותו בלילה כשר כל הלילה.אבל בהקטר מלבים ואברים עד מכמים עד מלת כלל, ולא נקט ליה כבאללה אלא להודיע שכל דבר שמלותו בלילה (ח): **כדי להרחיק את האדם מן העבירה.** שלא יבוא לאכול אחר שיעלה עמוד השחר ויתחייב כרת. וכן בקש שלא יאמר עדיין יש לי שהות ותעבור עונתה:

MISHNA

1. Mishna—see Talmud

2. Rabbeinu Ovadiah M'Bertinoro. *born c. 1450.*
An Italian, he spread the study of Torah in Salerno, Palermo and Naples. He was also active in Messina, Rhodes, Egypt, and in the land of Israel, where he helped establish real communal life. He set up a yeshiva in Jerusalem which ultimately became quite renowned. While in Jerusalem, he finished his commentary on the Mishna. It seeks to sum up as a digest the explanations

of the Talmud—thru Rashi, always with an eye toward simplifying the text.

3. Tosafot Yom Tov
Written by Rabbi Yom Tov (Ben Nathan) Lipman Heller. Born in 1579 in Wallerstein, Germany, he served in the most distinguished rabbinical posts of Europe. This is very much a work of erudition as well as intellectual force. The author's intention was to frame larger questions in the Mishna and to answer them with the Talmudic and Rishonic corpus.

MISHNA TORAH

1. Mishna Torah—*Rabbi Moses Ben Maimon (Rambam), 1135-1204.*

This work, one of the great codes, encompasses the entire written and oral law. It is based on the works of R. Yitzchak Alfasi and serves as the basis for all later codes. Maimonides was a student of the Ri' Migash. His work was divided into 14 parts; because 14 has the numerical value of the word 'yad' in Hebrew, which means hand, the text is often called 'The Yad'.

2. Magid Mishna—*Rabbi Vidal De Tulusa, c. 13th century.*

Explains the Rambam in difficult passages and establishes why he chose this or that opinion in the case of disagreement. Some have stated that Magid Mishna was a student of Rabbi Shlomo Ben Aderet (Rashba); Others claim that he was a student of the Ra'ah—Rabbi Aharon Halevy.

3. Kesef Mishna—*Rabbi Yosef Ben Efraim Karo, 1489-1575.*

Born in Spain and among the four ordained by Rabbi Yaacov Berav, the Bet Yosef, was so called for his great work on the Tur Shulchan Aruch. Two years before his death he sent the manuscript of Kesef Mishna to Venice for publication. An indispensable elucidation and analysis of sources and problems in the text of Maimonides' work.

4. Lechem Mishna—*Rabbi Avraham Ben Moshe di Boton, 1545-1588.*

This commentary on The Yad was first published in Venice in 1609. The author was a Greek Jew from Salonika whose work has been reprinted in almost every subsequent edition of the Rambam.

5. Mishna LaMelech—This work was edited by Rabbi Yaakov Culi (The Me'Am Loez) from the prior writings of the Chief Rabbi of Constantinople, Rabbi Yehudah Rosannes (1658—1727). Much of it is in the way of novellae and comments on Rambam and the implications of his decisions vis-a-vis other Rishonim.

6. Hagaot Maimoniot—Some ascribe this to Rabbi Meir Ben Baruch of Rottenberg, born in 1215 in Worms, Germany. One of the the German Tosafists, he was the Ashkenazic Torah authority par excellence. He spent seven years of his life in jail and only fourteen years after his death were his remains interred after being ransomed for an exorbitant sum. Others ascribe this work to Rabbi Meir Hakohen, a brother-in-law of Rav Mordecai Ashkenazy, "The Mordecai". Primarily this is a halachic work, not an analytical one.

7. Migdal Oz—This work was written by Rabbeinu Shem-Tov, a student of Rabbi Shlomo Ben Aderet (Rashba). He emigrated to the land of Israel in the 14th century. Very little else is known about him.

ט"ז מגן דוד   א'ח א הלכות הנהגות אדם בבוקר   מגן אברהם נ"י

א

טור אורח חיים

א דין השכמת הבוקר ובו ט' סעיפים

א א (א) יתגבר (b) כארי לעמוד בבוקר לעבודת בוראו (ג) שיהא הוא מעורר (נ) השחר :

ב ג ד * המשכים להתחנן לפני בוראו יכוין לשעות שמשתנות המשמרות שהן בשלישי הלילה ולסוף שני שלישי הלילה (ו) ולסוף הלילה [א] שהתפילה שיתפלל באותן השעות על החורבן ועל הגלות רצויה :

ג ** ד * ראוי לכל ירא שמים (ז) שיהא מיצר ודואג על ה חורבן בית המקדש :

ד ה (נ) טוב ו מעט תחנונים (ח) בכוונה מהרבות בלא כונה :

באר הגולה

עטרת זקנים

נתיב חיים

חתם סופר

שערי תשובה

אשל אברהם

ביאור הגר"א

הגהות ר' עקיבא איגר

מחצית השקל

באר היטב

יד אברהם

לבושי שרד

SHULCHAN ARUCH

1. Shulchan Aruch & R'ma

A. The Shulchan Aruch—(Lit. 'Set Table')
This is the code of Jewish law written by Rabbi Yosef Ben Efraim Karo, 1488-1575. Divided into four parts, it deals with every aspect of Jewish law which is applicable today. Rabbi Karo was a Spanish Jew who moved to Turkey and later to Safed, where he served as Chief Rabbi. The Shulchan Aruch was basically written with a Sephardic orientation. He was also the author of the Bet Yosef on the Tur.

B. Hagah (Lit. 'Note' or 'Comment') of the R'ma.
Acronym for Rabbi Moses Isserles, 1520-1575, Rabbi of Cracow, Poland. The R'ma wrote his comments with an Ashkenazik orientation and they were subsequently included in the text of the Shulchan Aruch as an addendum. The work is often referred to as the 'Mapah' (Lit.—'Tablecloth') as it complemented the 'Set Table'.

2. Magen David—*Rabbi David Ben Shmuel Halevi, (Taz),* born 1586, Ludmir, Poland. This commentary on Shulchan Aruch encompasses difficulties in other authorities as well as the Bet Yosef. While its aims differ widely in the four respective volumes, sometimes "pilpulistic" and at others legalistic, the work on "Yore Deah" is the one that claimed for its author immortality in the world of Halachic decision-making. The Taz died in 1667.

3. Magen Avraham—*Rabbi Avraham Evli Gumbiner,* d. 1683.
This work was begun by the author while only 38 years old. Six years later, as Dayan in Kalisz, Poland, he completed his explanation of the Shulchan Aruch to wide acclaim. It was so concise, however, that . . .

4. Rabbi Shmuel Halevi, d. 1827, had to write the Machatzit HaShekel to explain the Magen Avraham and show the sources upon which he based his Halachic decisions. He was an intimate of Rabbi Natan Adler and the Chasam Sofer.

5. Be'er Hetev
Rabbi Yehuda Ben Shimon Ashkenazi, Dayan, Tiktin, Poland. A more basic commentary devoted to an understanding of the text and its immediate ramifications.

6. Be'er Hagola—Rabbi Moshe Rivkis, mid-17th century. Gaon from Vilna, who lived (together with Rabbi Shabtai Cohen ('Shoch') through the upheavals of the Hetman Chmielnitzki massacre of Vilna Jewry. This source work that shows enormous erudition, traces every law in the Shulchan Aruch to its origin in the Talmudic corpus.

7. Yad Efraim—Rabbi Efraim Zalman Margolies of Brody. Born in 1761. This prolific Torah scholar ranged over the entire oral law with phenomenal depth and acumen as can be seen in this penetrating analysis. The Yad Efraim was a merchant, not a professional rabbi.

8. Sharei Tshuva—Rabbi Chaim Mordechai Margolies. Rav of Dubnow, Poland in the 18th-19th century, this Halachic authority makes mention of his brother, Rabbi Efraim Zalman Margolies. His comments are very valuable, among other things, as a summing up of the opinions of the later authorities in responsa literature by the Achronim and some of the newer problems which were resolved by them.

9. Be'ur Ha-gra—This is the classic work by Rabbi Eliyahu, the Gaon of Vilna (1720-1797). The commentary is difficult, incredibly erudite and so terse that it defies any simplistic attempt towards mastery. One is forced back to the Gaon's source material for exhaustive re-evaluation. Patience and skill are required.

53

"From the Beginning": A Modern Targum

Isaac Elchanan Mozeson

Genesis

1:1
From the beginning
of this creation for revelation
the Lord balanced
the spiritual and the material.
1:2
And this world was then
pure form and matter
in the dark about the depths,
yet the wind of the Lord
hovered with the wings
of a mother bird
over the open faces of Truth.
1:3
And the Lord willed energy
and it radiated.
1:4
And the Lord knew
energy when it was Edenic,
so the Lord separated
the positive and negative.
1:5
And the Lord summoned
the energies of day
and entropy of night;
and there was mingling
before examination
in millennium one.
1:6
And the Lord willed
an atmosphere of Truth
with a stratosphere
dividing truth from truth.
1:7
And the Lord developed
this sheet of division,
a babel of cultural values
below the more rarified perceptions:
And so it had to be.
1:8
And the Lord summoned
the sheet of heaven
which divided with water
the evil and righteous
in the destruction and rebirth
of the second millennium.
* * * * *

1:9
And the Lord willed
that terrestrial truth
flow to one place,
leaving dry continents
of the visible:
And so it had to be.
1:10
And the Lord summoned
to spiritual dryness
its earthiness,
and to those pools of truth
were called forth waterways:
And the Lord saw
when it was good.
1:11
And the Lord willed
vegetable from the mineral,
perennial greening:
fruition cultivated by Man
from divine seeds, genetic codes
in twisted ladders leading to heaven
but rooted in the earth:
And so it had to be.
1:12
And from regional creeds
sprang grass root concepts,
full bloomed cultures
perpetuated by tribe.
And the Lord saw them
when they solidified.
1:13
And after a darkness
dawned the wisdom of the One
which fruited full at Sinai
in the third millennium.
* * * * *

1:14
And the Lord willed
a double mirror of divine light
over the beaten silver of sky
to separate the rational and intuitive
and serve as metaphors,
historical witnesses
marking ellipses of time.
1:15
And they were to be
heavenly guides
for the lower spheres:
And so it had to be.
1:16
And the Lord developed
the two great mirrors
of divine energies;
the sun would power the visible
kingdom of the nations,
the moon would rule the invisible
empire of the chosen
and the stellar ones.
1:17
And the Lord gave them to Man
from an atmosphere above
to bathe all below
in cosmic rays.
1:18
To rule the rises
and falls of history
and to separate between
revolution and anarchy:
And the Lord saw
that it was well prepared.
1:19
And there was to be barbarity
before enlightenment
in the two Temple time
of the fourth millennium.
* * * * *
1:20
And the Lord willed
that there evolve from marine plants
motile, organic life;
amphibians emerging
until fin and wing would fly
through the skies below and above.
1:21
And the Lord created
the dinosaurs
and all reptilian life
that evolved from aquatic species
and all species of feathered birds:
and the Lord saw them
well prepared.
1:22
And the Lord charged their survival
with abilities to populate and colonize,
to fill the seas of oceans

and multiply flying sails 'round
the globe.
1:23
And there were dark ages
before the golden age
of emerging naval powers
in the fifth millennium.
*   *   *   *   *
1:24
And the Lord willed
the evolution of agrarian,
commercial and predatory states:
And so it had to be.
1:25
Just as the Lord developed
the carnivorous and herbivorous,
all species that roam the land:
And the Lord saw them
completed in their habitat.
1:26
And the Lord willed
that the material and spiritual
together
make up human form and essence;
and men would classify
the fish of the seas,
the birds of the sky,
the beasts and all creatures of the
earth.
1:27
And Cro-Magnon was created
from its Neanderthal mold,

body and soul a divine creature;
hermaphroditic were they created.
1:28
And the Lord charged them
and the Lord willed for them
to freely succeed generations,
to populate the globe and
landscape it;
and to submarine with the fish,
to plane the air with the birds
and to burrow beneath and track
across
like the animals of the earth.
1:29
And the Lord willed,
and behold it is given to you
all the seed grasses of contemplation
bearding the full face of the earth,
and the cores of conceptions
free fruiting to perpetuity;
for you it shall be sustenance.
1:30
For consumption by the beastly
barons of the earth
and by those who soar heavenward,
for those who roam the globe
searching
and for the vegetating masses:
And so it had to be.
1:31
And only the Lord understands
the ultimate synthesis

of energy and entropy
and the raven black night
and messianic dawn
in the ascent of Man
of the sixth millennium.
*   *   *   *   *
2:1
And spiritual and material history
in all their measures were set.
2:2
And the Lord shall finish
in the seventh millennium
all the divine patterns
that were spun;
in the sabbatical era
the evolutionary striving
will cease.
2:3
And the Lord shall charge
the seventh millennium
with prosperity
and make it distinct,
when then is completed
all the progression
that the Lord created
to unfold.
*   *   *   *   *

Note: This translation has been endorsed by
numerous rabbinic authorities, including
Rabbi Aharon Lichtenstein and Rabbi Aryeh
Kaplan, zt'l.

54

The Best of Physicians Is Destined for Gehenna

Fred Rosner, M.D.

Judaism has always held the physician in high esteem. Ancient and medieval Jewish writings are replete with expressions of admiration and praise for the "faithful physician." Therefore, it is not surprising that the at-first glance derogatory Talmudic statement "the best of physicians is destined for Gehenna"(Kiddushin 4:14) has generated extensive discussion and commentary throughout the centuries.

The Hebrew epigram *tov sheberofim legehinnom* is variously translated as "the best among physicians is destined to Gehinnom," "the best among physicians is destined for Gehenna, "the best of physicians is fit for Gehenna," "the best among doctors is for Gehenna," "the best of doctors are destined for Gehenna," "to hell with the best of the physicians," and "the best physician is destined to go to hell."

Jakobovits, in *Jewish Medical Ethics* (1959), points out that the Talmud does not comment on this epigram at all, which is as significant as it is unusual. Probably the earliest commentary on the Mishnaic assertion that "the best physicians are destined for Gehenna" is that of Rabbi Shlomo ben Yitzchok, popularly known as *Rashi* (1040-1105), who says that the reasons are because a physician "is not afraid of illness, and tells the patient to eat food fit for healthy people, and does not subdue his heart before God, and sometimes causes the death of people, and is able to heal the poor [free] but does not do so" (Kiddushin 82a). Physicians were thus censured for their overconfidence in their craft, which results in their trusting in it, and their haughtiness before God, instead of trusting in Him. They are further blamed for commercializing their profession, to the extent that they sometimes fail or refuse to attend the poor, which may indirectly cause the latter's death. Furthermore, according to *Rashi*, physicians may err in their treatment regiments and thus cause the death of patients. A descendant of *Rashi*, Rabbi Yitzchok Sen, known as *Tosafos Ri Hazaken,* simply states that physicians "cause the death of the patient."

Another Talmudic passage (Aboth de Rabbi Nathan 36:5) states that: "Seven have no portion in the world to come [if they do not conduct their affairs with the utmost caution and sincerity], viz, a scribe, a writer, the best of doctors, a city judge, a diviner, a communal official and a butcher . . .".

Rabbi Joshua Falk, in his commentary *Binyan Yehoshua* on this tractate, cites the aforementioned *Rashi* verbatim and then adds that he is critical of physicians because the physician treats the patient on the basis of his own knowledge and understanding and does not ask other physicians to join him in his deliberations. In monetary matters the sages state (Sanhedrin 7b) that it is proper to include in the deliberations all those rabbis who understand the case under consideration. If that is the case where money is at stake, how much more so when someone's life is at stake. To save one life one should consult with the whole world, if necessary. Falk continues by stating that there are many well-known and widely disseminated explanations of the phrase "the best of doctors is destined for Gehenna" and concludes "May the Lord save us from their hands." Preuss points out that Falk is only saying what Diodorus asserted about the famous Egyptian physicians: "We wish that we should not have need for any one of them."

Rabbi Menachem ben Shlomo Meiri, known simply as *Mei'ri* (1249-1316), in his Talmudic commentary, opines that "the best of physicians is destined for Gehenna" because "many times he sheds blood because he gives up and doesn't try hard enough in his medical art [to heal the patient]; or sometimes he doesn't know the cause of the patient's illness or how to treat it and considers himself to be an expert."

According to Kalonymus ben Kalonymus (1286-1328), a Provencal writer and philosopher, in his ethical treatise *Even Bochan* (The Touchstone), the epigram "physicians are fit only for Gehenna" refers not to genuine physicians but to quacks because "their art is lying and deception; all their boasting is empty falsehood; their hearts are turned away from God; and their hands are covered with blood."

Friedenwald states that an interesting explanation of this difficult sentence is to be found in Rabbi Solomon Ibn Verga's *Schevet Yehuda* in the course of a discussion between Pope Martin V and Don Samuel Abrabalia and Don Salomo ha-Levi, ambassadors of the Spanish Jews to Rome in 1418. The latter, in answering, said: " 'The best physician is fit for Gehenna', signifies that he should always see Gehenna opened before him should he cause the death of anyone whose health had been entrusted to him. As a consequence he must carefully consider [the treatment] and apply all his thought to it. It is well therefore that he should be mindful that he is destined for Gehenna if he does not give sufficient thought to his patients *(Shevet Yehuda,* chap. 41)." (Ibn Verga was a physician who lived in Seville in the second half of the 15th century.)

Also in the 15th century, Rabbi Simon Duran (1361-1444), in his Responsa *Tashbatz,* part 3, No. 82, believed the Mishnaic epigram sought to castigate only those physicians who maintained their own views in the presence of greater experts and who relied on their own experiments. A similar explanation was given by the Talmudist Rabbi Samuel Edels, known as *Maharsha* (1555-1631), who states that the condemning judgment of going to hell applies to the physician who considers himself to be the best and most expert among physicians and that there is none like him. He relies excessively on his own expertise because of his haughtiness. Sometimes he errs in his understanding of the nature or constitution of a specific patient and causes the patient's death with remedies that are harmful to that patient. Rather, he should consult with other physicians because it is a matter of life and death.

In the following century, Rabbi Jonathan Eybeschutz (1690-1764), in his famous *Kerethi Upelethi* (Section *Yoreh Deah* No. 188), related the dictum to his theory that the divine sanction of healing applies only to external injuries, whereas attempts to cure internal diseases were deprecated. His contemporary, Rabbi Isaac Lampronti (1678-1756), in his renowned *Pachad Yitzchok,* suggested that the condemnation was aimed at surgeons "because they vary the instructions of the wise [diagnosticians], and, in particular, they exceed, or fall short of, the proper measure when letting blood, according to their limited intelligence, thus killing their patients; and many times have I seen . . . such evil. . . ."

The famous Mishnah commentator Rabbi Yom Tov Lippman Heller (1578-1654), known as *Tosafoth Yom Tov,* and the two prominent commentators on the Jerusalem Talmud (Kiddushin 41a), Rabbi Moses Margoliot, known as *Pne Moshe* (died 1781), and Rabbi David Fraenkel, known as *Korban Ha'edah* (1707-1762), all cite the previously mentioned *Rashi* verbatim. Rabbi Eleazar Fleckeles (1754-1826), in his work *Teshuvah Meyahavah* (section III No. 336), reiterates the interpretation that physicians who are overly confident in their own skills and who profess that "good" (Hebrew: *tov*) or the "best" emanates from them rather than God are the ones to whom the epigram "the best of physicians is destined for Gehenna" is addressed.

In Jacob ibn Habib's famous *Eyn Yaakov,* one finds the commentary of Rabbi Hanokh Zundel ben Yoseph (died 1867), known as *Etz Yoseph,* on the famous epigram about physicians and Gehenna. *Etz Yoseph* asserts the following:

> It appears to me that this statement is not derogatory toward the physician. On the contrary, it is a compliment to an expert physician . . . He who thinks of himself as the most expert physician is destined for Gehenna because through his haughtiness he relies on his imperfect knowledge and doesn't consult with his colleagues . . . also because of his conceit he does not even consider the possibility of his being in error and does not delve adequately into medical books before he administers medicinal remedies. He is, therefore, not sufficiently acquainted with their side effects and does not administer them slowly as is required for dangerously ill patients.
>
> The text of the Mishnah does not say that the doctor is evil or will definitely go to hell. Rather, it states "to Gehenna" which implies that it is in a state of readiness and that by his action he might go to Gehenna. However, if he conducts himself properly [and consults with colleagues and refers the patient to experts when appropriate] he will, on the contrary, be rewarded and praised [and share in the world to come].

Rabbi Israel Lipschutz, known as *Tifereth Yisroel* (1792-1860), in his Mishnah commentary on Kiddushin 4:14, has nearly identical language as *Etz Yoseph* but also brings a long story to illustrate the meaning of the famous epigram.

Another view is that the dictum of the Mishnah is not directed against healing as such but against the "advanced" views held by physicians in those days. Zimmels suggests that the dictum might have been originally an ancient proverb censuring physicians for counteracting heavenly decrees. Friedenwald offers a Cabalistic philosophical interpretation of the Mishnah by the great Rabbi Loeb of Prague: Gehenna stands for the material world, which according to the doctrine of the Cabalists, is nothing but the negation of real existence, the spiritual. The physician or, in other words, the naturalist, who knows only the material world, will end in Gehenna, in "non-existence." . . . In the original form of the saying about the physician and the nether world the point made was that even the most skilled physician cannot save himself from death and it read accordingly, "The best of physicians has to descend to the dwelling of the nether world."

Both Friedenwald (*The Jews and Medicine, 1944*) and Jakobovits seem to be convinced that the association of physicians with hell, in its original form, was nothing but a pun, based on the assonance of *rophim,* meaning physicians, and *r'pho'im,* meaning the dwellers of the nether world. Several examples from Scriptures are cited by Friedenwald and Jakobovits to show how easily *rophim* and r'pho'im were confused.

Friedenwald also cites a personal communication from H. Malter who wrote:

> The ancient rabbis had foreseen that a time will come when there will be no more rabbis; doctors will replace them. Only doctors and no rabbis will reign; doctors who will cure the eyes, and leave the heart and soul sick, and in a burst of passion and jealousy they scolded these doctors, saying, "the best of the doctors should go to hell."

A novel interpretation of the epigram of the Mishnah "the best of physicians is destined for Gehenna," using the numerical value of the word "best" (the Hebrew word *tov* has the numerical value 17), is that of Rabbi Meir of Przemyslan in his *Margenitha di R. Meir.* The most important part of the daily prayer service is the recitation of The Eighteen (now 19) Benedictions (*Shemoneh Esreh* in Hebrew), known simply as *Tefillah* or prayer. The eighth benediction is a petition for healing for all who are ill, strength for all who are feeble, and relief for all who suffer pain. The benediction begins with the phrase: "Heal us, O Lord, and we shall be healed," and concludes with the phrase: "Blessed art thou O Lord, who healest the sick of thy people Israel." According to Rabbi Meir of Przemyslan, "the best of physicians is destined for Gehenna" refers to those physicians who only believe in 17 of the 18 benedictions in that they do not recognize that God is the true Healer of the ill. Although these physicians may recite all 18 benedictions, if their trust in themselves and conceit in their own medical skills preclude their acceptance of the eighth benediction, which acknowledges God as the trustworthy and merciful Healer, such physicians are considered as "the best" (Hebrew *tov*) and are destined for Gehenna.

A very recent writer offers yet other interpretations of the dictum of the Mishnah. He states that all knowledge is divided into two types: precise, objective, and scientific knowledge, and humanistic, philosophic, and historical knowledge. Medicine is a combination of both precise and imprecise knowledge. A human being is also composed of two parts: a physical body and a spiritual soul, which complement and supplement each other. Manipulation of either body or soul, of necessity, affects the other. On the other hand, no two human beings are alike either in physical features or in body temperaments. If a person is ill, the remedy to cure him may not be the same as the remedy for another individual with a similar illness. Host factors vary from patient to patient. There is thus room for wide variation in efficacy and toxicity of every therapeutic regimen employed by a physician. Therefore, how easy it is for even the best of physicians to unwittingly harm a patient by any given treatment. This is the meaning of "the best of physicians is destined for Gehenna."

Another explanation offered by the same writer is the following: since medicine was traditionally considered to be a praiseworthy profession, many Jewish scholars studied and practiced medicine. The Sages were concerned lest large numbers of the best minds in Israel forsake the study of the Torah to pursue careers in medicine. Hence, perhaps, to discourage this trend, the Sages enunciated the dictum "the best of physicians is destined for Gehenna."

Preuss adds that there is no dearth of other explanations of the famous epigram. In fact, he states that an entire book on the subject was written in 1724 by Reinecke. Two authors, Buxtorf and Schenkel, cited by Preuss, interpret the dictum to mean a general deprecation of physicians, whereas another author (Israels) considers it a vote of censure of physicians who follow Greek philosophy. Finally, Preuss quotes Landau who states that the phrase refers to the sect of Essenes.

Based on many of these interpretations, Jakobovits concludes that "to hell with the best of the physicians" was never understood as a denunciation of the conscientious practitioner. Physicians are among a group of communal servants who have heavy public responsibilities and are warned against the danger of negligence or error. The Talmudic epigram with its curse is thus limited to physicians who are overly confident in their craft, or are guilty of commercializing their profession, or lie and deceive as do quacks, or who fail to acknowledge God as the true Healer of the sick, or who fail to consult with colleagues or medical texts when appropriate, or who perform surgery without heeding proper advice from diagnosticians, or who fail to heal the poor and thus indirectly cause their death, or who fail to try hard enough to heal their patients, or who consider themselves to be the best in their field, or who otherwise fail to conduct themselves in an ethical and professional manner.

May the Lord remove all sickness from this world and heal all those who need physical or spiritual healing. In the meantime, may every physician practice his art with the approach cited in the morning prayers: "Heal us, O Lord, and we shall be healed; save us and we shall be saved; for Thou art our praise."

55

Definition of Death In Jewish Law

Fred Rosner

The first heart transplant was performed in 1967 and raised moral, religious, ethical, and legal problems relating to life and death, and especially the medical definition of death. The rapid advances in biomedical technology over the past two decades have provided the medical profession with life-support and life-sustaining equipment which becloud and make difficult the recognition of death in some patients.

Medicolegal definition of death

Medical and legal definitions of death, although similar in certain respects, differ in others. Even among physicians or medical groups there is neither unanimity of opinion nor uniformity in defining death, and religious definition may be at variance with either those of the medical or legal professions.

The criteria for defining death acceptable to many physicians include complete bilateral pupillary dilatation with no reaction to local constricting stimuli, complete abolition of reflexes, complete cessation of spontaneous respiration, absence of measurable blood pressure, and a flat electroencephalogram.

In 1968, guidelines for organ transplants were approved by the House of Delegates of the American Medical Association. Included was the following statement:

> When a vital single organ is to be transplanted, the death of the donor shall have been determined by at least one physician other than the recipient's physician. Death shall be determined by the clinical judgment of the physician. In making this determination, the ethical physician will use all available, currently accepted scientific tests.

How does one ascertain the irreversibility of the process of life? The Ad Hoc Committee of the Harvard Medical School to Examine the Definition of Brain Death arrived at the generally accepted definition of irreversible coma which included unreceptivity and unresponsivity, no movements or breathing, no reflexes, and a flat electroencephalogram.

At what point need a physician no longer attempt resuscitation? In 1968 the World Medical Association adopted a statement, which asserted in part that a physician's determination of death "should be based on clinical judgment, supplemented if necessary by diagnostic aids, of which the electroencephalograph is the current most helpful single one." Drafters of the statement admitted its indefiniteness and stressed that there are neither precise scientific criteria nor a definition for what is the moment of death.

In 1973 the American Medical Association reaffirmed its opposition to any "inflexible" statutory definition of death. The Conference of Royal Colleges and Faculties of the United Kingdom in 1976 endorsed a document which described in general terms the diagnosis of death and set out detailed diagnostic criteria for establishing when death has occurred in cases where vital functions are being maintained mechanically; commenting on the document, an editorial writer stated that:

> Some patients who are rescued from impending death after cardiorespiratory arrest are left with a dead brain, artificial ventilation, and a beating heart. Even when mechanical ventilation is maintained, progressive dissolution of the brain, and then of other organs, continues; and the heart will stop beating within a few days. This biological artefact, achieved by technological progress, is the state of brain death.

Because the 1976 document made no reference to organ transplantation, a supplementary memorandum was published in 1979. A brain death protocol appeared a year later. That same year, a BBC television program, *Panorama,* suggested that in Britain, kidneys may on occasion be removed from donors who would otherwise have lived. Much was made of three illustrative case histories from the United States—a man who had been unconscious after cardiac arrest, a woman with drug overdose, and a man with severe accidental injuries—in all of whom brain death was said to have been diagnosed, yet the patients recovered. The recurring motif was, "If the patient wasn't dead when he was wheeled into the operating theatre, he certainly is now." One writer to *The Lancet,* alarmed at the insufficient methods for defining brain death, tore up his donor card. Another pointed out the fact that an isoelectric electroencephalogram (EEG) can occur in hypothermic patients or in those treated with sedative or neuromuscular blocking drugs. Yet another posited the value of the EEG in assessing irreversible coma. Confusion was compounded by the use of terms such as "brain death," "cerebral death," and "brain stem death." The Code of British Practice which requires irreversible loss of brain stem function was firmly defended by some and resoundly criticized by others. In this respect, the much-quoted US Collaborative Study was also strongly criticized.

The controversy generated by the *Panorama* program reached fever pitch and resulted in the cancellation of a sequel program on brain death. Everyone seems to agree that the EEG is not 100% accurate and that flat EEGs can occur in a variety of situations in which the patient survives. Angiography and isotope angiography have been suggested as helpful aids in determining irreversible brain or brain stem death. Thirty sets of criteria for the diagnosis of brain death were recently reviewed. Is it not possible to diagnose brain stem death on the basis of critical criteria alone? Must this diagnosis be reinforced by EEG or angiography, or both?

In the United States, partially in response to pressures from Stanford University Medical Center where most of the world's heart transplants were and continue to be performed, California, in 1976, became the first state to enact a law defining death as brain death, irrespective of whether or not the heart is still beating. To date, at least 26 states have adopted statutory definitions of death based on four different models: (a) the Kansas Model in which alternative means for determining death are acceptable, (b) the Capron-Kass Model in which brain death pronouncements can be made only when heart and lung function are artificially maintained, (c) the American Bar Association Model in which irreversible cessation of total brain function equals death, and (d) the Uniform Brain Death Model which emphasizes irreversible cessation of brain stem function.

Two American medical journals have published review articles on medical, legal, ethical, and public opinion aspects of the definition and criteria of death. The President's Commission for the Study of Ethical Problems in Medicine and Bio-medical and Behavioral Research has recommended the adoption of a Uniform Determination of Death Act in which a person who has sustained either irreversible cessation of circulatory and respiratory functions, or irreversible cessation of all functions of the entire brain, including the brain stem, is dead. This Uniform Determination of Death Act was developed and approved by the American Bar Association, the American Medical Association, and the National Conference of Commissioners on Uniform State Laws. The law does not specify diagnostic tests or medical procedures acceptable for determining death, leaving the medical profession free to make use of new medical knowledge and diagnostic advances as they become available. The determination of death must thus be made in accordance with accepted medical standards.

Although the original impetus for equating human death with irreversible brain failure was initially stimulated by the rapidly expanding field of organ transplantation, in recent years the need for instituting a single organ (brain) definition of death from a scientific, theologic, and legal point of view has become paramount because of the difficulties surrounding the discontinuance of life-support systems in hopeless patient situations. One should also not confuse brain death and other forms of irreversible brain damage, particularly the vegetative state. Although such patients, best typified by Karen Ann Quinlan, may be thought to no longer function as human beings, bodily life can continue for months or even years. Such individuals are certainly not dead in the medical or biologic sense. How long is one obligated to maintain life-support systems for a brain-damaged person?

When is the dying patient beyond help? When is the physician guilty of a grave moral and religious sin by not doing everything possible to "maintain" his patient? Just as one cannot properly define health as the absence of disease, it seems totally inappropriate to define death as the absence of life. Although society in general and the medical and legal professions in particular are struggling to come up with an acceptable definition of death, it seems

desirable to review the Jewish religious definition of death.

Classic definition of death in Jewish law

The definition of death in Jewish law is first mentioned in the fifth century Babylonian Talmud. The Mishnah (Yoma 8:6-7) enumerates circumstances under which one may desecrate the Sabbath:

> ... every danger to human life suspends the [laws of the] Sabbath. If debris [of a collapsing building] falls on someone and it is doubtful whether he is there or whether he is not there, or if it is doubtful whether he is alive or whether he is dead or if it is doubtful whether he is an Israelite or a heathen, one must probe the heap of the debris for his sake [even on the Sabbath]. If one finds him alive, one should remove the debris but if he is dead, one leaves him there [until after the Sabbath].

The Talmud (*Yoma* 85a), commenting on the above Mishnah, states as follows:

> ... How far does one search [to ascertain whether he is dead or alive]? Until [one reaches] his nose. Some say: Up to his heart ... life manifests itself primarily through the nose as it is written: *In whose nostrils was the breath of the spirit of life* (Genesis 7:22) ...

The biblical and Talmudic commentator *Rashi* explains that if no air emanates from his nostrils, he is certainly dead. *Rashi* further explains that some people suggest the heart be examined for signs of life, but the respiration test is considered of greatest import.

The Palestinian Talmud (Yoma 8:5) quotes certain authorities who require "until one reaches the navel" but this is a minority viewpoint.

This rule from the Mishnah is codified by Maimonides as follows:

> If upon examination no sign of breathing can be detected at the nose, the victim must be left where he is [until after the Sabbath] because he is already dead ....

The famous Code of Jewish Law by Joseph Karo, known as *Shulkhan Arukh,* states:

> Even if the victim was found so severely injured that he cannot live for more than a short while, one must probe [the debris] until one reaches his nose. If one cannot detect signs of respiration at the nose, then he is certainly dead whether the head was uncovered first or whether the feet were uncovered first.

Neither Maimonides nor Karo seems to require examination of the heart or navel, both mentioned as minority opinions in the Babylonian and Palestinian Talmuds, respectively. Cessation of respiration seems to be the determining physical sign for the ascertainment of death.

Another pertinent passage found in Karo's Code states as follows:

> If a woman is sitting on the birthstool [i.e., about to give birth] and she dies, one brings a knife on the Sabbath, even through a public domain, and one incises her womb and removes the fetus since one might find it alive.

Rabbi Moses Isserles adds to this statement:

> However, today we do not conduct ourselves according to this [rule] even during the week [i.e., even *not* on the Sabbath] because we are not competent to recognize precisely the moment of maternal death. ...

Several commentators explain that Isserles is concerned that perhaps the mother only fainted and incising her abdomen might kill her. Maimonides, five centuries earlier, had already raised the problem of fainting complicating the recognition of death when he stated:

> . . . whosoever closes the eyes of the dying while the soul is about to depart is shedding blood. One should wait a while; perhaps he is only in a swoon. . . .

However, both Maimonides and Isserles agree that the Talmudic description of death for all practical purposes is the absence or cessation of respiration. We are not primarily concerned with the extremely rare case of someone recovering from what appears to be the deceased state. Such an example is described in the Talmud (Semachot 8:1). Rather, Jewish law follows the rule of the majority.

Recent rabbinic writings on definition of death

Recent rabbinic opinions support the classic Jewish legal definition that death is established when spontaneous respiration ceases. Since respiration was thought to be dependent on cardiac activity, the definition would thus include absence of a heartbeat. Such an opinion was first expressed by Rabbi Moses Schreiber who asserts that if a person is motionless like an inanimate stone and has no palpable pulse either in the neck or at the wrist, and also has no spontaneous respiration, his soul has certainly departed, but one should wait a short while to fulfill the requirement of Maimonides (*vide supra*) who was concerned that the patient may only be in a swoon. Rabbi Sholom Mordechai Schwadron states that if any sign of life is observed in limbs other than the heart and lungs, the apparent absence of spontaneous respiration is not conclusive in establishing death.

On the other hand, Rabbi Isaac Yehuda Unterman stated that one is dead when one has stopped breathing. Thus, most Talmudic and post-Talmudic sages agree that the absence of spontaneous respiration is the only sign needed to ascertain death. A minority would also require cessation of heart action. Thus a patient who has stopped breathing, says Unterman, and whose heart is not beating, is considered dead by Jewish law.

Rabbi Eliezer Yehuda Waldenberg also defines death as the cessation of respiration and cardiac activity. One must use all available medical means to ascertain that respiratory and cardiac functions have indeed ceased. A flat electroencephalogram in the face of a continued heartbeat is not an acceptable finding by itself to pronounce a patient dead. Even after death has been established one should wait a while before moving the deceased. Rabbi Waldenberg cites a work entitled *Divrei Shaul* in which the author states that "It is clear to me like the sun that if we observe a patient and he appears dead, and has no respiration and no heartbeat which are the signs of life as explained in tractate Yoma, he is not alive any more and has the [legal] status of a dead person in all respects." Rabbi Waldenberg also discusses the issue of whether the seat of the soul resides in the heart or in the brain and cites Rabbi Zvi ben Yaakov Ashkenazy, known as *Chacham Tzvi* (Responsum No. 77) who pointed out that this issue has been argued since the times of Galen, whose opinion was that the brain is the source of life, and Aristotle, who considered the heart to be more important than the brain.

Rabbi Moses Feinstein states that if the brain is not functioning, death will occur because breathing will stop. Until the latter occurs, physicians may be able to resuscitate the patient, or prayers to God may avail. Hence, if one kills someone with no brain function who is still breathing, it is murder. The Talmud and Codes of Jewish law do not indicate, continues Feinstein, that the signs of life are in the brain, and it is illogical to say that the nature of man changed since, even in Talmudic days, the brain controlled all life-sustaining functions (i.e., respiration) and, yet, cessation of brain activity was not considered to be the definition of death. In a patient without spontaneous respiration or heartbeat but with some electrical activity on an electroencephalogram, the rare possibility of resuscitation must be reckoned with. Although the respiration test is paramount, it is clear that "the nose is not the organ which gives life to a human being, nor is it the organ of respiration; rather the brain and the heart give life to man." The nose is the easiest place to recognize the presence of this life, concludes Feinstein, since a very weak pulse may not be detectable and brain activity is not easily measured on physical examination alone.

In a personal communication in 1967 a similar conclusion was expressed by Rabbi Immanuel Jakobovits who stated in part that "The classic definition of death as given in the Talmud and Codes is acceptable today and correct. However, this would be set aside in cases where competent medical opinion deems any prospects of resuscitation, however remote, at all feasible."

Rabbi Aaron Soloveitchik, in a very novel approach, states that death is a process that begins the moment spontaneous respiration ceases and ends when all bodily functions emanating from the controlling center, i.e., the brain, end. This means that:

> When a person in whom death is imminent becomes devoid of respiration but other bodily functions such as the brain are potentially operative, such a person is no longer completely alive but he is not yet dead; death has begun but the death process is not complete until the brain and heart completely cease to function. During this period, a person is in a state of semi-living, not fully alive but not fully dead. Anyone who kills such a person or who hastens his death is, therefore, guilty of murder. This is the reason why Maimonides rules that one is not allowed to move a dying person while his soul is departing until after one waits awhile. Maimonides refers to a person who is motionless and who has no spontaneous heartbeat or respiration. One must wait half an hour because his brain may still be operative and the patient potentially resuscitable. This "dying" person is in a semi-living state and, therefore, one is prohibited from doing anything which may hasten his death.

Rabbi J. David Bleich traces the Jewish legal attitude concerning the definition of death from Talmudic through recent rabbinic times. He posits that brain death and irreversible coma are not acceptable definitions of death insofar as Jewish law is concerned since the sole criterion of death accepted by Jewish law is total cessation of both cardiac and respiratory activity. Even when these indications are present, there is a definite obligation to resuscitate the patient, if at all feasible. Bleich also discusses the various time of death statutes already enacted into law in many states in this country and statutes being contemplated by other states. These statutes supplant the classical definition of death with more flexible criteria. Bleich voices concern about the fact that it is unlikely that Jewish opinion can succeed in stemming the legislative tide indefinitely. It is also unrealistic to believe that time-of-death statutes will accurately reflect even the most liberal of Jewish legal opinions. He expresses hope that civil and religious liberties be preserved by writing into such statutes a provision allowing for exemption from legislated definitions of death for reasons of conscience.

Several Jewish physicians, well-versed in Talmudic law and rabbinic writings, have written in detail about the Jewish legal definition of death. They conclude that today one requires all three criteria cited by Rabbi Moses Schreiber *(vide supra),* namely (1) absence of spontaneous respiration, (2) absence of a heartbeat in a patient who appears dead, and (3) being "motionless like an inanimate stone."

Rabbi Moses David Tendler introduced the concept of brain stem death as an acceptable criterion for the definition of death even if cardiac function has not ceased. Tendler points out:

> . . . that absent heartbeat or pulse was *not* considered a significant factor in ascertaining death in any early religious sources. Furthermore, the scientific fact that cellular death does not occur at the same time as the death of the human being is well recognized in the earliest biblical sources. The twitching of a lizard's amputated tail or the death throes of a decapitated man were never considered residual life but simply manifestations of cellular life that continued after death of the entire organism had occurred. In the situation of decapitation, death can be defined or determined by the decapitated state itself as recognized in the Talmud and the Code of Laws. Complete destruction of the brain, which includes loss of all integrative, regulatory, and other functions of the brain, can be considered physiological decapitation and thus a determinant per se of death of the person.
>
> Loss of the ability to breathe spontaneously is a crucial criterion for determining whether complete destruction of the brain has occurred. Earliest biblical sources recognized the ability to breathe independently as a prime index of life . . . destruction of the entire brain or brain death, and only that, is consonant with biblical pronouncements on what constitutes an acceptable definition of death, i.e., a patient who has all the appearances of lifelessness and who is no longer breathing spontaneously. Patients with irreversible total destruction of the brain fulfill this definition even if heart action and circulation are artificially maintained.

Thus, according to Tendler, if it can be definitely demonstrated that brain stem death, not cerebral cortex or "brain" death, but actual brain stem death, has occurred, then the patient is legally dead in Jewish law because he is equated with a decapitated individual whose heart may still be beating but whose brain stem is irreversibly "dead." Brain stem function can be evaluated medically by evoked potential studies, isotope flow investigations, angiography, and caloric studies.

The Tendler position that "complete and permanent absence of any brain-related vital bodily function is recognized as death by Jewish scholars" is supported by a recent responsum of Rabbi Moses Feinstein. The latter states that if by injecting a substance into the vein of a patient, physicians can ascertain that there is no circulation to the brain,

meaning no connection between the brain and the rest of the body, then the patient is legally dead in Judaism because he is equivalent to a decapitated person. Where the test is available, continues Feinstein, it should be used.

Tendler's arguments generated considerable discussion and controversy. Rabbi Aaron Soloveitchik attacked the Tendler position as a serious misinterpretation of Jewish law, an attack refuted by Tendler himself. An opposing viewpoint on brain death asserted that "cessation of total brain function, whether irreversible or not, is not necessarily linked to total destruction of the brain or to the death of the person. Further, to take vital organs or to otherwise treat people as though they were dead already on the basis of these recent criteria is morally unacceptable to most Orthodox Jews and Christians." This firm criticism of Tendler's thesis was somewhat tempered by an accompanying editorial and a response by Veith and Tendler. However, Tendler maintains his position that total and irreversible cessation of brain (stem) function as determined by the Harvard criteria or their more recent modifications is equivalent to total destruction of the brain and, hence, tantamount to functional or physiologic decapitation, a condition that most lay and religious ethicists—and indeed most persons—can equate with death.

Conclusion

Guidelines for the determination of death continue to be proposed, discussed, and debated. It is axiomatic in Judaism that human life is of infinite worth. The taking or the shortening of a human life is, therefore, ethically wrong and constitutes an act of murder. "When does life end" is an issue presently being actively discussed.

All rabbis agree that the classic definition of death in Judaism is the absence of spontaneous respiration and heartbeat in a patient with no bodily motion. A brief waiting period of a few minutes to one-half hour after breathing has ceased is also required. In the present era, when it is recognized that hypothermia or drug overdose can result in depression of the respiratory center with absence of spontaneous respiration and even heartbeat, this classic definition of death is insufficient. Hence, wherever resuscitation is deemed possible, no matter how remote the chance, it must be attempted. Cerebral death is not generally accepted by rabbinic scholars to be a criterion for establishing death other than to confirm death in a patient who already has irreversible absence of spontaneous respiration and no heartbeat. The only exception may be the situation of decapitation where immediate death is assumed even if the heart may still be briefly beating. Irreversible brain stem death as evidenced by sophisticated medical testing is the Jewish legal equivalent of decapitation and is presently a matter of intense debate in rabbinic circles.

The artificial heart

The implantation of an artificial heart into Dr. Barney Clark and others has raised many ethical and religious issues in regard to life and death and the "artificial" prolongation of life.

A basic tenet of Judaism is the supreme value of human life. This principle is based in part on the belief that man was created in the image of God. Jewish law requires the physician to do everything in his power to prolong life, but prohibits the use of measures that prolong the act of dying. To save a life all Jewish religious laws are automatically suspended, the only exceptions being idolatry, incest, and murder.

Organ transplantation is a praiseworthy activity in that it provides prolongation of life for most patients undergoing this procedure. Hence corneal, renal, and cardiac transplantation are sanctioned by most rabbis and even mandated by some but with permission of the deceased or next of kin. For kidney transplants, live donors may be used. When cadaver organs are to be used, the organ may not be removed for transplantation until the donor has been pronounced dead.

Euthanasia is opposed without qualification in Jewish law, which condemns any deliberate hastening of death, whether the physician acts with or without the patient's consent. Some Rabbinic views do not allow any relaxation of efforts, however artifical and hopeless, to prolong life. Others do not require the physician to resort to "heroic" methods, but sanction the omission of machines and artificial life support systems that only serve to draw out the dying patient's agony, provided, however, that basic care such as food, good nursing, and psychosocial support is provided. Jewish tradition views death as inevitable and just. It differentiates between the body and the soul, acknowledges resurrection for the former and immortality for the latter. Respect for death is mandated.

The concern for the patient's physical and mental welfare remains supreme to the end, and everything must be done to preserve both. Therefore, the implantation of an artificial heart is consonant with the basic axioms of Judaism relating to the sanctity and infinite value of human life. This sanctioning of such a complex and controversial experimental treatment in Judaism is also predicated on the fulfillment of Jewish principles governing human experimentation, such as the lack of availability of a standard therapy, the expertise of the experimental team, the testing of such experimental procedures in animal models, and the reasonable expectation of therapeutic efficacy weighed against the potential risks.

Should a Jew Sell Guns?

J. David Bleich

Mr. Isaac Goldstein, Proprietor
Rocky's Pawn-Shop
Elm Street
Dallas, Texas

Dear Mr. Goldstein:

Time Magazine reports that you are giving serious consideration to discontinuing the sale of handguns in your establishment. No doubt, the 1981 attempt upon the life of President Reagan is prompting such soulsearching not only on your part, as proprietor of the store which sold that particular gun, but on the part of countless other gun dealers as well. Permit me to draw your attention to one aspect of Jewish teaching which should figure prominently in such deliberations.

Maimonides (*Hilkhot Rotzeah* 12:12, paraphrasing *Avodah Zarah* 15b) declares: "It is forbidden to sell heathens weapons of war. Nor is it permitted to sharpen their spears, or to sell them knives, manacles, iron chains, bears, lions or any object which can endanger the public; but it is permitted to sell them shields which are only for defense."

Mr. Goldstein, a sticker on the door of your shop reads, "Guns Don't Cause Crime Any More Than Flies Cause Garbage." Maimonides disagrees emphatically. In explaining the premise upon which this provision of Jewish law is based, Maimonides tells us that in selling arms to a heathen "one strengthens the hands of an evil-doer and *causes him to transgress*" and "anyone who causes one who is blind with regard to a matter to stumble—or one who strengthens the hand of a person who is blind and does not see the path of truth because of the desire of his heart violates a negative precept as it is stated, "You shall not put a stumbling block before the blind."

This precept was understood by the Sages as an admonition designed to protect not only the physically blind, but the intellectually and morally blind as well. A Jew is forbidden to take advantage of another person's lack of awareness in a way which causes harm to that person or to others. The Torah forbids us to mislead the blind and thereby cause them to stumble. We are forbidden to give the uninformed misinformation or poor advice; we are forbidden to prey upon, or pander to, the predilections of the morally blind.

These restrictions are part of the Torah and accepted by Jews because such is the divine command, but they also happen to make good sense. Let me tell you a story.

Everyone remembers the assassination of Martin Luther King. Some, but probably not many, will remember the shooting of Martin Luther King's mother some time afterward. It is an event I am not likely to forget, not because of the event itself, but because of an incident which occurred subsequently.

A short time after the shooting, my wife and I were sitting in a cafe in Prague. A young, highly intelligent medical student struck up a conversation with us. As he began to feel comfortable in our company, he leaned across the table and, in a conspiratorial tone, asked why American intelligence had sought the death of Mrs. King. I hastened to assure him that Mrs. King was a very private person, not involved in political affairs, and that it was highly unlikely that anyone beyond her immediate circle of family and friends had been more than dimly aware of her existence. Moreover, there was cause to believe that the man responsible for her shooting was mentally incompetent.

Our young friend was incredulous. I assumed that he suspected a plot to be lurking behind every headline. No, he assured me, he understood well enough that in the West not everything is controlled by the government. But this incident must have been government-directed, came the clincher to the argument, because how would the assassin have come into possession of a gun!

We had come to Prague via Vienna. In Vienna, but several kilometers away, we stayed in a hotel off the *Graben on Dorotheergasse*. The street was rather narrow and easily overlooked. Returning from our outings, we recognized the turn by means of a large neon sign outside a store on the corner. The sign was emblazoned with but a single word—*"Waffen."* The young man's reaction to my account of how handguns are freely available in many Western nations was that either I must be a weaver of fancy tales or else Western society is plumb crazy!

The ease with which handguns can be acquired in some Western countries is simply incomprehensible to persons who live in a more circumscribed environment. To them this is not a sign of freedom of the West, of which they are jealous and which they would replicate if they but could, but of an irrationality of which they wish no part.

Jewish law recognizes that indiscriminate sale of weapons cannot fail to endanger the public. The daily newspaper confirms this deep-seated distrust far more often than is necessary. As the bearers of an ageless moral code Jews ought to be in the vanguard of those seeking to impress upon our legislators that handguns are indeed "stumbling blocks" which must not fall into the hands of the "blind." Criminals do commit crimes and it is precisely because "morally blind" criminals are disposed to crime that Judaism teaches that it is forbidden to provide them with the tools of their trade.

Yes, Mr. Goldstein, flies do not cause garbage, but garbage does attract flies. Guns may or may not cause crime, but crimes of violence cannot be committed without tools of violence. Self-restraint in the sale of weapons is a small enough price to pay for even marginal enhancement of public safety.

Sincerely yours,
J. David Bleich

Animal Experimentation: The Jewish View

Fred Rosner

The use of animals for research and teaching is an issue of great concern in the United States. In Britain, the 1876 Cruelty to Animals Act, still in effect, permits the government to license scientists, to regulate experimentation, and to carry out inspections. The act will be replaced and updated as soon as final agreement is reached on animal experiments. Animal protection groups continue to raise the consciousness and concerns about the humane treatment of experimental animals. These groups are concerned with the moral rights of animals not to be used as subjects for experiments. Scientists have become concerned with the ethical responsibility for the humane treatment of animals in experimentation. There is a delicate balance between scientists and animal protectionists; neither side is able to convince the other fully of the absolute merits of each other's positions and views.

Jewish law not only forbids cruelty to animals but also requires that we be kind to them, have compassion for them, and treat them humanely. Thus, if one sees an animal collapsing under a heavy burden, one must unload it (Exodus 23:5). One may not muzzle an animal to deprive it of food while it is working (Deuteronomy 25:4). In fact, one may not partake of any food until one has first assured the provision of food for one's animals (based on Deuteronomy 11:15). Animals may not work on the Sabbath (Exodus 20:10 and Deuteronomy 5:14). This rule is enunciated among the Ten Commandments, indicating that care of and kindness to animals are of profound importance for the humanizing of man. The All-Merciful One shows mercy over all His creatures, including animals (Psalms 145:9), and provides food for their sustenance (Psalms 147:9). A righteous man has regard for his animal (Proverbs 12:10). Balaam was strongly rebuked for smiting his ass (Numbers 22:32), a classic text for the preaching of humane treatment of animals.

These and other biblical and rabbinic moral and legal rules concerning the treatment of animals are based on the principle that animals are part of God's creation for which man bears responsibility. Moses Maimonides, the 12th century rabbi, philosopher, theologian, and codifier of Jewish law, offers an insight into these rules in that he states that the prohibition of causing suffering to animals was set down with a view to perfecting humans so that we do not acquire moral habits of cruelty. Rather, we should not inflict pain gratuitously without any utility, but should be kind and merciful even with a chance or stray animal. The reason why man is forbidden to eat a limb cut off from a living animal (Genesis 9:4 and Deuteronomy 12:23) is because this act would make one acquire the habit of cruelty. The same reason is given for the rule forbidding the slaughtering of an animal and its young on the same day (Leviticus 22:28) and the commandment to release the mother bird before taking the young (Deuteronomy 22:6-7).

There are many additional rules that the rabbis enacted to guard animals against hunger, overwork, disease, distress and suffering. Wanton hunting and killing of animals for sport is prohibited. It is forbidden to inflict a blemish on an animal. Numerous Sabbath laws relating to forbidden acts are waived when such acts are intended to relieve the pain of an animal. A person is not permitted to buy animals unless he can properly care and provide for them.

Judaism also espouses the concept that everything created in this world by God was created to serve mankind. Animals thus may be used as beasts of burden and for food, providing they are humanely slaughtered. It has been suggested that the Jewish method of ritual slaughter, particularly the laws that the knife be exceedingly sharp and without the slightest notch, were motivated by consideration for the animal because this method is the most painless. Scientific experiments on laboratory animals during the course of medical research designed to yield information that might lead to cure of disease are sanctioned by Jewish law as legitimate use of animals for the benefit of mankind. Wherever possible, however, pain or discomfort should be eliminated or minimized by analgesia, anesthesia, or other means. Otherwise, the pain does not serve to satisfy a legitimate human need and its infliction is prohibited. In addition, animal experimentation is only permissible by Jewish law if its purpose is to obtain practical benefits to mankind and not to simply satisfy intellectual curiosity. Furthermore, if alternate means, e.g., tissue culture studies, of obtaining the same information are available, animal experimentation might be categorized as unnecessary cruelty to animals and be prohibited.

"The Honey Jar"

Howard Spielman
Arnold Fine

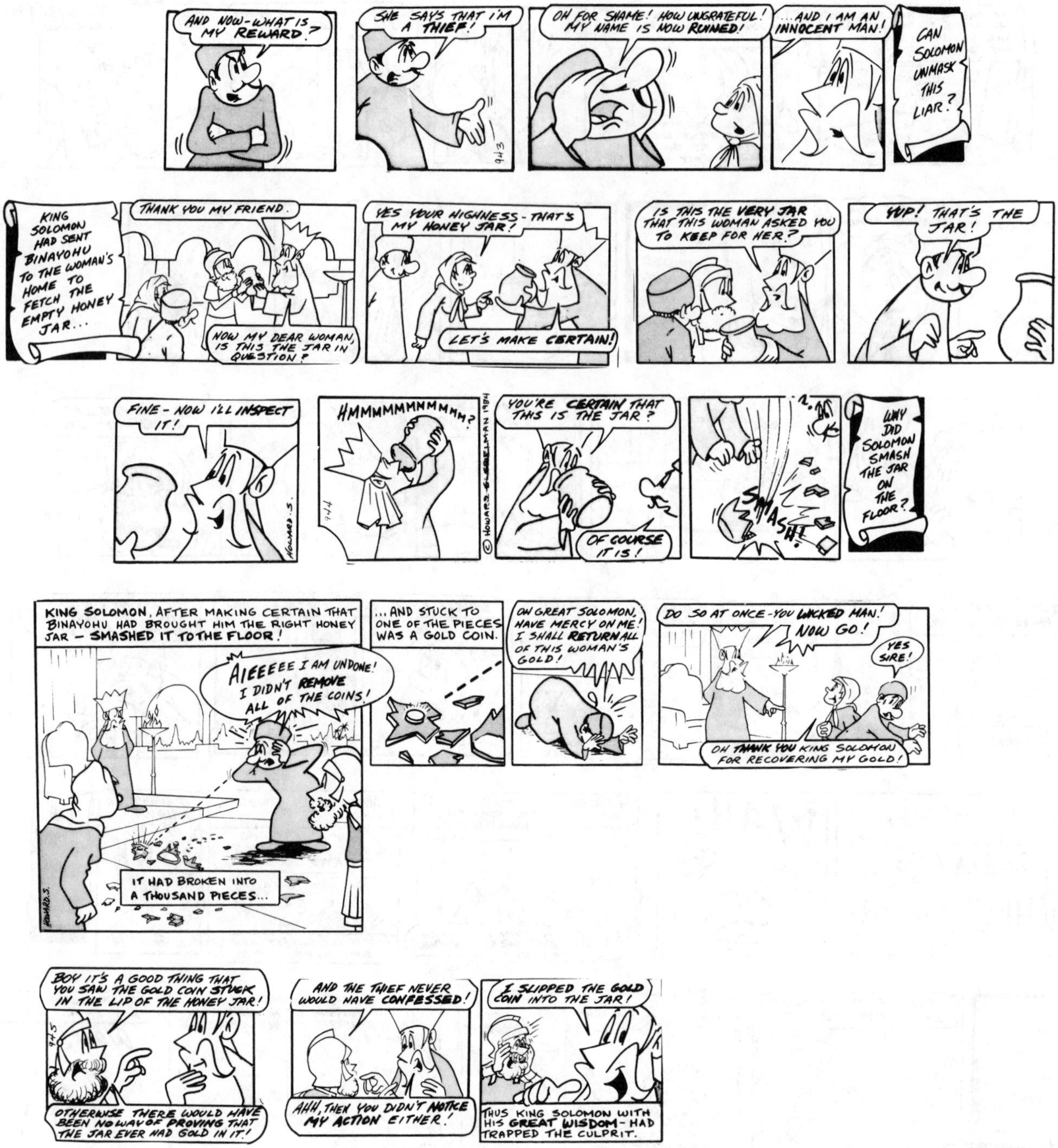

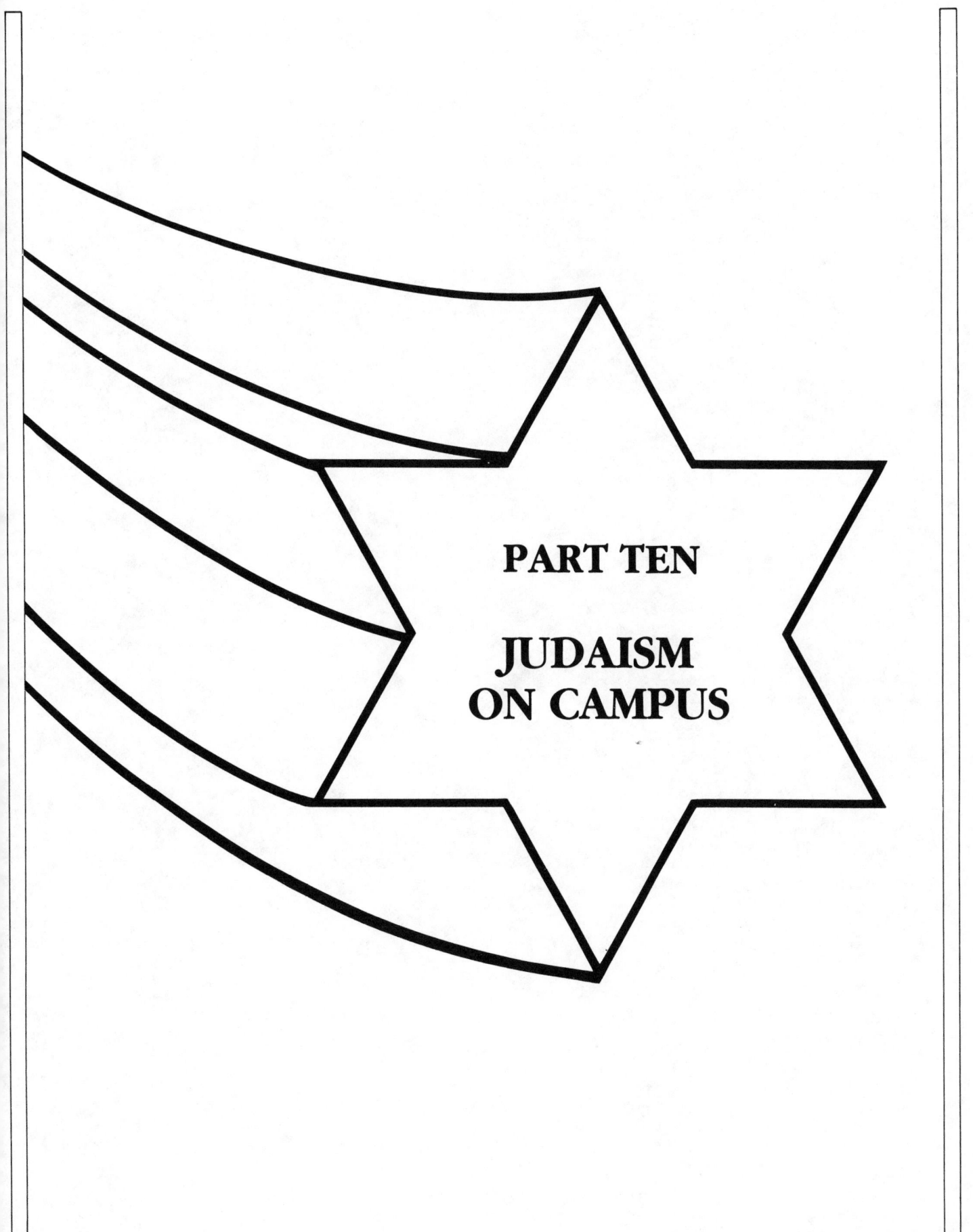

PART TEN

JUDAISM
ON CAMPUS

59

Judaism on Campus

	Enrollment (1985)	Estimated Jewish Enrollment	Judaica Courses; Major	Kosher Food
ALABAMA				
Auburn University Auburn, Alabama	18,000	70	—	—
University of Alabama Tuscaloosa, Alabama	17,000	350	3	Vegetarian Dining
University of Alabama in Birmingham Birmingham, Alabama	12,000	125	—	Dormitory Cooking
ARIZONA				
Arizona State University Tempe, Arizona	38,000	2,200	8; BA	Vegetarian Dining
Northern Arizona University Flagstaff, Arizona	13,000	150	1	Dormitory Cooking
Phoenix College Tempe, Arizona	7,700	100	1; BA	Kosher Meals by: Asu Hillel
University of Arizona Tucson, Arizona	30,000	2,500	13; BA, MA	Kosher Meals—Hillel Vegetarian Dining Dormitory Cooking
ARKANSAS				
University of Arkansas Fayetteville, Arkansas	16,000	60	—	Vegetarian Dining
CALIFORNIA				
California Institute of Technology Pasadena, California	1,500	250	—	Dormitory Cooking
California State University—Chico Chico, California	14,000	250	4	Dormitory Cooking Vegetarian Dining
California State Univ.—Dominguez Hills Los Angeles, California	8,700	150	—	—
California State Univ.—Fresno Fresno, California	15,000	70	2	—
California State Univ.—Fullerton Fullerton, California	25,000	1,250	5	—
California State Univ.—Hayward Hayward, California	11,000	250	—	—
California State Univ.—Long Beach Long Beach, California	33,000	3,000	9; BA	Local Chabad; Vegetarian Dining
California State Univ.—Los Angeles Los Angeles, California	25,000	500	1	—
California State Univ.—Northridge Northridge, California	28,000	8.000	10	—
California State Univ.—San Bernardino San Bernardino, California	—	—	—	—
Cerritos Community College Long Beach, California	20,000	100	—	—
Chapman College Orange, California	1,200	100	—	—
Claremont Colleges Claremont, California	5,500	800	6, BA, MA, PhD	Kosher Meals by Pomona Kitchen Ko-op. Vegetarian Dining Dormitory Cooking

	Enrollment (1985)	Estimated Jewish Enrollment	Judaica Courses; Major	Kosher Food
Cypress College Long Beach, California	12,000	—	—	—
El Camino College Los Angeles, California	28,000	1,000	—	—
Hastings College of Law San Francisco, California	—	400	—	—
Long Beach City College Long Beach, California	26,000	750	—	—
Los Angeles Harbor College Los Angeles, California	11,000	450	—	—
Los Angeles Pierce College Los Angeles, California	30,000	1,500	1	—
Los Angeles Valley College Van Nuys, California	20,000	4,000	5	—
Loyola Marymount University Los Angeles, California	5,500	100	—	—
Loyola University Law School Los Angeles, California	1,400	600	1	—
Mills College Oakland, California	930	50	—	—
Occidental College Los Angeles, California	1,500	120	1	Vegetarian Dining Dormitory Cooking
Pasadena City College Pasadena, California	—	—	—	—
San Diego State University San Diego, California	30,000	4,500	15; BA	Vegetarian Dining
San Francisco State University San Francisco, California	28,000	3,000	2	—
San Jose State University San Jose, California	25,000	1,000	15	Vegetarian Dining Dormitory Cooking
Santa Monica College Los Angeles, California	25,000	1,500	1	—
Southwestern Law School Los Angeles, California	1,700	—	—	—
Stanford University Stanford, California	12,000	1,500	4; BA	—
University of California Medical School San Francisco, California	—	500	—	—
University of California—Berkeley Berkeley, California	30,000	5,500	25; BA, MA, PhD	Kosher Meals by Hebrew Houses Vegetarian Dining Dormitory Cooking Hillel
University of California—Davis Davis, California	19,000	2,200	8; BA	
University of California—Irvine Tustin, California	13,000	1,000	—	—
University of California—Los Angeles Los Angeles, California	32,000	6,500	18; BA, MA, PhD	Vegetarian Dining Kosher Meals-Hillel Dormitory Cooking
University of California—Riverside Riverside, California	3,500	300	1	—
University of California—San Diego San Diego, California	10,000	2,000	5; BA	Vegetarian Dining Dormitory Cooking
University of California—Santa Barbara Goleta, California	16,000	1,000	15; BA	—
University of California—Santa Cruz Santa Cruz, California	7,000	1,500	6	Vegetarian Dining Dormitory Cooking
University of Judaism Los Angeles, California	160	160	35; BA, MA	Kosher Dining
University of Redlands Redlands, California	1,150	25	2	Vegetarian Dining
University of San Francisco San Francisco, California	—	425	—	—
University of Santa Clara San Jose, California	3,300	—	2	—

	Enrollment (1985)	Estimated Jewish Enrollment	Judaica Courses; Major	Kosher Food
University of Southern California Los Angeles, California	25,000	2,000	25; BA, MA, PhD	Kosher Meals by Jewish Bayit Dormitory Cooking
Whittier College Whittier, California	1,500	50	—	Dormitory Cooking
Whittier School of Law Los Angeles, California	—	—		—

COLORADO

Colorado State University Ft. Collins, Colorado	16,000	275	—	Hillel
United States Air Force Academy Colorado Springs, Colorado	4,500	35	—	—
University of Colorado Boulder, Colorado	22,500	1,500	6	Vegetarian Dining Dormitory Cooking
University of Denver Denver, Colorado	9,000	1,000	20; BA	Hillel Co-op
University of Northern Colorado Greeley, Colorado	10,500	150	—	Vegetarian Dining

CONNECTICUT

Central Connecticut State College New Britain, Connecticut	3,000	200	4	
Connecticut College New London, Connecticut	2,000	500	3	Vegetarian Dining
Quinnipiac College New Haven, Connecticut	2,000	100	—	—
Trinity College Hartford, Connecticut	1,700	150	8; BA	Vegetarian Dining
U.S. Coast Guard Academy New London, Connecticut	300	12	—	—
University of Bridgeport Bridgeport, Connecticut	7,500	2,000	4	Kosher Meals by: Dining Hall (Frozen) Dormitory Cooking
University of Connecticut Storrs, Connecticut	15,750	2,000	8; BA	Kosher Meals by: Hillel Kosher Co-Op Vegetarian Dining
University of Hartford West Hartford, Connecticut	8,000	1,500	6	Kosher Meals by A.R.A. Food Service Vegetarian Dining
Wesleyan University Middletown, Connecticut	2,600	900	11; BA	Kosher Meals by: Co-Op at Bayit Vegetarian Dining
Yale University New Haven, Connecticut	10,000	3,000	20; BA, MA, PhD	Kosher Meals by University Kosher Kitchen Vegetarian Dining

DELAWARE

University of Delaware Newark, Delaware	12,000	1,200	1	—

DISTRICT OF COLUMBIA

American University Washington, D.C.	9,100	2,700	10; BA	Vegetarian Dining Dormitory Cooking
Antioch Law School Washington, D.C.	—	100	—	—
Catholic University Washington, D.C.	7,000	300	8; MA, PhD	—
Gallaudet College Washington, D.C.	1,400	100	1	Frozen, on request
George Washington Univ. Washington, D.C.	18,000	5,000	15; BA, MA	Kosher Meals by: Hillel Vegetarian Dining

	Enrollment (1985)	Estimated Jewish Enrollment	Judaica Courses; Major	Kosher Food
Georgetown University Washington, D.C.	10,500	1,500	11; BA	Kosher Meals by: Jewish Student House Vegetarian Dining Dormitory Cooking
Howard University Washington, D.C.	13,000	150	—	—
Mt. Vernon College Washington, D.C.	460	30	—	—
FLORIDA				
Barry University Miami Shores, Florida	2,150	150	BA, MA	Vegetarian Dining
Broward Community College (3 campuses) Fort Lauderdale, Florida	22,000	4,000	1	
College of Boca Raton Pembroke Pines, Florida	450	56	—	
Eckerd College St. Petersburg, Florida	1,300	65	—	Vegetarian Dining Dormitory Cooking
Florida Atlantic Univ. Boca Raton, Florida	6,000	600	1	—
Florida International Univ. Miami, Florida	12,700	1,200	2	Vegetarian Dining
Florida International Univ. North Pembroke Pines, Florida	3,300	280	1	Vegetarian Dining
Florida Southern College Lakeland, Florida	2,000	15	—	—
Florida State University Tallahassee, Florida	22,000	2,000	4	Kosher Meals by: Hillel & FSU Vegetarian Dining
Jacksonville University Jacksonville, Florida	2,600	120	—	Vegetarian Dining Dormitory Cooking
Miami-Dade Community College, North Miami, Florida	24,000	1,000	1	—
Miami-Dade Community College, South Miami, Florida	17,000	1,000	2	Vegetarian Dining
Palm Beach Junior College Pembroke Pines, Florida	2,000	300	1	—
Rollins College Winter Park, Florida	1,350	105	1	Vegetarian Dining
University of Central Florida Orlando, Florida	1,500	400	—	—
University of Florida Gainesville, Florida	35,000	3,800	8; BA, MA, PhD	Kosher Meals by: Hillel
University of Miami Coral Gables, Florida	14,000	2,300	12; BA	Kosher Meals by: Hillel Vegetarian Dining Dormitory Cooking
University of North Florida Mandarin, Florida	4,500	150	1	—
University of South Florida Tampa, Florida	30,000	3,000	5; BA	Kosher Meals by : Hillel Vegetarian Dining
University of South Florida—New College Sarasota, Florida	500	50	—	Vegetarian Dining
University of Tampa Tampa, Florida	2,000	300	1	Vegetarian Dining Dormitory Cooking
GEORGIA				
Emory University Atlanta, Georgia	7,500	3,000	8; BA, MA	Dormitory Cooking
Georgia State University Atlanta, Georgia	23,000	1,000	1	—
Georgia Technical Institute Atlanta, Georgia	11,000	700	—	Dormitory Cooking
Oglethorpe University Atlanta, Georgia	700	125	—	—
University of Georgia Athens, Georgia	23,000	1,200	2	Kosher Meals by: Hillel

	Enrollment (1985)	Estimated Jewish Enrollment	Judaica Courses; Major	Kosher Food
ILLINOIS				
Bradley University Peoria, Illinois	5,100	400	1	—
Chicago Kent School of Law Chicago, Illinois	1,200	900	—	—
De Paul University Chicago, Illinois	1,000	100	BA	—
De Paul University School of Law Chicago, Illinois	800	100	—	—
Illinois State University Normal, Illinois	19,000	400	—	Dormitory Cooking
John Marshall Law School Chicago, Illinois	1,000	800	—	—
Loyola University Chicago, Illinois	11,750	600	BA, MA	Kosher Meals by: Food Service (frozen) Vegetarian Dining
Loyola University Law School Chicago, Illinois	600	60	—	—
Northeastern Illinois Univ. Evanston, Illinois	10,000	500	BA	—
Northern Illinois University DeKalb, Illinois	2,500	700	2	Kosher Meals by: Hillel
Northwestern University Evanston, Illinois	10,000	2,000	15; BA, MA, PhD	Kosher Meals by: Hillel Vegetarian Dining Dormitory Cooking
Northwestern Univ. Dental School Chicago, Illinois	40	30	—	—
Northwestern Univ. Medical School Chicago, Illinois	600	300	—	—
Oakton Community College Des Plaines, Illinois	8,600	2,000	1	—
Southern Illinois Univ. Carbondale, Illinois	23,000	750	—	—
University of Chicago Chicago, Illinois	8,000	1,500	10; BA, MA, PhD	Vegetarian Dining Dormitory Cooking
University of Illinois at Champaign Champaign, Illinois	35,000	3,500	10; BA	Kosher Meals by: Hillel
Univ. of Illinois at Chicago Health Sciences Chicago, Illinois	700	400	—	—
University of Illinois at Chicago Chicago, Illinois	22,000	3,000	BA	—
Western Illinois University Macomb, Illinois	11,000	200	1	—
William S. Scholl School of Podiatry Chicago, Illinois	800	500	—	—
INDIANA				
Indiana University Bloomington, Indiana	30,000	1,800	20; BA, MA, PhD	Vegetarian Dining Dormitory Cooking
Purdue University West Lafayette, Indiana	31,500	600	15	Kosher Meals by: Hillel
IOWA				
Briar Cliff College Sioux City, Iowa	700	40	—	Vegetarian Dining
Drake University Des Moines, Iowa	4,500	400	—	Vegetarian Dining
Grinnell College Grinnell, Iowa	1,200	350	7; BA	Vegetarian Dining
Iowa State University Ames Iowa	26,000	75	—	Vegetarian Dining
Morningside College Sioux City, Iowa	2,000	60	2	—
University of Iowa Iowa City, Iowa	23,000	1,000	7	Vegetarian Dining

	Enrollment (1985)	Estimated Jewish Enrollment	Judaica Courses; Major	Kosher Food
KANSAS				
Kansas State Univ.	19.000	230	5	—
Manhattan, Kansas				
University of Kansas	22,000	1,200	5; BA	Dormitory Cooking
Lawrence, Kansas				
KENTUCKY				
University of Kentucky	22,000	200	3	Dormitory Cooking
Lexington, Kentucky				
University of Louisville	20,000	300	3	Dormitory Cooking
Louisville, Kentucky				
LOUISIANA				
Louisiana State Univ.	30,000	200	2	—
Baton Rouge, Louisiana				
Louisiana Technical Univ.	10,000	12	—	Dormitory Cooking
Ruston, Louisiana				
Loyola University	4,500	125	2	Kosher Meals by: Hillel at Tulane
New Orleans, Louisiana				
Tulane Univ. & Newcomb College	9,000	3,000	12; BA	Kosher Meals by: Hillel
New Orleans, Louisiana				
University of New Orleans	14,000	200	2	Kosher Meals by: Hillel at Tulane
New Orleans, Louisiana				
MAINE				
Bates College	1,400	250	3	Vegetarian Dining Dormitory Cooking
Auburn, Maine				
Bowdoin College	1,400	120	2	Vegetarian Dining Dormitory Cooking
Brunswick, Maine				
Colby College	1,650	100	6	Vegetarian Dining
Waterville, Maine				
University of Maine	10,000	200	1	Vegetarian Dining
Orono, Maine				
MARYLAND				
Catonsville Community College	3,000	360	—	Vegetarian Dining
Catonsville, Maryland				
Goucher College	1,000	300	5	Kosher Meals by: Young Israel
Towson, Maryland				
Hood College	900	30	—	—
Frederick, Maryland				
Johns Hopkins University	3,000	600	15; BA, MA, PhD	Kosher Meals by: Young Israel Dormitory Cooking
Baltimore, Maryland				
Loyola College	5,000	35	1	—
Baltimore, Maryland				
Montgomery College	17,000	2,000	2	—
Rockville, Maryland				
Towson State University	15,000	1,000	3	Vegetarian Dining Dormitory Cooking
Towson, Maryland				
U.S. Naval Academy	4,200	40	—	—
Annapolis, Maryland				
Univ. of Maryland—Baltimore County	6,000	1,500	1	Dormitory Cooking
Baltimore, Maryland				
University of Maryland at Baltimore	6,350	800	—	Dormitory Cooking
Owings Mills, Maryland				
University of Maryland—College Park	35,000	6,000	20; BA, MA	Kosher Meals by: Hillel, Young Israel Vegetarian Dining
College Park, Maryland				
Western Maryland College	1,800	50	BA	Vegetarian Dining
Westminster, Maryland				
MASSACHUSETTS				
Amherst College	1,600	300	4; BA	Kosher Meals by: Food Services Vegetarian Dining
Amherst, Massachusetts				

	Enrollment (1985)	Estimated Jewish Enrollment	Judaica Courses; Major	Kosher Food
Babson College Wellesley, Massachusetts	2,950	800	—	—
Bentley College Waltham, Massachusetts	5,000	200	—	Kosher Meals by: Food Services Dormitory Cooking
Berkeley College of Music Boston, Massachusetts	850	100	—	—
Boston College Newton, Massachusetts	12,000	500	8; BA	—
Boston University Boston, Massachusetts	21,000	6,000	25; BA, MA, PhD	Kosher Meals by: YBU and Hillel
Brandeis University Waltham, Massachusetts	3,350	2,150	60; BA, MA, PhD	Kosher Meals by: Univ. Food Services Vegetarian Dining Dormitory Cooking
Clark University Worcester, Massachusetts	2,000	1,000	20; BA	Kosher Meals by: Clark Vegetarian Dining Dormitory Cooking
Curry College Milton, Massachusetts	850	325	—	Vegetarian Dining
Emerson College Boston, Massachusetts	1,600	500	—	Vegetarian Dining Dormitory Cooking
Harvard University and Radcliffe College Cambridge, Massachusetts	12,000	3,000	30; BA, MA, PhD	Kosher Meals by: Hillel Vegetarian Dining
Lesley College Cambridge, Massachusetts	1,640	380	1	Vegetarian Dining
Massachusetts Bay Community College Wellesley, Massachusetts	4,000	150	—	Dormitory Cooking
Massachusetts College of Art Boston, Massachusetts	1,200	200	—	—
Massachusetts College of Pharmacy Boston, Massachusetts	1,118	50	—	—
Massachusetts Institute of Technology Cambridge, Massachusetts	8,000	2,000	—	Kosher Meals by: MIT & Hillel Vegetarian Dining Dormitory Cooking
Mount Holyoke College South Hadley, Massachusetts	1,850	130	2	Vegetarian Dining Dormitory Cooking
New England Conservatory of Music Boston, Massachusetts	750	150	1	—
Northeastern University Boston, Massachusetts	50,000	5,000	1	Vegetarian Dining Dormitory Cooking
Salem State College Salem, Massachusetts	5,800	150	—	—
Simmons College Boston, Massachusetts	2,800	1,000	—	Kosher Meals by: Coop Kitchen
Smith College Northampton, Massachusetts	2,500	300	5; BA	Kosher Meals by: Food Service Vegetarian Dining
Southeastern Massachusetts Univ. N. Dartmouth, Massachusetts	5,000	200	—	Vegetarian Dining
Suffolk University Boston, Massachusetts	4,600	250	—	—
Tufts University Medford, Massachusetts	6,000	2,100	10; BA	Kosher Meals by: Hillel Co-op Vegetarian Dining
University of Lowell Lowell, Massachusetts	8,800	350	1	—
University of Massachusetts Amherst, Massachusetts	25,900	3,800	12; BA	Kosher Meals by: Food Service Vegetarian Dining
University of Massachusetts—Boston Harbor Boston, Massachusetts	2,220	90	1	—
Wellesley College Wellesley, Massachusetts	2,500	250	4; BA	Kosher Meals by: College Vegetarian Dining
Western New England College Springfield, Massachusetts	5,360	?	2	Univ.—frozen on request

	Enrollment (1985)	Estimated Jewish Enrollment	Judaica Courses; Major	Kosher Food
Westfield State College Westfield, Massachusetts	2,800	50	—	Kosher Meals by: Seiler Food Services Vegetarian Dining Dormitory Cooking
Wheelock College Boston, Massachusetts	700	70	—	Kosher Meals by: Simmons College Vegetarian Dining Dormitory Cooking
Williams College Williamstown, Massachusetts	1,900	170	5; BA	Kosher Meals by: College Jewish Assn. Vegetarian Dining
MICHIGAN				
Central Michigan University Mt. Pleasant, Michigan	16,000	100	4	locally available Vegetarian Dining
Michigan State Univ. E. Lansing, Michigan	39,000	2,500	4	Kosher Meals by: Hillel Co-op Vegetarian Dining Dormitory Cooking
Oakland University Rochester, Michigan	12,000	300	1	Vegetarian Dining
University of Michigan Ann Arbor, Michigan	35,000	6,000	15; BA, MA, PhD	Kosher Meals by: Hillel Vegetarian Dining Dormitory Cooking
Wayne State University Detroit, Michigan	30,000	1,500	3	Kosher Meals by: Public Restaurant
Western Michigan University Kalamazoo, Michigan	20,000	350	3	—
MINNESOTA				
Carleton College Northfield, Minnesota	1,500	86	5	Kosher Meals by: JSC
Macalester College St. Paul, Minnesota	1,500	150	3	Kosher Meals by: Hebrew House
University of Minnesota Minneapolis, Minnesota	47,000	1,800	12; BA	Kosher Meals by: Hillel Vegetarian Dining
MISSISSIPPI				
University of Mississippi University, Mississippi	9,000	45	—	—
MISSOURI				
St. Louis University St. Louis, Missouri	8,200	200	1	—
Stephens College Columbia, Missouri	990	100	1	Vegetarian Dining
University of Missouri—Columbia Columbia, Missouri	22,290	1,000	1	Kosher Meals by: Hillel
University of Missouri—St. Louis Clayton, Missouri	11,400	150	1	Vegetarian Dining
Washington University Clayton, Missouri	8,200	2,400	10; BA	Kosher Meals by: University Vegetarian Dining
Webster College St. Louis, Missouri	1,800	150	1	Dormitory Cooking
NEBRASKA				
Creighton University Omaha, Nebraska	4,100	150	2	Vegetarian Dining
University of Nebraska Lincoln, Nebraska	20,000	60	—	—
University of Nebraska Omaha, Nebraska	15,500	150	5; BA	Vegetarian Dining
NEVADA				
University of Nevada Las Vegas, Nevada	11,500	340	—	—

	Enrollment (1985)	Estimated Jewish Enrollment	Judaica Courses; Major	Kosher Food
University of Nevada Reno, Nevada	9,900	225	2	—
NEW HAMPSHIRE				
Dartmouth College Hanover, New Hampshire	4,600	450	6; BA	Kosher Meals by: Hillel Vegetarian Dining
University of New Hampshire Durham, New Hampshire	10,000	400	—	Vegetarian Dining
NEW JERSEY				
Atlantic Community College Mays Landing, New Jersey	1,500	150	—	—
Drew University Madison, New Jersey	1,850	160	2	—
Fairleigh Dickinson Univ. Newark, New Jersey	3,100	?	?	—
Glassboro State College Glassboro, New Jersey	10,000	1,000	1	Vegetarian Dining Frozen, on request
Kean College of New Jersey Union, New Jersey	13,400	2,000	6	—
Montclair State College Upper Montclair, New Jersey	14,000	375	3	—
Princeton University Princeton, New Jersey	5,700	1,000	12; BA	Kosher Meals by: Univ. and Young Israel Vegetarian Dining Dormitory Cooking
Rider College Trenton, New Jersey	4,000	500	—	—
Rutgers U. (incl. Douglass, Cook, Lvgstn.) New Brunswick, New Jersey	21,000	3,000	12; BA	Kosher Meals by: Hillel Vegetarian Dining
Rutgers University Newark, New Jersey	7,000	300	8	—
Stevens Institute of Technology Hoboken, New Jersey	3,100	400	—	Dormitory Cooking
Stockton State College Pomona, New Jersey	4,000	400	4	Vegetarian Dining
Trenton State College Trenton, N.J.	10,000	200	—	—
NEW MEXICO				
New Mexico State Univ. University Park, N.M.	12,000	100	3	Dormitory Cooking
University of New Mexico Albuquerque, N.M.	23,000	150	—	—
NEW YORK				
Adelphi University Garden City, New York	12,000	1,800	3	Kosher Meals by: University
Alfred University Alfred, New York	2,000	300	1	Vegetarian Dining Dormitory Cooking
Bramson ORT Technical Inst. New York, New York	225	150	2	—
C. W. Post Center of Long Island U. New York, New York	13,000	3,000	15; BA	—
Colgate University Hamilton, New York	2,600	450	3; BA	Kosher Meals By: Colgate Jewish Union Vegetarian Dining Dormitory Cooking
Columbia University and Barnard College New York, New York	18,000	7,000	35; BA, MA, PhD	Kosher Meals by: Barnard and Residences Vegetarian Dining
Cornell University Ithaca, New York	17,000	3,200	14; BA, MA, PhD	Kosher Meals by: Young Israel Vegetarian Dining Dormitory Cooking

	Enrollment (1985)	Estimated Jewish Enrollment	Judaica Courses; Major	Kosher Food
CUNY—Baruch College New York, New York	15,000	2,000	10; BA	—
CUNY—Brooklyn College Brooklyn, New York	25,000	15,000	50; BA, MA	Kosher Meals by: Public Facility
CUNY—City College New York, New York	13,000	1,000	30	Kosher Meals by: Hillel
CUNY—Hunter College New York, New York	17,800	3,000	17; BA	—
CUNY—Queens College Flushing, New York	16,000	8,000	25; BA	Kosher Meals by: Campus Restaurants
Hamilton College Clinton, New York	1,600	160	2; BA	Univ. (on request) Vegetarian Dining
Hobart & William Smith Colleges Geneva, New York	1,850	350	9; BA	Vegetarian Dining Dormitory Cooking
Hofstra University Hempstead, New York	9,500	2,500	7; BA	Kosher Meals by: ARA
Ithaca College Ithaca, New York	5,000	1,200	—	Vegetarian Dining Dormitory Cooking
New York Institute of Technology New York, New York	10,000	—	1	—
New York University New York, New York	40,000	15,000	30; BA, MA, PhD	Kosher Meals by: Kosher Kitchen Dormitory Cooking
Pace University—Downtown New York, New York	13,000	350	2	local restaurants
Pace University—Westchester Pleasantville, New York	3,700	250	—	Dormitory Cooking
Rensselaer Polytechnic Institute Troy, New York	6,000	800	—	Vegetarian Dining
Rochester Inst. of Tech./NTID Rochester, New York	16,000	1,125	—	Kosher Meals by: Co-op
Russell Sage College Troy, New York	1,400	300	—	—
Saint Lawrence Univ. Canton, New York	2,100	50	2	Kosher Meals by: Food Service Vegetarian Dining
Sarah Lawrence College Bronxville, New York	850	250	1	—
Skidmore College Saratoga Springs, New York	2,100	450	2	Vegetarian Dining
SUNY at Albany Albany, New York	16,000	5,000	19; BA	Kosher Meals by: Univ. Aux. Services Vegetarian Dining
SUNY at Binghamton Binghamton, New York	12,000	6,000	10; BA	Kosher Meals by: Campus Enterprises Vegetarian Dining Dormitory Cooking
SUNY at Buffalo Buffalo, New York	28,000	3,500	20; BA, MA	Vegetarian Dining Dormitory Cooking
SUNY at Cortland Cortland, New York	6,000	400	1	—
SUNY at New Paltz New Paltz, New York	7,000	1,000	5	Vegetarian Dining Dormitory Cooking
SUNY at Oswego Oswego, New York	6,500	1,000	1	Kosher Meals by: Food Service
SUNY at Stony Brook Stony Brook, New York	16,500	4,000	7; BA	Kosher Meals by: University Vegetarian Dining Dormitory Cooking
SUNY College at Brockport Brockport, New York	7,400	600	5	Kosher Meals by: Food Service Vegetarian Dining Dormitory Cooking
SUNY College at Buffalo Buffalo, New York	15,000	1,000	10; BA	Kosher Meals by: Hillel/JSU Vegetarian Dining
SUNY College at Purchase Purchase, New York	1,500	500	4	—

	Enrollment (1985)	Estimated Jewish Enrollment	Judaica Courses; Major	Kosher Food
Syracuse University Syracuse, New York	16,000	2,000	6	—
Union College Schenectady, New York	2,000	650	10	Kosher Meals by: Kosher Co-op
United States Military Academy West Point, New York	4,400	46	—	—
University of Rochester Rochester, New York	7,500	1,400	10; BA	Kosher Meals by: Food Service Vegetarian Dining Dormitory Cooking
Vassar College Poughkeepsie, New York	2,250	800	10	Vegetarian Dining Dormitory Cooking
Yeshiva University New York, New York	7,000	4,800	200; BA, MA, PhD.	Univ. Cafeterias

NORTH CAROLINA

Duke University Durham, North Carolina	8,800	2,000	10; BA, MA, PhD	Vegetarian Dining Dormitory Cooking
East Carolina Univ. Greenville, North Carolina	14,000	125	—	—
Guilford College Chapel Hill, North Carolina	1,675	40	—	—
North Carolina State University—Raleigh Raleigh, North Carolina	22,000	130	—	Dormitory Cooking
Univ. of North Carolina—Chapel Hill Chapel Hill, North Carolina	21,500	700	10; BA, MA, PhD	Dormitory Cooking
Univ. of North Carolina—Charlotte Chapel Hill, North Carolina	10,000	75	—	Dormitory Cooking
Univ. of North Carolina—Greensboro Greensboro, North Carolina	10,000	100	—	—

OHIO

Baldwin Wallace University Cleveland, Ohio	3,400	20	1	—
Bowling Green State University Bowling Green, Ohio	16,000	250	—	—
Case Western Reserve University Cleveland, Ohio	7,500	1,100	3; BA	Kosher Meals by: Hillel Co-op/Restaurant
Cleveland State University Cleveland, Ohio	19,000	800	—	—
College of Wooster Wooster, Ohio	1,875	24	1	Vegetarian Dining
Cuyahoga Community College Cleveland, Ohio	23,000	300	—	—
Denison University Granville, Ohio	2,200	100	4	Vegetarian Dining Dormitory Cooking
Hiram College Cleveland, Ohio	1,000	20	—	—
John Carroll University Cleveland, Ohio	4,000	200	4	—
Kent State University Kent, Ohio	20,000	1,000	10; BA	Dormitory Cooking
Kenyon College Gambier, Ohio	1,450	150	3	Vegetarian Dining
Miami University Oxford, Ohio	14,700	700	3	Kosher Meals by: Hillel Kosher Co-op
Oberlin College Oberlin, Ohio	2,750	1,100	4; BA	Kosher Meals by: University Vegetarian Dining
Ohio State University Columbus, Ohio	53,000	2,700	25; BA, MA, PhD	Kosher Meals by: Hillel
Ohio University Athens, Ohio	14,500	900	—	Kosher Meals by: Hillel Co-op
Ohio Wesleyan University Delaware, Ohio	2,240	150	4	Vegetarian Dining Dormitory Cooking
University of Cincinnati Cincinnati, Ohio	35,000	2,500	10; BA	Kosher Meals by: Hillel Dining Co-op

	Enrollment (1985)	Estimated Jewish Enrollment	Judaica Courses; Major	Kosher Food
University of Toledo Toledo, Ohio	19,000	450	1	—
OKLAHOMA				
University of Oklahoma Norman, Oklahoma	24,000	350	2	Kosher Meals by: Hillel Co-op
OREGON				
Oregon State University Corvallis, Oregon	16,500	300	—	—
University of Oregon Eugene, Oregon	15,000	700	5	Community Co-op Vegetarian Dining
PENNSYLVANIA				
Albright College Reading, Pennsylvania	1,300	110	—	Vegetarian Dining Dormitory Cooking
Allegheny College Meadville, Pennsylvania	1,950	50	1	—
Beaver College Jenkintown, Pennsylvania	800	200	—	—
Bryn Mawr College Haverford, Pennsylvania	800	200	4; BA	—
Bucknell University Lewisburg, Pennsylvania	3,400	240	6	—
Carnegie-Mellon Univ. Pittsburgh, Pennsylvania	5,000	600	3	Kosher Meals by: Hillel at Pitt.
Cedar Crest College Allentown, Pennsylvania	700	20	—	—
Chatham College Pittsburgh, Pennsylvania	600	100	—	Kosher Meals by: Hillel at Pitt.
Community College of Philadelphia Philadelphia, Pennsylvania	11,000	500	2	—
Dickinson College Carlisle, Pennsylvania	1,700	200	15; BA	—
Drexel University Philadelphia, Pennsylvania	11,000	2,000	1	Kosher Meals by: Hillel at Penn. Dormitory Cooking
Duquesne University Pittsburgh, Pennsylvania	7,700	800	1	Kosher Meals by: Hillel at Pitt.
Elizabethtown College Elizabethtown, Pennsylvania	1,450	20	1	Vegetarian Dining
Franklin & Marshall College Lancaster, Pennsylvania	2,000	500	3	Dormitory Cooking
Harcum Junior College Philadelphia, Pennsylvania	850	200	—	—
Haverford College Haverford, Pennsylvania	800	250	4; BA	Kosher Meals by: Hillel Co-op
Indiana University of Pa. Indiana, Pennsylvania	12,000	80	—	Vegetarian Dining
Kutztown State College Kutztown, Pennsylvania	5,500	50	—	Vegetarian Dining Dormitory Cooking
La Salle College Philadelphia, Pennsylvania	7,000	300	1	—
Lafayette College Easton, Pennsylvania	2,000	250	14; BA	Kosher Meals by: Hillel Co-op
Lehigh University Bethlehem, Pennsylvania	6,200	600	5	Kosher Meals by: University Dormitory Cooking
Millersville University Millersville, Pennsylvania	6,000	50	—	—
Moravian College Bethlehem, Pennsylvania	1,275	30	2	Dormitory Cooking
Muhlenberg College Allentown, Pennsylvania	1,500	375	6	Vegetarian Dining Dormitory Cooking
Pennsylvania State Univ. State College, Pennsylvania	33,000	3,200	4	Dormitory Cooking

	Enrollment (1985)	Estimated Jewish Enrollment	Judaica Courses; Major	Kosher Food
Pennsylvania State Univ.—Ogontz Philadelphia, Pennsylvania	1,500	600	—	—
Philadelphia College of Pharmacy & Science Philadelphia, Pennsylvania	1,100	100	—	Vegetarian Dining
Philadelphia College of Textiles & Science Philadelphia, Pennsylvania	2,800	700	—	Vegetarian Dining
Point Park College Pittsburgh, Pennsylvania	1,650	150	—	Kosher Meals by: Hillel at Pitt.
St. Joseph's College Philadelphia, Pennsylvania	?	200	—	—
Swarthmore College Philadelphia, Pennsylvania	1,275	150	3	Kosher Meals by: Co-op
Temple University—Main & Ambler Campus Philadelphia, Pennsylvania	33,000	6,000	25; BA, MA, PhD	Kosher Meals by: Hillel Vegetarian Dining
University of Pennsylvania Philadelphia, Pennsylvania	16,875	6,000	25; BA, MA	Kosher Meals by: Hillel Vegetarian Dining Dormitory Cooking
University of Pittsburgh Pittsburgh, Pennsylvania	31,600	4,000	6; BA, MA	Kosher Meals by: Hillel
Ursinus College Collegeville, Pennsylvania	1,100	70	—	Vegetarian Dining Dormitory Cooking
Villanova University Philadelphia, Pennsylvania	?	200	—	—
Washington & Jefferson College Washington, Pennsylvania	1,300	100	—	Vegetarian Dining Dormitory Cooking
West Chester University West Chester, Pennsylvania	9,300	500	5	Locally available Vegetarian Dining
Widener College Chester, Pennsylvania	4,200	60	—	Vegetarian Dining

RHODE ISLAND

Brown University Providence, Rhode Island	6,400	1,600	12; BA, MA, PhD	Kosher Meals by: Hillel & Young Israel Vegetarian Dining Dormitory Cooking
Bryant College Smithfield, Rhode Island	4,000	250	—	—
Rhode Island School of Design Providence, Rhode Island	—	—	2	Kosher Meals by: Brown Hillel Vegetarian Dining
University of Rhode Island Kingston, Rhode Island	8,000	800	4	Kosher Meals by: Hillel Vegetarian Dining

SOUTH CAROLINA

Clemson University Clemson, South Carolina	12,000	120	2	Dormitory Cooking
The Citadel-Military College of S.C. Charleston, South Carolina	1,900	18	—	—
University of South Carolina Columbia, South Carolina	20,000	650	12	Vegetarian Dining

TENNESSEE

George Peabody College for Teachers Nashville, Tennessee	1,500	100	—	—
Memphis State University Memphis, Tennessee	26,000	300	1	Kosher Meals by : JSU Dormitory Cooking
Rhodes College Memphis, Tennessee	1,000	?	—	JSU at Memphis State Univ.
Southern College of Optometry Memphis, Tennessee	600	?	—	Kosher Meals by: JSU
Southwestern University Memphis, Tennessee	1,000	—	—	Kosher Meals by: JSU
U. of Tenn.—Medical & Nursing Memphis, Tennessee	2,000	?	—	Kosher Meals by: JSU
University of Tennessee—Knoxville Knoxville, Tennessee	25,000	500	4	Vegetarian Dining

	Enrollment (1985)	Estimated Jewish Enrollment	Judaica Courses; Major	Kosher Food
University of Tennessee—Memphis Memphis, Tennessee	2,000	—	—	Kosher Meals by: JSU
Vanderbilt University Nashville, Tennessee	7,000	350	3	—
TEXAS				
Brookhaven College Dallas, Texas	7,500	90	—	—
North Texas State Univ. Denton, Texas	18,800	250	—	—
Rice University Houston, Texas	3,600	250	2	Vegetarian Dining
Richland College Dallas, Texas	14,000	90	—	—
Southern Methodist Univ. Dallas, Texas	9,200	400	2	—
Texas A & M University College Station, Texas	40,000	800	—	Hillel
Texas Medical Center (Baylor & V. T.) Houston, Texas	2,300	500	—	Hillel
Texas Tech University Lubbock, Texas	23,000	150	3	—
University of Houston Houston, Texas	35,000	2,000	3	Hillel
University of Texas—Austin Austin, Texas	49,000	3,200	15; BA, MA, PhD	Dormitory Cooking
University of Texas at Arlington Arlington, Texas	23,000	300	—	—
University of Texas at Dallas Dallas, Texas	10,000	75	—	—
UTAH				
University of Utah Salt Lake City, Utah	22,000	150	10; BA, MA, PhD	Synagogue Co-op
VERMONT				
Middlebury College Middlebury, Vermont	1,900	190	1	Vegetarian Dining Dormitory Cooking
University of Vermont Burlington, Vermont	10,000	800	5	—
VIRGINIA				
College of William & Mary Williamsburg, Virginia	6,000	200	3	Vegetarian Dining
George Mason University Fairfax, Virginia	8,000	150	—	Vegetarian Dining
James Madison University Harrisonburg, Virginia	9,000	200	3	—
Northern Virginia Community College Annandale, Virginia	20,000	100	—	Vegetarian Dining
Old Dominion University Norfolk, Virginia	14,000	300	—	Vegetarian Dining
University of Richmond Richmond, Virginia	2,857	65	2	Kosher Meals by: VCU Kosher Kitchen
University of Virginia Charlottesville, Virginia	16,000	1,100	4; BA, MA, PhD	Kosher Meals by: Hillel Kitchen Vegetarian Dining Dormitory Cooking
Virginia Commonwealth Univ. Richmond, Virginia	19,428	800	7	Kosher Meals by: Hillel Kitchen Vegetarian Dining Dormitory Cooking
Virginia Polytechnic Inst. & State U. Blacksburg, Virginia	21,000	550	—	Community Co-op
WASHINGTON				
University of Puget Sound Tacoma, Washington	4,000	50	—	—

	Enrollment (1985)	Estimated Jewish Enrollment	Judaica Courses; Major	Kosher Food
University of Washington Seattle, Washington	32,500	1,700	4; BA	—
Washington State University Pullman, Washington	17,000	200	—	Vegetarian Dining
WEST VIRGINIA				
West Virginia University Morgantown, West Virginia	22,000	450	1	Vegetarian Dining Dormitory Cooking
WISCONSIN				
Beloit College Beloit, Wisconsin	1,100	100	6; BA	Vegetarian Dining
University of Wis.—Milwaukee/Marquette Milwaukee, Wisconsin	27,000	650	6	Kosher Meals by: Hillel Kitchen Available
University of Wisconsin Madison, Wisconsin	42,000	3,600	13; BA, MA, PhD	Kosher Meals by: Kibbutz Langdon Vegetarian Dining
CANADA				
Carleton University Ottawa, Ontario K1N 7Y2	10,000	750	9	Vegetarian Dining
Concordia University—Sir George & Loyola Montreal, Que. H3A 1R8	10,000	600	20; BA, MA, PhD	Kosher Meals by: McGill Hillel
Dalhousie University Halifax, Nova Scotia	9,000	200	—	Locally available
Dawson Cegep Montreal, Que. H3A 1R8	8.000	600	—	—
Marianopolis Cegep Montreal, Que. H3A IR8	1,300	250	—	—
McGill University Montreal, Que. H3A 1R8	18,000	4,000	50; BA, MA, PhD	Kosher Meals by : Hillel Vegetarian Dining Dormitory Cooking
McMaster University Toronto, Ontario	?	300	—	—
Queen's University Kingston, Ontario	10,000	400	2	Hillel
University of Alberta Edmonton, Al. T6G 2E0	25,000	300	3	Kosher Meals by: Hillel
University of British Columbia Vancouver, B.C. V6T 1W5	23,000	400	4; BA, MA	Kosher Meals by: Hillel
University of Calgary Calgary, Alberta	20,000	400	—	JCC
University of Guelph Guelph, Ontario	?	300	—	—
University of Manitoba Winnipeg, Man. R3T 2N2	20,000	800	14; BA	—
University of Montreal Montreal, Que. H3A 1K8	—	500	10	—
University of Ottawa Ottawa, Ont. K1N 7Y2	17,000	750	2	Vegetarian Dining
University of Quebec/Cegep St. Laurent Montreal, Que. H3A 1K8	—	300	—	—
University of Toronto Toronto, Ont. M5S 2H4	37,000	3,000	50; BA	Kosher Meals by: Hillel and University Residents
University of Waterloo Waterloo, Ontario	?	300	—	—
University of Western Ontario London, Ontario	20,000	800	1	Hillel
University of Windsor Windsor, Ontario	?	300	—	—
University of Winnipeg Winnipeg, Manitoba	2,000	100	3	—
Vanier Cegep (St. Croix & Snowdown) Montreal, Que.	6,000	1,500	—	—
York University Downsview, Ont. M6C 1S3	20,000	3,500	8; BA	Kosher Meals by: Public Restaurant Vegetarian Dining

PART ELEVEN

SACRED
CYCLES:
JEWISH TIME

1985

5745/46   תשמ״ה / תשמ״ו

Day	January (Tevet)	February	March	April	May	June	July	August	September	October	November	December
1	8 Tevet	10	8	10	10	12 Naso	12	14	15	16 Hol ha-Mo'ed	17	18
2	9	11 Be-Shallah	9 Tezavveh / Zakhor	11	11	13	13	15	16	17	18 Va-Yera	19
3	10 Fast	12	10	12	12	14	14	16 Va-Ethannan	17	18	19	20
4	11	13	11	13	13 Aharei Mot / Kedoshim	15	15	17	18	19	20	21
5	12 Va-Yehi	14	12	14	14	16	16	18	19	20	21	22
6	13	15	13 Ta'anit Esther	15 Pesah	15	17	17 Balak	19	20	21 Hoshana Rabba	22	23
7	14	16	14 Purim	16 Omer	16	18	18 Fast	20	21 Ki Tavo	22 Shemini Azeret	23	24 Va-Yeshev
8	15	17	15 Shushan Purim	17 Hol ha-Mo'ed	17	19 Be-Ha'alotkha	19	21	22	23 Simhat Torah / Ve-Zot Ha-Berakhah	24	25 Hanukkah 1
9	16	18 Yitro	16 Ki Tissa	18	18 Lag ba-Omer	20	20	22	23	24	25 Hayyei Sarah	26 (2)
10	17	19	17	19	19	21	21	23 Ekev	24	25	26	27 (3)
11	18	20	18	20	20 Emor	22	22	24	25	26	27	28 (4)
12	19 Shemot	21	19	21 Pesah	21	23	23	25	26	27 Bereshit	28	29 (5)
13	20	22	20	22	22	24	24 Pinhas	26	27	28	29	1 Tevet R.H. (6)
14	21	23	21	23	23	25	25	27	28 Nizzavim	29	1 Kislev R.H.	2 Mi-Kez (7)
15	22	24	22	24	24	26 Shelah	26	28	29	30 R.H.	2	3 (8)
16	23	25 Mishpatim / Shekalim	23 Va-Yakhel Pekudei / Parah	25	25	27	27	29	1 Tishri Rosh Ha-Shanah	1 Heshvan R.H.	3 Toledot	4
17	24	26	24	26	26	28	28	30 R.H. Re'eh	2	2	4	5
18	25	27	25	27	27 Be-Har / Be-Hukkotai	29	29	1 Elul R.H.	3 Fast	3	5	6
19	26 Va-Era	28	26	28	28	30 R.H.	1 Av R.H.	2	4	4 Noah	6	7
20	27	29	27	29 Shemini	29	1 Tammuz R.H.	2 Mattot / Masei	3	5	5	7	8
21	28	30 R.H.	28	30 R.H.	1 Sivan R.H.	2	3	4	6 Va-Yelekh / Shabbat Shuvah	6	8	9 Va-Yiggash
22	29	1 Adar R.H.	29	1 Iyyar R.H.	2	3 Korah	4	5	7	7	9	10 Fast
23	1 Shevat R.H.	2 Terumah	1 Nisan R.H. Va-Yikra / Ha-Hodesh	2	3	4	5	6	8	8	10 Va-Yeze	11
24	2	3	2	3	4	5	6	7 Shofetim	9	9	11	12
25	3	4	3	4 Yom ha-Azma'ut	5 Be-Midbar	6	7	8	10 Yom Kippur	10	12	13
26	4 Bo	5	4	5	6 Shavuot	7	8	9	11	11 Lekh Lekha	13	14
27	5	6	5	6 Tazria / Mezora	7	8	9 Devarim / Tishah be-Av	10	12	12	14	15
28	6	7	6	7	8	9	10 Fast	11	13 Ha'azinu	13	15	16 Va-Yehi
29	7		7	8	9	10 Hukkat	11	12	14	14	16	17
30	8		8 Zav / Shabbat ha-Gadol	9	10	11	12	13	15 Sukkot	15	17 Va-Yishlah	18
31	9		9		11		13	14 Ki Teze		16		19

1986

5746/47   ה'תשמ״ו / ה'תשמ״ז

Day	January	February	March	April	May	June	July	August	September	October	November	December
1	20 Tevet	22 Yitro	20 Ki Tissa	21	22 Pesah	23	24	25	27	27	29 Bereshit	29
2	21	23	21	22	23	24	25	26 Mattot Masei	28	28	30 R.H.	30 R.H.
3	22	24	22	23	24 Aharei Mot	25	26	27	29	29	1 Heshvan R.H.	1 Kislev R.H.
4	23 Shemot	25	23	24	25	26	27	28	30 R.H.	1 Tishri Rosh Ha-Shanah	2	2
5	24	26	24	25 Shemini / Ha-Hodesh	26	27	28 Shelah	29	1 Elul R.H.	2	3	3
6	25	27	25	26	27	28	29	1 Av R.H.	2 Shofetim	3 Fast	4	4 Toledot
7	26	28	26	27	28	29 Be-Midbar	30 R.H.	2	3	4	5	5
8	27	29 Mishpatim	27 Va-Yakhel / Shekalim	28	29	1 Sivan R.H.	1 Tammuz R.H.	3	4	5	6 No'ah	6
9	28	30 R.H.	28	29	30 R.H.	2	2	4 Devarim	5	6	7	7
10	29	1 Adar I R.H.	29	1 Nisan R.H.	1 Iyyar R.H. / Kedoshim	3	3	5	6	7	8	8
11	1 Shevat R.H. / Va-Era	2	30 R.H.	2	2	4	4	6	7	8 Ha'azinu / Shabbat Shuvah	9	9
12	2	3	1 Adar II R.H.	3 Tazri'a	3	5	5 Korah	7	8	9	10	10
13	3	4	2	4	4	6 Shavuot	6	8	9 Ki Teze	10 Yom Kippur	11	11 Va-Yeze
14	4	5	3	5	5 Yom ha-Azma'ut	7 (Shavuot)	7	9 Tishah be-Av	10	11	12	12
15	5	6 Terumah	4 Pekudei	6	6	8	8	10	11	12	13 Lekh Lekha	13
16	6	7	5	7	7	9	9	11 Va-Ethannan	12	13	14	14
17	7	8	6	8	8 Emor	10	10	12	13	14	15	15
18	8 Bo	9	7	9	9	11	11	13	14	15 Sukkot	16	16
19	9	10	8	10 Mezora / Shabbat ha-Gadol	10	12	12 Hukkat / Balak	14	15	16 Hol ha-Mo'ed	17	17
20	10	11	9	11	11	13	13	15	16 Ki Tavo	17 Hol ha-Mo'ed	18	18 Va-Yishlah
21	11	12	10	12	12	14 Naso	14	16	17	18 Hol ha-Mo'ed	19	19
22	12	13 Tezavveh	11 Va-Yikra / Zakhor	13	13	15	15	17	18	19 Hol ha-Mo'ed	20 Va-Yera	20
23	13	14	12	14	14	16	16	18 Ekev	19	20 Hol ha-Mo'ed	21	21
24	14	15	13 Ta'anit Esther	15 Pesah	15 Be-Har	17	17 Fast	19	20	21 Hoshana Rabba	22	22
25	15 Be-Shallah	16	14 Purim	16 Omer	16	18	18	20	21	22 Shemini Azeret	23	23
26	16	17	15 Shushan Purim	17 Hol ha-Mo'ed	17	19	19 Pinhas	21	22	23 Simhat Torah / Ve-Zot Ha-Berakhah	24	24
27	17	18	16	18 Hol ha-Mo'ed	18 Lag ba-Omer	20	20	22	23 Nizzavim / va-Yelekh	24	25	25 Va-Yeshev / Hanukkah 1
28	18	19	17	19 Hol ha-Mo'ed	19	21 Be-Ha'alotkha	21	23	24	25	26	26 Hanukkah 2
29	19		18 Zav / Parah	20 Hol ha-Mo'ed	20	22	22	24	25	26	27 Hayyei Sarah	27 Hanukkah 3
30	20		19	21 Pesah	21	23	23	25 Re'eh	26	27	28	28 Hanukkah 4
31	21		20		22 Be-Hukkotai		24	26		28		29 Hanukkah 5

1987

5747/48 — תשמ״ז / תשמ״ח

	January	February	March	April	May	June	July	August	September	October	November	December
1	30 Kislev R. Ḥ. 6 Ḥanukkah	2	30 R. Ḥ.	2	2	4	4	6 Devarim	7	8	9	10
2	1 Tevet R. Ḥ. 7	3	1 Adar R. Ḥ.	3	3 Tazri'a Meẓora	5	5	7	8	9	10	11
3	2 Mi-Keẓ 8	4	2	4	4	6 Shavuot	6	8	9	10 Yom Kippur	11	12
4	3	5	3	5 Va-Yikra	5 Yom ha-Aẓma'ut	7	7 Ḥukkat	9 Tishah be-Av	10	11	12	13
5	4	6	4	6	6	8	8	10	11 Ki Teẓe	12	13	14 Va-Yishlaḥ
6	5	7	5	7	7	9 Naso	9	11	12	13	14	15
7	6	8 Bo	6 Terumah	8	8	10	10	12	13	14	15 Va-Yera	16
8	7	9	7	9	9	11	11	13 Va-Ethannan	14	15 Sukkot	16	17
9	8	10	8	10	10 Aḥarei Mot Kedoshim	12	12	14	15	16	17	18
10	9 Va-Yiggash	1i	9	11	11	13	13	15	16	17 Ḥol ha-Mo'ed	18	19
11	10 Fast	12	10	12 Ẓav Shabbat ha-Gadol	12	14	14 Balak	16	17	18	19	20
12	11	13	11 Ta'anit Esther	13	13	15	15	17	18 Ki Tavo	19	20	21 Va-Yeshev
13	12	14	12	14	14	16 Be-Ha'alotkha	16	18	19	20	21	22
14	13	15 Be-Shallaḥ	13 Teẓavveh Zakhor	15 Pesaḥ	15	17	17 Fast	19	20	21 Hoshana Rabba	22 Ḥayyei Sarah	23
15	14	16	14 Purim	16 Omer	16	18	18	20 Ekev	21	22 Shemini Aẓeret	23	24
16	15	17	15 Shushan Purim	17 Ḥol ha-Mo'ed	17 Emor	19	19	21	22	23 Simḥat Torah Ve-Zot Ha-Berakhah	24	25 Ḥanukkah 1
17	16 Va-Yeḥi	18	16	18	18 Lag ba-Omer	20	20	22	23	24 Bereshit	25	26 2
18	17	19	17	19	19	21	21 Pinḥas	23	24	25	26	27 3
19	18	20	18	20	20	22	22	24	25 Niẓẓavim Va-Yelekh	26	27	28 Mi-Keẓ 4
20	19	21	19	21 Pesaḥ	21	23 Shelaḥ	23	25	26	27	28	29 5
21	20	22 Yitro	20 Ki Tissa Parah	22	22	24	24	26	27	28	29 Toledot	30 R. Ḥ. 6
22	21	23	21	23	23	25	25	27 Re'eh	28	29	1 Kislev R. Ḥ.	1 Tevet R. Ḥ. 7
23	22	24	22	24	24 Be-Har Be-Ḥukkotai	26	26	28	29	30 R. Ḥ.	2	2 8
24	23 Shemot	25	23	25	25	27	27	29	1 Tishri Rosh Ha-Shanah	1 Ḥeshvan R. Ḥ. No'aḥ	3	3
25	24	26	24	26 Shemini	26	28	28 Mattot Masei	30 R. Ḥ.	2	2	4	4
26	25	27	25	27	27	29	29	1 Elul R. Ḥ.	3 Ha'azinu Shabbat Shuvah	3	5	5 Va-Yiggash
27	26	28	26	28	28	30 R. Ḥ. Koraḥ	1 Av R. Ḥ.	2	4 Fast	4	6	6
28	27	29 Mishpatim Shekalim	27 Va-Yakhel Pekudei Ha-Ḥodesh	29	29	1 Tammuz R. Ḥ.	2	3	5	5	7 Va-Yeẓe	7
29	28		28	30 R. Ḥ.	1 Sivan R. Ḥ.	2	3	4 Shofetim	6	6	8	8
30	29		29	1 Iyyar R. Ḥ.	2 Be-Midbar	3	4	5	7	7	9	9
31	1 Shevat R. Ḥ. Va-Era		1 Nisan R. Ḥ.		3		5	6		8 Lekh Lekha		10 Fast

1988

5748/49

התשמ"ח / התשמ"ט

#	January	February	March	April	May	June	July	August	September	October	November	December
1	11 Tevet	13	12	14	14	16	16	18	19	20 Hol ha-Mo'ed	21	22
2	12 Va-Yehi	14	13 Ta'anit Esther	15 Pesah	15	17	17 Balak	19	20	21 Hoshana Rabba	22	23
3	13	15	14 Purim	16 Omer	16	18	18 Fast	20	21 Ki Tavo	22 Shemini Azeret	23	24 Va-Yeshev
4	14	16	15 Shushan Purim	17 Hol ha-Mo'ed	17	19 Be-Ha'alotkha	19	21	22	23 Simhat Torah Ve-Zot Ha-Berakhah	24	25 Hanukkah 1
5	15	17	16 Ki Tissa	18	18 Lag ba-Omer	20	20	22	23	24	25 Hayyei Sarah	26 2
6	16	18 Yitro	17	19	19	21	21	23 Ekev	24	25	26	27 3
7	17	19	18	20	20 Emor	22	22	24	25	26	27	28 4
8	18	20	19	21 Pesah	21	23	23	25	26	27 Bereshit	28	29 5
9	19 Shemot	21	20	22 Pesah	22	24	24 Pinhas	26	27	28	29	1 Tevet R.H. 6
10	20	22	21	23	23	25	25	27	28 Nizzavim	29	1 Kislev R.H.	2 Mi-Kez 7
11	21	23	22	24	24	26 Shelah	26	28	29	30 R.H.	2	3 8
12	22	24	23 Va-Yakhel Pekudei Parah	25	25	27	27	29	1 Tishri Rosh Ha-Shanah	1 Heshvan R.H.	3 Toledot	4
13	23	25 Mishpatim Shekalim	24	26	26	28	28	30 R.H. Re'eh	2	2	4	5
14	24	26	25	27	27 Be-Har Be-Hukkotai	29	29	1 Elul R.H.	3 Fast	3	5	6
15	25	27	26	28	28	30	30	2	4	4 No'ah	6	7
16	26 Va-Era	28	27	29 Shemini	29	1 Tammuz	1 Av R.H.	3	5	5	7	8
17	27	29	28	30 R.H.	1 Sivan R.H.	2	2 Mattot Masei	4	6 Va-Yelekh Shabbat Shuvah	6	8	9 Va-Yiggash
18	28	30 R.H.	29	1 Iyyar R.H.	2	3 Korah	3	5	7	7	9 Va-Yeze	10 Fast
19	29	1 Adar R.H.	1 Nisan Va-Yikra R.H. Ha-Hodesh	2	3	4	4	6	8	8	10	11
20	1 Shevat R.H.	2 Terumah	2	3	4	5	5	7 Shofetim	9	9	11	12
21	2	3	3	4 Yom ha-Azma'ut	5 Be-Midbar	6	6	8	10 Yom Kippur	10	12	13
22	3	4	4	5	6 Shavuot	7	7	9	11	11 Lekh Lekha	13	14
23	4 Bo	5	5	6 Tazri'a Mezora	7	8	8	10	12	12	14	15
24	5	6	6	7	8	9	9 Tishah be-Av Devarim	11	13 Ha'azinu	13	15	16 Va-Yehi
25	6	7	7	8	9	10 Hukkat	10 Fast	12	14	14	16	17
26	7	8	8 Zav Shabbat ha-Gadol	9	10	11	11	13	15 Sukkot	15	17 Va-Yishlah	18
27	8	9 Tezavveh Zakhor	9	10	11	12	12	14 Ki Teze	16	16	18	19
28	9	10	10	11	12	13	13	15	17	17	19	20
29	10	11	11	12	13	14	14	16	18	18 Va-Yera	20	21
30	11 Be-Shallah		12	13 Aharei Mot Kedoshim	14	15	15	17	19	19	21	22
31	12		13		15		16 Va-Ethannan	18		20		23 Shemot

Day	January	February	March	April	May	June	July	August	September	October	November	December
1	24 Tevet	26	24	25 Shemini / Ha-Hodesh	26	27	28 Shelah	29	1 Elul R.H.	2 Rosh Ha-Shanah	3	3
2	25	27	25	26	27	28	29	1 Av R.H.	2 Shofetim	3 Fast	4	4 Toledot
3	26	28	26	27	28	29 / Be-Midbar	30 R.H.	2	3	4	5	5
4	27	29 Mishpatim	27 Va-Yakhel / Shekalim	28	29	1 Sivan R.H.	1 Tammuz R.H.	3	4	5	6 Noah	6
5	28	30 R.H.	28	29	30 R.H.	2	2	4 Devarim	5	6	7	7
6	29	1 Adar I R.H.	29	1 Nisan R.H.	1 Iyyar R.H. / Kedoshim	3	3	5	6	7	8	8
7	1 Shevat R.H. / Va-Era	2	30 R.H.	2	2	4	4	6	7	8 Ha'azinu / Shabbat Shuvah	9	9
8	2	3	1 Adar II R.H.	3 Tazri'a	3	5	5 Korah	7	8	9	10	10
9	3	4	2	4	4	6 Shavuot	6	8	9 Ki Teze	10 Yom Kippur	11	11 Va-Yeze
10	4	5	3	5	5 Yom ha-Azma'ut	7	7	9 Tishah be-Av	10	11	12	12
11	5	6 Terumah	4 Pekudei	6	6	8	8	10	11	12	13 Lekh Lekha	13
12	6	7	5	7	7	9	9	11 Va-Ethannan	12	13	14	14
13	7	8	6	8	8 Emor	10	10	12	13	14	15	15
14	8 Bo	9	7	9	9	11	11	13	14	15 Sukkot	16	16
15	9	10	8	10 Mezora / Shabbat ha-Gadol	10	12	12 Hukkat / Balak	14	15	16	17	17
16	10	11	9	11	11	13	13	15	16 Ki Tavo	17 Hol ha-Mo'ed	18	18 Va-Yishlah
17	11	12	10	12	12	14 Naso	14	16	17	18	19	19
18	12	13 Tezavveh	11 Va-Yikra / Zakhor	13	13	15	15	17	18	19	20 Va-Yera	20
19	13	14	12	14	14	16	16	18 Ekev	19	20	21	21
20	14	15	13 Ta'anit Esther	15 Pesah	15 Be-Har	17	17 Fast	19	20	21 Hoshana Rabba	22	22
21	15 Be-Shallah	16	14 Purim	16 Omer	16	18	18	20	21	22 Shemini Azeret	23	23
22	16	17	15 Shushan Purim	17 Hol ha-Mo'ed	17	19	19 Pinhas	21	22	23 Simhat Torah / Ve-Zot Ha-Berakhah	24	24
23	17	18	16	18	18 Lag ba-Omer	20	20	22	23 Nizzavim / Va-Yelekh	24	25	25 Hanukkah / Va-Yeshev [1]
24	18	19	17	19	19	21 Be-Ha'alotkha	21	23	24	25	26	26 [2]
25	19	20 Ki Tissa	18 Zav / Parah	20	20	22	22	24	25	26	27 Hayyei Sarah	27 [3]
26	20	21	19	21 Pesah	21	23	23	25 Re'eh	26	27	28	28 [4]
27	21	22	20	22	22 Be-Hukkotai	24	24	26	27	28	29	29 [5]
28	22 Yitro	23	21	23	23	25	25	27	28	29 Bereshit	30 R.H.	30 R.H. [6]
29	23		22	24 Aharei Mot	24	26	26 Mattot / Masei	28	29	30 R.H.	1 Kislev R.H.	1 Tevet R.H. [7]
30	24		23	25	25	27	27	29	1 Tishri Rosh Ha-Shanah	1 Heshvan R.H.	2	2 Mi-Kez [8]
31	25		24		26		28	30 R.H.		2		3

499

5750/51 — 1990 — תש״ן / תשנ״א

Day	January	February	March	April	May	June	July	August	September	October	November	December
1	4 Tevet	6	4	6	6	8	8	10	11 Ki Teze	12	13	14 Va-Yishlah
2	5	7	5	7	7	9 Naso	9	11	12	13	14	15
3	6	8 Bo	6 Terumah	8	8	10	10	12	13	14	15 Va-Yera	16
4	7	9	7	9	9	11	11	13 Va-Ethannan	14	15 Sukkot	16	17
5	8	10	8	10	10	12	12	14	15	16	17	18
6	9 Va-Yiggash	11	9	11	11	13	13	15	16	17	18	19
7	10 Fast	12	10	12 Shabbat ha-Gadol / Zav	12	14	14 Balak	16	17	18 Hol ha-Mo'ed	19	20
8	11	13	11 Ta'anit Esther	13	13	15	15	17	18 Ki Tavo	19	20	21 Va-Yeshev
9	12	14	12	14	14	16 Be-Ha'alotkha	16	18	19	20	21	22
10	13	15 Be-Shallah	13 Tezavveh / Zakhor	15 Pesah	15	17	17 Fast	19	20	21 Hoshana Rabbah	22 Hayyei Sarah	23
11	14	16	14 Purim	16 Omer	16	18	18	20 Ekev	21	22 Shemini Azeret	23	24
12	15	17	15 Shushan Purim	17	17 Emor	19	19	21	22	23 Simhat Torah / Ve-Zot Ha-Berakhah	24	25 Hanukkah
13	16 Va-Yehi	18	16	18	18 Lag ba-Omer	20	20	22	23	24 Bereshit	25	26
14	17	19	17	19	19	21	21 Pinhas	23	24	25	26	27
15	18	20	18	20	20	22	22	24	25 Nizzavim / Va-Yelekh	26	27	28 Mi-Kez
16	19	21	19	21 Pesah	21	23 Shelah	23	25	26	27	28	29
17	20	22 Yitro	20 Ki Tissa / Parah	22	22	24	24	26	27	28	29 Toledot	30 R.H. 6
18	21	23	21	23	23	25	25	27 Re'eh	28	29	1 Kislev R.H.	1 Tevet R.H. 7
19	22	24	22	24	24 Be-Har / Be-Hukkotai	26	26	28	29	30 R.H.	2	2
20	23 Shemot	25	23	25	25	27	27	29	1 Tishri Rosh Ha-Shaneh	1 Heshvan R.H. / No'ah	3	3
21	24	26	24	26 Shemini	26	28	28 Mattot / Masei	30 R.H.	2	2	4	4
22	25	27	25	27	27	29	29	1 Elul R.H.	3 Ha'azinu / Shabbat Shuvah	3	5	5 Va-Yiggash
23	26	28	26	28	28	30 R.H. / Korah	1 Av R.H.	2	4 → Fast	4	6	6
24	27	29 Mishpatim / Shekalim	27 Va-Yakhel Pekudei / Ha-Hodesh	29	29	1 Tammuz R.H.	2	3	5	5	7 Va-Yeze	7
25	28	30	28	30	1 Sivan R.H.	2	3	4 Shofetim	6	6	8	8
26	29	1 Adar R.H.	29	1 Iyyar R.H.	2 Be-Midbar	3	4	5	7	7	9	9
27	1 Shevat R.H. / Va-Era	2	1 Nisan R.H.	2	3	4	5	6	8	8 Lekh Lekha	10	10 Fast
28	2	3	2	3 Tazri'a / Mezora	4	5	6 Devarim	7	9	9	11	11
29	3		3	4	5	6	7	8	10 Yom Kippur	10	12	12 Va-Yehi
30	4		4	5 Yom ha-Azma'ut	6 Shavuot	7 Hukkat	8	9	11	11	13	13
31	5		5 Va-Yikra		7		9 Tishah be-Av	10		12		14

	January	February	March	April	May	June	July	August	September	October	November	December
1	15 Tevet	17	15 Shushan Purim	17 Hol ha-Mo'ed	17	19 Be-Ha'alotkha	19	21	22	23 Simhat Torah Ve-Zot Ha-Berakhah	24	24
2	16	18 Yitro	16 Ki Tissa	18	18 Lag ba-Omer	20	20	22	23	24	25 Hayyei Sarah	25 Hanukkah
3	17	19	17	19	19	21	21	23 Ekev	24	25	26	26
4	18	20	18	20	20 Emor	22	22	24	25	26	27	27
5	19 Shemot	21	19	21	21	23	23	25	26	27 Bereshit	28	28
6	20	22	20	22 Pesah	22	24	24 Pinhas	26	27	28	29	29
7	21	23	21	23	23	25	25	27	28 Nizzavim	29	30	30 R.H.
8	22	24	22	24	24	26 Shelah	26	28	29	30	1 Kislev R.H.	1 Tevet R.H. Mi-Kez
9	23	25 Mishpatim Shekalim	23 Va-Yakhel Pekudei Parah	25	25	27	27	29	1 Tishri Rosh Ha-Shanah	1 Heshvan R.H.	2 Toledot	2
10	24	26	24	26	26	28	28	30 R.H. Re'eh	2	2	3	3
11	25	27	25	27	27 Be-Har Be-Hukkotai	29	29	1 Elul R.H.	3 Fast	3	4	4
12	26 Va-Era	28	26	28	28	30	1 Av R.H.	2	4	4 Noah	5	5
13	27	29	27	29 Shemini	29	1 Tammuz R.H.	2 Mattot Masei	3	5	5	6	6
14	28	30 R.H.	28	30 R.H.	1 Sivan R.H.	2	3	4	6 Va-Yelekh Shabbat Shuvah	6	7	7
15	29	1 Adar R.H.	29	1 Iyyar R.H.	2	3 Korah	4	5	7	7	8	8
16	1 Shevat R.H.	2 Terumah	1 Nisan R.H. Va-Yikra Ha-Hodesh	2	3	4	5	6	8	8	9 Va-Yeze	9
17	2	3	2	3	4	5	6	7 Shofetim	9	9	10	10 Fast
18	3	4	3	4	5 Be-Midbar	6	7	8	10 Yom Kippur	10	11	11
19	4 Bo	5	4	5 Yom ha-Azma'ut	6 Shavuot	7	8	9	11	11 Lekh Lekha	12	12
20	5	6	5	6 Tazri'a Mezora	7	8	9 Devarim Tishah be-Av	10	12	12	13	13
21	6	7	6	7	8	9	10 Fast	11	13	13	14	14 Va-Yehi
22	7	8	7	8	9	10 Hukkat	11	12	14	14	15	15
23	8	9 Tezavveh Zakhor	8 Zav Shabbat ha-Gadol	9	10	11	12	13	15 Sukkot	15	16 Va-Yishlah	16
24	9	10	9	10	11	12	13	14 Ki Teze	16	16	17	17
25	10	11	10	11	12	13	14	15	17 Hol ha-Mo'ed	17	18	18
26	11 Be-Shallah	12	11	12	13	14	15	16	18	18 Va-Yera	19	19
27	12	13 Ta'anit Esther	12	13 Aharei Mot Kedoshim	14	15	16 Va-Ethannan	17	19	19	20	20
28	13	14 Purim	13	14	15	16	17	18	20	20	21	21 Shemot
29	14		14	15	16	17 Balak	18	19	21 Hoshana Rabba	21	22	22
30	15		15 Pesah	16	17	18 Fast	19	20	22 Shemini Azeret	22	23 Va-Yeshev	23
31	16		16 Omer		18		20	21 Ki Tavo		23		24

1992

5752/53 — תשנ״ב / תשנ״ג

	January (Tevet)	February	March	April (Nisan)	May	June	July	August	September	October	November	December
1	25 Tevet	27 *Mishpatim*	26	27	28	29	30	2 *Mattot Masei*	3	4	5	6
2	26	28	27	28	29 *Aharei Mot*	1 Sivan R.H.	1 Tammuz R.H.	3	4	5	6	7
3	27	29	28	29	30 R.H.	2	2 R.H.	4	5	6 *Va-Yelekh* / Shabbat Shuvah	7	8
4	28 *Va-Era*	30 R.H.	29	1 Nisan R.H. Ha-Hodesh *Tazria*	1 Iyyar R.H.	3	3 *Korah*	5	6	7	8	9
5	29	1 Adar I R.H.	30 R.H.	2	2	4	4	6	7 *Shofetim*	8	9	10 *Va-Yeze*
6	1 Shevat R.H.	2	1 Adar II R.H.	3	3	5 *Be-Midbar*	5	7	8	9	10	11
7	2	3	2 *Pekudei*	4	4 Yom ha-Azma'ut	6 Shavuot	6	8	9	10 Yom Kippur	11 *Lekh Lekha*	12
8	3	4 *Terumah*	3	5	5	7	7	9 *Devarim*	10	11	12	13
9	4	5	4	6	6 *Kedoshim*	8	8	10 Fast (Tishah be-Av)	11	12	13	14
10	5	6	5	7	7	9	9	11	12	13 *Ha'azinu*	14	15
11	6 *Bo*	7	6	8 *Mezora* / Shabbat ha-Gadol	8	10	10 *Hukkat*	12	13	14 Hol ha-Mo'ed	15	16
12	7	8	7	9	9	11	11	13	14 *Ki Teze*	15 Sukkot	16	17 *Va-Yishlah*
13	8	9	8	10	10	12 *Naso*	12	14	15	16	17	18
14	9	10	9 *Va-Ykra* / Zakhor	11	11	13	13	15	16	17 Hol ha-Mo'ed	18 *Va-Yera*	19
15	10	11 *Tezavveh*	10	12	12	14	14	16 *Va-Ethannan*	17	18 Hol ha-Mo'ed	19	20
16	11	12	11	13	13 *Emor*	15	15	17	18	19 Hol ha-Mo'ed	20	21
17	12	13	12	14	14	16	16	18	19	20 Hol ha-Mo'ed	21	22
18	13 *Be-Shallah*	14	13 Ta'anit Esther	15 Pesah	15	17	17 *Balak* / Fast	19	20	21 Hoshana Rabba	22	23
19	14	15	14 Purim	16 Omer	16	18	18 Fast	20	21 *Ki Tavo*	22 Shemini Azeret	23	24 *Va-Yeshev*
20	15	16	15 Shushan Purim	17 Hol ha-Mo'ed	17	19 *Be-Ha'alotkha*	19	21	22	23 Simhat Torah / *Ve-Zot Ha-Berakhah*	24	25 Hanukkah 1
21	16	17	16 *Zav*	18 Hol ha-Mo'ed	18 Lag ba-Omer	20	20	22	23	24	25 *Hayyei Sarah*	26 — 2
22	17	18 *Ki Tissa*	17	19 Hol ha-Mo'ed	19	21	21	23 *Ekev*	24	25	26	27 — 3
23	18	19	18	20 Hol ha-Mo'ed	20 *Be-Har*	22	22	24	25	26	27	28 — 4
24	19	20	19	21	21	23	23	25	26	27 *Bereshit*	28	29 — 5
25	20 *Yitro*	21	20	22 Pesah	22	24	24 *Pinhas*	26	27	28	29	1 Tevet R.H. — 6
26	21	22	21	23	23	25	25	27	28 *Nizzavim*	29	1 Kislev R.H.	2 *Mi-Kez* — 7
27	22	23	22	24	24	26 *Shelah*	26	28	29	30 R.H.	2	3 — 8
28	23	24	23 *Shemini* / Parah	25	25	27	27	29	1 Tishri Rosh Ha-Shanah	1 Heshvan R.H.	3 *Toledot*	4
29	24	25 *Va-Yakhel* / Shekalim	24	26	26	28	28	30 R.H. (*Re'eh*)	2	2	4	5
30	25		25	27	27 *Be-Hukkotai*	29	29	1 Elul R.H.	3 Fast	3	5	6
31	26		26		28		1 Av R.H.	2		4 *No'ah*		7

	January	February	March	April	May	June	July	August	September	October	November	December
1	8 Tevet	10	8	10	10 Aharei Mot Kedoshim	12	12	14	15	16	17	17
2	9 Va-Yiggash	11	9	11	11	13	13	15	16	17 Hol ha-Mo'ed	18	18
3	10 Fast	12	10	12 Zav Shabbat ha-Gadol	12	14	14 Balak	16	17	18	19	19
4	11	13	11 Ta'anit Esther	13	13	15	15	17	18 Ki Tavo	19	20	20 Va-Yeshev
5	12	14	12 Tezavveh Zakhor	14	14	16 Be-Ha'alotkha	16	18	19	20	21	21
6	13	15 Be-Shallah	13	15 Pesah	15	17	17 Fast	19	20	21 Hoshana Rabba	22 Hayyei Sarah	22
7	14	16	14 Purim	16 Omer	16 Emor	18	18	20 Ekev	21	22 Shemini Azeret	23	23
8	15	17	15 Shushan Purim	17	17	19	19	21	22	23 Simhat Torah Ve-Zot Ha-Berakhah	24	24
9	16 Va-Yehi	18	16	18	18 Lag ba-Omer	20	20	22	23	24 Bereshit	25	25 Hanukkah 1
10	17	19	17	19	19	21	21 Pinhas	23	24	25	26	26 2
11	18	20	18	20	20	22	22	24	25 Nizzavim Va-Yelekh	26	27	27 Mi-Kez 3
12	19	21	19	21 Pesah	21	23	23	25	26	27	28	28 4
13	20	22 Yitro	20 Ki Tissa Parah	22	22	24	24	26	27	28	29 Toledot	29 5
14	21	23	21	23	23	25	25	27 Re'eh	28	29	30 R.H.	30 R.H. 6
15	22	24	22	24	24 Be-Har Be-Hukkotai	26	26	28	29	30 R.H.	1 Kislev R.H.	1 Tevet R.H. 7
16	23 Shemot	25	23	25	25	27	27	29	1 Tishri Rosh Ha-Shanah	1 R.H. Heshvan No'ah	2	2 8
17	24	26	24	26 Shemini	26	28	28 Mattot Masei	30	2	2	3	3
18	25	27	25	27	27	29	29	1 Elul R.H.	3 Ha'azinu Shabbat Shuvah	3	4	4 Va-Yiggash
19	26	28	26	28	28	30 R.H. Korah	30 R.H.	2 R.H.	4 Fast	4	5	5
20	27	29 Mishpatim Shekalim	27 Va-Yakhel Pekudei Ha-Hodesh	29	29	1 Tammuz R.H.	1 Av R.H.	3	5	5	6 Va-Yeze	6
21	28	30 R.H.	28	30 R.H.	1 Sivan R.H.	2	2	4	6	6	7	7
22	29	1 Adar R.H.	1 Nisan R.H.	1 Iyyar R.H.	2 Be-Midbar	3	3	5	7	7	8	8
23	1 Shevat R.H. Va-Era	2	2	2	3	4	4 Devarim	6	8	8 Lekh Lekha	9	9
24	2	3	3	3 Tazri'a Mezora	4	5	5	7	9	9	10	10 Fast
25	3	4	4	4	5	6	6	8	10 Yom Kippur	10	11	11 Va-Yehi
26	4	5	5 Va-Yikra	5 Yom ha-Azma'ut	6 Shavuot	7	7	9	11	11	12	12
27	5	6 Terumah	6	6	7	8	8	10	12	12	13 Va-Yishlah	13
28	6	7	7	7	8	9	9 Tishah be-Av	11 Ki Teze	13	13	14	14
29	7		8	8	9 Naso	10	10	12	14	14	15	15
30	8 Bo		8	9	10	11	11	13	15 Sukkot	15 Va-Yera	16	16
31	9		9		11		12	14		16		17 Va-Yehi

1994

5754/55 · תשנ״ד / תשנ״ה

Jewish–Gregorian calendar (Hebrew dates, Sabbath portions and festivals shown against the Gregorian month and day).

Day	January	February	March	April	May	June	July	August	September	October	November	December
1	18 Tevet · *Shemot*	20	18	20 Hol ha-Mo'ed	20	22	22	24	25	26 · *Bereshit*	27	28
2	19	21	19	21 Pesaḥ	21	23	23 · *Pinḥas*	25	26	27	28	29
3	20	22	20	22	22	24	24	26	27 · *Niẓẓavim*	28	29	30 R.H. · *Mi-Keẓ*
4	21	23	21	23	23	25 · *Shelaḥ*	25	27	28	29	1 Kislev R.H.	1 Tevet R.H.
5	22	24 · *Mishpatim*	22 · *Va-Yakhel / Parah*	24	24	26	26	28	29	30 R.H.	2 · *Toledot*	2
6	23	25	23	25	25	27	27	29 · *Re'eh*	1 Tishri · Rosh Ha-Shanah	1 Heshvan R.H.	3	3
7	24	26	24	26	26 · *Be-Har / Be-Ḥukkotai*	28	28	30 R.H.	2	2	4	4
8	25 · *Va-Era*	27	25	27	27	29	29	1 Elul R.H.	3 · Fast	3 · *No'aḥ*	5	5
9	26	28	26	28 · *Shemini*	28	30 R.H.	1 Av R.H. · *Mattot / Masei*	2	4	4	6	6
10	27	29	27	29	29	1 Tammuz R.H.	2	3	5 · *Va-Yelekh / Shabbat Shuvah*	5	7	7 · *Va-Yiggash*
11	28	30 R.H.	28	30 R.H.	1 Sivan R.H.	2 · *Koraḥ*	3	4	6	6	8	8
12	29	1 Adar R.H. · *Terumah / Shekalim*	29 · *Pekudei / Ha-Hodesh*	1 Iyyar R.H.	2	3	4	5	7	7	9 · *Va-Yeẓe*	9
13	1 Shevat R.H.	2	1 Nisan R.H.	2	3	4	5	6 · *Shofetim*	8	8	10	10 · Fast
14	2	3	2	3 · Yom ha-Aẓma'ut	4 · *Be-Midbar*	5	6	7	9	9	11	11
15	3 · *Bo*	4	3	4	5	6	7	8	10 · Yom Kippur	10 · *Lekh Lekha*	12	12
16	4	5	4	5 · *Tazria / Meẓora*	6 · Shavuot	7	8 · *Devarim*	9	11	11	13	13
17	5	6	5	6	7	8	9 · Tishah be-Av	10	12 · *Ha'azinu*	12	14	14 · *Va-Yeḥi*
18	6	7	6	7	8	9	10	11	13	13	15	15
19	7	8 · *Tezaveh / Zakhor*	7 · *Va-Yikra*	8	9	10	11	12	14	14	16 · *Va-Yishlaḥ*	16
20	8	9	8	9	10	11	12	13 · *Ki-Teẓe*	15 · Sukkot	15	17	17
21	9	10	9	10	11 · *Naso*	12	13	14	16 · Hol ha-Mo'ed	16	18	18
22	10 · *Be-Shallaḥ*	11	10	11	12	13	14	15	17	17 · *Va-Yera*	19	19
23	11	12	11	12	13	14	15 · *Va-Ethannan*	16	18	18	20	20
24	12	13 · Ta'anit Esther	12	13	14	15	16	17	19	19	21	21 · *Shemot*
25	13	14 · Purim	13	14	15	16 · *Balak*	17	18	20	20	22	22
26	14	15 · *Ki Tissa / Shushan Purim*	14	15	16	17 · Fast	18	19	21 · Hoshana Rabba	21	23 · *Va-Yeshev*	23
27	15	16	15 Pesaḥ	16	17	18	19	20 · *Ki-Tavo*	22 · Shemini Aẓeret	22	24	24
28	16	17	16 Omer / Hol ha-Mo'ed	17	18 · *Be-Ha'alotkha*	19	20	21	23 · Simḥat Torah / *Ve-Zot Ha-Berakhah*	23	25 · Hanukkah 1	25
29	17 · *Yitro*		17	18 · Lag ba-Omer	19	20	21	22	24	24 · *Ḥayyei Sarah*	26	26
30	18		18	19 · *Emor*	20	21	22 · *Ekev*	23	25	25	27	27
31	19		19		21		23	24		26		28 · *Va-Era*

1995

5755/56 תשנ״ה / תשנ״ו

	January	February	March	April	May	June	July	August	September	October	November	December
1	29 **Tevet**	1 **Adar I** R. Ḥ.	29	**1** R. Ḥ. *Tazri'a* **Nisan** Ha-Hodesh	1 **Iyyar** R. Ḥ.	3	**3** *Koraḥ*	5	6	7	8	8
2	1 **Shevat** R. Ḥ.	2	30 R. Ḥ.	2	2	4	4	6	**7** *Shofetim*	8	9	**9** *Va-Yeẓe*
3	2	3	1 **Adar II** R. Ḥ.	3	3	**5** *Be-Midbar*	5	7	8	9	10	10
4	3	**4** *Terumah*	**2** *Pekudei*	4	4 Yom ha-Aẓma'ut	**6** Shavuot	6	8	9	**10** Yom Kippur	**11** *Lekh Lekha*	11
5	4	5	3	5	5	7	7	**9** *Devarim* Tishah be-Av	10	11	12	12
6	5	6	4	6	**6** *Kedoshim*	8	8	10 Fast	11	12	13	13
7	**6** *Bo*	7	5	7	7	9	9	11	12	**13** *Ha'azinu*	14	14
8	7	8	6	**8** *Meẓora* Shabbat ha-Gadol	8	10	**10** *Ḥukkat*	12	13	14	15	15
9	8	9	7	9	9	11	11	13	**14** *Ki Teẓe*	**15** Sukkot	16	**16** *Va-Yishlaḥ*
10	9	10	8	10	10	**12** *Naso*	12	14	15	16	17	17
11	10	**11** *Teẓavveh*	**9** *Va-Yikra* Zakhor	11	11	13	13	15	16	17 Ḥol ha-Mo'ed	**18** *Va-Yera*	18
12	11	12	10	12	12	14	14	**16** *Va-Etḥannan*	17	18	19	19
13	12	13	11	13	**13** *Emor*	15	15	17	18	19	20	20
14	**13** *Be-Shallaḥ*	14	12	14	14	16	16	18	19	**20**	21	21
15	14	15	13 Ta'anit Esther	**15** Pesaḥ	15	17	**17** *Balak*	19	20	21 Hoshana Rabba	22	22
16	15	16	14 Purim	16 Omer	16	18	18 Fast	20	**21** *Ki Tavo*	22 Shemini Aẓeret	23	**23** *Va-Yeshev*
17	16	17	15 Shushan Purim	17 Ḥol ha-Mo'ed	17	**19** *Be-Ha'alotkha*	19	21	22	23 Simḥat Torah *Ve-Zot Ha-Berakhah*	24	24
18	17	**18** *Ki Tissa*	**16** *Ẓav*	18	18 Lag ba-Omer	20	20	22	23	24	**25** *Ḥayyei Sarah*	25 Hanukkah 1
19	18	19	17	19	19	21	21	**23** *Ekev*	24	25	26	26 2
20	19	20	18	20	**20** *Be-Har*	22	22	24	25	26	27	27 3
21	**20** *Yitro*	21	19	21 Pesaḥ	21	23	23	25	26	**27** *Bereshit*	28	28 4
22	21	22	20	**22**	22	24	**24** *Pinḥas*	26	27	28	29	29 5
23	22	23	21	23	23	25	25	27	**28** *Niẓẓavim*	29	30 R. Ḥ.	**30** R. Ḥ. *Mi-Keẓ* 6
24	23	24	22	24	24	**26** *Shelaḥ*	26	28	29	30 R. Ḥ.	1 **Kislev** R. Ḥ.	1 **Tevet** R. Ḥ. 7
25	24	**25** *Va-Yakhel* Shekalim	**23** *Shemini* Parah	25	25	27	27	29	1 **Tishri** Rosh Ha-Shanah	1 **Heshvan** R. Ḥ.	**2** *Toledot*	2 8
26	25	26	24	26	26	28	28	**30** R. Ḥ. *Re'eh*	2	2	3	3
27	26	27	25	27	**27** *Be-Ḥukkotai*	29	29	1 **Elul** R. Ḥ.	3 Fast	3	4	4
28	**27** *Mishpatim*	28	26	28	28	30 R. Ḥ.	1 **Av** R. Ḥ.	2	4	**4** *No'aḥ*	5	5
29	28		27	**29** *Aḥarei Mot*	29	1 **Tammuz** R. Ḥ.	**2** *Mattot Masei*	3	5	5	6	6
30	29		28	30 R. Ḥ.	1 **Sivan** R. Ḥ.	2	3	4	**6** *Va-Yelekh* Shabbat Shuvah	6	7	**7** *Va-Yiggash*
31	30 R. Ḥ.		29		2		4	5		7		8

1996

5756/57 תשנ"ו / תשנ"ז

Day	January	February	March	April	May	June	July	August	September	October	November	December
1	9 Tevet	11	10	12	12	14 Naso	14	16	17	18	19	20
2	10 Fast	12	11	13	13	15	15	17	18	19	20 Va-Yera	21
3	11	13 Be-Shallaḥ	12	14	14	16	16	18 Ekev	19	20	21	22
4	12	14	13 Taʿanit Esther	15 Pesaḥ	15 Emor	17	17 Fast	19	20	21 Hoshana Rabba	22	23
5	13	15	14 Purim	16 Omer	16	18	18	20	21	22 Shemini Azeret / Hol ha-Moʿed	23	24
6	14 Va-Yeḥi	16	15 Shushan Purim	17	17	19	19 Pinḥas	21	22	23 Simḥat Torah / Ve-Zot Ha-Berakhah	24	25 Hanukkah 1
7	15	17	16	18	18 Lag ba-Omer	20	20	22	23 Nizzavim / Va-Yelekh	24	25	26 Va-Yeshev — 2
8	16	18	17	19	19	21 Be-Haʿalotkha	21	23	24	25	26	27 — 3
9	17	19	18 Ki Tissa / Parah	20	20	22	22	24	25	26	27 Hayyei Sarah	28 — 4
10	18	20 Yitro	19	21 Pesaḥ	21	23	23	25 Reʾeh	26	27	28	29 — 5
11	19	21	20	22	22 Be-Har / Be-Hukkotai	24	24	26	27	28	29	1 Tevet R.H. — 6
12	20	22	21	23	23	25	25	27	28	29 Bereshit	1 Kislev R.H.	2 — 7
13	21 Shemot	23	22	24 Shemini	24	26	26 Mattot / Masei	28	29	30 R.H.	2	3 — 8
14	22	24	23	25	25	27	27	29	1 Tishri / Rosh Ha-Shanah	1 Heshvan R.H.	3	4 Mi-Kez
15	23	25	24	26	26	28 Shelaḥ	28	30 R.H.	2	2	4	5
16	24	26	25 Va-Yakhel-Pekudei / Ha-Hodesh	27	27	29	29	1 Elul R.H.	3 Fast	3	5 Toledot	6
17	25 Mishpatim / Shekalim	27	26	28	28	30	1 Av R.H.	2 Shofetim	4	4	6	7
18	26	28	27	29	29 Be-Midbar	1 Tammuz R.H.	2 Devarim	3	5	5	7	8
19	27	29	28	30 R.H.	1 Sivan R.H.	2	3	4	6	6 Noʾaḥ	8	9
20	28 Va-Era	30 R.H.	29	1 Iyyar R.H.	2	3	4	5	7	7	9	10 Fast
21	29	1 Adar R.H.	1 Nisan R.H.	2	3	4	5	6	8 Haʾazinu / Shabbat Shuvah	8	10	11 Va-Yiggash
22	1 Shevat R.H.	2	2	3	4	5 Korah	6	7	9	9	11	12
23	2	3	3 Va-Yikra	4	5	6	7	8	10 Yom Kippur	10	12 Va-Yeze	13
24	3	4 Terumah	4	5 Yom ha-Azmaʾut	6	7	8	9 Ki Teze	11	11	13	14
25	4	5	5	6	7	8	9 Tishah be-Av	10	12	12	14	15
26	5	6	6	7	8	9	10	11	13	13 Lekh Lekha	15	16
27	6 Bo	7	7	8 Aharei Mot / Kedoshim	9	10	11 Va-Etḥannan	12	14	14	16	17
28	7	8 Tezavveh / Zakhor	8	9	10	11	12	13	15 Sukkot	15	17	18 Va-Yeḥi
29	8	9	9	10	11	12 Hukkat / Balak	13	14	16	16	18	19
30	9		10 Zav / Shabbat ha-Gadol	11	12	13	14	15	17 Hol ha-Moʿed	17	19 Va-Yishlaḥ	20
31	10		11		13		15	16 Ki Tavo		18		21

1997

5757/58 — ה׳תשנ״ז / ה׳תשנ״ח

R.H. = Rosh Hodesh. Bold dates and italic names indicate Sabbath Torah portions and festivals.

Day	January	February	March	April	May	June	July	August	September	October	November	December
1	22 Tevet	24 *Yitro*	22 *Ki Tissa*	23	24	25	26	27	29	29	1 Heshvan R.H. *Noah*	2
2	23	25	23	24	25	26	27	28 *Mattot Masei*	30 R.H.	1 Tishri Rosh Ha-Shanah	2	3
3	24	26	24	25	26 *Aharei Mot*	27	28	29	1 Elul R.H.	2 R.H. *Shabbat Shuvah*	3	4
4	25 *Shemot*	27	25	26	27	28	29	1 Av R.H.	2	3 Fast	4	5
5	26	28	26	27 *Shemini Ha-Hodesh*	28	29	30 R.H. *Korah*	2	3	4	5	6 *Va-Yeze*
6	27	29	27	28	29	1 Sivan R.H.	1 Tammuz R.H.	3	4 *Shofetim*	5	6	7
7	28	30 R.H.	28	29	30 R.H.	2 *Be-Midbar*	2	4	5	6	7	8
8	29	1 Adar I R.H. *Mishpatim*	29 *Va-Yakhel Shekalim*	1 Nisan R.H.	1 Iyyar R.H.	3	3	5	6	7	8 *Lekh Lekha*	9
9	1 Shevat	2	30 R.H.	2	2	4	4	6 *Devarim*	7	8	9	10
10	2	3	1 Adar II R.H.	3	3 *Kedoshim*	5	5	7	8	9	10	11
11	3 *Va-Era*	4	2	4	4	6 Shavuot	6	8	9	10 Yom Kippur	11	12
12	4	5	3	5 *Tazri'a*	5 Yom ha-Azma'ut	7 (Shavuot)	7 *Hukkat*	9 Tishah be-Av	10	11 *Ha'azinu*	12	13 *Va-Yishlah*
13	5	6	4	6	6	8	8	10	11 *Ki Teze*	12	13	14
14	6	7	5	7	7	9 *Naso*	9	11	12	13	14	15
15	7	8 *Terumah*	6 *Pekudei*	8	8	10	10	12	13	14	15 *Va-Yera*	16
16	8	9	7	9	9	11	11	13 *Va-Ethannan*	14	15 Sukkot	16	17
17	9	10	8	10	10 *Emor*	12	12	14	15	16	17	18
18	10 *Bo*	11	9	11	11	13	13	15	16	17 (Hol ha-Mo'ed)	18	19
19	11	12	10	12 *Mezora Shabbat ha-Gadol*	12	14	14 *Balak*	16	17	18	19	20 *Va-Yeshev*
20	12	13	11 Ta'anit Esther	13	13	15	15	17	18 *Ki Tavo*	19	20	21
21	13	14	12	14	14	16 *Be-Ha'alotkha*	16	18	19	20	21	22
22	14	15	13 *Va-Yikra Zakhor*	15 Pesah	15	17	17 Fast	19	20	21 Hoshana Rabba	22 *Hayyei Sarah*	23
23	15	16	14 Purim	16 Omer (Hol ha-Mo'ed)	16	18	18	20 *Ekev*	21	22 Shemini Azeret	23	24
24	16	17	15 Shushan Purim	17	17 *Be-Har*	19	19	21	22	23 Simhat Torah *Ve-Zot Ha-Berakhah*	24	25 Hanukkah
25	17 *Be-Shallah*	18	16	18	18 Lag ba-Omer	20	20	22	23	24 *Bereshit*	25	26
26	18	19	17	19 (Hol ha-Mo'ed)	19	21	21 *Pinhas*	23	24	25	26	27
27	19	20	18	20	20	22	22	24	25 *Nizzavim Va-Yelekh*	26	27	28 *Mi-Kez*
28	20	21	19	21 Pesah	21	23 *Shelah*	23	25	26	27	28	29
29	21		20 *Zav Parah*	22	22	24	24	26	27	28	29 *Toledot*	30 R.H.
30	22		21	23	23	25	25	27 *Re'eh*	28	29	1 Kislev R.H.	1 Tevet R.H.
31	23		22		24 *Be-Hukkotai*		26	28		30 R.H.		2

1998

5758/59 התשנ״ח / התשנ״ט

Day	January	February	March	April	May	June	July	August	September	October	November	December
1	3 Tevet	5	3	5	5	7	7	9 Tishah be-Av / Devarim	10	11	12	12
2	4	6	4	6	6 Tazri'a Mezora	8	8	10 Fast	11	12	13	13
3	5 Va-Yiggash	7	5	7	7	9	9	11	12	13 Ha'azinu	14	14
4	6	8	6	8 Zav / Shabbat ha-Gadol	8	10	10 Hukkat	12	13	14	15	15
5	7	9	7	9	9	11	11	13	14 Ki Teze	15 Sukkot	16	16 Va-Yishlah
6	8	10	8	10	10	12 Naso	12	14	15	16 (Hol ha-Mo'ed)	17	17
7	9	11 Be-Shallah	9 Tezavveh Zakhor	11	11	13	13	15	16	17	18 Va-Yera	18
8	10* Fast	12	10	12	12	14	14	16 Va-Ethannan	17	18	19	19
9	11	13	11	13	13	15	15	17	18	19	20	20
10	12 Va-Yehi	14	12	14	14	16	16	18	19	20	21	21
11	13	15	13 Ta'anit Esther	15 Pesah	15	17	17 Balak	19	20	21 Hoshana Rabba	22	22
12	14	16	14 Purim	16 Omer	16	18	18 Fast	20	21 Ki Tavo	22 Shemini Azeret	23	23 Va-Yeshev
13	15	17	15 Shushan Purim	17 Hol ha-Mo'ed	17	19 Be-Ha'alotkha	19	21	22	23 Simhat Torah / Ve-Zot Ha-Berakhah	24	24
14	16	18 Yitro	16 Ki Tissa	18	18 Lag ba-Omer	20	20	22	23	24	25 Hayyei Sarah	25 Hanukkah 1
15	17	19	17	19	19	21	21	23 Ekev	24	25	26	26 — 2
16	18	20	18	20	20 Emor	22	22	24	25	26	27	27 — 3
17	19 Shemot	21	19	21 Pesah	21	23	23	25	26	27 Bereshit	28	28 — 4
18	20	22	20	22	22	24	24 Pinhas	26	27	28	29	29 — 5
19	21	23	21	23	23	25	25	27	28 Nizzavim	29	30	30 R.H. — 6 Mi-Kez
20	22	24	22	24	24	26 Shelah	26	28	29	30 R.H.	1 Kislev R.H.	1 Tevet R.H. — 7
21	23	25 Mishpatim / Shekalim	23 Va-Yakhel Pekudei / Parah	25	25	27	27	29	1 Tishri Rosh Ha-Shanah	1 Heshvan R.H.	2 Toledot	2 — 8
22	24	26	24	26	26	28	28	30 R.H. Re'eh	2	2	3	3
23	25	27	25	27	27 Be-Har Be-Hukkotai	29	29	1 Elul R.H.	3 Fast	3	4	4
24	26 Va-Era	28	26	28	28	30 R.H.	1 Av R.H.	2	4	4 No'ah	5	5
25	27	29	27	29 Shemini	29	1 Tammuz R.H.	2 Mattot / Masei	3	5	5	6	6
26	28	30 R.H.	28	30	1 Sivan R.H.	2	3	4	6 Va-Yelekh / Shabbat Shuvah	6	7	7 Va-Yiggash
27	29	1 Adar R.H.	29	1 Iyyar R.H.	2	3 Korah	4	5	7	7	8	8
28	1 Shevat R.H.	2 Terumah	1 R.H. Va-Yikra / Nisan Ha-Hodesh	2	3	4	5	6	8	8	9 Va-Yeze	9
29	2		2	3	4	5	6	7 Shoftim	9	9	10	10 Fast
30	3		3	4 Yom ha-Azma'ut	5 Be-Midbar	6	7	8	10 Yom Kippur	10	11	11
31	4 Bo		4		6 Shavuot		8	9		11 Lekh Lekha		12

1999

5759/60   תשנ"ט / תש"ס

Day	January	February	March	April	May	June	July	August	September	October	November	December
1	13 Tevet	15	13 Ta'anit Esther	15 Pesah	15 Emor	17	17 Fast	19	20	21 Hoshana Rabba	22	22
2	14 Va-Yehi	16	14 Purim	16 Omer	16	18	18	20	21	22 Shemini Azeret	23	23
3	15	17	15 Shushan Purim	17 Hol ha-Mo'ed	17	19	19 Pinhas	21	22	23 Simhat Torah / Ve-Zot Ha-Berakhah	24	24
4	16	18	16	18	18 Lag ba-Omer	20	20	22	23 Nizzavim Va-Yelekh	24	25	25 Va-Yeshev Hanukkah
5	17	19	17	19	19	21 Be-Ha'alotkha	21	23	24	25	26	26
6	18	20 Yitro	18 Ki Tissa / Parah	20	20	22	22	24	25	26 No'ah	27 Hayyei Sarah	27
7	19	21	19	21 Pesah	21 Be-Har Be-Hukkotai	23	23	25 Re'eh	26	27	28	28
8	20	22	20	22	22 Be-Har Be-Hukkotai	24	24	26	27	28	29	29
9	21 Shemot	23	21	23	23	25	25	27	28	29 Bereshit	30	30 R.H.
10	22	24	22	24 Shemini	24	26	26 Mattot Mase'	28	29	30	1 Kislev R.H.	1 Tevet R.H.
11	23	25	23	25	25	27	27	29	1 Tishri Rosh Ha-Shanah	1 Heshvan (R.H.)	2	2 Mi-Kez
12	24	26	24	26	26	28	28	30 R.H.	2	2	3	3
13	25	27 Mishpatim / Shekalim	25 Va-Yakhel Pekudei / Ha-Hodesh	27	27	29	29	1 Elul R.H.	3 Fast	3	4 Toledot	4
14	26	28	26	28	28	30	1 Av R.H.	2	4	4	5	5
15	27	29	27	29	29	1 Tammuz R.H.	2	3	5	5	6	6
16	28 Va-Era	30 R.H.	28	30 R.H.	1 Sivan R.H.	2	3	4	6	6	7	7
17	29 R.H.	1 Adar R.H.	29	1 Iyyar R.H. / Tazri'a Mezora	2	3	4 Devarim	5	7	7	8	8
18	1 Shevat	2	1 Nisan R.H.	2	3	4	5	6	8 Ha'azinu Shabbat Shuvah	8	9	9 Va-Yiggash
19	2	3	2	3	4	5 Korah	6	7	9	9	10	10 Fast
20	3	4 Terumah	3 Va-Yikra	4	5	6	7	8	10 Yom Kippur	10	11	11
21	4	5	4	5 Yom ha-Azma'ut	6 Shavuot	7	8	9 Ki Teze	11	11	12	12
22	5	6	5	6	7	8	9 Tishah be-Av	10	12	12	13	13
23	6 Bo	7	6	7	8	9	10	11	13	13 Lekh Lekha	14	14
24	7	8	7	8 Aharei Mot Kedoshim	9	10	11 Va-Ethannan	12	14	14	15	15
25	8	9	8	9	10	11	12	13	15 Sukkot	15	16	16 Va-Yehi
26	9	10	9	10	11	12 Hukkat Balak	13	14	16	16	17	17
27	10	11 Tezavveh / Zakhor	10 Zav / Shabbat ha-Gadol	11	12	13	14	15	17	17	18 Va-Yishlah	18
28	11	12	11	12	13	14	15	16 Ki Tavo	18	18	19	19
29	12		12	13	14 Naso	15	16	17	19	19	20	20
30	13 Be-Shallah		13	14	15	16	17	18	20	20 Va-Yera	21	21
31	14		14		16		18 Ekev	19		21		22

Hal ha-Mo'ed (April, Pesah); Hal ha-Mo'ed (October, Sukkot)

2000

5760/61 תשס"א / תש"ס

#	January	February	March	April	May	June	July	August	September	October	November	December
1	23 Tevet *Shemot*	25	24	25 *Shemini* Ha-Hodesh	26	27	28	29	1 Elul R.H.	2 Rosh Ha-Shanah	3	4
2	24	26	25	26	27	28	29	1 Av R.H.	2 *Shofetim*	3 Fast	4	5 *Toledot*
3	25	27	26	27	28	29	30 R.H.	2	3	4	5	6
4	26	28	27 *Va-Yakhel* Shekalim	28	29	1 Sivan R.H.	1 Tammuz R.H.	3	4	5	6 *No'ah*	7
5	27	29 *Mishpatim*	28	29	30 R.H.	2	2	4 *Devarim*	5	6	7	8
6	28	30 R.H.	29	1 Nisan R.H.	1 Iyyar R.H. *Kedoshim*	3	3	5	6	7	8	9
7	29	1 Adar I R.H.	30 R.H.	2	2	4	4	6	7	8 *Ha'azinu* Shabbat Shuvah	9	10
8	1 Shevat R.H. *Va-Era*	2	1 Adar II R.H.	3 *Tazri'a*	3	5	5 *Shelah*	7	8	9	10	11
9	2	3	2	4	4	6 Shavuot	6	8	9 *Ki Teze*	10 Yom Kippur	11	12 *Va-Yeze*
10	3	4	3	5	5 Yom ha-Azma'ut	7	7	9 Tishah be-Av	10	11	12	13
11	4	5	4 *Pekudei*	6	6	8	8	10	11	12	13 *Lekh Lekha*	14
12	5	6 *Terumah*	5	7	7	9	9	11 *Va-Ethannan*	12	13	14	15
13	6	7	6	8	8 *Emor*	10	10	12	13	14	15	16
14	7	8	7	9	9	11	11	13	14	15	16	17
15	8 *Bo*	9	8	10 *Mezora* Shabbat ha-Gadol	10	12	12 *Korah*	14	15	16	17	18
16	9	10	9	11	11	13	13	15	16 *Ki Tavo*	17 Hol ha-Mo'ed	18	19 *Va-Yishlah*
17	10	11	10	12	12	14 *Naso*	14	16	17	18	19	20
18	11	12	11 *Va-Yikra* Zakhor	13	13	15	15	17	18	19	20 *Va-Yera*	21
19	12	13 *Tezavveh*	12	14	14	16	16	18 *Ekev*	19	20	21	22
20	13	14	13 Ta'anit Esther	15 Pesah	15 *Be-Har*	17	17 Fast	19	20	21 Hoshana Rabba	22	23
21	14	15	14 Purim	16 Omer	16	18	18	20	21	22 Shemini Azeret	23	24
22	15 *Be-Shallah*	16	15 Shushan Purim	17 Hol ha-Mo'ed	17	19	19 *Hukkat* Balak	21	22	23 Simhat Torah *Ve-Zot Ha-Berakhah*	24	25 Hanukkah
23	16	17	16	18	18 Lag ba-Omer	20	20	22	23 *Nizzavim* Va-Yelekh	24	25	26 *Va-Yeshev*
24	17	18	17	19	19	21 *Be-Ha'alotkha*	21	23	24	25	26	27
25	18	19	18 *Zav* Parah	20	20	22	22	24	25	26	27 *Hayyei Sarah*	28
26	19	20 *Ki Tissa*	19	21 Pesah	21	23	23	25 *Re'eh*	26	27	28	29
27	20	21	20	22	22 *Be-Hukkotai*	24	24	26	27	28	29	1 Tevet R.H.
28	21	22	21	23	23	25	25	27	28	29 *Bereshit*	1 Kislev R.H.	2
29	22 *Yitro*	23	22	24 *Aharei Mot*	24	26	26 *Pinhas*	28	29	30 R.H.	2	3
30	23		23	25	25	27	27	29	1 Tishri Rosh Ha-Shanah	1 Heshvan R.H.	3	4 *Mi-Kez*
31	24		24		26		28	30 R.H.		2		5

	January (Tevet)	February	March	April	May	June	July	August	September	October	November	December
1	6 Tevet	8	6	8	8	10	10	12	13 Ki Teze	14	15	16 Va-Yishlah
2	7	9	7	9	9	11 Naso	11	13	14	15 Sukkot	16	17
3	8	10	8 Terumah Zakhor	10	10	12	12	14	15	16 Sukkot	17 Va-Yera	18
4	9	11	9	11	11	13	13	15 Va-Ethannan	16	17 Hol ha-Mo'ed	18	19
5	10 Fast	12	10	12	12 Aharei Mot Kedoshim	14	14	16	17	18	19	20
6	11 Va-Yiggash	13	11	13	13	15	15	17	18	19	20	21
7	12	14	12	14 Zav Shabbat ha-Gadol	14	16	16 Balak	18	19	20	21 Hoshana Rabba	22
8	13	15	13 Ta'anit Esther	15 Pesah	15	17	17 Fast	19	20 Ki Tavo	21 Hoshana Rabba	22	23 Va-Yeshev
9	14	16	14 Purim	16 Omer	16	18 Be-Ha'alotkha	18	20	21	22 Shemini Azeret	23	24
10	15	17 Be-Shallah	15 Shushan Purim Tezavveh	17	17	19	19	21	22	23 Simhat Torah Ve-Zot Ha-Berakhah	24 Hayyei Sarah	25
11	16	18	16	18 Hol ha-Mo'ed	18 Lag ba-Omer	20	20	22 Ekev	23	24	25	26
12	17	19	17	19	19 Emor	21	21	23	24	25	26	27
13	18 Va-Yehi	20	18	20	20	22	22	24	25	26 Bereshit	27	28
14	19	21	19	21 Pesah	21	23	23 Pinhas	25	26	27	28	29
15	20	22	20	22 Pesah	22	24	24	26	27 Nizzavim	28	29	30 Mi-Kez
16	21	23	21	23	23	25 Shelah	25	27	28	29	1 Kislev R.H.	30 R.H. 1 Tevet R.H. 7
17	22	24 Yitro	22 Ki Tissa Parah	24	24	26	26	28	29	30	2 Toledot	2
18	23	25	23	25	25	27	27	29 Re'eh	1 Tishri Rosh Ha-Shanah	1 Heshvan R.H.	3	3
19	24	26	24	26	26 Be-Har Be-Hukkotai	28	28	30 R.H.	2	2 R.H.	4	4
20	25 Shemot	27	25	27	27	29	29	1 Elul R.H.	3 Fast	3 No'ah	5	5
21	26	28	26	28 Shemini	28	30 R.H.	30 R.H. Mattot Masei	2	4	4	6	6
22	27	29	27	29	29	1 Tammuz R.H.	1 Av R.H.	3	5 Va-Yelekh Shabbat Shuvah	5	7	7 Va-Yiggash
23	28	30 R.H.	28	30	1 Sivan R.H.	2 Korah	2	4	6	6	8	8
24	29	1 Adar R.H. Mishpatim Shekalim	29 Va-Yakhel Pekude Ha-Hodesh	1 Iyyar R.H.	2	3	3	5	7	7	9 Va-Yeze	9
25	1 Shevat R.H.	2	1 Nisan R.H.	2	3	4	4	6 Shofetim	8	8	10 Fast	10 Fast
26	2	3	2	3 Yom ha-Azma'ut	4 Be-Midbar	5	5	7	9	9	11	11
27	3 Va-Era	4	3	4	5	6	6	8	10 Yom Kippur	10 Lekh Lekha	12	12
28	4	5	4	5 Tazri'a Mezora	6 Shavuot	7	7	9	11	11	13	13
29	5		5	6	7 Shavuot	8	8 Devarim	10	12 Ha'azinu	12	14	14 Va-Yehi
30	6		6	7	8	9 Hukkat	9 Tishah be-Av	11	13	13	15	15
31	7		7 Va-Yikra		9		10	12		14		16

Candle Lighting Times

ATLANTA, GEORGIA

DAY	JAN.	FEB.	MAR.	APR.	MAY	JUNE	JULY	AUG.	SEPT.	OCT.	NOV.	DEC.
1	5:22 P.M.	5:51	6:16	6:40	7:03	7:25	7:34	7:20	6:46	6:04	5:28	5:11
2	5:23	5:52	6:17	6:41	7:03	7:25	7:34	7:19	6:44	6:03	5:27	5:11
3	5:24	5:53	6:18	6:42	7:04	7:26	7:34	7:18	6:43	6:02	5:26	5:11
4	5:25	5:54	6:19	6:42	7:05	7:26	7:34	7:17	6:42	6:00	5:25	5:11
5	5:25	5:55	6:19	6:43	7:06	7:27	7:34	7:16	6:40	5:59	5:24	5:11
6	5:26	5:55	6:20	6:44	7:06	7:27	7:33	7:16	6:39	5:58	5:23	5:11
7	5:27	5:56	6:21	6:44	7:07	7:28	7:33	7:15	6:38	5:56	5:23	5:11
8	5:28	5:57	6:22	6:45	7:08	7:28	7:33	7:14	6:36	5:55	5:22	5:11
9	5:29	5:58	6:23	6:46	7:09	7:29	7:33	7:13	6:35	5:54	5:21	5:12
10	5:30	5:59	6:23	6:47	7:09	7:29	7:32	7:12	6:33	5:53	5:20	5:12
11	5:31	6:00	6:24	6:47	7:10	7:30	7:32	7:11	6:32	5:51	5:20	5:12
12	5:31	6:01	6:25	6:48	7:11	7:30	7:32	7:10	6:31	5:50	5:19	5:12
13	5:32	6:02	6:26	6:49	7:12	7:31	7:32	7:08	6:29	5:49	5:18	5:12
14	5:33	6:03	6:27	6:50	7:12	7:31	7:31	7:07	6:28	5:48	5:18	5:13
15	5:34	6:04	6:27	6:50	7:13	7:31	7:31	7:06	6:27	5:46	5:17	5:13
16	5:35	6:05	6:28	6:51	7:14	7:32	7:30	7:05	6:25	5:45	5:16	5:13
17	5:36	6:06	6:29	6:52	7:15	7:32	7:30	7:04	6:24	5:44	5:16	5:14
18	5:37	6:07	6:30	6:53	7:15	7:32	7:29	7:03	6:22	5:43	5:15	5:14
19	5:38	6:08	6:30	6:53	7:16	7:33	7:29	7:02	6:21	5:42	5:15	5:14
20	5:39	6:08	6:31	6:54	7:17	7:33	7:28	7:01	6:20	5:40	5:14	5:15
21	5:40	6:09	6:32	6:55	7:17	7:33	7:28	6:59	6:18	5:39	5:14	5:15
22	5:41	6:10	6:33	6:56	7:18	7:33	7:27	6:58	6:17	5:38	5:14	5:16
23	5:42	6:11	6:33	6:56	7:19	7:33	7:27	6:57	6:15	5:37	5:13	5:16
24	5:43	6:12	6:34	6:57	7:20	7:34	7:26	6:56	6:14	5:36	5:13	5:17
25	5:44	6:13	6:35	6:58	7:20	7:34	7:25	6:54	6:13	5:35	5:13	5:17
26	5:45	6:14	6:36	6:59	7:21	7:34	7:25	6:53	6:11	5:34	5:12	5:18
27	5:46	6:14	6:36	7:00	7:22	7:34	7:24	6:52	6:10	5:33	5:12	5:19
28	5:47	6:15	6:37	7:00	7:22	7:34	7:23	6:51	6:09	5:32	5:12	5:19
29	5:48	6:16	6:38	7:01	7:23	7:34	7:22	6:49	6:07	5:31	5:12	5:20
30	5:49		6:39	7:02	7:23	7:34	7:22	6:48	6:06	5:30	5:11	5:21
31	5:50		6:39		7:24		7:21	6:47		5:29		5:21

BALTIMORE, MARYLAND

DAY	JAN.	FEB.	MAR.	APR.	MAY	JUNE	JULY	AUG.	SEPT.	OCT.	NOV.	DEC.
1	4:36 P.M.	5:09	5:41	6:12	6:41	7:09	7:19	7:01	6:20	5:32	4:48	4:26
2	4:37	5:10	5:42	6:13	6:42	7:09	7:19	7:00	6:18	5:30	4:47	4:26
3	4:38	5:12	5:43	6:14	6:43	7:10	7:19	6:59	6:17	5:29	4:46	4:26
4	4:39	5:13	5:44	6:15	6:44	7:11	7:18	6:58	6:15	5:27	4:45	4:26
5	4:40	5:14	5:45	6:16	6:45	7:11	7:18	6:56	6:14	5:25	4:44	4:26
6	4:41	5:15	5:46	6:17	6:46	7:12	7:18	6:55	6:12	5:24	4:43	4:26
7	4:42	5:16	5:47	6:18	6:47	7:13	7:18	6:54	6:10	5:22	4:42	4:26
8	4:43	5:17	5:48	6:19	6:48	7:13	7:17	6:53	6:09	5:21	4:41	4:26
9	4:44	5:19	5:49	6:20	6:49	7:14	7:17	6:52	6:07	5:19	4:40	4:26
10	4:45	5:20	5:50	6:21	6:50	7:14	7:17	6:51	6:06	5:18	4:39	4:26
11	4:46	5:21	5:51	6:22	6:51	7:15	7:16	6:49	6:04	5:16	4:38	4:26
12	4:47	5:22	5:52	6:23	6:52	7:15	7:16	6:48	6:02	5:15	4:37	4:26
13	4:48	5:23	5:53	6:24	6:53	7:16	7:15	6:47	6:01	5:13	4:36	4:26
14	4:49	5:24	5:54	6:25	6:54	7:16	7:15	6:46	5:59	5:12	4:35	4:26
15	4:50	5:26	5:55	6:26	6:55	7:16	7:14	6:44	5:58	5:10	4:34	4:27
16	4:51	5:27	5:56	6:27	6:56	7:17	7:14	6:43	5:56	5:09	4:34	4:27
17	4:52	5:28	5:57	6:28	6:57	7:17	7:13	6:42	5:54	5:07	4:33	4:27
18	4:53	5:29	5:58	6:29	6:57	7:17	7:12	6:40	5:53	5:06	4:32	4:28
19	4:54	5:30	5:59	6:30	6:58	7:18	7:12	6:39	5:51	5:05	4:32	4:28
20	4:55	5:31	6:00	6:31	6:59	7:18	7:11	6:37	5:49	5:03	4:31	4:29
21	4:57	5:32	6:01	6:32	7:00	7:18	7:10	6:36	5:48	5:02	4:30	4:29
22	4:58	5:33	6:02	6:33	7:01	7:18	7:10	6:35	5:46	5:01	4:30	4:30
23	4:59	5:34	6:03	6:34	7:02	7:19	7:09	6:33	5:45	4:59	4:29	4:30
24	5:00	5:36	6:04	6:35	7:03	7:19	7:08	6:32	5:43	4:58	4:29	4:31
25	5:01	5:37	6:05	6:36	7:03	7:19	7:07	6:30	5:41	4:57	4:28	4:31
26	5:02	5:38	6:06	6:37	7:04	7:19	7:06	6:29	5:40	4:55	4:28	4:32
27	5:03	5:39	6:07	6:38	7:05	7:19	7:06	6:27	5:38	4:54	4:28	4:33
28	5:05	5:40	6:08	6:39	7:06	7:19	7:05	6:26	5:37	4:53	4:27	4:33
29	5:06	5:41	6:09	6:40	7:07	7:19	7:04	6:24	5:35	4:52	4:27	4:34
30	5:07		6:10	6:40	7:07	7:19	7:03	6:23	5:33	4:50	4:27	4:35
31	5:08		6:11		7:08		7:02	6:21		4:49		4:35

BOSTON, MASSACHUSETTS

DAY	JAN.	FEB.	MAR.	APR.	MAY	JUNE	JULY	AUG.	SEPT.	OCT.	NOV.	DEC.
1	4:04 P.M.	4:40	5:16	5:52	6:26	6:56	7:07	6:46	6:01	5:08	4:20	3:55
2	4:05	4:41	5:17	5:53	6:27	6:57	7:07	6:45	5:59	5:07	4:19	3:55
3	4:06	4:43	5:18	5:54	6:28	6:58	7:06	6:44	5:57	5:05	4:17	3:54
4	4:07	4:44	5:20	5:55	6:29	6:58	7:06	6:42	5:56	5:03	4:16	3:54
5	4:08	4:45	5:21	5:56	6:30	6:59	7:06	6:41	5:54	5:01	4:15	3:54
6	4:09	4:47	5:22	5:57	6:31	7:00	7:06	6:40	5:52	5:00	4:14	3:54
7	4:10	4:48	5:23	5:59	6:32	7:00	7:05	6:39	5:50	4:58	4:13	3:54
8	4:11	4:49	5:24	6:00	6:33	7:01	7:05	6:37	5:49	4:56	4:12	3:54
9	4:12	4:51	5:25	6:01	6:34	7:02	7:05	6:36	5:47	4:55	4:10	3:54
10	4:13	4:52	5:27	6:02	6:35	7:02	7:04	6:35	5:45	4:53	4:09	3:54
11	4:14	4:53	5:28	6:03	6:36	7:03	7:04	6:33	5:43	4:51	4:08	3:54
12	4:15	4:54	5:29	6:04	6:37	7:03	7:03	6:32	5:42	4:50	4:07	3:54
13	4:16	4:56	5:30	6:05	6:39	7:04	7:03	6:31	5:40	4:48	4:06	3:54
14	4:18	4:57	5:31	6:06	6:40	7:04	7:02	6:29	5:38	4:46	4:05	3:54
15	4:19	4:58	5:32	6:08	6:41	7:05	7:01	6:28	5:36	4:45	4:05	3:54
16	4:20	5:00	5:34	6:09	6:42	7:05	7:01	6:26	5:35	4:43	4:04	3:55
17	4:21	5:01	5:35	6:10	6:43	7:05	7:00	6:25	5:33	4:42	4:03	3:55
18	4:22	5:02	5:36	6:11	6:44	7:06	6:59	6:23	5:31	4:40	4:02	3:55
19	4:24	5:03	5:37	6:12	6:45	7:06	6:59	6:22	5:29	4:38	4:01	3:56
20	4:25	5:05	5:38	6:13	6:46	7:06	6:58	6:20	5:28	4:37	4:01	3:56
21	4:26	5:06	5:39	6:14	6:47	7:06	6:57	6:19	5:26	4:35	4:00	3:57
22	4:27	5:07	5:41	6:15	6:48	7:07	6:56	6:17	5:24	4:34	3:59	3:57
23	4:29	5:08	5:42	6:17	6:49	7:07	6:55	6:15	5:22	4:32	3:59	3:58
24	4:30	5:10	5:43	6:18	6:49	7:07	6:54	6:14	5:21	4:31	3:58	3:58
25	4:31	5:11	5:44	6:19	6:50	7:07	6:53	6:12	5:19	4:30	3:57	3:59
26	4:32	5:12	5:45	6:20	6:51	7:07	6:52	6:11	5:17	4:28	3:57	4:00
27	4:34	5:13	5:46	6:21	6:52	7:07	6:51	6:09	5:15	4:27	3:56	4:00
28	4:35	5:15	5:47	6:22	6:53	7:07	6:50	6:07	5:13	4:25	3:56	4:01
29	4:36	5:16	5:48	6:23	6:54	7:07	6:49	6:06	5:12	4:24	3:56	4:02
30	4:38		5:50	6:24	6:55	7:07	6:48	6:04	5:10	4:23	3:55	4:02
31	4:39		5:51		6:55		6:47	6:02		4:21		4:03

CHICAGO, ILLINOIS

DAY	JAN.	FEB.	MAR.	APR.	MAY	JUNE	JULY	AUG.	SEPT.	OCT.	NOV.	DEC.
1	4:13 P.M.	4:48	5:23	5:58	6:30	7:00	7:11	6:51	6:06	5:15	4:27	4:03
2	4:13	4:49	5:24	5:59	6:31	7:01	7:11	6:50	6:05	5:13	4:26	4:03
3	4:14	4:50	5:25	6:00	6:33	7:02	7:11	6:48	6:03	5:11	4:25	4:02
4	4:15	4:52	5:26	6:01	6:34	7:03	7:10	6:47	6:01	5:10	4:24	4:02
5	4:16	4:53	5:27	6:02	6:35	7:03	7:10	6:46	6:00	5:08	4:23	4:02
6	4:17	4:54	5:29	6:03	6:36	7:04	7:10	6:45	5:58	5:06	4:21	4:02
7	4:18	4:55	5:30	6:04	6:37	7:05	7:09	6:44	5:56	5:05	4:20	4:02
8	4:19	4:57	5:31	6:05	6:38	7:05	7:09	6:42	5:55	5:03	4:19	4:02
9	4:20	4:58	5:32	6:06	6:39	7:06	7:09	6:41	5:53	5:01	4:18	4:02
10	4:21	4:59	5:33	6:07	6:40	7:06	7:08	6:40	5:51	5:00	4:17	4:02
11	4:22	5:01	5:34	6:09	6:41	7:07	7:08	6:38	5:49	4:58	4:16	4:02
12	4:23	5:02	5:35	6:10	6:42	7:07	7:07	6:37	5:48	4:57	4:15	4:02
13	4:25	5:03	5:37	6:11	6:43	7:08	7:07	6:36	5:46	4:55	4:14	4:02
14	4:26	5:04	5:38	6:12	6:44	7:08	7:06	6:34	5:44	4:53	4:13	4:03
15	4:27	5:06	5:39	6:13	6:45	7:09	7:06	6:33	5:42	4:52	4:12	4:03
16	4:28	5:07	5:40	6:14	6:46	7:09	7:05	6:31	5:41	4:50	4:12	4:03
17	4:29	5:08	5:41	6:15	6:47	7:09	7:04	6:30	5:39	4:49	4:11	4:03
18	4:30	5:09	5:42	6:16	6:48	7:10	7:04	6:28	5:37	4:47	4:10	4:04
19	4:32	5:11	5:43	6:17	6:49	7:10	7:03	6:27	5:36	4:46	4:09	4:04
20	4:33	5:12	5:44	6:18	6:50	7:10	7:02	6:25	5:34	4:44	4:09	4:05
21	4:34	5:13	5:46	6:19	6:51	7:11	7:01	6:24	5:32	4:43	4:08	4:05
22	4:35	5:14	5:47	6:21	6:52	7:11	7:01	6:22	5:30	4:41	4:07	4:06
23	4:36	5:15	5:48	6:22	6:53	7:11	7:00	6:21	5:29	4:40	4:07	4:06
24	4:38	5:17	5:49	6:23	6:54	7:11	6:59	6:19	5:27	4:38	4:06	4:07
25	4:39	5:18	5:50	6:24	6:55	7:11	6:58	6:18	5:25	4:37	4:05	4:07
26	4:40	5:19	5:51	6:25	6:56	7:11	6:57	6:16	5:23	4:35	4:05	4:08
27	4:41	5:20	5:52	6:26	6:56	7:11	6:56	6:15	5:22	4:34	4:04	4:09
28	4:43	5:21	5:53	6:27	6:57	7:11	6:55	6:13	5:20	4:33	4:04	4:09
29	4:44	5:22	5:54	6:28	6:58	7:11	6:54	6:11	5:18	4:31	4:04	4:10
30	4:45		5:55	6:29	6:59	7:11	6:53	6:10	5:17	4:30	4:03	4:11
31	4:46		5:57		7:00		6:52	6:08		4:29		4:12

CINCINNATI, OHIO

DAY	JAN.	FEB.	MAR.	APR.	MAY	JUNE	JULY	AUG.	SEPT.	OCT.	NOV.	DEC.
1	5:08 P.M.	5:41	6:12	6:43	7:13	7:40	7:50	7:32	6:51	6:03	5:20	4:58
2	5:09	5:42	6:13	6:44	7:14	7:41	7:50	7:31	6:50	6:02	5:18	4:58
3	5:10	5:43	6:14	6:45	7:15	7:41	7:50	7:30	6:48	6:00	5:17	4:58
4	5:11	5:44	6:16	6:46	7:16	7:42	7:49	7:29	6:46	5:58	5:16	4:57
5	5:12	5:45	6:17	6:47	7:17	7:43	7:49	7:28	6:45	5:57	5:15	4:57
6	5:12	5:47	6:18	6:48	7:17	7:43	7:49	7:27	6:43	5:55	5:14	4:57
7	5:13	5:48	6:19	6:49	7:18	7:44	7:49	7:25	6:42	5:54	5:13	4:57
8	5:14	5:49	6:20	6:50	7:19	7:44	7:48	7:24	6:40	5:52	5:12	4:57
9	5:15	5:50	6:21	6:51	7:20	7:45	7:48	7:23	6:39	5:51	5:11	4:57
10	5:16	5:51	6:22	6:52	7:21	7:45	7:48	7:22	6:39	5:49	5:10	4:57
11	5:17	5:52	6:23	6:53	7:22	7:46	7:47	7:21	6:35	5:48	5:09	4:58
12	5:18	5:54	6:24	6:54	7:23	7:46	7:47	7:19	6:34	5:46	5:09	4:58
13	5:19	5:55	6:25	6:55	7:24	7:47	7:46	7:18	6:32	5:45	5:08	4:58
14	5:20	5:56	6:26	6:56	7:25	7:47	7:46	7:17	6:31	5:43	5:07	4:58
15	5:21	5:57	6:27	6:57	7:26	7:48	7:45	7:16	6:29	5:42	5:06	4:58
16	5:23	5:58	6:28	6:58	7:27	7:48	7:45	7:14	6:27	5:40	5:05	4:59
17	5:24	5:59	6:29	6:59	7:28	7:48	7:44	7:13	6:26	5:39	5:05	4:59
18	5:25	6:00	6:30	7:00	7:29	7:49	7:44	7:12	6:24	5:38	5:04	4:59
19	5:26	6:01	6:31	7:01	7:30	7:49	7:43	7:10	6:22	5:36	5:03	5:00
20	5:27	6:03	6:32	7:02	7:30	7:49	7:42	7:09	6:21	5:35	5:03	5:00
21	5:28	6:04	6:33	7:03	7:31	7:49	7:42	7:07	6:19	5:33	5:02	5:01
22	5:29	6:05	6:34	7:04	7:32	7:50	7:41	7:06	6:18	5:32	5:01	5:01
23	5:30	6:06	6:35	7:05	7:33	7:50	7:40	7:04	6:16	5:31	5:01	5:02
24	5:32	6:07	6:36	7:06	7:34	7:50	7:39	7:03	6:14	5:29	5:00	5:02
25	5:33	6:08	6:37	7:07	7:35	7:50	7:38	7:02	6:13	5:28	5:00	5:03
26	5:34	6:09	6:38	7:08	7:35	7:50	7:38	7:00	6:11	5:27	5:00	5:04
27	5:35	6:10	6:39	7:09	7:36	7:50	7:37	6:59	6:10	5:26	4:59	5:04
28	5:36	6:11	6:40	7:10	7:37	7:50	7:36	6:57	6:08	5:24	4:59	5:05
29	5:37	6:12	6:41	7:11	7:38	7:50	7:35	6:56	6:06	5:23	4:59	5:06
30	5:38		6:42	7:12	7:38	7:50	7:34	6:54	6:05	5:22	4:58	5:06
31	5:40		6:43		7:39		7:33	6:53		5:21		5:07

CLEVELAND, OHIO

DAY	JAN.	FEB.	MAR.	APR.	MAY	JUNE	JULY	AUG.	SEPT.	OCT.	NOV.	DEC.
1	4:50 P.M.	5:25	6:00	6:34	7:07	7:36	7:47	7:27	6:43	5:52	5:05	4:41
2	4:51	5:27	6:01	6:35	7:08	7:37	7:47	7:26	6:41	5:50	5:04	4:41
3	4:52	5:28	6:02	6:36	7:09	7:38	7:46	7:25	6:40	5:48	5:02	4:40
4	4:53	5:29	6:03	6:38	7:10	7:38	7:46	7:23	6:38	5:47	5:01	4:40
5	4:54	5:30	6:04	6:39	7:11	7:39	7:46	7:22	6:36	5:45	5:00	4:40
6	4:55	5:32	6:06	6:40	7:12	7:40	7:46	7:21	6:35	5:43	4:59	4:40
7	4:56	5:33	6:07	6:41	7:13	7:40	7:45	7:20	6:33	5:42	4:58	4:40
8	4:57	5:34	6:08	6:42	7:14	7:41	7:45	7:18	6:31	5:40	4:57	4:40
9	4:58	5:35	6:09	6:43	7:15	7:42	7:45	7:17	6:29	5:38	4:56	4:40
10	4:59	5:37	6:10	6:44	7:16	7:42	7:44	7:16	6:28	5:35	4:55	4:40
11	5:00	5:38	6:11	6:45	7:17	7:43	7:44	7:15	6:26	5:34	4:54	4:40
12	5:01	5:39	6:12	6:46	7:18	7:43	7:43	7:13	6:24	5:32	4:53	4:40
13	5:02	5:40	6:14	6:47	7:19	7:44	7:43	7:12	6:23	5:30	4:52	4:40
14	5:03	5:42	6:15	6:48	7:20	7:44	7:42	7:10	6:21	5:29	4:51	4:40
15	5:05	5:43	6:16	6:49	7:21	7:44	7:42	7:09	6:19	5:27	4:50	4:41
16	5:06	5:44	6:17	6:50	7:22	7:45	7:41	7:08	6:17	5:26	4:49	4:41
17	5:07	5:45	6:18	6:52	7:23	7:45	7:40	7:06	6:16	5:24	4:48	4:41
18	5:08	5:47	6:19	6:53	7:24	7:46	7:40	7:05	6:14	5:23	4:48	4:42
19	5:09	5:48	6:20	6:54	7:25	7:46	7:39	7:03	6:12	5:21	4:47	4:42
20	5:10	5:49	6:21	6:55	7:26	7:46	7:38	7:02	6:11	5:20	4:46	4:42
21	5:12	5:50	6:22	6:56	7:27	7:46	7:37	7:00	6:09	5:18	4:46	4:43
22	5:13	5:51	6:23	6:57	7:28	7:46	7:36	6:59	6:07	5:17	4:45	4:43
23	5:14	5:53	6:25	6:58	7:29	7:47	7:36	6:57	6:05	5:16	4:44	4:44
24	5:15	5:54	6:26	6:59	7:30	7:47	7:35	6:56	6:04	5:14	4:44	4:45
25	5:17	5:55	6:27	7:00	7:31	7:47	7:34	6:54	6:02	5:13	4:43	4:45
26	5:18	5:56	6:28	7:01	7:31	7:47	7:33	6:53	6:00	5:11	4:43	4:46
27	5:19	5:57	6:29	7:02	7:32	7:47	7:32	6:51	5:59	5:10	4:42	4:46
28	5:20	5:59	6:30	7:03	7:33	7:47	7:31	6:49	5:57	5:09	4:42	4:47
29	5:22	6:00	6:31	7:04	7:34	7:47	7:30	6:48	5:55	5:07	4:41	4:48
30	5:23		6:32	7:06	7:35	7:47	7:29	6:46	5:53	5:06	4:41	4:49
31	5:24		6:33		7:36		7:28	6:44		5:06		4:49

DENVER, COLORADO

DAY	JAN.	FEB.	MAR.	APR.	MAY	JUNE	JULY	AUG.	SEPT.	OCT.	NOV.	DEC.
1	4:28 P.M.	5:01	5:34	6:06	6:36	7:04	7:14	6:55	6:14	5:25	4:40	4:18
2	4:29	5:03	5:35	6:07	6:37	7:04	7:14	6:54	6:12	5:23	4:39	4:18
3	4:30	5:04	5:36	6:08	6:38	7:05	7:14	6:53	6:11	5:22	4:38	4:18
4	4:31	5:05	5:37	6:09	6:39	7:06	7:13	6:52	6:09	5:20	4:37	4:18
5	4:32	5:06	5:38	6:10	6:40	7:06	7:13	6:51	6:07	5:19	4:36	4:17
6	4:32	5:07	5:39	6:11	6:41	7:07	7:13	6:50	6:06	5:17	4:35	4:17
7	4:33	5:09	5:40	6:12	6:42	7:08	7:13	6:49	6:04	5:15	4:34	4:17
8	4:34	5:10	5:41	6:13	6:43	7:08	7:12	6:48	6:03	5:14	4:33	4:17
9	4:35	5:11	5:42	6:14	6:44	7:09	7:12	6:46	6:01	5:12	4:32	4:17
10	4:36	5:12	5:43	6:15	6:45	7:09	7:12	6:45	5:59	5:11	4:31	4:17
11	4:37	5:13	5:44	6:16	6:46	7:10	7:11	6:44	5:58	5:09	4:30	4:18
12	4:38	5:14	5:45	6:17	6:47	7:10	7:11	6:43	5:56	5:08	4:29	4:18
13	4:39	5:16	5:46	6:18	6:48	7:11	7:10	6:41	5:54	5:06	4:28	4:18
14	4:41	5:17	5:48	6:19	6:48	7:11	7:10	6:40	5:53	5:05	4:27	4:18
15	4:42	5:18	5:49	6:20	6:49	7:12	7:09	6:39	5:51	5:03	4:27	4:18
16	4:43	5:19	5:50	6:21	6:50	7:12	7:09	6:37	5:50	5:02	4:26	4:19
17	4:44	5:20	5:51	6:22	6:51	7:12	7:08	6:36	5:48	5:00	4:25	4:19
18	4:45	5:21	5:52	6:23	6:52	7:13	7:07	6:35	5:46	4:59	4:24	4:19
19	4:46	5:23	5:53	6:24	6:53	7:13	7:07	6:33	5:45	4:57	4:24	4:20
20	4:47	5:24	5:54	6:25	6:54	7:13	7:06	6:32	5:43	4:56	4:23	4:20
21	4:48	5:25	5:55	6:26	6:55	7:13	7:05	6:30	5:41	4:55	4:22	4:21
22	4:50	5:26	5:56	6:27	6:56	7:14	7:05	6:29	5:40	4:53	4:22	4:21
23	4:51	5:27	5:57	6:28	6:57	7:14	7:04	6:27	5:38	4:52	4:21	4:22
24	4:52	5:28	5:58	6:29	6:57	7:14	7:03	6:26	5:36	4:51	4:21	4:22
25	4:53	5:29	5:59	6:30	6:58	7:14	7:02	6:24	5:35	4:49	4:20	4:23
26	4:54	5:30	6:00	6:31	6:59	7:14	7:01	6:23	5:33	4:48	4:20	4:23
27	4:55	5:32	6:01	6:32	7:00	7:14	7:00	6:21	5:32	4:47	4:19	4:24
28	4:57	5:33	6:02	6:33	7:01	7:14	6:59	6:20	5:30	4:45	4:19	4:25
29	4:58	5:34	6:03	6:34	7:01	7:14	6:58	6:18	5:28	4:44	4:19	4:26
30	4:59		6:04	6:35	7:02	7:14	6:57	6:17	5:27	4:43	4:18	4:26
31	5:00		6:05		7:03		6:56	6:15		4:42		4:27

DETROIT, MICHIGAN

DAY	JAN.	FEB.	MAR.	APR.	MAY	JUNE	JULY	AUG.	SEPT.	OCT.	NOV.	DEC.
1	4:54 P.M.	5:30	6:05	6:41	7:14	7:45	7:56	7:35	6:50	5:57	5:09	4:44
2	4:55	5:31	6:06	6:42	7:15	7:46	7:55	7:34	6:48	5:56	5:08	4:44
3	4:56	5:32	6:07	6:43	7:17	7:46	7:55	7:33	6:46	5:54	5:07	4:44
4	4:57	5:33	6:09	6:44	7:18	7:47	7:55	7:31	6:45	5:52	5:06	4:44
5	4:58	5:35	6:10	6:45	7:19	7:48	7:55	7:30	6:43	5:51	5:04	4:43
6	4:59	5:36	6:11	6:46	7:20	7:48	7:54	7:29	6:41	5:49	5:03	4:43
7	5:00	5:37	6:12	6:48	7:21	7:49	7:54	7:28	6:40	5:47	5:02	4:43
8	5:01	5:39	6:13	6:49	7:22	7:50	7:54	7:26	6:38	5:46	5:01	4:43
9	5:02	5:40	6:15	6:50	7:23	7:50	7:53	7:25	6:36	5:44	5:00	4:43
10	5:03	5:41	6:16	6:51	7:24	7:51	7:53	7:24	6:34	5:42	4:59	4:43
11	5:04	5:43	6:17	6:52	7:25	7:51	7:52	7:22	6:33	5:41	4:58	4:43
12	5:05	5:44	6:18	6:53	7:26	7:52	7:52	7:21	6:31	5:39	4:57	4:43
13	5:05	5:45	6:19	6:54	7:27	7:52	7:51	7:19	6:29	5:37	4:56	4:44
14	5:07	5:46	6:20	6:55	7:28	7:53	7:51	7:18	6:27	5:36	4:55	4:44
15	5:08	5:48	6:22	6:56	7:29	7:53	7:50	7:17	6:26	5:34	4:54	4:44
16	5:09	5:49	6:23	6:58	7:30	7:54	7:49	7:15	6:24	5:32	4:53	4:44
17	5:11	5:50	6:24	6:59	7:31	7:54	7:49	7:14	6:22	5:31	4:52	4:45
18	5:12	5:51	6:25	7:00	7:32	7:54	7:48	7:12	6:20	5:29	4:52	4:45
19	5:13	5:53	6:26	7:01	7:33	7:55	7:47	7:11	6:19	5:28	4:51	4:45
20	5:14	5:54	6:27	7:02	7:34	7:55	7:47	7:09	6:17	5:26	4:50	4:46
21	5:15	5:55	6:28	7:03	7:35	7:55	7:46	7:08	6:15	5:25	4:49	4:46
22	5:17	5:56	6:30	7:04	7:36	7:55	7:45	7:06	6:13	5:23	4:49	4:47
23	5:18	5:58	6:31	7:05	7:37	7:55	7:44	7:04	6:11	5:22	4:48	4:47
24	5:19	5:59	6:32	7:07	7:38	7:56	7:43	7:03	6:10	5:20	4:47	4:48
25	5:21	6:00	6:33	7:08	7:39	7:56	7:42	7:01	6:08	5:19	4:47	4:48
26	5:22	6:01	6:34	7:09	7:40	7:56	7:41	7:00	6:06	5:17	4:46	4:49
27	5:23	6:03	6:35	7:10	7:41	7:56	7:40	6:58	6:04	5:16	4:46	4:50
28	5:24	6:04	6:36	7:11	7:42	7:56	7:39	6:56	6:03	5:15	4:45	4:51
29	5:26	6:05	6:37	7:12	7:43	7:56	7:38	6:55	6:01	5:13	4:45	4:51
30	5:27		6:39	7:13	7:43	7:56	7:37	6:53	5:59	5:12	4:45	4:52
31	5:28		6:40		7:44		7:36	6:51		5:11		4:53

HOUSTON, TEXAS

DAY	JAN.	FEB.	MAR.	APR.	MAY	JUNE	JULY	AUG.	SEPT.	OCT.	NOV.	DEC.
1	5:15 P.M.	5:41	6:03	6:22	6:40	6:59	7:08	6:56	6:26	5:49	5:17	5:04
2	5:16	5:42	6:03	6:23	6:41	7:00	7:08	6:56	6:25	5:48	5:16	5:04
3	5:17	5:43	6:04	6:23	6:42	7:00	7:08	6:55	6:24	5:47	5:15	5:04
4	5:18	5:43	6:05	6:24	6:42	7:01	7:08	6:54	6:23	5:46	5:15	5:04
5	5:18	5:44	6:05	6:24	6:43	7:01	7:08	6:53	6:21	5:45	5:14	5:04
6	5:19	5:45	6:06	6:25	6:43	7:02	7:08	6:53	6:20	5:43	5:13	5:04
7	5:20	5:46	6:07	6:25	6:44	7:02	7:08	6:52	6:19	5:42	5:13	5:04
8	5:21	5:47	6:07	6:26	6:45	7:03	7:07	6:51	6:18	5:41	5:12	5:04
9	5:21	5:48	6:08	6:27	6:45	7:03	7:07	6:50	6:16	5:40	5:11	5:04
10	5:22	5:48	6:09	6:27	6:46	7:03	7:07	6:49	6:15	5:39	5:11	5:05
11	5:23	5:49	6:09	6:28	6:47	7:04	7:07	6:48	6:14	5:38	5:10	5:05
12	5:24	5:50	6:10	6:28	6:47	7:04	7:07	6:47	6:13	5:36	5:09	5:05
13	5:25	5:51	6:10	6:29	6:48	7:05	7:06	6:46	6:12	5:35	5:09	5:05
14	5:25	5:52	6:11	6:30	6:49	7:05	7:06	6:45	6:10	5:34	5:08	5:06
15	5:26	5:52	6:12	6:30	6:49	7:05	7:06	6:44	6:09	5:33	5:08	5:06
16	5:27	5:53	6:12	6:31	6:50	7:06	7:05	6:44	6:08	5:32	5:07	5:06
17	5:28	5:54	6:13	6:32	6:50	7:06	7:05	6:43	6:07	5:31	5:07	5:07
18	5:29	5:55	6:14	6:32	6:51	7:06	7:04	6:42	6:05	5:30	5:07	5:07
19	5:30	5:55	6:14	6:33	6:52	7:06	7:04	6:40	6:04	5:29	5:06	5:08
20	5:31	5:56	6:15	6:33	6:52	7:07	7:04	6:39	6:03	5:28	5:06	5:08
21	5:31	5:57	6:15	6:34	6:53	7:07	7:03	6:38	6:02	5:27	5:06	5:09
22	5:32	5:58	6:16	6:35	6:54	7:07	7:03	6:37	6:00	5:26	5:05	5:09
23	5:33	5:58	6:17	6:35	6:54	7:07	7:02	6:36	5:59	5:25	5:05	5:10
24	5:34	5:59	6:17	6:36	6:55	7:07	7:02	6:35	5:58	5:24	5:05	5:10
25	5:35	6:00	6:18	6:36	6:55	7:08	7:01	6:34	5:57	5:23	5:05	5:11
26	5:36	6:00	6:18	6:37	6:56	7:08	7:00	6:33	5:55	5:22	5:04	5:11
27	5:37	6:01	6:19	6:38	6:56	7:08	7:00	6:32	5:54	5:21	5:04	5:12
28	5:38	6:02	6:20	6:38	6:57	7:08	6:59	6:31	5:53	5:20	5:04	5:12
29	5:38	6:03	6:20	6:39	6:58	7:08	6:59	6:30	5:52	5:19	5:04	5:13
30	5:39		6:21	6:40	6:58	7:08	6:58	6:28	5:51	5:19	5:04	5:14
31	5:40		6:21		6:59		6:57	6:27		5:18		5:14

LOS ANGELES, CALIFORNIA

DAY	JAN.	FEB.	MAR.	APR.	MAY	JUNE	JULY	AUG.	SEPT.	OCT.	NOV.	DEC.
1	4:37 P.M.	5:05	5:31	5:56	6:19	6:41	6:50	6:36	6:01	5:20	4:42	4:26
2	4:37	5:06	5:32	5:56	6:19	6:42	6:50	6:35	6:00	5:18	4:41	4:26
3	4:38	5:07	5:33	5:57	6:20	6:42	6:50	6:34	5:58	5:17	4:41	4:25
4	4:39	5:08	5:34	5:58	6:21	6:43	6:50	6:33	5:57	5:15	4:40	4:25
5	4:40	5:09	5:34	5:59	6:22	6:43	6:50	6:32	5:56	5:14	4:39	4:25
6	4:41	5:10	5:35	5:59	6:22	6:44	6:50	6:31	5:54	5:13	4:38	4:25
7	4:41	5:11	5:36	6:00	6:23	6:44	6:49	6:30	5:53	5:11	4:37	4:26
8	4:42	5:12	5:37	6:01	6:24	6:45	6:49	6:29	5:52	5:10	4:36	4:26
9	4:43	5:13	5:38	6:02	6:25	6:45	6:49	6:28	5:50	5:09	4:36	4:26
10	4:44	5:14	5:39	6:02	6:26	6:46	6:49	6:27	5:49	5:07	4:35	4:26
11	4:45	5:15	5:39	6:03	6:26	6:46	6:48	6:26	5:47	5:06	4:34	4:26
12	4:46	5:16	5:40	6:04	6:27	6:47	6:48	6:25	5:46	5:05	4:33	4:26
13	4:47	5:17	5:41	6:05	6:28	6:47	6:48	6:24	5:45	5:04	4:33	4:27
14	4:48	5:18	5:42	6:05	6:29	6:47	6:47	6:23	5:43	5:02	4:32	4:27
15	4:49	5:19	5:43	6:06	6:29	6:48	6:47	6:22	5:42	5:01	4:31	4:27
16	4:50	5:20	5:43	6:07	6:30	6:48	6:46	6:21	5:40	5:00	4:31	4:27
17	4:51	5:21	5:44	6:08	6:31	6:48	6:46	6:20	5:39	4:59	4:30	4:28
18	4:52	5:21	5:45	6:08	6:32	6:49	6:46	6:19	5:38	4:57	4:30	4:28
19	4:52	5:22	5:46	6:09	6:32	6:49	6:45	6:17	5:36	4:56	4:29	4:29
20	4:53	5:23	5:46	6:10	6:33	6:49	6:44	6:16	5:35	4:55	4:29	4:29
21	4:54	5:24	5:47	6:11	6:34	6:49	6:44	6:15	5:33	4:54	4:28	4:30
22	4:55	5:25	5:48	6:12	6:34	6:50	6:43	6:14	5:32	4:53	4:28	4:30
23	4:56	5:26	5:49	6:12	6:35	6:50	6:43	6:13	5:31	4:52	4:28	4:31
24	4:57	5:27	5:49	6:13	6:36	6:50	6:42	6:11	5:29	4:51	4:27	4:31
25	4:58	5:28	5:50	6:14	6:37	6:50	6:41	6:10	5:28	4:49	4:27	4:32
26	4:59	5:29	5:51	6:15	6:37	6:50	6:41	6:09	5:26	4:48	4:27	4:32
27	5:00	5:29	5:52	6:15	6:38	6:50	6:40	6:08	5:25	4:47	4:26	4:33
28	5:01	5:30	5:53	6:16	6:38	6:50	6:39	6:06	5:24	4:46	4:26	4:34
29	5:02	5:31	5:53	6:17	6:39	6:50	6:38	6:05	5:22	4:45	4:26	4:34
30	5:03		5:54	6:18	6:40	6:50	6:38	6:04	5:21	4:44	4:26	4:35
31	5:04		5:55		6:40		6:37	6:02		4:43		4:36

MIAMI, FLORIDA

DAY	JAN.	FEB.	MAR.	APR.	MAY	JUNE	JULY	AUG.	SEPT.	OCT.	NOV.	DEC.
1	5:23 P.M.	5:46	6:04	6:19	6:34	6:50	6:58	6:49	6:22	5:50	5:21	5:11
2	5:24	5:47	6:05	6:20	6:34	6:50	6:58	6:48	6:21	5:49	5:20	5:11
3	5:25	5:48	6:05	6:20	6:35	6:51	6:58	6:48	6:20	5:48	5:20	5:11
4	5:25	5:49	6:06	6:21	6:35	6:51	6:58	6:47	6:19	5:46	5:19	5:11
5	5:26	5:49	6:07	6:21	6:36	6:52	6:58	6:46	6:18	5:45	5:19	5:12
6	5:27	5:50	6:07	6:22	6:36	6:52	6:58	6:46	6:17	5:44	5:18	5:12
7	5:27	5:51	6:08	6:22	6:37	6:52	6:58	6:45	6:16	5:43	5:18	5:12
8	5:28	5:51	6:08	6:23	6:37	6:53	6:58	6:44	6:15	5:42	5:17	5:12
9	5:29	5:52	6:09	6:23	6:38	6:53	6:58	6:43	6:14	5:41	5:17	5:12
10	5:30	5:53	6:09	6:23	6:39	6:54	6:58	6:43	6:13	5:40	5:16	5:13
11	5:30	5:53	6:10	6:24	6:39	6:54	6:57	6:42	6:12	5:39	5:16	5:13
12	5:31	5:54	6:10	6:24	6:40	6:54	6:57	6:41	6:10	5:38	5:15	5:13
13	5:32	5:55	6:11	6:25	6:40	6:55	6:57	6:40	6:09	5:37	5:15	5:13
14	5:33	5:55	6:11	6:25	6:41	6:55	6:57	6:39	6:08	5:36	5:14	5:14
15	5:33	5:56	6:12	6:26	6:41	6:55	6:56	6:38	6:07	5:35	5:14	5:14
16	5:34	5:57	6:12	6:26	6:42	6:56	6:56	6:38	6:06	5:34	5:14	5:14
17	5:35	5:57	6:12	6:27	6:42	6:56	6:56	6:37	6:05	5:34	5:13	5:15
18	5:36	5:58	6:13	6:27	6:43	6:56	6:56	6:36	6:04	5:33	5:13	5:15
19	5:37	5:59	6:13	6:28	6:43	6:56	6:55	6:35	6:03	5:32	5:13	5:16
20	5:37	5:59	6:14	6:28	6:44	6:57	6:55	6:34	6:02	5:31	5:12	5:16
21	5:38	6:00	6:14	6:29	6:44	6:57	6:54	6:33	6:01	5:30	5:12	5:17
22	5:39	6:00	6:15	6:29	6:45	6:57	6:54	6:32	5:59	5:29	5:12	5:17
23	5:40	6:01	6:15	6:30	6:45	6:57	6:54	6:31	5:58	5:28	5:12	5:18
24	5:40	6:02	6:16	6:30	6:46	6:57	6:53	6:30	5:57	5:27	5:12	5:18
25	5:41	6:02	6:16	6:31	6:46	6:58	6:53	6:29	5:56	5:27	5:12	5:19
26	5:42	6:03	6:17	6:31	6:47	6:58	6:52	6:28	5:55	5:26	5:11	5:19
27	5:43	6:03	6:17	6:32	6:47	6:58	6:52	6:27	5:54	5:25	5:11	5:20
28	5:43	6:04	6:18	6:32	6:48	6:58	6:51	6:26	5:53	5:24	5:11	5:21
29	5:44	6:04	6:18	6:33	6:48	6:58	6:51	6:25	5:52	5:24	5:11	5:21
30	5:45		6:18	6:33	6:49	6:58	6:50	6:24	5:51	5:23	5:11	5:22
31	5:46		6:19		6:49		6:49	6:23		5:22		5:22

NEW YORK, NEW YORK

DAY	JAN.	FEB.	MAR.	APR.	MAY	JUNE	JULY	AUG.	SEPT.	OCT.	NOV.	DEC.
1	4:21 P.M.	4:56	5:29	6:03	6:34	7:03	7:13	6:54	6:11	5:21	4:35	4:11
2	4:22	4:57	5:30	6:04	6:35	7:03	7:13	6:53	6:09	5:19	4:34	4:11
3	4:23	4:58	5:31	6:05	6:36	7:04	7:13	6:51	6:07	5:17	4:32	4:11
4	4:24	4:59	5:32	6:06	6:37	7:05	7:13	6:50	6:06	5:16	4:31	4:11
5	4:25	5:00	5:34	6:07	6:38	7:06	7:12	6:49	6:04	5:14	4:30	4:11
6	4:26	5:02	5:35	6:08	6:39	7:06	7:12	6:48	6:03	5:12	4:29	4:11
7	4:27	5:03	5:36	6:09	6:40	7:07	7:12	6:47	6:01	5:11	4:28	4:11
8	4:28	5:04	5:37	6:10	6:41	7:07	7:11	6:46	5:59	5:09	4:27	4:11
9	4:29	5:05	5:38	6:11	6:42	7:08	7:11	6:44	5:58	5:08	4:26	4:11
10	4:30	5:07	5:39	6:12	6:43	7:08	7:11	6:43	5:56	5:06	4:25	4:11
11	4:31	5:08	5:40	6:13	6:44	7:09	7:10	6:42	5:54	5:04	4:24	4:11
12	4:32	5:09	5:41	6:14	6:45	7:09	7:10	6:40	5:53	5:03	4:23	4:11
13	4:33	5:10	5:42	6:15	6:46	7:10	7:09	6:39	5:51	5:01	4:22	4:11
14	4:34	5:11	5:43	6:16	6:47	7:10	7:09	6:38	5:49	5:00	4:21	4:11
15	4:35	5:13	5:45	6:17	6:48	7:11	7:08	6:36	5:48	4:58	4:20	4:12
16	4:36	5:14	5:46	6:18	6:49	7:11	7:07	6:35	5:46	4:57	4:20	4:12
17	4:37	5:15	5:47	6:19	6:50	7:11	7:07	6:34	5:44	4:55	4:19	4:12
18	4:39	5:16	5:48	6:20	6:51	7:12	7:06	6:32	5:42	4:54	4:18	4:13
19	4:40	5:17	5:49	6:21	6:52	7:12	7:05	6:31	5:41	4:52	4:17	4:13
20	4:41	5:19	5:50	6:22	6:53	7:13	7:05	6:29	5:39	4:51	4:17	4:13
21	4:42	5:20	5:51	6:23	6:54	7:13	7:04	6:28	5:37	4:49	4:16	4:14
22	4:43	5:21	5:52	6:24	6:55	7:13	7:03	6:26	5:36	4:48	4:15	4:14
23	4:45	5:22	5:53	6:26	6:55	7:13	7:02	6:25	5:34	4:47	4:15	4:15
24	4:46	5:23	5:54	6:27	6:56	7:13	7:01	6:23	5:32	4:45	4:14	4:15
25	4:47	5:25	5:55	6:28	6:57	7:13	7:01	6:22	5:31	4:44	4:14	4:16
26	4:48	5:26	5:56	6:29	6:58	7:13	7:00	6:20	5:29	4:42	4:13	4:17
27	4:49	5:27	5:57	6:30	6:59	7:13	6:59	6:19	5:27	4:41	4:13	4:17
28	4:51	5:28	5:58	6:31	7:00	7:13	6:58	6:17	5:26	4:40	4:12	4:18
29	4:52	5:29	5:59	6:32	7:00	7:13	6:57	6:16	5:24	4:39	4:12	4:19
30	4:53		6:00	6:33	7:01	7:13	6:56	6:14	5:22	4:37	4:12	4:20
31	4:54		6:01		7:02		6:55	6:12		4:36		4:20

PHILADELPHIA, PENNSYLVANIA

DAY	JAN.	FEB.	MAR.	APR.	MAY	JUNE	JULY	AUG.	SEPT.	OCT.	NOV.	DEC.
1	4:29 P.M.	5:02	5:35	6:07	6:37	7:05	7:15	6:57	6:15	5:26	4:41	4:19
2	4:30	5:03	5:36	6:08	6:38	7:06	7:15	6:56	6:13	5:24	4:40	4:19
3	4:30	5:04	5:37	6:09	6:39	7:06	7:15	6:55	6:12	5:23	4:39	4:18
4	4:31	5:06	5:38	6:10	6:40	7:07	7:15	6:54	6:10	5:21	4:38	4:18
5	4:32	5:07	5:39	6:11	6:41	7:08	7:15	6:52	6:09	5:20	4:37	4:18
6	4:33	5:08	5:40	6:12	6:42	7:08	7:14	6:51	6:07	5:18	4:36	4:18
7	4:34	5:09	5:41	6:13	6:43	7:09	7:14	6:50	6:05	5:16	4:35	4:18
8	4:35	5:10	5:42	6:14	6:44	7:10	7:14	6:49	6:04	5:15	4:34	4:18
9	4:36	5:12	5:43	6:15	6:45	7:10	7:13	6:48	6:02	5:13	4:33	4:18
10	4:37	5:13	5:44	6:16	6:46	7:11	7:13	6:46	6:00	5:12	4:32	4:18
11	4:38	5:14	5:45	6:17	6:47	7:11	7:13	6:45	5:59	5:10	4:31	4:18
12	4:39	5:15	5:46	6:18	6:48	7:12	7:12	6:44	5:57	5:09	4:30	4:18
13	4:40	5:16	5:47	6:19	6:49	7:12	7:12	6:43	5:56	5:07	4:29	4:18
14	4:41	5:18	5:49	6:20	6:50	7:13	7:11	6:41	5:54	5:06	4:28	4:19
15	4:42	5:19	5:50	6:21	6:51	7:13	7:11	6:40	5:52	5:04	4:27	4:19
16	4:43	5:20	5:51	6:22	6:52	7:13	7:10	6:39	5:51	5:03	4:26	4:19
17	4:44	5:21	5:52	6:23	6:53	7:14	7:09	6:37	5:49	5:01	4:26	4:20
18	4:46	5:22	5:53	6:24	6:54	7:14	7:09	6:36	5:47	5:00	4:25	4:20
19	4:47	5:23	5:54	6:25	6:54	7:14	7:08	6:34	5:46	4:58	4:24	4:20
20	4:48	5:25	5:55	6:26	6:55	7:15	7:07	6:33	5:44	4:57	4:24	4:21
21	4:49	5:26	5:56	6:27	6:56	7:15	7:07	6:32	5:42	4:55	4:23	4:21
22	4:50	5:27	5:57	6:28	6:57	7:15	7:06	6:30	5:41	4:54	4:22	4:22
23	4:51	5:28	5:58	6:29	6:58	7:15	7:05	6:29	5:39	4:53	4:22	4:22
24	4:53	5:29	5:59	6:30	6:59	7:15	7:04	6:27	5:37	4:51	4:21	4:23
25	4:54	5:30	6:00	6:31	7:00	7:15	7:03	6:26	5:36	4:50	4:21	4:23
26	4:55	5:31	6:01	6:32	7:00	7:15	7:03	6:24	5:34	4:49	4:20	4:24
27	4:56	5:32	6:02	6:33	7:01	7:15	7:02	6:23	5:32	4:47	4:20	4:25
28	4:57	5:34	6:03	6:34	7:02	7:15	7:01	6:21	5:31	4:46	4:20	4:25
29	4:58	5:35	6:04	6:35	7:03	7:15	7:00	6:20	5:29	4:45	4:19	4:26
30	5:00		6:05	6:36	7:04	7:15	6:59	6:18	5:28	4:44	4:19	4:27
31	5:01		6:06		7:04		6:58	6:16		4:42		4:28

PHOENIX, ARIZONA

DAY	JAN.	FEB.	MAR.	APR.	MAY	JUNE	JULY	AUG.	SEPT.	OCT.	NOV.	DEC.
1	5:13 P.M.	5:41	6:07	6:30	6:53	7:14	7:24	7:10	6:36	5:55	5:19	5:02
2	5:14	5:42	6:07	6:31	6:53	7:15	7:24	7:09	6:35	5:54	5:18	5:02
3	5:15	5:43	6:08	6:32	6:54	7:16	7:24	7:08	6:33	5:52	5:17	5:02
4	5:16	5:44	6:09	6:32	6:55	7:16	7:24	7:07	6:32	5:51	5:16	5:02
5	5:16	5:45	6:10	6:33	6:56	7:17	7:23	7:07	6:31	5:50	5:15	5:02
6	5:17	5:46	6:11	6:34	6:56	7:17	7:23	7:06	6:29	5:48	5:14	5:02
7	5:18	5:47	6:11	6:35	6:57	7:18	7:23	7:05	6:28	5:47	5:13	5:02
8	5:19	5:48	6:12	6:35	6:58	7:18	7:23	7:04	6:27	5:46	5:13	5:02
9	5:20	5:49	6:13	6:36	6:59	7:19	7:23	7:03	6:25	5:44	5:12	5:02
10	5:21	5:50	6:14	6:37	6:59	7:19	7:22	7:02	6:24	5:43	5:11	5:03
11	5:21	5:51	6:15	6:38	7:00	7:20	7:22	7:01	6:22	5:42	5:10	5:03
12	5:22	5:52	6:15	6:38	7:01	7:20	7:22	7:00	6:21	5:41	5:10	5:03
13	5:23	5:53	6:16	6:39	7:02	7:20	7:21	6:59	6:20	5:39	5:09	5:03
14	5:24	5:54	6:17	6:40	7:02	7:21	7:21	6:58	6:18	5:38	5:08	5:03
15	5:25	5:54	6:18	6:41	7:03	7:21	7:21	6:56	6:17	5:37	5:08	5:04
16	5:26	5:55	6:18	6:41	7:04	7:21	7:20	6:55	6:16	5:36	5:07	5:04
17	5:27	5:56	6:19	6:42	7:05	7:22	7:20	6:54	6:14	5:35	5:07	5:04
18	5:28	5:57	6:20	6:43	7:05	7:22	7:19	6:53	6:13	5:33	5:06	5:05
19	5:29	5:58	6:21	6:44	7:06	7:22	7:19	6:52	6:11	5:32	5:06	5:05
20	5:30	5:59	6:21	6:44	7:07	7:23	7:18	6:51	6:10	5:31	5:05	5:06
21	5:31	6:00	6:22	6:45	7:07	7:23	7:18	6:50	6:09	5:30	5:05	5:06
22	5:32	6:01	6:23	6:46	7:08	7:23	7:17	6:48	6:07	5:29	5:04	5:07
23	5:33	6:02	6:24	6:47	7:09	7:23	7:17	6:47	6:06	5:28	5:04	5:07
24	5:34	6:02	6:24	6:47	7:09	7:23	7:16	6:46	6:05	5:27	5:04	5:08
25	5:35	6:03	6:25	6:48	7:10	7:24	7:15	6:45	6:03	5:26	5:03	5:08
26	5:36	6:04	6:26	6:49	7:11	7:24	7:15	6:44	6:02	5:24	5:03	5:09
27	5:37	6:05	6:27	6:50	7:11	7:24	7:14	6:42	6:00	5:23	5:03	5:10
28	5:37	6:06	6:27	6:50	7:12	7:24	7:13	6:41	5:59	5:22	5:03	5:10
29	5:38	6:07	6:28	6:51	7:13	7:24	7:12	6:40	5:58	5:21	5:03	5:11
30	5:39		6:29	6:52	7:13	7:24	7:12	6:38	5:56	5:20	5:02	5:12
31	5:40		6:30		7:14		7:11	6:37		5:19		5:12

PITTSBURGH, PENNSYLVANIA

DAY	JAN.	FEB.	MAR.	APR.	MAY	JUNE	JULY	AUG.	SEPT.	OCT.	NOV.	DEC.
1	4:46 P.M.	5:20	5:53	6:26	6:57	7:26	7:36	7:17	6:34	5:45	4:59	4:36
2	4:47	5:21	5:54	6:27	6:58	7:27	7:36	7:16	6:33	5:43	4:58	4:36
3	4:48	5:22	5:55	6:28	6:59	7:27	7:36	7:15	6:31	5:41	4:57	4:36
4	4:49	5:24	5:57	6:29	7:00	7:28	7:36	7:14	6:30	5:40	4:56	4:36
5	4:50	5:25	5:58	6:30	7:01	7:29	7:35	7:13	6:28	5:38	4:55	4:35
6	4:50	5:26	5:59	6:31	7:02	7:29	7:35	7:11	6:26	5:37	4:53	4:35
7	4:51	5:27	6:00	6:32	7:03	7:30	7:35	7:10	6:25	5:35	4:52	4:35
8	4:52	5:29	6:01	6:34	7:04	7:30	7:35	7:09	6:23	5:33	4:51	4:35
9	4:53	5:30	6:02	6:35	7:05	7:31	7:34	7:08	6:21	5:32	4:50	4:35
10	4:54	5:31	6:03	6:36	7:06	7:32	7:34	7:06	6:20	5:30	4:49	4:35
11	4:56	5:32	6:04	6:37	7:07	7:32	7:33	7:05	6:18	5:29	4:48	4:35
12	4:57	5:33	6:05	6:38	7:08	7:33	7:33	7:04	6:16	5:27	4:48	4:36
13	4:58	5:35	6:06	6:39	7:09	7:33	7:32	7:03	6:15	5:26	4:47	4:36
14	4:59	5:36	6:07	6:40	7:10	7:33	7:32	7:01	6:13	5:24	4:46	4:36
15	5:00	5:37	6:09	6:41	7:11	7:34	7:31	7:00	6:11	5:22	4:45	4:36
16	5:01	5:38	6:10	6:42	7:12	7:34	7:31	6:58	6:10	5:21	4:44	4:37
17	5:02	5:39	6:11	6:43	7:13	7:35	7:30	6:57	6:08	5:19	4:43	4:37
18	5:03	5:41	6:12	6:44	7:14	7:35	7:29	6:56	6:06	5:18	4:43	4:37
19	5:04	5:42	6:13	6:45	7:15	7:35	7:29	6:54	6:05	5:17	4:42	4:38
20	5:06	5:43	6:14	6:46	7:16	7:35	7:28	6:53	6:03	5:15	4:41	4:38
21	5:07	5:44	6:15	6:47	7:17	7:36	7:27	6:51	6:01	5:14	4:41	4:39
22	5:08	5:45	6:16	6:48	7:18	7:36	7:26	6:50	6:00	5:12	4:40	4:39
23	5:09	5:46	6:17	6:49	7:19	7:36	7:26	6:48	5:58	5:11	4:39	4:40
24	5:10	5:48	6:18	6:50	7:19	7:36	7:25	6:47	5:56	5:09	4:39	4:40
25	5:11	5:49	6:19	6:51	7:20	7:36	7:24	6:45	5:55	5:08	4:38	4:41
26	5:13	5:50	6:20	6:52	7:21	7:36	7:23	6:44	5:53	5:07	4:38	4:41
27	5:14	5:51	6:21	6:53	7:22	7:36	7:22	6:42	5:51	5:05	4:37	4:42
28	5:15	5:52	6:22	6:54	7:23	7:36	7:21	6:41	5:50	5:04	4:37	4:43
29	5:16	5:53	6:23	6:55	7:24	7:36	7:20	6:39	5:48	5:03	4:37	4:43
30	5:18		6:24	6:56	7:24	7:36	7:19	6:38	5:46	5:02	4:36	4:44
31	5:19		6:25		7:25		7:18	6:36·		5:00		4:45

ST. LOUIS, MISSOURI

DAY	JAN.	FEB.	MAR.	APR.	MAY	JUNE	JULY	AUG.	SEPT.	OCT.	NOV.	DEC.
1	4:32 P.M.	5:04	5:35	6:06	6:34	7:01	7:11	6:54	6:13	5:26	4:43	4:22
2	4:33	5:06	5:37	6:07	6:35	7:02	7:11	6:53	6:12	5:25	4:42	4:22
3	4:34	5:07	5:38	6:08	6:36	7:03	7:11	6:52	6:10	5:23	4:41	4:22
4	4:35	5:08	5:39	6:09	6:37	7:03	7:11	6:51	6:09	5:21	4:40	4:21
5	4:36	5:09	5:40	6:10	6:38	7:04	7:11	6:49	6:07	5:20	4:39	4:21
6	4:36	5:10	5:41	6:11	6:39	7:04	7:10	6:48	6:06	5:18	4:38	4:21
7	4:37	5:11	5:42	6:12	6:40	7:05	7:10	6:47	6:04	5:17	4:37	4:21
8	4:38	5:12	5:43	6:13	6:41	7:06	7:10	6:46	6:03	5:15	4:36	4:21
9	4:39	5:14	5:44	6:14	6:42	7:06	7:09	6:45	6:01	5:14	4:35	4:21
10	4:40	5:15	5:45	6:14	6:43	7:07	7:09	6:44	5:59	5:12	4:34	4:22
11	4:41	5:16	5:46	6:15	6:44	7:07	7:09	6:42	5:58	5:11	4:33	4:22
12	4:42	5:17	5:47	6:16	6:45	7:08	7:08	6:41	5:56	5:09	4:32	4:22
13	4:43	5:18	5:48	6:17	6:46	7:08	7:08	6:40	5:55	5:08	4:31	4:22
14	4:44	5:19	5:49	6:18	6:47	7:08	7:07	6:39	5:53	5:06	4:31	4:22
15	4:45	5:20	5:50	6:19	6:48	7:09	7:07	6:37	5:52	5:05	4:30	4:22
16	4:46	5:21	5:51	6:20	6:48	7:09	7:06	6:36	5:50	5:04	4:29	4:23
17	4:48	5:23	5:52	6:21	6:49	7:10	7:06	6:35	5:48	5:02	4:28	4:23
18	4:49	5:24	5:53	6:22	6:50	7:10	7:05	6:34	5:47	5:01	4:28	4:24
19	4:50	5:25	5:54	6:23	6:51	7:10	7:04	6:32	5:45	4:59	4:27	4:24
20	4:51	5:26	5:54	6:24	6:52	7:10	7:04	6:31	5:44	4:58	4:26	4:24
21	4:52	5:27	5:55	6:25	6:53	7:11	7:03	6:29	5:42	4:57	4:26	4:25
22	4:53	5:28	5:56	6:26	6:54	7:11	7:02	6:28	5:40	4:55	4:25	4:25
23	4:54	5:29	5:57	6:27	6:54	7:11	7:02	6:27	5:39	4:54	4:25	4:26
24	4:55	5:30	5:58	6:28	6:55	7:11	7:01	6:25	5:37	4:53	4:24	4:26
25	4:56	5:31	5:59	6:29	6:56	7:11	7:00	6:24	5:36	4:52	4:24	4:27
26	4:58	5:32	6:00	6:30	6:57	7:11	6:59	6:22	5:34	4:50	4:24	4:28
27	4:59	5:33	6:01	6:31	6:58	7:11	6:58	6:21	5:32	4:49	4:23	4:28
28	5:00	5:34	6:02	6:32	6:58	7:11	6:57	6:19	5:31	4:48	4:23	4:29
29	5:01	5:35	6:03	6:33	6:59	7:11	6:57	6:18	5:29	4:47	4:22	4:30
30	5:02		6:04	6:34	7:00	7:11	6:56	6:16	5:28	4:45	4:22	4:30
31	5:03		6:05		7:01		6:55	6:15		4:44		4:31

SAN FRANCISCO, CALIFORNIA

DAY	JAN.	FEB.	MAR.	APR.	MAY	JUNE	JULY	AUG.	SEPT.	OCT.	NOV.	DEC.
1	4:44 P.M.	5:15	5:45	6:14	6:42	7:08	7:17	7:01	6:21	5:35	4:53	4:33
2	4:44	5:16	5:46	6:15	6:43	7:08	7:17	7:00	6:20	5:34	4:52	4:33
3	4:45	5:17	5:47	6:16	6:44	7:09	7:17	6:59	6:18	5:32	4:51	4:33
4	4:46	5:18	5:48	6:17	6:45	7:10	7:17	6:57	6:17	5:31	4:50	4:33
5	4:47	5:20	5:49	6:18	6:46	7:10	7:17	6:56	6:15	5:29	4:49	4:33
6	4:48	5:21	5:50	6:19	6:46	7:11	7:17	6:55	6:14	5:28	4:48	4:33
7	4:49	5:22	5:51	6:20	6:47	7:11	7:16	6:54	6:12	5:26	4:47	4:33
8	4:50	5:23	5:52	6:21	6:48	7:12	7:16	6:53	6:11	5:25	4:46	4:33
9	4:51	5:24	5:53	6:22	6:49	7:12	7:16	6:52	6:09	5:23	4:45	4:33
10	4:52	5:25	5:54	6:23	6:50	7:13	7:15	6:51	6:08	5:22	4:44	4:33
11	4:52	5:26	5:55	6:23	6:51	7:13	7:15	6:50	6:06	5:20	4:44	4:33
12	4:53	5:27	5:56	6:24	6:52	7:14	7:15	6:48	6:05	5:19	4:43	4:33
13	4:54	5:28	5:57	6:25	6:53	7:14	7:14	6:47	6:03	5:17	4:42	4:33
14	4:55	5:29	5:58	6:26	6:54	7:15	7:14	6:46	6:01	5:16	4:41	4:34
15	4:57	5:31	5:59	6:27	6:54	7:15	7:13	6:45	6:00	5:15	4:41	4:34
16	4:58	5:32	6:00	6:28	6:55	7:15	7:13	6:43	5:58	5:13	4:40	4:34
17	4:59	5:33	6:01	6:29	6:56	7:16	7:12	6:42	5:57	5:12	4:39	4:34
18	5:00	5:34	6:02	6:30	6:57	7:16	7:12	6:41	5:55	5:10	4:38	4:35
19	5:01	5:35	6:02	6:31	6:58	7:16	7:11	6:40	5:54	5:09	4:38	4:35
20	5:02	5:36	6:03	6:32	6:59	7:17	7:10	6:38	5:52	5:08	4:37	4:36
21	5:03	5:37	6:04	6:33	6:59	7:17	7:10	6:37	5:51	5:06	4:37	4:36
22	5:04	5:38	6:05	6:34	7:00	7:17	7:09	6:36	5:49	5:05	4:36	4:37
23	5:05	5:39	6:06	6:34	7:01	7:17	7:08	6:34	5:47	5:04	4:36	4:37
24	5:06	5:40	6:07	6:35	7:02	7:17	7:07	6:33	5:46	5:03	4:35	4:38
25	5:07	5:41	6:08	6:36	7:03	7:17	7:07	6:31	5:44	5:01	4:35	4:38
26	5:08	5:42	6:09	6:37	7:03	7:18	7:06	6:30	5:43	5:00	4:34	4:39
27	5:10	5:43	6:10	6:38	7:04	7:18	7:05	6:29	5:41	4:59	4:34	4:40
28	5:11	5:44	6:11	6:39	7:05	7:18	7:04	6:27	5:40	4:58	4:34	4:40
29	5:12	5:45	6:12	6:40	7:06	7:18	7:03	6:26	5:38	4:57	4:34	4:41
30	5:13		6:13	6:41	7:06	7:18	7:02	6:24	5:37	4:56	4:33	4:42
31	5:14		6:13		7:07		7:01	6:23		4:54		4:43

WASHINGTON, DISTRICT OF COLUMBIA

DAY	JAN.	FEB.	MAR.	APR.	MAY	JUNE	JULY	AUG.	SEPT.	OCT.	NOV.	DEC.
1	4:39 P.M.	5:11	5:43	6:13	6:42	7:09	7:19	7:01	6:21	5:33	4:50	4:29
2	4:40	5:13	5:44	6:14	6:43	7:10	7:19	7:00	6:19	5:32	4:49	4:29
3	4:41	5:14	5:45	6:15	6:44	7:11	7:19	6:59	6:18	5:30	4:48	4:28
4	4:41	5:15	5:46	6:16	6:45	7:11	7:19	6:58	6:16	5:29	4:47	4:28
5	4:42	5:16	5:47	6:17	6:46	7:12	7:19	6:57	6:15	5:27	4:46	4:28
6	4:43	5:17	5:48	6:18	6:47	7:12	7:18	6:56	6:13	5:26	4:45	4:28
7	4:44	5:18	5:49	6:19	6:48	7:13	7:18	6:55	6:12	5:24	4:44	4:28
8	4:45	5:19	5:50	6:20	6:49	7:14	7:18	6:54	6:10	5:22	4:43	4:28
9	4:46	5:21	5:51	6:21	6:50	7:14	7:17	6:53	6:08	5:21	4:42	4:28
10	4:47	5:22	5:52	6:22	6:51	7:15	7:17	6:51	6:07	5:19	4:41	4:28
11	4:48	5:23	5:53	6:23	6:52	7:15	7:17	6:50	6:05	5:18	4:40	4:28
12	4:49	5:24	5:54	6:24	6:53	7:16	7:16	6:49	6:04	5:17	4:39	4:29
13	4:50	5:25	5:55	6:25	6:54	7:16	7:16	6:48	6:02	5:15	4:38	4:29
14	4:51	5:26	5:56	6:26	6:54	7:16	7:15	6:46	6:00	5:14	4:37	4:29
15	4:52	5:27	5:57	6:27	6:55	7:17	7:15	6:45	5:59	5:12	4:37	4:29
16	4:53	5:29	5:58	6:28	6:56	7:17	7:14	6:44	5:57	5:11	4:36	4:30
17	4:54	5:30	5:59	6:29	6:57	7:18	7:14	6:42	5:56	5:09	4:35	4:30
18	4:55	5:31	6:00	6:30	6:58	7:18	7:13	6:41	5:54	5:08	4:35	4:30
19	4:57	5:32	6:01	6:31	6:59	7:18	7:12	6:40	5:52	5:06	4:34	4:31
20	4:58	5:33	6:02	6:32	7:00	7:18	7:12	6:38	5:51	5:05	4:33	4:31
21	4:59	5:34	6:03	6:33	7:01	7:19	7:11	6:37	5:49	5:04	4:33	4:32
22	5:00	5:35	6:04	6:34	7:02	7:19	7:10	6:36	5:48	5:02	4:32	4:32
23	5:01	5:36	6:05	6:35	7:02	7:19	7:09	6:34	5:46	5:01	4:32	4:33
24	5:02	5:37	6:06	6:36	7:03	7:19	7:09	6:33	5:44	5:00	4:31	4:33
25	5:03	5:38	6:07	6:36	7:04	7:19	7:08	6:31	5:43	4:59	4:31	4:34
26	5:04	5:39	6:08	6:37	7:05	7:19	7:07	6:30	5:41	4:57	4:30	4:34
27	5:06	5:41	6:09	6:38	7:06	7:19	7:06	6:28	5:40	4:56	4:30	4:35
28	5:07	5:42	6:10	6:39	7:06	7:19	7:05	6:27	5:38	4:55	4:30	4:36
29	5:08	5:43	6:11	6:40	7:07	7:19	7:04	6:25	5:36	4:54	4:29	4:36
30	5:09		6:12	6:41	7:08	7:19	7:03	6:24	5:35	4:52	4:29	4:37
31	5:10		6:12		7:09		7:02	6:22		4:51		4:38

ISRAEL

BE'ER SHEVA

Jan.	1	4:32		17	5:33		31	6:22		14	6:08		28	4:39
	4	4:34		20	5:35	June	3	6:24		17	6:05		31	4:36
	7	4:36		23	5:37		6	6:25		20	6:02	Nov.	3	4:34
	10	4:39		26	5:39		9	6:27		23	5:59		6	4:32
	13	4:41		29	5:40		12	6:28		26	5:55		9	4:29
	16	4:44	Apr.	1	5:42		15	6:29		29	5:52		12	4:29
	19	4:46		4	5:44		18	6:30	Sept.	1	5:48		15	4:26
	22	4:49		7	5:46		21	6:31		4	5:44		18	4:24
	25	4:52		10	5:48		24	6:31		7	5:41		21	4:23
	28	4:55		13	5:50		27	6:32		10	5:37		24	4:22
	31	4:57		16	5:52		30	6:32		13	5:33		27	4:21
Feb.	3	5:00		19	5:54	July	3	6:32		16	5:29		30	4:21
	6	5:03		22	5:56		6	6:31		19	5:25	Dec.	3	4:21
	9	5:05		25	5:58		9	6:31		22	5:21		6	4:21
	12	5:08		28	6:00		12	6:30		25	5:17		9	4:21
	15	5:10	May	1	6:02		15	6:29		28	5:14		12	4:22
	18	5:13		4	6:04		18	6:28	Oct.	1	5:10		15	4:23
	21	5:15		7	6:06		21	6:27		4	5:06		18	4:24
	24	5:18		10	6:08		24	6:25		7	5:02		21	4:25
	27	5:20		13	6:10		27	6:23		10	4:59		24	4:26
Mar.	2	5:22		16	6:13		30	6:21		13	4:55		27	4:28
	5	5:24		19	6:14	Aug.	2	6:19		16	4:52		30	4:30
	8	5:26		22	6:16		5	6:17		19	4:48			
	11	5:28		25	6:18		8	6:14		22	4:45			
	14	5:31		28	6:20		11	6:11		25	4:42			

HAIFA

Jan.	1	4:27		17	5:31		31	6:24		14	6:09		28	4:36
	4	4:29		20	5:33	June	3	6:26		17	6:06		31	4:33
	7	4:31		23	5:35		6	6:27		20	6:03	Nov.	3	4:30
	10	4:34		26	5:37		9	6:29		23	5:59		6	4:28
	13	4:36		29	5:40		12	6:30		26	5:55		9	4:25
	16	4:39	Apr.	1	5:42		15	6:31		29	5:52		12	4:23
	19	4:42		4	5:44		18	6:32	Sept.	1	5:48		15	4:21
	22	4:45		7	5:46		21	6:33		4	5:44		18	4:20
	25	4:47		10	5:48		24	6:34		7	5:40		21	4:18
	28	4:50		13	5:50		27	6:34		10	5:36		24	4:17
	31	4:53		16	5:52		30	6:34		13	5:32		27	4:16
Feb.	3	4:56		19	5:54	July	3	6:34		16	5:28		30	4:16
	6	4:59		22	5:57		6	6:34		19	5:24	Dec.	3	4:16
	9	5:02		25	5:59		9	6:33		22	5:20		6	4:16
	12	5:04		28	6:01		12	6:32		25	5:16		9	4:16
	15	5:07	May	1	6:03		15	6:31		28	5:12		12	4:16
	18	5:10		4	6:05		18	6:30	Oct.	1	5:08		15	4:17
	21	5:12		7	6:08		21	6:29		4	5:04		18	4:18
	24	5:15		10	6:10		24	6:27		7	5:00		21	4:20
	27	5:17		13	6:12		27	6:25		10	4:56		24	4:21
Mar.	2	5:20		16	6:14		30	6:23		13	4:53		27	4:23
	5	5:22		19	6:16	Aug.	2	6:20		16	4:49		30	4:25
	8	5:24		22	6:18		5	6:18		19	4:45			
	11	5:26		25	6:20		8	6:15		22	4:42			
	14	5:29		28	6:22		11	6:12		25	4:39			

JERUSALEM

Jan.	1	4:28		17	5:30		31	6:21		14	6:07		28	4:36
	4	4:30		20	5:32	June	3	6:22		17	6:03		31	4:33
	7	4:32		23	5:34		6	6:24		20	6:00	Nov.	3	4:31
	10	4:35		26	5:36		9	6:25		23	5:57		6	4:28
	13	4:38		29	5:38		12	6:27		26	5:53		9	4:26
	16	4:40	Apr.	1	5:40		15	6:28		29	5:50		12	4:24
	19	4:43		4	5:42		18	6:29	Sept.	1	5:46		15	4:22
	22	4:46		7	5:44		21	6:30		4	5:42		18	4:21
	25	4:48		10	5:46		24	6:30		7	5:39		21	4:19
	28	4:51		13	5:48		27	6:30		10	5:35		24	4:18
	31	4:54		16	5:50		30	6:31		13	5:31		27	4:18
Feb.	3	4:57		19	5:52	July	3	6:31		16	5:27		30	4:17
	6	4:59		22	5:54		6	6:30		19	5:23	Dec.	3	4:17
	9	5:02		25	5:56		9	6:30		22	5:19		6	4:17
	12	5:05		28	5:59		12	6:29		25	5:15		9	4:17
	15	5:07	May	1	6:01		15	6:28		28	5:11		12	4:18
	18	5:10		4	6:03		18	6:27	Oct.	1	5:07		15	4:19
	21	5:12		7	6:05		21	6:25		4	5:03		18	4:20
	24	5:15		10	6:07		24	6:24		7	5:00		21	4:21
	27	5:17		13	6:09		27	6:22		10	4:56		24	4:23
Mar.	2	5:19		16	6:11		30	6:20		13	4:52		27	4:24
	5	5:21		19	6:13	Aug.	2	6:18		16	4:49		30	4:26
	8	5:24		22	6:15		5	6:15		19	4:45			
	11	5:26		25	6:17		8	6:12		22	4:42			
	14	5:28		28	6:19		11	6:10		25	4:39			

TEL AVIV

Month	Day	Time		Day	Time		Day	Time		Day	Time		Day	Time
Jan.	1	4:29		17	5:32		31	6:23		14	6:09		28	4:38
	4	4:31		20	5:34	June	3	6:25		17	6:06		31	4:35
	7	4:34		23	5:36		6	6:27		20	6:03	Nov.	3	4:32
	10	4:36		26	5:38		9	6:28		23	5:59		6	4:30
	13	4:39		29	5:40		12	6:29		26	5:56		9	4:27
	16	4:42	Apr.	1	5:42		15	6:31		29	5:52		12	4:25
	19	4:44		4	5:44		18	6:32	Sept.	1	5:48		15	4:24
	22	4:47		7	5:46		21	6:32		4	5:45		18	4:22
	25	4:50		10	5:48		24	6:33		7	5:41		21	4:21
	28	4:53		13	5:50		27	6:33		10	5:37		24	4:20
	31	4:55		16	5:53		30	6:33		13	5:33		27	4:19
Feb.	3	4:58		19	5:55	July	3	6:33		16	5:29		30	4:18
	6	5:01		22	5:57		6	6:33		19	5:25	Dec.	3	4:18
	9	5:04		25	5:59		9	6:32		22	5:21		6	4:18
	12	5:06		28	6:01		12	6:32		25	5:17		9	4:19
	15	5:09	May	1	6:03		15	6:31		28	5:13		12	4:19
	18	5:11		4	6:05		18	6:29	Oct.	1	5:09		15	4:20
	21	5:14		7	6:07		21	6:28		4	5:05		18	4:21
	24	5:16		10	6:10		24	6:26		7	5:01		21	4:22
	27	5:19		13	6:12		27	6:24		10	4:58		24	4:24
Mar.	2	5:21		16	6:14		30	6:22		13	4:54		27	4:26
	5	5:23		19	6:16	Aug.	2	6:20		16	4:50		30	4:28
	8	5:26		22	6:18		5	6:18		19	4:47			
	11	5:28		25	6:20		8	6:15		22	4:44			
	14	5:30		28	6:22		11	6:12		25	4:41			

CANADA

MONTREAL, QUEBEC

Month	Day	Time		Day	Time		Day	Time		Day	Time		Day	Time
Jan.	1	4:04		17	5:45		31	7:17		14	6:48		28	4:31
	4	4:07		20	5:49	June	3	7:19		17	6:43		31	4:27
	7	4:10		23	5:52		6	7:22		20	6:38	Nov.	3	4:23
	10	4:13		26	5:56		9	7:24		23	6:33		6	4:18
	13	4:17		29	6:00		12	7:26		26	6:27		9	4:15
	16	4:21	Apr.	1	6:04		15	7:27		29	6:22		12	4:11
	19	4:24		4	6:08		18	7:28	Sept.	1	6:16		15	4:08
	22	4:29		7	6:12		21	7:29		4	6:11		18	4:05
	25	4:33		10	6:16		24	7:30		7	6:05		21	4:02
	28	4:37		13	6:20		27	7:30		10	6:00		24	4:00
	31	4:41		16	6:24		30	7:30		13	5:54		27	3:58
Feb.	3	4:46		19	6:27	July	3	7:29		16	5:48		30	3:56
	6	4:50		22	6:31		6	7:28		19	5:42	Dec.	3	3:55
	9	4:54		25	6:35		9	7:27		22	5:36		6	3:54
	12	4:59		28	6:39		12	7:25		25	5:31		9	3:54
	15	5:03	May	1	6:43		15	7:23		28	5:25		12	3:54
	18	5:07		4	6:47		18	7:21	Oct.	1	5:19		15	3:54
	21	5:12		7	6:50		21	7:18		4	5:13		18	3:55
	24	5:16		10	6:54		24	7:16		7	5:08		21	3:56
	27	5:20		13	6:58		27	7:12		10	5:02		24	3:58
Mar.	2	5:24		16	7:01		30	7:09		13	4:57		27	4:00
	5	5:28		19	7:05	Aug.	2	7:05		16	4:51		30	4:02
	8	5:33		22	7:08		5	7:01		19	4:46			
	11	5:37		25	7:11		8	6:57		22	4:41			
	14	5:41		28	7:14		11	6:52		25	4:36			

TORONTO, ONTARIO

Month	Day	Time		Day	Time		Day	Time		Day	Time		Day	Time
Jan.	1	4:34		17	6:08		31	7:33		14	7:06		28	4:58
	4	4:36		20	6:11	June	3	7:35		17	7:02		31	4:54
	7	4:39		23	6:15		6	7:38		20	6:57	Nov.	3	4:50
	10	4:43		26	6:19		9	7:40		23	6:52		6	4:46
	13	4:46		29	6:22		12	7:41		26	6:47		9	4:42
	16	4:50	Apr.	1	6:26		15	7:43		29	6:42		12	4:39
	19	4:53		4	6:29		18	7:44	Sept.	1	6:37		15	4:36
	22	4:57		7	6:33		21	7:45		4	6:32		18	4:33
	25	5:01		10	6:37		24	7:45		7	6:26		21	4:31
	28	5:05		13	6:40		27	7:46		10	6:21		24	4:29
	31	5:09		16	6:44		30	7:45		13	6:16		27	4:27
Feb.	3	5:13		19	6:47	July	3	7:45		16	6:10		30	4:25
	6	5:17		22	6:51		6	7:44		19	6:05	Dec.	3	4:24
	9	5:21		25	6:54		9	7:43		22	5:59		6	4:24
	12	5:25		28	6:58		12	7:42		25	5:54		9	4:23
	15	5:29	May	1	7:01		15	7:40		28	5:48		12	4:23
	18	5:33		4	7:05		18	7:38	Oct.	1	5:43		15	4:24
	21	5:37		7	7:08		21	7:35		4	5:37		18	4:25
	24	5:41		10	7:12		24	7:32		7	5:32		21	4:26
	27	5:45		13	7:15		27	7:30		10	5:27		24	4:28
Mar.	2	5:49		16	7:18		30	7:26		13	5:22		27	4:30
	5	5:53		19	7:22	Aug.	2	7:23		16	5:17		30	4:32
	8	5:57		22	7:25		5	7:19		19	5:12			
	11	6:00		25	7:28		8	7:15		22	5:07			
	14	6:04		28	7:30		11	7:11		25	5:02			

VANCOUVER, BRITISH COLUMBIA

Jan. 1	4:07	17	6:01	31	7:48	14	7:13	28	4:42
4	4:10	20	6:06	June 3	7:51	17	7:08	31	4:36
7	4:13	23	6:10	6	7:54	20	7:02	Nov. 3	4:31
10	4:17	26	6:15	9	7:56	23	6:56	6	4:27
13	4:21	29	6:19	12	7:58	26	6:51	9	4:22
16	4:25	Apr. 1	6:24	15	8:00	29	6:44	12	4:18
19	4:30	4	6:28	18	8:01	Sept. 1	6:38	15	4:14
22	4:34	7	6:33	21	8:02	4	6:32	18	4:11
25	4:39	10	6:37	24	8:02	7	6:26	21	4:08
28	4:44	13	6:42	27	8:02	10	6:20	24	4:05
31	4:49	16	6:46	30	8:02	13	6:13	27	4:02
Feb. 3	4:54	19	6:51	July 3	8:01	16	6:07	30	4:00
6	4:59	22	6:55	6	8:00	19	6:00	Dec. 3	3:59
9	5:04	25	7:00	9	7:59	22	5:54	6	3:58
12	5:08	28	7:04	12	7:57	25	5:47	9	3:57
15	5:13	May 1	7:09	15	7:54	28	5:41	12	3:57
18	5:18	4	7:13	18	7:52	Oct. 1	5:35	15	3:57
21	5:23	7	7:17	21	7:48	4	5:28	18	3:58
24	5:28	10	7:22	24	7:45	7	5:22	21	3:59
27	5:33	13	7:26	27	7:41	10	5:16	24	4:00
Mar. 2	5:38	16	7:30	30	7:37	13	5:10	27	4:02
5	5:43	19	7:33	Aug. 2	7:33	16	5:04	30	4:05
8	5:47	22	7:38	5	7:28	19	4:58		
11	5:52	25	7:41	8	7:24	22	4:52		
14	5:57	28	7:45	11	7:18	25	4:47		

WINNIPEG, MANITOBA

Jan. 1	4:19	17	6:18	31	8:10	14	7:33	28	4:56
4	4:23	20	6:23	June 3	8:13	17	7:27	31	4:51
7	4:26	23	6:28	6	8:15	20	7:21	Nov. 3	4:46
10	4:30	26	6:32	9	8:18	23	7:16	6	4:41
13	4:34	29	6:37	12	8:20	26	7:09	9	4:36
16	4:38	Apr. 1	6:42	15	8:22	29	7:03	12	4:32
19	4:43	4	6:46	18	8:23	Sept. 1	6:57	15	4:28
22	4:48	7	6:51	21	8:24	4	6:51	18	4:24
25	4:53	10	6:56	24	8:24	7	6:44	21	4:21
28	4:57	13	7:01	27	8:24	10	6:38	24	4:18
31	5:03	16	7:05	30	8:24	13	6:31	27	4:15
Feb. 3	5:08	19	7:10	July 3	8:23	16	6:24	30	4:13
6	5:13	22	7:15	6	8:22	19	6:18	Dec. 3	4:12
9	5:18	25	7:19	9	8:20	22	6:11	6	4:10
12	5:23	28	7:24	12	8:18	25	6:04	9	4:10
15	5:28	May 1	7:29	15	8:16	28	5:58	12	4:09
18	5:33	4	7:33	18	8:13	Oct. 1	5:51	15	4:09
21	5:39	7	7:38	21	8:10	4	5:45	18	4:10
24	5:44	10	7:42	24	8:06	7	5:38	21	4:11
27	5:49	13	7:46	27	8:02	10	5:32	24	4:13
Mar. 2	5:53	16	7:51	30	7:58	13	5:26	27	4:15
5	5:59	19	7:55	Aug. 2	7:53	16	5:20	30	4:17
8	6:04	22	7:59	5	7:49	19	5:14		
11	6:08	25	8:03	8	7:44	22	5:08		
14	6:13	28	8:06	11	7:38	25	5:02		

INTERNATIONAL CITIES WITH LARGE JEWISH POPULATIONS

AMSTERDAM, THE NETHERLANDS

Jan. 1	4:19	17	6:29	31	8:33	14	7:51	28	5:02
4	4:23	20	6:35	June 3	8:36	17	7:45	31	4:56
7	4:26	23	6:40	6	8:39	20	7:39	Nov. 3	4:51
10	4:31	26	6:45	9	8:42	23	7:33	6	4:45
13	4:35	29	6:50	12	8:44	26	7:26	9	4:40
16	4:40	Apr. 1	6:55	15	8:46	29	7:19	12	4:36
19	4:45	4	7:01	18	8:48	Sept. 1	7:12	15	4:31
22	4:50	7	7:06	21	8:49	4	7:05	18	4:27
25	4:55	10	7:11	24	8:49	7	6:59	21	4:23
28	5:01	13	7:16	27	8:49	10	6:51	24	4:20
31	5:06	16	7:21	30	8:49	13	6:44	27	4:17
Feb. 3	5:12	19	7:27	July 3	8:48	16	6:37	30	4:14
6	5:17	22	7:32	6	8:46	19	6:30	Dec. 3	4:12
9	5:23	25	7:37	9	8:44	22	6:23	6	4:11
12	5:29	28	7:42	12	8:42	25	6:16	9	4:10
15	5:34	May 1	7:47	15	8:39	28	6:09	12	4:09
18	5:40	4	7:52	18	8:36	Oct. 1	6:02	15	4:09
21	5:46	7	7:57	21	8:32	4	5:55	18	4:10
24	5:51	10	8:02	24	8:28	7	5:48	21	4:11
27	5:57	13	8:07	27	8:24	10	5:41	24	4:12
Mar. 2	6:02	16	8:12	30	8:19	13	5:34	27	4:14
5	6:08	19	8:17	Aug. 2	8:14	16	5:28	30	4:17
8	6:13	22	8:21	5	8:09	19	5:21		
11	6:19	25	8:25	8	8:03	22	5:15		
14	6:24	28	8:29	11	7:57	25	5:08		

BUENOS AIRES, ARGENTINA

Jan.	1	6:52		17	5:52		31	4:33		14	5:04		28	6:01
	4	6:52		20	5:48	June	3	4:32		17	5:06		31	6:03
	7	6:52		23	5:44		6	4:32		20	5:08	Nov.	3	6:06
	10	6:52		26	5:40		9	4:31		23	5:10		6	6:09
	13	6:52		29	5:35		12	4:31		26	5:12		9	6:12
	16	6:51	Apr.	1	5:31		15	4:31		29	5:14		12	6:15
	19	6:50		4	5:27		18	4:32	Sept.	1	5:17		15	6:18
	22	6:49		7	5:23		21	4:32		4	5:19		18	6:21
	25	6:47		10	5:19		24	4:33		7	5:21		21	6:24
	28	6:46		13	5:15		27	4:34		10	5:23		24	6:27
	31	6:43		16	5:12		30	4:35		13	5:25		27	6:29
Feb.	3	6:41		19	5:08	July	3	4:36		16	5:27		30	6:32
	6	6:39		22	5:04		6	4:38		19	5:29	Dec.	3	6:35
	9	6:36		25	5:01		9	4:39		22	5:31		6	6:37
	12	6:33		28	4:57		12	4:41		25	5:34		9	6:40
	15	6:30	May	1	4:54		15	4:43		28	5:36		12	6:42
	18	6:27		4	4:51		18	4:45	Oct.	1	5:38		15	6:44
	21	6:23		7	4:49		21	4:47		4	5:40		18	6:46
	24	6:20		10	4:46		24	4:49		7	5:43		21	6:48
	27	6:16		13	4:43		27	4:51		10	5:45		24	6:49
Mar.	2	6:12		16	4:41		30	4:53		13	5:47		27	6:50
	5	6:08		19	4:39	Aug.	2	4:55		16	5:50		30	6:51
	8	6:04		22	4:37		5	4:57		19	5:53			
	11	6:00		25	4:36		8	4:59		22	5:55			
	14	5:56		28	4:34		11	5:01		25	5:58			

JOHANNESBURG, SOUTH AFRICA

Jan.	1	6:46		17	6:05		31	5:06		14	5:30		28	6:04
	4	6:47		20	6:02	June	3	5:06		17	5:31		31	6:06
	7	6:47		23	5:59		6	5:05		20	5:32	Nov.	3	6:08
	10	6:48		26	5:55		9	5:05		23	5:34		6	6:10
	13	6:48		29	5:52		12	5:05		26	5:35		9	6:12
	16	6:47	Apr.	1	5:49		15	5:06		29	5:36		12	6:14
	19	6:47		4	5:46		18	5:06	Sept.	1	5:37		15	6:16
	22	6:46		7	5:43		21	5:07		4	5:39		18	6:19
	25	6:45		10	5:40		24	5:07		7	5:40		21	6:21
	28	6:44		13	5:37		27	5:08		10	5:41		24	6:23
	31	6:43		16	5:34		30	5:09		13	5:42		27	6:25
Feb.	3	6:42		19	5:31	July	3	5:10		16	5:43		30	6:28
	6	6:40		22	5:28		6	5:11		19	5:45	Dec.	3	6:30
	9	6:38		25	5:26		9	5:12		22	5:46		6	6:32
	12	6:36		28	5:23		12	5:14		25	5:47		9	6:34
	15	6:34	May	1	5:21		15	5:15		28	5:48		12	6:36
	18	6:31		4	5:19		18	5:17	Oct.	1	5:50		15	6:38
	21	6:29		7	5:16		21	5:18		4	5:51		18	6:40
	24	6:26		10	5:15		24	5:19		7	5:53		21	6:41
	27	6:23		13	5:13		27	5:21		10	5:54		24	6:43
Mar.	2	6:21		16	5:11		30	5:22		13	5:55		27	6:44
	5	6:18		19	5:10	Aug.	2	5:24		16	5:57		30	6:45
	8	6:15		22	5:09		5	5:25		19	5:59			
	11	6:11		25	5:08		8	5:27		22	6:00			
	14	6:08		28	5:07		11	5:28		25	6:02			

KIEV, U.S.S.R.

Jan.	1	4:44		17	6:47		31	8:43		14	8:05		22	5:35
	4	4:47		20	6:52	June	3	8:46		17	7:59		25	5:29
	7	4:51		23	6:57		6	8:49		20	7:53		28	5:23
	10	4:55		26	7:02		9	8:52		23	7:47		31	5:18
	13	4:59		29	7:07		12	8:54		26	7:40	Nov.	3	5:12
	16	5:03	Apr.	1	7:12		15	8:56		29	7:34		6	5:07
	19	5:08		4	7:17		18	8:57	Sept.	1	7:28		9	5:02
	22	5:13		7	7:21		21	8:58		4	7:21		12	4:58
	25	5:18		10	7:26		24	8:59		7	7:14		15	4:54
	28	5:23		13	7:31		27	8:59		10	7:08		18	4:50
	31	5:28		16	7:36		30	8:58		13	7:01		21	4:46
Feb.	3	5:34		19	7:41	July	3	8:57		16	6:54		24	4:43
	6	5:39		22	7:46		6	8:56		19	6:47		27	4:40
	9	5:44		25	7:51		9	8:54		22	6:40		30	4:38
	12	5:50		28	7:56		12	8:52		25	6:33	Dec.	3	4:36
	15	5:55	May	1	8:00		15	8:49		28	6:27		6	4:35
	18	6:01		4	8:05		18	8:46	Oct.	1	6:20		9	4:34
	21	6:06		7	8:10		21	8:43		4	6:13		12	4:34
	24	6:11		10	8:15		24	8:39		7	6:07		15	4:34
	27	6:16		13	8:19		27	8:35		10	6:00		18	4:34
Mar.	2	6:22		16	8:24		30	8:31		13	5:53		21	4:35
	5	6:27		19	8:28	Aug.	2	8:26		16	5:47		24	4:37
	8	6:32		22	8:32		5	8:21		19	5:41		27	4:39
	11	6:37		25	8:36		8	8:16					30	4:42
	14	6:42		28	8:40		11	8:10						

525

LENINGRAD, U.S.S.R.

Jan. 1	3:45	17	6:41	31	9:44	14	8:39	28	4:57
4	3:49	20	6:53	June 3	9:50	17	8:30	31	4:49
7	3:54	23	7:00	6	9:54	20	8:22	Nov. 3	4:41
10	4:00	26	7:07	9	9:59	23	8:13	6	4:33
13	4:06	29	7:15	12	10:02	26	8:04	9	4:26
16	4:13	Apr. 1	7:22	15	10:05	29	7:55	12	4:19
19	4:20	4	7:29	18	10:08	Sept. 1	7:46	15	4:12
22	4:27	7	7:37	21	10:08	4	7:32	18	4:06
25	4:35	10	7:44	24	10:08	7	7:28	21	4:00
28	4:42	13	7:51	27	10:08	10	7:19	24	3:55
31	4:50	16	7:59	30	10:06	13	7:10	27	3:50
Feb. 3	4:58	19	8:06	July 3	10:04	16	7:01	30	3:45
6	5:06	22	8:14	6	10:02	19	6:52	Dec. 3	3:41
9	5:14	25	8:21	9	9:58	22	6:42	6	3:38
12	5:22	28	8:25	12	9:54	25	6:33	9	3:36
15	5:30	May 1	8:36	15	9:49	28	6:29	12	3:34
18	5:37	4	8:43	18	9:44	Oct. 1	6:15	15	3:33
21	5:45	7	8:51	21	9:38	4	6:06	18	3:33
24	5:53	10	8:58	24	9:31	7	5:46	21	3:34
27	6:01	13	9:05	27	9:26	10	5:43	24	3:36
Mar. 2	6:08	16	9:12	30	9:18	13	5:39	27	3:38
5	6:16	19	9:19	Aug. 2	9:10	16	5:31	30	3:42
8	6:23	22	9:26	5	9:03	19	5:22		
11	6:31	25	9:32	8	8:55	22	5:13		
14	6:38	28	9:39	11	8:47	25	5:05		

LONDON, ENGLAND

Jan. 1	3:43	17	5:49	31	7:48	14	7:08	28	4:24
4	3:47	20	5:54	June 3	7:51	17	7:02	31	4:18
7	3:50	23	5:59	6	7:54	20	6:56	Nov. 3	4:13
10	3:54	26	6:04	9	7:57	23	6:50	6	4:08
13	3:59	29	6:09	12	7:59	26	6:43	9	4:03
16	4:03	Apr. 1	6:14	15	8:01	29	6:37	12	3:58
19	4:08	4	6:19	18	8:02	Sept. 1	6:30	15	3:54
22	4:13	7	6:24	21	8:03	4	6:24	18	3:50
25	4:18	10	6:29	24	8:03	7	6:17	21	3:46
28	4:23	13	6:34	27	8:03	10	6:10	24	3:43
31	4:29	16	6:39	30	8:03	13	6:03	27	3:40
Feb. 3	4:34	19	6:44	July 3	8:02	16	5:56	30	3:38
6	4:40	22	6:49	6	8:01	19	5:49	Dec. 3	3:36
9	4:45	25	6:54	9	7:59	22	5:42	6	3:35
12	4:51	28	6:59	12	7:57	25	5:35	9	3:34
15	4:56	May 1	7:04	15	7:54	28	5:29	12	3:33
18	5:01	4	7:09	18	7:51	Oct. 1	5:22	15	3:33
21	5:07	7	7:14	21	7:47	4	5:15	18	3:34
24	5:12	10	7:18	24	7:43	7	5:08	21	3:35
27	5:18	13	7:23	27	7:39	10	5:01	24	3:37
Mar. 2	5:23	16	7:28	30	7:35	13	4:55	27	3:39
5	5:28	19	7:32	Aug. 2	7:30	16	4:48	30	3:41
8	5:33	22	7:36	5	7:25	19	4:42		
11	5:39	25	7:40	8	7:20	22	4:36		
14	5:44	28	7:44	11	7:14	25	4:30		

MELBOURNE, AUSTRALIA

Jan. 1	7:28	17	6:20	31	4:52	14	5:26	22	6:26
4	7:28	20	6:15	June 3	4:51	17	5:28	25	6:29
7	7:28	23	6:11	6	4:50	20	5:31	28	6:32
10	7:28	26	6:06	9	4:50	23	5:33	31	6:35
13	7:27	29	6:02	12	4:50	26	5:36	Nov. 3	6:39
16	7:26	Apr. 1	5:57	15	4:50	29	5:38	6	6:42
19	7:25	4	5:52	18	4:50	Sept. 1	5:41	9	6:45
22	7:23	7	5:48	21	4:50	4	5:43	12	6:48
25	7:22	10	5:44	24	4:51	7	5:46	15	6:52
28	7:19	13	5:39	27	4:52	10	5:48	18	6:55
31	7:17	16	5:35	30	4:53	13	5:51	21	6:58
Feb. 3	7:14	19	5:31	July 3	4:55	16	5:53	24	7:01
6	7:12	22	5:27	6	4:56	19	5:56	27	7:05
9	7:08	25	5:23	9	4:58	22	5:58	30	7:08
12	7:05	28	5:20	12	5:00	25	6:00	Dec. 3	7:10
15	7:02	May 1	5:16	15	5:02	28	6:04	6	7:13
18	6:58	4	5:13	18	5:05	Oct. 1	6:06	9	7:16
21	6:54	7	5:10	21	5:06	4	6:09	12	7:18
24	6:50	10	5:07	24	5:08	7	6:12	15	7:20
27	6:46	13	5:04	27	5:11	10	6:14	18	7:22
Mar. 2	6:42	16	5:01	30	5:13	13	6:17	21	7:24
5	6:38	19	4:59	Aug. 2	5:16	16	6:20	24	7:26
8	6:33	22	4:57	5	5:18	19	6:23	27	7:27
11	6:29	25	4:55	8	5:21			30	7:28
14	6:24	28	4:54	11	5:23				

MEXICO CITY, MEXICO

Date	Time	Date	Time	Date	Time	Date	Time	Date	Time
Jan. 1	5:51	17	6:28	31	6:52	14	6:47	28	5:46
4	5:53	20	6:29	June 3	6:53	17	6:45	31	5:45
7	5:55	23	6:30	6	6:54	20	6:43	Nov. 3	5:43
10	5:57	26	6:30	9	6:54	23	6:41	6	5:42
13	5:58	29	6:31	12	6:57	26	6:39	9	5:41
16	6:00	Apr. 1	6:32	15	6:58	29	6:36	12	5:41
19	6:02	4	6:33	18	6:58	Sept. 1	6:33	15	5:39
22	6:04	7	6:34	21	6:59	4	6:31	18	5:39
25	6:06	10	6:34	24	7:00	7	6:29	21	5:38
28	6:08	13	6:35	27	7:00	10	6:26	24	5:38
31	6:10	16	6:36	30	7:01	13	6:24	27	5:38
Feb. 3	6:11	19	6:37	July 3	7:01	16	6:21	30	5:38
6	6:13	22	6:38	6	7:01	19	6:18	Dec. 3	5:39
9	6:15	25	6:39	9	7:01	22	6:15	6	5:39
12	6:16	28	6:40	12	7:00	25	6:12	9	5:40
15	6:18	May 1	6:41	15	7:00	28	6:10	12	5:41
18	6:19	4	6:41	18	7:00	Oct. 1	6:06	15	5:42
21	6:20	7	6:43	21	6:59	4	6:05	18	5:43
24	6:22	10	6:44	24	6:58	7	6:02	21	5:45
27	6:22	13	6:45	27	6:57	10	5:59	24	5:46
Mar. 2	6:24	16	6:47	30	6:56	13	5:57	27	5:48
5	6:24	19	6:47	Aug. 2	6:55	16	5:55	30	5:50
8	6:25	22	6:49	5	6:53	19	5:53		
11	6:27	25	6:50	8	6:51	22	5:51		
14	6:27	28	6:51	11	6:50	25	5:49		

MOSCOW, U.S.S.R.

Date	Time	Date	Time	Date	Time	Date	Time	Date	Time
Jan. 1	3:48	17	6:23	31	8:49	14	7:58	22	5:01
4	3:57	20	6:29	June 3	8:53	17	7:51	25	4:54
7	4:01	23	6:35	6	8:57	20	7:44	28	4:47
10	4:06	26	6:42	9	9:00	23	7:37	31	4:40
13	4:11	29	6:48	12	9:03	26	7:29	Nov. 3	4:34
16	4:16	Apr. 1	6:55	15	9:05	29	7:21	6	4:28
19	4:22	4	7:00	18	9:06	Sept. 1	7:14	9	4:22
22	4:28	7	7:06	21	9:07	4	7:06	12	4:16
25	4:34	10	7:12	24	9:08	7	6:58	15	4:10
28	4:40	13	7:18	27	9:08	10	6:50	18	4:05
31	4:47	16	7:24	30	9:07	13	6:42	21	4:01
Feb. 3	4:53	19	7:30	July 3	9:06	16	6:34	24	3:57
6	5:00	22	7:37	6	9:04	19	6:26	27	3:53
9	5:06	25	7:43	9	9:01	22	6:18	30	3:50
12	5:13	28	7:49	12	8:58	25	6:10	Dec. 3	3:47
15	5:20	May 1	7:55	15	8:54	28	6:02	6	3:45
18	5:26	4	8:01	18	8:50	Oct. 1	5:54	9	3:43
21	5:33	7	8:07	21	8:46	4	5:47	12	3:42
24	5:39	10	8:13	24	8:41	7	5:39	15	3:42
27	5:45	13	8:18	27	8:36	10	5:31	18	3:43
Mar. 2	5:52	16	8:24	30	8:30	13	5:23	21	3:44
5	5:58	19	8:30	Aug. 2	8:24	16	5:16	24	3:45
8	6:05	22	8:35	5	8:18	19	5:08	27	3:47
11	6:11	25	8:40	8	8:12			30	3:50
14	6:17	28	8:45	11	8:02				

PARIS, FRANCE

Date	Time	Date	Time	Date	Time	Date	Time	Date	Time
Jan. 1	4:47	17	6:40	31	8:26	14	7:52	28	5:21
4	4:50	20	6:45	June 3	8:29	17	7:46	31	5:16
7	4:53	23	6:49	6	8:32	20	7:41	Nov. 3	5:11
10	4:57	26	6:54	9	8:34	23	7:35	6	5:06
13	5:01	29	6:58	12	8:36	26	7:29	9	5:02
16	5:05	Apr. 1	7:03	15	8:38	29	7:23	12	4:58
19	5:09	4	7:07	18	8:39	Sept. 1	7:17	15	4:54
22	5:14	7	7:12	21	8:40	4	7:11	18	4:50
25	5:19	10	7:16	24	8:40	7	7:05	21	4:47
28	5:23	13	7:21	27	8:40	10	6:58	24	4:45
31	5:28	16	7:25	30	8:40	13	6:52	27	4:42
Feb. 3	5:33	19	7:29	July 3	8:39	16	6:46	30	4:40
6	5:38	22	7:34	6	8:38	19	6:39	Dec. 3	4:39
9	5:43	25	7:38	9	8:37	22	6:33	6	4:37
12	5:48	28	7:43	12	8:35	25	6:26	9	4:37
15	5:53	May 1	7:47	15	8:32	28	6:20	12	4:37
18	5:58	4	7:51	18	8:30	Oct. 1	6:14	15	4:37
21	6:03	7	7:56	21	8:27	4	6:08	18	4:38
24	6:07	10	8:00	24	8:23	7	6:01	21	4:39
27	6:12	13	8:04	27	8:20	10	5:55	24	4:40
Mar. 2	6:17	16	8:08	30	8:16	13	5:49	27	4:42
5	6:22	19	8:12	Aug. 2	8:11	16	5:43	30	4:45
8	6:26	22	8:16	5	8:07	19	5:37		
11	6:31	25	8:20	8	8:02	22	5:32		
14	6:36	28	8:23	11	7:57	25	5:26		

RIO DE JANEIRO, BRAZIL

Mo.	Day	Time	Mo.	Day	Time	Mo.	Day	Time	Mo.	Day	Time	Mo.	Day	Time
Jan.	1	6:26		17	5:52		31	5:00		14	5:20		28	5:47
	4	6:27		20	5:48	June	3	4:59		17	5:22		31	5:48
	7	6:27		23	5:46		6	4:59		20	5:23	Nov.	3	5:50
	10	6:28		26	5:43		9	4:59		23	5:24		6	5:52
	13	6:28		29	5:40		12	4:59		26	5:25		9	5:53
	16	6:28	Apr.	1	5:37		15	5:00		29	5:26		12	5:56
	19	6:27		4	5:34		18	5:00	Sept.	1	5:26		15	5:58
	22	6:27		7	5:32		21	5:01		4	5:27		18	6:00
	25	6:27		10	5:29		24	5:02		7	5:28		21	6:01
	28	6:26		13	5:26		27	5:02		10	5:29		24	6:04
	31	6:25		16	5:24		30	5:03		13	5:31		27	6:05
Feb.	3	6:23		19	5:21	July	3	5:04		16	5:31		30	6:08
	6	6:22		22	5:18		6	5:05		19	5:32	Dec.	3	6:10
	9	6:21		25	5:17		9	5:06		22	5:33		6	6:12
	12	6:19		28	5:14		12	5:07		25	5:33		9	6:14
	15	6:17	May	1	5:12		15	5:08		28	5:35		12	6:16
	18	6:15		4	5:10		18	5:10	Oct.	1	5:35		15	6:18
	21	6:13		7	5:08		21	5:11		4	5:37		18	6:19
	24	6:11		10	5:07		24	5:12		7	5:38		21	6:21
	27	6:07		13	5:05		27	5:14		10	5:39		24	6:22
Mar.	2	6:05		16	5:05		30	5:15		13	5:40		27	6:24
	5	6:02		19	5:02	Aug.	2	5:17		16	5:41		30	6:25
	8	6:00		22	5:02		5	5:17		19	5:43			
	11	5:57		25	5:01		8	5:19		22	5:44			
	14	5:55		28	5:01		11	5:20		25	5:46			

ROME, ITALY

Mo.	Day	Time	Mo.	Day	Time	Mo.	Day	Time	Mo.	Day	Time	Mo.	Day	Time
Jan.	1	4:31		17	6:00		31	7:19		14	6:55		28	4:53
	4	4:34		20	6:03	June	3	7:22		17	6:51		31	4:49
	7	4:37		23	6:07		6	7:24		20	6:46	Nov.	3	4:45
	10	4:40		26	6:10		9	7:26		23	6:42		6	4:41
	13	4:43		29	6:13		12	7:26		26	6:37		9	4:38
	16	4:47	Apr.	1	6:17		15	7:29		29	6:32		12	4:35
	19	4:50		4	6:20		18	7:30	Sept.	1	6:27		15	4:32
	22	4:54		7	6:23		21	7:31		4	6:22		18	4:30
	25	4:57		10	6:27		24	7:31		7	6:17		21	4:27
	28	5:01		13	6:30		27	7:31		10	6:12		24	4:25
	31	5:05		16	6:33		30	7:31		13	6:07		27	4:24
Feb.	3	5:09		19	6:37	July	3	7:31		16	6:01		30	4:23
	6	5:13		22	6:40		6	7:30		19	5:56	Dec.	3	4:22
	9	5:17		25	6:43		9	7:29		22	5:51		6	4:21
	12	5:20		28	6:46		12	7:28		25	5:46		9	4:21
	15	5:24	May	1	6:50		15	7:26		28	5:40		12	4:21
	18	5:28		4	6:53		18	7:24	Oct.	1	5:35		15	4:22
	21	5:32		7	6:56		21	7:21		4	5:30		18	4:23
	24	5:35		10	6:59		24	7:19		7	5:25		21	4:24
	27	5:39		13	7:03		27	7:17		10	5:20		24	4:25
Mar.	2	5:43		16	7:06		30	7:14		13	5:15		27	4:27
	5	5:46		19	7:09	Aug.	2	7:10		16	5:10		30	4:29
	8	5:50		22	7:11		5	7:07		19	5:06			
	11	5:53		25	7:14		8	7:03		22	5:01			
	14	5:57		28	7:17		11	6:59		25	4:57			

SAO PAULO, BRAZIL

Mo.	Day	Time	Mo.	Day	Time	Mo.	Day	Time	Mo.	Day	Time	Mo.	Day	Time
Jan.	1	6:39		17	6:03		31	5:09		14	5:30		28	5:59
	4	6:40		20	5:59	June	3	5:08		17	5:32		31	6:01
	7	6:40		23	5:57		6	5:08		20	5:33	Nov.	3	6:03
	10	6:41		26	5:54		9	5:08		23	5:34		6	6:05
	13	6:41		29	5:51		12	5:08		26	5:35		9	6:06
	16	6:41	Apr.	1	5:48		15	5:09		29	5:36		12	6:09
	19	6:40		4	5:45		18	5:09	Sept.	1	5:37		15	6:10
	22	6:40		7	5:42		21	5:10		4	5:38		18	6:13
	25	6:39		10	5:39		24	5:11		7	5:39		21	6:14
	28	6:39		13	5:36		27	5:11		10	5:40		24	6:17
	31	6:37		16	5:34		30	5:12		13	5:41		27	6:18
Feb.	3	6:36		19	5:31	July	3	5:13		16	5:42		30	6:21
	6	6:35		22	5:28		6	5:14		19	5:43	Dec.	3	6:23
	9	6:33		25	5:26		9	5:15		22	5:44		6	6:25
	12	6:31		28	5:24		12	5:16		25	5:44		9	6:27
	15	6:29	May	1	5:22		15	5:18		28	5:46		12	6:29
	18	6:27		4	5:19		18	5:19	Oct.	1	5:46		15	6:31
	21	6:24		7	5:18		21	5:21		4	5:48		18	6:33
	24	6:23		10	5:16		24	5:22		7	5:49		21	6:34
	27	6:19		13	5:15		27	5:23		10	5:51		24	6:35
Mar.	2	6:17		16	5:14		30	5:24		13	5:52		27	6:37
	5	6:14		19	5:12	Aug.	2	5:26		16	5:53		30	6:39
	8	6:11		22	5:11		5	5:27		19	5:55			
	11	6:09		25	5:10		8	5:28		22	5:56			
	14	6:06		28	5:10		11	5:30		25	5:58			

STOCKHOLM, SWEDEN

Month	Day	Time	Month	Day	Time	Month	Day	Time	Month	Day	Time	Month	Day	Time
Jan.	1	2:40		17	5:35		31	8:27		14	7:25		28	3:49
	4	2:45		20	5:42	June	3	8:32		17	7:17		31	3:41
	7	2:50		23	5:49		6	8:37		20	7:08	Nov.	3	3:34
	10	2:55		26	5:56		9	8:41		23	7:00		6	3:26
	13	3:01		29	6:03		12	8:44		26	6:51		9	3:19
	16	3:08	Apr.	1	6:11		15	8:47		29	6:43		12	3:12
	19	3:14		4	6:18		18	8:49	Sept.	1	6:34		15	3:06
	22	3:21		7	6:25		21	8:50		4	6:25		18	3:00
	25	3:29		10	6:32		24	8:50		7	6:16		21	2:54
	28	3:36		13	6:39		27	8:50		10	6:07		24	2:49
	31	3:43		16	6:46		30	8:48		13	5:59		27	2:44
Feb.	3	3:51		19	6:53	July	3	8:47		16	5:50		30	2:40
	6	3:59		22	7:00		6	8:44		19	5:41	Dec.	3	2:37
	9	4:06		25	7:08		9	8:41		22	5:32		6	2:34
	12	4:14		28	7:15		12	8:37		25	5:23		9	2:32
	15	4:22	May	1	7:22		15	8:32		28	5:14		12	2:30
	18	4:29		4	7:29		18	8:27	Oct.	1	5:05		15	2:29
	21	4:37		7	7:36		21	8:21		4	4:56		18	2:29
	24	4:44		10	7:43		24	8:15		7	4:47		21	2:30
	27	4:52		13	7:50		27	8:09		10	4:39		24	2:32
Mar.	2	4:59		16	7:57		30	8:02		13	4:30		27	2:34
	5	5:05		19	8:03	Aug.	2	7:55		16	4:22		30	2:38
	8	5:14		22	8:10		5	7:48		19	4:13			
	11	5:21		25	8:16		8	7:40		22	4:05			
	14	5:28		28	8:22		11	7:33		25	3:57			

TOKYO, JAPAN

Month	Day	Time	Month	Day	Time	Month	Day	Time	Month	Day	Time	Month	Day	Time
Jan.	1	4:20		17	5:32		31	6:32		14	6:15		28	4:33
	4	4:23		20	5:34	June	3	6:34		17	6:11		31	4:30
	7	4:25		23	5:37		6	6:36		20	6:07	Nov.	3	4:27
	10	4:28		26	5:39		9	6:37		23	6:04		6	4:24
	13	4:31		29	5:42		12	6:39		26	6:00		9	4:21
	16	4:34	Apr.	1	5:44		15	6:40		29	5:56		12	4:19
	19	4:37		4	5:47		18	6:41	Sept.	1	5:52		15	4:17
	22	4:40		7	5:49		21	6:42		4	5:47		18	4:15
	25	4:43		10	5:51		24	6:42		7	5:43		21	4:13
	28	4:46		13	5:54		27	6:43		10	5:39		24	4:12
	31	4:49		16	5:56		30	6:43		13	5:34		27	4:11
Feb.	3	4:52		19	5:59	July	3	6:43		16	5:30		30	4:10
	6	4:55		22	6:01		6	6:42		19	5:26	Dec.	3	4:10
	9	4:58		25	6:04		9	6:41		22	5:21		6	4:10
	12	5:01		28	6:06		12	6:40		25	5:17		9	4:10
	15	5:04	May	1	6:09		15	6:39		28	5:12		12	4:10
	18	5:07		4	6:11		18	6:38	Oct.	1	5:08		15	4:11
	21	5:10		7	6:14		21	6:36		4	5:04		18	4:12
	24	5:13		10	6:16		24	6:34		7	5:00		21	4:13
	27	5:16		13	6:19		27	6:32		10	4:55		24	4:15
Mar.	2	5:19		16	6:21		30	6:30		13	4:51		27	4:17
	5	5:21		19	6:23	Aug.	2	6:27		16	4:47		30	4:19
	8	5:24		22	6:26		5	6:24		19	4:44			
	11	5:27		25	6:28		8	6:21		22	4:40			
	14	5:29		28	6:30		11	6:18		25	4:36			

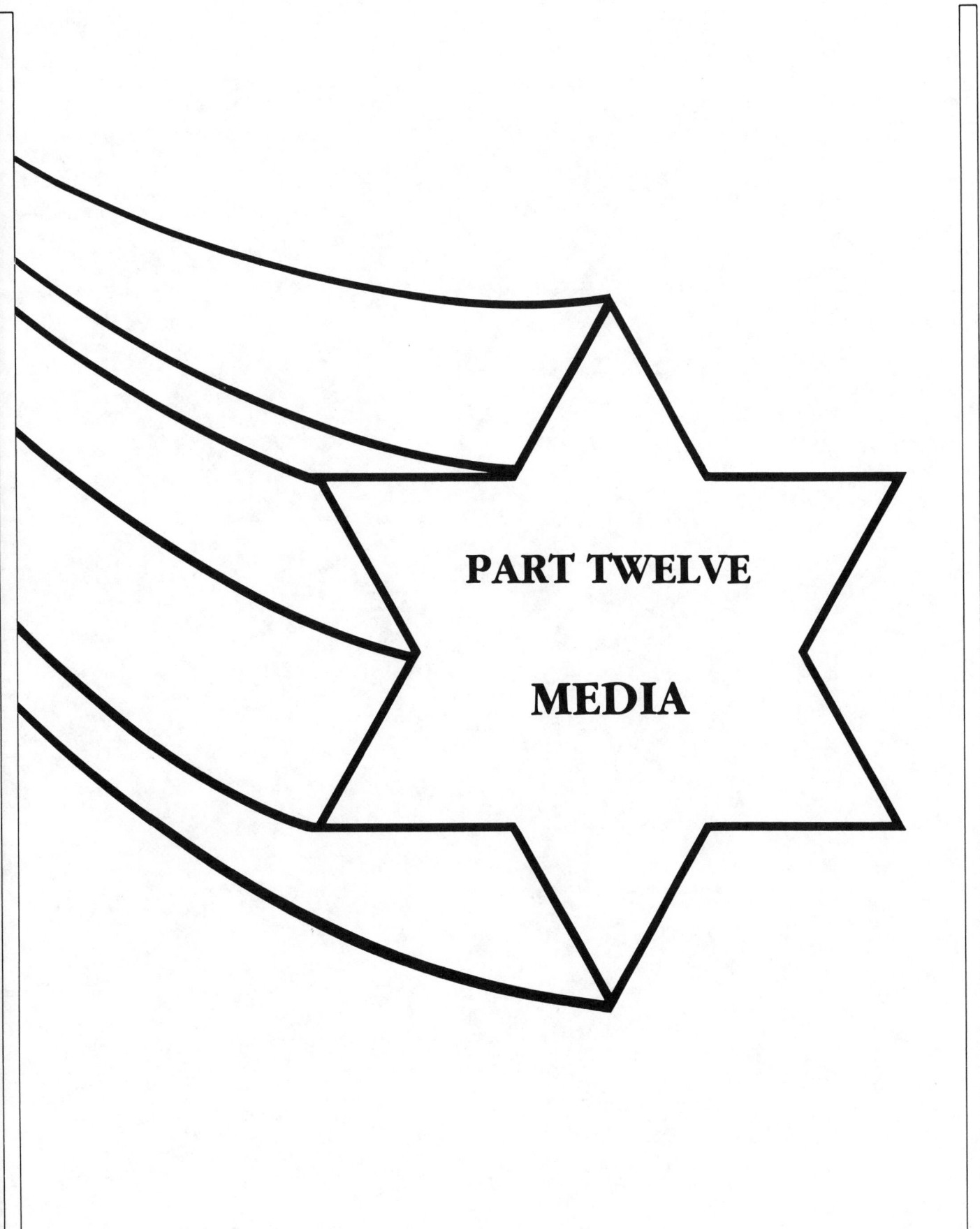

PART TWELVE

MEDIA

62

Jewish Books in Review

Indifference in the Face of Disaster

The Abandonment of the Jews: America and the Holocaust, 1941-1945. By David S. Wyman. Pantheon, New York, 1984. 444 pages. $19.95.

Reviewed by Monty Noam Penkower

In the last few years, a number of books have documented the many-faceted moral bankruptcy of the Christian West during Jewry's most anguished hour—the Holocaust. Aspects of the bystanders' conduct have been rewardingly explored by such specialists as Bernard Wasserstein, Walter Laqueur, and Martin Gilbert, with my own *The Jews Were Expendable* offering a first overview of free world diplomacy in the face of Germany's "Final Solution." Yet America's stance, analyzed much earlier in pioneering works by Arthur Morse, Henry Feingold, and Saul Friedman, had eluded comprehensive analysis. David Wyman, author of a formidable critique of U.S. foreign policy between 1938-1941 *(Paper Walls,* 1968) and the significant essay "Why Auschwitz Was Never Bombed" *(Commentary,* May 1978), now provides us with that study.

A publisher's hyperbole notwithstanding, dramatic revelations do not suffuse *The Abandonment of the Jews.* Those historians cited above and other scholars have unmasked the initial disbelief, then indifference, anti-Semitism, and political expediency which prevailed in the American State Department and British Foreign Office. Roosevelt's callousness; Allied aid to various nationalities under Nazi domination but not to the only people targeted for death in World War II; regrettable bickering among American Jewish organizations; heroic War Refugee Board activity—all have been well substantiated for the public record.

Wyman's valuable contribution lies in the amount of detail brought to the indictment of the United States within the covers of one book. Scrupulous research damns an entire society for not responding adequately to the ethical imperative of saving innocent human beings. With the exception of the Treasury Department under Henry Morgenthau, Jr., Washington officialdom in particular could have done far more in this regard, and without compromising the war effort. Novel here is Wyman's account of what visa and shipping possibilities did exist, even though a mere 21,000 refugees—10 per cent of the legal quotas—were admitted during the period in question.

Worthy of special note, too, is his sensitivity to anti-Semitic and nativist sentiment, reflected both nationwide and in the halls of Congress. The mass media and almost all of the Christian churches, never before examined as thoroughly as in this volume, maintained a near silence. So, too, did most American intellectuals, the political left, and the masses of organized labor.

Some gaps remain. Those interested in the individual activities of different Jewish organizations will have to look elsewhere. In addition, the very focus on American sources overlooks the fact, for example, that the ultimate saving of lives from the Balkans lay in the hands of a small Palestinian contingent—led by War Refugee Board delegate Ira Hirschmann—operating out of Istanbul.

As for American Jewry, the author credits its leaders with publicizing the catastrophe and pressing for government aid, yet he contends that their effectiveness was severely limited by disunity and the lack of sustained action. The Zionist establishment, striving at the August 1943 American Jewish Conference and beyond for a state in postwar Palestine, alienated other Jewish organizations committed to immediate rescue and abolishing Britain's restrictive White Paper quotas for Palestine. A tiny faction led by Hillel Kook (alias Peter Bergson), from Palestine, mustering grass-roots support and helping to create the War Refugee Board, suggests what a major, united campaign could have accomplished.

Lamentable this strife unquestionably was, but it should not obscure the overriding fact that the world powers capable of checking the tempo of the Holocaust had other priorities during World War II. American Jewish organizations did offer the Allies concrete, varied programs of rescue and relief—to scant avail. A moderate Palestine resolution at the American Jewish Conference would not have evoked a more humanitarian response: London adhered to the White Paper throughout, with Washington nodding approval. Nor did a representation to the War Refugee Board from the conference and all other established Jewish organizations in August 1944 secure any substantial aid on behalf of Hungarian Jewry, the last surviving Jewish community in Europe.

Wyman conclusively demonstrates that Roosevelt, in whom Jews placed their greatest trust, failed to champion an active rescue program. The president's indifference surfaced in other instances not discussed here, such as a personal report in July 1943 from eyewitness Jan Karski about the gassing of Jews at Belzec, eliciting only sympathetic generalities at the same moment that FDR approved a confidential joint Anglo-American statement aiming to maintain White Paper policy until the war's end. American Jewish unity would not have altered this overall attitude.

The major Western powers had no intention of relinquishing any control over policy. As a consequence, they sealed the fate of European Jewry. After reading *The Abandonment of the Jews* and other such judicious studies, we can better appreciate the crime of complacency and the urgent mandate for its prevention.

The Jewish Story—Shorter Version

Heritage: Civilization and the Jews. By Abba Eban. Summit Books/Simon and Schuster, New York. 1984. 354 pp. with many illustrations and index. $32.95.

Reviewed by David M. Szonyi

A companion to the recently televised, nine-part PBS series of the same title, *Heritage: Civilization and the Jews* attempts to provide an overview of more than 4,000 years of Jewish history in less than 340 pages. It largely succeeds, in part because of its organizing principle: like Chaim Potok in *Wanderings,* Abba Eban focuses on cultural symbiosis—the interaction of Jewish with a politically, theologically or intellectually "dominant" culture—rather than on an internal communal/institutional history, a la Salo Baron. This approach allows him to paint the Jewish story against the backdrop of world history, where it belongs, and thus make it easier for the general reader to grasp.

Eban also has a gift for succinctly and clearly stating complex ideas. He notes, for example, that the prophetic vision of a coming messianic age contrasted sharply with the stoic belief in a past "golden age," and that while Marcus Aurelius and other stoics were resigned to the idea of historical cyclicality, the prophets lay the foundation for the idea of progress by demanding human commitment to a better society in the here-and-now.

Heritage: Civilization and the Jews also relates the frequent convergence of Jewish and general history. Thus, the Magna Carta (1215), that landmark document of Western civil liberties, included a clause limiting the claims of Jewish moneylenders against the estates of landowners who had died in their debt.

Unlike many Israeli historians, Eban is careful not to provide short shrift to, or to stereotype, Diaspora history. To the contrary, he feels that "The Jews were exiled into survival . . . the diaspora became the essential precondition for the preservation of their creativity and identity."

Eban's telling of the Jews' epic story is considerably enhanced by the book's extensive and beautiful illustrations. Particularly striking are the reproductions of master works of Renaissance art based on biblical themes— paintings by Raphael of *Jacob's Dream* and by Caravaggio of *The Sacrifice of Isaac,* as well as a Donatello sculpture of *Jeremiah the Prophet* are among the many included here—an illumination of Pompey entering the Holy of Holies (from Josephus) by Jean Fouquet, and a series of maps which are models of clarity and usefulness.

Curiously, *Heritage* falters most in dealing with the last century of Jewish history. Eban's telling of the Russian Jewish story in effect ends, inexplicably, with 1917; there is no mention of the crushing of Hebrew and Yiddish culture during the 1920s and '30s, of the "Black Years" (1948-1953), of the recrudescence of Jewish consciousness during the 1960s and '70s, or of the exit of a quarter-million Jews and the plight of the "prisoners of conscience" since 1970.

Similarly, a chapter on American Jewry alludes, as usual, to Haym Salomon and such entrepreneurs as Levi Strauss and Julius Rosenwald (a co-founder of Sears, Roebuck), but tells the reader next to nothing about the founding of the reform and conservative movements or the growth of the federation movement. Mordecai Kaplan, Abraham Joshua Heschel, and J.B. Soloveitchik are among the names that go unmentioned. This is taking the "symbiotic" approach to Jewish history too far.

Even the concluding chapter on "Israel and World Jewry" limits mention of Menachem Begin's stunning 1977 electoral triumph, which ended thirty years of Labor rule, to a photo caption. In summing up the impressive achievements of the Jewish state during its first four decades, Eban also glosses over the tensions between the two "two Israels" (Ashkenazic/Sephardic and religious/secular).

Finally, *Heritage* contains a number of errors which, in a work of this importance, should have been caught. To cite three: Walter Rathenau, the German-Jewish foreign minister, was assassinated in 1922, not 1920; Tel Aviv unmistakably is Israel's largest, not "second most populous city," as a photo caption has it; the Falashas, the recently decimated black Jews of Ethiopia, number more like 20,000 than the 32,000 claimed by Eban.

Despite these flaws, the fluid writing and visual sumptuousness of *Heritage: Civilization and the Jews*—as well as its TV tie-in—guarantee it a large readership, though its format and price may also prompt many readers to relegate it to the coffee table. That would be a shame, for Abba Eban has written a good introduction to, if not a really comprehensive telling of, the Jewish saga. I hope it will serve as a spur to Jews everywhere to tackle more detailed academic or analytic works on their people's sometimes colorful, often tragic, ever richly varied past.

David Szonyi, Associate Director, The Radius Institute in New York, is contributing editor of the Baltimore Jewish Times *and* The Long Island Jewish World.

Abba Eban as Israeli Foreign Minister before the UN Security Council during the Six-Day War.

The Horrifying Record of a Futile Struggle for Survival

The Chronicle Of The Lodz Ghetto, 1941-1944. Edited by Lucjan Dobroszycki. Yale University Press, New Haven. 1984. 539 pp. $35.00.

Reviewed by Sylvia Rothchild

The Department of Archives in the Lodz ghetto was founded by Mordecai Chaim Rumkowski, the controversial Eldest of the Jews, who carried out the orders of the Gestapo and controlled the lives of all the Jews in the ghetto as if he were some feudal prince in the middle ages. He was described in private diaries as "a well-mannered man, tidy, peaceful, religious, a traditional Jew" and at the same time, "sordid, ridiculous . . . insidious, treacherous and murderous." His decision to keep a daily record of the news of the ghetto was both pretentious and self-serving. It provided a vehicle for establishing his importance and infallibility. He was described only with the respect accorded a beloved leader. All protests, strikes and demonstrations were attributed in the *Chronicle* to "irresponsible individuals intent on disturbing the law and public order created by the ghetto authorities who watched over the peace, safety and food supplies of the ghetto dwellers."

Rumkowski deceived himself with reports from the orphanages, schools, hospitals, and old-age homes that provided an aura of normalcy and later with the workshops and factories that provided Jewish workers for the German war effort. In a sealed ghetto without radios, newspapers, or any communication with the world outside its barbed wire enclosures and guards, it was possible to lull the inhabitants with promises of survival he could not keep.

The Germans were stationed in the center of the ghetto. The proclamations relayed by Rumkowski were about their orders to salute all Germans, their exhortations to turn in radios, furs, boots and gold objects with penalties of death or "resettlement" for those who dared to refuse.

There were 200,000 Jews in the Lodz ghetto when it was sealed off by the Nazis in 1940—and 870 Jews left when the city was liberated in 1944. In spite of the cautious language of the archivists who avoided mentioning the Germans and had only praise for Rumkowski; in spite of all their efforts to deny the ultimate fate of the inhabitants of the ghetto, the six archivists who wrote the daily reports left a horrifying record of a futile struggle for survival. Though diaries and memoirs of men and women from Lodz have already offered their personal tales of anguish (several stories about life in Lodz were included in my anthology *Voices From The Holocaust)*, there is much to be learned from these cool, censored daily reports.

The calm notices of the state of the weather, the births and deaths, the marriages, Bar Mitzvahs, graduations, and the announcements and reviews of concerts and entertainments are at first interspersed and later taken over by the reports of shootings, suicides, and the deportations to Auschwitz they called "resettlements." The information about medical care and services alternates with the reports of typhus epidemics and the problems of accumulated bodies that turned up faster than two hundred grave diggers could bury them. There are reports of mysterious shipments of bedding, used clothes and prayer shawls that came to Lodz for sorting before being sent to an unknown destination. The chroniclers were bewildered by truckloads of sewing machines and household goods but unwilling or unable to think about where they might have come from. The contemporary reader is likely to be shaken by the human capacity for denial and the power of authorities to deceive by controlling communication and sealing off an area.

Lucjan Dobroszycki, the historian who edited the *Chronicles,* was born in Poland. He was incarcerated in the Lodz ghetto at the age of fourteen and deported to Auschwitz where his parents and two younger brothers perished. He was liberated by the Russian Army in 1945 and returned to Lodz to study history at the university. He later was appointed Associate Professor at the Institute of History at the Polish Academy of Sciences in Warsaw, where he received his Ph.D. His introduction and footnotes are an invaluable addition to this macabre chronicle. Photographs taken by the Archive and street maps add immediacy and credibility to events it might still be tempting to deny.

Readers who are new to the subject will find an astonishing view from the inside of a closed and doomed ghetto. Those who are familiar with the details will find it impossible to forget the day-by-day record, kept by writers who knew too little and wrote about even less than they knew.

Sylvia Rothchild is the editor of Voices From The Holocaust *(NAL) and book columnist for* The Jewish Advocate, *Boston, Massachusetts.*

Life On The Western Frontier

We Lived There Too. Kenneth Libo and Irving Howe. St. Martin's/Marek, New York 1984. 344 pp.

Mid-America's Promise. Joseph P. Schultz, ed. The Jewish Community Foundation of Greater Kansas City and the American Jewish Historical Society. 1982. 405 pp.

Pioneer Jews. Harriet and Fred Rochlin. Houghton Mifflin Co. Boston. 1984. 244 pp.

Reviewed by Jeffrey S. Gurock

Having earned their "home and fortunes" as chroniclers of New York ghetto life and culture, Kenneth Libo and Irving Howe have now "turned (their) faces to the Great West" and in accord with Horace Greeley's century-old dictum have sought out new horizons for their considerable talents.

Their collection of documents, photographs, and ephemera offers a reminder to American historians, in an appropriate and non-triumphalist way, of the important role immigrants in general and Jews in particular played in the opening and development of the West. And it strongly argues to students of American Jewish history that the story of their people in this country extends beyond the borders of the Lower East Side and its sister ghettos of the East and Mid-West.

Sol (Eye) Berg Men's Store, El Paso, Texas, from We Lived There Too.

To be sure, Libo and Howe's correctives are not new; more than 40 years ago, Marcus Lee Hansen argued for the significance of the New American in the Manifest Destiny story. And for more than a generation, local Jewish Historical Societies from Kansas City to Colorado to California to Oregon have patiently collected the miscellanea that make up the texts of this book. Indeed, some of these

Price 25 cts. per year.   3 cts. per Copy.

דער אידישער פֿאַרמער

THE JEWISH FARMER

May 1912.
Vol. V., No. 5.

PUBLISHED BY
The Jewish Agricultural and Industrial Aid Society
174 Second Avenue, New York City, U. S. A.

From We Lived There Too.

documents have been published elsewhere: Abraham Kohn's peddler lament is, for example, one of the most widely quoted passages in American Jewish memoir literature. Libo and Howe's contribution lies rather in their uncommon abilities to assimilate and to masterfully introduce documents usually of interest only to scholars to large and appreciative lay audiences.

As noted above, Libo and Howe could not have done their work without books like *Mid-America's Promise,* a compilation of essays and documents on Kansas City Jewish history. A work typical of many produced by local historical societies over the last 30 years, it provides scholars possessed of sensitivities to national trends in Jewish economic life, politics, demographics, and religion with important case studies from whence they ultimately draw wider conclusions.

Finally, it should be noted that the spade work of Western Jewish history continues to be undertaken by loving and devoted members of historical societies. Harriet and Fred Rochlin's richly illustrated and handsomely produced record of Jewish life in the Far West is a case in point. *Pioneer Jews* covers much new ground even as it retells the sagas of Jewish peddlers and entrepreneurs in 19th-century frontier society.

Jeffrey S. Gurock is the author of When Harlem Was Jewish *(Columbia University Press).*

Major New Novels from Wiesel, Potok and Wouk

The Fifth Son. Elie Wiesel. Summit, New York. $15.95.

Davita's Harp. Chaim Potok. Knopf, New York. $16.95.

Inside, Outside. Herman Wouk. Little Brown, Boston. $19.95.

Reviewed by Benjamin Nelson.

Here are three new novels by authors who share a commonality of Jewish outlook, tradition, and sensibility. Despite these similarities, however, each writer speaks with a distinct voice out of a personal vision.

A survivor of the Holocaust and its most eloquent poet, Elie Wiesel has turned repeatedly to the issues and questions raised by the most traumatic event of our century. In his works he has given voice to the unspeakable in his explorations of the phenomena of faith and skepticism, hope and despair, life and death, good and evil. In his latest novel, *The Fifth Son,* Wiesel presents a stunning and disturbing image of the isolation and possible redemption of a second-generation Holocaust victim, the son of a survivor whose journey toward retribution and self-recognition is the central action of the book.

The story, told in overlapping narratives by four figures—the youth, his father, and two of the father's friends (also survivors)—shuttles back and forth in time from contemporary New York to a Nazi-enslaved ghetto in Europe of the 1940s. The underlying plot involves the unnamed son's plan to accomplish what his father had botched after the war: the execution of the sadistic SS officer who had terrorized the ghetto and brutally murdered the father's first son. For this young man, the execution will be both an act of retributive justice as well as a means of breaking through the barrier of incomprehensibility between his father and himself.

This is the stuff of powerful drama, and in terms of plot and structure, Wiesel handles it with consummate skill. The climax and resolution is perceptive and challenging. Nonetheless, something is missing in this complex morality tale: an emotional core to the characters who move through it.

Simcha, a friend of the youth's father, is described as "a merchant of shadows." The characters who people the novel are not only merchants of shadows; they are shadows themselves, abstractions, ghosts, haunted and haunting spectres out of the author's life and imagination. Their catastrophe is real enough, and certainly their creator's commitment to them and their anguish is unquestionable; but they lack physical and spatial dimension, and because they do, their drama lacks the emotional weight and power to move the heart as well as the mind. Consequently their story engages our thoughts but falls short of gripping us as deeply as it could and should.

For all its poetic beauty and moral seriousness, *The Fifth Son* is a curiously detached and isolate work, a dramatization of a thesis in which characters serve more as illustrations than human beings. The thesis is pertinent and profound, but the illustrations are still illustrations.

If Elie Wiesel's characters tend to shade toward the abstract, Chaim Potok's have often been mired in one-dimensionality. In *The Chosen,* the story was interesting enough to compensate for the lack of in-depth characterization, but in subsequent novels, in which the story became increasingly repetitive, the superficiality of the characters became increasingly obvious and, in the process, weakened the narrative. Potok was caught on a treadmill. With *Davita's Harp,* he has happily and successfully leaped off. Although the concerns in *Davita's Harp* are vintage Potok—the schism between tradition and modernism, faith and doubt, and the emotional and spiritual crises of a child moving toward adulthood—they are dramatized here with a skillful and imaginative quality that makes this his best book to date.

Ilana Davita Chandal is the daughter of a Christian father and Jewish mother who are both atheistic and suffused with a zealous commitment to Communist ideology and idealism so prevalent among the young intellectuals of the 1930s. The book dramatizes the young girl's loving but complex relationship with her parents, their struggles for survival and meaning, and her own process of maturation through pain, death, disillusionment and love.

Potok does not escape from some of the pitfalls of his previous works, and some of his characters, particularly Davita's father, never wholly break free from the bonds of stock characterization. However, in his portrayal of the girl and her mother Potok has created two of his finest characters. They are multi-faceted, believable, and deeply human. Their developments, which subtly parallel each other, are rendered with great insight and compassion.

The climactic, epiphanal moment in which Davita envisions the speech she would have given had not her yeshiva reneged (because of her sex) on awarding her a prize for Talmudic studies, is not only a gem of creative imagination, but a beautiful and wondrous synthesis of the themes of the novel in a single, poetic act of faith, courage and hope. Like the harp of its title, this novel, despite some flaws, gives off a sweet, pure and gentle sound.

On the last page of Herman Wouk's *Inside, Outside,* the first-person narrator, Israel David Goodkind, sums up the book. "It is a kaddish for my father . . . but in counterpoint it is also a torch song of the thirties, a sentimental Big Band number." It is that indeed—and more. It is also a kaddish, riotously and poignantly ambivalent, for Goodkind's mother, a presence in his life and memory even more dominant than Goodkind's much gentler and self-effacing father. It is also a story about Goodkind himself and the Inside/Outside equilibrium of his life. Here is Goodkind the Insider, the product of Jewish tradition, life and observance, and Goodkind the Outsider, university wit, bon vivant, tax attorney, and presidential advisor, trying to maintain this equilibrium throughout his life in a series of sometimes hilarious, sometimes deeply moving events and situations.

Inside, Outside is far from being a perfect novel. Like many of Wouk's previous books, it bogs down into woefully cliched situations, its language often flattens out into banalities, and some of its characters, particularly the women, remain predictable stereotypes. Ironically, the daughter of Goodkind, his "shikse" first love, and to an extent his embarrassingly indomitable mother have been treated more brilliantly and incisively in the novels of Philip Roth, a writer whom Wouk skewers hilariously in the person of a neurotic self-hating American-Jewish author who is a friend of Goodkind.

What lifts *Inside, Outside* above second-rate Philip Roth? The answer is simple: first-rate Herman Wouk, namely, his gifts as a story teller, to which must be added here, a warmth and remarkable sense of humor that are wholly captivating. Characters and sequences frequently burst into joyous life. An incident involving the making of sauerkraut and another about the purchase of a ghastly purple suit for young Israel David are comic masterpieces. Wouk's long but absorbing dramatization of Goodkind's immigrant parents and grandparents adjusting to America, the youth's career at Columbia College, and his apprenticeship to a precariously successful and garishly flamboyant gag writer in the 30s are all permeated with a sense of time, place and feeling that is both accurate and enthralling.

A Big Band kaddish indeed. *Inside, Outside* may not be as profound a work as Goodkind (and Wouk) may wish. It coagulates into too much banality, stereotype, and platitude. But at its best—and this is often—it is suffused with warmth and sentiment and joy. Mr. Wouk conducts his torch song-folk dance with gusto and with deserved pride, and eventually he has us swaying and stomping to his music. Dance. Read. Enjoy.

Benjamin Nelson is Professor of English and Comparative Literature at Fairleigh Dickinson University. He has written books on Arthur Miller and Tennessee Williams.

Like Family

Bums: An Oral History of the Brooklyn Dodgers. Peter Golenbock. G.P. Putnam's Sons, New York. 464 pp. $17.95

Bums is not a Jewish book. It is, however, the story of a ballclub that was idolized by most of Brooklyn's massive Jewish population during the 1940s and 1950s. The flight of the Dodgers from working-class Brooklyn to Los Angeles after the 1957 baseball season mirrored the flight of Brooklyn's Jewish population to the suburbs. Any study of the Brooklyn Dodgers' constituency would by necessity have to include a study of Jewish demographics. The Jews of New York were fiercely loyal to their Dodgers—particularly to *landsmen* Goody Rosen, Cal Abrams, long-time coach Jake Pitler and Sandy Koufax.

Exerpts from this oral history:

Larry King: "We were very Jewish, and we wanted Jewish ballplayers to do well. Before he died the comedian Godfrey Cambridge told me once, 'If the blacks could only learn Jewish public relations.' He said, 'I don't know if you have an international league of P.R., but when polio was cured, a guy called me and said, "Did you hear what happened today?" I said, "What?" He said, "A Jewish doctor cured polio." Not a doctor, a Jewish doctor. Sandy Koufax was a "Jewish pitcher." '

"We rooted for Ed Levy, who changed his name from some Polish name, and we rooted for Herschel Martin, who I thought was Jewish—he wasn't—but he had the name Herschel, so we rooted for him. Hank Greenberg was our hero. To this day any Jewish person will tell you that they never let Hank Greenberg hit a homer the last two weeks after he hit fifty-eight—he never got a pitch, they walked him every time—because he was Jewish. We were convinced of it. And of course we rooted for Al Rosen, and we loved Cal Abrams. Cal was a favorite. At first there was suspicion. Was he Jewish? Then we saw the picture. We saw the nose. He was Jewish. Cal had a lot of speed, and he was a good outfielder. But we uniformly despised him for the turn he took at third base in the final game against the Phillies in 1950. I loved Cal Abrams—until he got thrown out at home."

Back in the early 1940s, the Dodgers' Larry MacPhail had the notion that because of the 1,500,000 Jews living in Brooklyn, it would be good business for the Dodgers to have a Jewish presence. There should be someone to give the day off on the holy days of Rosh Hashanah and Yom Kippur during the pennant race. The Dodgers had had Goody Rosen, and after he left in 1946, Jake Pitler, the first base coach, became the Dodgers' Jewish presence. The Jewish fan didn't necessarily root for him, but Jake's being on the field would give him a sense of comfort.

Jack Newfield: "My mother would be so impressed when Jake Pitler would walk off the field in the seventh inning of a game when it got dark because it was Yom Kippur. She would say, 'That's a good Jewish man.' "

After MacPhail left the Dodgers for the Yankees, he went a little overboard, when failing to sign a real Jew, he made Ed Clarence Whitner change his name to Ed Levy to give the Waspy Yankees a Jewish player who was supposed to

compete with the greatest Jewish player to ever wear spikes, Hammerin' Hank Greenberg. Levy spent two seasons with the Yankees, 1942 and 1944, and then disappeared from the majors.

MacPhail was not the first to seek a Jewish Presence. Back in the 1920s, John McGraw of the Giants had coveted a Jewish ballplayer to help him attract the Jews who packed upper Manhattan and the South Bronx.

In 1923 a Giant scout brought to the Polo Grounds a youngster named Moses Solomon. Solomon had batted .421 and hit forty-nine home runs for Hutchinson, Kansas. Reporters immediately began calling Solomon the "Rabbi of Swat."

Solomon played exactly two games.

The other Jewish hope brought to McGraw was infielder Andy Cohen, who neither fielded nor batted well.

McGraw was in the habit after the game of going to the track with his friend, comedian Georgie Jessel. On one particular day, Cohen kicked two grounders, costing the Giants the game. At the track McGraw played a hot tip for the ninth race. His horse was ridden by a Jewish jockey. The horse lost in a photo finish.

Back in the limo, McGraw and Jessel rode back to Manhattan in silence. As they drove over the Queensboro Bridge, McGraw suddenly turned to Jessel and said, "They can't ride either."

The Giants never did have much luck finding a good one. In fact, almost nobody did. Hank Greenberg and Sandy Koufax were the best of the very few Jewish ballplayers.

Irving Rudd: "Jews were city people. Where could you play? On the concrete pavement? Stickball was the Jewish sport. And if you were good enough, you would have to go out of your way to find a place to play and a team to play on. Most of the guys on the teams were *goyim*. And maybe a Jewish kid couldn't fit in so well. And if the field was in Canarsie, maybe it was, 'What's the Jew-boy from Brownsville doing coming here to play?' Unless he was especially good, like Sid Gordon, who became a Giant, but long after McGraw had passed away.

"The power base in Brooklyn were the Brooklyn Jews who were the elite box-seat holders. In a borough of 3,000,000 people, there had to be 1,500,000 Jews. The Jews who bought the box seats were the same guys who went crazy at basketball games at the Garden. You had Abe Stark, who owned a clothing store. He owned a box. He was not a freeloading guy, even though he had paid for the sign out in right field, 'Hit Sign, Win a Free Suit.' There was a guy named Sam Abrams, who was the bossman of Esquire shoe polish. There was Judge Samuel Liebowitz, a noted judge and jurist and prior to that a very famous lawyer. And I had a friendship going with a kid named Buddy Hackett. He couldn't afford to buy. I had to smuggle him in.

"The Dodgers were looking for box office magic. When I was a kid, Eddie Cantor, Benny Leonard, these were the saints, the deities. Eddie Cantor was like the Pope. And a Jewish ballplayer or athlete was looked up to. How many were there? Al Schacht, Moe Berg, Johnny Kling, whose real name was Kline, Hank Greenberg, Sid Gordon, Goody Rosen, Al Rosen, Jimmy Reese, an old coach for the Yankees—his real name is Hymie Soloman, a Jew. And

Jake Pitler

Cal Abrams

Sandy Koufax

every Jew knew his name was Hymie Soloman. One thing you couldn't do was pass. It took one to know one. So obviously a Jew as a box office attraction had to be tremendous.

"What puzzles me to this day about Cal Abrams is this: How could the Dodgers have not taken full advantage of him? He was a Jew, and he was from Bröoklyn, for crying out loud. He wasn't a bad player. One year he was hitting .470 something, led the league in hitting in July. But then they stopped using him.

"There was something. I'll be very blunt about it. In the Dodger organization, the *goyim* did okay. Very true. They were tolerant, but it helped if you were Irish. As James Carter once said, 'Life isn't fair.' I was hired by the Dodgers at the time O'Malley took over, and in looking back in hindsight, I wonder if being Jewish didn't hurt me. I don't know. Did it hurt Cal? I wonder about that, too."

●

"Casey Stengel once said that Sandy was probably the best pitcher who ever lived. He said, 'Forget the other fellow,' meaning Walter Johnson. 'You can forget Waddell. The Jewish kid is probably the best of all of them.'"

●

Larry King: "What I remember most about Sandy, what the whole neighborhood knew, was that he was what we call a *heimisha* boy. He was a *mensch*. Unlike us, Sandy did not do crazy things. We'd sit in the PAL section in Ebbets Field and then sneak down into the box seats. Sandy, never.

"He was as close to being an Orthodox Jew as any of the neighborhood kids. Most of us observed the dietary laws, but Sandy wouldn't even drive a car on Saturday, and he always observed the High Holidays. To the end of his career, he wouldn't pitch on Yom Kippur.

"Once it was the day before Rosh Hashanah, and I was interviewing him, and this was right before the start of the World Series, and he said, 'Don't forget to remind everybody we taped this the day before.' He didn't want people to think that he would do an interview on Rosh Hashanah.

"We loved to tease Sandy even after he grew up. I remember it was spring training, and there was an annual Yankee-Dodger series just before the start of the season, and it was Passover, and we went to Ebbets Field, and we brought matzo sandwiches with chicken fat on it. Herbie Cohen and Hooha and I went down to the Dodger dugout, and we started calling, 'Sandy, hey, Sandy, we got matzo for you.' And Sandy's going, 'Go away. Go away.' And Russ Meyer, who was from Illinois, comes over and says to us, 'What's matzo?' So we gave him some matzo with chicken fat on it, and Meyer started giving some to one of the other Dodgers, and pretty soon all the Dodgers were eating matzo with chicken fat, and they're all saying, 'This is terrific.' Even Jackie Robinson. So the Dodgers are passing around the matzo, and Sandy is going, 'I don't know these guys.'

"Anyway, in the third inning, Meyer gives up eleven runs, I mean the Yankees bombed him, and Herbie Cohen, a Yankee fanatic, is going around saying, 'It was my plot. I planned it. I fed him matzo and chicken fat, and no man has ever pitched five innings with matzo and chicken fat in him.'"

The Animal Kingdom

A Jewish Bestiary: A Book of Fabulous Creatures Drawn from Hebraic Legend and Lore. By Mark Podwal. Jewish Publication Society, Philadelphia. 1984. 52 pages. $10.95

Our Rabbis said: Even those things which you may regard as completely superfluous to the creation of the world, such as fleas, gnats, and flies, even they too are included in the creation of the world, and the Holy One, blessed be He, carries out His purpose through everything, even through a snake, a scorpion, a gnat, or a frog.

Genesis Rabbah

The world of the animal kingdom has illumined the Jewish imagination throughout the centuries. Indeed, the earliest printed Jewish book, as far as is known, is a collection of illustrated medieval animal fables, *Meshal HaKadmoni* ("The Ancient Parable"). *A Jewish Bestiary* is a fit heir to this tradition.

Mark Podwal, the creator of *A Book of Hebrew Letters,* once again reveals a vital stream in the Jewish imagination by depicting twenty-five creatures, both real and fanciful, from among those which can be found in the traditional Jewish sources—biblical, talmudic, midrashic, and kabbalistic: from the ant to the ziz. Once more, the author and artist combines traditional Jewish themes with his own distinctive line. A spider plays on King David's harp. The "pious" stork is shown donning phylacteries. The despised swine is represented merely by a shadow. Each drawing is accompanied by a facing text that enhances our understanding and appreciation.

The resulting juxtaposition of art with Jewish legend and lore is indicative of Podwal's profound sensibility. Here are the creatures that exert a special force on the Jewish fancy.

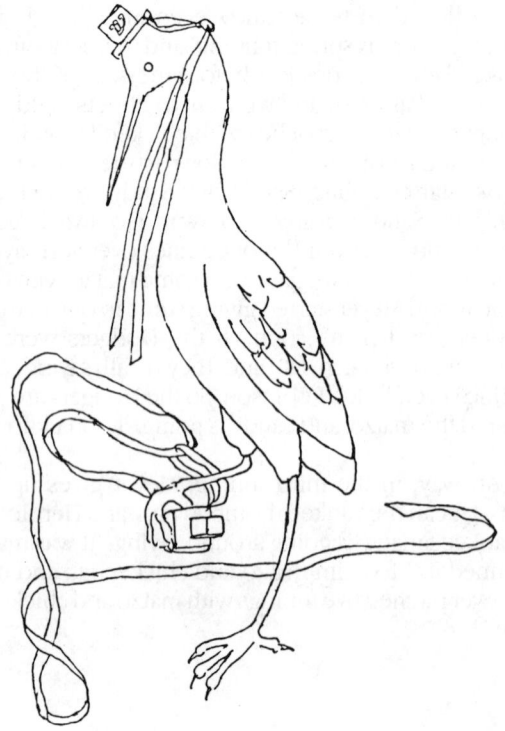

The Siddur

The Complete ArtScroll Siddur. Nosson Scherman, ed. Mesorah Publications, Brooklyn. 991 pp. $15.95.

This Hebrew-English *siddur* includes a new English translation, Torah readings, and services for weekdays, Sabbath and festivals.

The *siddur* is by far the most difficult and ambitious project ever undertaken by ArtScroll, and has taken production priority for the editorial and production staffs over the past two years.

Rabbis, synagogue and communal leaders from throughout the Jewish community were consulted at length. Numerous test editions were produced and circulated for comment and suggestions. Previous editions of the *siddur* were studied and analyzed for their faults and strengths. There were tremendous production challenges of typography and page design.

Many of the prayers had to be translated into English for the first time, since previous English translations of the *siddur* had only paraphrased them, or omitted them completely. Other sections were adapted from previous ArtScroll works on individual prayers or holidays.

The emphasis in the translation throughout is on the literal, overall meaning of the prayers. The comments on the bottom of each page are more concise than the usual ArtScroll treatment, and offer a more uniform point of view, concentrating on the inspirational content of the prayers. The overriding priority of the ArtScroll team was to produce, above all, a work that is convenient and practical for everyday use in the home and synagogue.

The finished pages are a historic Hebrew-English typographical achievement. Well-organized and comfortably readable, all instructions and Halakhic notes, in elaborate details, are inserted clearly into the text of the prayers, each at the exact point of application. Hazzan's notes are clear, but unobtrusive. All commentaries and their references in the text are readily available. Communal responses are translated in bold face. Special care is taken with the page breaks to maintain continuity, and all prayers are printed in order, even when repeated, eliminating the need to turn to other sections to find prayers. There are, in addition, numerous aesthetic touches in the typography and page design, to make the *ArtScroll Siddur* attractive as well as practical and complete.

Trivia Judaica

The Jewish Trivia and Information Book. Ian Shapolsky. Steimatzky, New York. 400 pp. $5.95 softcover, $4.95 pocketsize.

The Jewish Trivia & Information Book contains 1400 questions and answers divided into seven categories: Current Events, Arts and Culture, People, Religion, History, Language and Geography.

A sampler:

1. What did the Jewish scientist Judah Cresques, otherwise known as the "Map Jew" of medieval Spain, hypothesize before all others?

2. What and where is "Birobidjan"?

3. On June 7, 1981, Israeli planes attacked and destroyed this objective deep within hostile Arab territory.

4. What was planned for Grand Island in upstate New York, in the early 20th century?

5. What was Israel's "Operation Redemption," on July 4th, 1976?

6. In Michelangelo's famous sculpture, what non-human characteristic does Moses possess?

7. This famous fictional Jewish character said: "I am a Jew. Hath not a Jew eyes? Hath not a Jew hands, organs, dimensions, sense, affections, passions . . . ?"

8. Jacob Cohen is the original name of this always depressed and harassed comedian . . . ?

9. What was the *Machal,* formed in 1948?

10. What was the main inspiration for the Jewish flag's design?

11. What was the first country that the ancient Jews were foreigners in?

12. In 1941, the "Palmach" organization was formed in Palestine, in anticipation of this contingency . . . ?

13. What famous French Jewish painter was born with the name Moshe Segal?

ANSWERS

1. That the earth was round (200 years before Copernicus).

2. An area in the Eastern U.S.S.R., on the border of China, that was at one time designated by the Soviets for "autonomous" Jewish settlement.

3. An Iraqi nuclear reactor.

4. This was considered as a potential homeland for the Jews (it would have been called Ararat).

5. The raid on Entebbe Airport to rescue the hostages taken prisoner by pro-Palestinian hijackers.

6. A horned forehead. (Michelangelo misunderstood the use of the word "keren" which means both "to shine" and "horn," in his instructions. Moses' forehead was intended to shine, not to be horned.)

7. Shylock, from Shakespeare's *The Merchant of Venice.*

8. Rodney Dangerfield.

9. It was an organization of volunteers from the Diaspora, that came to aid Israel during the War of Independence.

10. The Jewish prayer shawl.

11. Egypt.

12. The invasion of Palestine by the German army of Field Marshal Rommel.

13. Marc Chagall.

63

The National Jewish Book Awards

National Jewish Book Award—Biography

Dr. Moses Leo Gitelson Award
1984—DAN KURZMAN, for *Ben Gurion: Prophet of Fire,* Simon & Schuster.
1985—MAURICE FRIEDMAN, for *Martin Buber's Life and Work: The Later Years, 1945-1965,* E.P. Dutton, Inc.

National Jewish Book Award—Children's Literature

Isaac Siegel Memorial Award
1952—SYDNEY TAYLOR, for *All-Of-A-Kind Family,* Wilcox and Follett.
1953—LILLIAN S. FREEHOF, for *Stories of King David,* Jewish Publication Society; and *Star Light Stories,* Bloch Publishing Co.
1954—DEBORAH PESSIN, for *The Jewish People: Book Three,* United Synagogue Commission on Jewish Education.
1955—NORA BENJAMIN KUBIE, for *King Solomon's Navy,* Harper and Brothers.
1956—SADIE ROSE WEILERSTEIN, for her cumulative contributions to Jewish juvenile literature.

Temple B'nai Jeshurun Award, Newark, N.J.
1957—ELMA E. LEVINGER, for her cumulative contributions to Jewish juvenile literature.

Pioneer Women's Hayim Greenberg Memorial Award
1958—NAOMI BEN ASHER and HAYIM LEAF, for *Jewish Junior Encyclopedia,* Shengold Publishers.

Isaac Siegel Memorial Award
1959—LLOYD ALEXANDER, for *Border Hawk: August Bondi,* Farrar, Straus and Cudahy; Jewish Publication Society
1960—SYLVIA ROTHCHILD, for *Keys to a Magic Door: Isaac Leib Peretz,* Farrar, Straus and Cudahy; Jewish Publication Society
1961—REGINA TOR, for *Discovering Israel,* Random House.
1962—SADIE ROSE WEILERSTEIN, for *Ten and a Kid,* Doubleday & Co.
1963—JOSEPHINE KAMM, for *Return to Freedom,* Abelard-Schuman.
1964—SULAMITH ISH-KISHOR, for *A Boy of Old Prague,* Pantheon Books.
1965—DOV PERETZ ELKINS and AZRIEL EISENBERG, for *Worlds Lost and Found,* Abelard-Schuman.
1966—BETTY SCHECHTER, for *The Dreyfus Affair,* Houghton-Mifflin.
1967—MEYER LEVIN, for *The Story of Israel,* G.P. Putnam's Sons.

Charles and Bertie G. Schwartz Juvenile Award
1970—CHARLIE MAY SIMON, for *Martin Buber: Widsom in Our Time,* E.P. Dutton.
　　—GERALD GOTTLIEB, for *The Story of Masada by Yigael Yadin: Retold for Young Readers,* Random House.
1971—SONIA LEVITIN, for *Journey to America,* Atheneum.
1972—SULAMITH ISH-KISHOR, for *The Master of Miracle: A New Novel of the Golem,* Harper & Row.

1973—JOHANNA REISS, for *The Upstairs Room,* Thomas Y. Crowell.
1974—YURI SUHL, for *Uncle Misha's Partisans,* Four Winds Press.
1975—BEA STADTLER, for *The Holocaust: A History of Courage and Resistance,* Behrman House.
1976—SHIRLEY MILGRIM, for *Haym Salomon: Liberty's Son,* Jewish Publication Society.
1977—CHAYA BURSTEIN, for *Rifka Grows Up,* Bonim Books/Hebrew Publishing Co.
1978—MILTON MELTZER, for *Never to Forget: The Jews of the Holocaust,* Harper & Row.
1979—IRENE NARELL, for *Joshua: Fighter for Bar Kochba,* Akiba Press.
1980—ARNOST LUSTIG, for *Dita Saxova,* Harper & Row.

William (Zev) Frank Memorial Award
Presented by Ellen and David Scheinfeld
1981—LEONARD EVERETT FISHER, for *A Russian Farewell,* Four Winds Press.
1982—KATHRYN LASKY, for *The Night Journey,* Frederick Warne & Co. Inc.
1983—BARBARA COHEN, for *King of the Seventh Grade,* Lothrop, Lee & Shepard Books.
1984—CHAYA M. BURSTEIN, for *The Jewish Kids Catalog,* Jewish Publication Society.
1985—GARY PROVOST and GAIL LEVINE-FREIDUS, for *Good If It Goes,* Bradbury Press.

National Jewish Book Award—Children's Picture Book

Marcia and Louis Posner Award
1983—BARBARA COHEN and MITCHELL J. DERANEY (illustrator), for *Yussel's Prayer: A Yom Kippur Story,* Lothrop, Lee & Shepard.
1985—AMY SCHWARTZ, for *Mrs. Moskowitz and the Sabbath Candlesticks,* Jewish Publication Society.

National Jewish Book Award—Fiction

Harry and Ethel Daroff Award
1949—HOWARD FAST, for *My Glorious Brothers,* Little, Brown.
1950—JOHN HERSEY, for *The Wall,* Alfred A. Knopf.
1951—SOMA MORGENSTERN, for *The Testament of the Lost Son,* Jewish Publication Society.
1952—ZELDA POPKIN, for *Quiet Street,* J.B. Lippincott.
1953—MICHAEL BLANKFORT, for *The Juggler,* Little, Brown.
1954—CHARLES ANGOFF, for *In the Morning Light,* Beechurst Press.
1955—LOUIS ZARA, for *Blessed is the Land,* Crown Publishers.
1956—JO SINCLAIR, for *The Changelings,* McGraw-Hill.
1957—LEON FEUCHTWANGER, for *Raquel: The Jewess of Toledo,* Julian Messner.
1958—BERNARD MALAMUD, for *The Assistant,* Farrar, Straus & Cudahy.
1959—LEON URIS, for *Exodus,* Doubleday & Co.
1960—PHILIP ROTH, for *Goodbye, Columbus,* Houghton Mifflin Co.
1961—EDWARD L. WALLANT, for *The Human Season,* Harcourt, Brace & Co.
1962—SAMUEL YELLEN, for *Wedding Band,* Atheneum Publishers.
1963—ISAAC BASHEVIS SINGER, for *The Slave,* Farrar, Straus & Cudahy.
1964—JOANNE GREENBERG, for *The King's Persons,* Holt, Rinehart and Winston.

1965—ELIE WIESEL, for *The Town Beyond the Wall,* Atheneum.
1966—MEYER LEVIN, for *The Stronghold,* Simon and Schuster.
1967—CHAIM GRADE, for *The Well,* Jewish Publication Society of America.
1969—DR. CHARLES ANGOFF, for *Memory of Autumn,* Thomas Yoseloff.
1970—DR. LEO LITWAK, for *Waiting for the News,* Doubleday & Co.
1972—CYNTHIA OZICK, for *The Pagan Rabbi and Other Stories,* Alfred A. Knopf.

William and Janice Epstein Award

1973—ROBERT KOTLOWITZ, for *Somewhere Else,* Charterhouse.
1974—FRANCINE PROSE, for *Judah the Pious,* Atheneum.
1975—JEAN KARSAVINA, for *White Eagle, Dark Skies,* Charles Scribner's Sons.
1976—JOHANNA KAPLAN, for *Other People's Lives,* Alfred A. Knopf.
1977—CYNTHIA OZICK, for *Bloodshed and Three Novellas,* Alfred A. Knopf.
1978—CHAIM GRADE, for *The Yeshiva, Vols. I and II,* Bobbs-Merrill Co.
1979—GLORIA GOLDREICH, for *Leah's Journey,* Harcourt Brace Jovanovich.
1980—DANIEL FUCHS, for *Apathetic Bookie Joint,* Methuen, Inc.
1981—JOHANNA KAPLAN, for *O, My America!,* Harper & Row.
1982—MARK HELPRIN, for *Ellis Island and Other Stories,* Delacorte Press.
1983—ROBERT GREENFIELD, for *Temple,* Summit Books.
1984—ARTHUR A. COHEN, for *An Admirable Woman,* David R. Godine.
1985—FREDERICK BUSCH, for *Invisible Mending,* David R. Godine.

National Jewish Book Award—Holocaust

Leon Jolson Award

1966—ZOSA SZAJKOWSKI, for *Analytical Franco-Jewish Gazetteer 1939-1945.*
1967—ABRAHAM KIN, MORDECAI KOSOVER and ISAIAH TRUNK, for their editorship of *Alqemeyne Entsiklopedye: Yidn VII (General Encyclopedia: Jews VII),* Dubnow Fund and Encyclopedia Committee.
1968—DR. JACOB ROBINSON, for *And The Crooked Shall be Made Straight: The Eichmann Trial, Jewish Catastrophe and Hannah Ahrendt's Narrative,* Macmillan.
1969—DR. JUDAH PILON, for *The Jewish Catastrophe in Europe,* American Association for Jewish Education.
  —NORA LEVIN, for *The Holocaust: The Destruction of European Jewry,* Thomas Y. Crowell.
1970—ZALMAN AYLBERCWEIG, for *Lexicon of the Yiddish Theater: Martyrs Volume,* Hebrew Actors Union of America.
1971—RABBI EPHRAIM OSHRY, for *Sheelot u-Teshuvot: Mi-Maamakim.*
1972—DR. HENRY L. FEINGOLD, for *The Politics of Rescue: The Roosevelt Administration and the Holocaust, 1938-1945,* Rutgers University Press.
1973—DR. AARON ZEITLIN, for *Veiterdike Lider Fun Hurban un Lider Fun Gloiben un Yanish Korshaks Letzte Gang* (More Poems of the Holocaust and Poems of Faith and Yanish Kortshak's Last Walk), New York, Bergen-Belsen Memorial Press.
1975—DR. ISAIAH TRUNK, for *Judenrat: The Jewish Councils in Eastern Europe Under Nazi Occupation,* Macmillan Co.
1976—LEYZER RAN, for *Yerushalayim de Lite: Jerusalem of Lithuania.*
1977—RABBI EPHRAIM OSHRY, for *Sefer Sheelot u-Teshuvot Mi-Maamakim: Part 4: Book of Questions and Answers from the Depths.*
1978—TERRENCE DES PRES, for *The Survivor: An Anatomy of Life in the Death Camp,* Oxford University Press.
1979—MICHAEL SELZER, for *Deliverance Day: The Last Hours at Dachau,* J.B. Lippincott Company.
1980—BENJAMIN B. FERENCZ, for *Less Than Slaves: Jewish Forced Labor and the Quest for Compensation,* Harvard University Press.
1981—RANDOLPH L. BRAHAM, for *The Politics of Genocide—The Holocaust in Hungary, 2 Vols.,* Columbia University Press.
1982—MICHAEL MARRUS AND ROBERT O. PAXTON, for *Vichy France and the Jews,* Basic Books Inc.

1983—IRVING ABELLA and HAROLD TROPER, for *None is Too Many: Canada and the Jews of Europe 1933-1948,* Lester & Orpen Dennys, Publishers.
1984—MARGUERITE DORIAN, for *The Quality of Witness: A Rumainian Diary 1937-44,* Jewish Publication Society.
1985—DAVID S. WYMAN, for *The Abandonment of the Jews: America and the Holocaust 1941-1945,* Pantheon.

National Jewish Book Award—Israel

Morris J. Kaplun Award

1974—ISAIAH FRIEDMAN, for *The Question of Palestine, 1914-1918: British-Jewish-Arab Relations,* Schocken Books.
1975—ARNOLD KRAMMER, for *The Forgotten Friendship: Israel and the Soviet Bloc, 1947-1953,* University of Illinois Press.
1976—MELVIN I. UROFSKY, for *American Zionism from Herzl to the Holocaust,* Doubleday & Co.
1977—HOWARD M. SACHAR, for *A History of Israel,* Alfred A. Knopf.
1978—HILLEL HALKIN, for *Letters to an American Jewish Friend,* Jewish Publication Society.
1979—RUTH GRUBER, for *Raquela: A Woman of Israel,* Coward, McCann & Geoghegan.
1980—EMANUEL LEVY, for *The Habima-Israel's National Theater 1917-1977: A Study of Cultural Nationalism,* Columbia University Press.
1981—No Award given.
1982—HOWARD M. SACHAR, for *Egypt and Israel,* Richard Marek Publishers.
1983—J. ROBERT MOSKIN, for *Among Lions: The Battle for Jerusalem June 5-7, 1967,* Arbor House Publishing Co.
1984—PETER GROSE, for *Israel in the Mind of America,* Alfred A. Knopf.
1985—JOAN PETERS, for *From Time Immemorial: The Origins of the Arab-Jewish Conflict Over Palestine,* Harper & Row.

National Jewish Book Award—
Jewish History

Bernard H. Marks Award

1973—ARTHUR J. ZUCKERMAN, for *A Jewish Princedom in Feudal France, 768-900,* Columbia University Press.
1974—BERNARD D. WEINRYB, for *The Jews of Poland: A Social and Economic History, 1100 to 1800,* Jewish Publication Society.
1975—SOLOMON ZEITLIN, for his cumulative contribution to Jewish history.
1976—RAPHAEL PATAI and JENNIFER PATAI WING, for *The Myth of the Jewish Race,* Charles Scribner's Sons.
1977—IRVING HOWE, for *World of Our Fathers,* Harcourt Brace Jovanovich.

Gerrard and Ella Berman Award

1978—CELIA S. HELLER, for *On the Edge of Destruction,* Columbia University Press.
1979—SALO W. BARON, for his cumulative contribution to Jewish historic research and thought. Columbia University Press and Jewish Publication Society.
1980—TODD M. ENDELMAN, for *The Jews of Georgian England, 1714-1830,* Jewish Publication Society.
1981—MARK R. COHEN, for *Jewish Self-Government in Medieval Egypt: The Origins of the Office of Head of the Jews, ca. 1065-1126,* Princeton University Press.
1982—PROF. DAVID RUDERMAN, for *The World of a Renaissance Jew,* Hebrew Union College.
1983—YOSEF HAYIM YERUSHALMI, for *Zakhor: Jewish History and Jewish Memory,* University of Washington Press.
1984—MICHAEL STANISLAWSKI, for *Tsar Nicholas I and the Jews: The Transformation of Jewish Society in Russia, 1825-1855,* Jewish Publication Society.
1985—NAOMI W. COHEN, for *Encounter with Emancipation: The German Jews in the United States, 1830-1914,* Jewish Publication Society.

National Jewish Book Award— Jewish Thought

Jewish Community Council of Washington, D.C. Award

1949—HARRY A. WOLFSON, for *Philo: Foundations of Religious Philosophy in Judaism, Christianity and Islam,* Harvard University Press.

Isadore Hershfield Memorial Award for Non-Fiction

1950—GUIDO KISCH, for *The Jews in Medieval Germany: A Study of Their Legal and Social Status.*

Frank and Ethel S. Cohen Non-Fiction Award

1963—MOSES RISCHIN, for *The Promised City: New York's Jews, 1870-1914,* Harvard University Press.

Frank and Ethel S. Cohen Award For A Book On Jewish Thought

1964—BEN ZION BOKSER, for *Judaism: Profile of a Faith,* Burning Bush Press and Alfred A. Knopf.

1965—ISRAEL EFROS, for *Ancient Jewish Philosophy,* Wayne State University Press.

1966—DAVID POLISH, for *The Higher Freedom: A New Turning Point in Jewish History,* Quadrangle Press.

1967—NAHUM M. SARNA, for *Understanding Genesis: The Heritage of Biblical Israel,* Jewish Theological Seminary of America.

1968—DR. MICHAEL A. MEYER, for *Origins of the Modern Jews,* Wayne State University Press.

1969—DR. EMIL L. FACKENHEIM, for *Quest for Past and Future: Essays in Jewish Theology,* University of Indiana Press.

1970—DR. ABRAHAM JOSHUA HESCHEL, for *Israel: An Echo of Eternity,* Farrar, Straus & Giroux, and for his cumulative contributions to Jewish thought.

1971—DR. MORDECAI M. KAPLAN, for *The Religion of Ethical Nationhood: Judaism's Contribution to World Peace,* Macmillan, and for his cumulative contributions to Jewish thought.

1972—DR. ABRAHAM E. MILLGRAM, for *Jewish Worship,* Jewish Publication Society.

1973—SAMUEL SANDMEL, for *Two Living Traditions: Essays on Religion and The Bible,* Wayne State University Press; and
    —ELIE WIESEL, for *Souls on Fire: Portraits and Legends of Hasidic Masters,* Random House.

1974—EUGENE BOROWITZ, for *The Masks Jews Wear: The Self-Deception of American Jewry,* Simon & Schuster.

1975—ELIEZER BERKOVITS, for *Major Themes in Modern Philosophies of Judaism,* Ktav Publishing.

1976—SOLOMON B. FREEHOF, for *Contemporary Reform Responsa,* Hebrew Union College Press.

1977—DAVID HARTMAN, for *Maimonides: Torah and Philosophic Quest,* Jewish Publication Society.

1978—RAPHAEL PATAI, for *The Jewish Mind,* Charles Scribner's Sons.

1979—ROBERT GORDIS, for *Love and Sex: A Modern Jewish Perspective,* Women's League for Conservative Judaism/Farrar, Straus & Giroux.

1980—DAVID BIALE, for *Gershom Scholem: Kabbalah and Counter-History,* Harvard University Press.

1981—ISADORE TWERSKY, for *Introduction to the Code of Maimonides (Mishneh Torah),* Yale University Press.

1982—ROBERT ALTER, for *The Art of Biblical Narrative,* Basic Books Inc.

1983—BERNARD SEPTIMUS, for *Hispano-Jewish Culture in Transition: The Career and Controversies of Ramah,* Harvard University Press.

1984—STEVEN T. KATZ, for *Post Holocaust Dialogues: Critical Studies in Modern Jewish Thought,* New York University Press.

1985—JOSEPH B. SOLOVEITCHIK, for *Halakhic Man,* Jewish Publication Society.

National Jewish Book Award—Poetry

Florence Kovner Memorial Poetry Awards English Poetry

1951—JUDAH STAMPFER, for *Jerusalem Has Many Faces,* Farrar, Straus & Giroux.

1952—A.M. KLEIN, for cumulative contributions to English-Jewish poetry.

1953—ISIDORE GOLDSTICK, for translation of *Poems of Yehoash.*

1954—HARRY H. FEIN, for cumulative contributions to English-Jewish poetry.

Harry and Florence Kovner Memorial Poetry Award

1959—GRACE GOLDIN, for *Come Under the Wings: A Midrash on Ruth,* Jewish Publication Society.

1960—AMY K. BLANK, for *The Spoken Choice,* Hebrew College Press.

1962—IRVING FELDMAN, for *Work and Days and Other Poems,* Little Brown & Co.

1963—CHARLES REZNIKOFF, for *By the Waters of Manhattan,* New Directions; San Francisco Review.

1966—RUTH FINER MINTZ, for *The Darkening Green,* Big Mountain Press.

1969—RUTH WHITMAN, for *The Marriage Wig and Other Poems,* Harcourt, Brace and World.

1971—RUTH FINER MINTZ, for *Traveler Through Time,* Jonathan David.

1974—HAROLD SCHIMMEL, for translation of Yehuda Amichai's *Songs of Jerusalem and Myself,* Harper & Row.

1977—MYRA SKLAREW, for *From the Backyard of the Diaspora,* Dryad Press.

National Jewish Book Award— Hebrew Poetry

1951—AARON ZEITLIN, for *Shirim u'Poemot* (Songs and Poems), Mossad Bialik.

1952—HILLEL BAVLI, for cumulative contributions to Hebrew poetry.

1953—A.S. SCHWARTZ, for cumulative contributions to Hebrew poetry.

1954—EPHRAIM E. LISITZKY, for *Be-Ohalei Kush* (In Negro Tents), Mossad Bialik.

1955—GABRIEL PREIL, for *Ner Mul Kochavim* (Candle Under the Stars) Mossad Bialik.

1956—HILLEL BAVLI, for *Aderet Ha-Shanim* (Mantle of Years), Mossad Bialik.

1957—MOSHE FEINSTEIN, for *Avraham Abulafia,* Mossad Bialik.

1958—AARON ZEITLIN, for *Bein ha-Esh veha-Esha* (Between the Man and The Woman), Yavneh.

1959—MOSHE BEN-MEIR, for *Tzil va-Tzel* (Sound and Shadow), Ogen Publishing House.

1960—EISIG SILBERSCHLAG, for *Kimron Yamai* (Arch of My Days), Kiryat Sefer.

1961—EPHRAIM E. LISITZKY, for *K'Mo Hayom Rad* (As the Day Wanes), Mahbarot Lesifrut.

1962—GABRIEL PREIL, for *Mapat Erev,* Dvir Publishing Co.

1964—ARNOLD BAND, for *Ha-Rei Boer ba-Esh* (The Mirror Burns in Fire), Jerusalem, Ogdan; New York, Ogen.

1966—SIMON HALKIN, for *Ma'avar Yabok* (Crossing the Yabok), Am Oved.

1967—LEONARD D. FRIEDLAND, for *Shirim be-Sulam Miner* (Poems in a Minor Key), M. Newman.

1969—REUVEN BEN YOSEF, for *Derech Eretz* (Respect), Hakebutz Hameuchad Publishing House.

1972—DR. EISIG SILBERSCHLAG, for *Igrotai El Dorot Aherim* (Letters to Other Generations), Kiryat Sefer.

1975—REUVEN BEN-YOSEF, for *Metim ve-Ohavim* (The Dead and Lovers), Masada Publishing Co.

1978—T. CARMI, for *El Eretz Aheret* (To Another Land), Dvir Publishing Co.

National Jewish Book Award— Yiddish Poetry

1951—BER LAPIN, for *Der Fuller Krug,* (The Brimming Jug), Ykuf.

1952—MORDECAI JAFFE, for editing and translation of *Antologia fun Der Hebraishe Poesie* (Anthology of Hebrew Poetry), CYCO (2 volumes)

1953—MARK SCHWEID, for *Collected Poems.*

1954—ELIEZER GREENBERG, for *Banachtiger Dialog* (Night Dialogue), Gezelten.

1955—ALTER ESSELIN, for *Lider Fun a Midbarnik* (Poems of a Hermit), Culture Club of the Peretz Hirschbein Folk Theater.

1956—NAFTALI GROSS, for cumulative contributions to Yiddish poetry.

1957—JACOB GLATSTEIN, for *Fun Mein Gantzer Mei: 1919-1956* (Of All My Toil: Collected Poems: 1919-1956).

1958—I.J. SCHWARTZ, for his cumulative contributions to Yiddish poetry.

1959—BENJAMIN I. BIALOSTOTZKY, for *Lid Tzu Lid* (Poem to Poem), CYCO.

1960—EPHRAIM AUERBACH, for *Gildene Shekia* (Golden Sunset), Kium.

1961—JOSEPH RUBINSTEIN, for *Megilath Russland* (Scroll of Russia), CYCO.

1962—ISRAEL EMIOT, for *In Nigun Eingebert* (In Melody Absorbed), Rochester Culture Council.

1963—CHAIM GRADE, for *Der Mentsh Fun Fier* (The Man of Fire), CYCO.

1964—AARON GLANZ-LEYELES, for *Amerike un Ich* (America and I), Der Kval.

1965—ALEPH KATZ, for *Di Emesse Hasunah* (Some Wedding), CYCO.

1966—KADIA MOLODOWSKY, for *Light fun Dorenboim* (Light from the Thornbush), Kium.

1967—JACOB GLATSTEIN, for *A Yid fun Lublin* (A Jew from Lublin), CYCO.

1968—AARON ZEITLIN, for *Lider fun Hurban un Lider fun Gloiben* (Poems of the Holocaust and Poems of Faith), World Federation of Bergen-Belsen.

1969—RACHEL H. KORN, for *Di Gnod fun Vort,* Hemenora Publishing House.

1970—ELIEZER GREENBERG, for *Eibiker Dorsht* (Eternal Thirst).

1973—MEIR STICKER, for *Yidishe Landshaft* (Jewish Landscape), Peretz Farlag.

1976—M. HUSID, for *A Shotn Trogt Main Kroin* (A Shadow Wears My Crown).

1979—MOISHE STEINGART, for *In Droisen fun der Velt* (Outside of the World), Shulsinger Brothers.

JWB Jewish Book Council Award for Poetry

1980—CHARLES REZNIKOFF, for the totality of his poetic achievement, (posthumously awarded).

1981—LOUIS SIMPSON, for *Caviare at the Funeral,* Franklin Watts, Inc.

National Jewish Book Award—Scholarship

Sarah H. Kushner Memorial Award

1983—JEREMY COHEN, for *The Friars and the Jews: The Evolution of Medieval Anti-Judaism,* Cornell University Press.

1984—S.D. GOITEN, for *A Mediterranean Society: The Jewish Community of the Arab World, As Portrayed in the Documents of the Cairo Geniza—Daily Life,* University of California Press.

1985—SEYMOUR FELDMAN, translator, for *The Wars of the Lord: Book One, Immortality of the Soul,* by Levi Ben Gershon (Gersonides), Jewish Publication Society.

National Jewish Book Award— Translation of a Jewish Classic

Rabbi Jacob Freedman Award

1975—MAX ARZT, BERNARD J. BAMBERGER, HARRY FREEDMAN, H.L. GINSBERG, SOLOMON GRAYZEL, and HARRY M. ORLINSKY, for *The Book of Isaiah,* Jewish Publication Society.

1976—WILLIAM G. BRAUDE and ISRAEL J. KAPSTEIN, for *Pesikta de-Rab Kahana: R. Kahana's Compilation of Discourses for Sabbaths and Festival Days,* Jewish Publication Society.

1977—ZVI L. LAMPEL, for *Maimonides' Introduction to the Talmud,* Judaica Press.

1979—WILLIAM M. BRINNER, for Nissim Ben Jacob ibn Shahin's *An Elegant Composition Concerning Relief After Adversity,* Yale University Press.

National Jewish Book Award—Visual Arts

Leon L. Gildesgame Award

1981—YESHIVA UNIVERSITY MUSEUM, for *Purim: The Face and the Mask.*

1982—JANET BLATTER and DR. SYBIL MILTON, for *Art of the Holocaust,* The Rutledge Press.

1983—ANDREW S. ACKERMAN and SUSAN L. BRAUNSTEIN, *Israel in Antiquity: From David to Herod,* The Jewish Museum.

1984—ROMAN VISHNIAC, for *A Vanished World,* Farrar, Straus & Giroux.

1985—EVELYN M. COHEN, *The Rothschild Mahzor: Florence, 1492,* The Library/The Jewish Theological Seminary of America.

National Jewish Book Award— Yiddish Literature

The Workmen's Circle Award

1980—PERETZ MIRANSKY, for *Tzwishn Shmeichl Un Trern* (Between Smiles and Tears).

1981—HYMAN BASS, for *Pathways in Yiddish Literature,* I.L. Peretz Publishing.

1982—JOSHUA A. FISHMAN, for *Never Say Die!,* Mouton Publishers.

1983—CHAIM SPILBERG and YAACOV ZIPPER, for *Kanader Yidisher Zamlbukh* (Canadian Jewish Anthology), National Committee for Yiddish at the Canadian Jewish Congress.

1984—CHAIM LEIB FOX, for *Tsu Di Himlen Arof* (To The Heavens Above), CYCO Publishing Company.

1985—SHEA TENENBAUM, for *Fun Ash Un Fayer Iz Dayn Kroyn* (From Ash and Fire Is Your Crown), CYCO Publishing Company.

64

Hollywood's Image of the Jew

Lester Friedman

The American film industry entered the eighties with confidence. 1979 had been a record year for Hollywood profits, with overall film receipts hitting the eight billion dollar mark. Novelist and scriptwriter Budd Schulberg's April 27, 1980 article in *The New York Times* provides some glimpses into the filmmaking business at the start of the new decade. Schulberg found the studios "ready to call themselves major again," buoyed up by electronic marvels "that will revolutionize the very nature of entertainment in America." Even venerable old MGM, which had essentially stopped making movies in the seventies, was setting up a separate production company to signal its return to the world of motion pictures. "The year 1980," concludes Schulberg, "is a watershed [for the film industry] not unlike 1930 when talking pictures were coming in."

But Schulberg and the confident Hollywood moguls he interviewed never imagined that their fiercest competition would come not from each other, but rather from an entirely unsuspected source: Home Box Office (HBO). HBO began its corporate life as a subsidiary of Time, Inc., and its initial function was simply to put theatrical films on cable television. Within a short ten years, however, HBO emerged as the world's largest financial backer of motion pictures, spending over $200 million a year to develop, purchase, and rent movies. In 1982 HBO invested in one-third of the major studio films in production, which translated into some seventy to one hundred pictures in various states of completion. In addition, HBO recently joined with CBS and Columbia Pictures to form Tri Star Productions, a company many insiders believe will soon become Hollywood's seventh major studio.

The secret of HBO's astonishingly successful assault on the movie industry was its awareness of America's changing film viewing habits. Traditionally, the twelve to twenty-four-year-old age group represents the largest theatergoing segment of society. Decreasing numbers in this age group have led to decreasing ticket sales at the box office. HBO predicted that older viewers would watch movies in the comfort of their own living rooms, even if they had to pay to do so. Along with its sister organization, Cinemax, HBO now services more than sixty percent of the country's movie-service subscribers, a figure which represents a built-in audience of over eighteen million people who pay from $8 to $12 monthly for a subscription. Such a broad base creates an excellent cash-flow income for HBO, which it in turn uses to invest in new productions of its own and to keep the river of Hollywood hits flowing into its subscribers' homes. So, ironically, HBO could be both a blessing and a curse for the established studios: it puts money into studio coffers by renting films for cable distribution, but it also presents a challenge by producing its own films.

In the sixties, when Hollywood responded to the country's growing obsession with ethnicity, filmmakers presented Jews in a number of new roles. The movies of the seventies continued in this direction, expanding their range and exploring their characters more fully. If the first years of the eighties prove an accurate indicator of Hollywood trends, Jews will continue to figure even more prominently on celluloid. Many Jewish characters have already appeared, some in the most unlikely of places. In *Fort Apache, The Bronx* (1981), an Orthodox sergeant, Applebaum (Irving Metzman) lectures the multi-ethnic cops of the beleaguered 41st precinct, and in *Sharkey's Machine* (1981), Burt Reynolds is aided by his Jewish boyhood friend, an electronics genius named Nosh (Richard Libertini). Arthur Rosenberg (Robert Balaban) assists Dr. Eddie Jessup (William Hurt) with his religious hallucinatory experiments during *Altered States* (1981). Seymour Goldfarb, Jr., playboy son of a wealthy girdle manufacturer and a competitor in *The Cannonball Run* (1981), pretends to be suave actor Roger Moore (who actually plays this role). Much to our surprise in *Rocky III* (1982), we discover that Mickey (Burgess Meredith), the Italian Stallion's long-time manager, is Jewish rather than Irish. A young American Jew (David Naughton) traveling in England gets bitten by a werewolf and turns into a savage beast in *An American Werewolf in London* (1981), and a young Jewish teacher from Toronto (Nick Mancuso)—whose father laments how he could never get him into a synagogue—gets sucked into a Moonie-like cult in *Ticket to Heaven* (1983). Mr. Blumenthal (Eli Wallach), the cynical and tightfisted bailbondsman in *The Hunter* (1980), provides bounty hunter Ralph Thorsen (Steve McQueen) with most of his assignments. *Ragtime* (1981) contains an interesting, if brief, portrait of a Jewish immigrant turned filmmaker (Mandy Patinkin), and *Reds* (1981) shows glimpses of the famous Jewish radical Emma Goldman (Maureen Stapleton). Jews even enter a new genre in the eighties, science-fiction films, though in comic rather than serious roles: the archetypal scientist from early serial days becomes a Jewish Dr. Hans Zarkov (Topol) in the campy, updated *Flash Gordon* (1980), a Jewish secretary is abducted by a lascivious robot in *Heavy Metal* (1981), and two segments of *The Twilight Zone, The Movie* (1983) deal with Jewish characters.

The Jewish characters in these films mentioned are mainly secondary figures, but the very fact that identified Jews function as commonplace inhabitants of the vastly different environments in these diverse pictures shows that much of the "exoticness" so evident in earlier movies is no longer a necessary component of Jewish celluloid portraits in the eighties. American filmmakers apparently feel confident that their audience will not find it strange or disconcerting to discover Jews almost anywhere, from the Harvard of *Altered States* to the alien planets of *Heavy Metal* and *Flash Gordon*.

In the eighties Jews are not relegated to minor roles. Ralph Bakshi's *American Pop* (1981) follows the saga of a family of Russian immigrants in the United States. *It's My Turn* (1980) presents a female protagonist, Kathy Gunsinger (Jill Clayburgh), who tries to assert herself in her professional and personal life, while *Fame* (1980) concentrates on a Jewish girl, Doris Feinsecker (Maureen Teefy), who tries to make it in show business. *Eyewitness* (1981) reverses the typical Jewish male/Irish female romance by having a cultured, upper-class Jewish reporter (Sigourney Weaver) become involved with a blond, working-class Irishman (William Hurt). Neil Diamond remakes *The Jazz Singer* (1980), this time with a rock score, and Alan King plays an egotistical Jewish tycoon in *Just Tell Me What You Want* (1980). In *Private Benjamin* (1980), Goldie Hawn struggles with her parents and the United States Army; in *Ordinary People* (1980), Judd Hirsch ministers to an ailing WASP family; and in *S.O.B.* (1981), Robert Preston plays a hip Beverly Hills physician. *My Favorite Year* (1982), a loving recreation of television's early days, stars Mark Linn-Baker as Benjy Stone (nee Benjamin Steinberg), a fledgling writer for a Sid Caesar-like comic. Though Jewish humor permeates the picture, it becomes pivotal in the unforgettable scene where Benjy takes Alan Swann, a drunken swashbuckling actor, home to Brooklyn to meet his parents and is humiliated by his domineering Jewish mother (Lainie Kazan). A trio of talented Jewish filmmakers make new movies in the eighties: Woody Allen *(Stardust Memories*, 1980, *Zelig*, 1983 and *The Purple Rose of Cairo*, 1985), Paul Mazursky *(Willy and Phil*, 1980), and Mel Brooks *(History of the World, Part One*, 1981 and *To Be or Not To Be*, 1983).

Three important and controversial films of the early eighties are: *Yentl* (1983), *Sophie's Choice* (1983), and *The Chosen* (1982). In spite of its aesthetic failures, *Yentl* stands as the most lavish film ever to feature a Jewish/female protagonist. Its star/director, Barbra Streisand, fought to do the film since 1968, when she first fell in love with I.B. Singer's wry tale of a Polish rabbi's daughter who disguises herself as a man to study in a yeshiva. Once there, the girl falls in love with one of her fellow students (Mandy Patinkin), who is in turn betrothed to a Jewish girl (Amy Irving). What follows is a number of seriocomic situations through which the characters all learn something about themselves and the traditional values they hold so dear. Streisand's preparation for the film engendered a return to her own cultural roots, culminating with her endowing a medical chair in her father's name, underwriting a Jewish elementary school, and funding a Center for Jewish Cultural Arts at UCLA. Unfortunately, her on-screen efforts were far less satisfying, as the picture suffers from too many bland songs, too shallow character development, and too little dramatic pacing.

Streisand's film was clearly a critical failure, but it raised far less debate within the Jewish community than did director Alan Pakula's film version of William Styron's best-selling novel, *Sophie's Choice*. Though more about the psychological trauma of a gentile Holocaust survivor than about the Holocaust itself, the film nonetheless drew fire from critics such as Alvin Rosenfeld who claimed it presented, "a generalized history of evil, for which no one in particular need be held accountable." More importantly, the film's major Jewish character, the demonic and insane Nathan (Kevin Kline), becomes one more brutal man who vents his rage on the long-suffering survivor, Sophie (Meryl Streep). He even succeeds where the Nazis have failed: he induces Sophie to her death. Nathan's deeply disturbed personality makes his brilliance and charm pall beside his vicious behavior and sadistic personal attacks on people who care about him.

The Chosen remains the most interesting picture of Jews to emerge from Hollywood, and the most "Jewish" commercial movie ever made. Director Jeremy Paul Kagan carefully delves into Jewish customs and traditions, as he skillfully recounts the deepening bond between two teenage boys (Robby Bensen/Barney Miller). Kagan refuses to apologize for the film's ethnicity, through which he develops the larger themes of youthful rebellion, painful adolescence, father/son conflicts, true friendship, and familial love. Together, the boys unite Jewish traditions of secular social activism and spiritual Torah scholarship. Each, for Kagan, enriches the other. In *The Chosen*, Judaism and Americanism are not mutually exclusive goals; in fact, one nurtures the other so that both grow and prosper. The characters in this film are American Jews seen equally as Jewish Americans.

Halfway through the eighties, therefore, we have seen many films that deal with Jewish problems, that contain Jewish characters, and that confront Jewish issues. Unfortunately, most lack the openness of the sixties films about Jews and the sophistication of the seventies movies. Instead, many directors and writers of the eighties fall back on outmoded stereotypes and simple solutions to difficult problems. As such, the movies of 1984 prove an equally uneven lot.

Stereotypes on the Screen

Stereotypes are a problem both on and off the screen in the eighties. Harold E. Quinley and Charles Y. Glock's *Anti-Semitism in America* (1979) concludes that "anti-Semitism today largely involves the harboring of negative images about Jews." It also provides the generation of Jews about to enter the eighties with some disconcerting news: while very few non-Jews favored overt discrimination, a third of the Gentile Americans surveyed viewed Jews with suspicion and distrust, seeing them as "deceitful and dishonest in business, clannish in their behavior toward others, pushy and aggressive, vain and conceited, and controlling or having disproportionate influence over the media, motion picture, and banking industries." Another poll, conducted during the last month of 1980, showed that one third of those surveyed believed Jews were more loyal to Israel than to the United States. For the Jewish-American community, therefore, the new decade brought an increased awareness of their "otherness," and a series of shocking and disturbing incidents testified to a renewed spirit of anti-Semitism in American life. In 1980, the Anti-

Defamation League of the B'nai B'rith reported a three-fold increase in anti-Semitic "episodes" in just one year, including arson, firebombings, and death threats. The resurgence of the Ku Klux Klan and the American Nazi Party, both of which ran somewhat successful candidates for public office in the last election, contributed to Jewish fears.

At least three basic causes can be seen as contributing to these renewed incidents of anti-Semitism. First, the country's continuing economic problems have brought some latent race hatred out into the open. "Times of distress, social unrest, and economic depression," says Rev. Edward H. Flannery (author of *The Anguish of the Jews*), "are often preludes to outbreaks of anti-Semitism. In hard times people find it comforting to have a scapegoat, and they have always looked in the direction of the Jews." Second, media coverage, according to New York City police official Patrick J. Murphy, allows such anti-Semitic incidents to feed off each other: "the kids read about themselves . . . and any dope can see himself immortalized."

Finally, and most difficult to combat, is the dynamic power of right wing, so-called "Moral Majority" politics. In early February of 1981, Rev. Dan C. Fore, Moral Majority leader in New York City, stated: "Jews have a God-given ability to make money, almost a supernatural ability. . . . They control this city." When the head of the Southern Baptist convention declared, "God Almighty does not hear the prayers of a Jew," none of the assembled Protestant ministers rose to dispute his point.

Another development calculated to cause Jews alarm in the eighties is the growing economic and political power of Arab countries. Using the vast riches gained from selling their oil to an energy-hungry world, Arabs have bought into American life. Some have purchased farm land in Iowa; others have invested heavily in U.S. corporations. Col. Muammar Kaddafi, the oil-rich dictator of Libya, recently gave Georgetown University a large grant to establish a chair in Islamic Studies. A similar grant from Saudi Arabia was rejected by the University of Southern California because it stipulated control over distribution of the money was to be left in Saudi hands, effectively creating an autonomous entity within the college. The April/May issue of *The Link,* a magazine published by an organization called "Americans for Middle East Understanding," is entirely devoted to attacking the media's negative portraits of Arabs, particularly in conjunction with positive images of Israelis. Editor Jack G. Shaheen, an American of Arab heritage, claims that "the creation of the State of Israel brought about a new Arab image in both motion pictures and on television," and goes on to "consider the possibility that stereotyping of Arabs is the result of a continuing campaign by pressure groups to discredit Arabs, thus preventing the development of American-Arab relations." *The Link* makes some valuable points about the gross caricatures of Arab figures in the mass media, but Shaheen's covert message that Jews are responsible for this distortion, perhaps even in an organized way as the tools of Israel, is a flight of fancy that is itself a stereotypical attack on the Jews for controlling the American media.

The Big Chill (1983) demonstrates that negative Jewish stereotypes remain alive and well in the Hollywood consciousness. The film presents a reunion of sixties archetypes for the funeral of their former leader, a brilliant

Mary Kay Place and Jeff Goldblum in The Big Chill.

student who has committed suicide. Among them is Michael (Jeff Goldblum), once a radical journalist, then a ghetto schoolteacher, and now a writer for *People* magazine. The plot consists of a series of gatherings over the ensuing weekend, as the group relives old times, resets nw priorities, and rearranges their relationships for middle age. Throughout this process, Michael—the Jewish intellectual who gave up serious writing for gossip reporting—fares the worst. For example, one old friend (Mary Kay Place) is a single lawyer so desperate for a child that she propositions all the men in the group—except Michael. Even when he volunteers to father her baby, she turns him down. In fact, everyone at one point or another makes love to someone else during the weekend to reaffirm their continued intimacy—except Michael. He sleeps in his childish airplane bed, an apt symbol of his emotional immaturity, bereft of both sexual passion and emotional fulfillment.

Another repugnant aspect of Michael's personality is his use of the funeral for business purposes. Obsessed with opening a chic New York City nightclub, Michael comes to the funeral looking to convince his now wealthy ex-roommates to back his dubious enterprise. Finally, in his most callous gesture, Michael even attempts to seduce his dead buddy's young girlfriend with a series of distasteful overtures. Though director/writer Lawrence Kasden gives Michael some of the movie's funniest lines, the audience quickly realizes that his cynical humor merely masks his basically superficial, and selfish, view of life. As a writer for *People* magazine, Michael sums up the existence of others in six short paragraphs, or as he puts it, in as much time as it takes for one toilet sitting. His artistic/radical writing aspirations have degenerated into excremental musings.

Though *The Big Chill* does not explore Michael's Jewishness or use it as an excuse for his obnoxious activities, he clearly remains the least likable character in the picture. At the conclusion of the film, when the other figures seem to have sorted out their lives at least a little bit, Michael remains essentially as shallow as when the weekend started. "I'm going to write a novel about this weekend," he proudly declares at their last meal together. "What were you going to write your last book about?" asks one of his friends. "Last weekend," he replies, barely recognizing the sad irony of his response.

Broadway Danny Rose (1984), another in a series of black and white films by director/writer/star Woody Allen, depicts another Jewish loser, this time as a hapless theatrical agent. It should be no surprise to any Allen-watcher that his Danny Rose represents some of the worst talent ever assembled, including a one-legged tap dancer, a blind xylophone player, a one-armed juggler, and a stuttering ventriloquist. But for one flickering moment all his bad luck seems over. Danny's best act is Lou Canova (Nick Forte), a once-popular singer who appears ready to ride the crest of the nostalgia craze to renewed prominence. Rose has been supporting Nick for years. In essence, he has become his Jewish mother, soothing his ego, building his confidence, and even paying his debts. Of course, when Nick does finally start to become popular once again, when he actually lands some jobs at second rather than his normal fifth rate-clubs, he immediately drops Danny and signs with a more prestigious agent.

Throughout Allen's career, critics have compared him to the most illustrious cinema clown of all, Charlie Chaplin. Allen, like Chaplin, continually treads the thin line between sentimentality and sweetness. *Broadway Danny Rose* again displays Allen's deft mingling of laughter and trembling which, as novelist Saul Bellow tells us, so often distinguishes the very best Jewish writings. The film shows Allen as a modern day Menashe Skulnik, a classical schlemiel preyed upon by society's more pragmatic members. Through his unique blend of laughter and trembling, of horror and humor, Allen shows us the world from the bottom up.

Horror and humor inform director Francis Ford Coppola's extravagant (estimates of its cost run from forty-five to sixty million dollars) story of crime and music in the legendary Harlem of the twenties and thirties, *The Cotton Club* (1984). As such, the movie displays a virtual compen-

Woody Allen and Nick Apollo Forte in Broadway Danny Rose.

Richard Gere and James Remar in The Cotton Club.

dium of ethnic groups battling for supremacy over New York City's crime world. Jews, Irishmen, Blacks, and Italians vie for power in the city's grimy backstreets and bustling nightclubs. But even here, in a world of sudden violence and deadly mayhem, the Jew remains an outsider. The most vicious portrait in the picture is of Dutch Schultz (James Remar), whose real name was Arthur Flegenheimer. For example, the most brutal moment in a picture dripping with violence is when Dutch almost literally cuts out the heart of his major rival. The motivation for his brutality is when the man declares, "A Jew is nothing but a nigger turned inside out!"

Dutch's main hitman is Sol Weinstein, played by the leader of the Experimental Living Theater, Julian Beck. Characterized by one of the other figures as "the golem," Sol is a chilling portrait of violence depicted with frigid understatement. Both Dutch and Sol remain alienated outsiders even in this realm of archetypal outsiders. The suave and savvy Italians who finally take over the territory view Dutch's violent outbursts as brutal and animalistic. Even more importantly, the Jewish gangsters don't operate under the same code of honor as do their Italian counterparts; they are not to be trusted. They cannot be counted upon to behave as "gentlemen" or abide by the rules that make it possible for these warring factions to co-exist, no matter how uneasily.

Warring factions that refuse to co-exist in the Middle East are the subject of director George Roy Hill's controversial adaptation of novelist John le Carre's bestseller, *The Little Drummer Girl* (1984). This film, much like last year's *Sophie's Choice,* sparked a great deal of Jewish ire. The convoluted tale follows the adventures of Charlie (Diane Keaton), a gullible actress, as she alternately takes sides with Palestinian terrorists and Israeli assassins. Much of the time both Charlie and the viewer are unsure who is on what side, as Israeli agents masquerade as Arab agents and Arab radicals pretend to be peace-loving diplomats. This is the "theater of the real," one Israeli tells Charlie, though separating the real from the unreal becomes one of the most difficult tasks in the film.

Two things about *The Little Drummer Girl* angered the Jewish community. First, it objected to the Palestinian point of view being depicted with such simplistic sympathy. In fact, one of the picture's ironies is that a war-weary

Diane Keaton in The Little Drummer Girl.

Israeli agent (Yorgo Voyagis) presents this position so effectively. Once Charlie goes on her undercover mission to the Palestinian training camp, she constantly encounters "freedom fighters" who proclaim themselves to be anti-Zionist rather than anti-Semitic. The filmmakers seem to accept their distinction as being both sincere and correct. Second, Jewish Americans denounced the movie's portrait of ruthless Israeli agents. They were particularly offended by the characterization of Kurtz (Klaus Kinski), a manipulating, almost psychotic, espionage chieftain. In one of the most emotionally brutal brainwashing sequences ever filmed, Kurtz breaks down Charlie's psychological and emotional defenses, eventually convincing her to seduce and finally to set up the murder of an elusive Arab leader, Khalil (Sami Frey). Once she has played her part, however, Charlie is left to her own shaky devices, now unable to function in her theatrical world because of the role she has played so well in the real world of betrayal, terrorism, and brutality.

Another world of betrayal, terrorism, and brutality is that created by director Sergio Leone in *Once Upon a Time in America* (1984), a sprawling film which traces the lives of some Lower East Side Jews from 1923 through 1933, and finally to 1968. Central are the criminal careers of David "Noodles" Aaronson (Robert DeNiro), a composite character based on Jewish gangsters Bugsy Siegel and Meyer Lansky, and Maximillian Bercovitz (James Woods), the

Robert DeNiro and James Woods in Once Upon A Time In America.

New York's Lower East Side in Once Upon A Time In America.

brilliant and ruthless leader of "the Company." What is perhaps most frustrating about this film is Leone's failure to investigate his Jewish character in any depth. In fact, except for a couple of expressions, mannerisms, and moments, the characters seem to have no connection to any discernible form of Judaism either religiously or culturally. It's as if Leone realized that one too many gangster films had been made about Italians, so he arbitrarily decided to shift the ethnic terrain to Jews, a culture about which he knew little and communicated even less. In addition, the presence of Robert DeNiro, so well-known for his *Godfather II* role as the young mobster Don Corleone, simply adds to one's feeling that there are very Italian Jews. *Once Upon a Time in America* remains a sadly misguided effort from a talented director, a film with snatches of visual beauty that mask a basically superficial viewpoint.

A misguided effort from a talented director is also an apt description for *King David* (1985), Bruce Beresford's bewildering biblical potboiler. Actually, the first hour of the picture depicts a rather interesting portrait of King Saul (Edward Woodward), as his attitude toward David (Richard Gere) evolves from admiration to affection to jealousy to fear to madness. But, once David becomes King of Israel, the movie meanders aimlessly from one incident to the next with little dramatic tension, character development, or even plot coherence. For example, director Beresford (along with writers Andrew Birkin and James Costigan) present only superficial interactions between David and his second-born Absalom (Jean-Marc Barr), so when the King rolls in the dirt and cries aloud to mourn his son's death his grief becomes absurdly histrionic. Other characters, such as David's eldest son Amnon (James Coombes) and his daughter Tamar (Gina Bellman), appear so fleetingly as to be almost non-existent. Even the lovely Bathsheba (Alice Krige) has little to do except stand around, look beautiful, and mumble some forgettable dialogue every so often. Never is the adultery between two of the Bible's lustiest sinners ever explored, analyzed, or even presented very erotically.

The saddest part of *King David* is that Beresford obviously strives to create a different kind of Biblical film, one unlike the silly costume epics so popular a generation ago. "I wanted to do the film in as realistic a way as possible," Beresford told an interviewer, and for a while it almost works. The world of King Saul is a brutal, primitive environment where religion and politics dominate daily life. When, for instance, the prophet Samuel (Denis Quilley) tells Saul to obliterate the Amalekite king, the infidel's head is immediately severed from his body. Later, Beresford shoots the famous battle between David and Goliath without special effects and in a very believable manner. Cinematographer Don McAlpine fills this section with dark and dismal scenes, and one can almost feel the oppressive atmosphere created by Saul's Lear-like descent into madness.

While Beresford captures the starkness of ancient Israel, as well as the political intrigue between Saul and David, he fails to incorporate a religious consciousness into the film. "This is not a film about religion," claims producer Martin Elfand. "It's about a large group of people trying to work things out and live their lives." Of course, Judaism was the center of their lives, so to ignore it is to misrepresent the very crux of their existence. Equally strange about Elfand's statement is the fact that the filmmakers employed two renowned religious experts as technical advisors. Dr. Jonathan Magonet, head of the Bible department at Leo Baeck College (London) worked with Gere, Woodward, and Krige, instructing them on the historical personages they portrayed in the movie. Rabbi Hillel Avidan was a constant observer of the actual filming, both in England and in Italy. At one point, he noted that a scroll used in one of the scenes was printed in the incorrect Hebrew script and spent several intensive days rewriting the artwork that would be seen on camera. Yet even with the expertise of Magonet and Avidan, *King David* remains devoid of a vibrant religious sensibility. The filmmakers may have captured the outer shell of Judaism, but they never present it as vital tradition which informs the characters and events in the picture.

The outnumbered Israelite troops face the might of the Philistines as they prepare to battle to the death in King David.

John Hurt in 1984.

Finally, we have the second screen version of George Orwell's classic dystopia, *1984* (1985). Director Michael Radford's picture remains quite faithful to Orwell's pessimistic vision. Featuring John Hurt as Winston Smith, Suzanna Hamilton as Julia, and Richard Burton (in his last role) as the nefarious O'Brien, the film's washed-out look becomes an appropriate visual equivalent for Orwell's bleak prediction of the future. Interestingly, the filmmakers chose not to update the technology Orwell imagined. No high-tech wizardry powers the Ministry of Truth, and Big Brother's propaganda spews out of black and white monitors. The result is to keep the film's focus on the people, not on the gadgets that dominate so many "science-fiction" features.

In his 1945 essay, "Notes on Nationalism," Orwell discusses the irrationality of anti-Semitism and points out that prejudice against Jews is only one form of a more widespread "disease . . . called nationalism." It should be no surprise, therefore, that when he wrote 1984 a few years later, he represented one extreme of Oceania's politics by a clearly Jewish name, Emmanuel Goldstein. Goldstein, like Big Brother, does not really exist, though he inspires much of the action in the novel. (Critics have assumed that Trotsky was Orwell's model for Goldstein, particularly since his book, *The Theory and Practice of Oligarchical Collectivism,* mimics Trotsky's style of using scientific references in non-scientific contexts.) The Party creates him as a focus for citizen aggression, and Orwell realizes that this is precisely the way various governments have used Jews for centuries. Goldstein is an archetypal Jewish scapegoat, a device to divert the masses from recognizing their true problems and demanding solutions from the people in power.

The Decades in Perspective

Some screen Jews realize success, riches, and happiness without losing their souls. Other screen Jews have not been so fortunate. Movies have chronicled the story of America's Jews from their immigrant days to the present time, and the early silent features have exhorted Jews to trade in their tarnished, Old-World customs for shiny, new American values. According to these films, an immigrant could make it in America—could partake of the American Dream—only by rejecting traditions, changing his name, and marrying the Gentile girl next door. Any hints of religious parochialism and duty were seen as outworn notions associated with foreign lands and bygone times; assimilation, not individuality, was the prevailing theme of silent pictures featuring Jews. Those who refused to adjust to American life became butts of humorous episodes, or hopeless reactionaries condemned to live as perennial outsiders. As Jakie Rabinowitz tells his father in *The Jazz Singer* (1927), "tradition is all right, but this is another day." These early Hollywood products, therefore, document the immigrant's experience in a new world and detail his headlong dash toward assimilation. They taught Jews what was expected of them in America, and made Americans more conscious of Jews.

The major lesson Jews learned in the silent pictures was that they should become more like their Christian neighbors, and in the films of the thirties Jews became almost indistinguishable from Gentiles. In fact, they nearly evaporated from American movie screens. Literary works containing Jews were made into movies that eliminated any ethnic references. Those few Jews who did appear became one-dimensional caricatures trapped in trite plots and plodding melodramas. From *Gunboat Ginsburg* (1930) to *The Life of Emile Zola* (1937), Jewish-American films of the thirties offer few insights into Jewish life and add little depth to Jewish characterizations. The decade's two best Jewish-American films, *Street Scene* (1931) and *Counsellor-at-Law* (1933), are simply one step above the rest of the period's dismal pictures. As such, the thirties represent the lowest point in the history of the Jewish-American cinema.

The films of the forties, however, played an important role in the evolution of the Jewish-American cinema. Americans became more aware of Hollywood's power to influence society during World War II, and consequently its images of minority group members were scrutinized with more care both by filmmakers and industry outsiders. In the grip of a wartime mentality, the film industry became even more dedicated to the concept of "the great melting pot," seeing one of its primary duties to be the democratization of America. As such, Jews engage in more diverse dramatic situations during this decade, and they are even more assimilated than their celluloid predecessors. Many Jews function as part of wartime, multi-ethnic platoons dedicated to defending America from her enemies, i.e., *The Purple Heart* (1944). These fighting men are Americans first and Jews as an afterthought. Other films such as *Address Unknown* (1944) show Jews as the victims of Nazi oppression.

Once the war ended, the American cinema entered a relatively short phase when problem pictures dominated the screen, and Jews play major roles in many of these films. Two pictures, *Crossfire* (1947) and *Gentleman's Agreement* (1947), confront the evils of anti-Semitism, showing that America is not immune from racism and bigotry. Despite all the films containing Jewish characters during this period, forties filmmakers almost totally ignored the two most crucial Jewish events of the decade: the Holocaust and Israel's formation. The former was too painful to deal with so quickly, and the latter too controversial. Still, the forties represented a giant leap forward

from the thirties, and once again Jews became part of Hollywood's cast of characters.

In the fifties, moviemakers added little new or interesting to the image of the Jews in the American cinema. Jews were relegated to smaller roles in fewer pictures than during the forties. Those who did surface were "safe" Jews whose ethnic blandness made them all but invisible. The Hollywood films of the decade, therefore, became a shield, not a mirror, for America's Jews. Trapped by sagging profits, government attacks on their industry, and fierce competition from television, fifties filmmakers retreated to noncontroversial topics and simple answers. If a Jew appeared at all, he was beyond reproach and never associated with a political position. Recycled war films, bloated biblical epics, and syrupy biographies of well-known personalities dominated what was left of the Jewish-American cinema of the fifties.

A few films, however, managed to strike out in new directions. For example, *Home Before Dark* (1958) introduced the sensitive Jewish male who would become so prominent in the pictures of later decades. *The Juggler* (1953) approached Israel as a homeland for displaced Jews. *Marjorie Morningstar* (1958) introduced the so-called Jewish-American Princess, a popular character in future films. But for the most part, the films of this decade are a relatively undistinguished group. In terms of their character development and thematic focus, they constitute a static period in the evolution of the Jewish-American cinema.

Such was not the case in the sixties. Freed from a studio system that produced fairly predictable pictures, and imbued with a growing sense of ethnic consciousness, sixties moviemakers fashioned a number of intriguing films. Jewish characters appear in a variety of roles, from gangster to prostitute to vampire to cop. In addition, some very new types of contemporary Jews entered the American cinema. The soldiers of *Exodus* (1960) and *Cast A Giant Shadow* (1966) showed Jews as fighters instead of victims. The arrival of Barbra Streisand in *Funny Girl* (1967) signaled pride in being Jewish, as she celebrated her heritage rather than discarded it. *The Pawnbroker* (1965) finally confronted the pain and the trauma of the Holocaust. At the end of the decade, *Goodbye, Columbus* (1969) raised the issue of what Jews have lost and what they have gained in their rapid rise from the urban ghettos to the country clubs of suburbia. Throughout the sixties, therefore, a great number of identifiable Jewish figures wrestled with difficult, and specifically Jewish, problems. The turbulent events of the decade forced the Jewish-American community to examine itself and its priorities, and many of the films of the sixties recorded that process with intelligence, candor, and compassion.

The films of the seventies continued this movement toward diversification begun in the sixties. Directors felt no compunction in placing Jewish characters just about anywhere, from Westerns to detective pictures to animated films. The wave of nostalgia that engulfed Hollywood during the seventies also swept through the Jewish-American cinema and resulted in sentimental movies like *Fiddler on the Roof* (1971) and *Hester Street* (1974). Some directors, however, refused to ignore the problems of the present: tension between Blacks and Jews, the plight of elderly

Jews, the search for identity, and the pain left over from the horrors of Nazi Germany. Most important for the evolutions of the Jewish-American cinema was the rise to prominence of two filmmakers, Woody Allen and Paul Mazursky, who infused their pictures with Jewish characters, a Jewish sensibility, and a unique perception of Jewish problems. In *Next Stop, Greenwich Village* (1976) and *Annie Hall* (1977), Mazursky and Allen raise the Jewish-American cinema to new heights of thematic sophistication and technical achievement.

To date, the films of the eighties have not matched the raw power of the sixties movies or the thematic sophistication of seventies pictures. The first years of the new decade, however, have been filled with films about Jews. Sadly, most of these Jewish characters have been negative, from the lost immigrants of *American Pop* (1981) to the immature professional of *It's My Turn* (1980), to the spoiled "JAP" of *Private Benjamin* (1980), to the tormented Nathan Landau of *Sophie's Choice* (1983). Most ominous of all is the picture of the suave but fanatical Israeli murderer in *Eyewitness* (1981), the first negative portrait of an Israeli in Hollywood history. The strongest positive images of Jews in the eighties have come in the form of the kindly psychiatrist of *Ordinary People* (1980), the Jewish cantor who becomes a rock star in *The Jazz Singer* (1980), the intrepid title character of *Yentl* (1983), and the struggling inhabitants of *The Chosen* (1983). All these figures strive for some meaningful union of the past and the present, the traditional and the new.

Throughout the history of Hollywood, therefore, celluloid Jews have been pilloried, chastised, praised, victimized, ridiculed, and admired. Hollyood filmmakers acknowledged their positive values, such as a dedication to a warm home life and a deep love of learning, as well as their more negative manifestations: the overbearing Jewish mother and the spoiled Jewish-American Princess. All became part of American culture, as easily recognizable as hot dogs and apple pie.

As they survived in the "real" world that at times threatened their very existence, so Jews have survived in the "reel" world of the cinema. The Jewish-American films discussed here have recorded the triumphs and the defeats of a people adjusting to an alien environment. They have measured what Jews were when they landed here, what they went through in the next eighty years, how they changed, and what they became. As such, these images frozen in time contribute to our concept of America as a nation of immigrants, of outsiders. They vividly depict the power of the American Dream to weave its spell over the hearts and minds of immigrants throughout the decades. Some found the Dream a shell of empty phrases and unfulfilled promises. Others found what they were looking for, captured it, and made it theirs. Like an endless Saturday matinee serial, the celluloid history of the American Jew always has one more chapter.

65

A Chronological Listing of Jewish-American Films

Title	Year	Director	Distributor/ Production Company	Title	Year	Director	Distributor/ Production Company
Features till 1919				The Copper & the Crook	1910		Yankee
				Cupid at Cohen's	1916	A. McMackin	Beauty
Absalom	1912		Pathe	Cupid Puts One Over on the Shadchen	1915		Vitagraph
Accused by Darkest Russia	1913		Liberty	Daniel	1913		Vitagraph
The Airship, or One Hundred Years Hence	1908		Vitagraph	A Daughter of Israel	1914	V. D. Brooke	Vitagraph
				David and Goliath	1908		Kalem
Arabian Jewish Dance	1903		Edison	David's War with Absalom	1912		N.Y. Film Co.
Athaliah	1911		Pathe	The Death of Saul	1912		Pathe
A Bad Day for Levinsky	1909		Precision	Deborah or The Jewish Maiden's Wrong	1914		Thanhouser
Bar Kochba-The Hero of a Nation	1913		Fox	The Deluge	1911		Vitagraph
The Barrier of Faith	1915	V. Brooke	Vitagraph	Disraeli	1917		Paul Cromelin
Becky Gets a Husband	1912		Lubin Films	The Embodied Thought	1916	E. Sloman	Lubin
The Bells	1913		Reliance	Escape From Siberia	1914		Great Players Feature Film Co.
The Bells	1914		Sawyer's				
Belshazar's Feast	1913		Gaumont	Esther	1914		Eclectic
Ben Hur	1907	F. O. Rose	Kalem	Esther and Mordecai	1910		Gaumont
Bizzy Izzy	1915		Gaumont	The Fable of How Weisenstein Did Not Lose Out to Buttinsky	1916	R. F. Baker	Essanay
The Black 107	1913	S. Golden	Ruby Features				
Bleeding Hearts or Jewish Freedom Under King Casimir of Poland	1913	S. Golden	Imperial	The Faith of Her Fathers	1914	E. Lewis	Reliance
				Faith of Her Fathers	1915		Universal
Blood of the Poor	1912		Champion	The Fall of Babylon	1919	D. W. Griffith	Wark
The Blood Red Tape of Charity	1913	E. August	Powers	Father and Son or The Curse of the Golden Land	1913		Vitagraph
The Broker's Daughter	1910		Yankee				
Business and Love	1914		Lubin	A Female Fagin	1913		Kalem
Business Is Business	1915		United Film Svc.	Fighting is No Business	1914		Universal
				The Firebug	1913		Keystone
Cain and Abel	1910		Gaumont	A Flurry in Diamonds	1913		Essanay
Cast into the Flame	1910		Gaumont	For Sale, A Baby	1916	P. N. Vekroff	C. K. Harris
A Child of the Ghetto	1910	D. W. Griffith	Biograph	For the Love of Mike and Rosie	1916		Universal
The Children of the Ghetto	1915	F. Powell	Fox				
Children of the Tenements	1913		Kalem	Foxy Izzy	1911		Lubin
				The Fur Coat	1916		Vitagraph
A Citizen in the Making	1912		Selig Polyscope	Gesture Fight in Hester Street	1903		Pathe
Cohen and Murphy	1910		Powers				
Cohen at Coney Island	1909		Vitagraph	Get Rich Quick Billington	1913		Pathe
Cohen Collects a Debt	1912	M. Sennett	Keystone	The Ghetto Seamstress	1910		Yankee
Cohen Saves the Flag	1913	F. Powell	Keystone	The Girl of the Ghetto	1910		Thanhouser
Cohen's Advertising Scheme	1904		Edison	Guaranteed Rainproof	1914		Lubin
				Gwendolyn	1914		Biograph
Cohen's Dream of Coney Island	1909		Vitagraph	The Heart of a Jewess	1913		Universal
				Her Condoned Sin	1917	D. W. Griffith	Biograph
Cohen's Fire Sale	1907		Edison	His First Long Trousers	1911		Selig Polyscope
Cohen's Generosity	1910		Defender	How Izzy Stuck to His Post	1914		Reliance
Cohen's Luck	1915	J. H. Collins	T. Edison				
Cohen's Outing	1913		Keystone				

Title	Year	Director	Distributor/ Production Company	Title	Year	Director	Distributor/ Production Company
How Izzy Was Saved	1914		Reliance	The Lily of Poverty Flat	1915		
How Mosha Came Back	1912		Chrystal-Universal	The Little Jewess	1914		Kinetophoto
				Little Old New York	1912		Champion
How the Jews Take Care of Their Poor	1913	S. Golden	Imperial	Love in the Ghetto	1913	O. Eagle	Selig-Polyscope
				Lucky Cohen	1914		Lubin
In the Czar's Name	1910		Yankee	The Maccabees	1911		Pathe
In the Days of King Solomon	1913		Feature Film Co.	The Man's A Man	1912		
				The Marriage of Esther	1910		Gaumont
Intolerance	1916	D. W. Griffith	Wark	The Melting Pot	1915	O. D. Bailey	Cort Film Corp.
Ireland and Israel	1912		Champion				
Isabella of Aragon	1910		Itala	The Merchant of Venice	1908		Vitagraph
Ivanhoe	1913	H. Brenon	Universal	The Merchant of Venice	1912		Champion
Izzy and His Rival	1914		Reliance	The Merchant of Venice	1912		Thanhouser
Izzy and the Diamond	1914		Reliance	The Merchant of Venice	1914	P. Smalley	Universal
Izzy's Night Out	1914		Reliance	Michael Strogoff	1914		Popular Plays & Players
Izzy the Detective	1914		Reliance				
Jephthah's Daughter	1909		Vitagraph	Mike and Jake as Heroes	1913		Joker
Jephthah's Daughter	1913	J.F. McDonald	Warner's Features	Mike and Jake as Pugilists	1913		Joker
				Mike and Jake in Mexico	1913		Joker
Jerusalem in the Time of Christ	1908		Kalem	Mike and Jake in Society	1913		Universal
				Mike and Jake in the Wild West	1913		Joker
The Jewess	1913		Nesster				
A Jewish Dance at Jerusalem	1903		Edison	The Miser's Heart	1911	D. W. Griffith	Biograph
				The Missing Diamond	1914		Lubin
The Jewish Maiden's Wrong	1913			The Money Lender	1914		Eclectic
				The Moneylender's Son	1910		Lux
The Jew's Christmas	1913	P. Smalley/L. Weber	Universal	The Monster of Fate or The Golem	1917		Hawk Film Co.
The Jew's Gratitude	1910		Yankee Film Co.	Mr. Isaacs and the Sporting Mice	1909		Cricks & Martin
Joseph and His Brethren	1915		Dormet	Murphy and the Mermaids	1914		Biograph
Joseph and His Coat of Many Colors	1914		Sawyer				
				The New Baby	1913		Keystone
Joseph in Egypt	1912		Cines	The New Fire Chief	1912		Universal
Joseph in the Land of Egypt	1914		Thanhouser	Nihilist Vengeance	1913		Victor
				Oh, Sammy	1913		Biograph
Joseph Sold by His Brethren	1910		Pathe	The Old Chess Players	1912		Lubin
				The Old Cobbler	1914		Bison
Joseph's Trials in Egypt	1914		Eclectic	Old Isaacs the Pawnbroker	1908	W. McCotchen	Biograph
The Judgment of Solomon	1909		Vitagraph				
				The Old Peddler	1911		Universal
Judith and Holofernes	1910		Gaumont	Old Women on the Streets of New York	1913		Kalem
Judith of Bethulia	1914	D. W. Griffith	Biograph				
The Kiss of Hate	1916	W. Nigh	Columbia	Oliver Twist	1909		Vitagraph
L'Chayim (Good Luck)	1911		Pathe	Oliver Twist	1910		Pathe
Leah, the Forsaken	1908		Vitagraph	Oliver Twist	1912		General
Leah, the Forsaken	1912	H. Brenon	Universal	Oliver Twist	1916		
Legally Dead	1910		Powers	The Pawnbroker's Daughter	1913		Kalem
Legend of the Erring Jew	1911		Eclair				
Levi and Cohen, The Irish Comedians	1903		American Mutoscope	A Passover Miracle	1914		Kalem
				The Pawnshop	1910		Solax
Levi and Family at Coney Island	1910		Atlas	The Pawnshop	1916	C. Chaplin	Mutual
				The Peddler's Find	1912		Reliance
Levi and McGuiness Running for Office	1913		Imperial	Pharaoh or Israel in Egypt	1910		Gaumont
Levi the Cop	1910		Atlas				
Levinsky's Gold Mine	1914		Imperial	The Question	1911		Power's Picture Plays
Levinsky's Holiday	1913		Majestic				
Levi's Dilemma	1910		Essanay	Rebecca the Jewess	1914		World's Leader Features
Levi's Luck	1914		Komic				
Levitsky Sees the Parade	1909		Independent	Regeneration	1915	R. Walsh	Fox
Levy's Seven Daughters	1915	W. Van Nostrand	Vitagraph	The Riot	1913		Keystone
				The Romance of the Jewess	1908	D. W. Griffith	Griffith
Life of Moses (5 parts)	1909-10	J. S. Blackton	Vitagraph				

Title	Year	Director	Distributor/ Production Company	Title	Year	Director	Distributor/ Production Company
Russia, the Land of Oppression	1910		Defender	Cohen on the Telephone	1929	R. Bloss	Universal
Samson	1914		Universal	The Cohens and Kellys	1926	H. Pollard	Universal
Samson's Betrayal	1910		Gaumont	The Cohens and Kellys in Atlantic City	1929	W. J. Craft	Universal
Samuel of Posen	1910		Selig Polyscope	The Cohens and Kellys in Paris	1928	W. Beaudine	Universal
Sandy and Shorty Work Together	1913		Vitagraph	A Daughter of Israel	1929	E. Jose	Bell
Saul and David	1911		Gaumont	The Delicatessen Kid	1929	W. Fabian	Universal
Saul and David	1909		Vitagraph	Disraeli	1921	H. Kolker	Distinctive Artists
Shylock	1913		Eclipse				
Solomon's Son	1912		Reliance	Disraeli	1929	A. Green	Warner Bros.
The Son of the Shunammite	1911		Gaumont	East Side Sadie	1929	H. Beaumont	Metro Pictures
				Fanny Lear	1920		Delac, Vandal & Co.
The Song of Solomon	1914	E. Boulder	Edison				
The Sorrows of Israel	1913	S. Golden	Imperial	The Five Dollar Baby	1922	H. Beaumont	Metro
A Stage Door Flirtation	1914		Lubin	Flying Romeo	1928	M. LeRoy	E. M. Asher
The Stone Heart	1915		Edison	Fool's Highway	1924	I. Cummings	Universal
Such a Business	1914		Royal	For the Love of Mike	1927	F. Capra	First National
Threads of Destiny	1914	J. W. Smiley	Lubin	Frisco Sally Levy	1927	W. Beaudine	MGM
Toplitsky and Co.	1913		Keystone	George Washington Cohen	1928	G. Archinbaud	Tiffany-Stahl
Tough Guy Levi	1912		Lubin				
Traffickers on Souls	1914		Universal	The Ghetto	1928	N. Laurog	Tiffany-Stahl
Two Overcoats	1911		Vitagraph	A Harp in Hock	1927	R. Hoffman	Pathe
The Ungrateful Daughter-in-Law	1910		Yankee	His People	1925	E. Sloman	Universal
				Humoresque	1920	F. Borzage	Paramount
Unto the Third Generation	1913	H. Salter	Universal	Hungry Hearts	1922	E. M. Hopper	Goldwyn
				In Hollywood with Potash and Perlmutter	1924	A. Green	Goldwyn
Uriel Acosta	1914		Great Players				
Vengeance of the Oppressed	1916		Lubin	Izzy and Lizzy	1926		
				The Jazz Singer	1927	A. Crosland	Warner Brothers
The Vow	1910		Gaumont				
When Tony Pawned Louisa	1913		Lubin	Jewish Prudence	1927	H. Roach	Pathe
				Just Around the Corner	1921	M. Frances	Cosmopolitan
The Wife of Cain	1913	C. L. Gaskill	Charles Fuller	Kosher Kitty Kelly	1926	J. Horn	R-C Pictures
A Woodland Christmas in California	1912		Melies	Little Miss Smiles	1922	J. Ford	Fox Films Corp.
The Yellow Passport	1916		World Films	Little Old New York	1923	S. Olcott	
The Yellow Ticket	1918	W. Parke	Pathe	Love's Blindness	1926	J. Dillon	MGM
The Yiddisher Cowboy	1909		N.Y. Motion Picture Co. Bison	The Magic Cup	1921	J. Robertson	Realart
				Mazel-Tov	1924		Listo-Picon
The Yiddisher Cowboy	1911		American Bank Flor	Millionaires	1926	H. Raymaker	Warner Brothers
				My Man	1929	A. Mayo	Warner Brothers
Features 1920-1929				New York	1927	L. Reed	Famous Players Lasky
Abie's Imported Bride	1925	R. Calneck	Temple				
Abie's Irish Rose	1928	V. Fleming	Paramount	Noah's Ark	1929	M. Curtiz	Warner Brothers
Adam and Eve	1920	R. Vignola	John Franklin Meyer	None So Blind	1923	B. King	Arrow
Auction of Souls	1922	O. Apfel	Associated First National	The Oath	1921	R. Walsh	Mayflower Photoplay
The Auctioneer	1927			Old Clothes	1925	E. Cline	MGM
The Bells	1925	J. Young	Universal	Oliver Twist	1922	F. Lloyd	Jackie Coogan Prod.
Ben Hur	1927	F. Niblo	MGM				
Blind Prejudice	1921	L. M. Allaire	Regal	Oliver Twist, Jr.	1921	W. Webb	Fox
Breaking Home Ties	1922	F. Seltzer/G. Rolands	Manheimer	One of the Bravest	1925	F. O'Conner	Lumas
				Orphans of the Ghetto	1922		Arista Film Corp.
Broadway Broke	1923	J. S. Dawley	Murray Garsson	Partners Again	1926	H. King	U.A.
Broken Hearts	1926	M. Schwartz	Jaffe Art Film Corp.	Pass the Gravy	1928	F. Guidol	MGM
				Pawn Ticket 210	1922	S. Dunlap	Fox
Cheated Love	1921	K. Baggot	Universal	Potash and Perlmutter	1923	C. Badger	Goldwyn
Children of Fate	1926		Ivan Abramson	Prejudice	1922	J. Belmont	Arista
Clancy's Kosher Wedding	1927	A. E. Gilstrom	R-C Pictures	Princess from Hoboken	1927		

Title	Year	Director	Distributor/ Production Company
Private Izzy Murphy	1926	L. Bacon	Warner Brothers
The Queen of Sheba	1921	J. G. Edwards	Fox
The Rag Man	1925	E. Kline	MGM
Raggedy Rose	1926	H. Roach	Pathe
The Rawhide Kid	1927		Universal
Rose of the Tenements	1926	P. Rosen	R-C Pictures
Sailor Izzy Murphy	1927	H. Lehrman	Warner Bros.
Sally in Our Alley	1927	W. Lang	Columbia
Salome of the Tenements	1925	S. Olcott	Famous Players
Second Hand Rose	1922	L. Ingraham	Universal
Shamrock and the Rose	1927	J. Nelson	Chadwick Prod.
The Shepherd King	1923	J. G. Edwards	Fox
Surrender	1927	E. Sloman	Universal
Sweet Daddies	1926	A. Santell	First National
A Tailor Made Man	1922	J. DeGrasse	Charles Ray
Talk of Hollywood	1929	M. Sandrick	Sono Art World Wide Pictures
Temperamental Tillie	1928		Warner Brothers
The Ten Commandments	1923	C. DeMille	Paramount
The Way of a Man	1922	C. C. Calvert	Gaumont
We Americans	1928	E. Sloman	Universal
Welcome Stranger	1924	J. Young	Belasco
The Women He Loved	1927	E. Sloman	J. L. Frothingham
The Younger Generation	1928	F. Capra	Columbia

Features 1930-1939

Title	Year	Director	Distributor/ Production Company
Around the Corner	1930	B. Glennon	Columbia
Be Yourself	1930	T. Freeland	United Artists
The Big Butter and Yegg Man	1931	Henry Lehrman	Universal
The Bowery	1933	R. Walsh	20th Century-Fox
Caught Cheating	1931	F. Strayer	Tiffany
The Cohens and Kellys in Africa	1930	V. Moore	Universal
The Cohens and Kellys in Hollywood	1932	J. F. Dillon	Universal
The Cohens and Kellys in Scotland	1930	W. J. Craft	Universal
The Cohens and Kellys in Trouble	1933	G. Stevens	Universal
Confessions of a Nazi Spy	1939	A. Litvak	First National Warner
Counsellor-at-Law	1933	W. Wyler	Universal
The Dreyfus Case	1934	F. Kraemer and M. Rosmer	Columbia
East of Fifth Avenue	1933	A. Rogell	Columbia
Gunboat Ginsburg	1930	M. Sandrich	RCA Photophone
The Heart of New York	1932	M. LeRoy	Warner Brothers
High Pressure	1932	M. LeRoy	Warner Brothers
Hitler's Reign of Terror	1934	M. Mindlin	Jewel Prod.
House of Rothschild	1934	A. Werker	20th Century Fox

Title	Year	Director	Distributor/ Production Company
The Kibitzer	1930	E. Sloman	Paramount-Famous Players-Lasky
Life of Emile Zola	1937	W. Dieterle	Warner Brothers
Light of Western Stars	1930	O. Brewer/E. Knopf	Paramount
Manhattan Melodrama	1934	Van Dyke	MGM
Manhattan Parade	1932	L. Bacon	Warner Brothers
Models and Wives	1931	C. Lamont	Universal
Night Class	1931	H. Fraser	RKO
No Greater Love	1932	L. Seiler	Columbia
Oliver Twist	1933	W. Cowen	Monogram
Power	1934	L. Mendez	Gaumont
Professor Mamlock	1938	A. Minkin/H. Rappaport	Brandon
Side Streets	1934	A. Green	First National
The S.S. Malaria	1931	H. Bretherton	Paramount
The Strange Case of Clara Deane	1932	L. Gasnier/M. Marcin	Paramount
Street Scene	1931	K. Vidor	United Artists
Subway Express	1931	F. Newmeyer	Columbia
Svengali	1931	A. Mayo	Warner Brothers
Symphony of Six Million	1932	G. La Cava	RKO
Taxi	1932	R. DelRuth	Warner Brothers
This Day and Age	1933	C. DeMille	Paramount
The Vice Squad	1931	J. Cromwell	Paramount
The Yellow Ticket	1931	R. Walsh	20th Century-Fox

Features 1940-1949

Title	Year	Director	Distributor/ Production Company
Abie's Irish Rose	1946	E. Sutherland	Bing Crosby
Action in the North Atlantic	1943	L. Bacon	Warner Brothers
Address Unknown	1944	W. C. Menzies	Columbia
Air Force	1943	H. Hawks	Warner Brothers
Bataan	1943	T. Garnett	MGM
Big City	1948	N. Taurog	MGM
Body & Soul	1947	R. Rossen	Somerset
Burning Cross	1947	W. Colmes	Screen Guild
Crossfire	1947	E. Dmytryk	RKO
The Dolly Sisters	1945	I. Cummings	20th Century-Fox
East Side, West Side	1949	M. LeRoy	MGM
Escape	1940	M. LeRoy	MGM
Gentleman's Agreement	1947	E. Kazan	20th Century-Fox
The Great Dictator	1940	C. Chaplin	Chaplin
Hitler's Children	1942	E. Dmytryk	RKO
The Hitler Gang	1944	J. Farrow	Paramount
Humoresque	1947	J. Negulesco	Warner Brothers
Jolson Sings Again	1949	H. Levin	Columbia
The Jolson Story	1946	A. E. Green	Columbia
Margin for Error	1943	O. Preminger	20th Century-Fox
Men of Boys Town	1941	N. Taurog	MGM
The Mortal Storm	1940	F. Borzage	MGM

Title	Year	Director	Distributor/Production Company
Mr. Skeffington	1945	V. Sherman	Warner Brothers
Night Train	1940	C. Reed	20th Century-Fox
None Shall Escape	1944	W. DeToth	Columbia
Objective-Burma	1945	R. Walsh	Warner Brothers
Oliver Twist	1948	D. Lean	Rank
Once Upon a Honeymoon	1942	L. McCarey	RKO
Open Secret	1948	J. Reinhardt	Marathon Pictures
Pride of the Marines	1945	D. Daves	Warner Brothers
The Purple Heart	1944	L. Milestone	20th Century-Fox
The Red Menace	1949	R. G. Springsteen	Republic
Rhapsody in Blue	1945	I. Rapper	Warner Brothers
Samson and Delilah	1949	C. DeMille	Paramount
Sands of Iwo Jima	1949	A. Dwan	Republic
Sealed Verdict	1948	L. Allen	Paramount
The Search	1947	F. Zinneman	MGM
The Seventh Cross	1944	F. Zinneman	MGM
The Sword in the Desert	1949	G. Sherman	Universal
Three Faces West	1940	B. Vorhaus	Republic
Till the Clouds Roll By	1947	R. Whorf	MGM
To Be or Not To Be	1942	E. Lubitsch	United Artists
Tomorrow the World	1944	L. Fenton	Lester Cowan
Winged Victory	1944	G. Cukor	20th Century-Fox

Features 1950-1959

Title	Year	Director	Distributor/Production Company
Attack	1956	R. Aldrich	United Artists
Battle Hymn	1957	D. Sirk	Universal
The Benny Goodman Story	1956	V. Davies	Universal
The Big Knife	1955	R. Aldrich	United Artists
A Bucket of Blood	1959	R. Corman	American International Pictures
Caine Mutiny	1954	E. Dmytryk	Columbia
Compulsion	1959	R. Fleischer	Zanuck
David and Bathsheba	1951	H. King	20th Century-Fox
The Deep Sea	1958	R. Mate	Jaguar
Detective Story	1951	W. Wyler	Paramount
Diary of Anne Frank	1959	G. Stevens	20th Century-Fox
The Eddie Cantor Story	1953	A. Green	Warner Brothers
Espresso Bongo	1959	V. Guest	Conquest
Garment Jungle	1957	V. Sherman	Columbia
Good Morning, Miss Dove	1955	H. Koster	20th Century-Fox
Home Before Dark	1958	M. LeRoy	Warner Brothers
I Accuse	1958	J. Ferrar	MGM
I Can Get It For You Wholesale or Only the Best	1951	M. Gordon	20th Century-Fox
It's a Big Country	1951	D. Schary	MGM

Title	Year	Director	Distributor/Production Company
Ivanhoe	1952	R. Thorpe	MGM
The Jazz Singer	1953	M. Curtiz	Warner Brothers
The Juggler	1953	E. Dmytryk	Columbia
The Last Angry Man	1959	D. Mann	Columbia
The Last Ten Days	1956	G. B. Pabst	Columbia
The Magnificent Yankee	1951	J. Sturges	MGM
Marjorie Morningstar	1958	I. Rapper	Beechwald
Me and the Colonel	1958	P. Glenville	Court Goetz
Middle of the Night	1959	D. Mann	Columbia
Molly	1951	Hart	Paramount
The Naked and the Dead	1958	R. Walsh	RKO
Never Love a Stranger	1958	R. Stevens	Allied Artists
Not as a Stranger	1955	S. Kramer	United Artists
The Prodigal	1955	R. Thorpe	MGM
The Proud Rebel	1958	M. Curtiz	Buena Vista
Say One For Me	1958	F. Tashlin	20th Century-Fox
Singing in the Dark	1956	M. Nosseck	A.N.O.
Solomon and Sheba	1959	K. Vidor	United Artists
Somebody Up There Likes Me	1956	R. Wise	MGM
Stalag 17	1953	W. Wilder	Paramount
The Sun Also Rises	1957	H. King	20th Century-Fox
The Sword in the Desert	1952	G. Sherman	Universal
The Ten Commandments	1956	C. DeMille	Paramount
Three Brave Men	1957	P. Dunne	20th Century-Fox
Titanic	1953	G. Negulesco	20th Century-Fox
The Young Lions	1958	E. Dmytryk	20th Century-Fox

Features 1960-1969

Title	Year	Director	Distributor/Production Company
Act One	1963	D. Schary	Warner Brothers
The Bible . . . In the Beginning	1966	J. Huston	20th Century-Fox
Bye Bye Braverman	1968	S. Lumet	Warner Brothers
Captain Newman, M.D.	1963	D. Miller	Universal
Cast a Giant Shadow	1966	M. Shavelson	Mirish-Llenroc-Batjac
Come Blow Your Horn	1963	B. Yorkin	Paramount
Dark at the Top of the Stairs	1960	D. Mann	Warner Brothers
The Detective	1968	Gordon Douglas	20th Century-Fox
Enter Laughing	1967	C. Reiner	Acre-Sajo Prod.
Esther and the King	1960	R. Walsh	20th Century-Fox
Exodus	1960	O. Preminger	Otto Preminger
The Fearless Vampire Killers	1967	R. Polanski	MGM
The Fixer	1968	J. Frankenheimer	MGM
The Fortune Cookie	1966	W. Wilder	United Artists
Freud	1962	J. Huston	Universal
Funny Girl	1968	W. Wyler	Columbia
Goldstein	1965	P. Kaufman/ B. Monaster	Montrose

Title	Year	Director	Distributor/ Production Company	Title	Year	Director	Distributor/ Production Company
Goodbye, Columbus	1969	L. Peerce	Willow Tree Prod.	Black Sunday	1977	J. Franken-heimer	Paramount
Hello, Dolly!	1969	G. Kelly	20th Century-Fox	Blazing Saddles	1974	M. Brooks	Warner Bros.
The Hoodlum Priest	1961	I. Kershner	Murr Woods	Bloodline	1979	T. Young	Paramount
A House Is Not a Home	1964	R. Rouse	Embassy	Blume in Love	1973	P. Mazursky	Warner Bros.
I Love You, Alice B. Toklas!	1968	H. Averback	Warner Brothers	Boardwalk	1979	S. Verona	Atlantic Releasing Co.
John Goldfarb, Please Come Home	1964	J. L. Thompson	20th Century-Fox	The Boys from Brazil	1979	F. Schaffner	20th Century-Fox
Judgment at Nuremberg	1961	S. Kramer	Roxlam	Cabaret	1972	R. Fosse	Allied Artists
Judith	1965	D. Mann	Paramount	California Suite	1978	H. Ross	Columbia
King of the Roaring Twenties: The Story of Arnold Rothstein	1961	J. Newman	Allied Artists	Children of Rage	1975	A. Seidelman	Emessee
				The Devil and Sam Silverstein	1975		
Lisa	1962	P. Dunne	20th Century-Fox	The Diary of a Mad Housewife	1970	F. Perry	Universal
The Little Shop of Horrors	1960	R. Corman	Film Group	The Duchess and The Dirtwater Fox	1976	M. Frank	20th Century-Fox
Luv	1967	C. Donner	Columbia	The Eagle Has Landed	1977	J. Sturges	Columbia
A Majority of One	1961	M. LeRoy	Warner Brothers	Everything You Always Wanted to Know About Sex But Were Afraid to Ask	1972	W. Allen	United Artists
Me, Natalie	1969	F. Loe	National General Pictures				
Night of the Generals	1967	A. Litvak	Columbia	Fiddler on the Roof	1971	N. Jewison	United Artists
The Night They Raided Minsky's	1968	W. Freidkin	Norman Lear	For Pete's Sake	1974	P. Yates	Columbia
No Way to Treat a Lady	1968	J. Smight	Paramount	The Frisco Kid	1979	R. Aldrich	Warner Bros.
Oliver!	1968	C. Reed	Columbia	Fritz The Cat	1972	R. Bakshi	Cinemation Industries
Operation Eichmann	1961	R. G. Springsteen	Allied Artists	The Front	1976	M. Ritt	Columbia
				Funny Lady	1975	H. Ross	Columbia
The Out-of-Towners	1969	A. Hiller	Paramount	The Gambler	1974	K. Reisz	Paramount
The Pawnbroker	1965	S. Lumet	Eli Landau	The Godfather, Pt. II	1974	F. F. Coppola	Paramount
The Producers	1968	M. Brooks	Embassy Pictures	Godspell	1973	D. Green	Columbia
The Saboteur: Code Name Mori	1965	B. Wicki	20th Century-Fox	Going in Style	1979	M. Brest	Warner Bros.
				The Great Gatsby	1974	J. Clayton	Paramount
Ship of Fools	1965	S. Kramer	Columbia	Harry and Tonto	1974	P. Mazursky	20th Century-Fox
The Spy Who Came In From the Cold	1965	Martin Ritt	Paramount	The Heartbreak Kid	1972	E. May	20th Century-Fox
The Story of Ruth	1960	H. Kostler	Fox	Hearts of the West	1975	H. Zieff	United Artists
Thoroughly Modern Millie	1967	G. R. Hill	Universal	Hester Street	1975	J. M. Silver	Midwest Film
Tobruk	1966	A. Hiller	Universal	Hit	1973	S. Furie	Paramount
Ulysses	1967	J. Strick	Continental	House Calls	1978	Howard Zeiff	Universal
Walk in the Shadow	1962	B. Dearden	Allied Film Makers	I Never Sang for My Father	1970	G. Cates	Columbia
				I Will . . . I Will . . . For Now	1975	N. Panama	20th Century-Fox
Features 1970-1979				The In-Laws	1979	A. Hiller	Warner Bros.
				Interiors	1978	W. Allen	United Artists
Alex in Wonderland	1970	P. Mazursky	MGM	The Jerusalem File	1971	J. Flynn	MGM
The All American Boy	1973	C. Eastman	Warner Bros.	Jesus Christ Superstar	1973	N. Jewison	Universal
All the President's Men	1976	A. Pakula	Warner Bros.	Julia	1977	F. Zinneman	20th Century-Fox
Americathon	1979	N. Israel	United Artists				
The Angel Levine	1970	J. Kadar	United Artists	Kelly's Heroes	1970	B. Hutton	MGM
Annie Hall	1977	W. Allen	United Artists	Kotch	1971	J. Lemmon	Cinerama
The Apprenticeship of Duddy Kravitz	1974	T. Kotcheff	Paramount	The Last Embrace	1979	J. Demme	United Artists
				Lenny	1974	R. Fosse	United Artists
The Assassination of Trotsky	1973	J. Losey	Cinerama	Lepke	1975	M. Golan	Warner Bros.
				Lies My Father Told Me	1975	J. Kadar	Columbia
Bananas	1971	W. Allen	United Artists	Little Murders	1971	A. Arkin	20th Century-Fox
The Big Fix	1978	J. P. Kagan	Universal	The Long Goodbye	1973	R. Altman	United Artists
				Love and Death	1975	W. Allen	United Artists

Title	Year	Director	Distributor/Production Company	Title	Year	Director	Distributor/Production Company
Love at First Bite	1979	S. Dragoti	American International	Bad Boys	1983	R. Rosenthal	EMI/Universal
Made for Each Other	1971	R. Bean	20th Century-Fox	The Big Chill	1983	L. Kasdan	Columbia
The Main Event	1979	H. Zieff	Warner Bros.	Broadway Danny Rose	1984	Woody Allen	United Artists
Making It	1971	A. Jacobs	20th Century-Fox	The Cannonball Run	1981	H. Needham	20th Century-Fox
The Man in the Glass Booth	1975	A. Hiller	American Film Theater	Chariots of Fire	1982	H. Hudson	Warner Bros./Ladd Co.
Manhattan	1979	W. Allen	United Artists	The Chosen	1982	J. Kagan	20th Century-Fox
Marathon Man	1976	J. Schlesinger	Paramount	The Cotton Club	1984	F.F. Coppola	Orion
Meatballs	1979	I. Reitman	Paramount	Daniel	1984	S. Lumet	20th Century-Fox
Mikey and Nicky	1976	E. May	Paramount				
Minnie and Moskowitz	1971	J. Cassavetes	Universal	Diner	1982	B. Levinson	MGM
A New Leaf	1970	E. May	Paramount	Endless Love	1981	F. Zefferelli	Universal
Next Stop, Greenwich Village	1976	P. Mazursky	20th Century-Fox	Eyewitness	1981	P. Yates	20th Century-Fox
Norma Rae	1979	M. Ritt	20th Century-Fox	Fame	1980	A. Parker	MGM
				Flash Gordon	1980	M. Hodges	Universal
The Owl and the Pussycat	1970	H. Ross	Columbia	Fort Apache, The Bronx	1981	D. Petrie	20th Century-Fox
Play It Again Sam	1972	H. Ross	Paramount	Four Friends	1981	A. Penn	Filmways Pictures
Play It As It Lays	1972	F. Perry	Universal				
Plaza Suite	1970	A. Hiller	Paramount	Frances	1982	G. Clifford	EMI
Portnoy's Complaint	1972	E. Lehman	Warner Bros.	Garbo Talks	1984	S. Lumet	
The Poseidon Adventure	1972	R. Neame	20th Century-Fox	Gilda Live	1980	M. Nichols	Warner Bros.
				Heavy Metal	1981	G. Potterton	Columbia
Prisoner of Second Avenue	1975	M. Frank	Warner Bros.	History of the World, Part I	1981	M. Brooks	20th Century-Fox
Romance of a Horsethief	1971	A. Polonsky	Allied Artists	The Hotel New Hampshire	1984	T. Richardson	Orion
Running	1979	S. H. Stern	Universal	The Hunter	1980	B. Kulik	Paramount
The Salzburg Connection	1972	L. Katzin	Fox	It's My Turn	1980	C. Weill	Columbia
Save the Tiger	1973	J. Avildsen	Paramount	The Jazz Singer	1981	R. Fleischer	Associated Film Development
Shampoo	1975	H. Ashby	Universal				
Sheila Levine is Alive and Well	1975	S. Furie	Paramount	Just Tell Me What You Want	1980	S. Lumet	Warner Bros.
Sleeper	1973	W. Allen	United Artists	King David	1985	B. Beresford	Paramount
Some of My Best Friends Are	1971	M. Nelson	American International	The King of Comedy	1983	M. Scorcese	20th Century-Fox
A Star is Born	1976	F. Pierson	Warner Bros.	The Little Drummer Girl	1984	G.R. Hill	Warner Bros.
Such Good Friends	1971	O. Preminger	Paramount	Lovesick	1983	M. Brickman	Warner Bros.
The Sunshine Boys	1975	H. Ross	MGM	Mommie Dearest	1981	Frank Perry	Paramount
An Unmarried Woman	1978	P. Mazursky	20th Century-Fox	Moscow on the Hudson	1984	P. Mazursky	Columbia
				My Favorite Year	1982	R. Benjamin	MGM
Voyage of the Damned	1979	S. Rosenberg	Auco Embassy	1984	1985	M. Radford	
Voices	1979	R. Markowitz	MGM	Once Upon a Time in America	1984	S. Leone	Ladd Co.
The Way We Were	1973	S. Pollack	Columbia				
Where's Poppa?	1970	C. Reiner	United Artists	Ordinary People	1980	R. Redford	Paramount
Who Is Harry Kellerman and Why Is He Saying Those Terrible Things About Me?	1971	U. Grosbard	National Gen. Pictures	Popeye	1980	R. Altman	Paramount
				Porky's	1982	Bob Clark	20th Century-Fox
				Porky's II	1984	Bob Clark	20th Century-Fox
Features 1980 to Present				Prince of The City	1981	S. Lumet	Warner Bros.
				Private Benjamin	1980	H. Zieff	Warner Bros.
Altered States	1981	K. Russell	Warner Bros.	Ragtime	1981	M. Forman	Paramount
The Amateur	1982	C. Jarrott	20th Century-Fox	Reds	1981	W. Beatty	Paramount
				Rocky III	1982	S. Stallone	United Artists
American Pop	1981	R. Bakshi	Columbia	Sharkey's Machine	1981	B. Reynolds	Orion
An American Werewolf in London	1981	J. Landis	Universal	Simon	1980	M. Brickman	Orion
				A Small Circle of Friends	1980	R. Cohen	United Artists
Baby, It's You	1983	J. Sayles	Paramount	S.O.B.	1981	B. Edwards	Paramount

Title	Year	Director	Distributor/ Production Company	Title	Year	Director	Distributor/ Production Company
So Fine	1982	A. Bergman	Warner Bros.	The Twilight Zone, The Movie (Pt. 1)	1983	J. Landis	Warner Bros.
Sophie's Choice	1983	A. Pakula	Universal	The Twilight Zone, The Movie (Pt. 2)	1983	S. Speilberg	Warner Bros.
Stardust Memories	1980	W. Allen	United Artists				
Tell Me A Riddle	1980	L. Grant	Filmways Pictures	Wholly Moses	1980	G. Weiss	Columbia
Those Lips, Those Eyes	1980	M. Pressman	United Artists	Willy and Phil	1980	P. Mazursky	20th Century Fox
Ticket to Heaven	1982	R. L. Thomas	United Artist Classics	Yentl	1983	B. Streisand	MGM
To Be or Not To Be	1983	A. Johnson	BrooksFilm	Zelig	1983	W. Allen	Warner Bros.

PART THIRTEEN

SPORTS

The Jewish Sports Hall of Fame

The Jewish Sports Hall of Fame was founded in 1979 to recognize Jewish men and women who achieve distinction in sports.

The Hall of Fame is located at the Wingate Institute for Physical Education and Sport, in Netanya, Israel. To be eligible, a candidate must have retired from sports.

Harold Abrahams, *Great Britain*—Track & Field 1981
Dr. Joseph Alexander, *USA*—Football 1984
Mel Allen, *USA*—Sportscaster 1980
Abe Attell, *USA*—Boxing 1982
Red Auerbach, *USA*—Basketball 1979
Victor Barna, *Hungary/Great Britain*—Table Tennis 1981
Isaac Berger, *USA*—Weightlifting 1980
Samuel Berger, *USA*—Boxing 1984
Richard Bergmann, *Austria*—Table Tennis 1982
Gyorgy Brody, *Hungary*—Water Polo 1982
Angela Buxton, *Great Britain*—Tennis 1981
Zephania Carmel/Lydia Lazarov, *Israel*—Yachting 1982
Lillian Copeland, *USA*—Track & Field 1980
Barney Dreyfuss, *USA*—Baseball 1980
Charlotte Epstein, *USA*—Swimming 1982
Jackie Fields, *USA*—Boxing 1979
Alfred Flatow, *Germany*—Gymnastics 1981
Benny Friedman, *USA*—Football 1979
Jeno Fuchs, *Hungary*—Fencing 1982
Marshall Goldberg, *USA*—Football 1980
Alexander Gomelsky, *USSR*—Basketball 1981
Eddie Gottlieb, *USA*—Basketball 1980
Hank Greenberg, *USA*—Baseball 1979
George Gulak, *USA*—Gymnastics 1983
Boris Gurevich, *USSR*—Wrestling 1982
Bela Guttmann, *Hungary*—Soccer 1981
Sir Ludwig Guttmann, *Germany/*
   Great Britain—Sports Medicine 1981
Alfred Hajos-Guttmann, *Hungary*—Swimming 1981
Hakoah-Vienna, *Austria*—Soccer 1982
Nat Holman, *USA*—Basketball 1979
Hirsch Jacobs, *USA*—Horse Racing 1979
Jim Jacobs, *USA*—Handball 1979
Irving Jaffe, *USA*—Ice Skating 1979
Alan Jay, *Great Britain*—Fencing 1984
Elias Katz, *Finland*—Track & Field 1981
Agnes Keleti, *Hungary*—Gymnastics 1981
Irena Kirszenstein, *Poland*—Track & Field 1981
Abel Kiviat, *USA*—Track & Field 1983
Sandy Koufax, *USA*—Baseball 1979
Lily Kronberger, *Hungary*—Figure Skating 1982

Benny Leonard, *USA*—Boxing 1979
Battling Levinsky, *USA*—Boxing 1982
Ted "Kid" Lewis, *Great Britain*—Boxing 1982
Alexandre Lippmann, *France*—Fencing 1983
Harry Litwack, *USA*—Basketball 1980
Sid Luckman, *USA*—Football 1979
Gyula Mandy, *Hungary*—Soccer 1982
Hugo Meisl, *Austria*—Soccer 1981
Faina Melnik, *USSR*—Track & Field 1983
Daniel Mendoza, *Great Britain*—Boxing 1981
Mark Midler, *USSR*—Fencing 1982
Walter Miller, *USA*—Horse Racing 1982
Ron Mix, *USA*—Football 1980
Sir Ivor Goldsmid Montagu, *England*—Table Tennis 1983
Lady Swathling, Gladys Goldsmid Montagu,
   England—Table Tennis 1984
Samuel Mosberg, *USA*—Boxing 1984
Lon Myers, *USA*—Track & Field 1980
Paul Neumann, *Austria*—Swimming 1983
Zvi Nishri, *Israel*—Physical Education 1981
Grigori Novak, *USSR*—Weightlifting 1984
Attila Petschauer, *Hungary*—Fencing 1984
Lipman Pike, *USA*—Baseball 1984
Myer Prinstein, *USA*—Track & Field 1982
Al Rosen, *USA*—Baseball 1980
Maxie Rosenbloom, *USA*—Boxing 1983
Fanny Rosenfeld, *Canada*—Track & Field 1981
Barney Ross, *USA*—Boxing 1979
Angelica Adelstein-Rozeanu, *Romania/Israel*—Table Tennis . . . 1981
Louis Rubenstein, *Canada*—Ice Skating 1981
Abe Saperstein, *USA*—Basketball 1979
Dick Savitt, *USA*—Tennis 1979
Dolph Schayes, *USA*—Basketball 1979
Jody Scheckter, *South Africa*—Auto Racing 1982
Frank Spellman, *USA*—Weightlifting 1982
Mark Spitz, *USA*—Swimming 1979
Eva Szekely, *Hungary*—Swimming 1981
Richard Weisz, *Hungary*—Wrestling 1982
Sylvia Wene Martin, *USA*—Bowling 1979
Henry Wittenberg, *USA*—Wrestling 1979
Max Zaslovsky, *USA*—Basketball 1982

67

Jewish Olympic Medalists

George Eisen

1896 (ATHENS)
Gold
Alfred Hajos-Guttman, Hungary, 100-meter freestyle swimming
Alfred Hajos-Guttman, Hungary, 1,500-meter freestyle swimming
Paul Neumann, Austria, 400-meter freestyle swimming
Alfred Flatow, Germany, gymnastics, parallel bars
Alfred Flatow, Germany, gymnastics, team parallel bars
Alfred Flatow, Germany, gymnastics, team horizontal bar
Gustav Felix Flatow, Germany, gymnastics, team parallel bars
Gustav Felix Flatow, Germany, gymnastics, team horizontal bar

Silver
Alfred Flatow, Germany, gymnastics, horizontal bar

Bronze
Otto Herschmann, Austria, 100-meter freestyle swimming

1900 (PARIS)
Gold
Myer Prinstein, USA, athletics, triple jump

Silver
Myer Prinstein, USA, athletics, long jump
Otto Wahle, Austria, 1000-meter freestyle swimming
Otto Wahle, Austria, 200-meter swimming obstacle race
Henri Cohen, Belgium, water polo
Jean Bloch, France, soccer

Bronze
Siegfried Flesch, Austria, fencing, individual saber

1904 (ST. LOUIS)
Gold
Myer Prinstein, USA, athletics, long jump
Myer Prinstein, USA, athletics, triple jump
Samuel Berger, USA, heavyweight boxing

Silver
Albert Lehman, USA, lacrosse
Philip Hess, USA, lacrosse
Daniel Frank, USA, athletics, long jump

Bronze
Otto Wahle, Austria, 400-meter freestyle swimming

1906 (ATHENS/unofficial)
Gold
Myer Prinstein, USA, athletics, long jump
Otto Scheff, Austria, 400-meter freestyle swimming
Henrik Hajos-Guttman, Hungary, 800-meter freestyle swimming relay

Silver
Edgar Seligman, Great Britain, fencing, team epee

Bronze
Hugo Friend, USA, athletics, long jump
Otto Scheff, Austria, 1,500-meter freestyle swimming

1908 (LONDON)
Gold
Richard Weisz, Hungary, Greco-Roman heavyweight wrestling
Jean Stern, France, fencing, team epee
Alexandre Lippmann, France, fencing, team epee
Dr. Jeno Fuchs, Hungary, fencing, individual saber
Dr. Jeno Fuchs, Hungary, fencing, team saber
Lajos Werkner, Hungary, fencing, team saber
Dr. Oszkar Gerde, Hungary, fencing, team saber

Silver
Edwin "Barney" Solomon, Great Britain (Ireland), rugby
Bethel "Bert" Solomon, Great Britain (Ireland), rugby
Harry Simon, USA, free rifle
Edgar Seligman, Great Britain, fencing, team epee
Alexandre Lippmann, France, fencing, individual epee

Bronze
Odon Bodor, Hungary, athletics, 1,600-meter relay
Charles "Clair" Jacobs, USA, athletics, pole vault
Otto Scheff, Austria, 400-meter freestyle swimming

1912 (STOCKHOLM)
Gold
Jacques Ochs, Belgium, fencing, team epee
Gaston Salmon, Belgium, fencing, team epee
Dr. Jeno Fuchs, Hungary, fencing, team saber
Dr. Oszkar Gerde, Hungary, fencing, team saber
Lajor Werkner, Hungary, fencing, team saber
Dr. Jeno Fuchs, Hungary, fencing, individual saber

Silver
Alvah T. Meyer, USA, athletics, 100-meter dash
Abel Kiviat, USA, athletics, 1,500-meter run
Imre Gellert, Hungary, gymnastics, team combined exercises
Ivan Osiier, Denmark, fencing, individual epee
Edgar Seligman, Great Britain, fencing, team epee
Dr. Otto Herschmann, Austria, fencing, team saber
Samu Fodi, Hungary, team gymnastics
Joszef Szalai, Hungary, team gymnastics

1920 (ANTWERP)
Gold
Samuel Mosberg, USA, lightweight boxing
Albert Schneider, Canada (USA citizen), welterweight boxing
Morris Fisher, USA, free rifle
Morris Fisher, USA, 300-meter team shooting
Morris Fisher, USA, prone team shooting

Silver
Gerard Blitz, Belgium, water polo
Maurice Blitz, Belgium, water polo
Samuel Gerson, USA, freestyle featherweight wrestling
Alexandre Lippmann, France, fencing, individual epee

Bronze
Gerard Blitz, Belgium, 100-meter backstroke swimming
Frederick Meyer, USA, freestyle heavyweight wrestling
Montgomery "Moe" Herscovitch, Canada, middleweight boxing
Alexandre Lippmann, France, fencing, team epee

1924 (Chamonix/PARIS)
Gold
Elias Katz, Finland, athletics, 3,000-meter steeplechase
Harold Abrahams, Great Britain, athletics, 100-meter dash
Louis Clarke, USA, athletics, 400-meter relay
Elias Katz, Finland, athletics, 3,000-meter team cross-country
John "Jackie" Fields, USA, featherweight boxing
Alexandre Lippmann, France, fencing, team epee
Morris Fisher, USA, free-rifle
Morris Fisher, USA, 300-meter team shooting

Silver
Harold Abrahams, Great Britain, athletics, 400-meter relay
Maurice Blitz, Belgium, water polo
Gerard Blitz, Belgium, water polo
Janos Garay, Hungary, fencing, team saber
Elias Katz, Finland, individual steeplechase

Bronze
Baron Umberto Luigi de Morpurgo, Italy, tennis singles
Janos Garay, Hungary, fencing, individual saber
Sidney Jelinek, USA, rowing, coxed-fours

1928 (St. Moritz/AMSTERDAM)
Gold
Fanny Rosenfeld, Canada, athletics, 400-meter relay
Dr. Sandor Gombos, Hungary, fencing, team saber
Attila Petschauer, Hungary, fencing, team saber
Janos Garay, Hungary, fencing, team saber

Silver
Fanny Rosenfeld, Canada, athletics, 100-meter dash
Lillian Copeland, USA, athletics, discus throw
Istvan Barta, Hungary, water polo
Attila Petschauer, Hungary, fencing, individual saber

Bronze
Ellis Smouha, Great Britain, athletics, 400-meter relay
Harry Isaacs, South Africa, bantamweight boxing
Harold Devine, USA, featherweight boxing
Samuel Rabin, Great Britain, freestyle middleweight wrestling

1932 (Lake Placid/LOS ANGELES)
Gold
Lillian Copeland, USA, athletics, discus throw
Irving Jaffee, USA, 5,000-meter speed skating
Irving Jaffee, USA, 10,000-meter speed skating
George Gulack, USA, gymnastics, rings
Gyorgy Brody, Hungary, water polo
Istvan Barta, Hungary, water polo
Miklos Sarkany, Hungary, water polo
Endre Kabos, Hungary, fencing, team saber
Attila Petschauer, Hungary, fencing, team saber

Silver
Karoly Karpati, Hungary, freestyle lightweight wrestling
Abraham Kurland, Denmark, Greco-Roman lightweight wrestling
Peter Jaffe, Great Britain, Star-class yachting
Phillip Erenberg, USA, gymnastics, club swinging

Bronze
Albert Schwartz, USA, 100-meter freestyle swimming
Nickolaus Herschl, Austria, freestyle heavyweight wrestling
Nickolaus Herschl, Austria, Greco-Roman heavyweight wrestling
Nathan Bor, USA, lightweight boxing
Endre Kabos, Hungary, fencing, individual saber
Rudolf Ball, Germany, ice hockey

1936 (Garmisch-Partenkirchen/BERLIN)
Gold
Samuel Balter, USA, basketball
Gyorgy Brody, Hungary, water polo
Miklos Sarkany, Hungary, water polo
Karoly Karpati, Hungary, lightweight freestyle wrestling
Endre Kabos, Hungary, fencing, individual saber
Endre Kabos, Hungary, fencing, team saber

Silver
Irving Maretzky, Canada, basketball

Bronze
Gerard Blitz, Belgium, water polo
Rudi Ball, Germany, ice hockey
Laszlo Szollas, Hungary, pair figure skating
Emilia Rotter, Hungary, pair figure skating

1948 (St. Moritz/LONDON)
Gold
Frank Spellman, USA, middleweight weightlifting
Henry Wittenberg, USA, freestyle light-heavyweight wrestling

Silver
Steve Seymour, USA, athletics, javelin throw

Bronze
James Fuchs, USA, athletics, shot put

1952 (Oslo/HELSINKI)
Gold
Eva Szekely, Hungary, 200-meter breaststroke swimming
Robert Antal, Hungary, water polo
Boris Gurevitsch, USSR, Greco-Roman flyweight wrestling
Claude Netter, France, fencing, team foil
Mikhail Perelman, USSR, gymnastics, team combined exercises
Agnes Keleti, Hungary, gymnastics, floor exercises
Sandor Geller, Hungary, soccer
Valeria Gyenge, Hungary, 400-meter freestyle swimming

Silver
Aleksandr Moiseyev, USSR, basketball
Grigoriy Novak, USSR, middle-heavyweight weightlifting
Henry Wittenberg, USA, light-heavyweight freestyle wrestling
Agnes Keleti, Hungary, gymnastics, team combined exercises

Bronze
James Fuchs, USA, athletics, shot put
Lev Vainschtein, USSR, free rifle
Agnes Keleti, Hungary, gymnastics, team exercise with portable apparatus
Agnes Keleti, Hungary, gymnastics, asymmetrical bars

1956 (Cortina d'Ampezzo/MELBOURNE)
Gold
Leon Rotman, Rumania, canoe, 1,000-meter Canadian singles
Leon Rotman, Rumania, canoe, 10,000-meter Canadian singles
Isaac Berger, USA, featherweight weightlifting
Agnes Keleti, Hungary, gymnastics, asymmetrical bars
Agnes Keleti, Hungary, gymnastics, floor exercises
Agnes Keleti, Hungary, gymnastics, balance beam
Agnes Keleti, Hungary, gymnastics, team exercise with portable apparatus
Aliz Kertesz, Hungary, gymnastics, team exercise with portable apparatus
Boris Rasinsky, USSR, soccer

Silver
Eva Szekely, Hungary, 200-meter breaststroke swimming
Claude Netter, France, fencing, team foil
Agnes Keleti, Hungary, gymnastics; individual combined exercises
Agnes Keleti, Hungary, gymnastics, team combined exercises
Aliz Kertesz, Hungary, gymnastics, team combined exercises
Rafael Gratsch, USSR, 500-meter speed skating

Bronze
Imre Farkas, Hungary, canoe, 10,000-meter Canadian pairs
Boris Goikhman, USSR, water polo
Yves Dreyfus, France, fencing, team epee
Armand Mouyal, France, fencing, team epee
Yakov Rylsky, USSR, fencing, team saber
David Tyschler, USSR, fencing, team saber

1960 (Squaw Valley/ROME)
Gold
Mark Midler, USSR, fencing, team foil

Silver

Boris Goikhman, USSR, water polo
Isaac Berger, USA, featherweight weightlifting
Allan Jay, Great Britain, fencing, individual epee
Allan Jay, Great Britain, fencing, team epee
Guy Nosbaum, France, rowing, coxed-fours
Jean Klein, France, rowing, coxed-fours
Vladimir Portnoi, USSR, gymnastics, team combined exercises

Bronze

Leon Rotman, Rumania, canoe, 1,000-meter Canadian singles
Imre Farkas, Hungary, canoe, 1,000-meter Canadian pairs.
Klara Fried-Banfalvi, Hungary, kayak, 500-meter pairs
Moyses Blas, Brazil, basketball
David Segal, Great Britain, athletics, 400-meter relay
Albert Axelrod, USA, fencing, individual foil
Robert Halperin, USA, Star-class yachting
Vladimir Portnoi, USSR, gymnastics, long horse vault
Rafael Gratsch, USSR, 500-meter speed skating

1964 (Innsbruck/TOKYO)
Gold

Lawrence Brown, USA, basketball
Gerald Ashworth, USA, athletics, 400-meter relay
Irena Kirszenstein, Poland, athletics, 400-meter relay
Mark Midler, USSR, fencing, team foil
Yakov Rylsky, USSR, fencing, team saber
Tamas Gabor, Hungary, team epee

Silver

Irena Kirszenstein, Poland, athletics, 200-meter dash
Irena Kirszenstein, Poland, athletics, long jump
Marilyn Ramenofsky, USA, 400-meter freestyle swimming
Nelly Abramova, USSR, volleyball
Isaac Berger, USA, featherweight weightlifting

Bronze

Yves Dreyfus, France, fencing, team epee
James Bregman, USA, middleweight judo

1968 (Grenoble/MEXICO CITY)
Gold

Irena Szewinska-Kirszenstein, Poland, athletics, 200-meter dash
Mark Spitz, USA, 400-meter freestyle swimming relay
Mark Spitz, USA, 800-meter freestyle swimming relay
Boris Gurevitsch, USSR, freestyle middleweight wrestling

Silver

Mark Spitz, USA, 100-meter butterfly swimming
Semyon Belits-Geiman, USSR, 400-meter freestyle swimming relay
Alain Calmat, France, figure skating

Bronze

Irena Szewinska-Kirszenstein, Poland, athletics, 100-meter dash
Mark Spitz, USA, 100-meter freestyle swimming
Semyon Belits-Geiman, USSR, 800-meter freestyle swimming relay

1972 (Sapporo/MUNICH)
Gold

Mark Spitz, USA, 100-meter freestyle swimming
Mark Spitz, USA, 200-meter freestyle swimming
Mark Spitz, USA, 100-meter butterfly swimming
Mark Spitz, USA, 200-meter butterfly swimming
Mark Spitz, USA, 400-meter freestyle swimming relay
Mark Spitz, USA, 400-meter medley swimming relay
Mark Spitz, USA, 800-meter freestyle swimming relay
Faina Melnik, USSR, athletics, discus throw
Sandor Erdoes, Hungary, fencing team epee

Silver

Andrea Gyarmati, Hungary, 100-meter backstroke swimming
Neal Shapiro, USA, equestrian team jumping

Bronze

Irena Szewinska, Poland, athletics, 200-meter dash
Andrea Gyarmati, Hungary, 100-meter butterfly swimming
Peter Asch, USA, water polo
Neal Shapiro, USA, equestrian individual jumping
Don Cohan, USA, Dragon-class yachting
Barry Weitzenberg, USA, water polo

1976 (Innsbruck/MONTREAL)
Gold

Ernest Grunfeld, USA, basketball
Irena Szewinska, Poland, athletics, 400-meter run

Silver

Nancy Lieberman, USA, basketball
Natalia Kushnir, USSR, volleyball

Bronze

Wendy Weinberg, USA, 800-meter freestyle swimming
Victor Zilbermann, Rumania, welterweight boxing
Edith Master, USA, equestrian team dressage

1980 (Lake Placid/MOSCOW)
Gold

Shamir Sabyrov, USSR, boxing
Svetlana Krachevskaja, USSR, track and field
John Harmanberg, Sweden, fencing

Silver

Vladimir Myshkin, USSR, ice hockey

1984 (Sarajevo/LOS ANGELES)
Gold

Mitch Gaylord, USA, team gymnastics

Silver

Mitch Gaylord, USA, vaulting
Bob Berland, USA, middleweight judo

Bronze

Mitch Gaylord, USA, rings
Mitch Gaylord, USA, parallel bars

68

Jews in Major League Baseball

PLAYER REGISTER

	Position	Years	Teams	Games	HR	RBI	BA
CAL ABRAMS / *Calvin Ross Abrams* (1924-) . . . . OF		1949-56	BKN, CIN, PIT, BAL, CHI (A)	567	32	138	.269
MORRIE ADERHOLT / *Morris Woodrow Aderholt* (1915-1955)	OF, 2B	1939-41, 44-45	WASH, BKN, BOS (N)	106	3	32	.267
MORRIE ARNOVICH / *Morris Arnovich* (1910-1959) . . . . . . OF		1936-41, 46	PHI (N)	590	22	261	.287
JAKE ATZ / *Jacob Henry Zimmerman* (1879-1945) . . . . 2B, SS		1902, 07-09	WASH, CHI (A)	208	0	49	.219
RICK AUERBACH / *Frederick Steven Auerbach* (1950-) SS, 2B, 3B		1971-81	MIL, LA(N), CIN, SEA	624	9	86	.220
STEVE BEHEL / *Stephen Arnold Douglas Behel* . . . . OF		1884, 86	MIL (U), NY (AA)	68	0	?	.210
JOE BENNETT / *Joseph Rosenblum Bennett* (1900-) 3B		1923	PHI (N)	1	0	0	—
MOE BERG / *Morris Berg* (1902-1972) . . . . C, SS		1923, 26-39	BKN, CHI (A), CLE, WASH, CLE, BOS (A)	662	6	206	.243
BOB BERMAN / *Robert Leon Berman* (1899-) C		1918	WASH	2	0	0	—
CY BLOCK / *Seymour Block* (1919-) 3B, 2B		1942, 45-46	CHI (N)	17	0	5	.302
RON BLOMBERG / *Ronald Mark Blomberg* (1948-) . . . . . 1B, OF, DH		1969, 71-76, 78	NY (A), CHI (A)	461	52	224	.293
SAMMY BOHNE / *Sammy Arthur Cohen* (1896-1977) . . . . . . 2B, SS, 3B		1916, 21-26	STL (N), CIN, BKN	663	16	228	.261
LOU BROWER / *Louis Lester Brower* (1900-) . . . . SS		1931	DET	21	0	6	.161
HARRY CHOZEN / *Harry Kenneth Chozen* (1915-) C		1937	CIN	1	0	0	.250
ALTA COHEN / *Albert Cohen* (1908-) . . . . OF		1931-33	BKN, PHI (N)	29	0	2	.194
ANDY COHEN / *Andrew Howard Cohen* (1904-) 2B		1926, 28-29	NY (N)	262	14	114	.281
PHIL COONEY / *Phillip Cohn* (1886-?) 3B		1905	NY (A)	1	0	0	.000
HARRY DANNING / *(Harry the Horse)* (1911-) C		1933-42	NY (N)	890	57	397	.285
IKE DANNING (1905-) C		1928	STL (A)	2	0	1	.500

Moe Berg

Ron Blomberg

Mike Epstein

Sidney Gordon   *Hank Greenberg*   *Benny Kauff*

	Position	Years	Teams	Games	HR	RBI	BA
MIKE EPSTEIN / *Michael Peter Epstein* (1943-) 1B		1966-74	BAL, WASH, OAK, TEX, CAL	907	130	380	.244
REUBEN EWING / *Reuben Cohen* (1899-1970) . . . . SS		1921	STL (N)	3	0	0	.000
AL FEDEROFF / *Alfred Federoff* (1924-) 2B		1951-52	DET	76	0	14	.238
EDDIE FEINBERG / *Edward (Itzy) Feinberg* (1918-) . . . . . SS, 2B, OF		1938-39	PHI (N)	16	0	0	.184
MURRAY FRANKLIN (1914-1978) . . . . SS, 2B		1941-42	DET	61	2	16	.262
MILT GALATZER / *Milton Galatzer* (1907-1976) . . . . OF		1933-36, 39	CLE, CIN	251	1	57	.268
JOE GINSBERG / *Myron Nathan Ginsberg* (1926-) C		1948, 50-54, 56-62	DET, CLE, KC, BAL, CHI (A), BOS (A), NY (N)	695	20	182	.241
JONAH GOLDMAN / *Jonah John Goldman* (1906-1980) . . . . SS, 3B		1928, 30-31	CLE	148	1	49	.224
LONNIE GOLDSTEIN / *Leslie Elmer Goldstein* (1918-) 1B		1943, 46	CIN	11	0	0	.100
JAKE GOODMAN / *Jacob Goodman* (1853-1890) 1B		1878, 82	MIL (N), PIT (AA)	70	1	27	.256
SID GORDON / *Sidney Gordon* (1917-1975) . . . . OF, 3B		1941-43, 46-55	NY (N), BOS (N), MIL (N), PIT (N), NY (N)	1475	202	805	.283
HERB GORMAN / *Herbert Allen Gorman* (1924-1953) . . . . . . —		1952	STL (N)	1	0	0	.000
HANK GREENBERG / *Henry Benjamin Greenberg* (1911-) 1B, OF Hall of Fame, 1956		1930, 33-41, 45-47	DET, PIT	1394	331	1276	.313
STEVE HERTZ / *Stephen Allan Hertz* (1945-) 3B		1964	HOU	5	0	0	.000
IZZY HOFFMAN / *Harry C. Hoffman* (1875-1942) . . . . OF		1904, 07	WASH, BOS (N)	29	0	4	.233
MERWIN JACOBSON (1894-1978) . . . . OF		1915-16, 26-27	NY (N), CHI (N), BKN	133	0	24	.230
BENNY KAUFF / *Benjamin Michael Kauff* (1890-1961) . . . . . OF		1912, 14-20	NY (A), IND (F), BKN (F), NY (N)	859	49	454	.311
JOHNNY KLING / *John Gradwohl Kling* (1875-1947) C		1900-08, 10-13	CHI (N), BOS (N), CIN	1260	20	513	.271
JIM LEVEY / *James Julius Levey* (1906- 1970) . . . . SS		1930-33	STL (A)	440	11	140	.230
LOU LIMMER / *Louis Limmer* (1925-) 1B		1951, 54	PHI (A)	209	19	62	.202
ELLIOTT MADDOX (1948-) . . . . OF, 3B		1970-80	DET, WASH, TEX, NY (A), BAL, NY (N)	1029	18	234	.261
SAM MAYER / *Samuel Frankel Erskine* (1893-1962) . . . . OF		1915	WASH	11	1	4	.241
LEVI MEYERLE / *Levi Samuel Meyerle* (1849-1921) . . . . IF		1876-77, 84	PHI (N), CIN, PHI (U)	85	0	49	.329
NORM MILLER / *Norman Calvin Miller* (1946-) . . . . OF		1965-74	HOU, ATL	540	24	159	.238
BUDDY MYER / *Charles Solomon Myer* (1904-1974) . . . . 2B, SS, 3B		1925-41	WASH, BOS (A), WASH	1923	38	850	.303
BILLY NASH / *William Mitchell Nash* (1865-1929) 3B		1884-98	RICH (AA), BOS (N), BOS (P), BOS (N), PHI (N)	1549	61	977	.275

	Position	Years	Teams	Games	HR	RBI	BA
JEFF NEWMAN / *Jeffrey Lynn Newman* (1948-) .... (record through 1984)	C, 1B	1976-	OAK, BOS (A)	735	63	233	.224
JAY PIKE	OF	1877	HART (N)	1	0	0	.250
LIP PIKE / *Lipman Emanuel Pike* (1845-1893) .... Generally acknowledged to be the first paid professional baseball player, 1866.	OF, 2B	1876-78, 81, 87	STL (N), CIN, PRO (N), WOR (N), NY (AA)	163-	5	88	.304
JAKE PITLER / *Jacob Albert Pitler* (1894-1968)	2B	1917-18	PIT	111	0	23	.232
JIMMY REESE / *James Hymie Soloman* (1904-)	2B	1930-32	NY (A), STL (N)	232	8	70	.278
AL RICHTER / *Allen Gordon Richter* (1927-)	SS	1951, 53	BOS (A)	6	0	0	.091
CHIEF ROSEMAN / *James J. Roseman* (1856-?)	OF	1882-87, 90	TROY (N), NY (AA), PHI (AA), NY (AA), BKN (AA), STL (AA), LOU (AA)	681	15	43	.263
AL ROSEN / *Albert Leonard Rosen* (1924-)	3B, 1B	1947-56	CLE	1044	192	717	.285
GOODY ROSEN / *Goodwin George Rosen* (1912-)	OF	1937-39, 44-46	BKN, NY (N)	551	22	197	.291
HARRY ROSENBERG (1909-)	OF	1930	NY (N)	9	0	0	.000
LOU ROSENBERG / *Louis C. Rosenberg* (1903-)	2B	1923	CHI (A)	3	0	0	.250
MAX ROSENFELD (1902-1969)	OF	1931-33	BKN	42	2	7	.298
SI ROSENTHAL (1903-1969)	OF	1925-26	BOS (A)	123	4	42	.266
MICKEY RUTNER / *Milton Rutner* (1920-)	3B	1947	PHI (A)	12	1	4	.250
IKE SAMUELS / *Samuel Earl Samuels* (1876-?)	3B	1895	STL (N)	24	0	5	.230
HEINIE SCHEER / *Henry William Scheer* (1900-1976)	2B, 3B	1922-23	PHI (A)	120	6	33	.212
RICHIE SCHEINBLUM / *Richard Alan Scheinblum* (1942-)	OF	1965, 67-69, 71-74	CLE, WASH, KC, CIN, CAL, KC, STL (N)	462	13	127	.263
MIKE SCHEMER / *Michael Schemer* (1917-)	1B	1945-46	NY (N)	32	1	10	.330
ART SHAMSKY / *Arthur Lewis Shamsky* (1941-)	OF, 1B	1965-72	CIN, NY (N), CHI (N), OAK	665	68	233	.253
DICK SHARON / *Richard Louis Sharon* (1950-)	OF	1973-75	DET, SD	242	13	46	.218
NORM SHERRY / *Norman Burt Sherry* (1931-)	C	1959-63	LA (N), NY (N)	194	18	69	.215
AL SILVERA / *Aaron Albert Silvera* (1935-)	OF	1955-56	CIN	14	0	2	.143
MIKE SIMON / *Michael Edward Simon* (1883-1963)	C	1909-15	PIT, STL (F), BKN (F)	378	1	90	.225
FRED SINGTON / *Frederick William Sington* (1910-)	OF	1934-39	WASH, BKN	181	7	85	.271
BROADWAY ALECK SMITH / .... *Alexander Benjamin Smith* (1871-1919)	C, OF	1897-1904, 06	BKN, BAL (N), BKN, NY (N), BAL (A), BOS (A), CHI (N), NY (N)	290	1	130	.263
MOE SOLOMON / *.Moses H. Solomon* (1900-1966)	OF	1923	NY (N)	2	0	1	.375
CHICK STARR / *William Starr* (1911-)	C	1935-36	WASH	13	0	1	.208

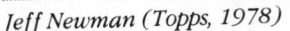

Jeff Newman (Topps, 1978)

Al Rosen.

Art Shamsky

George Stone

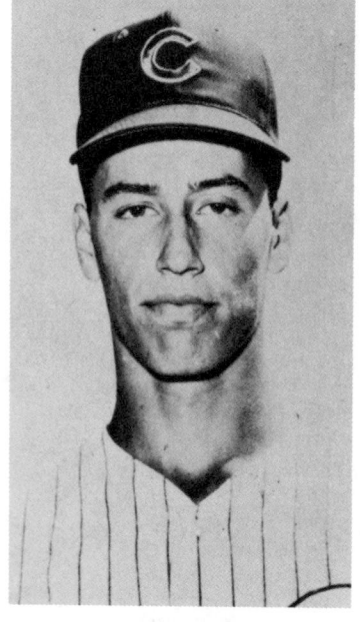

Ken Holtzman

Sandy Koufax

	Position	Years	Teams	Games	HR	RBI	BA
DAN STEARNS / *William Eckford Stearns* (1861-1944)......1B		1880-85, 89	BUF (N), DET (N), CIN (AA), BAL (AA), BUF (N), KC (AA)	509	7	109	.242
BEN STEINER / *Benjamin Saunders Steiner* (1921-) 2B		1945-47	BOS (A), DET	82	3	20	.256
GEORGE STONE (1876-1945).........................OF		1903, 05-10	BOS (A), STL (A)	848	23	268	.301
JOE STRAUSS / *Joseph Strauss* (?-?) ....OF		1884-86	KC (U), LOU (AA), BKN (AA)	101	1	?	.216
DON TAUSSIG / *Donald Franklin Taussig* (1932-).......OF		1958, 61-62	SF, STL (N), HOU	153	4	30	.262
EDDIE TURCHIN / *Edward Lawrence Turchin* (1917-)...3B, SS		1943	CLE	11	0	1	.231
PHIL WEINTRAUB / *Philip (Mickey) Weintraub* (1907-)..1B, OF		1933-35, 37-38, 44-45	NY (N), CIN, NY (N), PHI (N), NY (N)	444	32	207	.295

PITCHER REGISTER

	Years	Teams	Games	W	L	Pct.	ERA
LLOYD ALLEN / *Lloyd Cecil Allen* (1950-) 1969-75		CAL, TEX, CHI (A)	159	8	25	.242	4.70
ROSS BAUMGARTEN (1955-) 1978-82		CHI (A), PIT	90	22	36	.379	3.99
BO BELINSKY / *Robert Belinsky* (1936-) 1962-67, 69-70		LA (A), PHI (N), HOU, PIT, CIN	146	28	51	.354	4.10
CONRAD CARDINAL / *Conrad Seth Cardinal* (1942- 1963		HOU	6	0	1	.000	6.08
HY COHEN / *Hyman Cohen* (1931-)................1955		CHI (N)	7	0	0	—	7.94
SID COHEN / *Sydney Harry Cohen* (1908-) 1934, 36-37		WASH	55	3	7	.300	4.54
DICK CONGER / *Richard Conger* (1921-1970)..........1940-43		DET, PIT, PHI (N)	19	3	7	.300	5.14
MOE DRABOWSKY / *Myron Walter Drabowsky* (193?.....1956-72		CHI (N), MIL, CIN, KC, BAL, KC, BAL, STL, CHI (A)	589	88	105	.456	3.71
HARRY EISENSTAT (1915-)........................1935-42		BKN, DET, CLE	165	25	27	.481	3.84
HARRY FELDMAN (1919-1962).......................1941-46		NY (N)	143	35	35	.500	3.80
JULIE FREEMAN / *Julius B. Freeman* (1869-?) 1888		STL (AA)	1	0	1	.000	4.26
IZZY GOLDSTEIN / *Isadore Goldstein* (1908-) 1932		DET	16	3	2	.600	4.47
KEN HOLTZMAN / *Kenneth Dale Holtzman* (1945- 1965-79		CHI (N), OAK, BAL, NY (A), CHI (N)	451	174	150	.537	3.49
HAM IBURG / *Herman Edward Iburg* (1878-1945) 1902		PHI (N)	30	11	18	.379	3.89
HARRY KANE / *Harry Cohen "Klondike"* (1883-1932).....1902-03, 05-06		STL (A), DET, PHI (N)	15	2	7	.222	4.81
HERB KARPEL / *Herbert Karpel "Lefty"* (1917-) 1946		NY (A)	2	0	0	—	10.80
BOB KATZ / *Robert Clyde Katz* (1911-1962)............1944		CIN	6	0	1	.000	3.93

	Years	Teams	Games	W	L	Pct.	ERA
BILL KLING / *William Kling* (1867-1934)	1891-92, 95	PHI (N), BAL (N), LOU	15	4	4	.500	5.17
ALAN KOCH / *Alan Goodman Koch* (1938-)	1963-64	DET, WASH	42	4	11	.267	5.41
HOWIE KOPLITZ / *Howard Dean Koplitz* (1938-)	1961-62, 64-66	DET, WASH	54	9	7	.563	4.21
SANDY KOUFAX / *Sanford (Braun) Koufax* (1935-) ... Hall of Fame, 1971	1955-1966	BKN, LA (N)	397	165	87	.655	2.76
BARRY LATMAN / *Arnold Barry Latman* (1936-)	1957-67	CHI (A), CLE, LA (A), CAL, HOU	344	59	68	.465	3.91
DUKE MARKELL / *Harry Duquesne Makowsky* (1923-1984)	1951	STL (A)	5	1	1	.500	6.33
ED MAYER / *Edwin David Mayer* (1931-)	1957-58	CHI (N)	22	2	2	.500	4.31
ERSKINE MAYER / *James Erskine* (1891-1957)	1912-19	PHI (N), PIT, CHI (A)	245	91	70	.565	2.96
SAM MAYER / *Samuel Frankel Erskine* (1893-1962).......	1915	WASH	1	0	0	—	0.00
SAM NAHEM / *Samuel Ralph Nahem* (1915-)	1938, 41-42, 48	BKN, STL (N), PHI (N)	90	10	8	.556	4.69
BARNEY PELTY (1880-1939)	1903-12	STL (A), WASH	266	91	117	.438	2.62
STEVE RATZER / *Stephen Wayne Ratzer* (1953-)	1980-81	MON	13	1	1	.500	7.29
ED REULBACH / *Edward Marvin Reulbach* (1882-1961)...	1905-17	CHI (N), BKN, NWK (F), BOS (N)	399	185	104	.640	2.28
DAVE ROBERTS / *David Arthur Roberts* (1944-)........	1969-81	SD, HOU, DET, CHI (N), SF, PIT, SEA, NY (N)	445	103	125	.452	3.78
SAUL ROGOVIN / *Saul Walter Rogovin* (1922-)........	1949-57	DET, CHI (A), BAL, PHI (N)	150	48	48	.500	4.06
CHIEF ROSEMAN / *James J. Roseman* (1856-?)..........	1885-87	NY (AA), BKN (AA)	4	0	1	.000	7.88
MARV ROTBLATT / *Marvin Joseph Rotblatt* (1927-)	1948, 50-51	CHI (A)	35	4	3	.571	4.82
LARRY ROTHSCHILD / *Lawrence Lee Rothschild* (1954-) .	1981-82	DET	7	0	0	—	5.19
MOE SAVRANSKY / *Morris Savransky* (1929-)..........	1954	CIN	16	0	2	.000	4.88
AL SCHACHT / *Alexander Schacht* (1892-1984)	1919-21	WASH	53	14	10	.583	4.48
SID SCHACHT / *Sidney Schacht* (1918-)	1950-51	STL (A), BOS (N)	19	0	2	.000	14.34
LARRY SHERRY / *Lawrence Sherry* (1935-)	1958-1968	LA (N), DET, HOU, CAL	416	53	44	.546	3.67
HARRY SHUMAN (1916-)..........................	1942-44	PIT, PHI (N)	30	0	0	—	4.44
STEVE STONE / *Steven Michael Stone* (1947-)	1971-81	SF, CHI (A), CHI (N), CHI (A), BAL	320	107	93	.535	3.97
BUD SWARTZ / *Sherwin Merle Swartz* (1929-)	1947	STL (A)	5	0	0	—	6.75
ED WINEAPPLE / *Edward Wineapple "Lefty"* (1906-) ...	1929	WASH	1	0	0	—	4.50
RALPH WINEGARNER (1909-)......................	1932, 34-36, 49	CLE, STL (A)	70	8	6	.571	5.33
MELLIE WOLFGANG / *Meldon John Wolfgang* (1890-1947)	1914-18	CHI (A)	77	14	14	.500	2.18
LARRY YELLEN / *Lawrence Alan Yellen* (1943-)	1963-64	HOU	14	0	0	—	6.23

Erskine Mayer

Ed Reulbach

Al Schacht

MANAGERS

	Team/League	Years	Games	W	L	Pct.	Standing
ANDY COHEN / *Andrew Howard Cohen* . . . Philadelphia (N) (1904-)		1960	1	1	0	1.000	8
BENJAMIN J. FINE . . . . St. Louis (N)		1885					last
JUDGE FUCHS / *Emil Edwin Fuchs* . . . . Boston (N) (1878-1961)		1929	154	56	98	.364	8
LOUIE HEILBRONER (1861-1933) . . . . St. Louis (N)		1900	38	17	20	.459	5
JOHNNY KLING / *John Gradwohl Kling* . . . . Boston (N) (1875-1947)		1912	153	52	101	.340	8
JAKE MORSE (1860-1937) . . . . Boston (U)		1884	75	46	28	.622	5
BILLY NASH / *William Mitchell Nash* . . . . . . Philadelphia (N) (1865-1929)		1896	131	62	68	.477	8
LEFTY PHILLIPS / *Harold Ross Phillips* . . . . . California (A) (1919-1972)		1969	124	60	63	.488	6
		1970	162	86	76	.531	3
		1971	162	76	86	.469	4
			448	222	225	.497	
LIP PIKE / *Lipman Emanuel Pike* . . . . Cincinnati (N) (1845-1893)		1877	14	3	11	.214	6
CHIEF ROSEMAN / *James J. Roseman* . . . . . St. Louis (AA) (1856- ?)		1890	51	32	19	.627	4
NORM SHERRY / *Norman Burt Sherry* . . . . . California (A) (1931-)		1976	66	37	29	.561	4
		1977	81	39	42	.481	5
			147	76	71	.517	

69

Jews in Basketball

Haskell Cohen

ALL-AMERICA JEWISH COLLEGE BASKETBALL PLAYERS

Year	Player	College	Year	Player	College
1908	Ira Streusand	CCNY	1936	William Fleishman	Western Reserve
1909	Samuel Melitzer	Columbia	1937	Jules Bender	LIU
1916-17	Cyril Haas	Princeton	1937	Marvin Colen	Loyola (Ill.)
1918-19	Leon (Bob) Marcus	Syracuse	1938	Meyer (Mike) Bloom	Temple
1920-21	Maclyn (Mac) Baker	NYU	1938	Bernard Fliegel	CCNY
1922	Louis Farer	CCNY	1938-39	Irving Torgoff	LIU
1923	Samuel Pite	Yale	1939	Bernard Opper	Kentucky
1925-26	Emanuel (Menchy) Goldblatt	Pennsylvania	1939	Robert Lewis	NYU
1925	Pincus (Pinky) Match	CCNY	1939	John Bromberg	LIU
1926	Carl Loeb	Princeton	1939	Daniel Kaplowitz	LIU
1926	William (Red) Laub	Columbia	1939	Jack (Dutch) Garfinkel	St. John's (NY)
1929	Edward Wineapple	Providence	1940	Louis Possner	De Paul
1930	Max (Mac) Kinsbrunner	St. John's (NY)	1941	Oscar (Ossie) Schectman	LIU
1930, 32	Louis Bender	Columbia	1941	Moe Becker	Duquesne
1931	Max (Mack) Posnack	St. John's (NY)	1942	William (Red) Holzman	CCNY
1931	Louis Hayman	Syracuse	1943, 46	Harry Boykoff	St. John's (NY)
1932	Moe Spahn	CCNY	1943	Jerry Fleishman	NYU
1933	Jerry Nemer	Southern California	1944-45	Hyman (Hy) Gotkin	St. John's (NY)
1933	Nathan Lazar	St. John's (NY)	1946-47	Sid Tanenbaum	NYU
1934	Moe Goldman	CCNY	1946	Jackie Goldsmith	LIU
1936	Herbert Bonn	Duquesne	1948	Don Forman	NYU
1936	Milton Schulman	NYU	1948	Adolph Schayes	NYU
1936	Ben Kramer	LIU	1950	Irwin Dambrot	CCNY

Red Auerbach

Max Friedman

Eddie Gottlieb

Art Heyman

Nat Holman

Maurice Podoloff

Year	Player	College	Year	Player	College
1953	Irving Bemoras	Illinois	1963-64	Barry Kramer	NYU
1955-57	Leonard Rosenbluth	North Carolina	1964	Robert (Rick) Kaminsky	Yale
1957	Larry Friend	California	1965	Talbot (Tal) Brody	Illinois
1958-59	Alan Seiden	St. John's (NY)	1966	Dave Newmark	Columbia
1959	Don Goldstein	Louisville	1968-69	Neal Walk	Florida
1960-61	Jeff Cohen	William & Mary	1976-77	Ernest (Ernie) Grunfeld	Tennessee
1961	Howard Carl	De Paul	1978-80	Nancy Lieberman	Old Dominion
1961-63	Art Heyman	Duke	1981	Danny Schayes	Syracuse

JEWS IN PROFESSIONAL BASKETBALL

Player	Teams	Player	Teams
RED AUERBACH (1917-)	Boston Celtics (headcoach, gm)	LEO FISCHER (1897-1970)	President, National Basketball League
HERSHEL BALTIMORE	St. Louis Bombers		
DAVID "PRETZEL" BANKS (1901-1952)	Original Celtics	JEROME FLEISHMAN (1922-)	Philadelphia Warriors
MOE BECKER (1917-)	Baltimore, Pittsburgh, Boston, Detroit, etc.	DONALD J. FORMAN (1926-)	Minneapolis Lakers
		PHIL FOX	NBA referee
IRV BEMORAS	Milwaukee Hawks	NAT FRANKEL	Pittsburgh Ironmen
JULES BENDER (1914-)	Baltimore, etc.	MAX "MARTY" FRIEDMAN (1889-?)	New York Whirlwinds
LOUIS BENDER (1910-)		LAWRENCE FRIEND (1935-)	New York Knicks
BEN BERGER	Minneapolis Lakers (president)	JACK GARFINKEL (1920-)	Rochester Royals, Boston Celtics
MARK BINSTEIN	coach	EMANUEL GOLDBLATT (1904-)	
MIKE BLOOM	Baltimore Bullets	BEN GOLDFADEN	Washington Capitols
NELSON BOBB	Philadelphia Warriors	MOE GOLDMAN (1913-)	Philadelphia Sphas
HARRY BOYKOFF (1922-)	Boston Celtics, etc.	EDWARD B. GOTTLIEB (1898-1979)	Founder, NBA
TALBERT "TAL" BRODY (1943-)	Baltimore (draft only)		Philadelphia Warriors (owner and headcoach)
LARRY BROWN (1940-)	New Orleans, Oakland, Washington, Virginia, Denver, Carolina, Denver, New Jersey (as headcoach)	LEO GOTTLIEB	New York Knicks
		NORMAN GREKIN (1930-)	Philadelphia Warriors
		ERNIE GRUNFELD (1955-)	Milwaukee, Kansas City, New York
PHIL BROWNSTEIN	Chicago Stags (coach)		
NORMAN DRUCKER	NBA referee	LES HARRISON	Rochester Royals (coach)
LOU EISENSTEIN	NBA referee	ARNOLD HEFT	NBA referee; part owner Baltimore Bullets
PHIL FARBMAN	Philadelphia Warriors		
GEORGE FEIGENBAUM (1929-)	Baltimore, Milwaukee	SONNY HERTZBERG (1922-)	New York, Washington, Boston

Player	Teams	Player	Teams
ARTHUR HEYMAN (1941-)	New York, San Francisco, New Jersey, Pittsburgh, Minnesota, Miami	MAURICE PODOLOFF (1890-)	NBA Commissioner
		IRWIN RAIKEN	New York Knicks
		ALEXANDER ROSENBERG	Philadelphia Warriors
MEL HIRSCH (1921-)	Boston Celtics	LEONARD ROSENBLUTH (1933-)	Philadelphia Warriors
NAT HOLMAN (1896-)	New York Whirlwinds, Original Celtics	HENRY ROSENSTEIN	New York Knicks
		IRVING ROTHENBERG	Cleveland Rebels, Baltimore Bullets
RED HOLZMAN (1920-)	Rochester Royals, Milwaukee, St. Louis, New York (headcoach)	MARVIN ROTTNER	Chicago Stags
		MENDY RUDOLPH (1928-1979)	NBA referee
RALPH KAPLOWITZ (1920-)	Philadelphia, New York	ABE SAPERSTEIN (1901-1966)	creator and coach, Harlem Globetrotters
BEN KERNER (1917-)	owner, St. Louis Hawks		
HERMAN KLOTZ (1921-)	Baltimore Bullets	MARVIN SCHATZMAN	Syracuse Nationals
BARRY KRAMER (1942-)	New York (NBA & ABA), San Francisco	ADOLPH SCHAYES (1928-)	Syracuse, Philadelphia; Philadelphia, Buffalo (headcoach)
BENJAMIN KRAMER (1913-)	various teams; Baltimore (headcoach)		
		DAN SCHAYES (1959-)	Utah, Denver
JOEL KRAMER (1955-)	Phoenix Suns	OSSIE SCHECTMAN	New York Knicks
HERB KRAUTBLATT	Baltimore Bullets	BARNEY SEDRAN (1891-1969)	New York Whirlwinds
RUDY LARUSSO (1937-)	Minneapolis, Los Angeles Lakers	ARTHUR SPECTOR (1920-)	Boston Celtics
		LOUIS L. SUGARMAN (1890-1951)	
HENRY LEFKOWITZ	Cleveland Rebels	SIDNEY H. TANENBAUM (1925-)	New York, Baltimore
BARRY LEIBOWITZ	New Jersey, Pittsburgh	DAVID TOBEY (1898-)	
HARRY LITWACK (1907-)	Philadelphia (coach)	IRVING TORGOFF	Washington Capitols, Baltimore, Philadelphia
LIONEL MALAMED (1924-)	Indianapolis Jets		
JULIE MEYER	NBA referee	NEAL WALK (1948-)	Phoenix, New York
NATHAN MILITZOK	New York Knicks	RON WATTS	Boston Celtics
BORIS NACHAMKIN	Rochester Royals	GEORGE WOLFE (1905-1970)	Philadelphia Sphas
DAVE NEWMARK (1946-)	Atlanta Hawks	MAX ZASLOFSKY (1925-)	Chicago, New York, Baltimore, Milwaukee, Ft. Wayne
BERNARD OPPER (1918-)	Detroit, etc.		

Abe Saperstein

Dolph Schayes

Barney Sedran

70

Jews in Football

Haskell Cohen

ALL-AMERICA JEWISH COLLEGE FOOTBALL PLAYERS

Year	Player	College	Year	Player	College
1891-93	Phil King—Quarterback	Princeton	1932-33	Aaron Rosenberg—Guard	USC
1903-4	Sig Harris—Quarterback	Minnesota	1934	Isadore Weinstock—Fullback	Pittsburgh
1905-6	Israel Levene—End	Pennsylvania	1934	Dave Smukler—Fullback	Temple
1909-10	Joe Magidsohn—Halfback	Michigan	1937-38	Marshall Goldberg—Halfback, Fullback	Pittsburgh
1911-12	Arthur Bluethenthal—Center	Princeton	1937	Leroy Monsky—Guard	Alabama
1911	Leonard Frank—Tackle	Minnesota	1937-38	Sid Luckman—Halfback	Columbia
1911	Harry Kallet—End	Syracuse	1938	Sid Roth—Guard	Cornell
1918-20	Joe Alexander—Guard, Center	Syracuse	1943	Mervin Pregulman—Tackle, Guard	Michigan
1918	Victor Frank—Guard	Pennsylvania	1943	William Stein—Quarterback	Georgia Tech
1920	Arnold Horween—Fullback	Harvard	1944	Maurice Furchgott—Guard	Georgia Tech
1922	Max Kadesky—End	Iowa	1946	Hyman Harris—End	Oregon
1924	George Abramson—Guard	Minnesota	1947	Dan Dworsky—Center, Linebacker	Michigan
1925-26	Benny Friedman—Quarterback	Michigan	1950	Bernard Lemonick—Guard	Pennsylvania
1925	Milton Levy—Guard	Tulane	1952	Myron Berliner—End	UCLA
1927	Ray Baer—Guard	Michigan	1958	Alan Goldstein—End	No. Carolina
1927-29	Benny Lom—Halfback	California	1959	Ron Mix—Tackle	USC
1929	Louis Gordon—Tackle	Illinois	1967	Richard Stotter—Guard	Houston
1929	Louis Gordon—Lineman	Illinois	1967-68	Bob Stein—Defensive End	Minnesota
1929-30	Fred Sington—Tackle	Alabama	1971	Gary Wichard—Quarterback	C.W. Post
1930	Gabe Bromberg—Guard	Dartmouth	1973	Randy Grossman—Tight End	Temple
1931	John Grossman—Backfield	Rutgers	1978	Dave Jacobs—Placekicker	Syracuse
1932	Harry Newman—Quarterback	Michigan	1984	John Frank—Tight End	Ohio
1932	Franklin Meadow—End	Brown			

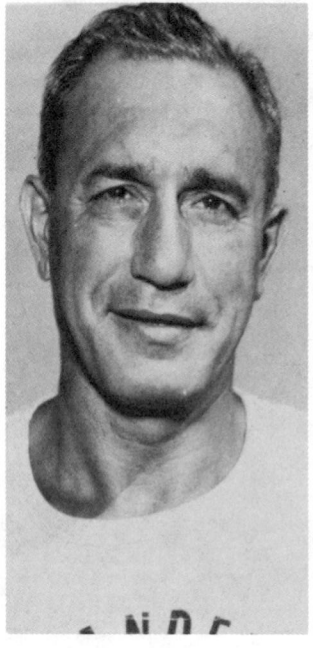

Benny Friedman

Aaron Rosenberg

Randy Grossman

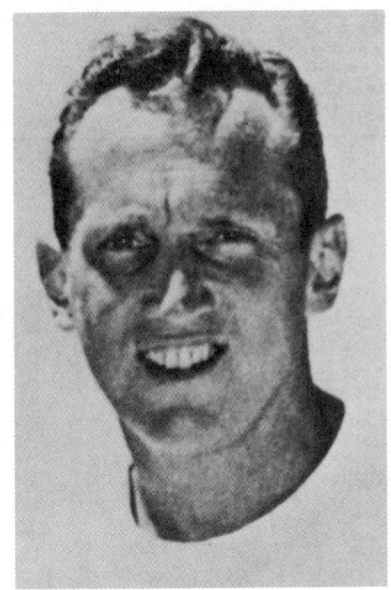
Al Davis

Sid Gillman

Marshall Goldberg

JEWS IN PROFESSIONAL FOOTBALL

	Position	Teams
GEORGE ABRAMSON (1903-)	guard	Green Bay Packers
JOSEPH A. ALEXANDER (1898-1975)	lineman, guard	New York Giants
	headcoach	New York Giants
LYLE ALZADO (1949-)	end	Denver Broncos
JOHN BARSHA (1900-)		
MORRIS BODENGER (1909-)	guard	Detroit Lions
NORMAN CAHN (1892-1965)	referee	NFL
AL DAVIS (1929-)	coach, gm	Oakland, L.A. Raiders
	commissioner	AFL, 1966
SAM FOX (1924-)	end	New York Giants
BENNY FRIEDMAN (1905-1982)	quarterback	Cleveland Bulldogs, Detroit Wolverines, New York Giants, Brooklyn Dodgers
	headcoach	Brooklyn Dodgers
SIDNEY GILLMAN (1911-)	headcoach	L.A. Rams, San Diego Chargers, Houston Oilers
MARSHALL GOLDBERG (1917-)	running back	Chicago Cardinals
CHARLES R. "BUCKETS" GOLDENBERG (1911-)	lineman	Green Bay Packers
LOUIS J. GORDON (1908-)	tackle	Green Bay Packers, Chicago Cardinals, Brooklyn Dodgers, Chicago Bears
JEROME GREEN (1936-)	end	Boston Patriots
RANDY GROSSMAN (1952-)	tight end	Pittsburgh Steelers
PHILIP J. "MOTSY" HANDLER (1908-1968)	lineman	Chicago Cardinals
	coach	Chicago Cardinals, Chicago Bears
ARNOLD HORWEEN (1898-)	back	Chicago Cardinals
	headcoach	Chicago Cardinals
RALPH HORWEEN (1896-)	running back	Chicago Cardinals
EDWIN B. "KING KONG" KAHN (1911-1945)	guard	Boston Patriots, Wash. Redskins
MIKE KATZ (1939-)	guard	New York Jets
IRVING KUPCINET (1912-)	back	Philadelphia Eagles
MARVIN D. LEVY (1928-)	headcoach	Kansas City Chiefs

	Position	Teams
BENJAMIN F. LINDHEIMER (1890-1960)	commissioner	All-America Conference 1946-47
SAMUEL J. LIPP (1889-1958)	referee	NFL
SIDNEY LUCKMAN (1916-)	quarterback	Chicago Bears
JOSEPH MAGIDSOHN (1888-?)	referee	NFL
RONALD J. MIX (1938-)	offensive lineman	San Diego Chargers
SAUL MIELZINER (1905-)		
ARTHUR B. MODELL (1925-)	owner	Cleveland Browns
	president	NFL 1967-70
ED NEWMAN (1953-)	guard	Miami Dolphins
HARRY NEWMAN (1909-)	quarterback	New York Giants
RED PEARLMAN (1898-)		Steubenville, others
MERVIN PREGULMAN (1922-)	lineman, guard	Green Bay Packers, Detroit Lions, Canton Bulldogs
HERBERT RICH (1928-)		
DONALD ROGERS (1936-)	center	San Diego Chargers
CARROLL ROSENBLOOM (1908-1978)	owner	Baltimore Colts, Los Angeles Rams
LEONARD SACHS (1897-1942)		
JACK SACK (1902-)	guard	
HERMAN "BIFF" SCHNEIDMAN (1913-)	halfback	Green Bay Packers, Chicago Cardinals
ALEXANDER "ALLIE" SHERMAN (1923-)	quarterback	Philadelphia Eagles
	headcoach	New York Giants
DAVID SMUKLER (1914-)	fullback	Philadelphia Eagles, Detroit Lions, Boston Yankees
MICHAEL SOMMER (1936-)		
SAMUEL STEIN (1906-1966)		
WILLIAM STEIN (1924-)	referee	NFL
PAUL "TWISTER" STEINBERG (1880-?)	running back	Phildelphia, Syracuse, Canton
ABRAHAM B. WATNER (1891-1961)	executive	Baltimore Colts
SAMUEL A. WEISS (1902-)	referee	NFL
SIDNEY YOUNGELMAN (1933-)	tackle	S.F. 49ers, Phila. Eagles, Cleveland Browns, N.Y. Titans, Buffalo Bills

71

Jews in Boxing

Irving Rudd

RAY ARCEL (1899-)	trainer of 20 world champions
BOB ARUM (1931-)	promoter
ABRAHAM ATTELL/*Albert Knoehr* (1884-1969)	Featherweight, World Champion, 1901-12
MONTE ATTELL/*M. Knoehr* (1885-1960)	Bantamweight, U.S. Champion, 1909-10
JACOB "SOLDIER" BARTFIELD (1892-1970)	Middleweight
BENNY BASS (1904-1975)	Featherweight, World Champion, 1927-28; Junior Lightweight, World Champion, 1929-31
JOE BENJAMIN (1899-)	Lightweight
JACKIE BERG/*Judah Bergman* (1909-)	Junior Welterweight, World Champion, 1930-31
SAMUEL BERGER (1884-1925)	Olympic Heavyweight, Gold Medal 1904 (U.S.)
JACK BERNSTEIN/*John Dodick* (1899-1945)	Junior Lightweight, World Champion, 1923
JOE BERNSTEIN (1877-1931)	
HARRY BLITMAN (1908-)	Bantamweight
PHIL BLOOM (1894-)	Lightweight
NATHAN BOR (1913-1972)	Olympic Lightweight, Bronze Medal 1932 (U.S.)
NEWSBOY BROWN/*David Montrose* (1904-)	Bantamweight, Flyweight
MUSHY CALLAHAN/*Vicente M. Scheer* (1905-)	Junior Welterweight, World Champion, 1926-30
JOE CHOYNSKI (1869-1943)	Heavyweight
GILBERT COHEN	Light-Middleweight, European Champion, 1978
ROBERT COHEN (1930-)	Bantamweight, World Champion, 1954-56
LEACH CROSS/*Louis C. Wallach* (1886-1957)	Lightweight
HARRY DEVINE (1909-)	Olympic Featherweight, Bronze Medal 1928 (U.S.)
SAMUEL "DUTCH SAM" ELIAS (1776-1816)	English champion; credited with invention of the uppercut
JACKIE FIELDS/*Jacob Finkelstein* (1908-)	Olympic Featherweight, Gold Medal 1924 (U.S.) Welterweight, World Champion, 1929-30, 32-33
NAT FLEISCHER (1887-1972)	Boxing historian; Founder and Editor of *Ring* magazine; initiated boxing's rating system
CHARLEY GOLDMAN (1887-1968)	Flyweight; Bantamweight
ABE GOLDSTEIN (1900-)	Bantamweight, World Champion, 1924
RUBY GOLDSTEIN (1907-1984)	Lightweight, later a championship referee
ALPHONSE HALIMI (1932-)	Bantamweight, World Champion, 1957-59

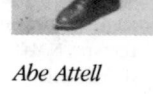

Abe Attell

Jackie Fields

Nat Fleischer

Benny Leonard

Daniel Mendoza

Maxie Rosenbloom

HARRY HARRIS (1880-1959)	Bantamweight, World Champion, 1901-02
SIG HART (1872-1963)	Bantamweight, later a leading manager
MONTGOMERY HERSCOVITZ	Olympic Middleweight, Gold Medal 1920 (Canada)
ABE "THE NEWSBOY" HOLLANDERSKY (1888-)	
HARRY ISAACS	Olympic Bantamweight, Bronze Medal 1928 (S. Africa)
WILLIE JACKSON/*Oscar Tobler* (1897-1961)	Lightweight
JOE JACOBS (1896-1940)	manager of Max Schmeling, others
MIKE JACOBS (1880-1953)	promoter
BEN JEBY/*Morris B. Jebaltowsky* (1907-)	Middleweight, World Champion, 1932-33
LOUIS "KID" KAPLAN (1902-1970)	Featherweight, World Champion, 1925-27
DANNY KRAMER (1900-)	Featherweight
SOLLY KRIEGER (1909-?)	Middleweight, World Champion, 1938-39
BENNY LEONARD/*Benjamin Leiner* (1896-1947)	Lightweight, World Champion, 1917-25
BATTLING LEVINSKY/*Barney Lebrowitz* (1891-1949)	Light-Heavyweight, World Champion, 1916-20
HARRY LEWIS (1886-1956)	Welterweight
TED LEWIS/*Gershon Mendeloff* (1894-1970)	Welterweight, World Champion, 1915, 1917-19
AL McCOY/*Al Rudolph* (1894-)	Middleweight, World Champion, 1914-17
HARRY MARKSON	promoter
DANIEL MENDOZA (1764-1836)	Heavyweight, World Champion (unofficial), 1792-95
RAY MILLER (1908-)	Lightweight; Welterweight
SAMUEL MOSBERG (1896-1967)	Olympic Lightweight, Gold Medal 1920 (U.S.)
HENRY NISSEN (1948-)	Flyweight, British Commonwealth Champion, 1971-74
BOB OLIN/*Robert Olinsky* (1908-1956)	Light-Heavyweight, World Champion, 1934-35
YOUNG PEREZ/*Victor Perez* (1911-1942)	Flyweight, World Champion, 1931-32
CHARLEY PHIL ROSENBERG/*Charles Green* (1902-1976)	Bantamweight, World Champion, 1925-27
DAVE ROSENBERG (1901-)	Welterweight, National AAU Champion, 1919
"SLAPSIE" MAXIE ROSENBLOOM (1904-1976)	Light-Heavyweight, World Champion, 1930-34
JOHNNY ROSNER (1895-)	Flyweight
BARNEY ROSS/*Barnet Rasofsky* (1909-1967)	Lightweight, World Champion, 1933-35; Junior Welterweight, World Champion, 1933-35; Welterweight, World Champion, 1934-38
MIKE ROSSMAN (1947-)	Light Heavyweight, World Champion, 1978-79
CORPORAL IZZY SCHWARTZ (1902-)	Flyweight, World Champion, 1927-29
AL SINGER (1907-1961)	Lightweight, World Champion, 1930
JACK SOLOMONS (1900-)	British promoter
LEW TENDLER (1898-?)	Lightweight, welterweight
SID TERRIS (1904-?)	Lightweight
MATT WELLS (1886-1953)	Lightweight and Welterweight Champion of Great Britain; Welterweight Champion of the British Empire
CHARLEY WHITE/*Charles Anschowitz* (1891-)	Lightweight
YOUNG OTTO/*Otto Susskind* (1886-1967)	Lightweight
YOUNG MONTREAL/*Morris Billingkoff* (1898-)	Flyweight

Ivan L. Tillem, Esq. was formerly associate general counsel of COLPA, the National Jewish Commission on Law and Public Affairs. An alumnus of Yeshiva University, ITRI and Sh'or Yoshuv Institute, he has written extensively on Jewish themes. A native of Far Rockaway, he practices law in New York and Boston.

Contributors

Dr. Philip D. Abramowitz is director of the New York Jewish Community Relations Council Task Force on Cults and Missionaries.

Charles R. Allen, Jr. is a prolific writer on the subject of anti-fascism. Formerly senior editor of *The Nation*, he is the author of *Heusinger of the Fourth Reich: The Step-by-Step Resurgence of the German General Staff*. His latest book is *From Hitler to Uncle Sam: How American Intelligence Used Accused Nazi War Criminals.*

American Jewish Congress.

American Zionist Federation.

Rabbi Dr. Marc D. Angel is rabbi of Congregation Shearith Israel (The Spanish-Portuguese Synagogue) in New York City. He is the author of *La America: The Sephardic Experience in the United States.*

Anti-Defamation League of B'nai B'rith.

Rhonda Barad is Director of Community Relations for the Simon Wiesenthal Center in New York.

Abraham J. Bayer is Director, International Commission, of the National Jewish Community Relations Advisory Council (NJCRAC).

Noah M. Bee has created weekly political cartoons for the Jewish Telegraphic Agency since 1959. In 1938, he held the first cartoon exhibit in Palestine under the sponsorship of the renowned Hebrew poet, Saul Tchernichowsky.

Shlomo Berger was born in Czechoslovakia and educated in this country at Shor Yoshuv Institute and the Kollel Gur Aryeh. He has taught courses on Jewish thought at Seton Hall University as well as other educational institutions in the Northeast.

Rabbi Dr. J. David Bleich is Rosh Yeshiva (Professor of Talmud) at Yeshiva University, and Professor of Law at the Benjamin N. Cardozo School of Law. He has written extensively on Jewish law and ethics.

Rabbi Abraham P. Bloch has been a practicing rabbi since 1937. He is the author of *The Biblical and Historical Background of the Jewish Holy Days* and *The Biblical and Historical Background of Jewish Customs and Ceremonies.* He also contributes a weekly column to *The Jewish Post and Opinion.*

B'nai B'rith International.

Aaron Breitbart is a senior researcher for the Simon Wiesenthal Center in Los Angeles.

Lillian N. Burg, a retired New York schoolteacher, lives in Los Angeles. She was the first president of the sisterhood of the Flatbush Park Jewish Center, where she organized and taught Hebrew school in the fledgling shul. Her interest in learning and research is never-ending.

Louis Burg, Esq. is a Los Angeles lawyer and private airplane pilot. He is a founder of the Flatbush Park Jewish Center. His interest in aviation and individual achievement resulted in *The First Stowaway.*

Central Bureau of Statistics, State of Israel.

The Coalition to Free Soviet Jews.

Haskell Cohen was public relations director of the National Basketball Association for 20 years. A two-term president of the U.S. Committee for Sports in Israel, two-term president of New York B'nai B'rith Sports Lodge and member of the Board of Trustees, U.S. Basketball Hall of Fame, he ghostwrote Joe Louis' *My Life Story.*

Rabbi Abraham Cooper has served as the Assistant Dean and Director of Outreach Programs of the Simon Wiesenthal Center, Los Angeles, since its inception in 1977.

Dr. George Eisen received his Ph.D. degree from the University of Maryland, and serves presently as a professor at the California State Polytechnic University at Pomona.

Encyclopaedia Judaica.

Facts on File.

Donald Feldstein is a community relations specialist.

Arnold Fine has been the editor of New York's *Jewish Press* since its inception. An educator with B.A. and M.A. degrees, he has taught on the elementary, jr. high school, high school and university levels, and has written on a wide range of subjects.

Leonard Fink, national director of public relations for Women's American ORT, was formerly director of public relations for the American Zionist Federation.

Ruth Frank is Director of the JWB Jewish Book Council.

Lester D. Friedman, Ph.D. lectures frequently on the cinematic view of Jews. He teaches film at Syracuse University and the humanities at SUNY Upstate Medical Center in Syracuse.

Jonathan Geffner is a member of the American Association of Professors of Yiddish. He lectures frequently on Yiddish language and literature.

Jane Gerber is Associate Professor of Jewish History at the Graduate School of the City University of New York and President of the Association for Jewish Studies. She is the author of *Jewish Society in Fez, Jews in Muslim Lands,* and *The Jewish People: Ethnographic Studies* and has served as Editor of *Shoah.*

Richard M. Goodman, M.D. is professor of human genetics at Sackler School of Medicine, Tel Aviv University and The Chaim Sheba Medical Center, Tel Hashomer, Israel.

David C. Gross, author and newspaper editor, has written and edited eight books of Jewish interest. His most recent was a 30-year update of the *Pictorial History of the Jewish People* by Nathan Ausubel.

Rachel Oestreicher Haspel is executive director of the Raoul Wallenberg Committee of the United States.

The Jerusalem Post.

Jewish Telegraphic Agency.

JWB Jewish Book Council.

Rabbi Benzion C. Kaganoff has for three decades been the rabbi of Congregation Ezras Israel in Chicago. He is the author of *A Dictionary of Jewish Names and Their History.*

Devorah Kleinbeast received her formal degrees at the Boston Museum School of Fine Arts. Having mastered New England, she returned to her native New York, where she currently resides and works.

Seymour Kleinman, Esq. is a senior partner with the New York law firm of Golenbock and Barell, and a nationally-known raconteur. His book, *The Bible According to the Nationally-Known Inquirer* is to be published shortly and he hopes 'longly' as well.

Dr. William Korey is Director of International Policy and Research, B'nai B'rith.

Dr. Norman Lamm, President of Yeshiva University, is a rabbi, philosopher, teacher, author and member of the United States Holocaust Memorial Council.

Rabbi Daniel Landes was ordained by the Rabbi Isaac Elchanan Theological Seminary, and receiving his M.A. from Yeshiva University. He is Assistant Professor of Talmud and Jewish Thought at YULA and Director of Research Projects at the Simon Wiesenthal Center. He is co-editor of the *Simon Wiesenthal Center Annual.*

Chaim J. Leibtag, manager of Goldheart Enterprises, earned his M.S.W. from Wurzweiler School of Social Work and was formerly assistant executive director of the Hartman YMHA in Far Rockaway, New York. He and his wife Sheila are parents of two children of Israel.

Israel E. Levine is Director of Communications for the American Jewish Congress.

Dr. Gerald Margolis is Director of the Simon Wiesenthal Center.

Martindale-Hubbell, Inc.

Isaac Elchanan Mozeson has taught at Yeshiva University and at Bramson ORT. He is the author of *The Watcher,* a collection of poetry.

National Foundation for Jewish Genetic Diseases.

National Jewish Community Relations Advisory Council (NJCRAC).

The New York Times.

Monty N. Penkower, Chairman of Touro College's History department, is author of *The Jews Were Expendable: Free World Diplomacy and the Holocaust* (University of Illinois Press, 1983) and *The Emergence of Zionist Thought* (Associated Faculty Press).

Dennis Prager was Director of the Brandeis-Bardin Institute in California from 1976 to 1983. He does political and social commentary nightly for KABC Radio in Los Angeles, and publishes his own national newsletter, *Ultimate Issues.*

Raoul Wallenberg Committee of the United States, in conjunction with the Anti-Defamation League of B'nai B'rith.

Aaron I. Reichel, Esq. is a rabbi, lawyer and editor. He serves as Attorney Editor for Prentice-Hall, Inc. He is the author of *The Maverick Rabbi,* the biography of Rabbi Herbert S. Goldstein.

Joseph L. Reichler, the preeminent baseball archivist, is a special assistant to the commissioner of baseball and is chairman of baseball's official records committee. His books include *The Baseball Encyclopedia* and *The Great All-Time Baseball Record Book.*

Shari Rosenfeld is Director of Media and Publications for the Coalition to Free Soviet Jews.

Fred Rosner, M.D. is Director, Department of Medicine, Long Island Jewish-Hillside Medical Center, and Professor of Medicine, School of Medicine, Health Services Center, State University of New York at Stony Brook. He is one of the world's leading authorities on Jewish bioethics.

Irving Rudd is Director of Publicity for Top Rank, Inc., the leading promoter of championship boxing matches.

Joan Samsen is Executive Director of the National Foundation for Jewish Genetic Diseases.

Arthur Schreiber.

Alan M. Schwartz is Assistant Director, Research Department of the Anti-Defamation League of B'nai B'rith.

Joseph Seigman is vice-president, West Coast region of the United States Committee Sports for Israel.

Franklin Sherman has been Tutor and Dean of Lutheran Students at Mansfield College, Oxford, England; a member of the Faculty of Theology of Oxford University; and Associate Professor, Professor of Christian Ethics, and Director of Graduate Studies at the Lutheran School of Theology in Chicago, where he is currently Dean of Faculty. His translation of Paul Tillich's book *Die Sozialistische Entscheidung (The Socialist Decision)* was published by Harper and Row in 1977.

The Simon Wiesenthal Center.

Howard Spielman, a graduate of Syracuse University, was formerly production director for the animated cartoon division at New York Institute of Technology in Westbury, N.Y.. He is the only cartoonist in the world to have had a continuous cartoon strip dealing with Jewish subject matter for over 20 years.

Marc D. Stern, Esq. is associate director, legal department of the American Jewish Congress.

Joseph Telushkin is an ordained rabbi and holds a Ph.D. in Jewish history from Columbia University. He is the former Education Director of the Brandeis-Bardin Institute. He now lives in Jerusalem, where he is a Jerusalem Fellow.

Nelly Toll was still a young child when the Nazis invaded her native city of Lw'ow, Poland. She is a painter and author of numerous articles and art reviews, and teaches art and lectures on art history.

Barry Weise is Director of the Ethiopia Desk of the National Jewish Community Relations Advisory Council (NJCRAC).

Elie Wiesel is Andrew W. Mellon Professor in the Humanities at Boston University. Among his many acclaimed books are *The Gates of the Forest* and most recently, *The Fifth Son.*

George Will is a columnist for *The Washington Post* and *Newsweek.*

Yaacov Salomon, Lipschutz & Co. are advocates and notaries with offices in Haifa and Tel Aviv.

Efraim Zuroff was Director of the Department for Overseas Activities at Yad Vashem and Assistant Editor of *Yad Vashem Studies* Vols. 10 and 11 (Hebrew and English editions). From 1978 to 1980, he was the first Director of the Simon Wiesenthal Center and a lecturer at Yeshiva University of Los Angeles. Currently, he is Israel Liaison to U.S. Department of Justice, Office of Special Investigations and correspondent for *Page One,* the Wiesenthal Center's national radio news program.

THE JEWISH DIRECTORY AND ALMANAC YELLOW PAGES

Corrections and additions are welcome for The 1987 Jewish Directory and Almanac. Rates for display advertising are described in our rate card. For a copy, write:
PACIFIC PRESS, DEPT. JD & A
501 FIFTH AVENUE, SUITE 2203
NEW YORK, NEW YORK 10017

The Jewish Directory and Almanac has attempted to verify the kashrut of all food products, manufacturers, and retailers listed herein; however, we cannot guarantee the kashrut of any listing.

TABLE OF CONTENTS

STATE AND PROVINCE CODES

AL	Alabama	HA	Hawaii	MN	Minnesota	NC	North Carolina	SK	Saskatchewan
AK	Alaska	IA	Iowa	MO	Missouri	ND	North Dakota	TN	Tennessee
AR	Arkansas	ID	Idaho	MS	Mississippi	OH	Ohio	TX	Texas
AT	Alberta	IL	Illinois	MT	Montana	OK	Oklahoma	UT	Utah
AZ	Arizona	IN	Indiana	NB	New Brunswick	ON	Ontario	VA	Virginia
BC	British Columbia	KS	Kansas	NE	Nebraska	OR	Oregon	VI	Virgin Islands
CA	California	KY	Kentucky	NF	Newfoundland	PA	Pennsylvania	VT	Vermont
CO	Colorado	LA	Louisiana	NH	New Hampshire	PR	Puerto Rico	WA	Washington
CT	Connecticut	MA	Massachusetts	NJ	New Jersey	PZ	Panama Canal Zone	WI	Wisconsin
DC	District of Columbia	MB	Manitoba	NM	New Mexico	QU	Quebec	WV	West Virginia
DE	Delaware	MD	Maryland	NS	Nova Scotia	RI	Rhode Island	WY	Wyoming
FL	Florida	ME	Maine	NV	Nevada	SC	South Carolina		
GA	Georgia	MI	Michigan	NY	New York	SD	South Dakota	IS	Israel

ADVERTISING AGENCIES

ALEF BES MEDIA GROUP P.O. BOX 96	BROOKLYN NY	11204	(718) 998-3201
BRENNER TRADE CONSULTATION & MEDIA SERVICE P.O. BOX 10	BROOKLYN NY	11230	(718) 339-4256
GOLDMARK GROUP, THE 6 WEST 18TH STREET	NEW YORK NY	10011	(212) 691-7111
J.J. GROSS & CO. 11 WEST 25TH STREET	NEW YORK NY	10010	(212) 989-9600
JERUSALEM POST ADVERTISING AGENCY, THE 120 E. 56TH STREET	NEW YORK NY	10022	(212) 355-4440
JOSEPH JACOBS ORGANIZATION, INC. 60 EAST 42ND STREET	NEW YORK NY	10165	(212) 687-6234
MARK WEISZ CORP. 175 FIFTH AVENUE	NEW YORK NY	10010	(212) 254-5170
NORMARK/NORTHEAST MARKETS INC. - JEWISH DIVISION			
110 WEST 34TH STREET	NEW YORK NY	10001	(212) 714-2935
DAUPHIN HARRIS ADVERTISING BOX 142	PORT ROYAL PA	17082	(717) 436-8916
JEWISH MARKET SERVICE 8050 N. PORT WASHINGTON	MILWAUKEE WI	53217	(800) 558-6908

AIRLINES TO ISRAEL

EL AL 1225 CONNECTICUT AVENUE N.W.	WASHINGTON DC	20036	(202) 296-5440
EL AL 407 LINCOLN ROAD, SUITE 4B	MIAMI BEACH FL	33139	(305) 532-5441
EL AL 174 NORTH MICHIGAN AVENUE, RM. 310	CHICAGO IL	60601	(312) 236-7264
EL AL 20 PARK PLAZA	BOSTON MA	02116	(617) 267-9220
EL AL:CARGO EXPORT JFK INT'L AIRPORT	JAMAICA NY	11430	(718) 656-2931
EL AL:CARGO IMPORT JFK INT'L AIRPORT	JAMAICA NY	11430	(718) 656-2921
EL AL:FLIGHT ARRIVAL INFORMATION JFK INT'L AIRPORT	JAMAICA NY	11430	(718) 656-7750
EL AL:PASSENGER SERVICE JFK INT'L AIRPORT	JAMAICA NY	11430	(718) 656-2900
EL AL JFK INTERNATIONAL AIRPORT	JAMAICA NY	11430	(718) 656-2900
AIR FRANCE 666 FIFTH AVENUE	NEW YORK NY	10019	(212) 247-0100
ALITALIA 666 FIFTH AVENUE	NEW YORK NY	10019	(212) 582-8900
ARISTA AIRLINES 1 EAST 42ND STREET	NEW YORK NY	10017	(212) 599-4455
ARKIA 350 FIFTH AVENUE	NEW YORK NY	10167	(212) 695-2998
ARKIA ISRAELI AIRLINES 350 FIFTH AVENUE	NEW YORK NY	10118	(212) 695-2998
AUSTRIAN AIRLINES 608 FIFTH AVENUE	NEW YORK NY	10019	(212) 307-6226
BRITISH AIRWAYS 245 PARK AVENUE	NEW YORK NY	10167	(212) 878-4500
EL AL:CARGO SALES 850 3RD AVENUE	NEW YORK NY	10022	(212) 940-0703
EL AL:INSURANCE & CLAIMS 850 3RD AVENUE	NEW YORK NY	10010	(212) 940-0634
EL AL RESERVATIONS & INFORMATION	NEW YORK NY		(212) 486-2600
EL AL TOLL FREE RESERVATIONS	NEW YORK NY		(800) 223-6700
EL AL ISRAEL AIRLINES 850 THIRD AVENUE	NEW YORK NY	10022	(212) 486-2600
EL AL - MAIN OFFICE 850 3RD AVENUE	NEW YORK NY	10022	(212) 486-2600
EL AL:N.Y. DISTRICT SALES OFFICES 850 3RD AVENUE	NEW YORK NY	10022	(212) 940-0708
IBERIAN AIRLINES OF SPAIN 565 FIFTH AVENUE	NEW YORK NY	11130	(212) 793-3300
KLM 437 MADISON AVENUE	NEW YORK NY	10022	(212) 759-3600
LUFTHANSA GERMAN AIRLINES 680 FIFTH AVENUE	NEW YORK NY	10022	(212) 397-9250
METRO INTERNATIONAL 90 PARK AVENUE	NEW YORK NY	10016	(212) 953-6400
OLYMPIC AIRWAYS 647 FIFTH AVENUE	NEW YORK NY	10022	(212) 838-3600
SAS SCANDINAVIAN AIRLINES 630 FIFTH AVENUE	NEW YORK NY	10111	(212) 841-0100
SABENA BELGIAN WORLD AIRLINES 720 FIFTH AVENUE	NEW YORK NY	10019	(212) 961-6200
SWISSAIR 608 FIFTH AVENUE	NEW YORK NY	10019	(212) 995-8400
TWA 605 THIRD AVENUE	NEW YORK NY	10016	(212) 290-2121
TAROM ROMANIAN AIR 200 EAST 38TH STREET	NEW YORK NY	10016	(212) 687-6013
TOWER AIR			(718) 917-8500
TOWER AIR			(800) 221-2500
EL AL 3 PENN CENTER, SUITE 922	PHILADELPHIA PA	19102	(215) 563-8011
EL AL 555 DORCHESTER BOULEVARD WEST	MONTREAL QU		(514) 875-8900
EL AL PASEO DE LA REFORMA	MEXICO CITY,DF		(905) 535-5617
EL AL 151 BLOOR STREET WEST, SUITE 860	TORONTO		(416) 864-9779

ALIYAH ORGANIZATIONS

ISRAEL ALIYAH CENTER 950 WEST 41ST AVENUE	VANCOUVER BC	V5Z 2N7	(604) 266-5366
ISRAEL ALIYAH CENTER 6505 WILSHIRE BLVD	LOS ANGELES CA	90048	(213) 655-7881
ISRAEL ALIYAH CENTER 870 MARKET STREET, SUITE 1083	SAN FRANCISCO CA	94102	(415) 392-8998
JEWISH COMMUNITY CENTER 4800 ALAMEDA AVE. P.O. BOX 6196 (80206)	DENVER CO	80206	(303) 399-2660
ISRAEL ALIYAH CENTER 4200 BISCAYNE BLVD	MIAMI FL	33137	(305) 573-2556
HADASSAH ZIONIST YOUTH COMMITTEE			
1655 PEACHTREE STREET NORTHEAST, SUITE 904	ATLANTA GA	30309	(404) 876-1554
ISRAEL ALIYAH CENTER 205 WEST WACKER DRIVE, ROOM 516	CHICAGO IL	60606	(312) 332-2709

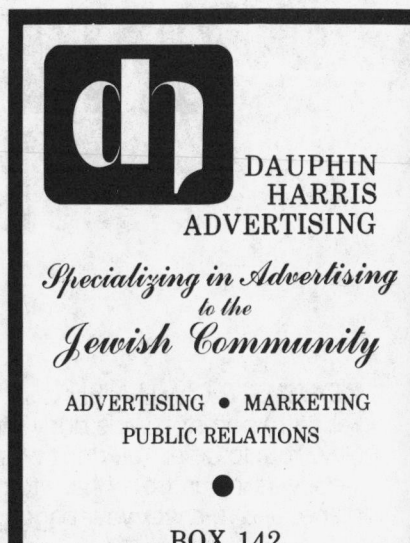

ISRAEL ALIYAH CENTER			
31 ST. JAMES AVENUE, PARK SQUARE BLDG., SUITE 450	BOSTON MA	02116	(617) 423-0868
ISRAEL ALIYAH CENTER 8730 GEORGIA AVENUE	SILVER SPRING MD	20910	(301) 589-6136
JEWISH COMMUNITY CENTER 6600 WEST MAPLE	WEST BLOOMFIELD MI	48033	(313) 661-1084
JEWISH COMMUNITY CENTER 4330 CEDAR LAKE ROAD SOUTH	MINNEAPOLIS MN	55416	(612) 377-8330
ISRAEL PROGRAM CENTER 760 NORTHFIELD AVENUE	WEST ORANGE NJ	07052	(201) 736-3200
ISRAEL ALIYAH CENTER 1416 AVENUE M	BROOKLYN NY	11230	(718) 336-1215
ISRAEL ALIYAH CENTER, MAIN OFFICE 515 PARK AVENUE	NEW YORK NY	10022	(212) 752-0600
KIBBUTZ ALIYAH DESK 27 WEST 20TH STREET	NEW YORK NY	10011	(212) 255-1338
NORTH AMERICAN ALIYAH MOVEMENT 515 PARK AVENUE	NEW YORK NY	10022	(212) 752-0600
ORTHODOX UNION ALIYAH DEPT., RABBI SHMUEL HIMELSTEIN			
45 W. 36TH STREET	NEW YORK NY	10018	(212) 563-4000
JEWISH COMMUNITY CENTER 1200 EDGEWOOD AVENUE	ROCHESTER NY	14618	(716) 461-2000
ISRAEL ALIYAH CENTER 13967 CEDAR ROAD, SUITE 201	CLEVELAND OH	44118	(216) 321-0757
ISRAEL ALIYAH CENTER 1110 FINCH AVENUE WEST, SUITE 700	DOWNSVIEW ON	M3J 2T2	(416) 665-7772
ISRAEL ALIYAH CENTER 225 S. 15TH STREET, SUITE 2528	PHILADELPHIA PA	19102	(215) 546-2088
ISRAEL ALIYAH CENTER 1310 GREENE AVENUE	MONTREAL QU	H3Z 2B2	(514) 934-0804
JEWISH COMMUNITY CENTER 6560 POPLAR AVENUE	MEMPHIS TN	38138	(901) 761-0810
ISRAEL ALIYAH CENTER 6420 HILLCROFT, SUITE 403	HOUSTON TX	77081	(713) 778-0643
JEWISH COMMUNITY CENTER 1400 NORTH PROSPECT AVENUE	MILWAUKEE WI	53202	(414) 276-0716

ANTIQUES & ANTIQUE JUDAICA

HERMAN BERMAN COMPANY 1025 N. VERMONT	LOS ANGELES CA	90029	(213) 666-6161
LEWIS A. SHEPARD 2 CONGRESS STREET	WORCHESTER MA	01609	(617) 756-0172
ADIR GALLERY 22 SOLHILL	NJ	08817	(201) 572-1751
DEGEN ENTERPRISES PO BOX 1557	NEW BRUNSWICK NJ	08903	
ALEXANDER OLAND 120 WEST 44TH STREET	NEW YORK NY	10036	(212) 582-3900

EL AL RELIEVES THE 10 MOST COMMON SYMPTOMS OF TRAVEL DISCOMFORT ON THE WAY TO ISRAEL.

HEADACHE: Only El Al has daily (except Sabbath) non-stop wide body service from New York to Israel. You don't waste time with stopovers in Europe, or have to change planes and re-check your baggage.

INDIGESTION: El Al serves only gourmet kosher meals on all flights, as well as our famous bagels and lox breakfast.

CRAMPS: El Al flies only wide body 747's, complete with first-run movies, stereo entertainment and room to stretch out and relax.

HANGOVER: Only El Al has a non-stop night flight from Tel-Aviv to New York so you don't have to "hang over" an extra day at your hotel. Instead, you can spend the extra day in New York on business or pleasure.

FOOT-TAPPING-ITIS: El Al has one of the best on-time departure records of any airline.

FRUSTRATION: El Al has one of the lowest baggage loss rates of any airline.

SHLEPPER'S ELBOW: El Al provides early check-in privileges in Tel Aviv, Jerusalem and Haifa on the day before your departure.

ANXIETY: El Al's concern for safety and security is unequalled by any other airline in the world.

PAIN-IN-THE-POCKET: El Al has the lowest scheduled fares to Israel of any airline.

FIRST TIME JITTERS: El Al is the airline of Israel, so we know Israel best. We can answer all your questions, assist with all your hotel and land arrangements and help make your trip to Israel the vacation of a lifetime.

Now that you know how El Al takes care of you, you probably feel better already. For more travel relief, reservations and information, take two minutes and call your travel agent in the morning. Or, if you prefer, call us any time at your convenience at our toll free number: 800-223-6700.

The Airline of Israel

BEN ARI ARTS LTD. 11 AVENUE A	NEW YORK	NY	10009	(212) 677-4730
EMANUEL WEISBERG ANTIQUE JUDAICA 45 ESSEX STREET	NEW YORK	NY	10002	(212) 674-1770
GRAND STERLING SILVER COMPANY 345 GRAND STREET	NEW YORK	NY	10002	(212) 674-6450
HA-ATIKOT-JUDAICA ANTIQUES 17 ESSEX ST.	NEW YORK	NY	10002	(212) 254-8395
HECKER SILVERSMITHS 605 FIFTH AVENUE (49TH STREET)	NEW YORK	NY	10017	(212) 593-2424
IN THE SPIRIT 460 EAST 79TH STREET	NEW YORK	NY	10021	(212) 662-6693
JEWISH FOLKLORE AND ETHNOLOGY NEWSLETTER, YIVO JEWISH RES.				
1048 FIFTH AVENUE	NEW YORK	NY	10028	(212) 535-6700
MORIAH ANTIQUE JUDAICA 699 MADISON AVENUE	NEW YORK	NY	10021	(212) 751-7090
THE JEWISH MUSEUM SHOP 1109 FIFTH AVENUE	NEW YORK	NY	10028	(212) 860-1888
PRESTIGE ANTIQUES 9931 65TH ROAD	REGO PARK	NY	11374	(718) 897-9503
R. ITTELSON 9931 65TH ROAD	REGO PARK	NY	11374	(718) 897-9503
CHARLES SESSLER, INC. 1308 WALNUT STREET	PHILADELPHIA	PA	19107	(215) 735-1086
BROBURY HOUSE GALLERY BROBURY	HEREFORDSHIRE	UK		

ARCHITECTS

SANFORD WERFEL STUDIOS 133 AVENEL STREET	AVENEL	NJ	07001	(201) 636-2320
ASCALON STUDIOS 206 CROSS KEYS ROAD	BERLIN	NJ	08009	(609) 768-3779
EMANUEL MILSTEIN R.D. 1, BOX 81C	MARLBORO	NJ	07746	(201) 946-8604
ERNA WEILL 886 ALPINE DRIVE	TEANECK	NJ	07666	(201) 837-1627
ARCHITECTS ADVISORY PANEL, UNION OF AMERICAN HEBREW CONG.				
838 FIFTH AVENUE	NEW YORK	NY	10021	(212) 249-0100
EFREM WEITZMAN 334 WEST 86TH STREET	NEW YORK	NY	10024	(212) 877-6500
TOBE PASCHER WORKSHOP, THE JEWISH MUSEUM				
1109 FIFTH AVENUE	NEW YORK	NY	10028	(212) 860-1864
ALBERT WOOD AND FIVE SONS, INC.				
ONE PLEASANT AVENUE	PORT WASHINGTON	NY	11050	(516) 767-0794
SHAMIR STUDIO 609 KAPPOCK STREET	RIVERDALE	NY	10463	(212) 695-5378

ARCHIVES & ARCHIVAL INSTITUTIONS

WESTERN JEWISH HISTORY CENTER OF THE JUDAH L. MAGNES MUSEUM				
2911 RUSSELL STREET	BERKELEY	CA	94705	(415) 849-2710
ROCKY MTN. JEWISH HIST. SOCIETY - IRA. M. BECK MEM. ARCHIVES				
UNIVERSITY OF DENVER	DENVER	CO	80208	(303) 753-1964
JEWISH HISTORICAL SOCIETY OF GREATER HARTFORD				
335 BLOOMFIELD AVENUE	WEST HARTFORD	CT	06117	(203) 236-4571

JEWISH HISTORICAL SOCIETY OF DELAWARE				
101 GARDEN OF EDEN ROAD	WILMINGTON	DE	19803	(302) 656-8558
CHICAGO JEWISH ARCHIVES - SPERTUS COLLEGE OF JUDAICA				
618 SOUTH MICHIGAN AVENUE	CHICAGO	IL	60605	(312) 922-9012
INDIANA JEWISH HISTORICAL SOCIETY, THE				
215 EAST BERRY STREET	FORT WAYNE	IN	46802	(219) 422-3862
HEBREW COLLEGE LIBRARY 43 HAWES STREET	BROOKLINE	MA	02146	(617) 232-8710
AMERICAN JEWISH HISTORICAL SOCIETY 2 THORNTON ROAD	WALTHAM	MA	02154	(617) 891-8110
BRANDEIS UNIVERSITY LIBRARY 215 SOUTH STREET	WALTHAM	MA	02254	(617) 647-2000
THE JEWISH HISTORICAL SOCIETY OF WESTERN CANADA				
402-365 BARGRAVE STREET	WINNIPEG	MB	3B 2K3	(204) 942-4822
CENTER FOR HOLOCAUST STUDIES - DOCUMENTATION & RESEARCH				
1610 AVENUE J	BROOKLYN	NY	11230	(718) 338-6494

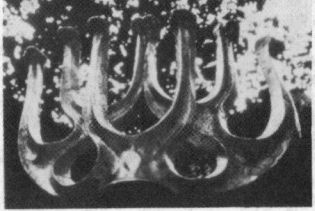

CHABAD RESEARCH CENTER 770 EASTERN PARKWAY .... BROOKLYN **NY** 11213   (718) 774-4001
AGUDATH ISRAEL OF AMERICA ARCHIVES FIVE BEEKMAN STREET ...... NEW YORK **NY** 10038   (212) 791-1800
BUND ARCHIVES OF THE JEWISH LABOR MOVEMENT
  25 EAST 78TH STREET .... NEW YORK **NY** 10021   (212) 535-1209
HADASSAH, THE WOMEN'S ZIONIST ORGANIZATION OF AMERICA
  50 WEST 58TH STREET .... NEW YORK **NY** 10019   (212) 355-7900
JEWISH THEOLOGICAL SEMINARY ARCHIVES 3080 BROADWAY .... NEW YORK **NY** 10027   (212) 678-8080
LEO BAECK INSTITUTE 129 EAST 73RD STREET .... NEW YORK **NY** 10021   (212) 744-6400
YESHIVA UNIVERSITY LIBRARY - ROOM 405 500 WEST 185 STREET ...... NEW YORK **NY** 10033   (212) 960-5400
YIVO ARCHIVES 1048 FIFTH AVENUE .... NEW YORK **NY** 10028   (212) 535-6700
ZIONIST ARCHIVES & LIBRARY/WORLD ZIONIST ORG.-AMER. SECTION
  515 PARK AVENUE .... NEW YORK **NY** 10022   (212) 753-2167
AMERICAN JEWISH ARCHIVES 3101 CLIFTON AVENUE .... CINCINNATI **OH** 45220   (513) 221-1875
AMERICAN JEWISH PERIODICAL CENTER 3101 CLIFTON AVENUE .... CINCINNATI **OH** 45220   (513) 221-1875
HEBREW UNION COLLEGE-JEWISH INST. OF RELIGION, KLAU LIBRARY
  3101 CLIFTON AVENUE .... CINCINNATI **OH** 45220   (513) 221-1875
CLEVELAND JEWISH ARCHIVES-WESTERN RESERVE HISTORICAL SOCIETY
  10825 EAST BLVD. .... CLEVELAND **OH** 44026   (216) 721-5722
OTTAWA JEWISH HISTORICAL SOCIETY 151 CHAPEL STREET .... OTTAWA **ON** K1N 7Y2   (613) 232-7306
CANADIAN JEWISH CONGRESS CENTRAL REGION ARCHIVES
  150 BEVERLY STREET .... TORONTO **ON** M5T 1Y6   (416) 977-3811
PHILADELPHIA JEWISH ARCHIVES CENTER
  CURTIS BLDG., 625 WALNUT STREET .... PHILADELPHIA **PA** 19106   (215) 923-2729
RECONSTRUCTIONIST RABBINICAL COLLEGE
  2308 NORTH BROAD STREET .... PHILADELPHIA **PA** 19132   (215) 221-9343
JEWISH PUBLIC LIBRARY 5151 COTE ST. CATHERINE ROAD .... MONTREAL **QU** H3W 1M6   (514) 735-6535
RHODE ISLAND JEWISH HISTORICAL ASSOCIATION
  130 SESSIONS STREET .... PROVIDENCE **RI** 02906   (401) 421-4111
SEATTLE JEWISH ARCHIVES UNIVERSITY OF WASHINGTON LIBRARY ..... SEATTLE **WA** 98195   (206) 543-9158
WISCONSIN JEWISH ARCHIVES 816 STATE STREET .... MADISON **WI** 53706   (608) 262-3266
'MASSUA'-MEM. TO MEMBERS OF ZIONIST YOUTH MOVEMENTS
  KIBBUTZ TEL ITZHAK, 45805 .... **IS**
GHETTO FIGHTERS' HOUSE IN MEMORY OF YIZHAK KATZNELSON
  AKKO POST OFFICE, KIBBUTZ LOHAMEI HAGHETAOT .... AKKO **IS**
ISRAEL LABOUR PARTY ARCHIVES KFAR SABA 44905 .... BEIT BERL **IS**
MILITARY (I.D.F.) & DEFENSE ESTABLISHMENT ARCHIVES
  JABOTINSKY STREET 50 .... GIVATAYIM **IS**
HAIFA CITY ARCHIVES HAGEFEN STREET 4 .... HAIFA **IS**
CENTRAL ARCHIVES FOR THE HISTORY OF THE JEWISH PEOPLE, THE
  HEBREW UNIV. CAMPUS GIVAT RAM. SPRINZAK BLDG. POB 1149 ...... JERUSALEM **IS**
CENTRAL ZIONIST ARCHIVES, THE
  BLDG. OF THE NATIONAL INSTITUTIONS, P.O. BOX 92 .... JERUSALEM **IS**
ISRAEL STATE ARCHIVES - GANSAKH HAMEDINAH
  PRIME MINISTER'S OFFICE, QIRYAT BEN-GURION, BUILDING 3 .... JERUSALEM **IS**
JERUSALEM MINICIPALITY HISTORICAL ARCHIVES
  28 AGRON STREET .... JERUSALEM **IS**
JEWISH NATL. & UNIV. LIB.-DEPT. OF MANUSCRIPTS & ARCHIVES, THE
  GIVAT RAM, P.O.B. 503 .... JERUSALEM **IS**
YAD VASHEM CENTRAL ARCHIVES HAR HAZIKARON, P.O. BOX 3477 .... JERUSALEM **IS**
ARCHIVES OF THE KIBBUTZ ARTZI HASHOMER HATZAIR
  POST OFFICE MERHAVIYA .... KIBBUTZ MERHAVIYA **IS**
WEIZMANN INSTITUTE ARCHIVES, THE
  THE WEIZMANN INSTITUTE OF SCIENCE, P.O. BOX 26 .... REHOVOT **IS**
ARCHIVES & MUSEUM OF THE ISRAEL LABOUR MOVEMENT
  34 WEIZMANN STREET, P.O.B. 21010 .... TEL AVIV **IS**
ARCHIVES OF THE ISRAEL TEACHERS' UNION, THE
  BEN SARUQ STREET 8 .... TEL AVIV **IS**
DIASPORA RESEARCH INSTITUTE, TEL AVIV UNIVERSITY RAMAT AVIV .... TEL AVIV **IS**
JABOTINSKY INSTITUTE IN ISRAEL
  38 KING GEORGE STREET, P.O. BOX 23110 .... TEL AVIV **IS**
TEL AVIV-YAFO MUNICIPALITY HISTORICAL ARCHIVES
  27 BIALIK ST., TEL AVIV-YAFO MUN., KIKAR MALKHEI ISRAEL .... TEL AVIV **IS**
ZVI NISHRI ARCHIVES ON PHYSICAL EDUCATION & SPORT, THE
  WINGATE INSTITUTE FOR PHYSICAL EDUCATION &
  SPORT .... WINGATE POST OFFICE **IS**
CENTRO DI DOCUMENTAZIONE EBRAICA CONTEMPORANEA
  6 VIA EUPILI, JEWISH CONTEMPORARY DOCUMENTATION CENTER .... MILANO **IT**
CENTRE DE DOCUMENTATION JUIVE CONTEMPORAINE
  17 RUE GEOFFROY L'ASNIER .... PARIS **FR**
CONSISTOIRE CENTRALE ISRAELITE DE FRANCE ET D'ALGERIE
  17 RUE SAINT GEORGES .... PARIS **FR**
CONSISTOIRE DE PARIS (ASSOCIATION CONSISTORIAL DE PARIS)
  17 RUE SAINT GEORGES .... PARIS **FR**
BIBLIOTHEQUE ET ARCHIVES DE L'ALLIANCE ISRAELITE UNIVERSELLE
  4K RUE BRUYERE, F 75425 .... PARIS CEDEX09 **FR**
JEVREJSKI ISTORIJSKI MUSEJ - JEWISH HISTORICAL MUSEUM
  7 JUL 71A/L, P.O. BOX 841 .... BELGRADE
MAGYAR ZSIDO LEVELTAR - HUNGARIAN JEWISH ARCHIVES
  27 JOZSEF KRT .... BUDAPEST
STATNI ZIDOWSKE MUZEUM-STATE JEWISH MUSEUM 3 JACHYMOVA .... PRAGUE 1
AUSTRALIAN JEWISH HISTORICAL SOCIETY
  166 CASTLEREAGH STREET .... SYDNEY, N.S.W. 2000
ZYDOWSKI INSTYTUT HISTORYCZNY W POLSCE
  AL. SWIECZEWSKIEGO 79, JEWISH HISTORICAL INSTITUTE .... WARSZAWA
ANGLO-JEWISH ARCHIVES
  MOCATTA LIBRARY, UNIVERSITY COLLEGE, GOWER STREET .... LONDON **UK**

ART GALLERIES & ART

BAT SHEVA IMPORTS 9884 GARDEN GROVE BLVD .... GARDEN GROVE **CA** 92644
GALLERY JUDAICA .... LOS ANGELES **CA**   (213) 459-2657

MICHAEL HITTLEMAN GALLERY 8797 BEVERLY BOULEVARD .... LOS ANGELES **CA** 90048   (213) 655-5364
SKIRBALL MUSEUM, HEBREW UNION COLLEGE
  3077 UNIVERSITY MALL .... LOS ANGELES **CA** 90007   (213) 749-3424
ALON GALLERY 1407 MONTANA AVENUE .... SANTA MONICA **CA** 90403   (213) 394-6545
THE JEWISH DEVELOPMENT COMPANY 18331-C IRVINE BOULEVARD .... TUSTIN **CA** 92680   (714) 730-1419
ALPERT AND CARTER MERCHANDISE MART .... CHICAGO **IL** 60654
PUCKER/SAFRAI GALLERY 171 NEWBURY STREET .... BOSTON **MA** 02116   (617) 267-0473
KOLBO 435 HARVARD STREET .... BROOKLINE **MA** 02146   (617) 731-8743
LIPMAN'S ART SHOP 300 E. DIAMOND AVENUE .... GATHERSBURG **MD** 20760
LIPMAN'S ART SHOP 8209 GEORGIA AVENUE .... SILVER SPRING **MD** 20910   (301) 587-5581
MR. B'S ART & FRAMING 7913 SANTA FE DRIVE .... KANSAS CITY **MO** 64100   (913) 649-3676
ADIR GALLERY 22 SOLHILL .... **NJ** 08817   (201) 572-1751
RAYE LANDIS ART CENTER 1050 GEORGE STREET .... NEW BRUNSWICK **NJ** 08901   (201) 249-7776
EDELWEISS CO. - GLASS STUDIO 1217 49 STREET .... BROOKLYN **NY** 11219   (718) 851-9687
THE CHASSIDIC ART INSTITUTE (CHAI) 375 KINGSTON AVENUE .... BROOKLYN **NY** 11213   (718) 774-9149
VISUAL DIMENSIONS-PAINTINGS AND LITHOGRAPHS
  1661 MCDONALD AVENUE .... BROOKLYN **NY** 11230   (718) 627-0903
MARLIN ART INCORPORATED 920 GRAND BOULEVARD .... DEER PARK **NY** 11729   (516) 242-3344
GOLDEN GRAPHICS 35 BRIDLE PATH .... GREAT NECK **NY** 11021   (516) 482-4282
WILLIAM HABER GALLERY 139-11 QUEENS BOULEVARD .... JAMAICA **NY** 11435   (212) 739-1000
BLD, LIMITED 118 EAST 25TH STREET .... NEW YORK **NY** 10010   (212) 460-8700
BEN ARI ARTS 11 AVENUE A .... NEW YORK **NY** 10009   (212) 677-4730
BEZALEL JEWISH ART GALLERY 11 ESSEX STREET .... NEW YORK **NY** 10002   (212) 228-5982

HA-ATIKOT-JUDAICA ANTIQUES 17 ESSEX STREET .... NEW YORK **NY** 10002   (212) 254-8395
HECKER SILVERSMITHS 605 FIFTH AVENUE (49TH STREET) .... NEW YORK **NY** 10017   (212) 593-2424
IN THE SPIRIT 460 EAST 79TH STREET .... NEW YORK **NY** 10021   (212) 662-6693
ISRA-ART PRODUCTIONS, INC. 157 WEST 57TH STREET .... NEW YORK **NY** 10019   (212) 246-3363
ISRAEL ARTS CENTER/AMERICAN-ISRAEL CULTURAL FOUNDATION
  4 EAST 54TH STREET .... NEW YORK **NY** 10022
ISRAEL CREATIONS 212 5TH AVENUE .... NEW YORK **NY** 10010   (212) 686-7005
ISRAELI GIFTS 575 7TH AVENUE .... NEW YORK **NY** 10018   (212) 391-4928
J. LEVINE CO. 58 ELDRIDGE STREET .... NEW YORK **NY** 10002   (212) 966-4460
JEWISH ART GALLERY 11 ESSEX STREET .... NEW YORK **NY** 10002
MURRAY S. GREENFIELD 21 WEST 39TH STREET .... NEW YORK **NY** 10018   (212) 391-8350
NECHEMIA GLEZER GALLERY 760 WEST END AVENUE .... NEW YORK **NY** 10025   (212) 684-0160
THE EAGLE'S NEST 142 11TH AVENUE .... NEW YORK **NY** 10011   (212) 929-9304
TRADITIONS-ART JUDAICA 23715 MERCANTILE ROAD A214 .... CLEVELAND **OH** 44122   (216) 831-3451
ELIJAH'S CUP 12306 MEADOW LAKE DR. .... HOUSTON **TX** 77077   (713) 497-2243
MILLIOUD INTERNATIONAL GALLERY WEST ALABAMA & BUFFALO .... HOUSTON **TX** 77027   (713) 621-3330
RACHEL DAVID GALLERY 2402 ADDISON .... HOUSTON **TX** 77030   (713) 664-4130

ARTISTS

JOE HARNIK 8110 LONGRIDGE AVENUE .... NORTH HOLLYWOOD **CA**   (818) 782-2548
CHICKY RAUCH 25 A SHALER LANE .... CAMBRIDGE **MA** 02138

World's largest archive
of photographs of
art and architecture for
research and reproduction.

With a section on Judaica, current
Jewish life and the
History of Jewish Art, derived from
the collections of the Jewish
Museum of New York and other sources.

Mané Katz, Rabbi with Torah, Geneva, Modern Art Foundation (Snark/Art Resource)

Exclusive representative for Scala Fine Arts
and Fratelli Alinari of Italy, Photographie
Giraudon of Paris, the Bildarchiv Foto
Marburg of Germany, and the Isabella
Stewart Gardner Museum of Boston.

ART
RESOURCE

65 Bleecker St. (9th floor) • New York, N.Y. 10012
Tel. (212) 505-8700 / (212) 673-4988—Tlx. 237053

FOR ONLY $500 WE'LL FLY YOU ROUND-TRIP TO ISRAEL,

feed you three meals a day, house you with Israelis and give you a chance to make a valuable contribution to Israeli society.

All you have to do is VOLUNTEER!

Can you spare three weeks?

Day after day, week after week, most people spend their time these days without changing their routine in any significant way. We dream of the new and exciting, the creative and worthwhile, the opportunity to do something — *anything* — that will refresh mind, body and soul. But what is there to turn to that is honestly different?

If you, your friends or any members of your family are looking for an answer to this question, maybe it's time you thought about volunteering for Israel.

The fact is, Israel needs help right now. There's a manpower shortage on, so whether you're an 18-year-old Jewish student or a 60-year-old able-bodied grandmother — or anything in between — there are critical jobs that have to be filled today.

And that's why, *if you volunteer*, we will subsidize your air fare, meals and housing to the tune of over $2000.

For only $500 and your three week commitment of time, you will:

- be flown from New York to Tel Aviv round-trip, via El Al Israel Airlines
- be transported to your lodging
- take up the challenge of a 5½ day work week, performing services vital to the strength of Israel
- be served three Kosher meals daily
- experience the beauty of a Shabbat (Sabbath) in the Jewish state
- participate in organized tours throughout the country
- meet Israeli families in Jerusalem and elsewhere — —

And, by the way, don't worry if you don't know Hebrew. Everyone knows *some* English and will be eager to practice on you as soon as you give them a chance.

So come. Pick your three weeks. *Any three weeks.* If you're lucky enough to have a few weeks free, take advantage of a genuine opportunity to do something important.

To apply, write or call:

VOLUNTEERS FOR ISRAEL

40 Worth Street, Rm. 710
New York, New York 10013
(212) 608-4848

Ask about the 15 credit, three-month student program.

KAREN FROSTIG 85 TROWBRIDGE STREET .... CAMBRIDGE MA 02138

JANIS PEROMSIK 47 HADWEN ROAD .... WORCESTER MA 01602 (617) 753-6781

ASCALON STUDIOS 206 CROSS KEYS ROAD .... BERLIN NJ 08009 (609) 768-3779

EMANUEL MILSTEIN R.D. 1, BOX 81C .... MARLBORO NJ 07746 (201) 946-8604

ROSLYN HOLLANDA 5 DOGWOOD DRIVE .... NEWTON NJ 07860 (201) 383-4966

MIRIAM ALEXENBERG 615 MAITLAND AVENUE .... TEANECK NJ 07666

BASSYA EIN 1534 53RD STREET .... BROOKLYN NY 11219

SHARON LEVINSON 5649 KINGS HIGHWAY .... BROOKLYN NY 11203 (718) 541-1151

SHARON GELLER METAL 144-15 78TH AVENUE .... FLUSHING NY 11367 (718) 969-0417

RENEE PULVER 67-10 108TH STREET .... FOREST HILLS NY 11367

JONATHAN CRAIG 1 SWALLOW LANE .... HAPPAUGE NY 11787 (516) 724-7250

LORRAINE ROSENBAUM 250-14 GASKILL ROAD .... LITTLE NECK NY 11363 (718) 428-3658

KAREN KAUFMAN 1918 GEORGE COURT .... MERRICK NY 11566 (516) 546-3843

HUGH MESIBOV 377 SADDLE RIVER ROAD .... MONSEY NY 10952 (914) 356-2610

CHARLES J. STANLEY PO BOX 1132, PETER STUYVESANT STATION ...... NEW YORK NY 10009 (212) 673-2705

EFREM WEITZMAN - SYNAGOGUE ARTIST 334 WEST 86TH STREET ...... NEW YORK NY 10024 (212) 877-6590

ELAINE SCHLACKMAN 645 WEST END AVENUE/#9A .... NEW YORK NY 10025

EZEKIEL SAAD 137 SULLIVAN STREET/#2C .... NEW YORK NY 10003

FERN AMPFER 375 RIVERSIDE DRIVE .... NEW YORK NY 10025

DR. MARK PODWAL 999 FIFTH AVENUE .... NEW YORK NY 10028 (212) 288-7488

NATIONAL COUNCIL ON ART IN JEWISH LIFE 15 E. 84TH STREET ...... NEW YORK NY 10028 (212) 879-4500

WENDY BURTON 7 1/2 JANE STREET .... NEW YORK NY 10014

ART & DESIGN STUDIO OF SARA SHAPIRO 13 DR. FRANK ROAD .... SPRING VALLEY NY 10977 (914) 352-3988

LAUREL PRESS 26 WEST FENIMORE STREET .... VALLEY STREAM NY 11580

CINDY BENJAMIN 11483 HESSLER COURT #6 .... CLEVELAND OH 44106

BEVERLY A. MOSLER 8629 ALGON AVENUE .... PHILADELPHIA PA 19142

FRUMA ROTHBERG 1990 BARCLAY AVENUE .... MONTREAL QU

BAKERIES - RETAIL

GOLD STAR BAKERY 3219 EAST CAMELBACK ROAD .... PHOENIX AZ 85018 (602) 955-7670

KARSH'S BAKERY 5539 NORTH 7TH STREET .... PHOENIX AZ 85016 (602) 264-4874

KARSH'S BAKERY 10893 NORTH SCOTTSDALE ROAD .... SCOTTSDALE AZ 85016 (602) 951-0202

HANSEN CAKES 193 SOUTH BEVERLY DRIVE .... BEVERLY HILLS CA 90212 (213) 878-0433

MICKEY'S KOSHER BAKERY 2298 SOUTH BASKIN AVENUE .... CAMPBELL CA 95008 (408) 371-5151

EILAT BAKERY 515 N. FAIRFAX .... LOS ANGELES CA 90036 (213) 653-5553

FAIRFAX BAKERY 431 NORTH FAIRFAX AVENUE .... LOS ANGELES CA 90036 (213) 653-2106

FAMOUS BAKERY 350-354 N. FAIRFAX AVENUE .... LOS ANGELES CA 90036 (213) 939-8367

FAMOUS BAKERY 354 NORTH FAIRFAX AVENUE .... LOS ANGELES CA 90036 (213) 939-8900

HAIMISH BAKERY 9100 WEST PICO BOULEVARD .... LOS ANGELES CA 90035 (213) 276-3116

HANSEN CAKES 1060 SOUTH FAIRFAX AVENUE .... LOS ANGELES CA 90019 (213) 936-4332

KING DAVID BAKERY 357 N. FAIRFAX AVENUE .... LOS ANGELES CA 90036 (213) 655-3021

LITTLE JERUSALEM 8971 WEST PICO BOULEVARD .... LOS ANGELES CA 90035 (213) 274-3598

MODEL 8377 WEST THIRD .... LOS ANGELES CA 90036 (213) 651-3938

SCHWARTZ BAKERY 441 N. FAIRFAX AVENUE .... LOS ANGELES CA 90036 (213) 653-1683

SCHWARTZ BAKERY 8616 W. PICO BOULEVARD .... LOS ANGELES CA 90035 (213) 854-0592

REUBENS CONTINENTAL BAKERY, INC.
12419 BURBANK BLVD. .... NORTH HOLLYWOOD CA 91607 (818) 762-5005

ERNIE'S INTERNATIONAL PASTRIES 3264 GRAND AVENUE .... OAKLAND CA 94610 (415) 444-8226

WEDEMEYER'S BAKERY 314 HARBOR WAY .... SOUTH SAN FRANCISCO CA 94080 (415) 873-1000

LEON'S BAKERIES 1359 DIXWELL AVENUE .... HAMDEN CT 06514 (203) 281-6560

REYMOND BAKING COMPANY 2457 EAST MAIN STREET .... WATERBURY CT 06702 (203) 756-7871

OTTENBERG'S BREAD 655 TAYLOR N.E. .... WASHINGTON DC 20019 (202) 529-5800

POSIN'S BAKERY-DELICATESSEN 5756 GEORGIA AVENUE N.W. ...... WASHINGTON DC 20027 (202) 726-4424

BUTTERFLAKE NEW YORK BAKERY 1349 WASHINGTON AVENUE ...... MIAMI BEACH FL 33139 (305) 532-4445

CARMEL HUNGARIAN BAKERY 847 WASHINGTON AVENUE .... MIAMI BEACH FL 33139 (305) 538-7592

COHEN'S BAKERY 955 WASHINGTON AVENUE .... MIAMI BEACH FL 33139 (305) 538-6142

FRIEDMAN'S BAKERY 685 WASHINGTON AVENUE .... MIAMI BEACH FL 33139 (305) 531-6173

PARAMOUNT BAKERY 1407 WASHINGTON AVENUE .... MIAMI BEACH FL 33139 (305) 534-2683

BEN ZION BAKERY 1360 N.E. 163 STREET .... N. MIAMI BEACH FL 33162 (305) 947-4092

GORDON'S OF NEW YORK 761 NORTH MIAMI BEACH BLVD. ...... N. MIAMI BEACH FL 33162 (305) 652-9176

PARAMOUNT BAKERY 757 NORTH MIAMI BEACH BLVD ...... N. MIAMI BEACH FL 33162 (305) 652-9176

GOLDBERG & SON 4383 ROSWELL ROAD N.E. .... ATLANTA GA 30329 (404) 256-3751

SUNSHINE BAKERY 1209 BROAD STREET .... AUGUSTA GA 30900 (404) 724-2302

DUNKIN' DONUTS (DAIRY/CRC) 3132 WEST DEVON .... CHICAGO IL 60659 (312) 262-4560

GITEL'S BAKERY 2745 W. DEVON AVENUE .... CHICAGO IL 60659 (312) 262-3701

KAREN'S PASTR SHOP 3113 N. BROADWAY .... CHICAGO IL 60657 (312) 525-5700

TEL AVIV KOSHER BAKERY 2944 WEST DEVON .... CHICAGO IL 60645 (312) 764-8877

DUNKIN' DONUTS (DAIRY/CRC) 3900 WEST DEMPSTER .... SKOKIE IL 60076 (312) 673-7099

KING DAVID'S KOSHER BAKERY 3309 WEST DEMPSTER .... SKOKIE IL 60076 (312) 677-4355

TEL AVIV 4956-60 WEST DEMPSTER .... SKOKIE IL 60077 (312) 675-1005

GREEN & FREEDMAN BAKERY ONE BOSTON PLACE .... BOSTON MA 02135 (617) 227-5111

MONTILLO'S BAKERY SHOP 33-35 FANUEIL HALL MARKET .... BOSTON MA 02115 (617) 267-4700

DUBIN'S BAKERY 1010 WEST ROXBURY PKWY .... BROOKLINE MA 02167 (617) 469-9241

PASTRYLANE PRODUCTS 305 HARVARD STREET .... BROOKLINE MA 02146 (617) 566-8136

TOWNE LYNNE BAKERY 12 WASHINGTON STREET .... CANTON MA 02021 (617) 828-2260

BREAD BASKET 151 COCHITUATE ROAD .... FRAMINGHAM MA 01701 (617) 875-9441

MONTILIO'S BAKERY SHOP 70 WATER STREET .... HINGHAM MA 02025 (617) 749-9851

M&M CAKE BOX 237 FERRY STREET .... MALDEN MA 02148 (617) 322-4447

EAGERMAN'S BAKERY 810 WORCESTER ROAD .... NATICK MA 01760 (617) 653-9474

NEEDHAM BAKERY 117 CHAPEL STREET .... NEEDHAM MA 02192 (617) 444-9619

DIAMOND'S BAKERY 1136 BEACON STREET .... NEWTON MA 02158 (617) 527-5100

HANNA'S BAKERY 551 COMMONWEALTH AVENUE .... NEWTON MA 02158 (617) 527-9503

LEDERMAN'S 1223 CENTRE STREET .... NEWTON MA 02158 (617) 527-7896

MONTILIO'S BAKERY SHOP 29 CHESTNUT STREET .... QUINCY MA 02169 (617) 773-2300

LIBERMAN'S BAKERY 108 SHIRLEY AVENUE .... REVERE MA 02151 (617) 289-0041

RAIN'S BAKERY 57 NICHOLAS ROAD .... SAXONVILLE MA 01701 (617) 877-3927

GOLDMAN'S KOSHER FANCY BAKERY 6848 REISTERSTOWN ROAD ...... BALTIMORE MD 21215 (301) 358-9625

KATZ'S SUPERMARKET 4860 BOILING BROOK PKWY .... ROCKVILLE MD 20852 (301) 468-0400

DELUXE BAKE SHOP WHITE OAK SHOPPING PLAZA .... SILVER SPRING MD 20910 (301) 593-6607

WOODEN SHOE BAKERY 11301 GEORGIA AVENUE .... WHEATON MD 20902 (301) 942-9330

ELIZABETH PASTRIES 13730 WEST NINE MILE ROAD .... OAK PARK MI 48237 (313) 545-6900

MERTZ BAKE SHOPPE 24770 COOLIDGE .... OAK PARK MI (313) 548-4835

MERTZ BAKE SHOPPE 23055 COOLIDGE .... OAK PARK MI (313) 547-3581

ZEMAN'S NEW YORK BAKERY 25258 GREENFIELD RD. .... OAK PARK MI (313) 967-3905

ZEMAN'S NEW YORK BAKERY 30760 SOUTHFIELD RD. .... SOUTHFIELD MI (313) 646-7159

CECIL'S KOSHER DELICATESSEN RESTAURANT & BAKERY
651 CLEVELAND SOUTH .... ST. LOUIS PARK MN 55416 (612) 698-6276

EPSTEIN KOSHER FOODS 403 WEST 79TH STREET .... KANSAS CITY MO 64119 (816) 361-0200

NEW YORK BAKERY 11451 OLIVE STREET ROAD .... ST. LOUIS MO 63108 (314) 567-7299

NEW YORK BAKERY 8625 OLIVE STREET ROAD .... ST LOUIS MO 63123 (314) 993-9922

PETROFSKY'S BAKERY 7649 DELMAR STREET .... ST. LOUIS MO 63108 (314) 721-9445

TEL AVIV DELICATESSEN BAKERY 11036 OLIVE STREET ROAD ...... ST. LOUIS MO 63131 (314) 567-4496

KOSHER DISH 437 PENNINGTON STREET .... ELIZABETH NJ 07702 (201) 527-1818

SPINDLER'S 247 BOULEVARD .... HASBROUCK HEIGHTS NJ 07604 (201) 288-1348

FISCHL BAKERY 110 N. MAPLE AVENUE .... RIDGEWOOD NJ 07450 (201) 445-0425

FISCHL BAKERY 156 ROCHELLE AVENUE .... ROCHELLE PARK NJ 07662 (201) 843-2462

GOLD BELL BAKERY 1133 ST. GEORGE AVENUE .... ROSSELLE NJ 07203 (201) 245-2172

GRATZEL'S BAKERY 474 CEDAR LANE .... TEANECK NJ 07666 (201) 836-4049

HOT BAGELS 573 CEDAR LANE .... TEANECK NJ 07666 (201) 836-9705

BAGEL BOX 642 EAGLE ROCK ROAD .... WEST ORANGE NJ 07052 (201) 731-4985

BAGEL DEN 212-47 26TH AVENUE .... BAYSIDE NY 11360 (718) 224-3579

BAGEL CORNER 581 WEST 235TH STREET .... BRONX NY 10463 (212) 549-9709

GRUENEBAUM'S BAKERY 741 LYDIG AVENUE .... BRONX NY 10461 (212) 822-9874

HEISLER PASTRY SHOP 3601 RIVERDALE AVENUE .... BRONX NY 10463 (212) 549-0770

1373 HEBREW BAKE SHOP 1373 CONEY ISLAND AVENUE .... BROOKLYN NY 11230 (718) 258-8822

13TH AVENUE BAGEL BAKERY CORP. 4807 13TH AVENUE .... BROOKLYN NY 11219 (718) 633-4009

AVENUE M KOSHER BAKERY 1218 AVENUE M .... BROOKLYN NY 11230 (718) 998-7819

BAGEL WHEEL 734 FLATBUSH AVENUE .... BROOKLYN NY 11226 (718) 284-9726

C.P.C. BAKERY CORP. 1506 ELM AVENUE .... BROOKLYN NY 11230 (718) 339-8138

CONGREGATION BETH ABRAHAM 210 CORTELYOU ROAD .... BROOKLYN NY 11218 (718) 438-9869

CONGREGATION SATMAR MATZOH BAKERY 427 BROADWAY ...... BROOKLYN NY 11211 (718) 388-4008

EUROPEAN STYLE KOSHER PRETZELS AND BAGELS
6516 BAY PARKWAY .... BROOKLYN NY 11204 (718) 232-5790

FEIGENBLUM'S BAKE SHOP 712 KINGS HIGHWAY .... BROOKLYN NY 11223 (718) 375-7651

FLATBUSH KOSHER HOMEMADE BAKERY 412 AVENUE M .... BROOKLYN NY 11230 (718) 375-5010

FRANCZOZ BAKERY 4623 13TH AVENUE .... BROOKLYN NY 11219 (718) 438-8978

FRANKEL'S 18TH AVENUE BAKE SHOP 4616 18TH AVENUE .... BROOKLYN NY 11204 (718) 436-6777

FREUND BAKERY 5014 12TH AVENUE .... BROOKLYN NY 11219 (718) 854-9582

FRIEDMAN, DOV 422 BEDFORD AVENUE .... BROOKLYN NY 11211 (718) 388-4044

HEBREW BAKE SHOP 1373 CONEY ISLAND AVENUE .... BROOKLYN NY 11230 (718) 258-8822

HIRSCH BROS. BAKERY 1079 CLARKSON AVENUE .... BROOKLYN NY 11212 (718) 498-7614

KORF'S MATZOS BAKERY 460 ALBANY AVENUE .... BROOKLYN NY 11213 (718) 778-7914

LECHEM BAKE SHOPS INC. 4814 13TH AVENUE .... BROOKLYN NY 11219 (718) 438-9752

LEE AVENUE KOSHER BAKERY 73 LEE AVENUE .... BROOKLYN NY 11211 (718) 387-4736

LOWEN'S BAKE SHOP 311 ROGERS AVENUE .... BROOKLYN NY 11225 (718) 467-3500

LOWEN'S BAKE SHOP 1419 CONEY ISLAND AVENUE .... BROOKLYN NY 11230 (718) 253-0462

MANDELBAUM BAKERY 4410 14TH AVENUE .... BROOKLYN NY 11219 (718) 853-7089

MOISHE'S BAKERY 902 CORTELYOU ROAD .... BROOKLYN NY 11218 (718) 941-4264

MOTEL'S BAKERY 2213 65TH STREET .... BROOKLYN NY 11204 (718) 837-0782

R & G KOSHER BAKERY 430 AVENUE P .... BROOKLYN NY 11223 (718) 998-7530

REISMAN'S 110 AVENUE O .... BROOKLYN NY 11204 (718) 331-2012

SABEL KOSHER BAKE SHOP 4518 FT. HAMILTON PARKWAY	BROOKLYN	**NY**	11219	(718) 633-2600
SCHICK'S BAKERY 4710 16TH AVENUE	BROOKLYN	**NY**	11204	(718) 436-8020
SHMURAH MATZOH BAKERY 1285 36TH STREET	BROOKLYN	**NY**	11218	(718) 438-9764
SHOMER SHABBOS BAKE SHOP 425 KINGSTON AVENUE	BROOKLYN	**NY**	11225	(718) 493-2627
SPITZER'S KOSHER BAKERY 657 BEDFORD AVENUE	BROOKLYN	**NY**	11211	(718) 875-0668
STRAUSS KOSHER BAKERY 5209 13TH AVENUE	BROOKLYN	**NY**	11219	(718) 851-7728
SZABO KOSHER BAKERY 702 AVENUE U	BROOKLYN	**NY**	11223	(718) 376-8003
WEISS BAKERY 5011 13TH AVENUE	BROOKLYN	**NY**	11219	(718) 436-3864
WEISS HEIMISHE BAKERY 123 LEE AVENUE	BROOKLYN	**NY**	11211	(718) 387-7708
WERZBERGER KOSHER BAKERY & CANDY SHOP 5502 13TH AVENUE	BROOKLYN	**NY**	11219	(718) 435-2490
WILLIAMSBURG KOSHER BAKE SHOP 159 LEE AVENUE	BROOKLYN	**NY**	11211	(718) 387-7411
SCHROEDER'S COSMOPOLITAN BAKERY 2971 DELAWARE	BUFFALO	**NY**	14217	(716) 874-2253
G & I KOSHER BAKERY 536 CENTRAL AVENUE	CEDARHURST	**NY**	11516	(516) 374-2525
BROADWAY BAGELS 1627 DUTCH BROADWAY	ELMONT	**NY**	11003	(516) 825-9696
G & I KOSHER BAKERY 72-22 MAIN STREET	FLUSHING	**NY**	11367	(718) 544-8736
G & I KOSHER BAKERY 69-72 MAIN STREET	FLUSHING	**NY**	11367	(718) 261-1155
KOSHER BAKERY 69-30 JEWEL AVENUE	FLUSHING	**NY**	11367	(718) 544-0225
MENORAH BAKERY 189-09 UNION TURNPIKE	FLUSHING	**NY**	11366	(718) 591-3510
STAR OF DAVID BAGELS 67-11 MAIN STREET	FLUSHING	**NY**	11367	(718) 520-8892
ABRAHAM'S KOSHER CAKELAND 64-17 108TH STREET	FOREST HILLS	**NY**	11375	(718) 897-7744
BAGEL HUT 485 MIDDLE NECK ROAD	GREAT NECK	**NY**	11023	(516) 482-8939
G&G KOSHER BAKE SHOP 81-72 LEFFERTS BLVD	KEW GARDENS	**NY**	11415	(718) 441-3417
G&I KOSHER BAKERIES 141-11 70TH ROAD	KEW GARDENS	**NY**	11367	(718) 544-9433
ZOMICK'S '2' 392 CENTRAL AVENUE	LAWRENCE	**NY**	11559	(516) 569-5520
EUROPEAN HOMEMADE FOODS 82 ROUTE 59	MONSEY	**NY**	10952	(914) 356-9555
MONSEY KOSHER BAKE SHOP 51 MAIN STREET	MONSEY	**NY**	10952	(914) 352-6435
SCHLESINGER'S BAKERY 18 MAIN STREET	MONSEY	**NY**	10952	(914) 352-4171
BIALYSTOKER KUCHEN BAKERY 367 GRAND STREET	NEW YORK	**NY**	10002	(212) 674-9747
EICHLER BAKERY 181 E. BROADWAY	NEW YORK	**NY**	10002	(212) 228-1110
GERTEL'S BAKE SHOP 53 HESTER STREET	NEW YORK	**NY**	10002	(212) 982-3250
GRUENEBAUM BAKERIES 2173 BROADWAY	NEW YORK	**NY**	10024	(212) 595-9251
GRUENEBAUM BAKERIES 725 W. 181ST STREET	NEW YORK	**NY**	10033	(212) 781-8813
GRUENEBAUM'S BAKERY 4484 BROADWAY	NEW YORK	**NY**	10040	(212) 567-9794
H & H BAGELS 2239 BROADWAY	NEW YORK	**NY**	10024	(212) 799-9680
ISRAEL BAGELS EAST BROADWAY KOSHER BAKERY				
181 EAST BROADWAY	NEW YORK	**NY**	10002	(212) 228-1110
JERUSALEM II 1375 BROADWAY	NEW YORK	**NY**	10018	(212) 398-1475
MOISHE'S BAKERY 181 EAST HOUSTON STREET	NEW YORK	**NY**	10002	(212) 475-9624
MOISHE'S SECOND AVENUE HOME MADE KOSHER BAKE SHOP				
115 SECOND AVENUE	NEW YORK	**NY**	10003	(212) 505-8555
ROYALE PASTRY SHOP 237 WEST 72ND STREET	NEW YORK	**NY**	10023	(212) 874-5642
TASTY PASTRY 4175 BROADWAY	NEW YORK	**NY**	10033	(212) 568-6800
YONAH SCHIMMEL KNISHERY 137 EAST HOUSTON	NEW YORK	**NY**	10002	(212) 477-2858
YONAH SCHIMMEL KNISHERY 1275 LEXINGTON AVENUE	NEW YORK	**NY**	10028	(212) 722-4049
ZARO'S BREAD BASKET 625 8TH AVENUE	NEW YORK	**NY**	10018	(212) 279-7663
ZARO'S BREAD BASKET GRAND CENTRAL TERMINAL	NEW YORK	**NY**	10017	(212) 599-1515
ZARO'S BREAD BASKET 32ND AND BROADWAY	NEW YORK	**NY**	10001	(212) 564-7968
PEARL'S BAKERY 26 MANETTO HILL MALL	PLAINVIEW	**NY**	11803	(516) 935-5225
DANKER'S QUALITY BAKERY 687 JOSEPH AVENUE	ROCHESTER	**NY**	14614	(714) 544-2100
ISRAEL BAKERY 1248 CLINTON AVENUE NORTH	ROCHESTER	**NY**	14612	(716) 342-6060
ELITE BAKE SHOP, THE 10 EAST CENTRAL AVENUE	SPRING VALLEY	**NY**	10952	(914) 352-9881
NOVELTY KOSHER PASTRY SHOP, INC. 10 HOFFMAN STREET	SPRING VALLEY	**NY**	10977	(914) 356-0428
FAMOUS KOSHER BAKERY 2208 VICTORY BOULEVARD	STATEN ISLAND	**NY**	10314	(718) 494-1411
KOLMAN'S KOSHER BAKERY 460 BRADLEY AVENUE	STATEN ISLAND	**NY**	10314	(718) 698-6425
BAGEL POLE, INC. 1075 OLD COUNTRY ROAD	WESTBURY	**NY**	11590	(516) 334-9466
WOODBOURNE BAKE MASTERS MAIN STREET	WOODBOURNE	**NY**	12788	(914) 434-6310
LAX & MANDEL KOSHER BAKERY 2070 SOUTH TAYLOR ROAD	CLEVELAND	**OH**	44118	(216) 932-6445
UNGAR'S BAKERY & FOOD SHOP 1831 S. TAYLOR ROAD	CLEVELAND	**OH**	44118	(216) 321-7176
ANITA BENGIO PATISSERIE 870 STEEPROCK DRIVE	TORONTO	**ON**		(416) 638-3051
CARMEL BAKERY 3856 BATHURST STREET	TORONTO	**ON**		(416) 633-5315
HERMES 2885 BATHURST STREET	TORONTO	**ON**		(416) 787-1234
HERMES 3543 BATHURST STREET	TORONTO	**ON**		(416) 787-1775
HERMES 924 ST. CLAIR AVENUE WEST	TORONTO	**ON**		(416) 654-4456
HERMES 652 SHEPPARD AVENUE WEST	TORONTO	**ON**		(416) 635-1932
ISACC'S 3390 BATHURST STREET	TORONTO	**ON**		(416) 789-7587
ISACC'S 221 WILMINGTON AVENUE	TORONTO	**ON**		(416) 633-8845
MIAMI KOSHER BAKERY AND DAIRY 3030 BATHURST STREET	TORONTO	**ON**		(416) 782-2786
MY ZAIDY'S BAGEL 3456 BATHURST STREET	TORONTO	**ON**		(416) 789-0785
OLDE FASHIONED BAGEL FACTORY 3385 BATHURST STREET	TORONTO	**ON**		(416) 781-4476
RICHMAN'S BAKERY 4119 BATHURST STREET	TORONTO	**ON**		(416) 636-9710
SILVERMAN'S 2839 BATHURST STREET	TORONTO	**ON**		(416) 787-6791
CAKEMASTERS 6404 STENTON AVENUE	PHILADELPHIA	**PA**	19138	(215) 464-6676
CAKEMASTERS 9373 KREWSTOWN ROAD	PHILADELPHIA	**PA**	19115	(215) 248-0178
GOLD MEDAL BAKING COMPANY 1101 N. 40TH STREET	PHILADELPHIA	**PA**	19104	(215) 627-5288
GREENBERG'S BAKERY 7594 HAVERFORD AVENUE	PHILADELPHIA	**PA**	19151	(215) 878-1127
ROSEN'S FAMOUS BAKERY 775 HUNTINGDON PIKE	ROCKLEDGE	**PA**	19111	(215) 379-4911
EUROPEAN BAKERIES 206 ST. VIATEUR WEST	MONTREAL	**QU**		(514) 276-2105
EUROPEAN BAKERIES 1587 VAN HORNE	MONTREAL	**QU**		(514) 272-3003
EUROPEAN BAKERIES 222 LAURIER WEST	MONTREAL	**QU**		(514) 277-5893
EUROPEAN BAKERIES 4595 CHRISTOPHER COLUMBUS	MONTREAL	**QU**		(514) 527-1249
HOME-MADE KOSHER BAKERY 5438 VICTORIA AVENUE	MONTREAL	**QU**		(514) 737-1751
HOME-MADE KOSHER BAKERY 1085 BERNARD WEST	MONTREAL	**QU**		(514) 342-1991
HOME-MADE KOSHER BAKERY 1465 VAN HORNE	MONTREAL	**QU**		(514) 279-2827
HOME-MADE KOSHER BAKERY 6685 VICTORIA AVENUE	MONTREAL	**QU**		(514) 733-4141
HOME-MADE KOSHER BAKERY 925 BEAUMONT	MONTREAL	**QU**		(514) 270-1366
KOSHER QUALITY BAKERY 5855 VICTORIA AVENUE	MONTREAL	**QU**		(514) 279-1366
KORB BAKING COMPANY 508 ARMISTICE BOULEVARD	PAWTUCKET	**RI**	02800	(401) 726-8983
KORB BAKING COMPANY 540 PAWTUCKET AVENUE	PAWTUCKET	**RI**	02800	(401) 421-9273
GUTTIN'S BAKERY 1095 BROAD STREET	PROVIDENCE	**RI**	02906	(401) 781-8929
KORB BAKING COMPANY 1617 WARWICK AVENUE	WARWICK	**RI**	02886	(401) 737-9625
BRENNER BAKERY 1200 E. BELLEVUE-REDMOND ROAD	BELLEVUE	**WA**	98110	(206) 454-0600

BAKERIES - WHOLESALE

IVERSON BAKING CO. P.O. BOX B	ROGERS	**AR**	72756	(501) 636-5904
LENDER'S BAGELS P.O. BOX 869	ORANGE	**CT**	06477	
PARAMOUNT BAKERY 1407 WASHINGTON AVENUE	MIAMI BEACH	**FL**	33139	(305) 534-2683
CRESCENT BAKING CORP. 427 IOWA STREET	DAVENPORT	**IA**	52801	(319) 322-3539
PITA BAKING CO. 6540 W. DIVERSEY AVENUE	CHICAGO	**IL**	60635	(312) 635-0556
RUBSCHLAGER BAKING CORPORATION 3220 WEST GRAND AVENUE	CHICAGO	**IL**	60651	(312) 826-1245
INTERNATIONAL BAKERS SERVICES, INC. 3839 PROGRESS DRIVE	SOUTH BEND	**IN**	46628	
H & S BAKERY 603 SOUTH BOND	BALTIMORE	**MD**	21231	(301) 276-7254
DEER PARK BAKING CO. P.O. BOX 500, S. EGG HARBOR	HAMMONTOWN	**NJ**	08037	(609) 561-2900
CHRISTINA'S STRUDEL, INC. 322 COMMERCIAL AVENUE	PALISADES PARK	**NJ**	07650	(201) 461-4064
ENTENMANN'S BAKERY INC. 1724 FIFTH AVENUE	BAY SHORE	**NY**	11706	(212) 273-6000
STELLO D'ORO BISCUIT COMPANY 184 WEST 237TH STREET	BRONX	**NY**	10463	(212) 549-3700
BLUE BAKING COMPANY 1003 METROPOLITAN AVENUE	BROOKLYN	**NY**	11232	(718) 782-4245
DAMASCUS BAKERY INC. - MIDDLE EASTERN BREADS & PASTRIES				
56 GOLD STREET	BROOKLYN	**NY**	11201	(718) 855-1457
EAST COAST PITA BAKERS 243 26TH STREET	BROOKLYN	**NY**	11232	(718) 499-1818
J.M.P. BAKERY COMPANY, INC. 508 JUNIUS	BROOKLYN	**NY**	11212	(718) 272-5400
JASON DAIRY PRODUCTS COMPANY 9204 DITMAS AVENUE	BROOKLYN	**NY**	11220	(718) 498-1881
KOSHER BAKERS INC. 814 BERGEN STREET	BROOKLYN	**NY**	11238	(718) 857-6464
MOSHA'S PUMPERNICKEL BAKERY 170 WYETH AVENUE	BROOKLYN	**NY**	11211	(718) 638-6100
PALAGONIA ITALIAN BREAD 508 JUNIUS STREET	BROOKLYN	**NY**	11218	(718) 272-5400
PECHTER-FIELD BAKING CORPORATION 800 PACIFIC STREET	BROOKLYN	**NY**	11238	(718) 638-6100
PITA HOUSE BAKERY, INC. 2610 AVENUE U	BROOKLYN	**NY**	11229	(718) 934-4717
POLLACK'S KOSHER COOKIE BAKERY INC. 5007 18TH AVENUE	BROOKLYN	**NY**	11204	(718) 435-3700
REISMAN BROTHERS BAKERY INC. 110 AVENUE O	BROOKLYN	**NY**	11204	(718) 331-2012
SAM'S FAMOUS KOSHER KNISHES 504 BRIGHTON BEACH AVENUE	BROOKLYN	**NY**	11235	(718) 646-5450
NATIONAL BAGEL CO., INC. 3100 N. TRIPHAMMER	LANSING	**NY**	14882	(607) 533-4265
FINK BAKING CORPORATION 5-35 54TH AVENUE	LONG ISLAND CITY	**NY**	11106	(718) 392-8300
THE CAKE STYLISTS, INC. 56-64 58TH PLACE	MASPETH	**NY**	11378	(718) 894-3494
BELLACICCO & SONS INC. 217-44 98TH AVENUE	QUEENS VILLAGE	**NY**	11429	(718) 479-5100
RESTIVO BROTHERS BAKERIES 1633 CENTRE STREET	RIDGEWOOD	**NY**	11385	(718) 456-0454
PHILADELPHIA BAKING CO. P.O. BOX 6914	PHILADELPHIA	**PA**	11915	(215) 464-4242

BANKS

BANK LEUMI LE-ISRAEL B.M. 9731 WILSHIRE BOULEVARD	BEVERLY HILLS	**CA**	90212	(213) 278-7001
ISRAEL DISCOUNT BANK, LTD. 9465 WILSHIRE BOULEVARD	BEVERLY HILLS	**CA**	90212	(213) 275-1411
BANK HAPOALIM B.M. 6501 WILSHIRE BOULEVARD	LOS ANGELES	**CA**	90048	(213) 658-7350
UNITED MIZRAHI BANK 727 WEST SEVENTH STREET	LOS ANGELES	**CA**	90017	(213) 623-7345
ISRAEL DISCOUNT BANK, LTD. 14 N.E. FIRST AVENUE	MIAMI	**FL**	33132	(305) 579-9200
BANK HAPOALIM/MIAMI BRANCH 407 LINCOLN ROAD	MIAMI BEACH	**FL**	33139	(305) 532-4476
BANK LEUMI LE-ISRAEL B.M. 407 LINCOLN ROAD MALL	MIAMI BEACH	**FL**	33139	(305) 531-3378
ISRAEL DISCOUNT BANK, LTD. 420 LINCOLN ROAD	MIAMI BEACH	**FL**	33139	(305) 579-9260
BANK HAPOALIM/CHICAGO BRANCH 174 NORTH MICHIGAN AVENUE	CHICAGO	**IL**	60601	(312) 621-0800
BANK LEUMI LE-ISRAEL B.M. 100 NORTH LASALLE STREET	CHICAGO	**IL**	60602	(312) 781-1800
BANK HAPOALIM/BOSTON BRANCH 70 FEDERAL STREET	BOSTON	**MA**	02110	(617) 482-7440
BANK LEUMI TRUST COMPANY OF NEW YORK 301 EAST FORDHAM ROAD	BRONX	**NY**	10458	(212) 220-5777
BANK LEUMI TRUST COMPANY OF NEW YORK 1321 KINGS HIGHWAY	BROOKLYN	**NY**	11229	(718) 998-6500
BANK LEUMI TRUST COMPANY OF NEW YORK				
3851 NOSTRAND AVENUE AT AVENUE Z	BROOKLYN	**NY**	11235	(718) 891-6700
BANK LEUMI TRUST COMPANY OF NEW YORK 4410 13TH AVENUE	BROOKLYN	**NY**	11219	(718) 854-1800
BANK LEUMI TRUST COMPANY OF NEW YORK 2095 RALPH AVENUE	BROOKLYN	**NY**	11234	(718) 968-7174
BANK LEUMI TRUST COMPANY OF NEW YORK				
188 MONTAGUE STREET	BROOKLYN	**NY**	11201	(718) 834-4800
BANK LEUMI TRUST COMPANY OF NEW YORK				
104-70 QUEENS BOULEVARD	FOREST HILLS	**NY**	11375	(718) 896-9200
BANK LEUMI TRUST COMPANY OF NEW YORK				
121 MIDDLE NECK ROAD	GREAT NECK	**NY**	11020	(516) 466-6270
BANK LEUMI TRUST COMPANY OF NEW YORK 1280 BROADWAY	HEWLETT	**NY**	11557	(516) 569-5400
BANK LEUMI TRUST COMPANY OF NEW YORK				
KENNEDY AIRPORT-EL AL TERMINAL	JAMAICA	**NY**	11430	(718) 656-4560
BANK HAPOALIM/HUNTINGTON BRANCH 445 BROAD HOLLOW ROAD	MELVILLE	**NY**	11747	(516) 752-7979
BANK DISCOUNT LE-ISRAEL 511 FIFTH AVENUE	NEW YORK	**NY**	10017	(212) 551-8500
BANK HAPOALIM B M - NEW YORK BRANCH 10 ROCKEFELLER PLAZA	NEW YORK	**NY**	10020	(212) 397-9650
BANK HAPOALIM B M, INTERNATIONAL DEPARTMENT				
10 ROCKEFELLER PLAZA	NEW YORK	**NY**	10020	(212) 397-7244
BANK HAPOALIM B M, LETTERS OF CREDIT 10 ROCKEFELLER PLAZA	NEW YORK	**NY**	10020	(212) 397-9670
BANK HAPOALIM B M, MONEY MARKET - OPERATIONS				
10 ROCKEFELLER PLAZA	NEW YORK	**NY**	10020	(212) 397-9602
BANK HAPOALIM B M, MONEY MARKET - TRADERS				
10 ROCKEFELLER PLAZA	NEW YORK	**NY**	10020	(212) 397-9490
BANK HAPOALIM B M, MONEY TRANSFER 10 ROCKEFELLER PLAZA	NEW YORK	**NY**	10020	(212) 397-8354
BANK HAPOALIM B M, SECURITIES DEPARTMENT				
10 ROCKEFELLER PLAZA	NEW YORK	**NY**	10020	(212) 397-8352
BANK HAPOALIM/ROCKEFELLER CENTER BRANCH				
10 ROCKEFELLER PLAZA	NEW YORK	**NY**	10020	(212) 397-9650
BANK LEUMI LE-ISRAEL B M NEW YORK AGENCY				
342 MADISON AVENUE	NEW YORK	**NY**	10017	(212) 850-9500
BANK LEUMI LE-ISRAEL B M NEW YORK AGENCY 562 FIFTH AVENUE	NEW YORK	**NY**	10017	(212) 832-5006
BANK LEUMI LE-ISRAEL B.M. 562 FIFTH AVENUE	NEW YORK	**NY**	10017	(212) 850-9500
BANK LEUMI LE-ISRAEL REGIONAL MANAGEMENT				
342 MADISON AVENUE	NEW YORK	**NY**	10017	(212) 850-9500
BANK LEUMI TRUST COMPANY 111 BROADWAY	NEW YORK	**NY**	10006	(212) 669-0333
BANK LEUMI TRUST COMPANY 1960 BROADWAY	NEW YORK	**NY**	10023	(212) 362-1443
BANK LEUMI TRUST COMPANY 605 THIRD AVENUE	NEW YORK	**NY**	10016	(212) 286-0860
BANK LEUMI TRUST COMPANY OF NEW YORK				
1660 SECOND AVENUE AT 86TH STREET	NEW YORK	**NY**	10028	(212) 534-8800

Into the ninth decade

The business of industrial development. The lifeline of Israel's future. And in the forefront Bank Leumi.

Bank Leumi has been actively financing and helping to develop international business for over 80 years. We began by offering loans and encouragement to the pioneers who built the foundation of Israel's economy.

Today, through our international network, we offer you the same professional approach and attention to clients' needs that helped to catapult Israel into the world arena.

Both in Israel and around the world, Bank Leumi offers you expertise: in cash management and foreign exchange, in import-export and correspondent banking, in acquisitions and mergers, financing through a full range of domestic and international banking services.

Our resources are considerable. With over 455 branches, offices and subsidiaries of which 74 are located overseas. Assets of more than US$24 billion. And experience, of over 80 years, has taught us how to use those resources for you.

Contact one of our conveniently located local offices or our Regional Management in New York for a copy of our annual report. And get the full story of what Bank Leumi can do for your business.

Regional Management
Western Hemisphere
342 Madison Ave.
Suite 1104
New York, NY 10173
Tel: (212)850-9500

Bank Leumi
Trust Company of New York*
579 Fifth Avenue
New York, NY 10017
Tel: (212) 382-4000
Telex: ITT 420968 Finut
    WUI 62856 Finyork
    RCA 232772 Finyur

27 branches

bank leumi le-israel בנק לאומי

Head Office:	New York*	Montreal	Nice	Punta del Este	Caracas
24-32 Yehuda Halevi St.	Los Angeles*	London	Zurich	Buenos Aires	Curaçao
Tel Aviv 65546	Encino*	Leeds	Geneva	São Paulo	Bahamas
Tel: (03)632111	Miami*	Paris	Frankfurt a/M	Santiago	Johannesburg
Telex: 33586 BLITA IL.	Chicago*	Marseille	Milan	Mexico City	Hong Kong
	Philadelphia*	Strasbourg	Antwerp	Panama City	Melbourne
	Toronto	Lyon	Montevideo	Cayman Islands	

*Member of FDIC

Bank Hapoalim B M

Head Office: 50 Rothschild Blvd., 65124 Tel Aviv, Israel.

Overseas Offices: Rockefeller Center, New York* • Plaza Branch, New York • Queens, New York* • Huntington, New York* • Miami, Florida
Boston, Massachusetts* • Los Angeles, California* • Chicago, Illinois* • Philadelphia, Pennsylvania* • London, West End, England
London, City, England • Manchester, England • Zurich, Switzerland • Luxembourg • Paris, France • Georgetown, Grand Cayman
Toronto, Canada • Montreal, Canada • Buenos Aires, Argentina • Sao Paulo, Brazil • Caracas, Venezuela • Punta del Este, Uruguay
Montevideo, Uruguay • Santiago, Chile • Panama City, Panama • Mexico City, Mexico
Regional Management — USA, 1 Rockefeller Plaza, Suite 1025, New York, New York.   *member F.D.I.C.

BANK LEUMI TRUST COMPANY OF NEW YORK
1148 THIRD AVENUE AT 67TH STREET .... NEW YORK **NY** 10021   (212) 570-2800
BANK LEUMI TRUST COMPANY OF NEW YORK
1960 BROADWAY AT LINCOLN SQUARE .... NEW YORK **NY** 10023   (212) 580-4000
BANK LEUMI TRUST COMPANY OF NEW YORK
845 THIRD AVENUE AT 52ND STREET .... NEW YORK **NY** 10022   (212) 935-7561
BANK LEUMI TRUST COMPANY OF NEW YORK
579 FIFTH AVENUE AT 47TH STREET............................ NEW YORK **NY** 10017   (212) 382-4407
BANK LEUMI TRUST COMPANY OF NEW YORK
562 FIFTH AVENUE AT 46TH STREET .... NEW YORK **NY** 10036   (212) 382-4193
BANK LEUMI TRUST COMPANY OF NEW YORK
535 SEVENTH AVENUE AT 39TH STREET .... NEW YORK **NY** 10018   (212) 382-4606
BANK LEUMI TRUST COMPANY OF NEW YORK
605 THIRD AVENUE AT 39TH STREET .... NEW YORK **NY** 10158   (212) 687-9666
BANK LEUMI TRUST COMPANY OF NEW YORK
301 THIRD AVENUE AT 23RD STREET .... NEW YORK **NY** 10010   (212) 679-5305
BANK LEUMI TRUST COMPANY OF NEW YORK
85 DELANCEY AT ORCHARD .... NEW YORK **NY** 10002   (212) 477-1150
BANK LEUMI TRUST COMPANY OF NEW YORK 177 EAST BROADWAY .... NEW YORK **NY** 10002   (212) 477-1201
BANK LEUMI TRUST COMPANY OF NEW YORK 25 BROAD STREET .... NEW YORK **NY** 10004   (212) 943-3400
BANK LEUMI TRUST COMPANY OF NEW YORK
111 BROADWAY (NEAR WALL STREET) .... NEW YORK **NY** 10006   (212) 669-0333

BANK LEUMI TRUST COMPANY OF NEW YORK - BROKERS LOAN
579 FIFTH AVENUE .... NEW YORK **NY** 10017   (212) 669-0327
BANK LEUMI TRUST COMPANY OF NEW YORK - COMMERCIAL FINANCE
579 FIFTH AVENUE .... NEW YORK **NY** 10017   (212) 382-4576
BANK LEUMI TRUST COMPANY OF NEW YORK-COMMERCIAL SERVICES
579 FIFTH AVENUE .... NEW YORK **NY** 10017   (212) 669-0257
BANK LEUMI TRUST COMPANY OF NEW YORK-EXECUTIVE OFFICES
579 FIFTH AVENUE .... NEW YORK **NY** 10017   (212) 382-4000
BANK LEUMI TRUST COMPANY OF NEW YORK-FOREIGN COLL. DEPT.
579 FIFTH AVENUE .... NEW YORK **NY** 10017   (212) 382-4070
BANK LEUMI TRUST COMPANY OF NEW YORK-INSTALLMENT LOANS
579 FIFTH AVENUE .... NEW YORK **NY** 10017   (212) 669-0219
BANK LEUMI TRUST COMPANY OF NEW YORK-LETTERS OF CR-ISSUE
579 FIFTH AVENUE .... NEW YORK **NY** 10017   (212) 382-4057
BANK LEUMI TRUST COMPANY OF NEW YORK-LETTERS OF CR-PAYMENT
579 FIFTH AVENUE .... NEW YORK **NY** 10017   (212) 382-4064
BANK LEUMI TRUST COMPANY OF NEW YORK-MONEY MARKET DEPT.
579 FIFTH AVENUE .... NEW YORK **NY** 10017   (212) 382-4503
BANK LEUMI TRUST COMPANY OF NEW YORK-PERSONNEL DEPT.
579 FIFTH AVENUE .... NEW YORK **NY** 10017   (212) 382-4451
BANK LEUMI TRUST COMPANY OF NEW YORK-PUBLIC RELATIONS
579 FIFTH AVENUE .... NEW YORK **NY** 10017   (212) 382-4494

BANK LEUMI TRUST COMPANY OF NEW YORK-TRUST DEPARTMENT 579 FIFTH AVENUE NEW YORK **NY** 10017 (212) 943-3613
BANK LEUMI TRUST COMPANY, COLLECTION DEPARTMENT 111 BROADWAY NEW YORK **NY** 10006 (212) 669-0200
ISRAEL DISCOUNT BANK OF N.Y. (MAIN OFFICE-COLLECTIONS) 511 FIFTH AVENUE NEW YORK **NY** 10017 (212) 551-8598
ISRAEL DISCOUNT BANK OF N.Y. (MAIN OFFICE-CREDIT INQUIRIES) 511 FIFTH AVENUE NEW YORK **NY** 10017 (212) 551-8573
ISRAEL DISCOUNT BANK OF N.Y. (MAIN OFFICE-ISRAEL INFO.) 511 FIFTH AVENUE NEW YORK **NY** 10017 (212) 551-8702
ISRAEL DISCOUNT BANK OF N.Y. (MAIN OFFICE-MONEY DESK) 511 FIFTH AVENUE NEW YORK **NY** 10017 (212) 551-8648
ISRAEL DISCOUNT BANK OF N.Y. (MAIN OFFICE-PERSONNEL) 511 FIFTH AVENUE NEW YORK **NY** 10017 (212) 551-8664
ISRAEL DISCOUNT BANK OF N.Y. (MAIN OFFICE-COMMERCIAL LOANS) 511 FIFTH AVENUE NEW YORK **NY** 10017 (212) 551-8532
ISRAEL DISCOUNT BANK OF N.Y. (MAIN OFFICE-INSTALLMENT LOANS) 511 FIFTH AVENUE NEW YORK **NY** 10017 (212) 551-8728
ISRAEL DISCOUNT BANK OF N.Y. (MAIN OFFICE-LETTERS OF CREDIT) 511 FIFTH AVENUE NEW YORK **NY** 10017 (212) 551-8590
ISRAEL DISCOUNT BANK OF N.Y. (MAIN OFFICE-MONEY TRANSFERS) 511 FIFTH AVENUE NEW YORK **NY** 10017 (212) 551-8617
ISRAEL DISCOUNT BANK OF N.Y. (MAIN OFFICE-NEW ACCOUNTS) 511 FIFTH AVENUE NEW YORK **NY** 10017 (212) 551-8709
ISRAEL DISCOUNT BANK OF NEW YORK 511 FIFTH AVENUE NEW YORK **NY** 10017 (212) 551-8500
ISRAEL DISCOUNT BANK OF NEW YORK 1350 BROADWAY NEW YORK **NY** 10018 (212) 551-8750
ISRAEL DISCOUNT BANK OF NEW YORK (MAIN OFFICE) 511 FIFTH AVENUE NEW YORK **NY** 10017 (212) 551-8500
NORTH AMERICAN BANK (TEL AVIV) 608 FIFTH AVENUE SUITE 403 NEW YORK **NY** 10020 (212) 245-2430
UMB BANK & TRUST COMPANY 630 FIFTH AVENUE NEW YORK **NY** 10020 (212) 541-8070
UMB BANK AND TRUST COMPANY ONE WORLD TRADE CENTER NEW YORK **NY** 10048 (212) 466-1114
UMB BANK AND TRUST COMPANY 350 FIFTH AVENUE NEW YORK **NY** 10118 (212) 947-3611
BANK LEUMI TRUST COMPANY OF NEW YORK 1105 OLD COUNTRY ROAD PLAINVIEW **NY** 11803 (516) 935-4800
BANK HAPOALIM B M - QUEENS BRANCH 97-77 QUEENS BOULEVARD REGO PARK **NY** 11374 (718) 544-7900
BANK HAPOALIM/QUEENS BRANCH 97-77 QUEENS BOULEVARD REGO PARK **NY** 11374 (718) 544-7900
BANK LEUMI TRUST COMPANY OF NEW YORK 97-03 QUEENS BOULEVARD REGO PARK **NY** 11374 (718) 896-7300
BANK HAPOALIM B.M. 3 PENN CENTER PLAZA PHILADELPHIA **PA** 19102 (215) 665-2200
BANK HAPOALIM/PHILADELPHIA BRANCH 3 PENN CENTER PLAZA PHILADELPHIA **PA** 19102 (215) 665-2200
BANK LEUMI LE-ISRAEL B.M. 1511 WALNUT STREET PHILADELPHIA **PA** 19102 (215) 299-4400

BATIK

ORA BATIK 1 TAYLOR LANE TROY **NY** 12180 (518) 274-0758

BET DIN - JEWISH COURT

RABBINICAL ASSEMBLY-WESTERN STATES REGION C/O UNIVERSITY OF JUDAISM, 15600 MULHOLLAND DRIVE LOS ANGELES **CA** 90077 (213) 476-9777
JEWISH CONCILIATION BOARD 163 SOUTH FAIRFAX AVENUE LOS ANGELES **CA** 90036 (213) 938-6271
BETH DIN, JEWISH COURT & ARBITRATION COMMITTEE 1850 ORTEGA STREET SAN FRANCISCO **CA** 94122 (415) 661-4055
BET DIN - RABBI DR. TIBOR H. STERN 1532 WASHINGTON AVENUE MIAMI BEACH **FL** 33139 (305) 534-1004
BET DIN C/O RABBI DAVID LEHRFIELD 1400 LENOX AVENUE MIAMI BEACH **FL** 33139 (305) 672-0894
BET DIN 5718 N. DRAKE AVENUE CHICAGO **IL** 60659 (312) 588-4252
BET DIN ZEDEK 2735 WEST DEVON CHICAGO **IL** 60659 (312) 764-0259
SYNAGOGUE COUNCIL OF MASSACHUSETTS 177 TREMONT STREET BOSTON **MA** 02115 (617) 426-1832
JEWISH BOARD OF ARBITRATION 319 WEST MONUMENT BALTIMORE **MD** 21201 (301) 752-2630
SUPREME RABBINIC COURT OF AMERICA 1401 ARCOLA AVENUE SILVER SPRING **MD** 20902 (301) 649-2799
RABBINIC COURT OF EAST FLATBUSH 333 EAST 52ND STREET BROOKLYN **NY** 11203 (718) 498-2801
RABBINICAL COURT OF BROOKLYN 1447 56TH STREET BROOKLYN **NY** 11219 (718) 851-2626
RABBINICAL COURT OF BROOKLYN 5424 16TH AVENUE BROOKLYN **NY** 11204 (718) 633-6378
BETH DIN OF AMERICA 275 SEVENTH AVENUE NEW YORK **NY** 10001 (212) 807-9042
BETH DIN OF THE U.S.A. 220 PARK AVENUE S. NEW YORK **NY** 10003 (212) 677-4030
JEWISH CONCILIATION BOARD OF AMERICA 120 W. 57TH STREET, SUITE 2600 NEW YORK **NY** 10019 (212) 582-3577
RABBINICAL ASSEMBLY 3080 BROADWAY NEW YORK **NY** 10027 (212) 678-8000
RABBINICAL COURT OF THE RABBINICAL ALLIANCE OF AMERICA 156 FIFTH AVENUE, ROOM 810 NEW YORK **NY** 10010 (212) 242-6420
BET DIN C/O RABBI PELBERG 904 WEST DUNCANNON STREET PHILADELPHIA **PA** 19140 (215) 745-4292
BETH DIN-RABBINICAL COURT 7926 ALGON AVENUE PHILADELPHIA **PA** 19111 (215) 722-6161
BET DIN C/O RABBI KENNETH HAIN-UNITED ORTHODOX SYNAGOGUES 4221 S. BRAESWOOD BLVD. HOUSTON **TX** 77096 (713) 723-3850

BEVERAGES

SYFO WATER CO., INC. 129 55 NE 14TH AVENUE NORTH MIAMI **FL** 33161 (305) 891-2200
ROYAL CROWN COLA 2550 GOLF ROAD, SUITE 500 ROLLING MEADOWS **IL** 60008 (800) 323-0338
MAYIM CHAIM BEVERAGE CORP. 626 WITTIER AVENUE BRONX **NY** 10450 (212) 378-2525
CORNELL BEVERAGES INC. 105 HARRISON PLACE BROOKLYN **NY** 11237 (718) 381-3000
CROWN BEVERAGE CORP. 458 COZINE AVENUE BROOKLYN **NY** 11208 (718) 257-2320

BIG BROTHER/BIG SISTER ORGANIZATIONS

JEWISH BIG BROTHERS ASSOCIATION 6505 WILSHIRE BLVD. LOS ANGELES **CA** 90048 (213) 852-1234
JEWISH BIG BROTHERS ASSOCIATION 6851 LENNOX AVENUE VAN NUYS **CA** 91405 (818) 785-8861
JEWISH BIG SISTERS 2451 NORTH SACRAMENTO CHICAGO **IL** 60647
JEWISH BIG BROTHER ASSOCIATION OF BOSTON 31 NEW CHARDON STREET BOSTON **MA** 02110 (617) 367-5818
BIG BROTHER LEAGUE OF BALTIMORE 5750 PARK HEIGHTS AVENUE BALTIMORE **MD** 21215 (301) 542-6300
JEWISH BIG BROTHER & BIG SISTER LEAGUE 5750 PARK HEIGHTS AVENUE BALTIMORE **MD** 21215 (301) 466-4242
BIG BROTHER OF JEWISH FAMILY SERVICE 20 BANTA PLACE HACKENSACK **NJ** 07601 (201) 488-8340
JEWISH BIG BROTHERS OF THE JEWISH BOARD OF GUARDIANS 120 WEST 57TH STREET NEW YORK **NY** 10019 (212) 582-9100
BIG BROTHER ASSOCIATION OF CINCINNATI 1580 SUMMIT ROAD CINCINNATI **OH** 45237 (513) 761-3200
THE JEWISH BIG BROTHERS AND BIG SISTERS ASSOCIATION 22001 FAIRMONT BOULEVARD CLEVELAND **OH** 44118 (216) 932-2800

BIKUR HOLIM SOCIETIES

BIKUR CHOLIM SHEVET ACHIM 278 WINTHROP AVENUE NEW HAVEN **CT** 06502 (203) 776-4997
BIKUR CHOLIM LODGE 1400 S. DES PLAINES AVENUE FOREST PARK **IL** 60130 (312) 366-4541
BIKUR CHOLIM 22 MARKET STREET PASSAIC **NJ** 07055
BIKUR CHOLIM MEDICAL OFFICE 566 BEDFORD AVENUE BROOKLYN **NY** 11211
BIKUR CHOLIM MEDICAL OFFICE 281 MARCY AVENUE BROOKLYN **NY** 11211
BIKUR CHOLIM OF REMSEN VILLAGE 9202 AVENUE A BROOKLYN **NY** 11236 (718) 338-6230
BIKUR CHOLIM VISITING SICK SOCIETY OF BROOKLYN 8656 21ST AVENUE BROOKLYN **NY** 11230 (718) 372-8848
BIKUR CHOLIM OF THE STATE OF NEW YORK 260 BROADWAY BROOKLYN **NY** 11211 (718) 387-3876
KUPATH CHOLIM 372 KINGSTON AVENUE BROOKLYN **NY** 11213 (718) 604-0900
KUPATH CHOLIM 1277 55TH STREET BROOKLYN **NY** 11210 (718) 438-2367
UNITED BIKUR CHOLIM OF WILLIAMSBURG 260 BROADWAY BROOKLYN **NY** 11211 (718) 387-4517
UNITED BIKUR CHOLIM OF WILLIAMSBURG 260 BROADWAY BROOKLYN **NY** 11211 (718) 387-4517
UNITED BIKUR CHOLIM OF WILLIAMSBURG 80 LEE AVENUE BROOKLYN **NY** 11211 (718) 387-4517
BIALYSTOKER CENTER & BIKUR CHOLIM 228 EAST BROADWAY NEW YORK **NY** 10002 (718) 475-7755
BIKUR HOLIM DAVID & JEROME ROADS TREVOSE **PA** 19047 (215) 357-7131
BIKUR CHOLIM 5145 S. MORGAN STREET SEATTLE **WA** 98102 (206) 723-0970
BIKUR CHOLIM 6500 52ND STREET SEATTLE **WA** 98102

BLIND, HOMES & ORGANIZATIONS FOR THE

CHICAGO RABBINICAL COUNCIL 3525 PETERSON AVENUE CHICAGO **IL** 60659 (312) 588-1600
HOME OF THE ASSOCIATION OF JEWISH BLIND 3525 WEST FOSTER CHICAGO **IL** 60625 (312) 478-7040
NEW YORK INSTITUTE FOR THE EDUCATION OF THE BLIND 999 PELHAM PARKWAY BRONX **NY** 10469 (212) 547-1234
AMERICAN-ISRAELI LIGHTHOUSE 30 EAST 60TH STREET NEW YORK **NY** 10023 (212) 838-5322
JEWISH BRAILLE INSTITUTE OF AMERICA 110 EAST 30TH STREET NEW YORK **NY** 10016 (212) 889-2525
JEWISH BRAILLE REVIEW (PUBLICATION) 110 EAST 30TH STREET NEW YORK **NY** 10016 (212) 889-2525
JEWISH GUILD FOR THE BLIND 15 W. 65TH STREET NEW YORK **NY** 10023 (212) 595-2000
KEREN-OR JERUSALEM INSTITUTE FOR THE BLIND, INC. 1133 BROADWAY NEW YORK **NY** 10010 (212) 255-1180
JEWISH GUILD FOR THE BLIND HOME 75 STRATTON STREET YONKERS **NY** 10701 (914) 963-4661

B'NAI B'RITH HILLEL FOUNDATIONS

AUBURN UNIVERSITY-B'NAI B'RITH HILLEL COUNSELORSHIP 442 CARY DRIVE AUBURN **AL** 36830 (205) 887-9550
UNIVERSITY OF ALABAMA IN BIRMINGHAM, HILLEL AFFILATE C/O HESSE, 3824 HALBROOK LANE BIRMINGHAM **AL** 35243 (205) 969-2801
UNIVERSITY OF ALABAMA-B'NAI B'RITH HILLEL FOUNDATION 728 10TH AVENUE TUSCALOOSA **AL** 35401 (205) 758-3280
UNIVERSITY OF ARKANSAS-B'NAI B'RITH HILLEL COUNSELORSHIP C/O FELDMAN-DEPARTMENT OF MATH FAYETTEVILLE **AR** 72701 (501) 575-3351
UNIVERSITY OF ALBERTA - B'NAI B'RITH HILLEL COUNSELORSHIP P.O. BOX 81 STUDENT UNION EDMONTON **AT** T6G 2E0 (403) 484-1917
NORTHERN ARIZONA UNIVERSITY-HILLEL C.U. BOX 15036 FLAGSTAFF **AZ** 86011 (602) 523-3613
ARIZONA STATE UNIVERSITY-B'NAI B'RITH HILLEL FOUNDATION 1012 SOUTH MILL TEMPE **AZ** 85281 (602) 967-7563
PHOENIX COLLEGE-B'NAI B'RITH HILLEL COUNSELORSHIP 1012 SOUTH MILL TEMPE **AZ** 85281 (602) 967-7563
UNIVERSITY OF ARIZONA-B'NAI B'RITH HILLEL FOUNDATION 1245 E. 2ND STREET, BOX 40523 TUCSON **AZ** 85719 (602) 624-6561
UNIV. OF BRIT. COL.-VANCOUVER B'NAI B'RITH HILLEL FOUNDATION BOX 43 SUB, UBC VANCOUVER **BC** V6T 1W5 (604) 224-4748
UNIV. OF CALIFORNIA-BERKELEY-B'NAI B'RITH HILLEL FOUNDATION 2736 BANCROFT WAY BERKELEY **CA** 94704 (415) 845-7793
CALIFORNIA STATE UNIV./CHICO-JEWISH STUDENT UNION BMU CHICO STATE CHICO **CA** 95929 (916) 895-6774
CLAREMONT COLLEGES-HILLEL AT THE CLAREMONT COLLEGES MCALISTER, 919 N. COLUMBIA CLAREMONT **CA** 91711 (714) 621-8000
UNIV. OF CALIFORNIA-DAVIS-B'NAI B'RITH HILLEL COUNSELORSHIP 328 A STREET DAVIS **CA** 95616 (916) 756-3708
CALIFORNIA STATE UNIVER./FRESNO-B'NAI B'RITH HILLEL COUNSEL. POST OFFICE BOX 1328 FRESNO **CA** 93710 (209) 264-2929
UNIV. OF CALIF.-SANTA BARBARA-B'NAI B'RITH HILLEL FOUNDATION URC. 770 CAMINO PESCADERO GOLETA **CA** 93017 (805) 968-1555
CALIFORNIA STATE UNIV./HAYWARD-HILLEL EXTENSION CSU HAYWARD **CA** 94542
CALIFORNIA STATE UNIV./LONG BEACH-JEWISH STUDENT SERVICES JCC 3801 E. WILLOW LONG BEACH **CA** 90815 (213) 426-7601
CERRITOS COMMUNITY COLLEGE-JEWISH COLLEGE STUDENT SERVICE JCC 3801 E. WILLOW LONG BEACH **CA** 90815 (213) 426-7601
CYPRESS COLLEGE-JEWISH COLLEGE STUDENT SERVICES JCC 3801 E. WILLOW LONG BEACH **CA** 90815 (213) 426-7601
LONG BEACH CITY COLLEGE-JEWISH COLLEGE STUDENT SERVICES JCC 3801 E. WILLOW LONG BEACH **CA** 90815 (213) 426-7601
CALIFORNIA STATE UNIV./DOMINGUEZ HILLS-SOUTH BAY HILLEL C/O LAHC 900 HILGARD AVENUE LOS ANGELES **CA** 90024 (213) 208-4427

CALIFORNIA STATE UNIV./LOS ANGELES-HILLEL EXTENSION
5151 STATE COLLEGE DRIVE .... LOS ANGELES **CA** (213) 224-0111
EL CAMINO COLLEGE-SOUTH BAY HILLEL
C/O LAHC, 900 HILGARD AVENUE .... LOS ANGELES **CA** 90024 (213) 208-4427
LOS ANGELES HARBOR COLLEGE-SOUTH BAY HILLEL
C/O LAHC, 900 HILGARD AVENUE .... LOS ANGELES **CA** 90024 (213) 208-4427
LOS ANGELES HILLEL COUNCIL 900 HILGARD AVENUE .... LOS ANGELES **CA** 90024 (213) 208-6639
LOS ANGELES PIERCE COLLEGE-HILLEL EXTENSION
C/O LAHC, 900 HILGARD AVENUE .... LOS ANGELES **CA** 90024 (213) 208-4427
LOYOLA MARYMOUNT U.-S. BAY HILLEL/JEWISH LAW STUDENT ASSOC.
C/O LAHC, 900 HILGARD AVENUE .... LOS ANGELES **CA** 90024 (213) 208-4427
OCCIDENTAL COLLEGE-HILLEL EXTENSION 1600 CAMPUS ROAD .... LOS ANGELES **CA** (213) 259-2621
SANTA MONICA COLLEGE-HILLEL EXTENSION
C/O LAHC, 900 HILGARD AVENUE .... LOS ANGELES **CA** 90024 (213) 208-4427
SOUTHWESTERN LAW SCHOOL-JEWISH LAW STUDENTS ASSOCIATION
C/O LAHC, 900 HILGARD AVENUE .... LOS ANGELES **CA** 90024 (213) 208-4427
UCLA-B'NAI B'RITH HILLEL FOUNDATION 900 HILGARD AVENUE .... LOS ANGELES **CA** 90024 (213) 208-3081
UNIV. OF CALIFORNIA-L.A.-B'NAI B'RITH HILLEL FOUNDATION
900 HILGARD AVENUE .... LOS ANGELES **CA** 90024 (213) 208-3081
UNIV. OF SOUTHERN. CAL.-B'NAI B'RITH HILLEL FOUNDATION
3300 S. HOOVER BLVD .... LOS ANGELES **CA** 90007 (213) 747-9135
WHITTIER SCHOOL OF LAW-JEWISH LAW STUDENTS ASSOCIATION
C/O LAHC, 900 HILGARD AVENUE .... LOS ANGELES **CA** 90024 (213) 208-4427
CALIFORNIA STATE UNIV./NORTHRIDGE-B'NAI B'RITH HILLEL FOUND.
17729 PLUMMER STREET .... NORTHRIDGE **CA** 91325 (818) 886-5101
MILLS COLLEGE-HILLEL EXTENSION 5000 MACARTHUR BLVD .... OAKLAND **CA** 94613
CALIFORNIA INSTITUTE OF TECHNOLOGY-HILLEL EXTENSION
1201 E. CALIFORNIA .... PASADENA **CA** 91109 (818) 356-6811
PASADENA CITY COLLEGE-HILLEL EXTENSION 1570 E. COLORADO .... PASADENA **CA** 91106 (818) 578-7391
UNIVERSITY OF REDLANDS-JEWISH STUDENT GROUP
COUNTY CENTER, 1200 E. COLTON AVENUE .... REDLANDS **CA** 92373 (714) 793-2121
UNIV. OF CALIF.-RIVERSIDE-B'NAI B'RITH HILLEL COUNSELORSHIP
2532 GONZAGA LANE .... RIVERSIDE **CA** 92507 (714) 682-6341
CALIFORNIA STATE UNIV./SAN BERNARDINO-HILLEL
6000 STATE COLLEGE PARKWAY .... SAN BERNARDINO **CA** 92404
SAN DIEGO STATE UNIVERSITY-JEWISH CAMPUS CENTERS
5742 MONTEZUMA ROAD .... SAN DIEGO **CA** 92115 (619) 583-6080
UNIV. OF CALIFORNIA-SAN DIEGO-JEWISH CAMPUS CENTERS
OFFICE OF RELIGIOUS AFFAIRS, UCSD .... SAN DIEGO **CA** 92037 (619) 452-2521
SAN FRANCISCO STATE UNIV.-B'NAI B'RITH HILLEL FOUNDATION
33 BANBURY DRIVE .... SAN FRANCISCO **CA** 94132 (415) 333-4922
SAN JOSE STATE UNIV.-B'NAI B'RITH HILLEL COUNSELORSHIP
300 S. 10TH STREET .... SAN JOSE **CA** 95112 (408) 267-2770
UNIVERSITY OF SANTA CLARA-HILLEL EXTENSION 300 S. 10TH STREET .... SAN JOSE **CA** 95112 (408) 267-2770
UNIV. OF CALIFORNIA-SANTA CRUZ-JEWISH STUDENT COALITION
TEMPLE BETH-EL, 920 BAY STREET .... SANTA CRUZ **CA** 95060 (408) 423-3012
STANFORD UNIVERSITY-B'NAI B'RITH HILLEL FOUNDATION
OLD UNION CLUBHOUSE, BOX 3034 .... STANFORD **CA** 94305 (415) 497-1602
CALIFORNIA STATE UNIV./FULLERTON-JEWISH STUDENT PROGRAM
13411 CROMWELL DRIVE .... TUSTIN **CA** 92680 (714) 838-2825
UNIV. OF CALIFORNIA-IRVINE-JEWISH STUDENT PROGRAM
13411 CROMWELL DRIVE .... TUSTIN **CA** 92680 (714) 838-2825
LOS ANGELES VALLEY COLLEGE-B'NAI B'RITH HILLEL FOUNDATION
13162 BURBANK BLVD .... VAN NUYS **CA** 91401 (818) 994-7443
WHITTIER COLLEGE-HILLEL EXTENSION 13500 PHILADELPHIA STREET .... WHITTIER **CA** 90608 (213) 693-0771
UNIV. OF COLORADO-B'NAI B'RITH HILLEL FOUNDATION
2795 COLORADO AVENUE .... BOULDER **CO** 80302 (303) 442-6571
UNIV. OF DENVER-B'NAI B'RITH HILLEL COUNSELORSHIP
CENTER FOR JUDAIC STUDIES-UNIVERSITY PARK .... DENVER **CO** 80208 (303) 753-2255
COLORADO STATE UNIV.-B'NAI B'RITH HILLEL COUNSELORSHIP .... FORT COLLINS **CO** 80523 (303) 394-2001
UNIV. OF NORTH. COLORADO-B'NAI B'RITH HILLEL COUNSELORSHIP
STUDENT CENTER .... GREELEY **CO** 80639 (303) 394-2001
UNIV. OF BRIDGEPORT-B'NAI B'RITH HILLEL COUNSELORSHIP
174 UNIVERSITY AVENUE .... BRIDGEPORT **CT** 06601 (203) 576-4532
TRINITY COLLEGE-B'NAI B'RITH HILLEL COUNSELORSHIP
30 CRESCENT STREET .... HARTFORD **CT** 06106 (213) 527-3151
UNIVERSITY OF HARTFORD-JEWISH STUDENT UNION
BOX 3027 TRINITY COLLEGE .... HARTFORD **CT** 06106 (213) 527-3151
WESLEYAN UNIVERSITY-HAVURAH
C/O DEPARTMENT OF RELIGION .... MIDDLETOWN **CT** 06457 (203) 347-9411
CENTRAL CONNECTICUT STATE COLLEGE-JEWISH STUDENT GROUP
1615 STANLEY STREET .... NEW BRITAIN **CT** 06053 (203) 223-6935
YALE UNIVERSITY-B'NAI B'RITH HILLEL FOUNDATION
1904A YALE STATION .... NEW HAVEN **CT** 06520 (203) 432-4174
CONNECTICUT COLLEGE-CONNECTICUT COLLEGE CHAVURAH
C/O JEWISH FEDERATION, 302 STATE STREET .... NEW LONDON **CT** 06320 (203) 442-8062
U.S. COAST GUARD ACADEMY-CONNECTICUT COLLEGE CHAVURAH
C/O JEWISH FEDERATION, 302 STATE STREET .... NEW LONDON **CT** 06320 (203) 442-8062
UNIV. OF CONNECTICUT-B'NAI B'RITH HILLEL FOUNDATION
N. EAGLEVILLE ROAD .... STORRS **CT** 06268 (203) 429-9007
AMERICAN UNIVERSITY-B'NAI B'RITH HILLEL FOUNDATION
KAY SPIRITUAL LIFE CENTER/AU .... WASHINGTON **DC** 20016 (202) 686-2390
ANTIOCH LAW SCHOOL-JEWISH COMMUNITY CAUCUS
2633 16TH STREET N.W. BOX 159 .... WASHINGTON **DC** 20009 (202) 667-2125
CATHOLIC UNIVERSITY-HILLEL COMMUNITY CAMPUS MINISTRY .... WASHINGTON **DC** 20064 (202) 269-6528
GALLAUDET COLLEGE-B'NAI B'RITH HILLEL COUNSELORSHIP
CAMPUS MINISTRIES/GALLAUDET .... WASHINGTON **DC** 20002 (202) 651-5347
GEORGE WASHINGTON UNIV.-B'NAI B'RITH HILLEL FOUNDATION
2129 F STREET N. W. .... WASHINGTON **DC** 20037 (202) 338-4747
GEORGETOWN UNIVERSITY-HILLEL-JSA
CAMPUS MINISTRIES-ONE HEALY .... WASHINGTON **DC** 20057 (202) 625-2694

INTERNATIONAL OFFICE 1640 RHODE ISLAND AVENUE, N.W. .... WASHINGTON **DC** 20036 (202) 857-6560
WASHINGTON, D.C.-JEWISH CAMPUS ACTIVITIES BOARD
2129 F STREET, N.W. .... WASHINGTON **DC** 20037 (202) 333-5923
UNIV. OF DELAWARE-B'NAI B'RITH HILLEL COUNSELORSHIP
TEMPLE BETH-EL .... NEWARK **DE** 19711 (302) 366-8330
FLORIDA ATLANTIC UNIVERSITY-HILLEL EXTENSION
UNITED CAMPUS MINISTRY SSB212 .... BOCA RATON **FL** 33431 (305) 395-5100
MIAMI/FLORIDA-B'NAI B'RITH HILLEL FOUNDATIONS OF GR. MIAMI
1100 STANFORD DRIVE .... CORAL GABLES **FL** 33146 (305) 661-8549
UNIVERSITY OF MIAMI-B'NAI B'RITH HILLEL FOUNDATION
1100 STANFORD DRIVE .... CORAL GABLES **FL** 33146 (305) 665-6948
BROWARD COMMUNITY COLLEGE-B'NAI B'RITH HILLEL EXTENSION
(3 CAMPUSES) .... FORT LAUDERDALE **FL** 33301
UNIVERSITY OF FLORIDA-B'NAI B'RITH HILLEL FOUNDATION
16 NW 18TH STREET .... GAINESVILLE **FL** 32603 (904) 372-2900
JACKSONVILLE UNIVERSITY-B'NAI B'RITH HILLEL COUNSELORSHIP
2800 UNIVERSITY BOULEVARD, N. .... JACKSONVILLE **FL** 32211 (904) 744-3950
FLORIDA SOUTHERN COLLEGE-HILLEL .... LAKELAND **FL** 33803
UNIVERSITY OF NORTH FLORIDA-B'NAI B'RITH HILLEL EXTENSION
11136 RIVER CK.DR.W .... MANDARIN **FL** 32217 (904) 268-7649
FLORIDA INT'L UNIVERSITY-B'NAI B'RITH HILLEL FOUNDATION
F.I.U. TAMIAMI TRAIL .... MIAMI **FL** 33199 (305) 554-2215
MIAMI-DADE COMMUNITY COLLEGE, NO.-B'NAI B'RITH HILLEL EXT. .... MIAMI **FL** 33167
MIAMI-DADE COMMUNITY COLLEGE, SO.-B'NAI B'RITH HILLEL EXT.
DEPT OF ARCH. MIAMI-DADE CC .... MIAMI **FL** 33176 (305) 596-1225
BARRY UNIVERSITY-HILLEL JEWISH STUDENT UNION
11300 N.E. SECOND AVENUE .... MIAMI SHORES **FL** 33161 (305) 758-3392
UNIVERSITY OF CENTRAL FLORIDA-B'NAI B'RITH HILLEL EXTENSION
P.O. BOX 26, 279 .... ORLANDO **FL** 32816 (305) 275-2233
COLLEGE OF BOCA RATON-HILLEL: JSU 10371 FAIRWAY ROAD .... PEMBROKE PINES **FL** 33026 (305) 432-6281
FLORIDA INT'L UNIVERSITY NORTH-HILLEL JSU
10371 FAIRWAY ROAD .... PEMBROKE PINES **FL** 33026 (305) 432-6287
PALM BEACH JUNIOR COLLEGE-HILLEL JSU
10371 FAIRWAY ROAD .... PEMBROKE PINES **FL** 33026 (305) 432-6281
UNIVERSITY OF S. FLORIDA/NEW COLLEGE-HILLEL EXTENSION
5700 N. TAMIAMI TRAIL, BOX 526 .... SARASOTA **FL** 33580 (813) 355-7671
ECKERD COLLEGE-HILLEL JEWISH STUDENT UNION
ECKERD COLLEGE-BOX J .... ST. PETERSBURG **FL** 33733 (813) 867-1166
FLORIDA STATE UNIVERSITY-B'NAI B'RITH HILLEL FOUNDATION
843 W. PENSACOLA STREET .... TALLAHASSEE **FL** 32304 (904) 222-5454
UNIVERSITY OF SOUTH FLORIDA-B'NAI B'RITH HILLEL FOUNDATION
5014 PATRICIA COURT, #172 .... TAMPA **FL** 33617 (813) 988-7076
UNIVERSITY OF TAMPA-JEWISH STUDENT ACTIVITIES ORGANIZATION
P.O. BOX 2599 .... TAMPA **FL** 33606 (813) 253-3117
ROLLINS COLLEGE-JEWISH STUDENT LEAGUE
PO BOX 2666 ROLLINS COLLEGE .... WINTER PARK **FL** 32789 (305) 646-2000
UNIVERSITY OF GEORGIA-B'NAI B'RITH HILLEL FOUNDATION
1155 S. MILLEDGE AVENUE .... ATHENS **GA** 30605 (404) 543-6393
EMORY UNIVERSITY-B'NAI B'RITH HILLEL FOUNDATION
DRAWER A. EMORY UNIVERSITY .... ATLANTA **GA** 30329 (404) 329-6490
GEORGIA STATE UNIVERSITY-B'NAI B'RITH HILLEL EXTENSION
DRAWER A. EMORY UNIVERSITY .... ATLANTA **GA** 30329 (404) 329-6490
GEORGIA TECHNICAL INSTITUTE-B'NAI B'RITH HILLEL EXTENSION
DRAWER A. EMORY UNIVERSITY .... ATLANTA **GA** 30329 (404) 329-6490
OGLETHORPE UNIVERSITY-B'NAI B'RITH HILLEL EXTENSION
DRAWER A. EMORY UNIVERSITY .... ATLANTA **GA** 30329 (404) 329-6490
IOWA STATE UNIVERSITY-B'NAI B'RITH HILLEL COUNSELORSHIP
C/O DEPT. OF ZOOLOGY-234 SCI 2 .... AMES **IA** 50011 (515) 294-1309
DRAKE UNIVERSITY-B'NAI B'RITH HILLEL COUNSELORSHIP
3303 UNIVERSITY .... DES MOINES **IA** 50311 (515) 274-5769
GRINNELL COLLEGE-ASSOCIATED JEWISH STUDENTS
STEINER HALL #20 .... GRINNELL **IA** 50112 (515) 236-2864
UNIVERSITY OF IOWA-B'NAI B'RITH HILLEL FOUNDATION
122 E. MARKET STREET .... IOWA CITY **IA** 52240 (319) 338-0778
SOUTHERN ILLINOIS UNIVERSITY-B'NAI B'RITH HILLEL FOUNDATION
913 SOUTH ILLINOIS .... CARBONDALE **IL** 62901 (618) 457-7279
UNIV. OF ILLINOIS AT CHAMPAIGN-B'NAI B'RITH HILLEL FOUND.
503 E. JOHN STREET .... CHAMPAIGN **IL** 61820 (217) 344-1328
CHICAGO/ILLINOIS-B'NAI B'RITH HILLEL FOUNDATIONS, JEWISH FD.
ONE SOUTH FRANKLIN ST., COLLEGE AGE YOUTH SERVICES OF IL .... CHICAGO **IL** 60606 (312) 346-6700
LOYOLA UNIVERSITY-LOYOLA JEWISH STUDENT ORGANIZATION
ASSISI CENTER, 1132 W. LOYOLA .... CHICAGO **IL** 60626 (312) 274-3000
UNIV. OF ILLINOIS AT CHICAGO-B'NAI B'RITH HILLEL FOUNDATION
516 CCC UNIV. OF ILLINOIS CIRCLE CAMPUS .... CHICAGO **IL** 60680 (312) 996-3385
UNIVERSITY OF CHICAGO-B'NAI B'RITH HILLEL FOUNDATION
5715 S. WOODLAWN AVENUE .... CHICAGO **IL** 60637 (312) 752-1127
NORTHERN ILLINOIS UNIVERSITY-B'NAI B'RITH HILLEL FOUNDATION
JCC 820 RUSSELL ROAD .... DEKALB **IL** 60115 (815) 758-4582
OAKTON COMMUNITY COLLEGE-GESHER 1600 EAST GOLF ROAD .... DES PLAINES **IL** 60016 (312) 635-1600
NORTHEASTERN ILLINOIS UNIVERSITY - HILLEL
1935 SHERMAN AVENUE .... EVANSTON **IL** 60201 (312) 328-0650
NORTHWESTERN UNIVERSITY-B'NAI B'RITH HILLEL FOUNDATION
1935 SHERMAN AVENUE .... EVANSTON **IL** 60201 (312) 328-0650
WESTERN ILLINOIS UNIVERSITY-HILLEL
DEPARTMENT OF LEARNING RESOURCES .... MACOMB **IL** 61455 (309) 298-1645
ILLINOIS STATE UNIVERSITY-B'NAI B'RITH HILLEL COUNSELORSHIP
225 N. UNIVERSITY STREET .... NORMAL **IL** 61761
BRADLEY UNIVERSITY-B'NAI B'RITH HILLEL COUNSELORSHIP
HILLEL HOUSE 1410 W. FREDONIA .... PEORIA **IL** 61606 (309) 676-7611
INDIANA UNIVERSITY-B'NAI B'RITH HILLEL FOUNDATION
730 EAST 3RD STREET .... BLOOMINGTON **IN** 47401 (812) 336-3824

PURDUE UNIVERSITY-B'NAI B'RITH HILLEL FOUNDATION				
912 W. STATE STREET	WEST LAFAYETTE	**IN**	47906	(317) 743-1293
UNIVERSITY OF KANSAS-B'NAI B'RITH HILLEL COUNSELORSHIP				
B-117 KANSAS UNION	LAWRENCE	**KS**	66045	(913) 864-3948
KANSAS STATE UNIVERSITY-B'NAI B'RITH HILLEL COUNSELORSHIP				
1509 WREATH AVENUE	MANHATTAN	**KS**	66502	(913) 539-9292
UNIVERSITY OF LOUISVILLE-B'NAI B'RITH HILLEL COUNSELORSHIP				
ECUMENICAL CENTER	LOUISVILLE	**KY**	40292	(502) 588-6598
LOUISIANA STATE UNIVERSITY-B'NAI B'RITH HILLEL COUNSELORSHIP				
PO BOX 116420A	BATON ROUGE	**LA**	70893	(504) 383-9082
LOYOLA UNIVERSITY-B'NAI B'RITH HILLEL EXTENSION				
912 BROADWAY	NEW ORLEANS	**LA**	70118	(504) 866-7060
TULANE-NEWCOMB UNIVERSITIES-B'NAI B'RITH HILLEL FOUNDATION				
912 BROADWAY	NEW ORLEANS	**LA**	70118	(504) 866-7060
UNIVERSITY OF NEW ORLEANS-B'NAI B'RITH HILLEL EXTENSION				
912 BROADWAY	NEW ORLEANS	**LA**	70118	(504) 866-7060
LOUISIANA TECHNICAL UNIVERSITY-JEWISH STUDENT ORGANIZATION				
C/O DEPT. OF PHYSICS-LTU	RUSTON	**LA**	71272	(318) 257-4670
AMHERST COLLEGE-B'NAI B'RITH HILLEL COUNSELORSHIP				
108 CHAPIN HALL	AMHERST	**MA**	01002	(413) 542-2181
UNIVERSITY OF MASSACHUSETTS-B'NAI B'RITH HILLEL FOUNDATION				
302 STUDENT UNION	AMHERST	**MA**	01003	(413) 545-2526
BOSTON UNIVERSITY-B'NAI B'RITH HILLEL FOUNDATION				
233 BAY STATE ROAD	BOSTON	**MA**	92215	(617) 266-3880
BOSTON-B'NAI B'RITH HILLEL COUNCIL OF METROPOLITAN BOSTON				
233 BAY STATE ROAD	BOSTON	**MA**	02215	(617) 266-3882
EMERSON COLLEGE-HILLEL EXTENSION 130 BEACON STREET	BOSTON	**MA**	02216	(617) 266-3882
MASSACHUSETTS COLLEGE OF PHARMACY-HILLEL EXTENSION				
111 LONGWOOD AVENUE	BOSTON	**MA**	02146	(617) 732-2855
NEW ENGLAND CONSERVATORY OF MUSIC-HILLEL EXTENSION				
290 HUNTINGTON AVENUE	BOSTON	**MA**	02115	(617) 262-1120
NORTHEASTERN UNIVERSITY-B'NAI B'RITH HILLEL FOUNDATION				
456 PARKER STREET	BOSTON	**MA**	02115	(617) 437-3937
SIMMONS COLLEGE-HILLEL EXTENSION 300 FENWAY	BOSTON	**MA**	02115	(617) 738-2000
SUFFOLK UNIVERSITY-HILLEL EXTENSION 41 TEMPLE STREET	BOSTON	**MA**		(617) 266-3882
UNIVERSITY OF MASS./BOSTON HARBOR-HILLEL EXTENSION				
UNIV. OF MASSACHUSETTS, HARBOR CAMPUS	BOSTON	**MA**		(617) 287-1900
WHEELOCK COLLEGE-B'NAI B'RITH HILLEL EXTENSION				
200 THE RIVERWAY	BOSTON	**MA**	02215	(617) 734-5200
HARVARD UNIV./RADCLIFFE COLLEGE-B'NAI B'RITH HILLEL FOUND.				
74 MT. AUBURN STREET	CAMBRIDGE	**MA**	02138	(617) 495-4696
LESLEY COLLEGE-HILLEL EXTENSION 29 EVERETT STREET	CAMBRIDGE	**MA**	02238	(617) 868-9600
MASS. INSTITUTE OF TECHNOLOGY-B'NAI B'RITH HILLEL FOUNDATION				
312 MEMORIAL DRIVE	CAMBRIDGE	**MA**	02139	(617) 253-2982
TUFTS UNIVERSITY-B'NAI B'RITH HILLEL FOUNDATION				
CURTIS HALL, 474 BOSTON AVENUE	MEDFORD	**MA**	02155	(617) 381-3242
BOSTON COLLEGE-HILLEL EXTENSION BOSTON COLLEGE CAMPUS	NEWTON	**MA**	02167	(617) 969-0100
SMITH COLLEGE-B'NAI B'RITH HILLEL FOUNDATION				
HELEN HILLS CHAPEL	NORTHAMPTON	**MA**	01063	(413) 584-2700
MOUNT HOLYOKE COLLEGE-JEWISH STUDENT UNION				
ELIOT HOUSE-MHC	SOUTH HADLEY	**MA**	01075	(413) 538-2054
BENTLEY COLLEGE-B'NAI B'RITH HILLEL EXTENSION				
STUDENT CENTER	WALTHAM	**MA**	92254	(617) 891-2194
BRANDEIS UNIVERSITY-B'NAI B'RITH HILLEL FOUNDATION				
133 USDAN STUDENT CENTER	WALTHAM	**MA**	02254	(617) 647-2177
BABSON COLLEGE-HILLEL EXTENSION BABSON PARK	WELLESLEY	**MA**	02157	(617) 235-1200
MASSACHUSETTS BAY COMMUNITY COLLEGE-HILLEL EXTENSION				
ROUTE 9	WELLESLEY	**MA**	02157	(617) 237-1100
WELLESLEY COLLEGE-B'NAI B'RITH HILLEL COUNSELORSHIP	WELLESLEY	**MA**	02181	(617) 235-0320
WESTFIELD STATE COLLEGE-JEWISH STUDENT ORGANIZATION				
C/O DEPT. OF HISTORY, WSC	WESTFIELD	**MA**	01086	(413) 568-3311
WILLIAMS COLLEGE-JEWISH ASSOCIATION S.U. BOX 3195	WILLIAMSTOWN	**MA**	01267	
CLARK UNIVERSITY-JEWISH STUDENT COALITION				
BOX A-84, CLARK UNIVERSITY	WORCESTER	**MA**	01610	(617) 793-7296
UNIVERSITY OF MANITOBA - JEWISH STUDENT ASSOCIATION				
ROOM 149, UNIVERSITY CENTER	WINNIPEG	**MB**	R3T 2N2	(204) 474-9325
UNIVERSITY OF WINNIPEG - JEWISH STUDENT ASSOCIATION				
515 PORTAGE AVENUE	WINNIPEG	**MB**		(204) 786-7811
U.S. NAVAL ACADEMY-L'CHAIM, 25TH COMPANY				
CHAPLAIN'S CENTER, MITSCHER	ANNAPOLIS	**MD**	21402	(301) 267-2703
JOHNS HOPKINS UNIVERSITY-JEWISH STUDENT ASSOCIATION				
CHARLES STREET	BALTIMORE	**MD**	21218	(301) 338-7973
LOYOLA COLLEGE-JEWISH STUDENT ASSOCIATION				
CHARLES STREET	BALTIMORE	**MD**	21218	(301) 542-4900
UNIV. OF MARYLAND AT BALTIMORE-JEWISH STUDENT ASSOCIATION				
C/O 5700 PARK HEIGHTS AVENUE	BALTIMORE	**MD**	21215	(301) 542-4900
UNIV. OF MARYLAND/BALTIMORE COUNTY-JEWISH STUDENTS ASSC.				
801 WILKEN AVENUE	BALTIMORE	**MD**	21228	(301) 455-2496
CATONSVILLE COMMUNITY COLLEGE-JEWISH STUDENT ASSOCIATION				
	CATONSVILLE	**MD**	21228	(301) 455-4506
UNIV. OF MARYLAND/COLLEGE PARK-B'NAI B'RITH HILLEL FOUND.				
7612 MOWATT LANE, BOX 187	COLLEGE PARK	**MD**	20740	(301) 422-6200
MONTGOMERY COLLEGE-HILLEL	ROCKVILLE	**MD**	20850	(301) 279-5247
GOUCHER COLLEGE-JEWISH STUDENT ASSOCIATION				
DULANEY VALLEY ROAD	TOWSON	**MD**	21204	(301) 337-6000
TOWSON STATE UNIVERSITY-JEWISH STUDENT ASSOCIATION				
PO BOX 1953	TOWSON	**MD**	21204	(301) 321-2270
WESTERN MARYLAND COLLEGE-JEWISH STUDENT UNION	WESTMINISTER	**MD**	21157	(301) 848-7000
BATES COLLEGE-B'NAI B'RITH HILLEL COUNSELORSHIP				
TEMPLE SHALOM 74 BRADMAN PO259	AUBURN	**ME**	04210	(207) 786-4201
BOWDOIN COLLEGE-BOWDOIN JEWISH ORGANIZATION	BRUNSWICK	**ME**	04011	(207) 725-8731

UNIVERSITY OF MAINE-B'NAI B'RITH HILLEL COUNSELORSHIP				
MEMORIAL UNION, UNIVERSITY OF MAINE	ORONO	**ME**	04473	(207) 866-2456
COLBY COLLEGE-B'NAI B'RITH HILLEL COUNSELORSHIP	WATERVILLE	**ME**	04901	(207) 873-1131
UNIVERSITY OF MICHIGAN-B'NAI B'RITH HILLEL FOUNDATION				
1429 HILL STREET	ANN ARBOR	**MI**	48104	(313) 663-3336
WAYNE STATE UNIVERSITY-B'NAI B'RITH HILLEL FOUNDATION				
667 STUDENT CENTER	DETROIT	**MI**	48202	(313) 577-3459
MICHIGAN STATE UNIVERSITY-B'NAI B'RITH HILLEL FOUNDATION				
402 LINDEN STREET	EAST LANSING	**MI**	48823	(517) 332-1916
WESTERN MICHIGAN UNIVERSITY-HILLEL				
DEPT. OF SOCIOLOGY-WESTERN MICHIGAN UNIVERSITY	KALAMAZOO	**MI**	49008	(616) 383-1734
OAKLAND UNIVERSITY-JEWISH STUDENTS ORGANIZATION				
OFFICE 34 OAKLAND CENTER	ROCHESTER	**MI**	48032	(313) 377-2020
UNIVERSITY OF MINNESOTA-B'NAI B'RITH HILLEL FOUNDATION				
1521 UNIVERSITY AVENUE, S.E.	MINNEAPOLIS	**MN**	55414	(612) 332-4691
CARLETON COLLEGE-JEWISH STUDENT CENTER				
JSC 100 NORTH UNION STREET	NORTHFIELD	**MN**	55057	(507) 663-4589
MACALESTER COLLEGE-MACALESTER HEBREW HOUSE				
GRAND & MACALESTER AVENUES	ST. PAUL	**MN**	55105	(612) 696-6464
UNIV. OF MISSOURI/ST. LOUIS-B'NAI B'RITH HILLEL EXTENSION	CLAYTON	**MO**	63105	
WASHINGTON UNIVERSITY-B'NAI B'RITH HILLEL FOUNDATION				
6300 FORSYTH BOULEVARD	CLAYTON	**MO**	63105	(314) 726-6177
STEPHENS COLLEGE-B'NAI B'RITH HILLEL EXTENSION BOX 2032	COLUMBIA	**MO**	65215	(314) 442-2211
UNIV. OF MISSOURI/COLUMBIA-B'NAI B'RITH HILLEL FOUNDATION				
1107 UNIVERSITY AVENUE	COLUMBIA	**MO**	65201	(314) 443-7460
ST. LOUIS UNIVERSITY-JEWISH STUDENTS ORGANIZATION				
BUSCH CENTER, ROOM 310	ST. LOUIS	**MO**	63103	(314) 658-2425
WEBSTER COLLEGE-B'NAI B'RITH HILLEL EXTENSION				
470 EAST LOCKWOOD AVENUE, C/O RELIGIOUS DEPARTMENT	ST. LOUIS	**MO**	63119	(314) 968-7047
UNIVERSITY OF MISSISSIPPI-B'NAI B'RITH HILLEL COUNSELORSHIP	UNIVERSITY	**MS**	38677	(601) 232-7271
GUILFORD COLLEGE-B'NAI B'RITH HILLEL COUNSELORSHIP				
210 WEST CAMERON AVENUE	CHAPEL HILL	**NC**	27514	(919) 942-4057
UNIV. OF NORTH CAROLINA/CHAPEL HILL-B'NAI B'RITH HILL FOUND.				
210 W. CAMERON AVENUE	CHAPEL HILL	**NC**	27514	(919) 942-4054
UNIV. OF NORTH CAROLINA/CHARLOTTE-B'NAI B'RITH HILLEL COUN.				
210 W. CAMERON AVENUE	CHAPEL HILL	**NC**	27514	(919) 942-4057
DUKE UNIVERSITY-B'NAI B'RITH HILLEL FOUNDATION DUKE CHAPEL	DURHAM	**NC**	27706	(919) 684-5955
UNIV. OF NORTH CAROLINA/GREENSBORO-B'NAI B'RITH HILLEL COUN.				
4102 REDWINE DRIVE	GREENSBORO	**NC**	27410	(919) 942-4057
EAST CAROLINA UNIVERSITY-B'NAI B'RITH HILLEL COUNSELORSHIP				
DEPT. OF FOREIGN LANGUAGES	GREENVILLE	**NC**	27834	(919) 757-6232
NORTH CAROLINA STATE U./RALEIGH-B'NAI B'RITH HILLEL FOUND.				
C/O KATZ. 2617 AVENT FERRY ROAD	RALEIGH	**NC**	27606	(919) 942-4057
CREIGHTON UNIVERSITY-JEWISH STUDENT ORGANIZATION				
333 S. 132 STREET	OMAHA	**NE**	68154	(402) 334-8200
UNIVERSITY OF NEBRASKA-B'NAI B'RITH HILLEL COUNSELORSHIP				
333 S. 132ND STREET	OMAHA	**NE**	68154	(402) 334-8200
UNIVERSITY OF NEW HAMPSHIRE-HILLEL/JEWISH STUDENT ORG.				
MEMORIAL UNION, UNH	DURHAM	**NH**	03824	(603) 862-1524
DARTMOUTH COLLEGE-B'NAI B'RITH HILLEL FOUNDATION				
COLLEGE HALL	HANOVER	**NH**	03755	(603) 646-3441
RUTGERS UNIVERSITY-B'NAI B'RITH HILLEL FOUNDATION				
CLIFTON AVENUE & RYDERS LANE	NEW BRUNSWICK	**NJ**	08901	(201) 545-2407
PRINCETON UNIVERSITY-B'NAI B'RITH HILLEL FOUNDATION				
MURRAY-DODGE HALL	PRINCETON	**NJ**	08544	(609) 452-3635
RIDER COLLEGE-B'NAI B'RITH HILLEL COUNSELORSHIP				
499 GREENWOOD AVENUE	TRENTON	**NJ**	08609	(609) 695-3479
TRENTON STATE COLLEGE-B'NAI B'RITH HILLEL COUNSELORSHIP				
499 GREENWOOD AVENUE	TRENTON	**NJ**	08609	(609) 695-3479
KEAN COLLEGE OF NEW JERSEY-JEWISH STUDENT UNION GREEN LANE	UNION	**NJ**	07083	(201) 351-5060
UNIVERSITY OF NEVADA-B'NAI B'RITH HILLEL COUNSELORSHIP				
4765 BRUSSELS AVENUE, CRL	LAS VEGAS	**NV**	89109	(702) 736-0887
SUNY AT ALBANY-JEWISH STUDENTS COALITION-HILLEL				
PO BOX 22249, 1400 WASHINGTON AVENUE	ALBANY	**NY**	12222	(518) 459-8000
ALFRED UNIVERSITY-B'NAI B'RITH HILLEL COUNSELORSHIP BOX 1217	ALFRED	**NY**	14802	(607) 871-2215
SUNY AT BINGHAMTON-JEWISH STUDENT UNION	BINGHAMTON	**NY**	13901	(607) 798-4980
SUNY COLLEGE AT BROCKPORT-B'NAI B'RITH HILLEL EXTENSION				
HAVURAH/HILLEL, SEYMOUR UNION	BROCKPORT	**NY**	14420	(716) 637-2310
SARAH LAWRENCE COLLEGE-JEWISH STUDENT UNION/JACY	BRONXVILLE	**NY**	10770	(914) 337-0700
CUNY/BROOKLYN COLLEGE-B'NAI B'RITH HILLEL FOUNDATION				
2901 CAMPUS	BROOKLYN	**NY**	11210	(718) 859-1151
SUNY COLLEGE AT BUFFALO-B'NAI B'RITH HILLEL COUNSELORSHIP				
B6 CASSITY HALL SUCB	BUFFALO	**NY**	14222	(716) 835-3832
SUNY AT BUFFALO-B'NAI B'RITH HILLEL OF BUFFALO				
40 CAPEN BOULEVARD	BUFFALO	**NY**	14214	(716) 835-3832
SAINT LAWRENCE UNIVERSITY-JEWISH STUDENTS ORGANIZATION				
CHAPLAIN'S OFFICE	CANTON	**NY**	13617	
SUNY AT CORTLAND-JEWISH STUDENT SOCIETY				
C/O DEPARTMENT OF HISTORY	CORTLAND	**NY**	13045	
CUNY/QUEENS COLLEGE-B'NAI B'RITH HILLEL FOUNDATION				
PO BOX 446	FLUSHING	**NY**	11367	(718) 793-2222
CUNY/QUEENS COLLEGE-B'NAI B'RITH HILLEL FOUNDATION				
PO BOX 446	FLUSHING	**NY**	11367	(718) 793-2222
ADELPHI UNIVERSITY-B'NAI B'RITH HILLEL FOUNDATION				
RELIGIOUS CENTER-EARLE HALL	GARDEN CITY	**NY**	11530	(516) 294-8700
HOBARD & WILLIAM SMITH COLLEGES - ATID - JEWISH STUDENTS ORG				
CHAPLAIN'S OFFICE	GENEVA	**NY**	14620	(212) 789-5500
HOBART & WILLIAM SMITH COLLEGES-ATID-JEWISH STUDENTS ORG.				
CHAPLAIN'S OFFICE	GENEVA	**NY**	14620	(315) 789-5500
COLGATE UNIVERSITY-B'NAI B'RITH HILLEL COUNSELORSHIP				
COLGATE JEWISH UNION	HAMILTON	**NY**	13346	(315) 824-1000

HOFSTRA UNIVERSITY-B'NAI B'RITH HILLEL FOUNDATION
CHAPLAIN'S OFFICE. HOFSTRA UNIVERSITY ....HEMPSTEAD NY 11550   (516) 560-6922
CORNELL UNIVERSITY-B'NAI B'RITH HILLEL FOUNDATION
G-34 ANABEL TAYLOR HALL ....ITHACA NY 14853   (607) 256-4227
ITHACA COLLEGE-B'NAI B'RITH HILLEL COUNSELORSHIP
MULLER CHAPEL, ITHACA COLLEGE ....ITHACA NY 14850   (607) 274-3323
SUNY AT NEW PALTZ-J.S.O. HILLEL S. U. B. BUILDING 427 ....NEW PALTZ NY 12561
C.W. POST CENTER OF LONG ISLAND UNIVERSITY-JACY
130 E. 59TH STREET ....NEW YORK NY 10022   (212) 688-0808
CUNY/BARUCH COLLEGE-HILLEL JEWISH STUDENT COUNCIL
17 LEXINGTON AVENUE ....NEW YORK NY 10010
CUNY/CITY COLLEGE-B'NAI B'RITH HILLEL FOUNDATION
475 W. 140TH STREET ....NEW YORK NY 10031   (212) 234-7317
CUNY/HUNTER COLLEGE-B'NAI B'RITH HILLEL FOUNDATION
695 PARK AVENUE ....NEW YORK NY 10021   (212) 734-2600
COLUMBIA UNIVERSITY/BARNARD COLLEGE-COUNCIL FOR JEWISH ORGS.
105 EARL HALL, COLUMBIA UNIVERSITY ....NEW YORK NY 10027   (212) 280-5111
NEW YORK CITY-JEWISH ASSOCIATION FOR COLLEGE YOUTH
130 EAST 59TH STREET ....NEW YORK NY 10022   (212) 688-0808
NEW YORK INSTITUTE OF TECHNOLOGY-JACY 130 E. 59TH STREET ..... NEW YORK NY 10022   (212) 688-0808
NEW YORK UNIVERSITY-JEWISH CULTURAL FOUNDATION, JACY
715 LOEB CENTER-566 LA GUARDIA ....NEW YORK NY 10012   (212) 598-3584
PACE UNIVERSITY/DOWNTOWN-JEWISH STUDENT ASSOCIATION/JACY
1 PACE PLAZA ....NEW YORK NY 10038   (212) 285-3590
SUNY AT OSWEGO-B'NAI B'RITH HILLEL COUNSELORSHIP
HEWITT UNION ....OSWEGO NY 13126
PACE UNIVERSITY - WESTCHESTER, JEWISH STUDENT ASSOC. - JACY
CAMPUS CENTER ..........PLEASANTVILLE NY 10570   (914) 769-3200
VASSAR COLLEGE-JEWISH STUDENT UNION BOX 180, VASSAR ..... POUGHKEEPSIE NY 12601   (914) 452-7000
SUNY COLLEGE AT PURCHASE-RUACH/JACY SUNY-PURCHASE ....PURCHASE NY 10577   (914) 253-9114
ROCHESTER INST. OF TECH/NTID-B'NAI B'RITH HILLEL EXTENSION
1 LOMB MEMORIAL DRIVE, CHAPLAIN'S OFFICE ....ROCHESTER NY 14623   (716) 475-2135
UNIVERSITY OF ROCHESTER-B'NAI B'RITH HILLEL FOUNDATION
INTERFAITH CHAPEL, WILSON BOULEVARD ....ROCHESTER NY 14627   (716) 275-4323
SKIDMORE COLLEGE-JEWISH STUDENT UNION ....SARATOGA SPRINGS NY 12866   (518) 584-5000
UNION COLLEGE-B'NAI B'RITH HILLEL COUNSELORSHIP
DEPARTMENT OF HISTORY ....SCHENECTADY NY 12308   (518) 370-6075
SUNY AT STONY BROOK-B'NAI B'RITH HILLEL FOUNDATION
HUMANITIES 165 ....STONY BROOK NY 11794   (516) 246-6842
SYRACUSE UNIVERSITY-B'NAI B'RITH HILLEL FOUNDATION
HENDRICKS MEMORIAL CHAPEL ....SYRACUSE NY 13210   (315) 423-2904
RENSSELAER POLYTECH. INST.-B'NAI B'RITH HILLEL COUNSELORSHIP
RPI STUDENT UNION, CHAPLAIN'S OFFICE ....TROY NY 12181   (518) 270-6517
RUSSELL SAGE COLLEGE-B'NAI B'RITH HILLEL COUNSELORSHIP
STUDENT UNION, RPI ....TROY NY 12181   (518) 270-6517
OHIO UNIVERSITY-B'NAI B'RITH HILLEL FOUNDATION 21 MILL STREET ..... ATHENS OH 45701   (614) 592-1173
BOWLING GREEN STATE UNIVERSITY-JEWISH STUDENT GROUP
DEPT. OF HISTORY ....BOWLING GREEN OH 43403   (419) 372-2940
UNIVERSITY OF CINCINNATI-B'NAI B'RITH HILLEL FOUNDATION
2615 CLIFTON AVENUE ....CINCINNATI OH 45220   (513) 221-6728
BALDWIN WALLACE UNIVERSITY-B'NAI B'RITH HILLEL EXTENSION
11291 EUCLID AVENUE ....CLEVELAND OH 44106   (216) 231-0040
CASE WESTERN RESERVE UNIVERSITY-B'NAI B'RITH HILLEL FOUND.
11291 EUCLID AVENUE ....CLEVELAND OH 44106   (216) 231-0040
CLEVELAND STATE UNIVERSITY-B'NAI B'RITH HILLEL EXTENSION
11291 EUCLID AVENUE ....CLEVELAND OH 44106   (216) 231-0040
CUYAHOGA COMMUNITY COLLEGE-B'NAI B'RITH HILLEL EXTENSION
11291 EUCLID AVENUE ....CLEVELAND OH 44106   (216) 231-0040
HIRAM COLLEGE-B'NAI B'RITH HILLEL EXTENSION
11291 EUCLID AVENUE ....CLEVELAND OH 44106   (216) 231-0040
JOHN CARROLL UNIVERSITY-B'NAI B'RITH HILLEL EXTENSION
11291 EUCLID AVENUE ....CLEVELAND OH 44106   (216) 231-0040
NORTHEASTERN OHIO-B'NAI B'RITH HILLEL FOUNDATIONS OF NE OHIO
11291 EUCLID AVENUE ....CLEVELAND OH 44106   (216) 231-0040
OHIO STATE UNIVERSITY-B'NAI B'RITH HILLEL FOUNDATION
46 EAST 16TH AVENUE ....COLUMBUS OH 43201   (614) 294-4797
OHIO WESLEYAN UNIVERSITY-JEWISH STUDENT GROUP, OWU
CHAPLAIN'S OFFICE ....DELAWARE OH 43015   (614) 369-4431
DENISON UNIVERSITY-DENISON JEWISH COMMUNITY ....GRANVILLE OH 43023   (614) 587-0810
KENT STATE UNIVERSITY-B'NAI B'RITH HILLEL FOUNDATION
202 NORTH LINCOLN ....KENT OH 44240   (216) 678-0397
OBERLIN COLLEGE, B'NAI B'RITH HILLEL FOUNDATION, WILDER HALL ..OBERLIN OH 44074   (216) 775-8128
MIAMI UNIVERSITY-B'NAI B'RITH HILLEL COUNSELORSHIP
11-15 E. WALNUT STREET, BERMAN CENTER ....OXFORD OH 45056   (513) 523-5190
UNIVERSITY OF TOLEDO-B'NAI B'RITH HILLEL COUNSELORSHIP
3436 GODDARD ROAD ....TOLEDO OH 43606   (419) 472-7238
COLLEGE OF WOOSTER-JEWISH STUDENTS ASSOCIATION
COLLEGE OF WOOSTER ....WOOSTER OH 44691   (216) 263-2000
UNIVERSITY OF OKLAHOMA-B'NAI B'RITH HILLEL FOUNDATION
494 ELM AVENUE ....NORMAN OK 73069   (405) 321-3703
YORK UNIVERSITY - JEWISH STUDENT FEDERATION
CS140B ROSS, 4700 KEALE STREET ....DOWNSVIEW ON M6C 1S3   (416) 667-3647
CARLETON UNIVERSITY - JEWISH STUDENT UNION 151 CHAPEL ....OTTAWA ON K1N 7Y2   (613) 232-7306
UNIVERSITY OF OTTAWA - JEWISH STUDENTS UNION-HILLEL
151 CHAPEL STREET ....OTTAWA ON K1N 7Y2   (613) 232-7306
UNIVERSITY OF TORONTO - B'NAI B'RITH HILLEL FOUNDATION
604 SPADINA AVENUE ....TORONTO ON M5S 2H4   (416) 923-9861
OREGON STATE UNIVERSITY-B'NAI B'RITH HILLEL COUNSELORSHIP
DEPARTMENT OF HISTORY, OSU ....CORVALLIS OR 97331   (506) 754-3421
UNIVERSITY OF OREGON-B'NAI B'RITH HILLEL COUNSELORSHIP
1414 KONIONIA CENTER ....EUGENE OR 97401   (503) 484-1707

CEDAR CREST COLLEGE-B'NAI B'RITH HILLEL COUNSELORSHIP ..... ALLENTOWN PA 18104
MUHLENBERG COLLEGE-B'NAI B'RITH HILLEL COUNSELORSHIP ..... ALLENTOWN PA 18104
LEHIGH UNIVERSITY-B'NAI B'RITH HILLEL COUNSELORSHIP
346 MAGINNES 9, LEHIGH ....BETHLEHEM PA 18105   (215) 861-3368
MORAVIAN COLLEGE-B'NAI B'RITH HILLEL COUNSELORSHIP
DEPARTMENT OF ENGLISH, MORAVIAN ....BETHLEHEM PA 18018   (215) 861-1391
DICKINSON COLLEGE-B'NAI B'RITH HILLEL COUNSELORSHIP BOX 135 ... CARLISLE PA 17013   (717) 245-1482
WIDENER COLLEGE - HILLEL CLUB
P. O. BOX 1184 - WIDENER UNIVERSITY ....CHESTER PA 19013   (215) 449-4375
URSINUS COLLEGE - ORGANIZATION OF JEWISH STUDENTS ........COLLEGEVILLE PA 19426   (215) 489-4111
LAFAYETTE COLLEGE-B'NAI B'RITH HILLEL COUNSELORSHIP
329 MCCARTNEY ....EASTON PA 18042   (215) 250-5174
BRYN MAWR COLLEGE-BRYN MAWR HAVERFORD HILLEL
YARNALL HOUSE, ROOM 113 ....HAVERFORD PA 19041   (215) 849-5584
HAVERFORD COLLEGE - BRYN MAWR-HAVERFORD HILLEL
YARNALL HOUSE, ROOM 13 ....HAVERFORD PA 19041   (215) 849-5584
BEAVER COLLEGE-HILLEL EXTENSION 1096 SPARROW ROAD .... JENKINTOWN PA 19046   (215) 886-1297
KUTZTOWN STATE COLLEGE-B'NAI B'RITH HILLEL COUNSELORSHIP ..KUTZTOWN PA 19530   (215) 683-4000
FRANKLIN & MARSHALL COLL.-B'NAI B'RITH HILLEL COUNSELORSHIP
P.O. BOX 3003 ....LANCASTER PA 17604   (717) 291-4060
BUCKNELL UNIVERSITY-B'NAI B'RITH HILLEL COUNSELORSHIP
MARTIN HOUSE, 532 ST. GEORGE ....LEWISBURG PA 17837   (717) 286-1127
ALLEGHENY COLLEGE-B'NAI B'RITH HILLEL COUNSELORSHIP
BOX 14, ALLEGHENY COLLEGE ....MEADVILLE PA 16335   (814) 724-2368
COMM. COLLEGE OF PHILADELPHIA-HILLEL JEWISH STUDENT UNION
6344 N. 8TH STREET, #206 ..........PHILADELPHIA PA 19126   (215) 549-8432
DREXEL UNIVERSITY-DREXEL HILLEL
224 CREESE ACTIVITY CENTER ..........PHILADELPHIA PA 19104   (215) 895-2531
LA SALLE COLLEGE-HILLEL EXTENSION, CAMPUS MINISTRY CENTER
6809 EMLEN ..........PHILADELPHIA PA 19119   (215) 848-2115
PENNSYLVANIA STATE UNIV.-OGONTZ - HILLEL EXTENSION
7000 LINCOLN DRIVE ..........PHILADELPHIA PA 19119   (215) 242-2913
PHILADELPHIA COLL. OF PHARM. & SCIENCE-HILLEL EXTENSION
MCNEILL BLDG. 43 & KINGSESSING, C/O ZANGER ..........PHILADELPHIA PA 19104   (215) 898-8265
PHILADELPHIA COLL. OF TEXTILES & SCIENCE-HILLEL EXTENSION
HENRY AVENUE & SCHOOLHOUSE LANE ..........PHILADELPHIA PA 19115   (215) 676-6897
PHILADELPHIA-JEWISH CAMPUS ACTIVITIES BOARD
202 SOUTH 36TH STREET ..........PHILADELPHIA PA 19104   (215) 898-8265
SWARTHMORE COLLEGE - HILLEL EXTENSION
C/O 259 W. JOHNSON STREET ..........PHILADELPHIA PA 19119   (215) 848-7310
TEMPLE UNIV.-MAIN & AMBLER CAMPUS-B'NAI B'RITH HILLEL FOUND.
2014 N. BROAD STREET ..........PHILADELPHIA PA 19121   (215) 769-1174
UNIVERSITY OF PENNSYLVANIA-B'NAI B'RITH HILLEL FOUNDATION
202 SOUTH 36TH STREET ..........PHILADELPHIA PA 19104   (215) 898-7391
CARNEGIE MELLON UNIVERSITY-B'NAI B'RITH HILLEL FOUNDATION
315 SOUTH BELLEFIELD AVENUE ....PITTSBURGH PA 15213   (412) 621-8875
CHATHAM COLLEGE-B'NAI B'RITH HILLEL EXTENSION
315 SOUTH BELLEFIELD AVENUE ....PITTSBURGH PA 15213   (412) 621-8875
DUQUESNE UNIVERSITY-B'NAI B'RITH HILLEL FOUNDATION
315 SOUTH BELLEFIELD AVENUE ....PITTSBURGH PA 15213   (412) 621-8875
POINT PARK COLLEGE-B'NAI B'RITH HILLEL EXTENSION
315 SOUTH BELLEFIELD AVENUE ....PITTSBURGH PA 15213   (412) 621-8875
UNIVERSITY OF PITTSBURGH-B'NAI B'RITH HILLEL FOUNDATION
315 SOUTH BELLEFIELD AVENUE ....PITTSBURGH PA 15213   (412) 621-8875
ALBRIGHT COLLEGE-B'NAI B'RITH HILLEL COUNSELORSHIP
P.O. BOX 516 ....READING PA 19603   (215) 921-8619
PENNSYLVANIA STATE UNIV.-B'NAI B'RITH HILLEL FOUNDATION
224 LOCUST LANE ....STATE COLLEGE PA 16801   (814) 237-2408
WASHINGTON & JEFFERSON COLLEGE - HILLEL SOCIETY ....WASHINGTON PA 15301   (412) 222-4400
CONCORDIA UNIV.-SIR GEORGE & LOYOLA-B'NAI B'RITH HILLEL EXT.
2070 MCKAY STREET NORTH EN 401 ....MONTREAL QU H3A 1R8   (514) 845-9171
DAWSON CEGEP - B'NAI B'RITH HILLEL EXTENSION
3460 STANLEY STREET ....MONTREAL QU H3A 1R8   (514) 845-9171
MARIANOPOLIS CEGEP - MCGILL HILLEL 3460 STANLEY STREET ....MONTREAL QU H3A 1R8   (514) 845-9171
MCGILL UNIVERSITY - B'NAI B'RITH HILLEL FOUNDATION
3460 STANLEY STREET ....MONTREAL QU H3A 1R8   (514) 845-9171
MONTREAL-B'NAI B'RITH HILLEL FOUNDATIONS OF MONTREAL, INC.
3460 STANLEY STREET ....MONTREAL QU H3A 1R8   (514) 845-9171
UNIVERSITY OF MONTREAL - CENTRE HILLEL
5186 COTE DES NEIGES SUITE 2 ....MONTREAL QU H3A 1K8   (514) 738-2655
UNIVERSITY OF QUEBEC/CEGEP ST. LAURENT - CENTRE HILLEL
5186 COTE DES NEIGES SUITE 2 ....MONTREAL QU H3A 1K8   (514) 738-2655
VANIER CEGEP (ST. CROIX & SNOWDON)-B'NAI B'RITH HILLEL EXT.
5160 DECAIRE BLVD ....MONTREAL QU   (514) 845-9171
UNIVERSITY OF RHODE ISLAND-B'NAI B'RITH HILLEL FOUNDATION
34 LOWER COLLEGE ROAD ....KINGSTON RI 02881   (401) 792-2740
BROWN UNIVERSITY - B'NAI B'RITH HILLEL FOUNDATION
80 BROWN STREET ....PROVIDENCE RI 02906   (401) 863-2805
RHODE ISLAND SCHOOL OF DESIGN-B'NAI B'RITH HILLEL EXTENSION
80 BROWN STREET ....PROVIDENCE RI 02906   (401) 863-2805
BRYANT COLLEGE - JEWISH STUDENTS ORGANIZATION
BRYANT COLLEGE ....SMITHFIELD RI 02917   (401) 231-1200
THE CITADEL-MILITARY COLL. OF SC-B'NAI B'RITH HILLEL COUNSL.
182 RUTLEDGE AVENUE ....CHARLESTON SC 29403   (803) 722-7261
CLEMSON UNIVERSITY - HILLEL-BRANDEIS STUDENT ORGANIZATION
CLEMSON UNIVERSITY ....CLEMSON SC 29631
UNIV. OF SOUTH CAROLINA-B'NAI B'RITH HILLEL COUNSELORSHIP
USC BOX 80128 ....COLUMBIA SC 29208   (803) 799-9132
UNIV. OF TENN.-KNOXVILLE-B'NAI B'RITH HILLEL COUNSELORSHIP
BOX 16204 ....KNOXVILLE TN 37996   (615) 974-5048
MEMPHIS STATE UNIVERSITY - JEWISH STUDENT UNION
3603 MYNDERS ....MEMPHIS TN 38111   (901) 452-2453

SOUTHERN COLLEGE OF OPTOMETRY-JEWISH STUDENT UNION
3603 MYNDERS .... MEMPHIS TN 38111   (901) 452-2453
SOUTHWESTERN UNIVERSITY - JEWISH STUDENT UNION
3603 MYNDERS .... MEMPHIS TN 38111   (901) 452-2453
UNIV. OF TENN.-MEMPHIS -JEWISH STUDENT UNION 3603 MYNDERS ...... MEMPHIS TN 38111   (901) 452-2453
GEORGE PEABODY COLLEGE FOR TEACHERS-JEWISH STUDENT UNION
BOX 6311-STA B .... NASHVILLE TN 37235   (615) 322-2457
VANDERBILT UNIVERSITY-JEWISH STUDENT UNION BOX 6311, STA B ... NASHVILLE TN 37235   (615) 322-2457
UNIV. OF TEXAS AT ARLINGTON - JEWISH STUDENT ORGANIZATION
C/O UNIV. OF TEXAS BOX 19348, #160 .... ARLINGTON TX 76019   (817) 275-3913
UNIV. OF TEXAS - AUSTIN - B'NAI B'RITH HILLEL FOUNDATION
2105 SAN ANTONIO, P.O. BOX H .... AUSTIN TX 78712   (512) 476-0125
TEXAS A & M UNIVERSITY-B'NAI B'RITH HILLEL FOUNDATION
800 JERSEY .... COLLEGE STATION TX 77840   (713) 696-7313
RICE UNIVERSITY - B'NAI B'RITH HILLEL EXTENSION
RELIGION CENTER, U. OF HOUSTON .... HOUSTON TX 77004   (713) 749-2271
TEXAS MEDICAL CENTER (BAYLOR & U.T.) - HILLEL EXTENSION
RELIGION CENTER, U. OF HOUSTON .... HOUSTON TX 77004   (713) 749-2271
UNIVERSITY OF HOUSTON-B'NAI B'RITH HILLEL FOUNDATION
RELIGION CENTER .... HOUSTON TX 77004   (713) 749-2271
TEXAS TECH. UNIVERSITY-B'NAI B'RITH HILLEL COUNSELORSHIP
MATHEMATICS DEPARTMENT TEXAS TECH .... LUBBOCK TX 79409   (806) 742-2566
UNIVERSITY OF UTAH - B'NAI B'RITH HILLEL COUNSELORSHIP
C/O FREEDMAN, MIDEAST CENTER .... SALT LAKE CITY UT 84112   (801) 581-7843
NORTHERN VIRGINIA COMMUNITY COLLEGE-JEWISH STUDENT CLUB
.... ANNANDALE VA 22003
VA. POLYTECHNIC INST. & STATE U.-B'NAI B'RITH HILLEL COUNSL.
PHYSICS DEPARTMENT, VPI & SU .... BLACKSBURG VA 24061   (703) 961-6525
UNIVERSITY OF VIRGINIA-B'NAI B'RITH HILLEL FOUNDATION
1824 UNIVERSITY CIRCLE .... CHARLOTTESVILLE VA 22903   (804) 295-4963
GEORGE MASON UNIVERSITY - JEWISH STUDENT GROUP .... FAIRFAX VA 22030
MARY WASHINGTON COLLEGE-B'NAI B'RITH HILLEL COUNSELORSHIP
COMBS HALL .... FREDERICKSBURG VA 22401   (703) 899-4731
JAMES MADISON UNIVERSITY-B'NAI B'RITH HILLEL COUNSELORSHIP
DEPARTMENT OF ECONOMICS, JMU .... HARRISONBURG VA 22801   (703) 433-6451
FERRUM COLLEGE - HILLEL C/O OHEV ZION 801 PARKVIEW ... MARTINSVILLE VA 24112   (703) 632-2828
OLD DOMINION UNIVERSITY-B'NAI B'RITH HILLEL COUNSELORSHIP
DEPARTMENT OF SOCIOLOGY, ODU .... NORFOLK VA 23508   (804) 440-3800
UNIVERSITY OF RICHMOND-B'NAI B'RITH HILLEL COUNSELORSHIP
1103 WEST FRANKLIN STREET .... RICHMOND VA 23220   (804) 353-6477
VIRGINIA COMMONWEALTH UNIV.-B'NAI B'RITH HILLEL FOUNDATION
1103 WEST FRANKLIN STREET .... RICHMOND VA 23220   (804) 353-6477
COLLEGE OF WILLIAM & MARY-B'NAI B'RITH HILLEL COUNSELORSHIP
DEPARTMENT OF ENGLISH, CWM .... WILLIAMSBURG VA 23185   (804) 229-8795
UNIVERSITY OF VERMONT-B'NAI B'RITH HILLEL COUNSELORSHIP
8127 LIVING/LEARNING CENTER .... BURLINGTON VT 05405   (802) 656-3488
MIDDLEBURY COLLEGE - B'NAI B'RITH HILLEL COUNSELORSHIP
BOX 2242 MIDDLEBURY COLLEGE .... MIDDLEBURY VT 05753   (802) 388-3711
WASHINGTON STATE UNIV.-B'NAI B'RITH HILLEL COUNSELORSHIP
JSO, COMPTON UNION BUILDING .... PULLMAN WA 99164
UNIVERSITY OF WASHINGTON-B'NAI B'RITH HILLEL FOUNDATION
4745 17TH AVENUE .... SEATTLE WA 98105   (206) 522-1060
UNIVERSITY OF PUGET SOUND - JEWISH STUDENT ASSOCIATION
C/O TEMPLE BETHEL 5975 S 12 STREET .... TACOMA WA 98465   (206) 564-7101
INTERNATIONAL ASSOCIATION OF HILLEL DIRECTORS
611 LANGDON STREET .... MADISON WI 53703   (608) 256-8361
UNIVERSITY OF WISCONSIN - B'NAI B'RITH HILLEL FOUNDATION
611 LANGDON STREET .... MADISON WI 53703   (608) 256-8361
U. OF WISC.-MILWAUKEE/MARQUETTE-B'NAI B'RITH HILLEL FOUND.
3035 N. STOWELL AVENUE .... MILWAUKEE WI 53211   (414) 961-2010
WEST VIRGINIA UNIVERSITY - B'NAI B'RITH HILLEL FOUNDATION
1420 UNIVERSITY AVENUE .... MORGANTOWN WV 26505   (304) 296-2660

BOARDS OF JEWISH EDUCATION

JEWISH EDUCATION COUNCIL 3310 N. TENTH AVENUE .... PHOENIX AZ 85013   (602) 279-7005
JEWISH EDUCATION SERVICE OF ORANGE COUNTY
12181 BUARO .... GARDEN GROVE CA 92640   (714) 537-2424
BUREAU OF JEWISH EDUCATION
6505 WILSHIRE BOULEVARD SUITE 710 .... LOS ANGELES CA 90048   (213) 852-1234
AGENCY FOR JEWISH EDUCATION 3245 SHEFFIELD AVENUE .... OAKLAND CA 94602   (415) 533-7032
BUREAU OF JEWISH EDUCATION 2351 WYDA WAY .... SACRAMENTO CA 95825   (916) 485-4151
SAN DIEGO BUREAU OF JEWISH EDUCATION 5511 EL CAJON BLVD ... SAN DIEGO CA 92115   (619) 583-8532
BUREAU OF JEWISH ED. OF SAN FRANCISCO, MARIN CTY & PENINSULA
639 14 AVENUE .... SAN FRANCISCO CA 94118   (415) 751-6983
CENTRAL AGENCY FOR JEWISH EDUCATION
300 SOUTH DAHLIA STREET (#207) .... DENVER CO 80222   (303) 321-3191
DEPT. OF JEWISH ED. OF THE NEW HAVEN JEWISH FEDERATION
1162 CHAPEL STREET .... NEW HAVEN CT 06511   (203) 562-3163
COMMITTEE ON JEWISH ED. OF GREATER HARTFORD JEWISH EDUCATION
333 BLOOMFIELD AVENUE .... WEST HARTFORD CT 06117   (203) 232-4483
CENTRAL AGENCY FOR JEWISH EDUCATION 4200 BISCAYNE BOULEVARD ... MIAMI FL 33137   (305) 576-4030
JEWISH FEDERATION OF PALM BEACH COUNTY
501 SOUTH FLAGLER DRIVE (SUITE 305) .... WEST PALM BEACH FL 33401   (305) 832-2120
ATLANTA BUREAU OF JEWISH EDUCATION
1745 PEACHTREE ROAD, NORTH EAST .... ATLANTA GA 30309   (404) 873-1248
BUREAU OF JEWISH LIVING 924 POLK BOULEVARD .... DES MOINES IA 50312   (515) 277-5566
ASSOCIATED TALMUD TORAHS OF CHICAGO
2828 WEST PRATT BOULEVARD .... CHICAGO IL 60645   (312) 973-2828
BOARD OF JEWISH EDUCATION OF METROPOLITAN CHICAGO
618 SOUTH MICHIGAN AVENUE .... CHICAGO IL 60605   (312) 427-5570

BUREAU OF JEWISH EDUCATION 6711 HOOVER ROAD .... INDIANAPOLIS IN 46260   (317) 255-3124
JEWISH EDUCATION COUNCIL OF GREATER KANSAS CITY
2210 WEST 75 STREET (SUITE 12) .... SHAWNEE MISSION KS 66208   (913) 722-2922
BUREAU OF JEWISH EDUCATION 3819 BARDSTOWN ROAD .... LOUISVILLE KY 40218   (502) 459-0927
JEWISH ED. COMMITTEE-JEWISH FED. OF GREATER NEW ORLEANS
3625 HOUMA BOULEVARD (#B) .... METAIRIE LA 70002   (504) 455-6434
BUREAU OF JEWISH EDUCATION OF GREATER BOSTON
333 NONANTUM STREET .... NEWTON MA 02159   (617) 965-7350
UNITED HEBREW SCHOOL 979 DICKINSON STREET .... SPRINGFIELD MA 01108   (413) 734-8215
WINNIPEG BOARD OF JEWISH EDUCATION 365 HARGRAVE STREET ... WINNIPEG MB R3B 2K3   (204) 949-1482
BOARD OF JEWISH EDUCATION 5800 PARK HEIGHTS AVENUE .... BALTIMORE MD 21215   (301) 367-8300
BOARD OF JEWISH EDUCATION OF GREATER WASHINGTON
9325 BROOKVILLE ROAD .... SILVER SPRING MD 20910   (301) 589-3180
UNITED HEBREW SCHOOLS OF METROPOLITAN DETROIT
21550 WEST TWELVE MILE ROAD .... SOUTHFIELD MI 48076   (313) 354-1050
TALMUD TORAH OF MINNEAPOLIS 8200 WEST 33 STREET ..... MINNEAPOLIS MN 55426   (612) 935-0316
CENTRAL AGENCY FOR JEWISH EDUCATION
12 MILLSTONE CAMPUS DRIVE .... ST. LOUIS MO 63146   (314) 432-0020
BUREAU OF JEWISH EDUCATION 333 SOUTH 123 STREET .... OMAHA NE 68154   (402) 334-8200
BUREAU OF JEWISH EDUCATION OF SOUTHERN NEW JERSEY
2393 WEST MARLTON PIKE .... CHERRY HILL NJ 08002   (609) 662-6300
JEWISH ED. SERVICES OF THE JEWISH COMMUNITY OF BERGEN COUNTY
111 KINDERMACK ROAD P.O. BOX 4176
NORTH HACKENSACK STATION .... RIVER EDGE NJ 07661   (201) 488-6800
BUREAU OF JEWISH EDUCATION OF NORTH JERSEY 1 PIKE DRIVE ...... WAYNE NJ 07470   (201) 595-0560
JEWISH EDUCATION ASSOCIATION 1 HENDERSON DRIVE ...... WEST CALDWELL NJ 07006   (201) 575-6050
BUREAU OF JEWISH EDUCATION OF GREATER BUFFALO, INC.
2640 NORTH FOREST ROAD .... GETZVILLE NY 14068   (716) 689-8844
BOARD OF JEWISH EDUCATION OF GREATER NEW YORK
426 WEST 58TH STREET .... NEW YORK NY 10019   (212) 245-8200
DEPARTMENT OF EDUCATION, UNION OF AMERICAN HEBREW CONGS.
838 FIFTH AVENUE .... NEW YORK NY 10021   (212) 249-0100
DEPARTMENT OF EDUCATION, UNITED SYNAGOGUE OF AMERICA
155 FIFTH AVENUE .... NEW YORK NY 10010   (212) 260-8450
NATIONAL COMMISSION ON TORAH EDUCATION, YESHIVA UNIVERSITY
500 WEST 185TH STREET .... NEW YORK NY 10033   (212) 960-5266
BUREAU OF JEWISH EDUCATION OF ROCHESTER, NEW YORK, INC.
50 CHESTNUT STREET .... ROCHESTER NY 14604   (716) 546-1468
BUREAU OF JEWISH EDUCATION 1580 SUMMIT ROAD .... CINCINNATI OH 45237   (513) 761-0203
BUREAU OF JEWISH EDUCATION OF CLEVELAND
2030 SOUTH TAYLOR ROAD .... CLEVELAND OH 44118   (216) 371-0446
THE COLUMBUS HEBREW SCHOOL 1125 COLLEGE AVENUE .... COLUMBUS OH 43209   (614) 231-7764
BUREAU OF JEWISH EDUCATION OF GREATER DAYTON
4501 DENLINGER ROAD .... DAYTON OH 45426   (513) 854-2021
TOLEDO BOARD OF JEWISH EDUCATION 2727 KENWOOD BOULEVARD ..... TOLEDO OH 43606   (419) 531-8969
COMMISSION FOR JEWISH EDUCATION
P.O. BOX 8021 3970 LOGAN WAY .... YOUNGSTOWN OH 44505   (216) 759-0452
BOARD OF JEWISH EDUCATION 4600 BATHURST STREET .... WILLOWDALE ON M2R 3V3   (416) 633-7770
DEPT. OF EDUCATION & CULTURE CANADIAN JEWISH CONGRESS
4600 BATHURST STREET (SUITE 232) .... WILLOWDALE ON M2R 3V2   (416) 635-2883
JEWISH EDUCATION ASSOCIATION
6651 SOUTH WEST CAPITOL HIGHWAY .... PORTLAND OR 97219   (503) 244-0126
DIVISION OF COMMUNITY SERVICES OF GRATZ COLLEGE
TENTH STREET AND TABOR ROAD .... PHILADELPHIA PA 19141   (215) 329-3363
HEBREW INSTITUTE OF PITTSBURGH 6401-07 FORBES AVENUE ...... PITTSBURGH PA 15217   (412) 521-1100
SCHOOL OF ADVANCED JEWISH STUDIES
315 SOUTH BELLEFIELD AVENUE .... PITTSBURGH PA 15213   (412) 681-1630
HILLEL ACADEMY 900 GIBSON STREET .... SCRANTON PA 18510   (717) 343-7837
JEWISH EDUCATION COUNCIL OF GREATER MONTREAL
5151 COTE STREET CATHERINE ROAD (ROOM 201) .... MONTREAL QU H3W 1M6   (514) 735-3541
BUREAU OF JEWISH EDUCATION OF RHODE ISLAND
130 SESSIONS STREET .... PROVIDENCE RI 02906   (401) 331-0956
COMMISSION FOR JEWISH EDUCATION
5603 SOUTH BRAESWOOD BOULEVARD .... HOUSTON TX 77096   (713) 729-7000
JEWISH EDUCATION COUNCIL 516 SECURITIES BUILDING .... SEATTLE WA 98101   (206) 625-0665
MILWAUKEE ASSOCIATION FOR JEWISH EDUCATION
4560 NORTH PORT WASHINGTON ROAD .... MILWAUKEE WI 53212   (414) 962-8860

BOOK CLUBS & SERVICES

ZIONIST BOOK CLUB 788 MARLEE AVENUE .... TORONTO ON
YONATHAN SHULTZ'S JEWISH PERIODICAL SUBSCRIPTION SERVICE
7518 LEXINGTON AVENUE .... LOS ANGELES CA 90046
PERCHIK'S - REUBEN CANNON 345 S. MC DOWELL BLVD .... PETALUMA CA 94952   (707) 763-2482
B'NAI B'RITH PAPERBACK SERVICE
1640 RHODE ISLAND AVENUE, N.W. .... WASHINGTON DC 20036   (202) 857-6600
YIDDISH BOOK CLUB COMMITTEE FOR JEWISH CULTURE IN ISRAEL
BNEI EPHRAIM STREET .... MAOZ AVIV, TEL AVIV IS
NATIONAL YIDDISH BOOK CENTER OLD E. ST. SCHOOL, P.O. BOX 969 .... AMHERST MA 01004   (413) 253-9201
MAAYAN: A WELLSPRING OF JEWISH BOOKS PO BOX 246 .... SUDBURY MA 01776   (617) 767-9450
THE INTERNATIONAL LIBRARY OF JEWISH LITERATURE
2115 NORTH CHARLES STREET .... BALTIMORE MD 21218   (301) 685-6615
JEWISH BOOKSHELF, THE PO BOX 434 .... TEANECK NJ
JUDAICA BOOK CLUB
C/O THE JONATHAN DAVID CO. 68-22 ELIOT AVENUE .... MIDDLE VILLAGE NY 11379   (212) 456-8611
BOOKAZINE CO., INC. 303 W. 10 STREET .... NEW YORK NY 10014
JEWISH BOOK CLUB 111 EIGHTH AVENUE .... NEW YORK NY 10011   (212) 924-6663
JEWISH BOOK COUNCIL OF THE JEWISH WELFARE BOARD
15 EAST 26TH STREET .... NEW YORK NY 10010   (212) 532-4949
PHILIPP FELDHEIM, INC. 96 EAST BROADWAY .... NEW YORK NY 10002   (212) 925-3180
UNITED SYNAGOGUE OF AMERICA BOOK SERVICE 155 FIFTH AVENUE ... NEW YORK NY 10010   (212) 533-7800

FOUR TIMES A YEAR, ONE OF THE BEST THINGS IN LIFE IS FREE

Four times a year, *Jewish Book World* is sent free to its subscribers. If you care about Jewish books, you will find *Jewish Book World* a vital source of news, opinion, and reviews—a book lover's treasure trove.

What's the Catch?

There isn't any. The JWB Jewish Book Council is a non-profit organization whose sole purpose is to promote the writing, publishing, and reading of Jewish books. For more than 40 years the Council has sponsored programs based on its conviction that books of Jewish interest make an invaluable contribution to the welfare of the Jewish people. *Jewish Book World* is just one of its many activities and subscriptions are available without charge. All you need do is send us your name and address—we'll be glad to add you to the mailing list. You will not be solicited for funds and your name will not be used for other mailing lists.

What Else Does the Council Do?

A lot. The Council has many programs to stimulate the interest in Jewish books. You probably have heard of the presti-gious **National Jewish Book Awards.** Since 1949 the Council has been conferring the Awards annually on the authors of books outstanding for their literary merit and scholarship. Award winners include Elie Wiesel, Isaac Bashevis Singer, Cynthia Ozick, Joseph B. Soloveitchik, and A.J. Heschel.

Another major activity is **Jewish Book Month.** This celebration of Jewish books is observed annually in communities throughout the United States and Canada during the month preceding Hanukkah. The Council provides educational and promotional materials, including posters, bookmarks, and book lists. The children's poster this year is by Maurice Sendak.

The Council also helps to coordinate book fairs, issues citations to Jewish libraries that meet its standards of excellence, and serves as a resource and clearing house for information on all aspects of Jewish publishing.

Are *All* the Council Publications So Inexpensive?

No. But every one of the Council's publications, from *Selected Jewish Children's Books* and *Large-Type Books of Jewish Interest* to *How to Organize a Jewish Library* and *Selected Readings on the Holocaust*, is authoritative and filled with valuable information and advice. The prices start at $3.00. The most expensive is only $18.00. For that amount you get the *Jewish Book Annual*, the indispensable source of information on Jewish literary creativity. The *Annual's* distinguished articles and comprehensive book lists make it the most valuable reference in the field. The 1985 Order Form with information on all of the Council's publications is available free on request.

Why Isn't There a Coupon in This Ad?

We value books and the good opinion of librarians too highly to put a tear-out coupon into a book. Just write or call. We look forward to hearing from you.

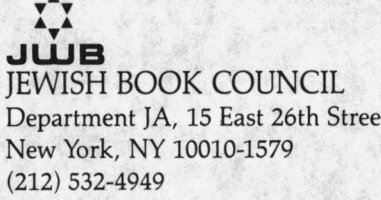

JWB
JEWISH BOOK COUNCIL
Department JA, 15 East 26th Street
New York, NY 10010-1579
(212) 532-4949

ENJOY-A-BOOK CLUB 1 STATION PLAZA	WOODMERE NY 11598	(516) 569-0830
ENJOY-A-BOOK CLUB P.O. BOX 101	WOODMERE NY 11598	(516) 569-0324
JEWISH PUBLICATION SOCIETY 1930 CHESTNUT STREET	PHILADELPHIA PA 19103	(215) 564-5925

BOOK DEALERS

ATARA'S 450 NORTH FAIRFAX AVENUE	LOS ANGELES CA 90036	(213) 655-3050
CALIFORNIA HOUSE OF ISRAEL BOX 48425	LOS ANGELES CA 90048	(213) 653-6757
CHABAD MID-CITY CENTER 420 NORTH FAIRFAX AVENUE	LOS ANGELES CA 90036	(213) 655-4734
HERSKOVITZ HEBREW BOOKSTORE 428 NORTH FAIRFAX AVENUE	LOS ANGELES CA 90036	(213) 852-9310
J. ROTH BOOKSELLER 9427 WEST PICO BOULEVARD	LOS ANGELES CA 90035	(213) 557-1848
JEWISH AMERICAN BOOK SHOP PO BOX 36185	LOS ANGELES CA 90035	(213) 557-1848
JEWISH AMERICAN BOOKSTORE 9427 PICO BOULEVARD	LOS ANGELES CA 90035	(213) 557-1848

JOSEPH HERSKOVITZ HEBREW BOOK STORE		
428 NORTH FAIRFAX AVENUE	LOS ANGELES CA 90036	(213) 852-9310
SKIRBALL MUSEUM GIFT SHOP, HEBREW UNION COLLEGE		
3077 UNIVERSITY MALL	LOS ANGELES CA 90007	(213) 749-3424
SOLOMON'S BOOKS & GIFTS 447 N. FAIRFAX AVENUE	LOS ANGELES CA 90036	(213) 653-9045
BOB & BOB BOOKS 151 FOREST AVENUE	PALO ALTO CA 94301	(415) 329-9050
PERCHIKS JUDAICA 345 S. MCDOWELL #115	PETALUMA CA 94952	(707) 763-2482
CHABAD HOUSE - LUBAVITCH 6115 MONTEZUMA ROAD	SAN DIEGO CA 92115	(619) 265-7700
LIEBER'S HEBREW-ENGLISH BOOK & GIFT STORE		
5445 GEARY BOULEVARD	SAN FRANCISCO CA 94121	(415) 387-3077
THE MERKAZ 2444 NORIEGA STREET	SAN FRANCISCO CA 94122	(415) 665-9090
JERUSALEM FAIR 14537 VENTURA BOULEVARD	SHERMAN OAKS CA 91423	(818) 995-0116
THE JEWISH DEVELOPMENT COMPANY 18331-C IRVINE BOULEVARD	TUSTIN CA 92680	(714) 730-1419
SELIGMAN / BENCHMARKS 307 ROSE AVENUE	VENICE CA 90291	(213) 392-1010
YTC SEFORIM STORE 1400 QUITMAN ST #4067	DENVER CO 80204	
MEDIA JUDAICA 1363 FAIRFIELD AVENUE	BRIDGEPORT CT 06605	(203) 384-2284
ISRAEL GIFT SHOP & HEBREW BOOK SHOP 262 S. WHITNEY STREET	HARTFORD CT 06105	(203) 232-2984
JEWISH BOOK SHOP & HEBREW BOOK SHOP 1162 CHAPEL STREET	NEW HAVEN CT 06511	(203) 562-3163
AMERICAN-ISRAELI SHOP 1357 WASHINGTON AVENUE	MIAMI BEACH FL 33139	(305) 531-7722
TORAH TREASURES 1202 WASHINGTON AVENUE	MIAMI BEACH FL 33139	(305) 673-6095
JUDAICA ENTERPRISES, INC. 1074 N.E. 163RD ST.	NORTH MIAMI BEACH FL 33162	(305) 945-5091
NER TAMID BOOK DISTRIBUTORS PO BOX 10401	RIVIERA BEACH FL 33404	(305) 686-9095
ANSLEY MALL BOOK STORE 1544 PIEDMONT AVENUE N.E.	ATLANTA GA 30320	(404) 875-6492
BAIS STAM 6343 NORTH CALIFORNIA	CHICAGO IL 60659	(312) 973-1311
HEBREW BOOK STORE 2942 WEST DEVON AVENUE	CHICAGO IL 60659	(312) 973-6636
HAMAKOR JUDAICA BOOK STORE 6112 N. LINCOLN AVENUE	CHICAGO IL 60659	(312) 463-6186
ROSENBLUM HEBREW BOOK STORE 2906 WEST DEVON AVENUE	CHICAGO IL 60659	(312) 262-1700
CHABAD BOOKS 7037 FRERET ST	NEW ORLEANS LA 70118	
ISRAEL BOOKSHOP INC. 410 HARVARD STREET	BROOKLINE MA 02146	(617) 566-7113
DAVIDSON'S HEBREW BOOK STORE 1106 N. MAIN STREET	NORTH RANDOLPH MA 02368	(617) 961-4989
JEWISH BOOK FINDER 30 WESTERN VIEW	SPRINGFIELD MA 01108	
EPHRAIM'S BOOK STORE 72 FRANKLIN STREET	WORCESTER MA 01608	(617) 755-9505
CENTRAL HEBREW BOOK STORE 228 REISTERSTOWN ROAD	BALTIMORE MD 21208	(301) 653-0550
PERN'S HEBREW BOOK & GIFT SHOP 7012 REISTERSTOWN ROAD	BALTIMORE MD 21215	(301) 653-2450
ABE'S JEWISH BOOKSTORE 11250 GEORGIA AVENUE	WHEATON MD 20902	(301) 942-2237
LISBON'S HEBREW BOOKS AND GIFTS		
2305 UNIVERSITY BOULEVARD WEST	WHEATON MD 20902	(301) 933-1800
JEWISH BOOK STORE OF GREATER WASHINGTON		
11250 GEORGIA AVENUE	WHEATON MD 20902	(301) 942-2237
BORENSTEIN'S BOOK STORE 25242 GREENFIELD ROAD	OAK PARK MI 48237	(313) 967-3920
SPITZER'S HEBREW BOOK AND GIFT CENTER		
21770 ELEVEN MILE ROAD	SOUTHFIELD MI 48076	(313) 356-6080
BROCHIN'S JEWISH BOOK & GIFT SHOP		
4813 MINNETONKA BOULEVARD	MINNEAPOLIS MN 54416	(612) 926-2011
MIDWEST JEWISH BOOK & GIFT CENTER 8318 OLIVE STREET ROAD	ST. LOUIS MO 63132	(314) 993-6300
SOURCE UNLIMITED 11044 OLIVE ST. RD	ST. LOUIS MO 63141	(314) 567-1925
JUDAIC SPECIALTIES 45 BROAD STREET	CARLSTADT NJ 07002	(201) 939-4522
HIGHLAND PARK JUDAICA 227 RARITAN AVENUE	HIGHLAND PARK NJ 08904	(201) 246-1690
SKY HEBREW BOOKSTORE 1923 SPRINGFIELD AVENUE	MAPLEWOOD NJ 07040	(201) 763-4244
THE JUDAICA HOUSE, LIMITED 412 CEDAR LANE	TEANECK NJ 07666	(201) 836-5284
PELHAM PARKWAY HEBREW BOOKSTORE 781 LYDIG AVENUE	BRONX NY 10462	(212) 892-2522
BIEGELEISEN SFORIM STORE 4409 16TH AVENUE	BROOKLYN NY 11204	(718) 436-1165
BLUM'S HEBREW BOOK STORE 169A ROSS STREET	BROOKLYN NY 11211	(718) 963-1234

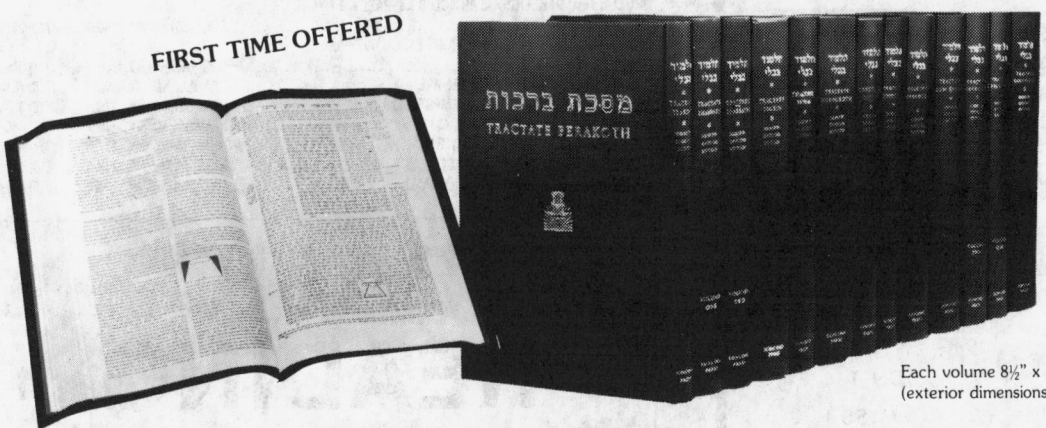

COHEN'S RELIGIOUS ARTICLES 5302 16TH AVENUE	BROOKLYN	NY	11204	(718) 851-4877
DRIMMERS 329 KINGSTON AVENUE	BROOKLYN	NY	11213	(718) 774-0198
EICHLER'S RELIGIOUS ARTICLES & GIFTS				
1429 CONEY ISLAND AVENUE	BROOKLYN	NY	11230	(718) 258-7643
FISHER'S BOOKS 5402 NEW UTRECHT	BROOKLYN			
FLOHR'S GIFTS & RELIGIOUS ARTICLES 4603 13TH AVENUE	BROOKLYN	NY	11219	(718) 854-0865
FLUSBERG'S HEBREW BOOK STORE 1276 47TH STREET	BROOKLYN	NY	11219	(718) 853-7302
FRANKEL'S BOOK STORE 4904 16TH AVENUE	BROOKLYN	NY	11204	(718) 851-7766
GRUNFELD HEBREW BOOK STORE 4624 16TH AVENUE	BROOKLYN	NY	11204	(718) 871-8885
HAICHAL HASEFORIM 4401 16TH AVENUE	BROOKLYN	NY	11204	(718) 438-8414
HEBREW PUBLISHING COMPANY 100 WATER STREET	BROOKLYN	NY	11201	(718) 858-6928
HECHT HEBREW BOOK & RELIGIOUS SUPPLIES				
1265 CONEY ISLAND AVENUE	BROOKLYN	NY	11230	(718) 258-9696
MERCAZ STAM 309 KINGSTON AVENUE	BROOKLYN	NY	11213	(718) 773-0090
PINTER'S HEBREW BOOKS 4408 14TH AVENUE	BROOKLYN	NY	11219	(718) 871-2260
REBECCA BENNET PUBLICATIONS 5409 18TH AVENUE	BROOKLYN	NY	11204	(718) 256-1954
RIGLER'S SEFORIM 1206 AVENUE M	BROOKLYN	NY	11230	(718) 627-3818
WISSBROT CHOIMIE HEBREW BOOKS 167 RODNEY STREET	BROOKLYN	NY	11211	(718) 782-9218
Z. BERMAN BOOKS 1340 53RD STREET	BROOKLYN	NY	11219	(718) 851-5372
ELBAUM JUDAICA 694 CENTRAL AVENUE	CEDARHURST	NY	11516	(516) 569-4577
KI-TOV/HEBREW BOOK & GIFT CENTER 1847 MOTT AVENUE	FAR ROCKAWAY	NY	11691	(718) 471-0963
SHAYA'S BOOK NOOK 1513 CENTRAL AVENUE	FAR ROCKAWAY	NY	11691	(718) 327-0163
HOUSE OF ISRAEL 100-23 QUEENS BLVD	FOREST HILLS	NY	11375	(718) 459-4556
THEODORE S. CINNAMON LIMITED 420 JERUSALEM AVENUE	HICKSVILLE	NY	11801	(516) 935-7480
HEBREW BOOK AND GIFT WORLD 72-20 MAIN STREET	KEW GARDENS HILLS	NY	11367	(718) 261-0233
SOURCE GIFT SHOP, INC. 307 CENTRAL AVENUE	LAWRENCE	NY	11559	(516) 569-1773
JONATHAN DAVID COMPANY 68-22 ELIOT AVENUE	MIDDLE VILLAGE	NY	11379	(718) 456-8611
HEBREW BOOK STORE (CONGREGATION VAYOEL MOSHE)				
214 MAPLE AVENUE	MONSEY	NY	10952	(914) 356-9807
MONSEY BOOK & RELIGIOUS ARTICLES 42 MAIN STREET	MONSEY	NY	10952	(914) 425-8530
SIMCHA SHOPPE, THE 18 HILLTOP LANE	MONSEY	NY	10952	(914) 352-4543
ZIEGELHEIM HEBREW BOOKS & RELIGIOUS ARTICLES 68 MAIN STREET	MONSEY	NY	10952	(914) 354-5842
TIFERES BOOKS 9 LINCOLN AVENUE	NEW SQUARE	NY	10952	(914) 362-0881
BEHRMAN HOUSE 1261 BROADWAY	NEW YORK	NY	10001	(212) 689-2020
BLOCH PUBLISHING COMPANY 19 WEST 21ST STREET	NEW YORK	NY	10010	(212) 989-9104
CENTRAL YIDDISH CULTURE ORGANIZATION - CYCO				
25 EAST 78TH STREET	NEW YORK	NY	10024	(212) 535-4320
GOLDMAN'S OTZAR HASEFARIM, INC. 33 CANAL STREET	NEW YORK	NY	10002	(212) 674-1707
H & M SKULLCAP CO. 46 HESTER STREET	NEW YORK	NY	10002	(212) 475-1910
ISRAELI GIFTS 23 ESSEX	NEW YORK	NY	10002	(212) 475-6075
ISRAELI GIFTS & BOOKSTORES 575 SEVENTH AVENUE	NEW YORK	NY	10018	(212) 391-4928
ISRAEL TRADE BOOKS 49 CANAL ST	NEW YORK	NY	10002	(212) 226-8020
ISRAEL WHOLESALE 21 ESSEX STREET	NEW YORK	NY	10002	(212) 477-2310
J. LEVINE CO. 58 ELDRIDGE STREET	NEW YORK	NY	10002	(212) 966-4460
JEWISH GIFT SHOP 2404 BROADWAY	NEW YORK	NY	10024	(212) 362-7846
JEWISH MUSEUM BOOKSHOP, THE 1109 FIFTH AVENUE	NEW YORK	NY	10028	(212) 860-1888
LEVINE RELIGIOUS SUPPLIES 58 ELDRIDGE STREET	NEW YORK	NY	10002	(212) 966-4460
LOUIS STAVSKY COMPANY, INC. 147 ESSEX STREET	NEW YORK	NY	10002	(212) 674-1289
MORGENSTERN BOOKS 150 EAST BROADWAY	NEW YORK	NY	10002	(212) 267-1332
OTZER SEFORIM 33 CANAL STREET	NEW YORK	NY	10002	(212) 674-1707
PHILIPP FELDHEIM 96 E. BROADWAY	NEW YORK	NY	10002	(212) 925-3180

RABBI MOSES EISENBACH BOOKSTORE 49 ESSEX STREET	NEW YORK	NY	10002	(212) 674-8840
SEFER ISRAEL, INC. 156 FIFTH AVENUE	NEW YORK	NY	10010	(212) 929-6411
SEPHER-HERMON PRES, INC. 53 PARK PLACE	NEW YORK	NY	10007	(212) 349-1860
SHALLER'S BOOKSTORE 2555 AMSTERDAM AVENUE	NEW YORK	NY	10033	(212) 928-2140
SHILO PUBLISHING COMPANY 73 CANAL STREET	NEWYORK	NY	10002	(212) 925-3468
SOLOMON RABINOWITZ HEBREW BOOK STORE 30 CANAL STREET	NEW YORK	NY	10002	(212) 267-2406
STAVSKY'S HEBREW BOOK STORE 147 ESSEX STREET	NEW YORK	NY	10002	(212) 674-1289
STEIMATZKY PUBLISHING OF NORTH AMERICA, INC.				
56 EAST 11TH STREET	NEW YORK	NY	10003	(212) 505-2505
THE JEWISH MUSEUM BOOKSHOP 1104 FIFTH AVENUE	NEW YORK	NY	10028	(212) 860-1888
WEST SIDE JUDAICA 2404 BROADWAY	NEW YORK	NY	10024	(212) 362-7846
ZIONTALIS/BOOK DIVISION 48 ELDRIDGE STREET	NEW YORK	NY	10002	(212) 925-8558
ORGEL'S JEWISH RELIGIOUS ARTICLES & ISRAEL GIFTWARE				
984 MONROE AVENUE	ROCHESTER	NY	14609	(716) 271-2310
PHILIPP FELDHEIM, INC. 200 AIRPORT EXECUTIVE PARK				
MITH ROAD	SPRING VALLEY	NY	10977	(914) 356-2282
CARMEL GIFT CENTER 10 CARMEL AVENUE	STATEN ISLAND	NY	10314	(718) 761-8480
JUDAICA UNLIMITED, INC. 433 HEMPSTEAD AVENUE	WEST HEMPSTEAD	NY	11552	(516) 486-3636
LONG ISLAND TEMPLE SUPPLIES 433 HEMPSTEAD AVENUE	WEST HEMPSTEAD	NY	11552	(516) 486-3636
HAKOL B'SEFER JUDAICA MAIN STREET	WOODBOURNE	NY	12788	(914) 434-2626
ENJOY-A-BOOK CLUB P.O. BOX 101	WOODMERE	NY	11598	(516) 569-0324
K'TONTON BOOK STORE 1 STATION PLAZA	WOODMERE	NY	11598	(516) 569-0830

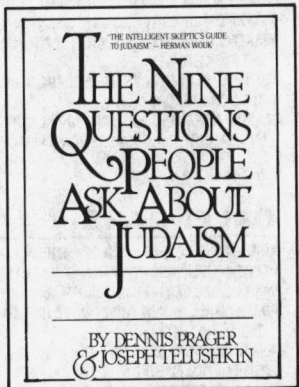

COMMENTS ON

FROM THE BEGINNING:
A MODERN TARGUM

"Most interesting and original, using the periphrastic approach of the ancient targum from a modern perspective."—
Prof. Robert Alter, UCLA
(The Art of Biblical Narrative)

"It reminds of Samson Raphael Hirsch as told to William Blake."
Dr. Shalom Carmy,
editor of TRADITION magazine, Yeshiva Univ.

"Your rendition of Bereshith was quite fascinating— almost kabbalistic."
Rabbi Aryeh Kaplan
(The Living Torah)

"Scholarship . . . a treasure trove of midrashic and traditional exegesis."
Rabbi Dr. Aaron Lichtenstein

Distributed by L. Stavsky   24 Fifth Avenue, NYC 10011

HEBREW UNION COLLEGE BOOKSTORE 3101 CLIFTON AVENUE .... CINCINNATI OH 45220   (513) 221-1875
FRANK'S HEBREW BOOK STORE 1647 LEE ROAD .... CLEVELAND OH 44118   (216) 321-6850
PAUL'S HEBREW BOOK STORE 13962 CEDAR ROAD .... CLEVELAND OH 44118   (216) 321-7200
ISRAEL'S...THE JUDAICA CENTRE 973 EGLINTON AVENUE WEST .... TORONTO ON M6C 2C3 (416) 789-2169
MATOV JEWISH BOOKS 3173A BATHURST ST. .... TORONTO ON M6A 2B1
MIRIAM'S BOOK STORE 2007 BATHURST STREET .... TORONTO ON   (416) 781-8261
NEGEV BOOK & GIFT STORE 3509 BATHURST STREET .... TORONTO ON M6A 2C5 (416) 781-9356
ZUCKER'S JEWISH BOOKS AND ART 3453 BATHURST STREET ...... TORONTO ON   (416) 781-2133
RABBI PIOTRKOWSKI'S JUDAICA CENTER
   289 MONTGOMERY AVENUE .... BALA CYNWYD PA 19004   (215) 664-1303
ROSENBERG HEBREW BOOK STORE 409 OLD YORK ROAD .... JENKINTOWN PA 19046   (215) 884-1728
ROSENBERG HEBREW BOOK STORE 6408 CASTOR AVENUE .... PHILADELPHIA PA 19149   (215) 744-5205
MILTON PINSKER 2028 MURRAY AVENUE .... PITTSBURGH PA 15217   (412) 421-3033
BOOK CENTER, INC. 1140 BEAULAC STREET .... MONTREAL QU   (514) 332-4154
BOOK CENTRE 5168 QUEEN MARY ROAD .... MONTREAL QU   (514) 481-5609
CAPLANSKY BOOK STORE 39-20 ST. KEVIN STREET .... MONTREAL QU   (514) 737-6237
RODAL'S HEBREW BOOK STORE 4689 VAN HORNE STREET .... MONTREAL QU   (514) 733-1876
THE KOTEL BOOKS 6414 VICTORIA AVENUE .... MONTREAL QU H3W Z56
VICTORIA GIFT SHOP & BOOK CENTRE 5869 VICTORIA AVENUE .... MONTREAL QU   (514) 738-1414
MELZER'S HEBREW BOOK STORE 742 HOPE STREET .... PROVIDENCE RI 02906   (401) 831-1710
MRS. FRED GLATZER 6630 NORTHPORT DRIVE .... DALLAS TX 75230   (214) 368-2479
HOUSE OF BOOKS 9215 STELLA LINK ROAD .... HOUSTON TX 77025   (713) 667-9434
SOURCE OF HOUSTON 9760 HILLCROFT .... HOUSTON TX 77096   (713) 721-4624
MERCAZ BOOKS 1716 E. OLIVE WAY .... SEATTLE WA 98102   (206) 324-2454
CHEVRAT SEFORIM 92 HOTHAM ST. .... BALACLAVA, AUSTRALIA
AMZALAH BOOKS 10 CASTLEFIELD STREET .... BOND, NEW SOUTH WALES AU 2026
JEWISH BOOK CENTER 25 ASHBOURNE GROVE .... MANCHESTER GB M70 DB
LUBAVITCH PUBLICATIONS P.O. BOX 39276.................... BRAMLEY SA 2018
KOLLEL BOOKSHOP P.O. BOX 27784 YEOVILLE 2143............. JOHANNESBURG SA
RUBIN BOOKSELLERS 34 GLENEAGLES RD., GREENSIDE 2193 ..... JOHANNESBURG SA

BOOK DEALERS - YIDDISH

YIDDISH BOOK CLUB COMMITTEE FOR JEWISH CULTURE IN ISRAEL
   BNEI EPHRAIM STREET............................ MAOS AVIV, TEL AVIV IS
NATIONAL YIDDISH BOOK EXCHANGE P.O. BOX 969 .... AMHERST MA 01004
CYCO - YIDDISH BOOK DISTRIBUTORS 25 EAST 78TH STREET .... NEW YORK NY 10021   (212) 535-4320

BURIAL SOCIETIES - CHEVRA KADISHA

CHEVRA KADISHA CHAPEL 12313 105TH AVENUE .... EDMONTON AT   (403) 482-3065
CHEVRA KADISHA 7832 SANTA MONICA BLVD.................... LOS ANGELES CA
JEWISH COMMUNITY BURIAL COMMITTEE 599 NORTH VERMONT .... LOS ANGELES CA 90004
JEWISH COMMUNITY BURIAL PROGRAM, JEWISH FAMILY SERVICE
   6505 WILSHIRE BOULEVARD .... LOS ANGELES CA 90048   (213) 852-1234
MOUNT ZION CEMETERY FUND, JEWISH FEDERATION COUNCIL
   6505 WILSHIRE BOULEVARD .... LOS ANGELES CA 90048   (213) 852-1234
THE JEWISH SACRED SOCIETY 415 NORTH STANLEY AVENUE ... LOS ANGELES CA 90036
JEWISH FAMILY SERVICE - FREE BURIAL & LOAN SERVICE
   3245 SHEFFIELD AVENUE.................................. OAKLAND CA 94602   (415) 532-6314
JEWISH FAMILY SERVICE - FREE BURIAL SERVICE
   3355 FOURTH AVENUE................................... SAN DIEGO CA 92103   (619) 291-0473
SHALOM GARDENS 2255 LOS GATOS-ALMADEN ROAD .... SAN JOSE CA 95124   (408) 356-4151
JEWISH BURIAL SOCIETY OF SOUTHERN COUNTIES
   13031 JUSTIN STREET .... SANTA ANA CA 92703   (714) 530-6636

DENVER RABBINICAL COUNCIL FREE BURIAL SERVICES
   C/O RODEF SHALOM SYNAGOGUE, 450 SOUTH KEARNEY .... DENVER CO 80222
INDEPENDENT TRUE BIKUR CHOLIM 726 CAPITAL AVENUE............ BRIDGEPORT CT 06606
HEBREW FUNERAL HOME - CHESED SHEL EMES
   1061 ALBANY AVENUE .... HARTFORD CT 06114
FREE BURIAL SOCIETY - CHEVRA KADISHA 31 WILLIAMSON DRIVE .... WATERBURY CT 06705
JEWISH FEDERATION OF DELAWARE-FREE BURIAL SERVICE
   101 GARDEN OF EDEN ROAD............................. WILMINGTON DE 19801   (302) 478-6200
MOUNT SINAI CEMETARY - FREE BURIAL SERVICE
   1125 N.W. 137TH STREET AND 11TH AVENUE .... MIAMI FL 33124   (305) 681-4432
CHEVRA KADISHO MACHZAIKAI HADAS 2040 W. DEVON AVENUE .... CHICAGO IL 60645   (312) 764-8760
JEWISH BURIAL SOCIETY 221 N. LASALLE .... CHICAGO IL 60659   (312) 346-7950
JEWISH FREE BURIAL SOCIETY 1300 WEST DEVON .... CHICAGO IL 60660   (312) 761-2400
JEWISH SACRED SOCIETY-CHEVRA KADISHA
   6633 NORTH SACRAMENTO .... CHICAGO IL 60645   (312) 743-0074
HEBREW CEMETERY ASSOCIATION - FREE BURIAL SERVICE
   3127 SHERIDAN ROAD .... PEORIA IL 61604
ORTHODOX JEWISH CEMETERY ASSOCIATION
   C/O FORT WAYNE JEWISH FEDERATION,
   227 E. WASHINGTON BLVD .... FORT WAYNE IN 46802   (219) 422-8566
JEWISH SOCIAL SERVICE AGENCY - FREE BURIAL SERVICE
   3640 DUTCHMAN'S LANE .... LOUISVILLE KY 40202   (502) 452-6341
JEWISH FAMILY & CHILDREN'S SERVICE - FREE BURIAL SERVICE
   2026 ST. CHARLES AVENUE .... NEW ORLEANS LA 70130   (504) 524-8475
CHEVRA KADISHA - FREE BURIAL SOCIETY 27 DICK DRIVE .... WORCESTER MA 01608
JEWISH CHILD & FAMILY SERVICE - FREE BURIAL SERVICE
   956 MAIN STREET .... WINNIPEG MB   (204) 943-6425
HEBREW BURIAL & SOCIAL SERVICE SOCIETY
   5750 PARK HEIGHTS AVENUE.............................. BALTIMORE MD 21215   (301) 466-9200
HEBREW BURIAL & SOCIAL SERVICE SOCIETY OF BALTIMORE
   319 W. MONUMENT STREET .... BALTIMORE MD 21201   (301) 727-4828
HEBREW ORTHODOX FREE BURIAL SOCIETY P.O. BOX 5778 .... BALTIMORE MD 21208   (301) 633-5806
HEBREW ORTHODOX MEMORIAL SOCIETY 6820 GERMAN HILL ROAD ... BALTIMORE MD 21216   (301) 633-5806
HEBREW BENEVOLENT SOCIETY (CHESED SHEL EMES)
   26640 GREENFIELD ROAD .... OAK PARK MI 48237   (313) 543-1622
JEWISH FAMILY & CHILDREN'S SERVICES - FREE BURIAL SERVICE
   1115 EAST 65TH STREET................................ KANSAS CITY MO 64110   (816) 333-1172
CHEVRA KADISHA 1601 NORTH AND SOUTH ROAD .... ST LOUIS MO 63123   (314) 427-0160
HEBREW FREE BURIAL SOCIETY C/O PHILIP APTER & SON
   1600 SPRINGFIELD AVENUE .... MAPLEWOOD NJ 07040
BOROUGH PARK HEBREW BURIAL ASSOCIATION 9322 AVENUE L........ BROOKLYN NY 11230
HEBREW BURIAL SOCIETY 1283 CONEY ISLAND AVENUE .... BROOKLYN NY 11230   (718) 776-8100
PINCUS MANDEL-CEMETERY CONSULTANT 1569 47TH STREET........ BROOKLYN NY 11219   (718) 855-5121
JEWISH FAMILY SERVICE OF ERIE COUNTY - FREE BURIAL ASSOC.
   2600 NORTH FOREST ROAD .... GETZVILLE NY   (716) 668-2321
ADATH ISRAEL OF NEW YORK, UNITED HEBREW COMMUNITY OF NEW YORK
   201 EAST BROADWAY .... NEW YORK NY 10002   (212) 674-3580
AUSTRO-HUNGARIAN HEBREW FREE BURIAL 245 EAST 63RD STREET ... NEW YORK NY 10021   (212) 838-1187
HEBREW FREE BURIAL ASSOCIATION INC. (EXECUTIVE OFFICES)
   1170 BROADWAY .... NEW YORK NY 10001   (212) 686-2433
UNITED HEBREW COMMUNITY OF N.Y., ADATH ISRAEL OF N.Y.
   201 EAST BROADWAY .... NEW YORK NY 10002   (212) 674-3580
WEIL FUNERAL HOME-FREE BURIAL SERVICE 3901 READING RD..... CINCINNATI OH 45229   (513) 281-0178
CHESED SHEL EMETH FREE BURIAL ASSOCIATION-FREE BURIAL SERVC.
   3740 RIDGE ROAD .... CLEVELAND OH 44114   (216) 631-4493
JEWISH FAMILY SERVICE - FREE BURIAL SERVICE 4501 DENLINGER .... DAYTON OH 45406   (513) 854-2944
JEWISH FAMILY SERVICE - FREE BURIAL SERVICE
   6525 SYLVANIA AVENUE .... SYLVANIA OH   (419) 885-2561
JEWISH CHILD & FAMILY SERVICE - FREE BURIAL SERVICE
   4600 BATHURST STREET .... TORONTO ON   (416) 638-7800
HEBREW BURIAL ASSOCIATION - FREE BURIAL SERVICE
   1000 LIBERTY AVENUE .... PITTSBURGH PA 15222
CHEVRA KADISHA-HOLY SOCIETY OF BUCKS COUNTY
   400 DAVID DRIVE .... TREVOSE PA 19047   (215) 357-7130
JEWISH FAMILY SERVICES OF THE BARON DE HIRSCH INSTITUTE
   FREE BURIAL SERVICES, 3600 VAN HORNE AVENUE .... MONTREAL QU   (514) 731-3881
CHARLESTON JEWISH SOCIAL SERVICE - FREE BURIAL SERVICE
   1645 WALLENBERG BOULEVARD .... CHARLESTON SC 29407   (803) 571-6565
JEWISH SOCIAL SERVICE FEDERATION - FREE BURIAL SERVICE
   8434 AHERN STREET .... SAN ANTONIO TX 78216   (512) 341-8234
HEBREW BURIAL SOCIETY - FREE BURIAL SERVICE
   814 RIVERSIDE DRIVE .... NEWPORT NEWS VA 23606
HEBREW LADIES CHARITY SOCIETY - FREE BURIAL SERVICE
   8065 BUFFALO AVENUE .... NORFOLK VA 23518
JEWISH FAMILY SERVICES - FREE BURIAL SERVICES
   7027-3 CHOPT ROAD .... RICHMOND VA 23200   (804) 282-5644
SEATTLE JEWISH CHAPEL - FREE BURIAL SERVICE
   104 12TH STREET (CONGREGATION BIKUR CHOLIM) .... SEATTLE WA 98144   (206) 323-7321

CALENDARS

ADVERTISING CORPORATION OF AMERICA 110 LYMAN STREET .... HOLYOKE MA 01040   (413) 533-7151
HEBREW PUBLISHING COMPANY 100 WATER STREET .... BROOKLYN NY 11201   (718) 858-6928
VAAD L'CHIZUK KIYUM HAMITZVOTH 4911 - 16TH AVENUE .... BROOKLYN NY 11204   (718) 851-1314
ADATH ISRAEL OF NEW YORK, UNITED HEBREW COMMUNITY OF NEW YORK
   201 EAST BROADWAY .... NEW YORK NY 10002   (212) 674-3580
ISRAEL DISCOUNT BANK 511 FIFTH AVENUE .... NEW YORK NY 10017   (212) 551-8500
JEWISH NATIONAL FUND STUDENT CALENDAR 42 EAST 69TH STREET .. NEW YORK NY 10021   (212) 879-9300
THE COMPREHENSIVE HEBREW CALENDAR, BEHRMAN HOUSE
   1261 BROADWAY .... NEW YORK NY 10001   (212) 689-2020

UNITED HEBREW COMMUNITY OF N.Y.-ADATH ISRAEL OF N.Y.				
201 EAST BROADWAY	NEW YORK	NY	10002	(212) 674-3580
UNITED SYNAGOGUE OF AMERICA - PROGRAM SUGGESTIONS				
3080 BROADWAY	NEW YORK	NY	10027	(212) 533-7800
UNIVERSE BOOKS 381 PARK AVENUE SOUTH	NEW YORK	NY	10016	(212) 685-7400
YAD L'ACHIM CALENDAR 156 FIFTH AVENUE	NEW YORK	NY	10010	(212) 624-2003
ZIONTALIS MANUFACTURING COMPANY 48 ELDRIDGE STREET	NEW YORK	NY	10002	(212) 925-8558

CALLIGRAPHERS

CALLIGRAPHERS II, JOY BLANK - TAMARA GREENSTEIN				
1101 SOUTH ROBERTSON BOULEVARD, SUITE 210	LOS ANGELES	CA	90035	(213) 278-5370
DAVID WILLNER, TOBY S. WILLNER	LOS ANGELES	CA		(213) 931-6298
ELLEN LAMPERT PO BOX 70025	LOS ANGELES	CA	90070	(213) 386-2341
EMANUEL COHEN ZEDEK 9760 WEST PICO BOULEVARD	LOS ANGELES	CA	90035	(213) 557-0826
GUY-PAUL BISMUTH, LINDA BISMUTH				
1432 SOUTH CRESCENT HEIGHTS BOULEVARD	LOS ANGELES	CA	90035	(213) 939-4713
JOANNE ABENSOUR	LOS ANGELES	CA		(213) 659-7329
JODY MYERS	LOS ANGELES	CA		(213) 397-4248
ORA COOPER 412 WEST SIXTH STREET, SUITE 615	LOS ANGELES	CA	90014	(213) 622-2823
ROBIN MUER 612 NORTH KINGS ROAD, APT 306	LOS ANGELES	CA	90048	(213) 653-0019
ROSETTE WEISEL 1211 SOUTH SHERBOURNE DRIVE, APT.2	LOS ANGELES	CA	90035	(213) 272-5310
SUSAN SREBO 9215 ALCOTT STREET	LOS ANGELES	CA	90035	(213) 550-7752
HEDY M. HARRIS 6325 BEN AVENUE	NORTH HOLLYWOOD	CA	91606	(818) 763-4339
CHARLES H. BAUM 72 CALHOUN AVENUE	TRUMBULL	CT	06611	(203) 268-2512
NANCY GREENBERG DESIGNS 7045 S.W. 110TH TERRACE	MIAMI	FL	33156	(305) 667-1324
GERSHON YUDKOWSKY 2927 WEST TOUHY AVENUE	CHICAGO	IL	60645	(312) 262-5700
HANNAH DRESNER 920 EAST 61ST STREET	CHICAGO	IL	60637	(312) 955-2882
JUDITH KANIN 833 WEST BUCKINGHAM	CHICAGO	IL	60657	(312) 348-8432
KADISH GAIBEL C/O JOSARAH ENTERPRISES 422 NORTH WELLS	CHICAGO	IL	60610	(312) 338-0235
ROSE ANN CHASMAN 6147 NORTH RICHMOND	CHICAGO	IL	60659	(312) 764-4169
NESSIE FRANK 1642 LINDEN AVENUE	HIGHLAND PARK	IL	60035	(312) 432-6668
YOCHANAN CENTER C/O NAJARIAN 22 SOUTH CHASE	LOMBARD	IL	60148	
SHARON SAVITSKY 20 PARK AVENUE	NEWTON	MA	02158	(617) 965-1940
MIRIAM KARP 17 BIGELOW STREET	BRIGHTON	MA	02135	
A.N. GOLDSTEIN C/O J.C.C. OF GREATER MINNEAPOLIS				
4330 CEDAR LAKE ROAD SOUTH	MINNEAPOLIS	MN	55416	(612) 698-0751
ANN ZAIMAN 7912 WINTERSET AVENUE	BALTIMORE	MD	21208	(301) 484-4377
MARSHA GOLDFINE 8486 SNOWDEN OAKS PLACE	LAUREL	MD	20708	(301) 953-9260
PEGGY H. DAVIS CALLIGRAPHY 3249 HENNEPIN AVE. SO. SUITE 144	MINNEAPOLIS	MN	55408	(612) 929-3362
ADIR GALLERY		NJ		(201) 572-1751
SIMCHA BACK STUDIOS 325 11TH STREET	LAKEWOOD	NJ	08701	(201) 363-4702
SIMCHA STUDIOS 325 11TH STREET	LAKEWOOD	NJ	08701	(201) 363-4702
EMANUEL MILSTEIN R.D. 1, BOX 81C	MARLBORO	NJ	07746	(201) 946-8604
ABIGAIL CHAPMAN 529 LAUREL ROAD	RIDGEWOOD	NJ	07450	(201) 652-7535
DOV BER SCHWARTZ	BROOKLYN	NY		(718) 387-1363
LIPOT FRIEDMAN 5501 15TH AVENUE	BROOKLYN	NY	11219	(718) 436-0901
NORMAN SAPOZNIK 2321 EAST 24TH STREET	BROOKLYN	NY	11229	(718) 769-2566
NUSACH 195 LEE AVENUE	BROOKLYN	NY	11211	(718) 782-3578
RAPHAEL POSNER 993 EAST 18TH STREET	BROOKLYN	NY	11230	(718) 253-7922
RENEE SANDRA GREENBERG 18 BRIGHTON 10 PATH	BROOKLYN	NY	11235	(718) 891-8846
SHIMON KATZMAN	BROOKLYN	NY		(718) 853-3014
SIMCHA ARTWORK 199 ROTH STREET	BROOKLYN	NY		(718) 387-0739
YEHUDAH CLAPMAN 719 MONTGOMERY STREET	BROOKLYN	NY	11213	(718) 774-9313
YEKUSIEL YEHUDA LAX	BROOKLYN	NY		(718) 946-2934
IRWIN RAPPAPORT	FAR ROCKAWAY	NY		(718) 474-7300
NECHAMA FELLER 740 MADOR COURT	FAR ROCKAWAY	NY	11691	(718) 337-5295
LEE FANKUSHEN 11 WEBB HILL ROAD	GREAT NECK	NY	11020	(516) 466-4660
LILI WRONKER 144-44 VILLAGE ROAD	JAMAICA	NY	11435	(718) 380-3990
CARA GOLDBERG MARKS 388 KENRIDGE ROAD	LAWRENCE	NY	11559	(516) 374-5574
NOAMI NADATA 39 STEVENS PLACE	LAWRENCE	NY	11559	(516) 239-0292
FRED SPINOWITZ KETUGOT 5 OVERLOOK ROAD	NEW ROCHELLE	NY	10804	(914) 632-9794
BETSY PLATKIN TEUTSCH 789 WEST END AVENUE, APT. 9C	NEW YORK	NY	10025	(212) 866-5448
JAY GREENSPAN PO BOX 914	NEW YORK	NY	10025	(212) 737-2444
JOAN MESZNIK 441 WEST END AVENUE, 15-C	NEW YORK	NY	10024	(212) 874-2645
KETUBOT ETC.	NEW YORK	NY		(212) 598-0393
NISSIM HIZME 82 CANAL STREET	NEW YORK	NY	10002	(212) 925-2922
S.T.M. SCRIBES 200 WEST 86TH STREET	NEW YORK	NY	10024	(212) 799-1510
SHEL BASSEL 305 PALMWOOD DRIVE	TROTWOOD	OH	45426	(513) 837-3439
SHARON BINDER, BETH TZEDEC CONGREGATION				
1700 BATHURST STREET	TORONTO	ON	M5P 3K3	(416) 781-3511
REEVA KIMBLE 2352 VAN NESS	EUGENE	OR	97439	(503) 345-8129
EMES EDITIONS 2001 LEVICK STREET	PHILADELPHIA	PA	19149	(215) 268-8787
MARCIA KAUNTER 50 SARGENT AVENUE	PROVIDENCE	RI	02906	(401) 331-0219

CAMPS

AMERICAN JEWISH SOCIETY FOR SERVICE				
15 EAST 26TH STREET ROOM 1304	NEW YORK	NY	10010	(212) 683-6178
ASSOCIATION OF JEWISH SPONSORED CAMPS, INC.				
130 EAST 59TH STREET	NEW YORK	NY	10022	(212) 751-0477
CAMP INFORMATION AGENCY 500 FIFTH AVENUE	NEW YORK	NY	10017	(212) 944-6200
CAMP INFORMATION ASSOCIATION 1 ROCKEFELLER PLAZA	NEW YORK	NY	10020	(212) 757-4440
DIVISION OF COMMUNITY SERVICES, YESHIVA UNIVERSITY				
185TH STREET AND AMSTERDAM AVENUE	NEW YORK	NY	10033	(212) 960-5400
UNION OF AMERICAN HEBREW CONGREGATIONS 838 FIFTH AVENUE	NEW YORK	NY	10021	(212) 249-0100

CAMPS - CHILDREN & TEENS

B'NAI B'RITH PINE LAKE, CAMP - ALBERTA 7200-156TH STREET	EDMONTON	AT	T5R IX3	(403) 487-0899
CAMP CHARLES PERLSTEIN C/O TEMPLE BETH ISRAEL				
3310 N. 10TH AVENUE	PHOENIX	AZ	85013	(602) 264-4428
CAMP TEVA C/O PHOENIX JEWISH COMMUNITY CENTER				
1718 W. MARYLAND	PHOENIX	AZ	85015	(602) 249-1832
CAMP HATIKVAH C/O ZIONIST ORGANIZATION OF CANADA				
950 WEST 41ST STREET	VANCOUVER	BC		(604) 266-9111
CAMP MIRIAM C/O ICHUD HABONIM 950 WEST 41ST STREET	VANCOUVER	BC		
CAMP ALONIM, BRANDEIS-BARDIN INSTITUTE				
1101 PEPPERTREE LANE	BRANDEIS	CA	93064	(213) 348-7201
CAMP YOUNG JUDEA C/O NORTHERN CALIFORNIA HADASSAH				
264 ARLINGTON AVENUE	KENSINGTON	CA	94707	
CAMP KOMAROFF 3801 EAST WILLOW AVENUE	LONG BEACH	CA	90815	(213) 424-8159
CAMP KOMAROFF C/O LONG BEACH JEWISH COMMUNITY CENTER				
3801 E. WILLOW	LONG BEACH	CA	90815	(213) 426-7601
CAMP GILBOA, HABONIM 8339 WEST THIRD STREET	LOS ANGELES	CA	90048	(213) 655-1858
CAMP HESS KRAMER, C/O WILSHIRE BOULEVARD TEMPLE				
3663 WILSHIRE BOULEVARD	LOS ANGELES	CA	90010	(213) 388-2401
CAMP JCA - HIGH SIERRAS 8455 BEVERLY BOULEVARD	LOS ANGELES	CA	90048	
CAMP JCA - MALIBU 8455 BEVERLY BOULEVARD	LOS ANGELES	CA	90048	
CAMP JCA OF JEWISH CENTER ASSOCIATION				
6505 WILSHIRE BLVD. #209	LOS ANGELES	CA	90048	(213) 653-4260
CAMP MAOZ 10400 WILSHIRE BOULEVARD	LOS ANGELES	CA	90024	(213) 474-1518
CAMP MAX STRAUS C/O JEWISH BIG BROTHERS ASSOCIATION				
6505 WILSHIRE BOULEVARD	LOS ANGELES	CA	90048	(213) 852-1234
CAMP MOSHAVA, B'NEI AKIVA 7269 BEVERLY BOULEVARD	LOS ANGELES	CA	90036	(213) 934-1854
CAMP NCSY C/O NATIONAL CONFERENCE OF SYNAGOGUE YOUTH				
7269 BEVERLY BOULEVARD	LOS ANGELES	CA	90048	(213) 938-6576
CAMP RAMAH IN CALIFORNIA 15600 MULHOLLAND DRIVE	LOS ANGELES	CA	90077	(213) 879-4114
CAMP SHOMRIA, HASHOMER HATZAIR				
1070 SOUTH CRESCENT HEIGHTS BOULEVARD	LOS ANGELES	CA	90036	(213) 655-7881
CAMP USY, UNITED SYNAGOGUE YOUTH				
15600 MULHOLLAND DRIVE	LOS ANGELES	CA	90077	(213) 879-4114

CAMP YOUNG JUDAEA C/O HADASSAH ZIONIST YOUTH COMMISSION				
6505 WILSHIRE BOULEVARD	LOS ANGELES	CA	90048	(213) 653-4771
CAMP YOUNG JUDEA, HASHACHAR 6505 WILSHRE BOULEVARD	LOS ANGELES	CA	90048	(213) 653-4771
CHABAD SUMMER YESHIVA 7215 WARING AVENUE	LOS ANGELES	CA	90036	(213) 937-3763
GINDLING HILLTOP CAMP, C/O WILSHIRE BOULEVARD TEMPLE				
3663 WILSHIRE BOULEVARD	LOS ANGELES	CA	90010	(213) 388-2401
HABONIM - CAMP GILBOA 8339 WEST 3RD STREET	LOS ANGELES	CA	90048	(213) 655-1868
YOUNG JUDEA-CAMP JUDEA 6505 WILSHIRE BLVD., #201	LOS ANGELES	CA	90048	(213) 653-4771
CAMP ARAZIM 1419 BROADWAY, SUITE 612	OAKLAND	CA	94612	(415) 839-6044
CAMP YOUNG JUDEA 1419 BROADWAY, SUITE 308	OAKLAND	CA	94612	(415) 832-8448
CAMP RAMAH IN CALIFORNIA 385 FAIRVIEW ROAD	OJAI	CA	93023	(805) 646-4301
CAMP ARAZIM C/O UNITED SYNAGOGUE OF AMERICA				
PO BOX 9154	SACRAMENTO	CA	95816	
CAMP ARAZIM 944 MARKET STREET, SUITE 604	SAN FRANCISCO	CA	94102	(415) 397-1730
CAMP TAWONGA 3195 CALIFORNIA STREET	SAN FRANCISCO	CA	94115	(415) 929-1986
CAMP TAWONGA C/O UNITED JEWISH COMMUNITY CENTERS-BAY AREA				
3200 CALIFORNIA STREET	SAN FRANCISCO	CA	94118	(415) 346-6040
UAHC SWIG CAMP INST. C/O UNION OF AMERICAN HEBREW CONGS.				
703 MARKET STREET	SAN FRANCISCO	CA	94103	(415) 392-7080
CAMP SHALOM 2300 CANOAS GARDEN ROAD	SAN JOSE	CA	95125	(408) 266-6317
UAHC SWIG CAMP INSTITUTE 24500 BIG BASIN WAY	SARATOGA	CA	95070	(415) 392-7080
J BAR DOUBLE C RANCH C/O JEWISH COMMUNITY CENTER				
PO BOX 6196, CHERRY CREEK STATION	DENVER	CO	80206	(303) 399-2660
RANCH CAMP, THE P. O. BOX 6196	DENVER	CO	80206	(303) 399-2660
CAMP HADAR 435 BROOKLAWN AVENUE	FAIRFIELD	CT	06432	(203) 333-0343
INT'L TORAH CAMPS-RABBI GERALD BRIEGER AT TEMPLE EMANUEL				
150 DERBY AVENUE	ORANGE	CT	06477	
B'NAI B'RITH BEBER CAMP (NAT'L OFFICE)				
1640 RHODE ISLAND AVENUE N.W.	WASHINGTON	DC	20036	(202) 857-6600
B'NAI B'RITH PERLMAN CAMP 1640 RHODE ISLAND N.W.	WASHINGTON	DC	20036	(202) 857-6600
CAMP TEL SHALOM C/O ADAS ISRAEL CONGREGATION				
2850 QUEBEC STREET N.W.	WASHINGTON	DC	20008	(202) 362-4433
CAMP COLEMAN, C/O UNION OF AMERICAN HEBREW CONGREGATIONS				
3785 NW 82 AVENUE	MIAMI	FL	33131	(305) 592-4792
UAHC COLEMAN CAMP INSTITUTE 119 E. FLAGLER STREET	MIAMI	FL	33131	(305) 379-4553
GAN ISRAEL DAY CAMP 1140 ALTON ROAD	MIAMI BEACH	FL	33139	(305) 673-5664
SAVAGE'S MT. LAKE (NORTH CAROLINA)				
PO BOX 4450, NORMANDY DRIVE	MIAMI BEACH	FL	33141	(305) 866-3045
CAMP BARNEY MEDINTZ C/O JEWISH COMMUNITY CENTER				
1745 PEACHTREE STREET, N.E.	ATLANTA	GA	30309	(404) 875-7881
CAMP JUDAEA 1655 PEACHTREE STREET N.W. ROOM 405	ATLANTA	GA	30309	(404) 876-1526
UAHC COLEMAN CAMP INSTITUTE ROUTE #3	CLEVELAND	GA	30528	(404) 865-3521
B'NAI B'RITH BEBER CAMP 8 SOUTH MICHIGAN, SUITE 2301	CHICAGO	IL	60603	(312) 782-4766
CAMP CHI 1 SOUTH FRANKLIN	CHICAGO	IL	60606	(312) 346-6700
CAMP MOSHAVA C/O BNEI AKIVA 6500 N. CALIFORNIA AVENUE	CHICAGO	IL	60645	(312) 338-2871
CAMP RAMAH (WISCONSIN) 59 EAST VAN BUREN	CHICAGO	IL	60605	(312) 939-2393
HARAND CAMP 708 CHURCH STREET	CHICAGO	IL	60605	(312) 864-1500
HENRY HORNER, CAMP 30 W. WASHINGTON STREET	CHICAGO	IL	60602	(312) 726-8891
RAMAH, CAMP 72ND E. 11TH STREET	CHICAGO	IL	60605	(312) 939-2393
UAHC OLIN-SANG-RUBY CAMP C/O UNION OF AMERICAN HEBREW CONG.				
100 WEST MONROE STREET	CHICAGO	IL	60603	(312) 782-1477
YEHUDAH, CAMP 6328 NORTH CALIFORNIA	CHICAGO	IL	60659	(312) 973-3232
CAMP GAN ISRAEL 2014 ORRINGTON	EVANSTON	IL	60201	(312) 869-8060
CAMP MENORAH 8 BLACKHAWK HILLS DRIVE	ROCK ISLAND	IL	61201	(309) 786-1866
HABONIM LABOR ZIONIST YOUTH				
HABONIM CAMP TAVOR, 3740 DEMPSTER	SKOKIE	IL	60076	(312) 676-9790
YOUNG JUDEA, CAMP 4155 W. MAIN STREET	SKOKIE	IL	60076	(312) 676-9790
UAHC MYRON S. GOLDMAN CAMP INSTITUTE 9349 MOORE ROAD	ZIONSVILLE	IN	46077	(317) 873-3361
KAMP ISRAEL 10910 NALL	OVERLAND PARK	KS	66204	
CAMP BEN F. WASHER C/O JEWISH COMMUNITY CENTER				
3600 DUTCHMANS LANE	LOUISVILLE	KY	40205	(502) 459-0660
GROSSMAN CAMP C/O ASSOC. JEWISH COMMUNITY CENTERS				
72 FRANKLIN STREET	BOSTON	MA	02110	(617) 329-9300
CAMP RAMAH IN NEW ENGLAND 1330 BEACON STREET	BROOKLINE	MA	02146	(617) 232-7400
CAMP YAVNEH C/O HEBREW COLLEGE 43 HAWES STREET	BROOKLINE	MA	02146	(617) 232-8710
INT'L TORAH CAMPS-RABBI DOV TAYLOR AT TEMPLE OHABEI SHALOM				
1187 BEACON STREET	BROOKLINE	MA	02147	(617) 277-6610
PIRCHAI DAY CAMP/BAIS SARAH DAY CAMP				
C/O NEW ENGLAND CHASSIDIC CENTER, 1710 BEACON STREET	BROOKLINE	MA	02146	
YAVNEH, CAMP C/O HEBREW COLLEGE 43 HAWES STREET	BROOKLINE	MA	01907	(617) 232-8710
CAMP BAUERCREST 10 PERKINS ROAD	CHELSEA	MA	02150	
UAHC EISNER CAMP INSTITUTE BROOKSIDE ROAD	GREAT BARRINGTON	MA	01230	(413) 528-1652
CAMP AVODA 11 ESSEX STREET	LYNNFIELD	MA	01940	
CAMP SHALOM LAKE GARFIELD	MONTEREY	MA	01245	
CAMP JOSEPH C/O JEWISH COMMUNITY CENTER CAMPS				
50 HUNT STREET	WATERTOWN	MA	02172	(617) 924-2030
CAMP NAOMI C/O JEWISH COMMUNITY CENTER CAMPS				
50 HUNT STREET	WATERTOWN	MA	02172	(617) 924-2030
CAMP YOUNG JUDAEA 81 KINGSBURY STREET	WELLESLEY	MA	02181	
JEWISH COMMUNITY CENTER DAY CAMP MANNING HOLD STREET	WORCESTER	MA	01602	(617) 756-7109
B'NAI B'RITH CAMPS 370 HARGRAVE STREET	WINNIPEG	MB		(204) 947-0601
CAMP AIRY C/O STRAUS FOUNDATION 5750 PARK HEIGHTS AVENUE	BALTIMORE	MD	21215	(301) 466-9010
CAMP LOUISE C/O STRAUS FOUNDATION				
5750 PARK HEIGHTS AVENUE	BALTIMORE	MD	21215	(301) 466-9010
CAMP MOSHAVA C/O ICHUD HABONIM 920 SLIGO AVENUE	SILVER SPRING	MD	20910	
CAMP TAMARACK C/O FRESH AIR SOCIETY				
6600 WEST MAPLE ROAD	WEST BLOOMFIELD	MI	48033	(313) 661-0600
CAMP TAVOR C/O HABONIM CAMP TAVOR 2005 MERRIL #5	YPSILANTI	MI	48197	
CAMP TIKVAH C/O JEWISH COMMUNITY CENTER OF GREATER MINN.				
4330 CEDAR LAKE ROAD SOUTH	MINNEAPOLIS	MN	55416	(612) 377-8330
CAMP HERZL 790 S. CLEVELAND #202	ST. PAUL	MN	55116	(612) 827-2108
GAN ISRAEL DAY CAMP 15 MONTCALM COURT	ST. PAUL	MN	55116	(612) 698-3858
HERZL CAMP 1698 GRAND AVENUE	ST. PAUL	MN	55116	(612) 698-3895
JEWISH COMMUNITY CENTER DAY CAMPS 1375 ST. PAUL AVENUE	ST. PAUL	MN	55116	(612) 698-0751
BARNEY GOODMAN CAMP - JCC 8201 HOLMES ROAD	KANSAS CITY	MO	64131	(816) 361-5200
CAMP SABRA C/O JEWISH COMMUNITY CENTERS ASSOCIATION				
2 MILLSTONE CAMPUS DRIVE	ST. LOUIS	MO	63146	(314) 432-5700
UAHC JACOBS CAMP INSTITUTE BOX C	UTICA	MS	39175	(601) 885-6042
BLUE STAR CAMPS KANUGA ROAD, PO BOX 1029	HENDERSONVILLE	NC	28739	(919) 692-3591
CAMP ESTHER F. NEWMAN C/O JEWISH FEDERATION OF OMAHA				
333 SOUTH 132ND STREET	OMAHA	NE	68154	(402) 334-8200
CAMP PEMBROKE C/O COHEN FOUNDATION CAMPS				
66 PROSPECT STREET	MANCHESTER	NH	03104	(603) 627-1100
CAMP TEL NOAR C/O COHEN FOUNDATION CAMPS				
66 PROSPECT STREET	MANCHESTER	NH	03104	(603) 627-1100
CAMP TEVYA C/O COHEN FOUNDATION CAMPS				
66 PROSPECT STREET	MANCHESTER	NH	03104	(603) 627-1100
YM/YMHA OF PASSAIC SCOLES AVENUE	CLIFTON	NJ		(201) 779-2980
NEW JERSEY YMHA/YWHA CAMPS C/O NEW JERSEY FEDERATION OF YS				
21 PLYMOUTH STREET	FAIRFIELD	NJ	07006	(201) 575-3333
YAC DAY CAMP WEST ST. GEORGES AVENUE AND ORCHARD TERRACE	LINDEN	NJ	07036	(201) 486-2866
CAMP-BY-THE-SEA OF THE JEWISH COMM. CENTER OF ATLANTIC CTY.				
501 N. JEROME AVENUE	MARGATE	NJ	08402	(609) 822-1167
CAMP KADIMAH C/O CANADIAN YOUNG JUDAEA				
1551 SOUTH PARK STREET	HALIFAX	NS		
LOUEMMA - R.D.2-SUSSEX, N.J.(55 MILES FROM NYC) 41-25 BELL BLVD	BAYSIDE	NY	11361	(718) 631-3747
BRONX HOUSE-EMANUEL-COPAKE, N.Y. (110 MILES FROM NYC)				
990 PELHAM PARKWAY SOUTH	BRONX	NY	10461	(212) 828-8952
BEER MORDECHAI SCHOOL & DAY CAMP 1670 OCEAN AVENUE	BROOKLYN	NY	11230	(718) 377-1838
BROAD CHANNEL DAY CAMP, YESHIVA OF FLATBUSH				
919 EAST 10TH STREET	BROOKLYN	NY	11230	(718) 377-4466
CAMP EMUNAH TINY TOTS C/O LUBAVITCH 824 EASTERN PKWY	BROOKLYN	NY	11213	(718) 735-0200
CAMP GAN ISRAEL 770 EASTERN PARKWAY	BROOKLYN	NY	11213	(718) 756-8007
CAMP GILA 1533 48TH STREET	BROOKLYN	NY	11219	
CAMP HASC C/O HEBREW ACADEMY FOR SPECIAL CHILDREN				
1311 55TH STREET	BROOKLYN	NY	11219	
CAMP HADAR HATORAH 1138 43RD STREET	BROOKLYN	NY	11219	
CAMP HUNTINGTON 1017 EAST 80TH STREET	BROOKLYN	NY	11236	
CAMP MOGEN AVRAHAM C/O YM/YWHA 575 BEDFORD AVENUE	BROOKLYN	NY	11211	
CAMP NAARIM 1726 45TH STREET	BROOKLYN	NY	11204	
CAMP NISSIAH C/O YM/YWHA OF WILLIAMSBURG				
575 BEDFORD AVENUE	BROOKLYN	NY	11211	
CAMP RALEIGH 1245 OCEAN AVENUE	BROOKLYN	NY	11230	
CAMP SDEI CHEMED INTERNATIONAL 1618 43RD STREET	BROOKLYN	NY	11204	(718) 633-1909
CAMP SPATT C/O YM/YWHA 575 BEDFORD AVENUE	BROOKLYN	NY	11211	
CAMP TORAH VODAATH 425 EAST 9TH STREET	BROOKLYN	NY	11218	(718) 941-8000
CAMP TORAS CHESED 3121 KINGS HIGHWAY	BROOKLYN	NY	11234	
DORA GOLDING - P.O.B. 531, R.D. #2 E. STROUDSBURG, PA(100MI)				
27 WEST END AVENUE	BROOKLYN	NY	11235	(718) 891-4800
HEBREW EDUCATIONAL SOCIETY - SUFFERN, N.Y. (45 MILES)				
9502 SEAVIEW AVENUE	BROOKLYN	NY	11236	(718) 241-3000
KINGS BAY DAY CAMP 2611 AVENUE Z	BROOKLYN	NY	11235	(718) 646-3447
MENUCHA DAY CAMP 841-853 OCEAN PKWY	BROOKLYN	NY	11230	(718) 434-5421
MIKAN-RECRO-ARDEN, N.Y. (50 MILES)				
1201 PENNSYLVANIA AVENUE (SUITE 1C)	BROOKLYN	NY	11239	(718) 642-1700
MORASHA - LAKE COMO, PA. (135 MILES)				
1364 CONEY ISLAND AVENUE	BROOKLYN	NY	11230	(718) 252-9696
MORASHA, CAMP 1277 EAST 14TH STREET	BROOKLYN	NY	11215	(718) 253-5742
NOAM DAY CAMP C/O YESHIVA CHSAN SOFER 1705 49TH STREET	BROOKLYN	NY	11204	(718) 853-8100
OCEAN PRIMARY SCHOOL & DAY CAMP 904 EAST 98TH STREET	BROOKLYN	NY	11236	(718) 649-1567
SHEVES ACHIM DAY CAMP 1818 54TH STREET	BROOKLYN	NY	11204	(718) 232-7800
YESHIVA ATERES YISROEL 8101 AVENUE K	BROOKLYN	NY	11236	(718) 251-9754
ELLA FOHS - NEW MILFORD, CONN. (80 MILES) 257 B. 17 STREET	FAR ROCKAWAY	NY	11691	(718) 327-5500
AGUDAH, CAMP	FERNDALE	NY	12734	(212) 736-4734
CAMP COEUR D'ALENE C/O YM/YMHA OF GREATER FLUSHING				
4535 KISSENA BOULEVARD	FLUSHING	NY	11355	(718) 461-3030
EDWARD ISAACS - HOLMES, N.Y. (65 MILES) 108-05 68 ROAD	FOREST HILLS	NY	11375	(718) 268-5011
FOREST HILLS SUMMER PLAY PROGRAM 71-02 113TH STREET	FOREST HILLS	NY	11375	(718) 261-9624
FOREST PARK DAY CAMP 102-35 63RD ROAD	FOREST HILLS	NY	11375	(718) 896-4444
SIMCHA DAY CAMP 1170 WILLIAM STREET	HEWLETT	NY	11557	
BETAR, CAMP 85-40 149TH STREET	KEW GARDENS	NY	11415	
CAMP HILLEL 33 WASHINGTON AVENUE	LAWRENCE	NY	11559	(516) 569-3370
CAMP SHALOM C/O ARONSKIND 60-29 264TH STREET	LITTLE NECK	NY	11363	
AVNET, CAMP 530 WEST BROADWAY, P. O. BOX 329	LONG BEACH	NY	11561	
CAMP KFAR MASADA C/O LONG ISLAND ZIONIST FOUNDATION				
381 SUNRISE HIGHWAY	LYNBROOK	NY	11563	(516) 593-9222
AGUDAH, CAMP (BOYS) 5 BEEKMAN STREET	NEW YORK	NY	10038	(212) 791-1832
AMERICAN ZIONIST YOUTH FOUNDATION 515 PARK AVENUE	NEW YORK	NY	10022	(212) 751-6070
ANNA HELLER - NARROWSBURG, N.Y. (100 MILES) 114 FIFTH AVENUE	NEW YORK	NY	10011	(212) 691-5548
ASSOCIATION OF JEWISH SPONSORED CAMPS, INC.				
130 EAST 59TH STREET	NEW YORK	NY	10022	(212) 751-0477
B'NAI B'RITH PERLMAN - STARLIGHT, PA.18461 (150 MI FROM NYC)				
823 UNITED NATIONS PLAZA	NEW YORK	NY	10017	(212) 490-3327
CAMP BETAR 55 WEST 42ND STREET	NEW YORK	NY	10036	
CAMP BETH JACOB 149 EAST BROADWAY	NEW YORK	NY	10002	
CAMP BNOS 5 BEEKMAN STREET	NEW YORK	NY	10038	(212) 791-1832
CAMP HAMSHEKH C/O UNITED SURVIVORS OF NAZI PERSECUTION				
25 EAST 78TH STREET	NEW YORK	NY	10021	
CAMP TEL ARI C/O LABOR ZIONIST YOUTH				
575 AVENUE OF THE AMERICAS	NEW YORK	NY	10011	
CAMP WILDWOOD C/O RECREATION ROOMS AND SETTLEMENT				
12 AVENUE D	NEW YORK	NY	10009	(212) 865-0925

CEJWIN - PORT JERVIS, N.Y. (80 MILES) 15 E. 26TH STREET ... NEW YORK **NY** 10010 (212) 696-1024

CHAVATZELETH - WOODBOURNE, N.Y.(100 MILES) 142 BROOME STREET ... NEW YORK **NY** 10002 (212) 473-4500

EISNER CAMP INSTITUTE - GREAT BARRINGTON, MASS. (120 MILES) 838 FIFTH AVENUE ... NEW YORK **NY** 10021 (212) 249-0100

KINDER RING - HOPEWELL JUNCTION, N.Y. (70 MILES) 45 E. 33RD STREET ... NEW YORK **NY** 10016 (212) 889-6800

KINDERLAND - TOLLAND, MASS. (130 MILES) 1 UNION SQUARE WEST ... NEW YORK **NY** 10003 (212) 255-6283

LEAH - BEAR MOUNTAIN, N.Y. (45 MILES) 197 EAST BROADWAY ... NEW YORK **NY** 10002 (212) 475-6061

MASSAD HEBREW CAMPS 426 WEST 58TH STREET ... NEW YORK **NY** 10019

MOGEN AVRAHAM CHAIM HELLER - SWAN LAKE, N.Y. (100 MILES) 114 FIFTH AVENUE ... NEW YORK **NY** 10011 (212) 691-5548

MOGEN AVRAHAM-STERNBERG-SPATT, INC. 114 FIFTH AVENUE ... NEW YORK **NY** 10011 (212) 691-5548

MORASHA, CAMP 2540 AMSTERDAM AVENUE ... NEW YORK **NY** 10033

MOSHAVA - INDIAN ORCHARD, PA. (110 MILES) 25 W. 26TH STREET ... NEW YORK **NY** 10010 (212) 683-4484

MOSHAVA OF BNAI AKIVA OF NORTH AMERICA, CAMP 25 W. 26TH STREET ... NEW YORK **NY** 10010 (212) 683-4484

NAALEH - ELIZAVILLE, N.Y. (95 MILES) 27 W. 20TH STREET ... NEW YORK **NY** 10011 (212) 255-1796

NATIONAL JEWISH WELFARE BOARD, DIRECTOR CAMPING SERVICES 15 EAST 26TH STREET ... NEW YORK **NY** 10010 (212) 532-4949

NATIONAL RAMAH 3080 BROADWAY ... NEW YORK **NY** 10027 (212) 749-8000

POYNTELLE-RAY HILL & LEWIS VILL. TEEN CAMP-POYNTELLE,PA(135) 253 W. 72ND STREET ... NEW YORK **NY** 10023 (212) 787-7974

RAMAH IN THE BERKSHIRES, INC.-WINGDALE, N.Y. (80 MILES) 3080 BROADWAY ... NEW YORK **NY** 10027 (212) 749-0754

RAMAH, CAMP BROADWAY & 122ND STREET ... NEW YORK **NY** 10027 (212) 749-8000

RECEIVE-A-GUEST OF LONDON - DEPT T 200 PINEHURST AVENUE ... NEW YORK **NY** 10033 (212) 568-0270

SENECA LAKE, CAMP 510 EAST 86TH STREET ... NEW YORK **NY** 10028 (212) 794-0105

SHOMRIA - LIBERTY, N.Y. (90 MILES) 150 FIFTH AVENUE (SUITE 709) ... NEW YORK **NY** 10011 (212) 929-4955

STERNBERG-NARROWSBURG, N.Y. (100 MILES) 114 FIFTH AVENUE ... NEW YORK **NY** 10011 (212) 691-5548

SUNRISE LAKE CAMP 225 PARK AVENUE SOUTH ... NEW YORK **NY** 10003

SURPRISE LAKE CAMP - COLD SPRING, N.Y. (60 MILES) 80 FIFTH AVENUE ... NEW YORK **NY** 10011 (212) 924-3131

SUSSEX LAKE CAMP - R.D.#5, SUSSEX, N.J. (55 MILES) 1140 BROADWAY ... NEW YORK **NY** 10001 (212) 683-8528

TEL YEHUDAH - BARRYVILLE, N.Y. (100 MILES) 50 W. 58TH STREET ... NEW YORK **NY** 10019 (212) 355-7900

TEL YEHUDAH, CAMP 817 BROADWAY ... NEW YORK **NY** 10003 (212) 260-4700

THE AMERICAN JEWISH SOCIETY FOR SERVICE 15 EAST 26TH STREET, ROOM 1302 ... NEW YORK **NY** 10010 (212) 683-6178

TORAH VAAVODAH INSTITUTE C/O BNEI AKIVA 25 WEST 26TH STREET ... NEW YORK **NY** 10010

UAHC EISNER CAMP INSTITUTE 838 FIFTH AVENUE ... NEW YORK **NY** 10021 (212) 249-0100

UAHC HENRY S. JACOBS CAMP INST. C/O UNION OF AMER HEB CONG. 838 FIFTH AVENUE ... NEW YORK **NY** 10021 (212) 249-0100

UAHC KUTZ CAMP INSTITUTE 838 FIFTH AVENUE ... NEW YORK **NY** 10021 (212) 249-0100

UNION CAMP INSTITUTE C/O UNION OF AMERICAN HEBREW CONGS. 838 FIFTH AVENUE ... NEW YORK **NY** 10021 (212) 249-0100

WEL-MET CAMPS-BARRYVILLE BRANCH C/O CHILD STUDY ASSOC. OF AMERICA, 50 MADISON AVENUE ... NEW YORK **NY** 10010

WEL-MET CAMPS-NARROWSBURG BRANCH C/O CHILD STUDY ASSOC. OF AMERICA, 50 MADISON AVENUE ... NEW YORK **NY** 10010

WEL-MET CAMPS-SILVER LAKE BRANCH C/O CHILD STUDY ASSOC. OF AMERICA, 50 MADISON AVENUE ... NEW YORK **NY** 10010

YOUNG JUDEA-SPROUT LAKE - VERBANK, N.Y. (75 MILES) 50 W. 58TH STREET ... NEW YORK **NY** 10019 (212) 355-7900

CAMP EAGLE COVE 164 LONGACRE ROAD ... ROCHESTER **NY** 14621 (716) 544-0600

CAMP MODIN FOR BOYS/GIRLS (CANAAN, ME) 791-T CENTRAL AVENUE ... SCARSDALE **NY** 10583 (914) 472-7713

CAMP TA-GO-LA 1 DOVER LANE ... SYOSSET **NY** 11791 (516) 921-5644

UAHC KUTZ CAMP INSTITUTE BOWEN ROAD ... WARWICK **NY** 10990 (914) 986-1174

CAMP LAKELAND C/O JEWISH CENTER OF GREATER BUFFALO 2600 N. FOREST ROAD ... WEST AMHERST **NY** 14228 (716) 688-4033

CAMP BETH JACOB ... WOODBOURNE **NY** 12788 (914) 434-4440

LAVI, CAMP 301 JORDAN AVENUE ... WOODMERE **NY** 11598 (718) 327-6565

MORRIS, CAMP ... WOODRIDGE **NY** 12789 (914) 434-7480

CAMP LIVINGSTON C/O JEWISH COMMUNITY CENTER 1580 SUMMIT ROAD ... CINCINNATI **OH** 45237 (513) 761-7500

JEWISH COMMUNITY CENTER 3505 MAYFIELD ROAD ... CLEVELAND **OH** 44118 (216) 382-4000

YOUNG ISRAEL - B'NEI AKIVA 14141 CEDAR ROAD ... CLEVELAND **OH** 44121 (216) 382-5740

CAMP WISE C/O JEWISH COMMUNITY CENTER 3505 MAYFIELD ROAD ... CLEVELAND HEIGHTS **OH** 44118 (216) 382-4000

JEWISH CENTER 125 COLLEGE AVENUE ... COLUMBUS **OH** 43209 (614) 231-2731

YOUNG ISRAEL MOSHEVET STONE 14141 CEDAR ROAD ... SOUTH EUCLID **OH** 44121 (216) 382-5740

CAMP REENA 100 ELDER STREET ... DOWNSVIEW **ON**

CAMP KADIMA 57 DELAWARE AVENUE ... HAMILTON **ON**

CAMP B'NAI B'RITH OF OTTAWA 34 ELM BANK CRESCENT ... OTTAWA **ON** (613) 825-3067

CAMP BILUIM C/O CANADIAN YOUNG JUDAEA 788 MARLEE AVENUE ... TORONTO **ON** (416) 787-5350

CAMP MACHAR C/O YOUNG JUDAEA AND ZIONIST ORG. OF CANADA 788 MARLEE AVENUE ... TORONTO **ON** (416) 787-5350

CAMP MASSAD 4140 BATHURST STREET ... TORONTO **ON**

CAMP MOSHAVA C/O BNEI AKIVA 86 VAUGHAN ROAD ... TORONTO **ON** (416) 630-7578

CAMP RAMAH IN CANADA C/O JEWISH THEOLOGICAL SOCIETY 3101 BATHURST STREET ... TORONTO **ON** (416) 789-2193

CAMP SHALOM C/O CANADIAN YOUNG JUDAEA 788 MARLEE AVENUE ... TORONTO **ON** (416) 787-5350

CAMP SOLELIM C/O CANADIAN YOUNG JUDAEA 788 MARLEE AVENUE ... TORONTO **ON** (416) 787-5350

CAMPS NORTHLAND, BNAI BRITH C/O JEWISH CAMP COUNCIL OF TOR. 750 SPADINA AVENUE ... TORONTO **ON** (416) 924-6211

GOOD FELLOWSHIP C/O JEWISH CAMP COUNCIL OF TORONTO 750 SPADINA AVENUE ... TORONTO **ON** (416) 924-6211

CAMP KVUTZA GALIL C/O MID-STATES HABONIM PO BOX 64 ... MERION **PA** 19066

ASSOCIATED CAMPING SERVICES 401 S. BROAD STREET ... PHILADELPHIA **PA** 19147 (215) 546-6600

CAMP JOSEPH & BETTY HARLAM C/O UNION OF AMER. HEB. CONGS. 117 S. 17TH STREET ... PHILADELPHIA **PA** 19103 (215) 563-8183

CAMP RAMAH IN THE POCONOS 1701 WALNUT STREET ... PHILADELPHIA **PA** 19103 (717) 798-2504

CAMP SAGINAW PENN SQUARE BUILDING, 1317 FILBERT STREET ... PHILADELPHIA **PA** 19107 (215) 649-7822

JYC CAMPS C/O JEWISH YS & CENTERS 401 S. BROAD STREET ... PHILADELPHIA **PA** 19147 (215) 545-4400

PINEMERE CAMP OF THE MIDDLE ATLANTIC REGION OF J.W.B. 438 W. TABOR ROAD (WINTER ADDRESS) ... PHILADELPHIA **PA** 19120 (215) 924-0402

S.G.F. VACATION CAMP C/O FEDERATION OF JEWISH AGENCIES 1511 WALNUT STREET ... PHILADELPHIA **PA** 19102 (215) 893-5600

CAMP EMMA KAUFMANN C/O JEWISH COMMUNITY CENTER 315 S. BELLEFIELD AVENUE ... PITTSBURGH **PA** 15213 (412) 621-6500

B'NAI B'RITH PERLMAN CAMP ... STARLIGHT **PA**

PINEMERE CAMP OF THE MIDDLE ATLANTIC REGION OF J.W.B. R.D.#3 ... STROUDSBURG **PA**

JYC CAMPS ARTHUR & REETA ... ZIEGLERVILLE **PA** 19492 (215) 545-4400

B'NAI B'RITH, CAMP 5151 COTE ST. CATHERINE ROAD ... MONTREAL **QU** H3W 1M6 (514) 735-3669

CAMP SHOMRAI C/O HASHOMER HATZAIR YOUTH ORGANIZATION 4970 MONPETIT #18 ... MONTREAL **QU**

CAMP WOODEN ACRES C/O JEWISH COMMUNITY CAMPS 5170 COTE STE. CATHERINE ROAD #203 ... MONTREAL **QU** (514) 739-2301

JEWISH LAURENTIAN FRESH AIR CAMP, C/O GOLDEN AGE ASSOCIATION 5700 WESTBURY ... MONTREAL **QU** (514) 739-4731

Y COUNTRY CAMP C/O YM/YWHA OF MONTREAL 5500 WESTBURY AVENUE ... MONTREAL **QU** (514) 737-6551

CAMP SHALOM C/O TEMPLE OHAVE SHALOM 305 HIGH STREET ... PAWTUCKET **RI** 02864

CAMP JORI C/O JEWISH FAMILY & CHILDREN'S SERVICE 229 WAYLAND AVENUE ... PROVIDENCE **RI** 02906 (401) 783-7000

UAHC GREENE FAMILY CAMP ... BRUCEVILLE **TX** 76630 (817) 859-5411

BEN G. BARNETT CAMP YOUNG JUDAEA 10921 CHIMNEY ROCK ... HOUSTON **TX** 77035

KLEIN CAMP 1010 NORTH BAYSHORE DRIVE ... LAPORTE **TX** 77571

CAMP BENBOW C/O SEATTLE JEWISH COMMUNITY CENTER 3801 E. MERCER WAY, PO BOX 779 ... MERCER ISLAND **WA** 98040 (206) 232-7115

GAN ISRAEL CAMP 4541 19TH AVENUE N.E. ... SEATTLE **WA** 98118

CAMP INTERLAKEN C/O JEWISH COMMUNITY CENTER 1400 NORTH PROSPECT AVENUE ... MILWAUKEE **WI** 53202 (414) 276-0716

B'NAI B'RITH BEBER CAMP ... MUKWONAGO **WI**

UAHC OLIN-SANG-RUBY CAMP INSTITUTE 600 LAC LA BELLE DRIVE ... OCONOMOWOC **WI** 53066 (414) 567-6277

CAMPS - HANDICAPPED

MAX STRAUS C/O JEWISH BIG BROTHERS ASSOCIATION 6505 WILSHIRE BOULEVARD ... LOS ANGELES **CA** 90048 (213) 852-1234

CAMP HENRY HORNER C/O YOUNG MEN'S JEWISH COUNCIL 30 WEST WASHINGTON STREET ... CHICAGO **IL** 60602 (312) 276-8891

CAMP RAMAH IN WISCONSIN 59 EAST VAN BUREN ... CHICAGO **IL** 60605 (312) 939-7400

CAMP RAMAH IN NEW ENGLAND 233 HARVARD ... BROOKLINE **MA** 02146 (617) 232-7400

CAMP TAMARACK C/O FRESH AIR SOCIETY 6600 WEST MAPLE ROAD ... WEST BLOOMFIELD **MI** 48033 (313) 627-2821

NEW JERSEY YM-YWHA CAMPS (ROUND LAKE CAMP, LAKE COMO, PA.) 21 PLYMOUTH STREET ... FAIRFIELD **NJ** 07006 (201) 575-3333

HEBREW ACADEMY FOR SPECIAL CHILDREN-PARKSVILLE NY (110 MI.) 1311 55TH STREET ... BROOKLYN **NY** 11219 (718) 851-6100

CUMMINGS CAMPGROUNDS - BREWSTER, N.Y. (65 MILES) 197 EAST BROADWAY ... NEW YORK **NY** 10002 (212) 475-6061

OAKHURST - OAKHURST, N.J. (61 MILES) 853 BROADWAY ... NEW YORK **NY** 10003 (212) 533-4020

RAINBOW - CROTON-ON-HUDSON, N.Y.(40 MILES) 33 W. 60TH STREET ... NEW YORK **NY** 10023 (212) 586-2900

RAMAPO ANCHORAGE - RHINEBECK, N.Y.(95 MILES) ... RHINEBECK **NY** 12572 (914) 876-4273

CAMP EMMA KAUFMANN C/O JEWISH COMMUNITY CENTER 315 SOUTH BELLEFIELD AVENUE ... PITTSBURGH **PA** 15213 (412) 521-8010

CAMPS - ISRAEL

SUMMER INST. IN ISRAEL FOR PROBLEM ADOLESCENTS & COLLEGE ST. 71-11 112TH STREET ... FOREST HILLS **NY** 11375 (718) 268-6060

AMERICAN ZIONIST YOUTH FOUNDATION 515 PARK AVENUE ... NEW YORK **NY** 10022 (212) 751-6070

CAMP NCSY 45 W. 36TH STREET ... NEW YORK **NY** 10018 (212) 563-4000

KIBBUTZ ALIYA DESK BOX 30 27 W 20 STREET ... NEW YORK **NY** 10011 (212) 255-1338

CAMPS - SENIOR CITIZENS

BRONX HOUSE-EMANUEL - COPAKE, N.Y. (110 MILES) 990 PELHAM PARKWAY SOUTH ... BRONX **NY** 10461 (212) 828-8952

BORO PARK Y - OLDER ADULT DAY CAMP 4912 14TH AVENUE ... BROOKLYN **NY** 11219 (718) 438-5921

ELLA FOHS - NEW MILFORD, CONN. 257 BEACH 17TH STREET ... FAR ROCKAWAY **NY** 11691 (718) 327-5500

BLOCK & HEXTER VACATION CENTER - POYNTELLE, PA. (160 MILES) 130 E. 59TH STREET ... NEW YORK **NY** 10022 (212) 751-8580

ISABELLA FREEDMAN - FALLS VILLAGE, CONN. 80 FIFTH AVENUE ... NEW YORK **NY** 10011 (212) 242-5586

KINDER RING - HOPEWELL JUNCTION, N.Y. (70 MILES) 45 E. 33RD STREET ... NEW YORK **NY** 10016 (212) 889-6800

SALOMON VACATION CENTER - BREWSTER, N.Y. (65 MILES) 197 EAST BROADWAY ... NEW YORK **NY** 10002 (212) 475-6061

CAMPS - TOURS

USY ON WHEELS 72 EAST 11TH STREET ... CHICAGO **IL** 60605 (312) 939-2353

92ND STREET Y BICYCLE TOURS YM/YWHA 92ND STREET & LEXINGTON AVENUE ... NEW YORK **NY** 10028 (212) 427-6000

NAOM 25 W. 26TH STREET ... NEW YORK **NY** 10010 (212) 684-6091

USY ON WHEELS 155 FIFTH AVENUE ... NEW YORK **NY** 10010 (212) 533-7800

CANDY

BEN MYERSON CANDY CO. 928 TOWNE AVENUE	LOS ANGELES	**CA**	90021	(213) 623-6266
BLUM'S 635 MARKET STREET	SAN FRANCISCO	**CA**	94105	(415) 777-9251
BARTON'S KOSHER CANDIES 2816 WEST DEVON AVENUE	CHICAGO	**IL**	60645	(312) 274-1273
KOSHER CHOCOLATE FACTORY 1827 WILLOW ROAD	NORTHFIELD	**IL**	60093	(312) 441-7110
BOGDON CANDY CO. 3034 HOLMES STREET	KANSAS CITY	**MO**	64109	(816) 561-4402
BIERMANN MARZIPAN CO. 5418 TONNELLE AVENUE	NORTH BERGEN	**NJ**	07047	(201) 863-2928
BARRY CHOCOLATE, INC. 1500 SUCKLE HIGHWAY	PENNSAUKEN	**NJ**	08110	(609) 665-4940
BANNER CANDY CORP. 700 LIBERTY AVENUE	BROOKLYN	**NY**	11208	(718) 647-4747
BLOOM PACKING CO. 4222 10TH AVENUE	BROOKLYN	**NY**	11219	(718) 853-6050
CANDY MAN (KOSHER CANDY, DRIED FRUITS, NUTS, ETC.) 4702 13TH AVENUE	BROOKLYN	**NY**	11219	(718) 438-5419
JOYVA CORP. 53 VARIK AVENUE	BROOKLYN	**NY**	11212	(718) 497-0170
LIEBER CHOCOLATE COMPANY 100 19TH STREET	BROOKLYN	**NY**	11232	(718) 499-0888
MADANIM CHOCOLATE 513 FLUSHING AVENUE	BROOKLYN	**NY**	11205	(718) 855-7876
PASKESZ CANDY CO. 125 51ST STREET	BROOKLYN	**NY**	11232	(718) 439-6222
PASKESZ KOSHER CANDIES 5315 13TH AVENUE	BROOKLYN	**NY**	11219	(718) 851-4657
SHUFRA 585 MANHATTAN AVENUE	BROOKLYN	**NY**	11222	(718) 383-5760
CROWN KOSHER CANDIES 10 RASON ROAD	CEDARHURST	**NY**	11516	(516) 239-0800
ASTOR CHOCOLATE CORP. 48-25 METROPOLITAN AVENUE	GLENDALE	**NY**	11385	(718) 386-7400
BARRICINI CANDIES 22-19 41ST AVENUE	LONG ISLAND CITY	**NY**	11101	(718) 429-8335
GOLDENBERG CANDY CO. 161 W. WYOMING AVENUE	PHILADELPHIA	**PA**	19140	(215) 455-7505
AMBROSIA CHOCOLATE CO. 1133 N. 5TH STREET	MILWAUKEE	**WI**	53203	(414) 271-2089

CANDY - ISRAELI

R.L. ALBERT & SON, INC., ALTRAY COMPANY 19 WEST ELM STREET	GREENWICH	**CT**	06830	(203) 622-8655
SOUTHEAST FOODS 1801 N.W. FIRST AVENUE	MIAMI	**FL**	33136	(305) 573-7313
HAMAKOR JUDAICA, INC. 6112 N. LINCOLN AVENUE	CHICAGO	**IL**	60659	(312) 463-6186
KOSHER PRODUCTS OF LOUISVILLE 3723 STANTON BLVD	LOUISVILLE	**KY**	40220	(502) 452-6519
EXPO-EL INC. 3000 TOWN CENTER	SOUTHFIELD	**MI**	48075	(313) 358-1560
THE KELLER FOOD CO. 2917 BROOKLYN AVENUE, P.O. BOX 4824	KANSAS CITY	**MO**	64109	(816) 921-3500
I. ROKEACH & SONS, INC. 560 SYLVAN AVENUE	ENGLEWOOD CLIFFS	**NJ**	07632	(201) 568-7550
I. ROKEACH & SONS, INC. WATER & CHESTNUT STREETS	FARMINGDALE	**NJ**	07727	(201) 938-6131
GOODISCO INC. 1045 PENN AVENUE	LINDEN	**NJ**	07036	(201) 925-7400
SPITZER DISTRIBUTOR CO., INC. 320 MANIDA STREET	BRONX	**NY**	10474	(212) 378-1470
ATALANTA CORPORATION 17 VARICK STREET	NEW YORK	**NY**	10013	(212) 431-9000
ISRAEL ASSORTED CONFECTIONS, INC. 212 FIFTH AVENUE	NEW YORK	**NY**	10010	(212) 686-7005
MIDLAND MARINE FOODS, INC. 4540 COMMERCE AVENUE	CLEVELAND	**OH**	44103	(216) 391-1005
REISER KOSHER WINE CO. 4834 NORTH BROAD STREET	PHILADELPHIA	**PA**	19141	(215) 329-3350

CANTORIAL INSTITUTIONS & SCHOOLS

JEWISH THEOLOGICAL SEMINARY CANTORIAL INSTITUTE 3080 BROADWAY	NEW YORK	**NY**	10027	(212) 678-8000
SCHOOL OF SACRED MUSIC, HUC-JIR 1 W. 4TH STREET	NEW YORK	**NY**	10012	(212) 873-0388
YESHIVA UNIVERSITY CANTORIAL INSTITUTE 500 W. 185TH STREET	NEW YORK	**NY**	10033	(212) 960-5400

CANTORIAL ORGANIZATIONS

AMERICAN CONFERENCE OF CANTORS, THE 838 FIFTH AVENUE	NEW YORK	**NY**	10021	(212) 249-0100
CANTORS ASSEMBLY-JEWISH THEOLOGICAL SEMINARY OF AMERICA 150 FIFTH AVENUE	NEW YORK	**NY**	10011	(212) 691-8020
JEWISH MINISTERS CANTORS ASSOCIATION OF AMERICA, INC. 3 W. 16TH STREET	NEW YORK	**NY**	10011	(212) 675-6601

CATERERS & CATERING HALLS

FEIG'S KOSHER FOODS 5071 E. 5TH STREET	TUCSON	**AZ**	85711	(602) 325-2255
HARTFORD KOSHER CATERERS HARTFORD HILTON-FORD & PEARL STREETS	HARTFORD	**CT**	06103	(203) 527-7770
GUTKIN CATERERS 363 WHALLEY AVENUE	NEW HAVEN	**CT**	06511	(203) 562-6184
M&T APPETIZERS & DELICATESSEN 1150 WHALLEY AVENUE	NEW HAVEN	**CT**	06515	(203) 389-5603
MR. OMELETTE 5020 LAGUNA ROAD	COLLEGE PARK	**MD**	20740	(202) 441-2695
GAMIEL BROTHERS DELICATESSEN & RESTAURANT 13 E. 7TH STREET	WILMINGTON	**DE**	19801	(302) 655-2748
MAZEL KOSHER CATERING 107 S. 20TH AVENUE	HOLLYWOOD	**FL**	33020	(305) 922-6666
MASTER HOST DINNER SERVICE 3095 N.W. 40TH STREET	MIAMI	**FL**	33142	(305) 635-5201
EMBASSY KOSHER STEAK HOUSE 1417 WASHINGTON AVENUE	MIAMI BEACH	**FL**	33139	(305) 538-7550
MADAN KOSHER CATERING AT FORTE TOWERS 1000 WEST AVENUE	MIAMI BEACH	**FL**	33139	(305) 944-6644
ROYAL HUNGARIAN KOSHER RESTAURANT & CATERERS SASSOON HOTEL	MIAMI BEACH	**FL**	33139	(305) 538-5401
KOSHER TREATS 1678 N.E. 164TH STREET	NORTH MIAMI BEACH	**FL**	33162	(305) 947-1800
DANZIGER 2932 WEST GREENLEAF	CHICAGO	**IL**	60645	(312) 743-4325
KOSHER KARRY 2828 WEST DEVON	CHICAGO	**IL**	60659	(312) 973-4355
POLSKI KOSHER CATERING	CHICAGO	**IL**		(312) 539-2288
TURNER KOSHER CATERERS 7771 S. EXCHANGE AVENUE	CHICAGO	**IL**	60649	(312) 721-8017
GOLDMAN-SEGAL KOSHER CATERERS 3411 WEST CHURCH	SKOKIE	**IL**	60076	(312) 338-4060
KOSHER GOURMET 3552 DEMPSTER	SKOKIE	**IL**	60077	(312) 679-0432
MAYER STIEBEL CATERERS 9599 SKOKIE BLVD	SKOKIE	**IL**	60076	(312) 679-7000
SIMCHAS' SIMCHAS 3552 W. DEMPSTER	SKOKIE	**IL**	60077	(312) 679-0432
CHATEAU GAROD 1581 BEACON STREET	BROOKLINE	**MA**	02146	(617) 232-8444
MYER'S KOSHER KITCHEN 168 SHIRLEY AVENUE	REVERE	**MA**	02151	(617) 289-2063
GREEN MANOR 80 MASSAPOAG AVENUE	SHARON	**MA**	02067	(617) 784-6000
GOLDMAN'S FANCY KOSHER BAKERY 6848 REISTERSTOWN ROAD	BALTIMORE	**MD**	21202	(301) 358-9625
MARION'S CUSTOM CATERING 2702 NAVARE DRIVE	CHEVY CHASE	**MD**		(301) 587-5820
KNISH SHOP 508 REISTERSTOWN ROAD	PIKESVILLE	**MD**		(301) 484-5850
SCHLEIDER CATERERS 1335 ROCKVILLE PIKE	ROCKVILLE	**MD**	20852	(301) 881-3787
CORNED BEEF STATION OCEAN PLAZA MALL, OCEAN HWY & 94TH STREET	SILVER SPRING	**MD**		(301) 723-3222
HALLMARK KOSHER CATERERS	SILVER SPRING	**MD**		(301) 622-2239
SHABAT, CATERING BY	SILVER SPRING	**MD**		(301) 621-5577
KOHN SIMON KOSHER MEAT MARKET 10424 OLD OLIVE STREET ROAD	ST. LOUIS	**MO**	64131	(314) 569-0727
SOL & ELY'S KOSHER MEAT MARKET 8627 OLIVE STREET ROAD	ST. LOUIS	**MO**	64132	(314) 993-9977
KEN'S DELICATESSEN STATE HIGHWAY 34	ABERDEEN TOWNSHIP	**NJ**		(201) 583-1111
GOODWILL PANTRY CATERING 815 BROADWAY	BAYONNE	**NJ**	07002	(201) 339-2392
KOSHER KITCHEN 5901 BROADWAY	BAYONNE	**NJ**	07002	(201) 437-1594
FOSTER VILLAGE KOSHER CATERING 469 SOUTH WASHINGTON	BERGENFIELD	**NJ**	07621	(201) 384-7100
MERION CATERERS U.S. HIGHWAY 130 & WYNWOOD DRIVE	CINNAMINSON	**NJ**	08077	(609) 829-2111
VICTOR MAYER & SONS 100 HEPBURN ROAD	CLIFTON	**NJ**	07012	(201) 471-5096
VILLAGE KOSHER CATERERS 389 PIAGET AVENUE	CLIFTON	**NJ**	07011	(201) 772-5387
MIN GOLDBLATT & SONS 211 ELIZABETH AVENUE	EAST LINDEN	**NJ**	07052	(201) 925-3869
KOSHER DISH 437 PENNINGTON STREET	ELIZABETH	**NJ**	07202	(201) 527-1818
KOSHER PARADISE 155 ELMORA AVENUE	ELIZABETH	**NJ**	07202	(201) 354-0448
NOSHER'S HEAVEN (DAIRY & VEGETARIAN) 437 PENNINGTON STREET	ELIZABETH	**NJ**	07202	(201) 527-1818
SUPERIOR DELI & APPETIZER COMPANY 150 ELMORE AVENUE	ELIZABETH	**NJ**	07202	(201) 352-0355
ENGLEWOOD KOSHER DELI 95 WEST PALISADE AVENUE	ENGLEWOOD	**NJ**	07631	(201) 567-0732
PETAK BROS. KOSHER DELICATESSEN 19-03 FAIR LAWN AVENUE	FAIR LAWN	**NJ**	07410	(201) 797-5010
SQUIRE KOSHER RESTAURANT & DELI 209 MAIN STREET	FT. LEE	**NJ**	07024	(201) 461-7410
ZELLY'S 1347 16TH STREET	FT. LEE	**NJ**	07024	(201) 224-4848
SHERATON HEIGHTS 650 HARRIS AVENUE	HASBROUCK HEIGHTS	**NJ**	07604	(201) 288-6100
FOX LIEBERMAN HOTEL 814 MADISON AVENUE	LAKEWOOD	**NJ**	08701	(201) 367-9199
DELI KING 628 ST. GEORGES AVENUE	LINDEN	**NJ**	07036	(201) 925-3909
EPPES ESSEN OF LIVINGSTON 105 MT PLEASANT AVENUE	LIVINGSTON	**NJ**	07039	(201) 994-1120
KEN'S DELICATESSEN STATE HIGHWAY 34	MATAWAN	**NJ**	07747	(201) 583-1111
GOVERNOR MORRIS INN, THE 2 WHIPPANY ROAD	MORRISTOWN	**NJ**	07960	(201) 539-7300
MIDDLEBROOK KOSHER DELICATESSEN 594 STATE HIGHWAY 35	OAKHURST	**NJ**	07755	(201) 493-8300
PATERSON CATERERS 12 MORTON STREET	PATERSON	**NJ**	07501	(201) 279-1941
LARRY'S KOSHER DELI RESTAURANT APPETIZERS & CATERERS 1353 SOUTH AVENUE	PLAINFIELD	**NJ**	07062	(201) 755-8013
SHORT HILLS CATERERS 610 MORRIS TURNPIKE	SHORT HILLS	**NJ**	07078	(201) 379-6950
TOMS RIVER KOSHER CATERERS 1065 MULBERRY PLACE	TOMS RIVER	**NJ**	08753	(201) 349-7914
QUALITY DELI & APPETIZERS 638 OCEAN AVENUE	WEST END	**NJ**	07740	(201) 222-9753
GOLDMAN CATERERS 350 PLEASANT VALLEY WAY	WEST ORANGE	**NJ**	07052	(201) 731-4408
WEST MONT COUNTRY CLUB RIFLE CAMP ROAD	WEST PATERSON	**NJ**	07424	(201) 256-2700
FOREMOST KOSHER CATERERS 58 JEFFERSON AVENUE	WESTWOOD	**NJ**	07090	(201) 664-2465
TABATCHNICK OF WESTWOOD KOSHER DELICATESSEN & APPETIZERS 226 FAIRVIEW AVENUE	WESTWOOD	**NJ**	07090	(201) 666-1051
BIRCHWOOD MANOR 111 NORTH JEFFERSON ROAD	WHIPPANY	**NJ**	07981	(201) 887-1414
GOLDENBERG CATERERS, INC.		**NY**		(516) 239-5652
D & D CATERERS 8 MAGNOLIA TERRACE	ALBANY	**NY**	12209	(518) 462-2510
KAYE'S CATERERS 22 WILLOW STREET	ALBANY	**NY**	12206	(518) 538-5275
PHIL BROADWAY KOSHER DELI & RESTAURANT 30-05 BROADWAY	ASTORIA	**NY**		(718) 728-4253
SANDS AT ATLANTIC BEACH 1395 BEACH BLVD	ATLANTIC BEACH	**NY**	11509	(516) 239-0660
SCHARF CATERERS, INC. 1395 BEECH BLVD	ATLANTIC BEACH	**NY**	11509	(516) 239-0900
BEN'S KOSHER GOURMET RESTAURANTS & CATERERS 933 ATLANTIC AVENUE	BALDWIN	**NY**	11510	(516) 868-2072
BAYSIDE JEWISH CENTER 203-05 32ND AVENUE	BAYSIDE	**NY**	11361	(718) 352-7900
LEDERMAN CATERERS LIMITED, BAYSIDE JEWISH CENTER 203-05 32ND AVENUE	BAYSIDE	**NY**	11363	(718) 461-6998
PRESTIGE CATERERS 61-35 220TH STREET	BAYSIDE	**NY**	11364	(718) 631-4217
SHORE TERRACE CATERERS, BAY TERRACE JEWISH CENTER 209TH STREET & CROSS ISLAND PARKWAY	BAYSIDE	**NY**	11364	(718) 224-5577
BELLE HARBOR JEWISH CENTER 134-01 ROCKAWAY BEACH BLVD	BELLE HARBOR	**NY**	11694	(718) 474-3300
LEVINE'S WASHINGTON HOTEL BEACH 125TH STREET & ROCKAWAY BEACH BLVD	BELLE HARBOR	**NY**	11694	(718) 634-4244
ZORN'S POULTRY FARMS 4321 HEMPSTEAD TURNPIKE	BETHPAGE	**NY**	11714	(516) 731-5500
CAL-TUV CATERERS 3483 JEROME AVENUE	BRONX	**NY**	10467	(212) 881-5770
KINGSBRIDGE KOSHER KITCHEN 58 WEST KINGSBRIDGE ROAD	BRONX	**NY**	10468	(212) 584-5688
KOL-TUV CATERERS 3483 JEROME AVENUE	BRONX	**NY**	10467	(212) 881-5770
LOESER'S KOSHER DELICATESSEN & CATERER 214 WEST 231ST STREET	BRONX	**NY**	10463	(212) 548-9735
MARINA DEL REY 2894 SCHURZ AVENUE	BRONX	**NY**	10465	(212) 931-6500
MEAL MART 798 LYDIG AVENUE	BRONX	**NY**	10462	(212) 931-2900
MOTHER'S GRAND KOSHER DELICATESSEN 2458 GRAND CONCOURSE	BRONX	**NY**		
PALACE KOSHER RESTAURANT & DELICATESSEN 122 EAST 188TH STREET	BRONX	**NY**	10458	(212) 933-0043
RIVERDALE CATERERS 27-40 JOHNSON AVENUE	BRONX	**NY**	10463	(212) 543-6750
S & O KOSHER DELICATESSEN 1596 WESTCHESTER AVENUE	BRONX	**NY**	10472	(212) 842-2214
SAMUEL ADLER & SONS 54 WEST KINGSBRIDGE ROAD	BRONX	**NY**	10463	(212) 367-3888
SCHWELLER'S KOSHER CATERERS 3411 JEROME AVENUE	BRONX	**NY**	10467	(212) 655-8649
SIMON'S KOSHER TAKE HOME FOODS 3532 JOHNSON AVENUE	BRONX	**NY**	10463	(212) 796-7530
ZION KOSHER DELICATESSEN & RESTAURANT 750 LYDIG AVENUE	BRONX	**NY**	10462	(212) 597-6360
ACH TOV KOSHER DAIRY RESTAURANT 5001-13TH AVENUE	BROOKLYN	**NY**	11219	(718) 438-8494
ADELMAN'S 4514-13TH AVENUE	BROOKLYN	**NY**	11219	(718) 853-5680
AHI EZER CONGREGATION 1885 OCEAN PARKWAY	BROOKLYN	**NY**	11223	(718) 376-4088
APERION MANOR 815 KINGS HIGHWAY	BROOKLYN	**NY**	11223	(718) 339-4466
ARMON TERRACE CATERERS 5120 NEW UTRECHT AVENUE	BROOKLYN	**NY**	11219	(718) 438-5700
AVENUE O JEWISH CENTER CATERERS 54 AVENUE O	BROOKLYN	**NY**	11204	(718) 232-3443
AVON CATERERS 17 EASTERN PARKWAY	BROOKLYN	**NY**	11238	(718) 836-6868
BAIS ROCHEL HALL 125 HEYWARD STREET	BROOKLYN	**NY**	11206	(718) 387-9022
BANQUETS BY LOCKER C/O YOUNG ISRAEL OF AVENUE K,2818 AVENUE K	BROOKLYN	**NY**	11229	(718) 258-7088
BANQUETS BY LOCKER C/O AVENUE O JEWISH CENTER,54 AVENUE O	BROOKLYN	**NY**		(718) 232-3443
CAN TAAM 4813-13TH AVENUE	BROOKLYN	**NY**	11219	(718) 436-0400
CAROUSEL SMOKED FISH COMPANY 1504 ALBANY AVENUE	BROOKLYN	**NY**	11210	(718) 434-0700
CHAP-A-NOSH 1426 ELM AVENUE	BROOKLYN	**NY**	11230	(718) 627-0072

CHEESE'N THINGS 1117 AVENUE J	BROOKLYN	NY	11230	(718) 377-4911
CHEF'S DELIGHT 4704-18TH AVENUE	BROOKLYN	NY		
CONTINENTAL GLATT KOSHER CATERERS 75 RUTLEDGE STREET	BROOKLYN	NY	11211	(718) 875-0400
CONTINENTAL HOUSE OF GOURMET FOODS				
2123 NOSTRAND AVENUE	BROOKLYN	NY	11210	(718) 859-9090
COTILLION TERRACE 7307 18TH AVENUE	BROOKLYN	NY	11204	(718) 436-2112
COUSINS KOSHER DELICATESSEN 5014 AVENUE D	BROOKLYN	NY	11203	(718) 629-0830
CROWN GLATT KOSHER CATERERS & RESTAURANT				
4909-13TH AVENUE	BROOKLYN	NY	11219	(718) 853-9000
DEAUVILLE CATERERS 3939 SHORE PARKWAY	BROOKLYN	NY	11235	(718) 743-2700
DEE & JAY KOSHER CATERERS 1902 UTICA AVENUE	BROOKLYN	NY	11234	(718) 968-8908
ELM CATERERS 1213 ELM AVENUE	BROOKLYN	NY	11230	(718) 851-5444
EMBASSY TERRACE 401 AVENUE U	BROOKLYN	NY	11223	(718) 449-4040
EMPRESS KOSHER DELICATESSEN 2210 86TH STREET	BROOKLYN	NY	11214	(718) 266-7679
FLATBUSH KOSHER TAKE HOME FOODS				
1383 CONEY ISLAND AVENUE	BROOKLYN	NY	11230	(718) 252-8888
GEORGE & SID KOSHER DELICATESSEN 2175 RALPH AVENUE	BROOKLYN	NY	11234	(718) 968-1622
GERSON CATERERS 1387 EAST 96TH STREET	BROOKLYN	NY	11236	(718) 251-1060
GLUCK'S TAKE HOME FOODS 2271-65TH STREET	BROOKLYN	NY	11204	(718) 232-1444
GOLDEN CATERERS 1416 AVENUE J	BROOKLYN	NY	11230	(718) 338-9865
GRABSTEIN BROS. 1845 ROCKAWAY PARKWAY	BROOKLYN	NY	11236	(718) 251-2280
GUTTMAN'S CATERING 5602-11TH AVENUE	BROOKLYN	NY	11219	(718) 851-7179
GUTTMAN'S GLATT KOSHER TAKE HOME & CATERING				
5120-13TH AVENUE	BROOKLYN	NY	11219	(718) 436-4830
IRWIN JAY'S DELICATESSEN 1121 AVENUE J	BROOKLYN	NY	11230	(718) 258-9363
JAFFA RESTAURANT 4210-18TH AVENUE	BROOKLYN	NY	11218	(718) 435-9661
JOE'S KOSHER DELICATESSEN CATERING 545 KINGS HIGHWAY	BROOKLYN	NY	11223	(718) 336-4040
KENERETH GLATT KOSHER CATERERS 1920 AVENUE U	BROOKLYN	NY	11229	(718) 743-2473
KINGS BAY STRICTLY KOSHER CATERERS 3692 NOSTRAND AVENUE	BROOKLYN	NY	11211	(718) 891-7178
KINGSWAY JEWISH CENTER 2902 KINGS HIGHWAY	BROOKLYN	NY	11229	(718) 338-5000
KOEGEL & JACOBS KOSHER CATERERS 4305-15TH AVENUE	BROOKLYN	NY	11219	(718) 871-4727
KOSHER DELIGHT 1223 AVENUE I	BROOKLYN	NY	11230	(718) 377-6873
KOSHER DELIGHT 13TH AVENUE,CORNER OF 46TH STREET	BROOKLYN	NY	11219	(718) 435-8500
KOTIMSKY & TUCHMAN 111 WEST END AVENUE	BROOKLYN	NY	11235	(718) 939-9000
LA MER 1060 OCEAN PARKWAY	BROOKLYN	NY	11230	(718) 252-9700
LA PERVILLE CATERERS 1815-65TH AVENUE	BROOKLYN	NY	11204	(718) 236-4600
LANDAU'S DELICATESSEN 65 LEE AVENUE	BROOKLYN	NY	11211	(718) 782-3700
LE GOURMET 1210 KINGS HIGHWAY	BROOKLYN	NY	11213	(718) 778-3999
LE PALAIS ISRAELI-GREEK RESTAURANT 923 KINGS HIGHWAY	BROOKLYN	NY	11223	(718) 336-2500
LEVENSTEIN & SARNOFF, KINGSWAY JEWISH CENTER				
2902 KINGS HIGHWAY	BROOKLYN	NY	11229	(718) 338-5000
LOWINGER & JACOB CATERERS 1982 53RD STREET	BROOKLYN	NY	11204	(718) 258-1175
MANN NATT HOLLYWOOD CATERERS 3311 AVENUE S	BROOKLYN	NY	11234	(718) 375-8433
MARARD CATERERS 1387 EAST 96TH STREET	BROOKLYN	NY		(718) 251-1060
MATAMIM GLATT KOSHER CATERERS 5815-20TH AVENUE	BROOKLYN	NY	11204	(718) 232-3701
MAZEL TOV CATERERS 114 WEBSTER AVENUE	BROOKLYN	NY	11230	(718) 871-1607
MEAL MART 1412 AVENUE J	BROOKLYN	NY	11230	(718) 338-8100
MEAL MART 1920 AVENUE M	BROOKLYN	NY	11230	(718) 998-0800
MEAL MART 5417 NEW UTRECHT AVENUE	BROOKLYN	NY	11219	(718) 851-8800
MEAL MART 510 BRIGHTON BEACH AVENUE	BROOKLYN	NY	11235	(718) 769-6800
MEAL MART 4722-16TH AVENUE	BROOKLYN	NY	11219	(718) 871-5335
MEAL MART 54 LEE AVENUE	BROOKLYN	NY	11211	(718) 387-8900
MEAL MART 4410 FT.HAMILTON PARKWAY	BROOKLYN	NY	11219	
MEAL MART 4621-13TH AVENUE	BROOKLYN	NY	11219	(718) 854-7800
MEAL MART 54 LEE AVENUE	BROOKLYN	NY	11211	(718) 387-1445
MEAL MART 502 FLUSHING AVENUE	BROOKLYN	NY	11205	(718) 855-9600
MEAL MART 206 DIVISION AVENUE	BROOKLYN	NY	11211	(718) 963-3450
MENASHE HIRSCH CATERERS 222 OCEAN PARKWAY	BROOKLYN	NY		
MENDELES & ABRAHAM 942 MCDONALD AVENUE	BROOKLYN	NY	11218	(718) 436-1702
MENORAH BALLROOM 5000 14TH AVENUE	BROOKLYN	NY	11219	(718) 438-6490
MENROSE CATERERS 1114-52ND STREET	BROOKLYN	NY	11219	(718) 438-5977
MERMELSTEIN CATERERS 351 KINGSTON AVENUE	BROOKLYN	NY	11213	(718) 778-3100
MOISHE'S TAKE HOME FOODS 1706 EAST 16TH STREET	BROOKLYN	NY	11229	(718) 627-9438
NEGEV HOME MADE FOODS INC. 1211 AVENUE J	BROOKLYN	NY	11230	(718) 258-8440
NEWMAN & LEVENTHAL KOSHER CATERERS 1625 OCEAN AVENUE	BROOKLYN	NY	11230	(718) 338-3800
OCEAN BREEZE HOTEL 3811 SURF AVENUE	BROOKLYN	NY	11224	(718) 372-9813
OCEAN PARKWAY JEWISH CENTER 550 OCEAN PARKWAY	BROOKLYN	NY	11218	(718) 436-4900
PALACE KOSHER CATERERS 1906 AVENUE M	BROOKLYN	NY	11230	(718) 339-2650
PALACE, THE 4910-13TH AVENUE	BROOKLYN	NY	11219	
PARADISE GLATT KOSHER CATERERS 1426 ELM AVENUE	BROOKLYN	NY	11230	(718) 627-0072
PARKSIDE GARDEN CATERERS 83 DIVISION AVENUE	BROOKLYN	NY	11211	(718) 388-4204
ROYALE, THE 770 MCDONALD AVENUE	BROOKLYN	NY	11218	(718) 435-1047
RUTHIE'S RESTAURANT 1427 CONEY ISLAND AVENUE	BROOKLYN	NY	11230	(718) 252-5308
RUTLAND KOSHER CATERING 1118 AVENUE J	BROOKLYN	NY	11230	(718) 377-9695
S & D MAYER CATERERS INC. 2030 OCEAN PARKWAY	BROOKLYN	NY	11223	(718) 376-1300
SAMMY'S BAGEL NOSH 533 KINGS HIGHWAY	BROOKLYN	NY	11223	(718) 266-5920
SARNOFF CATERERS 2902 KINGS HIGHWAY	BROOKLYN	NY	11228	(718) 338-5000
SCHICK'S MANOR 4901-12TH AVENUE	BROOKLYN	NY	11219	(718) 853-6329
SCHREIBER CATERERS,INC. 9024 FOSTER AVENUE	BROOKLYN	NY	11236	(718) 272-9184
SEAVIEW JEWISH CENTER 1440 EAST 99TH STREET	BROOKLYN	NY	11236	(718) 763-5600
SHANG CHAI RESTAURANT 2189 FLATBUSH AVENUE	BROOKLYN	NY	11234	(718) 377-6100
SILBER GLATT KOSHER CATERERS 135 ROSS STREET	BROOKLYN	NY	11211	(718) 384-8085
SIMCHA CATERERS - COTILLION TERRACE 7307-18TH AVENUE	BROOKLYN	NY	11204	(718) 436-2112
SIMON'S KOSHER CATERERS 391 CROWN STREET	BROOKLYN	NY	11211	(718) 773-1480
TAM-GAN EDEN 2363 RALPH AVENUE	BROOKLYN	NY		(718) 241-6102
TORAS EMES KAMENITZ 1650 56TH STREET	BROOKLYN	NY	11204	(718) 851-4735
TORATH MOSHE JEWISH CENTER 4314-10TH AVENUE	BROOKLYN	NY	11219	(718) 438-9578
TUVIA'S GLATT KOSHER TAKE OUT 1813 KINGS HIGHWAY	BROOKLYN	NY	11219	(718) 627-8626
TWO FRIENDS CATERERS (CHOLOV YISROEL)				
1017 EAST 29TH STREET	BROOKLYN	NY	11210	(718) 258-6018
YOUNG ISRAEL OF AVENUE K 2818 AVENUE K	BROOKLYN	NY	11229	(718) 258-8550
YUN KEE RESTAURANT & CATERERS 1416 ELM AVENUE	BROOKLYN	NY	11230	(718) 627-0072
ROSENTHAL CATERERS 283 TACOMA AVENUE	BUFFALO	NY		(716) 876-8888
PRESTIGE CATERERS 555 VANDERBILT PARKWAY	DIX HILLS	NY	11746	(516) 499-4515
BRODIE'S KOSHER DELICATESSEN 1518 FRONT	EAST MEADOW	NY	11545	(516) 483-5382
DELRAY CATERERS 354 LARKFIELD ROAD	EAST NORTHPORT	NY	11731	(516) 266-9801
KOTIMSKY & TUCHMAN 295 MAIN STREET	EAST ROCKAWAY	NY	11518	(516) 599-1330
BAYSWATER JEWISH CENTER CATERERS 23-55 HEALY AVENUE	FAR ROCKAWAY	NY	11691	(718) 471-5252
CONGREGATION KNESETH ISRAEL 728 EMPIRE AVENUE	FAR ROCKAWAY	NY	11691	(718) 327-7545
KARMEL'S TAKE HOME FOODS INC. 19-03 CORNAGA AVENUE	FAR ROCKAWAY	NY	11691	(718) 327-7317
CONTINENTAL HOSTS LTD. FLUSHING MEADOW PARK	FLUSHING	NY	11368	(718) 592-5000
ELECTRIC INDUSTRY,THE 158-11 JEWEL AVENUE	FLUSHING	NY	11365	(718) 591-2000
LINDEN HILL KOSHER DELICATESSEN & CATERERS				
29-20 UNION STREET	FLUSHING	NY	11355	(718) 762-1515
MAUZONE TAKE HOME FOOD 69-60 MAIN STREET	FLUSHING	NY	11367	(718) 261-7723
MEAL MART 72-10 MAIN STREET	FLUSHING	NY	11367	(718) 261-3300
MEHL CATERERS,TERRACE ON THE PARK FLUSHING MEADOW PARK	FLUSHING	NY	11368	(718) 592-7373
STAR CATERERS INC. 41-23 MURRAY AVENUE	FLUSHING	NY	11355	(718) 886-2800
TERRACE ON THE PARK FLUSHING MEADOW PARK	FLUSHING	NY	11368	(718) 592-5000
KNISH NOSH CATERERS 101-02 QUEENS BLVD	FOREST HILLS	NY	11374	(718) 897-5554
KOTIMSKY & TUCHMAN 106-06 QUEENS BLVD	FOREST HILLS	NY	11375	(718) 939-9000
PATRICIAN CATERERS 106-06 QUEENS BLVD	FOREST HILLS	NY	11375	(718) 939-9000
SHARMEL CATERERS 71-00 YELLOWSTONE BLVD	FOREST HILLS	NY	11375	(718) 793-1130
YOUNG ISRAEL OF FOREST HILLS 71-00 YELLOWSTONE BLVD	FOREST HILLS	NY	11375	(718) 268-7100
ROSEBROOKE KOSHER CATERERS 366 DOGWOOD AVENUE	FRANKLIN SQUARE	NY	10010	(516) 483-3361
PARKSIDE CATERERS, FOREST PARK JEWISH CENTER				
90-45 MYRTLE AVENUE	GLENDALE	NY	11385	(718) 849-8817
ALLISON KOSHER CATERERS GREAT NECK ROAD	GREAT NECK	NY		(516) 466-5263
JEM CATERERS OF NASSAU,INC. 26 OLD MILL ROAD	GREAT NECK	NY	11023	(212) 895-7165
LEONARD'S OF GREAT NECK 555 NORTHERN BLVD	GREAT NECK	NY	11021	(516) 487-7900
MENORAH RESTAURANT 75 NORTH STATION PLAZA	GREAT NECK	NY	11021	(516) 466-8181
PRUZANSKY FAMILY CATERERS-LEONARD'S OF GREAT NECK				
555 NORTHERN BLVD	GREAT NECK	NY	11021	(516) 851-5272
TEMPLE ISRAEL OF GREAT NECK 108 OLD MILL ROAD	GREAT NECK	NY		(516) 487-2230
BEN'S KOSHER GOURMET RESTAURANTS & CATERERS				
140 WHEATLEY PLAZA	GREENVALE	NY	11548	(516) 621-3340
EPSTEIN'S KOSHER DELICATESSEN & RESTAURANT				
387 CENTRAL AVENUE	HARTSDALE	NY	10712	(914) 428-5320
MONTI'S TOWN & COUNTRY 301 JERUSALEM AVENUE	HEMPSTEAD	NY		(516) 483-3352
VICTOR MAYER & SON CATERERS 1255 HEWLETT PLAZA	HEWLETT	NY	11557	(516) 374-6300
WOODRO KOSHER DELICATESSEN & RESTAURANT				
1342 PENINSULA BLVD	HEWLETT	NY	11557	(516) 791-4033
FELDWOOD KOSHER CATERING 428 SOUTH OYSTER BAY ROAD	HICKSVILLE	NY	11801	(516) 681-7766
HUNTINGTON TOWN HOUSE				
124 EAST JERICHO TURNPIKE	HUNTINGTON STATION	NY	11743	(516) 427-8485
HUNTINGTON TOWN HOUSE				
124 EAST JERICHO TURNPIKE	HUNTINGTON STATION	NY	11743	(516) 895-5855
GATE OF LIONS 4435 AUSTIN BLVD	ISLAND PARK	NY	11558	(516) 431-2222
A & B CATERING 182-69 WEXFORD TERRACE	JAMAICA	NY	11423	(718) 658-8900
BORENSTEIN CATERERS 179-29 150TH ROAD	JAMAICA	NY	11434	(718) 656-3600
FOUNTAINBLEU CATERERS JERICHO TURNPIKE	JERICHO	NY	11753	(516) 333-8585
HOST KOSHER CATERERS 287 NORTH BROADWAY	JERICHO	NY	11753	(516) 433-5223
COLONIAL CATERERS ROUTE 209	KERTHONKSON	NY	12446	(914) 647-7575
TAIN LEE CHOW 72-24 MAIN STREET	KEW GARDENS HILLS	NY	11367	(718) 268-0960
BETH SHALOM OF LAWRENCE BROADWAY & WASHINGTON AVENUE	LAWRENCE	NY	11559	(516) 569-1880
LEVENSTEIN & SARNOFF CATERERS 390 BROADWAY	LAWRENCE	NY	11559	(516) 569-1880
TEMPLE TORAH CATERERS 54-27 LITTLE NECK PARKWAY	LITTLE NECK	NY	11362	(718) 423-2100
JACKSON HOTEL 10 WEST BROADWAY	LONG BEACH	NY	11561	(516) 431-3700
MICHELE CATERERS PARK AVENUE AT ROOSEVELT BLVD	LONG BEACH	NY	11561	(516) 334-7681
TEMPLE ISRAEL OF LONG BEACH RIVERSIDE BLVD	LONG BEACH	NY	11561	(516) 432-1410
KOSHER CATALOGUE,INC. 2107 BORDEN AVENUE	LONG ISLAND CITY	NY	11101	(718) 784-6150
				(800) 5KO-SHER
BETH DAVID OF LYNBROOK 185 DENTON AVENUE	LYNBROOK	NY	11563	(516) 887-9595
JERRAND CATERERS 153 BROADWAY	LYNBROOK	NY	11563	(516) 887-1533
LEVENSTEIN & SARNOFF CATERERS 185 DENTON AVENUE	LYNBROOK	NY	11563	(516) 887-9595
MALVERNE KOSHER CATERERS 370 HEMPSTEAD AVENUE	MALVERNE	NY	11565	(516) 599-1070
NEWMAN & LEVENTHAL CATERERS 333 SEARINGTON ROAD	MANHASSET	NY	11030	(516) 621-8049
MILJAY KOSHER CATERERS 1282 HICKSVILLE ROAD	MASSAPEQUA	NY	11758	(516) 541-0402
BAIS YAAKOV OF SPRING VALLEY 11 SMOLLEY DRIVE	MONSEY	NY	10952	(914) 356-3113
BETH ROCHEL SADDLE RIVER ROAD	MONSEY	NY	10952	(914) 356-7985
EUROPEAN HOMEMADE FOODS,INC. 82 ROUTE 59	MONSEY	NY	10952	(914) 356-9555
LANDAU CATERERS 9 JEFFREY PLACE	MONSEY	NY	10952	(914) 425-2837
MEAL MART 41 C MAIN STREET	MONSEY	NY	10952	(914) 352-9008
RAM CATERERS,INC. 20B ROBERT PITT DRIVE	MONSEY	NY	10952	(914) 352-0733
YESHIVA OF SPRING VALLEY ROUTE 306 & MAPLE AVENUE	MONSEY	NY	10952	(914) 352-1247
DORNSTEIN'S BIG THREE CATERERS				
C/O TEMPLE EMANUEL,3315 HILLSIDE AVENUE	NEW HYDE PARK	NY	11040	(516) 747-8484
ROBBINS & ROBBINS 15 DRAKE AVENUE	NEW ROCHELLE	NY	10805	(914) 632-9115
BERNSTEIN'S ON ESSEX STREET 135 ESSEX STREET	NEW YORK	NY	10002	(212) 473-3900
CORAL KOSHER DELICATESSEN & RESTAURANT 1473 2ND AVENUE	NEW YORK	NY	10021	(212) 249-6480
DELI ART KOSHER DELICATESSEN 333 7TH AVENUE	NEW YORK	NY	10001	(212) 564-5994
DELI-GLATT KOSHER 150 FULTON STREET	NEW YORK	NY	10038	(212) 349-3622
EDNA'S RESTAURANT & DELI 401 GRAND STREET	NEW YORK	NY	10002	(212) 473-7630
FIFTH AVENUE SYNAGOGUE 5 EAST 62ND STREET	NEW YORK	NY	10021	(212) 838-2122
FINE & SCHAPIRO'S RESTAURANT 138 WEST 72ND STREET	NEW YORK	NY	10023	(212) 877-2874
G & M KOSHER CATERERS CO. 41 ESSEX STREET	NEW YORK	NY	10002	(212) 254-5370
HIRSCHFELD CATERERS 809 WEST 177TH STREET	NEW YORK	NY	10033	(212) 923-2148
KAY CATERERS 200 AMSTERDAM AVENUE	NEW YORK	NY	10023	(212) 362-5555
LEVANA'S CAFE & RESTAURANT 148 WEST 67TH STREET	NEW YORK	NY	10021	(212) 877-8457
LINCOLN SQUARE SYNAGOGUE CATERERS 200 AMSTERDAM AVENUE	NEW YORK	NY	10023	(212) 362-5555
LOU G. SIEGEL'S RESTAURANT 209 WEST 38TH STREET	NEW YORK	NY	10018	(212) 921-4433
MACCABEEM RESTAURANT 147 WEST 47TH STREET	NEW YORK	NY	10036	(212) 575-0226

MARCY KOSHER DELICATESSEN 2511 BROADWAY	NEW YORK	**NY**	10025	(212) 222-0700
MEAL MART 4403 BROADWAY	NEW YORK	**NY**	10040	(212) 568-7401
MEAL MART 2189 BROADWAY	NEW YORK	**NY**	10024	(212) 787-4720
MERMELSTEIN CATERERS,INC.	NEW YORK	**NY**		(212) 778-3100
MICHELE & JOEL KARMAZIN-COMET CATERING (DAIRY OR MEAT)		**NY**		(212) 362-0412
MT.SINAI JEWISH CENTER 135 BENNETT AVENUE	NEW YORK	**NY**	10040	(212) 928-9870
NEW YORK HILTON,THE AVENUE OF THE AMERICAS & 53RD STREET	NEW YORK	**NY**	10019	(212) 586-7000
NEW YORK PENTA 33RD STREET & 7TH AVENUE	NEW YORK	**NY**	10001	(212) 736-5000
NEW YORK UNIVERSITY-ARA 22 WASHINGTON SQUARE NORTH	NEW YORK	**NY**	10011	(212) 598-3396
NEWMAN & LEVENTHAL KOSHER CATERERS 45 WEST 81ST STREET	NEW YORK	**NY**	10024	(212) 362-9400
PAPILSKY CATERERS 305 WEST END AVENUE	NEW YORK	**NY**	10023	(212) 724-3761
PARAMOUNT GLATT CATERERS 23 WEST 73RD STREET	NEW YORK	**NY**	10023	(212) 362-8404
RATNER'S DAIRY RESTAURANT 138 DELANCEY STREET	NEW YORK	**NY**	10002	(212) 677-5588
SCHUSTER HALL 85-93 BENNETT AVENUE	NEW YORK	**NY**	10033	(212) 923-3582
SHAARE HATIKVAH AHAVATH TORAH,CONGREGATION 711 WEST 179TH STREET	NEW YORK	**NY**	10033	(212) 927-2720
SHALOM JAPAN,JAPANESE RESTAURANT & NITESPOT 22 WOOSTER STREET	NEW YORK	**NY**	10013	(212) 925-0930
STERN'S CATERERS 666 WEST END AVENUE	NEW YORK	**NY**	10025	(212) 873-0446
TEMPLE ISRAEL 112 EAST 75TH STREET	NEW YORK	**NY**	10021	(212) 249-5000
TOWN HOUSE CATERING 150 EAST 35TH STREET	NEW YORK	**NY**	10016	(212) 685-5468
ZISKIN CATERERS 23 WEST 73RD STREET	NEW YORK	**NY**	10023	(212) 362-8404
CHATEAU CATERERS,LTD. 1373 BELLMORE ROAD	NORTH BELLMORE	**NY**	11710	(516) 569-4447
CATERERS OF WOODMERE,INC. 410 HUNGRY HARBOR ROAD	NORTH WOODMERE	**NY**	11581	(516) 791-1414
TAPPAN ZEE TOWNE HOUSE MOUNTAIN VIEW AVENUE	NYACK	**NY**	10960	(914) 358-8400
MR. OMELETTE 3445 LAWSON BLVD	OCEANSIDE	**NY**	11572	(516) 766-1884
PELHAM CATERERS 299 WOLFS LANE	PELHAM	**NY**	10803	(914) 738-1617
FELDWOOD KOSHER CATERING 428 SOUTH OYSTER BAY ROAD	PLAINVIEW	**NY**	11803	(516) 681-7766
GALAXIE CATERERS 1600 ROUND SWAMP ROAD	PLAINVIEW	**NY**	11803	(516) 694-6200
RICHMAN CATERERS (AT PLAINVIEW JEWISH CENTER)	PLAINVIEW	**NY**	11803	(516) 938-1310
RYE TOWN HILTON 699 WESTCHESTER AVENUE	PORT CHESTER	**NY**	10573	(914) 939-6300
NORTH SHORE JEWISH CENTER NORWOOD AVENUE & OLD TOWN ROAD	PT.JEFFERSON STATION	**NY**		(516) 473-5525
FOREST PARK JEWISH CENTER 90-45 MYRTLE AVENUE	QUEENS	**NY**	11419	(718) 849-8817
CAFE BABA OF ISRAEL 91-33 63RD DRIVE	REGO PARK	**NY**	11374	(718) 275-2660
TOV CATERERS 97-22 63RD ROAD	REGO PARK	**NY**	11374	(718) 896-7788
BARDY KOSHER CATERERS 339 RUTGERS STREET	ROCHESTER	**NY**	14609	(716) 271-6948
BITTKER CATERERS 1700 EAST AVENUE	ROCHESTER	**NY**	14609	(716) 473-7635
BON APETIT CATERERS 444 WILLIS AVENUE	ROSLYN HEIGHTS	**NY**	11577	(516) 621-0402
ROSLYN COUNTRY CLUB CLUB DRIVE	ROSLYN HEIGHTS	**NY**	11577	(516) 621-0333
DUNOWITZ & LESSER CATERERS,TEMPLE ISRAEL 2655 CLUBHOUSE ROAD	S.MERRICK	**NY**	11566	(516) 379-7436
TEMPLE ISRAEL 2655 CLUBHOUSE ROAD	S.MERRICK	**NY**	11566	(516) 379-7436
FT.HILL COUNTRY CLUB 50 FT.HILL ROAD	SCARSDALE	**NY**		
CHEF-AH KOSHER CATERERS 33 MAPLE AVENUE	SPRING VALLEY	**NY**	10977	(914) 356-4410
GARTNER'S INN HUNGRY HOLLOW ROAD	SPRING VALLEY	**NY**	10977	(914) 356-0875
MAZEL GLATT CATERERS-SINGER'S HOTEL CENTRAL AVENUE	SPRING VALLEY	**NY**	10977	(914) 356-2306
ROYALE GOURMET CATERERS 23 ROOSEVELT AVENUE	SPRING VALLEY	**NY**	10977	(914) 354-3237
SINGER'S HOTEL CENTRAL AVENUE	SPRING VALLEY	**NY**	10977	(914) 356-2300
WILTON CATERERS,INC. 710 S.MAIN STREET	SPRING VALLEY	**NY**	10977	(914) 352-4800
KAPLAN'S KOSHER CATERING 20 TOWNLY AVENUE	STATEN ISLAND	**NY**	10314	(718) 442-3877
SHALIMAR 2380 HYLAN BLVD	STATEN ISLAND	**NY**	10306	(718) 987-4800
SIMCHA BY THE SEA 11 CAPODANNO BLVD	STATEN ISLAND	**NY**	10306	(718) 979-7400
YOUNG ISRAEL OF STATEN ISLAND WILLOWBROOK AT WOOLLEY	STATEN ISLAND	**NY**	10314	(718) 494-6700
HOLIDAY INN 3 EXECUTIVE BLVD	SUFFERN	**NY**	10901	(914) 357-4800
MEAL MART	SWAN LAKE	**NY**	12783	(914) 292-9439
NOAM CATERERS 310A SOUTH OYSTER BAY ROAD	SYOSSET	**NY**	11791	(516) 921-1800
RICHMAN CATERERS(AT EAST NASSAU JEWISH CENTER) 310 OYSTER BAY ROAD	SYOSSET	**NY**	11791	(516) 496-3390
RICHMAN CATERERS (AT MIDWAY JEWISH CENTER)	SYOSSET	**NY**	11791	(516) 433-6563
PICKLES UNLIMITED 4469 EAST GENESSEE	SYRACUSE	**NY**	13214	(315) 445-1294
HILTON INN 455 SOUTH BROADWAY	TARRYTOWN	**NY**	10591	(914) 631-5700
BEN & SOL KOSHER DELICATESSEN GREEN ACRES SHOPPING CENTER	VALLEY STREAM	**NY**	11581	(516) 825-2240
CONGREGATION TREE OF LIFE 502 NO. CENTRAL AVENUE	VALLEY STREAM	**NY**	11580	(516) 825-2090
JEM CATERERS OF NASSAU,INC. 1000 ROSEDALE ROAD	VALLEY STREAM	**NY**	11581	(212) 297-1240
CONCORD CATERERS 3710 WOODBINE AVENUE	WANTAGH	**NY**	11793	(516) 781-5577
FOUNTAINBLEAU JERICHO TURNPIKE	WESTBURY	**NY**	11753	(516) 333-8585
STOUFFER'S INN 80 WEST RED OAK LANE	WHITE PLAINS	**NY**	10604	(914) 694-5400
WOLLOWICK CATERING OF WHITESTONE 12-25 CLINTON STREET	WHITESTONE	**NY**		(718) 767-7000
CREST HOLLOW COUNTRY CLUB JERICHO TURNPIKE	WOODBURY	**NY**	11797	(516) 692-8000
LE CORDON BLEU 96-01 JAMAICA AVENUE	WOODHAVEN	**NY**	11421	(718) 441-8800
SONS OF ISRAEL,CONGREGATION 111 IRVING PLACE	WOODMERE	**NY**	11598	(516) 379-7436
BATTERMAN & HIRSCHEL CATERERS 311 CENTRAL PARK DRIVE	YONKERS	**NY**	10704	(914) 963-0602
EPSTEIN'S KOSHER DELICATESSEN & RESTAURANT 2369 CENTRAL PARK AVENUE	YONKERS	**NY**	10710	(914) 793-3131
ACADEMY PARTY CENTER CATERING 4182 MAYFIELD STREET	CLEVELAND	**OH**	44116	(216) 381-2066
DAVIS KOSHER CATERERS 1805 SOUTH TAYLOR STREET	CLEVELAND	**OH**	44116	(216) 321-7945
DISTINCTIVE CATERING CORPORATION/WORLD OF MOUTH C/O THE CIVIC 3130 MAYFIELD ROAD	CLEVELAND	**OH**	44118	(216) 371-1112
EXECUTIVE CATERERS 27629 CHAGRIN BOULEVARD	CLEVELAND	**OH**		(216) 831-1714
FISHMAN CATERING CORPORATION 3300 MAYFIELD STREET	CLEVELAND	**OH**	44118	(216) 291-1220
FISHMAN CATERING CORPORATION 2437 SOUTH GREEN ROAD	CLEVELAND	**OH**	44122	(216) 291-1220
PERSONAL TOUCH CATERING BY EVA 1926 SOUTH TAYLOR ROAD	CLEVELAND	**OH**	44118	(216) 932-7411
SIEGLE'S DELICATESSEN & FOOD MART 15 WEST BANCROFT	TOLEDO	**OH**		(419) 243-6261
SIEGLE'S DELICATESSEN & FOOD MART 2636 WEST CENTRAL	TOLEDO	**OH**		(419) 473-2791
BETH SHOLOM SYNAGOGUE CATERERS 1445 EGLINTON AVENUE WEST	TORONTO	**ON**		(416) 782-1549
MONTECASSINO PALACE 3710 CHESSWOOD DRIVE	TORONTO	**ON**		(416) 630-8100
ZUCHTER'S CATERING 3101 BATHURST STREET	TORONTO	**ON**		(416) 789-5397
BOLOTIN CATERING SERVICE YORK & ASBOURNE ROADS	ELKINS PARK	**PA**	19117	(215) 782-8660
DELUXE KOSHER MEAT MARKET 678 WEST STREET ROAD	FEASTERVILLE	**PA**	19047	(215) 322-2121
ROSENTHAL & KAUFMAN OLD LANCASTER ROAD AND HIGHLAND AVENUE	MERION	**PA**	19066	(215) 667-4050
BETTY THE CATERER 25 EAST WALNUT LANE	PHILADELPHIA	**PA**	19144	(215) 844-6798
NORM THE CATERER 5163 KERSHAW	PHILADELPHIA	**PA**	19131	(215) 878-6300
R.PRESSMAN KOSHER CATERING 4027 WEST GIRARD AVENUE	PHILADELPHIA	**PA**	19104	(215) 382-4971
ROTHSCHILD CATERING 610 STRATHAVEN AVENUE	SWARTHMORE	**PA**	19081	(215) 544-5915
ADAM THE CATERER 9800 MEILLEUR	MONTREAL	**QU**		(514) 381-2909
GOLDEN CATERERS 5500 WESTBURY	MONTREAL	**QU**		(514) 737-1182
PERLMAN'S KOSHER CATERERS 4655 COURTRAI	MONTREAL	**QU**		(514) 733-7141
SHALOM KOSHER CATERING 4693 VAN HORNE	MONTREAL	**QU**		(514) 342-0087

CHARITABLE ORGANIZATIONS

UNITED ORTHODOX SERVICES 202 E. BENRIDGE LANE	PHOENIX	**AZ**	85012	(602) 277-7479
ASSOCIATION FOR ETHIOPIAN JEWS 304 ROBIN HOOD LANE	COSTA MESA	**CA**	92627	(714) 642-8613
AMERICAN ASSOCIATION FOR ETHIOPIAN JEWS, NAT'L MATERIALS CTR. 6505 WILSHIRE BLVD., ROOM 802	LOS ANGELES	**CA**	90048	(213) 852-1234
JEWISH NATIONAL HOSPITAL AT DENVER 440 NORTH LA BREA	LOS ANGELES	**CA**	90036	(213) 938-7273
UNITED ORTHODOX SERVICES 150 NORTH GARDENER	LOS ANGELES	**CA**	90036	(213) 934-0849
UNITED ORTHODOX SERVICES 441 NORTH GENESSEE	LOS ANGELES	**CA**	90036	(213) 655-8373
UNITED ORTHODOX SERVICES 1850 ORTEGA STREET	SAN FRANCISCO	**CA**	94122	(415) 661-4055
STOCKTON JEWISH WELFARE FUND 5105 N. EL DORADO STREET	STOCKTON	**CA**	95204	
UNITED ORTHODOX SERVICES, INC. 175 MAPLE STREET	NEW HAVEN	**CT**	06511	(203) 865-0923
UNITED ORTHODOX SERVICES, INC. 18 PEARL STREET	NORWICH	**CT**	06360	(203) 889-1900
UNITED ORTHODOX SERVICES 876 FARMINGTON AVENUE	WEST HARTFORD	**CT**	06119	
DAVENPORT JEWISH WELFARE FUND 1115 MISSISSIPPI AVENUE	DAVENPORT	**IA**	52803	(319) 326-4419
JEWISH WELFARE FUND 1712 W. SUNSET DRIVE	CARBONDALE	**IL**	62901	
HIAS 130 NORTH WELLS	CHICAGO	**IL**	60606	(312) 263-6880
JEWISH STUDENTS SCHOLARSHIP FUND 10 S. LASALLE STREET, SUITE 1100	CHICAGO	**IL**	60603	(312) 346-4537
JEWISH UNITED FUND 1 S. FRANKLIN STREET	CHICAGO	**IL**	60606	(312) 346-6700
NATIONAL JEWISH WELFARE BOARD 127 NORTH DEARBORN, SUITE 510	CHICAGO	**IL**	60602	(312) 332-3302
UNITED ORTHODOX SERVICES, INC. 6342 NORTH TROY	CHICAGO	**IL**	60645	(312) 973-5161
DANVILLE JEWISH COMMUNITY CHEST 1655 NORTH VERMILION	DANVILLE	**IL**	61832	(217) 443-2063
UNITED JEWISH CHARITIES OF ROCK ISLAND COUNTY 1804 7TH AVENUE	ROCK ISLAND	**IL**	61201	
UNITED ORTHODOX SERVICES 7334 BERYL STREET	NEW ORLEANS	**LA**	70124	(504) 283-5840
NOAM SHABBOS ASSOCIATION 192 KELTON STREET	ALLSTON	**MA**	02134	
OHEL CHESED CHARITY FUND 26 PRISCILLA ROAD	BRIGHTON	**MA**	02135	(617) 254-5067
UNITED ORTHODOX SERVICES 119 SUTHERLAND ROAD, SUITE A	BRIGHTON	**MA**	02146	(413) 731-8316
HEBREW IMMIGRANT AID SOCIETY (HIAS) C/O H. ALPERT, 9 SEWALL AVENUE #115	BROOKLINE	**MA**	02146	
JEWISH PHILANTHROPIES CENTER 233 HARVARD STREET	BROOKLINE	**MA**	02140	
UNITED ORTHODOX SERVICES, INC. 1710 BEACON STREET	BROOKLINE	**MA**	02146	(617) 734-5101
COMBINED JEWISH PHILANTHROPIES 1793 MASSACHUSETTS AVENUE	LEXINGTON	**MA**	02173	(617) 861-1560
UNION OF COUNCILS FOR SOVIET JEWS 24 CRESCENT STREET, SUITE 3A	WALTHAM	**MA**	02154	
UNITED ORTHODOX SERVICES 69 S. FLAGG STREET	WORCESTER	**MA**	01602	(617) 754-3681
HIAS OF BALTIMORE, INC. 5750 PARK HEIGHTS AVENUE	BALTIMORE	**MD**	21215	(301) 466-9200
NATIONAL JEWISH HOSPITAL AT DENVER 6301 LINCOLN AVENUE	BALTIMORE	**MD**	21202	(301) 752-7207
UNITED ORTHODOX SERVICES 3800 LABYRINTH ROAD	BALTIMORE	**MD**	21215	(301) 764-6122
UNITED ORTHODOX SERVICES 1201 BALLARD STREET	SILVER SPRING	**MD**	20910	(301) 585-1720
UNITED ORTHODOX SERVICES, INC. 14 HOLWELL STREET	PORTLAND	**ME**	04103	(207) 773-1022
BETH ISRAEL SYNAGOGUE C 291 MAIN STREET	WATERVILLE	**ME**	04901	(207) 773-4453
SHABBOS-YOM TOV FUND 14000 WEST NINE MILE ROAD	OAK PARK	**MI**	48237	
UNITED ORTHODOX SERVICES 15030 SUTHERLAND	OAK PARK	**MI**	48237	(313) 967-3728
UNITED ORTHODOX SERVICES, INC. 24031 BEVERLY	OAK PARK	**MI**	48237	(313) 967-3728
ST. PAUL UNITED JEWISH FUND & COUNCIL 790 S. CLEVELAND, SUITE 201	MINNEAPOLIS	**MN**	55116	(612) 690-1707
UNITED ORTHODOX SERVICES 439 E. 80TH STREET	KANSAS CITY	**MO**	64131	(816) 363-6272
JEWISH FOUNDATION FOR RETARDED CHILDREN 6271 DELMAR	UNIVERSITY CITY	**MO**	63130	(314) 863-3913
UNITED JEWISH CHARITIES-HIGH POINT HEBREW CONGREGATION KENSINGTON DRIVE	HIGH POINT	**NC**	27260	
UNITED ORTHODOX SERVICES, INC. 225 HIGHLAND AVENUE	EDISON	**NJ**	08817	(201) 572-1936
UNITED ORTHODOX SERVICES 375 BROOK AVENUE	PASSAIC	**NJ**	07055	(201) 472-3203
UNITED ORTHODOX SERVICES 22 BENNETT AVENUE	BINGHAMTON	**NY**	13905	(607) 724-3900
ACADEMY FOR JEWISH RELIGION 250 STREET & HENRY HUDSON PARKWAY	BRONX	**NY**	10471	(212) 543-8400
AMERICAN JEWISH REFUGEE AID SOCIETY 2632 UNIVERSITY AVENUE	BRONX	**NY**	10468	(212) 364-9680
SHOLOM ALEICHEM FOLK INSTITUTE 3301 BAINBRIDGE AVENUE	BRONX	**NY**	10467	(212) 881-6555
CHESED L'ABRAHAM, INC. 118 HOOPER STREET	BROOKLYN	**NY**	11211	
FRIENDS OF REFUGEES OF EASTERN EUROPE 1383 PRESIDENT STREET	BROOKLYN	**NY**	11213	(718) 467-0860
HACHNOSAS KALLAH FUND 879 44TH STREET	BROOKLYN	**NY**	11220	(718) 633-0998
HACHNOSAS ORCHIM L'ANASHIM D'BORO PARK 1554 49TH STREET	BROOKLYN	**NY**	11219	(718) 851-6178
LISHKAS EZRAS ACHIM 688 LEFFERTS AVENUE	BROOKLYN	**NY**	11203	
OHR JOSEPH RABBINICAL SEMINARY IN FRANCE 1362 46TH STREET	BROOKLYN	**NY**	11219	(718) 871-4861
RAV TOV - NATIONAL COMMITTEE TO AID NEW IMMIGRANTS 125 HAYWARD STREET	BROOKLYN	**NY**	11206	(718) 875-8300
TOMCHE CHOLIM ASSOCIATION 543 BEDFORD AVENUE	BROOKLYN	**NY**	11211	
UNITED HEBREW COMMUNITY 1381 CONEY ISLAND AVENUE	BROOKLYN	**NY**	11230	(718) 377-2566
UNITED ORTHODOX SERVICES 1178 44TH STREET	BROOKLYN	**NY**	11219	(718) 854-1620
UNITED ORTHODOX SERVICES 1674 47TH STREET	BROOKLYN	**NY**	11204	(718) 854-1620
YAD L'ACHIM 4820 16TH AVENUE	BROOKLYN	**NY**	11204	(718) 633-0776
ZALMAN ARYEH HILSENRAD KEREN HACHESED 1746 E. 13TH STREET	BROOKLYN	**NY**	11229	
UNITED ORTHODOX SERVICES, INC. 129 COMMONWEALTH AVENUE	BUFFALO	**NY**	14216	(716) 876-9344

UNITED ORTHODOX SERVICES 14 WEST MAPLE AVENUE — MONSEY NY 10952 (914) 356-9523
ADATH ISRAEL OF NEW YORK, UNITED HEBREW COMMUNITY OF NEW YORK 201 EAST BROADWAY — NEW YORK NY 10002 (212) 674-3580
AMERICAN COUNCIL FOR JUDAISM PHILANTHROPIC FUND 386 PARK AVENUE SOUTH — NEW YORK NY 10016 (212) 684-1525
AMERICAN FRIENDS OF THE ALLIANCE ISRAELITE UNIVERSELLE INC. 135 WILLIAM STREET — NEW YORK NY 10038 (212) 349-0537
AMERICAN JEWISH JOINT DISTRIBUTION COMMITTEE 60 EAST 42ND STREET — NEW YORK NY 10017 (212) 687-6200
AMERICAN JEWISH SOCIETY FOR SERVICE 15 EAST 26TH STREET — NEW YORK NY 10010 (212) 683-6178
CENTRAL COMMITTEE KNESSETH ISRAEL 245 EAST BROADWAY — NEW YORK NY 10002 (212) 267-6969
DOROT 251 WEST 100TH STREET — NEW YORK NY 10025 (212) 864-7410
FRIENDS OF BELLEVUE HOSPITAL SYNAGOGUE FIRST & 27TH STREET — NEW YORK NY 10016 (212) 685-1376
JEWISH BOARD OF GUARDIANS 120 W. 57TH STREET — NEW YORK NY 10019 (212) 582-9100
JEWISH COMMUNAL FUND OF NEW YORK 745 FIFTH AVENUE — NEW YORK NY 10151 (212) 752-8277
JEWISH PHILANTHROPIC FUND OF 1933 INC. 570 SEVENTH AVENUE — NEW YORK NY 10018 (212) 921-3860
JEWISH UNMARRIED MOTHERS SERVICE 12 E. 94TH STREET — NEW YORK NY 10028 (212) 876-3050
JOINT DISTRIBUTION COMMITTEE 60 EAST 42ND STREET — NEW YORK NY 10165 (212) 687-6200
NATIONAL ASSOCIATION FOR THE JEWISH POOR, THE 234 FIFTH AVENUE, RM. 301 — NEW YORK NY 10001 (212) 687-2570
OZAR HATORAH 411 FIFTH AVENUE — NEW YORK NY 10016 (212) 684-4733
REFORM JEWISH APPEAL 838 FIFTH AVENUE — NEW YORK NY 10021 (212) 249-0100
THE JEWISH BRAILLE INSTITUTE OF AMERICA, INC. 110 EAST 30TH STREET — NEW YORK NY 10016 (212) 889-2525
UNITED HIAS SERVICE 200 PARK AVENUE S — NEW YORK NY 10003 (212) 674-6800
UNITED HEBREW COMMUNITY OF NEW YORK, ADATH ISRAEL OF NEW YORK 201 EAST BROADWAY — NEW YORK NY 10002 (212) 674-3580
UNITED JEWISH APPEAL 1290 AVENUE OF THE AMERICAS — NEW YORK NY 10019 (212) 757-1500
UNITED JEWISH APPEAL OF GREATER NEW YORK, INC. 130 EAST 59TH STREET — NEW YORK NY 10019 (212) 980-1000
UNITED RESTITUTION ORGANIZATION 570 SEVENTH AVENUE, 16TH FLOOR — NEW YORK NY 10018 (212) 921-3860
WEST POINT JEWISH CHAPEL FUND 342 MADISON AVENUE, #625 — NEW YORK NY 10017 (212) 986-4086
UNITED JEWISH CHARITIES P.O. BOX 168 — NEWBURGH NY 12550
UNITED JEWISH WELFARE FUND 440 MAIN STREET EAST — ROCHESTER NY 14604 (716) 325-3393
UNITED ORTHODOX SERVICES, INC. 107 UNIVERSITY PARK — ROCHESTER NY 14620 (716) 275-0489
UNITED ORTHODOX SERVICES, INC. 7866 GREENLAND — CINCINNATI OH 45237 (513) 761-2212
RUSSIAN IMMIGRANT AID SOCIETY 1924 LEE ROAD — CLEVELAND OH 44118
UNITED ORTHODOX SERVICES 3575 HARVEY ROAD — CLEVELAND OH 44118 (216) 321-5002
UNITED JEWISH CAMPAIGN (JESSE PHILLIPS BLDG.) 4501 DENLINGER ROAD — DAYTON OH 45426 (513) 854-4150
UNITED ORTHODOX SERVICES 1130 NORTH MAIN STREET — ALLENTOWN PA 18104 (215) 776-1935
UNITED ORTHODOX SERVICES 103 EDGE HILL ROAD — BALA CYNWYD PA 19004 (215) 664-4680
UNITED ORTHODOX SERVICES 1545 OHIO AVENUE — MCKEESPORT PA 15131 (412) 678-2725
UNITED ORTHODOX SERVICES 5534 RALEIGH STREET — PITTSBURGH PA 15217 (412) 421-4943
UNITED JEWISH CHARITIES 2300 MAHANTONGO STREET — POTTSVILLE PA 17901 (412) 622-5890
UNITED ORTHODOX SERVICES 441 MONROE STREET — SCRANTON PA 18510 (412) 846-8222
JEWISH IMMIGRANT AID SERVICES OF CANADA 5151 COTE ST. CATHERINE ROAD — MONTREAL QU H3W 1M6 (514) 342-9351
UNITED JEWISH RELIEF AGENCIES OF CANADA 1590 DOCTEUR PENFIELD AVENUE — MONTREAL QU H3G 1C5 (514) 931-7531
SOCIETY OF FRIENDS OF TOURO SYNAGOGUE 85 TOURO STREET — NEWPORT RI 02840 (401) 847-4794
UNITED ORTHODOX SERVICES 249 ROCHAMBEAU AVENUE — PROVIDENCE RI 02906 (401) 751-0192
UNITED ORTHODOX SERVICES 9602 GREENWILLOW — HOUSTON TX 77096 (713) 721-1594
UNITED ORTHODOX SERVICES 4404 A WEST FRANKLIN STREET — RICHMOND VA 23221 (804) 358-6895
UNITED ORTHODOX SERVICES 5218 S. HOLLY STREET — SEATTLE WA 98118 (206) 722-5574
UNITED ORTHODOX SERVICES 5237 57TH AVENUE SOUTH — SEATTLE WA 98118
UNITED ORTHODOX SERVICES 3259 NORTH 51ST BLVD — MILWAUKEE WI 53216 (414) 442-6983
FEDERATED JEWISH CHARITIES 1576 VIRGINIA STREET EAST — CHARLESTON WV 25311

CHARITABLE ORGANIZATIONS - ISRAEL

JEWISH NATIONAL FUND 1323 ANNAPOLIS AVENUE — ANCHORAGE AK 99504 (907) 278-2777
JEWISH NATIONAL FUND 2100 S. CUSHMAN STREET — FAIRBANKS AK 99701 (907) 452-1981
JEWISH NATIONAL FUND 3070 RIVERWOOD DRIVE — JUNEAU AK 99801 (907) 789-4638
JEWISH NATIONAL FUND 5039 N. 19TH AVENUE #5 — PHOENIX AZ 85015 (602) 246-7676
AMERICAN COMMITTEE FOR SHAARE ZEDEK HOSPITAL IN JERUSALEM 265 SOUTH ROBERTSON BOULEVARD, SUITE 5 — BEVERLY HILLS CA 90212 (213) 278-6050
AMERICAN FRIENDS OF ASSAF HAROFEH HOSPITAL OF ISRAEL 9701 WILSHIRE BOULEVARD, SUITE 800 — BEVERLY HILLS CA 90212 (213) 273-2402
AMERICAN FRIENDS OF HAIFA UNIVERSITY 9301 WILSHIRE BOULEVARD — BEVERLY HILLS CA 90210 (213) 273-4707
AMERICAN FRIENDS OF HEBREW UNIVERSITY 8665 WILSHIRE BLVD — BEVERLY HILLS CA 90221 (213) 657-6511
SHELTERS FOR ISRAEL 603 NORTH CAMDEN DRIVE — BEVERLY HILLS CA 90210 (213) 936-6321
TEL HASHOMER HOSPITAL-CHAIM SHEBA MEDICAL CENTER 9100 WILSHIRE BOULEVARD, SUITE 333 — BEVERLY HILLS CA 90212 (213) 278-6050
AMERICAN COMMITTEE FOR THE WEIZMANN INSTITUTE OF SCIENCE 1801 MURCHISON DRIVE — BURLINGAME CA 94010 (415) 697-3253
JEWISH NATIONAL COUNCIL 17337 VENTURA BOULEVARD — ENCINO CA 91316 (213) 990-0511
JEWISH NATIONAL FUND 17337 VENTURA BLVD. #216 — ENCINO CA 91316 (213) 990-0511
JEWISH NATIONAL FUND 12181 BUARO STREET — GARDEN GROVE CA 92640 (213) 638-4483
AMERICAN FRIENDS OF BOYS TOWN JERUSALEM — LOS ANGELES CA (213) 203-0300
AMERICAN FRIENDS OF HAIFA UNIVERSITY 9301 WILSHIRE BOULEVARD — LOS ANGELES CA 90210 (213) 273-4707
AMERICAN FRIENDS OF HEBREW UNIVERSITY 8665 WILSHIRE BOULEVARD — LOS ANGELES CA 90211 (213) 657-6511
AMERICAN FRIENDS OF KIRYAT SANZ-LANIADO HOSPITAL — LOS ANGELES CA (213) 825-5075
AMERICAN FRIENDS OF TEL AVIV UNIVERSITY 1900 AVENUE OF THE STARS — LOS ANGELES CA 90067 (213) 556-3141
AMERICAN RED MAGEN DAVID FOR ISRAEL 8230 BEVERLY BOULEVARD — LOS ANGELES CA 90048 (213) 655-1582
AMERICAN TECHNION SOCIETY 8170 BEVERLY BLVD — LOS ANGELES CA 90048 (213) 651-3321
BEN-GURION UNIVERSITY OF THE NEGEV 1801 AVENUE OF THE STARS, SUITE 701 — LOS ANGELES CA 90067 (213) 277-9787
BONDS FOR ISRAEL-DEVELOPMENT CORPORATION FOR ISRAEL 6380 WILSHIRE BOULEVARD — LOS ANGELES CA 90048 (213) 653-8400
FRIENDS OF PORYIAH HOSPITAL — LOS ANGELES CA (213) 858-8354
FUND FOR HIGHER EDUCATION IN ISRAEL 6404 WILSHIRE BOULEVARD — LOS ANGELES CA 90048 (213) 655-7850
ISRAEL HISTADRUT CAMPAIGN 8455 BEVERLY BOULEVARD, SUITE 308 — LOS ANGELES CA 90048 (213) 651-4892
JEWISH NATIONAL FUND 6420 WILSHIRE BLVD. #430 — LOS ANGELES CA 90048 (213) 655-8100
KEREN-OR CENTER FOR MULTI-HANDICAPPED BLIND CHILDREN 1317 NORTH CRESCENT HEIGHTS BOULEVARD — LOS ANGELES CA 90046 (213) 654-3109
WEST COAST FRIENDS OF BAR ILAN UNIVERSITY 6505 WILSHIRE BOULEVARD, SUITE 404 — LOS ANGELES CA 90048 (213) 658-6688
WEST COAST FRIENDS OF PONEVEZ YESHIVA & ISRAEL BOYS TOWN — LOS ANGELES CA (213) 655-2073
NEW ISRAEL FUND, THE 22 MILLER AVENUE — MILL VALLEY CA 94941 (415) 388-8820
JEWISH NATIONAL FUND 262 GRAND AVENUE #101 — OAKLAND CA 94610 (415) 465-0740
JEWISH NATIONAL FUND 6363 EL CAJON BLVD. #200 — SAN DIEGO CA 92115 (619) 287-3447
AMERICAN COMMITTEE FOR SHAARE ZEDEK IN JERUSALEM-NW REGION 1654 33RD AVENUE — SAN FRANCISCO CA 94122 (415) 661-2160
AMERICAN FRIENDS OF THE HEBREW UNIVERSITY OF JERUSALEM 717 MARKET STREET, SUITE 323 — SAN FRANCISCO CA 94103 (415) 391-9056
AMERICAN TECHNION SOCIETY 870 MARKET STREET, SUITE 542 — SAN FRANCISCO CA 94102 (415) 392-1032
JEWISH NATIONAL FUND 2266 GEARY BLVD — SAN FRANCISCO CA 94115 (415) 567-3440
LOS ANGELES COMMITTEE FOR THE WEIZMANN INSTITUTE OF SCIENCE 3235 BARRY DRIVE — STUDIO CITY CA 91604 (213) 654-0540
B.M.H. SYNAGOGUE 560 S. MONACO PARKWAY — DENVER CO 89224 (303) 333-0213
JEWISH NATIONAL FUND 65 COOPER PLACE — NEW HAVEN CT 06525 (203) 397-3767
JEWISH NATIONAL FUND 1430 'K' STREET, N.W. #701 — WASHINGTON DC 20005 (202) 783-8700
JEWISH NATIONAL FUND 800 W. OAKLAND PARK BLVD. #201 — FORT LAUDERDALE FL 33311 (305) 561-4812
AMERICAN COMMITTEE FOR SHAARE ZEDEK IN JERUSALEM-S.E. REGION 605 LINCOLN ROAD, SUITE 211 — MIAMI BEACH FL 33139 (305) 531-8329
AMERICAN FRIENDS OF HAIFA UNIVERSITY, THE 420 LINCOLN ROAD — MIAMI BEACH FL 33139 (305) 531-1174
JEWISH NATIONAL FUND 420 LINCOLN ROAD, #335 — MIAMI BEACH FL 33139 (305) 538-6464
JEWISH NATIONAL FUND 730 S. STERLING AVENUE #213 — TAMPA FL 33609 (813) 876-9327
JEWISH NATIONAL FUND 3 PIEDMONT CENTER, #416 — ATLANTA GA 30305 (404) 237-1132
AMERICAN COMMITTEE FOR SHAARE ZEDEK IN JERUSALEM-MIDWEST RGN 79 MONROE STREET — CHICAGO IL 60603 (312) 236-5778
AMERICAN FRIENDS OF HEBREW UNIVERSITY 4001 W. DEVON AVENUE, SUITE 208 — CHICAGO IL 60646 (312) 236-6395
AMERICAN SOCIETY FOR TECHNION-ISRAEL 59 E. VAN BUREN — CHICAGO IL 60605
EZRA CHAPTER OF MAGEN DAVID ADOM 1212 N. LAKE SHORE DRIVE, SUITE 23 — CHICAGO IL 60610 (312) 649-1583
HISTADRUT CAMPAIGN OF CHICAGO 320 SOUTH STATE — CHICAGO IL 60604 (312) 427-4086
JEWISH NATIONAL FUND 230 N. MICHIGAN AVENUE #420 — CHICAGO IL 60601 (312) 236-9100
MAGEN DAVID ADOM 6952 N. CALIFORNIA AVENUE — CHICAGO IL 60645 (312) 465-0664
MIZRACHI-HAPOEL HAMIZRACHI 6500 N. CALIFORNIA AVENUE — CHICAGO IL 60645 (312) 338-2871
JEWISH NATIONAL FUND 1265 W. 86TH STREET — INDIANAPOLIS IN 46260 (317) 253-5577
GUARDIANS OF THE WESTERN WALL, THE 18 AMOS STREET — JERUSALEM IS
JEWISH NATIONAL FUND 2210 W. 75TH STREET #18 — SHAWNEE MISSION KS 66208 (913) 432-9330
AMERICAN RED MAGEN DAVID FOR ISRAEL-DAVID BEN-GURION CHAPTER 1701 DRYADES STREET — NEW ORLEANS LA 70113 (504) 525-2971
JEWISH NATIONAL FUND 6227 ST. CHARLES AVENUE — NEW ORLEANS LA 70118 (504) 861-3693
AMERICAN PHYSICIANS FELLOWSHIP, INC. 2001 BEACON STREET — BROOKLINE MA 02146 (617) 232-5382
JEWISH NATIONAL FUND 1330 BEACON STREET, #202 — BROOKLINE MA 02146 (617) 731-6850
JEWISH NATIONAL FUND 14 OLD COURT ROAD — BALTIMORE MD 21208 (301) 486-3317
AMERICAN COMMITTEE FOR SHAARE ZEDEK IN JERUSALEM-DETROIT 13128 WALES — HUNTINGTON WOODS MI 48070 (313) 544-8412
JEWISH NATIONAL FUND 18877 W. TEN MILE ROAD — SOUTHFIELD MI 48075 (313) 557-6644
AMERICAN FRIENDS OF HAIFA UNIVERSITY, THE 8701 E. EIGHT MILE ROAD — WARREN MI 48089 (313) 758-1048
JEWISH NATIONAL FUND 425 HENNEPIN AVENUE, #210 — MINNEAPOLIS MN 55401 (612) 339-0862
ISRAEL HISTADRUT CAMPAIGN 8029 CLAYTON ROAD — ST. LOUIS MO 63117 (314) 727-9019
JEWISH NATIONAL FUND 8420 DELMAR ROAD, SUITE 5031-504 — ST. LOUIS MO 63124 (314) 991-0451
AMERICAN FRIENDS OF HAIFA UNIVERSITY, THE P.O. BOX 18137 — RALEIGH NC 27619 (919) 876-7270
JEWISH NATIONAL FUND 545 CEDAR LANE — TEANECK NJ 07666 (201) 836-6888
AMERICAN FRIENDS OF YESHIVA ZVI HATZADIK 3100 BRIGHTON 3RD STREET — BROOKLYN NY 11235
COLEL HIBATH JERUSALEM 1282 49TH STREET — BROOKLYN NY 11219 (718) 633-7112
DISKIN ORPHAN HOME OF ISRAEL 4305 18TH AVENUE — BROOKLYN NY 11204 (718) 851-2598
DONATE USED CLOTHING TO ISRAEL — BROOKLYN NY (718) 435-1041
FEDERATED COUNCIL OF ISRAEL INSTITUTIONS - FCLL 1475 47TH STREET — BROOKLYN NY 11219 (718) 462-0603
FRIENDS OF LUBAVITCH FOR SEFAD 625 MONTGOMERY STREET — BROOKLYN NY 11225 (718) 778-3962
GIDULEI YAAKOV KOLLEL IN JERUSALEM 1530 53RD STREET — BROOKLYN NY 11219 (718) 851-7676
JERUSALEM INSTITUTE OF TALMUDIC RESEARCH 1481 44TH STREET — BROOKLYN NY 11219 (718) 435-8877
JERUSALEM RABBINICAL ACADEMY, THE 1260 59TH STREET — BROOKLYN NY 11219 (718) 853-3273
JEWISH NATIONAL FUND 1369 CONEY ISLAND AVENUE — BROOKLYN NY 11230 (718) 338-4555
KOLLEL GIDULEI YAAKOV IN JERUSALEM 1530 53RD STREET — BROOKLYN NY 11219 (718) 851-7676
TCHECHENOV INSTITUTIONS IN ISRAEL 5916 18TH AVENUE — BROOKLYN NY 11204 (718) 232-0070
TSHEBINER YESHIVA KOHAV MIYAACOV OF JERUSALEM 1434 57TH STREET — BROOKLYN NY 11219 (718) 851-5474
YAD L'ACHIM-BORO PARK-FLATBUSH 4702 16TH AVENUE — BROOKLYN NY 11204 (718) 633-0776
AMERICAN RED MAGEN DAVID FOR ISRAEL 888 SEVENTH AVENUE — HEMPSTEAD NY 11552 (516) 757-1627
DEBORAH HOSPITAL FOUNDATION 135-25 NORTHERN BOULEVARD — LINDEN HILL NY 11354 (718) 762-1400
AM. FRIENDS/JERUSALEM MENTAL HEALTH CTR.-EZRATH NASHIM, INC. 10 E. 40TH STREET — NEW YORK NY 10016 (212) 725-8175

GESHER

We're helping to put Israel back together again.

Because somebody must do something about the splintering of Israeli society.

Ami-ad Family Seminars

Beit Gesher

B'nai Mitzvah Curricular Series

David Schoen Institute for Creative Jewish Education

Encounter Seminars for High School Youth

Encounter Seminars for Leading Israeli Artists

Gesher Coffee Houses

Gesher Computer Games

Jerusalem Productions

Jewish Identity Seminars for Business Executives

Livnot U'Lehibanot Work-Study Program

Midrashat Gesher

Seminars for Israel Defense Force Personnel

Shabbatonim

Weekly Study Circles

The Gesher Foundation
421 Seventh Avenue Suite 905 New York, N.Y. 10001 (212) 564-0338

AM. FRIENDS/YAD BENJAMIN-ED. CTR. OF POALE AGUDATH ISRAEL
147 W. 42ND STREET .... NEW YORK **NY** 10036 (212) 279-0816
AMERICAN ASSOCIATES BEN-GURION UNIVERSITY OF THE NEGEV
342 MADISON AVENUE, SUITE 1923 .... NEW YORK **NY** 10173 (212) 687-7721
AMERICAN ASSOCIATION FOR BIKUR CHOLIM HOSPITAL
119 FIFTH AVENUE .... NEW YORK **NY** 10021 (212) 260-4260
AMERICAN COLLEGE IN JERUSALEM 342 MADISON AVENUE .... NEW YORK **NY** 10017
AMERICAN COMM. FOR SHAARE ZEDEK HOSPITAL IN JERUSALEM, INC.
49 WEST 45TH STREET .... NEW YORK **NY** 10036 (212) 354-8801
AMERICAN COMMITTEE FOR THE ISRAEL FASHION COLLEGE INC.
855 AVENUE OF THE AMERICAS .... NEW YORK **NY** 10001 (212) 947-1597
AMERICAN COMMITTEE FOR THE NATIONAL SICK FUND OF ISRAEL
60 E. 42ND STREET, SUITE 1144 .... NEW YORK **NY** 10165 (212) 599-3670
AMERICAN COMMITTEE FOR THE WEIZMANN INST. OF SCIENCE, INC.
515 PARK AVENUE .... NEW YORK **NY** 10022 (212) 752-1300
AMERICAN FRIENDS OF BETH HATEFUTSOTH 515 PARK AVENUE .... NEW YORK **NY** 10022 (212) 752-0246
AMERICAN FRIENDS OF BOY'S TOWN JERUSALEM 22 W. 38TH STREET .. NEW YORK **NY** 10018 (212) 921-1380
AMERICAN FRIENDS OF HAIFA UNIVERSITY 206 FIFTH AVENUE .... NEW YORK **NY** 10010 (212) 696-4022
AMERICAN FRIENDS OF HEBRON YESHIVA IN JERUSALEM
1220 BROADWAY .... NEW YORK **NY** 10001 (212) 695-2230
AMERICAN FRIENDS OF JERUSALEM MENTAL HEALTH CENTER-EZ.NASHIM
10 EAST 40TH STREET .... NEW YORK **NY** 10016 (212) 725-8175
AMERICAN FRIENDS OF LANIADO KIRYAT SANZ HOSPITAL
580 FIFTH AVENUE .... NEW YORK **NY** 10017 (212) 944-2690
AMERICAN FRIENDS OF MICHLALAH 10 COLUMBUS CIRCLE .... NEW YORK **NY** 10019 (212) 586-1232
AMERICAN FRIENDS OF MIGDAL OHR (ISRAEL) 6 MAIDEN LANE .... NEW YORK **NY** 10038 (212) 227-5961
AMERICAN FRIENDS OF NEVEH YEHOSHUA 3 WEST 16TH STREET .... NEW YORK **NY** 10011 (212) 929-1836
AMERICAN FRIENDS OF OHR SOMAYACH 39 BROADWAY .... NEW YORK **NY** 10006 (212) 344-2000
AMERICAN FRIENDS OF YESHIVAT KEREM B'YAVNEH
6 EAST 45TH STREET .... NEW YORK **NY** 10017 (212) 687-0805
AMERICAN FRIENDS OF YESHIVAT NER MOSHE OF JERUSALEM
501 FIFTH AVENUE, SUITE 2203 .... NEW YORK **NY** 10017 (212) 687-0500
AMERICAN FRIENDS OF YESHIVAT SHA'ALVIM
156 FIFTH AVENUE, SUITE 811 .... NEW YORK **NY** 10010 (212) 924-9475
AMERICAN FRIENDS OF YESHIVOT BNEI AKIVA IN ISRAEL
50 WEST 34TH STREET .... NEW YORK **NY** 10001 (212) 947-6787
AMERICAN FRIENDS OF THE ALLIANCE ISRAELITE UNIVERSELLE
61 BROADWAY, ROOM 811 .... NEW YORK **NY** 10006 (212) 425-5171
AMERICAN FRIENDS OF THE HAIFA MARITIME MUSEUM, INC.
18 E. 74TH STREET, P.O. BOX 616 .... NEW YORK **NY** 10021 (212) 776-4509
AMERICAN FRIENDS OF THE HEBREW UNIVERSITY
11 EAST 69TH STREET .... NEW YORK **NY** 10021 (212) 472-9800
AMERICAN FRIENDS OF THE HEBREW UNIVERSITY
1140 AVENUE OF THE AMERICAS .... NEW YORK **NY** 10036 (212) 840-5820
AMERICAN FRIENDS OF THE ISRAEL MUSEUM
10 E. 40TH STREET, SUITE 1208 .... NEW YORK **NY** 10016 (212) 683-5190
AMERICAN FRIENDS OF THE ISRAEL PHILHARMONIC ORCHESTRA INC.
1715 BROADWAY .... NEW YORK **NY** 10019 (212) 581-4374
AMERICAN FRIENDS OF THE JERUSALEM ACADEMY & CONFERENCE CTR.
75 EAST 55TH STREET .... NEW YORK **NY** 10022 (212) 688-7979
AMERICAN FRIENDS OF THE JERUSALEM MENTAL HEALTH CENTER-
EZRATH NASHIM, 10 EAST 40TH STREET .... NEW YORK **NY** 10016 (212) 725-8175
AMERICAN FRIENDS OF THE KIBBUTZIM IN ISRAEL INC.
150 FIFTH AVENUE .... NEW YORK **NY** 10003 (212) 255-8760
AMERICAN FRIENDS OF THE MIRRER YESHIVA IN JERUSALEM
1133 BROADWAY .... NEW YORK **NY** 10010 (212) 243-3987
AMERICAN FRIENDS OF THE TEL AVIV UNIVERSITY INC.
342 MADISON AVENUE .... NEW YORK **NY** 10017 (212) 687-5651
AMERICAN HECHAL SHLOMO 358 FIFTH AVENUE .... NEW YORK **NY** 10016 (212) 736-4698
AMERICAN ISRAELI LIGHTHOUSE 30 E. 60TH STREET .... NEW YORK **NY** 10022 (212) 838-5322
AMERICAN MIZRACHI WOMEN 817 BROADWAY .... NEW YORK **NY** 10003 (212) 477-4720
AMERICAN RED MAGEN DAVID FOR ISRAEL 888 SEVENTH AVENUE .... NEW YORK **NY** 10019 (212) 757-1627
AMERICAN SOCIETY FOR CRIPPLED CHILDREN IN ISRAEL
19 WEST 44TH STREET .... NEW YORK **NY** 10036 (212) 869-0369
AMERICAN SOCIETY FOR TECHNION-ISRAEL INSTITUTE OF TECHNOLOGY
271 MADISON AVENUE .... NEW YORK **NY** 10016 (212) 889-2050
BIKUR CHOLIM HOSPITAL, JERUSALEM 119 FIFTH AVENUE .... NEW YORK **NY** 10011 (212) 260-4260
COLEL POLEN-RABBI MEIR BAAL HANESS JERUSALEM
373 FIFTH AVENUE .... NEW YORK **NY** 10016 (212) 689-4500
DISKIN ORPHAN HOME OF ISRAEL 156 FIFTH AVENUE .... NEW YORK **NY** 10010 (212) 924-0494
EMET-RABBI HERZOG WORLD ACADEMY 122 WEST 76TH STREET .... NEW YORK **NY** 10023 (212) 787-1051
ETZ CHAIM TORAH CENTER OF JERUSALEM 1141 BROADWAY .... NEW YORK **NY** 10001 (212) 683-3221
EZRAS TORAH FUND-TORAH RELIEF SOCIETY, INC.
235 EAST BROADWAY .... NEW YORK **NY** 10002 (212) 227-8960
EZRATH NASHIM JERUSALEM MENTAL HEALTH CENTER
10 EAST 40TH STREET .... NEW YORK **NY** 10016 (212) 725-8175
FEDERATED COUNCIL OF ISRAEL INSTITUTIONS, INC.
15 BEEKMAN STREET .... NEW YORK **NY** 10038 (212) 962-0603
FRIENDS OF DAVID YELLIN TEACHERS COLLEGE, INC.
1501 BROADWAY, SUITE 1715 .... NEW YORK **NY** 10036 (212) 391-8686
FRIENDS OF JERUSALEM 545 FIFTH AVENUE .... NEW YORK **NY** 10017 (212) 687-4187
FRIENDS OF YESHIVA SHALAVIM, INC. 156 FIFTH AVENUE .... NEW YORK **NY** 10010 (212) 924-9475
FUND FOR HIGHER EDUCATION IN ISRAEL, INC. 1500 BROADWAY .... NEW YORK **NY** 10036 (212) 354-4660
GENERAL ISRAEL ORPHANS HOME FOR GIRLS IN JERUSALEM
132 NASSAU STREET .... NEW YORK **NY** 10038 (212) 267-7222
GESHER FOUNDATION, THE 421 SEVENTH AVENUE .... NEW YORK **NY** 10001 (212) 564-0338
GREAT CHARITY CHAYE OLAM INSTITUTION OF JERUSALEM
5 BEEKMAN STREET .... NEW YORK **NY** 10038 (212) 962-0224
HADASSAH MEDICAL RELIEF ASSOCIATION INC.
50 WEST 58TH STREET .... NEW YORK **NY** 10019 (212) 355-7900
HADASSAH, THE WOMEN'S ZIONIST ORG. OF AMERICA
50 WEST 58TH STREET .... NEW YORK **NY** 10019 (212) 355-7900

HASHOMER HATZAIR, INC. 150 FIFTH AVENUE .... NEW YORK **NY** 10011 (212) 255-8760
HEBREW UNIVERSITY-TECHNION JOINT MAINTENANCE APPEAL
11 E. 69TH STREET .... NEW YORK **NY** 10021 (212) 472-9800
HEBRON YESHIVA IN JERUSALEM 1220 BROADWAY .... NEW YORK **NY** 10001 (212) 695-2230
HEICHAL HATALMUD OF TEL AVIV 217 EAST BROADWAY .... NEW YORK **NY** 10002 (212) 473-1912
HISTADRUT ISRAEL CAMPAIGN 33 EAST 67TH STREET .... NEW YORK **NY** 10021 (212) 628-1000
ISRAEL CANCER RESEARCH FUND 850 THIRD AVENUE .... NEW YORK **NY** 10022 (212) 752-3623
ISRAEL EDUCATION & BENEVOLENT RELIEF SOCIETY
203 EAST BROADWAY .... NEW YORK **NY** 10002 (212) 233-9275
ISRAEL EDUCATION FUND 51 WEST 51ST STREET .... NEW YORK **NY** 10019 (212) 757-1500
ISRAEL EDUCATIONAL & BENEVOLENT RELIEF SOCIETY
203 EAST BROADWAY .... NEW YORK **NY** 10002 (212) 475-7328
ISRAEL EDUCATIONAL & BENEVOLENT RELIEF SOCIETY
126 EAST BROADWAY .... NEW YORK **NY** 10002 (212) 233-9275
ISRAEL FOUNDATION FUND (KEREN HAYESOD), INC.
515 PARK AVENUE .... NEW YORK **NY** 10022 (212) 688-0800
ISRAEL HISTADRUT CAMPAIGN, INC. 33 EAST 67TH STREET .... NEW YORK **NY** 10021 (212) 628-1000
ISRAEL INSTITUTIONS FOR THE BLIND-KEREN-OR, INC.
1133 BROADWAY .... NEW YORK **NY** 10010 (212) 255-1180
JABOTINSKY FOUNDATION, INC., THE 261 FIFTH AVENUE .... NEW YORK **NY** 10016 (212) 679-6868
JERUSALEM ACADEMY FOR GIRLS 225 BROADWAY .... NEW YORK **NY** 10007 (212) 233-1500
JERUSALEM FOUNDATION, THE 500 FIFTH AVENUE .... NEW YORK **NY** 10110 (212) 840-1101
JERUSALEM INSTITUTION FOR THE BLIND-KEREN-OR, INC.
1133 BROADWAY .... NEW YORK **NY** 10110 (212) 255-1180
JEWISH NATIONAL FUND 42 E. 69TH STREET .... NEW YORK **NY** 10021 (212) 879-9300
KEREN KAYEMETH LE-ISRAEL, INC. (JEWISH NATIONAL FUND)
42 E. 69TH STREET .... NEW YORK **NY** 10021 (212) 879-9300
KEREN OR, INC. 1133 BROADWAY .... NEW YORK **NY** 10010 (212) 255-1180
KEREN YALDENU 51 EAST 42ND STREET .... NEW YORK **NY** 10017 (212) 490-2340
KEREN-OR JERUSALEM INSTITUTE FOR THE BLIND, INC.
1133 BROADWAY .... NEW YORK **NY** 10010 (212) 255-1180
KOLEL AMERICA TIFERETH JERUSALEM 132 NASSAU STREET .... NEW YORK **NY** 10038 (212) 349-3078
KOLEL SHOMRE HACHOMOS 5 BEEKMAN STREET .... NEW YORK **NY** 10038 (212) 732-0300
KUPATH RABBI MEIR HANESS JERUSALEM 373 FIFTH AVENUE .... NEW YORK **NY** 10016 (212) 691-1330
KUPATH RAMBAN COLEL POLEN JERUSALEM 373 FIFTH AVENUE .... NEW YORK **NY** 10016 (212) 691-1330
MIGDAL OHR 6 MAIDEN LANE .... NEW YORK **NY** 10038 (212) 227-5961
MIZRACHI PALESTINE FUND 200 PARK AVENUE S .... NEW YORK **NY** 10003 (212) 673-8100
NAT'L COMMITTEE FOR LABOR ISRAEL (ISRAEL HISTADRUT CAMPAIGN)
33 EAST 67TH STREET .... NEW YORK **NY** 10021 (212) 628-1000
NAT'L JEWISH HOSPITAL AT DENVER 49 WEST 45TH STREET .... NEW YORK **NY** 10036 (212) 382-0711
POALE AGUDATH ISRAEL OF AMERICA 156 FIFTH AVENUE .... NEW YORK **NY** 10010 (212) 924-9475
POALE AGUDATH ISRAEL OF AMERICA - WOMEN'S DIVISION
156 FIFTH AVENUE, SUITE 881 .... NEW YORK **NY** 10010 (212) 924-9475
RELIGIOUS ZIONISTS OF AMERICA 25 W. 26TH STREET .... NEW YORK **NY** 10010
TEL-HAI FUND, INC. 47 W. 34TH STREET .... NEW YORK **NY** 10001 (212) 594-2879
TORAH SCHOOLS FOR ISRAEL 167 MADISON AVENUE .... NEW YORK **NY** 10016 (212) 889-0606
UNITED CHARITY INSTITUTIONS OF JERUSALEM 1141 BROADWAY .... NEW YORK **NY** 10001 (212) 683-3221
UNITED ISRAEL APPEAL, INC. 515 PARK AVENUE .... NEW YORK **NY** 10022 (212) 688-0800
UNITED JEWISH APPEAL 1290 AVENUE OF THE AMERICAS .... NEW YORK **NY** 10104 (212) 757-1500
UNITED TIBERIAS INSTITUTIONS RELIEF SOCIETY 195 HENRY STREET .. NEW YORK **NY** 10002 (212) 349-8755
WOMEN'S LEAGUE FOR ISRAEL, INC. 1860 BROADWAY .... NEW YORK **NY** 10023 (212) 245-8742
YESHIVA BETH ABRAHAM OF JERUSALEM 73 WEST 47TH STREET .... NEW YORK **NY** 10036 (212) 819-0355
YESHIVA HEICHAL HATALMUD OF TEL AVIV 247 EAST BROADWAY .... NEW YORK **NY** 10002 (212) 608-3301
YESHIVA PETACH TIKVA ISRAEL 249 EAST BROADWAY .... NEW YORK **NY** 10002 (212) 349-1934
YESHIVA PONEVEZ 1133 BROADWAY .... NEW YORK **NY** 10010 (212) 675-9260
YESHIVA SFATH EMETH OF JERUSALEM 145 EAST BROADWAY .... NEW YORK **NY** 10002 (212) 964-2830
YESHIVAT HAR ETZION 310 MADISON AVENUE .... NEW YORK **NY** 10017 (212) 883-0883
YESHIVATH CHATAM SOFER TORAH CENTER 119 NASSAU STREET .... NEW YORK **NY** 10038 (212) 732-0301
YESHIVATH HANEGEV 860 WEST 181ST STREET .... NEW YORK **NY** 10033 (212) 568-1647
YESHIVATH SFATH EMETH OF JERUSALEM 150 FIFTH AVENUE .... NEW YORK **NY** 10011 (212) 929-3899
FEDERATED COUNCIL OF ISRAEL INSTITUTIONS, INC.
15 BEEKMAN STREET .... NEW YORK **NY** 10038 (212) 227-3152
P.E.F.ISRAEL ENDOWMENT FUNDS, INC. 342 MADISON AVENUE .... NEW YORK **NY** 10173 (212) 599-1260
JEWISH NATIONAL FUND 1400 WANTAGH AVENUE, SUITE L2 .... WANTAGH **NY** 11793 (516) 826-8700
JEWISH NATIONAL FUND 1720 SECTION ROAD .... CINCINNATI **OH** 45237 (513) 631-1796
AM. COMMITTEE FOR SHAARE ZEDEK IN JERUSALEM-MID-CENTRAL REG.
3507 WARRENSVILLE CENTER ROAD .... CLEVELAND **OH** 44122 (216) 283-9222
AMERICAN RED MAGEN DAVID ADOM FOR ISRAEL (ISRAEL RED CROSS)
3645 WARRENSVILLE CENTER ROAD, NO. 330 .... CLEVELAND **OH** 44122 (216) 752-6884
AMERICAN TECHNION SOCIETY - WOMEN'S DIVISION
2992 LINCOLN BLVD .... CLEVELAND **OH** 44118 (216) 321-4320
ANSHE GRODNO LADIES AUXILIARY 3351 DESOTA AVENUE .... CLEVELAND **OH** 44118 (216) 932-4138
CLEVELAND CHAPTER OF BEN-GURION UNIVERSITY .... CLEVELAND **OH** (216) 283-2400
CLEVELAND COMMITTEE FOR WEIZMANN INSTITUTE
23 PEPPER CREEK DRIVE .... CLEVELAND **OH** 44124 (216) 464-1103
CLEVELAND FRIENDS OF THE JERUSALEM BOTANICAL GARDENS
28950 GATES MILLS BLVD .... CLEVELAND **OH** 44124 (216) 464-3084
ISRAEL HISTADRUT CAMPAIGN 13969 CEDAR ROAD .... CLEVELAND **OH** 44118 (216) 321-4900
JEWISH NATIONAL FUND 14055 CEDAR ROAD, #304 .... CLEVELAND **OH** 44118 (216) 371-8733
JEWISH NATIONAL FUND 2700 E. MAIN STREET .... COLUMBUS **OH** 43209 (614) 231-1397
CANADIAN FRIENDS OF BAR-ILAN UNIVERSITY
333 WILSON AVENUE .... DOWNSVIEW **ON** M3H 1T2 (416) 635-1966
CANADIAN SOCIETY FOR THE WEIZMANN INSTITUTE OF SCIENCE
345 WILSON AVENUE, SUITE 403 .... DOWNSVIEW **ON** M3H 5W1
CANADIAN FRIENDS OF BAR-ILAN UNIVERSITY
825 EGLINTON AVENUE WEST, SUITE 314 .... TORONTO **ON** M5N 1E7 (416) 783-8546
CANADIAN FRIENDS OF OHR SOMAYACH
534 LAWRENCE AVENUE WEST, SUITE 205 .... TORONTO **ON** M6A 1A2 (416) 787-1681
CANADIAN FRIENDS OF THE HEBREW UNIVERSITY
2081 YORKDALE ROAD .... TORONTO **ON** M6A 3A1 (416) 789-2633
CANADIAN TECHNION SOCIETY 2828 BATHURST STREET, SUITE 502 .... TORONTO **ON** M6B 3A7
JEWISH NATIONAL FUND 5765 S.W. GLENBROOK ROAD .... BEAVERTON **OR** 97005 (503) 644-0944

AM. COMMITTEE FOR SHAARE ZEDEK IN JERUSALEM-MID-ATLANTIC RGN
1518 WALNUT STREET, SUITE 900 .... PHILADELPHIA **PA** 19102   (215) 735-3306
AMERICAN FRIENDS OF HAIFA UNIVERSITY, THE
226 W. RITTENHOUSE SQUARE, SUITE 2301 .... PHILADELPHIA **PA** 19103   (215) 735-8074
AMERICAN FRIENDS OF THE HEBREW UNIVERSITY
2400 LEWIS TOWER BLDG .... PHILADELPHIA **PA** 19102
JEWISH NATIONAL FUND 1405 LOCUST STREET, #1621 .... PHILADELPHIA **PA** 19102   (215) 545-6660
JEWISH NATIONAL FUND 6315 FORBES AVENUE .... PITTSBURGH **PA** 15217   (412) 521-6866
CANADIAN ASSOCIATION FOR LABOR ISRAEL 4770 KENT AVENUE ...... MONTREAL **QU** H3W 1H2 (514) 735-1593
CANADIAN FRIENDS OF THE ALLIANCE ISRAELITE UNIVERSELLE
5711 EDGEMORE AVENUE .... MONTREAL **QU** H4W 1V8 (514) 487-1243
CANADIAN SOCIETY FOR THE WEIZMANN INSTITUTE OF SCIENCE
5180 QUEEN MARY ROAD, SUITE 360 .... MONTREAL **QU**
CANPAL-CANADIAN ISRAEL CORP. LTD.
1550 MAISONNEUVE BOULEVARD WEST, SUITE 1030 .... MONTREAL **QU** H3G 1N2 (514) 935-6577
UNITED ISRAEL APPEAL OF CANADA, INC. 1310 GREENE AVENUE ..... WESTMOUNT **QU** H3Z 2B2 (514) 932-1431
JEWISH NATIONAL FUND 6584 POPLAR AVENUE #310 .... MEMPHIS **TN** 38138   (901) 682-2414
JEWISH NATIONAL FUND 11333 N. CENTRAL EXPRESSWAY .... DALLAS **TX** 75243   (214) 363-1498
JEWISH NATIONAL FUND 6006 BELLAIRE BLVD. #106 .... HOUSTON **TX** 77081   (713) 432-7070
JEWISH NATIONAL FUND 629 SECURITIES BUILDING .... SEATTLE **WA** 98101   (206) 624-8625
JEWISH NATIONAL FUND 1119 WEST KILBOURN .... MILWAUKEE **WI** 53233   (414) 276-0630

CHILDREN'S HOMES & SERVICES

CALIFORNIA HAMBURGER HOME 7357 HOLLYWOOD BOULEVARD .... LOS ANGELES **CA** 90046   (213) 876-0550
VISTA DEL MAR CHILD-CARE SERVICES 3200 MOTOR AVENUE .... LOS ANGELES **CA** 90034   (213) 836-1223
EMANU-EL RESIDENCE 300 PAGE STREET .... SAN FRANCISCO **CA** 94102
HOMEWOOD TERRACE 160 SCOTT STREET .... SAN FRANCISCO **CA** 94102   (415) 562-2788
JEWISH HOME FOR CHILDREN 152 TEMPLE STREET .... NEW HAVEN **CT** 06500   (203) 776-5130
JEWISH FOSTER HOME 1341 G STREET, N.W. .... WASHINGTON **DC** 20026
JEWISH FAMILY & CHILDREN'S SERVICE 1790 S.W. 27TH AVENUE .... MIAMI **FL** 33145   (305) 445-0555
JEWISH CHILDREN'S BUREAU 1 SOUTH FRANKLIN STREET .... CHICAGO **IL** 60606   (312) 346-6700
NICHOLAS J. PRITZKER CENTER-JEWISH CHILDREN'S BUREAU
800 E. 55TH STREET .... CHICAGO **IL** 60615   (312) 643-7300
VIRGINIA FRANK CHILD DEVELOPMENT CENTER 3033 WEST TOUHY ...... CHICAGO **IL** 60645   (312) 761-4550
JEWISH HOME FOR CONVALESCENT CHILDREN
1135 SOUTH 1ST STREET .... LOUISVILLE **KY** 40203
JEWISH CHILDREN'S HOME SERVICE
5342 ST. CHARLES AVENUE, PO BOX 15225 .... NEW ORLEANS **LA** 70115   (504) 897-0143
JEWISH CHILDREN'S REGIONAL SERVICE OF JEWISH CHILDREN'S HOME
5342 CHARLES AVENUE, P.O. BOX 15225 .... NEW ORLEANS **LA** 70175   (504) 889-1595
JEWISH FAMILY & CHILDREN'S SERVICE 107 CAMP STREET .... NEW ORLEANS **LA** 70130   (504) 524-8476
SHREVEPORT JEWISH FAMILY & CHILDREN'S SERVICES
2030 LINE AVENUE .... SHREVEPORT **LA** 71104   (318) 221-4129

JEWISH CHILD AND FAMILY SERVICE
228 NOTRE DAME STREET/SUITE 1001 .... WINNIPEG **MB** R3B 1N7 (204) 943-6425
JEWISH SOCIAL SERVICE AGENCY 6123 MONTROSE ROAD .... ROCKVILLE **MD** 20852   (301) 881-3700
JEWISH CHILDREN'S HOME 9385 OLIVE STREET ROAD .... ST. LOUIS **MO** 63100   (314) 993-0100
HEBREW BENEVOLENT & ORPHAN ASYLUM 161 MILLBURN AVENUE ...... MILLBURN **NJ** 07041   (201) 467-3300
BROOKLYN HEBREW ORPHAN ASYLUM
(CALL JEWISH CHILD CARE ASSOCIATION OF N.Y.) .... **NY**   (718) 490-9160
HEBREW CHILDREN'S HOME 1682 MONROE AVENUE .... BRONX **NY** 10457
CONEY ISLAND COMMUNITY SUPPORT SYSTEMS PROJECT
3312-30 SURF AVENUE .... BROOKLYN **NY**   (718) 372-3300
FAMILY COURT LIAISON OFFICE - BROOKLYN
283 ADAMS STREET, ROOM 304 .... BROOKLYN **NY** 11201   (718) 875-1841
IHB DAY TREATMENT CENTER AND RESIDENCE 1358 56TH STREET .... BROOKLYN **NY** 11219   (718) 851-8000
INFANTS HOME OF BROOKLYN JEWISH BOARD OF FAMILY SERVICES
1358 56TH STREET .... BROOKLYN **NY** 11219   (718) 851-8000
IRANIAN JEWISH PROGRAM 1113 AVENUE J .... BROOKLYN **NY** 11230   (718) 258-7700
JEWISH BOARD OF GUARDIANS 283 ADAMS STREET .... BROOKLYN **NY** 11201   (718) 875-5951
JEWISH BOARD OF GUARDIANS 1484 FLATBUSH AVENUE .... BROOKLYN **NY** 11210   (718) 434-4158
JEWISH BOARD OF GUARDIANS MENTAL HEALTH CENTER
1301 SURF AVENUE .... BROOKLYN **NY** 11224   (718) 226-5300
JEWISH BOARD OF GUARDIANS MIDWOOD ADOLESCENT PROJECT
1484 FLATBUSH AVENUE .... BROOKLYN **NY** 11210   (718) 434-6200
JEWISH CH. CARE ASSOC. OF N.Y.-KINGSBROOK RESIDENCE
150 E. 49TH STREET .... BROOKLYN **NY** 11203   (718) 756-1900
JEWISH CHILD CARE ASSOCIATION OF NEW YORK 663 RUGBY ROAD ... BROOKLYN **NY** 11230   (718) 859-7809
JEWISH CHILD CARE ASSOCIATION OF NEW YORK 1810 AVENUE H ...... BROOKLYN **NY** 11230   (718) 859-0503
MADELEINE BORG COUNSEL. SVCS. - THOMAS ASKIN YOUTH PROJECT
307 BRIGHTON BEACH AVENUE .... BROOKLYN **NY** 11235   (718) 934-8025
MADELEINE BORG COUNSEL. SVCS.-CAREY GARDENS EARLY CHILDHOOD
2964 WEST 23RD STREET .... BROOKLYN **NY**   (718) 372-4044
MADELEINE BORG COUNSELING SERVICES - BORO PARK OFFICE
1276 47TH STREET .... BROOKLYN **NY** 11219   (718) 435-5700
MADELEINE BORG COUNSELING SERVICES - CANARSIE OFFICE
164 CONKLIN AVENUE .... BROOKLYN **NY**   (718) 257-0002
MADELEINE BORG COUNSELING SERVICES - CONEY ISLAND OFFICE
2857 WEST 8 .... BROOKLYN **NY**   (718) 266-5300
MADELEINE BORG COUNSELING SERVICES - MID-BROOKLYN OFFICE
1113 AVENUE J .... BROOKLYN **NY** 11230   (718) 258-7700
MADELEINE BORG COUNSELING SERVICES - MONTAGUE STREET OFFICE
186 MONTAGUE STREET .... BROOKLYN **NY** 11201   (718) 855-6900
MADELEINE BORG COUNSELING SERVICES - STARRETT CITY OFFICE
1201 PENNSYLVANIA AVENUE .... BROOKLYN **NY**   (718) 642-8955
MIDWOOD ADOLESCENT PROJECT 1484 FLATBUSH AVENUE .... BROOKLYN **NY**   (718) 434-4158
MISHKON B'NAI YISROEL 4105 16TH AVENUE .... BROOKLYN **NY** 11219   (718) 851-6570
MONTAGUE SCHOOL 180 MONTAGUE STREET .... BROOKLYN **NY** 11201   (718) 858-0886

OHEL CHILDREN'S HOME 4423 16TH AVENUE	BROOKLYN **NY**	11204	(718) 851-6300
PROGRAM FOR RUSSIAN JEWISH IMMIGRANTS 2857 WEST 8TH	BROOKLYN **NY**		(718) 266-5300
TIFERETH SHLOMO BOYS INSTITUTIONS 5121 17TH AVENUE	BROOKLYN **NY**	11204	(718) 435-0206
JEWISH CH. CARE ASSOC. OF N.Y.-LEFRAK RESIDENCE			
98-25 HORACE HARDING EXPRESSWAY	CORONA **NY**	11368	(718) 592-0190
PRIDE OF JUDEA CHILDREN'S SERVICES 243-02 NORTHERN BLVD	DOUGLASTON **NY**	11363	
JEWISH CH. CARE ASSOC. OF N.Y.-REGO PARK RESIDENCE FOR BOYS			
94-30 60TH AVENUE	ELMHURST **NY**	11380	(718) 271-4555
JEWISH CH. CARE ASSOC. OF N.Y.-REGO PARK RESIDENCE FOR GIRLS			
94-31 60TH AVENUE	ELMHURST **NY**	11380	(718) 271-2199
JEWISH CH. CARE ASSOC. OF N.Y.-WOODHAVEN RESIDENCE			
94-30 59TH AVENUE	ELMHURST **NY**	11380	(718) 271-0228
HEBREW KINDERGARTEN AND INFANTS HOME			
310 BEACH 20TH STREET	FAR ROCKAWAY **NY**	11691	(718) 327-1140
JEWISH CH. CARE ASSOC./N.Y.-HARTMAN HOMECREST FAR ROCK. RES.			
25-32 BEACH CHANNEL DRIVE	FAR ROCKAWAY **NY**	11691	(718) 327-3300
JEWISH CH. CARE ASSOC. OF N.Y.-PROGRESS HOUSE FOR BOYS			
162-19 76TH AVENUE	FLUSHING **NY**	11366	(718) 591-2552
JEWISH CH. CARE ASSOC. OF N.Y.-PROGRESS HOUSE FOR GIRLS			
162-08 77TH AVENUE	FLUSHING **NY**	11366	(718) 591-9339
JEWISH CH. CARE ASSOC. OF N.Y.-VERNONDALE RESIDENCE			
111 N. 3RD AVENUE	MT. VERNON **NY**	10550	(914) 699-7324
JEWISH CH. CARE ASSOC./N.Y.-HARTMAN HOMECREST MT.VERNON RES.			
165 ESPLANADE AVENUE	MT. VERNON **NY**	10553	(914) 699-4083
ASSOCIATION OF JEWISH FAMILY & CHILDREN'S AGENCIES			
200 PARK AVENUE SOUTH	NEW YORK **NY**	10003	(212) 674-6659
COMMUNITY HOMEMAKER SERVICE 120 WEST 57TH STREET	NEW YORK **NY**	10019	(212) 582-9100
FAMILY LOCATION & LEGAL SERVICE 120 WEST 57TH STREET	NEW YORK **NY**	10019	(212) 582-9100
JEWISH BOARD OF FAMILY & CHILDREN'S SERVICES			
120 WEST 57TH STREET	NEW YORK **NY**	10019	(212) 582-9100
JEWISH BOARD OF GUARDIANS 120 WEST 57TH STREET	NEW YORK **NY**	10019	(212) 582-9100
JEWISH BOARD OF GUARDIANS CHILD GUIDANCE INSTITUTE			
120 WEST 57TH STREET	NEW YORK **NY**	10019	(212) 582-9100
JEWISH CH. CARE ASSOC. OF N.Y.-CHILDVILLE DIVISION			
440 E. 88TH STREET	NEW YORK **NY**	10028	(212) 490-9160
JEWISH CH. CARE ASSOC. OF N.Y.-CNTRL. INTAKE & REFERRAL SERV			
345 MADISON AVENUE	NEW YORK **NY**	10017	(212) 490-9161
JEWISH CH. CARE ASSOC. OF N.Y.-DIV./DEVELOPMENTALLY DISABLED			
345 MADISON AVENUE	NEW YORK **NY**	10017	(212) 490-9161
JEWISH CH. CARE ASSOC. OF N.Y.-EXECUTIVE & ADMIN. OFFICES			
345 MADISON AVENUE	NEW YORK **NY**	10017	(212) 490-9160
JEWISH CH. CARE ASSOC. OF N.Y.-FAMILY DAY CARE SERVICE			
345 MADISON AVENUE	NEW YORK **NY**	10017	(212) 490-9160
JEWISH CH. CARE ASSOC. OF N.Y.-FOSTER HOME DIVISION			
345 MADISON AVENUE	NEW YORK **NY**	10017	(212) 490-9160
JEWISH CH. CARE ASSOC. OF N.Y.-FRIENDLY HOME			
465 WEST END AVENUE	NEW YORK **NY**	10024	(212) 874-2522
JEWISH CH. CARE ASSOC. OF N.Y.-FRIENDLY HOME			
320 WEST END AVENUE	NEW YORK **NY**	10023	(212) 595-2620
JEWISH CH. CARE ASSOC. OF N.Y.-FRIENDLY HOME			
465 WEST END AVENUE	NEW YORK **NY**	10023	(212) 595-2620
JEWISH CH. CARE ASSOC. OF N.Y.-GROUP RESIDENCE DIVISION			
345 MADISON AVENUE	NEW YORK **NY**	10017	(212) 490-9160
JEWISH CH. CARE ASSOC. OF N.Y.-PREVENTIVE SERVICES			
2521 BROADWAY	NEW YORK **NY**	10025	(212) 864-5600
JEWISH CH. CARE ASSOC. OF N.Y.-TWO TOGETHER PROGRAM			
345 MADISON AVENUE	NEW YORK **NY**	10017	(212) 490-9160
JEWISH CH. CARE ASSOC. OF N.Y.-YOUTH RESIDENCE CENTER			
217 E. 87TH STREET	NEW YORK **NY**	10028	(212) 427-6655
JEWISH YOUTH SERVICES OF BROOKLYN			
CALL JEWISH CHILD CARE ASSOCIATION OF N.Y.	NEW YORK **NY**		(212) 490-9160
LOUISE WISE SERVICES 12 EAST 94TH STREET	NEW YORK **NY**	10028	(212) 876-3050
SERVICES TO THE WIDOWED 33 WEST 60TH STREET	NEW YORK **NY**	10023	(212) 586-2900
JEWISH CH. CARE ASSOC. OF N.Y.-EDENWALD CENTER			
ROUTE 141	PLEASANTVILLE **NY**	10570	(914) 769-7150
JEWISH CH. CARE ASSOC. OF N.Y.-PLEASANTVILLE COTTAGE SCHOOL			
BROADWAY	PLEASANTVILLE **NY**	10570	(914) 769-0164
JEWISH CH. CARE ASSOC. OF N.Y.-ELMHURST RESIDENCE FOR BOYS			
94-30 58TH AVENUE	REGO PARK **NY**	11374	(718) 592-8417
JEWISH CH. CARE ASSOC. OF N.Y.-ELMHURST RESIDENCE FOR GIRL			
94-30 60TH AVENUE	REGO PARK **NY**	11374	(718) 592-8316
JEWISH CH. CARE ASSOC. OF N.Y.-FAMILY DAY CARE SERVICE			
97-45 QUEENS BLVD.	REGO PARK **NY**	11374	(718) 268-8870
GELLER HOUSE - JEWISH BOARD OF GUARDIANS			
77 CHICAGO AVENUE	STATEN ISLAND **NY**	10305	(718) 442-7828
JEWISH CHILDREN'S BUREAU 21811 FAIRMOUNT	CLEVELAND **OH**	44118	(216) 932-2800
JEWISH CHILDREN'S BUREAU 22001 FAIRMOUNT BLVD.	CLEVELAND **OH**	44118	(216) 932-2800
JEWISH FAMILY AND CHILD SERVICE 4600 BATHURST STREET	WILLOWDALE **ON**	M2R-3V3	(416) 638-7800
ASSOCIATION FOR JEWISH CHILDREN 1301 SPENCER STREET	PHILADELPHIA **PA**	19141	(215) 549-9000
JEWISH HOME FOR BABIES AND CHILDREN 5808 FORBES AVENUE	PITTSBURGH **PA**	15200	(412) 441-0174
LUBAVITCH NURSERY SCHOOL 3109 NORTH LAKE DRIVE	MILWAUKEE **WI**	53211	(414) 962-2444
MILWAUKEE JEWISH CHILDREN'S HOME 1360 NORTH PROSPECT	MILWAUKEE **WI**	53202	(414) 273-6515

COINS & MEDALS

JEWISH-AMERICAN HALL OF FAME-JUDAH L. MAGNES MEMORIAL MUSEUM			
2911 RUSSEL STREET	BERKELEY **CA**	94705	(415) 849-2710
JOSEPH J. GOLDBERG, INC. 9454 WILSHIRE BOULEVARD	BEVERLY HILLS **CA**	90212	(213) 273-4452
BICK INTERNATIONAL P.O.BOX 854	VAN NUYS **CA**	91408	(818) 997-6496
ISRAEL NUMISMATIC SOCIETY OF ILLINOIS P.O. BOX 427	SKOKIE **IL**	60076	(312) 673-8514

HY GOLDBERG, CALHOUN COLLECTOR'S SOCIETY
  CALHOUN CENTER .... MINNEAPOLIS **MN** 55435   (612) 835-0300
AARON C. OPPENHEIM, INC.
  P.O. BOX 709 ROCKEFELLER CENTER STATION .... NEW YORK **NY** 10185   (212) 568-0342
ABRAHAM NACHMANY COINS PO BOX 1193/ANSONIA STATION .... NEW YORK **NY** 10023   (212) 246-6233
HECKER SILVERSMITHS 605 FIFTH AVENUE (49TH STREET) .... NEW YORK **NY** 10017   (212) 593-2424
ISRAEL GOVERNMENT COINS & MEDALS CORP., LTD.
  350 FIFTH AVENUE .... NEW YORK **NY** 10118   (212) 560-0690

COLLEGES & UNIVERSITIES

HEBREW UNION COLLEGE - JEWISH INSTITUTE OF RELIGION
  3077 UNIVERSITY AVENUE .... LOS ANGELES **CA** 90007   (213) 749-3424
JEWISH THEOLOGICAL SEMINARY OF AMERICA
  15600 MULHOLLAND DRIVE .... LOS ANGELES **CA** 90077   (213) 879-4114
UNIVERSITY OF JUDAISM 15600 MULHOLLAND DRIVE .... LOS ANGELES **CA** 90077   (213) 476-9777
YESHIVA UNIVERSITY OF LOS ANGELES
  9760 WEST PICO BOULEVARD .... LOS ANGELES **CA** 90035   (213) 553-4478
CENTER FOR JUDAIC STUDIES UNIVERSITY OF DENVER .... DENVER **CO** 80208   (303) 753-2068
CENTER FOR JUDAIC STUDIES, THE - UNIVERSITY OF DENVER
  UNIVERSITY PARK .... DENVER **CO** 80208   (303) 753-1964
SPERTUS COLLEGE OF JUDAICA 618 S. MICHIGAN AVENUE .... CHICAGO **IL** 60605   (312) 922-9012
HEBREW THEOLOGICAL COLLEGE 7135 N. CARPENTER ROAD .... SKOKIE **IL** 60077   (312) 267-9800
HEBREW COLLEGE 43 HAWES STREET .... BROOKLINE **MA** 02146   (617) 232-8710
BRANDEIS UNIVERSITY .... WALTHAM **MA** 02254   (617) 647-2177
BALTIMORE HEBREW COLLEGE & LIBRARY
  5800 PARK HEIGHTS AVENUE .... BALTIMORE **MD** 21215   (301) 367-8300
COLLEGE OF JEWISH STUDIES OF GREATER WASHINGTON
  9325 BROOKVILLE ROAD .... SILVER SPRING **MD** 20910   (301) 589-3180
MIDRASHA COLLEGE OF JEWISH STUDIES
  21550 W. TWELVE MILE ROAD .... SOUTHFIELD **MI** 48076   (313) 352-7117
PHILIP & FLORENCE DWORSKY CTR./JEWISH STUDIES, UNIV. OF MINN
  178 KLABER CT., 320 16TH AVENUE S.E. .... MINNEAPOLIS **MN** 55455   (612) 373-2851
ALBERT EINSTEIN COLLEGE OF MEDICINE-YESHIVA UNIV. BRONX CTR.
  EASTCHESTER ROAD & MORRIS PARK AVENUE .... BRONX **NY** 10461   (212) 430-2000
JACK & PEARL GERONTOLOGY CTR. ALBERT EINSTEIN COLLEGE OF MED
  BRONX CENTER, EASTCHESTER RD. & MORRIS PARK AVENUE .... BRONX **NY** 10461   (212) 430-2900
YESHIVA UNIVERSITY-ALBERT EINSTEIN COLLEGE HOSPITAL
  1825 EASTCHESTER ROAD .... BRONX **NY** 10461   (212) 430-2000
YESHIVA UNIVERSITY-ALBERT EINSTEIN COLLEGE OF MEDICINE
  1300 MORRIS PARK AVENUE .... BRONX **NY** 10461   (212) 430-2000
YESHIVA UNIVERSITY-BELFER INST. FOR ADV. BIOMEDICAL STUDIES
  1300 MORRIS PARK AVENUE .... BRONX **NY** 10461   (212) 430-2801
YESHIVA UNIVERSITY-FERKAUF GRAD. SCHOOL OF PSYCHOLOGY
  1165 MORRIS PARK AVENUE .... BRONX **NY** 10461   (212) 430-4204
YESHIVA UNIVERSITY-FERKAUF GRAD. SCHOOL/PSYCH. (ADMIN.)
  1165 MORRIS PARK AVENUE .... BRONX **NY** 10461   (212) 430-4207
YESHIVA UNIVERSITY-FERKAUF GRAD. SCHOOL/PSYCH. (REGISTRAR)
  1165 MORRIS PARK AVENUE .... BRONX **NY** 10461   (212) 430-4206
YESHIVA UNIVERSITY-FERKAUF GRAD. SCHOOL/PSYCH: FACULTY & OFF.
  1165 MORRIS PARK AVENUE .... BRONX **NY** 10461   (212) 430-4201
YESHIVA UNIVERSITY-FERKAUF GRAD.SCHOOL/PSYCH: STUDENT FINANCE
  1165 MORRIS PARK AVENUE .... BRONX **NY** 10461   (212) 430-4208
YESHIVA UNIVERSITY-SUE GOLDING GRAD. DIV. OF MEDICAL SCIENCE
  1300 MORRIS PARK AVENUE .... BRONX **NY** 10461   (212) 430-2107
BETH JACOB TEACHERS SEMINARY OF AMERICA 132 S. 8TH STREET .... BROOKLYN **NY** 11211   (718) 388-2701
TOURO COLLEGE - LAW SCHOOL 300 NASSAU ROAD .... HUNTINGTON **NY** 11743   (516) 421-2244
TOURO COLLEGE - TECHNION MEDICAL EDUCATION PROGRAM
  300 NASSAU ROAD .... HUNTINGTON **NY** 11743   (516) 421-2246
TOURO COLLEGE - PHYSICAL THERAPY PROGRAM
  300 NASSAU ROAD .... HUNTINGTON **NY** 11743   (516) 421-2244
BAR-ILAN UNIVERSITY IN ISRAEL 527 MADISON AVENUE .... NEW YORK **NY** 10022   (212) 751-6366
BEIT MIDRASH L'TORAH, JERUSALEM TORAH COLLEGE FOR MEN
  TORAH DEPT., WORLD ZIONIST ORGANIZATION, 515 PARK AVENUE ... NEW YORK **NY** 10022   (212) 752-0600
BENJAMIN N. CARDOZO SCHOOL OF LAW - YESHIVA UNIVERSITY
  55 FIFTH AVENUE .... NEW YORK **NY** 10003   (212) 790-0463
BERNARD REVEL GRADUATE SCHOOL-YESHIVA UNIVERSITY
  500 W. 185TH STREET .... NEW YORK **NY** 10033   (212) 960-5253
BRANDEIS UNIVERSITY 12 EAST 77TH STREET .... NEW YORK **NY** 10021   (212) 472-1501
HEBREW UNION COLLEGE - JEWISH INSTITUTE OF RELIGION
  1 WEST FOURTH STREET .... NEW YORK **NY** 10003   (212) 764-5300
HERZLIAH - JEWISH TEACHERS SEMINARY 69 BANK STREET .... NEW YORK **NY** 10014   (212) 575-1819
HERZLIAH HEBREW TEACHERS INST. & JEW. TEACHERS SEMINARY &
  PEOPLE'S UNIV. 333 W. 17TH STREET .... NEW YORK **NY** 10011   (212) 741-0220
HORACE M. KALLEN CENTER FOR JEWISH STUDIES 69 BANK STREET ... NEW YORK **NY** 10014   (212) 575-1819
JEWISH THEOLOGICAL SEMINARY OF AMERICA, THE 3080 BROADWAY .. NEW YORK **NY** 10027   (212) 678-8000
MACHON GOLD COLLEGE FOR WOMEN
  TORAH DEPT. WORLD ZIONIST ORGANIZATION 515 PARK AVENUE ..... NEW YORK **NY** 10022   (212) 752-0600
MOUNT SINAI SCHOOL OF MEDICINE OF CUNY, THE
  100TH STREET & FIFTH AVENUE .... NEW YORK **NY** 10029   (212) 650-6500
MT. SINAI SCHOOL OF MEDICINE OF CUNY, THE (FUND DEVELOPMENT)
  100TH STREET & FIFTH AVENUE .... NEW YORK **NY** 10029   (212) 650-6976
RABBI ISAAC ELCHANAN THEOLOGICAL SEMINARY
  2540 AMSTERDAM AVENUE .... NEW YORK **NY** 10033   (212) 960-5346
RECONSTRUCTIONIST RABBINICAL COLLEGE
  432 PARK AVENUE SOUTH .... NEW YORK **NY** 10016   (212) 889-9080
STERN COLLEGE FOR WOMEN 245 LEXINGTON AVENUE .... NEW YORK **NY** 10016   (212) 340-7700
STERN COLLEGE FOR WOMEN 245 LEXINGTON AVENUE .... NEW YORK **NY** 10016   (212) 255-5600
STONE-SAPIRSTEIN CENTER FOR JEWISH EDUCATION-YESHIVA UNIV.
  500 W. 185TH STREET .... NEW YORK **NY** 10033   (212) 960-5400

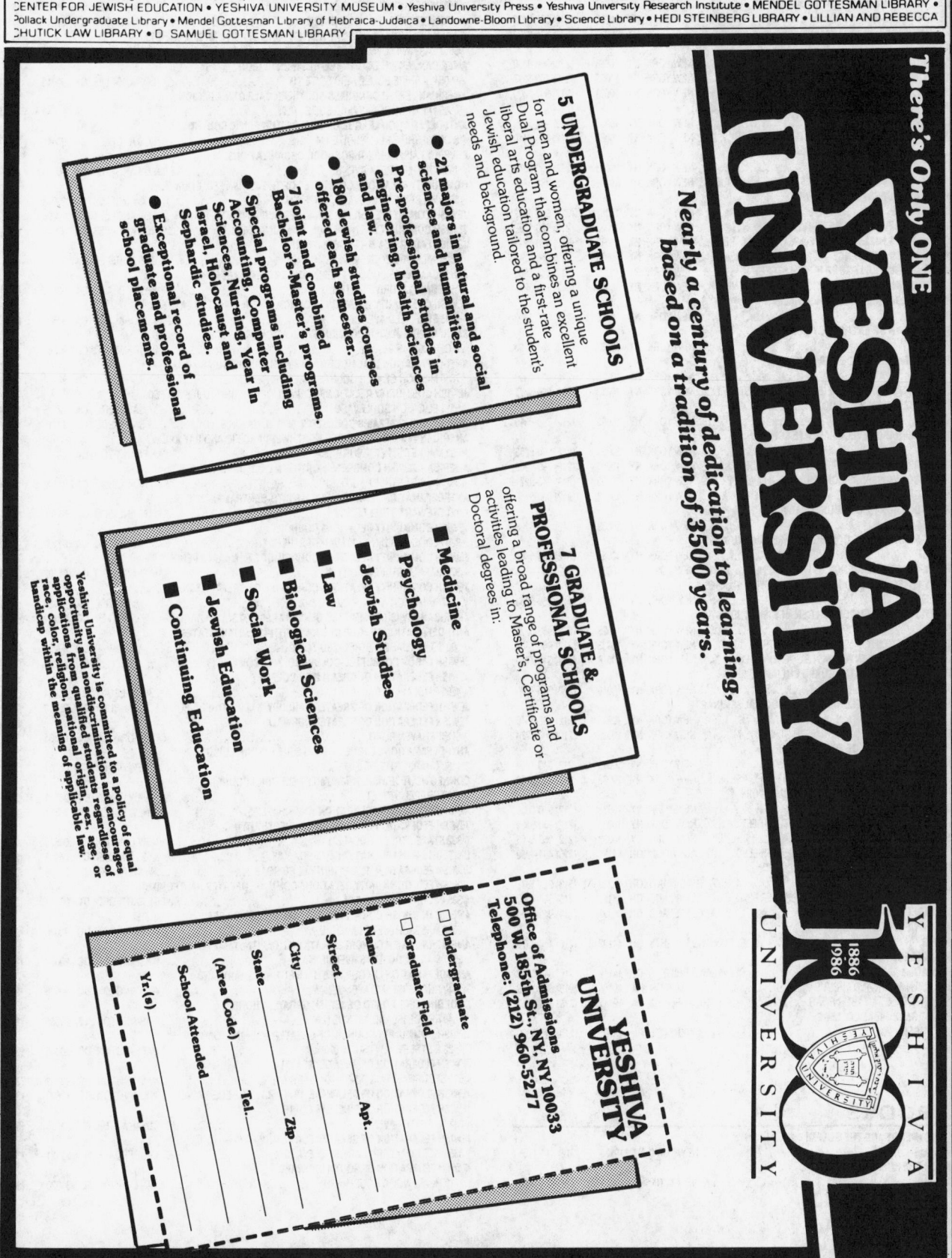

TEACHERS INSTITUTE - SEMINARY COLLEGE OF JEWISH STUDIES
3080 BROADWAY ... NEW YORK **NY** 10027 (212) 678-8000
TOURO COLLEGE 30 WEST 44TH STREET ... NEW YORK **NY** 10036 (212) 575-0190
TOURO COLLEGE - DEAN OF FACULTIES 30 WEST 44TH STREET ... NEW YORK **NY** 10036 (212) 575-0190
TOURO COLLEGE - DEAN OF STUDENTS 30 WEST 44TH STREET ... NEW YORK **NY** 10036 (212) 221-2296
TOURO COLLEGE - FINANCIAL AID 30 WEST 44TH STREET ... NEW YORK **NY** 10036 (212) 575-0190
TOURO COLLEGE - GRADUATE PROGRAM - JEWISH STUDIES
30 WEST 44TH STREET ... NEW YORK **NY** 10036 (212) 575-0190
TOURO COLLEGE - JEWISH PEOPLE'S UNIVERSITY OF THE AIR
30 WEST 44TH STREET ... NEW YORK **NY** 10036 (212) 575-0190
TOURO COLLEGE - OFFICE OF ADMISSIONS 30 WEST 44TH STREET ... NEW YORK **NY** 10036 (212) 719-9865
TOURO COLLEGE - PHYSICIAN'S ASSISTANT PROGRAM
30 WEST 44TH STREET ... NEW YORK **NY** 10036 (212) 575-0190
TOURO COLLEGE - REGISTRAR 30 WEST 44TH STREET ... NEW YORK **NY** 10036 (212) 575-0190
WURZWEILER SCHOOL OF SOCIAL WORK-YESHIVA UNIVERSITY
500 W. 185TH STREET ... NEW YORK **NY** 10033 (212) 960-0800
YESHIVA UNIVERSITY 500 WEST 185TH STREET ... NEW YORK **NY** 10033 (212) 960-5277
YESHIVA UNIVERSITY 500 WEST 185TH STREET ... NEW YORK **NY** 10033 (212) 960-5400
YESHIVA UNIVERSITY - COMMENTATOR (YESHIVA COLLEGE NEWSPAPER)
2525 AMSTERDAM AVENUE ... NEW YORK **NY** 10033 (212) 928-1292
YESHIVA UNIVERSITY - DINING HALLS 2501 AMSTERDAM AVENUE ... NEW YORK **NY** 10033 (212) 568-2440
YESHIVA UNIVERSITY - HIGH SCHOOL FOR BOYS
2540 AMSTERDAM AVENUE ... NEW YORK **NY** 10033 (212) 960-5345
YESHIVA UNIVERSITY - HIGH SCHOOL FOR GIRLS 425 FIFTH AVENUE ... NEW YORK **NY** 10016 (212) 481-3746
YESHIVA UNIVERSITY - MORGENSTERN RESIDENCE
2525 AMSTERDAM AVENUE ... NEW YORK **NY** 10033 (212) 960-5249
YESHIVA UNIVERSITY - MUSEUM 2520 AMSTERDAM AVENUE ... NEW YORK **NY** 10033 (212) 960-5390
YESHIVA UNIVERSITY - RIETS HALL RESIDENCE 526 W. 187TH STREET ... NEW YORK **NY** 10033 (212) 960-5249
YESHIVA UNIVERSITY - RUBIN RESIDENCE 2501 AMSTERDAM AVENUE ... NEW YORK **NY** 10033 (212) 960-5249
YESHIVA UNIVERSITY - STERN COLLEGE 50 E. 34TH STREET ... NEW YORK **NY** 10016 (212) 686-5900
YESHIVA UNIVERSITY - WOMEN'S ORGANIZATION 55 FIFTH AVENUE ... NEW YORK **NY** 10003 (212) 790-0371
YESHIVA UNIVERSITY - BROOKDALE RESIDENCE HALL
50 E. 34TH STREET ... NEW YORK **NY** 10016 (212) 686-5900
YESHIVA UNIVERSITY - 185TH ST. EMERGENCY GUARD
500 WEST 185TH STREET ... NEW YORK **NY** 10033 (212) 960-5200
YESHIVA UNIVERSITY-34TH ST. GUARD EMERGENCY
50 EAST 34TH STREET ... NEW YORK **NY** 10016 (212) 481-0593
YESHIVA UNIVERSITY-ADMISSIONS OFFICE 500 WEST 185TH STREET ... NEW YORK **NY** 10033 (212) 960-5277
YESHIVA UNIVERSITY - BENJAMIN N. CARDOZO SCHOOL OF LAW
55 FIFTH AVENUE ... NEW YORK **NY** 10003 (212) 790-0310
YESHIVA UNIVERSITY-BERNARD REVEL GRADUATE SCHOOL
500 W. 185TH STREET ... NEW YORK **NY** 10033 (212) 960-5253
YESHIVA UNIVERSITY-BROOKDALE CENTER 55 FIFTH AVENUE ... NEW YORK **NY** 10003 (212) 790-0200
YESHIVA UNIVERSITY-CONNOISSEURS CORNER 55 FIFTH AVENUE ... NEW YORK **NY** 10003 (212) 243-9271
YESHIVA UNIVERSITY-DINING HALLS 2501 AMSTERDAM AVENUE ... NEW YORK **NY** 10033 (212) 960-5248
YESHIVA UNIVERSITY-DIVISION OF COMMUNAL SERVICES
500 W. 185TH STREET ... NEW YORK **NY** 10033 (212) 960-5265
YESHIVA UNIVERSITY-ERNA MICHAEL COLLEGE OF HEBRAIC STUDIES
500 W. 185TH STREET ... NEW YORK **NY** 10033 (212) 960-5347
YESHIVA UNIVERSITY-GUARD EMERGENCY OFFICE 55 FIFTH AVENUE ... NEW YORK **NY** 10003 (212) 790-0303
YESHIVA UNIVERSITY-H FISCHEL SCHOOL OF HIGHER JEWISH STUDIES
500 W. 185TH STREET ... NEW YORK **NY** 10033 (212) 960-5253
YESHIVA UNIVERSITY-J. STRIAR SCHOOL FOR GEN. JEWISH STUDIES
500 W. 185TH STREET ... NEW YORK **NY** 10033 (212) 960-5225
YESHIVA UNIVERSITY-MAIN CENTER 500 WEST 185TH STREET ... NEW YORK **NY** 10033 (212) 960-5400
YESHIVA UNIVERSITY-MIDTOWN CENTER 245 LEXINGTON AVENUE ... NEW YORK **NY** 10016 (212) 340-7700
YESHIVA UNIVERSITY-MIDTOWN CENTER GUARD EMERGENCY
245 LEXINGTON AVENUE ... NEW YORK **NY** 10016 (212) 340-7700
YESHIVA UNIVERSITY-RABBI ISAAC ELCHANAN THEOLOGICAL SEMINARY
2540 AMSTERDAM AVENUE ... NEW YORK **NY** 10033 (212) 960-5346
YESHIVA UNIVERSITY-REGISTRAR 500 WEST 185TH STREET ... NEW YORK **NY** 10033 (212) 960-5274
YESHIVA UNIVERSITY-STERN COLLEGE FOR WOMEN
245 LEXINGTON AVENUE ... NEW YORK **NY** 10016 (212) 340-7700
YESHIVA UNIVERSITY-STUDENT FINANCE 500 WEST 185TH STREET ... NEW YORK **NY** 10033 (212) 960-5269
YESHIVA UNIVERSITY-WURZWEILER SCHOOL OF SOCIAL WORK
2495 AMSTERDAM AVENUE ... NEW YORK **NY** 10033 (212) 960-0800
YESHIVA UNIVERSITY-YESHIVA COLLEGE 500 W. 185TH STREET ... NEW YORK **NY** 10033 (212) 960-5124
YESHIVA UNIVERSITY 500 W. 185TH STREET ... NEW YORK **NY** 10033 (212) 960-5285
CLEVELAND COLLEGE OF JEWISH STUDIES 26500 SHAKER BLVD. ... BEACHWOOD **OH** 44122 (216) 464-4050
HEBREW UNION COLLEGE-JEWISH INSTITUTE OF RELIGION
3101 CLIFTON AVENUE ... CINCINNATI **OH** 45220 (513) 221-1875
CLEVELAND COLLEGE OF JEWISH STUDIES 26500 SHAKER BLVD. ... CLEVELAND **OH** 44122 (216) 464-4050
TELSHE YESHIVA COLLEGE 28400 EUCLID AVENUE ... CLEVELAND **OH** 44092 (216) 943-5300
CLEVELAND COLLEGE OF JEWISH STUDIES
26500 SHAKER BLVD ... CLEVELAND HEIGHTS **OH** 44122 (216) 464-4370
YAVNE TEACHER'S COLLEGE FOR WOMEN
1970 S. TAYLOR ROAD ... CLEVELAND HEIGHTS **OH** 44118 (216) 943-5300
DROPSIE COLLEGE 250 N. HIGHLAND AVENUE ... MERION **PA** 19066 (215) 667-1830
GRATZ COLLEGE 10TH STREET & TABOR ROAD ... PHILADELPHIA **PA** 19141 (215) 329-3363
RECONSTRUCTIONIST RABBINICAL COLLEGE
CHURCH ROAD AT GREENWOOD ... WYNCOTE **PA** 19095 (215) 576-0800

COMIC BOOKS

MENDY ENTERPRISES (MENDY AND THE GOLEM)
450 SEVENTH AVENUE ... NEW YORK **NY** 10123 (212) 410-1155
MENDY ENTERPRISES-THE KOSHER COMIC BOOK
450 SEVENTH AVENUE ... NEW YORK **NY** 10001 (718) 774-4660

COMMUNITY RELATIONS ORGANIZATIONS

JEWISH COMMUNITY COUNCIL
P.O. BOX 9157 3960 MONTCLAIR ROAD ... BIRMINGHAM **AL** 36213 (205) 849-0416
AMERICAN JEWISH COMMITTEE-PHOENIX AREA
4710 NORTH 16TH STREET ... PHOENIX **AZ** 85012 (602) 279-9695
COMMUNITY RELATIONS COMMITTEE OF GREATER PHOENIX JEWISH FED.
1718 WEST MARYLAND AVENUE ... PHOENIX **AZ** 95015 (602) 249-1845
COMMUNITY RELATIONS COMMITTEE OF THE TUCSON J.C.C.
102 NORTH PLUMER ... TUCSON **AZ** 85719 (602) 884-8921
CANADIAN JEWISH CONGRESS-PACIFIC REGION
950 WEST 41ST STREET ... VANCOUVER **BC** V5Z 2N7 (604) 261-8101
JEWISH FEDERATION OF ORANGE COUNTY 12181 BUARO ... GARDEN GROVE **CA** 92640 (714) 530-6636
JEWISH COMMUNITY FED. OF GREATER LONG BEACH & W. ORANGE CTY
3801 EAST WILLOW STREET ... LONG BEACH **CA** 90815 (213) 426-7601
AMERICAN JEWISH COMMITTEE-WESTERN REGION
6505 WILSHIRE BOULEVARD SUITE 315 ... LOS ANGELES **CA** 90048 (213) 655-7071
AMERICAN JEWISH CONGRESS-SOUTHERN CALIFORNIA REGION
6505 WILSHIRE BOULEVARD SUITE 1103 ... LOS ANGELES **CA** 90048 (213) 651-4601
ANTI-DEFAMATION LEAGUE OF B'NAI B'RITH-PACIFIC SOUTHWEST
6505 WILSHIRE BLVD., SUITE 814 ... LOS ANGELES **CA** 90048 (213) 655-8205
BEVERLY FAIRFAX NEIGHBORHOOD ORGANIZATIONS
163 SOUTH FAIRFAX AVENUE ... LOS ANGELES **CA** 90036 (213) 931-1511
COMMUNITY RELATIONS COMMITTEE OF THE JEWISH FED. COUNCIL
6505 WILSHIRE BOULEVARD, SUITE 802 ... LOS ANGELES **CA** 90048 (213) 852-1234
JEWISH COMMITTEE FOR PERSONAL SERVICE 1891 EFFIE STREET ... LOS ANGELES **CA** 90026 (213) 666-0171
JEWISH COMMUNITY FOUNDATION 6505 WILSHIRE BLVD ... LOS ANGELES **CA** 90048 (213) 852-1234
JEWISH LABOR COMMITTEE-CALIFORNIA
6505 WILSHIRE BOULEVARD, SUITE 403 ... LOS ANGELES **CA** 90048 (213) 653-3501
AMERICAN JEWISH COMMITTEE-ORANGE COUNTY AREA
4500 CAMPUS DRIVE SUITE 420 ... NEWPORT BEACH **CA** 92660 (714) 546-2914
JEWISH COMMUNITY RELATIONS COUNCIL OF THE GREATER EAST BAY
3245 SHEFFIELD AVENUE ... OAKLAND **CA** 94602 (415) 533-7462
SACRAMENTO JEWISH COMMUNITY RELATIONS COUNCIL
P.O. BOX 254589 ... SACRAMENTO **CA** 95865 (916) 486-0906
ANTI-DEFAMATION LEAGUE OF B'NAI B'RITH-SAN DIEGO-ARIZONA
7850 MISSION CENTER COURT STREET ... SAN DIEGO **CA** 92108 (619) 293-3370
JEWISH COMMUNITY RELATIONS COUNCIL OF THE UNITED JEWISH FED.
5511 EL CAJON BOULEVARD ... SAN DIEGO **CA** 92115 (619) 582-2483
JEWISH PUBLIC AFFAIRS COMMITTEE 5511 EL CAJON BLVD. ... SAN DIEGO **CA** 92115 (619) 582-2483
AMERICAN JEWISH COMMITTEE-NORTHWEST PACIFIC AND BAY AREA
703 MARKET STREET, SUITE 1500 ... SAN FRANCISCO **CA** 94103 (415) 392-1892
AMERICAN JEWISH CONGRESS-NORTHERN CALIFORNIA REGION
942 MARKET STREET SUITE 501 ... SAN FRANCISCO **CA** 94102 (415) 391-6590
ANTI-DEFAMATION LEAGUE OF B'NAI B'RITH-CENTRAL PACIFIC
121 STEWART STREET ... SAN FRANCISCO **CA** 94105 (415) 391-0200
JEWISH COMMUNITY RELATIONS COUNCIL
920 FLOOD BUILDING 870 MARKET STREET ... SAN FRANCISCO **CA** 94102 (415) 391-4655
JEWISH COMMUNITY RELATIONS COUNCIL OF S.F., MARIN & PENIN.
870 MARKET STREET, SUITE 920 ... SAN FRANCISCO **CA** 94102 (415) 391-4655
JEWISH COMMUNITY RELATIONS COMMITTEE OF GREATER SAN JOSE
1777 HAMILTON AVENUE, SUITE 210 ... SAN JOSE **CA** 95125 (408) 267-2770
AMERICAN JEWISH COMMITTEE-DENVER AREA 300 SOUTH DAHLIA ... DENVER **CO** 80203 (303) 320-1742
ANTI-DEFAMATION LEAGUE OF B'NAI B'RITH-MOUNTAIN STATES
300 SOUTH DAHLIA STREET, SUITE 202 ... DENVER **CO** 80222 (303) 321-7177
JEWISH LABOR COMMITTEE-COLORADO 346 ACOMA ... DENVER **CO** 80223 (303) 759-3439
JEWISH FEDERATION OF GREATER BRIDGEPORT
4200 PARK AVENUE ... BRIDGEPORT **CT** 06604 (203) 372-6504
JEWISH FEDERATION OF GREATER DANBURY 5 MAIN STREET, SUITE E ... DANBURY **CT** 06810 (203) 792-6353
JEWISH FEDERATION OF GREATER NORWALK
SHOREHAVEN ROAD ... EAST NORWALK **CT** 06885 (203) 853-3440
ANTI-DEFAMATION LEAGUE OF B'NAI B'RITH-CONNECTICUT
1162 CHAPEL STREET ... NEW HAVEN **CT** 06511 (203) 787-4281
CONNECTICUT JEWISH COMMUNITY RELATIONS COUNCIL
1162 CHAPEL STREET ... NEW HAVEN **CT** 06511 (203) 562-2137
NEW HAVEN JEWISH FEDERATION 1162 CHAPEL STREET ... NEW HAVEN **CT** 06511 (203) 562-2137
JEWISH FEDERATION OF EASTERN CONNECTICUT, INC.
302 STATE STREET, ROOM 221 ... NEW LONDON **CT** 06320 (203) 442-8062
UNITED JEWISH FEDERATION P.O. BOX 3038 ... STAMFORD **CT** 06905 (203) 322-6935
JEWISH FEDERATION 1020 COUNTY CLUB ROAD ... WATERBURY **CT** 06708 (203) 758-2441
JEWISH FED. COMMUNITY RELATIONS COMM. OF GREATER HARTFORD
333 BLOOMFIELD AVENUE ... WEST HARTFORD **CT** 06117 (203) 232-4483
AMERICAN JEWISH COMMITTEE-CENTRAL ATLANTIC AREA
2027 MASSACHUSETTS AVENUE, NW ... WASHINGTON **DC** 20036 (202) 387-8641
AMERICAN JEWISH CONGRESS-NATIONAL CAPITAL CHAPTER
2027 MASSACHUSETTS AVENUE, NW ... WASHINGTON **DC** 20036 (202) 332-3888
ANTI-DEFAMATION LEAGUE OF B'NAI B'RITH-D.C.-MARYLAND
1640 RHODE ISLAND AVENUE, NW ... WASHINGTON **DC** 20036 (202) 960-0342
COORDINATING BOARD OF JEWISH ORGANIZATIONS
1640 RHODE ISLAND AVENUE N.W. ... WASHINGTON **DC** 20036 (202) 857-6600
JEWISH COMMUNITY COUNCIL OF GREATER WASHINGTON
1522 K STREET, N.W., SUITE 920 ... WASHINGTON **DC** 20005 (202) 347-4628
JEWISH FEDERATION OF GREATER SEATTLE
510 SECURITIES BUILDING, 1904 THIRD AVENUE ... WASHINGTON **DC** 98101 (206) 622-8211
JEWISH FEDERATION OF DELAWARE 101 GARDEN OF EDEN ROAD ... WILMINGTON **DE** 19803 (302) 478-6200
JEWISH FEDERATION OF PINELLAS COUNTY
302 S. JUPITER AVENUE ... CLEARWATER **FL** 33515 (813) 446-1033
JEWISH FEDERATION OF GREATER FORT LAUDERDALE
8358 WEST OAKLAND PARK BOULEVARD ... FORT LAUDERDALE **FL** 33321 (305) 748-8200
JEWISH FEDERATION OF SOUTH BROWARD
2719 HOLLYWOOD BOULEVARD ... HOLLYWOOD **FL** 33020 (305) 921-8810

JACKSONVILLE JEWISH FEDERATION
10829-1 OLD STREET, AUGUSTINE ROAD .... JACKSONVILLE FL 32223   (904) 262-2800
JEWISH FEDERATION OF GREATER ORLANDO
P.O. BOX 1508 851 N. MAITLAND AVENUE .... MAITLAND FL 32751   (305) 645-5933
AMERICAN JEWISH COMMITTEE-SOUTHEAST REGION 300 BISCAYNE BLVD .. MIAMI FL 33137   (305) 576-4240
AMERICAN JEWISH CONGRESS-SOUTHWEST REGION
4200 BISCAYNE BOULEVARD .... MIAMI FL 33137   (305) 576-4330
ANTI-DEFAMATION LEAGUE OF B'NAI B'RITH-FLORIDA
150 S.E. 2ND AVENUE .... MIAMI FL 33131   (305) 373-6306
GREATER MIAMI JEWISH FEDERATION 4200 BISCAYNE BOULEVARD .... MIAMI FL 33137   (305) 576-4000
AMERICAN JEWISH COMMITTEE-PALM BEACH AREA
120 SOUTH OLIVE AVENUE, SUITE 614 .... PALM BEACH FL 33480   (305) 655-5118
ANTI-DEFAMATION LEAGUE OF B'NAI B'RITH-PALM BEACH COUNTY
120 S. OLIVE AVENUE, SUITE 614 .... PALM BEACH FL 33401   (305) 832-7144
SARASOTA-MANATEE JEWISH FEDERATION
2197 RINGLING BOULEVARD .... SARASOTA FL 33577   (813) 365-4410
JEWISH FEDERATION OF PALM BEACH
SUITE 305 501 SOUTH FLAGLER DRIVE .... WEST PALM BEACH FL 33401   (305) 832-2120
AMERICAN JEWISH COMMITTEE-ATLANTA AREA
1649 TULLY CIRCLE, N.E. .... ATLANTA GA 30329   (404) 233-5501
ANTI-DEFAMATION LEAGUE OF B'NAI B'RITH-SOUTHEAST
805 PEACHTREE STREET, NE SUITE 633 .... ATLANTA GA 30308   (404) 523-3391
ATLANTA JEWISH FEDERATION, INC. 1753 PEACHTREE ROAD, N.E. .... ATLANTA GA 30309   (404) 873-1661
JEWISH LABOR COMMITTEE-GEORGIA
1000 RHODES HAVERTY BLDG. 134 PEACHTREE STREET, NW .... ATLANTA GA 30303
SAVANNAH JEWISH COUNCIL 5111 ABERCORN STREET .... SAVANNAH GA 31499   (912) 355-8111
JEWISH FEDERATION OF GREATER IOWA 910 POLK BOULEVARD .... DES MOINES IA 50312   (515) 277-6321
AMERICAN JEWISH COMMITTEE-MIDWESTERN REGION
55 JACKSON BOULEVARD SUITE 1870 .... CHICAGO IL 60604   (312) 663-5500
AMERICAN JEWISH CONGRESS-CHICAGO COUNCIL, MIDWEST REGION
22 WEST MONROE STREET SUITE 2101 .... CHICAGO IL 60603   (312) 332-7355
ANTI-DEFAMATION LEAGUE OF B'NAI B'RITH-MIDWEST
222 WEST ADAMS STREET .... CHICAGO IL 60606   (312) 782-5080
JEWISH LABOR COMMITTEE-ILLINOIS
JEWELRY WORKERS LOCAL 4A 1640 N. WELLS STREET .... CHICAGO IL 60603   (312) 642-3151
JEWISH LABOR COMMITTEE-ILLINOIS
54 WEST RANDOLPH STREET, ROOM 703 .... CHICAGO IL 60602   (312) 641-5086
PUBLIC AFFAIRS COMM. OF JEWISH UNITED FUND OF METRO CHICAGO
ONE SOUTH FRANKLIN STREET .... CHICAGO IL 60606   (312) 346-6700
JEWISH FEDERATION OF PEORIA 3100 N. KNOXVILLE, SUITE 17 .... PEORIA IL 61603   (309) 686-0611
SPRINGFIELD JEWISH FEDERATION 730 EAST VEIN STREET .... SPRINGFIELD IL 62703   (217) 528-3446
INDIANA JEWISH COMMUNITY RELATIONS COUNCIL
1100 WEST 42ND STREET .... INDIANAPOLIS IN 46208   (317) 926-2935
INDIANAPOLIS JEWISH COMMUNITY RELATIONS COUNCIL
1100 WEST 42ND STREET .... INDIANAPOLIS IN 46208   (317) 926-2935
JEWISH FEDERATION OF ST. JOSEPH VALLEY, INC.
804 SHERLAND BUILDING .... SOUTH BEND IN 46601   (219) 233-1164
JEWISH COMMUNITY FEDERATION P.O. BOX 33035 .... LOUISVILLE KY 40232   (502) 451-8840
ANTI-DEFAMATION LEAGUE OF B'NAI B'RITH-SOUTH CENTRAL
535 GRAVIER STREET SUITE 806 .... NEW ORLEANS LA 70130   (504) 522-9534
JEWISH FEDERATION OF GREATER NEW ORLEANS
1539 JACKSON AVENUE .... NEW ORLEANS LA 70130   (504) 525-0673
SHREVEPORT JEWISH FEDERATION 2030 LINE AVENUE .... SHREVEPORT LA 71104   (318) 221-4129
AMERICAN JEWISH COMMITTEE-NEW ENGLAND REGION
72 FRANKLIN STREET ROOM 403 .... BOSTON MA 02110   (617) 426-7415
AMERICAN JEWISH CONGRESS-NEW ENGLAND REGION
72 FRANKLIN STREET .... BOSTON MA 02110   (617) 542-0265
ANTI-DEFAMATION LEAGUE OF B'NAI B'RITH-NEW ENGLAND
72 FRANKLIN STREET, SUITE 504 .... BOSTON MA 02110   (617) 542-4977
JEWISH COMMUNITY COUNCIL OF METROPOLITAN BOSTON
72 FRANKLIN STREET, SUITE 406 .... BOSTON MA 02110   (617) 542-7525
JEWISH FEDERATION OF NORTH SHORE,INC. 4 COMMUNITY ROAD .. MARBLEHEAD MA 01945   (617) 745-4222
JEWISH FEDERATION OF GREATER NEW BEDFORD, INC.
467 HAWTHORN STREET .... N. DARTMOUTH MA 02747   (617) 997-7417
SPRINGFIELD JEWISH FEDERATION 1160 DICKINSON STREET .... SPRINGFIELD MA 01108   (413) 737-4313
WORCESTER JEWISH FEDERATION 633 SALISBURY STREET .... WORCESTER MA 01609   (617) 756-1543
CANADIAN JEWISH CONGRESS-MANITOBA REGION
370 HARGRAVE STREET .... WINNIPEG MB R3B 2K1
AMERICAN JEWISH COMMITTEE-BALTIMORE AREA
829 MONSEY BOULEVARD FAYETTE & CALVERT STREETS .... BALTIMORE MD 21201   (301) 539-4777
AMERICAN JEWISH CONGRESS-MARYLAND REGION
7504 SEVEN MILE ROAD .... BALTIMORE MD 21208   (301) 484-8863
BALTIMORE JEWISH COUNCIL 101 WEST MOUNT ROYAL, SUITE 208 .... BALTIMORE MD 21201   (301) 752-2630
JEWISH LABOR COMMITTEE-WASHINGTON, D.C. 7106 WILSON LANE .... BETHESDA MD 22034   (301) 229-0683
JEWISH FEDERATION-COMMUNITY COUNCIL OF SOUTHERN MAINE
57 ASHMONT STREET .... PORTLAND ME 04103   (207) 773-7254
AMERICAN JEWISH COMMITTEE-MICHIGAN-INDIANA AREA
163 MADISON AVENUE .... DETROIT MI 48226   (313) 965-3353
ANTI-DEFAMATION LEAGUE OF B'NAI B'RITH-MICHIGAN
163 MADISON AVENUE, SUITE 120 .... DETROIT MI 48226   (313) 962-9686
JEWISH COMMUNITY COUNCIL OF METROPOLITAN DETROIT
163 MADISON AVENUE .... DETROIT MI 48226   (313) 962-1880
JEWISH LABOR COMMITTEE-MICHIGAN 163 MADISON AVENUE .... DETROIT MI 48226   (313) 965-3939
FLINT JEWISH FEDERATION 120 WEST KEARSLEY .... FLINT MI 48502   (313) 767-5922
AMERICAN JEWISH CONGRESS-MICHIGAN REGION
21550 WEST 12 MILE ROAD .... SOUTHFIELD MI 48076   (313) 357-2766
ANTI-DEFAMATION LEAGUE OF B'NAI B'RITH-MINNESOTA-DAKOTAS
15 SOUTH 9TH STREET BUILDING .... MINNEAPOLIS MN 55402   (612) 338-7816
JEWISH COMMUNITY RELATIONS COUNCIL
15 SOUTH 9TH STREET BLDG., SUITE 400 .... MINNEAPOLIS MN 55402   (612) 338-7816
JEWISH COMMUNITY RELATIONS COUNCIL, ADL OF MINN. & DAKOTAS
15 S. 9TH STREET BUILDING, SUITE 400 .... MINNEAPOLIS MN 55402   (612) 338-7816

ANTI-DEFAMATION LEAGUE OF B'NAI B'RITH-MISSOURI-S. ILLINOIS
225 SOUTH MERAMEC .... CLAYTON MO 63105   (314) 726-3303
AMERICAN JEWISH COMMITTEE-KANSAS CITY AREA
C/O JEWISH FAMILY & CHILDREN'S SERVICES 1115 EAST 65 ST ...... KANSAS CITY MO 64114   (816) 333-1172
JEWISH COMMUNITY RELATIONS BUREAU OF GREATER KANSAS CITY
25 EAST 12TH STREET, 10TH FLOOR .... KANSAS CITY MO 64106   (816) 421-5808
AMERICAN JEWISH COMMITTEE-WEST CENTRAL AREA
7750 CLAYTON ROAD .... ST. LOUIS MO 63101   (314) 647-2519
AMERICAN JEWISH CONGRESS-SOUTHWEST REGION
8420 DELMAR, SUITE 201 .... ST. LOUIS MO 63124   (314) 993-5505
JEWISH COMMUNITY RELATIONS COUNCIL
722 CHESTNUT STREET, SUITE 1019 .... ST. LOUIS MO 63101   (314) 241-2584
JEWISH COMMUNITY RELATIONS COUNCIL
12 MILLSTONE CAMPUS DRIVE .... ST. LOUIS MO 63146   (314) 432-0020
JEWISH LABOR COMMITTEE-MISSOURI 10353 CORBELL .... ST. LOUIS MO 63141
ADL/COMMUNITY RELATIONS COMMITTEE OF THE JEW. FED. OF OMAHA
333 SOUTH 132ND STREET .... OMAHA NE 68154   (402) 333-1303
ANTI-DEFAMATION LEAGUE OF B'NAI B'RITH-PLAIN STATES
333 S. 132ND STREET .... OMAHA NE 68154   (412) 392-2274
JEWISH COMMUNITY RELATIONS COUNCIL OF THE JEW FED OF S. N.J.
2393 W. MARLTON PIKE .... CHERRY HILL NJ 08002   (609) 665-6100
UNITED JEWISH FEDERATION OF METROWEST
60 GLENWOOD AVENUE .... EAST ORANGE NJ 07017   (201) 673-6800
JEWISH FEDERATION OF NORTHERN MIDDLESEX COUNTY, NEW JERSEY
100 MENLO PARK, SUITE 101-102 .... EDISON NJ 08837   (201) 494-3920
JEWISH FEDERATION OF RARITAN VALLEY
2 SOUTH ADELAIDE AVENUE .... HIGHLAND PARK NJ 09804   (201) 246-1905
ANTI-DEFAMATION LEAGUE OF B'NAI B'RITH-NEW JERSEY
513 WEST MOUNT PLEASANT AVENUE .... LIVINGSTON NJ 07039   (201) 994-4546
JEWISH LABOR COMMITTEE-NEW JERSEY 63 OAKWOOD AVENUE .... LIVINGSTON NJ 07039   (201) 992-4709
AMERICAN JEWISH COMMITTEE-NEW JERSEY AREA
303 MILBURN AVENUE .... MILBURN NJ 07041   (201) 379-7844
AMERICAN JEWISH CONGRESS-NEW JERSEY REGION
24 COMMERCE STREET .... NEWARK NJ 02110   (201) 623-4754
JEWISH COMMUNITY RELATIONS COMM. OF UNITED JEWISH COMMUNITY
111 KINDERKAMACK ROAD (BERGEN) .... RIVER EDGE NJ 07661   (201) 488-6800
JEWISH FEDERATION OF CENTRAL NEW JERSEY GREEN LANE .... UNION NJ 07083   (201) 351-5060
FEDERATION OF JEWISH AGENCIES OF ATLANTIC COUNTY
5321 ATLANTIC AVENUE .... VENTNOR CITY NJ 08406   (609) 822-7122
JEWISH FEDERATION OF NORTH JERSEY 1 PIKE DRIVE .... WAYNE NJ 07470   (201) 595-0555
COMMUNITY RELATIONS COMMITTEE OF ALBUQUERQUE
12800 LOMAS, N.E. SUITE F .... ALBUQUERQUE NM 87112   (505) 292-1061
CANADIAN JEWISH CONGRESS-ATLANTIC REGION
5675 SPRING GARDEN ROAD .... HALIFAX NS B3J 1H1
GREATER ALBANY JEWISH FEDERATION 350 WHITE HALL ROAD .... ALBANY NY 12208   (518) 459-8000
JEWISH FEDERATION OF BROOME COUNTY
500 CLUB HOUSE ROAD .... BINGHAMTON NY 13903   (607) 724-2332
AMERICAN JEWISH CONGRESS-BRONX REGION 2510 VALENTINE AVENUE .. BRONX NY 10458   (212) 367-1500
BROOKLYN JEWISH COMMUNITY COUNCIL 16 COURT STREET .... BROOKLYN NY 11201   (718) 332-4459
COUNCIL OF JEWISH ORGANIZATIONS OF BORO PARK
4616 13TH AVENUE .... BROOKLYN NY 11219   (718) 436-5800
CROWN HEIGHTS JEWISH COMMUNITY COUNCIL
1695 PRESIDENT STREET .... BROOKLYN NY 11213   (718) 467-0166
CROWN HEIGHTS JEWISH COMMUNITY COUNCIL
387 KINGSTON AVENUE .... BROOKLYN NY 11225   (718) 778-8808
NATIONAL COMMITTEE ORTHODOX JEWISH COMMUNITIES
260 BROADWAY .... BROOKLYN NY 11211   (718) 936-1911
UNITED JEWISH ORGANIZATIONS OF WILLIAMSBURG
454 BEDFORD AVENUE .... BROOKLYN NY 11211   (718) 387-1888
JEWISH FEDERATION OF GREATER BUFFALO 787 DELAWARE AVENUE .... BUFFALO NY 14209   (716) 886-7750
ANTI-DEFAMATION LEAGUE OF B'NAI B'RITH-LONG ISLAND
2310 HEMPSTEAD TURNPIKE .... EAST MEADOW NY 11554   (516) 731-3400
ELMIRA JEWISH WELFARE FUND P.O. BOX 3087 .... ELMIRA NY 14905   (607) 734-8122
AMERICAN JEWISH COMMITTEE-LONG ISLAND AREA
5 BOND STREET .... GREAT NECK NY 11201   (516) 466-2980
AMERICAN JEWISH CONGRESS-NORTH & SOUTH SHORE REGION
33 GREAT NECK ROAD .... GREAT NECK NY 11021   (516) 466-4650
JEWISH FEDERATION OF GREATER KINGSTON 159 GREEN STREET ...... KINGSTON NY 12401   (914) 338-8131
AGUDATH ISRAEL WORLD ORGANIZATION 5 BEEKMAN STREET ... NEW YORK NY 10038   (212) 791-1800
AGUDATH ISRAEL OF AMERICA 5 BEEKMAN STREET .... NEW YORK NY 10038   (212) 964-1620
AMERICAN JEWISH COMMITTEE 165 EAST 56TH STREET .... NEW YORK NY 10022   (212) 751-4000
AMERICAN JEWISH COMMITTEE-METROPOLITAN NEW YORK REGION
165 EAST 56TH STREET .... NEW YORK NY 10022   (212) 751-4000
AMERICAN JEWISH CONGRESS 15 EAST 84TH STREET .... NEW YORK NY 10028   (212) 879-4500
AMERICAN JEWISH CONGRESS-NEW YORK METROPOLITAN COUNCIL
15 EAST 84TH STREET .... NEW YORK NY 10028   (212) 879-4500
AMERICAN JEWISH PUBLIC RELATIONS SOCIETY 234 FIFTH AVENUE .... NEW YORK NY 10016   (212) 697-5895
ANTI-DEFAMATION LEAGUE OF B'NAI B'RITH
823 UNITED NATIONS PLAZA .... NEW YORK NY 10017   (212) 490-2525
COMMISSION ON SOCIAL ACTION OF REFORM JUDAISM
838 FIFTH AVENUE .... NEW YORK NY 10021   (212) 249-0100
CONFERENCE OF JEWISH COMMUNAL SERVICE, THE
15 E. 26TH STREET .... NEW YORK NY 10010   (212) 683-8056
CONSULTATIVE COUNCIL OF JEWISH ORGANIZATIONS
61 BROADWAY .... NEW YORK NY 10006   (212) 425-5170
COUNCIL OF JEWISH ORGANIZATIONS IN CIVIL SERVICE, INC.
45 E. 33RD STREET .... NEW YORK NY 10016   (212) 689-2015
INTERNATIONAL CENTER OF THE ANTI-DEFAMATION LEAGUE FOUND.
823 UNITED NATIONS PLAZA .... NEW YORK NY 10017   (212) 986-8371
INTERNATIONAL CONFERENCE OF JEWISH COMMUNAL SERVICE
15 E. 26TH STREET .... NEW YORK NY 10010   (212) 683-8056

INTERNATIONAL COUNCIL OF B'NAI B'RITH
823 UNITED NATIONS PLAZA .... NEW YORK **NY** 10017 (212) 557-0018
JEWISH COMMUNITY COUNCIL SERVICES COMMISSION, INC.
15 PARK ROW .... NEW YORK **NY** 10038 (212) 233-2500
JEWISH COMMUNITY COUNCIL OF WASHINGTON HEIGHTS IN INWOOD
121 BENNETT AVENUE .... NEW YORK **NY** 10033 (212) 568-5450
JEWISH COMMUNITY RELATIONS COUNCIL OF NEW YORK
111 WEST 40TH STREET, SUITE 2600 .... NEW YORK **NY** 10018 (212) 221-1535
JEWISH DEFENSE LEAGUE (EXEC. & ADMN. OFFICES)
34 WEST 38TH STREET, 6TH FLOOR .... NEW YORK **NY** 10018 (212) 382-3333
JEWISH LABOR COMMITTEE 25 EAST 78TH STREET .... NEW YORK **NY** 10021 (212) 535-3700
JEWISH LABOR COMMITTEE-NEW YORK (NATIONAL OFFICE)
25 EAST 78TH STREET .... NEW YORK **NY** 10021 (212) 535-3700
JEWISH MOBILIZATION COMMITTEE 3 W. 16TH STREET .... NEW YORK **NY** 10011 (212) 929-1525
JEWISH POVERTY COORDINATING COUNCIL 15 PARK ROW .... NEW YORK **NY** 10038 (212) 267-9500
JEWISH RIGHTS COUNCIL 501 W. 123RD STREET .... NEW YORK **NY** 10027 (212) 362-3353
JOINT COMM. ON SOC. ACTION/COMM. ON JEW. COMMUNITY & PUB. POL
155 FIFTH AVENUE .... NEW YORK **NY** 10010 (212) 533-7800
NATIONAL JEWISH COMMUNITY RELATIONS ADVISORY COUNCIL
443 PARK AVENUE S .... NEW YORK **NY** 10016 (212) 684-6950
NEW JEWISH AGENDA 150 FIFTH AVENUE, #1002 .... NEW YORK **NY** 10011 (212) 620-0828
SOUTHERN BKLYN COMMUNITY ORG. (SBCO)
C/O AGUDATH ISRAEL OF AMERICA, 5 BEEKMAN STREET .... NEW YORK **NY** 10038 (212) 964-1620
UNITED JEWISH COUNCIL OF THE EAST SIDE 235 EAST BROADWAY .... NEW YORK **NY** 10002 (212) 233-6037
WORLD JEWISH CONGRESS ONE PARK AVENUE, SUITE 418 .... NEW YORK **NY** 10016 (212) 679-0600
WORLD JEWISH CONGRESS 15 EAST 84TH STREET .... NEW YORK **NY** 10028 (212) 879-4500
JEWISH COMMUNITY FEDERATION OF ROCHESTER, N.Y., INC.
50 CHESTNUT STREET 1200 CHESTNUT PLAZA .... ROCHESTER **NY** 14604 (716) 325-3393
JEWISH FEDERATION OF GREATER SCHENECTADY
2565 BALLTOWN ROAD .... SCHENECTADY **NY** 12309 (518) 393-1136
SYRACUSE JEWISH FEDERATION
2223 E. GENESSEE STREET P.O. BOX 5004 .... SYRACUSE **NY** 13250 (315) 422-4104
ANTI-DEFAMATION LEAGUE OF B'NAI B'RITH-NY STATE REGIONAL
65 SOUTH BROADWAY .... TARRYTOWN **NY** 10591 (914) 332-1166
JEWISH COMMUNITY COUNCIL 2310 ONEIDA STREET .... UTICA **NY** 13501 (315) 733-2343
AMERICAN JEWISH COMMITTEE-NEW JERSEY-NEW YORK REGION
48 MAMARONECK AVENUE .... WHITE PLAINS **NY** 10601 (914) 948-5585
JEWISH COUNCIL OF YONKERS 122 SOUTH BROADWAY .... YONKERS **NY** 10701 (914) 423-5009
AKRON JEWISH COMMUNITY FEDERATION 750 WHITE POND DRIVE .... AKRON **OH** 44320 (216) 867-7850
AMERICAN JEWISH CONGRESS-NORTHERN OHIO REGION
23715 MERCANTILE ROAD .... BEACHWOOD **OH** 44122 (216) 464-5244
JEWISH COMMUNITY FEDERATION 2631 HARVARD AVENUE, N.W. .... CANTON **OH** 44709 (216) 452-6444
AMERICAN JEWISH COMMITTEE-CINCINNATI AREA
105 WEST FOURTH STREET SUITE 818 .... CINCINNATI **OH** 45202 (513) 621-4020
JEWISH COMMUNITY RELATIONS COUNCIL
105 WEST FOURTH STREET, SUITE 614 .... CINCINNATI **OH** 45202 (513) 241-5620
AMERICAN JEWISH COMMITTEE-OHIO-KENTUCKY AREA
1220 EAST HURON ROAD, SUITE 703 .... CLEVELAND **OH** 44115 (216) 781-6035
JEWISH COMMUNITY FEDERATION 1750 EUCLID AVENUE .... CLEVELAND **OH** 44115 (216) 566-9200
JEWISH LABOR COMMITTEE-OHIO 1980 S. GREEN ROAD .... CLEVELAND **OH** 44121 (216) 381-4515
ANTI-DEFAMATION LEAGUE OF B'NAI B'RITH-OHIO-KENTUCKY
1175 COLLEGE AVENUE .... COLUMBUS **OH** 43209 (614) 239-8414
COMMUNITY RELATIONS COMMITTEE OF THE COLUMBUS JEWISH FED.
1175 COLLEGE AVENUE .... COLUMBUS **OH** 42209 (614) 237-7686
COMMUNITY RELATIONS COUNCIL (JESSE PHILIPS BLDG.)
4501 DENLINGER ROAD .... DAYTON **OH** 45426 (513) 854-4150
JEWISH FEDERATION OF GREATER DAYTON 4501 DENLINGER ROAD .... DAYTON **OH** 45426 (513) 854-4150
JEWISH WELFARE FEDERATION OF TOLEDO 6505 SYLVANIA AVENUE .... SYLVANIA **OH** 43560 (419) 885-4461
YOUNGSTOWN AREA JEWISH FEDERATION
505 GYPSY LANE, P.O. BOX 449 .... YOUNGSTOWN **OH** 44501 (216) 746-3251
JEWISH COMMUNITY COUNCIL
3022 N.W. EXPRESSWAY, SUITE 116 .... OKLAHOMA CITY **OK** 73112 (405) 949-0111
JEWISH FEDERATION OF TULSA 2021 E. 71ST STREET .... TULSA **OK** 74136 (918) 495-1100
CANADIAN JEWISH CONGRESS-ONTARIO REGION
150 BEVERLEY STREET .... TORONTO **ON** M5T 1Y6
NATIONAL JOINT COMMUNITY RELATIONS COMMITTEE
150 BEVERLEY STREET .... TORONTO **ON** M5T 1Y6 (416) 869-3811
AMERICAN JEWISH COMMITTEE-PORTLAND AREA
1220 S.W. MORRISON, SUITE 930 .... PORTLAND **OR** 97205 (503) 295-6761
JEWISH FEDERATION OF PORTLAND
4850 S.W. SCHOLLS FERRY ROAD, SUITE 304 .... PORTLAND **OR** 97225 (503) 297-8104
JEWISH FEDERATION OF ALLENTOWN 702 N. 22ND STREET .... ALLENTOWN **PA** 18104 (215) 821-5500
JEWISH COMMUNITY COUNCIL
702 G. DANIEL BALDWIN BUILDING, 1001 STATE STREET .... ERIE **PA** 16501 (814) 455-5575
JEWISH FEDERATION OF THE DELAWARE VALLEY
28 N. PENNSYLVANIA AVENUE .... MORRISVILLE **PA** 19067 (215) 736-8022
AMERICAN JEWISH COMMITTEE-MIDDLE ATLANTIC REGION
1411 WALNUT STREET, SUITE 1004 .... PHILADELPHIA **PA** 19102 (215) 735-6182
AMERICAN JEWISH CONGRESS-PENNSYLVANIA REGION
255 SOUTH 16TH STREET .... PHILADELPHIA **PA** 19102 (215) 546-4366
ANTI-DEFAMATION LEAGUE OF B'NAI B'RITH-PA.-WEST VA.-DEL.
225 S. 15TH STREET, SUITE 614 .... PHILADELPHIA **PA** 19102 (215) 735-4267
JEWISH COMMUNITY RELATIONS COUNCIL OF GREATER PHILADELPHIA
1520 LOCUST STREET, 5TH FLOOR .... PHILADELPHIA **PA** 19102 (215) 545-8430
JEWISH LABOR COMMITTEE-PENNSYLVANIA
1211 CHESTNUT STREET .... PHILADELPHIA **PA** 19107 (215) 568-4770
AMERICAN JEWISH COMMITTEE-WESTERN PENNSYLVANIA AREA
128 NORTH CRAIG STREET SUITE 215 .... PITTSBURGH **PA** 15213 (412) 683-7927
JEWISH LABOR COMMITTEE-PENNSYLVANIA
5260 CENTRE AVENUE, SUITE 312 .... PITTSBURGH **PA** 15232 (412) 687-6857
UNITED JEWISH FEDERATION OF PITTSBURGH 234 MCKEE PLACE .... PITTSBURGH **PA** 15213 (412) 681-8000
SCRANTON-LACKAWANNA JEWISH FEDERATION, THE
601 JEFFERSON AVENUE .... SCRANTON **PA** 18510 (717) 961-2300
JEWISH FEDERATION OF GREATER WILKES-BARRE
60 S. RIVER STREET .... WILKES-BARRE **PA** 18702 (717) 822-4146
CANADIAN JEWISH CONGRESS 1590 AVENUE DOCTEUR PENFIELD .... MONTREAL **QU** H3G 1C5 (514) 931-7531
COMBINED JEWISH ORGANIZATIONS OF MONTREAL
4180 DE COURTRAI, SUITE 218 .... MONTREAL **QU** H3S 1C3 (514) 735-6577
JEWISH FEDERATION OF RHODE ISLAND 130 SESSIONS STREET .... PROVIDENCE **RI** 02906 (401) 421-4111
CHARLESTON JEWISH FEDERATION
1645 RAOUL WALLENBERG BLVD., P.O. BOX 31298 .... CHARLESTON **SC** 29206 (803) 787-2023
JEWISH COMMUNITY RELATIONS COUNCIL 6560 POPLAR AVENUE .... MEMPHIS **TN** 38183 (901) 767-5161
MEMPHIS JEWISH FEDERATION 6505 POPLAR AVENUE, P.O. BOX 38268 .... MEMPHIS **TN** 38138 (901) 767-7100
JEWISH FEDERATION OF NASHVILLE & MIDDLE TENNESSEE
3500 WEST END AVENUE .... NASHVILLE **TN** 37205 (615) 269-0729
JEWISH COMMUNITY COUNCIL OF AUSTIN
5758 BALCONES DRIVE, SUITE 104 .... AUSTIN **TX** 78731 (512) 451-6435
AMERICAN JEWISH COMMITTEE-SOUTHWEST REGION
12870 HILLCREST ROAD .... DALLAS **TX** 75201 (214) 387-2943
AMERICAN JEWISH CONGRESS-DALLAS CHAPTER P.O. BOX 12826 .... DALLAS **TX** 75225 (214) 368-2731
ANTI-DEFAMATION LEAGUE OF B'NAI B'RITH-DALLAS
12800 HILLCREST ROAD SUITE 219 .... DALLAS **TX** 75230 (214) 960-0342
JEWISH FEDERATION OF GREATER DALLAS
7800 NORTHAVEN, SUITE 104 .... DALLAS **TX** 75203 (214) 369-3313
JEWISH COMMUNITY RELATIONS COMMITTEE
405 MARDI GRAS DRIVE, P.O. BOX 12097 .... EL PASO **TX** 79912 (915) 584-4437
JEWISH FEDERATION OF FORTH WORTH & TARRANT COUNTY
6801 DAN DANCIGER ROAD .... FORT WORTH **TX** 76133 (817) 292-3081
AMERICAN JEWISH COMMITTEE-HOUSTON AREA 3930 KIRBY DRIVE .... HOUSTON **TX** 77098 (713) 524-4789
ANTI-DEFAMATION LEAGUE OF B'NAI B'RITH-SOUTHWEST-HOUSTON
4211 SOUTHWEST FREEWAY SUITE 209 .... HOUSTON **TX** 77027 (713) 627-3490
JEWISH FEDERATION OF GREATER HOUSTON
5603 SOUTH BRAESWOOD .... HOUSTON **TX** 77096 (713) 729-7000
JEWISH FEDERATION OF SAN ANTONIO 8434 AHERN DRIVE .... SAN ANTONIO **TX** 78216 (512) 341-8234
UNITED JEWISH COMMUNITY 2700 SPRING ROAD, P.O. BOX 6680 .. NEWPORT NEWS **VA** 23606 (804) 595-5544
UNITED JEWISH FEDERATION OF TIDEWATER, THE
7300 NEWPORT AVENUE, P.O. BOX 9776 .... NORFOLK **VA** 23505 (804) 489-8040
ANTI-DEFAMATION LEAGUE OF B'NAI B'RITH-N. CAROLINA-VIRGINIA
3311 W. BROAD STREET .... RICHMOND **VA** 23230 (804) 355-2884
JEWISH COMMUNITY FEDERATION OF RICHMOND
P.O. BOX 8237, 5403 MONUMENT AVENUE .... RICHMOND **VA** 23226 (804) 288-0045
AMERICAN JEWISH COMMITTEE-SEATTLE AREA
729 JOSEPH VANCE BLDG .... SEATTLE **WA** 98101 (206) 622-6315
ANTI-DEFAMATION LEAGUE OF B'NAI B'RITH-PACIFIC NORTHWEST
1809 7TH AVENUE, SUITE 1609 .... SEATTLE **WA** 98101 (206) 624-5750
MADISON JEWISH COMMUNITY COUNCIL 310 N. MIDVALE BLVD .... MADISON **WI** 53705 (608) 231-3426
AMERICAN JEWISH COMMITTEE-MILWAUKEE AREA
759 NORTH MILWAUKEE STREET .... MILWAUKEE **WI** 53202 (414) 273-6833
ANTI-DEFAMATION LEAGUE OF B'NAI B'RITH-WISC.-UPPER MIDWEST
1360 N. PROSPECT AVENUE .... MILWAUKEE **WI** 53202 (414) 276-7920
MILWAUKEE JEWISH COUNCIL 1360 N. PROSPECT AVENUE .... MILWAUKEE **WI** 53202 (414) 276-7920

COMPUTER SERVICES

DAVKA CORPORATION 845 NORTH MICHIGAN AVENUE, SUITE 843 .... CHICAGO **IL** 60611 (312) 944-4070
ANTHRO-DIGITAL, INC. P.O. BOX 1385 .... PITTSFIELD **MA** 01202 (413) 448-8278
BRAMSON ORT 44 E. 23RD STREET .... NEW YORK **NY** 10010 (212) 677-7420
CLAL TRADING (N.Y.) INC. 440 PARK AVENUE SOUTH .... NEW YORK **NY** 10016 (212) 889-7750

CONVERSION ORGANIZATIONS

NAT'L JEWISH INFO. SERVICE FOR THE PROPAGATION OF JUDAISM
5174 WEST 8TH STREET .... LOS ANGELES **CA** 90036
RABBI SAMUEL KATZ, RABBINICAL COUNCIL OF CALIFORNIA 525 SOUTH FAIRFAX
AVENUE, C/O CONGREGATION OHEV SHALOM .... LOS ANGELES **CA** 90036 (213) 653-7190
CHICAGO BOARD OF RABBIS 1 SOUTH FRANKLIN .... CHICAGO **IL** 60606 (312) 427-5863
CHICAGO RABBINICAL COUNCIL 3525 WEST PETERSON .... CHICAGO **IL** 60659 (312) 588-1600
JEWISH CONVERSION CENTER 752 STELTON STREET .... TEANECK **NJ** 07666 (201) 837-7552
CONVERSION CLASSES-NEW YORK FEDERATION OF REFORM SYNAGOGUES
838 FIFTH AVENUE .... NEW YORK **NY** 10021 (212) 249-0100
JEWISH NEWCOMER SERVICE 6651 S.W. CAPITAL HIGHWAY .... PORTLAND **OR** 97201 (503) 244-0111

CORRESPONDENCE COURSES

ALTERNATIVES IN RELIGIOUS EDUCATION 3945 ONEIDA STREET .... DENVER **CO** 80237 (303) 363-7779
SPERTUS COLLEGE OF JUDAICA 618 SOUTH MICHIGAN AVENUE .... CHICAGO **IL** 60605 (312) 922-9012
HEINLE & HEINLE ENTERPRISES 29 LEXINGTON ROAD .... CONCORD **MA** 01742 (617) 369-7525
THE JEWISH CENTER FOR SPECIAL EDUCATION 430 KENT AVENUE .... BROOKLYN **NY** 11211 (718) 782-0064
ACADEMY FOR JEWISH STUDIES WITHOUT WALLS, THE
165 E. 56TH STREET .... NEW YORK **NY** 10022 (212) 751-4000
AMERICAN ASSOCIATION FOR JEWISH EDUCATION
114 FIFTH AVENUE .... NEW YORK **NY** 10011 (212) 675-5656
TARBUTH FOUNDATION 129 WEST 67TH STREET .... NEW YORK **NY** 10023 (212) 874-7837
THE COMMISSION ON JEWISH AFFAIRS, AMERICAN JEWISH CONGRESS
15 EAST 84TH STREET .... NEW YORK **NY** 10028 (212) 879-4500
WORLD ZIONIST ORGANIZATION, PUBLICATIONS DEPARTMENT
515 PARK AVENUE .... NEW YORK **NY** 10022 (212) 752-0600

COUNSELING

VALLEY BETH SHALOM COUNSELING CENTER
  15739 VENTURA BOULEVARD .... ENCINO CA 91436   (213) 788-6000
ALCOHOLISM PROGRAM, JEWISH FAMILY SERVICE
  6505 WILSHIRE BOULEVARD .... LOS ANGELES CA 90048   (213) 852-1234
CHABAD DRUG REHABILITATION AND MENTAL HEALTH PROGRAMS
  6333 WILSHIRE BOULEVARD .... LOS ANGELES CA 90048   (213) 653-9230
CHAPLAINCY SERVICE, BOARD OF RABBIS OF SOUTHERN CALIFORNIA
  6505 WILSHIRE BOULEVARD .... LOS ANGELES CA 90048   (213) 852-1234
JULIA SINGER PRE-SCHOOL PSYCHIATRIC CENTER
  8730 ALDEN DRIVE .... LOS ANGELES CA 90048   (213) 855-5000
ONE PARENT INFORMATION NETWORK 8857 SATURN STREET .... LOS ANGELES CA 90035   (213) 556-1687
THE CULT CLINIC, JEWISH FAMILY SERVICE
  6505 WILSHIRE BOULEVARD .... LOS ANGELES CA 90048   (213) 852-1234
THE WIDOWS CENTER .... LOS ANGELES CA 90064   (213) 933-5411
JEWISH CAREER COUNSELING & EMPLOYMENT SERVICE
  703 MARKET STREET, ROOM 2007 .... SAN FRANCISCO CA 94103   (415) 777-2022
TEMPLE JUDEA COMMUNITY OUTREACH CENTER
  5429 LINDLEY AVENUE .... TARZANA CA 91356   (213) 780-4994
B'NAI B'RITH CAREER & COUNSELING SERVICES
  1640 RHODE ISLAND AVENUE N.W. .... WASHINGTON DC 20036   (202) 857-6600
TAMPA JEWISH SOCIAL SERVICE 2808 HORATIO .... TAMPA FL 33609   (813) 872-4451
ARK, THE 3509 W. LAWRENCE AVENUE .... CHICAGO IL 60625   (312) 478-9600
ROFEH 1710 BEACON STREET .... BROOKLINE MA 02146   (617) 566-9182
ASSOCIATED PLACEMENT & GUIDANCE SERVICE
  5750 PARK HEIGHTS AVENUE .... BALTIMORE MD 21215   (301) 466-9200
CENTER FOR COUNSELING REFERRAL, THE 6 WYNKOOP COURT .... BETHESDA MD 20034
JEWISH SOCIAL SERVICE AGENCY & JEWISH FOSTER HOME
  6123 MONTROSE ROAD .... ROCKVILLE MD 20852   (301) 881-3700
CHAPLAINCY SERVICE TO STATE INSTITUTIONS
  2640 QUENTIN AVENUE S .... ST. LOUIS PARK MN 55426   (612) 922-0322
JEWISH COUNSELING SERVICE 161 MILLBURN AVENUE .... MILLBURN NJ 07041   (201) 467-3300
RABBINIC CENTER FOR RESEARCH & COUNSELING
  128 E. DUDLEY AVENUE .... WESTFIELD NJ 07090   (201) 233-0419
INTERBOROUGH CONSULTATION CENTER 1402 AVENUE N .... BROOKLYN NY 11230   (718) 375-1200
OHEL CHILDREN'S HOME & FAMILY SERVICES 4423 16TH AVENUE ...... BROOKLYN NY 11204   (718) 851-6300
SHALVA COUNSELING CENTER 1402 AVENUE N .... BROOKLYN NY 11230   (718) 375-1200
JEWISH COMMUNITY SERVICES OF LONG ISLAND
  1600 CENTRAL AVENUE .... FAR ROCKAWAY NY 11691   (718) 327-1600
JEWISH COMMUNITY SERVICES OF LONG ISLAND
  50 CLINTON STREET .... HEMPSTEAD NY 11550   (516) 485-5710
WESTCHESTER JEWISH COMMUNITY SERVICES, INC.
  9 W. PROSPECT AVENUE .... MT. VERNON NY 10550   (914) 668-8938
B'NAI B'RITH - CAREER & COUNSELING SERVICES
  823 UNITED NATIONS PLAZA .... NEW YORK NY 10017   (212) 490-0677
COUNSELING CENTER OF N.Y. FEDERATION OF REFORM SYNAGOGUES
  838 FIFTH AVENUE .... NEW YORK NY 10021   (212) 249-7700
JACS FOUNDATION (JEWISH ALCOHOLICS) 10 EAST 73RD STREET ...... NEW YORK NY 10021   (212) 737-6261
JEWISH CONCILLIATION BOARD OF AMERICA 120 WEST 57TH STREET .. NEW YORK NY 10019   (212) 582-3577
JEWISH CONSULTATION SERVICE .... NEW YORK NY   (212) 752-2406
JEWISH UNMARRIED MOTHERS SERVICE 12 E. 94TH STREET .... NEW YORK NY 10028   (212) 876-3050
LOSS & BEREAVEMENT CENTER OF N.Y. 170 EAST 83RD STREET .... NEW YORK NY 10028   (212) 879-5655
MID-WAY COUNSELING CENTER 27 E. 20TH STREET .... NEW YORK NY 10003   (212) 475-7081
JEWISH COMMUNITY SERVICES OF LONG ISLAND
  97-45 QUEENS BLVD. .... REGO PARK NY 11374   (718) 896-9090
JEWISH COMMUNITY SERVICES OF LONG ISLAND
  22 LAWRENCE AVENUE .... SMITHTOWN NY 11787   (516) 724-6300
JEWISH COMMUNITY SERVICES OF LONG ISLAND
  175 JERICHO TURNPIKE .... SYOSSET NY 11791   (516) 364-8040

CULTURAL ORGANIZATIONS

BRANDEIS-BARDIN INSTITUTE, THE 1101 PEPPERTREE LANE .... BRANDEIS CA 93064   (213) 348-7201
PATRONS ART SOCIETY 4455 LOS FELIZ BLVD., SUITE 804 .... LOS ANGELES CA 90027   (213) 664-7703
SEPHARDIC HEBREW CENTER 4911 W. 59TH STREET .... LOS ANGELES CA 90056   (213) 295-5541
B'NAI B'RITH INTERNATIONAL 1640 RHODE ISLAND AVENUE N.W. .... WASHINGTON DC 20036   (202) 857-6600
JEWISH CULTURAL ORGANIZATION 429 LENOX AVENUE .... MIAMI BEACH FL 33139   (305) 673-9079
AMERICA-ISRAEL CULTURAL FOUNDATION 79 WEST MONROE .... CHICAGO IL 60611   (312) 726-4672
JEWISH CULTURAL CLUBS OF CHICAGO 1740 WEST GREENLEAF .... CHICAGO IL 60626   (312) 338-9283
VLADECK EDUCATIONAL CENTER WORKMEN'S CIRCLE
  6500 NORTH CALIFORNIA .... CHICAGO IL 60645   (312) 274-5400
ARTHUR SIDNEY MENDEL EDUCATIONAL CENTER
  BROADWAY & DELAWARE .... BENTON HARBOR MI 49022   (616) 925-8021
JEWISH EDUCATIONAL CENTER 1602 E. 2ND STREET .... DULUTH MN 55812   (218) 724-8857
KOLLEL ZECHER NAFTALI, THE 1550 SUMMIT AVENUE .... HILLSIDE NJ 07205   (201) 923-6191
JEWISH ACADEMY OF ARTS & SCIENCES, INC.
  123 GREGORY AVENUE .... WEST ORANGE NJ 07052   (201) 731-1137
SHOLEM ALEICHEM FOLK INSTITUTE, INC. 3301 BAINBRIDGE AVENUE ...... BRONX NY 10467   (212) 881-6555
AKIVA JEWISH CULTURE CLUBS OF THE N.Y.C. PUBLIC HIGH SCHOOLS
  1577 CONEY ISLAND AVENUE .... BROOKLYN NY 11230   (718) 258-3585
HEBREW EDUCATIONAL SOCIETY 9502 SEAVIEW AVENUE .... BROOKLYN NY 11236   (718) 241-3000
CENTER FOR RETURN 85-35 117TH STREET .... KEW GARDENS NY 11418   (718) 849-6787
AMERICAN BIBLICAL ENCYCLOPEDIA SOCIETY 24 W. MAPLE AVENUE ..... MONSEY NY 10952   (914) 428-8079
JEWISH COMMUNITY CENTER OF MONTICELLO
  PARK AVENUE, BOX 208 .... MONTICELLO NY 12701   (914) 794-4560
ABRAHAM GOODMAN HOUSE 129 WEST 67TH STREET .... NEW YORK NY 10023   (212) 362-8060
AMERICAN ACADEMY FOR JEWISH RESEARCH 3080 BROADWAY .... NEW YORK NY 10027   (212) 678-8864
AMERICAN HISTADRUT CULTURAL EXCHANGE INSTITUTE
  33 E. 67TH STREET .... NEW YORK NY 10021   (212) 628-1000

AMERICAN JEWISH INSTITUTE 250 W. 57TH STREET .... NEW YORK NY 10019   (212) 582-5318
ASSOC. OF JEWISH LIBRARIES, C/O NAT'L FOUND. JEWISH CULTURE
  122 E. 42ND STREET, ROOM 1512 .... NEW YORK NY 10168   (212) 490-2280
CENTRAL YIDDISH CULTURE ORGANIZATION 25 EAST 78TH STREET .... NEW YORK NY 10021   (212) 535-4320
CONFERENCE ON JEWISH SOCIAL STUDIES
  250 W. 57TH STREET, ROOM 904 .... NEW YORK NY 10019   (212) 247-4718
CONFERENCE ON JEWISH SOCIAL STUDIES, INC. 2112 BROADWAY .... NEW YORK NY 10023   (212) 724-5336
CONGRESS FOR JEWISH CULTURE 25 E. 21ST STREET .... NEW YORK NY 10010   (212) 505-8040
DEPARTMENT OF EDUCATION & CULTURE-WORLD ZIONIST ORGANIZATION
  515 PARK AVENUE .... NEW YORK NY 10022   (212) 752-0600
EDUCATIONAL ALLIANCE 197 EAST BROADWAY .... NEW YORK NY 10002   (212) 475-6200
ELIAS A. COHEN INSTITUTE 251 W. 100 STREET .... NEW YORK NY 10025
HEBREW ARTS SCHOOL FOR MUSIC & DANCE 129 WEST 67TH STREET .. NEW YORK NY 10023   (212) 362-8060
HEBREW CULTURE FOUNDATION 1776 BROADWAY .... NEW YORK NY 10019   (212) 247-0741
HEBREW CULTURE FOUNDATION 515 PARK AVENUE .... NEW YORK NY 10022   (212) 752-0600
HEBREW CULTURE SERV. COMM. FOR AM. HIGH SCHOOLS & COLLEGES
  1776 BROADWAY .... NEW YORK NY 10019   (212) 247-0741
HEBREW LANGUAGE & CULTURE ASSOCIATION 1841 BROADWAY ...... NEW YORK NY 10023   (212) 581-5151
HINENI 155 E 38TH STREET .... NEW YORK NY 10016   (212) 557-1190
INSTITUTE FOR JEWISH EXPERIENCE, THE 157 W. 57TH STREET .... NEW YORK NY 10019   (212) 265-0370
INSTITUTE OF ADULT JEWISH STUDIES 270 W. 89TH STREET .... NEW YORK NY 10024   (212) 787-7600
INSTITUTE OF JEWISH HUMANITIES 47 BEEKMAN STREET .... NEW YORK NY 10038   (212) 227-7800
ISRAEL-IBEROAMERICAN CULTURAL INSTITUTE 515 PARK AVENUE .... NEW YORK NY 10022   (212) 752-0600
JEWISH BOOK COUNCIL OF JWB 15 E. 26TH STREET .... NEW YORK NY 10010   (212) 532-4949
JEWISH CULTURAL CLUBS & SOCIETIES 1133 BROADWAY .... NEW YORK NY 10010   (212) 675-8854
JEWISH HISTORICAL SOCIETY OF NEW YORK 8 W. 70TH STREET .... NEW YORK NY 10023   (212) 873-0300
JEWISH MINORITIES RESEARCH 16 E. 85TH STREET .... NEW YORK NY 10028
JEWISH MUSIC COUNCIL 15 E. 26TH STREET .... NEW YORK NY 10010   (212) 532-4949
JEWISH PROGRAM SERVICE COMMITTEE 1133 BROADWAY .... NEW YORK NY 10010   (212) 675-8854
JEWISH WELFARE BOARD 15 E. 26TH STREET .... NEW YORK NY 10011   (212) 532-4949
JEWISH WELFARE BOARD-ARMED FORCES & VETERANS SERVICE
  15 E. 26TH STREET .... NEW YORK NY 10010   (212) 532-4949
JEWISH WELFARE BOARD-COMMISSION ON JEWISH CHAPLAINCY
  15 E. 26TH STREET .... NEW YORK NY 10010   (212) 532-4949
JEWISH WELFARE BOARD-JEWISH BOOK COUNCIL 15 E. 26TH STREET .. NEW YORK NY 10010   (212) 532-4949
JEWISH WELFARE BOARD-JEWISH LECTURE BUREAU
  15 E. 26TH STREET .... NEW YORK NY 10010   (212) 532-4949
JEWISH WELFARE BOARD-JEWISH MEDIA SERVICE 15 E. 26TH STREET .. NEW YORK NY 10010   (212) 532-4949
JEWISH WELFARE BOARD-JEWISH MUSIC COUNCIL
  15 E. 26TH STREET .... NEW YORK NY 10010   (212) 532-4949
JEWISH WELFARE BOARD-NATIONAL OFFICE 15 E. 26TH STREET ...... NEW YORK NY 10010   (212) 532-4949
JEWISH WELFARE BOARD-WOMEN'S ORGANIZATIONS SERVICE
  15 E. 26TH STREET .... NEW YORK NY 10010   (212) 532-4949
LEO BAECK INSTITUTE, INC. 129 E. 73RD STREET .... NEW YORK NY 10021   (212) 744-6400
MAX WEINREICH CENTER FOR ADVANCED STUDIES
  1048 FIFTH AVENUE .... NEW YORK NY 10028   (212) 535-6700
MEMORIAL FOUNDATION FOR JEWISH CULTURE 15 E. 26TH STREET .... NEW YORK NY 10010   (212) 679-4074
MESORAH INSTITUTE 111 EIGHTH AVENUE .... NEW YORK NY 10011   (212) 691-0894
NATIONAL FOUNDATION FOR JEWISH CULTURE
  408 CHANIN BUILDING, 122 EAST 42ND STREET .... NEW YORK NY 10017   (212) 490-2280
NATIONAL HEBREW CULTURE COUNCIL 14 E. 4TH STREET .... NEW YORK NY 10012   (212) 674-8412
NATIONAL JEWISH MUSIC COUNCIL 15 E. 26TH STREET .... NEW YORK NY 10010   (212) 532-4949
NATIONAL JEWISH RESOURCE CENTER 421 SEVENTH AVENUE .... NEW YORK NY 10001   (212) 714-9500
NATIONAL JEWISH WELFARE BOARD 15 EAST 26TH STREET .... NEW YORK NY 10010   (212) 532-4949
NEW YORK UNIVERSITY JEWISH CULTURAL FOUNDATION
  LOEB STUDENT CENTER ROOM 715, 566 LA GUARDIA PLACE ...... NEW YORK NY 10012   (212) 598-3584
RESEARCH INSTITUTE OF RELIGIOUS JEWRY 471 WEST END AVENUE ... NEW YORK NY 10024
SAM & ESTHER MINSKOFF CULTURAL CENTER 164 E. 68TH STREET ..... NEW YORK NY 10021   (212) 737-1196
SINAI HERITAGE CENTER 350 5TH AVENUE SUITE 6809 .... NEW YORK NY 10118   (212) 967-8060
USDAN CENTER FOR CREATIVE & PERFORMING ARTS
  315 WEST 57TH STREET .... NEW YORK NY 10019   (212) 757-5015
WORKMEN'S CIRCLE 175 EAST BROADWAY .... NEW YORK NY 10002   (212) 674-3400
WORKMEN'S CIRCLE COMMUNITY CENTER 45 EAST 33RD STREET ..... NEW YORK NY 10016   (212) 889-6800
YIVO INSTITUTE FOR JEWISH RESEARCH 1048 FIFTH AVENUE .... NEW YORK NY 10028   (212) 535-6700
YIDDISHER KULTUR FARBAND - YKUF 1123 BROADWAY .... NEW YORK NY 10019   (212) 692-0708
CANADA-ISRAEL CULTURAL FOUNDATION
  60 BLOOR STREET WEST, SUITE 1003 .... TORONTO ON M4W 3B8   (416) 921-2103
CANADIAN FOUNDATION FOR JEWISH CULTURE
  150 BEVERLEY STREET .... TORONTO ON M5T 1Y6   (416) 869-3811
SOCIETY FOR THE SOCIOLOGICAL STUDY OF JEWRY, THE
  3718 LOCUST WALK .... PHILADELPHIA PA 19104

DAIRY PRODUCTS

MOSER FARMS DAIRY 58 WEST ROAD .... ROCKVILLE CT 06066   (203) 872-8346
RASKAS DAIRY 25 NORTH BRENTWOOD .... ST. LOUIS MO 63105   (800) 325-0071
CHEESE'N THINGS 1117 AVENUE J .... BROOKLYN NY 11230   (212) 377-4911
GOLD STAR ICE CREAM COMPANY, INC.
  921 EAST NEW YORK AVENUE .... BROOKLYN NY 11203   (212) 756-1500
J & J DAIRY PRODUCTS, INC 72 STEUBEN STREET .... BROOKLYN NY 11205   (212) 636-1888
JASON DAIRY PRODUCTS CO., INC. 9204 DITMAS AVENUE .... BROOKLYN NY 11236   (212) 498-1881
LA GVINA CHEESE CORP. 379 KINGSTON AVENUE .... BROOKLYN NY 11213   (212) 604-0200
METRO KOSHER ICES 147 METROPOLITAN AVENUE .... BROOKLYN NY 11212   (212) 388-1323
TAAM-TOV FOODS, INC. 344 AVENUE Y .... BROOKLYN NY 11223   (212) 376-5400
BISON FOODS COMPANY 196 SCOTT STREET .... BUFFALO NY 14204   (716) 854-8400
LEIBEL'S KOSHER SPECIALTIES 27 1/2 ESSEX STREET .... NEW YORK NY 10002   (212) 254-0335
MILLER'S CHEESE CORP. 174 DUANE STREET .... NEW YORK NY 10013   (212) 925-1773
MILLER'S CHEESE 2192 BROADWAY .... NEW YORK NY 10023   (212) 595-6736
WORLD CHEESE COMPANY 172 DUANE STREET .... NEW YORK NY 10013   (212) 925-8855

[njrc] Educating Leaders for Jewish Leadership

NATIONAL JEWISH RESOURCE CENTER

421 SEVENTH AVENUE
NEW YORK, NEW YORK 10001
(212) 714-9500

The Center for Learning and Leadership . . .

The NJRC offers a year-round program of retreats, Shabbatonim, institutes, and family weekends. We are currently establishing a national retreat center in the New York area to expand our programs and activities.

NJRC: A Unique Education/Training Center . . .

NJRC conducts leadership study groups, institutes and retreats, conferences and colloquia, using advanced communications media.

Building Jewish LAY Leadership . . .

At the Resouce Center, Jewish lay leaders renew their purpose and enhance their Jewish consciousness and identity, while they contribute to the Center's effectiveness for others. And the Center helps identify, nurture and motivate talented new individuals to assume the obligations and responsibilities of leadership in the Jewish community.

As a result of Center programs, Jewish consciousnes, experience and memories are evoked and deepened.

Building Jewish RELIGIOUS Leadership . . .

The National Jewish Resource Center serves as a systematic training center for scholars and rabbis to confront the religious issue of contemporary Jewish life.

Building Jewish PROFESSIONAL Leadership . . .

Professionals make significant contributions to Jewish community, cultural family and organizational life. NJRC conducts intensive leadership development programs for Federations, UJA and other Jewish organization staffs.

NJRC: A Resource for Holocaust Study . . .

Perhaps no one organization has played as varied and decisive a role as NJRC in incorporating consciousness and developing the implications of the Holocaust for Jewish life in America.

Holocaust Center Model:

ZACHOR, NJRC's Holocaust Resource Center, developed a community memorial center model for educating Jewry on the Holocaust and its implications, and worked with local groups to create such centers. Many cities have now set up this new Jewish institution-in-the-making.

President's Commission on the Holocaust:

Based on its expertise, reputation and performance, NJRC was chosen to staff and guide the President's Commission, which is now the permanent United States Holocaust Memorial Council, charged to set up a national memorial center.

Research and Education:

NJRC created and publishes "SHOAH, a Journal of Resources on the Holocaust," devoted to scholarship, pedagogy and community education; assessed major Holocaust curricula for the National Endowment for the Humanities (Published as Mary Glynn, et. al., "American Youth and the Holocaust"); organizes Faculty Seminars, in which leading academics explore the frontier issues of Holocaust scholarship.

Holocaust Study Media:

NJRC produced "Witness to the Holocaust," a series of seven teaching films on the Holocaust with accompanying study guides. This powerful documentary series serves as the core of a course of study in public, private and religious high schools, in colleges, adult education and interfaith programs, and in Yom HaShoah (Holocaust Remembrance Day) activities. The Center also released "A Time to Remember," a 20-minute overview film on the Holocaust from the perspective of four survivors. It traces the rise of Nazism through the 'Final Solution' of the death camps.

MILLER'S CHEESE MAIN STREET ..... SOUTH FALLSBURG **NY**

BALLAS EGG PRODUCTS CORPORATION 40 NORTH 2ND STREET ..... ZANESVILLE **OH** 43701 (614) 453-0386

ZAUSNER FOODS CORP. 254 S. CUSTARD AVENUE ..... NEW HOLLAND **PA** 17557 (717) 354-4411

DANCE

HLOMO BACHAR 3638 GREEN VISTA DRIVE ..... ENCINO **CA** (213) 907-0147

HOMREL TARBUT DANCERS C/O SHALOM CONCERT BUREAU PO BOX 35092 ..... LOS ANGELES **CA** 90036 (213) 931-6125

SRAEL YAKOVEE PO BOX 3194 ..... VAN NUYS **CA** 91407 (818) 994-5432

NN BARZEL 3950 LAKE SHORE DRIVE ..... CHICAGO **IL** 60613 (312) 935-7458

R MAYER GRUBER 618 S. MICHIGAN AVENUE ..... CHICAGO **IL** 60605 (312) 922-9012

ENNY BRICHTA 2707 W. ALBION ..... CHICAGO **IL** 60645 (312) 262-1569

HLOMO BARCHECHAT 4522 NORTH ASHLAND ..... CHICAGO **IL** 60640 (312) 769-4529

HIL MOSS 2341 MEADOW LANE SOUTH ..... WILMETTE **IL** 60091 (312) 251-2676

EFFREY MARC ROCKLAND 106 FRANCIS STREET ..... BROOKLINE **MA** 02146 (617) 735-9050

IRIAM ROSENBLUM 73 COOLIDGE STREET ..... BROOKLINE **MA** 02146 (617) 739-1826

EREN SHEMESH ISRAELI DANCE GROUP C/O MIT HILLEL 312 MEMORIAL DRIVE ..... CAMBRIDGE **MA** 02139 (617) 253-2982

ERRY KAPLAN 73 MORAN AVENUE ..... PRINCETON **NJ** 98540 (609) 924-6370

DINA KAUFMAN 3755 HENRY HUDSON PARKWAY ..... BRONX **NY** 10463

ELIX FIBICH 50 WEST 97TH STREET ..... NEW YORK **NY** 10025 (212) 865-3935

SRAEL FOLK DANCE INST.-AMERICAN ZIONIST YOUTH FOUNDATION 515 PARK AVENUE ..... NEW YORK **NY** 10022 (212) 751-6070

SRAEL FOLK DANCE INSTITUTE 515 PARK AVENUE ..... NEW YORK **NY** 10022 (212) 371-5650

MOSHE ESKAYO 99 HILLSIDE AVENUE ..... NEW YORK **NY** 10040 (212) 942-0274

NATIONAL JEWISH WELFARE BOARD 15 EAST 26TH STREET ..... NEW YORK **NY** 10010 (212) 532-4949

AKDANEEM, ROBERTA KAPLAN 100 EAST END AVENUE, #7E ..... NEW YORK **NY** 10028 (212) 734-5062

WORLDTONE MUSIC, INC., RECORD LOFT INTERNATIONAL 230 SEVENTH AVENUE ..... NEW YORK **NY** 10011 (212) 691-1934

DINA KAUFMAN 64 ELDERWOOD DRIVE ..... TORONTO **ON** M5P 1X4 (416) 549-0529

AKDANEEM, ROBERTA KAPLAN 552 NORTH NEVILLE STREET ..... PITTSBURGH **PA** 15213

EFFREY MARC ROCKLAND PO BOX 488, VIRGINIA INTERMONT COLLEGE ..... BRISTOL **VA** 24201

DAY CARE CENTERS & NURSERIES

TEMPLE BETH ISRAEL NURSERY & DAY SCHOOL 3310 NORTH 10TH AVENUE ..... PHOENIX **AZ** 85103 (602) 264-4429

JEWISH COMMUNITY CENTER DAY CARE PRE-SCHOOL 38-22 EAST RIVER ROAD ..... TUCSON **AZ** 85718

TEMPLE BETH EMET PRESCHOOL 1770 WEST CERRITOS STREET ..... ANAHEIM **CA** (714) 772-2770

TEMPLE BETH TIKVAH OF NORTH ORANGE COUNTY TEMPLE SCHOOL 1600 NORTH ACACIA ..... FULLERTON **CA** 92634 (714) 871-9555

ISTA DEL MAR CHILD CARE SERVICE 3200 MOTOR AVENUE ..... LOS ANGELES **CA** 90034 (213) 836-1223

BRANDEIS HILLEL NURSERY 655 BROTHERHOOD WAY ..... SAN FRANCISCO **CA** (415) 344-9841

HEBREW ACADEMY OF SAN FRANCISCO NURSERY 763 25TH AVENUE ..... SAN FRANCISCO **CA** 94121 (415) 752-9583

TEMPLE BETH SHALOM COMMUNITY NURSERY SCHOOL 13031 TUSTIN ..... SANTA ANA **CA** (714) 633-1984

EZRA TORAH INSTITUTE 1525 CLEARVIEW ROAD ..... SANTA BARBARA **CA** 93101 (805) 968-0515

HEBREW ACADEMY OF GREATER HARTFORD 53 GABB ROAD ..... BLOOMFIELD **CT** 06002 (203) 243-8333

HILLEL ACADEMY 4200 PARK ROAD ..... BRIDGEPORT **CT** 06601 (203) 374-6147

NORWALK JEWISH CENTER SHORE HAVEN ROAD ..... NORWALK **CT** 06851 (203) 838-7504

EMANUEL SYNAGOGUE NURSERY SCHOOL 160 MEHEGAN DRIVE ..... WEST HARTFORD **CT** 06117 (203) 233-2774

TEMPLE ISRAEL NURSERY SCHOOL 14 COLEYTOWN ROAD ..... WESTPORT **CT** 06880 (203) 227-1293

BETH SHOLEM NURSERY 13TH AND EASTERN AVENUE N.W. ..... WASHINGTON **DC** 20012 (202) 723-9202

GAN YELADINE PRE-SCHOOL 13TH & EASTERN AVENUES, NW ..... WASHINGTON **DC** (202) 723-3466

JEWISH COMMUNITY CENTER 101 GARDEN OF EDEN ROAD ..... WILMINGTON **DE** 19802 (302) 478-5660

TEMPLE BETH SHALOM KINDERGARTEN & NURSERY SCHOOL 4601 ARTHUR ..... HOLLYWOOD **FL** 33020 (305) 966-2200

TEMPLE SINAI JEWISH COMMUNITY CENTER 1201 JOHNSON STREET ..... HOLLYWOOD **FL** 33020 (305) 920-1577

TEMPLE ISRAEL OF MIRAMAR 6920 S.W. 35TH STREET ..... MIRAMAR **FL** 33023 (305) 961-1700

AKIBA-SOUTHSIDE SCHOOL 5200 HYDE PARK BOULEVARD ..... CHICAGO **IL** 60615 (312) 493-8880

HILLEL TORAH NORTH SUBURBAN DAY SCHOOL 3003 WEST TOUHY AVENUE ..... CHICAGO **IL** 60645 (312) 262-2010

ROGERS PARK JEWISH COMMUNITY CENTER 7101 NORTH GREENVIEW .. CHICAGO **IL** 60626 (312) 274-0920

TRI-CON CHILD CARE CENTER 425 LAUREL AVENUE ..... HIGHLAND PARK **IL** 60635 (312) 433-1450

MAYER KAPLAN JEWISH COMMUNITY CENTER 5050 CHURCH STREET ..... SKOKIE **IL** 60077 (312) 675-2200

SOUTH BEND HEBREW DAY SCHOOL 206 WEST 8TH STREET ..... MISHAWAKAU **IN** 46544 (219) 255-3351

SOUTH SHORE HEBREW ACADEMY 144 BELMONT AVENUE ..... BROCKTON **MA** 02401 (617) 583-0717

YAL-DAY-NEW 62 GREEN STREET ..... BROOKLINE **MA** 02146 (617) 232-6019

ASSOCIATED JEWISH COMMUNITY CENTERS (PRESCHOOL) 1 BLUE HILL AVENUE ..... CANTON **MA** 02021 (617) 828-3507

TEMPLE BETH AM KINDERGARTEN & NURSERY 300 PLEASANT STREET ..... FRAMINGHAM **MA** 01701 (617) 872-3622

TEMPLE BETH SHALOM NURSERY SCHOOL PAMELA ROAD ..... SAXONVILLE **MA** 01701 (617) 877-2540

BAIS YAAKOV SCHOOL FOR GIRLS SEVEN MILE LANE ..... BALTIMORE **MD** 21209 (301) 363-3300

BETH TFILOH CONGREGATION 3300 OLD COURT ROAD ..... BALTIMORE **MD** 21208 (301) 486-1900

GAN YELADIM 6300 PARK HEIGHTS AVENUE ..... BALTIMORE **MD** (301) 764-7640

BAIS YAAKOV SCHOOL FOR GIRLS 11111 PARK HEIGHTS AVENUE ... OWINGS MILLS **MD** 21117 (301) 363-3300

SOUTHEAST HEBREW CONGREGATION NURSERY SCHOOL C/O TEITELBAUM, 11556 LOCKWOOD DRIVE ..... SILVER SPRING **MD** 20904 (301) 593-2120

JEWISH COMMUNITY CENTER ASSOC. DAY CARE CENTER 7400 OLIVE STREET ROAD ..... ST. LOUIS **MO** 63132 (314) 432-5700

GOLDBERG CHILD CARE CENTER 410 CENTER AVENUE ..... WESTWOOD **NJ** 07675 (201) 664-4013

KINNERET DAY SCHOOL 2510 VALENTINE AVENUE ..... BRONX **NY** 10453 (212) 548-0900

YESHIVA KINDERGARTEN & NURSERY 1925 GRAND CONCOURSE ..... BRONX **NY** 10453 (212) 588-5800

BAIS ISAAC ZVI 1019 46TH STREET ..... BROOKLYN **NY** 11219 (718) 854-7777

BEER MORDECHAI 1670 OCEAN AVENUE ..... BROOKLYN **NY** 11230 (718) 377-1838

BETH AM-LABOR ZIONIST CENTER & DAY SCHOOL 1182 BRIGHTON BEACH AVENUE ..... BROOKLYN **NY** 11235 (718) 743-4442

BETH JACOB DAY SCHOOL FOR GIRLS 550 OCEAN PARKWAY ..... BROOKLYN **NY** 11218 (718) 375-7771

BETH KIRSCH PRE-SCHOOL & DAY CAMP 1014 E. 15TH STREET ..... BROOKLYN **NY** 11230 (718) 377-8426

DAY CARE NURSERY OF THE INSTITUTE OF ADAS ISRAEL 1454 OCEAN PARKWAY ..... BROOKLYN **NY** (718) 375-9292

OCEAN PRIMARY SCHOOL & DAY CAMP 904 EAST 98TH STREET ..... BROOKLYN **NY** 11212 (718) 649-1567

OHOLEI TORAH 1267 EASTERN PARKWAY ..... BROOKLYN **NY** 11213 (718) 778-3340

YESHIVA IMREI YOSEF SPINKA 1460 56TH STREET ..... BROOKLYN **NY** 11219 (718) 851-1600

YESHIVA MAHARYATS MARGARETEN 7902 15TH AVENUE ..... BROOKLYN **NY** 11228 (718) 259-0423

YESHIVA TORAS EMES KAMENITZ 53RD STREET AND 14TH AVENUE ..... BROOKLYN **NY** 11219 (718) 435-3973

YESHIVA TORAS EMES KAMENITZ 1167 EAST 13TH STREET ..... BROOKLYN **NY** 11230 (718) 851-4735

BNOS ISRAEL INSTITUTE 612 BEACH 9TH STREET ..... FAR ROCKAWAY **NY** 11691 (718) 327-0196

HEBREW KINDERGARTEN & INFANTS HOME 210 BEACH 20TH STREET ..... FAR ROCKAWAY **NY** 11691 (718) 327-1140

YESHIVA DARCHEI TORAH 257 BEACH 17TH STREET ..... FAR ROCKAWAY **NY** 11691 (718) 337-5880

YOUNG ISRAEL OF KEW GARDEN HILLS PRIMARY SCHOOL 150-05 70TH ROAD ..... FLUSHING **NY** 11367 (718) 261-9723

TEMPLE SINAI NURSERY SCHOOL 70-35 112TH STREET ..... FOREST HILLS **NY** 11375 (718) 261-2900

YESHIVA DOV REVEL OF FOREST HILLS 71-02 113TH STREET ..... FOREST HILLS **NY** 11375 (718) 261-9624

HEBREW ACADEMY OF WEST QUEENS 34-25 82ND STREET ..... JACKSON HEIGHTS **NY** 11372 (718) 899-9193

JEWISH NURSERY SCHOOL 82-17 LEFFERTS BOULEVARD ..... KEW GARDENS **NY** 11415 (718) 849-7988

YESHIVA BAIS YITZCHOK 184 MAPLE AVENUE ..... MONSEY **NY** 10952 (914) 356-3113

CENTRAL SYNAGOGUE NURSERY 123 EAST 55TH STREET ..... NEW YORK **NY** 10022 (212) 838-5122

FRIENDLY HOME JEWISH CHILD CARE ASSOC. OF NEW YORK 465 WEST END AVENUE ..... NEW YORK **NY** 10024 (212) 874-2522

FRIENDLY HOME JEWISH CHILD CARE ASSOC. OF NEW YORK 320 WEST END AVENUE ..... NEW YORK **NY** 10023 (212) 595-2620

JEWISH CHILD CARE ASSOCIATION OF NEW YORK 345 MADISON AVENUE ..... NEW YORK **NY** 10017 (212) 490-9160

YESHIVA DAY SCHOOL OF SOUTH QUEENS 115-70 LEFFERTS BOULEVARD ..... OZONE PARK **NY** 11420 (718) 641-0100

JEWISH FOUNDATION SCHOOL NURSERY 835 FOREST HILL ROAD ..... STATEN ISLAND **NY** 10314 (718) 494-7477

YESHIVA OF WILLOWBROOK 61 RUPERT AVENUE ..... STATEN ISLAND **NY** 10314 (718) 494-7477

JEWISH COMMUNITY CENTER OF WEST HEMPSTEAD-NURSERY SCHOOL 711 DOGWOOD AVENUE ..... WEST HEMPSTEAD **NY** 11552 (516) 481-7448

ADATH ISRAEL-JARSON EDUCATIONAL CENTER 3201 EAST GALBRAITH ROAD ..... CINCINNATI **OH** 45236 (513) 793-1805

YAVNEH DAY SCHOOL 1636 SUMMIT ROAD ..... CINCINNATI **OH** 45237 (513) 984-3770

AGNON PRESCHOOL/PREKINDERGARTEN 26500 SHAKER BLVD ..... CLEVELAND **OH** 44122 (216) 464-4055

FAIRMOUNT TEMPLE PRESCHOOL 23737 FAIRMOUNT BLVD ..... CLEVELAND **OH** 44122 (216) 464-1330

FAMILY PLACE JEWISH COMMUNITY CENTER,3505 MAYFIELD ROAD .... CLEVELAND **OH** 44118 (216) 382-4000

GANON GIL PRESCHOOL 25400 FAIRMOUNT BLVD ..... CLEVELAND **OH** 44122 (216) 464-0536

GANON GIL PRESCHOOL 1960 LANDER ROAD ..... CLEVELAND **OH** 44124 (216) 442-6414

HEBREW ACADEMY OF CLEVELAND 1860 SOUTH TAYLOR ROAD ..... CLEVELAND **OH** 44118 (216) 321-5838

JEWISH COMMUNITY CENTER PRESCHOOL 3505 MAYFIELD ROAD ..... CLEVELAND **OH** 44118 (216) 382-4000

JEWISH DAY NURSERY DAY CARE CENTER 22201 FAIRMOUNT BLVD .... CLEVELAND **OH** 44118 (216) 932-2802

KINDER RING WORKMEN'S CIRCLE PRESCHOOL 1980 SOUTH GREEN ROAD ..... CLEVELAND **OH** 44121 (216) 381-4515

LILLIAN RATNER MONTESSORI PRESCHOOL 4900 ANDERSON ROAD ... CLEVELAND **OH** 44124 (216) 291-0033

PARK SYNAGOGUE NURSERY SCHOOL 3300 MAYFIELD ROAD ..... CLEVELAND **OH** 44118 (216) 371-4177

TAYLOR ROAD SYNAGOGUE NURSERY 1970 SOUTH TAYLOR ROAD .... CLEVELAND **OH** 44118 (216) 321-4875

TORAH NURSERY (CHABAD) 1825 SOUTH GREEN ROAD ..... CLEVELAND **OH** 44121 (216) 381-9178

YOUNG ISRAEL SHULAMITH NURSERY 14141 CEDAR ROAD ..... CLEVELAND **OH** 44121 (216) 381-7526

JEWISH CENTER NURSERY 1821 EMERSON STREET ..... DAYTON **OH** 45406 (513) 854-4014

GAN YELADIM 100 ELDER ST ..... DOWNSVIEW **ON** (416) 638-1796

KENESETH ISRAEL NURSERY SCHOOL YORK ROAD AND TOWNSHIP LINE ..... ELKINS PARK **PA** 19117 (215) 855-2425

BETH DAVID NURSERY SCHOOL 5220 WYNNEFIELD AVENUE ..... PHILADELPHIA **PA** 19131

DOWNTOWN CHILDREN'S CENTER 366 SNYDER AVENUE ..... PHILADELPHIA **PA** 19148 (215) 389-1018

FEDERATION DAY CARE SERVICES JAMISON AVENUE & GARTH ROAD ..... PHILADELPHIA **PA** 19116 (215) 676-7550

NORTHEAST FAMILY DAY CARE JAMISON AVENUE & GARTH ROAD ..... PHILADELPHIA **PA** 19116

NORTHERN HEBREW DAY NURSERY 10800 JAMISON AVENUE ..... PHILADELPHIA **PA** 19116

NORTHERN HEBREW DAY SCHOOL NURSERY 10TH AND RUSCOMB ..... PHILADELPHIA **PA** 19141 (215) 677-7191

SAMUEL PALEY DAY CARE CENTER STRABLE & HORROCKS STREETS ..... PHILADELPHIA **PA** 19152 (215) 725-8930

TEMPLE SINAI NURSERY SCHOOL 30 HAGAN AVENUE ..... CRANSTON **RI** 02920 (401) 942-8350

DAY SCHOOLS

BIRMINGHAM JEWISH DAY SCHOOL 3960-A MONTCLAIR ROAD - P.O. BOX 9206 ..... BIRMINGHAM **AL** 35213 (205) 879-1068

HEBREW INSTITUTE OF ARIZONA AT MESA 104 WEST FIRST STREET ..... MESA **AZ** 85201 (602) 249-6338

ARIZONA TORAH HIGH SCHOOL-BOYS 1123 W.GEORGIA ..... PHOENIX **AZ** 85013 (602) 266-2586

ARIZONA TORAH HIGH SCHOOL-GIRLS 1123 W.GEORGIA ..... PHOENIX **AZ** 85013 (602) 277-3389

HEBREW INSTITUTE OF ARIZONA 935 WEST MARYLAND AVENUE ..... PHOENIX **AZ** 85013 (602) 249-6338

PHOENIX HEBREW ACADEMY 515 EAST BETHANY HOME ROAD ..... PHOENIX **AZ** 85012 (602) 277-7479

TUCSON HEBREW ACADEMY 5550 EAST 5TH STREET ..... TUCSON **AZ** 85711 (602) 745-5592

EMANUEL COMMUNITY DAY SCHOOL 8844 BURTON WAY ..... BEVERLY HILLS **CA** 90211 (213) 274-6388

HILLEL HEBREW ACADEMY 9120 WEST OLYMPIC BLVD ..... BEVERLY HILLS **CA** 90212 (213) 276-6135

KADIMA HEBREW ACADEMY 22600 SHERMAN WAY ..... CANOGA PARK **CA** 91307 (818) 346-0849

VALLEY BETH SHALOM DAY SCHOOL 15739 VENTURA BOULEVARD ..... ENCINO **CA** 91436 (818) 788-6000

EZRA TORAH INSTITUTE 7631 EVERGREEN DRIVE ..... GOLETA **CA** 93117 (805) 968-3768

LONG BEACH HEBREW ACADEMY 3981 ATLANTIC AVENUE	LONG BEACH	CA	90807	(213) 424-9787
AKIBA ACADEMY 10400 WILSHIRE BOULEVARD	LOS ANGELES	CA	90024	(213) 475-6401
BAIS YAAKOV SCHOOL FOR GIRLS 461 NORTH LA BREA AVENUE	LOS ANGELES	CA	90036	(213) 938-3231
HERZL SCHOOLS 1039 SOUTH LA CIENEGA BOULEVARD	LOS ANGELES	CA	90035	(213) 652-1854
JEWISH ACADEMY OF LOS ANGELES, NEW JEWISH HIGH SCHOOL 1317 NORTH CRESCENT HEIGHTS BOULEVARD	LOS ANGELES	CA	90046	(213) 656-5020
NEW JEWISH HIGH SCHOOL 1317 N.CRESCENT HEIGHTS BLVD	LOS ANGELES	CA	90046	
SAMUEL A.FRYER YAVNEH ACADEMY 7353 BEVERLY BLVD	LOS ANGELES	CA	90036	(213) 938-2636
SEPHARDIC HEBREW ACADEMY 310 NORTH HUNTLEY DRIVE	LOS ANGELES	CA	90048	(213) 659-2456
SHALOM HEBREW ACADEMY 1419 SOUTH BEVERLY DRIVE	LOS ANGELES	CA	90035	(213) 275-2457
SHAPELL-FEINTECH JUNIOR HIGH SCHOOL,STEPHEN S.WISE TEMPLE 1550 STEPHEN S.WISE DRIVE	LOS ANGELES	CA	90077	(213) 788-7554
STEPHEN S.WISE DAY SCHOOL 15500 STEPHEN S.WISE DRIVE	LOS ANGELES	CA	90077	(213) 788-7554
TEMPLE BETH AM DAY SCHOOL 1039 SOUTH LA CIENEGA BOULEVARD	LOS ANGELES	CA	90035	(213) 655-6401
WEST COAST TALMUDICAL SEMINARY-YESHIVA OHR ELCHONON CHABAD 7215 WARING AVENUE	LOS ANGELES	CA	90046	(213) 937-3763
YAVNEH HEBREW ACADEMY 7353 BEVERLY BOULEVARD	LOS ANGELES	CA	90036	(213) 938-2636
YESHIVA GEDOLA OF LOS ANGELES 5822 WEST THIRD	LOS ANGELES	CA	90036	(213) 938-2071
YESHIVA OHR ELCHONON 7215 WARING AVENUE	LOS ANGELES	CA	90046	(213) 937-3763
YESHIVA OHR ELCHONON CHABAD/WEST COAST TALMUDICAL SEMINARY 7215 WARING AVENUE	LOS ANGELES	CA	90046	(213) 937-3763
YESHIVA RAV ISACSOHN/YESHIVATH TORATH EMETH 540 NORTH LA BREA AVENUE	LOS ANGELES	CA	90036	(213) 938-8147
YESHIVA RAV ISACSON-TORATH EMETH ACADEMY 540 NORTH LA BREA AVENUE	LOS ANGELES	CA	90036	(213) 939-1148
YESHIVA UNIVERSITY OF LOS ANGELES HIGH SCHOOLS 9760 WEST PICO BLVD	LOS ANGELES	CA	90035	(213) 553-1574
YESHIVA UNIVERSITY OF LOS ANGELES, BOY'S DIVISION 9760 WEST PICO BOULEVARD	LOS ANGELES	CA	90035	(213) 553-4478
YESHIVA UNIVERSITY OF LOS ANGELES, GIRL'S DIVISION 10345 WEST PICO BOULEVARD	LOS ANGELES	CA	90035	(213) 552-0513
ADAT ARI EL DAY SCHOOL 5540 LAUREL CANYON BOULEVARD	NORTH HOLLYWOOD	CA	91607	(818) 766-3506
EMEK HEBREW ACADEMY 12732 CHANDLER BLVD	NORTH HOLLYWOOD	CA	91607	(818) 980-0155
EMEK HIGH SCHOOL, BOY'S DIVISION 12326 RIVERSIDE DRIVE	NORTH HOLLYWOOD	CA	91607	(818) 980-0155
EMEK HIGH SCHOOL, GIRL'S DIVISION 12422 CHANDLER BOULEVARD	NORTH HOLLYWOOD	CA	91607	(818) 980-0155
UNION HEBREW HIGH SCHOOL 13107 VENTURA BLVD	NORTH HOLLYWOOD	CA	91604	(818) 872-3550
VALLEY TORAH CENTER-STANLEY M.LINTZ HIGH SCHOOL-BOY'S DIV 12003 RIVERSIDE DRIVE	NORTH HOLLYWOOD	CA	91607	(818) 984-1805
VALLEY TORAH CENTER-STANLEY M.LINTZ HIGH SCHOOL-GIRL'S DIV 12326 RIVERSIDE DRIVE	NORTH HOLLYWOOD	CA	91607	(818) 985-8682
ABRAHAM J. HESCHEL DAY SCHOOL 17701 DEVONSHIRE STREET	NORTHRIDGE	CA	91325	(818) 368-5781
HILLEL ACADEMY OF EAST BAY 3778 PARK BLVD	OAKLAND	CA	94610	(415) 482-3470
ETZ CHAIM HEBREW INSTITUTE OF CALIFORNIA 13609 TWIN PEAKS RD	SAN DIEGO	CA	90264	(619) 748-7750
SAN DIEGO HEBREW DAY SCHOOL 6880 MOHAWK STREET	SAN DIEGO	CA	92115	(619) 460-3300
HEBREW ACADEMY OF SAN FRANCISCO 763 25TH AVENUE	SAN FRANCISCO	CA	94121	(415) 752-9583
KEREM YESHIVA 250 HOWARD DRIVE	SANTA CLARA	CA	95051	(408) 247-1722
PACIFIC JEWISH CENTER DAY SCHOOL 1515 MAPLE STREET	SANTA MONICA	CA	91405	(213) 396-8780
MIDRASHA KEREM 1030 ASTORIA DRIVE	SUNNYVALE	CA	94087	(408) 735-0921
SOUTH PENINSULA HEBREW DAY SCHOOL 1030 ASTORIA DRIVE	SUNNYVALE	CA	94087	(408) 738-3060
EMANUEL STREISAND JEWISH DAY SCHOOL 720 ROSE AVENUE	VENICE	CA	90291	(213) 399-0303
SAN GABRIEL/POMONA VALLEYS JEWISH DAY SCHOOL 3508 EAST TEMPLE WAY	WEST COVINA	CA	91791	(818) 967-3881
HEBREW ACADEMY, THE - LUBAVITCH 1401 WILLOW LANE	WESTMINSTER	CA	92683	(714) 898-0051
BETH JACOB HIGH SCHOOL OF DENVER 5100 WEST 14TH AVENUE	DENVER	CO	80204	(303) 893-1333
HILLEL ACADEMY OF DENVER 450 SOUTH HUDSON STREET	DENVER	CO	80222	(303) 333-1511
ROCKY MOUNTAIN HEBREW ACADEMY 560 S.MONACO PARKWAY	DENVER	CO	80224	(303) 355-7642
YESHIVA TORAS CHAIM 1400 QUITMAN STREET	DENVER	CO	80204	(303) 629-8200
THE BESS AND PAUL SIGEL HEBREW ACADEMY OF GREATER HARTFOD 53 GABB ROAD	BLOOMFIELD	CT	06002	(203) 243-8333
HILLEL ACADEMY 4200 PARK AVENUE	BRIDGEPORT	CT	06604	(203) 347-6147
HILLEL ACADEMY 1571 STRATFIELD ROAD	FAIRFIELD	CT	06432	(203) 347-6147
NEW ENGLAND ACADEMY FOR JEWISH STUDIES 155 PENDLETON ST	NEW HAVEN	CT	06511	(203) 397-2791
THE GAN SCHOOL 765 ELM STREET	NEW HAVEN	CT	06511	(203) 777-2200
TORAH ACADEMY HIGH SCHOOL FOR GIRLS 570 WHALLEY AVE	NEW HAVEN	CT	06515	(203) 397-1808
TORAH ACADEMY OF CONNECTICUT-YESHIVA MAOR HATORAH 330 BLAKE STREET	NEW HAVEN	CT	06515	(203) 397-3243
HEBREW DAY SCHOOL OF EASTERN CONNECTICUT 2 BROAD STREET	NORWICH	CT	06360	(203) 889-9169
BETH CHANA ACADEMY H.S. FOR GIRLS AND BOYS H.S. OF CONN. 261 DERBY AVENUE	ORANGE	CT	06477	(203) 795-5261
LUBAVITCH YESHIVAH 261 DERBY AVENUE	ORANGE	CT	06477	(203) 795-5261
YESHIVA ACHEI TMIMIM LUBAVITCH NEW HAVEN HEBREW DAY SCHOOL 261 DERBY AVENUE	ORANGE	CT	06477	(203) 795-5261
BI-CULTURAL DAY SCHOOL 2186 HIGH RIDGE ROAD	STAMFORD	CT	06903	(203) 329-2186
BI-CULTURAL DAY SCHOOL BRANCH 2186 HIGH RIDGE ROAD	STAMFORD	CT	06903	(203) 329-1761
YESHIVA BAIS BINYOMIN 132 PROSPECT STREET	STAMFORD	CT	06710	(212) 582-1540
EZRA ACADEMY RIMMON ROAD	WOODBRIDE	CT	06525	(203) 389-5500
ALBERT EINSTEIN HEBREW ACADEMY 300 LEA BLVD	WILMINGTON	DE	19802	
BETH SHOLOM ACADEMY 1400 N 46 AVENUE	HOLLYWOOD	FL	33021	(305) 966-2000
SOUTH DADE HEBREW ACADEMY 11801 S.W. 74TH AVENUE	MIAMI	FL	33156	(305) 253-2300
SOUTH DADE HEBREW ACADEMY 5950 N.KENDALL DRIVE	MIAMI	FL	33156	(305) 667-6667
TORAS EMES ACADEMY 16020 N.W. 2ND AVENUE	MIAMI	FL	33169	(305) 947-8074
AGUDATH ISRAEL HEBREW INSTITUTE-YESHIVA TORAS CHAIM 7801 CARLYLE AVENUE, P.O. BOX 4443	MIAMI BEACH	FL	33141	(305) 865-0243
BAIS YAAKOV OF MIAMI 7055 BONITA DRIVE	MIAMI BEACH	FL	33141	(305) 865-0763
HEBREW ACADEMY 2400 PINE TREE DRIVE	MIAMI BEACH	FL	33140	(305) 532-6421
LUBAVITCH YESHIVA-CHEDER OF GREATER MIAMI 1140 ALTON ROAD	MIAMI BEACH	FL	33139	(305) 673-5664
MESIVTA HIGH SCHOOL 1965 ALTON ROAD	MIAMI BEACH	FL	33139	(305) 538-5543
RABBI ALEXANDER S. GROSS HEBREW ACADEMY OF GREATER MIAMI 2400 PINE TREE DRIVE	MIAMI BEACH	FL	33140	(305) 532-6421
RABBI ALEXANDER S. GROSS JUNIOR AND SENIOR HIGH SCHOOL 2425 PINE TREE DRIVE	MIAMI BEACH	FL	33140	(305) 532-6421
TORAS EMES ACADEMY 7902 CARLYLE AVENUE	MIAMI BEACH	FL	33141	(305) 868-1388
SAMUEL SCHECK HILLEL COMMUNITY DAY SCHOOL 19000 N.E. 25 AVENUE	NORTH MIAMI BEACH	FL	33180	(305) 931-2831
HEBREW DAY SCHOOL OF CENTRAL FLORIDA 4917 ELI STREET	ORLANDO	FL	32804	(305) 647-0713
HILLEL SCHOOL OF TAMPA 2801 BAYSHORE BLVD	TAMPA	FL	33609	(813) 839-7047
HEBREW ACADEMY OF ATLANTA 1892 NORTH DRUID HILLS ROAD	ATLANTA	GA	30319	(404) 634-7388
YESHIVA HIGH SCHOOL OF ATLANTA 1745 PEACHTREE ROAD, N.E.	ATLANTA	GA	30309	(404) 873-1492
SAVANNAH HEBREW DAY SCHOOL 5111 ABERCORN STREET	SAVANNAH	GA	31499	(912) 355-8111
DES MOINES JEWISH ACADEMY 954 CUMMINS PARKWAY	DES MOINES	IA	50312	(515) 274-0453
AKIBA JEWISH DAY SCHOOL 5200 SOUTH HYDE PARK BLVD	CHICAGO	IL	60615	(312) 493-8880
BAIS YAAKOV HEBREW PAROCHIAL SCHOOL 2447 WEST GRANVILLE AVENUE	CHICAGO	IL	60659	(312) 465-3770
BAIS YAAKOV OF CHICAGO-BOYS DIVISION 6122 NORTH CALIFORNIA	CHICAGO	IL	60659	(312) 465-9878
BIAS YAAKOV OF CHICAGO - BOYS DIVISION 6526 NORTH CALIFORNIA AVENUE	CHICAGO	IL	60659	(312) 465-5761
HANNA SACKS GIRLS HIGH SCHOOL/IDA CROWN JEWISH ACADEMY 3021 WEST DEVON AVENUE	CHICAGO	IL	60659	(312) 338-9222
HILLEL TORAH NORTH SUBURBAN DAY SCHOOL 3021 WEST DEVON AVENUE	CHICAGO	IL	60659	(312) 262-2010
IDA CROWN JEWISH ACADEMY 2828 W PRATT AVENUE	CHICAGO	IL	60645	(312) 973-1450
TELSHE YESHIVA OF CHICAGO 3535 WEST FOSTER AVENUE	CHICAGO	IL	60625	(312) 463-7738
YESHIVAS BRISK 2956 WEST PETERSON AVENUE	CHICAGO	IL	60659	(312) 275-5166
YESHIVAS TIFERES TZVI 6122 NORTH CALIFORNIA AVE	CHICAGO	IL	60659	(312) 764-1170
PEORIA HEBREW DAY SCHOOL 3616 NORTH SHERIDAN ROAD	PEORIA	IL	61604	(309) 688-2821
ARI E CROWN HEBREW DAY SCHOOL 8150 NORTH TRIPP AVENUE	SKOKIE	IL	60076	(312) 982-9192
HILLEL TORAH NORTH SUBURBAN DAY SCHOOL 8825 EAST PRAIRIE	SKOKIE	IL	60076	(312) 677-1021
HILLEL TORAH NORTH SUBURBAN DAY SCHOOL 7120 NORTH LARAMIE AVENUE	SKOKIE	IL	60077	(312) 674-6533
YESHIVA H.S.-PREP. DIV. OF THE HEBREW THEOLOGICAL COLLEGE 7135 NORTH CARPENTER ROAD	SKOKIE	IL	60077	(312) 674-7750
YESHIVAS BRISK 9000 FORESTVIEW ROAD	SKOKIE	IL	60203	(312) 674-4652
HEBREW ACADEMY OF INDIANAPOLIS 6602 HOOVER ROAD	INDIANAPOLIS	IN	46260	(317) 251-1261
SOUTH BEND HEBREW DAY SCHOOL 206 WEST 8TH STREET	MISHAWAKA	IN	46544	(219) 255-3351
HYMAN BRAND HEBREW ACADEMY 5901 COLLEGE BLVD	OVERLAND PARK	KS	66211	(913) 649-1993
LOUISVILLE JEWISH DAY SCHOOL/ELI AHU ACADEMY 3600 DUTCHMANS LANE	LOUISVILLE	KY	40205	(502) 459-4554
LAKESHORE HEBREW DAY SCHOOL 5210 WEST ESPLANADE AVENUE	METAIRIE	LA	70002	(504) 885-4532
NEW ENGLAND HEBREW ACADEMY-LUBAVITCH YESHIVA 1845 COMMONWEALTH AVENUE	BRIGHTON	MA	02135	(617) 787-0020
SOUTH SHORE HEBREW ACADEMY 144 BELMONT AVENUE	BROCKTON	MA	02401	(617) 583-0717
BROOKLINE I.L. PERETZ SCHOOL OF THE WORKMEN'S CIRCLE 1762 BEACON STREET	BROOKLINE	MA	02146	
GAN TORAH 1611 BEACON STREET	BROOKLINE	MA	02146	(800) 343-0470
MAIMONIDES SCHOOL PHILBRICK ROAD	BROOKLINE	MA	02146	(617) 232-4452
NEW ENGLAND HEBREW ACADEMY-LUBAVITCH YESHIVA 9 PRESCOTT STREET	BROOKLINE	MA	02146	(617) 731-5330
SOUTH AREA JEWISH COMMUNITY CENTER MASORET PROGRAM 1 BLUE HILL RIVER ROAD	CANTON	MA	02021	(617) 773-3000
HERITAGE ACADEMY 594 CONGRESS STREET	LONGMEADOW	MA	01106	(413) 567-1517
LUBAVITCHER YESHIVA ACADEMY 1148 CONVERSE STREET	LONGMEADOW	MA	01106	(413) 736-9420
MERRIMACK VALLEY HEBREW ACADEMY 460 WESTFORD STREET	LOWELL	MA	01851	(617) 459-9400
SHALOH HOUSE OHOLEI TORAH 68 SMITH ROAD	MILTON	MA	02186	(617) 333-0477
LUBAVITCHER YESHIVA ACADEMY 15 ELWOOD DRIVE	SPRINGFIELD	MA	01108	(413) 373-7998
SHALOH HOUSE OHOLEI TORAH 50 ETHYL WAY	STOUGHTON	MA	02072	(617) 333-0477
HILLEL ACADEMY OF THE NORTH SHORE 837 HUMPHREY STREET	SWAMPSCOTT	MA	01907	(617) 599-3837
BAIS CHANA JUNIOR AND SENIOR H.S. AND DORMITORY FOR GIRLS 9 MIDLAND STREET	WORCESTER	MA	01602	(617) 752-0904
YESHIVA ACHEI TMIMIM ACADEMY 22 NEWTON AVENUE	WORCESTER	MA	01602	(617) 752-0904
BETH TFILOH COMMUNITY DAY SCHOOL 3300 OLD COURT ROAD	BALTIMORE	MD	21208	(301) 486-1905
NER ISRAEL HIGH SCHOOL 400 MT WILSON LANE	BALTIMORE	MD	21208	(301) 484-7200
YESHIVA INSTITUTE OF BALTIMORE (EDUCATIONAL CENTER) 3605 CORONADO ROAD	BALTIMORE	MD	21207	(301) 922-0547
YESHIVA INSTITUTE OF BALTIMORE (EXECUTIVE CENTER) 6216 BALTIMORE AVENUE	BALTIMORE	MD	21215	(301) 358-9330
YESHIVA KOCHAV YITZCHAK 4300 BEDFORD AVENUE	BALTIMORE	MD	21208	(301) 484-2340
YESHIVAS CHOFETZ CHAIM 4445 OLD COURT ROAD	BALTIMORE	MD	21208	(301) 484-6600
BAIS YAAKOV SCHOOL FOR GIRLS 11111 PARK HEIGHTS AVENUE	OWINGS MILLS	MD	21117	(301) 363-3300
SILVER SPRING HEBREW DAY INSTITUTE 4511 BESTOR DRIVE	ROCKVILLE	MD	20853	(301) 460-7070
HEBREW ACADEMY OF GREATER WASHINGTON 2010 LINDEN LANE	SILVER SPRING	MD	20910	(301) 587-4100
HEBREW DAY SCHOOL OF MONTGOMERY COUNTY 1401 ARCOLA AVENUE	SILVER SPRING	MD	20902	(301) 649-5400
YESHIVA HIGH SCHOOL OF GREATER WASHINGTON INC.-GIRLS DIV. 8915 COLESVILLE RD.	SILVER SPRING	MD	20910	(301) 587-6187
YESHIVA HIGH SCHOOL OF GREATER WASHINGTON, INC.-BOYS DIV. 1216 ARCOLA AVENUE	SILVER SPRING	MD	20902	(301) 649-7077
HEBREW ACADEMY OF BANGOR 28 SOMERSET STREET	BANGOR	ME	04401	(207) 945-5631
THE ABRAHAM S. AND FANNIE B. LEVEY HEBREW DAY SCHOOL 76 NOYES STREET	PORTLAND	ME	04103	(207) 773-0693
SALLY ALLAN ALEXANDER BETH JACOB SCHOOL FOR GIRLS 32605 BELLVINE TRAIL	BIRMINGHAM	MI	48010	(313) 644-3113
YESHIVAT AKIVA-THE AKIVA HEBREW DAY SCHOOL 27700 SOUTHFIELD ROAD	LATHRUP VILLAGE	MI	48076	(313) 552-9690
YESHIVA GEDOLAH OF METROPOLITAN DETROIT-DIV. OF BETH YEHUDA 24600 GREENFIELD ROAD	OAK PARK	MI	48237	(313) 968-4270
YESHIVA BETH YEHUDA 15751 WEST LINCOLN DRIVE	SOUTHFIELD	MI	48076	(313) 557-6750
TORAH ACADEMY 2800 JOPPA AVENUE, SOUTH	MINNEAPOLIS	MN	55416	(612) 920-6630

LUBAVITCH HOUSE CHEDER 1758 FORD PKWY ST. PAUL **MN** 55116 (612) 698-0556
RABBI H.F. EPSTEIN HEBREW ACADEMY 1138 NORTH WARSON ROAD ST. LOUIS **MO** 63132 (314) 994-7856
TORAH ACADEMY FOR GIRLS 8630 OLIVE ST ROAD ST. LOUIS **MO** 63132
YESHIVA HIGH SCHOOL OF ST. LOUIS 9723 GRANDVIEW DRIVE ST. LOUIS **MO** 63132 (314) 997-3940
YESHIVA OF ST. LOUIS RABBINICAL COLLEGE 7400 OLIVE ST ST. LOUIS **MO** 63130 (314) 727-1379
B'NAI ISRAEL SYNAGOGUE, DAY SCHOOL P.O. BOX 10214 GREENSBORO **NC** 27404 (919) 855-5091
HILLEL SCHOOL 7400 FALLS OF THE NEUSE ROAD RALEIGH **NC** 27609 (919) 847-8986
TALMUDICAL ACADEMY OF NEW JERSEY ROUTE 524 ALELPHIA **NJ** 07710 (201) 431-1600
YESHIVA OF HUDSON COUNTY 5 BERGEN COURT BAYONNE **NJ** 07002 (201) 865-2484
BAIS KALLA TORAH PREPARATORY HIGH SCHOOL 503 - 11TH AVENUE BELMAR **NJ** 07719 (201) 681-9400
HEBREW ACADEMY OF MORRIS COUNTY 219 HILL STREET BOONTON **NJ** 07005 (201) 335-9009
HILLEL HIGH SCHOOL 100 GRANT AVE DEAL PARK **NJ** 07723 (201) 531-9300
MORRIS NAMIAS SHALOM TORAH ACADEMY
639 ABBINGTON DRIVE-TWIN RIVERS TOWN CENTER EAST WINDSOR **NJ** 08520 (609) 443-4877
RABBI PESACH RAYMON YESHIVA ACADEMY 2 HARRISON STREET EDISON **NJ** 08817 (201) 572-5052
BRURIAH HIGH SCHOOL FOR GIRLS 35 NORTH AVENUE ELIZABETH **NJ** 07208 (201) 351-6315
JEWISH EDUCATIONAL CENTER 330 ELMORA AVENUE ELIZABETH **NJ** 07208 (201) 353-4446
MORIAH SCHOOL OF ENGLEWOOD 53 S. WOODLAND STREET ENGLEWOOD **NJ** 07631 (201) 567-0208
ROGOSIN YESHIVA HIGH SCHOOL 25 COTTAGE STREET JERSEY CITY **NJ** 07306 (201) 798-0055
BEZALEL HEBREW DAY SCHOOL 419 5TH STREET LAKEWOOD **NJ** 08701 (201) 363-1748
LAKEWOOD CHEDER SCHOOL 901 MADISON AVENUE LAKEWOOD **NJ** 08701 (201) 364-1552
LAKEWOOD CHEDER SCHOOL-BAIS YAAKOV OF LAKEWOOD
602 7TH STREET LAKEWOOD **NJ** 08701 (201) 363-5070
LIMUD LEARNING CENTER 414 YESHIVA PLAZA, APT 4A LAKEWOOD **NJ** 08701 (201) 364-1877
MESIVTA OF LAKEWOOD 215 PRIVATE WAY LAKEWOOD **NJ** 08701 (201) 367-7345
YESHIVA YETEV LEV SATMAR 405 FOREST AVENUE LAKEWOOD **NJ** 08701 (201) 363-9746
THE HEBREW ACADEMY
C/O CONGREGATION SONS OF ISRAEL-GORDONS CORNER ROAD MANALAPAN **NJ** 07726
HEBREW ACADEMY OF ATLANTIC COUNTY
601 NORTH JEROME AVENUE, PO BOX 3163 MARGATE **NJ** 08402 (609) 823-6681
HILLEL ACADEMY P.O. BOX 287 METUCHEN **NJ** 08840
TORAH ACADEMY OF TEANECK 435 RIVER ROAD NEW MILFORD **NJ** 07646 (201) 265-0600
HILLEL YESHIVA 1025 DEAL ROAD OCEAN **NJ** 07712 (201) 493-9300
THE FRISCH SCHOOL-YESHIVA H.S. OF NORTHERN NEW JERSEY
EAST 243 FRISCH COURT PARAMUS **NJ** 07652 (201) 845-0555
YAVNEH ACADEMY 155 FAIRVIEW AVENUE PARAMUS **NJ** 07652 (201) 262-8494
HILLEL ACADEMY 565 BROADWAY PASSAIC **NJ** 07055 (201) 777-0735
HEBREW FREE SCHOOLS 660 14TH AVENUE PATERSON **NJ** 07504 (201) 742-9345
REGIONAL HIGH SCHOOL OF JEWISH STUDIES
152 VAN HOUTEN STREET PATERSON **NJ** 07505
YAVNEH ACADEMY 413 12TH AVENUE PATERSON **NJ** 07514 (201) 274-7005
TORAH ACADEMY OF TEANECK NORTH STREET AND ELM TEANECK **NJ** 07666 (201) 836-8005
YESHIVA OF HUDSON COUNTY/BERGEN BRANCH 800 BROAD STREET TEANECK **NJ** 07666 (201) 833-0203
MESIVTA SANZ OF HUDSON COUNTY 3400 NEW YORK AVENUE UNION CITY **NJ** 07087 (201) 867-8690
YESHIVA OF HUDSON COUNTY 2501 NEW YORK AVENUE UNION CITY **NJ** 07087 (201) 865-2484
JEWISH DAY SCHOOL ORCHARD ROAD VINELAND **NJ** 08360
KADIMAH TORAH SCHOOL OF SOUTH NEW JERSEY
321 GRAPE STREET VINELAND **NJ** 08360
HILLEL SCHOOL OF THE SHORE AREA
LOGAN ROAD AND PARK BLVD WANAMASSA **NJ** 07712 (201) 531-1220
REGIONAL H.S. OF JEWISH STUDIES 1 PIKE DRIVE WAYNE **NJ** 07470 (201) 595-0560
HEBREW YOUTH ACADEMY OF ESSEX COUNTY
1 HENDERSON DRIVE WEST CALDWELL **NJ** 07006 (201) 575-1194
YESHIVA TALMIDEI TELSHE 111 WASHINGTON WESTWOOD **NJ** 07675 (201) 358-0900
NEW MEXICO HEBREW ACADEMY 4800 EUBANK N.E. ALBUQUERQUE **NM** 87111 (505) 296-5553
MAIMONIDES HEBREW DAY SCHOOL OF THE CAPITAL DISTRICT
18 FEDERAL STREET ALBANY **NY** 12209 (518) 449-5889
OHAEL SHMUEL, YESHIVA 165 HAINES ROAD BEDFORD HILLS **NY** 10507 (914) 241-2700
YESHIVAH OF BELLE HARBOR 134-01 ROCKAWAY BEACH BLVD BELLE HARBOR **NY** 11694 (718) 945-0309
HILLEL ACADEMY OF BROOME COUNTY DEERFIELD PLACE BINGHAMTON **NY** 13903 (607) 722-9274
BETH JACOB HIGH SCHOOL OF THE BRONX 2058 WALLACE AVENUE BRONX **NY** 10462 (212) 547-7860
BETH JACOB-BETH MIRIAM 2126 BARNES AVENUE BRONX **NY** 10462 (212) 892-1476
BETH JACOB-BETH MIRIAM HIGH SCHOOL OF THE BRONX
3006 WILLIAMSBRIDGE ROAD BRONX **NY** 10467 (212) 583-8993
BRONX YESHIVA HIGH SCHOOL 1328 ALLERTON AVENUE BRONX **NY** 10469 (212) 653-1363
BRONX YESHIVA HIGH SCHOOL 1524 PARKER STREET BRONX **NY** 10462 (212) 829-4570
HEBREW DAY NURSERY 5720 MOSHOLU AVENUE BRONX **NY** 10471 (212) 884-1101
KINNERET DAY SCHOOL 2600 NETHERLAND AVENUE BRONX **NY** 10463 (212) 548-0900
LUBAVITCHER YESHIVA ACHEI TMIMIM 3415 OLINVILLE AVENUE BRONX **NY** 10467 (212) 654-5318
SALANTER AKIBA RIVERDALE ACADEMY 655 WEST 254 STREET BRONX **NY** 10471 (212) 549-5160
TORAH V'EMUNAH YESHIVA 1778 EAST 172 STREET BRONX **NY** 10472 (212) 829-4701
ACHPRI TEVUAH, YESHIVA 1449 50TH STREET BROOKLYN **NY** 11219 (718) 436-5555
AHAVAS ISRAEL, YESHIVA 6 LEE AVENUE BROOKLYN **NY** 11211 (718) 388-0848
AHI EZER YESHIVA 2433 OCEAN PARKWAY BROOKLYN **NY** 11235 (718) 648-6100
AHI EZER YESHIVA ANNEX 293 NEPTUNE AVENUE BROOKLYN **NY** 11235 (718) 332-7000
ALTERNATIVE SCHOOL-BAIS SHOLOM, YESHIVA
555 REMSEN AVENUE BROOKLYN **NY** 11236 (718) 495-2100
ARUGATH HABOSEM, YESHIVA 171 HOOPER STREET BROOKLYN **NY** 11211 (718) 388-7534
ASSOCIATED BETH RIVKAH SCHOOLS 310 CROWN STREET BROOKLYN **NY** 11225 (718) 735-0400
ATERES YISRAEL, YESHIVA 8101 AVENUE K BROOKLYN **NY** 11236 (718) 763-6777
BAIS ISAAC ZVI 1019 46 STREET BROOKLYN **NY** 11219 (718) 854-7887
BAIS ROCHEL SCHOOL FOR GIRLS 225 PATCHEN AVENUE BROOKLYN **NY** 11233 (718) 453-0250
BAIS YAACOV D'KHAL ADAS YEREIM 563 BEDFORD AVENUE BROOKLYN **NY** 11211 (718) 782-2486
BAIS YAAKOV D'CHASSIDEI GUR 1480 43RD STREET BROOKLYN **NY** 11219 (718) 633-3335
BAIS YAAKOV KHAL ADAS YEREIM KINDERGARTEN
574 BEDFORD AVENUE BROOKLYN **NY** 11211 (718) 384-7187
BAIS YAAKOV OF 18TH AVENUE 4419 18TH AVENUE BROOKLYN **NY** 11204 (718) 633-6050
BAIS YAAKOV OF BROOKLYN 1362 49 STREET BROOKLYN **NY** 11219 (718) 435-7776
BAIS YAAKOV OF BROOKLYN ANNEX 4910 14TH AVENUE BROOKLYN **NY** 11219 (718) 854-1219
BAIS YAAKOV OF FERNDALE 1676 52TH STREET BROOKLYN **NY** 11204 (718) 851-5180
BAIS YITZCHAK FOR BOYS 1413 45TH AVENUE BROOKLYN **NY** 11219 (718) 851-6959
BAIS YITZCHAK FOR BOYS 4722 18TH AVENUE BROOKLYN **NY** 11204 (718) 854-0800
BE'ER HAGOLAH INST.-ADMINISTRATIVE OFFICES AND GIRLS H.S.
1709 KINGS HIGHWAY BROOKLYN **NY** 11229 (718) 627-7800
BE'ER HAGOLAH INSTITUTE 1709 KINGS HIGHWAY BROOKLYN **NY** 11229 (718) 627-7800
BE'ER HAGOLAH INSTITUTES 2810 NOSTRAND AVENUE BROOKLYN **NY** 11229 (718) 377-8423
BE'ER HAGOLAH INSTITUTES 2114 BROWN STREET BROOKLYN **NY** 11229 (718) 934-9247
BE'ER HAGOLAH INSTITUTES HIGH SCHOOL
1542 CONEY ISLAND AVENUE BROOKLYN **NY** 11230 (718) 338-0724
BE'ER MORDECAI 1670 OCEAN AVENUE BROOKLYN **NY** 11230 (718) 338-6064
BE'ER SHMUEL MESIVTA 4407 12TH AVENUE BROOKLYN **NY** 11219 (718) 853-1376
BE'ER SHMUEL, YESHIVA & MESIVTA 1363 50TH STREET BROOKLYN **NY** 11219 (718) 438-6100
BEN YEHUDA SCHOOL 405 81ST STREET BROOKLYN **NY** 11209 (718) 238-1504
BETH AM-LABOR ZIONIST CENTER & DAY SCHOOL
1182 BRIGHTON BEACH AVENUE BROOKLYN **NY** 11235 (718) 743-4442
BETH CHANA ELEMENTARY AND HIGH SCHOOL
620 BEDFORD AVENUE BROOKLYN **NY** 11211 (718) 552-7422
BETH CHANA ELEMENTARY AND HIGH SCHOOL 204 KEAP STREET BROOKLYN **NY** 11211 (718) 338-5491
BETH CHANA SCHOOL FOR GIRLS 204 KEAP STREET BROOKLYN **NY** 11211 (718) 522-7422
BETH EL ELEMENTARY SCHOOL 457 GRAND AVENUE BROOKLYN **NY** 11238 (718) 789-1259
BETH EL TALMUDIC INSTITUTE 1981 HOMECREST AVENUE BROOKLYN **NY** 11229 (718) 339-9117
BETH HAMEDRASH SHAAREI YOSHER 4102 16TH AVENUE BROOKLYN **NY** 11204 (718) 854-2290
BETH HATAIMUD 2127 82ND STREET BROOKLYN **NY** 11219 (718) 259-2525
BETH HILLEL OF KRASNA, YESHIVA 1364 66 42ND STREET BROOKLYN **NY** 11219 (718) 871-0210
BETH JACOB ACADEMY HIGH SCHOOL OF BROOKLYN
4419 18TH AVENUE BROOKLYN **NY** 11204 (718) 435-8478
BETH JACOB DAY SCHOOL FOR GIRLS 85 PARKVILLE BROOKLYN **NY** 11230 (718) 633-6555
BETH JACOB DAY SCHOOL FOR GIRLS 550 OCEAN PARKWAY BROOKLYN **NY** 11218 (718) 633-6555
BETH JACOB ELEMENTARY SCHOOL 4412 15TH STREET BROOKLYN **NY** 11219 (718) 851-2900
BETH JACOB ELEMENTARY SCHOOL 616 BEDFORD AVENUE BROOKLYN **NY** 11211 (718) 782-7117
BETH JACOB HIGH SCHOOL 4421 15TH AVENUE BROOKLYN **NY** 11219 (718) 851-2255
BETH JACOB PAROCHIAL HIGH SCHOOL 4121 CROWN STREET BROOKLYN **NY** 11219 (718) 851-2900
BETH JACOB SCHOOL 616 BEDFORD AVENUE BROOKLYN **NY** 11211 (718) 625-8390
BETH JACOB OF BORO PARK 1371 46TH STREET BROOKLYN **NY** 11219 (718) 436-7300
BETH JACOB OF BORO PARK 1413 45TH STREET BROOKLYN **NY** 11219 (718) 853-7197
BETH JACOB OF FLATBUSH 1823 OCEAN PARKWAY BROOKLYN **NY** 11223 (718) 375-7771
BETH JACOB OF FLATBUSH 1823 OCEAN PARKWAY BROOKLYN **NY** 11223 (718) 645-2009
BETH JACOB OF MIDWOOD-OCEAN PRIMARY SCHOOL
904 EAST 98TH STREET BROOKLYN **NY** 11236 (718) 649-1567
BETH KIRSH NURSERY 1014 EAST 15TH STREET BROOKLYN **NY** 11230 (718) 377-8426
BETH MOSHE COMMUNITY SCHOOL 910 48TH STREET BROOKLYN **NY** 11219 (718) 633-1591
BETH RACHEL SCHOOL FOR GIRLS 62 HARRISON AVENUE BROOKLYN **NY** 11211 (718) 963-9593
BETH RACHEL SCHOOL FOR GIRLS 277 MARCY AVENUE BROOKLYN **NY** 11211 (718) 384-4923
BETH RACHEL SCHOOL FOR GIRLS 165 CLYMER STREET BROOKLYN **NY** 11211 (718) 782-8811
BETH RACHEL SCHOOL FOR GIRLS-PRE-SCHOOL 960 49TH STREET BROOKLYN **NY** 11219 (718) 438-7822
BETH RACHEL SCHOOL OF BORO PARK 5301 14TH AVENUE BROOKLYN **NY** 11219 (718) 438-7822
BETH RIVKA ELEMENTARY SCHOOL 2270 CHURCH AVENUE BROOKLYN **NY** 11226 (718) 856-4451
BETH RIVKA SCHOOLS 2270 CHURCH AVENUE BROOKLYN **NY** 11226 (718) 771-9000
BETH RIVKAH HIGH SCHOOL 310 CROWN STREET BROOKLYN **NY** 11225 (718) 771-9000
BETH RIVKAH SCHOOLS 310 CROWN STREET BROOKLYN **NY** 11225 (718) 771-9000
BETH SARAH SCHOOL 5801 16TH AVENUE BROOKLYN **NY** 11204 (718) 851-5198
BETH SHEARIM YESHIVA 5306 16TH AVENUE BROOKLYN **NY** 11204 (718) 851-0089
BETH YEHUDA V'CHAIM D'BETLAN YESHIVA 52-62 KEAP STREET BROOKLYN **NY** 11211 (718) 855-3546
BETH YITZCHOK D'SPINKA, YESHIVA 192 KEAP STREET BROOKLYN **NY** 11211 (718) 387-4597
BIALIK SCHOOL, THE 500 CHURCH AVENUE BROOKLYN **NY** 11218 (718) 853-7100
BNOS ISRAEL OF EAST FLATBUSH 9214 AVENUE B BROOKLYN **NY** 11236 (718) 498-1991
BNOS ISRAEL OF EAST FLATBUSH 2818 AVENUE K BROOKLYN **NY** 11210 (718) 253-9141
BNOS JERUSALEM-BELZ GIRLS SCHOOL 12 FRANKLIN AVENUE BROOKLYN **NY** 11211 (718) 852-5551
BNOS YAAKOV EDUCATIONAL CENTER FOR GIRLS
62 HARRISON STREET BROOKLYN **NY** 11211 (718) 855-8275
BNOS YAAKOV EDUCATIONAL CENTER FOR GIRLS 95 PENN STREET BROOKLYN **NY** 11211 (718) 387-6880
BNOS YAAKOV EDUCATIONAL CENTER FOR GIRLS
5000 14TH AVENUE BROOKLYN **NY** 11219 (718) 438-3080
BNOS YAKOV SCHOOL FOR GIRLS 174 PACIFIC STREET BROOKLYN **NY** 11201 (718) 963-3940
BNOS YISROEL SCHOOL FOR GIRLS 2 LEE AVENUE BROOKLYN **NY** 11211 (718) 388-0848
BNOS ZION OF BOBOV 5000 14TH AVENUE BROOKLYN **NY** 11219 (718) 438-3080
BNOS ZION OF BOBOV 5220 13TH AVENUE BROOKLYN **NY** 11219 (718) 853-7182
BOBOVER YESHIVA 1533 48TH STREET BROOKLYN **NY** 11219 (718) 438-8411
BOBOVER YESHIVA BNEI ZION 1533 48TH STREET BROOKLYN **NY** 11219 (718) 871-0300
BOBOVER YESHIVA BNEI ZION 4715 15TH AVENUE BROOKLYN **NY** 11219 (718) 436-3479
BORO PARK TORAH INSTITUTE 1417 49TH STREET BROOKLYN **NY** 11219 (718) 438-7633
BRIGHTON YESHIVA 293 NEPTUNE AVENUE BROOKLYN **NY** 11235 (718) 332-7000
BROOKLYN SCHOOL FOR SPECIAL CHILDREN 376 BAY 44TH STREET BROOKLYN **NY** 11234 (718) 946-9700
BROOKLYN, YESHIVA OF 1462-66 OCEAN PARKWAY BROOKLYN **NY** 11230 (718) 376-3775
BROOKLYN, YESHIVA OF (BOYS) 1210 OCEAN PARKWAY BROOKLYN **NY** 11230 (718) 376-3775
BROOKLYN, YESHIVA OF (GIRLS) 1470 OCEAN PARKWAY BROOKLYN **NY** 11230 (718) 376-3775
CENTRAL YESHIVA TOMCHEI TMIMIM LUBAVITCH
841-853 OCEAN PARKWAY BROOKLYN **NY** 11230 (718) 859-7600
CH'SAN SOFER YESHIVA-RABBI SOLOMON KLUGER
1876 50TH STREET BROOKLYN **NY** 11204 (718) 236-1171
CHANOCH LENAAR, YESHIVA 876 EASTERN PARKWAY BROOKLYN **NY** 11213 (718) 774-8456
CHATZAR HAKODESH, YESHIVA 1450 50TH STREET BROOKLYN **NY** 11219 (718) 436-1234
CHESED YISRAEL, YESHIVA 2422 AVENUE K BROOKLYN **NY** 11210 (718) 338-8300
COMMUNITY SCHOOL BETH MOSHE 910 48TH STREET BROOKLYN **NY** 11219 (718) 633-1591
CROWN HEIGHTS, YESHIVA OF 6363 AVENUE U BROOKLYN **NY** 11234 (718) 444-5800
CROWN OF ISRAEL TALMUD TORAH 1769 56TH STREET BROOKLYN **NY** 11204 (718) 232-4827
DARKEI TSHUVA OF MUNKATSCH, YESHIVA 240 KEAP STREET BROOKLYN **NY** 11211
DEJESHER YESHIVA, MAGLE ZEDEK 1223 35TH STREET BROOKLYN **NY** 11219 (718) 436-0239
DERECH EMUNOH 1554 49TH STREET BROOKLYN **NY** 11219 (718) 851-6774
EDUCATIONAL INSTITUTE OHOLEI TORAH 667 EASTERN PARKWAY BROOKLYN **NY** 11213 (718) 778-3340
EITZ CHAIM OF BOBOV-BOBOVER YESHIVA 1533 48TH STREET BROOKLYN **NY** 11219 (718) 871-0300
EZRA ACADEMY C/O RABBI GREENWALD, 20 AMHERST STREET BROOKLYN **NY** 11235

FLATBUSH, YESHIVA OF 919 EAST 10TH STREET	BROOKLYN	**NY**	11230	(718) 377-4466
FLATBUSH, YESHIVA OF-JOEL BRAVERMAN HIGH SCHOOL 1609 AVENUE J	BROOKLYN	**NY**	11230	(718) 377-4466
FREE SCHOOL 1383 PRESIDENT STREET	BROOKLYN	**NY**	11213	(718) 467-0860
GERER YESHIVA & MESIFTA-MACHZEIKI HADATH 5407 16TH AVENUE	BROOKLYN	**NY**	11204	(718) 438-7700
HARAMA, YESHIVA 2600 OCEAN AVENUE	BROOKLYN	**NY**	11229	(718) 743-3141
HADAR HATORAH 824 EASTERN PARKWAY	BROOKLYN	**NY**	11213	(718) 735-0200
HAICHEL HATORAH, MESIVTA 2449 OCEAN AVENUE	BROOKLYN	**NY**	11229	(718) 648-1150
HARMA INSTITUTE SEPHARDIC COMMUNITY HIGH SCHOOL 2600 OCEAN AVENUE	BROOKLYN	**NY**	11229	(718) 743-3141
HARMA RELIGIOUS INST. OF SEC EDUC-YESHIVA H.S. FOR GIRLS 2600 OCEAN AVENUE	BROOKLYN	**NY**	11229	(718) 743-3141
HEBREW ACADEMY FOR SPECIAL CHILDREN 1311 55TH STREET	BROOKLYN	**NY**	11219	(718) 851-6100
HEBREW INSTITUTE FOR THE DEAF & EXCEPTIONAL CHILDREN 2025 67TH STREET	BROOKLYN	**NY**	11204	(718) 259-2626
HEBREW INSTITUTE OF BORO PARK 4702 15TH AVENUE	BROOKLYN	**NY**	11219	(718) 853-1600
HEBREW MIDRASHA OF BROOKLYN 1609 AVENUE J	BROOKLYN	**NY**	11230	
IMREI YOSEF SPINKA, YESHIVA 1460 56TH STREET	BROOKLYN	**NY**	11219	(718) 851-1600
INSTITUTE FOR OLEI RUSSYA 4901 11TH AVENUE	BROOKLYN	**NY**	11219	(718) 633-6244
INSTITUTE OF ADAS ISRAEL 1454 OCEAN PARKWAY	BROOKLYN	**NY**	11230	
JESODE HATORAH NACHLAS YAKOV, YESHIVA 1350 50TH STREET	BROOKLYN	**NY**	11219	(718) 851-6462
JESODE HATORAH OF ADAS YEREIM, YESHIVA 505 BEDFORD AVENUE	BROOKLYN	**NY**	11211	(718) 384-6393
JEWISH CENTER FOR SPECIAL EDUCATION 430 KENT AVENUE	BROOKLYN	**NY**	11211	(718) 782-0064
JOSEPH S. GRUSS HIGH SCHOOL-TORAS EMES OF KAMINETZ 1650 56TH STREET	BROOKLYN	**NY**	11204	(718) 851-4735
KARLIN STOLIN, YESHIVA 1818 54TH STREET	BROOKLYN	**NY**	11204	(718) 232-7800
KEHILATH YAKOV, YESHIVA 206 WILSON STREET	BROOKLYN	**NY**	11211	(718) 963-3940
KESSER MALKA 1315 43RD STREET	BROOKLYN	**NY**	11219	(718) 854-2528
KESSER MALKA 1315 43RD STREET	BROOKLYN	**NY**	11219	(718) 854-7777
KHAL ADAS PAYE, YESHIVA 296 MARCY AVENUE	BROOKLYN	**NY**	11211	(718) 387-2231
KINGS BAY, YESHIVA OF 2611 AVENUE Z	BROOKLYN	**NY**	11235	(718) 646-8500
KINGSWAY ACADEMY 2810 NOSTRAND AVENUE	BROOKLYN	**NY**	11229	(718) 258-3344
LEV SOMEACH, YESHIVA 674 EAST 2ND STREET	BROOKLYN	**NY**	11218	(718) 338-3929
M'KOR CHAIM, MESIFTA 1571 55TH STREET	BROOKLYN	**NY**	11219	(718) 851-0183
MACHZIKE TALMUD TORAH OF BORO PARK 4622 14TH AVENUE	BROOKLYN	**NY**	11219	(718) 436-8690
MACHZIKEI HADAS, YESHIVA 1601 42ND STREET	BROOKLYN	**NY**	11204	(718) 436-4445
MACHZIKEI TORAH, YESHIVA 630 BEDFORD AVENUE	BROOKLYN	**NY**	11211	(718) 875-2164
MAGEN DAVID YESHIVA 50 AVENUE P	BROOKLYN	**NY**	11204	(718) 236-5905
MANHATTAN BEACH, YESHIVA OF 60 WEST END AVENUE	BROOKLYN	**NY**	11235	(718) 743-5511
MESIVTA EITZ CHAIM OF BOBOV 1573 48TH STREET	BROOKLYN	**NY**	11219	(718) 438-2018
MESIVTA HAICHEL HATORAH 2449 OCEAN AVENUE	BROOKLYN	**NY**	11229	(718) 648-1150
MESIVTA M'KOR CHAIM 1571 55TH STREET	BROOKLYN	**NY**	11219	(718) 851-0197
MESIVTA NACHLAS YAKOV 185 WILSON STREET	BROOKLYN	**NY**	11211	(718) 388-1751
MESIVTA RABBI CHAIM BERLIN 1593 CONEY ISLAND AVENUE	BROOKLYN	**NY**	11230	(718) 377-0777
MESIVTA SHAAREI EMUNAH 1631 42ND STREET	BROOKLYN	**NY**	11204	(718) 853-1898
MESIVTA TORAH VODAATH 425 EAST 9TH STREET	BROOKLYN	**NY**	11218	(718) 941-8000
MIDWOOD INSTITUTE OF TORAH 1286 E 10TH STREET	BROOKLYN	**NY**	11230	(718) 252-6168
MINCHAS ELUZAR D'MUNKACS, YESHIVA 1377 42ND STREET	BROOKLYN	**NY**	11219	(718) 438-5246
MIRRER YESHIVA 1791 OCEAN PARKWAY	BROOKLYN	**NY**	11223	(718) 645-0536
MIRRER YESHIVA CENTRAL INST.-MORRIS MORGENSTERN HIGH SCHOOL 1795 OCEAN PARKWAY	BROOKLYN	**NY**	11223	(718) 645-0536
MIZRACHI L'BONIM 2114 BROWN STREET	BROOKLYN	**NY**	11229	(718) 934-3663
NACHLAS YAAKOV OF ADAS YEREIM, MESIFTA 185 WILSON STREET	BROOKLYN	**NY**	11211	(718) 388-1751
NODAH B'YEHUDA, INC. 750 REMSEN AVENUE	BROOKLYN	**NY**	11236	
OHEL MOSHE, YESHIVA 7914 BAY PARKWAY	BROOKLYN	**NY**	11214	(718) 236-4003
OHEL SOROH SCHOOL 771 CROWN STREET	BROOKLYN	**NY**	11213	(718) 756-8300
OHOLEI TORAH 706 EASTERN PARKWAY	BROOKLYN	**NY**	11213	(718) 778-3340
OHOLEI TORAH 667 EASTERN PARKWAY	BROOKLYN	**NY**	11213	(718) 778-3340
OHOLEI TORAH 417 TROY AVENUE	BROOKLYN	**NY**	11213	(718) 773-9658
PHILIP HIRTH ACADEMY 4419 18TH STREET	BROOKLYN	**NY**	11204	(718) 435-8478
PHILIP HIRTH ACADEMY OF BROOKLYN 1213-1223 ELM STREET	BROOKLYN	**NY**	11230	(718) 339-4747
PROSPECT PARK YESHIVA 1202 AVENUE P	BROOKLYN	**NY**	11229	(718) 645-7800
PROSPECT PARK YESHIVA 1609 AVENUE R	BROOKLYN	**NY**	11229	(718) 376-0004
RABBI CHAIM BERLIN, MESIVTA 1302 AVENUE I	BROOKLYN	**NY**	11230	(718) 277-0777
RABBI CHAIM BERLIN, YESHIVA 1302 AVENUE I	BROOKLYN	**NY**	11230	(718) 253-1000
RABBI HARRY HALPERN DAY SCHOOL/EAST MIDWOOD JEWISH CENTER 1625 OCEAN AVENUE	BROOKLYN	**NY**	11230	(718) 338-3800
RABBI HIRSH DACHOWITZ SCHOOL R'TZAHD YESHIVA 1800 UTICA AVENUE	BROOKLYN	**NY**	11234	(718) 763-5500
RABBINICAL SEMINARY OF MUNKACS 1377 42ND STREET	BROOKLYN	**NY**	11219	(718) 438-5246
RAMBAM, YESHIVA 3300 KINGS HIGHWAY	BROOKLYN	**NY**	11234	(718) 338-6918
SARA SCHENIRER HIGH SCHOOL AND TEACHERS SEMINARY 4622 14TH AVENUE	BROOKLYN	**NY**	11219	(718) 633-8557
SAVE RUSSIAN JEWRY 2324 WEST 13TH STREET	BROOKLYN	**NY**	11223	(718) 449-6741
SEPHARDIC HIGH SCHOOL 511 AVENUE R	BROOKLYN	**NY**	11223	(718) 998-8171
SEPHARDIC INSTITUTE 511 AVENUE R	BROOKLYN	**NY**	11223	(718) 998-8171
SHAAREI EMUNAH, MESIVTA 153 OCEAN AVENUE	BROOKLYN	**NY**	11225	(718) 287-4700
SHAAREI YOSHER, YESHIVA 4104 16TH AVENUE	BROOKLYN	**NY**	11204	(718) 854-2290
SHAREI ZEDEK, YESHIVA 3701 SURF AVENUE	BROOKLYN	**NY**	11224	(718) 266-4604
SHEVET YEHUDA, YESHIVA 5220 13TH AVENUE	BROOKLYN	**NY**	11219	(718) 342-6878
SHEVET YEHUDAH RESNICK INSTITUTE OF TECHNOLOGY 5220 13TH AVENUE	BROOKLYN	**NY**	11219	(718) 853-1212
SHULAMITH SCHOOL FOR GIRLS 1350-1353 50TH STREET	BROOKLYN	**NY**	11219	(718) 853-7070
SHULAMITH SCHOOL FOR GIRLS 1277 EAST 14TH STREET	BROOKLYN	**NY**	11230	(718) 338-4000
SHULAMITH SCHOOL FOR GIRLS 60 WEST END AVENUE	BROOKLYN	**NY**	11235	(718) 338-4000
SOLOMON SCHECHTER HIGH SCHOOL OF BROOKLYN 500 CHURCH AVENUE	BROOKLYN	**NY**	11218	(718) 854-3500
TALMUD TORAH TIFERES BUNIM 5202 13TH AVENUE	BROOKLYN	**NY**	11219	(718) 436-6868
TALMUD TORAH TOLDOS YAKOV YOSEF 1383 44TH STREET	BROOKLYN	**NY**	11219	(718) 436-2550
TALMUD TORAH TOLDOS YAKOV YOSEF 105 HEYWARD ST (MAIL:GPO BOX 1721, BKLN 11206)	BROOKLYN	**NY**	11211	(718) 852-0502
TALMUD TORAH TOLDOS YAKOV YOSEF 94 WILSON	BROOKLYN	**NY**	11237	(718) 387-1130
TALMUD TORAH TOMCHAI TORAH 1722 AVENUE N	BROOKLYN	**NY**	11230	(718) 336-8072
TALMUDICAL HIGH SCHOOL OF BROOKLYN 1182 BRIGHTON BEACH AVENUE	BROOKLYN	**NY**	11235	(718) 796-4646
THE JEWISH CENTER FOR SPECIAL EDUC-YESHIVA LIMUDEI HASHEM 430 KENT AVENUE	BROOKLYN	**NY**	11211	(718) 782-0064
TIFERES BUNIM 5202 13TH AVENUE	BROOKLYN	**NY**	11219	(718) 436-6870
TIFERES ELIMELICH, YESHIVA 54 AVENUE O	BROOKLYN	**NY**	11204	(718) 236-1001
TINOK SCHOOL 1440 E 99TH STREET	BROOKLYN	**NY**	11236	(718) 436-5555
TOMER D'VORA SCHOOL FOR GIRLS 1413 45TH STREET	BROOKLYN	**NY**	11219	(718) 853-9400
TOMER DVORA HIGH SCHOOL 1462 50TH STREET	BROOKLYN	**NY**	11219	(718) 438-4600
TOMER DVORA SCHOOL FOR GIRLS 4500 9TH AVENUE	BROOKLYN	**NY**	11219	(718) 853-9400
TORAH ACADEMY OF BROOKLYN 1540 CONEY ISLAND AVENUE	BROOKLYN	**NY**	11230	(718) 998-0110
TORAH TEMIMAH, YESHIVA 555 OCEAN PARKWAY	BROOKLYN	**NY**	11218	(718) 853-8500
TORAH UMESORAH HEADSTART PROGRAM 1315 43RD STREET	BROOKLYN	**NY**	11219	(718) 851-0402
TORAH V'YIRAH FOR GIRLS, YESHIVA 5301 14TH STREET	BROOKLYN	**NY**	11219	(718) 438-7822
TORAH VODAATH, YESHIVA 425 EAST 9TH STREET	BROOKLYN	**NY**	11218	(718) 941-8000
TORAS EMES OF KAMINETZ, YESHIVA 1650 56TH STREET	BROOKLYN	**NY**	11204	(718) 851-4735
TZE ULMAD 1725 E. 27TH STREET	BROOKLYN	**NY**	11229	
UNGVARER YESHIVA 5306 16TH AVENUE	BROOKLYN	**NY**	11219	(718) 851-0806
UNITED LUBAVITCHER YESHIVAH HIGH SCHOOL 841 OCEAN PARKWAY	BROOKLYN	**NY**	11230	(718) 434-0795
UNITED LUBAVITCHER YESHIVOTH 841 OCEAN PARKWAY	BROOKLYN	**NY**	11230	(718) 434-0795
UNITED LUBAVITCHER YESHIVOTH 841 OCEAN PARKWAY	BROOKLYN	**NY**	11230	(718) 859-7600
UNITED TALMUDICAL ACADEMY/BETH RACHEL SCHOOL FOR GIRLS 62 HARRISON AVENUE	BROOKLYN	**NY**	11211	(718) 963-9260
UNITED TALMUDICAL ACADEMY HIGH SCHOOL 227 MARCY AVENUE	BROOKLYN	**NY**	11211	(718) 963-9260
UNITED TALMUDICAL ACADEMY TORAH V'YIRAH 5301 14TH AVENUE	BROOKLYN	**NY**	11219	(718) 438-7822
UNITED TALMUDICAL ACADEMY TORAH V'YIRAH 94 THROOP AVENUE	BROOKLYN	**NY**	11206	(718) 963-9290
UNITED TALMUDICAL ACADEMY TORAH V'YIRAH 236-238 MARCY AVENUE	BROOKLYN	**NY**	11211	(718) 563-0658
UNITED TALMUDICAL ACADEMY TORAH V'YIRAH 212 WILLIAMSBURG STREET EAST	BROOKLYN	**NY**	11211	(718) 963-9288
UNITED TALMUDICAL ACADEMY TORAH V'YIRAH 165 CLYMER STREET	BROOKLYN	**NY**	11211	(718) 384-9585
UNITED TALMUDICAL ACADEMY/TORAH V'YIRAH FOR BOYS, YESHIVA 82 LEE AVENUE	BROOKLYN	**NY**	11211	(718) 963-9260
YAGDIL TORAH, YESHIVA 5110 18TH AVENUE	BROOKLYN	**NY**	11204	(718) 871-9100
YESHIVA & BETH JACOB OF CANARSIE 904 E. 98TH STREET	BROOKLYN	**NY**	11234	(718) 649-1567
YESHIVA & MESIFTA BEER SHMUEL 4407 12TH AVENUE	BROOKLYN	**NY**	11219	(718) 853-1376
YESHIVA & MESIVTA BAIS YITZCHOCK D'CHASIDEI SKWERE 4722 18TH AVENUE	BROOKLYN	**NY**	11204	(718) 436-9434
YESHIVA ACH PRI TEVUAH 1449 50 STREET	BROOKLYN	**NY**	11219	
YESHIVA AHAVAS YISROEL 6 LEE AVENUE	BROOKLYN	**NY**	11211	(718) 388-0848
YESHIVA ATERES YISROEL 8101 AVENUE K	BROOKLYN	**NY**	11236	(718) 763-6777
YESHIVA ATERET TORAH 1020 OCEAN PARKWAY	BROOKLYN	**NY**	11230	(718) 258-1776
YESHIVA BAIS EPHRAIM 2802 AVENUE J	BROOKLYN	**NY**	11210	(718) 377-8448
YESHIVA BAIS HILLEL MOSES 229 NEPTUNE AVENUE	BROOKLYN	**NY**	11235	
YESHIVA BAIS JEHUDO OF BORO PARK 1383 44TH STREET	BROOKLYN	**NY**	11219	
YESHIVA BAIS YITZCHOK 1334 47TH AVENUE	BROOKLYN	**NY**	11219	
YESHIVA BAIS YITZCHOK D'SPINKA 182 KEAP STREET	BROOKLYN	**NY**	11211	(718) 387-4597
YESHIVA BAIS YITZCHOK D'SPINKA 191 RODNEY STREET	BROOKLYN	**NY**	11211	(718) 387-4597
YESHIVA BETH HATALMUD 2127 82ND STREET	BROOKLYN	**NY**	11214	(718) 259-2525
YESHIVA BETH HILLEL OF KRASNE 1364 42ND STREET	BROOKLYN	**NY**	11219	(718) 871-0210
YESHIVA BETH REUVEN 1111 55TH STREET	BROOKLYN	**NY**	11219	(718) 435-2535
YESHIVA BETH YITZCHAK SPINK 205 HOOPER STREET	BROOKLYN	**NY**	11211	
YESHIVA CHANOCH LENAAR 876 EASTERN PARKWAY	BROOKLYN	**NY**	11213	(718) 774-8456
YESHIVA CHATZAR HAKODESH SANZ-KLAUSENBERG 1420 50TH STREET	BROOKLYN	**NY**	11219	(718) 436-1234
YESHIVA CHESSED YISROEL 2422 AVENUE K	BROOKLYN	**NY**	11210	(718) 338-8300
YESHIVA DARKEI TSHIVO OF MUNKATSH 240 KEAP STREET	BROOKLYN	**NY**	11211	
YESHIVA FARM SETTLEMENT 194 DIVISION AVENUE	BROOKLYN	**NY**	11211	(718) 387-0422
YESHIVA HAICHEL HATORAH 2449 OCEAN AVENUE	BROOKLYN	**NY**	11229	
YESHIVA HARAMA HIGH SCHOOL FOR GIRLS 2600 OCEAN AVENUE	BROOKLYN	**NY**	11229	(718) 743-3142
YESHIVA HARAMA TIFERETH ZVI 319 CROWN STREET	BROOKLYN	**NY**	11225	(718) 773-5530
YESHIVA HARBOTZAS TORAH 239 HAVEMEYER STREET	BROOKLYN	**NY**	11211	
YESHIVA IMREI YOSEF SPINKA 5801 15TH AVENUE	BROOKLYN	**NY**	11219	(718) 851-1600
YESHIVA IMREI YOSEF SPINKA 1460 56TH STREET	BROOKLYN	**NY**	11219	(718) 851-1600
YESHIVA INSTITUTE 6414 BAY PARKWAY	BROOKLYN	**NY**	11204	(718) 259-1432
YESHIVA JESODE HATORAH OF BORO PARK 1350 50TH STREET	BROOKLYN	**NY**	11219	(718) 851-6462
YESHIVA JESODE HATORAH OF BORO PARK 5402 14TH AVENUE	BROOKLYN	**NY**	11219	
YESHIVA KAHAL MAGLEI ZEDEK DEJ 1223 45TH STREET	BROOKLYN	**NY**	11219	
YESHIVA KEHILATH YAAKOV 206 WILSON STREET	BROOKLYN	**NY**	11211	(718) 963-3940
YESHIVA KETANA OF OCEAN AVENUE 2449 OCEAN AVENUE	BROOKLYN	**NY**	11229	(718) 648-1152
YESHIVA M'KOR CHAIM 1571 55TH STREET	BROOKLYN	**NY**	11219	(718) 851-0183
YESHIVA MACHZIKEI HADAS BELZ 1601 42ND STREET	BROOKLYN	**NY**	11204	(718) 436-4445
YESHIVA MACHZIKEI TORAH D'CHASSIDEI BELZ 630 BEDFORD AVENUE	BROOKLYN	**NY**	11211	(718) 237-1818
YESHIVA MEOR HATORAH 2221 OCEAN AVENUE	BROOKLYN	**NY**	11229	
YESHIVA NACHLAS HALEVYIM 544 E. 92ND STREET	BROOKLYN	**NY**	11236	
YESHIVA NESEVOS OLUM 205 HEWES STREET	BROOKLYN	**NY**	11211	
YESHIVA OHR MOLEH KOSON 1645 53RD STREET	BROOKLYN	**NY**	11204	
YESHIVA R'TZAHD - THE RABBI HIRSH DACHOWITZ DAY SCHOOL 1800 UTICA AVENUE	BROOKLYN	**NY**	11234	(718) 763-5500
YESHIVA RABBI CHAIM BERLIN 1302 AVENUE I	BROOKLYN	**NY**	11230	(718) 253-1000
YESHIVA RABBI CHAIM BERLIN 1569 CONEY ISLAND AVENUE	BROOKLYN	**NY**	11230	(718) 252-7190
YESHIVA RABBI DAVID LEIBOWITZ 9102 CHURCH AVENUE	BROOKLYN	**NY**	11236	
YESHIVA RABBI HACOHEN 289 EAST 53RD STREET	BROOKLYN	**NY**	11203	
YESHIVA RABBI SOLOMON KLUGER-MESIVTA CHASAN SOFER 1876 50TH STREET	BROOKLYN	**NY**	11204	(718) 236-1171
YESHIVA RAMBAM 3300 KINGS HIGHWAY	BROOKLYN	**NY**	11234	(718) 338-6918

YESHIVA SHAAREI SIMCHA 4619 13TH AVENUE	BROOKLYN	**NY**	11219	
YESHIVA SHAAREI TORAH 1326 OCEAN PARKWAY	BROOKLYN	**NY**	11230	(718) 998-3883
YESHIVA SHAAREI YOSHER 4102 16TH AVENUE	BROOKLYN	**NY**	11204	(718) 854-2290
YESHIVA SHAREI ZEDEK IN SEA GATE 3701 SURF AVENUE	BROOKLYN	**NY**	11224	(718) 266-4604
YESHIVA SHARIE HAYOSHER 1440 E. 99TH STREET	BROOKLYN	**NY**	11236	(718) 436-5555
YESHIVA TIFERES ELIMELECH 54 AVENUE O	BROOKLYN	**NY**	11204	(718) 236-1001
YESHIVA TIFERETH AVROHOM 2997 OCEAN PARKWAY	BROOKLYN	**NY**	11235	
YESHIVA TOLDOS YAKOV YOSEF CHASIDEI SQVERE 1383 44TH STREET	BROOKLYN	**NY**	11219	(718) 436-2550
YESHIVA TORAH 5114 18TH AVENUE	BROOKLYN	**NY**	11204	
YESHIVA TORAH M'ZION 1440 E. 99TH STREET	BROOKLYN	**NY**	11236	
YESHIVA TORAH V'YIRAH OF BORO PARK 1356 53RD STREET	BROOKLYN	**NY**	11219	
YESHIVA TORAH VODAATH 425 EAST 9TH STREET	BROOKLYN	**NY**	11218	(718) 941-8000
YESHIVA TORAS EMES KAMENITZ 1650 56TH STREET	BROOKLYN	**NY**	11204	(718) 851-4735
YESHIVA TORAS EMES KAMENITZ-JOSEPH S. GRUSS HIGH SCHOOL 1650 56TH STREET	BROOKLYN	**NY**	11204	(718) 851-4735
YESHIVA TORAS EMES KAMENITZ-JOSEPH S. GRUSS HIGH SCHOOL 1310 53RD STREET	BROOKLYN	**NY**	11219	(718) 851-4735
YESHIVA TORAS EMES KAMENITZ-JOSEPH S. GRUSS HIGH SCHOOL 321 AVENUE N	BROOKLYN	**NY**	11230	(718) 851-4735
YESHIVA YAGDIL TORAH 5110 18TH AVENUE	BROOKLYN	**NY**	11204	(718) 871-9100
YESHIVA YESODE HATORAH 187 HOOPER STREET	BROOKLYN	**NY**	11211	(718) 387-6242
YESHIVA YESODE HATORAH 131 LEE AVENUE	BROOKLYN	**NY**	11211	(718) 384-1611
YESHIVA YESODE HATORAH SHEARITH HAPLETA 131 LEE AVENUE	BROOKLYN	**NY**	11211	
YESHIVA YESODE HATORAH OF ADAS YEREIM 505 BEDFORD AVENUE	BROOKLYN	**NY**	11211	(718) 384-6393
YESHIVA YESODEI HACHAIM HIGH SCHOOL 4514 11TH AVENUE	BROOKLYN	**NY**	11219	(718) 851-5755
YESHIVA YESODEI HATORAH (WEINER YESHIVA) 1350 50TH STREET	BROOKLYN	**NY**	11219	(718) 851-6462
YESHIVA ZICHRON ELIEZER MESKIN 725 CROWN STREET	BROOKLYN	**NY**	11213	(718) 773-1298
YESHIVA ZICHRON YOSEF ARYEH 4911 16TH AVENUE	BROOKLYN	**NY**	11204	
YESHIVA AND MESIVTA ARUGATH HABOSEM 171-173 HOOPER STREET	BROOKLYN	**NY**	11211	(718) 388-7534
YESHIVA AND MESIVTA BAIS SHOLOM ALTERNATIVE SCHOOL 555 REMSEN AVENUE	BROOKLYN	**NY**	11236	(718) 494-2100
YESHIVA AND MESIVTA BAIS YITZCHOK 4314 10TH AVENUE	BROOKLYN	**NY**	11220	(718) 851-6959
YESHIVA AND MESIVTA BE'ER SCHMUEL 4407 12TH AVENUE	BROOKLYN	**NY**	11219	(718) 853-1376
YESHIVA AND MESIVTA BE'ER SCHMUEL 1363 50TH STREET	BROOKLYN	**NY**	11219	(718) 438-6100
YESHIVA AND MESIVTA KARLIN STOLIN 1818 54TH STREET	BROOKLYN	**NY**	11204	(718) 232-7800
YESHIVA AND MESIVTA MAHARYATS MARGARETEN 7902 15TH AVENUE	BROOKLYN	**NY**	11228	(718) 259-0423
YESHIVA AND MESIVTA TORAH TEMIMAH 555 OCEAN PARKWAY	BROOKLYN	**NY**	11218	(718) 853-8500
YESHIVA OF BENSONHURST, INC. 2025 79TH STREET	BROOKLYN	**NY**	11214	(718) 232-7400
YESHIVA OF BRIGHTON 293 NEPTUNE AVENUE	BROOKLYN	**NY**	11235	
YESHIVA OF BROOKLYN 1470-1476 OCEAN PARKWAY	BROOKLYN	**NY**	11230	(718) 376-3775
YESHIVA OF BROOKLYN-BOYS DIVISION 1210 OCEAN PARKWAY	BROOKLYN	**NY**	11230	(718) 376-3775
YESHIVA OF BROOKLYN-GIRLS HIGH SCHOOL DIVISION 1470-1476 OCEAN PARKWAY	BROOKLYN	**NY**	11230	(718) 376-3775
YESHIVA OF CANARSIE 904 EAST 98TH STREET	BROOKLYN	**NY**	11236	(718) 649-1567
YESHIVA OF CROWN HEIGHTS 6363 AVENUE U	BROOKLYN	**NY**	11234	(718) 444-5800
YESHIVA OF FLATBUSH 919 E. 10TH STREET	BROOKLYN	**NY**	11230	(718) 377-4466
YESHIVA OF FLATBUSH ELEMENTARY SCHOOL 919 EAST 10TH STREET	BROOKLYN	**NY**	11230	(718) 377-4466
YESHIVA OF FLATBUSH HIGH SCHOOL 1609 AVENUE J	BROOKLYN	**NY**	11230	(718) 377-4466
YESHIVA OF FLATBUSH-JOEL BRAVERMAN HIGH SCHOOL & ELEMENTARY 1609 AVENUE J	BROOKLYN	**NY**	11230	(718) 377-4466
YESHIVA OF KINGS BAY 2611 AVENUE Z	BROOKLYN	**NY**	11235	(718) 646-8500
YESHIVA OF MANHATTAN BEACH 60 WEST END AVENUE	BROOKLYN	**NY**	11235	(718) 743-5511
YESHIVA OF MIDWOOD 904 EAST 98TH STREET	BROOKLYN	**NY**	11203	
YESHIVAH MAGEN DAVID 50 AVENUE P	BROOKLYN	**NY**	11204	
YESHIVAH OHEL MOSHE 7914 BAY PARKWAY	BROOKLYN	**NY**	11214	(718) 236-4003
YESHIVAS CH'SAN SOFER 1876 50TH STREET	BROOKLYN	**NY**	11204	(718) 236-1171
YESHIVAT MIZRACHI L'BANIM 2114 BROWN STREET	BROOKLYN	**NY**	11229	(718) 252-3579
YESHIVATH CHACHMEY LUBLIN 1404 E. 7TH STREET	BROOKLYN	**NY**	11230	
YESOD HACHAIM YESHIVA 4514 11TH AVENUE	BROOKLYN	**NY**	11219	(718) 851-5755
YESODE HATORAH, YESHIVA SHEARITH HAPLETAH 204 KEAP STREET	BROOKLYN	**NY**	11211	(718) 384-1611
ZICHRON MEILECH OF EASTERN PARKWAY, YESHIVA 3121 KINGS HIGHWAY	BROOKLYN	**NY**	11234	(718) 338-6100
HEBREW ACADEMY OF BUFFALO-YESHIVA LUBAVITZ 85 SARANAC AVENUE	BUFFALO	**NY**	14216	
HEBREW ACADEMY OF FIVE TOWNS AND ROCKAWAYS CEDARHURST AND LOCUST AVENUE	CEDARHURST	**NY**	11516	(516) 569-3807
HEBREW ACADEMY OF THE FIVE TOWNS AND THE ROCKAWAYS CENTRAL & LOCUST AVENUES	CEDARHURST	**NY**	11516	(516) 569-3370
SOLOMON SCHECTER DAY SCHOOL OF SUFFOLK COUNTY 74 HAUPPAUGE ROAD	COMMACK	**NY**	11725	
L.I. PERETZ JEWISH SCHOOL 574 NEWBRIDGE AVENUE	EAST MEADOW	**NY**	11554	(516) 542-9640
BNOS ISRAEL INSTITUTE 612 BEACH 9TH STREET	FAR ROCKAWAY	**NY**	11691	(718) 327-8007
MAIMONIDES INSTITUTE 3401 MOTT AVENUE	FAR ROCKAWAY	**NY**	11691	(718) 471-0100
SH'OR YOSHUV INSTITUTE 1526 CENTRAL AVENUE	FAR ROCKAWAY	**NY**	11691	(718) 327-2048
SIACH YITZCHOK (BOYS) 1513-17 CENTRAL AVENUE	FAR ROCKAWAY	**NY**	11691	(718) 327-2048
TAPEINU 1284 CENTRAL AVENUE	FAR ROCKAWAY	**NY**	11691	(718) 327-9273
TAPEINU ELEMENTARY SCHOOL (GIRLS) 1284 CENTRAL AVENUE	FAR ROCKAWAY	**NY**	11691	(718) 327-8305
TORAH ACADEMY FOR GIRLS 444 BEACH 6TH STREET	FAR ROCKAWAY	**NY**	11691	(718) 471-8444
YESHIVA DARCHEI TORAH 257 BEACH 17TH STREET	FAR ROCKAWAY	**NY**	11691	(718) 337-5880
YESHIVA OF FAR ROCKAWAY-DERECH AYSON 802 HICKSVILLE ROAD	FAR ROCKAWAY	**NY**	11691	(718) 327-7600
BETH SHOSHANA ACADEMY OF QUEENS 75-09 MAIN STREET	FLUSHING	**NY**	11367	(718) 268-2626
CENTRAL QUEENS, YESHIVA OF 147-37 70TH ROAD	FLUSHING	**NY**	11367	(718) 793-8500
EZRA ACADEMY OF QUEENS 71-25 MAIN STREET	FLUSHING	**NY**	11367	(718) 263-5500
SOLOMON SCHECHTER DAY SCHOOL 76-16 PARSONS BOULEVARD	FLUSHING	**NY**	11366	(718) 591-9800
YESHIVA OF CENTRAL QUEENS (INCORP. MAX & ROSE HELLER ACADEMY) 147-37 70TH ROAD	FLUSHING	**NY**	11367	(718) 793-8500
YOUNG ISARAEL OF KEW GARDEN HILLS PRIMARY SCHOOL 150-05 70TH ROAD	FLUSHING	**NY**	11367	(718) 261-9723
FOREST HILLS, MESIVTA OF 108-55 69TH AVENUE	FOREST HILLS	**NY**	11375	(718) 263-1445
FOREST PARK SCHOOL-BETH JACOB EDUCATIONAL CENTER 102-35 63RD RD	FOREST HILLS	**NY**	11375	(718) 896-4444
MAX & DOROTHY COHN HIGH SCHOOL FOR GIRLS-OHR TORAH 66-35 108TH STREET	FOREST HILLS	**NY**	11375	(718) 268-3444
MESIVITA OF FOREST HILLS 68-54 KESSEL STREET	FOREST HILLS	**NY**	11375	(718) 263-1445
OHR TORAH INSTITUTE 66-35 108TH STREET	FOREST HILLS	**NY**	11375	(718) 268-3444
OHR YISROEL, MESIFTA 66-20 THORNTON PLACE	FOREST HILLS	**NY**	11374	(718) 263-6242
OHR YISROEL, YESHIVA 66-20 THORNTON PLACE	FOREST HILLS	**NY**	11375	(718) 263-6242
RABBI DOV REVEL YESHIVA OF FOREST HILLS 71-02 113TH STREET	FOREST HILLS	**NY**	11375	(718) 261-9624
YESHIVA CHOFETZ CHAIM 68-54 KESSEL STREET	FOREST HILLS	**NY**	11375	(718) 263-1445
YESHIVA CHOFETZ CHAIM-MESIVTA OF FOREST HILLS 92-15 69TH AVENUE	FOREST HILLS	**NY**	11375	(718) 263-1445
YESHIVA SHUVAY YISROEL 100-09 METROPOLITAN AVENUE	FOREST HILLS	**NY**	11375	(718) 544-7960
YESHIVA AND MESIVTA OHR YISROEL 66-20 THORNTON PLACE	FOREST HILLS	**NY**	11374	(718) 263-6242
BUREAU OF JEWISH ED./INSTITUTE & H.S. OF JEWISH STUDIES 2640 NORTH FOREST ROAD	GETZVILLE	**NY**	14068	(718) 689-8844
TORAH TEMIMAH SCHOOL 2501 NORTH FOREST ROAD	GETZVILLE	**NY**	14068	(716) 688-6524
NORTH SHORE HEBREW ACADEMY 26 OLD MILL ROAD	GREAT NECK	**NY**	11023	(516) 487-9163
NORTH SHORE HEBREW ACADEMY 16 CHERRY LANE	GREAT NECK	**NY**	11024	(516) 487-8687
NORTH SHORE HEBREW ACADEMY 26 OLD MILL ROAD	GREAT NECK	**NY**	11023	(516) 487-8694
BETH SHRAGA HEBREW ACADEMY 2211-A WESTERN AVENUE	GUILDERLAND	**NY**	12084	(914) 456-6816
TORAS CHAIM OF SOUTH SHORE, YESHIVA 1170 WILLIAM STREET	HEWLETT	**NY**	11557	(516) 374-7363
YESHIVA AND MESIVTA TORAS CHAIM AT SOUTH SHORE 1170 WILLIAM STREET	HEWLETT	**NY**	11557	(516) 374-7363
SAMUEL H. WANG YESHIVA HIGH SCHOOL OF QUEENS 86-86 PALO ALTO STREET	HOLLISWOOD	**NY**	11423	(718) 479-8550
YESHIVA HIGH SCHOOL OF QUEENS, OHR TORAH 86-86 PALO ALTO STREET	HOLLISWOOD	**NY**	11423	(718) 479-8550
HEBREW ACADEMY OF WEST QUEENS 34-25 82ND STREET	JACKSON HEIGHTS	**NY**	11372	(718) 899-9193
SOLOMON SCHECTER DAY SCHOOL OF NASSAU COUNTY BARBARA LANE	JERICHO	**NY**	11753	(516) 935-1441
BAIS YAAKOV ACADEMY OF QUEENS 124-50 METROPOLITAN AVENUE	KEW GARDENS	**NY**	11415	(718) 847-5352
SHAAREY BNOS CHAYIL-SHEVAVH HIGH SCHOOL 124-27 85TH AVENUE	KEW GARDENS	**NY**	11415	(718) 847-4402
SHEVACH HIGH SCHOOL 124-27 85TH STREET	KEW GARDENS	**NY**	11415	(718) 847-4402
TIFERETH MOSHE, YESHIVA 83-06 ABINGDON ROAD	KEW GARDENS	**NY**	11415	(718) 846-7300
YESHIVA SHAAR HATORAH 83-96 117 STREET	KEW GARDENS	**NY**	11418	(718) 846-1940
YESHIVA TIFERETH MOSHE 83-06 ABINGDON ROAD	KEW GARDENS	**NY**	11415	(718) 846-7300
HEBREW DAY SCHOOL OF SULLIVAN AND ULSTER COUNTY ROUTE 42	KIAMESHA LAKE	**NY**	12751	(914) 794-7890
BRANDEIS SCHOOL 25 FROST LANE	LAWRENCE	**NY**	11559	(516) 371-4747
HEBREW ACADEMY OF FIVE TOWNS AND ROCKAWAY 44 FROST LANE	LAWRENCE	**NY**	11559	(516) 569-3488
HEBREW ACADEMY OF FIVE TOWNS AND ROCKAWAY 33 WASHINGTON AVENUE	LAWRENCE	**NY**	11559	(516) 569-3370
HEBREW ACADEMY OF LONG BEACH 530 WEST BROADWAY	LONG BEACH	**NY**	11561	(516) 432-8285
MESIVTA OF LONG BEACH 205 WEST BEECH STREET	LONG BEACH	**NY**	11561	(516) 431-7414
TORAH HIGH SCHOOL OF LONG BEACH 205 W. BEECH STREET	LONG BEACH	**NY**	11561	(516) 431-7414
KEHILATH YAAKOV, MESIFTA 33-23 GREENPOINT AVENUE	LONG ISLAND CITY	**NY**	11101	(718) 963-3940
YESHIVA KEHILATH YAAKOV 33-23 GREENPOINT AVENUE	LONG ISLAND CITY	**NY**	11101	(718) 729-9857
WESTCHESTER DAY SCHOOL 856 ORIENTA AVENUE	MAMARONECK	**NY**	10543	(914) 698-8900
WESTCHESTER HEBREW HIGH SCHOOL 856 ORIENTA AVENUE	MAMARONECK	**NY**	10543	(914) 698-0806
HEBREW DAY SCHOOL OF ORANGE COUNTY 195 WATKINS AVENUE	MIDDLETOWN	**NY**	10940	(914) 343-8588
BAIS ROCHEL SCHOOL BAKERTOWN ROAD	MONROE	**NY**	10950	(914) 782-5889
YESHIVA TORAH V'YIRAH D'RABBEINU YOEL D'SATMAR SCHUNEMUNK ROAD	MONROE	**NY**	10950	(914) 782-0844
ADOLPH H. SCHREIBER HEBREW ACADEMY OF ROCKLAND COUNTY 70 HIGHVIEW ROAD	MONSEY	**NY**	10952	(914) 357-1515
BAIS MIKRA 23 WEST MAPLE AVENUE	MONSEY	**NY**	10952	(914) 356-1239
BAIS YAAKOV H.S. 11 SMOLLEY DRIVE-P.O. BOX 116	MONSEY	**NY**	10952	(914) 356-3113
BAIS YITZCHOK, YESHIVA 184 MAPLE AVENUE	MONSEY	**NY**	10952	(914) 352-9635
BETH DAVID, YESHIVA 20 WEST MAPLE AVENUE, P.O. BOX 136	MONSEY	**NY**	10952	(914) 352-2111
BETH JACOB HIGH SCHOOL FOR GIRLS 11 SMOLLEY DRIVE, P.O. BOX 116	MONSEY	**NY**	10952	(914) 356-3113
BETH ROCHEL SCHOOL FOR GIRLS P.O. BOX 302, 145 SADDLE RIVER ROAD	MONSEY	**NY**	10952	(914) 352-5000
BETH ROCHEL SCHOOL FOR GIRLS 145 SADDLE RIVER ROAD - P.O. BOX 302	MONSEY	**NY**	10952	(914) 352-7654
BETH SHRAGA, MESIVTA 28 SADDLE RIVER ROAD, P.O. BOX 412	MONSEY	**NY**	10952	(914) 356-1980
BNOS YISROEL GIRLS SCHOOL OF VIZNITZ 73 MAIN STREET	MONSEY	**NY**	10952	(914) 356-1010
BNOS YISROEL GIRLS SCHOOL OF VIZNITZ 73 MAIN STREET	MONSEY	**NY**	10952	(914) 356-2322
HADAR, YESHIVAT 70 HIGHVIEW ROAD	MONSEY	**NY**	10952	
MESIVTA BETH SHRAGA 145 SADDLE RIVER ROAD - P.O. BOX 412	MONSEY	**NY**	10952	(914) 356-1980
MESIVTA HIGH SCHOOL 207 MAPLE AVENUE	MONSEY	**NY**	10952	(914) 356-5929
ROCKLAND HEBREW DAY SCHOOL 101 ROUTE 306	MONSEY	**NY**	10952	(914) 352-6629
SHAAREI TORAH OF ROCKLAND COUNTY 1 SCHOOL TERRACE	MONSEY	**NY**	10952	(914) 356-4773
SPRING VALLEY, YESHIVA OF 229-230 MAPLE AVENUE	MONSEY	**NY**	10952	(914) 356-1400
UNITED TALMUDICAL ACADEMY 89 SOUTH MAIN STREET - P.O. BOX 188	MONSEY	**NY**	10952	(914) 425-0392
VIZNITZ, YESHIVA P.O. BOX 446	MONSEY	**NY**	10952	(914) 356-1010
YESHIVA BETH DAVID 20 WEST MAPLE AVENUE - P.O. BOX 136	MONSEY	**NY**	10952	(914) 352-2111
YESHIVA VIZNITZ 20 ASHEL LANE	MONSEY	**NY**	10952	(914) 356-1010
YESHIVA OF SPRING VALLEY - BAIS SARAH 230 MAPLE AVENUE	MONSEY	**NY**	10952	(914) 356-1400
YESHIVA K'TANA OF MOUNTAINDALE P.O. BOX 118	MOUNTAINDALE	**NY**	12763	(914) 434-3612
BETH MIRIAM-LEAH PINES BRIDGE ROAD	MT KISCO	**NY**	10549	(212) 387-0422
FARM SETTLEMENT OF NITRA, YESHIVA PINESBRIDGE ROAD	MT KISCO	**NY**	10549	(914) 666-8746
TALMUD TORAH BAIS YECHIEL-YESHIVA OF NITRA PINES BRIDGE ROAD	MT KISCO	**NY**	10549	(212) 387-0422

YESHIVA FARM SETTLEMENT SCHOOL R.D. 4 BOX 428	MT KISCO	**NY**	10549	(212) 387-0422
SOLOMON SCHECHTER DAY SCHOOL OF ROCKLAND COUNTY ROUTE 45	NEW CITY	**NY**	10956	(914) 354-5500
OHR HAMEIR HIGH SCHOOL 3 BOULEVARD	NEW ROCHELLE	**NY**	10801	(914) 632-6192
OHR HAMEIR THEOLOGICAL SEMINARY AND H.S. 3 BOULEVARD	NEW ROCHELLE	**NY**	10801	(212) 828-6520
GRUSS GIRLS SCHOOL OF NEW SQUARE 15 ROOSEVELT AVENUE	NEW SQUARE	**NY**	10977	(914) 354-5778
YESHIVA OF NEW SQUARE 91 WASHINGTON AVENUE	NEW SQUARE	**NY**	10977	(914) 354-5591
BETH JACOB SCHOOL 142 BROOME STREET	NEW YORK	**NY**	10002	(212) 473-4500
BNAI JESHURUN DAY SCHOOL 270 WEST 89TH STREET	NEW YORK	**NY**	10024	(212) 787-7600
CHOFETZ CHAIM, MESIVTA 346 WEST 89TH STREET	NEW YORK	**NY**	10024	(212) 362-1435
LINCOLN SQUARE SYNAGOGUE NURSERY SCHOOL 200 AMSTERDAM AVENUE	NEW YORK	**NY**	10023	(212) 874-6100
MANHATTAN DAY SCHOOL-YESHIVA OHR TORAH 310 WEST 75TH STREET	NEW YORK	**NY**	10023	(212) 595-6800
MESIVTA RABBI SAMSON RAPHAEL HIRSCH 220 BENNETT AVENUE	NEW YORK	**NY**	10040	(212) 568-6200
MESIVTA TIFERETH JERUSALEM 141-7 EAST BROADWAY	NEW YORK	**NY**	10002	(212) 964-2830
PARK EAST DAY SCHOOL-EAST SIDE HEBREW INSTITUTE 164 EAST 68TH STREET	NEW YORK	**NY**	10021	(212) 737-6900
PARK EAST-ESHI DAY SCHOOL 164 EAST 68TH STREET	NEW YORK	**NY**	10021	(212) 737-6900
RABBI JOSEPH KONVITZ, YESHIVA 313 HENRY STREET	NEW YORK	**NY**	10002	(212) 473-5078
RABBI MOSES SOLOVEICHIK, YESHIVA 560 WEST 185TH STREET	NEW YORK	**NY**	10033	(212) 923-2900
RABBI SAMSON RAPHAEL HIRSCH, MESIVTA 91 BENNETT AVENUE	NEW YORK	**NY**	10033	(212) 568-6200
RABBI SAMSON RAPHAEL HIRSCH, YESHIVA 85-91 BENNETT AVENUE	NEW YORK	**NY**	10033	(212) 568-6200
RAMAZ UPPER SCHOOL 60 EAST 78TH STREET	NEW YORK	**NY**	10028	(212) 427-1000
RAMAZ-LOWER SCHOOL 125 EAST 85TH STREET	NEW YORK	**NY**	10028	(212) 427-1000
RODEPH SHOLOM DAY SCHOOL 10 WEST 84TH STREET	NEW YORK	**NY**	10024	(212) 362-8800
RODEPH SHOLOM DAY SCHOOL 10 WEST 84TH STREET	NEW YORK	**NY**	10024	(212) 362-8769
SOLOMON SCHECTER DAY SCHOOL ASSOCIATION 155 FIFTH AVENUE	NEW YORK	**NY**	10010	(212) 533-7800
THE RABBI JOSEPH H.LOOKSTEIN UPPER SCHOOL OF RAMAZ 60 EAST 78TH STREET	NEW YORK	**NY**	10021	(212) 427-1000
THE RAMAZ LOWER SCHOOL 125 EAST 85TH STREET	NEW YORK	**NY**	10028	(212) 427-1000
TIFERETH JERUSALEM, MESIVTA 147 EAST BROADWAY	NEW YORK	**NY**	10002	(212) 964-2830
TIFERETH JERUSALEM, YESHIVA 145 EAST BROADWAY	NEW YORK	**NY**	10002	(212) 964-2830
TONYA SOLOVEITCHIK-YESHIVA UNIVERSITY H.S. FOR GIRLS 425 5TH AVENUE	NEW YORK	**NY**	10016	(212) 481-3746
YESHIVA CHOFETZ CHAIM 346 WEST 89TH STREET	NEW YORK	**NY**	10024	(212) 363-1435
YESHIVA HECHAL MOSHE-BETH JACOB SCHOOL 303 WEST 91ST STREET	NEW YORK	**NY**	10024	(212) 877-8709
YESHIVA RABBI JOSEPH KONVITZ 313 HENRY STREET	NEW YORK	**NY**	10002	(212) 473-1000
YESHIVA RABBI MOSES SOLOVEITCHIK 560 WEST 185TH STREET	NEW YORK	**NY**	10033	(212) 923-2900
YESHIVA RABBI SAMSON RAPHAEL HIRSCH 85-93 BENNETT AVENUE	NEW YORK	**NY**	10033	(212) 568-6200
YESHIVA RABBI SAMSON RAPHAEL HIRSCH-BETH JACOB HIGH SCHOOL 85-93 BENNETT AVENUE	NEW YORK	**NY**	10033	(212) 568-6200
YESHIVA UNIVERSITY HIGH SCHOOL FOR BOYS 2540 AMSTERDAM AVENUE	NEW YORK	**NY**	10033	(212) 960-5345
YESHIVA UNIVERSITY HIGH SCHOOL FOR GIRLS 425 FIFTH AVENUE	NEW YORK	**NY**	10016	(212) 481-3746
HEBREW DAY SCHOOL OF ORANGE COUNTY 290 NORTH STREET	NEWBURGH	**NY**	12550	(914) 343-8588
YESHIVA DAY SCHOOL OF QUEENS 107-01 CROSS BAY BLVD	OZONE PARK	**NY**	11417	
YESHIVA DAY SCHOOL OF SOUTH QUEENS 115-70 LEFFERTS BLVD	OZONE PARK	**NY**	11420	(718) 641-0100
HANC MID-ISLAND HEBREW DAY SCHOOL JOYCE ROAD	PLAINVIEW	**NY**	11803	(516) 681-5922
HEBREW ACADEMY OF NASSAU COUNTY-MID-ISLAND SCHOOL JOYCE ROAD	PLAINVIEW	**NY**	11803	(516) 681-5922
MESORAT YISRAEL ACADEMY 98-12 66TH AVENUE	REGO PARK	**NY**	11374	(718) 459-1274
KINNERET DAY SCHOOL 2600 NETHERLAND AVENUE	RIVERDALE	**NY**	10463	(212) 584-0900
SAR ACADEMY 655 W. 254TH STREET	RIVERDALE	**NY**	10471	(212) 549-5160
SALANTER AKIBA RIVERDALE ACADEMY 655 WEST 254 STREET	RIVERDALE	**NY**	10471	(212) 549-5160
HILLEL SCHOOL OF ROCHESTER 191 FAIRFIELD DRIVE	ROCHESTER	**NY**	14620	(716) 271-6877
TALMUDICAL INSTITUTE OF UPSTATE NEW YORK 769 PARK AVENUE	ROCHESTER	**NY**	14607	(716) 473-2810
ROBERT GORDIS DAY SCHOOL OF TEMPLE BETH EL 445 BEACH 135TH STREET	ROCKAWAY PARK	**NY**	11694	(718) 634-7711
HEBREW ACADEMY OF SUFFOLK COUNTY 525 VETERANS HIGHWAY	SMITHTOWN	**NY**	11787	(516) 543-3377
YESHIVA GEDOLAH ZICHRON MOSHE ELEMENTARY AND HIGH SCHOOL LAUREL PARK ROAD	SOUTH FALLSBURG	**NY**	12779	(914) 434-5240
BETH ESTHER D'SATMAR 89 SOUTH MAIN STREET, P.O. BOX 188	SPRING VALLEY	**NY**	10977	(914) 425-6758
BETH ESTHER D'SATMAR 5502 COMMERCE STREET	SPRING VALLEY	**NY**	10977	(914) 425-6758
UNITED TALMUDICAL ACADEMY 89 SOUTH MAIN STREET, P.O. BOX 188	SPRING VALLEY	**NY**	10977	(914) 425-0392
UNITED TALMUDICAL BOYS ACADEMY 89 SOUTH MAIN	SPRING VALLEY	**NY**	10977	(914) 356-4480
UNITED TALMUDICAL GIRLS ACADEMY 206 VIOLA ROAD	SPRING VALLEY	**NY**	10977	(914) 425-6758
JEWISH FOUNDATION SCHOOL 20 PARK HILL CIRCLE	STATEN ISLAND	**NY**	10304	(718) 981-6700
MESIVTA OF STATEN ISLAND 1870 DRUMGOOLE ROAD, E	STATEN ISLAND	**NY**	10309	(718) 356-2101
RABBI JACOB JOSEPH SCHOOL 3495 RICHMOND ROAD	STATEN ISLAND	**NY**	10306	(718) 979-6333
YESHIVA TIFERET SHMUEL EZRA JEWISH FOUNDATION SCHOOL OF S.I. 20 PARK HILL CIRCLE	STATEN ISLAND	**NY**	10304	(718) 981-6700
YESHIVA TIFERETH SHMUEL EZRA 20 PARK HILL CIRCLE	STATEN ISLAND	**NY**	10304	(718) 981-6700
YESHIVA OF STATEN ISLAND 1870 DRUMGOOLE ROAD EAST	STATEN ISLAND	**NY**	10309	(718) 356-4323
BAS TORAH ACADEMY 4 CAMPBELL AVENUE	SUFFERN	**NY**	10901	(914) 357-0774
CHOFETZ CHAIM, YESHIVA 24 HIGHVIEW ROAD	SUFFERN	**NY**	10901	(914) 357-9821
MAX GILBERT HEBREW ACADEMY 5655 THOMPSON ROAD - P.O. BOX 189	SYRACUSE	**NY**	13214	(315) 446-1900
KADIMAH SCHOOL OF BUFFALO 300 FRIES ROAD	TONAWANDA	**NY**	14150	(716) 836-6903
HEBREW ACADEMY 215 OAK STREET	UNIONDALE	**NY**	11553	(516) 538-8161
HEBREW ACADEMY OF NASSAU COUNTY 215 OAK STREET	UNIONDALE	**NY**	11553	(516) 538-8161
HEBREW ACADEMY OF NASSAU COUNTY - BROOKDALE HIGH SCHOOL 215 OAK STREET	UNIONDALE	**NY**	11553	(516) 538-8161
HEBREW ACADEMY OF NASSAU COUNTY - MOSES HORNSTEIN JR. H.S. 215 OAK STREET	UNIONDALE	**NY**	11553	(516) 538-8161
HILLEL DAY SCHOOL 2310 ONEIDA STREET	UTICA	**NY**	13501	(315) 724-7317
HEBREW ACADEMY OF NASSAU COUNTY 609 HEMPSTEAD AVENUE	WEST HEMPSTEAD	**NY**	11552	(516) 485-7786
SOLOMON SCHECHTER SCHOOL OF WESTCHESTER 30 DELLWOOD ROAD	WHITE PLAINS	**NY**	10605	(914) 948-3111
MESIVTA OF YONKERS 63 HAMILTON AVENUE	YONKERS	**NY**	10705	(914) 963-1951
HILLEL ACADEMY OF AKRON 750 WHITE POND DRIVE	AKRON	**OH**	44320	(216) 836-0419
AGNON SCHOOL, THE 26500 SHAKER BLVD	BEACHWOOD	**OH**	44122	(216) 464-4055
CINCINNATI HEBREW DAY SCHOOL 7855 DAWN ROAD	CINCINNATI	**OH**	45237	(513) 761-1614
YAVNEH DAY SCHOOL 1636 SUMMIT ROAD	CINCINNATI	**OH**	45237	(513) 984-3770
AGNON SCHOOL 26500 SHAKER BLVD	CLEVELAND	**OH**	44122	(216) 464-4055
AKIVA HIGH SCHOOL 26500 SHAKER BLVD	CLEVELAND	**OH**	44122	(216) 464-4370
HEBREW ACADEMY OF CLEVELAND 1860 SOUTH TAYLOR ROAD	CLEVELAND	**OH**	44118	(216) 382-6495
MOSDOS OHR HATORAH - BOYS DIVISION 1508 WARRENSVILLE CENTER ROAD	CLEVELAND	**OH**	44121	(216) 382-6248
MOSDOS OHR HATORAH - GIRLS DIVISION 3246 DESOTA AVENUE	CLEVELAND	**OH**	44118	(216) 321-1547
RATNER DAY SCHOOL 4900 ANDERSON ROAD	CLEVELAND	**OH**	44124	(216) 291-0034
TEISHE HIGH SCHOOL 28400 EUCLID AVENUE	CLEVELAND	**OH**	44092	(216) 944-0299
YESHIVATH ADATH BNAI ISRAEL 2308 WARRENSVILLE CENTER ROAD	CLEVELAND	**OH**	44118	(216) 932-7664
HEBREW ACADEMY OF CLEVELAND 1860 SOUTH TAYLOR ROAD	CLEVELAND HEIGHTS	**OH**	44118	(216) 321-5838
HEBREW ACADEMY OF CLEVELAND-FOREIGN DIVISION (RUSSIANS) 1970 SOUTH TAYLOR ROAD	CLEVELAND HEIGHTS	**OH**	44118	(216) 321-2941
MOSDOS OR HATORAH 1508 WARRENSVILLE CENTER ROAD	CLEVELAND HEIGHTS	**OH**	44121	(216) 382-6248
YAVNE HIGH SCHOOL FOR GIRLS 1860 SOUTH TAYLOR ROAD	CLEVELAND HEIGHTS	**OH**	44118	(216) 321-5838
COLUMBUS TORAH ACADEMY 181 NOE-BIXBY ROAD	COLUMBUS	**OH**	43213	(614) 864-0299
HILLEL ACADEMY OF DAYTON 100 EAST WOODBURY DRIVE	DAYTON	**OH**	45415	(513) 277-8966
MESIVTA HIGH SCHOOL OF HEBREW ACADEMY OF CLEVELAND 1975 LYNDWAY	LYNDHURST	**OH**	44121	(216) 382-6495
HEBREW ACADEMY OF TOLEDO 2727 KENWOOD BLVD	TOLEDO	**OH**	43606	(419) 531-8960
TELSHE HIGH SCHOOL 28400 EUCLID AVENUE	WICKLIFFE	**OH**	44092	(216) 943-5300
HERITAGE ACADEMY 1719 SOUTH OWASSO	TULSA	**OK**	74120	(918) 584-2596
HILLEL ACADEMY OF PORTLAND 920 N.W. 25TH AVENUE	PORTLAND	**OR**	97210	(503) 223-0155
JEWISH DAY SCHOOL OF ALLENTOWN 2313 PENNSYLVANIA STREET	ALLENTOWN	**PA**	18104	(215) 437-0721
TORAH ACADEMY OF GREATER PHILADELPHIA WYNNEWOOD AND ARGYLE ROADS	ARDMORE	**PA**	19003	(215) 642-7870
BETH JACOB SCHOOLS OF PHILADELPHIA HIGH SCHOOL ROAD AND MONTGOMERY AVENUE	ELKINS PARK	**PA**	19117	(215) 635-6805
YESHIVA ACADEMY OF HARRISBURG 100 VAUGHN STREET	HARRISBURG	**PA**	17110	(717) 238-2074
ISRAEL BEN ZION ACADEMY THIRD AVENUE AND INSTITUTE LANE	KINGSTON	**PA**	18704	(717) 287-9608
LANCASTER JEWISH DAY SCHOOL 22 SPENCER AVENUE	LANCASTER	**PA**	17604	(717) 397-0183
AKIBA HEBREW ACADEMY 223 N. HIGHLAND AVENUE	MERION STATION	**PA**	19066	(215) 839-3540
BETH JACOB - LOWER GIRLS SCHOOL PENWAY & FRIENDSHIP STREETS	PHILADELPHIA	**PA**	19111	
BETH JACOB SCHOOL HIGHSCHOOL ROAD & MONTGOMERY AVENUE	PHILADELPHIA	**PA**	19124	(215) 635-6805
HEBREW ACADEMY OF N.E. PHILADELPHIA 97-68 VERREE ROAD	PHILADELPHIA	**PA**	19115	(215) 969-3956
TALMUDICAL YESHIVA OF PHILADELPHIA 6063 DREXEL ROAD	PHILADELPHIA	**PA**	19131	(215) 477-1000
HEBREW INSTITUTE OF PITTSBURGH 6401-07 FORBES AVENUE	PITTSBURGH	**PA**	15217	(412) 521-1100
HILLEL ACADEMY OF PITTSBURGH 5685 BEACON STREET	PITTSBURGH	**PA**	15217	(412) 521-8131
NECHAMA MINSKY SCHOOL FOR GIRLS 2100 WIGHTMAN STREET	PITTSBURGH	**PA**	15217	(412) 422-7779
YESHIVA ACHEI TMIMIM FOR BOYS 2410 5TH AVENUE	PITTSBURGH	**PA**	15213	(412) 681-2446
BAIS YAAKOV INSTITUTE 901 OLIVE STREET	SCRANTON	**PA**	18510	(717) 342-4247
HILLEL ACADEMY 900 GIBSON STREET	SCRANTON	**PA**	18510	(717) 343-7837
SCRANTON HEBREW DAY SCHOOL 540 MONROE AVENUE	SCRANTON	**PA**	18510	(717) 346-1576
YESHIVA BETH MOSHE 930 HICKORY STREET - P.O. BOX 1141	SCRANTON	**PA**	18505	(717) 346-1747
ABRAMS HEBREW ACADEMY 31 WEST COLLEGE AVENUE	YARDLEY	**PA**	19067	
NEW ENGLAND ACADEMY OF TORAH 450 ELMGROVE AVENUE	PROVIDENCE	**RI**	02906	(401) 331-5327
PROVIDENCE HEBREW DAY SCHOOL 450 ELMGROVE AVENUE	PROVIDENCE	**RI**	02906	(401) 331-5327
ADDLESTONE HEBREW ACADEMY 182 RUTLEDGE AVENUE	CHARLESTON	**SC**	29403	(803) 577-6597
CHATTANOOGA JEWISH DAY SCHOOL 5326 LYNNLAND TERRACE	CHATTANOOGA	**TN**	37411	(615) 892-2337
BAIS YAACOV 392 CONWELL ROAD	MEMPHIS	**TN**	38117	(901) 685-7451
MEMPHIS HEBREW ACADEMY 390 SOUTH WHITE STATION ROAD - P.O. BOX 171154	MEMPHIS	**TN**	38117	(901) 682-2409
YESHIVA OF THE SOUTH 5255 MEADOWCREST COVE	MEMPHIS	**TN**	38117	(901) 767-4140
AKIVA SCHOOL 3600 WEST END AVENUE	NASHVILLE	**TN**	37205	(615) 292-6614
AKIBA ACADEMY OF DALLAS 6210 CHURCHILL WAY	DALLAS	**TX**	75230	(214) 239-7248
TORAH ACADEMY HIGH SCHOOL OF TEXAS 7120 SPRING VALLEY ROAD	DALLAS	**TX**	75240	(214) 386-9213
TORAH HIGH SCHOOL OF TEXAS 7120 SPRING VALLEY ROAD	DALLAS	**TX**	75240	(214) 233-6766
EL PASO HEBREW DAY SCHOOL 220 EAST CLIFF STREET	EL PASO	**TX**	79902	(915) 532-4484
HEBREW ACADEMY 5435 SOUTH BRAESWOOD	HOUSTON	**TX**	77096	(713) 723-7170
TORAH DAY SCHOOL OF HOUSTON-LUBAVITCH 10900 FONDREN ROAD	HOUSTON	**TX**	77096	(713) 777-2000
THE JEWISH DAY SCHOOL OF SAN ANTONIO 703 TRAFALGAR ROAD	SAN ANTONIO	**TX**	78216	(512) 341-0735
HENRIETTA KURZER HEBREW ACADEMY 1815 CHESTNUT AVENUE	NEWPORT NEWS	**VA**	23607	
THE JOSEPH AND FANNIE RUDLIN TORAH ACADEMY 6801 PATTERSON AVENUE	RICHMOND	**VA**	23226	(804) 288-7610
HEBREW ACADEMY OF TIDEWATER 1244 THOMPKINS LANE	VIRGINIA BEACH	**VA**	23464	(804) 424-4327
SEATTLE HEBREW ACADEMY 1617 INTERLAKEN DRIVE EAST	SEATTLE	**WA**	98112	(206) 323-5750
YESHIVAT OR HAZAFON 1617 INTERLAKEN DRIVE EAST	SEATTLE	**WA**	98112	(206) 323-5750
HILLEL ACADEMY 4650 NORTH PORT WASHINGTON ROAD	MILWAUKEE	**WI**	53212	(414) 962-9545
TORAH ACADEMY OF MILWAUKEE 1144 EAST HENRY CLAY	MILWAUKEE	**WI**	53217	(414) 963-0621
WISCONSIN INSTITUTE FOR TORAH STUDY 3288 NORTH LAKE DRIVE	MILWAUKEE	**WI**	53211	(414) 963-9317
AKIVA ACADEMY 19-2323 OAKMOOR DRIVE	CALGARY	**AT**	T2V HT2	(403) 252-0339
EDMONTON TALMUD TORAH 1312 106TH AVENUE	EDMONTON	**AT**	T5N 1A3	(403) 455-9114
UNITED TALMUD TORAHS OF MONTREAL 931 EMERSON DRIVE	CHOMEDEY, LAVAL		H7W 3Y5	(514) 681-9146
HEBREW ACADEMY OF MONTREAL 8205 MACKLE ROAD	COTE ST. LUC		H4W 1B1	(514) 489-8289
UNITED TALMUD TORAHS OF MONTREAL 5554 ROBINSON AVENUE	COTE ST. LUC		H4W 2P8	(514) 484-1151
HEBREW FOUNDATION SCHOOL OF CONGREGATION BETH TIKVAH 2 HOPE DRIVE	DOLLARD DES ORMEAUX		H9A 2V5	(514) 684-6270

ASSOCIATED HEBREW SCHOOLS OF TORONTO - BETH DAVID BRANCH
55 YEOMANS ROAD .... DOWNSVIEW M3H 3J7 (416) 630-4162
RAMAH HEBREW SCHOOL 705 LANKARK STREET .... WINNIPEG **MB** R3N 1M4 (204) 453-4136
TORAH ACADEMY 620 BROCK STREET .... WINNIPEG **MB** R3N 0Z4 (204) 489-6262
WINNIPEG HEBREW SCHOOLS 427-437 MATHESON AVENUE .... WINNIPEG **MB** R2W 0E1 (204) 586-5822
BETH ISRAEL RELIGIOUS SCHOOL 1480 OXFORD STREET .... HALIFAX **NS** (902) 422-1301
OHR CHAIM BNAI AKIVA YESHIVA HIGH SCHOOL
159 ALMORE AVENUE .... DOWNSVIEW **ON** M3H 2H9 (416) 630-6772
ULPANAT OROT 45 CANYON AVENUE .... DOWNSVIEW **ON** M3H 3S4 (416) 638-5434
ULPANAT OROT GIRL'S SCHOOL-NACHMAN SOKOL TORAH CENTRE
45 CANYON AVENUE .... DOWNSVIEW **ON** M3H 3S4 (416) 638-5434
YESHIVA OR CHAIM-ISRAEL & GOLDA KOSCHITZKY TORAH CENTER
159 ALMORE AVENUE .... DOWNSVIEW **ON** M3H 2H9 (416) 630-6772
HILLEL ACADEMY 1400 COLDREY AVENUE .... OTTAWA **ON** K1Z 7P9 (613) 728-1759
HILLEL ACADEMY-OTTAWA TALMUD TORAH BOARD
453 RIDEAY STREET .... OTTAWA **ON** K1N 5Z3 (613) 235-1841
OTTAWA TORAH INSTITUTE 2310 VIRGINIA DRIVE .... OTTAWA **ON** K1H 6S2 (613) 521-9700
ASSOCIATED HEBREW SCHOOLS OF TORONTO
3630 BATHURST STREET .... TORONTO **ON** M6A 2E3 (416) 789-7471
BIALIK HEBREW DAY SCHOOL 12 VIEWMOUNT AVENUE .... TORONTO **ON** M6C 1S6 (416) 783-3346
ASSOCIATED HEBREW SCHOOLS OF TORONTO-HURWICH EDUCATION CNTR.
252 FINCH AVENUE WEST .... WILLOWDALE **ON** M2R 1M9 (416) 223-4845
ASSOCIATED HEBREW SCHOOLS OF TORONTO - BETH EMETH BRANCH
100 ELDER STREET .... DOWNSVIEW M3H 5G7 (416) 223-4845
OR HAEMET SEFARDIC SCHOOL 210 WILSON STREET .... DOWNSVIEW M5M 3B1 (416) 630-3216
EDMONTON TALMUD TORAH HEBREW DAY SCHOOL
13212-106 AVENUE .... EDMONTON T5N 1A3 (403) 455-9114
HAMILTON HEBREW ACADEMY 60 DOW AVENUE .... HAMILTON L8S 1W4 (416) 528-0330
LONDON COMMUNITY HEBREW DAY SCHOOL 247 EPWORTH AVENUE .... LONDON N6A 2M2 (519) 439-8419
BAIS MALKA 1495 DUCHARME AVENUE .... OUTREMENT H2V 1E8 (514) 279-8033
BNOS YERUSHALAYLM 1495 DUCHARME AVENUE .... OUTREMENT H2V 1E8 (514) 271-9464
HEBREW ACADEMY OF MONTREAL 1500 DUCHARME AVENUE .... OUTREMENT H2V 1G1 (514) 274-3573
UNITED ORTHODOX JEWISH SCHOOL 1495 DUCHARME AVENUE .... OUTREMENT H2V 1E8 (514) 273-1698
BAIS YAAKOV OF TORONTO 85 STORMONT AVENUE .... TORONTO M5N 2C3 (416) 781-3073
BETH JACOB HIGH SCHOOL FOR GIRLS 410 LAWRENCE AVENUE WEST .. TORONTO M5M 1C2 (416) 787-4949
EITZ CHAIM YESHIVA 1 VIEWMOUNT AVENUE .... TORONTO M6M 1T2 (416) 789-4366
YESHIVA YESODEL HATORAH 567 LAWRENCE AVENUE WEST .... TORONTO M6A 1A5 (416) 789-1891
THE AKIVA SCHOOL 1000 LUCERNE ROAD .... TOWN OF MT. ROYAL H3R 2H9 (514) 731-3491
VANCOUVER TALMUD TORAH 998 WEST 26TH AVENUE .... VANCOUVER V5Z 2G1 (604) 736-7307
SEPHARDIC ACADEMY OF MONTREAL (ECOLE SEPHARDE)
805 TASSE .... VILLE ST. LAURENT 4HL 1N8 (514) 744-2861
ASSOCIATED HEBREW SCHOOLS OF TORONTO - LESLIE BRANCH
6100 LESLIE STREET .... WILLOWDALE M2H 3J1 (416) 491-5232
EITZ CHAIM YESHIVA-WILLOWDALE 475 PATRICIA AVENUE .... WILLOWDALE M6B 1T2 (416) 225-1187
NER ISRAEL YESHIVA COLLEGE OF TORONTO
625 FINCH AVENUE WEST .... WILLOWDALE M2R 1N8 (416) 636-2360
JOSEPH WOLINSKY COLLEGIATE 437 MATHESON AVENUE .... WINNIPEG R2W 0E1 (204) 589-4311
WINNIPEG HEBREW SCHOOLS TALMUD TORAH
427 MATHESON AVENUE .... WINNIPEG R2W 0E1 (204) 586-5822
BETH ESTHER SCHOOL 5402 PARK AVENUE .... MONTREAL **QU** H2V 3G7 (514) 272-4998
BETH JACOB SCHOOL OF MONTREAL 1750 GLENDALE AVENUE .... MONTREAL **QU** H2V 1B3 (514) 739-3614
BETH RIVKAH ACADEMY FOR GIRLS 5001 VEZINA AVENUE .... MONTREAL **QU** H3W 1C2 (514) 731-3681
BETH ZION HEBREW ACADEMY 5740 HUDSON AVENUE .... MONTREAL **QU** H4W 2K5 (514) 489-8411
BIALIK H.S. OF THE JEWISH PEOPLE'S SCHOOL & PERETZ SCHOOLS
7946 WAVELL ROAD .... MONTREAL **QU** (514) 489-8291
FIRST MESIVTA OF CANADA 2325 EKERS AVENUE .... MONTREAL **QU** (514) 342-0977
HERZLIAH HIGH SCHOOL 805 DORAIS .... MONTREAL **QU** H4M 2A2 (514) 336-7490
HERZLIAH HIGH SCHOOL 4840 ST. KEVIN AVENUE .... MONTREAL **QU** H3W 1P2 (514) 739-2291
JEWISH PEOPLE'S SCHOOLS & PERETZ SCHOOLS
570 VAN HORNE AVENUE .... MONTREAL **QU** H3W 1J6 (514) 731-7741
MEOR HAGOLA RABBINICAL COLLEGE OF CANADA
5815 JEANNE MANCE AVENUE .... MONTREAL **QU** H2V 4K9 (514) 274-8467
RABBINICAL COLLEGE OF CANADA - TOMCHE TMIMIM LUBAVITCH
6405 WESTBURY AVENUE .... MONTREAL **QU** H3W 2X5 (514) 735-2201
UNITED TALMUD TORAHS OF MONTREAL 4850 ST. KEVIN AVENUE .... MONTREAL **QU** H3W 1P2 (514) 739-2291
UNITED TALMUD TORAHS OF MONTREAL 2250 RUE DE L'EGLISE .... MONTREAL **QU** H3M 1G5 (514) 337-4566
UNITED TALMUD TORAHS OF MONTREAL 4894 ST. KEVIN AVENUE .... MONTREAL **QU** H3W 1P2 (514) 739-2291
YESHIVA CHASIDEI BELZ 5340 JEANNE MANCE STREET .... MONTREAL **QU** H2V 4K4 (514) 270-5086
YESHIVA GEDOLA MERKAZ HATORAH 6155 DEACON ROAD .... MONTREAL **QU** H3S 2P4 (514) 735-6611
YESHIVA TORAS MOSHE 5214 ST. URBAIN .... MONTREAL **QU** (514) 273-1698

DAY SCHOOLS - SOLOMON SCHECHTER

UNITED SYNAGOGUE DAY SCHOOL (N-9) 1700 BATHURST STREET .... TORONTO M5P 3K3 (416) 781-5658
UNITED SYNAGOGUE DAY SCHOOL BAYVIEW BRANCH (N-6)
3080 BAYVIEW AVENUE .... WILLOWDALE (416) 225-1144
SOLOMON SCHECHTER DAY SCHOOL OF TUCSON 8016 E. 7TH STREET .... TUCSON **AZ** 85710 (704) 366-6390
JEWISH STUDIES INSTITUTE DAY SCHOOL 1770 W. CERRITOS AVENUE .... ANAHEIM **CA** 92804 (714) 535-3665
KADIMA HEBREW ACADEMY (K-7) 22600 SHERMAN WAY .... CANOGA PARK **CA** 91307 (213) 346-0849
JEWISH STUDIES INSTITUTE DAY SCHOOL (N-7)
12181 BUARO STREET .... GARDEN GROVE **CA** 92640 (714) 636-3361
AKIBA ACADEMY (K-7) 10400 WILSHIRE BLVD .... LOS ANGELES **CA** 90024 (213) 475-6401
GOLDA MEIR ACADEMY NEW JEWISH HIGH SCHOOL
1317 N. CRESCENT HTS. .... LOS ANGELES **CA** 90046 (213) 656-3060
HERZL SCHOOLS (7-9) 1039 S. LA CIENEGA BLVD .... LOS ANGELES **CA** 90035 (213) 652-1854
ADAT ARI EL DAY SCHOOL (K-6) 5540 LAUREL CANYON BLVD .... N. HOLLYWOOD **CA** 91607 (818) 766-3506
YAVNEH DAY SCHOOL 19700 PROSPECT RD. .... SARATOGA **CA** 95070 (408) 446-2956
ETZ CHAIM DAY SCHOOL PO BOX 246 .... WALNUT CREEK **CA** 94596 (415) 934-9449
SOLOMON SCHECHTER ACADEMY OF NEW LONDON COUNTY (K-6)
660 OCEAN AVENUE .... NEW LONDON **CT** 06320 (203) 443-5589
SOLOMON SCHECHTER DAY SCHOOL OF GREATER HARTFORD (K-6)
160 MOHEGAN DRIVE .... WEST HARTFORD **CT** 06117 (203) 233-1418
EZRA ACADEMY (K-8) 75 RIMMON ROAD .... WOODBRIDGE **CT** 06525 (203) 389-5500
SOLOMON SCHECHTER DAY SCHOOL - JACKSONVILLE JEWISH CTR. (N-7)
10101 SAN JOSE BLVD., P.O. BOX 23886 .... JACKSONVILLE **FL** 32217 (904) 268-6736
BETH DAVID SOLOMON SCHECHTER DAY SCHOOL (N-6)
7500 S.W. 120TH STREET .... MIAMI **FL** 33156 (305) 238-2601
LEHRMAN DAY SCHOOL OF TEMPLE EMANU-EL (N-9)
727 77TH STREET .... MIAMI BEACH **FL** 33141 (305) 866-2771
SARASOTA HEBREW DAY SCHOOL (K-6) 1050 S. TUTTLE AVENUE .... SARASOTA **FL** 33577 (813) 955-8121
PINELLAS COUNTY JEWISH DAY SCHOOL (K-3)
301 59TH STREET N. .... ST. PETERSBURG **FL** 33710 (813) 381-8111
HARRY EPSTEIN SCHOOL (1-8) 600 PEACHTREE BATTLE AVENUE N.W. .... ATLANTA **GA** 30327 (404) 351-7623
AKLBA-SCHECHTER JEWISH DAY SCHOOL (1-3)
5200 S. HYDE PARK BLVD .... CHICAGO **IL** 60615 (312) 493-8880
SAGER SOLOMON SCHECHTER DAY SCHOOL (K-6) 350 LEE ROAD .... NORTHBROOK **IL** 60062 (312) 498-2100
SOLOMON SCHECHTER DAY SCHOOL OF SKOKIE (K-6)
9301 GROSS POINT ROAD .... SKOKIE **IL** 60076 (312) 679-6270
SOLOMON SCHECHTER SECONDARY EDUCATION DEPARTMENT (7-12)
9301 GROSS POINT ROAD .... SKOKIE **IL** 60076 (312) 679-6270
SOLOMON SCHECHTER DAY SCHOOL OF THE MERRIMACK VALLEY
514 MAIN STREET .... HAVERHILL **MA** 01830 (617) 887-9790
SOLOMON SCHECHTER DAY SCHOOL 60 STEIN CIRCLE .... NEWTON CENTRE **MA** 02159 (617) 964-7765
HILLEL ACADEMY OF THE NORTH SHORE (K-9)
837 HUMPHREY STREET .... SWAMPSCOTT **MA** 01907 (617) 599-3837
SOLOMON SCHECHTER DAY SCHOOL OF WORCESTER (K-6)
633 SALISBURY STREET .... WORCESTER **MA** 01609 (617) 799-7888
SOLOMON SCHECHTER DAY SCHOOL (K-2) 8100 STEVENSON ROAD .... BALTIMORE **MD** 21208 (301) 486-6400
CHARLES E. SMITH JEWISH DAY SCHOOL (9-12)
1901 E. JEFFERSON STREET .... ROCKVILLE **MD** 20852 (301) 881-1408
CHARLES E. SMITH JEWISH DAY SCHOOL (K-6)
1901 E. JEFFERSON STREET .... ROCKVILLE **MD** 20852 (301) 881-1403
HEBREW DAY SCHOOL OF ANN ARBOR (K-6) 1920 AUSTIN .... ANN ARBOR **MI** 48104 (313) 668-6770
HILLEL DAY SCHOOL (K-9) 32200 MIDDLEBELT ROAD .... FARMINGTON **MI** 48018 (313) 851-2394
SOLOMON SCHECHTER DAY SCHOOL OF ST. LOUIS (K-2)
324 S. MASON ROAD .... ST. LOUIS **MO** 63141 (314) 576-6177
JEWISH DAY SCHOOL OF OMAHA 12604 PACIFIC ST. .... OMAHA **NE** 68154 (402) 334-0517
NORTH CAROLINA HEBREW DAY ACADEMY (K-6) P.O.B. 220176 .... CHARLOTTE **NC** 28222 (704) 366-6390
B'NAI SHALOM SYNAGOGUE DAY SCHOOL (K-6)
904 WINVIEW DRIVE .... GREENSBORO **NC** 27410 (919) 855-5091
SOLOMON SCHECHTER DAY SCHOOL OF CENTRAL NEW JERSEY (K-1)
NORTH BRIDGE STREET, P.O. BOX 6007 .... BRIDGEWATER **NJ** 08807 (201) 722-2089
HARRY B. KELLMAN ACADEMY (N-8) 2901 WEST CHAPEL AVENUE .... CHERRY HILL **NJ** 08002 (609) 667-1300
SOLOMON SCHECHTER DAY SCHOOL OF ESSEX & UNION (K-8)
721 ORANGE AVENUE .... CRANFORD **NJ** 07016 (201) 272-3400
SOLOMON SCHECHTER HIGH SCHOOL OF ESSEX & UNION (9-12)
721 ORANGE AVENUE .... CRANFORD **NJ** 07016 (201) 272-3400
SOLOMON SCHECHTER DAY SCHOOL OF EAST BRUNSWICK (N-6)
511 RYDERS LANE .... EAST BRUNSWICK **NJ** 08816 (201) 238-7971
SOLOMON SCHECHTER DAY SCHOOL OF BERGEN COUNTY (K-7)
153 TENAFLY ROAD .... ENGLEWOOD **NJ** 07631 (201) 879-1152
SOLOMON SCHECHTER ACADEMY OF OCEAN & MONMOUTH COUNTIES (K-8)
101 KENT ROAD .... HOWELL **NJ** 07731 (201) 370-1767
SOLOMON SCHECHTER DAY SCHOOL OF MARLBORO PO BOX 203 .... MARLBORO **NJ** 07746 (201) 431-5525
SOLOMON SCHECHTER DAY SCHOOL OF MARLBORO (N-2)
P.O. BOX 94 .... MORGANVILLE **NJ** 07751
THE HEBREW ACADEMY OF THE SHORE AREA
PO BOX 324 301 MONMOUTH ROAD .... OAKHURST **NJ** 07755 (201) 531-0300
HEBREW ACADEMY OF MORRIS COUNTY (N-8)
146 DOVER-CHESTER ROAD .... RANDOLPH **NJ** 07869 (201) 584-5530
BIALIK SCHOOL (N-8) 500 CHURCH AVENUE .... BROOKLYN **NY** 11218 (718) 853-7100
RABBI HARRY HALPERN DAY SCHOOL (N-8) 1625 OCEAN AVENUE .... BROOKLYN **NY** 11230 (718) 338-3800
SOLOMON SCHECHTER HIGH SCHOOL (9-12) 500 CHURCH AVENUE .... BROOKLYN **NY** 11218 (718) 854-3500
SOLOMON SCHECHTER SCHOOL OF SUFFOLK COUNTY
74 HAUPPAUGE RD. .... COMMACK **NY** 11725 (516) 462-5999
SOLOMON SCHECHTER DAY SCHOOL OF QUEENS (K-9)
76-16 PARSONS BLVD .... FLUSHING **NY** 11366 (718) 591-9800
HEBREW ACADEMY OF THE CAPITAL DISTRICT (K-8)
2211A WESTERN AVENUE .... GUILDERLAND **NY** 12084 (518) 456-6816
SOLOMON SCHECHTER DAY SCHOOL OF NASSAU COUNTY (K-8)
BARBARA LANE .... JERICHO **NY** 11753 (516) 935-1441
THE BRANDEIS SCHOOL (N-8) 25 FROST LANE .... LAWRENCE **NY** 11559 (516) 371-4747
THE BRANDEIS SCHOOL-LAWRENCE EVAN SLOATE HIGH SCHOOL (9-12)
25 FROST LANE .... LAWRENCE **NY** 11559 (516) 371-4747
SOLOMON SCHECHTER DAY SCHOOL OF ROCKLAND COUNTY (N-8)
ROUTE 45 .... NEW CITY **NY** 10956 (914) 353-5500
B'NAI JESHURUN DAY SCHOOL (N-8) 270 WEST 89TH STREET .... NEW YORK **NY** 10024
MID-HUDSON HEBREW DAY SCHOOL (K-6) 110 GRAND AVENUE .... POUGHKEEPSIE **NY** 12603 (914) 454-0474
ROBERT GORDIS DAY SCHOOL (N-8) 445 BEACH 135TH STREET .... ROCKAWAY PARK **NY** 11694 (718) 634-7711
SOLOMON SCHECHTER DAY SCHOOL OF WESTCHESTER (N-8)
30 DELLWOOD ROAD .... WHITE PLAINS **NY** 10605 (914) 948-3111
SOLOMON SCHECHTER DAY SCHOOL OF CLEVELAND (K-3)
3557 WASHINGTON BLVD. .... CLEVELAND HEIGHTS **OH** 44118 (216) 371-1364
SOLOMON SCHECHTER DAY SCHOOL OF CLEVELAND
1825 GREEN RD. .... SOUTH EUCLID **OH** 44121 (216) 371-1364
SOLOMON SCHECHTER DAY SCHOOL OF PHILADELPHIA (K-6)
971 OLD YORK ROAD .... ABINGTON **PA** 19001 (215) 886-2355
SOLOMON SCHECHTER DAY SCHOOL
OLD LANCASTER & HIGHLAND RDS. .... BALA CYNWYD **PA** 19004 (215) 664-5480
FORMAN HEBREW DAY SCHOOL (K-6)
OLD YORK & FOXCROFT ROADS .... ELKINS PARK **PA** 19117 (215) 887-6981

SOLOMON SCHECHTER DAY SCHOOL OF GREATER PITTSBURGH (K-1)
1900 COCHRAN RD .... PITTSBURGH PA 15220 (412) 344-5877
SOLOMON SCHECHTER ACADEMY (N-7) 5555 COTE ST. LUC ROAD ...... MONTREAL QU H3X 2C9 (514) 481-7719
SOLOMON SCHECHTER DAY SCHOOL OF RHODE ISLAND (K-4)
99 TAFT AVENUE .... PROVIDENCE RI 02906 (401) 751-2470
I. WEINER SECONDARY SCHOOL (6-10) 4610 BELLAIRE AVENUE .... BELLAIRE TX 77401 (713) 668-0393
SOLOMON SCHECHTER ACADEMY OF DALLAS (K-3)
9401 DOUGLAS AVENUE .... DALLAS TX 75225 (214) 369-8237
I. WEINER SECONDARY SCHOOL 12583 S. GESSNER .... HOUSTON TX 77071 (713) 668-0393
WILLIAM S. MALEV SCHOOL OF RELIGIOUS STUDIES (N-6)
4525 BEECHNUT BLVD .... HOUSTON TX 77096 (713) 666-1884

DEAF, ORGANIZATIONS FOR THE

TEMPLE BETH SOLOMON OF THE DEAF 13580 OSBOURNE STREET .... ARLETA CA 91331 (213) 899-2202
CHABAD HOUSE-WEST COAST 741 GAYLEY AVE .... LOS ANGELES CA 90024
LOS ANGELES HAD 458 N. DETROIT AVENUE .... LOS ANGELES CA 90036
TEMPLE BETH SOLOMON O/T DEAF 8936 LANGDON .... SAN FERNANDO CA 91343
GALLAUDET COLLEGE HILLEL CLUB, THE HILLEL CLUB, C/O OFF OF CAMPUS
MINISTRIES, GALLAUDET CLG .... WASHINGTON DC 20002 (202) 651-5106
JEWISH COMM CTR ASSN J FERSHLEISER CENT VILL V D79 .... DEERFIELD FL 33441
CONGREGATION BENE SHALOM OF THE HEBREW ASSOC. OF THE DEAF
5920 NORTH KENMORE .... CHICAGO IL 60660
BENE SHOLOM, CONGREGATION - HEBREW ASSOCIATION FOR THE DEAF
4435 WEST OAKTON .... SKOKIE IL 60076 (312) 677-3330
BOSTON HAD 154 SALISBURY ROAD .... BROOKLINE MA 02146
BALTIMORE JSD 5709 GREENSPRING .... BALTIMORE MD 21209
NATIONAL CONGRESS OF JEWISH DEAF 9102 EDMONSTON CT. #302 ... GREENBELT MD 20770
WASHINGTON SOCIETY OF THE JEWISH DEAF 6610 23 AVENUE....... WEST HYATTS MD 20782
TEMPLE BETH OR OF THE DEAF 195 PRINCETON DRIVE .... RIVER EDGE NJ 07661
BETH TORAH O/T DEAF 1949 E 21ST ST .... BROOKLYN NY 11229
B'KLYN HSD/SISTERHOOD 1230 AVENUE Y .... BROOKLYN NY 11235
HEBREW INSTITUTE FOR THE DEAF & EXCEPTIONAL CHILDREN
2025 67TH STREET .... BROOKLYN NY 11204 (718) 259-2626
TEMPLE BETH OR O/T DEAF R GEFFEN-TREAS 582 BENTON RD...... EAST MEADOW NY 11554
NEW YORK SOCIETY FOR THE DEAF (PHONE FOR THE HEARING PERSON)
344 E. 14TH STREET .... NEW YORK NY 10003 (212) 673-6500
NEW YORK SOCIETY FOR THE DEAF(TELETYPEWRITER PHONE FOR DEAF)
344 E. 14TH STREET .... NEW YORK NY 10003 (212) 673-6974
HEARING IMPAIRED CHAVURA 199 DORKING RD .... ROCHESTER NY 14610
HEBREW ASSOCIATION OF THE DEAF - JEWISH COMMUNITY CENTER
3505 MAYFIELD ROAD .... CLEVELAND OH 44118 (216) 382-4000
HAD - CLEVELAND P.O. BOX 29114 .... PARMA OH 44129
HAD - PHILADELPHIA 7005 CALVERT STREET .... PHILADELPHIA PA 19149
PHILADELPHIA HAD 9801 HALDEMAN AVENUE APT. D204 .... PHILADELPHIA PA 19115
TORONTO JEWISH DEAF SOCIETY JACK OSTEN 58 SUMERSIDE CR... WILLOWDALE ON M2H 1X1

DRIVER EDUCATION

PROSPECT PARK YESHIVAH HIGH SCHOOL 1609 AVENUE R .... BROOKLYN NY 11229 (718) 376-0006
YESHIVAH OF FLATBUSH 1609 AVENUE J .... BROOKLYN NY 11230 (718) 377-4466
HEBREW ACADEMY OF FIVE TOWNS & ROCKAWAY
33 WASHINGTON AVENUE .... LAWRENCE NY 11559 (516) 569-3370
RAMAZ DAY SCHOOL 60 EAST 78TH STREET .... NEW YORK NY 10021 (212) 427-1000
HEBREW ACADEMY OF NASSAU COUNTY 215 OAK STREET .... UNIONDALE NY 11553 (516) 538-8161

EDUCATIONAL ORGANIZATIONS

BRANDEIS-BARDIN INSTITUTE, THE 1101 PEPPERTREE LANE .... BRANDEIS CA 93064 (805) 348-7201
BUREAU OF JEWISH EDUCATION 6505 WILSHIRE BLVD .... LOS ANGELES CA 90048 (213) 852-1234
AMERICAN FRIENDS OF THE HEBREW UNIVERSITY OF JERUSALEM
717 MARKET STREET, SUITE 323 .... SAN FRANCISCO CA 94103 (415) 391-9056
BRANDEIS-BARDIN INSTITUTE 1101 PEPPERTREE LANE .... SIMI VALLEY CA 93064 (805) 523-1131
ASSOCIATED TALMUD TORAH 2828 W. PRATT BLVD .... CHICAGO IL 60645 (312) 973-2828
TEACHER CENTER 415 GREEN BAY ROAD .... WILMETTE IL 60091 (312) 256-6056
JEWISH EDUCATIONAL ASSOCIATION 6711 HOOVER ROAD.......... INDIANAPOLIS IN 46260 (317) 255-3124
JEWISH EDUCATIONAL VENTURES, THE 462 BOYLSTON STREET .... BOSTON MA 02116 (617) 536-6252
ASSOCIATION FOR JEWISH STUDIES
WIDENER LIBRARY, HARVARD UNIVERSITY..................... CAMBRIDGE MA 02138 (617) 495-2985
UNITED HEBREW SCHOOLS 15110 W. TEN MILE ROAD .... OAK PARK MI 48237 (313) 548-4747
UNITED HEBREW SCHOOLS OF DETROIT
21550 W. TWELVE MILE ROAD .... SOUTHFIELD MI 48076 (313) 354-1050
CENTRAL AGENCY FOR JEWISH EDUCATION
225 SOUTH MERAMEC, SUITE 400........................... ST. LOUIS MO 63105 (314) 862-0606
ASSOCIATION OF ORTHODOX JEWISH TEACHERS
1577 CONEY ISLAND AVENUE .... BROOKLYN NY 11230 (718) 258-3585
EDUCATIONAL INSTITUTE OHOLEI TORAH 667 EASTERN PARKWAY ...... BROOKLYN NY 11213 (718) 778-3340
JEWISH EDUCATION PROGRAM 425 E. 9TH STREET .... BROOKLYN NY 11218 (718) 941-2600
MERKOS L'INYONEI CHINUCH, CENTRAL ORG. FOR JEWISH EDUCATION
770 EASTERN PARKWAY .... BROOKLYN NY 11213 (718) 493-9250
NATIONAL COMMITTEE FOR THE FURTHERANCE OF JEWISH EDUCATION
824 EASTERN PARKWAY .... BROOKLYN NY 11213 (718) 735-0200
NATIONAL COUNCIL OF BETH JACOB SCHOOLS
1415 EAST 7TH STREET .... BROOKLYN NY 11230 (718) 375-3533
NATIONAL COUNCIL OF BETH JACOB SCHOOLS, INC.
1415 E. 7TH STREET .... BROOKLYN NY 11230 (718) 979-7400
P'TACH - PARENTS FOR TORAH FOR ALL CHILDREN
4612 13TH AVENUE .... BROOKLYN NY 11219 (718) 436-5125

AMERICAN BIBLICAL ENCYCLOPEDIA SOCIETY 24 WEST MAPLE AVENUE ..MONSEY NY 10952 (914) 352-4609
AGUDAS ISRAEL WORLD ORGANIZATION 471 WEST END AVENUE .... NEW YORK NY 10024 (212) 874-7979
AMERICAN ASSOCIATION FOR JEWISH EDUCATION
114 FIFTH AVENUE .... NEW YORK NY 10011 (212) 675-5656
AMERICAN COUNCIL FOR JUDAISM 307 FIFTH AVENUE .... NEW YORK NY 10001 (212) 889-1312
AMERICAN ORT FEDERATION 817 BROADWAY .... NEW YORK NY 10003 (212) 677-4400
ASSOCIATION OF ADVANCED RABBINICAL & TALMUDIC SCHOOLS
175 FIFTH AVENUE .... NEW YORK NY 10010 (212) 477-0950
COALITION FOR ALTERNATIVES IN JEWISH EDUCATION
468 PARK AVENUE SOUTH SUITE 904 .... NEW YORK NY 10016 (212) 696-0740
COMMISSION ON JEWISH EDUCATION OF U.S.A.
427 WEST 58TH STREET .... NEW YORK NY 10019 (212) 245-8200
DEPARTMENT OF EDUCATION & CULTURE-WORLD ZIONIST ORGANIZATION
515 PARK AVENUE .... NEW YORK NY 10022 (212) 752-0600
FEDERATED COUNCIL OF BETH JACOB SCHOOLS
142 BROOME STREET .... NEW YORK NY 10002 (212) 473-4500
FUND FOR HIGHER EDUCATION 1500 BROADWAY, SUITE 1900 .... NEW YORK NY 10036 (212) 354-4660
ISRAEL EDUCATION FUND 51 WEST 51ST STREET .... NEW YORK NY 10019 (212) 757-1500
JEWISH CHAUTAUQUA SOCIETY 838 FIFTH AVENUE .... NEW YORK NY 10021 (212) 570-0707
JEWISH EDUCATION SERVICE OF NORTH AMERICA, INC.
114 FIFTH AVENUE .... NEW YORK NY 10011 (212) 675-5656
JEWISH FOLK SCHOOLS 575 AVENUE OF AMERICAS .... NEW YORK NY 10011
JEWISH FOUNDATION FOR EDUCATION OF GIRLS
120 W. 57TH STREET .... NEW YORK NY 10019 (212) 265-2565
JEWISH FOUNDATION FOR EDUCATION OF WOMEN
120 W. 57TH STREET .... NEW YORK NY 10019 (212) 265-2565
JEWISH NATIONAL FUND - YOUTH & EDUCATION DEPARTMENT
42 EAST 69TH STREET .... NEW YORK NY 10021 (212) 879-9300
JEWISH RECONSTRUCTIONIST FOUNDATION, EDUCATION DEPARTMENT
15 W. 86 STREET .... NEW YORK NY 10024 (212) 316-3011
NAT'L COUNCIL FOR JEWISH EDUCATION 114 FIFTH AVENUE .... NEW YORK NY 10011 (212) 675-5656
NATIONAL ACADEMY FOR ADULT JEWISH STUDIES 155 FIFTH AVENUE .. NEW YORK NY 10010 (212) 260-8450
NATIONAL COMMISSION ON TORAH EDUCATION
2540 AMSTERDAM AVENUE .... NEW YORK NY 10033 (212) 960-5400
NATIONAL COMMITTEE OF JEWISH FOLK SCHOOLS 575 6TH AVENUE ... NEW YORK NY 10011
NATIONAL CONFERENCE OF YESHIVA PRINCIPALS 160 BROADWAY ..... NEW YORK NY 10038 (212) 406-4190
NATIONAL COUNCIL FOR JEWISH EDUCATION 114 FIFTH AVENUE ...... NEW YORK NY 10011 (212) 675-5656
NATIONAL COUNCIL FOR TORAH EDUCATION
C/O RELIGIOUS ZIONISTS OF AMERICA, 25 W. 26TH STREET .... NEW YORK NY 10011 (212) 289-1414
OZAR HATORAH 411 FIFTH AVENUE .... NEW YORK NY 10016 (212) 684-4130
P'EYLIM - AMERICAN YESHIVA STUDENT UNION 3 WEST 16TH STREET .. NEW YORK NY 10011 (212) 989-2500
RESEARCH INSTITUTE OF RELIGIOUS JEWRY, INC.
471 WEST END AVENUE .... NEW YORK NY 10024 (212) 874-7979
RESHET - TORAH EDUCATION NETWORK
5 BEEKMAN STREET, ROOM 910 .... NEW YORK NY 10038 (212) 791-1800
STONE-SAPIRSTEIN CENTER FOR JEWISH EDUCATION-YESHIVA UNIV.
500 W. 185TH STREET .... NEW YORK NY 10033 (212) 960-5400
TORAH UMESORAH 160 BROADWAY, 4TH FLOOR-EAST BUILDING .... NEW YORK NY 10038 (212) 406-4190
UNITED PARENT-TEACHERS ASSOCIATION OF JEWISH SCHOOLS
426 W. 58TH STREET .... NEW YORK NY 10019 (212) 245-8200
UNITED SYNAGOGUE DEPT. OF EDUCATION/COMMISSION OF JEWISH ED.
155 FIFTH AVENUE .... NEW YORK NY 10010 (212) 533-7800
UNITED HEBREW SCHOOLS & YESHIVOS OF PHILADELPHIA
701 BYBERRY ROAD .... PHILADELPHIA PA 19116 (215) 677-7261
PITTSBURGH JEWISH PUBLICATION & EDUCATION FOUNDATION
315 S. BELLEFIELD AVENUE .... PITTSBURGH PA 15213 (412) 687-1000
EDUCATIONAL HORIZONS 126 SOUTH GLENDALE AVENUE .... GLENDALE CA 91316 (213) 500-4828

OZAR HATORAH

WORLD SEPHARDI EDUCATIONAL NETWORK

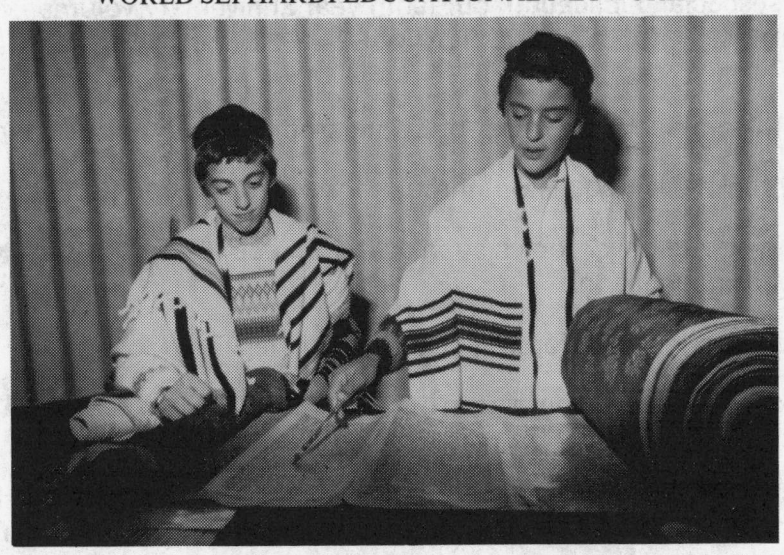

INTERNATIONAL HEADQUARTERS
411 FIFTH AVENUE - 4th FLOOR
NEW YORK, NY 10016
(212) 684-4733

•

FOUNDED IN 1945 BY
ISAAC SHALOM

•

Serving the educational needs of three continents:
North Africa, Europe and Middle East

•

Educated over 250,000 children

•

President - Joseph Shalom
International President - Rabbi Solomon D. Sassoon
Executive Vice-President - Rabbi H. Augenbaum

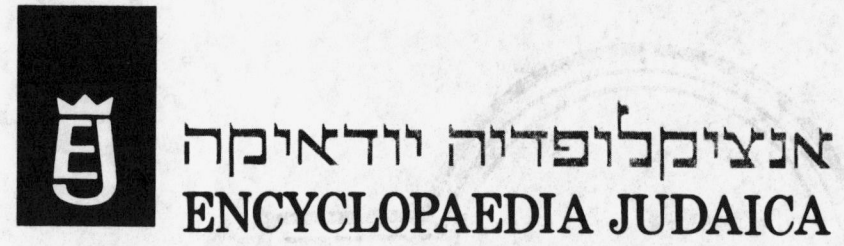

ENCYCLOPAEDIA JUDAICA

אנציקלופדיה יודאיקה

PUBLISHED BY
KETER PUBLISHING HOUSE LTD.
JERUSALEM, ISRAEL

ACT NOW!

ENCYCLOPAEDIA JUDAICA DECENNIAL BOOK 1973-1982

As the proud owner of the **ENCYCLOPAEDIA JUDAICA** you appreciate and are aware of the beauty and value of the set. And because we are certain that you want to keep your **JUDAICA** as up to date as possible, we continue to supplement the original set of sixteen volumes.

DON'T MISS the latest special publication, our tenth year anniversary volume—the **ENCYCLOPAEDIA JUDAICA DECENNIAL BOOK 1973-1982.**

- ✔ Combines and integrates the Calendar of Events from all the previous Year Books.

- ✔ Continues to chronicle Jewish history through the years 1978, 1979, 1980, and 1981!

- ✔ New articles and entries cover topics such as the Entebbe Raid, the Yom Kippur War and the Israel-Egypt peace negotiations.

- ✔ Extensively illustrated text in color and black-and-white.

- ✔ No duplication of any articles appearing in the **ENCYCLOPAEDIA JUDAICA** or its supplements.

We invite you to obtain NOW the **ENCYCLOPAEDIA JUDAICA DECENNIAL BOOK 1973-1982.** Please take a minute to complete the attached form and send your prepaid order today.

Immediate delivery from our New York Office upon receipt of your order!

- -

Please send me:

____ Copies of the **ENCYCLOPAEDIA JUDAICA DECENNIAL BOOK 1973-1982** at @ U.S. $39.00 U.S. $_____
For New York State deliveries please add appropriate sales tax .... U.S. $_____
Shipping and handling charges... U.S. $____4.75____

Enclosed please find my check/money order (in U.S. funds or Canadian equivalent)
    in the amount of... U.S. $_____

NAME_____

ADDRESS_____

CITY_____ STATE_____ ZIP_____

TEL. _____

I would like information on:
- ☐ the purchase of a complete set of the **ENCYCLOPAEDIA JUDAICA**
- ☐ previous Year Books
- ☐ other Keter publications

Please make your check/money order payable to:
KETER, INC. 440 PARK AVENUE SOUTH, NEW YORK, N.Y. 10016 TEL.: (212) 889-7750 TELEX: 233705

EDUCATIONAL RESOURCES

EKS PUBLISHING 5336 COLLEGE AVENUE — OAKLAND **CA** 94618 (415) 653-5183
EDUCATIONAL RESOURCES 24010 OXNARD STREET — WOODLAND HILLS **CA** 91367 (213) 992-6330
ALTERNATIVES IN RELIGIOUS EDUCATION, INC. 3945 SOUTH ONEIDA — DENVER **CO** 80237 (303) 363-7779
THE LEARNING PLANT 6950 COUNTRY PLACE ROAD — WEST PALM BEACH **FL** 33411
KOHL JEWISH TEACHER CENTER 161 GREEN BAY ROAD — WILMETTE **IL** 60091 (312) 256-6056
HEINLE & HEINLE ENTERPRISES 29 LEXINGTON ROAD — CONCORD **MA** 01742 (617) 369-7525
TORAH MICROFICHE LIBRARY - THE RUDMAN FOUNDATION
1051 BAY 25TH STREET — FAR ROCKAWAY **NY** 11691 (718) 634-8000
BEHRMAN HOUSE INC. 1261 BROADWAY — NEW YORK **NY** 10001 (212) 689-2020
BOARD OF JEWISH EDUCATION 426 WEST 58TH STREET — NEW YORK **NY** 10019 (212) 245-8200
UNION OF AMERICAN HEBREW CONGREGATIONS 838 FIFTH AVENUE — NEW YORK **NY** 10021 (212) 249-0100
UNITED SYNAGOGUE OF AMERICA 155 FIFTH AVENUE — NEW YORK **NY** 10010 (212) 533-7800
B. ARBIT BOOKS 8050 NORTH PORT WASHINGTON ROAD — MILWAUKEE **WI** 53217 (414) 352-4404

EDUCATORS ORGANIZATIONS

JEWISH EDUCATORS ASSOCIATION 6505 WILSHIRE BOULEVARD — LOS ANGELES **CA** 90048 (213) 852-1234
HEBREW TEACHERS FEDERATION PO BOX 824 — VAN NUYS **CA** 91408 (818) 980-2191
COALITION FOR ALTERNATIVES IN JEWISH EDUCATION
468 PARK AVENUE SOUTH, SUITE 904 — NEW YORK **NY** 10016 (212) 696-0740
JEWISH EDUCATORS ASSEMBLY OF AMERICA 155 FIFTH AVENUE — NEW YORK **NY** 10010 (212) 533-7800
JEWISH TEACHERS ASSOCIATION - MORIM 45 E. 33RD STREET — NEW YORK **NY** 10010 (212) 260-8450
NATIONAL ASSOCIATION OF HEBREW DAY SCHOOL ADMINISTRATORS
160 BROADWAY — NEW YORK **NY** 10038 (212) 406-4190
NATIONAL ASSOCIATION OF TEMPLE ADMINISTRATORS
838 FIFTH AVENUE — NEW YORK **NY** 10021 (212) 249-0100
NATIONAL ASSOCIATION OF TEMPLE EDUCATORS 838 FIFTH AVENUE — NEW YORK **NY** 10021 (212) 249-0100
NATIONAL CONFERENCE OF YESHIVA PRINCIPALS 160 BROADWAY — NEW YORK **NY** 10038 (212) 406-4190
NATIONAL COUNCIL FOR JEWISH EDUCATION 114 FIFTH AVENUE — NEW YORK **NY** 10011 (212) 675-5656

EMERGENCY SERVICES

HATZOLOH GENERAL P.O. BOX 3500 — BROOKLYN **NY** 11202 (718) 387-1750

EMPLOYMENT AGENCIES

AIDES TO THE ELDERLY 330 NORTH FAIRFAX AVENUE — LOS ANGELES **CA** 90048 (213) 760-1423
PROJECT GELT 128 LABREN STREET — LOS ANGELES **CA** 90036 (213) 658-5111
YOUNG ISRAEL EMPLOYMENT SERVICE — LOS ANGELES **CA** 90007 (213) 936-6101
BUREAU OF JEWISH EMPLOYMENT PROBLEMS
220 SOUTH STATE STREET, SUITE 1703 — CHICAGO **IL** 60603 (312) 663-9470
BUREAU OF JEWISH EMPLOYMENT PROBLEMS 220 S. STATE STREET — CHICAGO **IL** 60604 (312) 663-9470
FEDERATION EMPLOYMENT & GUIDANCE SERVICE
1 THORNTON STREET — BROOKLYN **NY** 11206 (718) 782-6060
FEDERATION EMPLOYMENT & GUIDANCE SERVICE
3312-30 SURF AVENUE — BROOKLYN **NY** 11224 (718) 449-4000
FEDERATION EMPLOYMENT & GUIDANCE SERVICE
1622 MERMAID AVENUE — BROOKLYN **NY** 11224 (718) 449-7900
KOLLEL EMPLOYMENT SERVICE P.O. BOX 255, 125 HEYWARD STREET — BROOKLYN **NY** 11211 (718) 388-7118
REMBRANDT PERSONNEL AGENCY 1422 AVENUE J — BROOKLYN **NY** 11230 (718) 258-9202
COUNCIL OF JEWISH MANPOWER ASSOCIATION 299 BROADWAY — NEW YORK **NY** 10013 (212) 233-8333
TRADITION PERSONNEL 8 W. 40TH STREET — NEW YORK **NY** 10018 (212) 391-2614
YOUNG ISRAEL EMPLOYMENT AGENCIES 3 WEST 16TH STREET — NEW YORK **NY** 10011 (212) 929-1525

ENCYCLOPEDIA JUDAICA

AMER. COMMITTEE FOR SHAARE ZEDEK HOSPITAL IN JERUSALEM, INC.
49 WEST 45TH STREET — NEW YORK **NY** 10036 (212) 354-8801
KETER, INC. 440 PARK AVENUE SOUTH — NEW YORK **NY** 10016 (212) 889-7750

ENDOWMENTS & FOUNDATIONS

JEWISH ENDOWMENT FOUNDATION 211 CAMP STREET — NEW ORLEANS **LA** 70130 (504) 525-0673
AMERICA CHAI TRUST 350 FIFTH AVENUE — NEW YORK **NY** 10118 (212) 736-3633
AMERICAN COUNCIL FOR JUDAISM PHILANTHROPIC FUND
386 PARK AVENUE SOUTH — NEW YORK **NY** 10016 (212) 684-1525
AMERICAN HISTADRUT DEVELOPMENT FOUNDATION
33 EAST 67TH STREET — NEW YORK **NY** 10021 (212) 628-1000
BARON DE HIRSCH FUND 386 PARK AVENUE SOUTH — NEW YORK **NY** 10016 (212) 532-7088
ISRAEL ENDOWMENT FUNDS 342 MADISON AVENUE — NEW YORK **NY** 10173 (212) 599-1260
ISRAEL ENDOWMENT FUNDS, INC. 511 FIFTH AVENUE — NEW YORK **NY** 10017 (212) 687-2400
JEWISH PHILANTHROPIC FUND OF 1933 570 SEVENTH AVENUE — NEW YORK **NY** 10018
MEMORIAL FOUNDATION FOR JEWISH CULTURE
15 EAST 26TH STREET — NEW YORK **NY** 10010 (212) 679-4074
NAT'L FOUNDATION FOR JEWISH CULTURE, INC.
122 EAST 42ND STREET — NEW YORK **NY** 10017 (212) 490-2280

FEDERATIONS, WELFARE FUNDS & COMMUNITY COUNCILS

BIRMINGHAM JEWISH FEDERATION, THE PO BOX 9157 — BIRMINGHAM **AL** 35213 (205) 879-0416
MOBILE JEWISH WELFARE FUND, INC. 404 C ONE OFFICE PARK — MOBILE **AL** 36609 (205) 343-7197
JEWISH FEDERATION OF MONTGOMERY, INC. PO BOX 1150 — MONTGOMERY **AL** 36101 (205) 263-7674
JEWISH FEDERATION OF LITTLE ROCK DONAGHEY BLDG — LITTLE ROCK **AR** 72201 (501) 372-3571
JEWISH FEDERATION OF GREATER PHOENIX
1718 WEST MARYLAND AVENUE — PHOENIX **AZ** 85015 (602) 249-1845
JEWISH COMMUNITY COUNCIL 102 N. PLUMER — TUCSON **AZ** 85719 (602) 884-8921
CALGARY JEWISH COMMUNITY COUNCIL 1607 90TH AVENUE S.W. — CALGARY **AT** T2V 4V7 (403) 253-8600
EDMONTON JEWISH COMMUNITY COUNCIL, INC.
7200-156TH STREET — EDMONTON **AT** T5R 1X3 (403) 487-5120
JEWISH COMMUNITY FUND & COUNCIL OF VANCOUVER
950 WEST 41ST AVENUE — VANCOUVER **BC** V5Z 2N7 (604) 266-8371
JEWISH COMMUNITY FUND & COUNCIL OF VANCOUVER
950 WEST 41ST AVENUE — VANCOUVER **BC** V5Z 2N7 (604) 261-8101
JFC EASTERN REGION OFFICE 801 WEST SAN BERNARDINO ROAD — COVINA **CA** 91822 (213) 686-0631
JEWISH FEDERATION COUNCIL-EASTERN REGION
801 WEST SAN BERNARDINO ROAD — COVINA **CA** 91722 (213) 444-4584
JEWISH WELFARE FEDERATION 2014 TULARE ST. SUITE 424 — FRESNO **CA** 93721 (209) 264-9429
JEWISH FED. OF ORANGE COUNTY-UNITED JEWISH WELFARE FUND
12181 BUARO — GARDEN GROVE **CA** 92640 (714) 530-6636
JEWISH COMMUNITY FED. OF GREATER LONG BEACH & W. ORANGE CO.
3801 EAST WILLOW STREET — LONG BEACH **CA** 90815 (213) 426-7601
JFC METROPOLITAN REGION OFFICE 6505 WILSHIRE BOULEVARD — LOS ANGELES **CA** 90048 (213) 852-1234
JEWISH FEDERATION COUNCIL OF GREATER LOS ANGELES
6505 WILSHIRE BLVD — LOS ANGELES **CA** 90048 (213) 852-1234
JEWISH FEDERATION OF THE GREATER EAST BAY
3245 SHEFFIELD AVENUE — OAKLAND **CA** 94602 (415) 533-7462
JEWISH FEDERATION OF PALM SPRINGS - DESERT AREA
611 SOUTH PALM CANYON DRIVE, SUITE 215 — PALM SPRINGS **CA** 92262 (619) 325-7281
JEWISH FEDERATION OF SACRAMENTO PO BOX 254589 — SACRAMENTO **CA** 95865 (916) 486-0906
SAN BERNARDINO UNITED JEWISH WELFARE FUND, INC.
3512 NO. 'E' STREET, CONGREGATION EMANU-EL — SAN BERNARDINO **CA** 92405 (714) 886-4818
CJF WESTERN AREA OFFICE 2831 CAMINO DEL RIO SOUTH, SUITE 217 — SAN DIEGO **CA** 92108 (619) 296-2949
UNITED JEWISH FEDERATION OF SAN DIEGO COUNTY
5511 EL CAJON BLVD — SAN DIEGO **CA** 92115 (619) 582-2483
JEWISH COM. FED. OF SAN FRANCISCO, MARIN CO. & THE PENINSULA
254 SUTTER STREET — SAN FRANCISCO **CA** 94108 (415) 781-3082
JEWISH FEDERATION OF GREATER SAN JOSE
1777 HAMILTON AVENUE, SUITE 210 — SAN JOSE **CA** 95125 (408) 267-2770
SANTA BARBARA JEWISH FEDERATION, THE PO BOX 6782 — SANTA BARBARA **CA** 93111
JFC WESTERN REGION OFFICE 2811 WILSHIRE BOULEVARD — SANTA MONICA **CA** 90403 (213) 828-9521
JFC SAN FERNANDO VALLEY REGION OFFICE
15477 VENTURA BOULEVARD, SUITE 300 — SHERMAN OAKS **CA** 91403 (818) 986-7900
STOCKTON JEWISH WELFARE FUND
5105 NORTH EL DORADO STREET — STOCKTON **CA** 95207 (209) 477-9306
JFC SOUTHERN REGION OFFICE 3848 CARSON STREET, SUITE 101 — TORRANCE **CA** 90503 (213) 772-9186
VENTURA COUNTY JEWISH COUNCIL, TEMPLE BETH TORAH
7620 FOOTHILL ROAD — VENTURA **CA** 93004 (805) 647-4181
ALLIED JEWISH FEDERATION OF DENVER-ALLIED JEWISH CAMPAIGN
300 SOUTH DAHLIA STREET — DENVER **CO** 80222 (303) 321-3399
JEWISH FEDERATION OF GREATER BRIDGEPORT, INC., UJ CAMPAIGN
4200 PARK AVENUE — BRIDGEPORT **CT** 06604 (203) 372-6504
JEWISH FEDERATION OF GREATER DANBURY
54 MAIN STREET, SUITE E — DANBURY **CT** 06810 (203) 792-6353
JEWISH FEDERATION OF GREATER NORWALK, INC.
SHOREHAVEN ROAD — EAST NORWALK **CT** 06855 (203) 853-3440
GREENWICH JEWISH FEDERATION
22 WEST PUTNAM AVENUE, SUITE 18 — GREENWICH **CT** 06830 (203) 622-1434
JEWISH FED. OF MERIDEN/MERIDEN JEWISH WELFARE FUND, INC.
127 EAST MAIN STREET — MERIDEN **CT** 06450 (203) 235-2581
NEW HAVEN JEWISH FEDERATION 1162 CHAPEL STREET — NEW HAVEN **VT** 06511 (203) 562-2137
JEWISH FEDERATION OF EASTERN CONNECTICUT, INC.
302 STATE STREET — NEW LONDON **CT** 06320 (203) 442-8062
UNITED JEWISH FEDERATION 1035 NEWFIELD AVENUE, PO BOX 3038 — STAMFORD **CT** 06905 (203) 322-6935
JEWISH FEDERATION OF WATERBURY, INC.
1020 COUNTRY CLUB ROAD — WATERBURY **CT** 06708 (203) 758-2441
GREATER HARTFORD JEWISH FEDERATION
333 BLOOMFIELD AVENUE — WEST HARTFORD **CT** 06117 (203) 232-4483
CJF WASHINGTON ACTION OFFICE
227 MASSACHUSETTS AVE. N.E. SUITE 120 — WASHINGTON **DC** 20002 (202) 547-0020
JEWISH FEDERATION OF DELAWARE, INC.
101 GARDEN OF EDEN ROAD — WILMINGTON **DE** 19803 (302) 478-6200
SOUTH COUNTY JEWISH FEDERATION
2200 N. FEDERAL HIGHWAY, SUITE 206 — BOCA RATON **FL** 33432 (305) 368-2737
JEWISH FEDERATION OF PINELLAS COUNTY, INC.
302 SOUTH JUPITER AVENUE — CLEARWATER **FL** 33515 (813) 446-1033
BREVARD COUNTY JEWISH COMMUNITY COUNCIL PO BOX 1816 — MERRITT ISLAND **FL** 32952 (305) 453-4695
JEWISH FEDERATION OF VOLUSIA & FLAGLER COUNTIES, INC.
637 NORTH GRANDVIEW AVENUE — DAYTONA BEACH **FL** 32018 (904) 255-6260
JEWISH FEDERATION OF GREATER FORT LAUDERDALE
8360 WEST OAKLAND PARK BLVD — FORT LAUDERDALE **FL** 33321 (305) 748-8200
JEWISH FEDERATION OF LEE COUNTY P.O. BOX 06465 — FT. MYERS **FL** 33906 (813) 772-1777
JEWISH FEDERATION OF SOUTH BROWARD, INC.
2719 HOLLYWOOD BLVD — HOLLYWOOD **FL** 33020 (305) 921-8810
JACKSONVILLE JEWISH FEDERATION, THE
10829-1 OLD ST. AUGUSTINE ROAD, PO BOX 24508 — JACKSONVILLE **FL** 32223 (904) 262-2800
THE JEWISH FEDERATION OF GREATER ORLANDO
851 NORTH MAITLAND AVENUE, P.O. BOX 1508 — MAITLAND **FL** 32751 (305) 645-5933
GREATER MIAMI JEWISH FEDERATION, INC. 4200 BISCAYNE BLVD — MIAMI **FL** 33137 (305) 576-4000
PENSACOLA FEDERATED JEWISH CHARITIES 1320 EAST LEE STREET — PENSACOLA **FL** 32503 (904) 438-1464
SARASOTA-MANATEE JEWISH FEDERATION 2197 RINGLING BLVD — SARASOTA **FL** 33577 (813) 365-4410
TAMPA JEWISH FEDERATION 2808 HORATIO — TAMPA **FL** 33609 (813) 875-1618
JEWISH FEDERATION OF PALM BEACH COUNTY, INC.
501 SOUTH FLAGLER DRIVE, SUITE 305 — WEST PALM BEACH **FL** 33401 (305) 832-2120
ATLANTA JEWISH FEDERATION 1753 PEACHTREE ROAD N.E. — ATLANTA **GA** 30309 (404) 873-1661

FEDERATION OF JEWISH CHARITIES P.O. BOX 3251, SILBEY ROAD AUGUSTA **GA** 30904 (404) 736-1818
JEWISH WELFARE FEDERATION OF COLUMBUS, INC. P.O. BOX 6313 COLUMBUS **GA** 31907 (404) 563-4766
SAVANNAH JEWISH COUNCIL-UJA-FEDERATION CAMPAIGN
5111 ABERCORN STREET SAVANNAH **GA** 31405 (912) 355-8111
JEWISH FEDERATION OF HAWAII 817 COOKE STREET HONOLULU **HI** 96813 (808) 536-7228
JEWISH FEDERATION OF GREATER DES MOINES 910 POLK BLVD DES MOINES **IA** 50312 (515) 277-6321
JEWISH FEDERATION 525 14TH STREET SIOUX CITY **IA** 51105 (712) 258-0618
JEWISH FEDERATION OF SOUTHERN ILLINOIS
6464 WEST MAIN, SUITE 7A BELLEVILLE **IL** 62223 (618) 398-6100
CHAMPAIGN-URBANA JEWISH FEDERATION 503 EAST JOHN STREET CHAMPAIGN **IL** 61820 (217) 356-5907
JEWISH FEDERATION OF METROPOLITAN CHICAGO
ONE SOUTH FRANKLIN STREET CHICAGO **IL** 60606 (312) 346-6700
DECATUR JEWISH FEDERATION, C/O TEMPLE B'NAI ABRAHAM
1326 WEST ELDORADO DECATUR **IL** 62522 (217) 429-5740
ELGIN AREA JEWISH WELFARE CHEST 330 DIVISION STREET ELGIN **IL** 60120 (312) 741-5656
JOLIET JEWISH WELFARE CHEST 250 NORTH MIDLAND AVENUE JOLIET **IL** 60435 (815) 741-4600
JEWISH FEDERATION OF PEORIA 3100 NORTH KNOXVILLE, SUITE 17 PEORIA **IL** 61603 (309) 686-0611
JEWISH FEDERATION OF THE QUAD CITIES
224 18TH STREET, SUITE 511 ROCK ISLAND **IL** 61201 (309) 793-1300
ROCKFORD JEWISH COMMUNITY COUNCIL 1500 PARKVIEW AVENUE ROCKFORD **IL** 61107 (815) 399-5497
SPRINGFIELD JEWISH FEDERATION 730 EAST VINE STREET SPRINGFIELD **IL** 62703 (217) 528-3446
EVANSVILLE JEWISH COMMUNITY COUNCIL, INC. P.O. BOX 5026 EVANSVILLE **IN** 47715 (812) 477-7050
FORT WAYNE JEWISH FEDERATION 227 E. WASHINGTON BLVD FORT WAYNE **IN** 46802 (219) 422-8566
THE JEWISH FEDERATION, INC. 2939 JEWETT STREET HIGHLAND **IN** 46322 (219) 972-2251
JEWISH WELFARE FEDERATION, INC.
615 NORTH ALABAMA STREET INDIANAPOLIS **IN** 46204 (317) 637-2473
FEDERATED JEWISH CHARITIES P.O. BOX 708 LAFAYETTE **IN** 47902 (317) 742-9081
MICHIGAN CITY UNITED JEWISH WELFARE FUND
2800 FRANKLIN STREET MICHIGAN CITY **IN** 46360 (219) 874-4477
JEWISH FEDERATION OF ST. JOSEPH VALLEY 804 SHERLAND BLDG SOUTH BEND **IN** 46601 (219) 233-1164
TOPEKA-LAWRENCE JEWISH FEDERATION
3237 SOUTHWEST WESTOVER ROAD TOPEKA **KS** 66604 (913) 357-4244
MID-KANSAS JEWISH FEDERATION, INC.
400 NORTH WOODLAWN, SUITE 8 WICHITA **KS** 67208 (316) 686-4741
CENTRAL KENTUCKY JEWISH ASSOCIATION
258 PLAZA DRIVE, SUITE 208 LEXINGTON **KY** 40503 (606) 277-8048
JEWISH COMMUNITY FEDERATION OF LOUISVILLE, INC., UJ CAMPAIGN
P.O. BOX 33035, 3630 DUTCHMANS LANE LOUISVILLE **KY** 40232 (502) 451-8840
THE JEWISH WELFARE FED. & COMMUNITY COUNCIL OF CENTRAL LA
1262 HEYMAN LANE ALEXANDRIA **LA** 71301 (318) 442-1264
JEWISH FEDERATION OF GREATER BATON ROUGE
P.O. BOX 80827 BATON ROUGE **LA** 70898 (504) 769-0561
UNITED JEWISH CHARITIES OF NORTHEAST LOUISIANA
2400 ORREL PLACE MONROE **LA** 71201 (318) 387-0730
JEWISH FEDERATION OF GREATER NEW ORLEANS
1539 JACKSON AVENUE NEW ORLEANS **LA** 70130 (504) 525-0673
SHREVEPORT JEWISH FEDERATION 2030 LINE AVENUE SHREVEPORT **LA** 71104 (318) 221-4129
COMBINED JEWISH PHILANTHROPIES OF GREATER BOSTON, INC.
72 FRANKLIN STREET BOSTON **MA** 02110 (617) 542-8080
JEWISH FEDERATION OF FITCHBURG 40 BOUTELLE STREET FITCHBURG **MA** 01420 (617) 342-2227
GREATER FRAMINGHAM JEWISH FEDERATION
76 SALEM END ROAD FRAMINGHAM **MA** 01701 (617) 879-3301
HAVERHILL UNITED JEWISH APPEAL, INC. 514 MAIN STREET HAVERHILL **MA** 01830 (617) 373-3861
JEWISH COMMUNITY COUNCIL OF GREATER LAWRENCE
580 HAVERHILL STREET LAWRENCE **MA** 01841 (617) 686-4157
LEOMINSTER JEWISH COMMUNITY COUNCIL, INC.
268 WASHINGTON STREET LEOMINSTER **MA** 01453 (617) 534-6121
JEWISH FEDERATION OF THE NORTH SHORE, INC.
4 COMMUNITY ROAD MARBLEHEAD **MA** 01945 (617) 598-1810
JEWISH FEDERATION OF GREATER NEW BEDFORD, INC.
467 HAWTHORN STREET NEW BEDFORD **MA** 02747 (617) 977-7471
JEWISH FEDERATION OF THE BERKSHIRES 235 EAST STREET PITTSFIELD **MA** 01201 (413) 442-4360
SPRINGFIELD JEWISH FEDERATION, INC., UJ WELFARE FUND
1160 DICKINSON SPRINGFIELD **MA** 01108 (413) 737-4313
WORCESTER JEWISH FEDERATION, INC., JEWISH WELFARE FUND
633 SALISBURY STREET WORCESTER **MA** 01609 (617) 756-1513
WINNIPEG JEWISH COMMUNITY COUNCIL 370 HARGRAVE STREET WINNIPEG **MB** R3B 2K1 (204) 943-0406
ANNAPOLIS JEWISH WELFARE FUND 601 RIDGLEY AVENUE ANNAPOLIS **MD** 21401
ASSOCIATED JEWISH CHARITIES & WELFARE FUND
101 W. MOUNT ROYAL AVENUE BALTIMORE **MD** 21201 (301) 727-4828
UNITED JEWISH APPEAL FED. OF GREATER WASHINGTON, INC.
6935 ARLINGTON ROAD BETHESDA **MD** 20814 (301) 652-6480
LEWISTON-AUBURN JEWISH FEDERATION, UJA
74 BRADMAN STREET, P.O. BOX 259 AUBURN **ME** 04210 (207) 786-4201
JEWISH COMMUNITY COUNCIL & JEWISH FEDERATION OF BANGOR
28 SOMERSET STREET BANGOR **ME** 04401 (207) 945-5631
JEWISH FEDERATION COMMUNITY COUNCIL OF SOUTHERN MAINE, UJA
57 ASHMONT STREET PORTLAND **ME** 04103 (207) 773-7254
JEWISH WELFARE FEDERATION OF DETROIT, ALLIED JEWISH CAMPAIGN
163 MADISON, FRED M. BUTZEL MEMORIAL BLDG DETROIT **MI** 48226 (313) 965-3939
GREATER LANSING JEWISH WELFARE FEDERATION PO BOX 975 EAST LANSING **MI** 48823 (517) 351-3197
FLINT JEWISH FEDERATION 120 WEST KEARSLEY STREET FLINT **MI** 48502 (313) 767-5922
JEWISH COMMUNITY FUND OF GRAND RAPIDS
1121 KENEBERRY WAY S.E. GRAND RAPIDS **MI** 49506 (616) 949-5238
KALAMAZOO JEWISH FEDERATION C/O CONGREGATION OF MOSES
2501 STADIUM DRIVE KALAMAZOO **MI** 49008 (616) 375-5715
SAGINAW JEWISH WELFARE FEDERATION
1424 SOUTH WASHINGTON AVENUE SAGINAW **MI** 48601 (517) 753-5230
JEWISH FEDERATION AND COMMUNITY COUNCIL
1602 EAST SECOND STREET DULUTH **MN** 55812 (218) 724-8857
MINNEAPOLIS FEDERATION FOR JEWISH SERVICES
811 LASALLE AVENUE MINNEAPOLIS **MN** 55402 (612) 339-7491

UNITED JEWISH FUND & COUNCIL 790 SOUTH CLEVELAND ST. PAUL **MN** 55116 (612) 690-1707
JEWISH FEDERATION OF GREATER KANSAS CITY
25 EAST 12TH STREET, 10TH FLOOR KANSAS CITY **MO** 64106 (816) 421-5808
UNITED JEWISH FUND OF ST. JOSEPH 1124 NORTH 26TH STREET ST. JOSEPH **MO** 64507 (816) 364-6507
JEWISH FEDERATION OF ST. LOUIS 10957 SCHUETZ ROAD ST. LOUIS **MO** 63141 (314) 432-0200
JACKSON JEWISH WELFARE FUND, INC. P.O. BOX 12329 JACKSON **MS** 39211 (601) 956-6215
FEDERATED JEWISH CHARITIES OF ASHEVILLE, INC.
236 CHARLOTTE STREET ASHEVILLE **NC** 28801 (704) 253-0701
DURHAM-CHAPEL HILL JEWISH FEDERATION & COMMUNITY COUNCIL
1509 CRESTWOOD LANE CHAPEL HILL **NC** 27514 (919) 933-6810
CHARLOTTE JEWISH FEDERATION P.O. BOX 220188 CHARLOTTE **NC** 28222 (704) 366-0358
GREENSBORO JEWISH FEDERATION
713-A NORTH GREENE STREET GREENSBORO **NC** 27401 (919) 272-3189
HIGH POINT JEWISH FEDERATION P.O. BOX 2063 HIGH POINT **NC** 27261 (919) 431-7101
WINSTON-SALEM JEWISH COMMUNITY COUNCIL
620 LANKASHIRE ROAD WINSTON-SALEM **NC** 27106 (919) 765-6685
LINCOLN JEWISH WELFARE FEDERATIONS, INC., THE P.O. BOX 80014 LINCOLN **NE** 68501 (402) 435-0230
JEWISH FEDERATION OF OMAHA 333 SOUTH 132ND STREET OMAHA **NE** 68154 (402) 334-8200
JEWISH FEDERATION OF GREATER MANCHESTER
698 BEECH STREET MANCHESTER **NH** 03104 (603) 627-7679
BAYONNE JEWISH COMMUNITY COUNCIL 1050 KENNEDY BLVD BAYONNE **NJ** 07002 (201) 436-6900
JEWISH FEDERATION OF SOUTHERN NEW JERSEY
2393 WEST MARLTON PIKE CHERRY HILL **NJ** 08002 (609) 665-6100
JEWISH FEDERATION OF GREATER CLIFTON-PASSAIC, UJ CAMPAIGN
199 SCOLES AVENUE CLIFTON **NJ** 07012 (201) 777-7031
JEWISH FEDERATION OF GREATER MONMOUTH COUNTY 100 GRANT AVENUE,
P.O.BOX 210 DEAL PARK **NJ** 07723 (201) 531-6200
JEWISH COMMUNITY FEDERATION OF METROPOLITAN NEW JERSEY-UJA
60 GLENWOOD AVENUE EAST ORANGE **NJ** 07017 (201) 673-6800
JEWISH FEDERATION OF NORTHERN MIDDLESEX COUNTY-UJA
1775 OAK TREE ROAD EDISON **NJ** 08820 (201) 494-3920
JEWISH FEDERATION OF RARITAN VALLEY
2 SOUTH ADELAIDE AVENUE HIGHLAND PARK **NJ** 08904 (201) 246-1905
UNITED JEWISH APPEAL 71 BENTLEY AVENUE JERSEY CITY **NJ** 07304 (201) 332-6644
OCEAN COUNTY JEWISH FEDERATION 301 MADISON AVENUE LAKEWOOD **NJ** 08701 (201) 363-0530
UNITED JEWISH COMMUNITY OF BERGEN COUNTY
111 KINDERKAMACK ROAD, P. O. BOX 176, HACKENSACK STATION RIVER EDGE **NJ** 07661 (201) 488-6800
JEWISH FEDERATION OF SOMERSET COUNTY
2 DIVISION STREET, PO BOX 874 SOMERVILLE **NJ** 08876 (201) 725-6994
JEWISH FEDERATION OF CENTRAL NEW JERSEY, UJ CAMPAIGN
GREEN LANE UNION **NJ** 07083 (201) 351-5060
FEDERATION OF JEWISH AGENCIES OF ATLANTIC COUNTY
5321 ATLANTIC AVENUE VENTNOR CITY **NJ** 08406 (609) 822-7122
THE JEWISH FEDERATION OF CUMBERLAND COUNTY
629 WOOD STREET, SUITE 204 VINELAND **NJ** 08360 (609) 696-4445
JEWISH FEDERATION OF NORTH JERSEY- UJA DRIVE ONE PIKE DRIVE WAYNE **NJ** 07470 (201) 595-0555
JEWISH COMMUNITY COUNCIL OF ALBUQUERQUE
12800 LOMAS N.E., SUITE F ALBUQUERQUE **NM** 87112 (505) 292-1061
JEWISH FEDERATION OF LAS VEGAS 1030 EAST TWAIN AVENUE LAS VEGAS **NV** 89109 (702) 732-0556
GREATER ALBANY JEWISH FEDERATION 350 WHITEHALL ROAD ALBANY **NY** 12208 (518) 459-8000
THE JEWISH FEDERATION OF BROOME COUNTY
500 CLUBHOUSE ROAD BINGHAMTON **NY** 13903 (607) 724-2332
JEWISH FEDERATION OF GREATER BUFFALO, INC
787 DELAWARE AVENUE BUFFALO **NY** 14209 (716) 886-7750
ELMIRA JEWISH WELFARE FUND, INC.
P.O. BOX 3087, GRANDVIEW ROAD EXT ELMIRA **NY** 14905 (607) 734-8122
QUEENS JEWISH COMMUNITY COUNCIL
114-18 QUEENS BOULEVARD FOREST HILLS **NY** 11375 (718) 544-9033
GREATER GLEN FALLS JEWISH WELFARE FUND P.O. BOX 177 GLEN FALLS **NY** 12401 (914) 338-8131
JEWISH WELFARE FUND OF HUDSON, N.Y. JOSLEN BLVD HUDSON **NY** 12354 (518) 828-6848
JEWISH FEDERATION OF GREATER KINGSTON, INC.
159 GREEN STREET KINGSTON **NY** 12401 (914) 338-8131
COUNCIL OF JEWISH FEDERATIONS & WELFARE FUNDS, INC.
730 BROADWAY NEW YORK **NY** 10003 (212) 475-5000
FEDERATION OF JEWISH PHILANTHROPIES OF NEW YORK
130 EAST 59TH STREET NEW YORK **NY** 10022 (212) 980-1000
INTERNATIONAL COUNCIL ON JEWISH SOCIAL & WELFARE SERVICES
200 PARK AVENUE S NEW YORK **NY** 10003 (212) 674-6800
UNITED JEWISH APPEAL OF GREATER NEW YORK, INC.
130 EAST 59TH STREET NEW YORK **NY** 10022 (212) 980-1000
UNITED JEWISH COUNCIL OF THE EAST SIDE, INC.
235 EAST BROADWAY NEW YORK **NY** 10002 (212) 233-6037
JEWISH FEDERATION OF GREATER ORANGE COUNTY
360 POWELL AVENUE NEWBURGH **NY** 12550 (914) 562-7860
JEWISH FEDERATION OF NIAGARA FALLS, NEW YORK, INC. TEMPLE BETH ISRAEL,
ROOM #5, COLLEGE & MADISON AVENUES NIAGARA FALLS **NY** 14305 (716) 284-4575
JEWISH WELFARE FUND OF DUTCHESS COUNTY
110 GRAND AVENUE POUGHKEEPSIE **NY** 12603 (914) 471-9811
JEWISH COMMUNITY FEDERATION OF ROCHESTER, NY INC.
441 EAST AVENUE ROCHESTER **NY** 14607 (716) 461-0490
JEWISH FEDERATION OF GREATER SCHENECTADY
2565 BALLTOWN ROAD SCHENECTADY **NY** 12309 (518) 393-1136
SYRACUSE JEWISH FEDERATION, INC
2223 EAST GENESEE STREET, PO BOX 5004 SYRACUSE **NY** 13214 (315) 422-4104
TROY JEWISH COMMUNITY COUNCIL, INC. 2430 21ST STREET TROY **NY** 12180 (518) 274-0700
JEWISH FEDERATION OF UTICA, NEW YORK, INC. 2310 ONEIDA STREET UTICA **NY** 13501 (315) 733-2343
AKRON JEWISH COMMUNITY FEDERATION 750 WHITE POND DRIVE AKRON **OH** 44320 (216) 867-7850
CANTON JEWISH COMMUNITY FEDERATION
2631 HARVARD AVENUE N.W. CANTON **OH** 44709 (216) 452-6444
JEWISH FEDERATION OF CINCINNATI AND VICINITY
200 WEST 4TH STREET CINCINNATI **OH** 45202 (513) 381-5800

JEWISH COMMUNITY FEDERATION OF CLEVELAND
1750 EUCLID AVENUE .... CLEVELAND **OH** 44115   (216) 566-9200
COLUMBUS JEWISH FEDERATION 1175 COLLEGE AVENUE .... COLUMBUS **OH** 43209   (614) 237-7686
JEWISH FEDERATION OF GREATER DAYTON 4501 DENLINGER ROAD .... DAYTON **OH** 45426   (513) 854-4150
FEDERATED JEWISH CHARITIES OF LIMA DISTRICT
2417 WEST MARKET STREET .... LIMA **OH** 45805   (419) 224-8941
JEWISH COMMUNITY COUNCIL P.O. BOX 472 .... STEUBENVILLE **OH** 43952   (614) 282-9031
JEWISH WELFARE FEDERATION OF GREATER TOLEDO
6505 SYLVANIA AVENUE, P.O. BOX 587 .... SYLVANIA **OH** 43560   (419) 885-4461
YOUNGSTOWN AREA JEWISH FEDERATION
P.O. BOX 449, 505 GYPSY LANE .... YOUNGSTOWN **OH** 44501   (216) 746-3251
JEWISH COMMUNITY COUNCIL 11032 QUAIL CREEK ROAD #201 ... OKLAHOMA CITY **OK** 73120   (405) 755-6030
JEWISH FEDERATION OF TULSA 2021 EAST 71ST STREET .... TULSA **OK** 74136   (918) 495-1100
HAMILTON JEWISH FEDERATION 57 DELAWARE AVENUE .... HAMILTON **ON** L8M 1T6   (416) 528-8570
LONDON JEWISH COMMUNITY COUNCIL 532 HURON STREET .... LONDON **ON** N5Y 4J5   (519) 432-6337
JEWISH COMMUNITY COUNCIL OF OTTAWA 151 CHAPEL STREET ...... OTTAWA **ON** K1N 7Y2   (613) 232-7306
TORONTO JEWISH CONGRESS 150 BEVERLY STREET .... TORONTO **ON** M5T 1Y6   (416) 977-3811
CJF CANADIAN OFFICE 4600 BATHURST STREET SUITE 251 .... WILLOWDALE **ON** M2R 3V3   (416) 635-9567
JEWISH COMMUNITY COUNCIL 1641 QUELLETTE AVENUE .... WINDSOR **ON** N8X 1K9   (519) 254-7558
JEWISH FEDERATION OF PORTLAND
4850 SOUTHWEST SCHOLLS FERRY ROAD, SUITE 304 .... PORTLAND **OR** 97225   (503) 297-8104
JEWISH FEDERATION OF ALLENTOWN, INC.
702 NORTH 22ND STREET .... ALLENTOWN **PA** 18104   (215) 821-5500
FEDERATION OF JEWISH PHILANTHROPIES 1308 17TH STREET .... ALTOONA **PA** 16601   (814) 944-4072
BUTLER JEWISH WELFARE FUND 148 HAVERFORD DRIVE .... BUTLER **PA** 16001   (412) 287-3814
JEWISH COMMUNITY COUNCIL OF ERIE
701 G. DANIEL BALDWIN BLDG., 1001 STATE STREET .... ERIE **PA** 16501   (814) 455-4474
UNITED JEWISH FEDERATION OF GREATER HARRISBURG
100 VAUGHN STREET .... HARRISBURG **PA** 17110   (717) 236-9555
JEWISH COMMUNITY COUNCIL LAUREL & HEMLOCK STREETS .... HAZELTON **PA** 18201   (717) 454-3528
UNITED JEWISH FEDERATION OF JOHNSTOWN
1334 LUZERNE STREET EXT .... JOHNSTOWN **PA** 15905   (814) 255-1447
LANCASTER JEWISH FEDERATION 2120 OREGON PIKE .... LANCASTER **PA** 17601   (717) 569-7352
JEWISH FEDERATION OF DELAWARE VALLEY
20-28 NORTH PENNSYLVANIA AVENUE .... MORRISVILLE **PA** 19067   (215) 736-8022
UNITED JEWISH APPEAL OF NEW CASTLE, PENNSYLVANIA
P.O. BOX 5050 .... NEW CASTLE **PA** 16105   (412) 658-8389
TIFERES ISRAEL JEWISH CENTER 1541 POWELL STREET .... NORRISTOWN **PA** 19401   (215) 275-8797
FEDERATION OF JEWISH AGENCIES OF GREATER PHILADELPHIA
226 SOUTH 16TH STREET .... PHILADELPHIA **PA** 19102   (215) 893-5600
UNITED JEWISH FEDERATION OF GREATER PITTSBURGH
234 MCKEE PLACE .... PITTSBURGH **PA** 15213   (412) 681-8000
UNITED JEWISH CHARITIES 2300 MAHANTONGO STREET .... POTTSVILLE **PA** 17901   (717) 622-5890
JEWISH FEDERATION OF READING, PENNSYLVANIA, INC.
1700 CITY LINE STREET .... READING **PA** 19604   (215) 921-2766
SCRANTON-LACKAWANNA JEWISH FEDERATION
601 JEFFERSON AVENUE .... SCRANTON **PA** 18510   (717) 961-2300
JEWISH FEDERATION OF GREATER WILKES-BARRE
60 SOUTH RIVER STREET .... WILKES-BARRE **PA** 18702   (717) 824-4646
YORK COUNCIL OF JEWISH CHARITIES, INC. 120 EAST MARKET STREET ...... YORK **PA** 17401   (717) 843-0918
ALLIED JEWISH COMMUNITY SERVICES
5151 COTE ST. CATHERINE ROAD .... MONTREAL **QU** H3W 1M6   (514) 735-3541
JEWISH FEDERATION OF RHODE ISLAND 130 SESSIONS STREET ...... PROVIDENCE **RI** 02906   (401) 421-4111
CHARLESTON JEWISH FEDERATION
1645 RAOUL WALLENBERG BLVD., P.O. BOX 31298 .... CHARLESTON **SC** 29407   (803) 571-6565
COLUMBIA UNITED JEWISH WELFARE FEDERATION
4540 TRENHOLM ROAD .... COLUMBIA **SC** 29206   (803) 787-2023
JEWISH WELFARE FUND NATIONAL RESERVE BLDG .... SIOUX FALLS **SD** 57102   (605) 336-2880
CHATTANOOGA JEWISH FEDERATION 5326 LYNNLAND TERRACE .. CHATTANOOGA **TN** 37411   (615) 894-1317
JEWISH WELFARE FUND, INC. 6800 DEANE HILL DRIVE, P.O. BOX 10882 .. KNOXVILLE **TN** 37919   (615) 693-5837
MEMPHIS JEWISH FEDERATION 6560 POPLAR AVENUE, P.O. BOX 38268 .... MEMPHIS **TN** 38138   (901) 767-5161
JEWISH FEDERATION OF NASHVILLE & MIDDLE TENNESSEE
3500 WEST END AVENUE .... NASHVILLE **TN** 37205   (615) 269-0729
JEWISH COMMUNITY COUNCIL OF AUSTIN
5758 BALCONES DRIVE, SUITE 104 .... AUSTIN **TX** 78731   (512) 451-6435
BEAUMONT JEWISH FEDERATION OF TEXAS, INC. P.O. BOX 1981 .... BEAUMONT **TX** 77704   (713) 833-5427
CORPUS CHRISTI JEWISH COMMUNITY COUNCIL
750 EVERHART ROAD .... CORPUS CHRISTI **TX** 78411   (512) 855-6239
JEWISH FEDERATION OF GREATER DALLAS
7800 NORTHHAVEN ROAD, SUITE A .... DALLAS **TX** 75230   (214) 369-3313
JEWISH FEDERATION OF EL PASO, INC. 405 MARDI GRAS, P.O. BOX 12097 .. EL PASO **TX** 79912   (915) 584-4437
JEWISH FEDERATION OF FORT WORTH & TARRANT COUNTY
6801 DAN DANCIGER ROAD .... FORT WORTH **TX** 76133   (817) 292-3081
GALVESTON COUNTY JEWISH WELFARE ASSOCIATION P.O. BOX 146 .. GALVESTON **TX** 77553   (713) 744-8295
JEWISH FEDERATION OF GREATER HOUSTON
5603 SOUTH BRAESWOOD BLVD .... HOUSTON **TX** 77096   (713) 729-7000
JEWISH FEDERATION OF SAN ANTONIO 8434 AHERN DRIVE .... SAN ANTONIO **TX** 78216   (512) 341-8234
FEDERATION OF JEWISH WELFARE FUND P.O. BOX 8601 .... TYLER **TX** 75711
JEWISH WELFARE COUNCIL OF WACO P.O. BOX 8031 .... WACO **TX** 76710   (817) 776-3740
UNITED JEWISH COUNCIL & SALT LAKE JEWISH WELFARE FUND
2416 EAST 1700 SOUTH .... SALT LAKE CITY **UT** 84108   (801) 581-0098
JEWISH FEDERATION OF THE VIRGINIA PENINSULA, INC.
2700 SPRING ROAD, P.O. BOX 6680 .... NEWPORT NEWS **VA** 23606   (804) 595-5544
UNITED JEWISH FEDERATION OF TIDEWATER
7300 NEWPORT AVENUE, P.O. BOX 9776 .... NORFOLK **VA** 23505   (804) 489-8040
JEWISH COMMUNITY FEDERATION OF RICHMOND
P.O. BOX 8237, 5403 MONUMENT AVENUE .... RICHMOND **VA** 23226   (804) 288-0045
JEWISH COMMUNITY COUNCIL P.O. BOX 1074 .... ROANOKE **VA** 24005   (703) 774-2828
JEWISH FEDERATION OF GREATER SEATTLE
510 SECURITIES BLDG., 1904 THIRD AVENUE .... SEATTLE **WA** 98101   (206) 622-8211
JEWISH COMMUNITY COUNCIL OF SPOKANE 521 PARKADE PLAZA .... SPOKANE **WA** 99201   (509) 838-4261

UNITED JEWISH CHARITIES OF APPLETON
3131 NORTH MEADE STREET .... APPLETON **WI** 54911   (414) 733-1848
GREEN BAY JEWISH WELFARE FUND P.O. BOX 335 .... GREEN BAY **WI** 54305   (414) 432-9347
KENOSHA JEWISH WELFARE FUND 6537 7TH AVENUE .... KENOSHA **WI** 53140   (414) 658-8635
MADISON JEWISH COMMUNITY COUNCIL, INC.
310 NORTH MIDVALE BLVD., SUITE 325 .... MADISON **WI** 53705   (608) 231-3426
MILWAUKEE JEWISH FEDERATION, INC. 1360 N. PROSPECT AVENUE ... MILWAUKEE **WI** 53202   (414) 271-8338
RACINE JEWISH WELFARE COUNCIL 944 SOUTH MAIN STREET .... RACINE **WI** 53403   (414) 633-7093
JEWISH WELFARE COUNCIL OF SHEBOYGAN 1404 NORTH AVENUE .... SHEBOYGAN **WI** 53081
FEDERATED JEWISH CHARITIES OF CHARLESTON, INC.
P.O. BOX 1613 .... CHARLESTON **WV** 25326   (304) 346-7500
FEDERATED JEWISH CHARITIES P.O. BOX 947 .... HUNTINGTON **WV** 25713   (304) 523-9326
CJF ISRAEL OFFICE 11 PINSKER STREET .... JERUSALEM **IS** 92228

FILMS & FILM STRIPS

BUREAU OF JEWISH EDUCATION 590 NORTH VERMONT AVENUE ..... LOS ANGELES **CA** 90004
BUREAU OF JEWISH EDUCATION 6505 WILSHIRE BOULEVARD ...... LOS ANGELES **CA** 90048   (213) 852-1234
HEBREW UNION COLLEGE-JEWISH INSTITUTE OF RELIGION
3077 UNIV. MALL, EDUCATION LABORATORY & LEARNING CNTR. ... LOS ANGELES **CA** 90007   (213) 749-2434
CONTEMPORARY FILMS 1714 STOCKTON STREET .... SAN FRANCISCO **CA** 94133
TELEVISUALS 4224 ELLENITA AVENUE .... TARZANA **CA** 91356
LIVING ARCHIVES LIMITED PO BOX 86 .... BARRINGTON **IL** 60010   (312) 381-3736
BOARD OF JEWISH EDUCATION 618 SOUTH MICHIGAN AVENUE ... CHICAGO **IL** 60605   (312) 427-5570
CHICAGO BOARD OF RABBIS 1 SOUTH FRANKLIN .... CHICAGO **IL** 60605   (312) 444-2896
MIDWEST FILM CONFERENCE 800 CUSTER AVENUE .... EVANSTON **IL** 60602   (312) 869-0600
NATIONAL EDUCATIONAL TELEVISION FILM LIBRARY
INDIANA UNIVERSITY .... BLOOMINGTON **IN** 47401   (812) 332-0211
MIRAMAR FILM LIBRARY 19 CORNELL STREET .... NEWTON **MA** 02162
MODI'IN PRODUCTIONS 415 SOUTH STREET .... WALTHAM **MA** 02154
RUTTENBERG & EVERETT YIDDISH FILM LIBRARY
BRANDEIS UNIVERSITY .... WALTHAM **MA** 02154   (617) 647-2000
JEWISH MEDIA SERVICE OF THE INSTITUTE FOR JEWISH LIFE
65 WILLIAM STREET .... WELLESLEY **MA** 02181
MEDIA RESOURCES CNTR. UNIV. OF MICHIGAN, EDUC. FILM LIBRARY
416 FOURTH STREET .... ANN ARBOR **MI** 48104   (313) 764-1817
MICHIGAN STATE UNIVERSITY AUDIO-VISUAL DEPARTMENT .... EAST LANSING **MI** 48824   (517) 355-6532
CONTEMPORARY FILMS PRINCETON ROAD .... HIGHTSTOWN **NJ** 08520   (609) 488-1700
KOL REE ASSOCIATES 1923 SPRINGFIELD AVENUE .... MAPLEWOOD **NJ** 07040   (201) 763-4244
ALDEN FILMS 7820 20TH AVENUE .... BROOKLYN **NY** 11214   (718) 331-1045
JEWISH EDUCATIONAL MEDIA 784 EASTERN PARKWAY .... BROOKLYN **NY** 11213   (718) 774-6000
TARYAG MEDIA INC. 719 CROWN STREET .... BROOKLYN **NY** 11213   (718) 467-3077
ZELMAN STUDIOS, LTD. 623 CORTELYOU ROAD .... BROOKLYN **NY** 11218   (718) 941-5500
TORAH MICROFICHE LIBRARY-THE RUDMAN FOUNDATION
1051 BAY 25TH STREET .... FAR ROCKAWAY **NY** 11691   (718) 634-8000
MACMILLAN AUDIO-BRANDON FILMS
34 MACQUESTEN PARKWAY SOUTH .... MT. VERNON **NY** 10550
AMERICAN ASSOCIATION FOR JEWISH EDUCATION
114 FIFTH AVENUE .... NEW YORK **NY** 10011   (212) 675-5656
AMERICAN FRIENDS OF THE ALLIANCE ISRAELITE UNIVERSELLE
61 BROADWAY .... NEW YORK **NY** 10006   (212) 349-0537
AMERICAN JEWISH CONGRESS, COMMISSION ON JEWISH AFFAIRS
15 EAST 84TH STREET .... NEW YORK **NY** 10028   (212) 879-4500
AMERICAN LIBRARY COLOR SLIDE COMPANY 222 WEST 23RD STREET .. NEW YORK **NY** 10011   (212) 255-5356
AMERICAN ZIONIST YOUTH FOUNDATION 515 PARK AVENUE .... NEW YORK **NY** 10022   (212) 751-6070
ANTI-DEFAMATION LEAGUE OF B'NAI B'RITH
823 UNITED NATIONS PLAZA .... NEW YORK **NY** 10017   (212) 490-2525
BEHRMAN HOUSE INC. 1261 BROADWAY .... NEW YORK **NY** 10001   (212) 689-2020
BEN-LAR PRODUCTIONS 311 WEST 24TH STREET .... NEW YORK **NY** 10011   (212) 255-5553
CONTEMPORARY FILMS - MCGRAW HILL
1221 AVENUE OF THE AMERICAS .... NEW YORK **NY** 10020   (212) 997-4100
ETERNAL LIGHT C/O UNITED SYNAGOGUE OF AMERICA
155 FIFTH AVENUE .... NEW YORK **NY** 10010   (212) 533-7800
FRIENDSHIP PRESS 475 RIVERSIDE DRIVE .... NEW YORK **NY** 10027   (212) 870-2586
HADASSAH FILM LIBRARY 50 W. 58TH STREET .... NEW YORK **NY** 10016   (212) 355-7900
INTERNATIONAL FILM EXCHANGE LIMITED 159 WEST 53RD STREET .. NEW YORK **NY** 10019   (212) 582-4318
ISRA-ART 157 WEST 57TH STREET .... NEW YORK **NY** 10019   (212) 246-4500
ISRAEL EDUCATIONAL MATERIALS & GAMES, C/O ISRAEL TRADE CNTR.
111 WEST 40TH STREET .... NEW YORK **NY** 10018

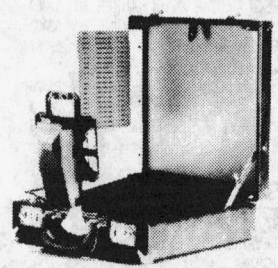
ISRAEL FILM CENTER 515 PARK AVENUE	NEW YORK NY	10022	(212) 688-0800
ISRAEL GOVERNMENT TOURIST OFFICE 350 FIFTH AVENUE	NEW YORK NY	10001	(212) 560-0600
ISRAEL GOVERNMENT TRADE OFFICE 350 FIFTH AVENUE	NEW YORK NY	10001	(212) 560-0600
ISRAEL PHILATELIC AGENCY IN AMERICA 116 WEST 32ND STREET	NEW YORK NY	10001	(212) 695-0008
J. LEVINE COMPANY 58 ELDRIDGE STREET	NEW YORK NY	10002	(212) 966-4460
JWB LECTURE BUREAU, THE NATIONAL JEWISH WELFARE BOARD			
15 EAST 26TH STREET	NEW YORK NY	10010	(212) 532-4949
JEWISH AGENCY 515 PARK AVENUE	NEW YORK NY	10022	(212) 752-0600
JEWISH BOOK COUNCIL, THE NATIONAL JEWISH WELFARE BOARD			
15 EAST 26TH STREET	NEW YORK NY	10010	(212) 532-4949
JEWISH CHAUTAUQUA SOCIETY, FILM DISTRIBUTION CENTER			
838 FIFTH AVENUE	NEW YORK NY	10021	(212) 249-0100
JEWISH EDUCATION COMMITTEE 426 WEST 58TH STREET	NEW YORK NY	10019	(212) 245-8200
JEWISH EDUCATION PRESS 426 WEST 58TH STREET	NEW YORK NY	10019	(212) 245-8200
JEWISH MEDIA SERVICE, THE NATIONAL JEWISH WELFARE BOARD			
15 EAST 26TH STREET	NEW YORK NY	10010	(212) 532-4949
JEWISH NATIONAL FUND - DEPT. OF YOUTH & EDUCATION			
42 EAST 69TH STREET	NEW YORK NY	10021	(212) 879-9300
JEWISH THEOLOGICAL SEMINARY OF AMERICA, DEPT. OF RADIO & TV			
3080 BROADWAY	NEW YORK NY	10027	(212) 678-8000
MARQUIS FILM DISTRIBUTOR 416 WEST 45TH STREET	NEW YORK NY	10036	(212) 245-8900
MAXI COHEN 31 GREEN STREET	NEW YORK NY	10013	(212) 966-6326
MIZRACHI 817 BROADWAY	NEW YORK NY	10003	(212) 477-4720
NAT'L ACADEMY FOR ADULT JEWISH STUDIES OF THE U. SYN. OF AM.			
155 FIFTH AVENUE	NEW YORK NY	10010	(212) 260-8450
NATIONAL COMMITTEE FOR LABOR ISRAEL 33 EAST 67TH STREET	NEW YORK NY	10021	(212) 628-1000
NATIONAL JEWISH WELFARE BOARD 15 EAST 26TH STREET	NEW YORK NY	10010	(212) 532-4949
NEW JEWISH MEDIA PROJECT C/O NORTH AMERICAN JEWISH STUDENTS			
36 WEST 37TH STREET	NEW YORK NY	10017	
NEW YORK BOARD OF RABBIS 10 EAST 73RD STREET	NEW YORK NY	10021	(212) 879-8415
PHOENIX FILMS, INC. 470 PARK AVENUE SOUTH, SUITE 802	NEW YORK NY	10016	(212) 684-5910
PIONEER WOMEN 200 MADISON AVENUE	NEW YORK NY	10016	(212) 725-8010
STUDENT STRUGGLE FOR SOVIET JEWRY 210 WEST 91ST STREET	NEW YORK NY	10024	(212) 799-8900
TARBUTH FOUNDATION 129 WEST 67TH STREET	NEW YORK NY	10023	(212) 874-7837
TORAH UMESORAH 160 BROADWAY	NEW YORK NY	10038	(212) 406-4190
UNION OF AMERICAN HEBREW CONGREGATIONS 838 FIFTH AVENUE	NEW YORK NY	10021	(212) 249-0100
UNITED JEWISH APPEAL 1290 AVENUE OF THE AMERICAS	NEW YORK NY	10019	(212) 757-1500
UNITED SYNAGOGUE OF AMERICA 155 FIFTH AVENUE	NEW YORK NY	10010	(212) 260-8450
WOMEN'S AMERICAN ORT 1250 BROADWAY	NEW YORK NY	10001	(212) 594-8500
YIVO SLIDE BANK, MAX WEINREICH CENTER 1048 FIFTH AVENUE	NEW YORK NY	10028	(212) 535-6700
THE CENTER FOR JEWISH MEDIA LIMITED 48 URBAN AVENUE	WESTBURY NY	11590	(516) 333-5300
ROBERT BINDER - B'YAD HAYOTZER 24 WARWICK AVENUE	TORONTO ON	M6C 1T6	(416) 979-3393
AMIN PRODUCTIONS 425 ASHBOURNE ROAD	ELKINS PARK PA	11917	
GRATZ COLLEGE, DIVISION OF COMMUNITY SERVICES			
1000 WEST TABOR ROAD	PHILADELPHIA PA	19141	(215) 329-3363
LAURENCE SALZMANN 3607 BARING STREET	PHILADELPHIA PA	19104	(215) 382-1410
FELIX LAZARUS 441 DUFFERIN ROAD	MONTREAL QU		
RARIG'S FILM SERVICE 1941 AURORA NORTH	SEATTLE WA	98109	(206) 282-1941

FISH

FLORIDA SMOKED FISH CO. 111 NW 159TH DRIVE	MIAMI FL	33169	(305) 625-5112
STOLLER FISHERIES, INC. BOX B	SPIRIT LAKE IA	51360	(712) 336-1750
VITA FOOD PRODUCTS INC. 2222 WEST LAKE	CHICAGO IL	60612	(312) 738-4500
BLUE RIBBON SMOKED FISH CO. 5901 FOSTER AVENUE	BROOKLYN NY	11234	(718) 251-9100
DAGIM TAHORIM CO., INC. 1644 52ND STREET	BROOKLYN NY	11204	(718) 851-1006

DANY'S KOSHER FISH MARKET 4104 18TH AVENUE	BROOKLYN NY		(718) 853-7816
NOVA SCOTIA FOOD PRODUCTS CORP. 77 LOMBARDY STREET	BROOKLYN NY	11222	(718) 388-2876
KINERET FOOD CORP. 24 JERICHO TPKE.	JERICHO NY	11753	(516) 333-2626
BELNORD FISH MARKET 544 AMSTERDAM AVENUE	NEW YORK NY	10024	(212) 724-4214
NEWMARK'S KOSHER FISH MARKET 13897 CEDAR ROAD	CLEVELAND OH	44118	(216) 321-1048

FLOWERS

KENNICOTT BROTHERS COMPANY 1317 WEST RANDOLPH STREET	CHICAGO IL	60607	(312) 421-0465
FLORAGRAM CO. 295 MADISON AVENUE	NEW YORK NY	10017	(212) 532-4444
N'SHEI AHAVAS CHESED 1549 46TH STREET	BROOKLYN NY	11219	(212) 438-0211
AGREXCO U.S.A. LTD. 149-32 132ND STREET	S. OZONE PARK NY	11420	(718) 529-4411
MILWAUKEE FLORIST EXCHANGE 1130 WATER STREET	MILWAUKEE WI	53202	(414) 273-4903

FOOD PRODUCTS

KING SALMON, INC. 171 N. GREEN STREET	CHICAGO IL	60607	(312) 666-3226
TULKOFF'S HORSERADISH PRODUCTS CO., INC. 1101 S. CONKLIN	BALTIMORE MD	21224	(301) 327-6585
GREENFIELD NOODLE & SPECIALTY CO. 600 CUSTER AVENUE	DETROIT MI	48202	(313) 873-2212
I. ROKEACH & SONS 560 SYLVAN AVENUE	ENGLEWOOD CLIFFS NJ	07632	(201) 568-7550
MACABEE FOODS, INC. 107 PINK STREET	HACKENSACK NJ	07601	(201) 489-4343
B. MANISHEWITZ CO. ONE MANISCHEWITZ PLAZA	JERSEY CITY NJ	07302	(212) 344-0330
MOTHER'S FOOD PRODUCTS INC. 80 AVENUE K	NEWARK NJ	07105	(201) 589-5297
MALLMAR KOSHER FOODS P.O. BOX 125	BRONX NY	10461	(212) 824-5040
MRS. WEINBERG'S FOOD PRODUCTS INC. 1303 HERSCHELL STREET	BRONX NY	10461	(212) 824-6940
STELLA D'ORO BISCUIT CO, INC. 184 WEST 237TH STREET	BRONX NY	10463	(212) 549-3700
ADLER'S FOOD CORP. 902 ESSEX STREET	BROOKLYN NY	11208	(718) 649-9121

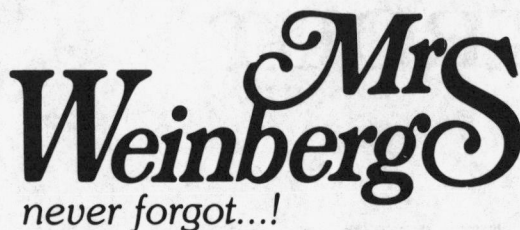
BATAMPTE PICKLE PRODUCTS INC.
77 BROOKLYN TERMINAL MARKET .... BROOKLYN NY 11236 (718) 251-2100
GOLD PURE FOOD PRODUCTS CO., INC. 895 MCDONALD AVENUE ...... BROOKLYN NY 11218 (718) 435-1910
LEIBOWITZ DIVISION-VLASIC FOODS, INC. 9301 DITMAS AVENUE .... BROOKLYN NY 11236 (718) 342-4886
LIEBER'S KOSHER FOOD SPECIALTIES 100 19 STREET .... BROOKLYN NY 11232 (718) 499-0888
OLD DUTCH MUSTARD CO., INC. 80 METROPOLITAN AVENUE .... BROOKLYN NY 11211 (718) 387-9155
VICTOR VICTOR CORP. 401 MARCY AVENUE .... BROOKLYN NY 11206 (718) 384-1777
KINERET FOOD CORP. 24 JERICHO TPKE .... JERICHO NY 11753 (516) 333-2626
KOSHERIFIC FOODS 24 JERICHO TPKE. .... JERICHO NY 11753 (516) 333-2626
HOROWITZ-MARGARETEN KOSHER FOODS
29-00 REVIEW AVENUE .... LONG ISLAND CITY NY 11101 (718) 729-5420
HEBREW NATIONAL FOODS 58-80 MAURICE AVENUE .... MASPETH NY 11378 (718) 894-4300
CANTON NOODLE MANUFACTURING COMPANY, INC.
101 MOTT STREET .... NEW YORK NY 10013 (718) 226-3276
EMPIRE KOSHER FOODS, INC. R.D. #3 P.O. BOX 165 .... MIFFLINTOWN PA 17059 (717) 436-2131

FREE CLOTHES

JEWISH SALVAGE BUREAU 130 NORTH WELLS .... CHICAGO IL 60606 (312) 346-5883
JEWISH FREE STORE - MALBISH ARUMIM 306 WEST 37TH STREET .... NEW YORK NY 10018

FREE LOAN SOCIETIES

PHOENIX JEWISH FREE LOAN ASSOCIATION
1718 WEST MARYLAND AVENUE .... PHOENIX AZ 85015 (602) 249-1832
HEBREW FREE LOAN ASSOCIATION 4032 EAST WHITTIER .... TUCSON AZ 85712
FEDERATION FREE LOAN ASSOCIATION 2601 GRAND AVENUE .... LONG BEACH CA 90815
JEWISH FREE LOAN ASSOCIATION
6505 WILSHIRE BLVD., SUITE 614 .... LOS ANGELES CA 90048 (213) 655-6922
JEWISH FAMILY SERVICE 3245 SHEFFIELD AVENUE .... OAKLAND CA 94602 (415) 532-6314
HEBREW FREE LOAN ASSOCIATION
703 MARKET STREET, SUITE 445 .... SAN FRANCISCO CA 94103 (415) 982-3177
MAX GORDON MEMORIAL LOAN FUND OF THE JEWISH COMMUNITY COUNC.
1024 EMORY STREET .... SAN JOSE CA 95126
HEBREW FREE LOAN ASSOCIATION 187 EATON STREET .... BRIDGEPORT CT 06604
HEBREW FREE LOAN ASSOCIATION 34 GILBERT AVENUE .... NEW HAVEN CT 06511 (203) 562-0584
HEBREW FREE LOAN ASSOCIATION 19 AVALON CIRCLE .... WATERBURY CT 06710
JEWISH FAMILY SERVICE 2105 WASHINGTON STREET .... WILMINGTON DE 19802 (302) 478-9411
HEBREW FREE LOAN 500 S.W. 17TH AVENUE .... MIAMI FL 33160
GREATER MIAMI HEBREW FREE LOAN ASSOCIATION, THE
1545 ALTON ROAD .... MIAMI BEACH FL 33139 (305) 532-1392
HEBREW GEMILATH CHESED SOCIETY PO BOX 6546 .... SAVANNAH GA 31408
FREE LOAN FUND 525 14TH STREET .... SIOUX CITY IA 51105 (712) 258-0618
GEMILAS CHESED - FREE LOAN FUND 3453 WEST FOSTER .... CHICAGO IL 60625
HEBREW FREE LOAN ASSOCIATION 262 WASHINGTON STREET .... BOSTON MA 02108
HEBREW FREE LOAN ASSOCIATION 2 ATWATER STREET .... WORCESTER MA 01602
HEBREW FREE LOAN ASSOCIATION 5752 PARK HEIGHTS AVENUE ...... BALTIMORE MD 21215 (301) 466-9206

Pick·a·Pack of Quality
Empire ✓

PICK-A-PACK
OF KOSHER
GOODNESS...
EMPIRE KOSHER

CHICKEN ITEMS

- ☐ CHICKEN IN BROTH
- ☐ CHICKEN LEGS
- ☐ CHICKEN BREASTS
- ☐ CHICKEN WINGS
- ☐ CHICKEN THIGHS
- ☐ 3 LEGGED CUT-UP
- ☐ WHOLE CUT-UP
- ☐ 1/2 lb. CHICKEN LIVER
- ☐ 1/2 lb. CHICKEN FAT
- ☐ GOURMETTES
- ☐ RST. DRUMSTICKS
- ☐ ROCK CORNISH CHICKEN
- ☐ FRYERS (all sizes)
- ☐ PULLETS (all sizes)
- ☐ ROASTERS (all sizes)
- ☐ QUARTERED PULLETS
- ☐ QUARTERED ROASTERS
- ☐ FOWL (Stewing Chicken)
- ☐ QUARTERED FOWL
- ☐ DUCKS (all sizes)
- ☐ FRIED CHICKEN NUGGETS
- ☐ FRIED CHICKEN PATTIES
- ☐ FRIED CHICKEN STIX
- ☐ FRIED CUTLETS
- ☐ FRIED WHOLE CUT-UP
- ☐ FRIED DRUMSTICK & THIGH
- ☐ FRIED WINGS
- ☐ FRIED BREAST
- ☐ BBQ CHICKEN
- ☐ BBQ DRUM & THIGH
- ☐ CHICKEN ROLLS (all sizes)
- ☐ SMOKED DRUM & THIGH
- ☐ CHICKEN CHOW MEIN
- ☐ CHICKEN POT PIE
- ☐ CHICKEN DINNER

- ☐ BBQ CUT-UP CHICKEN
- ☐ SANDWICH BBQ
- ☐ MINI CHICKEN BREAST
- ☐ CHICKEN FRANKS
- ☐ CHICKEN KIEV
- ☐ CHICKEN a'la JOCELYN
- ☐ CHICKEN a'la MAURICE
- ☐ CHICKEN FLORENTINE

BEEF ITEMS

- ☐ BEEF SALAMI
- ☐ BEEF POT PIE
- ☐ BEEF LIVER (sliced)
- ☐ COCKTAIL FRANKS
- ☐ CHOPPED LIVER
- ☐ BEEF KNOCKWURST
- ☐ BEEF FRANKS
- ☐ BEEF BOLOGNA

FOOD ITEMS

- ☐ TV DINNERS
- ☐ PIZZAS
- ☐ BAGEL PIZZA
- ☐ MUFFIN PIZZA
- ☐ 6 BAGELS
- ☐ EGG ROLLS
- ☐ BLINTZES
- ☐ GARLIC BREAD 2 loaf
- ☐ BREADED ZUCCHINI
- ☐ CORN ON THE COB
- ☐ POTATO LATKES
- ☐ BREADED MUSHROOMS
- ☐ CHEESE CAKE
- ☐ PIE CRUSTS
- ☐ SOUPS
- ☐ BELGIAN WAFFLES
- ☐ MUSTARDS
- ☐ NOVA LOX
- ☐ CROISSANTS
- ☐ FRENCH FRIES
- ☐ SAUCES
- ☐ SPICES

TURKEY ITEMS

- ☐ TURKEY DINNER
- ☐ WHITE TURKEY ROLL
- ☐ DARK TURKEY ROLL
- ☐ TURKEY PASTRAMI
- ☐ TURKEY SALAMI
- ☐ MINI TURKEY BREAST
- ☐ TURKEY SLICES (all kinds)
- ☐ WHITE TURKEY PAN ROAST
- ☐ CHINESE TURKEY PAN ROAST
- ☐ WHITE & DARK PAN ROAST
- ☐ COOKED TURKEY BREAST
- ☐ SMOKED TURKEY BREAST
- ☐ TURKEY NUGGETS
- ☐ SMOKED WINGS
- ☐ TURKEY BURGER
- ☐ TURKEY-TACO
- ☐ TURKEY MEATLOAF
- ☐ SMOKED 1/2 HEN BREAST
- ☐ HEN TURKEYS (6 lbs.-16 lbs.)
- ☐ TOM TURKEYS (16 lbs. and up)
- ☐ BBQ TURKEYS
- ☐ SMOKED WHOLE TURKEY
- ☐ SMOKED DRUMSTICKS
- ☐ CRYOVAC DRUMSTICKS
- ☐ CRYOVAC THIGHS
- ☐ CRYOVAC BREASTS
- ☐ TURKEY PATTIES
- ☐ TURKEY FRANKS
- ☐ CHOPPED LIVER SPREAD
- ☐ TURKEY POT PIE
- ☐ FRIED TURKEY NUGGETS
- ☐ FRIED TURKEY PATTIES

KOSHER Empire FOODS

Empire Kosher Poultry, Inc.   (800) 233-7177

Telex: 754869 EKP MFLT UD

The Most Trusted Name in
Kosher Poultry and Foods.

HEBREW FREE LOAN ASSOCIATION 341 CUMBERLAND ROAD	PORTLAND	ME	04101
HEBREW FREE LOAN ASSOCIATION 18100 MEYERS ROAD	DETROIT	MI	48235
HEBREW FREE LOAN ASSOCIATION 457 CENTER STREET	ORANGE	NJ	07079
HEBREW FREE LOAN ASSOCIATION 152 VAN HOUTEN	PATERSON	NJ	07505	(201) 742-8395
HEBREW FREE LOAN ASSOCIATION 457 CENTER	SOUTH ORANGE	NJ	07079
HEBREW FREE LOAN ASSOCIATION 1418 WEST STATE STREET	TRENTON	NJ	08618
HEBREW BENEVOLENT LOAN ASSOCIATION 787 DELAWARE AVENUE	BUFFALO	NY	14209	(716) 886-7750
GEMILUTH CHESSED OF GREATER NEW YORK, INC.			
717 W. 177TH STREET	NEW YORK	NY	10033	(212) 923-8701
HEBREW FREE LOAN SOCIETY INC. (MAIN OFFICE)			
205 EAST 42ND STREET	NEW YORK	NY	10017	(212) 687-0188
HEBREW FREE LOAN ASSOCIATION 1220 HURON ROAD, #709	CLEVELAND	OH	44115	(216) 771-7349
HEBREW FREE LOAN ASSOCIATION			
ARCADE BUILDING, 338 THE ARCADE	CLEVELAND	OH	44143	(216) 771-7349
LADIES FREE LOAN ASSOCIATION 3351 DESOTA AVENUE	CLEVELAND	OH	44118	(216) 932-4138
JEWISH FAMILY SERVICE 184 SALEM AVENUE	DAYTON	OH	45406
JEWISH FAMILY SERVICE 2247 COLLINGWOOD BOULEVARD	TOLEDO	OH	43620
FREE LOAN COMMITTEE			
JEWISH COMMUNITY COUNCIL, 200 MCBIRNEY BUILDING	TULSA	OK	74103
HEBREW RE-ESTABLISHMENT SERVICES 150 BEVERLY STREET	TORONTO	ON	
TORONTO HEB. RE-ESTABLISHMENT SERVICE-GMILATH CHASODIM ASSOC			
3199 BATHURST STREET, ROOM 205	TORONTO	ON	M6A 2B2	(416) 789-1844
HEBREW FREE LOAN ASSOCIATION 234 MCKEE PLACE	PITTSBURGH	PA	15213	(412) 681-8000

A.B. COHEN HEBREW FREE LOAN SOCIETY 601 JEFFERSON AVENUE	SCRANTON	PA	18510	(717) 961-2300
HEBREW FREE LOAN ASSOCIATION 5775 VICTORIA AVENUE	MONTREAL	QU		
HEBREW FREE LOAN ASSOCIATION 128 NORTH MAIN STREET	PROVIDENCE	RI	02906	
SOUTH PROVIDENCE HEBREW FREE LOAN 1027 BROAD STREET	PROVIDENCE	RI	02905	
HEBREW BENEVOLENT SOCIETY 105 BROAD STREET	CHARLESTON	SC	29402	
HEBREW FREE LOAN ASSOCIATION 701 NORTH CHAPARRAL	CORPUS CHRISTI	TX	78401	
HEBREW FREE LOAN ASSOCIATION 2821 CANAL	HOUSTON	TX	77003	
HEBREW FREE LOAN ASSOCIATION 107 SOUTH PECOS STREET	SAN ANTONIO	TX	78207	
HEBREW FREE LOAN ASSOCIATION P.O. BOX 12131	SAN ANTONIO	TX	78212	
FREE LOAN SOCIETY 113 LONGWOOD DRIVE	NEWPORT NEWS	VA	23606	
HEBREW LADIES CHARITY SOCIETY 1416 WEST PRINCESS ANNE ROAD	NORFOLK	VA	23507	
HEBREW LADIES FREE LOAN SOCIETY 1110 HARVARD STREET	SEATTLE	WA	89115	
SEATTLE HEBREW FREE LOAN 1501 17TH AVENUE	SEATTLE	WA	89104	

FREE SHELTER

HEBREW SHELTERING HOME 699 WEST JACKSON AVENUE	BRIDGEPORT	CT	06605	
HEBREW LADIES SHELTERING HOME-INDEPENDENT TRANSIENT SERVICE				
922 ALBANY AVENUE	HARTFORD	CT	06614	
JEWISH SHELTER HOUSE 5050 N. KIMBALL AVENUE	CHICAGO	IL	60625	(312) 539-6956
KANSAS CITY KANSAS RELIEF - INDEPENDENT TRANSIENT SERVICE				
726 MINNESOTA AVENUE	KANSAS CITY	KS	66101	
HEBREW SHELTERING HOME 53 WHEELER STREET	LYNN	MA	01908	
HEBREW SHELTERING SOCIETY 744 SILVER SPRING AVENUE	SILVER SPRING	MD	20910	(301) 585-5108
JEWISH SHELTERING HOME 1231 N. & S. ROADS	ST. LOUIS	MO	63123	
HEBREW FREE SHELTERING HOME 65 QUINCY	PASSAIC	NJ	07055	
HEBREW SHELTERING HOME-INDEPENDENT TRANSIENT SERVICE				
138 NORTH PARK AVENUE	BUFFALO	NY	14216	
HEBREW SHELTER HOME 1775 SOUTH TAYLOR ROAD	CLEVELAND	OH	44105	(216) 321-3650
JEWISH RELIEF & BENEVOLENT SOCIETY-INDEPENDENT TRANSIENT SVC				
6651 S.W. CAPITOL HIGHWAY	PORTLAND	OR	97218	
HEBREW SHELTERING LADIES AID SOCIETY - IND. TRANSIENT SVC.				
C/O 540 WESTMORELAND AVENUE	KINGSTON	PA	18704	
HEBREW FRIENDLY INN - INDEPENDENT TRANSIENT SERVICE				
2126 OAK AVENUE	NEWPORT NEWS	VA	23607	

FROCKS

BROADWAY CLOTHING CORP. 234 KEAP STREET	BROOKLYN	NY	11211	(718) 387-2004
FRANKFURTER QUALITY CLOTHING 4203 13TH AVENUE	BROOKLYN	NY	11219	(718) 435-7223
FRANKFURTER QUALITY CLOTHING 314 ROEBLING STREET	BROOKLYN	NY	11211	(718) 387-2977
LEE AVENUE CLOTHING 122 LEE AVENUE	BROOKLYN	NY	11211	(718) 522-6792
REINHOLD CLOTHIERS 4421 14TH AVENUE	BROOKLYN	NY	11219	(718) 438-9342
ROTH CLOTHING 300 PENN STREET	BROOKLYN	NY	11211	(718) 384-4927
SINGER'S CLOTHING 116 LEE AVENUE	BROOKLYN	NY	11211	(718) 384-6200
STUHL CLOTHING 59 LEE AVENUE	BROOKLYN	NY	11211	(718) 387-3213

FUND RAISING

CELEBRITY ART AUCTIONS				
10511 ANDORA AVENUE, DEPARTMENT N	CHATSWORTH	CA	91311	(818) 341-7373
ART AUCTION, J. RICHARDS GALLERY 64 EAST PALISADE AVENUE	ENGLEWOOD	NJ	07631	(201) 871-1050
AGENTS CARD & GIFT COMPANY 4543 THIRD AVENUE	BRONX	NY	10458	(212) 933-1080
FLARE 2884 NOSTRAND AVENUE	BROOKLYN	NY	11229	(718) 258-8860
DEVELOPMENT CONSULTANTS OF AMERICA, INC. 1776 BROADWAY	NEW YORK	NY	10019	(212) 265-8333
HECKER SILVERSMITHS 605 FIFTH AVENUE (49TH STREET)	NEW YORK	NY	10017	(212) 593-2424
ISRAEL AMERICAN FUND RAISING CORP. 315 FIFTH AVENUE	NEW YORK	NY	10016	(212) 532-2757

FUNERAL DIRECTORS

THE PARK MEMORIAL CHAPEL 2401 STEELES AVENUE WEST	TORONTO			(416) 663-9060
SINAI MORTUARY OF ARIZONA 4538 N. 16TH STREET	PHOENIX	AZ	85016	(602) 248-0030
CHEVRA KADISHA MORTUARY 7209 ALABAMA	CANOGA PARK	CA	91303	(818) 884-4008
GLASBAND-WILLEN LONG BEACH MORTUARY				
638 ATLANTIC AVENUE	LONG BEACH	CA	90810	(213) 436-1273
CHEVRA KADISHA MORTUARY 7832 SANTA MONICA BLVD.	LOS ANGELES	CA	90046	(213) 653-8886
GLASBAND-WILLEN MEMORIAL CHAPELS				
7700 SANTA MONICA BLVD	LOS ANGELES	CA	90046	(213) 656-6260
GROMAN EDEN MORTUARY 11500 NORTH SEPULVEDA BLVD	LOS ANGELES	CA	91340	(213) 877-0335
GROMAN MORTUARY 830 WEST WASHINGTON BLVD	LOS ANGELES	CA	90015	(213) 748-2201
MALINOW & SILVERMAN MORTUARY 850 VENICE BLVD	LOS ANGELES	CA	90015	(213) 749-1051
MT. SINAI MEMORIAL PARK & MORTUARY				
5950 FOREST LAWN DRIVE	LOS ANGELES	CA	90028	(213) 469-6000
AM ISRAEL MORTUARY 6316 EL CAJON BLVD	SAN DIEGO	CA	92115	(619) 583-8850
HOME OF PEACE SANCTUARIES 3668 IMPERIAL	SAN DIEGO	CA	92115	(619) 264-0832
SINAI MEMORIAL CHAPEL 1501 DIVISADERO STREET	SAN FRANCISCO	CA	94115	(415) 921-3636
CHEVRA KADISHA MORTUARY 1218 SANTA MONICA MALL #3	SANTA MONICA	CA	90401	(213) 393-7942
FELDMAN FUNERAL HOME 17TH AND YORK	DENVER	CO	80206	(303) 322-7764
ABRAHAM L. GREEN & SONS 927 GRAND STREET	BRIDGEPORT	CT	06604	(203) 334-8893
HEBREW FUNERAL ASSOCIATION 906 FARMINGTON WEST	HARTFORD	CT	06091	(203) 527-3890
WEINSTEIN MORTUARY 640 FARMINGTON AVENUE	HARTFORD	CT	06105	(203) 233-2675
ROBERT E. SHURE FUNERAL HOME, INC. 543 GEORGE STREET	NEW HAVEN	CT	06511	(203) 562-8244
WELLER FUNERAL HOME, INC. 425 GEORGE STREET	NEW HAVEN	CT	06511	(203) 624-6912
DONALD M. STEIN HEBREW MEMORIAL FUNERAL HOME, INC.				
232 CARROLL STREET, N.W.	WASHINGTON	DC	20012	(202) 726-4222
SCHOENBERG MEMORIAL CHAPEL, INC. 519 PHILADELPHIA PIKE	WILMINGTON	DE	19809	(302) 762-0334
BELKOFF JEWISH MEMORIAL CHAPEL		FL		(305) 865-0638
MAX SUGARMAN MEMORIAL CHAPEL		FL		(305) 861-9066
SCHWARTZ BROTHERS MEMORIAL CHAPEL, INC.		FL		(305) 949-1656
STANETSKY MEMORIAL CHAPELS (REPRESENTED BY MENORAH CHAPELS)		FL		(305) 742-6000
GARLICK FUNERAL HOMES, INC.	BROWARD COUNTY	FL		(305) 925-2209
GARLICK FUNERAL HOMES, INC.	DADE COUNTY	FL		(305) 947-2229
MENORAH CHAPELS 2305 WEST HILLSBORO BLVD	DEERFIELD BEACH	FL	33441	(800) 327-9192
PISER MENORAH CHAPELS 2305 W. HILLSBORO BLVD	DEERFIELD BEACH	FL	33441	(305) 427-4700
MENORAH CHAPELS 6800 WEST OAKLAND PARK BLVD	FT. LAUDERDALE	FL	33313	(800) 327-9192
PISER MENORAH CHAPELS 6800 W. OAKLAND PARK BLVD	FT. LAUDERDALE	FL	33313	(305) 742-6000
RUBIN-ZILBERT MEMORIAL CHAPEL 100 S. DIXIE HWY	HALLANDALE	FL	33009	(305) 456-4011
BERNHEIM-GOLDSTICKER 5801 HOLLYWOOD BOULEVARD	HOLLYWOOD	FL	33020	(305) 922-2101
JEFFER FUNERAL HOMES, INC.-FLORIDA 1921 PEMBROKE ROAD	HOLLYWOOD	FL	33020	(305) 925-2743
LEVITT-WEINSTEIN MEMORIAL CHAPELS 1921 PEMBROKE ROAD	HOLLYWOOD	FL	33020	(305) 921-7200
RIVERSIDE MEMORIAL CHAPEL, INC. 2230 HOLLYWOOD BLVD	HOLLYWOOD	FL	33020	(305) 531-1151
MENORAH CHAPELS 5915 PARK DRIVE AT U.S. 441	MARGATE	FL	33063	(800) 327-9192
BERNHEIM-GOLDSTICKER 1717 S.W. 37TH AVENUE	MIAMI	FL	33145	(305) 922-2101
BERNHEIM-GOLDSTICKER 16480 N.E. 19TH AVENUE	MIAMI	FL	33162	(305) 922-2101
GORDON FUNERAL HOME 710 S.W. 12TH AVENUE	MIAMI	FL	33130	(305) 858-5566
JEFFER FUNERAL HOMES, INC.-FLORIDA 13385 W. DIXIE HWY	MIAMI	FL	33161	(305) 947-1185
RIVERSIDE MEMORIAL CHAPEL, INC.				
DOUGLAS ROAD AT S.W. 17TH AVENUE	MIAMI	FL		(305) 531-1151
BERNHEIM-GOLDSTICKER 1920 ALTON ROAD	MIAMI BEACH	FL	33139	(305) 531-1151
BERNHEIM-GOLDSTICKER 1250 NORMANDY DRIVE	MIAMI BEACH	FL	33139	(305) 531-1151
BLASBERG FUNERAL CHAPEL 720 71ST STREET	MIAMI BEACH	FL	33141	(305) 865-2353
NEWMAN FUNERAL HOME 1333 DADE BLVD	MIAMI BEACH	FL	33139	(305) 531-7677
PARKSIDE MEMORIAL CHAPELS, INC.	MIAMI BEACH	FL		(212) 896-9000
RIVERSIDE MEMORIAL CHAPEL, INC. 1920 ALTON ROAD	MIAMI BEACH	FL	33139	(305) 531-1151
RIVERSIDE MEMORIAL CHAPEL, INC. 1250 NORMANY DRIVE	MIAMI BEACH	FL	33139	(305) 531-1151
RUBIN-ZILBERT MEMORIAL CHAPEL 1701 ALTON ROAD	MIAMI BEACH	FL	33139	(305) 538-6371
GARLICK FUNERAL HOMES 18840 WEST DIXIE HIGHWAY	NORTH MIAMI BEACH	FL	33161	(305) 947-2229
JEFFER FUNERAL HOMES 18840 WEST DIXIE HIGHWAY	NORTH MIAMI BEACH	FL	33161	(305) 947-1185
LEVITT-WEINSTEIN MEMORIAL CHAPELS				
18840 WEST DIXIE HIGHWAY	NORTH MIAMI BEACH	FL	33161	(305) 949-6315
MENORAH CHAPELS 20955 BISCAYNE BLVD	NORTH MIAMI BEACH	FL	33180	(800) 327-9192
PISER MENORAH CHAPELS				
BISCAYNE BLVD. AND 209TH STREET	NORTH MIAMI BEACH	FL	33180	(305) 945-3939
RIVERSIDE MEMORIAL CHAPEL, INC.				
16480 N.E. 19TH AVENUE	NORTH MIAMI BEACH	FL		(305) 531-1151
LEVITT-WEINSTEIN MEMORIAL CHAPELS				
7500 NORTH STATE ROAD 7	POMPANO BEACH	FL	33067	(305) 427-6500
MENORAH CHAPELS 5915 PARK DRIVE AT U.S. 441	POMPANO BEACH	FL	33063	(800) 327-9192
ARNOLD & GRUNDWAG, INC. 4100 16TH STREET NORTH	ST. PETERSBURG	FL	33703	(813) 521-2444
DAVID C. GROSS FUNERAL HOME, INC. 6366 CENTRAL AVENUE	ST. PETERSBURG	FL	33707	(813) 381-4911
RIVERSIDE MEMORIAL CHAPEL, INC. 1171 NORTHWEST 61ST AVENUE	SUNRISE	FL		(305) 531-1151
RIVERSIDE MEMORIAL CHAPEL 6701 COMMERCIAL BLVD	TAMARAC	FL	33319	(305) 523-5801
LEVITT-WEINSTEIN MEMORIAL CHAPELS				
5411 OKEECHOBEE BLVD	WEST PALM BEACH	FL	33409	(305) 689-8700
MENORAH GARDENS AND FUNERAL CHAPEL				
9321 MEMORIAL PARK ROAD	WEST PALM BEACH	FL	33410	(305) 627-2277
RIVERSIDE MEMORIAL CHAPEL 4714 OKEECHOBEE BLVD	WEST PALM BEACH	FL	33409	(305) 683-8676
FURTH & CO. 5206 NORTH BROADWAY	CHICAGO	IL	60640	(312) 784-4300
HARTMAN-MILLER, INC. 6130 NORTH CALIFORNIA AVENUE	CHICAGO	IL	60659	(312) 463-5000
KATZ-LEVE MEMORIALS 4350 NORTH HARLEM AVENUE	CHICAGO	IL	60634	(312) 761-3334
ORIGINAL WEINSTEIN MENORAH CHAPELS				
3019 WEST PETERSON ROAD	CHICAGO	IL	60659	(312) 561-1890
ORIGINAL WEINSTEIN MENORAH CHAPELS 5206 BROADWAY	CHICAGO	IL	60640	(312) 561-1890
PAUL BRENNER 6450 W. CORTLAND	CHICAGO	IL	60635	(312) 666-8811
PISER MEMORIAL CHAPELS 5206 NORTH BROADWAY	CHICAGO	IL	60649	(312) 561-4740
PISER MENORAH CHAPELS 6130 NORTH CALIFORNIA AVENUE	CHICAGO	IL	60659	(312) 338-2300
WEINSTEIN BROS., INC. 1300 WEST DEVON AVENUE	CHICAGO	IL	60660	(312) 761-2400
WEINSTEIN MENORAH CHAPELS 3019 WEST PETERSON AVENUE	CHICAGO	IL		(312) 561-1890
WEINSTEIN MENORAH CHAPELS 5206 NORTH BROADWAY	CHICAGO	IL	60649	(312) 561-1890
ORIGINAL WEINSTEIN MENORAH CHAPELS 9200 SKOKIE BLVD	SKOKIE	IL	60077	(312) 673-1891
PISER MENORAH CHAPELS 9200 SKOKIE BLVD	SKOKIE	IL	60077	(312) 679-4740
WEINSTEIN BROS., INC. 111 SKOKIE BLVD	WILMETTE	IL	60091	(312) 256-5700
AARON-RUBEN-NELSON MERIDIAN HILLS MORTUARY				
1328 WEST 86TH STREET	INDIANAPOLIS	IN	46260	(317) 846-6501
HERMAN MEYER & SON, INC. 1338 ELLISON AVENUE	LOUISVILLE	KY	40204	(502) 458-9569
THARP-SONTHEIMER-THARP, INC.				
4127 SOUTH CLAIBORNE AVENUE	NEW ORLEANS	LA	70125	(504) 821-8411
STANETSKY MEMORIAL CHAPELS	BOSTON	MA		() 232-9300
LEVINE CHAPEL, INC. 470 HARVARD STREET	BROOKLINE	MA	02146	(617) 277-8300
STANETSKY MEMORIAL CHAPELS 1668 BEACON STREET	BROOKLINE	MA	02146	(617) 232-9300
SCHLOSSBERG-GOLDMAN-SOLOMON MEMORIAL CHAPELS				
824 WASHINGTON STREET	CANTON	MA	02021	(617) 828-6990
TORF FUNERAL SERVICE, INC. 151 WASHINGTON AVENUE	CHELSEA	MA	02150	(617) 889-2900
LEVINE CHAPELS 394 WASHINGTON STREET	DORCHESTER	MA	02146	(617) 436-1550
FISHER MEMORIAL CHAPEL 422 NORTH MAIN STREET	FALL RIVER	MA	02723	(617) 678-6300
IRVING FISHER MEMORIAL CHAPEL, INC.				
LOWELL AT WARREN STREET	LAWRENCE	MA	01841	(617) 683-2411
SCHLOSSBERG-GOLDMAN-SOLOMON MEMORIAL CHAPELS				
174 FERRY STREET	MALDEN	MA	02148	(617) 324-1122
LEVINE-BRISS FUNERAL HOME, INC. 84 MAZZEO DRIVE	RANDOLPH	MA	02368	(617) 963-2900
STANETSKY-HYMANSON MEMORIAL CHAPELS 10 VINNIN STREET	SALEM	MA	01970	(617) 581-2300
HAROLD R. ASCHER & SON MEMORIAL CHAPEL, INC.				
44 SUMNER AVENUE	SPRINGFIELD	MA	01108	(413) 734-5229
PERLMAN FUNERAL HOME, INC. 1026 MAIN STREET	WORCESTER	MA	01603	(617) 756-2200
SOL LEVINSON & BROS., INC. 6010 REISTERSTOWN ROAD	BALTIMORE	MD	21215	(301) 358-1700
DANZANSKY-GOLDBERG MEMORIAL CHAPELS, INC.				
1170 ROCKVILLE PIKE	ROCKVILLE	MD	20852	(301) 340-1400
JEWISH FUNERAL DIRECTORS OF AMERICA 1170 ROCKVILLE PIKE	ROCKVILLE	MD	20852	(301) 340-1400
HEBREW MEMORIAL CHAPEL 26640 GREENFIELD ROAD	OAK PARK	MI	48237	(313) 543-1622
IRA KAUFMAN CHAPEL, INC., THE 18325 W. NINE MILE ROAD	SOUTHFIELD	MI	48075	(313) 569-0020
AARON HODROFF & SONS FUNERAL CHAPEL 126 EAST FRANKLIN	MINNEAPOLIS	MN	55404	(612) 698-8311
DUBE FUNERAL HOME 2730 HENNEPIN AVENUE SOUTH	MINNEAPOLIS	MN	55408	(612) 872-1600
AARON HODROFF & SONS FUNERAL CHAPEL				
671 SOUTH SNELLING AVENUE	ST. PAUL	MN	55116	(612) 698-8311
LOUIS MEMORIAL CHAPEL 6830 TROOST AVENUE	KANSAS CITY	MO	64131	(816) 361-5211
BERGER MEMORIAL CHAPEL 4715 MCPHERSON AVENUE	ST. LOUIS	MO	63108	(314) 361-0622
HERMAN RINDSKOPF, INC. 5216 DELMAR BLVD	ST. LOUIS	MO	63108	(314) 367-0438
MAYER FUNERAL HOME 4356 LINDELL STREET	ST. LOUIS	MO	63108	(314) 371-9067
JEWISH FUNERAL CHAPEL 1912 CUMING STREET	OMAHA	NE	68104	(402) 346-1184
ROTH MEMORIAL CHAPEL 116 PACIFIC AVENUE	ATLANTIC CITY	NJ	08401	(609) 344-9004
PLATT MEMORIAL CHAPELS, INC.				
2001 HADDONFIELD-BERLIN ROAD	CHERRY HILL	NJ	08003	(609) 428-9442
KREITZMAN'S MEMORIAL HOME 1055 EAST JERSEY STREET	ELIZABETH	NJ	07201	(201) 351-4414
WIEN & WIEN 129 ENGLE STREET	ENGLEWOOD	NJ	07631	(201) 569-2404
LOUIS SUBURBAN CHAPELS 13-01 BROADWAY	FAIR LAWN	NJ	07410	(201) 278-4126
GUTTERMAN-MUSICANT 402 PARK STREET	HACKENSACK	NJ	07601	(201) 489-3800
BERNHEIM-GOLDSTICKER MEMORIAL HOME 1200 CLINTON AVENUE	IRVINGTON	NJ	07111	(201) 375-2400
EPSTEIN & SONS, INC. 34 LORETTO STREET	IRVINGTON	NJ	07111	(201) 923-1818
GUTTERMAN-MUSICANT 2030 KENNEDY BOULVARD	JERSEY CITY	NJ	07304	(201) 433-6500
WIEN & WIEN 2030 KENNEDY BLVD	JERSEY CITY	NJ	07305	(201) 333-8360
BELKOFF JEWISH MEMORIAL CHAPEL 313 SECOND STREET	LAKEWOOD	NJ	08701	(201) 364-0900
BLOOMFIELD-COOPER FUNERAL CHAPEL				
2130 STATE HIGHWAY 35	OCEAN TOWNSHIP	NJ	07712	(201) 493-4343
ROBERT SCHOEM'S MENORAH CHAPEL W-150, ROUTE 4	PARAMUS	NJ	07652	(201) 843-9090
JEWISH MEMORIAL CHAPEL 66 HOWE AVENUE	PASSAIC	NJ	07056	(201) 779-3048
DAVID A. BERSCHLER FUNERAL CHAPELS				
5341 STATE HIGHWAY NO. 38	PENNSAUKEN	NJ	08110	(609) 665-5401
ORLAND'S EWING MEMORIAL CHAPEL, INC. 1534 PENNINGTON ROAD	TRENTON	NJ	08618	(609) 883-1400
RIVERSIDE MEMORIAL CHAPELS, INC. 1009 WHITEHEAD ROAD EXT	TRENTON	NJ	08638	(609) 771-9109
LEVINE MEMORIAL CHAPEL, INC. 649 WASHINGTON AVENUE	ALBANY	NY	12206	(518) 438-1002
SWARTZ MEMORIAL CHAPEL, INC. 864 MADISON AVENUE	ALBANY	NY	12208	(518) 482-5355
GARLICK FUNERAL HOMES, INC. 1439 UNIONPORT ROAD	BRONX	NY	10462	(212) 892-9400
GUTTERMAN'S, INC. 1345 JEROME AVENUE	BRONX	NY	10452	(212) 681-2033
HIRSEN & SONS 1225 JEROME AVENUE	BRONX	NY	10452	(212) 473-2050
PARKSIDE MEMORIAL CHAPELS 1345 JEROME AVENUE	BRONX	NY	10452	(212) 588-7970
RIVERSIDE MEMORIAL CHAPEL, INC. 1963 GRAND CONCOURSE	BRONX	NY		(212) 362-6600
BOULEVARD-PARK WEST CHAPELS, INC. 1901 FLATBUSH AVENUE	BROOKLYN	NY	11210	(718) 633-0400
GARLICK FUNERAL HOMES, INC. 1700 CONEY ISLAND AVENUE	BROOKLYN	NY	11230	(718) 377-4848
GUTTERMAN'S, INC. 2576 FLATBUSH AVENUE	BROOKLYN	NY	11234	(718) 284-1500
I.J. MORRIS, INC. 1895 FLATBUSH AVENUE AT KINGS HIGHWAY	BROOKLYN	NY		(718) 377-8610
JACK YABLOKOFF KINGSWAY MEMORIAL CHAPEL, INC.				
1978 CONEY ISLAND AVENUE	BROOKLYN	NY	11223	(718) 654-9800
JEFFER COMMUNITY CHAPELS 4620 FT. HAMILTON PKWY	BROOKLYN	NY	11219	(718) 853-4000
JEFFER FUNERAL HOMES 1283 CONEY ISLAND AVENUE	BROOKLYN	NY	11230	(718) 716-8100
JEFFER NORMAN L. COMMUNITY CHAPELS, INC.				
4620 FORT HAMILTON PARKWAY	BROOKLYN	NY	11219	(718) 853-4000
KIRSCHENBAUM BROS., INC., WESTMINSTER CHAPELS				
1153 CONEY ISLAND AVENUE	BROOKLYN	NY	11230	(718) 859-2020

edelweiss co.
GLASS STUDIO
1217 - 49th Street
Brooklyn, N.Y. 11219
Tel: (718) 851-9687 - 435-6920
Judaica and Modern Art, drawn on Glass

MAALIN BAKODESH SOCIETY 4511 FT. HAMILTON PARKWAY .... BROOKLYN **NY** 11219 (718) 435-6100
MIDWOOD MEMORIAL CHAPEL 1625 CONEY ISLAND AVENUE .... BROOKLYN **NY** (718) 377-2700
NIEBERG MIDWOOD CHAPEL, INC. 1625 CONEY ISLAND AVENUE .... BROOKLYN **NY** 11230 (718) 377-2700
PARKSIDE MEMORIAL CHAPELS, INC. 2576 FLATBUSH AVENUE .... BROOKLYN **NY** 11234 (718) 338-1500
PINCUS B. MANDEL 1569 47TH STREET .... BROOKLYN **NY** 11219 (718) 436-6088
RIVERSIDE MEMORIAL CHAPEL, INC.
ONE OCEAN PARKWAY AT PROSPECT PARK .... BROOKLYN **NY** 11218 (718) 854-2000
SHERMAN'S FLATBUSH MEMORIAL CHAPEL, INC.
1283 CONEY ISLAND AVENUE .... BROOKLYN **NY** 11230 (718) 377-7300
SHOMREI HADAS CHAPELS, INC. 4511 FT. HAMILTON PKWY .... BROOKLYN **NY** 11219 (718) 436-8700
WEST END FUNERAL CHAPEL 1283 CONEY ISLAND AVENUE .... BROOKLYN **NY** 11230 (718) 854-6900
YEREIM ORTHODOX CHAPEL 93 BROADWAY .... BROOKLYN **NY** 11211 (718) 384-7684
DELAWARE PARK MEMORIAL CHAPEL, INC. 2141 DELAWARE AVENUE ..... BUFFALO **NY** 14216 (716) 873-2141
I.J. MORRIS, INC. 21 EAST DEER PARK ROAD .... DIX HILLS **NY** (516) 864-6060
RIVERSIDE MEMORIAL CHAPEL, INC. 1250 CENTRAL AVENUE .... FAR ROCKAWAY **NY** 11691 (718) 327-7100
TEMPLE MEMORIAL 134-35 NORTHERN BOULEVARD .... FLUSHING **NY** 11354 (718) 359-1010
GUTTERMAN'S, INC. QUEENS BLVD. AT 66TH AVENUE .... FOREST HILLS **NY** (718) 896-5252
PARKSIDE MEMORIAL CHAPELS, INC. 98-60 QUEENS BLVD .... FOREST HILLS **NY** 11374 (718) 896-9000
SCHWARTZ BROS. MEMORIAL CHAPEL, INC. 114-03 QUEENS BLVD ... FOREST HILLS **NY** 11375 (718) 263-7600
SINAI CHAPELS (RESNICK & BUCHBINDER)
162-05 HORACE HARDING EXPRESSWAY .... FRESH MEADOWS **NY** 11365 (718) 445-0300
PARKSIDE MEMORIAL CHAPELS, INC. 14 CALVERT STREET .... HARRISON **NY** (212) 896-9000
I.J. MORRIS, INC. 46 GREENWICH STREET .... HEMPSTEAD **NY** (516) 486-2500
BOULEVARD-PARK WEST CHAPELS, INC. 1450 BROADWAY .... HEWLETT **NY** 11557 (516) 295-3100
JEFFER FUNERAL HOMES HILLSIDE AVENUE AND 188TH STREET .... HOLLIS **NY** 11363 (718) 776-8100
SUNSET CHAPELS, INC. 1285 NORTHERN BLVD .... MANHASSET **NY** 11030 (516) 482-3600
GARLICK FUNERAL HOMES, INC. 186 BROADWAY .... MONTICELLO **NY** 12701 (914) 794-7474
PARKSIDE MEMORIAL CHAPELS 195 BROADWAY .... MONTICELLO **NY** 12701 (914) 794-1141
THE WESTCHESTER RIVERSIDE MEMORIAL CHAPEL, INC.
21 WEST BROAD STREET .... MT. VERNON **NY** 10502 (914) 664-6800
ABRAHAM BLAU MEMORIAL CHAPELS, INC. 153 EAST BROADWAY .... NEW YORK **NY** 10002 (212) 226-1617
BOULEVARD-PARK WEST CHAPELS, INC. 115 WEST 79TH STREET .... NEW YORK **NY** 10024 (212) 362-3600
BROADWAY MEMORIAL CHAPEL, INC. 4120 BROADWAY .... NEW YORK **NY** 10033 (212) 927-2250
GUTTERMAN'S INC. 331 AMSTERDAM AVENUE .... NEW YORK **NY** 10023 (212) 873-3500
HARRY NEIBERG & SONS .... NEW YORK **NY** (212) 674-3600
JEWISH FUNERAL DIRECTORS OF AMERICA 122 E. 42ND STREET .... NEW YORK **NY** 10017 (212) 370-0024
MIDWOOD MEMORIAL CHAPELS 141 LUDLOW STREET .... NEW YORK **NY** 10002 (212) 674-3600
NAGEL ISADOR & SONS 152 SECOND AVENUE .... NEW YORK **NY** 10003 (212) 674-3200
PARK WEST CHAPELS 333 AMSTERDAM AT 76TH STREET .... NEW YORK **NY** 10023 (212) 362-3600
PARK WEST CHAPELS 115 WEST 79TH STREET .... NEW YORK **NY** 10024 (212) 362-3600
PARKSIDE MEMORIAL CHAPELS, INC.
400 COLUMBUS AVENUE (AT WEST 79TH STREET) .... NEW YORK **NY** 10024 (212) 896-9000
RESNICK FUNERAL HOME 156 EAST BROADWAY .... NEW YORK **NY** 10002 (212) 349-1166
RIVERSIDE MEMORIAL CHAPEL, INC. 180 WEST 76TH STREET .... NEW YORK **NY** 10023 (212) 362-6600
WEST END FUNERAL CHAPELS
91ST STREET AND AMSTERDAM AVENUE .... NEW YORK **NY** 10024 (212) 724-0600
WIEN & WIEN 152 SECOND AVENUE .... NEW YORK **NY** 10003 (212) 285-9659
GARLICK FUNERAL HOMES, INC. 38-08 DITMARS BLVD .... QUEENS **NY** (718) 274-1050
PARSKY FUNERAL HOME, INC. 1125 ST. PAUL STREET .... ROCHESTER **NY** 14621 (716) 423-0220
GUTTERMAN'S, INC. 175 NORTH LONG BEACH ROAD .... ROCKVILLE CENTRE **NY** 11570 (516) 764-9400
PARKSIDE MEMORIAL CHAPELS, INC.
175 LONG BEACH ROAD .... ROCKVILLE CENTRE **NY** 11570 (212) 896-9000
HEBREW COMMUNITY CHAPEL, INC. 15 STATE STREET .... SPRING VALLEY **NY** 10977 (914) 425-2228
MENORAH CHAPELS, INC. 2145 RICHMOND AVENUE .... STATEN ISLAND **NY** 10314 (212) 494-7700
BIRNBAUM FUNERAL SERVICE, INC. 1909 E. FAYETTE STREET .... SYRACUSE **NY** 13210 (315) 472-5291
SURRIDGE & JACOBSON MEMORIAL HOME, INC. 2212 GENESEE STREET ..... UTICA **NY** 13502 (315) 797-9121
GUTTERMAN'S, INC. 8000 JERICHO TURNPIKE .... WOODBURY **NY** 11797 (516) 921-5757
PARKSIDE MEMORIAL CHAPELS, INC. 8000 JERICHO TPKE .... WOODBURY **NY** 11797 (212) 896-9000
GARLICK FUNERAL HOMES, INC. 1091 YONKERS AVENUE .... YONKERS **NY** 10704 (914) 237-3300
GORDON MEMORIAL HOME, INC. 1260 COLLIER ROAD .... AKRON **OH** 44320 (216) 836-7989
WEIL FUNERAL HOME 3901 READING ROAD .... CINCINNATI **OH** 45229 (513) 281-0178
CLEVELAND TEMPLE MEMORIAL HOME 1985 SOUTH TAYLOR ROAD .... CLEVELAND **OH** 44118 (216) 421-8484
JEWISH SACRED SOCIETY 3492 SEVERN ROAD .... CLEVELAND **OH** 44118 (216) 371-5717
PLYMOUTH MEMORIAL COMPANY 1936 SOUTH TAYLOR ROAD .... CLEVELAND **OH** 44118 (216) 321-1800
SIDNEY DEUTSCH CHAPEL 27570 CHAGRIN .... CLEVELAND **OH** 44118 (216) 831-1300
BARNETT BOOKATZ CLEVELAND TEMPLE MEMORIAL
1985 SOUTH TAYLOR ROAD .... CLEVELAND HEIGHTS **OH** 44118 (216) 421-8484
BERKOWITZ-KUMIN, INC. 1985 SOUTH TAYLOR ROAD .... CLEVELAND HEIGHTS **OH** 44118 (216) 932-7900
EPSTEIN MEMORIAL CHAPELS 3230 EAST MAIN STREET .... COLUMBUS **OH** 43213 (614) 235-3232
BRADFORD-CONNELLY & GLICKLER FUNERAL HOME
1849 SALEM AVENUE .... DAYTON **OH** 45406 (513) 278-4287

ZIMMERMAN-WICK MEMORIAL CHAPEL, INC. 2221 JEFFERSON AVENUE .... TOLEDO **OH** 43624 (419) 241-7168
BENJAMIN'S PARK MEMORIAL CHAPEL 2401 STEELES AVENUE WEST ..... TORONTO **ON** M3J 2P1 (416) 663-9060
IRWIN M. JUDD FUNERAL HOME 1314 HAMILTON STREET .... ALLENTOWN **PA** 18102 (215) 434-5555
BERSCHLER FUNERAL CHAPELS 4300 NORTH BROAD STREET .... PHILADELPHIA **PA** 19140 (215) 329-2900
GOLDSTEIN'S FUNERAL DIRECTORS, INC.
6410 NORTH BROAD STREET .... PHILADELPHIA **PA** 19126 (215) 927-5800
J. LEVINE & SONS MEMORIAL CHAPEL
7112 NORTH BROAD STREET .... PHILADELPHIA **PA** 19126 (215) 927-2700
RAPHAEL SACKS MEMORIAL CHAPEL, INC
4720 NORTH BROAD STREET .... PHILADELPHIA **PA** 19141 (215) 455-0100
REISMAN-GOLD FUNERAL CHAPEL, INC.
2315-17 NORTH BROAD STREET .... PHILADELPHIA **PA** 19132 (215) 223-5100
ROSENBERG'S CHAPEL 4720 NORTH BROAD STREET .... PHILADELPHIA **PA** 19141 (215) 455-0100
STILLMAN'S MEMORIAL CHAPEL 4324 NORTH BROAD STREET .... PHILADELPHIA **PA** 19140 (215) 324-8800
BLANK BROTHERS 3222 FORBES AVENUE .... PITTSBURGH **PA** 15213 (412) 682-4000
BURTON L. HIRSCH FUNERAL HOME, INC. 2704 MURRAY AVENUE ..... PITTSBURGH **PA** 15217 (412) 521-2600
RALPH SCHUGAR, INC. 5509 CENTRE AVENUE .... PITTSBURGH **PA** 15232 (412) 621-8282
ZIMAN FUNERAL HOME 612 GIBSON STREET .... SCRANTON **PA** 18510 (717) 344-1716
ROSENBERG FUNERAL CHAPEL 348 SOUTH RIVER STREET .... WILKES BARRE **PA** 18702 (717) 822-1210
CHESED SHEL EMES FUNERAL HOME 935 BEAUMONG .... MONTREAL **QU** (514) 273-3211
PAPERMAN & SONS, INC. 5605 COTE DES NEIGES ROAD .... MONTREAL **QU** H3T 1Y8 (514) 733-7101
MAX SUGARMAN FUNERAL HOME, INC. 458 HOPE STREET .... PROVIDENCE **RI** 02906 (401) 331-8094
SINAI MEMORIAL CHAPEL 825 HOPE STREET .... PROVIDENCE **RI** 02906 (401) 331-3337
FISHER MEMORIAL CHAPELS 972 WEST SHORE ROAD .... WARWICK **RI** 02888 (401) 738-5300
LEVY FUNERAL DIRECTORS, INC. 1402 CLEBURNE AT AUSTIN STREET ... HOUSTON **TX** 77004 (713) 529-6179
H.D. OLIVER FUNERAL APARTMENTS *COLONIAL AND SHIRLEY AVENUE* .. NORFOLK **VA** 23523 (804) 622-7353
HEBREW CEMETERY 4TH AND HOSPITAL .... RICHMOND **VA** 23221 (804) 648-2289
JEWISH FUNERAL CHAPEL 162 12TH STREET .... SEATTLE **WA** 98101 (206) 323-7321
GOODMAN-BENSMAN FUNERAL HOME
5831 WEST BURLEIGH STREET .... MILWAUKEE **WI** 53210 (414) 964-3111
GOODMAN-BENSMAN WHITEFISH BAY FUNERAL HOME
4750 NORTH SANTA MONICA BLVD .... MILWAUKEE **WI** 53211 (414) 964-3111

FUNERAL SUPPLIES - SHROUDS

A & G MFRS., INC. 183 LORRAINE STREET .... BROOKLYN **NY** 11231 (718) 875-6297
KLEIN BROS. FUNERAL SUPPLIES 4104 14TH AVENUE .... BROOKLYN **NY** 11219 (718) 633-4490
GEMILAS CHESED ZICHRON YESHIVA ZVI P.O. BOX 95 .... MONROE **NY** 10950 (914) 783-1680
MIRIAM FUNERAL SUPPLIES, INC. 48 CANAL STREET .... NEW YORK **NY** 10002 (212) 925-9272
ROSE SOLOMON, INC. 6 EAST 2ND STREET .... NEW YORK **NY** 10003 (212) 473-0404

GAMES & TOYS - IMPORTERS (ISRAEL)

EXECUTIVE SPORTS PROMOTERS 2029 CENTURY PARK EAST,
2029 CENTURY PLAZA, SUITE 600 .... LOS ANGELES **CA** 90067 (213) 924-5788
SHARON PRODUCTS P.O. BOX 55-7579 .... MIAMI **FL** 33155 (305) 266-4595
HAMAKOR JUDAICA, INC. 6112 NORTH LINCOLN AVENUE .... CHICAGO **IL** 60659 (312) 463-6186
SCHWARTZ-ROSENBLUM INC. 2906 WEST DEVON AVENUE .... CHICAGO **IL** 60659 (312) 338-3919
TIC & TUC 1 O'NEIL PLACE, P.O. BOX 51 .... BRIGHTON **MA** (617) 782-4423
EXPO-EL, INC. 3000 TOWN CENTER .... SOUTHFIELD **MI** 48075 (313) 358-1560
CHILDCRAFT EDUCATION CORP. 20 KILMER ROAD .... EDISON **NJ** 08817 (201) 572-6118
DRYBRANCH INC. P.O. BOX 83 .... ALBERTSON **NY** 11507 (516) 681-7000
PUPPET LOVERS COMPANY 406 SEVENTH STREET .... BROOKLYN **NY** 11215 (718) 965-2765
NATHAN NEUMANN-ISRAEL NOVELTIES 75-71 UTOPIA PARKWAY .... FLUSHING **NY** 11366 (718) 969-7740
GLENOIT MILLS INC. 111 WEST 40TH STREET .... NEW YORK **NY** 10018 (212) 391-3915
ISRAEL CREATIONS INC. 212 FIFTH AVE .... NEW YORK **NY** 10010 (212) 686-7005
MARVEL EDUCATION CORP. 212 FIFTH AVENUE, SUITE 1303 .... NEW YORK **NY** 10010 (212) 662-7005
HOKUS POKUS AMERICA, INC. P.O.BOX 376 .... SOUTHAMPTON **PA** 18966 (215) 947-6175

GAMES & TOYS—PRODUCERS

THE DREIDEL FACTORY 2445 PRINCE STREET .... BERKELEY **CA** 94705
JUDAICA UNLIMITED P.O.BOX 6394 .... ORANGE **CA** 92667 (714) 630-9064
ALTERNATIVES IN RELIGIOUS EDUCATION, INC. 3945 S. ONEIDA .... DENVER **CO** 80237 (303) 363-7779
LUCKEY EDUCATIONAL PUBLICATIONS 89 ABBOTSFORD ROAD .... BROOKLINE **MA** 02146
PEOPLE PENCILS & GOODIES NOVELTIES
12825 EPPING TERRACE .... SILVER SPRING **MD** 20906 (301) 949-3629
KTAV PUBLISHING HOUSE INC. 900 JEFFERSON ST .... HOBOKEN **NJ** 07030 (201) 963-9524

SELCHOW & RIGHTER COMPANY, (SCRABBLE IN HEBREW)	BAY SHORE NY 11706	(516) 666-7390
AMCOR GROUP, LTD., THE 350 FIFTH AVENUE, SUITE 1907	NEW YORK NY 10118	(212) 736-7711
BEHRMAN HOUSE 1261 BROADWAY	NEW YORK NY 10001	(212) 689-2020
BOARD OF JEWISH EDUCATION 426 WEST 58TH STREET	NEW YORK NY 10019	(212) 245-8200
TORAH TOYS, J. LEVINE COMPANY 58 ELDRIDGE STREET	NEW YORK NY 10002	(212) 966-4460
ARBIT BOOKS 8050 NORTH PORT WASHINGTON ROAD	MILWAUKEE WI 53217	(414) 352-4404

GENEALOGY

JEWISH GENEALOGICAL SOCIETY OF LOS ANGELES		
P.O. BOX 25245	LOS ANGELES CA 90025	
WORLD JEWISH GENEALOGY ORGANIZATION: THE YOCHSIN INSTITUTE		
1533 60TH STREET	BROOKLYN NY 11219	
JEWISH GENEALOGY RESEARCH SERVICE P.O. BOX 126	FLUSHING NY 11367	(718) 261-0525
GENEALOGY SERVICE 190 WEST NECK ROAD	HUNTINGTON NY 11743	(516) 673-5430
CHARLES TUCKER 111A NETHER STREET	FINCHLEY, LONDON UK N.12	

GENETIC DISEASES

TAY SACHS DISEASE PREVENTION PROGRAM, UNIV. OF CAL. MED CTR.,		
HEALTH SCIENCE WEST, HSW 1475	SAN FRANCISCO CA 94143	(415) 666-4157
TAY-SACHS DISEASE SCREENING-HARBOR GENERAL HOSPITAL, E 4		
1124 WEST CARSON STREET, PROFESSIONAL STAFF ASSOCIATES	TORRANCE CA 90502	(213) 775-7333
NATIONAL TAY-SACHS & ALLIED DISEASES ASSOCIATION		
92 WASHINGTON AVENUE	CEDARHURST NY 11516	(516) 569-4300
DYSAUTONOMIA FOUNDATION 370 LEXINGTON AVENUE	NEW YORK NY 10028	(212) 889-0370
NATIONAL FOUNDATION FOR JEWISH GENETIC DISEASES		
250 PARK AVENUE	NEW YORK NY 10017	(212) 682-5550

GIFT SERVICES & MAIL ORDER

THE JEWISH DEVELOPMENT COMPANY 18331-C IRVINE BOULEVARD	TUSTIN CA 92680	(714) 730-1419
POTPOURRI OF GIFTS INC. 12356 S.W. 117 CT.	MIAMI FL 33186	(305) 252-2094
TO ISRAEL WITH LOVE 61-08 218TH STREET	BAYSIDE NY 11364	(718) 261-4850
CHADISH MEDIA 453 EAST 9 STREET	BROOKLYN NY 11218	(718) 856-3882

KOSHER CATALOGUE, INC. 2107 BORDEN AVENUE	LONG ISLAND CITY NY 11101	(718) 784-6150
KOSHER CATALOGUE, INC. 2107 BORDEN AVENUE	LONG ISLAND CITY NY 11101	(800) 5KOSHER
BEN ARI ARTS LTD. 11 AVENUE A	NEW YORK NY 10009	(212) 677-4730
BEN-EZER (CITRUS) 440 PARK AVENUE	NEW YORK NY 10016	(212) 532-7097
HECKER SILVERSMITHS 605 FIFTH AVENUE (49TH STREET)	NEW YORK NY 10017	(212) 593-2424
JEWISH NATIONAL FUND (TREES) 42 EAST 69TH STREET	NEW YORK NY 10021	(212) 879-9300
SHOP-AT-HOME JUDAICA/ZIONTALIS 48 ELDRIDGE STREET	NEW YORK NY 10002	(212) 925-8558
MEAT SERVICE C/O MRS. IRVING FREISTAT (TO ISRAEL)		
1 NORTH DAWES AVENUE	KINGSTON PA 18704	(717) 288-4002
TEMPO DESIGNS (JUDAICA) 42 LADD STREET	EAST GREENWICH RI 02818	(401) 884-2443
JERUSALEM PRODUCTS CORPORATION (TORAH SCROLLS)		
BOX 76, DEPARTMENT K	WAITSFIELD VT 05673	(802) 496-3751

GLASSWORK

EDELWEISS CO. - GLASS STUDIO 1217 49 STREET	BROOKLYN NY 11219	(718) 851-9687
EAGLE MIRROR, GLASS & BLIND, INC.-STAINED GLASS, ETC.		
75 SUNSET AVENUE	LYNBROOK NY 11563	(718) 327-6764

GREETING CARDS

MARCEL SCHURMAN COMPANY, INC. 954 60TH STREET	OAKLAND CA 94608	(415) 428-0200
HANUCRAFT 8271 N.W. 56TH STREET	MIAMI FL 33166	(305) 592-1552
CHICAGO CHAPTER MDA OFFICES 6952 N. CALIFORNIA AVENUE	CHICAGO IL 60645	(312) 465-0664
ROSE ANN CHASMAN 6147 NORTH RICHMOND	CHICAGO IL 60659	(312) 764-4169
ARTFORMS CARD CORPORATION 1207 GLENCOE AVENUE	HIGHLAND PARK IL 60035	(312) 433-0532
PUCKER/SAFRAI GALLERY 171 NEWBURY STREET	BOSTON MA 02116	(617) 267-9473
TIC & TUC 1 O'NEIL PLACE, P.O. BOX 51	BRIGHTON MA	(617) 782-4423
AMERICAN JEWISH HISTORICAL SOCIETY 2 THORNTON ROAD	WALTHAM MA 02154	(617) 891-8110
RUTTENBERG & EVERETT YIDDISH FILM LIBRARY-LOWN BUILDING		
415 SOUTH STREET	WALTHAM MA 02154	(617) 647-2000
BINAH BINDELL, 'SILENT STORIES ART CREATIONS'		
19 OAKWOOD STREET	ALBANY NY 12208	(518) 438-1889
AGENTS CARD & GIFT 4543 THIRD AVENUE	BRONX NY 10458	(212) 933-1080
SHULSINGER BROTHERS 50 WASHINGTON STREET	BROOKLYN NY 11205	(718) 852-0042
NATHAN NEUMANN-ISRAEL NOVELTIES 75-71 UTOPIA PARKWAY	FLUSHING NY 11366	(718) 969-7740

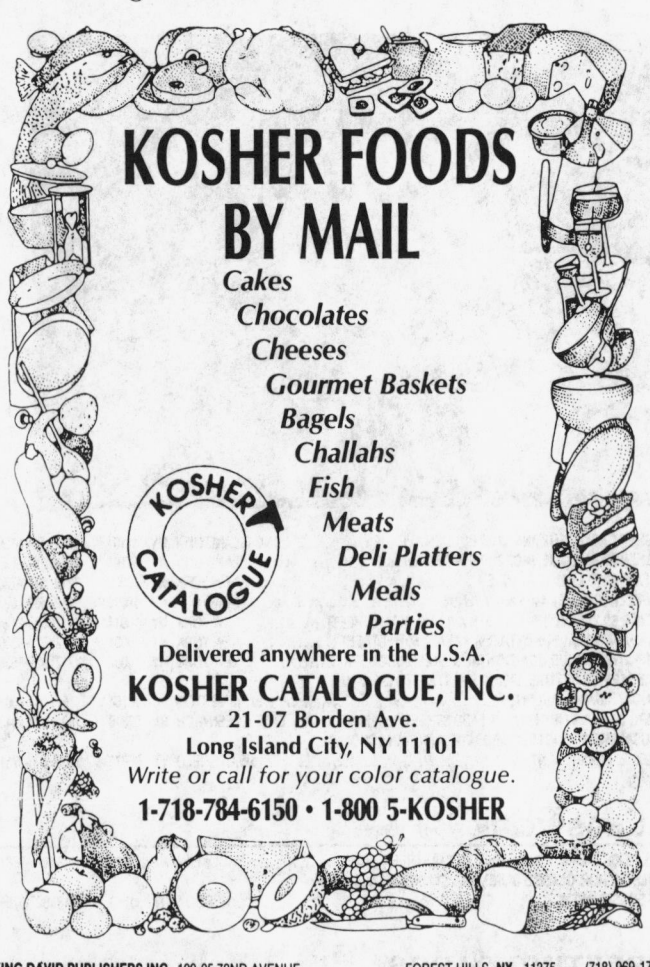

KOSHER FOODS BY MAIL

Cakes
Chocolates
Cheeses
Gourmet Baskets
Bagels
Challahs
Fish
Meats
Deli Platters
Meals
Parties

KOSHER CATALOGUE

Delivered anywhere in the U.S.A.

KOSHER CATALOGUE, INC.

21-07 Borden Ave.
Long Island City, NY 11101

Write or call for your color catalogue.

1-718-784-6150 • 1-800 5-KOSHER

KING DAVID PUBLISHERS INC. 109-05 72ND AVENUE	FOREST HILLS	NY	11375	(718) 969-1772
KOSHER CARDS 125 EAST 93RD STREET	NEW YORK	NY	10128	(212) 860-4422
WORKMEN'S CIRCLE EDUCATION DEPARTMENT				
45 EAST 33RD STREET	NEW YORK	NY	10016	(212) 889-6600
YIVO INSTITUTE FOR JEWISH RESEARCH 1048 FIFTH AVENUE	NEW YORK	NY	10028	(212) 535-6700
REJOICERS 2795 LOSANTIRIDGE AVE.	CINCINNATI	OH	45213	(513) 631-5478

HASIDIC CENTERS

CONGREGATION OHEL DAVID, RABBI ELIEZER ADER				
7067 BEVERLY BOULEVARD	LOS ANGELES	CA	90007	
GERER BET MEDRASH 7575 MELROSE AVENUE	LOS ANGELES	CA	90024	
RABBI LEVI HOROWITZ; RABBI MEIER HOROWITZ				
NEW ENGLAND CHASSIDIC CENTER, 1710 BEACON STREET	BROOKLINE	MA	02146	
TALNER BETH DAVID 64 COREY ROAD	BROOKLINE	MA	02146	
BELZER BET MIDRASH 662 EASTERN PARKWAY	BROOKLYN	NY	11213	
BELZER BET MIDRASH 4814 16TH AVENUE	BROOKLYN	NY	11219	
GERER SHTIBEL 1327 49TH STREET	BROOKLYN	NY	11219	
KAPISHNITZER BET MEDRASH 1415 55TH STREET	BROOKLYN	NY	11219	
MUNKATCHER BET MEDRASH 1377 42ND STREET	BROOKLYN	NY	11219	
PUPOVER CHASSIDIM 656 BEDFORD AVENUE	BROOKLYN	NY	11211	
RABBI L.Y. GRUNWALD 559 BEDFORD AVENUE	BROOKLYN	NY	11211	
RABBI LEO ROSENFELD; RABBI GEDALIA FLEER 864 44TH STREET	BROOKLYN	NY	11219	
RABBI SHEINGARTEN'S SHTIBEL 1520 49TH STREET	BROOKLYN	NY	11219	
SIGETER CHASSIDIM 152 HEWES STREET	BROOKLYN	NY	11211	
SKULENER REBBE - RABBI PORTUGAL 420 CROWN STREET	BROOKLYN	NY	11213	
SKVERER CHASSIDIM 571 BEDFORD AVENUE	BROOKLYN	NY	11211	
STOLINER BET MEDRASH 1818 54TH STREET	BROOKLYN	NY	11219	
THE BOBOVER REBBE-RABBI HALBERSTAM-YESHIVA BNAI ZION				
4909 15TH STREET	BROOKLYN	NY	11219	
SKVERER TOWN	NEW SQUARE	NY	10977	

HATS

MODERN HATTERS 313 THIRD STREET	JERSEY CITY	NJ		(201) 659-9300
BENCRAFT HATTERS 236 BROADWAY	BROOKLYN	NY	11211	(718) 384-8956
HAT RACK, THE 5416 16TH AVENUE	BROOKLYN	NY	11204	(718) 871-2278
KOVA QUALITY HATTERS 4311 13TH AVENUE	BROOKLYN	NY	11219	(718) 871-2944
M. HIRSHFELD 225 DIVISION AVENUE	BROOKLYN	NY	11211	(718) 387-3265
SELCO HATTERS 228 BROADWAY	BROOKLYN	NY	11211	(718) 388-6848
THE HAT RACK 5416 16TH AVENUE	BROOKLYN	NY	11204	(718) 871-2278
FELTY HATS 97 ORCHARD STREET	NEW YORK	NY	10002	(212) 226-0322
MOE PENN HATS 395 GRAND STREET	NEW YORK	NY	10002	(212) 475-4156

HEBREW SOFTWARE

ANTHRO-DIGITAL, INC. P.O. BOX 1385	PITTSFIELD	MA	01202	(413) 448-8278

HISTORICAL SOCIETIES

WESTERN JEWISH HISTORY CTR. OF THE JUDAH I. MAGNES MEM. MUS.				
2911 RUSSELL AVENUE	BERKELEY	CA	94705	(415) 849-2710
SOUTHERN CALIFORNIA JEWISH HISTORICAL SOCIETY				
590 NORTH VERMONT AVENUE	LOS ANGELES	CA	90004	
JEWISH HISTORICAL SOCIETY OF NEW HAVEN, INC., THE				
169 DAVENPORT AVENUE	NEW HAVEN	CT	06519	(203) 787-3183
JEWISH HISTORICAL SOCIETY OF GREATER HARTFORD, THE				
24 CLIFFMORE ROAD	WEST HARTFORD	CT	06117	(203) 236-4571
JEWISH HISTORICAL SOCIETY OF GREATER WASHINGTON				
701 3RD STREET	WASHINGTON	DC		(202) 789-0900
JEWISH HISTORICAL SOCIETY OF DELAWARE				
101 GARDEN OF EDEN ROAD	WILMINGTON	DE		(302) 656-8558
SOUTH FLORIDA JEWISH HISTORICAL SOCIETY				
C/O A.S. ROSICHAN, 50 SHORE DRIVE W.	MIAMI	FL	33133	(305) 854-0450
JEWISH HISTORICAL SOCIETY OF SOUTH FLORIDA				
605 LINCOLN ROAD	MIAMI BEACH	FL	33139	(305) 538-6213
CHICAGO JEWISH HISTORICAL SOCIETY, THE				
618 S. MICHIGAN AVENUE	CHICAGO	IL	60635	(312) 663-5634
ISRAEL HISTORICAL SOCIETY 1 S. WACKER DRIVE	CHICAGO	IL	60606	(312) 782-8920
INDIANA JEWISH HISTORICAL SOCIETY				
215 E. BERRY STREET, ROOM 303	FORT WAYNE	IN	46802	(219) 422-3862
AMERICAN JEWISH HISTORICAL SOCIETY 21 BLAKE ROAD	BROOKLINE	MA	02146	
AMERICAN JEWISH HISTORICAL SOCIETY 2 THORNTON ROAD	WALTHAM	MA	02154	(617) 891-8110
GREATER BOSTON JEWISH HISTORICAL SOCIETY				
TWO THORNTON ROAD	WALTHAM	MA	02154	(617) 891-8110
JEWISH HISTORICAL SOCIETY OF ANNAPOLIS 24 ROMAR STREET	ANNAPOLIS	MD	21403	
JEWISH HISTORICAL SOCIETY OF MARYLAND				
5800 PARK HEIGHTS AVENUE	BALTIMORE	MD	21215	(301) 466-4443
JEWISH HISTORICAL SOCIETY OF MARYLAND 3809 CLARK'S LANE	BALTIMORE	MD	21215	(301) 358-9417
JEWISH HISTORICAL SOCIETY OF MICHIGAN 163 MADISON STREET	DETROIT	MI	48226	
JEWISH HISTORICAL SOCIETY OF MICHIGAN 24680 RENSSELAER	OAK PARK	MI	48237	(313) 548-9176
JEWISH HISTORICAL SOCIETY OF RARITAN VALLEY				
1050 GEORGE STREET	NEW BRUNSWICK	NJ	08901	(201) 247-0288
JEWISH HISTORICAL SOCIETY OF RARITAN VALLEY				
185 WESTWOOD AVENUE	RIVER VALE	NJ	07675	(201) 666-2370
JEWISH HISTORICAL SOCIETY OF TRENTON				
999 LOWER FERRY ROAD/PO BOX 7249	TRENTON	NJ	08628	
SOCIETY FOR THE HISTORY OF CZECHOSLOVAK JEWS, INC.				
C/O LEWIS WEINER, 87-08 SANTIAGO STREET	HOLLISWOOD	NY	11423	(718) 468-6841
SOCIETY FOR THE HISTORY OF CZECHOSLOVAK JEWS				
25 MAYHEW AVENUE	LARCHMONT	NY	10538	(914) 834-4333
AM. JEWISH HISTORY CENTER OF THE JEWISH THEOLOGICAL SEMINARY				
3080 BROADWAY	NEW YORK	NY	10027	(212) 749-8000
JEWISH HISTORICAL SOCIETY OF NEW YORK 8 WEST 70TH STREET	NEW YORK	NY	10023	(212) 873-0300
CANADIAN JEWISH CONGRESS 150 BEVERLY STREET	TORONTO	ON		(416) 977-3811
OREGON JEWISH HISTORICAL SOCIETY 6651 S.W. CAPITOL HIGHWAY	PORTLAND	OR	97219	(503) 246-9844
PHILADELPHIA JEWISH ARCHIVES CENTER 625 WALNUT STREET	PHILADELPHIA	PA	19106	
RHODE ISLAND JEWISH HISTORICAL SOCIETY				
130 SESSIONS STREET	PROVIDENCE	RI	02926	
SOUTHERN JEWISH HISTORICAL SOCIETY-C/O CONG. BETH AHABAH				
1111 WEST FRANKLIN STREET	RICHMOND	VA	23220	(401) 358-6757

HOLOCAUST RESOURCES

MARTYRS MEMORIAL AND MUSEUM OF THE HOLOCAUST				
6505 WILSHIRE BLVD	LOS ANGELES	CA	90048	(213) 852-1234
SIMON WIESENTHAL CENTER NATIONAL HEADQUARTERS				
9760 WEST PICO BOULEVARD	LOS ANGELES	CA	90035	(213) 553-9036
SIMON WIESENTHAL CENTER FOR HOLOCAUST STUDIES				
9760 W. PICO BLVD	LOS ANGELES	CA	90035	(213) 553-9035
THE 1939 CLUB CHAIR IN HOLOCAUST STUDIES UNIVERSITY OF CALIFORNIA				
AT LOS ANGELES, DEPT OF HISTORY	LOS ANGELES	CA	90024	(213) 825-4601
HOLOCAUST LIBRARY & RESEARCH CENTER 601-14TH AVENUE	SAN FRANCISCO	CA	94118	(415) 751-6040
ALTERNATIVES IN RELIGIOUS EDUCATION, INC.				
3945 SOUTH ONEIDA STREET	DENVER	CO	80237	(303) 363-7779
YAD V'KIDUSH HASHEM, HOUSE OF MARTYRS				
4200 SHERIDAN AVENUE	MIAMI BEACH	FL	33140	(305) 532-0363
ROSENBUSH PRODUCTIONS 6033 NORTH SHERIDAN ROAD, SUITE 43D	CHICAGO	IL	60660	
SIMON WIESENTHAL CENTER 5715 NORTH LINCOLN AVE.	CHICAGO	IL	60659	(312) 989-0022
SPERTUS COLLEGE OF JUDAICA 618 SOUTH MICHIGAN AVENUE	CHICAGO	IL	60605	(312) 922-9012
FACING HISTORY AND OURSELVES RESOURCE CENTER				
25 KENNARD ROAD	BROOKLINE	MA	02146	(617) 232-1595
DAVID BERGMAN 23011 PARKLAWN	OAK PARK	MI	48237	(313) 557-2440
REMEMBERANCE EDUCATION MEDIA PO BOX 37111	OAK PARK	MI	48237	(313) 557-2440
HOLOCAUST MEMORIAL CENTER 6602 WEST MAPLE ROAD	WEST BLOOMFIELD	MI	48033	(313) 661-0840
ST. LOUIS CENTER FOR HOLOCAUST STUDIES 10957 SCHUETZ ROAD	ST. LOUIS	MO	63141	(314) 432-0020
JUDAIC RESEARCH INSTITUTE 747 LIVINGSTON ROAD	ELIZABETH	NJ	07208	
SECOND GENERATION OF NORTH JERSEY P.O. BOX 141	FAIR LAWN	NJ	07410	
RESOURCE CTR./HOLOCAUST & GENOCIDE STUDIES-RAMAPO COLLEGE				
505 RAMAPO VALLEY ROAD	MAHWAH	NJ	07430	(201) 825-0550
CENTER FOR HOLOCAUST STUDIES 1609 AVENUE J	BROOKLYN	NY	11230	(718) 338-6494
INTERNATIONAL BOOKS AND RECORDS 40-11 24TH STREET	LONG ISLAND CITY	NY	11101	(718) 786-2966
BOARD OF JEWISH EDUCATION 426 WEST 58TH STREET	NEW YORK	NY	10019	(212) 245-8200
HOLOCAUST PUBLICATIONS 216 WEST 18TH STREET	NEW YORK	NY	10011	(212) 691-9220

The Simon Wiesenthal Center

National Headquarters
9760 West Pico Boulevard
Los Angeles, California 90035
(213) 553-9036

8 King Street East
Suite 204
Toronto, Ontario M5C 1B5
Canada
(416) 864-9735

5715 N. Lincoln Avenue
Suite 16
Chicago, Illinois 60659
(312) 989-0022

342 Madison Avenue
Suite 437
New York, NY 10017
(212) 370-0320

HOLOCAUST SURVIVORS MEMORIAL FOUNDATION 350 FIFTH AVENUE	NEW YORK	NY	10118	(212) 594-8765
JEWISH DOCUMENTATION CENTER, INC. 666 FIFTH AVENUE	NEW YORK	NY	10103	(212) 581-1100
JEWISH MEDIA SERVICE OF J.W.B. 15 EAST 26TH STREET	NEW YORK	NY	10010	(212) 532-4949
JEWISH PEOPLE'S UNIVERSITY OF THE AIR 30 WEST 44TH STREET	NEW YORK	NY	10036	
NEW YORK CITY HOLOCAUST MEMORIAL COMMISSION 111 WEST 40TH STREET	NEW YORK	NY	10018	(212) 221-1574
PHOENIX FILMS 470 PARK AVENUE SOUTH	NEW YORK	NY	10016	(212) 684-5910
SIMON WIESENTHAL CENTER-N.Y. OFFICE 342 MADISON AVENUE SUITE 437	NEW YORK	NY	10017	(212) 370-0320
WORLD FEDERATION OF BERGEN-BELSEN ASSOCIATES P.O. BOX 333	NEW YORK	NY	10021	(212) 752-0600
ZACHOR, HOLOCAUST STUDY/COMMEMORATION-NATL JEW. RESOURCE CTR 421 SEVENTH AVENUE	NEW YORK	NY	10001	(212) 714-9500
SIMON WIESENTHAL CENTER 8 KING STREET EAST, SUITE 204	TORONTO	ON	M5C 1B5	(416) 864-9735
JEWISH IDENTITY CENTER 1453 LEVICK STREET	PHILADELPHIA	PA	19149	
HOLOCAUST CENTER OF GREATER PITTSBURGH 234 MCKEE PLACE	PITTSBURGH	PA	15213	(412) 681-8000
CANADIAN JEWISH CONGRESS 1590 AVENUE DR. PENFIELD	MONTREAL	QU	H3G 1C5	(514) 931-7531

HOLOCAUST SURVIVOR ORGANIZATIONS

1939 CLUB 435 SOUTH PALM DRIVE, SUITE 6	BEVERLY HILLS	CA	90212	
SHELTERS FOR ISRAEL 603 NORTH CAMDEN DRIVE	BEVERLY HILLS	CA	90210	
UNITED NOWY-DWOR SOCIETY 422 SOUTH MAPLE DRIVE, #4	BEVERLY HILLS	CA	90212	
WOLYNER SOCIETY OF LOS ANGELES 329 SOUTH REXFORD DRIVE, SUITE 8	BEVERLY HILLS	CA	90212	
AMER. CONGRESS/JEWS FROM POLAND & SURV./CONCENTRATION CAMPS 6534 MOORE DRIVE	LOS ANGELES	CA	90048	(213) 938-7881
AMERICAN ROMANIAN JEWISH AID SOCIETY	LOS ANGELES	CA		(213) 653-2109
BELGIAN JEWISH SOCIETY 715 NORTH SPAULDING AVENUE	LOS ANGELES	CA	90048	
COUNCIL OF POSTWAR JEWISH ORG'S.-SURVIVORS OF THE NAZI HOLO. 6205 ORANGE STREET	LOS ANGELES	CA	90048	
JEWISH CLUB OF 1933 112 SOUTH ROBERTSON BOULEVARD, SUITE 6	LOS ANGELES	CA	90035	(213) 271-6873
LODZER ORGANIZATION OF AMERICA 1241 SOUTH HOLT AVENUE	LOS ANGELES	CA	90035	
LUBLINER ORGANIZATION 1136 SOUTH ORLANDO AVENUE	LOS ANGELES	CA	90035	
LUKVOR MEZRICHER SOCIETY 337 1/2 NORTH HAYWORTH AVENUE	LOS ANGELES	CA	90048	
NASHELSKER SOCIETY 418 NORTH DETROIT STREET	LOS ANGELES	CA	90036	
SECOND GENERATION-MARTYRS MEMORIAL & MUSEUM OF THE HOLOCAUST 6505 WILSHIRE BOULEVARD	LOS ANGELES	CA	90048	(213) 852-1234
SEPHARDIC ASSOC. MAX NORDAU, C/O AMERICAN SEPHARDIC FED. 6505 WILSHIRE BOULEVARD	LOS ANGELES	CA	90048	
THE GENERATION AFTER, JEWISH FAMILY SERVICE 11646 WEST PICO BOULEVARD	LOS ANGELES	CA	90064	(213) 478-8241
WILNO VICINITY AND FRIENDS 6310 ORANGE STREET	LOS ANGELES	CA	90048	
LOS ANGELES CHILD DEVELOPMENT CENTER 225 26TH STREET, ROOM 2	SANTA MONICA	CA	90402	(213) 394-4069
JEWISH LITHUANIAN ORGANIZATION 4631 CEDROS AVENUE	SHERMAN OAKS	CA	91403	
SECOND GENERATION OF NORTH JERSEY P.O. BOX 141	FAIR LAWN	NJ	07410	
SURVIVORS OF NAZI CAMPS & RESISTANCE FIGHTERS 2747 THROOP AVENUE	BRONX	NY	10469	(212) 231-5456
AMERICAN FEDERATION FOR POLISH JEWS 1 UNION SQUARE	NEW YORK	NY	10003	(212) 691-7415
AMERICAN FEDERATION OF JEWS FROM CENTRAL EUROPE INC. 570 SEVENTH AVENUE	NEW YORK	NY	10036	(212) 921-3860
ASSOCIATION OF YUGOSLAV JEWS IN THE U.S., INC. 247 WEST 99TH STREET	NEW YORK	NY	10025	(212) 865-2211
COMMISSION ON STATUS OF JEWISH WAR ORPHANS IN EUROPE 47 BEEKMAN STREET	NEW YORK	NY	10038	(212) 227-7800
CONFERENCE ON JEWISH MATERIAL CLAIMS AGAINST GERMANY 15 E. 26TH STREET	NEW YORK	NY	10010	(212) 679-4704
FEDERATION OF POLISH JEWS, INC. 342 MADISON AVENUE	NEW YORK	NY	10017	(212) 986-3693
HERITAGE OF POLISH JEWS FOUNDATION 12 WEST 44TH STREET	NEW YORK	NY	10036	(212) 921-8011
THANKS TO SCANDINAVIA 745 FIFTH AVENUE	NEW YORK	NY		(212) 486-8600
KOL ISRAEL FOUNDATION 14462 E. CARROLL BLVD	CLEVELAND	OH	44122	(216) 382-7597

HOSPITALS & MEDICAL CENTERS

LEO N. LEVI NATIONAL ARTHRITIS HOSPITAL 300 PROSPECT	HOT SPRINGS PARK	AR	71901	(501) 321-9496
SUN AIR FEDERATION AND HOME FOR ASTHMATIC CHILDREN 221 N. ROBERTSON BLVD	BEVERLY HILLS	CA	90212	(213) 272-4371
CEDARS-SINAI MEDICAL CENTER 8700 BEVERLY BOULEVARD	LOS ANGELES	CA	90048	(213) 855-5000
JEWISH NATIONAL HOSPITAL AT DENVER 4929 WILSHIRE BLVD	LOS ANGELES	CA	90010	(213) 938-7263
SINAI MEDICAL CENTER 8720 BEVERLY BLVD	LOS ANGELES	CA	90048	(213) 652-5000
MOUNT ZION HOSPITAL & MEDICAL CENTER 1600 DIVISADERO STREET	SAN FRANCISCO	CA		(415) 567-6600
HOPE CENTER FOR THE RETARDED 3601 E. 32ND AVENUE	DENVER	CO	80205	(303) 388-4801
JEWISH NATIONAL HOME, THE-HOME FOR ASTHMATIC CHILDREN 1989 JULIAN STREET	DENVER	CO	80204	(303) 458-1999
NAT'L JEWISH HOSPITAL & RESEARCH CTR.-NATIONAL ASTHMA CENTER 3800 E. COLFAX AVENUE	DENVER	CO	80206	(303) 388-4461
NATIONAL JEWISH HOSPITAL/NATIONAL ASTHMA CENTER 3800 E. COLFAX AVENUE	DENVER	CO	80206	(800) 222-5864
CANCER RESEARCH CENTER & HOSPITAL 6401 W. COLFAX AVENUE	LAKEWOOD	CO	80214	(303) 233-6501
MOUNT SINAI HOSPITAL 500 BLUE HILLS AVENUE	HARTFORD	CT	06112	(203) 243-1441
MICHAEL REESE HOSPITAL & MEDICAL CENTER 2929 S. ELLIS AVENUE	CHICAGO	IL	60616	(312) 791-2330
SCHWAB REHABILITATION HOSPITAL 1401 S. CALIFORNIA BLVD	CHICAGO	IL	60608	(312) 522-2010
THE ARK 2341 W. DEVON	CHICAGO	IL	60659	(312) 973-1000
TOURO INFIRMARY 1401 FOUCHER STREET	NEW ORLEANS	LA	70115	(504) 897-3311
BETH ISRAEL HOSPITAL 330 BROOKLINE AVENUE	BOSTON	MA	02215	(617) 735-4431
LEVINDALE HEBREW GERIATRIC CENTER & HOSPITAL BELVEDERE & GREENSPRING AVENUE	BALTIMORE	MD	21215	(301) 466-8700
SINAI HOSPITAL OF BALTIMORE BELVEDERE AVENUE AT GREENSPRING	BALTIMORE	MD	21215	(301) 367-7800
SINAI HOSPITAL OF DETROIT 6767 W. OUTER DRIVE	DETROIT	MI	48235	(313) 493-5500
MOUNT SINAI HOSPITAL OF MINNEAPOLIS 2215 PARK AVENUE	MINNEAPOLIS	MN	55404	(612) 339-1692
MENORAH MEDICAL CENTER 4949 ROCKHILL ROAD	KANSAS CITY	MO	64110	(816) 276-8000
JEWISH HOSPITAL AND REHABILITATION CENTER OF NEW JERSEY HUDSON CITY COMPLEX, 198 STEVENS AVENUE	JERSEY CITY	NJ	07305	(201) 451-9000
NEWARK BETH ISRAEL MEDICAL CENTER 201 LYONS AVENUE	NEWARK	NJ	07112	(201) 926-7175
ALBERT EINSTEIN COLLEGE HOSPITAL 1825 EASTCHESTER ROAD	BRONX	NY	10461	(212) 430-2000
ALBERT EINSTEIN COLLEGE OF MEDICINE OF YESHIVA UNIVERSITY 1300 MORRIS PARK AVENUE	BRONX	NY	10461	(212) 430-2000
BETH ABRAHAM HOSPITAL 612 ALLERTON AVENUE	BRONX	NY	10467	(212) 920-5881
HEBREW HOSPITAL FOR CHRONIC SICK, INC. 2200 GIVAN AVENUE	BRONX	NY	10475	(212) 379-5020
BROOKDALE HOSPITAL MEDICAL CENTER 1275 LINDEN BOULEVARD & ROCKAWAY PARKWAY	BROOKLYN	NY	11212	(718) 240-5000
KINGSBROOK JEWISH MEDICAL CENTER RUTLAND ROAD & E. 49TH STREET	BROOKLYN	NY	11203	(718) 756-9700
KINGSBROOK JEWISH MEDICAL CENTER 585 SCHENECTADY AVENUE	BROOKLYN	NY	11203	(718) 756-9700
MAIMONIDES MEDICAL CENTER 4802 TENTH AVENUE	BROOKLYN	NY	11219	(718) 270-7679
MOUNT SINAI HOSPITAL-CITY HOSPITAL AT ELMHURST AFFILLATE 79-01 BROADWAY	ELMHURST	NY	11380	(718) 830-1515
L.I. JEWISH-HILLSIDE MEDICAL CENTER 1554 NORTHERN BOULEVARD	MANHASSET	NY	11030	(212) 539-9800
LONG ISLAND JEWISH-HILLSIDE MEDICAL CENTER 270-05 76TH AVENUE	NEW HYDE PARK	NY	11040	(212) 343-6700
ALBERT EINSTEIN COLLEGE OF MEDICINE OF YESHIVA UNIVERSITY 55 FIFTH AVENUE	NEW YORK	NY	10003	(212) 790-0200
AMERICAN ASSOCIATION FOR BIKUR CHOLIM HOSPITAL 119 FIFTH AVENUE	NEW YORK	NY	10021	(212) 260-4260
AMERICAN COMM. FOR SHAARE ZEDEK HOSPITAL IN JERUSALEM, INC. 49 WEST 45TH STREET	NEW YORK	NY	10036	(212) 354-8801
BETH ISRAEL MEDICAL CENTER 10 NATHAN D. PERLMAN PLACE	NEW YORK	NY	10003	(212) 420-2000
BETH ISRAEL MEDICAL CENTER-ALCOHOLISM TREATMENT PROGRAM 50 COOPER SQUARE	NEW YORK	NY	10003	(212) 420-4300
JEWISH MEMORIAL HOSPITAL BROADWAY & 196TH STREET	NEW YORK	NY	10040	(212) 569-4700
MOUNT SINAI MEDICAL CENTER, THE FIFTH AVENUE & 100TH STREET, ONE GUSTAVE L. LEVY PLACE	NEW YORK	NY	10029	(212) 650-6500
JEWISH HOSPITAL OF CINCINNATI, THE 3212 BURNET AVENUE	CINCINNATI	OH	45229	(513) 872-3220
MOUNT SINAI MEDICAL CENTER, THE UNIVERSITY CIRCLE	CLEVELAND	OH	44106	(216) 795-6000
EAGLEVILLE HOSPITAL & REHABILITATION CENTER 100 EAGLEVILLE ROAD, P.O. BOX 45	EAGLEVILLE	PA	19408	(215) 539-6000
HERZL FAM. PRACTICE CTR.-SIR MORTIMER DAVIS JEWISH GEN. HOS. 5750 COTE DES NEIGES	MONTREAL	QU	H3T 1E2	(514) 739-6371
JEWISH HOSPITAL OF HOPE CENTRE 7745 EST RUE SHERBROOKE STREET EAST	MONTREAL	QU	H1L 1A3	(514) 352-3120
MAIMONIDES HOSPITAL & HOME FOR THE AGED 5795 CALDWELL AVENUE	MONTREAL	QU	H4W 1W3	(514) 488-2301
MIRIAM HOSPITAL, THE 164 SUMMIT AVENUE	PROVIDENCE	RI	02906	(401) 274-3700
MT. SINAI MEDICAL CENTER 950 NORTH 12TH STREET	MILWAUKEE	WI	53233	(414) 289-8200

HOTELS & MOTELS

BEVERLY ARISTOCRAT 7257 BEVERLY BOULEVARD	LOS ANGELES	CA	90036	(213) 939-1653
SHALOM KOSHER HOTEL 330 NORTH HAYWORTH	LOS ANGELES	CA	90024	(213) 655-1500
GRAND LAKE LODGE	LEBANON	CT	06249	(203) 642-6512
VOYAGER GLATT KOSHER HOTEL 2424 NORTH ATLANTIC AVENUE	DAYTONA BEACH	FL	32018	(800) 874-1824
ASTOR HOTEL 956 WASHINGTON AVENUE	MIAMI BEACH	FL	33139	(305) 534-8536
BARCELONA HOTEL COLLINS AT 43RD STREET	MIAMI BEACH	FL	33140	(305) 532-3311
BLACKSTONE HOTEL 8TH STREET AT WASHINGTON AVENUE	MIAMI BEACH	FL	33139	(305) 538-1811
CARIBBEAN HOTEL 3737 COLLINS AVENUE	MIAMI BEACH	FL	33140	(305) 531-0061
CROWN HOTEL 4041 COLLINS AVENUE	MIAMI BEACH	FL	33140	(305) 531-5771
MARSEILLES HOTEL 1741 COLLINS AVENUE	MIAMI BEACH	FL	33139	(305) 538-5711
ROYAL PALM HOTEL 1545 COLLINS AVENUE	MIAMI BEACH	FL	33139	(800) 327-3195
SASSON HOTEL ON THE OCEAN AT 20TH STREET	MIAMI BEACH	FL	33139	(212) 436-8820
SAXONY HOTEL 3201 COLLINS AVENUE	MIAMI BEACH	FL	33140	(305) 538-6811
SEA ISLE HOTEL OF MIAMI BEACH 3001 COLLINS AVENUE	MIAMI BEACH	FL	33140	(305) 538-7841
SEAGULL HOTEL OCEAN AND 21ST STREET	MIAMI BEACH	FL	33139	(305) 538-6631
SHORE CLUB 19TH STREET AND COLLINS AVENUE	MIAMI BEACH	FL	33139	(305) 538-7811
SOVEREIGN HOTEL ON THE OCEAN AT 44TH STREET	MIAMI BEACH	FL	33140	(800) 327-4733
SURREY HOTEL 4390 COLLINS AVENUE	MIAMI BEACH	FL	33140	(305) 534-2227
TARLETON HOTEL 25TH STREET AND COLLINS AVENUE	MIAMI BEACH	FL	33140	(305) 538-5721
TIDES HOTEL 1222 OCEAN DRIVE	MIAMI BEACH	FL	33139	(305) 531-6701
VERSAILLES HOTEL 34 STREET AND COLLINS AVENUE	MIAMI BEACH	FL	33140	(305) 531-4213
WALDMAN'S HOTEL 4299 COLLINS AVENUE	MIAMI BEACH	FL	33140	(305) 538-5731
LAFAYETTE INN 109 SOUTH NORTH CAROLINA AVENUE	ATLANTIC CITY	NJ	08404	(609) 345-3251
TEPLITZKY'S INTERNATIONAL MOTEL BOARDWALK-END OF CHELSEA AVENUE	ATLANTIC CITY	NJ	08401	(609) 344-7071
FOX & LIEBERMAN HOTEL 814 MADISON AVENUE	LAKEWOOD	NJ	08701	(201) 367-9199
HARBOR ISLAND SPA 701 OCEAN AVENUE	LONG BRANCH	NJ	07740	(201) 222-2600
PARK HOTEL 123 WEST 7TH STREET	PLAINFIELD	NJ	07060	(201) 754-2211
LEVINE'S WASHINGTON HOTEL 124-19 ROCKAWAY BEACH BOULEVARD	BELLE HARBOR	NY	11694	(718) 634-4244
PARK HOUSE HOTEL 1206 48TH STREET	BROOKLYN	NY	11219	(718) 871-8100
FALLSVIEW	ELLENVILLE	NY	12428	(914) 647-5100
NEVELE COUNTRY CLUB NEVELE ROAD	ELLENVILLE	NY	12428	(914) 647-6000
REGAL HOTEL BOX C	FALLSBURG	NY	12733	(914) 434-7788
HY-SA-NA LODGE	FERNDALE	NY	12734	(914) 292-7330

PEAR HOTEL (FORMERLY HOTEL SHALOM) .... FERNDALE **NY** 12734	(914) 272-4464
OPPENHEIMER'S REGIS HOTEL .... FLEISCHMANNS **NY** 12430	(914) 254-5080
ZUCKER'S GLEN WILD HOTEL .... GLEN WILD **NY** 12738	(914) 434-7470
TAMARACK LODGE .... GREENFIELD PARK **NY** 12435	(914) 647-7000
GROSSINGER'S HOTEL AND COUNTRY CLUB .... GROSSINGER **NY** 12734	(914) 292-5000
BROOKSIDE HOTEL .... KERHONKSON **NY** 12446	(914) 626-7311
CONCORD HOTEL ....KIAMESHA LAKE **NY** 12751	(914) 794-4000
HOTEL GIBBER P.O. BOX G ....KIAMESHA LAKE **NY** 12751	(914) 794-6900
BROWN'S HOTEL ROUTE 52 EAST .... LOCH SHELDRAKE **NY** 12759	(914) 434-5151
DELMAR HOTEL .... LOCH SHELDRAKE **NY** 12759	(914) 292-5234
JACKSON HOTEL 10 WEST BROADWAY ....LONG BEACH **NY** 11561	(516) 431-3700
KUTSHER'S COUNTRY CLUB .... MONTICELLO **NY** 12701	(914) 794-6000
CAMBRIDGE HOUSE 333 WEST 86TH STREET .... NEW YORK **NY** 10024	(212) 873-8800
DAN HOTELS GROUP 120 EAST 56TH STREET .... NEW YORK **NY** 10022	(212) 752-6120
ESPLANADE HOTEL 305 WEST END AVENUE .... NEW YORK **NY** 10023	(212) 874-5000
H. SHIFF ISRAEL LEADING HOTELS, INC. 420 LEXINGTON AVENUE .... NEW YORK **NY** 10170	(212) 986-5782
HAIFA DAN CARMEL HOTEL 120 EAST 56TH STREET .... NEW YORK **NY** 10022	(212) 752-6120
HERZLIA ACCADIA GRAND HOTEL 120 EAST 56TH STREET .... NEW YORK **NY** 10022	(212) 752-6120
ISRAEL HOTEL REPRESENTATIVES, INC. 120 EAST 56TH STREET .... NEW YORK **NY** 10022	(212) 752-6120
ISRAEL LEADING HOTELS, INC. 420 LEXINGTON AVENUE .... NEW YORK **NY** 10017	(212) 986-5782
JERUSALEM KING DAVID HOTEL 120 EAST 56TH STREET .... NEW YORK **NY** 10022	(212) 752-6120
MORIAH HOTELS, LTD. 10 ROCKEFELLER PLAZA....................... NEW YORK **NY** 10020	(212) 541-5009
RAMADA SHALOM HOTEL JERUSALEM 370 EAST 76TH STREET .... NEW YORK **NY** 10021	(212) 570-0606
SHORE CLUB HOTEL OF MIAMI 1775 BROADWAY .... NEW YORK **NY** 10019	(212) 757-1660
PARAMOUNT HOTEL .... PARKSVILLE **NY** 12768	(914) 252-6700
THE TANZVILLE .... PARKSVILLE **NY** 12768	(914) 292-4020
HOTEL COLUMBIA .... SHARON SPRINGS **NY** 13459	(518) 284-2220
YARKONY'S ADLER HOTEL .... SHARON SPRINGS **NY** 13459	(518) 284-2220
AVON LODGE .... SOUTH FALLSBURG **NY** 12779	(914) 434-9110
BRICKMAN HOTEL BRICKMAN ROAD .... SOUTH FALLSBURG **NY** 12779	(914) 434-5000
PINES HOTEL .... SOUTH FALLSBURG **NY** 12779	(914) 434-6000
RALEIGH HOTEL .... SOUTH FALLSBURG **NY** 12779	(914) 434-7000
HOMOWACK LODGE .... SPRING GLEN **NY** 12483	(914) 647-8800
BADERS LAKE STREET .... SPRING VALLEY **NY** 10977	(914) 356-7700
GARTNER'S INN HUNGRY HOLLOW ROAD .... SPRING VALLEY **NY** 10977	(914) 356-0875
SINGER'S HOTEL CENTRAL AVENUE .... SPRING VALLEY **NY** 10977	(914) 356-2300
WEISMAN'S HOTEL 42 CLINTON STREET .... SPRING VALLEY **NY** 10977	(914) 356-2131
WHITE HOUSE 180 NORTH PASCAK ROAD .... SPRING VALLEY **NY** 10977	(914) 356-0964
SIMCHA BY THE SEA	
111 CAPODAMO BOULEVARD, MIDLAND BEACH .... STATEN ISLAND **NY**	(718) 979-7400
STEVENSVILLE HOTEL & COUNTRY CLUB .... SWAN LAKE **NY** 12783	(914) 292-8000

ALADDIN HOTEL	WOODBOURNE NY	12788	(914) 434-7700
CHALET VIM CHESTER ROAD	WOODBOURNE NY	12788	(914) 434-5786
LAKE HOUSE HOTEL LAKE HOUSE ROAD	WOODRIDGE NY	12789	(914) 434-7800
SUNNY OAKS HOTEL	WOODRIDGE NY	12789	(914) 434-7580
VEGETARIAN HOTEL BOX 457	WOODRIDGE NY	12789	(914) 434-4455
POCMONT LODGE HOTEL	BUSHKILL PA	18324	(800) 762-6668

HOTLINES

VALLEY BETH SHALOM COUNSELING CENTER			
14739 VENTURA BOULEVARD	ENCINO CA	91436	(818) 788-6000
ALCOHOLICS ANONYMOUS	LOS ANGELES CA		(213) 387-8316
CEDARS-SINAI MEDICAL EMERGENCY	LOS ANGELES CA		(213) 855-6517
CEDARS-SINAI PSYCHIATRY EMERGENCY	LOS ANGELES CA		(213) 855-6527
ISRAEL HOTLINE	SAN FRANCISCO CA		(415) 392-6397
MEZUZAH HOTLINE 305 KINGSTON AVENUE	BROOKLYN NY	11213	(718) 774-1780
CULT CLINIC HOTLINE (JBFCS) 1651 THIRD AVENUE	NEW YORK NY	10028	(212) 860-8533
JEWISH CENTER HOT LINE 1125 COLLEGE STREET	COLUMBUS OH	43209	(614) 231-2731

IMPORT & EXPORT - AMERICAN - ISRAELI TRADE

AMERICAN-ISRAEL CHAMBER OF COMMERCE			
6399 WILSHIRE BLVD	LOS ANGELES CA	90048	(213) 658-7910
AMERICAN-ISRAEL CHAMBER OF COMMERCE/FLORIDA REGION			
3950 BISCAYNE BLVD	MIAMI FL	33137	(305) 573-0668
AMERICAN-ISRAEL CHAMBER OF COMMERCE & INDUSTRY, INC.			
180 NORTH MICHIGAN AVENUE	CHICAGO IL	60601	(312) 641-2937
NEW ENGLAND-ISRAEL CHAMBER OF COMMERCE & INDUSTRY, INC.			
P.O. BOX 40	CHESTNUT HILL MA	02167	(617) 738-5344
SEABOARD AMERICA-ISRAEL CHAMBER OF COMMERCE			
1000 HAVERHILL ROAD	BALTIMORE MD	21229	(301) 525-2110
AMERICAN-ISRAEL CHAMBER OF COMMERCE & INDUSTRY OF MINN., INC.			
130 SOUTH 10TH STREET	MINNEAPOLIS MN	55403	(612) 332-1284
HOD LAVAN TURKEY PRODUCTS, LIMITED 149-32 132ND STREET	JAMAICA NY	11430	(718) 529-4411
AMERICAN-ISRAEL CHAMBER OF COMMERCE & INDUSTRY, INC.			
500 FIFTH AVENUE	NEW YORK NY	10110	(212) 354-6510
AMERICAN-ISRAELI GAS CORP. 55 WEST 42ND STREET	NEW YORK NY	10036	(212) 687-6377
AMERICAN-ISRAELI SHIPPING COMPANY, INC.			
1 WORLD TRADE CENTER	NEW YORK NY	10048	(212) 432-0300
ATALANTA CORPORATION 17 VARICK STREET	NEW YORK NY	10013	(212) 431-9000
DISTRIBUTOR'S CENTER FOR ISRAELI BOOKS LTD. 350 FIFTH AVENUE	NEW YORK NY	10118	(212) 736-9888
GOVT. OF ISRAEL TRADE CENTER, S. BEN-TOVIM, CONSUL & COMM.			
350 FIFTH AVENUE	NEW YORK NY	10118	(212) 560-0660
ISRAEL AIRCRAFT INDUSTRIES INTERNATIONAL, INC.			
50 WEST 23 STREET	NEW YORK NY	10011	(212) 620-4400
ISRAEL PRODUCTS, INC. 212 FIFTH AVENUE	NEW YORK NY	10010	(212) 686-7005
ISRAEL WHOLESALERS IMPORT CO., INC. 21 1/2 ESSEX STREET	NEW YORK NY	10002	(212) 228-1661
ISRAELI COAT CORP. OF AMERICA 512 SEVENTH AVENUE	NEW YORK NY	10018	(212) 354-7110

ISRAELI HANDICRAFT IMPORTING CO. 168 FIFTH AVENUE	NEW YORK NY	10003	(212) 929-4928
AMERICAN-ISRAEL CHAMBER OF COMMERCE & INDUSTRY, INC.			
10800 BROOKPARK ROAD	CLEVELAND OH	44130	(216) 267-1200
AMERICAN-ISRAEL CHAMBER OF COMMERCE & INDUSTRY, INC.			
1845 WALNUT STREET	PHILADELPHIA PA	19103	(215) 299-1700
CANADA-ISRAEL CHAMBER OF COMMERCE & INDUSTRY			
FIRST CANADIAN PLACE, P.O. BOX 31, 100 KING STREET	TORONTO ON	M5X 1A9	(416) 362-7424

INFORMATION BUREAUS

NATIONAL JEWISH HOSPITALITY COMMITTEE AND INFORMATION CENTER			
TEMPLE AKIBA, 5249 S. SEPULVEDA BLVD	CULVER CITY CA	90230	(213) 398-5783
FREDA MOHR MULTISERVICE CENTER 351 FAIRFAX AVENUE	LOS ANGELES CA	90036	(213) 655-5141
NAT'L JEW. INFO. SERVICE FOR THE PROPAGATION OF JUDAISM, INC			
5174 W. 8TH STREET	LOS ANGELES CA	90036	(213) 936-6033
REFORM SYNAGOGUE INFORMATION 13107 VENTURA BLVD	NORTH HOLLYWOOD CA	91606	(818) 872-3550
JEWISH ACTIVIST FRONT-ISRAEL INFORMATION CENTER			
800 21ST STREET N.W., ROOM 417	WASHINGTON DC	20006	(202) 686-7574
RUBIN R. DOBIN, 'JEWS FOR JEWS'			
17720 NORTH BAY ROAD, SUITE 8D	N. MIAMI BEACH FL	33160	
JEWS FOR JEWS ORGANIZATION P.O. BOX 6194	SURFSIDE FL	33154	(305) 931-0001
JEWISH INFORMATION SOCIETY 1129 THORN TREE	HIGHLAND PARK IL	60035	
MID-EAST INFORMATION RESOURCE 871 MARION AVENUE	HIGHLAND PARK IL	60035	(312) 432-1735
NATIONAL KASHRUS DATA BASE 1204 AVENUE U, BOX 1179	BROOKLYN NY	11229	(718) 376-1470
AMERICAN JEWISH PUBLIC RELATIONS SOCIETY 234 FIFTH AVENUE	NEW YORK NY	10001	(212) 697-5895
BLACK-JEWISH INFORMATION CENTER 16 E. 85TH STREET	NEW YORK NY	10028	(212) 879-4577
CAMP INFORMATION AGENCY 500 FIFTH AVENUE	NEW YORK NY	10017	(212) 944-6200
CAMP INFORMATION ASSOCIATION 1 ROCKEFELLER PLAZA	NEW YORK NY	10020	(212) 757-4440
JEWISH INFORMATION & REFERRAL SERVICE-FEDERATION			
130 E. 59TH STREET	NEW YORK NY	10022	(212) 753-2288
JEWISH INFORMATION BUREAU, INC. 250 W. 57TH STREET	NEW YORK NY	10019	(212) 582-5318
JEWISH STATISTICAL BUREAU 1182 BROADWAY	NEW YORK NY	10001	(212) 685-3359
JEWISH INFORMATION SERVICE 2030 SOUTH TAYLOR ROAD	CLEVELAND OH	44118	(216) 371-3999
JEWISH INFORMATION SERVICE 2953 BATHURST STREET, SUITE 104	TORONTO ON	M6B 3B2	(416) 789-7278
JEWISH INFORMATION BUREAU 234 MCKEE PLACE	PITTSBURGH PA	15213	(412) 681-8000

INTERFAITH ORGANIZATIONS

ARK. COUNCIL ON BROTHERHOOD/NAT'L CONF. OF CHRISTIANS & JEWS			
350 TOWER BUILDING	LITTLE ROCK AR	72205	(501) 372-5129
NATIONAL CONFERENCE OF CHRISTIANS & JEWS			
6711 E. 9TH STREET	LONG BEACH CA	90815	
NATIONAL CONFERENCE OF CHRISTIANS & JEWS			
3580 WILSHIRE BLVD	LOS ANGELES CA	90010	(213) 385-0491
NATIONAL CONFERENCE OF CHRISTIANS & JEWS			
730 MARKET STREET, SUITE 809	SAN FRANCISCO CA	94103	(415) 391-2850
NATIONAL CONFERENCE OF CHRISTIANS & JEWS			
777 NORTH FIRST STREET, SUITE 620	SAN JOSE CA	95112	(408) 286-9663
SECRETARIAT FOR CATHOLIC-JEWISH RELATIONS	NATIONAL CONFERENCE OF CHRISTIANS & JEWS 111 PEARL STREET	HARTFORD CT 06103	(203) 522-4231
1312 MASSACHUSETTS AVENUE N.W.	WASHINGTON DC	20005	(202) 659-6857
NATIONAL CONFERENCE OF CHRISTIANS & JEWS			
9300 S. DADELAND BLVD, SUITE 511	MIAMI FL	33156	
NATIONAL CONFERENCE OF CHRISTIANS & JEWS 203 NORTH WABASH	CHICAGO IL	60601	(312) 236-9272
NATIONAL CONFERENCE OF CHRISTIANS & JEWS			
512 INSURANCE BUILDING	WICHITA KS	67202	(316) 264-0356
NATIONAL CONFERENCE OF CHRISTIANS & JEWS			
407 FINCASTLE BUILDING	LOUISVILLE KY	40202	
NATIONAL CONFERENCE OF CHRISTIANS & JEWS			
612 INTERNATIONAL BUILDING	NEW ORLEANS LA	70130	
NATIONAL CONFERENCE OF CHRISTIANS & JEWS			
1031 DUDLEY DRIVE	SHREVEPORT LA	71104	
NATIONAL CONFERENCE OF CHRISTIANS & JEWS			
88 TREMONT STREET, ROOM 610	BOSTON MA	02108	(617) 532-7510
NATIONAL CONFERENCE OF CHRISTIANS & JEWS 150 W. BOSTON BLVD	DETROIT MI	48202	(313) 869-6306
NATIONAL CONFERENCE OF CHRISTIANS & JEWS 721 OLIVE STREET	ST. LOUIS MO	63101	
NATIONAL CONFERENCE OF CHRISTIANS & JEWS 423 CENTER BUILDING	OMAHA NE	68105	(402) 346-3357
NATIONAL CONFERENCE OF CHRISTIANS & JEWS P.O. BOX 3165	ALBUQUERQUE NM	87110	(505) 266-4964
NATIONAL CONFERENCE OF CHRISTIANS & JEWS			
4220 S. MARYLAND PARK, 304	LAS VEGAS NV	89109	
BROTHERHOOD RESEARCH INSTITUTE, INC. 2879 W. 12TH STREET	BROOKLYN NY	11224	(718) 372-5280
NATIONAL CONFERENCE OF CHRISTIANS & JEWS 43 W. 57TH STREET	NEW YORK NY	10019	(212) 688-7530
NATIONAL CONFERENCE OF CHRISTIANS & JEWS			
175 MAIN STREET	WHITE PLAINS NY	10601	(914) 946-1604
NATIONAL CONFERENCE OF CHRISTIANS & JEWS 617 VINE STREET	CINCINNATI OH	45202	(513) 381-4660
NATIONAL CONFERENCE OF CHRISTIANS & JEWS			
621 NORTH ROBINSON	OKLAHOMA CITY OK	73102	(405) 232-3861
NATIONAL CONFERENCE OF CHRISTIANS & JEWS 309 CENTER BLDG	TULSA OK	74127	(918) 583-1361
NATIONAL CONFERENCE OF CHRISTIANS & JEWS			
141 WAYLAND AVENUE	PROVIDENCE RI	02906	(401) 351-5120
NATIONAL CONFERENCE OF CHRISTIANS & JEWS			
3373 POPLAR AVENUE-414	MEMPHIS TN	38111	(901) 327-0010
NATIONAL CONFERENCE OF CHRISTIANS & JEWS			
409 EXECUTIVE CENTER-SUITE 202	EL PASO TX	79902	(915) 532-6637
NATIONAL CONFERENCE OF CHRISTIANS & JEWS			
4848 GUITON-SUITE 212	HOUSTON TX	77027	(713) 960-9244
NATIONAL CONFERENCE OF CHRISTIANS & JEWS			
118 BROADWAY #623	SAN ANTONIO TX	78205	(713) 960-9244

NATIONAL CONFERENCE OF CHRISTIANS & JEWS 3808 HAYNSWORTH PLACE	FAIRFAX	VA	22030	(703) 591-6024
NATIONAL CONFERENCE OF CHRISTIANS & JEWS 2317 WESTWOOD AVENUE	RICHMOND	VA	23230	

INVESTMENT - ISRAEL

ISRAEL INVESTMENT AUTHORITY 6404 WILSHIRE BLVD	LOS ANGELES	CA	90048	(213) 658-8721
ISRAEL INVESTMENT AUTHORITY 174 NORTH MICHIGAN AVENUE	CHICAGO	IL	60601	(312) 332-2160
ISRAEL INVESTMENT AUTHORITY 20 PROVIDENCE STREET	BOSTON	MA	02116	(617) 426-3636
DEVELOPMENT CORPORATION FOR ISRAEL 3803 NAUTILUS AVENUE	BROOKLYN	NY	11224	(718) 677-9650
AMERICAN-ISRAELI INVESTORS LTD. 345 EAST 46TH STREET	NEW YORK	NY	10017	(212) 599-0868
AMPAL-AMERICAN ISRAEL CORPORATION 10 ROCKEFELLER PLAZA, 8TH FLOOR	NEW YORK	NY	10020	(212) 586-3232
CAPITAL FOR ISRAEL 215 PARK AVENUE SOUTH	NEW YORK	NY	10003	(212) 673-5500
DEVELOPMENT CORPORATION FOR ISRAEL 215 PARK AVENUE SOUTH	NEW YORK	NY	10003	(212) 677-9650
GOVERNMENT OF ISRAEL INVESTMENT AUTHORITY EMPIRE STATE BUILDING, 350 FIFTH AVENUE	NEW YORK	NY	10118	
ISRAEL GOVERNMENT INVESTMENT AUTHORITY 850 THIRD AVENUE	NEW YORK	NY	10022	(212) 940-9400
ISRAEL INVESTMENT FUND 120 WALL STREET	NEW YORK	NY	10005	(212) 344-6676
ISRAEL INVESTORS CORP. 10 ROCKEFELLER PLAZA	NEW YORK	NY	10020	(212) 582-8431
ISRAEL INVESTORS REPORT, ISRAEL COMMUNICATIONS 110 EAST 59TH STREET	NEW YORK	NY	10022	(212) 582-8431
LEUMI SECURITIES CORPORATION 18 EAST 48TH STREET	NEW YORK	NY	10017	(212) 759-1310
PEC ISRAEL ECONOMIC CORPORATION 511 FIFTH AVENUE	NEW YORK	NY	10017	(212) 687-2400
STATE OF ISRAEL BONDS 215 PARK AVENUE SOUTH	NEW YORK	NY	10003	(212) 677-9650
ISRAEL INVESTMENT AUTHORITY 180 BLOOR STREET, SUITE 700	TORONTO	ON	M5S 1M8	(416) 961-1242
ISRAEL INVESTMENT AUTHORITY LEWIS TOWER BLDG	PHILADELPHIA	PA	12102	(215) 546-4300
ISRAEL INVESTMENT AUTHORITY 2085 UNION STREET, SUITE 675	MONTREAL	QU	H3A 1B9	(514) 288-9276
ISRAEL INVESTMENT AUTHORITY 1 GREENWAY PLAZA EAST, SUITE 722	HOUSTON	TX	77042	(713) 840-0510

ISRAEL - CENTERED ORGANIZATIONS

COMMITTEE FOR PROGRAMS IN ISRAEL 6505 WILSHIRE BOULEVARD	LOS ANGELES	CA	90048	(213) 852-1234
HISTADRUT ISRAEL CAMPAIGN 8455 BEVERLY BLVD., #308	LOS ANGELES	CA	90048	(213) 651-4892
INTERNS FOR PEACE 3875 WILSHIRE BOULEVARD, ROOM 407	LOS ANGELES	CA	90010	(213) 381-6621
AMERICAN FRIENDS OF RELIGIOUS FREEDOM IN ISRAEL P.O. BOX 5888	WASHINGTON	DC	20014	(301) 530-1737
AMERICAN ISRAEL PUBLIC AFFAIRS COMMITTEE 444 N CAPITOL STREET N.W., SUITE 412	WASHINGTON	DC	20001	(202) 638-2256
B'NAI B'RITH ISRAEL COMMISSION 1640 RHODE ISLAND AVENUE, N.W.	WASHINGTON	DC	20036	(202) 857-6580
NATIONAL CHRISTIAN LEADERSHIP CONFERENCE FOR ISRAEL 1629 K STREET N.W., SUITE 700	WASHINGTON	DC	20006	(202) 223-4016
GOVERNMENT OF ISRAEL TRADE CENTER & ECONOMIC OFFICE 111 EAST WACKER DRIVE	CHICAGO	IL	60611	(312) 565-3300
AMERICAN EDUCATIONAL LEAGUE FOR A SECURE ISRAEL 101 GREYSTONE	KANSAS CITY	KS	66103	(913) 342-1393
MIZRACHI HAPOEL HAMIZRACHI 611 WASHINGTON STREET	BOSTON	MA	02111	(617) 426-9148
ISRAEL HISTADRUT COUNCIL 6810 PARK HEIGHTS AVENUE	BALTIMORE	MD	21215	(301) 358-1533
DISKIN ORPHAN HOME OF ISRAEL 4305 18TH AVENUE	BROOKLYN	NY	11218	
HA'VAADA L'DOVREI IVRIT 788 EASTERN PARKWAY	BROOKLYN	NY	11213	(718) 774-9847
JORDAN IS PALESTINE COMMITTEE P.O. BOX 2003	NEW HYDE PARK	NY	11040	
AMERICA ISRAEL FRIENDSHIP LEAGUE 136 EAST 39TH STREET	NEW YORK	NY	10016	(212) 679-4822
AMERICA-ISRAEL CULTURAL FOUNDATION 485 MADISON AVENUE	NEW YORK	NY	10022	(212) 751-2700
AMERICAN ASSOCIATES BEN-GURION UNIVERSITY OF NEGEV INC. 342 MADISON AVENUE	NEW YORK	NY	10017	(212) 687-7721
AMERICAN ASSOCIATION FOR BIKUR CHOLIM HOSPITAL 119 FIFTH AVENUE	NEW YORK	NY	10021	(212) 260-4260
AMERICAN COMM. FOR SHAARE ZEDEK HOSPITAL IN JERUSALEM, INC. 49 WEST 45TH STREET	NEW YORK	NY	10036	(212) 354-8801
AMERICAN COMMITTEE FOR THE ISRAEL FASHION COLLEGE INC. 855 AVENUE OF THE AMERICAS	NEW YORK	NY	10001	(212) 947-1597
AMERICAN COMMITTEE FOR THE WEIZMANN INST. OF SCIENCE, INC. 515 PARK AVENUE	NEW YORK	NY	10022	(212) 752-1300
AMERICAN FRIENDS OF ISRAEL 850 THIRD AVENUE	NEW YORK	NY	10022	(212) 582-8431
AMERICAN FRIENDS OF THE STATE OF ISRAEL 3 WEST 16TH STREET	NEW YORK	NY	10011	(212) 929-1525
AMERICAN HISTADRUT CULTURAL EXCHANGE INSTITUTE 33 E. 67TH STREET	NEW YORK	NY	10020	(212) 628-1000
AMERICAN ISRAEL CORPORATION-AMPAL 10 ROCKEFELLER PLAZA	NEW YORK	NY	10019	(212) 586-3232
AMERICAN JEWISH ALTERNATIVES TO ZIONISM, INC. 133 EAST 73RD STREET	NEW YORK	NY	10021	(212) 628-2727
AMERICAN JEWISH LEAGUE FOR ISRAEL 30 EAST 60TH STREET	NEW YORK	NY	10022	(212) 371-1583
AMERICAN MIZRACHI WOMEN 817 BROADWAY	NEW YORK	NY	10003	(212) 477-4720
AMERICAN PROFESSORS FOR PEACE IN THE MIDDLE EAST 330 SEVENTH AVENUE	NEW YORK	NY	10001	(212) 563-2580
AMERICAN RED MAGEN DAVID FOR ISRAEL 888 SEVENTH AVE.	NEW YORK	NY	10106	(212) 757-1627
AMERICAN TRADE UNION COUNCIL FOR HISTADRUT 33 E. 67TH STREET	NEW YORK	NY	10021	(212) 628-1000
AMERICAN ZIONIST FEDERATION 515 PARK AVENUE	NEW YORK	NY	10022	(212) 371-7750
AMERICAN ZIONIST YOUTH FOUNDATION 515 PARK AVENUE	NEW YORK	NY	10022	(212) 751-6070
AMERICAN-ISRAEL CHAMBER OF COMMERCE 500 FIFTH AVENUE	NEW YORK	NY	10017	(212) 354-6510
AMERICAN-ISRAEL CULTURAL FOUNDATION 485 MADISON AVENUE	NEW YORK	NY	10022	(212) 751-2700
AMERICAN-ISRAEL FRIENDSHIP HOUSE 136 EAST 39TH STREET	NEW YORK	NY	10016	(212) 371-1583
AMERICAN-ISRAELI TORAH CENTER 5 BEEKMAN STREET	NEW YORK	NY	10038	(212) 964-4851
AMERICAN-JEWISH LEAGUE FORUM: AMERICAN-ISRAEL FRIENDSHIP-HOUSE 136 EAST 39TH STREET	NEW YORK	NY	10016	(212) 371-1583
AMERICANS FOR PROGRESSIVE ISRAEL 150 FIFTH AVENUE	NEW YORK	NY	10011	(212) 255-8760
AMERICANS FOR A SAFE ISRAEL INC. 147 EAST 76TH STREET	NEW YORK	NY	10021	(212) 988-2121
AMPAL-AMERICAN ISRAEL CORP. 10 ROCKEFELLER PLAZA	NEW YORK	NY	10020	(212) 586-3232
BEIT TRUMPELDOR, BETAR 136 DUANE STREET	NEW YORK	NY	10013	
CONFERENCE OF PRESIDENTS OF MAJOR AMERICAN JEWISH ORGS. 515 PARK AVENUE	NEW YORK	NY	10022	(212) 752-1616
COUNCIL FOR A BEAUTIFUL ISRAEL 350 FIFTH AVENUE	NEW YORK	NY	10118	(212) 947-5709
FREELAND LEAGUE-JEWISH TERRITORIAL COLONIZATION 200 W. 72ND STREET	NEW YORK	NY	10023	(212) 767-7765
GARIN YARDIN-YOUNG KIBBUTZ MOVEMENT 215 PARK AVENUE SOUTH #1806	NEW YORK	NY	10003	(212) 777-9388
GOVERNMENT BUREAU FOR ISRAELI PROFESSIONALS 800 SECOND AVENUE	NEW YORK	NY	10017	(212) 986-6360
GOVERNMENT OF ISRAEL ECONOMIC OFFICE 111 WEST 40TH STREET	NEW YORK	NY	10017	(212) 560-0600
GOVERNMENT OF ISRAEL TRADE CENTER & ECONOMIC OFFICE 111 WEST 40TH STREET	NEW YORK	NY	10017	(212) 560-0660
HADASSAH-WOMEN'S ZIONIST ORGANIZATION OF AMERICA 50 WEST 58TH STREET	NEW YORK	NY	10019	(212) 355-7900
HERUT-USA 41 E. 42ND STREET	NEW YORK	NY	10017	(212) 687-4502
HERZL FOUNDATION 515 PARK AVENUE	NEW YORK	NY	10022	(212) 752-0600
HISTADRUTH IVRITH OF AMERICA 1841 BROADWAY	NEW YORK	NY	10023	(212) 581-5151
ICHUD HABONIM LABOR ZIONIST YOUTH 27 WEST 40TH STREET	NEW YORK	NY	10018	(212) 255-1796
INSTITUTE OF STUDENTS & FACULTY ON ISRAEL 55 W. 42ND STREET	NEW YORK	NY	10036	(212) 997-1812
ISRAEL DEVELOPMENT CORP. 10 ROCKEFELLER PLAZA	NEW YORK	NY	10020	(212) 586-3232
ISRAEL FOUNDATION FUND (KEREN HAYESOD), INC. 515 PARK AVENUE	NEW YORK	NY	10022	(212) 688-0800
ISRAELI COMMITTEE OF MIZRACHI-HAPOEL HAMIZRACHI 25 WEST 26TH STREET	NEW YORK	NY	10001	(212) 679-2050
JEWISH AGENCY AMERICAN SECTION, INC. 515 PARK AVENUE	NEW YORK	NY	10022	(212) 752-0600
JEWISH AMERICAN POLITICAL ACTION COMMITTEE 220 EAST 57TH STREET	NEW YORK	NY	10022	(212) 980-1519
LABOR ZIONIST ALLIANCE 275 7TH AVENUE	NEW YORK	NY	10001	(212) 989-0300
LEAGUE FOR LABOR ISRAEL 275 7TH AVENUE	NEW YORK	NY	10001	(212) 989-0300
MERCAZ (THE MOVEMENT TO REAFFIRM CONSERVATIVE ZIONISM) 155 FIFTH AVENUE	NEW YORK	NY	10010	(212) 533-7800
NATIONAL COMMITTEE FOR LABOR ISRAEL 33 E. 67TH STREET	NEW YORK	NY	10021	(212) 628-1000
NEW JEWISH AGENDA 1123 BROADWAY, ROOM 1217	NEW YORK	NY	10010	(212) 620-0828
PEC ISRAEL ECONOMIC CORPORATION 511 FIFTH AVENUE	NEW YORK	NY	10017	(212) 687-2400
PIONEER WOMEN-WOMEN'S LABOR ZIONIST ORGANIZATION 200 MADISON AVENUE	NEW YORK	NY	10016	(212) 725-8010
POALE AGUDATH ISRAEL OF AMERICA 156 FIFTH AVENUE	NEW YORK	NY	10010	(212) 924-9475
RELIGIOUS ZIONISTS OF AMERICA 25 WEST 26TH STREET	NEW YORK	NY	10010	(212) 689-1414
SERVIS-ERETZ YISRAEL MOVEMENT 210 WEST 91 STREET	NEW YORK	NY	10024	(212) 595-6890
SHERUT LA'AM 515 PARK AVENUE	NEW YORK	NY	10022	(212) 753-0230
UNITED ISRAEL APPEAL 515 PARK AVENUE	NEW YORK	NY	10022	(212) 688-0800
UNITED ISRAEL WORLD UNION 507 FIFTH AVENUE, ROOM 903	NEW YORK	NY	10017	(212) 688-7557
UNITED STATES COMMITTEE SPORTS FOR ISRAEL, INC. 823 UNITED NATIONS PLAZA	NEW YORK	NY	10017	(212) 687-9625
WOMEN'S LEAGUE FOR ISRAEL 515 PARK AVENUE	NEW YORK	NY	10022	(212) 838-1997
WOMEN'S SOCIAL SERVICE FOR ISRAEL 240 W. 98TH STREET	NEW YORK	NY	10025	(212) 666-7880
WORLD CONFEDERATION OF UNITED ZIONISTS 595 MADISON AVENUE	NEW YORK	NY	10022	(212) 371-1452
WORLD ZIONIST ORGANIZATION-AMERICAN SECTION 515 PARK AVENUE	NEW YORK	NY	10022	(212) 752-0600
YOUTH CENTERS OF ISRAEL, INC. 51 EAST 42ND STREET	NEW YORK	NY	10017	(212) 490-2340
YOUTH ZIONIST ORGANIZATION-DROR 215 PARK AVENUE SOUTH	NEW YORK	NY	10003	(212) 751-6070
ZIONIST ORGANIZATION OF AMERICA 4 EAST 34TH STREET	NEW YORK	NY	10016	(212) 481-1500
JEWISH PEACE FELLOWSHIP P.O. BOX 271	NYACK	NY	10960	(914) 358-4601
AMERICAN ISRAEL PUBLIC AFFAIRS COMMITTEE (AIPAC) 23700 MERCANTILE ROAD	CLEVELAND	OH	44122	(216) 464-2353
ASSOCIATION OF PARENTS OF AMERICAN ISRAELIS 2567 LAFAYETTE ROAD	CLEVELAND	OH	44118	(216) 932-5269
CLEVELAND COMMITTEE FOR ECONOMIC GROWTH IN ISRAEL 10800 BROOKPARK ROAD	CLEVELAND	OH	44130	(216) 267-1200
CONSUMERS FOR ISRAELI PRODUCTS 2162 SOUTH TAYLOR ROAD	CLEVELAND	OH	44118	(216) 371-1138
VOLUNTEERS FOR CLEVELANDERS IN ISRAEL 1414 SOUTH GREEN ROAD, #309	CLEVELAND	OH	44121	(216) 291-2218
PALESTINE ECONOMIC CORPORATION OF CANADA, LTD. 50 WINGOLD AVENUE	TORONTO	ON		
UNITED STATES COMMITTEE, SPORTS FOR ISRAEL 341 S. 18TH STREET	PHILADELPHIA	PA	19103	(215) 546-4700
CANADA-ISRAEL COMMITTEE-NATIONAL OFFICE 1310 GREENE AVENUE	MONTREAL	QU	H3Z 2B2	(514) 934-0771
FRIENDS OF PIONEERING ISRAEL (MAPAM) 600 COTE ST. LUC ROAD	MONTREAL	QU		
COMMITTEE FOR THE ECONOMIC GROWTH OF ISRAEL P.O. BOX 2053, 5301 NORTH IRONWOOD ROAD	MILWAUKEE	WI	53201	(414) 961-1000

ISRAEL BONDS

ISRAEL BONDS CITY FEDERAL BUILDING	BIRMINGHAM	AL	35203	(205) 871-6161
BONDS FOR ISRAEL-DEVELOPMENT CORPORATION FOR ISRAEL 6380 WILSHIRE BOULEVARD	LOS ANGELES	CA	90048	(213) 653-8400
STATE OF ISRAEL BONDS DEVELOPMENT CORPORATION FOR ISRAEL 47 KEARNY STREET, SUITE 705	SAN FRANCISCO	CA	94108	(415) 781-3212
ISRAEL BONDS 470 S. COLORADO BOULEVARD	DENVER	CO	80202	(303) 321-2921
ISRAEL BONDS 740 N. MAIN STREET	HARTFORD	CT	06117	(203) 236-4523
ISRAEL BONDS 419 WHALLEY AVENUE	NEW HAVEN	CT	06511	(203) 624-9975
STATE OF ISRAEL BONDS 4601 W. KENNEDY BLVD., SUITE 118	TAMPA	FL	33609	(813) 978-8850
ISRAEL BONDS 230 N. MICHIGAN AVENUE	CHICAGO	IL	60601	(312) 558-9400
ISRAEL BONDS 1 INDIANA SQUARE, SUITE 3370	INDIANAPOLIS	IN	46204	(317) 848-2000
ISRAEL BONDS BARONNE BUILDING, 305 BARONNE STREET	NEW ORLEANS	LA	70112	(504) 524-8756

ISRAEL BONDS 262 WASHINGTON STREET	BOSTON	MA		(617) 723-2400
ISRAEL BONDS 645 CHANDLER STREET	WORCESTER	MA	01602	(617) 752-2864
ISRAEL BONDS 200 EAST LEXINGTON	BALTIMORE	MD	21202	(301) 484-6670
ISREAL BONDS	BETHESDA	MD		(301) 654-6575
ISRAEL BONDS 24123 GREENFIELD ROAD	OAK PARK	MI	48237	(313) 557-2900
STATE OF ISRAEL BONDS 1488 NORTHWESTERN BANK BUILDING	MINNEAPOLIS	MN	55402	(612) 338-8475
ISRAEL BONDS 916 WALNUT STREET	KANSAS CITY	MO	64106	(913) 642-5800
ISRAEL BONDS 225 S. MERAMEC AVENUE	ST. LOUIS	MO	63105	(314) 721-7866
ISRAEL BONDS 920 CITY NATIONAL BANK, 405 S. 16TH STREET	OMAHA	NE	68102	(402) 341-1177
ISRAEL BONDS 701 NEWARK AVENUE	ELIZABETH	NJ	07201	(201) 354-5400
ISRAEL BONDS 1425 PLAZA ROAD	FAIRLAWN	NJ	07505	(201) 794-1050
ISRAEL BONDS 28 WEST STATE STREET	TRENTON	NJ	08608	(609) 882-9290
ISRAEL BONDS 28 COLVIN	ALBANY	NY	12207	(518) 489-2509
ISRAEL BONDS 775 MAIN STREET	BUFFALO	NY	14203	(716) 856-3464
ISRAEL BONDS WHOLESALERS 120 WALL STREET	NEW YORK	NY	10005	(212) 344-6676
LEUMI SECURITIES CORPORATION 18 EAST 48TH STREET	NEW YORK	NY	10017	(212) 759-1310
OSCAR GRUSS & SONS 80 PINE STREET	NEW YORK	NY	10005	(212) 943-6313
STATE OF ISRAEL BOND ORGANIZATION 730 BROADWAY	NEW YORK	NY	10003	(212) 677-9650
ISRAEL BONDS 94 N. MAIN STREET	SPRING VALLEY	NY	10977	(914) 352-3550
STATE OF ISRAEL BONDS 3645 WARRENSVILLE CENTER ROAD	CLEVELAND	OH	44122	(216) 751-3984
ISRAEL BONDS 2375 E. MAIN STREET	COLUMBUS	OH	43209	(614) 239-7212
ISRAEL BONDS 825 EGLINTON AVENUE WEST	TORONTO	ON		(416) 789-3351
ISRAEL BONDS 200 S.W. MARKET	PORTLAND	OR	97201	(503) 228-8541
ISRAEL BONDS 801 HAMILTON STREET	ALLENTOWN	PA	18101	(215) 435-8095
ISRAEL BONDS 1405 LOCUST STREET	PHILADELPHIA	PA	19102	(215) 546-1022
ISRAEL BONDS 717 LIBERTY AVENUE	PITTSBURGH	PA	15222	(412) 521-6500
ISRAEL BONDS CONNELL BUILDING	SCRANTON	PA	18503	(717) 346-7418
ISRAEL BOND ORGANIZATION 1255 UNIVERSITY STREET #1120	MONTREAL	QU	H3B 3W7	(514) 878-1871
ISRAEL BONDS 6 BRAYMAN STREET	PROVIDENCE	RI	02903	(401) 751-6767
ISRAEL BONDS 81 MADISON BUILDING	MEMPHIS	TN	38103	(901) 682-7841
STATE OF ISRAEL BONDS 5118 PARK AVENUE, P.O. BOX 17008	MEMPHIS	TN	38117	(901) 682-7841
ISRAEL BONDS 12810 HILLCREST ROAD	DALLAS	TX	75231	(214) 661-9191
ISRAEL BONDS 112 MEYERLAND PLAZA MALL	HOUSTON	TX	77035	(713) 666-0221
ISRAEL BONDS 740 DUKE	NORFOLK	VA	23510	(804) 622-4631
ISRAEL BONDS 1940 THIRD AVENUE	SEATTLE	WA	98101	(206) 624-0910
ISRAEL BONDS 212 W. WISCONSIN AVENUE	MILWAUKEE	WI	53203	(414) 273-7425

ISRAEL GOVERNMENT TOURIST OFFICES

WEST COAST 6380 WILSHIRE AVENUE	LOS ANGELES	CA	90048	(213) 658-7462
MIDWEST REGION 5 SOUTH WABASH AVENUE	CHICAGO	IL	60603	(312) 782-4306
EASTERN REGION 350 FIFTH AVENUE	NEW YORK	NY	10118	(212) 560-0620

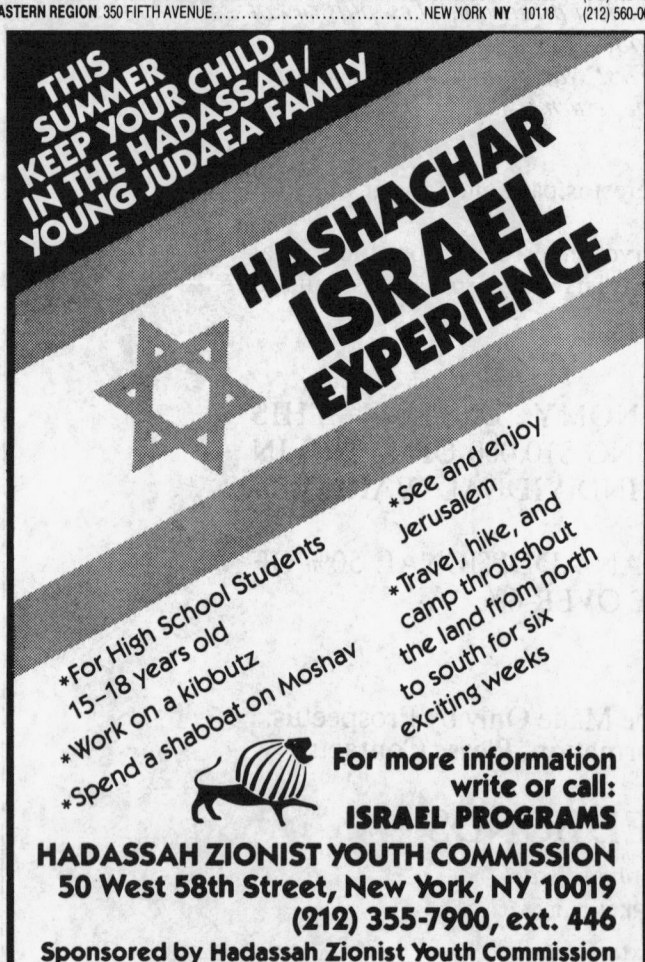

UZI MICHAELI, COMMISSIONER OF TOURISM, ISRAEL MIN. OF TOUR.				
350 FIFTH AVENUE	NEW YORK	NY	10118	(212) 560-0620
SOUTHERN REGION 4151 S.W. FREEWAY.,	HOUSTON	TX	77027	(713) 850-9341

ISRAEL GOVERNMENT TRADE CENTERS

ABRAHAM ROSENTAL 6404 WILSHIRE BLVD	LOS ANGELES	CA	90048	(213) 658-7924
DAN HALPERIN, ECONOMIC MINISTER, EMBASSY OF ISRAEL				
3514 INTERNATIONAL DRIVE N.W.	WASHINGTON	DC	20009	(202) 364-5500
MOSHE NETANEL, ISRAEL GOV'T INVESTMENT & EXPORT AUTHORITY				
330 BISCAYNE BLVD	MIAMI	FL	33132	(305) 358-8140
AMI TALMOR 174 N. MICHIGAN AVENUE	CHICAGO	IL	60601	(312) 332-2160
AMOS WOHL 20 PROVIDENCE STREET, STATLER OFFICE BUILDING	BOSTON	MA	02116	(617) 426-3636
ARIE SHEER, CHIEF FISCAL OFFICER, DEP'T OF THE TREASURY				
350 FIFTH AVENUE, GOVERNMENT OF ISRAEL	NEW YORK	NY	10118	(212) 560-0640
DIRECTOR, INVESTMENT AUTHORITY, GOV'T OF ISRAEL				
350 FIFTH AVENUE	NEW YORK	NY	10118	(212) 560-0610
ISRAEL PICKOL, ECONOMIC MINISTER, GOVERNMENT OF ISRAEL				
350 FIFTH AVENUE	NEW YORK	NY	10118	(212) 560-0630
JOSEPH MAZUR, SUPPLY MISSION, GOVERNMENT OF ISRAEL				
350 FIFTH AVENUE, GOVERNMENT OF ISRAEL	NEW YORK	NY	10118	(212) 560-0680
SHMUEL BEN-TOVIM, CONSUL & TRADE COMMISSIONER TO THE U.S.				
350 FIFTH AVENUE	NEW YORK	NY	10118	(212) 560-0660
MEIR DAYAN 225 S. 15TH STREET	PHILADELPHIA	PA	19102	(215) 546-4300
AVRAHAM GOLAN 1 GREENWAY PLAZA E.	HOUSTON	TX	77046	(713) 840-0510

ISRAEL MISSIONS IN THE UNITED STATES

ISRAELI EMBASSY 3514 INTERNATIONAL DRIVE, N.W.	WASHINGTON	DC	20008	(202) 364-5500
PERMANENT MISSION TO THE UNITED NATIONS				
800 SECOND AVENUE	NEW YORK	NY	10017	(212) 697-5500

ISRAEL PROGRAMS

AMPAL (ISRAEL DEVELOPMENT) 6505 WILSHIRE BLVD. #203	LOS ANGELES	CA	90048	(213) 653-5633
COMMITTEE FOR PROGRAMS IN ISRAEL				
6505 WILSHIRE BOULEVARD	LOS ANGELES	CA	90048	(213) 852-1234
HISTADRUT ISRAEL CAMPAIGN 8455 BEVERLY BLVD., #308	LOS ANGELES	CA	90048	(213) 651-4892
ISRAEL PROGRAMS OFFICE 4200 BISCAYNE BLVD	MIAMI	FL	33137	(305) 576-4000
FELLOWSHIP IN ISRAEL FOR ARAB-JEWISH YOUTH				
45 FRANCIS AVENUE	CAMBRIDGE	MA	02138	(617) 354-1198
PROGRAMS IN ISRAEL COMMITTEE				
MN JCC, 4330 S. CEDAR LAKE RD	MINNEAPOLIS	MN	55455	(612) 377-8330
AMERICAN JEWISH LEAGUE FOR ISRAEL 595 MADISON AVENUE	NEW YORK	NY	10022	(212) 371-1583
CENTER FOR STUDY IN ISRAEL 60 EAST 42ND STREET	NEW YORK	NY	10017	(212) 286-9474
GARIN YARDIN-YOUNG KIBBUTZ MOVEMENT				
215 PARK AVENUE SOUTH #1806	NEW YORK	NY	10003	(212) 777-9388
ISRAEL PROGRAM CENTER 515 PARK AVENUE	NEW YORK	NY	10022	(212) 751-6070
ISRAEL SEMINARS FOUNDATION 515 PARK AVENUE	NEW YORK	NY	10022	(212) 371-7761
NOAM-BAR ILAN SUMMER PROGRAM 25 WEST 26TH STREET	NEW YORK	NY	10010	
SHERUT LA'AM COLL. GRAD. PROGRAM, AMER. ZIONIST YOUTH FOUND.				
515 PARK AVENUE	NEW YORK	NY	10022	(212) 751-6070
USY PILGRIMAGE (YOUTH) 155 FIFTH AVENUE	NEW YORK	NY	10010	(212) 533-7800
UNITED SYNAGOGUE TOUR SERVICE (ADULTS) 155 FIFTH AVENUE	NEW YORK	NY	10010	(212) 533-7800
YOUTH & HECHALUTZ DEPARTMENT (ISRAEL PROGRAM CENTRE)				
788 MARLEE AVENUE	TORONTO	ON	M6B 3K1	(416) 783-4722
YOUTH & HECHALUTZ DEPARTMENT (ISRAEL PROGRAM CENTRE)				
1310 GREENE AVENUE	WESTMOUNT	QU	H3Z 2B2	(514) 934-0804

ISRAELI CONSULATES IN THE UNITED STATES

ISRAEL CONSULATE 6380 WILSHIRE BLVD	LOS ANGELES	CA	90048	(213) 651-5700
ISRAEL CONSULATE 105 MONTGOMERY STREET	SAN FRANCISCO	CA	94101	(415) 981-2786
ECONOMIC MINISTER, EMBASSY OF ISRAEL				
3514 INTERNATIONAL DRIVE N.W.	WASHINGTON	DC	20008	(202) 364-5500
ISRAEL CONSULATE 805 PEACHTREE STREET, N.E.	ATLANTA	GA	30308	(404) 875-7851
ISRAEL CONSULATE 111 EAST WACKER DRIVE	CHICAGO	IL	60601	(312) 565-3300
ISRAEL CONSULATE				
450 PARK SQUARE BUILDING, 31 ST. JAMES AVENUE	BOSTON	MA	02116	(617) 266-3800
ISRAEL CONSULATE 800 SECOND AVENUE	NEW YORK	NY	10017	(212) 697-5500
ISRAEL CONSULATE				
1720 LEWIS TOWER BUILDING, 225 SOUTH 15TH STREET	PHILADELPHIA	PA	19102	(215) 546-2555
ISRAEL CONSULATE 1 GREENWAY PLAZA EAST	HOUSTON	TX	77046	(713) 627-3780

ISRAELI GOVERNMENT

ISRAEL GOVERNMENT MINISTRY OF DEFENSE 850 THIRD AVENUE	NEW YORK	NY	10022	(212) 940-9400
ISRAEL GOVERNMENT TOURISM ADMINISTRATION 350 FIFTH AVENUE	NEW YORK	NY	10118	(212) 560-0620
ISRAEL GOVERNMENT TOURIST OFFICE 350 FIFTH AVENUE	NEW YORK	NY	10118	(212) 560-0650
ISRAEL GOVERNMENT-BEQUESTS & LEGACIES 350 FIFTH AVENUE	NEW YORK	NY	10118	(212) 560-0635
ISRAEL GOVERNMENT-COINS & MEDALS 350 FIFTH AVENUE	NEW YORK	NY	10118	(212) 560-0690
ISRAEL GOVERNMENT-ECONOMIC MINISTER 350 FIFTH AVENUE	NEW YORK	NY	10118	(212) 560-0630
ISRAEL GOVERNMENT-ECONOMIC OFFICES 350 FIFTH AVENUE	NEW YORK	NY	10118	(212) 560-0600
ISRAEL GOVERNMENT-INVESTMENT AUTHORITY 350 FIFTH AVENUE	NEW YORK	NY	10118	(212) 560-0610
ISRAEL GOVERNMENT-MINISTRY OF FINANCE 350 FIFTH AVENUE	NEW YORK	NY	10118	(212) 560-0640
ISRAEL GOVERNMENT-SUPPLY MISSION 350 FIFTH AVENUE	NEW YORK	NY	10118	(212) 560-0680
ISRAEL GOVERNMENT-TRADE CENTER 350 FIFTH AVENUE	NEW YORK	NY	10118	(212) 560-0660

The United Jewish Appeal

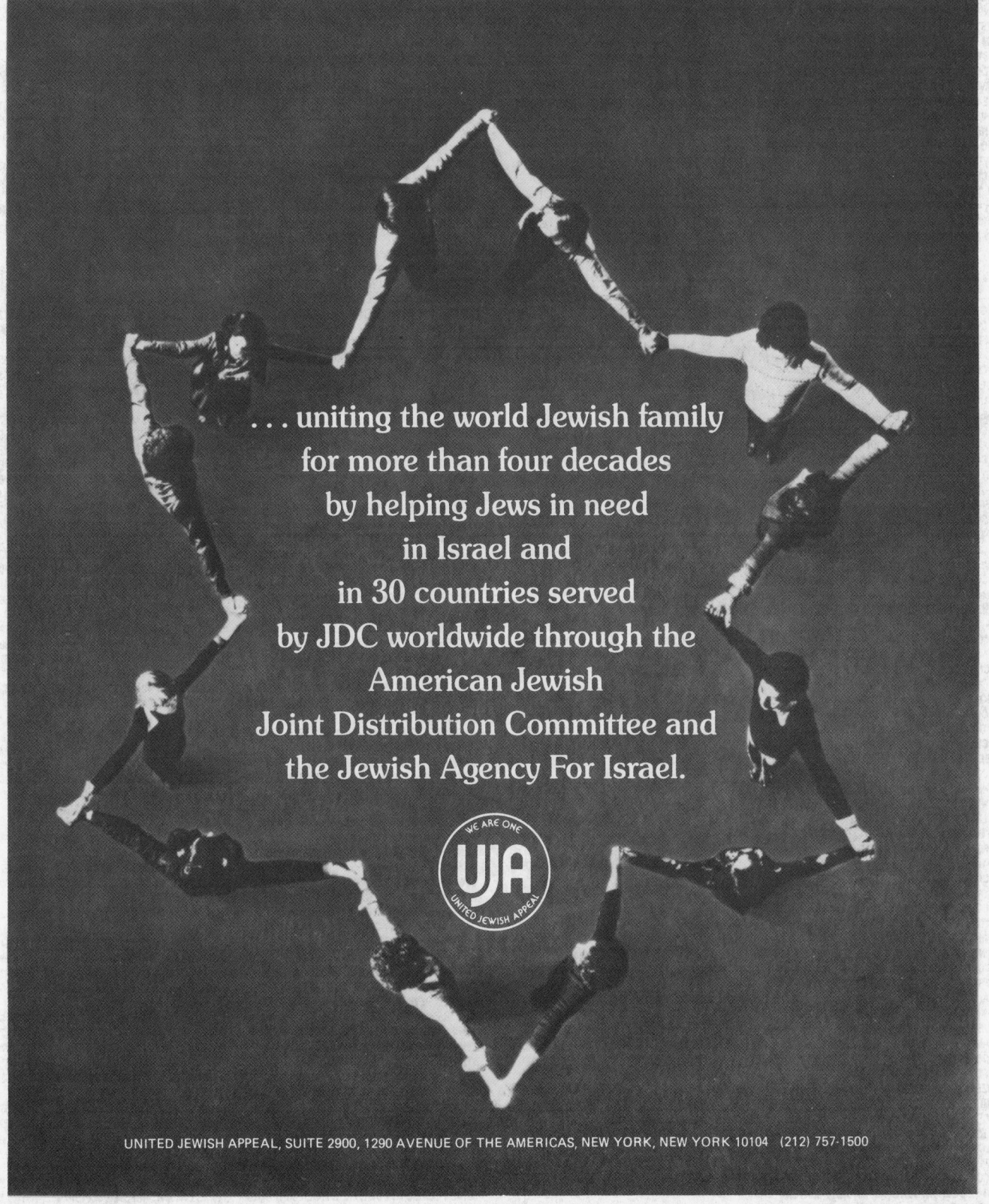

... uniting the world Jewish family
for more than four decades
by helping Jews in need
in Israel and
in 30 countries served
by JDC worldwide through the
American Jewish
Joint Distribution Committee and
the Jewish Agency For Israel.

UNITED JEWISH APPEAL, SUITE 2900, 1290 AVENUE OF THE AMERICAS, NEW YORK, NEW YORK 10104　(212) 757-1500

JEWELRY

LAOR JEWELRY 4605 13TH AVENUE ... BROOKLYN **NY** 11219 (212) 436-5055
SOURCE GIFT SHOP 307 CENTRAL AVENUE ... LAWRENCE **NY** 11559 (516) 569-1773
DUMAY JEWELERS 166 ROUTE 59 ... MONSEY **NY** 10952 (914) 356-2833
JEWELRY DIAMONDS & COIN EXCHANGE 94 ROUTE 59 ... MONSEY **NY** 10952 (914) 356-7104
JEWELRY SHOWROOM, THE 4 COLLEGE ROAD ... MONSEY **NY** 10952 (914) 352-6622
SIMCHA SHOPPE, THE 18 HILLTOP LANE ... MONSEY **NY** 10952 (914) 352-4543
BEN ARI ARTS LTD. 11 AVENUE A ... NEW YORK **NY** 10009 (212) 677-4730
DIAMOND DEALERS ALLIANCE, INC. 580 FIFTH AVENUE ... NEW YORK **NY** 10036 (212) 757-4589
DIAMOND DEALERS CLUB, INC. 30 WEST 47TH STREET ... NEW YORK **NY** 10036 (212) 840-4660
DIAMOND DEALERS INFORMATION SERVICE, INC.
22 WEST 48TH STREET ... NEW YORK **NY** 10036 (212) 997-0015
GIA GEM TRADE LABORATORY, INC 580 FIFTH AVENUE ... NEW YORK **NY** 10036 (212) 221-5858
GEM INSTRUMENTS 1180 AVENUE OF THE AMERICAS ... NEW YORK **NY** 10036 (212) 354-2970
GEMOLOGICAL INSTITUTE OF AMERICA, INC.-ED. & CLASSROOM
1180 AVENUE OF THE AMERICAS ... NEW YORK **NY** 10036 (212) 944-5900
GOLDHEART ENTERPRISES, INC 576 FIFTH AVENUE ... NEW YORK **NY** 10036 (212) 764-6060
HIZME NISSIM HEBREW JEWELRY, INC. (WORKSHOP)
80 CANAL STREET ... NEW YORK **NY** 10002 (212) 925-2922
HOWARD SLOCHOWSKY GOLDHEART ENTERPRISES, INC.
576 FIFTH AVENUE ... NEW YORK **NY** 10036 (212) 764-6060
ISRAEL CREATIONS 212 FIFTH AVENUE ... NEW YORK **NY** 10010 (212) 686-7005
ISRAELI GIFTS 575 7TH AVENUE ... NEW YORK **NY** 10018 (212) 391-4928
MORIAH ART CRAFTS INCORPORATED 699 MADISON AVENUE ... NEW YORK **NY** 10021 (212) 751-7090
WHITE HOUSE JEWELERS, THE 78 ROUTE 59 ... SPRING VALLEY **NY** 10977 (914) 425-2565
SARAH'S JEWELRY ROUTE 59 & AIRMONT ROAD ... SUFFERN **NY** 10901 (914) 357-6663

JEWISH COMMUNITY CENTERS

JEWISH COMMUNITY CENTER P.O. BOX 9157 ... BIRMINGHAM **AL** 35213 (205) 879-0416
JEWISH COMMUNITY CENTER 6150 AIRPORT BLVD ... MOBILE **AL** 36608 (205) 342-1450
JEWISH FEDERATION OF LITTLE ROCK, THE
226 DONAGHEY BLDG., MAIN AT 7TH STREET ... LITTLE ROCK **AR** 72201 (501) 372-3571
JEWISH COMMUNITY CENTER - TRI-CITY BRANCH
1720 WEST SOUTHERN, SUITE C-6 ... MESA **AR** 85202 (602) 962-0441
JEWISH COMMUNITY CENTER OF GREATER PHOENIX
1718 WEST MARYLAND AVENUE ... PHOENIX **AR** 85015 (602) 249-1832
JEWISH COMMUNITY CENTER - EAST VALLEY BRANCH
7119 EAST SHEA BLVD., SUITE 101 ... SCOTTSDALE **AR** 85253 (602) 998-9145
JEWISH COMMUNITY CENTER 3822 EAST RIVER ROAD ... TUCSON **AR** 85715 (602) 323-7167
CALGARY JEWISH CENTRE 1607 90TH AVENUE, S.W. ... CALGARY **AT** T2V 4V7 (403) 253-8600
JEWISH COMMUNITY CENTRE, HILLCREST FOUNDATION
7200 156TH STREET ... EDMONTON **AT** T5R 1X3 (403) 487-0585
JEWISH COMMUNITY CENTER OF GREATER PHOENIX
PHOENIX BRANCH, 1718 WEST MARYLAND AVENUE ... PHOENIX **AZ** 85015 (602) 249-1832
JEWISH COMMUNITY CENTRE 950 WEST 41ST AVENUE ... VANCOUVER **BC** V5Z 2N7 (604) 266-9111
PENINSULA JCC 2440 CARLMONT DRIVE ... BELMONT **CA** 94002 (415) 591-4438
JEWISH COMMUNITY CENTER OF BERKELEY-RICHMOND
1414 WALNUT ... BERKELEY **CA** 94709 (415) 848-0237
MACCABEE ATHLETIC CLUB 239 E. LA CIENEGA BLVD ... BEVERLY HILLS **CA** 90211
WEST VALLEY JCC 22622 VANOWEN ... CANOGA PARK **CA** 91307 (818) 346-3003
NORTH COUNTY JCC 2725 JEFFERSON STREET, #8-B ... CARLSBAD **CA** 92008 (619) 729-5932
NORTH VALLEY JCC 16601 RINALDI STREET ... GRANADA HILLS **CA** 91324 (213) 701-7601
NORTH CITY JCC 8950 VILLA LA JOLLA DRIVE, SUITE 2131 ... LA JOLLA **CA** 92037 (619) 460-9937
JEWISH COMMUNITY CENTER OF SOUTH ORANGE COUNTY
298 BROADWAY ... LAGUNA BEACH **CA** 92651 (714) 497-2070
JEWISH COMMUNITY CENTER 3801 EAST WILLOW AVENUE ... LONG BEACH **CA** 90815 (213) 426-7601
HOLLYWOOD-LOS FELIZ JCC 1110 BATES AVENUE ... LOS ANGELES **CA** 90029 (213) 663-2255
JEWISH CENTERS ASSOCIATION 5870 WEST OLYMPIC BLVD ... LOS ANGELES **CA** 90036 (213) 938-2531
WESTSIDE JCC 5870 WEST OLYMPIC BLVD ... LOS ANGELES **CA** 90036 (213) 938-2531
JEWISH COMMUNITY CENTER OF OAKLAND-PIEDMONT
3245 SHEFFIELD AVENUE ... OAKLAND **CA** 94602 (415) 533-9222
JEWISH WELFARE FEDERATION OF PALM SPRINGS - DESERT AREA
611 SOUTH PALM CANYON DRIVE ... PALM SPRINGS **CA** 92262 (619) 325-7281
SOUTH PENINSULA JCC 830 EAST MEADOW DRIVE ... PALO ALTO **CA** 94303 (415) 494-2511
JEWISH FEDERATION OF SACRAMENTO
2351 WYDA WAY, P.O. BOX 25489 ... SACRAMENTO **CA** 95865 (916) 486-0906
JEWISH COMMUNITY CENTER - CENTRAL OFFICE
7510 CLAIREMONT, MESA BLVD ... SAN DIEGO **CA** 92111 (619) 565-0280
JEWISH COMMUNITY CENTER - COLLEGE AREA BRANCH
4079 54TH STREET ... SAN DIEGO **CA** 92105 (619) 583-3300
BROTHERHOOD WAY CENTER 655 BROTHERHOOD WAY ... SAN FRANCISCO **CA** 94132 (415) 334-7474
KOSHER NUTRITION PROGRAM 3200 CALIFORNIA STREET ... SAN FRANCISCO **CA** 94118 (415) 346-6040
MONTEFIORE SENIOR CENTER 3200 CALIFORNIA STREET ... SAN FRANCISCO **CA** 94118 (415) 921-3275
RETIRED SENIOR VOLUNTEER PROGRAM
3195 CALIFORNIA STREET ... SAN FRANCISCO **CA** 94115 (415) 346-1812
SAN FRANCISCO CENTER 3200 CALIFORNIA STREET ... SAN FRANCISCO **CA** 94118 (415) 346-6040
UNITED JEWISH COMMUNITY CENTERS
3272 CALIFORNIA STREET ... SAN FRANCISCO **CA** 94118 (415) 929-1986
JEWISH COMMUNITY CENTER 2300 CANOAS GARDEN ROAD ... SAN JOSE **CA** 95125 (408) 266-6317
MARIN JCC 200 NORTH SAN PEDRO ROAD ... SAN RAFAEL **CA** 94903 (415) 479-2000
BAY CITIES JCC 2601 SANTA MONICA BLVD ... SANTA MONICA **CA** 90404 (213) 870-8883
COMMUNITY SERVICES DIVISION 3848 CARSON STREET, SUITE 101 ... TORRANCE **CA** 90503 (213) 540-2631
VALLEY CITIES JCC 13164 BURBANK BLVD ... VAN NUYS **CA** 91401 (818) 786-6310
ISRAEL LEVIN SENIOR ADULT CENTER 201 OCEAN FRONT WALK ... VENICE **CA** 90291 (213) 399-9584
CONTRA COSTA JEWISH COMMUNITY CENTER
1355 CREEKSIDE DRIVE ... WALNUT CREEK **CA** 94596 (415) 938-7800
JEWISH COMMUNITY CENTER P.O. BOX 6196, 4800 ALAMEDA AVENUE ... DENVER **CO** 80206 (303) 399-2660
GREATER BRIDGEPORT JEWISH COMMUNITY CENTER
4200 PARK AVENUE ... BRIDGEPORT **CT** 06604 (203) 372-6567
JEWISH COMMUNITY CENTER SHOREHAVEN ROAD, P.O. BOX 483 ... EAST NORWALK **CT** 06855 (203) 838-7504
JEWISH COMMUNITY CENTER 1156 CHAPEL STREET ... NEW HAVEN **CT** 06511 (203) 865-5181
JEWISH COMMUNITY CENTER, THE
P.O. BOX 3326, NEWFIELD AVENUE AT VINE ROAD ... STAMFORD **CT** 06905 (203) 322-7900
JEWISH FEDERATION OF WATERBURY 1020 COUNTRY CLUB ROAD ... WATERBURY **CT** 06708 (203) 758-2441
JEWISH COMMUNITY CENTER 335 BLOOMFIELD AVENUE ... WEST HARTFORD **CT** 06117 (203) 236-4571
D.C. OFFICE 2027 MASSACHUSETTS AVENUE N.W. ... WASHINGTON **DC** 20036 (202) 966-3236
JEWISH COMMUNITY CENTER 101 GARDEN OF EDEN ROAD ... WILMINGTON **DE** 19803 (302) 478-5660
JEWISH COMMUNITY CENTER OF GREATER FT. LAUDERDALE
6501 WEST SUNRISE BLVD ... FT. LAUDERDALE **FL** 33313 (305) 792-6700
JEWISH COMMUNITY CENTER OF SOUTH BROWARD
2838 HOLLYWOOD BLVD ... HOLLYWOOD **FL** 33020 (305) 921-6511
JACKSONVILLE JEWISH FEDERATION
5846 MOUNT CARMEL TERRACE ... JACKSONVILLE **FL** 32216 (904) 733-7613
JEWISH COMMUNITY CENTER OF CENTRAL FL
851 N. MAITLAND AVE., P.O. BOX 1508 ... MAITLAND **FL** 32751 (305) 645-5933
JEWISH COMMUNITY CENTERS OF SOUTH FLORIDA, CENTRAL OFFICE
4200 BISCAYNE BLVD ... MIAMI **FL** 33137 (305) 576-1660
SOUTH DADE JCC 12401 S.W. 102 AVE ... MIAMI **FL** 33176 (305) 251-1394
MIAMI BEACH JCC 25 WASHINGTON AVENUE ... MIAMI BEACH **FL** 33139 (305) 673-6060
MICHAEL-ANN RUSSELL JCC 18900 N.E. 25TH AVENUE ... NORTH MIAMI BEACH **FL** 33180 (305) 932-4200
PENSACOLA FEDERATED JEWISH CHARITIES 1320 E. LEE STREET ... PENSACOLA **FL** 32503 (904) 438-1772
SARASOTA JEWISH FEDERATION 1900 MAIN STREET, SUITE 315 ... SARASOTA **FL** 33577 (813) 365-4410
JEWISH COMMUNITY CENTER OF PINELLAS COUNTY
8167 ELBOW LANE NORTH ... ST. PETERSBURG **FL** 33710 (813) 344-5795
JEWISH COMMUNITY CENTER 2808 HORATIO STREET ... TAMPA **FL** 33609 (813) 872-4451
JEWISH COMMUNITY CENTER OF THE PALM BEACHES, INC.
2415 OKEECHOBEE BLVD ... WEST PALM BEACH **FL** 33409 (305) 689-7700
EUROPEAN ASSOC. OF JEWISH COMMUNITY CENTERS 4 BIS RUE DE LOTA ... PARIS **FR** 75116 () 553-3126
FONDS SOCIAL JUIF UNIFIE 19 RUE DE TEHERAN ... PARIS **FR** 75008 () 563-1728
JEWISH COMMUNITY CENTER 1745 PEACHTREE ROAD N.E. ... ATLANTA **GA** 30309 (404) 875-7881
JEWISH COMMUNITY CENTER P.O. BOX 3251 ... AUGUSTA **GA** 30904 (404) 736-1918
ZABAN BRANCH 5342 TILLY MILL ROAD N.E. ... DUNWOODY **GA** 30338 (404) 396-3250
MIDDLE GEORGIA FEDERATION OF JEWISH CHARITIES P.O. BOX 5276 ... MACON **GA** 31208
JEWISH EDUCATIONAL ALLIANCE 5111 ABERCORN STREET ... SAVANNAH **GA** 31405 (912) 355-8111
JEWISH FEDERATION OF HAWAII 817 COOKE STREET ... HONOLULU **HA** 96813 (808) 536-7228
BUREAU FOR JEWISH LIVING BRANCH 954 CUMMINS PARKWAY ... DES MOINES **IA** 50311 (515) 274-3467
BUREAU FOR JEWISH LIVING-EDUCATION-CULTURE-RECREATION
924 POLK BLVD ... DES MOINES **IA** 50312 (515) 277-5566
JEWISH FEDERATION 525 14TH STREET ... SIOUX CITY **IA** 51105 (712) 258-0618
JEWISH FEDERATION OF SOUTH ILLINOIS 6464 WEST MAIN, SUITE 7A ... BELLEVILLE **IL** 62223 (618) 271-2400
BERNARD HORWICH JCC 3003 WEST TOUHY AVENUE ... CHICAGO **IL** 60645 (312) 761-9100
HYDE PARK JCC 1100 EAST HYDE PARK BLVD ... CHICAGO **IL** 60615 (312) 268-4600
JEWISH COMMUNITY CENTERS 1 SOUTH FRANKLIN STREET ... CHICAGO **IL** 60606 (312) 346-6700
LINCOLN PARK-LAKEVIEW JCC 524 WEST MELROSE ... CHICAGO **IL** 60657 (312) 871-6780
ROGERS PARK JCC 7101 NORTH GREENVIEW AVENUE ... CHICAGO **IL** 60626 (312) 274-0920
SENIOR ADULT DEPARTMENT 3003 WEST TOUHY AVENUE ... CHICAGO **IL** 60645 (312) 761-9100
YOUNG MEN'S JEWISH COUNCIL 30 WEST WASHINGTON STREET ... CHICAGO **IL** 60602 (312) 726-8891
ANITA M. STONE JCC 18600 GOVERNORS HIGHWAY ... FLOSSMOOR **IL** 60422 (312) 799-7650
NORTH SUBURBAN JCC 459 CENTRAL STREET ... HIGHLAND PARK **IL** 60035 (312) 433-6424
JEWISH FEDERATION OF PEORIA 3100 NORTH KNOXVILLE, SUITE 17 ... PEORIA **IL** 61603 (309) 686-0611
JEWISH FEDERATION OF THE QUAD CITIES
224-18 STREET, SUITE 511 ... ROCK ISLAND **IL** 61201 (309) 793-1300
PHILIP BEHR JCC 1500 PARKVIEW AVENUE ... ROCKFORD **IL** 61107 (815) 399-5497
MAYER KAPLAN JCC 5050 CHURCH STREET ... SKOKIE **IL** 60076 (312) 675-2200
SPRINGFIELD JEWISH FEDERATION
730 EAST VINE STREET, ROOM 212 ... SPRINGFIELD **IL** 62704 (217) 528-3446
NORTH LAKE COUNTY FEDERATED JEWISH CHARITIES
1500 SUNSET AVENUE ... WAUKEGAN **IL** 60087 (312) 336-9110
NORTHWEST SUBURBAN JCC 3316 NORTH SCHOENBECK ROAD ... WHEELING **IL** 60090
JEWISH COMMUNITY COUNCIL P.O. BOX 5026 ... EVANSVILLE **IN** 47715 (812) 425-8222
JEWISH COMMUNITY CENTER ASSOCIATION 6701 HOOVER ROAD ... INDIANAPOLIS **IN** 46260 (317) 251-9467
JEWISH FEDERATION OF ST. JOSEPH VALLEY 804 SHERLAND BLDG ... SOUTH BEND **IN** 46601 (219) 233-1164
HAIM ZIPORI J.D.C. HILL ... JERUSALEM **IS** 91080
ISRAEL FEDERATION OF COMMUNITY CENTERS 12 HESS STREET ... JERUSALEM **IS** 91080
MID-KANSAS JEWISH WELFARE FEDERATION, INC.
400 NORTH WOODLAWN, SUITE 8 ... WICHITA **KA** 67208 (316) 686-4741
CENTRAL KENTUCKY JEWISH ASSOCIATION, INC.
258 PLAZA DRIVE, #208 ... LEXINGTON **KY** 40503 (606) 277-8048
JEWISH COMMUNITY CENTER 3600 DUTCHMANS LANE ... LOUISVILLE **KY** 40205 (502) 459-0660
JEWISH COMMUNITY CENTER 5342 ST. CHARLES AVENUE ... NEW ORLEANS **LA** 70175 (504) 897-0143
SHREVEPORT JEWISH FEDERATION 2030 LINE AVENUE ... SHREVEPORT **LA** 71104 (318) 221-4129
JEWISH COMMUNITY CENTER OF GREATER BOSTON
72 FRANKLIN STREET ... BOSTON **MA** 02110 (617) 542-1870
SOUTH AREA JEWISH COMMUNITY CENTER 71 LEGION PARKWAY ... BROCKTON **MA** 02401 (617) 586-6404
BROOKLINE-BRIGHTON-NEWTON JCC 50 SUTHERLAND ROAD ... BROOKLINE **MA** 02146 (617) 734-0800
JEWISH YOUNG ADULT CENTER 1120 BEACON STREET ... BROOKLINE **MA** 02146 (617) 566-5946
CHELSEA/REVERE JEWISH COMMUNITY CENTER
19 CRESCENT AVENUE ... CHELSEA **MA** 02150 (617) 884-5672
JEWISH COMMUNITY COUNCIL 56 NORTH MAIN STREET ... FALL RIVER **MA** 02720 (617) 673-7791
JEWISH COMMUNITY CENTER 76 SALEM END ROAD ... FRAMINGHAM **MA** 01701 (617) 879-3300
TEMPLE EMANU-EL COMMUNITY CENTER 514 MAIN STREET ... HAVERHILL **MA** 01830 (617) 373-3861
JEWISH COMMUNITY CENTER 580 HAVERHILL STREET ... LAWRENCE **MA** 01841 (617) 686-4157
NORTH SHORE JEWISH COMMUNITY CENTER
4 COMMUNITY ROAD ... MARBLEHEAD **MA** 01945 (617) 631-8330
CENTRAL AREA EXTENSION 601 WINCHESTER STREET ... NEWTON **MA** 02161 (617) 969-0733
JEWISH COMMUNITY CENTER ON THE CAMPUS
333 NAHANTON STREET ... NEWTON CENTRE **MA** 02159
JEWISH COMMUNITY CENTER 1160 DICKINSON STREET ... SPRINGFIELD **MA** 01108 (413) 739-4715
KINGS PLAZA JCC LOWELL STREET AT RUSSELL STREET ... WEST PEABODY **MA** 01960 (617) 535-2968
JEWISH COMMUNITY CENTER 633 SALISBURY STREET ... WORCESTER **MA** 01609 (617) 756-7109
YMHA JEWISH COMMUNITY CENTRE 370 HARGRAVE STREET ... WINNIPEG **MB** R3B 2K1 (204) 947-0601

WISH COMMUNITY CENTER OF GREATER BALTIMORE
ARK HEIGHTS BLDG., 5700 PARK HEIGHTS AVENUE BALTIMORE **MD** 21215 (301) 542-4900
WISH COMMUNITY CENTER
506 GWYNNBROOK AVENUE, DALSHEIMER BLDG OWINGS MILLS **MD** 21117 (301) 356-5200
WISH COMMUNITY CENTER OF GREATER WASHINGTON
25 MONTROSE ROAD ROCKVILLE **MD** 20852 (301) 881-0100
WISH COMMUNITY CENTER 28 SOMERSET STREET BANGOR **ME** 04401 (207) 945-5631
WISH COMMUNITY CENTER 57 ASHMONT STREET PORTLAND **ME** 04103 (207) 772-1959
WISH COMMUNITY FUND 1121 KENEBERRY WAY S.E. GRAND RAPIDS **MI** 49506 (616) 949-5238
MILE BRANCH 15110 W. TEN MILE ROAD OAK PARK **MI** 48237 (313) 967-4030
WISH COMMUNITY CENTER OF METROPOLITAN DETROIT
600 WEST MAPLE ROAD WEST BLOOMFIELD **MI** 48033 (313) 661-1000
WISH COMMUNITY CENTER OF GREATER MINNEAPOLIS
330 SOUTH CEDAR LAKE ROAD MINNEAPOLIS **MN** 55416 (612) 377-8330
WISH COMMUNITY CENTER 1375 ST. PAUL AVENUE ST. PAUL **MN** 55116 (612) 698-0751
WISH COMMUNITY CENTER 8201 HOLMES ROAD KANSAS CITY **MO** 64131 (816) 361-5200
WISH COMMUNITY CENTERS ASSN. 2 MILLSTONE CAMPUS DRIVE ST. LOUIS **MO** 63146 (314) 432-5700
WISH COMMUNITY CENTER 236 CHARLOTTE STREET ASHEVILLE **NC** 28801 (704) 253-0701
WISH COMMUNITY CENTER 600 NORTH SHARON AMITY ROAD CHARLOTTE **NC** 28211 (704) 366-0357
H POINT JEWISH FEDERATION 1308 LONG CREEK HIGH POINT **NC** 27260 (919) 431-7101
WISH COMMUNITY CENTER 333 SOUTH 132ND STREET OMAHA **NE** 68154 (402) 334-8200
WISH COMMUNITY CENTER 698 BEECH STREET MANCHESTER **NH** 03104 (603) 627-7679
WISH COMMUNITY CENTER 1050 KENNEDY BLVD BAYONNE **NJ** 07002 (201) 436-6900
WISH COMMUNITY CENTER OF SOUTHERN NEW JERSEY
395 WEST MARLTON PIKE CHERRY HILL **NJ** 08002 (609) 662-8800
SSAIC-CLIFTON YM-YWHA 199 SCOLES AVENUE CLIFTON **NJ** 07012 (201) 779-2980
WISH COMMUNITY CENTER OF GREATER MONMOUTH COUNTY
00 GRANT AVENUE DEAL PARK **NJ** 07723 (201) 531-9100
WISH COMMUNITY CENTER OF MIDDLESEX COUNTY
775 OAK TREE ROAD EDISON **NJ** 08820 (201) 494-3232
GIONAL YM & YWHA OF RARITAN VALLEY
SOUTH ADELAIDE AVENUE HIGHLAND PARK **NJ** 08904 (201) 249-2221
YWHA OF MORRIS-SUSSEX 500 ROUTE 10 LEDGEWOOD **NJ** 07852 (201) 584-1851
WISH COMMUNITY CENTER OF ATLANTIC COUNTY
01 NORTH JEROME AVENUE MARGATE **NJ** 08402 (609) 822-1167
YWHA OF WESTERN MONMOUTH COUNTY, MARLBORO BRANCH
.O. BOX 53, RTE. 79 & TENNENT ROAD MORGANVILLE **NJ** 07751 (201) 591-1777
YWHA OF BERGEN COUNTY EAST 285 MIDLAND AVENUE PARAMUS **NJ** 07652 (201) 967-8810
YWHA OF NORTH JERSEY - SCHNEIDER BRANCH
6 EAST 39TH STREET PATERSON **NJ** 07514 (201) 279-5528
YWHA 316 MADISON AVENUE PERTH AMBOY **NJ** 08861 (201) 442-0365
WISH COMMUNITY CENTER OF SOMERSET COUNTY
DIVISION STREET, P.O. BOX 874 SOMERVILLE **NJ** 08876 (201) 725-2231
WISH COMMUNITY CENTER ON THE PALISADES
1 EAST CLINTON AVENUE TENAFLY **NJ** 07670 (201) 569-7900
C OF THE DELAWARE VALLEY
.O. BOX 7365, 999 LOWER FERRY ROAD TRENTON **NJ** 08628 (609) 883-9550
STERN UNION COUNTY YM-YWHA GREEN LANE UNION **NJ** 07083 (201) 289-8112
& YWHA OF NORTH JERSEY 1 PIKE DRIVE WAYNE **NJ** 07470 (201) 595-0100
YWHA OF METROPOLITAN NEW JERSEY - NORTHWEST BRANCH
HENDERSON DRIVE WEST CALDWELL **NJ** 07006 (201) 736-3200
YWHA OF METROPOLITAN NEW JERSEY
60 NORTHFIELD AVENUE WEST ORANGE **NJ** 07052 (201) 736-3200
WISH COMMUNITY CENTER OF CENTRAL N.J.
22 SOUTH AVENUE, WEST WESTFIELD **NJ** 07090 (201) 889-8800
LANTIC JEWISH COUNCIL 5675 SPRING GARDEN ROAD HALIFAX **NS** B3J 1H1 (902) 422-7491
WISH COMMUNITY CENTER 340 WHITEHALL ROAD ALBANY **NY** 12208 (518) 438-6651
TORIA CENTER OF ISRAEL 27-35 CRESCENT STREET ASTORIA **NY** 11102 (718) 278-2680
UTH SHORE YM & YWHA 806 MERRICK ROAD BALDWIN **NY** 11510 (516) 623-9393
WISH CENTER 203-05 32ND AVENUE BAYSIDE **NY** 11361 (718) 352-7900
& YWHA OF NORTHERN WESTCHESTER
29 PLAINFIELD AVENUE BEDFORD HILLS **NY** 10507 (914) 241-2064
WISH COMMUNITY CENTER OF BROOME COUNTY
0 CLUBHOUSE ROAD BINGHAMTON **NY** 13903 (607) 724-2417
ONX HOUSE 990 PELHAM PARKWAY SOUTH BRONX **NY** 10461 (212) 792-1800
COB H. SCHIFF CENTER 2510 VALENTINE AVENUE BRONX **NY** 10458 (212) 295-2510
WISH CENTER OF WILLIAMSBRIDGE 2910 BARNES AVENUE BRONX **NY** 10467 (212) 655-4077
GSBRIDGE HEIGHTS JEWISH CENTER 124 EAMES PLACE BRONX **NY** 10468 (212) 549-4120
SHOLU JEWISH CENTER 3044 HULL AVENUE BRONX **NY** 10467 (212) 547-1515
SHOLU-MONTEFIORE COMMUNITY CENTER 3450 DEKALB AVENUE BRONX **NY** 10467 (212) 882-4000
ERDALE YM-YWHA 450 WEST 250TH STREET BRONX **NY** 10471 (212) 548-8200
OOKLYN JEWISH CENTER, THE 667 EASTERN PARKWAY BROOKLYN **NY** 11213 (718) 493-8800
NGREGATION SHEIRIS ISRAEL BAY RIDGE JEWISH CENTER
05 81ST STREET BROOKLYN **NY** 11209 (718) 836-3103
BREW EDUCATIONAL SOCIETY 9502 SEAVIEW AVENUE BROOKLYN **NY** 11236 (718) 241-3000
WISH COMMUNAL CENTER 1302 AVENUE I BROOKLYN **NY** 11210 (718) 377-9281
WISH COMMUNITY HOUSE OF BENSONHURST 7802 BAY PARKWAY BROOKLYN **NY** 11214 (718) 331-6800
GS BAY YM-YWHA 3495 NOSTRAND AVENUE BROOKLYN **NY** 11229 (718) 648-7703
CREATION ROOMS & SETTLEMENT 715 EAST 105TH STREET BROOKLYN **NY** 11236 (718) 649-1461
PHARDIC COMMUNITY CENTER 1901 OCEAN PARKWAY BROOKLYN **NY** 11223 (718) 627-4300
OREFRONT YM-YWHA OF BRIGHTON-MANHATTAN BEACH
300 CONEY ISLAND AVENUE BROOKLYN **NY** 11235 (718) 646-1444
& YWHA OF BORO PARK 4912 14TH AVENUE BROOKLYN **NY** 11219 (718) 438-5921
WISH CENTER OF GREATER BUFFALO, INC. 787 DELAWARE AVENUE BUFFALO **NY** 14209 (716) 886-3145
TH EL, TEMPLE BROADWAY & LOCUST AVENUE CEDARHURST **NY** 11516 (516) 569-2700
EATER FIVE TOWNS YM-YWHA
07 GROVE AVENUE, P.O. BOX 191 CEDARHURST **NY** 11516 (516) 569-6733
& YWHA OF SUFFOLK 74 HAUPPAUGE ROAD COMMACK **NY** 11725 (516) 462-9800
WISH COMMUNITY CENTER OF SYRACUSE, INC.
655 THOMPSON ROAD, P.O. BOX 29 DEWITT **NY** 13214 (315) 445-2360
WISH COMMUNITY CENTER, THE
.O. BOX 3087, GRANDVIEW ROAD EXT ELMIRA **NY** 14905 (607) 734-8122

GUSTAVE HARTMAN YM & YWHA 1742 SEAGIRT BLVD FAR ROCKAWAY **NY** 11691 (718) 471-9600
GUSTAVE HARTMAN YM & YWHA 710 HARTMAN LANE FAR ROCKAWAY **NY** 11691 (718) 471-0200
HILLCREST JEWISH CENTER 183-02 UNION TURNPIKE FLUSHING **NY** 11366 (718) 380-4145
YM-YWHA OF GREATER FLUSHING 45-35 KISSENA BLVD FLUSHING **NY** 11355 (718) 461-3030
CENTRAL QUEENS YM-YWHA 67-09 108TH STREET FOREST HILLS **NY** 11375 (718) 268-5011
FOREST HILLS JEWISH CENTER 106-06 QUEENS BLVD FOREST HILLS **NY** 11375 (718) 263-7000
JEWISH CENTER OF GREATER BUFFALO 2640 NORTH FOREST ROAD GETZVILLE **NY** 14068 (716) 688-4033
JEWISH COMMUNITY CENTER 28 EAST FULTON STREET GLOVERSVILLE **NY** 12078 (518) 725-3161
HUNTINGTON HEBREW CONGREGATION 510 PARK AVENUE HUNTINGTON **NY** 11743 (516) 427-1089
JEWISH CENTER OF JACKSON HEIGHTS 35-25 82 STREET JACKSON HEIGHTS **NY** 11372 (718) 429-1150
SAMUEL FIELD YM-YWHA 58-20 LITTLE NECK PARKWAY LITTLE NECK **NY** 11362 (718) 225-6750
BEACH YM & YWHA 310 NATIONAL BLVD LONG BEACH **NY** 11561 (516) 431-2929
TEMPLE ISRAEL 305 RIVERSIDE BLVD LONG BEACH **NY** 11561 (516) 432-1410
SUNNYSIDE JEWISH CENTER 45-46 43RD STREET LONG ISLAND CITY **NY** 11104 (718) 786-3576
MERRICK JEWISH CENTER 225 FOX BLVD MERRICK **NY** 11566 (516) 379-8650
YM & YWHA OF LOWER WESTCHESTER 30 OAKLEY AVENUE MOUNT VERNON **NY** 10550 (914) 664-0500
92ND STREET YM-YWHA 1395 LEXINGTON AVENUE NEW YORK **NY** 10028 (212) 427-6000
ANCHE CHESED, TEMPLE 251 WEST 100 STREET NEW YORK **NY** 10025 (212) 865-0600
ASSOCIATED YM-YWHA'S OF GREATER NEW YORK
130 EAST 59TH STREET NEW YORK **NY** 10022 (212) 751-8880
EDUCATIONAL ALLIANCE, THE 197 EAST BROADWAY NEW YORK **NY** 10002 (212) 475-6200
EMANU-EL MIDTOWN YM-YWHA 344 EAST 14TH STREET NEW YORK **NY** 10003 (212) 674-7200
JWB 15 EAST 26TH STREET NEW YORK **NY** 10010 (212) 532-4949
YM & YWHA OF WASHINGTON HEIGHTS & INWOOD 54 NAGLE AVENUE NEW YORK **NY** 10040 (212) 569-6200
MID-ISLAND YM & YWHA 45 MANETTO HILL ROAD PLAINVIEW **NY** 11803 (516) 822-3535
UNITED JEWISH Y'S OF LONG ISLAND 55 MANETTO HILL ROAD PLAINVIEW **NY** 11803 (516) 938-4600
JEWISH COMMUNITY CENTER 110 SOUTH GRAND AVENUE POUGHKEEPSIE **NY** 12603 (914) 471-0430
REGO PARK JEWISH CENTER 97-30 QUEENS BLVD REGO PARK **NY** 11374 (718) 459-1000
JEWISH COMMUNITY CENTER OF GREATER ROCHESTER, INC.
1200 EDGEWOOD AVENUE ROCHESTER **NY** 14618 (716) 461-2000
NORTH SHORE YM & YWHA REMSEN AVENUE, P.O. BOX 393 ROSLYN **NY** 11576 (516) 484-1545
YM & YWHA OF MID WESTCHESTER 999 WILMOT ROAD SCARSDALE **NY** 10583 (914) 472-3300
JEWISH COMMUNITY CENTER 2565 BALLTOWN ROAD SCHENECTADY **NY** 12309 (518) 377-8803
JEWISH COMMUNITY CENTER 475 VICTORY BLVD STATEN ISLAND **NY** 10301 (718) 981-1500
MAILMAN MEM. CENTER OF THE JEWISH COMMUNITY CENTER ASSN.
2310 ONEIDA STREET UTICA **NY** 13501 (315) 733-2343
CONGREGATION SONS OF ISRAEL 111 IRVING PLACE WOODMERE **NY** 11598 (516) 374-0655
JEWISH COMMUNITY CENTER 122 SOUTH BROADWAY YONKERS **NY** 10701 (914) 963-8457
JEWISH CENTER 750 WHITE POND DRIVE AKRON **OH** 44320 (216) 867-7850
JEWISH COMMUNITY CENTER 2631 HARVARD AVENUE N.W. CANTON **OH** 44709 (216) 453-0132
JEWISH COMMUNITY CENTER 1580 SUMMIT ROAD CINCINNATI **OH** 45237 (513) 761-7500
JEWISH COMMUNITY CENTER 3505 MAYFIELD ROAD CLEVELAND HEIGHTS **OH** 44118 (216) 382-4000
LEO YASSENOFF JEWISH CENTER 1125 COLLEGE AVENUE COLUMBUS **OH** 43209 (614) 231-2731
DAYTON JEWISH CENTER 4501 DENLINGER ROAD DAYTON **OH** 45426 (513) 854-4014
JEWISH FEDERATION, INC. 667 STEWART LANE MANSFIELD **OH** 44907 (419) 756-7347
JEWISH COMMUNITY CENTER 6465 SYLVANIA AVENUE SYLVANIA **OH** 43560 (419) 885-4485
JEWISH COMMUNITY CTR. OF THE YOUNGSTOWN AREA-JEWISH FED.
P.O. BOX 449, 505 GYPSY LANE YOUNGSTOWN **OH** 44501 (216) 746-3251
JEWISH COMMUNITY COUNCIL
3022 NORTHWEST EXPRESSWAY #116 OKLAHOMA CITY **OK** 73112 (405) 755-6030
JEWISH COMMUNITY CENTER 2021 EAST 71ST STREET TULSA **OK** 74136 (918) 495-1111
JEWISH COMMUNITY CENTRE 57 DELAWARE AVENUE HAMILTON **ON** L8M 1T6 (416) 528-8577
JEWISH COMMUNITY CENTRE 532 HURON STREET LONDON **ON** N5Y 4J5 (519) 432-6337
JEWISH COMMUNITY CENTER 151 CHAPEL STREET OTTAWA **ON** K1N 7Y2 (613) 232-7306
BLOOR BRANCH 750 SPADINA AVENUE TORONTO **ON** M5S 2J2 (416) 493-8866
JEWISH COMMUNITY CENTRE 4588 BATHURST STREET WILLOWDALE **ON** M2R 1W6 (416) 636-1880
KOFFLER CENTRE OF THE ARTS 4588 BATHURST STREET WILLOWDALE **ON** M2R 1W6 (416) 636-1880
LEAH POSLUNS THEATRE 4588 BATHURST STREET WILLOWDALE **ON** M2R 1W6 (416) 636-1880
NORTH EAST BRANCH 1091 FINCH AVENUE EAST WILLOWDALE **ON** M2J 2X3 (416) 493-8866
NORTHERN BRANCH 4588 BATHURST STREET WILLOWDALE **ON** M2R 1W6 (416) 636-1880
JEWISH COMMUNITY COUNCIL 1641 OUELLETTE AVENUE WINDSOR **ON** N8X 1K9 (519) 254-7558
MITTLEMAN JCC 6651 SOUTHWEST CAPITOL HIGHWAY PORTLAND **OR** 97219 (503) 244-0111
JEWISH COMMUNITY CENTER 722 NORTH 22ND STREET ALLENTOWN **PA** 18104 (215) 435-3571
BRITH SHOLOM COMMUNITY CENTER
BRODHEAD & PACKER AVENUES, P.O. BOX 5323 BETHLEHEM **PA** 18015 (215) 866-8009
JEWISH COMMUNITY CENTER 100 VAUGHN STREET HARRISBURG **PA** 17110 (717) 236-9555
JEWISH COMMUNITY CENTER ASSOCIATION 2120 OREGON PIKE LANCASTER **PA** 17601 (717) 569-7352
JCC OF THE DELAWARE VALLEY 501 TRENTON ROAD LANGHORNE **PA** 19047 (215) 493-2900
JEWISH COMMUNITY CENTER 1541 POWELL STREET NORRISTOWN **PA** 19401 (215) 275-8797
DAVID G. NEUMAN SENIOR CENTER 6600 BUSTLETON AVENUE PHILADELPHIA **PA** 19149 (215) 338-9800
JEWISH YS AND CENTERS OF GREATER PHILADELPHIA
401 SO. BROAD STREET PHILADELPHIA **PA** 19147 (215) 545-4400
KAISERMAN BRANCH CITY LINE & HAVERFORD AVENUE PHILADELPHIA **PA** 19151 (215) 896-7770
KLEIN BRANCH RED LION ROAD & JAMISON AVENUE PHILADELPHIA **PA** 19116 (215) 698-7300
MULTI-SERVICE CENTER MARSHALL & PORTER STREETS PHILADELPHIA **PA** 19148 (215) 468-6285
SENIOR ADULT SERVICES AND RESEARCH
401 SOUTH BROAD STREET PHILADELPHIA **PA** 19147 (215) 545-4400
YM & YWHA BRANCH 401 SO. BROAD STREET PHILADELPHIA **PA** 19147 (215) 545-4400
JCC SQUIRREL HILL 5738 FORBES AVENUE PITTSBURGH **PA** 15217 (412) 521-8010
JEWISH COMMUNITY CENTER 315 SOUTH BELLEFIELD AVENUE PITTSBURGH **PA** 15213 (412) 621-6500
JEWISH COMMUNITY CENTER 1700 CITY LINE STREET READING **PA** 19604 (215) 921-0624
JEWISH COMMUNITY CENTER 601 JEFFERSON AVENUE SCRANTON **PA** 18510 (717) 346-6595
JEWISH COMMUNITY CENTER 60 SOUTH RIVER STREET WILKES-BARRE **PA** 18702 (717) 824-4646
JEWISH COMMUNITY CENTER 120 EAST MARKET STREET YORK **PA** 17401 (717) 843-0918
USO-JEWISH COMMUNITY ARMED FORCES CENTER, INC. BOX 105 BALBOA **PZ** 52-5972
DAVIS YM-YWHA 5700 KELLERT AVENUE, COTE ST. LUC., P.Q. MONTREAL **QU** H4W 1T4 (514) 482-0730
LAVAL JEWISH COMMUNITY CENTRE
755 DU SABLON, CHOMEDEY, LAVAL, P.Q. MONTREAL **QU** H7W 4H5 (514) 688-8961
NEIGHBORHOOD HOUSE SERVICES 5480 WESTBURY AVENUE MONTREAL **QU** H3W 3G2 (514) 735-5565
SAIDYE BRONFMAN CENTRE 5170 COTE ST. CATHERINE ROAD MONTREAL **QU** H3W 1M7 (514) 739-2301
SNOWDON BRANCH 5500 WESTBURY AVENUE MONTREAL **QU** H3W 2W8 (514) 737-6551
YM-YWHA & NHS 5500 WESTBURY AVENUE MONTREAL **QU** H3W 2W8 (514) 737-6551

JEWISH COMMUNITY CENTER OF RHODE ISLAND 401 ELMGROVE AVENUE ... PROVIDENCE **RI** 02906 (401) 861-8800

JEWISH COMMUNITY CENTER 1645 WALLENBERG BLVD., P.O. BOX 31298 ... CHARLESTON **SC** 29407 (803) 571-6565

JEWISH COMMUNITY CENTER 4540 TRENHOLM ROAD ... COLUMBIA **SC** 29206 (803) 787-2023

JEWISH COMMUNITY CENTER 5326 LYNNLAND TERRACE ... CHATTANOOGA **TN** 37411 (615) 894-1317

ARNSTEIN JEWISH COMMUNITY CENTER 6800 DEANE HILL DRIVE, P.O. BOX 10882 ... KNOXVILLE **TN** 37919 (615) 690-6343

JEWISH COMMUNITY CENTER P.O. BOX 38349 ... MEMPHIS **TN** 38138 (901) 761-0810

JEWISH COMMUNITY CENTER 3500 WEST END AVENUE ... NASHVILLE **TN** 37205 (615) 297-3588

JEWISH COMMUNITY COUNCIL OF AUSTIN 5758 BALCONES DRIVE ... AUSTIN **TX** 78731 (512) 451-6435

JEWISH COMMUNITY COUNCIL 750 EVERHART ROAD ... CORPUS CHRISTI **TX** 78411 (512) 855-6239

JEWISH COMMUNITY CENTER 7900 NORTHHAVEN ROAD ... DALLAS **TX** 75230 (214) 739-2737

JEWISH FED. & JEWISH COMMUNITY CENTER P.O. BOX 12097, 405 MARDI GRAS DRIVE ... EL PASO **TX** 79912 (915) 584-4438

DAN DANCIGER JCC 6801 GRANBURY ROAD ... FT. WORTH **TX** 76133 (817) 292-3111

JCC MEMORIAL CENTER 783 COUNTRY PLACE ... HOUSTON **TX** 77024 (713) 496-0283

JEWISH COMMUNITY CENTER 5601 SOUTH BRAESWOOD ... HOUSTON **TX** 77096 (713) 729-3200

JEWISH COMMUNITY CENTER 103 WEST RAMPART DRIVE ... SAN ANTONIO **TX** 78216 (512) 344-3453

FEDERATED JEWISH WELFARE FUND P.O. BOX 8601 ... TYLER **TX** 75711

ASSOCIATION OF JEWISH YOUTH 50 LINDLEY STREET ... LONDON **UK** E1 3AX () 790-6407

JEWISH COMMUNITY CENTER 2416 EAST 1700 SOUTH ... SALT LAKE CITY **UT** 84108 (801) 581-0098

NORTHERN VIRGINIA JCC 8822 LITTLE RIVER TURNPIKE ... FAIRFAX **VA** 22031 (703) 323-0880

JEWISH COMMUNITY CENTER OF THE VIRGINIA PENINSULA 2700 SPRING ROAD, P.O. BOX 1680 ... NEWPORT NEWS **VA** 23606 (804) 595-5544

JEWISH COMMUNITY CENTER OF TIDEWATER 7300 NEWPORT AVENUE ... NORFOLK **VA** 23505 (804) 489-1371

JEWISH COMMUNITY CENTER 5403 MONUMENT AVENUE ... RICHMOND **VA** 23226 (804) 288-6091

SAMUEL & ALTHEA STROUM JEWISH COMM. CTR. OF GREATER SEATTLE P.O. BOX 779, 3801 EAST MERCER WAY ... MERCER ISLAND **WA** 98040 (206) 232-7115

MADISON JEWISH COMMUNITY COUNCIL, INC. 310 NORTH MIDVALE BLVD., SUITE 325 ... MADISON **WI** 53705

JEWISH COMMUNITY CENTER 1400 NORTH PROSPECT AVENUE ... MILWAUKEE **WI** 53202 (414) 276-0716

FEDERATION JEWISH CHARITIES OF CHARLESTON, INC. 723 KANAWHA BLVD E. ... CHARLESTON **WV** 25326 (304) 346-7500

ARGENTINE FEDERATION OF MACCABI COMMUNITY CENTERS 2233 SARMIENTO ... BUENOS AIRES **AG** ()48-5880

JEWISH FAMILY SERVICES

JEWISH FAMILY SERVICE, HOUSE OF ISRAEL BUILDING, ROOM 1 102 18TH AVENUE S.E. ... CALGARY **AT** (403) 252-8136

JEWISH FAMILY SERVICES 606 MCLEOD BUILDING, 10136 100TH STREET ... EDMONTON **AT** T5J 0P1 (403) 424-6346

JEWISH FAMILY & CHILDREN'S SERVICE 20-39 N. SEVENTH STREET ... PHOENIX **AZ** 85006 (602) 257-1904

JEWISH FAMILY SERVICES OF TUCSON JEWISH COMMUNITY COUNCIL 102 NORTH PLUMER AVENUE ... TUCSON **AZ** 85719 (602) 792-3641

JEWISH FAMILY SERVICE AGENCY WEST 42ND AVENUE ... VANCOUVER **BC** (604) 266-2396

JEWISH FAMILY & CHILDREN'S SERVICES 490 EL CAMINO REAL ... BELMONT **CA** 94002 (415) 591-8991

JEWISH FAMILY SERVICE OF ORANGE COUNTY 121-81 BUARO STREET ... GARDEN GROVE **CA** 92640 (714) 537-4980

JEWISH FAMILY SERVICE 3801 EAST WILLOW ... LONG BEACH **CA** 90815 (213) 427-7916

JEWISH FAMILY SERVICE 11646 WEST PICO BLVD ... LOS ANGELES **CA** 90064 (213) 879-0910

JEWISH FAMILY SERVICE OF LOS ANGELES 6505 WILSHIRE BLVD., SUITE 614 ... LOS ANGELES **CA** 90048 (213) 852-1234

JEWISH FAMILY SERVICE, FREDA MOHR MULTISERVICE CENTER 351 NORTH FAIRFAX AVENUE ... LOS ANGELES **CA** 90036 (213) 655-5141

JEWISH FAMILY SERVICE OF THE GREATER EAST BAY 3245 SHEFFIELD AVENUE ... OAKLAND **CA** 94602 (415) 532-6314

JEWISH FAMILY AND CHILDREN'S SERVICES 299 CALIFORNIA STREET ... PALO ALTO **CA** 94306 (415) 326-6696

JEWISH FAMILY SERVICE 3355 4TH AVENUE ... SAN DIEGO **CA** 92103 (619) 291-0473

JEWISH FAMILY & CHILDREN'S SERVICES 160 SCOTT STREET ... SAN FRANCISCO **CA** 94115 (415) 567-8860

JEWISH FAMILY SERVICE OF SANTA CLARA COUNTY 2075 LINCOLN AVENUE, SUITE C ... SAN JOSE **CA** 95125 (408) 264-7140

JEWISH FAMILY AND CHILDREN'S SERVICES 1330 LINCOLN AVENUE, ROOM 204 ... SAN RAFAEL **CA** 94901 (415) 456-7554

JEWISH FAMILY SERVICE OF SANTA MONICA 1424 4TH STREET ... SANTA MONICA **CA** 90401 (213) 393-0732

JEWISH FAMILY SERVICE OF SANTA MONICA 2811 WILSHIRE BOULEVARD ... SANTA MONICA **CA** 90401 (213) 828-9521

JEWISH FAMILY CENTER, SAN FERNANDO VALLEY 6851 LENNOX ... VAN NUYS **CA** 91405 (818) 873-1520

JEWISH FAMILY & CHILDREN'S SERVICE OF COLORADO 1375 DELAWARE STREER ... DENVER **CO** 80204 (303) 321-3115

JEWISH FAMILY SERVICES 300 S. DAHLIA STREET 101 ... DENVER **CO** 80222 (303) 321-3115

JEWISH FAMILY SERVICE 144 GOLDEN HILL STREET ... BRIDGEPORT **CT** 06603 (203) 366-5438

JEWISH FAMILY SERVICE 2370 PARK AVENUE ... BRIDGEPORT **CT** 06604 (203) 366-5438

JEWISH FAMILY SERVICE 50 GILLETT STREET ... HARTFORD **CT** 06105 (203) 236-1927

JEWISH FAMILY SERVICE OF NEW HAVEN 52 TEMPLE STREET ... NEW HAVEN **CT** 06510 (203) 777-6641

JEWISH FAMILY SERVICE NEWFIELD AVENUE & VINE ROAD, P.O. BOX 3038 ... STAMFORD **CT** 06905 (203) 322-6938

JEWISH FAMILY SERVICE 333 BLOOMFIELD AVENUE ... WEST HARTFORD **CT** 06117

JEWISH FAMILY SERVICE TALLEYVILLE SHOPPING CENTER, 3617 SILVERSIDE ROAD ... WILMINGTON **DE** 19803 (302) 478-5111

JEWISH FAMILY SERVICE 101 GARDEN OF EDEN ROAD ... WILMINGTON **DE** 19803 (302) 478-9411

GULF COAST JEWISH FAMILY SERVICE, INC. 304 S. JUPITER AVENUE ... CLEARWATER **FL** 33515 (813) 446-1005

GULF COAST JEWISH FAMILY SERVICE, INC. DADE CITY HALL, 612 E. MERIDIAN AVENUE ... DADE CITY **FL** 33525 (904) 567-7657

JEWISH FAMILY SERVICE 1909 HARRISON STREET ... HOLLYWOOD **FL** 33020 (305) 922-1144

JEWISH FAMILY & CHILDRENS SERVICE 1415 LASALLE STREET ... JACKSONVILLE **FL** 32207 (904) 396-2941

JEWISH FAMILY & CHILDREN'S SERVICE 1790 S.W. 27TH AVENUE ... MIAMI **FL** 33145 (305) 445-0555

GULF COAST JEWISH FAMILY SERVICE, INC. 1718 W. KENNEDY BLVD ... PORT RICHEY **FL** 33568 (813) 848-517

GULF COAST JEWISH FAMILY SERVICE, INC. 8167 ELBOW LANE N ... ST. PETERSBURG **FL** 33710 (813) 381-237

GULF COAST JEWISH FAMILY SERVICE, INC. TRILBY ADULT & COMMUNITY SCHOOL, OLD TRILBY ROAD ... TRILBY **FL** 33593 (904) 583-342

JEWISH FAMILY & CHILDREN'S BUREAU OF THE ATLANTIC JEWISH WELFARE FEDERATION, 41 EXCHANGE PLACE S.E. ... ATLANTA **GA** 30303 (404) 881-185

JEWISH FAMILY & CHILDRENS BUREAU 1753 PEACHTREE ROAD N.E. ... ATLANTA **GA** 30309 (404) 873-227

JEWISH FAMILY & COMMUNITY SERVICE 1 SOUTH FRANKLIN STREET ... CHICAGO **IL** 60606 (312) 346-670

JEWISH FAMILY & COMMUNITY SERVICE 210 SKOKIE VALLEY ROAD ... HIGHLAND PARK **IL** 60035 (312) 831-422

JEWISH FAMILY & CHILDREN'S SERVICES 1475 WEST 86TH STREET ... INDIANAPOLIS **IN** 46260 (317) 872-664

JEWISH SOCIAL SERVICE AGENCY 118 SOUTH SECOND STREET ... LOUISVILLE **KY** 40202 (502) 452-634

JEWISH FAMILY & CHILDREN'S SERVICE 107 CAMP STREET ... NEW ORLEANS **LA** 70130 (504) 524-847

SHREVEPORT JEWISH FAMILY & CHILDREN'S SERVICES 2030 LINE AVENUE ... SHREVEPORT **LA** 71104 (318) 221-412

JEWISH FAMILY & CHILDREN'S SERVICE 31 NEW CHARDON STREET ... BOSTON **MA** 02114 (617) 227-664

JEWISH FAMILY SERVICE 71 LEGION PARKWAY ... BROCKTON **MA** 02401 (617) 588-732

JEWISH FAMILY SERVICE 430 NORTH CANAL STREET ... LAWRENCE **MA** 01840 (617) 683-671

JEWISH FAMILY SERVICE OF GREATER SPRINGFIELD 367 PINE STREET ... SPRINGFIELD **MA** 01105 (413) 737-260

JEWISH FAMILY SERVICE 25 WEST STREET ... WORCESTER **MA** 01609 (617) 755-310

JEWISH CHILD & FAMILY SERVICES 228 NOTRE DAME AVENUE, SUITE 1001 ... WINNIPEG **MB** (204) 943-642

JEWISH FAMILY & CHILDREN'S SERVICES 5750 PARK HEIGHTS AVENUE ... BALTIMORE **MD** 21215 (301) 466-920

JEWISH SOCIAL SERVICE AGENCY 6123 MONTROSE ROAD ... ROCKVILLE **MD** 20852 (301) 881-370

JEWISH FAMILY & CHILDREN'S SERVICE 24123 GREENFIELD ... SOUTHFIELD **MI** (313) 559-150

JEWISH FAMILY & CHILDREN'S SERVICE 404 SOUTH 8TH STREET, ROOM 244 ... MINNEAPOLIS **MN** 55404 (612) 338-877

JEWISH FAMILY SERVICE 1546 ST. CLAIR AVENUE ... ST. PAUL **MN** 55105 (612) 698-076

JEWISH FAMILY & CHILDREN'S SERVICE 1115 EAST 65TH STREET ... KANSAS CITY **MO** 64131 (816) 333-117

JEWISH FAMILY & CHILDREN'S SERVICE 9385 OLIVE BOULEVARD ... ST. LOUIS **MO** 63132 (314) 993-100

FAMILY SERVICE DEPARTMENT OF THE JEWISH FEDERATION 101 NORTH 20TH STREET ... OMAHA **NE** 68102 (402) 330-202

FEDERATION FAMILY SERVICE 31 SOUTH SURREY AVENUE ... ATLANTIC CITY **NJ** 08406 (609) 822-110

JEWISH FAMILY & COUNSELING SERVICE OF JERSEY CITY-BAYONNE 1050 KENNEDY BLVD ... BAYONNE **NJ** 07002 (201) 436-129

JEWISH FAMILY SERVICE 2393 W. MARLTON PIKE ... CHERRY HILL **NJ** 08002 (609) 662-861

JEWISH FAMILY SERVICE 199 SCOLES AVENUE ... CLIFTON **NJ** 07012 (201) 777-763

JEWISH FAMILY SERVICE AGENCY OF UNION COUNTY GREEN LANE ... ELIZABETH **NJ** 07083 (201) 352-837

FAMILY SERVICE OF THE JEWISH WELFARE COUNCIL 20 BANTA PLACE ... HACKENSACK **NJ** 07601 (201) 488-834

JEWISH COUNSELING & SERVICE AGENCY 161 MILLBURN AVENUE ... JERSEY CITY **NJ** 07041 (201) 436-129

JEWISH FAMILY SERVICE ... PATERSON **NJ** 07501 (201) 777-703

JEWISH FAMILY SERVICE 255 EAST HANOVER STREET ... TRENTON **NJ** 08608 (609) 822-931

JEWISH FAMILY SERVICE OF ATLANTIC COUNTY 31 S. SURREY AVENUE ... VENTNOR **NJ** 08406 (201) 822-110

JEWISH FAMILY SERVICE 2 E. RIVER DRIVE ... WILLINGBORO **NJ** 08046 (609) 871-145

JEWISH FAMILY SERVICE AGENCY 1555 E. FLAMINGO ROAD, SUITE 125 ... LAS VEGAS **NV** 89109 (702) 732-030

JEWISH FAMILY SERVICE 291 STATE STREET ... ALBANY **NY** 12210 (518) 462-429

JEWISH BD. OF FAMILY & CH. SERVICES-BRIGHTWATERS GROUP HOME 556 MANATUCK BLVD ... BRIGHTWATERS **NY** 11718 (516) 665-818

JEWISH BOARD OF FAM. & CHILDREN'S SVCS.-CO-OP CITY OUTPOST 140-26 CARVER LOOP ... BRONX **NY** 10475 (212) 379-707

JEWISH FAMILY SERVICE 305 EAST KINGSBRIDGE ROAD ... BRONX **NY** 10458 (212) 933-280

BETH DAVID COMMUNAL SERVICE 1145 45TH STREET ... BROOKLYN **NY** 11219 (718) 854-162

BORO PARK CONSULTATION CTR.-JEWISH BD./FAM. & CHILDREN'S SVC 1276 47TH STREET ... BROOKLYN **NY** 11221

JEWISH BOARD OF FAM. & CHILDRENS'S SVCS.-CONEY ISLAND SUPPORT SYSTEMS PROJECT 3312 SURF AVENUE ... BROOKLYN **NY** 11224 (718) 372-330

JEWISH FAMILY SERVICE 283 ADAMS STREET ... BROOKLYN **NY** 11201 (718) 625-080

JEWISH FAMILY SERVICE 3679 NOSTRAND AVENUE ... BROOKLYN **NY** 11229 (718) 769-332

JEWISH FAMILY SERVICE - FAMILY COUNSELING 164 CONKLIN AVENUE ... BROOKLYN **NY** 11236 (718) 257-000

JEWISH FAMILY SERVICE - FAMILY COUNSELING 186 MONTAGUE STREET ... BROOKLYN **NY** 11201 (718) 855-690

JEWISH FAMILY SERVICE CONSULTATION CENTER 4917 12TH AVENUE ... BROOKLYN **NY** 11219 (718) 435-570

MACHNE ISRAEL 770 EASTERN PARKWAY ... BROOKLYN **NY** 11213 (718) 493-925

OHEL CHILDREN'S HOME & FAMILY SERVICES 4423 16TH AVENUE ... BROOKLYN **NY** 11204 (718) 851-630

JEWISH FAMILY SERVICE 775 MAIN STREET ... BUFFALO **NY** 14203 (716) 853-995

JEWISH FAMILY SERVICE OF ERIE COUNTY 70 BARKER STREET ... BUFFALO **NY** 14203 (716) 883-191

JEWISH COMMUNITY SERVICE OF LONG ISLAND 1600 CENTRAL AVENUE ... FAR ROCKAWAY **NY** 11691 (718) 327-160

JEWISH COMMUNITY SERVICES OF LONG ISLAND 50 CLINTON STREET ... HEMPSTEAD **NY** 11550 (516) 485-571

JEWISH COMMUNITY SERVICES 76 NORTH BROADWAY ... HICKSVILLE **NY** 11801 (516) 931-711

FAMILY STUDIES CENTER 161 E. MAIN STREET ... HUNTINGTON **NY** 11743 (516) 423-337

JEWISH COMMUNITY SERVICES 9 WEST PROSPECT AVENUE ... MOUNT VERNON **NY** 10550 (914) 668-893

WESTCHESTER JEWISH COMMUNITY SERVICES, INC. 271 NORTH AVENUE ... NEW ROCHELLE **NY** 10802 (914) 632-643

ALTRO HEALTH & REHABILITATION SERVICES, INC. 345 MADISON AVENUE ... NEW YORK **NY** 10017 (212) 684-060

ASSOCIATION OF JEWISH FAMILY & CHILDREN'S AGENCIES 200 PARK AVENUE S ... NEW YORK **NY** 10003 (212) 674-665

CONFERENCE OF JEWISH COMMUNAL SERVICES 15 EAST 26TH STREET ... NEW YORK **NY** 10010 (212) 683-805

FAMILY LOCATION & LEGAL SERVICES OF JEW. FAMILY SERVICE INC. 33 WEST 60TH STREET ... NEW YORK **NY** 10023 (212) 586-427

EWISH BD. OF FAMILY & CH. SERVICES-CHILD DEVELOPMENT CENTER
120 W. 57TH STREET...NEW YORK **NY** 10019 (212) 582-6300
EWISH BOARD OF FAM. & CH. SERVICES-ADMINISTRATION & INFO.
120 WEST 57TH STREET...NEW YORK **NY** 10019 (212) 582-9100
EWISH BOARD OF FAM. & CHILDREN'S SVCS.-CHILD DEVELOPMENT CENTER
2720 BROADWAY...NEW YORK **NY** 10025 (212) 662-1591
EWISH BOARD OF FAM. & CHILDREN'S SVCS.-COMM. HOMEMAKER SVC
120 W. 57TH STREET...NEW YORK **NY** 10019 (212) 582-9100
EWISH BOARD OF FAM. & CHILDREN'S SVCS.-COURT SERVICES
120 W. 57TH STREET...NEW YORK **NY** 10019 (212) 582-9100
EWISH BOARD OF FAM. & CHILDREN'S SVCS.-CULT HOT-LINE & CLINIC
1651 THIRD AVENUE...NEW YORK **NY** 10028 (212) 860-8533
EWISH BOARD OF FAM. & CHILDREN'S SVCS.-DEPT. OF JEWISH ED.
120 W. 57TH STREET...NEW YORK **NY** 10019 (212) 582-9100
EWISH BOARD OF FAM. & CHILDREN'S SVCS.-ED. THERAPY DEPT.
33 W. 60TH STREET..NEW YORK **NY** 10023 (212) 586-2900
EWISH BOARD OF FAM. & CHILDREN'S SVCS.-EDUCATIONAL INST.
120 W. 57TH STREET...NEW YORK **NY** 10019 (212) 582-9100
EWISH BOARD OF FAM. & CHILDREN'S SVCS.-EMPLOYEE COUNSELING
120 W. 57TH STREET...NEW YORK **NY** 10019 (212) 582-9100
EWISH BOARD OF FAM. & CHILDREN'S SVCS.-INFANT CARE CENTER
201 W. 93RD STREET...NEW YORK **NY** 10025 (212) 865-8200
EWISH BOARD OF FAM. & CHILDREN'S SVCS.-PRE-SCHOOL COMM. PGM
120 W. 57TH STREET...NEW YORK **NY** 10019 (212) 582-6300
EWISH BOARD OF FAMILY & CHILDREN SERVICES-AFTERCARE UNIT
33 W. 60TH STREET..NEW YORK **NY** 10023 (212) 586-2900
EWISH BOARD OF FAMILY & CHILDREN'S SVCS.-APPLICATION & SVCS
120 W. 57TH STREET...NEW YORK **NY** 10019 (212) 582-9100
EWISH FAMILY SERVICE 120 WEST 57TH STREET ....NEW YORK **NY** 10019 (212) 592-9100
EWISH FAMILY SERVICE 33 W. 60TH STREET ....NEW YORK **NY** 10023 (212) 586-2900
EWISH WELFARE BOARD 15 E. 26TH STREET ....NEW YORK **NY** 10010 (212) 532-4949
EWISH COMMUNITY SERVICE OF LONG ISLAND 97-45 QUEENS BLVD .. REGO PARK **NY** 11374 (718) 896-9090
EWISH FAMILY SERVICE 130 EAST MAIN STREET...............ROCHESTER **NY** 14604 (716) 232-5440
EWISH COMMUNITY SERVICE 22 LAWRENCE AVENUE .... SMITHTOWN **NY** 11787 (516) 724-6300
EWISH BOARD OF FAM. & CHILDREN'S SVCS.-GELLER HOUSE
77 CHICAGO AVENUE..STATEN ISLAND **NY** 10305 (718) 442-7828
EWISH FAMILY SERVICE BUREAU 316 SOUTH WARREN STREET........ SYRACUSE **NY** 13202 (315) 445-0820
EWISH FAMILY SERVICE BUREAU 4101 EAST GENESEE STREET......... SYRACUSE **NY** 13214 (315) 445-0820
WESTCHESTER JEWISH COMMUNITY SERVICES, INC.
475 TUCKAHOE ROAD...YONKERS **NY** 10710 (914) 793-3565
WESTCHESTER JEWISH COMMUNITY SERVICES, INC.
20 SOUTH BROADWAY..YONKERS **NY** 10701 (914) 423-4433
WESTCHESTER JEWISH COMMUNITY SERVICES, INC.
2000 MAPLE HILL STREET .... YORKTOWN HEIGHTS **NY** 10598 (914) 632-6433
JEWISH FAMILY SERVICE 73 EAST MILL STREET ....AKRON **OH** 44308 (216) 867-3388
JEWISH FAMILY SERVICE 750 WHITE POND DRIVE ....AKRON **OH** 44320 (216) 867-3388
JEWISH FAMILY SERVICE 1710 SECTION ROAD ....CINCINNATI **OH** 45237 (513) 351-3680
JEWISH FAMILY SERVICE ASSOCIATION 2060 SOUTH TAYLOR ROAD ... CLEVELAND **OH** 44118 (216) 371-2600
JEWISH FAMILY SERVICE 1175 COLLEGE AVENUE ....COLUMBUS **OH** 43209 (614) 231-1890
JEWISH FAMILY SERVICE-DIV. OF THE JEWISH FED. OF GTR. DAYTON
4501 DENLINGER ROAD..DAYTON **OH** 45426 (513) 854-2944
JEWISH FAMILY SERVICE 2247 COLLINGWOOD BOULEVARD................TOLEDO **OH** 43620 (419) 885-2561
JEWISH FAMILY SERVICE ASSOCIATION 28790 CHAGRIN BLVD .... WOODMERE **OH** 44122 (216) 292-3999
JEWISH FAMILY & CHILDREN'S SERVICE OF THE JEWISH FEDERATION
505 GYPSY LANE, PO BOX 449 ....YOUNGSTOWN **OH** 44501 (216) 746-3251
JEWISH SOCIAL SERVICES 57 DELAWARE AVENUE ....HAMILTON **ON**   (416) 528-8579
JEWISH FAMILY & CHILD SERVICE 150 BEVERLY STREET ....TORONTO **ON**   (416) 977-3811
JEWISH FAMILY & CHILD SERVICE 316 MAISER BUILDING................PORTLAND **OR** 97205 (503) 226-7079
JEWISH FAMILY & CHILD SERVICE 1130 S.W. MORRISON, 316........PORTLAND **OR** 97205 (503) 226-7090
JEWISH FAMILY SERVICE OF HARRISBURG 3332 N. 2ND STREET ......HARRISBURG **PA** 17110 (717) 233-1681
JEWISH FAMILY SERVICE OF PHILADELPHIA 1610 SPRUCE STREET .. PHILADELPHIA **PA** 19103 (215) 545-3290
JEWISH FAMILY & CHILDREN'S SERVICE OF PITTSBURGH
234 MCKEE PLACE...PITTSBURGH **PA** 15213 (412) 683-4900
JEWISH FAMILY SERVICE OF LACKAWANNA COUNTY
615 JEFFERSON AVENUE..SCRANTON **PA** 18510 (717) 344-1186
JEWISH WELFARE AGENCY 60 SOUTH RIVER STREET ....WILKES-BARRE **PA** 18701 (717) 782-4646
JEWISH FAMILY SERVICES OF THE BARON DE HIRSCH INSTITUTE
5151 COTE ST. CATHERINE ROAD ....MONTREAL **QU** H3W 1M6 (714) 731-3882
JEWISH FAMILY & CHILDREN'S SERVICE 229 WATERMAN ......PROVIDENCE **RI** 02906 (401) 331-1244
CHARLESTON JEWISH SOCIAL SERVICE RAOUL WALLENBERG .... CHARLESTON **SC** 29407 (803) 571-6565
JEWISH SERVICE AGENCY 6560 POPLAR AVENUE ....MEMPHIS **TN** 38183 (901) 767-5161
WEST END SYNAGOGUE-KHAL KODESH ADATH ISRAEL C
3500 WEST END AVENUE..NASHVILLE **TN** 37205 (615) 269-4927
JEWISH FAMILY SERVICE 1416 COMMERCE, SUITE 614 ....DALLAS **TX** 75201 (214) 696-6400
JEWISH FAMILY SERVICE 11333 NORTH CENTRAL EXPY. 219 ....DALLAS **TX** 75231 (214) 369-8612
JEWISH FAMILY SERVICE 4131 SOUTH BRAESWOOD BOULEVARD ....HOUSTON **TX** 77025 (713) 667-9336
JEWISH FAMILY SERVICE, THE 8438 AHERN ....SAN ANTONIO **TX** 78216 (512) 349-5481
JEWISH FAMILY SERVICE OF TIDEWATER, INC. 7300 NEWPORT AVENUE .. NORFOLK **VA** 23505 (804) 489-3111
JEWISH FAMILY SERVICE 7027-3 CHOP ROAD ....RICHMOND **VA** 23230 (804) 282-5644
JEWISH FAMILY & CHILD SERVICE 1214 BOLSTON ....SEATTLE **WA** 98102 (206) 447-3240
JEWISH FAMILY & CHILDREN'S SERVICE 1110 HARVARD-#201 ...... SEATTLE **WA** 98122 (206) 323-1421
JEWISH FAMILY & CHILDREN'S SERVICE
1360 NORTH PROSPECT AVENUE.................................MILWAUKEE **WI** 53202 (414) 273-6515

JUDAICA & GIFT SHOPS

M.D.G. ISRAELI IMPORTS LTD. 51 WOODBROOK WAY S.W. ....CALGARY **AT** T2W 4E7
MIDBAR IMPORTS 6125 EAST INDIAN SCHOOL ROAD ....SCOTTSDALE **AZ** 85251 (602) 949-0004
JUDAH L. MAGNES MEMORIAL MUSEUM-JEWISH MUSEUM OF THE WEST
2911 RUSSEL STREET..BERKELEY **CA** 94705 (415) 849-2710
SHALOM HOUSE 19757 SHERMAN WAY ....CANOGA PARK **CA** 91303 (818) 882-7399

BET SHIVA IMPORTS-SHOWROOM & WAREHOUSE
10428 STANFORD AVENUE..GARDEN GROVE **CA** 92640 (714) 636-6151
ARYE IMPORTS 6380 WILSHIRE BLVD ....LOS ANGELES **CA** 90048 (213) 651-4809
ATARA'S 450 N. FAIRFAX AVENUE..................................LOS ANGELES **CA** 90036 (213) 655-3050
HATAKLIT 436 NORTH FAIRFAX AVENUE.........................LOS ANGELES **CA** 90036 (213) 655-1242
HERMAN BERMAN COMPANY 1025 N. VERMONT ....LOS ANGELES **CA** 90029 (213) 666-6161
HERSKOVITZ BOOKS & GIFTS 428 NORTH FAIRFAX AVENUE ....LOS ANGELES **CA** 90036 (213) 852-9310
KOL-BO STAM-RABBI D. MISHULOVIN 152 1/2 N. LA BREA AVENUE.... LOS ANGELES **CA** 90036 (213) 933-8093
SKIRBALL MUSEUM GIFT GALLERY 3077 UNIVERSITY AVENUE ....LOS ANGELES **CA** 90007 (213) 749-3424
SOLOMON'S BOOKS & JEWELRY 447 NORTH FAIRFAX AVENUE ....LOS ANGELES **CA** 90036 (213) 653-9045
HOUSE OF DAVID 12826 VICTORY BOULEVARD ....NORTH HOLLYWOOD **CA** 91602 (818) 763-2070
ALLCREST ENTERPRISES ....RESEDA **CA** 91335 (818) 345-5507
HELENE WILSON, SAN FRANCISCO WESTERN MERCHANDISE MART
1355 MARKET STREET ....SAN FRANCISCO **CA** 94103 (415) 552-2311
ISRAEL IMPORTS 5542 GEARY BOULEVARD ....SAN FRANCISCO **CA** 94121 (415) 752-5546
EYTAN'S JERUSALEM FAIR 14537 VENTURA BLVD ....SHERMAN OAKS **CA** 91403 (818) 995-0116
THE JEWISH DEVELOPMENT COMPANY 18331-C IRVINE BOULEVARD ....TUSTIN **CA** 92680 (714) 730-1419
EMBASSY IMPORTS 14250 OXNARD STREET ....VAN NUYS **CA** 91401 (818) 785-8464
YA-EL IMPORTS INC. 137 MAIN STREET ....DANBURY **CT** 06810 (203) 748-6062
ISRAEL GIFT SHOP & HEBREW BOOK SHOP
262 SOUTH WHITNEY STREET ....HARTFORD **CT** 06105 (203) 232-3984
B'NAI B'RITH MUSEUM SHOP AND BOOKSTORE
1640 RHODE ISLAND AVENUE, N.W. ....WASHINGTON **DC** 20036 (202) 857-6583
CHERYL'S GIFTS & CARDS 242 HOLLYWOOD MALL ....HOLLYWOOD **FL** 33020 (305) 987-6059
POTPOURRI OF GIFTS INC. 12356 S.W. 117 CT. ....MIAMI **FL** 33186 (305) 252-2094

AMERICAN ISRAELI RELIGIOUS STORE 1357 WASHINGTON AVENUE	MIAMI BEACH	FL	33139	(305) 531-7722
JERUSALEM GALLERY 764 41ST STREET	MIAMI BEACH	FL	33140	(305) 538-3618
NATIONAL HEBREW-ISRAEL GIFT SHOP				
1507 WASHINGTON AVENUE	MIAMI BEACH	FL	33139	(305) 532-2210
TORAH TREASURES 1202 WASHINGTON AVENUE	MIAMI BEACH	FL	33139	(305) 673-6095
JUDAICA 1074 N.E. 163RD STREET	N. MIAMI BEACH	FL	33162	(305) 945-5091
HAMAKOR JUDAICA, INC. 6112 N. LINCOLN AVENUE	CHICAGO	IL	60659	(312) 463-6186
SCHWARTZ-ROSENBLUM, INC. 2906 WEST DEVON AVENUE	CHICAGO	IL	60659	(312) 338-3919
THE MUSEUM STORE, SPERTUS MUSEUM OF JUDAICA				
618 SOUTH MICHIGAN AVENUE	CHICAGO	IL	60605	(312) 922-9012
CHARLES GELLES AND SON	CANTON	MA		(617) 828-1866
JANET KAPLAN 105 TACONIC AVENUE	GREAT BARRINGTON	MA	01230	(413) 528-1907
NORMAN GORDON 2 TAMARACK WAY	SHARON	MA	02067	(617) 784-5228
CAROL LEBEAUX 15 MONADNOCK DRIVE	SHREWSBURY	MA	01545	(617) 842-8730
CENTRAL HEBREW BOOK STORE 228 REISTERSTOWN ROAD	BALTIMORE	MD	21208	(301) 653-0550
PERN'S HEBREW BOOK & GIFT SHOP 7012 REISTERSTOWN ROAD	BALTIMORE	MD	21215	(301) 653-2450
ISRAELI ACCENTS 11641 BOILING BROOK PLACE	ROCKVILLE	MD	20852	(301) 231-7999
MAZEL TOV GIFTS 13837 DOWLAIS DRIVE	ROCKVILLE	MD	20853	(301) 460-0626
ISRAELI ACCENTS BY LESLIE KANNER IMPORTS				
613 PERSHING DRIVE	SILVER SPRING	MD	20910	(301) 588-5481
KAR-BEN COPIES 11713 AUTH LANE	SILVER SPRING	MD	20902	(301) 984-8733
GOODMAN'S HEBREW BOOK & GIFT				
2305 UNIVERSITY BOULEVARD WEST	WHEATON	MD	30902	(301) 933-1800
BORENSTEIN'S BOOK & MUSIC STORE 25242 GREENFIELD ROAD	OAK PARK	MI	48237	(313) 967-3920
BROCHIN'S JEWISH BOOK & GIFT SHOP				
4813 MINNETONKA BOULEVARD	MINNEAPOLIS	MN	55416	(612) 926-2011
OLSON'S CLOTHING STORE 617 WEST BROADWAY	MINNEAPOLIS	MN	55411	(612) 529-2222
MR. B'S ART & FRAMING 7919 SANTA FE	KANSAS CITY	MO	64106	(816) 649-3676
MIDWEST JEWISH BOOK & GIFT CENTER 8318 OLIVE STREET ROAD	ST. LOUIS	MO	63132	(314) 993-6300
GILAH INDIAN HILLS PLAZA, 8901 WEST DODGE ROAD	OMAHA	NE	68114	(402) 391-3500
JUDAICA SPECIALTIES 45 BROAD STREET	CARLSTADT	NJ	07072	(201) 939-4522
CNS JUDAICA 111 LAKEVIEW AVENUE	CLIFTON	NJ		(201) 772-3141
TRIO ISRAELI GIFTS 246 RARETON AVENUE	HIGHLAND PARK	NJ		(201) 828-9555
A & C ISRAELI IMPORTS 1061 FAIRVIEW PLACE	HILLSIDE	NJ	07205	(201) 354-0885
TIV-TOV HEBREW GIFT CENTER 208 CLIFTON	LAKEWOOD	NJ	08701	(201) 364-8716
SKY HEBREW BOOK STORE 1923 SPRINGFIELD AVENUE	MAPLEWOOD	NJ	07040	(201) 763-4244
EMANUEL MILSTEIN R.D. 1, BOX 81C	MARLBORO	NJ	07746	(201) 946-8604

THE JUDAICA HOUSE, LIMITED 412 CEDAR LANE	TEANECK	NJ	07666	(201) 836-5264
ISRAEL CREATIONS 3404 BAILEY AVENUE	BRONX	NY	10463	(212) 796-9100
PELHAM PARKWAY HEBREW BOOKSTORE 781 LYDIG AVENUE	BRONX	NY	10462	(212) 892-2522
A GIFT OF GOLD 1753 53RD STREET	BROOKLYN	NY	11204	(718) 633-7842
A.J. WEISS 276 PENN STREET	BROOKLYN	NY	11211	(718) 387-4065
AVIV JUDAICA IMPORTS, LTD. 4726 NEW UTRECHT AVENUE	BROOKLYN	NY	11219	(718) 435-6201
BERGER GIFT SHOP 106 LEE AVENUE	BROOKLYN	NY	11211	(718) 387-2130
CHAIM O. EINHORN 114 LEE AVENUE	BROOKLYN	NY	11211	(718) 782-7782
COHEN'S RELIGIOUS ARTICLES 5302 16TH AVENUE	BROOKLYN	NY	11204	(718) 851-4877
DAVID SICHERMAN 68 LEE AVENUE	BROOKLYN	NY	11211	(718) 388-8215
DRIMMER GIFT CENTER 329 KINGSTON AVENUE	BROOKLYN	NY	11213	(718) 773-8483
EDELWEISS CO.-GLASS STUDIO 1217 49 STREET	BROOKLYN	NY	11219	(718) 851-9687
EICHLER'S RELIGIOUS ARTICLES & GIFTS				
1429 CONEY ISLAND AVENUE	BROOKLYN	NY	11230	(718) 258-7643
EICHLER'S RELIGIOUS ARTICLES AND GIFTS 4908 13 AVENUE	BROOKLYN	NY	11219	(718) 633-1505
ENGRAVING UNLIMITED 1533 CARROLL STREET	BROOKLYN	NY	11213	(718) 756-5307
FLOHR'S 4603 13TH AVENUE	BROOKLYN	NY	11219	(718) 854-0865
FLUSBERG'S HEBREW BOOK STORE 1276 47TH STREET	BROOKLYN	NY	11219	(718) 853-7302
FRANKEL'S HEBREW BOOK STORE 4904 16TH AVENUE	BROOKLYN	NY	11204	(718) 851-7766
HEBREW PUBLISHING COMPANY 100 WATER STREET	BROOKLYN	NY	11201	(718) 858-6928
KOHN'S WATCH & GIFT CENTER 171 RODNEY STREET	BROOKLYN	NY	11211	(718) 384-0920
MATANA GALLERY 4906 18 AVENUE	BROOKLYN	NY	11204	(718) 851-4448
MATONO GIFT CENTER 190 LEE AVENUE	BROOKLYN	NY	11211	(718) 625-9807
MERCAZ STAM 309 KINGSTON AVENUE	BROOKLYN	NY	11213	(718) 773-1120
PRESENT PLACE, THE 4607 16TH AVENUE	BROOKLYN	NY	11204	(718) 438-4785
R & W 1442 45TH STREET	BROOKLYN	NY	11219	(718) 853-6570
SHELBANK JEWISH GIFT SHOP 2121 BRAGG STREET	BROOKLYN	NY	11229	(718) 891-8666
SISU RELIGIOUS ARTICLES 632 KINGS HIGHWAY	BROOKLYN	NY	11223	(718) 645-8185
TOV GIFT & DECORATING 5015 13TH AVENUE	BROOKLYN	NY	11219	(718) 435-1451
THE JUDAICA HOUSE, LIMITED 694 CENTRAL AVENUE	CEDARHURST	NY	11516	(516) 569-4577
KI-TOV/HEBREW BOOK & GIFT CENTER 1847 MOTT AVENUE	FAR ROCKAWAY	NY	11691	(718) 471-0963
NATHAN NEUMANN ISRAEL NOVELTIES 75-71 UTOPIA PARKWAY	FLUSHING	NY	11366	(718) 969-7740
HOUSE OF ISRAEL 100-23 QUEENS BLVD.	FOREST HILLS	NY	11375	(718) 459-4556
ZION LION LTD. 212 WEST JERICHO TPKE.	HUNTINGTON	NY	11746	(516) 549-5155
GIFT WORLD & RELIGIOUS CENTER 72-20 MAIN STREET	KEW GARDENS HILLS	NY	11367	(718) 261-0233
SOURCE GIFT SHOP 307 CENTRAL AVENUE	LAWRENCE	NY	11559	(516) 569-1773
SHALOM 363 E. PARK AVENUE	LONG BEACH	NY	11561	(516) 889-0554
ATERES GIFT & TOY CENTER 4 RITA AVENUE	MONSEY	NY	10952	(914) 425-9140
BIRNHACK, TZIREL	MONSEY	NY	10952	(914) 356-5133
DAVID A FISHMAN 12 CAMEO RIDGE ROAD	MONSEY	NY	10952	(914) 425-1653
SIMCHA SHOPPE, THE 18 HILLTOP LANE	MONSEY	NY	10952	(914) 352-4543
MAZEL TOV GIFT SHOP 4 EISENHOWER AVENUE	NEW SQUARE	NY	10952	(914) 354-1183
ALEXANDER OLAND 120 WEST 44TH STREET	NEW YORK	NY	10036	(212) 730-7903
BEN ARI ARTS 11 AVENUE A	NEW YORK	NY	10009	(212) 677-4730
BLOCH PUBLISHING CO. 915 BROADWAY	NEW YORK	NY	10010	(212) 673-7910
BLUMENTHAL, ZELIG 13 ESSEX STREET	NEW YORK	NY	10002	(212) 267-8370
CONCORDIA GIFTS 141 EAST 44TH STREET	NEW YORK	NY	10017	(212) 972-1326
CRADLE GIFTS 27 WEST 38TH STREET	NEW YORK	NY	10018	(212) 221-6466
EASTERN ORIGINS 510 SECOND AVENUE	NEW YORK	NY	10016	(212) 684-6628
EASTERN SILVER COMPANY 54 CANAL STREET	NEW YORK	NY	10002	(212) 226-5708
ELECTRO-SCULPTURE LTD. 168 FIFTH AVENUE	NEW YORK	NY	10010	(212) 929-2999
FAR-N-WIDE 175 EAST 86TH STREET	NEW YORK	NY	10028	(212) 369-0920
GENE SINGER ARTS 577 GRAND ST.	NEW YORK	NY	10002	(212) 673-9669
GRAND STERLING COMPANY, INC. 345 GRAND STREET	NEW YORK	NY	10002	(212) 674-6450
HA-ATIKOT-JUDAICA ANTIQUES 17 ESSEX STREET	NEW YORK	NY	10002	(212) 254-8395
HEBREW RELIGIOUS ARTICLES 45 ESSEX STREET	NEW YORK	NY	10002	(212) 674-1770
HECKER SILVERSMITHS 605 FIFTH AVENUE (49TH STREET)	NEW YORK	NY	10017	(212) 593-2424
HOUSE OF DAVIAN 6 WEST 32ND STREET	NEW YORK	NY	10001	(212) 868-8336
IMPORT PRODUCT SALES CO. 1140 BROADWAY	NEW YORK	NY	10001	(212) 685-4115
IN THE SPIRIT 460 EAST 79TH STREET	NEW YORK	NY	10021	(212) 662-6693
ISRAEL CREATIONS 212 FIFTH AVENUE	NEW YORK	NY	10010	(212) 686-7005
ISRAEL GIFT & ERGO MANUFACTURING CO. 29 CANAL STREET	NEW YORK	NY	10002	(212) 677-1670
ISRAEL GIFT CENTER 23 ESSEX STREET	NEW YORK	NY	10002	(212) 475-6035

SRAEL GIFTS 575 SEVENTH AVENUE	NEW YORK NY	10018	(212) 391-4928
SRAEL RELIGIOUS ART, INC. 43 WEST 61ST STREET	NEW YORK NY	10023	(212) 582-1768
SRAELI ART & CRAFT CENTER 485 MADISON AVENUE	NEW YORK NY	10022	(212) 757-2700
SRAELI GIFTS 575 SEVENTH AVENUE	NEW YORK NY	10018	(212) 391-4928
SRAELI HANDICRAFTS IMPORTING CO. 168 FIFTH AVENUE	NEW YORK NY	10010	(212) 929-2999
M. LEVINE RELIGIOUS SUPPLIES 58 ELDRIDGE STREET	NEW YORK NY	10002	(212) 966-4460
JACOB BEN-EZER LIMITED 440 PARK AVENUE SOUTH	NEW YORK NY	10016	(212) 532-7097
JERUSALEM GIFT CO. 48 CANAL STREET	NEW YORK NY	10002	(212) 966-0466
JEWISH MUSEUM BOOKSHOP 1109 FIFTH AVENUE	NEW YORK NY	10028	(212) 860-1888
KIBBUTZ STORE, THE 856 LEXINGTON AVENUE	NEW YORK NY	10021	(212) 772-6644
LIEBERMAN'S JEWISH GIFT SHOPS 2404 BROADWAY	NEW YORK NY	10024	(212) 362-7846
MIRIAM RELIGIOUS SUPPLIES MANUFACTURING CORPORATION			
48 CANAL STREET	NEW YORK NY	10002	(212) 925-9272
ORIGINALS ONLY COMPANY 5 WHITE STREET	NEW YORK NY	10013	(212) 966-6464
SHALLER'S ISRAEL GIFT BOOK & RECORD CENTER			
2555 AMSTERDAM AVENUE	NEW YORK NY	10033	(212) 928-2140
SHOVAL GALLERIE JUDAICA			
915 BROADWAY, CORNER OF 21ST STREET	NEW YORK NY	10010	(212) 505-2580
STAVSKY'S BOOK STORE 147 ESSEX STREET	NEW YORK NY	10002	(212) 674-1289
THE GIFT OF EDUCATION 10 ROCKEFELLER PLAZA	NEW YORK NY	10020	(212) 541-7568
THE HECKER CORPORATION 605 FIFTH AVENUE	NEW YORK NY	10017	(212) 593-2424
THE JEWISH MUSEUM SHOP 1109 FIFTH AVENUE	NEW YORK NY	10028	(212) 860-1888
WEST SIDE JEWISH GIFT STORE 2404 BROADWAY	NEW YORK NY	10024	(212) 362-7846
ZIONTALIS MANUFACTURING COMPANY 48 ELDRIDGE STREET	NEW YORK NY	10002	(212) 925-8558
ABBERBOCK RELIGIOUS SUPPLIES 3405 OCEANSIDE ROAD	OCEANSIDE NY	11572	(516) 764-2593
P. ITTELSON 9931 65TH ROAD	REGO PARK NY	11374	(718) 897-9503
ORGEL'S JEWISH RELIGIOUS ARTICLES & ISRAEL GIFTWARE			
984 MONROE AVENUE	ROCHESTER NY	14609	(716) 271-2310
CHAI & MAZEL GIFT SHOP 220 W. MAIN STREET	SMITHTOWN NY		(516) 360-3331
GIFT GALLERY, THE 74 WEST ROUTE 59	SPRING VALLEY NY	10977	(914) 356-4988
JUDAICA HOME & GIFT CENTER 26 S. CENTRAL AVENUE	SPRING VALLEY NY	10977	(914) 425-9399
MAZEL TOV 833 ENGELWOOD AVENUE	TONAWANDA TWP NY	14150	(716) 838-5900
JUDAICA UNLIMITED, INC. 433 HEMPSTEAD AVENUE	WEST HEMPSTEAD NY	11552	(516) 486-3636
LONG ISLAND TEMPLE SUPPLIES 433 HEMPSTEAD AVENUE	WEST HEMPSTEAD NY	11552	(516) 486-3636
ENJOY-A-BOOK CLUB P.O. BOX 101	WOODMERE NY	11598	(516) 569-0324
FRANK'S HEBREW BOOK STORE 1647 LEE ROAD	CLEVELAND OH	44118	(216) 321-6850
OHIO POSTER COMPANY 14077 CEDAR ROAD	CLEVELAND OH	44118	(216) 371-5905
PAUL'S HEBREW BOOK STORE 13962 CEDAR ROAD	CLEVELAND OH	44114	(216) 371-7200
MIRIAM'S GIFT GALLERY 3007 BATHURST STREET	TORONTO ON		(416) 781-8261
NEGEV BOOK & GIFT STORE 3509 BATHURST STREET	TORONTO ON		(416) 781-9356
ZUCKER JEWISH BOOKS & ART 3543 BATHURST STREET	TORONTO ON		(416) 781-2133
PIOTRKOWSKI'S JUDAICA CENTER 289 MONTGOMERY AVENUE	BALA CYNWYD PA	19004	(215) 664-1303
TREE OF LIFE, INC. 858 SUSSEX BLVD	BROOMALL PA	19008	(215) 544-9900
ROSENBERG HEBREW BOOKS 409 OLD YORK ROAD	JENKINTOWN PA	19046	(215) 884-1728
ANNA SCHACTER GIFTS 629 SOUTH FOURTH STREET	PHILADELPHIA PA	19147	(215) 533-9250
ART ASSOCIATE 726 N. THIRD STREET	PHILADELPHIA PA	19123	(215) 925-8121

ERLICH ISRAEL IMPORTS 9 N. THIRD STREET .... PHILADELPHIA PA 19106   (215) 592-0404
FOR THE CHILDREN 8420 BUSTLETON AVE .... PHILADELPHIA PA 19152   (215) 745-2290
HEBREW BOOK & ART CENTER 6743 CASTOR AVENUE .... PHILADELPHIA PA 19149   (215) 742-2397
ISRAEL DESIGNS 45 NORTH SECOND STREET .... PHILADELPHIA PA 19106   (215) 925-1600
ROSENBERG HEBREW BOOKS & GIFTS 6743 CASTOR AVENUE .... PHILADELPHIA PA 19149   (215) 742-2397
DESIGNS BY BRENDA 1110 GROUSE DRIVE .... PITTSBURGH PA 15243   (412) 276-6602
ISAAC SKULL CAP COMPANY 3553 ST. LAWRENCE .... MONTREAL QU   (514) 274-8403
RODAL'S HEBREW BOOK STORE & GIFT SHOP 4689 VAN HORNE .... MONTREAL QU   (514) 733-1876
VICTORIA GIFT SHOP & BOOK CENTER 5865 VICTORIA AVENUE .... MONTREAL QU   (514) 738-1414
ELIJAH'S CUP 12306 MEADOW LAKE DRIVE .... HOUSTON TX 77077   (713) 497-2243
JERUSALEM PRODUCTS CORPORATION
  PO BOX 76, DEPARTMENT CC .... WAITSFIELD VT 05673   (802) 496-3751
EZRA BESSAROTH GIFTS 4217 SOUTH BRANDON .... SEATTLE WA 98102   (206) 722-5500
JUDAICA SHOP OF TEMPLE DE HIRSCH SINAI 1511 EAST PIKE STREET .... SEATTLE WA 98103   (206) 323-8488

JUDAICA APPRAISALS

APPRAISAL CONSULTANTS P.O. BOX 249 .... MONSEY NY 10952   (914) 352-9170
BELLE ROSENBAUM, A.S.A., C.F.A.A., I.S.A. 15 HIGHVIEW ROAD ..... MONSEY NY 10952   (914) 352-9170
HECKER SILVERSMITHS 605 FIFTH AVENUE (49TH STREET) .... NEW YORK NY 10017   (212) 593-2424

KADDISH

LUBAVITCH YOUTH ORGANIZATION 770 EASTERN PARKWAY .... BROOKLYN NY 11213   (718) 778-4270
KOLEL AMERICA/AMERICAN RABBI MEIR BAAL HANESS CHARITY
  132 NASSAU STREET .... NEW YORK NY 10038   (212) 871-4111

KASHRUT SUPERVISION & INFORMATION

KOSHER OVERSEAS ASSOCIATION OF AMERICA, INC.
  DR. HAROLD SCHARFMAN, P.O. BOX 1321 .... BEVERLY HILLS CA 90213   (213) 870-0011
IGUD HAKASHRUT 360 NORTH CURSON AVENUE .... LOS ANGELES CA 90036   (213) 935-2499
KEHILA DE LOS ANGELES 186 NORTH CITRUS .... LOS ANGELES CA 90030   (213) 935-3838
RABBINICAL COUNCIL IN CALIFORNIA
  9760 WEST PICO BOULEVARD .... LOS ANGELES CA 90035   (213) 938-2619
KOSHER HOTLINE .... SAN JOSE CA   (408) 243-6640
ORTHODOX RABBINICAL COUNCIL OF NORTHERN CALIFORNIA
  1851 NORIEGA STREET .... SAN FRANCISCO CA 94122   (415) 564-5665
CHICAGO RABBINICAL COUNCIL 3525 W. PETERSON AVE., SUITE 45 ...... CHICAGO IL 60659   (312) 588-1600
VAAD HORABONIM (VAAD HAKASHRUS) OF MASSACHUSETTS
  177 TREMONT AVENUE .... BOSTON MA 02111   (617) 426-6268
KASHRUTH SUPERVISION SERVICE 7111 PARK HEIGHTS AVENUE ...... BALTIMORE MD 21215
VAAD HAKASHRUS OF THE ORTHODOX JEWISH COUNCIL OF BALTIMORE
  7504 SEVEN MILE LANE .... BALTIMORE MD 21209   (301) 484-4110
VAAD HORABONIM OF GREATER DETROIT AND MERKAZ
  17071 WEST TEN MILE ROAD .... SOUTHFIELD MI 48075   (313) 559-5005
METROPOLITAN KASHRUTH COUNCIL OF MICHIGAN
  6533 POST OAK DRIVE, ... WEST BLOOMFIELD MI 48033   (313) 855-4324
KASHRUTH INSPECTION SERVICE OF THE VAAD HOEIR OF ST. LOUIS
  4 MILLSTONE CAMPUS, ... ST. LOUIS MO 63146   (314) 569-2770
THE BOARD OF RABBIS, 143 BAY STREET, POB 214, ... JERSEY CITY NJ 07303   (201) 333-3700
KOSHER SUPERVISION SERVICE 1144 QUEEN ANNE ROAD .... TEANECK NJ 07666   (201) 342-7400
AGUDATH VAAD HAKASHRUTH 750 REMSEN AVENUE .... BROOKLYN NY 11236   (718) 629-1802
CENTRAL RABBINICAL CONGRESS (HISACHDUS HORABONIM)
  85 DIVISION AVENUE .... BROOKLYN NY 11211   (718) 384-6765
CONGREGATION BETH MEDRASH HAGODOL 1350 56TH STREET, ... BROOKLYN NY 11219   (718) 854-8047
KASHRUS NEWSLETTER PO BOX 96 .... BROOKLYN NY 11204   (718) 375-8611
KASHRUT CENTER 1649 PRESIDENT STREET .... BROOKLYN NY 11213   (718) 774-3025
LUBAVITCH HEADQUARTERS 770 EASTERN PARKWAY .... BROOKLYN NY 11213   (718) 493-9250
NATIONAL KASHRUS DATA BASE 1204 AVENUE U P.O.BOX 1179 .... BROOKLYN NY 11229   (718) 376-1470
ORGANIZED KASHRUS LABORATORIES POB 218 .... BROOKLYN NY 11204   (718) 851-6528
SEPHARDIC RABBINICAL COUNCIL OF AMERICA SHAARE ZION CONGREGATION
  2030 OCEAN PARKWAY .... BROOKLYN NY   (718) 376-0009
THE JEWISH HOMEMAKER PO BOX 324 .... BROOKLYN NY 11204
VAAD HAKASHRUS OF KHAL BES MEDRASH HAGADOL
  1350 56TH STREET .... BROOKLYN NY 11219   (718) 854-8047
VAAD HARABBONIM OF FLATBUSH 1618 CONEY ISLAND AVENUE ...... BROOKLYN NY 11230   (718) 951-8585
QUALITY KASHRUS LABORATORY 92-15 69TH AVENUE, SUITE 205 .... FLUSHING NY 11375   (718) 849-7006
RABBI SOLOMON B. SHAPIRO 73-09 136TH STREET .... FLUSHING NY 11367   (718) 263-1574
NATIONAL KASHRUTH 1 ROUTE 306 .... MONSEY NY 10952   (914) 352-4448
UNITED KOSHER SUPERVISION POB 122 .... MONSEY NY 10952   (914) 352-0630
BETH DIN OF KHAL ADATH JESHURUN (BREUER'S)
  85-93 BENNETT AVENUE .... NEW YORK NY 10133   (212) 923-3592
KASHRUTH ALLIANCE OF THE RABBINICAL ALLIANCE OF AMERICA/
  IGUD HORABONIM ROOM 805, 156 FIFTH AVENUE .... NEW YORK NY 10010   (212) 675-5803
KASHRUTH SUPERVISOR'S UNION LOCAL 621 37 UNION SQUARE .... NEW YORK NY 10003   (212) 691-9494
KOSHER OVERSEAS ASSOCIATION OF AMERICA, INC.
  565 FIFTH AVENUE .... NEW YORK NY 10017   (212) 697-7400
UNION OF ORTHODOX JEWISH CONGREGATIONS OF AMERICA
  45 WEST 36TH STREET .... NEW YORK NY 10018   (212) 564-8330
VAAD HAKASHRUS OF BUFFALO 76 N. MAPLEMERE .... WILLIAMSVILLE NY 14221   (716) 634-3990
BNAI EMUNASH KASHRUT COMMITTEE 1719 SOUTH OWASSO AVENUE .... TULSA OK 74120   (918) 584-2156
CANADIAN JEWISH CONGRESS OF TORONTO
  4600 BATHURST STREET .... DOWNSVIEW ON   (416) 635-2883
KO KOSHER SERVICE 5871 DREXEL ROAD .... PHILADELPHIA PA 19131   (215) 879-1100
PENNSYLVANIA KASHRUS ASSOCIATION
  7718 SUMMERDALE AVENUE .... PHILADELPHIA PA 19111   (215) 725-3773
RABBI DR. BERNARD POUPKO 2533 BEACHWOOD BLVD .... PITTSBURGH PA 15217   (412) 421-2442

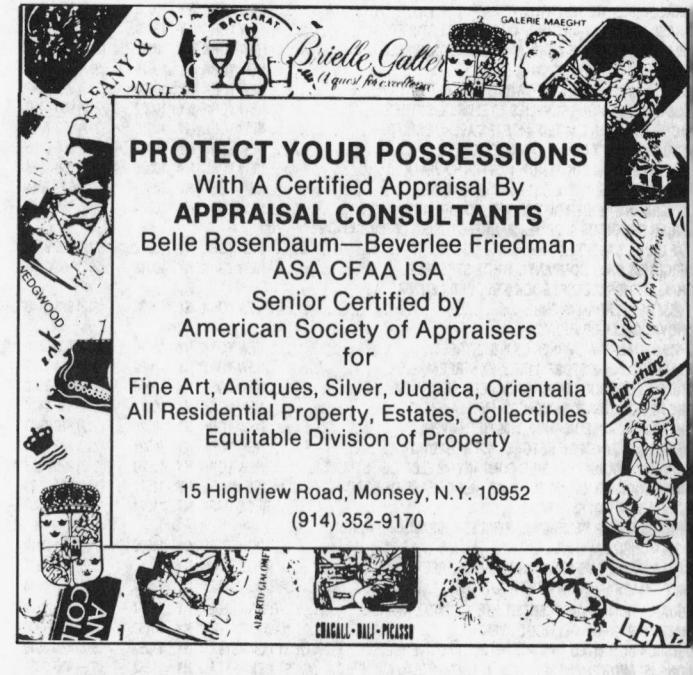

VAAD HAKASHRUS OF DELAWARE VALLEY 400 DAVID DRIVE .... TREVOSE PA 19047   (215) 357-7130
MONTREAL VAAD HAIR 5491 VICTORY AVENUE .... MONTREAL QU   (514) 739-6363
DALLAS KASHRUTH COUNCIL POB 30511 .... DALLAS TX 75230   (214) 387-4778
RABBI SAUL A. PERL POB 30662 .... DALLAS TX 75230
MANCHESTER BETH DIN 435 CHEETHAM HILL ROAD .... MANCHESTER 8 GB   (061) 740-9711
KASHRUS DEPARTMENT OF THE BETH DIN OF JOHANNESBURG OF
  THE FEDERATION OF SYNAGOGUES OF S AFRICA
  24 RALEIGH ST., YEOVILLE 2198 .... JOHANNESBURG SA   () 648-9136

LECTURE BUREAUS

AMERICAN ISRAEL PUBLIC AFFAIRS COMMITTEE
  444 NORTH CAPITAL .... WASHINGTON DC   (202) 638-2256
B'NAI B'RITH LECTURE BUREAU 1640 RHODE ISLAND AVENUE N.W. ... WASHINGTON DC 20036   (213) 857-6600
B'NAI B'RITH LECTURE BUREAU - TRAVELING EXHIBIT SERVICE
  1640 RHODE ISLAND AVENUE, N.W. .... WASHINGTON DC 20036   (202) 857-6600
ASSOCIATION OF JEWISH CLERGYMEN P.O. BOX 317 .... MONSEY NY 10952   (914) 352-0630
AMERICAN PROFESSORS FOR PEACE IN THE MIDDLE EAST
  330 SEVENTH AVENUE .... NEW YORK NY 10017   (212) 563-2980
ANTI-DEFAMATION LEAGUE OF B'NAI B'RITH-LECTURE BUREAU
  823 UN PLAZA .... NEW YORK NY 10017   (212) 490-2525
CONSULATE GENERAL OF ISRAEL SPEAKERS BUREAU
  800 2ND AVENUE .... NEW YORK NY 10017   (212) 697-5500
ISRA-ART PRODUCTIONS, INC 157 WEST 57TH STREET .... NEW YORK NY 10022   (212) 724-1500
JWB LECTURE BUREAU, THE NATIONAL JEWISH WELFARE BOARD
  15 EAST 26TH STREET .... NEW YORK NY 10010   (212) 532-4949
STATE OF ISRAEL BOND ORGANIZATION 215 PARK AVENUE SOUTH..... NEW YORK NY 10003   (212) 677-9650
UNITED JEWISH APPEAL SPEAKERS BUREAU 1290 6TH AVE....... NEW YORK NY 10019   (212) 757-1500
UNIVERSITY SERVICE DEPARTMENT 515 PARK AVENUE .... NEW YORK NY 10022   (212) 751-6070
ZIONIST ACADEMIC COUNCIL 330 SEVENTH AVE., SUITE 606 .... NEW YORK NY 10001   (212) 563-2980

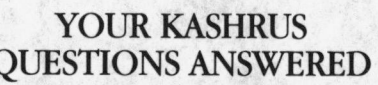

The Kashrus Newsletter
The bimonthly magazine for the kosher consumer.

Can You Pass This Kashrus Quiz?

TRUE OR FALSE:

1. There are over 200 acceptably kosher cereals, many without any rabbinic supervision.

2. The "K" means that some rabbi or supervisory organization certifies the product as kosher.

3. All kashrus organizations have the same standards.

4. A kosher symbol on a product is the consumer's guarantee that the product is kosher.

Answers:

1. True. **The Kashrus Newsletter** recently printed such a recommended cereal list.

2. False. A company need not have rabbinic supervision in order to display a "K" symbol. The company's own management may claim kashrus status.

3. The methods of koshering equipment, the standards of industrial products used as ingredients and the regularity of kosher supervision vary widely from one supervisory agency to another. **The Kashrus Newsletter** features reports on the various supervisory organizations.

4. False. Last year alone nearly 100 products were either mislabeled or bore an unauthorized kosher symbol. There are also many package markings that are look-alikes for kosher symbols.

WHO'S BEHIND THESE 33 SYMBOLS?

Inside each bimonthly **40** page issue of The Kashrus Newsletter you'll find features like:

* **"Consumer Alert"** — listing all products that are mislabeled, bear unauthorized symbols, have a supervision change, whose pareve/dairy status needs clarification, is kosher even if no kosher symbol is on the label, plus dozens of other clarifications.

* **Kosher services provided by kashrus organizations countrywide** — telephone kashrus hotlines, radio shows, lectures, books and booklets, newsletters, classes, video presentations, etc.

* **Indepth research articles on current kashrus issues** — "Hotel Catering," "The New Vegetable Wax Coating," "Insect Infestation in Vegetables," "The Kashrus Standards of Packaged Baked Goods," "Recommended Kosher Cereals," "Report on Caterers," and "Who's Who In Kosher Supervision."

* **Travel reports on the Jewish communities worldwide** — with specific attention paid to the kosher food available and whom to contact.

* **Health, Nutrition and Pharmaceuticals** — by Dr. Philip Zimmerman, Chief Chemist at Freeda Vitamins.

LEGAL SERVICES

BET TZEDEK LEGAL SERVICES 7966 BEVERLY BOULEVARD, SUITE 210	LOS ANGELES	CA	90048	(213) 658-8930
LEGAL AID SOCIETY OF LOS ANGELES 1550 WEST 8TH STREET	LOS ANGELES	CA	90015	(213) 487-3320
INTERNATIONAL ASSN. OF JEWISH LAWYERS AND JURISTS 600 NEW JERSEY AVENUE, N.W.	WASHINGTON	DC	20001	(202) 624-8083
ARK, THE 3509 W. LAWRENCE AVENUE	CHICAGO	IL	60645	(312) 463-4545
THE ARK 2341 W. DEVON	CHICAGO	IL	60659	(312) 973-1000
COMMUNITY ACTION FOR LEGAL SERVICES 606 BRIGHTON BEACH	BROOKLYN	NY	11235	(718) 934-2989
COMMISSION ON LAW & SOCIAL ACTION OF THE AM. JEWISH CONGRESS 15 EAST 84TH STREET	NEW YORK	NY	10028	(212) 879-4500
NATIONAL JEWISH COMMISSION ON LAW & PUBLIC AFFAIRS (COLPA) 450 SEVENTH AVENUE	NEW YORK	NY	10001	(212) 563-0100

LIBRARIES

ASSOCIATION OF JEWISH LIBRARIES, C/O NATIONAL FOUNDATION FOR JEWISH CULTURE, 122 EAST 42ND STREET, ROOM 1512	NEW YORK	NY	10168	
JEWISH PUBLIC LIBRARY OF TORONTO 22 GLEN PARK AVENUE	TORONTO	ON	M6B 2B9	(416) 363-3289
JEWISH PUBLIC LIBRARY OF MONTREAL 5151 COTE ST. CATHERINE ROAD	MONTREAL	QU	H3W 1M6	(514) 735-6535

LUBAVITCH CENTERS / CHABAD

CHABAD LUBAVITCH 3348 STONERIDGE LANE	MOUNTAINBROOK	AL	35243	(205) 967-4417
LUBAVITCH 92 HOTHAM STREET, EAST S. KILDA 3183	MELBOURNE	AU		
YESHIVA GEDOLAH 67 ALEXANDRA STREET, EAST S. KILDA 3183	MELBOURNE	AU		
YESHIVA GEDOLAH 67A PENKIUL STREET, BONDI 2026	SYDNEY	AU		
CHABAD LUBAVITCH 1536 EAST MARYLAND	PHOENIX	AZ	85014	(602) 274-5377
LUBAVITCH CENTER 915 W. 14TH STREET	TEMPE	AZ	85281	(602) 966-4649
CHABAD LUBAVITCH 6200 N. ORACLE ROAD, #213	TUCSON	AZ	85704	(602) 297-8150
CHABAD HOUSE 497 WEST 39TH STREET	VANCOUVER	BC		(604) 324-2406
CHABAD HOUSE 5750 OAK STREET	VANCOUVER	BC	V6M 2V7	(604) 266-1313
CHABAD OF ANAHEIM 518 S. BROOKHURST ST	ANAHEIM	CA	92804	(714) 520-0770
CHABAD HOUSE 2340 PIEDMONT AVENUE	BERKELEY	CA	94704	(415) 845-7791
CHABAD HOUSE 409 NORTH FOOTHILL	BEVERLY HILLS	CA	90210	(213) 859-3948
CHABAD OF THE VALLEY 4915 HAYVENHURST AVENUE	ENCINO	CA	91436	(818) 784-9985
CHABAD OF IRVINE 4872 ROYCE ROAD	IRVINE	CA	92715	(714) 786-5000
CHABAD HOUSE 8950 VILLA LA JOLLA DRIVE	LA JOLLA	CA	92037	(619) 455-1670
CHABAD HOUSE 24412 NARBONNE AVENUE	LOMITA	CA	90717	(213) 326-8234
CONGREGATION LUBAVITCH 3981 ATLANTIC AVENUE	LONG BEACH	CA	91807	(213) 434-6338
CHABAD HOUSE 741 GAYLEY AVENUE	LOS ANGELES	CA	90024	(213) 208-7511
CHABAD HOUSE, MID-CITY 420 NORTH FAIRFAX	LOS ANGELES	CA	90036	(213) 655-4739
CHABAD HOUSE, WEST COAST HEADQUARTERS 741 GAYLEY AVENUE	LOS ANGELES	CA	90024	(213) 272-7113
CONGREGATION LUBAVITCH 9017 W. PICO BLVD	LOS ANGELES	CA	90035	(213) 208-7511
LUBAVITCH 101 N. EDINBURG AVENUE	LOS ANGELES	CA	90048	(213) 931-0913
OHR ELCHONON 7215 WARING AVENUE	LOS ANGELES	CA	90046	(213) 937-3763
RUSSIAN CENTER 221 S. LA BREA AVENUE	LOS ANGELES	CA	90036	(213) 938-1837
TREATMENT CENTER 1952 ROBERTSON BLVD	LOS ANGELES	CA	90034	(213) 204-3196
CHABAD HOUSE 425 AVENIDA ORTEGA	PALM SPRINGS	CA	92262	(619) 325-0774
CHABAD HOUSE 2850 COWPER #15	PALO ALTO	CA	94306	(415) 322-4700
CHABAD HOUSE 6115 MONTEZUMA ROAD	SAN DIEGO	CA	92115	(619) 265-7700
CHABAD HOUSE 2415 VAN NESS AVENUE, #203	SAN FRANCISCO	CA	94109	(415) 928-0165
CHABAD HOUSE 4141 STATE STREET #F1	SANTA BARBARA	CA	93110	(805) 683-1544
CHABAD BAY AREA 1428 17TH STREET	SANTA MONICA	CA	90401	(213) 829-5620
CHABAD HOUSE 1247 LINCOLN BLVD	SANTA MONICA	CA	90403	(213) 395-4470
CHABAD OF LAGUNA 21452 WESLEY	SO. LAGUNA	CA		(714) 786-5000
BLAUNER YOUTH CENTER 18211 BURBANK BLVD	TARZANA	CA	92356	(818) 881-2352
CHABAD HOUSE 24248 CRENSHAW	TORRANCE	CA	90506	(805) 326-8234
CHABAD HOUSE 13079 CHANDLER BOULEVARD	VAN NUYS	CA	91401	(818) 989-9539
CHABAD OF CONEJO 741 LAKEFIELD ROAD #E	WESTLAKE VILLAGE	CA	91361	(805) 497-9635
HEBREW ACADEMY 14401 WILLOW LANE	WESTMINSTER	CA	92683	(714) 895-2015
CHABAD HOUSE 85 FOREST STREET	DENVER	CO	80220	(303) 329-0211
HEBREW ACADEMY 111 ALDEN AVENUE	NEW HAVEN	CT	06511	(203) 387-8468
LUBAVITCH YOUTH ORGANIZATION 152 GOFFE TERRACE	NEW HAVEN	CT	06511	(203) 865-3649
LUBAVITCH 17 MORTON	NEW LONDON	CT	06320	(203) 444-1005
LUBAVITCH YESHIVAH 261 DERBY AVENUE	ORANGE	CT	06477	(203) 795-5261
CHABAD HOUSE 798 FARMINGTON AVENUE	WEST HARTFORD	CT	06119	(203) 233-5912
CHABAD HOUSE 1540 ALBENGA AVENUE	CORAL GABLES	FL	33146	(305) 661-7642
CONGREGATION LEVI YITZCHOK 1504 WILEY	HOLLYWOOD	FL	33020	(305) 923-1707
CHABAD SYNAGOGUE 13830 S.W. 73RD STREET	MIAMI	FL	33183	
CHABAD HOUSE 1401 ALTON ROAD	MIAMI BEACH	FL	33139	(305) 672-8947
MERKOS 1140 ALTON ROAD	MIAMI BEACH	FL	33139	(305) 673-5664
CHABAD OF NORTH DADE 2590 N.E. 202ND STREET	NORTH MIAMI BEACH	FL	33180	(305) 932-7770
CHABAD OF INVERRARY 7770 NORTHWEST 44TH STREET	SUNRISE	FL	33321	(305) 748-1777
CHABAD HOUSE 3645 COLLEGE PARK CIRCLE	TAMPA	FL	33612	(813) 971-6768
CHABAD HOUSE 13104 N. 50TH STREET	TAMPA	FL	33617	(813) 985-7926
CHABAD HOUSE CTR217, UC BOX 2463, UNIVERSITY OF SOUTH FLORIDA	TAMPA	FL	33617	(813) 971-6768
CHABAD HOUSE 2923 UNIVERSITY AVENUE	DES MOINES	IA	50311	(515) 277-0770
CHABAD HOUSE 2014 ORRINGTON	EVANSTON	IL	60201	(312) 869-8060
NORTH SUBURBAN CHABAD 1871 SHEAHAN COURT	HIGHLAND PARK	IL	60035	(312) 433-1567
CHABAD OF SKOKIE 3912 CHURCH	SKOKIE	IL	60076	(312) 679-1649
CHABAD LUBAVITCH 816 WEST 64TH STREET	INDIANAPOLIS	IN	46260	(317) 251-5573
CHABAD HOUSE 7037 FRERET STREET	NEW ORLEANS	LA	70118	(504) 866-5164
CHABAD HOUSE 30 N. HADLEY ROAD	AMHERST	MA	01002	(413) 253-9040
CHABAD HOUSE 491 COMMONWEALTH AVENUE	BOSTON	MA	02215	(617) 424-1190
LUBAVITCH YOUTH ORGANIZATION 42 KIRKWOOD ROAD	BRIGHTON	MA	02135	(617) 787-2667
LUBAVITCH YESHIVA 9 PRESCOTT STREET	BROOKLINE	MA	02146	(617) 731-5330
CHABAD HOUSE 74 JOSEPH ROAD	FRAMINGHAM	MA	01701	(617) 877-8888
LUBAVITCH YOUTH ORGANIZATION 74 JOSEPH ROAD	FRAMINGHAM	MA	01761	(617) 877-5313
CHABAD HOUSE 1148 CONVERSE STREET	LONG MEADOW	MA	01106	(413) 253-9040
SHALOM HOUSE 68 SMITH ROAD	MILTON	MA	02186	(617) 333-0477
CONGREGATION LUBAVITCH 100 WOODCLIFF	SOUTH BROOKLINE	MA	02167	(617) 469-9007
LUBAVITCH 15 ELWOOD DRIVE	SPRINGFIELD	MA	01108	(413) 567-8665
LUBAVITCH YOUTH ORGANIZATION 15 ELWOOD DRIVE	SPRINGFIELD	MA	01108	(413) 737-7998
LUBAVITCH YOUTH ORGANIZATION 24 CRESWELL	WORCESTER	MA	01602	(617) 752-5791
CHABAD LUBAVITCH 532 INKSTER BOULEVARD	WINNIPEG	MB	R2W 0K9	(204) 586-1867
LUBAVITCH 6711 WELLS PARKWAY	HYATTSVILLE	MD	20872	(301) 422-6200
CHABAD HOUSE 311 WEST MONTGOMERY AVENYE	ROCKVILLE	MD	20850	(301) 340-6858
CHABAD HOUSE 715 HILL STREET	ANN ARBOR	MI	48104	(313) 995-3276
CHABAD HOUSE 32276 TAREYTON	FARMINGTON HILLS	MI	48018	(313) 626-3194
CHABAD HOUSE 1549 MICHIGAN N.E.	GRAND RAPIDS	MI	49503	(616) 458-6575
CHABAD LUBAVITCH 14000 WEST NINE MILE ROAD	OAK PARK	MI	48237	(313) 548-2666
LUBAVITCH 7189 COTTONWOOD KNOLL	WEST BLOOMFIELD	MI	48033	
MERKOS L'INYONEI CHINUCH LUBAVITCH 15 MONTCALM CT.	ST. PAUL	MN	55116	(612) 698-3858
CHABAD HOUSE 8901 HOLMES STREET	KANSAS CITY	MO	64131	(816) 333-7117
CHABAD LUBAVITCH 921 GAY AVENUE	ST. LOUIS	MO	63130	(314) 863-3516
LUBAVITCH OF NORTH CAROLINA 6500 NEWHALL ROAD	CHARLOTTE	NC	28226	(704) 366-3984
CHABAD HOUSE 2801 PACIFIC AVENUE	ATLANTIC CITY	NJ	08410	(609) 345-6102
LIBAVITCH 410 NORTH 8TH AVENUE	EDISON	NJ	08817	(201) 572-3523
FRIENDS OF LUBAVITCH 409 GRAND AVENUE, #7	ENGLEWOOD	NJ	07631	(201) 568-9423
LUBAVITCH 12 BEVERLY ROAD	LIVINGSTON	NJ	07039	(201) 994-0262
LUBAVITCH 12 WELLESLEY ROAD	MAPLEWOOD	NJ	07040	(201) 762-6628
LUBAVITCH 16 IRONDALE ROAD	MORRIS PLAINS	NJ	07950	(201) 538-6321
LUBAVITCH STUDENTS ORGANIZATION 226 SUSSEX AVENUE	MORRISTOWN	NJ	07960	(201) 540-0877
RABBINICAL COLLEGE 226 SUSSEX AVENUE	MORRISTOWN	NJ	07960	(201) 267-9404
CHABAD HOUSE 8 SICARD STREET	NEW BRUNSWICK	NJ	08901	(201) 828-7374
LUBAVITCH 6 MANOR ROAD	PATERSON	NJ	07514	(201) 271-2250
LUBAVITCH 2202 SUNSET AVENUE	WANAMASSA	NJ	07712	(201) 774-5921
CHABAD HOUSE 1801 SIGMI CHI	ALBUQUERQUE	NM	87106	(505) 242-2231
CHABAD HOUSE 122 SOUTH MAIN AVENUE	ALBANY	NY	12208	(518) 465-5638
LUBAVITCH WORLD HDQ. MERKOS L'INYANEL CHINUCH MACHNE ISRAEL 770 EASTERN PARKWAY	BROOKLYN	NY	11213	(718) 493-9250
LUBAVITCH WORLD HEADQUARTERS 770 EASTERN PARKWAY	BROOKLYN	NY	11213	(718) 774-4000
SHABBOS CANDLE CAMPAIGN 603 LEFFERTS AVENUE	BROOKLYN	NY	11203	(718) 774-2060
CHABAD HOUSE 3292 MAIN STREET	BUFFALO	NY	14214	(716) 833-8334
CHABAD HOUSE 74 HAUPPAUGUE ROAD	COMMACK	NY	11725	(516) 462-6640
CHABAD HOUSE 2501 NORTH FOREST ROAD	GETZVILLE	NY	14068	(716) 688-1642
CHABAD HOUSE 4 PHYLISS TERRACE	MONSEY	NY	10952	(914) 352-7642
EDUCATION CENTER 59E HERITAGE ROAD	NEW CITY	NY	10956	(914) 638-4458
CHABAD HOUSE 550 WEST 110TH STREET	NEW YORK	NY	10025	(212) 866-3401
CHABAD LUBAVITCH 36 LATTIMORE ROAD	ROCHESTER	NY	14620	(716) 244-4324
CHABAD HOUSE 211 LOCKWOOD ROAD	SYRACUSE	NY	13214	(315) 446-8340
CHABAD HOUSE 2306 15TH STREET	TROY	NY	12180	(518) 274-5572
LUBAVITCH 43 THOMPSON STREET	WELLINGTON 1	NZ		
CHABAD HOUSE 1636 SUMMIT ROAD	CINCINNATI	OH	45237	(513) 821-5100
LUBAVITCH 1542 BEAVERTON	CINCINNATI	OH	45237	(513) 761-5200
CHABAD HOUSE 2004 SOUTH GREEN ROAD	CLEVELAND	OH	44121	(216) 382-5050
CHABAD HOUSE 2057 CORNELL ROAD	CLEVELAND	OH	44106	(216) 721-5050
HOUSE OF TRADITION 57 EAST 14TH AVENUE	COLUMBUS	OH	43201	(614) 294-3296
CHABAD HOUSE 44 EDINBURGH DRIVE	DOWNSVIEW	ON	M3N 1B4	(416) 633-8020
CHABAD LUBAVITCH 87 WESTWOOD AVENUE	HAMILTON	ON	L8S 2B1	(416) 529-7458
DR. Y. BLOCK 1059 WILLIAMS STREET	LONDON	ON		(519) 439-4828
LUBAVITCH 312 ROBIN LANE	OTTAWA	ON	K1Z 7J8	(613) 820-9484
RABBI M. BERGER 690 MELBOURNE STREET	OTTAWA	ON	K2A 1XA	(613) 722-5029
CHABAD HOUSE, RABBI Y. HECHT 1059 DOUGALL	WINDSOR	ON		(519) 258-1225
LUBAVITCH 102 THIRD AVENUE	KINGSTON	PA	18704	(717) 287-6336
LUBAVITCH CENTER 7622 CASTOR AVENUE	PHILADELPHIA	PA	19152	(215) 725-2030
CHABAD HOUSE 315 SOUTH BELLFIELD, ROOM 416	PITTSBURGH	PA	15213	(412) 681-6473
LUBAVITCH YOUTH ORGANIZATION 5819 DOUGLAS STREET	PITTSBURGH	PA	15213	(412) 521-5252
YESHIVA ACHEL TMIMIM 5717 HOBART	PITTSBURGH	PA	15217	(412) 681-2446
CHABAD HOUSE 3429 PEEL STREET	MONTREAL	QU	H3A 1W7	(514) 842-6616
CHABAD LUBAVITCH 48 SAVOY STREET	PROVIDENCE	RI	02906	(401) 273-7238
CONGREGATION SHERITH ISRAEL 3730 WHITLAND AVENUE	NASHVILLE	TN	37205	(615) 385-3730
CHABAD HOUSE 2101 NEUCES AVENUE	AUSTIN	TX	78705	(512) 472-3900
FRIENDS OF LUBAVITCH 3924 PERSIMMON DRIVE	FAIRFAX	VA	22031	(703) 323-0233
CHABAD LUBAVITCH 5311 WEST FRANKLIN STREET	RICHMOND	VA	23226	(804) 288-0588
LUBAVITCH CENTER 212 GASKINS ROAD	RICHMOND	VA	23229	(804) 740-2000
CHABAD LUBAVITCH 609 NICKLAUS	VIRGINIA BEACH	VA	23462	(804) 467-4980
CHABAD HOUSE 4541 19TH AVENUE NORTHEAST	SEATTLE	WA	98105	(206) 527-1411
CHABAD HOUSE 613 HOWARD PLACE	MADISON	WI	53703	(608) 251-6022
TZEIRE AGUDATH JABAD CORRIENTES 2470 20 '1'	BUENOS AIRES	AG	1046	()47-1593
JABAD LUBAVITCH D. P. GARAT 437 (3200)	CONCORDIA, E. RIOS	AG		(045) 215-995
JABAD LUBAVITCH LAMADRID 752 (4000)	TUCUMAN	AG		(081) 225-429
LUBAVITCH YOUTH ORGANIZATION 49 PLANTIJN EN MORETUSLES 2026	ANTWERP	BE	B2000	
LUBAVITCH 1A AVENUE REINE MARIE HENRIETTE 1090	BRUSSELS	BE		(345) 052-2
BEIT CHABAD R. AMERICO DIAMANTINO, 78, BELLO HORIZONTE	MINAS GERAIS	BZ		(221) 996-6
CHABAD RUA BEUNOS AIRES 144, CURITIBA PORTO ALEGRE	PARANA	BZ		(232) 252-3
BEIT CHABAD R. PROF JULIO FERRIERA, DE MELO 756/401, RECIFE	PERNAMBUICO	BZ		(325) 370-3
YESHIVA COLEGIAL SCP 372	PETROPOLIS, R.J.	BZ		(345) 052-2
BEIT CHABAD F. FELIPE CAMARAO 72 # APT 22, PORTO ALEGRE	RIO GRANDE DO SUL	BZ		(255) 966-
RABINO R. BLUMENFELD R. SANTA CLARA	RIO DE JANEIRO	BZ	ZC07	(236) 024-9
BEIT CHABAD RUA CHABAD 60	SAO PAULO	BZ	01417	(280) 181-9
LUBAVITCH CALLE 92 #9A-20 (405)	BOGOTA	CM		(257) 043-6
LUBAVITCH 34 RUE DE GOULET, 93300	AUBERVILLES	FR		

YESHIVA TOMCHEI TMIMIM LUBAVITCH 2 AVENUE DU PETIT CHATEAU ....BRUNOY FR 92800 (046) 314-6
LUBAVITCH 727 RUE JULIETTE SAVAR, 94000 ....CRETEIL FR
CHABAD 3 IMPASSE CAZENOVE ....LYON, ARENOVE FR 69003 (890) 832-
BETH LOBAVITCH 8 RUE LAMARTINE ....PARIS FR 75009 (526) 876-0
BUREAU EUROPEEN DE LOUBAVITCH 8 RUE MESLAY....PARIS FR 75003
HADAR HATORA 5 RUE DUC ....PARIS FR 75018
BETH RIVKAH ECOLE DE FILLES 49 RUE RAYMOND POINCARE ....YERRES FR (948) 460-1
BETH RIVKAH SEMINARY FILLES 49 RUE RAYMOND POINCARE ....YERRES FR (948) 178-5
LUBAVITCH 101 OPERAWEG ....AMERSFOOT HD (033) 262-04
LUBAVITCH VLASCHAARDE 59 ....AMSTELVEEN HD (020) 441-402
LUBAVITCH GREVELINGEN STR. 20 ....AMSTERDAM HD (020) 794-455
CHABAD HOUSE VIA DAGNINI 24 ....BOLOGNA IT Y0129 (051) 340-936
LUBAVITCH VIA G. UHERTI 41 ....MILAN IT 20129 (022) 720-01
CHABAD VIA GENOVA 26, LAISPOLI ....ROMA IT 00055 (992) 644-7
LUBAVITCH VIA LORENZO IL MAGNIFICO 23 ....ROME IT (424) 696-2
CHABAD 10 WASHINGTON AVENUE ....CASABLANCA MC (222) 146-2
CHABAD 174 BD. ZIRAOUI ....CASABLANCA MC (221) 204-2
CHABAD 27 RUE VERLES HANUS ....CASABLANCA MC (279) 218-
RABBI C. SUED MOLIERE 311 P.B. ....MX 5 D.F (424) 696-2
RABBI S. SCHABBES MOLIERE 88-301 ....MX 507 (424) 696-2
LUBAVITCH FOUNDATION 31 ARTHURS ROAD, SEAPOINT, 8001 ....CAPETOWN SA (443) 740-
LUBAVITCH FOUNDATION 33 HARLEY STREET, YEOVILLE, 2198 ....JOHANNESBURG SA (648) 125-3
CHABAD OF SANDTON PO BOX 7861, GALLO MANOR 2052 ....SANDTON SA
LUBAVITCH CALLE GENERAL, SANJURJO, 22 APT, 5B ....MADRID 3 SP (441) 543-0
LUBAVITCH FOUNDATION 8 ORCHARD DRIVE ....GIFFNOCK, GLASGOW ST 7NR (041) 638-6116
LUBAVITCH PO BOX 565 ....ZURICH SW 8018
CHABAD 65 AV. TAIEB MEHIRI ....TUNIS TU (280) 900-
LUBAVITCH CENTER 10900 FONDREN ROAD ....HOUSTON TX 77096 (713) 777-2000
LUBAVITCH CENTRE, RABBI S. ARKUSH 95 WILLOWS ROAD ....BIRMINGHAM UK (021) 440-5853
LEEDS LUBAVITCH, RABBI Y, ANGYALFI 594 STONEGATE ROAD ....LEEDS UK
LUBAVITCH FOUNDATION, RABBI N. SUDAK 107-115 STAMFORD HILL ....LONDON UK (018) 000-022
LUBAVITCH HOUSE, RABBI C. FARRO
　62 SINGLETON ROAD....SALFORD, NANCHESTER UK M7OLU
CHABAD LUBAVITCH APPARTADO 5454 ....CARACAS VZ 101

MAPS

ISRAEL OFFICE OF INFORMATION 800 SECOND AVENUE ....NEW YORK NY 10017

MARKET RESEARCH

NORMARK / NORTHEAST MARKETS INC. JEWISH DIVISION
110 W. 34TH STREET....NEW YORK NY 10001 (212) 714-2935

MEALS - ON - WHEELS

KOSHER MEALS FOR THE ELDERLY 7711 MELROSE AVENUE ....LOS ANGELES CA 90036 (213) 653-8682
THE ARK 3509 W. LAWRENCE AVENUE ....CHICAGO IL 60625 (312) 478-9600
JEWISH HOME OF EASTERN PENNSYLVANIA, THE 1101 VINE STREET ....SCRANTON PA 18510 (717) 344-6177
NATIONAL COUNCIL OF JEWISH WOMEN, MONTREAL SECTION
　5775 VICTORIA....MONTREAL QU (514) 733-7589
JEWISH COMMUNITY CENTER 7300 NEWPORT AVENUE ....NORFOLK VA 23523 (804) 489-1371

MEAT & POULTRY - RETAIL

KOSHER STAR MARKET 4182 NORTH 19TH AVENUE....PHOENIX AZ (602) 265-3762
SEGAL'S KOSHER MARKET 2905 NORTH 16TH STREET ....PHOENIX AZ (602) 277-5769
FEIG'S KOSHER FOODS 5071 EAST 5TH STREET....TUCSON AZ 85711 (602) 325-2255
ENCINO KOSHER MEATS 17942 VENTURA BOULEVARD ....ENCINO CA 91316 (818) 343-7900
SAM'S KOSHER MEAT MARKET 12432 LAMPTON STREET....GARDEN GROVE CA 92640 (714) 534-5621
COMMUNITY KOSHER MEAT MARKET 2325 EAST ANAHEIM STREET ....LONG BEACH CA 90804 (213) 439-8652
L GOLDSTEIN KOSHER MEATS 3815 SANTA ROSALIA DRIVE ....LOS ANGELES CA 90008 (213) 294-8067
KASTOMSKI'S KOSHER MEAT MARKET 7667 BEVERLY BOULEVARD ....LOS ANGELES CA 90036 (213) 933-4040
BEVERLYWOOD KOSHER MEATS 9126 WEST PICO BOULEVARD ....LOS ANGELES CA 90035 (213) 274-3650
CARMEL KOSHER MEATS 8914 WEST PICO BOULEVARD ....LOS ANGELES CA 90035 (213) 278-6347
CENTURY CITY MEATS 8973 WEST PICO BOULEVARD ....LOS ANGELES CA 90035 (213) 278-1754
DOHENY KOSHER MEATS 9213 WEST PICO BOULEVARD ....LOS ANGELES CA 90035 (213) 276-7232
MES KOSHER MEATS 2627 SOUTH LA CIENEGA BOULEVARD ....LOS ANGELES CA 90034 (213) 836-0535
HAZAN 415 NORTH FAIRFAX AVENUE ....LOS ANGELES CA 90036 (213) 655-5554
H & K 8702 WEST PICO BOULEVARD ....LOS ANGELES CA 90035 (213) 652-4747
G & L KOSHER MEAT MARKET 10657 WEST PICO BOULEVARD ....LOS ANGELES CA 90064 (213) 475-3253
H & M 501 NORTH FAIRFAX AVENUE ....LOS ANGELES CA 90036 (213) 651-3034
HADAR KOSHER MEAT MARKET 440 NORTH FAIRFAX AVENUE ....LOS ANGELES CA 90036 (213) 655-0250
HAYOT & HAYOT KOSHER MEAT 7605 BEVERLY BOULEVARD ....LOS ANGELES CA 90035 (213) 939-0529
KOTLAR'S 8622 WEST PICO BOULEVARD ....LOS ANGELES CA 90035 (213) 652-5355
KUROSH-DAVID'S 8365 WEST THIRD STREET ....LOS ANGELES CA 90048 (213) 655-2265
L. KULKIN 7605 BEVERLY BOULEVARD ....LOS ANGELES CA 90048 (213) 653-6929
M & D KOSHER MEAT MARKET 8365 WEST THIRD ....LOS ANGELES CA 90048 (213) 655-2265
MARY & SAM KOSHER MEATS 445 NORTH FAIRFAX AVENUE ....LOS ANGELES CA 90036 (213) 651-2474
MAX'S KOSHER MEATS 10608 WEST PICO BOULEVARD ....LOS ANGELES CA 90064 (213) 837-4147
HAZEL FOODS KOSHER MEAT & POULTRY MARKETS
　6151 WEST PICO BOULEVARD ....LOS ANGELES CA (213) 653-8244
MEHADRIN KOSHER MEAT MARKET 7613 BEVERLY BOULEVARD ....LOS ANGELES CA 90035 (213) 934-2196
PRIME KOSHER MEAT MARKET
　7919 BEVERLY BOULEVARD, IN MERLO'S MARKET ....LOS ANGELES CA 90036 (213) 655-0057
R.K.F. 7862 SANTA MONICA BOULEVARD ....LOS ANGELES CA 90046 (213) 936-7119
REAL KOSHER MEAT MARKET 7965 BEVERLY BOULEVARD ....LOS ANGELES CA 90048 (213) 653-8355
SAM & MARTY'S 455 NORTH FAIRFAX AVENUE ....LOS ANGELES CA 90036 (213) 651-2474

SHALOM KOSHER MEATS 7605 BEVERLY BOULEVARD ....LOS ANGELES CA 90036 (213) 939-0529
SHELLY'S 345 NORTH FAIRFAX AVENUE....LOS ANGELES CA 90036 (213) 655-1835
SOL'S 1458 SOUTH ROBERTSON BOULEVARD ....LOS ANGELES CA 90035 (213) 276-0830
SOLOMON'S KOSHER MEAT MARKET
　1053 SOUTH FAIRFAX AVENUE ....LOS ANGELES CA 90019 (213) 935-7314
WILSHIRE KOSHER MEATS 5407 1/2 WILSHIRE BOULEVARD ....LOS ANGELES CA 90036 (213) 936-6283
H. DREXLER 12519 BURBANK BOULEVARD ....NORTH HOLLYWOOD CA 91607 (818) 761-6405
SUPERIOR KOSHER MEATS 12820 VICTORY BOULEVARD ....NORTH HOLLYWOOD CA 91606 (818) 671-9500
VALLEY MARKET 9561 LAUREL CANYON BOULEVARD....NORTH HOLLYWOOD CA 91607 (818) 764-0363
HENRY'S KOSHER MEAT MARKET 3256 GRAND AVENUE ....OAKLAND CA 94610 (415) 451-3885
ZION KOSHER MEATS 18236 SHERMAN WAY ....RESEDA CA 91335 (818) 881-1777
ISRAEL KOSHER MEAT MARKET 5621 GEARY BOULEVARD ....SAN FRANCISCO CA 94121 (415) 752-3064
JACOB'S KOSHER MEAT MARKET 2435 NORIEGA STREET ....SAN FRANCISCO CA 94122 (415) 564-7482
TEL AVIV KOSHER MEAT MARKET 1301 NORIEGA STREET ....SAN FRANCISCO CA 94122 (415) 661-7588
WILLOW GLEN 1185 LINCOLN AVENUE ....SAN JOSE CA 95125 (408) 297-6604
ELLIOT'S KOSHER MEATS 4609 1/2 VAN NUYS BOULEVARD ....SHERMAN OAKS CA 91403 (818) 783-7190
MURRAY'S KOSHER MEATS 14539 VENTURA BOULEVARD ....SHERMAN OAKS CA 91403 (818) 784-8722
ROZ KOSHER MEATS 12910 RIVERSIDE DRIVE ....SHERMAN OAKS CA 91403 (818) 984-1102
SHERMAN OAKS KOSHER MEATS 14054 VENTURA BOULEVARD....SHERMAN OAKS CA 91403 (818) 784-4987
VENTURA KOSHER MEATS 18357 VENTURA BOULEVARD ....TARZANA CA 91356 (818) 881-3717
G & L KOSHER MEATS 10657 WEST PICO BOULEVARD ....WESTWOOD CA 90064 (213) 475-3253
MEYER'S KOSHER MEAT MARKET 3211 EAST COLFAX AVENUE ....DENVER CO 80206 (303) 377-2729
WEST HILL GROCERY 3933 WEST COLFAX AVENUE ....DENVER CO 80204 (303) 892-1180
COPACO KOSHER MEAT DEPARTMENT COTTAGE GROVE ROAD ....BLOOMFIELD CT 06002 (203) 242-5521
BENNY LEVINE MEATS 1115 MADISON AVENUE ....BRIDGEPORT CT 06606 (203) 335-2216
RUBENSTEIN BROTHERS KOSHER MEAT MARKET
　982 MADISON AVENUE ....BRIDGEPORT CT 06606 (203) 333-0420
STATE KOSHER MARKET 1147 MADISON AVENUE ....BRIDGEPORT CT 06606 (203) 579-1699
ESTRYN'S KOSHER MEAT MARKET 300 WHALLEY AVENUE ....NEW HAVEN CT 06511 (203) 787-5348
M & J KOSHER MEAT MARKET 418 WHALLEY AVENUE ....NEW HAVEN CT 06511 (203) 777-1656
TEITELMAN KOSHER MEAT MARKET 376 WHALLEY AVENUE ....NEW HAVEN CT 06515 (203) 387-8885
SOLTZ KOSHER MEAT MARKET 300 BANK STREET ....NEW LONDON CT 06320 (203) 443-4734
BLUE RIBBON PROVISION COMPANY 5646 THIRD STREET N.E. ....WASHINGTON DC 20011 (202) 526-4940
POSIN'S KOSHER MARKET 5756 GEORGIA AVENUE N.W. ....WASHINGTON DC 20011 (202) 726-4424
ROLAND FOODS 135 R STREET S.W. ....WASHINGTON DC 20024 (202) 488-0888
SAVAL DIRECTOR 2266 25TH PLACE N.E. ....WASHINGTON DC 20001 (202) 832-9400
FOOD FAIR STORES 6500 NORTH ANDREWS AVENUE ....FORT LAUDERDALE FL (305) 371-6008
HARRISON'S KOSHER MEAT MARKET
　8330 WEST OAKLAND PARK BOULEVARD ....FORT LAUDERDALE FL (305) 741-0855
STAR OF DAVID KOSHER BUTCHER
　3570 NORTH STATE ROAD 7 ....FORT LAUDERDALE FL (305) 484-6272
TOM-TOV KOSHER BUTCHER & APPETIZER
　2610 WEST ATLANTIC AVENUE ....FORT LAUDERDALE FL (305) 741-1995
TRI KOSHER MEAT INCORPORATED
　6600 WEST ATLANTIC AVENUE ....FORT LAUDERDALE FL (305) 496-0966
KEZREH, INC. 1025 E. HALLANDALE BEACH BOULEVARD ....HALLANDALE FL 33009 (305) 454-5776
SYON KOSHER MEATS
　17G-1 EAST HALLANDALE BEACH BOULEVARD ....HALLANDALE FL 33009 (305) 454-5659
HOLLYWOOD KOSHER MEATS 2009 HARRISON ....HOLLYWOOD FL 33020 (305) 922-1697
WEST HOLLYWOOD KOSHER MEATS 142 SOUTH STATE ROAD 7 ....HOLLYWOOD FL 33020 (305) 962-5018
SUPERIOR KOSHER MEATS 677 NORTH ORLANDO ....MAITLAND FL 32751 (305) 645-1704
MEYERS ROYAL KOSHER MEAT MARKET 5987 SW 8TH STREET ....MIAMI FL 33144 (305) 264-0691
RUBINDALE KOSHER MEAT & POULTRY 10021 S.W. 72ND STREET ....MIAMI FL 33136 (305) 279-1568
ZION CORPORATION 1717 N.W. 7TH AVENUE ....MIAMI FL 33136 (305) 324-1855
ADAM'S STRICTLY KOSHER MEAT & POULTRY
　1403 1/2 WASHINGTON AVENUE ....MIAMI BEACH FL 33139 (305) 532-0103
COMMUNITY KOSHER 525 41ST STREET, ARTHUR GODFREY ROAD ....MIAMI BEACH FL 33140 (305) 531-7691
FREDDY'S MEAT MARKET 1419 WASHINGTON AVENUE ....MIAMI BEACH FL 33139 (305) 531-1267
GOLDSTEIN & SONS PRIME MEAT 7443 COLLINS AVENUE ....MIAMI BEACH FL 33141 (305) 865-4981
KARL & ALLEN QUALITY MEATS 1321 WASHINGTON AVENUE ....MIAMI BEACH FL 33139 (305) 531-4800
M & L FOOD CENTER 7446 COLLINS AVENUE ....MIAMI BEACH FL 33141 (305) 865-2648
MENDELSON & SONS KOSHER MEAT MARKET
　953 WASHINGTON AVENUE ....MIAMI BEACH FL 33139 (305) 532-2426
NORMANDY KOSHER MEAT MARKET 1112 71ST STREET ....MIAMI BEACH FL 33141 (305) 866-5223
S & W KOSHER MEATS 1255 WASHINGTON AVENUE ....MIAMI BEACH FL 33139 (305) 534-8863
SURF KOSHER MEAT & POULTRY 7432 COLLINS AVENUE ....MIAMI BEACH FL 33141 (305) 868-0559
NORMANDY KOSHER MEAT MARKET 1112 NORMANDY DRIVE... NORMANDY ISLAND FL 33141 (305) 866-5223
KLEINMAN'S STRICTLY KOSHER MARKET
　18315 N.E. 19TH AVENUE ....NORTH MIAMI BEACH FL 33162 (305) 932-5611
MENDELSON & SONS KOSHER MEAT MARKET
　1354 N.E. 163RD STREET ....NORTH MIAMI BEACH FL 33162 (305) 945-6451
NEW DEAL KOSHER MEAT MARKET & POULTRY
　1362 N.E. 163RD STREET ....NORTH MIAMI BEACH FL 33162 (305) 945-2512
SOUTH FLORIDA KOSHER MEATS
　1320-24 NE 163RD STREET ....NORTH MIAMI BEACH FL 33162 (305) 949-6068
ARTHUR'S KOSHER MEAT MARKET 2166 BRIARCLIFFE ROAD N.E. ....ATLANTA GA 30329 (404) 634-6881
ARGYLE KOSHER MEAT MARKET 1009 WEST ARGYLE ....CHICAGO IL (312) 561-4550
COHEN & HOROWITZ KOSHER MEATS & POULTRY
　3341 NORTH BROADWAY ....CHICAGO IL (312) 528-6565
DEVON KOSHER MEAT MARKET 2255 WEST DEVON ....CHICAGO IL (312) 274-6198
EBNER'S KOSHER MEAT AND POULTRY MARKET 2649 W. DEVON ....CHICAGO IL (312) 764-1446
FINE'S KOSHER MEAT MARKETS 3310 NORTH BROADWAY ....CHICAGO IL (312) 248-5599
HUNGARIAN KOSHER DELI & SAUSAGE COMPANY
　2613 WEST DEVON AVENUE ....CHICAGO IL 60636 (312) 973-5991
J & N KOSHER MEAT MARKET 1009 WEST ARGYLE ....CHICAGO IL (312) 274-2220
JACOB MILLER & SONS 2727 WEST DEVON AVENUE ....CHICAGO IL 60636 (312) 761-4200
KOSHER KARRY OUT 2828 WEST DEVON AVENUE ....CHICAGO IL 60659 (312) 973-4355
KOSHER ZION 5529 NORTH KEDZIE AVENUE ....CHICAGO IL 60625 (312) 463-3351
LIPMAN KOSHER MEATS 2255 WEST DEVON ....CHICAGO IL (312) 338-6120
MILLER JACOB & SONS MEAT MARKET & POULTRY 2727 WEST DEVON ....CHICAGO IL (312) 761-4200
RAPOPORT KOSHER MEAT MARKET 3920 WEST LAWRENCE ....CHICAGO IL (312) 463-2434

ROMANIAN KOSHER SAUSAGE 7200 NORTH CLARK	CHICAGO	**IL**	60659	(312) 761-4141
ROSENBLUM'S MEATS 2906 WEST DEVON AVENUE	CHICAGO	**IL**	60636	(312) 262-1700
SAVITZKY & MILLSTEIN KOSHER MEAT MARKET 2604 WEST DEVON	CHICAGO	**IL**		(312) 274-0430
TOUHY KOSHER MARKET 2811 WEST TOUHY	CHICAGO	**IL**		(312) 274-2132
REISWERG'S KOSHER MEAT MARKET 6334 GUILFORD AVENUE	INDIANAPOLIS	**IN**	46220	(317) 257-0422
KOSHER FOODS 2307 TAYLORSVILLE ROAD	LOUISVILLE	**KY**	40205	(502) 452-6519
STAN'S KOSHER MEAT MARKET 2423 BARDSTOWN ROAD	LOUISVILLE	**KY**	40205	(502) 458-3679
RALPH'S KOSHER MEAT & DELICATESSEN 4518 FRERET STREET	NEW ORLEANS	**LA**	70115	(504) 891-8476
BRIGHTON KOSHER MEAT MARKET 1620 COMMONWEALTH AVENUE	BRIGHTON	**MA**	02135	(617) 277-0786
BROCKTON 217 BELMONT STREET	BROCKTON	**MA**	02401	(617) 588-6170
SAMS'S 31 PLEASANT	BROCKTON	**MA**	02401	(617) 583-3748
AL'S KOSHER MEAT 415 HARVARD STREET	BROOKLINE	**MA**	02146	(617) 277-0780
ALTER BROTHERS 1620 COMMONWEALTH	BROOKLINE	**MA**		(617) 566-9010
BEACON KOSHER 1671 BEACON STREET	BROOKLINE	**MA**	02146	(617) 277-6551
NATHAN'S 400 HARVARD STREET	BROOKLINE	**MA**	02146	(617) 566-7888
PARKWAY 1004 W. ROXBURY PARKWAY	BROOKLINE	**MA**	02146	(617) 469-9100
SHAFRAN'S 423 HARVARD STREET	BROOKLINE	**MA**	02146	(617) 566-9622
THE BUTCHERIE 428 HARVARD STREET	BROOKLINE	**MA**	02146	(617) 731-9888
WARD-BEACON 1671 BEACON STREET	BROOKLINE	**MA**	02146	(617) 277-3502
SOLOMON & TUTIN 827 WASHINGTON STREET	CANTON	**MA**		(617) 838-3530
TRI KOSHER MEATS 110 WASHINGTON STREET	CANTON	**MA**		(617) 838-3530
ARLINGTON 139 ARLINGTON STREET	CHELSEA	**MA**	02150	(617) 884-9538
LARRY LEVINE'S KOSHER MARKET 35 CENTRAL AVENUE	CHELSEA	**MA**	02150	(617) 884-1406
SEA-LECT FOODS 5 CHARLES STREET, PO BOX 86	CHELSEA	**MA**	02150	(617) 884-7222
DELI-TIZER 147 COCHITUATE ROAD	FRAMINGHAM	**MA**	01701	(617) 875-3048
HURWITZ KOSHER MEAT MARKET 326 CONCORD STREET, ROUTE 126	FRAMINGHAM	**MA**	01701	(617) 875-0481
BENDELL'S 6 WILLOW STREET	MALDEN	**MA**	02148	(617) 324-0780
AMERICAN KOSHER 1188 BLUE HILL AVENUE	MATTAPAN	**MA**	02126	(617) 296-5605
DELI-TIZER 1657 BEACON STREET	NEWTON	**MA**	02146	(617) 566-5933
DELI-TIZER 1134 BEACON STREET	NEWTON	**MA**	02158	(617) 527-7826
FOUR CORNERS 52 COMMONWEALTH	NEWTON	**MA**	02158	(617) 527-3913
GORDON & ALPERIN 552 COMMONWEALTH	NEWTON	**MA**	02158	(617) 332-4170
SOLOMON & TUTIN'S 827 WASHINGTON STREET	NEWTON	**MA**	02158	(617) 332-7577
STAR KOSHER MEATS 1138 BEACON STREET	NEWTON	**MA**	02158	(617) 961-1177
MYER'S 412 CENTER STREET	RANDOLPH	**MA**		(617) 986-6880
RANDOLPH 41 NORTH MAIN STREET	RANDOLPH	**MA**	02368	(617) 961-2931
J. KOOR MEAT MARKET 103 SHIRLEY AVENUE	REVERE	**MA**	02151	(617) 284-9766
S & M KOSHER MEAT MARKET 168 SHIRLEY AVENUE	REVERE	**MA**	02151	(617) 289-2063
SAM'S 76 SHIRLEY AVENUE	REVERE	**MA**	02151	(617) 284-1397
B. COHEN KOSHER MARKET 413 CHANDLER STREET	WORCESTER	**MA**	01602	(617) 752-2047
ACME PRODUCE 525 JARVIS	WINNIPEG	**MB**		(204) 586-4709
L. OMNITSKY & SONS 1428 MAIN STREET	WINNIPEG	**MB**		(204) 582-4494
ZIPURSKY'S KOSHER MEAT MARKET 1836 GRANT AVENUE	WINNIPEG	**MB**		(204) 489-9596
AYRDALE LIBERTY KOSHER MEAT MARKET 8122 LIBERTY ROAD	BALTIMORE	**MD**	21207	(301) 922-2030
CAPLAN BROTHERS KOSHER MEAT MARKET 6970 REISTERTOWN	BALTIMORE	**MD**	21207	(301) 358-5868
POSNER & SONS 6719 REISTERSTOWN	BALTIMORE	**MD**	21215	(301) 764-1991
WASSERMAN & LEMBERGER KOSHER MARKET 610 REISTERSTOWN	BALTIMORE	**MD**	21215	(301) 486-4191
WEINTRAUB'S KOSHER MEAT MARKET 607 REISTERSTOWN	BALTIMORE	**MD**	21208	(301) 486-2726
B. SUROSKY & SONS 106 REISTERSTOWN ROAD	PIKESVILLE	**MD**		(301) 653-2000
PIKESVILLE KOSHER MEAT & FISH MARKET 1013 REISTERSTOWN ROAD	PIKESVILLE	**MD**		(301) 486-5220
WASSERMAN & LEMBERGER 610 REISTERSTOWN ROAD	PIKESVILLE	**MD**		(301) 486-4191
SHAPIRO'S SUPER MARKETS 8515 LIBERTY ROAD	RANDALLSTOWN	**MD**	21133	(301) 922-1600
KATZ KOSHER SUPERMARKET 4860 BOWLING BROOK PARKWAY	ROCKVILLE	**MD**		(301) 468-0400
SHALOM STRICTLY KOSHER MEATS 2307 UNIVERSITY BOULEVARD WEST	WHEATON	**MD**	20902	(301) 946-6500
SHAUL'S KOSHER MEAT MARKET 11238 GEORGIA AVENUE	WHEATON	**MD**		(301) 949-8477
MORRIS KOSHER MEAT MARKET 7134 WEST SEVEN MILE ROAD	HAZEL PARK	**MI**	48221	(313) 545-7600
FRANKLIN KOSHER MEAT MARKET 32930 MIDDLEBELT RD	FARMINGTON	**MI**		(313) 855-1020
CARL'S KOSHER MEAT MARKET 26020 GREENFIELD RD	OAK PARK	**MI**	48237	(313) 968-7450
DEXTER-DAVISON KOSHER MEAT MARKET 24760 COOLIDGE RD	OAK PARK	**MI**	48237	(313) 548-6800
LOUIS COHEN & SON 24721 COOLIDGE	OAK PARK	**MI**	48237	(313) 543-8860
NORTHGATE KOSHER MEAT & POULTRY 25254 GREENFIELD	OAK PARK	**MI**	48237	(313) 548-4887
SINGER'S MEAT MARKET 13721 WEST SEVEN MILE ROAD	OAK PARK	**MI**	48237	(313) 547-8111
STRICT KOSHER MEAT CENTER 13831 WEST 9 MILE RD	OAK PARK	**MI**	48237	(313) 543-7092
SUPERIOR KOSHER MEAT MARKET 23057 COOLIDGE	OAK PARK	**MI**	48237	(313) 547-3900
DEXTER-DAVIDSON KOSHER MEAT MARKET 19835 WEST 12 MILE ROAD	SOUTHFIELD	**MI**	48076	(313) 557-7677
HARVARD ROW KOSHER MEAT MARKET 21780 WEST 11 MILE RD	SOUTHFIELD	**MI**	48076	(313) 356-5110
DUBEN & ADLER FARMER JACK MARKET 6565 ORCHARD LAKE RD	W. BLOOMFIELD	**MI**		(313) 851-4175
FEINBERG DISTRIBUTING 2200 SUMMER AVENUE	MINNEAPOLIS	**MN**	55413	(612) 623-1300
L. FIDELMAN KOSHER MEAT MARKET 540 NORTH WINNETKA AVENUE	MINNEAPOLIS	**MN**	55427	(612) 544-5215
MILT'S MARKET 4000 MINNETONKA BOULEVARD	MINNEAPOLIS	**MN**	55417	(612) 926-5611
RUBIN'S KOSHER MEAT MARKET 934 SELBY AVENUE	ST. PAUL	**MN**	55104	(612) 690-5837
TEL-AVIV KOSHER MEATS 2056 MARSHALL AVENUE	ST. PAUL	**MN**	55104	(612) 690-4367
EPSTEIN KOSHER FOODS 403 WEST 79TH STREET	KANSAS CITY	**MO**	64114	(816) 361-0200
KELLER FOOD COMPANY 2917 BROADWAY	KANSAS CITY	**MO**	64108	(816) 921-3500
KOSHER CONNECTION INCORPORATION 5333 W. 94 TERRACE	KANSAS CITY	**MO**		(816) 383-9533
ARKY'S KOSHER MEAT MARKET 965 MIDLAND BOULEVARD	ST. LOUIS	**MO**	63130	(314) 721-0062
DIAMANT'S KOSHER MEAT MARKET 618 NORTH AND SOUTH BOULEVARD	ST. LOUIS	**MO**	63130	(314) 721-9624
GALLER'S KOSHER MEAT MARKET 8502 OLIVE BOULEVARD	ST. LOUIS	**MO**	63132	(314) 993-4535
TALISMIK & SON KOSHER MEAT MARKET 6602 DELMAR STREET	ST. LOUIS	**MO**	64130	(314) 726-1177
SCHANDLER'S 50 BROADWAY	ASHEVILLE	**NC**	28802	(704) 253-5626
NEBRASKA KOSHER MEAT MARKET 4902 HAMILTON STREET	OMAHA	**NE**	68154	(402) 558-5262
K & Z KOSHER MEAT MARKET 1014 MAIN STREET	ASBURY PARK	**NJ**	07712	(201) 775-1240
REITNER & BLOCK 590 BROADWAY	BAYONNE	**NJ**	07002	(201) 437-1594
CALDWELL KOSHER MEAT MARKET 412 BLOOMFIELD AVENUE	CALDWELL	**NJ**	07006	(201) 226-0843
VILLAGE KOSHER MEATS 403 PIAGET AVENUE	CLIFTON	**NJ**	07011	(201) 772-5100
MORRIS COUNTY MEATS 303 SOUTH SALEM	DOVER	**NJ**	07801	(201) 361-1888
J & J KOSHER MEAT & POULTRY MARKET EVERGREEN ROAD	EDISON	**NJ**	08817	(201) 549-3707
ELIZABETH KOSHER MEAT & POULTRY MARKET 149 ELMORA AVENUE	ELIZABETH	**NJ**	07202	(201) 353-5448
FARKAS BROTHERS 179 ELMORA AVENUE	ELIZABETH	**NJ**	07202	(201) 352-3756
GREENSPAN'S KOSHER MEAT & LIVE POULTRY 81 WEST PALISADE AVENUE	ENGLEWOOD	**NJ**	07631	(201) 567-2868
CENTER KOSHER PRIME MEAT & POULTRY MARKET 12-76 RIVER ROAD	FAIRLAWN	**NJ**	07410	(201) 797-7928
HAROLD'S KOSHER MEATS 1911 FAIRLAWN AVENUE	FAIRLAWN	**NJ**	07410	(201) 796-0003
BLUE RIBBON SELF SERVICE KOSHER MEAT MARKET 1363 INWOOD TERRACE	FT. LEE	**NJ**	07024	(201) 224-3220
SEROFF'S KOSHER MEAT MARKET 29 MILL ROAD	IRVINGTON	**NJ**	07111	(201) 399-3741
SINGER KOSHER MEAT MARKET 59 NORTH BEAVERWYCK ROAD	LAKE HIAWATHA	**NJ**	07034	(201) 263-3220
KERN Z 299 RIDGE AVENUE	LAKEWOOD	**NJ**	08201	(201) 363-0009
COUNTY KOSHER MEAT & POULTRY 1171 WEST ST. GEORGES AVENUE, LINDEN PLAZA	LINDEN	**NJ**	07036	(201) 925-4050
LIVINGSTON KOSHER MEAT MARKET 57 EAST MT. PLEASANT AVENUE	LIVINGSTON	**NJ**	07039	(201) 992-2313
MOISHAS BUTCHER & PROVISIONS 105 WILLIAM STREET	MIDDLESEX	**NJ**	08846	(201) 560-1919
E & F KOSHER MEAT 7531 BERGEN LINE	NORTH BERGEN	**NJ**		(201) 869-1832
HAROLD'S KOSHER MEATS 67A EAST RIDGEWOOD AVENUE	PARAMUS	**NJ**	07652	(201) 262-0030
BROOK KOSHER MEAT MARKET 222 BROOK AVENUE	PASSAIC	**NJ**	07055	(201) 773-1910
MARTIN HERMAN 516 PARK AVENUE	PATERSON	**NJ**	07504	(201) 345-1311
COHEN LEMPERT M & M COMPANY 719 MOUNTAIN AVENUE	SPRINGFIELD	**NJ**	07081	(201) 379-6643
MARTY & HARRY'S SELF SERVICE KOSHER MEATS & DELI 205 MORRIS AVENUE	SPRINGFIELD	**NJ**	08736	(201) 376-4711
BERGEN COUNTY KOSHER MEATS 456 CEDAR LANE	TEANECK	**NJ**	07666	(201) 837-1422
CEDAR LANE KOSHER MEATS & POULTRY 445 CEDAR LANE	TEANECK	**NJ**	07666	(201) 836-6700
KURTS KOSHER MEAT 206 WEST ENGLEWOOD AVENUE	TEANECK	**NJ**	07666	(201) 386-8400
MAPLE KOSHER MEAT MARKET 2933 VAUXHALL ROAD	VAUXHALL	**NJ**	07088	(201) 688-2080
COUNTY KOSHER MEAT CENTER 1111 ST. GEORGES AVENUE	WEST LINDEN	**NJ**	07036	(201) 925-4050
LINDEN KOSHER MEAT & POULTRY MARKET 712 ST. GEORGES AVENUE	WEST LINDEN	**NJ**	07036	(201) 925-0088
FRANK GREENBERG KOSHER 500 PLEASANT VALLEY WAY	WEST ORANGE	**NJ**	07052	(201) 731-4426
NEW PLEASANTDALE KOSHER SELF SERVICE 470 PLEASANT VALLEY WAY	WEST ORANGE	**NJ**	07052	(201) 731-3216
SEGAL'S KOSHER MEATS	LAS VEGAS	**NV**		(702) 734-9540
HAGELU 544 DELAWARE AVENUE	ALBANY	**NY**	12209	(518) 434-3354
KAGAN & SONS 216 SOUTH PEARL STREET	ALBANY	**NY**		(518) 449-7961
SALE ON KOSHER MEATS 1044 WILLIS AVENUE	ALBERTSON	**NY**	11507	(516) 621-9615
JERRY FAYNE & MORRIS WEIDEN 3312 BROADWAY	ASTORIA	**NY**	11102	
HA-MAR KOSHER MEATS 18-48 PARK STREET	ATLANTIC BEACH	**NY**	11509	(516) 371-2900
LEDERMAN & BOYER ATLANTIC BEACH 1848 PARK STREET	ATLANTIC BEACH	**NY**	11509	(516) 371-4410
MAZUR KOSHER MEATS 909 ATLANTIC AVENUE	BALDWIN	**NY**	11510	(516) 623-8252
SAHBRA PACKING COMPANY 1757 GRAND AVENUE	BALDWIN	**NY**	11510	(516) 223-3721
MERRICK PACKING CORPORATION OF BAY TERRACE 23-06 BELL BOULEVARD	BAY TERRACE	**NY**	11360	(718) 224-7577
SUSSMAN'S MEATS 47-36 BELL BOULEVARD	BAY TERRACE	**NY**	11360	(718) 223-2300
AMERICAN FEDERATION OF RETAIL KOSHER BUTCHERS 212-01A 48TH AVENUE	BAYSIDE	**NY**		(718) 428-4638
BASS & SCHWEITZER 214-22 73RD AVENUE	BAYSIDE	**NY**	11364	(718) 464-8421
BAYSIDE KOSHER FOODS, INCORPORATED 47-36 BELL BOULEVARD	BAYSIDE	**NY**	11362	(718) 224-2300
D & W KOSHER MEATS 6142 SPRINGFIELD BOULEVARD	BAYSIDE	**NY**	11364	(718) 225-1550
JOMAN, INC. 6123 SPRINGFIELD BOULEVARD	BAYSIDE	**NY**	11364	(718) 224-8149
MERRICK PACKING CORPORATION 2366 BELL BOULEVARD	BAYSIDE	**NY**	11360	(718) 224-7577
NEW BELL KOSHER CATERERS 214-22 73RD AVENUE	BAYSIDE	**NY**	11364	(718) 464-8421
STAR OF DAVID 214-22 73RD AVENUE	BAYSIDE	**NY**	11364	(718) 464-8421
AND-HOW KOSHER MEATS 450 BEACH 129TH STREET	BELLE HARBOR	**NY**	11694	(718) 474-4638
GLEN OAKS KOSHER MEAT MARKET 248-18 UNION TPKE	BELLEROSE	**NY**		(718) 343-6410
BINGHAMTON KOSHER MARKETS 14-16 CONKLIN AVENUE	BINGHAMTON	**NY**	13903	(607) 723-5331
ABRAHAM COHEN 49 EAST KINGSBRIDGE ROAD	BRONX	**NY**	10468	(212) 933-3933
BEE & SEY KOSHER MEAT INC. 2100 WHITE PLAINS ROAD	BRONX	**NY**	10462	(212) 822-4658
BLUE RIBBON MEATS 101 DREISER LOOP	BRONX	**NY**	10475	(212) 379-4300
BOB & SAM 27 EAST KINGSBRIDGE ROAD	BRONX	**NY**	10468	(212) 367-6261
BRETTSCHNEIDER MEATS 246 WEST 231ST STREET	BRONX	**NY**	10463	(212) 548-0866
BRONX STAR KOSHER MEAT MARKET 132 EINSTEIN LOOP	BRONX	**NY**	10475	(212) 379-3283
BURKE KOSHER MEAT 700 BURKE AVENUE	BRONX	**NY**		(212) 547-2646
CARL HOCHSTEIN 153 EAST 181ST STREET	BRONX	**NY**	10453	(212) 367-7555
DAVE & JOE KOSHER MEAT 936 SHERIDAN AVENUE	BRONX	**NY**		(212) 293-2639
DAVE DAVITZ 700 BURKE AVENUE	BRONX	**NY**	10467	(212) 547-2646
DAVID GEIER 1478 WHITE PLAINS ROAD	BRONX	**NY**	10460	(212) 863-9686
FRUCHTER & STEIN 791 LYDIG AVENUE	BRONX	**NY**	10462	(212) 863-5909
G & S KOSHER 305 EAST 204TH STREET	BRONX	**NY**	10467	(212) 652-2554
GLATT SHOP OF RIVERDALE INC. 3711 RIVERDALE AVENUE	BRONX	**NY**		(212) 884-1200
GLUCKSMAN BROTHERS 73 EAST KINGSBRIDGE ROAD	BRONX	**NY**	10468	(212) 933-2620
H & G KOSHER MEATS 779 LYDIG AVENUE WEST	BRONX	**NY**	10462	(212) 829-0643
HANS BROTHERS KOSHER MEAT 2232 WHITE PLAINS ROAD	BRONX	**NY**		(212) 547-4998
HERBIE & LEO'S KOSHER MEAT 305 EAST 204TH STREET	BRONX	**NY**	10467	(212) 654-7993
HILLSIDE MEAT MARKET 3099 BAINBRIDGE AVENUE	BRONX	**NY**	10469	(212) 519-1580
HOCHSTEIN'S MEATS 3407 JEROME AVENUE	BRONX	**NY**	10467	(212) 367-7555
IRVING LUBIN 3478 JEROME AVENUE	BRONX	**NY**	10468	(212) 881-0448
JACK MUCHA 743 ALLERTON AVENUE	BRONX	**NY**	10467	(212) 231-1050
JOSEPH SCHULLMAN 758 LYDIG AVENUE	BRONX	**NY**	10462	(212) 863-3077
KAROUSEL 550 WEST 235TH STREET	BRONX	**NY**	10463	(212) 884-4000
KLEIN & FRUCTER MEATS 791 LYDIG AVENUE	BRONX	**NY**	10462	(212) 863-5909
KRAMES & ROSEHAM MEATS 27 EAST KINGSBRIDGE ROAD	BRONX	**NY**	10468	(212) 367-6261
L & L KOSHER MEATS 731 ALLERTON AVENUE	BRONX	**NY**	10467	(212) 231-3272
LEO BERMAN 206 EAST 198TH STREET	BRONX	**NY**	10468	(212) 365-6640
LUBIN'S OF KINGSBRIDGE ROAD 7 EAST KINGSBRIDGE ROAD	BRONX	**NY**	10468	(212) 584-1195
LYDIG MEAT 716 LYDIG AVENUE	BRONX	**NY**	10462	(212) 822-1681
MANNHEIMER'S MEATS 3711 RIVERDALE AVENUE	BRONX	**NY**		(212) 884-1200

MAX KOSHER MEAT MARKET 673 ALLERTON AVENUE	BRONX	**NY**		(212) 547-4197
MAYER HERBLUM 634 LYDIG AVENUE	BRONX	**NY**	10462	(212) 829-4822
MORHY & KING 2232 WHITE PLAINS ROAD	BRONX	**NY**	10467	(212) 547-4998
PELHAM KOSHER 732 LYDIG AVENUE	BRONX	**NY**	10462	(212) 838-0170
RADZIMINSKY 2037 BARTOW AVENUE	BRONX	**NY**	10475	(212) 671-0195
RIVERDALE KOSHER MEATS 246 WEST 231ST STREET	BRONX	**NY**	10463	(212) 548-2131
ROSENHEIMER & SCHWARTZ 570 WEST 235TH STREET	BRONX	**NY**	10463	(212) 548-1723
S & L MEAT MARKET INCORPORATED 116 EAST 170TH STREET	BRONX	**NY**		(212) 293-2156
SSS KOSHER 131 EINSTEIN LOOP	BRONX	**NY**	10475	(212) 379-3283
SCHULMAN BROTHERS 743 ASTOR AVENUE	BRONX	**NY**	10467	(212) 654-9688
SIEGEL KOSHER MEATS 936 SHERIDAN AVENUE	BRONX	**NY**	10451	(212) 293-2639
SKYVIEW KOSHER MEATS 550 WEST 235TH STREET	BRONX	**NY**		(212) 884-4000
SPECTOR & KAUFMAN 3421 JEROME AVENUE	BRONX	**NY**	10468	(212) 655-0571
STANLEY & HARVEY KOSHER MEAT 761 LYDIG AVENUE	BRONX	**NY**	10462	(212) 892-5355
STARR & ERBST 761 LYDIG AVENUE	BRONX	**NY**	10462	(212) 892-5355
VALUE PLUS KOSHER MEATS 5676 BROADWAY	BRONX	**NY**	10463	(212) 549-9602
4004D KOSHER MEATS 4815 13TH AVENUE	BROOKLYN	**NY**	11219	(718) 871-4455
AARON WEINSTOCK 128 LEE AVENUE	BROOKLYN	**NY**	11211	
ABE NADLER & SON KOSHER MEATS 613 BRIGHTON BEACH AVENUE	BROOKLYN	**NY**	11235	(718) 648-6900
ABRAHAM JERUSALEM 5211 13TH AVENUE	BROOKLYN	**NY**	11219	(718) 436-3134
ADLER & MERMELSTEIN KOSHER MEAT 4501-14TH AVENUE	BROOKLYN	**NY**	11219	(718) 853-6115
APEX KOSHER MEATS 1817 AVENUE M	BROOKLYN	**NY**	11212	(718) 377-9081
ARUGATH HABBOSEM MEAT MARKET 67 LEE AVENUE	BROOKLYN	**NY**	11211	(718) 782-4457
BLUE CREST KOSHER MEATS 68 AVENUE O	BROOKLYN	**NY**	11204	(718) 837-4500
BOB SCHELINS KOSHER MEATS 1944 RALPH AVENUE	BROOKLYN	**NY**	11234	(718) 251-2880
CHAIMOVITZ KOSHER BUTCHERS 1203 AVENUE J	BROOKLYN	**NY**	11230	(718) 377-8142
COHN & GRUNBAUM 314 MARCY AVENUE	BROOKLYN	**NY**	11211	(718) 387-8545
DANTER'S MEATS 4220 12TH AVENUE	BROOKLYN	**NY**	11219	(718) 854-3744
DAVE & JOE JOSHER MEATS 2807 NOSTRAND AVENUE	BROOKLYN	**NY**	11229	(718) 252-6302
DEBRECZINER BUTCHER CORP. 4922 FORT HAMILTON PKWY	BROOKLYN	**NY**	11219	(718) 851-2917
DORF'S MEATS 5021 AVENUE D	BROOKLYN	**NY**	11204	(718) 629-1325
E & S MEAT CORPORATION 1148 CONEY ISLAND AVENUE	BROOKLYN	**NY**	11230	(718) 859-0203
ECKHAUS BROTHERS KOSHER MEATS 497 NEPTUNE AVENUE	BROOKLYN	**NY**	11224	(718) 996-1991
EDELSTEIN, JACOB 5009 17TH AVENUE	BROOKLYN	**NY**	11204	(718) 851-0400
EMANUEL FRIED 5704 NEW UTRECHT AVENUE	BROOKLYN	**NY**	11219	(718) 633-0239
EMMEL PACKING COMPANY 1817 AVENUE M	BROOKLYN	**NY**	11230	(718) 253-5429
FAMOUS KOSHER 1391 CONEY ISLAND AVENUE	BROOKLYN	**NY**	11230	(718) 377-3900
FELDMAN & TAUB, INC. 511 BRIGHTON BEACH AVENUE	BROOKLYN	**NY**	11235	(718) 332-2555
FREIDMAN MEATS 950 NOSTRAND AVENUE	BROOKLYN	**NY**	11225	(718) 756-0949
G & G MEATS-BENEFELD 4411 16TH AVENUE	BROOKLYN	**NY**	11204	(718) 436-2265
GANZ KOSHER MEATS 4620 AVENUE J	BROOKLYN	**NY**	11234	(718) 377-3284
GEORGETOWN KOSHER MEATS 2157 RALPH AVENUE	BROOKLYN	**NY**	11234	(718) 531-6100
GLATT KOSHER MEAT MARKET 117 LEE AVENUE	BROOKLYN	**NY**	11211	(718) 387-8618
GLATT MART 1205 AVENUE M	BROOKLYN	**NY**	11230	(718) 338-4040
GLATT MART KOSHER MEATS 1205 AVENUE M	BROOKLYN	**NY**	11230	(718) 338-4040
GLATT PACK KOSHER MEATS 4815 13TH AVENUE	BROOKLYN	**NY**	11219	(718) 633-6346
GLENWOOD KOSHER MEATS 1665 RALPH AVENUE	BROOKLYN	**NY**	11236	(718) 251-4444
GLICK BROTHERS 448 AVENUE F	BROOKLYN	**NY**	11236	(718) 376-9556
GLICK BROTHERS 2259 86TH STREET	BROOKLYN	**NY**	11214	(718) 236-9752
GLICK BROTHERS 1875 ROCKAWAY PARKWAY	BROOKLYN	**NY**	11236	(718) 444-9570
GLICK BROTHERS 3719 NOSTRAND AVENUE	BROOKLYN	**NY**	11235	(718) 769-7705
GLICK KOSHER MEATS 520 NEPTUNE AVENUE	BROOKLYN	**NY**	11224	(718) 372-9394
GOLDMAN, SHIMON 1421 CONEY ISLAND AVENUE	BROOKLYN	**NY**		(718) 338-7661
GOTTESMAN'S MEAT MARKET 626 AVENUE U	BROOKLYN	**NY**	11223	(718) 375-3634
GREENBAUM BUTCHER SHOP 154 LEE AVENUE	BROOKLYN	**NY**	11211	(718) 624-7697
GRODKO KOSHER MEATS 8402 20TH AVENUE	BROOKLYN	**NY**	11214	
GROSSMAN'S MEAT MARKET 1919 KINGS HIGHWAY	BROOKLYN	**NY**	11229	(718) 375-3320
H A S KOSHER MEATS & POULTRY 421 BRIGHTON BEACH AVENUE	BROOKLYN	**NY**	11235	(718) 743-3900
HARRY GLAZER 8022 20TH AVENUE	BROOKLYN	**NY**	11214	(718) 236-1785
HERBST MEHADRIN MEAT MARKET 4809 18TH AVENUE	BROOKLYN	**NY**	11204	(718) 871-0444
HOLTZMAN & PARIS KOSHER MEATS 5513 13TH AVENUE	BROOKLYN	**NY**	11219	(718) 851-9270
HOUSE OF GLATT 385 KINGSTON AVENUE	BROOKLYN	**NY**		(718) 467-9411
ISRAEL GLATT KOSHER MEATS 4907 13TH AVENUE	BROOKLYN	**NY**	11219	(718) 436-2948
J & L PRIME MEATS 1840 FLATBUSH AVENUE	BROOKLYN	**NY**	11210	(718) 338-1254
JACK & JOE'S KOSHER MEATS 621 BRIGHTON BEACH AVENUE	BROOKLYN	**NY**	11235	(718) 934-0809
JACK'S KOSHER MEATS 2145 KNAPP STREET	BROOKLYN	**NY**	11235	(718) 934-4179
JERRY LEBOWITZ KOSHER MEATS 482 AVENUE P	BROOKLYN	**NY**		(718) 339-9890
JERUSALEM & SHAFRAN 5211 13TH AVENUE	BROOKLYN	**NY**	11219	(718) 436-3134
JERUSALEM GLATT 710 KINGS HIGHWAY	BROOKLYN	**NY**		(718) 375-8879
JERUSALEM KOSHER MEAT MARKET 4516 FORT HAMILTON PKWY	BROOKLYN	**NY**	11219	(718) 633-5555
JOSEPH CHARATAN & SIDNEY KAPLAN, J & S 1321 AVENUE Z	BROOKLYN	**NY**	11235	
JOSEPH COHEN & SONS 9410 CHURCH AVENUE	BROOKLYN	**NY**	11212	(718) 495-1335
KASCON KOSHER MEATS 1917 AVENUE U	BROOKLYN	**NY**	11229	(718) 934-8948
KLENETSKY MEAT MARKET 4321 18TH AVENUE	BROOKLYN	**NY**	11218	(718) 854-3307
KOSHER CITY FOODS CORP. 2104 RALPH AVENUE	BROOKLYN	**NY**	11236	
LAMM'S MEATS 76 LEE AVENUE	BROOKLYN	**NY**	11211	(718) 384-6315
LANDMARK KOSHER MEATS 2104 RALPH AVENUE	BROOKLYN	**NY**	11234	(718) 531-7250
LEHRMAN MEAT & POULTRY 1809 SCHENECTADY AVENUE	BROOKLYN	**NY**	11234	(718) 353-5031
LEO MENAKER & LEIB LAKMUS 321 CHURCH AVENUE	BROOKLYN	**NY**	11218	(718) 435-2605
LEON HERZEK & LEONARD KRIEGER 423 CHURCH AVENUE	BROOKLYN	**NY**	11218	
LEON PUPKO MEAT MARKET 6914 BAY PARKWAY	BROOKLYN	**NY**	11204	(718) 236-2795
LIEBERMAN & RUBASHKIN GLATT KOSHER 4308 14TH AVENUE	BROOKLYN	**NY**	11219	(718) 436-5511
LITTMAN'S MEATS 8017 FLATBUSH AVENUE	BROOKLYN	**NY**	11236	(718) 763-4444
LOWY'S MEHADRIN GLATT KOSHER 502 FLUSHING AVENUE	BROOKLYN	**NY**	11205	(718) 625-2121
M & M KOSHER MEAT MARKET 1724 AVENUE M	BROOKLYN	**NY**	11230	(718) 998-7744
M & M KOSHER MEAT MARKET 1624 CORTELYOU ROAD	BROOKLYN	**NY**	11226	(718) 462-9144
M & M KOSHER MEATS 557 KINGS HIGHWAY	BROOKLYN	**NY**	11223	(718) 339-6667
M&D KOSHER MEAT MARKET 4004 13TH AVENUE	BROOKLYN	**NY**	11218	(718) 871-4455
MARTIN & VICTOR KOSHER MEAT MARKET 1917 AVENUE U	BROOKLYN	**NY**	11229	(718) 743-4927
MAX BROOKER 1624 CORTELYOU ROAD	BROOKLYN	**NY**	11226	
MEAL MART 54 LEE AVENUE	BROOKLYN	**NY**	11211	(718) 854-7800
MEAL MART 206 DIVISION AVENUE	BROOKLYN	**NY**	11211	(718) 963-3450
MEHADRIN GLATT KOSHER BUTCHER 1317 55TH AVENUE	BROOKLYN	**NY**	11219	(718) 851-7342
MENDEL WEINSTOCK 54 LEE AVENUE	BROOKLYN	**NY**	11211	
MENDEL'S KOSHER MEAT MARKET 4620 AVENUE J	BROOKLYN	**NY**		(718) 252-7354
MOISHES MEAT MARKET 1706 EAST 16TH STREET	BROOKLYN	**NY**	11229	(718) 627-9438
MORRIS ZUHLER 1717 AVENUE M	BROOKLYN	**NY**	11230	
MOSES GLATT KOSHER MEAT CENTER 4602 18TH AVENUE	BROOKLYN	**NY**	11204	(718) 633-0493
MOSKOWITZ BUTCHER SHOP 4535 16TH AVENUE	BROOKLYN	**NY**	11219	(718) 853-0623
MURRAY BRAUN 771 FLATBUSH AVENUE	BROOKLYN	**NY**	11226	
MURRAY TEICHER KOSHER MEATS 549 KINGS HIGHWAY	BROOKLYN	**NY**	11223	
NADLER'S KOSHER MEAT & POULTRY 613 BRIGHTON BEACH AVENUE	BROOKLYN	**NY**	11235	(718) 648-6900
NETZACH ISRAEL SELF-SERVICE MEAT & POULTRY 4924 16TH AVENUE	BROOKLYN	**NY**	11204	(718) 851-0051
NETZACH ISRAEL MEAT & POULTRY 5010 16TH AVENUE	BROOKLYN	**NY**	11204	(718) 851-0288
NETZACH ISRAEL MEAT MARKET 4310 16TH AVENUE	BROOKLYN	**NY**	11219	(718) 435-1128
PARKWAY KOSHER MEAT CENTER 423 CHURCH AVENUE	BROOKLYN	**NY**	11218	(718) 436-4321
PASTERNAK KOSHER BUTCHER 422 DITMAS AVENUE	BROOKLYN	**NY**	11218	(718) 438-4411
PIC-N-PAY KOSHER MEATS 1907 AVENUE M	BROOKLYN	**NY**	11230	(718) 377-4050
PICK-N-SAVE KOSHER MEATS 2052 ROCKAWAY PARKWAY	BROOKLYN	**NY**	11236	(718) 251-3420
R&W GLATT KOSHER BUTCHER COMPANY 1501 CONEY ISLAND AVENUE	BROOKLYN	**NY**	11230	(718) 377-7391
R. GLICK MEATS 1875 ROCKAWAY PARKWAY	BROOKLYN	**NY**	11230	(718) 377-7391
RAN LEE KOSHER MEATS 3805 NOSTRAND AVENUE	BROOKLYN	**NY**	11236	(718) 444-9570
RETAIL KOSHER BUTCHER ASSOCIATION OF NEW YORK 1109 UTICA AVENUE	BROOKLYN	**NY**		(718) 629-1014
REUBEN GLAZER 8022 20TH AVENUE	BROOKLYN	**NY**	11214	(718) 236-1785
ROSNER KOSHER MEATS 719 AVENUE U	BROOKLYN	**NY**	11223	(718) 645-8486
SAM & HARRY'S KOSHER MEAT MARKET 557 KINGS HIGHWAY	BROOKLYN	**NY**		(718) 339-6668
SAM FOX MEATS 2233 86TH STREET	BROOKLYN	**NY**	11214	(718) 232-3234
SAM GLICK & SONS INC. 2259 86TH STREET	BROOKLYN	**NY**	11214	(718) 236-9752
SAM WEISS & BROS SURKIS 1403 FOSTER AVENUE	BROOKLYN	**NY**	11230	
SAMUEL LITTMAN 8017 FLATLANDS AVENUE	BROOKLYN	**NY**	11236	(718) 436-5511
SASSON & FARRAH INCORPORATED 710 KINGS HIGHWAY	BROOKLYN	**NY**	11223	(718) 376-7443
SATMAR BUTCHER & MEAT MARKET 82 LEE AVENUE	BROOKLYN	**NY**	11211	(718) 963-1100
SATMAR MEATS 5109 NEW UTRECHT AVENUE	BROOKLYN	**NY**	11219	(718) 435-8200
SCHNEPS KOSHER MEATS 421 BRIGHTON BEACH AVENUE	BROOKLYN	**NY**	11235	
SCHNITZER'S GLATT KOSHER MEAT 4602 18TH AVENUE	BROOKLYN	**NY**	11204	(718) 853-2801
SIMON BUTCHER SHOP 539 KINGS HIGHWAY	BROOKLYN	**NY**	11223	(718) 339-4570
SPERBER'S MEATS 4535 16TH AVENUE	BROOKLYN	**NY**	11204	(718) 854-7335
STAR OF DAVID KOSHER MEATS 2440 NOSTRAND AVENUE	BROOKLYN	**NY**	11210	(718) 252-0208
SYM'S KOSHER MEATS 1913 KINGS HIGHWAY	BROOKLYN	**NY**		(718) 375-2677
SYMS KOSHER MEATS 2318 NOSTRAND AVENUE	BROOKLYN	**NY**	11210	(718) 951-7459
TAUB'S MEATS 211 CHURCH AVENUE	BROOKLYN	**NY**	11218	(718) 438-0422
WEISS GLATT KOSHER MEATS 5520 13TH AVENUE	BROOKLYN	**NY**	11219	(718) 871-5442
WERKER'S KOSHER MEATS 2802 AVENUE U	BROOKLYN	**NY**	11229	(718) 646-5927
ZAKEN'S KOSHER MEATS 3100 OCEAN PARKWAY	BROOKLYN	**NY**	11235	
COHEN'S MEAT MARKET 1258 HERTEL	BUFFALO	**NY**	14216	(716) 875-4690
KORNMEHL KOSHER MARKET 1440 HERTEL	BUFFALO	**NY**	14216	(716) 838-2429
GOURMET GLATT KOSHER MEATS 460 CENTRAL AVENUE	CEDARHURST	**NY**	11516	(516) 569-2662
LAWRENCE KOSHER MEAT MARKET 415 CENTRAL AVENUE	CEDARHURST	**NY**	11516	(516) 569-3683
COMMACK KOSHER MEATS 132 EAST JERICHO TURNPIKE	COMMACK	**NY**	11725	(516) 543-2300
EAST MEADOW KOSHER MEAT & POULTRY 495 BELLMORE AVENUE	EAST MEADOW	**NY**	11554	(516) 481-3335
SAV-ON KOSHER MEATS 713 WHITE PLAINS ROAD	EASTCHESTER	**NY**	10583	(914) 725-0565
ABE LEVINE & SONS 104 CENTER STREET	ELLENVILLE	**NY**	12428	(914) 647-5630
KING'S MEAT-O-MART 96-23 57TH AVENUE	ELMHURST	**NY**	11373	(718) 271-8501
MORRIS OBERMAN'S MEATS BOX 437	FALLSBURG	**NY**	12733	(914) 434-4510
BERNARD BIRNBAUM 2152 MOTT AVENUE	FAR ROCKAWAY	**NY**	11691	
ERP'S MEATS 1813 MOTT AVENUE	FAR ROCKAWAY	**NY**	11691	(718) 471-3099
MENORAH POULTRY 1813 MOTT AVENUE	FAR ROCKAWAY	**NY**	11691	(718) 471-5166
NAGLER & SMALL MEATS 1905 MOTT AVENUE	FAR ROCKAWAY	**NY**	11691	(718) 327-2822
NOAM FOOD SERVICE-GLATT KOSHER BEEF & VEAL 1216 BRUNSWICK AVENUE	FAR ROCKAWAY	**NY**	11691	(718) 471-3456
SMALL KOSHER MEAT MARKET 18-49 MOTT AVENUE	FAR ROCKAWAY	**NY**	11691	(718) 327-1972
WAVECREST KOSHER MEATS 237 BEACH 20TH STREET	FAR ROCKAWAY	**NY**	11691	
BLOCH & FALK FINE FOODS 73-04 37TH AVENUE	FLUSHING	**NY**	11367	(718) 429-2379
BRACH'S GLATT SELF SERVICE MEAT MARKET 72-49 MAIN STREET	FLUSHING	**NY**	11367	(718) 544-7448
EDEN KOSHER MEAT & POULTRY 79-09 MAIN STREET	FLUSHING	**NY**	11367	(718) 381-1386
EMMETT PACKING COMPANY INC. 7226 MAIN STREET	FLUSHING	**NY**	11367	(718) 544-1950
GLICK BROTHERS 72-09 KISSENA BLVD	FLUSHING	**NY**		(718) 658-9479
HERSHKOWITZ'S MEATS 71-26 MAIN STREET	FLUSHING	**NY**	11367	(718) 263-1279
LORI KOSHER 68-24 MAIN STREET	FLUSHING	**NY**	11367	(718) 263-4696
MARIN'S KOSHER MEAT 184-08 HORACE HARDING EXPRESSWAY	FLUSHING	**NY**		(718) 358-3223
MITCHELL GARDENS KOSHER MEATS 2820 UNION STREET	FLUSHING	**NY**	11354	(718) 463-5709
PAULINE GLASS 172-07 67TH AVENUE	FLUSHING	**NY**	11365	
PRIDE KOSHER MEATS 6833 FRESH MEADOW LANE	FLUSHING	**NY**	11365	(718) 461-9844
R. GLICK MEATS 7209 KISSENA BOULEVARD	FLUSHING	**NY**	11367	(718) 658-9479
REGENCY KOSHER MEATS 77-34 VLEIGH PLACE	FLUSHING	**NY**		(718) 297-1205
RUBIN ARON 188-18 UNION TURNPIKE	FLUSHING	**NY**	11367	
TRU VALUE KOSHER MEATS 25-17 PARSONS BOULEVARD	FLUSHING	**NY**	11354	(718) 886-0444
TURNPIKE GLATT KOSHER MEATS 189-23 UNION TURNPIKE	FLUSHING	**NY**	11366	(718) 776-7727
YOUR KOSHER BUTCHERS, INC. 4185 MAIN STREET	FLUSHING	**NY**	11355	(718) 886-4464
CROFT KOSHER MEAT MARKET 65-49 99TH STREET	FOREST HILLS	**NY**		(718) 459-8480
ABE'S GLATT KOSHER MEATS, INCORPORATED 98-106 QUEENS BOULEVARD	FOREST HILLS	**NY**	11374	(718) 459-5820
CHAI KOSHER MEATS 6437 108TH STREET	FOREST HILLS	**NY**	11375	(718) 897-9619
CONTINENTAL MEATS 22-73 31 AUSTIN STREET	FOREST HILLS	**NY**	11375	(718) 721-1900
CROFT MEAT & POULTRY MARKET 65-49 99TH STREET	FOREST HILLS	**NY**		(718) 459-8480
D & A MEATS 164-08 69TH STREET	FOREST HILLS	**NY**	11365	(718) 591-0750
FINEST KOSHER MEAT MARKET 6371 108TH STREET	FOREST HILLS	**NY**	11375	(718) 897-3053
HERMAN GLICK'S SONS 101-15 QUEENS BOULEVARD	FOREST HILLS	**NY**	11365	(718) 896-7736

JOE STARK 6355 108TH STREET	FOREST HILLS	**NY**	11375	
KISSENA KOSHER MEATS INCORPORATED				
103-35 QUEENS BOULEVARD	FOREST HILLS	**NY**	11375	(718) 897-8996
LAZAR'S PACKING CORP. 100-30 QUEENS BOULEVARD	FOREST HILLS	**NY**	11375	(718) 897-6635
PAUL & LUDWIG ZIEGLER 115-16 QUEENS BOULEVARD	FOREST HILLS	**NY**	11375	(718) 263-3093
SIMON'S KOSHER BUTCHER 115-06 QUEENS BOULEVARD	FOREST HILLS	**NY**	11375	(718) 261-7463
SIMON'S KOSHER MEAT & POULTRY 87-48 PARSONS BLVD	FOREST HILLS	**NY**	11375	(718) 739-6066
ZIEGLER P & L KOSHER MEAT 115-16 QUEENS BOULEVARD	FOREST HILLS	**NY**	11375	(718) 362-2975
GEL OF GREAT NECK 503 MIDDLE NECK ROAD	GREAT NECK	**NY**	11023	(516) 487-5886
GREAT NECK KOSHER MEATS 65 MIDDLE NECK ROAD	GREAT NECK	**NY**	11021	(516) 482-0266
JAY'S KOSHER MEAT 503 MIDDLE NECK ROAD	GREAT NECK	**NY**	11023	(516) 487-7353
COHEN'S KOSHER MEATS & POULTRY 1330 BROADWAY	HEWLETT	**NY**	11557	(516) 374-1129
FIVE TOWN KOSHER PACKING 1324 PENINSULA BOULEVARD	HEWLETT	**NY**	11557	(516) 791-9877
FELDWOOD KOSHER MEATS 4285 OYSTER BAY ROAD	HICKSVILLE	**NY**	11801	(516) 681-7766
JERUSALEM KOSHER MEATS 412 JERUSALEM AVENUE	HICKSVILLE	**NY**	11801	(516) 935-2238
LINDENWOOD KOSHER BUTCHER 82-09 153RD AVENUE	HOWARD BEACH	**NY**	11414	(718) 641-2227
R & A KOSHER MEATS INCORPORATED				
156-30 CROSS BAY BOULEVARD	HOWARD BEACH	**NY**	11414	(718) 641-1308
BERGER'S KOSHER MEATS 13 NEW FIFTH STREET	HUNTINGTON STATION	**NY**	11746	(516) 423-0960
BEACHHAVEN KOSHER MEATS & POULTRY CORPORATION				
75-11 37TH AVENUE	JACKSON HEIGHTS	**NY**	11372	(718) 898-0600
BRIARWOOD KOSHER MEATS 138-09 QUEENS BLVD	JAMAICA	**NY**	11435	(718) 237-7340
E&Z KOSHER MEAT 188-18 UNION TPKE	JAMAICA	**NY**		(718) 465-2664
JERICHO KOSHER MEATS 441 HICKSVILLE ROAD	JERICHO	**NY**	11753	(516) 938-7900
H & W GLATT KOSHER MEATS 118-29A METROPOLITAN AVENUE	KEW GARDENS	**NY**	11415	(718) 441-1140
METROPOLITAN KOSHER MEAT MARKET				
116-10 METROPOLITAN AVENUE	KEW GARDENS	**NY**	11415	(718) 441-1880
EDEN KOSHER MEAT 79-09 MAIN STREET	KEW GARDENS	**NY**	11367	(718) 380-1366
SUPERSOL LTD. 330 CENTRAL AVENUE	LAWRENCE	**NY**	11559	(516) 295-3300
VALUE PLUS KOSHER MEATS 290 BURNSIDE AVENUE	LAWRENCE	**NY**	11559	(516) 239-5458
MITCHELL GARDENS KOSHER MEAT & POULTRY MARKET				
28-20 UNION STREET	LINDEN HILL	**NY**	11354	(718) 463-5709
LITTLE NECK SELF SERVICE 254-51 HORACE HARDING BOULEVARD	LITTLE NECK	**NY**	11362	(718) 428-5000
GORDON MEAT MARKET 220 WEST PARK AVENUE	LONG BEACH	**NY**	11561	(516) 431-4540
ISRAEL KOSHER MEATS 261 WEST PARK AVENUE	LONG BEACH	**NY**	11561	(516) 431-4120
PICK-N-SAVE KOSHER MEATS 172 EAST PARK AVENUE	LONG BEACH	**NY**	11561	(516) 889-2828
BROADWAY KOSHER MEAT 33-12 BROADWAY	LONG ISLAND CITY	**NY**		(718) 728-5658
M.F. MEAT INC. 33-15 BROADWAY	LONG ISLAND CITY	**NY**		(718) 728-1626
MALVERNE KOSHER MEAT & POULTRY 370 HEMPSTEAD AVENUE	MALVERNE	**NY**	11565	(516) 599-1070
G&M KOSHER MEATS INC. 2065 MERRICK ROAD	MERRICK	**NY**		(516) 378-6463
MENDLOWITZ'S MEATS 42 MAIN STREET	MONSEY	**NY**	10952	(914) 356-2376
LASHINSKY'S 338 BROADWAY	MONTICELLO	**NY**	12701	(914) 794-6140
LENK'S MEATS 380 BROADWAY	MONTICELLO	**NY**	12701	(914) 794-7380
LUNGEN'S MEATS 292 BROADWAY	MONTICELLO	**NY**	12701	(914) 794-4990
WESTCHESTER KOSHER MEAT & POULTRY MARKET				
11 EAST PROSPECT AVENUE	MOUNT VERNON	**NY**	10552	(914) 664-4313
NEW HYDE PARK KOSHER MEATS 1620 MARCUS AVENUE	NEW HYDE PARK	**NY**	11040	(516) 484-3396
BROADWAY KOSHER MEATS 13 QUAKER RIDGE ROAD	NEW ROCHELLE	**NY**	10804	(914) 235-2500
EPPY'S FOOD CORPORATION 1291 NORTH AVENUE	NEW ROCHELLE	**NY**	10804	(914) 636-4241
ATLAS MEATS 860 WASHINGTON	NEW YORK	**NY**	10014	(212) 255-3030
BENDER BROTHERS 1 BENNETT AVENUE	NEW YORK	**NY**	10033	(212) 798-0716
BLOCH & FALK MEAT PRODUCTS 152 NAGLE AVENUE	NEW YORK	**NY**	10040	(212) 927-5010
EIGHTH AVENUE KOSHER MEAT & POULTRY, INC.				
327 EIGHTH AVENUE	NEW YORK	**NY**	10001	(212) 929-8870
ERNST FLEISCHMAN 150 SHERMAN AVENUE	NEW YORK	**NY**	10040	(212) 567-2030
FISCHER BROTHERS & LESLIE 230 WEST 72ND STREET	NEW YORK	**NY**	10023	(212) 787-1715
GARY TURKEL 152 ESSEX STREET	NEW YORK	**NY**	10002	(212) 477-0146
GOLDBERG BUTCHER STORE 500 GRAND STREET	NEW YORK	**NY**	10002	(212) 475-6915
GRUENSPECHT & SONS 2830 BROADWAY	NEW YORK	**NY**	10032	(212) 568-5656
GUTMANN & MAYER MEATS 4229-4231 BROADWAY	NEW YORK	**NY**	10033	(212) 923-1989
H & M FELDSTEIN 2370 BROADWAY	NEW YORK	**NY**	10025	(212) 873-3560
HY-GRADE KOSHER MEAT 1200 MADISON AVENUE	NEW YORK	**NY**	10028	(212) 722-6379
I. SALZMAN 1384 SECOND AVENUE	NEW YORK	**NY**	10021	(212) 650-1996
INWOOD KOSHER 587 WEST 207TH STREET	NEW YORK	**NY**	10034	(212) 567-3088
IRVING BERGER 202 EAST 87TH STREET	NEW YORK	**NY**	10028	(212) 289-7234
JOE KARTIN 327 EIGHTH AVENUE	NEW YORK	**NY**	10001	(212) 929-8870
JONAS STERN & SONS-GLATT KOSHER 229 WEST 100TH STREET	NEW YORK	**NY**	10024	(212) 662-7081
KOESTRICH BROTHERS 4092 BROADWAY	NEW YORK	**NY**	10033	(212) 795-1670
MARTIN THAU 736 WEST 181ST STREET	NEW YORK	**NY**	10033	(212) 923-9319
MURRAY SCHEIN 507 GRAND STREET	NEW YORK	**NY**	10002	(212) 254-0180
P. FELDSTEIN BUTCHERS 2370 BROADWAY	NEW YORK	**NY**	10024	(212) 873-3560
PARK EAST KOSHER 1163 MADISON AVENUE	NEW YORK	**NY**	10028	(212) 787-3545
PERL'S BROADWAY KOSHER MEAT MARKET 2251 BROADWAY	NEW YORK	**NY**	10024	(212) 877-9640
PHILIP LEVITCH 807 WEST 181ST STREET	NEW YORK	**NY**	10033	(212) 923-9826
RICK BROTHERS MEATS 557 GRAND STREET	NEW YORK	**NY**	10002	(212) 677-9230
ROSEN BROTHERS 2411 BROADWAY	NEW YORK	**NY**	10025	(212) 724-0220
ROSEN BROTHERS (IDEE CORP.) 2254 12TH AVENUE	NEW YORK	**NY**	10024	(212) 281-5750
SCHILD BROTHERS INC. 4191 BROADWAY	NEW YORK	**NY**	10033	(212) 927-5997
SHEDLETSKY'S MEATS 221 EAST BROADWAY	NEW YORK	**NY**	10002	(212) 964-1232
SIDNEY SISSUN 4230 BROADWAY	NEW YORK	**NY**	10033	(212) 927-8188
SMALLS MEAT & POULTRY 221 EAST BROADWAY	NEW YORK	**NY**	10002	(212) 964-1232
STAHL KOSHER MEATS 62 AVENUE A	NEW YORK	**NY**	10009	(212) 228-2668
WARSHAYCHIK'S MEATS 181 CLINTON STREET	NEW YORK	**NY**	10002	(212) 982-1040
WERNER'S MEATS 4316 BROADWAY	NEW YORK	**NY**	10033	(212) 927-0463
PARKMERE KOSHER MEATS 951 ROSEDALE ROAD	NORTH WOODMERE	**NY**	11581	(516) 791-4683
D & W KOSHER MEAT & POULTRY MARKET				
61-42 SPRINGFIELD BLVD	OAKLAND GARDENS	**NY**	11364	(718) 255-1550
COHEN'S KOSHER MEATS 351 LONG BEACH ROAD	OCEANSIDE	**NY**	11572	(516) 766-1714
OCEANSIDE KOSHER MEAT MARKET 18 ATLANTIC AVENUE	OCEANSIDE	**NY**	11572	(516) 766-5252
JOE'S MEAT MARKET 17-11 101TH AVENUE	OZONE PARK	**NY**		(718) 845-3060
KOSHER MEAT FARM OF PLAINVIEW 365A SOUTH OYSTER BAY ROAD	PLAINVIEW	**NY**	11803	(516) 931-6446
PLAINVIEW KOSHER MEATS 1113 OLD COUNTRY ROAD	PLAINVIEW	**NY**	11803	(516) 681-4410
STAR MARKET 73 PONINGO STREET	PORT CHESTER	**NY**	10573	(914) 937-8007
IRVAL KOSHER MEATS 93-05 63RD DRIVE	QUEENS	**NY**	11374	
IDEAL KOSHER MEATS & POULTRY 97-18 63RD ROAD	REGO PARK	**NY**	11375	(718) 459-2815
LAZAR'S PACKING 110-30 QUEENS BOULEVARD	REGO PARK	**NY**	11375	(718) 897-6635
MID-QUEENS KOSHER MEAT CORPORATION 94-05 63RD DRIVE	REGO PARK	**NY**	11374	(718) 896-2927
SIDNEY REISS 6360 SAUNDERS STREET	REGO PARK	**NY**	11374	(718) 459-9722
GUSS' MEATS 113-17 LIBERTY AVENUE	RICHMOND HILL	**NY**	11419	(718) 843-1993
GLATT STOP OF RIVERDALE 3711 RIVERDALE AVENUE	RIVERDALE	**NY**	10471	(212) 884-1200
GORONKINS MEAT MARKET 515 RIDGE ROAD EAST	ROCHESTER	**NY**	14615	(716) 476-4270
LIPMAN'S KOSHER MEAT 1482 MONROE AVENUE	ROCHESTER	**NY**	14618	(716) 271-7886
COHEN'S KOSHER MEAT				
115-06 ROCKAWAY BEACH BOULEVARD	ROCKAWAY PARK	**NY**	11694	(718) 634-1349
G & K MEAT MARKET 115-06 ROCKAWAY BEACH BOULEVARD	ROCKAWAY PARK	**NY**	11694	(718) 474-5704
GREYSTONE KOSHER MEATS				
176 NORTH LONG BEACH ROAD	ROCKVILLE CENTRE	**NY**	11570	(516) 766-0099
S & W KOSHER MEATS 16 SOUTH PARK AVENUE	ROCKVILLE CENTRE	**NY**	11570	(516) 766-1771
SAVON KOSHER MEATS 713 WHITE PLAINS ROAD	SCARSDALE	**NY**	10709	(914) 725-0565
KING KOSHER MEATS 1087 HICKSVILLE ROAD	SEAFORD	**NY**	11783	(516) 735-8490
LAZAR'S MEAT MONTEGO PLAZA	SOUTH FALLSBURG	**NY**	12701	(914) 434-7300
HELLMAN'S MEATS 52 NORTH MAIN STREET	SPRING VALLEY	**NY**	10977	(914) 356-0715
HERBIES KOSHER MEATS 30 SOUTH CENTRAL AVENUE	SPRING VALLEY	**NY**	10977	(914) 425-3113
HILLCREST KOSHER MEATS 285A NORTH MAIN STREET	SPRING VALLEY	**NY**	10977	(914) 352-3626
L & D 303A NORTH MAIN STREET	SPRING VALLEY	**NY**	10977	(914) 352-9444
M & S 94 NORTH MAIN STREET	SPRING VALLEY	**NY**	10977	(914) 356-1607
DAVID'S KOSHER BUTCHERS 1989 VICTORY BOULEVARD	STATEN ISLAND	**NY**	10314	(718) 442-3920
KOSHER ISLAND GLATT TAKE HOME 2206 VICTORY BOULEVARD	STATEN ISLAND	**NY**		(718) 698-5800
STATEN ISLAND BUTCHERS 1919 VICTORY BOULEVARD	STATEN ISLAND	**NY**	10314	(718) 442-3920
TIKVA KOSHER MEATS & POULTRY 2845 RICHMOND AVENUE	STATEN ISLAND	**NY**	10314	(718) 698-2603
ADLER'S KOSHER MARKET 41 LAFAYETTE AVENUE	SUFFERN	**NY**	10901	(914) 357-1637
GLATT STOP 191 ROUTE 59	SUFFERN	**NY**	10977	(914) 357-9594
MEAL MART ROUTE 55	SWAN LAKE	**NY**	12783	(914) 292-9439
MARTIN TENENBAUM KOSHER MEATS 2914 EAST GENESEE	SYRACUSE	**NY**	13224	(315) 446-3254
PARKMERE KOSHER MEATS 951 ROSEDALE ROAD	VALLEY STREAM	**NY**	11581	(516) 791-3086
SHUB & NOVICK 355 NORTH CENTRAL AVENUE	VALLEY STREAM	**NY**	11580	(516) 825-8171
SUNRISE KOSHER MEAT MARKET 355 CENTRAL AVENUE	VALLEY STREAM	**NY**	11580	(212) 276-3166
KOSHER MEAT FARM #2 1172 WANTAGH AVENUE	WANTAGH	**NY**	11793	(516) 781-6296
NORTH NASSAU KOSHER MEATS 598 OLD COUNTRY ROAD	WESTBURY	**NY**	11590	(516) 333-1616
SATMAR MEATS & POULTRY C/O CONGREGATION YETEV LEV	WHITE LAKE	**NY**	12786	(914) 583-7020
KEN-MAR MEATS 333 MAMARONECK AVENUE	WHITE PLAINS	**NY**	10605	(914) 761-8046
CLEARVIEW KOSHER 160-32 WILLETS POINT BOULEVARD	WHITESTONE	**NY**	11357	(718) 352-2099
K & K 20-11 UTOPIA PARKWAY	WHITESTONE	**NY**	11357	(718) 352-2776
WOODMERE KOSHER MEATS 1017 BROADWAY	WOODMERE	**NY**	11598	(516) 374-4058
KESSLER'S & SONS MAIN STREET	WOODRIDGE	**NY**	12789	(914) 434-7550
NAT KAGEN MEATS & POULTRY GREEN AVENUE	WOODRIDGE	**NY**	12789	(914) 434-4334
BAKER HILL PACKING COMPANY 2558 CENTRAL PARK AVENUE	YONKERS	**NY**	10704	(914) 779-8100
CENTUCK 622 TUCKAHOE ROAD	YONKERS	**NY**	10710	(914) 779-3683
HENRY'S KOSHER MEATS 636 MCLEAN AVENUE	YONKERS	**NY**	10705	(914) 965-5802
SYON MEATS 2558 CENTRAL AVENUE	YONKERS	**NY**	10710	(914) 779-8100
VALUE PLUS MEATS OF YONKERS 1733 CENTRAL PARK AVENUE	YONKERS	**NY**		(914) 961-2048
BONEM'S KOSHER MEAT MARKET 7377 BROOKCREST DRIVE	CINCINNATI	**OH**		(513) 351-3144
PILDER'S KOSHER FOODS 7601 READING	CINCINNATI	**OH**	45237	(513) 821-7050
SIMON'S KOSHER MEAT MARKET 1436 SECTION ROAD	CINCINNATI	**OH**	45237	(513) 761-1864
A & W FOODS 4900 CRAYTON AVENUE	CLEVELAND	**OH**	44104	(216) 431-8000
ALTMAN'S KOSHER MEAT MARKET 2185 SOUTH GREEN ROAD	CLEVELAND	**OH**	44121	(216) 381-7615
BASCH'S KOSHER MEAT MARKET 1944 SOUTH TAYLOR ROAD	CLEVELAND	**OH**	44118	(216) 321-1911
BERGER'S QUALITY KOSHER MEAT MARKET				
BERGER'S QUALITY KOSHER MEAT MARKET	CLEVELAND	**OH**	44121	(216) 382-6560
BORIS' KOSHER MEAT 14406 CEDAR ROAD	CLEVELAND	**OH**	44118	(216) 382-5330
COVENTRY POULTRY 1825 COVENTRY ROAD	CLEVELAND	**OH**	44118	(216) 371-0555
IRVING'S KOSHER MEAT MARKET 13938½ CEDAR STREET	CLEVELAND	**OH**	44118	(216) 321-5660
LEO'S KOSHER MEAT MARKET 1839 SOUTH TAYLOR ROAD	CLEVELAND	**OH**	44118	(216) 932-9212
SAM & JACK'S KOSHER MEAT MARKET 2110 SOUTH TAYLOR ROAD	CLEVELAND	**OH**	44118	(216) 321-7322
SILVERMAN BROTHERS KOSHER MEAT MARKETS				
26301 RICHMOND ROAD	CLEVELAND	**OH**	44118	(216) 292-3720
MARTIN'S KOSHER FOODS 3685 EAST BROAD STREET	COLUMBUS	**OH**	43213	(614) 231-3653
SIEGLE'S DELICATESSEN & FOOD MART 2636 WEST CENTRAL	TOLEDO	**OH**	43606	(419) 473-2791
SIEGLE'S DELICATESSEN & FOOD MART 15 WEST BANCROFT	TOLEDO	**OH**	43620	(419) 243-6264
ABRAM'S KOSHER MART - LOBLAWS 270 WILSON AVENUE	TORONTO	**ON**		(416) 635-5004
BATHURST MEAT MARKET 3774 BATHURST STREET	TORONTO	**ON**		(416) 636-4440
COMMUNITY KOSHER FOODS LTD. 7335 YONGE STREET	TORONTO	**ON**		(416) 881-8820
COMMUNITY KOSHER MEATS LTD. 3862 BATHURST STREET	TORONTO	**ON**		(416) 638-6898
B. GOLDSTEIN 308 WILSON AVENUE	TORONTO	**ON**		(416) 633-9642
J & S MEAT 366 MARLEE AVENUE	TORONTO	**ON**		(416) 781-2733
JOE KIRSHEN'S KOSHER MEAT MARKET 3544 BATHURST STREET	TORONTO	**ON**		(416) 781-7767
MANOR KOSHER MEAT MARKET 662 SHEPPARD AVENUE WEST	TORONTO	**ON**		(416) 636-2000
H. PERL 3013 BATHURST STREET	TORONTO	**ON**		(416) 787-4234
SPRINGER'S 3393 BATHURST STREET	TORONTO	**ON**		(416) 787-3971
STROLI'S 3459 BATHURST STREET	TORONTO	**ON**		(416) 789-5333
SUNNYBROOK FOODS LTD				
241 WILMINGTON AVENUE (BATHURST MANOR PLAZA)	TORONTO	**ON**		(416) 635-5987
YOSSI'S FINE FOODS 4117 BATHURST STREET	TORONTO	**ON**		(416) 635-9509
ABE'S & SONS 7410 BUSTLETON AVENUE	PHILADELPHIA	**PA**	19120	(215) 742-3800
BLACK'S KOSHER MEAT & POULTRY 1601 EAST WADSWORTH	PHILADELPHIA	**PA**	19150	(215) 247-0215
MODERN KOSHER MEAT MARKET 5948 OGONTZ AVENUE	PHILADELPHIA	**PA**	19141	(215) 924-8259
RHAWNHURST KOSHER PRIME MEATS 8261 BUSTLETON AVENUE	PHILADELPHIA	**PA**		(215) 742-5287
PRIME KOSHER FOODS 1916 MURRAY AVENUE	PITTSBURGH	**PA**	15217	(412) 421-1015
SAUL KRONZEK MEATS 5719 BRYANT STREET	PITTSBURGH	**PA**	15206	(412) 661-3377
TEL AVIV KOSHER MEAT MARKET 1716 MURRAY AVENUE	PITTSBURGH	**PA**	15217	(412) 421-4450
GOTTESMAN'S KOSHER MEAT & POULTRY MARKET				
1216 MULBERRY STREET	SCRANTON	**PA**	18510	(717) 342-3886

ROBINSON KOSHER MEAT MARKET 1502 VINE STREET ....SCRANTON PA 18510   (717) 961-9760
CONTINENTAL KOSHER MEAT POULTRY & DELICATESSEN PRODUCTS
  230 FAIRMOUNT WEST ....MONTREAL QU   (514) 274-5491
GATT'S KOSHER MEATS 7015 COTE ST LUC ROAD ....MONTREAL QU   (514) 482-6227
GLATT KOSHER MEATS 175 LAURIER WEST........................MONTREAL QU   (514) 274-9477
GLATT'S KOSHER MEATS 5897 VICTORIA...........................MONTREAL QU   (514) 737-3228
MARTY WEISSMAN KOSHER MEAT MARKET 88½ ROLFE STREET ....CRANSTON RI 02910   (401) 467-8903
FRED SPIGEL'S KOSHER MEAT MARKET & DELI APPETIZER
  243 RESERVOIR AVENUE ....PROVIDENCE RI 02907   (401) 461-0425
STONE'S HOPE STREET KOSHER MEAT MARKET 780 HOPE STREET....PROVIDENCE RI 02906   (401) 421-0271
KIPPERT'S KOSHER FOODS 4965 SUMMER AVENUE ....MEMPHIS TN 38122   (901) 682-3801
MANNY'S KOSHER MEAT & DELICATESSEN
  215 PRESTON ROYAL SHOPPING CENTER ....DALLAS TX 75225   (214) 943-5895
REICHMAN'S KOSHER MEAT & DELICATESSEN
  215 PRESTON ROYAL SHOPPING CENTER ....DALLAS TX 75225   (214) 368-2847
JIM JAMAIL & SONS 3114 KIRBY DRIVE ....HOUSTON TX 77006   (713) 523-5535
MARTIN POULTRY EGG & FROZEN FOOD COMPANY 2002 WHITE..........HOUSTON TX 77007   (713) 869-6191
UNITED FOODS 5901 BEVERLY HILLS ....HOUSTON TX   (713) 789-0301
SIDNEY PERLIN'S KOSHER MEAT MARKET 619 WEST 35TH STREET ....NORFOLK VA 23508   (804) 622-5196
RICHMOND KOSHER MEAT MARKET 3109 WEST CARY STREET ....RICHMOND VA 23221   (804) 358-6905
KOSHER MEAT KLUB 4731 WEST BURLEIGH ....MILWAUKEE WI 53210   (414) 871-3273
RABINOWITZ BROTHERS KOSHER MEAT MARKET
  4622 WEST BURLEIGH...MILWAUKEE WI 53210   (414) 871-3273

MEAT & POULTRY - WHOLESALE

EMES KOSHER MEAT PRODUCTS
  2627 SOUTH LA CIENEGA BOULEVARD ....LOS ANGELES CA   (213) 836-0535
HY-GRADE MEAT SPECIALTIES COMPANY 3462 LARIMER ....DENVER CO 80205   (303) 292-6328
SUPERVISED PRODUCTS 3890 ADAMS STREET, PO BOX 16432 ....DENVER CO 80216   (303) 321-7033
ROLAND FOODS 135 R STREET S.W. ....WASHINGTON DC 20023   (202) 488-0888
SAVAL DIRECTOR 925 FIFTH STREET N.W. ....WASHINGTON DC 20023   (202) 832-9400
GOLDBERG BROTHERS SOUTH MARKET STREET ....WILMINGTON DE 19801   (302) 655-5301
AMERICAN KOSHER PROVISIONS 6988 N.W. 36TH AVENUE ....MIAMI FL 33147   (305) 653-4496
HEBREW NATIONAL KOSHER, J & J PURVEYORS 2140 N.W. 13TH AVENUE .....MIAMI FL 33142   (305) 592-0300
ZION CORPORATION 1717 N.W. SEVENTH AVENUE ....MIAMI FL 33125   (305) 324-1855
BEST KOSHER SAUSAGE COMPANY ....CHICAGO IL 60608   (312) 738-2100
KOSHER STAR SAUSAGE MANUFACTURING COMPANY
  1000 WEST PERSHING STREET ....CHICAGO IL 60645   (312) 927-2810
KOSHER ZION SAUSAGE COMPANY 1455 SOUTH ABERDINE ....CHICAGO IL 60636   (312) 738-2208
SINAI KOSHER FOODS CORP. 1000 WEST PERSHING ROAD ....CHICAGO IL 60609   (312) 927-2810
UNITED KOSHER FOODS, INC. 711 W. GRAND AVENUE ....CHICAGO IL 60610   (312) 243-3473
STRATHMOOR KEY DISTRIBUTING COMPANY
  2733 BARDSTOWN ROAD ....LOUISVILLE KY 40205   (502) 458-2276
MORRISON & SCHIFF P.O. BOX 248...............................BOSTON MA 02135
SNIDER'S DRESSED BEEF COMPANY 219 SUMMER STREET ....WORCESTER MA 01608   (617) 755-5225
EUROPEAN KOSHER PROVISION MANUFACTURING
  6 SOUTH SPRING STREET ....BALTIMORE MD 21231   (301) 342-2002
EUROPEAN KOSHER PROVISIONS MANUFACTURING CO.
  1419 EAST BALTIMORE STREET ....BALTIMORE MD 21231   (301) 342-2002
EMPIRE PACKING COMPANY 8648 FENKELL ....DETROIT MI 48221   (313) 345-6565
LANDY PACKING CO. P.O. BOX 670...............................ST CLOUD MN 56301   (612) 252-1331
FEINBERG DISTRIBUTING 323 SOUTH 9TH STREET ....OMAHA NE 69154   (800) 247-7402
POSNOCK KOSHER FOODS 1713 ELIZABETH AVENUE ....EAST LINDEN NJ 07036   (201) 925-5400
SHOFAR KOSHER FOODS, INC. 219 EMMET STREET ....NEWARK NJ 07114   (201) 242-2434
ABELES & HEYMANN, INC. 3498 THIRD AVENUE ....BRONX NY 10456   (212) 589-0100
ISAAC GELLIS, INC. 968 LONGFELLOW AVENUE....................BRONX NY 10474   (212) 589-1770
MOGEN DAVID KOSHER MEAT PRODUCTS CORP.
  968 LONGFELLOW AVENUE ....BRONX NY 10474   (212) 589-1770
PARKSIDE KOSHER MEATS INC. 1197 BRYANT AVENUE ....BRONX NY   (212) 328-6999
ZION KOSHER DELICATESSEN COMPANY 968 LONGFELLOW AVENUE ...BRONX NY 10474   (212) 589-1770
A TO Z KOSHER PRODUCTS 123 GRAND STREET ....BROOKLYN NY   (718) 384-7400
ALLE PROCESSING CORP. 502 FLUSHING AVENUE ....BROOKLYN NY 11205   (718) 855-1811
AMERICAN KOSHER PROVISIONS INC. 39 NORMAN AVENUE ....BROOKLYN NY 11222   (718) 963-1700
GOLDEN SIMCHA POULTRY 1602 TROY AVENUE ....BROOKLYN NY   (718) 253-7733
HOROWITZ KOSHER PROVISIONS INC. 258 EAST 87TH STREET ......BROOKLYN NY   (718) 629-9820
SCHMULKA BERNSTEIN & CO. INC. 1100 UTICA AVENUE ....BROOKLYN NY 11203   (718) 345-0050
YERUSHALAYIM KOSHER PROVISIONS INC. 502 FLUSHING AVENUE ....BROOKLYN NY   (718) 855-4811
D. JACOBSON SONS 163 ADAMS STREET ....BUFFALO NY 14216   (716) 854-1150
METROPOLITAN KOSHER FOOD SERVICE
  HUNTS POINT COOPERATIVE MARKET ....HUNTS POINT NY   (212) 893-3500
FALLS POULTRY CORP. SCHOOL ROAD ....LIVINGSTON MANOR NY 12578   (212) 594-7826
HEBREW NATIONAL FOODS 58-80 MAURICE AVENUE ....MASPETH NY 11378   (718) 894-4300
HOD CARMEL KOSHER PROVISION COMPANY 58-80 MAURICE AVENUE...MASPETH NY 11378   (718) 894-4300
ISRAEL FINE FOOD IMPORTS INC. P.O. BOX 76 ....MONSEY NY 10952   (914) 352-0123
EUROPEAN KOSHER PROVISION MANUFACTURING COMPANY, INC.
  15 RIVINGTON STREET ....NEW YORK NY 10002   (212) 254-5994
REAL KOSHER SAUSAGE CO., INC. 15 RIVINGTON STREET ....NEW YORK NY 10002   (212) 254-5994
FALLS POULTRY CORP. MAIN STREET ....S. FALLSBURG NY 12779   (914) 434-5000
HEBREW NATIONAL KOSHER FOODS INC. - SALES AND DISTRIBUTION
  58-65 52ND ROAD..WOODSIDE NY   (718) 779-3600
KOSHER KING PRODUCTS 58-65 52ND ROAD ....WOODSIDE NY   (718) 779-3600
H.J.P. WHOLESALE KOSHER MEATS, INC. 636 MCLEAN AVENUE ....YONKERS NY 10705   (914) 965-5802
GILDER'S KOSHER MEAT MARKET 14406 CEDAR ....CLEVELAND OH 44121   (216) 382-5330
SIDNEY CROSS WHOLESALE MEATS 7707 SYCAMORE AVENUE ...ELKINS PARK PA 19117   (215) 782-1400
EMPIRE KOSHER FOODS, INC. R.D. #3, P.O. BOX 165 ....MIFFLINTOWN PA 17059   (717) 436-2131
LUNDY'S & SONS 934 NORTH THIRD STREET .................PHILADELPHIA PA 19140   (215) 627-2050
SAMUEL SANDLER MANUFACTURING COMPANY
  2207 NORTH 30TH STREET ...............................PHILADELPHIA PA 19140   (215) 232-4700
ALBER & LEFF FOOD COMPANY 405 COLLEGE AVENUE ....PITTSBURGH PA 15232   (412) 321-7700
WEISS PROVISION COMPANY 1114 MURIEL STREET..............PITTSBURGH PA 15203   (412) 431-3270

MEDIA

AISH HATORAH ON THE AIR ....LOS ANGELES CA   (213) 980-6934
JEWISH TELEVISION NETWORK
  617 SOUTH OLIVE STREET, SUITE 515 ....LOS ANGELES CA 90014   (213) 614-0972
ISRAEL TODAY MEDIA GROUP 10340 ROSEDA BLVD ....NORTHRIDGE CA 91326   (818) 786-4000
ISRAEL BROADCASTING AUTHORITY 1101 30TH STREET ....WASHINGTON DC 20007   (202) 338-6091
IDF RADIO ISRAEL GALEI ZAHAL 1110 FIDLER LANE ....SILVER SPRING MD 20911   (301) 565-3027
JEWISH SPECTRUM (RADIO SHOW) 621 W. MT. PLEASANT AVENUE .....LIVINGSTON NJ 07039   (212) 349-1111
TELE-ISRAEL CABLEVISION OF WESTCHESTER (YONKERS)-CHANNEL 25 .... NY   (212) 620-7041
TELE-ISRAEL UA COLUMBIA (BERGEN)-CHANNEL K/24 .... NY   (212) 620-7041
TELE-ISRAEL UA COLUMBIA (WESTCHESTER)-CHANNEL 23 .... NY   (212) 620-7041
TELE-ISRAEL CABLEVISION OF L.I. (NASSAU)-CHANNEL 25 .... NY   (212) 620-7041
JEWISH EDUCATIONAL MEDIA 784 EASTERN PARKWAY ....BROOKLYN NY 11213   (718) 774-6000
DIAL-A-JEWISH-STORY ....LONG ISLAND NY   (516) 432-7811
DIAL-A-DAF, TORAH COMMUNICATIONS NETWORK 1618 43RD STREET .. NEW YORK NY 11204   (212) 436-4999
HEBREW HOUR, THE (HEBREW) 227 E. 45TH STREET ....NEW YORK NY 10017   (212) 697-8354
ISRAEL BROADCASTING AUTHORITY INTERNATIONAL RELATIONS
  10 ROCKEFELLER PLAZA ....NEW YORK NY 10020   (212) 489-6180
ISRAEL BROADCASTING AUTHORITY RADIO & TELEVISION
  10 ROCKEFELLER PLAZA ....NEW YORK NY 10020   (212) 265-6330
ISRAEL COMMUNICATIONS, INC. 575 LEXINGTON AVENUE ....NEW YORK NY 10022   (212) 486-8835
ISRAEL COMMUNICATIONS, INC. 350 FIFTH AVENUE..............NEW YORK NY 10118   (212) 695-2998
JEWISH BROADCASTING SERVICE 2130 BROADWAY ....NEW YORK NY 10023
JEWISH MEDIA SERVICE-J W B 15 E. 26TH STREET ....NEW YORK NY 10010   (212) 532-4949
JEWISH VIDEO WORKSHOP-TORAH VISION, INC. 576 FIFTH AVENUE .....NEW YORK NY 10036   (212) 921-2175
KAN ISRAEL - WEVD RADIO, N.Y. (HEBREW) 1700 BROADWAY ....NEW YORK NY 10019   (212) 427-1218
MESSAGE OF ISRAEL 123 EAST 55TH STREET, CENTRAL SYNAGOGUE ... NEW YORK NY 10022
NIGHT-RAP RADIO PROGRAM CHANNEL J-MANHATTAN.................NEW YORK NY   (212) 434-1928

TELE-ISRAEL MANHATTAN CABLE-CHANNEL M ... NEW YORK **NY** (212) 620-7041
TELE-ISRAEL GROUP W-CHANNEL L/25 ... NEW YORK **NY** (212) 620-7041
WEVD RADIO FORWARD ASSOCIATION 770 BROADWAY ... NEW YORK **NY** 10003 (212) 777-7900
JEWISH SCENE IN CLEVELAND - JEWISH COMMUNITY CENTER
3505 MAYFIELD ROAD ... CLEVELAND **OH** 44118 (216) 382-4000
JEWISH VIDEO CLEVELAND - JEWISH COMMUNITY FEDERATION
1750 EUCLID AVENUE ... CLEVELAND **OH** 44115 (216) 566-9200
ISRAEL RADIO BOX 204 ... CHELTENHAM **PA** 19012

MEMORIAL INFORMATION

MEMORIAL INFORMATION SYSTEMS 21412 HILLTOP ... SOUTHFIELD **MI** (313) 358-1818

MEZUZOT

VAAD MISHMERES STAM 4902 16TH AVENUE ... BROOKLYN **NY** 11204 (718) 438-4963

MIKVAOT

KNESSETH ISRAEL SYNAGOGUE 3225 MONTEVALLO ROAD ... BIRMINGHAM **AL** 35223 (205) 879-1664
CONGREGATION AGUDATH ISRAEL 3525 CLOVERDALE ROAD ... MONTGOMERY **AL** 36111 (205) 281-7998
MIKVAH, CHAPEL TWO, BUILDING #8-760
8TH & J STREET, ELMENDORF AFB ... ANCHORAGE **AK** 99506 (907) 752-2202
CONGREGATION AGUDATH ACHIM 7901 WEST 5TH STREET ... LITTLE ROCK **AR** 72205 (501) 225-1683
MIKVAH (CALGARY HEBREW SCHOOL) 1415 GLENMORE TRAIL ... CALGARY **AT** T2V 4Y8 (403) 455-9114
BETH ISRAEL SYNAGOGUE 10205-119TH STREET ... EDMONTON **AT** (403) 488-2840
MIKVAH SOCIETY 515 EAST BETHANY HOME ROAD ... PHOENIX **AZ** 85012 (602) 277-7479
YOUNG ISRAEL SYNAGOGUE 2443 EAST 4TH STREET ... TUCSON **AZ** 85716 (602) 795-1267
CHABAD MIKVAH 5750 OAK STREET ... VANCOUVER **BC** V6M 2V7 (604) 266-5295
CONGREGATION SCHARA TZEDEK 3476 OAK STREET ... VANCOUVER **BC** (604) 736-7607
MIKVAH TAHARAS ISRAEL 2520 WARRING AVENUE ... BERKELEY **CA** 94705 (415) 848-7221
MIKVAH YISROEL 3847 ATLANTIC AVENUE ... LONG BEACH **CA** 90807 (213) 427-1360
MIKVAH SOCIETY 9548 WEST PICO BOULEVARD ... LOS ANGELES **CA** 90035 (213) 550-9124
MOGEN ABRAHAM SYNAGOGUE 356 NORTH LA BREA AVENUE ... LOS ANGELES **CA** 90036 (213) 937-9690
OHEL DAVID SYNAGOGUE 7967 BEVERLY BOULEVARD ... LOS ANGELES **CA** 90035 (213) 939-9239
VALLEY MIKVAH SOCIETY 12800 CHANDLER BOULEVARD ... NORTH HOLLYWOOD **CA** 91607 (818) 763-2285
BETH JACOB SYNAGOGUE 3778 PARK BOULEVARD ... OAKLAND **CA** 94602 (415) 482-1147
MIKVAH ISRAEL 5170 LA DORNA ... SAN DIEGO **CA** 92115 (619) 287-6411
MIKVAH 1404 QUITMAN ... DENVER **CO** 80204 (303) 893-5315
MIKVAH ISRAEL 1326 STRATFIELD ROAD ... FAIRFIELD **CT** 06604 (203) 374-2191
NEW HAVEN MIKVAH SOCIETY 86 HUBINGER STREET ... NEW HAVEN **CT** 06511 (203) 387-2184
CONGREGATION BROTHERS OF JOSEPH 2 BROAD STREET ... NORWICH **CT** 06360 (203) 889-1900
CONGREGATION AGUDATH SHOLOM
301 STRAWBERRY HILL AVENUE ... STAMFORD **CT** 06902 (203) 754-4159
CONGREGATION BNAI SHOLOM 135 ROSELAND AVENUE ... WATERBURY **CT** 06710 (203) 754-4159
MIKVAH OF GREATER HARTFORD 61 NORTH MAIN STREET ... WEST HARTFORD **CT** 06107 (203) 521-9446
MIKVEH ETZ CHAIM 5864 UNIVERSITY BOULEVARD WEST ... JACKSONVILLE **FL** 32216 (904) 733-0720
DAUGHTER OF ISRAEL RITUALARIUM 151 MICHIGAN AVENUE ... MIAMI BEACH **FL** 33139 (305) 672-3500
MIKVAH MIAMI GARDENS DRIVE AND 10TH AVENUE ... NORTH MIAMI BEACH **FL** (305) 944-1334
MIKVAH ISRAEL OF TAMPA BAY 3600 E. FLETCHER AVE. ... TAMPA **FL** 33612 (813) 971-6768
CONGREGATION BETH JACOB 1855 LA VISTA ROAD N.E. ... ATLANTA **GA** 30329 (404) 633-0551
CONGREGATION ADAS YESHURUN 935 JOHNS ROAD ... AUGUSTA **GA** 30904 (404) 733-9491
CONGREGATION BNAI BRITH JACOB 5444 ABERCORN ... SAVANNAH **GA** 31405 (912) 355-3406
BETH EL JACOB SYNAGOGUE 954 CUMMINS PARKWAY ... DES MOINES **IA** 50312 (515) 274-1551
JEWISH COMMUNITY CENTER 14TH & NEBRASKA ... SIOUX CITY **IA** 55105 (712) 258-2618
MIKVAH 3110 WEST TOUHY AVENUE ... CHICAGO **IL** 60645 (312) 274-7425
CONGREGATION YEHUDA MOSHE 4721 WEST TOUHY AVENUE ... LINCOLNWOOD **IL** 60646 (312) 674-0820
CONGREGATION AGUDAS ACHIM 3616 NORTH SHERIDAN ROAD ... PEORIA **IL** 61604 (309) 688-4800
TRI-CITY JEWISH CENTER 2715 30TH STREET ... ROCK ISLAND **IL** 61201 (309) 788-3426
CONGREGATION BNAI TORAH 6510 HOOVER ROAD ... INDIANAPOLIS **IN** 46260 (317) 253-5253
HEBREW ORTHODOX CONGREGATION 3207 HIGH STREET ... SOUTH BEND **IN** 46614 (219) 289-3988
AHAVATH ACHIM CONGREGATION 1850 NORTH WOODLAWN ... WICHITA **KS** 67208 (316) 685-1339
ANSHEI SFARD SYNAGOGUE 3700 DUTCHMANS LANE ... LOUISVILLE **KY** 40205 (502) 451-3122
BETH ISRAEL SYNAGOGUE 7000 CANAL BOULEVARD ... NEW ORLEANS **LA** 70124 (504) 282-4916
DAUGHTERS OF ISRAEL 101 WASHINGTON STREET ... BRIGHTON **MA** 02135 (617) 782-9433
BETH PINCAS 1710 BEACON STREET ... BROOKLINE **MA** 02146 (617) 566-9182
MIKVAH 146 WALNUT STREET ... CHELSEA **MA** 02150 (617) 884-5169
MIKVAH ISRAEL 1104 CONVERSE STREET ... LONGMEADOW **MA** 01106 (413) 567-1607
RITUALARIUM OF THE NORTH SHORE (CONGREGATION AHABAT SHOLOM)
151 OCEAN STREET ... LYNN **MA** 09102 (617) 595-9492
MIKVEH ORGANIZATION OF THE SOUTH SHORE, (YOUNG ISRAEL OF SHARON)
9 DUNBAR STREET ... SHARON **MA** 02067 (617) 784-7444
MIKVAH 57 HUNTLEY ... WORCESTER **MA** 01604 (617) 754-5495
CHABAD MIKVAH N.E. CORNER MCGREGOR & HARTFORD AVENUES ... WINNIPEG **MB** (204) 334-1680
MIKVAH (BAIS HAMIDRASH KHAL ARUGAS HABOSEM)
6615 PARK HEIGHTS AVE. ... BALTIMORE **MD** 21215
MIKVAH 3500 WEST ROGERS AVENUE ... BALTIMORE **MD** 21215 (301) 466-9719
MIKVAH 8901 GEORGIA AVENUE ... SILVER SPRING **MD** 20907 (301) 587-2014
SILVER SPRING JEWISH CENTER 1401 ARCOLA AVENUE ... SILVER SPRING **MD** 20902 (301) 649-4425
BANGOR MIKVAH-C/O RABBI ISAACS ... BANGOR **ME** (207) 945-5940
SHAARAY TEFILOH SYNAGOGUE 76 NOYES STREET ... PORTLAND **ME** 04103 (207) 733-2611
MIKVAH, CHABAD HOUSE 715 HILL STREET ... ANN ARBOR **MI** 48104 (313) 995-3276
MIKVAH ISRAEL 15150 WEST TEN MILE ROAD ... OAK PARK **MI** 48231 (313) 968-9715
MIKVAH IN EAST GRAND FORKS ... GRAND FORKS **MN** (218) 773-9394
KNESSETH ISRAEL SYNAGOGUE 4330 WEST 28TH STREET ... MINNEAPOLIS **MN** 55416 (612) 920-2183
CHABAD MIKVAH 15 MONTCALM COURT ... ST PAUL **MN** 55116 (612) 698-3858
MIKVAH ASSOCIATION 1618 RANDOLPH AVENUE ... ST PAUL **MN** 55105 (612) 698-6163
KEHILATH ISRAEL SYNAGOGUE 800 EAST MEYER BOULEVARD ... KANSAS CITY **MO** 64131 (816) 333-1992
MIKVAH ISRAEL 8901 HOLMES RD. ... KANSAS CITY **MO** 64131 (816) 333-7117
MIKVAH 10977 SCHEUTZ ROAD ... ST LOUIS **MO** 63141 (314) 721-8990
SYLVIA GREEN MIKVAH 4 MILLSTONE CAMPUS ... ST LOUIS **MO** 63146 (314) 569-2774
MIKVAH (LUBAVITCH OF NORTH CAROLINA) 6500 NEWHALL RD. ... CHARLOTTE **NC** 28226 (704) 366-3984
CONGREGATION SHAAREI ISRAEL 7400 FALLS OF THE NEUSE ROAD ... RALEIGH **NC** 27609 (919) 847-6286
OMAHA MIKVAH 333 SOUTH 132 STREET ... OMAHA **NE** 68154 (402) 333-5166
BETH EL SYNAGOGUE CORNER ELIZABETH & DOWNING AVENUES ... ST JOHN'S **NF** A1B 1S3 (709) 726-0480
MIKVAH LEWIS HILL ROAD ... BETHLEHEM **NH** 03574 (603) 869-3962
MIKVAH SONS OF ISRAEL 720 COOPER LANDING ROAD ... CHERRY HILL **NJ** 08002 (609) 667-9700
MIKVAH 35 NORTH AVENUE ... ELIZABETH **NJ** 07208 (201) 352-5048
MIKVAH 112 FIRST AVENUE SOUTH ... HIGHLAND PARK **NJ** 08904 (201) 249-2411
MIKVAH 705 MADISON AVENUE ... LAKEWOOD **NJ** 08701 (201) 363-9593
MIKVAH NEAR GERSHEL AVENUE ... NORMA **NJ** 08347 (609) 691-7191
SHORE AREA MIKVAH 201 JEROME AVENUE ... OAKHURST **NJ** 07755 (201) 531-1712
SHAARAY TEFILOH SYNAGOGUE 15 MARKET STREET ... PERTH AMBOY **NJ** 08862 (201) 826-2977
MIKVAH ASSOCIATION 1726 WINDSOR ROAD ... TEANECK **NJ** 07666 (201) 837-8220
MIKVAH ISRAEL OF NORTH HUDSON 412 34TH STREET ... UNION CITY **NJ** 07087 (201) 866-0690
MIKVAH 717 PLEASANT VALLEY WAY ... WEST ORANGE **NJ** 07052 (201) 731-1427
BETH ISRAEL SYNAGOGUE 1480 OXFORD STREET ... HALIFAX **NS** B3H 3Y8 (902) 422-1301
CONGREGATION SGOOLAI ISRAEL 168 WESTMORLAND STREET ... FREDERICTON **NB** (506) 455-8425
CONGREGATION SHAAREI ZEDEK ... ST JOHN **NB** (506) 657-1962
MIKVAH 4800 EUBANK N.E. ... ALBUQUERQUE **NM** 87111 (505) 296-6060
MIKVAH 190 ELM STREET ... ALBANY **NY** 12202 (518) 482-5781
BETH DAVID SYNAGOGUE 39 RIVERSIDE DRIVE ... BINGHAMTON **NY** 13905 (607) 722-1793
AITZ CHAIM 708 MACE AVENUE ... BRONX **NY** 10465 (212) 798-6173
AGUDAS TAHARAS HAMISHPACHAH OF CROWN HEIGHTS
1608 UNION STREET ... BROOKLYN **NY** 11211 (718) 493-2661
CANARSIE COMMUNITY MIKVAH FLATLANDS & REMSEN STREETS ... BROOKLYN **NY** 11236 (718) 251-5084
CONGREGATION ARUGAS HABOSEM 135 RODNEY STREET ... BROOKLYN **NY** 11211 (718) 782-6608
CONGREGATION KEHILAS MORIYOH-SEA GATE
3740 OCEANIC AVENUE ... BROOKLYN **NY** 11224 (718) 372-6706
KEHILAS YAAKOV 110-112 PENN STREET ... BROOKLYN **NY** 11211 (718) 625-8795
KEHILAS YAAKOV 115 RUTLEDGE ... BROOKLYN **NY** 11211 (718) 624-9262
MIKVAH 2965 OCEAN PARKWAY ... BROOKLYN **NY** 11235 (718) 891-4286
MIKVAH INFORMATION - FAMILY SANCTITY
780 MONTGOMERY STREET ... BROOKLYN **NY** 11213 (718) 778-1070
MIKVAH ISRAEL OF BENSONHURST 48 BAY 28 STREET ... BROOKLYN **NY** 11214 (718) 372-9563
MIKVAH ISRAEL OF BORO PARK 1351 46TH STREET ... BROOKLYN **NY** 11219 (718) 871-6866
MIKVAH ISRAEL OF BRIGHTON 245 NEPTUNE AVENUE ... BROOKLYN **NY** 11235 (718) 760-8599
MIKVAH OF BORO PARK 1249 52ND STREET ... BROOKLYN **NY** 11219 (718) 438-9808
MIKVAH-CONGREGATION HAMAOR 5012 18TH AVENUE ... BROOKLYN **NY** 11204 (718) 633-7724
RITUALARIUM OF EAST FLATBUSH 340 EAST 52ND STREET ... BROOKLYN **NY** 11203 (718) 385-7707
RITUALARIUM OF EASTERN PARKWAY 1506 UNION STREET ... BROOKLYN **NY** 11213 (718) 773-8826
SEPHARDIC MIKVAH ISRAEL 810 AVENUE S ... BROOKLYN **NY** 11223 (718) 339-4600
TAHARATH ISRAEL OF EAST FLATBUSH 1013 EAST 15TH STREET ... BROOKLYN **NY** 11226 (718) 377-9813
Y.I. OF BEDFORD BAY 2113 HARING STREET ... BROOKLYN **NY** 11229 (718) 332-4120
YETEV LEV D'SATMAR 212 WILLIAMSBURG STREET ... BROOKLYN **NY** 11211 (718) 387-9388
MIKVAH 1248 KENMORE ... BUFFALO **NY** 14216 (716) 875-8451
CONGREGATION EZRATH ISRAEL 31 CENTER STREET ... ELLENVILLE **NY** 12428 (914) 647-8740
HEBREW COMMUNITY SERVICE 1121 BAYPORT PLACE ... FAR ROCKAWAY **NY** 11691 (718) 327-9727
FLEISCHMANNS ... FLEISCHMANNS **NY** 12430 (914) 254-4595
MIKVAH (CONG. OF GEORGIAN JEWS FROM RUSSIA)
102-58 63RD AVENUE ... FOREST HILLS **NY** 11375 (212) 897-6139
MIKVAH OF QUEENS 75-48 GRAND CENTRAL PARKWAY ... FOREST HILLS **NY** 11375 (718) 261-6380
MIKVAH ASSOCIATION OF GREAT NECK 26 OLD MILL ROAD ... GREAT NECK **NY** 11023 (516) 487-2726
MIKVAH SOUTH SHORE, CONGREGATION 1156 PENINSULA BLVD ... HEWLETT **NY** 11557 (516) 569-5514
MIKVAH ISRAEL 71-11 VLEIGH PLACE ... KEW GARDEN HILLS **NY** 11367 (718) 268-6500
MIKVAH 37 LINCOLN PLACE ... LIBERTY **NY** 12754 (914) 292-9733
HOTEL AISHEL ... LIVINGSTON MANOR **NY** 12758 (914) 439-5161
SCHARF MANOR 274 WEST BROADWAY ... LONG BEACH **NY** 11561 (516) 431-7758
CONGREGATION YETEV LEV 20 QUICKWAY ROAD ... MONROE **NY** 10950 (914) 783-3451
MIKVAH ISRAEL MAPLE LEAF ROAD ... MONSEY **NY** 10952 (914) 356-1000
MIKVAH 16 NORTH STREET ... MONTICELLO **NY** 12701 (914) 794-6757
YESHIVA FARM SETTLEMENT MIKVAH PINES BRIDGE ROAD ... MOUNT KISCO **NY** 10549 (914) 666-5321
MIKVAH ... MOUNTAINDALE **NY** 12763 (914) 434-9192
MIKVAH OF EAST SIDE 313 EAST BROADWAY ... NEW YORK **NY** 10002 (212) 475-8514
MIKVAH OF MID-MANHATTAN 234 WEST 78TH STREET ... NEW YORK **NY** 10024 (212) 799-1520
MIKVAH OF WASHINGTON HEIGHTS 536 WEST 187TH STREET ... NEW YORK **NY** 10033 (212) 923-9548
MIKVAH 3397 PARK AVENUE ... OCEANSIDE **NY** 11572 (516) 766-3242
SHOMREI ISRAEL SYNAGOGUE 18 PARK AVENUE ... POUGHKEEPSIE **NY** 12603 (914) 454-4078
MIKVAH 3710 HENRY HUDSON PARKWAY ... RIVERDALE **NY** 10463 (212) 549-8336
BETH HAKNESES HACHODOSH 27 ST. REGIS DRIVE N ... ROCHESTER **NY** 14618 (716) 244-4888
Y.I. OF SCARSDALE 1313 WEAVER STREET ... SCARSDALE **NY** 10583 (914) 636-8686
MIKVAH 33 TRUMAN AVENUE ... SPRING VALLEY **NY** 10977 (914) 354-6578
MIKVAH ISRAEL 61 RUPERT AVENUE ... STATEN ISLAND **NY** 10314 (718) 698-4066
YOUNG ISRAEL SYNAGOGUE 2200 EAST GENESEE STREET ... SYRACUSE **NY** 13210 (315) 472-8411
CONGREGATION ANSHEI HASHARON THOMPKINS STREET ... TANNERSVILLE **NY** 12485 (518) 589-5830
MIKVAH IN UTICA 110 MEMORIAL PKWY ... UTICA **NY** 13501 (315) 724-8357
MIKVAH ASSOCIATION OF NASSAU COUNTY
775 HEMPSTEAD AVENUE ... WEST HEMPSTEAD **NY** 11552 (516) 489-9358
MIKVAH EAST POND ROAD ... WOODRIDGE **NY** 12789 (914) 434-9726
MIKVAH GREEN RD ... BEECHWOOD **OH** 44122 (216) 381-9178
MIKVAH 1546 KENOVA AVENUE ... CINCINNATI **OH** 45237 (513) 821-6679
MIKVAH 1774 LEE ROAD ... CLEVELAND HEIGHTS **OH** 44118 (216) 321-0270
CONGREGATION BETH JACOB 1223 COLLEGE AVENUE ... COLUMBUS **OH** 43209 (614) 237-8641
MIKVAH 556 KENWOOD AVENUE ... DAYTON **OH** 45406 (513) 277-6754
AITZ CHAIM SYNAGOGUE 3853 WOODLEY ROAD ... TOLEDO **OH** 43606 (419) 473-8838
CHILDREN OF ISRAEL 1702 FIFTH AVENUE ... YOUNGSTOWN **OH** 44504 (216) 744-1754
CONGREGATION BNAI EMUNAH ... TULSA **OK** (918) 583-7121
LUBAVITCH MIKVAH 42A EDINBURGH DRIVE ... DOWNSVIEW **ON** (416) 633-4608
MIKVAH SOCIETY 694 SHEPPARD AVENUE WEST ... DOWNSVIEW **ON** (416) 633-4729
ADAS ISRAEL RITUALARIUM OF HAMILTON 128 CLINE AVENUE SOUTH ... HAMILTON **ON** (416) 525-3768

BETH ISRAEL SYNAGOGUE 116 CENTRE STREET	KINGSTON	**ON**		(613) 542-5012
CONGREGATION BETH TEFILOH ADELAIDE STREET	LONDON	**ON**		(519) 433-7081
RITUALARIUM (IN SYNAGOGUE) 151 CHAPEL STREET	OTTAWA	**ON**		(613) 232-7306
CONGREGATION SHAAREY ZEDEK 610 GILES BLVD. EAST	WINDSOR	**ON**		(519) 252-1594
JEWISH RITUALARIUM 1425 S.W. HARRISON STREET	PORTLAND	**OR**	97201	(503) 222-7069
MIKVAH 1836 WHITEHALL STREET	ALLENTOWN	**PA**	18102	(215) 434-3809
PHILADELPHIA MIKVAH ASSN. WYNNEWOOD & ARGYLE RDS.	ARDMORE	**PA**	19003	(215) 642-8679
MIKVAH 3601 NORTH 4TH STREET	HARRISBURG	**PA**	17110	(717) 232-2023
CONGREGATION OHEV SHOLOM 20 EAST THIRD STREET	LEWISTOWN	**PA**	17044	(717) 248-8070
CONGREGATION GEMILAS CHESED 1545 OHIO AVENUE	MCKEESPORT	**PA**	15131	(412) 678-8859
MIKVAH 4600 OLD YORK ROAD	PHILADELPHIA	**PA**	19140	(215) 455-0699
JEWISH WOMEN'S LEAGUE 2336 SHADY AVENUE	PITTSBURGH	**PA**	15217	(412) 422-7110
MACHZIKEH HADAS MADISON AVENUE & VINE STREET	SCRANTON	**PA**	18510	(717) 344-5138
MIKVAH 3RD AVENUE AND INSTITUTE LANE	WILKES-BARRE	**PA**	18704	(717) 287-2032
OHEV SHALOM CHERRY & BELMONT STREETS	WILLIAMSPORT	**PA**	17701	(717) 322-7050
MIKVE KIRYAT THAS AVE. BET HALEVI	BOISBRIAND	**QU**		(514) 430-4114
MIKVAH ISRAEL 7015 KILDARE, COTE ST. LUC	MONTREAL	**QU**		
MIKVAH MAYEN (CONGREGATION YETEV LEV) 5214 ST. URBAIN STREET	MONTREAL	**QU**		(514) 279-9443
MIKVAH TAHARATH HAMISHPACHA 5124 ST. URBAIN STREET	MONTREAL	**QU**		(514) 277-7013
MIKVAH OF MONTREAL 6235 HILLSDALE ROAD	MONTREAL	**QU**		(514) 737-2625
CONGREGATION SHAARE ZEDEK 688 BROAD STREET	PROVIDENCE	**RI**	02907	(401) 751-4936
BRITH SHOLOM BETH ISRAEL 182 RUTLEDGE	CHARLESTON	**SC**	29403	(803) 577-6599
CONGREGATION BETH JACOB 1640 VICTORIA AVENUE	REGINA	**SK**		(306) 527-8643
JEWISH COMMUNITY CENTER 715 MCKINNON AVENUE	SASKATOON	**SK**		(306) 343-7023
BETH SHOLOM CONGREGATION 20 PISGAH AVENUE	CHATTANOOGA	**TN**	37411	(615) 894-0801
BARON HIRSCH CONGREGATION 1740 VOLLINTINE AVENUE	MEMPHIS	**TN**	38107	(901) 274-3525
CONGREGATION SHERITH ISRAEL 3600 WEST END AVENUE	NASHVILLE	**TN**	37205	(615) 292-6614
ANSHE SPHARD-BETH EL EMETH 120 EAST YATES DRIVE NORTH	NORTH MEMPHIS	**TN**	38117	(901) 682-1611
CONGREGATION TIFERETH ISRAEL 10909 HILLCREST ROAD	DALLAS	**TX**	75230	(214) 691-3611
MIKVAH (CONG. BNAI ZION) 905 CHERRY HILL LANE	EL PASO	**TX**	79912	(915) 532-3137
MIKVAH ISRAEL OF HOUSTON 109-00 FONDERN	HOUSTON	**TX**	77096	(713) 981-1000
UNITED ORTHODOX SYNAGOGUE 4221 SOUTH BRAESWOOD BOULEVARD	HOUSTON	**TX**	77096	(713) 723-3850
CONGREGATION RODFEI SHOLOM 115 EAST LAUREL	SAN ANTONIO	**TX**	78212	(512) 227-6040
CONGREGATION ETZ CHAIM 720 WILSON STREET	DANVILLE	**VA**	24541	
CONGREGATION ADATH JESHURUN 1815 CHESTNUT AVENUE	NEWPORT NEWS	**VA**	23607	(804) 245-7485
CONGREGATION BNAI ISRAEL 420 SPOTSWOOD AVENUE	NORFOLK	**VA**	23517	(804) 627-7358
CONGREGATION KOL EMES 4811 PATTERSON AVENUE	RICHMOND	**VA**	23226	(804) 353-5831
MIKVAH 168 ARCHIBALD STREET	BURLINGTON	**VT**	05401	(802) 658-2962
MIKVAH 5140 SOUTH HOLLY STREET	SEATTLE	**WA**	98118	(206) 723-3644
CONGREGATION AGUDAS ACHIM 5820 WEST BURLEIGH	MILWAUKEE	**WI**	53210	(414) 447-9239
CONGREGATION BETH JEHUDA 2700 NO. 54TH STREET	MILWAUKEE	**WI**	53210	(414) 447-7727
MIKVAH (LUBAVITCH HOUSE) 3109 N. LAKE DRIVE	MILWAUKEE	**WI**	53211	(414) 962-0566
BNAI JACOB SYNAGOGUE VIRGINIA & ELIZABETH STREETS	CHARLESTON	**WV**	25311	(304) 346-4722
MT. SINAI CONGREGATION 2610 PIONEER AVENUE	CHEYENNE	**WY**	82001	(307) 634-3052
MIKVAH (IN SYNAGOGUE) JOACHIMSTALERSTRASSE 13	1 BERLIN 15			() 881-9300
MIKVAH (ASHKENAZI) HEINZSTR. 3	AMSTERDAM			
MIKVAH (SEPHARDI) J.D. MEYERPLEIN 7	AMSTERDAM			
MIKVAH STEENBOKSTRAAT 22	ANTWERP			
MIKVAH ANTHEON & KAMELION STREETS, SUBURB OF P. PSIHICO	ATHENS			
MIKVAH (BETH ISRAEL) GREY'S AVENUE	AUCKLAND			
MIKVAH JUDISCHE KURHOTEL, FRANKFURTERSTR. 63-65	BAD NAUHEIM			() 817-26
MIKVAH (IN SYNAGOGUE) KARLSTRASSE 34	BAD NAUHEIM			() 560-5
MIKVAH (IN SYNAGOGUE) CALLE PORVENIR 24	BARCELONA			() 200-6148
MIKVAH LEIMENSTR. 24	BASEL			
MIKVAH, WOLFSON CENTRE 49 SOMERTON ROAD	BELFAST			(232) 777-974
MIKVAH BOURNEVILLE LANE BATHS	BIRMINGHAM			(021) 440-1019
MIKVAH (BLOEMFONTEIN HEBREW CONGREGATION) CORNER OF FAIRVIEW & UNION ROAD	BLOEMFONTEIN			
MIKVAH CALLE 25 N. 27A 39	BOGOTA			
MIKVAH CALLE 79N. 9-66	BOGOTA			
MIKVAH (IN SYNAGOGUE) VIA MARIO FINZI	BOLOGNA			(051) 340-936
MIKVAH (BOURNEMOUTH HEBREW CONGREGATION) WOOTTON GARDENS	BOURNEMOUTH			(202) 278-47
MACHSIKE HADASS 67A RUE DE LA CLINIQUE	BRUSSELS			() 521-1289
MIKVAH (IN SYNAGOGUE) STR. MAMULARI 21	BUCHAREST			
MIKVAH, VII KAZINCZY UTCA 16	BUDAPEST			
MIKVAH BOGOTA 3015 (FLORES)	BUENOS AIRES			() 612-4905
MIKVAH MOLDES 2449 (BELGRANO)	BUENOS AIRES			() 781-4859
MIKVAH LARREA 730-732 (ONCE)	BUENOS AIRES			
MIKVAH (HEBREW CONGREGATION) P.O. BOX 337, ABERCORN STREET	BULAWAYO			
CALGARY HEBREW SCHOOL 1415 GLENMORE TRAIL	CALGARY			(403) 253-3992
MIKVAH (BETH DIN) P.O. BOX 543	CAPETOWN			
MIKVAH (UNION ISRAELITA SYNAGOGUE) AV. MARQUES DEL TORO. SAN BERNARDINO	CARACAS			
MIKVAH WALES EMPIRE POOL BUILDING	CARDIFF			
MIKVAH (ECOLE LUBAVITCH) 174 BLVD. ZIRAOUI	CASABLANCA			
MIKVAH (EN HABANIM 14 RUE LUSITANIA	CASABLANCA			
MIKVAH (OZAR HATORAH) 59 RUE VERLET HANUS	CASABLANCA			
MIKVAH (IN SYNAGOGUE) ROONSTRASSE 50	COLOGNE			
JEWISH COMMUNITY CENTER 6 NY KONGENSGADE 1472 K	COPENHAGEN			
MIKVAH (IN SYNAGOGUE) UL. MIODOWA 24	CRACOW			
MIKVAH ETANIA SANATORIUM	DAVOS			
MIKVAH 37 ADELAIDE ROAD	DUBLIN			
MIKVAH (GREAT SYNAGOGUE) ESSENWOOD ROAD, BEREA	DURBAN			
MIKVAH (IN SYNAGOGUE) ZEITENSTRASSE 50	DUSSELDORF			
MIKVAH PRINSESTRAAT 16	ENSCHEDE			
MIKVAH 465 CRANBROOK ROAD, ILFORD	ESSEX			554-8532

MIKVAH (IN SYNAGOGUE) VIA L.C. FARINI 4	FLORENCE		270-763
MIKVAH (IN SYNAGOGUE) FREIHERR VON STEINSTRASSE 30	FRANKFURT-AM-MAIN		721-568
MIKVAH (IN SYNAGOGUE) JULIENSTRASSE 2	FUERTH		
MIKVAH PARTIZANSKA 907	GALANTA		
MIKVAH (IN SYNAGOGUE) 180 BEWICK ROAD	GATESHEAD		(632) 781-472
MIKVAH (HEKHAL HANESS) 54 TER ROUTE DE MALGNOU	GENEVA		
MIKVAH 10 BOMB HOUSE LANE	GIBRALTAR		431-6
MIKVAH (GIFFNOCK & NEWLANDS SYNAGOGUE) MARYVILLE AVENUE	GIFFNOCK, GLASGOW		(041) 638-6600
MIKVAH KAHN'S SILBERHORN HOTEL	GRINDELWALD		
MIKVAH KENAUPARK 7	HAARLEM		143-42
MIKVAH (IN SYNAGOGUE) HOHE WEIDE 34	HAMBURG		
MIKVAH (IN SYNAGOGUE) HAECKELSTRASSE 10	HANOVER		
MIKVAH 70 ROBINSON ROAD	HONG KONG		
MIKVAH, CAGALOGLU KADINLAR HAMAMI CAGALOGLU	ISTANBUL		440-472
MIKVAH (ADATH JESHURUN SYNAGOGUE) 34 FORTESCUE ROAD, YEOVILLE	JOHANNESBURG		433-380
MIKVAH (BETH DIN) 24 RALEIGH STREET, YEOVILLE	JOHANNESBURG		432-161
MIKVAH VRIDELNI 59	KARLSBAD		
MIKVAH	KNOKKE		
MIKVAH (JEWISH COMMUNITY OF JAPAN) 66-1, KITANO-CHO, 4-CHOME. IKUTA-KU	KOBE 650		221-7236
MIKVAH (CONGREGATION SHOMREI HADASS) 368 HARROGATE ROAD	LEEDS		(532) 685-119
MIKVAH (CHILDWALL SYNAGOGUE PRECINCT) DUNBABIN ROAD	LIVERPOOL		(051) 722-2079
MIKVAH 62 FILEY AVENUE	LONDON, N. 16		800-8534
NORTH LONDON MIKVAH 40 QUEEN ELIZABETH'S WALK	LONDON, N. 16		(01) 802-2554
STAMFORD HILL MIKVAH MARGARET STREET (LAMPARD GORVE)	LONDON, N. 16		(01) 806-3880
NORTH WEST LONDON COMMUNAL MIKVAH 10 SHIREHALL LANE	LONDON, N.W.4		(01) 202-8517
MIKVAH BRUCHSTR. 51	LUCERNE		
MIKVAH (IN SYNAGOGUE) 11 VIA MADERNO	LUGANO		
MIKVAH (IN SYNAGOGUE) CALLE BALMES	MADRID		445-9843
MIKVAH	MALAGA		214-875
MIKVAH (JEWISH COMMUNITY CENTER) KAMERGATAN 11	MALMO		
COMMUNITY MIKVAH BROOM HOLME, TETLOW LANE, SALFORD 7	MANCHESTER		(061) 740-4333
MANCHESTER & DISTRICT MIKVAH SEDGLEY PARK ROAD, PRESTWICH	MANCHESTER		(061) 733-1537
MIKVAH (ADAS ISRAEL SYNAGOGUE) 24 GLEN EIRA AVENUE, RIPPONLEA, ST. KILDA	MELBOURNE		523-5587
MIKVAH CAMPECHE 255, COLONIA HIPODROMO	MEXICO CITY		574-2224
MIKVAH (MOGEN DAVID SYNAGOGUE) PRESIDENTE MASARYK & BERNARD SHAW, COLONIA POLANCO	MEXICO CITY		540-3492
MIKVAH VIA SALLY MEYER 4-6	MILAN		412-1539
MIKVAH (IN SYNAGOGUE) VIA GUASTALLA 19	MILAN		791-892
MIKVAH MALDONADO 1168	MONTEVIDEO		981-405
MIKVAH MARCELINO BERTELOT 1884	MONTEVIDEO		257-09
MIKVAH (IN SYNAGOGUE) REICHENBACHSTRASSE 27	MUNICH		
MIKVAH (IN SYNAGOGUE) POSSARTSTRASSE 15	MUNICH		
MIKVAH BERGSTIEN 15	OSLO		
MIKVAH 55 ROOSEVELT ROAD, GLENGINNINGVALE	PORT ELIZABETH		331-332
MIKVAH RUA FRANCISCO FERRER 170	PORTO ALEGRE		
MIKVAH ZAMOCKA 49A	PRESSBURG		
MIKVAH (GREAT SYNAGOGUE) 717 PRETORIUS STREET	PRETORIA		742-069
MIKVAH RUA GENERAL CANABARRA 454	RIO DE JANEIRO		
MIKVAH (IN SYNAGOGUE) VIA BALBO 33	ROME		475-9881
MIKVAH (IN SYNAGOGUE) LUNGOTEVERE CENCI 9	ROME		
MIKVAH (IN SYNAGOGUE) A.B.N. DAVIDSPLEIN 4	ROTTERDAM		
MIKVAH LASSERSTRASSE 8	SALZBURG		
MIKVAH, NEXT TO CONGREGATION CHEVRA KADISHA	SANTIAGO		465-927
MIKVAH RUA HADDOCK LOBO 1279	SAO PAOLO		
MIKVAH BOM RETIRO, RUA TENENTE PENA 310	SAO PAOLO		
MIKVAH (CONGREGATION KHAL CHASIDIM) RUA MAMORE 597	SAO PAOLO		220-1735
MIKVAH (KHAL MACHZIKEI HADASS) RUA PADRE JOAO MANOEL 693	SAO PAOLO		282-6762
MIKVAH, SISLI SINAJONU EFE SOKATE NO. 4	SISLI-ISTANBUL		
MIKVAH (SOUTHPORT HEBREW CONGREGATION) ARNSIDE ROAD	SOUTHPORT		(704) 261-89
MIKVAH HOTEL EDELWEISS	ST. MORITZ		(082) 355-33
MIKVAH (JEWISH COMMUNITY CENTER) NYBROGATAN 19	STOCKHOLM		636-566
MIKVAH (IN SYNAGOGUE) HOSPITALSTRASSE 36	STUTTGART		295-665
MIKVAH (BAIS 'AMEDRASH) MOWBRAY ROAD	SUNDERLAND		(783) 574-17
MIKVAH 117 GLENAYR AVENUE, BONDI	SYDNEY		302-509
MIKVAH (IN SYNAGOGUE) WAGENSTR. 101	THE HAGUE		450-417
MIKVAH (JEWISH COMMUNITY CENTER) 8-8, HIROO 3-CHOME. SHIBUYA-KU	TOKYO 150		(400) 255-9
MIKVAH (LUBAVITCH) IN TUNIS 65 AV. TAIEB MEHIRI	TUNIS		280-900
MIKVAH SPRINGWEG 164	UTRECHT		314-742
MIKVAH, JEWISH REST HOME SHETTO NUOVO 2874	VENICE		201-92
MIKVAH FLEISCHMARKT 22	VIENNA I		
MIKVAH DOBLINGER GURTEL 11	VIENNA XIX		
MIKVAH (WELLINGTON HEBREW CONGREGATION) 80 WEBB STREET	WELLINGTON		845-081
MIKVAH GENESTA ROAD, AT REAR OF SATANITA ROAD	WESTCLIFF		(702) 449-00
MIKVAH VALENTIN-BECKERSTRASSE 11	WURZBURG		
MIKVAH (IN SYNAGOGUE) FREIGUTSTRASSE 37	ZURICH		201-6746
MIKVAH (IN SYNAGOGUE) FREIGUST STATION 37	ZURICH		201-6746
MIKVAH, PAVILLION SALVATOR RUE DE PRESIDENT ROOSEVELT	AIX-LES-BAINS	**FR**	352-808
MIKVAH (IN SYNAGOGUE) 3 RUE MONTPERRIN	AIX-EN-PROVENCE	**FR**	266-939
MIKVAH (IN SYNAGOGUE) RUE GANBETTA	ARACHON	**FR**	213-875
MIKVAH 213 RUE STE. CATHERINE	BORDEAUX	**FR**	
MIKVAH 28 AVENUE DE NEWBURN	CHOISY-LE-ROI	**FR**	853-4827
MIKVAH 3 RUE DE LA SYNAGOGUE	COLMAR	**FR**	413-829
MIKVAH RUE DU 8 MAI 1945	CRETEIL	**FR**	207-3782

MIKVAH (IN SYNAGOGUE) 11 RUE MAGINOT	GRENOBLE	**FR**		870-280
MIKVAH 317 RUE DUGUESCLIN	LYON	**FR**		
MIKVAH 45 RUE A. BOUTIN	LYON VILLEURBANNE	**FR**		
MIKVAH 45A RUE CONSOLAT	MARSEILLES	**FR**		
MIKVAH 73 RUE DE LA PALUD	MARSEILLES	**FR**		
MIKVAH 41 RUE AUX ARENES	METZ	**FR**		
MIKVAH RUE DE LA SYNAGOGUE	MEUDON-LA-FORET	**FR**		630-8284
MIKVAH 19 RUE DE LA SYNAGOGUE	MULHOUSE	**FR**		
MIKVAH (IN SYNAGOGUE) 5 IMPASSE COPERNIC	NANTES	**FR**		734-892
MIKVAH 1 BIS RUE BOISSY D'ANGLAS	NICE	**FR**		805-896
MIKVAH 22 RUE MICHELET	NICE	**FR**		
MIKVAH 176 RUE DU TEMPLE	PARIS	**FR**	75003	271-8928
MIKVAH 50 RUE DU FAUBOURG ST. MARTIN	PARIS	**FR**	75010	206-4395
MIKVAH 74 AVENUE PAUL VALERY	SARCELLES	**FR**		992-1180
MIKVAH RUE GEORGE V	SARRAGUEMINES	**FR**		
MIKVAH LA RUE RENE HIRSCHLER	STRASBOURG	**FR**		356-135
MIKVAH 15 RUE FRANCISQUE SARCEY	TOULOUSE	**FR**		804-542
MIKVAH (IN SYNAGOGUE) 5 RUE BRUNNEVAL	TROYES	**FR**		
MIKVAH RUE CHARLOT	VICHY	**FR**		
MIKVAH GIVAT HAMOREH, SHCHUNAT YAAR EXTENSION	AFULA	**IS**		
MIKVAH RECHOV KINAMON (OPPOSITE FOOTBALL FIELD)	AFULA	**IS**		
MIKVAH SHIKUN RASSCO	AFULA LLIT	**IS**		
MIKVAH DERECH HAARBAAH (NEWAR EGGED BUS STATION)	AKKO	**IS**		
MIKVAH SHIKUN GIMMEL	AKKO	**IS**		
MIKVAH NEAR YOUTH HOSTEL, OPPOSITE EMPLOYMENT OFFICE	ARAD	**IS**		
MIKVAH DISTRICT A, NEAR RAMBAM SCHOOL	ASHDOD	**IS**		
MIKVAH SHCHUNAT HAPOLANIM	ASHKELON	**IS**		
MIKVAH 38 HALPER STREET	BAT YAM	**IS**		
MIKVAH KIRYAT BOBOV	BAT YAM	**IS**		
MIKVAH HAVRADIM ST., RAMAT YOSEF	BAT YAM	**IS**		
MIKVAH SHCHUNA DALED, HAKNIZI CIRCLE,				
NEAR THE OLD CENTER	BEERSHEVA	**IS**		
MIKVAH RECHOV CHOFETZ CHAIM, CORNER MAHARSHAL	BNEI BRAK	**IS**		787-479
MIKVAH RECHOV RAMBAM	BNEI BRAK	**IS**		
MIKVAH SHIKUN VISHNITZ	BNEI BRAK	**IS**		
MIKVAH NEXT TO THE CENTRAL SYNAGOGUE	EILAT	**IS**		
MIKVAH 55 TIBER STREET	GIVATAYIM	**IS**		
MIKVAH 2 MENORAH STREET	GIVATAYIM	**IS**		
MIKVAH RECHOV HAGIBORIM, ENTER FROM YOVEL STREET	HADERA	**IS**		
CENTRAL MIKVAH, RECHOV ARLOZOROV, WOMEN'S ENTRANCE				
2 BEZALEL STREET	HAIFA	**IS**		
MIKVAH 5 RECHOV TZFAT				
(CORNER HANEVIIM & HERZLIA STREETS) HADAR	HAIFA	**IS**		
MIKVAH NEAR CENTRAL SYNAGOGUE. KIRYAT SHMUEL	HAIFA	**IS**		712-926
MIKVAH (CARMEL CENTRAL SYNAGOGUE)				
10 DERECH HAYAM., MT. CARMEL	HAIFA	**IS**		817-72
MIKVAH (IN SYNAGOGUE) 16 SDEROT SINAI. ACHUZA	HAIFA	**IS**		
MIKVAH SIRKIN STREET, NEAR CENTRAL SYNAGOGUE	HERZLIA	**IS**		
MIKVAH NEAR CENTRAL SYNAGOGUE, RAMATAYIM	HOD HASHARON	**IS**		
MIKVAH RECHOV SOKOLOV, MAGDIEL	HOD HASHARON	**IS**		
MIKVAH NEAR ASHKENAZI SYNAGOGUE, GANEI ZVI	HOD HASHARON	**IS**		
MIKVAH RECHOV SHIMON HATZADIK, NEVEI NE'EMAN	HOD HASHARON	**IS**		
MIKVAH EDNA INSTITUTE, 9 RAV KOOK ST., AGROBANK	HOLON	**IS**		848-759
MIKVAH SHCHUNAT G. COHEN, RECHOV HASANHEDRIN	HOLON	**IS**		
MIKVAH 3 RECHOV FLORENTIN. KIRYAT HAYOVEL	JERUSALEM	**IS**		417-110
MIKVAH 1 RECHOV PANIM MEIROT. KIRYAT MATTERSDORF	JERUSALEM	**IS**		521-019
MIKVAH 5 RECHOV HA'ARI. RECHAVIA	JERUSALEM	**IS**		327-83
MIKVAH 7 RECHOV HAMATZOR. KATAMON	JERUSALEM	**IS**		
MIKVAH 13 RECHOV YEHUDA HANASI. KATAMON HEH	JERUSALEM	**IS**		363-52
MIKVAH ORENSTEIN BUILDINGS. ZICHRON MOCHE	JERUSALEM	**IS**		
MIKVAH 8 RECHOV HANATZIV. SHCHUNAT BATEI RAND	JERUSALEM	**IS**		
MIKVAH 22 RECHOV HARAV BLAU, SANHEDRIA	JERUSALEM	**IS**		
MIKVAH NEAR CENTRAL SYNAGOGUE, SHCHUNAT MEKOR CHAIM	JERUSALEM	**IS**		
MIKVAH (CENTRAL HOTEL) 6 PINES STREET	JERUSALEM	**IS**		223-111
MIKVAH (CENTRAL SHEPHARDI SYNAGOGUE)				
RECHOV BAYIT VEGAN 9	JERUSALEM	**IS**		225-560
MIKVAH TAL 7 RECHOV GID'ON. SHCHUNAT BAK'A	JERUSALEM	**IS**		375-97
MIKVAH YISROEL OFF STRAUSS STREET	JERUSALEM	**IS**		234-791
MIKVAH 23 RECHOV HATIKVAH	KFAR SABA	**IS**		
MIKVAH RECHOV HAMEYASDIM	KIRYAT ATTA	**IS**		
MIKVAH 15 RECHOV REUVEN	KIRYAT BIALIK	**IS**		
MIKVAH RECHOV BET GURBIN-				
NEXT TO BET YISROEL V'DAMESEK ELIEZER	KIRYAT GAT	**IS**		
MIKVAH SHUCHUNAT NACHALAT HAR-CHABAD,				
NEXT TO KUPAT CHOLIM CLINI	KIRYAT MALACHI	**IS**		
MIKVAH RECHOV EILAT, NEXT TO CENTER FOR THE AGED	KIRYAT MALACHI	**IS**		
MIKVAH RAMBAM STREET, NEXT TO MAON WIZO	KIRYAT MALACHI	**IS**		
MIKVAH 1 RECHOV GRUSHKEVITZ	KIRYAT MOTZKIN	**IS**		
MIKVAH 53 RECHOV JABOTINSKY	KIRYAT ONO	**IS**		
MIKVAH RECHOV S.Y. AGNON	KIRYAT ONO	**IS**		
MIKVAH SHIKUN CHABAD, SHCHUNAT HARAKEVET	LOD	**IS**		
MIKVAH RECHOV ELPAEL, CORNER RECHOV NATAN SCHWARTZ	LOD	**IS**		
MIKVAH RECHOV AHAD HA'AM	NAHARIYA	**IS**		
MIKVAH NEAR HAGALIL CIRCLE, NEXT TO KINDERGARTEN	NAZARETH LLLIT	**IS**		
MIKVAH 29 RECHOV HA'ATZMAUT	NES ZIONA	**IS**		
CENTRAL MIKVAH 25 YEHUDA HALEVI	NETANYA	**IS**		918-39
MIKVAH KIRYAT ZANS	NETANYA	**IS**		
MIKVAH KIRYAT NORDAU	NETANYA	**IS**		
MIKVAH RECHOV HAMACHABIM, CORNER OF ORLOV,				
NEXT TO CENTRAL BUS ST	PETACH TIKVAH	**IS**		
MIKVAH RECHOV HERZL, CENTER OF TOWN	RA'ANANA	**IS**		
MIKVAH 7 HAGIBORIM STREET	RAMAT GAN	**IS**		
MIKVAH 5 RECHOV UZIEL	RAMAT GAN	**IS**		789-340
MIKVAH RECHOV AZNEL, NEXT TO SCHOOL, RAMAT HASHIKMAH	RAMAT GAN	**IS**		769-9256
MIKVAH SHCHUNAT WEIZMAN	RAMLAH	**IS**		
MIKVAH RECHOV MOTZKIN	RAMLAH	**IS**		
MIKVAH RECHOV HASHOFTIM, CENTER OF TOWN,				
NEAR TNUVA DELIVERY CE	RECHOVO	**IS**		
CENTRAL MIKVAH RECHOV NECHAMA,				
NEAR CENTRAL SYNAGOGUE	RISHON LEZION	**IS**		
MIKVAH SHCHUNAT MIZRACH RECHOV YOSEF HANASI	RISHON LEZION	**IS**		
MIKVAH SHCHUNAT RAMAT ELIAHU, RECHOV TORAH V'AVODAH	RISHON LEZION	**IS**		
MIKVAH SHIKUN DAROM, RECHOV HERZL, OPPOSITE RASSCO	SAFED	**IS**		
MIKVAH HAMAGINIM CIRCLE	SAFED	**IS**		
MIKVAH 202 BNEI EPHRAIM STREET. HADAR YOSEF	TEL AVIV	**IS**		
MIKVAH 24 PINES STREET	TEL AVIV	**IS**		548-53
MIKVAH 5 RECHOV HATECHIYA. YAFO	TEL AVIV	**IS**		827-142
MIKVAH SDEROT HACHAYAL. YAD ELIAHU	TEL AVIV	**IS**		372-56
MIKVAH 10 RECHOV YAVNE	TEL AVIV	**IS**		296-512
MIKVAH 8 RECHOV HAKOVSHIM	TEL AVIV	**IS**		
MIKVAH (ICHUD SHAVEI ZION SYNAGOGUE) 86 RECHOV BEN YEHUDA	TEL AVIV	**IS**		228-188
MIKVAH RECHOV HAYARKON, IN LOWER CITY	TIBERIAS	**IS**		
MIKVAH SHIKUN DALED, ON STREET OF DAN HALL	TIBERIAS	**IS**		
MIKVAH END OF RECHOV HARAV VERNER, KIRYAT SHMUEL	TIBERIAS	**IS**		
MIKVAH SHIKUN DROMI, OPPOSITE SCHOOL	ZICHRON YAAKOV	**IS**		
MIKVAH RECHOV HAMEYASDIM, CENTER OF TOWN,				
OPPOSITE SCHOOL	ZICHRON YAAKOV	**IS**		

MONUMENTS

LODGE MEMORIALS 1247 S. FAIRFAX AVENUE	LOS ANGELES	**CA**	90019	(213) 931-1081
ALPINE MONUMENTS 1240 SOUTH KALAMATH	DENVER	**CO**		(303) 777-1034
ARTCRAFT MEMORIALS 1450 MAIN STREET	HARTFORD	**CT**		(203) 247-3054
LICHTENSTEIN COMPANY 100 LEGION AVENUE	NEW HAVEN	**CT**		(203) 397-1336
GELB MONUMENTS 140 S.W. 57TH AVENUE	MIAMI	**FL**		(305) 266-2888
SAM CANTOR & SONS 47 EVERETT AVENUE	CHELSEA	**MA**	02150	(617) 889-1562
S. SLOTNICK MONUMENTAL WORKS 232 FULLER STREET	EVERETT	**MA**	02149	(617) 387-3980
EDEN MEMORIALS MAIN STREET	WINNIPEG	**MB**		(204) 586-8579
SHELDON GRANITE COMPANY 19800 WOODWARD AVENUE	DETROIT	**MI**	48203	(313) 368-3550
MONUMENT CENTER 661 EAST EIGHT MILE ROAD	FERNDALE	**MI**	48220	(313) 542-8266
BERG & URBACH MONUMENT WORKS 13405 CAPITAL	OAK PARK	**MI**	48203	(313) 544-2212
DETROIT MONUMENT WORKS 14441 WEST ELEVEN MILE ROAD	OAK PARK	**MI**	49835	(313) 399-2711
MINNEAPOLIS GRANITE & MARBLE COMPANY				
4400 CHICAGO AVENUE	MINNEAPOLIS	**MN**		(612) 822-3135
AARON MONUMENT COMPANY 1799 HILLCREST	ST. PAUL	**MN**	55116	(612) 698-6262
KANSAS CITY MONUMENT COMPANY 6842 TROOST	KANSAS CITY	**MO**	64100	(816) 333-0075
ROSENBLOOM MONUMENT COMPANY	ST. LOUIS	**MO**		(314) 721-5070
J.F. BLOOM MONUMENT COMPANY 4431 NORTH 20TH STREET	OMAHA	**NE**		(402) 451-6000
J.F. BLOOM MONUMENT COMPANY 2701 NORTH 90TH STREET	OMAHA	**NE**		(402) 393-6222
BRONZE & GRANITE MEMORIALS 45 SAMWORTH ROAD	CLIFTON	**NJ**		(201) 473-3922
GOODMAN BROTHERS MONUMENTS 402 PARK STREET	HACKENSACK	**NJ**	07601	(201) 487-3810
LIMAN'S NEWARK MEMORIALS 358 GROVE STREET	NEWARK	**NJ**		(201) 373-6514
ORLOVSKY MEMORIALS 284 SOUTH 20TH STREET	NEWARK	**NJ**		(201) 372-6487
HAIMM GARDEN MEMORIAL CENTER U.S. HIGHWAY 1	WOODBRIDGE	**NJ**	07095	(201) 634-8500
BRONX MEMORIAL CORP. 1888 WASHINGTON AVENUE	BRONX	**NY**	10457	(212) 733-5400
HASKELL, BENJAMIN & SON 1888 WASHINGTON AVENUE	BRONX	**NY**	10457	(212) 294-3848
PARKWAY MONUMENTS 764 LYDIG AVENUE	BRONX	**NY**	10457	(212) 583-6461
TREMONT MONUMENT WORKS 1811 WASHINGTON AVENUE	BRONX	**NY**	10457	(212) 294-2626
BRENNER MONUMENTS CORP. 1572 CONEY ISLAND AVENUE	BROOKLYN	**NY**	11230	(718) 438-0500
GREENBAUM MONUMENTS 4509 14TH AVENUE	BROOKLYN	**NY**	11219	(718) 436-2411
HASKEL BROTHERS 1572 CONEY ISLAND AVENUE	BROOKLYN	**NY**	11230	(718) 258-3230
J. GOLDSTEIN & SONS 826 JAMAICA AVENUE	BROOKLYN	**NY**	11208	(718) 277-2937
RABBI PREMOCK	BROOKLYN	**NY**	11204	(718) 851-1314
WEISS MONUMENTS 2223 AVENUE U	BROOKLYN	**NY**		(718) 646-0300
WILLIAM ROSEN MONUMENTS 1912 FLATBUSH AVENUE	BROOKLYN	**NY**	11210	(718) 951-6900
HEBREW MEMORIAL COMPANY 1640 EAST DELAVAN AVENUE	BUFFALO	**NY**		(716) 893-2500
TEL-AVIV MEMORIALS 314 ELMONT ROAD	ELMONT	**NY**	11003	(516) 481-3700
GOODMAN BROTHERS MONUMENTS				
130-30 HORACE HARDING BOULEVARD	FLUSHING	**NY**	11367	(718) 359-3724
GINSBERG MEMORIAL 1285 NORTHERN BOULEVARD	MANHASSET	**NY**		(516) 821-7330
ADLER'S MONUMENTS 148 EAST 57TH STREET	NEW YORK	**NY**	10022	(212) 753-6330
BLEVITZKY BROTHERS MONUMENTS 210-212 FORSYTH STREET	NEW YORK	**NY**	10002	(212) 477-9908
DUBIN & STEINBERG 245 EAST HOUSTON STREET	NEW YORK	**NY**	10002	(212) 475-7697
L. NEUMANN MONUMENTS 219 EAST THIRD STREET	NEW YORK	**NY**	10002	(212) 228-7530
M. GOLDFINGER MONUMENTS 172 SUFFOLK STREET	NEW YORK	**NY**	10002	(212) 473-2288
WEINREB BROTHERS & GROSS 172 SUFFOLK STREET	NEW YORK	**NY**	10002	(212) 254-2360
WEITZNER BROTHERS & PAPPER 25 SECOND AVENUE	NEW YORK	**NY**	10003	(212) 254-8826
WENIG MONUMENT WORKS 351 EAST HOUSTON STREET	NEW YORK	**NY**	10002	(212) 228-7250
GALLE MEMORIAL STUDIOS 1481 LAKE AVENUE	ROCHESTER	**NY**		(716) 458-5302
GOLDENBERG MONUMENTS 12 YOUNG AVENUE	YONKERS	**NY**		(914) 779-3717
FRIEDMAN MONUMENTS 1900 SOUTH TAYLOR ROAD	CLEVELAND	**OH**	44118	(216) 932-9122
GOLDBERG MONUMENTS 2687 BATHURST STREET	TORONTO	**ON**		(416) 781-6669
KILVINGTON BROTHERS 2751 BLOOR STREET WEST	TORONTO	**ON**		(416) 233-5531
SAM IZENBERG MONUMENTS 3173 BATHHURST STREET	TORONTO	**ON**		(416) 787-0319
ART MONUMENT COMPANY 4709 NORTH BROAD STREET	PHILADELPHIA	**PA**	19141	(215) 324-5006
G. A. KAEPPIER & SONS 2540 WEST CHELTENHAM AVENUE	PHILADELPHIA	**PA**	19150	(215) 924-1130
NATHAN SHAPIRO MONUMENTS 7056 BUSTLETON AVENUE	PHILADELPHIA	**PA**	19152	(215) 745-7220
QUALITY MONUMENT 1869 COTTMAN AVENUE	PHILADELPHIA	**PA**		(215) 745-3333
REIBSTEIN MEMORIALS 4709 NORTH BROAD STREET	PHILADELPHIA	**PA**	19141	(215) 324-6400
WERTHEIMER MONUMENTS 6720 BUSTLETON AVENUE	PHILADELPHIA	**PA**	19152	(215) 333-1222
FALEDER MONUMENTS 2414 FIFTH AVENUE	PITTSBURGH	**PA**	15215	(412) 682-5500

URBACH MONUMENTAL WORKS 2635 MURRAY AVENUE .... PITTSBURGH **PA** 15215 (412) 421-8655
MOUNT SINAI MEMORIAL MONUMENT COMPANY 825 HOPE STREET ..PROVIDENCE **RI** 02906 (401) 331-3337
SUGARMAN MONUMENT COMPANY 458 HOPE STREET .... PROVIDENCE **RI** 02906 (401) 331-8094
QUIRING MONUMENTS 9608 AURORO NORTH .... SEATTLE **WA** (206) 522-8400
UNIVERSAL MONUMENT WORKS 6339 WEST APPLETON AVENUE .... MILWAUKEE **WI** (414) 445-5330

MUSEUMS

BETH ZEDEK MUSEUM 1700 BATHURST .... TORONTO (416) 781-3511
TEMPLE BETH ISRAEL 3310 NORTH 10TH AVENUE .... PHOENIX **AZ** 85031 (602) 264-4428
JUDAH L. MAGNES MEMORIAL MUSEUM 2911 RUSSELL STREET .... BERKELEY **CA** 94705 (415) 849-2710
HEBREW UNION COLLEGE-SKIRBALL MUSEUM
 3077 UNIVERSITY AVENUE .... LOS ANGELES **CA** 90007 (213) 749-3424
MARTYRS MEMORIAL & MUSEUM OF THE HOLOCAUST JEWISH FEDERATION
 COUNCIL 6505 WILSHIRE BOULEVARD .... LOS ANGELES **CA** 90048 (213) 852-1234
B'NAI B'RITH KLUTZNICK EXHIBIT HALL
 1640 RHODE ISLAND AVENUE N.W. .... WASHINGTON **DC** 20036 (202) 857-6583
B'NAI B'RITH KLUTZNICK MUSEUM
 1640 RHODE ISLAND AVENUE N.W. .... WASHINGTON **DC** 20036 (202) 857-6600
MORTON WEISS MEMORIAL MUSEUM OF JUDAICA-K.A.M. ISAIAH ISRAEL
 1110 EAST HYDE PARK BOULEVARD .... CHICAGO **IL** 60615 (312) 924-1234
RODFEI ZEDEK CONGREGATION MUSEUM 5200 HYDE PARK .... CHICAGO **IL** 60615 (312) 752-2770
SPERTUS MUSEUM OF JUDAICA 618 SOUTH MICHIGAN AVENUE .... CHICAGO **IL** 60605 (312) 922-9012
AMERICAN JEWISH HISTORICAL SOCIETY 2 THORTON ROAD .... WALTHAM **MA** 02154 (617) 891-8110
CHIZUK AMUNO CONGREGATION 8100 STEVENSON ROAD .... BALTIMORE **MD** 21208 (301) 486-6400
LLOYD STREET SYNAGOGUE MUSEUM BALTIMORE HEBREW COLLEGE,
 5800 PARK HEIGHTS AVENUE .... BALTIMORE **MD** 21215 (301) 588-2808
HOLOCAUST MEMORIAL CENTER 6602 WEST MAPLE ROAD ..... WEST BLOOMFIELD **MI** 48033 (313) 661-0840
TEMPLE-CONGREGATION B'NAI JEHUDA 712 EAST 69TH STREET ...... KANSAS CITY **MO** 64131 (816) 363-1050
JUDAICA MUSEUM 5961 PALISADE AVENUE .... BRONX **NY** 10471 (212) 548-1006
FERKAUF MUSEUM OF THE INTERNATIONAL SYNAGOGUE
 JFK INTERNATIONAL AIRPORT .... JAMAICA **NY** 11430 (718) 656-5044
CONGREGATION EMANU-EL MUSEUM 1 EAST 65TH STREET .... NEW YORK **NY** 10021 (212) 744-1400
JEWISH MUSEUM, THE 1109 FIFTH AVENUE .... NEW YORK **NY** 10028 (212) 860-1888
JEWISH MUSIC COUNCIL 15 E. 26TH STREET .... NEW YORK **NY** 10010 (212) 532-4949
JEWISH RECORD SHOP 147 ESSEX STREET .... NEW YORK **NY** 10002 (212) 674-1289
YIVO 1048 FIFTH AVENUE .... NEW YORK **NY** 10028 (212) 535-6700
YESHIVA UNIVERSITY MUSEUM 2520 AMSTERDAM AVENUE .... NEW YORK **NY** 10033 (212) 920-5390
TEMPLE B'RITH KODESH MUSEUM 2131 ELMWOOD AVENUE .... ROCHESTER **NY** 14618 (716) 244-7060
TEMPLE BETH SHOLOM, JUDAICA MUSEUM
 ROSLYN ROAD AT NORTHERN STATE PARKWAY .... ROSLYN **NY** 11577 (516) 621-2288
GALLERY OF ART AND ARTIFACTS-HEBREW UNION COLLEGE
 3101 CLIFTON AVENUE .... CINCINNATI **OH** 42522 (513) 221-1875
TEMPLE MUSEUM OF RELIGIOUS ART, THE
 UNIVERSITY CIRCLE AND SILVER PARK .... CLEVELAND **OH** 44106
REVECCA AND GERSHON FENSTER GALLERY OF JEWISH ART
 1223 EAST 17TH PLACE .... TULSA **OK** 74120 (918) 582-3732
BETH TZEDEC MUSEUM 1700 BATHURST STREET .... TORONTO **ON** M5P 3K3 (416) 781-5658
MUSEUM OF AMERICAN JEWISH HISTORY
 INDEPENDENCE MALL E., 55TH N. 5TH STREET .... PHILADELPHIA **PA** 19106 (215) 923-3811
ASSOCIATED AMERICAN JEWISH MUSEUMS, INC. 303 LEROI ROAD .... PITTSBURGH **PA** 15208
TEMPLE MUSEUM OF RELIGIOUS ART/TEMPLE EMANUEL
 4100 SHERBROOKE STREET WEST .... MONTREAL **QU** (514) 937-3575
BETH YESHURIN JEWISH MUSEUM 4525 BEECHNUT .... HOUSTON **TX** 77000 (713) 666-1381

MUSIC

THE KLEZMORIM 1846 SPRUCE, 23 .... BERKELEY **CA** 94709 (415) 540-5501
THE KLEZMORIM 87 EDGECROFT .... KENSINGTON **CA** 94707 (415) 540-5501
AMERICAN JEWISH CORAL SOCIETY .... LOS ANGELES **CA** (213) 653-1041
BARUCH COHON, SHALOM CONCERT BUREAU PO BOX 35092 .... LOS ANGELES **CA** 90035 (213) 931-6125
SHALOM CONCERT BUREAU PO BOX 35092 .... LOS ANGELES **CA** 90035 (213) 931-6125
HUGHES DULCIMER COMPANY, INC. 441 WEST COLFAX AVENUE .... DENVER **CO** 80204 (303) 572-3753
SHIRU SHIR CHADASH C/O TEMPLE SHEARITH ISRAEL
 46 PEACEABLE STREET .... RIDGEFIELD **CT** 06877 (203) 438-6589
NEW ENGLAND JEWISH MUSIC FORUM C/O MARY WOLFMAN EPSTEIN
 327 ST. PAUL STREET .... BROOKLINE **MA** 02146 (617) 566-4042
KADIMA C/O HAL KATZMAN 34 IRVING STREET .... NEWTON CENTRE **MA** 02158 (617) 969-1926
DAVID SHNEYER 2307 FOREST GLEN ROAD .... SILVER SPRING **MD** 20910 (301) 565-9422
SHANACHIE RECORDS CORPORATION DALEBROOK PARK .... HO-HO-KUS **NJ** 07423 (201) 445-5561
KAPELYE C/O HENRY SAPOZNIK 2018 VOORHIES AVENUE, #B24 .... BROOKLYN **NY** 11235 (718) 934-3859
MERKOS L'INYONEI CHINUCH, INC. 770 EASTERN PARKWAY .... BROOKLYN **NY** 11213 (718) 493-9250
ISRAEL MUSIC FOUNDATION 109 CEDARHURST AVENUE .... CEDARHURST **NY** 11516 (516) 569-1541
TARA PUBLICATIONS 29 DERBY AVENUE .... CEDARHURST **NY** 11516 (516) 295-2290
MOSHE SHUR, HILLEL FOUNDATION, STUDENT SERVICES CORPORATION
 PO BOX 446 .... FLUSHING **NY** 11367 (718) 793-2222
PAUL ZIM P.O. BOX 310 .... FOREST HILLS **NY** 11375 (718) 520-0666
RAMIE & MERRI ARIAN, ETZ CHAIM CREATIVE JEWISH MUSIC
 736 FOREST AVENUE .... LARCHMONT **NY** 10538 (914) 834-2813
AMERICAN SOCIETY FOR JEWISH MUSIC 155 FIFTH AVENUE .... NEW YORK **NY** 10010 (212) 533-2601
AMERICAN ZIONIST YOUTH FOUNDATION-EDUCATION DEPARTMENT
 515 PARK AVENUE .... NEW YORK **NY** 10022 (212) 308-4733
BALKAN ARTS CENTER 325 SPRING STREET .... NEW YORK **NY** 10013 (212) 691-9510
BOARD OF JEWISH EDUCATION OF GREATER NEW YORK
 426 WEST 58TH STREET .... NEW YORK **NY** 10019 (212) 245-8200
DIASPORA YESHIVA BAND, B'NAI B'RITH LECTURE BUREAU
 823 U.N. PLAZA .... NEW YORK **NY** 10017 (212) 490-1170
GLORIA FEIDMAN, B'NAI B'RITH LECTURE BUREAU 823 U.N. PLAZA ...... NEW YORK **NY** 10017 (212) 490-1170
HEBREW ARTS SCHOOL FOR MUSIC & DANCE 129 WEST 67TH STREET .. NEW YORK **NY** 10023 (212) 787-0650

HERSHMAN MUSICAL INSTRUMENT CO., INC. 135 WEST 29TH STREET ... NEW YORK **NY** 10001 (212) 564-0252
JEWISH MUSIC & RECORD SHOP 147 ESSEX STREET .... NEW YORK **NY** 10002 (212) 674-1289
JEWISH MUSIC ALLIANCE 1 UNION SQUARE .... NEW YORK **NY** 10003 (212) 924-8311
JEWISH MUSIC COUNCIL, NATIONAL JEWISH WELFARE BOARD
 15 EAST 26TH STREET .... NEW YORK **NY** 10010 (212) 532-4949
JEWISH MUSIC SOCIETY 315 W. 36TH STREET .... NEW YORK **NY** 10018 (212) 594-1690
MERKIN CONCERT HALL-ABRAHAM GOODMAN HOUSE
 129 WEST 67TH STREET .... NEW YORK **NY** 10023 (212) 944-9300
NAT'L FEDERATION OF TEMPLE YOUTH-UNION OF AMER. HEBR. CONG.
 838 FIFTH AVENUE .... NEW YORK **NY** 10021 (212) 249-0100
NAT'L JEWISH MUSIC COUNCIL OF THE NAT'L JEWISH WELFARE BOARD
 15 EAST 26TH STREET .... NEW YORK **NY** 10010 (212) 532-4949
SHERWOOD GOFFIN 142 WEST END AVENUE .... NEW YORK **NY** 10023 (212) 799-1393
THE JEWISH MUSIC SOCIETY 315 WEST 37TH STREET .... NEW YORK **NY** 10018 (212) 594-1690
TRANSCONTINENTAL MUSIC PUBLISHING, UNION OF AMER. HEBR. CONG
 838 FIFTH AVENUE .... NEW YORK **NY** 10021 (212) 249-0100
UNITED SYNAGOGUE, DEPARTMENT OF MUSIC 155 FIFTH AVENUE .... NEW YORK **NY** 10010 (212) 533-7800
WORDTONE MUSIC, INC., RECORD LOFT INTERNATIONAL
 230 SEVENTH AVENUE .... NEW YORK **NY** 10011 (212) 691-1934
WORKMEN'S CIRCLE, EDUCATION DEPARTMENT
 45 EAST 33RD STREET .... NEW YORK **NY** 10016 (212) 889-6800
WORLD ZIONIST ORGANIZATION, DEPT. OF EDUCATION AND CULTURE
 515 PARK AVENUE .... NEW YORK **NY** 10022 (212) 752-0600
JOSEPH BACH 1432 NORTH 49TH STREET .... ALLENTOWN **PA** 18104 (215) 398-2494
JAY M. BURMAN MUSIC 3 GREENWAY PLAZA EAST, SUITE B110 .... HOUSTON **TX** 77024 (713) 776-8183

NEEDLEWORK

STITCHERY BY HENYE 5710 W. MARIPOSA #19 .... PHOENIX **AZ** 85031
DOROTHY LOTSTEIN 26 BERWYN ROAD .... WEST HARTFORD **CT** 06107 (203) 561-1137
BONNIE YALES 23 DANE ROAD .... LEXINGTON **MA** 02173 (617) 861-8125
ALICE NUSSBAUM 2835 SALEM AVENUE SOUTH .... MINNEAPOLIS **MN** 55416 (612) 922-3531
BETTY WINTER SAMUELS 390 WEST HUDSON AVENUE .... ENGLEWOOD **NJ** 07631 (201) 567-8468
JANE BEARMAN 30 SPIER DRIVE .... LIVINGSTON **NJ** 07039 (201) 992-3369
THE POMEGRANATE GUILD OF JUDAIC NEEDLEWORK
 12 BAYVIEW AVENUE, C/O GILDA HECHT, VP MEMBERSHIP .... GREAT NECK **NY** 11021 (914) 245-3244
THE POMEGRANATE GUILD OF JUDAIC NEEDLEWORK
 289 LINDEN PLACE .... YORKTOWN HEIGHTS **NY** 10598 (914) 245-3244

NEWS SERVICES & SYNDICATES

LUBAVITCH NEWS SERVICE 784 EASTERN PARKWAY .... BROOKLYN **NY** 11213 (718) 774-4000
INTERNATIONAL JEWISH PRESS BUREAU 5 BEEKMAN STREET .... NEW YORK **NY** 10038 (212) 267-5450
JEWISH NEWSPAPER AGENCY 1 PENN PLAZA .... NEW YORK **NY** 10119 (212) 760-5555
JEWISH STUDENT PRESS SERVICE 15 E. 26TH STREET .... NEW YORK **NY** 10010 (212) 679-1411
JEWISH TELEGRAPHIC AGENCY 165 WEST 46TH STREET, ROOM 511 ..... NEW YORK **NY** 10036 (212) 575-9370
SEVEN ARTS FEATURE SYNDICATE & WORLD-WIDE NEWS SERVICE
 165 WEST 46TH STREET, ROOM 511 .... NEW YORK **NY** 10036 (212) 575-9370
AMERICAN JEWISH PRESS ASSOCIATION P.O. BOX 742 .... FORT WORTH **TX** 76101 (817) 927-2831

NEWSPAPERS & PERIODICALS

CONTEMPORARY JEWRY (SEMI-ANNUAL)
DEPT. OF SOCIOLOGY/UNIVERSITY OF ALABAMA .... BIRMINGHAM AL 35294   (205) 934-4011
JEWISH MONITOR P.O. BOX 396 .... SHEFFIELD AL 35660   (205) 766-0508
JEWISH STAR (SEMI-WEEKLY) 2315 98TH AVE. SW .... CALGARY AT T2V 4S7   (403) 238-0010
THE JEWISH STAR (MONTHLY) 7200 156 STREET .... EDMONTON AT T5R 1X3   (403) 238-0010
PHOENIX JEWISH NEWS (BIWEEKLY) CIRC. 4,300 (ENG.) EST. 1947
1530 WEST THOMAS ROAD .... PHOENIX AZ 85015   (602) 264-0536
ARIZONA POST (FORTNIGHTLY) CIRC. 3,400 (ENG.) EST. 1946
102 NORTH PLUMER AVENUE .... TUCSON AZ 85719   (602) 791-9962
CHABAD TIMES (MONTHLY 11X) CIRCULATION 10,000 (ENGLISH) .... TUCSON AZ
CANADIAN JEWISH OUTLOOK 2414 MAIN STREET #4 .... VANCOUVER BC V5T 3E3   (604) 874-1323
JEWISH WESTERN BULLETIN 3268 HEATHER STREET .... VANCOUVER BC V5Z 3K5   (604) 879-6575
SHMATE (BI-MONTHLY) P.O. BOX 4228 .... BERKELEY CA 94704
ISRAEL TODAY (WEEKLY) CIRC. 104,000 (ENGLISH) EST. 1973
16661 VENTURA BLVD. .... ENCINO CA 91436   (818) 786-4000
B'NAI B'RITH MESSENGER (WEEKLY) CIRC. 65,200 (ENG) EST. 1897
2510 WEST SEVENTH STREET .... LOS ANGELES CA 90057   (213) 380-5000
CALIFORNIA JEWISH PRESS 6399 WILSHIRE BLVD. #511 .... LOS ANGELES CA 90048   (213) 651-2230
HA'AM (6X YEAR) CIRC. 10,000 (ENGLISH)
112 KH/308 WESTWOOD PLAZA .... LOS ANGELES CA 90024
HERITAGE-SOUTHWEST (WEEKLY) CIRC. 15,000 (ENG.) EST. 1914
2130 SOUTH VERMONT AVENUE .... LOS ANGELES CA 90007   (213) 737-2122
JEWISH COMMUNITY BULLETIN 6505 WILSHIRE BLVD .... LOS ANGELES CA 90048   (213) 852-1234
JEWISH DAILY FORWARD 1161 N. OGDEN DRIVE .... LOS ANGELES CA 90046   (213) 659-0861
LIFE IN ISRAEL (6 TIMES/YR. L.A. TIMES)
CIRCULATION 198,000 (ENGLISH) .... LOS ANGELES CA
ULTIMATE ISSUES (QUARTERLY)
2265 WESTWOOD BLVD. SUITE 508 .... LOS ANGELES CA 90064   (213) 204-4290
JEWISH OBSERVER OF THE EAST BAY (FORTNIGHTLY) EST. 1967
3245 SHEFFIELD AVENUE .... OAKLAND CA 94602   (415) 533-7462
JEWISH STAR (MONTHLY) CIRC. 2,000 (ENGLISH) EST. 1956
693 MISSION STREET, #305 .... SAN FRANCISCO CA 94105   (415) 421-4874
NORTH CALIFORNIA JEWISH BULLETIN
121 STEUART ST. SUITE 302 .... SAN FRANCISCO CA 94105   (415) 957-9340
SAN FRANCISCO JEWISH BULLETIN (WEEKLY) CIRC. 22,900 EST. 1946
670 MARKET STREET, SUITE 954 .... SAN FRANCISCO CA 94102   (415) 391-9444
JEWISH COMMUNITY NEWS 1777 HAMILTON AVENUE, SUITE 210 .... SAN JOSE CA 95125   (408) 267-2770
JEWISH SPECTATOR (QUARTERLY) CIRC. 17,500, EST. 1935
PO BOX 2016 .... SANTA MONICA CA 90406   (213) 929-2484
WESTERN STATES JEWISH HISTORICAL QUARTERLY (QUARTERLY)
2429 23RD STREET .... SANTA MONICA CA 90405   (213) 399-3585
INTERMOUNTAIN JEWISH NEWS (WEEKLY) CIRC9 10,000 (ENGLISH)
1275 SHERMAN STREET, SUITE 215-217, ESTABLISHED 1913 .... DENVER CO 80203   (303) 861-2235
JEWISH DIGEST (MONTHLY) ESTABLISHED 1955
1363 FAIRFIELD AVENUE .... BRIDGEPORT CT 06605   (203) 384-2284
CONNECTICUT JEWISH LEDGER (WEEKLY) CIRC. 25,000 (ENGLISH)
PO BOX 1688, ESTABLISHED 1929 .... HARTFORD CT 06101   (203) 233-2148
THE JEWISH LEADER (BIWEEKLY) CIRC. 2,000 (ENGLISH)
302 STATE STREET .... NEW LONDON CT 06320   (203) 442-7677

ALERT, ESTABLISHED 1970 1411 K STREET, N.W., SUITE 402 .... WASHINGTON DC 20005   (202) 393-4117
JERUSALEM POST WASHINGTON BUREAU
2139 WISCONSIN AVE., NW .... WASHINGTON DC 20007   (202) 338-4553
JEWISH VETERAN (5X/YR.) CIRC. 55,800 (ENG.) EST 1896
1811 R STREET NW .... WASHINGTON DC 20009   (202) 265-6200
JEWISH WEEK CIRC. 16,000 (ENG.) EST. 1965 1317 F STREET NW .... WASHINGTON DC 20004   (202) 783-7200
MENORAH (MONTHLY) EST. 1979
1747 CONNECTICUT AVENUE, N.W. .... WASHINGTON DC 20009
NEAR EAST REPORT (WEEKLY) CIRC. 28,000, EST. 1957
444 NORTH CAPITOL STREET, N.W./SUITE 412 .... WASHINGTON DC 20001   (202) 638-1225
SHOFAR (8X/YR.) CIRC. 33,000-B'NAI B'RITH YOUTH ORG.
1640 RHODE ISLAND AVENUE, N.W. .... WASHINGTON DC 20036   (202) 857-6644
THE B'NAI B'RITH INTERNATIONAL JEWISH MONTHLY (MONTHLY)
1640 RHODE ISLAND AVENUE, N.E. CIRC.200,000, EST. 1886 ..... WASHINGTON DC 20036   (202) 857-6645
WOMEN'S WORLD (BI-MONTHLY) CIRC. 137,000-B'NAI B'RITH WOM.
1640 RHODE ISLAND AVENUE, N.W. .... WASHINGTON DC 20036   (202) 857-6640
JEWISH VOICE 101 GARDEN OF EDEN ROAD .... WILMINGTON DE 19803   (302) 478-6200
HERITAGE FLORIDA JEWISH NEWS P.O. BOX 742 .... FERN PARK FL 32730   (813) 224-0700
JEWISH JOURNAL P.O. BOX 23909 .... FORT LAUDERDALE FL 33307   (305) 563-3311
SOUTHERN JEWISH WEEKLY, CIRC 28,500 (ENG.) EST. 1924
PO BOX 3297 .... JACKSONVILLE FL 32206   (904) 355-3459
JEWISH FLORIDIAN NEWSPAPERS (WEEKLY) CIRC. 54,700 (ENGLISH)
PO BOX 012973 .... MIAMI FL 33101   (305) 373-4605
THE JEWISH FLORIDIAN & SHOFAR OF GR. HOLLYWOOD (26X YEAR)
JEWISH FLORIDIAN GROUP/PO BOX 012973, CIRC. 12,000 (ENGL .... MIAMI FL 33101   (305) 373-4605
THE JEWISH FLORIDIAN OF MIAMI BEACH (WEEKLY) CIRC. 25,000
JEWISH FLORIDIAN GROUP/PO BOX 012973 .... MIAMI FL 33101   (305) 373-4605
THE JEWISH FLORIDIAN OF PALM BEACH COUNTY (26X YEAR)
JEWISH FLORIDIAN GROUP/PO BOX 012973, CIRC. 10,000 (ENGL .... MIAMI FL 33101   (305) 373-4605
JEWISH FLORIDIAN OF GREATER FORT LAUDERDALE (WEEKLY) CIRC. 24,000
8358 WEST OAKLAND PARK BLVD. P.O. BOX 26810 .... TAMARAC FL 33320   (305) 748-8400
THE JEWISH FLORIDIAN OF TAMPA (WEEKLY) CIRC. 2,500 (ENGLISH)
3655 HENDERSON BOULEVARD .... TAMPA FL 33609   (813) 872-4470
JEWISH WORLD (WEEKLY) CIRC. 2,000 (ENGLISH)
2405 MERCER AVENUE .... WEST PALM BEACH FL 33409   (305) 659-5311
SOUTHERN ISRAELITE (WEEKLY) CIRC. 7200 (ENG.) EST. 1925
PO BOX 77388 .... ATLANTA GA 30357   (404) 876-8249
HAWAII JEWISH NEWS (MONTHLY) CIRC. 2,000 (ENGLISH)
817 COOKE STREET .... HONOLULU HI 96813   (808) 536-7228
M'GODOLIM/THE JEWISH QUARTERLY 621 HOLD .... IOWA CITY IA 52240   (206) 322-1431
SOUTHERN ILLINOIS JEWISH NEWS (MONTHLY) (EST. 1945)
6464 W. MAIN, SUITE 7A .... BELLEVILLE IL 62223   (618) 271-2400
JUF NEWS (MONTHLY) (CIRC. 48,000)
ONE SOUTH FRANKLIN, ROOM 702 .... CHICAGO IL 60606   (312) 444-2863

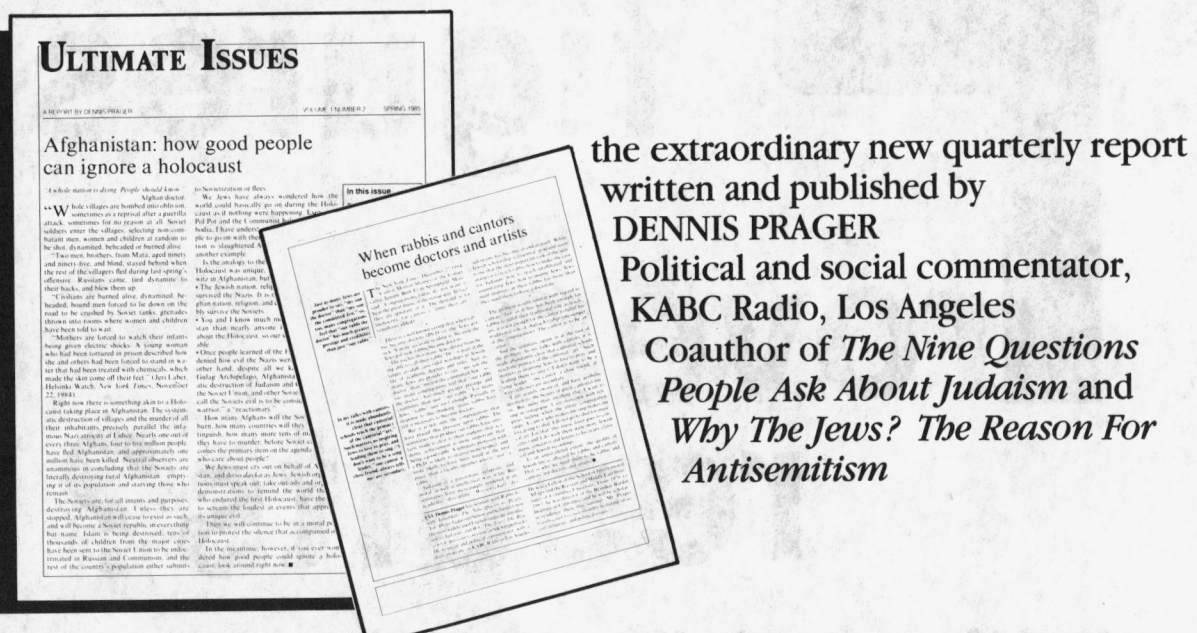

SENTINEL (WEEKLY) CIRC. 26,000 (ENG.) EST. 1911
  323 SOUTH FRANKLIN STREET .... CHICAGO IL 60606 (312) 663-1101
D'VAR SHALOM P.O. BOX 554 .... HIGHLAND PARK IL 60035
CHICAGO JEWISH POST AND OPINION, THE 6350 NORTH ALBANY .... SKOKIE IL 60659 (312) 677-5451
INDIANA JEWISH POST (WEEKLY) CIRC. 2,000, EST. 1935
  611 NORTH PARK AVENUE... INDIANAPOLIS IN 46204 (317) 634-1307
JEWISH POST AND OPINION (WEEKLY) CIRC. 10,000
  611 NORTH PARK AVENUE... INDIANAPOLIS IN 46204 (317) 634-1307
KANSAS CITY JEWISH CHRONICLE (WEEKLY) CIRC. 12,200 EST. 1920
  7375 W 107TH STREET .... OVERLAND PARK KS 66212 (913) 381-1010
KANSAS CITY JEWISH CHRONICLE 7375 W. 107TH STREET .... SHAWNEE MISSION KS 66212 (913) 648-4620
COMMUNITY (BI-WEEKLY) CIRC. 5,400 (ENGLISH) PO BOX 33035 .... LOUISVILLE KY 40232
KENTUCKY JEWISH POST AND OPINION (WEEKLY) CIRC. 4,500
  1551 BARDSTOWN ROAD .... LOUISVILLE KY 40205 (502) 459-1914
JEWISH TIMES (BIWEEKLY) CIRC. 10,700 (ENG.) EST. 1945 .... NEW ORLEANS LA 70130 (504) 524-3147
THE JEWISH CIVIC PRESS (BIWEEKLY) CIRC. 7,000 (ENG) EST. 1965
  PO BOX 15500 .... NEW ORLEANS LA 70175 (504) 524-3147
GENESIS 2 (8X ANNUALLY) CIRC. 15,000 (ENGLISH)
  99 BISHOP ALLEN DRIVE .... CAMBRIDGE MA 02139 (617) 576-1801
JEWISH ADVOCATE (WEEKLY) CIRC. 25,200 (ENG.) EST. 1902
  251 CAUSEWAY STREET .... BOSTON MA 02114 (617) 227-5130
MOMENT (MONTHLY) CIRC. 23,000, EST. 1975
  462 BOYLSTON STREET, SUITE 301 .... BOSTON MA 02116 (617) 536-6252
JEWISH TIMES (WEEKLY) CIRC. 5,000 (ENG.) EST. 1974
  118 CYPRESS STREET .... BROOKLINE MA 02146 (617) 566-7710
JEWISH SPORTS REVIEW 198 MT. VERNON STREET .... DEDHAM MA 02026 (617) 326-0938
JEWISH REPORTER (MONTHLY) CIRC. 5,300 (ENG.) EST. 1970
  76 SALEM END ROAD .... FRAMINGHAM MA 01701 (617) 879-3300
JOURNAL, THE 140 WASHINGTON STREET.................................... SALEM MA 01970 (617) 744-5675
THE JOURNAL OF THE NORTH SHORE JEWISH COMMUNITY CENTER
  209 WASHINGTON STREET .... SALEM MA 01970 (617) 741-1558
JEWISH WEEKLY NEWS, CIRC. 8,530 (ENG.) EST. 1945
  PO BOX 1569/38 HAMPDEN STREET................................... SPRINGFIELD MA 01103 (413) 739-4771
AMERICAN JEWISH HISTORY (QUARTERLY) CIRC. 3,500, ETS. 1893
  2 THORNTON ROAD .... WALTHAM MA 02154 (617) 891-8110
JEWISH CHRONICLE LEADER (SEMIMONTHLY) CIRC. 4,700 (ENGLISH)
  340 MAIN STREET, SUITE 551 .... WORCESTER MA 01608 (617) 752-2512
JEWISH CIVIC LEADER 11 HARVARD STREET .... WORCESTER MA 01609 (617) 791-0953
JEWISH POST P.O. BOX 3777 .... WINNIPEG MB R2W 3R6 (204) 633-5575
WESTERN JEWISH NEWS P.O. BOX 87, 400-259 PORTAGE AVENUE........ WINNIPEG MB R3C 2G6 (204) 942-6361
YIDDISH PRESS 230 CATHEDRAL AVENUE .... WINNIPEG MB
BALTIMORE JEWISH TIMES (WEEKLY) CIRC. 19,000 (ENG.) EST. 1919
  9104 NORTH CHARLES STREET.. BALTIMORE MD 21218 (301) 752-3504

WASHINGTON INTERNATIONAL REPORT 5608 GREENTREE ROAD .... BETHESDA MD 20014 (703) 573-7192
WASHINGTON JEWISH WEEK 9030 COMPRINT COURT .... GAITHERSBURG MD 20879 (301) 258-9435
AMERICAN JEWISH JOURNAL (QUARTERLY) CIRC. 8,000, EST. 1944
  1220 BLAIR MILL ROAD .... SILVER SPRING MD 20910 (301) 585-1756
JEWISH WEEK 8630 FENTON STREET, SUITE 611 .... SILVER SPRING MD 20910 (301) 565-9336
MICHIGAN JEWISH HISTORY (SEMI-ANNUAL) EST. 1960
  24680 RENSSELAER .... OAK PARK MI 48237 (313) 548-9176
DETROIT JEWISH NEWS 17515 W. NINE MILE ROAD, SUITE 865 .... SOUTHFIELD MI 48075 (313) 424-8833
AMERICAN JEWISH WORLD (WEEKLY) CIRC. 6,200 (ENG.) EST. 1912
  4509 MINNETONKA .... MINNEAPOLIS MN 55416 (612) 920-7000
AMERICAN JEWISH PRESS ASSOCIATION C/O ST. LOUIS JEWISH LIGHT,
  12 MILLSTONE CAMPUS DRIVE .... ST. LOUIS MO 63146 (314) 432-3353
MISSOURI JEWISH POST AND OPINION (WEEKLY) CIRC. 3,500
  8235 OLIVE STREET .... ST. LOUIS MO 63132 (314) 993-2842
ST. LOUIS JEWISH LIGHT (BIWEEKLY) CIRC 17,300 (ENG) EST. 1947
  12 MILLSTONE CAMPUS DRIVE .... ST. LOUIS MO 63146 (314) 432-3353
AMERICAN JEWISH TIMES OUTLOOK (MONTHLY) CIRC. 2,400 (ENG.)
  PO BOX 10674 .... CHARLOTTE NC 28234 (704) 372-3296

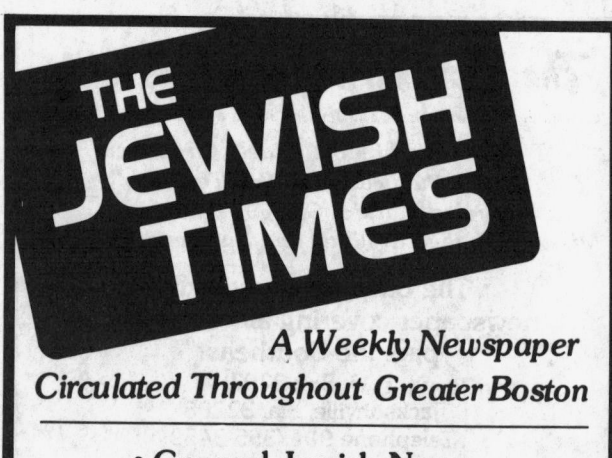

THE JEWISH TIMES

A Weekly Newspaper
Circulated Throughout Greater Boston

- **General Jewish News**
- **Coverage of Israel**
- **Local Organization News**
- **Arts. . .Business. . .Lifestyle**

Subscription: $12.00 One Year, 20.00 Two years

THE JEWISH TIMES
118 Cypress St. P.O. Box 403
Brookline, MA 02146

FEDERATION NEWS 713-A N. GREENE ST. . . . . GREENSBORO **NC** 27401   (919) 272-3189
THE JEWISH PRESS (WEEKLY) CIRC.3,700 (ENG.) EST.1921
   333 SOUTH 132ND STREET . . . . OMAHA **NE** 68154   (402) 334-8200
JEWISH RECORD (WEEKLY) CIRC.5,000 (ENG.) EST. 1939
   1537 ATLANTIC AVENUE . . . . ATLANTIC CITY **NJ** 08401   (609) 344-5119
BERGEN JEWISH NEWS (MONTHLY)
   CIRCULATION 25,000 (ENGLISH) . . . . BERGEN COUNTY **NJ**
THE JEWISH VOICE (BIWEEKLY) CIRC. 10,000, EST. 1941
   2393 WEST MARLTON PIKE . . . . CHERRY HILL **NJ** 08002   (609) 665-6100
THE JEWISH VOICE 100 GRANT AVENUE . . . . DEAL PARK **NJ** 07723   (201) 531-6200
JEWISH NEWS (WEEKLY) CIRC. 24,000 (ENG.) EST. 1947
   60 GLENWOOD AVENUE . . . . EAST ORANGE **NJ** 07017   (201) 678-3900
JEWISH VOICE (BIWEEKLY) CIRC. 5,000 (ENG.) EST. 1975
   100 MENLO PARK, SUITE 101-102 . . . . EDISON **NJ** 08837   (201) 494-3920
JEWISH COMMUNITY NEWS (MONTHLY 11X)
   CIRCULATION 3,700 (ENGLISH) . . . . GR. CLIFTON/PASSAIC **NJ**
JEWISH JOURNAL (SEMIMONTHLY) CIRC. 8,000 (ENG.) EST. 1956
   2 SOUTH ADELAIDE AVENUE . . . . HIGHLAND PARK **NJ** 08904   (201) 246-1905
JEWISH STANDARD (WEEKLY) CIRC. 10,000 (ENG.) EST. 1931
   40 JOURNAL SQUARE . . . . JERSEY CITY **NJ** 07306   (201) 653-6330
MORRIS/SUSSEX JEWISH NEWS (MONTHLY) CIRC. 6,800 (ENGLISH)
   500 ROUTE 10 . . . . LEDGEWOOD **NJ** 07852   (201) 584-1850
THE JEWISH VOICE (24XYEAR) CIRC. 6,500 (ENGLISH)
   574A SOMERSET STREET . . . . NORTH PLAINFIELD **NJ** 07060   (201) 561-0988
BERGEN JEWISH NEWS 111 KINDERKAMACK ROAD . . . . RIVER EDGE **NJ** 07661   (201) 488-6800
JEWISH HORIZON (WEEKLY) CIRC. 12,000 (ENG.) EST. 1939 GREEN LANE . . . . . UNION **NJ** 07083   (201) 351-1473
THE JEWISH COMMUNITY NEWS (WEEKLY)
   GREEN LANE, CIRCULATION 14,000 (ENGLISH) . . . . UNION **NJ** 07083   (201) 351-5060
THE JEWISH CHRONICLE 629 WOOD ST., SUITE 204 . . . . VINELAND **NJ** 08360   (609) 696-4445
FEDERATION NEWS (SEMI-MONTHLY) CIRCULATION 8,400 (ENGLISH) . . . . . . WAYNE **NJ**
JEWISH REPORTER (MONTHLY) ESTABLISHED 1976
   1030 EAST TWAIN AVENUE . . . . LAS VEGAS **NV** 89109   (702) 732-0556
LAS VEGAS ISRAELITE (WEEKLY) CIRC. 19,800 (ENG.) EST. 1965
   PO BOX 14096 . . . . LAS VEGAS **NV** 89114   (702) 876-1255
ALBANY JEWISH WORLD 1104 CENTRAL AVENUE . . . . ALBANY **NY** 12205   (518) 459-8455
THE REPORTER (WEEKLY) CIRC. 1,500 (ENGLISH)
   500 CLUBHOUSE ROAD . . . . BINGHAMTON **NY** 13903   (607) 724-2360
KINDER JOURNAL, EST. 1920 3301 BAINBRIDGE AVENUE . . . . BRONX **NY**   (212) 881-3588
A THOUGHT FOR THE WEEK - LUBAVITCH 784 EASTERN PARKWAY . . . . . . BROOKLYN **NY** 11213   (718) 774-7200
BORO PARK VOICE 4616 13TH AVENUE . . . . BROOKLYN **NY** 11219   (718) 436-5800
CROWN HEIGHTS CHRONICLE, THE - KEREN PUBLICATIONS
   G.P.O. BOX 2007 . . . . BROOKLYN **NY** 11202   (718) 282-9041
DER YID (WEEKLY) CIRC. 8,000 (YIDDISH) 260 BROADWAY . . . . . . BROOKLYN **NY** 11211   (718) 387-8600
DI YIDDISH HEIM (QUARTERLY) CIRC. 3,000 (ENG-YID) EST. 1958
   770 EASTERN PARKWAY . . . . BROOKLYN **NY** 11213   (718) 493-9250
ESRA - THE WOMEN'S INTEREST GUIDE 774 E. 8TH STREET . . . . BROOKLYN **NY** 11230   (718) 434-2712
JEWISH AMERICAN RECORD P.O. BOX 1100, 271 CAMDEN PLAZA E . . . . BROOKLYN **NY** 11201   (718) 646-5184

JEWISH GUARDIAN (QUARTERLY) CIRC. 10,000, EST. 1974
   PO BOX 2143 . . . . BROOKLYN **NY** 11202   (718) 384-4661
JEWISH JOURNAL (WEEKLY) CIRC. 45,000 (ENG.) EST. 1970
   16 COURT STREET . . . . BROOKLYN **NY** 11201
JEWISH PRESS (WEEKLY) CIRC. 209,000 (ENG.) EST. 1950
   338 THIRD AVENUE . . . . BROOKLYN **NY** 11215   (718) 858-3300
KASHRUS - BIMONTHLY, CIRC. 7,000 P.O. BOX 96 . . . . BROOKLYN **NY** 11204   (718) 998-3201
LONG ISLAND JEWISH WORLD 1029 BRIGHTON BEACH AVENUE . . . . BROOKLYN **NY** 11235   (718) 769-6000
MOSHIACH TIMES 1304 PRESIDENT STREET . . . . BROOKLYN **NY** 11213   (718) 769-6000
SHMUESSEN MIT KINDER IN YUGENT (MONTHLY) EST. 1942
   770 EASTERN PARKWAY . . . . BROOKLYN **NY** 11213   (718) 493-9250
SVET (LIGHT)(MONTHLY) CIRC. 25,000 (RUSSIAN)
   455 ALBANY AVENUE . . . . BROOKLYN **NY** 11213   (718) 774-0065
TALKS AND TALES (MONTHLY) EST. 1942, LUBAVITCH PUBLICATION
   770 EASTERN PARKWAY . . . . BROOKLYN **NY** 11213   (718) 493-9250
THE JEWISH HOMEMAKER (5X/YEAR) CIRC. 43,000 (ENGLISH)
   PO BOX 218 . . . . BROOKLYN **NY** 11204   (718) 851-6428
THE UFORATZTO JOURNAL (QUARTERLY) CIRC. 20,000
   770 EASTERN PARKWAY . . . . BROOKLYN **NY** 11213   (718) 778-4270
YAGDIL TORAH 770 EASTERN PARKWAY . . . . BROOKLYN **NY** 11213   (718) 774-4001
BUFFALO JEWISH REVIEW (WEEKLY) CIRC. 3,800 (ENG.) EST. 1918
   15 E. MOHAWK STREET . . . . BUFFALO **NY** 14203   (716) 854-2192
JEWISH WORLD OF LONG ISLAND AND QUEENS (EVERY OTHER WEEK)
   1 OLD INDIAN HEAD ROAD CIRC. 12,500-NEWSPAPER (ENGLISH) . . . COMMACK **NY** 11725   (516) 543-2427
JEWISH OBSERVER 2223 EAST GENESEE STREET P.O. BOX 510 . . . . DEWITT **NY** 13214   (315) 422-4104
JEWISH CURRENT EVENTS (BIWEEKLY) EST. 1959 430 KELLER AVENUE . . . . . ELMONT **NY** 11003
CONTEMPORARY JEWRY (SEMI-ANNUAL) EST. 1974
   65-30 KISSENA BOULEVARD-QUEENS CLG, DEPT. OF SOCIOLOGY . . . . . . FLUSHING **NY** 11367   (718) 222-3699
MODERN JEWISH STUDIES ANNUAL, QUEENS COLLEGE, EST. 1977
   65-30 KISSENA BOULEVARD . . . . FLUSHING **NY** 11367   (718) 520-7067
YIDDISH QUEENS COLLEGE ACADEMY (QUARTERLY) ESTABLISHED 1973
   65-30 KISSENA BOULEVARD . . . . FLUSHING **NY** 11367   (718) 520-7067
LONG ISLAND GREAT NECK RECORD (WEEKLY) CIRC. 5,000 (ENGLISH)
   1 GREAT NECK ROAD . . . . GREAT NECK **NY** 11021   (516) 482-4490

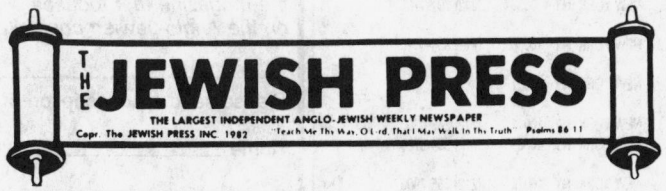

LONG ISLAND JEWISH WORLD 115 MIDDLE NECK ROAD .... GREAT NECK **NY** 11021 (516) 429-4000
JEWISH VIEW - BIWEEKLY CIRC. 12,000 P.O. BOX 309 .... ISLAND PARK **NY** 11558 (516) 431-6109
SHOFAR 43 NORTHCOTE DRIVE .... MELVILLE **NY** 11747 (516) 643-4598
EDUCATION MEDIA EXPOSITION SOCIETY, INC. PO BOX 122 .... MONSEY **NY** 10952 (914) 352-0630
AFN SHVEL (QUARTERLY) CIRC. 1,000 (YIDDISH) EST. 1941
  200 WEST 72ND STREET .... NEW YORK **NY** 10023 (212) 787-6675
ALGEMEINER JOURNAL (WEEKLY) CIRC. 20,000 (YIDDISH) EST. 1972
  404 PARK AVENUE SOUTH .... NEW YORK **NY** 10016 (212) 689-3390
ALIYON/THE JEWISH AGENCY (6X/YR.) CIRC. 4,000 (ENGLISH)
  515 PARK AVENUE .... NEW YORK **NY** 10022 (212) 752-0600
AMERICAN JEWISH YEARBOOK (ANNUAL) EST. 1899
  165 EAST 56TH STREET .... NEW YORK **NY** 10022 (212) 751-4000
AMERICAN ZIONIST (BIMONTHLY) CIRC. 47,000 (ENG.) EST. 1910
  4 EAST 34TH STREET .... NEW YORK **NY** 10016 (212) 481-1500
AMIT WOMEN (8X/YR.) CIRC. 25,000 (ENG.) EST. 1925 817 BROADWAY .... NEW YORK **NY** 10003 (212) 477-4720
AUFBAU (WEEKLY) CIRC. 13,400 (GERMAN) EST. 1934 2121 BROADWAY . NEW YORK **NY** 10023 (212) 873-7400
B'NAI YIDDISH (BIMONTHLY) CIRC. 1,500-ENGLISH-YIDDISH
  41 UNION SQUARE .... NEW YORK **NY** 10003 (212) 989-3162
B. B. INT'L JEWISH MONTHLY (10X/YR.) CIRC. 189,000 (ENGLISH)
  823 UNITED NATIONS PLAZA .... NEW YORK **NY** 10016 (212) 243-0308
BITZARON (BIMONTHLY) CIRC. 19,000 (HEBREW) EST. 1939
  1141 BROADWAY, COOPER STATION, PO BOX 798 .... NEW YORK **NY** 10003 (212) 598-3209
BOOKS IN REVIEW (BIMONTHLY) BOOK REVIEWS
  15 EAST 26TH STREET .... NEW YORK **NY** 10010 (212) 532-4949
BROTHERHOOD (QUARTERLY) CIRC. 70,000 (ENGLISH) REL/EDUC.
  838 FIFTH AVENUE .... NEW YORK **NY** 10021 (212) 249-0100
COMMENTARY (MONTHLY) CIRC. 60,000 (ENG.) EST. 1945
  165 EAST 56TH STREET .... NEW YORK **NY** 10022 (212) 751-4000
CONGRESS MONTHLY (8X/YR.) CIRC. 31,600 (ENG.) EST. 1933
  15 EAST 84TH STREET .... NEW YORK **NY** 10028 (212) 879-4500
CONSERVATIVE JUDAISM (QUARTERLY) CIRC. 2,400, EST. 1945
  3080 BROADWAY .... NEW YORK **NY** 10027 (212) 678-8863
DER WECKER (BIMONTHLY) YIDDISH, EST. 1921 45 EAST 33RD STREET . NEW YORK **NY** 10016 (212) 686-1538
DI ZUKUNFT (MONTHLY) CIRC. 3,430, EST. 1892 25 EAST 78TH STREET ... NEW YORK **NY** 10021
DOS YIDDISHE VORT (MONTHLY) YIDDISH, EST. 1953
  5 BEEKMAN STREET .... NEW YORK **NY** 10038 (212) 791-1181
ECONOMIC HORIZONS (QUARTERLY) CIRC. 3,000, EST. 1953
  500 FIFTH AVENUE .... NEW YORK **NY** 10036 (212) 354-6510
EMUNAH WOMAN (QUARTERLY) CIRC. 40,000 (ENGLISH)
  370 SEVENTH AVENUE .... NEW YORK **NY** 10001
FARBAND NEWS (IRREGULAR) CIRC. 26,000 - LABOR ZIONISM
  575 SIXTH AVENUE .... NEW YORK **NY** 10011 (212) 989-0300
HADAROM (SEMI-ANNUAL) CIRC. 1,500, EST. 1957 1250 BROADWAY ...... NEW YORK **NY** 10001 (212) 594-3780
HADASSAH MAGAZINE (MONTHLY) CIRC. 370,000 (ENG.) EST. 1921
  50 WEST 58TH STREET .... NEW YORK **NY** 10019 (212) 355-7900
HADOAR (WEEKLY) CIRC. 5,300 (HEBREW) EST. 1921 1841 BROADWAY ... NEW YORK **NY** 10023 (212) 581-5151
IMPACT (QUARTERLY) ENGLISH - HEBREW JOURNAL FOR EDUCATORS
  155 FIFTH AVENUE .... NEW YORK **NY** 10010 (212) 533-7800
ISRA-LAMED (BIMONTHLY) RIGHTS OF THE JEWISH PEOPLE
  515 PARK AVENUE .... NEW YORK **NY** 10022 (212) 752-0600
ISRAEL HORIZONS (BIMONTHLY) CIRC. 3,000, EST. 1952
  150 FIFTH AVENUE, SUITE 1002 .... NEW YORK **NY** 10011 (212) 255-8760
ISRAEL QUALITY (QUARTERLY) CIRC. 15,000, EST. 1976
  500 FIFTH AVENUE .... NEW YORK **NY** 10110 (212) 354-6510
ISRAEL SCENE (MONTHLY) CIRCULATION 9,000 (ENGLISH)
  515 PARK AVENUE .... NEW YORK **NY** 10022
ISRAEL SHELANU (WEEKLY) CIRC. 46,800 (HEBREW)
  933 EAST 17TH STREET .... NEW YORK **NY** 11230 (212) 258-8696

ISRAEL TODAY (DAILY 5X) CIRC. 100,000
  205 WEST 34TH STREET, SUITE 2306 .... NEW YORK **NY** 10001 (212) 695-1581
JASA BROOKDALE NEWS (BIMONTHLY) CIRC. 25,000-NEWSLETTER
  222 PARK AVENUE SOUTH .... NEW YORK **NY** 10003 (212) 677-2530
JDC WORLD 60 E. 42ND ST. .... NEW YORK **NY** 10165 (212) 687-6200
JWB CIRCLE (BIMONTHLY) CIRC. 28,000, EST. 1946
  15 EAST 26TH STREET .... NEW YORK **NY** 10010 (212) 532-4949
JERUSALEM POST, THE 120 EAST 56TH STREET .... NEW YORK **NY** 10022 (212) 355-4440
JEWISH ACTION (QUARTERLY) CIRC. 50,000, EST. 1950
  45 WEST 36TH STREET .... NEW YORK **NY** 10018 (212) 563-4000
JEWISH AMERICAN RECORD (MONTHLY) EST. 1973 G.P.O. BOX 317 ...... NEW YORK **NY** 10116
JEWISH BOOK ANNUAL, CIRC. 18,000, EST. 1942 15 EAST 26TH STREET . NEW YORK **NY** 10010 (212) 532-4949
JEWISH BOOKS IN REVIEW, EST. 1945, JEWISH BOOK COUNCIL
  15 EAST 26TH STREET .... NEW YORK **NY** 10010 (212) 532-4949
JEWISH BRAILLE INSTITUTE VOICE (10X/YR.) EST. 1978
  110 EAST 30TH STREET .... NEW YORK **NY** 10016 (212) 889-2525
JEWISH BRAILLE REVIEW (10X/YR.) CIRC. 2,000, EST. 1931
  110 EAST 30TH STREET .... NEW YORK **NY** 10016 (212) 889-2525
JEWISH CHRONICLE NEWS SERVICE 235 WEST 102ND STREET .... NEW YORK **NY** 10025 (212) 866-6139
JEWISH CURRENTS (MONTHLY) CIRC. 4,500 (ENG.) EST. 1946
  22 EAST 17TH STREET, SUITE 601 .... NEW YORK **NY** 10003 (212) 924-5740
JEWISH DAILY FORWARD   CIRC. 20,000 (YIDDISH) EST. 1897
  45 EAST 33RD STREET .... NEW YORK **NY** 10016 (212) 889-8200
JEWISH EDUCATION (QUARTERLY) EST. 1929 114 FIFTH AVENUE .... NEW YORK **NY** 10011 (212) 675-5656
JEWISH EDUCATION DIRECTORY (TRIENNIAL) EST. 1951
  114 FIFTH AVENUE .... NEW YORK **NY** 10011 (212) 675-5656
JEWISH EDUCATION NEWS (IRREGULAR) CIRC. 2,000, EST. 1939
  114 FIFTH AVENUE .... NEW YORK **NY** 10011 (212) 675-5656
JEWISH EXAMINER 1 PARK AVENUE .... NEW YORK **NY** 10016 (212) 686-2320
JEWISH FRONTIER (MONTHLY) CIRC. 13,500 (ENG.) EST. 1934
  114 FIFTH AVENUE .... NEW YORK **NY** 10011 (212) 243-2741
JEWISH JOURNAL 1841 BROADWAY, ROOM 315 .... NEW YORK **NY** 10023 (212) 265-3274
JEWISH LIFE (QUARTERLY) CIRC. 20,700 (ENG.) EST. 1946
  116 EAST 27TH STREET .... NEW YORK **NY** 10016 (212) 563-4000
JEWISH MUSIC NOTES (SEMI-ANNUAL) CIRC. 18,000, EST. 1945
  15 EAST 26TH STREET .... NEW YORK **NY** 10010 (212) 532-4949
JEWISH OBSERVER (MONTHLY) CIRC. 13,700 (ENG.) EST. 1963
  5 BEEKMAN STREET .... NEW YORK **NY** 10038 (212) 791-1814
JEWISH PARENT, THE 229 PARK AVENUE SOUTH .... NEW YORK **NY** 10003 (212) 674-6700
JEWISH POST OF NEW YORK (WEEKLY) CIRC. 88,000 (ENG) EST. 1977
  101 FIFTH AVENUE .... NEW YORK **NY** 10003 (212) 989-6262

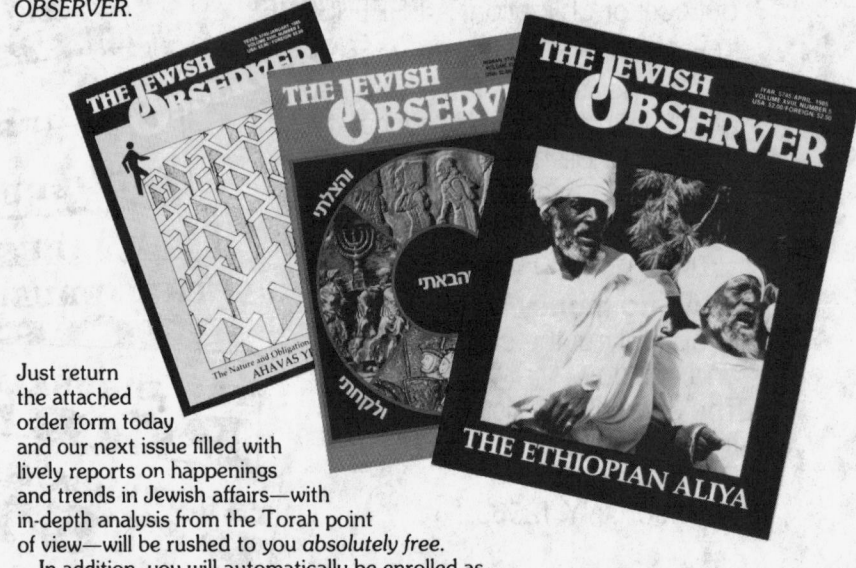

ALL THE NEWS THAT'S FIT TO PRINT ABOUT JEWS ISN'T IN THE NEW YORK TIMES
(OR THE WASHINGTON POST OR ON CBS)

Some of our best friends report for the general press. But when they write on the critical questions of Jewish survival and the future shape of Judaism they write for Present Tense, published by the American Jewish Committee.

In every issue there is news about Jewish life—written from the heart and the spirit—found nowhere else in the world. Here is a sample of the knowledge $10 a year buys:

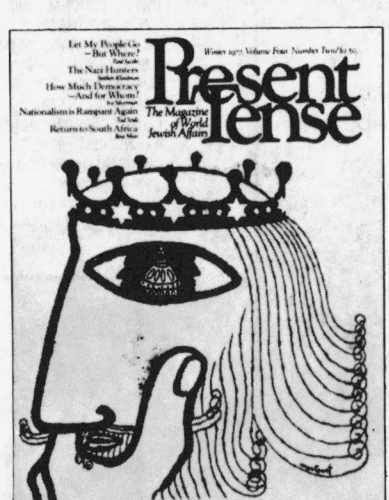

On American Jews: "For the first time in American history, American Jews feel secure enough in their Jewishness and in their Americanism to challenge major aspects of this country's foreign policy." Stephen Isaacs.

On Soviet Jews: "The historic turning-point was the trial in 1970 of eleven foolish, naive young people who hoped to steal a small airplane and fly to freedom in Scandinavia." Murray Seeger.

On searching for roots in Eastern Europe: "Where was my mother's home? Where was the path she must have walked to the Narew River she had told me about? Where was the synagogue and where was the market place?" Sigmund Diamond.

On Jerusalem: "No place on earth offers so many delights to the eye, the ear and the mind as Kollek's Jerusalem, but one must find the time to stand and stare." Chaim Bermant.

On renewed interest in Judaica among young Americans: "The young people perceived themselves as survivors of the failures of Jewish education and the false values of America." Sylvia Rothchild.

On Israel's Nature Reserves: "It may be that General Yoffe's animals will somehow lead the people of the Middle East to peace one day. But the tanks were in the mountains, waiting. The real beast in the desert was still man." Robert Spero.

On being a Jewish poet: "The truest Jewish poetry will be written out of the inward preoccupations of people who happen to be Jews." M. L. Rosenthal.

On the Persian Gulf arms race: "The ramifications of what is happening...extend from the Caspian Sea to the Suez Canal and from the African Coast to Pakistan." Tad Szulc.

On Israel's Arab intellectuals: "I am an Israeli but I cannot be a Jew." Naomi Shepherd.

On American foreign policy: "American companies, which for so long we have considered 'our companies,' have in fact become the policing agents of the Arabs' boycott against the U.S." Paul Dickson.

On South Africa: "To live with such a system of laws, with certificates of racial purity, with leaders who admired Hitler, to live in South Africa as a Jew and to be silent and happy takes some special skills." Rose Moss.

Present Tense: 1 Year: $14

PRESENT TENSE
165 East 56th Street New York. N.Y. 10022
Yes. enter my subscription

Name_____

Address _____

City _____

State_____ Zip_____

☐ **Payment enclosed** (I am entitled to an extra issue FREE!)

☐ **2 years (8 issues) $24**   ☐ **1 year (4 issues) $14**

☐ **Bill me later Charge my** ☐ **American Express** ☐ **Master Charge**

American Express: ☐☐☐☐☐☐☐☐☐☐☐☐☐☐

Master Charge: ☐☐☐☐☐☐☐☐☐☐☐☐☐☐

Signature / Credit Card Expiration Date

PRESENT TENSE
The Magazine of World Jewish Affairs

JEWISH PRESS FEATURES (MONTHLY) EST. 1970
15 EAST 26TH STREET, SUITE 1350 .... NEW YORK **NY** 10010   (212) 679-1411
JEWISH SINGLES NEWSLETTER (MONTHLY) EVENTS CALENDAR
130 EAST 59TH STREET .... NEW YORK **NY** 10022   (212) 751-1000
JEWISH SOCIAL STUDIES 2112 BROADWAY .... NEW YORK **NY** 10023   (212) 724-5336
JEWISH SOCIAL STUDIES (QUARTERLY) CIRC. 1,500, EST. 1939
250 WEST 57TH STREET .... NEW YORK **NY** 10019
JEWISH STUDENT PRESS SERVICE 15 E. 26TH ST. STE 1350 .... NEW YORK **NY** 10010   (212) 679-1411
JEWISH TELEGRAPHIC AGENCY COMMUNITY NEWS REPORTER (WEEKLY)
165 WEST 46TH STREET, ROOM 511 .... NEW YORK **NY** 10036   (212) 575-9370
JEWISH TELEGRAPHIC AGENCY DAILY NEWS BULLETIN
165 WEST 46TH STREET, ROOM 511 .... NEW YORK **NY** 10036   (212) 575-9370
JEWISH TELEGRAPHIC AGENCY WEEKLY NEWS DIGEST
165 WEST 46TH STREET, ROOM 511 .... NEW YORK **NY** 10036   (212) 575-9370
JEWISH TELEGRAPHIC AGENCY, INC. (DAILY) EST. 1917
165 WEST 46TH STREET, ROOM 511 .... NEW YORK **NY** 10036   (212) 575-9370
JEWISH WEEK (WEEKLY) CIRC. 100,000 (ENG) EST 1876, REORG 1970
1 PARK AVENUE .... NEW YORK **NY** 10016   (212) 686-2320
JOURNAL OF JEWISH COMMUNAL SERVICE (QUARTERLY) EST. 1899
15 EAST 26TH STREET .... NEW YORK **NY** 10010   (212) 683-8056
JOURNAL OF JEWISH CONSERVATIVE EDUCATION (QUARTERLY)EST. 1942
155 FIFTH AVENUE .... NEW YORK **NY** 10010
JOURNAL OF PSYCHOLOGY-JUDAISM (QUARTERLY)
72 FIFTH AVENUE .... NEW YORK **NY** 10011
JOURNAL OF REFORM JUDAISM (QUARTERLY) CIRC. 2,200, EST. 1953
21 EAST 40TH STREET .... NEW YORK **NY** 10016   (212) 684-4990
JUDAICA BOOK NEWS (SPRING & FALL) 303 WEST 10 STREET .... NEW YORK **NY** 10014   (212) 691-3817
JUDAISM (QUARTERLY) CIRC. 3,500, (ENG.) EST. 1952
15 EAST 84TH STREET .... NEW YORK **NY** 10028   (212) 879-4500
KEEPING POSTED (7X/YR.) CIRC. 56,000 - ADULT EDUCATION
838 FIFTH AVENUE .... NEW YORK **NY** 10021   (212) 249-0100
KEEPING POSTED (BIMONTHLY) CIRC. 10,000-YOUTH PUBLICATION
116 EAST 27TH STREET .... NEW YORK **NY** 10016   (212) 725-3420
KINDER ZEITUNG (BIMONTHLY) EST. 1930 45 EAST 33RD STREET .... NEW YORK **NY** 10016   (212) 889-6800

KOL HAT'NUAH (MONTHLY) HASHACHAR, EST. 1943
50 WEST 58TH STREET .... NEW YORK **NY** 10019   (212) 355-7900
KOL YAVNEH, CIRC. 18,000, EST. 1960, (JEWISH STUDENT INT.)
25 WEST 26TH STREET .... NEW YORK **NY** 10010   (212) 679-4574
KULTUR UN LEBN-CULTURE LIFE (QUARTERLY) CIRC. 13,000
45 EAST 33RD STREET .... NEW YORK **NY** 10016   (212) 889-6800
LILITH-THE JEWISH WOMEN'S MAGAZINE (QUARTERLY) CIRC. 15,000
250 WEST 57TH STREET, SUITE 1328 .... NEW YORK **NY** 10019   (212) 757-0818
LONG ISLAND JEWISH WORLD (WEEKLY) CIRC 45,000 (ENG) EST 1971
115 MIDDLE NECK ROAD .... NEW YORK **NY** 11021   (516) 829-4000
METROPOLITAN STAR (MONTHLY) COMB. FEB-MAR, NOV-DEC
823 UNITED NATIONS PLAZA, CIRC. 70,000-GENERAL NEWS .... NEW YORK **NY** 10017   (212) 490-2525
MIDSTREAM (MONTHLY) CIRC. 13,000 (ENG.) EST. 1954
515 PARK AVENUE .... NEW YORK **NY** 10022   (212) 752-0600
MORGEN FREIHEIT (WEEKLY) CIRC. 10,000 (YIDDISH) EST. 1922
22 WEST 21ST STREET .... NEW YORK **NY** 10010   (212) 255-7661
NCJW JOURNAL (BIMONTHLY 6X) CIRC. 90,000 15 EAST 26TH STREET ... NEW YORK **NY** 10010   (212) 532-1740
OU INSTITUTIONAL & INDUSTRIAL KOSHER PRODUCTS DIRECTORY
45 WEST 36TH STREET .... NEW YORK **NY** 10018   (212) 563-4000
OU KOSHER PRODUCTS DIRECTORY (IRREGULAR) EST. 1925
45 WEST 36TH STREET .... NEW YORK **NY** 10018   (212) 563-4000
OU NEWS REPORTER(IRREGULAR) NEW FOODS UNDER OU SUPERVISION
45 WEST 36TH STREET .... NEW YORK **NY** 10018   (212) 563-4000
OU PASSOVER PRODUCTS DIRECTORY (ANNUAL) EST. 1923
45 WEST 36TH STREET .... NEW YORK **NY** 10018   (212) 563-4000
OLOMEINU-OUR WORLD (MONTHLY) CIRC. 15,000 (ENG/HEB)EST. 1945
160 BROADWAY .... NEW YORK **NY** 10038   (212) 406-4190
OR CHADASH (2-4X/YR.) EST. 1981, JEWISH BRAILLE INST. OF AM.
110 EAST 30TH STREET .... NEW YORK **NY** 10016   (212) 889-2525

PEDAGOGIC REPORTER (QUARTERLY) EST. 1949, JEWISH EDUC. SVCE.
114 FIFTH AVENUE .... NEW YORK **NY** 10011   (212) 675-5656
PIONEER WOMAN (5X/YR.) CIRC. 26,800 (ENG.) EST. 1926
200 MADISON AVENUE .... NEW YORK **NY** 10016   (212) 725-8010
PRESENT TENSE (QUARTERLY) CIRC. 25,000 (ENG.) EST. 1973
165 EAST 56TH STREET .... NEW YORK **NY** 10022   (212) 751-4000
PROCEEDINGS OF THE AMERICAN ACADEMY FOR JEWISH RESEARCH (AN)
3080 BROADWAY .... NEW YORK **NY** 10027
RABBINICAL COUNCIL RECORD (QUARTERLY) CIRC. 1,200, EST.1953
1250 BROADWAY .... NEW YORK **NY** 10001   (212) 594-3780
RECONSTRUCTIONIST (MONTHLY) CIRC. 6,400, EST. 1935
31 EAST 28TH STREET .... NEW YORK **NY** 10016   (212) 889-9080
RECORD-UNITED JEWISH APPEAL 1290 AVENUE OF THE AMERICAS ..... NEW YORK **NY** 10019   (212) 757-1500
REFORM JUDAISM (8X/YR) CIRC. 265,000 (ENG.) EST. 1972
838 FIFTH AVENUE .... NEW YORK **NY** 10021   (212) 249-0100
RESPONSE (QUARTERLY) EST. 1967 610 WEST 113TH STREET .... NEW YORK **NY** 10025   (212) 621-3000
SAFRA: JEWISH SCHOOL MATERIALS REVIEW (SEMI-ANNUAL) EST. 1980
114 FIFTH AVENUE .... NEW YORK **NY** 10011
SEVEN ARTS FEATURE SYNDICATE AND WORLD WIDE NEWS SERVICE
165 WEST 46TH STREET, ROOM 511 .... NEW YORK **NY** 10036   (212) 247-3595
SHEVILEY HAHINUCH (QUARTERLY) EST. 1939 114 FIFTH AVENUE .... NEW YORK **NY** 10011   (212) 675-5656
SHOAH (3X/YR.) CIRC. 3,500, EST. 1977
250 WEST 57TH STREET, ROOM 216 .... NEW YORK **NY** 10107   (212) 582-6116
SPECTRUM, NORTH AMERICAN JEWISH STUDENT NETWORK CIRC. 20,000
1 PARK AVENUE SUITE 418 .... NEW YORK **NY** 10016   (212) 689-0790
SYNAGOGUE LIGHT (QUARTERLY) CIRC. 19,000 (ENG.) EST. 1933
47 BEEKMAN STREET .... NEW YORK **NY** 10038   (212) 227-7800
THE CALL (BIMONTHLY) CIRC. 53,000, EST. 1932 45 EAST 33RD STREET .. NEW YORK **NY** 10016   (212) 889-6800
THE JEWISH FUNERAL DIRECTOR 122 EAST 42ND STREET, SUITE 1120 .. NEW YORK **NY** 10168   (212) 370-0024
THE NEW AMERICAN (WEEKLY) CIRCULATION 11,000 (RUSSIAN) .... NEW YORK **NY**   (212) 255-1390
TOLEDOT: THE JOURNAL OF JEWISH GENEALOGY
155 EAST 93RD STREET, SUITE 3C .... NEW YORK **NY** 10028
TORCHLIGHT (QUARTERLY) CIRC, 36,000 474 RIVERSIDE DRIVE ——— NEW YORK **NY** 10027   (212) 749-8100
TRADITION (QUARTERLY) CIRC. 4,000, EST. 1958
275 SEVENTH AVENUE....................................... NEW YORK **NY** 10001   (212) 807-7888
UJA RECORD 1290 AVENUE OF THE AMERICAS .... NEW YORK **NY** 10019   (212) 757-1500
UNITED SYNAGOGUE REVIEW (QUARTERLY) CIRC. 230,000 (ENGLISH)
155 FIFTH AVENUE .... NEW YORK **NY** 10010   (212) 533-7800
UNSER TSAIT (MONTHLY) ESTABLISHED 1941, YIDDISH
25 EAST 78TH STREET .... NEW YORK **NY** 10021   (212) 535-0850
WOMEN'S AMERICAN ORT REPORTER (QUARTERLY) CIRC. 148,800
1250 BROADWAY .... NEW YORK **NY** 10001   (212) 594-8500
WOMEN'S LEAGUE OUTLOOK (QUARTERLY) CIRC. 144,900, EST. 1930
48 EAST 74TH STREET .... NEW YORK **NY** 10021   (212) 628-1600
WORLD OVER (MONTHLY) CIRC. 65,000, EST. 1940
426 WEST 58TH STREET .... NEW YORK **NY** 10019   (212) 245-8200
YIVO ANNUAL OF JEWISH SOCIAL SCIENCE (BI-ANNUAL)CIRC. 2,700
1048 FIFTH AVENUE .... NEW YORK **NY** 10028   (212) 535-6700
YIVO BLETER (IRREGULAR) ESTABLISHED 1931 1048 FIFTH AVENUE ..... NEW YORK **NY** 10028   (212) 535-6700
YAVNEH REVIEW (ANNUAL) CIRC. 5,000, EST. 1963
25 WEST 26TH STREET .... NEW YORK **NY** 10010   (212) 679-4574
YEARBOOK OF THE CENTRAL CONFERENCE OF AMERICAN RABBIS
21 EAST 40TH STREET .... NEW YORK **NY** 10016   (212) 684-4990
YIDDISHE KULTUR (MONTHLY) CIRC. 3,000 JEWISH LITERATURE
1123 BROADWAY, ROOM 203............................ NEW YORK **NY** 10010   (212) 691-0708
YIDDISHE SHPRAKH (ANNUAL) CIRC. 2,500 (YIDDISH) EST. 1941
1048 FIFTH AVENUE .... NEW YORK **NY** 10028   (212) 231-7905
YIDDISHER KEMFER (WEEKLY) CIRC. 3,000 (YIDDISH) EST. 1906
575 SIXTH AVENUE .... NEW YORK **NY** 10011   (212) 675-7808
YOUNG ISRAEL VIEWPOINT (8X/YR.) CIRC. 33,000 (ENG) EST. 1952
3 WEST 16TH STREET .... NEW YORK **NY** 10011   (212) 929-1525
YOUNG JUDAEAN (MONTHLY) CIRC. 8,000 EST. 1912
50 WEST 58TH STREET .... NEW YORK **NY** 10019   (212) 355-7900
YOUTH AND NATION (QUARTERLY) CIRC. 1,500, EST. 1933
150 FIFTH AVENUE .... NEW YORK **NY** 10011   (212) 929-4955
JEWISH DIGEST (MONTHLY) CIRC. 15,500 3459 FREDERICK STREET ..... OCEANSIDE **NY** 11572   (516) 764-6250
SH'MA (BIWEEKLY) CIRC. 9,000, EST. 1970 BOX 567 .... PORT WASHINGTON **NY** 11050   (516) 944-9791
LONG ISLAND JEWISH PRESS (MONTHLY) CIRC. 12,700, EST. 1942
95-20 63RD ROAD .... REGO PARK **NY** 11374
WESTCHESTER JEWISH TRIBUNE (MONTHLY) CIRC. 15,000, EST. 1942
95-20 63RD ROAD .... REGO PARK **NY** 11374
JEWISH LEDGER (WEEKLY) CIRC. 24,000 (ENG.) EST. 1924
721 MONROE AVENUE .... ROCHESTER **NY** 14607   (716) 275-9090
THE SCARSDALE INQUIRER (WEEKLY) CIRC. 10,000 (ENGLISH)
HARWOOD BUILDING .... SCARSDALE **NY** 10583   (914) 725-2500
ALBANY JEWISH WORLD (WEEKLY) CIRC. 5,400 (ENG.) EST. 1965
416 SMITH STREET .... SCHENECTADY **NY** 12305   (212) 459-8455
SYRACUSE JEWISH OBSERVER (BIWEEKLY) CIRC. 4,000, EST. 1978
PO BOX 510/2223 EAST GENESEE STREET .... SYRACUSE **NY** 13214   (315) 422-4104
STARK JEWISH NEWS, INCORPORATED (5X/YR.) CIRC. 2,000 (ENG.)
PO BOX 9112 .... CANTON **OH** 44711   (216) 494-7792
AMERICAN JEWISH ARCHIVES (SEMI-ANNUAL) CIRC 5,000, EST. 1947
3101 CLIFTON AVENUE .... CINCINNATI **OH** 45220   (513) 221-1875
HEBREW UNION COLLEGE ANNUAL, ENGLISH, HEBREW, FRENCH, GERMAN
3101 CLIFTON AVENUE .... CINCINNATI **OH** 45220   (513) 221-1875
STUDIES IN BIBLIOGRAPHY AND BOOKLORE (IRREGULAR) HUC-JIR
3101 CLIFTON AVENUE .... CINCINNATI **OH** 45220   (513) 221-1875
THE AMERICAN ISRAELITE (WEEKLY) CIRC. 5,100 (ENG.) EST. 1854
906 MAIN STREET, ROOM 505 .... CINCINNATI **OH** 45202   (513) 621-3145
THE CHABAD TIMES (MONTHLY) CIRC.20,000 (ENGLISH)
1636 SUMMIT ROAD .... CINCINNATI **OH**

CLEVELAND JEWISH NEWS (WEEKLY) CIRC. 18,000(ENG.) EST. 1964
13910 CEDAR ROAD .... CLEVELAND **OH** 44118   (216) 371-0800
INDEX TO JEWISH PERIODICALS (SEMI-ANNUALLY) EST. 1963
PO BOX 18570 .... CLEVELAND HEIGHTS **OH** 44118   (216) 321-7296
OHIO JEWISH CHRONICLE (WEEKLY) CIRC. 2,950 (ENG.) EST. 1921
2831 MAIN STREET .... COLUMBUS **OH** 43209   (614) 237-4296
DAYTON JEWISH CHRONICLE (WEEKLY) CIRC. 1,550 (ENG) EST. 1961
118 SALEM AVENUE .... DAYTON **OH** 45405   (513) 222-0783
TOLEDO JEWISH NEWS (MONTHLY) CIRC. 3,000(ENG.) EST. 1951
5151 MONROE STREET .... TOLEDO **OH** 43604   (419) 241-8913
YOUNGSTOWN JEWISH TIMES (FORTNIGHTLY) CIRC. 9,000, EST. 1935
PO BOX 777 .... YOUNGSTOWN **OH** 44501   (216) 746-6192
SOUTHWEST JEWISH CHRONICLE (QUARTERLY) EST. 1929
324 NORTH ROBINSON STREET, SUITE 313 .... OKLAHOMA CITY **OK** 73102   (405) 236-4226
TULSA JEWISH REVIEW (MONTHLY) ENGLISH EST. 1930
2205 EAST 51ST STREET .... TULSA **OK** 74105   (918) 749-7751
CANADIAN JEWISH NEWS 562 EAST EGLINTON AVENUE, SUITE 401 .... TORONTO **ON** M4P 1P1   (416) 481-6434
JEWISH STANDARD 67 MOWAT AVENUE, SUITE 319 .... TORONTO **ON** M6K 3E3   (416) 363-3289
THE PORTLAND JEWISH REVIEW P.O. BOX 10105 .... PORTLAND **OR** 97210   (503) 297-8104
JEWISH COMMUNITY VOICE (BIWEEKLY) CIRCULATION 10,300 (ENGLISH) .... **PA**
JEWISH EXPERIENCE (MONTHLY) CIRCULATION 3,500 (ENGLISH) .... **PA**
JEWISH REPORTER (MONTHLY 11X)
CIRCULATION 6,700 (ENGLISH) .... DELAWARE VALLEY **PA**
AMERICAN JEWISH PRESS ASSOCIATION 226 S. 16TH STREET .... PHILADELPHIA **PA** 19102   (215) 893-5700
EXPO-THE CONTEMPORARY JEWISH MAGAZINE (6X/YR.) EST. 1979
226 SOUTH 16TH STREET, CIRCULATION 130,000 .... PHILADELPHIA **PA** 19102   (215) 893-5757
INSIDE MAGAZINE (QUARTERLY) CIRC. 85,000 (ENGLISH)
226 SOUTH 16TH STREET .... PHILADELPHIA **PA** 19102   (215) 893-5700
JEWISH NEWSPAPER GROUP OF GREATER PHILADELPHIA (WEEKLIES)
2417 WELSH ROADCIRC. 150,000 (ENGLISH) .... PHILADELPHIA **PA** 19114   (215) 464-3900
JEWISH QUARTERLY REVIEW (QUARTERLY) CIRC. 1,000, EST. 1910
BROAD & YORK STREETS .... PHILADELPHIA **PA** 19132   (215) 229-0110
JEWISH TIMES OF THE GREATER NORTHEAST (WEEKLY) CIRC. 40,000
2417 WELSH ROAD .... PHILADELPHIA **PA** 19114   (215) 464-3900
THE JEWISH EXPONENT (WEEKLY) CIRC. 72,000(ENG.) EST. 1887
226 SOUTH 16TH STREET .... PHILADELPHIA **PA** 19102   (215) 893-5740
JEWISH CHRONICLE (WEEKLY) CIRC. 14,250 (ENG.) EST. 1962
315 SOUTH BELLEFIELD AVENUE .... PITTSBURGH **PA** 15213   (412) 687-1000
JEWISH LIFE MAGAZINE (QUARTERLY) CIRC. 10,000 (ENGLISH)
BOX 573 ESTABLISHED 1977 .... READING **PA** 19602
CANADIAN JEWISH HERALD
17 ANSELME LAVIGNE BOULEVARD .... DOLLARD DES ORMEAUX **QU** H9A 1N3   (514) 684-7667

FEDERATION VOICE (MONTHLY) CIRC. 7,000(ENGLISH)
C/O JEWISH FEDERATION OF RHODE ISLAND, 130 SESSIONS ST ..... PROVIDENCE RI   (401) 421-4111
RHODE ISLAND JEWISH HISTORICAL NOTES (ANNUAL) EST. 1954
130 SESSIONS STREET .... PROVIDENCE RI 02906
CENTER TALK 1645 WALLENBERG BLVD P.O. BOX 31298 .... CHARLESTON SC 29407
THE HEBREW WATCHMAN (WEEKLY) CIRC. 2,400 (ENG.) EST. 1925
277 JEFFERSON AVENUE .... MEMPHIS TN 38103   (901) 526-2215
OBSERVER P.O. BOX 2632 .... NASHVILLE TN 37221   (615) 256-0012
TEXAS JEWISH POST (F) 11333 N. CENTRAL EXPRESSWAY .... DALLAS TX 75231   (214) 692-7283
TEXAS JEWISH POST (WEEKLY) CIRC. 4,400 (ENG.) EST. 1947
PO BOX 742 .... FORT WORTH TX 76101   (817) 927-2831
JEWISH CIVIC PRESS (MONTHLY) CIRC. 4,800, EST. 1971 PO BOX 35656 ... HOUSTON TX 77035   (713) 721-8901
JEWISH HERALD-VOICE (WEEKLY) CIRC. 7,500 (ENG.) EST. 1908
PO BOX 153 .... HOUSTON TX 77001   (713) 661-3116
NOAH'S ARK (MONTHLY) CIRC. 60,000 - MAGAZINE FOR CHILDREN
6330 GULFTON #220 .... HOUSTON TX 77018   (713) 771-7143
THE JEWISH JOURNAL OF SAN ANTONIO (MONTHLY) CIRC. 2,500 ENG.
8434 AHERN DRIVE .... SAN ANTONIO TX 78216   (512) 341-8234
UJF NEWS (WEEKLY) CIRC. 4,900 (ENGLISH) EST. 1973
7300 NEWPORT AVENUE .... NORFOLK VA 23505   (804) 489-8040
THE JEWISH NEWS (WEEKLY) CIRC. 3,900 - GENERAL NEWS (ENGLISH
PO BOX 8228 .... RICHMOND VA 23226   (804) 282-5567
THE JEWISH TRANSCRIPT (BIMONTHLY) CIRC. 3,300 EST. 1924
SECURITIES BUILDING, ROOM 929 .... SEATTLE WA 98101   (206) 624-0136
WISCONSIN JEWISH CHRONICLE (WEEKLY) CIRC. 3,900 EST. 1921
1360 NORTH PROSPECT AVENUE .... MILWAUKEE WI 53202   (414) 271-2992

NEWSPAPERS - HEBREW & ISRAELI

DAVAR 913 NATIONAL PRESS BUILDING .... WASHINGTON DC 20054
JERUSALEM POST & AL HAMISHMAR
615 NATIONAL PRESS BUILDING .... WASHINGTON DC 20045   (202) 783-1161
MA'ARIV 2939 VAN NESS STREET, N.W. .... WASHINGTON DC   (202) 362-8526
HA'ARETZ 4515 S. WILLARD AVENUE .... CHEVY CHASE MD 20015   (301) 951-0182
YEDIOT ACHARONOT 4824 DERUSSEY PARKWAY .... CHEVY CHASE MD 20015   (301) 652-3230
HA'ARETZ-INDEPENDENT MORNING DAILY 24 TEHAMA STREET .. BROOKLYN NY 11218   (718) 581-5151
HAZOFE-NEWSPAPER OF ISRAEL'S NATIONAL RELIGIOUS PARTY
785 E. SECOND STREET .... BROOKLYN NY 11218   (718) 436-9153
ISRAEL SHELANU - WEEKLY (HEBREW) 993 E. 17TH STREET .... BROOKLYN NY 11230   (718) 258-8696
AL HAMISHMAR 301 W. 108TH STREET .... NEW YORK NY 10025   (212) 758-5125
HA'ARETZ 350 FIFTH AVENUE, 19TH FL .... NEW YORK NY 10118   (212) 695-2998
HADOAR HEBREW WEEKLY 1841 BROADWAY .... NEW YORK NY 10023   (212) 581-5151
JERUSALEM POST, THE 120 EAST 56TH STREET .... NEW YORK NY 10022   (212) 355-4440

JEWISH TELEGRAPHIC AGENCY, GLOBAL NEWS 165 W. 46TH STREET ... NEW YORK NY 10036   (212) 575-9370
LAMISHPAHA ILLUSTRATED HEBREW MONTHLY 1841 BROADWAY .... NEW YORK NY 10023   (212) 581-5151
M. DWORKIN AND CO. 150 FIFTH AVENUE .... NEW YORK NY 10011   (212) 924-5788
MA'ARIV-INDEPENDENT EVENING DAILY 130 W. 67TH STREET .... NEW YORK NY 10023   (212) 580-8099
MAARIV ISRAEL NEWSPAPER 350 FIFTH AVENUE .... NEW YORK NY 10001   (212) 695-2998
OMER-DAVER ISRAEL NEWSPAPERS 150 FIFTH AVENUE .... NEW YORK NY 10010   (212) 564-5165
YEDIOT ACHARONOT - INDEPENDENT EVENING DAILY
230 E. 44TH STREET .... NEW YORK NY 10017   (212) 687-6086
YEDIOT AHARANOT C/O M. DWORKIN & COMPANY 350 FIFTH AVENUE .. NEW YORK NY 10001   (212) 564-5165

NEWSPAPERS
YIDDISH & FOREIGN LANGUAGE

JEWISH FORWARD 1161 NORTH OGDEN DRIVE .... LOS ANGELES CA 90046   (213) 659-0861
JEWISH MORNING FREIHEIT 163 SOUTH FAIRFAX AVENUE #4 .... LOS ANGELES CA 90036   (213) 937-5017
DE YIDDISH HEIM/THE JEWISH HOME 770 EASTERN PARKWAY ...... BROOKLYN NY 11213   (718) 493-0571
DER YID 543 BEDFORD AVENUE .... BROOKLYN NY 11211   (718) 782-4900
SHMUESSEN MIT KINDER UN YUGENT 770 EASTERN PARKWAY .... BROOKLYN NY 11213   (718) 774-4000
SVET (LIGHT)(MONTHLY) CIRC. 25,000 (RUSSIAN)
455 ALBANY AVENUE .... BROOKLYN NY 11213   (718) 774-0065
YID: VOICE OF AMERICAN ORTHODOX JEWRY YID PUB ASSOCIATION
260 BROADWAY .... BROOKLYN NY 11211
ALGEMEINER JOURNAL 404 PARK AVE. SOUTH .... NEW YORK NY 10016   (212) 689-3390
AUFBAU 2121 BROADWAY .... NEW YORK NY 10023   (212) 873-7400
JEWISH FORWARD, THE 45 EAST 33RD STREET .... NEW YORK NY 10016   (212) 889-8200
JEWISH FORWARD, THE-CLASSIFIED ADVERTISEMENT DEPT.
45 EAST 33RD STREET .... NEW YORK NY 10016   (212) 689-5505
JEWISH MORNING FREIHEIT 22 WEST 21ST STREET .... NEW YORK NY 10010   (212) 255-7661

NURSING HOMES, REST HOMES &
OLD AGE HOMES

JEWISH HOME FOR THE AGED 3560 BATHURST STREET .... TORONTO M6A 2E1   (416) 789-5131
THE LOUIS BRIER HOME AND HOSPITAL 1055 WEST 41 AVENUE .... VANCOUVER   (604) 261-9376
THE SHARON HOME BOX 3537 STATION B .... WINNIPEG R2W 3R4   (204) 582-5583
KIVEL NURSING HOME 3020 NORTH 36 STREET .... PHOENIX AZ 85018   (602) 956-3110
HANDMAKER JEWISH GERIATRIC CENTER 2221 NO. ROSEMONT BLVD .....TUCSON AZ 85712   (602) 881-2323
HOME FOR JEWISH PARENTS 2780 26TH AVENUE .... OAKLAND CA 94601   (415) 536-4604
JEWISH HOMES FOR THE AGING OF GREATER L.A.
18855 VICTORY BOULEVARD .... RESEDA CA 91335   (818) 881-4411
SAN DIEGO HEBREW HOME FOR THE AGED 4075 54TH STREET ... SAN DIEGO CA 92105   (619) 582-5168
JEWISH HOME FOR THE AGED 302 SILVER AVENUE .... SAN FRANCISCO CA 94112   (415) 334-2500
MENORAH PARK 3365 SACRAMENTO STREET .... SAN FRANCISCO CA 94118   (415) 929-7912
PINECREST 320 SILVER AVENUE .... SAN FRANCISCO CA 94112   (415) 587-4666
BETH ISRAEL 1620 MEADA WAY .... DENVER CO 80209   (303) 825-2190
JEWISH HOME FOR THE ELDERLY OF FAIRFIELD COUNTY
175 JEFFERSON STREET .... FAIRFIELD CT 06432   (203) 347-9461
HEBREW HOME & HOSPITAL 615 TOWER AVENUE .... HARTFORD CT 06112   (203) 242-6207
JEWISH HOME FOR THE AGED, INC. 169 DAVENPORT AVENUE .... NEW HAVEN CT 06519   (203) 788-1650
THE MILTON & HATTIE KUTZ HOME, INC. 704 RIVER ROAD .... WILMINGTON DE 19809   (302) 764-7000
RIVER GARDEN HEBREW HOME 1800 STOCKTON STREET .... JACKSONVILLE FL 32204   (904) 389-3665
MIAMI JEWISH HOME AND HOSPITAL FOR THE AGED
151 N.E. 52ND STREET .... MIAMI FL 33137   (305) 751-8626
HEBREW HOME FOR THE AGED OF MIAMI BEACH
320 COLLINS AVENUE .... MIAMI BEACH FL 33139   (305) 672-6464
KINNERET, INC. 515-517 S. DELANEY AVENUE .... ORLANDO FL 32801   (305) 425-4537
THE JEWISH HOME TOWER INC. 3160 HOWELL MILL ROAD N.W. .... ORLANDO FL 32801   (305) 425-4537
JEWISH HOME FOR AGED 501 S. FLAGLER DRIVE, SUITE 305 .... WEST PALM BEACH FL 33401
THE JEWISH HOME 3150 HOWELL MILL ROAD, N.W. .... ATLANTA GA 30327   (404) 351-8410
IOWA JEWISH HOME 1620 PLEASANT .... DES MOINES IA 50312   (515) 288-1001
NORTHWEST HOME FOR AGED 6300 N. CALIFORNIA .... CHICAGO IL 60645   (312) 973-1900
GEORGE J. GOLDMAN MEMORIAL HOME FOR THE AGED 6601 W. TOUHY ..... NILES IL 60648   (312) 647-9875
JACOB & MARCELLE LIEBERMAN GERIATRIC CENTRE
9700 GROSS POINT ROAD .... SKOKIE IL 60076   (312) 674-7210
INDIANAPOLIS JEWISH HOME, INC. (HOOVERWOOD)
7001 HOOVER ROAD .... INDIANAPOLIS IN 46260   (317) 251-2261
JEWISH WELFARE FED. HOUSING CORP.-PARK REGENCY
8851 COLBY BLVD .... INDIANAPOLIS IN 46268   (317) 875-5763
FOUR COURTS (THE LOUISVILLE HEBREW HOME)
2100 MILLVALE ROAD .... LOUISVILLE KY 40205   (502) 451-0990
WILLOW WOOD HOME FOR JEWISH AGED 3701 BEHRMAN PLACE.... NEW ORLEANS LA 70114   (504) 367-5640
CHELSEA JEWISH NURSING HOME 17 LAFAYETTE AVENUE .... CHELSEA MA 02150   (617) 884-3658
FALL RIVER JEWISH HOME 199 HANOVER STREET .... FALL RIVER MA 02720
SPRINGFIELD JEWISH HOME FOR THE AGED
770 CONVERSE STREET .... LONGMEADOW MA 01106   (413) 567-6211
NEW BEDFORD JEWISH CONVALESCENT HOME, INC.
200 HAWTHORN STREET .... NEW BEDFORD MA 02740   (617) 997-9314
H.R.C.A. HOUSING FOR ELDERLY - REVERE HOUSE
420 REVERE BEACH BLVD .... REVERE MA 01108   (617) 289-4505
HEBREW REHABILITATION CENTER FOR AGED
1200 CENTRE STREET .... ROSLINDALE MA 02131   (617) 325-8000
RECUPERATIVE CENTER, THE 1245 CENTRE STREET .... ROSLINDALE MA 02131   (617) 325-5400
NEW ENGLAND SINAI HOSPITAL 150 YORK STREET (BOX 647) .... STOUGHTON MA 02072
JEWISH REHABILITATION CENTER FOR AGED OF THE NORTH SHORE
330 PARADISE ROAD .... SWAMPSCOTT MA 01907   (617) 598-5061
JEWISH HOME FOR AGED OF WORCESTER COUNTY
629 SALISBURY STREET .... WORCESTER MA 01609   (617) 798-8653

HURWITZ HOUSE 133 SLADE AVENUE................................BALTIMORE MD 21208   (301) 466-8700
JEWISH CONVALESCENT & NURSING HOME
  7920 SCOTTS LEVEL ROAD ....BALTIMORE MD 21208   (301) 521-3600
JEWISH CONVALESCENT & NURSING HOME 4601 PALL MALL ROAD .... BALTIMORE MD 21208   (301) 521-3600
LEVENDALE HEBREW HOME & INFIRMARY
  BELVEDERE AND GREENSPRING ....BALTIMORE MD 21215   (301) 466-8700
HEBREW HOME OF GREATER WASHINGTON 6121 MONTROSE ROAD .... ROCKVILLE MD 20852   (301) 881-0300
JEWISH HOME FOR THE AGED P.O. BOX 446 DTS .... PORTLAND ME 04112
JEWISH HOME FOR AGED 19100 WEST SEVEN MILE ROAD .... DETROIT MI   (313) 532-7112
JEWISH FEDERATION APARTMENTS, INC. 15100 WEST TEN MILE......... OAK PARK MI 48237   (313) 967-4240
COMMUNITY HOUSING & SERVICE CORP. - MENORAH PLAZA APARTMENTS
  4925 MINNETONKA BLVD. ....ST. LOUIS PARK MN 55416   (612) 927-0460
SHOLOM HOME, INC. 1554 MIDWAY PARKWAY .... ST. PAUL MN 55108   (612) 646-6311
JEWISH CENTER FOR AGED 13190 SOUTH OUTER 40 ROAD .... CHESTERFIELD MO 63017   (314) 434-3330
JEWISH GERIATRIC & CONVALESCENT CENTER 7801 HOLMES .... KANSAS CITY MO 64131   (816) 333-7800
BLUMENTHAL JEWISH HOME FOR THE AGED, INC. P.O. BOX 38 .... CLEMONS NC 27012   (919) 766-6401
DR. PHILIP SHER JEWISH HOME 4801 NORTH 52ND STREET .... OMAHA NE 68104
SEASHORE GARDENS/HEBREW OLD AGE CENTER
  3850 ATLANTIC AVENUE ....ATLANTIC CITY NJ 08401   (609) 345-5941
JEWISH GERIATRIC HOME 3025 WEST CHAPEL AVENUE .... CHERRY HILL NJ 08034   (609) 667-3100
DAUGHTERS OF MIRIAM CENTER FOR THE AGED 155 HAZEL STREET ..... CLIFTON NJ 07015   (201) 772-3700
WORKMEN'S CIRCLE HOME FOR AGED & INFIRM OF NJ, BRANCHES INC.
  225 WEST JERSEY STREET ....ELIZABETH NJ 07202   (201) 353-1220
JEWISH HOSPITAL & REHABILITATION CENTER OF N.J.
  198 STEVENS AVENUE ....JERSEY CITY NJ 07305   (201) 451-9000
CHARLES BIERMAN HOME FOR AGED 10 MADISON AVENUE .... MONTCLAIR NJ 07042   (201) 744-6333
JEWISH HOME FOR THE AGED 380 DE MOTT LANE .... SOMERSET NJ 08873   (201) 873-2000
GREENWOOD HOUSE, HOME FOR JEWISH AGED 53 WALTER STREET ..... TRENTON NJ 08628   (609) 883-5391
DAUGHTERS OF ISRAEL GERIATRIC CENTER
  1155 PLEASANT VALLEY WAY ....WEST ORANGE NJ 07052   (201) 731-5100
DAUGHTERS OF SARAH HOME WASHINGTON AVENUE & RAPP ROAD .... ALBANY NY 12203   (518) 456-7831
BETH ABRAHAM HOSPITAL 612 ALLERTON AVENUE .... BRONX NY 10467   (212) 920-6001
DAUGHTERS OF JACOB NURSING HOME 1160 TELLER AVENUE .... BRONX NY 10456   (212) 293-1500
HEBREW HOME FOR THE AGED AT RIVERDALE, THE
  5901 PALISADE AVENUE ....BRONX NY 10471   (212) 549-8700
HEBREW HOSPITAL FOR CHRONIC SICK 2200 GIVAN AVENUE .... BRONX NY 10475   (212) 379-5020
HOME & HOSPITAL OF THE DAUGHTERS OF JACOB 321 E 167TH STREET ... BRONX NY 10456   (212) 293-1500
JEWISH HOME & HOSPITAL FOR AGED, THE (KINGSBRIDGE CENTER)
  100 W KINGSBRIDGE ROAD ....BRONX NY 10468   (212) 579-0500
UNITED ODDFELLOW AND REBEKAH HOME 1072 HAVEMEYER AVENUE ...... BRONX NY 10462   (212) 863-6200
WORKMAN'S CIRCLE HOME 3155 GRACE AVENUE .... BRONX NY 10469   (212) 379-8100
AISHEL AVRAHAM RHF INC. 40 HEYWARD STREET .... BROOKLYN NY 11211   (718) 858-6200
DAVID MINKIN REHABILITATION INSTITUTE (RUTLAND NURSING HOME)
  585 SCHENECTADY AVENUE ....BROOKLYN NY 11203   (718) 756-9700
JHMCB CENTER FOR NURSING & REHABILITATION
  520 PROSPECT PLACE ....BROOKLYN NY   (718) 636-1000
JEWISH GERIATRIC CENTER WEST 29TH STREET & BOARDWALK .... BROOKLYN NY 11224
LEMBERG HOME & GERIATRIC INSTITUTE, INC. 8629 BAY PARKWAY ..... BROOKLYN NY 11214   (718) 606-0901
MENORAH HOME 871 BUSHWICK AVENUE .... BROOKLYN NY 11221   (718) 443-3000
METROPOLITAN JEWISH GERIATRIC CENTER 4915 TENTH AVENUE ...... BROOKLYN NY 11219   (718) 346-7000
SEPHARDIC HOME 2265 CROPSEY AVENUE .... BROOKLYN NY 11214   (718) 266-6100
ROSA COPLON JEWISH HOME AND INFIRMARY 10 SYMPHONY CIRCLE .... BUFFALO NY 14201   (716) 885-3311
FAIRFIELD DIVISION-HEBREW HOME
  3220 HENRY HUDSON PARKWAY ....EAST BRONX NY 10463   (212) 549-9400
BEZALEL HEALTH RELATED FACILITY
  29-38 FAR ROCKAWAY BLVD......................................FAR ROCKAWAY NY 11691   (718) 471-2600
MARGARET TIETZ CENTER FOR NURSING CARE
  164-11 CHAPIN PARKWAY ....JAMAICA NY 11432   (718) 523-6400
CHARLES T SITRIN NURSING HOME CO., INC
  RD 1 BOX 318 TILDEN AVENUE ....NEW HARTFORD NY 13413   (315) 797-3114
JIGC NURSING HOME CO., INC 271-11 76TH AVENUE .... NEW HYDE PARK NY 11042   (718) 343-2100
UNITED HOME FOR AGED HEBREWS 60 WILLOW DRIVE.............. NEW ROCHELLE NY 10805   (914) 632-2804
BIALYSTOKER HOME FOR AGED 228 EAST BROADWAY .... NEW YORK NY 10002   (212) 475-7755
CENTRAL BUREAU FOR JEWISH AGED 80 FIFTH AVENUE .... NEW YORK NY 10011   (212) 929-3999
HOME OF THE SAGES OF ISRAEL 25 WILLETT STREET .... NEW YORK NY 10002   (212) 673-8500
JEWISH ASSOCIATION FOR SERVICES 40 WEST 68TH STREET .... NEW YORK NY 10023
JEWISH HOME & HOSPITAL FOR AGED, THE (ZEMAN CENTER)
  120 W. 106TH STREET ....NEW YORK NY 10025   (212) 870-5000
HEBREW HOME HOUSING DEV. FUND CO., INC. - RIVER HOUSE WEST
  5961 PALISADE AVENUE ....RIVERDALE NY 10471   (212) 543-9600
JEWISH HOME & INFIRMARY OF ROCHESTER, N.Y., INC.
  1180 ST. PAUL STREET ....ROCHESTER NY 14621   (716) 467-0843
JEWISH HOME OF CENTRAL NEW YORK 4101 EAST GENESEE STREET ... SYRACUSE NY 13214   (315) 446-9111
JEWISH FED. HOUSING DEV. FUND CO., INC.-JEWISH FED. HOUSING
  275 ESSJAY ROAD ....WILLIAMSVILLE NY 14221   (716) 631-8471
HOME FOR AGED BLIND 5 STRATTON STREET .... YONKERS NY 10701   (204) 582-5583
MENORAH PARK-JEWISH HOME FOR THE AGED
  27100 CEDAR ROAD ....BEACHWOOD OH 44122   (216) 831-6500
R.H. MEYERS APARTMENTS 27200 CEDAR ROAD .... BEACHWOOD OH 44122   (216) 831-6515
HOME FOR JEWISH AGED 6969 GLENMEADOW LANE .... CINCINNATI OH 45237
ORTHODOX JEWISH HOME FOR THE AGED 1171 TOWNE STREET .... CINCINNATI OH 45216   (513) 242-1360
MENORAH PARK - JEWISH HOME FOR AGED 27100 CEDAR ROAD .... CLEVELAND OH 44122   (216) 831-6500
COUNCIL GARDENS 2501 N. TAYLOR ROAD .... CLEVELAND HEIGHTS OH 44118   (216) 382-8625
THE MONTEFIORE HOME, INC. 3151 MAYFIELD ROAD .... CLEVELAND HEIGHTS OH 44118   (216) 371-5500
HERITAGE TOWER - JEWISH COMM. SR. CITIZENS HOUSING CORP.
  1145 COLLEGE AVENUE ....COLUMBUS OH 43209   (614) 237-2521
HERITAGE VILLAGE 1151 COLLEGE AVENUE .... COLUMBUS OH 43209   (614) 237-7417
COVENANT HOUSE 4911 COVENANT HOUSE DRIVE .... DAYTON OH 45426   (513) 837-2651
DARLINGTON HOUSE, TOLEDO JEWISH HOME FOR AGED
  2735 DARLINGTON ROAD ....TOLEDO OH   (419) 531-4465
TOLEDO JEWISH HOME FOR THE AGED - PELHAM MANOR
  2700 PELHAM ROAD ....TOLEDO OH 43606   (419) 537-1515

HERITAGE MANOR 517 GYPSY LANE, P.O. BOX 449 .... YOUNGSTOWN OH 44501   (216) 746-1076
HILLEL LODGE 125 WURTEMBURG STREET .... OTTAWA ON K1N 8L9
ROBINSON JEWISH HOME FOR AGED 6125 S.W. BOUNDARY STREET...... PORTLAND OR 97221
JEWISH HOME OF GREATER HARRISBURG
  4000 LINGLESTOWN ROAD.......................................HARRISBURG PA 17112   (717) 657-0700
FEDERATION HOUSING, INC. 8900 ROOSEVELT BLVD .... PHILADELPHIA PA 19115   (215) 673-6446
PHILADELPHIA GERIATRIC CENTER 5301 OLD YORK ROAD .... PHILADELPHIA PA 19141   (215) 455-6100
UPTOWN HOME FOR THE AGED 7800 BUSTLETON AVENUE .... PHILADELPHIA PA 19152   (215) 722-2300
YORK HOUSE INC. - YORK HOUSE NORTH AND SOUTH
  5325 OLD YORK ROAD ....PHILADELPHIA PA 19141   (215) 455-6100
JEWISH HOME & HOSPITAL FOR AGED 4724 BROWN'S HILL ROAD ...... PITTSBURGH PA 15217   (412) 521-5900
THE JEWISH HOME OF EASTERN PENNSYLVANIA 1101 VINE STREET..... SCRANTON PA 18510   (717) 344-6177
JEWISH NURSING HOME 3939 CURATTEAU STREET .... MONTREAL QU H1K 4A6
MAIMONIDES HOSPITAL GERIATRIC CENTER
  5795 CALDWELL AVENUE ....MONTREAL QU H4W 1W3 (514) 483-2121
JEWISH HOME FOR THE AGED OF RHODE ISLAND
  99 HILLSIDE AVENUE ....PROVIDENCE RI 02906   (401) 351-4750
B'NAI B'RITH HOME FOR AGED 131 N. TUCKER STREET .... MEMPHIS TN 38104   (504) 367-5640
DALLAS HOME FOR JEWISH AGED (GOLDEN ACRES)
  2525 CENTERVILLE ROAD ....DALLAS TX 75228   (214) 327-4503
ECHAD, INC. - ECHAD APARTMENTS 2620 RUIDOSA .... DALLAS TX 75228   (214) 321-2130
NORTH AMERICAN ASSOC. OF JEWISH HOMES & HOUSING FOR THE AGED
  2525 CENTERVILLE ROAD ....DALLAS TX 75228   (214) 327-4503
B'NAI B'RITH SEN. CITIZENS HOUSING COMM. OF HOUSTON, INC.
  10909 FONDREN ROAD ....HOUSTON TX 77096   (713) 771-2417
JEWISH HOME FOR THE AGED - 'SEVEN ACRES'
  6200 NORTH BRAESWOOD ....HOUSTON TX 77074   (713) 771-4111
GOLDEN MANOR 130 SPENCER LANE .... SAN ANTONIO TX 78201   (512) 736-4544
BETH SHOLOM HOME OF CENTRAL VIRGINIA
  5700 FITZHUGH AVENUE ....RICHMOND VA 23226   (804) 282-5471
BETH SHOLOM HOUSING CORP. - BETH SHOLOM WOODS
  2027 LAUDERDALE ROAD ....RICHMOND VA 23233   (804) 741-4691
BETH SHOLOM HOME OF EASTERN VIRGINIA
  6401 AUBURN DRIVE ....VIRGINIA BEACH VA 23464   (804) 420-2512
THE CAROLINE KLINE GALLAND HOME
  7500 STEWARD PARK AVENUE SOUTH ....SEATTLE WA 98118   (206) 725-8800
MILWAUKEE JEWISH CONVALESCENT CENTER 5555 N. 51ST BLVD...... MILWAUKEE WI 53218   (414) 464-2300
MILWAUKEE JEWISH HOME 1414 N. PROSPECT AVENUE .... MILWAUKEE WI 53202   (414) 276-2627

NUTRITION & HEALTH

KOSHER NUTRITION PROJECT 320 15TH .... SAN FRANCISCO CA 94105   (415) 221-1025
JEWISH VOCATIONAL SERVICE NUTRITIONAL PROJECT
  920 ALTON ROAD..MIAMI BEACH FL 33139   (305) 672-6263
ADWE BEAUTY & HEALTH AIDS (INC. KOSHER FOR PASSOVER)
  141 20TH STREET ....BROOKLYN NY 11232   (718) 788-6838
PRECISION VITAMINS 1524 47TH ST. .... BROOKLYN NY 11219   (718) 435-4333
START FRESH - UNIQUE KOSHER WEIGHT CONTROL PROGRAM
  1173 50TH STREET ....BROOKLYN NY 11219   (718) 851-0081
FAR ROCKAWAY HEALTH FOOD CENTER 1815 MOTT AVENUE ...... FAR ROCKAWAY NY 11691   (718) 327-9087
KOSHER CATALOGUE, INC. 2107 BORDEN AVENUE .... LONG ISLAND CITY NY 11101   (718) 784-6150
KOSHER CATALOGUE, INC. 2107 BORDEN AVENUE .... LONG ISLAND CITY NY 11101   (800) 5KOSHER
FREEDA VITAMINS (INC. KOSHER FOR PASSOVER)
  36 EAST 41ST STREET ....NEW YORK NY 10017   (212) 685-8980
LOIS LANE'S NINTH & NATURAL 580 NINTH AVENUE CORNER 42ND ST... NEW YORK NY 10036   (212) 695-5055

ORCHESTRAS

CINDY PALEY ABOODY ....LOS ANGELES CA   (213) 785-8273
DAVE & GILA BELL ....LOS ANGELES CA   (213) 931-6125
DAVID KAMENIR ORCHESTRA ....LOS ANGELES CA   (213) 990-7802
EVERETT COVIN ORCHESTRAS ....LOS ANGELES CA   (213) 822-8404
HAL BREGMAN ORCHESTRAS ....LOS ANGELES CA   (213) 393-4813
HAL SANDACK ORCHESTRAS ....LOS ANGELES CA   (213) 934-3610
HERB SILVER ORCHESTRAS ....LOS ANGELES CA   (213) 981-9293
JAY SAUNDERS MUSIC ....LOS ANGELES CA   (213) 347-5600
JERRY ROSEN ORCHESTRAS ....LOS ANGELES CA   (213) 939-2027
JOEY SHARPE ORCHESTRAS ....LOS ANGELES CA   (213) 987-3249
KOL ECHAD CHORALE 1620 CORNING STREET ....LOS ANGELES CA   (213) 859-1057
LIONEL AMES ORCHESTRAS ....LOS ANGELES CA   (213) 985-0010
LOS ANGELES MANDOLIN ORCHESTRA ....LOS ANGELES CA   (213) 731-2353
LUDDY DREYFUSS ....LOS ANGELES CA   (213) 931-6125
MANNY HARMON ORCHESTRAS ....LOS ANGELES CA   (213) 656-8720
MERRILL LISH ORCHESTRAS ....LOS ANGELES CA   (213) 992-6330
MICKEY KATZ & HIS CAPITOL RECORDING ORCHESTRA ....LOS ANGELES CA   (213) 271-0256
MURRAY KORDA STRINGS & ORCHESTRAS ....LOS ANGELES CA   (213) 274-3404
NEIL SEIDEL ....LOS ANGELES CA   (213) 852-1035
QUABAL BAND ....LOS ANGELES CA   (213) 876-3285
SHALOM SHERMAN ....LOS ANGELES CA   (213) 931-6125
SIMCHA ORCHESTRA ....LOS ANGELES CA   (213) 399-0211
THE NAMA ORCHESTRA AND SINGERS ....LOS ANGELES CA   (213) 475-6262
THE SABRAS BAND ....LOS ANGELES CA   (213) 999-4193
EILAT ORCHESTRAS ....NJ   (201) 471-9179
ALBERT WARMAN & HIS CORDOVOX ....NY   (718) 531-9767
DAVID NULMAN ORCHESTRAS ....NY   (718) 252-0308
ED MEYERS ENTERTAINMENT ....NY   (516) 781-0383
ELI LIPSKER ORCHESTRA ....NY   (718) 774-5174
EZRA INTERNATIONAL ENTERTAINER ....NY   (718) 268-8707
FOR WOMEN ONLY ....NY   (718) 377-4154
FREILACH ORCHESTRA ....NY   (718) 436-3106

HAROLD DAVIS MUSIC	NY	(516) 764-7876
ISRA ART PRODUCTIONS	NY	(212) 246-4500
JERRY MARKOWITZ ORCHESTRA	NY	(718) 698-9380
JERUSALEM ORCHESTRA (MOTTY PERL)	NY	(718) 438-0406
JERRY KING ORCHESTRAS	NY	(718) 217-0326
JOEL BERNARD - ONE MAN BAND	NY	(914) 794-7069
JOSH GOLDBERG	NY	
KOL CHODOSH ORCHESTRA	NY	(718) 851-4620
KOL ZAHAV ORCHESTRA (ZEV AND ARI)	NY	(718) 896-2606
LEIB GILDIN ORCHESTRA	NY	(718) 251-4213
MARVIN B'SIMCHA	NY	(718) 633-4298
MESSENGERS ORCHESTRA, THE	NY	(718) 471-2801
MEYER DAVIS ORCHESTRA	NY	(212) 247-6161
MIZMOR SHIR ORCHESTRA (ELI KLEINMAN)	NY	(718) 339-2218
NAT EPSTEIN MUSIC	NY	(718) 229-4343
NAT SAMBERG DISCO PRODUCTIONS	NY	(212) 379-6572
NEGINAH ORCHESTRA	NY	(718) 854-2911
NESHOMA ORCHESTRAS	NY	(718) 376-6122
NOBLEMEN ORCHESTRAS	NY	(516) 731-9810
PAUL GLASSER ORCHESTRA, THE	NY	(718) 544-2361
PAUL ZAHN ORCHESTRA	NY	(516) 484-0077
RAYA MEHEMNA ORCHESTRA (YITZCHOK BATON)	NY	(718) 467-4947
RUACH (SAM KLAVER, IRA SILBER)	NY	(718) 854-2059
RUACH ORCHESTRA & SINGERS (ALAN FREISHTAT)	NY	(718) 435-3285
RUACH REVIVAL ORCHESTRA (JOEY FISHOF, YOSSI ROSENBERG)	NY	(516) 374-6444
RUDY TEPEL	NY	(718) 377-0655
SHELLEY LANG ORCHESTRA	NY	(718) 438-3402
SHEMESH ORCHESTRA, THE (ZALMAN UMLAS)	NY	(718) 263-9431
SHIRIM ORCHESTRAS (SHRAGIE SONTAG)	NY	(914) 356-4366
SHLOMO RABINOWITZ ORCHESTRA	NY	(718) 332-7825
SHMUEL BEIM ORCHESTRAS	NY	(718) 436-9255
SHMUEL GOLDMAN ORCHESTRA	NY	(718) 604-1234
SIMCHA SOUND ORCHESTRA	NY	(516) 489-0880
SIMCHATONE ORCHESTRAS	NY	(718) 853-5284
STANLEY MILLER BAND, THE	NY	(516) 569-2374
STONE & STUART 'DUO' OR 'TRIO'	NY	(718) 763-0394
SY MANDEL ORCHESTRA	NY	(718) 268-6400
TZAHALAH ORCHESTRA (MEIR SHERMAN)	NY	(718) 438-3648
ZIMRIAH ORCHESTRAS	NY	(718) 544-2602
KEN JAMES ORCHESTRAS	NY	(516) 829-6480

OVERSEAS AID

AMERICAN ASSOCIATION OF ETHIOPIAN JEWS
304 ROBIN HOOD LANE .... COSTA MESA **CA** 92627 (714) 642-8613
AMERICAN ASSOCIATION FOR ETHIOPIAN JEWS, NAT'L MATERIALS CTR.
6505 WILSHIRE BLVD., ROOM 802 .... LOS ANGELES **CA** 90048 (213) 852-1234
AMERICAN ASSOCIATION FOR ETHIOPIAN JEWS
2789 OAK STREET .... HIGHLAND PARK **IL** 60035 (312) 433-8150
HATZILU RESCUE ORGANIZATION 1770 PITKIN AVENUE .... BROOKLYN **NY** 11212 (718) 389-5538
ARIF - ASSOCIATION POUR LA RETABLISSEMENT DES INSTITUTIONS
ET OEUVRES ISRAELITES EN FRANCE, 119 EAST 95TH STREET .... NEW YORK **NY** 10028
ALLIANCE ISRAELITE UNIVERSELLE, AMERICAN FRIENDS OF
61 BROADWAY .... NEW YORK **NY** 10006 (212) 349-0537
AMERICAN COMMITTEE FOR RESCUE & RESETTLEMENT OF IRAQI JEWS
1200 FIFTH AVENUE .... NEW YORK **NY** 10029 (212) 427-1246
AMERICAN COUNCIL FOR JEWISH PHILANTHROPIC FUND
386 PARK AVENUE SOUTH .... NEW YORK **NY** 10016 (212) 684-1525
AMERICAN FRIENDS OF THE ALLIANCE ISRAELITE UNIVERSELLE
135 WILLIAM STREET .... NEW YORK **NY** 10038 (212) 349-0537
AMERICAN JEWISH JOINT DISTRIBUTION COMMITTEE, INC.
60 E. 42ND STREET .... NEW YORK **NY** 10017 (212) 687-6200
AMERICAN ORT FEDERATION-ORG. FOR REHABIL. THROUGH TRAINING
817 BROADWAY .... NEW YORK **NY** 10003 (212) 677-4400
AMERICAN PRO-FALASHA COMMITTEE 507 FIFTH AVENUE .... NEW YORK **NY** 10017 (212) 697-5895
CONFERENCE ON JEWISH MATERIAL CLAIMS AGAINST GERMANY
15 EAST 26TH STREET .... NEW YORK **NY** 10010
FREELAND LEAGUE FOR JEWISH TERRITORIAL COLONIZATION
200 WEST 72ND STREET .... NEW YORK **NY** 10023
INTERNATIONAL LEAGUE FOR REPATRIATION OF RUSSIAN JEWS
315 CHURCH STREET .... NEW YORK **NY** 10013 (212) 431-6789
JEWISH RESTITUTION SUCCESSOR ORGANIZATION
15-19 EAST 26TH STREET .... NEW YORK **NY** 10010
JOINT DISTRIBUTION COMMITTEE 60 EAST 42ND STREET .... NEW YORK **NY** 10165 (212) 687-6200
NORTH AMERICAN CONFERENCE ON ETHIOPIAN JEWRY
C/O LINCOLN SQUARE SYNAGOGUE, 200 AMSTERDAM AVENUE .... NEW YORK **NY** 10023 (212) 595-1759
RELIEF COMMITTEE OF GENERAL JEWISH WORKERS - POLAND
25 EAST 78TH STREET .... NEW YORK **NY** 10021
UNITED HIAS SERVICE 200 PARK AVENUE SOUTH .... NEW YORK **NY** 10003 (212) 674-6800
UNITED JEWISH APPEAL 1290 AVENUE OF THE AMERICAS ..... NEW YORK **NY** 10019 (212) 757-1500
WOMEN'S SOCIAL SERVICE FOR ISRAEL 240 WEST 98TH STREET .... NEW YORK **NY** 10025 (212) 666-7880
AMERICAN ASSOCIATION FOR ETHIOPIAN JEWS 340 CORLIES AVENUE .... PELHAM **NY** 10803 (914) 738-0956

PASSOVER PRODUCTS

B. MANISCHEWITZ CO. 9 CLINTON STREET .... JERSEY CITY **NJ** 07302 (201) 333-3700
MOTHER'S - A DIVISION OF VITA FOODS HUNTS POINT FOOD CENTER ...... BRONX **NY** 10468 (212) 796-5676
ADWE LABS 141 20TH STREET .... BROOKLYN **NY** 11232 (718) 788-6838

BELZER SHMURA MATZOH BAKERY 4312 NEW UTRECHT AVENUE ...... BROOKLYN **NY** 11219 (718) 854-0597
CONGREGATION YETEV LEV MATZOH BAKERY 152 RODNEY ...... BROOKLYN **NY** 11230 (718) 384-7449
OAKDALE'S PASSOVER SUPERMARKET 1253 CONEY ISLAND AVENUE ... BROOKLYN **NY** 11230 (718) 377-8866
PUPOVER MATZAH BAKERY 658 BEDFORD AVENUE .... BROOKLYN **NY** 11211
SATMAR MATZOH BAKERY 427 BROADWAY .... BROOKLYN **NY** 11211
SCHICK'S BAKERY 4710 16TH AVENUE .... BROOKLYN **NY** 11219 (718) 436-8020
SHATZER MATZOS 210 CORTELYOU ROAD .... BROOKLYN **NY** 11230 (718) 435-2873
SOLOMON SALTZMAN - MATZAH 9821 FOSTER AVENUE .... BROOKLYN **NY** 11236
GOODMAN & SONS .... LONG ISLAND CITY **NY** 11101
HOROWITZ MARGARETEN COMPANY 29-00 REVIEW AVENUE .... LONG ISLAND CITY **NY** 11101 (718) 729-5420
FREEDA VITAMINS 36 EAST 41ST STREET .... NEW YORK **NY** 10017 (212) 685-8980
GERTEL'S BAKERY 53 HESTER STREET .... NEW YORK **NY** 10002 (212) 982-3250
JOINT PASSOVER ASSOCIATION 197 EAST BROADWAY .... NEW YORK **NY** 10002 (212) 260-6360
JOINT PASSOVER ASSOCIATION OF THE CITY OF NEW YORK
33 W. 60TH STREET .... NEW YORK **NY** 10023 (212) 586-2900
STREIT'S INC. 150-54 RIVINGTON STREET .... NEW YORK **NY** 10002 (212) 475-7000
FOODTOWN PASSOVER STORE 123 FROST STREET .... WESTBURY **NY** 11590 (516) 334-9730
JEWISH RELIEF SOCIETY 1775 SOUTH TAYLOR ROAD .... CLEVELAND **OH** 44118 (216) 321-3650

PEN PALS

INTERNATIONAL JEWISH CORRESPONDENCE/CORRESPONDANCE JUIVE
INTERNATIONALE 1590 AVE. DR. PENFIELD .... MONTREAL **QU** H3G 1C5

PERIODICALS - HISTORICAL & SCHOLARLY

SHIRIM A JEWISH POETRY JOURNAL
C/O HILLEL EXTENSION 900 HILGARD AVE. .... LOS ANGELES **CA** 90024
WESTERN STATES JEWISH HISTORICAL QUARTERLY
2429 23RD STREET .... SANTA MONICA **CA** 90405
AMERICAN JEWISH HISTORICAL QUARTERLY 2 THORNTON ROAD ...... WALTHAM **MA** 02154 (617) 891-8110
MICHIGAN JEWISH HISTORY 1036 WHITNEY BUILDING .... DETROIT **MI** 48226
LIKKUTEI SICHOT (SCHOLARLY-LUBAVITCH) 784 EASTERN PARKWAY... BROOKLYN **NY** 11213 (718) 774-7200
SICHOS IN ENGLISH 784 EASTERN PARKWAY .... BROOKLYN **NY** 11213 (718) 778-5436
JEWISH SOCIAL STUDIES 2112 BROADWAY .... NEW YORK **NY** 10025 (212) 724-5336
PROCEEDINGS OF THE AMERICAN ACADEMY OF JEWISH RESEARCH
3080 BROADWAY .... NEW YORK **NY** 10027
YIVO ANNUAL OF JEWISH SOCIAL SCIENCE 1048 FIFTH AVENUE.......... NEW YORK **NY** 10028 (212) 535-6700
AMERICAN JEWISH ARCHIVES 3101 CLIFTON AVENUE .... CINCINNATI **OH** 45220 (513) 221-1875
STUDIES IN BIBLIOGRAPHY & BOOKLORE 3101 CLIFTON AVENUE ...... CINCINNATI **OH** 45220
JEWISH QUARTERLY REVIEW BROAD AND YORK STREETS .... PHILADELPHIA **PA** 19132 (215) 229-0110
RHODE ISLAND JEWISH HISTORICAL NOTES 209 ANGELL STREET..... PROVIDENCE **RI** 02906 (401) 331-0956

PERIODICALS-ISRAELI & ISRAEL-CENTERED

ISRAEL TODAY 16661 VENTURA BOULEVARD .... ENCINO **CA** 91396 (818) 786-4000
NEAR EAST REPORT 444 NORTH CAPITOL .... WASHINGTON **DC** 20005 (202) 638-1225
AMERICAN ZIONIST 515 PARK AVENUE .... NEW YORK **NY** 10016 (212) 371-7750
HADOAR 220 PARK AVENUE SOUTH .... NEW YORK **NY** 10003 (212) 581-5151
HISTADRUT 33 EAST 67TH STREET .... NEW YORK **NY** 10021 (212) 628-1000
ISRAEL HORIZONS 150 FIFTH AVENUE .... NEW YORK **NY** 10011 (212) 255-8760
ISRAEL JOURNAL OF MEDICAL SCIENCES 114 EAST 32ND STREET..... NEW YORK **NY** 10018 (212) 889-8040

PERIODICALS - YIDDISH & FOREIGN LANGUAGE

MACCABEE PUBLISHING 14 WEST FOREST AVENUE .... ENGLEWOOD **NJ** 07631 (201) 569-8700
DE YIDDISH HEIM / THE JEWISH HOME 770 EASTERN PARKWAY ... BROOKLYN **NY** 11213 (718) 493-0571
DER YID 543 BEDFORD AVENUE .... BROOKLYN **NY** 11211 (718) 782-4900
MESORAH PUBLICATIONS 1969 CONEY ISLAND AVENUE .... BROOKLYN **NY** 11223 (718) 339-1700
SHMUESSEN MIT KINDER UN YUGENT 770 EASTERN PARKWAY .... BROOKLYN **NY** 11213
ASSOCIATION OF JEWISH ANTI-POVERTY WORKERS
141 EAST 44TH STREET, ROOM 802 .... NEW YORK **NY** 10017
BNAI YIDDISH 22 EAST 17TH STREET .... NEW YORK **NY** 10003
DER WECKER 175 EAST BROADWAY .... NEW YORK **NY** 10002
DOS YIDDISHE VORT 5 BEEKMAN STREET .... NEW YORK **NY** 10038
KINDER ZEITUNG 41 UNION SQUARE WEST .... NEW YORK **NY** 10003
KULTURE UN LEBN 175 EAST BROADWAY .... NEW YORK **NY** 10002
NCSY/ORTHODOX UNION 45 WEST 36TH STREET .... NEW YORK **NY** 10018 (212) 563-4000
OYFN SHVEL 200 WEST 72ND STREET .... NEW YORK **NY** 10023
UNSER TSAIT 25 EAST 21 STREET .... NEW YORK **NY** 10010 (212) 505-8040
VISTA CORE, JEWISH ASSOCIATION FOR COLLEGE YOUTH
30 WEST 60TH STREET .... NEW YORK **NY** 10023
YIVO BLETER 1048 FIFTH AVENUE .... NEW YORK **NY** 10028 (212) 535-6700
YIDDISHE KULTUR 1123 BROADWAY .... NEW YORK **NY** 10011 (212) 691-0708
YIDISHE SHPRAKH 1048 FIFTH AVENUE .... NEW YORK **NY** 10028 (212) 535-6700
ZUKUNFT 25 EAST 21 STREET .... NEW YORK **NY** 10010 (212) 505-8040
UNDZER VEG 272 CODSELL AVENUE.................... TORONTO **ON**

PHOTOGRAPHERS

STEVE GOLDBERG P.O. BOX 493 .... HALLANDALE **FL** 33009 (305) 940-6629
ROBERT CUMINS 140 HEPBURN STREET, SUITE 14A .... CLIFTON **NJ** 07012 (201) 778-9279
SUE STEMBER 8 HONEY BROOK DRIVE .... PRINCETON **NJ** 08540 (609) 737-2380

AURA STUDIOS LTD. 819 KINGS HIGHWAY .... BROOKLYN **NY** 11223 | (718) 627-6969
ELITE PHOTOGRAPHERS LTD.
516 KINGS HIGHWAY .... BROOKLYN **NY** 11223 | (718) 627-0499
FOCUS STUDIO (ABRAHAM HOLD) 4419 13TH AVENUE .... BROOKLYN **NY** 11219
LIONEL STUDIO 1723 AVENUE M .... BROOKLYN **NY** 11230 | (718) 252-0702
MORGEN STUDIOS (SHLOMO STROH) 3913 13TH AVENUE .... BROOKLYN **NY** 11218 | (718) 435-0323
NISSEN STUDIO & RECORDING (SHLOMO NISSEN) 200 ROSS STREET ... BROOKLYN **NY** 11211 | (718) 384-0205
ONLY WEDDINGS (SID PERRIS) 1716 EAST 7TH STREET .... BROOKLYN **NY** 11223 | (718) 627-8956
OSCAR ISRAELOWITZ P.O. BOX 228 .... BROOKLYN **NY** 11229 | (718) 951-7072
SILVIO BUCHRIS: PHOTOGRAPHER 3021 AVENUE I .... BROOKLYN **NY** 11210 | (718) 377-4518
TRAINER STUDIO 5321 13TH AVENUE .... BROOKLYN **NY** 11219 | (718) 851-0600
ZELMAN STUDIOS 623 CORTELYOU ROAD .... BROOKLYN **NY** 11218 | (718) 941-5500
JERRY MEYERS STUDIOS 147-53 77TH ROAD .... FLUSHING **NY** 11367 | (718) 591-7079
FIRST ROW VIDEO (MARK HERSLY) 96-09 67TH AVENUE .... FOREST HILLS **NY** 11374 | (718) 263-9629
BATYA AND ROCHEL .... MONSEY **NY** 10952 | (914) 356-3540
LENI SONNENFELD 552 RIVERSIDE DRIVE .... NEW YORK **NY** 10027 | (212) 222-0445
MIKE GOLDBERG 600 WEST END AVENUE .... NEW YORK **NY** 10025 | (212) 874-3285
THREE STAR PHOTOGRAPHERS LTD. .... STATEN ISLAND **NY** | (718) 494-3249
VILLAGE STUDIO 1 DUTCH COURT .... WEST NYACK **NY** 10994 | (914) 353-0412

PLAQUES AND PRESENTATIONS

ARCHITECTURAL BRONZE & ALUMINUM CORPORATION
3638 OAKTON STREET .... SKOKIE **IL** 60076 | (312) 674-3638
EMANUEL MILSTEIN R.D. 1, BOX 81C .... MARLBORO **NJ** 07746 | (201) 946-8604
BEN ARI ARTS LTD. 11 AVENUE A .... NEW YORK **NY** 10009 | (212) 677-4730
GENE SINGER ARTS 577 GRAND ST .... NEW YORK **NY** 10002 | (212) 673-9669
HECKER SILVERSMITHS 605 FIFTH AVENUE (49TH STREET) .... NEW YORK **NY** 10017 | (212) 593-2424
IN THE SPIRIT 460 EAST 79TH STREET .... NEW YORK **NY** 10021 | (212) 662-6693
UNITED STATES BRONZE SIGN COMPANY 101 WEST 31ST STREET ... NEW YORK **NY** 10001 | (212) 563-5670
W & E BAUM BRONZE TABLET CORPORATION 524 WEST 43RD STREET .. NEW YORK **NY** 10036 | (212) 279-5341
EMES EDITIONS LIMITED 2001 LEVICK STREET .... PHILADELPHIA **PA** 19149 | (215) 288-8787

POOR & ELDERLY, AID FOR THE

FREDA MOHR CENTER 330 NORTH FAIRFAX .... LOS ANGELES **CA** 90024 | (213) 937-5901
COUNCIL FOR JEWISH ELDERLY 1415 WEST MORSE .... CHICAGO **IL** 60645 | (312) 973-6065
COUNCIL FOR THE JEWISH ELDERLY 1 SOUTH FRANKLIN STREET ... CHICAGO **IL** 60606 | (312) 973-6065
THE ARK 2341 W. DEVON .... CHICAGO **IL** 60659 | (312) 973-1000
COUNCIL FOR JEWISH ELDERLY 1015 W. HOWARD STREET ..... EVANSTON **IL** 60202 | (312) 973-4105
JEWISH COUNCIL FOR THE AGING 6111 MONTROSE ROAD ...... ROCKVILLE **MD** 20852
JEWISH ASSOCIATION FOR SERVICES FOR THE AGED
3450 DEKALB AVENUE .... BRONX **NY** 10467 | (212) 231-1234
JEWISH ASSOCIATION FOR SERVICES FOR THE AGED
2488 GRAND CONCOURSE .... BRONX **NY** 10458 | (212) 365-4044
BOARD FOR LEGAL ASSISTANCE - JEWISH POOR
130 CLINTON STREET .... BROOKLYN **NY** 11201

Phototeque

Over half a million rare and original photographs from the lively arts. Vintage to current portraits, scenes and production stills in black and white and color for editorial and advertising use. Expert researchers. Call 242-6406 for appointment

COLEL TIFERES ZKEINIM - LEVI YITZCHAK 779 EASTERN PARKWAY ..... BROOKLYN **NY** 11213 | (718) 778-4270
JEWISH ASSOCIATION FOR SERVICES FOR THE AGED
575 BEDFORD AVENUE .... BROOKLYN **NY** 11211 | (718) 387-6695
JEWISH ASSOCIATION FOR SERVICES FOR THE AGED
555 REMSEN AVENUE .... BROOKLYN **NY** 11236 | (718) 385-0010
JEWISH ASSOCIATION FOR SERVICES FOR THE AGED
2410 SURF AVENUE .... BROOKLYN **NY** 11224 | (718) 449-9600
JEWISH ASSOCIATION FOR SERVICES FOR THE AGED
242 GRAHAM AVENUE .... BROOKLYN **NY** 11206 | (718) 384-3354
JEWISH ASSOCIATION FOR SERVICES FOR THE AGED
202 GRAHAM AVENUE .... BROOKLYN **NY** 11206 | (718) 388-6865
JEWISH ASSOCIATION FOR SERVICES FOR THE AGED
2211 CHURCH AVENUE .... BROOKLYN **NY** 11226 | (718) 693-7606
JEWISH ASSOCIATION FOR SERVICES FOR THE AGED 158 3RD STREET ... MINEOLA **NY** 11501 | (516) 742-2050
CENTRAL BUREAU FOR THE JEWISH AGED 80 FIFTH AVENUE ...... NEW YORK **NY** 10003 | (212) 929-3999
CENTRAL BUREAU OF THE JEWISH AGED 31 UNION SQUARE W ...... NEW YORK **NY** 10003 | (212) 924-5454
COUNCIL FOR THE JEWISH POOR 141 E. 44 SUITE 802 .... NEW YORK **NY** 10017
JEWISH ASSOCIATION FOR SERVICES FOR THE AGED
40 WEST 68TH STREET .... NEW YORK **NY** 10023 | (212) 724-3200
JEWISH ASSOCIATION FOR SERVICES FOR THE AGED
222 PARK AVENUE S .... NEW YORK **NY** 10003 | (212) 677-2530
JEWISH POVERTY COORDINATING COUNCIL 15 PARK ROW .... NEW YORK **NY** 10038 | (212) 267-9500
METROPOLITAN N.Y. COORDINATING COUNCIL OF JEWISH POVERTY
21 E. 40TH STREET, ROOM 1207 .... NEW YORK **NY** 10016 | (212) 685-0032
PROJECT EZRA 197 EAST BROADWAY .... NEW YORK **NY** 10002 | (212) 982-3700

POSTERS

HEINLE & HEINLE ENTERPRISES 29 LEXINGTON ROAD .... CONCORD **MA** 01742 | (617) 369-7525
JEWISH COMMUNITY CENTER 633 SALISBURY STREET .... WORCESTER **MA** 01609 | (617) 756-7109
THE EXHUMATION PO BOX 2057 .... PRINCETON **NJ** 08540 | (609) 921-2339
GOLDEN GRAPHICS INC. 35 BRIDLE PATH .... GREAT NECK **NY** 11021 | (516) 482-4282
CENTRAL CONFERENCE OF AMERICAN RABBIS 21 EAST 40TH STREET .. NEW YORK **NY** 10021 | (212) 684-4990
EL AL ISRAEL AIRLINES 850 THIRD AVENUE .... NEW YORK **NY** 10022 | (212) 940-0708
ISRAEL GOVERNMENT TOURIST OFFICE 488 MADISON AVENUE ...... NEW YORK **NY** 10022 | (212) 560-0650
ISRAEL OFFICE OF INFORMATION, JEWISH AGENCY
515 PARK AVENUE .... NEW YORK **NY** 10022 | (212) 752-0600
NATIONAL CONFERENCE ON SOVIET JEWRY 10 EAST 40TH STREET ..... NEW YORK **NY** 10016 | (212) 679-6122
YIVO INSTITUTE FOR JEWISH RESEARCH 1048 FIFTH AVENUE ...... NEW YORK **NY** 10028 | (212) 535-6700
OHIO POSTER COMPANY 14077 CEDAR ROAD .... CLEVELAND **OH** 44118 | (216) 371-5905

PREPARED FOODS

HEBREW NATIONAL KOSHER FOOD 625 SOUTH SANTA FE .... SANTA ANA **CA** | (714) 558-8651
SUPERVISED PRODUCTS 3890 ADAMS STREET, PO BOX 16432 .... DENVER **CO** 80216 | (303) 321-7033
POSINS 5756 GEORGIA AVENUE, N.W. .... WASHINGTON **DC** | (202) 726-4424
SPECIALTY FOOD SALES 58013 20TH AVENUE SOUTH .... GULFPORT **FL** 33062 | (813) 321-3847
NATURALLY KOSHER BRAND PREPARED FOODS 132 N.W. 24TH STREET .... MIAMI **FL** 33127 | (305) 576-6060
EVERYTHING'S KOSHER 1344 WASHINGTON AVENUE .... MIAMI BEACH **FL** 33139 | (305) 672-4154
H & M STEIN DELI 1141 WASHINGTON AVENUE .... MIAMI BEACH **FL** 33139 | (305) 534-2557
PARAMOUNT BAKERY 1407 WASHINGTON AVENUE .... MIAMI BEACH **FL** 33139 | (305) 534-2683
KOSHER TREATS 1678 N.E. 164TH STREET .... NORTH MIAMI BEACH **FL** 33162 | (305) 947-1800

HUNGARIAN KOSHER SAUSAGE COMPANY 2613 WEST DEVON AVENUE	CHICAGO	IL	60659	(312) 973-5991
SINAI KOSHER SAUSAGE CORP. 1000 WEST PERSHING ROAD	CHICAGO	IL	60601	(312) 927-2810
KOSHER GOURMET 3552 W. DEMPSTER	SKOKIE	IL		(312) 679-0432
SIMCHAS' SIMCHAS 3552 W. DEMPSTER	SKOKIE	IL		(312) 679-0432
MYER'S KOSHER KITCHEN 168 SHIRLEY AVENUE	REVERE	MA	02151	(617) 289-2063
BLUEFELD'S BUTLER'S PANTRY 401 REISTERSTOWN ROAD	PIKESVILLE	MD		(301) 486-2100
SCHLEIDER CATERERS OF GREATER WASHINGTON	ROCKVILLE	MD		(301) 881-3787
EPSTEIN KOSHER FOODS 403 WEST 79TH STREET	KANSAS CITY	MO	64114	(816) 361-0200
SCHANDLER'S PICKLE BARREL 50 BROADWAY	ASHEVILLE	NC	28801	(704) 253-5626
GOODWILL PANTRY CATERING 815 BROADWAY	BAYONNE	NJ	07002	(201) 339-2392
KOSHER DISH 437 PENNINGTON STREET	ELIZABETH	NJ	07202	(201) 527-1818
DEER PARK BAKING COMPANY	HAMMONTON	NJ	08037	(609) 561-2900
ZANIO'S EGG MARKET 308 MENAUL ROAD	ALBUQUERQUE	NM		(505) 843-9292
MAUZONE HOME KOSHER PRODUCTS 61-36 SPRINGFIELD BOULEVARD	BAYSIDE	NY	11361	(212) 225-1188
KINGSBRIDGE KOSHER KITCHEN, INC. 58 W. KINGSBRIDGE ROAD	BRONX	NY	10468	(212) 584-5688
MRS. WEINBERG'S FOOD PRODUCTS CORP. 1303 HERSCHELL	BRONX	NY	10461	(212) 824-6940
ZION KOSHER DELICATESSEN & RESTAURANT 750 LYDIG AVENUE	BRONX	NY	10469	(212) 597-6360
ERBA FOOD PRODUCTS 624 COURT STREET	BROOKLYN	NY	11231	(718) 522-1800
ISRAEL'S TAKE HOME FOODS 409 BRIGHTON BEACH AVENUE	BROOKLYN	NY	11235	
KENERETH GLATT KOSHER CATERERS 1920 AVENUE D	BROOKLYN	NY	11226	(718) 743-2473
LEON & MARK TAKE HOME FOODS 1877 ROCKAWAY PARKWAY	BROOKLYN	NY	11236	
MAUZONE 4901 16TH AVENUE	BROOKLYN	NY	11204	(718) 851-1162
MEAL MART 206 DIVISION AVENUE	BROOKLYN	NY	11211	(718) 963-3450
MEAL MART 510 BRIGHTON BEACH AVENUE	BROOKLYN	NY	11235	(718) 769-6800
MEAL MART 4621 13TH AVENUE	BROOKLYN	NY	11219	(718) 854-7800
MEAL MART 54 LEE AVENUE	BROOKLYN	NY	11211	(718) 387-1445
MEAL MART 128 LEE AVENUE	BROOKLYN	NY	11211	(718) 855-9368
MEAL MART 4410 FT. HAMILTON PARKWAY	BROOKLYN	NY	11219	(718) 853-3900
MEAL MART 1101 BRIGHTON BEACH AVENUE	BROOKLYN	NY	11235	(718) 769-6800
MEAL MART 1920 AVENUE M	BROOKLYN	NY	11230	(718) 998-0800
MEAL MART 5417 NEW UTRECHT AVENUE	BROOKLYN	NY	11219	(718) 851-8800
MEAL MART 502 FLUSHING AVENUE	BROOKLYN	NY	11211	(718) 855-9600
MEAL MART 1412 AVENUE J	BROOKLYN	NY	11230	(718) 338-8100
MEAL MART 4722 16TH AVENUE	BROOKLYN	NY	11219	(718) 871-5335
MELROSE TAKE HOME FOODS 924 KINGS HIGHWAY	BROOKLYN	NY	11223	(718) 336-7500
MELROSE TAKE HOME FOODS 407 BRIGHTON BEACH AVENUE	BROOKLYN	NY	11235	
MRS. ADLER'S FOOD CORPORATION 902 ESSEX STREET	BROOKLYN	NY	11208	(718) 649-9121
NEGEV KOSHER HOMEMADE FOOD 1211 AVENUE J	BROOKLYN	NY	11230	(718) 258-8440
OLD FASHIONED KITCHENS FOODS 401 MARCY AVENUE	BROOKLYN	NY	11211	(718) 388-1132
ONEG TAKE HOME FOODS 4911 12TH AVENUE	BROOKLYN	NY	11219	(718) 438-3388
RUTLAND TAKE HOME FOODS 1120 AVENUE J	BROOKLYN	NY	11230	(718) 377-9695
SCHECHTER'S TAKE HOME FOODS 509 BRIGHTON BEACH AVENUE	BROOKLYN	NY	11235	(718) 743-5900
SCHREIBER CATERERS 9024 FOSTER AVENUE	BROOKLYN	NY	11236	(718) 272-9184
SEUDA FOODS 705 KINGS HIGHWAY	BROOKLYN	NY	11223	(718) 375-1500

TAAM KOSHER PRODUCTS 344 AVENUE Y	BROOKLYN	NY	11235	(718) 376-5400
TAM-GAN EDEN 1780 RALPH AVENUE	BROOKLYN	NY	11236	(718) 241-6102
MAZEL TAKE HOME FOODS 119 CEDARHURST AVENUE	CEDARHURST	NY	11516	(516) 569-1666
MAUZONE HOME KOSHER PRODUCTS 69-60 MAIN STREET	FLUSHING	NY	11367	(718) 261-7723
MEAL MART 72-10 MAIN STREET	FLUSHING	NY	11367	(718) 261-3300
NEW FOREST TAKE HOME FOODS 64-20 108TH STREET	FOREST HILLS	NY	11375	(718) 275-9793
HOROWITZ BROTHERS & MARGARETEN				
29-00 REVIEW AVENUE	LONG ISLAND CITY	NY	11106	(718) 729-5420
KOSHER CATALOGUE, INC. 2107 BORDEN AVENUE	LONG ISLAND CITY	NY	11101	(718) 784-6150
KOSHER CATALOGUE, INC. 2107 BORDEN AVENUE	LONG ISLAND CITY	NY	11101	(800) 5KOSHER
KOSHER KONNECTION 1284 NORTH AVENUE	NEW ROCHELLE	NY	10804	(914) 636-5636
KOSHER DESSERTS, INC. 8 W. 28TH STREET	NEW YORK	NY	10001	(212) 685-4672
LEIBEL BISTRITZKY 27-1/2 ESSEX STREET	NEW YORK	NY	10002	(212) 254-0335
MEAL MART 2189 BROADWAY	NEW YORK	NY	10024	(212) 787-4720
MEAL MART 4403 BROADWAY	NEW YORK	NY	10033	(212) 568-7401
YONAH SCHIMMEL'S KNISHES BAKERY 137 E. HOUSTON STREET	NEW YORK	NY	10002	(212) 477-2858
MEAL MART MAIN STREET	SOUTH FALLSBURG	NY		(914) 434-3689
KOSHER ISLAND TAKE HOME FOODS 2206 VICTORY BLVD.	STATEN ISLAND	NY	10314	(718) 698-5800
MEAL MART	SWAN LAKE	NY	12783	(914) 292-9439
PERL'S 3013 BATHURST STREET	TORONTO	ON		(416) 787-4234
STROLI'S 3459 BATHURST STREET	TORONTO	ON		(416) 789-5333
RHAWNHURST 8261 BUSTLETON AVENUE	PHILADELPHIA	PA		(215) 742-5287
ALBER & LEFF FOOD COMPANY 405 COLLEGE AVENUE	PITTSBURGH	PA	15237	(412) 321-7700
CANTON & SMOLAR COMPANY 1816 BEDFORD AVENUE	PITTSBURGH	PA	15212	(412) 261-4777
MILLER'S DELICATESSEN 776 HOPE STREET	PROVIDENCE	RI	02906	(401) 521-0368

PRINTERS & PRINT SERVICES

GOTTLIEB TORAH GRAPHICS 406 YESHIVA PLAZA	LAKEWOOD	NJ	08701	(201) 363-8025
ARTYPE PRINTING 1778 JEROME AVENUE	BRONX	NY	10453	(212) 731-3900
DAVE'S PRINTING 1279 44TH STREET	BROOKLYN	NY	11219	(718) 853-1919
GOLDSTEIN PRESS 4602 16TH AVENUE	BROOKLYN	NY	11204	(718) 853-7444
HADDAR PRINTING 195 LEE AVENUE	BROOKLYN	NY	11211	(718) 384-4249
MASH PRINTING 1305 43RD STREET	BROOKLYN	NY	11219	(718) 436-1543
MODERN LINOTYPE COMPANY 371 EAST 98TH STREET	BROOKLYN	NY	11212	(718) 498-7580
NATIONAL PRINTING & STATIONERY 5314 13TH AVENUE	BROOKLYN	NY	11219	(718) 438-7200
SHALLER PRINTERS	BROOKLYN	NY		(718) 859-0281
KLASS PUBLICATIONS, INC. 112 BROADWAY	MALVERNE	NY	11565	(516) 887-7878
ARTSCROLL STUDIOS	MONSEY	NY	10952	(914) 352-2207
ENQUIRE PRINTING & PUBLISHING CO. 601 WEST 54TH STREET	NEW YORK	NY	10019	(212) 581-5050
GOLDMARK GROUP, THE 6 W. 18TH STREET	NEW YORK	NY	10011	(212) 691-7111
KETER INC. 440 PARK AVENUE SOUTH	NEW YORK	NY	10016	(212) 889-9360

KING TYPOGRAPHIC SERVICE 305 EAST 46TH STREET .... NEW YORK NY 10017　(212) 754-9595
KING TYPOGRAPHIC SERVICE 240 WEST 40TH STREET .... NEW YORK NY 10018　(212) 754-9595
MENORAH PRINTING COMPANY 51 WEST 21ST STREET .... NEW YORK NY 10010　(212) 691-2050
OLIVESTONE PUBLISHING SERVICES 6 W. 18TH STREET .... NEW YORK NY 10011　(212) 691-8420
SOLOGRAPHIC PHOTOCOMPOSITION SERVICE 6 WEST 18TH STREET ... NEW YORK NY 10011　(212) 924-9300
INVITATIONS PLUS 600 WEST 246TH STREET .... RIVERDALE NY 10471　(212) 548-3900
INVITATIONS PLUS 600 WEST 246TH STREET .... RIVERDALE NY 10471　(800) INV-PLUS

PRISONERS ASSISTANCE

COMMITTEE FOR JEWISH PRISONERS PO BOX 31265 .... SAN FRANCISCO CA 94131
BNAI BRITH COMMISSION ON COMMUNITY AND VETERANS SERVICE
　1640 RHODE ISLAND AVENUE N.W. .... WASHINGTON DC 20036　(202) 857-6600
NORTH SHORE JEWISH COMMUNITY CENTER C/O ROBERTA KALECHOFSKY
　2 COMMUNITY ROAD .... MARBLEHEAD MA 01945　(617) 631-8338
AMERICAN JEWISH CORRECTIONAL CHAPLAINS ASSOCIATION
　10 E. 73RD STREET .... NEW YORK NY 10021　(212) 879-8415
JEWISH BOARD OF GUARDIANS, VOLUNTEER SERVICES DEPARTMENT
　120 WEST 57TH STREET .... NEW YORK NY 10019　(212) 582-9100
JEWISH IDENTITY CENTER-UNION OF JEWISH PRISONERS
　1133 BROADWAY, SUITE 302 .... NEW YORK NY 10010
NAT'L COUNCIL OF JEWISH WOMEN-JUSTICE FOR CHILDREN TASK FRCE
　1 WEST 47TH STREET .... NEW YORK NY 10036　(212) 532-1740
ALLENWOOD JEWISH CONGREGATION PO BOX 1000 .... MONTGOMERY PA 17752

PROFESSIONAL ORGANIZATIONS

HEBREW TEACHERS FEDERATION PO BOX 824 .... VAN NUYS CA 91408　(818) 980-2191
INTERNATIONAL ASSOCIATION OF HILLEL DIRECTORS
　5715 SOUTH WOODLAWN AVENUE .... CHICAGO IL 60637　(312) 752-1127
JEWISH FUNERAL DIRECTORS OF AMERICA 1170 ROCKVILLE PIKE ...... ROCKVILLE MD 20852　(301) 340-1400
NAT'L ASSOC. OF JEWISH FAMILY, CHILDREN'S & HEALTH PROF.
　24123 GREENFIELD .... SOUTHFIELD MI 48075　(313) 559-1500
UNITED KOSHER MEAT & POULTRY DEALERS 3053 KLUGERT AVENUE .... BRONX NY 10467
ASSOCIATION OF ORTHODOX JEWISH TEACHERS
　1577 CONEY ISLAND AVENUE .... BROOKLYN NY 11230　(718) 258-3586
NATIONAL JEWISH CIVIL SERVICE EMPLOYEES P.O. BOX 525 .... BROOKLYN NY 11202　(718) 646-8366
AMERICAN ASSOCIATION OF PROFESSORS OF YIDDISH
　A1309 QUEENS COLLEGE .... FLUSHING NY 11367　(718) 520-7067
JEWISH ALLIANCE OF BUSINESSMEN 10-25 44TH AVENUE .... LONG ISLAND CITY NY 11101　(718) 937-9813
ASSOCIATION OF JEWISH CLERGYMEN P.O. BOX 317 .... MONSEY NY 10952　(914) 352-0630
AMERICAN ACADEMIC ASSOCIATION FOR PEACE IN THE MIDDLE EAST
　330 SEVENTH AVENUE .... NEW YORK NY 10001　(212) 563-2580

AMERICAN JEWISH CORRECTIONAL CHAPLAINS ASSOCIATION
　10 EAST 73RD STREET .... NEW YORK NY 10021　(212) 879-8415
ASSOCIATION OF JEWISH ANTI-POVERTY WORKERS
　18 E. 41ST STREET, ROOM 806 .... NEW YORK NY 10017　(212) 686-2777
ASSOCIATION OF JEWISH BOOK PUBLISHERS 1646 FIRST AVENUE ... NEW YORK NY 10028　(212) 799-6517
ASSOCIATION OF JEWISH BOOK PUBLISHERS 838 FIFTH AVENUE .... NEW YORK NY 10021　(212) 249-0100
ASSOCIATION OF JEWISH CENTER WORKERS 15 E. 26TH STREET .... NEW YORK NY 10010　(212) 532-4949
ASSOCIATION OF JEWISH CHAPLAINS OF THE ARMED FORCES - JWB
　15 EAST 26TH STREET .... NEW YORK NY 10010　(212) 532-4949
ASSOCIATION OF JEWISH COMMUNITY RELATIONS WORKERS
　15 EAST 26TH STREET .... NEW YORK NY 10010　(212) 532-4949
ASSOCIATION OF ORTHODOX JEWISH NURSES 116 E. 27TH STREET .... NEW YORK NY 10016　(212) 889-1364
ASSOCIATION OF ORTHODOX JEWISH SCIENTISTS
　45 WEST 36TH STREET .... NEW YORK NY 10018　(212) 695-7525
ASSOCIATION OF ORTHODOX JEWISH TEACHERS 3 W. 16TH STREET.... NEW YORK NY 10011　(212) 436-0440
DIAMOND DEALERS ALLIANCE, INC. 580 FIFTH AVENUE .... NEW YORK NY 10036　(212) 757-4589
DIAMOND DEALERS CLUB, INC. 30 WEST 47TH STREET .... NEW YORK NY 10036　(212) 840-4660
GOVERNMENT BUREAU FOR ISRAELI PROFESSIONALS
　800 SECOND AVENUE .... NEW YORK NY 10017　(212) 986-6360
HEBREW ACTORS UNION 31 E. SEVENTH STREET .... NEW YORK NY 10003　(212) 674-1923
HEBREW BUTCHER WORKERS UNION 37 UNION SQUARE .... NEW YORK NY 10003
JEWISH FUNERAL DIRECTORS OF AMERICA 122 E. 42ND STREET ...... NEW YORK NY 10168　(212) 370-0024
JEWISH OCCUPATIONAL COUNCIL 114 FIFTH AVENUE .... NEW YORK NY 10011
JEWISH POSTAL WORKERS WELFARE LEAGUE 363 7TH AVENUE .... NEW YORK NY 10001　(212) 594-1488
JEWISH TEACHER'S ASSOCIATION 45 E. 33RD STREET .... NEW YORK NY 10016　(212) 684-0556
JEWISH THEATRICAL GUILD 1501 BROADWAY .... NEW YORK NY 10036　(212) 221-1848
KASHRUTH SUPERVISOR'S UNION LOCAL 621 37 UNION SQUARE .... NEW YORK NY 10003　(212) 691-9494
NATIONAL ASSOCIATION OF JEWISH CENTER WORKERS
　15 E. 26TH STREET .... NEW YORK NY 10010　(212) 532-4949
NATIONAL ASSOCIATION OF JEWISH VOCATIONAL SERVICES
　386 PARK AVENUE .... NEW YORK NY 10022　(212) 685-8355
NATIONAL CONFERENCE OF JEWISH COMMUNAL SERVICE
　15 EAST 26TH STREET .... NEW YORK NY 10010
NATIONAL CONFERENCE OF YESHIVA PRINCIPALS 160 BROADWAY ..... NEW YORK NY 10038　(212) 406-4190
YESHIVA ENGLISH PRINCIPALS ASSOCIATION 426 WEST 58TH STREET .. NEW YORK NY 10019　(212) 245-8200
INTERNATIONAL ASSOCIATION OF HILLEL DIRECTORS
　611 LANGDON STREET .... MADISON WI 53703　(608) 256-8361

PUBLISHERS

UNIVERSITY OF ALABAMA PRESS BOX 2877 .... UNIVERSITY AL 35486　(205) 348-6010
UNIVERSITY OF ARIZONA PRESS 1615 EAST SPEEDWAY BOULEVARD .... TUCSON AZ 85719　(602) 621-1441
BEN MIR BOOKS 570 VISTAMONTE AVE .... BERKELEY CA 94708　(415) 527-0266
HAMOROH PRESS P.O. BOX 48862 .... LOS ANGELES CA 90048
TZE ULMAD PRESS 2265 WESTWOOD BOULEVARD SUITE 508 .... LOS ANGELES CA 90064　(213) 204-4290

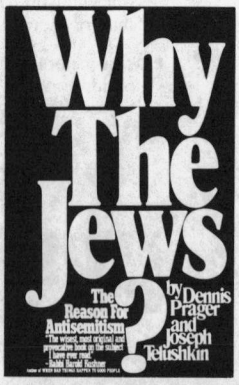

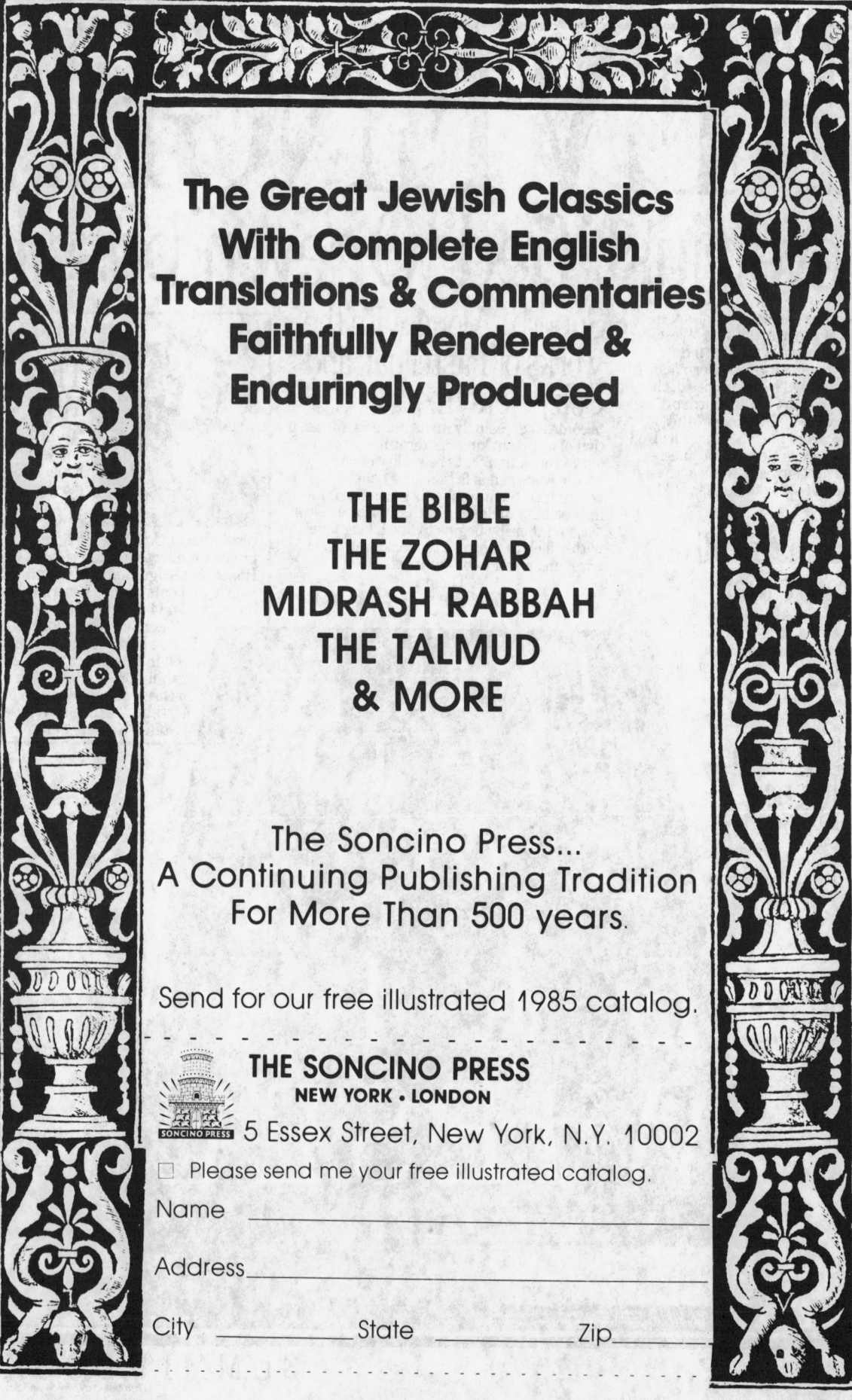

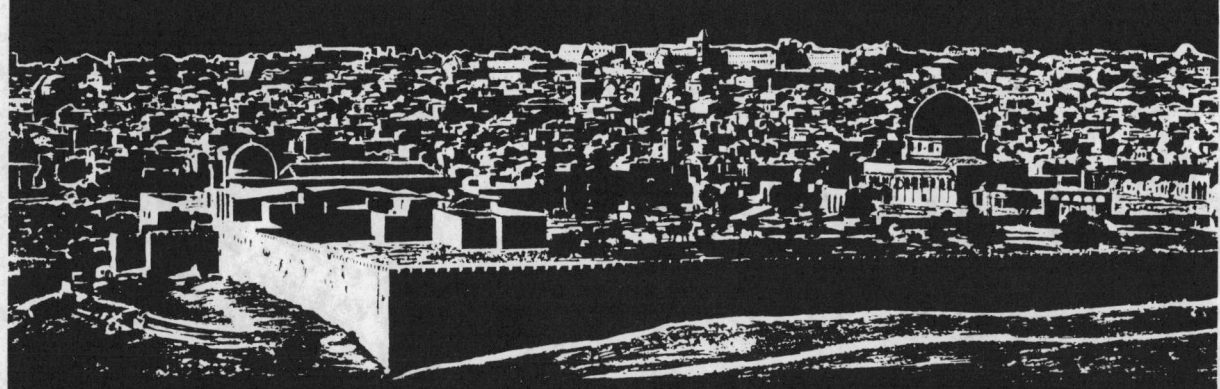

THE MAVERICK RABBI

by Rabbi Aaron I. Reichel, Esq.

Rabbi Herbert S. Goldstein, DD

Goldstein's Institutional Synagogue . . . "a Camelot in American Orthodoxy". . .
—Jewish Journal, NYC

". . . fiery young Goldstein's idealistic aspirations . . . comparable to the vision-like aspirations of early Zionists, or the Hasidic and Kabbalistic movements . . ."
—Jewish Post & Renaissance

". . . lifelong pioneer . . . who . . . left an indelible mark . . . in America and in Israel . . ."
—Chief Rabbi Immanuel Jakobovits

". . . combined loyalty in tradition with a sophisticated modern mind . . ."   *—Herman Wouk*

Book describes *"modus operandi* of . . . master orator, organizer, and fund raiser" (—Alumni Review, Yeshiva U.); "claims that sound too good to be true are . . . too well established to be denied" (—Jewish Press, NYC); formulae for organizational and personal success implemented by dynamic precedent-setter; The story of Rabbi Herbert S. Goldstein, nat'l pres. of RCA, SCA, UOJCA; leader at Yeshiva University, Central Jewish Institute, Kehilath Jeshurun, National Conference of Christians and Jews, B'nai B'rith, Agudah, and Mizrachi.

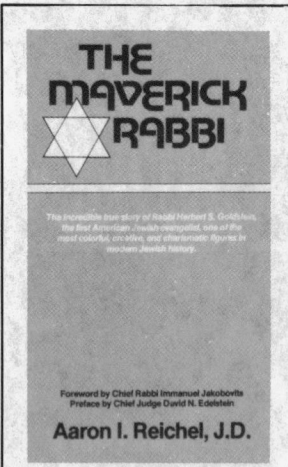

THE MAVERICK RABBI

The incredible true story of Rabbi Herbert S. Goldstein, the first American Jewish evangelist, one of the most colorful, creative, and charismatic figures in modern Jewish history.

Foreword by Chief Rabbi Immanuel Jakobovits
Preface by Chief Judge David N. Edelstein

Aaron I. Reichel, J.D.

Special features:
* Foreword by Immanuel Jakobovits, Chief Rabbi, England;
* Preface by David N. Edelstein, Fed. Chief Judge, NYC;
* Index that includes dozens of entries under "women," illustrating positive roles *within* Orthodox framework;
* introducing "camouflaged footnotes"

Available in hardcover and paperback in bookstores and by mail from Donning Co.
5659 Virginia Beach Blvd., Norfolk, VA 23502

Rabbi Aaron I. Reichel, JD (rabbi, attorney, editor, former nat'l pres., Yavneh) accepting speaking engagements
(212) 874-2062; 230 W. 79 St./NYC 10024

UNIVERSITY OF CALIFORNIA PRESS 1428 HARBOUR WAY SOUTH	RICHMOND CA	94804	(415) 231-9400
ALTERNATIVES IN RELIGIOUS EDUCATION, INC.			
3945 SOUTH ONEIDA STREET	DENVER CO	80237	(303) 363-7779
PRAYER BOOK PRESS, THE 1363 FAIRFIELD AVENUE	BRIDGEPORT CT	06605	(203) 384-2284
YALE UNIVERSITY PRESS 92A YALE STATION	NEW HAVEN CT	06520	(203) 436-8926
B'NAI B'RITH YOUTH ORGANIZATION			
1640 RHODE ISLAND AVENUE N.W.	WASHINGTON DC	20036	(202) 857-6633
UNIVERSITY OF IOWA PRESS GRAPHIC SERVICES BUILDING	IOWA CITY IA	52242	(319) 353-2121
UNIVERSITY OF ILLINOIS PRESS			
54 EAST GREGORY DRIVE, BOX 5081 - STATION A	CHAMPAIGN IL		(217) 333-0950
FLYING FISH RECORDS	CHICAGO IL		(312) 528-5455
UNIVERSITY OF CHICAGO PRESS 5801 SOUTH ELLIS AVENUE	CHICAGO IL	60637	(312) 962-7700
INDIANA UNIVERSITY PRESS 10TH AND MORTON STREETS	BLOOMINGTON IN	47405	(812) 335-4203
DAVID R. GODINE 306 DARTMOUTH ST	BOSTON MA	02116	(617) 536-0761
MICAH PUBLICATIONS 255 HUMPHREY STREET	MARBLEHEAD MA	01945	(617) 631-7601
THE BEATE KLARSFELD FOUNDATION BOX 157	SOUTH DEERFIELD MA	01373	() 948-8733
KAR-BEN COPIES 11216 EMPIRE LANE	ROCKVILLE MD	20852	(301) 948-8733
UNIVERSITY OF NORTH CAROLINA PRESS PO BOX 2288	CHAPEL HILL NC	27514	(919) 966-3561
ASHLEY PUBLICATIONS 263 VETERANS ROAD	CARLSTAD NJ		(201) 935-1113
MACCABEE PUBLISHING HOUSE 14 WEST FOREST AVENUE	ENGLEWOOD NJ	07631	(201) 569-8700
KTAV PUBLISHING HOUSE 900 JEFFERSON ST. PO BOX 6249	HOBOKEN NJ	07030	(201) 963-9524
M.P. PRESS 317 ST. PAULS AVENUE	JERSEY CITY NJ	07306	(201) 656-9173
SHIMON EIDER PUBLICATIONS 418 TWELFTH STREET	LAKEWOOD NJ	08701	(201) 363-3965
FAIRLEIGH DICKINSON UNIVERSITY PRESS 285 MADISON AVENUE	MADISON NJ	07940	(201) 377-4700
PAULIST PRESS 545 ISLAND ROAD	RAMSEY NJ	07446	(201) 825-7300
OPTIONS PUBLISHING BOX 311	WAYNE NJ	07470	(201) 694-2327
CENTER FOR HOLOCAUST STUDIES 1609 AVENUE J	BROOKLYN NY	11230	(718) 338-6494
HEBREW PUBLISHING COMPANY 100 WATER STREET	BROOKLYN NY	11201	(718) 858-6902
JEP (JEWISH EDUCATION PROGRAM) PUBLICATIONS			
425 EAST 9TH STREET	BROOKLYN NY	11218	(718) 941-2600
JEWISH COMBATANTS PUBLISHERS HOUSE P. O. BOX 323	BROOKLYN NY	11236	
KEHOT PUBLICATIONS SOCIETY 770 EASTERN PARKWAY	BROOKLYN NY	11213	(718) 774-4000
MERKOS L'INYONEI CHINUCH 770 EASTERN PARKWAY	BROOKLYN NY	11213	(718) 774-4000
MESORAH PUBLICATIONS 1969 CONEY ISLAND AVENUE	BROOKLYN NY	11223	(718) 339-1700
MOZNAIM PUBLISHING CORPORATION 4304 TWELFTH AVENUE	BROOKLYN NY	11219	(718) 853-0525
OTZAR HACHASSIDIM 770 EASTERN PARKWAY	BROOKLYN NY	11213	(718) 774-4000
TRADITIONAL PRESS, INC. 1306 40TH STREET	BROOKLYN NY	11218	(718) 435-4411
ZUNDEL BERMAN BOOKS 4520 17TH AVENUE	BROOKLYN NY	11204	
BIBLIO PRESS P.O. BOX 22	FRESH MEADOWS NY	11365	
ADAMA BOOKS 306 W. 38TH ST.	NEW YORK NY	10018	(212) 594-5770
ALFRED A. KNOPF, INC. 201 EAST 50TH STREET	NEW YORK NY	10022	(212) 751-2600
AMERICAN JEWISH COMMITTEE-INST. OF HUMAN RELATIONS PRESS			
165 E. 56TH STREET	NEW YORK NY	10022	(212) 751-4000
AMERICAN MIZRACHI WOMEN 817 BROADWAY	NEW YORK NY	10016	
ANTI-DEFAMATION LEAGUE OF B'NAI B'RITH			
823 UNITED NATIONS PLAZA	NEW YORK NY	10017	(212) 490-2525
ASSOCIATION OF JEWISH BOOK PUBLISHERS 838 FIFTH AVENUE	NEW YORK NY	10021	(212) 249-1000
ASSOCIATION OF JEWISH BOOK PUBLISHERS 1646 FIRST AVENUE	NEW YORK NY	10028	(212) 799-6517
BANTAM BOOKS 666 FIFTH AVENUE	NEW YORK NY	10019	(212) 765-6500
BASIC BOOKS, INC. 10 EAST 53RD STREET	NEW YORK NY	10022	(212) 207-7057
BEHRMAN HOUSE 1261 BROADWAY	NEW YORK NY	10019	(212) 689-2020
BLOCH PUBLISHING COMPANY 19 WEST 21ST STREET	NEW YORK NY	10010	(212) 989-9104
BURNING BUSH PRESS 155 FIFTH AVENUE	NEW YORK NY	10010	
CENTRAL CONFERENCE OF AMERICAN RABBIS 21 E. 40TH STREET	NEW YORK NY	10010	(212) 684-4990
COLUMBIA UNIVERSITY PRESS 562 W. 113TH ST.	NEW YORK NY	10025	(212) 316-7130
CONGRESS FOR JEWISH CULTURE & CYCO PUBLISHERS			
25 E. 78TH STREET	NEW YORK NY	10021	(212) 879-2232
DODD, MEAD & COMPANY 79 MADISON AVENUE	NEW YORK NY	10016	(212) 685-6464
DOUBLEDAY & COMPANY, INC. 245 PARK AVENUE	NEW YORK NY	10167	(212) 953-4561
EMET-RABBI HERZOG WORLD ACADEMY 122 W. 76TH STREET	NEW YORK NY	10023	(212) 435-0115
FARRAR, STRAUS & GIROUX 19 UNION SQ. WEST	NEW YORK NY	10003	(212) 741-6900
HARPER & ROW 10 E. 53RD STREET	NEW YORK NY	10010	(212) 593-7000
HERZI PRESS 515 PARK AVENUE	NEW YORK NY	10022	(212) 752-0600
HIPPOCRENE BOOKS, INC. 171 MADISON AVENUE	NEW YORK NY	10016	(212) 685-4371
HOLIDAY HOUSE 18 EAST 53RD STREET	NEW YORK NY	10022	(218) 688-0085
HOLOCAUST LIBRARY 216 WEST 18TH STREET	NEW YORK NY	10011	(212) 691-9220
HOLOCAUST PUBLICATIONS, INC. 216 WEST 18TH STREET	NEW YORK NY	10011	(212) 691-9220
JWB JEWISH BOOK COUNCIL 15 EAST 26TH STREET	NEW YORK NY	10010	(212) 532-4949
JEWISH EDUCATION OF GREATER NEW YORK 426 WEST 58TH STREET	NEW YORK NY	10019	(212) 245-8200
JEWISH MUSEUM 1109 FIFTH AVENUE	NEW YORK NY	10028	(212) 860-1888
JEWISH PUBLICATION SOCIETY OF AMERICA 60 EAST 42ND STREET	NEW YORK NY	10017	(212) 687-0809
JEWISH RADIO THEATER 175 FIFTH AVENUE	NEW YORK NY	10010	
JEWISH THEOLOGICAL SEMINARY 3080 BROADWAY	NEW YORK NY	10020	(212) 678-8074
JUDAICA PRESS 33 CANAL	NEW YORK NY		(212) 260-0520
KETER PUBLICATIONS, INC. 440 PARK AVENUE SOUTH	NEW YORK NY	10016	(212) 696-0460
KETER PUBLICATIONS, INC. 440 PARK AVENUE SOUTH	NEW YORK NY	10016	(212) 889-7750
KINDERBUCH PUBLICATIONS 1133 BROADWAY, ROOM 1023	NEW YORK NY	10010	
KTAV PUBLISHING HOUSE 900 JEFFERSON STREET	HOBOKEN NJ		(201) 963-9524
LEO BAECK INSTITUTE, INC. 129 EAST 73RD STREET	NEW YORK NY	10021	(212) 744-6400
MENDY PUBLICATIONS 450 SEVENTH AVENUE	NEW YORK NY	10001	(212) 410-1155
MENORAH RECORD DISTRIBUTORS 36 ELDRIDGE STREET	NEW YORK NY	10002	(212) 925-7573
NCSY/OU PUBLICATIONS 45 WEST 36TH STREET	NEW YORK NY	10018	(212) 563-4000
NEW AMERICAN LIBRARY, INC. 1633 BROADWAY	NEW YORK NY	10019	(212) 397-8000
NEW YORK TIMES BOOK COMPANY 3 PARK AVENUE	NEW YORK NY	10002	(212) 725-2050
NEW YORK UNIVERSITY PRESS 70 WASHINGTON SQ. SOUTH	NEW YORK NY	10012	(212) 598-2886
PACIFIC PRESS 501 FIFTH AVENUE, SUITE 2203	NEW YORK NY	10017	(212) 687-0500
PANTHEON BOOKS 201 E. 50TH ST.	NEW YORK NY	10022	(212) 751-2600
PHILLIP FELDHEIM, INC. 96 EAST BROADWAY	NEW YORK NY	10002	(212) 925-3180
PHILOSOPHICAL LIBRARY 200 W. 57TH ST.	NEW YORK NY	10019	(212) 265-6050
PILGRIM PRESS 132 WEST 31ST ST	NEW YORK NY	10018	(212) 594-8555
POCKET BOOKS			
SIMON & SCHUSTER BUILDING-1230 AVENUE OF THE AMERICAS	NEW YORK NY	10020	(212) 246-2121

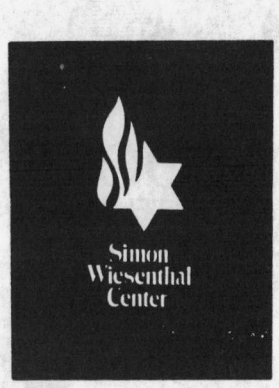

THE SIMON WIESENTHAL CENTER ANNUAL
Volume 2
Edited by Sybil Milton and Henry Friedlander.

"This annual is fascinating, horrifying, and informative. It assumes prior knowledge of the Holocaust, but even general readers may not be able to put it down. College and university libraries should place a standing order now."

– CHOICE, January 1985

The **Simon Wiesenthal Center Annual** is the first serial publication in the United States focusing on the scholarly study of the Holocaust. The editors' definition of the Holocaust in its widest context includes: European Jewry during World War II: Refugees, Rescue, and Immigration; Displaced Persons and Postwar Trials; and Modern Antisemitism.

Volume 2 provides various articles and review essays on a wide range of topics such as the American response to Nazi book-burning, destruction of the Polish ghettos, survival and hiding, and the Fedorenko case.

Corresponding editors include Zvi Bacharach, Wolfgang Benz, and Daniel Landes.

Standing or Continuation Orders accepted. All standing order customers receive a 10% discount.

White Plains, N.Y., 1985
Price to be announced.

For more information or to place an order, please write or call:

KRAUS INTERNATIONAL PUBLICATIONS
A Division of Kraus-Thomson Ltd.
One Water Street
White Plains, New York 10601
(914) 761-9600

REBECCA BENNET PUBLICATIONS, INC. 5409 18TH AVENUE	NEW YORK	NY	11204	(212) 256-1954
SACRED MUSIC PRESS, HUC-JIR 1 W. 4TH STREET	NEW YORK	NY	10012	(212) 873-0388
SCARF PRESS 825 THIRD AVENUE	NEW YORK	NY	10028	(212) 832-2508
SCHOCKEN BOOKS, INC. 200 MADISON AVENUE	NEW YORK	NY	10016	(212) 685-6500
SEPHER-HERMON PRESS, INC. 53 PARK PLACE, SUITE 503	NEW YORK	NY	10007	(212) 349-1860
SHENGOLD PUBLISHERS, INC. 23 W. 45TH STREET	NEW YORK	NY	10036	(212) 944-2555
SIMON & SCHUSTER 1230 AVENUE OF THE AMERICAS	NEW YORK	NY	10020	(212) 245-6400
SONCINO 5 ESSEX STREET	NEW YORK	NY		(212) 673-9751

STEIMATZKY PUBLISHING OF NORTH AMERICA, INC.

56 EAST 11TH STREET	NEW YORK	NY	10003	(212) 505-2505
SUMMIT BOOKS 1230 AVE. OF THE AMERICAS	NEW YORK	NY	10020	(212) 246-2471
UNION OF AMERICAN HEBREW CONGREGATIONS 838 FIFTH AVENUE	NEW YORK	NY	10021	(212) 249-0100
UNITED SYNAGOGUE BOOK SERVICE 155 FIFTH AVENUE	NEW YORK	NY	10010	(212) 533-7800
VIKING PENGUIN, INC. 40 W. 23RD ST.	NEW YORK	NY	10010	(212) 807-7300
WORKMEN'S CIRCLE PUBLICATIONS 45 EAST 33RD STREET	NEW YORK	NY	10016	(212) 889-6800
YIVO INSTITUTE FOR JEWISH RESEARCH 1048 FIFTH AVENUE	NEW YORK	NY	10028	(212) 535-6700
YESHIVA UNIVERSITY PRESS 500 WEST 185TH STREET	NEW YORK	NY	10033	(212) 960-5400
ZIONTALIS/BOOK DIVISION 48 ELDRIDGE STREET	NEW YORK	NY	10002	(212) 925-8558
PHILIPP FELDHEIM INC. 200 AIRPORT EXECUTIVE PARK	SPRING VALLEY	NY	10977	(914) 356-2282
SYRACUSE UNIVERSITY PRESS 1600 JAMESVILLE AVENUE	SYRACUSE	NY	13210	(315) 423-1870
SIMCHA PUBLISHING COMPANY, INC. 1 COVE DRIVE	WOODMERE	NY	11598	(516) 569-0830
WRITERS DIGEST BOOKS 9933 ALLIANCE ROAD	CINCINNATI	OH	45242	(513) 984-0717

HEBREW ACADEMY OF CLEVELAND PUBLISHING HOUSE

1860 SOUTH TAYLOR ROAD	CLEVELAND HEIGHTS	OH	44118	

INSTITUTE FOR THE STUDY OF HUMAN ISSUES

3401 MARKET STREET, SUITE 252	PHILADELPHIA	PA	19104	(215) 387-9002

JEWISH PUBLICATION SOCIETY OF AMERICA

1930 CHESTNUT STREET	PHILADELPHIA	PA	19103	(215) 564-5925
UNIVERSITY OF WISCONSIN PRESS 114 NORTH MURRAY STREET	MADISON	WI	53715	(608) 262-4928

PUBLISHERS - ISRAEL

MASSADA PUBLISHERS, LTD/PELI PRINTING WORKS, LTD.

11-15 TFUTSOT ISRAEL	GIVATAYIM	IS	53583	(037) 408-11
BIALIK INSTITUTE, THE PO BOX 92	JERUSALEM	IS	91920	(022) 271-89

CARTA, THE ISRAEL MAP AND PUBLISHING COMPANY

4/6 YAD HARUTZIM ST, INDUSTL ZONE, TALPIOT, POB 2500	JERUSALEM	IS	92014	(027) 135-367
DOMINO PRESS, LTD., THE P.O. BOX 4143	JERUSALEM	IS	94041	(026) 608-68
ISRAEL ACADEMY OF SCIENCES & HUMANITIES P.O. BOX 4040	JERUSALEM	IS	91040	(026) 362-11

ISRAEL EXPLORATION SOCIETY

3 SHMUEL HANAGID STREET, P.O. BOX 7041	JERUSALEM	IS	91070	(022) 279-91

JERUSALEM PUBLISHING HOUSE, LTD., THE

39 TCHERNICHOVSKY STREET, P.O. BOX 7147	JERUSALEM	IS	91071	(026) 677-44

KETER PUBLISHING HOUSE JERUSALEM, LTD.

INDUSTRIAL ZONE, GIVAT SHAUL B, P.O. BOX 7145	JERUSALEM	IS	91071	(025) 212-01
LA SEMANA PUBLISHING CO. LTD. P.O. BOX 2427	JERUSALEM	IS	91023	(026) 367-65
MAGNES PRESS, THE THE HEBREW UNIVERSITY	JERUSALEM	IS	91904	(026) 603-41
MASSADA PRESS, LTD. 46 BETHLEHEM ROAD, P.O. BOX 1232	JERUSALEM	IS	91012	(027) 194-415

SHIKMONA PUBLISHING COMPANY, LTD.

33 HERZOG STREET, P.O. BOX 4044	JERUSALEM	IS	91040	(026) 601-88
VAN LEER JERUSALEM FOUNDATION, THE P.O. BOX 4070	JERUSALEM	IS	91040	

WEIZMANN SCIENCE PRESS OF ISRAEL, THE

8A HORKANIA, P.O. BOX 801	JERUSALEM	IS	91007	(026) 632-03
ZALMAN SHAZAR CENTRE 22 RASHBA STREET, P.O. BOX 4179	JERUSALEM	IS	91041	(026) 371-71
MASSADA PRESS, LTD. 21 JABOTINSKY ROAD, P.O. BOX 3154	RAMAT GAN	IS	52131	(037) 342-03
SETTLEMENT STUDY CENTER (SSC) P.O. BOX 2355	REHOVOT	IS	76120	(054) 741-11

BOOK PUBLISHERS ASSOCIATION OF ISRAEL, THE

29 CARLEBACH STREET, P.O. BOX 20123	TEL AVIV	IS	61201	

BOOK AND PRINTING CENTER OF THE ISRAEL EXPORT INSTITUTE

29 HAMERED STREET, P.O. BOX 50084	TEL AVIV	IS	68125	(036) 308-58
GAALYAH CORNFELD PUBLISHERS 185 HAYARKON STREET	TEL AVIV	IS	63453	(032) 217-37
I.L. PERETZ PUBLISHING 14 BRENNER ST.	TEL AVIV	IS	65246	(032) 817-51

INSTITUTE FOR THE TRANSLATION OF HEBREW LITERATURE, LTD., THE

66 SHLOMO HAMELECH STREET	TEL AVIV	IS	64511	(032) 448-79
ISRAEL MUSIC INSTITUTE 6 CHEN BLVD., P.O. BOX 11253	TEL AVIV	IS	61112	(032) 843-97

MINISTRY OF DEFENCE PUBLISHING HOUSE

27 DAVID ELAZAR STREET, HAKIRYA, P.O. BOX 7103	TEL AVIV	IS	67673	(032) 179-40
MOSADOT PUBLICATIONS, INC. 6 BEN ZION BLVD	TEL AVIV	IS	64285	(032) 954-79
SADAN PUBLISHING HOUSE, LTD. 1 DAVID HAMELECH STREET	TEL AVIV	IS	64953	(032) 675-43

SHILOAH CENTER FOR MIDDLE EASTERN & AFRICAN STUDIES

TEL AVIV UNIVERSITY, RAMAT AVIV, PO BOX 39012	TEL AVIV	IS	69978	(034) 206-46
SINAI PUBLISHING 72 ALLENBY ROAD	TEL AVIV	IS		(036) 236-22
STEIMATZKY, LTD. P.O. BOX 628	TEL AVIV	IS	61006	(036) 120-60

TAMMUZ PUBLISHING HOUSE, LTD

3 TCHERNICHOVSKY STREET, PO BOX 23029	TEL AVIV	IS	63291	(036) 578-68
TERRA SANCTA ARTS, LTD. 522 DIZENGOFF CENTER, P.O. BOX 10009	TEL AVIV	IS	61100	(032) 896-30
YACHDAV UNITED PUBLISHERS COMPANY 29 CARLEBACH STREET	TEL AVIV	IS	67132	(032) 841-91

PUPPETRY

RED RUG PUPPET THEATRE, BETH KATZ, PUPPETEER 434 BUTTERFIELD	LANSING	MI	48906	(517) 332-8442
ROBERT BINDER, B'YAD HAYOTZER 24 WARWICK AVENUE	TORONTO	ON	M6C 1T6	(416) 979-3393

RABBINICAL ORGANIZATIONS

BOARD OF RABBIS 6505 WILSHIRE BLVD	LOS ANGELES	CA	90048	(213) 852-1234

BOARD OF RABBIS OF NORTHERN CALIFORNIA

870 MARKET STREET, SUITE 977	SAN FRANCISCO	CA	94102	(415) 788-3630
DENVER RABBINICAL COUNCIL 450 S. KEARNEY	DENVER	CO	80222	(303) 399-0035
BRIDGEPORT BOARD OF RABBIS 85 ARLINGTON STREET	BRIDGEPORT	CT	06606	

BRIDGEPORT BOARD OF RABBIS 1200 FAIRFIELD WOODS ROAD .... FAIRFIELD CT 06430
RABBINICAL COUNCIL 7826 EASTERN AVENUE N.W. .... WASHINGTON DC 20036 (202) 291-6052
RABBINICAL ASSOCIATION OF MIAMI 4200 BISCAYNE BLVD .... MIAMI FL 33137 (305) 576-4000
CHICAGO BOARD OF RABBIS ONE SOUTH FRANKLIN. .... CHICAGO IL 60606 (312) 444-2896
CHICAGO RABBINICAL COUNCIL 3525 W. PETERSON AVENUE .... CHICAGO IL 60659 (312) 588-1600
MERKAZ HARABONIM 6500 N. CALIFORNIA AVENUE .... CHICAGO IL 60645 (312) 761-3800
AMERICAN ASSOCIATION OF RABBIS 705 W. WILDWOOD AVENUE .....FORT WAYNE IN 46807
JEWISH CHAPLAINCY COUNCIL 177 TREMONT STREET ....BOSTON MA 02111 (617) 426-1832
MASSACHUSETTS BOARD OF RABBIS 177 TREMONT STREET ....BOSTON MA 02115 (617) 426-2139
MASSACHUSETTS COUNCIL OF RABBIS 611 WASHINGTON STREET ....BOSTON MA 02111 (617) 426-9586
ORTHODOX RABBINICAL COUNCIL OF GREATER BOSTON
  611 WASHINGTON STREET, ROOM 507 ....BOSTON MA 02111 (617) 426-9148
RABBINICAL COUNCIL OF MASSACHUSETTS (VAAD HARABONIM)
  177 TREMONT STREET ....BOSTON MA 02111 (617) 426-2139
COUNCIL OF ORTHODOX RABBIS OF DETROIT
  17071 W. TEN MILE ROAD. .... SOUTHFIELD MI 48075 (313) 559-5005
MINNESOTA RABBINICAL ASSOCIATION; TEMPLE OF AARON CONG.
  616 S. MISSISSIPPI RIVER BLVD. .... ST. PAUL MN 55116 (612) 698-8874
VAAD HOEIR OF ST. LOUIS 10977 SCHUETZ ROAD .... ST. LOUIS MO 63141 (314) 569-2770
CENTRAL RABBINICAL CONGRESS OF U.S. AND CANADA
  85 DIVISION AVENUE ....BROOKLYN NY 11211 (718) 384-6765
INTERNATIONAL RABBINICAL COUNCIL 4000 MANHATTAN AVENUE .....BROOKLYN NY 11224 (718) 372-4863
KNESSET HORABONIM RABBINICAL SOCIETY 1537 41ST STREET ...... BROOKLYN NY 11218 (718) 871-1754
LIKUTEI HALACHOS 537 EAST 4TH STREET .... BROOKLYN NY 11218 (718) 633-3521
NATIONAL ASSOCIATION OF RABBIS P.O. BOX 111 .... BROOKLYN NY 11219 (718) 853-3273
NATIONAL COMMITTEE ORTHODOX JEWISH COMMUNITIES
  260 BROADWAY ....BROOKLYN NY 11211 (718) 936-1911
RABBINICAL BOARD OF BAY RIDGE 4723 SEVENTH AVENUE .... BROOKLYN NY 11220 (718) 633-6378
VAAD RABONEI LUBAVITCH 333A KINGSTON AVENUE .... BROOKLYN NY 11213 (718) 493-4061
ATID-UNITED SYNAGOGUE OF AMERICA 155 FIFTH AVENUE .... NEW YORK NY 10010 (212) 533-7800
AGUDATH HORABONIM-UNION OF ORTHODOX RABBIS OF U.S. & CANADA
  235 EAST BROADWAY .... NEW YORK NY 10002 (212) 964-6337
AMERICAN ASSOCIATION OF RABBIS 350 FIFTH AVENUE .... NEW YORK NY 10001 (212) 244-3350
AMERICAN JEWISH CORRECTIONAL CHAPLAINS ASSOCIATION
  10 E. 73RD STREET .... NEW YORK NY 10021 (212) 879-8415
ASSOCIATION OF JEWISH CHAPLAINS OF THE ARMED FORCES
  15 E. 26TH STREET .... NEW YORK NY 10010 (212) 532-4949
ASSOCIATION OF RABBIS OF AMERICA 504 FIFTH AVENUE .... NEW YORK NY 10017 (212) 697-5895
CENTRAL CONFERENCE OF AMERICAN RABBIS 21 E. 40TH STREET...... NEW YORK NY 10016 (212) 684-4990
COMMISSION ON JEWISH CHAPLAINCY 15 E. 26TH STREET .... NEW YORK NY 10010 (212) 532-4949
COUNCIL OF YOUNG ISRAEL RABBIS 3 W. 16TH STREET .... NEW YORK NY 10011 (212) 929-1525
JEWISH MINISTERS CANTORS ASSOCIATION OF AMERICA
  3 W. 16TH STREET .... NEW YORK NY 10011 (212) 675-6601
JEWISH RECONSTRUCTIONIST FOUNDATION 432 PARK AVENUE S ..... NEW YORK NY 10016 (212) 889-9080
JEWISH WELFARE BOARD COMMISSION ON JEWISH CHAPLAINCY
  15 E. 26TH STREET .... NEW YORK NY 10010 (212) 532-4949
NEW YORK BOARD OF RABBIS 10 EAST 73RD STREET .... NEW YORK NY 10021 (212) 879-8415
RABBINICAL ALLIANCE OF AMERICA-IGUD HARABONIM
  156 FIFTH AVENUE, SUITE 807 .... NEW YORK NY 10010 (212) 242-6420
RABBINICAL ASSEMBLY 3080 BROADWAY .... NEW YORK NY 10027 (212) 749-8000
RABBINICAL COUNCIL OF AMERICA, INC. 1250 BROADWAY .... NEW YORK NY 10001 (212) 594-3780
RECONSTRUCTIONIST RABBINICAL ASSOCIATION
  423 PARK AVENUE SO., SUITE 1206-08 .... NEW YORK NY 10016 (212) 889-9080
UNION OF CHASIDIC RABBIS OF AMERICA 47 BEEKMAN STREET ..... NEW YORK NY 10038
UNION OF ORTHODOX RABBIS OF THE U.S. & CANADA, INC.
  235 EAST BROADWAY .... NEW YORK NY 10002 (212) 964-6837
CLEVELAND BOARD OF RABBIS 3557 WASHINGTON BLVD .... CLEVELAND OH 44118 (216) 321-1000
ORTHODOX RABBINICAL COUNCIL 1970 SOUTH TAYLOR ROAD ...... CLEVELAND OH 44118 (216) 321-4875
COLUMBUS BOARD OF RABBIS 1226 COLLEGE AVENUE .... COLUMBUS OH 43209
BOARD OF RABBIS OF GREATER PHILADELPHIA
  117 S. 17TH STREET, ROOM 903. .... PHILADELPHIA PA 19103 (215) 563-1463
JEWISH CHAPLAINCY OF BUCKS COUNTY 800 DAVID DRIVE .... TREVOSE PA 19047 (215) 357-7131
HOUSTON RABBINICAL ASSOCIATION 4610 BELLAIRE BLVD .... BELLAIRE TX 77401 (713) 667-9201

REAL ESTATE

AMBASSADOR REAL ESTATE & INVESTMENTS COMPANY
  23 REHOV RAMBAN. .... JERUSALEM IS 92422 (026) 391-64
ISRAEL HOMES & REAL ESTATE CORP. LTD. 800 SECOND AVENUE....... NEW YORK NY 10017 (212) 684-2219
ISRALOM-ISRAEL HOMES & REAL ESTATE CORP., LTD.
  440 PARK AVENUE SOUTH. .... NEW YORK NY 10016 (212) 684-2219
ISRALOM-ISRAEL HOMES & REAL ESTATE CORP., LTD.
  440 PARK AVENUE SOUTH. .... NEW YORK NY 10016 (212) 582-0844
HERITAGE INVESTMENTS 13 S. RIGAUD ROAD .... SPRING VALLEY NY 10977 (914) 356-6432

RECORDS, SHEET MUSIC & TAPES

LYRON MUSIC ENTERPRISES PO BOX 6103 ....BEVERLY HILLS CA 90212
HATAKLIT 436 NORTH FAIRFAX ....LOS ANGELES CA 90036 (213) 655-1242
NAMA RECORDS 2367 GLENDON AVENUE ....WESTWOOD CA 90064 (213) 475-6262
HEBREW PUBLISHING COMPANY 100 WATER STREET ....BROOKLYN NY 11201 (718) 858-6928
KEHOT MUSIC DEPARTMENT 770 EASTERN PARKWAY ....BROOKLYN NY 11213 (718) 774-4000
TORAH TAPES 1814 50 STREET......................BROOKLYN NY 11204 (718) 438-3904
TARA PUBLICATIONS 29 DERBY AVENUE ....CEDARHURST NY 11516 (516) 295-2290
BLOCH PUBLISHING 19 WEST 21ST STREET ....NEW YORK NY 10010 (212) 989-9104
HOUSE OF MENORAH, INC. 36 ELDRIDGE STREET ....NEW YORK NY 10002 (212) 925-7573
ISRAELI PRODUCTIONS 322 WEST 57TH STREET ....NEW YORK NY 10019 (212) 245-3463
J. LEVINE CO. 58 ELDRIDGE STREET ....NEW YORK NY 10002 (212) 966-4460
MUSIC MASTERS UPTOWN 25 WEST 43RD STREET ....NEW YORK NY 10036 (212) 840-1958

RABBINICAL ALLIANCE OF AMERICA 156 FIFTH AVENUE, SUITE 807 ..... NEW YORK NY 10010 (212) 242-6420
WORKMEN'S CIRCLE, EDUCATIONAL DEPARTMENT
  45 EAST 33RD STREET .... NEW YORK NY 10016 (212) 889-6800
YESHIVA UNIVERSITY, RABBINIC ALUMNI OFFICE
  500 WEST 185TH STREET .... NEW YORK NY 10033 (212) 960-5400
ELITE RECORDS 214-18 WHITEHALL TERRACE .... QUEENS VILLAGE NY 11427
HEBRAICA RECORD DISTRIBUTORS 50 ANDOVER ROAD .... ROSLYN HEIGHTS NY 11577 (516) 484-4006

RELIGIOUS ORGANIZATIONS

UNITED SYNAGOGUE OF AMERICA-PACIFIC SOUTHWEST REGION
  15600 MULHOLLAND DRIVE ....LOS ANGELES CA 90024 (213) 879-4114
UNION OF AMERICAN HEBREW CONGREGATIONS-PACIFIC SOUTHWEST
  13197 VENTURA BOULEVARD ....NORTH HOLLYWOOD CA 91604
UNITED SYNAGOGUE OF AMERICA-NORTHERN CALIFORNIA REGION
  1419 BROADWAY SUITE 612 .... OAKLAND CA 94612 (415) 839-6333
UNITED SYNAGOGUE OF AMERICA-PACIFIC NORTHWEST REGION
  1419 BROADWAY .... OAKLAND CA 94612 (415) 839-6333
UNION OF AMERICAN-HEBREW CONGREGATIONS-N. CAL. & PACIFIC NW
  703 MARKET STREET, SUITE 705 ....SAN FRANCISCO CA 94103 (415) 392-7080
SYNAGOGUE COUNCIL OF AMERICA
  1776 MASSACHUSETTS AVENUE, N W ....WASHINGTON DC 20036
UNION OF AMERICAN HEBREW CONGREGATIONS-MID ATLANTIC COUNCIL
  2027 MASSACHUSETTS AVENUE, N.W. ....WASHINGTON DC 20036 (202) 387-2800
UNION OF AMERICAN HEBREW CONGREGATIONS-SOUTHEAST COUNCIL
  3785 NW 82ND AVENUE #210 ....MIAMI FL 33166 (305) 592-4792
UNITED SYNAGOGUE OF AMERICA-SOUTHEAST REGION
  282 S. UNIVERSITY DRIVE, SUITE 216 ....PLANTATION FL 33324 (305) 947-6094
JEWS FOR JEWS ORGANIZATION P.O. BOX 6194 ....SURFSIDE FL 33154 (305) 931-0001
UNITED SYNAGOGUE OF AMERICA-CENTRAL STATES & PROVINCES REG.
  525 14TH STREET ....SIOUX CITY IA 51105 (712) 258-6007
UNION OF AMERICAN HEBREW CONGREGATIONS-GREAT LAKES COUNCIL
  100 WEST MONROE STREET ROOM 312 ....CHICAGO IL 60603 (312) 782-1477
UNITED SYNAGOGUE OF AMERICA-MIDWEST REGION
  180 N. MICHIGAN ....CHICAGO IL 60605 (312) 726-1802
ASSOCIATED SYNAGOGUES OF MASSACHUSETTS
  177 TREMONT STREET ....BOSTON MA 02111 (617) 426-1832
MIZRACHI-HAPOEL HAMIZRACHI OF NEW ENGLAND
  611 WASHINGTON STREET ....BOSTON MA 02111 (617) 426-9148
ASSOCIATED SYNAGOGUES OF MASSACHUSETTS
  177 TREMONT STREET ....BROOKLINE MA 02111 (617) 426-1832

Now There's an Easier Way to Get Into Jewish Learning

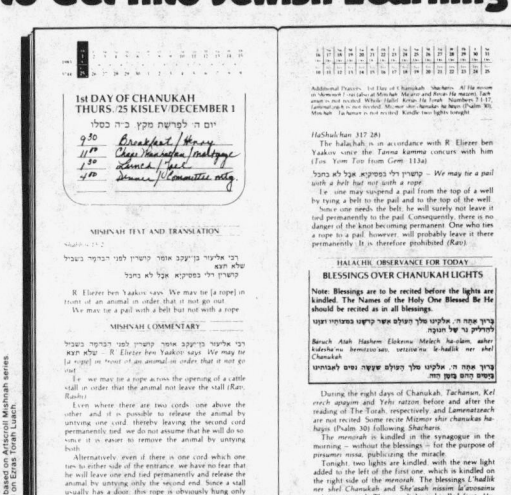

WITH LUACH & LIMUD YOU'LL NEVER MISS YOUR MOST IMPORTANT APPOINTMENT

Start your next month on the right track with Luach & Limud—the daily diary for businessmen, professionals and anyone else who doesn't want a day to go by without Torah.

Luach & Limud reminds you of all your regular business and social appointments, *and* it features a concise daily Torah lesson.

Luach & Limud provides a luach, daily Sabbath and Holiday laws and observances, candle lighting, and end of Sabbath times for 20 cities.

Luach & Limud is pocket size and is delivered to your home or office each month. So it's never too late (or too soon) to enter your subscription.

For only $24 you can assure yourself of 12 uninterrupted months of Luach & Limud. Subscribe now.

This way you'll never miss the most important appointment of all.

YES. I want every day to be a Torah day.
Please enter my subscription to Luach & Limud

NAME
ADDRESS
CITY/STATE/ZIP
TELEPHONE

☐ Enclosed is my check for $ 24 (Canada/foreign $ 32 U.S.)
☐ Please bill me through ☐ Mastercard ☐ Visa

Account #
Exp date

Signature of credit card holder. Valid only with full signature

Please make checks payable to:
Luach & Limud, P.O. Box 6749, Syracuse, NY 13217

Luach & Limud TORAH DIARY

UNION OF AMERICAN HEBREW CONGREGATIONS-NORTHEAST COUNCIL			
1330 BEACON STREET	BROOKLINE **MA** 02146	(617) 277-1655
UNITED SYNAGOGUE OF AMERICA-NEW ENGLAND REGION			
180 BLUE HILL AVENUE	MILTON **MA** 02186	(617) 698-0085
COUNCIL OF ORTHODOX SYNAGOGUES OF GREATER WASHINGTON			
801 WHITTINGTON TERRACE	SILVER SPRING **MD** 20901	
UNITED SYNAGOGUE OF AMERICA-SEABOARD REGION			
420 UNIVERSITY BOULEVARD, E	SILVER SPRING **MD** 20901	(301) 434-6650
THE SOCIETY FOR HUMANISTIC JUDAISM			
28611 WEST TWELVE MILE ROAD	FARMINGTON HILLS **MI** 48018	(313) 478-7610
UNITED SYNAGOGUE OF AMERICA-MICHIGAN REGION			
29901 MIDDLEBELT ROAD	FARMINGTON HILLS **MI** 48018	(313) 855-5950
UNION OF AMERICAN HEBREW CONGREGATIONS-MIDWEST COUNCIL			
8420 DELMAR, SUITE 304	ST. LOUIS **MO** 63124	(314) 997-7566
UNITED SYNAGOGUE OF AMERICA-NEW JERSEY REGION			
910 SALEM AVENUE	HILLSIDE **NJ** 07205	(201) 353-8844
UNITED ORTHODOX SYNAGOGUES 75 SOMERSET STREET	NORTH PLAINFIELD **NJ** 07060	
UNITED SYNAGOGUE OF AMERICA-EMPIRE REGION			
18 PINE STREET	AMSTERDAM **NY** 12010	(518) 842-2829
AGUDATH ISRAEL OF AMERICA 813 AVENUE H	BROOKLYN **NY** 11230	(718) 434-8670
BETH SHIFRA INSTITUTIONS 3044 CONEY ISLAND AVENUE	BROOKLYN **NY** 11235	(718) 449-1397
CENTRAL RABBINICAL CONGRESS 85 DIVISION	BROOKLYN **NY** 11211	(718) 384-6766
COMMITTEE FOR THE FURTHERANCE OF TORAH OBSERVANCE			
1430 57TH STREET	BROOKLYN **NY** 11219	(718) 851-6428
MACHNE ISRAEL 770 EASTERN PARKWAY	BROOKLYN **NY** 11213	(718) 493-9250
MITZVAH CAMPAIGN-LUBAVITCH 770 EASTERN PARKWAY	BROOKLYN **NY** 11213	(718) 493-9250
ORGANIZATION FOR TORAH ETHICS, THE 928 46TH STREET	BROOKLYN **NY** 11219	(718) 438-1574
PHYSICIANS FOR TORAH OBSERVANCE 4718 12TH AVENUE	BROOKLYN **NY** 11219	(718) 438-3090
SIMAN UMESORAH INSTITUTE 1448 50TH STREET	BROOKLYN **NY** 11219	(718) 435-8171
TZIVOS HASHEM 770 EASTERN PARKWAY	BROOKLYN **NY** 11213	(718) 467-6630
AMERICAN TORAH SHELEMAH COMMITTEE 24 W. MAPLE AVENUE	MONSEY **NY** 10952	(914) 352-4609
ACADEMY FOR JEWISH RELIGION 112 E. 88TH STREET	NEW YORK **NY** 10028	(212) 722-5811
AGUDAS ISRAEL WORLD ORGANIZATION 471 WEST END AVENUE	NEW YORK **NY** 10024	(212) 874-7979
AGUDATH ISRAEL OF AMERICA 5 BEEKMAN STREET	NEW YORK **NY** 10038	(212) 791-1800
FEDERATION OF RECONSTRUCTIONIST CONGREGATIONS AND HAVUROT			
2521 BROADWAY	NEW YORK **NY** 10025	(212) 316-3011
JEWISH RECONSTRUCTIONIST FOUNDATION 2521 BROADWAY	NEW YORK **NY** 10025	(212) 316-3011
LEAGUE FOR SAFEGUARDING THE FIXITY OF THE SABBATH			
122 W. 76TH STREET	NEW YORK **NY** 10023	(212) 877-7652

NATIONAL ASSOCIATION FOR THE ADVANCEMENT OF ORTHODOX JUDAISM			
132 NASSAU STREET	NEW YORK **NY** 10038	(212) 964-7829
NATIONAL COUNCIL OF YOUNG ISRAEL 3 WEST 16TH STREET	NEW YORK **NY** 10011	(212) 929-1525
NEW YORK FEDERATION OF REFORM SYNAGOGUES			
838 FIFTH AVENUE	NEW YORK **NY** 10021	(212) 249-0100
OZAR HATORAH, INC. 411 FIFTH AVENUE	NEW YORK **NY** 10016	(212) 684-4733
POALE AGUDATH ISRAEL OF AMERICA, INC.			
156 FIFTH AVENUE, SUITE 811	NEW YORK **NY** 10010	(212) 924-9475
RABBINICAL COUNCIL OF AMERICA 1250 BROADWAY	NEW YORK **NY** 10001	(212) 594-3780
RECONSTRUCTIONIST FEDERATION OF CONGREGATIONS & FELLOWSHIPS			
432 PARK AVENUE S	NEW YORK **NY** 10016	(212) 889-9080
SHOFAR ASSOCIATION OF AMERICA, INC. 234 FIFTH AVENUE	NEW YORK **NY** 10001	(212) 687-2570
SOCIETY FOR THE ADVANCEMENT OF JUDAISM			
15 WEST 86TH STREET	NEW YORK **NY** 10024	(212) 724-7000
SYNAGOGUE COUNCIL OF AMERICA 327 LEXINGTON AVENUE	NEW YORK **NY** 10016	(212) 686-8670
UNION OF AMERICAN HEBREW CONGREGATIONS 838 FIFTH AVENUE	NEW YORK **NY** 10021	(212) 249-0100

Books From Ⓤ
Orthodox Union/NCSY Publications

NEW BOOK! Tzitzith–A Thread of Light
by Aryeh Kaplan

Aryeh Kaplan delves into the mystery of the commandment of tzitzis to reveal the link between tzitzis and the ability of mankind to overcome sin and reach towards God. This rewarding book covers every aspect of this daily commandment–from the practical to the mystical.

112 pages   **$3.50**

JUST REPRINTED!
Maimonides' Principles
The Fundamentals of Jewish Faith
by Aryeh Kaplan

An anthology of Maimonides' own writings, newly translated and compiled with special emphasis and explanations given to the thirteen Principles of Faith.

106 pages   **$3.95**

Jerusalem, Eye of the Universe
by Aryeh Kaplan

What is the significance of the city of Jerusalem? Why should it be so all-important a place to the Jewish people? This book explores the uniqueness of Jerusalem and provides an understanding of just what the holy city represents.

112 pages   **$3.50**

Sabbath–Day of Eternity
by Aryeh Kaplan

An introduction to the underlying thought and ideology of the Sabbath and a survey of its laws and customs presented in a concise, straightforward manner. Special emphasis on "why keep the Sabbath," the meaning of Sabbath rest, and the "39 categories of work."

48 pages   **$2.50**

SHIPPING: $1.50 for orders totalling $30 and under.

For a complete Publications Catalogue, with information about volume discounts, call or write the Orthodox Union/NCSY Publications Department, 45 West 36 Street, New York, N.Y. 10018, (212) 563-4000.

ORTHODOX UNION/NCSY PUBLICATION
45 West 36 Street, New York, N.Y. 10018

Please send me the following Ⓤ publications:
☐ Maimonides' Principles ☐ Tzitzith–A Thread of Light ☐ Jerusalem ☐ Sabbath.

Name
Address
City/State/Zip

All orders must be prepaid in full (U.S. funds only, please). Please make check payable to: Orthodox Union

UNION OF AMERICAN HEBREW CONGREGATIONS-NJ-W. HUDSON COUNCIL 838 FIFTH AVENUE	NEW YORK	**NY**	10021	(212) 249-0100
UNION OF AMERICAN HEBREW CONGREGATIONS-NY FEDERATION 838 FIFTH AVENUE	NEW YORK	**NY**	10021	(212) 249-0100
UNION OF ORTHODOX JEWISH CONGREGATIONS OF AMERICA 45 WEST 36TH STREET	NEW YORK	**NY**	10018	(212) 563-4000
UNION OF SEPHARDIC CONGREGATIONS 8 WEST 70TH STREET	NEW YORK	**NY**	10023	(212) 873-0300
UNITED SYNAGOGUE OF AMERICA 155 FIFTH AVENUE	NEW YORK	**NY**	10010	(212) 533-7800
UNITED SYNAGOGUE OF AMERICA-CONNECTICUT VALLEY REGION 155 FIFTH AVENUE	NEW YORK	**NY**	10010	(212) 533-7800
UNITED SYNAGOGUE OF AMERICA-NEW YORK METROPOLITAN REGION 155 FIFTH AVENUE	NEW YORK	**NY**	10010	(212) 533-7800
UNITED SYNAGOGUE OF AMERICA-OHIO REGION 155 FIFTH AVENUE	NEW YORK	**NY**	10010	(212) 533-7800
UNITED SYNAGOGUE OF AMERICA-WESTERN PENNSYLVANIA REGION 155 FIFTH AVENUE	NEW YORK	**NY**	10010	(212) 533-7800
WORLD COUNCIL OF SYNAGOGUES 155 FIFTH AVENUE	NEW YORK	**NY**	10010	(212) 533-7800
WORLD UNION FOR PROGRESSIVE JUDAISM 838 FIFTH AVENUE	NEW YORK	**NY**	10021	(212) 249-0100
UNION OF AMERICAN HEBREW CONGREGATIONS-DETROIT & NORTHEAST 25550 CHAGRIN ROAD	BEACHWOOD	**OH**	44122	(216) 831-6722
UNION OF AMERICAN HEBREW CONGREGATIONS-CANADIAN COUNCIL 534 LAWRENCE AVENUE W	TORONTO	**ON**	M6A 1A2	(416) 787-9838
UNITED SYNAGOGUE OF AMERICA-ONTARIO-CANADA REGION 3199 BATHURST STREET, SUITE 200	TORONTO	**ON**	M6A 2B2	(416) 781-6908
UNION OF AMERICAN HEBREW CONGREGATIONS-PA COUNCIL 117 SOUTH 17TH STREET	PHILADELPHIA	**PA**	19103	(215) 563-8726
UNITED SYNAGOGUE OF AMERICA-E. PA. & DEL. VALLEY REGION 1701 WALNUT STREET	PHILADELPHIA	**PA**	19103	(215) 563-8809
UNITED SYNAGOGUE OF AMERICA-EASTERN CANADA REGION 875 MARLBORO DRIVE	MONTREAL	**QU**	H4P 1B7	(514) 733-7217
UNION OF AMERICAN HEBREW CONGREGATIONS-SOUTHWEST COUNCIL 13773 N. CENTRAL EXPRESSWAY	DALLAS	**TX**	75243	(214) 699-0656
UNITED SYNAGOGUE OF AMERICA-SOUTH WEST REGION 8525 STELLA LINK ROAD	HOUSTON	**TX**	77025	(713) 661-4520

RESTAURANTS & DELICATESSENS

SEGAL'S KOSHER MARKET 2905 NORTH 16TH STREET	PHOENIX	**AZ**	85018	(602) 277-5769
FEIG KOSHER FOODS 5071 EAST 5TH STREET	TUCSON	**AZ**	85711	(602) 325-2255
BEAUMONT KOSHER KETTLE 17614 VENTURA BOULEVARD	ENCINO	**CA**	91316	(818) 995-1484
MASADA GLATT KOSHER RESTAURANT 12181 BUARO (NEAR DISNEYLAND)	GARDEN GROVE	**CA**	92640	(714) 956-0544
HANCOCK PARK GOURMET 129 NORTH LA BREA AVENUE	LOS ANGELES	**CA**	90036	(213) 936-7372
JUDY'S LAPETITE 129 N. LA BREA	LOS ANGELES	**CA**	90036	(213) 936-7372
KOLDODY KOSHER BURGERS 8965 WEST PICO BOULEVARD	LOS ANGELES	**CA**	90035	(213) 274-6534
KOSHER CUTTING BOARD 6505 WILSHIRE BOULEVARD	LOS ANGELES	**CA**	90048	(213) 653-7774
KOSHER EXPRESS 363 S. FAIRFAX AVENUE	LOS ANGELES	**CA**	90036	(213) 651-0147
KOSHER KOLONEL 9301 WEST PICO BOULEVARD	LOS ANGELES	**CA**	90035	(213) 858-0111
KOSHER NOSTRA 365 SOUTH FAIRFAX AVENUE	LOS ANGELES	**CA**	90036	(213) 655-1994
KOSHER PIZZA NOSH 8844 WEST PICO BOULEVARD	LOS ANGELES	**CA**	90035	(213) 276-8708
LA BRIUT 448 NORTH FAIRFAX AVENUE	LOS ANGELES	**CA**	90036	(213) 653-2090
LA GLATT 446 NORTH FAIRFAX AVENUE	LOS ANGELES	**CA**	90036	(213) 651-0242
MARCELLE'S CUISINE 448 N. FAIRFAX	LOS ANGELES	**CA**	90036	(213) 653-2090
MILKY WAY 9108 WEST PICO BOULEVARD	LOS ANGELES	**CA**	90035	(213) 859-0004
PICO KOSHER DELI 8826 WEST PICO BOULEVARD	LOS ANGELES	**CA**	90035	(213) 273-9381
RAPHY'S 9303 WEST PICO BOULEVARD	LOS ANGELES	**CA**	90035	(213) 275-6265
SUPER-CHEF 363 NORTH FAIRFAX AVENUE	LOS ANGELES	**CA**	90036	(213) 651-0147
TWO WORLDS HEALTH FOOD RESTAURANT 8022 WEST THIRD STREET	LOS ANGELES	**CA**	90048	(213) 653-4212
UNIVERSITY OF JUDAISM 15600 MULHOLLAND DRIVE	LOS ANGELES	**CA**	90077	(213) 476-9777
WESTERN KOSHER 426 NORTH FAIRFAX AVE.	LOS ANGELES	**CA**	90036	(213) 655-8870
YESHIVA UNIVERSITY OF LOS ANGELES 9760 WEST PICO BOULEVARD	LOS ANGELES	**CA**	90035	(213) 277-9924
DREXLER'S 12519 1/2 BURBANK BOULEVARD	NORTH HOLLYWOOD	**CA**	91607	(818) 761-6405
LA PIZZA RISTORANTE 4454 VAN NUYS BOULEVARD	SHERMAN OAKS	**CA**	91403	(818) 986-0581
MOISHE'S KOSHER DELICATESSEN BAKERY 2081 BLACK ROCK TURNPIKE	FAIRFIELD	**CT**	06430	(203) 333-3059
HARTFORD KOSHER CATERERS FORD AND PEARL	HARTFORD	**CT**	06111	(203) 527-7770

M & T APPETIZERS & DELICATESSEN 1150 WHALLEY AVENUE	NEW HAVEN	**CT**		(203) 389-5603
BEE BEE DAIRY RESTAURANT TOWN STREET	NORWICH	**CT**	06360	(203) 887-4101
DELI-LAND KOSHER DELICATESSEN 850 HIGH RIDGE ROAD	STAMFORD	**CT**		(203) 322-3649
POSINS' BAKERY-DELI 5756 GEORGIA AVENUE N.W.	WASHINGTON	**DC**	20008	(202) 726-4424
EMBASSY NORTH 1025 E. HALLANDALE BEACH BLVD	HALLANDALE	**FL**	33009	(305) 456-7550
SAGE BAGEL & APPETIZER SHOP 800 EAST HALLANDALE BEACH BOULEVARD	HALLANDALE	**FL**	33009	(305) 456-7499
WORMAN'S BAKERY & DELICATESSEN 1712 SAN MARCO BOULEVARD	JACKSONVILLE	**FL**		(904) 396-0393
WORMAN'S BAKERY & DELICATESSEN 204 BROAD STREET	JACKSONVILLE	**FL**		(904) 354-5702
BERNARD WACHTEL'S TOWER SUITE 4101 PINE TREE DRIVE	MIAMI BEACH	**FL**	33140	(305) 673-8308
CASABLANCA RESTAURANT & TAKE-OUT 6345 COLLINS AVENUE	MIAMI BEACH	**FL**	33141	(305) 868-4565
DAIRY PATCH 534 41ST STREET	MIAMI BEACH	**FL**	33140	(305) 531-1511
DELI NOSH 420 ARTHUR GODFREY ROAD, 41ST STREET	MIAMI BEACH	**FL**	33140	(305) 538-9104
EMBASSY 41 534 41ST STREET	MIAMI BEACH	**FL**	33140	(305) 538-7550
EMBASSY KOSHER STEAK HOUSE 1417 WASHINGTON AVENUE	MIAMI BEACH	**FL**	33139	(305) 538-7550
H & M STEIN DELI 1141 WASHINGTON AVENUE	MIAMI BEACH	**FL**	33139	(305) 534-2557
KING DAVID DELICATESSEN 1339 WASHINGTON AVENUE	MIAMI BEACH	**FL**	33139	(305) 534-0197
ROYAL HUNGARIAN SASSON HOTEL-OCEAN AT 20TH STREET	MIAMI BEACH	**FL**	33139	(305) 538-5401
SARA'S RESTAURANT 534 41ST STREET	MIAMI BEACH	**FL**	33140	(305) 531-1511
SEA GULL KOSHER STEAK HOUSE ON THE OCEAN AT 21ST STREET	MIAMI BEACH	**FL**	33139	(305) 531-4114
SHLOMI'S FAMOUS VEGETARIAN RESTAURANT 753 41ST STREET	MIAMI BEACH	**FL**	33140	(305) 538-7333
TOWER SUITE 4101 PINE TREE DRIVE	MIAMI BEACH	**FL**	33140	(305) 673-8308
DAIRY PATCH 9802 N.E. 2ND AVENUE	MIAMI SHORES	**FL**	33138	(305) 758-4821
SARAH'S PIZZA 2214 NE. 123RD ST.	NORTH MIAMI	**FL**		(305) 891-3312
AVI'S STEAK HOUSE 175 SUNNY ISLES BLVD	N. MIAMI BEACH	**FL**	33160	(305) 947-4781
LA DIFFERENCE 1344 N.E. 163 STREET	N. MIAMI BEACH	**FL**	33162	(305) 949-4552
SHIPUDAY AHUVA ISRAELI RESTAURANT 133024 N.E. 163RD STREET	N. MIAMI BEACH	**FL**	33162	
KATZ'S DELICATESSEN 2205 CHESHIRE BRIDGE ROAD N.E.	ATLANTA	**GA**		(404) 321-7444
SABRA 2712 WEST PRATT	CHICAGO	**IL**	60645	(312) 764-3563
TEL AVIV KOSHER PIZZA & DAIRY RESTAURANT 6349 NORTH CALIFORNIA	CHICAGO	**IL**	60659	(312) 764-3776
SELIG'S KOSHER DELICATESSEN 309 SKOKIE VALLEY ROAD	HIGHLAND PARK	**IL**	60035	(312) 831-5560
FALAFEL KING 4507 WEST OAKTON	SKOKIE	**IL**	60076	(312) 677-6020
KOSHER GOURMENT 3552 DEMPSTER	SKOKIE	**IL**	60076	(312) 679-0432
SHAPIRO'S DELICATESSEN 808 SOUTH MERIDIAN	INDIANAPOLIS	**IN**		(317) 631-4041
EPSTEIN'S 403 WEST 79TH STREET	KANSAS CITY	**KS**	66102	(816) 361-0200
YESHIVA ACADEMY CAFETERIA 22 NEWTON AVENUE	WORCESTER	**MA**		(617) 752-0904
THE KNISH SHOP 508 REISTERSTOWN ROAD	BALTIMORE	**MD**	21208	(301) 484-5850
THE GARDEN 7723 WISCONSIN AVENUE	BETHESDA	**MD**		(301) 654-3511
MARION'S CUSTOM CATERING 2702 NAVARE DRIVE	CHEVY CHASE	**MD**	20815	(301) 587-5820
LIEBES KOSHER DELI 607 REISTERSTOWN ROAD	PIKESVILLE	**MD**	21208	(301) 653-1977
CECIL'S KOSHER DELICATESSEN RESTAURANT & BAKERY 651 CLEVELAND AVENUE SOUTH	ST. PAUL	**MN**	55416	(612) 698-6276
EPSTEIN'S KOSHER FOOD 403 WEST 79TH	KANSAS CITY	**MO**		(816) 361-0200
M & M BAKERY & DELICATESSEN 1721 EAST 31ST STREET	KANSAS CITY	**MO**		(816) 924-9172
GOODWILL KOSHER DELICATESSEN & APPETIZERS 815 BROADWAY	BAYONNE	**NJ**	07002	(201) 339-2392
KOSHER KITCHEN 5901 BROADWAY	BAYONNE	**NJ**	07002	(201) 437-1594
FOSTER VILLAGE KOSHER DELICATESSEN 469 S. WASHINGTON	BERGENFIELD	**NJ**	07621	(201) 384-7100
BRADLEY KOSHER DELICATESSEN 401 MAIN STREET	BRADLEY BEACH	**NJ**	07720	(201) 775-1081
JERUSALEM II PIZZA 106 NORWOOD AVENUE	DEAL	**NJ**	07723	(201) 531-9800
KOSHER IRISHMAN DELI 392 CENTRAL AVENUE	EAST ORANGE	**NJ**	07011	(201) 673-2407
KOSHER DISH 437 PENNINGTON	ELIZABETH	**NJ**		(201) 527-1818
SUPERIOR DELI & APPETIZER CO. 150 ELMORA AVENUE	ELIZABETH	**NJ**		(201) 352-0355
ENGLEWOOD KOSHER DELI 95 WEST PALISADE AVENUE	ENGLEWOOD	**NJ**	07632	(201) 567-0732
KOSHER PARADISE 14-20 PLAZA ROAD	FAIRLAWN	**NJ**	07410	(201) 797-0100
MIDDLEBROOK KOSHER DELICATESSEN 1594 STATE HIGHWAY 35	OAKHURST	**NJ**	07755	(201) 493-8300
LARRY'S KOSHER DELI RESTAURANT - APPETIZERS & CATERERS 1353 SOUTH AVENUE	PLAINFIELD	**NJ**		(201) 755-8013
DELI KING 628 ST. GEORGES AVENUE	WEST LINDEN	**NJ**	07036	(201) 925-3909
TABATCHNIK WESTWOOD DELI & APPETIZERS 226 FAIRVIEW AVENUE	WESTWOOD	**NJ**	07675	(201) 666-1051
PHIL BROADWAY KOSHER DELICATESSEN & RESTAURANT 30-05 BROADWAY	ASTORIA	**NY**	11102	(718) 728-4253
BEN'S KOSHER GOURMET RESTAURANTS & CATERERS 933 ATLANTIC AVENUE	BALDWIN	**NY**	11510	(516) 868-2072
NEW DELSEN'S KOSHER DELICATESSEN 43 EAST MAIN STREET	BAY SHORE	**NY**	11706	(516) 665-4203
WINDSOR PARK KOSHER DELI 215-01 73RD AVENUE	BAYSIDE	**NY**	11364	(718) 229-3380
WOLFMAN'S KOSHER DELI 256-01 UNION TURNPIKE	BAYSIDE	**NY**	11364	(718) 347-7310
SAM'S FAMOUS KNISHES (DAIRY) 504 BRIGHTON BEACH AVENUE	BRIGHTON BEACH	**NY**	11235	(718) 646-5450
FLASH KOSHER PIZZA 3702 RIVERDALE AVENUE	BRONX	**NY**	10463	(212) 543-1811
K & G KOSHER DELICATESSEN 772 ALLERTON AVENUE	BRONX	**NY**	10467	(212) 655-9424
LEVINE'S KOSHER DELICATESSEN RESTAURANT 2144 WHITE PLAINS ROAD	BRONX	**NY**	10462	(212) 409-9600
LIEBMAN'S KOSHER DELICATESSEN & CATERING 552 WEST 235TH STREET	BRONX	**NY**	10463	(212) 548-4534
LOESSER'S KOSHER DELICATESSEN & CATERER 214 WEST 231ST STREET	BRONX	**NY**	10463	(212) 548-9735
OTHER'S KOSHER DELI GRAND CONCOURSE AT EAST 188TH STREET	BRONX	**NY**		
PALACE KOSHER DELICATESSEN 122 EAST 188TH STREET	BRONX	**NY**	10468	(212) 933-0043
S & O KOSHER DELICATESSEN 1596 WESTCHESTER AVENUE	BRONX	**NY**	10472	(212) 842-2214
SCHWELLER'S KOSHER CATERERS 3411 JEROME AVENUE	BRONX	**NY**	10467	(212) 655-8649
SIMON'S KOSHER TAKE HOME FOODS 3532 JOHNSON AVENUE	BRONX	**NY**		(212) 796-7530
SKYVIEW KOSHER DELICATESSEN & CATERERS 5665 RIVERDALE AVENUE	BRONX	**NY**	10471	(212) 796-8596
ZION KOSHER DELICATESSEN 968 LONGFELLOW AVENUE	BRONX	**NY**	10462	(212) 589-1770
ZION KOSHER DELICATESSEN & RESTAURANT 750 LYDIG AVENUE	BRONX	**NY**	10462	(212) 597-6360
18TH AVENUE KOSHER PIZZA 4418 18TH AVENUE	BROOKLYN	**NY**	11204	
A-1 ELLAT RESTAURANT 4823 18TH AVENUE	BROOKLYN	**NY**	11204	(718) 853-9501

ACH TOV KOSHER DAIRY RESTAURANT 5001-13TH AVENUE	BROOKLYN	NY	11219	(718) 438-8494
ADELMAN'S DELI 1906 KINGS HIGHWAY	BROOKLYN	NY	11229	(718) 336-4915
AVENUE U KOSHER PIZZA 2117 AVENUE U	BROOKLYN	NY	11229	(718) 646-9740
BERNAT BERKOWITZ RESTAURANT 1427 CONEY ISLAND AVENUE	BROOKLYN	NY	11229	(718) 252-5308
BERWIE'S BAR-B-Q 123 CHURCH AVENUE	BROOKLYN	NY	11218	(718) 854-3340
BOROUGH PARK KOSHER PIZZA 4303 19TH AVENUE	BROOKLYN	NY	11204	(718) 436-1064
BOROUGH PARK KOSHER PIZZA 4923 18TH AVENUE	BROOKLYN	NY	11204	(718) 438-8542
BRIGHTON BEACH DAIRY RESTAURANT				
410 BRIGHTON BEACH AVENUE	BROOKLYN	NY	11235	(718) 646-7421
B'TEYAVON RESTAURANT & DELI 1427 CONEY ISLAND AVENUE	BROOKLYN	NY	11230	(718) 252-5308
CAN TAAM 4813-13TH AVENUE	BROOKLYN	NY	11219	(718) 436-0400
CHAP-A-NOSH 1426 ELM AVENUE	BROOKLYN	NY	11230	(718) 627-0072
CHEF'S DELIGHT 4704-18TH AVENUE	BROOKLYN	NY	11204	(718) 871-1515
COURT GARDEN 187 STATE STREET	BROOKLYN	NY	11201	(718) 875-9746
COUSIN'S KOSHER DELI 5014 AVENUE D	BROOKLYN	NY	11203	(718) 451-9811
CROWN GLATT KOSHER CATERERS & RESTAURANT				
4909-13TH AVENUE	BROOKLYN	NY	11219	(718) 853-9000
DAGAN DAIRY RESTAURANT 4820 16TH AVENUE	BROOKLYN	NY	11204	
DAVID'S SYRIAN & ISRAELI RESTAURANT 547 KINGS HIGHWAY	BROOKLYN	NY	11223	(718) 998-8600
EDNA'S GLATT KOSHER DELICATESSEN & RESTAURANT				
125 CHURCH AVENUE	BROOKLYN	NY	11218	(718) 438-8207
EILAT RESTAURANT 4823 18TH AVENUE	BROOKLYN	NY	11204	(718) 853-9501
ELITE RESTAURANT 1622 E. 16TH STREET	BROOKLYN	NY	11229	(718) 376-9862
EMIL FRIEDMAN 1555 48TH STREET	BROOKLYN	NY	11219	(718) 854-3456
EMPRESS KOSHER DELI 2210 86TH STREET	BROOKLYN	NY	11214	(718) 266-7679
ESS & BENCH 299 KINGSTON AVENUE	BROOKLYN	NY	11213	
FAMOUS DAIRY RESTAURANT 4818-13TH AVENUE	BROOKLYN	NY	11219	(718) 435-4201
FRANKEL'S 5301 NEW UTRECHT AVENUE	BROOKLYN	NY	11219	(718) 853-2040
GOTTLIEB'S GLATT KOSHER DELICATESSEN 352 ROEBLING STREET	BROOKLYN	NY	11211	(718) 384-9037
GRABSTEIN BROS. 1845 ROCKAWAY PARKWAY	BROOKLYN	NY	11236	(718) 251-2280
GUTTMAN'S RESTAURANT 5120-13TH AVENUE	BROOKLYN	NY	11219	(718) 436-4830
H & S KOSHER DELI 1654 SHEEPSHEAD BAY ROAD	BROOKLYN	NY	11235	(718) 646-9032
HIGHWAY ISRAELI GREEK RESTAURANT, THE 1811 KINGS HIGHWAY	BROOKLYN	NY	11229	(718) 627-9516
IMPERIAL 4910 13TH AVENUE	BROOKLYN	NY	11219	(718) 851-7550
IRVINGS KNISHERY & KOSHER PIZZA 7922 FLATLANDS AVENUE	BROOKLYN	NY	11236	(718) 451-1645
IRWIN JAY'S DELI 1121 AVENUE J	BROOKLYN	NY	11230	(718) 258-9363
ISRAEL KOSHER PIZZA & FALAFEL 4810 13TH AVENUE	BROOKLYN	NY	11219	(718) 438-9872
ITZU'S DAIRY RESTAURANT 45 LEE AVENUE	BROOKLYN	NY	11211	
JACK'S KOSHER DELI 116 COURT STREET	BROOKLYN	NY	11201	(718) 875-0225
JACK'S KOSHER PIZZA 709 KINGS HIGHWAY	BROOKLYN	NY	11223	
JAY'S KOSHER DELI 1416 AVENUE J	BROOKLYN	NY	11230	(718) 253-7440
JERUSALEM II KOSHER PIZZA 1312 AVENUE J	BROOKLYN	NY	11230	(718) 338-8156
JERUSALEM II PIZZA 1424 AVENUE M	BROOKLYN	NY	11230	(718) 645-4753
JERUSALEM RESTAURANT 5209 13TH AVENUE	BROOKLYN	NY	11219	
JOE'S KOSHER PIZZA 545 KINGS HIGHWAY	BROOKLYN	NY	11223	(718) 336-4040
KING ARTHUR'S KOSHER DELI 9732 SEAVIEW AVENUE	BROOKLYN	NY	11236	(718) 763-2233
KOSHER COUNTRY-BROOKLYN COLLEGE				
AVENUE H & BEDFORD AVENUE	BROOKLYN	NY	11210	(718) 434-9798
KOSHER DELIGHT 1223 AVENUE J	BROOKLYN	NY	11230	(718) 377-6873
KOSHER DELIGHT 13TH AVENUE AT 46TH STREET	BROOKLYN	NY	11219	(718) 435-8500
KOSHER DELIGHT 710 BRIGHTON BEACH AVENUE	BROOKLYN	NY	11235	(718) 332-1150
KOSHER HUT 709 KINGS HIGHWAY	BROOKLYN	NY	11223	(718) 376-8996
KOSHER PIZZA 5114 13TH AVENUE	BROOKLYN	NY	11219	
KOSHER PRIDE 4924 13TH AVENUE	BROOKLYN	NY	11219	
LA GVINA PIZZARIA 379 KINGSTON AVENUE	BROOKLYN	NY	11213	(718) 778-9500
LANDAU'S GLATT KOSHER DELICATESSEN 65 LEE AVENUE	BROOKLYN	NY	11211	(718) 782-3700
LE GOURMET - GLATT KOSHER 1210 KINGS HIGHWAY	BROOKLYN	NY	11229	(718) 376-8600
LE PALAIS ISRAELI - GREEK RESTAURANT 923 KINGS HIGHWAY	BROOKLYN	NY	11223	(718) 336-2500
LEE KOSHER PIZZA 108 LEE AVENUE	BROOKLYN	NY	11211	(718) 384-9380
LEVY'S KOSHER PIZZA 4810 13TH AVENUE	BROOKLYN	NY	11219	(718) 438-9872
LOU'S KOSHER DELI 514 KINGS HIGHWAY	BROOKLYN	NY	11223	(718) 339-9353
LULU'S KOSHER DELI 107 BRIGHTON BEACH AVENUE	BROOKLYN	NY	11235	
M & D KOSHER PIZZA 380 KINGSTON AVENUE	BROOKLYN	NY	11225	
MASADA RESTAURANT 2178 NOSTRAND AVENUE	BROOKLYN	NY	11223	(718) 434-9835
MCDANIEL'S KOSHER PIZZA 555 KINGS HIGHWAY	BROOKLYN	NY	11223	(718) 627-9668
MENDELES & ABRAHAM 942 MCDONALD AVENUE	BROOKLYN	NY	11218	(718) 436-1702
MILL BASIN KOSHER DELI 5823 AVENUE T	BROOKLYN	NY	11234	(718) 241-4910
NATANYA PIZZA 1506 AVENUE J	BROOKLYN	NY	11230	(718) 258-5160
NATANYA PIZZA 1383 CONEY ISLAND AVENUE	BROOKLYN	NY	11230	
NEW PALACE KOSHER DELI 1906 AVENUE M	BROOKLYN	NY	11230	(718) 339-2650
NOSHERIA FAST FOOD, INC. 4813-13TH AVENUE	BROOKLYN	NY	11219	(718) 436-0400
NOSHIN' GOOD DONUTS 1217 AVENUE J	BROOKLYN	NY	11230	(718) 252-3731

LEVANA ®K
RESTAURANT - CAFE

148 West 67th Street
New York City, N.Y.
(212) 877-8457

full menu and all
baked goods available
for catering and take-out

P & K KOSHER DELI 2001 AVENUE U	BROOKLYN	NY	11229	(718) 646-9700
PALACE, THE 4910-13TH AVENUE	BROOKLYN	NY	11219	(718) 871-7660
RACHEL'S KOSHER LUNCHEONETTE 4926 NEW UTRECHT AVENUE	BROOKLYN	NY	11219	
REGENCY 4910 13 AVENUE	BROOKLYN	NY	11219	(718) 851-7550
REICH'S KOSHER DAIRY RESTAURANT 702 KINGS HIGHWAY	BROOKLYN	NY	11223	
RUTHIE'S RESTAURANT 1427 CONEY ISLAND AVENUE	BROOKLYN	NY	11230	(718) 252-5308
SAM'S KNISHES 504 BRIGHTON BEACH AVENUE	BROOKLYN	NY	11235	(718) 646-5450
SAM'S FAMOUS KNISHES & PIZZA 5006 13TH AVENUE	BROOKLYN	NY	11219	(718) 871-2100
SAMUEL'S RESTAURANT 5508-16TH AVENUE	BROOKLYN	NY	11204	(718) 438-8927
SCHICK'S RESTAURANT 4901-12TH AVENUE	BROOKLYN	NY	11219	(718) 853-6329
SHALOM ISRAELI ORIENTAL FOODS 538 KINGS HIGHWAY	BROOKLYN	NY	11223	(718) 339-8085
SHANG CHAI RESTAURANT 2189 FLATBUSH AVENUE	BROOKLYN	NY	11234	(718) 377-6100
SHARONE KOSHER PIZZA 4916 13TH AVENUE	BROOKLYN	NY	11219	(718) 438-8800
SHAY'S RESTAURANT 4819 16TH AVENUE	BROOKLYN	NY	11204	
SHELANU ISRAELI & SYRIAN RESTAURANT 521 KINGS HIGHWAY	BROOKLYN	NY	11223	(718) 339-0612
SHMUEL'S PIZZA 162 KINGS HIGHWAY	BROOKLYN	NY	11223	
WEISS KOSHER DAIRY RESTAURANT 1369 CONEY ISLAND AVENUE	BROOKLYN	NY	11230	(718) 253-9494
WILLIAMSBURG KOSHER PIZZA 216 WILLIAMSBURG STREET W.	BROOKLYN	NY	11211	(718) 384-2540
WILLIAMSBURG RESTAURANT 214 ROSS STREET	BROOKLYN	NY	11211	(718) 384-2540
WINDSOR KOSHER DELI 2281 NOSTRAND AVENUE	BROOKLYN	NY	11210	(718) 377-1476
YUN KEE 1424 ELM AVENUE	BROOKLYN	NY	11230	(718) 627-0072
ZEL-MAR KOSHER DELI 509 BRIGHTON BEACH AVENUE	BROOKLYN	NY	11235	(718) 646-9751
MASTMAN'S KORNER DELICATESSEN 1322 HERTEL AVENUE	BUFFALO	NY	14216	(716) 877-9446
BURGER NOSH 530 CENTRAL AVENUE	CEDARHURST	NY	11559	(516) 569-6183
DELICIOUS KOSHER DAIRY RESTAURANT 698 CENTRAL AVENUE	CEDARHURST	NY	11559	(516) 569-6725
JACOB'S LADDER 83 SPRUCE STREET	CEDARHURST	NY	11559	(516) 569-3373
KING DAVID RESTAURANT & CATERERS 550 CENTRAL AVENUE	CEDARHURST	NY	11516	(516) 569-2920
SABRA KOSHER PIZZA 560 CENTRAL AVENUE	CEDARHURST	NY	11516	(516) 569-1563
BRODIE'S KOSHER DELICATESSEN 1518 FRONT	EAST MEADOW	NY	11554	(516) 483-5382
BENJY'S KOSHER PIZZA 72-72 MAIN STREET	FLUSHING	NY	11367	(718) 268-0791
DAVID'S KNISHES 67-11 MAIN STREET	FLUSHING	NY	11367	(718) 520-8892
LEVY'S KOSHER PIZZA 68-28 MAIN STREET	FLUSHING	NY	11367	
LINDEN HILLS KOSHER DELI 29-20 UNION STREET	FLUSHING	NY	11354	(718) 762-1515
NAOMI LEVY'S KOSHER PIZZA 68-28 MAIN STREET	FLUSHING	NY	11367	
NATURE'S NOSH 67-03 MAIN STREET	FLUSHING	NY	11367	(718) 268-4010
QUEENS COLLEGE KOSHER CAFETERIA KISSENA BLVD	FLUSHING	NY	11367	
SURREY KOSHER DELICATESSEN & RESTAURANT				
179-08 UNION TURNPIKE	FLUSHING	NY	11366	(718) 658-9243
BERSO 64-20 108 STREET	FOREST HILLS	NY	11375	(718) 275-9793
BOULEVARD KOSHER DELI 98-02 QUEENS BLVD	FOREST HILLS	NY	11374	(718) 896-0900
JOMAN KOSHER DELI 97-20 QUEENS BLVD	FOREST HILLS	NY	11374	
KATZ'S KOSHER DELI 98-102 QUEENS BLVD	FOREST HILLS	NY	11374	(718) 896-0900
KNISH NOSH 101-02 QUEENS BLVD	FOREST HILLS	NY	11374	(718) 897-5554
LEVY'S KOSHER PIZZA 93-01 63RD DRIVE	FOREST HILLS	NY	11374	
SAM'S ZION KOSHER PIZZA 63-45 108TH STREET	FOREST HILLS	NY	11375	(718) 897-0907
STARK'S KOSHER RESTAURANT 63-55 108TH STREET	FOREST HILLS	NY	11375	
ZION PIZZA CORP 63-46 108TH STREET	FOREST HILLS	NY	11375	(718) 897-0907
CAFE SHALOM 188-02 UNION TURNPIKE	FRESH MEADOWS	NY	11366	(718) 479-2600
DELI-MASTERS KOSHER DELICATESSEN & RESTAURANT				
184-02 HORACE HARDING BOULEVARD	FRESH MEADOWS	NY	11365	(718) 353-3030
MENORAH RESTAURANT 178 MIDDLE NECK ROAD	GREAT NECK	NY	11023	(516) 466-8181
BEN'S KOSHER GOURMET RESTAURANTS & CATERERS				
140 WHEATLEY PLAZA	GREENVALE	NY		(516) 621-3340
EPSTEIN'S KOSHER DELICATESSEN & RESTAURANT				
389 CENTRAL AVENUE	HARTSDALE	NY	10530	(914) 428-5320
WOODRO KOSHER DELICATESSEN & RESTAURANT				
1342 PENINSULA BLVD	HEWLETT	NY	11557	(516) 791-4033
HAPPY'S KOSHER DELI & APPETIZING 82-41 153RD AVENUE	HOWARD BEACH	NY	11433	(718) 641-4007
PATIO KOSHER DELICATESSEN & RESTAURANT				
78-16A LINDEN BLVD	HOWARD BEACH	NY	11433	(718) 296-3064
MURRAY'S KOSHER DELI 75-16 37TH AVENUE	JACKSON HEIGHTS	NY	11377	(718) 639-8016
SUTPHIN KOSHER DELICATESSEN 87-71 SUTPHIN BLVD	JAMAICA	NY	11435	(718) 526-9591
BURGER NOSH 69-74 MAIN STREET	KEW GARDENS HILLS	NY	11367	(718) 793-6927
NOT JUST DONUTS 72-04A MAIN STREET	KEW GARDENS HILLS	NY	11367	(718) 268-7830
SHIMON'S KOSHER PIZZA FALAFEL 71-24 MAIN STREET	KEW GARDENS HILLS	NY	11367	(718) 793-1491
TAIN LEE CHOW 72-24 MAIN STREET	KEW GARDENS HILLS	NY	11367	(718) 268-0960
B & H KOSHER DELI 4811 43RD AVENUE	LONG ISLAND CITY	NY	11377	(718) 457-9052
WILLY'S KOSHER DELICATESSEN				
75-12 METROPOLITAN AVENUE	MIDDLE VILLAGE	NY	11379	(718) 326-7358

EUROPEAN HOMEMADE FOODS 82 ROUTE 59 . . . . MONSEY NY 10952   (914) 356-9555
KOSHER DELIGHT 82 ROUTE 59 . . . . MONSEY NY 10952   (914) 356-9555
TOV TAAM DAIRY RESTAURANT 32 MAIN STREET . . . . MONSEY NY 10952   (914) 352-0207
B'TEAVON LUNCHEONETTE, INC. 2549 AMSTERDAM AVENUE . . . . NEW YORK NY 10033   (212) 496-5018
BENJAMIN OF TUDELA 307 AMSTERDAM AVENUE . . . . NEW YORK NY 10023   (212) 496-5018
BERNSTEIN'S ON ESSEX STREET 135 ESSEX STREET . . . . NEW YORK NY 10002   (212) 473-3900
BOYCHIK'S 19 WEST 45TH STREET . . . . NEW YORK NY 10036   (212) 719-5999
BROWNIE'S CREATIVE COOKERY 21 EAST 16TH STREET . . . . NEW YORK NY 10003   (212) 255-2838
CAFE MASADA 1239 FIRST AVENUE AT 67 ST . . . . NEW YORK NY 10021   (212) 988-0950
CAFE MISADAH 49 WHITE STREET . . . . NEW YORK NY 10013   (212) 966-7141
CALDRON RESTAURANT 308 EAST 6TH STREET . . . . NEW YORK NY 10003   (212) 473-9543
CHANDRA GARDENS VEGETARIAN RESTAURANT
   310 E. 86TH STREET (BTWN. 1ST & 2ND AVENUE) . . . . NEW YORK NY 10028   (212) 628-2642
CHOPSIE'S PIZZA 2500 AMSTERDAM AVENUE . . . . NEW YORK NY 10033   (212) 568-1637
CONTINENTAL KOSHER DELICATESSEN & RESTAURANT
   732 WEST 181ST STREET . . . . NEW YORK NY 10033   (212) 928-9661
CORNUCOPIA KOSHER DELICATESSEN & APPETIZERS
   1651 SECOND AVENUE . . . . NEW YORK NY 10028   (212) 879-0733
DAIRY PLANET 182 BROADWAY (CORNER JOHN STREET) . . . . NEW YORK NY 10038   (212) 227-8252
DELI CITY 7 WEST 47TH STREET . . . . NEW YORK NY 10036   (212) 819-0202
DELI GLATT CORPORATION 152 FULTON STREET . . . . NEW YORK NY 10038   (212) 349-3622
DELI-ART KOSHER DELICATESSEN 333 SEVENTH AVENUE . . . . NEW YORK NY 10001   (212) 564-5994
DIAMOND KOSHER DAIRY LUNCHEONETTE 4 WEST 47TH STREET . . . . NEW YORK NY 10036   (212) 719-2694
EDNA'S RESTAURANT & DELI 401 GRAND STREET . . . . NEW YORK NY 10002   (212) 473-7630
EL AVRAM 80 GROVE STREET . . . . NEW YORK NY 10014   (212) 243-9661
ELI'S GLATT KOSHER DELI & BAKERY 1026 AVENUE OF THE AMERICAS . . NEW YORK NY 10018   (212) 382-2494
ESTHER'S DAIRY RESTAURANT 165 MADISON AVENUE . . . . NEW YORK NY 10016   (212) 685-7290
FAMOUS RESTAURANT (DAIRY) 222 WEST 72ND STREET . . . . NEW YORK NY 10023   (212) 595-8487
FINE & SHAPIRO 138 WEST 72ND STREET . . . . NEW YORK NY 10023   (212) 877-2874

FRIEDMAN'S KOSHER DAIRY RESTAURANT 43 CANAL STREET . . . . NEW YORK NY 10002   (212) 226-9444
GEFEN KOSHER DAIRY RESTAURANT 297 7TH AVENUE . . . . NEW YORK NY 10001   (212) 929-6476
GIRLCHIK'S 155 W. 47TH STREET . . . . NEW YORK NY 10036   (212) 391-2033
GLATT NOSH 884 AVENUE OF THE AMERICAS . . . . NEW YORK NY 10001   (212) 684-0530
GRANDMA'S COOKIE JAR 2543 AMSTERDAM AVENUE . . . . NEW YORK NY 10033   (212) 568-4855
GREAT AMERICAN HEALTH BAR
   55 JOHN ST. (BET. NASSAU & WILLIAM) . . . . NEW YORK NY 10038   (212) 227-6100
GREAT AMERICAN HEALTH BAR
   2 PARK AVENUE (BET. 32ND & 33RD STREETS) . . . . NEW YORK NY 10016   (212) 685-7117
GREAT AMERICAN HEALTH BAR
   154 E. 43RD ST. (BET. 3RD & LEX. AVES. GRAND CENTRAL) . . . . NEW YORK NY 10017   (212) 682-5656
GREENER PASTURES 117 EAST 60TH STREET . . . . NEW YORK NY 10022   (212) 832-3212
GROSS' DAIRY RESTAURANT 1372 BROADWAY . . . . NEW YORK NY 10018   (212) 921-1969
HENRY'S KOSHER DELICATESSEN & RESTAURANT
   195 EAST HOUSTON STREET . . . . NEW YORK NY 10002   (212) 674-2200
HERSHEY'S DAIRY RESTAURANT 167 WEST 29TH STREET . . . . NEW YORK NY 10001   (212) 868-6988
JERUSALEM II 1375 BROADWAY . . . . NEW YORK NY 10018   (212) 398-1475
JERUSALEM II 112 FULTON STREET . . . . NEW YORK NY 10038   (212) 732-6523
JEWISH THEOLOGICAL SEMINARY 3080 BROADWAY . . . . NEW YORK NY 10027   (212) 678-8000
JUST-A-BITE 106 GREENWICH STREET . . . . NEW YORK NY 10006   (212) 425-5470
KOSHER DELIGHT 1359 BROADWAY . . . . NEW YORK NY 10036   (212) 563-3366
KOSHER HUT 866 6TH AVENUE . . . . NEW YORK NY 10001   (212) 686-8319
KOSHER INN #2, INC. 2500 AMSTERDAM AVENUE . . . . NEW YORK NY 10033   (212) 927-5858
LA DIFFERENCE - HOTEL ROOSEVELT
   MADISON AVENUE & 45TH STREET . . . . NEW YORK NY 10017   (212) 697-7000
LA FRELLA 121 UNIVERSITY PLACE . . . . NEW YORK NY 10003   (212) 420-1300
LEVANA RESTAURANT-CAFE 148 WEST 67TH STREET . . . . NEW YORK NY 10023   (212) 877-8457
LOIS LANE'S NINTH & NATURAL 580 9TH AVENUE AT 42 ST. . . . . NEW YORK NY   (212) 695-5055
LOU G. SIEGEL'S 209 WEST 38TH STREET . . . . NEW YORK NY 10018   (212) 921-4433

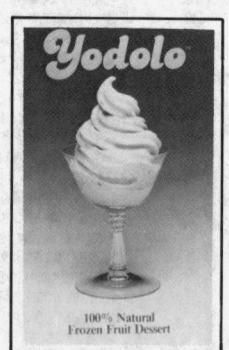

MACCABEEM RESTAURANT 147 WEST 47TH STREET	NEW YORK	NY	10036	(212) 575-0226
MARCY KOSHER DELICATESSEN 2511 BROADWAY	NEW YORK	NY	10025	(212) 222-0700
MARRAKESH WEST 149 BLEEKER STREET	NEW YORK	NY	10012	(212) 777-8911
MCDOVID'S 2502 AMSTERDAM AVENUE	NEW YORK	NY	10033	(212) 928-4497
MEAL MART 2189 BROADWAY	NEW YORK	NY	10024	(212) 787-4720
MOSHE PEKING 40 WEST 37TH STREET	NEW YORK	NY	10018	(212) 594-6500
N.Y. PITA DEPOT 267 AMSTERDAM AVENUE	NEW YORK	NY	10023	(212) 724-6000
NOGA - MEDITERRANEAN CABARET 40 WEST 8TH STREET	NEW YORK	NY	10011	(212) 473-3361
RATNER'S DAIRY RESTAURANT 138 DELANCEY STREET	NEW YORK	NY	10002	(212) 677-5588
SAM'S FAMOUS KNISHES (DAIRY) 25 CANAL STREET	NEW YORK	NY	10002	(212) 598-9186
SAM'S KOSHER DELICATESSEN 37 ESSEX STREET	NEW YORK	NY	10002	(212) 674-0980
SECOND AVENUE DELICATESSEN & RESTAURANT 156 SECOND AVENUE	NEW YORK	NY	10003	(212) 677-0606
SHALOM JAPAN 22 WOOSTER STREET	NEW YORK	NY	10013	(212) 925-0930
SOMEPLACE SPECIAL DELI-RESTAURANT 401 GRAND STREET	NEW YORK	NY	10002	(212) 674-0980
STEINBERG'S DAIRY RESTAURANT 21 ESSEX STREET	NEW YORK	NY	10002	(212) 254-7787
STERN COLLEGE CAFETERIA 245 LEXINGTON AVENUE	NEW YORK	NY	10016	(212) 481-0560
WEST 35TH ST. DAIRY 218 W. 35 STREET	NEW YORK	NY	10001	(212) 947-2167
YAHALOM RESTAURANT 49 WEST 47TH STREET	NEW YORK	NY	10036	(212) 575-1699
YESHIVA UNIVERSITY CAFETERIA 2501 AMSTERDAM AVENUE	NEW YORK	NY	10033	(212) 960-5390
HUNKI'S KOSHER PIZZA & FALAFEL 3300 LONG BEACH ROAD	OCEANSIDE	NY	11572	(516) 766-3666
PELHAM KOSHER RESTAURANT 91 WOLF LANE	PELHAM	NY		(914) 738-1617
BEN'S KOSHER DELICATESSEN & RESTAURANT 96-40 QUEENS BLVD.	REGO PARK	NY	11374	(718) 897-1700
CAFE BABA OF ISRAEL 91-33 63RD DRIVE	REGO PARK	NY	11374	(718) 275-2660
FLAME-LAPID, THE 97-04 QUEENS BLVD	REGO PARK	NY	11374	(718) 275-1403
MAMA'S PLACE 97-28 63RD RD.	REGO PARK	NY	11374	(718) 896-9627
PIZZA FALAFEL OF QUEENS 93-01 63RD DRIVE	REGO PARK	NY	11374	(718) 897-5111
FLASH KOSHER PIZZA 3602 RIVERDALE AVENUE	RIVERDALE	NY	10463	(212) 543-1811
CHOLOV YISROEL PIZZA MAIN STREET	SOUTH FALLSBURG	NY	12779	(914) 434-5845
ROADSIDE DAIRY RESTAURANT ROUTE 42	SOUTH FALLSBURG	NY	12779	
GARTNER'S INN HUNGRY HOLLOW ROAD	SPRING VALLEY	NY	10977	(914) 356-0875
HERSHEY'S KOSHER RESTAURANT 33 MAPLE AVENUE	SPRING VALLEY	NY	10977	(914) 352-9720
CAFE NETANYA 2811 RICHMOND AVENUE	STATEN ISLAND	NY	10314	(718) 494-4484
MEL'S MILCHIG DINER 2016 VICTORY BLVD	STATEN ISLAND	NY	10314	(718) 273-6593
PICKLES UNLIMITED 4469 EAST GENESEE	SYRACUSE	NY		(315) 445-1294
BAGEL CRAFT OF HEMPSTEAD 118 HEMPSTEAD TPKE	WEST HEMPSTEAD	NY	11552	(516) 485-2314
KOSHER COTTAGE 338 HEMPSTEAD AVENUE	WEST HEMPSTEAD	NY	11552	(516) 486-8362
SQUARE KOSHER DELICATESSEN 20-14 FRANCIS LEWIS BLVD	WHITESTONE	NY	11435	(718) 746-9222
DELI COUNTRY MAIN STREET	WOODBOURNE	NY	12788	(914) 434-2298
WOODBOURNE KOSHER PIZZA 398 MAIN STREET	WOODBOURNE	NY	12788	(914) 434-4790
PIZZA PIOUS 1063 BROADWAY	WOODMERE	NY	11598	(516) 295-2050
PILDERS KOSHER FOODS 7601 READING STREET	CINCINNATI	OH	45215	(513) 821-7050
DELI CELLAR 11291 EUCLID AVENUE, HILLEL BUILDING - CWRU	CLEVELAND	OH	44106	(216) 231-0040
KINNERET KOSHER RESTAURANT 1869 SOUTH TAYLOR ROAD	CLEVELAND	OH	44118	(216) 321-1404
KOSHER KORNER 1026 SOUTH TAYLOR ROAD	CLEVELAND	OH	44118	(216) 321-6308
THE DELI 1805 SOUTH TAYLOR ROAD	CLEVELAND	OH	44118	(216) 321-9545
THE DINING ROOM 1805 SOUTH TAYLOR ROAD	CLEVELAND	OH	44118	(216) 321-9545
VEGETARIA 2057 CORNELL ROAD	CLEVELAND	OH	44118	(216) 791-9914
HARRY'S APPETIZER & DELICATESSEN 2072 SOUTH TAYLOR ROAD	CLEVELAND HEIGHTS	OH	44118	(216) 932-5000
SIEGLER'S DELICATESSEN & FOOD MARKET 15 WEST BANCROFT	TOLEDO	OH	43603	(419) 243-6264
SIEGLER'S DELICATESSEN & FOOD MARKET 2636 WEST CENTRAL	TOLEDO	OH	43603	(419) 473-2791
KRAVITZ'S DELICATESSEN 3135 BELMONT	YOUNGSTOWN	OH		(216) 544-3842
NEWPORT DELICATESSEN & SANDWICH SHOP 4609 HILLMAN WAY	YOUNGSTOWN	OH		(216) 782-4213
SPIEGLE'S DELICATESSEN & GOURMET SHOP UNION SQUARE	YOUNGSTOWN	OH		(216) 746-1993
BAYCREST JEWISH CENTRE HOME FOR THE AGED 3560 BATHURST STREET	TORONTO	ON		(416) 789-5131
MALKAT PEKING 2436 BATHURST STREET	TORONTO	ON		(416) 783-9345
MALKAT PEKING 3426 BATHHURST STREET	TORONTO	ON		(416) 783-9345
MARKY'S DELICATESSEN 280 WILSON	TORONTO	ON		(416) 638-1081
MATI'S FALAFEL HOUSE 3430 BATHURST STREET	TORONTO	ON		(416) 783-9505
PERL'S MEAT & DELICATESSEN PRODUCTS 3013 BATHURST STREET	TORONTO	ON		(416) 787-4234
GOLD CUTS 245 S. 17TH STREET	PHILADELPHIA	PA		(212) 735-4762
ABE'S DELICATESSEN & RESTAURANT 325 PENN AVENUE	SCRANTON	PA		(717) 342-4517
DELI PEKING 6900 DECARIE BLVD	MONTREAL	QU		(514) 738-2844
DAVIS' DAIRY PRODUCTS COMPANY 721 HOPE STREET	PROVIDENCE	RI	02906	(401) 331-4239
JEWISH COMMUNITY CENTER KOSHER RESTAURANT 1400 WEST PROSPECT AVENUE	MILWAUKEE	WI		(414) 276-0716

RETIREMENT HOMES

KIVEL MANOR 3040 NORTH 36TH STREET	PHOENIX	AZ	85018	(602) 956-0150
BETH AVOT 7721 BEVERLY BOULEVARD	LOS ANGELES	CA	90048	(213) 932-8889
BEVERLY HILLS CARMEL RETIREMENT HOTEL 8750 BURTON WAY	LOS ANGELES	CA	90048	(213) 278-9720
BEVERLY HILLS GARDENS 1470 SOUTH ROBERTSON BOULEVARD	LOS ANGELES	CA	90035	(213) 273-3668
BEVERLY SINAI TOWERS 8435 BEVERLY BOULEVARD	LOS ANGELES	CA	90048	(213) 852-9237
FLORA TERRACE RETIREMENT HOTEL 6070 WEST PICO BOULEVARD	LOS ANGELES	CA	90035	(213) 653-5565
GOLDEN STATE RETIREMENT HOTEL 4340 LOCKWOOD	LOS ANGELES	CA	90036	(213) 663-2153
SHALOM KOSHER HOTEL 330 NORTH HAYWORTH	LOS ANGELES	CA	90036	(213) 655-1500
ROYAL BELLINGHAM 12229 CHANDLER BOULEVARD	NORTH HOLLYWOOD	CA	91607	(818) 980-2997
BEACH FRONT GUEST HOME 20 OZONE AVENUE	VENICE	CA	90291	(213) 396-0206
MOUNT CARMEL GARDENS 5846 MT. CARMEL TERRACE	JACKSONVILLE	FL	33216	(904) 733-6696
WILTON HOTEL 1039 WEST LAWRENCE	CHICAGO	IL	60640	(312) 561-1133
DELCREST 8350 DELCREST DRIVE	ST. LOUIS	MO	63124	(314) 991-2055
MIRIAM APARTMENTS 127 HAZEL STREET	CLIFTON	NJ	07011	(201) 772-9383
QUEEN ESTHER HOME FOR ADULTS 124-05 ROCKAWAY BEACH BOULEVARD	BELLE HARBOR	NY	11694	(718) 474-0400
HARBOR VIEW HOTEL 3900 SHORE PARKWAY	BROOKLYN	NY	11235	(718) 769-9700
OCEAN BREEZE HOTEL 3811 SURF AVENUE	BROOKLYN	NY	11235	(718) 266-1456
PARK SHORE MANOR 1555 ROCKAWAY PARKWAY	BROOKLYN	NY	11236	(718) 498-6400
SCHAROME MANOR 631 FOSTER AVENUE	BROOKLYN	NY	11230	(718) 859-2499
SCHARF MANOR HOME FOR ADULTS 112-14 CORONA AVENUE	CORONA	NY	11368	(718) 699-4100
ROCKAWAY MANOR HOME 145 BEACH 8TH STREET	FAR ROCKAWAY	NY	11691	(718) 327-6300
HOMESTEAD HOME 82-45 GRENFELL STREET	KEW GARDENS	NY	11415	(718) 441-2000
AMBASSADOR MANOR 351 WEST BROADWAY	LONG BEACH	NY	11561	(516) 431-2200
ATLANTIC HOME FOR ADULTS 125 EAST BROADWAY	LONG BEACH	NY	11561	(516) 432-6300
BRIGHTON MANOR HOME 403 EAST BROADWAY	LONG BEACH	NY	11561	(516) 431-0200
BROADWAY MANOR 165 EAST BROADWAY	LONG BEACH	NY	11561	(516) 431-5400
CROWN HOME FOR ADULTS 172 WEST BROADWAY	LONG BEACH	NY	11561	(516) 889-8900
KING DAVID MANOR 80 WEST BROADWAY	LONG BEACH	NY	11561	(516) 889-1300
LINCOLN HOME FOR ADULTS 405 EAST BROADWAY	LONG BEACH	NY	11561	(516) 889-7100
PALACE HOTEL 275 EAST BROADWAY	LONG BEACH	NY	11561	(516) 432-9000
PROMENADE HOME FOR ADULTS 102 WEST BROADWAY	LONG BEACH	NY	11561	(516) 431-0100
SCHARF MANOR 274 WEST BROADWAY	LONG BEACH	NY	11561	(516) 431-1400
PHILADA APARTMENTS 7732 GREENLAND PLACE	CINCINNATI	OH	45237	(513) 761-5544
COUNCIL GARDENS 2501 TAYLOR ROAD	CLEVELAND	OH	44118	(216) 382-8625
YORK HOUSE YORK ROAD AND SOMERVILLE AVENUE	PHILADELPHIA	PA	19141	(215) 456-2906
RIVERVIEW APARTMENTS GARETTA STREET	PITTSBURGH	PA	15217	(412) 521-7876
ROSE GARDEN SENIOR CITIZENS HOME 4387 BURRET	MONTREAL	QU		(514) 733-6625
JEWISH COMMUNITY COUNCIL 5601 SOUTH BRAESWOOD BOULEVARD	HOUSTON	TX	77035	(713) 729-3200

RETREAT CENTER & SITES

NATIONAL JEWISH RESOURCE CENTER 421 SEVENTH AVENUE	NEW YORK	NY	10001	(212) 714-9500
DR. ELLIOT UDELL (PROFESSIONAL SINGLES)	PLAINVIEW	NY		(516) 349-7125

RUBBER STAMPS

COMMERCIAL STAMP COMPANY 106 DEKALB AVENUE	BROOKLYN	NY	11215	(718) 858-3880

SAFES - ISRAELI

ACME SAFE COMPANY 150 LAFAYETTE STREET	NEW YORK	NY	10013	(212) 226-2500
I. S. M. (MAXIMUM SECURITY SAFES FROM ISRAEL) 103 GRAND STREET	NEW YORK	NY	10002	(212) 226-1969
ISM-RICHARD KRASILOVSKY 103 GRAND STREET	NEW YORK	NY	10002	(212) 226-1969
ISRAEL SAFES MANUFACTURING CO.,LTD. 103 GRAND STREET	NEW YORK	NY	10002	(212) 226-1969

SCHOOLS - ART

HEBREW ARTS SCHOOL 129 WEST 67TH STREET	NEW YORK	NY	10023	(212) 362-8060
SAIDYE BRONFMAN CENTRE 5170 COTE ST. CATHERINE	MONTREAL	QU	H3W 1M7	(514) 739-2301

SCHOOLS - SPECIAL EDUCATION & LEARNING DISABILITY

GATEWAYS HOSPITAL & COMMUNITY MENTAL HEALTH CENTER 1891 EFFIE STREET	LOS ANGELES	CA	90026	(213) 666-0171
HOPE CENTER FOR THE RETARDED 3601 EAST 32ND AVENUE	DENVER	CO	80205	(303) 388-4308
JEWISH CHILDREN'S BUREAU 1 SOUTH FRANKLIN STREET	CHICAGO	IL	60606	(312) 346-6700
MICHAEL REESE HOSPITAL & MEDICAL CENTER 29TH STREET AND ELLIS AVENUE	CHICAGO	IL	60616	(312) 791-2000
TEMPLE KEHILATH ISRAEL D. CARE/EDUC. SVCS. FOR RETARDED CHLDN 384 HARVARD STREET	BROOKLINE	MA	02146	(617) 277-9155
TORAH WORKSHOP DAY CARE/EDUC. SERVICE FOR RETARDED CHILDREN 1 HENDERSON	WEST CALDWELL	NJ		(201) 575-6050
SHIELD INSTITUTE FOR RETARDED CHILDREN 1800 ANDREWS AVENUE	BRONX	NY	10453	(212) 731-0481
BROOKLYN HEBREW SCHOOL FOR SPECIAL CHILDREN 376 BAY 44TH STREET	BROOKLYN	NY	11214	(718) 946-9700
CAMP HUNTINGTON C/O DR. KURTZER 1017 EAST 80TH STREET	BROOKLYN	NY	11236	(718) 633-1591
COMMUNITY SCHOOL BETH MOSHE 913 49TH STREET	BROOKLYN	NY	11219	
HEBREW ACADEMY FOR SPECIAL CHILDREN 1311 55TH STREET	BROOKLYN	NY	11219	(718) 851-6100
HEBREW INSTITUTE FOR THE DEAF 2025 67TH STREET	BROOKLYN	NY	11204	(718) 259-2626
ORTHODOX TORAH SERVICES & ADVOCACY FOR THE RETARDED 1717 15TH STREET	BROOKLYN	NY	11229	(718) 376-0557
PTACH 1363 49TH STREET	BROOKLYN	NY	11219	(718) 854-8600
PESHA SOLOVEICHIK DAY SCHOOL - SPECIAL CHILDREN 376 BAY 44TH STREET	BROOKLYN	NY	11214	
PRIDE OF JUDEA CHILDREN'S SERVICES 1000 DUMONT AVENUE	BROOKLYN	NY	11208	
THE JEWISH CENTER FOR SPECIAL EDUCATION 430 KENT AVENUE	BROOKLYN	NY	11211	(718) 782-0064
YESHIVA BAIS SHALOM ALTERNATIVE SCHOOL 555 REMSEN AVENUE	BROOKLYN	NY	11236	(718) 495-2100
YESHIVA CHESED YISROEL 2422 AVENUE K	BROOKLYN	NY	11230	(718) 338-8300
MAIMONIDES SCHOOL FOR EXCEPTIONAL CHILDREN 3401 MOTT AVENUE	FAR ROCKAWAY	NY	11691	(718) 471-0100
MAIMONIDES DAY SCHOOL & RESIDENTIAL CENTER FOR SPECIAL CHILDREN	MONTICELLO	NY	12701	
NATIONAL COMMISSION ON TORAH EDUCATION 500 WEST 185TH STREET	NEW YORK	NY	10033	(212) 960-5400
PTACH PROGRAM, MARSHA STERN TALMUDICAL ACADEMY, YU HIGH SCH AMSTERDAM AVENUE & 186TH STREET	NEW YORK	NY	10033	(212) 960-5337
SHALAYIM, UNITED SYNAGOGUE DEPARTMENT OF EDUCATION 155 FIFTH AVENUE	NEW YORK	NY	10010	(212) 553-7800
TIKVAH PROGRAM, NATIONAL RAMAH COMMISSION 3080 BROADWAY	NEW YORK	NY	10027	

HEBREW ACADEMY FOR SPECIAL CHILDREN ... PARKSVILLE **NY** 12768
SUBURBAN EAST SCHOOL OF PVA 3031 MONTICELLO BOULEVARD ... CLEVELAND **OH** 44118
WOODS SCHOOLS, THE ROUTE 213 ... LANGHORNE **PA** 19047 (215) 757-3731
HAR ZION RELIGIOUS SCHOOL HAGYS FORK AT HOLLOW ROAD ... PENN VALLEY **PA** 19072 (215) 667-5002
ADATH ZION BRANCH OF THE UNITED HEBREW SCHOOLS PENNWAY & FRIENDSHIP STREETS ... PHILADELPHIA **PA** 19111 (215) 742-8500
BETH T'FILLAH BRANCH OF THE UNITED HEBREW SCHOOLS 7630 WOODBINE AVENUE ... PHILADELPHIA **PA** 19151 (215) 477-9146
PENNSYLVANIA SCHOOL FOR THE DEAF 7500 GERMANTOWN AVENUE ... PHILADELPHIA **PA** 19119 (215) 247-9700
PHILADELPHIA PSYCHIATRIC CENTER FORD ROAD AND MONUMENT AVENUE ... PHILADELPHIA **PA** 19131
SCHOOL OF OBSERVATION & PRACTICE 701 BYBERRY ROAD ... PHILADELPHIA **PA** 19116 (215) 677-7261
CAMP WOODEN ACRES C/O JEWISH COMMUNITY CAMPS 5151 COTE STE. CATHERINE ROAD #203 ... MONTREAL **QU**
MIRIAM HOME FOR THE EXCEPTIONAL CHILD 4321 GUIMONT ... MONTREAL **QU**

SCHOOLS - TECHNICAL

COPE INSTITUTE 4419 18TH AVENUE ... BROOKLYN **NY** 11204 (718) 436-1700
SHEVET Y'HUDAH RESNICK INSTITUTE OF TECHNOLOGY 670 ROCKAWAY PARKWAY ... BROOKLYN **NY** 11236 (718) 342-6878
SYRIT COMPUTER SCHOOL 5220 13TH AVENUE ... BROOKLYN **NY** 11219 (718) 853-1212
BRAMSON ORT 44 E. 23 STREET ... NEW YORK **NY** 10010 (212) 677-7420

SCIENTIFIC ORGANIZATIONS

ASSOCIATION OF ORTHODOX JEWISH SCIENTISTS 45 WEST 36TH STREET ... NEW YORK **NY** 10018 (212) 695-7525
SOCIETY OF JEWISH SCIENCE P.O. BOX 114, 825 ROUND SWAMP ROAD ... OLD BETHPAGE **NY** 11804 (516) 249-6262

SCOUTING

NATIONAL JEWISH COMMITTEE ON SCOUTING-BOY SCOUTS OF AMERICA ... NEW BRUNSWICK **NJ** 08902 (201) 249-6000
BOY SCOUTS OF AMERICA, NATIONAL DIRECTOR OF JEWISH RELATIONS ... NORTH BRUNSWICK **NJ** 08902 (201) 821-6500
JEWISH COMM. ON SCOUTING-BERGEN COUNCIL, BOY SCOUTS OF AMER. 1060 MAIN STREET ... RIVER EDGE **NJ** 07661
JEWISH COMMITTEE ON SCOUTING 4314 SILSBY ROAD ... CLEVELAND **OH** 44118 (216) 381-6788
NATIONAL JEWISH COMMITTEE ON SCOUTING P.O. BOX 61030 ... DALLAS-FT WORTH AIRP **TX** 75261 (214) 659-2000

SCULPTORS

EMANUEL MILSTEIN R.D. 1, BOX 81C ... MARLBORO **NJ** 07746 (201) 946-8604
JANE TELLER 200 PROSPECT AVENUE ... PRINCETON **NJ** 08540 (619) 924-6371
PHIL KUZNEZOFF 773 TOBIA ROAD ... SOMERVILLE **NJ** 08876 (201) 725-1333
ERNA WEILL 886 ALPINE DRIVE ... TEANECK **NJ** 07666 (201) 837-1627
EDELWEISS CO. - GLASS STUDIO 1217 49TH STREET ... BROOKLYN **NY** 11219 (718) 851-9687
SAMPSON SEYMOUR ENGOREN 11 HOLMES PLACE ... LYNBROOK **NY** 11563 (516) 599-3173
EFREM WEITZMAN - SYNAGOGUE ART 334 WEST 86TH STREET ... NEW YORK **NY** 10024 (212) 877-6590
SHAMIR STUDIO 609 KAPPOCK STREET ... RIVERDALE **NY** 10463 (212) 695-5378

SEA TRAVEL

ADRIATICA 437 MADISON ... NEW YORK **NY** 10017 (212) 838-2113
CHANDRIS CRUISES 666 FIFTH AVENUE ... NEW YORK **NY** 10022 (212) 586-8370
EPIROTIKI LINES 551 FIFTH AVENUE ... NEW YORK **NY** 10017 (212) 599-1750
HELLENIC MEDITERRANEAN LINES 200 PARK AVENUE ... NEW YORK **NY** 10017 (212) 697-4220
PRUDENTIAL LINES 1 WORLD TRADE CENTER ... NEW YORK **NY** 10005 (212) 775-0550
ZIM PASSENGER LINES 1 WORLD TRADE CENTER ... NEW YORK **NY** 10047 (212) 432-0300

SECURITIES

AMPAL-AMERICAN ISRAEL CORPORATION 6501 WILSHIRE BOULEVARD ... LOS ANGELES **CA** 90048 (213) 653-5633
AMPAL SECURITIES CORPORATION 10 ROCKEFELLER PLAZA ... NEW YORK **NY** 10020 (212) 586-3232
AMPAL-AMERICAN ISRAEL CORPORATION 10 ROCKEFELLER PLAZA ... NEW YORK **NY** 10020 (212) 586-3232
H.L.WOLF & COMPANY 120 WALL STREET, SUITE 1044 ... NEW YORK **NY** 10005 (212) 425-2315
ISRAEL BOND DISCOUNTERS 120 WALL STREET ... NEW YORK **NY** 10005 (212) 344-6676
ISRAEL SECURITIES 10 ROCKEFELLER PLAZA ... NEW YORK **NY** 10020 (212) 541-7568
LEUMI SECURITIES CORPORATION 18 EAST 48TH STREET ... NEW YORK **NY** 10017 (212) 759-1310
TRANSMITTAL SECURITIES CORP. 82 WALL STREET ... NEW YORK **NY** 10005 (212) 344-8245

SEMINARIES

BAIS CHANA WOMEN'S INSTITUTE 15 MONTCALM COURT ... ST. PAUL **MN** 55116 (612) 698-3858
BETH JACOB TEACHERS SEMINARY OF AMERICA 132 S. 8TH STREET ... BROOKLYN **NY** 11211 (718) 388-2701
MACHON CHANA WOMAN'S INSTITUTE 733 EASTERN PARKWAY ... BROOKLYN **NY** 11213 (718) 735-0217
MAIMONIDES HEBREW TEACHER'S COLLEGE 701 48TH STREET ... BROOKLYN **NY** 11220 (718) 871-0913
SARA SCHENIRER HIGH SCHOOL & TEACHERS SEMINARY 4622 14TH AVENUE ... BROOKLYN **NY** 11219 (718) 633-8557
AYELET HASHACHAR TEACHERS SEMINARY 1284 CENTRAL AVENUE ... FAR ROCKAWAY **NY** 11691 (718) 471-2182
LONG ISLAND SEMINARY OF JEWISH STUDIES FOR WOMEN 540 JARVIS AVENUE ... FAR ROCKAWAY **NY** 11691 (718) 471-8444
RIKA BREUER TEACHERS SEMINARY 91 BENNETT AVENUE ... NEW YORK **NY** 10033 (212) 675-9260
RIKA BREUER TEACHERS SEMINARY 95-103 BENNETT AVENUE ... NEW YORK **NY** 10033 (212) 568-6200
UNITED JEWISH TEACHERS' SEMINARY 5237 CLANRANALD AVENUE ... MONTREAL **QU** H3X 2S5 (514) 489-4401

SENIOR CITIZENS

FREDA-MOHR CENTER 446 NORTH FAIRFAX AVENUE ... LOS ANGELES **CA** 90004 (213) 937-5901
JEWISH FAMILY SERVICE DROP-IN CENTER 4451 30TH STREET ... SAN DIEGO **CA** (619) 291-0473
AGED SERVICE CENTER 1751 EAST 55TH STREET ... CHICAGO **IL** 60615 (312) 939-1399
AGED SERVICE CENTER 1345 WEST JARVIS ... CHICAGO **IL** 60626 (312) 939-1399
AGED SERVICE CENTER 6400 WEST DEVON AVENUE ... CHICAGO **IL** 60626 (312) 939-1399
AGED SERVICE CENTER 1415 WEST MORSE ... CHICAGO **IL** 60626 (312) 939-1399
COUNCIL FOR JEWISH ELDERLY 1 SOUTH FRANKLIN STREET ... CHICAGO **IL** 60606 (312) 346-6700
JEWISH FAMILY & CHILDREN'S SERVICE 31 NEW CHARDON STREET ... BOSTON **MA** 02114 (617) 227-6641
JEWISH SERVICE CENTER FOR OLDER ADULTS 1030 PLEASANT STREET ... WORCESTER **MA** 01602 (617) 756-4363
JEWISH COUNCIL FOR THE AGING 6111 MONTROSE ROAD ... ROCKVILLE **MD** 20852 (301) 881-8782
CO-OP CITY OUTREACH CENTER 1356 EINSTEIN LOOP ... BRONX **NY** 10467 (212) 671-4959
EAST CONCOURSE LUNCHEON CLUB 236 EAST TREMONT AVENUE ... BRONX **NY** 10467 (212) 731-6300
JASA-BRONX BOROUGH SERVICE CENTER 2488 GRAND CONCOURSE ... BRONX **NY** 10458 (212) 365-4044
JASA-BRONX HOME CARE PROGRAM 2166 MATTHEWS AVENUE ... BRONX **NY** 10462 (212) 823-2121
JASA-CO-OP CITY OUTREACH CENTER 135 EINSTEIN LOOP ... BRONX **NY** 10475 (212) 671-4959
JASA-EAST CONCOURSE LUNCHEON CLUB 236 E. TREMONT AVENUE ... BRONX **NY** 10457 (212) 731-6300
JASA-MOSHOLU SERVICE CENTER 3450 DEKALB AVENUE ... BRONX **NY** 10467 (212) 231-1234
JASA-PELHAM SERVICE CENTER 2166 MATTHEWS AVENUE ... BRONX **NY** 10462 (212) 829-7150
JASA-THROGS NECK LUNCHEON CLUB 2705 SCHLEY AVENUE ... BRONX **NY** 10465 (212) 823-1623
AGUDATH ISRAEL OF AMERICA 803 KINGS HIGHWAY ... BROOKLYN **NY** 11223 (718) 627-3500
BROOKLYN BOROUGH SERVICE CENTER 44 COURT ... BROOKLYN **NY** 11201 (718) 852-0880
FLATBUSH YM/YWHA 1401 FLATBUSH AVENUE ... BROOKLYN **NY** 11210 (718) 469-8100
HABER HOUSES SERVICE CENTER 2410 SURF AVENUE ... BROOKLYN **NY** 11235 (718) 449-9600
JASA - BRIGHTON BEACH SERVICE CENTER 2915 BRIGHTON 6 STREET ... BROOKLYN **NY** 11235 (718) 769-5669
JASA-ASSOCIATION FOR SERVICES FOR THE AGED 2211 CHURCH AVENUE ... BROOKLYN **NY** 11226 (718) 941-2200
JASA-BOROUGH PARK SERVICE CENTER 4116 14TH AVENUE ... BROOKLYN **NY** 11219 (718) 854-3535
JASA-BROOKLYN BORO SERVICE CENTER 44 COURT STREET ... BROOKLYN **NY** 11201 (718) 852-0880
JASA-CONEY ISLAND MEALS ON WHEELS 3601 SURF AVENUE ... BROOKLYN **NY** 11224 (718) 996-4874
JASA-EAST FLATBUSH COMMUNITY SERVICES FOR THE ELDERLY 666 REMSEN AVENUE ... BROOKLYN **NY** 11236 (718) 342-5454
JASA-HARBER HOUSES SERVICES CENTER 2410 SURF AVENUE ... BROOKLYN **NY** 11224 (718) 449-9600
JASA-SCHEUER HOUSE GROUP CENTER & SCHEUER HOUSE COMMISSARY 1360 SURF AVENUE ... BROOKLYN **NY** 11224 (718) 373-3954
JASA-SHOREFRONT SERVICE CENTER 3212 CONEY ISLAND AVENUE ... BROOKLYN **NY** 11235 (718) 769-3100
JASA-STARRETT CITY CENTER 11325 SEAVIEW AVENUE ... BROOKLYN **NY** 11239 (718) 642-1300
JASA-STARRETT CITY GROUP CENTER 1540 VAN SICLEN AVENUE ... BROOKLYN **NY** 11239 (718) 642-1010
JASA-WILLIAMSBURG GROUP CENTER 202 GRAHAM AVENUE ... BROOKLYN **NY** 11206 (718) 388-6865
KINGS BAY YM/YWHA SENIOR CITIZEN CENTER 3643 NOSTRAND AVENUE ... BROOKLYN **NY** 11226 (718) 648-2053
SEPHARDIC MULTI-SERVICE CITIZENS CENTER 2165 71ST STREET ... BROOKLYN **NY** 11204 (718) 259-0100
WILLIAMSBURG GROUP CENTER 202 GRAHAM AVENUE ... BROOKLYN **NY** 11211 (718) 388-6805
WILLIAMSBURG YM/YWHA SERVICE CENTER 575 BEDFORD AVENUE ... BROOKLYN **NY** 11211 (718) 782-2315
JASA-BROOKDALE VILLAGE SENIOR CENTER 131 BEACH 19 STREET ... FAR ROCKAWAY **NY** 11691 (718) 471-3200
JASA-QUEENS BORO SERVICE CENTER 97-45 QUEENS BLVD ... FOREST HILLS **NY** 11375 (718) 263-4700
JASA-ROCHDALE VILLAGE LUNCHEON CLUB 169-65 137 AVENUE ... JAMAICA **NY** 11434 (718) 525-2800
JASA-BROOKDALE CENTER OF LONG BEACH-TEMPLE BETH EL 570 W. WALNUT ... LONG BEACH **NY** 11561 (516) 432-5555
JASA-LONG BEACH SERVICE CENTER 72 W. PARK AVENUE ... LONG BEACH **NY** 11561 (516) 432-0570
JASA-NASSAU DISTRICT SERVICE CENTER 158 3RD STREET ... MINEOLA **NY** 11501 (516) 742-2050
NASSAU DISTRICT SERVICE CENTER 158 THIRD STREET ... MINEOLA **NY** 11501 (516) 742-2050
JEWISH INSTITUTE OF GERIATRIC CARE 271-11 76TH AVENUE ... NEW HYDE PARK **NY** 11040 (516) 437-0090
CENTRAL BUREAU FOR THE JEWISH AGED 130 EAST 59TH STREET ... NEW YORK **NY** 10022 (212) 308-7316
FEDERATION JOINT SERVICES OF THE LOWER EAST SIDE 197 EAST BROADWAY ... NEW YORK **NY** 10002 (212) 475-6200
JASA-CENTRAL ADMINISTRATION 40 W. 68 STREET ... NEW YORK **NY** 10023 (212) 724-3200
JASA-FEDERATION JOINT SERVICES OF THE EAST SIDE ED. ALLIANCE 197 E. BROADWAY ... NEW YORK **NY** 10002 (212) 475-6200
JASA-MANHATTAN BOROUGH SERVICES CENTER 40 W. 68 STREET ... NEW YORK **NY** 10023 (212) 724-3200
JASA-MARSEILLES SENIOR CENTER 230 W. 103 STREET ... NEW YORK **NY** 10025 (212) 663-6000
JASA-WASHINGTON HEIGHTS SERVICE 711 W. 179TH STREET ... NEW YORK **NY** 10033 (212) 928-0100
JASA-WEST SIDE SENIOR CITIZEN CENTER 40 W. 68 STREET ... NEW YORK **NY** 10023 (212) 724-3200
JEWISH ASSOCIATION FOR SERVICES FOR THE AGED 40 WEST 68TH STREET ... NEW YORK **NY** 10023 (212) 724-3200
MANHATTAN BOROUGH SERVICE CENTER 40 WEST 68TH STREET ... NEW YORK **NY** 10023 (212) 724-3200
PROJECT EZRA 197 EAST BROADWAY ... NEW YORK **NY** 10002 (212) 982-3700
WASHINGTON HEIGHTS SERVICE CENTER C/O SELF HELP 717 WEST 177TH STREET ... NEW YORK **NY** 10033 (212) 928-0010
JASA-QUEENS LEGAL SERVICE FOR THE ELDERLY 97-45 QUEENS BLVD. ... REGO PARK **NY** 11374 (718) 897-2515
JEWISH INFORMATION SERVICE FOR THE AGING 5418 WEST BURLEIGH ... MILWAUKEE **WI** (414) 445-4014

SEPHARDIC ORGANIZATIONS

AMERICAN SEPHARDI FEDERATION-LOS ANGELES CHAPTER
6505 WILSHIRE BOULEVARD, SUITE 208 ....LOS ANGELES **CA** 90048　(213) 653-8177
IRANIAN JEWISH FEDERATION
6505 WILSHIRE BOULEVARD, SUITE 1101 ....LOS ANGELES **CA** 90048　(213) 852-1272
KAHAL JOSEPH CONGREGATION
10505 SANTA MONICA BOULEVARD ....LOS ANGELES **CA** 90025　(213) 474-0559
MIDRASH OD YOSEF HAI 420 NORTH FAIRFAX AVENUE ....LOS ANGELES **CA** 90036　(213) 653-5163
SEPHARDIC ASSOC. MAX NORDAU, C/O AMERICAN SEPHARDI FED.
6505 WILSHIRE BOULEVARD, SUITE 208 ....LOS ANGELES **CA** 90048　(213) 653-8177
SEPHARDIC CONGREGATION KEHAL YOSEPH
10505 SANTA MONICA BLVD ....LOS ANGELES **CA** 90025　(213) 474-0559
SEPHARDIC HEBREW ACADEMY 310 NORTH HUNTLEY DRIVE ....LOS ANGELES **CA** 90048　(213) 659-2456
SEPHARDIC HEBREW CENTER 4911 WEST 59TH STREET ....LOS ANGELES **CA** 90034　(213) 295-5541
SEPHARDIC MAGEN DAVID CONGREGATION
7454 MELROSE AVENUE ....LOS ANGELES **CA** 90046　(213) 655-3441
SEPHARDIC TEMPLE TIFERETH ISRAEL
10500 WILSHIRE BOULEVARD ....LOS ANGELES **CA** 90024　(213) 475-7311
SEPHARDIC WOMEN'S DIVISION-UJWF
6505 WILSHIRE BOULEVARD, SUITE 1002 ....LOS ANGELES **CA** 90048　(213) 852-1234
SEPHARDIC YOUTH AND YOUNG ADULTS
6505 WILSHIRE BOULEVARD, SUITE 208 ....LOS ANGELES **CA** 90048　(213) 653-8177
TIFARET TEIMAN, CONGREGATION OF YEMENITE JEWS
1940 LINDA FLORA DRIVE ....LOS ANGELES **CA** 90024　(213) 479-4114
ADAT YESHURUN VALLEY SEPHARDIC CONGREGATION
6348 WHITSETT AVENUE ....NORTH HOLLYWOOD **CA** 91606　(818) 766-4682
CONGREGATION EM HABANIM 12052 CALIFA STREET ....NORTH HOLLYWOOD **CA** 91607　(818) 762-7779
SEPHARDIC CONGREGATION OF GREATER HARTFORD
21 TUMBLEBROOK LANE ....WEST HARTFORD **CT** 06117　(203) 233-1888
CUBAN SEPHARDIC HEBREW CONGREGATION
1200 NORMANDY DRIVE ....MIAMI BEACH **FL** 33141　(305) 531-4732
MAGEN DAVID SEPHARDIC CONGREGATION P.O. BOX 41019 ....BETHESDA **MD** 20014　(301) 588-0446
SEPHARDIC COMMUNITY OF GREATER DETROIT 21830 BEVERLY ....OAK PARK **MI** 48237　(313) 968-8393
SEPHARDIC JEWISH BROTHERHOOD 116 EAST 169TH STREET ....BRONX **NY** 10452
SEPHARDIC JEWISH CENTER OF THE BRONX, INC. O
116 EAST 169TH STREET ....BRONX **NY** 10452
SEPHARDIC SHAARE RAHAMIM OF EAST BRONX, INC. O
100 CO-OP CITY BLVD ....BRONX **NY** 10475　(212) 671-8882
ADELANTRE-THE JUDEZMO SOCIETY 4594 BEDFORD AVENUE ....BROOKLYN **NY** 11235
SEPHARDIC CENTER OF MAPLETON 7216 BAY PARKWAY ....BROOKLYN **NY** 11204
SEPHARDIC HOME, THE 2266 CROPSEY AVENUE ....BROOKLYN **NY** 11214　(718) 266-6100
SEPHARDIC INSTITUTE 511 AVENUE R ....BROOKLYN **NY** 11223　(718) 998-8171
SEPHARDIC JEWISH CENTER OF CANARSIE O
9320 FLATLANDS AVENUE ....BROOKLYN **NY** 11236　(718) 257-0400
SEPHARDIC TEMPLE TORAH O 60 BRIGHTON 11 STREET ....BROOKLYN **NY** 11235　(718) 743-4616
SEPHARDIC JEWISH CENTER OF FOREST HILLS O
67-67 108TH STREET ....FOREST HILLS **NY** 11375　(718) 268-2100
SEPHARDIC CONGREGATION OF LONG BEACH
161 LAFAYETTE BLVD., P.O. BOX 779 ....LONG BEACH **NY** 11561　(516) 432-9224
AMERICAN SEPHARDI FEDERATION 521 FIFTH AVENUE ....NEW YORK **NY** 10017　(212) 697-1845
AMERICAN SOCIETY OF SEPHARDIC STUDIES 500 W. 185TH STREET ....NEW YORK **NY** 10033　(212) 960-5236
CENTRAL SEPHARDIC JEWISH COMMUNITY OF AMERICA
8 W. 70TH STREET ....NEW YORK **NY** 10023　(212) 787-2850
FOUND. FOR ADVANCEMENT OF SEPHARDIC STUDIES & CULTURE, INC.
599-601 BROADWAY ....NEW YORK **NY** 10012
SEPHARDIC HOUSE AT THE CONG. SHEARITH ISRAEL
8 W. 70TH STREET ....NEW YORK **NY** 10023　(212) 873-0300
SEPHARDIC STUDIES PROGRAM - YESHIVA UNIVERSITY
500 WEST 185 STREET ....NEW YORK **NY** 10033　(212) 960-5235
UNION OF SEPHARDIC CONGREGATIONS, INC. 8 WEST 70TH STREET ....NEW YORK **NY** 10023　(212) 873-0300
WORLD INSTITUTE FOR SEPHARDIC STUDIES 310 WEST 72ND STREET ....NEW YORK **NY** 10023
SEPHARDIC JEWISH BROTHERHOOD OF AMERICA, INC.
97-29 64TH ROAD ....REGO PARK **NY** 11374　(718) 459-1600
SEPHARDIC COMMUNITY OF NEW ROCHELLE-SCARSDALE, THE O
C/O YOUNG ISRAEL OF SCARSDALE, 1313 DAISY FARMS ROAD ....SCARSDALE **NY** 10583　(914) 723-6273
SEPHARDIC GROUP OF SYRACUSE
C/O MR. HABIB, 119 DOLL PARKWAY ....SYRACUSE **NY** 13214　(315) 446-0760
SEPHARDIC BETH SHALOM CONGREGATION P.O. BOX 37431 ....CINCINNATI **OH** 45222　(513) 793-6936
SEPHARDIC CONGREGATION AHAVAT ACHIM
3225 S.W. BARBUR BLVD ....PORTLAND **OR** 97201　(503) 227-0010
CANADIAN SEPHARDI FEDERATION 1310 GREENE AVENUE ....MONTREAL **QU** H3Z 2B2　(514) 934-0804
MAGEN DAVID SEPHARDIC CONGREGATION O 9112 BOWLER DRIVE ....FAIRFAX **VA** 22031　(703) 251-0766
SEPHARDIC BIKUR HOLIM CONGREGATION 6500 52ND STREET SOUTH ....SEATTLE **WA** 98118　(206) 723-9661

SHATNES TESTING

SHATNES LABORATORY OF TORAH AND MITZVOTH, J. ROSENBERG-FOUNDER
203 LEE AVENUE ....BROOKLYN **NY** 11206　(718) 387-8520
SHATNEZ TESTING ....CLEVELAND **OH**　(216) 932-4313

SHIPPING

ZIM CONTAINER SERVICE 3450 WILSHIRE BOULEVARD ....LOS ANGELES **CA** 90010　(213) 385-2400
ZIM CONTAINER SERVICE 100 CALIFORNIA STREET ....SAN FRANCISCO **CA** 94111　(415) 986-5717
T.D.Y. FREIGHT SERVICES, LTD. P.O. BOX 630132 ....MIAMI **FL** 33163　(305) 653-8338
ZIM CONTAINER SERVICE 1644 TULLIE CIRCLE, SUITE 111 ....ATLANTA **GA** 30329　(404) 325-4100
ZIM CONTAINER SERVICE 24 DRAYTON STREET, PO BOX 8547 ....SAVANNAH **GA** 31402　(912) 236-4263

ZIM - AMERICAN-ISRAELI SHIPPING COMPANY, INC.
10600 WEST HIGGINS ROAD, SUITE 410 ....ROSEMONT **IL** 60018　(312) 298-9700
ZIM - AMERICAN-ISRAELI SHIPPING COMPANY, INC.
203 CARONDELET STREET, SUITE 1000 ....NEW ORLEANS **LA** 70130　(504) 524-1184
FARRELL LINES, INC. ONE WHITEHALL STREET ....NEW YORK **NY** 10004　(212) 440-4200
FLEET LINES 440 PARK AVENUE SOUTH ....NEW YORK **NY** 10016　(212) 696-5210
MARITIME OVERSEAS CORPORATION 511 FIFTH AVENUE ....NEW YORK **NY** 10017　(212) 953-4100
P.E.C. 511 FIFTH AVENUE ....NEW YORK **NY** 10017　(212) 687-2400
YORK SHIPPING CORPORATION 342 MADISON AVENUE ....NEW YORK **NY** 10017　(212) 697-9510
ZIM - AMERICAN-ISRAELI SHIPPING COMPANY, INC.
1 WORLD TRADE CENTER, SUITE 2969 ....NEW YORK **NY** 10048　(212) 432-0300
BURLINGTON NORTHERN AIR FREIGHT
145 HOOK CREEK BOULEVARD ....ROSEDALE **NY** 11422　(718) 889-7750
E. ROSEMAN COMPANY 829 N. SECOND ST. ..............PHILADELPHIA **PA** 19123　(215) 627-0539
ZIM CONTAINER SERVICE 201 COTTON EXCHANGE ....DALLAS **TX** 75201　(214) 742-1693
ZIM - AMERICAN-ISRAELI SHIPPING COMPANY, INC.
1314 TEXAS AVENUE, SUITE 812 ....HOUSTON **TX** 77002　(713) 224-9461

SINGLES

NEW JEWISH SINGLES - ORANGE COUNTY P.O. BOX 631 ....ARTESIA **CA** 90701　(714) 761-1870
NORTH PENINSULA JCC SINGLES (25-37) ....BELMONT **CA**　(415) 591-4438
BERKELEY/RICHMOND JCC SINGLES & SINGLES PARENTS ....BERKELEY **CA**　(415) 848-0237
NEW SHUL SINGLES 9454 WILSHIRE BLVD ....BEVERLY HILLS **CA** 90212　(213) 276-9338
BRANDEIS - BARDIN YOUNG ADULTS (AGE 25-35) ....BRANDEIS **CA** 93064　(213) 348-7201

BETH AM 30 PLUS .... CUPERTINO **CA** (408) 886-5350
LONG BEACH JEWISH CONNECTION 3801 EAST WILLOW .... LONG BEACH **CA** 90815 (213) 426-7601
30'S PLUS SINGLES, CONGREGATION BETH AM .... LOS ALTOS **CA** (415) 592-7759
DEPARTMENT OF SINGLE ADULTS, JEWISH FEDERATION COUNCIL
  6505 WILSHIRE BOULEVARD .... LOS ANGELES **CA** 90048 (213) 852-1234
JASS-JEWISH ASSOCIATION OF SINGLES SERVICES
  6505 WILSHIRE BOULEVARD .... LOS ANGELES **CA** 90048 (213) 852-1234
JASSLINE (AGES 21-35) 6505 WILSHIRE BOULEVARD .... LOS ANGELES **CA** 90048 (213) 852-0909
JASSLINE (AGES 35 UP) 6505 WILSHIRE BOULEVARD .... LOS ANGELES **CA** 90048 (213) 651-4420
JEWISH SINGLES COMPUTER SERVICE 15600 MULHOLLAND DRIVE ... LOS ANGELES **CA** 90077 (213) 471-3055
JEWISH SINGLES CONNECTION, JEWISH CENTERS ASSOC., JCC
  5870 WEST OLYMPIC BOULEVARD .... LOS ANGELES **CA** 90036 (213) 272-1073
MARINA DEL REY YOUNG SINGLES 6505 WILSHIRE BLVD .... LOS ANGELES **CA** 90048 (213) 651-4602
NEW BEGINNINGS BOX 241622 .... LOS ANGELES **CA** 90024 (213) 458-1101

THE JEWISH SINGLES GUIDE TO LOS ANGELES, DEPT/SINGLE ADULTS
  6505 WILSHIRE BOULEVARD .... LOS ANGELES **CA** 90048 (213) 852-1234
VIP CLUB 9831 WEST PICO BOULEVARD #12A .... LOS ANGELES **CA** 90035 (213) 553-6642
MALIBU SINGLES HAVURAH P.O. BOX 4063 .... MALIBU **CA** 90265 (213) 457-2979
TEMPLE BETH ABRAHAM SINGLES .... OAKLAND **CA** (415) 832-0936
JASSLINE ORANGE COUNTY (AGE 21=) .... ORANGE COUNTY **CA** (714) 537-JASS
YOUNG JEWISH SINGLES OF BETH AM (21-29) .... PALO ALTO **CA** (415) 325-6405
JEWISH DATING 1742 UNION STREET .... SAN FRANCISCO **CA** 94123 (415) 346-6229
L'CHAIM & MID-PENINSULA JEWISH SINGLES .... SAN FRANCISCO **CA** (415) 341-2462
MARIN JEWISH SINGLES .... SAN FRANCISCO **CA** (415) 479-2000
SAN FRANCISCO JCC ADULT GROUP PROGRAMS .... SAN FRANCISCO **CA** (415) 346-6040
YOUNG ADULT DIVISION, JEWISH COMMUNITY FEDERATION OF SAN FR.
  .... SAN FRANCISCO **CA** (415) 781-3082
EMET JEWISH YOUNG PROFESSIONALS 6467 VAN NUYS BLVD. #300 .. VAN NUYS **CA** 91401 (818) 988-7278
JEWISH INTRODUCTIONS, INC. .... DADE, BROWARD **FL** (305) 923-0777
JEWISH DATING CENTER .... **NJ** (201) 778-3461
NATIONAL DIRECTORY OF JEWISH SINGLES, THE .... **NY** (718) 258-9797
JEWISH COMPUTER DATING SERVICE 1314 AVENUE P .... BROOKLYN **NY** 11229 (718) 336-7911
JEWISH SINGLES REGISTRY 4911 16TH AVENUE .... BROOKLYN **NY** 11204 (718) 851-1314
YOUNG ADULTS, YOUNG ISRAEL OF FLATBUSH 1012 AVENUE I .... BROOKLYN **NY** 11230
FEDERATION OF JEWISH PHILANTHROPIES 130 EAST 59TH STREET ... NEW YORK **NY** 10022 (212) 980-1000
FIELDS MATRIMONIAL BROKER SERVICE 41 EAST 42ND STREET ..... NEW YORK **NY** 10017 (212) 391-2233
JEWISH PROFESSIONAL SINGLES .... NEW YORK **NY** (212) 734-5566
JEWISH SINGLES DATE PHONE 301 E. 49TH STREET .... NEW YORK **NY** 10017 (212) 755-3008
JEWISH SINGLES HOT LINE 301 E. 49TH STREET .... NEW YORK **NY** 10017 (212) 753-7282
JEWISH SINGLES INTRODUCTION SERVICE
  UNITED SYNAGOGUE OF AMERICA, 155 FIFTH AVENUE .... NEW YORK **NY** 10010 (212) 533-7800
LE JUDA (TAPE RECORDING OF CURRENT PARTY INFO.) .... NEW YORK **NY** (212) 753-7282
TASK FORCE ON JEWISH SINGLES, FED. OF JEWISH PHILANTHROPIES
  130 EAST 59TH STREET .... NEW YORK **NY** 10022 (212) 980-1000
TZEMED-HELENA, INC. 400 MADISON AVENUE .... NEW YORK **NY** 10017 (212) 759-9009
YOUNG ISRAEL SINGLES—YOUNG ADULTS 3 WEST 16TH STREET ... NEW YORK **NY** 10011 (212) 929-1525
DR. ELLIOT UDELL—SINGLES RETREATS .... PLAINVIEW **NY** (516) 349-7125
MARRIAGE ENCOUNTER JEWISH EXPRESSION
  365 WOODMERE BOULEVARD .... WOODMERE **NY** 11598 (516) 374-6430
SINGLES CENTER OF THE GREATER FIVE TOWNS
  207 GROVE STREET .... WOODMERE **NY** 11598 (516) 569-6733
FAIRMOUNT TEMPLE SINGLES 3666 TOWNLEY ROAD .... CLEVELAND **OH** 44122 (216) 491-9275
FAIRMOUNT TEMPLE SINGLES 24650 S. WOODLAND ROAD .... CLEVELAND **OH** 44122 (216) 464-2583
HATIKVAH YOUNG ISRAEL ADULT GROUP 13817 CEDAR ROAD ..... CLEVELAND **OH** (216) 371-2244
PARK SINGLES .... CLEVELAND **OH** (216) 371-2244
RAVAKIM 1369 FORD ROAD .... CLEVELAND **OH** 44124 (216) 449-3797
JEWISH DATING SERVICE P.O.BOX 14393 .... PHILADELPHIA **PA** 19115 (215) 342-9951

SOCIAL, COMMUNAL & FRATERNAL ORGANIZATIONS

B'NAI B'RITH—DISTRICT 4 6300 WILSHIRE BOULEVARD, SUITE 1717 ... LOS ANGELES **CA** 90048 (213) 655-8994
JEWISH WAR VETERANS OF THE U.S.A.—CALIFORNIA
  6505 WILSHIRE BOULEVARD, ROOM 401 .... LOS ANGELES **CA** 90048 (213) 635-4752
LABOR ZIONIST ALLIANCE (YIDDISHER NAZIONALER ARBETER FARBAND)
  8339 WEST THIRD STREET .... LOS ANGELES **CA** 90048 (213) 655-2842
MACCABEE ATHLETIC CLUB, INC. 6399 WILSHIRE BOULEVARD ..... LOS ANGELES **CA** 90048 (213) 651-3182
WORKMEN'S CIRCLE (ARBEITER RING)
  1525 SOUTH ROBERTSON BOULEVARD .... LOS ANGELES **CA** 90035 (213) 522-2007
B'NAI B'RITH 1640 RHODE ISLAND AVENUE, N.W. .... WASHINGTON **DC** 20036 (202) 857-6600
B'NAI B'RITH INTERNATIONAL 1640 RHODE ISLAND AVENUE, N.W. ... WASHINGTON **DC** 20036 (202) 857-6600
JEWISH WAR VETERANS OF THE UNITED STATES OF AMERICA
  1811 R STREET .... WASHINGTON **DC** 20009 (202) 265-6280
LEADERSHIP CONFERENCE ON CIVIL RIGHTS
  2027 MASSACHUSETTS AVENUE N.W. .... WASHINGTON **DC** 20036 (202) 667-1780
WORKMEN'S CIRCLE 311 LINCOLN ROAD, ROOM 217 .... MIAMI BEACH **FL** 33139
NATIONAL JEWISH CIVIL SERVICE EMPLOYEES
  1451 N.E. 169TH STREET .... NORTH MIAMI BEACH **FL** 33162
B'NAI B'RITH—DISTRICT 5
  P.O. BOX 54386, 3379 PEACHTREE ROAD, N.E. .... ATLANTA **GA** 30308 (404) 876-3681
BUREAU FOR JEWISH LIVING 924 POLK BLVD .... DES MOINES **IA** 50312 (515) 277-5566
ARK, THE 3509 W. LAWRENCE AVENUE .... CHICAGO **IL** 60625 (312) 478-9600

WHO'S INTERNATIONAL BUT NOT LEFT THE NEIGHBORHOOD?

The Young Israel movement, founded in 1912 by a handful of idealistic young men and women who fostered a successful synthesis of the authentic traditions of Judaism and the American experience, has had a profound influence upon the development of the American Orthodox community of the 20th century.

We cordially invite you to participate in one of our many public programs, to join the Young Israel synagogue in your community, and to support our many important activities on the college campus, in Israel, and throughout the Jewish community.

NATIONAL COUNCIL OF YOUNG ISRAEL

3 WEST 16 STREET
NEW YORK, NY 10011
212•929•1525

Yes!

Please send me information on the following Young Israel project of activity:

☐ Youth Activities
☐ Achva Summer Mission to Israel
☐ Collegiate and Young Adult Programs
☐ Campus and Kosher Dining Clubs
☐ Public Affairs Committee

☐ Torah Tape Library
☐ Eretz Israel Commission
☐ National Convention
☐ Nearest Young Israel Synagogue
☐ Womens' League

NATIONAL COUNCIL OF YOUNG ISRAEL

Please accept my enclosed donation to support your activities:

☐ $25 National Council of Young Israel membership
☐ $18 Eretz Israel Commission membership
☐ $_____ To support Young Israel's campus work
(Please make checks payable to: National Council of Young Israel, Dept. A, 3 West 16th Street, New York, NY 10011)

Name _____

Address _____

City _____ State _____ Zip _____

Telephone _____

Call the Young Israel Public Affairs Mobilization Hotline: (212) 924-5424

FREE SONS OF ISRAEL 6335 NORTH CALIFORNIA	CHICAGO	**IL**	60659	(312) 338-9810
JEWISH CIVIL SERVICE EMPLOYEES IN CHICAGO				
7064 N. SHERIDAN ROAD	CHICAGO	**IL**	60626	(312) 973-4558
JEWISH DEFENSE LEAGUE 22 WEST MADISON, SUITE 900	CHICAGO	**IL**	60626	(312) 973-4558
JEWISH DEFENSE LEAGUE 22 WEST MADISON, SUITE 900	CHICAGO	**IL**	60602	(312) 338-3800
JEWISH WAR VETERANS 536 S. CLARK STREET, SUITE 484	CHICAGO	**IL**	60605	(312) 353-2872
MACCABI SPORT CLUB 6237 NORTH SACRAMENTO	CHICAGO	**IL**	60659	(312) 338-7597
NATIONAL JEWISH CIVIL SERVICE EMPLOYEES				
7075 N. PAULINA STREET	CHICAGO	**IL**	60626	(312) 973-6125
YOUNG MEN'S JEWISH COUNCIL 30 W. WASHINGTON STREET	CHICAGO	**IL**	60602	(312) 726-8891
NATIONAL FEDERATION OF JEWISH MEN'S CLUBS				
9129 WAUKEGAN	MORTON GROVE	**IL**	60053	(312) 965-7202
B'NAI B'RITH—DISTRICT 6 9933 LAWLER STREET, SUITE 100	SKOKIE	**IL**	60077	(312) 676-0011
SHALOM ORGANIZATION OF CHICAGO 4050 TOWER CIRCLE	SKOKIE	**IL**	60076	(312) OR6-9408
JEWISH WAR VETERANS OF THE U.S.A.—MASSACHUSETTS				
JFK FEDERAL BUILDING, GOVERNMENT CENTER, ROOM E314A	BOSTON	**MA**	02203	(617) 223-4580
COUNCIL OF CONCERNED JEWISH CITIZENS				
113 WASHINGTON STREET	BRIGHTON	**MA**	02135	(617) 254-1334
NEW ENGLAND CHASSIDIC CENTER 2720 BEACON STREET	BROOKLINE	**MA**	02146	(617) 566-9182
ROFEH 1710 BEACON STREET	BROOKLINE	**MA**	02146	(617) 566-9182
CONCORD AREA JEWISH GROUP P.O. BOX 1339	CONCORD	**MA**	01742	
JEWISH SURVIVAL LEGION 388 N. MAIN STREET	SHARON	**MA**	02067	
JEWISH ARMED SERVICES COMM. 5750 PARK HEIGHTS AVENUE	BALTIMORE	**MD**	21215	(301) 466-4242
JEWISH WAR VETERANS OF THE U.S.A.-MARYLAND				
31 HAPKINS PLAZA	BALTIMORE	**MD**	21201	(301) 752-3526
JEWISH ATHLETIC & CULTURAL ASSOCIATION				
1118 CHICKASAW DRIVE	SILVER SPRING	**MD**	20903	(301) 431-1077
WORKMEN'S CIRCLE 5790 CLEVELAND AVENUE, SUITE 225	ST. PAUL	**MN**	55116	(612) 699-5146
NORTH CAROLINA ASSOCIATION OF JEWISH MEN P.O. BOX 10628	CHARLOTTE	**NC**	28201	
PAULSBORO JEWISH COMMUNITY CLUB 39 W. BROAD	PAULSBORO	**NJ**	08066	
VAN CORTLANDT WORKMEN'S CIRCLE COMMUNITY HOUSE				
3990 HILLMAN AVENUE	BRONX	**NY**	10463	
JEWISH ATHLETIC CLUB OF BROOKLYN				
P.O. BOX 190, GRAVESEND STATION	BROOKLYN	**NY**	11223	(718) 376-9683
AMERICAN VETERANS OF ISRAEL				
C/O SIDNEY RABINOVICH, 110-23 63RD AVENUE	FOREST HILLS	**NY**	11375	
AMERICAN VETERANS OF ISRAEL 548 E. WALNUT STREET	LONG BEACH	**NY**	11561	(516) 431-8316
ABRAHAM GOODMAN HOUSE 129 WEST 67TH STREET	NEW YORK	**NY**	10023	(212) 362-8060
ADATH ISRAEL OF NEW YORK, UNITED HEBREW COMMUNITY OF NEW YORK				
201 EAST BROADWAY	NEW YORK	**NY**	10002	(212) 674-3580
AGUDAS ISRAEL WORLD ORGANIZATION 471 WEST END AVENUE	NEW YORK	**NY**	10024	(212) 874-7979
AM. FED. OF JEWISH FIGHTERS, CAMP INMATES & NAZI VICTIMS, INC				
823 UNITED NATIONS PLAZA	NEW YORK	**NY**	10017	(212) 490-2525
AM. VETERANS OF THE JEWISH LEGION-HAGDUD HAIVRI LEAGUE, INC.				
C/O DR. JUDAH LAPSON, 1776 BROADWAY	NEW YORK	**NY**	10019	(212) 245-8200
AMERICAN CONGREGATION OF JEWS FROM AUSTRIA				
188 W. 95TH STREET	NEW YORK	**NY**	10025	(212) 663-1920
AMERICAN COUNCIL FOR JUDAISM 307 FIFTH AVENUE	NEW YORK	**NY**	10016	(212) 889-1313
AMERICAN FAR EASTERN SOCIETY 259 W. 30TH STREET	NEW YORK	**NY**	10001	(212) 244-6225
AMERICAN FEDERATION OF JEWS FROM CENTRAL EUROPE, INC.				
570 SEVENTH AVENUE	NEW YORK	**NY**	10018	(212) 921-3871
AMERICAN FRIENDS OF THE ALLIANCE ISRAELITE UNIVERSELLE				
61 BROADWAY, ROOM 811	NEW YORK	**NY**	10006	(212) 425-5171
AMERICAN JEWISH LEAGUE AGAINST COMMUNISM, INC.				
39 EAST 68TH STREET	NEW YORK	**NY**	10021	(212) 472-1400
AMERICAN JEWISH SOCIETY FOR SERVICE 15 E. 26TH STREET	NEW YORK	**NY**	10010	(212) 683-6178
AMERICAN VETERANS OF ISRAEL 15 E. 26TH STREET	NEW YORK	**NY**	10010	(212) 532-4949
ASSOCIATION OF YUGOSLAV JEWS IN THE U.S.A. 247 W. 99TH STREET	NEW YORK	**NY**	10025	(212) 865-2211
B'NAI B'RITH-DISTRICT 1 823 UNITED NATIONS PLAZA	NEW YORK	**NY**	10017	(212) 490-2525
COMMISSION ON STATUS OF JEWISH WAR ORPHANS IN EUROPE-AM.				
47 BEEKMAN STREET	NEW YORK	**NY**	10038	(212) 227-7800
EDUCATIONAL ALLIANCE, INC., THE 197 EAST BROADWAY	NEW YORK	**NY**	10002	(212) 475-6200
FEDERATION OF POLISH JEWS, INC. 342 MADISON AVENUE	NEW YORK	**NY**	10017	(212) 986-3693
FREE SONS OF ISRAEL 932 BROADWAY	NEW YORK	**NY**	10010	(212) 260-4222
FREE SONS OF ISRAEL-CREDIT UNION 932 BROADWAY	NEW YORK	**NY**	10010	(212) 475-2200
FREE SONS OF ISRAEL-FOUNDATION FUND 932 BROADWAY	NEW YORK	**NY**	10010	(212) 475-2150
FREE SONS OF ISRAEL-INSURANCE DEPARTMENT 932 BROADWAY	NEW YORK	**NY**	10010	(212) 228-1070
FRIENDS OF BELLEVUE HOSPITAL SYNAGOGUE				
FIRST AVENUE & 27TH STREET	NEW YORK	**NY**	10016	(212) 685-1376
HIAS, INC. 200 PARK AVENUE S	NEW YORK	**NY**	10003	(212) 674-6800
HINENI 155 E. 38TH STREET	NEW YORK	**NY**	10016	(212) 557-1190
HISTADRUTH IVRITH OF AMERICA 1841 BROADWAY	NEW YORK	**NY**	10023	(212) 581-5151
ISRAELI COMMUNITY OF MIZRACHI-HAPOEL HAMIZRACHI				
25 W. 26TH STREET	NEW YORK	**NY**	10010	(212) 679-2050
JEWISH ASSOCIATION FOR SERVICES FOR THE AGED				
40 W. 68TH STREET	NEW YORK	**NY**	10023	(212) 724-3200
JEWISH DEFENSE LEAGUE 76 MADISON AVENUE	NEW YORK	**NY**	10016	(212) 686-3041
JEWISH LABOR BUND 25 E. 78TH STREET, SUITE 501	NEW YORK	**NY**	10021	(212) 535-0850
JEWISH LABOR COMMISSION 25 E. 78TH STREET	NEW YORK	**NY**	10021	(212) 535-3700
JEWISH POSTAL EMPLOYEES WELFARE LEAGUE OF MANHATTAN & BRONX, INC.				
45 E. 33RD STREET	NEW YORK	**NY**	10016	(212) 689-1629
JEWISH RESTITUTION SUCCESSOR ORGANIZATION				
15 E. 26TH STREET	NEW YORK	**NY**	10010	(212) 679-4074
JEWISH SOCIALIST VERBAND OF AMERICA 45 EAST 33RD STREET	NEW YORK	**NY**	10016	(212) 686-1536
JEWISH WAR VETERANS OF THE U.S.A.-COMMUNITY RELATIONS OFFICE				
1457 BROADWAY	NEW YORK	**NY**	10036	(212) 234-3000
JEWISH WAR VETERANS OF THE U.S.A.-DEPT.OF NEW YORK JWV				
51 CHAMBERS STREET, ROOM 1411	NEW YORK	**NY**	10007	(212) 349-6640
JEWISH WAR VETERANS OF THE U.S.A.-NEW YORK				
VETERANS ADMINISTRATION 252 SEVENTH AVENUE	NEW YORK	**NY**	10001	(212) 924-7590
JEWISH WAR VETERANS OF THE USA-DEPT. OF N.Y.-(SHOW DIV.)				
51 CHAMBERS STREET	NEW YORK	**NY**	10007	(212) 349-6420
JEWISH WAR VETERANS OF THE USA-DEPT. OF N.Y.-COUNTY COUNCIL				
346 BROADWAY	NEW YORK	**NY**	10013	(212) 962-2176
JEWISH WELFARE BOARD 15 E. 26TH STREET	NEW YORK	**NY**	10010	(212) 532-4949
MEDEM JEWISH SOCIALISTS GROUP 25 E. 78TH STREET	NEW YORK	**NY**	10021	(212) 535-0850
NATIONAL COUNCIL OF YOUNG ISRAEL 3 W. 16TH STREET	NEW YORK	**NY**	10011	(212) 929-1525
NATIONAL FEDERATION OF JEWISH MENS CLUBS, INC.				
475 RIVERSIDE DRIVE, SUITE 244	NEW YORK	**NY**	10115	(212) 749-8100
NATIONAL FEDERATION OF TEMPLE BROTHERHOODS-CHAUTAUQUA SOC.				
838 FIFTH AVENUE	NEW YORK	**NY**	10021	(212) 249-0100
NATIONAL JEWISH WELFARE BOARD 15 EAST 26TH STREET	NEW YORK	**NY**	10010	(212) 532-4949
NEW WORLD CLUB 2121 BROADWAY	NEW YORK	**NY**	10023	(212) 873-7400
RABBI ISAAC ELCHANAN THEOLOGICAL SEMINARY-DIV./COMMUNAL SVS.				
2540 AMSTERDAM AVENUE	NEW YORK	**NY**	10033	(212) 960-5265
ROUMANIAN JEWISH FEDERATION OF AMERICA, INC.				
210 W. 101 STREET	NEW YORK	**NY**	10025	(212) 866-2214
SELFHELP COMMUNITY SERVICES 44 E. 23RD STREET	NEW YORK	**NY**	10010	(212) 533-7100
UNITED HEBREW COMMUNITY OF NEW YORK, ADATH ISRAEL OF NEW YORK				
201 EAST BROADWAY	NEW YORK	**NY**	10002	(212) 674-3580
UNITED HEBREW TRADES OF THE STATE OF NEW YORK				
853 BROADWAY	NEW YORK	**NY**	10003	(212) 674-2573
UNITED ORDER TRUE SISTERS, INC. 150 W. 85TH STREET	NEW YORK	**NY**	10024	(212) 362-2520
UNITED PARENT-TEACHERS ASSOCIATION OF JEWISH SCHOOLS				
426 W. 58TH STREET	NEW YORK	**NY**	10019	(212) 245-8200
UNITED ROUMANIAN JEWS OF AMERICA 485 FIFTH AVENUE	NEW YORK	**NY**	10017	(212) 867-9696
UNITED SONS OF ISRAEL 41 UNION SQUARE	NEW YORK	**NY**	10003	(212) 255-6648
WORKMEN'S CIRCLE 45 EAST 33RD STREET	NEW YORK	**NY**	10016	(212) 889-6800
WORLD FEDERATION OF BERGEN-BELSEN ASSOCIATES P.O. BOX 333	NEW YORK	**NY**	10021	(212) 752-0600
WORLD FEDERATION OF HUNGARIAN JEWS 136 E. 39TH STREET	NEW YORK	**NY**	10016	(212) 683-5377
WORLD JEWISH CONGRESS 15 EAST 84TH STREET	NEW YORK	**NY**	10028	(212) 879-4500
WORLD ORG. FOR JEWS FROM ARAB COUNTRIES, INC. (EXEC. OFFICE)				
165 E. 56TH STREET	NEW YORK	**NY**	10022	(212) 751-4000
WORLD ORGANIZATION FOR JEWS FROM ARAB COUNTRIES, INC.				
1200 FIFTH AVENUE	NEW YORK	**NY**	10022	(212) 427-1246
JEWISH PEACE FELLOWSHIP P.O. BOX 271	NYACK	**NY**	10960	(914) 358-4601
WESTCHESTER JEWISH COMMUNITY SERVICES, INC.				
475 TUCKAHOE ROAD	YONKERS	**NY**	10710	(914) 793-3565
WESTCHESTER JEWISH COMMUNITY SERVICES, INC.				
20 SOUTH BROADWAY	YONKERS	**NY**	10701	(914) 423-4433
B'NAI B'RITH-DISTRICT 2 7750 MONTGOMERY ROAD	CINCINNATI	**OH**	45236	(513) 891-2880
WORKMEN'S CIRCLE 1980 S. GREEN ROAD	CLEVELAND	**OH**	44121	(216) 381-4515
B'NAI B'RITH-DISTRICT 22 15 HOVE STREET, SUITE 200	DOWNSVIEW	**ON**	M3H 4YS	(416) 633-6224
B'NAI B'RITH-DISTRICT 3 230 SOUTH 15TH STREET	PHILADELPHIA	**PA**	19102	(215) 732-6400
BRITH SHOLOM 3939 CONSHOHOCKEN AVENUE	PHILADELPHIA	**PA**	19131	(215) 878-5696
JWB ARMED SERVICES COMMITTEE 401 S. BROAD STREET	PHILADELPHIA	**PA**	19147	(215) 545-4400
MULTI-SERVICE CENTER MARSHALL & PORTER STREETS	PHILADELPHIA	**PA**	19148	(215) 468-6285
JEWISH WAR VETERANS OF THE U.S.A.-PENNSYLVANIA				
1000 LIBERTY AVENUE FEDERAL BUILDING	PITTSBURGH	**PA**	15222	(412) 644-6797
CANADIAN MACCABIAH ASSOCIATION 1225 HODGE STREET	MONTREAL	**QU**		(514) 748-7711
JEWISH WAR VETERANS OF THE U.S.A-RHOE ISLAND				
VETERANS ADMINISTRATION 321 SOUTH MAIN STREET	PROVIDENCE	**RI**	02903	(401) 528-4416
B'NAI B'RITH-DISTRICT 7				
ROYAL CENTER TOWER, 11300 N CENTRAL EXPRESSWAY, #604	DALLAS	**TX**	75243	(214) 691-6190

SOFRIM

FLUMENBAUM, RABBI M. 8 NORTH 2ND STREET	HIGHLAND PARK	**NJ**	08904	(201) 246-1690
BERGER, RABBI D. 418 7TH STREET, G-29	LAKEWOOD	**NJ**	08701	(201) 363-5725
PINCUS, RABBI Z. 602 5TH STREET	LAKEWOOD	**NJ**	08701	(201) 998-2053
ROTHSCHILD, RABBI Z. 230 PRIVATE WAY	LAKEWOOD	**NJ**	08701	(201) 370-8052
BEN DOVID, RABBI Y. 3326 PALISADES AVENUE, #B6	UNION CITY	**NJ**	07087	(201) 866-1269
BERKOWITZ, RABBI AVROHOM Y. 1470 CONEY ISLAND AVENUE	BROOKLYN	**NY**	11230	(718) 377-3664
BETH HASOFRIM 5009 16TH AVENUE	BROOKLYN	**NY**	11204	(718) 851-1637
BIXENSPAN, RABBI YITZCHOK 185 RODNEY STREET	BROOKLYN	**NY**	11211	(718) 384-6755
BODNER, RABBI S. 1620 45TH STREET	BROOKLYN	**NY**	11204	(718) 438-7036
BRITZ, RABBI SHAYA 1364 58TH STREET	BROOKLYN	**NY**	11219	(718) 435-7788
COHEN, AMRAM 238 KEAP STREET	BROOKLYN	**NY**	11211	(718) 384-7173
ECKSTEIN, YEHOSHUA 190 WILSON STREET	BROOKLYN	**NY**	11211	(718) 388-0091
FELDMAN, RABBI N. 711 AVENUE S	BROOKLYN	**NY**	11223	(718) 375-1576
FINKEL, RABBI Y. 1444 50TH STREET	BROOKLYN	**NY**	11219	(718) 851-0815
FRIED, MORDECHAI 1554 39TH STREET	BROOKLYN	**NY**	11210	(718) 853-2182
FRIEDMAN, RABBI LIPOT 1311 43RD STREET	BROOKLYN	**NY**	11219	(718) 853-8432
FRIEDMAN, RABBI Y. 4519 16TH AVENUE	BROOKLYN	**NY**	11204	(718) 633-1884
GRUNFELD, RABBI E. 80 ROSS STREET	BROOKLYN	**NY**	11211	(718) 384-2317
GRUNHUT, RABBI S. 104 ROSS STREET	BROOKLYN	**NY**	11211	(718) 387-7030
HABERFELD, RABBI N. 1673 55TH STREET	BROOKLYN	**NY**	11204	(718) 851-0352
HALBERSTAM, RABBI MOSHE SHEA 1519 52ND STREET	BROOKLYN	**NY**	11219	(718) 633-0069
HIRSCHFELD, RABBI DOVID 94 ROSS STREET	BROOKLYN	**NY**	11211	(718) 387-7066
HOROWITZ, RABBI Y. 5324 12TH AVENUE	BROOKLYN	**NY**	11219	(718) 853-0621
HOUSE OF THE SOFRIM (CERTIFIED BY VAAD MISHMERES STAM)				
5009 16TH AVENUE	BROOKLYN	**NY**	11204	(718) 851-1637
KASNETT, RABBI B. 4815 16TH AVENUE	BROOKLYN	**NY**	11204	(718) 436-0543
KATZ, RABBI EZRA 1336 53RD STREET	BROOKLYN	**NY**	11219	(718) 851-9683
KATZ, RABBI YITZCHOK 217 ROSS STREET	BROOKLYN	**NY**	11211	(718) 388-6719
KATZ, YESOSHUA 1349 53RD STREET	BROOKLYN	**NY**	11219	(718) 436-8885
KLEIN BROTHERS 4104 16TH AVENUE	BROOKLYN	**NY**	11204	(718) 633-4490
KLEIN, AKIVA 135 HEYWARD STREET	BROOKLYN	**NY**	11206	(718) 875-6096
KLEINMAN, RABBI Y'SHAYA 1678 57TH STREET	BROOKLYN	**NY**	11204	(718) 236-0206
KREIMAN, RABBI P. 1158 53RD STREET	BROOKLYN	**NY**	11219	(718) 435-7708
LAUFER, YITZCHOK 112 DIVISION STREET	BROOKLYN	**NY**	11211	(718) 388-6570
LENCHEVSKY, RABBI NATHAN 1122 45TH STREET	BROOKLYN	**NY**	11219	(718) 851-6508
LIPOT FRIEDMAN 5501 15TH AVENUE	BROOKLYN	**NY**	11219	(718) 436-0901

בס"ד

MAYBLOOM, RABBI A. 1819 AVENUE O	BROOKLYN	**NY**	11230	(718) 336-5604
PINCUS, RABBI ZVI CHAIM 1376 EAST 10TH STREET	BROOKLYN	**NY**	11230	(718) 645-4916
POLLACK, RABBI ARON 220 HOOPER STREET	BROOKLYN	**NY**	11211	(718) 384-5248
POLLACK, RABBI Y. 185 RODNEY STREET	BROOKLYN	**NY**	11211	(718) 388-3012
RABBI Y. MISHULOVIN 309 KINGSTON AVENUE	BROOKLYN	**NY**	11213	(718) 773-1120
ROSENBERG, RABBI MENACHEM 917 50TH STREET	BROOKLYN	**NY**	11219	(718) 851-0966
SCHECHTER, RABBI A. 1553 41ST STREET	BROOKLYN	**NY**	11218	(718) 871-5477
SCHERTZER, RABBI DAVID 924 EAST 13TH STREET	BROOKLYN	**NY**	11215	(718) 258-2595
SEREBROWSKI, RABBI P. 7402 BAY PARKWAY	BROOKLYN	**NY**	11204	(718) 331-5287
SHARABI, RABBI M. 1736 EAST 4TH STREET	BROOKLYN	**NY**	11223	(718) 645-2974
SHUSHAN, RABBI A. 1435 40TH STREET	BROOKLYN	**NY**	11218	(718) 438-3207
SIFREI KODESH STAM 1525 55TH STREET	BROOKLYN	**NY**	11219	(718) 436-1697
TEITELBAUM, RABBI L. 547 BEDFORD AVENUE	BROOKLYN	**NY**	11211	(718) 963-0497
TEITELBAUM, RABBI M. 140 WILSON STREET	BROOKLYN	**NY**	11211	(718) 387-0290
TWERSKY, RABBI NACHUM 5721 13TH AVENUE	BROOKLYN	**NY**	11218	
TZVI BARNETT 802 MONTGOMERY STREET	BROOKLYN	**NY**	11213	(718) 493-1243
WALKENFELD, RABBI S. 1651 42ND STREET	BROOKLYN	**NY**	11204	(718) 871-2585
WEIDER, RABBI P. 74 ROSS STREET	BROOKLYN	**NY**	11211	(718) 388-8393
YEHUDAH CLAPMAN 719 MONTGOMERY STREET	BROOKLYN	**NY**	11213	(718) 774-9313
ZOLDAN, RABBI S. 210 ROSS STREET	BROOKLYN	**NY**	11211	(718) 782-6178
BRAUNSDORFER, RABBI C. 5 WALTER DRIVE	MONSEY	**NY**	10952	(914) 352-2855
EIDENSOHN, RABBI DAVID 2 PHYLLIS TERRACE	MONSEY	**NY**	10952	(914) 352-7267
FEIG, RABBI YITZCHOK 28 RITA AVENUE	MONSEY	**NY**	10952	(914) 352-0825
FREIDUS, KALMAN 28 CARLTON ROAD	MONSEY	**NY**	10952	(914) 352-7363
FRIEDMAN, RABBI N. 4 ELYON ROAD	MONSEY	**NY**	10952	(914) 356-7572
GALANDER, ISSAMAR TUVIA 18 RITA AVENUE	MONSEY	**NY**	10952	(914) 352-1647
LEITNER, M. 18 RITA AVENUE	MONSEY	**NY**	10952	(914) 356-7807
MORRIS, RABBI MENDEL 9 ORCHARD	MONSEY	**NY**	10952	(914) 352-6876
TEICHER, AVROHOM S. 12 EDWIN LANE	MONSEY	**NY**	10952	(914) 425-8242
UNGER, RABBI MOSHE 20 JACKSON AVENUE	MONSEY	**NY**	10952	(914) 354-5542
VICENTOWSKY, RABBI D. 37 MAIN STREET	MONSEY	**NY**	10952	(914) 356-1390
WUDOWSKY, RABBI SHMUEL 25 ORCHARD STREET	MONSEY	**NY**	10952	(914) 356-6124
YAKTER, RABBI CHAIM 134 WEST CENTRAL AVENUE	MONSEY	**NY**	10952	(914) 352-6561
FISHER, YITZCHOK 38 LINCOLN AVENUE	NEW SQUARE	**NY**	10952	(914) 354-6467
BLUMENTHAL, ZELIG 13 ESSEX STREET	NEW YORK	**NY**	10002	(212) 267-8370
BODENHEIM, RABBI S. 121 BENNETT AVENUE	NEW YORK	**NY**	10033	(212) 781-5385
DEUTSCH, RABBI LAZAR 47 ESSEX STREET	NEW YORK	**NY**	10002	(212) 254-1400
EISENBACH, RABBI MOSHE 49 ESSEX STREET	NEW YORK	**NY**	10002	(212) 674-8840
LASDUN, RABBI Y. 80 BENNETT AVENUE	NEW YORK	**NY**	10033	(212) 927-1655
LUBART, RABBI M. 50 CANAL STREET	NEW YORK	**NY**	10002	(212) 966-0526
SOFER 3320 DESOTA AVENUE	CLEVELAND	**OH**		(216) 932-6186

SOLDIERS & SAILORS

ASSOCIATION OF JEWISH CHAPLAINS OF ARMED FORCES 15 E. 26TH STREET	NEW YORK	**NY**	10010	(212) 532-4949
JEWISH WELFARE BOARD-ASSOC. WELFARE SOLDIERS IN ISRAEL 15 E. 26TH STREET	NEW YORK	**NY**	10010	(212) 532-4949
JWB ARMED SERVICES COMMITTEE 401 S. BROAD STREET	PHILADELPHIA	**PA**	19147	(215) 545-4400

SOVIET JEWRY

ALABAMA COUNCIL TO SAVE SOVIET JEWS 3113 JASMINE RD	MONTGOMERY	**AL**	36111	(205) 264-3101
ARIZONA COUNCIL ON SOVIET JEWS 421 EAST LA MAR RD	PHOENIX	**AZ**	85012	(602) 264-2325
VANCOUVER SOVIET JEWRY ACTION COMMITTEE 950 WEST 41ST AVENUE	VANCOUVER	**BC**	V5Z 2N7	(604) 261-8101
SOUTHERN CALIFORNIA COUNCIL FOR SOVIET JEWS PO BOX 113; 8621 WILSHIRE BLVD	BEVERLY HILLS	**CA**	90211	(213) 556-2598
SAN DIEGO COUNCIL FOR SOVIET JEWRY 1770 AVENUE, DEL MUNDO 902	CORONADO	**CA**	92118	(619) 435-5519
CALIFORNIA STUDENTS FOR SOVIET JEWS 900 HIGARD AVENUE	LOS ANGELES	**CA**	90026	
BAY AREA COUNCIL ON SOVIET JEWRY 106 BADEN STREET	SAN FRANCISCO	**CA**	94131	(415) 585-1400
SOVIET EMBASSY 2790 GREEN STREET	SAN FRANCISCO	**CA**	94123	(415) 922-6642
COLORADO COMMITTEE OF CONCERN FOR SOVIET JEWRY 22 S. JERSEY ST	DENVER	**CO**	80224	(303) 377-7859
CONNECTICUT COMMITTEE FOR SOVIET JEWS 502 FOUNTAIN ST., #3A	NEW HAVEN	**CT**	06515	(203) 387-4526
NATIONAL CONFERENCE ON SOVIET JEWRY 2027 MASSACHUSETTS AVENUE N.W.	WASHINGTON	**DC**	20036	(202) 265-8114
SOVIET EMBASSY 1511 K STREET N.W.	WASHINGTON	**DC**	20005	(202) 628-9693
UNION OF COUNCILS FOR SOVIET JEWS 1411 K STREET N.W. SUITE 402	WASHINGTON	**DC**	20005	(202) 393-4117
WASHINGTON COMMITTEE FOR SOVIET JEWRY 2129 F STREET	WASHINGTON	**DC**	20037	
JEWISH FEDERATION OF SOUTH BROWARD 2719 HOLLYWOOD BOULEVARD	HOLLYWOOD	**FL**	33020	(305) 921-8810
SOUTH FLORIDA CONFERENCE ON SOVIET JEWRY 4200 BISCAYNE BLVD	MIAMI	**FL**	33161	(305) 576-4000
SARASOTA COUNCIL ON SOVIET JEWRY PO BOX 2778	SARASOTA	**FL**	33578	(813) 349-5725
WEST PALM BEACH-JEWISH FEDERATION OF PALM BEACH COUNTY 120 SOUTH OLIVE STREET	WEST PALM BEACH	**FL**	33401	(305) 832-2120
DES MOINES ACTION COMMITTEE FOR SOVIET JEWRY 705 41ST ST	WEST DES MOINES	**IA**	50265	(515) 223-1247
NATIONAL INTERRELIGIOUS TASK FORCE ON SOVIET JEWRY 1307 SOUTH WABASH	CHICAGO	**IL**	60605	(312) 922-1983
CHICAGO ACTION FOR SOVIET JEWRY 1724 FIRST STREET	HIGHLAND PARK	**IL**	60035	(312) 433-0144
SOVIET JEWRY COMMITTEE, JEWISH FEDERATION OF SOUTH BEND 1105 N. IRONWOOD DR	SOUTH BEND	**IN**	46615	(219) 234-3829
ASSOC. FOR DISSEMINATION OF THE HEBREW LANGUAGE IN THE USSR PO BOX 3897	JERUSALEM	**IS**	91037	
KANSAS CITY COUNCIL FOR SOVIET JEWRY 5812 W. 100TH ST	OVERLAND PARK	**KS**	66207	(913) 649-0290
NEW ENGLAND STUDENT STRUGGLE FOR SOVIET JEWRY 233 BAY STATE ROAD	BOSTON	**MA**	02215	(617) 267-8250
PITTSFIELD COUNCIL FOR SOVIET JEWRY 22 MARLBORO DR	PITTSFIELD	**MA**	01201	(413) 448-8043
SOVIET JEWRY COMMITTEE OF THE NORTH SHORE 1000 LORING AVENUE, #C91	SALEM	**MA**	01970	(617) 745-5453
BOSTON ACTION FOR SOVIET JEWRY 24 CRESCENT STREET, SUITE 3B	WALTHAM	**MA**	02154	(617) 893-2331
MEDICAL MOBILIZATION FOR SOVIET JEWRY 24 CRESCENT STREET	WALTHAM	**MA**	02154	(617) 893-2331
SOVIET JEWRY LEGAL ADVOCACY CENTER 24 CRESCENT STREET, #2G	WALTHAM	**MA**	02154	(617) 893-2331
BALTIMORE COUNCIL FOR SOVIET JEWRY 6503 PARK HEIGHTS AVE., APT 1-C	BALTIMORE	**MD**	21215	(301) 764-7242
WASHINGTON COMMITTEE FOR SOVIET JEWRY 8402 FREYMAN DR	CHEVY CHASE	**MD**	20815	(301) 587-4455
DETROIT SOVIET JEWRY COMMITTEE OF THE JCC 163 MADISON AVENUE	DETROIT	**MI**	58226	(313) 962-1880
MINNESOTA-DAKOTAS ACTION COMM. FOR SOVIET JEWRY 15 SOUTH 9TH ST	MINNEAPOLIS	**MN**	55402	(612) 338-7816
GREENSBORO ACTION FOR SOVIET JEWRY 222 MISTLETOE DRIVE	GREENSBORO	**NC**	27403	(919) 282-1710
OMAHA COMMITTEE FOR SOVIET JEWRY 11217 WOOLWORTH PLAZA	OMAHA	**NE**	68144	(402) 334-1055
LOS ALAMOS COMMITTEE ON SOVIET ANTI-SEMITISM 9 VILLAGE PL.; WHITE ROCK VILLAGE	LOS ALAMOS	**NM**	87544	(505) 672-3783
ASSOCIATION OF SOVIET JEWS IN AMERICA 1050 OCEAN AVENUE	BROOKLYN	**NY**	11226	(718) 434-4518
FREE FRIENDS OF REFUGEES OF EASTERN EUROPE 1383 PRESIDENT STREET	BROOKLYN	**NY**	11213	(718) 467-0860
OCEANFRONT COUNCIL FOR SOVIET JEWRY 4089 OCEAN AVENUE	BROOKLYN	**NY**	11235	(718) 891-9685
STUDENT STRUGGLE FOR SOVIET JEWRY 1118 AVENUE J	BROOKLYN	**NY**	11230	(718) 253-3800
LONG ISLAND COMMITTEE FOR SOVIET JEWRY ONE OLD COUNTRY ROAD, SUITE 393	CARLE PLACE	**NY**	11514	(516) 294-8181
SOVIET JEWRY HOT LINE 98 CUTTER MILL ROAD	GREAT NECK	**NY**	11021	(516) 466-4699
LONG ISLAND COMMITTEE FOR SOVIET JEWRY 134 JACKSON STREET	HEMPSTEAD	**NY**	11550	(516) 538-5454
LONG ISLAND MEDICAL/DENTAL/HEALTH COMMITTEE FOR SOVIET JEWRY 91 NORTH FRANKLIN	HEMPSTEAD	**NY**	11550	(516) 538-5454
ACADEMIC COMMITTEE ON SOVIET JEWRY 345 E 46TH STREET	NEW YORK	**NY**	10017	(212) 557-9013
CENTER FOR RUSSIAN JEWRY 210 W 91ST STREET	NEW YORK	**NY**	10024	(212) 799-8900
COMMITTEE FOR DEFENSE OF SOVIET POLITICAL PRISONERS 254 WEST 31ST STREET	NEW YORK	**NY**	10001	(212) 695-3895
CTR FOR RUSSIAN JEWRY-STUDENT STRUGGLE FOR SOVIET JEWRY, THE 210 W 91ST STREET	NEW YORK	**NY**	10024	(212) 799-8900
COALITION TO FREE SOVIET JEWS 8 WEST 40TH STREET, SUITE 602	NEW YORK	**NY**	10018	(212) 354-1316
24 HOUR SOVIET JEWRY ACTIONLINE	NEW YORK	**NY**		(212) 391-0954
JACOB BIRNBAUM-CENTER FOR RUSSIAN AND EAST EUROPEAN JEWRY 240 CABRINI BLVD	NEW YORK	**NY**	10033	(212) 928-7451
INTERNATIONAL LEAGUE FOR REPATRIATION OF RUSSIAN JEWS 315 CHURCH STREET	NEW YORK	**NY**	10013	(212) 431-6789
INTERNATIONAL LEAGUE FOR REPATRIATION OF RUSSIAN JEWS 41 E 42ND STREET, SUITE 515	NEW YORK	**NY**	10017	(212) 682-7865
INTERNATIONAL LEAGUE FOR THE REPATRIATION OF RUSSIAN JEWS 315 CHURCH STREET	NEW YORK	**NY**	10013	(212) 431-6866
JOINT COMM. ON SOC. ACTION/COMM. ON JEW. COMMUNITY & PUB. POL 155 FIFTH AVENUE	NEW YORK	**NY**	10010	(212) 533-7800
NATIONAL CONFERENCE ON SOVIET JEWRY 10 E. 40TH STREET, SUITE 907	NEW YORK	**NY**	10016	(212) 679-6122
NATIONAL CONFERENCE ON SOVIET JEWRY 10 W. 40TH STREET	NEW YORK	**NY**	10016	(212) 679-6122
PROJECT RISE-RUSSIAN IMMIGRANT SERVICES & EDUCATION 5 BEEKMAN STREET	NEW YORK	**NY**	10038	(212) 864-1620
PROJECT RISE-A DIVISION OF AGUDATH ISRAEL 5 BEEKMAN STREET	NEW YORK	**NY**	10038	(212) 791-1830
RUSSIAN IMMIGRANT RESCUE FUND 5 BEEKMAN STREET	NEW YORK	**NY**	10038	(212) 964-8262
SOVIET JEWRY RESEARCH BUREAU-NAT'L CONF. ON SOVIET JEWRY 10 E. 40TH STREET, SUITE 907	NEW YORK	**NY**	10016	(212) 679-6122
SOVIET UN MISSION 136 EAST 67TH STREET	NEW YORK	**NY**	10021	(212) 861-4900
STUDENT STRUGGLE FOR SOVIET JEWRY 210 WEST 91ST STREET	NEW YORK	**NY**	10024	(212) 799-8900
TASS NEWS AGENCY 50 ROCKEFELLER PLAZA	NEW YORK	**NY**	10020	(212) 245-4250
CINCINNATI COUNCIL FOR SOVIET JEWRY 2615 CLIFTON AVE	CINCINNATI	**OH**	45220	(513) 221-7134
CLEVELAND COUNCIL ON SOVIET ANTI-SEMITISM (CCSA, INC.) 6325 ALDENHAM DRIVE	CLEVELAND	**OH**	44143	(216) 449-3662
OKLAHOMA COMMISSION FOR SOVIET JEWRY 5633 SOUTH GARY	TULSA	**OK**	74105	(918) 747-6390
GREATER PHILADELPHIA COUNCIL FOR SOVIET JEWS PO BOX 83	BALA CYNWYD	**PA**	19004	
SOVIET JEWRY ACTION COUNCIL OF HARRISBURG 3560 GREEN STREET	HARRISBURG	**PA**	17110	(717) 238-5673
SOVIET JEWRY COUNCIL OF THE JCRC 1520 LOCUST ST	PHILADELPHIA	**PA**	19102	(215) 545-8430
PITTSBURGH VOICE ON SOVIET JEWRY 234 MCKEE PLACE	PITTSBURGH	**PA**	15213	(412) 681-8000
CANADIAN 35'S 118 ABERDEEN AVENUE	WESTMONT	**QU**		(518) 891-3319
KNOXVILLE-OAK RIDGE COUNCIL FOR SOVIET JEWS 7113 CHESHIRE DR	KNOXVILLE	**TN**	37919	(615) 584-6042
HOUSTON ACTION FOR SOVIET JEWRY 9107 TIMBERSIDE DRIVE	HOUSTON	**TX**	77025	(713) 665-6753
WACO COUNCIL OF CONCERN ON SOVIET JEWRY 5501 FAIRVIEW DR	WACO	**TX**	76710	(817) 772-8929
NEWPORT NEWS SOVIET JEWRY COMMITTEE UNITED JEWISH FEDERATION 317 LYNCHBURG DRIVE	NEWPORT NEWS	**VA**	23606	(804) 599-5546
SEATTLE ACTION FOR SOVIET JEWRY 5229 S. MORGAN	SEATTLE	**WA**	98118	(206) 723-6897
LONDON 35'S (WOMEN'S CAMPAIGN FOR SOVIET JEWRY) 755A FINCHLEY ROAD	LONDON	**GB**		
COMITE DES QUINZE 14 RUE DE LONGCHAMP	9200 NEUILLY	**FR**		

SPORTS

INTERNATIONAL JEWISH SPORTS HALL OF FAME-USA 9200 SUNSET BOULEVARD, SUITE 1010	LOS ANGELES	**CA**	90069	(213) 276-1014
MACCABEE ATHLETIC CLUB, INC 6399 WILSHIRE BOULEVARD	LOS ANGELES	**CA**	90048	(213) 651-3182
UNITED STATES COMMITTEE SPORTS FOR ISRAEL PO BOX 37604	WASHINGTON	**DC**	20013	
ISRAEL TENNIS CENTER COMMITTEE 350 FIFTH AVENUE	NEW YORK	**NY**	10118	(212) 594-5250
UNITED STATES COMMITTEE SPORTS FOR ISRAEL, INC 275 SOUTH 19TH STREET	PHILADELPHIA	**PA**	19103	(215) 546-4700

STAINED GLASS

ASCALON STUDIOS 206 CROSS KEYS ROAD	BERLIN	NJ	08009	(609) 768-3779
EDELWEISS CO - GLASS STUDIO 1217 49 STREET	BROOKLYN	NY	11219	(718) 851-9687
EAGLE MIRROR, GLASS & BLIND, INC-STAINED GLASS, ETC. 75 SUNSET AVENUE	LYNBROOK	NY	11563	(718) 327-6764
CLEVELAND CHAPTER OF THE SOCIETY OF ISRAEL PHILATELISTS 24355 TUNBRIDGE LANE	CLEVELAND	OH	44122	(216) 292-3843
ISRAEL NUMISMATIC SOCIETY OF CLEVELAND 614 W. SUPERIOR ROAD, #600	CLEVELAND	OH	44113	(216) 241-2258
SOCIETY OF ISRAEL PHILATELISTS 3619 CLEVELAND AVENUE	CLEVELAND	OH	44118	
AMERICAN TOPICAL ASSOCIATION 5014 WEST CENTER	MILWAUKEE	WI	53216	(414) 873-8280

STAMPS

SOCIETY OF ISRAEL PHILATELISTS 1125 EAST CARSON STREET #2	LONG BEACH	CA	90807	(213) 595-9224
FRANK STEINER 199 SOUTH LA JOLLA AVENUE	LOS ANGELES	CA	90048	(213) 655-2695
SOCIETY OF ISRAEL PHILATELISTS	LOS ANGELES	CA	90025	(213) 345-7645
BICK INTERNATIONAL PO BOX 854	VAN NUYS	CA	91408	(818) 997-6496
ISRAEL STAMP COLLECTORS SOCIETY PO BOX 854	VAN NUYS	CA	91408	(818) 997-6496
B'NAI B'RITH PHILATELIC SERVICE 1640 RHODE ISLAND AVENUE N.W.	WASHINGTON	DC	20036	(202) 857-6600
KLUTZNICK EXHIBIT HALL 1640 RHODE ISLAND AVENUE N.W.	WASHINGTON	DC	20036	(202) 857-6600
ISRAEL NUMISMATIC SOCIETY PO BOX 427	SKOKIE	IL	60035	
JEWISH ASSOCIATION FOR SERVICES FOR THE AGED 155 BEACH 19TH STREET	FAR ROCKAWAY	NY	11691	(718) 471-6677
GAREL COMPANY PO BOX 374	HEWLETT	NY	11557	(516) 374-2909
AMERICAN ZIONIST YOUTH FOUNDATION 515 PARK AVENUE	NEW YORK	NY	10022	(212) 751-6070
COLLECTOR'S CLUB 22 EAST 35TH STREET	NEW YORK	NY	10016	(212) 683-0559
ISRAEL PHILATELIC AGENCY IN AMERICA, INC. 116 WEST 32ND STREET	NEW YORK	NY	10001	(212) 695-0008
ISRAEL PHILATELIC AGENCY IN AMERICA 41 WEST 25TH STREET	NEW YORK	NY	10001	(212) 807-6044
JUDAICA HISTORICAL PHILATELIC SOCIETY PO BOX 484, COOPER STATION	NEW YORK	NY	10003	
MOSDEN STAMP COMPANY 232 EAST 54TH STREET	NEW YORK	NY	10022	(212) 758-7818
SAM MALAMUD, IDEAL STAMP COMPANY 48 WEST 48TH STREET	NEW YORK	NY	10036	(212) 869-5545
JUDAICA HISTORICAL PHILATELIC SOCIETY 80 BRUCE AVENUE	YONKERS	NY	10705	

STREIMELS

EINHORN MOSHE 50-18 14TH AVENUE	BROOKLYN	NY	11219	(718) 853-5599
KESER SHTREIMLICH (M. HERZL) 1769 50TH STREET	BROOKLYN	NY	11204	(718) 633-3563
KOPITCH, AVROHOM DOVID 155 ROSS STREET	BROOKLYN	NY	11211	
KRAUSS, SHMUEL 202 KEAP STREET	BROOKLYN	NY	11211	(718) 387-7832
ONE-HA-STREIMEL 193 LEE AVENUE	BROOKLYN	NY	11211	
ONEG SHTREIMLICH (GESTETNER) 110 LEE AVENUE	BROOKLYN	NY	11211	(718) 387-0218
SCHWARTZ, YISROEL NECHEMIA 190 ROSS STREET	BROOKLYN	NY	11211	(718) 387-4491
SELCO HATTERS 228 BROADWAY	BROOKLYN	NY	11211	(718) 388-6848
SHMUEL KRAUSS 167 PENN STREET	BROOKLYN	NY	11211	
KLEIN, CHAIM YEHUDA 24 RALPH BOULEVARD	MONSEY	NY	10952	(914) 425-1068

STUDENT, YOUNG ADULT & YOUTH ORGANIZATIONS

BRANDEIS-BARDIN YOUNG ADULTS 1101 PEPPERTREE LANE	BRANDEIS	CA	93064	(213) 348-7201
JEWISH COMMUNITY CENTER OF LONG BEACH, COLLEGE STUDENT SERV. 3801 EAST WILLOW	LONG BEACH	CA	90815	(213) 426-7601
HA'AM 112 E KERCKHOFF HALL, 308 WESTWOOD PLAZA	LOS ANGELES	CA	90024	
JEWISH YOUTH DEPT. 6505 WILSHIRE BLVD	LOS ANGELES	CA	90048	(213) 852-1234
NITZAN CHAPTER FOR YOUNG CAREER WOMEN 1494 S ROBERTSON BLVD	LOS ANGELES	CA	90035	(213) 275-5345
NORTHERN PACIFIC COAST, HASHACHAR-YOUNG JUDEA 1419 BROADWAY, SUITE 308	OAKLAND	CA	94612	(415) 832-8448
LUBAVITCH YOUTH ORGANIZATION 152 GOFFE TERR	NEW HAVEN	CT	06511	(203) 865-3649
B'NAI B'RITH YOUTH ORGANIZATION 1640 RHODE ISLAND AVENUE N.W.	WASHINGTON	DC	20036	(202) 857-6600
FLORIDA UNION OF JEWISH STUDENTS C/O MIAMI HILLEL 100 MILLER DRIVE	CORAL GABLES	FL	33146	(305) 661-8549
BNEI AKIVA OF CHICAGO 6500 NORTH CALIFORNIA	CHICAGO	IL	60645	(312) 338-6569
CHICAGO JEWISH YOUTH COUNCIL 3003 W. TOUHY AVENUE	CHICAGO	IL	60645	(312) 961-9100
DEBORAH BOYS CLUB 3201 W. AINSLIE STREET	CHICAGO	IL	60625	(312) 539-5907
FEDERATION OF TEMPLE YOUTH 100 WEST MONROE	CHICAGO	IL	60603	(312) 782-1477
YOUNG MEN'S JEWISH COUNCIL 30 WEST WASHINGTON	CHICAGO	IL	60602	(312) 726-8891
LUBAVITCH YOUTH ORGANIZATION 42 KIRKWOOD ROAD	BRIGHTON	MA	02135	(617) 787-2667
FELLOWSHIP IN ISRAEL FOR ARAB-JEWISH YOUTH 45 FRANCIS AVENUE	CAMBRIDGE	MA	02138	(617) 354-1198
LUBAVITCH YOUTH ORGANIZATION 74 JOSEPH ROAD	FRAMINGHAM	MA	01761	(617) 877-5313
NANTASKET YOUTH CENTER 7 WILSON STREET	HULL	MA	02045	(413) 925-4445
LUBAVITCH YOUTH ORGANIZATION 15 ELWOOD DRIVE	SPRINGFIELD	MA	01108	(413) 737-7998
EMANUEL, TEMPLE R 280 MAY STREET	WORCESTER	MA	01602	(617) 755-1257
LUBAVITCH YOUTH ORGANIZATION 24 CRESWELL	WORCESTER	MA	01602	(617) 752-5791
NAT'L CONFERENCE OF SYNAGOUE YOUTH-ATLANTIC SEABOARD REGION 5713 PARK HEIGHTS AVENUE	BALTIMORE	MD	21215	(301) 542-8678
JEWISH STUDENTS OF CARLETON CARLETON COLLEGE	NORTHFIELD	MN	55057	(507) 645-4431
LUBAVITCH STUDENTS ORGANIZATION 226 SUSSEX AVENUE	MORRISTOWN	NJ	07960	(201) 540-0877
YUGNTRUF 3328 BAINBRIDGE AVENUE	BRONX	NY	10467	(212) 654-8540
AKIVA JEWISH CULTURE CLUBS OF THE N.Y.C. PUBLIC HIGH SCHOOLS 1577 CONEY ISLAND AVENUE	BROOKLYN	NY	11230	(718) 258-3585
JEWISH ORTHODOX YOUTH, INC. 563 BEDFORD AVENUE	BROOKLYN	NY	11211	(718) 384-0461
JEWISH STUDENT UNION OF BROOKLYN LAW SCHOOL 250 JORALEMON STREET	BROOKLYN	NY	11201	(718) 625-2200
LUBAVITCH YOUTH ORGANIZATION 770 EASTERN PARKWAY	BROOKLYN	NY	11213	(718) 625-2200
TZIVOS HASHEM 770 EASTERN PARKWAY	BROOKLYN	NY	11213	(718) 467-6630
LUBAVITCH OF LONG ISLAND 74 HAPPAUGE ROAD	COMMACK	NY	11725	(516) 462-6640
QUEENS COLLEGE UNION B-42 COUNCIL OF JEWISH ORGANIZATIONS 65-30 KISSENA BLVD BOX 24	FLUSHING	NY	11367	(718) 591-8978
AMERICAN JEWISH SOCIETY FOR SERVICE 15 E 26TH STREET	NEW YORK	NY	10010	(212) 683-6178
AMERICAN ZIONIST YOUTH FOUNDATION 515 PARK AVENUE	NEW YORK	NY	10022	(212) 751-6070
BETAR 41 EAST 42ND STREET	NEW YORK	NY	10017	(212) 687-4502
BETAR 116 NASSAU STREET	NEW YORK	NY	10038	
BNEI AKIVA OF NEW YORK 25 W. 26TH STREET	NEW YORK	NY	10010	(212) 889-5992
BNEI AKIVA OF NORTH AMERICA 25 WEST 26TH STREET	NEW YORK	NY	10010	(212) 889-5260
BNOS AGUDATH ISRAEL 5 BEEKMAN STREET	NEW YORK	NY	10038	(212) 964-1620
COLLEGE YOUTH FOR TORAH 116 E. 27TH STREET	NEW YORK	NY	10016	(212) 725-3420
DEPT. OF YOUTH ACTIVITIES/USY, KADIMA 155 FIFTH AVENUE	NEW YORK	NY	10010	(212) 533-7800
DROR YOUNG KIBBUTZ MOVEMENT 27 WEST 20TH STREET	NEW YORK	NY	10011	(212) 675-1168
HABONIM LABOR ZIONIST YOUTH 27 WEST 20TH STREET	NEW YORK	NY	10011	(212) 255-1796
HAMAGSHIMIM 50 WEST 58TH STREET	NEW YORK	NY	10019	(212) 355-7900
HASHACHAR 50 W. 58TH STREET	NEW YORK	NY	10019	(212) 355-7900
HASHOMER HATZAIR SOCIALIST ZIONIST YOUTH MOVEMENT 150 FIFTH AVENUE, #710	NEW YORK	NY	10011	(212) 929-4955
ICHUD HABONIM LABOR ZIONIST YOUTH 27 W. 20 STREET	NEW YORK	NY	10011	(212) 255-1796
ISRAEL SUMMER SEMINAR 1776 BROADWAY	NEW YORK	NY	10019	(212) 247-0741
ISRAELI STUDENTS' ORGANIZATION IN THE U.S. & CANADA 515 PARK AVENUE	NEW YORK	NY	10022	(212) 688-6796
JEWISH ASSOCIATION FOR COLLEGE YOUTH 130 EAST 59TH STREET	NEW YORK	NY	10022	(212) 688-0808
JEWISH MEDIA SERVICE 15 EAST 26TH STREET	NEW YORK	NY	10010	(212) 532-4949
JEWISH STUDENT APPEAL 15 EAST 26TH STREET	NEW YORK	NY	10010	(212) 679-2293
JEWISH STUDENT PRESS SERVICE 15 E. 26TH STREET, SUITE 1350	NEW YORK	NY	10010	(212) 679-1411
LUBAVITCH YOUTH ORGANIZATION 770 EASTERN PARKWAY	NEW YORK	NY	11213	(212) 493-0571
MESORAH 45 W 36TH STREET	NEW YORK	NY	10018	(212) 563-4000
METROPOLITAN UNION OF JEWISH STUDENTS 515 PARK AVENUE	NEW YORK	NY	10022	
NATIONAL CONFERENCE OF SYNAGOGUE YOUTH (NCSY) 45 WEST 36TH STREET	NEW YORK	NY	10018	(212) 563-4000
NATIONAL FEDERATION OF TEMPLE YOUTH 838 FIFTH AVENUE	NEW YORK	NY	10021	(212) 249-0100
NETWORK 36 WEST 37TH STREET	NEW YORK	NY	10018	
NEW JEWISH MEDIA PROJECT 36 WEST 37TH STREET	NEW YORK	NY	10018	
NOAR MIZRACHI 25 WEST 26TH STREET	NEW YORK	NY	10010	(212) 684-6091
NORTH AMERICAN FEDERATION OF TEMPLE YOUTH 838 FIFTH AVENUE	NEW YORK	NY	10021	(212) 249-0100
NORTH AMERICAN JEWISH STUDENTS NETWORK, INC. 1 PARK AVENUE	NEW YORK	NY	10016	(212) 689-0790
NORTH AMERICAN JEWISH YOUTH COUNCIL 515 PARK AVENUE	NEW YORK	NY	10022	
ORT YOUTH FELLOWSHIP 315 PARK AVENUE SOUTH	NEW YORK	NY	10010	(212) 505-7700
ORT YOUTH FELLOWSHIP 1250 BROADWAY	NEW YORK	NY	10001	
P'EYLIM-AMERICAN YESHIVA STUDENT UNION 3 W. 16TH STREET	NEW YORK	NY	10011	(212) 989-2500
PIRCHEI AGUDATH ISRAEL 5 BEEKMAN STREET	NEW YORK	NY	10038	(212) 964-1620
SEIXAS-MENORAH SOCIETY OF COLUMBIA & BARNARD 102 EARL HALL-COLUMBIA UNIVERSITY	NEW YORK	NY	10027	
STUDENT STRUGGLE FOR SOVIET JEWRY 210 WEST 91ST STREET	NEW YORK	NY	10024	(212) 799-8900
STUDENTS ON SCHOLARSHIP/NAT'L. COUNCIL OF YOUNG ISRAEL 3 WEST 16TH STREET	NEW YORK	NY	10011	(212) 929-1525
UNITED SYNAGOGUE YOUTH 155 FIFTH AVENUE	NEW YORK	NY	10010	(212) 533-7800
YAVNEH - NATIONAL RELIGIOUS STUDENTS ASSOCIATION 156 FIFTH AVENUE	NEW YORK	NY	10010	(212) 929-5434
YAVNEH-NATIONAL RELIGIOUS JEWISH STUDENTS ASSOCIATION 25 W. 26TH STREET	NEW YORK	NY	10010	(212) 679-4574
YISRAEL HATZAIR-YOUNG ISRAEL SYNAGOGUE YOUTH 3 WEST 16TH STREET	NEW YORK	NY	10011	(212) 929-1525
YOUNG ISRAEL MASSORAH COLLEGIATE COUNCIL 3 WEST 16TH STREET	NEW YORK	NY	10011	(212) 929-1525
ZEIREI ADUDATH ISRAEL OF AMERICA 5 BEEKMAN STREET	NEW YORK	NY	10038	(212) 791-1820
HEBREW UNION COLLEGE STUDENT ASSOCIATION 3101 CLIFTON AVENUE	CINCINNATI	OH	45220	(513) 221-1875
ETHIC, THE 3246 DESOTA AVENUE	CLEVELAND	OH	44118	(216) 932-0206
NEW OHIO UNION OF JEWISH STUDENTS 11291 EUCLID AVENUE	CLEVELAND	OH	44106	
ISRAEL YOUTH PROGRAM CENTRE 1000 FINCH AVENUE WEST	DOWNSVIEW	ON		(416) 665-7733
CANADIAN YOUNG JUDEA ZIONIST YOUTH MOVEMENT 788 MARLEE AVENUE	TORONTO	ON	M6B 3K1	(416) 787-5350
YOUNG HERUT 3417 BATHURST STREET	TORONTO	ON		
HASHACHAR YOUNG JUDAEA 1825 SPRUCE STREET	PHILADELPHIA	PA	19103	(215) 545-6270
PENNSYLVANIA FED. OF TEMPLE YOUTH, PA COUNCIL UAHC 2111 ARCHITECTS BLDG., 117 S. 17TH STREET	PHILADELPHIA	PA	19103	(215) 563-8183
WESTERN PENNSYLVANIA HASHACHAR-YOUNG JUDEA 6328 FORBES AVENUE	PITTSBURGH	PA	15217	(412) 521-4877
B'NAI ISRAEL, CONGREGATION O 7 EAST SUNBURY STREET	SHAMOKIN	PA	17872	(717) 648-2281
BNEI AKIVA OF MONTREAL 5497A VICTORIA AVENUE, SUITE 103	MONTREAL	QU	H3W 2R1	(514) 739-1119
BRITH TRUMPELDOR BETAR OF AMERICA 5234 CLANRANALD AVENUE	MONTREAL	QU		(514) 486-8926
CANADIAN YOUNG JUDEA 5319 DECARIE BOULEVARD	MONTREAL	QU		(514) 481-8910
YOUNG HERUT 5234 CLANRANALD AVENUE	MONTREAL	QU	H3X 2S4	
SHERUT LA'AM 1310 GREENE AVENUE	WESTMOUNT	QU	H3Z 2B2	(514) 934-0804
STUDENT ZIONIST ORGANIZATIONS 1310 GREENE AVENUE	WESTMOUNT	QU	H3Z 2B2	(514) 934-0804
YOUTH & HECHALUTZ DEPARTMENT (ISRAEL PROGRAM CENTRE) 1310 GREENE AVENUE	WESTMOUNT	QU	H3Z 2B2	(514) 934-0804

THE NEW YORK TIMES, WEDNESDAY, OCTOBER 3, 1984

The third largest Jewish organization

בה

in America* was established in 1980 and has over 100,000 members, all under 13 years of age

Four and a half years ago a new organization appeared on the American Jewish landscape. Tzivos Hashem.

It is a restricted organization. Restricted to boys and girls aged 13 years old and younger. Its purpose is to guarantee that there will be a Jewish tomorrow.

We live in an era of extreme assimilation. Most Jewish organizations are experiencing serious decline in membership. Recruiting new members is difficult if not impossible.

Yet Tzivos Hashem has in three short years become the third largest independent Jewish organization in America. And with over 100,000 members it is the fastest growing Jewish organization in recent history. This despite the fact that each year 20% of its members leave the organization when they reach the retirement age of 13.

What is Tzivos Hashem?

It is children. Children united for a Jewish tomorrow.

Why is Tzivos Hashem so successful?

Tzivos Hashem was founded by the Lubavitcher Rebbe, Rabbi Menachem M. Schneerson. He recognized that children, because they are more in touch with themselves and therefore with G-d, often have a greater sense of destiny than adults. Such wisdom is fragile, however, and often erodes with age.

Tzivos Hashem unites these children, providing the information and inspiration needed to grow in a Jewish direction.

After all, a young child is like a young tree. He can grow straight and erect or bowed and bent. She can reach for the heavens or grow warped and misdirected.

Whether today's Jewish child grows up with eternal values or grows up to worship the idols of pop culture—or worse yet, to subjugate himself to a cult—is not a matter of fate but a matter of faith. Tzivos Hashem *is* faith. Faith in today's children and faith in their future as Jews.

If you have a child of your own, or know of a Jewish boy or girl who does not yet belong to Tzivos Hashem, let us know and we will send them a Tzivos Hashem starter kit.

And if you believe that we must work today for a Jewish tomorrow, please make your most generous contribution to Tzivos Hashem. The reward will be eternal.

Tzivos Hashem

718 - 467-6630

For more information about Tzivos Hashem, or to support its work, please return the coupon below to:
Tzivos Hashem, 770 Eastern Parkway, Brooklyn, NY

☐ Please send me more information about Tzivos Hashem
☐ Please enroll the child listed below in Tzivos Hashem:

Name _____ Age _____

Address _____

City / State / Zip _____

☐ Enclosed is my contribution of $_____ to help Tzivos Hashem guarantee a Jewish tomorrow

Name _____

Address _____

City / State / Zip _____

*Hadassah and Bnai Brith are first and second

This advertisement made possible by Friends of Tzivos Hashem.

SUKKOT SUPPLIES

ATARAH	LOS ANGELES CA	90036	(213) 655-3050
TORAH TREASURES 1202 WASHINGTON AVENUE	MIAMI BEACH FL	33139	(305) 673-6095
JUDAICA ENTERPRISES	NORTH MIAMI BEACH FL		(305) 945-5091
CRAFTWOOD LUMBER COMPANY 1590 OLD DEERFIELD ROAD	HIGHLAND PARK IL	60035	(312) 831-2800
R. KROCHMAL 71 MONASTERY RD.	BRIGHTON MA	02135	(617) 254-1760
GOODMAN'S HEBREW BOOK SHOP	BALTIMORE MD		(301) 933-1800
CUSTOM SUKKAHS	BERGEN COUNTY NJ		(201) 568-9423
8TH AVENUE LUMBER 5002 8TH AVENUE	BROOKLYN NY	11220	(718) 854-0401
BORO PARK 4717 13TH AVENUE	BROOKLYN NY	11219	(718) 853-8888
BORO PARK LUMBER & HOME CENTER 4601 NEW UTRECHT AVENUE	BROOKLYN NY	11219	(718) 853-3100
CERTIFIED LUMBER COMPANY 470 KENT AVENUE	BROOKLYN NY	11211	(718) 387-1233
CUSTOM SUKKAHS 4511 16TH AVENUE	BROOKLYN NY	11204	
EICHLER'S 1429 CONEY ISLAND AVENUE	BROOKLYN NY	11230	(718) 258-7643
F & F SUKKAH FACTORY & SHOWROOM 32 LYNCH STREET	BROOKLYN NY	11206	(718) 596-0597
F & F SUKKAH FACTORY & SHOWROOM 1271 56TH STREET	BROOKLYN NY	11219	(718) 435-5433
HADAR ESSROGIM 4717 13TH AVENUE	BROOKLYN NY	11219	(718) 853-8888
LEITER'S, THE SOURCE 4301 14TH AVENUE	BROOKLYN NY	11219	(718) 436-0303
RABBI LEIB PURETZ 1571 CONEY ISLAND AVENUE	BROOKLYN NY	11230	(718) 252-7532
SUKKAS SHOLOM 196 LEE AVENUE	BROOKLYN NY	11211	(718) 855-1163
FRANK SUPPLY COMPANY 21-07 CORNAGA AVENUE	FAR ROCKAWAY NY	11691	(718) 471-2663
GIFT WORLD 72-20 MAIN STREET	FLUSHING NY	11367	(718) 261-0233
PRI ETROG COMPANY, THE 69-66 MAIN STREET	FLUSHING NY	11367	(718) 263-6040
HECKER SILVERSMITHS 605 FIFTH AVENUE (49TH STREET)	NEW YORK NY	10017	(212) 593-2424
ISRAEL ETROG CENTER 38 CANAL STREET	NEW YORK NY	10002	(212) 431-4140
J. LEVINE CO. 58 ELDRIDGE STREET	NEW YORK NY	10002	(212) 966-4460
MOSHE TARLOW 45 CANAL STREET	NEW YORK NY	10002	(212) 226-8115
S. GOLDMAN OTZAR HASEFRIM, JACOB D. GOLDMAN			
38 CANAL STREET	NEW YORK NY	10002	(212) 674-1707
ROSENBERG 413 YORK ROAD	JENKINTOWN PA		(215) 884-1728
ROSENBERG 6408 CASTOR AVENUE	PHILADELPHIA PA		(215) 744-5205

SUPERMARKETS

E & S GROCERY MARKET 370 N. FAIRFAX AVENUE	LOS ANGELES CA	90036	(213) 938-1512
FAIRFAX KOSHER MARKET 439 NORTH FAIRFAX AVENUE	LOS ANGELES CA	90036	(213) 653-2530
KOSHER BASKET 8664 WEST PICO BOULEVARD	LOS ANGELES CA	90035	(213) 854-0447
KOTLAR'S KOSHER MARKET 8622 WEST PICO BOULEVARD	LOS ANGELES CA	90035	(213) 652-5355
LITTLE JERUSALEM 8971 WEST PICO BOULEVARD	LOS ANGELES CA	90035	(213) 858-8361
DREXLER'S 12519 1/2 BURBANK BOULEVARD	NORTH HOLLYWOOD CA	91607	(818) 761-6405
EVERYTHING'S KOSHER 1344 WASHINGTON AVENUE	MIAMI BEACH FL	33139	(305) 672-4154
SOUTH FLORIDA KOSHER MEATS 1320-24 NE 163RD STREET	N MIAMI BEACH FL	33162	(305) 949-6068
HUNGARIAN KOSHER DELICATESSEN & FRESH MEAT CO.			
2613 W DEVON	CHICAGO IL		(313) 973-5991
JACK'S GROCERY & DELICATESSEN 6311 REISTERSTOWN ROAD	PIKESVILLE MD		(301) 764-1616
KATZ KOSHER SUPERMARKET 4860 BOILING BROOK PARKWAY	ROCKVILLE MD	20852	(301) 468-0400
SHALOM KOSHER SUPERMARKET 2307 UNIVERSITY BLVD	WEST SILVER SPRING MD		(301) 946-6500
SIMON NUNBERG'S STRICTLY KOSHER SUPERMARKET & DELI			
11238 GEORGIA	WHEATON MD	20902	(301) 949-8477
KOSHER CITY 1590 RALPH AVENUE (BTWN.FARRAGUT & FOSTER)	BROOKLYN NY	11236	(718) 763-4992
KOSHER REVOLUTION, THE 3910 13TH AVENUE RETAIL MARKET	BROOKLYN NY	11218	(718) 633-0649
SUPERSOL 330 CENTRAL AVENUE	LAWRENCE NY	11559	(516) 295-3300
SEMEL'S OF WOODBOURNE MAIN STREET	WOODBOURNE NY	12788	(914) 434-2402

SYNAGOGUE INTERIORS

JUDSON STUDIES 200 SOUTH AVENUE 66	LOS ANGELES CA	90042	(213) 255-0130
EDWARD GOLDMAN 50 ELM STREET	SAXONVILLE MA		(617) 877-2188
STAINED GLASS ASSOCIATES PO BOX 1531	RALEIGH NC	27602	(919) 266-2493
ASCALON STUDIOS 206 CROSS KEYS ROAD	BERLIN NJ	08009	(609) 768-3779
EMANUEL MILSTEIN RD #1 BOX 81 C	MARLBORO NJ	07746	(201) 946-8604
CARVED GLASS & SIGNS 697 EAST 132ND STREET	BRONX NY	10456	(212) 665-6240
EDELWEISS CO.- GLASS STUDIO 1217 49 STREET	BROOKLYN NY	11219	(718) 851-9687
SAMPSON SEYMOUR ENGOREN 11 HOLMES PLACE	LYNBROOK NY	11563	(516) 599-3173
EFRAIM WEITZMAN 334 WEST 86TH STREET	NEW YORK NY	10024	(212) 877-6590
ELVAIGH CARMEN & AHRONN 463 WEST STREET	NEW YORK NY	10014	(212) 691-0099
HECKER SILVERSMITHS 605 FIFTH AVENUE (49TH STREET)	NEW YORK NY	10017	(212) 593-2424
J LEVINE CO. 58 ELDRIDGE STREET	NEW YORK NY	10002	(212) 966-4460
ALBERT WOOD & FIVE SONS INC. ONE PLEASANT AVENUE	PORT WASHINGTON NY	11050	(516) 767-0794
BETTY GOLDSTEIN 35 BENEDICT ROAD	SCARSDALE NY	10583	(914) 723-9552
ART & DESIGN STUDIO OF SARA SHAPIRO 13 DR. FRANK ROAD	SPRING VALLEY NY	10977	(914) 352-3988
WILLET STAINED GLASS COMPANY 10 EAST MORELAND AVENUE	PHILADELPHIA PA	19118	(215) 247-5721

SYNAGOGUES

BETH EL, TEMPLE R P.O.BOX 1364	ANNISTON AL	36202	(205) 236-9249
BETH EL, TEMPLE C 2179 HIGHLAND AVENUE S	BIRMINGHAM AL	35256	(205) 933-2740
EMANU-EL, TEMPLE R 2100 HIGHLAND AVENUE P.O.BOX 3303-A	BIRMINGHAM AL	35205	(205) 933-8037
KNESSETH ISRAEL CONGREGATION O 3225 MONTEVALLO ROAD	BIRMINGHAM AL	35223	(205) 879-1664
B'NAI JESHURUN, CONGREGATION R P.O.BOX 340	DEMOPOLIS AL	36732	(205) 289-2378
EMANU-EL, TEMPLE R P.O.BOX 37 AVENUE	DOTHAN AL	36302	(205) 792-5001
B'NAI ISRAEL, TEMPLE R 201 HAWTHORNE STREET	FLORENCE AL	35630	(205) 764-9242
BETH ISRAEL, CONGREGATION R			
P.O.BOX 1616, 761 CHESTNUT STREET	GADSDEN AL	35902	(205) 546-3223
B'NAI SHOLOM, TEMPLE R 103 LINCOLN STREET S.E.	HUNTSVILLE AL	35801	(205) 536-4771
ETZ CHAYIM - HUNTSVILLE CONSERVATIVE SYNAGOGUE C			
7705 BAILEY COVE ROAD S.E.	HUNTSVILLE AL	35802	(205) 881-6260

EMANUEL, TEMPLE R 1501 FIFTH AVENUE, P.O.BOX 1627	JASPER AL	35501	(205) 221-4000
AHAVAS CHESED CONGREGATION - DAUPHIN STREET SYNAGOGUE C			
1717 DAUPHIN STREET	MOBILE AL	36604	(205) 476-6010
SPRING HILL AVENUE TEMPLE, CONGREGATION SHA'ARAI SHOMAYIM R			
1769 SPRING HILL AVENUE	MOBILE AL	36607	(205) 478-0415
AGUDATH ISRAEL SYNAGOGUE C 3525 CLOVERDALE ROAD	MONTGOMERY AL	36111	(205) 281-7394
BETH OR, TEMPLE R P.O.BOX 6180, 2246 NARROW LANE ROAD	MONTGOMERY AL	36106	(205) 272-3314
ETZ AHAYEM SYNAGOGUE C 725 AUGUSTA STREET	MONTGOMERY AL	36111	(205) 281-9819
MISHKAN ISRAEL CONGREGATION R			
C/O SEYMOUR COHN, HOUSTON PARK	SELMA AL	36701	(205) 874-9811
EMANUEL, TEMPLE R P.O.BOX 5607	TUSCALOOSA AL	35405	(205) 553-3286
BETH SHALOM, CONGREGATION 1000 W. 20TH AVENUE	ANCHORAGE AK	99510	(907) 272-8874
ISRAEL, TEMPLE R 1500 WEST CHICKASAWBA	BLYTHEVILLE AR	72315	(501) 763-4148
BETH ISRAEL, TEMPLE R P.O.BOX 570	EL DORADO AR	71730	
SHALOM, TEMPLE R	FAYETTEVILLE AR		(501) 521-7357
UNITED HEBREW CONGREGATION O P.O.BOX 785	FORT SMITH AR	72315	(501) 452-1468
BETH EL, TEMPLE R 406 PERRY STREET	HELENA AR	72342	(501) 338-6654
BETH JACOB, CONGREGATION O 200 QUPAW AVENUE	HOT SPRINGS AR	71901	(501) 623-9335
HOUSE OF ISRAEL, CONGREGATION R 300 QUAPAW AVENUE	HOT SPRINGS AR	71901	(501) 623-5821
ISRAEL, TEMPLE R 203 W. OAK, P.O.BOX 293	JONESBORO AR	72401	(501) 932-9333
AGUDATH ACHIM, CONGREGATION R 7901 W. 5TH STREET	LITTLE ROCK AR	72205	(501) 225-1683
B'NAI ISRAEL, CONGREGATION R 3700 RODNEY PARHAM ROAD	LITTLE ROCK AR	72212	(501) 225-9700
MEIR CHAYIM, TEMPLE R 210 N. 4TH	MCGEHEE AR	71654	(501) 222-4399
ANSHE EMETH, TEMPLE R P.O.BOX 6022	PINE BLUFF AR	71611	(501) 534-3853
B'NAI TIKVAH, TEMPLE R 7211 11TH STREET S.W.	CALGARY AT	T2V IN2	(403) 252-1654
BETH ISRAEL CONGREGATION C 1325 GLENMORE TERRACE S.W.	CALGARY AT	T2V 4Y8	(403) 255-6868
BETH ISRAEL SYNAGOGUE O 10219 119TH STREET	EDMONTON AT	T5K IZ3	(403) 482-2470
BETH ORA CONGREGATION, TEMPLE R 7200 156TH STREET	EDMONTON AT	TSR IX3	(403) 456-9616
BETH SHALOM SYNAGOGUE C 10219 119TH STREET	EDMONTON AT	T5K IZ3	(403) 482-2470
EDMONTON BETH SHALOM CONGREGATION 11916 JASPER AVENUE	EDMONTON AT	T5K OM9	(403) 488-6333
BETH SHOLOM, TEMPLE C 104 WEST FIRST STREET	MESA AZ	85201	(602) 964-1981
AHAVAT TORAH C 10427 NORTH SCOTTSDALE	PHOENIX AZ	85258	(602) 991-5645
BETH EL, CONGREGATION C 1118 WEST GLENDALE AVENUE	PHOENIX AZ	85021	(602) 944-3359
BETH HEBREW CONGREGATION C 4003 EAST ORANGEWOOD	PHOENIX AZ	85021	(602) 934-0124
BETH ISRAEL, TEMPLE R 3310 N. 10TH AVENUE	PHOENIX AZ	85013	(602) 264-4428
CHAI, TEMPLE R 16026 N. 32ND STREET	PHOENIX AZ	85032	(602) 971-1234
TORAT MOSHE MINYAN, CONGREGATION O			
337 E. BETHANY HOME ROAD	PHOENIX AZ	85012	(602) 277-8858
HAR ZION CONGREGATION C 5929 EAST LINCOLN DRIVE	SCOTTSDALE AZ	85258	(602) 991-0720
SOLEL, TEMPLE R 6805 EAST MCDONALD DRIVE	SCOTTSDALE AZ	85253	(602) 991-7414
BETH EMETH CONGREGATION C 10810 EL DORADO DRIVE	SUN CITY AZ	85351	(602) 977-1786
BETH SHALOM, TEMPLE R 12202 101ST AVENUE	SUN CITY AZ	85351	(602) 977-3240
TEMPLE EMANUEL OF TEMPE R 5801 S. RURAL ROAD	TEMPE AZ	85283	(602) 838-1414
ANSHEI ISRAEL CONGREGATION C 5550 E. 5TH STREET	TUCSON AZ	85711	(602) 745-5550

CHAVERIM, CONGREGATION R
C/O MR. E.C.KAPLAN 6121 E. 30TH STREET .... TUCSON **AZ** 85711 (602) 790-9541
EMANU-EL, TEMPLE R 225 NORTH COUNTRY CLUB ROAD, P.O.BOX 42887 ... TUCSON **AZ** 85733 (602) 327-4501
YOUNG ISRAEL OF TUCSON 2443 EAST 4TH STREET .... TUCSON **AZ** 85716 (602) 326-8352
BETH TIKVAH CONGREGATION & CENTRE ASSOCIATION C
P.O.BOX 94374 .... RICHMOND **BC** V6Y 2A8 (604) 271-6262
BETH TIKVAH SYNAGOGUE OF RICHMOND C 9711 GEAL ROAD .... RICHMOND **BC** V6Y 2A8 (604) 271-6262
BETH HAMIDRASH, CONGREGATION O 3231 HEATHER STREET .... VANCOUVER **BC** V5Z 3K4 (604) 872-4222
BETH ISRAEL, CONGREGATION C 4350 OAK STREET .... VANCOUVER **BC** V6H 2N4 (604) 731-4161
SHOLOM, TEMPLE R 4426 WEST TENTH AVENUE .... VANCOUVER **BC** V6R 2H9 (604) 224-1381
ISRAEL, TEMPLE C 2268 ALAMEDA AVENUE .... ALAMEDA **CA** 94501 (415) 522-9355
BETH TORAH, TEMPLE C 225 S. ATLANTIC BLVD .... ALHAMBRA **CA** 91801 (818) 283-2053
BETH EMET, TEMPLE C 1770 W. CERRITOS AVENUE .... ANAHEIM **CA** 92804 (714) 772-4720
FOOTHILL JEWISH TEMPLE-CENTER C 550 S. 2ND AVENUE .... ARCADIA **CA** 91006 (818) 445-0810
SHAAREI TIKVAH, TEMPLE C 550 S. SECOND AVENUE .... ARCADIA **CA** 91006 (818) 445-0810
BETH SOLOMON OF THE DEAF, TEMPLE R 13580 OSBORNE STREET .... ARLETA **CA** 91331 (213) 889-2202
B'NAI JACOB, CONGREGATION C 600 17TH STREET .... BAKERSFIELD **CA** 93301 (805) 325-8017
BETH EL, TEMPLE R 2906 LOMA LINDA ROAD .... BAKERSFIELD **CA** 93305 (805) 322-7607
BETH ISRAEL, CONGREGATION R 2009 BARCELONA AVENUE .... BARSTOW **CA** 92311 (619) 256-7693
BETH EL, CONGREGATION R 2301 VINE STREET .... BERKELEY **CA** 94708 (415) 848-3988
BETH ISRAEL, CONGREGATION O 1630 BANCROFT WAY .... BERKELEY **CA** 94703 (415) 843-5246
BETH JACOB, CONGREGATION O 9030 W. OLYMPIC BLVD .... BEVERLY HILLS **CA** 90211 (213) 278-1911
EMANUEL OF BEVERLY HILLS, TEMPLE R 8844 BURTON WAY .... BEVERLY HILLS **CA** 90211 (213) 274-6388
TANYA, TEMPLE 133 S. ALMOUNT DRIVE .... BEVERLY HILLS **CA** 90211
YOUNG ISRAEL OF BEVERLY HILLS 8701 PICO BOULEVARD .... BEVERLY HILLS **CA** 90035 (213) 275-3020
B'NAI EMUNAH, CONGREGATION O 4001 W. MAGNOLIA BLVD .... BURBANK **CA** 91505 (408) 843-9248
BURBANK TEMPLE EMANU-EL C 1302 N. GLENOAKS BLVD .... BURBANK **CA** 91504 (408) 845-1734
PENINSULA TEMPLE SHOLOM R 1655 SEBASTIAN DRIVE .... BURLINGAME **CA** 94010 (415) 697-2266
BETH KODESH, CONGREGATION C 7401 SHOUP AVENUE .... CANOGA PARK **CA** 91307 (818) 346-0811
SOLAEL, TEMPLE R 6601 VALLEY CIRCLE BLVD .... CANOGA PARK **CA** 91307 (818) 348-3885
SHIR AMI, CONGREGATION R 4529 MALABAR AVENUE .... CASTRO VALLEY **CA** 94546 (415) 538-9660
BETH ISRAEL, CONGREGATION C 1336 HEMLOCK STREET, P.O.BOX 3266 ... CHICO **CA** 95927 (916) 342-6146
ALL-FAITH CHAPEL, HEBREW CONGREGATION R
NAVAL WEAPONS CENTER .... CHINA LAKE **CA** 93555 (619) 939-3506
BETH SHOLOM, TEMPLE C 208 MADRONA STREET .... CHULA VISTA **CA** 92010 (619) 420-6040
BETH SHOLOM, TEMPLE C 823 SOUTH SHERIDAN .... CORONA **CA** 91720 (714) 737-9322
ISAIAH OF NEWPORT BEACH/IRVINE, TEMPLE C
P.O.BOX 10414, 2401 IRVINE AVENUE .... COSTA MESA **CA** 92627 (714) 540-1310
TEMPLE SHARON C 617 W. HAMILTON .... COSTA MESA **CA** 92627 (714) 631-3262
AKIBA, TEMPLE R 5249 S. SEPULVEDA BLVD .... CULVER CITY **CA** 90230 (213) 870-6575
B'NAI ISRAEL, CONGREGATION C 1575 ANNIE STREET .... DALY CITY **CA** 94015 (415) 756-5430
NOVE SHOLOM, CONGREGATION C
66-777 E. PIERSON BLVD .... DESERT HOT SPRINGS **CA** 92240 (619) 329-5168
NER TAMID, TEMPLE R 10629 LAKEWOOD BLVD .... DOWNEY **CA** 90241 (213) 861-9276
EILAT, TEMPLE C 24432 MUIRLANDS BLVD .... EL TORO **CA** 92630 (714) 770-9606
HEBREW CONGREGATION, THE O P.O.BOX 245 .... ELSINORE **CA** 92330 (714) 674-3046
SINAI, TEMPLE C 677 SANTA FE DRIVE .... ENCINITAS **CA** 92024
SOLEL, TEMPLE R 890 BALOUR DRIVE .... ENCINITAS **CA** 92024
CHABAD OF THE VALLEY O 4915 HAYVENHURST AVENUE .... ENCINO **CA** 91436 (818) 784-9985
MAAREV, TEMPLE C 5180 YARMOUTH AVENUE .... ENCINO **CA** 91436 (818) 345-7833
VALLEY BETH SHALOM C 15739 VENTURA BLVD .... ENCINO **CA** 91436 (818) 788-6000
BETH EL, TEMPLE R HODGSON & T STREETS, P.O.BOX 442 .... EUREKA **CA** 95501 (707) 422-9686
ISRAEL, TEMPLE C 14795 MERRILL .... FONTANA **CA** 92335
CONGREGATION B'NAI TZEDEK R 9669 TALBERT AVENUE .... FOUNTAIN VALLEY **CA** 92708 (714) 963-4611
BETH TORAH, TEMPLE R 42000 PASEO PADRE PARKWAY, P.O.BOX 6017 ... FREMONT **CA** 94538 (415) 656-7141
BETH ISRAEL, TEMPLE C P.O.BOX 1328 .... FRESNO **CA** 93715 (209) 264-2929
BETH JACOB, CONGREGATION C
406 WEST SHIELDS AVENUE, P.O.BOX 6017 .... FRESNO **CA** 93705 (209) 222-0664
BETH TIKVAH OF NORTH ORANGE COUNTY, TEMPLE R
1600 NORTH ACACIA AVENUE .... FULLERTON **CA** 92631 (714) 871-3535
SINAI, TEMPLE R 1212 PACIFIC AVENUE .... GLENDALE **CA** 91202 (818) 246-8101
HUNTINGTON PARK HEBREW CONGREGATION C
P.O.BOX 867, 2877 EAST FLORENCE AVENUE .... HUNTINGTON PARK **CA** 90255 (213) 585-4436
IRVINE JEWISH COMMUNITY R P.O.BOX 4420 .... IRVINE **CA** 92716 (714) 786-0823
BETH EL, CONGREGATION C 8745 LA JOLLA SCENIC DRIVE .... LA JOLLA **CA** 90237 (619) 452-1734
TIFERETH ISRAEL SYNAGOGUE 9019-A PARK PLAZA DRIVE .... LA MESA **CA** 92041 (619) 697-0181
BETH OHR, TEMPLE R 15721 E. ROSECRANS BLVD .... LA MIRADA **CA** 90638 (714) 521-6765
ISAIAH, TEMPLE R 3800 MT. DIABLO BLVD .... LAFAYETTE **CA** 94549 (415) 283-8575
TEMPLE JUDEA 24512 MOULTON PARKWAY .... LAGUNA HILLS **CA** 92653 (714) 830-0470
BETH ZION-SINAI, TEMPLE C 6440 DEL AMO BLVD .... LAKEWOOD **CA** 90713 (213) 429-0715
BETH KNESSET BAMIDBAR R P.O.BOX 1008, 1611 EAST AVENUE J .... LANCASTER **CA** 93534 (805) 942-4415
LANCASTER HEBREW CONGREGATION 1611 AVENUE J .... LANCASTER **CA** 93535
KOL SHOFAR C 20 MAGNOLIA AVENUE .... LARKSPUR **CA** 94939 (415) 924-6081
BETH EMEK, CONGREGATION R 1886 COLLEGE AVENUE, P.O.BOX 722 ... LIVERMORE **CA** 94550 (415) 443-1689
BETH EL, TEMPLE C 853 LINDEN AVENUE .... LONG BEACH **CA** 90813 (213) 447-4430
BETH SHALOM, TEMPLE C 3635 ELM AVENUE .... LONG BEACH **CA** 90807 (213) 426-6413
BETH ZION - TEMPLE SINAI C 6440 DEL AMO BLVD .... LONG BEACH **CA** 90713 (213) 429-0715
ISRAEL, TEMPLE R 3538 E. 3RD STREET, P.O.BOX 14406 .... LONG BEACH **CA** 90814 (213) 434-0996
LUBAVITCH, CONGREGATION O 3977 ATLANTIC AVENUE .... LONG BEACH **CA** 90807 (213) 774-3747
BETH AM, CONGREGATION R 26790 ARASTRADERO ROAD .... LOS ALTOS HILLS **CA** 94022 (415) 493-4661
AATZEI CHAIM, CONGREGATION O 8018 W. 3RD STREET .... LOS ANGELES **CA** 90048 (213) 653-9104
ADAS CHASAM SOFER, CONGREGATION O 8013 MELROSE AVENUE ... LOS ANGELES **CA** 90046 (213) 653-2918
ADAT MOSHE, CONGREGATION 110 SOUTH VISTA .... LOS ANGELES **CA** 90036
ADAT SHALOM C 3030 WESTWOOD BLVD .... LOS ANGELES **CA** 90034 (213) 475-4985
AGUDATH ISRAEL OF LOS ANGELES O
501 SOUTH FAIRFAX AVENUE .... LOS ANGELES **CA**
AHAVATH ISRAEL, CONGREGATION O 5454 VIRGINIA AVENUE .... LOS ANGELES **CA** 90029 (213) 464-3885
ANSHE-EMET SYNAGOGUE O 1490 S. ROBERTSON BLVD .... LOS ANGELES **CA** 90035 (213) 275-5640
B'NAI DAVID-JUDEA, CONGREGATION O 8906 WEST PICO BLVD .... LOS ANGELES **CA** 90035 (213) 272-7223
B'NAI TIKVAH, CONGREGATION C 5820 W. MANCHESTER BLVD .... LOS ANGELES **CA** 90045 (213) 776-5933
BAIS HACHASIDIM D-GUR, CONGREGATION O
7575 MELROSE AVENUE .... LOS ANGELES **CA** 90046 (213) 653-3237

BETH AM, TEMPLE C 1039 S LA CIENEGA BLVD .... LOS ANGELES **CA** 90035 (213) 652-7353
BETH CHAYIM CHADASHIM, TEMPLE R 6000 W. PICO BLVD .... LOS ANGELES **CA** 90035 (213) 931-7023
BETH HATIKVA-CITY OF HOPE MEDICAL CENTER, CONGREGATION
208 W. 8TH STREET .... LOS ANGELES **CA** 90014 (213) 656-4611
BETH ISRAEL OF HIGHLAND PARK-EAGLE ROCK, TEMPLE C
5711 MONTE VISTA STREET .... LOS ANGELES **CA** 90042 (213) 255-5416
BETH ISRAEL, CONGREGATION O 8056 BEVERLY BLVD .... LOS ANGELES **CA** 90048 (213) 651-4022
BETH TORAH, TEMPLE C 11827 VENICE BLVD .... LOS ANGELES **CA** 90066 (213) 398-4536
BETH ZION, TEMPLE C 5555 W. OLYMPIC BLVD .... LOS ANGELES **CA** 90036 (213) 933-9136
BEVERLY ISRAEL SYNAGOGUE C 447 N. FAIRFAX AVENUE .... LOS ANGELES **CA** 90036 (213) 651-2227
BNAI JACOB, CONGREGATION O 2833 FAIRMOUNT STREET .... LOS ANGELES **CA** 90033 (213) 261-2788
ETZ JACOB, CONGREGATION O 7659 BEVERLY BLVD .... LOS ANGELES **CA** 90036 (213) 938-2619
HOLLYWOOD TEMPLE BETH EL C
1317 N. CRESCENT HEIGHTS BLVD .... LOS ANGELES **CA** 90046 (213) 474-1518
ISAIAH, TEMPLE R 10345 W. PICO BLVD .... LOS ANGELES **CA** 90064 (213) 277-2772
ISRAEL, TEMPLE R 7300 HOLLYWOOD BLVD .... LOS ANGELES **CA** 90046 (213) 876-8330
JEREMIAH, TEMPLE R 8333 AIRPORT BLVD .... LOS ANGELES **CA** 90045 (213) 776-4074
KEHILATH YITZCHOK, CONGREGATION O 7711 BEVERLY BLVD .... LOS ANGELES **CA** 90036 (213) 936-4232
KNESSET ISRAEL OF HOLLYWOOD 1260 N. VERMONT AVENUE .... LOS ANGELES **CA** 90029 (213) 665-5171
LEO BAECK, TEMPLE R 1300 N. SEPULVEDA BLVD .... LOS ANGELES **CA** 90049 (213) 476-2861
MAGEN DAVID, CONGREGATION O 9717 WEST PICO BLVD .... LOS ANGELES **CA** 90035 (213) 879-3681
MISHKAN YICHESKE, CONGREGATION O 8344 MELROSE AVENUE ... LOS ANGELES **CA** 90069 (213) 938-9292
MOGEN ABRAHAM, CONGREGATION O 354 N. ORANGE DRIVE .... LOS ANGELES **CA** 90036 (213) 937-9690
NER ISRAEL, CONGREGATION O 5822 W. 3RD STREET .... LOS ANGELES **CA** 90036 (213) 933-3405
NETZACH ISRAEL, CONGREGATION O 4117 BEVERLY BLVD .... LOS ANGELES **CA** 90004 (213) 663-2383
OHEL DAVID, CONGREGATION O 7967 BEVERLY BLVD .... LOS ANGELES **CA** 90048 (213) 655-0973
OHEV SHALOM CONGREGATION O 525 SOUTH FAIRFAX AVENUE .... LOS ANGELES **CA** 90036 (213) 653-7190
SEPHARDIC CONGREGATION KEHAL YOSEPH O
10505 SANTA MONICA BLVD .... LOS ANGELES **CA** 90025 (213) 474-0559
SEPHARDIC MAGEN DAVID, CONGREGATION O
7454 MELROSE AVENUE .... LOS ANGELES **CA** 90046 (213) 655-3441
SEPHARDIC TEMPLE TIFERETH ISRAEL O 10500 WILSHIRE BLVD .... LOS ANGELES **CA** 90024 (213) 475-7311
SHAAREI TEFILA, CONGREGATION O 7269 BEVERLY BLVD .... LOS ANGELES **CA** 90028 (213) 938-7147
SHAAREY ELIMELECH, CONGREGATION 6111 W. OLYMPIC BLVD .... LOS ANGELES **CA** 90048
SHYERIT SHAARE TORAH, CONGREGATION O 220 W. 8TH STREET ... LOS ANGELES **CA** 90057 (213) 389-3181
SINAI, TEMPLE C 10400 WILSHIRE BLVD .... LOS ANGELES **CA** 90024 (213) 474-1518
STEPHEN S. WISE TEMPLE R 15500 STEPHEN WISE DRIVE .... LOS ANGELES **CA** 90024 (213) 476-8561
TALMUD TORAH, CONGREGATION O 247 N. BREED STREET .... LOS ANGELES **CA** 90033 (213) 262-3922
TIFERETH ZVI, CONGREGATION O 7561 BEVERLY BLVD .... LOS ANGELES **CA** 90048 (213) 931-3252
UNIVERSITY SYNAGOGUE R 11960 SUNSET BLVD .... LOS ANGELES **CA** 90049 (213) 472-1255
VISTA DEL MAR TEMPLE 3200 MOTOR AVENUE .... LOS ANGELES **CA** 90034 (213) 836-1223
WILSHIRE BOULEVARD TEMPLE R 3663 WILSHIRE BLVD .... LOS ANGELES **CA** 90010 (213) 388-2401
YOUNG ISRAEL OF BEVERLY HILLS 8701 WEST PICO BLVD. .... LOS ANGELES **CA** 90035 (213) 275-3020
YOUNG ISRAEL OF CENTURY CITY 9315 W. PICO BLVD. .... LOS ANGELES **CA** 90035 (213) 273-6954
YOUNG ISRAEL OF HANCOCK PARK 225 SOUTH LA BREA AVENUE ... LOS ANGELES **CA** 90036 (213) 931-4030
YOUNG ISRAEL OF LOS ANGELES 660 NORTH SPAULDING AVENUE .. LOS ANGELES **CA** 90036 (213) 655-0300
SHIR HADASH, CONGREGATION R P.O.BOX 1635 .... LOS GATOS **CA** 95030 (408) 227-8880
MALIBU JEWISH CENTER & SYNAGOGUE RE POB 4063 .... MALIBU **CA** 90265 (213) 457-2979
JEWISH COMMUNITY CENTER OF MERCED CO., R P.O.BOX 2531 .... MERCED **CA** 95344 (209) 722-0530
EILAT, TEMPLE C P.O.BOX 2004 .... MISSION VIEJO **CA** 92675 (714) 830-1001
TEMPLE BETH EL R 28261 MARGUERITE PARKWAY .... MISSION VIEJO **CA** 92692 (714) 495-2332
TEMPLE OHAVEI SHALOM 27276 VIA AVILA .... MISSION VIEJO **CA** 92675 (714) 855-4823
BETH SHOLOM OF MODESTO, CONGREGATION
1705 SHERWOOD AVENUE, P.O.BOX 4082 .... MODESTO **CA** 94941 (209) 522-5613
B'NAI EMET, TEMPLE C 482 NORTH GARFIELD AVENUE .... MONTEBELLO **CA** 90640 (213) 721-7064
BETH ISRAEL, CONGREGATION R 151 PARK AVENUE .... MONTEREY **CA** 93940 (408) 675-2759
BETH SHOLOM, CONGREGATION C 1455 ELM STREET .... NAPA **CA** 94558
BETH SHALOM OF THE SANTA CLARITA VALLEY, CONGREGATION
P.O.BOX 39 .... NEWHALL **CA** 91321 (805) 259-4975
BAT YAHM, TEMPLE R 1011 CAMELBACK STREET .... NEWPORT BEACH **CA** 92660 (714) 644-1999
SHIR HAMA'ALOT R 2100 A MAR VISTA .... NEWPORT BEACH **CA** 92660 (714) 644-7203
TEMPLE ISAIAH OF NEWPORT BEACH C 2401 IRVINE AVENUE .... NEWPORT BEACH **CA** 92660 (714) 548-6900
ADAT ARI EL C 5540 LAUREL CANYON BLVD .... NORTH HOLLYWOOD **CA** 91607 (818) 766-9426
BETH HILLEL, TEMPLE R
12326 RIVERSIDE ROAD, SAN FERNANDO VALLEY .... NORTH HOLLYWOOD **CA** 91670 (818) 763-9148
MISHKAN ISRAEL, CONGREGATION O 6450 BELLINGHAM .... NORTH HOLLYWOOD **CA** 91606 (818) 769-8043
SHAAREY ZEDEK, CONGREGATION O
12800 CHANDLER BLVD .... NORTH HOLLYWOOD **CA** 91607 (818) 984-3878
VALLEY JEWISH COMMUNITY CENTER & TEMPLE C
5540 LAUREL CANYON BLVD .... NORTH HOLLYWOOD **CA** 91607 (818) 877-0666
AHAVAT SHALOM, TEMPLE R 18200 RINALDI PLACE .... NORTHRIDGE **CA** 91326 (818) 360-2258
RAMAT ZION, TEMPLE C 17655 DEVONSHIRE STREET .... NORTHRIDGE **CA** 91325 (818) 360-1881
YOUNG ISRAEL NORTHRIDGE 17332 DEARBORNE .... NORTHRIDGE **CA** 91325
BETH ABRAHAM, TEMPLE C 327 MACARTHUR BLVD .... OAKLAND **CA** 94610 (415) 832-0936
BETH JACOB CONGREGATION O 3778 PARK BLVD .... OAKLAND **CA** 94610 (415) 482-1147
SINAI, TEMPLE R 2808 SUMMIT STREET .... OAKLAND **CA** 94609 (415) 451-3263
SHOLOM OF ONTARIO, TEMPLE C 936 W. 6TH STREET .... ONTARIO **CA** 91762 (714) 983-9661
JEWISH CONGREGATION OF PACIFIC PALISADES RE
16019 SUNSET BLVD .... PACIFIC PALISADES **CA** 90272 (213) 459-2328
KEHILLATH ISRAEL 16019 SUNSET BLVD .... PACIFIC PALISADES **CA** 90272 (213) 454-9130
BETH AMI, CONGREGATION 2015 TACHEVAH .... PALM SPRINGS **CA** 92262
ISAIAH, TEMPLE R PALM SPRINGS JEWISH COMMUNITY CENTER,
332 WEST ALEJO RD .... PALM SPRINGS **CA** 92662 (619) 325-2281
KOL EMETH, CONGREGATION C 4175 MANUELA AVENUE .... PALO ALTO **CA** 94306 (415) 948-7498
NER TAMID OF SOUTH BAY, CONGREGATION
5721 CRESTRIDGE ROAD .... PALOS VERDES **CA** 90274 (213) 377-4482
PASADENA JEWISH TEMPLE C 1434 NORTH ALTADENA DRIVE .... PASADENA **CA** 91107 (818) 798-1161
BETH ISRAEL, TEMPLE R 3033 N. TOWNE AVENUE .... POMONA **CA** 91767 (714) 626-1277
ADAT SHALOM, TEMPLE R 15847 POMERDO ROAD .... POWAY **CA** 92046 (619) 489-1918
NER TAMID OF SOUTH BAY, CONGREGATION C
5721 CRESTRIDGE ROAD .... RANCHO PALOS VERDES **CA** 90274 (213) 377-6986
BETH ISRAEL, CONGREGATION R P.O.BOX 201 .... REDDING **CA** 96001 (916) 243-4159

MENORA, TEMPLE R 1101 CAMINO REAL	REDONDO BEACH	CA	90277	(213) 316-8444
BETH JACOB, TEMPLE C 1550 ALAMEDA DE LAS PULGAS	REDWOOD CITY	CA	94061	(415) 366-8481
BETH AMI, TEMPLE C 18449 KITTRIDGE STREET	RESEDA	CA	91335	(818) 343-4624
BETH HILLEL, TEMPLE R 801 PARK CENTRAL	RICHMOND	CA	94803	(415) 223-2560
BETH EL, TEMPLE R 2675 CENTRAL AVENUE	RIVERSIDE	CA	92506	(714) 684-4511
SONOMA COUNTY SYNAGOGUE CENTER RE POB 1066	ROHNERT PARK	CA	94928	(707) 763-7508
B'NAI ISRAEL, TEMPLE R 3600 RIVERSIDE BLVD	SACRAMENTO	CA	95818	(916) 446-4861
BETH SHALOM, CONGREGATION 525 FULTON AVENUE	SACRAMENTO	CA	95825	
MOSAIC LAW CONGREGATION C 1300 SIERRA BLVD	SACRAMENTO	CA	95825	(916) 488-1122
BETH EL, TEMPLE R 1212 RIKER STREET	SALINAS	CA	93901	(408) 424-9151
EMANU-EL, CONGREGATION R 3512 NORTH 'E' STREET	SAN BERNARDINO	CA	92405	(714) 886-4818
BETH ISRAEL, TEMPLE R 2512 THIRD AVENUE AT LAUREL STREET	SAN DIEGO	CA	92103	(619) 239-0149
BETH JACOB, CONGREGATION O 4855 COLLEGE AVENUE	SAN DIEGO	CA	92115	(619) 287-9890
BETH TEFILAH, CONGREGATION 4967 69TH STREET	SAN DIEGO	CA	92115	(619) 463-0391
DOR HADASH RE 2504 QUIDDE AVENUE	SAN DIEGO	CA	92127	(619) 450-9588
EMANU-EL, TEMPLE R 6299 CAPRI DRIVE	SAN DIEGO	CA	92120	(619) 286-2555
TIFERETH ISRAEL SYNAGOGUE 6660 COWLES MOUNTAIN BLVD	SAN DIEGO	CA	92119	(619) 697-6001
ADATH ISRAEL 1851 NORIEGA STREET	SAN FRANCISCO	CA	94122	(415) 564-5665
ANSHEY SFARD, CONGREGATION O 1500 CLEMENT STREET	SAN FRANCISCO	CA	94118	(415) 752-4979
B'NAI DAVID, CONGREGATION 3535 19TH STREET	SAN FRANCISCO	CA	94110	(415) 826-2595
B'NAI EMUNAH, CONGREGATION C 3595 TARAVEL STREET	SAN FRANCISCO	CA	94116	(415) 664-7373
B'NAI ISRAEL, CONGREGATION 590 WASHINGTON	SAN FRANCISCO	CA	94111	(415) 756-5430
BETH ISRAEL, CONGREGATION C 625 BROTHERHOOD WAY	SAN FRANCISCO	CA	94132	(415) 586-8833
BETH SHOLOM C 14TH AVENUE & CLEMENT STREET	SAN FRANCISCO	CA	94118	
CHEVRA THILIM, CONGREGATION O 751 25TH AVENUE	SAN FRANCISCO	CA	94121	(415) 752-2866
EMANU-EL, CONGREGATION R P.O.BOX 18247, ARQUELLO BLVD. & LAKE STREET	SAN FRANCISCO	CA	94118	(415) 751-2535
KEHILATH JACOB HOUSE OF LOVE & PRAYER, CONGREGATION O 1456 9TH AVENUE	SAN FRANCISCO	CA	94122	(415) 731-9507
KENESETH ISRAEL, CONGREGATION O 1255 POST	SAN FRANCISCO	CA	94109	(415) 771-3420
MAGAIN DAVID SEPHARDIM, CONGREGATION O 351 4TH AVENUE	SAN FRANCISCO	CA	94118	(415) 752-9095
NER TAMID, CONGREGATION C 1250 QUINTARA STREET	SAN FRANCISCO	CA	94118	(415) 752-9095
SAN FRANCISCO BAY AREA RECONSTRUCTIONIST HAVURAH C/O SHANA WINOKUR	SAN FRANCISCO	CA		(415) 655-7776
SHAAR ZAHAV, CONGREGATION R P.O.BOX 5640	SAN FRANCISCO	CA	94101	(415) 621-2871
SHERITH ISRAEL, CONGREGATION R 2266 CALIFORNIA STREET	SAN FRANCISCO	CA	94115	(415) 346-1720
UNITED TALMUD TORAH CONGREGATION O 1822 26TH AVENUE	SAN FRANCISCO	CA	94107	(415) 564-5672
AM ECHAD, CONGREGATION O 1537 A MERIDIAN AVENUE	SAN JOSE	CA	95125	(408) 267-2591
BETH SHOLOM, TEMPLE R 325 CHEYNOWETH AVENUE	SAN JOSE	CA	95136	(408) 224-1009
EMANU-EL, TEMPLE R 1010 UNIVERSITY AVENUE	SAN JOSE	CA	95126	(408) 292-0939
SHIR HADASH, CONGREGATION R 13500 QUITO ROAD	SAN JOSE	CA	95130	(408) 379-7522
SINAI, CONGREGATION T 1532 WILLOWBRAE AVENUE	SAN JOSE	CA	95125	(408) 264-8542
YOUNG ISRAEL SAN JOSE 1975 HAMILTON AVE., SUITE #5	SAN JOSE	CA	95125	(408) 265-9255
BETH SHOLOM, TEMPLE C 642 DOLORES AVENUE	SAN LEANDRO	CA	94577	(415) 357-8505
BETH DAVID, CONGREGATION R 2932 AUGUSTA STREET	SAN LUIS OBISPO	CA	93401	(805) 544-0760
PENINSULA TEMPLE BETH EL R 1700 ALAMEDA DE LAS PULGAS	SAN MATEO	CA	94403	(415) 341-7701
BETH EL & CENTER, TEMPLE R 1435 W. 7TH STREET	SAN PEDRO	CA	90732	(213) 833-2467
KOL SHOFAR, CONGREGATION C P.O.BOX 1235	SAN RAFAEL	CA	94902	(415) 456-1515
BETH SHOLOM, TEMPLE - ORANGE COUNTY R 13031 TUSTIN AVENUE	SANTA ANA	CA	92705	(714) 532-6724
B'NAI B'RITH, CONGREGATION R 900 SAN ANTONIO CREEK ROAD	SANTA BARBARA	CA	93111	(805) 964-7869
YESHIVAT & MIDRASHA KEREM 250 HOWARD DRIVE	SANTA CLARA	CA	95051	(408) 247-1722
BETH EL, TEMPLE R 920 BAY STREET	SANTA CRUZ	CA	95060	(408) 423-3012
BETH EL, TEMPLE R 1501 E. ALVIN	SANTA MARIA	CA	93454	(805) 925-9028
BETH SHOLOM, TEMPLE R 1827 CALIFORNIA AVENUE	SANTA MONICA	CA	90403	(213) 453-3361
PACIFIC JEWISH CENTER O 3115 6TH STREET	SANTA MONICA	CA	90405	(213) 392-8512
YOUNG ISRAEL OF SANTA MONICA 216 MARINE STREET	SANTA MONICA	CA	90405	(213) 452-0488
BETH AMI, CONGREGATION C 4676 MAYETTE AVENUE	SANTA ROSA	CA	95405	(707) 545-4334
SHOMREI TORAH, CONGREGATION R 1717 YULUPA AVENUE	SANTA ROSA	CA	95405	(707) 539-6127
BETH DAVID, CONGREGATION C 19700 PROSPECT AVENUE	SARATOGA	CA	95070	(408) 257-3333
SHOLOM OF LEISURE WORLD, CONGREGATION C 13044 DEL MONTE DRIVE #34A	SEAL BEACH	CA	90740	(213) 596-3188
BETH TORAH, TEMPLE 8936 LANGDON AVENUE	SEPULVEDA	CA	91343	
BETH TORAH, TEMPLE R 8756 WOODLEY AVENUE	SEPULVEDA	CA	91343	(213) 893-3756
B'NAI HAYIM, TEMPLE C 4302 VAN NUYS BLVD	SHERMAN OAKS	CA	91403	(818) 788-4664
BETH DALIAH, TEMPLE C 13754 VENTURA BLVD	SHERMAN OAKS	CA	91403	(818) 784-3914
B'NAI EMET, CONGREGATION R P.O.BOX 878	SIMI VALLEY	CA	93065	(805) 581-3723
NER TAMID, TEMPLE C 3050 LOS ANGELES AVENUE	SIMI VALLEY	CA	93065	(805) 522-4747
ADAS YESHURUN, CONGREGATION O 427 E. FREMONT STREET	STOCKTON	CA	95202	
ISRAEL, TEMPLE R 5105 NORTH EL DORADO STREET	STOCKTON	CA	95207	(209) 477-9306
BETH MEIRER, CONGREGATION C 11725 MOORPARK STREET	STUDIO CITY	CA	91604	(818) 769-0515
BETH OHR, CONGREGATION RE 12355 MOORPARK	STUDIO CITY	CA	91604	(818) 766-3826
VALLEY BETH ISRAEL C 13060 ROSCOE BLVD	SUN VALLEY	CA	91352	(818) 782-2281
BETH AMI, TEMPLE C 19258 BERNETTA PLACE	TARZANA	CA	91356	(818) 343-4624
JUDEA, TEMPLE R 5429 LINDLEY AVENUE	TARZANA	CA	91356	(213) 987-2616
BETH DAVID OF THE SAN GABRIEL VALLEY, TEMPLE R 9677 E. LONGDEN AVENUE	TEMPLE CITY	CA	91780	(818) 287-9994
ADAT ELOHIM, TEMPLE R 2420 E. HILLCREST DRIVE	THOUSAND OAKS	CA	91360	(805) 497-7101
ETZ CHAIM, TEMPLE C 1080 E. JANSS ROAD	THOUSAND OAKS	CA	91360	(805) 497-6891
VERDUGO HILLS HEBREW CENTER C 10275 TUJUNGA CANYON BLVD	TUJUNGA	CA	91040	(818) 352-3171
B'NAI ISRAEL, CONGREGATION C 13112 NEWPORT AVENUE, SUITE H	TUSTIN	CA	92680	(714) 730-9693
BNAI ISRAEL, CONGREGATION C 1256 NEBRASKA STREET	VALLEJO	CA	94590	(707) 642-6526
BETH DAVID, TEMPLE C 7452 HAZELTINE AVENUE	VAN NUYS	CA	91405	(818) 780-4141
NER TAMID, TEMPLE C 15339 SATICOY STREET	VAN NUYS	CA	91406	(818) 782-9010
BAY CITIES SYNAGOGUE O 505 OCEAN FRONT WALK	VENICE	CA	90291	(213) 390-8868
MISHKON TEPHILO, TEMPLE C 206 MAIN STREET	VENICE	CA	90291	(213) 828-2445
BETH TORAH, TEMPLE R VENTURA CITY JEWISH COUNCIL, 7620 FOOTHILL ROAD	VENTURA	CA	93004	(805) 647-4181
VENTURA COUNTY JEWISH COUNCIL-TEMPLE BETH TORAH R 7620 FOOTHILL ROAD	VENTURA	CA	93003	(805) 647-4181
B'NAI DAVID, CONGREGATION R P.O.BOX 3822	VISALIA	CA	93278	(209) 732-7196
JUDEA, TEMPLE C 1930 SUNSET DRIVE	VISTA	CA	92083	(619) 724-8318
B'NAI SHOLOM, CONGREGATION C 74 ECKLEY LANE	WALNUT CREEK	CA	94598	(415) 934-9446
BETH AMI, TEMPLE C 3508 E. TEMPLE WAY	WEST COVINA	CA	91791	(818) 331-0515
SHALOM, TEMPLE R 1912 W. MERCED AVENUE	WEST COVINA	CA	91790	(818) 337-6500
BETH DAVID OF ORANGE COUNTY, TEMPLE R 6100 HEFLEY STREET	WESTMINSTER	CA	92683	(714) 892-6623
BETH SHALOM OF WHITTIER C 14564 E. HAWES STREET	WHITTIER	CA	90604	(213) 941-8744
WHITTIER RECONSTRUCTIONIST HAVURAH C/O LEONARD HALE	WHITTIER	CA		(714) 694-1123
ALLYAH, TEMPLE C 6025 VALLEY CIRCLE BLVD	WOODLAND HILLS	CA	91367	(818) 346-3545
EMET, TEMPLE R 20400 VENTURA BLVD	WOODLAND HILLS	CA	91364	(818) 348-0670
HAR HASHEM, CONGREGATION 3950 BASELINE ROAD	BOULDER	CO	80303	(303) 499-7077
SHALOM, TEMPLE C & R 1523 E. MONUMENT	COLORADO SPRINGS	CO	80909	(303) 634-5311
BETH HAMEDROSH HAGODOL, CONGREGATION O 560 S. MONACO PARKWAY	DENVER	CO	80222	(303) 355-7321
BETH JOSEPH CONGREGATION 825 IVANHOE STREET	DENVER	CO	80220	(303) 355-7341
COLORADO JEWISH RECONSTRUCTIONIST FEDERATION 6565 EAST EVANS, SUITE 104	DENVER	CO	80222	(303) 753-1610
EAST DENVER ORTHODOX CONGREGATION O 198 SOUTH HOLLY	DENVER	CO	80222	(303) 322-7943
EMANUEL, CONGREGATION R 51 GRAPE STREET	DENVER	CO	80220	(303) 388-4013
HEBREW EDUCATIONAL ALLIANCE, CONGREGATION O 1555 STUART STREET	DENVER	CO	80204	(303) 629-0410
MICAH, CONGREGATION R 2600 LEYDEN STREET	DENVER	CO	80207	(303) 388-4239
MICAH, TEMPLE 195 S. MONACO PARKWAY	DENVER	CO	80222	
RODEPH SHALOM, CONGREGATION C 450 S. KEAMEY STREET	DENVER	CO	80224	(303) 399-0035
SINAI, TEMPLE R 8050 E. DARTMOUTH AVENUE	DENVER	CO	80231	(303) 750-3006
ZERA ABRAHAM, CONGREGATION O 1560 WINONA COURT	DENVER	CO	80204	(303) 825-7517
ZERA ISRAEL, CONGREGATION O 3934 W. 14TH AVENUE	DENVER	CO	80204	(303) 244-6772
BETH SHALOM, CONGREGATION C 2280 E. NOBLE PLACE	LITTLETON	CO	80120	(303) 794-6643
EMANUEL, TEMPLE R 1325 N. GRAND AVENUE	PUEBLO	CO	81003	(303) 544-6448
UNITED HEBREW CENTER C 106 W. 15TH STREET	PUEBLO	CO	81003	(303) 544-9897
AARON, CONGREGATION R THIRD & MAPLE	TRINIDAD	CO	81082	(303) 846-3193
UNITED BRETHREN SYNAGOGUE	AMSTON	CT	06231	
BETH HILLEL SYNAGOGUE C 160 WINTONBURY AVENUE	BLOOMFIELD	CT	04002	(203) 242-5561
TEFERES ISRAEL, CONGREGATION O 27 BROWN STREET	BLOOMFIELD	CT	06002	(203) 243-1719
TIKVOH CHADOSHOH, CONGREGATION C 180 STILL ROAD	BLOOMFIELD	CT	06002	(203) 236-2010
BETH TIKVAH, TEMPLE R 64 MEADOW WOOD ROAD	BRAMFORD	CT	06405	
ADATH ISRAEL, CONGREGATION O 540 E. WASHINGTON AVENUE	BRIDGEPORT	CT	06608	
ADATH YESHURAN, CONGREGATION O 246 LENOX AVENUE	BRIDGEPORT	CT	06605	
AGUDAS ACHIM, CONGREGATION O 85 ARLINGTON STREET	BRIDGEPORT	CT	06606	(203) 335-6353
B'NAI ISRAEL, CONGREGATION R 2710 PARK AVENUE	BRIDGEPORT	CT	06604	(203) 336-1858
BIKUR CHOLIM, CONGREGATION O P.O.BOX 3462	BRIDGEPORT	CT	06605	
RODEPH SHOLOM, CONGREGATION C PARK & CAPITOL AVENUES	BRIDGEPORT	CT	06604	(203) 334-0159
SHAARE TORAH, CONGREGATION O 3050 MAIN STREET	BRIDGEPORT	CT	06606	(203) 372-6513
BETH ISRAEL SYNAGOGUE C 339 W STREET	BRISTOL	CT	06010	(203) 583-6293
BETH DAVID, TEMPLE R 3 MAIN STREET, P.O.BOX 274	CHESHIRE	CT	06410	(203) 272-0037
AHAVATH ACHIM SYNAGOGUE C LEBANON AVENUE	COLCHESTER	CT	06415	(203) 537-2809
AGUDATH ACHIM, CONGREGATION O	COLUMBIA	CT	06237	
CLAPBOARD RIDGE SYNAGOGUE-CONGREGATION B'NAI ISRAEL C P.O.BOX 1060, 193 CLAPBOARD RIDGE ROAD	DANBURY	CT	06810	(203) 792-6161
UNITED JEWISH CENTER R 141 DEER HILL AVENUE	DANBURY	CT	06810	(203) 748-3355
BETH ISRAEL, TEMPLE C KILLINGLY DRIVE	DANIELSON	CT	06239	(203) 774-9874
BETH ISRAEL SYNAGOGUE CENTER C 300 ELIZABETH STREET	DERBY	CT	06418	(203) 734-3361
SONS OF ISRAEL, CONGREGATION C 6 ANSON STREET	DERBY	CT	06418	
RODFE ZEDEK, CONGREGATION C ORCHARD ROAD	EAST HADDAM	CT	06423	(203) 873-8061
BETH TEFILAH, TEMPLE C 465 OAK STREET	EAST HARTFORD	CT	06118	(203) 569-0670
KENESSETH ISRAEL, CONGREGATION O PINNEY STREET	ELLINGTON	CT	06029	(203) 875-3623
AHAVATH ACHIM, CONGREGATION O 1571 STRATFIELD ROAD	FAIRFIELD	CT	06432	(203) 372-6529
BETH EL, CONGREGATION C 1200 FAIRFIELD WOODS ROAD	FAIRFIELD	CT	06430	(203) 374-5544
SHOLOM, TEMPLE C 300 E. PUTNAM AVENUE	GREENWICH	CT	06830	(203) 869-7191
EMANU-EL, TEMPLE R 16 FORT STREET	GROTON	CT	06340	(203) 442-4955
BETH SHOLOM, TEMPLE C 1809 WHITNEY AVENUE	HAMDEN	CT	06517	(203) 288-7748
MISHKAN ISRAEL, CONGREGATION R 785 RIDGE ROAD	HAMDEN	CT	06517	(203) 288-3877
ADOS ISRAEL, CONGREGATION O 215 PEARL	HARTFORD	CT	06103	(203) 525-3590
AGUDAS ACHIM, CONGREGATION O 1244 N. MAIN STREET	HARTFORD	CT	06117	(203) 233-6241
ANSHE SHOLOM, TEMPLE 130 W. RIDGE DRIVE	HARTFORD	CT	06117	
BETH EL, TEMPLE C 2626 ALBANY AVENUE	HARTFORD	CT	06117	
BETH ISRAEL, CONGREGATION R 701 FARMINGTON AVENUE	HARTFORD	CT	06119	(203) 233-8215
UNITED SYNAGOGUES OF GREATER HARTFORD O 840 N. MAIN STREET	HARTFORD	CT	06117	(203) 236-3338
JEWISH CONGREGATION	LEBANON	CT	06249	
BETH TIKVAH, TEMPLE R 196 DURHAM ROAD, P.O.BOX 523	MADISON	CT	06443	(203) 245-7028
BETH SHOLOM, TEMPLE C 400 E. MIDDLE TURNPIKE	MANCHESTER	CT	06040	(203) 643-9563
B'NAI ABRAHAM, TEMPLE C 127 E. MAIN STREET	MERIDEN	CT	06450	(203) 235-2581
ADATH ISRAEL, CONGREGATION C P.O.BOX 337	MIDDLETOWN	CT	06457	(203) 346-8780
B'NAI SHALOM, TEMPLE C 88 NOBLE AVENUE	MILFORD	CT	06460	(203) 874-5910
RODFE ZEDEK, CONGREGATION C P.O.BOX 38A, SILLIMANVILLE ROAD	MOODUS	CT	06469	(203) 873-8061
B'NAI ISRAEL, TEMPLE C 265 W. MAIN STREET	NEW BRITAIN	CT	06052	(203) 224-0479
TIPHERETH ISRAEL, CONGREGATION O P.O.BOX 490, 76 WINTER STREET	NEW BRITAIN	CT	06052	(203) 229-1485
B'NAI JACOB, CONGREGATION C RIMMON ROAD	NEW HAVEN	CT	06525	(203) 389-2111
BETH EL, CONGREGATION - KESER ISRAEL C 85 HARRISON STREET	NEW HAVEN	CT	06515	(203) 389-2108
BETH HAMEDROSH HAGODOL B'NAI ISRAEL-WESTVILLE SYNAGOGUE O 74 W. PROSPECT STREET	NEW HAVEN	CT	06515	(203) 389-9513
BETH ISRAEL, CONGREGATION O 232 ORCHARD STREET	NEW HAVEN	CT	06511	(203) 776-1468
BIKUR CHOLIM SHEVET ACHIM, CONGREGATION O 279 WINTHROP AVENUE	NEW HAVEN	CT	06510	(203) 776-4997
YOUNG ISRAEL OF NEW HAVEN 292 NORTON STREET	NEW HAVEN	CT	06511	(203) 776-4212
BETH EL C 660 OCEAN AVENUE	NEW LONDON	CT	06320	(203) 442-0418
OHAVE SHOLOM, CONGREGATION 109 BLINMAN STREET	NEW LONDON	CT	06230	
SHOLOM, TEMPLE R P.O.BOX 509	NEW MILFORD	CT	06776	(203) 354-0273

B'NAI SHOLOM R 26 CHURCH STREET	NEWINGTON	CT	06111	(203) 667-0826
SINAI, TEMPLE R 41 W. HARTFORD ROAD	NEWINGTON	CT	06111	(203) 561-1055
ADATH ISRAEL, CONGREGATION C HUNTINGTON ROAD	NEWTOWN	CT	06470	(203) 426-6309
BETH EL, CONGREGATION C 109 E AVENUE	NORWALK	CT	06851	(203) 838-2710
BETH ISRAEL SYNAGOGUE O 40 KING STREET	NORWALK	CT	06851	(203) 866-0534
SHALOM, TEMPLE R 259 RICHARDS AVENUE	NORWALK	CT	06850	(203) 866-0148
BETH JACOB SYNAGOGUE C 400 NEW LONDON TURNPIKE	NORWICH	CT	06360	(203) 886-2459
BETH JACOB, CONGREGATION C 63 CHURCH STREET	NORWICH	CT	06360	(203) 887-8331
BROTHERS OF JOSEPH, CONGREGATION O 2 BROAD STREET	NORWICH	CT	06360	(203) 887-3777
B'NAI SHALOM, TEMPLE - ORANGE SYNAGOGUE CENTER C 205 OLD GRASSY HILL ROAD	ORANGE	CT	06477	(203) 795-2341
EMANUEL, TEMPLE R P.O.BOX 897, 150 DERBY AVENUE	ORANGE	CT	06477	(203) 397-3000
SONS OF ZION, CONGREGATION C CHURCH STREET	PUTNAM	CT	06260	(203) 928-4496
SHEARITH ISRAEL, TEMPLE R 46 PEACEABLE STREET	RIDGEFIELD	CT	06877	(203) 438-6589
B'NAI ISRAEL C 54 TALCOTT AVENUE	ROCKVILLE	CT	06066	(203) 875-5685
FARMINGTON VALLEY JEWISH CONGREGATION R 55 BUSHY HILL ROAD, P.O.BOX 261	SIMSBURY	CT	06070	(203) 658-1075
BETH HILLEL, TEMPLE R P.O.BOX 403, 1001 FOSTER STREET	SOUTH WINDSOR	CT	06074	(203) 644-8466
AGUDATH SHOLOM, CONGREGATION O 301 STRAWBERRY HILL AVENUE	STAMFORD	CT	06902	(203) 325-3501
BETH EL, TEMPLE C 350 ROXBURY ROAD	STAMFORD	CT	06902	(203) 322-6901
SINAI, TEMPLE R LAKESIDE DRIVE	STAMFORD	CT	06903	(203) 322-1649
STAMFORD RECONSTRUCTIONIST HAVURAH	STAMFORD	CT		(203) 322-5042
YOUNG ISRAEL OF STAMFORD P.O.BOX 2124	STAMFORD	CT	06906	(203) 323-3390
BETH SHOLOM, TEMPLE C 275 HUNTINGTON ROAD	STRATFORD	CT	06497	(203) 378-6175
BETH EL SYNAGOGUE C 124 LITCHFIELD STREET	TORRINGTON	CT	06790	(203) 482-8263
B'NAI TORAH, CONGREGATION C 5700 MAIN STREET	TRUMBULL	CT	06611	(203) 268-6940
BETH ISRAEL, CONGREGATION C 22 N. ORCHARD STREET	WALLINGFORD	CT	06492	(203) 269-5983
B'NAI SHALOM SYNAGOGUE O 135 ROSELAND AVENUE	WATERBURY	CT	06710	(203) 754-4159
BETH EL SYNAGOGUE C 359 COOKE STREET	WATERBURY	CT	06710	(203) 749-4659
ISRAEL, TEMPLE R 100 WILLIAMSON DRIVE	WATERBURY	CT	06710	(203) 754-0187
SHARES ISRAEL, CONGREGATION 94 RANDOLPH AVENUE	WATERBURY	CT	06710	
EMANU-EL, TEMPLE 29 DAYTON ROAD, P.O.BOX 288	WATERFORD	CT	06835	(203) 443-3069
BETH DAVID SYNAGOGUE O 20 DOVER ROAD	WEST HARTFORD	CT	06119	(203) 236-1241
BETH EL TEMPLE OF WEST HARTFORD C 2626 ALBANY AVENUE	WEST HARTFORD	CT	06117	(203) 233-9696
BETH ISRAEL, TEMPLE R 701 FARMINGTON AVENUE	WEST HARTFORD	CT	06119	(203) 233-8215
EMANUEL SYNAGOGUE C 160 MOHEGAN DRIVE	WEST HARTFORD	CT	06117	(203) 236-1275
SEPHARDIC CONGREGATION OF GREATER HARTFORD 21 TUMBLEBROOK LANE	WEST HARTFORD	CT	06117	(203) 233-1888
YOUNG ISRAEL OF HARTFORD 1137 TROUT BROOK DRIVE	WEST HARTFORD	CT	06107	(203) 523-7804
YOUNG ISRAEL OF WEST HARTFORD 2240 ALBANY AVENUE	WEST HARTFORD	CT	06117	(203) 523-8670
ISRAEL, TEMPLE R 14 COLEYTOWN ROAD	WESTPORT	CT	06880	(203) 227-1293
BETH TORAH, TEMPLE C 130 MAIN STREET	WETHERSFIELD	CT	06109	(203) 529-2410
B'NAI ISRAEL, TEMPLE C 345 JACKSON STREET	WILLIMANTIC	CT	06226	(203) 423-3743
B'NAI CHAIM, TEMPLE R P.O.BOX 764	WILTON	CT	06897	(203) 762-8852
BETH AHM, CONGREGATION C 362 PALISADO AVENUE	WINDSOR	CT	06095	(203) 688-9989
BETH ISRAEL, TEMPLE C 74 PARK PLACE	WINSTED	CT	06098	
B'NAI JACOB, CONGREGATION C 75 RIMMON ROAD	WOODBRIDGE	CT	06525	(203) 389-2111
ADAS ISRAEL HEBREW CONGREGATION C 2850 QUEBEC STREET NW	WASHINGTON	DC	20008	(202) 362-4433
AGUDATH ACHIM, CONGREGATION T 6343 13TH STREET N.W.	WASHINGTON	DC	20011	
BETH EL CONGREGATION & TALMUD TORAH C/O LEVINSON, 6101 16TH STREET	WASHINGTON	DC	20011	
BETH JOSHUA, CONGREGATION O 6045 16TH STREET N.W.	WASHINGTON	DC	20012	
BETH SHOLOM CONGREGATION O EASTERN AVENUE N.W.	WASHINGTON	DC	20012	(202) 726-3869
GALLAUDET COLLEGE HILLEL CLUB, THE C/O OFF OF CAMPUS MINISTRIES, GALLAUDET COLLEGE	WASHINGTON	DC	20002	(202) 651-5106
KESHER ISRAEL, CONGREGATION O 2801 N. STREET N.W.	WASHINGTON	DC	20007	
MICAH, TEMPLE R 600 M STREET S.W.	WASHINGTON	DC	20024	(202) 554-3099
OHEV SHOLOM TALMUD TORAH CONGREGATION O 1600 JONQUIL STREET N.W.	WASHINGTON	DC	20012	(202) 882-7225
RECONSTRUCTIONIST FELLOWSHIP OF GREATER WASHINGTON C/O HARRIET OSTROFF	WASHINGTON	DC		(301) 770-3591
SINAI, TEMPLE R 3100 MILITARY ROAD N W	WASHINGTON	DC	20015	(202) 363-6394
TIFERETH ISRAEL CONGREGATION C 7701 26TH STREET N.W.	WASHINGTON	DC	20012	(202) 882-1605
WASHINGTON HEBREW CONGREGATION R 3935 MACOMB STREET N.W.	WASHINGTON	DC	20016	(202) 362-7100
BETH SHOLOM, CONGREGATION C NORTH QUEEN & CLARA STREETS, BOX 223	DOVER	DE	19901	(302) 734-5578
BETH-EL, TEMPLE 70 AMSTEL AVENUE	NEWARK	DE	19711	(302) 366-8330
BETH EMETH, CONGREGATION R 300 W. LEA BLVD	WILMINGTON	DE	19802	(302) 764-2393
BETH SHALOM C 18TH & BAYNARD BLVD	WILMINGTON	DE	19802	(302) 654-4462
SHUL OF BAL HARBOR 9955 COLLINS AVENUE	BAL HARBOR	FL	33154	(305) 868-1411
B'NAI TORAH CONGREGATION C 1401 N.W. 4TH AVENUE	BOCA RATON	FL	33432	(305) 392-8566
BETH EL, TEMPLE R 333 S.W. 4TH AVENUE	BOCA RATON	FL	33432	(305) 391-8900
ETERNAL LIGHT, TEMPLE 499 N.W. 13TH STREET, P.O. BOX 3	BOCA RATON	FL	33432	(305) 391-1111
FREE SYNAGOGUE CENTER, THE 499 N.W. 13TH STREET, P.O. BOX 3	BOCA RATON	FL	33432	(305) 368-1600
BETH EL, TEMPLE C 2209 75TH STREET W	BRADENTON	FL	33529	(813) 792-0870
BETH-EL, TEMPLE R 2721 DEL PRADO BLVD	CAPE CORAL	FL	33904	(305) 574-5115
B'NAI ISRAEL, TEMPLE R 1685 S. BELCHER ROAD	CLEARWATER	FL	33516	(813) 531-5829
BETH SHALOM C 1325 S. BELCHER ROAD	CLEARWATER	FL	33516	(813) 531-1418
BETH ORR, TEMPLE R P.O. BOX 8242, 2151 RIVERSIDE DRIVE	CORAL GABLES	FL	33065	(305) 753-3232
JUDEA, TEMPLE R 5500 GRANADA BLVD	CORAL GABLES	FL	33146	(305) 667-5657
ZAMORA, TEMPLE C 44 ZAMORA AVENUE	CORAL GABLES	FL	33134	
CORAL SPRINGS HEBREW CONGREGATION R P.O. BOX 8242	CORAL SPRINGS	FL	33060	
BETH EL, TEMPLE R 507 FIFTH AVENUE	DAYTONA BEACH	FL	32018	(904) 252-1248
ISRAEL OF DAYTONA BEACH, TEMPLE C 1400 S. PENINSULA DRIVE	DAYTONA BEACH	FL	32018	(904) 252-3097
BETH ISRAEL, TEMPLE C 200 CENTURY BLVD	DEERFIELD BEACH	FL	33441	(305) 421-7060
YOUNG ISRAEL OF DEERFIELD BEACH 1640 WEST HILLSBORO BOULEVARD	DEERFIELD BEACH	FL	33441	(305) 421-1367
EMETH, TEMPLE C 5780 W. ATLANTIC AVENUE	DELRAY BEACH	FL	33445	(305) 498-3536
SINAI, TEMPLE R P.O. BOX 1901	DELRAY BEACH	FL	33446	(305) 276-6161
SHALOM, TEMPLE R P.O. BOX 132, 1785 ELKCAM BLVD	DELTONA	FL	32725	(904) 789-2202
AHAVAT SHOLOM, TEMPLE R 2000 MAIN STREET	DUNEDIN	FL	33528	(813) 734-9428
BETH ISRAEL, TEMPLE 7100 W. OAKLAND PARK BLVD	FORT LAUDERDALE	FL	33313	
EMANU-EL, TEMPLE R 3245 W. OAKLAND PARK BLVD	FORT LAUDERDALE	FL	33311	(305) 731-2310
OHEL B'NAI RAPHAEL, TEMPLE 4351 W. OAKLAND PARK BLVD	FORT LAUDERDALE	FL	33313	(305) 733-7684
YOUNG ISRAEL OF HOLLYWOOD 3291 STIRLING ROAD	FORT LAUDERDALE	FL	33312	(305) 966-7877
BETH EL, TEMPLE R 4600 OLEANDER AVENUE	FORT PIERCE	FL	33450	(305) 461-7428
B'NAI ISRAEL C 3830 N.W. 16TH BLVD	GAINESVILLE	FL	32605	(904) 376-1508
BETH SHOLOM OF GULFPORT, CONGREGATION C 1844 54TH STREET S.	GULFPORT	FL	33707	(305) 345-7232
HALLANDALE JEWISH CENTER C 416 N.E. 8TH AVENUE	HALLANDALE	FL	33009	(305) 454-9100
TIFERETH JACOB, TEMPLE C 951 E. 4TH AVENUE	HIALEAH	FL	33010	
BETH EL, TEMPLE R 1351 S. 14TH AVENUE	HOLLYWOOD	FL	33020	(305) 920-8225
BETH SHALOM, TEMPLE C 1400 N. 46TH AVENUE	HOLLYWOOD	FL	33021	(305) 981-6111
SINAI, TEMPLE C 1201 JOHNSON STREET	HOLLYWOOD	FL	33019	(305) 920-1577
SOLEL, TEMPLE R 5100 SHERIDAN STREET	HOLLYWOOD	FL	33021	(305) 989-0205
HOMESTEAD JEWISH CENTER 183 N.E. 8TH STREET	HOMESTEAD	FL	33023	
AHAVATH CHESED, CONGREGATION R 8727 SAN JOSE BLVD	JACKSONVILLE	FL	32217	(904) 733-7078
BETH SHALOM C 4072 SUNBEAM ROAD	JACKSONVILLE	FL	32217	(904) 268-0404
ETZ CHAIM SYNAGOGUE O 5864 UNIVERSITY BLVD. W.	JACKSONVILLE	FL	32216	(904) 733-0720
ETZ CHAIM SYNAGOGUE - SAN JOSE BRANCH O 10167 SAN JOSE BLVD.	JACKSONVILLE	FL	32217	(904) 262-3565
JACKSONVILLE JEWISH CENTER C P.O. BOX 23886, 10101 SAN JOSE BLVD	JACKSONVILLE	FL	32217	(904) 268-6736
BETH SHOLOM, TEMPLE 315 NORTH A STREET, P.O. BOX 1209	LAKE WORTH	FL	33460	(305) 585-5020
EMANUEL, TEMPLE C 730 LAKE HOLLINGSWORTH DRIVE	LAKELAND	FL	33803	(813) 682-8616
BETH AM, TEMPLE C 7205 ROYAL PALM BLVD	MARGATE	FL	33063	(305) 974-8650
BETH HILLEL, CONGREGATION C 7640 MARGATE BLVD	MARGATE	FL	33063	(305) 974-3090
NER TAMID, CONGREGATION C 820 E. STRAWBRIDGE AVENUE	MELBOURNE	FL	32901	(305) 723-9112
ISRAEL, TEMPLE R P.O. BOX 592	MERRITT ISLAND	FL	32952	(305) 636-4920
AHAVAT SHALOM, CONGREGATION O 985 S.W. 67TH AVENUE	MIAMI	FL	33144	
ANSHEI EMES, CONGREGATION C 2533 S.W. 19TH AVENUE	MIAMI	FL	33133	
AVENTURA JEWISH CENTER C 2972 AVENTURA BLVD	MIAMI	FL	33180	(305) 932-0666
B'NAI ISRAEL & GREATER MIAMI YOUTH SYNAGOGUE P.O. BOX 161542	MIAMI	FL	33116	(305) 595-9336
BET BREIRA, CONGREGATION R 9075 S.W. 87TH AVENUE	MIAMI	FL	33176	(305) 595-1500
BETH AM, TEMPLE R 5950 N. KENDALL DRIVE	MIAMI	FL	33156	
BETH DAVID CONGREGATION C 2625 S.W. THIRD AVENUE	MIAMI	FL	33129	(305) 854-3911
BETH KODESH, CONGREGATION C 1101 S.W. 12TH AVENUE	MIAMI	FL	33129	(305) 858-6334
BETH MOSHE, CONGREGATION C 2225 N.E. 121 STREET	MIAMI	FL	33181	(305) 801-5508
BETH TOV, TEMPLE C 6438 S.W. 8TH STREET	MIAMI	FL	33144	
CONGREGATION SHAARE TEFILLAH OF KENDALL O 15410 S.W. 75TH CIRCLE LANE	MIAMI	FL	33193	(305) 382-3343
ISRAEL OF GREATER MIAMI, TEMPLE R 137 N.E. 19TH STREET	MIAMI	FL	33132	(305) 573-5900
ISRAELITE CENTER TEMPLE, THE C 3175 S.W. 25TH STREET	MIAMI	FL	33133	(305) 445-1529
KENDALL LAKES, SYNAGOGUE OF - CHABAD O 14456 KENDALL LAKES BLVD	MIAMI	FL	33183	(305) 271-8277
OR OLAM, TEMPLE C 8755 S.W. 16TH STREET	MIAMI	FL	33165	(305) 221-9131
SAMU-EL, TEMPLE C 9353 S.W. 152ND AVENUE	MIAMI	FL	33196	(305) 382-3668
TEMPLE BETH OR RE POB 160081	MIAMI	FL	33116	(305) 596-4523
TIFERETH ISRAEL, TEMPLE C 6500 N. MIAMI AVENUE	MIAMI	FL	33150	
ZION, TEMPLE C 8000 MILLER ROAD	MIAMI	FL	33155	(305) 271-2311
AGUDATH ISRAEL HEBREW INSTITUTE 7801 CARLYLE AVE	MIAMI BEACH	FL	33141	(305) 866-5226
AHAVAS ISRAEL, CONGREGATION 525 78TH STREET	MIAMI BEACH	FL	33141	
ALL PEOPLES REFORM SYNAGOGUE 7455 COLLINS AVENUE	MIAMI BEACH	FL	33141	(305) 861-5554
BEIS HAMEDRASH LEVI YITZCHAK, CONGREGATION O 1140 ALTON ROAD	MIAMI BEACH	FL	33139	(305) 673-5664
BETH EL, TEMPLE O 2400 PINE TREE DRIVE	MIAMI BEACH	FL	33140	(305) 532-6421
BETH ISRAEL CONGREGATION O 770 40TH STREET	MIAMI BEACH	FL	33140	(305) 534-1461
BETH JACOB, CONGREGATION O 311 WASHINGTON AVENUE	MIAMI BEACH	FL	33139	(305) 672-6150
BETH RAPHAEL, TEMPLE C 1545 JEFFERSON AVENUE	MIAMI BEACH	FL	33139	(305) 538-4112
BETH SHOLOM, TEMPLE R 4144 CHASE AVENUE	MIAMI BEACH	FL	33140	(305) 538-7231
BETH TFILAH, CONGREGATION O 935 EUCLID AVENUE	MIAMI BEACH	FL	33139	(305) 538-1521
CONGREGATION OHR CHAIM 317 W. 47 ST	MIAMI BEACH	FL	33140	(305) 674-1326
CUBAN HEBREW CONGREGATION 1700 MICHIGAN AVENUE	MIAMI BEACH	FL	33139	(305) 534-7213
CUBAN SEPHARDIC HEBREW CONGREGATION O 1200 NORMANDY DRIVE	MIAMI BEACH	FL	33141	(305) 531-4732
EMANU-EL, TEMPLE C 1701 WASHINGTON AVENUE	MIAMI BEACH	FL	33139	(305) 538-2503
ETZ CHAIM, CONGREGATION 1544 WASHINGTON AVENUE	MIAMI BEACH	FL	33139	(305) 674-1326
JACOB J. COHEN COMMUNITY CONGREGATION O 1532 WASHINGTON AVENUE	MIAMI BEACH	FL	33139	(305) 534-0271
JEWISH CULTURAL CENTER 429 LENOX AVENUE	MIAMI BEACH	FL	33139	(305) 672-7784
KING SOLOMON TEMPLE C 910 LINCOLN ROAD	MIAMI BEACH	FL	33139	(305) 534-9776
KNESETH ISRAEL, CONGREGATION O 1415 EUCLID AVENUE	MIAMI BEACH	FL	33139	(305) 538-2741
LUBAVITCH, CONGREGATION 1220 OCEAN AVENUE	MIAMI BEACH	FL	33139	(305) 673-1800
LUBAVITCH, CONGREGATION O 1120 COLLINS AVENUE	MIAMI BEACH	FL	33139	(305) 673-1800
MENORAH, TEMPLE C 620 75TH STREET	MIAMI BEACH	FL	33141	(305) 866-0221
MOGAN DAVID OF SURFSIDE, CONGREGATION O 9348 HARDING AVENUE (SURFSIDE)	MIAMI BEACH	FL	33154	(305) 865-9714
NER TAMID, TEMPLE C 7902 CARLYLE STREET	MIAMI BEACH	FL	33141	(305) 866-9833
NORTH BAY VILLAGE JEWISH CENTER C 1720 79TH STREET CAUSEWAY	MIAMI BEACH	FL	33141	(305) 861-4005
OHEV SHALOM CONGREGATION O 7055 BONITA DRIVE	MIAMI BEACH	FL	33141	(305) 865-9851
SEPHARDIC JEWISH CENTER OF GREATER MIAMI 645 COLLINS AVENUE	MIAMI BEACH	FL	33139	(305) 534-4092
TEMPLE HATIKVAH ISRAEL 800 71 STREET	MIAMI BEACH	FL	33141	(305) 865-0479
YOUNG ISRAEL OF SUNNY ISLES, O 17420 COLLINS AVENUE	MIAMI BEACH	FL	33160	(305) 932-4433
ISRAEL OF MIRAMAR, TEMPLE C 6920 S.W. 35TH STREET	MIRAMAR	FL	33023	(305) 961-1700
BETH MOSHE, TEMPLE C 2225 N.E. 121ST STREET	NORTH MIAMI	FL	33181	(305) 891-5508
ADATH YESHURUN, TEMPLE C 1025 N.E. MIAMI GARDENS	NORTH MIAMI BEACH	FL	33162	

B'NAI RAPHAEL, CONGREGATION C				
1401 N.W. 183RD STREET	NORTH MIAMI BEACH	FL	33169	
BETH TORAH CONGREGATION C				
1051 N. MIAMI BEACH BLVD	NORTH MIAMI BEACH	FL	33162	(305) 947-7528
ETZ CHAIM, CONG. - METRO COMMUNITY SYN. OF GREATER MIAMI R				
19094 W. DIXIE HIGHWAY	NORTH MIAMI BEACH	FL	33180	(305) 931-9318
KOL YISRAEL CHAVERIM, CONGREGATION				
17720 N. BAY ROAD, SUITE 8D	NORTH MIAMI BEACH	FL	33160	(305) 931-0001
METROPOLITAN COMM. SYN./GREATER MIAMI, CONG. ETZ CHAIM,				
19094 W. DIXIE HIGHWAY	NORTH MIAMI BEACH	FL	33180	(305) 931-9318
SINAI OF NORTH DADE, TEMPLE R 18801 N.E. 22ND AVENUE	NORTH MIAMI BEACH	FL	33180	(305) 932-9010
SKY LAKE SYNAGOGUE O 18151 N.E. 19TH AVENUE	NORTH MIAMI BEACH	FL	33162	
YOUNG ISRAEL OF GREATER MIAMI 990 N.E. 171ST STREET	NORTH MIAMI BEACH	FL	33162	(305) 651-3591
YOUNG ISRAEL OF SKY LAKE 1850 N.E. 183RD STREET	NORTH MIAMI BEACH	FL	33179	(305) 945-8712
BETH DAVID OF NORTHERN PALM BEACH COUNTY, TEMPLE C				
321 NORTHLAKE BLVD	NORTH PALM BEACH	FL	33408	(305) 845-1134
ISRAEL, TEMPLE C 4917 ELI STREET	ORLANDO	FL	32804	(305) 647-3055
LIBERAL JUDAISM CONGREGATION R 928 MALONE DRIVE	ORLANDO	FL	32810	(305) 645-0444
OHEV SHALOM C 5015 GODDARD AVENUE	ORLANDO	FL	32810	(305) 298-4650
EMANU-EL OF PALM BEACH, TEMPLE C 190 N. CITY ROAD	PALM BEACH	FL	33480	(305) 832-0804
BETH EMET, TEMPLE R P.O. BOX 8842	PEMBROKE PINES	FL	33024	(305) 431-3638
IN THE PINES, TEMPLE C 9730 STIRLING ROAD	PEMBROKE PINES	FL	33024	(305) 431-5100
B'NAI ISRAEL SYNAGOGUE C P.O. BOX 9002, 1909 N. 9TH AVENUE	PENSACOLA	FL	32503	(904) 433-7311
BETH EL, TEMPLE R 800 N. PALAFOX STREET	PENSACOLA	FL	32501	(904) 438-3321
KOL AMI, TEMPLE - PLANTATION JEWISH CONGREGATION				
8200 PETERS ROAD	PLANTATION	FL	33324	(305) 472-1988
RAMAT SHALOM RECONSTRUCTIONIST SYNAGOGUE				
11301 W. BROWARD BLVD	PLANTATION	FL	33325	(305) 472-3600
SHOLOM, TEMPLE C 132 S.E. 11TH AVENUE	POMPANO BEACH	FL	33060	(305) 942-6410
BETH SHOLOM, TEMPLE C 1050 S. TUTTLE AVENUE	SARASOTA	FL	33577	(813) 955-8121
EMANU-EL, TEMPLE R 151 S. MCINTOSH ROAD	SARASOTA	FL	33582	(813) 371-2788
BETH SHOLOM, TEMPLE C P.O. BOX 2253 (N.E. THIRD STREET)	SATELLITE BEACH	FL	32937	(305) 773-3039
BETH CHAI C P.O. BOX 3235	SEMINOLE	FL	33542	(813) 393-5525
B'NAI ISRAEL C 301 59TH STREET N	ST. PETERSBURG	FL	33710	(813) 381-4900
BETH EL, TEMPLE R 400 S. PASADENA AVENUE	ST. PETERSBURG	FL	33707	(813) 347-6136
BETH ISRAEL, TEMPLE C 7100 W. OAKLAND PARK BLVD	SUNRISE	FL	33313	(305) 742-4040
ISRAEL, TEMPLE R P.O. BOX 3343	TALLAHASSEE	FL	32303	(904) 877-3517
BETH TORAH, TEMPLE - TAMARAC JEWISH CENTER C				
9101-15 N.W. 57TH STREET	TAMARAC	FL	33321	(305) 721-7660
BETH ISRAEL, CONGREGATION C 2111 SWANN AVENUE	TAMPA	FL	33606	
DAVID, TEMPLE C 2001 SWANN AVENUE	TAMPA	FL	33609	(813) 251-4215
KOL AMI, CONGREGATION C P.O. BOX 270444	TAMPA	FL	33688	(813) 885-3356
RODEPH SHOLOM, CONGREGATION C 2713 BAYSHORE	TAMPA	FL	33609	(813) 837-1911
SHAARAI ZEDEK, TEMPLE R 3303 SWANN AVENUE	TAMPA	FL	33609	(813) 876-2377
BETH SHALOM, TEMPLE R P.O. BOX 2113	VERO BEACH	FL	32960	(305) 569-1082
BETH EL, TEMPLE C 2815 N. FLAGLER DRIVE	WEST PALM BEACH	FL	33407	(305) 833-0339
BETH TORAH, TEMPLE R 1125 JACKPINE STREET	WEST PALM BEACH	FL	33411	(305) 793-2700
ISRAEL, TEMPLE R 1901 N. FLAGLER DRIVE	WEST PALM BEACH	FL	33407	(305) 833-8421
ALBANY HEBREW CONGREGATION R P.O. BOX 3288	ALBANY	GA	31706	(912) 432-6536
CHILDREN OF ISRAEL R DUDLEY DRIVE, P.O. BOX 5694	ALBANY	GA	30604	(912) 549-4192
AHAVATH ACHIM SYNAGOGUE C				
600 PEACHTREE BATTLE AVENUE N.W.	ATLANTA	GA	30327	(404) 355-5222
ANSHEI SFARD, CONGREGATION O 1324 N. HIGHLAND AVENUE N.E.	ATLANTA	GA	30312	
BETH JACOB, CONGREGATION O 1855 LA VISTA ROAD, N.E.	ATLANTA	GA	30329	(404) 633-0551
BETH SHALOM, CONGREGATION C 3147 CHAMBLEE-TUCKER ROAD	ATLANTA	GA	30341	(404) 458-0489
B'NAI TORAH T 700 MT. VERNON HIGHWAY	ATLANTA	GA	30358	(404) 257-0537
EMANU-EL, TEMPLE R 120 COPELAND ROAD, SUITE 254	ATLANTA	GA	30342	(404) 257-0633
HEBREW BENEVOLENT CONGREGATION; THE TEMPLE				
1589 N.E. PEACHTREE ROAD	ATLANTA	GA	30367	(404) 873-1731
ISRAEL, TEMPLE OF 891 MAYSON TURNER AVENUE N.W.	ATLANTA	GA	30309	(404) 524-7952
KEHILLAT CHAIM R 141 W. WIEUCA ROAD, N.W. SUITE 202-A	ATLANTA	GA	30342	(404) 252-4441
OR VESHALOM, CONGREGATION O 1681 N. DRUID HILLS ROAD N.E.	ATLANTA	GA	30319	(404) 633-1737
SHEARITH ISRAEL, CONGREGATION C 1180 UNIVERSITY DRIVE N.E.	ATLANTA	GA	30306	(404) 873-1743
SINAI, TEMPLE R 5645 N.W. DUPREE DRIVE	ATLANTA	GA	30327	(404) 252-3073
CHILDREN OF ISRAEL, CONGREGATION - WALTON WAY TEMPLE R				
3005 WALTON WAY	AUGUSTA	GA	30909	(404) 736-3140
BETH EL, TEMPLE R P.O. BOX 476	BAINBRIDGE	GA	31717	(912) 432-6536
BETH TEFILLOT, TEMPLE R P.O. BOX 602	BRUNSWICK	GA	31521	(912) 265-7575
ISRAEL, TEMPLE R P.O. BOX 5086	COLUMBUS	GA	31906	(404) 323-1617
SHEARITH ISRAEL CONGREGATION C				
2550 WYNNTON ROAD, P.O. BOX 5515	COLUMBUS	GA	31906	(404) 323-1443
BETH EL, TEMPLE C VALLEY DRIVE	DALTON	GA	30720	(404) 278-6798
EMANU-EL, TEMPLE R 1580 SPALDING DRIVE	DUNWOODY	GA	30338	(404) 395-1340
FITZGERALD HEBREW CONGREGATION C ROUTE 4 BOX 520	FITZGERALD	GA	31750	
BETH-EL, CONGREGATION C				
C/O ISAAC STRULETZ, 200 SPRINGDALE DRIVE	LA GRANGE	GA	30240	
BETH ISRAEL, TEMPLE R 892 CHERRY STREET	MACON	GA	31201	(912) 745-6727
SHERAH ISRAEL C 611 FIRST STREET	MACON	GA	31201	(912) 745-4571
ETZ CHAIM, CONGREGATION C 1190 INDIAN HILLS PARKWAY	MARIETTA	GA	30067	(404) 973-0137
TEMPLE KOL EMETH R P.O. BOX 71031	MARIETTA	GA	30067	
B'NAI ISRAEL R P.O. BOX 383	RIVERDALE	GA	30274	
RODEPH SHOLOM, TEMPLE R 406 E. FIRST STREET	ROME	GA	30161	(404) 291-6315
AGUDATH ACHIM C P.O. BOX 14317, 9 LEE BLVD	SAVANNAH	GA	31406	(912) 352-4737
B'NAI B'RITH JACOB, CONGREGATION O				
5444 ABERCORN STREET, P.O. BOX 6326	SAVANNAH	GA	31405	
MIKVE ISRAEL, TEMPLE R 20 E. GORDON STREET	SAVANNAH	GA	31405	(912) 233-1547
TEMPLE BETH DAVID R P.O. BOX 865	SNELLVILLE	GA	30278	(404) 979-2773
ISRAEL, TEMPLE C 511 BAYTREE ROAD	VALDOSTA	GA	31601	(912) 244-1813
VALDOSTA HEBREW CONGREGATION-TEMPLE ISRAEL C				
600 WEST PARK	VALDOSTA	GA	31601	(912) 242-2590
EMANU-EL, TEMPLE R 2550 PALI HIGHWAY	HONOLULU	HA	96817	(808) 595-7521
SOF MA'ARAV, CONGREGATION C P.O. BOX 11154	HONOLULU	HA	96828	(808) 923-5563
ALOHA JEWISH CHAPEL C NAVAL STATION, BOX 47	PEARL HARBOR	HA	96860	(808) 471-0050
AMES JEWISH CONGREGATION R 6712 CALHOUN	AMES	IA	50010	(515) 233-1347
ISRAEL, TEMPLE R 830 DIVISION	BURLINGTON	IA	52601	(319) 752-1138
JUDAH, TEMPLE R 3221 S.E. LINDSAY LANE	CEDAR RAPIDS	IA	52403	(319) 362-1261
B'NAI ISRAEL SYNAGOGUE C 618 MYNSTER STREET	COUNCIL BLUFFS	IA	51501	(712) 322-4705
EMANUEL, TEMPLE R 1115 MISSISSIPPI AVENUE	DAVENPORT	IA	52803	(319) 326-4419
B'NAI JESHURUN, TEMPLE R 5101 GRAND AVENUE	DES MOINES	IA	50312	(515) 274-4679
BETH EL JACOB, CONGREGATION O 954 CUMMINS PARKWAY	DES MOINES	IA	50312	(515) 274-1551
CHILDREN OF ISRAEL, CONGREGATION 1816 61ST STREET	DES MOINES	IA	50322	
TIFERETH ISRAEL C 924 POLK BLVD	DES MOINES	IA	50312	(515) 255-1137
BETH EL, CONGREGATION R 475 W. LOCUST STREET, P.O. BOX 185	DUBUQUE	IA	52001	(319) 583-3473
BETH EL, CONGREGATION C 507 N. 12TH STREET	FORT DODGE	IA	50501	(515) 576-2024
AGUDAS ACHIM C 602 E. WASHINGTON STREET	IOWA CITY	IA	52240	(319) 337-3813
B'NEI ISRAEL, CONGREGATION 302 EAST WASHINGTON	IOWA CITY	IA	52240	
SONS OF ISRAEL C 211 W. CHURCH STREET	MARSHALLTOWN	IA	50158	(515) 753-7870
ADAS ISRAEL, CONGREGATION C 396 WILLOWBROOK DRIVE	MASON CITY	IA	50401	
B'NAI JACOB C 529 E. MAIN STREET	OTTUMWA	IA	52501	(515) 684-7465
MOUNT SINAI TEMPLE R P.O. BOX 2128 NS STATION	SIOUX CITY	IA	51104	(712) 252-4265
SHAARE ZION SYNAGOGUE C 1522 DOUGLAS STREET	SIOUX CITY	IA	51105	(712) 252-4057
SONS OF JACOB SYNAGOGUE C 411 MITCHELL AVENUE	WATERLOO	IA	50702	(319) 233-9448
AHAVATH ISRAEL SYNAGOGUE C 2620 BANNOCK STREET	BOISE	ID	83702	(208) 343-6601
BETH ISRAEL, CONGREGATION R P.O. BOX 353	BOISE	ID	83701	(208) 343-6601
ADAT YISRAEL CONGREGATION C				
2550 N. ARLINGTON HEIGHTS RD.	ARLINGTON HEIGHTS	IL	60004	(312) 885-1569
B'NAI ISRAEL, TEMPLE C 400 NORTH EDGELAWN	AURORA	IL	60506	(312) 892-2450
BETH ISRAEL, TEMPLE 225 N. HIGH STREET	BELLEVILLE	IL	62220	
UNITED HEBREW TEMPLE C P.O. BOX 160	BENTON	IL	62812	
MOSES MONTEFIORE R 102 ROBIN HOOD LANE	BLOOMINGTON	IL	61701	(309) 662-3182
BETH JUDEA, CONGREGATION C P.O. BOX 763	BUFFALO GROVE	IL	60090	(312) 634-0777
MISHPAHA-OUR FAMILY C 760 CHECKER DRIVE	BUFFALO GROVE	IL	60090	(312) 459-3279
MONTEFIORE TEMPLE C 3014 ELM STREET	CAIRO	IL	62914	
BETH JACOB, CONGREGATION C P.O. BOX 1042	CARBONDALE	IL	62901	(618) 529-1409
SOLOMON, TEMPLE R C/O MR. LINKON, ROUTE 161 E.	CENTRALIA	IL	62801	(618) 532-8749
SINAI CONGREGATION R 3104 W. WINDSOR ROAD	CHAMPAIGN	IL	61820	(217) 352-8140
A.G. BETH ISRAEL T 3635 WEST DEVON	CHICAGO	IL	60659	(312) 539-9060
ADAS BNAI ISRAEL O 6200 NORTH KIMBALL	CHICAGO	IL	60659	(312) 583-8141
ADAS YESCHURUN O 2949 W. TOUHY	CHICAGO	IL	60645	(312) 465-2288
ADATH HATIKVAH CONGREGATION C				
6327 N. WASHTENAW AVENUE, P.O. BOX 59056	CHICAGO	IL	60659	
AGUDAS ACHIM NORTH SHORE, CONGREGATION T				
5029 N. KENMORE AVENUE	CHICAGO	IL	60640	(312) 561-0435
AGUDAS ANSHEI LUBAVITCH, CONGREGATION O				
7424 NORTH PAULINA	CHICAGO	IL	60626	(312) 274-0623
AGUDATH ACHIM - BIKUR CHOLIM O 8927 S. HOUSTON	CHICAGO	IL	60617	(312) 768-7685
AGUDAH ISRAEL OF CHICAGO O 3540 WEST PETERSON	CHICAGO	IL	60659	(312) 588-5085
ALBANY PARK HEBREW CONGREGATION C				
4601 N. LAWNDALE AVENUE	CHICAGO	IL	60625	
ANSHE EMET SYNAGOGUE C 3760 PINE GROVE AVENUE	CHICAGO	IL	60613	(312) 281-1423
ANSHE KNESSESS ISRAEL, CONGREGATION O 2357 E. 75TH STREET	CHICAGO	IL	60649	
ANSHE MIZRACH, CONGREGATION O 627 W. PATTERSON AVENUE	CHICAGO	IL	60613	(312) 525-4034
ANSHE MOTELE O 6520 N. CALIFORNIA AVENUE	CHICAGO	IL	60645	(312) 743-2420
ANSHE SHOLOM BNAI ISRAEL CONGREGATION O				
540 W. MELROSE STREET	CHICAGO	IL	60657	(312) 248-9200
ANSHIE LUBAVITCH, CONGREGATION O 4928 RIDGEWAY AVENUE	CHICAGO	IL	60625	
ATERES YEHOSHUA CONGREGATION O 2819 W. TOUHY	CHICAGO	IL	60645	
AUSTRIAN GALICIAN BETH ISRAEL CONGREGATION T				
3635 WEST DEVON	CHICAGO	IL	60645	
B'NAI DAVID-SHAARE ZEDEK, CONGREGATION C				
2508 W. FITCH AVENUE	CHICAGO	IL	60625	(312) 764-8825
B'NAI JACOB CONGREGATION OF WEST ROGERS PARK C				
2447 W. GRANVILLE AVENUE	CHICAGO	IL	60659	
B'NAI JACOB, CONGREGATION C 6200 N. ARTESIAN AVENUE	CHICAGO	IL	60659	(312) 274-1586
B'NAI YAKOV, CONGREGATION O 2700 W. HADDON AVENUE	CHICAGO	IL	60622	
B'NAI ZION, CONGREGATION C 6759 N. GREENVIEW AVENUE	CHICAGO	IL	60626	(312) 465-2161
BETH AM, THE PEOPLE'S SYNAGOGUE R 3480 N. LAKE SHORE	CHICAGO	IL	60657	
BETH DAVID O 4830 N. ST. LOUIS AVENUE	CHICAGO	IL	60625	
BETH EL OF CHICAGO, TEMPLE R 3050 W. TOUHY STREET	CHICAGO	IL	60645	(312) 274-0341
BETH EL OF ROGERS PARK, CONGREGATION O				
7612 N. ROGERS AVENUE	CHICAGO	IL	60626	
BETH HAKNESSETH, CONGREGATION O 5000 NORTH LAWNDALE	CHICAGO	IL	60625	
BETH HAMEDROSH HAGODOL KESSER MAARIV, CONGREGATION				
6418 N. GREENVIEW AVENUE	CHICAGO	IL	60626	(312) 764-5370
BETH ISRAEL ANSHE YANOVA, CONGREGATION O				
1328 W. MORSE AVENUE	CHICAGO	IL	60626	
BETH ISRAEL, TEMPLE R 4850 N. BERNARD STREET	CHICAGO	IL	60625	(312) 677-0915
BETH ITZCHOK OF ALBANY PARK, CONGREGATION O				
4645 NORTH DRAKE	CHICAGO	IL	60625	(312) 478-6416
BETH ITZCHOK OF WEST ROGERS PARK, CONGREGATION O				
6716 NORTH WHIPPLE	CHICAGO	IL	60645	(312) 973-2522
BETH JACOB OF ALBANY PARK, CONGREGATION O				
4926 N. KIMBALL AVENUE	CHICAGO	IL	60625	
BETH SHOLOM AHAVAS ACHIM, CONGREGATION O				
5665 N. JERSEY AVENUE	CHICAGO	IL	60659	(312) 267-9055
BETH SHOLOM OF ROGERS PARK, CONGREGATION T				
1233 W. PRATT BLVD	CHICAGO	IL	60626	(312) 743-4160
BNAI DAVID, CONGREGATION C 2626 W. FOSTER AVENUE	CHICAGO	IL	60625	
BNAI ISRAEL, CONGREGATION O 1814 FARWELL AVENUE	CHICAGO	IL	60626	
BNEI RUVEN, CONGREGATION O 6350 N. WHIPPLE STREET	CHICAGO	IL	60659	(312) 743-5434
CENTRAL SYNAGOGUE OF THE SOUTH SIDE HEBREW CONGREGATION C				
30 E. CEDAR STREET	CHICAGO	IL	60611	(312) 787-0450

CHESSED L'AVROHOM NACHLAS DAVID, CONGREGATION O
6342 N. TROY STREET .... CHICAGO IL 60659 (312) 743-2156
CHEVRA KADISHO MACHZIKAI HADAS O 2040 W. DEVON AVENUE .... CHICAGO IL 60645 (312) 764-8760
CHICAGO COMMUNITY KOLLEL O 6506 N. CALIFORNIA .... CHICAGO IL 60645 (312) 262-4160
CHICAGO LOOP SYNAGOGUE T 16 S. CLARK STREET .... CHICAGO IL 60603 (312) 346-7370
CHICAGO SINAI CONGREGATION R 5350 S. SHORE DRIVE .... CHICAGO IL 60615 (312) 288-1600
CONGREGATION HAKAFA R .... CHICAGO IL (312) 441-6020
DREXEL HOME TEMPLE R 6140 S. DREXEL AVENUE .... CHICAGO IL 60637 (312) 643-2384
EMANUEL CONGREGATION R 5959 N. SHERIDAN ROAD .... CHICAGO IL 60660 (312) 561-5173
ETHIOPIAN HEBREWS, CONGREGATION OF 6734 SOUTH ABERDEEN ..... CHICAGO IL 60621
EZRA-HABONIM, CONGREGATION C 2620 W. TOUHY AVENUE .... CHICAGO IL 60645 (312) 743-0154
EZRAS ISRAEL, CONGREGATION T 7001 N. CALIFORNIA AVENUE .... CHICAGO IL 60645 (312) 764-8320
FREE FRIENDS OF REFUGEES OF EASTERN EUROPE
6418 N. GREENVIEW .... CHICAGO IL 60626 (312) 274-5123
GARFIELD RIDGE HEBREW CONGREGATION T
6524 W. ARCHER AVENUE .... CHICAGO IL 60638 (312) 586-7108

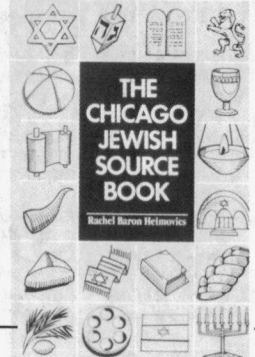
K.I.N.S. OF WEST ROGERS PARK, CONGREGATION T
2800 W. NORTH SHORE AVENUE .... CHICAGO IL 60645 (312) 761-4000
KAM ISAIAH ISRAEL CONGREGATION R 1100 E. HYDE PARK BLVD .... CHICAGO IL 60615 (312) 924-1234
KEHILAT JESHURUN, CONGREGATION C 3707 W. AINSLIE STREET........ CHICAGO IL 60625 (312) 539-7776
KEHILATH JACOB BETH SAMUEL CONGREGATION O
3701 W. DEVON AVENUE .... CHICAGO IL 60659 (312) 539-7779
KOL-AMI, CONGREGATION R 233 E. ERIE STREET .... CHICAGO IL 60611 (312) 644-6900
KOLLEL TORAS CHESED O 2938 W. ARTHUR .... CHICAGO IL 60645 (312) 262-0666
LAKE SHORE DRIVE SYNAGOGUE T 70 EAST ELM .... CHICAGO IL 60611 (312) 337-6811
LAKEVIEW ANSHE SHOLOM BNAI ISRAEL O 540 W. MELROSE AVENUE .... CHICAGO IL 60613
LAWN MANOR HEBREW CONGREGATION C 6601 S. KEDZIE AVENUE .... CHICAGO IL 60629 (312) 476-2924
LEV SOMEACH, CONGREGATION O 5555 N. BERNARD STREET .... CHICAGO IL 60625 (312) 267-4390
MENORAH TEMPLE R 2800 W. SHERWIN AVENUE .... CHICAGO IL 60645 (312) 761-5700
MEYER & ANNIE HANDELSMAN SYNAGOGUE 2828 PRATT BLVD .... CHICAGO IL 60645
MIKRO KODESH ANSHE TIKTIN, CONGREGATION O
2832 W. FOSTER AVENUE .... CHICAGO IL 60625 (312) 784-1010
MISHNA UGMORO, CONGREGATION O 6045 N. CALIFORNIA AVENUE ..., CHICAGO IL 60659 (312) 465-1433
MIZPAH, TEMPLE R 1615 W. MORSE AVENUE .... CHICAGO IL 60626
MOUNT SINAI, CONGREGATION O 4710 N. KEDZIE AVENUE .... CHICAGO IL 60625 (312) 478-8545
NACHLAS DOVID, CONGREGATION O 3135 W. DEVON AVENUE .... CHICAGO IL 60659 (312) 465-3616
NER TAMID CONGREGATION C 2754 W. ROSEMONT AVENUE .... CHICAGO IL 60659 (312) 465-6090
NORTH SHERIDAN HEBREW CONGREGATION ADATH ISRAEL
6301 N. SHERIDAN ROAD .... CHICAGO IL 60660 (312) 262-0330
NUSACH ARIE, CONGREGATION O 4706 N. MONTICELLO AVENUE .... CHICAGO IL 60625 (312) 588-9520
OIR ISRAEL, CONGREGATION O 4610 N. KEDZIE AVENUE .... CHICAGO IL 60625 (312) 463-9325
PARK SYNAGOGUE OF CHICAGO, THE O 505 N. MICHIGAN AVENUE .... CHICAGO IL 60611 (312) 467-5928
PARK VIEW HOME C 1401 S. CALIFORNIA AVENUE .... CHICAGO IL 60622 (312) 278-6420
POALIE ZEDECK, CONGREGATION O 2801 WEST ALBION .... CHICAGO IL 60645 (312) 764-5680
RODFEI ZEDEK, CONGREGATION C 5200 HYDE PARK BLVD .... CHICAGO IL 60615 (312) 752-2770
SHAARE TIKVAH, CONGREGATION C 5800 N. KIMBALL AVENUE......... CHICAGO IL 60659 (312) 539-2202
SHAAREI TORAH ANSHEI MAARIV, CONGREGATION O
2756 W. MORSE AVENUE .... CHICAGO IL 60645 (312) 262-6819
SHEARITH ISRAEL O 2938 W. ARTHUR .... CHICAGO IL 60645
SHEVET ACHIM, CONGREGATION O 730 W. WAVELAND AVENUE .... CHICAGO IL 60613
SHOLOM, TEMPLE R 3480 LAKE SHORE DRIVE .... CHICAGO IL 60657 (312) 525-4707
SINAI OF ROGERS PARK, CONGREGATION O 6905 N. SHERIDAN ROAD ... CHICAGO IL 60626 (312) 764-0042
SOUTHSIDE SENIOR ADULT JEWISH CENTER 1642 E. 56TH STREET .... CHICAGO IL 60637 (312) 667-7373
SOUTHTOWN ANSHE EMET CONGREGATION O 8100 S. LOOMIS BLVD .... CHICAGO IL 60605
SOVEREIGN SYNAGOGUE CONGREGATION KESER TORAH O
6159 N. KENMORE AVENUE .... CHICAGO IL 60626
TIFERETH MOSHE, CONGREGATION O 6308 N. FRANCISCO AVENUE ...... CHICAGO IL 60659 (312) 764-5322
WARSAW BICKUR CHOLIM O 3541 WEST PETERSON .... CHICAGO IL 60659 (312) 588-0021
YOUNG ISRAEL OF CHICAGO 4931 KIMBALL STREET .... CHICAGO IL 60659 (312) 478-8650
ISRAEL SYNAGOGUE, CONGREGATION C 949 N. WALNUT STREET......... DANVILLE IL 61832 (217) 442-6643
B'NAI ABRAHAM, TEMPLE R 1326 W. ELDORADO STREET............... DECATUR IL 62522 (217) 429-5740
B'NAI TIKVAH, CONGREGATION C 795 WILMONT ROAD .... DEERFIELD IL 60015 (312) 945-0470
BETH OR, CONGREGATION R 2075 DEERFIELD ROAD BOX 234 .... DEERFIELD IL 60015 (312) 945-0477
MORIAH CONGREGATION C 200 HYACINTH LANE .... DEERFIELD IL 60015 (312) 948-5340
INDEPENDENT TEMPLE O 355 BELLAIRE DR .... DES PLAINES IL 60016 (312) 296-5641
MAINE TOWNSHIP JEWISH CONGREGATION C 8800 BALLARD ROAD .. DES PLAINES IL 60016 (312) 297-2006
AGUDAS ACHIM, CONGREGATION 425 N. 88 STREET............ EAST ST. LOUIS IL 62201
KNESETH ISRAEL, CONGREGATION C 330 DIVISION STREET.................. ELGIN IL 60120 (312) 741-5656
AGUDATH JACOB, CONGREGATION T 633 HOWARD .... EVANSTON IL 60202 (312) 475-9317
BETH EMETH, THE FREE SYNAGOGUE R 1224 DEMPSTER .... EVANSTON IL 60202 (312) 869-4230
JEWISH RECONSTRUCTIONIST CONGREGATION RE
2525 HARTREY AVENUE .... EVANSTON IL 60201 (312) 328-7678
MIKDOSH EL HAGRO HEBREW CENTER C 303 DODGE AVENUE .... EVANSTON IL 60202 (312) 328-9677
SEPHARDIC CONGREGATION O 1819 W. HOWARD .... EVANSTON IL 60202 (312) 475-9287
ANSHE SHOLOM, TEMPLE 707 ELM STREET .... FLOSSMOOR IL 60422
SHOLOM, TEMPLE R
CORNER NORTH & MONROE STREETS, P.O. BOX 501 .... GALESBURG IL 61401 (309) 343-3323
AM SHALOM R 614 SHERIDAN ROAD .... GLENCOE IL 61401 (312) 835-4800
NORTH SHORE CONGREGATION ISRAEL R 1185 SHERIDAN ROAD .... GLENCOE IL 60022 (312) 835-4800
AM CHAI, CONGREGATION C 292 NORTH BRANDON .... GLENDALE HEIGHTS IL 60137 (312) 980-6699
B'NAI JEHOSHUA BETH ELOHIM R 901 MILWAUKEE AVENUE .... GLENVIEW IL 60025 (312) 729-7575
ISRAEL, TEMPLE R 1414 WEST DELMAR .... GODFREY IL 62035 (618) 466-4641
UNITED HEBREW CONGREGATION
C/O LOUIS COHEN 2300 ILLINOIS AVENUE .... GRANITE CITY IL 62040
UNITED HEBREW TEMPLE OF BENTON R 120 N. PARK AVENUE............. HERRIN IL 62948 (618) 439-3521
B'NAI TORAH, CONGREGATION R 2789 OAK STREET .... HIGHLAND PARK IL 60035 (312) 433-7100
LAKESIDE CONGREGATION FOR REFORM JUDAISM R
1221 CITY LINE ROAD .... HIGHLAND PARK IL 60035 (312) 432-7950
NORTH SUBURBAN SYNAGOGUE BETH EL C
1175 SHERIDAN ROAD .... HIGHLAND PARK IL 60035 (312) 432-8900
SOLEL, CONGREGATION R 1301 CLAVEY ROAD .... HIGHLAND PARK IL 60035 (312) 433-3555
BETH TIKVA CONGREGATION R 300 HILLCREST BLVD .... HOFFMAN ESTATES IL 60195 (312) 885-4545
B'NAI YEHUDA, TEMPLE R 1424 W. 183RD STREET .... HOMEWOOD IL 60430 (312) 799-4110
JOLIET JEWISH CONGREGATION C 250 N. MIDLAND .... JOLIET IL 60435 (815) 725-7078
B'NAI ISRAEL, TEMPLE C 600 S. HARRISON AVENUE .... KANKAKEE IL 60901 (815) 933-7814
OR SHALOM R P.O. BOX 773............................. LIBERTYVILLE IL 60048 (312) 680-9696
BETH TORAH O 4721 WEST TOUHY .... LINCOLNWOOD IL 60646
LINCOLNWOOD JEWISH CONGREGATION O
7117 N. CRAWFORD AVENUE .... LINCOLNWOOD IL 60646 (312) 676-0491
YEHUDAH MOSHE, CONGREGATION O 4721 W. TOUHY AVENUE .... LINCOLNWOOD IL 60646 (312) 673-5870
ETZ CHAIM, CONGREGATION R 1710 S. HIGHLAND AVENUE .... LOMBARD IL 60148 (312) 627-3912
CHAI, TEMPLE R ROUTE 6, P.O. BOX 423 .... LONG GROVE IL 60047 (312) 537-1771
MATTOON JEWISH CENTER R P.O. BOX 881 .... MATTOON IL 61938 (312) 537-1771
ADAS SHALOM CONGREGATION R 6945 DEMPSTER .... MORTON GROVE IL 60053 (312) 965-1880
NORTHWEST SUBURBAN JEWISH CONGREGATION C
7800 WEST LYONS .... MORTON GROVE IL 60053 (312) 965-0900
BETH AM R 2005 KIOWA LANE............................. MT. PROSPECT IL 60056 (312) 827-7599

CONGREGATION BETH SHALOM RE 21 EAST FRANKLIN AVENUE	NAPERVILLE	**IL**	60540	(312) 961-1818
BETH SHALOM C 3433 WALTERS AVENUE	NORTHBROOK	**IL**	60062	(312) 498-4100
B'NAI ISRAEL 601 SKOKIE BLVD.	NORTHBROOK	**IL**	60062	(312) 480-0092
EZRA HABONIM OF NORTHBROOK C 2095 LANDWEHR RD.	NORTHBROOK	**IL**	60062	(312) 480-1690
AM YISROEL CONSERVATIVE CONGREGATION OF THE NORTH SHORE 4 HAPP ROAD	NORTHFIELD	**IL**	60093	(312) 446-7215
JEREMIAH TEMPLE R P.O. BOX N 193, 937 HAPP ROAD	NORTHFIELD	**IL**	60093	(312) 441-5760
CONGREGATION SHIR AMI C P.O. BOX 1094	OAK PARK	**IL**	60304	(312) 386-4408
OAK PARK TEMPLE R 1235 N. HARLEM AVENUE	OAK PARK	**IL**	60302	(312) 386-3937
ANSHE SHOLOM, TEMPLE - BETH TORAH R 20820 WESTERN AVENUE	OLYMPIA FIELDS	**IL**	60461	(312) 748-6010
AM ECHAD, CONGREGATION C 160 WESTWOOD	PARK FOREST	**IL**	60466	(312) 747-9513
BETH SHOLOM, CONGREGATION R 1 DOGWOOD	PARK FOREST	**IL**	60466	(312) 747-3040
AGUDAS ACHIM, CONGREGATION C 3616 N. SHERIDAN ROAD	PEORIA	**IL**	61604	(309) 688-5720
ANSHAI EMETH, CONGREGATION R 5614 N. UNIVERSITY STREET	PEORIA	**IL**	61614	(309) 691-3323
B'NAI SHOLOM TEMPLE C 427 NORTH 9TH	QUINCY	**IL**	62301	
WEST SUBURBAN TEMPLE HAR ZION C 1040 N. HARLEM AVENUE	RIVER FOREST	**IL**	60305	(312) 366-9000
TRI-CITY JEWISH CENTER C 2715 30TH STREET	ROCK ISLAND	**IL**	61201	(309) 788-3426
BETH EL, TEMPLE R 1203 COMANCHE DRIVE	ROCKFORD	**IL**	61107	(815) 398-5020
OHAVE SHOLOM SYNAGOGUE C 3730 GUILFORD ROAD	ROCKFORD	**IL**	61107	(815) 226-4900
OR CHADASH TRADITIONAL CONGREGATION T 664 S. ROSELLE RD.	SCHAUMBERG	**IL**	60172	(312) 529-6390
B'NAI EMUNAH, CONGREGATION C 9131 NILES CENTER ROAD, P.O. BOX 272	SKOKIE	**IL**	60076	(312) 674-9292
BENE SHALOM, CONGREGATION - HEBREW ASSN. FOR THE DEAF R 4435 OAKTON	SKOKIE	**IL**	60076	(312) 677-3330
BETH ISRAEL, TEMPLE R 3939 W. HOWARD STREET	SKOKIE	**IL**	60076	(312) 675-0951
HYDE PARK HEBREW CENTER T 3661 DAVIS STREET	SKOKIE	**IL**	60076	
IRAN HEBREW CONGREGATION O 3820 MAIN STREET	SKOKIE	**IL**	60076	(312) 674-5444
JUDEA MIZPAH, TEMPLE R 8610 NILES CENTER ROAD	SKOKIE	**IL**	60077	(312) 676-1566
KOL EMETH C 5130 W. TOUHY AVENUE	SKOKIE	**IL**	60077	(312) 673-3370
NILES TOWNSHIP JEWISH CONGREGATION, THE C 4500 DEMPSTER STREET	SKOKIE	**IL**	60076	(312) 675-4141
OR TORAH, CONGREGATION O 3740 WEST DEMPSTER	SKOKIE	**IL**	60076	(312) 674-3695
SKOKIE CENTRAL TRADITIONAL CONGREGATION T 4040 MAIN STREET	SKOKIE	**IL**	60076	(312) 674-4117
SKOKIE VALLEY TRADITIONAL SYNAGOGUE 8825 E. PRAIRIE ROAD	SKOKIE	**IL**	60076	(312) 674-3473
B'RITH SHALOM, TEMPLE R 1004 S. 4TH STREET	SPRINGFIELD	**IL**	62703	(217) 525-1360
ISRAEL, TEMPLE C 1140 WEST GOVERNOR	SPRINGFIELD	**IL**	62704	(217) 546-2481
SHOLOM, TEMPLE R 21956 RIDGE ROAD, ROUTE #2	STERLING	**IL**	61081	(815) 625-2599
AM ECHOD C 1500 SUNSET AVENUE	WAUKEGAN	**IL**	60085	(312) 336-9110
B'NAI ISRAEL OF PROVISO, CONGREGATION O 10216 KITCHENER	WESTCHESTER	**IL**	60153	(312) 343-0288
B'NAI SHALOM TRADITIONAL P.O. BOX 173	WHEELING	**IL**	60090	(312) 541-1460
BETH HILLEL CONGREGATION C 3220 BIG TREE LANE	WILMETTE	**IL**	60091	(312) 256-1213
B'NAI SHOLOM CONGREGATION C 4508 BARING AVENUE	EAST CHICAGO	**IN**	46312	(219) 397-3106
ADATH B'NAI ISRAEL R 3600 WASHINGTON AVENUE	EVANSVILLE	**IN**	47715	(812) 425-8222
ADATH ISRAEL, TEMPLE C 3600 WASHINGTON AVENUE	EVANSVILLE	**IN**	47715	(812) 477-1577
WASHINGTON AVENUE TEMPLE R 100 WASHINGTON AVENUE	EVANSVILLE	**IN**	47713	
ACHDUTH VESHOLOM, CONGREGATION R 5200 OLD MILL ROAD	FORT WAYNE	**IN**	46807	(219) 744-4245
B'NAI JACOB, CONGREGATION C 2340 FAIRFIELD AVENUE	FORT WAYNE	**IN**	46807	(219) 744-2183
ISRAEL, TEMPLE R 601 N. MONTGOMERY STREET	GARY	**IN**	46403	(219) 938-5232
BETH EL, TEMPLE R 6947 HOHMAN AVENUE	HAMMOND	**IN**	46324	(219) 932-3754
BETH ISRAEL, CONGREGATION C 7105 HOHMAN AVENUE	HAMMOND	**IN**	46324	(219) 931-1312
KNESETH ISRAEL, CONGREGATION C 7105 HOHMAN AVENUE	HAMMOND	**IN**	46324	(219) 931-1312
B'NAI TORAH, CONGREGATION O 6510 HOOVER ROAD	INDIANAPOLIS	**IN**	46260	(317) 253-5253
BETH EL ZEDEK, CONGREGATION C 600 W. 70TH STREET	INDIANAPOLIS	**IN**	46260	(317) 253-3441
INDIANAPOLIS HEBREW CONGREGATION R 6501 N. MERIDIAN STREET	INDIANAPOLIS	**IN**	46260	(317) 255-6647
UNITED ORTHODOX HEBREW CONGREGATION O 5879 CENTRAL AVENUE	INDIANAPOLIS	**IN**	46220	
B'NAI ISRAEL, TEMPLE R 618 W. SUPERIOR STREET, P.O. BOX 1290	KOKOMO	**IN**	46901	(317) 452-0383
ISRAEL, TEMPLE R 620 CUMBERLAND AVENUE	LAFAYETTE	**IN**	47906	(317) 463-3455
SONS OF ABRAHAM, CONGREGATION T 661 N. 7TH STREET	LAFAYETTE	**IN**	47901	(317) 742-2113
SINAI TEMPLE R 1001 EUCLID AVENUE	MARION	**IN**	46952	(317) 664-4453
SINAI TEMPLE R 2800 FRANKLIN STREET	MICHIGAN CITY	**IN**	46360	(219) 874-4477
BETH EL TEMPLE R P.O. BOX 2395, 525 W. JACKSON STREET	MUNCIE	**IN**	47302	(317) 288-4662
BETH BORUK TEMPLE R 3040 PARKWOOD DRIVE	RICHMOND	**IN**	47374	(317) 962-6501
BETH EL, TEMPLE R 305 W. MADISON STREET	SOUTH BEND	**IN**	46601	(219) 234-4402
B'NAI ISRAEL CONGREGATION RE POB 1091	SOUTH BEND	**IN**	46624	(219) 289-5636
SINAI SYNAGOGUE O 1102 E. LASALLE AVENUE	SOUTH BEND	**IN**	46617	(317) 234-8584
SONS OF ISRAEL, CONGREGATION O 420 S. WILLIAM STREET	SOUTH BEND	**IN**	46601	(317) 289-5636
UNITED HEBREW CONGREGATIONS R 540 S. 6TH STREET	TERRE HAUTE	**IN**	47807	(812) 232-5988
ISRAEL, TEMPLE C 22 WASHINGTON STREET	VALPARAISO	**IN**	46383	
ISRAEL, TEMPLE R 620 CUMBERLAND	WEST LAFAYETTE	**IN**	47906	(317) 463-3455
B'NAI JUDAH, CONGREGATION C P.O. BOX 233, 1549 DAVIS AVENUE	WHITTING	**IN**	46394	(317) 659-0797
MANHATTAN JEWISH CONGREGATION R 1509 WREATH	MANHATTAN	**KS**	66502	(913) 539-8462
BETH EL, TEMPLE R 9400 NALL AVENUE	OVERLAND PARK	**KS**	66207	(913) 642-8707
YOUNG ISRAEL OF OVERLAND PARK 8716 WOODWARD	OVERLAND PARK	**KS**	66212	(913) 341-1597
OHEV SHOLOM, CONGREGATION O 5311 W. 75TH STREET	PRAIRIE VILLAGE	**KS**	66208	(913) 642-6460
BETH SHOLOM, TEMPLE R 4200 MUNSON	TOPEKA	**KS**	66604	(913) 272-6040
EMANU-EL, TEMPLE R 7011 EAST CENTRAL	WICHITA	**KS**	67206	(316) 684-5148
HEBREW CONGREGATION O 1850 WOODLAWN	WICHITA	**KS**	67208	(316) 685-1339
AGUDAT ACHIM, TEMPLE R 805 CLARA	ASHLAND	**KY**	41101	(606) 329-1840
ADATH ISRAEL, CONGREGATION 100-102 E. 6TH STREET	HOPKINSVILLE	**KY**	42240	
JEWISH CONGREGATION P.O. BOX 17	HOPKINSVILLE	**KY**	42240	
ADATH ISRAEL, TEMPLE R 124 N. ASHLAND AVENUE	LEXINGTON	**KY**	40502	(606) 266-3251
LEXINGTON HAVURAH C 3379 SUTHERLAND DRIVE	LEXINGTON	**KY**	40502	(606) 272-1459
OHAVAY ZION, CONGREGATION T 120 W. MAXWELL STREET	LEXINGTON	**KY**	40508	
ADATH ISRAEL, CONGREGATION R 834 S. THIRD STREET	LOUISVILLE	**KY**	40203	
ADATH ISRAEL-BRITH SHOLOM'R 1649 COWLING AVENUE	LOUISVILLE	**KY**	40205	(502) 451-4050
ADATH JESHURUN, CONGREGATION C 2401 WOODBOURNE AVENUE	LOUISVILLE	**KY**	40205	(502) 458-5359
ANSHEI SFARD, CONGREGATION O 3700 DUTCHMANS LANE	LOUISVILLE	**KY**	40205	(502) 451-3122
KENESETH ISRAEL CONGREGATION O P.O. BOX 5295	LOUISVILLE	**KY**	40205	(502) 459-2780
SHALOM, TEMPLE R 4220 TAYLORSVILLE ROAD	LOUISVILLE	**KY**	40220	(502) 458-4739
TEMPLE, THE R 5101 BROWNSBORD ROAD	LOUISVILLE	**KY**	40222	(502) 423-1818
ADATH ISRAEL, TEMPLE R 429 DAVIES STREET	OWENSBORO	**KY**	42301	(502) 683-9723
ISRAEL, TEMPLE R 330 JOE CLIFTON DRIVE, P.O. BOX 1141	PADUCAH	**KY**	42001	(502) 442-4104
B'NAI ISRAEL SYNAGOGUE C P.O. BOX 5086, VANCE & HICKORY STREETS	ALEXANDRIA	**LA**	71301	(318) 445-4586
GEMILUTH CHASSODIM R P.O. BOX 863, 2021 TURNER STREET	ALEXANDRIA	**LA**	71301	(318) 445-3655
B'NAI ISRAEL, TEMPLE R 3354 KLEINERT AVENUE	BATON ROUGE	**LA**	70806	(504) 343-0111
LIBERAL SYNAGOGUE R 9111 JEFFERSON HIGHWAY	BATON ROUGE	**LA**	70800	(504) 924-6773
BETH EL JEWISH CENTER, CONGREGATION P.O. BOX 1207	BOGALUSA	**LA**	70427	
RODEPH SHOLOM, TEMPLE R 603 LEE AVENUE, P.O. BOX 2564	LAFAYETTE	**LA**	70501	(318) 234-3760
YESHURUN SYNAGOGUE R P.O. BOX 53711 OCS, 1520 KALISTE SALOOM ROAD	LAFAYETTE	**LA**	70505	(318) 984-1775
SINAI, TEMPLE R 713 HODGES STREET	LAKE CHARLES	**LA**	70601	(318) 439-2866
GATES OF PRAYER R 4000 W. ESPLANADE AVENUE	METAIRIE	**LA**	70002	(504) 885-2600
TIKVAT SHALOM CONSERVATIVE CONGREGATION C 3737 W. ESPLANADE AVENUE	METAIRIE	**LA**	70002	(504) 899-1144
YOUNG ISRAEL METAIRIE 4428 COURTLAND DRIVE	METAIRIE	**LA**	70002	(504) 887-6997
B'NAI ISRAEL, CONGREGATION R 2400 ORELL PLACE	MONROE	**LA**	71201	(318) 387-0730
SHAARE ZEDEK, TEMPLE R P.O. BOX 329	MORGAN CITY	**LA**	70380	(318) 385-2552
GATES OF PRAYER, CONGREGATION R P.O. BOX 488	NEW IBERIA	**LA**	70560	(318) 364-1218
A.A. ANSHE SFARD, CONGREGATION O 2230 CARONDELET STREET	NEW ORLEANS	**LA**	70130	(504) 522-4714
BETH ISRAEL, CONGREGATION O 7000 CANAL BLVD	NEW ORLEANS	**LA**	70124	(504) 283-4366
CHEVRA THILIM, CONGREGATION O 4429 S. CLAIBORNE AVENUE	NEW ORLEANS	**LA**	70125	(504) 895-7987
GATES OF PRAYER, CONGREGATION R 4000 W. ESPLANADE AVENUE	NEW ORLEANS	**LA**	70119	(504) 885-2600
SINAI, TEMPLE R 6227 ST. CHARLES AVENUE	NEW ORLEANS	**LA**	70118	(504) 861-3693
TIKVAT SHALOM CONGREGATION C 923 NAPOLEON AVENUE	NEW ORLEANS	**LA**	70115	
TOURO SYNAGOGUE R ST. CHARLES AT GENERAL PERSHING	NEW ORLEANS	**LA**	70115	(504) 895-4843
AGUDATH ACHIM, CONGREGATION C 9401 VILLAGE GREEN DRIVE	SHREVEPORT	**LA**	71115	(318) 797-6401
B'NAI ZION CONGREGATION R 175 SOUTHFIELD ROAD	SHREVEPORT	**LA**	70115	(318) 861-2122
SHAARAY SHALOM, CONGREGATION R P.O. BOX 15	ACCORD	**MA**	02018	(617) 749-8103
EMANUEL, TEMPLE R 7 HAGGETTS POND ROAD	ANDOVER	**MA**	01810	(617) 470-1356
ISRAEL, TEMPLE C 107 WALNUT STREET	ATHOL	**MA**	01331	
AGUDAS ACHIM, CONGREGATION C TONER & KELLEY BLVDS	ATTLEBORO	**MA**	02703	(617) 222-2243
ANSHE SHOLOM, CONGREGATION	AYER	**MA**	01432	
BETH CHAVERIM, CONGREGATION 16 YVONNE ROAD	BELLINGHAM	**MA**	02019	
BETH EL TEMPLE CENTER R 2 CONCORD AVENUE	BELMONT	**MA**	02178	(617) 484-6668
B'NAI ABRAHAM, TEMPLE C 200 E. LOTHROP STREET	BEVERLY	**MA**	01915	(617) 927-3211
OHAV SHOLOM, CONGREGATION O 3 BECKFORD STREET	BEVERLY	**MA**	01915	
ASSOCIATED SYNAGOGUES CHAPEL 177 TREMONT STREET	BOSTON	**MA**	02111	
B'NAI JACOB, CONGREGATION 100 BLUE HILLS PARKWAY	BOSTON	**MA**	02187	
CHARLES RIVER PARK SYNAGOGUE O 55 MARTHA ROAD (AMY CT)	BOSTON	**MA**	02114	(617) 523-0453
ISRAEL, TEMPLE R LONGWOOD AVENUE AT PLYMOUTH STREET	BOSTON	**MA**	02215	(617) 566-3960
B'NAI SHALOM, TEMPLE C 41 STORES AVENUE	BRAINTREE	**MA**	02184	(617) 843-3687
AGUDATH ISRAEL OF BOSTON 81 WALLINGFORD ROAD	BRIGHTON	**MA**	02135	(617) 254-0260
ANSHE LUBAVITCH, CONGREGATION O 241 CHESTNUT HILL ROAD	BRIGHTON	**MA**	02135	
B'NAI MOSHE, TEMPLE C 1845 COMMONWEALTH AVENUE	BRIGHTON	**MA**	02135	(617) 254-3620
BETH DAVID, CONGREGATION O 64 COREY ROAD	BRIGHTON	**MA**	02460	
KADIMAH-TORAS MOSHE, CONGREGATION O 113 WASHINGTON STREET	BRIGHTON	**MA**	02135	(617) 254-1333
AGUDAS ACHIM, CONGREGATION O 144 BELMONT AVENUE	BROCKTON	**MA**	02401	
BETH EMUNAH, TEMPLE C TORREY & PEARL STREETS	BROCKTON	**MA**	02401	(617) 583-5810
ISRAEL, TEMPLE R 184 W. ELM STREET	BROCKTON	**MA**	02401	(617) 587-4130
BETH ISRAEL, CONGREGATION 114 WILLARD ROAD	BROOKLINE	**MA**	02146	
BETH PINCHAS, CONGREGATION O 1710 BEACON STREET	BROOKLINE	**MA**	02146	(617) 566-9182
BETH ZION, TEMPLE C 1566 BEACON STREET	BROOKLINE	**MA**	02146	(617) 566-8171
CHAI ODOM, CONGREGATION O 77 ENGLEWOOD AVENUE	BROOKLINE	**MA**	02146	(617) 277-8794
EMETH, TEMPLE 194 GROVE	BROOKLINE	**MA**	02146	
GREATER BOSTON RECONSTRUCTIONIST HAVURAH POB 1197	BROOKLINE	**MA**	02146	(617) 964-2791
KADDISHA OF BOSTON, CONGREGATION 156 LONGWOOD AVENUE	BROOKLINE	**MA**	02146	
KEHILLATH ISRAEL, CONGREGATION C 384 HARVARD STREET	BROOKLINE	**MA**	02146	(617) 277-9155
OHABEI SHALOM, TEMPLE R 1187 BEACON STREET	BROOKLINE	**MA**	02146	(617) 277-6610
SINAI, TEMPLE R 50 SEWALL AVENUE	BROOKLINE	**MA**	02146	(617) 277-5888
YOUNG ISRAEL OF BROOKLINE 62 GREEN STREET	BROOKLINE	**MA**	02146	(617) 734-0276
SHALOM EMETH, TEMPLE R P.O. BOX 216	BURLINGTON	**MA**	01803	(617) 272-7454
ASHKENAZ, TEMPLE C 8 TREMONT STREET	CAMBRIDGE	**MA**	02139	
BETH SHALOM, TEMPLE 8 TREMONT STREET	CAMBRIDGE	**MA**	02139	
BETH ABRAHAM, TEMPLE C 1301 WASHINGTON STREET	CANTON	**MA**	02021	
BETH DAVID OF SOUTH SHORE, TEMPLE R 250 RANDOLPH	CANTON	**MA**	02021	
SHALOM, CONGREGATION RICHARDSON ROAD	CHELMSFORD	**MA**	01824	
AGUDAS SHALOM, CONGREGATION 145 WALNUT STREET #265	CHELSEA	**MA**	02150	
AHAVAS ACHIM ANSHE SFARD, CONGREGATION O 48 WASHINGTON AVENUE	CHELSEA	**MA**	02150	(617) 884-7945
ELM STREET SYNAGOGUE 48 WASHINGTON AVENUE	CHELSEA	**MA**	02150	
EMANUEL, TEMPLE C 16 CARY AVENUE	CHELSEA	**MA**	02150	
SHAARE ZION, CONGREGATION O 76 ORANGE STREET	CHELSEA	**MA**	02150	
SHOMREI LINATH HAZEDEK, CONGREGATION O 140 SHURTLEFF STREET	CHELSEA	**MA**	02150	
YOUNG ISRAEL OF CHELSEA 40 CRESCENT AVENUE	CHELSEA	**MA**	02150	(617) 889-2992
EMETH, TEMPLE C 194 GROVE STREET	CHESTNUT HILL	**MA**	02167	(617) 738-5344
MISHKAN TEFILA, CONGREGATION C 300 HAMMOND POND PARKWAY	CHESTNUT HILL	**MA**	02167	(617) 332-7770
SHAARI ZEDECK, CONGREGATION C WATER STREET	CLINTON	**MA**	01510	
SONS OF ISRAEL, CONGREGATION O 43 W. MAIN STREET	DUDLEY	**MA**	01570	
TIFERETH ISRAEL COMMUNITY CENTRE, CONGREGATION O 34 MALDEN STREET	EVERETT	**MA**	02149	
ADAS ISRAEL, CONGREGATION O 1647 ROBESON	FALL RIVER	**MA**	02720	
AGUDAS MACHZIKAY HORAV, CONGREGATION O 470 MADISON STREET	FALL RIVER	**MA**	02720	
AMERICAN BROTHERS OF ISRAEL, CONGREGATION O P.O. BOX 1215	FALL RIVER	**MA**	02722	

BETH EL, TEMPLE C 385 HIGH STREET	FALL RIVER	**MA**	02720	(617) 674-3529
FALMOUTH JEWISH CONGREGATION, THE P.O. BOX 9	FALMOUTH	**MA**	02541	
AGUDATH ACHIM, CONGREGATION C 122 LINCOLN STREET	FITCHBURG	**MA**	01420	
BAIS CHABAD, CONGREGATION O 74 JOSEPH ROAD	FRAMINGHAM	**MA**	01761	(617) 877-8888
BETH AM, TEMPLE R 300 PLEASANT STREET	FRAMINGHAM	**MA**	01701	(617) 872-8300
BETH SHOLOM, TEMPLE C PAMELA ROAD	FRAMINGHAM	**MA**	01701	(617) 877-2540
OHAVE SHOLOM, CONGREGATION C 152 PLEASANT STREET	GARDNER	**MA**	01440	(617) 632-2779
AHAVATH ACHIM, TEMPLE C 86 MIDDLE STREET	GLOUCESTER	**MA**	01930	(617) 281-0739
LOVE OF PEACE, CONGREGATION R 29 NORTH STREET	GREAT BARRINGTON	**MA**	01230	
GREENFIELD HEBREW CONGREGATION C 89 BURNHAM ROAD	GREENFIELD	**MA**	01301	
ISRAEL OF GREENFIELD, INC., TEMPLE C 27 PIERCE STREET	GREENFIELD	**MA**	01301	(413) 773-5884
EMANU-EL, TEMPLE R 514 MAIN STREET	HAVERHILL	**MA**	01830	(617) 373-3861
SHA'ARAY SHALOM, CONGREGATION 1112 MAIN STREET	HINGHAM	**MA**	02043	
BETH TORAH, TEMPLE R WASHINGTON STREET	HOLLISTON	**MA**	01746	
RODPHEY SHOLOM, CONGREGATION O 1800 NORTHAMPTON STREET	HOLYOKE	**MA**	01040	(413) 533-6556
SONS OF ZION, CONGREGATION C 378 MAPLE STREET	HOLYOKE	**MA**	01040	(413) 534-3369
BETH SHOLOM, TEMPLE C 600 NANTASKET AVENUE	HULL	**MA**	02045	(617) 925-0091
ISRAEL OF NANTASKET, TEMPLE SAMOSET AVENUE & WILSON STREET	HULL	**MA**	02045	
CAPE COD SYNAGOGUE R 145 WINTER STREET, P.O. BOX 61	HYANNIS	**MA**	02601	(617) 775-2988
ADAS HADRATH ISRAEL, TEMPLE C 28 ARLINGTON STREET	HYDE PARK	**MA**	02136	(617) 364-2661
GEORGETOWN, CONGREGATION O 412 GEORGETOWN DRIVE	HYDE PARK	**MA**	02136	
ANSHAI SFARD AND SONS OF ISRAEL, CONGREGATION C 492 LOWELL STREET	LAWRENCE	**MA**	01841	(617) 686-0391
ANSHAI SHOLOM, CONGREGATION O 411 HAMPSHIRE STREET	LAWRENCE	**MA**	01841	
EMANUEL, TEMPLE R 483 LOWELL STREET	LAWRENCE	**MA**	01841	(413) 682-8443
SONS OF ISRAEL, CONGREGATION 380 ELM STREET	LAWRENCE	**MA**	01841	
AGUDAT ACHIM C 268 WASHINGTON STREET	LEOMINSTER	**MA**	01453	(617) 534-6121
EMUNAH, TEMPLE C 9 PIPER ROAD	LEXINGTON	**MA**	02139	(617) 861-0300
ISAIAH, TEMPLE R 55 LINCOLN STREET	LEXINGTON	**MA**	02173	(617) 862-7160
B'NAI JACOB C 2 EUNICE DRIVE	LONGMEADOW	**MA**	01106	(413) 567-0058
BETH ISRAEL, CONGREGATION 1280 WILLIAMS STREET	LONGMEADOW	**MA**	01106	(413) 567-3210
BETH EL, TEMPLE C 105 PRINCETON BLVD	LOWELL	**MA**	01851	(617) 453-0073
EMANUEL, TEMPLE R 101 W. FOREST STREET	LOWELL	**MA**	01851	(617) 454-1372
MONTEFIORE SYNAGOGUE O 460 WESTFORD AVENUE	LOWELL	**MA**	01851	(617) 455-5264
AHABAT SHOLOM, CONGREGATION O 151 OCEAN STREET	LYNN	**MA**	01902	(617) 595-9492
ANSHE SFARD, CONGREGATION O 150 S. COMMON STREET	LYNN	**MA**	01905	
CHEVRA TEHILLEM, CONGREGATION O 12 BREED STREET	LYNN	**MA**	01902	(617) 598-2964
AGUDAS ACHIM, CONGREGATION T 160 HARVARD STREET	MALDEN	**MA**	01248	
BETH ISRAEL, CONGREGATION O 10 DEXTER STREET	MALDEN	**MA**	02148	
EZRATH ISRAEL, TEMPLE C 245 BRYANT STREET	MALDEN	**MA**	02148	(617) 322-7205
TEFERETH ISRAEL, TEMPLE R 3539 SALEM STREET	MALDEN	**MA**	02148	(617) 322-2794
YOUNG ISRAEL OF MALDEN 45 HOLYOKE AVENUE	MALDEN	**MA**	02148	(617) 322-9438
EMANU-EL, TEMPLE R 393 ATLANTIC AVENUE	MARBLEHEAD	**MA**	01945	(617) 631-9300
SINAI, TEMPLE C 1 COMMUNITY ROAD	MARBLEHEAD	**MA**	01945	(617) 631-7539
EMANUEL, TEMPLE C 150 BERLIN ROAD, P.O. BOX 596	MARLBOROUGH	**MA**	01752	(617) 485-7565
OHEL TORAH, CONGREGATION O 149 GREENFIELD ROAD	MATTAPAN	**MA**	02126	
SHALOM, TEMPLE - MEDFORD JEWISH COMMUNITY CENTER C 475 WINTHROP STREET	MEDFORD	**MA**	02155	(617) 396-3262
AGUDATH ACHIM, CONGREGATION C 13 HOLLISTON STREET	MEDWAY	**MA**	02053	
MELROSE JEWISH CENTER R 21 E. FOSTER STREET	MELROSE	**MA**	02176	(617) 665-4520
BETH SHALOM-MILFORD HEBREW ASSOCIATION, CONGREGATION O P.O. BOX 30 PINE STREET	MILFORD	**MA**	01757	
HOUSE OF JACOB, CONGREGATION O VILLAGE STREET	MILLIS	**MA**	02054	
B'NAI JACOB, CONGREGATION O 159 TOURO LANE	MILTON	**MA**	02186	
SHALOM HOUSE 68 SMITH ROAD	MILTON	**MA**	02186	(617) 333-0477
SHALOM OF MILTON, TEMPLE C 180 BLUE HILL AVENUE	MILTON	**MA**	02186	(617) 698-3394
ISRAEL OF NATICK, TEMPLE C 145 HARTFORD STREET	NATICK	**MA**	01760	(617) 653-8591
ALIYAH, TEMPLE C 1664 CENTRAL AVENUE	NEEDHAM	**MA**	01292	(617) 444-8522
BETH SHALOM, TEMPLE R HIGHLAND AVENUE AT WEBSTER STREET	NEEDHAM	**MA**	02194	(617) 444-0077
AHAVATH ACHIM, CONGREGATION O 385 COUNTY STREET	NEW BEDFORD	**MA**	02740	(617) 994-1760
TIFERETH ISRAEL CONGREGATION C 145 BROWNELL AVENUE	NEW BEDFORD	**MA**	02740	(617) 997-3171
AHAVAS ACHIM, CONGREGATION O OLIVE & WASHINGTON STREETS	NEWBURYPORT	**MA**	01950	
BETH EL-ATERETH ISRAEL, CONGREGATION 561 WARD	NEWTON	**MA**	02159	(617) 244-7233
CHEVRA SHA'AS, CONGREGATION O 35 MORSELAND AVENUE	NEWTON	**MA**	02159	
EMANUEL, TEMPLE C 385 WARD STREET	NEWTON	**MA**	02159	(617) 332-5770
REYIM, TEMPLE C 1860 WASHINGTON STREET	NEWTON	**MA**	02166	(617) 527-2410
SHALOM, TEMPLE R 175 TEMPLE STREET	NEWTON	**MA**	02165	(617) 332-9550
BETH AVODAH, TEMPLE R 45 PUDDING STONE LANE	NEWTON CENTER	**MA**	02159	(617) 527-0045
BETH ISRAEL, CONGREGATION C 265 CHURCH STREET	NORTH ADAMS	**MA**	01247	(413) 663-5830
SHALOM, CONGREGATION R RICHARDSON ROAD	NORTH CHELMSFORD	**MA**	01863	(617) 251-8091
SINAI, TEMPLE R P.O. BOX 188	NORTH DARTMOUTH	**MA**	02747	
B'NAI ISRAEL, CONGREGATION C 253 PROSPECT STREET	NORTHAMPTON	**MA**	01060	(413) 584-3593
SHAARE TEFILAH, TEMPLE C 556 NICHOLS STREET	NORWOOD	**MA**	02602	(617) 762-8670
BETH ISRAEL OF ONSET, CONGREGATION O	ONSET	**MA**	02558	
BETH SHALOM, TEMPLE R 489 LOWELL STREET	PEABODY	**MA**	01960	(617) 535-2100
NER TAMID, TEMPLE C 368 LOWELL STREET	PEABODY	**MA**	01960	(617) 532-1293
TIFERETH ISRAEL, CONGREGATION PIERPONT STREET	PEABODY	**MA**	01960	
AHAVATH SHOLEM CONGREGATION O P.O. BOX 1061	PITTSFIELD	**MA**	01201	(413) 442-2885
ANSHE AMUNIM, TEMPLE R 26 BROAD STREET, P.O. BOX 544	PITTSFIELD	**MA**	01202	(413) 443-9400
KNESSET ISRAEL, CONGREGATION C 16 COLT ROAD	PITTSFIELD	**MA**	01960	(413) 445-4872
BETH JACOB, CONGREGATION R 8 PLEASANT STREET, P.O. BOX 284	PLYMOUTH	**MA**	02361	(617) 746-1575
ADAS SHALOM C 435 ADAMS STREET	QUINCY	**MA**	02169	(617) 471-1818
BETH EL, TEMPLE C 1001 HANCOCK STREET	QUINCY	**MA**	02169	(617) 479-4309
BETH ISRAEL SYNAGOGUE O 33 GRAFTON STREET	QUINCY	**MA**	02169	(617) 472-6796
BETH AM, TEMPLE C 871 N. MAIN STREET	RANDOLPH	**MA**	02368	(617) 963-0440
BETH DAVID OF THE SOUTH SHORE, TEMPLE R P.O. BOX 284	RANDOLPH	**MA**	02368	(617) 828-2275
YOUNG ISRAEL OF MATTAPAN-RANDOLPH 374 NORTH MAIN STREET	RANDOLPH	**MA**	02368	(617) 961-9817
AHAVAS ACHIM, CONGREGATION O 89 WALNUT AVENUE	REVERE	**MA**	02151	
B'NAI ISRAEL, TEMPLE C 1 WAVE AVENUE	REVERE	**MA**	02151	
TIFERETH ISRAEL, CONGREGATION O P.O. BOX 81	REVERE	**MA**	02151	
SHALOM, TEMPLE C 287 LAFAYETTE STREET	SALEM	**MA**	01970	(617) 744-9709

AHAVAS SHOLOM, CONGREGATION C 36 HURD AVENUE	SAUGUS	**MA**	01906	
ADATH SHARON, TEMPLE C 18 HARDING STREET	SHARON	**MA**	02067	(617) 784-2517
ISRAEL, TEMPLE C 125 POND STREET	SHARON	**MA**	02067	(617) 784-3986
SINAI, TEMPLE R 100 AMES STREET, P.O. BOX 414	SHARON	**MA**	02067	(617) 784-6081
TIKVAS ISRAEL, CONGREGATION 7 SUNSET DRIVE	SHARON	**MA**	02067	
YOUNG ISRAEL OF SHARON 9 DUNBAR STREET	SHARON	**MA**	02067	(617) 784-6112
B'NAI BRITH, TEMPLE C 201 CENTRAL STREET	SOMERVILLE	**MA**	02145	
HAVURAT SHALOM CONGREGATION 113 COLLEGE AVENUE	SOMERVILLE	**MA**	02144	(617) 623-3376
BETH EL, TEMPLE C 979 DICKINSON STREET	SPRINGFIELD	**MA**	01108	(413) 733-4149
BETH ISRAEL, CONGREGATION O 565 CHESTNUT STREET, P.O. BOX 874	SPRINGFIELD	**MA**	01107	
KESSER ISRAEL SYNAGOGUE O 19 OAKLAND STREET	SPRINGFIELD	**MA**	01108	(413) 732-8492
KODIMOH, CONGREGATION O 124 SUMNER AVENUE	SPRINGFIELD	**MA**	01108	
SINAI TEMPLE R 1100 DICKINSON STREET	SPRINGFIELD	**MA**	01108	(413) 736-3619
JUDEA, TEMPLE C 188 FRANKLIN STREET	STONEHAM	**MA**	02180	(617) 665-5752
AHAVATH TORAH CONGREGATION C 1179 CENTRAL AVENUE	STOUGHTON	**MA**	02072	(617) 344-8733
B'NAI TORAH, CONGREGATION P.O. BOX 195	SUDBURY	**MA**	01776	
BETH EL, CONGREGATION R HUDSON ROAD	SUDBURY	**MA**	01176	(617) 443-9622
BETH EL, TEMPLE C 55 ATLANTIC AVENUE	SWAMPSCOTT	**MA**	01907	(617) 599-8005
ISRAEL OF SWAMPSCOTT & MARBLEHEAD, TEMPLE C 837 HUMPHREY STREET	SWAMPSCOTT	**MA**	01907	(617) 595-6636
AGUDATH ACHIM, CONGREGATION C 36 WINTHROP STREET	TAUNTON	**MA**	02780	(617) 822-3230
MARTHAS VINEYARD HEBREW CENTER C CENTER STREET	VINEYARD HAVEN	**MA**	02568	(617) 693-0745
EMANUEL, TEMPLE C 120 CHESTNUT STREET	WAKEFIELD	**MA**	01880	(617) 245-1886
BETH ISRAEL, TEMPLE R 25 HARVARD STREET	WALTHAM	**MA**	02154	
WARE HEBREW CONGREGATION C 89 MAIN STREET	WARE	**MA**	01082	
SHIR TIKVA, TEMPLE R P.O. BOX 265	WAYLAND	**MA**	01778	(617) 358-7719
SONS OF ISRAEL, CONGREGATION 281 MAIN STREET	WEBSTER	**MA**	01570	
BETH ELOHIM, TEMPLE R 10 BETHEL ROAD	WELLESLEY HILLS	**MA**	02181	(617) 235-8419
AGUDATH ACHIM, CONGREGATION 40 MILO STREET	WEST NEWTON	**MA**	02165	
SHALOM OF NEWTON, TEMPLE 175 TEMPLE STREET	WEST NEWTON	**MA**	02165	(617) 332-9550
ADATH JESHURUN, CONGREGATION O 5230 WASHINGTON STREET	WEST ROXBURY	**MA**	02132	
B'NAI TORAH HILLEL C 120 COREY STREET	WEST ROXBURY	**MA**	02132	(617) 323-0486
B'NAI SHALOM, CONGREGATION R 9 CHARLES STREET	WESTBOROUGH	**MA**	01581	(617) 366-7191
BETH DAVID OF DEDHAM, TEMPLE - EAST WESTWOOD R 40 POND STREET, P.O. BOX 459	WESTWOOD	**MA**	02090	(617) 329-1938
TIFERETH ABRAHAM, CONGREGATION 283 SHIRLEY STREET	WINTHROP	**MA**	02152	
TIFERETH ISRAEL, TEMPLE O 93 VETERANS ROAD	WINTHROP	**MA**	02152	(617) 846-1390
SHALOM EMETH, TEMPLE R 14 GREEN STREET	WOBURN	**MA**	01801	
AGUDAS SONS OF JACOB, CONGREGATION O 14 WOODFORD STREET	WORCESTER	**MA**	01604	
B'NAI ZION, CONGREGATION 56 GRANITE STREET	WORCESTER	**MA**	01604	
BETH ISRAEL, CONGREGATION C JAMESBURY DRIVE & KINNICUTT ROAD	WORCESTER	**MA**	01609	(617) 756-6204
BETH JUDAH, CONGREGATION O 889 PLEASANT STREET	WORCESTER	**MA**	01602	(617) 754-3681
MOGEN DAVID, CONGREGATION O 1029 PLEASANT STREET	WORCESTER	**MA**	01602	
SHAARAI TORAH, CONGREGATION O 123 DORCHESTER STREET	WORCESTER	**MA**	01604	
SINAI, TEMPLE R 661 SALISBURY STREET	WORCESTER	**MA**	01609	(617) 755-2519
TIFERETH ISRAEL, CONGREGATION O 22 NEWTON AVENUE	WORCESTER	**MA**	01602	
BETH ISRAEL CONGREGATION C 1007 SINCLAIR STREET	WINNIPEG	**MB**	R2V 3J5	(204) 582-2352
HERZLIA-ADAS YESHURUN CONGREGATION O 620 BROCK STREET	WINNIPEG	**MB**	R3N OZ4	(204) 489-6262
ROSH PINA CONGREGATION C P.O. BOX 3586, STATION B, 123 MATHESON AVENUE	WINNIPEG	**MB**	R2W 3R4	(204) 589-6306
SHAAREY ZEDEK, CONGREGATION C 561 WELLINGTON CRESCENT	WINNIPEG	**MB**	R3M OA6	(204) 452-3711
SHALOM, TEMPLE R 921 ASH STREET	WINNIPEG	**MB**	R3N OS1	(204) 453-8260
HARFORD JEWISH CENTER R 402 PARADISE ROAD	ABERDEEN	**MD**	21001	(301) 272-8316
KNESETH ISRAEL, CONGREGATION O P.O. BOX 626, HILLTOP LANE & SPA ROAD	ANNAPOLIS	**MD**	21403	(301) 269-0740
BETH SHOLOM, TEMPLE R P.O. BOX 1461, OLD ANNAPOLIS ROAD	ARNOLD	**MD**	21012	(301) 974-0900
KOL AMI C 517 MYSTIC LANE	ARNOLD	**MD**	21012	(301) 268-9254
AGUDATH ISRAEL OF BALTIMORE 5719 NARCISSUS AVENUE	BALTIMORE	**MD**	21215	(301) 358-4985
B'NAI JACOB, CONGREGATION O 6605 LIBERTY ROAD	BALTIMORE	**MD**	21207	
BALTIMORE HEBREW CONGREGATION R 7401 PARK HEIGHTS AVENUE	BALTIMORE	**MD**	21208	(301) 764-1587
BETH ABRAHAM ANSHEI SEFARD, CONGREGATION O 6210 WALLIS AVENUE	BALTIMORE	**MD**	21215	
BETH EL C 8101 PARK HEIGHTS AVENUE	BALTIMORE	**MD**	21208	(301) 484-0411
BETH ISAAC ADATH ISRAEL, CONGREGATION 4398 CREST HEIGHTS ROAD	BALTIMORE	**MD**	21215	
BETH JACOB WISHEER, CONGREGATION O 1016 HILLEN STREET	BALTIMORE	**MD**	21202	
BETH JACOB, CONGREGATION O 5713 PARK HEIGHTS AVENUE	BALTIMORE	**MD**	21215	
BETH TFILOH CONGREGATION O 330 OLD COURT ROAD	BALTIMORE	**MD**	21208	(301) 486-1900
BNAI ISRAEL CONGREGATION O 3701 SOUTHERN AVENUE	BALTIMORE	**MD**	21206	(301) 426-3534
CHIZUK AMUNO CONGREGATION C 8100 STEVENSON ROAD	BALTIMORE	**MD**	21208	(301) 486-6400
CHOFETZ CHAIM ADATH BNEI ISRAEL, CONGREGATION O 3702 W. ROGERS AVENUE	BALTIMORE	**MD**	21215	
CONGREGATION BEIT TIKVAH RE C/O DORI GRASSO	BALTIMORE	**MD**		(301) 325-2159
EMANUEL, TEMPLE R 3301 MILFORD MILL ROAD	BALTIMORE	**MD**	21207	(301) 922-3642
HAR SINAI CONGREGATION R 6300 PARK HEIGHTS AVENUE	BALTIMORE	**MD**	21215	(301) 764-2882
LLOYD STREET SYNAGOGUE S LLOYD & WATSON STREETS	BALTIMORE	**MD**	21215	(301) 358-9417
MACHZIKEI TORAH, CONGREGATION O 6216 BILTMORE AVENUE	BALTIMORE	**MD**	21215	(301) 358-4630
MOGEN ABRAHAM, CONGREGATION O 3114C PARKINGTON AVENUE	BALTIMORE	**MD**	21215	
MOSES MONTEFIORE EMUNATH ISRAEL WOODMOOR HEBREW CONG. O 3605 CORONADO ROAD	BALTIMORE	**MD**	21207	(301) 655-4484
NER TAMID GREENSPRING VALLEY SYNAGOGUE & CENTER O 6214 PIMLICO ROAD	BALTIMORE	**MD**	21209	
OHEB SHALOM, TEMPLE R 7310 PARK HEIGHTS AVENUE	BALTIMORE	**MD**	21208	(301) 358-0105
OHEL YAKOV, CONGREGATION O 3200 GLEN AVENUE	BALTIMORE	**MD**	21215	
OHR KNESSETH ISRAEL ANSHE SPHARD, CONGREGATION O 3910 W. ROGERS AVENUE	BALTIMORE	**MD**	21215	

PICKWICK JEWISH CENTER-HAR ZION PETACH TIKVAH O 6221 GREENSPRING AVENUE	BALTIMORE	**MD**	21209	(301) 358-9660
SHAAREI TFILOH, CONGREGATION O 7504 SEVEN MILE LANE	BALTIMORE	**MD**	21208	
SHAAREI ZION CONGREGATION O 6602 PARK HEIGHTS AVENUE	BALTIMORE	**MD**	21215	(301) 764-6810
SYNAGOGUE CENTER O 7124 PARK HEIGHTS AVENUE	BALTIMORE	**MD**	21215	(301) 764-2735
TZEMACH ZEDEK V'SHOMREI HADAS, CONGREGATION O 7037 SURREY DRIVE	BALTIMORE	**MD**	21215	(301) 764-8213
BETH EL OF MONTGOMERY COUNTY, CONGREGATION C 8215 OLD GEORGETOWN ROAD	BETHESDA	**MD**	20014	(301) 652-2606
BETHESDA JEWISH CONGREGATION R 6601 BRADLEY BLVD	BETHESDA	**MD**	20817	(301) 469-8636
MAGEN DAVID SEPHARDIC CONGREGATION P.O. BOX 41019	BETHESDA	**MD**	20014	(301) 588-0446
NEVEY SHALOM C 12218 TORAH LANE	BOWIE	**MD**	20715	(301) 262-9020
SOLEL, TEMPLE R P.O. BOX 578	BOWIE	**MD**	20715	(301) 262-7878
OHR KODESH CONGREGATION C 8402 FREYMAN DRIVE	CHEVY CHASE	**MD**	20815	(301) 589-3880
SHALOM, TEMPLE R 8401 GRUBB ROAD	CHEVY CHASE	**MD**	20815	(301) 587-2273
ISAIAH, TEMPLE R 5885 ROBERT OLIVER PLACE	COLUMBIA	**MD**	21045	(301) 730-8277
MEETING HOUSE, THE - TEMPLE BETH SHALOM C 5885 ROBERT OLIVER PLACE	COLUMBIA	**MD**	21045	(301) 730-4090
BER CHAYIM CONGREGATION R 107 UNION STREET	CUMBERLAND	**MD**	21502	(301) 722-5688
BETH JACOB C 11 COLUMBIA STREET	CUMBERLAND	**MD**	21502	(301) 722-6570
B'NAI ISRAEL, TEMPLE C ADKINS AVENUE	EASTON	**MD**	21601	
BETH SHOLOM C 925 STREAKER ROAD	ELDERSBURG	**MD**	21784	
BETH SHOLOM, CONGREGATION C 20 W. 2ND STREET	FREDERICK	**MD**	21701	
GAITHERSBURG HEBREW CONGREGATION C 9915 APPLE RIDGE ROAD	GAITHERSBURG	**MD**	20760	(301) 869-7699
MISHKAN TORAH CONGREGATION C RIDGE & WESTWAY ROADS	GREENBELT	**MD**	20770	(301) 474-4223
NATIONAL CONGRESS OF JEWISH DEAF 9102 EDMONSTON CT. #302	GREENBELT	**MD**	20770	
B'NAI ABRAHAM R 53 E. BALTIMORE STREET	HAGERSTOWN	**MD**	21740	(301) 733-5039
HARTFORD JEWISH CENTER R 8 N. EARLTON ROAD	HAVRE DE GRACE	**MD**	21078	(301) 939-9673
EMANUEL, TEMPLE R 10101 CONNECTICUT AVENUE	KENSINGTON	**MD**	20895	(301) 942-2000
CONGREGATION OSEH SHALOM RE POB 387	LAUREL	**MD**	20810	(301) 725-9795
BETH ISRAEL, CONGREGATION C 335 MIDWAY DRIVE	LEXINGTON PARK	**MD**	20653	(301) 863-8886
B'NAI SHALOM OF OLNEY C 3701 OLNEY-LAYTONSVILLE ROAD	OLNEY	**MD**	20832	(301) 774-0879
ISRAEL, CONGREGATION OF C THIRD STREET	POCOMOKE CITY	**MD**	21851	
BETH SHOLOM OF POTOMAC 11285 SEVEN LOCKS ROAD	POTOMAC	**MD**	20854	(301) 882-5666
HAR SHALOM, CONGREGATION C 11510 FALLS ROAD	POTOMAC	**MD**	20854	(301) 299-7087
ANSHE AMUNAH-AITZ CHAIM-LIBERTY JEWISH CENTER O 8615 CHURCH LANE	RANDALLSTOWN	**MD**	21133	
BETH ISRAEL MIKRO KODESH CONGREGATION C 9411 LIBERTY ROAD	RANDALLSTOWN	**MD**	21133	(301) 922-6565
MOGEN ABRAHAM, CONGREGATION O 3800 PIKESWOOD DRIVE	RANDALLSTOWN	**MD**	21133	
RANDALLSTOWN SYN. CTR; AHAVAS SHOLOM-AGUDAS ACHIM-SEPHARDIC O 8729 CHURCH LANE	RANDALLSTOWN	**MD**	21133	(301) 655-6665
WINANDS ROAD SYNAGOGUE CENTER O 8701 WINANDS ROAD	RANDALLSTOWN	**MD**	21133	
B'NAI ISRAEL CONGREGATION C 6301 MONTROSE ROAD	ROCKVILLE	**MD**	20852	(301) 649-3440
BETH AMI, TEMPLE R 800 HURLEY AVENUE	ROCKVILLE	**MD**	20850	(301) 340-6818
BETH TIKVAH C 2200 BALTIMORE ROAD	ROCKVILLE	**MD**	20853	(301) 762-7338
BETHESDA-CHEVY CHASE JEWISH COMMUNITY GROUP 6125 MONTROSE ROAD	ROCKVILLE	**MD**	20858	
BETH ISRAEL CONGREGATION C CAMDEN AVENUE & WICOMICO STREET	SALISBURY	**MD**	21801	(301) 742-2564
B'NAI ISRAEL C 10500 GEORGIA AVENUE	SILVER SPRING	**MD**	20902	
HAR TZEON AGUDATH ACHIM, CONGREGATION C 1840 UNIVERSITY BLVD. W	SILVER SPRING	**MD**	20902	(301) 649-3800
ISRAEL, TEMPLE C 420 UNIVERSITY BLVD E	SILVER SPRING	**MD**	20901	(301) 439-3600
OHAVEI ZEDEK CONGREGATION O 1100 EAST-WEST HIGHWAY	SILVER SPRING	**MD**	20910	
SHAARE TEFILA CONGREGATION C 11120 LOCKWOOD DRIVE	SILVER SPRING	**MD**	20901	(301) 593-3410
SILVER SPRING JEWISH CENTER; SILVER SPRING HEBREW DAY INST. O 1401 ARCOLA AVENUE	SILVER SPRING	**MD**	20902	(301) 649-4425
SOUTHEAST HEBREW CONGREGATION 10900 LOCKWOOD DRIVE	SILVER SPRING	**MD**	20901	
SUMMIT HILL CONGREGATION O 8512 16TH STREET	SILVER SPRING	**MD**	20910	
YOUNG ISRAEL SHOMREI EMUNAH 1132 ARCOLA BLVD.	SILVER SPRING	**MD**	20902	(301) 593-4465
SHAARE TIKVAH, CONGREGATION C 5404 OLD TEMPLE HILLS ROAD	TEMPLE HILLS	**MD**	20031	(301) 894-4303
BETH ABRAHAM C MAIN STREET & LAUREL AVENUE	AUBURN	**ME**	04210	(207) 783-1302
BETH ABRAHAM, CONGREGATION O 145 YORK STREET	BANGOR	**ME**	04401	
BETH ISRAEL, CONGREGATION T 144 YORK STREET	BANGOR	**ME**	04401	(207) 945-3433
TOLDOS ITZCHOK, CONGREGATION O 142 YORK STREET	BANGOR	**ME**	04401	
BETH ISRAEL CONGREGATION C WASHINGTON STREET	BATH	**ME**	04530	(207) 443-5181
ETZ CHAIM, CONGREGATION C P.O. BOX 473	BIDDEFORD	**ME**	04005	
BETH JACOB, CONGREGATION O SHAWMUT & SABBATUS STREETS	LEWISTON	**ME**	04240	
BETH ISRAEL, CONGREGATION O EAST GRAND AVENUE	OLD ORCHARD BEACH	**ME**	04064	
BETH EL, TEMPLE C 400 DEERING AVENUE	PORTLAND	**ME**	04103	(207) 774-2649
SHAAREY TPHILOH, CONGREGATION O 76 NOYES STREET	PORTLAND	**ME**	04103	(207) 773-0693
BETH EL, TEMPLE R 610 S. 3RD STREET	ALPENA	**MI**	49707	(517) 354-5106
BETH EMETH, TEMPLE R 2309 PACKARD ROAD	ANN ARBOR	**MI**	48104	(313) 665-4744
BETH ISRAEL CONGREGATION C 2000 WASHTENAW	ANN ARBOR	**MI**	48104	(313) 663-5543
BETH EL, TEMPLE R 306 CAPITAL AVENUE N.E.	BATTLE CREEK	**MI**	49107	(616) 963-4921
ISRAEL, TEMPLE C 2300 CENTER AVENUE	BAY CITY	**MI**	48706	(517) 893-7811
B'NAI SHALOM, TEMPLE C 2050 BROADWAY	BENTON HARBOR	**MI**	49022	(616) 925-8021
BETH EL, TEMPLE R 7400 TELEGRAPH ROAD	BIRMINGHAM	**MI**	48010	(313) 851-1100
BETH ABRAHAM HILLEL MOSES, CONGREGATION T 5075 W. MAPLE ROAD	BLOOMFIELD	**MI**	48033	(616) 851-6880
SOLEL, CONGREGATION R 304 W. WASHINGTON STREET	BRIGHTON	**MI**	48843	(517) 546-2527
CONGREGATION T'CHIYA 1035 ST. ANTOINE	DETROIT	**MI**		(313) 353-1569
DOWNTOWN SYNAGOGUE C 1457 GRISWOLD	DETROIT	**MI**	48226	(313) 961-9328
ISRAEL, TEMPLE R 17400 MANDERSON ROAD	DETROIT	**MI**	48235	(313) 863-7769
KEHILLAT ISRAEL C 855 GROVE STREET	EAST LANSING	**MI**	48823	(517) 315-3221
SHAAREY ZEDEK, CONGREGATION C 1924 COOLIDGE ROAD	EAST LANSING	**MI**	48823	(517) 351-3570
ADAT SHALOM SYNAGOGUE C 29901 MIDDLEBELT	FARMINGTON HILLS	**MI**	48018	(313) 851-5100
BIRMINGHAM TEMPLE, THE R 28611 W. TWELVE MILE ROAD	FARMINGTON HILLS	**MI**	48018	(313) 477-1410
BETH EL, TEMPLE R 501 S. BALLENGER HIGHWAY	FLINT	**MI**	48504	(313) 232-3138
BETH ISRAEL, CONGREGATION C 5240 CALKINS ROAD	FLINT	**MI**	48504	(313) 732-6310
AHAVAS ISRAEL, CONGREGATION C 2727 MICHIGAN N.E.	GRAND RAPIDS	**MI**	49506	(616) 949-2840
EMANUEL, TEMPLE R 1715 E. FULTON STREET	GRAND RAPIDS	**MI**	49503	(616) 459-5976
FIRST ISRAEL CONGREGATION C 113 W. HOUGHTON AVENUE	HOUGHTON	**MI**	49931	
ANSHE KNESSETH ISRAEL, CONGREGATION C P.O. BOX 218, KIMBERLY & A STREET	IRON MOUNTAIN	**MI**	49801	
BETH SHOLOM, TEMPLE R C/O DR. DANIEL ARNOLD, 80 EDGEWOOD DRIVE	ISHPEMING	**MI**	49855	(906) 486-6246
BETH ISRAEL, TEMPLE R 801 W. MICHIGAN AVENUE	JACKSON	**MI**	49202	(517) 784-3862
B'NAI ISRAEL, CONGREGATION R 2232 CROSSWIND DRIVE	KALAMAZOO	**MI**	49008	(616) 344-9762
MOSES, CONGREGATION OF C 2501 STADIUM DRIVE	KALAMAZOO	**MI**	49008	(616) 312-5463
LIVONIA JEWISH CONGREGATION C 31840 W. SEVEN MILE ROAD	LIVONIA	**MI**	48152	(313) 477-8974
BETH EL, TEMPLE C 2505 BAY CITY ROAD	MIDLAND	**MI**	48640	(517) 496-3720
BETH TEPHILATH MOSES, CONGREGATION O 53 S. AVENUE, P.O. BOX 842	MOUNT CLEMENS	**MI**	48043	(313) 465-0641
BENJAMIN, TEMPLE C 502 N. BROWN STREET, P.O. BOX 246	MOUNT PLEASANT	**MI**	48858	
B'NAI ISRAEL, CONGREGATION R 391 WEST WEBSTER	MUSKEGON	**MI**	49441	(616) 722-2702
B'NAI ISRAEL BETH YEHUDA O 15400 W. TEN MILE ROAD	OAK PARK	**MI**	48237	(313) 967-3969
B'NAI MOSHE, CONGREGATION C 14390 W. TEN MILE ROAD	OAK PARK	**MI**	48237	(313) 548-9000
B'NAI ZION O 15250 W. NINE MILE ROAD	OAK PARK	**MI**	48237	(313) 968-2414
BETH SHALOM, CONGREGATION C 14601 W. LINCOLN ROAD	OAK PARK	**MI**	48237	(313) 547-7970
DOVID BEN NUCHIM, CONGREGATION O 14800 LINCOLN ROAD	OAK PARK	**MI**	48237	(313) 398-1017
EMANU-EL, TEMPLE R 14450 W. TEN MILE ROAD	OAK PARK	**MI**	48237	(313) 967-4020
MISHKAN ISRAEL LUBAVITCHER CENTER, CONGREGATION O 14000 W. NINE MILE ROAD	OAK PARK	**MI**	48237	(313) 548-2666
SEPHARDIC COMMUNITY OF DETROIT O 24021 MARLOW	OAK PARK	**MI**	48237	(313) 967-4414
SHAAREY SHOMAIM, CONGREGATION O 14131 VICTORIA	OAK PARK	**MI**	48237	(313) 542-4444
YOUNG ISRAEL OF GREENFIELD O 15140 W. TEN MILE ROAD	OAK PARK	**MI**	48237	(313) 967-3655
YOUNG ISRAEL OF OAK WOODS O 24061 COOLIDGE	OAK PARK	**MI**	48237	(313) 398-1177
B'NAI ISRAEL CONGREGATION R CORNER WAVKAZOO & MICHIGAN	PETOSKEY	**MI**	49770	
B'NAI ISRAEL, CONGREGATION C 143 ONEIDA ROAD	PONTIAC	**MI**	48053	
BETH JACOB, TEMPLE R 79 ELIZABETH LAKE ROAD	PONTIAC	**MI**	48053	(313) 332-3212
MOUNT SINAI, CONGREGATION O P.O. BOX 794	PORT HURON	**MI**	48060	
B'NAI ISRAEL, TEMPLE C 1424 S. WASHINGTON AVENUE	SAGINAW	**MI**	48601	(517) 753-5230
BETH EL, TEMPLE R C/O MR. LEO A. KAHAN, 100 S. WASHINGTON	SAGINAW	**MI**	48607	(517) 754-5171
FIRST HEBREW CONGREGATION O 249 BROADWAY	SOUTH HAVEN	**MI**	49090	
B'NAI DAVID, CONGREGATION O 24350 SOUTHFIELD ROAD	SOUTHFIELD	**MI**	48075	(313) 557-8210
BETH ACHIM, CONGREGATION C 21100 W. TWELVE MILE ROAD	SOUTHFIELD	**MI**	48076	(313) 352-8670
BETH TEFILAH, CONGREGATION O 24225 GREENFIELD ROAD	SOUTHFIELD	**MI**		(313) 557-6828
BNEI ISRAEL, CONGREGATION O 15751 W. 10 1/2 MILE ROAD	SOUTHFIELD	**MI**	48075	(313) 559-6354
KOLLEL INSTITUTE O 15230 W. LINCOLN BLVD.	SOUTHFIELD	**MI**		(313) 645-2585
MOGEN ABRAHAM, CONGREGATION O 15751 W. TEN MILE ROAD	SOUTHFIELD	**MI**	48075	(313) 557-6750
SHAAREY ZEDEK, CONGREGATION C 27375 BELL ROAD	SOUTHFIELD	**MI**	48076	(313) 357-5544
SHOMREY EMUNAH, CONGREGATION O 25451 SOUTHFIELD ROAD	SOUTHFIELD	**MI**	48075	(313) 559-1533
YOUNG ISRAEL OF DETROIT 15894 HARDEN CIRCLE	SOUTHFIELD	**MI**	48075	(313) 557-4047
YOUNG ISRAEL OF SOUTHFIELD 27705 LAHSER ROAD	SOUTHFIELD	**MI**	48034	(313) 358-0154
BETH EL, CONGREGATION R 3545 ORCHARD VIEW	TRAVERSE CITY	**MI**	49685	(616) 946-9586
BETH EL, TEMPLE 311 S. PARK STREET	TRAVERSE CITY	**MI**	49684	(313) 946-1913
BETH ISAAC, CONGREGATION C 2730 EDSEL DRIVE	TRENTON	**MI**	48183	(313) 675-0355
B'NAI ISRAEL C 4200 WALNUT LAKE ROAD	WEST BLOOMFIELD	**MI**	48033	(313) 681-5353
BETH ABRAHAM-HILLEL-MOSES, CONGREGATION 5075 W. MAPLE ROAD	WEST BLOOMFIELD	**MI**	48033	(313) 851-6880
ISRAEL, TEMPLE R 5725 WALNUT LAKE ROAD	WEST BLOOMFIELD	**MI**	48033	(313) 661-5700
KOL AMI, TEMPLE R 5085 WALNUT LAKE ROAD	WEST BLOOMFIELD	**MI**	48033	(313) 661-0040
ADAS ISRAEL CONGREGATION O 302 E. 3RD STREET	DULUTH	**MN**	55805	(218) 722-6459
ISRAEL, TEMPLE R 1602 E. 2ND STREET	DULUTH	**MN**	55812	(218) 724-2956
AGUDATH ACHIM SYNAGOGUE C 2320 SECOND AVENUE W	HIBBING	**MN**	55746	(218) 263-9237
ADATH JESHURUN CONGREGATION C 3400 DUPONT AVENUE	MINNEAPOLIS	**MN**	55408	(612) 824-2685
B'NAI ABRAHAM-MIKRO TIFERETH SYNAGOGUE C OTTAWA AVENUE SOUTH & HIGHWAY 7	MINNEAPOLIS	**MN**	55416	
B'NAI EMET SYNAGOGUE C 1804 NEVADA SOUTH	MINNEAPOLIS	**MN**	55416	(612) 545-8131
BET SHALOM, CONGREGATION R 1559 PENNSYLVANIA AVENUE N	MINNEAPOLIS	**MN**	55427	(612) 336-4391
BETH EL SYNAGOGUE C 5224 W. 26TH STREET	MINNEAPOLIS	**MN**	55416	(612) 920-3512
HILLEL, CONGREGATION 1521 UNIVERSITY AVENUE S.E.	MINNEAPOLIS	**MN**	55414	
ISRAEL, TEMPLE R 2324 EMERSON AVENUE S	MINNEAPOLIS	**MN**	55405	(612) 377-8680
KENESSETH ISRAEL CONGREGATION O 4330 W. 28TH STREET	MINNEAPOLIS	**MN**	55416	(612) 920-2183
MIKRO KODESH TIFERETH B'NAI JACOB, CONGREGATION C OTTAWA AVENUE SOUTH & HIGHWAY 7	MINNEAPOLIS	**MN**	55416	
MINNESOTA RECONSTRUCTIONIST HAVURAH C/O HOWARD BRIN	MINNEAPOLIS	**MN**		(612) 377-3887
SHAREI-CHESED CONGREGATION O 2734 RHODE ISLAND AVENUE S	MINNEAPOLIS	**MN**	55426	(612) 929-2734
B'NAI ISRAEL SYNAGOGUE R 621 2ND STREET S.W.	ROCHESTER	**MN**	55901	(507) 288-5825
B'NAI EMET SYNAGOGUE C 3115 OTTAWA AVENUE S	ST. LOUIS PARK	**MN**	55416	(612) 927-7309
SHAARE SHALOM CONGREGATION C 2524 AQUILA AVENUE S	ST. LOUIS PARK	**MN**	55426	(612) 546-4022
AARON, TEMPLE OF C 616 S. MISSISSIPPI RIVER BLVD	ST. PAUL	**MN**	55116	(612) 698-8874
ADATH ISRAEL ORTHODOX SYNAGOGUE O 2337 EDGCUMBE ROAD	ST. PAUL	**MN**	55116	(612) 698-8300
MOUNT ZION HEBREW CONGREGATION R 1300 SUMMIT AVENUE	ST. PAUL	**MN**	55105	(612) 698-3881
SHAARE SHALOM CONGREGATION C 1922 SARGENT	ST. PAUL	**MN**	55105	(612) 699-1014
SONS OF JACOB CONGREGATION C 1466 PORTLAND AVENUE	ST. PAUL	**MN**	55104	(612) 646-0498
UNITED ORTHODOX SERVICES 1530 HARTFORD AVENUE	ST. PAUL	**MN**	55116	(612) 699-0592
B'NAI ABRAHAM, CONGREGATION O P.O. BOX 1174	VIRGINIA	**MN**	55792	
TPHERIS ISRAEL CHEVRA KADISHA CONGREGATION O 14550 LADUE ROAD	CHESTERFIELD	**MO**	63017	(314) 469-7060
TRADITIONAL CONGREGATION OF MISSOURI T 12437 LADUE ROAD	CREVE COEUR	**MO**	63141	(314) 576-5230
BETH EL, TEMPLE R 1005 ADAMS STREET	JEFFERSON CITY	**MO**	65101	(314) 636-3821
UNITED HEBREW CONGREGATION R 702 SERGEANT STREET	JOPLIN	**MO**	64801	(417) 624-1181
BETH ISRAEL, CONGREGATION O ABRAHAM & VOLINER, 8310 HOLMES	KANSAS CITY	**MO**	64131	(816) 444-5747
BETH SHALOM CONGREGATION C 9400 WORNALL ROAD	KANSAS CITY	**MO**	64114	(816) 361-2990

CONGREGATION B'NAI JEHUDAH, THE TEMPLE R
712 E. 69TH STREET ... KANSAS CITY **MO** 64131 (816) 363-1050
KEHILATH ISRAEL SYNAGOGUE T 800 E. MEYER BLVD ... KANSAS CITY **MO** 64131 (816) 333-1992
NEW REFORM TEMPLE, THE R 7100 MAIN STREET AT GREGORY ... KANSAS CITY **MO** 64114 (816) 523-7809
GENESIS OF ST. LOUIS R 14 HIGH ACRES ... OLIVETTE **MO** 63132 (314) 994-0787
BRITH SHOLOM KNESETH ISRAEL, CONGREGATION C
1107 LINDEN AVENUE ... RICHMOND HEIGHTS **MO** 63117
BETH EL, TEMPLE R 232 S. DUNDEE STREET ... SEDALIA **MO** 65301 (816) 826-3392
UNITED HEBREW CONGREGATION R 931 S. KICKAPOO ... SPRINGFIELD **MO** 65804 (417) 866-4760
ADATH JOSEPH, TEMPLE R 17TH & FELIX STREETS ... ST. JOSEPH **MO** 64501 (816) 279-3179
B'NAI SHOLOM C 615 N. 10TH STREET ... ST. JOSEPH **MO** 64501
B'NAI AMOONA, CONGREGATION C 324 S. MASON ROAD ... ST. LOUIS **MO** 63141 (314) 576-9990
B'NAI EL TEMPLE R 11411 HIGHWAY 40 ... ST. LOUIS **MO** 63131 (314) 432-6393
BAIS ABRAHAM CONGREGATION O 6910 DEMAR ... ST. LOUIS **MO** 63130 (314) 721-3030
BETH HAMEDROSH HAGODOL, CONGREGATION O
1227 NORTH & SOUTH ROAD ... ST. LOUIS **MO** 63130
BETH TEPHILAH, CONGREGATION O 6912 DELMAR ... ST. LOUIS **MO** 63130
BRITH SHOLOM KNESETH ISRAEL CONGREGATION
1107 LINDEN AVENUE ... ST. LOUIS **MO** 63117 (314) 725-6230
CHESED SHEL EMETH, CONGREGATION O
700 NORTH & SOUTH ROADS ... ST. LOUIS **MO** 63130
EMANUEL, TEMPLE R 12166 CONWAY ROAD ... ST. LOUIS **MO** 63141 (314) 432-5877
ISRAEL, TEMPLE R 10675 LADUE ROAD ... ST. LOUIS **MO** 63141 (314) 432-8050
KOL AM, CONGREGATION R 11155 CLAYTON ROAD ... ST. LOUIS **MO** 63131 (314) 569-0797
MERCHANDISE MART SYNAGOGUE C 1000 WASHINGTON AVENUE ... ST. LOUIS **MO** 63101 (314) 241-5668
MISHKAN ISRAEL, CONGREGATION O 7205 DORSET STREET ... ST. LOUIS **MO** 63130
RECONSTRUCTIONIST HAVURAH OF ST. LOUIS C/O DAVID GAD-HARF ... ST. LOUIS **MO** (314) 432-0020
SHAARE EMETH, TEMPLE R 11645 LADUE ROAD ... ST. LOUIS **MO** 63141 (314) 569-0010
UNITED HEBREW CONGREGATION R 225 S. SKINNER BLVD ... ST. LOUIS **MO** 63105 (314) 726-4666
YOUNG ISRAEL OF ST. LOUIS 7800 GROBY ROAD ... ST. LOUIS **MO** 63130 (314) 727-1880
NUSACH HARI-B'NAI ZION CONGREGATION O 8630 OLIVE BLVD ... UNIVERSITY CITY **MO** 63132 (314) 991-2100
SHAARE ZEDEK C 829 N. HANLEY ROAD ... UNIVERSITY CITY **MO** 63130 (314) 727-1747
BETH ISRAEL, CONGREGATION C
CAMILLIA & SOUTHERN AVENUE, P.O. BOX 851 ... BILOXI **MS** 39533 (601) 388-5574
B'NAI SHOLOM, TEMPLE R P.O. BOX 622 ... BROOKHAVEN **MS** 39601
B'NAI ISRAEL, CONGREGATION R P.O. BOX 284 ... CANTON **MS** 39046
BETH ISRAEL, CONGREGATION R
P.O. BOX 165, 401 CATALPA STREET ... CLARKSDALE **MS** 38614 (601) 624-5862
ADATH ISRAEL R 201 S. BOLIVAR AVENUE ... CLEVELAND **MS** 38732 (601) 843-2005
B'NAI ISRAEL R 717 SECOND AVENUE NORTH ... COLUMBUS **MS** 39701 (601) 328-8355
HEBREW UNION CONGREGATION R P.O. BOX 212, 504 MAIN STREET .. GREENVILLE **MS** 38701 (601) 332-4153
AHAVATH RAYIM, CONGREGATION O P.O. BOX 1235 ... GREENWOOD **MS** 38930 (601) 453-7537
BETH ISRAEL, CONGREGATION R 506 E. HARDING STREET ... GREENWOOD **MS** 38930 (601) 453-5749
B'NAI ISRAEL, CONGREGATION R P.O. BOX 1753 ... HATTIESBURG **MS** 39401 (601) 583-0375
BETH ISRAEL CONGREGATION R P.O. BOX 12329 ... JACKSON **MS** 39211 (601) 956-6215
BETH EL, TEMPLE R 224 COURT STREET S ... LEXINGTON **MS** 39095
BETH ISRAEL, CONGREGATION R P.O. BOX 3456 ... MERIDIAN **MS** 39301 (601) 483-3193
OHEL JACOB, CONGREGATION O P.O. BOX 766 ... MERIDIAN **MS** 39302
B'NAI ISRAEL, CONGREGATION R P.O. BOX 1003 ... NATCHEZ **MS** 39120 (601) 445-5407
GEMILUTH CHASADIM, CONGREGATION R ... PORT GIBSON **MS** 39150
B'NAI ISRAEL, TEMPLE C MARSHALL & HAMLIN STREETS, P.O. BOX 515 ... TUPELO **MS** 38801 (601) 842-9169
ANSHE CHESED, TEMPLE R 2414 GROVE STREET ... VICKSBURG **MS** 39280 (601) 636-1126
BETH AARON R 1148 NORTH BROADWAY ... BILLINGS **MT** 59101 (406) 248-6412
B'NAI ISRAEL CONGREGATION C 327 W. GALENA STREET ... BUTTE **MT** 59701 (406) 792-9330
SGOOLAI ISRAEL SYNAGOGUE WESTMORLAND STREET ... FREDERICTON **NB** E3B 2V5
TIFERES ISRAEL SYNAGOGUE 50 STEADMAN STREET ... MONCTON **NB** (506) 382-8324
SHAAREI ZEDEK, CONGREGATION C
P.O. BOX 2041, 76 CARLETON STREET ... ST. JOHN **NB** E2L 3T5 (506) 657-4790
B'NAI JESHURUN, CONGREGATION R 20TH & SOUTH STREETS ... LINCOLN **NE** 68502 (402) 435-8004
TIFERETH ISRAEL, CONGREGATION C 3219 SHERIDAN BLVD ... LINCOLN **NE** 68502 (402) 423-8569
B'NAI JACOB ADASS YESURIN, CONGREGATION O 3028 CUMING STREET ... OMAHA **NE** 68102
BETH EL SYNAGOGUE C 210 S. 49TH STREET ... OMAHA **NE** 68132 (402) 553-3221
BETH ISRAEL, CONGREGATION O 1502 N. 59TH STREET ... OMAHA **NE** 68132
ISRAEL, CONGREGATION OF 1802 N. 56TH STREET ... OMAHA **NE** 68104
ISRAEL, TEMPLE R 7023 CASS STREET ... OMAHA **NE** 68132 (402) 556-6536
BETH ISRAEL, CONGREGATION 141 CHURCH STREET ... BERLIN **NH** 03570
BETH ISRAEL, CONGREGATION EXCHANGE STREET ... BERLIN **NH** 03570
BETHLEHEM HEBREW CONGREGATION C
P.O. BOX 167 STRAWBERRY HILL STREET ... BETHLEHEM **NH** 03574 (603) 869-5747
MEYER DAVID, TEMPLE C HIGH STREET ... CLAREMONT **NH** 03843 (603) 542-6773
BETH JACOB, TEMPLE R 67 BROADWAY ... CONCORD **NH** 03301 (603) 228-8581
ISRAEL, TEMPLE C 4 & GROVE STREETS ... DOVER **NH** 03820 (603) 742-3976
B'NAI ISRAEL, TEMPLE R 208 COURT STREET ... LACONIA **NH** 03246 (603) 524-1276
ADATH YESHURUN, TEMPLE R 152 PROSPECT STREET ... MANCHESTER **NH** 03104 (603) 669-5650
ISRAEL, TEMPLE C 678 PINE STREET ... MANCHESTER **NH** 03104 (603) 622-6171
BETH ABRAHAM, TEMPLE C 4 RAYMOND STREET ... NASHUA **NH** 03060 (603) 883-8184
ISRAEL, TEMPLE C 200 STATE STREET ... PORTSMOUTH **NH** 03801 (603) 436-5301
BETH AHM, TEMPLE C 550 LLOYD ROAD ... ABERDEEN **NJ** 07747 (201) 583-1700
SHALOM, TEMPLE R 5 AYRMONT LANE ... ABERDEEN **NJ** 07747 (201) 566-2621
SONS OF ISRAEL, CONGREGATION O 412 ASBURY AVENUE ... ASBURY PARK **NJ** 07712 (201) 775-1964
BETH JACOB AMUNATH ISRAEL, CONGREGATION O
506 PACIFIC AVENUE ... ATLANTIC CITY **NJ** 08401
CHELSEA HEBREW CONGREGATION C 4001 ATLANTIC AVENUE ... ATLANTIC CITY **NJ** 08401
COMMUNITY SYNAGOGUE C 901-903 PACIFIC AVENUE ... ATLANTIC CITY **NJ** 08401 (609) 345-3282
RODEF SHOLOM, CONGREGATION O 2016 PACIFIC AVENUE ... ATLANTIC CITY **NJ** 08401
SONS OF JACOB, CONGREGATION LORD STREET ... AVENEL **NJ** 07001
BETH ABRAHAM, CONGREGATION O 42 W. 21ST STREET ... BAYONNE **NJ** 07002
BETH AM, TEMPLE R 111 AVENUE B ... BAYONNE **NJ** 07002 (201) 858-2020
EMANU-EL OF BAYONNE, TEMPLE C 735 KENNEDY BLVD ... BAYONNE **NJ** 07002 (201) 436-4499
OHAB SHOLOM, CONGREGATION O 1016-22 AVENUE C ... BAYONNE **NJ** 07002
OHAV ZEDEK, CONGREGATION O 912 AVENUE C ... BAYONNE **NJ** 07002

OHAVE SHOLOM ANSHE SFARD, CONGREGATION O 190 AVENUE B ... BAYONNE **NJ** 07002
TALMUD TORAH, CONGREGATION O 489 KENNEDY BLVD ... BAYONNE **NJ** 07002
UPTOWN SYNAGOGUE O 49TH STREET & AVENUE C ... BAYONNE **NJ** 07002
AHAVATH ACHIM C 125 ACADEMY STREET ... BELLEVILLE **NJ** 07109 (201) 759-9731
SONS OF ISRAEL, CONGREGATION O P.O. BOX 298 ... BELMAR **NJ** 07719
BERGENFIELD-DUMONT JEWISH CENTER C
169 N. WASHINGTON AVENUE ... BERGENFIELD **NJ** 07621 (201) 384-3911
MENORAH, TEMPLE R 936 BROAD STREET ... BLOOMFIELD **NJ** 07003 (201) 338-6482
NER TAMID, TEMPLE C & R 936 BROAD STREET ... BLOOMFIELD **NJ** 07003 (201) 338-6482
BETH SHOLOM, TEMPLE C HARRISON STREET ... BOONTON **NJ** 07005 (201) 334-2714
B'NAI ABRAHAM, CONGREGATION C 58 CROSSWICK STREET ... BORDENTOWN **NJ** 08505
KNESSETH ISRAEL, CONGREGATION C 229 MOUNTAIN AVENUE ... BOUND BROOK **NJ** 08805 (201) 356-1634
AGUDATH ACHIM, CONGREGATION O 301 MCCABE AVENUE ... BRADLEY BEACH **NJ** 07720
MAGEN DAVID CONGREGATION O 101 5TH AVENUE ... BRADLEY BEACH **NJ** 07720
BETH OR, TEMPLE C 200 VAN ZILE ROAD ... BRICKTOWN **NJ** 08723 (201) 458-4700
BETH ABRAHAM, CONGREGATION C
FAYETTE STREET & BELMONT AVENUE ... BRIDGETON **NJ** 08302 (609) 451-7652
SHOLOM, TEMPLE C P.O. BOX 6007, N. BRIDGE STREET ... BRIDGEWATER **NJ** 08807
AGUDATH ISRAEL OF WEST ESSEX, CONGREGATION C
20 ACADEMY ROAD ... CALDWELL **NJ** 07006 (201) 226-3600
SHALOM OF WEST ESSEX, TEMPLE R 760 POMPTON AVENUE ... CEDAR GROVE **NJ** 07009 (201) 239-1321
BETH EL, CONGREGATION C
P.O. BOX 481, 2901 W. CHAPEL AVENUE ... CHERRY HILL **NJ** 08003 (609) 677-1300
EMANUEL, TEMPLE R COOPER RIVER PARKWAY & DONAHUE ... CHERRY HILL **NJ** 08002 (609) 665-0888
SONS OF ISRAEL, CONGREGATION O 720 COOPER LANDING ROAD ... CHERRY HILL **NJ** 08034 (609) 667-9700
SINAI, TEMPLE C NEW ALBANY ROAD & ROUTE 130 ... CINNAMINSON **NJ** 08077 (609) 829-0658
BETH OR, TEMPLE C 111 VALLEY ROAD ... CLARK **NJ** 07066 (201) 381-8403
SONS OF ISRAEL, CONGREGATION C EAST CENTER STREET ... CLAYTON **NJ** 08312
ISRAEL COMMUNITY CENTER, TEMPLE C 207 EDGEWATER ROAD .. CLIFFSIDE PARK **NJ** 07010 (201) 945-7310
BETH SHOLOM REFORM TEMPLE R 733 PASSAIC AVENUE ... CLIFTON **NJ** 07012 (201) 773-0355
CLIFTON JEWISH CENTER C 18 DELAWARE STREET ... CLIFTON **NJ** 07011 (201) 772-3131
BETH EL, TEMPLE R 211 SCHRAALENBURGH ROAD ... CLOSTER **NJ** 07624 (201) 768-5112
BETH AM, TEMPLE C 220 TEMPLE WAY ... COLONIA **NJ** 07067
OHEV SHALOM, TEMPLE C 220 TEMPLE WAY ... COLONIA **NJ** 07067 (201) 388-7222
BETH EL, TEMPLE C 338 WALNUT AVENUE ... CRANFORD **NJ** 07016 (201) 276-9231
ADATH ISRAEL-DOVER JEWISH CENTER C 18 THOMPSON AVENUE ... DOVER **NJ** 07801 (201) 366-0179
EAST BRUNSWICK JEWISH CENTER C 511 RYDERS LANE ... EAST BRUNSWICK **NJ** 08816 (201) 257-7070
EAST BRUNSWICK REFORM TEMPLE R P.O. BOX 337 ... EAST BRUNSWICK **NJ** 08816 (201) 251-4300
YOUNG ISRAEL OF EAST BRUNSWICK
195 DUNHAMS CORNER ROAD ... EAST BRUNSWICK **NJ** 08816 (201) 254-1860
SHAREY TEFILO, TEMPLE R 57 PROSPECT STREET ... EAST ORANGE **NJ** 07017 (201) 678-0005
BETH EL SYNAGOGUE C 50 MAPLE STREAM ROAD ... EAST WINDSOR **NJ** 08520 (609) 443-4454
EDISON JEWISH COMMUNITY CENTER-CONGREGATION BETH EL C
91 JEFFERSON BLVD ... EDISON **NJ** 08817 (201) 985-7272
EMANU-EL, TEMPLE R 100 JAMES STREET ... EDISON **NJ** 08817 (201) 549-4442
BETH MIRIAM, TEMPLE R P.O. BOX 2097 ... ELBERON **NJ** 07740 (201) 222-3754
BROTHERS OF ISRAEL, CONGREGATION O 250 PARK AVENUE ... ELBERON **NJ** 07740 (201) 222-6666
ADATH JESHURUN, CONGREGATION O 200 MURRAY STREET ... ELIZABETH **NJ** 07202 (201) 355-6723
B'NAI ISRAEL, CONGREGATION C 1005 E. JERSEY STREET ... ELIZABETH **NJ** 07201
BAIS YITZCHOK CHEVRA THILLIM, CONGREGATION O
153 BELLEVUE STREET ... ELIZABETH **NJ** 07202 (201) 354-4789
BETH EL, TEMPLE R 1374 NORTH AVENUE ... ELIZABETH **NJ** 07208 (201) 354-3021
ELMORA HEBREW CENTER O 420 WEST END AVENUE ... ELIZABETH **NJ** 07202 (201) 353-1740
JEWISH EDUCATIONAL CENTER SYNAGOGUE O 330 ELMORA AVENUE .. ELIZABETH **NJ** 07208 (201) 353-4446
JEWISH EDUCATIONAL CENTER SYNAGOGUE O 1391 NORTH AVENUE .. ELIZABETH **NJ** 07208 (201) 354-6058
ELMWOOD PARK JEWISH CENTER C 100 GILBERT AVENUE ... ELMWOOD PARK **NJ** 07407 (201) 797-7320
EMERSON JEWISH CENTER C P.O. BOX 591, 53 PALISADE AVENUE ... EMERSON **NJ** 07630 (201) 261-9692
AHAVATH TORAH OF ENGLEWOOD, N.J., CONGREGATION O
240 BROAD AVENUE ... ENGLEWOOD **NJ** 07631 (201) 569-1315
EMANU-EL, TEMPLE C 147 TENAFLY ROAD ... ENGLEWOOD **NJ** 07631 (201) 567-1300
SHOMEREI EMUNAH, CONGREGATION O
273 VAN NOSTRAND AVENUE ... ENGLEWOOD **NJ** 07631 (201) 568-7932
SHAARI EMETH, TEMPLE R P.O. BOX 393 ... ENGLISHTOWN **NJ** 07726 (201) 462-7744
SONS OF ISRAEL, CONGREGATION O
4 PARK AVENUE, P.O. BOX 306 GORDON'S CORNER ROAD ... ENGLISHTOWN **NJ** 07726 (201) 446-3000
AVODA, TEMPLE R 10-10 PLAZA ROAD ... FAIR LAWN **NJ** 07410 (201) 797-9716
B'NAI ISRAEL, CONGREGATION C PINE AVENUE & 30TH STREET ... FAIR LAWN **NJ** 07410 (201) 797-9735
BETH SHOLOM, TEMPLE C 40-25 FAIR LAWN AVENUE ... FAIR LAWN **NJ** 07410 (201) 797-9321
EMANUEL, TEMPLE C 151 E. 33RD STREET ... FAIR LAWN **NJ** 07514 (201) 684-5565
FAIR LAWN JEWISH CENTER C 10-10 NORMA AVENUE ... FAIR LAWN **NJ** 07410 (201) 796-5040
ORTHODOX CONGREGATION OF FAIR LAWN-SHOMREI TORAH O
19-09 MORLOT AVENUE ... FAIR LAWN **NJ** 07410 (201) 791-7910
MOUNT OLIVE JEWISH CENTER C P.O. BOX 152, PLEASANT HILL ROAD ... FLANDERS **NJ** 07836 (201) 584-0212
FLEMINGTON JEWISH COMMUNITY CENTER C P.O. BOX 567 ... FLEMINGTON **NJ** 08822 (201) 782-6410
JEWISH COMMUNITY CENTER OF FORT LEE C
1449 ANDERSON AVENUE ... FORT LEE **NJ** 07024 (201) 947-1735
YOUNG ISRAEL FORT LEE 1610 PARKER AVE ... FORT LEE **NJ** 07024 (201) 592-1518
SONS OF ISRAEL, CONGREGATION OAK STREET ... FRANKLIN **NJ** 07416
AGUDATH ACHIM, CONGREGATION O BROAD & STOKES STREETS ... FREEHOLD **NJ** 07728 (201) 462-0254
JEWISH COMMUNITY CENTER C 537 HARRISON AVENUE ... GARFIELD **NJ** 07026
GLEN ROCK JEWISH CENTER C 682 HARRISTOWN ROAD ... GLEN ROCK **NJ** 07452 (201) 652-6624
BETH EL, TEMPLE C 280 SUMMIT AVENUE ... HACKENSACK **NJ** 07601 (201) 342-2045
BETH SHOLOM, TEMPLE C
WHITE HORSE PIKE & GREEN STREET ... HADDON HEIGHTS **NJ** 08035 (609) 593-6113
SHOLOM, TEMPLE GREEN STREET & WHITE HORSE PIKE ... HADDON HEIGHTS **NJ** 08035 (201) 547-6113
BETH EL, TEMPLE C BELLEVUE AVENUE ... HAMMONTON **NJ** 08037
ETZ CHAIM, CONGREGATION O 230 DENNISON STREET ... HIGHLAND PARK **NJ** 08904
HIGHLAND PARK CONSERVATIVE TEMPLE & CENTER C
201 S. 3RD AVENUE ... HIGHLAND PARK **NJ** 08904 (201) 545-6482
OHAV EMETH, CONGREGATION O P.O. BOX 1399 ... HIGHLAND PARK **NJ** 08904 (201) 247-3038
BETH CHAIM, CONGREGATION R P.O. BOX 128 ... HIGHTSTOWN **NJ** 08520 (609) 799-9401

HILLSIDE JEWISH CENTER O 1550 SUMMIT AVENUE HILLSIDE **NJ** 07205 (201) 923-6191
SHOMREI TORAH, TEMPLE C 910 SALEM AVENUE HILLSIDE **NJ** 07205 (201) 351-1945
SINAI TORATH CHAIM, CONGREGATION O 1531 MAPLE AVENUE HILLSIDE **NJ** 07205 (201) 923-9500
UNITED SYNAGOGUE OF HOBOKEN T 830 HUDSON STREET HOBOKEN **NJ** 07030 (201) 659-2614
LAKE HOPATCONG JEWISH COMMUNITY CENTER C P.O. BOX 333 HOPATCONG **NJ** 07843 (201) 398-8700
JEWISH COMMUNITY CENTER-CONGREGATION AHAVAT ACHIM C P.O. BOX 344 HOWELL **NJ** 07731 (201) 367-1677
AGUDATH ISRAEL, CONGREGATION O 1125 STUYVESANT AVENUE IRVINGTON **NJ** 07111 (201) 372-1780
AHAVATH ACHIM BIKUR CHOLIM, CONGREGATION O 644 CHANCELLOR AVENUE IRVINGTON **NJ** 07111
B'NAI ISRAEL, TEMPLE C 706 NYE AVENUE IRVINGTON **NJ** 07111 (201) 327-9656
CHEVRA ANSHE LUBOWITZ, CONGREGATION O 74 MILL ROAD IRVINGTON **NJ** 07111 (201) 399-1199
CHEVRA THILIM TIFERETH ISRAEL, CONGREGATION O 745 CHANCELLOR AVENUE IRVINGTON **NJ** 07111 (201) 371-6699
BETH SHOLOM C 90 COOPER AVENUE ISELIN **NJ** 08830 (201) 283-0239
AGUDATH SHOLOM, CONGREGATION O 472 BERGEN AVENUE JERSEY CITY **NJ** 07304
B'NAI JACOB C 176 WEST SIDE AVENUE JERSEY CITY **NJ** 07305 (201) 435-5725
BERGEN HEBREW INSTITUTE-TALMUD TORAH AGUDATH SHOLEM 2-8 OXFORD AVENUE JERSEY CITY **NJ** 07304 (201) 432-9022
BETH EL, TEMPLE R 2419 KENNEDY BLVD JERSEY CITY **NJ** 07304 (201) 333-4229
EMANU-EL, CONGREGATION C 633 BERGEN AVENUE JERSEY CITY **NJ** 07304
MOUNT SINAI, CONGREGATION O 128 SHERMAN AVENUE JERSEY CITY **NJ** 07307 (201) 659-4267
MOUNT ZION, CONGREGATION O 233 WEBSTER AVENUE JERSEY CITY **NJ** 07307
OHAB SHALOM, CONGREGATION O 225 CLAREMONT AVENUE JERSEY CITY **NJ** 07305
SONS OF ISRAEL, CONGREGATION 35 COTTAGE JERSEY CITY **NJ** 07306 (201) 798-0172
SONS OF ISRAEL, CONGREGATION O 294 GROVE STREET JERSEY CITY **NJ** 07302 (201) 332-3212
B'NAI ISRAEL OF KEARNY & NORTH ARLINGTON C 780 KEARNY AVENUE KEARNY **NJ** 07032 (201) 998-3813
BETH SHALOM, TEMPLE C 9 STANWOOD ROAD KENDALL PARK **NJ** 08824
LAKE HIAWATHA JEWISH CENTER C LINCOLN AVENUE LAKE HIAWATHA **NJ** 07034 (201) 334-0959
LAKE HOPATCONG JEWISH COMMUNITY CENTER C P.O. BOX 333 LAKE HOPATCONG **NJ** 07834 (201) 398-8700
AHAVAT SHALOM, CONGREGATION C FOREST AVENUE & 11TH STREET LAKEWOOD **NJ** 08701 (201) 363-5190
ANSHEI SEFARD, CONGREGATION O MADISON AVENUE LAKEWOOD **NJ** 08701 (201) 364-9309
BETH AM, TEMPLE R MADISON AT CAREY LAKEWOOD **NJ** 08701 (201) 363-2800
CHEVRA LOMDEI TORAH O 617 5TH STREET LAKEWOOD **NJ** 08701 (201) 367-6393
SONS OF ISRAEL, CONGREGATION O MADISON AVENUE & 6TH STREET LAKEWOOD **NJ** 08701 (201) 364-2230
TALMUD TORAH-CONGREGATION SONS OF ISRAEL 6TH STREET & MADISON AVENUE LAKEWOOD **NJ** 08701 (201) 364-2230
YOUNG ISRAEL OF LAWRENCEVILLE 25 TEXAS AVENUE LAWRENCEVILLE **NJ** 08648 (609) 883-8833
ADAS EMUNO, CONGREGATION R 254 BROAD AVENUE LEONIA **NJ** 07605 (201) 461-4045
SONS OF ISRAEL, CONGREGATION C 150 GRAND AVENUE LEONIA **NJ** 07605 (201) 592-9700
ANSHE CHESED, CONGREGATION O ORCHARD TERRACE AT ST. GEORGE AVENUE LINDEN **NJ** 07036 (201) 486-8616
BETH DAVID, CONGREGATION O P.O. BOX 185 LINDEN **NJ** 07036
SUBURBAN JEWISH CENTER-TEMPLE MEKOR CHAYIM C DEERFIELD ROAD & ACADEMY TERRACE LINDEN **NJ** 07036 (201) 925-2283
B'NAI ABRAHAM, TEMPLE C 300 E. NORTHFIELD ROAD LIVINGSTON **NJ** 07039 (201) 994-2290
BETH SHALOM, TEMPLE C 193 MT. PLEASANT AVENUE LIVINGSTON **NJ** 07039 (201) 992-3600
EMANU-EL, TEMPLE R 264 W. NORTHFIELD ROAD LIVINGSTON **NJ** 07039 (201) 992-5560
SUBURBAN TORAH CENTER, SYNAGOGUE OF THE O 85 W. MT. PLEASANT AVENUE LIVINGSTON **NJ** 07039 (201) 994-0122
BROTHERS OF ISRAEL, CONGREGATION O 85 2ND AVENUE LONG BRANCH **NJ** 07740
LYNDHURST HEBREW CENTER C 333 VALLEY BROOK AVENUE LYNDHURST **NJ** 07071 (201) 438-9582
BETH HAVERIM R P.O. BOX 332, 59 MASONICUS ROAD MAHWAH **NJ** 07430 (201) 327-4333
TEMPLE BETH SHALOM 108 FREEHOLD ROAD MANALAPAN **NJ** 07726 (201) 446-1200
AHAVATH ZION, CONGREGATION O 421 BOYDEN AVENUE MAPLEWOOD **NJ** 07040 (201) 761-5444
ANSHE RUSSIA, CONGREGATION O 14 HAUSEMAN COURT MAPLEWOOD **NJ** 07040
BETH EPHRAIM-MAPLEWOOD JEWISH CENTER O 520 PROSPECT STREET, P.O. BOX 279 MAPLEWOOD **NJ** 07040 (201) 762-5722
ATERES TZVI, CONGREGATION O 419 N. ESSEX AVENUE MARGATE **NJ** 08402
BETH EL, TEMPLE C 500 N. JEROME AVENUE MARGATE **NJ** 08402 (609) 823-2725
BETH ISRAEL, CONGREGATION R 8401 VENTNOR AVENUE, P.O. BOX 1 MARGATE **NJ** 08402 (609) 823-4116
EMETH SHALOM, TEMPLE R 8501 VENTNOR AVENUE MARGATE **NJ** 08402 (609) 822-4343
OHAV SHALOM C P.O. BOX 98 MARLBORO **NJ** 07746 (609) 536-2300
BETH TIKVAH-MT. LAUREL C EVESBORO-MEDFORD ROAD MARLTON **NJ** 08053 (609) 983-8090
BET TEFILAH, CONGREGATION O 110 DEERFIELD LANE MATAWAN **NJ** 07747 (201) 583-6262
BETH AHM, TEMPLE C 550 LLOYD ROAD (ABERDEEN) MATAWAN **NJ** 07747 (201) 583-1700
SHALOM OF MATAWAN, TEMPLE R 5 AYRMONT LANE MATAWAN **NJ** 07747 (201) 566-2621
UNITED HEBREW CONGREGATION - TEMPLE BETH AHM 550 LLOYD ROAD MATAWAN **NJ** 07747
BETH ISRAEL, TEMPLE C 34 W. MAGNOLIA AVENUE MAYWOOD **NJ** 07607 (201) 845-7550
SHALOM, TEMPLE R P.O. BOX 93 MCAFEE **NJ** 07428 (201) 827-5655
BETH JACOB, CONGREGATION C 109 E. MAPLE AVENUE MERCHANTVILLE **NJ** 08109 (609) 662-4509
NEVE SHALOM, TEMPLE - JCC C 250 GROVE AVENUE METUCHEN **NJ** 08840 (201) 548-2238
B'NAI ISRAEL, CONGREGATION C 160 MILLBURN AVENUE MILLBURN **NJ** 07041 (201) 379-3811
BETH HILLEL, TEMPLE C 3RD & OAK STREETS MILLVILLE **NJ** 08332
CONGREGATION B'NAI KESHET RE 87-89 VALLEY ROAD MONTCLAIR **NJ** 07043 (201) 746-4489
SHOMREI EMUNAH, CONGREGATION C 67 PARK STREET MONTCLAIR **NJ** 07042 (201) 746-5031
RODEPH TORAH, TEMPLE R P.O. BOX 23 MORGANVILLE **NJ** 07751 (201) 536-2417
B'NAI OR, TEMPLE R OVERLOOK ROAD MORRISTOWN **NJ** 07960 (201) 539-4539
MORRISTOWN JEWISH COMMUNITY CENTER C 177 SPEEDWELL AVENUE MORRISTOWN **NJ** 07960 (201) 538-9292
MOUNT FREEDOM JEWISH CENTER O SUSSEX TURNPIKE MOUNT FREEDOM **NJ** 07970
HAR-ZION, TEMPLE C HIGH & RIDGWAY STREETS MT. HOLLY **NJ** 08060 (609) 267-0660
M'KOR SHALOM, CONGREGATION R CHURCH & FELLOWSHIP ROADS MT. LAUREL **NJ** 08054 (609) 235-0590
ANSHE EMETH MEMORIAL TEMPLE R 222 LIVINGSTON AVENUE NEW BRUNSWICK **NJ** 08901 (201) 545-6484
POALE ZEDEK, CONGREGATION T 145 NEILSON STREET, P.O. BOX 166 NEW BRUNSWICK **NJ** 08901
BETH TIKVA-NEW MILFORD JEWISH CENTER C 435 RIVER ROAD NEW MILFORD **NJ** 07646 (201) 261-4847

B'NAI MOSHE, CONGREGATION O 19-29 ROSS STREET NEWARK **NJ** 07114
B'NAI ZION, CONGREGATION O 215 CHANCELLOR AVENUE NEWARK **NJ** 07112
BETH DAVID JEWISH CENTER C 828 SANFORD AVENUE NEWARK **NJ** 07106 (201) 372-9360
CHEBRA ANSHE LUBAWITZ, CONGREGATION O P.O. BOX 416 NEWARK **NJ** 07101
MOUNT SINAI CONGREGATION OF IVY HILL O 250 MT. VERNON PLACE (IVY HILL) NEWARK **NJ** 07106 (201) 372-3551
JEWISH CENTER OF SUSSEX COUNTY C 13 WASHINGTON STREET, P.O. BOX 334 NEWTON **NJ** 07860 (201) 383-4570
NORMA CONGREGATION BROTHERHOOD O P.O. BOX 56 NORMA **NJ** 08347 (201) 691-4740
BETH ABRAHAM, TEMPLE O 8410 FOURTH AVENUE NORTH BERGEN **NJ** 07047 (201) 869-2425
BETH-EL, TEMPLE O 7501 HUDSON AVENUE NORTH BERGEN **NJ** 07047
ZEMACH DAVID, CONGREGATION O 8402 FIRST AVENUE NORTH BERGEN **NJ** (201) 869-2480
B'NAI TIKVAH, CONGREGATION C BOX 3028 NORTH BRUNSWICK **NJ** 08902 (201) 297-0696
SHARRI SHOLOM, CONGREGATION C R.F.D. #4-BOX 454E, GEORGES ROAD NORTH BRUNSWICK **NJ** 08902
B'NAI ISRAEL, TEMPLE C 192 CENTRE STREET NUTLEY **NJ** 07110 (201) 667-3713
BETH EL, TEMPLE C 301 MONMOUTH ROAD OAKHURST **NJ** 07755 (201) 531-0300
BETH TORAH, TEMPLE C 1200 RODELD AVENUE OCEAN **NJ** 07712 (201) 531-4410
BETH OHR C 300 ROUTE 516 OLD BRIDGE **NJ** 08857 (201) 257-9867
BETH TORAH, CONGREGATION C 270 REYNOLDS TERRACE ORANGE **NJ** 07050 (201) 678-1269
SONS OF ISRAEL, CONGREGATION BROAD & EDSALL AVENUES, P.O. BOX 2 PALISADES PARK **NJ** 07650
BETH TEFILLAH, CONGREGATION O 241 MIDLAND AVENUE PARAMUS **NJ** 07652 (201) 265-4100
JEWISH COMMUNITY CENTER OF PARAMUS C E. 304 MIDLAND AVENUE PARAMUS **NJ** 07652 (201) 262-7691
BETH SHOLOM, TEMPLE C P.O. BOX 104, 32 PARK AVENUE PARK RIDGE **NJ** 07656
OHAV SHALOM, TEMPLE - SAYREVILLE JEWISH CENTER C P.O. BOX 341 PARLIN **NJ** 08859 (201) 727-4334
AHAVAT TORAH OF PARSIPPANY, CONGREGATION O 1180 HIGHWAY 46 PARSIPPANY **NJ** 07054
BETH AM, TEMPLE R P.O. BOX 50, 879 S. BEVERWYCK ROAD PARSIPPANY **NJ** 07504 (201) 887-0046
ADAS ISRAEL, CONGREGATION O 565 BROADWAY PASSAIC **NJ** 07055 (201) 773-7272
AHAVAS ISRAEL, CONG.-PASSAIC PARK JEWISH COMMUNITY CTR. T 181 VAN HOUTEN AVENUE PASSAIC **NJ** 07055 (201) 777-5929
B'NAI JACOB, CONGREGATION O P.O. BOX 293 PASSAIC **NJ** 07055
BIKUR CHOLIM, CONGREGATION O 22 MARKET STREET PASSAIC **NJ** 07055
CHEVRAH THILIM, CONGREGATION O 132 SPRING STREET PASSAIC **NJ** 07055 (201) 473-0263
EMANUEL, TEMPLE C 181 LAFAYETTE AVENUE PASSAIC **NJ** 07055
HUNGARIAN HEBREW MEN, CONGREGATION C 71 DAYTON AVENUE PASSAIC **NJ** 07055
TIFERETH ISRAEL, CONGREGATION O 180 PASSAIC AVENUE PASSAIC **NJ** 07055
YOUNG ISRAEL OF PASSAIC-CLIFTON 200 BROOK AVENUE PASSAIC **NJ** 07055 (201) 778-7117
ANSHAI LUBAVITZ, CONGREGATION O 427 11TH AVENUE PATERSON **NJ** 07514
B'NAI ISRAEL AHAVATH JOSEPH, CONGREGATION O 561 PARK AVENUE PATERSON **NJ** 07504
B'NAI JESHURUN, CONGREGATION R 152 DERROM AVENUE PATERSON **NJ** 07504 (201) 279-2111
BETH HAMEDROSH HAGODOL, CONGREGATION O 115 VREELAND AVENUE PATERSON **NJ** 07504
COMMUNITY SYNAGOGUE C 660 14TH AVENUE PATERSON **NJ** 07504 (201) 742-9345
EASTSIDE HEBREW CENTER O 467 E. 37TH STREET PATERSON **NJ** 07504
EMANUEL OF NORTH JERSEY, TEMPLE C 151 E. 33RD STREET PATERSON **NJ** 07514 (201) 684-5564
ISRAEL CENTER O 115 VREELAND AVENUE PATERSON **NJ** 07504
UNITED BROTHERHOOD HENRY RAMER O 100 HAMILTON PLACE PATERSON **NJ** 07505
YAVNEH ACADEMY SYNAGOGUE O 413 12TH AVENUE PATERSON **NJ** 07514
SHARI TZADEK, CONGREGATION C N. BROAD STREET PENNS GROVE **NJ** 08069
BETH ISRAEL, CONGREGATION O 166 JEFFERSON STREET PERTH AMBOY **NJ** 08861
BETH MORDECAI, CONGREGATION C 224 HIGH STREET PERTH AMBOY **NJ** 08862 (201) 442-2431
SHAAREY TEFILOH, CONGREGATION O 15 MARKET STREET, P.O. BOX 633 PERTH AMBOY **NJ** 08862 (201) 826-2977
PINE BROOK JEWISH CENTER C CHANGEBRIDGE ROAD PINE BROOK **NJ** 07058 (201) 227-3520
CONGREGATION B'NAI ISRAEL PISCATAWAY JEWISH COMMUNITY CONGREGATION RE POB 965 PISCATAWAY **NJ** 08854 (201) 981-1096
BETH EL, TEMPLE C 225 E. 7TH STREET PLAINFIELD **NJ** 07060 (201) 756-2333
SHOLOM, TEMPLE R 815 W. 7TH STREET PLAINFIELD **NJ** 07063 (201) 756-6447
B'NAI ISRAEL, CONGREGATION C W. JERSEY AVENUE & FRANKLIN BLVD PLEASANTVILLE **NJ** 08232
BETH SHALOM, CONGREGATION C 21 PASSAIC AVENUE POMPTON LAKES **NJ** 07442 (201) 835-9785
POMPTON LAKES JEWISH CENTER 525 WANAQUE AVENUE POMPTON LAKES **NJ** 07442
JEWISH CENTER, THE C 457 NASSAU STREET PRINCETON **NJ** 08540 (609) 921-0100
YAVNEH HOUSE 83 PROSPECT AVENUE PRINCETON **NJ** 08540 (609) 452-3610
BETH TORAH, TEMPLE - RAHWAY HEBREW CONGREGATION C 1365 BRYANT STREET RAHWAY **NJ** 07065 (201) 574-8432
BETH SHOLOM C MAPLE STREET & PLAZA LANE RAMSEY **NJ** 07446 (201) 327-7759
B'NAI ISRAEL, CONGREGATION P.O. BOX 252 RED BANK **NJ** 07701 (201) 842-1800
BETH SHALOM, CONGREGATION O P.O. BOX 186 RED BANK **NJ** 07701
EMANUEL, TEMPLE C 120 PARK STREET RIDGEFIELD PARK **NJ** 07660 (201) 440-9464
ISRAEL OF RIDGEWOOD, TEMPLE C 475 GROVE STREET RIDGEWOOD **NJ** 07450 (201) 444-9320
LAKELAND HILLS JEWISH CENTER C P.O. BOX 115 RINGWOOD **NJ** 07456 (201) 835-4786
SHOLOM, TEMPLE R 385 HOWLAND AVENUE RIVER EDGE **NJ** 07661 (201) 489-2463
UNITED JEWISH COMMUNITY OF BERGEN COUNTY 111 KINDERKAMACK ROAD, P.O. BOX 176, N. HACKENSACK STA. RIVER EDGE **NJ** 07661 (201) 488-6800
OHAV SHALOM, CONGREGATION C 385 W. PASSAIC STREET ROCHELLE PARK **NJ** 07662 (201) 845-6882
WHITE MEADOW TEMPLE C 153 WHITE MEADOW ROAD ROCKAWAY **NJ** 07866 (201) 627-4500
ANSHEI ROOSEVELT, CONGREGATION O 20 HOMESTEAD LANE ROOSEVELT **NJ** 08555 (201) 448-2526
B'NAI ISRAEL, CONGREGATION C HANCE & RIDGE ROADS RUMSON **NJ** 07760 (201) 842-1800
BETH EL, TEMPLE C 185 MONTROSS AVENUE RUTHERFORD **NJ** 07070 (201) 438-4931
OHEB SHOLOM SYNAGOGUE C 240 GRANT STREET SALEM **NJ** 08079
ISRAEL OF SCOTCH PLAINS & FANWOOD, TEMPLE C 1920 CLIFFWOOD STREET SCOTCH PLAINS **NJ** 07076 (201) 889-1830
B'NAI JESHURUN, CONGREGATION R 1025 S. ORANGE AVENUE SHORT HILLS **NJ** 07078 (201) 379-1555
BETH EL, TEMPLE C 1495 AMWELL ROAD SOMERSET **NJ** 08873 (201) 873-2225
BETH EL, TEMPLE R 67 RTE. 206 SOUTH SOMERVILLE **NJ** 08876 (201) 722-0674
BETH EL OF THE ORANGES & MAPLEWOOD C 222 IRVINGTON AVENUE SOUTH ORANGE **NJ** 07079 (201) 763-0111

ISRAEL OF THE ORANGES & MAPLEWOOD, TEMPLE R				
432 SCOTLAND ROAD	SOUTH ORANGE	**NJ**	07079	(201) 763-4116
MONROE TOWNSHIP JEWISH CENTER R P.O. BOX 71	SOUTH ORANGE	**NJ**	08884	(201) 251-0594
OHEB SHALOM, CONGREGATION C 170 SCOTLAND ROAD	SOUTH ORANGE	**NJ**	07079	(201) 762-7067
ANSHE EMETH & JEWISH COMMUNITY CENTER O 88 MAIN STREET	SOUTH RIVER	**NJ**	08882	(201) 257-4190
BETH AHM, TEMPLE C 60 BALTUSROL WAY & TEMPLE DRIVE	SPRINGFIELD	**NJ**	07081	(201) 376-0539
ISRAEL OF SPRINGFIELD, CONGREGATION O				
339 MOUNTAIN AVENUE	SPRINGFIELD	**NJ**	07081	(201) 376-6806
SHA-AREY SHALOM, TEMPLE R 78 S. SPRINGFIELD AVENUE	SPRINGFIELD	**NJ**	07081	(201) 379-5387
SHALOM, TEMPLE R 215 S. HILLSIDE AVENUE	SUCCASUNNA	**NJ**	07876	(201) 584-5666
SINAI, TEMPLE R 208 SUMMIT AVENUE	SUMMIT	**NJ**	07901	(201) 273-4921
SUMMIT JEWISH COMMUNITY CENTER C 67 KENT PLACE BLVD	SUMMIT	**NJ**	07901	(201) 273-8130
B'NAI YESHURUN, CONGREGATION O 641 W. ENGLEWOOD AVENUE	TEANECK	**NJ**	07666	
BETH AM, CONGREGATION R 510 CLAREMONT AVENUE	TEANECK	**NJ**	07666	(201) 836-5752
BETH SHOLOM, CONGREGATION C RUGBY ROAD & RUTLAND AVENUE	TEANECK	**NJ**	07666	(201) 833-2620
EMETH, TEMPLE R 1666 WINDSOR ROAD	TEANECK	**NJ**	07666	(201) 833-1322
JEWISH CENTER OF TEANECK C 70 STERLING PLACE	TEANECK	**NJ**	07666	(201) 833-0515
BETH CHAVAIRUTH, CONGREGATION R 49 LEONARD AVENUE	TENAFLY	**NJ**	07670	(201) 569-8323
SINAI OF BERGEN COUNTY, TEMPLE R 1 ENGLE STREET	TENAFLY	**NJ**	07670	(201) 568-3035
MONMOUTH REFORM TEMPLE R 332 HANCE AVENUE	TINTON FALLS	**NJ**	07724	(201) 747-9365
B'NAI ISRAEL, CONGREGATION C 1488 OLD FREEHOLD ROAD	TOMS RIVER	**NJ**	08753	(201) 349-1244
ADATH ISRAEL CONGREGATION C 715 BELLEVUE AVENUE	TRENTON	**NJ**	08618	(609) 599-2591
AHAVATH ISRAEL, CONGREGATION C 1130 LOWER FERRY ROAD	TRENTON	**NJ**	08618	(201) 882-3092
BROTHERS OF ISRAEL, CONGREGATION C 499 GREENWOOD AVENUE	TRENTON	**NJ**	08609	(609) 695-3479
HAR SINAI HEBREW CONGREGATION R 491 BELLEVUE AVENUE	TRENTON	**NJ**	08618	(609) 392-7143
PEOPLE OF TRUTH CONGREGATION JESHURUN O				
1201 W. STATE STREET	TRENTON	**NJ**	08618	
BETH SHALOM, CONGREGATION C VAUXHALL ROAD & PLANE STREET	UNION	**NJ**	07083	(201) 686-6773
ISRAEL OF UNION, TEMPLE C 2372 MORRIS AVENUE	UNION	**NJ**	07083	(201) 687-2120
BETH JACOB, CONGREGATION O 325 4TH STREET	UNION CITY	**NJ**	07087	(201) 863-3114
ISRAEL EMANUEL, TEMPLE O 33 STREET & NEW YORK AVENUE	UNION CITY	**NJ**	07087	
MESIVTA SANZ O 3400 NEW YORK AVENUE	UNION CITY	**NJ**		(201) 867-6890
BETH JUDAH, CONGREGATION C 6725 VENTNOR AVENUE	VENTNOR	**NJ**	08406	(609) 822-7116
JEWISH COMMUNITY CENTER OF VERONA C 56 GROVE AVENUE	VERONA	**NJ**	07044	(201) 239-0754
AHAVAS ACHIM, CONGREGATION O 618 PLUM STREET	VINELAND	**NJ**	08360	
BETH ISRAEL CONGREGATION C 1015 PARK AVENUE, P.O. BOX 465	VINELAND	**NJ**	08360	(609) 691-0852
SONS OF JACOB, CONGREGATION O 321 GRAPE STREET	VINELAND	**NJ**	08360	
MOUNTAIN JEWISH CENTER 104 MT. HOREB ROAD	WARREN	**NJ**	07060	(201) 356-8777
BETH OR, TEMPLE R 56 RIDGEWOOD ROAD	WASHINGTON TOWNSHIP	**NJ**	07675	(201) 664-7422
BETH TIKVAH, TEMPLE R P.O. BOX 3182, 950 PREAKNESS AVENUE	WAYNE	**NJ**	07470	(201) 595-6565
EMANUEL, TEMPLE 1412 ALPS ROAD	WAYNE	**NJ**	07470	
WAYNE CONSERVATIVE CONGREGATION C 8 MAYFAIR DRIVE	WAYNE	**NJ**	07470	(201) 696-2500
YOUNG ISRAEL METROPOLITAN NEW JERSEY				
1 HENDERSON DRIVE	WEST CALDWELL	**NJ**	07006	(201) 575-1194
B'NAI SHOLOM, CONGREGATION C 213 LENOX AVENUE	WEST END	**NJ**	07740	(201) 229-2700
TALMUD TORAH, CONGREGATION O 5308 PALISADE AVENUE	WEST NEW YORK	**NJ**	07093	
AHAVAS ACHIM, B'NAI JACOB & DAVID, CONGREGATION O				
700 PLEASANT VALLEY WAY	WEST ORANGE	**NJ**	07052	(201) 736-1407
JEWISH CENTER OF WEST ORANGE C 300 PLEASANT VALLEY WAY	WEST ORANGE	**NJ**	07052	(201) 731-0160
YOUNG ISRAEL OF WEST ORANGE 567 PLEASANT VALLEY WAY	WEST ORANGE	**NJ**	07052	(201) 731-3383
EMANU-EL OF WESTFIELD, TEMPLE R 756 E. BROAD STREET	WESTFIELD	**NJ**	07090	(201) 232-6770
RABBINIC CENTER SYNAGOGUE 128 E. DUDLEY AVENUE	WESTFIELD	**NJ**	07090	(201) 233-0419
BETH OR, TEMPLE R 56 RIDGEWOOD ROAD	WESTWOOD	**NJ**	07675	(201) 644-7422
EMANUEL, TEMPLE 111 WASHINGTON AVENUE	WESTWOOD	**NJ**	07675	(201) 664-2880
BETH JUDAH SYNAGOGUE C SPENCER & PACIFIC AVENUE	WILDWOOD	**NJ**	08260	(201) 522-7541
BETH TORAH, CONGREGATION C BEVERLY-RANCOCAS ROAD	WILLINGBORO	**NJ**	08046	(609) 877-4214
EMANU-EL, TEMPLE R JOHN F. KENNEDY WAY	WILLINGBORO	**NJ**	08046	(609) 871-1736
WOODBINE BROTHERHOOD, CONGREGATION O				
614 WASHINGTON AVENUE	WOODBINE	**NJ**	08270	
ADATH ISRAEL, CONGREGATION C				
424 AMBOY AVENUE & S. PARK DRIVE	WOODBRIDGE	**NJ**	07095	(201) 634-9601
BETH ISRAEL C P.O. BOX 143, HIGH & WARNER STREETS	WOODBURY	**NJ**	08096	(609) 848-7272
EMANUEL, TEMPLE - PASACK VALLEY C 87 OVERLOOK DRIVE	WOODCLIFF LAKE	**NJ**	07675	(201) 664-2880
BETH RISHON, TEMPLE 585 RUSSELL AVENUE BOX 345	WYCKOFF	**NJ**	07481	(201) 891-4466
ALBERT, CONGREGATION R 1006 LEAD AVENUE S.E.	ALBUQUERQUE	**NM**	87106	(505) 243-3533
B'NAI ISRAEL, CONGREGATION C 4401 INDIAN SCHOOL RD., N.E.	ALBUQUERQUE	**NM**	87110	(505) 266-0115
BETH EL, TEMPLE P.O. BOX 1029	LAS CRUCES	**NM**	88003	(505) 524-3380
LOS ALAMOS JEWISH CENTER 2400 CANYON ROAD	LOS ALAMOS	**NM**	87544	(505) 662-2140
B'NAI ISRAEL, CONGREGATION C 8TH & WASHINGTON STREETS	ROSWELL	**NM**	88201	
SONS OF ISRAEL, CONGREGATION PRINCE STREET	GLACE BAY	**NS**	B1A 2J6	
SHAAR SHALOM CONGREGATION C 1981 OXFORD STREET	HALIFAX	**NS**	B3H 4A4	(902) 422-2580
BETH SHOLOM, TEMPLE C 1600 E. OAKEY BLVD	LAS VEGAS	**NV**	89104	(702) 384-5070
NER TAMID, CONGREGATION R 4412 S. MARYLAND PARKWAY	LAS VEGAS	**NV**	89109	(702) 733-6292
EMANU-EL, TEMPLE C				
1031 MANZANITA LANE, AT THE CORNER OF LAKESIDE DRIVE	RENO	**NV**	89509	(702) 825-5600
SINAI, TEMPLE R P.O. BOX 3114	RENO	**NV**	89505	(702) 747-9927
B'NAI SHOLOM, THE NEW REFORM CONGREGATION R				
420 WHITEHALL ROAD	ALBANY	**NY**	12208	(518) 482-5283
BETH ABRAHAM-JACOB, CONGREGATION O 66 HACKETT BLVD	ALBANY	**NY**	12209	(518) 449-7813
BETH EMETH, TEMPLE R 100 ACADEMY ROAD	ALBANY	**NY**	12208	(518) 436-9761
CHABAD LUBAVITCH O 122 S. MAIN STREET	ALBANY	**NY**	12208	(518) 482-5781
ISRAEL, TEMPLE C 600 NEW SCOTLAND AVENUE	ALBANY	**NY**	12208	(518) 438-7858
OHEV SHOLOM, CONGREGATION C NEW KRUMKILL ROAD	ALBANY	**NY**	12208	(518) 489-4706
RECONSTRUCTIONIST HAVURAH OF THE CAPITAL DISTRICT				
C/O PAUL GREENBERG	ALBANY	**NY**		(518) 439-5870
BETH DAVID CONGREGATION R P.O. BOX 76	AMENIA	**NY**	12501	(914) 373-8264
SINAI, TEMPLE R 50 ALBERTA DRIVE	AMHERST	**NY**	14226	(716) 834-0708
BETH SHOLOM CENTER OF AMITYVILLE & THE MASSAPEQUAS C				
79 CITY LINE ROAD	AMITYVILLE	**NY**	11701	(516) 264-2891
ISRAEL, TEMPLE OF R 166 LOCUST AVENUE	AMSTERDAM	**NY**	12010	
SONS OF ISRAEL 355 GUY PARK AVENUE	AMSTERDAM	**NY**	12010	(518) 842-8691

B'NAI YISRAEL, CONGREGATION R				
485 BEDFORD ROAD, BOX 766 LOCUST AVENUE	ARMONK	**NY**	10504	(914) 273-2220
ANSHE SFARD, CONGREGATION O 208-10 BEACH 75TH STREET	ARVERNE	**NY**	11692	
DERECH EMUNOH, CONGREGATION O 199 BEACH 67TH STREET	ARVERNE	**NY**	11692	(718) 634-2288
BETH EL OF ASTORIA, CONGREGATION O 30-85 35TH STREET	ASTORIA	**NY**	11103	(718) 278-8930
BETH JACOB OF ASTORIA, CONGREGATION O 22-51 29TH STREET	ASTORIA	**NY**	11105	(718) 278-4170
MISHKAN ISRAEL, CONGREGATION O 27-31 CRESCENT STREET	ASTORIA	**NY**	11102	
JEWISH CENTER OF ATLANTIC BEACH O				
PARK STREET & NASSAU AVENUE	ATLANTIC BEACH	**NY**	11509	(516) 371-0972
B'NAI ISRAEL, CONGREGATION C P.O. BOX 101, 8 JOHN SMITH AVENUE	AUBURN	**NY**	13021	(315) 253-6675
BETH SHOLOM, CONGREGATION C 441 DEER PARK AVENUE	BABYLON	**NY**	11702	(516) 587-5650
BALDWIN JEWISH CENTER C 885 E. SEAMAN AVENUE	BALDWIN	**NY**	11510	(516) 223-5599
CENTRAL SYNAGOGUE OF NASSAU COUNTY R 430 DEMOTT AVENUE	BALDWIN	**NY**	11510	(516) 766-4300
SOUTH BALDWIN JEWISH CENTER-CONGREGATION SHAAREI SHALOM C				
2959 GRAND AVENUE	BALDWIN	**NY**	11510	(516) 223-8688
EMANU-EL, TEMPLE C 124 BANK STREET	BATAVIA	**NY**	14020	(716) 343-7027
AGUDAS ISRAEL OF RIDGEWOOD, CONGREGATION O				
52 PINE BROOK PLACE	BAY SHORE	**NY**	11706	
JEWISH CENTRE OF BAY SHORE C 34 N. CLINTON AVENUE	BAY SHORE	**NY**	11706	(516) 665-1140
SINAI REFORM TEMPLE R 39 BRENTWOOD ROAD	BAY SHORE	**NY**	11706	(516) 665-5755
BAY TERRACE JEWISH CENTER C				
209 STREET & CROSS ISLAND PARKWAY	BAYSIDE	**NY**	11360	(718) 428-6363
BAYSIDE JEWISH CENTER C 203-05 32ND AVENUE	BAYSIDE	**NY**	11361	(718) 352-7900
BAYSIDE-OAKS JEWISH CENTER C 50-35 CLOVERDALE BLVD	BAYSIDE	**NY**	11364	(718) 631-0100
JEWISH CENTER OF BAYSIDE HILLS C 48TH AVENUE & 212TH STREET	BAYSIDE	**NY**	11364	(718) 225-5301
OAKLAND JEWISH CENTER 61-35 220TH STREET	BAYSIDE	**NY**	11364	(718) 225-7800
YOUNG ISRAEL OF BAYSIDE 209-34 26TH AVENUE	BAYSIDE	**NY**	11360	(718) 423-3720
YOUNG ISRAEL OF WINDSOR PARK 67-45 215TH STREET	BAYSIDE	**NY**	11364	(718) 224-2100
BEACON HEBREW ALLIANCE C 55 FISHKILL AVENUE	BEACON	**NY**	12508	(914) 831-2012
OHEL SHMUEL, YESHIVAH O HAINES ROAD	BEDFORD	**NY**	10507	(914) 241-2700
SHAARAY TEFILA, TEMPLE R P.O. BOX 416	BEDFORD	**NY**	10506	(914) 666-3133
B'NAI DAVID, CONGREGATION 567 BEACH 130TH STREET	BELLE HARBOR	**NY**	11694	
BETH EL OF ROCKAWAY PARK, TEMPLE C				
445 BEACH 135TH STREET	BELLE HARBOR	**NY**	11694	(718) 634-8100
CONGREGATION SHAARE TEFILA OF BELLE HARBOR				
214 BEACH 120TH STREET	BELLE HARBOR	**NY**	11694	(718) 945-2298
OHAB ZEDEK, CONGREGATION O				
134-01 ROCKAWAY BEACH BLVD	BELLE HARBOR	**NY**	11694	(718) 474-3300
YOUNG ISRAEL OF BELLE HARBOR 505 BEACH 129TH STREET	BELLE HARBOR	**NY**	11694	(718) 474-9223
SHOLOM, TEMPLE 80-63 249TH STREET	BELLEROSE	**NY**	11426	
BELLMORE JEWISH CENTER C 2550 CENTRE AVENUE	BELLMORE	**NY**	11710	(516) 781-3072
BETH EL, TEMPLE C 1373 BELLMORE ROAD	BELLMORE	**NY**	11710	(516) 781-2650
SHAAREI SHALOM, THE EAST BAY REFORM TEMPLE R				
2569 MERRICK ROAD	BELLMORE	**NY**	11710	(516) 781-5599
BETHPAGE JEWISH COMMUNITY CENTER C 600 BROADWAY	BETHPAGE	**NY**	11714	(516) 938-7909
BETH DAVID, CONGREGATION O 39 RIVERSIDE DRIVE	BINGHAMTON	**NY**	13905	(607) 722-1793
CONCORD, TEMPLE R 9 RIVERSIDE DRIVE	BINGHAMTON	**NY**	13905	(607) 723-7355
ISRAEL, TEMPLE C DEERFIELD PLACE	BINGHAMTON	**NY**	13903	(607) 723-7461
BETH ELOHIM, TEMPLE R ROUTE 22	BREWSTER	**NY**	10509	(914) 279-4585
CHAVURAH BETH CHAI (MAHOPAC) R RFD 6 BREWSTER HILL ROAD	BREWSTER	**NY**	10509	(914) 279-8307
PUTNAM COUNTY TEMPLE, JEWISH CENTER R ROUTE 22	BREWSTER	**NY**	10509	(914) 279-4585
CONGREGATION SONS OF ISRAEL C				
1666 PLEASANTVILLE ROAD	BRIARCLIFF MANOR	**NY**	10510	(914) 762-2700
AHAV TSEDEK OF KINGSBRIDGE C 3425 KINGSBRIDGE AVENUE	BRONX	**NY**	10463	(212) 543-6969
ANSHE AMAS, CONGREGATION O 713 EAST 222 STREET	BRONX	**NY**	10467	(212) 231-5036
B'NAI ISRAEL OF BRONX, CONGREGATION O 1570 WALTON AVENUE	BRONX	**NY**	10452	(212) 583-8993
B'NAI ISRAEL OF EDENWALD, CONGREGATION 1014 E. 227TH STREET	BRONX	**NY**	10466	(212) 881-4921
BEEKMAN AVENUE CONGREGATION O 335 BEEKMAN AVENUE	BRONX	**NY**	10454	
BETH EL OF CITY ISLAND, TEMPLE 480 CITY ISLAND AVENUE	BRONX	**NY**	10464	(212) 885-9865
BETH EL CO-OP CITY, TEMPLE R 920-1 BAYCHESTER AVENUE	BRONX	**NY**	10475	(212) 671-9719
BETH EL, THE HOUSE OF YAH 1231 FRANKLIN AVENUE	BRONX	**NY**	10465	(212) 681-4912
BETH JACOB, CONGREGATION O 1461 LELAND AVENUE	BRONX	**NY**	10460	(212) 892-1339
BETH SHRAGA INSTITUTE O 2757 MORRIS AVENUE	BRONX	**NY**	10468	(212) 295-3160
BRONX HOUSE 990 PELHAM PARKWAY SOUTH	BRONX	**NY**	10461	(212) 792-1800
BRONX PARK EAST CHOTINER JEWISH CENTER O 2256 BRONX PARK E.	BRONX	**NY**	10451	(212) 655-9934
CASTLE HILL JEWISH COMMUNITY CENTER O 486 HOWE AVENUE	BRONX	**NY**	10473	(212) 892-2372
CHEVRA MACHZIKEI HORAV O 3417 KNOX PLACE	BRONX	**NY**	10467	
CHOTINER JEWISH CENTER O 2256 BRONX PARK EAST	BRONX	**NY**	10467	(212) 655-9934
CO-OP CITY JEWISH CENTER C 900 CO-OP CITY BLVD	BRONX	**NY**	10475	(212) 671-4579
COMMUNITY CENTER OF ISRAEL C 2440 ESPLANADE	BRONX	**NY**	10469	(212) 882-2400
CONCOURSE CENTER OF ISRAEL O 2323 GRAND CONCOURSE	BRONX	**NY**	10468	
CONSERVATIVE SYNAGOGUE ADATH ISRAEL OF RIVERDALE C				
250TH STREET & HENRY HUDSON PARKWAY	BRONX	**NY**	10471	(212) 543-8400
EAST CONCOURSE HEBREW CENTER O 236 EAST TREMONT AVENUE	BRONX	**NY**	10457	(212) 294-1594
EDUCATIONAL JEWISH CENTER O 805 ASTOR AVENUE	BRONX	**NY**	10467	(212) 655-9865
EMANUEL AT PARKCHESTER, TEMPLE C 2000 BENEDICT AVENUE	BRONX	**NY**	10462	(212) 828-3400
FIRST VAN NEST HEBREW CONGREGATION O 1712 GARFIELD STREET	BRONX	**NY**	10460	
GHETTO LITZMANNSTADT (LODZ) MEMORIAL SYNAGOGUE O				
2435 KINGSLAND AVENUE	BRONX	**NY**	10469	
GUN HILL JEWISH CENTER O 3380 RESERVOIR OVAL E	BRONX	**NY**	10467	(212) 652-6700
HEBREW CENTER OF EAST BRONX O 1276 COMMONWEALTH AVENUE	BRONX	**NY**	10472	(212) 829-1772
HEBREW INSTITUTE OF UNIVERSITY HEIGHTS				
3700 HENRY HUDSON PARKWAY	BRONX	**NY**	10463	(212) 796-4730
HEBREW TABERNACLE O 2150 HOLLAND AVENUE	BRONX	**NY**	10462	(212) 822-8756
HOPE OF ISRAEL, CONGREGATION O 843 WALTON AVENUE	BRONX	**NY**	10451	(212) 292-6667
INTERVALE JEWISH CENTER OF THE BRONX O 1024 INTERVALE AVENUE	BRONX	**NY**	10459	(212) 842-5238
JACOB H. SCHIFF CENTER C 2510 VALENTINE AVENUE	BRONX	**NY**	10457	(212) 295-2510
JEWISH CENTER OF HIGHBRIDGE O 1178 NELSON AVENUE	BRONX	**NY**	10452	
JEWISH CENTER OF PELHAM BAY O 1807 MAHAN AVENUE	BRONX	**NY**	10461	(212) 892-8171
JEWISH CENTER OF UNIONPORT O 2137 ELLIS AVENUE	BRONX	**NY**	10462	(212) 822-8601
JEWISH CENTER OF VIOLET PARK O 3356 SEYMOUR AVENUE	BRONX	**NY**	10469	(212) 654-2712

JEWISH CENTER OF WAKEFIELD & EDENWALD O 641 EAST 233 STREET ...... BRONX NY 10466
JEWISH CENTER OF WILLIAMSBRIDGE O 2910 BARNES AVENUE .... BRONX NY 10467 (212) 655-4077
JOSEPH BEN MAYER, CONGREGATION O 80 WEST KINGSBRIDGE ROAD ... BRONX NY 10468
JUDEA, TEMPLE R 615 REISS PLACE .... BRONX NY 10467 (212) 881-5118
KHAL ADATH YESHURUN, CONGREGATION O 2222 CRUGER AVENUE .... BRONX NY 10467 (212) 653-4698
KINGSBRIDGE CENTER OF ISRAEL O 3115 CORLEAR AVENUE .... BRONX NY 10463 (212) 548-1678
KINGSBRIDGE HEIGHTS JEWISH CENTER O 124 EAMES PLACE .... BRONX NY 10468 (212) 549-4120
LANZUTER BETH DAVID, CONGREGATION R 2364 WOODHULL AVENUE...... BRONX NY 10469
LINAS HAZEDEK, CONGREGATION O 1115 WARD AVENUE .... BRONX NY 10472
LUBAVITCH OF THE BRONX, CONGREGATION O 3415 OLINVILLE AVENUE ... BRONX NY 10467 (212) 654-5318
MERCAZ HARAV, CONGREGATION O 2832 VALENTINE AVENUE .... BRONX NY 10458
MORRIS PARK HEBREW CENTER O 1812 PAULDING AVENUE .... BRONX NY 10461 (212) 822-8669
MOSHOLU JEWISH CENTER O 3044 HULL AVENUE .... BRONX NY 10467 (212) 547-1515
MOUNT EDEN CENTER O 1660 MORRIS AVENUE .... BRONX NY 10457
MOUNT HOREB, CONGREGATION O 1042 STEBBINS AVENUE .... BRONX NY 10459 (212) 589-2651
NATHAN STRAUS JEWISH CENTER O 3512 DEKALB AVENUE .... BRONX NY 10467 (212) 547-1616
OHEL MOSHE B'NAI JOSEPH, CONGREGATION O 2144 MULINER AVENUE ... BRONX NY 10462
OHEL TORAH SYNAGOGUE 629 W. 239TH STREET .... BRONX NY 10463
PELHAM PARKWAY JEWISH CENTER C 900 PELHAM PARKWAY S .... BRONX NY 10462 (212) 792-6450
RIVERDALE JEWISH CENTER O 3700 INDEPENDENCE AVENUE .... BRONX NY 10463 (212) 548-1850
RIVERDALE TEMPLE R 4545 INDEPENDENCE AVENUE .... BRONX NY 10471 (212) 548-3800
ROOSEVELT SYNAGOGUE & COMMUNITY CENTER O
2060 WALLACE AVENUE .... BRONX NY 10462 (212) 863-5200
SEPHARDIC SHAARE RAHAMIM CONGREGATION, INC. O
100 CO-OP CITY BLVD .... BRONX NY 10463 (212) 671-8882
SHARAY TEFILAH, CONGREGATION O 1744 EASTBURN AVENUE .... BRONX NY 10457
SHIELD OF DAVID INSTITUTE C 1800 ANDREWS AVENUE.................. BRONX NY 10453 (212) 731-0481
SONS OF ISRAEL, CONGREGATION O 2521 CRUGER AVENUE .... BRONX NY 10467 (212) 231-6213
THROGGS NECK JEWISH CENTER 2918 LAFAYETTE AVENUE .... BRONX NY 10465 (212) 822-9829
TORAS CHAIM 620A BAYCHESTER AVENUE .... BRONX NY 10475 (212) 671-0310
TORAS CHAIM OF CO-OP CITY, CONGREGATION
620 BAYCHESTER AVENUE .... BRONX NY 10475 (212) 671-0310
TOREI ZOHOV, CONGREGATION O 2341 WALLACE AVENUE............... BRONX NY 10467
TRADITIONAL SYNAGOGUE OF CO-OP CITY T 115 EINSTEIN LOOP .... BRONX NY 10475 (212) 379-6920
TREMONT TEMPLE GATES OF MERCY R 2064 GRAND CONCOURSE .... BRONX NY 10457
UNITED ODD FELLOW & REBEKAH HOME SYNAGOGUE
1072 HAVEMEYER AVENUE .... BRONX NY 10462
VAN CORTLANDT JEWISH CENTER O 3880 SEDGEWICK AVENUE.......... BRONX NY 10463 (212) 884-6105
YOUNG ISRAEL OF ASTOR GARDENS 1328 ALLERTON AVENUE .... BRONX NY 10469 (212) 653-1363
YOUNG ISRAEL OF BAYCHESTER 115 EINSTEIN LOOP .... BRONX NY 10475 (212) 379-6920
YOUNG ISRAEL OF CO-OP CITY 147 DREISER LOOP .... BRONX NY 10475 (212) 671-2300
YOUNG ISRAEL OF CONCOURSE 1040 GRAND CONCOURSE .... BRONX NY 10465 (212) 293-9700
YOUNG ISRAEL OF MOSHOLU PARKWAY 100 EAST 208TH STREET .... BRONX NY 10467 (212) 882-8181
YOUNG ISRAEL OF PARKCHESTER 1375 VIRGINIA AVENUE .... BRONX NY 10462 (212) 822-9576
YOUNG ISRAEL OF PELHAM PARKWAY 2126 BARNES AVENUE .... BRONX NY 10462 (212) 824-0630
YOUNG ISRAEL OF RIVERDALE 4502 HENRY HUDSON PARKWAY .... BRONX NY 10471 (212) 548-4765
ZION, TEMPLE 1925 GRAND CONCOURSE .... BRONX NY 10453 (212) 588-5800
ADAS YEREIM, CONGREGATION O LEE AVENUE & ROEBLING............ BROOKLYN NY 11211
ADATH ISRAEL, CONGREGATION O 672 LEFFERTS AVENUE............... BROOKLYN NY 11203
ADATH JACOB, CONGREGATION O 1569 47TH STREET .... BROOKLYN NY 11219 (718) 438-9230
ADATH YESHURUN OF FLATBUSH, CONGREGATION O
3418 AVENUE N. .... BROOKLYN NY 11234
ADUDATH YISROEL OF FLATBUSH 1302 OCEAN PARKWAY................ BROOKLYN NY 11236 (718) 375-2706
AGUDAS ACHIM ANSHEI MEREDITZ & KLOIZ, CONGREGATION O
45 RANDALLS PARK N.W. .... BROOKLYN NY 11205
AGUDAS ACHIM OF EAST FLATBUSH, CONGREGATION O
902 LENOX ROAD .... BROOKLYN NY 11203
AGUDATH ACHIM TALMUD TORAH, CONGREGATION O
865 50TH STREET .... BROOKLYN NY 11220
AGUDATH CHASIDEI SPINKA, CONGREGATION O 1460 56TH STREET .... BROOKLYN NY 11219
AGUDATH ISRAEL BRANCH CHOFETZ CHAIM, CONGREGATION O
5413 18TH AVENUE .... BROOKLYN NY 11218
AGUDATH ISRAEL BROOKLYN COMMUNITY CENTER O
803 KINGS HIGHWAY .... BROOKLYN NY 11223
AGUDATH ISRAEL OF 18TH AVENUE O 5413 18TH AVENUE .... BROOKLYN NY 11204 (718) 236-9578
AGUDATH ISRAEL OF BORO PARK O 4511 14TH AVENUE .... BROOKLYN NY 11219 (718) 438-6508
AGUDATH ISRAEL OF BORO PARK WEST O 867 50TH STREET .... BROOKLYN NY 11220
AGUDATH ISRAEL OF BORO PARK, CONGREGATION O
4909 16TH AVENUE .... BROOKLYN NY 11204
AGUDATH ISRAEL OF CROWN HEIGHTS O 456 CROWN STREET .... BROOKLYN NY 11225 (718) 778-7195
AGUDATH ISRAEL OF EAST MIDWOOD O 3120 BEDFORD .... BROOKLYN NY 11210
AGUDATH ISRAEL OF EIGHTEENTH AVENUE O 5413 18TH AVENUE ..... BROOKLYN NY 11204 (718) 236-9578
AGUDATH ISRAEL OF FLATBUSH 1032 OCEAN PARKWAY .... BROOKLYN NY 11230
AGUDATH ISRAEL OF FLATBUSH/SOUTH O 803 KINGS HIGHWAY .... BROOKLYN NY 11223
AGUDATH ISRAEL OF KINGS HIGHWAY 1796 EAST 7TH STREET .... BROOKLYN NY 11223 (718) 375-1630
AGUDATH ISRAEL OF MIDWOOD O 817 AVENUE H .... BROOKLYN NY 11230
AGUDATH ISRAEL OF SIXTEENTH AVENUE O 4906 16TH AVENUE ...... BROOKLYN NY 11204
AGUDATH ISRAEL OF WILLIAMSBURG O 616 BEDFORD AVENUE .... BROOKLYN NY 11211
AGUDATH SHOLOM OF FLATBUSH, CONGREGATION O
3714 18TH AVENUE .... BROOKLYN NY 11218 (718) 854-2226
AHABA VE AHVA, CONGREGATION O 2022 66TH STREET................ BROOKLYN NY 11204
AHAVAS ACHIM ANSHEI SFARD, CONGREGATION O
1385 E. 94TH STREET (NEAR AVENUE L) .... BROOKLYN NY 11236 (718) 272-6933
AHAVAS MOISCHE, CONGREGATION O 612 MAPLE STREET............. BROOKLYN NY 11203 (718) 771-7365
AHAVATH ACHIM ANSHEI CANARSIE, CONGREGATION O
9420 GLENWOOD ROAD .... BROOKLYN NY 11236 (718) 257-9586
AHAVATH ACHIM OF FLATBUSH, CONGREGATION O
549 EAST 2 STREET .... BROOKLYN NY 11218 (718) 853-1959
AHAVATH ACHIM, CONGREGATION C 151 WOODRUFF AVENUE .... BROOKLYN NY 11226
AHAVATH ACHIM, CONGREGATION O 1750 E. 4TH STREET.............. BROOKLYN NY 11223 (718) 375-3895
AHAVATH ISRAEL OF GREENPOINT SYNAGOGUE, CONGREGATION O
108 NOBLE STREET... BROOKLYN NY 11222 (718) 383-8475

AHAVATH ISRAEL, CONGREGATION O 2818 AVENUE K.................. BROOKLYN NY 11210 (718) 258-6666
AHAVATH SHALOM, CONGREGATION O
1495 CONEY ISLAND AVENUE .... BROOKLYN NY 11230
AHAVATH SHOLOM, TEMPLE R 1609 AVENUE R .... BROOKLYN NY 11229 (718) 375-4500
AHAVATH TORAH, INC. 1630 50TH STREET .... BROOKLYN NY 11204
AHI EZER CONGREGATION O 1885 OCEAN PARKWAY .... BROOKLYN NY 11223 (718) 376-4088
ANSHE SHOLOM, CONGREGATION - AVENUE U EDUCATIONAL CENTER O
2066 EAST 9TH STREET... BROOKLYN NY 11223
ANSHEI LUBAWITZ, CONGREGATION O 4204 12TH AVENUE .... BROOKLYN NY 11218 (718) 436-2200
ANSHEI SEFARD, CONGREGATION O 8214 21ST AVENUE................ BROOKLYN NY 11214 (718) 837-2145
ARUGATH HABOSEM, CONGREGATION O 559 BEDFORD AVENUE.......... BROOKLYN NY 11211
ATERETH ZVI-LISKER KOLLEL, CONGREGATION O 1449 50TH STREET ... BROOKLYN NY 11219 (718) 854-5555
ATZEI CHAIM SIGET, CONGREGATION 4915 15TH AVENUE .... BROOKLYN NY 11219 (718) 438-9126
ATZEI CHAIM, CONGREGATION O 152 HEWES STREET.................. BROOKLYN NY 11211
AVENUE N JEWISH COMMUNITY CENTER 321 AVENUE N................ BROOKLYN NY 11230 (718) 339-7747
AVENUE Z JEWISH CENTER O 875 AVENUE Z............................ BROOKLYN NY 11235 (718) 646-9874
AVRECHEL GUR, CONGREGATION O 1573 51ST STREET .... BROOKLYN NY 11219 (718) 435-2070
AVREICHEI GUR, CONGREGATION O 4622 16TH AVENUE................ BROOKLYN NY 11204 (718) 871-8683
B'NAI ABRAHAM, CONGREGATION 409 E. 53RD STREET................. BROOKLYN NY 11203 (718) 495-2660
B'NAI ABRAHAM, CONGREGATION O 1415 55TH STREET................ BROOKLYN NY 11219 (718) 851-9849
B'NAI ADATH KOL BETH ISRAEL, CONGREGATION O
1006 GREENE AVENUE.. BROOKLYN NY 11221
B'NAI ISAAC, CONGREGATION O 54 AVENUE O .... BROOKLYN NY 11204 (718) 232-3466
B'NAI ISRAEL JEWISH CENTER 3192 BEDFORD AVENUE .... BROOKLYN NY 11210 (718) 258-2784
B'NAI ISRAEL JEWISH CENTER 357 REMSEN AVENUE .... BROOKLYN NY 11212 (718) 342-4554
B'NAI ISRAEL OF LINDEN HEIGHTS, CONGREGATION O
4502 9TH AVENUE .... BROOKLYN NY 11220
B'NAI ISRAEL OF MIDWOOD, CONGREGATION O 1800 UTICA AVENUE ... BROOKLYN NY 11234 (718) 763-5500
B'NAI ISRAEL OF MIDWOOD, CONGREGATION O 4815 AVENUE I .... BROOKLYN NY 11234 (718) 763-5500
B'NAI ISRAEL, CONGREGATION 859 HENDRIX STREET .... BROOKLYN NY 11207 (718) 649-1144
B'NAI ISRAEL, CONGREGATION 1455 GENEVA LOOP .... BROOKLYN NY 11239 (718) 642-8804
B'NAI ISRAEL, CONGREGATION O 3007 OCEAN AVENUE .... BROOKLYN NY 11235 (718) 332-6231
B'NAI JACOB OF FLATBUSH, CONGREGATION O
3017 GLENWOOD ROAD .... BROOKLYN NY 11210 (718) 434-8855
B'NAI JONAH, CONGREGATION O 858 STANLEY AVENUE .... BROOKLYN NY 11208
B'NAI JOSEF, CONGREGATION O 1616 OCEAN PARKWAY .... BROOKLYN NY 11223 (718) 627-9861
B'NAI TORAH INSTITUTE CONGREGATION O 4722 18TH AVENUE .... BROOKLYN NY 11204
BAIS AVROHAM, CONGREGATION O 1719 AVENUE P................... BROOKLYN NY 11229
BAIS CHASIDIM D'GUR-YAGDIL O 5110 18TH AVENUE .... BROOKLYN NY 11204 (718) 633-6809
BAIS EPHRAIM, CONGREGATION O 2802 AVENUE J .... BROOKLYN NY 11210
BAIS HAMEDRASH AVREICHEI T.V. O 1580 53RD STREET .... BROOKLYN NY 11219 (718) 633-9459
BAIS HAMEDRASH YESHIAS ISRAEL, CONGREGATION O
1315 54TH STREET .... BROOKLYN NY 11219
BAIS HAYOTZER CONGREGATION O 628 BEDFORD AVENUE .... BROOKLYN NY 11211 (718) 852-0619
BAIS ISAAC ZVI O 1019 46TH STREET .... BROOKLYN NY 11219

BAIS YISROEL OF RUGBY, CONGREGATION 1821 OCEAN PARKWAY	BROOKLYN	**NY**	11223	(718) 376-9689
BAITH ISRAEL ANSHEI EMES, CONGREGATION C 236 KANE STREET	BROOKLYN	**NY**	11231	(718) 875-1550
BAY RIDGE JEWISH CENTER - CONGREGATION SHEIRIS ISRAEL C 405-81ST STREET	BROOKLYN	**NY**	11209	(718) 835-3103
BAYONER KLOYS, CONGREGATION O 260 MARCY AVENUE	BROOKLYN	**NY**	11211	
BE'ER MOSHE OF GROSSWARDEIN, CONGREGATION O 4617 10TH AVENUE	BROOKLYN	**NY**	11219	
BEACH HAVEN JEWISH CENTER O 723 AVENUE Z	BROOKLYN	**NY**	11223	(718) 375-5200
BELZ, CONGREGATION O 186 ROSS STREET	BROOKLYN	**NY**	11211	(718) 384-8193
BELZER BETH MEDRASH O 1411 45TH STREET	BROOKLYN	**NY**	11219	(718) 438-2890
BERLINER CONGREGATION KAHAL KENESETH ISRAEL O 1420 OCEAN PARKWAY	BROOKLYN	**NY**	11230	(718) 375-3955
BETH AARON V'ISRAEL CHASIDEI STOLIN, CONGREGATION O 4609 16TH AVENUE	BROOKLYN	**NY**	11204	(718) 438-8190
BETH AARON OF FLATBUSH CONGREGATION O 1670 OCEAN AVENUE	BROOKLYN	**NY**	11230	(718) 338-6064
BETH AARON, CONGREGATION O 2261 BRAGG STREET	BROOKLYN	**NY**	11229	
BETH AARON, CONGREGATION O 18TH AVENUE & 49TH STREET	BROOKLYN	**NY**	11204	(718) 435-2087
BETH ABRAHAM OF FLATBUSH, CONGREGATION 1089 CONEY ISLAND AVENUE	BROOKLYN	**NY**	11230	
BETH ABRAHAM OF FLATLANDS, CONGREGATION O 720 EAST 91ST STREET	BROOKLYN	**NY**	11235	(718) 495-4900
BETH ABRAHAM, CONGREGATION O 2997 OCEAN PARKWAY	BROOKLYN	**NY**	11235	(718) 373-4533
BETH ABRAHAM, TEMPLE C 301 SEA BREEZE AVENUE	BROOKLYN	**NY**	11224	(718) 266-6544
BETH AHARON, CONGREGATION O 649 BEDFORD AVENUE	BROOKLYN	**NY**	11211	
BETH AM CENTER C 1182 BRIGHTON BEACH AVENUE	BROOKLYN	**NY**	11235	(718) 743-4442
BETH AM JEWISH CENTER C 3574 NOSTRAND AVENUE	BROOKLYN	**NY**	11229	(718) 646-5467
BETH DAVID GERSHON TALMUD TORAH O 450 NEW YORK AVENUE	BROOKLYN	**NY**	11225	
BETH DAVID OF CROWN HEIGHTS, CONGREGATION O 442 CROWN STREET	BROOKLYN	**NY**	11225	(718) 774-2699
BETH DAVID, INC., CONGREGATION 802 44TH STREET	BROOKLYN	**NY**	11220	(718) 851-8829
BETH DOVID, CONGREGATION O 1248 49TH STREET	BROOKLYN	**NY**	11219	
BETH EL JEWISH CENTER OF FLATBUSH C 1981 HOMECREST AVENUE	BROOKLYN	**NY**	11229	(718) 375-0120
BETH EL OF BENSONHURST, TEMPLE C 1656 W. 10TH STREET	BROOKLYN	**NY**	11223	(718) 232-0019
BETH EL OF BOROUGH PARK, CONGREGATION O 4802 15TH AVENUE	BROOKLYN	**NY**	11219	(718) 435-9020
BETH EL OF FLATBUSH, CONGREGATION O 2181 E. 3RD STREET	BROOKLYN	**NY**	11223	(718) 336-1926
BETH EL OF MANHATTAN BEACH, TEMPLE C 111 WEST END AVENUE	BROOKLYN	**NY**	11235	(718) 891-3500
BETH ELIYOHU, CONGREGATION 111 RUTLEDGE STREET	BROOKLYN	**NY**	11211	(718) 855-0091
BETH ELOCHIM, CONGREGATION R 8TH AVENUE & GARFIELD PLACE	BROOKLYN	**NY**	11215	(718) 768-3814
BETH EMETH, TEMPLE R 83 MARLBOROUGH ROAD	BROOKLYN	**NY**	11226	(718) 282-1596
BETH GERSHON RABENU, CONGREGATION O 1537 41ST STREET	BROOKLYN	**NY**	11218	
BETH HAMEDRASH OHOLEI TORAH, CONGREGATION O 1267-71 EASTERN PARKWAY	BROOKLYN	**NY**	11213	
BETH HAMEDRASH SHOMREI HADATH BIKUR CHOLIM O 1327 41ST STREET	BROOKLYN	**NY**	11219	
BETH HAMEDROSH HAGODOL OF EAST FLATBUSH, CONGREGATION O 777 SCHENECTADY AVENUE	BROOKLYN	**NY**	11203	
BETH HATALMUD O 2127 82ND STREET	BROOKLYN	**NY**	11214	
BETH ISAAC, CONGREGATION O 1719 AVENUE P	BROOKLYN	**NY**	11229	
BETH ISRAEL V'DAMESEK ELIEZER O 179 TAYLOR STREET	BROOKLYN	**NY**	11211	
BETH ISRAEL OF BORO PARK, CONGREGATION O 5602 11TH AVENUE	BROOKLYN	**NY**	11219	(718) 853-1720
BETH ISRAEL, CONGREGATION 1424 51ST STREET	BROOKLYN	**NY**	11219	(718) 438-9087
BETH JACOB OHEV SHOLOM, CONGREGATION O 284 RODNEY STREET	BROOKLYN	**NY**	11211	(718) 384-8715
BETH JESHAYE, CONGREGATION O 711 EASTERN PARKWAY	BROOKLYN	**NY**	11213	(718) 744-2068
BETH JUDAH, CONGREGATION 1960 SCHENECTADY AVENUE	BROOKLYN	**NY**	11234	(718) 338-3968
BETH MEDRASH CHEMED OF NITRA, CONGREGATION O 2 LEE AVENUE	BROOKLYN	**NY**	11211	(718) 384-9546
BETH MEDRASH GOVOHA MINYAN O 5113 16TH AVENUE	BROOKLYN	**NY**	11204	(718) 853-9209
BETH MEDRASH HAGADOL, THE - MISHKON CHILDREN'S HOME, INC. 1358 56TH STREET	BROOKLYN	**NY**	11219	(718) 438-9384
BETH MOSES, CONGREGATION 124 WEST END AVENUE	BROOKLYN	**NY**	11235	(718) 769-9794
BETH SAMUEL, CONGREGATION O 5216 13TH AVENUE	BROOKLYN	**NY**	11219	(718) 633-5742
BETH SHALOM OF KINGS BAY, CONGREGATION C 2710 AVENUE X	BROOKLYN	**NY**	11235	(718) 891-4500
BETH SHALOM, CONGREGATION O 730 WILLOUGHBY AVENUE	BROOKLYN	**NY**	11206	
BETH SHOLOM PEOPLES TEMPLE R BAY PARKWAY & BENSON AVENUE	BROOKLYN	**NY**	11214	(718) 372-7164
BETH TALMUD TORAH, CONGREGATION O 25 BOERUM STREET, APT. 9R	BROOKLYN	**NY**	11206	
BETH TIKVAH, INC., CONGREGATION O 8800 SEA VIEW AVENUE	BROOKLYN	**NY**	11236	(718) 763-5577
BETH TORAH, CONGREGATION O 1061 OCEAN PARKWAY	BROOKLYN	**NY**	11230	(718) 252-9840
BETH TORAH, CONGREGATION O 3574 NOSTRAND AVENUE	BROOKLYN	**NY**	11229	
BETH YEHUDA, INC., CONGREGATION O 62 KEAP STREET	BROOKLYN	**NY**	11211	(718) 625-8732
BETH-EL TEMPLE 470 LAFAYETTE AVENUE	BROOKLYN	**NY**	11205	
BIKUR CHOLIM ANSHEI LUBASHOW, CONGREGATION O 72 EAST 89TH STREET	BROOKLYN	**NY**	11236	
BIKUR CHOLIM HYMAN JOSEPH, CONGREGATION O 255 PENN STREET	BROOKLYN	**NY**	11211	
BNEI YEHUDAH, CONGREGATION O 5311 16TH AVENUE	BROOKLYN	**NY**	11204	(718) 851-9199
BORO PARK PROGRESSIVE SYNAGOGUE CONGREGATION B'NAI SHOLOM R 1515 46TH STREET	BROOKLYN	**NY**	11219	(718) 436-5082
BOSTONER BETH MEDRASH-NETZACH ISRAEL O 1535 49TH STREET	BROOKLYN	**NY**	11219	(718) 853-6570
BOULEVARD JEWISH CENTER O 1380 LINDEN BLVD	BROOKLYN	**NY**	11212	
BOYANER BETH MEDRASH O 4405 14TH AVENUE	BROOKLYN	**NY**	11219	
BROOKLYN HEIGHTS SYNAGOGUE R 117 REMSEN STREET	BROOKLYN	**NY**	11201	(718) 522-2070
BROOKLYN JEWISH CENTER, THE C 667 EASTERN PARKWAY	BROOKLYN	**NY**	11213	(718) 493-8800
CANARSIE JEWISH CENTER 965 E. 107TH STREET	BROOKLYN	**NY**	11236	(718) 272-2484
CHAMDATH TORAH V'CHESSED, CONGREGATION O 1640 50TH STREET	BROOKLYN	**NY**	11204	
CHASIDEI BELZ OF BOROUGH PARK, CONGREGATION O 4814 16TH AVENUE	BROOKLYN	**NY**	11204	(718) 851-5345
CHASIDEI BELZ, CONGREGATION O 662 EASTERN PARKWAY	BROOKLYN	**NY**	11213	(718) 773-8561
CHASIDEI BELZ, CONGREGATION O 4814 16TH AVENUE	BROOKLYN	**NY**	11204	(718) 851-9890
CHASIDEI GUR, CONGREGATION 5104 18TH AVENUE	BROOKLYN	**NY**	11204	(718) 438-8818
CHASIDEI GUR, CONGREGATION O 1317 49TH STREET	BROOKLYN	**NY**	11219	(718) 438-8199
CHEISHEK SHLOMO OF YOKA, CONGREGATION O 1243 55TH STREET	BROOKLYN	**NY**	11219	(718) 853-0070
CHEVRA AHAVATH ACHIM ANSHEI SFARD, CONGREGATION O 489 EMPIRE BLVD	BROOKLYN	**NY**	11225	
CHEVRA B'NEI ISRAEL OF BORO PARK, CONGREGATION O 4304 15TH AVENUE	BROOKLYN	**NY**	11219	
CHEVRA BIKUR CHOLIM O 2953 WEST 31ST STREET	BROOKLYN	**NY**	11224	
CHEVRA GEMILUTH CHESED, CONGREGATION 771 MCDONALD AVENUE	BROOKLYN	**NY**	11218	(718) 435-4218
CHEVRA SHAAS & MISHNAYOTH OF FLATBUSH, CONGREGATION O 1706 MCDONALD AVENUE	BROOKLYN	**NY**	11230	
CHEVRA SHOMREI EMUNEI ANSHE LOMZA O 474 E. 96TH STREET	BROOKLYN	**NY**	11212	(718) 343-8401
CHEVRA SHOMREI SHABBOS 4404 14TH AVENUE	BROOKLYN	**NY**	11219	(718) 871-8118
CHEVRA THILIM OHEL MOSHE LUBAVITCH, CONGREGATION O 841 OCEAN PARKWAY	BROOKLYN	**NY**	11230	(718) 859-7600
CHEVRA TORAH ANSHE CHESED V'ANSHEI RADISHKOW O 731 MONTAUK STREET	BROOKLYN	**NY**	11235	(718) 934-8116
CHOVEVEI TORAH, CONGREGATION O 329 KINGSTON AVENUE	BROOKLYN	**NY**	11213	
COMMUNITY TEMPLE BETH OHR R 1010 OCEAN AVENUE	BROOKLYN	**NY**	11226	(718) 284-5760
CONGREGATION CHASIDEI RADOMSK O 14 AVENUE & 42 STREET	BROOKLYN	**NY**	11219	
CONGREGATION KEREN ORAH O 592 DITMAS AVENUE	BROOKLYN	**NY**	11218	(212) 436-5715
CONGREGATION YEREIM OF SEA GATE, INC. 3868 POPLAR AVENUE	BROOKLYN	**NY**	11224	(718) 372-9385
CONGREGATION YETEV LEV BIKUR CHOLIM 152 RODNEY STREET	BROOKLYN	**NY**	11211	(718) 387-0546
CROWN HEIGHTS OF ISRAEL 310 CROWN STREET	BROOKLYN	**NY**	11225	(718) 773-6520
CROWN OF ISRAEL TALMUD TORAH O 1769 56TH STREET	BROOKLYN	**NY**	11204	(718) 232-4827
EAST FLATBUSH JEWISH COMMUNITY CENTER O 661 LINDEN BLVD	BROOKLYN	**NY**	11203	
EAST MIDWOOD JEWISH CENTER C 1625 OCEAN AVENUE	BROOKLYN	**NY**	11230	(718) 338-3800
EAST NEW YORK JEWISH CENTER O 965 EAST 107TH STREET	BROOKLYN	**NY**	11236	
EIGHTEENTH AVENUE JEWISH CENTER 3714 18TH AVENUE	BROOKLYN	**NY**	11218	(718) 438-9131
ELIEZER OF EAST NEW YORK, CONGREGATION O 133 HINSDALE STREET	BROOKLYN	**NY**	11207	
EMANU-EL OF BORO PARK, TEMPLE C 1362 49TH STREET	BROOKLYN	**NY**	11219	(718) 871-4200
EMANU-EL OF CANARSIE, TEMPLE R 1880 ROCKAWAY PARKWAY	BROOKLYN	**NY**	11236	(718) 251-0450
EMUNAS YISROEL, CONGREGATION O 4420 14TH AVENUE	BROOKLYN	**NY**	11219	(718) 853-9249
ETZ CHAIM OF BORO PARK, CONGREGATION O 5000 13TH AVENUE	BROOKLYN	**NY**	11219	
ETZ CHAIM OF FLATBUSH, CONGREGATION O 1649 E. 13TH STREET	BROOKLYN	**NY**	11229	(718) 339-4886
FIRST CONGREGATION ANSHE SFARD OF BOROUGH PARK O 4502 14TH AVENUE	BROOKLYN	**NY**	11219	(718) 436-2691
FLATBUSH & SHAARE TORAH JEWISH CENTER C 500 CHURCH AVENUE	BROOKLYN	**NY**	11218	(718) 871-5200
FLATBUSH JEWISH CENTER 222 OCEAN PARKWAY	BROOKLYN	**NY**	11218	
FLATBUSH PARK JEWISH CENTER O 6363 AVENUE U	BROOKLYN	**NY**	11234	
FOREST PARK JEWISH CENTER O 90-45 MYRTLE AVENUE	BROOKLYN	**NY**	11227	(718) 847-6273
GLENWOOD JEWISH CENTER O 888 EAST 56TH STREET	BROOKLYN	**NY**	11234	(718) 251-5335
GVODZITZ-SADAGURA BETH MEDRASH O 1254 49TH STREET	BROOKLYN	**NY**	11219	(718) 854-2075
HAYM SALOMON COMMUNITY CONGREGATION O 2300 CROPSEY AVENUE	BROOKLYN	**NY**	11214	(718) 373-1700
HAYOSHOR V'HATOV, CONGREGATION O 1345 46TH STREET	BROOKLYN	**NY**	11219	
HEBREW ALLIANCE OF BRIGHTON BY THE SEA O 2915 BRIGHTON 6 STREET	BROOKLYN	**NY**	11235	
HILLEL OF FLATLANDS, TEMPLE C 2164 RALPH AVENUE	BROOKLYN	**NY**	11234	(718) 763-2400
ISRAEL CENTER OF CANARSIE O 1234 EAST 87TH STREET	BROOKLYN	**NY**	11236	(718) 251-9891
ISRAEL OF KINGS BAY, CONGREGATION O 3903 NOSTRAND AVENUE	BROOKLYN	**NY**	11235	(718) 934-5176
JEWISH CENTER NACHLATH ZION O 2201 EAST 23RD STREET	BROOKLYN	**NY**	11229	(718) 648-4865
JEWISH CENTER OF BRIGHTON BEACH O 2915 OCEAN PARKWAY	BROOKLYN	**NY**	11235	(718) 769-7400
JEWISH CENTER OF FORT GREENE O 209 CLERMONT AVENUE	BROOKLYN	**NY**	11205	
JEWISH CENTER OF HYDE PARK O 779 EAST 49TH STREET	BROOKLYN	**NY**	11203	(718) 629-1040
JEWISH CENTER OF KINGS HIGHWAY C 1202 AVENUE P	BROOKLYN	**NY**	11229	(718) 645-9000
JEWISH CENTER OF MAPLETON PARK, CONG. BETH HAMEDRASH HAGODOL 1477 W. 8TH STREET	BROOKLYN	**NY**	11204	(718) 837-8875
JEWISH COMMUNAL CENTER OF FLATBUSH C 1302 AVENUE I	BROOKLYN	**NY**	11230	(718) 258-2411
JEWISH COMMUNITY CENTRE OF BENSONHURST O 6222 23RD AVENUE	BROOKLYN	**NY**	11204	(718) 236-4767
JEWISH FRIENDS CONGREGATION 1410 CONEY ISLAND AVENUE	BROOKLYN	**NY**	11230	(718) 253-0974
JEWISH RECONSTRUCTIONIST SOCIETY RE 2701 NECK ROAD	BROOKLYN	**NY**	11229	(718) 332-5700
JUDEA CENTER SYNAGOGUE O 2059 BEDFORD AVENUE	BROOKLYN	**NY**	11226	
K'HAL CHASSIDIM, CONGREGATION O 4820 15TH AVENUE	BROOKLYN	**NY**	11219	(718) 871-0110
K'HAL YESODEL HATORAH O 4918 16TH AVENUE	BROOKLYN	**NY**	11204	(718) 851-5193
K'HALL BNEI EMUNIM, CONGREGATION O 215 HEWES STREET	BROOKLYN	**NY**	11211	
KAHAL ADATH KRASA, CONGREGATION O 1654 43RD STREET	BROOKLYN	**NY**	11204	(718) 438-8880
KAHAL ADATH YEREYIM O 672 LEFFERTS AVENUE	BROOKLYN	**NY**	11203	
KAHAL YERAIM OF BOROUGH PARK, CONGREGATION O 1184 53RD STREET	BROOKLYN	**NY**	11219	(718) 438-9499
KAHAL YESODE HATORAH, CONGREGATION O 4914 16TH AVENUE	BROOKLYN	**NY**	11204	(718) 851-9858
KAPITSHNITZER KLOIZ, CONGREGATION O 1415 55TH STREET	BROOKLYN	**NY**	11219	
KAV CHAIM, CONGREGATION O 1642 54TH STREET	BROOKLYN	**NY**	11204	(718) 851-7442
KEHAL RAATZFERT, CONGREGATION O 182 DIVISION AVENUE	BROOKLYN	**NY**	11211	(718) 387-2217
KEHILATH KODESH D'KOHANIM O 2879 WEST 12TH STREET	BROOKLYN	**NY**	11224	(718) 372-5280
KEHILATH YAKOV, CONGREGATION O 1137 53RD STREET	BROOKLYN	**NY**	11219	(718) 871-0149
KEHILATH YAKOV, CONGREGATION O 654 BEDFORD AVENUE	BROOKLYN	**NY**	11211	
KESSER ISRAEL, CONGREGATION O 1769 56TH STREET	BROOKLYN	**NY**	11204	
KESSER TORAH, CONGREGATION O 2310 CORTELYOU ROAD	BROOKLYN	**NY**	11226	(718) 282-3958
KHAL ADAS YISROEL, CONGREGATION 4712 14TH AVENUE	BROOKLYN	**NY**	11219	(718) 633-2305
KHAL CHASIDEI SKWERE, CONGREGATION O 1334 47TH STREET	BROOKLYN	**NY**	11219	
KHAL CHASIDIM OF BROOKLYN, CONGREGATION O 4820 15TH AVENUE	BROOKLYN	**NY**	11219	(718) 871-0110
KHAL TORATH CHAIM, CONGREGATION O 6 LEE AVENUE	BROOKLYN	**NY**	11211	
KHAL UNGVAR, CONGREGATION O 5305 16TH AVENUE	BROOKLYN	**NY**	11204	(718) 252-0005

KHALL MACHNEKA HADAS O 1631 50TH STREET	BROOKLYN	**NY**	11204	
KINGSWAY JEWISH CENTER O 2810 NOSTRAND AVENUE	BROOKLYN	**NY**	11229	(718) 258-3344
KLAUZENBERG B.M. CHATZOR HAKODESH O 1420 50TH STREET	BROOKLYN	**NY**	11219	(718) 435-2626
KNESES ISRAEL OF SEAGATE, CONGREGATION O 3803 NAUTILUS AVENUE	BROOKLYN	**NY**	11224	(718) 372-1668
KNESETH ISRAEL KLAUS, CONGREGATION O 95 DIVISION AVENUE	BROOKLYN	**NY**	11211	
KNESSET HORABONIM, CONGREGATION O 701 48TH STREET	BROOKLYN	**NY**	11220	(718) 633-6378
KOL ISRAEL CONGREGATION 3211 BEDFORD AVENUE	BROOKLYN	**NY**	11210	
KOL ISRAEL, CONGREGATION O 603 ST. JOHNS PLACE	BROOKLYN	**NY**	11238	(718) 638-6583
KOLEL BNEI YAAKOV O 1546 47TH STREET	BROOKLYN	**NY**	11219	
KOLEL TIFERETH MENACHEM O 241 MARCY AVENUE	BROOKLYN	**NY**	11211	
KOLLEL TIFERETH ZVI, CONGREGATION O 4122 14TH AVENUE	BROOKLYN	**NY**	11219	
KRULER MIKVA, CONGREGATION O 5102 11TH AVENUE	BROOKLYN	**NY**	11219	
LANZUT, CONGREGATION OF O 159 RODNEY STREET	BROOKLYN	**NY**	11211	(718) 384-3132
LOMDAI TORAH, CONGREGATION O 2209 63RD STREET	BROOKLYN	**NY**	11204	
MACHNAH LOMDAI TORAH O 239 HAVEMEYER STREET	BROOKLYN	**NY**	11211	
MACHNE ISRAEL, CONGREGATION O 2413 EAST 23RD STREET	BROOKLYN	**NY**	11235	(718) 332-8788
MACHNE ISRAEL, INC. O 770 EASTERN PARKWAY	BROOKLYN	**NY**	11213	(718) 493-9250
MACHNE TORAH O 1375 57TH STREET	BROOKLYN	**NY**	11219	
MACHZIKEI HADAS, CONGREGATION O 150 OCEAN PARKWAY	BROOKLYN	**NY**	11218	
MACHZIKEI HADAS, CONGREGATION O 1636 49TH STREET	BROOKLYN	**NY**	11204	(718) 871-5986
MACHZIKEI TALMUD TORAH, CONGREGATION O 4622 14TH AVENUE	BROOKLYN	**NY**	11219	
MACHZIKEI TORAH, CONGREGATION O 1016 BEVERLY ROAD	BROOKLYN	**NY**	11218	
MADISON JEWISH CENTER C 2989 NOSTRAND AVENUE	BROOKLYN	**NY**	11229	(718) 375-2271
MAGEN DAVID CONGREGATION O P.O. BOX 78, PARKVILLE STATION	BROOKLYN	**NY**	11204	(718) 236-6122
MAGEN DAVID OF OCEAN PARKWAY, CONGREGATION O 1616 OCEAN PARKWAY	BROOKLYN	**NY**	11233	
MANHATTAN BEACH JEWISH CENTER O 60 WEST END AVENUE	BROOKLYN	**NY**	11235	(718) 891-8700
MAPLETON PARK HEBREW INSTITUTE O 2022 66TH STREET	BROOKLYN	**NY**	11204	(718) 236-5551
MARINE PARK JEWISH CENTER O 3311 AVENUE S	BROOKLYN	**NY**	11234	(718) 376-5200
MARLBORO JEWISH CENTER O 2324 WEST 13TH STREET	BROOKLYN	**NY**	11223	(718) 996-5558
MEAH SHEARIM, CONGREGATION O 1061 OCEAN PARKWAY	BROOKLYN	**NY**	11230	
MENORAH SYNAGOGUE OF MENORAH HOME & HOSPITAL O 871 BUSHWICK AVENUE	BROOKLYN	**NY**	11221	(718) 443-3000
MENUCHAT USHER, CONGREGATION O 582 MONTGOMERY STREET	BROOKLYN	**NY**	11225	
MESIFTA HEICHAL HAKODESH 851 47TH STREET	BROOKLYN	**NY**	11220	(718) 438-9097
MESIVTA BAIS YISROEL (GUR) O 5407 16TH AVENUE	BROOKLYN	**NY**	11204	(718) 633-2472
MIFAL TORAH VODAATH, CONGREGATION O 4116 16TH AVENUE	BROOKLYN	**NY**	11204	(718) 438-2206
MIKVAH ISRAEL OF BORO PARK, CONGREGATION O 1351 46TH STREET	BROOKLYN	**NY**	11219	
MINCHAS ELUZER MINKATSCH, CONGREGATION O 1377 42ND STREET	BROOKLYN	**NY**	11219	
MINYAN MIR O 5401 16TH AVENUE	BROOKLYN	**NY**	11204	(718) 438-9173
MINYAN SFARD OF BORO PARK, CONGREGATION O 803 46TH STREET	BROOKLYN	**NY**	11220	
MIRRER YESHIVA SYNAGOGUE O 1791 OCEAN PARKWAY	BROOKLYN	**NY**	11223	(718) 645-0536
MIZRACHI HAPOEL HAMIZRACHI, CONGREGATION O 378 KINGSTON AVENUE	BROOKLYN	**NY**	11225	
MOUNT SINAI, CONGREGATION C 305 SCHERMERHORN STREET	BROOKLYN	**NY**	11217	(718) 875-9124
NACHLAS ISRAEL, CONGREGATION O 745 CROWN STREET	BROOKLYN	**NY**	11213	(718) 756-4593
NEW BRIGHTON JEWISH CENTER O 184 BRIGHTON 11 STREET	BROOKLYN	**NY**	11235	(718) 332-9689
NEW LOTS, CONGREGATION O 4320 16TH AVENUE	BROOKLYN	**NY**	11204	
NOVOMINSKER BETH MEDRASH O 1569 47TH STREET	BROOKLYN	**NY**	11204	(718) 633-4861
OCEAN AVENUE JEWISH CENTER-CONGREGATION PRI ETZ CHAIM O 2600 OCEAN AVENUE	BROOKLYN	**NY**	11229	(718) 743-5533
OCEAN AVENUE SYNAGOGUE O 1057 EAST 28TH STREET	BROOKLYN	**NY**	11210	
OCEAN PARKWAY JEWISH CENTER C 550 OCEAN PARKWAY	BROOKLYN	**NY**	11218	(718) 436-4900
OCEANVIEW JEWISH CENTER 3100 BRIGHTON STREET	BROOKLYN	**NY**	11235	(718) 646-9639
OHEL AVROHOM, CONGREGATION O 4907 18TH AVENUE	BROOKLYN	**NY**	11204	
OHEL ELIMELECH, CONGREGATION O 5120 FT. HAMILTON PARKWAY	BROOKLYN	**NY**	11219	(718) 871-5226
OHEL SHALOM, CONGREGATION OF O 4419 12TH AVENUE	BROOKLYN	**NY**	11219	(718) 854-7240
OHELEY SHEM, CONGREGATION O 5206 12TH AVENUE	BROOKLYN	**NY**	11219	
OHEV SHEM YESHIVA CONGREGATION 5206 12TH AVENUE	BROOKLYN	**NY**	11219	(718) 435-1639
OHEV SHOLOM ANSHEI MARMOROSH, CONGREGATION O 1266 47TH STREET	BROOKLYN	**NY**	11219	
OHR TORAH, CONGREGATION O 1520 48TH STREET	BROOKLYN	**NY**	11219	
PARK SLOPE JEWISH CENTER O 8TH AVENUE & 14TH STREET	BROOKLYN	**NY**	11215	(718) 508-4153
PETACH TIKVAH, CONGREGATION O 971 E. 10TH STREET	BROOKLYN	**NY**	11230	
POALEI AGUDATH ISRAEL O 4820 16TH AVENUE	BROOKLYN	**NY**	11204	(718) 436-6556
PORTUGAL CRETIENBERGER, CONGREGATION O 4924 16TH AVENUE	BROOKLYN	**NY**	11204	
PRIDE OF ISRAEL ANSHE BRISK, CONGREGATION O 274 KEAP STREET	BROOKLYN	**NY**	11211	(718) 384-6283
PROGRESSIVE SHAARI ZEDEK SYNAGOGUE R 1395 OCEAN AVENUE	BROOKLYN	**NY**	11230	(718) 377-1818
PROSPECT PARK TEMPLE ISAAC 1419 DORCHESTER ROAD	BROOKLYN	**NY**	11226	(718) 248-8032
RABBI ARIA LEIB TEITELBAUM - AITZ CHAIM CONGREGATION O 4822 11TH AVENUE	BROOKLYN	**NY**	11219	
RABBI HOROWITZ, CONGREGATION O 1706 47TH STREET	BROOKLYN	**NY**	11204	
RABBI MOSHE BICK, CONGREGATION O 1545 55TH STREET	BROOKLYN	**NY**	11219	
RACHMISTRIVKER BETH MEDRASH O 1223 45TH STREET	BROOKLYN	**NY**	11219	(718) 435-7802
REFUGEES DEB'AY D'MIZRACH EUROPE, CONGREGATION O 711 EASTERN PARKWAY	BROOKLYN	**NY**	11213	
REMSEN HEIGHTS JEWISH CENTER C 115 E. 87TH STREET	BROOKLYN	**NY**	11236	(718) 763-2244
RODFEH ZEDEK, CONGREGATION 2080 77TH STREET	BROOKLYN	**NY**	11214	
ROZENOYER ADAS KODEISHEM, CONGREGATION 1510 OCEAN PARKWAY	BROOKLYN	**NY**	11230	(718) 336-1195
SANZ KLAUZENBURG, CONGREGATION 1420 50TH STREET	BROOKLYN	**NY**	11219	(718) 438-9611
SARATOGA JEWISH CENTER & TALMUD TORAH O 163 PARKVILLE AVENUE	BROOKLYN	**NY**	11230	
SEA BREEZE JEWISH CENTER O 311 SEA BREEZE AVENUE	BROOKLYN	**NY**	11224	(718) 372-9749
SEAVIEW JEWISH CENTER O 1440 EAST 99TH STREET	BROOKLYN	**NY**	11236	(718) 251-1900
SEFARD ANSHEI POLEN, CONGREGATION O 216 KEAP STREET	BROOKLYN	**NY**	11211	
SEFAS EMES, CONGREGATION O 1337 42ND STREET	BROOKLYN	**NY**	11219	(718) 853-5371
SEPHARDIC CENTER OF MAPLETON O 7216 BAY PARKWAY	BROOKLYN	**NY**	11204	
SEPHARDIC INSTITUTE O 511 AVENUE R	BROOKLYN	**NY**	11223	(718) 998-8171
SHAARE EMETH ANNEX, TEMPLE 6012 FARRAGUT ROAD	BROOKLYN	**NY**	11226	(718) 444-9519
SHAARE EMETH, CONGREGATION C 6012 FARRAGUT ROAD	BROOKLYN	**NY**	11236	(718) 444-3223
SHAARE TEFILO OF KINGS HIGHWAY O 1679 WEST 1ST STREET	BROOKLYN	**NY**	11223	(718) 375-3095
SHAARE TORAH OF FLATBUSH, CONGREGATION C 305 EAST 21ST STREET	BROOKLYN	**NY**	11226	(718) 496-5300
SHAARE TORAH, CONGREGATION O 1061 OCEAN PARKWAY	BROOKLYN	**NY**	11230	
SHAARE ZION CONGREGATION O 2030 OCEAN PARKWAY	BROOKLYN	**NY**	11223	(718) 376-0009
SHAARI ISRAEL, CONGREGATION C 810 E. 49TH STREET	BROOKLYN	**NY**	11203	(718) 629-0476
SHAREI ZEDEK, CONGREGATION O 3701 SURF AVENUE	BROOKLYN	**NY**	11224	
SHAREI ZEDEK-SEA GATE SISTERHOOD & T.T.O 2301 MERMAID AVENUE	BROOKLYN	**NY**	11224	(718) 372-2731
SHAREI ZION, CONGREGATION O 1533 48TH STREET	BROOKLYN	**NY**	11219	
SHELLBANK JEWISH CENTER C 2121 BRAGG STREET	BROOKLYN	**NY**	11229	(718) 891-8666
SHEVES ACHIM, CONGREGATION O 1184 EAST 14TH STREET	BROOKLYN	**NY**	11230	(718) 252-1998
SHOLOM OF FLATBUSH, TEMPLE C 2075 E. 68TH STREET	BROOKLYN	**NY**	11234	(718) 251-0370
SHOMREI EMUNAH, CONGREGATION O 5202 14TH AVENUE	BROOKLYN	**NY**	11219	(718) 851-8586
SHOMREI HADATH OF BORO PARK, CONGREGATION O 1327 41ST STREET	BROOKLYN	**NY**	11218	(718) 438-0066
SHOMREI SHABOS ANSHEI SFARD, CONGREGATION O 1280 53RD STREET	BROOKLYN	**NY**	11219	
SHORE PARK JEWISH CENTER C 2959 AVENUE Y	BROOKLYN	**NY**	11235	(718) 648-2900
SHORE PARKWAY JEWISH CENTER C 8885 26TH AVENUE	BROOKLYN	**NY**	11214	(718) 449-6530
SHOTZER SASSOWER CONGREGATION O 143 RODNEY STREET	BROOKLYN	**NY**	11211	
SINAI OF BROOKLYN, TEMPLE C 24 ARLINGTON AVENUE	BROOKLYN	**NY**	11207	(718) 827-8695
SKVARER BETH MEDRASH O 12TH AVENUE & 54TH STREET	BROOKLYN	**NY**	11219	
SONS OF JUDAH, CONGREGATION O 5311 16TH AVENUE	BROOKLYN	**NY**	11204	(718) 851-9828
TABERNACLE BETH EL 85 FOUNTAIN AVENUE	BROOKLYN	**NY**	11208	(718) 277-8035
TALMUD TORAH AHAVATH ACHIM, CONGREGATION O 1750 E. 4TH STREET	BROOKLYN	**NY**	11223	(718) 375-3895
TALMUD TORAH BETH JUDAH COMMUNITY CENTER O 1960 SCHENECTADY AVENUE	BROOKLYN	**NY**	11234	
TALMUD TORAH OHEV SHALOM, CONGREGATION O 1387 E. 96TH STREET	BROOKLYN	**NY**	11236	(718) 251-1430
TALMUD TORAH SONS OF ISRAEL, CONGREGATION O 2115 BENSON AVENUE	BROOKLYN	**NY**	11214	(718) 372-4830
TALMUD TORAH TIFERES BUNIM O 1377 42ND STREET	BROOKLYN	**NY**	11219	(718) 436-6868
TALMUD TORAH TIFERETH ELCHANAN O 5311 16TH AVENUE	BROOKLYN	**NY**	11204	(718) 851-9828
TALMUD TORAH TIFERETH ISRAEL O 1915 WEST 7TH STREET	BROOKLYN	**NY**	11223	(718) 339-1927
TALMUD TORAH TOLDOIS YAAKOV YOSEF O 105 HEYWARD	BROOKLYN	**NY**	11206	(718) 852-0502
TALMUD TORAH TOMCHAI TORAH O 1320 SUTTER AVENUE	BROOKLYN	**NY**	11208	
TALMUD TORAH TOMCHAI TORAH O 8807 AVENUE A	BROOKLYN	**NY**	11236	
TALMUD TORAH ZICHRON MENACHEM LEVI, CONGREGATION O 1424 58TH STREET	BROOKLYN	**NY**	11219	
TALMUD TORAH OF FLATBUSH O 1305 CONEY ISLAND AVENUE	BROOKLYN	**NY**	11230	(718) 377-2528
TALMUD TORAH, CONGREGATION O 64 TEHAMA STREET	BROOKLYN	**NY**	11218	
TEFERETH TZVI, CONGREGATION O 2174 85TH STREET	BROOKLYN	**NY**	11214	(718) 266-3878
TELSHE ALUMNI BAIS HAMEDRASH, INC. O 5218 16TH AVENUE	BROOKLYN	**NY**	11204	(718) 438-8937
TIFERETH ISRAEL OF BENSONHURST, CONGREGATION O 1835 BAY RIDGE PARKWAY	BROOKLYN	**NY**	11204	(718) 236-8283
TIFERETH ISRAEL OF MAPLETON PARK, CONGREGATION O 2025 64TH STREET	BROOKLYN	**NY**	11204	
TIFERETH ISRAEL OF WILLIAMSBURG, CONGREGATION O 491 BEDFORD AVENUE	BROOKLYN	**NY**	11211	(718) 384-8145
TIFERETH ISRAEL, CONGREGATION O 2025 64TH STREET	BROOKLYN	**NY**	11204	(718) 236-9884
TIFERETH TORAH OF BENSONHURST, CONGREGATION O 23 AVENUE & 83RD STREET	BROOKLYN	**NY**	11214	(718) 236-6646
TIFERETH YEHUDAH, CONGREGATION O 347 EAST 49TH STREET	BROOKLYN	**NY**	11203	
TOLDAS YAKOV, CONGREGATION O 551 BEDFORD AVENUE	BROOKLYN	**NY**	11211	
TOLDOS YAKOV YOSEF 5323 12TH AVENUE	BROOKLYN	**NY**	11219	(718) 438-8312
TORAH ISRAEL, TEMPLE O 60 BRIGHTON 11 STREET	BROOKLYN	**NY**	11235	
TORAH TEMIMAH, CONGREGATION O 1575 50TH STREET	BROOKLYN	**NY**	11219	
TORAS CHAIM VIZNITZ, CONGREGATION O 5228 NEW UTRECHT AVENUE	BROOKLYN	**NY**	11219	(718) 853-6010
TORAS EMES SYNAGOGUE O 1650 56TH STREET	BROOKLYN	**NY**	11204	
TORAS YISROEL, CONGREGATION O 5311 NEW UTRECHT AVENUE	BROOKLYN	**NY**	11219	
TORATH MOSHE JEWISH CENTER O 4314 10TH AVENUE	BROOKLYN	**NY**	11219	(718) 438-9578
UNION TEMPLE R 17 EASTERN PARKWAY	BROOKLYN	**NY**	11238	(718) 638-7600
WALLERSTEIN INSTITUTE 750 REMSEN AVENUE	BROOKLYN	**NY**	11236	
WALTON AVENUE SYNAGOGUE O 1486 OCEAN PARKWAY	BROOKLYN	**NY**	11230	(718) 627-3777
YAGDIL TORAH, CONGREGATION O 5110 18TH AVENUE	BROOKLYN	**NY**	11204	
YESHIVA ATERES YISROEL O 8101 AVENUE K	BROOKLYN	**NY**	11236	(718) 763-6777
YESHIVA BETH SHEARIM CONGREGATION O 5306 16TH AVENUE	BROOKLYN	**NY**	11204	(718) 851-9809
YESHIVA BIRKAS REUVEN O 4911 16TH AVENUE	BROOKLYN	**NY**	11204	(718) 998-3201
YESHIVA LEV SOMEACH, INC., CONGREGATION O 674 E. 2ND STREET	BROOKLYN	**NY**	11218	(718) 438-4800
YESHIVA RABBI DAVID LEIBOWITZ, SYNAGOGUE OF O 9102 CHURCH AVENUE	BROOKLYN	**NY**	11236	
YESHIVA RABBI MEYER SIMCHE HACOHEN, CONGREGATION O 289 EAST 53RD STREET	BROOKLYN	**NY**	11203	(718) 385-7100
YESHIVA YESHURIN OF FLATBUSH, CONGREGATION 1454 OCEAN PARKWAY	BROOKLYN	**NY**	11230	(718) 375-9292
YESHIVAT ERETZ ISRAEL CONGREGATION O 1666 EAST 7TH STREET	BROOKLYN	**NY**	11230	
YESHIVATH YAVNE, CONGREGATION O 510 DAHILL ROAD	BROOKLYN	**NY**	11218	
YESHURIN-ADAS ISRAEL, CONGREGATION O 1454 OCEAN PARKWAY	BROOKLYN	**NY**	11230	(718) 375-9292
YETEV LEV, CONGREGATION 4507 10TH AVENUE	BROOKLYN	**NY**	11219	(718) 438-8144
YETEV LEV, CONGREGATION O 4514 15TH AVENUE	BROOKLYN	**NY**	11219	(718) 438-9638
YOUNG ISRAEL OF AVENUE J 1721 AVENUE J	BROOKLYN	**NY**	11230	(718) 338-2056
YOUNG ISRAEL OF AVENUE K 2818 AVENUE K	BROOKLYN	**NY**	11210	(718) 258-6666
YOUNG ISRAEL OF AVENUE U 2119 HOMECREST AVENUE	BROOKLYN	**NY**	11229	(718) 375-6942
YOUNG ISRAEL OF BEDFORD BAY 2114 BROWN STREET	BROOKLYN	**NY**	11229	(718) 332-4120

YOUNG ISRAEL OF BENSONHURST 48 BAY 28TH STREET	BROOKLYN	NY	11214	(718) 372-5610
YOUNG ISRAEL OF BORO PARK 1349 50TH STREET	BROOKLYN	NY	11219	(718) 438-1464
YOUNG ISRAEL OF BRIGHTON BEACH 293 NEPTUNE AVENUE	BROOKLYN	NY	11235	(718) 332-7000
YOUNG ISRAEL OF BROOKLYN 563 BEDFORD AVENUE	BROOKLYN	NY	11211	(718) 384-0461
YOUNG ISRAEL OF CANARSIE 1265 EAST 108TH STREET	BROOKLYN	NY	11236	(718) 251-2600
YOUNG ISRAEL OF CONEY ISLAND 2801 SURF AVENUE	BROOKLYN	NY	11224	(718) 449-1949
YOUNG ISRAEL OF EAST FLATBUSH 66 EAST 89TH STREET	BROOKLYN	NY	11236	(718) 495-2600
YOUNG ISRAEL OF EASTERN PARKWAY 937 EASTERN PARKWAY	BROOKLYN	NY	11213	(718) 774-6555
YOUNG ISRAEL OF FLATBUSH 1012 AVENUE I	BROOKLYN	NY	11230	(718) 377-4400
YOUNG ISRAEL OF KENSINGTON 305 CHURCH AVENUE	BROOKLYN	NY	11218	(718) 871-4543
YOUNG ISRAEL OF MAPLETON PARK 1400 WEST 6TH STREET	BROOKLYN	NY	11204	(718) 256-1060
YOUNG ISRAEL OF MIDWOOD 1694 OCEAN AVENUE	BROOKLYN	NY	11230	(718) 253-6266
YOUNG ISRAEL OF MILL BASIN 2082 EAST 58TH STREET	BROOKLYN	NY	11234	(718) 253-1016
YOUNG ISRAEL OF OCEAN PARKWAY 1781 OCEAN PARKWAY	BROOKLYN	NY	11223	(718) 376-6305
YOUNG ISRAEL OF PROSPECT PARK 2170 BEDFORD AVENUE	BROOKLYN	NY	11226	(718) 287-9432
YOUNG ISRAEL OF REDWOOD 619-621 E. 76TH STREET	BROOKLYN	NY	11236	(718) 763-8040
YOUNG ISRAEL OF REMSEN 9302 AVENUE B	BROOKLYN	NY	11236	(718) 345-7810
YOUNG ISRAEL OF SHEEPSHEAD BAY 2546 EAST 7TH STREET	BROOKLYN	NY	11235	(718) 891-6767
YOUNG ISRAEL OF VANDERVEER PARK 2811-15 FARRAGUT ROAD	BROOKLYN	NY	11210	(718) 434-2910
ZEMACH DAVID CHASIDEI SQUARE, CONGREGATION O 571 BEDFORD AVENUE	BROOKLYN	NY	11211	
ZIV YISROEL D'GUR, CONGREGATION O 4904 16TH AVENUE	BROOKLYN	NY	11204	(718) 436-8515
ZVI LEZADIK (BLUSHEV), CONGREGATION O 1431 58TH STREET	BROOKLYN	NY	11219	(718) 851-1361
AHAVAS ACHIM LUBAVITZ SYNAGOGUE O 345 TACOMA AVENUE	BUFFALO	NY	14216	(716) 877-5790
AMHERST SYNAGOGUE, THE O 504 FRANKHAUSER ROAD	BUFFALO	NY	14221	(716) 634-5255
BETH ABRAHAM, CONGREGATION O 1073 ELMWOOD AVENUE	BUFFALO	NY	14222	
BETH AM TEMPLE R 4660 SHERIDAN DRIVE	BUFFALO	NY	14221	(716) 633-8877
BETH EL OF GREATER BUFFALO, TEMPLE C 2368 EGGERT ROAD	BUFFALO	NY	14150	(716) 836-3762
BETH ZION TEMPLE R 805 DELAWARE AVENUE	BUFFALO	NY	14209	(716) 886-7150
BRITH ISRAEL ANSHE EMES, CONGREGATION O 1237 HERTEL AVENUE	BUFFALO	NY	14126	(716) 877-4601
BRITH SHOLEM, CONGREGATION O 787 DELAWARE AVENUE	BUFFALO	NY	14209	(716) 885-7848
CHAVURAH CONGREGATION R 11 HUXLEY DRIVE	BUFFALO	NY	14226	
SHAAREY ZEDEK, TEMPLE C 621 GETZVILLE ROAD	BUFFALO	NY	14226	(716) 838-3232
SINAI, TEMPLE R 50 ALBERTA DRIVE	BUFFALO	NY	14226	(716) 834-0708
ISRAEL, TEMPLE R SPRING STREET	CATSKILL	NY	12414	(518) 943-5758
BETH EL, TEMPLE C BROADWAY & LOCUST AVENUE	CEDARHURST	NY	11516	(516) 569-2700
SEPHARDIC TEMPLE BRANCH BLVD. AT HALEY DRIVE	CEDARHURST	NY	11516	(516) 295-4644
YOUNG ISRAEL OF LAWRENCE-CEDARHURST 26 COLUMBIA STREET	CEDARHURST	NY	11516	(516) 569-0163
JEWISH CENTER OF THE MORICHES P.O. BOX 127	CENTER MORICHES	NY	11934	(516) 878-0388
ETZ HAYYIM, TEMPLE O P.O. BOX 90	CENTRAL ISLIP	NY	11722	
BETH EL, TEMPLE R 220 BEDFORD ROAD	CHAPPAQUA	NY	10514	(914) 238-3928
BETH SHALOM, CONGREGATION C P.O. BOX 82, CLIFTON PARK CENTER	CLIFTON PARK	NY	12065	(518) 371-0608
KEHILLATH SHALOM, CONGREGATION 58 GOOSE HILL ROAD	COLD SPRING HARBOR	NY	11724	(516) 234-0548
BETH DAVID, TEMPLE R 100 HAUPPAUGE ROAD	COMMACK	NY	11725	(516) 499-0915
COMMACK JEWISH CENTER C 83 SHIRLEY COURT	COMMACK	NY	11725	(516) 543-3311
YOUNG ISRAEL OF COMMACK 40 KINGS PARK RD.	COMMACK	NY	11725	
TIFERETH ISRAEL ANSHEI-CORONA O 109-18 54TH AVENUE	CORONA	NY	11368	(718) 592-6254
CONGREGATION ANSHE DORSHE EMES RE POB 626	CROTON	NY	10562	(914) 941-9687
ISRAEL OF NORTHERN WESTCHESTER, TEMPLE R GLENGARY ROAD	CROTON-ON-HUDSON	NY	10520	(914) 271-4705
BETH SHOLOM, CONGREGATION C 5205 JAMESVILLE ROAD	DEWITT	NY	13214	(315) 446-9570
SUFFOLK JEWISH CENTER C 330 CENTRAL AVENUE	DEER PARK	NY	11729	(516) 667-7695
BETH TORAH, TEMPLE R 35 BAGATELLE ROAD	DIX HILLS	NY	11746	(516) 643-1200
DIX HILLS JEWISH CENTER C VANDERBILT PARKWAY & DEFOREST ROAD	DIX HILLS	NY	11746	(516) 499-6644
GREENBURGH HEBREW CENTER C 515 BROADWAY	DOBBS FERRY	NY	10522	(914) 693-4260
MARATHON JEWISH COMMUNITY CENTER C 245-37 60TH AVENUE	DOUGLASTON	NY	11362	(718) 428-1580
BETH EL, TEMPLE C 507 WASHINGTON AVENUE	DUNKIRK	NY	14048	(716) 366-6646
TIFERETH ISRAEL OF JACKSON HEIGHTS, CONGREGATION O 88TH STREET & 32ND AVENUE	EAST ELMHURST	NY	11369	(718) 429-4100
JEWISH CENTER OF THE HAMPTONS R 44 WOODS LANE, P.O. BOX 871	EAST HAMPTON	NY	11937	(516) 324-9858
EAST MEADOW JEWISH CENTER C 1400 PROSPECT AVENUE	EAST MEADOW	NY	11554	(516) 483-4205
EMANU-EL OF EAST MEADOW, TEMPLE R 123 MERRICK AVENUE	EAST MEADOW	NY	11554	(516) 794-8911
SUBURBAN PARK JEWISH CENTER C 400 OLD WESTBURY ROAD	EAST MEADOW	NY	11554	(516) 796-2626
EAST NORTHPORT JEWISH CENTER C 328 ELWOOD ROAD	EAST NORTHPORT	NY	11731	(516) 368-6474
YOUNG ISRAEL OF EAST NORTHPORT 547 LARKFIELD RD.	EAST NORTHPORT	NY	11731	(516) 368-5880
HEWLETT-EAST ROCKAWAY JEWISH CENTER, CONGREGATION ETZ CHAIM 295 MAIN STREET	EAST ROCKAWAY	NY	11518	(516) 599-2634
EZRATH ISRAEL, CONGREGATION O 31 CENTER STREET	ELLENVILLE	NY	12428	(914) 647-4450
EMANU-EL OF QUEENS R 91-15 CORONA AVENUE	ELMHURST	NY	11373	(718) 592-1343
B'NAI ISRAEL, TEMPLE R 900 W. WATER STREET	ELMIRA	NY	14905	(607) 734-7735
SHOMRAY HADATH, CONGREGATION C COBBLES PARK	ELMIRA	NY	14905	(607) 732-7410
B'NAI ISRAEL, TEMPLE R ELMONT ROAD, BAYLIS AVENUE	ELMONT	NY	11003	(516) 354-1156
ELMONT JEWISH CENTER O 500 ELMONT ROAD	ELMONT	NY	11003	(516) 488-1616
BETH EL-ENDICOTT JEWISH COMMUNITY CENTER C 119 JEFFERSON AVENUE	ENDICOTT	NY	13760	(914) 785-3840
AGUDATH ISRAEL OF LONG ISLAND O 1121 SAGE STREET	FAR ROCKAWAY	NY	11691	(718) 471-4861
BAYSWATER JEWISH CENTER-CONGREGATION DARCHAY NOAM C 2355 HEALY AVENUE	FAR ROCKAWAY	NY	11691	(718) 471-7771
KNESETH ISRAEL, CONGREGATION O 728 EMPIRE AVENUE	FAR ROCKAWAY	NY	11691	(718) 327-7545
SHAARE ZEDEK OF EDGEMERE, CONGREGATION O 315 BEACH 30TH STREET	FAR ROCKAWAY	NY	11691	(718) 327-0830
SH'OR YOSHUV INSTITUTE O 1526 CENTRAL AVE.	FAR ROCKAWAY	NY	11691	(718) 327-2048
TIFERETH CHAIM, CONGREGATION O 29-04 FAR ROCKAWAY BLVD.	FAR ROCKAWAY	NY	11691	(718) 337-5685
YESHIVA DARCHEI TORAH CONGREGATION 257 BEACH 17TH STREET	FAR ROCKAWAY	NY	11691	(718) 337-5880
YOUNG ISRAEL OF FAR ROCKAWAY O 716 BEACH 9TH STREET	FAR ROCKAWAY	NY	11691	(718) 471-6724
YOUNG ISRAEL OF WAVECREST & BAYSWATER 2360 BROOKHAVEN AVENUE	FAR ROCKAWAY	NY	11691	(718) 327-8606
FARMINGDALE JEWISH CENTER C 425 FULTON STREET	FARMINGDALE	NY	11735	(516) 694-2343
BNAI ISRAEL, CONGREGATION C	FLEISHMANNS	NY	12430	(914) 254-9837
BELLEROSE JEWISH CENTER C 254-04 UNION TURNPIKE	FLORAL PARK	NY	11004	(718) 343-9001
FLORAL PARK JEWISH CENTER C 26 NORTH TYSON AVENUE	FLORAL PARK	NY	11001	(718) 354-6980
SHOLOM, TEMPLE R 263-10 UNION TURNPIKE	FLORAL PARK	NY	11004	(718) 343-8660
BETH SHALOM, TEMPLE - HEBREW COMMUNITY CENTER R ROOSEVELT AVENUE	FLORIDA	NY	10921	(914) 651-7817
B'NAI ABRAHAM, CONGREGATION O 75-09 MAIN STREET	FLUSHING	NY	11367	
BETH HILLEL OF JACKSON HEIGHTS, CONGREGATION R 23-38 81ST STREET	FLUSHING	NY	11373	(718) 899-6666
BETH OR OF THE DEAF, TEMPLE R 171-39 NORTHERN BLVD	FLUSHING	NY	11358	(718) 776-4400
BETH SHOLOM OF REGO PARK, CONGREGATION O 55-36 97TH STREET	FLUSHING	NY	11368	(718) 699-4510
BETH SHOLOM, TEMPLE R 171-39 NORTHERN BLVD	FLUSHING	NY	11358	(718) 463-4143
DEGEL MORDECAI, CONGREGATION O 73-09 136TH STREET	FLUSHING	NY	11367	(718) 263-1575
EITZ CHAIM, CONGREGATION 54-96 KISSENA BLVD	FLUSHING	NY	11355	(718) 762-2323
ELECTCHESTER JEWISH CENTER, INC. C 65-15 164TH STREET	FLUSHING	NY	11365	(718) 886-4454
EMUNA SHLEIMA, CONGREGATION O 69-69 MAIN STREET	FLUSHING	NY	11367	
FLUSHING JEWISH CENTER T 43-00 171 STREET	FLUSHING	NY	11358	(718) 358-7071
FREE SYNAGOGUE OF FLUSHING R 41-60 KISSENA BLVD	FLUSHING	NY	11355	(718) 961-0030
HILLCREST JEWISH CENTER, THE C 183-02 UNION TURNPIKE	FLUSHING	NY	11366	(718) 380-4145
HILLCREST JEWISH CENTER, THE C 210-10 UNION TURNPIKE	FLUSHING	NY	11364	(718) 776-3500
ISRAEL CENTER OF HILLCREST MANOR C 167-11 73RD AVENUE	FLUSHING	NY	11366	(718) 969-8085
JEWISH CENTER OF KEW GARDENS HILLS, THE C 71-25 MAIN STREET	FLUSHING	NY	11367	(718) 263-6500
JEWISH CENTER OF TORAH EMETH O 78-15 PARSONS BLVD	FLUSHING	NY	11366	(718) 591-4240
KISSENA JEWISH CENTER O 43-43 BOWNE STREET	FLUSHING	NY	11355	(718) 461-1871
MACHZEKEI HADATH, CONGREGATION O 147-30 73RD AVENUE	FLUSHING	NY	11367	
QUEENSBORO HILL JEWISH CENTER C 156-03 HORACE HARDING BLVD	FLUSHING	NY	11367	(718) 445-4141
SHAARAI TEFILA-TEMPLE GATES OF PRAYER, CONGREGATION C 38-20 PARSONS BLVD	FLUSHING	NY	11354	(718) 359-1160
TIFERETH ISRAEL OF CORONA, CONGREGATION O 109-18 54TH AVENUE	FLUSHING	NY	11368	
UTOPIA JEWISH CENTER C 64-41 UTOPIA PARKWAY	FLUSHING	NY	11365	(718) 461-8347
YOUNG ISRAEL OF HILLCREST 169-07 JEWEL AVENUE	FLUSHING	NY	11365	(718) 969-2990
YOUNG ISRAEL OF QUEENS VALLEY 141-55 77TH AVENUE	FLUSHING	NY	11367	(718) 263-3921
AHAVATH ACHIM, CONGREGATION O 67-62 BURNS STREET	FOREST HILLS	NY	11375	
AHAVATH SHOLOM, CONGREGATION O 75-02 113TH STREET	FOREST HILLS	NY	11375	(718) 263-1949
BETH SHOLOM, CONGREGATION O 103-11 68TH DRIVE	FOREST HILLS	NY	11375	
CHOFETZ CHAIM, CONGREGATION O 92-15 69TH AVENUE	FOREST HILLS	NY	11375	(718) 544-4662
FOREST HILLS JEWISH CENTER, THE C 106-06 QUEENS BLVD	FOREST HILLS	NY	11375	(718) 263-7000
ISAIAH, TEMPLE R 75-24 GRAND CENTRAL PARKWAY	FOREST HILLS	NY	11375	(718) 544-2800
JEWISH EDUCATIONAL CENTER 102-35 63RD ROAD	FOREST HILLS	NY	11375	(718) 896-4444
MACHNE CHODOSH, CONGREGATION O 67-29 108TH STREET	FOREST HILLS	NY	11375	(718) 793-5656
MISHKAN ISRAEL, CONGREGATION O 67-04 AUSTIN STREET	FOREST HILLS	NY	11375	(718) 896-3077
QUEENS JEWISH CENTER & TALMUD TORAH O 66-05 108TH STREET	FOREST HILLS	NY	11375	(718) 459-8432
SEPHARDIC JEWISH CONGREGATION & CENTER OF QUEENS O 101-17 67TH DRIVE	FOREST HILLS	NY	11375	(718) 544-6932
SINAI, TEMPLE R 71-11 112TH STREET	FOREST HILLS	NY	11375	(718) 261-2900
YOUNG ISRAEL OF FOREST HILLS 7100 YELLOWSTONE BLVD.,	FOREST HILLS	NY	11375	(718) 268-7100
FRANKLIN SQUARE JEWISH CENTER C PACIFIC & LLOYD STREETS	FRANKLIN SQUARE	NY	11010	(516) 354-2322
B'NAI ISRAEL OF FREEPORT, CONGREGATION C 91 N. BAYVIEW AVENUE	FREEPORT	NY	11520	(516) 623-4200
UNION REFORM TEMPLE R 475 N. BROOKSIDE AVENUE	FREEPORT	NY	11520	(516) 623-1810
FRESH MEADOWS JEWISH CENTER C 193-10 PECK AVENUE	FRESH MEADOWS	NY	11365	(718) 357-5100
GARDEN CITY JEWISH CENTER R 168 NASSAU BLVD.	GARDEN CITY	NY	11530	(516) 248-9180
BETH EL, TEMPLE R 755 S. MAIN STREET	GENEVA	NY	14456	(315) 789-9710
NORTH COUNTRY REFORM TEMPLE R CRESCENT BEACH ROAD	GLEN COVE	NY	11542	(516) 671-4760
TIFERETH ISRAEL, CONGREGATION C HILL STREET & LANDING ROAD	GLEN COVE	NY	11542	(516) 676-5080
BETH EL, TEMPLE R 3 MARION AVENUE	GLEN FALLS	NY	12801	(518) 792-4364
SHAAREY TEFILA C 68 BAY STREET	GLEN FALLS	NY	12801	(518) 792-4945
GLEN WILD JEWISH SYNAGOGUE	GLEN WILD	NY	12738	
FOREST PARK JEWISH CENTER O 90-45 MYRTLE AVENUE	GLENDALE	NY	11385	(718) 847-6273
KNESSETH ISRAEL SYNAGOGUE C 34 E. FULTON STREET	GLOVERSVILLE	NY	12078	(518) 725-0649
BETH EL, TEMPLE R 5 OLD MILL ROAD	GREAT NECK	NY	11023	(516) 487-0900
BETH JOSEPH, TEMPLE 1 LINDEN PLACE	GREAT NECK	NY	11021	
EMANUEL, TEMPLE R 150 HICKS LANE	GREAT NECK	NY	11024	(516) 482-5701
GREAT NECK SYNAGOGUE O 26 OLD MILL ROAD	GREAT NECK	NY	11023	(516) 487-6100
ISAIAH OF GREAT NECK, TEMPLE R P.O. BOX 229	GREAT NECK	NY	11022	(516) 487-8709
ISRAEL OF GREAT NECK, TEMPLE C 108 OLD MILL ROAD	GREAT NECK	NY	11023	(516) 582-7800
LONG ISLAND RECONSTRUCTIONIST HAVURAH POB 2023	GREAT NECK	NY	11022	(516) 482-6532
YOUNG ISRAEL OF GREAT NECK 236 MIDDLE NECK ROAD	GREAT NECK	NY	11023	(516) 829-6040
TIFERETH ISRAEL, TEMPLE C 4TH STREET	GREENPORT	NY	11944	
BETH SHALOM, TEMPLE R 740 NORTH BROADWAY	HASTINGS-ON-HUDSON	NY	10706	(914) 478-3833
BETH CHAI, TEMPLE C 870 TOWNLINE ROAD	HAUPPAUGE	NY	11787	
BETH ISRAEL, CONGREGATION C 94 FULTON AVENUE	HEMPSTEAD	NY	11550	(516) 489-1818
NASSAU COMMUNITY TEMPLE R 240 HEMPSTEAD AVENUE	HEMPSTEAD	NY	11552	(516) 485-1811
BETH AM, TEMPLE C 3249 E. HENRIETTA ROAD, P.O. BOX 177	HENRIETTA	NY	14467	(716) 334-4855
BETH JOSEPH, TEMPLE C 327 N. PROSPECT STREET	HERKIMER	NY	13350	(315) 866-4270
BETH EMETH, CONGREGATION C 36 FRANKLIN AVENUE	HEWLETT	NY	11557	(516) 374-9220
HICKSVILLE JEWISH CENTER C 6 MAGLIE DRIVE	HICKSVILLE	NY	11801	(516) 931-9323
SHAARI ZEDEK, CONGREGATION O OLD COUNTRY & NEW SOUTH ROAD	HICKSVILLE	NY	11801	(516) 938-0420
ISRAEL OF JAMAICA, TEMPLE R 188-15 MCLAUGHLIN AVENUE	HOLLIS	NY	11423	(718) 776-4400
MISHKAN ISRAEL 153-14 90TH AVENUE	HOLLIS	NY	11423	
BETH EL, TEMPLE C 12 CHURCH STREET	HORNELL	NY	14843	(607) 324-2236
HOWARD BEACH JEWISH CENTER C 162-05 90TH STREET	HOWARD BEACH	NY	11414	(718) 845-9443

JUDEA, TEMPLE R 151-44 80TH STREET	HOWARD BEACH	NY	11414	(718) 848-0999
ROCKWOOD PARK JEWISH CENTER O 156-45 84TH STREET	HOWARD BEACH	NY	11414	(718) 641-5822
ANSHE KOL ISRAEL, CONGREGATION O	HUNTER	NY	12442	
BETH EL OF HUNTINGTON, TEMPLE R 660 PARK AVENUE	HUNTINGTON	NY	11743	(516) 421-5835
HUNTINGTON HEBREW CONGREGATION C 510 PARK AVENUE	HUNTINGTON	NY	11743	(516) 427-1089
SOUTH HUNTINGTON JEWISH CENTER C 2600 NEW YORK AVENUE	HUNTINGTON STATION	NY	11747	(516) 421-3224
ANSHEI HURLEYVILLE, CONGREGATION O	HURLEYVILLE	NY	12747	
JEWISH COMMUNITY CENTER O BAYSWATER BLVD & ELM ROAD	INWOOD	NY	11696	
BETH EMETH JEWISH CENTER, CONGREGATION C 191 LONG BEACH ROAD	ISLAND PARK	NY	11558	(516) 432-6706
BETH EL, TEMPLE COURT & TIOGA STREETS	ITHACA	NY	14850	(607) 273-5775
YOUNG ISRAEL OF CORNELL 106 WEST AVENUE	ITHACA	NY	14850	(607) 272-5810
BETH HILLEL CONGREGATION R 23-38 81ST STREET	JACKSON HEIGHTS	NY	11370	(718) 899-6666
ELMHURST JEWISH CENTER O 37-53 90TH STREET	JACKSON HEIGHTS	NY	11372	(718) 426-5642
JEWISH CENTER OF JACKSON HEIGHTS C 34-25 82ND STREET	JACKSON HEIGHTS	NY	11372	(718) 429-1150
NORTHSIDE HEBREW CONGREGATION C 90-11 35TH AVENUE	JACKSON HEIGHTS	NY	11372	
TIFERETH ISRAEL OF JACKSON HEIGHTS, CONGREGATION O 88TH STREET & 32ND AVENUE	JACKSON HEIGHTS	NY	11369	(718) 429-4100
YOUNG ISRAEL OF JACKSON HEIGHTS 86-15 37TH AVENUE	JACKSON HEIGHTS	NY	11372	(718) 639-8888
BRIARWOOD JEWISH CENTER C 139-06 86TH AVENUE	JAMAICA	NY	11435	(718) 657-5151
CONSERVATIVE SYNAGOGUE OF JAMAICA C 182-69 WEXFORD TERRACE	JAMAICA	NY	11432	(718) 739-7500
FIRST HEBREW CONGREGATION O 90-21 160TH STREET	JAMAICA	NY	11432	
INTERNATIONAL SYNAGOGUE OF JOHN F. KENNEDY AIRPORT, THE JFK AIRPORT	JAMAICA	NY	11430	(718) 656-5044
ROCHDALE VILLAGE JEWISH CENTER C 167-10 137TH AVENUE	JAMAICA	NY	11434	(718) 528-0200
SANHEDRIN JEWISH COMMUNITY CENTER O 103-06 131ST STREET	JAMAICA	NY	11419	
YOUNG ISRAEL OF BRIARWOOD 84-75 DANIELS STREET	JAMAICA	NY	11435	(718) 657-2880
YOUNG ISRAEL OF JAMAICA ESTATES 83-10 188 STREET	JAMAICA	NY	11423	(718) 454-1152
HESED ABRAHAM, TEMPLE R 215 HALL AVENUE	JAMESTOWN	NY	14701	(716) 484-1800
JERICHO JEWISH CENTER C NORTH BROADWAY	JERICHO	NY	11753	(516) 933-2540
OR ELOKIM, TEMPLER 18 TOBIE LANE	JERICHO	NY	11753	(516) 433-9888
BETH TORAH, TEMPLE C 243 CONTIAGUE ROCK ROAD	JERICHO GARDENS	NY	11590	(516) 334-7979
BETH EL, TEMPLE C P.O. BOX 682	KAUNEONGA	NY	12749	(914) 583-4442
TIFERETH YEHUDA YISROEL, CONGREGATION O P.O. BOX 295	KERHONKSON	NY	12446	
ADAS YEREIM, CONGREGATION O 122-25 METROPOLITAN AVENUE	KEW GARDENS	NY	11415	
KEW GARDENS ANSHE SHOLOM JEWISH CENTER C 82-52 ABINGDON ROAD	KEW GARDENS	NY	11415	(718) 441-2470
KEW GARDENS SYNAGOGUE ADATH YESHURUN O 82-17 LEFFERTS BLVD	KEW GARDENS	NY	11415	(718) 846-7541
TIFERETH AL-OZER V'YESHIVA DEGEL-HATORAH, CONGREGATION O 82-61 BEVERLY ROAD	KEW GARDENS	NY	11415	(718) 441-3862
AGUDATH ISRAEL OF KEW GARDENS O 147-37 70TH ROAD	KEW GARDENS HILLS	NY	11367	
B'NAI ABRAHAM, CONGREGATION C 75-09 MAIN STREET	KEW GARDENS HILLS	NY	11367	(718) 261-4580
YOUNG ISRAEL OF KEW GARDENS HILLS 70-11 150TH STREET	KEW GARDENS HILLS	NY	11367	(718) 261-9723
ETZ CHAIM OF KINGS PARK, CONGREGATION O 44 MEADOW ROAD	KINGS PARK	NY	11754	(516) 269-9666
KINGS PARK JEWISH CENTER, INC. C ROUTE 25A, P.O. BOX 301	KINGS PARK	NY	11754	(516) 269-1133
AGUDAS ACHIM, CONGREGATION O 254 LUCAS AVENUE, P.O. BOX 3573	KINGSTON	NY	12401	(914) 331-1176
AHAVATH ISRAEL, CONGREGATION C 100 LUCAS AVENUE	KINGSTON	NY	12401	(914) 338-4409
EMANUEL, TEMPLE R 243 ALBANY AVENUE, P.O. BOX 1421	KINGSTON	NY	12401	(914) 338-4271
TALMUD TORAH OF KINGSTON 100 LUCAS AVENUE	KINGSTON	NY	12401	
LAKE GROVE JEWISH CENTER 821 HAWKINS AVENUE	LAKE GROVE	NY	11755	(516) 585-9710
RONKONKOMA JEWISH CENTER C P.O. BOX 20	LAKE GROVE	NY	11755	(516) 585-0521
LAKE PLACID SYNAGOGUE T 30 SARANAC AVENUE	LAKE PLACID	NY	12946	(518) 523-3876
LAKE SUCCESS JEWISH CENTER C 354 LAKEVILLE ROAD	LAKE SUCCESS	NY	11020	(516) 466-0569
NORTH SHORE JEWISH CENTER C 354 LAKEVILLE ROAD	LAKE SUCCESS	NY	11020	
BETH EMETH SYNAGOGUE C 2111 BOSTON POST ROAD	LARCHMONT	NY	10538	(914) 834-1093
LARCHMONT TEMPLE R 75 LARCHMONT AVENUE	LARCHMONT	NY	10538	(914) 834-6120
BETH EL OF LAURELTON, TEMPLE R 133-21 232ND STREET	LAURELTON	NY	11413	(718) 528-6378
LAURELTON JEWISH CENTER C 139-49 228TH STREET	LAURELTON	NY	11413	(718) 527-0400
BETH SHOLOM, CONGREGATION O 390 BROADWAY	LAWRENCE	NY	11559	(516) 569-3600
ISRAEL, TEMPLE R 140 CENTRAL AVENUE	LAWRENCE	NY	11559	(516) 239-1140
KOL YISROEL CHAVERIM, CONGREGATION O 124 RICHMOND PLACE	LAWRENCE	NY	11559	(516) 239-1033
SHAARAY TEFILA, CONGREGATION O CENTRAL & LORD AVENUE	LAWRENCE	NY	11559	(516) 239-2444
SINAI OF LONG ISLAND, TEMPLE R 131 WASHINGTON AVENUE	LAWRENCE	NY	11559	(516) 569-0267
ISRAEL COMMUNITY CENTER OF LEVITTOWN C 3235 HEMPSTEAD TURNPIKE	LEVITTOWN	NY	11756	(516) 731-2580
AHAVATH ISRAEL, CONGREGATION O 39 CHESTNUT STREET	LIBERTY	NY	12754	(914) 292-8843
FERNDALE SYNAGOGUE O LIBERTY GARDENS, A-3	LIBERTY	NY	12754	(914) 292-6709
LIDO BEACH JEWISH CENTER O ONE FAIRWAY ROAD	LIDO BEACH	NY	11561	(516) 889-9650
BNEI ABRAHAM, CONGREGATION O 33-01 UNION STREET	LINDEN HILL	NY	11354	(718) 539-7742
LINDENHURST HEBREW CONGREGATION 225 NORTH FOURTH STREET	LINDENHURST	NY	11757	(516) 226-2022
LITTLE NECK JEWISH CENTER C 49-10 LITTLE NECK PARKWAY	LITTLE NECK	NY	11362	(718) 224-0404
MARATHON JEWISH COMMUNITY CENTER C 245-37 60TH AVENUE	LITTLE NECK	NY	11362	(718) 428-1580
MENORAH OF LITTLE NECK, TEMPLE R 252-00 H. HARDING EXPRESSWAY	LITTLE NECK	NY	11362	(718) 321-1920
TORAH OF LITTLE NECK, TEMPLE C 54-27 LITTLE NECK PARKWAY	LITTLE NECK	NY	11362	(718) 423-2100
AGUDAS ACHIM, CONGREGATION	LIVINGSTON MANOR	NY	12758	
BETH EL OF LONG BEACH, TEMPLE O 570 W. WALNUT STREET	LONG BEACH	NY	11561	(516) 432-1678
BETH SHOLOM OF LONG BEACH & LIDO, CONGREGATION C 700 E. PARK AVENUE	LONG BEACH	NY	11561	(516) 432-7464
EAST END SYNAGOGUE EAST PARK AVENUE AT ROOSEVELT BLVD	LONG BEACH	NY	11561	
EMANU-EL, TEMPLE R 455 NEPTUNE BLVD	LONG BEACH	NY	11561	(516) 431-4060
ISRAEL OF LONG BEACH, TEMPLE T 305 RIVERSIDE BLVD	LONG BEACH	NY	11561	(516) 432-1410
MUSMACH YESHUAH SYNAGOGUE O 369 EAST BEECH STREET	LONG BEACH	NY	11561	(516) 432-6841
SEPHARDIC CONGREGATION OF LONG BEACH O 161 LAFAYETTE BLVD, P.O. BOX 779	LONG BEACH	NY	11561	(516) 432-9224
YOUNG ISRAEL OF LONG BEACH 158 LONG BEACH BLVD	LONG BEACH	NY	11561	(516) 431-2404
ZION, TEMPLE O 62 MARYLAND AVENUE, P.O. BOX 389	LONG BEACH	NY	11561	(516) 432-5657
ADATH ISRAEL, CONGREGATION O 36-02 14TH STREET	LONG ISLAND CITY	NY	11106	
ASTORIA CENTER OF ISRAEL C 27-35 CRESCENT STREET	LONG ISLAND CITY	NY	11102	(718) 278-2680
ASTORIA HEIGHTS JEWISH CENTER 32-49 49TH STREET	LONG ISLAND CITY	NY	11103	(718) 728-1012
BNEY ISRAEL, CONGREGATION O P.O. BOX 1215, 45-11 21ST STREET	LONG ISLAND CITY	NY	11101	
SONS OF ISRAEL, CONGREGATION O 33-21 CRESCENT STREET	LONG ISLAND CITY	NY	11106	(718) 274-2125
SUNNYSIDE JEWISH CENTER C 45-46 43RD STREET	LONG ISLAND CITY	NY	11104	(718) 729-9176
YOUNG ISRAEL OF SUNNYSIDE 41-12 45TH STREET	LONG ISLAND CITY	NY	11104	(718) 786-4103
BETH DAVID CONGREGATION C 188 VINCENT AVENUE	LYNBROOK	NY	11563	(516) 599-9464
EMANU-EL, TEMPLE R SAPERSTEIN PLAZA	LYNBROOK	NY	11563	(516) 593-4004
JEWISH CENTER OF THE MAHOPACS-TEMPLE BETH SHALOM C ROAD 10, P.O. BOX 245	MAHOPAC	NY	10541	(914) 628-6133
MALVERNE JEWISH CENTER C 1 NORWOOD AVENUE	MALVERNE	NY	11564	(516) 593-6364
WESTCHESTER JEWISH CENTER C ROCKLAND & PALMER AVENUE	MAMARONECK	NY	10543	(914) 698-2960
JUDEA, TEMPLE R 333 SEARINGTOWN ROAD	MANHASSET	NY	11030	(516) 621-8049
MASPETH JEWISH CENTER O 66-64 GRAND AVENUE	MASPETH	NY	11378	(718) 639-7559
BETH EL, CONGREGATION C 99 JERUSALEM AVENUE	MASSAPEQUA	NY	11758	(516) 541-0740
HILLEL HEBREW CONGREGATION C 1066 HICKSVILLE ROAD, P.O. BOX 244	MASSAPEQUA	NY	11758	(516) 799-0616
JUDEA, TEMPLE R JERUSALEM & CENTRAL AVENUE	MASSAPEQUA	NY	11758	(516) 798-5444
SINAI, TEMPLE R 270 CLOCK BLVD	MASSAPEQUA	NY	11758	(516) 795-5015
ADATH ISRAEL CONGREGATION C P.O. BOX 196	MASSENA	NY	13662	(315) 769-6878
MASTIC BEACH HEBREW CENTER NEIGHBORHOOD ROAD	MASTIC BEACH	NY	11951	
SOUTH HUNTINGTON JEWISH CENTER C 2600 NEW YORK AVENUE	MELVILLE	NY	11747	(516) 421-3224
BETH AM, TEMPLE R MERRICK & KIRKWOOD AVENUE	MERRICK	NY	11566	(516) 378-3477
ISRAEL OF SOUTH MERRICK, TEMPLE C 2655 CLUBHOUSE ROAD	MERRICK	NY	11566	(516) 378-1963
MERRICK JEWISH CENTER-CONGREGATION OHR TORAH C 225 FOX BLVD	MERRICK	NY	11566	(516) 379-8650
OHAV SHOLOM, CONGREGATION O 145 SOUTH MERRICK AVENUE	MERRICK	NY	11566	(516) 378-1988
REFORM JEWISH CONGREGATION OF MERRICK R MERRICK & KIRKWOOD AVENUES	MERRICK	NY	11566	
JEWISH CENTER OF FOREST HILLS C 63-25 DRY HARBOR ROAD	MIDDLE VILLAGE	NY	11379	(718) 639-2110
SONS OF ISRAEL AHAVATH ACHIM O 75-27 67TH DRIVE	MIDDLE VILLAGE	NY	11379	
SINAI, TEMPLE C (MIDDLETOWN HEBREW ASSOCIATION) 75 HIGHLAND AVENUE	MIDDLETOWN	NY	10940	(914) 343-1861
BETH SHOLOM, CONGREGATION C 261 WILLIS AVENUE	MINEOLA	NY	11501	(516) 756-3211
BAIS NAFTULY, CONGREGATION O 5 KENNEDY COURT	MONROE	NY	10950	(914) 782-6192
BETH EL-MONROE TEMPLE OF LIBERAL JUDAISM, TEMPLE R 314 N. MAIN STREET	MONROE	NY	10950	(914) 783-2626
BETH ROPSHITZ & CONGREGATION KAHAL KDUSHAS YOM TOV O 4 RAYWOOD DRIVE	MONROE	NY	10950	(914) 782-5494
EITZ CHAIM, CONGREGATION C 251 SPRING STREET	MONROE	NY	10950	(914) 783-7424
KEDDUSHAS YOM TOV, CONGREGATION O 4 RAYWOOD DRIVE	MONROE	NY	10950	(914) 782-5494
MHARY ASHKENAZY, CONGREGATION O ROAD 5, P.O. BOX 157 4-A FOREST ROAD	MONROE	NY	10950	(914) 783-9033
MONROE-WOODBURY JEWISH COMMUNITY CENTER & CONG. EITZ CHAIM 251 SPRING STREET	MONROE	NY	10950	(914) 783-7424
YETEV LEV MONROE DIVISION, CONGREGATION P.O. BOX 566	MONROE	NY	10950	(914) 782-5149
YETEV LEV, CONGREGATION O P.O. BOX 420	MONROE	NY	10950	(914) 782-7546
AGUDATH ISRAEL OF MONSEY O	MONSEY	NY	10952	
AYSHEL AVRAHAM, CONGREGATION O P.O. BOX 317	MONSEY	NY	10952	(914) 352-0630
B'NAI JESHURUN SYNAGOGUE OF MONSEY N.Y. O PARK LANE, P.O. BOX 423	MONSEY	NY	10952	(914) 352-3239
COMMUNITY SYNAGOGUE OF MONSEY O 15 CLOVERDALE LANE	MONSEY	NY	10952	
HADAR, CONGREGATION O 70 HIGHVIEW ROAD	MONSEY	NY	10952	(914) 357-1515
K'HAL TORATH CHAIM, CONGREGATION O P.O. BOX 446, PHYLLIS TERRACE	MONSEY	NY	10952	(914) 356-6666
MACHZIKEI TORAH, CONGREGATION O 3 RALPH BLVD	MONSEY	NY	10952	
MONSEY JEWISH CENTER C 101 ROUTE 306	MONSEY	NY	10952	(914) 352-6444
SHAAREI TORAH OF ROCKLAND 1 SCHOOL TERRACE	MONSEY	NY	10952	(914) 356-9773
TORAS CHAIM, CONGREGATION O PHYLLIS TERRACE	MONSEY	NY	10952	
VAJOEL MOSHE, CONGREGATION O 214 MAPLE AVENUE	MONSEY	NY	10952	(914) 356-9807
HEBREW CONGREGATION OF MOUNTAINDALE O P.O. BOX 117	MONTICELLO	NY	12763	(914) 434-9306
SHOLOM, TEMPLE R PORT JERVIS & E. DILLON ROADS, P.O. BOX 664	MONTICELLO	NY	12701	(914) 794-8731
TIFERETH ISRAEL, CONGREGATION O 18 LANDFIELD AVENUE	MONTICELLO	NY	12701	(914) 794-8470
BET TORAH C 60 SMITH AVENUE	MOUNT KISCO	NY	10549	(914) 241-0608
BETH MEDRASH CHEMED, CONGREGATION O PINES BRIDGE ROAD	MOUNT KISCO	NY	10549	
SHAARAY TEFILA, TEMPLE R ROUTE 172	MOUNT KISCO	NY	10549	(914) 666-3133
BROTHERS OF ISRAEL, CONGREGATION O 116 CRARY AVENUE	MOUNT VERNON	NY	10550	(914) 667-1302
EMANU-EL JEWISH CENTER C 261 E. LINCOLN AVENUE	MOUNT VERNON	NY	10552	(914) 667-0161
FLEETWOOD SYNAGOGUE O 11 EAST BROAD STREET	MOUNT VERNON	NY	10552	(914) 664-7643
FREE SYNAGOGUE OF WESTCHESTER R 500 N. COLUMBUS AVENUE	MOUNT VERNON	NY	10552	(914) 664-1727
JEWISH CENTER C 261 EAST LINCOLN AVENUE	MOUNT VERNON	NY	10552	(914) 667-0161
SINAI TEMPLE R 132 CRARY AVENUE	MOUNT VERNON	NY	10550	(914) 668-9471
NANUET HEBREW CENTER C 34 S. MIDDLETOWN ROAD	NANUET	NY	10954	(914) 623-3735
WEST END TEMPLE-CONGREGATION SINAI R 147-02 NEWPORT AVENUE	NEPONSIT	NY	11694	(718) 634-0301
BETH SHOLOM, TEMPLE R 228 NEW HEMPSTEAD ROAD	NEW CITY	NY	10956	(914) 638-0770
NEW CITY JEWISH CENTER C OLD SCHOOLHOUSE ROAD	NEW CITY	NY	10956	(914) 634-6140
EMANUEL, TEMPLE R 3315 HILLSIDE AVENUE	NEW HYDE PARK	NY	11040	(516) 746-1120
NEW HYDE PARK JEWISH COMMUNITY CENTER C 100 LAKEVILLE ROAD	NEW HYDE PARK	NY	11040	(516) 354-7583
YOUNG ISRAEL OF NEW HYDE PARK 264-15 77TH AVENUE	NEW HYDE PARK	NY	11040	(718) 343-0496

AHAVATH ACHIM C CHURCH STREET ... NEW PALTZ **NY** 12561 (914) 255-9817
ANSHE SHOLOM, CONGREGATION O 50 NORTH AVENUE ... NEW ROCHELLE **NY** 10805 (914) 632-9220
BETH EL SYNAGOGUE OF NEW ROCHELLE, INC. C
NORTHFIELD ROAD AT N AVENUE ... NEW ROCHELLE **NY** 10804 (914) 235-2700
ISRAEL, TEMPLE R 1000 PINEBROOK BLVD ... NEW ROCHELLE **NY** 10804 (914) 235-1800
YOUNG ISRAEL OF WESTCHESTER 1228 NORTH AVENUE ... NEW ROCHELLE **NY** 10804 (914) 636-2215
ADAS BNEI ISRAEL, CONGREGATION - THE HEBREW LEAGUE O
257 EAST BROADWAY ... NEW YORK **NY** 10002
ADATH ISRAEL OF NEW YORK, UNITED HEBREW COMMUNITY OF NEW YORK O
201 EAST BROADWAY ... NEW YORK **NY** 10002 (212) 674-3580
AGUDAS CHAVERIM ANSHEI MARMAROS, CONGREGATION O
215 EAST BROADWAY ... NEW YORK **NY** 10002
AGUDATH ANSHEI MAMOD HOUSE OF SAGES, INC., CONGREGATION O
283 EAST BROADWAY ... NEW YORK **NY** 10002 (212) 732-3131
AGUDATH ANSHEI MAMOD, CONGREGATION 152 HENRY STREET ... NEW YORK **NY** 10002
AGUDATH ISRAEL OF EAST SIDE O 233 EAST BROADWAY ... NEW YORK **NY** 10002
AGUDATH ISRAEL OF WASHINGTON HEIGHTS O 617 W. 179TH STREET .. NEW YORK **NY** 10033 (212) 927-5404
AHAVATH CHESED, CONGREGATION O 309 W. 89TH STREET ... NEW YORK **NY** 10024 (212) 724-8065
AHAVATH ISRAEL, CONGREGATION O 502 W. 157TH STREET ... NEW YORK **NY** 10032 (212) 927-5696
AMERICAN CONGREGATION OF JEWS FROM AUSTRIA
118 WEST 95TH STREET ... NEW YORK **NY** 10025 (212) 663-1920
ANSCHE CHESED, CONGREGATION C 251 WEST 100TH STREET ... NEW YORK **NY** 10025 (212) 864-6637
ANSHE TASHKANVEH, CONGREGATION O 241 EAST BROADWAY ... NEW YORK **NY** 10002
ANSHEI LEBEDOWE-RADZILOWE MANSE, CONGREGATION O
266 EAST BROADWAY ... NEW YORK **NY** 10002 (212) 254-2384
ANSHEI LIBOVNEH VILLIN-SHOMER SHABBOS, CONGREGATION O
237 EAST BROADWAY ... NEW YORK **NY** 10002
ANSHEI VEISKAW, CONGREGATION O 257 EAST BROADWAY ... NEW YORK **NY** 10002
AUSTRIA HUNGARY ANSCHE SFARD, CONGREGATION O
239 EAST BROADWAY ... NEW YORK **NY** 10002 (212) 227-6145
B'NAI ISRAEL CHAIM, CONGREGATION O 353 W. 84TH STREET ... NEW YORK **NY** 10024 (212) 874-0644
B'NAI ISRAEL SHEARITH JUDAH, TEMPLE O 610 W. 149TH STREET ... NEW YORK **NY** 10031
B'NAI ISRAEL, CONGREGATION 335 E. 77TH STREET ... NEW YORK **NY** 10021 (212) 570-6650
B'NAI JESHURUN 270 W. 89TH STREET ... NEW YORK **NY** 10024 (212) 787-7600
BAYONER KLOYS, CONGREGATION O 247 EAST BROADWAY ... NEW YORK **NY** 10002
BETH AM, THE PEOPLE'S TEMPLE R 178 BENNETT AVENUE ... NEW YORK **NY** 10040 (212) 927-2230
BETH HACHASSIDIM DE POLEN, CONGREGATION O
233 EAST BROADWAY ... NEW YORK **NY** 10002 (212) 673-5191
BETH HAMEDRASH HAGODOL OF WASHINGTON HEIGHTS, CONGREGATION O
610 W. 175TH STREET ... NEW YORK **NY** 10033 (212) 927-6000
BETH HAMEDRASH HAGODOL, CONGREGATION O
60 NORFOLK STREET ... NEW YORK **NY** 10002 (212) 674-3330
BETH HAMEDRASH OF INWOOD, CONGREGATION
1781 RIVERSIDE DRIVE ... NEW YORK **NY** 10034 (212) 567-9776
BETH HILLEL & BETH ISRAEL, INC., CONGREGATION C
571 W. 182ND STREET ... NEW YORK **NY** 10033 (212) 568-3933
BETH ISRAEL, CONGREGATION O 347 WEST 34TH STREET ... NEW YORK **NY** 10001 (212) 279-0016
BETH SHOLOM OF WASHINGTON HEIGHTS, TEMPLE C
PINEHURST AVENUE & 179TH STREET ... NEW YORK **NY** 10033
BETH TOMCHEI TORAH V'ZIKNEI YISROEL-HOME/SAGES ISRAEL CONG O
25 WILLETT STREET ... NEW YORK **NY** 10002 (212) 673-8500
BIALYSTOKER SYNAGOGUE O 7-11 WILLETT STREET ... NEW YORK **NY** 10002 (212) 475-0165
BNAI ISAAC ANSHEI LECHOWITZ, CONGREGATION O
217 HENRY STREET ... NEW YORK **NY** 10002
BNAI ISRAEL, CONGREGATION 335 EAST 77TH STREET ... NEW YORK **NY** 10021 (212) 570-6650
BNAI MOSES JOSEPH, CONGREGATION 317 E. 8TH STREET ... NEW YORK **NY** 10009
BNAI SHOLOM, TEMPLE R 4580 BROADWAY ... NEW YORK **NY** 10040
BROTHERHOOD SYNAGOGUE, THE C 28 GRAMERCY PARK S ... NEW YORK **NY** 10003 (212) 674-5750
CENTRAL SYNAGOGUE R 123 E. 55TH STREET ... NEW YORK **NY** 10022 (212) 838-5122
CHAI ODOM MINSKI, CONGREGATION O 145 EAST BROADWAY ... NEW YORK **NY** 10002 (212) 964-2830
CHASAM SOPHER, CONGREGATION O 8 CLINTON STREET ... NEW YORK **NY** 10002 (212) 777-5140
CHATHAM JEWISH CENTER-CONGREGATION BETH SHOLOM C
217 PARK ROW ... NEW YORK **NY** 10038 (212) 233-0428
CHEVRA ANSHI STUZINER VEI-ANSHI GREIVER O
257 EAST BROADWAY ... NEW YORK **NY** 10002
CHEVRA BECHURIM B'NAI MENASHE AHAVAS ACHIM O
225 EAST BROADWAY ... NEW YORK **NY** 10002 (212) 349-0089
CIVIC CENTER SYNAGOGUE CONGREGATION SHAARE ZEDEK O
49 WHITE STREET ... NEW YORK **NY** 10013 (212) 966-7141
COMMUNITY SYNAGOGUE CENTER O 325 E. 6TH STREET ... NEW YORK **NY** 10003 (212) 473-3665
CONSERVATIVE SYNAGOGUE OF FIFTH AVENUE C
11 EAST 11TH STREET ... NEW YORK **NY** 10003 (212) 929-6954
COVENANT, TEMPLE OF THE R 612 W. 180TH STREET ... NEW YORK **NY** 10033
DARECH AMUNO, CONGREGATION O 53 CHARLES STREET ... NEW YORK **NY** 10014 (212) 242-6425
DOWNTOWN TALMUD TORAH SYNAGOGUE O 142 BROOME STREET ... NEW YORK **NY** 10002
EAST 55TH STREET CONSERVATIVE SYNAGOGUE C
308 E. 55TH STREET ... NEW YORK **NY** 10022 (212) 752-1200
EAST END TEMPLE R 398 SECOND AVENUE ... NEW YORK **NY** 10010 (212) 254-8515
EAST SIDE TORAH CENTER O 313 HENRY STREET ... NEW YORK **NY** 10002 (212) 473-1000
EDATH LEI ISRAEL ANSHEI MESARITZ, CONGREGATION O
P.O. BOX 124 ... NEW YORK **NY** 10002
EITZ CHAIM ANSHEI WOLOZIN, CONGREGATION O
209 MADISON STREET ... NEW YORK **NY** 10002
ELDRIDGE STREET SYNAGOGUE O 12 ELDRIDGE STREET ... NEW YORK **NY** 10002 (212) 219-0888
EMANU-EL OF THE CITY OF NEW YORK, CONGREGATION R
1 E. 65TH STREET ... NEW YORK **NY** 10021 (212) 744-1400
EMES WOZEDEK, INC., CONGREGATION O 560 W. 166TH STREET ... NEW YORK **NY** 10032 (212) 928-9785
EMUNATH ISRAEL, CONGREGATION O 236 WEST 23RD STREET ... NEW YORK **NY** 10011 (212) 242-9882
ERSTE LUTOWISKA MACHZIKA HADAS, CONGREGATION
262 DELANCEY STREET ... NEW YORK **NY** 10002 (212) 982-0007
EZRATH ISRAEL, CONGREGATION-THE ACTOR'S TEMPLE C
339 WEST 47TH STREET ... NEW YORK **NY** 10036 (212) 245-6975

FIFTH AVENUE SYNAGOGUE O 5 E. 62ND STREET ... NEW YORK **NY** 10021 (212) 838-2122
FIRST ROUMANIAN AMERICAN CONGREGATION O
89 RIVINGTON STREET ... NEW YORK **NY** 10002 (212) 673-2835
FORT TRYON JEWISH CENTRE C 524 FORT WASHINGTON AVENUE ... NEW YORK **NY** 10033 (212) 795-1391
FORT WASHINGTON SYNAGOGUE R 555 W. 182ND STREET ... NEW YORK **NY** 10033
FREE SYNAGOGUE R 30 WEST 68TH STREET ... NEW YORK **NY** 10023 (212) 877-4050
FRIENDS OF BELLEVUE HOSPITAL SYNAGOGUE
FIRST AVENUE & 27TH STREET ... NEW YORK **NY** 10016 (212) 685-1376
FUR CENTER SYNAGOGUE O 228 W. 29TH STREET ... NEW YORK **NY** 10001 (212) 560-9236
GARMENT CENTER CONGREGATION O 205 W. 40TH STREET ... NEW YORK **NY** 10018 (212) 391-6966
GATES OF ISRAEL, CONGREGATION O 560 WEST 185TH STREET ... NEW YORK **NY** 10033 (212) 923-2900
HABONIM, CONGREGATION R 44 W. 66TH STREET ... NEW YORK **NY** 10023 (212) 787-5347
HAVURAH HADASHAH RE ... NEW YORK **NY** (212) 646-9009
HEBREW TABERNACLE CONGREGATION R
551 FORT WASHINGTON AVENUE ... NEW YORK **NY** 10033 (212) 568-8304
HOUSE OF SAGES, INC. O 283 E. BROADWAY ... NEW YORK **NY** 10002 (212) 732-3131
INWOOD HEBREW CONGREGATION C 111 VERMILYEA AVENUE ... NEW YORK **NY** 10034 (212) 569-4010
INWOOD JEWISH CENTER & TALMUD TORAH, INC.
12 ELLWOOD STREET ... NEW YORK **NY** 10040 (212) 569-4311
ISRAEL OF THE CITY OF NEW YORK, TEMPLE R 112 E. 75TH STREET ... NEW YORK **NY** 10021 (212) 249-5000
JEWISH BOARD OF GUARDIANS RESIDENCE 74 ST. MARKS PLACE ... NEW YORK **NY** 10003 (212) 582-9100
JEWISH CENTER, THE O 131 W. 86TH STREET ... NEW YORK **NY** 10024 (212) 724-2700
JEWISH THEOLOGICAL SEMINARY, SYNAGOGUE OF THE C
3080 BROADWAY ... NEW YORK **NY** 10027 (212) 749-8000
JOSHUA JACOB ANSHEI HORODETZ, CONGREGATION O
253 EAST BROADWAY ... NEW YORK **NY** 10002
K'HAL ADATH JESHURUN, CONGREGATION O 90 BENNETT AVENUE ... NEW YORK **NY** 10033 (212) 923-8984
K'HAI ADATH JESHURUN, CONGREGATION O 85 BENNETT AVENUE ... NEW YORK **NY** 10033 (212) 923-3582
KAHAL MINCHAS CHINUCH, CONGREGATION O 321 W. 100TH STREET .. NEW YORK **NY** 10025
KEHILATH ISRAEL CHOFETZ CHAIM, CONGREGATION O
310 W. 103RD STREET ... NEW YORK **NY** 10025 (212) 222-3787
KEHILATH JACOB, CONGREGATION C 150 WEST 72ND STREET ... NEW YORK **NY** 10023 (212) 787-8680
KEHILATH JACOB, CONGREGATION O 305 W. 79TH STREET ... NEW YORK **NY** 10024 (212) 749-0159
KEHILATH JESHURUN, CONGREGATION O 125 EAST 85TH STREET ... NEW YORK **NY** 10028 (212) 427-1000
KOL ISRAEL, CONGREGATION 865 WEST END AVENUE ... NEW YORK **NY** 10025
LEBEDONE RADZILOWE, CONGREGATION O 225 EAST BROADWAY ... NEW YORK **NY** 10002
LINCOLN SQUARE SYNAGOGUE O 200 AMSTERDAM AVENUE ... NEW YORK **NY** 10023 (212) 874-6100
LITTLE SYNAGOGUE, THE C 27 E. 20TH STREET ... NEW YORK **NY** 10003 (212) 475-7081
MACHZEH ABRAHAM, CONGREGATION O 2581 BROADWAY ... NEW YORK **NY** 10025
MACHZIKEI TORAH, CONGREGATION 851 W. 181ST STREET ... NEW YORK **NY** 10033 (212) 927-6740
MANHATTAN RECONSTRUCTIONIST HAVURAH
C/O ETHEL EPSTEIN/FRITZI JACOBS ... NEW YORK **NY** (212) 362-5819
MASSAS BENJAMIN ANSHEI PODHAJCE, CONGREGATION O
108 E. 1ST STREET ... NEW YORK **NY** 10009
METROPOLITAN SYNAGOGUE OF NEW YORK R 40 E. 35TH STREET ... NEW YORK **NY** 10016 (212) 679-8580
MILLINERY CENTER SYNAGOGUE C 1025 SIXTH AVENUE ... NEW YORK **NY** 10018 (212) 921-1580
MIZRACHI HAPOEL HAMIZRACHI, CONGREGATION O
249 EAST BROADWAY ... NEW YORK **NY** 10002 (212) 964-6111
MORYA, CONGREGATION O 2228 BROADWAY ... NEW YORK **NY** 10024 (212) 729-6909
MOUNT NEBOH, CONGREGATION R 130 W. 79TH STREET ... NEW YORK **NY** 10024
MOUNT SINAI JEWISH CENTER O 135 BENNETT AVENUE ... NEW YORK **NY** 10040 (212) 568-9090
MT. SINAI ANSHE EMETH, CONGREGATION 135 BENNETT AVENUE ... NEW YORK **NY** 10040 (212) 928-9870
NODAH B'YEHUDA, CONGREGATION O
392 FORT WASHINGTON AVENUE ... NEW YORK **NY** 10033 (212) 795-1552
OHAB ZEDEK, CONGREGATION O 118 WEST 95TH STREET ... NEW YORK **NY** 10025 (212) 749-5150
OHAV SHALOM, CONGREGATION 270 W. 84TH STREET ... NEW YORK **NY** 10024 (212) 877-5850
OHAV SHOLAUM, CONGREGATION O 4624 BROADWAY ... NEW YORK **NY** 10040 (212) 567-0900
OLD BROADWAY SYNAGOGUE O 15 OLD BROADWAY ... NEW YORK **NY** 10027 (212) 662-8086
ORACH CHAIM, CONGREGATION O 1459 LEXINGTON AVENUE ... NEW YORK **NY** 10028 (212) 722-6566
PARK AVENUE SYNAGOGUE C 50 E. 87TH STREET ... NEW YORK **NY** 10028 (212) 369-2600
PARK EAST SYNAGOGUE O 163 E. 67TH STREET ... NEW YORK **NY** 10021 (212) 737-6900
PORT WASHINGTON SYNAGOGUE R
C/O MR. BAKER-25C, 1751 SECOND AVENUE ... NEW YORK **NY** 10028
RADIO CITY SYNAGOGUE O 49 W. 47TH STREET ... NEW YORK **NY** 10036 (212) 581-2839
RAMATH ORAH, CONGREGATION O 550 W. 110TH STREET ... NEW YORK **NY** 10025 (212) 222-2470
RODEPH SHOLOM CONGREGATION R 7 W. 83RD STREET ... NEW YORK **NY** 10024 (212) 362-8800
SHAARAY TEFILA, CONGREGATION R 250 E. 79TH STREET ... NEW YORK **NY** 10021 (212) 535-8008
SHAARE HATIKVAH AHAVATH TORAH V'TIKVOH CHADOSHOH, INC., CONG.
711 W. 179TH STREET ... NEW YORK **NY** 10033 (212) 927-2720
SHAARE TORAH, CONGREGATION O 15 W. 73RD STREET ... NEW YORK **NY** 10023 (212) 874-6322
SHAARE ZEDEK, CONGREGATION C 212 W. 93RD STREET ... NEW YORK **NY** 10025 (212) 874-7005
SHAARY TEFILA, CONGREGATION 250 EAST 79TH STREET ... NEW YORK **NY** 10021 (212) 535-8008
SHEARITH ADAS ISRAEL MINHAG SFARD, CONGREGATION O
237 EAST BROADWAY ... NEW YORK **NY** 10002
SHEARITH ISRAEL, CONGREGATION O 8 W. 70TH STREET ... NEW YORK **NY** 10023 (212) 873-0300
SHEVETH ACHIM ANSHEI SLONIM, CONGREGATION O
172 NORFOLK STREET ... NEW YORK **NY** 10002
SHMUEL JOSEF VCHAYAH, CONGREGATION
587B FORT WASHINGTON AVENUE ... NEW YORK **NY** 10033 (212) 927-9012
SIENEWER CHEVRAH O 217 HENRY STREET ... NEW YORK **NY** 10002
SMUEL JOSEF VCHAYAH, CONGREGATION
587-B FORT WASHINGTON AVENUE ... NEW YORK **NY** 10033 (212) 927-9012
SOCIETY FOR THE ADVANCEMENT OF JUDAISM RE
15 W. 86TH STREET ... NEW YORK **NY** 10024 (212) 724-7000
SONS OF ISRAEL KALWARIA, CONGREGATION O 13 PIKE STREET ... NEW YORK **NY** 10002
SPANISH-PORTUGUESE SYNAGOGUE R 8 W. 70TH STREET ... NEW YORK **NY** 10023 (212) 873-0300
STEPHEN WISE FREE SYNAGOGUE R 30 W. 68TH STREET ... NEW YORK **NY** 10023 (212) 877-4050
SUTTON PLACE SYNAGOGUE C 225 E. 51ST STREET ... NEW YORK **NY** 10022 (212) 593-3300
SYNAGOGUE COUNCIL OF AMERICA 432 PARK AVENUE S ... NEW YORK **NY** 10016 (212) 686-8670
TALMUD TORAH ADERETH EL, CONGREGATION O 135 E. 29TH STREET .. NEW YORK **NY** 10016 (212) 685-0241
TEL AVIV, CONGREGATION 27 EAST 20TH STREET ... NEW YORK **NY** 10003 (212) 475-7081

TIKVATH ISRAEL OF HARLEM, CONGREGATION O 160 E. 112TH STREET	NEW YORK	NY	10029	(212) 289-9677
TORAH VA'AVODAH INSTITUTE O 25 W. 26TH STREET	NEW YORK	NY	10010	(212) 683-4484
TORATH CHAIM, CONGREGATION 489 WEST END AVENUE	NEW YORK	NY	10024	(212) 874-3823
TOWN & VILLAGE SYNAGOGUE-TEMPLE TIFERETH ISRAEL C 334 E. 14TH STREET	NEW YORK	NY	10003	(212) 677-8090
UNION OF SEPHARDIC CONGREGATIONS 8 W. 70TH STREET	NEW YORK	NY	10023	(212) 873-0300
UNITED HEBREW COMMUNITY OF NEW YORK, ADATH ISRAEL OF NEW YORK O 201 EAST BROADWAY	NEW YORK	NY	10002	(212) 674-3580
UNIVERSAL JUDAISM, TEMPLE-CONGREGATION DAAT ELOHIM R 1010 PARK AVENUE	NEW YORK	NY	10028	(212) 673-1810
UNIVERSAL JUDAISM, TEMPLE OF 15 RUTHERFORD PLACE	NEW YORK	NY	10003	(212) 673-1810
VILLAGE TEMPLE R 33 E. 12TH STREET	NEW YORK	NY	10003	(212) 674-2340
WALL STREET SYNAGOGUE O 47 BEEKMAN STREET	NEW YORK	NY	10038	(212) 227-7800
WASHINGTON HEIGHTS CONGREGATION O 815 W. 179TH STREET	NEW YORK	NY	10033	(212) 923-4407
WASHINGTON MARKET SYNAGOGUE O 410 W. 14TH STREET	NEW YORK	NY	10014	(212) 243-2507
WEST SIDE INSTITUTIONAL SYNAGOGUE O 120-138 W. 76TH STREET	NEW YORK	NY	10023	(212) 877-7652
YORKVILLE SYNAGOGUE B'NAI JEHUDA O 352 E. 78TH STREET	NEW YORK	NY	10021	(212) 249-0760
YOUNG ISRAEL OF FIFTH AVENUE 3 WEST 16TH STREET	NEW YORK	NY	10011	(212) 929-1525
YOUNG ISRAEL OF MANHATTAN 225 EAST BROADWAY	NEW YORK	NY	10002	(212) 732-0966
YOUNG ISRAEL OF WEST SIDE 210 WEST 91ST STREET	NEW YORK	NY	10024	(212) 787-7513
ZEMACH TZEDEK, CONGREGATION O 241 EAST BROADWAY	NEW YORK	NY	10002	
ZICHRON EPHRAIM, CONGREGATION 163 E. 67TH STREET	NEW YORK	NY	10021	(212) 737-6900
ZICHRON MOSHE, CONGREGATION O 342 E. 20TH STREET	NEW YORK	NY	10003	(212) 475-9330
AGUDAS ISRAEL, CONGREGATION O 290 NORTH STREET	NEWBURGH	NY	12550	(914) 562-5604
BETH JACOB, TEMPLE R 344 GIDNEY AVENUE	NEWBURGH	NY	12550	(914) 562-5516
BETH EL, TEMPLE R 720 ASHLAND AVENUE	NIAGARA FALLS	NY	14302	(716) 282-2717
BETH ISRAEL, TEMPLE C COLLEGE & MADISON AVENUE	NIAGARA FALLS	NY	14305	(716) 285-9894
BETH EL OF BELLMORE, TEMPLE C 1373 BELLMORE ROAD	NORTH BELLMORE	NY	11710	(516) 781-2650
YOUNG ISRAEL OF NORTH BELLMORE 2428 HAMILTON ROAD	NORTH BELLMORE	NY	11710	(516) 826-0048
NER TAMID, CONGREGATION C P.O. BOX 126 5061 WEST TAFT ROAD	NORTH SYRACUSE	NY	13212	(315) 458-2022
OHR TORAH O 410 HUNGRY HARBOR ROAD	NORTH WOODMERE	NY	11581	(516) 791-2130
YOUNG ISRAEL OF NORTH WOODMERE-LAURELTON 785 GOLF DRIVE	NORTH WOODMERE	NY	11581	(516) 791-5099
NORWICH JEWISH CENTER R 72 SOUTH BROAD	NORWICH	NY	13815	(607) 334-2691
SONS OF ISRAEL, CONGREGATION C 300 NORTH BROADWAY	NYACK	NY	10960	(914) 358-3767
B'NAI ISRAEL REFORM TEMPLE R 96 BILTMORE AVENUE	OAKDALE	NY	11769	(516) 589-8948
JEWISH CENTER OF BAYSIDE OAKS C 50-35 CLOVERDALE BLVD	OAKLAND GARDENS	NY	11364	(718) 321-0300
OAKLAND JEWISH CENTER C 61-35 220TH STREET	OAKLAND GARDENS	NY	11364	(718) 225-7800
AVODAH, TEMPLE R 3050 OCEANSIDE ROAD	OCEANSIDE	NY	11572	(516) 766-6809
JEWISH CENTER OF OCEAN HARBOR C ROYAL & WEIDNER AVENUES	OCEANSIDE	NY	11572	(516) 536-6481
OCEANSIDE JEWISH CENTER C 2860 BROWER AVENUE	OCEANSIDE	NY	11572	(516) 764-4213
SHAAR HASHAMAYIM, CONGREGATION O 3309 SKILLMAN AVENUE	OCEANSIDE	NY	11572	(516) 764-6888
YOUNG ISRAEL OF OCEANSIDE 150 WAUKENA AVENUE	OCEANSIDE	NY	11572	(516) 764-1099
ANSHE ZOPHEN, CONGREGATION C 416 GREENE STREET	OGDENSBURG	NY	13669	(315) 393-3787
BETH ELOHIM, TEMPLE R 926 ROUND SWAMP ROAD	OLD BETH PAGE	NY	11804	(516) 694-4544
SOCIETY OF JEWISH SCIENCE & SYNAGOGUE 825 ROUND SWAMP ROAD	OLD BETH PAGE	NY	11804	(516) 249-6262
BETH ELOHIM, TEMPLE R 926 ROUND SWAMP ROAD	OLD BETHPAGE	NY	11804	(516) 694-4544
OLD WESTBURY HEBREW CONGREGATION C 21 OLD WESTBURY ROAD	OLD WESTBURY	NY	11590	(516) 333-7977
B'NAI ISRAEL, CONGREGATION R 127 S. BARRY STREET	OLEAN	NY	14760	(716) 372-3431
BETH EL C 83 CHESTNUT STREET	ONEONTA	NY	13802	(607) 432-5522
ORANGETOWN JEWISH CENTER C INDEPENDENCE AVENUE	ORANGEBURG	NY	10962	(914) 359-5920
ANSHE DORSHE EMES, CONGREGATION RE 100 S. HIGHLAND AVENUE	OSSINING	NY	10562	
ADATH ISRAEL, CONGREGATION C EAST THIRD & ONEIDA AVENUE	OSWEGO	NY	13126	(315) 342-0371
OYSTER BAY JEWISH CENTER C BERRY HILL ROAD	OYSTER BAY	NY	11771	(516) 922-6650
OZONE PARK JEWISH CENTER O 107-01 CROSS BAY BLVD	OZONE PARK	NY	11417	(718) 848-4096
SONS OF JACOB, TEMPLE C 97-44 75TH STREET	OZONE PARK	NY	11416	(718) 296-8334
GEMILUTH CHESSED, CONGREGATION OAK TREE ROAD	PALISADES	NY	10964	
TIFERETH ISRAEL, CONGREGATION - ANSHE PARKSVILLE	PARKSVILLE	NY	12768	
BETH EL OF PATCHOGUE, TEMPLE C 45 OAK STREET	PATCHOGUE	NY	11772	(516) 475-1882
PATCHOGUE, YOUNG ISRAEL OF O 28 MOWBRAY STREET	PATCHOGUE	NY	11772	(516) 654-0882
YOUNG ISRAEL OF PATCHOGUE 28 MOWBRAY STREET	PATCHOGUE	NY	11772	(516) 654-0882
BETH AM TEMPLE R 60 E. MADISON AVENUE, P.O. BOX 236	PEARL RIVER	NY	10965	(914) 735-5858
FIRST HEBREW CONGREGATION C 1821 E. MAIN STREET, P.O. BOX 590	PEEKSKILL	NY	10566	(914) 739-0500
ISRAEL, TEMPLE LAKE DRIVE	PEEKSKILL	NY	10537	(914) 528-2305
PELHAM JEWISH CENTER C 451 ESPLANADE	PELHAM	NY	10803	(914) 738-0870
BETH ELOHIM, TEMPLE R 926 ROUND SWAMP ROAD	PLAINVIEW	NY	11803	(516) 694-4544
MANETTO HILL JEWISH CENTER C 244 MANETTO HILL ROAD	PLAINVIEW	NY	11803	(516) 935-5454
PLAINVIEW JEWISH CENTER C 95 FLORAL DRIVE	PLAINVIEW	NY	11803	(516) 938-9610
YOUNG ISRAEL OF PLAINVIEW 132 SOUTHERN PARKWAY	PLAINVIEW	NY	11803	(516) 433-4811
BETH ISRAEL, TEMPLE R BOWMAN & MARCY LANE	PLATTSBURGH	NY	12901	(518) 563-3343
POMONA JEWISH CENTER C 106 POMONA ROAD	POMONA	NY	10970	(914) 354-2226
KNESSET TIFERETH ISRAEL, CONGREGATION C 575 KING STREET	PORT CHESTER	NY	10573	(914) 939-1004
NORTH SHORE JEWISH CENTER C 385 OLD TOWN ROAD	PORT JEFFERSON	NY	11776	(516) 928-3737
BETH EL C 88 E. MAIN STREET	PORT JERVIS	NY	12271	(914) 856-1722
BETH ISRAEL, TEMPLE C TEMPLE DRIVE	PORT WASHINGTON	NY	11050	(516) 767-1708
COMMUNITY SYNAGOGUE R 150 MIDDLE NECK ROAD	PORT WASHINGTON	NY	11050	(516) 883-3144
PORT JEWISH CENTER R P.O. BOX 852	PORT WASHINGTON	NY	11050	(516) 883-5117
BETH EL, CONGREGATION C 81 MARKET STREET	POTSDAM	NY	13676	
BETH EL, TEMPLE C 118 GRAND AVENUE	POUGHKEEPSIE	NY	12603	(914) 454-0570
BRETHREN OF ISRAEL, CONGREGATION - VASSAR TEMPLE R 140 HOOKER AVENUE	POUGHKEEPSIE	NY	12601	(914) 454-2570
SHOMRE ISRAEL, CONGREGATION O 18 PARK AVENUE	POUGHKEEPSIE	NY	12603	(914) 454-2890
VASSAR TEMPLE R 140 HOOKER AVENUE	POUGHKEEPSIE	NY	12601	(914) 454-2570
REFORM TEMPLE OF PUTNAM VALLEY R P.O. BOX 232, CHURCH ROAD	PUTNAM VALLEY	NY	10579	(914) 528-9721
AHAVATH ISRAEL, CONGREGATION O P.O. BOX 25	QUEENS VILLAGE	NY	11429	
BELL PARK JEWISH CENTER C 231-10 HILLSIDE AVENUE	QUEENS VILLAGE	NY	11427	(718) 464-9144
HOLLISWOOD JEWISH CENTER O 86-25 FRANCIS LEWIS BLVD	QUEENS VILLAGE	NY	11427	(718) 776-8500
QUEENS JEWISH CENTER C 94-34 HOLLIS COURT BLVD	QUEENS VILLAGE	NY	11428	(718) 465-4993
ATERES ZVI, CONGREGATION O 63-34 99TH STREET	REGO PARK	NY	11374	
BETH ISRAEL, CONGREGATION O 90-14 63RD DRIVE	REGO PARK	NY	11374	
BETH JACOB, CONGREGATION O 6602 SAUNDERS STREET	REGO PARK	NY	11374	(718) 897-8331
JEWISH COMMUNITY CENTER OF QUEENS O 99-07 66TH AVENUE	REGO PARK	NY	11374	(718) 896-6695
LEFRAK CITY JEWISH CENTER 98-54 HORACE HARDING EXPRESSWAY	REGO PARK	NY	11374	(718) 699-7752
PLAZA TORAH CENTER O 98-54 HORACE HARDING EXPRESSWAY	REGO PARK	NY	11374	(718) 699-7752
REGO PARK JEWISH CENTER C 97-30 QUEENS BLVD	REGO PARK	NY	11374	(718) 459-1000
AGUDATH ISRAEL OF KEW GARDENS 117-01 PARK LANE SO	RICHMOND HILL	NY	11418	
BETH ISRAEL, CONGREGATION C 88-01 102ND STREET	RICHMOND HILL	NY	11418	(718) 847-9688
JEWISH CENTER OF RICHMOND HILL O 101-54 117TH STREET	RICHMOND HILL	NY	11419	(718) 849-2507
OHEL TORAH SYNAGOGUE O 629 WEST 239TH STREET	RIVERDALE	NY	10463	(212) 543-5618
RIVERDALE TEMPLE R 246TH STREET & INDEPENDENCE AVENUE	RIVERDALE	NY	10471	(212) 548-3800
ISRAEL OF RIVERHEAD, TEMPLE C 490 NORTHVILLE TURNPIKE	RIVERHEAD	NY	11901	(516) 727-3191
TRADITIONAL SYNAGOGUE OF ROCHDALE VILLAGE O 165-27 BAISLEY BLVD	ROCHDALE VILLAGE	NY	11434	(718) 525-3610
AHAVAS ACHI, ASHEI KIPEL VOLIN, CONGREGATION O 703 JOSEPH AVENUE	ROCHESTER	NY	14621	(716) 544-9261
B'NAI ISRAEL, CONGREGATION O 692 JOSEPH AVENUE	ROCHESTER	NY	14621	(716) 544-9261
B'RITH KODESH, TEMPLE R 2131 ELMWOOD AVENUE	ROCHESTER	NY	14618	(716) 244-7060
BETH DAVID, TEMPLE C 3200 ST. PAUL BLVD	ROCHESTER	NY	14617	(716) 266-3223
BETH EL, TEMPLE C 139 WINTON ROAD S	ROCHESTER	NY	14610	(716) 473-1770
BETH HAKNESSES HACHODOSH O 19 ST. REGIS DRIVE N.	ROCHESTER	NY	14618	(716) 271-5390
BETH HAMEDRESH BETH ISRAEL C 1369 EAST AVENUE	ROCHESTER	NY	14610	(716) 244-2060
BETH JOSEPH CENTER O 1150 ST. PAUL STREET	ROCHESTER	NY	14621	(716) 266-1331
BETH SHALOM, CONGREGATION O 1161 MONROE AVENUE	ROCHESTER	NY	14620	(716) 473-1625
EMANU-EL OF IRONDEQUOIT, TEMPLE R 2956 ST. PAUL BLVD	ROCHESTER	NY	14617	(716) 266-1978
LIGHT OF ISRAEL, CONGREGATION O 206 NORTON STREET	ROCHESTER	NY	14621	
SINAI, TEMPLE R 363 PENFIELD ROAD	ROCHESTER	NY	14625	(716) 381-6890
TIPHERETH ISRAEL, CONGREGATION O 271 DARTMOUTH STREET	ROCHESTER	NY	14607	
VAAD HAKOLEL, CONGREGATION O P.O. BOX 362	ROCHESTER	NY	14602	
DERECH EMUNAH, CONGREGATION 199 BEACH 67TH STREET	ROCKAWAY BEACH	NY	11692	(718) 634-2288
ISRAEL, TEMPLE OF C 188 BEACH 84TH STREET	ROCKAWAY BEACH	NY	11693	(718) 327-6420
B'NAI SHOLOM, TEMPLE C 100 HEMPSTEAD AVENUE	ROCKVILLE CENTRE	NY	11570	(516) 764-4100
CENTRAL SYNAGOGUE R 430 DEMOTT AVENUE	ROCKVILLE CENTRE	NY	11570	(516) 766-4300
ADAS ISRAEL C 705 HICKORY STREET	ROME	NY	13440	(315) 337-3170
YOUNG ISRAEL OF ROOSEVELT ISLAND 560-1 MAIN STREET	ROOSEVELT ISLAND	NY	10044	(212) 826-6390
ROSEDALE JEWISH CENTER C 247-11 FRANCIS LEWIS BLVD	ROSEDALE	NY	11422	(718) 528-3988
BETH SHOLOM, TEMPLE C ROSLYN ROAD & N. STATE PARKWAY	ROSLYN HEIGHTS	NY	11577	(516) 621-2288
RECONSTRUCTIONIST SYNAGOGUE 1 WILLOW STREET	ROSLYN HEIGHTS	NY	11577	(516) 621-5540
SHELTER ROCK JEWISH CENTER C SEARINGTON & SHELTER ROCK ROADS	ROSLYN HEIGHTS	NY	11577	(516) 741-4305
SINAI OF ROSLYN, TEMPLE R 425 ROSLYN ROAD	ROSLYN HEIGHTS	NY	11577	(516) 621-6800
COMMUNITY SYNAGOGUE R 200 FOREST AVENUE	RYE	NY	10550	(914) 967-6262
EMANU-EL OF WESTCHESTER, CONGREGATION R WESTCHESTER AVENUE & KENILWORTH ROAD	RYE	NY	10580	(914) 967-4382
SONS OF ISRAEL, CONGREGATION O 127 STREET & FOCH BLVD	S. OZONE PARK	NY	11420	
TALMUD TORAH OF RICHMOND HILL O 109-25 114TH STREET	S. OZONE PARK	NY	11420	
ADAS ISRAEL, TEMPLE R ELIZABETH STREET & ATLANTIC AVENUE	SAG HARBOR	NY	11963	(516) 725-0054
COMMUNITY SYNAGOGUE, THE 150 MIDDLE NECK ROAD	SANDS POINT	NY	11021	(516) 883-3144
SINAI, TEMPLE R 509 BROADWAY, P.O. BOX 224	SARATOGA SPRINGS	NY	12866	(518) 584-8730
SHALOM, TEMPLE C 225 GREELEY AVENUE	SAYVILLE	NY	11782	(516) 567-3207
SCARSDALE SYNAGOGUE-TREMONT TEMPLE R 2 OGDEN ROAD	SCARSDALE	NY	10583	(914) 725-5175
SCARSDALE, YOUNG ISRAEL OF O 1313 DAISY FARMS ROAD	SCARSDALE	NY	10583	(914) 723-6273
SEPHARDIC COMMUNITY OF NEW ROCHELLE-SCARSDALE, THE O C/O YOUNG ISRAEL OF SCARSDALE, 1313 DAISY FARMS ROAD	SCARSDALE	NY	10583	(914) 723-6273
WESTCHESTER REFORM TEMPLE R 255 MAMARONECK ROAD	SCARSDALE	NY	10583	(914) 723-7727
YOUNG ISRAEL OF SCARSDALE 1313 WEAVER STREET P.O.B. 103H	SCARSDALE	NY	10583	(914) 636-8686
ADATH ISRAEL, CONGREGATION 872 ALBANY STREET	SCHENECTADY	NY	12307	
AGUDAT ACHIM, CONGREGATION C 2117 UNION STREET	SCHENECTADY	NY	12309	
BETH ISRAEL, CONGREGATION O 2195 EASTERN PARKWAY	SCHENECTADY	NY	12309	(518) 377-3700
GATES OF HEAVEN, CONGREGATION R 852 ASHMORE AVENUE	SCHENECTADY	NY	12309	(518) 374-8173
HEBREW CONGREGATION OF SOMERS, INC. C MERVYN DRIVE & CYPRESS LANE	SHENOROCK	NY	10587	(914) 248-5166
BETH SHOLOM OF SMITHTOWN, TEMPLE C P.O. BOX 764, EDGEWOOD AVENUE & RIVER ROAD	SMITHTOWN	NY	11787	(516) 724-0424
SOUTH FALLSBURG HEBREW ASSOCIATION P.O. BOX 457	SOUTH FALLSBURG	NY	12279	(914) 434-9675
SOUTH SHORE LONG ISLAND HAVURAH RE C/O FLATOW	SOUTH SHORE	NY		(516) 766-7390
AYSHEL AVRAHAM, CONGREGATION O 111 SOUTH MADISON AVENUE	SPRING VALLEY	NY	10977	(914) 352-0630
B'NAI YECHIEL, CONGREGATION 80 WASHINGTON AVENUE	SPRING VALLEY	NY	10977	
BETH EL, TEMPLE R 415 VIOLA ROAD	SPRING VALLEY	NY	10977	(914) 356-2000
JEWISH COMMUNITY CENTER OF SPRING VALLEY C 250 N. MAIN STREET	SPRING VALLEY	NY	10977	(914) 356-3710
NEW SQUARE, YESHIVA OF 766 NORTH MAIN STREET	SPRING VALLEY	NY	10977	(914) 354-2237
OHEV SHOLOM, CONGREGATION O 14 LINDEN AVENUE	SPRING VALLEY	NY	10977	
SHAAREY TFILOH, CONGREGATION C 972 S. MAIN STREET	SPRING VALLEY	NY	10977	(914) 356-2225
SONS OF ISRAEL, CONGREGATION C 80 WILLIAMS AVENUE	SPRING VALLEY	NY	10977	(914) 352-6767
YOUNG ISRAEL OF CLARKSTOWN 11 ELLEN STREET	SPRING VALLEY	NY	10977	(914) 352-8654
YOUNG ISRAEL OF SPRING VALLEY 23 UNION ROAD	SPRING VALLEY	NY	10977	(914) 356-3363
ZEMACH DAVID OF NEW SQUARE, CONGREGATION O	SPRING VALLEY	NY	10977	(914) 354-9736
RAMAT TORAH JEWISH COMMUNITY HOUSE, CONGREGATION C 221-03 137TH AVENUE	SPRINGFIELD GARDENS	NY	11413	
CAMBRIA HEIGHTS JEWISH CENTER 222-05 116TH AVENUE	ST. ALBANS	NY	11412	
AGUDAS SHOMREI HADAS O 98 RUPERT AVENUE	STATEN ISLAND	NY	10314	(718) 698-4066

AGUDATH ACHIM ANSHE CHESED, CONGREGATION O 641 DELAFIELD AVENUE	STATEN ISLAND	**NY**	10310	(718) 442-9445
AGUDATH ISRAEL OF STATEN ISLAND O 207 WARWICK AVENUE	STATEN ISLAND	**NY**		
AHAVATH ISRAEL, CONGREGATION C 7630 AMBOY ROAD	STATEN ISLAND	**NY**	10307	(718) 984-2113
AHAVATH SHALOM, CONGREGATION C 2044 RICHMOND AVENUE	STATEN ISLAND	**NY**	10314	(718) 761-8446
B'NAI ISRAEL, CONGREGATION C 45 TWOMBLY AVENUE	STATEN ISLAND	**NY**	10306	(718) 987-8188
B'NAI JESHURUN CONGREGATION C 275 MARTLING AVENUE	STATEN ISLAND	**NY**	10314	(718) 981-5550
BETH SHLOIME OF STATEN ISLAND, CONGREGATION O 84 OAKVILLE STREET	STATEN ISLAND	**NY**	10314	(718) 761-5559
EMANU-EL OF STATEN ISLAND, TEMPLE C 984 POST AVENUE	STATEN ISLAND	**NY**	10302	(718) 942-5966
ISRAEL, TEMPLE R 315 FOREST AVENUE	STATEN ISLAND	**NY**	10301	(718) 727-2231
TIFERETH ISRAEL, TEMPLE C 119 WRIGHT STREET	STATEN ISLAND	**NY**	10304	
YOUNG ISRAEL OF ELTINGVILLE 374 RIDGEWOOD AVENUE	STATEN ISLAND	**NY**	10312	(718) 948-1993
YOUNG ISRAEL OF STATEN ISLAND 835 FOREST HILL ROAD	STATEN ISLAND	**NY**	10314	(718) 494-6700
ISAIAH, TEMPLE R 1404 STONYBROOK ROAD	STONY BROOK	**NY**	11790	(516) 751-8518
REFORM TEMPLE OF SUFFERN R 70 HAVERSTRAW ROAD, P.O. BOX 472	SUFFERN	**NY**	10901	(914) 357-5872
SONS OF ISRAEL, CONGREGATION C SUFFERN PLACE	SUFFERN	**NY**	10901	(914) 357-9827
AHAVAS SHULEM, CONGREGATION O	SWAN LAKE	**NY**	12783	
AHAVATH ACHIM, CONGREGATION 1207 ALMOND STREET	SWAN LAKE	**NY**	13210	
EAST NASSAU HEBREW CONGREGATION O 310-A SOUTH OYSTER BAY ROAD	SYOSSET	**NY**	11791	(516) 921-1800
MIDWAY JEWISH CENTER C 330 S. OYSTER BAY ROAD	SYOSSET	**NY**	11791	(516) 938-8390
NORTH SHORE CONGREGATION R 83 MUTTONTOWN ROAD	SYOSSET	**NY**	11791	(516) 921-2282
ADATH YESHURUN, TEMPLE C 450 KIMBER ROAD	SYRACUSE	**NY**	13224	(315) 445-0002
ANSHE SFARD, CONGREGATION O 3528 EAST GENESEE STREET	SYRACUSE	**NY**	13214	
BETH SHOLOM-CHEVRA SHAS, CONGREGATION C 5205 JAMESVILLE ROAD	SYRACUSE	**NY**	13214	(315) 446-9570
SEPHARDIC GROUP OF SYRACUSE O 119 DOLL PARKWAY	SYRACUSE	**NY**	13214	(315) 446-0760
SOCIETY OF CONCORD, TEMPLE R 910 MADISON STREET	SYRACUSE	**NY**	13210	(315) 475-9952
YOUNG ISRAEL OF SYRACUSE 2200 EAST GENESSEE	SYRACUSE	**NY**	13210	(315) 472-8411
BETH ABRAHAM, TEMPLE R 25 LEROY AVENUE	TARRYTOWN	**NY**	10591	(914) 631-1770
BETH EL OF GREATER BUFFALO, TEMPLE C 2368 EGGERT ROAD	TONAWANDA	**NY**	14150	(716) 836-3762
BERITH SHOLOM, CONGREGATION R 167 THIRD STREET	TROY	**NY**	12180	(518) 272-8872
BETH EL, TEMPLE C 409 HOOSICK STREET	TROY	**NY**	12180	(518) 272-6113
BETH ISRAEL BIKUR CHOLIM, CONGREGATION 27 CENTERVIEW DRIVE	TROY	**NY**	12181	
BETH TEPHILA, CONGREGATION O 82 RIVER STREET	TROY	**NY**	12181	(518) 272-3182
GENESIS-AGUDAS ACHIM C 25 OAKLAND AVENUE	TUCKAHOE	**NY**	10707	(914) 961-3766
UNIONDALE JEWISH CENTER C 760 JERUSALEM AVENUE	UNIONDALE	**NY**	11553	(516) 486-8788
BETH TORAH, TEMPLE R ROUTE 9W	UPPER NYACK	**NY**	10960	(914) 358-2248
SONS OF ISRAEL, CONGREGATION C 300 NORTH BROADWAY	UPPER NYACK	**NY**	10960	(914) 358-3767
BETH EL, TEMPLE C 1607 GENESEE STREET	UTICA	**NY**	13501	(315) 724-4751
EMANU-EL, TEMPLE R 2710 GENESEE STREET	UTICA	**NY**	13502	(315) 724-4177
HOUSE OF JACOB, CONGREGATION O 14 CLINTON PLACE	UTICA	**NY**	13501	(315) 724-8357
ZVI JACOB, CONGREGATION O 313 JAMES STREET	UTICA	**NY**	13501	(315) 724-8357
BETH SHOLOM, CONGREGATION - SUNRISE JEWISH CENTER O 550 ROCKAWAY AVENUE	VALLEY STREAM	**NY**	11581	(516) 561-9245
GATES OF ZION, TEMPLE C 322 N. CORONA AVENUE	VALLEY STREAM	**NY**	11580	(516) 561-2308
HILLEL, TEMPLE - SOUTHSIDE JEWISH CENTER C 1000 ROSEDALE ROAD	VALLEY STREAM	**NY**	11581	(516) 791-6344
TREE OF LIFE, CONGREGATION C 502 NORTH CENTRAL AVENUE	VALLEY STREAM	**NY**	11580	(516) 825-2090
BETH HILLEL, CONGREGATION O 20 PINE STREET	WALDEN	**NY**	12586	
SUBURBAN TEMPLE, THE R 2900 JERUSALEM AVENUE	WANTAGH	**NY**	11793	(516) 221-2370
WANTAGH JEWISH CENTER C 3710 WOODBINE AVENUE	WANTAGH	**NY**	11793	(516) 785-2445
DEGEL ISRAEL, CONGREGATION C 557 THOMPSON BLVD	WATERTOWN	**NY**	13601	(315) 782-2860
BETH ISRAEL, CONGREGATION C 339 BROAD STREET	WAVERLY	**NY**	14892	
WOODSTOCK RECONSTRUCTIONIST HAVURAH C/O STEWART MAURER	WEST HARLEY	**NY**	12491	(914) 331-0319
ANSHEI SHALOM O 453 HEMPSTEAD AVENUE	WEST HEMPSTEAD	**NY**	11552	(516) 489-8112
JEWISH COMMUNITY CENTER OF WEST HEMPSTEAD C 711 DOGWOOD AVENUE	WEST HEMPSTEAD	**NY**	11552	(516) 481-7448
NASSAU COMMUNITY TEMPLE R 240 HEMPSTEAD AVENUE	WEST HEMPSTEAD	**NY**	11552	(516) 485-1811
YOUNG ISRAEL OF WEST HEMPSTEAD 630 HEMPSTEAD AVENUE	WEST HEMPSTEAD	**NY**	11552	(516) 481-7429
AGUDATH ISRAEL OF FAR ROCKAWAY 1 BALSAM COURT	WEST LAWRENCE	**NY**	11691	(718) 471-4861
BETH TORAH, CONGREGATION C 243 CANTIAGUE ROAD	WESTBURY	**NY**	11590	(516) 334-7979
COMMUNITY REFORM TEMPLE R 712 THE PLAIN ROAD	WESTBURY	**NY**	11590	(516) 333-1839
SHOLOM, TEMPLE C 675 BROOKSIDE COURT	WESTBURY	**NY**	11590	(516) 334-2800
WESTBURY HEBREW CONGREGATION C P.O. BOX B, 21 OLD WESTBURY ROAD	WESTBURY	**NY**	11590	
BETH AM SHALOM, CONGREGATION RE 295 SOUNDVIEW AVENUE	WHITE PLAINS	**NY**	10606	
HEBREW INSTITUTE OF WHITE PLAINS O 20 GREENRIDGE AVENUE	WHITE PLAINS	**NY**	10605	(914) 948-3095
ISRAEL CENTER OF WHITE PLAINS, TEMPLE C 280 OLD MAMARONECK ROAD	WHITE PLAINS	**NY**	10605	(914) 948-2800
JEWISH COMMUNITY CENTER OF WHITE PLAINS R 252 SOUNDVIEW AVENUE	WHITE PLAINS	**NY**	10606	(914) 949-4717
WOODLANDS COMMUNITY TEMPLE R 50 WORTHINGTON ROAD	WHITE PLAINS	**NY**	10607	(914) 592-7070
AGUDAS ACHIM, CONGREGATION 21-08 UTOPIA PARKWAY	WHITESTONE	**NY**	11377	
CLEARVIEW JEWISH CENTER C 16-50 UTOPIA PARKWAY	WHITESTONE	**NY**	11357	(718) 352-6670
GARDEN JEWISH CENTER T 24-20 PARSONS BLVD	WHITESTONE	**NY**	11357	
WHITESTONE HEBREW CENTER C 12-45 CLINTONVILLE STREET	WHITESTONE	**NY**	11357	(718) 767-1500
HAVURAH, CONGREGATION R 6320 MAIN STREET	WILLIAMSVILLE	**NY**	14221	(716) 634-3010
YOUNG ISRAEL OF GREATER BUFFALO 105 MAPLE ROAD	WILLIAMSVILLE	**NY**	14221	(716) 634-0212
BNAI ISRAEL OF WOODHAVEN JEWISH CENTER O 89-07 ATLANTIC AVENUE	WOODHAVEN	**NY**	11421	
WOODSIDE JEWISH CENTER O 89-07 ATLANTIC AVENUE	WOODHAVEN	**NY**	11421	
SONS OF ISRAEL, CONGREGATION O 111 IRVING PLACE	WOODMERE	**NY**	11598	(516) 374-0655
YOUNG ISRAEL OF WOODMERE 859 PENINSULA BOULEVARD	WOODMERE	**NY**	11598	(516) 295-0150
OHAVE SHOLEM, CONGREGATION O	WOODRIDGE	**NY**	12789	
BNEI ISRAEL, CONGREGATION 48-53 44TH STREET	WOODSIDE	**NY**	11377	
EMANU-EL, TEMPLE R 306 RUMSEY ROAD ON THE PARKWAY	YONKERS	**NY**	10705	(914) 963-0575
GREYSTONE JEWISH CENTER O 600 NORTH BROADWAY	YONKERS	**NY**	10701	(914) 963-8888
LINCOLN PARK JEWISH CENTER C 311 CENTRAL PARK AVENUE	YONKERS	**NY**	10704	(914) 965-7119
MIDCHESTER JEWISH CENTER C 236 GRANDVIEW BLVD	YONKERS	**NY**	10710	(914) 779-3660
NORTHEAST JEWISH CENTER C 11 SALISBURY ROAD	YONKERS	**NY**	10710	(914) 337-0268
OHEB ZEDEK OF YONKERS N.Y., CONGREGATION O 63 HAMILTON AVENUE	YONKERS	**NY**	10705	(914) 963-1951
SONS OF ISRAEL, CONGREGATION O 105 RADFORD STREET	YONKERS	**NY**	10705	(914) 969-4453
YOUNG ISRAEL OF NORTH RIVERDALE 25 CLIFTON AVENUE	YONKERS	**NY**	10705	(914) 963-9448
BETH AM, TEMPLE R CHURCH STREET, P.O. BOX 433	YORKTOWN HEIGHTS	**NY**	10598	(914) 962-7500
YORKTOWN JEWISH CENTER C 2966 CROMPOND ROAD	YORKTOWN HEIGHTS	**NY**	10598	(914) 245-2324
BETH HA-TEPHILA, CONGREGATION R 43 N. LIBERTY STREET	ASHEVILLE	**NC**	28801	(704) 253-4911
BETH ISRAEL SYNAGOGUE C 229 MURDOCK AVENUE	ASHEVILLE	**NC**	28804	(704) 252-8431
BETH EL, TEMPLE R 1727 PROVIDENCE ROAD	CHARLOTTE	**NC**	28207	(704) 366-1948
BETH SHALOM, TEMPLE R 3600 FAIRVIEW ROAD	CHARLOTTE	**NC**	28211	(704) 366-5560
ISRAEL, TEMPLE C 1014 DILWORTH ROAD	CHARLOTTE	**NC**	28203	(704) 376-2796
BETH EL CONGREGATION C P.O. BOX 1762, WATTS & MARKHAM AVENUE	DURHAM	**NC**	27702	(919) 682-1238
JUDEA REFORM CONGREGATION R 2115 CORNWALLIS ROAD	DURHAM	**NC**	27705	(919) 489-7062
RECONSTRUCTIONIST HAVURAH IN DURHAM, NC 1004 WATTS STREET	DURHAM	**NC**	27701	(919) 682-1238
BETH ISRAEL, CONGREGATION C 2204 MORGANTON ROAD, P.O. BOX 44	FAYETTEVILLE	**NC**	28303	(919) 484-4612
EMANUEL, TEMPLE R 320 SOUTH STREET	GASTONIA	**NC**	28052	(704) 865-1541
OHEB SHOLOM, TEMPLE R P.O. BOX 2063	GOLDSBORO	**NC**	27530	(919) 867-9975
B'NAI ISRAEL SYNAGOGUE 804 WINVIEW DRIVE, P.O.BOX 10214	GREENSBORO	**NC**	27404	(919) 855-5091
B'NAI ISRAEL SYNAGOGUE C 713 NORTH GREEN STREET, P.O. BOX 5426	GREENSBORO	**NC**	27403	
B'NAI SHOLOM SYNAGOGUE C P.O. BOX 10214	GREENSBORO	**NC**	27408	(919) 855-5091
BETH DAVID SYNAGOGUE C 804 WINEVIEW DRIVE	GREENSBORO	**NC**	27410	(919) 297-0007
EMANUEL, TEMPLE R 713 N. GREENE STREET	GREENSBORO	**NC**	27401	(919) 275-6316
AGUDAS ISRAEL, CONGREGATION C P.O. BOX 668, 328 N. KING STREET	HENDERSONVILLE	**NC**	28793	(704) 693-9838
HICKORY JEWISH CENTER C P.O. BOX 1032, 4 STREET DRIVE & 11TH AVENUE N.W.	HICKORY	**NC**	28601	(704) 327-4081
HIGH POINT B'NAI ISRAEL SYNAGOGUE C 1207 KENSINGTON DRIVE	HIGH POINT	**NC**	27260	(919) 883-1966
JACKSONVILLE HEBREW CONGREGATION C P.O. BOX 430	JACKSONVILLE	**NC**	28540	
ISRAEL, TEMPLE R P.O. BOX 903	KINSTON	**NC**	28501	(919) 523-2057
BETH EL, TEMPLE C P.O. BOX 16	LUMBERTON	**NC**	28358	(919) 739-6576
B'NAI SHOLEM CONGREGATION R 505 MIDDLE STREET	NEW BERN	**NC**	28560	(919) 637-5663
BETH MEYER SYNAGOGUE C P.O. BOX 2045, 806 W. JOHNSON STREET	RALEIGH	**NC**	27602	(919) 832-6498
BETH OR, TEMPLE R 5315 CREEDMOOR ROAD	RALEIGH	**NC**	27612	(919) 781-4895
BETH EL, TEMPLE R SUNSET AVENUE AT PINE, P.O. BOX 291	ROCKY MOUNT	**NC**	27801	(919) 446-7675
ISRAEL, TEMPLE C P.O. BOX 815, 1600 BRENNER AVENUE	SALISBURY	**NC**	28144	(704) 633-1152
EMANUEL, CONGREGATION C P.O. BOX 5171, KELLY STREET & WEST END AVENUE	STATESVILLE	**NC**	28677	(704) 873-7611
EMANU-EL, TEMPLE R EIGHTH & SYCAMORE STREETS	WELDON	**NC**	27890	
BETH ISRAEL, CONGREGATION C P.O. BOX 911	WHITEVILLE	**NC**	28472	(919) 642-4039
B'NAI ISRAEL, CONGREGATION C 2601 CHESTNUT STREET, P.O. BOX 3752	WILMINGTON	**NC**	28401	(919) 762-4117
ISRAEL, TEMPLE OF R 1 S. 4TH STREET	WILMINGTON	**NC**	28401	(919) 762-0000
BETH JACOB CONGREGATION C 1833 ACADEMY STREET	WINSTON-SALEM	**NC**	27103	(919) 725-3880
EMANUEL, TEMPLE R 201 OAKWOOD DRIVE	WINSTON-SALEM	**NC**	27103	(919) 722-6640
BISMARCK HEBREW CONGREGATION N. 5TH STREET	BISMARCK	**NC**	58501	(701) 223-1768
BETH EL, TEMPLE R 809 S. 11TH AVENUE	FARGO	**ND**	58103	(701) 232-0441
B'NAI ISRAEL SYNAGOGUE 601 COTTONWOOD AVENUE	GRAND FORKS	**ND**	58201	(701) 775-5124
BETH ISRAEL, TEMPLE 6TH STREET & FIRST AVENUE S.E.	MINOT	**ND**	58701	(701) 838-8798
MINOT HEBREW CONGREGATION C 205 8TH STREET	MINOT	**ND**	58701	
AHAVAS ZEDEK, CONGREGATION 189 OWASSO	AKRON	**OH**	44313	
ANSHE SFARD, CONGREGATION O 646 NORTH REVERE ROAD	AKRON	**OH**	44313	
BETH EL CONGREGATION C 464 S. HAWKINS AVENUE	AKRON	**OH**	44320	(216) 864-2105
ISRAEL, TEMPLE R 133 MERRIMAN ROAD	AKRON	**OH**	44303	(216) 762-8617
NEW HEBREW CONGREGATION O 1500 ROWLES DRIVE	AKRON	**OH**	44313	(216) 867-3407
REVERE ROAD SYNAGOGUE O 646 NORTH REVERE ROAD	AKRON	**OH**	44313	(216) 867-7292
TIFERETH ISRAEL CONGREGATION R 713 PROSPECT AVENUE, P.O. BOX 739	ASHTABULA	**OH**	44004	
BETH AYNU, CONGREGATION C 25400 FAIRMOUNT BLVD	BEACHWOOD	**OH**	44122	
GREEN ROAD SYNAGOGUE O 2437 SOUTH GREEN ROAD	BEACHWOOD	**OH**	44122	(216) 381-4757
SUBURBAN TEMPLE, THE R 22401 CHAGRIN BLVD	BEACHWOOD	**OH**	44122	(216) 991-0700
AGUDAS ACHIM, CONGREGATION 34TH STREET & NORTH BELMONT	BELLAIRE	**OH**	43906	
AHAVAS SHOLOM, CONGREGATION O 2568 EAST BROAD STREET	BEXLEY	**OH**	43209	(614) 252-4815
AGUDAS ACHIM, CONGREGATION O 929 CHERRY AVENUE N.E.	CANTON	**OH**	44704	(216) 456-8781
ISRAEL, TEMPLE R 333 25TH STREET N.W.	CANTON	**OH**	44709	(216) 455-5179
SHAARAY TORAH SYNAGOGUE, THE C 432 30TH STREET N.W.	CANTON	**OH**	44709	(216) 492-0310
YOUNG ISRAEL OF CANTON 2508 N. MARKET STREET	CANTON	**OH**	44714	(216) 456-8781
ADATH ISRAEL CONGREGATION C 3201 E. GALBRAITH ROAD	CINCINNATI	**OH**	45236	(513) 793-1800
AGUDAS ISRAEL, CONGREGATION O 6442 STOVER AVENUE	CINCINNATI	**OH**	45237	
AGUDATH ACHIM ROSELAWN SYNAGOGUE O 7600 READING ROAD	CINCINNATI	**OH**	45237	(513) 761-7755
B'NAI TZEDEK, CONGREGATION C 1580 SUMMIT ROAD	CINCINNATI	**OH**	45237	(513) 821-0941
BETH HAMEDRASH HAGODOL, BOND HILL SYNAGOGUE O 4906 READING	CINCINNATI	**OH**	45237	
BETH JACOB SYNAGOGUE 3770 ST. LAWRENCE AVENUE	CINCINNATI	**OH**	45205	
DOWNTOWN SYNAGOGUE-ENQUIRER BUILDING 617 VINE	CINCINNATI	**OH**	45202	(513) 241-3576
ISAAC M. WISE TEMPLE R 8329 RIDGE ROAD	CINCINNATI	**OH**	45236	(513) 793-2556
K.K. BENE ISRAEL-ROCKDALE TEMPLE R 8501 RIDGE ROAD	CINCINNATI	**OH**	45236	(513) 891-9900
KNESETH ISRAEL, CONGREGATION O 1515 SECTION ROAD	CINCINNATI	**OH**	45237	(513) 948-2209
NEW HOPE CONGREGATION O 1625 CREST HILL AVENUE	CINCINNATI	**OH**	45237	(513) 821-6274
NORTH AVONDALE SYNAGOGUE 3870 READING	CINCINNATI	**OH**	45229	(513) 281-3243
NORTHERN HILLS SYNAGOGUE-CONGREGATION B'NAI AVRAHAM C 715 FLEMING ROAD	CINCINNATI	**OH**	45231	(513) 931-6038
OHAV SHALOM, CONGREGATION O 1834 SECTION ROAD	CINCINNATI	**OH**	45237	(513) 531-4676
PRICE HILL BETH JACOB, CONGREGATION R ST. LAWRENCE & RAPIDS AVENUES	CINCINNATI	**OH**	45205	
ROCKDALE TEMPLE, K K BENE ISRAEL R 8501 RIDGE ROAD	CINCINNATI	**OH**	45236	(513) 891-9900
ROSELAWN SYNAGOGUE 7600 READING	CINCINNATI	**OH**	45237	(513) 761-7755

SEPHARDIC BETH SHALOM CONGREGATION P.O. BOX 37431	CINCINNATI	**OH**	45222	(513) 793-6936
SHOLOM, TEMPLE R 3100 LONGMEADOW LANE	CINCINNATI	**OH**	45236	(513) 791-1330
VALLEY TEMPLE, THE R 145 SPRINGFIELD PIKE	CINCINNATI	**OH**	45220	(513) 761-3555
YAD CHARUTZIM-TIFERES ISRAEL CONGREGATION O 3870 READING	CINCINNATI	**OH**	45229	
AGUDATH ISRAEL OF CLEVELAND O 3840 SEVERN ROAD	CLEVELAND	**OH**	44118	(216) 321-9718
AHAVATH ISRAEL O 3448 EUCLID HEIGHTS BLVD	CLEVELAND	**OH**	44118	(216) 371-3665
B'NAI JESHURUN (TEMPLE ON THE HEIGHTS) C 27501 FAIRMOUNT BLVD	CLEVELAND	**OH**	44124	(216) 831-6555
BETH AM, CONGREGATION C 3557 WASHINGTON BLVD	CLEVELAND	**OH**	44118	(216) 321-1000
BETH EL O 15808 CHAGRIN BLVD	CLEVELAND	**OH**	44120	(216) 991-6044
BETH ISRAEL-THE WEST TEMPLE R 14308 TRISKETT ROAD	CLEVELAND	**OH**	44111	(216) 941-8882
BETHAYNU C 25400 FAIRMOUNT BLVD	CLEVELAND	**OH**	44122	(216) 292-2931
BRITH EMETH R 27575 SHAKER BLVD	CLEVELAND	**OH**	44124	(216) 831-5363
CONGREGATIONAL PLENUM OF GREATER CLEVELAND 26000 SHAKER BLVD	CLEVELAND	**OH**	44122	(216) 831-3233
EMANU-EL, TEMPLE R 2200 S. GREEN ROAD	CLEVELAND	**OH**	44121	(216) 381-6600
ETZ CHAYIM (TREE OF LIFE CONGREGATION) C MAYFIELD HEIGHTS COMMUNITY CENTER, 6803 MARSOL ROAD	CLEVELAND	**OH**	44124	(216) 382-8925
FAIRMOUNT TEMPLE R 23737 FAIRMOUNT BLVD	CLEVELAND	**OH**	44122	(216) 464-1330
GREEN ROAD SYNAGOGUE O 2437 GREEN ROAD	CLEVELAND	**OH**	44122	(216) 381-4757
HEIGHTS JEWISH CENTER O 14270 CEDAR ROAD	CLEVELAND	**OH**	44121	(216) 382-1958
HEIGHTS JEWISH CENTER O 14274 SUPERIOR ROAD	CLEVELAND	**OH**	44118	(216) 932-7424
K'HAL YEREIM O 1771 SOUTH TAYLOR ROAD	CLEVELAND	**OH**	44118	(216) 321-9554
K'HAL YEREIM O 2203 S. GREEN	CLEVELAND	**OH**	44121	
MAYFIELD HILLCREST SYNAGOGUE C 1732 LANDER ROAD	CLEVELAND	**OH**	44124	(216) 449-6200
NER TAMID, TEMPLE (EUCLID JEWISH CENTER) R 24950 LAKE SHORE BLVD	CLEVELAND	**OH**	44132	(216) 261-2280
OER-CHODOSH ANSHE SFARD O 3466 WASHINGTON BLVD	CLEVELAND	**OH**	44118	(216) 932-7739
OHEB ZEDEK - THE TAYLOR ROAD SYNAGOGUE O 1970 S. TAYLOR ROAD	CLEVELAND	**OH**	44118	(216) 321-4875
PARK SYNAGOGUE, THE C 3300 MAYFIELD ROAD	CLEVELAND	**OH**	44118	(216) 371-2244
SHAAREI TORAH, CONGREGATION 2436 BEECHWOOD AVENUE	CLEVELAND	**OH**	44118	
SHOMRE SHABOTH O 1801 SOUTH TAYLOR ROAD	CLEVELAND	**OH**	44118	(216) 932-2619
SINAI SYNAGOGUE O 3246 DESOTA AVENUE	CLEVELAND	**OH**	44118	(216) 932-0206
SUBURBAN TEMPLE, THE R 22401 CHAGRIN BLVD	CLEVELAND	**OH**	44122	(216) 991-0700
TAYLOR ROAD SYNAGOGUE O 1970 SOUTH TAYLOR ROAD	CLEVELAND	**OH**	44118	
TEMPLE ON THE HEIGHTS C 27501 FAIRMOUNT BLVD	CLEVELAND	**OH**	44124	(216) 831-6555
TEMPLE, THE R UNIVERSITY CIRCLE & SILVER PARK	CLEVELAND	**OH**	44106	(216) 791-7755
TIFERETH ISRAEL - THE TEMPLE R UNIVERSITY CIRCLE AT SILVER PARK	CLEVELAND	**OH**	44106	(216) 791-7755
TORAH U'TEFILAH O 1970 SOUTH TAYLOR ROAD	CLEVELAND	**OH**	44118	(216) 371-5872
UNITED JEWISH RELIGIOUS SCHOOLS 25400 FAIRMOUNT BLVD	CLEVELAND	**OH**	44122	(216) 464-8050
WARRENSVILLE CENTER SYNAGOGUE O 1508 WARRENSVILLE CENTER ROAD	CLEVELAND	**OH**	44121	(216) 382-6566
ZEMACH ZEDEK O 1922 LEE ROAD	CLEVELAND	**OH**	44118	(216) 321-5169
AGUDAS ACHIM, CONGREGATION O 2767 EAST BROAD STREET	COLUMBUS	**OH**	43209	(614) 237-2747
AHAVAS SHOLOM, CONGREGATION 2568 E. BROAD STREET	COLUMBUS	**OH**	43209	(614) 258-4815
BETH JACOB, CONGREGATION O 1223 COLLEGE AVENUE	COLUMBUS	**OH**	43209	(614) 237-8641
BETH SHALOM, TEMPLE R 3100 E. BROAD STREET	COLUMBUS	**OH**	43209	(614) 231-4598
BETH TIKVAH, CONGREGATION R 6121 OLENTANGY RIVER ROAD	COLUMBUS	**OH**	43214	(614) 885-6286
ISRAEL, TEMPLE R 5419 E. BROAD STREET	COLUMBUS	**OH**	43213	(614) 866-0010
TIFERETH ISRAEL, CONGREGATION C 1354 E. BROAD STREET	COLUMBUS	**OH**	43205	(614) 253-8523
BETH ABRAHAM SYNAGOGUE C 1306 SALEM AVENUE	DAYTON	**OH**	45406	(513) 275-7403
BETH JACOB SYNAGOGUE 7020 N. MAIN STREET	DAYTON	**OH**	45415	(513) 274-2149
ISRAEL, TEMPLE R 1821 EMERSON AVENUE	DAYTON	**OH**	45406	(513) 278-9621
ISRAEL, TEMPLE - SOUTH BRANCH R 1136 W. CENTERVILLE ROAD	DAYTON	**OH**	45959	(513) 434-9067
SHOMREI EMUNAH YOUNG ISRAEL O 1706 SALEM AVENUE	DAYTON	**OH**	45406	(513) 274-6941
YOUNG ISRAEL OF DAYTON 1706 SALEM AVENUE	DAYTON	**OH**	45406	(513) 274-6941
BETH SHALOM, CONGREGATION R P.O. BOX 309	EAST LIVERPOOL	**OH**	43920	(216) 386-6820
BNAI ISRAEL, CONGREGATION P.O. BOX 309	EAST LIVERPOOL	**OH**	43920	
B'NAI ABRAHAM, TEMPLE C P.O. BOX 530, GULF ROAD	ELYRIA	**OH**	44036	(216) 366-1177
NER TAMID, TEMPLE R 24950 LAKE SHORE DRIVE	EUCLID	**OH**	44132	(216) 261-2280
BETH ISRAEL, TEMPLE C 514 BIRCHARD AVENUE	FREMONT	**OH**	43420	(419) 332-6302
OHEV ISRAEL TEMPLE R 324 MT. PARNASSUS	GRANVILLE	**OH**	43023	(614) 326-4501
ETZ CHAYIM, CONGREGATION P.O. BOX 2882	KENWOOD	**OH**	43606	
BETH ISRAEL, TEMPLE R LAKEWOOD AVENUE AT GLENWOOD	LIMA	**OH**	45805	(419) 223-9616
AGUDATH B'NAI ISRAEL C 1715 MEISTER ROAD AT POLE AVENUE	LORAIN	**OH**	44053	(216) 282-3307
B'NAI JACOB CONGREGATION R 973 LARCHWOOD ROAD	MANSFIELD	**OH**	44907	(419) 756-7355
EMANUEL, TEMPLE R COOK ROAD AT LARCHWOOD, P.O. BOX 1665	MANSFIELD	**OH**	44901	(419) 756-7266
BNEI ISRAEL, CONGREGATION O 522 4TH STREET	MARIETTA	**OH**	45750	
ISRAEL, TEMPLE R 730 HARDING ROAD	MARION	**OH**	43302	(614) 382-3629
B'NAI JESHURUN CONGREGATION C 1732 LANDER ROAD	MAYFIELD	**OH**	44124	(216) 449-6200
MAYFIELD HILLCREST CONGREGATION C 1732 LANDER ROAD	MAYFIELD HEIGHTS	**OH**	44124	(216) 449-6200
NER TAMID, TEMPLE - EUCLID JEWISH CENTER EAST 250TH & LAKE SHORE BLVD	MAYFIELD HEIGHTS	**OH**	44132	(216) 261-2280
AM SHALOM (LAKE COUNTY JEWISH CENTER) R P.O. BOX 454	MENTOR	**OH**	44060	(216) 953-1315
BETH SHOLOM, TEMPLE R 610 GLADYS DRIVE	MIDDLETOWN	**OH**	45042	(513) 422-8313
B'NAI JESHURUN CONGREGATION-THE TEMPLE ON THE HEIGHTS C 27501 FAIRMOUNT BLVD	PEPPER PIKE	**OH**	44124	(216) 831-6555
BRITH EMETH TEMPLE R 27575 SHAKER BLVD	PEPPER PIKE	**OH**	44124	
ANSHE EMETH CONGREGATION R C/O MR. HERMAN BARR, 1409 NICKLIN	PIQUA	**OH**	45356	(513) 773-4253
B'NAI ABRAHAM, CONGREGATION R 325 MASONIC BLDG	PORTSMOUTH	**OH**	45662	(614) 354-1671
OHEB SHALOM CONGREGATION R 1521 E. PERKINS AVENUE	SANDUSKY	**OH**	44870	(419) 433-6051
YOUNG ISRAEL OF CLEVELAND 14141 CEDAR ROAD	SOUTH EUCLID	**OH**	44121	(216) 382-5740
BETH EL SYNAGOGUE C 2424 N. LIMESTONE STREET	SPRINGFIELD	**OH**	45505	(513) 399-7512
SHOLOM, TEMPLE R 2424 N. LIMESTONE STREET	SPRINGFIELD	**OH**	45503	(513) 399-1231
BETH ISRAEL, TEMPLE R 300 LOVERS LANE	STEUBENVILLE	**OH**	43952	(614) 264-5514
BNAI ISRAEL, CONGREGATION C 128 S. 5TH STREET	STEUBENVILLE	**OH**	43952	
CONGREGATION SHOMER EMUNIM, THE TEMPLE R 6453 SYLVANIA AVENUE	SYLVANIA	**OH**	43560	(419) 885-3341
B'NAI ISRAEL, TEMPLE C 2727 KENWOOD BLVD	TOLEDO	**OH**	43606	(419) 531-1677
BNAI JACOB-SHAREI ZEDECK O P.O. BOX 2882	TOLEDO	**OH**	43606	
ETZ CHAYIM, CONGREGATION O 3853 WOODLEY ROAD	TOLEDO	**OH**	43606	(419) 473-2401
BETH SHALOM, TEMPLE R P.O. BOX 315	TWINSBURG	**OH**	44087	
BETH ISRAEL TEMPLE CENTER C 2138 E. MARKET STREET	WARREN	**OH**	44483	(216) 395-3877
AGUDATH ISRAEL OF WICKLIFFE O 2606 BISHOP ROAD	WICKLIFFE	**OH**	44092	(216) 913-4162
KNESSETH ISRAEL, TEMPLE C 1670 CLEVELAND ROAD	WOOSTER	**OH**	44691	(216) 262-3516
BETH TIKVA, CONGREGATION R 6121 OLENTANGY RIVER ROAD	WORTHINGTON	**OH**	43085	(614) 885-6286
ANSHE EMETH, TEMPLE C FIFTH & FAIRGREEN	YOUNGSTOWN	**OH**	44504	
EL EMETH, TEMPLE C FIFTH & FAIRGREEN	YOUNGSTOWN	**OH**	44515	(216) 744-5055
OHEV TZEDEK-SHAAREI TORAH C 5245 GLENWOOD AVENUE	YOUNGSTOWN	**OH**	44512	(216) 758-2321
RODEF SHOLOM, CONGREGATION R ELM & WOODBINE STREETS	YOUNGSTOWN	**OH**	44505	(216) 744-5001
BETH ABRAHAM, CONGREGATION C 1740 BLUE AVENUE	ZANESVILLE	**OH**	43701	(614) 453-5391
KNESETH ISRAEL, CONGREGATION 522 WEST HIGHLAND	ZANESVILLE	**OH**	43701	
EMETH, TEMPLE R 421 STANLEY	ARDMORE	**OK**	73401	(405) 223-3064
STAR OF DAVID, TEMPLE R P.O. BOX 1624	BARTLESVILLE	**OK**	74003	(918) 333-1735
BETH AHABA, TEMPLE R 4131 SOUTH ROBB	MUSKOGEE	**OK**	74401	(918) 682-1432
B'NAI ISRAEL, TEMPLE R 4901 N. PENNSYLVANIA AVENUE	OKLAHOMA CITY	**OK**	73112	(405) 848-0965
EMANUEL SYNAGOGUE C 900 N.W. 47TH STREET	OKLAHOMA CITY	**OK**	73118	(405) 528-2113
EMANUEL, TEMPLE R P.O. BOX 1081	PONCA CITY	**OK**	74601	(405) 765-5898
B'NAI EMUNAH, CONGREGATION C 1719 S. OWASSO AVENUE, P.O. BOX 52430	TULSA	**OK**	74152	(918) 583-7121
ISRAEL, TEMPLE R 2004 E. 22ND PLACE	TULSA	**OK**	74114	(918) 747-1309
ADATH ISRAEL CONGREGATION C 37 SOUTHBOURNE AVENUE	DOWNSVIEW	**ON**	M3H 1A4	(416) 635-5340
BETH DAVID B'NAI ISRAEL, BETH AM SYNAGOGUE C 55 YEOMANS ROAD	DOWNSVIEW	**ON**	M3H 3J7	(416) 633-5500
BETH EMETH BAIS YEHUDA SYNAGOGUE C 100 ELDER STREET	DOWNSVIEW	**ON**	M3H 5G7	(416) 633-3838
BETH JACOB V'ANSHE DRILDZ SYNAGOGUE O 147 OVERBROOK PLACE	DOWNSVIEW	**ON**		(416) 638-5955
CONGREGATION DARCHEI NOAM, RECONSTRUCTIONIST SYNAGOGUE OF TORONTO 15 HOVE STREET	DOWNSVIEW	**ON**	M3H 4Y8	(416) 633-3526
ANSHE SHOLOM, TEMPLE R 215 CLINE AVENUE N	HAMILTON	**ON**	L85 4A1	(416) 528-0121
BETH JACOB SYNAGOGUE C 375 ABERDEEN AVENUE	HAMILTON	**ON**	L8P 2R7	(416) 522-1351
IYR HA-MELECH R 842 MILFORD DRIVE	KINGSTON	**ON**	K7P 1AB	(613) 544-3088
SHALOM, TEMPLE R 1284 OTTAWA STREET S	KITCHENER	**ON**	N2E 1M1	(519) 743-0401
BETH TEFILAH, CONGREGATION O 1210 ADELAIDE STREET N	LONDON	**ON**	N5Y 4T6	(519) 433-7081
OR SHALOM, CONGREGATION C 534 HURON STREET	LONDON	**ON**	N5Y 4J5	(519) 438-3081
SOLEL CONGREGATION R 2399 FOLKWAY DRIVE	MISSISSAUGA	**ON**	L5L 2M6	(416) 828-5915
B'NAI JACOB, CONGREGATION C 5328 FERRY STREET	NIAGARA FALLS	**ON**		(416) 354-3934
BETH EL CONGREGATION 186 MORRISON ROAD	OAKVILLE	**ON**	L6J 4J4	(416) 845-0837
ADATH SHALOM CONGREGATION C P.O. BOX 106, POSTAL STATION B	OSHAWA	**ON**	K1P 6C3	(613) 225-7081
BETH ZION CONGREGATION OF OSHAWA C 144 KING STREET EAST	OSHAWA	**ON**	L1H 1C2	
AGUDATH ISRAEL CONGREGATION C 1400 COLDREY AVENUE	OTTAWA	**ON**	K1Z 7P9	(613) 728-3501
ISRAEL, TEMPLE R 1301 PRINCE OF WALES DRIVE	OTTAWA	**ON**	K2C 1N2	(613) 224-1802
YOUNG ISRAEL OF OTTAWA 627 KIRKWOOD AVENUE	OTTAWA	**ON**	K2U 5X5	(613) 722-8394
BETH ISRAEL CONGREGATION C WELLER STREET	PETERBOROUGH	**ON**		(705) 745-7483
B'NAI ISRAEL C 190 CHURCH STREET	SAINT CATHERINES	**ON**	L2R 4C4	(416) 685-6767
TIKVAH, TEMPLE R 83 CHURCH STREET, P.O. BOX 484	SAINT CATHERINES	**ON**	L2R 6Y9	(416) 682-4191
AHAVAS ISAAC SYNAGOGUE C 202 COBDEN STREET	SARNIA	**ON**		
HAR ZION, TEMPLE R 7360 BAYVIEW AVENUE	THORNHILL	**ON**	L3T 2R7	(416) 889-2252
AGUDATH ISRAEL OF TORONTO O 129 MCGILLIVRAY	TORONTO	**ON**		
BAYCREST TERRACE REFORM CONGREGATION R 3560 BATHURST	TORONTO	**ON**	M6A 2E1	(416) 789-5131
BETH SHOLOM SYNAGOGUE C 1445 EGLINTON AVENUE W	TORONTO	**ON**	M6C 2E6	(416) 783-6103
BETH TORAH CONGREGATION C 47 GLENBROOK AVENUE	TORONTO	**ON**	M6B 2L7	(416) 782-3561
BETH TZEDEC CONGREGATION C 1700 BATHURST STREET	TORONTO	**ON**	M5P 3K3	(416) 781-3511
HABONIM 3101 BATHURST STREET, SUITE 305	TORONTO	**ON**		
HOLY BLOSSOM TEMPLE R 1950 BATHURST STREET	TORONTO	**ON**	M5P 3K9	(416) 781-9185
SHAAREI SHOMAYIM CONGREGATION O 470 GLENCAIRN AVENUE	TORONTO	**ON**	M5N 1V8	(416) 789-3213
SINAI, TEMPLE R 210 WILSON AVENUE	TORONTO	**ON**	M5M 3B1	(416) 487-4161
BETH TIKVAH C 3080 BAYVIEW AVENUE	WILLOWDALE	**ON**	M2N 5L3	(416) 221-3433
EMANU-EL, TEMPLE R 120 OLD COLONY ROAD	WILLOWDALE	**ON**	M2L 2K2	(416) 449-3880
YOUNG ISRAEL SHAAREI ZION OF TORONTO 325 GOLDENWOOD ROAD	WILLOWDALE	**ON**		
BETH EL, CONGREGATION R 2525 MARK AVENUE	WINDSOR	**ON**	N9E 2W2	(519) 969-2422
BETH ISRAEL, TEMPLE C 2550 PORTLAND STREET	EUGENE	**OR**	97401	(503) 485-7218
ROGUE VALLEY JEWISH COMMUNITY CONGREGATION R P.O. BOX 1094	MEDFORD	**OR**	97501	(503) 779-7648
AHAVATH ACHIM, CONGREGATION 3225 S.W. BARBUR BLVD	PORTLAND	**OR**	97215	(503) 227-0010
BETH ISRAEL, TEMPLE R 1931 N.W. FLANDERS STREET	PORTLAND	**OR**	97209	(503) 222-1069
HAVURAH SHALOM, R 8085 S.W. RIDGEWAY DRIVE	PORTLAND	**OR**	97225	
NEVEH SHALOM, CONGREGATION C 2900 S.W. PEACEFUL LANE	PORTLAND	**OR**	97201	(503) 246-8831
SHAARIE TORAH, CONGREGATION O 920 N.W. 25TH AVENUE	PORTLAND	**OR**	97210	(503) 226-6131
TIFERETH ISRAEL, CONGREGATION C 4744 N.E. 15TH AVENUE	PORTLAND	**OR**	97211	(503) 288-1659
SALEM JEWISH CONGREGATION-TEMPLE BETH SHOLOM C 1795 BROADWAY N.E.	SALEM	**OR**	97308	
OLD YORK ROAD TEMPLE BETH AM R 971 OLD YORK ROAD	ABINGTON	**PA**	19001	(215) 886-8000
BETH EL, TEMPLE C 17TH & HAMILTON STREETS	ALLENTOWN	**PA**	18104	(215) 435-3521
CONGREGATION AM HASKALAH RE	ALLENTOWN	**PA**	18104	(215) 435-3775
KENESETH ISRAEL, CONGREGATION R 2227 CHEW STREET	ALLENTOWN	**PA**	18104	(215) 435-9074
SONS OF ISRAEL, CONGREGATION O 2715 TILGHMAN STREET	ALLENTOWN	**PA**	18104	(215) 433-6089
AGUDATH ACHIM SYNAGOGUE C 1306 17TH STREET	ALTOONA	**PA**	16601	(814) 944-5317
BETH ISRAEL, TEMPLE R 3004 UNION AVENUE	ALTOONA	**PA**	16602	(814) 942-0057
BETH SAMUEL JEWISH CENTER C P.O. BOX 219, 810 KENNEDY DRIVE	AMBRIDGE	**PA**	15003	(412) 266-9871
BNAI ISRAEL, CONGREGATION	BARNESBORO	**PA**	15714	
AGUDATH ACHIM CONGREGATION C P.O. BOX 293	BEAVER FALLS	**PA**	15010	(412) 846-5696
BETH SHOLOM CONGREGATION R 1409 EIGHTH AVENUE	BEAVER FALLS	**PA**	15010	(412) 846-0068
NES AMI PENN VALLEY CONGREGATION C 50 ASHLAND AVENUE	BELMONT HILLS	**PA**	19127	
TIFERETH ISRAEL OF LOWER BUCKS COUNTY, CONGREGATION C 2909 BRISTOL ROAD	BENSALEM	**PA**	19020	(215) 752-3468
OHEV SHOLOM, CONGREGATION C 1401 HOLLY DRIVE	BERWICK	**PA**	18603	
AGUDATH ACHIM, CONGREGATION O 1555 LINWOOD STREET	BETHLEHEM	**PA**	18016	

BRITH SHOLOM COMMUNITY CENTER C
P.O. BOX 5323, BRODHEAD & PACKER AVENUE — BETHLEHEM **PA** 18015 (215) 866-8000
BETH ISRAEL CONGREGATION C 144 E. 4TH STREET — BLOOMSBURG **PA** 17815 (717) 784-5778
BETH EL, TEMPLE R P.O. BOX 538, 111 JACKSON AVENUE — BRADFORD **PA** 16701 (814) 368-8204
BRISTOL JEWISH CENTER C 216 POND STREET — BRISTOL **PA** 19007 (215) 788-4995
BETH EL SUBURBAN, CONGREGATION C 715 PAXON HOLLOW ROAD — BROOMALL **PA** 19008 (215) 246-8700
SHOLOM, TEMPLE R 55 N. CHURCH ROAD — BROOMALL **PA** 19008 (215) 356-5165
B'NAI ABRAHAM C 519 N. MAIN STREET — BUTLER **PA** 16001 (412) 287-5806
AGUDATH SHOLOM, CONGREGATION O 51 1/2 PIKE STREET — CARBONDALE **PA** 18407
AHAVATH ACHIM C LYDIA & CHESTNUT STREETS — CARNEGIE **PA** 15106 (412) 276-9777
SONS OF ISRAEL, CONGREGATION C
KING & SECOND STREETS — CHAMBERSBURG **PA** 17201 (717) 264-2915
MELROSE B'NAI ISRAEL, CONGREGATION C
2ND STREET AT CHELTENHAM AVENUE — CHELTENHAM **PA** 19012
BETH ISRAEL CONGREGATION C
FIFTH AVENUE & HARMONY STREETS — COATESVILLE **PA** 19320 (215) 384-1978
AHAVATH SHOLOM TEMPLE R FLEMING STREET & VANCE AVENUE — CORAOPOLIS **PA** 15108 (412) 264-4100
OHAV SHOLOM, CONGREGATION O THOMPSON AVENUE — DONORA **PA** 15033 (412) 379-9943
JUDEA OF BUCKS COUNTY, TEMPLE R SWAMP ROAD, P.O. BOX 215 — DOYLESTOWN **PA** 18901 (215) 348-5022
SINAI, TEMPLE C LIMEKILN PIKE & DILLON ROAD — DRESHER **PA** 19025 (215) 643-6510
BETH JACOB, CONGREGATION O 431 CATHERINE STREET — DUQUESNE **PA** 15110
OHAB ZEDEK, CONGREGATION C ELECTRIC AVENUE — EAST PITTSBURGH **PA** 15112
ISRAEL, TEMPLE C P.O. BOX 368, 660 WALLACE STREET — EAST STROUDSBURG **PA** 18360 (717) 421-8781
BNAI ABRAHAM SYNAGOGUE C 16TH & BUSHKILL STREETS — EASTON **PA** 18042 (215) 258-5343
COVENANT OF PEACE, TEMPLE R 1451 NORTHAMPTON STREET — EASTON **PA** 18042 (215) 253-2031
ADATH JESHURUN, CONGREGATION C
YORK & ASHBOURNE ROADS — ELKINS PARK **PA** 19117 (215) 635-6611
BETH SHOLOM CONGREGATION C OLD YORK & FOXCROFT ROADS — ELKINS PARK **PA** 19117 (215) 887-3625
KENESETH ISRAEL, CONGREGATION R
YORK ROAD & TOWNSHIP LINE — ELKINS PARK **PA** 19117 (215) 887-8700
RODEPH SHALOM R 8201 HIGH SCHOOL ROAD — ELKINS PARK **PA** 19117 (215) 324-1010
TREE OF LIFE CONGREGATION C BEATTY STREET — ELLWOOD CITY **PA** 16617 (412) 758-7329
BETH TIKVAH-B'NAI JESHURUN C 1001 PAPER MILL ROAD — ERDENHEIM **PA** 19118 (215) 836-5677
ANSHE HESED, TEMPLE R 10TH & LIBERTY STREETS — ERIE **PA** 16502 (814) 454-2426
BRITH SHOLOM, CONGREGATION C 3207 STATE STREET — ERIE **PA** 16508 (814) 454-2431
BETH CHAIM, CONGREGATION C 350 EAST STREET — FEASTERVILLE **PA** 19047 (215) 355-3626
KNESSETH ISRAEL CONGREGATION 416 FORD STREET — FORD CITY **PA** 16226 (412) 762-2621
B'NAI ISRAEL, CONGREGATION C WEST FRACK STREET — FRACKVILLE **PA** 17931
EMANU-EL ISRAEL, CONGREGATION R 222 N. MAIN STREET — GREENSBURG **PA** 15601 (412) 834-0560
HANOVER HEBREW CONGREGATION C 179 SECOND AVENUE — HANOVER **PA** 17331
BETH EL C 2637 N. FRONT STREET — HARRISBURG **PA** 17110 (717) 232-0556
CHISUK EMUNA CONGREGATION C FIFTH & DIVISION STREETS — HARRISBURG **PA** 17110 (717) 232-4851
KESHER ISRAEL, CONGREGATION O 2500 NORTH 3RD STREET — HARRISBURG **PA** 17110 (717) 238-0736
REFORM TEMPLE OHEV SHOLOM R 2345 N. FRONT STREET — HARRISBURG **PA** 17110 (717) 233-6459
UNITED JEWISH COMMUNITY OF GREATER HARRISBURG
100 VAUGHN STREET — HARRISBURG **PA** 17110 (717) 236-9555
SUBURBAN JEWISH COMMUNITY CENTER, B'NAI AARON C
560 MILL ROAD — HAVERTOWN **PA** 19083 (215) 528-5011
AGUDAS ISRAEL CONGREGATION C PINE & OAK STREETS — HAZELTON **PA** 18201 (717) 454-9294
BETH ISRAEL CONGREGATION R 98 N. CHURCH STREET — HAZELTON **PA** 18201 (717) 455-3971
HOMESTEAD HEBREW CONGREGATION RODEF SHALOM O
331 10TH AVENUE — HOMESTEAD **PA** 15120 (412) 461-9251
BETH ISRAEL, CONGREGATION R P.O. BOX 311 — HONESDALE **PA** 18431 (717) 253-2222
AGUDATH ACHIM, CONGREGATION C 1009 WASHINGTON STREET — HUNTINGTON **PA** 16652
BETH ISRAEL CONGREGATION C 5TH & WASHINGTON STREETS — INDIANA **PA** 15701 (412) 465-6721
BETH SHOLOM CONGREGATION FOXCROFT & OLD YORK STREETS — JENKINTOWN **PA** 19117 (215) 924-2223
BETH SHOLOM CONGREGATION R 700 INDIANA AVENUE — JOHNSTOWN **PA** 15905 (814) 536-0647
RODEF SHOLOM, CONGREGATION C 100 DARTMOUTH AVENUE — JOHNSTOWN **PA** 15905
BETH JACOB, CONGREGATION — KANE **PA** 16735
BRITH ACHIM, TEMPLE R 481 S. GULPH ROAD, P.O. BOX 168 — KING OF PRUSSIA **PA** 19406 (215) 337-2222
B'NAI B'RITH OF WILKES BARRE, TEMPLE R 408 WYOMING AVENUE — KINGSTON **PA** 18704 (717) 287-9606
OR AMI, CONGREGATION R P.O. BOX 156, 708 RIDGE PIKE — LAFAYETTE HILL **PA** 19444 (215) 828-9066
BETH EL, TEMPLE C 25 N. LINE STREET — LANCASTER **PA** 17602 (717) 392-1379
DEGEL ISRAEL SYNAGOGUE O 1120 COLUMBIA AVENUE — LANCASTER **PA** 17603 (717) 397-0183
SHAARAI SHOMAYIM, TEMPLE R 508 N. DUKE STREET — LANCASTER **PA** 17602 (717) 397-5575
BETH ISRAEL, CONGREGATION C 1080 SUMNEYTOWN PIKE — LANSDALE **PA** 19446 (215) 855-8328
BETH ISRAEL C 414 WELDON STREET — LATROBE **PA** 15650 (412) 539-1450
BETH ISRAEL, CONGREGATION C 411 S. 8TH STREET — LEBANON **PA** 17042 (717) 273-6669
ISRAEL, TEMPLE C BANKWAY STREET — LEHIGHTON **PA** 18235 (215) 377-0400
BETH EL, CONGREGATION C 21 PENN VALLEY ROAD — LEVITTOWN **PA** 19055 (215) 945-1172
SHALOM, TEMPLE R EDGELY ROAD OFF MILL CREEK PARKWAY — LEVITTOWN **PA** 19057 (215) 945-4154
BETH YEHUDA SYNAGOGUE R 320 W. CHURCH STREET — LOCK HAVEN **PA** 17745 (717) 748-3908
B'NAI ISRAEL, TEMPLE R 536 SHAW AVENUE — MCKEESPORT **PA** 15132 (412) 678-6181
GEMILAS CHESED, CONGREGATION O 1400 SUMMIT STREET — MCKEESPORT **PA** 15131 (412) 678-8859
TEMPLE BETH SHALOM RE 913 ALLENDALE ROAD — MECHANICSBURG **PA** 17055 (717) 697-2662
BETH ISRAEL, CONGREGATION RE GAYLEY TERRACE — MEDIA **PA** 19063 (215) 566-4645
ADATH ISRAEL OF THE MAIN LINE, TEMPLE C
OLD LANCASTER ROAD & HIGHLAND AVENUE — MERION STATION **PA** 19066 (215) 664-5150
BETH AM, TEMPLE R 1000 WATKINS AVENUE — MONESSEN **PA** 15062 (412) 684-8290
BETH AM, TEMPLE R
C/O MR. SIDNEY ACKERMAN, ROUTE 1, P.O. BOX 615 — MONONGAHELA **PA** 15063 (412) 379-5312
DAVID, TEMPLE R 4415 NORTHERN PIKE — MONROEVILLE **PA** 15146 (412) 372-1200
TIFERETH ISRAEL, CONGREGATION O
135 SOUTH MAPLE STREET — MOUNT CARMEL **PA** 17851
TREE OF LIFE, CONGREGATION O CHURCH STREET — MOUNT PLEASANT **PA** 15666
BETH AM ISRAEL C 1301 HAGYS FORK ROAD — NARBERTH **PA** 19072 (215) 667-1651
ISRAEL, TEMPLE R 908 HIGHLAND AVENUE — NEW CASTLE **PA** 16101 (412) 652-7551
TIFERETH ISRAEL, CONGREGATION C
403 EAST MOODY AVENUE, P.O. BOX 1432 — NEW CASTLE **PA** 16101 (412) 658-3321
BETH JACOB CONGREGATION C 1040 KENNETH AVENUE — NEW KENSINGTON **PA** 15068 (412) 335-8525
SHIR AMI, BUCKS COUNTY JEWISH CONGREGATION R
101 RICHBORO ROAD — NEWTOWN **PA** 18940 (215) 968-3400

TIFERES ISRAEL CONGREGATION-JEWISH COMMUNITY CENTER C
1541 POWELL STREET — NORRISTOWN **PA** 19401 (215) 275-8797
TREE OF LIFE, CONGREGATION C 316 W. 1ST STREET — OIL CITY **PA** 16301
BICKOR CHOILIM, CONGREGATION O 302 LACKAWANNA AVENUE — OLYPHANT **PA** 18447 (717) 489-1955
BETH AM ISRAEL C 1301 HAGYSFORD ROAD — PENN VALLEY **PA** 19072 (215) 667-1651
HAR ZION TEMPLE C HAGYS FORK ROAD AT HOLLOW ROAD — PENN VALLEY **PA** 19072 (215) 667-1651
ADATH SHALOM C MARSHALL & RITNER STREETS — PHILADELPHIA **PA** 19148 (215) 463-2224
ADATH TIKVAH MONTEFIORE CONGREGATION C
HOFFNAGLE STREET & SUMMERDALE AVENUE — PHILADELPHIA **PA** 19152 (215) 752-9191
AGUDATH ISRAEL OF PHILADELPHIA O 2401 N. 59TH STREET — PHILADELPHIA **PA** 19131 (215) 473-4397
AHAVATH ISRAEL OF OAK LANE C 6735 N. 16TH STREET — PHILADELPHIA **PA** 19126 (215) 924-7675
AHAVATH ISRAEL, CONGREGATION O
2302 NORTH MASCHER STREET — PHILADELPHIA **PA** 19133
AITZ CHAIM SYNAGOGUE CENTER O 7600 SUMMERDALE AVENUE — PHILADELPHIA **PA** 19111 (215) 742-4870
ANSHEI VILNA, CONGREGATION O 509 PINE STREET — PHILADELPHIA **PA** 19106
B'NAI ABRAHAM JEWISH CENTER C 9037 EASTVIEW ROAD — PHILADELPHIA **PA** 19152
B'NAI ISRAEL OHAVE ZEDEK, CONGREGATION O
8201 CASTOR AVENUE — PHILADELPHIA **PA** 19152 (215) 742-0400
B'NAI JESHURUN AHAVAS CHESED, CONGREGATION C
1001 PAPER MILL ROAD — PHILADELPHIA **PA** 19118
B'NAI JESHURUN, CONGREGATION C 6826 ROOSEVELT BLVD — PHILADELPHIA **PA** 19149
B'NAI JESHURUN, CONGREGATION O 2029 N. 33RD STREET — PHILADELPHIA **PA** 19121 (215) 763-9616
B'NAI TORAH, CONGREGATION C 11082 KNIGHTS ROAD — PHILADELPHIA **PA** 19154
B'NAI YITZHOK, CONGREGATION O B & ROOSEVELT BLVD — PHILADELPHIA **PA** 19120 (215) 329-3712
BETH AHAVAH, CONGREGATION P.O. BOX 7566 — PHILADELPHIA **PA** 19101 (215) 922-3872
BETH AMI, TEMPLE C 9201 BUSTLETON AVENUE — PHILADELPHIA **PA** 19115 (215) 673-2511
BETH DAVID REFORM CONGREGATION R
5220 WYNNEFIELD AVENUE — PHILADELPHIA **PA** 19131 (215) 473-8438
BETH EMETH CONGREGATION C BUSTLETON & UNRUH AVENUE — PHILADELPHIA **PA** 19149 (215) 338-1533
BETH HAMEDROSH OF OVERBROOK PARK O
7505 BROOKHAVEN ROAD — PHILADELPHIA **PA** 19151 (215) 473-9671
BETH JACOB, CONGREGATION O 6018 LARCHWOOD AVENUE — PHILADELPHIA **PA** 19143 (215) 747-3116
BETH JUDAH OF LOGAN C 4820-30 N. 11TH STREET — PHILADELPHIA **PA** 19141 (215) 329-4545
BETH MIDRASH HARAV, CONGREGATION O 7926 ALGON AVENUE — PHILADELPHIA **PA** 19111 (215) 722-6161
BETH T'FILLAH OF OVERBROOK PARK, CONGREGATION C
7630 WOODBINE AVENUE — PHILADELPHIA **PA** 19151 (215) 477-2415
BETH TEFILATH ISRAEL OF PENNYPACK PARK C
2605 WELSH ROAD — PHILADELPHIA **PA** 19114 (215) 464-1242
BETH TIKVAH, CONGREGATION C 1001 PAPER MILL ROAD — PHILADELPHIA **PA** 19118
BETH TORAH, TEMPLE R 608 WELSH ROAD — PHILADELPHIA **PA** 19115 (215) 677-1555
BETH TOVIM, CONGREGATION O 5871 DREXEL ROAD — PHILADELPHIA **PA** 19131 (215) 879-1100
BETH UZIEL, CONGREGATION C
ROBAT STREET & WYOMING AVENUE — PHILADELPHIA **PA** 19120 (215) 329-0250
BETH ZION BETH ISRAEL, TEMPLE C
S.W. CORNER 18TH & SPRUCE STREETS — PHILADELPHIA **PA** 19103 (215) 735-5148
BNAI ABRAHAM, CONGREGATION O 527 LOMBARD STREET — PHILADELPHIA **PA** 19147 (215) 627-3123
BNAI YOSHIA, CONGREGATION O
5000 WYNNEFIELD, KENWYN APARTMENTS 17-C — PHILADELPHIA **PA** 19131
BRITH ISRAEL, CONGREGATION C
ROOSEVELT BLVD. & D STREETS — PHILADELPHIA **PA** 19120 (215) 329-2230
BUSTLETON SOMERTON SYNAGOGUE C
TOMLINSON ROAD & FERNDALE STREET — PHILADELPHIA **PA** 19116 (215) 677-6886
EMANU-EL, CONGREGATION C
OLD YORK ROAD & STENTON AVENUE — PHILADELPHIA **PA** 19141 (215) 548-1658
FOX CHASE JEWISH COMMUNITY CENTER C 7816 HALSTEAD — PHILADELPHIA **PA** 19111 (215) 342-4722
GERMANTOWN JEWISH CENTER C
LINCOLN DRIVE & ELLET STREET — PHILADELPHIA **PA** 19119 (215) 814-1507
ISRAEL, TEMPLE - WYNNEFIELD C 901 WOODBINE AVENUE — PHILADELPHIA **PA** 19131 (215) 877-3200
JUDEA, TEMPLE R 6928 OLD YORK ROAD — PHILADELPHIA **PA** 19126 (215) 224-3040
KESHER ISRAEL, CONGREGATION O 412 LOMBARD STREET — PHILADELPHIA **PA** 19147
KNESES ISRAEL, CONGREGATION C 2101 FRIENDSHIP — PHILADELPHIA **PA** 19144
LENAS HAZEDEK, CONGREGATION O
WOODSIDE JEWISH CENTER, 2749 CRANSTON ROAD — PHILADELPHIA **PA** 19131
LUBAVITCHER CENTRE O 7622 CASTOR AVENUE — PHILADELPHIA **PA** 19152 (215) 725-2030
MENORAH OF THE NORTHEAST JEWISH COMMUNITY CENTER, TEMPLE C
ALGARD & TYSON AVENUE — PHILADELPHIA **PA** 19135 (215) 624-9600
MENORAH, TEMPLE C 4301 TYSON AVENUE — PHILADELPHIA **PA** 19149 (215) 624-9600
MIKVEH ISRAEL, CONGREGATION C 44 N. 4TH STREET — PHILADELPHIA **PA** 19106 (215) 922-5446
NER ZEDEK-EZRATH ISRAEL C BUSTLETON & OAKMONT STREETS — PHILADELPHIA **PA** 19152 (215) 728-1155
NEZINER, CONGREGATION C 771 SOUTH 2ND STREET — PHILADELPHIA **PA** 19147
OHEL JACOB, CONGREGATION O
CASTOR & LONGSHORE AVENUES — PHILADELPHIA **PA** 19152 (215) 728-9488
OXFORD CIRCLE JEWISH COMMUNITY CENTER C
1009 UNRUH AVENUE — PHILADELPHIA **PA** 19111 (215) 352-2400
PHILADELPHIA RECONSTRUCTIONIST HAVURAH
C/O FRED HOFKIN — PHILADELPHIA **PA** (215) 886-4780
RAIM AHUVIM, CONGREGATION O 5854 DREXEL ROAD — PHILADELPHIA **PA** 19131 (215) 473-3634
RAMAT EL, CONGREGATION C JOHNSON & ARDLEIGH STREETS — PHILADELPHIA **PA** 19119 (215) 549-8800
RHAWNHURST JEWISH CENTER C
SUMMERDALE AVENUE & HOFFNABLE — PHILADELPHIA **PA** 19152
RODEPH SHALOM SUBURBAN CENTER R
8201 HIGH SCHOOL ROAD — PHILADELPHIA **PA** 19117 (215) 635-2500
RODEPH SHALOM, CONGREGATION R 615 N. BROAD STREET — PHILADELPHIA **PA** 19123 (215) 627-6747
RODEPH ZEDEK, TEMPLE O 10TH & RUSCOMB STREETS — PHILADELPHIA **PA** 19141 (215) 329-1114
SHAARE SHAMAYIM, CONGREGATION C 9768 VERREE ROAD — PHILADELPHIA **PA** 19115
SHAREI ELI, CONGREGATION O 8 & PORTER STREETS — PHILADELPHIA **PA** 19148
SHARI ISRAEL, CONGREGATION O
2445 SOUTH MARSHALL STREET — PHILADELPHIA **PA** 19148
SHOLOM, TEMPLE C LARGE STREET & ROOSEVELT BLVD — PHILADELPHIA **PA** 19149 (215) 288-7600
SOCIETY HILL SYNAGOGUE-AGUDATH AHIM/OHR HADASH C
418 SPRUCE STREET — PHILADELPHIA **PA** 19106 (215) 922-6590
SONS OF ISRAEL, CONGREGATION O SPRUCE & 6TH STREETS — PHILADELPHIA **PA**

TIKVOH CHADOSHOH C 5364 W. CHECO AVENUE	PHILADELPHIA	**PA**	19138	(215) 438-1508
YM/YMHA BRANCH, CONGREGATION OF THE C 401 SOUTH BROAD STREET	PHILADELPHIA	**PA**	19147	(215) 545-4400
YAGDIL TORAH OF OAK LANE, CONGREGATION O 5701 NORTH 13 STREET	PHILADELPHIA	**PA**	19141	
YOUNG ISRAEL OF OXFORD CIRCLE 6427 LARGE STREET	PHILADELPHIA	**PA**	19149	(215) 535-9328
YOUNG ISRAEL OF WYNNEFIELD 5300 WYNNEFIELD AVENUE	PHILADELPHIA	**PA**	19131	(215) 473-3511
YOUNG PEOPLES CONGREGATION SHARI ELI C 728 W. MOYAMENSING AVENUE WEST	PHILADELPHIA	**PA**	19148	(215) 339-9897
ZEMACH DAVID, CONGREGATION O 4900 NORTH 8TH STREET	PHILADELPHIA	**PA**	19120	
ZION, TEMPLE R 1620 PINE ROAD	PHILADELPHIA	**PA**	19115	
B'NAI JACOB, CONGREGATION C STARR & MANAVON STREETS	PHOENIXVILLE	**PA**	19460	(215) 933-5550
ADATH ISRAEL, CONGREGATION O 3257 WARD STREET	PITTSBURGH	**PA**	15213	(412) 682-6020
ADATH JESHURUN, CONG. - CONGREGATION KNESSETH ISRAEL O 5643 E. LIBERTY BLVD	PITTSBURGH	**PA**	15206	(412) 361-0173
B'NAI EMUNOH, CONGREGATION O 4315 MURRAY AVENUE	PITTSBURGH	**PA**	15217	(412) 521-1477
B'NAI ISRAEL, CONGREGATION C 327 N. NEGLEY AVENUE	PITTSBURGH	**PA**	15206	(412) 661-0252
BAIS YOSEF CONGREGATION O 6225 NICHOLSON STREET	PITTSBURGH	**PA**	15217	(412) 422-7437
BETH EL, CONGREGATION C 1900 COCHRAN ROAD	PITTSBURGH	**PA**	15220	(412) 561-1168
BETH HAMEDRASH HAGODOL-BETH JACOB CONGREGATION O 1230 COLWELL STREET	PITTSBURGH	**PA**	15219	
BETH ISRAEL CENTER C P.O. BOX 10873, GILL HALL ROAD	PITTSBURGH	**PA**	15236	(412) 655-9253
BETH ISRAEL, CONGREGATION C 1023 REBECCA AVENUE	PITTSBURGH	**PA**	15221	
BETH JACOB, CONGREGATION 1512 MURRAY AVENUE	PITTSBURGH	**PA**	15217	
BETH SHALOM, CONGREGATION C 5915 BEACON STREET AT SHADY AVENUE	PITTSBURGH	**PA**	15217	(412) 421-2288
CHOFETZ CHAIM, CONGREGATION O 5807 BEACON STREET	PITTSBURGH	**PA**	15217	
DOR HADASH RE P.O. BOX 8223	PITTSBURGH	**PA**	15217	(412) 421-9594
EMANUEL, TEMPLE R 1520 BOWER HILL ROAD	PITTSBURGH	**PA**	15243	(412) 279-7600
KETHER TORAH, CONGREGATION O 5706 BARTLETT STREET	PITTSBURGH	**PA**	15217	(412) 521-9992
MACHSIKEI HADAS, CONGREGATION O 814 NORTH NEGLEY AVENUE	PITTSBURGH	**PA**	15206	
NEW LIGHT CONGREGATION C 1700 BEECHWOOD BLVD	PITTSBURGH	**PA**	15217	(412) 421-1017
OHAVE ZEDECK OF OAKLAND, CONGREGATION O 356 CRAFT AVENUE	PITTSBURGH	**PA**	15213	
PARKWAY JEWISH CENTER C 300 PRINCETON DRIVE	PITTSBURGH	**PA**	15235	(412) 823-4338
POALE ZEDECK, CONGREGATION O PHILLIPS & SHADY AVENUES	PITTSBURGH	**PA**	15217	(412) 421-9786
RODEF SHALOM CONGREGATION R FIFTH & MOREWOOD AVENUE	PITTSBURGH	**PA**	15213	(412) 621-6566
SHAARAY TEFILLAH, CONGREGATION O 5741 BARTLETT	PITTSBURGH	**PA**	15217	(412) 521-9911
SHAARE TORAH, CONGREGATION O 2319 MURRAY AVENUE	PITTSBURGH	**PA**	15217	(412) 421-8855
SHAARE ZEDEK, CONGREGATION O 5751 BARTLETT	PITTSBURGH	**PA**	15217	
SINAI, TEMPLE R 5505 FORBES AVENUE	PITTSBURGH	**PA**	15217	(412) 421-9715
TORATH CHAIM, CONGREGATION O 729 NORTH NEGLEY AVENUE	PITTSBURGH	**PA**	15206	
TREE OF LIFE C WILKINS & SHADY AVENUE	PITTSBURGH	**PA**	15217	(412) 521-6788
YOUNG ISRAEL OF GREATER PITTSBURGH 5751 BARTLETT STREET	PITTSBURGH	**PA**	15217	(412) 421-9757
YOUNG PEOPLES SYNAGOGUE OF PITTSBURGH O 6401 FORBES AVENUE	PITTSBURGH	**PA**	15217	
MERCY & TRUTH, CONGREGATION C 575 N. KEIM STREET	POTTSTOWN	**PA**	19464	(215) 326-1717
OHEB ZEDEK SYNAGOGUE CENTER C 2300 MAHANTONGO STREET	POTTSVILLE	**PA**	17901	(717) 622-4320
CHEVRA AGUDATH ACHIM O CHURCH STREET	PUNXSUTAWNEY	**PA**	15767	
HAR ZION TEMPLE C 639 COUNTY LINE ROAD	RADNOR	**PA**	19087	
BETH JACOB, CONGREGATION 955 NORTH 10TH STREET	READING	**PA**	19604	(215) 372-8508
KESHER ZION SYNAGOGUE C 1245 ECKERT & PERKIOMEN AVENUE	READING	**PA**	19602	(215) 372-3818
MORRIS HASSEL RELIGIOUS SCHOOL C 1245 PERKIOMEN AVENUE	READING	**PA**	19602	(215) 372-3818
OHEB SHOLOM, CONGREGATION R 13TH STREET & PERKIOMEN AVENUE	READING	**PA**	19602	(215) 373-4623
SHOMREI HABRITH CONGREGATION O P.O. BOX 1394	READING	**PA**	19603	(215) 921-0881
OHEV SHALOM OF BUCKS COUNTY C 944 2ND STREET PIKE	RICHBORO	**PA**	18954	(215) 322-9595
BETH ISRAEL, TEMPLE 202 LINCOLN STREET	SAYRE	**PA**	18840	
BETH SHALOM, CONGREGATION O CLAY AVENUE & VINE STREET	SCRANTON	**PA**	18510	(717) 346-0502
HARRIS CHAPEL-JEWISH HOME OF EAST PENNSYLVANIA T 1101 VINE STREET	SCRANTON	**PA**	18510	(717) 344-6177
HESED, TEMPLE R LAKE SCRANTON ROAD & KNOX STREET	SCRANTON	**PA**	18505	(717) 344-7201
ISRAEL, TEMPLE C GIBBON STREET & MONROE AVENUE	SCRANTON	**PA**	18510	(717) 342-0350
MACHZIKEI HADAS, CONGREGATION 501 MADISON AVENUE	SCRANTON	**PA**	18510	(717) 342-6271
MADISON AVENUE TEMPLE R LAKE SCRANTON ROAD & KNOX STREET	SCRANTON	**PA**	18505	
OHEV ZEDEK, CONGREGATION O 1432 MULBERRY STREET	SCRANTON	**PA**	18510	
PENN MONROE SYNAGOGUE 901 OLIVE STREET	SCRANTON	**PA**	18510	(412) 347-3704
YOUNG ISRAEL OF SCRANTON 501 MADISON AVENUE	SCRANTON	**PA**	18510	(717) 342-6271
BETH ISRAEL, TEMPLE R 840 HIGHLAND ROAD	SHARON	**PA**	16146	(412) 346-4754
KEHILAT ISRAEL, CONGREGATION O 35 SOUTH JARDIN STREET	SHENANDOAH	**PA**	17976	
BETH OR R PENLLYN PIKE & DAGER ROAD	SPRING HOUSE	**PA**	19477	(215) 646-5806
DELAWARE COUNTY JCC-CONGREGATION NER TAMID C 300 W. WOODLAND AVENUE, P.O. BOX 266	SPRINGFIELD	**PA**	19064	(215) 543-4241
ISRAEL, TEMPLE C WALLACE STREET	STROUDSBURG	**PA**	18360	(717) 421-8781
BETH EL, CONGREGATION C 249 ARCH STREET	SUNBURY	**PA**	17801	(717) 286-9197
B'NAI YOSHIA, CONGREGATION O DAVID DRIVE & JEROME ROAD	TREVOSE	**PA**	19047	(215) 357-7131
ISRAEL, TEMPLE R 119 E. FAYETTE STREET	UNIONTOWN	**PA**	15401	(412) 437-6431
TREE OF LIFE, CONGREGATION C P.O. BOX 264, PENNSYLVANIA AVENUE	UNIONTOWN	**PA**	15401	(412) 437-6431
ISRAEL OF UPPER DARBY, TEMPLE C BYWOOD AVENUE & WALNUT STREET	UPPER DARBY	**PA**	19082	(215) 352-2125
OHEV SHALOM, CONGREGATION C 2 CHESTER ROAD, P.O. BOX 157	WALLINGFORD	**PA**	19086	(215) 874-1465
WARREN HEBREW CONGREGATION O 112 CONEWANGO AVENUE, P.O. BOX 365	WARREN	**PA**	16365	(814) 723-7122
BETH ISRAEL, CONGREGATION C 265 NORTH AVENUE	WASHINGTON	**PA**	15301	(215) 225-7080
OR SHALOM, THE CONSERVATIVE SYNAGOGUE OF THE MAIN LINE C P.O. BOX 476	WAYNE	**PA**	19087	(215) 296-3041
KESHER ISRAEL SYNAGOGUE C 206 NORTH CHURCH STREET, P.O. BOX 170	WEST CHESTER	**PA**	19380	(215) 696-7210
AGUDATH ACHIM, TEMPLE C	WEST PITTSTON	**PA**	18643	
TREE OF LIFE SFARD CONGREGATION C 2025 CYPRESS DRIVE	WHITE OAK	**PA**	15131	(215) 673-0938
ANSHEI EMES, CONGREGATION O 13 SOUTH WELLES STREET	WILKES-BARRE	**PA**	18702	
ANSHEI SFARD, CONGREGATION 53 SOUTH WELLES STREET	WILKES-BARRE	**PA**	18702	
ISRAEL, TEMPLE C 236 RIVER STREET	WILKES-BARRE	**PA**	18702	(717) 824-8927
OHAV ZEDEK SYNAGOGUE O 242 S. FRANKLIN STREET	WILKES-BARRE	**PA**	18702	(717) 825-6619
BETH HA-SHOLOM R 425 CENTER STREET	WILLIAMSPORT	**PA**	17701	(717) 323-7751
OHEV SHALOM CONGREGATION C CHERRY & BELMONT	WILLIAMSPORT	**PA**	17701	(717) 322-4209
EAST LANE TEMPLE C 501 CEDARBROOK HILL	WYNCOTE	**PA**	19095	(717) 884-4555
BETH HILLEL-BETH EL, TEMPLE C REMINGTON ROAD & LANCASTER AVENUE	WYNNEWOOD	**PA**	19096	(215) 649-5300
MAIN LINE REFORM TEMPLE, BETH ELOHIM R 410 MONTGOMERY AVENUE	WYNNEWOOD	**PA**	19096	(215) 649-7800
BETH TEFILAH-YEADON JEWISH COMMUNITY CENTER C WHITBY AVENUE & WEST COBBS CORK	YEADON	**PA**	19050	(215) 625-2156
BETH ISRAEL, TEMPLE R 2090 HOLLYWOOD DRIVE	YORK	**PA**	17403	(717) 843-2676
OHEV SHOLOM SYNAGOGUE C 2251 EASTERN BLVD	YORK	**PA**	17402	(717) 755-2714
BETH SHALOM, TEMPLE R 900 PONCE DE LEON AVENUE	SANTURCE	**PR**	00907	
SHAAR SHALOM, CONGREGATION C 4880 NOTRE DAME BOULEVARD	CHOMEDAY	**QU**	H7W 1V4	(418) 688-8100
YOUNG ISRAEL OF CHOMEDY 1025 ELIZABETH BOULEVARD	CHOMEDY	**QU**	H7W 3J7	(514) 681-2571
TIFERETH BETH DAVID JERUSALEM SYNAGOGUE 6519 BAILY ROAD	COTE ST. LUC	**QU**		(514) 484-3841
BETH TIKVAH, CONGREGATION 136 WESTPARK BOULEVARD	DOLLARD DES ORMEAUX	**QU**	H9A 2K2	(514) 683-5610
RODEPH SHALOM, TEMPLE R 96 FREDMIR BOULEVARD	DOLLARD DES ORMEAUX	**QU**	H9A 2R3	(514) 626-2173
ADATH ISRAEL CONGREGATION O 223 HARROW CRESCENT	HAMPSTEAD	**QU**	H3X 3X7	(514) 482-4252
YOUNG ISRAEL OF CHOMEDEY 1025 ELIZABETH BOULEVARD	LAVAL	**QU**	H7W 3J7	(514) 681-2571
CONGREGATION DORSHEI EMET, RECONSTRUCTIONIST SYNAGOGUE OF MONTREAL 18 CLEVE ROAD	MONTREAL	**QU**	H3X 1A6	(514) 486-9400
EMANU-EL BETH SHOLOM, TEMPLE R 4100 SHERBROOKE STREET WEST	MONTREAL	**QU**	H3Z 1A5	(514) 937-3575
SHAARE ZEDEK CONGREGATION C 5305 ROSEDALE AVENUE	MONTREAL	**QU**	H4V 2H7	(514) 484-1122
SHAARE ZION CONGREGATION C 5575 COTE ST. LUC ROAD	MONTREAL	**QU**	H3X 2C9	(514) 481-7727
YOUNG ISRAEL OF MONTREAL 6235 HILLSDALE ROAD	MONTREAL	**QU**		(514) 737-6589
YOUNG ISRAEL OF VAL ROYAL 2855 VICTOR DORE	MONTREAL	**QU**		(514) 334-4610
BETH EL, CONGREGATION C 1000 LUCERNE ROAD	MOUNT ROYAL	**QU**	H3R 2H9	(418) 738-4766
AGUDATH ISRAEL OF MONTREAL O 1819 GLENDALE AVENUE, #3	OUTREMOND	**QU**	H2V 1B3	
SHAAR HASHOMAYIM C 450 KENSINGTON AVENUE	WESTMOUNT	**QU**	H3Y 3A2	(514) 937-9471
BARRINGTON JEWISH CENTER R 147 COUNTY ROAD	BARRINGTON	**RI**	02806	
HABONIM, TEMPLE R 165 MEADOW ROAD	BARRINGTON	**RI**	02806	(401) 245-6536
BETH TORAH, TEMPLE C 330 PARK AVENUE	CRANSTON	**RI**	02905	(401) 785-1800
SINAI, TEMPLE R 30 HAGEN STREET	CRANSTON	**RI**	02920	(401) 942-8350
TORAT YISRAEL, TEMPLE C 330 PARK AVENUE	CRANSTON	**RI**	02905	
SHALOM, TEMPLE C 221 VALLEY ROAD, P.O. BOX 372	MIDDLETOWN	**RI**	02840	(401) 846-9002
AHAVAS ACHIM, CONGREGATION O 136 KAY STREET	NEWPORT	**RI**	02840	
OHAVE SHALOM, CONGREGATION O EAST AVENUE	PAWTUCKET	**RI**	02860	
BETH DAVID ANSHE KOVNO, TEMPLE C 145 OAKLAND AVENUE	PROVIDENCE	**RI**	02908	
BETH EL, TEMPLE R 70 ORCHARD AVENUE	PROVIDENCE	**RI**	02906	(401) 331-6070
BETH ISRAEL, TEMPLE C 155 NIAGARA STREET	PROVIDENCE	**RI**	02907	
BETH SHOLOM, TEMPLE C 275 CAMP STREET	PROVIDENCE	**RI**	02906	
EMANU-EL, TEMPLE C 99 TAFT AVENUE	PROVIDENCE	**RI**	02906	(401) 331-1616
MISHKON TFILOH, CONGREGATION O 203 SUMMIT AVENUE, P.O. BOX 9592	PROVIDENCE	**RI**	02906	(401) 521-1616
SHAARE ZEDEK-SONS OF ABRAHAM, CONGREGATION O 688 BROAD STREET	PROVIDENCE	**RI**	02907	(401) 751-4936
SONS OF JACOB, CONGREGATION O 24 DOUGLAS AVENUE	PROVIDENCE	**RI**	02908	(401) 274-5260
BETH AM-BETH DAVID, TEMPLE C 40 GARDINER STREET	WARWICK	**RI**	02888	(401) 463-7944
SHARAH ZEDEK, CONGREGATION C UNION STREET	WESTERLY	**RI**	02891	
B'NAI ISRAEL, CONGREGATION C 224 PROSPECT STREET	WOONSOCKET	**RI**	02895	(401) 765-3651
ADATH JESHURUN CONGREGATION C GREENVILLE STREET N.W., P.O. BOX 398	AIKEN	**SC**	29801	
B'NAI ISRAEL, TEMPLE R OAKLAND AVENUE, P.O. BOX 491	ANDERSON	**SC**	29622	(803) 226-0310
BETH ISRAEL C P.O. BOX 387	BEAUFORT	**SC**	29003	
BETH EL, CONGREGATION R P.O. BOX 496	CAMDEN	**SC**	29020	
BRITH SHOLOM-BETH ISRAEL O 182 RUTLEDGE AVENUE, P.O. BOX 2248	CHARLESTON	**SC**	29401	(803) 577-6599
EMANU-EL, SYNAGOGUE C 5 WINDSOR DRIVE	CHARLESTON	**SC**	29407	(803) 571-3264
KAHAL KADOSH BETH ELOHIM R 90 HASELL STREET	CHARLESTON	**SC**	29401	(803) 723-1090
BETH SHALOM, CONGREGATION C P.O. BOX 11482	COLUMBIA	**SC**	29211	(803) 782-2500
BETH SHOLOM, SYNAGOGUE C 5827 TRENHOLM ROAD	COLUMBIA	**SC**	29206	(803) 782-2500
TREE OF LIFE CONGREGATION R 2701 HEYWARD STREET	COLUMBIA	**SC**	29205	(803) 799-2485
OHAV SHALOM, CONGREGATION C CALHOUN STREET	DILLON	**SC**	29536	
BETH ISRAEL, TEMPLE R 316 PARK AVENUE, P.O. BOX 3008	FLORENCE	**SC**	29502	(803) 669-9724
BETH ELOHIM, TEMPLE R C/O SYLVAN ROSEN, ATTY. AT LAW, SCREVEN STREET	GEORGETOWN	**SC**	29440	(803) 546-7925
BETH ISRAEL, CONGREGATION C 425 SUMMIT DRIVE, P.O. BOX 83	GREENVILLE	**SC**	29602	(803) 232-9031
ISRAEL, TEMPLE R 115 BUIST AVENUE	GREENVILLE	**SC**	29609	(803) 233-2421
BETH OR C 107 HIRSCH STREET	KINGSTREE	**SC**	29556	(803) 354-6425
EMANU-EL, TEMPLE C P.O. BOX 1171	MYRTLE BEACH	**SC**	29577	(803) 449-5552
B'NAI ISRAEL, CONGREGATION C 145 HEYWOOD AVENUE	SPARTANBURG	**SC**	29302	(803) 582-7087
SINAI, TEMPLE R 11 CHURCH STREET, P.O. BOX 1673	SUMTER	**SC**	29150	(803) 773-2122
MOUNT SINAI, TEMPLE C P.O. BOX 506	WALTERBORO	**SC**	29488	(803) 549-5770
B'NAI ISAAC, CONGREGATION C P.O. BOX 91, 202 NORTH KLINE	ABERDEEN	**SD**	57401	(605) 225-3404
HILLS, SYNAGOGUE OF THE R P.O. BOX 391	RAPID CITY	**SD**	57709	(605) 342-3875
MOUNTAIN ZION CONGREGATION R 523 W. 14TH STREET	SIOUX FALLS	**SD**	57104	(605) 338-5454
SONS OF ISRAEL, CONGREGATION C 1207 SOUTH PHILLIPS AVENUE	SIOUX FALLS	**SD**	57105	
BETH JACOB, CONGREGATION 1640 VICTORIA AVENUE	REGINA	**SK**	S4P 0P7	(306) 527-8643
AGUDAS ISRAEL 715 MCKINNON AVENUE	SASKATOON	**SK**	S7H 2G2	(306) 527-8643
JEWISH COMMUNITY CENTRE, CONGREGATION AGUDAS ISRAEL C 715 MCKINNON AVENUE	SASKATOON	**SK**	S7H 2G2	(306) 343-7023
B'NAI SHOLOM, CONGREGATION R MT. TUCKER ADDITION, RT. 6	BLOUNTVILLE	**TN**	37617	(615) 323-7596

B'NAI SHOLOM, CONGREGATION C P.O.	BRISTOL	TN	37620	(615) 669-9199
ADAS ISRAEL CONGREGATION R N. WASHINGTON STREET	BROWNSVILLE	TN	38012	
B'NAI ZION SYNAGOGUE C 114 MCBRIEN ROAD	CHATTANOOGA	TN	37411	(615) 894-8900
BETH SHALOM CONGREGATION O 20 PISGAH AVENUE	CHATTANOOGA	TN	37411	(615) 894-0801
MIZPAH CONGREGATION R 923 MCCALLIE AVENUE	CHATTANOOGA	TN	37403	(615) 267-9771
B'NAI ISRAEL, CONGREGATION R P.O. BOX 278, 401 W. GRAND STREET	JACKSON	TN	38301	(901) 427-6141
BETH EL, TEMPLE R P.O. BOX 3037, KINGSTON PIKE	KNOXVILLE	TN	37919	(615) 524-3521
HESKA AMUNA SYNAGOGUE C 3811 KINGSTON PIKE	KNOXVILLE	TN	37919	(615) 522-0701
ANSHEL SPHARD BETH EL EMETH CONGREGATION O 120 E. YATES ROAD N	MEMPHIS	TN	38117	(901) 682-1611
BARON HIRSCH CONGREGATION O 5631 SHADY GROVE ROAD	MEMPHIS	TN	38117	(901) 683-4767
BARON HIRSCH CONGREGATION O 1740 VOLLINTINE AVENUE	MEMPHIS	TN	38107	(901) 274-3525
BETH SHALOM SYNAGOGUE C 482 S. MENDENHALL ROAD	MEMPHIS	TN	38117	(901) 683-3591
ISRAEL, TEMPLE R 1376 EAST MASSEY ROAD	MEMPHIS	TN	38119	(901) 761-3130
OHABAI SHOLOM, CONGREGATION R 5015 HARDING ROAD	NASHVILLE	TN	37205	(615) 352-7620
SHERITH ISRAEL, CONGREGATION O 3600 WEST END AVENUE	NASHVILLE	TN	37205	(615) 292-6614
WEST END SYNAGOGUE, KHAL KODESH ADATH ISRAEL C 3814 WEST END AVENUE	NASHVILLE	TN	37205	(615) 269-4592
BETH EL, CONGREGATION C W. MADISON LANE	OAK RIDGE	TN	37830	(615) 483-4284
JEWISH CONGREGATION OF OAK RIDGE C P.O. BOX 3248, 101 WEST MADISON	OAK RIDGE	TN	37830	(615) 483-3581
MIZPAH, TEMPLE R 849 CHESTNUT, P.O. BOX 1283	ABILENE	TX	79604	(915) 672-8225
B'NAI ISRAEL, TEMPLE R 4316 ALBERT	AMARILLO	TX	79106	(806) 352-7191
AGUDAS ACHIM, CONGREGATION C 4300 BULL CREEK ROAD	AUSTIN	TX	78758	(512) 459-3287
BETH ISRAEL, TEMPLE R 3901 SHOAL CREEK BLVD	AUSTIN	TX	78756	(512) 454-6806
EMANUEL, TEMPLE R P.O. BOX 423	BEAUMONT	TX	77704	(713) 832-6131
KOL ISRAEL, CONGREGATION C P.O. BOX 423	BEAUMONT	TX	77704	
BRITH SHALOM, CONGREGATION C 4610 BELLAIRE BLVD	BELLAIRE	TX	77401	(713) 667-9201
BETH ISRAEL, TEMPLE 1317 CYPRESS STREET	BRECKENRIDGE	TX	76024	
BETH EL, TEMPLE R P.O. BOX 3851	BROWNSVILLE	TX	78520	(512) 542-5263
BETH SHALOM, CONGREGATION R P.O. BOX 3523	BRYAN	TX	77801	(817) 846-7313
B'NAI ISRAEL SYNAGOGUE C 3434 FORT WORTH STREET	CORPUS CHRISTI	TX	78411	(512) 855-7308
BETH EL, TEMPLE R 1315 CRAIG STREET, P.O. BOX 3214	CORPUS CHRISTI	TX	78404	(512) 883-0831
AGUDAS ACHIM, CONGREGATION O PARK AVENUE & 19TH STREET	CORSICANA	TX	75110	(214) 874-3045
BETH-EL, TEMPLE R 208 SOUTH 15TH STREET	CORSICANA	TX	75110	
AGUDAS ACHIM, CONGREGATION 5810 FOREST LANE	DALLAS	TX	75230	
EMANU-EL, TEMPLE R 8500 HILLCREST ROAD	DALLAS	TX	75225	(214) 368-3613
SHALOM, TEMPLE R 6930 ALPHA ROAD	DALLAS	TX	75240	(214) 661-1810
SHEARITH ISRAEL, CONGREGATION C 9401 DOUGLAS AVENUE	DALLAS	TX	75225	(214) 361-6606
TIFERET ISRAEL CONGREGATION O 10909 HILLCREST ROAD	DALLAS	TX	75230	(214) 691-3611
YOUNG ISRAEL OF DALLAS 1450 PRESTON FOREST SQUARE SUITE 218	DALLAS	TX	75230	(214) 934-1263
B'NAI ZION, CONGREGATION C 210-220 E. CLIFF DRIVE	EL PASO	TX	79902	(915) 532-3137
MOUNT SINAI, TEMPLE R 4408 NORTH STANTON	EL PASO	TX	79902	(915) 532-5959
AHAVATH SHOLOM C 1600 WEST MYRTLE	FORT WORTH	TX	76401	
AHAVATH SHOLOM, CONGREGATION T 4050 SOUTH HULEN	FORT WORTH	TX	76109	(817) 923-7379
BETH EL, CONGREGATION R 207 WEST BROADWAY	FORT WORTH	TX	76104	(817) 332-7141
B'NAI ISRAEL, CONGREGATION R 3008 AVENUE O	GALVESTON	TX	77550	(713) 765-5796
BETH JACOB, CONGREGATION C 2401 AVENUE K	GALVESTON	TX	77550	(713) 762-7267
ISRAEL OF SCHULENBURG, TEMPLE R C/O MR. ARMAND G. SCHWARTZ, P.O. BOX 385	HALLETSVILLE	TX	77964	(713) 743-3864
BETH ISRAEL, TEMPLE R 1702 EAST JACKSON, P.O. BOX 611	HARLINGEN	TX	78550	
BETH AM, CONGREGATION C 1431 BRITTMOORE ROAD	HOUSTON	TX	77043	(713) 461-7725
BETH ISRAEL, CONGREGATION R 5600 N. BRAESWOOD BLVD	HOUSTON	TX	77906	(713) 771-6221
BETH YESHURUN, CONGREGATION C 4525 BEECHNUT	HOUSTON	TX	77906	(713) 666-1881
EMANU-EL, CONGREGATION R 1500 SUNSET BLVD	HOUSTON	TX	77005	(713) 529-5771
HOUSTON CONGREGATION FOR REFORM JUDAISM R P.O. BOX 27151	HOUSTON	TX	77027	(713) 782-4162
JEWISH COMMUNITY NORTH P.O. BOX 90448	HOUSTON	TX	77090	(713) 376-0016
SHAAR HASHALOM, CONGREGATION C 16020 EL CAMINO REAL	HOUSTON	TX	77062	(713) 488-5861
SINAI, TEMPLE R P.O. BOX 42888, SUITE 111	HOUSTON	TX	77042	(713) 496-5950
UNITED ORTHODOX SYNAGOGUES OF HOUSTON O 9001 GREENWILLOW	HOUSTON	TX	77096	(713) 723-3850
YOUNG ISRAEL OF HOUSTON 11523 BOB WHITE	HOUSTON	TX	77056	(713) 728-8128
AGUDAS ACHIM C LAREDO & MALINCHE STREETS	LAREDO	TX	78040	(713) 723-4435
B'NAI ISRAEL, TEMPLE R C/O MRS DEAN SANDITEN, 2120 MUSSER STREET	LAREDO	TX	78040	
EMANU-EL TEMPLE R 1205 EDEN DRIVE, P.O. BOX 423	LONGVIEW	TX	75601	(214) 753-6512
SHAARETH ISRAEL, CONGREGATION R P.O. BOX 6192, 1706 23RD STREET	LUBBOCK	TX	79413	(806) 744-6084
MOSES MONTEFIORE, TEMPLE R P.O. BOX 1146	MARSHALL	TX	75670	
EMANUEL, TEMPLE R 1410 REDWOOD, P.O. BOX 896	MCALLEN	TX	78501	(512) 686-9432
RODEF SHALOM, CONGREGATION R 3984 PROCTER STREET	PORT ARTHUR	TX	77640	(713) 985-7616
BETH TORAH, CONGREGATION C 810 LOOKOUT DRIVE	RICHARDSON	TX	75080	(214) 234-1541
BETH TSIYON, CONGREGATION 401 CANYON CREEK	RICHARDSON	TX	75080	
AGUDAS ACHIM, CONGREGATION C 1201 DONALDSON AVENUE	SAN ANTONIO	TX	78228	(512) 736-4216
BETH EL, TEMPLE R 211 BELKNAP PLACE	SAN ANTONIO	TX	78212	(512) 733-9135
NEW JEWISH CONGREGATION OF SAN ANTONIO R C/O DR. D. SHAPIRO, 9214 OLD HOMESTEAD	SAN ANTONIO	TX	78320	
RODFEI SHOLOM, CONGREGATION O 115 EAST LAUREL STREET	SAN ANTONIO	TX	78212	
ISRAEL, TEMPLE R 508 BAUMGARTEN STREET	SCHULENBURG	TX	78956	
BETH EMETH, TEMPLE R 304 NORTH RUSK STREET	SHERMAN	TX	75090	(214) 892-9326
MOUNT SINAI CONGREGATION R 1310 WALNUT STREET	TEXARKANA	TX	75501	(214) 792-2394
AHAVATH ACHIM C 1014 WEST HOUSTON STREET	TYLER	TX	75702	(214) 597-4284
BETH EL, TEMPLE R 1102 SOUTH AUGUSTA	TYLER	TX	75701	(214) 597-2917
B'NAI ISRAEL, TEMPLE R P.O. BOX 2088	VICTORIA	TX	77901	(512) 578-5140
AGUDATH JACOB C 4925 HILLCREST DRIVE	WACO	TX	76710	(817) 772-1451
RODEF SHOLOM, TEMPLE R 1717 NORTH 41ST STREET	WACO	TX	76707	(817) 754-3703
SHEARITH ISRAEL, CONGREGATION C 219 HOLLIS STREET	WHARTON	TX	77488	
HOUSE OF JACOB, CONGREGATION C 2624 AMHERST	WICHITA FALLS	TX	76308	(817) 692-2326
ISRAEL, TEMPLE R P.O. BOX 952	WICHITA FALLS	TX	76307	
KOL AMI, CONGREGATION C & R 2425 EAST HERITAGE WAY	SALT LAKE CITY	UT	84109	(801) 484-1501
AGUDAS ACHIM CONGREGATION C 2908 VALLEY DRIVE	ALEXANDRIA	VA	22302	(703) 548-4122
BETH EL HEBREW CONGREGATION R 3830 SEMINARY ROAD	ALEXANDRIA	VA	22304	(703) 370-9400
ARLINGTON-FAIRFAX JEWISH CONGREGATION C 2920 ARLINGTON BOULEVARD	ARLINGTON	VA	22204	(703) 979-4466
BETH ISRAEL, CONGREGATION R THIRD & JEFFERSON STREETS	CHARLOTTESVILLE	VA	22902	(804) 295-6382
AETZ CHAYIM, CONGREGATION O 168 STATFORD PLACE	DANVILLE	VA	24541	
BETH SHOLOM, TEMPLE R 127 SUTHERLIN AVENUE	DANVILLE	VA	24541	(804) 792-3489
OLAM TIKVAH, CONGREGATION C 3800 GLENBROOK ROAD	FAIRFAX	VA	22030	(703) 978-3333
RODEF SHALOM, TEMPLE R 2100 WESTMORELAND STREET	FALLS CHURCH	VA	22043	(703) 532-2217
FORT BELVOIR JEWISH CONGREGATION	FORT BELVOIR	VA	22060	(703) 664-1218
BETH SHOLOM, TEMPLE R P.O. BOX 481	FREDERICKSBURG	VA	22404	(703) 373-4834
B'NAI ISRAEL SYNAGOGUE O 3116 KECOUGHTAN ROAD	HAMPTON	VA	23661	
RODEF SHOLOM, CONGREGATION C 318 WHEALTON ROAD	HAMPTON	VA	23666	(804) 826-5894
BETH EL, CONGREGATION R P.O. BOX 845	HARRISONBURG	VA	22801	(703) 434-2744
AGUDATH SHOLOM, CONGREGATION R P.O. BOX 2262	LYNCHBURG	VA	24501	(804) 846-0739
OHEV ZION CONGREGATION R 801 PARKVIEW AVENUE	MARTINSVILLE	VA	24112	(703) 632-2828
ADATH JESHURUN SYNAGOGUE O 1815 CHESTNUT AVENUE	NEWPORT NEWS	VA	23607	(804) 245-7485
RODEF SHOLOM, TEMPLE C P.O. BOX 5726	NEWPORT NEWS	VA	23605	(804) 826-5894
SINAI, TEMPLE R 11620 WARWICK BOULEVARD	NEWPORT NEWS	VA	23601	(804) 596-8352
B'NAI ISRAEL, CONGREGATION O 420 SPOTSWOOD AVENUE	NORFOLK	VA	23517	(804) 627-7358
BETH EL C 422 SHIRLEY AVENUE, P.O. BOX 11206	NORFOLK	VA	23517	(804) 625-7821
ISRAEL, TEMPLE C 7255 GRANBY STREET	NORFOLK	VA	23505	(804) 489-4550
MIKVE KODESH CONGREGATION O P.O. BOX 1035	NORFOLK	VA	23501	
OHEV SHOLOM, TEMPLE R 530 RALEIGH AVENUE, STOCKLEY GARDENS	NORFOLK	VA	23507	(804) 625-4295
BRITH ACHIM, CONGREGATION C 314 SOUTH BOULEVARD	PETERSBURG	VA	23805	(804) 732-3968
GOMLEY CHESED CONGREGATION C 3110 STERLING POINT DRIVE	PORTSMOUTH	VA	23703	(804) 484-1019
SINAI, TEMPLE R 4401 HATTON POINT ROAD	PORTSMOUTH	VA	23703	(804) 484-1730
NORTH VIRGINIA HEBREW CONGREGATION R 1441 WIEHLE AVENUE, P.O. BOX 2758	RESTON	VA	22090	(703) 437-7733
B'NAI SHALOM CONGREGATION C 6007 WEST CLUB LANE	RICHMOND	VA	23226	(804) 270-7011
BETH AHABAH, CONGREGATION R 1111 WEST FRANKLIN STREET	RICHMOND	VA	23220	(804) 358-6757
BETH EL, TEMPLE C 3330 GROVE AVENUE	RICHMOND	VA	23221	(804) 355-3564
BETH SHOLOM, CONGREGATION R 5100 MONUMENT AVENUE	RICHMOND	VA	23223	
KENESETH BETH ISRAEL CONGREGATION O 6300 PATTERSON AVENUE	RICHMOND	VA	23226	(804) 288-7953
KOL EMES, CONGREGATION O 4811 PATTERSON AVENUE	RICHMOND	VA	23226	(804) 353-5831
OR AMI, CONGREGATION R 3406 NORTH HUGUENOT ROAD	RICHMOND	VA	23226	(804) 272-0017
BETH ISRAEL SYNAGOGUE C 920 FRANKLIN ROAD SW	ROANOKE	VA	24016	(703) 343-0289
EMANUEL, TEMPLE R 1163 PERSINGER ROAD SW	ROANOKE	VA	24015	(703) 342-3378
HOUSE OF ISRAEL, TEMPLE R MOUNTAINSIDE FARMS, RT. 1 BOX 1896	STAUNTON	VA	24401	(703) 885-6878
EMANUEL, TEMPLE C 25TH STREET & BALTIC AVENUE	VIRGINIA BEACH	VA	23451	(804) 428-2591
KEHILLAT BET HAMIDRASH C 740 ARTHUR AVENUE	VIRGINIA BEACH	VA	23452	(804) 424-9715
BETH EL CONGREGATION R 528 FAIRMONT AVENUE, P.O. BOX 1041	WINCHESTER	VA	22601	(703) 667-1043
NER TAMID, CONGREGATION R P.O. BOX 54	WOODBRIDGE	VA	22194	(703) 494-3251
HEBREW CONGREGATION O CHARLOTTE AMALIE	ST. THOMAS	VI	00801	
HEBREW CONGREGATION OF ST. THOMAS R P.O. BOX 266	ST. THOMAS	VI	00801	(809) 774-4312
BETH EL, TEMPLE C 151 NORTH STREET	BENNINGTON	VT	05201	
OHAVI ZEDEK SYNAGOGUE 188 NORTH PROSPECT STREET	BURLINGTON	VT	05401	(802) 864-0128
RUTLAND JEWISH CENTER C 96 GROVE STREET	RUTLAND	VT	05701	(802) 773-3455
SINAI, TEMPLE R 899 DORSET STREET	SOUTH BURLINGTON	VT	05401	(802) 862-5125
JEWISH CONGREGATION 55 HIGH STREET	ST. ALBANS	VT	05478	
BETH EL, CONGREGATION 76 RAILROAD STREET	ST. JOHNSBURY	VT	05819	
BETH ISRAEL, TEMPLE R 1801 SHERWOOD LANE	ABERDEEN	WA	98520	(206) 532-7485
BETH ISRAEL, CONGREGATION C 1320 LAKEWAY DRIVE, APARTMENT 127	BELLINGHAM	WA	98225	
B'NAI TORAH, TEMPLE R 6195 92ND AVENUE SE	MERCER ISLAND	WA	98040	(206) 232-7243
HERZI-NER TAMID CONSERVATIVE CONGREGATION C P.O. BOX 574, 3700 EAST MERCER WAY	MERCER ISLAND	WA	98040	(206) 232-8555
BETH SHOLOM, CONGREGATION P.O. BOX 761	RICHLAND	WA	99352	(509) 943-9457
B'NAI TORAH, TEMPLE 6195 92ND SE MERCER ISLAND	SEATTLE	WA	98112	(206) 232-7243
BETH AM, TEMPLE R 8015 27TH AVENUE NORTHEAST	SEATTLE	WA	98115	(206) 525-0915
BETH SHALOM, CONGREGATION C 6800 35TH AVENUE NORTHEAST	SEATTLE	WA	98115	(206) 524-0075
BIKUR CHOLIM MACHZIKAY HADATH CONGREGATION O 5145 SOUTH MORGAN STREET	SEATTLE	WA	98118	(206) 723-0970
DE HIRSCH SINAI, TEMPLE R 1511 EAST PIKE STREET	SEATTLE	WA	98122	(206) 323-8486
EMANUEL CONGREGATION O 3412 NE 65TH STREET	SEATTLE	WA	98115	(206) 525-1055
EZRA BESSAROTH, CONGREGATION O 5217 SOUTH BRANDON STREET	SEATTLE	WA	98118	(206) 725-3770
SEPHARDIC BIKUR HOLIM CONGREGATION O 6500 52ND STREET SOUTH	SEATTLE	WA	98118	(206) 723-9661
BETH SHALOM, TEMPLE C P.O. BOX 8013, EAST 1322 30TH AVENUE	SPOKANE	WA	99203	(509) 747-3304
BETH EL, TEMPLE R 5975 SOUTH 12TH STREET	TACOMA	WA	98465	(206) 564-7101
MOSES MONTEFIORE SYNAGOGUE C 3131 NORTH MEADE STREET	APPLETON	WI	54911	(414) 733-1848
ZION, CONGREGATION R 1751 NORTH DIVISION	APPLETON	WI	54911	
B'NAI ABRAHAM R P.O. BOX 964	BELOIT	WI	53511	(608) 364-4916
SHOLOM, TEMPLE C 1223 EMERY STREET	EAU CLAIRE	WI	54701	(715) 834-4667
BETH ISRAEL, TEMPLE C	FOND DU LAC	WI	54935	
CNESSES ISRAEL, CONGREGATION C P.O. BOX 1252, 222 SOUTH BAIRD STREET	GREEN BAY	WI	54301	(414) 437-4841
B'NAI ZEDEK, CONGREGATION C 1600 56TH STREET	KENOSHA	WI	53140	
BETH HILLEL TEMPLE R LIBRARY SQUARE	KENOSHA	WI	53140	(414) 654-2716
SONS OF ABRAHAM, CONGREGATION O 1820 MAIN STREET	LA CROSSE	WI	54601	
BETH EL, TEMPLE R 2702 ARBOR DRIVE	MADISON	WI	53711	(608) 238-3123
BETH ISRAEL CENTER C 1406 MOUND STREET	MADISON	WI	53711	(608) 256-7763
ANSHE POALE ZEDEK, CONGREGATION O 1422 WASHINGTON STREET	MANITOWOC	WI	54220	
MONTEFIORE & SONS OF JACOB, CONGREGATION O P.O. BOX 224	MARINETTE	WI	54143	
AGUDAS ACHIM, CONGREGATION O 5820 WEST BURLEIGH STREET	MILWAUKEE	WI	53210	(414) 447-9239
ANSHAI LEBOWITZ, CONGREGATION O 3100 NORTH 52ND STREET	MILWAUKEE	WI	53216	
ANSHE EMETH, CONGREGATION C 8057 WEST APPLETON AVENUE	MILWAUKEE	WI	53218	(414) 463-7680

ANSHE SFARD, CONGREGATION O 3447 NORTH 51ST BOULEVARD ..... MILWAUKEE WI 53216 (414) 444-9640
BETH EL NER TAMID SYNAGOGUE C
3725 NORTH SHERMAN BOULEVARD .... MILWAUKEE WI 53216 (414) 442-4520
BETH ISRAEL, CONGREGATION C 6880 NORTH GREEN BAY AVENUE ... MILWAUKEE WI 53209 (414) 352-7310
BETH JEHUDAH, CONGREGATION O 2700 NORTH 54TH STREET .... MILWAUKEE WI 53210
BNAI JACOB, CONGREGATION O 3056 NORTH 55TH STREET .... MILWAUKEE WI 53210
EMANU-EL B'NE JESHURUN, CONGREGATION R
2419 EAST KENWOOD BOULEVARD, P.O. BOX 11698 .... MILWAUKEE WI 53211 (414) 964-4100
MENORAH, TEMPLE C 9363 NORTH 76TH STREET .... MILWAUKEE WI 53223 (414) 355-1120
SHALOM, CONGREGATION R
7630 NORTH SANTA MONICA BOULEVARD .... MILWAUKEE WI 53217 (414) 352-9288
SINAI, CONGREGATION R 8223 NORTH PORT WASHINGTON ROAD ... MILWAUKEE WI 53217 (414) 352-2970
B'NAI ISRAEL, TEMPLE R 1121 ALGOMA BOULEVARD .... OSHKOSH WI 54901 (414) 235-4270
BETH ISRAEL SINAI CONGREGATION C 944 SOUTH MAIN STREET .... RACINE WI 53403 (414) 633-7093
BETH EL, CONGREGATION C 1007 NORTH AVENUE .... SHEBOYGAN WI 53081 (414) 452-5828
BETH EL OF SUPERIOR HEBREW CONGREGATION, TEMPLE C
603 FAXON AVENUE .... SUPERIOR WI 54880 (715) 392-4279
EMANUEL, CONGREGATION R 830 WEST MORELAND BOULEVARD ...... WAUKESHA WI 53186
MOUNT SINAI CONGREGATION R 622 4TH STREET .... WAUSAU WI 54401 (715) 845-7461
BETH EL, TEMPLE R BELLVIEW LANE, P.O. BOX 1363 .... BECKLEY WV 25801 (304) 253-9421
AHAVATH SHOLOM, CONGREGATION R 632 ALBEMARLE STREET .... BLUEFIELD WV 24701 (304) 325-9372
B'NAI JACOB, CONGREGATION O VIRGINIA & ELIZABETH STREETS .. CHARLESTON WV 25311
TREE OF LIFE SYNAGOGUE C 5TH & WEST PIKE STREETS .... CLARKSBURG WV 26301 (304) 622-3453
FAIRMONT JEWISH COMMUNITY CENTER R 216 BROADVIEW AVENUE ... FAIRMONT WV 26554 (304) 363-5630
B'NAI ISRAEL, CONGREGATION C 900 9TH STREET, P.O. BOX 847 ..... HUNTINGTON WV 25712
B'NAI SHOLOM CONGREGATION C & R
P.O. BOX 2004, 10TH AVENUE & 10TH STREET..................... HUNTINGTON WV 25720 (304) 522-2980
OHEV SHOLOM, TEMPLE R P.O. BOX 2004 .... HUNTINGTON WV 25720
B'NAI EL, CONGREGATION R P.O. BOX 899 .... LOGAN WV 25601 (304) 752-2275
BETH JACOB, CONGREGATION R
126 WEST MARTIN STREET, P.O. BOX 1147 .... MARTINSBURG WV 25401 (304) 267-4347
TREE OF LIFE, TEMPLE R P.O. BOX 791 .... MORGANTOWN WV 26505
B'NAI ISRAEL, CONGREGATION R 1703 20TH STREET .... PARKERSBURG WV 26101 (304) 428-1192
BETH ISRAEL, CONGREGATION O 500 BROOKLINE DRIVE .... WEIRTON WV 26062
EMANUEL CONGREGATION R .... WELCH WV 24801 (304) 436-4768
ISRAEL, SYNAGOGUE OF C 115 1/2 EDGINTON LANE................... WHEELING WV 26003
SHALOM, TEMPLE-CONGREGATION LESHEM SHOMAYIM R
23 BETHANY PIKE .... WHEELING WV 26003 (304) 233-4870
B'NAI ISRAEL R P.O. BOX 21 .... WILLIAMSON WV 25661 (304) 235-2947
MT. SINAI CONGREGATION 2610 PIONEER AVENUE .... CHEYENNE WV 82001 (307) 634-3052

TALLITOT & KIPPOT

ROSA FISCHER MISRACH 1709 SHATTUCK AVENUE .... BERKELEY CA 94709 (415) 849-2089
DEBORAH PESSA OLES 3649 JAMINE AVENUE .... LOS ANGELES CA 90034 (213) 837-9898
IRENE TABATSKY 231 PARKER STREET .... MANCHESTER CT 06040 (203) 647-9578
JUDY TSUKROFF, SUN PORCH WEAVING STUDIO .... NORFOLK CT 06058
MR. E. E.HOISINGTON 1227 S.E. 12TH STERRACE .... DEERFIELD BEACH FL 33441 (305) 421-6704
ALTMAN. S. 193 BROADWAY .... BROOKLYN NY 11211 (718) 384-7528
BORO PARK JUDAICA 5413 NEW UTRECHT AVENUE .... BROOKLYN NY 11219 (718) 435-4465
CHUSTER TALIS MANUFACTURING CO. 141 DIVISION STREET .... BROOKLYN NY 11211 (718) 384-3146
WEISS'S TALIS & TEFILIN BAGS 541 WYTHE AVENUE .... BROOKLYN NY 11211 (718) 387-7742
BOOK NOOK - BENTCHERS & YAMULKES 802 CORNAGA AVENUE ..FAR ROCKAWAY NY 11691 (718) 327-0163
TIRTZAH, TALLITOT FOR WOMEN BOX 220 .... GUILDERLAND NY 12084
RIKMAH .... LONG BEACH NY 11561 (212) 377-2466
SIMCHA SHOPPE, THE 18 HILLTOP LANE. .... MONSEY NY 10952 (914) 352-4543
CHARISMA, MANUFACTURER OF SKULL CAPS 3 BURROWS COURT .... NEW CITY NY 10956 (914) 354-3103
BEN ARI ARTS LTD. 11 AVENUE A .... NEW YORK NY 10009 (212) 677-4730
H & M SKULL CAP (OFFICE) 61 HESTER STREET .... NEW YORK NY 10002 (212) 777-2280
H & M SKULL CAP MANUFACTURING CO. 46 HESTER STREET .... NEW YORK NY 10002 (212) 475-1910
J. LEVINE CO. 58 ELDRIDGE STREET .... NEW YORK NY 10002 (212) 966-4460
MIRIAM MANUFACTURING COMPANY 48 CANAL STREET .... NEW YORK NY 10002 (212) 925-9272
MUNKACZER TALIS MANUFACTURING 87 EAST BROADWAY .... NEW YORK NY 10002 (212) 267-0540
RONA RONES - THE LOOM ROOM 607 WEST END AVENUE .... NEW YORK NY 10024 (212) 873-5276
S & W SKULL CAP COMPANY 45 ESSEX STREET .... NEW YORK NY 10002 (212) 673-3330
ZIONTALIS MANUFACTURING COMPANY, INC. 48 ELDRIDGE STREET .... NEW YORK NY 10002 (212) 925-8558
INVITATIONS PLUS 600 WEST 246TH STREET .... RIVERDALE NY 10471 (212) 548-3900
INVITATIONS PLUS 600 WEST 246TH STREET .... RIVERDALE NY 10471 (800) INV-PLUS
ANITA FREIMARK 7054 ROUNDELAY ROAD, NORTH .... REYNOLDSBURG OH 43068 (614) 864-7784
PHYLLIS KANTOR 250 EAST 38TH STREET .... EUGENE OR 97405 (503) 421-6704
RABBI PIOTRLOWSKI'S JUDAICA CENTER
289 MONTGOMERY AVENUE....................................... BALA CYNWYD PA 19004 (215) 887-0343
DORETTE BOEHM 411 NORTH STERLING ROAD .... ELKINS PARK PA 19117 (215) 635-2442
ZALMAN SCHACTER, C/O RELIGION DEPT. TEMPLE UNIVERSITY .... PHILADELPHIA PA 19121 (215) 849-5385
ROSE S. BANK 3 ROSELAWN TERRACE .... PITTSBURGH PA 15213 (412) 681-2863
ELSA WACHS 2 SOUTH PROVIDENCE ROAD .... WALLINGFORD PA 19086 (215) 566-5693
ISAAC SKULL CAP COMPANY 3553 ST. LAWRENCE .... MONTREAL QU (514) 274-8403

TALMUD TORAH & SUPPLEMENTARY SCHOOLS

TEMPLE BETH TORAH 225 SOUTH ATLANTIC BOULEVARD	ALHAMBRA	**CA**	91801	(818) 723-2978
TEMPLE SHAAREI TIKVAH 550 SOUTH SECOND AVENUE	ARCADIA	**CA**	91006	(818) 445-0810
MIDRASHA, EAST BAY COMMUNITY HIGH SCHOOL 2301 VINE STREET	BERKELEY	**CA**	94708	(415) 848-3988
TEMPLE EMANUEL 8844 BURTON WAY	BEVERLY HILLS	**CA**	90211	(213) 274-6388
TEMPLE BETH EMET 600 NORTH BUENA VISTA	BURBANK	**CA**	91505	(818) 843-9444
CONGREGATION BETH KODESH 7401 SHOUP AVENUE	CANOGA PARK	**CA**	91307	(818) 346-0811
TEMPLE SOLAEL 6600 VALLEY CIRCLE BOULEVARD	CANOGA PARK	**CA**	91340	(818) 348-3885
TEMPLE NER TAMID, BRANCH SCHOOL				
10824 TOPANGA CANYON BOULEVARD	CHATSWORTH	**CA**	91311	(818) 341-1270
TEMPLE AKIBA 5249 SEPULVEDA BOULEVARD	CULVER CITY	**CA**	90230	(213) 398-5783
TEMPLE NER TAMID 10629 LAKEWOOD BOULEVARD	DOWNEY	**CA**	90241	(213) 861-9276
MAAREV TEMPLE 5180 YARMOUTH AVENUE	ENCINO	**CA**	91316	(818) 345-7833
VALLEY BETH SHALOM 15739 VENTURA BOULEVARD	ENCINO	**CA**	91436	(818) 788-6000
TEMPLE SINAI OF GLENDALE 1212 NORTH PACIFIC AVENUE	GLENDALE	**CA**	91202	(818) 246-8101
TEMPLE BETH OHR 15721 EAST ROSECRANS AVENUE	LA MIRADA	**CA**	90638	(714) 521-6765
BETH KNESSEL BAMIDBAR 1611 EAST AVENUE J, PO BOX 1008	LANCASTER	**CA**	93534	(805) 942-4415
CHABAD OF SOUTH BAY 24412 NARBONNE AVENUE	LOMITA	**CA**	90717	(213) 326-8234
ADAT SHALOM 3030 WESTWOOD BOULEVARD	LOS ANGELES	**CA**	90034	(213) 475-4985
B'NAI DAVID-JUDEA CONGREGATION				
8906 WEST PICO BOULEVARD	LOS ANGELES	**CA**	90035	(213) 272-7223
B'NAI TIKVAH CONGREGATION 5820 MANCHESTER AVENUE	LOS ANGELES	**CA**	90045	(213) 645-6262
CHABAD COMMUNITY TALMUD TORAH 7215 WARING AVENUE	LOS ANGELES	**CA**	90048	(213) 937-3763
CONGREGATION MOGEN DAVID 9717 WEST PICO BOULEVARD	LOS ANGELES	**CA**	90035	(213) 879-3861
ETZ JACOB CONGREGATION 7659 BEVERLY BOULEVARD	LOS ANGELES	**CA**	90036	(213) 938-2619
HOLLYWOOD TEMPLE BETH EL				
1317 NORTH CRESCENT HEIGHTS BOULEVARD	LOS ANGELES	**CA**	90046	(213) 656-3150
INSTITUTE OF JEWISH EDUCATION 3889 WEST THIRD STREET	LOS ANGELES	**CA**	90048	(213) 655-1341
JEWISH ACADEMY OF LOS ANGELES - LA HEBREW HIGH SCHOOL				
1317 NORTH CRESCENT HEIGHTS BOULEVARD	LOS ANGELES	**CA**	90046	(213) 656-3060
LEO BAECK TEMPLE 1300 NORTH SEPULVEDA BOULEVARD	LOS ANGELES	**CA**	90049	(213) 879-0368
SEPHARDIC TALMUD TORAH OF LOS ANGELES				
420 NORTH FAIRFAX AVENUE	LOS ANGELES	**CA**	90036	
SEPHARDIC TEMPLE TIFERETH ISRAEL				
10500 WILSHIRE BOULEVARD	LOS ANGELES	**CA**	90024	(213) 475-7311
SHIR SHALOM PO BOX 67487	LOS ANGELES	**CA**	90067	(213) 471-1643
SINAI TEMPLE 10400 WILSHIRE BOULEVARD	LOS ANGELES	**CA**	90024	(213) 474-1518
STEPHEN S. WISE TEMPLE 15500 STEPHEN S. WISE DRIVE	LOS ANGELES	**CA**	90077	(213) 788-7554
TEMPLE BETH AM 1039 SOUTH LA CIENEGA BOULEVARD	LOS ANGELES	**CA**	90035	(213) 655-6401
TEMPLE BETH TORAH 11827 VENICE BOULEVARD	LOS ANGELES	**CA**	90066	(213) 398-4536
TEMPLE ISAIAH 10345 WEST PICO BOULEVARD	LOS ANGELES	**CA**	90064	(213) 879-2191
TEMPLE ISRAEL OF HOLLYWOOD 7300 HOLLYWOOD BOULEVARD	LOS ANGELES	**CA**	90046	(213) 876-8330
UNIVERSITY SYNAGOGUE 11960 SUNSET BOULEVARD	LOS ANGELES	**CA**	90049	(213) 272-3650
WILSHIRE BOULEVARD TEMPLE 3663 WILSHIRE BOULEVARD	LOS ANGELES	**CA**	90010	(213) 388-2401
MALIBU JEWISH CENTER 28925 PACIFIC COAST HIGHWAY #6	MALIBU	**CA**	90265	(213) 457-2979
CONGREGATION TIFERETH JACOB 1613 SIXTH STREET	MANHATTAN BEACH	**CA**	90266	(213) 644-6900
TEMPLE B'NAI EMET 482 NORTH GARFIELD AVENUE	MONTEBELLO	**CA**	90640	(213) 723-2978
CONGREGATION BETH SHALOM PO BOX 39	NEWHALL	**CA**	91321	(805) 259-4975
ADAT ARI EL 5440 LAUREL CANYON BOULEVARD	NORTH HOLLYWOOD	**CA**	91607	(818) 877-4881
SHAAREY ZEDEK CONGREGATION				
12800 CHANDLER BOULEVARD	NORTH HOLLYWOOD	**CA**	91607	(818) 763-0560
SOUTH BAY HEBREW HIGH SCHOOL, UNION HEBREW HIGH SCHOOL				
13107 VENTURA BOULEVARD	NORTH HOLLYWOOD	**CA**	91604	(818) 872-3550
TEMPLE BETH HILLEL 12326 RIVERSIDE DRIVE	NORTH HOLLYWOOD	**CA**	91607	(818) 877-3431
TEMPLE AHAVAT SHALOM 18200 RINALDI PLACE	NORTHRIDGE	**CA**	91324	(818) 360-6349
TEMPLE RAMAT ZION 17655 DEVONSHIRE STREET	NORTHRIDGE	**CA**	91324	(818) 360-1881
TEMPLE SHOLOM 963 EAST SIXTH STREET	ONTARIO	**CA**	91764	(714) 983-9661
KEHILLATH ISRAEL 16019 SUNSET BOULEVARD	PACIFIC PALISADES	**CA**	90272	(213) 459-2328
PALO ALTO SCHOOL FOR JEWISH EDUCATION 830 E. MEADOW	PALO ALTO	**CA**	94303	(415) 494-2511
PASADENA JEWISH TEMPLE-CENTER 1434 NORTH ALTADENA DRIVE	PASADENA	**CA**	91107	(818) 798-1164
TEMPLE BETH ISRAEL 333 NORTH TOWNE AVENUE	POMONA	**CA**	91767	(714) 521-6765
CONGREGATION NER TAMID OF SOUTH BAY				
5721 CRESTRIDGE ROAD	RANCHO PALOS VERDES	**CA**	90274	(213) 377-6986
TEMPLE MENORAH 1101 CAMINO REAL	REDONDO BEACH	**CA**	90277	(213) 316-8444
TEMPLE BETH AMI 18449 KITTRIDGE STREET	RESEDA	**CA**	91335	(818) 343-4624
TEMPLE BETH EL 1435 WEST SEVENTH STREET	SAN PEDRO	**CA**	90732	(213) 833-2467
BETH SHOLOM TEMPLE 1827 CALIFORNIA AVENUE	SANTA MONICA	**CA**	90403	(213) 451-1361
KEHILLAT MA'ARAV 2210 WILSHIRE BOULEVARD, PO BOX 287	SANTA MONICA	**CA**	90403	(213) 393-4507
TEMPLE BETH TORAH 8756 WOODLEY AVENUE	SEPULVEDA	**CA**	91343	(213) 893-3756
TEMPLE B'NAI HAYIM 4302 VAN NUYS BOULEVARD	SHERMAN OAKS	**CA**	91403	(818) 788-4664
TEMPLE NER TAMID 3050 LOS ANGELES AVENUE	SIMI VALLEY	**CA**	93065	(805) 522-4747
VALLEY BETH ISRAEL 12060 ROSCOE BOULEVARD	SUN VALLEY	**CA**	91352	(818) 782-2281
TEMPLE JUDEA 5429 LINDLEY AVENUE	TARZANA	**CA**	91356	(213) 342-3177
TEMPLE BETH DAVID 9677 EAST LONGDEN AVENUE	TEMPLE CITY	**CA**	91780	(818) 287-9994
ADAT ELOHIM 2420 EAST HILLCREST DRIVE	THOUSAND OAKS	**CA**	91360	(805) 497-7101
TEMPLE ETZ CHAIM 1080 JANSS ROAD	THOUSAND OAKS	**CA**	91360	(805) 497-6891
TEMPLE NER TAMID 15339 SATICOY STREET	VAN NUYS	**CA**	91406	(818) 782-9010
CONGREGATION MISHKON TEPHILO 206 MAIN STREET	VENICE	**CA**	90291	(213) 399-1432
TEMPLE BETH AMI 3508 EAST TEMPLE WAY	WEST COVINA	**CA**	91791	(818) 331-0515
TEMPLE SHALOM 1921 WEST MERCED AVENUE	WEST COVINA	**CA**	91790	(818) 337-6500
BETH SHALOM 14564 EAST HAWES STREET	WHITTIER	**CA**	90604	(213) 941-8744
TEMPLE ALIYAH 6025 VALLEY CIRCLE BOULEVARD	WOODLAND HILLS	**CA**	91367	(818) 346-3545
TEMPLE EMET 20400 VENTURA BOULEVARD	WOODLAND HILLS	**CA**	91364	(818) 348-0670
BMH-BJ HEBREW SCHOOL 560 SOUTH MONACO PARKWAY	DENVER	**CO**	80220	(303) 388-4203
HEBREW COMMUNITY SCHOOL OF SAVANNAH, THE				
5111 ABECORN STREET	SAVANNAH	**GA**	31405	(912) 355-8111
COMMISSION OF JEWISH EDUCATION-COMMUNAL HEBREW SCHOOL				
1631 CALHOUN STREET	NEW ORLEANS	**LA**	70118	(504) 861-7508
TIFERETH ISRAEL RELIGIOUS SCHOOL, TEMPLE R 3539 SALEM STREET	MALDEN	**MA**	02148	(617) 322-2794

MIDRASHA COMMUNITY HEBREW HIGH SCHOOL OF GREATER WASHINGTON				
9325 BROOKVILLE ROAD	SILVER SPRING	**MD**	20910	(301) 589-3180
UNITED HEBREW SCHOOLS 21550 W. TWELVE MILE ROAD	SOUTHFIELD	**MI**	48076	(313) 354-1050
TALMUD TORAH LOF MINNEAPOLIS, THE 8200 W. 33RD STREET	MINNEAPOLIS	**MN**	55426	(612) 935-0316
TALMUD TORAH OF ST. PAUL, THE 636 S. MISSISSIPPI RIVER BLVD	ST PAUL	**MN**	55116	(612) 698-8807
COMMUNITY JEWISH SCHOOL PO BOX 961	NEW BRUNSWICK	**NJ**	08903	(201) 545-6484
BETH SHALOM CENTER 79 COUNTY LINE ROAD	AMITYVILLE	**NY**	11701	(516) 264-2891
JEWISH CENTER OF ATLANTIC BEACH				
PARK STREET & NASSAU AVENUE	ATLANTIC BEACH	**NY**	11509	(516) 371-0972
BETH SHALOM, CONGREGATION 441 DEER PARK AVENUE	BABYLON	**NY**	11702	(516) 587-5650
JEWISH CENTER OF BALDWIN 885 EAST SEAMAN AVENUE	BALDWIN	**NY**	11510	(516) 223-5599
SHOLOM ALEICHEM FOLKSHULE #32				
C/O SOUTH SHORE YMHA-806 MERRICK ROAD	BALDWIN	**NY**	11510	(516) 678-5092
SOUTH BALDWIN JEWISH CENTER 2959 GRAND AVENUE	BALDWIN	**NY**	11510	(516) 223-8688
BAY SHORE JEWISH CENTER-MARY SELEY MEMORIAL SCHOOL				
26 NORTH CLINTON AVENUE	BAY SHORE	**NY**	11706	(516) 665-1140
SINAI REFORM TEMPLE/HARRIET S. LEVIN RELIGIOUS SCHOOL				
39 BRENTWOOD ROAD	BAY SHORE	**NY**	11706	(516) 665-5755
BAY TERRACE JEWISH CENTER				
209TH STREET & WILLETS POINT BOULEVARD	BAYSIDE	**NY**	11360	(718) 428-6363
BAYSIDE HILLS JEWISH CENTER 212-22 48TH AVENUE	BAYSIDE	**NY**	11364	(718) 229-2372
BAYSIDE JEWISH CENTER 203-05 32ND AVENUE	BAYSIDE	**NY**	11361	(718) 352-7900
OAKLAND JEWISH CENTER 61-35 220TH STREET	BAYSIDE	**NY**	11364	(718) 225-7800
SHAARAY TEFILA OF NORTH WESTCHESTER ROUTE 172	BEDFORD	**NY**	10549	(914) 666-3133
BETH EL OF ROCKAWAY PARK, TEMPLE 445 B. 135TH STREET	BELLE HARBOR	**NY**	11694	(718) 634-8110
OHAV ZEDEK, CONGREGATION				
134-01 ROCKAWAY BEACH BOULEVARD	BELLE HARBOR	**NY**	11694	(718) 474-3300
SHAAREI SHALOM, TEMPLE 2579 MERRICK ROAD	BELLMORE	**NY**	11710	(516) 781-5599
BETHPAGE JEWISH COMMUNITY CENTER 600 BROADWAY	BETHPAGE	**NY**	11714	(516) 938-7909
SONS OF ISRAEL, CONGREGATION 1666 PLEASANTVILLE ROAD	BRIARCLIFF	**NY**	10510	(914) 762-2700
BRONX HOUSE NURSERY 2222 WALLACE AVENUE	BRONX	**NY**	10467	(212) 792-1800
CO-OP CITY JEWISH CENTER 900 CO-OP CITY BOULEVARD	BRONX	**NY**	10475	(212) 671-4579
COMMUNITY CENTER OF ISRAEL 2440 ESPLANADE AVENUE	BRONX	**NY**	10469	(212) 882-2400
CONSERVATIVE SYNAGOGUE ADATH ISRAEL OF RIVERDALE				
250TH STREET-HENRY HUDSON PARKWAY	BRONX	**NY**	10471	(212) 543-8400
JACOB H. SCHIFF CENTER-EVA BECKER HEBREW SCHOOL				
2510 VALENTINE AVENUE	BRONX	**NY**	10458	(212) 295-2510
KINGSBRIDGE CENTER OF ISRAEL 3115 CORLEAR AVENUE	BRONX	**NY**	10463	(212) 548-1678
KINGSBRIDGE HEIGHTS JEWISH CENTER 124 EAMES PLACE	BRONX	**NY**	10468	(212) 549-4120
MOSHOLU MONTEFIORE NURSERY 3450 DEKALB AVENUE	BRONX	**NY**	10467	(212) 882-4000
NATHAN STRAUSS JEWISH CENTER 3512 DEKALB AVENUE	BRONX	**NY**	10467	(212) 547-1617
PELHAM PARKWAY JEWISH CENTER 900 PELHAM PARKWAY SOUTH	BRONX	**NY**	10462	(212) 792-6458
RIVERDALE JEWISH CENTER 3700 INDEPENDENCE AVENUE	BRONX	**NY**	10463	(212) 548-2922
RIVERDALE TEMPLE 4545 INDEPENDENCE AVENUE	BRONX	**NY**	10471	(212) 548-3800
TEMPLE BETH EL OF CO-OP CITY 920-1 BAYCHESTER AVENUE	BRONX	**NY**	10475	(212) 671-9719
TRADITIONAL SYNAGOGUE OF CO-OP CITY 115 EINSTEIN LOOP NORTH	BRONX	**NY**	10475	(212) 379-6920
VAN CORTLANDT JEWISH CENTER 3880 SEDGWICK AVENUE	BRONX	**NY**	10463	(212) 844-6105
WORKMEN'S CIRCLE AMALGAMATED NURSERY SCHOOL				
3980 ORLOFF AVENUE	BRONX	**NY**	10463	(212) 543-8688
WORKMEN'S CIRCLE SCHOOL #3 3990 HILLMAN AVENUE	BRONX	**NY**	10463	(212) 548-2217
YM-YWHA RIVERDALE NURSERY 450 WEST 250 STREET	BRONX	**NY**	10471	(212) 548-8200
YOUNG ISRAEL OF PARKCHESTER 1375 VIRGINIA AVENUE	BRONX	**NY**	10462	(212) 822-9576
YOUNG ISRAEL OF PELHAM PARKWAY 2126 BARNES AVENUE	BRONX	**NY**	10462	(212) 824-0630
AHAVATH SHOLOM, TEMPLE 1609 AVENUE R	BROOKLYN	**NY**	11229	(718) 375-4500
ATERES YISROEL TALMUD TORAH 8101 AVENUE K	BROOKLYN	**NY**	11229	(718) 763-6777
AVENUE Z JEWISH CENTER 875 AVENUE Z	BROOKLYN	**NY**	11235	(718) 646-9874
B'NAI ISRAEL CONGREGATION 1540 VAN SICLEN AVENUE	BROOKLYN	**NY**	11239	(718) 642-8804
B'NAI ISRAEL OF MIDWOOD-BERNICE FISHKIND HEBREW SCHOOL				
1800 UTICA AVENUE	BROOKLYN	**NY**	11234	(718) 763-5500
BAY RIDGE JEWISH CENTER-SHEARITH ISRAEL 405 81ST STREET	BROOKLYN	**NY**	11209	(718) 745-4366
BEACH HAVEN JEWISH CENTER 723 AVENUE Z	BROOKLYN	**NY**	11223	(718) 375-5200
BETH ABRAHAM, TEMPLE 301 SEA BREEZE AVENUE	BROOKLYN	**NY**	11224	(718) 266-6544
BETH EL OF MANHATTAN BEACH 111 WEST END AVENUE	BROOKLYN	**NY**	11235	(718) 891-3500
BETH ELOHIM, CONGREGATION 8 AVENUE & GARFIELD PLACE	BROOKLYN	**NY**	11215	(718) 768-3814
BETH EMETH, TEMPLE 83 MARLBORO ROAD	BROOKLYN	**NY**	11226	(718) 282-1596
BETH OHR COMMUNITY TEMPLE 1010 OCEAN AVENUE	BROOKLYN	**NY**	11226	(718) 284-5760
BETH SHALOM HEBREW SCHOOL 2710 AVENUE X	BROOKLYN	**NY**	11235	(718) 891-4500
BETH SHALOM PEOPLE'S TEMPLE BAY PARKWAY & BENSON AVENUE	BROOKLYN	**NY**	11214	(718) 372-0933
BETH TIKVA TALMUD TORAH 8800 SEAVIEW AVENUE	BROOKLYN	**NY**	11236	(718) 763-5577
BETH TORAH OF SHEEPSHEAD BAY 3574 NOSTRAND AVENUE	BROOKLYN	**NY**	11229	(718) 646-5467
BRIGHTON BEACH JEWISH CENTER 2915 OCEAN PARKWAY	BROOKLYN	**NY**	11235	(718) 769-7400
BROOKLYN HEIGHTS SYNAGOGUE 117 REMSEN STREET	BROOKLYN	**NY**	11201	(718) 522-2070
CANARSIE JEWISH CENTER 965 EAST 107TH STREET	BROOKLYN	**NY**	11236	(718) 272-2848
CENTRAL TALMUD TORAH 1305 CONEY ISLAND AVENUE	BROOKLYN	**NY**	11230	(718) 377-4400
COMMUNITY TALMUD TORAH 2115 BENSON AVENUE	BROOKLYN	**NY**	11214	(718) 372-4830
EAST MIDWOOD JEWISH CENTER 1625 OCEAN AVENUE	BROOKLYN	**NY**	11230	(718) 338-3800
EMANU-EL OF CANARSIE, TEMPLE 1880 ROCKAWAY PARKWAY	BROOKLYN	**NY**	11236	(718) 251-0450
FLATBUSH JEWISH CENTER - HILLEL SCHOOL 500 CHURCH AVENUE	BROOKLYN	**NY**	11218	(718) 871-5200
FLATBUSH PARK JEWISH CENTER 6363 AVENUE U	BROOKLYN	**NY**	11234	(718) 444-6868
HEBREW EDUCATIONAL SOCIETY NURSERY 9502 SEAVIEW AVENUE	BROOKLYN	**NY**	11236	(718) 241-3000
HILLEL OF FLATLANDS, TEMPLE 2164 RALPH AVENUE	BROOKLYN	**NY**	11234	(718) 763-2400
JEWISH COMMUNITY HOUSE OF BENSONHURST 7802 BAY PARKWAY	BROOKLYN	**NY**	11214	(718) 331-6800
KINGS HIGHWAY JEWISH CENTER 1202 AVENUE P	BROOKLYN	**NY**	11229	(718) 645-9000
MADISON JEWISH CENTER 2989 NOSTRAND AVENUE	BROOKLYN	**NY**	11234	(718) 339-7755
MANHATTAN BEACH JEWISH CENTER 60 WEST END AVENUE	BROOKLYN	**NY**	11235	(718) 891-8700
MARINE PARK JEWISH CENTER 3311 AVENUE S	BROOKLYN	**NY**	11234	(718) 376-5200
OCEAN AVENUE JEWISH CENTER 2600 OCEAN AVENUE	BROOKLYN	**NY**	11229	(718) 743-5534
OCEAN PARKWAY JEWISH CENTER 550 OCEAN PARKWAY	BROOKLYN	**NY**	11218	(718) 436-4900
OCEANVIEW JEWISH CENTER 3100 BRIGHTON 4 STREET	BROOKLYN	**NY**	11235	(718) 648-6662
OHEV SHOLOM TALMUD TORAH 1387 EAST 96TH STREET	BROOKLYN	**NY**	11236	(718) 251-1430
PROGRESSIVE SYNAGOGUE 1395 OCEAN AVENUE	BROOKLYN	**NY**	11230	(718) 377-1818

REMSEN HEIGHTS JEWISH CENTER 8700 AVENUE K	BROOKLYN	**NY**	11236	(718) 763-2244
SEAVIEW JEWISH CENTER 1440 EAST 99TH STREET	BROOKLYN	**NY**	11236	(718) 251-1900
SEPHARDIC JEWISH CENTER OF CANARSIE 9320 FLATLANDS AVENUE	BROOKLYN	**NY**	11236	(718) 257-0400
SHAARE EMETH, TEMPLE 6012 FARRAGUT ROAD	BROOKLYN	**NY**	11236	(718) 444-3222
SHELLBANK JEWISH CENTER 2121 BRAGG STREET	BROOKLYN	**NY**	11229	(718) 891-8666
SHOLOM OF FLATBUSH, TEMPLE 2075 EAST 68TH STREET	BROOKLYN	**NY**	11234	(718) 251-0370
SHORE PARK JEWISH CENTER 2959 AVENUE Y	BROOKLYN	**NY**	11235	(718) 648-2900
SHORE PARKWAY JEWISH CENTER 8885 26TH AVENUE	BROOKLYN	**NY**	11214	(718) 449-6530
TALMUD TORAH AHAVATH ACHIM, CONGREGATION O				
1750 E. 4TH STREET	BROOKLYN	**NY**	11223	(718) 375-3895
UNION TEMPLE 17 EASTERN PARKWAY	BROOKLYN	**NY**	11238	(718) 638-7600
YM-YWHA-SHOREFRONT 3300 CONEY ISLAND AVENUE	BROOKLYN	**NY**	11235	(718) 646-1444
YM-YWHA NURSERY OF KINGS BAY 3643 NOSTRAND AVENUE	BROOKLYN	**NY**	11229	(718) 648-7703
YM-YWHA OF CONEY ISLAND 3312-30 SURF AVENUE	BROOKLYN	**NY**	11224	(718) 449-1000
YESHIVA INSTITUTE 6414 BAY PARKWAY	BROOKLYN	**NY**	11204	(718) 259-1432
YOUNG ISRAEL OF BEDFORD BAY 21-14 BROWN STREET	BROOKLYN	**NY**	11229	(718) 332-4120
YOUNG ISRAEL OF SHEEPSHEAD BAY 2546 EAST 7TH STREET	BROOKLYN	**NY**	11225	(718) 449-1397
BETH EL, TEMPLE BROADWAY & LOCUST AVENUE	CEDARHURST	**NY**	11516	(516) 569-2700
SEPHARDIC TEMPLE, THE BRANCH BOULEVARD	CEDARHURST	**NY**	11516	(516) 295-4644
MORICHES, JEWISH CENTER OF THE PO BOX 127	CENTER MORICHES	**NY**	11934	(516) 878-0388
BETH EL, TEMPLE 220 SOUTH BEDFORD ROAD	CHAPPAQUA	**NY**	10514	(914) 238-3928
KEHILAT SHALOM RELIGIOUS SCHOOL				
58 GOOSE HILL ROAD	COLD SPRING HARBOR	**NY**	11724	(516) 595-3347
BETH DAVID, TEMPLE 100 HAUPPAUGE ROAD	COMMACK	**NY**	11725	(516) 499-0915
COMMACK JEWISH CENTER 83 SHIRLEY COURT	COMMACK	**NY**	11725	(516) 543-3311
ISRAEL, TEMPLE GLENGARY ROAD	CROTON-ON-HUDSON	**NY**	10520	(914) 271-8006
SUFFOLK JEWISH CENTER-SAMUEL BERKOWITZ RELIGIOUS SCHOOL				
330 CENTRAL AVENUE	DEER PARK	**NY**	11729	(516) 667-7695
DIX HILLS JEWISH CENTER DEFOREST ROAD & VANDERBILT PARKWAY	DIX HILLS	**NY**	11746	(516) 499-6644
SHOLOM ALEICHEM SCHOOL #41				
C/O MS. ROSEMAN-83 MCCULLOCH DRIVE	DIX HILLS	**NY**	11746	(516) 864-2387
BETH TORAH, TEMPLE 35 BAGATELLE ROAD	DIX HILLS SOUTH	**NY**	11746	(516) 271-1657
GREENBURGH HEBREW CENTER 515 NORTH BROADWAY	DOBBS FERRY	**NY**	10522	(914) 693-4260
MARATHON JEWISH COMMUNITY CENTER 245-37 60TH STREET	DOUGLASTON	**NY**	11362	(718) 428-1580
HAMPTONS, JEWISH CENTER OF THE 44 WOODS LANE	EAST HAMPTON	**NY**	11937	(516) 324-9858
EAST MEADOW JEWISH CENTER 1400 PROSPECT AVENUE	EAST MEADOW	**NY**	11554	(516) 483-4205
EMANUEL, TEMPLE 123 MERRICK AVENUE	EAST MEADOW	**NY**	11554	(516) 794-8937
SUBURBAN PARK JEWISH CENTER 400 OLD WESTBURY ROAD	EAST MEADOW	**NY**	11554	(516) 796-2626
WORKMEN'S CIRCLE SCHOOL-I.L. PERETZ SCHOOL OF NASSAU				
574 NEWBRIDGE AVENUE	EAST MEADOW	**NY**	11554	(516) 542-9640
EAST NORTHPORT JEWISH CENTER 328 ELWOOD ROAD	EAST NORTHPORT	**NY**	11731	(516) 368-6474
HEWLETT-EAST ROCKAWAY JEWISH CENTER 295 MAIN STREET	EAST ROCKAWAY	**NY**	11518	(516) 599-0424
EMANU-EL, TEMPLE 91-15 CORONA AVENUE	ELMHURST	**NY**	11373	(718) 592-4343
B'NAI ISRAEL, TEMPLE ELMONT ROAD & BAYLIS AVENUE	ELMONT	**NY**	11003	(516) 354-1156
ELMONT JEWISH CENTER 500 ELMONT ROAD	ELMONT	**NY**	11003	(516) 437-3937
BAYSWATER JEWISH CENTER 2355 HEALY AVENUE	FAR ROCKAWAY	**NY**	11691	(718) 471-7771
YM-YWHA, GUSTAV HARTMAN 710 HARTMAN LANE	FAR ROCKAWAY	**NY**	11691	(718) 471-0200
FARMINGDALE JEWISH CENTER 425 FULTON STREET	FARMINGDALE	**NY**	11735	(516) 694-2343
BELLEROSE JEWISH CENTER 254-04 UNION TPKE	FLORAL PARK	**NY**	11004	(718) 343-9001
SHOLOM, TEMPLE 263-10 UNION TURNPIKE	FLORAL PARK	**NY**	11004	(718) 343-8660
BAYSIDE OAKS, JEWISH CENTER OF 50-35 CLOVERDALE BOULEVARD	FLUSHING	**NY**	11364	(718) 631-0100
BETH OR OF THE DEAF, TEMPLE				
C/O TEMPLE BETH SHOLOM, 171 NORTHERN BOULEVARD	FLUSHING	**NY**	11358	(718) 463-4143
BETH SHOLOM, TEMPLE 171-39 NORTHERN BOULEVARD	FLUSHING	**NY**	11358	(718) 463-4143
ELECTCHESTER JEWISH CTR.-HENRY F. FISCHBAUM RELIGIOUS SCHOOL				
65-15 164TH STREET	FLUSHING	**NY**	11365	(718) 886-4454
FLUSHING JEWISH CENTER 43-00 171ST STREET	FLUSHING	**NY**	11358	(718) 358-7071
FREE SYNAGOGUE OF FLUSHING 41-60 KISSENA BOULEVARD	FLUSHING	**NY**	11355	(718) 961-0030
FRESH MEADOWS - UTOPIA JEWISH CENTER 193-10 PECK AVENUE	FLUSHING	**NY**	11365	(718) 357-5100
GARDEN JEWISH CENTER 24-20 PARSONS BOULEVARD	FLUSHING	**NY**	11357	(718) 445-1317
GATES OF PRAYER, TEMPLE 38-20 PARSONS BOULEVARD	FLUSHING	**NY**	11354	(718) 359-7641
HILLCREST JEWISH CENTER 183-02 UNION TPKE	FLUSHING	**NY**	11366	(718) 380-4145
HOLLIS HILLS JEWISH CENTER 210-10 UNION TPKE	FLUSHING	**NY**	11364	(718) 776-3500
ISRAEL CENTER OF HILLCREST MANOR 167-11 73RD AVENUE	FLUSHING	**NY**	11366	(718) 591-5353
JEWISH CENTER OF TORATH EMETH 78-15 PARSONS BOULEVARD	FLUSHING	**NY**	11366	(718) 591-4240
KEW GARDENS HILLS, JEWISH CENTER OF 71-25 MAIN STREET	FLUSHING	**NY**	11367	(718) 263-6500
WORKMEN'S CIRCLE SCHOOL-FLUSHING 45-25 KISSENA BOULEVARD	FLUSHING	**NY**	11355	()-
YM-YWHA OF GREATER FLUSHING 45-35 KISSENA BOULEVARD	FLUSHING	**NY**	11355	(718) 461-3030
FOREST HILLS JEWISH CENTER 106-06 QUEENS BOULEVARD	FOREST HILLS	**NY**	11375	(718) 263-7000
ISAIAH, TEMPLE 75-24 GRAND CENTRAL PARKWAY	FOREST HILLS	**NY**	11375	(718) 544-2800
QUEENS JEWISH CENTER 66-05 108 STREET	FOREST HILLS	**NY**	11375	(718) 459-8432
SINAI, TEMPLE-HORTENSE LIEBMAN SCHOOL 71-11 112 STREET	FOREST HILLS	**NY**	11375	(718) 261-2900
YM-YWHA OF CENTRAL QUEENS 108-05 68 ROAD	FOREST HILLS	**NY**	11375	(718) 268-5011
YOUNG ISRAEL OF FOREST HILLS				
7100 YELLOWSTONE BOULEVARD	FOREST HILLS	**NY**	11375	(718) 268-7100
B'NAI ISRAEL, CONGREGATION 91 NORTH BAYVIEW AVENUE	FREEPORT	**NY**	11520	(516) 623-4200
UNION REFORM TEMPLE 475 NORTH BROOKSIDE AVENUE	FREEPORT	**NY**	11520	(516) 623-1810
GARDEN CITY JEWISH CENTER 168 NASSAU BOULEVARD	GARDEN CITY	**NY**	11530	(516) 248-9180
NORTH COUNTY REFORM TEMPLE CRESCENT BEACH ROAD	GLEN COVE	**NY**	11542	(516) 671-4760
TIFERETH ISRAEL, CONGREGATION HILL STREET & LANDING	GLEN COVE	**NY**	11542	(516) 676-5080
BETH EL OF GREAT NECK, TEMPLE 5 OLD MILL ROAD	GREAT NECK	**NY**	11023	(516) 487-0900
BETH HAGAN NURSERY				
C/O TEMPLE ISRAEL, TEMPLE COURT & OLD MILL ROAD	GREAT NECK	**NY**	11023	(516) 482-7821
EMANUEL, TEMPLE 150 HICKS LANE	GREAT NECK	**NY**	11024	(516) 482-5701
GREAT NECK SYNAGOGUE 26 OLD MILL ROAD	GREAT NECK	**NY**	11023	(516) 487-6100
HEBREW HIGH SCHOOL OF TEMPLE ISRAEL 108 OLD MILL ROAD	GREAT NECK	**NY**	11023	(516) 482-4399
ISAIAH, TEMPLE PO BOX 229-OLD VILLAGE STATION	GREAT NECK	**NY**	11023	(516) 487-8709
ISRAEL, TEMPLE 108 OLD MILL ROAD	GREAT NECK	**NY**	11023	(516) 482-7800
JEWISH COMMUNITY CENTER 349 UNION AVENUE	HARRISON	**NY**	10528	(914) 835-2860
BETH SHALOM, TEMPLE 740 NORTH BROADWAY	HASTINGS-ON-HUDSON	**NY**	10706	(914) 478-3833
BETH CHAI, TEMPLE PO BOX 74	HAUPPAUGE	**NY**	11787	(516) 724-5807

BETH EMETH, TEMPLE 36 FRANKLIN AVENUE	HEWLETT	**NY**	11557	(516) 374-9220
HICKSVILLE JEWISH CENTER JERUSALEM AVENUE & MAGLIE DRIVE	HICKSVILLE	**NY**	11801	(516) 374-9220
SHARREI ZEDEK, CONGREGATION				
NEW SOUTH & OLD COUNTRY ROADS	HICKSVILLE	**NY**	11801	(516) 938-0420
ISRAEL OF JAMAICA, TEMPLE 188-15 MCLAUGHLIN AVENUE	HOLLISWOOD	**NY**	11423	(718) 776-4400
HOWARD BEACH JEWISH CENTER 162-05 90TH STREET	HOWARD BEACH	**NY**	11414	(718) 845-9444
ROCKWOOD PARK JEWISH CENTER 156-45 84 STREET	HOWARD BEACH	**NY**	11414	(718) 641-5822
WORKMEN'S CIRCLE SCHOOL-SUFFOLK COUNTY				
C/O KAPLAN-19 LARKIN STREET	HUNGTINGTON STATION	**NY**	11746	(516) 421-3049
BETH EL, TEMPLE 660 PARK AVENUE	HUNTINGTON	**NY**	11743	(516) 421-5836
HUNTINGTON JEWISH CENTER 510 PARK AVENUE	HUNTINGTON	**NY**	11743	(516) 427-1089
SOUTH HUNTINGTON JEWISH CENTER				
2600 NEW YORK AVENUE	HUNTINGTON STATION	**NY**	11746	(516) 421-3244
ISLAND PARK, JEWISH CENTER OF 191 LONG BEACH ROAD	ISLAND PARK	**NY**	11558	(516) 432-6706
JACKSON HEIGHTS, JEWISH CENTER OF 34-25 82ND STREET	JACKSON HEIGHTS	**NY**	11372	(718) 429-1150
BRIARWOOD JEWISH CENTER 139-06 86TH AVENUE	JAMAICA	**NY**	11435	(718) 657-5151
HOLLISWOOD JEWISH CENTER 86-25 FRANCIS LEWIS BOULEVARD	JAMAICA	**NY**	11427	(718) 776-8500
ROCHDALE VILLAGE JEWISH CENTER 167-10 137 AVENUE	JAMAICA	**NY**	11434	(718) 528-0200
CONSERVATIVE SYNAGOGUE OF JAMAICA				
182-69 WEXFORD TERRACE	JAMAICA ESTATES	**NY**	11432	(718) 526-6275
JERICHO JEWISH CENTER NORTH BROADWAY	JERICHO	**NY**	11753	(516) 938-2540
OR ELOHIM, TEMPLE-IRVING WEINER RELIGIOUS SCHOOL				
18 TOBIE LANE	JERICHO	**NY**	11753	(516) 433-9888
KEW GARDENS ANSHE SHOLOM JEWISH CENTER				
82-52 ABINGDON ROAD, BOX 21	KEW GARDENS	**NY**	11415	(718) 441-2470
KEW GARDENS SYNAGOGUE ADATH JESHURUN				
82-17 LEFFERTS BOULEVARD	KEW GARDENS	**NY**	11415	(718) 849-7988
COMMUNITY TALMUD TORAH AT YOUNG ISRAEL OF KEW GARDENS HILLS				
151-01 70TH ROAD	KEW GARDENS	**NY**	11367	(718) 261-9723
QUEENSBORO HILLS JEWISH CENTER				
156-03 HORACE HARDING BOULEVARD	KEW GARDENS	**NY**	11367	(718) 445-4141
ETZ CHAIM, CONGREGATION 44 MEADOW ROAD	KINGS PARK	**NY**	11754	(516) 269-9666
KINGS PARK JEWISH CENTER ROUTE 25-A	KINGS PARK	**NY**	11754	(516) 269-1133
LAKE GROVE JEWISH CENTER 821 HAWKINS AVENUE	LAKE GROVE	**NY**	11755	(516) 585-0521
RONKONKOMA JEWISH CENTER 821 HAWKINS AVENUE, PO BOX 20	LAKE GROVE	**NY**	11755	(516) 585-0521
LAKE SUCCESS JEWISH CENTER 354 LAKEVILLE ROAD	LAKE SUCCESS	**NY**	11020	(516) 466-0569
BETH EMETH, CONGREGATION 2111 BOSTON POST ROAD	LARCHMONT	**NY**	10543	(914) 834-2543
LARCHMONT TEMPLE 75 LARCHMONT AVENUE	LARCHMONT	**NY**	10538	(914) 834-6121
WORKMEN'S CIRCLE SCHOOL-WESTCHESTER				
C/O MIRIAM CREEMER-1 CREST AVENUE	LARCHMONT	**NY**	10538	(914) 834-6041
BETH SHOLOM CONGREGATION 390 BROADWAY	LAWRENCE	**NY**	11559	(516) 569-3600
HEBREW HIGH SCHOOL OF FIVE TOWNS 25 FROST LANE	LAWRENCE	**NY**	11559	(516) 239-1116
ISRAEL, TEMPLE 140 CENTRAL AVENUE	LAWRENCE	**NY**	11559	(516) 239-9213
SINAI, TEMPLE 131 WASHINGTON AVENUE	LAWRENCE	**NY**	11559	(516) 569-0267
ISRAEL COMMUNITY CENTER 3235 HEMPSTEAD TURNPIKE	LEVITTOWN	**NY**	11756	(516) 731-2580
CHAVURAT BETH CHAI LINCOLN HALL	LINCOLNDALE	**NY**	10540	(914) 628-5848
LINDENHURST HEBREW CONGREGATION				
224 NORTH FOURTH STREET, PO BOX 100	LINDENHURST	**NY**	11757	(516) 226-2022
LITTLE NECK JEWISH CENTER 49-10 LITTLE NECK PARKWAY	LITTLE NECK	**NY**	11362	(718) 225-9699
TORAH, TEMPLE 54-27 LITTLE NECK PARKWAY	LITTLE NECK	**NY**	11362	(718) 423-1235
BETH SHOLOM OF LONG BEACH & LIDO, CONGREGATEION				
700 EAST PARK AVENUE, BOX 599	LONG BEACH	**NY**	11561	(516) 432-7464
COMMUNITY HEBREW SCHOOL OF LONG BEACH & LIDO				
570 WEST WALNUT STREET/75 EAST WALNUT STREET	LONG BEACH	**NY**	11561	(516) 432-1678
EMANUEL, TEMPLE 455 NEPTUNE BOULEVARD	LONG BEACH	**NY**	11561	(516) 431-4060
SEPHARDIC CONGREGATION OF LONG BEACH				
161 LAFAYETTE BOULEVARD	LONG BEACH	**NY**	11561	(516) 432-9224
ASTORIA CENTER OF ISRAEL 27-35 CRESCENT STREET	LONG ISLAND CITY	**NY**	11102	(718) 278-2680
SUNNYSIDE JEWISH CENTER 45-46 43 STREET	LONG ISLAND CITY	**NY**	11104	(718) 729-9716
BETH DAVID, CONGREGATION 188 VINCENT AVENUE	LYNBROOK	**NY**	11563	(516) 599-9464
EMANU-EL, TEMPLE ROSS PLAZA	LYNBROOK	**NY**	11563	(516) 593-4004
MALVERNE-WEST HEMPSTEAD RELIGIOUS SCHOOL				
1 NORWOOD AVENUE	MALVERNE	**NY**	11565	(516) 593-6364
WESTCHESTER JEWISH CENTER ROCKLAND & PALMER AVENUES	MAMARONECK	**NY**	10543	(914) 698-2966
JUDEA, TEMPLE 333 SEARINGTON ROAD	MANHASSET	**NY**	11030	(516) 621-8049
MASPETH JEWISH CENTER 66-64 GRAND AVENUE	MASPETH	**NY**	11378	(718) 639-7559
BETH EL, CONGREGATION 99 JERUSALEM AVENUE	MASSAPEQUA	**NY**	11758	(516) 541-0740
JUDEA, TEMPLE JERUSALEM & CENTRAL AVENUES	MASSAPEQUA	**NY**	11758	(516) 798-5444
BETH AM, TEMPLE KIRKWOOD & MERRICK AVENUES	MERRICK	**NY**	11566	(516) 378-3477
ISRAEL OF SOUTH MERRICK, TEMPLE 2655 CLUBHOUSE ROAD	MERRICK	**NY**	11566	(516) 378-1963
MERRICK JEWISH CENTER-RABBI SOLOMON LIPMAN RELIGIOUS SCHOOL				
225 FOX BOULEVARD	MERRICK	**NY**	11566	(516) 378-8384
MERRICK-BELLMORE SYNAGOGUE, OHAV SHOLOM OF MERRICK				
145 SOUTH MERRICK AVENUE	MERRICK	**NY**	11566	(516) 378-1988
FOREST HILLS W., JEWISH CENTER OF				
63-25 DRY HARBOR ROAD	MIDDLE VILLAGE	**NY**	11379	(718) 639-2110
BETH SHOLOM, CONGREGATION 261 WILLIS AVENUE	MINEOLA	**NY**	11501	(516) 746-3211
BET TORAH 60 SMITH AVENUE	MOUNT KISCO	**NY**	10549	(914) 666-7595
EMANUEL-FLEETWOOD RELIGIOUS SCHOOL				
261 EAST LINCOLN AVENUE	MT VERNON	**NY**	10552	(914) 664-4587
FREE SYNAGOGUE OF WESTCHESTER				
500 NORTH COLUMBUS AVENUE	MT VERNON	**NY**	10552	(914) 664-1727
SINAI TEMPLE 132 CRARY AVENUE	MT VERNON	**NY**	10550	(914) 668-9471
YM-YWHA, MT VERNON 30 OAKLEY AVENUE	MT VERNON	**NY**	10550	(914) 664-0500
WEST END TEMPLE 147-02 NEWPORT AVENUE	NEPONSIT	**NY**	11694	(718) 634-0301
EMANUEL, TEMPLE 3315 HILLSIDE AVENUE	NEW HYDE PARK	**NY**	11580	(516) 746-1120
NEW HYDE PARK JEWISH CENTER 100 LAKEVILLE ROAD	NEW HYDE PARK	**NY**	11040	(516) 354-7583
YOUNG ISRAEL OF NEW HYDE PARK 264-15 77 AVENUE	NEW HYDE PARK	**NY**	11040	(516) 343-0496
ANSHE SHOLOM, CONGREGATION 50 NORTH AVENUE	NEW ROCHELLE	**NY**	10805	(914) 632-9220
BETH EL SYNAGOGUE NORTH AVENUE & NORTHFIELD ROAD	NEW ROCHELLE	**NY**	10804	(914) 235-2700
COMMUNITY HEBREW HIGH SCHOOL OF NEW ROCHELLE				
NORTH AVENUE & NORTHFIELD ROAD	NEW ROCHELLE	**NY**	10804	(914) 235-2700

ISRAEL, TEMPLE 1000 PINEBROOK BOULEVARD .... NEW ROCHELLE NY 10804   (914) 235-1800
BROTHERHOOD SYNAGOGUE 28 GRAMERCY PARK S..................... NEW YORK NY 10003   (212) 674-5750
CENTRAL SYNAGOGUE 123 EAST 55TH STREET .... NEW YORK NY 10022   (212) 838-5122
COMM. HEBREW SCHOOL-FT TYRON J.C./HEBREW TABERNACLE CONG.
  524 FORT WASHINGTON AVENUE .... NEW YORK NY 10033   (212) 795-1391
CONSERVATIVE SYNAGOGUE OF FIFTH AVENUE
  11 EAST 11TH STREET .... NEW YORK NY 10003   (212) 929-6954
DARCHEI SHOLOM 344 EAST 14TH STREET .... NEW YORK NY 10003   (212) 677-8090
EAST END TEMPLE 398 SECOND AVENUE .... NEW YORK NY 10010   (212) 254-8518
EDUCATIONAL ALLIANCE 197 EAST BROADWAY .... NEW YORK NY 10002   (212) 475-6200
EMANU-EL, CONGREGATION 1 EAST 65TH STREET .... NEW YORK NY 10021   (212) 744-1400
FIFTH AVENUE SYNAGOGUE 5 EAST 62ND STREET .... NEW YORK NY 10021   (212) 838-2122
HABONIM, CONGREGATION 44 WEST 66TH STREET .... NEW YORK NY 10023   (212) 787-5347
ISRAEL, TEMPLE 112 EAST 75TH STREET .... NEW YORK NY 10021   (212) 249-5000
LINCOLN SQUARE SYNAGOGUE & GUSTAV STERN HEBREW HIGH SCHOOL
  200 AMSTERDAM AVENUE .... NEW YORK NY 10023   (212) 874-6100
PARK AVENUE SYNAGOGUE 50 EAST 87TH STREET .... NEW YORK NY 10028   (212) 369-2600
PARK EAST SYNAGOGUE 164 EAST 68TH STREET .... NEW YORK NY 10021   (212) 737-6900
PROZDOR OF THE JEWISH THEOLOGICAL SEMINARY
  3080 BROADWAY .... NEW YORK NY 10027   (212) 749-8000
RODEPH SHOLOM, CONGREGATION 7 WEST 83RD STREET .... NEW YORK NY 10023   (212) 362-8800
SHAARAY TEFILA, TEMPLE 250 EAST 79TH STREET .... NEW YORK NY 10021   (212) 535-8008
SHEARITH ISRAEL 8 WEST 70TH STREET .... NEW YORK NY 10023   (212) 873-0300
SOCIETY FOR THE ADVANCEMENT OF JUDAISM
  15 WEST 86TH STREET .... NEW YORK NY 10024   (212) 724-7000
STEPHEN WISE FREE SYNAGOGUE 30 WEST 68TH STREET .... NEW YORK NY 10023   (212) 877-4050
VILLAGE TEMPLE 33 EAST 12TH STREET .... NEW YORK NY 10003   (212) 674-2340
YM-YWHA NINETY-SECOND STREET 1395 LEXINGTON AVENUE ..... NEW YORK NY 10028   (212) 427-6000
YM-YWHA OF INWOOD & WASHINGTON HEIGHTS 54 NAGLE AVENUE .... NEW YORK NY 10040   (212) 569-6200
AGUDAS ISRAEL 290 NORTH STREET .... NEWBURGH NY 12550   (914) 562-5604
BETH-EL, TEMPLE 1373 BELLMORE ROAD .... NORTH BELLMORE NY 11710   (516) 781-6923
OHR TORA, NORTH WOODMERE JEWISH CENTER
  410 HUNGRY HARBOR ROAD .... NORTH WOODMERE NY 11581   (516) 791-2346
BNAI ISRAEL REFORM TEMPLE
  PO BOX 158-IDLE HOUR BOULEVARD & BILTMORE AVENUE ..... OAKDALE NY 11769   (516) 589-8948
AVODAH, TEMPLE 3050 OCEANSIDE ROAD .... OCEANSIDE NY 11572   (516) 766-6835
CENTRAL HEBREW HIGH SCHOOL 2860 BROWER AVENUE .... OCEANSIDE NY 11572   (516) 766-3412
OCEAN HARBOR, JEWISH CENTER OF ROYAL & WEIDNER AVENUES.... OCEANSIDE NY 11572   (516) 536-6144
OCEANSIDE JEWISH CENTER 2860 BROWER AVENUE .... OCEANSIDE NY 11572   (516) 764-4213
SHAARY HASHOMAIM 3309 SKILLMAN .... OCEANSIDE NY 11572   (516) 764-9379
SOUTH SHORE HEBREW SCHOOL FOR SPECIAL CHILDREN
  3369 PARK AVENUE .... OCEANSIDE NY 11572   (516) 764-2529
YOUNG ISRAEL OF OCEANSIDE 150 WAUKENA AVENUE .... OCEANSIDE NY 11572   (516) 764-1099
BETH ELOHIM, TEMPLE 926 ROUND SWAMP ROAD .... OLD BETHPAGE NY 11804   (516) 694-4544
SOCIETY OF JEWISH SCIENCE 825 ROUND SWAMP ROAD .... OLD BETHPAGE NY 11804   (516) 249-6262
WESTBURY HEBREW CONGREGATION 21 OLD WESTBURY ROAD ... OLD WESTBURY NY 11568   (516) 333-7977
OYSTER BAY JEWISH CENTER BERRY HILL ROAD .... OYSTER BAY NY 11771   (516) 922-6650
BNAI JACOB RELIGIOUS SCHOOL 80-05 101ST AVENUE .... OZONE PARK NY 11416   (718) 296-8334
OZONE PARK JEWISH CENTER 107-01 CROSS BAY BOULEVARD ..... OZONE PARK NY 11417   (718) 848-4096
BETH EL OF PATCHOGUE, TEMPLE 45 OAK STREET.................. PATCHOGUE NY 11772   (516) 475-1882
FIRST HEBREW CONGREGATION 1821 EAST MAIN STREET .... PEEKSKILL NY 10566   (914) 739-0500
PELHAM JEWISH CENTER 451 ESPLANADE .... PELHAM MANOR NY 10803   (914) 738-9765
MANETTO HILL JEWISH CENTER 244 MANETTO HILL ROAD .... PLAINVIEW NY 11803   (516) 935-5454
PLAINVIEW JEWISH CENTER 95 FLORAL DRIVE .... PLAINVIEW NY 11803   (516) 938-8610
KNESES TIFERETH ISRAEL 575 KING STREET .... PORT CHESTER NY 10573   (914) 939-1004
SUFFOLK COUNTY INSTITUTE FOR JEWISH STUDIES
  BOX 363, HUNTINGTON STATION 7 .... PORT JEFFERSON NY 11776   (516) 462-9839
NORTH SHORE JEWISH CENTER 385 OLD TOWN ROAD ..... PORT JEFFERSON STA. NY 11776   (516) 928-3737
BETH ISRAEL, CONGREGATION TEMPLE DRIVE .... PORT WASHINGTON NY 11050   (516) 767-1708
COMMUNITY SYNAGOGUE 150 MIDDLE NECK ROAD .... PORT WASHINGTON NY 11050   (516) 883-3144
PORT JEWISH CENTER PO BOX 852 .... PORT WASHINGTON NY 11050   (516) 883-5174
HABONIM, CONGREGATION 63-44 WETHEROLE STREET .... REGO PARK NY 11374   (718) 897-0693
RANANAH NURSERY SCHOOL 90-14 63RD DRIVE .... REGO PARK NY 11374   (718) 275-5668
REGO PARK JEWISH CENTER 97-30 QUEENS BOULEVARD .... REGO PARK NY 11374   (718) 459-1000
ISRAEL, TEMPLE 490 NORTHVILLE TURNPIKE .... RIVERHEAD NY 11901   (516) 727-3191
B'NAI SHOLOM, TEMPLE 100 HEMPSTEAD AVENUE .... ROCKVILLE CENTRE NY 11570   (516) 764-4100
CENTRAL SYNAGOGUE OF NASSAU COUNTY
  430 DEMOTT AVENUE .... ROCKVILLE CENTRE NY 11570   (516) 766-4300
ROOSEVELT ISLAND, JEWISH CONGREGATION OF
  555 MAIN STREET .... ROOSEVELT ISLAND NY 10044
ROSEDALE JEWISH CENTER 247-11 FRANCIS LEWIS BOULEVARD .... ROSEDALE NY 11422   (718) 528-3988
SHELTER ROCK JEWISH CENTER
  SHELTER ROCK & SEARINGTON ROADS .... ROSLYN NY 11576   (516) 741-4305
BETH SHOLOM, TEMPLE
  ROSLYN ROAD AT NORTHERN STATE PARKWAY .... ROSLYN HEIGHTS NY 11577   (516) 484-4980
RECONSTRUCTIONIST SYNAGOGUE 1 WILLOW STREET .... ROSLYN HEIGHTS NY 11577   (516) 621-5540
SINAI, TEMPLE 425 ROSLYN ROAD .... ROSLYN HEIGHTS NY 11577   (516) 621-6800
COMMUNITY SYNAGOGUE 200 FOREST AVENUE......................... RYE NY 10580   (914) 967-6262
EMANU-EL, CONGREGATION
  WESTCHESTER AVENUE AND KENILWORTH ROAD .... RYE NY 10580   (914) 967-7977
SAYVILLE JEWISH CENTER 225 GREENLEY AVENUE..................... SAYVILLE NY 11782   (516) 589-9722
SCARSDALE SYNAGOGUE 2 OGDEN ROAD .... SCARSDALE NY 10583   (914) 725-5175
WESTCHESTER REFORM TEMPLE 255 MAMARONECK ROAD .... SCARSDALE NY 10583   (914) 723-7727
YM-YWHA, MID-WESTCHESTER 999 WILMOT ROAD .... SCARSDALE NY 10583   (914) 472-3300
YOUNG ISRAEL OF SCARSDALE 1313 WEAVER ROAD-PO BOX 103H ... SCARSDALE NY 10583   (914) 636-8686
SEAFORD JEWISH CENTER 2343 SOUTH SEAMANS NECK ROAD, BOX 81 ... SEAFORD NY 11783   (516) 785-4570
BETH SHOLOM, TEMPLE-LAWRENCE KARP RELIGIOUS SCHOOL
  PO BOX 764 .... SMITHTOWN NY 11787   (516) 724-0424
JEWISH CENTER OF BELLMORE 25-50 CENTER AVENUE .... SOUTH BELLMORE NY 11710   (516) 781-3072
AGUDAS ACHIM ANSHE CHESED, CONGREGATION
  641 DELAFIELD AVENUE .... STATEN ISLAND NY 10310   (718) 727-5920

B'NAI ISRAEL, CONGREGATION 45 TROMBLEY AVENUE............. STATEN ISLAND NY 10306   (718) 987-8188
B'NAI JESHURUN, CONGREGATION 275 MARTLING AVENUE .... STATEN ISLAND NY 10314   (718) 981-5550
EMANUEL OF STATEN ISLAND, TEMPLE 984 POST AVENUE .... STATEN ISLAND NY 10302   (718) 442-5966
ISRAEL, TEMPLE 315 FOREST AVENUE .... STATEN ISLAND NY 10301   (718) 727-2231
JEWISH COMMUNITY CENTER 475 VICTORY BOULEVARD .... STATEN ISLAND NY 10301   (718) 981-1500
YOUNG ISRAEL OF ELTINGVILLE, INCORPORATED
  374 RIDGEWOOD AVENUE .... STATEN ISLAND NY 10308   (718) 984-8393
YOUNG ISRAEL OF STATEN ISLAND 835 FOREST HILL ROAD .... STATEN ISLAND NY 10314   (718) 698-7041
ISAIAH, TEMPLE 1404 STONY BROOK ROAD......................... STONY BROOK NY 11790   (516) 751-8518
EAST NASSAU HEBREW CONGREGATION
  310A SOUTH OYSTER BAY ROAD .... SYOSSET NY 11791   (516) 921-1800
MIDWAY HEBREW HIGH SCHOOL #18 330 SOUTH OYSTER BAY ROAD ...... SYOSSET NY 11791   (516) 822-3639
MIDWAY JEWISH CENTER - DR. FELIX BERGER SCHOOL
  330 SOUTH OYSTER BAY ROAD..................................... SYOSSET NY 11791   (516) 938-8390
NORTH SHORE SYNAGOGUE 83 MUTTONTOWN ROAD .... SYOSSET NY 11791   (516) 921-2282
BETH ABRAHAM, TEMPLE 25 LEROY AVENUE .... TARRYTOWN NY 10591   (914) 631-1770
GENESIS HEBREW CENTER 25 OAKLAND AVENUE .... TUCKAHOE NY 10707   (914) 961-3766
UNIONDALE JEWISH CENTER 760 JERUSALEM AVENUE .... UNIONDALE NY 11553   (516) 486-8788
BETH SHOLOM CONGREGATION-SUNRISE JEWISH CENTER
  550 ROCKAWAY AVENUE .... VALLEY STREAM NY 11581   (516) 561-9245
GATES OF ZION, TEMPLE 322 NORTH CORONA AVENUE .... VALLEY STREAM NY 11580   (516) 262-6193
HILLEL, TEMPLE 1000 ROSEDALE ROAD .... VALLEY STREAM NY 11581   (516) 791-6344
SUBURBAN TEMPLE 2900 JERUSALEM AVENUE .... WANTAGH NY 11793   (516) 221-2370
WANTAGH JEWISH CENTER 3710 WOODBINE AVENUE .... WANTAGH NY 11973   (516) 221-1650
NASSAU COMMUNITY TEMPLE-BETH EL
  240 HEMPSTEAD AVENUE .... WEST HEMPSTEAD NY 11552   (516) 485-1811
WEST HEMPSTEAD JEWISH CENTER 711 DOGWOOD AVENUE.... WEST HEMPSTEAD NY 11552   (516) 481-7448
BETH TORAH, TEMPLE 243 CANTIAGUE ROAD .... WESTBURY NY 11590   (516) 334-7979
COMMUNITY REFORM TEMPLE 712 THE PLAIN ROAD .... WESTBURY NY 11590   (516) 333-1839
SHOLOM, TEMPLE 675 BROOKSIDE CENTER .... WESTBURY NY 11590   (516) 334-2800
BET AM SHALOM SYNAGOGUE 295 SOUNDVIEW AVENUE .... WHITE PLAINS NY 10606   (914) 946-8851
HEBREW INSTITUTE OF WHITE PLAINS 20 GREENRIDGE AVENUE ... WHITE PLAINS NY 10605   (914) 948-3095
ISRAEL CENTER, TEMPLE 280 OLD MAMARONECK ROAD .... WHITE PLAINS NY 10605   (914) 779-3782
JEWISH COMMUNITY CENTER-LAWRENCE W. SCHWARTZ SCHOOL
  252 SOUNDVIEW AVENUE .... WHITE PLAINS NY 10606   (914) 949-4717
WOODLANDS COMMUNITY TEMPLE 50 WORTHINGTON ROAD .... WHITE PLAINS NY 10607   (914) 592-7070
CLEARVIEW JEWISH CENTER 1650 UTOPIA PARKWAY............... WHITESTONE NY 11357   (718) 352-6670
WHITESTONE HEBREW CENTER 12-45 CLINTONVILLE STREET ..... WHITESTONE NY 11357   (718) 767-7852
SONS OF ISRAEL, CONGREGATION 111 IRVING PLACE .... WOODMERE NY 11598   (516) 374-0805
EMANU-EL, TEMPLE 306 RUMSEY ROAD .... YONKERS NY 10705   (914) 963-0575
LINCOLN PARK JEWISH CENTER-NORTHEAST JEWISH CENTER
  311 CENTRAL PARK AVENUE .... YONKERS NY 10704   (914) 965-7119
MIDCHESTER JEWISH CENTER 236 GRANDVIEW BOULEVARD .... YONKERS NY 10710   (914) 779-3660
NORTHEAST JEWISH CENTER 11 SALISBURY ROAD .... YONKERS NY 10710   (914) 337-0268
SONS OF ISRAEL 105 RADFORD STREET .... YONKERS NY 10705   (914) 423-2070
YORKTOWN JEWISH CENTER 2966 CROMPOND ROAD .... YORKTOWN NY 10598   (914) 245-2324
BETH AM TEMPLE CHURCH & SUMMIT STREETS .... YORKTOWN HEIGHTS NY 10598   (914) 962-7500
ANSHE CHESED (FAIRMOUNT TEMPLE) 23737 FAIRMOUNT BLVD .... CLEVELAND OH 44122   (216) 464-5890
B'NAI JESHURUN (TEMPLE ON THE HEIGHTS)
  27501 FAIRMOUNT BLVD .... CLEVELAND OH 44124   (216) 831-6555
BETH AM (COMMUNITY TEMPLE) 3557 WASHINGTON BLVD .... CLEVELAND OH 44118   (216) 321-1247
BETH ISRAEL (THE WEST TEMPLE) 14308 TRISKETT ROAD .... CLEVELAND OH 44111   (216) 941-8882
BETH TORAH - BETH AM CONGREGATION 3557 WASHINGTON BLVD ... CLEVELAND OH 44124   (216) 371-9313
BETHAYNU 25400 FAIRMOUNT BLVD .... CLEVELAND OH 44122   (216) 292-2931
BRITH EMETH 27575 SHAKER BLVD .... CLEVELAND OH 44124   (216) 831-5363
EMANU-EL, TEMPLE 2200 SOUTH GREEN ROAD .... CLEVELAND OH 44121   (216) 381-6600
MAYFIELD HILLCREST SYNAGOGUE 1732 LANDERS ROAD .... CLEVELAND OH 44124   (216) 449-6200
PARK SYNAGOGUE 3300 MAYFIELD ROAD .... CLEVELAND OH 44118   (216) 371-2244
SUBURBAN TEMPLE 22401 CHAGRIN BLVD .... CLEVELAND OH 44122   (216) 991-0700
TAYLOR ROAD SYNAGOGUE 1970 SOUTH TAYLOR ROAD .... CLEVELAND OH 44118   (216) 321-5875
WARRENSVILLE CENTER SYNAGOGUE
  1508 WARRENSVILLE CENTER ROAD .... CLEVELAND OH 44121   (216) 382-6566
COLUMBUS HEBREW SCHOOL 1125 COLLEGE AVENUE .... COLUMBUS OH 43209   (614) 231-7764
COMMUNITY HEBREW SCHOOL 4501 DENLINGER ROAD .... DAYTON OH 45426   (513) 854-2021
AM SHALOM (LAKE COUNTY JEWISH CENTER) R P.O. BOX 454 ...... MENTOR OH 44060   (216) 953-1315
BETH SHALOM, TEMPLE P.O. BOX 315.......................... TWINSBURG OH 44087   (216) 266-3161
OTTAWA TALMUD TORAH AFTERNOON SCHOOL 453 RIDEAU STREET ...... OTTAWA ON K1N 5Z3
HEBREW SUNDAY SCHOOL SOCIETY OF GREATER PHILADELPHIA, THE
  1729 PINE STREET .... PHILADELPHIA PA 19103   (215) 735-7972

TEACHERS ASSOCIATIONS

JEWISH TEACHERS ASSOCIATION 45 E. 33RD STREET .... NEW YORK NY 10016   (212) 684-0556
YESHIVA ENGLISH PRINCIPALS ASSOCIATION 426 WEST 58TH STREET .. NEW YORK NY 10019   (212) 245-8200

THEATRE

A TRAVELING JEWISH THEATRE, COREY FISCHER .... LOS ANGELES CA   (213) 650-7063
SHALOM CONCERT BUREAU BOX 35092 .... LOS ANGELES CA 90035   (213) 931-6125
THE NEW ARTEF PLAYERS PO BOX 345 .... LOS ANGELES CA 90048   (213) 655-1697
NORMAN J. FEDDER, THEATER PROGRAM, SPEECH DEPARTMENT
  KANSAS STATE UNIVERSITY .... MANHATTAN KS 66506   (913) 532-6011
FOLKSBIENE THEATER 123 EAST 55TH STREET .... NEW YORK NY 10022   (212) 755-2231
HEBREW ACTORS' UNION 31 EAST 7TH STREET .... NEW YORK NY 10003   (212) 674-1923
JEWISH REPERTORY THEATRE 344 E. 14TH STREET .... NEW YORK NY 10003   (212) 674-7200
JEWISH THEATRE ASSOCIATION 122 E. 44TH STREET .... NEW YORK NY 10017   (212) 490-2280
JEWISH THEATRE FOR CHILDREN 426 W. 58TH STREET .... NEW YORK NY 10019   (212) 245-8200
LIVELY & YIDDISH CO., INC. (PRODUCER OF YIDDISH SHOWS)
  45 EAST 33RD STREET.. NEW YORK NY 10016   (212) 686-3535

SASHA NANUS C/O LECTURE BUREAU J.W.B. 15 EAST 26TH STREET	NEW YORK	NY 10010	(212) 532-4949
YESHIVA COLLEGE DRAMATICS SOCIETY 2475 AMSTERDAM AVENUE	NEW YORK	NY 10033	(212) 928-0181
SALLY FOX, JEWISH INVOLVEMENT THEATRE			
PO BOX 3309, OSU STATION	COLUMBUS	OH 43210	

TOURS & TRAVEL PROGRAMS

FOREIGN/SHARON TOURS 9300 WILSHIRE BOULEVARD	BEVERLY HILLS	CA 90212	(213) 273-8872
TRAVEL CENTER OF BEVERLY HILLS - LEVY SPITZER			
291 S. LA CIENEGA BLVD. SUITE 101	BEVERLY HILLS	CA 90211	(213) 652-3434
BESTWAY TRAVEL SERVICE 334 NO. FAIRFAX AVENUE	LOS ANGELES	CA 90036	(213) 937-1565
ISRAEL GOVERNMENT TOURIST OFFICE			
6380 WILSHIRE BOULEVARD	LOS ANGELES	CA 90048	(213) 658-7462
MADAN TRAVEL SERVICE 7970 BEVERLY BOULEVARD	LOS ANGELES	CA 90048	(213) 651-3155
B'NAI B'RITH TOURS 1640 RHODE ISLAND AVENUE	WASHINGTON	DC 20036	(202) 857-6600
HERITAGE TOURS 3305 MACOMB STREET, N.W.	WASHINGTON	DC 20008	(202) 362-4367
ISRAEL GOVERNMENT TOURIST OFFICE 795 PEACHTREE STREET N.E.	ATLANTA	GA 30308	(404) 875-7851
ISRAEL GOVERNMENT TOURIST OFFICE 5 SOUTH WABASH AVENUE	CHICAGO	IL 60603	(312) 782-4306
CERTIFIED TRAVEL 4311 18TH AVENUE	BROOKLYN	NY 11204	(718) 633-1707
EXECUTIVE MOTOR TOURS 81 BROOKFIELD	BROOKLYN	NY 11204	(718) 436-1385
HARIM KOSHER TOURS 1736 E. 4TH ST.	BROOKLYN	NY 11223	(718) 645-2974
SWEET SIXTEEN TRAVEL 1706 E. 16TH STREET	BROOKLYN	NY 11229	(718) 627-0097
J.T.A. TOURS 527 CHESTNUT STREET	CEDARHURST	NY 11516	(718) 476-0900
TULI TRAVEL 69-54 MAIN STREET	FLUSHING	NY 11367	(718) 544-2000
AMBASSADOR KOSHER TOURS 25 WEST 43RD STREET	NEW YORK	NY 10036	(212) 575-8840
AMIT TRAVEL 817 BROADWAY	NEW YORK	NY 10003	(212) 477-4720
AGUDATH ISRAEL TRAVEL DEPARTMENT 5 BEEKMAN STREET	NEW YORK	NY 10038	(212) 791-1800
AMERICAN FRIENDS OF HAIFA UNIVERSITY 206 FIFTH AVENUE	NEW YORK	NY 10010	(212) 696-4022
AMERICAN FRIENDS OF HEBREW UNIVERSITY 11 EAST 69TH STREET	NEW YORK	NY 10021	(212) 472-9800
AMERICAN FRIENDS OF TEL AVIV UNIVERSITY 342 MADISON AVENUE	NEW YORK	NY 10017	(212) 687-5651
AMERICAN JEWISH CONGRESS, OVERSEAS TRAVEL DEPARTMENT			
15 EAST 84TH STREET	NEW YORK	NY 10028	(212) 879-4588
AMERICAN ORGANIZATION OF TOUR OPERATORS TO ISRAEL			
310 MADISON AVENUE	NEW YORK	NY 10017	(212) 599-2323
ARCHAEOLOGICAL TOURS OF ISRAEL 1560 BROADWAY	NEW YORK	NY 10019	(212) 719-5500
BAR/BAT MITZVAH PILGRIMAGE - WORLD ZIONIST ORGANIZATION			
515 PARK AVENUE	NEW YORK	NY 10022	(212) 752-0600
B'NAI B'RITH TOURS 823 U.N. PLAZA	NEW YORK	NY 10017	(212) 490-2525
COMPASS TRAVEL BUREAU, INC. 70 WEST 40TH STREET	NEW YORK	NY 10018	(212) 354-6868
DAPHNA TRAVEL BUREAU, INC. 444 MADISON AVENUE	NEW YORK	NY 10022	(800) 223-6874
E.T.S. TOURS 5 PENN PLAZA (8TH AVENUE & 34TH STREET)	NEW YORK	NY 10001	(212) 563-0780
EASTOURS, INC. 461 EIGHTH AVENUE	NEW YORK	NY 10001	(212) 947-9595
EMUNAH TOURS/EMUNAH WOMEN OF AMERICA			
370 SEVENTH AVENUE	NEW YORK	NY 10001	(212) 947-5454
FOREIGN/SHARON TOURS 461 EIGHTH AVENUE	NEW YORK	NY 10001	(212) 947-9595
GELLER-HOWARD TRAVEL 630 THIRD AVENUE	NEW YORK	NY 10017	(212) 599-0888
HABONIM LABOR ZIONIST YOUTH 27 WEST 20TH STREET	NEW YORK	NY 10011	(212) 255-1796
HADASSAH 50 WEST 58TH STREET	NEW YORK	NY 10022	(212) 355-7900
HADASSAH ZIONIST YOUTH COMMISSION 50 WEST 58TH STREET	NEW YORK	NY 10022	(212) 355-7900
HAPOEL-MIZRACHI WOMEN'S ORGANIZATION 370 7TH AVENUE	NEW YORK	NY 10001	(212) 564-9045
HASHOMER HATZAIR ZIONIST YOUTH ORGANIZATION			
150 FIFTH AVENUE	NEW YORK	NY 10011	(212) 242-0532
HISTADRUT FOUNDATION FOR EDUCATIONAL TRAVEL			
630 THIRD AVENUE	NEW YORK	NY 10017	(212) 697-6822
HISTADRUT TOURS 630 THIRD AVENUE	NEW YORK	NY 10017	(212) 697-6822
ISRAM WHOLESALE TOURS & TRAVEL, LTD. 630 THIRD AVENUE	NEW YORK	NY 10017	(212) 661-1193
ISRAEL AIR GROUP TRAVEL INFORMATION 20 EAST 49TH STREET	NEW YORK	NY 10017	(212) 688-5170
ISRAEL GOVERNMENT TOURIST OFFICE EMPIRE STATE BUILDING	NEW YORK	NY 10001	(212) 560-0560
ISRAEL HOTEL REPRESENTATIVES 120 EAST 56TH STREET	NEW YORK	NY 10022	(212) 752-6120
ISRAEL TRAVEL CENTER FOR STUDENTS 1140 BROADWAY	NEW YORK	NY 10001	(212) 691-2200
JEWISH EDUCATIONAL VENTURES, INC.			
ONE PARK AVENUE/SUITE 1900	NEW YORK	NY 10016	(212) 684-2010
KO-TOURS 183 MADISON AVENUE, SUITE 716	NEW YORK	NY 10016	(212) 725-4800
KOPEL TOURS, LTD. 40 EAST 49TH STREET	NEW YORK	NY 10017	(212) 838-0500
LABOR ZIONIST ALLIANCE, KIBBUTZ ALIYAH DESK			
275 SEVENTH AVENUE	NEW YORK	NY 10001	(212) 989-0300
NATIONAL HEBREW CULTURE COUNCIL 1776 BROADWAY	NEW YORK	NY 10019	(212) 247-0741
NATIONAL JEWISH WELFARE BOARD 15 EAST 26TH STREET	NEW YORK	NY 10010	(212) 532-4949
NOAM - HAMISHMERET 25 WEST 26TH STREET	NEW YORK	NY 10010	(212) 684-6091
ORIENT FLEXI-PAX TOURS 630 THIRD AVENUE	NEW YORK	NY 10017	(212) 692-9550
ORIENT FLEXI-PAX TOURS 630 THIRD AVENUE	NEW YORK	NY 10017	(800) 545-5540
TEK TRAVEL 45 EAST 17TH STREET	NEW YORK	NY 10003	(212) 673-6610
TRIPMASTERS 1140 BROADWAY	NEW YORK	NY 10001	(212) 689-7600
USY ON WHEELS, USY PILGRIMAGE (YOUTH) 155 FIFTH AVENUE	NEW YORK	NY 10010	(212) 533-7800
UNION OF AMERICAN HEBREW CONGREGATIONS 838 FIFTH AVENUE	NEW YORK	NY 10021	(212) 249-0100
UNITED SYNAGOGUE TOUR SERVICE (ADULT) 155 FIFTH AVENUE	NEW YORK	NY 10010	(212) 533-7800
UNITED SYNAGOGUE-ISRAEL TOUR DEPARTMENT 630 THIRD AVENUE	NEW YORK	NY 10017	(212) 697-8555
WOMEN'S AMERICAN ORT 162 WEST 56TH STREET	NEW YORK	NY 10019	(212) 247-4640
WORLD ZIONIST ORGANIZATION 515 PARK AVENUE	NEW YORK	NY 10022	(212) 752-0600
YOUNG ISRAEL TOURS 3 WEST 16TH STREET	NEW YORK	NY 10011	(212) 929-1525
ZIONIST ORGANIZATION OF AMERICA - ISRAEL SUMMER PROGRAMS			
4 EAST 34TH STREET	NEW YORK	NY 10016	(212) 481-1500
LEISURE TIME TOURS 145-98 GUY BREWER BLVD	QUEENS	NY 11434	(718) 528-0700
CANADIAN FRIENDS OF HEBREW UNIVERSITY			
1506 MCGREGOR AVENUE	MONTREAL	QU	(514) 932-2133

TRANSLATIONS

'A' CERTIFIED TRANSLATIONS 21-07 CORNAGA AVENUE	FAR ROCKAWAY	NY 11691	(718) 471-2711
HEBREW TRANSLATIONS SERVICE 22 CORNELIA STREET	NEW YORK	NY 10014	(212) 242-2469

TRAVEL TO THE SOVIET UNION

AMERICAN JEWISH CONGRESS 15 EAST 84TH STREET	NEW YORK	NY 10028	(212) 879-4500
INTOURIST 630 FIFTH AVENUE	NEW YORK	NY 10111	(212) 757-3884
NATIONAL CONFERENCE ON SOVIET JEWRY 10 EAST 40TH STREET	NEW YORK	NY 10036	(212) 679-6122
STUDENT STRUGGLE FOR SOVIET JEWRY 210 WEST 91ST STREET	NEW YORK	NY 10024	(212) 799-8900

ULPAN

HEBREW ULPAN CENTER 515 PARK AVENUE	NEW YORK	NY 10022	(212) 752-0600
KEREN HATARBUT INSTITUTE 788 MARLEE AVENUE	TORONTO	ON	(416) 787-0197

VEGETARIANS

JEWISH VEGETARIAN SOCIETY P.O. BOX 5722	BALTIMORE	MD 21208	(301) 521-3061
THE JEWISH VEGETARIAN SOCIETY-AMERICAN SECRETARIAT			
68-38 YELLOWSTONE BOULEVARD,			
C/O SAMUEL JUDAH GROSSBERG	FOREST HILLS	NY 11375	(718) 459-1014
JEWISH VEGETARIAN SOCIETY			
C/O MR. J. WOLF, 210 RIVERSIDE DRIVE	NEW YORK	NY 10025	(212) 666-6216

VITAMINS

PRECISION VITAMINS 1524 47TH ST.	BROOKLYN	NY 11219	(718) 435-4333
FREEDA VITAMINS 36 EAST 41ST STREET	NEW YORK	NY 10017	(212) 685-4980
LOIS LANE'S NINTH & NATURAL 580 NINTH AVENUE AT 42ND ST.	NEW YORK	NY 10036	(212) 695-5055

VOCATIONAL SERVICES

JEWISH VOCATIONAL SERVICE 6505 WILSHIRE BLVD	LOS ANGELES	CA 90048	(213) 655-8910
JEWISH VOCATIONAL SERVICE 6505 WILSHIRE BOULEVARD	LOS ANGELES	CA 90048	(213) 852-1234
JEWISH VOCATIONAL & CAREER COUNSELING SERVICE			
870 MARKET STREET, ROOM 872	SAN FRANCISCO	CA 94102	(415) 391-3595
JEWISH FAMILY & CHILDREN'S SERVICE 300 SOUTH DAHLIA STREET	DENVER	CO 80222	(303) 321-3115
JEWISH VOCATIONAL SERVICE 318 N.W. 25TH STREET	MIAMI	FL 33137	(305) 576-3220
JEWISH VOCATIONAL SERVICE OF THE ATLANTA JEWISH FEDERATION			
1745 PEACHTREE ROAD N.E.	ATLANTA	GA 30309	(404) 876-5872
JEWISH VOCATIONAL SERVICE 1 S. FRANKLIN STREET	CHICAGO	IL 60606	(312) 346-6700
JEWISH VOCATIONAL SERVICES 702 MARION E. TAYLOR BUILDING	LOUISVILLE	KY 40202	(502) 584-8336
JEWISH VOCATIONAL SERVICE 31 NEW CHARDON STREET	BOSTON	MA 02114	(617) 723-2846

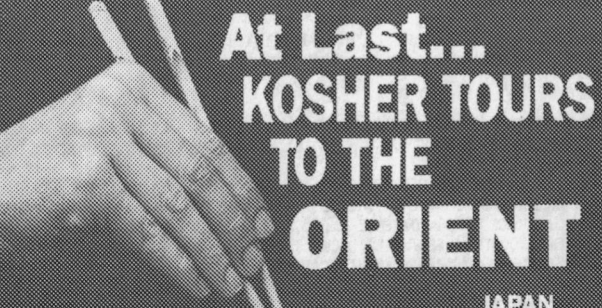

Man-O-Manischewitz, What Wines

In this ever changing world, a lot of companies have compromised their standards just to keep pace. Not us. We're Manischewitz Wine Company. And, we've been loyally serving our customers in exactly the same way–maintaining strict adherence to Kashruth and quality.

Starting back in 1937, we entered into an arrangement with The B. Manischewitz Company, to use their world famous name to produce Manischewitz kosher wine. This union allowed us to market our quality wines under a traditionally respected name–Manischewitz. Since that time, Americans have enjoyed their Jewish heritage, celebrating Simchas and holidays throughout the year with Manischewitz kosher wines.

Manischewitz wines are sent to all our United States Armed Forces around the world, to be enjoyed and to give them a comforting taste of home.

From the gathering and crushing of the grapes to the final bottling, there is strict supervision by Rabbi Dr. Joseph I. Singer, Manhattan Beach Jewish Center, Brooklyn, N.Y., Rabbi Solomon B. Shapiro, Congregation B'nai Abraham, Queens, N.Y., and their qualified staff of Mashgichim supervisors. They, along with the diligent technicians and enologists who oversee every stage of our winemaking process, ensure that from harvesting to bottling and labeling, the Kashruth and quality never varies.

We're proud of our history, our operation and our products. We're Manischewitz Wine Company. And, Man-O-Manischewitz, what wines!

© 1985 Manischewitz Wine Company, Brooklyn, N.Y. 11232

JEWISH VOCATIONAL SERVICE 5750 PARK HEIGHTS AVENUE	BALTIMORE MD 21215	(301) 466-9200
JEWISH VOCATIONAL SERVICE 4250 WOODWARD	DETROIT MI 48201	(313) 833-8100
JEWISH VOCATIONAL OFFICE		
LOWER CONCOURSE-811 LASALLE COURT BUILDING	MINNEAPOLIS MN 55402	(612) 338-8771
JEWISH VOCATIONAL SERVICES 1821 UNIVERSITY AVENUE	ST. PAUL MN 55104	(612) 645-9377
JEWISH VOCATIONAL SERVICE 1516 GRAND AVENUE	KANSAS CITY MO 64108	(816) 471-2808
JEWISH EMPLOYMENT & VOCATIONAL SERVICE 1727 LOCUST STREET	ST. LOUIS MO 63103	(314) 241-3464
WORK EXPERIENCE CENTER OF JEWISH EMPLOYMENT VOCATIONAL SERV.		
2545 SOUTH HANLEY	ST. LOUIS MO 63144	
JEWISH VOCATIONAL SERVICE 67 N. CLINTON STREET	EAST ORANGE NJ 07017	(201) 674-2415
JEWISH VOCATIONAL SERVICE 454 WILLIAM STREET	EAST ORANGE NJ 07017	(201) 674-2415
JEWISH VOCATIONAL SERVICE OF METROPOLITAN NEW JERSEY		
111 PROSPECT	EAST ORANGE NJ 07017	(201) 674-6330
ALTRO WORK SHOPS 3600 JEROME AVENUE	BRONX NY 10467	(212) 881-7600
OHEL CHILDREN'S HOME & FAMILY SERVICES 4423 16TH AVENUE	BROOKLYN NY 11204	(718) 851-6300
SHEVET Y'HUDAH RESNICK INSTITUTE OF TECHNOLOGY		
670 ROCKAWAY PARKWAY	BROOKLYN NY 11236	(718) 342-6878
BRAMSON ORT TECHNICAL INSTITUTE 44 EAST 23RD STREET	NEW YORK NY 10010	(212) 677-7420
BRAMSON ORT TRADE SCHOOL 817 BROADWAY	NEW YORK NY 10003	(212) 228-9560
COPE VOCATIONAL INSTITUTE: BUSINESS SKILLS DIVISION		
5 BEEKMAN STREET	NEW YORK NY 10038	(212) 587-9257
COPE VOCATIONAL INSTITUTE: VOCATIONAL SKILLS DIVISION		
5 BEEKMAN STREET	NEW YORK NY 10038	(215) 587-9259
COUNCIL JEWISH MANPOWER ASSOCIATES 299 BROADWAY	NEW YORK NY 10007	(212) 233-8448
FEDERATION EMPLOYMENT & GUIDANCE SERVICE 114 FIFTH AVENUE	NEW YORK NY 10011	(212) 741-7110
HEBREW TECHNICAL INSTITUTE 235 PARK AVENUE S	NEW YORK NY 10003	
JEWISH OCCUPATIONAL COUNCIL 114 FIFTH AVENUE	NEW YORK NY 10011	(212) 741-7110
NATIONAL ASSOCIATION OF JEWISH VOCATIONAL SERVICES		
225 PARK AVENUE S., 16TH FLOOR	NEW YORK NY 10003	(212) 475-2400
NEW YORK ASSOCIATES FOR NEW AMERICANS 225 PARK AVENUE S	NEW YORK NY 10003	(212) 674-7400
PROJECT COPE-DIVISION OF AGUDATH ISRAEL		
5 BEEKMAN STREET, SUITE 814	NEW YORK NY 10038	(212) 587-9250
VOCATIONAL INSTITUTE & PROJECT COPE 5 BEEKMAN STREET	NEW YORK NY 10038	(212) 964-1620
PROJECT COPE OF AGUDATH ISRAEL OF AMERICA		
98-12 66TH AVENUE, SUITE 4	REGO PARK NY 11374	
JEWISH VOCATIONAL SERVICE 13878 CEDAR ROAD	UNIVERSITY HEIGHTS OH 44118	(216) 321-1381
JEWISH VOCATIONAL SERVICE 74 TYCOS DRIVE	TORONTO ON	(416) 787-1151
JEWISH EMPLOYMENT & VOCATIONAL SERVICE, THE		
1624 LOCUST STREET	PHILADELPHIA PA 19103	(215) 893-5900
JEWISH VOCATIONAL SERVICE 5151 COTE STE. CATHERINE ROAD	MONTREAL QU	(514) 735-3541
JEWISH VOCATIONAL COUNSELING SERVICES		
11300 NORTH CRESCENT EXWY., SUITE 402	DALLAS TX 75231	

JEWISH VOCATIONAL SERVICES 7800 NORTHHAVEN ROAD-#C	DALLAS TX 75230	(214) 369-4211
VOCATIONAL GUIDANCE SERVICE 2529 SAN JACINTO	HOUSTON TX 77002	(713) 225-0053
JEWISH VOCATIONAL SERVICE 1339 NORTH MILWAUKEE STREET	MILWAUKEE WI 53202	(414) 272-1344

WINES & SPIRITS

HAGAFEN CELLARS PO BOX 3035	NAPA CA 94558	(707) 252-0781
BEST BRANDS 10700 EAST 40TH AVENUE	DENVER CO 80239	(303) 371-2750
GEFFEN WINES	BROOKLYN NY 11218	(718) 840-1828
KEDEM ROYAL WINE CORP. 420 KENT AVENUE	BROOKLYN NY 11211	(718) 384-2400
MANISCHEWITZ WINE COMPANY 4500 SECOND AVENUE	BROOKLYN NY 11232	(718) 965-8800
MONARCH WINE COMPANY, INC. 4500 SECOND AVENUE	BROOKLYN NY 11232	(718) 965-8800
PEERLESS IMPORTERS 16 BRIDGEWATER STREET	BROOKLYN NY 11222	(718) 383-5500
ROYAL WINE CORP. 420 KENT AVENUE	BROOKLYN NY 11211	(718) 384-2400
KEDEM ROYAL WINERY DOCK ROAD	MILTON NY 12547	(914) 795-2240
CARMEL WINE COMPANY 271 MADISON AVENUE	NEW YORK NY 10016	(212) 532-4016
EIN GUEDI IMPORT COMPANY 271 MADISON AVENUE	NEW YORK NY 10016	(212) 532-4016
GANELES KOSHER WINE COMPANY 107 NORFOLK STREET	NEW YORK NY 10002	(212) 477-5797
GENERAL WINE & SPIRITS COMPANY 375 PARK AVENUE	NEW YORK NY 10022	(212) 572-7000
GROSS WINES & LIQUORS 204 WEST END AVENUE	NEW YORK NY 10023	(212) 724-3007
JOSEPH E. SEAGRAMS, INC. 375 PARK AVENUE	NEW YORK NY 10022	(212) 572-7000
KEDEM KOSHER WINES 107 NORFOLK STREET	NEW YORK NY 10002	(212) 673-2780
PARK AVENUE IMPORTS 375 PARK AVENUE	NEW YORK NY 10022	(212) 572-7642
SCHAPIRO WINE CO. 126 RIVINGTON STREET	NEW YORK NY 10002	(212) 674-4404
TIROSH WINE COMPANY	NEW YORK NY	(212) 475-1165
MARGULIS 719 S. 4TH STREET	PHILADELPHIA PA	(215) 925-3118

WOMEN'S ORGANIZATIONS

DEBORAH, THE JEWISH WOMEN'S GROUP
C/O WIZO, DWARSLAAN 18, 126 B.B.BLARICUM .... AMSTERDAM
LONDON JEWISH FEMINIST GROUP
C/O MARGARET GREEN, FLAT 7, CALLCOTT COURT, CALLCOTT RD ..... LONDON

PIONEER WOMEN-NA'AMAT 1-703 56TH AVENUE S.W.	CALGARY	**AT**	T2V 0G9	(403) 253-9060
PIONEER WOMEN-NA'AMAT 950 WEST 41ST STREET, ROOM G	VANCOUVER	**BC**	V5Z 2N7	(604) 266-8308
NATIONAL COUNCIL OF JEWISH WOMEN, INC.-WESTERN DISTRICT 2734 A. COLLEGE AVENUE	BERKELEY	**CA**	94705	(415) 549-0788
WOMEN'S AMERICAN ORT,INC.-PACIFIC NORTHWEST 75 SOUTHGATE AVENUE, SUITE 10	DALY CITY	**CA**	94015	(415) 994-2002
AIDES TO GATEWAYS HOSPITAL 1891 EFFIE STREET	LOS ANGELES	**CA**	90026	(213) 666-0171
AMERICAN MIZRACHI WOMEN 6505 WILSHIRE BOULEVARD, SUITE 405	LOS ANGELES	**CA**	90048	(213) 653-6606
AMERICAN SOCIETY FOR TECHNION-WOMEN'S DIVISION 8170 BEVERLY BOULEVARD, SUITE 108	LOS ANGELES	**CA**	90048	(213) 651-3321
B'NAI B'RITH WOMEN 6399 WILSHIRE BOULEVARD, SUITE 706	LOS ANGELES	**CA**	90048	(213) 651-4924
BRANDEIS UNIV. NAT'L WOMEN'S CMTEE.C/O JFC WOMEN'S CONF. 6505 WILSHIRE BOULEVARD, SUITE 1002	LOS ANGELES	**CA**	90048	(213) 852-1234
BUILDERS OF SCOPUS 8665 WILSHIRE BOULEVARD	LOS ANGELES	**CA**	90211	(213) 657-6511
CEDARS-SINAI MEDICAL CENTER 8700 BEVERLY BOULEVARD	LOS ANGELES	**CA**	90048	(213) 855-3674
EMMA LAZARUS JEWISH WOMEN'S CLUBS 7213 BEVERLY BOULEVARD	LOS ANGELES	**CA**	90036	(213) 934-4866
GATEWAYS ASSOCIATES 1891 EFFIE STREET	LOS ANGELES	**CA**	90026	(213) 666-0171
HADASSAH 6505 WILSHIRE BOULEVARD	LOS ANGELES	**CA**	90048	(213) 653-9727
IDA MAYER CUMMINGS AUXILIARY-LA JEWISH HOMES FOR THE AGING 6505 WILSHIRE BOULEVARD	LOS ANGELES	**CA**	90048	(213) 658-7145
JEWISH CENTERS ASSOCIATES 5870 WEST OLYMPIC BOULEVARD	LOS ANGELES	**CA**	90036	(213) 938-2531
JEWISH PROFESSIONAL WOMEN'S CLUB, C/O WOMEN'S CONF. OF JFC 6505 WILSHIRE BOULEVARD, SUITE 1002	LOS ANGELES	**CA**	90048	(213) 852-1234
JEWISH WAR VETERAN'S WOMEN'S AUXILIARY 6505 WILSHIRE BOULEVARD, SUITE 401	LOS ANGELES	**CA**	90048	(213) 655-4752
LOS ANGELES LADIES BIKUR CHOLIM SOCIETY	LOS ANGELES	**CA**		(213) 655-7891
LOS ANGELES MIKVAH SOCIETY 9548 WEST PICO BOULEVARD	LOS ANGELES	**CA**	90035	(213) 550-9124
NASHEI CHABAD 741 GAYLEY AVENUE	LOS ANGELES	**CA**	90024	(213) 208-7511
NATIONAL COUNCIL OF JEWISH WOMEN 543 NORTH FAIRFAX AVENUE	LOS ANGELES	**CA**	90036	(213) 651-2930
NITZAN CHAPTER FOR YOUNG CAREER WOMEN 1494 S. ROBERTSON BLVD.	LOS ANGELES	**CA**	90035	(213) 275-5345
ON GUARD 6505 WILSHIRE BOULEVARD, SUITE 315	LOS ANGELES	**CA**	90048	(213) 655-7071
PIONEER WOMEN-NA'AMAT 5820 WILSHIRE BLVD.	LOS ANGELES	**CA**	90036	(213) 275-5345
PIONEER WOMEN-NA'AMAT 1494 S. ROBERTSON BLVD	LOS ANGELES	**CA**	90035	(213) 275-5345
THE WOMEN OF BRANDEIS-BARDIN PO BOX 24B89	LOS ANGELES	**CA**	90024	(213) 348-7201
UNION OF ORTHODOX HEBREW CONGREGATIONS OF AMERICA-WOMEN'S BR 7269 BEVERLY BOULEVARD	LOS ANGELES	**CA**	90036	(213) 857-1206
UNITED ORDER OF TRUE SISTERS 977 SOUTH WESTERN AVENUE	LOS ANGELES	**CA**	90029	(213) 737-9854
UNIVERSITY WOMEN 15600 MULHOLLAND DRIVE	LOS ANGELES	**CA**	90077	(213) 476-9777
VISTA DEL MAR ASSOCIATES/JUNIOR ASSOCIATES 3200 MOTOR AVENUE	LOS ANGELES	**CA**	90034	(213) 826-1223
WOMEN FOR BAR ILAN 6505 WILSHIRE BOULEVARD, SUITE 402	LOS ANGELES	**CA**	90048	(213) 658-6668
WOMEN'S AMERICAN ORT, INC.-PACIFIC SOUTHWEST 6505 WILSHIRE BOULEVARD, SUITE 512	LOS ANGELES	**CA**	90036	(213) 655-2911
WOMEN'S CONFERENCE OF JFC 6505 WILSHIRE BOULEVARD, SUITE 1002	LOS ANGELES	**CA**	90048	(213) 852-1234
WOMEN'S DIVISION OF AMERICAN JEWISH CONGRESS 6505 WILSHIRE BOULEVARD, SUITE 1102	LOS ANGELES	**CA**	90048	(213) 651-4601
WOMEN'S DIVISION-UNITED JEWISH WELFARE FUND 6505 WILSHIRE BOULEVARD, SUITE 1002	LOS ANGELES	**CA**	90048	(213) 852-1234
WOMEN'S LEAGUE FOR CONSERVATIVE JUDAISM 15600 MULHOLLAND DRIVE	LOS ANGELES	**CA**	90024	(213) 476-9777
NATIONAL FEDERATION OF TEMPLE SISTERHOODS 13107 VENTURA BOULEVARD	NORTH HOLLYWOOD	**CA**	91604	(718) 986-5720
VALLEY MIKVAH SOCIETY 12800 CHANDLER BOULEVARD	NORTH HOLLYWOOD	**CA**	91607	(718) 506-0996
WESTERN FEDERATION OF TEMPLE SISTERHOODS 13107 VENTURA BLVD	NORTH HOLLYWOOD	**CA**	91604	(718) 872-3550
WOMEN'S INSTITUTE FOR CONTINUING JEWISH EDUCATION 4079 54TH STREET	SAN DIEGO	**CA**	92105	
PIONEER WOMEN BRACHA CLUB 3240 GEARY BLVD	SAN FRANCISCO	**CA**	94118	(415) 387-3077
WOMEN'S CAMPAIGN FOR SOVIET JEWRY-35'S 111 SANTA MONICA BOULEVARD	SANTA MONICA	**CA**	90401	(213) 393-6751
PIONEER WOMEN-NA'AMAT 13609 VICTORY BLVD	VAN NUYS	**CA**	91401	(718) 780-4165
B'NAI B'RITH WOMEN 1640 RHODE ISLAND AVENUE N.W.	WASHINGTON	**DC**	20036	(202) 857-6600
NAT'L LADIES AUXILIARY JEWISH WAR VETERANS OF THE USA, INC. 1712 NEW HAMPSHIRE AVENUE N.W.	WASHINGTON	**DC**	20009	(202) 667-9061
NATIONAL COUNCIL OF JEWISH WOMEN, INC.-EA.PA.-DE-MD-VA-NC-DC 1346 CONNECTICUT AVENUE, NW	WASHINGTON	**DC**	20036	(202) 785-0222
WOMEN'S AMERICAN ORT, INC.-DISTRICT 6/SOUTHEAST FLORIDA 2101 E. HALLANDALE BEACH BOULEVARD, SUITE 301	HALLANDALE	**FL**	33009	(305) 458-1557
PIONEER WOMEN-NA'AMAT 1303 N. STATE ROAD 7	MARGATE	**FL**	33063	(305) 979-3311
NATIONAL COUNCIL OF JEWISH WOMEN, INC.-SOUTHERN DISTRICT 5220 BISCAYNE BOULEVARD, #202	MIAMI	**FL**	33137	(305) 757-1305
MIZRACHI WOMEN'S ORGANIZATION 420 LINCOLN ROAD, SUITE 402	MIAMI BEACH	**FL**	33139	(305) 531-7996
PIONEER WOMEN-NA'AMAT 605 LINCOLN ROAD	MIAMI BEACH	**FL**	33139	(305) 538-6213
WOMEN'S LEAGUE FOR ISRAEL, INC 5975 W. SUNRISE BLVD	SUNRISE	**FL**	33313	(305) 791-4840
AMERICAN MIZRACHI WOMEN 3018 W. DEVON AVENUE	CHICAGO	**IL**	60659	(312) 973-0688
CONFERENCE OF JEWISH WOMEN'S ORGANIZATIONS 2840 WEST COYLE	CHICAGO	**IL**	60645	(312) 764-5636
EMMA LAZARUS JEWISH WOMEN'S CLUBS 1673 W. PRATT BLVD	CHICAGO	**IL**	60626	(312) 761-1336
NATIONAL COUNCIL OF JEWISH WOMEN, INC.-CENTRAL DIST.-MIDWEST 53 WEST JACKSON, SUITE 724	CHICAGO	**IL**	60604	(312) 965-5156
PIONEER WOMEN-NA'AMAT 220 S. STATE STREET	CHICAGO	**IL**	60604	(312) 922-3736
WOMEN'S AMERICAN ORT,INC.-DISTRICT 8/MIDWEST 111 N. WABASH-GARLAND BUILDING, SUITE 1205	CHICAGO	**IL**	60602	(312) 726-6466
PIONEER WOMEN-NA'AMAT 466 CENTRAL AVENUE	NORTHFIELD	**IL**	60093	(312) 446-7275
PIONEER WOMEN-NA'AMAT 294 WASHINGTON STREET	BOSTON	**MA**	02108	(617) 426-1059
WOMEN'S AMERICAN ORT, INC.- DISTRICT 1/NEW ENGLAND 990 WASHINGTON STREET	DEDHAM	**MA**	02026	(617) 329-6693
NATIONAL COUNCIL OF JEWISH WOMEN, INC.-UPSTATE NY & N. ENG. 950 BOYLSTON STREET	NEWTON HIGHLANDS	**MA**	02161	(617) 244-8000
BRANDEIS UNIVERSITY NATIONAL WOMEN'S COMMITTEE BRANDEIS UNIVERSITY	WALTHAM	**MA**	02254	(617) 647-2194
PIONEER WOMEN-NA'AMAT 1727 MAIN STREET	WINNIPEG	**MB**	R2V 1Z4	(204) 334-3637
PIONEER WOMEN-NA'AMAT 6810 PARK HEIGHTS	BALTIMORE	**MD**	21215	(301) 358-3337
PIONEER WOMEN-NA'AMAT OHR KODESH SYNAGOGUE, 8402 FREYMAN DRIVE	CHEVY CHASE	**MD**	20815	(301) 565-3130
AMERICAN MIZRACHI WOMEN-SARAH RIBAKOW CHAPTER 8415 ALLENSWOOD ROAD	RANDALLSTOWN	**MD**	21133	(301) 655-4141
PIONEER WOMEN-NA'AMAT 25900 GREENFIELD, ROOM 205D	OAK PARK	**MI**	48237	(313) 967-4750
BAIS CHANA WOMEN'S INSTITUTE 15 MONTCALM COURT	ST. PAUL	**MN**	55116	(612) 698-3858
PIONEER WOMEN-NA'AMAT 8123 DELMAR BLVD	ST. LOUIS	**MO**	63130	(314) 721-5856
MIZRACHI WOMEN'S ORGANIZATION OF AMERICA 615 NYE AVENUE	IRVINGTON	**NJ**	07111	(201) 399-1127
WOMEN'S AMERICAN ORT, INC.-DISTRICT 3/NEW JERSEY 1767 MORRIS AVENUE	UNION	**NJ**	07083	(201) 686-4660
HADASSAH-THE WOMEN'S ZIONIST ORG. OF AMERICA: BRONX CHAPTER 2534 MARION AVENUE	BRONX	**NY**	10458	(212) 654-8800
AGUDAS NSHEI UB'NOS CHABAD 770 EASTERN PARKWAY	BROOKLYN	**NY**	11213	(718) 493-9250
LADIES HEBREW BENEVOLENT SOCIETY 285 SCHERMERHORN STREET	BROOKLYN	**NY**	11217	(718) 875-7753
LUBAVITCH WOMEN'S COOKBOOK 852 EASTERN PARKWAY	BROOKLYN	**NY**	11213	(718) 604-2785
LUBAVITCH WOMEN'S ORGANIZATION 770 EASTERN PARKWAY	BROOKLYN	**NY**	11213	(718) 493-0571
N'SHEI AHAVAS CHESED 1680 47TH STREET	BROOKLYN	**NY**	11204	(718) 438-0211
PIONEER WOMEN-NA'AMAT 3858 NOSTRAND AVENUE	BROOKLYN	**NY**	11229	(718) 769-9604
PIONEER WOMEN-NA'AMAT 1931 MOTT AVENUE	FAR ROCKAWAY	**NY**	11691	(718) 471-8453
PIONEER WOMEN-NA'AMAT 45 CONKLIN STREET	FARMINGDALE	**NY**	11735	(516) 735-2675
U.S./ISRAEL WOMEN-TO-WOMEN AND COALITION FOR WOMEN IN ISRAEL 35-24 78TH STREET, APT. B-39	JACKSON HEIGHTS	**NY**	11372	
AMIT WOMEN 817 BROADWAY	NEW YORK	**NY**	10003	(212) 477-4720
AMERICAN MIZRACHI WOMEN - AMIT 817 BROADWAY	NEW YORK	**NY**	10003	(212) 477-4720
B'NAI B'RITH - WOMEN EMPIRE REGION 823 U.N. PLAZA	NEW YORK	**NY**	10017	(212) 599-2123
BRANDEIS UNIVERSITY NATIONAL WOMEN'S COMMITTEE 215 EAST 68TH STREET	NEW YORK	**NY**	10021	(212) 249-4827
EMUNAH WOMEN OF AMERICA 370 SEVENTH AVENUE, SUITE 11N	NEW YORK	**NY**	10001	(212) 564-9045
FEDERATION OF JEWISH WOMEN'S ORGANIZATIONS, INC. 415 LEXINGTON AVENUE	NEW YORK	**NY**	10017	(212) 661-8090
HADASSAH 50 WEST 58TH STREET	NEW YORK	**NY**	10022	(212) 355-7900
HADASSAH-THE WOMEN'S ZIONIST ORG. OF AMERICA: N.Y.CHAPTER 250 W. 57TH STREET	NEW YORK	**NY**	10107	(212) 765-7050
HAPOEL HAMIZRACHI WOMEN'S ZIONIST ORGANIZATION 370 SEVENTH AVENUE	NEW YORK	**NY**	10001	(212) 564-9045
INTERNATIONAL COUNCIL OF JEWISH WOMEN 15 E. 26TH STREET	NEW YORK	**NY**	10010	(212) 532-1740
JEWISH FOUNDATION FOR EDUCATION OF WOMEN 120 W. 57TH STREET	NEW YORK	**NY**	10019	(212) 265-2565
JEWISH WOMEN'S CLUB 234 W. 78TH STREET	NEW YORK	**NY**	10024	(212) 799-1520
JEWISH WOMEN'S RESOURCE CENTER, 92ND STREET YM/YWHA LIBRARY 1395 LEXINGTON AVENUE	NEW YORK	**NY**	10028	
JEWISH WOMENS SOCIAL SERVICE FOR ISRAEL 265 RIVERSIDE DRIVE	NEW YORK	**NY**	10025	(212) 666-7880
LEADERSHIP CONFERENCE OF NAT'L JEWISH WOMEN'S ORGANIZATIONS 838 FIFTH AVENUE	NEW YORK	**NY**	10021	(212) 249-0100
LEADERSHIP CONFERENCE-JEWISH WOMEN'S ORGANIZATIONS 15 E. 84TH STREET	NEW YORK	**NY**	10028	
LILITH MAGAZINE 250 W. 57TH STREET	NEW YORK	**NY**	10019	(212) 757-0818
MIZRACHI WOMEN'S ORGANIZATION 817 BROADWAY	NEW YORK	**NY**	10003	(212) 477-4720
NAT'L COUNCIL OF JEWISH WOMEN, INC. 15 E. 26TH STREET	NEW YORK	**NY**	10010	(212) 532-1740
NAT'L COUNCIL OF JEWISH WOMEN-COUNCIL THRIFT SHOP 842 9TH AVENUE	NEW YORK	**NY**	10019	(212) 535-5900
NAT'L COUNCIL OF JEWISH WOMEN-COUNCIL WKSHOP/SENIOR CITIZENS 915 BROADWAY	NEW YORK	**NY**	10010	(212) 674-8010
NAT'L COUNCIL OF JEWISH WOMEN-KATHERINE ENGEL CENTER 241 WEST 72ND STREET	NEW YORK	**NY**	10023	(212) 799-7205
NAT'L COUNCIL OF JEWISH WOMEN-N.Y.SECTION 241 WEST 72ND STREET	NEW YORK	**NY**	10023	(212) 535-5900
NATIONAL BUREAU OF FEDERATED JEWISH WOMEN'S ORGANIZATIONS 55 W. 42ND STREET	NEW YORK	**NY**	10036	(212) 736-0240
NATIONAL COUNCIL OF JEWISH WOMEN 15 EAST 26TH STREET	NEW YORK	**NY**	10010	(212) 532-1740
NATIONAL COUNCIL OF JEWISH WOMEN, INC.-MIDDLE ATLANTIC, NJ 15 EAST 26TH STREET	NEW YORK	**NY**	10010	(212) 532-1740
NATIONAL COUNCIL OF JEWISH WOMEN, INC.-NORTHERN DISTRICT 15 EAST 26TH STREET	NEW YORK	**NY**	10010	(212) 532-1740
NATIONAL FEDERATION OF TEMPLE SISTERHOODS 838 FIFTH AVENUE	NEW YORK	**NY**	10021	(212) 249-0100
NATIONAL JEWISH WELFARE BOARD-WOMEN'S ORGANIZATIONAL SVCS. 15 E. 26TH STREET	NEW YORK	**NY**	10010	(212) 539-4949
NEW YORK STATE FOUNDATION OF TEMPLE SISTERHOODS 838 FIFTH AVENUE	NEW YORK	**NY**	10010	(212) 249-0100
PAOLE AGUDATH ISRAEL OF AMERICA 156 FIFTH AVENUE	NEW YORK	**NY**	10010	(212) 924-9475
PIONEER WOMEN-NA'AMAT 200 MADISON AVENUE	NEW YORK	**NY**	10016	(212) 725-8010
U.S./ISRAEL WOMEN-TO-WOMEN 4 SNIFFEN COURT, 156 E. 36TH STREET	NEW YORK	**NY**	10016	
UNION OF ORTHODOX JEWISH CONGREGATIONS-WOMEN'S BRANCH 45 W. 36TH STREET	NEW YORK	**NY**	10018	(212) 563-4000
UNITED ORDER OF TRUE SISTERS 150 WEST 85TH STREET	NEW YORK	**NY**	10024	(212) 362-2502
WOMEN'S AMERICAN ORT, INC. 315 PARK AVENUE SOUTH	NEW YORK	**NY**	10010	(212) 505-7700
WOMEN'S AMERICAN ORT, INC.-DISTRICT 2/NY STATE 254 WEST 31ST STREET 10TH FLOOR	NEW YORK	**NY**	10001	(212) 695-1772
WOMEN'S DIVISION OF AMERICAN JEWISH CONGRESS 15 EAST 84TH STREET	NEW YORK	**NY**	10028	(212) 879-4500

WOMEN'S DIVISION OF JEWISH LABOR COMMITTEE
25 EAST 78TH STREET ... NEW YORK **NY** 10021 (212) 535-3700
WOMEN'S DIVISION OF UNITED JEWISH APPEAL
130 EAST 59TH STREET ... NEW YORK **NY** 10022 (212) 980-1000
WOMEN'S DIVISION, COUNCIL OF JEWISH FED. & WELFARE FUNDS
575 LEXINGTON AVENUE ... NEW YORK **NY** 10022 (212) 751-1311
WOMEN'S DIVISION, UNITED JEWISH APPEAL
1290 AVENUE OF THE AMERICAS ... NEW YORK **NY** 10019 (212) 757-1500
WOMEN'S LEAGUE FOR CONSERVATIVE JUDAISM 48 E. 74TH STREET ... NEW YORK **NY** 10021 (212) 628-1600
WOMEN'S LEAGUE FOR ISRAEL 515 PARK AVENUE ... NEW YORK **NY** 10022 (212) 838-1997
WOMEN'S LEAGUE FOR ISRAEL, INC. 1860 BROADWAY ... NEW YORK **NY** 10023 (212) 245-8742
WOMEN'S ORGANIZATION OF HAPOEL HAMIZRACHI
370 SEVENTH AVENUE ... NEW YORK **NY** 10001 (212) 564-9045
WOMEN'S ORGANIZATION OF YESHIVA UNIVERSITY 55 FIFTH AVENUE ... NEW YORK **NY** 10003 (212) 790-0371
WOMEN'S SOCIAL SERVICE FOR ISRAEL 240 W. 98TH STREET ... NEW YORK **NY** 10025 (212) 666-7880
AMERICAN MIZRACHI WOMEN 2260 WARRENSVILLE CENTER ROAD ... CLEVELAND **OH** 44118 (216) 932-8656
DAUGHTERS BIKUR CHOLIM 1585 MALLARD DRIVE ... CLEVELAND **OH** (216) 449-6301
MIZRACHI WOMEN'S ORGANIZATIONS 4170 BAYARD ROAD ... CLEVELAND **OH** 44121 (216) 291-3108
NATIONAL COUNCIL OF JEWISH WOMEN - CLEVELAND SECTION
3535 LEE ROAD ... CLEVELAND **OH** 44120 (216) 283-1500
PIONEER WOMEN-NA'AMAT 13969 CEDAR ROAD, ROOM 208 ... CLEVELAND **OH** 44418 (216) 321-2002
WOMEN'S AMERICAN ORT, INC.-DISTRICT 7/MI, OH, W.PA., NW NY
SHAKER BLDG. 3645 WARRENSVILLE CENTER ROAD ... SHAKER HEIGHTS **OH** 44122 (216) 921-0228
PIONEER WOMEN-NA'AMAT 272 CODSELL AVENUE ... DOWNSVIEW **ON** M3H3X2 (416) 636-5425
HERUT WOMEN 3417 BATHURST STREET ... TORONTO **ON**
AMERICAN MIZRACHI WOMEN 1015 CHESTNUT STREET ... PHILADELPHIA **PA** 19107 (215) 925-8550
PIONEER WOMEN-NA'AMAT 1405 LOCUST STREET, ROOM 1117 ... PHILADELPHIA **PA** 19102 (215) 545-1328
WOMEN'S AMERICAN ORT, INC.-DISTRICT 4/PA, VA, DC, MD, DE
1405 LOCUST STREET, SUITE 300 ... PHILADELPHIA **PA** 19102 (215) 546-8888
PIONEER WOMEN-NA'AMAT 6328 FORBES AVENUE ... PITTSBURGH **PA** 15217 (412) 521-5253
HERUT WOMEN 5234 CLANRANALD AVENUE ... MONTREAL **QU** H3X 2S4
PIONEER WOMEN-NA'AMAT 4770 KENT AVENUE, SUITE 304 ... MONTREAL **QU** H3W 1H2 (514) 735-6253
WOMEN'S AMERICAN ORT, INC.-DISTRICT 9
4740 INGERSOLL SE GEN. BUILDING, SUITE 100 ... HOUSTON **TX** 77027 (713) 961-3759
HEBREW LADIES CHARITY SOCIETY 1321 NOBLE STREET ... NORFOLK **VA** 23518
PHILANTHROPIC FOCUS, INC.-CONSULTANTS IN CHARITABLE GIVING
10701 WEST NORTH AVENUE ... MILWAUKEE **WI** 53226 (414) 453-8282
SECOND SEX PUBLISHING COMPANY, THE 55 RECHOV SHENKIN ... GIVATAYIM **IS** 53298
KOL HAISHAH - THE WOMAN'S VOICE 4 HAHISTADRUT STREET ... JERUSALEM **IS** 94320 (022) 439-71
NATIONAL COUNCIL OF JEWISH WOMEN, INC.-ISRAEL OFFICE
NJCW RESEARCH INSTITUTE HEBREW UNIVERSITY-MT. SCOPUS ... JERUSALEM **IS**
NOGA P.O. BOX 21376 ... TEL AVIV **IS**

YESHIVOT

JEWISH LEARNING EXCHANGE
5322 WILSHIRE BLVD., SUITE 230 P.O. BOX 36B05 ... LOS ANGELES **CA** 90036 (213) 857-0923
KOLLEL OF LOS ANGELES 314 N. GARDNER STREET ... LOS ANGELES **CA** 90036 (213) 655-2631
WEST COAST TALMUDICAL SEMINARY (YESHIVA OHR ELCHONON CHABAD)
7215 WARING AVENUE ... LOS ANGELES **CA** 90046 (213) 937-3763
YESHIVA GEDOLAH OF LOS ANGELES 5822 WEST THIRD ... LOS ANGELES **CA** 90036 (213) 938-2071
BETH MIDRASH KETER TORAH 1898 MERIDIAN AVENUE, APT 42 ... SAN JOSE **CA** 95125
YESHIVAT & MIDRASHA KEREM 250 HOWARD DRIVE ... SANTA CLARA **CA** 95051 (408) 247-1722
TALMUDIC RESEARCH INSTITUTE 4634 W. 14TH AVENUE ... DENVER **CO** 80204 (303) 623-8466
YESHIVA TORAS CHAIM 1400 QUITMAN STREET ... DENVER **CO** 80204 (303) 629-9746
GIBORIM RABBINICAL SEMINARY 29 FAIRFIELD BOARD ... ENFIELD **CT** 06082
TALMUDIC UNIVERSITY OF FLORIDA 4014 CHASE AVENUE ... MIAMI BEACH **FL** 33140 (305) 534-7050
YESHIVAS BRISK 9000 FORESTVIEW ROAD ... SKOKIE **IL** 60203 (312) 674-4652
LUBAVITCH YESHIVA 9 PRESCOT STREET ... BROOKLINE **MA** 02146 (617) 731-5330
TORAH INSTITUTE OF NEW ENGLAND 1710 BEACON STREET ... BROOKLINE **MA** 02146 (617) 734-5100
YESHIVAT OHR YISROEL 1730 BEACON STREET ... BROOKLINE **MA** 02146 (617) 731-5720
NER ISRAEL RABBINICAL COLLEGE 400 MT. WILSON LANE ... BALTIMORE **MD** 21208 (301) 484-7200
TALMUDICAL ACADEMY OF BALTIMORE, THE
4445 OLD COURT ROAD ... BALTIMORE **MD** 21208 (301) 484-6600
YESHIVAH KOLLEL 17266 HILTON ... SOUTHFIELD **MI** 48075
ST. LOUIS RABBINICAL COLLEGE 7400 OLIVE ... ST. LOUIS **MO** 63130
YESHIVATH RABBI ZACHARIA JOSEPH 1236 NORTH & SOUTH ROADS ... ST. LOUIS **MO** 63130
BETH MEDRASH GOVOHA OF AMERICA 617 6TH STREET ... LAKEWOOD **NJ** 08701 (201) 367-1060
RABBINICAL COLLEGE OF AMERICA 226 SUSSEX AVENUE ... MORRISTOWN **NJ** 07960 (201) 267-9404
RABBINICAL COLLEGE OF QUEENS
141-20 GRAND CENTRAL PARKWAY ... BRIARWOOD **NY** 11435 (212) 291-1336
BEER SHMUEL TALMUDICAL ACADEMY 1363 59TH STREET ... BROOKLYN **NY** 11219
BELZER YESHIVA MACHZIKEI TORAH SEMINARY
632 BEDFORD AVENUE ... BROOKLYN **NY** 11211
BETH HAMEDRASH SHAAREI YOSHER INSTITUTE
4102-10 16TH AVENUE ... BROOKLYN **NY** 11204
BETH HAMEDRASH TORAS CHEMED NITRA 1462 50TH STREET ... BROOKLYN **NY** 11219 (718) 871-9847
BETH HAMEDRASH YAAKOV MOSHE MOSAD BNEI TORAH
4722 18TH AVENUE ... BROOKLYN **NY** 11204
BETH HATALMUD 2127 82ND STREET ... BROOKLYN **NY** 11214 (718) 259-2525
BETH MEDRASH & YESHIVA EMEK HALACHA 1763 63RD STREET ... BROOKLYN **NY** 11204 (718) 232-1600
BETH MEDRASH GOVOHA 314 MCDONALD AVENUE ... BROOKLYN **NY** 11218 (718) 638-8300
BNAI TORAH INSTITUTE 4722 18TH AVENUE ... BROOKLYN **NY** 11204
CENTRAL YESHIVA BETH JOSEPH RABBINICAL SEMINARY
1427 49TH STREET ... BROOKLYN **NY** 11219 (718) 436-7591
CENTRAL YESHIVA TOMCHEI TMIMIM LUBAVITCH
841-53 OCEAN PARKWAY ... BROOKLYN **NY** 11230 (718) 859-7600
EDUCATION INSTITUTE OHOLEI TORAH 667 EASTERN PARKWAY ... BROOKLYN **NY** 11213 (718) 778-3340
HADAR HATORAH RABBINICAL SEMINARY 824 EASTERN PARKWAY ... BROOKLYN **NY** 11213
ISRAEL TORAH RESEARCH INSTITUTE 1712 43RD STREET ... BROOKLYN **NY** 11204
KEHILATH YAKOV RABBINICAL SEMINARY 638 BEDFORD AVENUE ... BROOKLYN **NY** 11211
KOL ARYEH RESEARCH INSTITUTE 1642 54TH STREET ... BROOKLYN **NY** 11204 (718) 871-7442
KOLEL MAREI YECHESKEL & YESHIVA MAGLEI ZEDEK
1223 45TH STREET ... BROOKLYN **NY** 11219 (718) 436-0239
KOLLEL BAIS TORAH 1636 49TH STREET ... BROOKLYN **NY** 11204
KOLLEL NACHLAS YISROEL MOSHE 25 CHURCH AVENUE ... BROOKLYN **NY** 11218
MECHON HAHOYROA 4533 16 AVENUE ... BROOKLYN **NY** 11204 (718) 438-2100
MESIVTA EASTERN PARKWAY RABBINICAL SEMINARY
418 EAST 45TH STREET ... BROOKLYN **NY** 11203
MESIVTA TORAH VODAATH SEMINARY 425 EAST 9TH STREET ... BROOKLYN **NY** 11218 (718) 941-8000
MESIVTA YESHIVA RABBI CHAIM BERLIN RABBINICAL ACADEMY
1571 CONEY ISLAND AVENUE ... BROOKLYN **NY** 11230 (718) 377-9184
MIRRER YESHIVA CENTRAL INSTITUTE 1791-5 OCEAN PARKWAY ... BROOKLYN **NY** 11223 (718) 645-0536
OHR TORAH 239 HAVEMEYER STREET ... BROOKLYN **NY** 11211 (718) 387-9749
RABBINICAL ASSEMBLY COLLEGE, THE
48TH STREET AT SEVENTH AVENUE ... BROOKLYN **NY** 11220 (718) 633-6378
RABBINICAL COLLEGE CHSAN SOFER NEW YORK 1876 50TH STREET ... BROOKLYN **NY** 11204
RABBINICAL COLLEGE OF KAMENITZ YESHIVA 1315 43RD STREET ... BROOKLYN **NY** 11219
RABBINICAL SEMINARY ADAS YEREIM 185 WILSON STREET ... BROOKLYN **NY** 11211
RABBINICAL SEMINARY MIKOR CHAIM 1571 55TH STREET ... BROOKLYN **NY** 11219
RABBINICAL SEMINARY NETZACH ISRAEL
3044 CONEY ISLAND AVENUE ... BROOKLYN **NY** 11235 (718) 656-1997
RABBINICAL SEMINARY OF MUNKACS 1377 42ND STREET ... BROOKLYN **NY** 11219 (718) 438-5246
UNITED TALMUDICAL ACADEMY 500 BEDFORD AVENUE ... BROOKLYN **NY** 11211 (718) 384-9034
YAVNE HEBREW THEOLOGICAL SEMINARY 510 DAHILL ROAD ... BROOKLYN **NY** 11218 (718) 436-5610
YESHIVA BETH SHEARIM MISHNE HALACHOTH GEDOLOTH RABBIN. INST.
5306 16TH AVENUE ... BROOKLYN **NY** 11204 (718) 851-9809
YESHIVA BIRKAS REUVEN 1221 AVENUE S ... BROOKLYN **NY** 11204 (718) 375-8611
YESHIVA GEDOLA OF BORO PARK 1456 46TH STREET ... BROOKLYN **NY** 11219
YESHIVA TORAH VODAATH OF FLATBUSH 425 E. 9TH STREET ... BROOKLYN **NY** 11219 (718) 941-8000
YESHIVA TORAS YISROEL & RABBINICAL SEMINARY
5311 NEW UTRECHT AVENUE ... BROOKLYN **NY** 11219 (718) 633-5306
YESHIVA OF NITRA RABBINICAL COLLEGE 194 DIVISION AVENUE ... BROOKLYN **NY** 11211 (718) 384-5460
YESHIVAH SHAAREI TORAH RABBINICAL INSTITUTE
1164 E. 12TH STREET ... BROOKLYN **NY** 11230 (718) 377-9005
YESHIVAS HAMATMONIM 4320 16TH AVENUE ... BROOKLYN **NY** 11204 (718) 252-5524
YESHIVAT TORAH VODAATH & MESIVTA RABBINICAL SEMINARY
425 E. 9TH STREET ... BROOKLYN **NY** 11218 (718) 941-8000
DERECH AYSON RABBINICAL SEMINARY 802 HICKSVILLE ROAD ... FAR ROCKAWAY **NY** 11691 (718) 327-7600
SH'OR YOSHUV RABBINICAL COLLEGE-INSTITUTE FOR JEWISH STUDIES
1526 CENTRAL AVENUE ... FAR ROCKAWAY **NY** 11691 (718) 327-2048
PNIMIM TEACHERS COLLEGE ... FERNDALE **NY** 12734
YESHIVA CHOFETZ CHAIM 68-54 KESSEL STREET ... FLUSHING **NY** 11375 (718) 263-1445
OHR TORAH INSTITUTE 66-35 108 STREET ... FOREST HILLS **NY** 11375 (718) 268-3444
RABBINICAL SEMINARY OF AMERICA 92-15 69TH AVENUE ... FOREST HILLS **NY** 11375 (718) 268-4700
RABBINICAL COLLEGE OF QUEENS 141-20 GRAND CENTRAL PARKWAY ... JAMAICA **NY** 11435 (718) 291-1335
BETH MEDRASH EEYON HATALMUD 216 VIOLA ROAD ... MONSEY **NY** 10952 (914) 352-9837
BETH MEDROSH ELYON 73 MAIN STREET ... MONSEY **NY** 10952 (914) 356-9711
JEWISH LEARNING EXCHANGE 142 ROUTE 306, PO BOX 462 ... MONSEY **NY** 10952 (914) 352-7600
OHR SOMAYACH/CENTRAL CAMPUS 142 ROUTE 306, PO BOX 344 ... MONSEY **NY** 10952 (914) 425-1370
RABBINICAL COLLEGE BETH SHRAGA 30 SADDLE RIVER ROAD ... MONSEY **NY** 10952 (914) 578-9623
YESHIVA FARM SETTLEMENT - NITRA YESHIVA
PINES BRIDGE ROAD ... MOUNT KISCO **NY** 10549 (914) 666-9705
OHR HAMEIR THEOLOGICAL SEMINARY 3 BOULEVARD ... NEW ROCHELLE **NY** 10801 (914) 633-9655
ASSOCIATION OF ADVANCED RABBINICAL & TALMUDICAL SCHOOLS
175 FIFTH AVENUE ... NEW YORK **NY** 10003 (212) 477-0950
BEIT MIDRASH L'TORAH, JERUSALEM TORAH COLLEGE FOR MEN
TORAH DEPT., WORLD ZIONIST ORGANIZATION, 515 PARK AVENUE ... NEW YORK **NY** 10022 (212) 752-0600
MESIVTA TIFERETH JERUSALEM OF AMERICA 145 EAST BROADWAY ... NEW YORK **NY** 10002 (212) 964-2830
RABBI ISAAC EICHANAN THEOLOGICAL SEMINARY
2540 AMSTERDAM AVENUE ... NEW YORK **NY** 10033 (212) 960-5346
YESHIVA CHOFETZ CHAIM 346 WEST 89TH STREET ... NEW YORK **NY** 10024 (212) 362-1435
YESHIVA HAICHAL HATORAH 630 RIVERSIDE DRIVE ... NEW YORK **NY** 10031 (212) 283-6000
YESHIVA RABBI SAMSON RAPHAEL HIRSCH 85-93 BENNETT AVENUE ... NEW YORK **NY** 10033 (212) 568-6200
YESHIVA TIFERETH ISRAEL OF RIZHIN 247 EAST BROADWAY ... NEW YORK **NY** 10002 (212) 732-3660
YESHIVAT RADIN 314 WEST 100TH STREET ... NEW YORK **NY** 10025 (212) 222-4141
YESHIVA GEDOLAH ZICHRON MOSHE LAUREL PARK ROAD ... SOUTH FALLSBURG **NY** 12779 (914) 434-5240
RABBINICAL SEMINARY OF NEW SQUARE 766 N. MAIN ... SPRING VALLEY **NY** 10977 (914) 354-2237
RABBINICAL COLLEGE OF TELSHE, INC. 28400 EUCLID AVENUE ... WICKLIFFE **OH** 44092 (216) 943-5300
OHR SOMAYACH/JEP 534 LAWRENCE AVENUE WEST, SUITE 205 ... TORONTO **ON** M6A 1A2 (416) 787-1681
TALMUDICAL YESHIVA OF PHILADELPHIA 6063 DREXEL ROAD ... PHILADELPHIA **PA** 19131 (215) 477-1000
SCHOOL OF ADVANCED JEWISH STUDIES
315 SOUTH BELLEFIELD AVENUE ... PITTSBURGH **PA** 15213 (412) 681-1630
YESHIVAH ACHAI TMIMIM 2410 FIFTH AVENUE ... PITTSBURGH **PA** 15213 (412) 681-2446

YIDDISH ORGANIZATIONS

LOS ANGELES FRIENDS OF YIVO 1311 NORTH KENTER AVENUE ... LOS ANGELES **CA** 90049 (213) 472-6111
LOS ANGELES YIDDISH CULTURE CLUB 8339 WEST THIRD STREET ... LOS ANGELES **CA** 90048 (213) 934-9195
SHOLOM ALEICHEM YIDDISH CLUB
LOS ANGELES VALLEY COLLEGE ... LOS ANGELES **CA** (213) 454-4081
NORTHRIDGE YIDDISH CULTURE CLUB ... NORTHRIDGE **CA** (818) 886-7657
NATIONAL YIDDISH BOOK CENTER OLD E. ST. SCHOOL, P.O. BOX 969 ... AMHERST **MA** 01004 (413) 253-9201
SHOLEM ALEICHEM FOLK INSTITUTE, INC. 3301 BAINBRIDGE AVENUE ... BRONX **NY** 10467 (212) 881-6555
YUGNTRUF 3328 BAINBRIDGE AVENUE ... BRONX **NY** 10467 (212) 654-8540
ADELANTRE! - THE JUDEZMO SOCIETY 4594 BEDFORD AVENUE ... BROOKLYN **NY** 11235
AMERICAN ASSOCIATION OF PROFESSORS OF YIDDISH
QUEENS COLLEGE KILEY 802 ... FLUSHING **NY** 11367 (718) 520-7067
B'NAI YIDDISH SOCIETY 41 UNION SQUARE ... NEW YORK **NY** 10003 (212) 989-3162

CENTRAL YIDDISH CULTURE ORGANIZATION (CYCO)
25 EAST 78TH STREET ... NEW YORK **NY** 10021 (212) 535-4320
COMM. FOR THE IMPLEMENTATION/STANDARDIZED YIDD. ORTHOGRAPHY
PHILOSOPHY HALL, COLUMBIA UNIV., ROOM 406 ... NEW YORK **NY** 10027
CONGRESS FOR JEWISH CULTURE 25 EAST 21 STREET ... NEW YORK **NY** 10010 (212) 505-8040
LEAGUE FOR YIDDISH, INC. 200 W. 72ND STREET, SUITE 40 ... NEW YORK **NY** 10023 (212) 787-6675
MAX WEINREICH CENTER FOR ADVANCED STUDIES
1048 FIFTH AVENUE ... NEW YORK **NY** 10028 (212) 535-6700
WORKMEN'S CIRCLE 45 EAST 33RD STREET ... NEW YORK **NY** 10016 (212) 889-6800
YIVO INSTITUTE FOR JEWISH RESEARCH 1048 FIFTH AVENUE ... NEW YORK **NY** 10028 (212) 535-6700
YIDDISHE SHPRAKH 1048 FIFTH AVENUE ... NEW YORK **NY** 10028 (212) 535-6700
YIDDISHER KULTUR FARBAND 853 BROADWAY, #2121 ... NEW YORK **NY** 10003 (212) 673-4631
YIDDISHER KULTUR FARBAND 853 BROADWAY ... NEW YORK **NY** 10003 (212) 228-1955
YIDDISHER KULTUR FARBAND-YKUF 1123 BROADWAY ... NEW YORK **NY** 10010 (212) 691-0708
YIVO INSTITUTE FOR JEWISH RESEARCH 1048 FIFTH AVENUE ... NEW YORK **NY** 10028 (212) 535-6700

ZIONIST ORGANIZATIONS

PIONEER WOMEN-NA'AMAT 1-703 56TH AVENUE S.W. ... CALGARY **AT** T2V 0G9 (403) 253-9060
CANADIAN ZIONIST FEDERATION-WESTERN, THE
7200-156TH STREET ... EDMONTON **AT** T5N 3R4 (403) 487-0901
CANADIAN ZIONIST FEDERATION-PACIFIC, THE
950 WEST 41ST AVENUE ... VANCOUVER **BC** V5Z 2N7 (604) 266-5366
PIONEER WOMEN-NA'AMAT 950 WEST 41ST STREET, ROOM G ... VANCOUVER **BC** V5Z 2N7 (604) 266-8308
AMERICAN ZIONIST FEDERATION 6505 WILSHIRE BOULEVARD ... LOS ANGELES **CA** 90048 (213) 655-4636
AMERICAN ZIONIST YOUTH FOUNDATION
6505 WILSHIRE BOULEVARD ... LOS ANGEES **CA** 90048 (213) 655-9828
AMERICAN ZIONIST YOUTH FOUNDATION - WEST COAST REGION
6505 WILSHIRE BLVD ... LOS ANGELES **CA** 90048 (213) 655-4636
AMERICANS FOR PROGRESSIVE ISRAEL
319 NORTH ORANGE DRIVE ... LOS ANGELES **CA** 90036 (213) 933-5358
ASSOCIATION OF PARENTS OF AMERICAN ISRAELIS
1706 GARTH AVENUE ... LOS ANGELES **CA** 90035 (213) 870-8435
B'NAI ZION 6351 WILSHIRE BOULEVARD, SUITE 211 ... LOS ANGELES **CA** 90048 (213) 655-9128
DOR CHAPTER 6351 WILSHIRE BLVD, SUITE 211 ... LOS ANGELES **CA** 90048 (213) 655-9128
JEWISH PEACE ALLIANCE 3208 CAHUENGA BOULEVARD WEST ... LOS ANGELES **CA** 90068 (213) 828-6589
LABOR ZIONIST ALLIANCE 8339 WEST THIRD STREET ... LOS ANGELES **CA** 90048 (213) 655-2842
PIONEER WOMEN-NA'AMAT 5820 WILSHIRE BLVD ... LOS ANGELES **CA** 90036 (213) 938-9149
PIONEER WOMEN-NA'AMAT 1494 S. ROBERTSON BLVD ... LOS ANGELES **CA** 90035 (213) 275-5345
TELEM 6505 WILSHIRE BOULEVARD, SUITE 811 ... LOS ANGELES **CA** 90048 (213) 658-5021
ZIONIST ORGANIZATION OF AMERICA
5225 WILSHIRE BOULEVARD, SUITE 717 ... LOS ANGELES **CA** 90036 (213) 938-9183
PIONEER WOMEN-NA'AMAT 5511 EL CAJON BLVD., UJF BUILDING ... SAN DIEGO **CA** 92115 (619) 265-1325
ZIONIST ORGANIZATION OF AMERICA 46 KEARNY STREET ... SAN FRANCISCO **CA** 94108 (415) 391-7741
GRASP PO BOX 5433 ... SHERMAN OAKS **CA** 91403
ASSOC. OF REFORM ZIONISTS OF AMERICA - UAHC
13107 VENTURA BOULEVARD ... STUDIO CITY **CA** 91604 (213) 986-5720
PIONEER WOMEN-NA'AMAT 13609 VICTORY BLVD ... VAN NUYS **CA** 91401 (818) 780-4165
JEWISH ACTIVIST FRONT-ISRAEL INFORMATION CENTER
800 21ST STREET N.W. ROOM 417 ... WASHINGTON **DC** 20006 (202) 686-7574
PIONEER WOMEN-NA'AMAT 1303 N. STATE ROAD 7 ... MARGATE **FL** 33063 (305) 979-3311
FARBAND LABOR ZIONIST ALLIANCE 1 LINCOLN ROAD, SUITE 320 ... MIAMI BEACH **FL** 33139 (305) 532-1887
PIONEER WOMEN-NA'AMAT 605 LINCOLN ROAD ... MIAMI BEACH **FL** 33139 (305) 538-6213
CHICAGO ZIONIST FEDERATION 220 S. STATE STREET ... CHICAGO **IL** 60604 (312) 922-5282
PIONEER WOMEN-NA'AMAT 220 S. STATE STREET ... CHICAGO **IL** 60604 (312) 922-3736
ZIONIST ORGANIZATION OF CHICAGO 6328 N. CALIFORNIA AVENUE ... CHICAGO **IL** 60659 (312) 973-3232
PIONEER WOMEN-NA'AMAT 466 CENTRAL AVENUE ... NORTHFIELD **IL** 60093 (312) 446-7275
MIZRACHI-HAPOEL HAMIZRACHI OF NEW ENGLAND
611 WASHINGTON STREET ... BOSTON **MA** 02111 (617) 426-9148
NEW ENGLAND ZIONIST FEDERATION 17 COMMONWEALTH AVENUE ... BOSTON **MA** 02116 (617) 267-2235
PIONEER WOMEN-NA'AMAT 294 WASHINGTON STREET ... BOSTON **MA** 02108 (617) 426-1059
RELIGIOUS ZIONISTS OF AMERICA-N.E. REGION
611 WASHINGTON STREET, ROOM 507 ... BOSTON **MA** 02110 (617) 426-9148
ZIONIST HOUSE-ISRAEL CULTURAL CENTER
17 COMMONWEALTH AVENUE ... BOSTON **MA** 02116 (617) 267-3600
ZIONIST ORGANIZATION OF AMERICA-NEW ENGLAND REGION
17 COMMONWEALTH AVENUE ... BOSTON **MA** 02116 (617) 437-1647
HERUT-UNITED ZIONIST REVISIONISTS OF AMERICA
388 N. MAIN STREET ... SHARON **MA** 02067
CANADIAN ZIONIST FEDERATION-MIDWEST, THE
365 HARGRAVE STREET ... WINNIPEG **MB** R3B 2K3 (204) 943-6494
PIONEER WOMEN-NA'AMAT 1727 MAIN STREET ... WINNIPEG **MB** R2V 1Z4 (204) 334-3637
PIONEER WOMEN-NA'AMAT 6810 PARK HEIGHTS ... BALTIMORE **MD** 21215 (301) 358-3337
PIONEER WOMEN-NA'AMAT
OHR KODESH SYNAGOGUE, 8402 FREYMAN DRIVE ... CHEVY CHASE **MD** 20815 (301) 565-3130
AMERICAN MIZRACHI WOMEN-SARAH RIBAKOW CHAPTER
8415 ALLENSWOOD ROAD ... RANDALLSTOWN **MD** 21133 (301) 655-4141
PIONEER WOMEN-NA'AMAT 25900 GREENFIELD, ROOM 205D ... OAK PARK **MI** 48237 (313) 967-4750
DETROIT ZIONIST FEDERATION, THE 6600 W. MAPLE ROAD ... WEST BLOOMFIELD **MI** 48033 (313) 661-1000
HISTADRUT ISRAEL LABOR CAMPAIGN 4517 MINNETONKA BLVD ... MINNEAPOLIS **MN** 55416 (612) 927-4927
ZIONIST ORGANIZATION OF AMERICA 1595 HIGHLAND PARKWAY ... ST. PAUL **MN** 55116 (612) 698-3234
PIONEER WOMEN-NA'AMAT 8123 DELMAR BLVD ... ST. LOUIS **MO** 63130 (314) 721-5856
ZIONIST ORGANIZATION OF AMERICA 2816 MORRIS AVENUE ... UNION CITY **NJ** 07083 (201) 964-0100
CANADIAN ZIONIST FEDERATION-ATLANTIC, THE
5675 SPRING GARDEN ROAD ... HALIFAX **NS** B3J 1H1 (902) 422-7491
BRIT TRUMPELDOR BETAR OF AMERICA, INC.
85-40 149TH STREET ... BRIARWOOD MANOR **NY** 11435 (718) 526-3310
BETH AM-LABOR ZIONIST CENTER 1182 BRIGHTON BEACH AVENUE ... BROOKLYN **NY** 11235 (718) 646-9409
PIONEER WOMEN-NA'AMAT 3858 NOSTRAND AVENUE ... BROOKLYN **NY** 11229 (718) 769-9604
PIONEER WOMEN-NA'AMAT 1931 MOTT AVENUE ... FAR ROCKAWAY **NY** 11691 (718) 471-8453
PIONEER WOMEN-NA'AMAT 45 CONKLIN STREET ... FARMINGDALE **NY** 11735 (516) 735-2675
ARZA-ASSOCIATION OF REFORM ZIONISTS OF AMERICA
838 FIFTH AVENUE ... NEW YORK **NY** 10021 (212) 249-0100
AMERICA ISRAEL FRIENDSHIP HOUSE OF BNAI ZION
136 EAST 39TH STREET ... NEW YORK **NY** 10016 (212) 725-1211
AMERICAN JEWISH ALTERNATIVES TO ZIONISM
133 E. 73RD STREET, SUITE 404 ... NEW YORK **NY** 10021 (212) 628-2727
AMERICAN JEWISH LEAGUE FOR ISRAEL 595 MADISON AVENUE ... NEW YORK **NY** 10022 (212) 371-1583
AMERICAN ZIONIST FEDERATION 515 PARK AVENUE ... NEW YORK **NY** 10022 (212) 371-7750
AMERICAN ZIONIST YOUTH COUNCIL 515 PARK AVENUE ... NEW YORK **NY** 10022 (212) 751-6070
AMERICAN ZIONIST YOUTH FOUNDATION RESOURCE CENTER
515 PARK AVENUE ... NEW YORK **NY** 10022 (212) 751-6070
AMERICANS FOR PROGRESSIVE ISRAEL-HASHOMER HATZAIR
150 FIFTH AVENUE ... NEW YORK **NY** 10003 (212) 255-8760
ASSOCIATION OF REFORM ZIONISTS OF AMERICA 838 FIFTH AVENUE ... NEW YORK **NY** 10021 (212) 249-0100
B'NAI ZION 136 E. 39TH STREET ... NEW YORK **NY** 10016 (212) 725-1211
BAR/BAT MITZVAH PILGRIMAGE - WORLD ZIONIST ORGANIZATION
515 PARK AVENUE ... NEW YORK **NY** 10022 (212) 752-0600
BNAI ZION-AMERICAN FRATERNAL ZIONIST ORGANIZATION
136 EAST 39TH STREET ... NEW YORK **NY** 10016 (202) 725-1211
BNEI AKIVA OF NORTH AMERICA 25 W. 26TH STREET ... NEW YORK **NY** 10010 (212) 889-5260
CONTINUING SEMINAR ON ZIONIST THOUGHT 9 EAST 40TH STREET ... NEW YORK **NY** 10016 (212) 532-5615
DOR HEMSHECH, UNITED STATES 515 PARK AVENUE ... NEW YORK **NY** 10022 (212) 752-0600
DROR YOUNG ZIONIST ORGANIZATIONS 215 PARK AVENUE S ... NEW YORK **NY** 10003 (212) 777-9388
FARBAND LABOR ZIONIST ORDER 575 6TH AVENUE ... NEW YORK **NY** 10011 (212) 989-0300
HAPOEL HAMIZRACHI WOMEN'S ZIONIST ORGANIZATION
370 SEVENTH AVENUE ... NEW YORK **NY** 10001 (212) 564-9045
HASHACHAR 50 W. 58TH STREET ... NEW YORK **NY** 10019 (212) 355-7900
HASHOMER HATZAIR SOCIALIST ZIONIST YOUTH MOVEMENT
150 FIFTH AVENUE, #710 ... NEW YORK **NY** 10011 (212) 929-4955
HERUT-U.S.A. (UNITED REVISIONISTS OF AMERICA)
41 EAST 42ND STREET ... NEW YORK **NY** 10017 (212) 687-4502
ICHUD HABONIM LABOR ZIONIST YOUTH 575 SIXTH AVENUE ... NEW YORK **NY** 10011 (212) 255-1796
ICHUD HABONIM LABOR ZIONIST YOUTH 27 W. 20 STREET ... NEW YORK **NY** 10011 (212) 255-1796
JABOTINSKY FOUNDATION, INC., THE 261 FIFTH AVENUE ... NEW YORK **NY** 10016 (212) 679-6868
LABOR ZIONIST ALLIANCE 114 FIFTH AVENUE ... NEW YORK **NY** 10011 (212) 989-0300
LABOR ZIONIST ORGANIZATION OF AMERICA - POALE ZION
575 6TH AVENUE ... NEW YORK **NY** 10011
LEAGUE FOR THE NATIONAL LABOR IN ISRAEL 60 EAST 42ND STREET ... NEW YORK **NY** 10165 (212) 599-3670
LEAGUE OF FRIENDS OF LABOR ISRAEL 114 FIFTH AVENUE ... NEW YORK **NY** 10011 (212) 675-7192
LEAGUE OF RELIGIOUS SETTLEMENTS, INC. 156 FIFTH AVENUE ... NEW YORK **NY** 10010 (212) 924-9475
NATIONAL COUNCIL FOR TORAH EDUCATION
C/O RELIGIOUS ZIONISTS OF AMERICA, 25 W. 26TH STREET ... NEW YORK **NY** 10010 (212) 289-1414
PIONEER WOMEN-NA'AMAT 200 MADISON AVENUE ... NEW YORK **NY** 10016 (212) 725-8010
RELIGIOUS ZIONISTS OF AMERICA (MIZRACHI-HAPOEL HAMIZRACHI)
25 WEST 26TH STREET ... NEW YORK **NY** 10010 (212) 689-1414
THEODOR HERZL FOUNDATION 515 PARK AVENUE ... NEW YORK **NY** 10022 (212) 752-0600
THEODOR HERZL INSTITUTE 515 PARK AVENUE ... NEW YORK **NY** 10022 (212) 752-0600
UNITED LABOR ZIONIST PARTY 305 BROADWAY ... NEW YORK **NY** 10007
UNITED ZIONIST REVISIONISTS OF AMERICA-HERUT, U.S.A.
41 EAST 42ND STREET ... NEW YORK **NY** 10017 (212) 687-4502
WORLD CONFEDERATION OF UNITED ZIONISTS-HEAD OFFICE
595 MADISON AVENUE, ROOM 1004 ... NEW YORK **NY** 10022 (212) 371-1452
WORLD UNION OF GENERAL ZIONISTS ZOA HOUSE, 4 E. 34TH STREET ... NEW YORK **NY** 10016 (212) 481-1500
WORLD ZIONIST ORGANIZATION-AMERICAN SECTION
515 PARK AVENUE ... NEW YORK **NY** 10022 (212) 752-0600
ZIONIST ARCHIVES & LIBRARY/WORLD ZIONIST ORG.-AMER. SECTION
515 PARK AVENUE ... NEW YORK **NY** 10022 (212) 753-2167
ZIONIST ORGANIZATION OF AMERICA - ZOA HOUSE
4 EAST 34TH STREET ... NEW YORK **NY** 10016 (212) 481-1500
ASSOCIATION OF REFORM ZIONISTS OF AMERICA - ARZA
19425 VAN AKEN BLVD ... CLEVELAND **OH** 44122 (216) 283-1276
LABOR ZIONIST ALLIANCE 1708 BEACONWOOD DRIVE ... CLEVELAND **OH** 44121 (216) 241-2258
LABOR ZIONIST ALLIANCE 3715 WARRENSVILLE CENTER ROAD ... CLEVELAND **OH** 44122 (216) 752-2907
PIONEER WOMEN-NA'AMAT 13969 CEDAR ROAD, ROOM 208 ... CLEVELAND **OH** 44418 (216) 321-2002
UNITED ZIONIST REVISIONISTS OF CLEVELAND
23759 WENDOVER DRIVE ... CLEVELAND **OH** 44122 (216) 381-3967
ZIONIST ORGANIZATION OF AMERICA 25400 FAIRMOUNT BLVD ... CLEVELAND **OH** 44122 (216) 321-6131
ACHDUT HAAVODA-POALE ZION OF CANADA 272 CODSELL AVENUE ... DOWNSVIEW **ON** M3H 3X2 (416) 636-4021
PIONEER WOMEN-NA'AMAT 272 CODSELL AVENUE ... DOWNSVIEW **ON** M3H 3X2 (416) 636-5425
CANADIAN ZIONIST FEDERATION-CENTRAL, THE 788 MARLEE AVENUE ... TORONTO **ON** M6B 3K1 (416) 787-6171
LABOR ZIONIST ALLIANCE 14 VIEWMOUNT AVENUE ... TORONTO **ON** M6B 1T3 (416) 787-0339
LABOR ZIONIST MOVEMENT OF CANADA
3101 BATHURST STREET, SUITE 305 ... TORONTO **ON** M6A 2A6 (416) 783-8440
ZIONIST ORGANIZATION OF CANADA 788 MARLEE AVENUE ... TORONTO **ON** M6B 3K1 (416) 781-3571
ZIONIST REVISIONIST ORGANIZATION OF CANADA
3417 BATHURST STREET ... TORONTO **ON**
PIONEER WOMEN-NA'AMAT 1405 LOCUST STREET, ROOM 1117 ... PHILADELPHIA **PA** 19102 (215) 545-1328
PIONEER WOMEN-NA'AMAT 6328 FORBES AVENUE ... PITTSBURGH **PA** 15217 (412) 521-5253
CANADIAN ZIONIST FEDERATION, THE 1310 GREENE AVENUE ... MONTREAL **QU** H3Z 2B2 (514) 934-0804
HASHOMER HATZAIR 5234 CLANRANALD AVENUE ... MONTREAL **QU** H3X 2S4
JEWISH COLONISATION ASSOCIATION OF CANADA
5151 COTE ST. CATHERINE ROAD ... MONTREAL **QU** H3W 1M6
LABOR ZIONIST MOVEMENT OF CANADA 4770 KENT AVENUE ... MONTREAL **QU** H3W 1H2 (514) 735-1593
MIZRACHI-HAPOEL HAMIZRACHI ORGANIZATION OF CANADA
5497A VICTORIA AVENUE, SUITE 101 ... MONTREAL **QU** H3W 2R1 (514) 739-4748
PIONEER WOMEN-NA'AMAT 4770 KENT AVENUE, SUITE 304 ... MONTREAL **QU** H3W 1H2 (514) 735-6253
ZIONIST REVISIONIST ORGANIZATIONS OF CANADA
5234 CLANRANALD AVENUE ... MONTREAL **QU** H3X 2S4
STUDENT ZIONIST ORGANIZATIONS 1310 GREENE AVENUE ... WESTMOUNT **QU** H3Z 2B2 (514) 934-0804